WHAT
HISTORICAL
NOVEL
DO I READ NEXT?

VOLUME 2
INDEXES

(cis)

WHAT HISTORICAL NOVEL

DO I READ NEXT?

VOLUME 2
INDEXES

DANIEL S. BURT, PH.D

GALE

Detroit

New York

Toronto

London

Daniel S. Burt, Ph.D.

Gale Research Staff

Senior Editor: Debra M. Kirby
Associate Editors: Victoria A. Coughlin and Lydia Fink
Contributing Editors: Kathleen Dallas, Nancy Franklin, Arlene Johnson, Prindle
LaBarge, Sharon McGilvray, Charles B. Montney and Dana Shonta
Managing Editor: Ann V. Evory

Production Director: MaryBeth Trimper
External Production Assistant: Shanna Heilveil
Product Design Manager: Cynthia Baldwin
Graphic Designer: Mary Krzewinski

Manager Data Entry Services: Eleanor Allison
Data Entry Coordinator: Gwendolyn S. Tucker
Data Entry Associates: Maleka Imrana, Beverly Jendrowski

Manager, Technical Support Services: Theresa Rocklin
Programmer/Analyst: Joshua E. Cohen

Library of Congress Cataloging-in-Publication Data
Burt, Daniel S.
     What historical novel do I read next? / Daniel S. Burt.
         p.   cm.
     Includes indexes.
     ISBN 0-7876-0388-0 (set : alk. paper). -- ISBN
0-7876-1542-0 (vol. 2 : alk. paper)
         1. Historical fiction--Bibliography.   I. Title.
Z5917.H6B87   1997
[PN3441]
016.80863'81--dc21   97-10702
                                                                                          CIP

™ This book is printed on acid-free paper that meets the minimum requirements of
American National Standard for Information Sciences—Permanence Paper for
Printed Library Materials, ANSI Z39.48-1984.

ISBN 0-7876-0388-0 (Complete set)
ISBN 0-7876-1541-2 (Volume 1)
ISBN 0-7876-1542-0 (Volume 2)
ISSN 1052-2212

Printed in the United States of America

Contents

Volume 1

Preface vii

About the Author x

Introduction xi

The Most Popular Historical Novels xvi

Pulitzer Prize Winning Historical Novels xx

Recommended Historical Novels xxi

The Most Popular Time Periods, Settings, Subjects, and Historical Figures xxxii

Suggestions for Further Reading xxxiv

What Historical Novel Do I Read Next? 3

Volume 2

Time Period Index 3

Geographic Index 45

Subject Index 111

Fictional Character Name Index 195

Historical Character Name Index 311

Character Description Index 389

Author Index 609

Title Index 653

WHAT HISTORICAL NOVEL

DO I READ NEXT?

VOLUME 2
INDEXES

Time Period Index

This index chronologically lists the time periods in which the featured books take place. Main headings refer to centuries; the 18th through 20th centuries are broken down into decades when possible. (Note: The first decade of a century is the the ——00s, thus 1700s means 1701-1709, not the entire 18th century.) Titles that cover large spans of time are listed under *Multiple Time Periods*; when no specific time is given, the headings *Indeterminate* and *Indeterminate Past* are used. Featured titles are listed alphabetically beneath each heading, with author names and entry numbers also provided.

MULTIPLE TIME PERIODS

Alaska - James A. Michener 4364
American Beauty - Edna Ferber 2060
Annapolis - William Martin 4137
The Anthem - Noel B. Gerson 2361
Antonietta - John Hersey 2868
Articles of Faith - Ronald Harwood 2770
Back Bay - William Martin 4138
Bayou - Pamela Jekel 3183
Bless This House - Norah Lofts 3835
The Book of Abraham - Marek Halter 2665
The Books of Rachel - Joel Gross 2600
The Brahmins - Eileen Lottman 3901
Brazil - Errol Lincoln Uys 6395
The Bridge on the Drina - Ivo Andric 151
Cajun - Elizabeth Nell Dubus 1751
Cannibal Eliot and the Lost Histories of San Francisco - Hilton Obenzinger 4660
Cape Cod - William Martin 4139
Caribbean - James A. Michener 4365
Centennial - James A. Michener 4366
Chatterton - Peter Ackroyd 17
Chesapeake - James A. Michener 4367
The Children of the First Man - James Alexander Thom 6230
Columbia - Pamela Jekel 3184
The Covenant - James A. Michener 4368
Crossing over Jordan - Linda Beatrice Brown 725
Crossing the River - Caryl Phillips 4984
Cry of the Peacock - Gina Barkhordar Nahai 4552
Darker Grows the Valley - Harry Harrison Kroll 3556
The Great Alone - Janet Dailey 1454
The Harp and the Shadow - Alejo Carpentier 905
The Haunting of Lamb House - Joan Aiken 48
Hawaii - James A. Michener 4370
I Am England - Patricia Wright 6881
I Remember Love - Mollie Hardwick 2694
Isle of Woman - Piers Anthony 167
Jordan County: A Landscape in Narrative - Shelby Foote 2152
Joshua Moore, American - George Frederick Hummel 3078
The Lives of Rachel - Joel Gross 2601
Massachusetts: A Novel - Nancy Zaroulis 6956
Mexico - James A. Michener 4372
The Near and Distant Place - Patricia Wright 6883
The Nonsuch Lure - Mary M. Luke 3924
Orlando - Virginia Woolf 6866
Poland - James A. Michener 4373
The Prescott Chronicles - Albert Fried 2232
A Quest for Love - Jacquetta Hawkes 2781

Remembrance Rock - Carl Sandburg 5583
The Rock: A Novel about Gibraltar - John Masters 4179
Russka: The Novel of Russia - Edward Rutherfurd 5535
Sarum: The Novel of England - Edward Rutherfurd 5536
The Savage Brood - Martha Rofheart 5430
The Seven Ages - Eva Figes 2084
Shame of Man - Piers Anthony 168
The Source - James A. Michener 4374
Texas - James A. Michener 4375
Theo and Matilda - Rachel Billington 498
Those the Sun Has Loved - Rose Jourdain 3309
The Three Black Pennys - Joseph Hergesheimer 2855
The Tides of Malvern - Francis Griswold 2595
Ulverton - Adam Thorpe 6278
A Wayside Tavern - Norah Lofts 3862
Wind From the Carolinas - Robert Wilder 6751
The Winthrop Covenant - Louis Auchincloss 235

INDETERMINATE PAST

Abraham and Sarah: The Long Journey - Roberta Kells Dorr 1694
Amber Princess - Henry Treece 6325
And Abram Journeyed - Harry Simonhoff 5858
The Animal Wife - Elizabeth Marshall Thomas 6243
Beyond the Sea of Ice - William Sarabande 5595
Charioteer: A Story of Old Egypt in the Days of Joseph - Gertrude Eberle 1835
Children of the Dawn - Patricia Rowe 5516
Children of the Ice - Charlotte Prentiss 5166
Children of the Lion - Peter Danielson 1464
The Clan of the Cave Bear - Jean M. Auel 236
Corridor of Storms - William Sarabande 5596
Dance of the Tiger: A Novel of the Ice Age - Bjorn Kurten 3566
The Dark Way - Robert J. Conley 1241
Dawn Land - Joseph Bruchac III 734
The Death of Kings - Peter Danielson 1465
Deirdre - James Stephens 5996
Departed Glory - Peter Danielson 1466
Dido, Queen of Hearts - Gertrude Atherton 223
The Eagle King - Henry Treece 6327
The Edge of the World - William Sarabande 5597
Face of the Rising Sun - William Sarabande 5598
Finn Mac Cool - Morgan Llywelyn 3818
Fire Queen - Deborah Grabien 2503
First Knight - Elizabeth Chadwick 966
Forbidden Land - William Sarabande 5599
The Goddess - Miranda Seymour 5763

Hagar - Lois T. Henderson 2824
Hagar - Cothburn O'Neal 4737
The Horsemasters - Joan Wolf 6840
Husband of Delilah - Eric Linklater 3802
The Inheritors - William Golding 2455
Jacob - Jean Cabries 844
Jacob: An Autobiography - Irving Fineman 2088
The Jaguar Princess - Clare Bell 421
Jason - Henry Treece 6331
Jezebel - Dorothy Clarke Wilson 6802
Joseph of Egypt - Thomas Mann 4065
Joseph the Provider - Thomas Mann 4066
Keepers of the Misty Time - Patricia Rowe 5517
Lot's Wife - Marie Ley-Piscator 3767
The Mammoth Hunters - Jean M. Auel 237
The Maze Maker - Michael Ayrton 250
Medea - Miranda Seymour 5764
Merari - Gloria Howe Bremkamp 656
The Once and Future King - T.H. White 6705
Out of the House of Life - Chelsea Quinn Yarbro 6903
The Painted Queen - Olga Hesky 2871
People of the Mesa - Charlotte Prentiss 5168
Pillar of the Sky - Cecelia Holland 2994
The Plains of Passage - Jean M. Auel 238
The Private Life of Helen of Troy - John Erskine 1957
The Promise - Esther Kellner 3395
Prophets and Warriors - Peter Danielson 1473
The Reindeer Hunters - Joan Wolf 6841
Reindeer Moon - Elizabeth Marshall Thomas 6244
Return of the Stranger - Dorothy James Roberts 5377
Return to Ithaca - Eyvind Johnson 3224
Rhinegold - Stephan Grundy 2607
Ruth - Irving Fineman 2089
The Sacred Stones - William Sarabande 5600
Scandal in Troy - Eva Hemmer Hansen 2679
Shadow of the Watching Star - William Sarabande 5601
Shadows on the Stones - Moyra Caldecott 847
The Shattered Horse - S.P. Somtow 5945
The Shepherd Kings - Peter Danielson 1475
The Shining King - Peter Danielson 1476
Shiva: An Adventure of the Ice Age - J.H. Brennan 657
Singletusk - Bjorn Kurten 3567
The Son of Laughter - Frederick Buechner 764
The Sorceress - Nathaniel Norsen Weinreb 6602
Table in the Wilderness - Norton S. Parker 4806
The Tales of Jacob - Thomas Mann 4068
The Tall Stones - Moyra Caldecott 848
The Temple of the Sun - Moyra Caldecott 849

Three Ships and Three Kings - Georgia Sallaska 5573
Thunder in the Sky - William Sarabande 5602
Troy - Richard Matturro 4194
The Trumpet and the Sword - Peter Danielson 1479
The Valley of Horses - Jean M. Auel 239
The Voyage Home - Ernst Schnabel 5644
Walkers of the Wind - William Sarabande 5603
The Way of the Priests - Robert J. Conley 1253
The White Path - Robert J. Conley 1254
Wolves of the Dawn - William Sarabande 5604
The Year of the Horsetails - R.F. Tapsell 6162
Young Joseph - Thomas Mann 4069

180th CENTURY B.C.

The Last Mammoth - Margaret Allan 89
The Mammoth Stone - Margaret Allan 90

130th CENTURY B.C.

People of the Sea - W. Michael Gear 2339
People of the Wolf - W. Michael Gear 2341

80th CENTURY B.C.

People of the Fire - W. Michael Gear 2335

71th CENTURY B.C.

Brother Wind - Sue Harrison 2748
Mother Earth, Father Sky - Sue Harrison 2749
My Sister, the Moon - Sue Harrison 2750

50th CENTURY B.C.

The Deer Dancers - Amanda Cockrell 1146
People of the Lightning - W. Michael Gear 2337

44th CENTURY B.C.

The Year the Horses Came - Mary Mackey 3993

40th CENTURY B.C.

Winged Pharaoh - Joan Grant 2536

37th CENTURY B.C.

The Last Warrior Queen - Mary Mackey 3992

31th CENTURY B.C.

The Earth Goddess - Richard Herley 2856

30th CENTURY B.C.

The Flint Lord - Richard Herley 2857
People of the Earth - W. Michael Gear 2334
The Stone Arrow - Richard Herley 2858

26th CENTURY B.C.

Gilgamesh the King - Robert Silverberg 5853

21st CENTURY B.C.

No Other Gods - Wilder Penfield 4901

20th CENTURY B.C.

Abram, Son of Terah - Florence M. Bauer 378
The Bull From the Sea - Mary Renault 5295
The Covenant: A Novel of the Life of Abraham the Prophet - Zofja Kossak-Szczucka 3543
Death Comes as the End - Agatha Christie 1076

The Golden Strangers - Henry Treece 6328
The King Must Die - Mary Renault 5298
River God - Wilbur Smith 5928

16th CENTURY B.C.

Pharaoh - Eloise Jarvis McGraw 4276

15th CENTURY B.C.

Child of the Morning - Pauline Gedge 2343
The Golden Balance - Arthur Dana Hall 2646
Pharaoh - Eloise Jarvis McGraw 4276

14th CENTURY B.C.

The Egyptian - Mika Waltari 6552
A God Against the Gods - Allen Drury 1738
The Goddess Queen: A Novel Based on the Life of Nefertiti - Nicole Vidal 6494
The Golden Pharaoh - Peter Danielson 1468
The Hittite - Noel B. Gerson 2373
King and Goddess - Judith Tarr 6166
King of the Two Lands: The Pharaoh Akhenaten - Jacquetta Hawkes 2780
King Tut's Private Eye - Lee Levin 3739
The Lion in Egypt - Peter Danielson 1470
Murder at the Feast of Rejoicing - Lynda S. Robinson 5407
Murder at the God's Gate - Lynda S. Robinson 5408
Murder in the Place of Anubis - Lynda S. Robinson 5409
On a Balcony - David Stacton 5973
Pillar of Fire - Judith Tarr 6168
The Prophecy - Peter Danielson 1472
Return to Thebes - Allen Drury 1739
The Twelfth Transforming - Pauline Gedge 2347
Vengeance of the Lion - Peter Danielson 1480

13th CENTURY B.C.

All the Trumpets Sounded: A Novel Based on the Life of Moses - W.G. Hardy 2701
Alone Atop the Mountain - Samuel Sandmel 5591
Ancient Evenings - Norman Mailer 4035
Daughter of the Red Deer - Joan Wolf 6838
The Exodus - Konrad Bercovici 473
The Exodus - Peter Danielson 1467
The Firebrand - Marion Zimmer Bradley 624
Her-Bak: The Living Face of Ancient Egypt - Isha Schwaller de Lubicz 5676
Hercules, My Shipmate - Robert Graves 2545
The Miracle Hater - Shulamith Hareven 2704
Moses - Sholem Asch 199
Moses, Prince of Egypt - Howard Fast 2039
On Eagles' Wings - Arthur E. Southon 5951
Paris of Troy - George Baker 273
Prince of Egypt - Dorothy Clarke Wilson 6805
The River and the Stone: Moses' Early Years in Egypt - Kathleen Jenks 3192
The Scapegoat: A Life of Moses - Joan Lawrence 3684
Sword of Glory - Peter Danielson 1477
Tables of the Law - Thomas Mann 4067
Whom the Gods Would Destroy - Richard Powell 5148

12th CENTURY B.C.

Akhnaton, King of Egypt - Dmitri Merezhkovski 4337
Ancient Evenings - Norman Mailer 4035
Fires in the Sky - Phillip Parotti 4816
The Greek Generals Talk: Memoirs of the Trojan War - Phillip Parotti 4817
The Invaders - Peter Danielson 1469
Lady of the Reeds - Pauline Gedge 2345

The Promised Land - Peter Danielson 1471
Scarlet Cord: A Novel of the Woman of Jericho - Frank G. Slaughter 5899
The Trojan Generals Talk: Memoirs of the Greek War - Phillip Parotti 4818

11th CENTURY B.C.

David: Warrior and King - Frank G. Slaughter 5885
Earth Giant - Edison Marshall 4106
The Prophet and the King - Shirley Watkins 6582
The Sea Peoples - Peter Danielson 1474
The Song of Ruth: A Love Story of the Old Testament - Frank G. Slaughter 5901

10th CENTURY B.C.

After Goliath - R.V. Cassill 955
Bathsheba - Roberta Kells Dorr 1695
Children of the Sun - Charlotte Prentiss 5167
David and Bathsheba - Ari Ibn-Sahav 3098
David at Olivet - Wallace Hamilton 2671
David of Jerusalem - Louis De Wohl 1564
David the King - Gladys Schmitt 5641
David's Stranger - Moshe Shamir 5771
Giant Killer - Elmer Holmes Davis 1518
King David - Gwyn Jenkins 3191
The King David Report - Stefan Heym 2910
King of Kings: A Novel of the Life of David - Malachi Martin 4134
The Lily and the Bull - Moyra Caldecott 846
Love and Wisdom: A Novel about Solomon - Richard G. Hubler 3064
The Queen of Sheba - Roberta Kells Dorr 1696
Rizpah - Charles E. Israel 3124
Solomon and Sheba - Faye Levine 3740
Solomon and Sheba - Jay Williams 6774
Solomon and the Queen of Sheba - Czenzi Ormonde 4751
Solomon's Song - Roberta Kells Dorr 1697
Tamar - Ann Chamberlin 975
Triumph of the Lion - Peter Danielson 1478
The Trojan - Noel B. Gerson 2386
The Unanointed - Laurene Chinn 1070
The Valley of Vision: A Novel of King Solomon and His Time - Vardis Fisher 2113

9th CENTURY B.C.

The Curse of Jezebel: A Novel of the Biblical Queen of Evil - Frank G. Slaughter 5884
Dara, the Cypriot - Louis Paul 4842
The Purple Quest: A Novel of Seafaring Adventure in the Ancient World - Frank G. Slaughter 5896

8th CENTURY B.C.

Children of the Wolf - Alfred Duggan 1762
The Herdsman - Dorothy Clarke Wilson 6801
Homer's Daughter - Robert Graves 2546
The Horse Goddess - Morgan Llywelyn 3820
The Valley of God - Irene Steinman Patai 4825
Years of the City - George Rippey Stewart 6028

7th CENTURY B.C.

The Assyrian - Nicholas Guild 2610
The Blood Star - Nicholas Guild 2611
The Laughter of Aphrodite - Peter Green 2570
My Name Is Sappho - Martha Rofheart 5429
The Other Sappho - Ellen Frye 2240
Years of the City - George Rippey Stewart 6028

6th CENTURY B.C.

Babylon - Anthony Esler 1959
The Babylonians - Nathaniel Norsen Weinreb 6600

The Fabulist - John Vornholt 6512
Judith - Stella Wilchek 6748
Lady of the Lotus - William E. Barrett 353
The Laughter of Aphrodite - Peter Green 2570
Persian Conqueror - George Sidney Hellman 2822
The Praise Singer - Mary Renault 5302
The Prophet - Sholem Asch 201
The Yellow Robe: A Novel of the Life of Buddha -
   Robert Payne 4856

5th CENTURY B.C.

Achilles His Armour - Peter Green 2569
Alcibiades, Beloved of Gods - Vincenz Brun 735
Anabasis: A Journey to the Interior - Ellen
   Gilchrist 2408
Creation - Gore Vidal 6486
The Dragon of the Ishtar Gate - L. Sprague De
   Camp 1555
Esther - Nathaniel Norsen Weinreb 6601
Esther: The Star and the Sceptre - Gina
   Andrews 146
The Etruscan - Mika Waltari 6553
Farewell Great King: A Novel of Ancient Greece - Jill
   Paton Walsh 4829
The Flowers of Adonis - Rosemary Sutcliff 6122
Gate to the Sea - Bryher 743
Glory and the Lightning - Taylor Caldwell 856
Goat Song: A Novel of Ancient Greece - Frank
   Yerby 6920
Goatsong - Tom Holt 3009
The Immortal Marriage - Gertrude Atherton 225
Lady of the Lotus - William E. Barrett 353
*The Magnificent Traitor: A Novel of Alcibiades and
   the Golden Age of Pericles* - Lynn Poole 5092
*Nicanor of Athens: The Autobiography of an Unknown
   Citizen* - Owen Francis Grazebrook 2563
Pericles the Athenian - Rex Warner 6566
The Praise Singer - Mary Renault 5302
The Private and Public Life of Socrates - Rene
   Kraus 3552
The Serpent's Tooth - Diana L. Paxson 4846
The Shining - Stephen Marlowe 4097
*So Great a Queen: The Story of Esther, Queen of
   Persia* - Paul Frischauer 2235
Soldier of the Mist - Gene Wolfe 6843
The Walled Orchard - Tom Holt 3010
The Yellow Robe: A Novel of the Life of Buddha -
   Robert Payne 4856

4th CENTURY B.C.

Alexander in Babylon - Jakob Wassermann 6576
Alexander of Macedon: The Journey to World's End -
   Harold Lamb 3607
Alexander the God - Maurice Druon 1731
Alexander the God - Robert Payne 4849
The Arrows of Hercules - L. Sprague De Camp 1553
Bard: The Odyssey of the Irish - Morgan
   Llywelyn 3816
The Bronze God of Rhodes - L. Sprague De
   Camp 1554
A Choice of Murder - Peter Vansittart 6429
The Conqueror: A Novel of Alexander the Great -
   Edison Marshall 4104
An Elephant for Aristotle - L. Sprague De
   Camp 1556
The Escape of Socrates - Robert Pick 4993
Fire From Heaven - Mary Renault 5296
Funeral Games - Mary Renault 5297
The Golden Lyre - Noel B. Gerson 2371
Lord of the Two Lands - Judith Tarr 6167
The Mask of Apollo - Mary Renault 5300
*North to Thule: An Imagined Narrative of the Famous
   "Lost" Voyage of Pytheas of Massalla in the
   Fourth Century B.C.* - John Frye 2241
The Persian Boy - Mary Renault 5301

The Private and Public Life of Socrates - Rene
   Kraus 3552
Star of Macedon - Karl V. Eiker 1901
The Torch - Wilder Penfield 4902

3rd CENTURY B.C.

Besieger of Cities - Alfred Duggan 1761
The Chinese Emperor - Jean Levi 3733
The Coin of Carthage - Bryher 740
The Corn King and the Spring Queen - Naomi
   Mitchison 4419
The Dream of Confucius - Jean Levi 3734
Funeral Games - Mary Renault 5297
Hannibal - Ross Leckie 3704
Hannibal of Carthage - Mary Dolan 1686
Salammbo - Gustave Flaubert 2123
Swords Against Carthage - Friedrich Donauer 1689

2nd CENTURY B.C.

The Corn King and the Spring Queen - Naomi
   Mitchison 4419
The First Man in Rome - Colleen McCullough 4234
The Golden Wind - C.L. Grace 2507
Hannibal - Ross Leckie 3704
Hannibal of Carthage - Mary Dolan 1686
Horses of Heaven - Gillian Bradshaw 630
*The Island of the Innocent: A Novel of Greek and Jew
   in the Time of the Maccabees* - Vardis
   Fisher 2108
The Scarlet Beast - Francis Gerard 2357
The Seeking - Robert S. Elegant 1906
The Winds of Sinhala - Colin De Silva 1562
Winter Quarters - Alfred Duggan 1775

1st CENTURY B.C.

The Alexandrian - Martha Rofheart 5425
The Altar and the Crown - Marian Niven 4631
Arena: A Novel of Spartacus and Crassus - Maurice
   Ghnassia 2391
Arms of Nemesis - Steven Saylor 5623
Augustus - Allan Massie 4167
Augustus - John Williams 6785
Caesar - Mirko Jelusich 3188
Caesar - Allan Massie 4168
Caesar's Women - Colleen McCullough 4233
Catalina's Riddle - Steven Saylor 5624
The Catiline Conspiracy - John Maddox
   Roberts 5379
Chantefable - Eldorous L. Dayton 1546
The City of Libertines - W.G. Hardy 2702
Cleopatra - H. Rider Haggard 2637
Clodia - Robert DeMaria 1606
The Conquered - Naomi Mitchison 4418
The Death of Virgil - Hermann Broch 699
Death on the Appian Way - Kenneth Benton 463
Dreams of Empire - Jeanne Mackin 3994
Druids - Morgan Llywelyn 3817
Epicurus My Master - Max Radin 5233
Farewell, Catullus - Pierson Dixon 1651
Fortune's Favorite - Colleen McCullough 4235
Freedom, Farewell - Phyllis Bentley 461
Gaul Is Divided - Esther Fisher Brown 721
The Gift of Rome - John Wagner 6520
The Gladiators - Arthur Koestler 3532
A Goddess to a God - John Lloyd Balderston 278
The Gods Are Not Mocked - Anna Taylor 6177
Golden Peacock - Gertrude Atherton 224
The Grass Crown - Colleen McCullough 4236
I, Claudius - Robert Graves 2547
I Loved Tiberius - Elisabeth Dored 1692
The Ides of March - Thornton Wilder 6753
Imperial Caesar - Rex Warner 6565
The Key - Benita Kane Jaro 3169
The King of Flesh and Blood - Moshe Shamir 5772
A Murder on the Appian Way - Steven Saylor 5625

A Pillar of Iron - Taylor Caldwell 861
Prepare Them for Caesar - Mary Louise
   Mabie 3954
Purple Pirate - Talbot Mundy 4514
Red Branch - Morgan Llywelyn 3824
Roman Blood - Steven Saylor 5626
Roman Shadows - Ron Burns 804
The Sacrilege - John Maddox Roberts 5380
Spartacus - Howard Fast 2044
SPQR - John Maddox Roberts 5381
*Sword of Pleasure: Being the Memoirs of the Most
   Illustrious Lucius Cornelius Sulla* - Peter
   Green 2571
Swords in the North - Paul Lewis Anderson 138
The Temple of the Muses - John Maddox
   Roberts 5382
That Egyptian Woman - Noel B. Gerson 2384
Three's Company - Alfred Duggan 1774
Throne of Isis - Judith Tarr 6170
Tiberius: The Memoirs of the Emperor - Allan
   Massie 4169
Tros of Samothrace - Talbot Mundy 4515
Turn Back the River - W.G. Hardy 2703
Two From Galilee: A Love Story - Marjorie
   Holmes 3005
The Venus Throw - Steven Saylor 5627
Woman of Andros - Thornton Wilder 6754
The Young Caesar - Rex Warner 6567

1st CENTURY

According to Mary: A Novel of the Magdalene - Willa
   Gibbs 2398
According to Thomas - Gladys Malvern 4053
Agrippa's Daughter - Howard Fast 2025
*And Walk on Love: A Novel Based on the Life of the
   Apostle Paul* - Henrietta Buckmaster 759
The Antagonists - Ernest K. Gann 2276
Antioch Actress: A Novel of Pagan Against Christian -
   Jacob Randolph Perkins 4913
The Apostle - Sholem Asch 197
As Sure as the Dawn - Francine Rivers 5352
Augustus - Allan Massie 4167
Augustus - John Williams 6785
Barabbas - Par Lagerkvist 3585
Barabbas: A Dream of the World's Tragedy - Marie
   Corelli 1327
Barabbas: A Novel of the Time of Jesus - Emery
   Bekessy 417
Behold the Man - Toyohiko Kagawa 3321
Behold the Man - N. Richard Nash 4556
Behold Your King - Florence M. Bauer 379
Ben Hur: A Tale of the Christ - Lew Wallace 6536
Beware of Caesar - Vincent Sheean 5786
The Big Fisherman - Lloyd C. Douglas 1702
Blood of the Martyrs - Naomi Mitchison 4417
Bloody Poet - Deszo Kosztolanyi 3546
The Bond and the Free - Charles Dunscomb 1813
The Bride of Pilate - Esther Kellner 3393
The Brother - Dorothy Clarke Wilson 6799
The Brother - Chayym Zeldis 6958
Brothers of Vengeance - LeGette Blythe 556
Canis the Warrior - James Sinclair 5864
The Captive Princess - Maxine Shore 5831
Caravan to China - Frank Stanley Stuart 6085
The Centurion - Leonard Wibberley 6729
A Certain Woman: The Story of Mary Magdalene -
   Victor MacClure 3959
Claudius the God - Robert Graves 2543
The Conspiracy - John Hersey 2870
The Crows of War - Steven Rayson 5276
The Dark Island - Henry Treece 6326
Daughter of Jairus - Paul Hervey Fox 2196
Dear and Glorious Physician - Taylor Caldwell 853
Dogheaded Death - Ray Faraday Nelson 4581
The Eagle and the Crown - Hubertus
   Loewenstein 3832
The Eagle and the Raven - Pauline Gedge 2344

The Eighth Veil - Ellis Kadison 3320
The Emperor's Physician - Jacob Randolph
   Perkins 4914
Empire of the Eagle - Andre Norton 4649
The Fates Are Laughing - William Crozier 1439
First the Blade - Drayton Mayrant 4212
Fisher of Men: A Novel of Simon Peter - Kurt
   Frieberger 2231
The Flames of Rome - Paul L. Maier 4033
The Forest House - Marion Zimmer Bradley 625
Fourth King - Norbert Coulehan 1373
The Galileans - Frank G. Slaughter 5888
The Gifts: A Story of the Boyhood of Jesus - Dorothy
   Clarke Wilson 6800
The Gladiator - Thames Ross Williamson 6790
The Glorious Folly: A Novel of the Time of St. Paul -
   Louis De Wohl 1565
God Was Born in Exile - Vintila Horia 3033
God's Warrior - Frank G. Slaughter 5889
Gold for the Caesars - Florence A. Seward 5759
The Good Tidings - William Sidney 5843
The Gospel According to Gamaliel - Gerald
   Heard 2801
The Gospel According to Pontius Pilate - James R.
   Mills 4408
The Gospel of Corax - Paul Park 4802
Great Lion of God - Taylor Caldwell 858
He Came From Galilee - Daniel A. Poling 5083
Hear Me, Pilate! - LeGette Blythe 557
Hidden Victory: A Novel of Jesus - Herbert Francis
   Smith 5921
Hortensius, Friend of Nero - Edith Pargeter 4798
How Far to Bethlehem? - Norah Lofts 3846
I Am a Barbarian - Edgar Rice Burroughs 807
I, Claudius - Robert Graves 2547
I, Judas - Taylor Caldwell 859
I, Nathanael, Knew Jesus - William Gilbert Van Tassel
   Sutpen 6133
I, Paul - Rex Miller 4401
If I Forget Thee - Robert S. Deropp 1621
The Illusionist - Anita Mason 4144
An Imaginary Life - David Malouf 4047
The Imperial Governor - George Shipway 5828
The Iron Hand of Mars - Lindsey Davis 1528
The Jew of Rome - Lion Feuchtwanger 2071
Josephus - Lion Feuchtwanger 2072
Josephus and the Emperor - Lion
   Feuchtwanger 2073
Judas - Igal Mossinsohn 4500
Justus - Arthur L. Lapham 3663
King Jesus - Robert Graves 2549
The Kingdom of the Wicked - Anthony Burgess 778
The Knifeman: A Novel of Judas Iscariot - William
   Rayner 5271
The Lance of Longinus - Hubertus Loewenstein 3833
Last Act in Palmyra - Lindsey Davis 1529
The Last Days - William Rayner 5272
The Last Days of Pompeii - Edward Bulwer-
   Lytton 768
The Last Temptation of Christ - Nikos
   Kazantzakis 3384
The Last World: A Novel with an Ovidian Repertory -
   Christoph Ransmayr 5253
Lazarus - Alain Absire 15
The Letters of Nicodemus - Jan Dobraczynski 1655
The Life of Jesus: An Apocryphal Novel - Toby
   Olson 4731
The Light Bearer - Donna Gillespie 2419
Live From Golgotha - Gore Vidal 6491
The Lord Jesus - Robert Payne 4854
The Lost Eagles - Ralph Graves 2542
The Lost Legion - H. Warner Munn 4516
A Love Divine - Alexandra Ripley 5340
The Magdalene Gospel - Mary Ellen Ashcroft 203
Man Before the Morning - Cecil Maiden 4032
Man of Nazareth - Anthony Burgess 779
Man on Fire: A Novel on the Life of St. Paul -
   LeGette Blythe 558
Marcus - Laurene Chinn 1068

Martha, Martha - Patricia McGerr 4274
Mary - Sholem Asch 198
Mary of Magdala - Anne C. Williman 6791
Mary of Nazareth - Esther Kellner 3394
The Master - Max Brod 702
The Messiah - Marjorie Holmes 3003
The Moon under Her Feet - Ceysta Kinstler 3503
The Nazarene - Sholem Asch 200
Nero - Mary Teresa Ronalds 5437
No King but Caesar - Anne Powers 5151
Octavia: A Tale of Ancient Rome - Seymour Van
   Santvoord 6428
People of the Lakes - W. Michael Gear 2336
The Pirate From Rome - John V.D.
   Southworth 5952
Pontius Pilate: A Biographical Novel - Paul L.
   Maier 4034
Pontius Pilate Reflects - Werner Koch 3529
Poseidon's Gold - Lindsey Davis 1530
Quo Vadis - Henryk Sienkiewicz 5848
Red Queen, White Queen - Henry Treece 6332
Refuge in Avalon - Marguerite Steedman 5984
Road From Olivet - Edward Francis Murphy 4523
*The Road to Bithynia: A Novel of Luke, the Beloved
   Physician* - Frank G. Slaughter 5897
The Robber: A Tale of the Time of the Herods -
   Bertram Brooker 706
The Robe - Lloyd C. Douglas 1703
The Roman - Mika Waltari 6554
Saint Paul: A Historical Novel of His Life - Leon
   Poirier 5081
Salome, Princess of Galilee - Henry Denker 1611
The Salt of the Earth - Carlo Monterosso 4437
The Same Scourge - John Goldthorpe 2464
The Scarlet Lily - Edward Francis Murphy 4524
Scorpus the Moor - Leslie Turner White 6690
The Secret of the Kingdom - Mika Waltari 6555
Shadows in Bronze - Lindsey Davis 1531
The Shepherd - Robert Payne 4855
The Silver Chalice - Thomas B. Costain 1370
The Silver Pigs - Lindsey Davis 1532
*The Sins of Herod: A Novel of Rome and the Early
   Church* - Frank G. Slaughter 5900
Son of Judah - Dan Levin 3738
The Soothsayer - Laurene Chinn 1069
Soul Flame - Barbara Wood 6850
A Tear for Judas - LeGette Blythe 559
The Tenth Measure - Brenda Lesley Segal 5721
The Tentmaker - Julius Berstl 486
The Testament of Theophilus - Leonard
   Wibberley 6730
The Thorn of Arimathea - Frank G. Slaughter 5905
Three From Galilee: The Young Man From Nazareth -
   Marjorie Holmes 3004
The Three Legions - Gregory Solon 5941
Tiberius: The Memoirs of the Emperor - Allan
   Massie 4169
A Time for Judas - Morley Callaghan 866
Time to Depart - Lindsey Davis 1533
The Triumph - Ernest K. Gann 2280
Two From Galilee: A Love Story - Marjorie
   Holmes 3005
Two Thieves - Manuel Komroff 3535
*Upon This Rock: A Novel of Simon Peter, Prince of
   Apostles* - Frank G. Slaughter 5906
Upon This Rock: The Life of St. Peter - Walter F.
   Murphy 4526
Venus in Copper - Lindsey Davis 1534
The Voices of Masada - David Kossoff 3545
Warrior Queen - James Sinclair 5865
The Way - J.M. Hartley 2761
Who Came by Night - Roland Nicholas 4608
The Wolf of Masada - John Fredman 2220
A Woman of Samaria - James W. Ingles 3104
The Word and the Sword - Theo Lang 3662
Yeshua: The Gospel of St. Thomas - Alan Decker
   McNarie 4306
Candle in the Window - Christina Dodd 1662
Wyvern - A.A. Attanasio 227

Myself, Christopher Wren - David Weiss 6606

2nd CENTURY

As a Driven Leaf - Milton Steinberg 5992
Behold, We Live - Charles Dunscomb 1812
Between Eternities - Robert H. Pilpel 5001
The Crow Goddess - Patricia Finney 2094
*The Equinox: A Novel of Rome in the Time of
   Commodus* - Carol Saylor 5622
A Fig in Winter - Willa Gibbs 2400
Hadrian's Memoirs - Marguerite Yourcenar 6947
If I Forget Thee - Brenda Lesley Segal 5720
Lady of Conquest - Teresa Medeiros 4322
Marius the Epicurean - Walter Pater 4826
Prince of Israel - Elias Gilner 2422
Roman Nights - Ron Burns 803
The Second Crucifixion - Maurice Samuel 5579
A Shadow of Gulls - Patricia Finney 2096
The Side of the Moon - Amanda Prantera 5162
Simon Bar Cochba: Rebellion in Judea - Merton
   Finch 2086
The Soldier and the Sage: A Novel about Akiba -
   Richard G. Hubler 3065
*Street of the Sandalmakers: A Tale of Rome in the
   Time of Marcus Aurelius* - Nis Peterson 4977
The Sword and the Promise - Benjamin Siegel 5845
Votan - John James 3162
Lady of Conquest - Teresa Medeiros 4322

3rd CENTURY

Caesar of the Narrow Seas - John Gloag 2433
Confessors of the Name - Gladys Schmitt 5640
Family Favorites - Alfred Duggan 1766
Harkfast: The Making of the King - Hugh C.
   Rae 5238
The Living Wood - Louis De Wohl 1571
Origen: A Historical Novel - Theodore Vrettos 6515
Queen of the East - Alexander Baron 336
Roman Wall - Bryher 745

4th CENTURY

The Beacon of Alexandria - Gillian Bradshaw 627
The Centurion - Jan de Hartog 2762
Constantine: The Miracle of the Flaming Cross -
   Frank G. Slaughter 5883
The Converts: A Historical Novel - Rex
   Warner 6564
The Death of the Gods - Dmitri Merezhkovski 4338
The Deer Cry - William Greenough Schofield 5650
Dominic - Kathleen Robinson 5405
Golden Fire - Jonathan Fast 2047
Imperial Renegade - Louis De Wohl 1567
Julian - Gore Vidal 6489
The Last Athenian - Viktor Rydberg 5543
The Last Romans - Teodor Jeske-Choinski 3216
The Living Wood - Louis De Wohl 1571
The Man on the White Horse - Warwick
   Deeping 1577
The Restless Flame - Louis De Wohl 1573
The Skystone: The Forging of Arthur's Britain - Jack
   Whyte 6726
Son of Tears - Henry W. Coray 1320
Threshold of Fire - Hella S. Haasse 2633

5th CENTURY

Arthur - Stephen R. Lawhead 3679
Arthur Rex: A Legendary Novel - Thomas
   Berger 477
Attila's Treasure - Stephan Grundy 2606
Brendan - Frederick Buechner 762
Bury Me in Ravenna - Agnes Carr Vaughan 6432
Captive of Rome - Theodora McCormick Du
   Bois 1740
The Chessboard Queen - Sharan Newman 4597

Child of the Northern Spring - Persia Woolley 6867
The Coming of the King - Nikolai Tolstoy 6296
Conscience of the King - Alfred Duggan 1763
The Crimson Chalice - Victor Canning 882
The Crystal Cave - Mary Stewart 6029
Darkness and the Dawn - Thomas B. Costain 1364
The Death of Attila - Cecelia Holland 2986
The Deer Cry - William Greenough Schofield 5650
Druid's Enchantment - Millie J. Ragosta 5240
The Duke of War - Walter O'Meara 4734
Eagle in the Snow - Wallace Breem 654
The Eagles Depart - John Gloag 2434
The Emperor Arthur - Godfrey Turton 6368
The Four Rivers of Paradise - Helen Constance
   White 6678
Guinevere - Sharan Newman 4600
Guinevere Evermore - Sharan Newman 4601
Guinevere: The Legend in Autumn - Persia
   Woolley 6868
Heaven's Only Daughter - Kathleen Robinson 5406
The Hollow Hills - Mary Stewart 6030
Hypatia - Charles Kingsley 3498
The Idylls of the Queen - Phyllis Ann Karr 3367
Imperial Purple - Gillian Bradshaw 631
In the Shadow of the Oak King - Courtway
   Jones 3271
The Kingmaking - Helen Hollick 3000
The Last Enchantment - Mary Stewart 6031
The Last of the Wine - Mary Renault 5299
The Lion and the Cross - Joan Lesley
   Hamilton 2669
The Little Emperors - Alfred Duggan 1770
Merlin - Stephen R. Lawhead 3681
The Mists of Avalon - Marion Zimmer Bradley 626
The Pagan King - Edison Marshall 4109
Pendragon - Stephen R. Lawhead 3682
Pendragon's Banner - Helen Hollick 3001
The Prince and the Pilgrim - Mary Stewart 6032
Queen of the Summer Stars - Persia Woolley 6869
The Queen's Knight - Marvin Borowsky 585
The Restless Flame - Louis De Wohl 1573
The Road to Avalon - Joan Wolf 6842
Roman Go Home! - Adam Fergusson 2065
Sign of the Pagan - Don Tracy 6312
The Singing Sword - Jack Whyte 6725
The Sinner of Saint Ambrose - Robert
   Raynolds 5275
The Skystone: The Forging of Arthur's Britain - Jack
   Whyte 6726
Son of Tears - Henry W. Coray 1320
Sword at Sunset - Rosemary Sutcliff 6125
Taliesin - Stephen R. Lawhead 3683
Threshold of Fire - Hella S. Haasse 2633
Throne of the World - Louis De Wohl 1575
To Love Again - Bertrice Small 5913
The Twelve Pictures - Edith Simon 5857
The Wicked Day - Mary Stewart 6033
The Winter King - Bernard Cornwell 1351
Witch of the North - Courtway Jones 3272
The Wolf and the Raven - Diana L. Paxson 4848

6th CENTURY

Artorius Rex - John Gloag 2432
Basilissa: A Tale of the Empress Theodora - John
   Masefield 4142
The Bearkeeper's Daughter - Gillian Bradshaw 628
Beloved Exile - Parke Godwin 2446
Born of the Sun - Joan Wolf 6837
Brendan - Frederick Buechner 762
Citadel of God: A Novel of Saint Benedict - Louis De
   Wohl 1563
A Connecticut Yankee in King Arthur's Court - Mark
   Twain 6371
Conscience of the King - Alfred Duggan 1763
Count Belisarius - Robert Graves 2544
The Fair - Robert Nathan 4559

The Female: A Novel of Another Time - Paul I.
   Wellman 6617
Firelord - Parke Godwin 2447
A Flame in Byzantium - Chelsea Quinn Yarbro 6899
Fleet Surgeon to Pharaoh - Sheldon Jacobson 3140
The Great Captains - Henry Treece 6329
The Green Man - Henry Treece 6330
Gregory the Great - Gerhart Ellert 1913
Hawk of May - Gillian Bradshaw 629
In Winter's Shadow - Gillian Bradshaw 632
Isle of Glory - Jane Oliver 4723
Kingdom of Summer - Gillian Bradshaw 633
Last of Britain - Meriol Trevor 6343
The Last Pendragon - Robert Rice 5316
Lest Darkness Fall - L. Sprague De Camp 1557
Paradise - Dikkon Eberhart 1831
The Pendragon - Catherine Christian 1075
People of the River - W. Michael Gear 2338
Ruan - Bryher 746
Theodora - Samuel Edwards 1891
Theodora and the Emperor - Harold Lamb 3608
The Tower of Beowulf - Parke Godwin 2450
The Unspeakables: A Tale of Lombardy - Laverne
   Gay 2326
The Vandal - Richard O'Connor 4687
The Voice of Allah - Edwin P. Hoyt 3062
The White Raven - Diana L. Paxson 4847
Women in the Wall - Julia O'Faolain 4691

7th CENTURY

Absolution by Murder - Peter Tremayne 6334
Bride of the Spear - Kathleen Herbert 2851
The Chinese Nail Murders - Robert van Gulik 6413
Deception - Eleanor Cooney 1295
The Emperor's Pearl - Robert van Gulik 6414
Empress - Evelyn McCune 4238
Green Dragon, White Tiger - Annette Motley 4501
Gregory the Great - Gerhart Ellert 1913
The Haunted Monastery - Robert van Gulik 6415
The Jade Stalk - Jonathan Fast 2048
The Lacquer Screen - Robert van Gulik 6416
Lady Wu - Yutang Lin 3782
The Monkey and the Tiger - Robert van Gulik 6417
Murder in Canton - Robert van Gulik 6418
Necklace and Calabash - Robert van Gulik 6419
The Phantom of the Temple - Robert van Gulik 6420
Queen of the Lightning - Kathleen Herbert 2852
The Red Pavilion - Robert van Gulik 6421
The Vision of Stephen: An Elegy - Lolah
   Burford 775
The Voice of Allah - Edwin P. Hoyt 3062
The Willow Pattern - Robert van Gulik 6422

8th CENTURY

The Court of the Lion - Eleanor Cooney 1294
Deception - Eleanor Cooney 1295
Go Ask the River - Evelyn Eaton 1826
Silk Road - Jeanne Larsen 3670
Swords of Anjou - Mario Pei 4890
Tikal: A Novel about the Maya - Daniel Peters 4947
The Vermilion Bridge - Shelley Mydans 4539
Winter Cherry - Keith West 6632

9th CENTURY

The Adversary - Jan Widgery 6738
The Belt of Gold - Cecelia Holland 2984
By Love Enslaved - Phoebe Conn 1255
The Edge of Light - Joan Wolf 6839
The Emerald Crown - Theodora McCormick Du
   Bois 1741
The Flame in the Dark - Basil Bonallack 568
Go Ask the River - Evelyn Eaton 1826
The Hammer and the Cross - Harry Harrison 2736
Joanna the Pope - Daniel Panger 4785
The King Liveth - Jeffrey Farnol 2013

The Marsh King - C. Walter Hodges 2975
Pope Joan - Donna Woolfolk Cross 1433
The Price of Blood - Doris Sutcliffe Adams 24
Raven's Wind - Victor Canning 883
The Right Line of Cedric - Alfred Duggan 1773
Tikal: A Novel about the Maya - Daniel Peters 4947
The Tyrant of Bagdhad - Glenn Pierce 4996
The Viking - Edison Marshall 4113
The Viking's Woman - Heather Graham 2520
The Winter Servant - M.H. Davis 1537

10th CENTURY

Avalon - Anya Seton 5748
Bathsheba - Torgny Lindgren 3789
Beguiled - Alice Borchardt 577
Better in the Dark - Chelsea Quinn Yarbro 6894
Byzantium - Stephen R. Lawhead 3680
The Cross and the Sword - Evangeline Walton 6558
Devoted - Alice Borchardt 578
The Eagle's Daughter - Judith Tarr 6165
Eaters of the Dead - Michael Crichton 1425
Fire in the Ice - Dorothy James Roberts 5375
The Gallowglass - Howard Breslin 666
The Gentle Conqueror - Mary Ellen Gronau 2597
The Harp and the Blade - John Myers 4543
In the Falcon's Claw: A Novel of the Year 1000 -
   Chet Raymo 5257
The Long Ships - Frans Gunnar Bengtsson 442
Lord of Hawkfell Island - Catherine Coulter 1376
The Lord of the Last Days: Visions of the Year 1000 -
   Homero Aridjis 188
Passionate Warriors - Mary Ellen Gronau 2598

11th CENTURY

The Bastard King - Jean Plaidy 5004
The Battle-Ax of God - Le Roy MacLeod 4007
Belmarch: A Legend of the First Crusade -
   Christopher Davis 1514
Bond of Honour - Catherine Todd 6284
*A Booke of Days: A Journal of the Crusade by Roger,
   Duke of Lunel* - Stephen J. Rivele 5351
The Breath of Kings - Gene Farrington 2019
Byzantium - Michael Ennis 1945
The Conqueror - Georgette Heyer 2881
The Conqueror's Wife - Noel B. Gerson 2363
Count Bohemond - Alfred Duggan 1764
Count Robert of Paris - Sir Walter Scott 5695
The Cunning of the Dove - Alfred Duggan 1765
The Disputed Crown - Valerie Anand 128
The Dragons of Archenfield - Edward Marston 4119
The Exile Way - Ann Woodward 6865
The Firedrake - Cecelia Holland 2988
Flambard's Confession - Marilyn Durham 1816
*Fortune's Knave: The Making of William the
   Conqueror* - Mary Lide 3774
The Foster Brothers - Edward Frankland 2202
The Fourteenth of October - Bryher 742
The Gallowglass - Howard Breslin 666
Gildenford - Valerie Anand 130
God's Equal - Alain Absire 14
The Golden Warrior: The Story of Harold and William
   - Hope Muntz 4517
Great Maria - Cecelia Holland 2989
Gudrid's Saga - Constance Irwin 3115
Harold, the Last of the Saxon Kings - Edward Bulwer-
   Lytton 767
Harold Was My King - Hilda Lewis 3749
Hereward the Wake - Charles Kingsley 3497
The Ice Shirt - William T. Vollmann 6509
In the Falcon's Claw: A Novel of the Year 1000 -
   Chet Raymo 5257
The Infidel - Georgia Elizabeth Taylor 6182
The Infidels - Chloe Gartner 2308
The Invention of Truth - Marta Morazzoni 4449
The Iron Crown - Clare Barroll 354
King Hereafter - Dorothy Dunnett 1802

King of the Wood - Valerie Anand 131
The Kings in Winter - Cecelia Holland 2991
Knight with Armour - Alfred Duggan 1767
The Lady for Ransom - Alfred Duggan 1768
Lady Godiva and Master Tom - Raoul Cohen Faure 2052
Lady of Moray - Bonnie Copeland 1318
The Last Englishman: The Story of Hereward the Wake - Hebe Weenolsen 6596
The Lion of Ireland - Morgan Llywelyn 3822
The Lion of Justice - Jean Plaidy 5031
The Lions of the North - Edward Marston 4121
Madselin - Norah Lofts 3853
A Moment in Time - Bertrice Small 5911
The Norman Pretender - Valerie Anand 132
Not Built with Hands - Helen Constance White 6679
The Paladin - George Shipway 5830
The Physician - Noah Gordon 2482
Pilgermann - Russell Hoban 2960
Pride of Lions - Morgan Llywelyn 3823
Princess of Fire - Shannon Drake 1718
Princess of the Veil - Helen Mittermeyer 4420
The Proud Villeins - Valerie Anand 133
The Ravens of Blackwater - Edward Marston 4126
Red Lion and Gold Dragon - Rosemary Sprague 5969
Robin and the King - Parke Godwin 2448
Runestone - Don Coldsmith 1186
The Saxon Tapestry - Sile Rice 5317
Shards of Empire - Susan Schwartz 5677
Sherwood - Parke Godwin 2449
Silver Leopard - F. van Wyck Mason 4160
Sing Morning Star - Jane Oliver 4727
Son of Dust - H.F.M. Prescott 5171
This January Tale - Bryher 747
This Land Fulfilled - Charles Andrew Brady 636
The Trees of the Folkungs - Verner Von Heidenstam 2817
Under the Winter Moon - Teresa Brooke 705
A Viking's Daughter - John Andrews 147
West with the Vikings - Edison Marshall 4114
Wife to the Bastard - Hilda Lewis 3753
The Wild Hunt - Elizabeth Chadwick 969
The Wind From Hastings - Morgan Llywelyn 3825
Wine of Satan - Laverne Gay 2327
The Wolves of Savernake - Edward Marston 4130

12th CENTURY

Against the Fall of Night - Michael Arnold 193
Alamut - Judith Tarr 6164
Ann of Cambray - Mary Lide 3772
Banners of Gold - Pamela Kaufman 3371
Beloved Enemy: The Passions of Eleanor of Aquitaine - Ellen Jones 3288
Below the Salt - Thomas B. Costain 1362
The Betrothed - Sir Walter Scott 5691
Bird of Fire: A Tale of Francis of Assisi - Helen Constance White 6676
The Blue Falcon - Robyn Carr 935
Bond of Blood - Roberta Gellis 2349
The Bride - Julie Garwood 2311
Bronze Mirror - Jeanne Larsen 3668
Brother Cadfael's Penance - Ellis Peters 4955
Champion - L. Christian Balling 285
The Confessions of Brother Halvin - Ellis Peters 4956
The Courts of Love - Jean Plaidy 5010
The Courts of Love: A Romance of Medieval France - Peter Bourne 592
Crusader's Torch - Chelsea Quinn Yarbro 6897
Dead Man's Ransom - Ellis Peters 4957
Death Comes as Epiphany - Sharan Newman 4598
Death of the Red King - Pamela Bennetts 448
Defy Not the Heart - Johanna Lindsey 3794
The Devil Is Loose - Graham Shelby 5790
The Devil's Door - Sharan Newman 4599
The Devil's Novice - Ellis Peters 4958

The Doctor From Cordova: A Biographical Novel about the Great Philosopher Maimonides - Herbert Le Porrier 3693
The Earl - Cecelia Holland 2987
The Earth Is the Lord's: A Tale of the Rise of Genghis Khan - Taylor Caldwell 855
Eleanor the Queen - Norah Lofts 3842
Emerald Fire - Laurie Grant 2537
An Excellent Mystery - Ellis Peters 4959
The Fatal Crown - Ellen Jones 3289
Fitzempress' Law - Diana Norman 4644
The Fool of Venus - George William Cronyn 1428
The Garden of Persephone - Cesar J. Rotondi 5510
Gay Crusader - Cleone Knox 3528
Gilded Spurs - Grace Ingram 3105
The Godforgotten - Gladys Schmitt 5642
Godric - Frederick Buechner 763
The Golden Knight - George Challis 971
Harp into Battle - Cecil Maiden 4031
The Heart of the Lion - Jean Plaidy 5020
The Heike Story - Eiji Yoshikawa 6934
The Heirs of the Kingdom - Zoe Oldenbourg 4716
Here Be Dragons - Sharon Kay Penman 4904
The Heretic's Apprentice - Ellis Peters 4960
The Hermit of Eyton Forest - Ellis Peters 4961
The Holy Thief - Ellis Peters 4962
Ivanhoe - Sir Walter Scott 5699
Jerusalem - Cecelia Holland 2990
The Journal of Hildegard of Bingen - Barbara Lachman 3578
Kingdom of the Grail - A.A. Attanasio 226
King's Man - C.M. Edmondston 1880
The Kings of Vain Intent - Graham Shelby 5791
The King's Persons - Joanne Greenberg 2573
Kinsmen of the Grail - Dorothy James Roberts 5376
The Knight - George Shipway 5829
Knight's Honor - Roberta Gellis 2351
The Knights of Dark Renown - Graham Shelby 5792
Lady of Hay - Barbara Erskine 1955
The Leopard Unleashed - Elizabeth Chadwick 967
The Leper King - Zofja Kossak-Szczucka 3544
The Leper of St. Giles - Ellis Peters 4963
The Lion of Christ - Margaret Butler 823
The Lion of England - Margaret Butler 824
The Lion of Justice - Margaret Butler 825
The Lion of Justice - Jean Plaidy 5031
Lionheart!: A Novel of Richard I, King of England - Martha Rofheart 5428
Locksley - Nicholas Chase 1003
The Love of Fingin O'Lea - Theodora McCormick Du Bois 1743
The Lute Player - Norah Lofts 3852
Men Like Shadows - Dorothy Charques 1000
Monk's Hood - Ellis Peters 4964
A Morbid Taste for Bones - Ellis Peters 4965
The Morning Gift - Diana Norman 4645
Mortal Love: A Novel of Eleanor of Aquitaine - Linda Hutchins 3090
My Beautiful White Roses - Michael Lechner 3703
My Life for My Sheep - Alfred Duggan 1772
My Lord Brother the Lionheart - Molly Costain Haycraft 2795
No Man's Son - Doris Sutcliffe Adams 23
One Corpse Too Many - Ellis Peters 4966
Ordeal by Silence - Prudence Andrew 142
The Paladin - George Shipway 5830
The Passionate Enemies - Jean Plaidy 5039
People of the Silence - W. Michael Gear 2340
The Perfect Joy of St. Francis - Felix Timmermans 6281
Peter Abelard: A Novel - Helen Waddell 6517
The Pilgrim of Hate - Ellis Peters 4967
The Pillars of the Earth - Ken Follett 2149
The Plantagenet Prelude - Jean Plaidy 5041
The Potter's Field - Ellis Peters 4968
The Prince of Darkness - Jean Plaidy 5044
The Proud Villeins - Valerie Anand 133
Queen of Swords - Judith Tarr 6169
The Queen's Man - Sharon Kay Penman 4905

The Queen's War: A Novel of Eleanor of Aquitaine - Jeanne Mackin 3996
The Rain Maiden - Jill M. Phillips 4985
The Raven in the Foregate - Ellis Peters 4969
Red Adam's Lady - Grace Ingram 3106
The Revolt of the Eaglets - Jean Plaidy 5057
Richard and the Knights of God - Pamela Bennetts 454
Ride Home Tomorrow - Evan John 3221
The Ronin - William Dale Jennings 3212
The Rose Rent - Ellis Peters 4970
A Royal Quest - Mary Lide 3777
Ruler of the Sky: A Novel of Genghis Khan - Pamela Sargent 5606
The Running Vixen - Elizabeth Chadwick 968
St. Peter's Fair - Ellis Peters 4971
The Sanctuary Sparrow - Ellis Peters 4972
The Saracen Blade - Frank Yerby 6926
A Search for a King: A 12th-Century Legend - Gore Vidal 6492
Shield of Three Lions - Pamela Kaufman 3372
Sir Pagan - Henry John Colyton 1222
Stealing Heaven: The Love Story of Heloise and Abelard - Marion Meade 4317
Stephen and the Sleeping Saints - Pamela Bennetts 457
The Stones of the Abbey - Fernand Pouillon 5144
Strong as Death - Sharan Newman 4602
The Summer of the Danes - Ellis Peters 4973
The Sword of Hachiman - Lynn Guest 2608
The Swords of December - Robert York 6933
The Talisman - Sir Walter Scott 5708
The Tall One - Barbara Jefferis 3175
Their Most Serene Majesties - Ange Vlachos 6505
Thomas: A Novel of the Life, Passions, and Miracles of Becket - Shelley Mydans 4538
Time of the Unicorn - Barbara Jefferis 3176
To Keep This Oath - Hebe Weenolsen 6597
Tomorrow's Fire - Jay Williams 6775
Trail and Triumph: A Novel about Maimonides - Lester M. Morrison 4485
The Troubadour's Romance - Robyn Carr 940
The True Cross - Carlo Scarfoglio 5629
Two Ravens - Cecelia Holland 2997
The Unhurrying Chase - H.F.M. Prescott 5172
The Virgin in the Ice - Ellis Peters 4974
The Walking Drum - Louis L'Amour 3632
The Wandering Arm - Sharan Newman 4603
When Christ and His Saints Slept - Sharon Kay Penman 4908
When God Slept - Peter Bourne 597
Where Magic Dwells - Rexanne Becnel 411
The Wild Hunt - Elizabeth Chadwick 969
Wine of Satan - Laverne Gay 2327
The Wrong Horse - Jean Bassan 374

13th CENTURY

Alexander the Glorious - Jane Oliver 4719
Angel of Death - P.C. Doherty 1670
Antichrist: A Novel of the Emperor Frederick II - Cecelia Holland 2982
Ardent Flame - Frances Winwar 6829
An Army of Children - Evan H. Rhodes 5306
The Axe - Sigrid Undset 6378
The Barons of Runnymede - Pamela Bennetts 445
The Battle of the Queens - Jean Plaidy 5005
Below the Salt - Thomas B. Costain 1362
Bernadin, My Love - Leonard Rossiter 5506
Bird of Fire: A Tale of Francis of Assisi - Helen Constance White 6676
The Black Rose - Thomas B. Costain 1363
Blessed Are the Meek: A Novel about St. Francis of Assisi - Zofja Kossak-Szczucka 3542
Bodin, 1349: An Epic Novel of Christians and Jews in the Plague Years - Roberta Kalechofsky 3322
Braveheart - Randall Wallace 6538
The Briar Rose - Linda Neale 4561

The Brothers of Gwynedd - Edith Pargeter 4796
Caravan to Kanadu: A Novel of Marco Polo - Edison Marshall 4103
Cities of the Flesh - Zoe Oldenbourg 4713
Concordia - Frances Fleetwood 2124
The Cornerstone - Zoe Oldenbourg 4714
Cross, Sword, and Arrow - Gladys H. Barr 340
The Crown in Darkness - P.C. Doherty 1671
Crusader's Torch - Chelsea Quinn Yarbro 6897
The De Montfort Legacy - Pamela Bennetts 447
Deep Are the Valleys - Hannah Closs 1129
Destiny of Fire - Zoe Oldenbourg 4715
The Devil's Cross - Walter O'Meara 4733
Doctor Mirabilis - James Blish 550
A Dragon for Edward - Pamela Bennetts 450
Eagle of the Gredos - Claude Jack Osgood 4761
Earth Song - Catherine Coulter 1374
Elizabeth's Greetings - Rosemary Haughton 2774
The Emperor, the Sages and Death - Rachel Berdach 475
The Falcon and the Flower - Virginia Henley 2826
Falconer's Crusade - Ian Morson 4493
Falconer's Judgement - Ian Morson 4494
Falls the Shadow - Sharon Kay Penman 4903
The Follies of the King - Jean Plaidy 5014
The Golden Exile - Lawrence Schoonover 5664
The Great Infidel - Joseph Jay Deiss 1582
Hammer of the Scots - Jean Plaidy 5018
The Heaven Tree Trilogy - Edith Pargeter 4797
Here Be Dragons - Sharon Kay Penman 4904
High Are the Mountains - Hannah Closs 1130
In the Shadow of Midnight - Marsha Canham 880
Invisible Cities - Italo Calvino 867
The Journeyer - Gary Jennings 3194
The Joyful Beggar: A Novel of St. Francis of Assisi - Louis De Wohl 1568
The Keys of England - William Victor Cooke 1271
The King's Daughters - Molly Costain Haycraft 2793
Knights - Linda Lael Miller 4399
Lady of the Forest - Jennifer Roberson 5368
Leopards and Lilies - Alfred Duggan 1769
Let the Drum Speak: A Novel of Ancient America - Linda Lay Shuler 5837
The Lion of England - Eve Trevaskis 6336
Lionheart!: A Novel of Richard I, King of England - Martha Rofheart 5428
Lord Geoffrey's Fancy - Alfred Duggan 1771
The Lost Flight - H.F.M. Prescott 5169
The Lost Lands - Peter Vansittart 6430
The Marriage of Meggotta - Edith Pargeter 4799
Masques of Gold - Roberta Gellis 2352
Messer Marco Polo - Donn Byrne 840
Mirage - Pauline Gedge 2346
Mortal Love: A Novel of Eleanor of Aquitaine - Linda Hutchins 3090
My Beautiful White Roses - Michael Lechner 3703
My Gallant Enemy - Rexanne Becnel 409
Myself as Witness - James Goldman 2458
Orlok - Don Dandrea 1461
Our Lives Have Just Begun - Henry Myers 4541
Path of the Eclipse - Chelsea Quinn Yarbro 6905
The Perfect Joy of St. Francis - Felix Timmermans 6281
The Prince of Darkness - Jean Plaidy 5044
The Queen From Provence - Jean Plaidy 5047
The Quiet Light - Louis De Wohl 1572
The Reckoning - Sharon Kay Penman 4906
Rosehaven - Catherine Coulter 1380
Ruler of the Sky: A Novel of Genghis Khan - Pamela Sargent 5606
The Ruthless Yeomen - Valerie Anand 134
Saint Francis - Nikos Kazantzakis 3385
Sakuran: A Novel of Medieval Japan - Edward Tolosko 6292
The Saracen Blade - Frank Yerby 6926
Satan in St. Mary's - P.C. Doherty 1676
Satan's Fire - P.C. Doherty 1677
The Scottish Chiefs - Jane Porter 5135

Secret Song - Catherine Coulter 1381
The Seven Hills of Paradise - Rosemary Simpson 5859
She Who Remembers - Linda Lay Shuler 5838
The Sheriff of Nottingham - Richard Kluger 3512
Shield of Honor - Alice Walworth Graham 2511
Shike: Time of Dragons - Robert Shea 5784
The Siege - Jay Williams 6773
The Silent Tarn - Hannah Closs 1131
A Silver Mirror - Roberta Gellis 2353
Sing to the Sun - Lucille Borden 579
The Snake Pit - Sigrid Undset 6383
Sons of the Steppe: The Story of How the Conqueror Genghis Khan Was Overcome - Hans Baumann 380
The Spire - William Golding 2457
Spy in Chancery - P.C. Doherty 1680
Sybille - Marion Meade 4318
This Bright Sword - Donald Barr Chidsey 1066
The Trees of the Folkungs - Verner Von Heidenstam 2817
True Thomas - Nigel Tranter 6322
The Trumpet of God - David Duncan 1784
The Unholy Pilgrim - R.F. Tapsell 6161
Until the Sun Falls - Cecelia Holland 2998
Voice of the Eagle - Linda Lay Shuler 5839
Vows of the Peacock - Alice Walworth Graham 2513
The Wanderer: A Novel of Dante and Beatrice - Nathan Schachner 5633
The White Cutter - David Pownall 5158
Witness to Treason - Millie J. Ragosta 5244
The Wolf at the Door - Graham Shelby 5793
The Woman in the Cloak - Pamela Hill 2949

14th CENTURY

The Age of Miracles - Catherine MacCoun 3960
An Ancient Evil - C.L. Grace 2504
The Apothecary Rose - Candace M. Robb 5364
The Bloody Field - Edith Pargeter 4795
Bodin, 1349: An Epic Novel of Christians and Jews in the Plague Years - Roberta Kalechofsky 3322
Braveheart - Randall Wallace 6538
Brazen Whispers - Jane Feather 2055
The Bridal Wreath - Sigrid Undset 6379
By Right of Arms - Robyn Carr 937
Castle Dangerous - Sir Walter Scott 5694
The Constant Star - Prudence Andrew 139
The Corner That Held Them - Sylvia Townsend Warner 6568
The Cross - Sigrid Undset 6380
The Death of a King - P.C. Doherty 1672
Desire and Deceive - Cordia Byers 832
Don Pedro's Captain - Pamela Bennetts 449
Falstaff - Robert Nye 4653
The Gentle Falcon - Hilda Lewis 3747
The Gentle Knight - Philip Lindsay 3791
Glendower Country - Martha Rofheart 5427
The Golden Hand - Edith Simon 5856
Good King Harry - Denise Giardina 2393
The Good Yeomen - Jay Williams 6771
The Greenlanders - Jane Smiley 5915
Guns Forever Echo - Kenneth M. Ellis 1925
Harlot Queen - Hilda Lewis 3748
The House of Kanze - Nobuko Albery 64
The Image of Our Lord - Edward Burman 790
In a Dark Wood Wandering - Hella S. Haasse 2631
In Pursuit of the Green Lion - Judith Merkle Riley 5334
In the Wilderness - Sigrid Undset 6381
The Iron King - Maurice Druon 1732
Isabel the Fair - Margaret Campbell Barnes 323
The Journeyer - Gary Jennings 3194
Katherine - Anya Seton 5752
Kingdom of Shadows - Barbara Erskine 1954
The King's Bishop - Candace M. Robb 5365
Ladies Whose Bright Eyes - Ford Madox Ford 2162

The Lady Chapel - Candace M. Robb 5366
The Lady Royal - Molly Costain Haycraft 2794
Lay Siege to Heaven: A Novel of Saint Catherine of Siena - Louis De Wohl 1570
The Lily and the Lion - Maurice Druon 1733
The Lion and the Leopard - Mary Ellen Johnson 3226
The Lion Is Come - Jane Oliver 4725
The Lords of Lancaster - Pamela Bennetts 452
The Lords of Vaumartin - Cecelia Holland 2992
The Love Knot - Catherine Darby 1482
Marjorie of Scotland - Pamela Hill 2939
Master of the World - Cothburn O'Neal 4738
The Mistress of Husaby - Sigrid Undset 6382
Morality Play - Barry Unsworth 6387
Mortal Pageant - Johan Fabricius 1993
My Lord John - Georgette Heyer 2895
The Name of the Rose - Umberto Eco 1850
The Nightingale Gallery - Paul Harding 2684
The Nun's Tale - Candace M. Robb 5367
Passage to Pontefract - Jean Plaidy 5038
The Peacock and the Pearl - Jennifer Lang 3661
The Poisoned Crown - Maurice Druon 1734
The Prince of Darkness - P.C. Doherty 1675
Red Slayer: Being the Second of the Sorrowful Mysteries of Brother Athelstan - Paul Harding 2685
Richard Whittington, London's Mayor - Gwynedd Sudworth 6112
Riddle Me a Murder - Duane Crowley 1435
Ride East! Ride West!: A Romance of the Hundred Years' War - Anne Powers 5154
Rienzi, or The Last of the Tribunes - Edward Bulwer-Lytton 770
Riot at Gravesend: A Novel of Wat Tyler's Rebellion - William Howard Woods 6864
Robert the Bruce: The Path of the Hero King - Nigel Tranter 6318
Robert the Bruce: The Price of the King's Peace - Nigel Tranter 6319
Robert the Bruce: The Steps to the Empty Throne - Nigel Tranter 6320
The Royal Succession - Maurice Druon 1735
The Ruthless Yeomen - Valerie Anand 134
The Saint - Fritz von Unruh 6385
The Scottish Chiefs - Jane Porter 5135
Segaki - David Stacton 5975
The She-Wolf - Pamela Bennetts 456
The She-Wolf of France - Maurice Druon 1736
Simple Prayers - Michael Golding 2452
The Snake Pit - Sigrid Undset 6383
The Son Avenger - Sigrid Undset 6384
The Song of a Dark Angel - P.C. Doherty 1679
The Spanish Doctor - Matt Cohen 1159
A Sparkle From the Coal - Prudence Andrew 144
The Spire - William Golding 2457
The Star of Lancaster - Jean Plaidy 5065
The Strangled Queen - Maurice Druon 1737
A Tapestry of Murders - C.L. Grace 2510
The Teutonic Knights - Henryk Sienkiewicz 5849
Trumpet at the Gate - Jan Widgery 6739
The Ugly Duchess - Lion Feuchtwanger 2075
An Unholy Alliance - Susanna Gregory 2586
A Vision of Light - Judith Merkle Riley 5337
The Vow on the Heron - Jean Plaidy 5074
Vows of the Peacock - Alice Walworth Graham 2513
A Walk with Love and Death - Hans Koning 3539
Who Was Then the Gentleman - Charles E. Israel 3125
Within the Hollow Crown - Margaret Campbell Barnes 331
Witness to Treason - Millie J. Ragosta 5244
The Woman in the Cloak - Pamela Hill 2949
The Year of the Death - Reuben R. Merliss 4343

15th CENTURY

1492 - Newton Frolich   2236
1492 - Mary Johnston   3228
1492: The Life and Times of Juan Cabezon of Castile - Homero Aridjis   187
The Agony and the Ecstasy - Irving Stone   6054
Anne of Geierstein - Sir Walter Scott   5689
An Army of Angels: A Novel of Joan of Arc - Pamela Marcantel   4079
The Autobiography of Henry VIII - Margaret George   2355
Axe for an Abbot - Elizabeth Eyre   1989
Bay of Arrows - Jay Parini   4800
La Belle Sorel - Jacques Carton   949
Beloved Lady - Barbara Jefferis   3174
Bianca - Mabel Conquist   1257
The Bishop's Tale - Margaret Frazer   2215
The Black Arrow - Robert Louis Stevenson   6008
Blood of the Boar - Margaret Abbey   2
Blood Royal - Mollie Hardwick   2690
The Bloody Field - Edith Pargeter   4795
The Book of Shadows - C.L. Grace   2505
The Borgia Prince - Pamela Bennetts   446
Borgia Testament - Nigel Balchin   277
The Boy's Tale - Margaret Frazer   2216
The Bravo - James Fenimore Cooper   1298
Bravo for the Bride - Elizabeth Eyre   1990
The Bride of Sforza - Miranda Seymour   5760
The Broken Sword - Rhoda S. Edwards   1885
The Burnished Blade - Lawrence Schoonover   5661
Caressa - Linda Lang Bartell   363
Catalina - William Somerset Maugham   4197
Chain of Destiny - Nigel Tranter   6314
The Chancellor - Lawrence Schoonover   5662
Chivalry - Rafael Sabatini   5548
The Cloister and the Hearth - Charles Reade   5279
The Coil of the Serpent - Dexter Allen   94
Columbus: A Romance - Rafael Sabatini   5549
A Comedy of Murders - George Herman   2861
Condottiere - Jan Westcott   6644
The Conquest - Jude Deveraux   1630
Court of Shadows - Cynthia Morgan   4450
The Courts of Illusion - Rosemary Hawley Jarman   3165
Crippled Splendour - Evan John   3219
Crouchback - Carola Oman   4732
Crown in Candlelight - Rosemary Hawley Jarman   3166
Crown of Aloes - Norah Lofts   3840
Crown of Roses - Valerie Anand   127
Daimon - Abel Posse   5140
The Dark Angel - Mika Waltari   6551
Daughter of Shadows - Miranda Seymour   5762
The Daughter of Time - Josephine Tey   6209
Death and the Chapman - Kate Sedley   5715
Doctor Copernicus - John Banville   296
The Dogs of Paradise - Abel Posse   5141
The Dragon and the Rose - Roberta Gellis   2350
The Dragon Waiting: A Masque of History - John M. Ford   2165
Duchess of Milan - Michael Ennis   1946
Epitaph for Three Women - Jean Plaidy   5012
The Eve of Saint Hyacinth - Kate Sedley   5716
The Everlasting Covenant - Robyn Carr   939
The Eye of God - C.L. Grace   2506
Falcon: The Autobiography of His Grace James IV, King of Scots - A.J. Stewart   6021
Falstaff - Robert Nye   4653
The Fate of Princes - P.C. Doherty   1673
Ferdinand and Isabella - Hermann Kesten   3474
Fire and Morning - Francis W. Leary   3696
The Florentine - Sandra Shulman   5840
Fortune Made His Sword - Martha Rofheart   5426
Fortune's Wheel - Rhoda S. Edwards   1886
The Gentle Fury: A Novel of Margaret of Austria - Paul Lewis   3758
The Gentle Infidel - Lawrence Schoonover   5663
Gerait's Daughter - Millie J. Ragosta   5241

Glendower Country - Martha Rofheart   5427
The Golden Chain - Jean Gamo   2275
The Golden Porcupine - Muriel Ray Bolton   567
The Golden Yoke: A Novel of the War of the Roses - Olive Eckerson   1837
The Goldsmith's Wife - Jean Plaidy   5017
Good King Harry - Denise Giardina   2393
The Green Madonna - C.E. L'Ami   3617
Harry of Monmouth - A.M. Maughan   4199
The Heart Is a Traitor - Margaret Abbey   4
The Hepburn - Jan Westcott   6645
Here Lies Margot - Pamela Hill   2935
The Holy Innocents - Kate Sedley   5717
The Homecoming - Norah Lofts   3844
The Hooded Falcon - Prudence Andrew   140
The Hunchback of Notre Dame - Victor Hugo   3076
In a Dark Wood Wandering - Hella S. Haasse   2631
The Inquisitors - Jerzy Andrzejewski   153
The Jaguar and the Golden Stag - Dexter Allen   95
James and Joan - Anne Fremantle   2221
Katharine: The Virgin Widow - Jean Plaidy   5025
The Killing of Richard the Third - Robert Farrington   2020
The King's Bed - Margaret Campbell Barnes   324
The King's Grey Mare - Rosemary Hawley Jarman   3167
The King's Pleasure - Norah Lofts   3847
Knight's Acre - Norah Lofts   3848
The Lady Cicely - Sandra Wilson   6813
The Lady in the Mask - Anne Green   2564
Lady of Monkton - Elizabeth Byrd   835
The Last of the Barons - Edward Bulwer-Lytton   769
Leonardo's Judas - Leo Perutz   4941
Less Fortunate than Fair - Sandra Wilson   6814
Light on Lucrezia - Jean Plaidy   5029
The Lily and the Leopard - Susan Wiggs   6745
The Lodestar - Pamela Belle   432
The Lonely Furrow - Norah Lofts   3849
Lord of the Kongo - Peter Forbath   2155
The Luck of Huemac: A Novel about the Aztecs - Daniel Peters   4946
Madonna of the Seven Hills - Jean Plaidy   5034
Magnificent Enemies - Edgar Maas   3951
The Mapmaker: A Novel of the Days of Prince Henry, the Navigator - Frank G. Slaughter   5893
Martin Valliant - Warwick Deeping   1578
Mass for Arras - Andrzej Szczypiorski   6153
Master of Castile - Samuel Edwards   1888
The Master Painter - Edwin Mullins   4513
The Medici Emerald - Martin Woodhouse   6851
The Medici Guns - Martin Woodhouse   6852
The Medici Hawks - Martin Woodhouse   6853
The Memoirs of Christopher Columbus - Stephen Marlowe   4096
The Memory Cathedral: A Secret History of Leonardo Da Vinci - Jack Dann   1481
Mercedes of Castile - James Fenimore Cooper   1304
The Merchant of Death - C.L. Grace   2508
Merchant of the Ruby - Alice Harwood   2766
The Merchant Prince - Henry Christopher Bailey   267
Michelangelo the Florentine - Sidney Alexander   86
Mistress of the Eagles - Elona Malterre   4052
Mona Lisa: The Woman in the Portrait - Sara Mayfield   4206
The Moneyman - Thomas B. Costain   1368
The Monk - Matthew Gregory Lewis   3756
Monk in Armour - Gladys H. Barr   342
My Lord John - Georgette Heyer   2895
My Master Columbus - Cedric Belfrage   418
The Naked Sword: The Story of Lucretia Borgia - F.W. Kenyon   3456
Niccolo Rising - Dorothy Dunnett   1803
The Novice's Tale - Margaret Frazer   2217
The Outlaw's Tale - Margaret Frazer   2218
Owen Glendower - John Cowper Powys   5159
The Palace - Chelsea Quinn Yarbro   6904
A Passion in the Blood - Genevieve Davis   1519

Personal Recollections of Joan of Arc - Mark Twain   6372
The Plymouth Cloak - Kate Sedley   5718
The Private Life of Mona Lisa - Pierre La Mure   3577
The Queen's Cross: A Biographical Romance of Queen Isabella of Spain - Lawrence Schoonover   5666
The Queen's Secret - Jean Plaidy   5053
The Queen's Sister - Sandra Wilson   6815
Quentin Durward - Sir Walter Scott   5705
A Question of Choice - Prudence Andrew   143
Race of Scorpions - Dorothy Dunnett   1806
Red Rose of Anjou - Jean Plaidy   5054
The Reluctant Queen: The Story of Anne of York - Jean Plaidy   5056
Richard III: The Last Plantagenet - Tyler Whittle   6722
Richard Whittington, London's Mayor - Gwynedd Sudworth   6112
Rogue's Legacy: A Novel about Francois Villon - Babette Deutsch   1629
The Romance of Leonardo Da Vinci - Dmitri Merezhkovski   4339
Romola - George Eliot   1910
The Rose at Harvest End - Eleanor Fairburn   2003
The Royal Pawn - Antonia Ridge   5327
Royal Sword at Agincourt - Pamela Bennetts   455
Scales of Gold - Dorothy Dunnett   1808
Sea of Darkness - Roland Huntford   3086
The Serpent Amongst the Lilies - P.C. Doherty   1678
The Servant's Tale - Margaret Frazer   2219
A Shrine of Murders - C.L. Grace   2509
Simon the Coldheart - Georgette Heyer   2901
The Sins of the Lion - Annette Motley   4503
The Son of York - Margaret Abbey   5
The Spanish Doctor - Matt Cohen   1159
The Spider King - Lawrence Schoonover   5668
The Spitfire - Bertrice Small   5912
The Spring of the Ram - Dorothy Dunnett   1809
Stage of Fools - Charles Andrew Brady   635
The Star of Lancaster - Jean Plaidy   5065
A Stolen Tongue - Sheri Holman   3002
The Summer Queen - Alice Walworth Graham   2512
The Sun in Splendour - Jean Plaidy   5066
The Sunne in Splendour - Sharon Kay Penman   4907
Sunset at Noon - Jane Oliver   4728
The Swan and the Rose - Francis W. Leary   3697
The Sword of Il Grande - Will Creed   1424
The Taming - Jude Deveraux   1633
Taras Bulba - Nikolai V. Gogol   2451
The Tears of the Madonna - George Herman   2862
The Teutonic Knights - Henryk Sienkiewicz   5849
The Thistle and the Rose - Jean Plaidy   5069
The Time Returns - Alexandra Ripley   5343
Titian - Dario Cecchi   965
To Lie with Lions - Dorothy Dunnett   1810
To the Indies - C.S. Forester   2183
Torquemada - Howard Fast   2045
The Town House - Norah Lofts   3861
The Traitors of Bosworth - Robert Farrington   2021
Tudor Agent - Robert Farrington   2022
The Tudor Rose - Margaret Campbell Barnes   329
Uneasy Lies the Head - Jean Plaidy   5071
The Unicorn Hunt - Dorothy Dunnett   1811
An Unknown Welshman - Jean Stubbs   6100
The Velvet Doublet - James H. Street   6082
The Venetian - David Weiss   6611
The Voice and the Light - Edwin Fadiman   1995
Walk with Peril - Dorothy V.S. Jackson   3132
The Warwick Heiress - Margaret Abbey   6
We Speak No Treason - Rosemary Hawley Jarman   3168
The Weaver's Tale - Kate Sedley   5719
Web of Lucifer: A Novel of the Borgia Fury - Maurice Samuel   5580
The White Boar - Marian Palmer   4780
The White Company - Sir Arthur Conan Doyle   1716
The White Queen - Lesley J. Nickell   4611

The White Rose - Jan Westcott 6648
The Whyte Harte - P.C. Doherty 1681
Wife to Henry V - Hilda Lewis 3752
The Winter Rose - Millie J. Ragosta 5243
Wolf's Embrace - Gail Link 3801
Women of Ashdon - Valerie Anand 135
The World, the Flesh, and the Devil - Reay Tannahill 6159
Written in the Stars: A Novel about Albrecht Durer - Frances Hope Fisher 2103
The Wrong Plantagenet - Marian Palmer 4781

16th CENTURY

1492 - Mary Johnston 3228
The Abbot - Sir Walter Scott 5688
Absolute Elizabeth - Joanna Dessau 1624
The Abyss - Marguerite Yourcenar 6946
The Adventurer - Mika Waltari 6550
Against This Rock - Louis Zara 6948
The Agony and the Ecstasy - Irving Stone 6054
The Alchymist's Journal - Evan S. Connell 1256
All the Queen's Men - Evelyn Anthony 157
Among the Innocent - Elizabeth Borton de Trevino 6339
Anne Boleyn - Evelyn Anthony 158
Anne of the Thousand Days - Edward Fenton 2059
Armada - Charles Gidley 2404
At the Moon's Inn - Andrew Lytle 3944
The Autobiography of Henry VIII - Margaret George 2355
Aztec - Gary Jennings 3193
The Bait and the Trap - George Challis 970
Balboa: Conquistador - Omar V. Garrison 2303
Baton Sinister - Carl J. Spinatelli 5967
Beauvallet - Georgette Heyer 2876
The Best House in Stratford - Edward Fisher 2100
The Bisley Boy - Christopher Hunt 3080
The Black Duchess - Alanna Knight 3514
The Blade of Castlemayne - Anthony Esler 1960
The Blanket of the Dark - John Buchan 749
The Blood Countess - Andrei Codrescu 1149
Blood Royal - Mollie Hardwick 2690
Bold Encounter: A Novel Based on the Life of St. John of the Cross - Peter-Thomas Rohrbach 5433
Borgia Testament - Nigel Balchin 277
The Bride of Suleiman - Aileen Crawley 1421
Bride of the Conqueror - Hartzell Spence 5961
Brief Gaudy Hour - Margaret Campbell Barnes 322
A Brood of Vipers - Michael Clynes 1133
Bruegel, or, The Workshop of Dreams - Claude Henri Rocquet 5422
Buccaneer Surgeon - C.V. Terry 6205
Buffalo Medicine - Don Coldsmith 1171
Captain Bashful - Donald Barr Chidsey 1059
Captain for Elizabeth - Jan Westcott 6643
Captain From Castile - Samuel Shellabarger 5794
Captain General - John P. Stevenson 6007
Captain of the Medici - John J. Pugh 5206
The Captive Queen of Scots - Jean Plaidy 5008
Caravaggio - Robert Payne 4851
A Cardinal of the Medici - Susan Hicks Beach 393
Carnival of Saints - George Herman 2860
The Chancellor - Lawrence Schoonover 5662
Chase the Heart - Maggie Osborne 4760
Checkmate - Dorothy Dunnett 1799
Child of the Mist - Kathleen Morgan 4451
The Children of the Sun - Oakley Hall 2652
Circle in the Water - Susan Wiggs 6742
City of God: A Novel of the Borgias - Cecelia Holland 2985
City of Light - Alison Macleod 4001
Cloak of Folly - Burke Boyce 606
Color From a Light Within: A Novel Based on the Life of El Greco - Donald Braider 641
Come Rack! Come Rope! - Robert Hugh Benson 458
Command of the King - Mary Lide 3773
The Concubine - Norah Lofts 3839

The Constant Star - Dorothy Norris Foote 2151
Copilli, Aztec Prince - Miguel Aleman Velasco 75
Cortez and Marina - Edison Marshall 4105
Courtesan - Diane Haeger 2635
Cradle of the Sun - John Clagett 1083
Croatan - Mary Johnston 3231
The Cross and the Sword - Manuel de Jesus Galvan 2274
A Crossbowman's Story of the First Exploration of the Amazon - George Millar 4379
The Crown and the Shadow: The Story of Francoise d'Aubigne, Marquise de Maintenon - Pamela Hill 2930
A Crown in Darkness: A Novel about Lady Jane Grey - Margaret Mullally 4512
Crown of Aloes - Norah Lofts 3840
Curtains for the Cardinal - Elizabeth Eyre 1991
Daimon - Abel Posse 5140
Daishi-San: A Novel - Robert P. Lund 3925
The Dark Fire - Linda Murray 4537
Darker Jewels - Chelsea Quinn Yarbro 6898
Daughter of Satan - Jean Plaidy 5011
Daughter of the Eagle - Don Coldsmith 1173
A Dead Man in Deptford - Anthony Burgess 776
The Death and Life of Miguel De Cervantes - Stephen Marlowe 4094
Death of the Duchess - Elizabeth Eyre 1992
Death of the Fifth Sun - Robert Somerlott 5944
Death of the Fox - George Garrett 2300
Deborah - Colette Davenat 1498
Deborah and the Many Faces of Love - Colette Davenat 1499
Deborah and the Siege of Paris - Colette Davenat 1500
The Disorderly Knights - Dorothy Dunnett 1800
Divine Mistress - Frank G. Slaughter 5886
Doctor Copernicus - John Banville 296
Don Pedro and the Devil - Edgar Maas 3948
The Dreamer of the Vine - Liz Greene 2574
Duchess of Milan - Michael Ennis 1946
Edmund Campion - Evelyn Waugh 6585
Elizabeth and the Prince of Spain - Margaret Irwin 3117
Elizabeth, Captive Princess - Margaret Irwin 3118
Elizabeth: Queen & Woman - Helen Thorpe 6279
Elizabeth, the Woman - Amanda Mae Ellis 1917
The Elk-Dog Heritage - Don Coldsmith 1174
Entered From the Sun - George Garrett 2301
Envoy From Elizabeth - Pamela Bennetts 451
An Epic Joy: A Novel Based on the Life of Rubens - Donald Braider 642
Evergreen Gallant - Jean Plaidy 5013
The Examination - Malcolm Bosse 587
The Fair God - Lew Wallace 6537
The Faith and the Flame - June Dimmit Houston 3054
Falcon: The Autobiography of His Grace James IV, King of Scots - A.J. Stewart 6021
The Fall of the King - Johannes Vilhelm Jensen 3214
A Famine of Horses - P.F. Chisholm 1071
Faust - Robert Nye 4654
Feast in the Morning - Hugh Preston 5175
Ferdinand and Isabella - Hermann Kesten 3474
Feversham - Diane Davidson 1503
The Fifth Queen - Ford Madox Ford 2161
Fire Opal - Pamela Hill 2932
Fire over England - A.E.W. Mason 4143
The Firedrake's Eye - Patricia Finney 2095
The First Gentleman of America: A Comedy of Conquest - James Branch Cabell 841
Five Black Ships: A Novel of Discoverers - Napoleon Baccino Ponce de Leon 5089
Flame of Fire - Jane Oliver 4722
The Flame of the Borgias - Jean Briggs 680
The Flight of the Kestrel - Margaret Abbey 3
The Florentine - Carl J. Spinatelli 5968
Follow the Wind - Don Coldsmith 1176
For Love of a Pirate - Anthony Esler 1961

For One Sweet Grape - Kate O'Brien 4681
The Fourth Queen - Isabel Paterson 4827
Frobisher's Savage - Leonard Tourney 6299
The Gallows Murder - Michael Clynes 1134
The Game of Kings - Dorothy Dunnett 1801
The Gay Galliard - Margaret Irwin 3119
Gay Lord Robert - Jean Plaidy 5015
The Gentle Fury: A Novel of Margaret of Austria - Paul Lewis 3758
Gentleman of Stratford - John Brophy 708
The Glittering Strand - Judith Lennox-Smith 3716
Goa - Kara Dalkey 1458
God's Man: A Novel on the Life of John Calvin - Duncan Norton-Taylor 4650
Gods on Horseback - Samuel G. Baggett 263
Golden Admiral - F. van Wyck Mason 4150
The Golden Eagle - John Edward Jennings 3201
The Golden Princess - Alexander Baron 335
The Golden Thread - Louis De Wohl 1566
The Goliath Head - Charles J. Calitri 865
The Grail Murders - Michael Clynes 1135
Grania: She-King of the Irish Seas - Morgan Llywelyn 3819
The Great White Gods - Eduard Stucken 6102
The Greek of Toledo: A Romantic Narrative of El Greco - Elizabeth Borton 586
Green Darkness - Anya Seton 5751
The Green Salamander - Pamela Hill 2933
The Grove of Eagles - Winston Graham 2526
The Hand of Michelangelo - Sidney Alexander 85
The Hands of Cantu - Tom Lea 3694
Heart of a Queen - Josephine Delves-Broughton 1603
The Heart of Jade - Salvador de Madariaga 4024
The Heidenmauer - James Fenimore Cooper 1301
The Heir of Allington - Philippa Wiat 6727
Henry VIII and His Six Wives - Maureen Peters 4975
Henry, King of France - Heinrich Mann 4061
Her Majesty's Captain - Derek Wilson 6797
Her Royal Destiny - Carol Maxwell Eady 1820
Here Comes the King - Philip Lindsay 3792
The Heretic - Alison Macleod 4002
High Carnival - John J. Pugh 5207
Highland Belle - Patricia Grasso 2541
The Hireling - Alison Macleod 4003
The Horn and the Roses: A Novel Based on the Life of Peter Paul Rubens - Ira Jan Wallach 6542
The Hounds of God - Rafael Sabatini 5551
The House at Old Vine - Norah Lofts 3845
I Am Mary Tudor - Hilda Lewis 3750
I, Elizabeth - Rosalind Miles 4378
I, the King - Howard Clewes 1112
I, the King - Hermann Kesten 3475
Immortal Queen - Elizabeth Byrd 834
In the House of the King - Louis Zara 6951
In the Shadow of the Crown - Jean Plaidy 5022
The Incas - Daniel Peters 4945
The Indian Chronicles - Jose Barreiro 349
Islands of Unwisdom - Robert Graves 2548
The Italian Garden - Judith Lennox-Smith 3717
The Italian Woman - Jean Plaidy 5024
The Ivy Crown: A Biographical Novel of Queen Katherine Parr - Mary M. Luke 3923
James, by the Grace of God - Nigel Tranter 6315
Jewel of the Sea - Susan Wiggs 6743
Juan Ortiz: Gentleman of Seville - Mary Bethell Alfriend 88
Katharine: The Virgin Widow - Jean Plaidy 5025
Katheryn, the Wanton Queen - Maureen Peters 4976
Kathryn: In the Court of Six Queens - Anne Merton Abbey 1
Kenilworth - Sir Walter Scott 5700
A Kind of Justice - Benjamin Siegel 5844
King in Hell: A Novel of Bothwell and Mary, Queen of Scots - Beverly Balin 282
Kingdom of Gold - Susan Wiggs 6744
The King's Achievement - Robert Hugh Benson 459
The King's Cavalier - Samuel Shellabarger 5795

King's Fool - Margaret Campbell Barnes   325
The King's Good Servant - Olive White   6696
The King's Pleasure - Norah Lofts   3847
The King's Pleasure - Jean Plaidy   5026
The King's Secret Matter - Jean Plaidy   5027
The King's Vixen - Pamela Hill   2937
The Knight and the Dove - Lori Wick   6732
A Knight in Shining Armor - Jude Deveraux   1631
Lady Defiant - Suzanne Robinson   5412
Lady Gallant - Suzanne Robinson   5413
The Lady in the Tower - Jean Plaidy   5028
Lady in Waiting - Rosemary Sutcliff   6123
Lady Rich - Elizabeth Boatwright Coker   1166
Lamia: A Witch - Georgia Elizabeth Taylor   6183
The Last Crusader - Louis De Wohl   1569
The Last Princess - Charles O. Locke   3826
Late Harvest - Olive White   6697
Legacy - Susan Kay   3374
The Legend of Tyl Ulenspiegel - Charles Theodore Henri De Coster   1558
Leo Africanus - Amin Maalouf   3947
Life as Carola - Joan Grant   2535
Light on Lucrezia - Jean Plaidy   5029
The Lily and the Leopards - Alice Harwood   2765
The Lion and the Rose - Jane Oliver   4724
The Lion Triumphant - Philippa Carr   922
Liza Bowe - Shirley Barker   313
The Longest Night - Ada Cook Lewis   3744
Lord of Darkness - Robert Silverberg   5854
Lord of the Kongo - Peter Forbath   2155
Lords of the Dance - Robin Lloyd-Jones   3815
The Lost Colony - Edison Marshall   4108
Lost Love Found - Bertrice Small   5910
Lover of Life - Zsolt de Harsanyi   2756
Love's Labour's Won - Edward Fisher   2101
The Luck of Huemac: A Novel about the Aztecs - Daniel Peters   4946
The Mad Courtesan - Edward Marston   4122
Madame Serpent - Jean Plaidy   5033
Magnus the Magnificent - Leslie Turner White   6688
Maid of Honour: A Novel Set in the Court of Mary, Queen of Scots - Elizabeth Byrd   836
A Man Called Cervantes - Bruno Frank   2201
Man of the Shadows - Don Coldsmith   1178
The Man on a Donkey - H.F.M. Prescott   5170
A Mapmaker's Dream - James Cowan   1391
Mary of Scotland - F.W. Kenyon   3454
Mary, Queen of Scotland and the Isles - Margaret George   2356
The Master of Geneva: A Novel Based on the Life of John Calvin - Gladys H. Barr   341
The Master of Gray Trilogy - Nigel Tranter   6316
The Memoirs of Christopher Columbus - Stephen Marlowe   4096
The Mercenary - Charles Durbin   1814
Mermaid Tavern - George William Cronyn   1429
The Merry Devils - Edward Marston   4123
The Merrymaid - Mollie Hardwick   2696
Michelangelo the Florentine - Sidney Alexander   86
Mine Is the Kingdom - Jane Oliver   4726
The Miracle at St. Bruno's - Philippa Carr   925
Mistress Anne - Carolly Erickson   1952
The Monastery - Sir Walter Scott   5701
Monk in Armour - Gladys H. Barr   342
Mrs. Shakespeare: The Complete Works - Robert Nye   4656
Murder Most Royal - Jean Plaidy   5036
Musashi: An Epic Novel of the Samurai Era - Eiji Yoshikawa   6935
The Muscovite - Alison Macleod   4004
My Dear Lover England - Pamela Bennetts   453
My Enemy the Queen - Victoria Holt   3017
My Lady Glamis - Pamela Hill   2940
My Lady Greensleeves - Constance Beresford-Howe   476
My Lady of Cleves - Margaret Campbell Barnes   328
My Lord Essex - Olive Eckerson   1838
My Lord of Canterbury - Godfrey Turton   6369
My Lord the Fox - Robert York   6932

My Master Columbus - Cedric Belfrage   418
The Naked Sword: The Story of Lucretia Borgia - F.W. Kenyon   3456
The Near and the Far - Leopold Hamilton Myers   4547
The Needle-Watcher - Richard Blaker   540
The Negotiators - Francis Walder   6526
Nicholas Cooke: Actor, Soldier, Physician, Priest - Stephanie Cowell   1393
Nicodemus: The Roman Years of Michelangelo Buonarroti, 1534-1564 - Sidney Alexander   87
The Nine Giants - Edward Marston   4124
No Smoke Without Fire - Alice Harwood   2767
No Wall So High - Anne Powers   5152
Nothing Like the Sun - Anthony Burgess   781
The Nunnery - Dorothy Charques   1001
Oh! Where Are Bloody Mary's Earrings? - Robert Player   5079
The Old Priory - Norah Lofts   3855
Out on Any Limb - John Myers   4545
Parcel of Rogues - Jane Lane   3656
Pawn in Frankincense - Dorothy Dunnett   1804
Physician Extraordinary: A Novel of the Life and Times of William Harvey - David Weiss   6608
The Players' Boy Is Dead - Leonard Tourney   6303
The Poisoned Chalice - Michael Clynes   1136
The Pope's Rhinoceros - Lawrence Norfolk   4642
The Prince and the Pauper - Mark Twain   6373
Prince of Foxes - Samuel Shellabarger   5797
Prince of Outlaws - Alexey Tolstoy   6294
Prisoner of the Queen - Alison Macleod   4006
The Prisoner of Tordesillas - Lawrence Schoonover   5665
The Private Life of Mona Lisa - Pierre La Mure   3577
Private Renaissance - Maria Bellonci   436
Prophecies - Helena Soister   5937
The Proud Man - Elizabeth Linington   3800
The Quality of Mercy - Faye Kellerman   3391
Les Quarant Cinq - Alexandre Dumas   1779
The Queen and the Gypsy - Constance Heaven   2810
Queen Anne Boleyn - Francis Hackett   2634
Queen Jezebel - Jean Plaidy   5049
Queen Margot - Alexandre Dumas   1780
Queen of the Reformation - Charles Ludwig   3922
Queen of This Realm: The Story of Queen Elizabeth I - Jean Plaidy   5050
Queen's Caprice - Marjorie Bowen   599
The Queen's Grace - Jan Westcott   6646
The Queen's Head - Edward Marston   4125
Queen's Play - Dorothy Dunnett   1805
The Queen's Ward - Hebe Elsna   1933
Rakossy - Cecelia Holland   2995
Ralegh's Fair Bess: The Story of Bess Throckmorton - Judy Turner   6365
The Red-Haired Brat - Joanna Dessau   1627
Reluctant Cavalier - Donald Barr Chidsey   1064
The Reluctant Queen - Molly Costain Haycraft   2796
The Ringed Castle - Dorothy Dunnett   1807
The Riven Realm - Nigel Tranter   6317
Roanoke Hundred - Inglis Fletcher   2138
Roanoke Renegade - Don Tracy   6311
The Roaring Boy - Edward Marston   4127
The Robsart Affair - Jennette Letton   3729
The Rogue From Padua - Jay Williams   6772
The Romance of Leonardo Da Vinci - Dmitri Merezhkovski   4339
The Rose Without a Thorn - Jean Plaidy   5058
Roses for Mexico - Ethel Cook Eliot   1907
Royal Nonesuch: A Tudor Tapestry - Beatrice White   6674
Royal Road to Fotheringay - Jean Plaidy   5059
The Sage and the Olive - Florence Whitfield Barton   369
St. Thomas's Eve - Jean Plaidy   5060
The Scarlet City - Hella S. Haasse   2632
The Scarlet Cloak - Jean Plaidy   5061
The Sea Beggars - Cecelia Holland   2996
Sea of Lentils - Antonio Benitez-Rojo   443

A Season of Knives - P.F. Chisholm   1072
Seats of the Mighty: A Novel of James Stuart, Brother of Mary, Queen of Scots - Alice Harwood   2768
Serenissima: A Novel of Venice - Erica Jong   3300
The Serpent Garden - Judith Merkle Riley   5336
Set All Afire: A Novel of St. Francis Xavier - Louis De Wohl   1574
The Seven Cities of Gold - Virginia Davis Hersch   2865
Shadow in the Sun: A Novel of Elizabeth I, the Virgin Queen - F.W. Kenyon   3460
The Shadow of God - Aileen Crawley   1422
The Shadow of the Earth - Lee Wichelns   6731
The Shadow of the Pomegranate - Jean Plaidy   5062
Shakespeare & Son - Edward Fisher   2102
The Siege - Peter Vansittart   6431
A Signal Victory - David Stacton   5976
The Signore: Shogun of the Warring States - Kunio Tsuji   6357
The Silent Woman - Edward Marston   4128
Silver Cross - Mary Johnston   3239
Sir Rogue - Leslie Turner White   6691
Sister to Jane: The Story of Lady Katharine Grey - Beatrice May   4202
The Sixth Wife - Jean Plaidy   5063
The Slicing Edge of Death - Judith Cook   1263
Snared Nightingale - Geoffrey Trease   6324
So Far From Malabar - Joy DeWeese Wehen   6599
So Merciful a Queen, So Cruel a Woman - Alice Harwood   2769
Sofia - Ann Chamberlin   974
Soldier in Paradise - Burton Wohl   6835
The Spanish Bridegroom - Jean Plaidy   5064
Stage of Fools - Charles Andrew Brady   635
A Stake in the Kingdom - Nigel Tranter   6321
The Star-Gazer - Zsolt de Harsanyi   2757
Strange Devices of the Sun and Moon - Lisa Goldstein   2463
The Strong Room - Jere Hungerford Wheelwright   6671
The Succession: A Novel of Elizabeth and James - George Garrett   2302
The Sun, He Dies: A Novel about the End of the Aztec World - Jamake Highwater   2919
Sunset at Noon - Jane Oliver   4728
Superstition Corner - Sheila Kaye-Smith   3379
Sweet Will - Eric Malpass   4050
The Sword and the Flame - Pamela Hill   2945
The Sword and the Sun: The Story of the Spanish Civil Wars in Peru - Gerald Green   2566
The Sword of the Golem - Abraham Rothberg   5509
The Sword of Truth - Gilbert Morris   4472
Taiko - Eiji Yoshikawa   6936
Take Heed of Loving Me: A Novel about John Donne - Elizabeth Gray Vining   6502
Takers of the City - Hoffman Reynolds Hays   2800
A Tale for Midnight - Frederic Prokosch   5195
Tansy Taniard - Myrtle Strode-Jackson   6084
Tatham Mound - Piers Anthony   169
The Ten-Day Queen - Lozania Prole   5199
Then and Now - William Somerset Maugham   4198
They Are Coming: The Conquest of Mexico - Jose Lopez Portillo y Pacheco   3896
Three Years to Play - Colin MacInnes   3983
The Tides of Dawn - Emma Louise Mally   4044
Till the Day Goes Down - Judith Lennox-Smith   3719
A Time for the Death of a King - Ann Dukthas   1777
Titian - Dario Cecchi   965
To Be a King - Robert DeMaria   1607
To Love a Queen - Lawrence Schoonover   5669
To the Indies - C.S. Forester   2183
Too Near the Throne - Molly Costain Haycraft   2797
The Tower and the Dream - Jan Westcott   6647
The Tower of London - William Harrison Ainsworth   58
Towers in the Mist - Elizabeth Goudge   2495
A Trail of Blood - Jeremy Potter   5143
Trail of the Spanish Bit - Don Coldsmith   1193

The Trip to Jerusalem - Edward Marston 4129
Trust and Treason - Margaret Birkhead 506
Tudor Underground - Denis Meadows 4320
Two Loves Have I - Clara Longworth de Chambrun 985
Uneasy Lies the Head - Jean Plaidy 5071
Vagabond Prophet - Allene Symons 6149
Vain Shadow - Hartzell Spence 5962
The Valiant Lady - Brigid Knight 3523
Valley of Eagles - Dexter Allen 96
The Venetian - David Weiss 6611
Vittoria - Robert Merle 4342
The Wanderer - Mika Waltari 6556
Warm Wind, West Wind - Anne Irwin Matthew 4188
Westward Ho! - Charles Kingsley 3499
The White Queen - Frederic Fallon 2011
The White Rose Murders - Michael Clynes 1137
Will Shakespeare: The Untold Story - John Mortimer 4495
The Wind Dancer - Iris Johansen 3218
The Wind in His Fists - John Edward Jennings 3210
Windsor Castle - William Harrison Ainsworth 59
The Wise Virgin - Hebe Elsna 1934
The Witch From the Sea - Philippa Carr 933
The Witches - Jay Williams 6776
Wolfshead - Jere Hungerford Wheelwright 6672
Women of Ashdon - Valerie Anand 135
Written in the Stars: A Novel about Albrecht Durer - Frances Hope Fisher 2103
You, My Brother - Philip Burton 809
Young Bess - Margaret Irwin 3123
The Young Elizabeth - Jennette Letton 3730
Young Henry of Navarre - Heinrich Mann 4062
Zayni Barakat - Gamal Ahitani 42
The Border Lord - Jan Westcott 6641

17th CENTURY

The Adventures of Don Juan - Richard Gardner 2289
The Affairs of Nicholas Culpepper - Mabel L. Tyrrel 6375
Alethea - Pamela Belle 429
All My Sins: A Novel of the Life and Loves of Ninon de Lenclos - Norbert Estey 1965
All the Golden Gifts - Iola Fuller 2251
All the King's Ladies - Janice Law 3678
All the Living: A Novel of One Year in the Life of William Shakespeare - Henrietta Buckmaster 758
Always a River - Drayton Mayrant 4211
Angelique - Sergeanne Golon 2465
Angelique and the Demon - Sergeanne Golon 2466
Angelique and the Ghosts - Sergeanne Golon 2467
Angelique and the King - Sergeanne Golon 2468
Angelique in Barbary - Sergeanne Golon 2469
Angelique in Love - Sergeanne Golon 2470
Angelique in Revolt - Sergeanne Golon 2471
Annie - Gloria Jahoda 3141
The Arm and the Darkness - Taylor Caldwell 850
Artemesia - Anna Banti 295
Arthur Dimmesdale - Charles R. Larson 3671
Ashes in the Wilderness - William Greenough Schofield 5649
Ask No Quarter - George Tracy Marsh 4099
Ballenrose - Mallory Burgess 783
Baneful Sorceries, or The Countess Bewitched - Joan Sanders 5585
The Bartholomew Fair Murders - Leonard Tourney 6297
The Bastard - Brigitte Von Tessin 6208
Bear His Mild Yoke - Ethel White 6675
The Bellerose Bargain - Robyn Carr 934
Bennett's Welcome - Inglis Fletcher 2132
The Betrothed - Alessandro Manzoni 4078
The Big Chariot - Charmian Clift 1118
The Big Drum - Elizabeth Boatwright Coker 1162
Black Angels - C.T. Ritchie 5348
Black Robe - Brian Moore 4441
Blackrobe - Charles Corcoran 1323

Blessed Is the Land - Louis Zara 6949
Blood Royal - Robert Payne 4850
Blossom Like the Rose - Norah Lofts 3836
The Bondswoman - Caryl Ledner 3705
The Bracegirdle - Burris Atkins Jenkins 3189
The Braeswood Tapestry - Robyn Carr 936
The Bride of Lammermoor - Sir Walter Scott 5693
Bride of the MacHugh - Jan Cox Speas 5956
The Bride of the Wilderness - Charles McCarry 4220
The Bright Face of Danger - Clifford Sublette 6108
Bronze Christ - Yoshiro Nagaya 4551
Buccaneer - Dudley Pope 5093
Bundori - Laura Joh Rowland 5519
Call Lady Purbeck - Hilda Lewis 3745
Campion Towers - John Beatty 401
A Candle for D'Artagnan - Chelsea Quinn Yarbro 6895
A Candle in the Wilderness - Irving A. Bacheller 256
The Cannaways - Graham Shelby 5789
Captain Blood - Rafael Sabatini 5546
Captain Fantom - Charles Underhill 6377
The Captive Bride - Gilbert Morris 4457
The Cardinal and the Queen - Evelyn Anthony 159
Caribbee - Thomas Hoover 3025
Caribee - Christopher Nicole 4614
The Carmelite - Elgin Groseclose 2599
The Cat and the King - Louis Auchincloss 229
Catherine - Hilda Lewis 3746
Catherwood - Marly Youmans 6937
The Chains of Fate - Pamela Belle 430
The Changeling - Alison Macleod 4000
Charles the King - Evelyn Anthony 160
Chelynne - Robyn Carr 938
Christopher Humble - Charles Burnet Judah 3310
Cinq-Mars - Alfred Victor de Vigny 6495
Circle of Pearls - Rosalind Laker 3593
The Cleopatra Boy - Eric Malpass 4048
Cloak of Folly - Burke Boyce 606
Color From a Light Within: A Novel Based on the Life of El Greco - Donald Braider 641
Come Home at Even - Le Grand Cannon 884
Coromandel! - John Masters 4172
The Countess Angelique - Sergeanne Golon 2472
Countess Carrots - Molly Costain Haycraft 2792
Covenant of Grace - Jane Gilmore Rushing 5527
The Crown and the Shadow: The Story of Francoise d'Aubigne, Marquise de Maintenon - Pamela Hill 2930
A Crowning Mercy - Susannah Kells 3396
Cup of Gold - John Steinbeck 5991
Cutlass Empire - F. van Wyck Mason 4148
Daishi-San: A Novel - Robert P. Lund 3925
A Dancer in Darkness - David Stacton 5971
Daneclere - Pamela Hill 2931
A Dangerous Innocence - Victoria Lincoln 3787
Daniel Du Luth - Everett McNeil 4307
The Dark Dancer - Frederic Prokosch 5193
The Dark Fire - Linda Murray 4537
The Dark Rose - Maurice Walsh 6549
The Dark Stranger - Dorothy Charques 999
Dark Torrent of Glencoe - Edward Grierson 2590
Daughter of Eve - Noel B. Gerson 2366
Daughter of Fortune - Carla Kelly 3398
Daughter of Satan - Jean Plaidy 5011
Daughters of England - Philippa Carr 919
The Death and Life of Miguel De Cervantes - Stephen Marlowe 4094
Death of the Fox - George Garrett 2300
The Deluge - Henryk Sienkiewicz 5846
The Descent of the Idol - Jaroslav Durych 1818
The Devil and the Mathers - Edward E. Elliott 1914
The Devil in Velvet - John Dickson Carr 909
The Devil's Marchioness - William Fifield 2082
The Devil's Own - Christopher Nicole 4615
The Diary of William Harvey: The Imaginary Journal of the Physician Who Revolutionized Medicine - Jean Hamburger 2667
The Dispossessed - Dell Shannon 5773

The Disturber - L.S. Davidson Jr. 1505
The Doom Trail - Arthur Douglas Smith 5917
The Drowning Room - Michael Kenneth Pye 5212
A Durable Fire - Virginia Bernhard 480
The Dutchman - Maan Meyers 4351
The Dutchman's Dilemma - Maan Meyers 4352
The Echoing Cliffs - Hjalmar P. Thesen 6219
Elegant Witch - Robert Neill 4568
Elizabeth, the Woman - Amanda Mae Ellis 1917
The Elusive Crown - Hebe Elsna 1931
An Epic Joy: A Novel Based on the Life of Rubens - Donald Braider 642
Evergreen Gallant - Jean Plaidy 5013
Exiled - Helene Holt 3007
Exit Lady Masham - Louis Auchincloss 230
The Faithful Lovers - Valerie Anand 129
A Falling Star - Pamela Belle 431
Familiar Spirits - Leonard Tourney 6298
Fathers and Crows - William T. Vollmann 6508
The Favourite - Francoise Mallet-Joris 4040
Fire in the Steppe - Henryk Sienkiewicz 5847
The Fireflower - Edith Layton 3687
The Flight - Ruth Walgreen Stephan 5994
Flight of the Crow - Paul Clayton 1103
The Flower in the Mountains - Don Coldsmith 1175
For My Great Folly - Thomas B. Costain 1365
Forest Cavalier: A Romance of America's First Frontier and of Bacon's Rebellion - Roy Catesby Flannagan 2122
Forever Amber - Kathleen Winsor 6822
Forever Possess - Alexandra Phillips 4982
The Fortunes of Nigel - Sir Walter Scott 5696
The Franciscan - Forrester Blake 532
Frenchman's Creek - Daphne Du Maurier 1744
Gallant Warrior - Helen R. Mann 4063
Galleon - Dudley Pope 5095
Gallows Hill - Frances Winwar 6831
Gentleman of Stratford - John Brophy 708
The Ghost of Monsieur Scarron - Janet Lewis 3755
The Gilded Torch - Iola Fuller 2252
The Glory and the Dream - F.W. Kenyon 3450
The Golden Coast - Philip Rooney 5441
The Golden Days - Robert Neill 4569
The Golden Feather - Theda Kenyon 3462
The Golden Hawk - Frank Yerby 6921
The Golden Tulip - Rosalind Laker 3596
The Goliath Head - Charles J. Calitri 865
Graham of Claverhouse - Constance Dodge 1665
The Greater Hunger - Barbara Dodge Borland 581
The Greek of Toledo: A Romantic Narrative of El Greco - Elizabeth Borton 586
Hawk of Detroit - Arthur Pound 5145
A Health Unto His Majesty - Jean Plaidy 5019
Heart of a Queen - Josephine Delves-Broughton 1603
Hellbane - Anthony Esler 1963
Henry Esmond - William Makepeace Thackeray 6212
Here Lies Our Sovereign Lord - Jean Plaidy 5021
Heritage of the River - Muriel Elwood 1937
Hester - Christopher Bigsby 496
The Highland Hawk - Leslie Turner White 6682
Hilton Head - Josephine Pinckney 5003
The Holder of the World - Bharati Mukherjee 4510
The Honorable Imposter - Gilbert Morris 4463
Hope Leslie; or, Early Times in Massachusetts - Catharine Maria Sedgewick 5714
The Horn and the Roses: A Novel Based on the Life of Peter Paul Rubens - Ira Jan Wallach 6542
The House at Old Vine - Norah Lofts 3845
A House of Women - Eric Malpass 4049
I, Elizabeth - Rosalind Miles 4378
I, John Mordaunt - Virgil Scott 5687
I, Rembrandt - David Weiss 6605
I Seek a City - Gilbert Rees 5289
I, the King - Frances Parkinson Keyes 3479
I, Tituba, Black Witch of Salem - Maryse Conde 1233

The Imposter - Noel B. Gerson 2375
In Adam's Fall - Constance Dodge 1666
The Incredible Brazilian: The Native - Zulfikar Ghose 2392
The Island of the Day Before - Umberto Eco 1849
James, by the Grace of God - Hugh Williamson Ross 5499
John Inglesant - John Henry Shorthouse 5833
John Milton - Edmund Fuller 2249
Jubal Sackett - Louis L'Amour 3620
Katherine Christian - Hugh Walpole 6546
Kepler: A Novel - John Banville 297
The King Breaker - Elizabeth Linington 3797
The King James Version - Stanley N. Stewart 6035
King's Agent - Justus Kent Clark 1090
The King's Bastard - Hebe Elsna 1932
The King's Brat - Constance Gluyas 2441
The King's General - Daphne Du Maurier 1748
The King's Messenger - Samuel Edwards 1887
King's Minion - Rafael Sabatini 5552
The King's Passenger - Nathan Schachner 5631
The King's Rogue - Max Peacock 4859
The King's Way - Francoise Chandernagor 986
Knaves Templar - Leonard Tourney 6300
The Lacemaker - Janine Montupet 4438
A Lady at Bay - Edgar Maas 3950
Lady in Waiting - Rosemary Sutcliff 6123
Lady of the Glen - Jennifer Roberson 5369
Lady on the Coin - Margaret Campbell Barnes 326
Lady Rich - Elizabeth Boatwright Coker 1166
Lament for a Lost Lover - Philippa Carr 921
The Land Beyond the Tempest - Drayton Mayrant 4213
The Land Is Bright - Noel B. Gerson 2376
Land of the Beautiful River - Helmer Linderholm 3788
The Last Prince of Ireland - Morgan Llywelyn 3821
The Last Valley - J.B. Pick 4992
Late Harvest - Olive White 6697
The Laughing Hangman - Edward Marston 4120
Legacy - Susan Kay 3374
Legacy - Robert Vaughan 6448
The Legion of the Lost - Donald Barr Chidsey 1062
Lillibullero - Robert Neill 4571
Lily of the Mohawks - Jack Casey 952
Lion Rampant - Bernard Shrimsley 5836
Log Cabin Noble - F. van Wyck Mason 4153
Look to Your Geese: A Novel of the Deflowering of New England - Jacquin Sanders 5584
Lorna Doone - R.D. Blackmore 528
Lover of Life - Zsolt de Harsanyi 2756
Lovestorm - Judith E. French 2222
Low Treason - Leonard Tourney 6301
Malefice - Leslie Wilson 6810
A Man Called Cervantes - Bruno Frank 2201
Man Cannot Tell - Philip Lightfoot Scruggs 5711
Manchu - Robert S. Elegant 1904
Mansions of Darkness - Chelsea Quinn Yarbro 6902
Margaret Brent, Adventurer - Dorothy Grant 2533
Marlborough's Unfair Lady - Lozania Prole 5197
The Marquis - Joan Sanders 5586
The Marranos - Liliane Webb 6588
Mary's Land - Lucia St. Clair Robson 5415
Masquerade for the King - Marina Oliver 4729
Medicine Knife - Don Coldsmith 1179
Micah Clarke - Sir Arthur Conan Doyle 1715
Milton in America - Peter Ackroyd 20
Mine Is the Kingdom - Jane Oliver 4726
Ming: A Novel of Seventeeth Century China - Robert B. Oxnam 4772
A Mirror for Witches - Esther Forbes 2157
Mistress of the Boards - Richard Sumner 6118
Mistress of The Highlands - Chloe Gartner 2309
The Moghul - Thomas Hoover 3026
Monsieur Moliere - Michael O'Shaughnessy 4762
The Moon in the Water - Pamela Belle 433
Moon of Thunder - Don Coldsmith 1180
Most Secret - John Dickson Carr 912
Mr. Pepys of Seething Lane - Cecil Abernethy 10

The Murder in the Tower - Jean Plaidy 5035
The Murder of Sir Edmund Godfrey - John Dickson Carr 913
Musashi: An Epic Novel of the Samurai Era - Eiji Yoshikawa 6935
My Crown, My Love - Ruth Walgreen Stephan 5995
My Lady Benbrook - Constance Gluyas 2442
My Lord Essex - Olive Eckerson 1838
My Lord Foxe - Constance Gluyas 2443
My Lord Monleigh - Jan Cox Speas 5957
Myself, Christopher Wren - David Weiss 6606
Myself My Enemy - Jean Plaidy 5037
The Needle-Watcher - Richard Blaker 540
Nicholas Cooke: Actor, Soldier, Physician, Priest - Stephanie Cowell 1393
Night of Decision: A Novel of Colonial New York - Dorothy Grant 2534
No Bed for Bacon - Caryl Brahms 640
No Other Place - John Gould 2497
O Western Wind - John Anthony Devon 1634
Old Mortality - Sir Walter Scott 5702
The Old Priory - Norah Lofts 3855
Old St. Paul's - William Harrison Ainsworth 57
Old Saxon Blood - Leonard Tourney 6302
The Oracle Glass - Judith Merkle Riley 5335
Our Jo, or The Chronicle of a Coming Man - Kenneth M. Cameron 868
The Palace of Wisdom - Bob Marshall-Andrews 4118
Pale Star - Don Coldsmith 1181
Paradise - Esther Forbes 2158
Pargeters - Norah Lofts 3857
Peace, My Daughters - Shirley Barker 314
The Peaceable Kingdom - Jan de Hartog 2763
Pearl - Christopher Bigsby 497
People of the Book - David Stacton 5974
Peter the Great - Alexey Tolstoy 6293
Peveril of the Peak - Sir Walter Scott 5703
The Phoenix Rising - Jean Evans 1984
Physician Extraordinary: A Novel of the Life and Times of William Harvey - David Weiss 6608
The Physician of London - Stephanie Cowell 1394
The Pilgrim Prince - Gladys H. Barr 343
Pilgrims: A Novel of the Mayflower - Gerard Mac 3955
Pilgrims in Paradise - Frank G. Slaughter 5895
The Pirate - Sir Walter Scott 5704
The Pirate and the Pagan - Virginia Henley 2827
A Place of Ravens - Pamela Hill 2942
The Player's Boy - Bryher 744
The Pleasures of Love - Jean Plaidy 5042
The Plymouth Adventure - Ernest Gebler 2342
Pocahontas - Susan Donnell 1691
Pocahontas; or, The Nonpareil of Virginia - David Garnett 2297
The Pointless Knife - Constance Dodge 1667
Poison - Kathryn Harrison 2737
The Portingale - Alison Macleod 4005
The Power and the Glory - Phyllis Bentley 462
The Power and the Glory - Gilbert Parker 4805
The Power and the Passion - Christina Nicholson 4609
Powhatan's Daughter - John Clarke Bowman 605
The Princess of Celle - Jean Plaidy 5045
Prisoners of Hope: A Tale of Colonial Virginia - Mary Johnston 3238
Prisons - Mary Lee Settle 5757
The Privateer - Gordon Daviot 1510
The Proud Servant: The Story of Montrose - Margaret Irwin 3120
Purple Passage: A Novel about a Lady Both Famous and Fantastic - Emily Hahn 2638
The Pyrates - George MacDonald Fraser 2212
Queen of This Realm: The Story of Queen Elizabeth I - Jean Plaidy 5050
The Queen's Husband - Samuel Edwards 1889
The Quickenberry Tree - Annette Motley 4502
Quietly My Captain Waits - Evelyn Eaton 1829

Ralegh's Fair Bess: The Story of Bess Throckmorton - Judy Turner 6365
Rebel Heiress - Robert Neill 4573
Reckless Angel - Jane Feather 2056
Rembrandt - Gladys Schmitt 5643
The Renegade - Donald Clayton Porter 5122
Restoration: A Novel of Seventeenth-Century England - Rose Tremain 6333
Return to the River - Don Coldsmith 1184
Rider on a White Horse - Rosemary Sutcliff 6124
Riding Shotgun - Rita Mae Brown 729
River and Empty Sea - Louis Vaczek 6396
River of Swans - Don Coldsmith 1185
Rivers Parting - Shirley Barker 315
The Road and the Star - Berkely Mather 4182
Road to Lendor - Esther Hammon 1966
The Rogue and the Witch - John Edward Newton 4605
The Rose and the Flame - Jonreed Lauritzen 3676
The Rose Crossing - Nicholas Jose 3306
The Royal City - Les Savage Jr. 5621
Royal Escape - Georgette Heyer 2900
Royal Flush: The Story of Minette - Margaret Irwin 3121
Running Proud - Nicholas Monsarrat 4432
The Sable Lion - Jan Van Dorp 6405
Sackett's Land - Louis L'Amour 3628
The Sacred Hills - Don Coldsmith 1187
La Salle - John Vernon 6458
Salute to Adventurers - John Buchan 752
The Samurai - Shusaku Endo 1941
Saraband for Two Sisters - Philippa Carr 928
Scapegoat for a Stuart - Kate Kirby 3504
Scarlet Cockerel - Clifford Sublette 6110
The Scarlet Letter - Nathaniel Hawthorne 2786
Scent of Cloves - Norah Lofts 3859
The Sea 'Venture - F. van Wyck Mason 4159
The Secret Wife - Alice Acland 22
Seek the Fair Land - Walter Macken 3989
Seventeen of Leyden - John James 3160
The Severed Crown - Jane Lane 3657
The Shadow Flies - Rose Macaulay 3956
Shadow in the Sun: A Novel of Elizabeth I, the Virgin Queen - F.W. Kenyon 3460
Shadow of a Star - Jamie Lee Cooper 1315
The Shadow of the Sun - Sylvia Pell 4891
Shadows on the Rock - Willa Cather 959
Shakespeare's Dog - Leon Rooke 5439
The Shepherd's Crook - Paul Frischauer 2234
Shin Ju - Laura Joh Rowland 5520
Shogun - James Clavell 1101
Silver Nutmeg - Norah Lofts 3860
The Silver Oar - Howard Breslin 669
The Silver Plume - Arthur Meeker 4323
Silver Shoals - Hamilton Cochran 1142
Simplicissimus the Vagabond - J.J.C. Grimmelshausen 2594
The Slave - Isaac Bashevis Singer 5866
The Slave Ship - Mary Johnston 3240
Soldier in Paradise - Burton Wohl 6835
Soldiers of Fortune - Peter Bourne 595
Song of the Rock - Don Coldsmith 1189
The Song of the Siren - Philippa Carr 929
Sorrow by Day - Marjorie Coryn 1359
The Spoils of Eden - Robert H. Fowler 2193
Sporting with Amaryllis - Paul West 6635
The Star-Gazer - Zsolt de Harsanyi 2757
Stately Timber - Rupert Hughes 3075
The Storms of Fate - Patricia Wright 6885
The Strange Death of Mistress Coffin - Robert J. Begiebing 415
The Stranger Prince - Margaret Irwin 3122
The Street of Kings - Charles Dexter 1637
The Stuart Legacy - Robert Kerr 3472
The Succession: A Novel of Elizabeth and James - George Garrett 2302
The Swan of Usk - Helen Ashton 220
Sweet Ransom - Linda Madl 4026
Sweet Will - Eric Malpass 4050

Take Heed of Loving Me: A Novel about John Donne - Elizabeth Gray Vining 6502

Taos - Irwin R. Blacker 527

The Temptation of Angelique - Sergeanne Golon 2473

Thanksgiving - Terry Coleman 1207

This Widowed Land - Kathleen O'Neal Gear 2331

Three Came to Ville Marie - Alan Sullivan 6114

The Three Crowns - Jean Plaidy 5070

The Three Musketeers - Alexandre Dumas 1782

Three Years to Play - Colin MacInnes 3983

Thunder on St. Paul's Day - Jane Lane 3658

Time of Parting - Anton Donchev 1690

To Dance with Kings - Rosalind Laker 3601

To Have and to Hold - Mary Johnston 3241

To Love a Queen - Lawrence Schoonover 5669

To the Far Blue Mountains - Louis L'Amour 3630

Touched with Fire - John William Tebbel 6195

The Tower and the Dream - Jan Westcott 6647

Trail From Taos - Don Coldsmith 1192

Traitor's Moon - Robert Neill 4574

Treason's Gift - Pamela Belle 434

The Tree of Knowledge - Eva Figes 2085

The Trial of Jenny Sykes - Hebe Weenolsen 6598

Tristram Bent - Henry Barnard Safford 5560

Twenty Years After - Alexandre Dumas 1783

Two Loves Have I - Clara Longworth de Chambrun 985

Uncharted Ways - Caroline Snedeker 5935

Unicorn Rampant - Nigel Tranter 6323

Until the Winds - Jean Clark 1089

Valley in Arms: A Novel of the Settlement of Connecticut - Earl Schenck Miers 4376

Venture in the East - Bruce Lancaster 3648

The Voyage of the Destiny - Robert Nye 4657

The Wandering Prince - Jean Plaidy 5075

War Chief - Donald Clayton Porter 5130

The Warrior's Path - Louis L'Amour 3633

The Water Witch - James Fenimore Cooper 1311

We Stood for Freedom - Iris Morley 4455

Weep in the Sun - Jeanne Wilson 6809

The Wept of Wish-Ton-Wish - James Fenimore Cooper 1312

White Indian - Donald Clayton Porter 5134

White Rising - Zane Kotker 3548

The White Witch - Elizabeth Goudge 2496

The Wickedest Pilgrim - Donald Barr Chidsey 1067

Wife to Great Buckingham - Hilda Lewis 3751

Wife to Mr. Milton - Robert Graves 2553

Wild Jasmine - Bertrice Small 5914

William's Wife - Jean Plaidy 5077

Windward Passage - Hamilton Cochran 1143

Wintercombe - Pamela Belle 435

The Winthrop Woman - Anya Seton 5754

The Witch and the Priest - Hilda Lewis 3754

The Witch From the Sea - Philippa Carr 933

With All My Heart - Margaret Campbell Barnes 330

With Fire and Sword - Henryk Sienkiewicz 5850

Witness of Bones - Leonard Tourney 6304

Witnesses - Marcy Moran Heidish 2820

Woman Astride - Nora Purtscher-Wydenbruch 5209

The Woman Who Fell From the Sky - Barbara Riefe 5330

Woodstock; or, The Cavalier - Sir Walter Scott 5710

World and Paradise - Edgar Maas 3953

You, My Brother - Philip Burton 809

The Young and Lonely King - Jane Lane 3659

The Young Emperor - Robert Payne 4857

1640s

The Bride - Margaret Irwin 3116

Mary of Carisbrooke - Margaret Campbell Barnes 327

1650s

The Bride - Margaret Irwin 3116

18th CENTURY

1812 - David Nevin 4586

The Abandoned Woman - Richard Condon 1235

Abigail - Mary Louise Aswell 221

The Absorbing Fire: The Byron Legend - F.W. Kenyon 3445

Adams of the Bounty - Erle Wilson 6807

Adrienne - Barbara Levy 3742

The Adventures of Long John Silver - Denis Judd 3317

Alexander Hamilton's Wife - Alice Curtis Desmond 1623

All in Good Time - Marguerite Allis 106

The Angel: A Novel Based on the Life of Alexander I of Russia - William James Blech 543

Angelica - Samuel A. Schreiner Jr. 5671

Anna Zenger: Mother of Freedom - Kent Cooper 1316

Anne Bonny - Chloe Gartner 2306

Anthony Adverse - Hervey Allen 98

Arc d'X - Steve Erickson 1953

Ashanu - E.P. Roesch 5424

Ashes - Stefan Zeromski 6960

At the Sign of the Reine Pedauque - Anatole France 2198

Audrey - Mary Johnston 3229

Bearer of the Pipe - Don Coldsmith 1169

Beauty's Daughter - Mollie Hardwick 2689

Becky Landers, Frontier Warrior - Constance Skinner 5879

Bed in Hell - Elfrida Vipont 6504

Being Met Together - William Vaughan Wilkins 6756

Beyond the Blue Mountains - Jean Plaidy 5006

The Big Family - Vina Delmar 1600

Birthright - Robert E. Wall 6533

Black Body - H.C. Turk 6361

Black Forest - Meade Minnigerode 4411

The Black Moth - Georgette Heyer 2877

Black Triumvirate: A Novel of Haiti - Benjamin H. Levin 3736

The Blacksmith's Daughter - Joanna Dessau 1625

The Blue Heaven Bends Over All - Jane Oliver 4720

Boone: A Novel Based on the Life and Times of Daniel Boone - Cameron Judd 3311

The Border Captains - Jason Manning 4072

The Bounty Lands - William Donohue Ellis 1927

Bride of Glory - Bradda Field 2078

Bright to the Wanderer - Bruce Lancaster 3638

Bring Larks and Heroes - Thomas Keneally 3410

Brother Owl - Al Hine 2953

Buckskin Cavalier - John Clagett 1082

Burning Gold - Robert Hardy Andrews 148

Burr - Gore Vidal 6485

By Our Beginnings - Jean Stubbs 6092

By Reason of Strength - Gerald White Johnson 3225

The Cannaways - Graham Shelby 5789

Captain Adam - Donald Barr Chidsey 1058

Captain Lightfoot - William R. Burnett 792

Captain of the Sands - Keith Dewhurst 1636

Captain Paul - Edward Ellsberg 1930

Caroline the Queen - Jean Plaidy 5009

The Castle of Fratta - Ippolito Nievo 4625

The Castrato - Lawrence Goldman 2459

The Cat and the King - Louis Auchincloss 229

The Cavalier of Tennessee - Meredith Nicholson 4610

The Changeling - Alison Macleod 4000

The Cherished Wives - Valerie Anand 126

Child of the Dead - Don Coldsmith 1172

Child of the Snapping Turtle, Mike Fink - Julian Lee Rayford 5256

Circle of Pearls - Rosalind Laker 3593

Citizen Tom Paine - Howard Fast 2028

The Colors of Vaud - Bryher 741

Colossus: A Novel about Goya and a World Gone Mad - Stephen Marlowe 4093

The Conqueror - John William Tebbel 6194

The Conqueror: Being the True and Romantic Story of Alexander Hamilton - Gertrude Atherton 222

The Conquerors - Allen W. Eckert 1839

Consuelo - George Sand 5582

The Corsair: A Biographical Novel of Jean Lafitte, Hero of the Battle of New Orleans - Madeleine Fabiola Kent 3444

The Countess - March Cost 1360

Creek Mary's Blood - Dee Brown 712

Crockett of Tennessee: A Novel Based on the Life and Times of David Crockett - Cameron Judd 3314

Crompton Way - Thomas Thompson 6270

Cry to Heaven - Anne Rice 5313

Crystal - Helen Ashfield 205

Damaris - Jane Sheridan 5810

The Dark Stranger - Constance Dodge 1664

A Daughter of Liberty - Allan Cole 1196

The Deadly Lady of Madagascar - C.V. Terry 6206

Dear Mrs. Boswell - Marie Muir 4508

Deep Summer - Gwen Bristow 696

Deepwater: A Novel of the Carolinas - Pamela Jekel 3185

Delilah's Mountain - Gloria Jahoda 3142

Desiree - Annemarie Selinko 5741

Devil Child - Jo Germany 2359

Devil Water - Anya Seton 5749

Die the Long Day - Orlando Patterson 4833

Dr. Johnson's Dear Mistress - Winifred Carter 948

Dolley - Rita Mae Brown 727

Don Juan McQueen - Eugenia Price 5181

D'ri and I - Irving A. Bacheller 257

Drums of Destiny - Peter Bourne 593

The Drums of Monmouth - Emma Gelders Sterne 5998

The Eagle and the Rock - Frances Winwar 6830

Echo of the Flute - Mildred A. Jordan 3304

Edward, Edward - Lolah Burford 772

Eliza's Daughter - Joan Aiken 44

Emma - F.W. Kenyon 3448

Emperor's Ladies - Noel B. Gerson 2367

The Enchantress - Suyin Han 2673

Eroica: A Novel about Beethoven - Carl von Pidoll 4994

Erskine Dale, Pioneer - John Fox 2195

Exit Lady Masham - Louis Auchincloss 230

A Fair Wind Home - Ruth Moore 4443

Fairoaks - Frank Yerby 6915

The Faithful Lovers - Valerie Anand 129

The Fallon Blood - Reagan O'Neal 4741

Fanny: Being the True History of the Adventures of Fanny Hackabout-Jones - Erica Jong 3299

The Fatal Friendship: Marie Antoinette, Count Fersen and the Flight to Varennes - Stanley Loomis 3895

Fathers and Crows - William T. Vollmann 6508

The Favored Child - Philippa Gregory 2582

A Fiddle, a Sword, and a Lady - Albert Spalding 5953

The Firekeeper - Robert Moss 4498

The Flames of Time - Baynard Kendrick 3409

Foes - Mary Johnston 3233

Fool of God: A Novel Based on the Life of Alexander Campbell - Louis Cochran 1144

Footman in Powder - Helen Ashton 216

The Forest and the Fort - Hervey Allen 100

Free Man - Conrad Richter 5320

Freedom's Dues - Robert H. Abel 9

The Frenchwoman - Jeanne Mackin 3995

Friday - Michel Tournier 6305

The Frigate Captain - Showell Styles 6103

From Sea to Shining Sea - James Alexander Thom 6232

The Frontiersmen - Allen W. Eckert 1841

Gallant Captain - Pearl Frye 2242

Gateway to Empire - Allen W. Eckert 1842

A Generation of Leaves - Robert S. Bloom 552

The Gentleman From America - Polan Banks 293

The Gila River - Gary McCarthy 4223

Gilded Splendour - Rosalind Laker 3595

Give Me Liberty - Noel B. Gerson 2369

Give Me Liberty: The Story of an Innocent Man - John Erskine 1956
Give Me the Wind - Jan Jordan 3302
Give Me Your Golden Hand - Evelyn Eaton 1825
The Glass-Blowers - Daphne Du Maurier 1745
The Glory and the Dream - F.W. Kenyon 3450
Goddess of the Green Room - Jean Plaidy 5016
The Golden Harlot - Jeanne Wilson 6808
The Golden Quill: A Novel Based on the Life of Mozart - Bernard Grun 2605
The Golden Season - Oriana Akinson 60
Golden Venus - David Mynders Smythe 5933
Good-Bye My Son - Marjorie Coryn 1356
The Governor's Daughter - Denton Whitson 6718
The Governor's Lady - Thomas H. Raddall 5228
Great Black Russian - John Oliver Killens 3484
The Great Valley - Mary Johnston 3234
Griffith Gaunt - Charles Reade 5280
Hanta Yo - Ruth Beebe Hill 2951
Haym Solomon, Son of Liberty - Howard Fast 2032
Heart in Pilgrimage - Evelyn Eaton 1827
Heaven Is Too High - Mildred Masterson McNeilly 4309
Heir to Polventon - Marjorie Watson 6583
Heiress of Ardara - Margaret Evans Porter 5137
Henry Esmond - William Makepeace Thackeray 6212
High Towers - Thomas B. Costain 1366
A High Wind Rising - Elsie Singmaster 5867
His Was the Fire - Showell Styles 6104
Home to Kentucky: A Novel of Henry Clay - Alfred Leland Crabb 1399
The Horn and the Forest - Jamie Lee Cooper 1313
A House in Peiking - Robert Payne 4853
I, Madame Tussaud - Sylvia Martin 4135
I'll Storm Hell - Noel B. Gerson 2374
An Imperfect Joy - Jean Stubbs 6097
Imperial Venus: A Novel of Napoleon's Favorite Sister - Edgar Maas 3949
In the Blazing Light - Max White 6693
In the Days of Poor Richard - Irving A. Bacheller 259
The Interpreter - Robert Moss 4499
The Irish Boy: A Romantic Biography - Naomi Jacob 3137
Israel Potter - Herman Melville 4334
Jack Sheppard - William Harrison Ainsworth 56
Jackson: A Novel - Max Byrd 837
Jarrett's Jade - Frank Yerby 6923
Jesters - David Markish 4090
John Howard Payne, Skywalker - Maude Barragan 348
Johnny Logan: Shawnee Spy - Allen W. Eckert 1843
Judith Paris - Hugh Walpole 6545
Kentucky Home - Betty Layman Receveur 5283
King of the Bastards - Sarah Gertrude Millin 4405
Kingdom of This World - Alejo Carpentier 906
The King's Orchard - Agnes Sligh Turnbull 6363
The King's Way - Francoise Chandernagor 986
Knave of Hearts - Philippa Carr 920
Lady Washington - Dorothy Clarke Wilson 6803
Lancet - Garet Rogers 5431
The Last Mutiny: The Further Adventures of Captain Bligh - Bill Collett 1208
Let My Name Stand Fair - Shirley Seifert 5727
The Life and Times of Horatio Hornblower - C. Northcote Parkinson 4813
Lindeman's Daughters - Synnove Christensen 1073
Lisbon - Valerie Sherwood 5825
Long Knife - James Alexander Thom 6233
Look to the Mountain - Le Grand Cannon 885
Lord Fancy - Leslie Turner White 6686
Louis the Well-Beloved - Jean Plaidy 5032
Louisiana Purchase - A.E. Hotchner 3039
The Lovely Lynchs - Magdalen King-Hall 3490
Loving Emma - Nigel Foxell 2197
Madame Casanova - Gaby von Schonthan 5659
Madame Geneva - Jane Lane 3655
The Maid of Sker - R.D. Blackmore 529

The Malvie Inheritance - Pamela Hill 2938
Manchu Palaces - Jeanne Larsen 3669
Marie Antoinette - F.W. Kenyon 3453
Marlborough's Unfair Lady - Lozania Prole 5197
The Marriage Bed - Jean Clark 1088
Mary Anne - Daphne Du Maurier 1749
The Masked Man - P.C. Doherty 1674
Master of Bengal: A Novel of Robert Clive of India - Norman Partington 4821
The Masters of Bow Street - John Creasy 1423
The Measure of the Years - Alice Mary Colver 1218
The Medicine Horn - Jory Sherman 5820
Mirabeau, Lover and Stateman - Pierre Nezelof 4606
Miracles - Marcy Moran Heidish 2818
Mister Christian - William Kinsolving 3502
Mistress Nancy - Barbara Bentley 460
Mistress of Fortune - Sheila Lancaster 3651
Monsieur Beaucaire - Booth Tarkington 6163
Monsieur Janvier - Elizabeth Linington 3799
Mr. Christian! - Stanley Miller 4402
Mr. Oddity, Samuel Johnson - Charles Norman 4643
Murder in Grub Street - Bruce Alexander 77
My Brother Napoleon: The Confessions of Caroline Bonaparte - F.W. Kenyon 3455
My Grand Enemy - Jean Stubbs 6098
My Love Must Wait: The Story of Matthew Flinders - Ernestine Hill 2922
My Name Is Clary Brown - Charlotte Keppel 3466
The Naked Maja - Noel B. Gerson 2378
Nantucket Woman - Diana Gaines 2269
Napoleon Symphony - Anthony Burgess 780
Natchez: A Novel of the Deep South - Pamela Jekel 3186
The Nelson Touch - Paul Lewis 3759
Nethergate - Norah Lofts 3854
Norah - Pamela Hill 2941
Notorious Eliza - Basil Beyea 489
O Beulah Land - Mary Lee Settle 5756
O Genesee - Janet O'Daniel 4688
Oh, Promised Land - James H. Street 6079
O'Higgins and Don Bernardo - Edna Deu Pree Nelson 4578
O'Houlihan's Jest - Rohan O'Grady 4702
Old Glory - Christopher Nicole 4618
Old Hickory - Noel B. Gerson 2379
Old Mortality - Sir Walter Scott 5702
One Red Rose Forever - Mildred A. Jordan 3305
The Overmountain Men - Cameron Judd 3315
Palaces of Desire - Kate Alexander 81
Panther in the Sky - James Alexander Thom 6234
Parson Austen's Daughter - Helen Ashton 219
Passage to Natchez - Cameron Judd 3316
The Peacock's Feather - Sarah Woodhouse 6855
Peg Woffington - Charles Reade 5281
Perfume: The Story of a Murderer - Patrick Suskind 6120
Peter the Great - Alexey Tolstoy 6293
The Pleasure Garden - Leon Garfield 2293
The Porcelain Dove - Delia Sherman 5815
Portrait of Emma - Lillian Cheatham 1010
The President's Lady - Irving Stone 6063
The Princess of Celle - Jean Plaidy 5045
The Prospering - Elizabeth Speare 5954
Proud Heritage - Ilse Bischoff 510
Put Off Thy Shoes - Ethel Lillian Voynich 6513
Queen Dolley: The Life and Times of Dolley Madison - Dorothy Clarke Wilson 6806
Queen in Waiting - Jean Plaidy 5048
The Queen of Hearts - Joan Rees 5290
The Queen's Favourites - Jean Plaidy 5051
The Queen's Physician - Edgar Maas 3952
Quietly My Captain Waits - Evelyn Eaton 1829
Rage in Silence: A Novel Based on the Life of Goya - Donald Braider 643
Raleigh's Eden - Inglis Fletcher 2137
Ram: Being the Tale of One Ramillies Anstruther - Winchombe Taylor 6193
Rasero - Francisco Rebolledo 5282

The Rationalist - Warwick Collins 1217
Rebel Princess - Evelyn Anthony 164
Regency Royal - Michael Hardwick 2687
Renown - Frank Olney Hough 3045
Return to Treasure Island - Denis Judd 3318
The Revolutionary - Lawrence Schoonover 5667
The Riven Heart - Genevieve Gennari 2354
The River Devils - Carter A. Vaughan 6437
Roanoke Warrior - Carter A. Vaughan 6438
Roger Sudden - Thomas H. Raddall 5232
Rogue Herries - Hugh Walpole 6547
A Rose for Virtue - Norah Lofts 3858
The Rose of Malmaison: The Turbulent Life of the Beautiful Josephine - Gaby von Schonthan 5660
Royal Merry-Go-Round - F.W. Kenyon 3459
Royal William - Doris Leslie 3728
Running Proud - Nicholas Monsarrat 4432
The Sable Lion - Jan Van Dorp 6405
Sacajawea of the Shoshones - Della F. Emmons 1940
Sacred and Profane: A Novel of the Life and Times of Mozart - David Weiss 6609
The Salem Frigate - John Edward Jennings 3205
Sally Hemings - Barbara Chase-Riboud 1006
Sara Dane - Catherine Gaskin 2316
The Scimitar - Samuel Edwards 1890
The Sea Officer - Showell Styles 6105
The Sea Panther: A Novel about the Commander of the U.S.S. Constitution - Philip Vail 6397
The Sea Stands Watch - Helen Parker Mudgett 4507
Sea Star: The Private Life of Anne Bonny, Pirate - Pamela Jekel 3187
The Secret Memoirs of Lord Byron - Christopher Nicole 4622
The Secret Wife - Alice Acland 22
The Seekers - John Jakes 3153
Segu - Maryse Conde 1234
Sergeant Lamb's America - Robert Graves 2552
Shadow of the Moon - Douglas C. Jones 3284
Silas Marner - George Eliot 1911
The Silver Touch - Rosalind Laker 3599
Sir William - David Stacton 5977
So Much as Beauty Does - Muriel Elwood 1938
So Perish the Roses - Neil Bell 423
A Sorrow in Our Heart - Allen W. Eckert 1844
The Sot-Weed Factor - John Barth 364
The Sound of Coaches - Leon Garfield 2295
Sound of the Trumpet - Gilbert Morris 4471
The Spanish Bride - Walter O'Meara 4735
Speranza - Sven Delblanc 1584
The Spy: A Tale of the Neutral Ground - James Fenimore Cooper 1310
Storm of Time - Eleanor Dark 1494
The Storms of Fate - Patricia Wright 6885
The Strange Case of Madamoiselle P. - Patrick Ireland 3109
Stranger's Forest - Pamela Hill 2943
Strife Before Dawn - Mary Schumann 5675
The Stuart Legacy - Robert Kerr 3472
The Sugar Pavilion - Rosalind Laker 3600
Sultana - Michael, Prince of Greece 4358
The Sun Is God - Michael Noonan 4636
The Sunshine Patriot: A Novel of Benedict Arnold - Norman Partington 4822
The Swamp Fox, Francis Marion - Noel B. Gerson 2383
Sweet Marie-Antoinette - Lozania Prole 5198
A Tale of Two Cities - Charles Dickens 1642
Taste of Glory - Carleton Beals 394
Tell Your Sons: A Novel of the Napoleonic Era - Willa Gibbs 2402
The Tempestuous Petticoat - Mary Ann Gibbs 2397
That Dark and Bloody River - Allen W. Eckert 1845
There Is a Season - Alice Mary Colver 1219
The Third George - Jean Plaidy 5068
This Is the House - Deborah Hill 2921
This Land Is Ours - Louis Zara 6953
This Promised Land - Robert Easton 1824

Those Who Go Against the Current - Shirley Seifert 5734
Those Who Love - Irving Stone 6064
Through the Green Valley - Barbara Gowdy 2498
Thunderstick - Don Coldsmith 1190
Tidewater Dynasty: A Biographical Novel of the Lees of Stratford Hall - Carey Roberts 5372
Time and the Wind - Erico Verissimo 6451
To Dance with Kings - Rosalind Laker 3601
To Fame Unknown - Clifford Lindsey Alderman 67
To Keep Us Free - Marguerite Allis 115
To Seize a Dream - Virginia Davis Hersch 2866
To Spit Against the Wind - Benjamin H. Levin 3737
To the End of the World - Helen Constance White 6680
Track of the Bear - Don Coldsmith 1191
Treason - Robert Gessner 2389
Treasures on Earth - Jessica Stirling 6049
The Tree of Liberty - Elizabeth Page 4773
The Trees - Conrad Richter 5326
Tsar's Woman - Pamela Hill 2946
Turn of the Dice - Janet Edmonds 1870
The Twisted Saber: A Biographical Novel of Benedict Arnold - Philip Vail 6398
Up Country: A Story of the Vanguard - Donald Culross Peattie 4881
Up She Rises - David Garnett 2298
The Upstart - Edison Marshall 4112
Valide: A Novel of the Harem - Barbara Chase-Riboud 1007
The Valley of Decision - Edith Wharton 6653
Vice Avenged: A Moral Tale - Lolah Burford 774
Vindication - Frances Sherwood 5824
A Virginia Scout - Hugh Pendexter 4899
The Virginians - William Makepeace Thackeray 6214
The Volcano Lover - Susan Sontag 5946
Voltaire! Voltaire! - Guy Endore 1943
Wave High the Banner - Dee Brown 714
Weep in the Sun - Jeanne Wilson 6809
West to the Setting Sun - Harvey Chalmers 973
Whittling Boy: The Story of Eli Whitney - Roger Burlingame 789
Wideacre - Philippa Gregory 2585
Wild Geese - Eilis Dillon 1647
Wilderness Empire - Allen W. Eckert 1847
The Wilderness War - Allen W. Eckert 1848
The Wind That Shakes the Barley - James Barke 305
Wine of Life - Charles Orson Gorham 2489
Wolves Against the Moon - Julia Cooley Altrocchi 123
The Woman of Catawba - Hilda Stahl 5978
World of Silence - Don Coldsmith 1195
Yankee Doodle Dandy - Noel B. Gerson 2387
Yankee Trader - Stanley Morton 4496
Young Catherine - E.M. Almedingen 118
Young Hickory - Stanley Young 6942
Young Pitt - A.M. Maughan 4200

1700s
The Black Dwarf - Sir Walter Scott 5692
The Charlatan - Carter A. Vaughan 6433
The Cold Journey - Grace Zaring Stone 6052
Dark Possession - Alice Alison Lide 3771
For Love of Two Eagles - Barbara Riefe 5328
The Forest Lord - Noel B. Gerson 2368
Fort De Chastaigne - Don Coldsmith 1177
The Headsman; or, The Abbaye des Vignerons - James Fenimore Cooper 1300
The Long Sun - Janice Lucas 3920
The Lords of Loone - John James 3159
The Mohawk Ladder - Noel B. Gerson 2377
Moonfeather - Judith E. French 2223
Quest for the White Bull - Don Coldsmith 1182
The Red Marten - Peter William Nisser 4630
The Sachem - Donald Clayton Porter 5124
Savage Gentleman - Noel B. Gerson 2381
The Swedish Cavalier - Leo Perutz 4943

The Tokaido Road: A Novel of Feudal Japan - Lucia St. Clair Robson 5417
Ward of the Sun King - Mildred Allen Butler 826

1710s
Black William - Robert Neill 4567
Boon Island - Kenneth Roberts 5384
The Bridge of San Luis Rey - Thornton Wilder 6752
The Cannaway Concern - Graham Shelby 5788
Carolina Corsair - Don Tracy 6307
La Dame De Sainte Hermine - Grace King 3485
Deeper the Heritage - Muriel Elwood 1936
The Gamester - Rafael Sabatini 5550
Indian Brother - Hubert Coryell 1354
Katrina - Jeramie Price 5190
Lusty Wind for Carolina - Inglis Fletcher 2134
Men of Albemarle - Inglis Fletcher 2135
Mohawk Woman - Barbara Riefe 5329
On Stranger Tides - Tim Powers 5156
A Pirate's Pleasure - Heather Graham 2518
Ride the Red Earth - Paul I. Wellman 6620
Rob Roy - Sir Walter Scott 5707
Rogue's Holiday - Hamilton Cochran 1141
Running West - James Houston 3052
Through a Glass Darkly - Karleen Koen 3531
Tomorrow the New Moon - Shirley Barker 319
Will You Love Me in September? - Philippa Carr 932
Wind From the Main - Anne Osborne 4759
The Yemassee - William Gilmore Simms 5855

1720s
Atala - Francois Rene de Chateaubriand 1008
A Bride for New Orleans - Edward Francis Murphy 4522
Bride of the Morning Star - Don Coldsmith 1170
The Cannaway Concern - Graham Shelby 5788
Cormorant's Brood - Inglis Fletcher 2133
Katrina - Jeramie Price 5190
Lusty Wind for Carolina - Inglis Fletcher 2134
Now Face to Face - Karleen Koen 3530
Renno - Donald Clayton Porter 5123
Return of the Spanish - Don Coldsmith 1183
Through a Glass Darkly - Karleen Koen 3531
Violent Friends - Winston Clewes 1113
Walks in the Sun - Don Coldsmith 1194
White Man - Peter Freuchen 2228
Wind From the Main - Anne Osborne 4759

1730s
Blackrobe - Robert E. Wall 6534
Dark Sails - Helen Topping Miller 4388
The Devil and Ben Franklin - Theodore Mathieson 4184
Gamble's Hundred - Clifford Dowdey 1705
The Glory and the Dream - Katharine Dunlap 1789
The Heart of Midlothian - Sir Walter Scott 5698
The Holy Lover - Marie Oemler 4690
A New Creature - Prudence Andrew 141
Passion and the Sword - Harald Hornborg 3034
Rascal's Heaven - F. van Wyck Mason 4157
The Ravishers - Elizabeth Richards 5318
Royal Yankee - Victor Suthren 6132
Summer Thunder - Willie Snow Ethridge 1982
Take Her, Mr. Wesley - John W. Drakeford 1719
Tomahawk - Donald Clayton Porter 5129
The Villains: A Haunting Tale of the Marshes - Charlotte Keppel 3467
Yankee Rogue - Dana Fuller Ross 5496
Young Titan - F. van Wyck Mason 4165

1740s
Admiral of Fear - Victor Suthren 6126
Ask Me No Questions - Patricia Veryan 6459
The Black Cockade - Victor Suthren 6127
Blackrobe - Robert E. Wall 6534
The Blood of Roses - Marsha Canham 879
Bloodbrothers - Robert E. Wall 6535
Born to Be King - Constance Gluyas 2440
Candleshine No More - Jane Oliver 4721
Captain Monsoon - Victor Suthren 6128

Charlie Is My Darling - Mollie Hardwick 2691
Cherished Enemy - Patricia Veryan 6460
Clandara - Evelyn Anthony 161
Commander of the Mists - D.L. Murray 4527
The Dark Mile - Dorothy Kathleen Broster 709
Dark Sails - Helen Topping Miller 4388
A Day of Battle - Vincent Sheean 5787
The Dedicated Villain - Patricia Veryan 6461
The Deerslayer - James Fenimore Cooper 1299
The Double Man - Elinor Pryor 5205
Dragonfly in Amber - Diana Gabaldon 2262
The Drayton Legacy - Rona Randall 5247
The Flight of the Heron - Dorothy Kathleen Broster 710
Gennie the Huguenot Woman - Bette M. Ross 5464
The Golden Galleon - Victor Suthren 6129
The Golden Ocean - Patrick O'Brian 4665
Had We Never Loved - Patricia Veryan 6463
Hang for Treason - Robert Newton Peck 4886
Highlands Rebel - Sally Watson 6584
The Highwayman - Noel B. Gerson 2372
Hotel Transylvania - Chelsea Quinn Yarbro 6900
I Came to the Highlands: A Novel of Suspense - Velda Johnston 3263
In Perilous Seas - Victor Suthren 6130
The Indentured Heart - Gilbert Morris 4464
The Invincibles - Carter A. Vaughan 6436
Journey to Enchantment - Patricia Veryan 6464
A King's Ransom - Victor Suthren 6131
Lady of the Mohawks - Margaret Widdemer 6736
The Long Day Closes - Beatrice Tunstall 6360
Lord of Misrule - Gareth Jones 3290
Love Alters Not - Patricia Veryan 6467
MacLyon - Lolah Burford 773
Manila Galleon - F. van Wyck Mason 4154
The Masqueraders - Georgette Heyer 2894
The Master of Ballantrae: A Winter's Tale - Robert Louis Stevenson 6011
Midwinter - John Buchan 751
Mistress of Willowvale - Patricia Veryan 6471
The Mists of Manittoo - Lois Swann 6135
Never Doubt I Love - Patricia Veryan 6473
Outlander - Diana Gabaldon 2264
Practice to Deceive - Patricia Veryan 6475
The Pride of Lions - Marsha Canham 881
A Prince, a Piper, and a Rose - John Scalzo 5628
Rascal's Heaven - F. van Wyck Mason 4157
Red Cloak Flying - Margaret Widdemer 6737
Restless Are the Sails - Evelyn Eaton 1830
The Savage City - Jean Paradise 4787
Seasons of Fear - Philip McFarland 4272
A Shadow's Bliss - Patricia Veryan 6477
The Silver Saber - Carter A. Vaughan 6441
Time's Fool - Patricia Veryan 6479
Torbeg - Grace Campbell 873
Torn Covenants - Lois Swann 6136
Treasure Island - Robert Louis Stevenson 6012
The Tyrant - Patricia Veryan 6480
The Unknown Shore - Patrick O'Brian 4678
The Villains: A Haunting Tale of the Marshes - Charlotte Keppel 3467
Voyager - Diana Gabaldon 2265
The Wagered Widow - Patricia Veryan 6481
Waverley - Sir Walter Scott 5709
The Wilderness - Carter A. Vaughan 6442
Wilderness Adventure - Elizabeth Page 4774
The Willing Maid - C.T. Ritchie 5349
The Woman from The Glen - Chloe Gartner 2310
The Yankee Brig - Carter A. Vaughan 6443
Yankee Rogue - Dana Fuller Ross 5496
The Young Man From Mount Vernon - Arthur Stanwood Pier 4995
Young Titan - F. van Wyck Mason 4165

1750s
The Adulteress - Philippa Carr 916
Ambush - Donald Clayton Porter 5113
Barry Lyndon - William Makepeace Thackeray 6210

Benjamin Franklin and a Case of Artful Murder - Robert Lee Hall 2654

Benjamin Franklin and a Case of Christmas Murder - Robert Lee Hall 2655

Benjamin Franklin Takes the Case - Robert Lee Hall 2656

Bloodbrothers - Robert E. Wall 6535

The Bright Battalions - Howard Breslin 664

Catriona - Robert Louis Stevenson 6009

Charming Sally - Maude Hart Lovelace 3903

Commander of the Mists - D.L. Murray 4527

The Double Man - Elinor Pryor 5205

The Drayton Legacy - Rona Randall 5247

Drums Against Frontenac - Harvey Chalmers 972

Eagle Fur - Robert Newton Peck 4884

Eden's Gate - Karen Harper 2711

Edge of Greatness - Winthrop Neilson 4575

Eugene Aram - Edward Bulwer-Lytton 766

Fawn - Robert Newton Peck 4885

Fire Along the Sky: A Novel of America - Robert Moss 4497

Follow the River - James Alexander Thom 6231

The French Bride - Evelyn Anthony 163

Gentleman Ranker - John Edward Jennings 3200

Ghost Fox - James Houston 3051

The Golden Wildcat - Margaret Widdemer 6735

His Majesty's Highlanders - Leslie Turner White 6683

The Indentured Heart - Gilbert Morris 4464

Jason McGee - Robert H. Fowler 2190

Juniata Valley - Virginia C. Cassel 954

Kidnapped - Robert Louis Stevenson 6010

The Last of the Mohicans - James Fenimore Cooper 1302

Lord Johnnie - Leslie Turner White 6687

Lord Vanity - Samuel Shellabarger 5796

The Master of Ballantrae: A Winter's Tale - Robert Louis Stevenson 6011

Miss Philadelphia Smith - Paula Allardyce 91

Morning of a Hero - Burke Boyce 608

Murder at Drury Lane - Robert Lee Hall 2659

Murder by the Waters - Robert Lee Hall 2661

Next to Valour - John Edward Jennings 3202

The Ninth Statue - Roseleen Milne 4410

Northwest Passage - Kenneth Roberts 5388

The Pathfinder; or, The Inland Sea - James Fenimore Cooper 1305

The Peaceable Kingdom - Jan de Hartog 2763

The Plains of Abraham - James Oliver Curwood 1452

Power - Lion Feuchtwanger 2074

The Prince and the Quakeress - Jean Plaidy 5043

Prince Charlie's Bluff - Donald Thomas 6241

Red Morning - Ruby Frazier Frey 2230

The Red Road: A Romance of Braddock's Defeat - Hugh Pendexter 4898

Sacred Hunter - Barry Unsworth 6389

Sarah Camberwell Tring - Janet Edmonds 1869

The Seneca Hostage - Carter A. Vaughan 6440

Song of the Susquehanna - Herbert Stover 6071

Tavern in the Town - Cecile Hulse Matschat 4187

These Old Shades - Georgette Heyer 2906

Thunder in the East - Mike Roarke 5362

The Vast Memory of Love - Malcolm Bosse 588

War Cry - Donald Clayton Porter 5132

War in the Golden Weather - Stephen Longstreet 3892

War Paint and Rouge - Robert W. Chambers 983

Web of Destiny - Muriel Elwood 1939

Westward to Laughter - Colin MacInnes 3984

The White Cockade - Vincent O'Brien 4683

Whitton's Folly - Pamela Hill 2948

The Woodsman - Don Wright 6880

The Young Man From Mount Vernon - Arthur Stanwood Pier 4995

1760s

Barry Lyndon - William Makepeace Thackeray 6210

Bedford Village - Hervey Allen 99

Blind Justice - Bruce Alexander 76

Brimstone Club - F. van Wyck Mason 4147

The Case of Kitty Ogilvie - Jean Stubbs 6093

Charco Harbour - Godfrey Blunden 554

City of Golden Cages - Jo Germany 2358

Drums of Autumn - Diana Gabaldon 2263

Fire Along the Sky: A Novel of America - Robert Moss 4497

The Fires of July - Sharon Salvato 5576

The First Rebel - Neil Harmon Swanson 6137

Follow the River - James Alexander Thom 6231

Hatchet in the Sky - Margaret Cooper Gay 2328

In What Torn Ship - Evelyn Eaton 1828

The Judas Tree - Neil Harmon Swanson 6139

The Kentuckians - Janice Holt Giles 2413

The Light in the Forest - Conrad Richter 5322

The Lost Queen - Norah Lofts 3850

The Love Child - Philippa Carr 923

Lucy - Hester W. Chapman 992

Maria - Eugenia Price 5184

Nine Days of Father Serra - Isabelle Gibson Ziegler 6961

The Ninth Statue - Roseleen Milne 4410

Nobody's Angel - Karen Robards 5363

A Place Called Freedom - Ken Follett 2150

The Prince and the Quakeress - Jean Plaidy 5043

Prince Charlie's Bluff - Donald Thomas 6241

Red Gauntlet - Sir Walter Scott 5706

The Red Road: A Romance of Braddock's Defeat - Hugh Pendexter 4898

Richard Carvel - Winston Churchill 1081

River out of Eden - Shirley Seifert 5732

The Silent Drum - Neil Harmon Swanson 6141

Silent Drums - Mike Roarke 5361

Starrbelow - China Thompson 6248

Strange Wives - Shirley Barker 317

The Sun Is My Undoing - Marguerite Steen 5988

Temple Bells - Marjorie McEvoy 4271

Thunder in the Wilderness - Charles Granville Hamilton 2668

Toward the Morning - Hervey Allen 101

The Unconquered - Neil Harmon Swanson 6142

The Virginia Comedians - John Esten Cooke 1269

The War Chest - Porter Hill 2950

Watery Grave - Bruce Alexander 78

Weathercock - Constance Dodge 1668

1770s

Alice of Old Vincennes - Maurice Thompson 6268

April Morning - Howard Fast 2027

The Arch of Stars - Clifford Lindsey Alderman 66

Arundel - Kenneth Roberts 5383

Barnaby Rudge: A Tale of the Riots of Eighty - Charles Dickens 1641

The Bastard - John Jakes 3144

Be My Love - Harriet Hinsdale 2955

Bend Your Heads All - Rowena Rutherford Farrar 2015

Benjamin Blake - Edison Marshall 4102

Beyond the Blue Sierra - Honore Morrow 4486

The Big Knives - Bruce Lancaster 3635

The Bonnet Laird's Daughter - Barbara Annandale 154

The Border Men - Cameron Judd 3312

The Braintree Mission - Nicholas E. Wyckoff 6887

Bride of Liberty - Frank Yerby 6909

Brother to the Enemy - Bart Spicer 5964

Buckskin Baronet - Margaret Widdemer 6734

By Force of Arms - James L. Nelson 4579

By the King's Command - Shirley Seifert 5723

Cannon's Call - Adam Rutledge 5537

Captain Ironhand - Rosamond Marshall 4116

Captain Nash and the Honour of England - Ragan Butler 827

Captain Nash and the Wroth Inheritance - Ragan Butler 828

The Captain's Daughter - Alexander Pushkin 5210

Cardigan - Robert W. Chambers 976

The Carolinian - Rafael Sabatini 5547

Celia Garth - Gwen Bristow 695

Cherokee - Donald Clayton Porter 5115

A City for St. Francis - Evelyn Wells 6621

Clear for Action: A Novel about John Paul Jones - Clements Ripley 5344

Clouds of Destiny - Lou Ellen Davis 1535

The Coat I Wore - Lucile Finlay 2090

Come Spring - Ben Ames Williams 6764

Conceived in Liberty - Howard Fast 2029

Concord Bridge - Howard Horne 3035

The Court Martial of Daniel Boone - Allen W. Eckert 1840

The Cross and the Sword - Jonreed Lauritzen 3674

The Crossing - Winston Churchill 1080

Crown Without Sceptre - William Vaughan Wilkins 6758

The Culper Spy Ring - Lynn Groh 2596

Dawn's Early Light - Elswyth Thane 6215

The Day Before Thunder - Bart Spicer 5965

The Day Must Dawn - Agnes Sligh Turnbull 6362

Day of Battle - Frederic F. Van de Water 6402

Denis Duval - William Makepeace Thackeray 6211

Don't Tread on Me - Walter Karig 3366

Dragon Cove - Carter A. Vaughan 6434

Drums - James Boyd 611

Drums Along the Mohawk - Walter D. Edmonds 1874

The Drums of April - Charles Mergendahl 4340

Drums of Autumn - Diana Gabaldon 2263

The Drums of December - Sharon Salvato 5575

The Drums of Winter - Sandra Paretti 4790

Dust on the King's Highway - Helen Constance White 6677

The Eagle and the Wind - Herbert Stover 6068

Eagle of Niagara: The Story of David Harper and His Indian Captivity - John Brick 671

Eagles Where I Walk - Stephen Longstreet 3885

East to Bagaduce - Willard Wallace 6539

The Edge of Piracy - Donald Barr Chidsey 1060

Enough Good Men - Charles Mercer 4336

The Exquisite Siren - Edwin Haines 2639

Faith and Honor - Robin Maderich 4025

Farewell to Valley Forge - David Taylor 6178

Fire and the Hammer - Shirley Barker 311

The Firelands - Karen Harper 2712

The Fires of Glenlochy - Constance Heaven 2806

The Fires of July - Sharon Salvato 5576

The Forbidden Ground - Neil Harmon Swanson 6138

Fortress Fury - Carter A. Vaughan 6435

Freedom's Way - Theodora McCormick Du Bois 1742

The Gentle Rebel - Gilbert Morris 4461

Gilman of the Redford - William Stearns Davis 1541

The Great Meadow - Elizabeth Madox Roberts 5378

The Green Mountain Boys - Daniel Pierce Thompson 6249

The Guernseyman - C. Northcote Parkinson 4812

Guns for Rebellion - F. van Wyck Mason 4151

Guns of Burgoyne - Bruce Lancaster 3640

Hand of Glory - Glen Petrie 4980

Hang for Treason - Robert Newton Peck 4886

Hannah Fowler - Janice Holt Giles 2411

Harvest of Dreams - Jaroldeen Edwards 1884

Hearts of Fire - Christina Savage 5616

Henry Lunt and the Ranger - Tom McNamara 4304

Hidden Children - Robert W. Chambers 978

His Majesty's Highwayman - Donald Barr Chidsey 1061

His Majesty's Yankees - Thomas H. Raddall 5230

Hugh Wynne, Free Quaker - Silas Weir Mitchell 4416

The Hunting Shirt - Mary Johnston 3235

If Not Victory - Frank Olney Hough 3043

In Gallant Company - Alexander Kent 3433

In the Hands of the Senecas - Walter D. Edmonds 1876

Inherit the Earth - Margaret Shaw 5778

The Iron Chain - Jim DeFelice 1579

Janice Meredith - Paul Leicester Ford   2166

Jeremiah Martin: A Revolutionary War Novel - Robert H. Fowler   2191

Journey to Nashville - Alfred Leland Crabb   1402

Judas Flowering - Jane Aiken Hodge   2965

The Kentuckians - Janice Holt Giles   2413

Kentucky Stand - Jere Hungerford Wheelwright   6670

The Kentucky Trace: A Novel of the American Revolution - Harriette Simpson Arnow   195

The King's Iron - Robert Newton Peck   4888

The King's Rebel - James David Horan   3030

The Kingsbridge Plot - Maan Meyers   4355

The Lady From Yorktown - Eva McDonald   4260

The Land Breakers - John Ehle   1895

Land for My Sons - Maribelle Cormack   1331

The Last Gentleman - Shirley Barker   312

The Last Voyage: Captain Cook's Lost Diary - Hammond Innes   3108

The Latter Adventures of Tom Jones - Bob Coleman   1200

Let the King Beware! - Honore Morrow   4489

Let the Spring Come - Henry Schindall   5637

Liberty Tavern - Thomas Fleming   2129

Life and Liberty - Adam Rutledge   5538

The Life and Times of Captain N. - Douglas Glover   2436

Lionel Lincoln; or, The Leaguer of Boston - James Fenimore Cooper   1303

Little Red Foot - Robert W. Chambers   979

The Long March - Jane Barry   358

The Long Naked Descent into Boston - William Eastlake   1823

The Long Watch - Elizabeth Linington   3798

The Lost Queen - Norah Lofts   3850

Love Not a Rebel - Heather Graham   2516

Love's Tender Fury - Jennifer Wilde   6749

Lucifer Land - Mildred B. Davis   1538

The Lure of the Falcon - Juliette Benzoni   465

The Maddest Idea - James L. Nelson   4580

Man From Mt. Vernon - Burke Boyce   607

Maria - Eugenia Price   5184

The Marquis and Miss Jones - Helen Ashfield   208

Mars' Butterfly - Henry Pleasants   5080

The Master of Chaos - Irving A. Bacheller   262

Master of Morholm - Timothy R. Wilson   6817

Meggy MacIntosh - Elizabeth Janet Gray   2555

Men in Buckskin - Herbert Stover   6069

The Michaelmas Tree - Helen Ashfield   209

Midshipman Bolitho and the Avenger - Alexander Kent   3435

Mistaken Virtues - Joanna Trollope   6349

Mistress Devon - Virginia Coffman   1156

Monmouth - Charles Bracelen Flood   2144

Morning in America - Willard Wiener   6741

Murfy's Men - Gerald Green   2565

My Thomas: A Novel of Martha Jefferson's Life - Roberta Grimes   2593

Nantucket Rebel - Edouard A. Stackpole   5970

The Navigator: The Story of Nathaniel Bowditch - Alfred Stanford   5979

The Neutral Ground - Frank Olney Hough   3044

Never No More: The Story of Rebecca Boone - Shirley Seifert   5730

Night Wind's Woman - Shirl Henke   2825

Oh, Kentucky! - Betty Layman Receveur   5284

Oliver Wiswell - Kenneth Roberts   5389

Painted Minx - Robert W. Chambers   980

Patriot's Dream - Barbara Michaels   4360

Patriot's Progress - Joseph G.E. Hopkins   3027

The Perilous Night - Burke Boyce   609

The Pilot - James Fenimore Cooper   1306

The Price of Liberty - Joseph G.E. Hopkins   3028

The Prize Master - Harvey Haislip   2642

Proceed, Sergeant Lamb - Robert Graves   2550

The Queen's Confession - Victoria Holt   3019

Rabble in Arms - Kenneth Roberts   5390

The Raid - John Brick   673

The Rebel and the Turncoat - Malcolm Decker   1576

Rebel Guns - Adam Rutledge   5539

The Rebel Loyalist - Charles William Gordon   2480

The Rebels - John Jakes   3152

The Red Rover - James Fenimore Cooper   1309

Redcoat - Bernard Cornwell   1337

The Redemptioner - Isaac Rusling Pennypacker   4910

Reluctant Rebel - Frederic F. Van de Water   6403

Retreat and Recall - Joseph G.E. Hopkins   3029

The Return of Lono: A Novel of Captain Cook's Last Voyage - Oswald Andrew Bushnell   816

Richard Bolitho—Midshipman - Alexander Kent   3437

Richard Carvel - Winston Churchill   1081

Richard Pryne: A Novel of the American Revolution - Cyril Harris   2718

The Rifleman - John Brick   675

The Rival Shores - Arthur Beverly-Giddings   487

Rivers of Glory - F. van Wyck Mason   4158

The Road to Bunker Hill - Shirley Barker   316

Rogue's March - Maristan Chapman   993

Sailor Named Jones - Harvey Haislip   2643

The Saintly Buccaneer - Gilbert Morris   4469

Scarlet Ribbons - Judith E. French   2224

The Scotswoman - Inglis Fletcher   2140

Scoundrels' Brigade - Carter A. Vaughan   6439

The Sea Eagles - John Edward Jennings   3206

Seneca - Donald Clayton Porter   5127

The Shadow and the Glory - John Edward Jennings   3207

Shadow of the Long Knives - Thomas Alexander Boyd   615

Shadows on the Long House - Mike Roarke   5360

Sloop of War - Alexander Kent   3439

Something Gleamed - Theda Kenyon   3463

Song of a Strange Child - Gilbert Morris   4470

Sons of Liberty - Adam Rutledge   5540

Spanish Bayonet - Stephen Vincent Benet   441

Stand into Danger - Alexander Kent   3440

Stars and Stripes - Adam Rutledge   5541

Stars on the Sea - F. van Wyck Mason   4161

Storm Against the Wind - Helen Hull Jacobs   3138

Strange Wives - Shirley Barker   317

The Strong Men - John Brick   677

Swear by Apollo - Shirley Barker   318

That Bennington Mob - Henry Barnard Safford   5558

Thomas Forty - Edward Stanley   5982

Three Fields to Cross - Francis Tysen Nutt   4651

Three Harbors - F. van Wyck Mason   4162

Three Sides of Agiochook - Eric Kelly   3400

A Toast to the King - Elizabeth Coatsworth   1139

Toil of the Brave - Inglis Fletcher   2141

Tory Tavern - Henry Barnard Safford   5559

The Traitor - Dan Sherman   5814

Trumpet in the Sky - Helen Topping Miller   4397

Trumpet to Arms - Bruce Lancaster   3647

Trumpets at Dawn - Cyril Harris   2719

Two Crowns for America - Katherine Kurtz   3568

The Unvanquished - Howard Fast   2046

Valiant Libertine - John Gordon Bryson   748

Valley Forge - MacKinlay Kantor   3364

The Venetian Mask - Rosalind Laker   3603

Waters of the Wilderness - Shirley Seifert   5737

Weathercock - Constance Dodge   1668

The Weeping Ash - Joan Aiken   54

Westward the Tide - Harold Sinclair   5863

Wild Horizon - F. van Wyck Mason   4164

The Wind in the Forest - Inglis Fletcher   2143

Wings of the Morning - Frederic F. Van de Water   6404

The Yankee Rascals - Carter A. Vaughan   6444

Yorktown - Burke Davis   1513

1780s

Alabama Empire - Welbourn Kelley   3392

Apache - Donald Clayton Porter   5114

Balisand - Joseph Hergesheimer   2853

Barnaby Rudge: A Tale of the Riots of Eighty - Charles Dickens   1641

Battle Lanterns - Merrit Parmalee Allen   102

The Black Consul - Anatolii Vinogradov   6503

Blind Journey - Bruce Lancaster   3636

The Bonnet Laird's Daughter - Barbara Annandale   154

The Border Men - Cameron Judd   3312

Botany Bay - Charles Nordhoff   4637

Bridal Journey - Dale Van Every   6406

Bride of Liberty - Frank Yerby   6909

Captain Barney - Jan Westcott   6642

The Captive Witch - Dale Van Every   6407

The Captives - Don Wright   6878

The Carolinians - Jane Barry   357

A Case of Curiosities - Allen Kurzweil   3569

Catch a Falling Star - Frederic F. Van de Water   6401

Cato's War - Guy Wheeler   6655

Celia Garth - Gwen Bristow   695

Choctaw - Donald Clayton Porter   5116

Christmas at Mount Vernon - Helen Topping Miller   4385

City of Darkness, City of Light - Marge Piercy   4998

Cockades: A Romance - Meade Minnigerode   4412

Come Spring - Ben Ames Williams   6764

Command a King's Ship - Alexander Kent   3428

The Convenient Marriage - Georgette Heyer   2882

Crest of the Broken Wave - James Barke   302

The Crossing - Winston Churchill   1080

The Culper Spy Ring - Lynn Groh   2596

Dark Hills to Westward - Harry M. Caudill   964

Dawn's Early Light - Elswyth Thane   6215

The Days of the King - Bruno Frank   2200

Demelza - Winston Graham   2524

The Devil on Horseback - Victoria Holt   3014

Devil's Cub - Georgette Heyer   2885

The Devil's Laughter - Frank Yerby   6913

Dr. Guillotine: The Eccentric Exploits of an Early Scientist - Herbert Lom   3867

Don't Tread on Me - Walter Karig   3366

Drums - James Boyd   611

Drums Along the Mohawk - Walter D. Edmonds   1874

The Drums of December - Sharon Salvato   5575

The Drums of Winter - Sandra Paretti   4790

Eagle in the Sky - F. van Wyck Mason   4149

Eagles Where I Walk - Stephen Longstreet   3885

Faith and Honor - Robin Maderich   4025

Farewell the Tranquil - R.F. Delderfield   1585

Father of Waters - Donald Clayton Porter   5118

Fear No More - Hester W. Chapman   990

A Few Painted Feathers - Stephen Longstreet   3886

Flight From Avatchez - Frank G. Slaughter   5887

Flintlock - Jason Manning   4073

The French Admiral - Dewey Lambdin   3609

Friendly Cove - Irving Brant   651

Fruit in His Season - Helen C. Barney   333

The General's Lady - Esther Forbes   2156

The Gods Are Thirsty - Tanith Lee   3710

The Great Meadow - Elizabeth Madox Roberts   5378

The Guernseyman - C. Northcote Parkinson   4812

The Gun Ketch - Dewey Lambdin   3610

H.—: The Story of Heathcliff's Journey Back to Wuthering Heights - Lin Haire-Sargeant   2641

Hangman's Cliff - Robert Neill   4570

Harp of a Thousand Strings - Harold Lenoir Davis   1522

The Hawks of Hawk-Hollow - Robert Montgomery Bird   504

Hearts and Bones - Margaret Lawrence   3685

Hearts of Fire - Christina Savage   5616

The Hessian - Howard Fast   2033

Hester - Brian Cleeve   1107

H.M.S. Bounty - Alexander McKee   4280

Horseshoe Robinson, a Tale of the Tory Ascendancy - John P. Kennedy   3418

Hugh Wynne, Free Quaker - Silas Weir Mitchell   4416

The Hunting Shirt - Mary Johnston   3235

If This Be Magic - Ellen Marsh   4098

The Incorruptible - Helma De Bois   1551

The Ironmaster - Anne Powers   5150

Janice Meredith - Paul Leicester Ford 2166

Jefferson: A Novel - Max Byrd 838

Jeremiah Martin: A Revolutionary War Novel - Robert H. Fowler 2191

Journey to Nashville - Alfred Leland Crabb 1402

The Kidnapped Surgeon - Alexander Knox 3527

The King's Coat - Dewey Lambdin 3612

The King's Commission - Dewey Lambdin 3614

King's Masque - Evan John 3220

Kings Mountain - Florette Henri 2838

The Lady From Yorktown - Eva McDonald 4260

Lady of Paris - William Vaughan Wilkins 6760

The Land Beyond the Mountains - Janice Holt Giles 2414

The Land Breakers - John Ehle 1895

Lantern for the Dark - Jessica Stirling 6045

Lempriere's Dictionary - Lawrence Norfolk 4641

The Life and Times of Captain N. - Douglas Glover 2436

Little Red Foot - Robert W. Chambers 979

The Lonely Strangers - Charity Blackstock 531

The Long March - Jane Barry 358

The Long Watch - Elizabeth Linington 3798

Lucifer Land - Mildred B. Davis 1538

The Lure of the Falcon - Juliette Benzoni 465

Major Andre - Anthony Bailey 265

Man From Mt. Vernon - Burke Boyce 607

Manitou - Donald Clayton Porter 5120

The Marquis and Miss Jones - Helen Ashfield 208

Mars' Butterfly - Henry Pleasants 5080

Men Against the Sea - Charles Nordhoff 4638

Mistress of Darkness - Christopher Nicole 4617

Morning in America - Willard Wiener 6741

Morning Time - Charles Kendall O'Neill 4743

Mozart on the Way to Prague - Eduard Friedrich Morike 4454

Mr. Arnold - Francis Lynde 3935

Murfy's Men - Gerald Green 2565

Mutiny on the Bounty - Charles Nordhoff 4639

My Thomas: A Novel of Martha Jefferson's Life - Roberta Grimes 2593

The Neutral Ground - Frank Olney Hough 3044

Nick of the Woods; or, The Jibbenainosay - Robert Montgomery Bird 505

Now We Are Free - Marguerite Allis 112

Oh, Kentucky! - Betty Layman Receveur 5284

Oliver Wiswell - Kenneth Roberts 5389

Othneil Jones - John Adams Leland 3715

Painted Minx - Robert W. Chambers 980

Passage to Mutiny - Alexander Kent 3436

Perdita's Prince - Jean Plaidy 5040

The Perilous Night - Burke Boyce 609

Phantom Fortress - Bruce Lancaster 3643

The Pilot - James Fenimore Cooper 1306

A Place of Greater Safety - Hilary Mantel 4077

Playing the Jack - Mary Brown 726

The Playmaker - Thomas Keneally 3414

Poor Richard's Game - G.J.A. O'Toole 4766

Portrait of a Scoundrel - Nathaniel Benchley 438

Powder Mission - Herbert Stover 6070

The Prisoners of September - Leon Garfield 2294

Proceed, Sergeant Lamb - Robert Graves 2550

The Proud and the Free - Howard Fast 2042

The Queen's Confession - Victoria Holt 3019

Queen's Gift - Inglis Fletcher 2136

The Queen's Necklace - Alexandre Dumas 1781

The Ragged Ones - Burke Davis 1511

The Rebel Loyalist - Charles William Gordon 2480

The Rebels - John Jakes 3152

Red Belts - Hugh Pendexter 4897

The Red Doe - Drayton Mayrant 4214

The Regulators - William Degenhard 1580

The Renegade: A Novel of Cornwall, 1783-1787 - Winston Graham 2529

A Respectable Trade - Philippa Gregory 2584

Riders of the Long Road - Stephen E. Bransford 649

The Rifleman - John Brick 675

The Road to Glory - Darwin Le Ora Teilhet 6199

Rogue's March - Maristan Chapman 993

The Saintly Buccaneer - Gilbert Morris 4469

Sangaree - Frank G. Slaughter 5898

Scaramouche - Rafael Sabatini 5554

Scarlet Feather - Dale Van Every 6409

The Sea Eagles - John Edward Jennings 3206

Sea Road to Yorktown - Harvey Haislip 2644

The Secret Road - Bruce Lancaster 3646

Seminole - Donald Clayton Porter 5126

Shad Run - Howard Breslin 668

Shadows on the Long House - Mike Roarke 5360

Slow Dies the Thunder - Helen Topping Miller 4395

The Smile of the Stranger - Joan Aiken 53

Song in the Green Thorn Tree - James Barke 303

The Sounds of Chariots: A Novel of John Sevier and the State of Franklin - Helen Topping Miller 4396

Spirit Knife - Donald Clayton Porter 5128

The Sprig of Hemlock: A Novel about Shays' Rebellion - Robert Muir 4509

Storm the Last Rampart - David Taylor 6180

Storm Winds - Iris Johansen 3217

The Strange Case of Deacon Brodie - Forbes Bramble 646

Sweet Lass of Richmond Hill - Jean Plaidy 5067

Sycamore Men - David Taylor 6181

Tallien: A Brief Romance - Frederic Tuten 6370

Tennessee Hazard - Maristan Chapman 994

They Had a Glory - Davenport Steward 6018

Thomas Forty - Edward Stanley 5982

To Glory We Steer - Alexander Kent 3442

To the Ends of the Earth - Michael Talbot 6155

Tomorrow the Harvest - Viola Paradise 4789

The Traitor - Dan Sherman 5814

Tricolour - Mark Logan 3866

Trumpet to Arms - Bruce Lancaster 3647

Trumpets at Dawn - Cyril Harris 2719

The Twelfth Physician - Willa Gibbs 2403

The Venetian Mask - Rosalind Laker 3603

Veronique - Virginia Coffman 1158

The Voyagers - Dale Van Every 6412

War Drums - Donald Clayton Porter 5133

Waters of the Wilderness - Shirley Seifert 5737

The Way to the Lantern - Audrey Erskine Lindop 3790

The White Cockade - Charles James Louis Gilson 2423

Wicked Lady - Inglis Fletcher 2142

Wide Is the Water - Jane Aiken Hodge 2973

Wild Horizon - F. van Wyck Mason 4164

A Wilful Woman - Michael Talbot 6156

Windover - Jane Aiken Hodge 2974

Wonder of All the Gay World - James Barke 306

The World Turned Upside Down - William Rayner 5273

Yankee - Dana Fuller Ross 5495

The Year of the French - Thomas Flanagan 2121

Yorktown - Burke Davis 1513

1790s

Adam Bede - George Eliot 1908

Afternoon of a Autocrat - Norah Lofts 3834

Alabama Empire - Welbourn Kelley 3392

All Souls' Rising - Madison Smartt Bell 422

Alone Among Men - Marjorie Coryn 1355

American Captain - Edison Marshall 4101

The Angry Tide - Winston Graham 2521

The Antiquary - Sir Walter Scott 5690

As Runs the Glass - Evan John David 1502

Asylum for the Queen - Mildred A. Jordan 3303

Balisand - Joseph Hergesheimer 2853

Before the Wind - Lloyd M. Moxon 4506

Billy Budd - Herman Melville 4333

The Bizarre Sisters - Jay Walz 6559

The Black Consul - Anatolii Vinogradov 6503

The Black Moon - Winston Graham 2522

Blake's Reach - Catherine Gaskin 2313

The Brittle Glass - Norah Lofts 3837

Broadsides - Robert Welter Daly 1459

Brumaire - Mark Logan 3864

The Canebrake Men - Cameron Judd 3313

A Chance for Glory - Constance Wright 6877

City of Darkness, City of Light - Marge Piercy 4998

Claire - Elizabeth Lyle 3931

Conjuror's Journal - Frances L. Shine 5826

The Council of Europe - Leonardo Sciascia 5678

Cousin Susannah - Hazel Hucker 3066

Crest of the Broken Wave - James Barke 302

The Cumberland Rifles - Noel B. Gerson 2365

The Dark Palazzo - Virginia Coffman 1151

The Delectable Country - Leland Dewitt Baldwin 280

Devil to Pay - C. Northcote Parkinson 4810

The Devil's Laughter - Frank Yerby 6913

Dr. Guillotine: The Eccentric Exploits of an Early Scientist - Herbert Lom 3867

Dreams of Empire - Jeanne Mackin 3994

Drumbeat - Dudley Pope 5094

Drums at Dusk - Arna Bontemps 575

The Duke's Mistress: The Story of Mary Ann Clarke - F.W. Kenyon 3447

East Indiaman - Frank Pollard 5087

The Emperor's Lady: A Novel Based on the Life of the Empress Josephine - F.W. Kenyon 3449

Enemy in Sight! - Alexander Kent 3429

The Fallen Angels - Susannah Kells 3397

Fear No More - Hester W. Chapman 990

A Finger to Her Lips - Evelyn Berckman 472

The Fireship - C. Northcote Parkinson 4811

First Lieutenant - Kenneth Maynard 4208

The Flag Captain - Alexander Kent 3430

Follow the River - Albert Mayer 4203

Form Line of Battle! - Alexander Kent 3431

Forty Centuries Look Down - Frederick Britten Austin 245

The Four Swans - Winston Graham 2525

Friendly Cove - Irving Brant 651

A Game for Empires - Pearl Frye 2243

Genesee Fever - Carl Lamson Carmer 898

The Gods Are Thirsty - Tanith Lee 3710

The Golden Mistress - Basil Beyea 488

Governor Ramage, R.N. - Dudley Pope 5096

Guillotine - Mark Logan 3865

Harp of a Thousand Strings - Harold Lenoir Davis 1522

Hawthorn Hill - Doris Shannon 5777

Heroic Dust - Theodora Dehon 1581

Hester - Brian Cleeve 1107

H.M.S. Bounty - Alexander McKee 4280

H.M.S. Cockerel - Dewey Lambdin 3611

The Holy Warrior - Gilbert Morris 4462

The House by the Churchyard - Joseph Sheridan Le Fanu 3688

I Thee Wed - Gilbert Wolf Gabriel 2267

If This Be Magic - Ellen Marsh 4098

The Incorruptible - Marjorie Coryn 1357

The Incorruptible - Helma De Bois 1551

Jamaica Inn - Daphne Du Maurier 1747

Judith - Brian Cleeve 1108

Kate - Brian Cleeve 1109

A King Reluctant - William Vaughan Wilkins 6759

A King's Commander - Dewey Lambdin 3613

King's Masque - Evan John 3220

The King's Privateer - Dewey Lambdin 3615

Lady of Paris - William Vaughan Wilkins 6760

Lamb in Command - Kenneth Maynard 4209

The Land Beyond the Mountains - Janice Holt Giles 2414

The Last Gamble - Winston Graham 2527

Lieutenant Lamb - Kenneth Maynard 4210

Lord Elgin's Lady - Theodore Vrettos 6514

Lord Libertine - Anthony Esler 1964

Loving Sands, Deadly Sands - Charlotte Keppel 3465

The Man Who Killed the King - Dennis Wheatley 6654

Marianne - Juliette Benzoni 466

The Marriage of Josephine - Marjorie Coryn 1358

Master-At-Arms - Rafael Sabatini 5553

Matthew Early - Alexander Laing 3589

The Memoirs of Elizabeth Frankenstein - Theodore Roszak 5508
Midnight Moon - Jeanne Montague 4436
Mirage - Ruth McKenney 4283
Mistress of the Forge - David Taylor 6179
Monsieur Yankee - Leslie Turner White 6689
A Most Extraordinary Pair - Jean Detre 1628
Mr. Midshipman Hornblower - C.S. Forester 2180
Mutiny - Frank Tilsley 6280
Mutiny Run - Frank Eccles 1836
A Night with Casanova - Wolf Mankowitz 4060
Now We Are Free - Marguerite Allis 112
Oldtown Folks - Harriet Beecher Stowe 6072
Pandora's Galley - Macdonald Harris 2727
The Pioneers; or, The Sources of the Susquehanna - James Fenimore Cooper 1307
Pitcairn's Island - Charles Nordhoff 4640
Portrait of a Scoundrel - Nathaniel Benchley 438
Pride's Fancy - Thomas H. Raddall 5231
The Prince Lost to Time - Ann Dukthas 1776
The Prisoners of September - Leon Garfield 2294
The Private Adventures of Captain Shaw - Edith Shay 5783
The Proud Canaries - David Johnson 3222
Ramage - Dudley Pope 5097
Ramage's Prize - Dudley Pope 5107
The Red Rover - James Fenimore Cooper 1309
The Road to Glory - Frederick Britten Austin 246
The Rock Cried Out - Edward Stanley 5981
Ruby - Helen Ashfield 213
Sachem's Son - Donald Clayton Porter 5125
Scaramouche - Rafael Sabatini 5554
Scaramouche the King-Maker - Rafael Sabatini 5555
The Scarlet Pimpernel - Baroness Emma Orczy 4745
The Sea Treasure - Elisabeth Barr 338
A Season of Mists - Sarah Woodhouse 6856
Seed of Mischief - Willa Gibbs 2401
The Settlers - William Stuart Long 3878
Shadow of a Lady - Jane Aiken Hodge 2971
Signal—Close Action! - Alexander Kent 3438
The Silver Highways - Malcolm Macdonald 3972
The Sleeping Sword: A Biographical Novel - Pearl Frye 2244
Soldier of the Sea - Robert Welter Daly 1460
Sons of Thunder - Barbara Fitz Vroman 6516
Sylvia's Lovers - Elizabeth Gaskell 2312
The Talisman Ring - Georgette Heyer 2905
Tallien: A Brief Romance - Frederic Tuten 6370
Thaddeus of Warsaw - Jane Porter 5136
That Far Paradise - Gene Markey 4088
The Thieftaker - J.G. Jeffreys 3180
This Other Eden - Marilyn Harris 2733
The Timeless Land - Eleanor Dark 1495
Touch and Go - C. Northcote Parkinson 4815
The Triton Brig - Dudley Pope 5110
The Twelfth Physician - Willa Gibbs 2403
La Vendee - Anthony Trollope 6346
Venture Once More - Winston Graham 2532
Veronique - Virginia Coffman 1158
Voices in a Haunted Room - Philippa Carr 931
Walford's Oak - Jill M. Phillips 4986
Water Music - T. Coraghessan Boyle 619
The Way to the Lantern - Audrey Erskine Lindop 3790
Well of the Silent Harp - James Barke 304
West Goes the Road - Tim Pridgen 5192
Where Glory Waits - Gertrude Crownfield 1437
The White Cockade - Henry Farrand Griffin 2592
The Wild Ohio - Bart Spicer 5966
The Wind From the Sea - Constance Heaven 2812
Windover - Jane Aiken Hodge 2974
The Wine Princes - Margaret Mackay 3987
Yankee - Dana Fuller Ross 5495
Yankee Pasha - Edison Marshall 4115

19th CENTURY

54-40 or Fight - Emerson Hough 3040

1812 - David Nevin 4586
The Abandoned Woman - Richard Condon 1235
Abe Lincoln of Pigeon Creek - William Edward Wilson 6818
Abigail - Malcolm Macdonald 3962
Absalom, Absalom! - William Faulkner 2049
The Absorbing Fire: The Byron Legend - F.W. Kenyon 3445
Across the Bitter Sea - Eilis Dillon 1646
Adversary in the House - Irving Stone 6053
Against the Tide - Muriel Elwood 1935
Agotime, Her Legend - Judith Gleason 2430
Albany - Laura Black 519
Albert's Victoria - Tyler Whittle 6719
Alexander Hamilton's Wife - Alice Curtis Desmond 1623
Alice and Edith: A Biographical Novel of the Two Wives of Theodore Roosevelt - Dorothy Clarke Wilson 6798
The Alien Light - Iain Crichton Smith 1427
All Desires Known - Malcolm Macdonald 3963
All for Love: Baby Doe and Silver Dollar - John Vernon 6456
All God's Children - Alston Anderson 136
All in Good Time - Marguerite Allis 106
All Their Kingdoms - Madeleine Polland 5084
All This, and Heaven Too - Rachel Field 2080
The Amazing Mrs. Bonaparte - Harnett T. Kane 3351
The American - Howard Fast 2026
The American Cowboy - Will James 3163
And Tell of Time - Laura Krey 3554
And the Stars Shall Fall - True Bowen 603
The Angel: A Novel Based on the Life of Alexander I of Russia - William James Blech 543
Angel of the Delta - Edward Francis Murphy 4521
The Angel with the Trumpet - Ernst Lothar 3898
Angelica - Samuel A. Schreiner Jr. 5671
Angle of Repose - Wallace Stegner 5989
Animating Maria - Marion Chesney 1015
Annie's Captain - Kathryn Hulme 3077
Anthony Adverse - Hervey Allen 98
Anthony Trant - John Hyatt Downing 1713
Apache - Will Comfort 1226
Apache Autumn - Robert Skimin 5875
Apple Tree Lean Down - Mary E. Pearce 4860
Apprentice to the Sea - Philip McCutchan 4240
The Architecture of the Arkansas Ozarks - Donald Harington 2708
The Ardent Years - Janet Stevenson 6003
Arfive - A.B. Guthrie Jr. 2623
Arizona Ecstasy - Rosanne Bittner 511
The Arkansas River - Jory Sherman 5816
Arne - Bjornstjerne Bjornson 518
The Artist - Norman Garbo 2281
The Artist's Daughter - Leslie O'Grady 4698
Ashana - E.P. Roesch 5424
Ashes - Stefan Zeromski 6960
At the Sign of the Golden Pineapple - Marion Chesney 1016
Aurora Rose - Anne Worboys 6870
The Autobiography of Miss Jane Pittman - Ernest J. Gaines 2270
Autumn Lace - Eileen Jackson 3133
Back to Malachi - Robert J. Conley 1237
Bagatelle - Maurice Denuziere 1613
The Ballad of Typhoid Mary - Jurg Federspiel 2057
Band of Angels - Robert Penn Warren 6572
The Bank - Stephen Longstreet 3882
The Banishment - Marion Chesney 1018
The Bannaman Legacy - Catherine Cookson 1272
Banners Against the Wind - John Edward Jennings 3198
Banners of Silk - Rosalind Laker 3592
The Baroness of Bow Street - Gail Clark 1085
Beatrice Goes to Brighton - Marion Chesney 1019
Beau Barron's Lady - Helen Ashfield 204
Beauty for Ashes - Timothy R. Wilson 6816
Beauty From Ashes - Eugenia Price 5177

Beauty's Daughter - Mollie Hardwick 2689
The Beckoning Waters - Robert Carse 944
Beecher: A Novel - Dan McCall 4218
Before My Time - Niccolo Tucci 6358
Being Met Together - William Vaughan Wilkins 6756
Belinda Goes to Bath - Marion Chesney 1020
The Bellamy Saga - John Pearson 4878
La Belle - Elizabeth Boatwright Coker 1161
Belle Starr - Deborah Camp 870
Beloved - Vina Delmar 1599
The Beloved Invader - Eugenia Price 5179
Benton's Row - Frank Yerby 6908
Bertie, Albert Edward, Prince of Wales - Tyler Whittle 6720
Between Earth and Sky - Karen Osborn 4758
Beulah Land - Lonnie Coleman 1202
Beyond Desire: A Novel Based on the Life of Felix and Cecille Mendelssohn - Pierre La Mure 3574
Beyond the Blue Mountains - Jean Plaidy 5006
Beyond the Stars - David William Ross 5497
Bide Me Fair - Harvey Howells 3060
The Big Family - Vina Delmar 1600
Big River, Big Man - Thomas William Duncan 1786
Billy the Kid - Edwin Corle 1330
Bittersweet - Leslie Li 3769
The Black Angels - Maude Hart Lovelace 3902
The Black Candle - Catherine Cookson 1273
Black Feather - Harold Titus 6283
Black Jack Davy - John Oskison 4763
The Black Sheep's Daughter - Carola Dunn 1791
Black Triumvirate: A Novel of Haiti - Benjamin H. Levin 3736
The Blacksmith's Daughter - Joanna Dessau 1625
Blood Brother - Elliott Arnold 190
The Blood Endures - Robert Inman 3107
Blood on the Snow - John Elliott 1916
The Blood Seed - Andrew Ward 6561
A Bloodsmoor Romance - Joyce Carol Oates 4658
The Bloody Benders - Robert H. Adelman 35
Blue Camellia - Frances Parkinson Keyes 3477
The Blue Heaven Bends Over All - Jane Oliver 4720
Blunted Lance - Max Hennessy 2829
The Border Captains - Jason Manning 4072
Born Strangers - Helen Topping Miller 4384
Borrowed Plumes - Roseleen Milne 4409
The Bounty Lands - William Donohue Ellis 1927
The Bourlotas Fortune - Nicholas Gage 2268
Brandywine - Jack Rowe 5513
Brave Kingdom - Frances Murray 4534
A Bride for Donnigan - Janette Oke 4705
Bride of Ae - Pamela Hill 2928
Bride of Fortune - Harnett T. Kane 3352
Bride of Glory - Bradda Field 2078
Bride of the River - Laura B. Harris 2723
The Bridge - Marguerite Allis 108
Bright Journey - August Derleth 1614
The Bright Land - Janet Fairbank 2000
Bright to the Wanderer - Bruce Lancaster 3638
The Brocken - Pamela Hill 2929
Bronte - Glyn Hughes 3073
Brothers Three - John Oskison 4764
Brules - Harry Combs 1223
Buffalo Woman - Dorothy M. Johnson 3223
Buller's Guns - Richard Hough 3048
The Burning Man - Stephen Longstreet 3883
Burr - Gore Vidal 6485
Butcher's Broom - Neil Gunn 2620
Butcher's Crossing - John Williams 6786
Buttes Landing - Jean Rikhoff 5331
By Reason of Strength - Gerald White Johnson 3225
Bygones - Frank Wilkinson 6762
Byron: A Novel - Sigrid Combuchen 1225
Cain and His Brother - Anne Perry 4922
Calamity Jane of Deadwood Gulch - Ethel Hueston 3068
California Gold - John Jakes 3145
The Californian - Todhunter Ballard 284
The Californios - Louis L'Amour 3618

Call of the Arctic - Robert Steelman 5987

Call the Beast Thy Brother - William Oliver
  Turner 6366

Call the Darkness Light - Nancy Zaroulis 6954

Cambridge - Caryl Phillips 4983

The Candlesticks and the Cross - Ruth Freeman
  Solomon 5940

Captain Grant - Shirley Seifert 5724

Captain Jack - Gene Shelton 5800

Captain Paul - Edward Ellsberg 1930

Captains and the Kings - Taylor Caldwell 851

The Captive - Victoria Holt 3011

Cardigan Square - Alexandra Manners 4070

Caroline and Julia - Clare Darcy 1484

Casey - Ramona Stewart 6034

Cashelmara - Susan Howatch 3058

Castle Garden - Bill Albert 63

The Castle of Fratta - Ippolito Nievo 4625

The Cavalier of Tennessee - Meredith
  Nicholson 4610

Century in Scarlet - Lajos Zilahy 6962

Ceremony of the Innocent - Taylor Caldwell 852

Certain Harvest: A Novel of the Time of Peter Cooper
  - Ruth Adams Knight 3525

Certain People of Importance - Kathleen
  Norris 4647

The Chandler Heritage - Ben Haas 2629

Charity, Colorado - Chelsea Quinn Yarbro 6896

Charles - Victoria Lincoln 3786

Charleston - Alexandra Ripley 5338

Chelsea - Nancy Fitzgerald 2114

The Cherished Wives - Valerie Anand 126

Cherokee Rose: A Novel of America's First Cowgirl -
  Judy Alter 119

The Chess Player: A Novel of New Orleans and Paris
  - Frances Parkinson Keyes 3478

Chief Joseph - Bill Dugan 1756

Child of the Snapping Turtle, Mike Fink - Julian Lee
  Rayford 5256

Children of God - Vardis Fisher 2106

The Children of Segu - Maryse Conde 1232

*Children of the Vampire: The Diaries of the Family
  Dracul* - Jeanne Kalogridis 3326

China Saga - C.Y. Lee 3706

Christopher Strange - Ruth Eleanor McKee 4281

Cimarron - Edna Ferber 2061

Circle of Gold - Karen Harper 2710

Citizen Tom Paine - Howard Fast 2028

Clair De Lune: A Novel about Claude Debussy -
  Pierre La Mure 3575

Clear for Action! - Noel B. Gerson 2362

Cloud on the Land - Julia Davis 1526

Colliers Row - Jan Webster 6592

The Colors of Vaud - Bryher 741

*Colossus: A Novel about Goya and a World Gone
  Mad* - Stephen Marlowe 4093

Come Slowly Eden: A Novel about Emily Dickinson -
  Laura Benet 440

Come Winter - Douglas C. Jones 3275

Concert Grand - Howard Breslin 665

Confessions of Johnny Ringo - Geoff Aggeler 40

A Connecticut Yankee in Criminal Court - Peter J.
  Heck 2814

Conquering Horse - Frederick F. Manfred 4055

*The Conqueror: Being the True and Romantic Story of
  Alexander Hamilton* - Gertrude Atherton 222

The Consuming Flame: The Story of George Eliot -
  F.W. Kenyon 3446

*The Corsair: A Biographical Novel of Jean Lafitte,
  Hero of the Battle of New Orleans* - Madeleine
  Fabiola Kent 3444

Cosette: The Sequel to Les Miserables - Laura
  Kalpakian 3329

The Country Gentleman - Fiona Hill 2924

Country People - Ruth Suckow 6111

Crazy Horse - Bill Dugan 1757

Crazy Snake - Robert J. Conley 1240

Creek Mary's Blood - Dee Brown 712

Crescent City - Belva Plain 5078

Cressida - Clare Darcy 1485

*Crockett of Tennessee: A Novel Based on the Life and
  Times of David Crockett* - Cameron Judd 3314

Crompton Way - Thomas Thompson 6270

Crossings - Earl Rovit 5512

The Crown Prince - John Barchilon 300

The Cry and the Covenant - Morton Thompson 6269

Cry of the Rain Bird - Patricia Shaw 5779

Crystal - Helen Ashfield 205

Cunningham's Revenge - Duncan MacNeil 4012

The Curse of the Kings - Victoria Holt 3012

Damaris - Jane Sheridan 5810

*Damned Shall Be Desire: The Passionate Life of Guy
  de Maupassant* - Stephen Coulter 1384

The Dance of Death - Jeremy Potter 5142

Dance on the Wind - Terry C. Johnston 3249

Dancing at the Rascal Fair - Ivan Doig 1682

A Dangerous Fortune - Ken Follett 2147

Dark at Noon - Jill Tattersall 6173

Dark Quartet: The Story of the Brontes - Lynne Reid
  Banks 290

Dark Rider - Louis Zara 6950

Dark Winds - Virginia Coffman 1152

The Darkness of Corn - Caroline Stickland 6037

Darken Ship - Nicholas Monsarrat 4431

Darktown Strutters - Wesley Brown 732

A Daughter of Liberty - Allan Cole 1196

Daughter of Marignac - Constance Heaven 2805

Daughter of Strangers - Elizabeth Boatwright
  Coker 1164

Daughter of Time - Nelia Gardner White 6695

Daughters of the New World - Susan Richards
  Shreve 5835

Day Is Coming - William Cameron 869

The Days of the Butterfly - Norah Lofts 3841

Dear Lily - Malcolm W. Greenough Jr. 2575

Death Comes for the Archbishop - Willa Cather 957

Death of a Legend - Will Henry 2840

The Death of Artemio Cruz - Carlos Fuentes 2246

Deborah Goes to Dover - Marion Chesney 1023

*Deep in My Heart: A Story Based on the Life of
  Sigmund Romberg* - Elliott Arnold 192

The Delusson Family - Jacques Ducharme 1753

Depths of Glory - Irving Stone 6055

Desiree - Annemarie Selinko 5741

The Devil Inside: A Novel of Dostoevsky's Life -
  Stephen Coulter 1385

Devil's Fire, Love's Revenge - Barbara Paul 4836

The Devil's Rainbow - J.C. Furnas 2257

Devil's Yard - Ivo Andric 152

Diamond Six - William Fielding Smith 5932

Diamond Wedding - Wilbur Daniel Steele 5986

Dim the Flaring Lamps - Jan Jordan 3301

Disraeli Rising - Maurice Edelman 1852

Distant Music - Harold Lenoir Davis 1521

Distant Trails - Bill Gulick 2612

Distant Trumpet - Paul Horgan 3032

Divine Average - Elithe Hamilton Kirkland 3505

Doc Holliday's Woman - Jane Candia Coleman 1201

Doctor in Buckskin - T.D. Allen 103

Dr. Johnson's Dear Mistress - Winifred Carter 948

Dolley - Rita Mae Brown 727

Dominion - Jack Rowe 5514

Don Gaucho - Alyce Pollock 5088

Don Juan McQueen - Eugenia Price 5181

Double Wedding Ring - Patricia Wendorf 6624

The Dream Seekers - Stephen Longstreet 3884

Dream Time - Parris Afton Bonds 570

Dream West - David Nevin 4587

Dreams of Gold - Lewis Orde 4748

D'ri and I - Irving A. Bacheller 257

Drum - Kyle Onstott 4744

Drums of Destiny - Peter Bourne 593

The Drums of Morning - Philip Van Doren
  Stern 5997

The Duchess of Vidal - Dawn Lindsey 3793

The Dukes: A Novel - Malcolm Ross 5503

Dulcie Bligh - Gail Clark 1086

Dynasty of Death - Taylor Caldwell 854

The Eagle and the Rock - Frances Winwar 6830

The Earl and the Heiress - Barbara Metzger 4345

The Earth Abideth - George Dell 1595

The Earth and All It Holds - V.J. Banis 287

Earthshaker - Robert Wilson Krepps 3553

East of the Giants - George Rippey Stewart 6027

Eden - Julie Ellis 1918

Eden and Honor - Marilyn Harris 2729

Edward, Edward - Lolah Burford 772

Eleanora Duse - Jean Stubbs 6095

Elegant Journey - John Selby 5740

Eli's Road - Lucas Webb 6589

Elizabeth and Alexandra - Antony Lambton 3616

Eliza's Daughter - Joan Aiken 44

Elyza - Clare Darcy 1486

The Emancipist: An Unforgettable Epic of Australia -
  Veronica Geoghegan Sweeney 6147

Emily Goes to Exeter - Marion Chesney 1027

Emma - F.W. Kenyon 3448

The Emperor Franz Joseph - Ottokar
  Janetschek 3164

The Emperor Story: A Historical Romance - George
  Sava 5615

Emperor's Ladies - Noel B. Gerson 2367

Empire of Heaven - Linda Ching Sledge 5907

The Enduring Years - Claire Rayner 5263

Enlightening Delilah - Marion Chesney 1028

Eroica: A Novel about Beethoven - Carl von
  Pidoll 4994

Estella - Alanna Knight 3519

Eugenie - Hester W. Chapman 989

Evermore - Barbara Steward 6014

Evil Mark - Graham Miles 4377

An Excess of Love - Cathy Cash Spellman 5959

Exit Sherlock Holmes - Robert Lee Hall 2657

Eye of the Hawk - David William Ross 5498

Eye of the Hurricane - Fergus Reid Buckley 757

*The Eye of the Lion: A Novel Based on the Life of
  Mata Hari* - Lael Tucker Wertenbaker 6626

Fairoaks - Frank Yerby 6915

The Fall River Line - Daoma Winston 6824

Fallen Angel - Deborah Camp 872

Falls of Gard - Laura Black 520

Familiar Acts - June Barraclough 345

Family - J. California Cooper 1297

The Family of Women - Richard Peck 4883

Far Flies the Eagle - Evelyn Anthony 162

Far Mountains - Frank O'Rourke 4752

The Far-Off Rhapsody - Anne-Marie Sheridan 5808

The Far Pavilions - M.M. Kaye 3376

The Far Side of the Hill - Nancy Livingston 3811

The Far Tribes - Richard S. Wheeler 6658

A Fatal Assignation - Alice Chetwynd Ley 3764

A Father and His Fate - Ivy Compton-Burnett 1228

The Favored Child - Philippa Gregory 2582

The Feather and the Stone - Patricia Shaw 5780

Felding Castle - Edith De Born 1552

The Fifth Horseman - Jose Antonio Villarreal 6496

The Financier - Theodore Dreiser 1720

Finessing Clarissa - Marion Chesney 1029

Fire Opal - Pamela Hill 2932

Firewind - Bill Pronzini 5200

The First Rebellion - Marion Chesney 1030

The Five-Minute Marriage - Joan Aiken 46

Flames of Empire - Peter Bourne 594

The Flames of Time - Baynard Kendrick 3409

Flight of the Swan - Margaret Ann Hubbard 3063

The Flint Anchor - Sylvia Townsend Warner 6569

Flowers in the Blood - Gay Courter 1387

Follow the Free Wind - Leigh Brackett 621

*Fool of God: A Novel Based on the Life of Alexander
  Campbell* - Louis Cochran 1144

Footman in Powder - Helen Ashton 216

For the Love of Robert E. Lee - M.A. Harper 2715

For They Shall Inherit - Malcolm Macdonald 3964

Forbidden City - Muriel Molland Jernigan 3215

Forefathers - Nancy Cato 960

The Forge - Thomas S. Stribling 6083

Fort Worth - Leonard Sanders 5588

The Fortunate Marriage - Meriol Trevor 6342
The Fortune Hunter - Ira J. Morris 4477
Fortune Is a Woman - Elizabeth Adler 39
Fortune's Legacy - Jack Rowe 5515
Foundation Stone - Lella Warren 6571
The Fox-Red Hills - Cynthia S. Roberts 5374
The Foxes of Harrow - Frank Yerby 6917
Free Enterprise - Michelle Cliff 1116
The Free Frenchman - Piers Paul Read 5277
Freedom's Banner - Teresa Crane 1415
The French Lieutenant's Woman - John Fowles 2194
The French Woman - Barbara Paul 4837
The Frenchwoman - Jeanne Mackin 3995
The Frigate Captain - Showell Styles 6103
The Frog Earl - Carola Dunn 1792
From Fields of Gold - Alexandra Ripley 5339
From Sea to Shining Sea - James Alexander
Thom 6232
From the Terrace - John O'Hara 4703
The Frontiersmen - Allen W. Eckert 1841
Fur Brigade - Hal George Evarts 1985
The Furies - John Jakes 3146
The Gallery of His Dreams - Kristine Kathryn
Rusch 5525
The Gallows Land - Bill Pronzini 5201
Galveston - Suzanne Morris 4482
Gateway to Empire - Allen W. Eckert 1842
Gathering Storm - Bill Gulick 2613
The Gaudy Empire - Alfred Neumann 4584
A Generation of Leaves - Robert S. Bloom 552
The Gentleman From Chicago - John Cashman 953
Georgina - Clare Darcy 1488
Geronimo - Bill Dugan 1758
Ghost Woman - Lawrence Thornton 6275
Give Me the Wind - Jan Jordan 3302
The Glass-Blowers - Daphne Du Maurier 1745
Goddess of the Green Room - Jean Plaidy 5016
Gold Mountain - Charlotte Paul 4841
Gold of Their Bodies: A Novel about Gauguin -
Charles Orson Gorham 2488
The Golden Harlot - Jeanne Wilson 6808
The Golden Honeycomb - Kamala Markandaya 4086
Golden Isle - Frank G. Slaughter 5890
The Golden Lady - Dorothy Gardiner 2283
The Golden Season - Oriana Akinson 60
The Golden Veil - Paddy Kitchen 3507
Gone the Dreams and the Dancing - Douglas C.
Jones 3279
Gone to Texas - Don Worcester 6871
Good-Bye My Son - Marjorie Coryn 1356
A Good Day to Die - Del Barton 368
The Good Earth - Pearl S. Buck 754
Good Morning, Young Lady - Ardyth Kennelly 3424
The Gorgeous Hussy - Samuel Hopkins Adams 30
Grand Parade - G.B. Lancaster 3649
The Grandmothers - Glenway Westcott 6640
The Grassman - Len Fulton 2256
Great Black Russian - John Oliver Killens 3484
Great Elephant - Alan Scholefield 5654
The Greenlander - Mark Adlard 38
Greenstone - Yvonne Kalman 3324
Gunman - Loren D. Estleman 1971
The Half Breed - Maurice Constantin-Weyer 1261
The Handsome Road - Gwen Bristow 697
The Hangings - Bill Pronzini 5202
Hanta Yo - Ruth Beebe Hill 2951
Hard Money - Clarence Budington Kelland 3389
Hardacre - C.L. Skelton 5872
The Harrogate Secret - Catherine Cookson 1278
The Hawkeye - Herbert Quick 5222
The Healers - Henry Denker 1610
Heart in Pilgrimage - Evelyn Eaton 1827
The Heart of O. Henry - Dale Kramer 3550
Heart of the Country - Greg Matthews 4190
The Heart of the Rose - June Barraclough 346
The Heatherton Heritage - Pamela Hill 2934
Heaven Is Too High - Mildred Masterson
McNeilly 4309
The Hedge of Thorns - Helen Ashton 217

Heir to Kuragin - Constance Heaven 2807
Heirs of the Motherland - Judith Pella 4893
Henry and Clara - Thomas Mallon 4042
Her Grace's Passion - Marion Chesney 1033
A Heritage and Its History - Ivy Compton-
Burnett 1229
The Hesitant Heart - Anne Edwards 1882
High Heroic - Constantine FitzGibbon 2118
A High Wind in Jamaica - Richard Hughes 3074
His Was the Fire - Showell Styles 6104
The History of Rome Hanks - Joseph Stanley
Pennell 4909
Home to Kentucky: A Novel of Henry Clay - Alfred
Leland Crabb 1399
Home to the Hermitage - Alfred Leland Crabb 1401
The Homesman - Glendon Swarthout 6143
The Horn and the Forest - Jamie Lee Cooper 1313
Horne's Law - Jory Sherman 5819
Horses of War - Duff Hart-Davis 2760
The House of Cray - Pamela Hill 2936
The House of Five Talents - Louis Auchincloss 231
The House on the Mound - August Derleth 1616
The House That Tai Ming Built - Virginia Lee 3711
How Do I Love Thee - Lucille Iremonger 3110
How Green Was My Valley - Richard
Llewellyn 3813
Hungarian Rhapsody: The Life of Franz Liszt - Jean
Rousselot 5511
Hungry Hill - Daphne Du Maurier 1746
I Give You Oscar Wilde - Desmond Hall 2647
I, Jack Swilling - John Myers 4544
I, James McNeill Whistler - Lawrence
Williams 6787
I, Madame Tussaud - Sylvia Martin 4135
I Never Came to You in White - Judith Farr 2014
I, Rachel - March Cost 1361
I Speak for Thaddeus Stevens - Elsie
Singmaster 5868
I Take This Land - Richard Powell 5147
I, the Supreme - Augusto Antonio Roa Bastos 5353
I, Victoria - Cynthia Harrod-Eagles 2755
If a Lion Could Talk - Mildred Walker 6532
The Immigrants - Howard Fast 2034
Immortal Wife - Irving Stone 6057
An Imperfect Joy - Jean Stubbs 6097
Imperial Courtesan - F.W. Kenyon 3452
Imperial Venus: A Novel of Napoleon's Favorite Sister
- Edgar Maas 3949
Imperial Waltz - William M. Abrahams 13
Imperial Woman - Pearl S. Buck 755
Impressionist: A Novel of Mary Cassatt - Joan
King 3486
In Still and Stormy Waters - Reay Tannahill 6157
In the Season of the Wild Rose - Clara Rising 5347
In Those Days - Harvey Fergusson 2068
The Infinite Woman - Edison Marshall 4107
Inherit the Sun - Maxwell Grant 2539
The Inner Voice - Nina Wilcox Putnam 5211
The Intrigue - Marion Chesney 1034
Ippolita - Alberto Denti di Pirajno 1612
The Irish Boy: A Romantic Biography - Naomi
Jacob 3137
The Iron Mistress - Paul I. Wellman 6618
Israel Potter - Herman Melville 4334
It Began in Vauxhall Gardens - Jean Plaidy 5023
Jackson: A Novel - Max Byrd 837
Jade - Pat Barr 344
The Jealous House - Clarence Budington
Kelland 3390
*Jessie: A Novel Based on the Life of Jessie Benton
Fremont* - Judy Alter 120
Jewel of the Sea - Ellen Argo 185
Johanna: A Novel of the Van Gogh Family - Claire
Cooperstein 1317
John Bonwell - Charles K. Pulse 5208
John Crews - Arthur Chapman 988
John Howard Payne, Skywalker - Maude
Barragan 348
John Ruskin's Wife - Eva McDonald 4259

The Jonah Man - Henry Carlisle 895
Joseph - Mervyn Jones 3292
The Journal of Colonel De Lancey - James Warner
Bellah 426
The Journey of August King - John Ehle 1894
Journey Proud - Thomasine McGehee 4273
Jubilee - Margaret Walker 6531
The Judas Kiss - Victoria Holt 3015
Judith Paris - Hugh Walpole 6545
Julia's Last Hope - Janette Oke 4708
Kagami - Elizabeth Kata 3369
Kean: The Imaginary Memoirs of an Actor - Julius
Berstl 485
Kelly Blue - Peter Bowen 601
Kentucky Home - Betty Layman Receveur 5283
*Kid Curry: The Life and Times of Harvey Logan and
the Wild Bunch* - F. Bruce Lamb 3606
King of Paris - Guy Endore 1942
King of the Bastards - Sarah Gertrude Millin 4405
Know Nothing - Mary Lee Settle 5755
The Lady and the Arsenic - Marjorie Bowen 598
A Lady in Doubt - Annabel Wynne 6891
Lady Jane - Norma Lee Clark 1092
Lady Jane - Leslie O'Grady 4699
The Lady of Arlington - Harnett T. Kane 3354
A Lady of Repute - Janice James 3158
Lady Pamela - Clare Darcy 1491
Lady Washington - Dorothy Clarke Wilson 6803
Lady's Maid - Margaret Forster 2188
Ladysmead: A Novel in the Jane Austen Tradition -
Jane Gillespie 2420
Lakota - G. Clifton Wisler 6833
Lamb in His Bosom - Caroline Miller 4380
The Land Was Ours: A Novel of the Great Plains -
Charles W. Bailey 266
The Land Where the Sun Dies - Henry Carlisle 896
Last Gun: The Legend of John Selman - Gene
Shelton 5801
Last Letter Home - Vilhelm Moberg 4423
*The Last Mutiny: The Further Adventures of Captain
Bligh* - Bill Collett 1208
The Last Warpath - Will Henry 2844
Lavender Lady - Carola Dunn 1794
The Law in Charity - Chelsea Quinn Yarbro 6901
A Leaf in the Wind - Marie Joseph 3307
The Legacy of Beulah Land - Lonnie Coleman 1203
Legacy of the Wolf - Jean Raynes 5274
Lenin: The Novel - Alan Brien 679
The Leopard - Giuseppe di Lampedusa 3634
Letty - Helen Ashton 218
Levi Coffin and the Underground Railroad - Charles
Ludwig 3921
The Life and Times of Horatio Hornblower - C.
Northcote Parkinson 4813
Light on the Mountain - Leonard Sanders 5589
Lilith - Jean Plaidy 5030
Lillie - David Butler 818
Limmerston Hall - Hester W. Chapman 991
Lincoln's Mothers: A Story of Nancy and Sally Lincoln
- Dorothy Clarke Wilson 6804
Little Big Man - Thomas Berger 478
The Little Victoria - Lozania Prole 5196
The Living - Annie Dillard 1644
The Living Reed - Pearl S. Buck 756
Long Knife - James Alexander Thom 6233
Long Pig - Russell Foreman 2168
The Long Shadow - Anna Gilbert 2406
The Long Trail North - Robert J. Conley 1245
Look to the Rose - Shirley Seifert 5728
The Loon Feather - Iola Fuller 2253
Lord Iverbrook's Heir - Carola Dunn 1795
Lord of the Ladies - Joanna Dessau 1626
Lord Raven's Widow - Leslie O'Grady 4700
Lord Richard's Passion - Mervyn Jones 3293
The Lost Wagon - James Arthur Kjelgaard 3509
The Lost Years: A Biographical Fiction - Oscar
Lewis 3757
Lotus Land - Monica Highland 2917
Louisiana Purchase - A.E. Hotchner 3039

Love Is a Wild Assault - Elithe Hamilton Kirkland 3506

Love Is Eternal - Irving Stone 6058

Love Is My Vocation: An Imaginative Study of St. Therese of Lisieux - Tom Clarkson 1098

A Love So Wild - Deborah Chester 1056

The Lovely Lynchs - Magdalen King-Hall 3490

Lovers All Untrue - Norah Lofts 3851

Loving Belle Star - Robert Taylor 6187

Loving Emma - Nigel Foxell 2197

Lucinda Brayford - Martin Boyd 613

Lust for Life - Irving Stone 6059

The Maclarens - C.L. Skelton 5873

Madame Casanova - Gaby von Schonthan 5659

Madame Castel's Lodger - Frances Parkinson Keyes 3480

Maggie Craig - Marie Joseph 3308

The Magic Bow - Manuel Komroff 3534

Magic Fire: Scenes around Richard Wagner - Bertita Harding 2683

Magnificent Destiny - Paul I. Wellman 6619

The Maid of Sker - R.D. Blackmore 529

Malkeh and Her Children - Marjorie Edelson 1853

The Mallen Lot - Catherine Cookson 1281

The Maltese Angel - Catherine Cookson 1283

Mamaw - Susan Dodd 1663

A Man and His Mountain: The Life of Paul Cezanne - Hugh McLeave 4285

A Man Called Grant - Helen Todd 6285

Man of Montmartre: A Novel Based on the Life of Maurice Utrillo - Stephen Longstreet 3888

Manchu Empress - Bluebell Matilda Hunter 3081

Mandalay - Alexandra Jones 3269

Mandarin - Robert S. Elegant 1905

The Manly-Hearted Woman - Frederick F. Manfred 4057

A Man's Reach - Charles Morrow Wilson 6796

Many a Voyage - Loula Grace Erdman 1951

The Marburg Chronicles - Alfred Coppel 1319

Margaret's Story - Eugenia Price 5183

Marianne - Glen Petrie 4981

Marrying Harriet - Marion Chesney 1036

Mary Anne - Daphne Du Maurier 1749

Mary Dove - Jane Gilmore Rushing 5529

Mary Reilly - Valerie Martin 4136

Masquerade of Vengeance - Alice Chetwynd Ley 3765

The Masters of Bow Street - John Creasy 1423

The Matrix - Maria Thompson Daviess 1509

Max - Howard Fast 2038

The Medicine Horn - Jory Sherman 5820

The Melancholy Virgin - Annabel Laine 3587

Members of the Tribe - Richard Kluger 3511

Memoirs of a Victorian Gentleman: William Makepeace Thackeray - Margaret Forster 2189

Metello - Vasco Pratolini 5163

Mi Amigo - William R. Burnett 795

Miami: A Saga - Evelyn Wilde Mayerson 4204

Michael Torey - Janet Mathewson 4183

The Midnight Gardener: A Novel about Baudelaire - Max White 6694

The Mill on the Po - Riccardo Bacchelli 254

Miracles - Marcy Moran Heidish 2818

Miss Bishop - Bess Streeter Aldrich 71

Miss Davenport's Christmas - Marion Chesney 1039

Miss Delicia Allen - Mary Johnston 3237

Miss Fiona's Fancy - Marion Chesney 1040

Miss Hartwell's Dilemma - Carola Dunn 1796

The Mississippi Run - Paul Darcy Boles 565

Mister Christian - William Kinsolving 3502

Mistress - Amanda Quick 5215

Mistress Nancy - Barbara Bentley 460

Mistress of Fortune - Sheila Lancaster 3651

Modigliani: Prince of Montparnasse - Tadeusz Wittlin 6834

Molly - Teresa Crane 1417

Monday's Child - Mollie Hardwick 2697

Montana Hitch - Richard S. Wheeler 6661

Monte Walsh - Jack Schaefer 5635

The Moreland Legacy - Diana Haviland 2777

Mortal Hunger: A Novel Based on the Life of Lafcadio Hearn - Harry E. Wedeck 6594

Mother and Son - Ivy Compton-Burnett 1231

Moulin Rouge: A Novel Based on Henri de Toulouse-Lautrec - Pierre La Mure 3576

The Mountain of Immoderate Desires - Leslie Wilson 6811

Mr. Audubon's Lucy - Lucy Kennedy 3419

Mr. Lincoln's Wife - Anne Colver 1221

Mrs. Betsy, or Widowed and Wed - Francis Marton 4141

Mrs. Jeffries Stands Corrected - Emily Brightwell 688

The Mullah From Kashmir - Duncan MacNeil 4016

Music for God - Theresa Weiser 6603

The Mutual Friend - Frederick Busch 811

My Brother Napoleon: The Confessions of Caroline Bonaparte - F.W. Kenyon 3455

My Love Must Wait: The Story of Matthew Flinders - Ernestine Hill 2922

My Pride, My Folly - Suzanne Butler 830

My Savage Muse: The Story of My Life: Edgar Allan Poe, an Imaginative Work - Bernhardt J. Hurwood 3087

Mysteries of Winterthurn - Joyce Carol Oates 4659

Naked Came I: A Novel of Rodin - David Weiss 6607

The Naked Maja - Noel B. Gerson 2378

The Nancy Flyer - Ernest Poole 5091

Napoleon and His Son - Pierre Nezelof 4607

Napoleon Symphony - Anthony Burgess 780

Natchez: A Novel of the Deep South - Pamela Jekel 3186

Neighboring Lives - Thomas M. Disch 1648

The Nelson Touch - Paul Lewis 3759

A Nest of Simple Folk - Sean O'Faolain 4692

Nethergate - Norah Lofts 3854

Never Victorious, Never Defeated - Taylor Caldwell 860

The New Confessions - William Boyd 617

New Day - Victor Stafford Reid 5291

The New England Story - Henry Beetle Hough 3046

New Moon Rising - Eugenia Price 5185

New Orleans Woman: A Biographical Novel of Myra Clark Gaines - Harnett T. Kane 3355

New Road - Merle Estes Colby 1168

Niagara - Robert Lewis Taylor 6189

No Resting Place - William Humphrey 3079

North and South - John Jakes 3151

The Northern Correspondent - Jean Stubbs 6099

Nothing New under the Sun - Riccardo Bacchelli 255

Notorious Eliza - Basil Beyea 489

A Notorious Woman - Malcolm Macdonald 3969

O Genesee - Janet O'Daniel 4468

Of Lizards and Angels: A Saga of Sioux Land - Frederick F. Manfred 4058

Officer and Gentleman - Josephine Delves-Broughton 1604

Oh Glittering Promise - Anne Fisher 2099

Oh, Promised Land - James H. Street 6079

O'Higgins and Don Bernardo - Edna Deu Pree Nelson 4578

Ol' Prophet Nat - Daniel Panger 4786

Old Hickory - Noel B. Gerson 2379

Old Miss - Thomas Campbell 877

Oldest Living Confederate Widow Tells All - Allan Gurganus 2621

On the Long Tide - Laura Krey 3555

On the Night of the Seventh Moon - Victoria Holt 3018

On to Oregon! - Honore Morrow 4490

On Trial for My Country - Stanlake Samkange 5578

One-Eyed Dream - Terry C. Johnston 3253

One Smart Indian - Robert J. Seidman 5722

The Origin - Irving Stone 6060

Ourselves to Know - John O'Hara 4704

Out of the Dark - Norah Lofts 3856

Out of This Furnace - Thomas Bell 425

Outlaw - Warren Kiefer 3482

Pageant - G.B. Lancaster 3650

Paint the Wind - Cathy Cash Spellman 5960

Painted Lady: Eliza Jumel, Her Life and Times - Leonard Falkner 2009

Painting the Darkness - Robert Goddard 2445

Palaces of Desire - Kate Alexander 81

Palais-Royale - Richard Sennett 5747

Paloverde - Jacqueline Briskin 693

Panther in the Sky - James Alexander Thom 6234

Paradise - Sarah Neilan 4566

Paradise Falls - Don Robertson 5399

Paradise Reclaimed - Halldor Laxness 3686

The Parfit Knight - Juliet Blyth 555

Parson Austen's Daughter - Helen Ashton 219

The Parson's Daughter - Catherine Cookson 1286

Passage Home - Alison McLeay 4286

Passage to Natchez - Cameron Judd 3316

The Passionate Journey - Irving Stone 6061

Passionate Rebel: The Story of Hector Berlioz - F.W. Kenyon 3457

The Passions of the Mind - Irving Stone 6062

Pastora - Joanna Barnes 321

Pathetic Symphony: A Novel about Tchaikovsky - Klaus Mann 4064

Peace at Bowling Green - Alfred Leland Crabb 1405

Pearl - Anne Leaton 3701

The Pearl Pagoda - Susannah Broome 707

The Pecos River - Fred Bean 399

Pemberley, or Pride and Prejudice Continued - Emma Tennant 6201

Penelope Goes to Portsmouth - Marion Chesney 1043

Penhally - Caroline Gordon 2479

The People of Juvik - Olav Dunn 1798

The Pepper Tree - John Edward Jennings 3203

Perfecting Fiona - Marion Chesney 1044

Phantom - Susan Kay 3375

The Piano - Jane Campion 878

The Pistoleer - James Carlos Blake 536

The Place of Dead Roads - William S. Burroughs 808

Playing the Game - Ian Buruma 810

The Plums Hang High - Gertrude E. Finney 2091

Pomp and Circumstance - Fred Mustard Stewart 6025

Power in the Blood - Greg Matthews 4191

The Power of Black - M.B. Longman 3880

Prairie - Anna Lee Waldo 6528

Precious Bane - Mary Webb 6590

The President's Daughter - Barbara Chase-Riboud 1005

The President's Lady - Irving Stone 6063

Presumption: An Entertainment - Julia Barrett 350

Pride's Castle - Frank Yerby 6925

The Prime Minister's Wife - Doris Leslie 3727

The Prince of Eden - Marilyn Harris 2732

Princess in Amber - Evelyn Wilde Mayerson 4205

Princess Sophia - Edison Marshall 4110

The Prison Notebooks of Ricardo Flores Magon - Douglas Day 1545

Private Knowledge - Betty Palmer Nelson 4576

The Private Life of Florence Nightingale - Richard Gordon 2485

A Prologue to Love - Taylor Caldwell 862

The Proprietor - Ann Schlee 5638

The Proselyte - Susan Ertz 1958

The Proud Breed - Celeste De Blasis 1547

The Quade Inheritance - Barbara Ker Wilson 3469

Quanah Parker - Bill Dugan 1759

Queen Dolley: The Life and Times of Dolley Madison - Dorothy Clarke Wilson 6806

The Queen of Hearts - Joan Rees 5290

The Queen's Husband - Jean Plaidy 5052

The Questing Heart: A Romantic Novel about George Sand - F.W. Kenyon 3458

Quiet Lady - Norman Collins 1216

The Quiet Life of Mrs. General Lane - Victoria Case 951

Quinn's Book - William Kennedy 3423

Rabbit Boss - Thomas Sanchez 5581

Raccoon John Smith - Louis Cochran 1145

Rachel - Anne Powers 5153

A Rage Against Heaven - Fred Mustard Stewart 6026

Rage in Silence: A Novel Based on the Life of Goya - Donald Braider 643

The Raider - Jesse Hill Ford 2164

The Rainbird - Sara Lidman 3780

The Rainbow Promise - Lisa Gregory 2580

Raintree County - Ross Lockridge Jr. 3827

Rapaho - Jamie Lee Cooper 1314

Rasero - Francisco Rebolledo 5282

The Raven - Chancellor Williams 6769

Ravenshoe - Henry Kingsley 3500

Rawhider - Gene Shelton 5802

The Rector of Justin - Louis Auchincloss 233

Red Barbarian - Margaret Gaan 2260

Red Plush: The Story of the Moorhouse Family - Guy McCrone 4232

Redemption - Leon Uris 6393

Refining Felicity - Marion Chesney 1048

Refugio, They Named You Wrong - Susan Clark Schofield 5647

Regency Royal - Michael Hardwick 2687

Regent Square - Forbes Bramble 645

The Regiment - Christopher Nicole 4620

The Regiment - C.L. Skelton 5874

Reigning Passions - Kathrin Perutz 4940

The Reluctant Heiress - Annabel Laine 3588

Restless Is the River - August Derleth 1617

Restless Voyage - Stanley David Porteus 5138

Return of the Stranger - Reay Tannahill 6158

Reunion at Chattanooga - Alfred Leland Crabb 1406

Richard Walden's Wife - Eleanor Kelly 3399

The Richlands - Agnes Sligh Turnbull 6364

Ride the Wind - Lucia St. Clair Robson 5416

Riders of Judgment - Frederick F. Manfred 4059

The Riven Heart - Genevieve Gennari 2354

The River Devils - Carter A. Vaughan 6437

River of Dreams - Gay Courter 1390

Rivers of Gold - Janet Edmonds 1868

The Robber Bridegroom - Eudora Welty 6623

Roman - Douglas C. Jones 3281

Rose - Martin Cruz Smith 5923

A Rose for Virtue - Norah Lofts 3858

The Rose of Malmaison: The Turbulent Life of the Beautiful Josephine - Gaby von Schonthan 5660

Royal William - Doris Leslie 3728

The Running Iron - Rachel Ann Fish 2097

Sacajawea - Anna Lee Waldo 6529

Sacajawea of the Shoshones - Della F. Emmons 1940

The Saga of Henry Starr - Robert J. Conley 1250

St. John's Wood - Nancy Fitzgerald 2116

The Saint of Montparnasse: A Novel Based on the Life of Constantin Brancusi - Peter Neagoe 4560

The Salamanca Drum - Dorothy Eden 1861

The Salem Frigate - John Edward Jennings 3205

Sally Hemings - Barbara Chase-Riboud 1006

The Salt and the Savor - Howard William Troyer 6354

Sam Chance - Benjamin Capps 888

Sam Houston - Noel B. Gerson 2380

The Sam Houston Story - Dean Owen 4770

Samuel Brannan and the Golden Fleece - Reva Scott 5686

San Antone - V.J. Banis 288

Sara Dane - Catherine Gaskin 2316

Sarah - Joel Gross 2603

Saturday City - Jan Webster 6593

Savage Prodigal - Konrad Bercovici 474

The Scandalous Lady Wright - Marion Chesney 1049

The Scandalous Marriage - Marion Chesney 1050

Scarborough House - Sharon Salvato 5577

The Scottish Marriage - Karen Lynn 3942

The Sea of Grass - Conrad Richter 5323

The Sea Officer - Showell Styles 6105

The Sea Panther: A Novel about the Commander of the U.S.S. Constitution - Philip Vail 6397

The Sea Stands Watch - Helen Parker Mudgett 4507

The Seadon Fortune - Leonard St. Clair 5563

The Searchers - Alan Le May 3691

Season for War - P.F. Kluge 3510

A Season of Swans - Celeste De Blasis 1548

Season of Yellow Leaf - Douglas C. Jones 3283

Seasons - Anna Dillon 1645

The Seasons of Heroes - Paxton Davis 1539

Seattle Green - Jane Adams 26

The Second Sister - Leslie O'Grady 4701

The Second Son of Heaven: A Novel of Nineteenth-Century China - C.Y. Lee 3707

The Secret Annie Oakley - Marcy Moran Heidish 2819

The Secret Life of Laszlo, Count Dracula - Roderick Anscombe 156

The Secret Memoirs of Lord Byron - Christopher Nicole 4622

The Seducer - Henrik Stangerup 5980

The Seekers - John Jakes 3153

Segu - Maryse Conde 1234

Serpent and Staff - Frank Yerby 6927

Seven Tempest - William Vaughan Wilkins 6761

The Shadow in the Glass - August Derleth 1618

Shadow of the Moon - Douglas C. Jones 3284

Shadows and Images - Meriol Trevor 6344

The Shalimar - Betty Hale Hyatt 3091

Shaman - Noah Gordon 2483

She Rode a Yellow Stallion - Walter Reed 5286

The Ship's Clock - Catherine M. Rae 5237

Show Boat - Edna Ferber 2063

Show Me a Land - Clark McMeekin 4293

Signorina - Henry Myers 4542

The Silent People - Walter Macken 3990

The Silver Dolphin - Velda Johnston 3264

Sir William - David Stacton 5977

Sisters and Brothers - Janet Stevenson 6005

Sitting Bull - Bill Dugan 1760

Slave - William Malliol 4041

The Slender Reed - Noel B. Gerson 2382

The Smiths - Janet Fairbank 2002

The Smoky Hill - Don Coldsmith 1188

Snow-Water - Dorothy Gardiner 2285

So Free We Seem - Helen Todd 6286

So Much as Beauty Does - Muriel Elwood 1938

So Perish the Roses - Neil Bell 423

Soldier of the Queen - Max Hennessy 2837

Son of the Gamblin' Man: The Youth of an Artist - Mari Sandoz 5593

The Song of Bernadette - Franz Werfel 6625

Song of the Cheyenne - Jory Sherman 5822

Sophie - Geoffrey Wagner 6519

A Sorrow in Our Heart - Allen W. Eckert 1844

Southern Cross - Terry Coleman 1206

Southern Discomfort - Rita Mae Brown 730

Spangle - Gary Jennings 3196

Speak to Me of Love - Dorothy Eden 1862

The Spirit and the Flesh: A Novel Inspired by the Life of Isadora Duncan - David Weiss 6610

The Splendor Stays: An Historic Novel Based on the Lives of the Seven Hart Sisters of Saybrook - Marguerite Allis 114

The Spoils of War - Thomas Fleming 2131

Spring Came on Forever - Bess Streeter Aldrich 73

Spring Moon: A Novel of China - Bette Bao Lord 3897

The Spring of the Tiger - Victoria Holt 3021

The Spy: A Tale of the Neutral Ground - James Fenimore Cooper 1310

Stacey's Flyer - Patricia Burns 800

The Stanbroke Girls - Fiona Hill 2925

Stand We at Last - Zoe Fairbairns 1999

Star of Empire: A Novel of Old San Antonio - Leonard Sanders 5590

A Star Pointed North - Edmund Fuller 2250

Steamboat Gothic - Frances Parkinson Keyes 3481

Stone Song: A Novel of the Life of Crazy Horse - Winfred Blevins 548

The Store - Michael Pearson 4879

Storm Before Sunrise - June Wyndham Davies 1507

Storm Center: A Novel about Andy Johnson - Joseph Walker McSpadden 4312

Storm of Time - Eleanor Dark 1494

Storm to the South - Thelma Strabel 6073

Storming Heaven - Denise Giardina 2394

A Story of Deep Delight - Thomas McNamee 4305

The Story of Gosta Berling - Selma Lagerlof 3586

Stranger at Wildings - Madeleine Brent 663

Stranger in Two Worlds - Hugh Clevely 1111

The Street Sparrows - Rose Ayers 249

The Sugar Pavilion - Rosalind Laker 3600

Sultana - Michael, Prince of Greece 4358

The Sun Is God - Michael Noonan 4636

Sunshine and Shadow - Antonia Van-Loon 6426

The Sunshine Patriot: A Novel of Benedict Arnold - Norman Partington 4822

The Sutburys - Pamela Hill 2944

Swan's Chance - Celeste De Blasis 1549

The Swedish Nightingale: Jenny Lind - Elizabeth Kyle 3571

Sweet's Folly - Fiona Hill 2926

A Tale of the Wind: A Novel of Nineteenth-Century France - Kay Nolte Smith 5922

The Talking Rifle - Glenn R. Vernam 6454

Tall Ships to Cathay - Helen Augur 240

The Tall Woman - Wilma Dykeman 1819

The Taverners' Place - Joanna Trollope 6351

Tell Your Sons: A Novel of the Napoleonic Era - Willa Gibbs 2402

Tempered Blade - Monte Barrett 352

The Tenants of Time - Thomas Flanagan 2120

Teresa, or Her Demon Lover - Austin K. Gray 2554

Testimony of Two Men - Taylor Caldwell 863

Teverton Hall - Jane Gillespie 2421

That Skipper From Stonington - Theda Kenyon 3464

That Spanish Woman - F.W. Kenyon 3461

That Sweet and Savage Land - Emma Drummond 1728

Theirs Was the Kingdom - R.F. Delderfield 1590

Theory of War - Joan Brady 637

These Latter Days - Laura Kalpakian 3330

These Were the Brontes - Dorothy Helen Cornish 1332

They Called Her Mrs. Doc. - Janette Oke 4709

They Were Dreamers - James F. Murphy Jr. 4525

Thine Is the Glory - Samuel A. Schreiner Jr. 5672

Things Fall Apart - Chinua Achebe 16

The Third Sister - Julia Barrett 351

This Is the House - Deborah Hill 2921

This Land Is Ours - Louis Zara 6953

This Old Bill - Loren D. Estleman 1980

This Splendid Earth - V.J. Banis 289

Those Who Go Against the Current - Shirley Seifert 5734

Those Who Love - Irving Stone 6064

Thousand Years of Gold - Ruthanne Lum McCunn 4239

The Three-Cornered Hat - Pedro Antonio de Alarcon 62

Three-Headed Angel - Roark Bradford 623

The Three Lives of Elizabeth - Shirley Seifert 5735

Threescore and Ten - Walter Allen 105

Through the Green Valley - Barbara Gowdy 2498

Thunder on the River - Charlton Laird 3590

Tidewater Dynasty: A Biographical Novel of the Lees of Stratford Hall - Carey Roberts 5372

Time and the Wind - Erico Verissimo 6451

Time in Its Flight - Susan Fromberg Schaeffer 5636

The Time of the Hunter's Moon - Victoria Holt 3022

Time out of Mind - Rachel Field 2081

The Tin Drum - Gunther Grass 2540

To Fell the Giants - Bill Hotchkiss 3038

To Keep Us Free - Marguerite Allis 115

To Make a Killing - Robert J. Conley 1252
To Seize a Dream - Virginia Davis Hersch 2866
To Seize the Passing Dream - Ted Berkman 479
To Spit Against the Wind - Benjamin H. Levin 3737
Tolbecken - Samuel Shellabarger 5798
The Tontine - Thomas B. Costain 1371
Too Long a Stranger - Janette Oke 4710
TR - Noel B. Gerson 2385
Trail-Makers of the Middle Border - Hamlin
  Garland 2296
The Trail to Ogallala - Benjamin Capps 889
Trail's End - Fred Bean 400
Trapper's Moon - Jory Sherman 5823
Treasure in Hell's Canyon - Bill Gulick 2619
The Treasure of the Chisos - John H. Culp 1446
Treasures on Earth - Jessica Stirling 6049
The Tree of Liberty - Elizabeth Page 4773
The Trees - Conrad Richter 5326
Trinity - Leon Uris 6394
Triptych - Dora Landey 3652
Troubled Border - T.D. Allen 104
Troy Chimneys - Margaret Kennedy 3421
True Women - Janice Woods Windle 6820
Trumpets of Silver - Norma Harris 2735
Twilight of Empire - Allen W. Eckert 1846
*The Twisted Saber: A Biographical Novel of Benedict
  Arnold* - Philip Vail 6398
Two Corinthians - Carola Dunn 1797
The Tynedale Daughters - Norma Lee Clark 1093
Ulysses: A Biographical Novel - Robert Skimin 5878
Under the Fifth Sun: A Novel of Pancho Villa - Earl
  Shorris 5832
*An Unequal Marriage; or Pride and Prejudice Twenty
  Years Later* - Emma Tennant 6202
Up She Rises - David Garnett 2298
Utrillo's Mother - Sarah Baylis 391
El Vago - Laurence Gonzales 2474
Vale of Tyranny - Suzanne Butler 831
Valide: A Novel of the Harem - Barbara Chase-
  Riboud 1007
The Valley - Clifford Irving 3114
Valley of the Shadow - Charles Marquis
  Warren 6570
Vandemark's Folly - Herbert Quick 5223
Vanessa - Hugh Walpole 6548
Vanity Fair - William Makepeace Thackeray 6213
The Vengeance Trail of Josey Wales - Forrest
  Carter 946
Very Young Mrs. Poe - Cothburn O'Neal 4740
The Viceroy of Ouidah - Bruce C. Chatwin 1009
Victoire - Clare Darcy 1493
Victoria and Albert - Evelyn Anthony 166
Victoria in the Wings - Jean Plaidy 5072
Victoria Victorious - Jean Plaidy 5073
The View From Coyaba - Peter Abrahams 11
Vincent: A Novel Based on the Life of Van Gogh -
  Joost Poldermans 5082
Vindication - Frances Sherwood 5824
The Vines of Yarrabee - Dorothy Eden 1864
The Vivian Inheritance - Jean Stubbs 6101
A Voice in the Streets - John William Tebbel 6196
The Volcano Lover - Susan Sontag 5946
Voodoo Dreams: A Novel of Marie Laveau - Jewell
  Parker Rhodes 5310
Voss - Patrick White 6698
Walk in My Soul - Lucia St. Clair Robson 5418
Wallis: The Novel - Anne Edwards 1883
Walt Whitman's Secret - Ben Aronin 196
Wanderers Eastward, Wanderers West - Kathleen
  Winsor 6823
Watch for Me on the Mountain - Forrest Carter 947
Watchfires - Louis Auchincloss 234
Water over the Dam - Marguerite Allis 116
Watson's Apology - Beryl Bainbridge 271
Wave High the Banner - Dee Brown 714
The Way West - A.B. Guthrie Jr. 2628
The Wayfarer - Shirley Seifert 5738
We Must March: A Novel of the Winning of Oregon -
  Honore Morrow 4491

West to Eden - Gloria Goldreich 2461
Western: A Saga of the Great Plains - Frank
  Yerby 6930
Westfield - Roderick Thorp 6277
Westward the Sun - Brigid Knight 3524
The Whip - Catherine Cookson 1291
Whirlwind in Petticoats - Beril Becker 406
Whisper of the Wolf - Terry C. Johnston 3261
A Whistle in the Wind - John H. Culp 1447
The White King - Samuel Bertram Harrison 2747
White Poppy - Margaret Gaan 2261
The White Slave - Fanny Howe 3059
Whittling Boy: The Story of Eli Whitney - Roger
  Burlingame 789
Wide Sargasso Sea - Jean Rhys 5312
The Widow of Windsor - Jean Plaidy 5076
The Widow of Windsor - Tyler Whittle 6723
*Wild Decembers: A Biographical Portrait of the
  Brontes* - Hilda Crystal White 6681
Wild Earth's Nobility - Frank Waters 6578
Wild Swan - Celeste De Blasis 1550
Wild Times - Brian Garfield 2291
Wilford's Daughter - Alexandra Manners 4071
The Wind Leaves No Shadow - Ruth Laughlin 3672
Winds of Spring - Walter Havighurst 2776
Wine of Life - Charles Orson Gorham 2489
The Wine Widow - Tessa Barclay 301
The Witch of Manga Reva - Garland Roark 5359
Wives of the Wind - Marjorie Jarrett 3170
The Wolf and the Buffalo - Elmer Kelton 3408
Wolves Against the Moon - Julia Cooley
  Altrocchi 123
A Woman by Design - Frances Kennett 3426
A Woman Called Moses - Marcy Moran
  Heidish 2821
Woman Chief - Benjamin Capps 892
A Woman Named Damaris - Janette Oke 4711
A Woman of Texas - R.T. Stevens 6002
A Woman of the People - Benjamin Capps 893
Woman's Own - Robyn Carr 941
Wyatt Earp - Dan Gordon 2481
The Yankee From Tennessee - Noel B. Gerson 2388
Yankee Woman - Frederic Baume 381
The Yellowstone - Winfred Blevins 549
Yellowstone Kelly - Peter Bowen 602
Young Pitt - A.M. Maughan 4200
The Young Victoria - Tyler Whittle 6724
Yvonne Goes to York - Marion Chesney 1054

1800s
1805 - Richard Woodman 6857
The African - Harold Courlander 1386
An Air of Glory - Sarah Neilan 4563
All Souls' Rising - Madison Smartt Bell 422
Angel - Carola Dunn 1790
Anna - Cynthia Harrod-Eagles 2752
Antipodes Jane: A Novel of Jane Austen in Australia -
  Barbara Ker Wilson 3468
Arabella - Georgette Heyer 2874
Arctic Treachery - Richard Woodman 6858
A Balance of Dangers - Anthony Forrest 2184
Baltic Mission - Richard Woodman 6859
The Battle of Wagram - Gilles Lapouge 3664
Beat to Quarters - C.S. Forester 2170
The Believers - Janice Holt Giles 2409
Black Sheep - Georgette Heyer 2878
Black Thunder - Arna Bontemps 574
Blood and Sand - Rosemary Sutcliff 6121
The Bomb Vessel - Richard Woodman 6860
Bosnian Chronicle - Ivo Andric 150
The Brittle Glass - Norah Lofts 3837
Broadsides - Robert Welter Daly 1459
A Calf for Venus - Norah Lofts 3838
Captain Bolton's Corpse - J.G. Jeffreys 3178
Captain Cut-Throat - John Dickson Carr 908
Captain Justice - Anthony Forrest 2185
The Caretaker Wife - Barbara Whitehead 6706
Castaway - Frances Murray 4535
Charles O'Malley - Charles James Lever 3731

Clear for Action! - Simon White 6699
Coasts of Folly - Joel Williams 6784
Colors Aloft! - Alexander Kent 3427
Corner the Moon - Shirley Barker 310
Cotillion - Georgette Heyer 2883
Cousin Kate - Georgette Heyer 2884
Damnation Reef - Jill Tattersall 6172
Dead Reckoning - C. Northcote Parkinson 4809
Decision at Trafalgar - Richard Woodman 6861
The Dedicated - Willa Gibbs 2399
Desolation Island - Patrick O'Brian 4662
Draw Near to Battle - Jere Hungerford
  Wheelwright 6667
The Duke's Mistress: The Story of Mary Ann Clarke -
  F.W. Kenyon 3447
Eagle Song - James Houston 3050
The East Indiaman - Ellis K. Meacham 4313
An Embarrassment of Riches - James Howard
  Kunstler 3565
The Emperor's Duchess - R.G. Waldeck 6524
*The Emperor's Lady: A Novel Based on the Life of the
  Empress Josephine* - F.W. Kenyon 3449
The English Captain - Simon White 6700
The English Wife - Charity Blackstock 530
Expedition! - Dana Fuller Ross 5473
The Fallon Pride - Reagan O'Neal 4742
Farewell the Stranger - Saliee O'Brien 4682
Faro's Daughter - Georgette Heyer 2887
Father and Son - Donald Clayton Porter 5117
First Night - Jane Aiken Hodge 2963
Fleeting Fancy - Rosemary Edghill 1866
Flintlock - Jason Manning 4073
The Folly - Marion Chesney 1031
Forest of the Night - Madison Jones 3291
Forward the Nation - Donald Culross Peattie 4880
The Free Fishers - John Buchan 750
Free Lance - George Shipway 5827
Friday's Child - Georgette Heyer 2890
The Fur Masters - Alan Sullivan 6113
The Gates of the Mountains - Will Henry 2842
The Grandissimes - George W. Cable 842
A Great Lord - Paul Frischauer 2233
Guy Mannering - Sir Walter Scott 5697
The Hastening Wind - Edward Grierson 2591
Hawk's Journey - Donald Clayton Porter 5119
Hawthorn Hill - Doris Shannon 5777
He Brings Great News - Clemence Dane 1462
The High Constable - Maan Meyers 4353
H.M.S. Surprise - Patrick O'Brian 4666
The Holy Warrior - Gilbert Morris 4462
Honor This Day - Alexander Kent 3432
Hornblower and the Atropos - C.S. Forester 2175
Hornblower and the Hotspur - C.S. Forester 2176
Hornblower During the Crisis - C.S. Forester 2177
In Distant Waters - Richard Woodman 6862
The Inshore Squadron - Alexander Kent 3434
Jane and the Man of the Cloth - Stephanie
  Barron 355
Jane and the Unpleasantness at Scargrave Manor -
  Stephanie Barron 356
Jane Fairfax - Joan Aiken 50
Jennie about to Be - Elisabeth Ogilvie 4694
Jonathan Blair, Bounty Lands Lawyer - William
  Donohue Ellis 1929
Katya - Lucy Cores 1328
The Last of the Vikings - Johan Bojer 563
The Last Portrait of the Duchess of Alba - Antonio
  Larreta 3666
Lieutenant Hornblower - C.S. Forester 2178
Lighthouse - Eugenia Price 5182
The Long Fight - D.A. Rayner 5270
Lord Elgin's Lady - Theodore Vrettos 6514
The Lost Garden - Jane Aiken Hodge 2966
Louisa Brancusi - Darrell Husted 3088
Lydia Bailey - Kenneth Roberts 5387
The Man of the Storm - Ethel Hueston 3069
The Man Who Thought He Was Messiah - Curt
  Leviant 3735
Mansfield Revisited - Joan Aiken 51

Marianne - Juliette Benzoni   466

Marianne and the Masked Prince - Juliette Benzoni   469

Marianne and the Privateer - Juliette Benzoni   470

Marry in Haste - Jane Aiken Hodge   2967

Master and Commander - Patrick O'Brian   4669

Matthew Early - Alexander Laing   3589

The Mauritius Command - Patrick O'Brian   4670

The Medicine Man - Shirley Seifert   5729

Meridon - Philippa Gregory   2583

Midsummer Masque - Jill Tattersall   6174

The Miser of Mayfair - Marion Chesney   1038

My Lady Innkeeper - Barbara Metzger   4346

My Theodosia - Anya Seton   5753

Napoleon Must Die - Quinn Fawcett   2054

The Native Air - Sarah Woodhouse   6854

No Place on Earth - Christa Wolf   6836

The Nonesuch - Georgette Heyer   2896

Not by Any Single Man - Brigid Knight   3522

On the Company's Service - Ellis K. Meacham   4315

The Pandora Secret - Anthony Forrest   2186

Paths of Fortune - Susan Moore   4444

Pitcairn's Island - Charles Nordhoff   4640

Plain Jane - Marion Chesney   1045

Polonaise - Jane Aiken Hodge   2968

Post Captain - Patrick O'Brian   4672

The Prairie - James Fenimore Cooper   1308

A Private Revenge - Richard Woodman   6863

Promises to Keep - Jocelyn Stirling   6051

The Proud Canaries - David Johnson   3222

Pull Down to New Orleans - Zachary Ball   283

Ramage and the Dido - Dudley Pope   5098

Ramage and the Guillotine - Dudley Pope   5099

Ramage and the Rebels - Dudley Pope   5100

Ramage and the Saracens - Dudley Pope   5101

Ramage at Trafalgar - Dudley Pope   5102

The Ramage Touch - Dudley Pope   5103

Ramage's Devil - Dudley Pope   5104

Ramage's Diamond - Dudley Pope   5105

Ramage's Mutiny - Dudley Pope   5106

Ramage's Prize - Dudley Pope   5107

Ramage's Signal - Dudley Pope   5108

Ramage's Trial - Dudley Pope   5109

The Raven and the Rose - Susan Wiggs   6746

Reckon with the River - Clark McMeekin   4292

The Reluctant Widow - Georgette Heyer   2899

The Return of the Gypsy - Philippa Carr   927

Ride with Me - Thomas B. Costain   1369

Rio Grande - Jory Sherman   5821

River to the West: A Novel of the Astor Adventure - John Edward Jennings   3204

The Rock Cried Out - Edward Stanley   5981

Rogue's Harbor - Inglis Fletcher   2139

The Running of the Tide - Esther Forbes   2160

Saragossa - Benito Perez Galdos   4912

The Scalpel and the Sword - Dell Shannon   5774

A Season of Mists - Sarah Woodhouse   6856

The Settlers - William Stuart Long   3878

Seven Men of Gascony - R.F. Delderfield   1589

Shadows on the Shore - Jessica Stirling   6048

Sharpe's Eagle - Bernard Cornwell   1341

Sharpe's Rifles - Bernard Cornwell   1347

The Sherbrooke Bride - Catherine Coulter   1382

The Shining Mountains - Dale Van Every   6410

The Sleeping Sword: A Biographical Novel - Pearl Frye   2244

So Great a Man - David Pilgrim   5000

So Near So Far - C. Northcote Parkinson   4814

The Spanish Bride - Georgette Heyer   2902

Star of the West - Ethel Hueston   3070

Success to the Brave - Alexander Kent   3441

Sylvia's Lovers - Elizabeth Gaskell   2312

Tale of Valor - Vardis Fisher   2112

This Savage Race - Douglas C. Jones   3285

Tide of Empire - Bates Baldwin   279

A Time for Titans - Vina Delmar   1602

Tom Burke of Ours - Charles James Lever   3732

Topaz - Helen Ashfield   215

Touch and Go - C. Northcote Parkinson   4815

A Tradition of Victory - Alexander Kent   3443

Trail: The Story of the Lewis and Clark Expedition - Louis Charbonneau   998

The Traitors - William Stuart Long   3879

Tree of Gold - Rosalind Laker   3602

The Trumpet Major - Thomas Hardy   2700

The Twilighters - Noel M. Loomis   3894

Under Two Flags - Ouida   4767

Venetian Masque - Rafael Sabatini   5556

Vision of the Eagle - Kay L. McDonald   4263

Voices in a Haunted Room - Philippa Carr   931

War and Peace - Leo Tolstoy   6295

War Clouds - Donald Clayton Porter   5131

Water Music - T. Coraghessan Boyle   619

West Goes the Road - Tim Pridgen   5192

Westward! - Dana Fuller Ross   5492

The Wicked Godmother - Marion Chesney   1053

A Wicked Way to Die - J.G. Jeffreys   3182

Wilderness - Roger Zelazny   6957

The Wind From the Sea - Constance Heaven   2812

The World of Jennie G. - Elisabeth Ogilvie   4696

Written in Sand - Josephine Case   950

Yankee Pasha - Edison Marshall   4115

1810s

The Adventuress - Marion Chesney   1014

All Ye People - Merle Estes Colby   1167

Allegra - Clare Darcy   1483

An American, Sir - Corwin Root   5459

Anna - Cynthia Harrod-Eagles   2752

April Lady - Georgette Heyer   2873

As Long as the Rivers Run - Sam J. Slate   5882

The Asherwood Protegee - Mary A. Garratt   2299

The Autumn Rose - Fiona Hill   2923

Back in Society - Marion Chesney   1017

Bath Tangle - Georgette Heyer   2875

Beyond the Shining Mountains - Doris Shannon   5775

Black Dawn - Christopher Nicole   4613

Black Ivory - Polan Banks   292

Black Thunder - Arna Bontemps   574

The Bluestocking - June Drummond   1729

Bosnian Chronicle - Ivo Andric   150

Brave Pursuit - Marguerite Allis   107

Bride of the Unicorn - Kasey Michaels   4363

Bright Captivity - Eugenia Price   5180

The Brooks Legend - William Donohue Ellis   1928

The Brotherhood of the Red Poppy - Henri Troyat   6353

Call the New World - John Edward Jennings   3199

Called Away - Perdita Buchan   753

The Campaign - Carlos Fuentes   2245

Captain Caution - Kenneth Roberts   5385

The Captain From Connecticut - C.S. Forester   2171

Cassy - Elizabeth Lyle   3930

The Castle of the Winds - Jeanne Montague   4434

Charity Girl - Georgette Heyer   2879

Charles O'Malley - Charles James Lever   3731

The Charterhouse of Parma - Stendhal   5993

The Citadel of the Lakes - Myron David Orr   4754

A Civil Contract - Georgette Heyer   2880

Close Quarters - William Golding   2453

Colonel Sandhurst to the Rescue - Marion Chesney   1021

Come Be My Love - Diana Brown   717

The Commodore - Patrick O'Brian   4661

Commodore Hornblower - C.S. Forester   2172

Commodore Manifred - Miranda Seymour   5761

The Court Martial of Commodore Perry - James A. Rhodes   5307

Creature Comforts - Jessica Stirling   6041

Crimson Is the Eastern Shore - Don Tracy   6308

The Cross of Frankenstein - Robert J. Myers   4548

The Cry of Dolores - Herbert Gorman   2492

Dangerous - Amanda Quick   5213

Daphne - Marion Chesney   1022

Dead Reckoning - C. Northcote Parkinson   4809

Death at the French Creek - Raymond C. Borel   580

Deception - Amanda Quick   5214

Deirdre and Desire - Marion Chesney   1024

The Desirable Duchess - Marion Chesney   1025

Diana the Huntress - Marion Chesney   1026

Double Masquerade - Karen Lynn   3938

Drums of War - Roy Clews   1114

Eliza Stanhope - Joanna Trollope   6347

The Emerald Necklace - Diana Brown   718

Emma Watson - Joan Aiken   45

The Emperor's Duchess - R.G. Waldeck   6524

Enslaved - Ron Burns   801

Erie Water - Walter D. Edmonds   1875

Escapade - Jane Aiken Hodge   2962

Eugenia - Clare Darcy   1487

The Explorers - William Stuart Long   3872

The Fallon Pride - Reagan O'Neal   4742

False Colours - Georgette Heyer   2886

The Far Side of the World - Patrick O'Brian   4663

Feast of the Jesters - Manuel Komroff   3533

Feather Castles - Patricia Veryan   6462

Fire Down Below - William Golding   2454

The Fleet in the Forest - Carl Daniel Lane   3654

Fleeting Fancy - Rosemary Edghill   1866

The Flight of the Eagle - Donald Thomas   6239

Flying Colours - C.S. Forester   2173

For King and Company - Ellis K. Meacham   4314

The Fortune of War - Patrick O'Brian   4664

The Foundling - Georgette Heyer   2888

Frankenstein Unbound - Brian Aldiss   68

Frederica in Fashion - Marion Chesney   1032

French Dragoon - Roger Rudigoz   5523

French Slippers - Deborah Chester   1055

Fury in the Earth: A Novel of the New Madrid Earthquake - Harry Harrison Kroll   3557

The Gentleman From America - Paul Benton   464

The Girl Who Was Never Queen: A Biographical Novel of Princess Charlotte of Wales - Mary Main   4037

The Golden Fleece - Norah Lofts   3843

The Golden Years: A Novel Based on the Life and Loves of Percy Bysshe Shelley - F.W. Kenyon   3451

Gothic Romance - Emmanuel Carrere   942

The Grand Sophy - Georgette Heyer   2891

A Great Lord - Paul Frischauer   2233

The Gun - C.S. Forester   2174

Gwendolen - Clare Darcy   1489

Hangman's Beach - Thomas H. Raddall   5229

The Happy Parrot - Robert W. Chambers   977

Hate - Arthur Douglas Smith   5918

Haunted Summer - Anne Edwards   1881

The Hawthorne Legacy - Teresa Crane   1416

Hearts of Gold - Jessica Stirling   6044

Hearts of Hickory - John Trotwood Moore   4442

The Heiress Bride - Catherine Coulter   1375

Here Comes a Candle - Jane Aiken Hodge   2964

Here I Stay - Elizabeth Coatsworth   1138

Holy Week - Louis Aragon   182

Horseshoe Bend - Bruce Palmer   4779

The House of Kuragin - Constance Heaven   2808

I, James Lewis - Gilbert Wolf Gabriel   2266

If I Were You - Joan Aiken   49

An Infamous Army - Georgette Heyer   2892

The Ionian Mission - Patrick O'Brian   4667

Jonathan Dearborn: A Novel of the War of 1812 - Willard Wallace   6540

Lady Fortescue Steps Out - Marion Chesney   1035

Lady in the Briars - Carola Dunn   1793

Lady of Quality - Georgette Heyer   2893

Lanterns - Patricia Veryan   6465

The Last Love - Thomas B. Costain   1367

Leafy Rivers - Jessamyn West   6630

Letter of Marque - Andrew Hepburn   2849

The Letter of Marque - Patrick O'Brian   4668

Letty - Clare Darcy   1491

Lighthouse - Eugenia Price   5182

The Limits of Glory: A Novel of Waterloo - James McDonough   4265

The Lively Lady - Kenneth Roberts   5386

Logic of the Heart - Patricia Veryan 6466
Long Pennant - Oliver La Farge 3573
Lord Byron's Doctor - Paul West 6634
Lord Hornblower - C.S. Forester 2179
Lord Rivington's Lady - Eileen Jackson 3134
Lovers Meeting - Mollie Hardwick 2695
Love's Children - Judith Chernaik 1013
Love's Duet - Patricia Veryan 6468
Luise - Dawn Stewart Field 2079
Lustre in the Sky - R.G. Waldeck 6525
Lydia, or Love in Town - Clare Darcy 1492
Marcel Armand - Sallie Bell 424
Marianne and the Crown of Fire - Juliette
   Benzoni 467
Marianne and the Lords of the East - Juliette
   Benzoni 468
Marianne and the Rebels - Juliette Benzoni 471
The Marquis of Bolibar - Leo Perutz 4942
Married Past Redemption - Patricia Veryan 6469
Marsanne - Virginia Coffman 1155
Masque of Jade - Emma Merritt 4344
Masque of Sapphire - Deana James 3156
The Medicine Man - Shirley Seifert 5729
The Memoirs of Lord Byron - Robert Nye 4655
Men Were Deceivers Ever - Patricia Veryan 6470
Midsummer Moon - Karen Lynn 3940
The Mill on Mad River - Howard Clark 1087
The Miller's Dance - Winston Graham 2528
Minerva - Marion Chesney 1037
Miss Tonks Turns to Crime - Marion Chesney 1041
Mission to Mackinac - Myron David Orr 4755
Mrs. Budley Falls From Grace - Marion
   Chesney 1042
My Blood and My Treasure - Mary Schumann 5674
My Dear Cousin - Peggy Hoffmann 2977
My Love, My Enemy - Jan Cox Speas 5958
My Sister, My Love - Lucille Iremonger 3111
My Theodosia - Anya Seton 5753
The Mysterious Death of Meriwether Lewis - Ron
   Burns 802
Nanette - Patricia Veryan 6472
Napoleon and the Cossacks - Peter N.
   Krassnoff 3551
*Nephew to the Emperor: A Novel Based on the Life of
   Beethoven* - Jacques Brenner 658
The New Hope - Joseph C. Lincoln 3784
A Night in Cold Harbor - Margaret Kennedy 3420
Night Shadow - Catherine Coulter 1377
Night Storm - Catherine Coulter 1378
The Nightingale Legacy - Catherine Coulter 1379
No Brighter Glory - Armstrong Sperry 5963
The Noblest Frailty - Patricia Veryan 6474
The Nutmeg of Consolation - Patrick O'Brian 4671
The Olympians - Guy Bolton 566
Outpost! - Dana Fuller Ross 5486
The Pangersbourne Murders - J.G. Jeffreys 3179
Patience and Sarah - Isabel Miller 4398
Pelican Coast - Alan Le May 3690
Pemmican - Vardis Fisher 2111
Polonaise - Jane Aiken Hodge 2968
The Prince Lost to Time - Ann Dukthas 1776
The Prince Regent's Silver Bell - Gladys
   McGorian 4275
Promises to Keep - Jocelyn Stirling 6051
The Quality of Mercy - Anne Miller Downes 1712
Quicksilver Lady - Barbara Whitehead 6707
The Quiet Gentleman - Georgette Heyer 2897
Rainbird's Revenge - Marion Chesney 1046
The Rake - Karen Lynn 3941
The Rake and the Hussy - Robert W. Chambers 981
The Rake and the Rebel - Ira J. Morris 4478
Rake's Progress - Marion Chesney 1047
Rake's Ransom - Barbara Metzger 4347
Ravished - Amanda Quick 5216
Rebel Heiress - Jane Aiken Hodge 2969
Reckless - Amanda Quick 5217
The Red Lances - Arturo Uslar Pietri 4999
Red Stick - Donald Clayton Porter 5121
Regency Buck - Georgette Heyer 2898

Regency Rogue - Helen Ashfield 212
The Regent's Daughter - Jean Plaidy 5055
Rendezvous - Amanda Quick 5218
A Reputation Dies - Alice Chetwynd Ley 3766
Retreat From the Dolphin - Darwin Le Ora
   Teilhet 6198
The Return of the Gypsy - Philippa Carr 927
The Reverse of the Medal - Patrick O'Brian 4673
Ride with Me - Thomas B. Costain 1369
Rifleman Dodd - C.S. Forester 2181
Rites of Passage - William Golding 2456
River to the West: A Novel of the Astor Adventure -
   John Edward Jennings 3204
River's Run - Jane Ludlow Abbot 7
Rogue's Harbor - Inglis Fletcher 2139
The Rose and the Sword - Sandra Paretti 4792
The Running of the Tide - Esther Forbes 2160
Salvation - Sholem Asch 202
The Sandalwood Fan - Diana Brown 720
Sanguinet's Crown - Patricia Veryan 6476
Sara - Brian Cleeve 1110
Savannah - Eugenia Price 5186
Scalpdancers - Kerry Newcomb 4592
Scandal - Amanda Quick 5219
The Sea and the Sand - Christopher Nicole 4621
Seduction - Amanda Quick 5220
Seven Men of Gascony - R.F. Delderfield 1589
Sharpe's Battle - Bernard Cornwell 1338
Sharpe's Company - Bernard Cornwell 1339
Sharpe's Enemy - Bernard Cornwell 1342
Sharpe's Gold - Bernard Cornwell 1343
Sharpe's Honour - Bernard Cornwell 1344
Sharpe's Regiment - Bernard Cornwell 1345
Sharpe's Revenge - Bernard Cornwell 1346
Sharpe's Siege - Bernard Cornwell 1348
Sharpe's Sword - Bernard Cornwell 1349
Ship of the Line - C.S. Forester 2182
Silk and Steel - Stephen Alter 122
A Single Summer with Lord B. - Derek
   Marlowe 4092
Sir Philip's Folly - Marion Chesney 1051
So Brief a Spring - Claude Manceron 4054
Some Brief Folly - Patricia Veryan 6478
*Song of Metamoris: A Story That Remains of a People
   Who Passed This Way* - Milford E. Anness 155
Sons of Texas - Tom Early 1822
Sprig Muslin - Georgette Heyer 2903
The Storm Witch - Elisabeth Barr 339
The Strange Brigade - John Edward Jennings 3209
The Stranger From the Sea - Winston Graham 2530
The Stress of Her Regard - Tim Powers 5157
Stronghold - Donald Barr Chidsey 1065
The Surgeon's Mate - Patrick O'Brian 4674
Surrender - Amanda Quick 5221
Sword of Vengeance - Kerry Newcomb 4593
Sylvester; or, The Wicked Uncle - Georgette
   Heyer 2904
The Taming of Annabelle - Marion Chesney 1052
The Thirteen Gun Salute - Patrick O'Brian 4675
The Thousand Fires - Anne Powers 5155
Thread of Scarlet - Ben Ames Williams 6767
Tish - Cissie Miller 4381
The Toll-Gate - Georgette Heyer 2907
Tom Burke of Ours - Charles James Lever 3732
Treason's Harbour - Patrick O'Brian 4676
Tree of Gold - Rosalind Laker 3602
The Tree of Life - Hugh Nissenson 4629
The Trembling Earth - Dale Van Every 6411
The Truelove - Patrick O'Brian 4677
Trumpet in the Wilderness - Robert S. Harper 2717
The Twisted Sword - Winston Graham 2531
Two of a Kind: An English Trifle - Rosemary
   Edghill 1867
The Unknown Ajax - Georgette Heyer 2908
Valentina - Evelyn Anthony 165
The Valiant and the Daunted - Roy Clews 1115
Venetia - Georgette Heyer 2909
Version and Diversion - Judith Terry 6207
Vision of the Eagle - Kay L. McDonald 4263

Visions of a Heart - Emily Carmichael 899
A Visit to Highbury - Joan Austen-Leigh 243
The Wanton Fires - Meriol Trevor 6345
War and Peace - Leo Tolstoy 6295
Watch for the Dawn - Stuart Cloete 1128
Waterloo - Bernard Cornwell 1350
Waterloo - Manuel Komroff 3536
Waterloo - Frederic E. Smith 5920
Whispering - Jane Aiken Hodge 2972
Why Waterloo? - Alan Patrick Herbert 2850
The Wine-Dark Sea - Patrick O'Brian 4679
A World Too Wide - Susan Moore 4445
The Yellow Admiral - Patrick O'Brian 4680

1820s
Admiral Hornblower in the West Indies - C.S.
   Forester 2169
The Adventurers - William Stuart Long 3869
Allegheny Captive - Caroline Bourne 591
As Long as the Rivers Run - Sam J. Slate 5882
The Assassination of Mozart - David Weiss 6604
The Astrov Legacy - Constance Heaven 2802
Beau Blackstone - Richard Falkirk 2005
Ben Retallick - E.V. Thompson 6263
The Black Velvet Gown - Catherine Cookson 1274
Blackstone - Richard Falkirk 2006
Blackstone and the Scourge of Europe - Richard
   Falkirk 2007
Blackstone's Fancy - Richard Falkirk 2008
Blood Fury - David Thompson 6252
The Braganza Pursuit - Sarah Neilan 4564
A Broken Vessel - Kate Ross 5500
Buffalo Palace - Terry C. Johnston 3245
Call the New World - John Edward Jennings 3199
Canal Town - Samuel Hopkins Adams 29
Captain Marooner - Louis B. Davidson 1504
Charity Strong - Marguerite Allis 109
The Colonists - William Stuart Long 3870
Come Be My Love - Diana Brown 717
Crown of Grass - Charles Andrew Brady 634
Cut to the Quick - Kate Ross 5501
The Czar's Madman - Jaan Kross 3560
The Death of Napoleon - Simon Leys 3768
The Deceivers - John Masters 4173
Erie Water - Walter D. Edmonds 1875
Fairacres - Gladys Waters 6579
The Fields - Conrad Richter 5319
Fire, Burn! - John Dickson Carr 910
Fonthill - Aubrey Menen 4335
For Us the Living - Bruce Lancaster 3639
The Fortress - Hugh Walpole 6544
The Fourth King - Glen Petrie 4979
Frederica - Georgette Heyer 2889
*The Golden Years: A Novel Based on the Life and
   Loves of Percy Bysshe Shelley* - F.W.
   Kenyon 3451
The Hawthorne Legacy - Teresa Crane 1416
Hellfire Jackson - Garland Roark 5355
*Her Christmas at the Hermitage: A Tale about Rachel
   and Andrew Jackson* - Helen Topping Miller 4389
High Country - Jason Manning 4075
High Freedom - Earl Murray 4530
The High Missouri - Winfred Blevins 545
I Am Vidocq - Vincent McConnor 4225
In the Season of the Sun - Kerry Newcomb 4590
Indian Hater - Glenn R. Vernam 6452
Jennie Glenroy - Elisabeth Ogilvie 4695
Johnny Osage - Janice Holt Giles 2412
Kezzy - Patricia Burns 799
Kindred Spirits - June Barraclough 347
King of the Mountain - David Thompson 6255
Kingkill - Thomas Gavin 2325
Lady in the Briars - Carola Dunn 1793
The Last Love - Thomas B. Costain 1367
The Last Portrait of the Duchess of Alba - Antonio
   Larreta 3666
A London Season - Anthea Bell 420
The Long Rifle - Stewart Edward White 6702
Lord Grizzly - Frederick F. Manfred 4056

Lord of Ravensley - Constance Heaven 2809
Lord of the Dead: The Secret History of Byron - Tom
    Holland 2999
Lord of the Isles - Donald Barr Chidsey 1063
The Lord's Anointed - Ruth Eleanor McKee 4282
Lure of the Wind - David Thompson 6256
Manuela, La Caballeresa Del Sol - Demetrio Aguilera
    Malta 41
The Massacre at Fall Creek - Jessamyn West 6631
The Medicine Calf - Bill Hotchkiss 3037
The Memoirs of Lord Byron - Robert Nye 4655
Michael Beam - Richard Hallet 2663
The Missolonghi Manuscript - Frederic
    Prokosch 5194
The Morning River - W. Michael Gear 2333
My Sister, My Love - Lucille Iremonger 3111
Nephew to the Emperor: A Novel Based on the Life of
    Beethoven - Jacques Brenner 658
The Olympians - Guy Bolton 566
Out of the House of Life - Chelsea Quinn
    Yarbro 6903
Perilous Journey: A Tale of the Mississippi River and
    the Natchez Trace - Clifford Sublette 6109
The Pilgrim Soul - Anne Miller Downes 1711
The Quincunx - Charles Palliser 4778
Rainbow Road - Davenport Steward 6016
Ramillies - Barbara Whitehead 6708
The Rape of the Fair Country - Alexander
    Cordell 1325
Ratoon - Christopher Nicole 4619
The Raven's Bride - Elizabeth Crook 1431
The Real David Copperfield - Robert Graves 2551
The Red Lances - Arturo Uslar Pietri 4999
The Remarkable Young Man - Cecil Roberts 5373
Retreat From the Dolphin - Darwin Le Ora
    Teilhet 6198
Rivers West - Louis L'Amour 3626
Rogues' Company: A Novel of John Murrell - Harry
    Harrison Kroll 3559
Sam Patch: Ballad of a Jumping Man - William
    Getz 2390
Sapphire - Helen Ashfield 214
Savannah - Eugenia Price 5186
Savannah Purchase - Jane Aiken Hodge 2970
Sharpe's Devil - Bernard Cornwell 1340
The Shining Trail - Iola Fuller 2254
Sons of Texas - Tom Early 1822
Strange Adventure of Jonathan Drew - Christopher
    Ward 6562
The Stress of Her Regard - Tim Powers 5157
The Thistlewood Plot - J.G. Jeffreys 3181
The Thousand Fires - Anne Powers 5155
Thunder Before Seven - Anna Brand 648
Tomahawk Revenge - David Thompson 6260
The Unsuitable Miss Pelham - June
    Drummond 1730
The Vision of Stephen: An Elegy - Lolah
    Burford 775
Voyage to Santa Fe - Janice Holt Giles 2418
Warwyck's Woman - Rosalind Laker 3604
Where Shadows Go - Eugenia Price 5189
Whom the Gods Love - Kate Ross 5502
Wild Dog Running - Alan Scholefield 5658
Wilderness - Roger Zelazny 6957
The Wings of the Morning - Thomas Tryon 6356
A World Too Wide - Susan Moore 4445
Yankee Rover - Christopher Ward 6563
The Year of December - Lucy Cores 1329

1830s

Across the Shining Mountains - Christian
    McCord 4226
All the Brave Rifles - Clarke Venable 6450
Amistad: The Thunder of Freedom - David
    Pesci 4944
Ammahabas - Bill Hotchkiss 3036
And Never Yield - Elinor Pryor 5204
Apache Blood - David Thompson 6250
Avery's Knot - Mary Cable 843

Banner by the Wayside - Samuel Hopkins Adams 28
Benjy Boone - Maurice Dolbier 1687
Beyond All Frontiers - Emma Drummond 1722
The Big Sky - A.B. Guthrie Jr. 2624
The Big Wind - Beatrice Coogan 1262
Black Plume: The Supressed Memoirs of Edgar Allan
    Poe - David Madsen 4027
Blackfoot Massacre - David Thompson 6251
Blood on the Divide - William W. Johnstone 3265
Blood Truce - David Thompson 6253
Borderlords - Terry C. Johnston 3244
Boy with a Pack - Stephen Warren Meader 4319
Bridle the Wind - Julia Davis 1525
Bright Feather - Robert Wilder 6750
The Buckstones - Paul I. Wellman 6615
The Bugles Are Silent: A Novel of the Texas
    Revolution - John R. Knaggs 3513
Call of the Mountains - Cornelia Meigs 4326
Captain Sutter's Gold - Jonreed Lauritzen 3673
The Captive of Kensington Palace - Jean
    Plaidy 5007
Carry the Wind - Terry C. Johnston 3246
Castle of Doves - Constance Heaven 2803
Chad Hanna - Walter D. Edmonds 1873
Charity Strong - Marguerite Allis 109
The Color of Blood - E. Ralph Rundell 5524
Comes an Echo on the Breeze - Edward J.
    Ryan 5542
The Confessions of Nat Turner - William
    Styron 6106
Coniston - Winston Churchill 1078
Coronation Summer - Angela Thirkell 6220
Crum Elbow Folks - Percy Raymond Barnes 332
The Czar's Madman - Jaan Kross 3560
The Dahomean - Frank Yerby 6911
Disraeli in Love - Maurice Edelman 1851
Dizzy's Woman - George MacBeth 3957
The Eagle and the Raven - James A. Michener 4369
Eagles of Destiny - Jory Sherman 5817
Early Candlelight - Maude Hart Lovelace 3904
East by Day - Blair Niles 4626
Echo of Lions - Barbara Chase-Riboud 1004
Emerald - Helen Ashfield 206
Emmeline - Judith Rossner 5507
Empire of Bones: A Novel of Sam Houston and the
    Texas Revolution - Jeff Long 3868
Eyes of Eagles - William W. Johnstone 3266
The Fiercest Heart - Stuart Cloete 1122
Fire in the Heart - Henrietta Buckmaster 761
Flashman - George MacDonald Fraser 2204
The Floral Companion - Anthea Bell 419
For Us the Living - Bruce Lancaster 3639
The Fortress - Hugh Walpole 6544
Forty Guns West - William W. Johnstone 3267
The Fourth King - Glen Petrie 4979
Gabriel's Search - Della Lutes 3927
Garnet - Helen Ashfield 207
The General in His Labyrinth - Gabriel Garcia
    Marquez 2282
Give Us This Valley - Tom Ham 2666
Gone to Texas - Jason Manning 4074
Gower Street - Claire Rayner 5264
The Great Adventure - Janice Holt Giles 2410
The Great Tide - Rubylea Hall 2662
Harpoon in Eden - F. van Wyck Mason 4152
Hawken Fury - David Thompson 6254
The Haymarket - Claire Rayner 5265
Hellfire Jackson - Garland Roark 5355
Hong Kong - Mona Gardner 2288
Hope of Earth - Jane Gilmore Rushing 5528
The Horseman on the Roof - Jean Giono 2424
Hue and Cry - Elizabeth Yates 6907
The Impudent Rifle - Richard Pearce 4872
Independence! - Dana Fuller Ross 5476
An Insular Position - Timothy Mo 4421
The Island Harp - Jeanne Williams 6779
Jemmy Button - Benjamin Subercaseaux 6107
Johnny Christmas - Forrester Blake 533

Journey to the Sky: A Novel about the True Adventures
    of Two Men in Search of the Lost Maya Kingdom -
    Jamake Highwater 2918
Kings of the Missouri - Hugh Pendexter 4895
Lord of Ravensley - Constance Heaven 2809
A Man for the Ages - Irving A. Bacheller 261
Mandarin Gold - James Leasor 3700
Manuela, La Caballeresa Del Sol - Demetrio Aguilera
    Malta 41
The Medicine Calf - Bill Hotchkiss 3037
The Men of Gonzales - John H. Culp 1442
The Men That God Forgot - Richard Butler 829
Michael Beam - Richard Hallet 2663
Middlemarch - George Eliot 1909
Midsummer's Eve - Philippa Carr 924
Mississippi Belle - Clements Ripley 5346
Mountain Devil - David Thompson 6257
Mountain Windsong - Robert J. Conley 1246
Nebraska! - Dana Fuller Ross 5480
Northwest Passage - David Thompson 6258
Oregon! - Dana Fuller Ross 5484
Pearl - Helen Ashfield 211
The Peculiar People - Jan de Hartog 2764
The Phantom Emperor - Neil Harmon
    Swanson 6140
Plume Rouge: A Novel of the Pathfinders - John Upton
    Terrell 6203
Princess Pamela - Ray Russell 5534
Promised Lands - Elizabeth Crook 1430
The Proud and the Free - Janet Dailey 1456
Pushing the Bear: A Novel of the Trail of Tears -
    Diane Glancy 2426
The Queen and Lord M - Jean Plaidy 5046
The Railway King - Margaret Mayhew 4207
Ranchero - Stewart Edward White 6703
The Rape of the Fair Country - Alexander
    Cordell 1325
The Real David Copperfield - Robert Graves 2551
The Rebels - Alfred Neumann 4585
The Red Cock Crows - Frances Gaither 2272
The Reluctant Bridegroom - Gilbert Morris 4467
Republic: A Novel of Texas - E.V. Thompson 6266
The Restless Border - Richard Pearce 4873
The Rising Storm - Marguerite Allis 113
River in the Wind - Edith Pope 5111
River of Sky - Karen Harper 2713
The Road to Baltimore - Robert S. Harper 2716
The Road to San Jacinto - James F. Davis 1524
The Road to San Jacinto - Leonard L.
    Foreman 2167
Rockspring - R.G. Vliet 6506
Rogues' Company: A Novel of John Murrell - Harry
    Harrison Kroll 3559
The Romance of Charles Dickens - Ursula
    Bloom 553
Runaway - Heather Graham 2519
Savanna - Janice Holt Giles 2416
Say These Names (Remember Them) - Betty Sue
    Cummings 1448
Seminole - Theodore Pratt 5164
Shadows in the Dusk - John Edward Jennings 3208
The Shining Trail - Iola Fuller 2254
Signals of Distress - Jim Crace 1408
The Snake River - Winfred Blevins 547
Soldier in Buckskin - Ray Hogan 2981
Some Lose Their Way - Eloise S. Liddon 3770
The Soul of Ann Rutledge - Bernie Babcock 252
The Southern Cross - Peter French 2226
Sow the Seeds of Hemp - Gary Jennings 3195
Spring Symphony - Eleanor Painter 4777
Star in the Rigging: A Novel of the Texas Navy -
    Garland Roark 5358
Star of the Wilderness - Karle Wilson Baker 274
Steamboat on the River - Darwin Le Ora
    Teilhet 6200
The Still Storm - Francoise Sagan 5562
Sunrise to Sunset - Samuel Hopkins Adams 32
Swift Rivers - Cornelia Meigs 4328
Tenderfoot - David Thompson 6259

There Was a Season: A Biographical Novel of Jefferson Davis - Theodore Olsen 4730
They Seek a Country - Francis Brett Young 6941
The Thing about Clarissa - Roberta St. Clair Cook 1264
This Land I Hold - Virginia Myers 4550
The Thomas Street Horror - Raymond Paul 4843
Thunder Before Seven - Anna Brand 648
Tidewater - Clifford Dowdey 1709
Tilly - Catherine Cookson 1288
To Heaven on Horseback - Paul F. Cranston 1419
To See Your Face Again - Eugenia Price 5188
The Tragedy at Tinkerton: An Historical Novel of Murder - Raymond Paul 4844
Trail of Tears - Williams Forrest 2187
Trail of Tears - Frances Patton Statham 5983
Trapper's Blood - David Thompson 6261
The Turning Wheels - Stuart Cloete 1127
Viola Gwyn - George Barr McCutcheon 4258
The Wedding Journey - Walter D. Edmonds 1878
West of the River - Charlton Laird 3591
Where Shadows Go - Eugenia Price 5189
While Rivers Flow - Glen H. Fleischmann 2125
Wild Conquest - Peter Abrahams 12
The Wild Yazoo - John Myers 4546
The Wildcliffe Bird - Constance Heaven 2811
Wind over Wisconsin - August Derleth 1620
The Wine of San Lorenzo - Herbert Gorman 2493
Winterkill - David Thompson 6262
Wolf Song - Harvey Fergusson 2069
The World From Rough Stones - Malcolm Macdonald 3979
Wyoming! - Dana Fuller Ross 5494
Young Ames - Walter D. Edmonds 1879

1840s
Adios! - Lanier Bartlett 366
The American River - Gary McCarthy 4222
And Never Yield - Elinor Pryor 5204
And the Wild Birds Sing - Lola Irish 3112
The Argonauts - Yvonne Schoell 5645
Bayonets in the Sun - William Moore 4446
The Bear Flag: A Novel of the Birth of California - Cecelia Holland 2983
The Beckoning Road - Caroline Snedeker 5934
Before Darkness Falls - Eugenia Price 5178
Beyond All Frontiers - Emma Drummond 1722
The Big Freeze - Bellamy Partridge 4823
The Big Sky - A.B. Guthrie Jr. 2624
The Big Wind - Beatrice Coogan 1262
Birthright - Phillip Finch 2087
Black Plume: The Supressed Memoirs of Edgar Allan Poe - David Madsen 4027
Brazos Dreamer - Gene Shelton 5799
Bridle the Wind - Julia Davis 1525
Bright Feather - Robert Wilder 6750
The Brightwood Expedition - Kay L. McDonald 4261
The Buried Self: A Background to the Poems of Matthew Arnold - Isobel MacDonald 3961
The Cabin at the Trail's End - Sheba Hargreaves 2706
Calico Palace - Gwen Bristow 694
California! - Dana Fuller Ross 5467
Captain Sutter's Gold - Jonreed Lauritzen 3673
Captain Vinegar's Commission - Philip Glazebrook 2428
Carmen of the Rancho - Frank H. Spearman 5955
Castle Dor - Sir Arthur Thomas Quiller-Couch 5226
Castle of Eagles - Constance Heaven 2804
Chant of the Hawk - John Harris 2720
The Chisholms - Evan Hunter 3082
The Comancheros - Paul I. Wellman 6616
Consort for Victoria - William Vaughan Wilkins 6757
Covenant with the Vampire: The Diaries of the Family Dracul - Jeanne Kalogridis 3327
Covered Wagon - Emerson Hough 3041
The Crystal Star - Ellen Argo 184

The Dahomean - Frank Yerby 6911
Dan'l Boone Kissed Me - Felix Holt 3006
Dark Inheritance - Carola Salisbury 5568
The Darkening Leaf - Caroline Stickland 6036
Dead Man's Walk - Larry McMurtry 4297
Desert Hawks - Frank Burleson 786
Diana Stair - Floyd Dell 1594
Dizzy's Woman - George MacBeth 3957
Doniphan's Ride - Les Savage Jr. 5620
Dragonwyck - Anya Seton 5750
The Dream Ends in Fury - Samuel Anthony Peeples 4889
Drumm's War - Bill Bragg 638
Each Bright River - Mildred Masterson McNeilly 4308
Eagle in the Sun - Hoffman Birney 508
Eagle on the Sun - Julia Davis 1527
Eagles Fly West - Edward Maddin Ainsworth 55
The Earthbreakers - Ernest Haycox 2789
Echo of Lions - Barbara Chase-Riboud 1004
The Emigrants - Vilhelm Moberg 4422
The Everlasting Fire - Jonreed Lauritzen 3675
Eyes of Eagles - William W. Johnstone 3266
Famine - Liam O'Flaherty 4693
The Famished Land - Elizabeth Byrd 833
The Far Country - Marthedith Furnas 2258
The Feast of All Saints - Anne Rice 5314
The Fever Called Living - Barbara Moore 4439
Fire in the Heart - Henrietta Buckmaster 761
Fire in the Sky - J.A. Shears 5785
Flash for Freedom - George MacDonald Fraser 2203
Flashman - George MacDonald Fraser 2204
Flashman and the Mountain of Light - George MacDonald Fraser 2207
Flashman and the Redskins - George MacDonald Fraser 2208
Flashman's Lady - George MacDonald Fraser 2210
Folded Hills - Stewart Edward White 6701
Free Flows the River - Earl Murray 4529
Free Soil - Marguerite Allis 110
The Further Adventures of Huckleberry Finn - Greg Matthews 4189
The Glorious Three - June Wetherell 6651
The God-Seeker - Sinclair Lewis 3763
The Golden Eagle - Noel B. Gerson 2370
Golden Shore - George Shaftel 5769
The Great Tide - Rubylea Hall 2662
Greygallows - Barbara Michaels 4359
Grim Journey - Hoffman Birney 509
Gringo Gold - Dane Coolidge 1293
H.—: The Story of Heathcliff's Journey Back to Wuthering Heights - Lin Haire-Sargeant 2641
Hacey Miller - James Sherburne 5805
Harvest of the Sun - E.V. Thompson 6265
Heroine of the Prairies: A Romance of the Oregon Trail - Sheba Hargreaves 2707
Hill of the Hawk - Scott O'Dell 4689
The Hills Stand Watch - August Derleth 1615
Hoffman's Row - Walter Carnahan 902
Hong Kong - Mona Gardner 2288
In the Fire of Spring - Thomas Tryon 6355
In the Season of the Sun - Kerry Newcomb 4590
In the Shadow of the Brontes - Louise Brindley 690
An Insular Position - Timothy Mo 4421
The Iron Roads - Forbes Bramble 644
Java Head - Joseph Hergesheimer 2854
John Barry - Donald F. Bedford 412
Johnny Christmas - Forrester Blake 533
Jornada - Robert L. Duffus 1754
Journey by the River - John Prescott 5173
Journey to the Sky: A Novel about the True Adventures of Two Men in Search of the Lost Maya Kingdom - Jamake Highwater 2918
Jubilee Trail - Gwen Bristow 698
Judith Lankester - Marjorie Allee 93
Last Love of Camille - Frances Winwar 6832
The Last Mystery of Edgar Allan Poe - Manny Meyers 4356
El Lazo - L. Jay Martin 4132

Leaves From the Valley - Joanna Trollope 6348
Light in the Clearing - Irving A. Bacheller 260
The Lighthouse at the End of the World - Stephen Marlowe 4095
Lights Along the Shore - Diane Austell 241
Listen for the Voices - Anne Colver 1220
The Live Goat - Cecil Dawkins 1542
Lord of the River - Bernard Clavel 1099
The Magnolias - Julie Ellis 1922
A Man for the Ages - Irving A. Bacheller 261
Masque of Enchantment - Charlene Cross 1432
Masts to Spear the Stars - Stephen Longstreet 3889
Men of No Property - Dorothy Davis 1517
Midnight Is a Place - Joan Aiken 52
The Mills of Colne - Robert Neill 4572
Monday's Warriors - Maurice Shadbolt 5767
The Mothers - Vardis Fisher 2109
Mountains Ahead - Martha Ferguson McKeown 4284
Nickajack - Robert J. Conley 1248
Night Wind - Roberta Jean Mountjoy 4504
The No-Return Trail - Sonia Levitin 3741
No Road Too Long - Hildegarde Hawthorne 2785
North-West by South - Nancy Cato 962
The Ocean Mistress - Peter French 2225
Oh, Valley Green - John H. Culp 1443
Olivia and Jai - Rebecca Ryman 5544
The Overland Trail - Wendi Lee 3712
Paddington Green - Claire Rayner 5266
Path to the Silent Country - Lynne Reid Banks 291
Pathway to the Stars - Harnett T. Kane 3356
Pearl - Helen Ashfield 211
Peter Ibbetson - George Du Maurier 1750
The Pilgrimage - Ann B. Ross 5463
Pinto and Sons - Leslie Epstein 1947
The Pioneers - Courtney Ryley Cooper 1296
The Proud Way - Shirley Seifert 5731
The Queen and Lord M - Jean Plaidy 5046
The Railway King - Margaret Mayhew 4207
The Rich Are with You Always - Malcolm Macdonald 3971
Ride the Blue Riband - Rosalind Laker 3598
Ride the River - Louis L'Amour 3625
The Rifles - William T. Vollmann 6510
River in the Wind - Edith Pope 5111
The Roads to Guadalupe - Robert Lewis Taylor 6190
Rogers' Folly - Albert E. Idell 3102
Royal Flash - George MacDonald Fraser 2213
Royal Street - Walter Adolphe Roberts 5393
Rush to Destroy - L. Jay Martin 4133
The Russian River - Gary McCarthy 4224
Salt Lake City - A.R. Reife 5292
Sassafras - Jack Matthews 4193
The Second Kiss - Gayle Rogers 5432
Seneca Falls Inheritance - Miriam Grace Monfredo 4429
A Singular Conspiracy - Barry Perowne 4915
The Sleep of Life - Richard Gordon 2486
Soldier in Buckskin - Ray Hogan 2981
Spirit Lake - MacKinlay Kantor 3363
Stranger at the Wedding - Frances Lynch 3934
The Straw Man - Jean Giono 2425
The Stuart Women - Matt Braun 652
Surprise - Brian Burland 785
Swandowne - Daniel Farson 2024
Sweet Mountain Magic - Rosanne Bittner 516
Tai-Pan - James Clavell 1102
Talleyman - John James 3161
Tamarack Tree - Howard Breslin 670
Tamsen - David Galloway 2273
Texas! - Dana Fuller Ross 5490
This Land Is Mine - Frances Casey Kerns 3470
Tide of Empire - Peter S. Kyne 3572
Tilly Wed - Catherine Cookson 1290
Time and Chance - Gwen Davenport 1501
To Heaven on Horseback - Paul F. Cranston 1419
Too Late! Too Late! The Maiden Cried - Joan Fleming 2128

Trade Imperial - Alan Lloyd　3814
Trask - Don Berry　483
The Treasure of Pleasant Valley - Frank Yerby　6928
The Turquoise Trail - Shirley Seifert　5736
The Two Farms - Mary E. Pearce　4865
The Ungodly: A Novel of the Donner Party - Richard Rhodes　5311
The Vision Is Fulfilled - Kay L. McDonald　4262
Vollands - Pamela Hill　2947
Voyage to the First of December - Henry Carlisle　897
Wagons West - Leslie Turner White　6692
Warriors of the Night - Kerry Newcomb　4594
Wheels West - Homer Croy　1438
Where the River Runs - Richard S. Wheeler　6664
Wild Orchid - Isabel Dick　1640
Wilderness Passage - Forrester Blake　534
The Wine of San Lorenzo - Herbert Gorman　2493
Winter Harvest - Norah Lofts　3863

1850s
Abigail - Joan Druett　1721
The Adventure of "Horse" Barnsby - Philip D. Stong　6065
After the Rainbow - Yvonne Kalman　3323
The American - Louis Dodge　1669
The American River - Gary McCarthy　4222
Artemia - Pamela Hill　2927
Artillery of Time - Chard Powers Smith　5919
Badge of Glory - Douglas E. Reeman　5287
The Barbarian - Willard Price　5191
Beauty Beast - MacKinlay Kantor　3361
Bedford Row - Claire Rayner　5259
Beulah Land - Harold Lenoir Davis　1520
Bighorn Legacy - W. Michael Gear　2332
Blackwater Spirits - Miriam Grace Monfredo　4427
The Blue and the Gray - John Leekley　3713
The Bluestocking - David Delman　1598
Bound for the Promised Land - Richard Marius　4083
Brave Captains - Vivian Stuart　6086
Brazos Dreamer - Gene Shelton　5799
The Brightwood Expedition - Kay L. McDonald　4261
The Brothers of Uterica - Benjamin Capps　887
The Buckskin Girl: A Novel of the California Trail in the Mid-Nineteenth Century - Gwen Moffat　4426
The Buried Self: A Background to the Poems of Matthew Arnold - Isobel MacDonald　3961
Burton and Speke - William Harrison　2751
Calico Palace - Gwen Bristow　694
California! - Dana Fuller Ross　5467
Captain Vinegar's Commission - Philip Glazebrook　2428
Castle of Foxes - Alanna Knight　3516
Cedarhaven - Patricia Campbell　874
Chase the Wind - E.V. Thompson　6264
The Chateau - Stephen Coulter　1383
City of Illusion - Vardis Fisher　2107
Clara Reeve - Leonie Hargrave　2705
Claudine's Daughter - Rosalind Laker　3594
The Closest Possible Union - Joanna Scott　5680
A Clouded Star - Anne Parrish　4819
Cock of the Walk - Roy Lewis　3762
Colorado! - Dana Fuller Ross　5471
Cordelia Chantrell - Meade Minnigerode　4413
The Corinthians - Nicholas E. Wyckoff　6888
Cracksman on Velvet - Francis Selwyn　5743
The Crisis - Winston Churchill　1079
The Crystal Star - Ellen Argo　184
Dando on Delhi Ridge - William Clive　1119
A Dangerous Mourning - Anne Perry　4926
A Darkness at Ingraham's Crest: A Tale of the Slaveholding South - Frank Yerby　6912
Dean's Watch - Elizabeth Goudge　2494
Deep River - Henrietta Buckmaster　760
Defend and Betray - Anne Perry　4928
Departure - Janet Stevenson　6004
Destiny in Dallas - Shirley Seifert　5725

The Detective and Mr. Dickens - William J. Palmer　4782
The Devil's Wind: Nana Saheb's Story - Manohar Malgonkar　4039
Devilseed - Frank Yerby　6914
Dina's Book - Herbjorg Wassmo　6577
Dinner at Belmont - Alfred Leland Crabb　1398
The Distant Lands - Julian Green　2567
Double Moscadine - Frances Gaither　2271
A Dream of Kings - Davis Grubb　2604
The Drummer Was the First to Die - Liza Pennywitt Taylor　6186
Drury Randall - Mary Johnston　3232
Eagles Fly West - Edward Maddin Ainsworth　55
The Eden Passion - Marilyn Harris　2730
Elixir of Life - A.E. Cowdrey　1392
Except for Me and Thee - Jessamyn West　6628
Fabulous Valley - Cornelia Stratton Parker　4803
The Face of a Stranger - Anne Perry　4929
Fair Land, Fair Land - A.B. Guthrie Jr.　2625
The Fancher Train - Amelia Bean　395
Farewell, My General - Shirley Seifert　5726
The Father - Katharine Holland Brown　724
Fevre Dream - George R.R. Martin　4131
Fire Bell in the Night - Constance Robertson　5395
Flashman and the Angel of the Lord - George MacDonald Fraser　2205
Flashman at the Charge - George MacDonald Fraser　2209
Fleur - Cynthia Harrod-Eagles　2754
Floodtide - Frank Yerby　6916
Follow the Drum - James Leasor　3699
Forget the Glory - Emma Drummond　1725
The Fortress - Catherine Gavin　2320
Fortune, Smile Once More - Mary Floyd Williams　6788
Forty Pounds of Gold - Philip D. Stong　6066
Free Soil - Margaret Lynn　3943
The Gallant - William Stuart Long　3873
The Gallant Mrs. Stonewall - Harnett T. Kane　3353
Gallows Way - Daoma Winston　6825
Gentlemen—The Regiment! - Hugh Talbot　6154
The Girl - Catherine Cookson　1277
The Girl From Paris - Joan Aiken　47
God Is an Englishman - R.F. Delderfield　1587
Gods and Generals - Jeff Shaara　5765
God's Angry Man - Leonard Ehrlich　1898
The Gold Seekers - William Stuart Long　3874
Golden Destiny - June Wyndham Davies　1506
Grant of Kingdom - Harvey Fergusson　2067
Great Day in the Morning - Robert Hardy Andrews　149
The Great Hunger - Johan Bojer　562
The Great Train Robbery - Michael Crichton　1426
Greenyards - Joan Lingard　3796
Hacey Miller - James Sherburne　5805
Harpoon - C.W. Nicol　4612
Hazard of Huntress - Vivian Stuart　6087
Hazard's Command - Vivian Stuart　6088
Heartland - Robert Douglas Mead　4316
Heaven Trees - Stark Young　6943
The Highwayman and Mr. Dickens - William J. Palmer　4783
House Divided - Ben Ames Williams　6765
The House of Cards - Leon Garfield　2292
The Hoydens and Mr. Dickens - William J. Palmer　4784
I Am Lidian - Naomi Lane Babson　253
I Know My Love - Catherine Gaskin　2315
The Imagination of the Heart - Judith Glover　2437
Indigo - Nicholas Carnac　900
Iron Ships, Iron Men - Christopher Nicole　4616
John Barry - Donald F. Bedford　412
Julie - Jane Kesner Morris　4479
Ka'a'awa: A Novel about Hawaii in the 1850s - Oswald Andrew Bushnell　814
The Keeper of the House - Harry Harrison Kroll　3558
Kingdom Come - Virginia Sorensen　5950

The Lady and the Deep Blue Sea - Garland Roark　5356
Lady Hellfire - Suzanne Robinson　5414
The Land Is Bright - Archie Binns　501
A Land to Tame - Zola Helen Ross　5505
A Lantern in Her Hand - Bess Streeter Aldrich　69
The Law of Larion - Peter Freuchen　2227
Law of the Land - Marguerite Allis　111
Leaves From the Valley - Joanna Trollope　6348
The Legend of Ben Tree - Paul Hawkins　2784
Light in the Clearing - Irving A. Bacheller　260
The Light Infantry Ball - Hamilton Basso　375
The Lincoln Hunters - Wilson Tucker　6359
The Lion's Skin - Darwin Le Ora Teilhet　6197
Listen for the Voices - Anne Colver　1220
The Long Night - Andrew Lytle　3945
Look Away - Harold Coyle　1395
Madeleine - Pamela Elizabeth West　6633
The Magnificent Savages - Fred Mustard Stewart　6024
The Mallen Streak - Catherine Cookson　1282
The Mask - Stuart Cloete　1125
Massacre at Cawnpore - Vivian Stuart　6089
Mayfair - Nancy Fitzgerald　2115
McKay's Bees - Thomas McMahon　4289
Memories of the Ford Administration - John Updike　6391
Men of No Property - Dorothy Davis　1517
Mighty Mountain - Archie Binns　502
Mists of Heaven - Yvonne Kalman　3325
Moontrap - Don Berry　481
Mountain Laurel - Jude Deveraux　1632
Mountain Man - Vardis Fisher　2110
My Father's World - Michael Phillips　4989
The Nation Thief - Robert Houston　3057
New Orleans Legacy - Alexandra Ripley　5341
Nightrunners of Bengal - John Masters　4176
North Star Conspiracy - Miriam Grace Monfredo　4428
The Notorious Angel - Patricia Maxwell　4201
The Old Maid - Edith Wharton　6652
Old Misery - Hugh Pendexter　4896
One Small Candle - Mary Linehan MacKinnon　3998
One Wore Blue - Heather Graham　2517
Opal - Helen Ashfield　210
Oregon Bride - Rosanne Bittner　514
Orphan Train - James Magnuson　4029
Pacific Street - Cecelia Holland　2993
The Pagoda Tree - Berkely Mather　4181
Paiute - Sessions S. Wheeler　6666
Papa La-Bas - John Dickson Carr　914
The Paper Mistress - Dorothea Malm　4045
The Passionate Pilgrim - Charles Terrot　6204
Path to the Silent Country - Lynne Reid Banks　291
The Patriot - Antonio Fogazzaro　2146
Pendragon: Late of Prince Albert's Own - Robert Trevelyan　6337
Pendragon...The Montenegran Plot - Robert Trevelyan　6338
Peter Ashley - DuBose Heyward　2911
Pillar of Cloud - Jackson Burgess　782
Pioneer Breed - Glenn R. Vernam　6453
The Pool of St. Branok - Philippa Carr　926
Powderkeg - Richard Vetterli　6482
The Predators - F.A. Parker　4804
The Pride of the Trevallions - Carola Salisbury　5570
Queen Victoria's Bomb - Ronald Clark　1094
The Rag Nymph - Catherine Cookson　1287
Rainbow in the Royals - Garland Roark　5357
Rainbow on the Road - Esther Forbes　2159
Raising Holy Hell - Bruce Olds　4718
Rebels of the Heavenly Kingdom - Katherine Paterson　4828
Rhine Journey - Ann Schlee　5639
The Rich Are with You Always - Malcolm Macdonald　3971
Ride the River - Louis L'Amour　3625
The River Witch - Margerie McIntyre　4278
A Roaring in the Wind - Robert Lewis Taylor　6191

The Robber Baroness - William Kendall Clarke 1097
The Romance of Charles Dickens - Ursula Bloom 553
Rome Haul - Walter D. Edmonds 1877
The Rookery: A Novel of the Victorian Underworld - Hugh C. Rae 5239
The Royal Ann Tree - Patricia Campbell 875
The Running Thread - Drayton Mayrant 4215
Sapphira and the Slave Girl - Willa Cather 958
Savage Frontier - Frank Burleson 787
Savage Oaks - Julie Ellis 1924
Savages and Saints - Cora Older 4717
The Sea Runners - Ivan Doig 1685
Secret for a Nightingale - Victoria Holt 3020
The Senator's Lady - Shirley Seifert 5733
Sergeant Verity and the Imperial Diamond - Francis Selwyn 5745
The Settlers - Vilhelm Moberg 4424
Shadow of the Moon - M.M. Kaye 3377
The Siege of Krishnapur - J.G. Farrell 2016
The Sin of the Prophet - Truman Nelson 4582
The Sins of the Wolf - Anne Perry 4937
Sister Wives - Cleo Jones 3270
Sisters & Lovers - Nicola Thorne 6274
Six-Horse Hitch - Janice Holt Giles 2417
The Slave of Frankenstein - Robert J. Myers 4549
The Slave Stealer - Boyd Upchurch 6390
The Sleeping Tiger - Marjorie McEvoy 4269
The Slow Awakening - Catherine Marchant 4082
Soho Square - Claire Rayner 5268
Sojourn of a Stranger - Walter Sullivan 6115
Song of the Bayou - Elinor Lynley 3936
Song of Years - Bess Streeter Aldrich 72
Sons of Fortune - Malcolm Macdonald 3973
A Space of the Heart - Patricia Wright 6884
Spirit Lake - MacKinlay Kantor 3363
The Stallion Man - Judith Glover 2438
Star of Randevi - Marjorie McEvoy 4270
Stranger in Savannah - Eugenia Price 5187
The Strangers on the Island - Brand Whitlock 6714
Strathgallant - Laura Black 523
The Sun Shines West - Nathan Schachner 5632
The Surveyor - Truman Nelson 4583
Sweetwater Fever - Robert H. Adelman 36
Swords of Steel - Elsie Singmaster 5870
Tap Roots - James H. Street 6080
Tarnished Angel - Phyllis Leonard 3723
The Taste of Time - Ferol Egan 1892
This Dark Monarchy - Francis W. Leary 3698
Through a Gold Eagle - Miriam Grace Monfredo 4430
Thunder on the Plains - Rosanne Bittner 517
Tilly Alone - Catherine Cookson 1289
Timothy Larkin - Jane Hutchens 3089
To Build a Ship - Don Berry 482
The Town - Conrad Richter 5325
The Treasure of Pleasant Valley - Frank Yerby 6928
Trumpeter, Sound! - D.L. Murray 4528
The Two Medicine River - Richard S. Wheeler 6663
The Undiscovered Country - Jay Walz 6560
Until the Colors Fade - Tim Jeal 3173
Unto a Good Land - Vilhelm Moberg 4425
The Valiant Sailors - Vivian Stuart 6090
Victory at Sebastopol - Vivian Stuart 6091
Vigilante - Richard Summers 6116
War Eagles - Frank Burleson 788
The Way to Fort Pillow - James Sherburne 5807
The White Rajah - Nicholas Monsarrat 4433
Whole Hog - David Wagoner 6523
The Wide House - Taylor Caldwell 864
Willowwood - Elizabeth Savage 5619
Wind Like a Bugle - Leonard Nathan 3722
The Wings of Morning - Karen Harper 2714
The Winter Bride - Carola Salisbury 5572
The World in His Arms - Rex Beach 392
The Yankee Girl - Ellen Argo 186
Zemindar - Valerie Fitzgerald 2117
The Woman Question - Dorothea Malm 4046

1860s

The Able McLaughlins - Margaret Wilson 6812
Action at Aquila - Hervey Allen 97
The Adventurers - Ernest Haycox 2787
After the Glory - Helen Topping Miller 4383
Aide to Glory - Louis Devon 1635
Ain't Goin' to Glory - David Delman 1597
Albuquerque - Sara Orwig 4757
American Falls - John Calvin Batchelor 376
The Amulet - Hal Borland 582
And One Rode West - Heather Graham 2514
And One Wore Gray - Heather Graham 2515
And Wait for the Night - John William Corrington 1352
Andersonville - MacKinlay Kantor 3359
Angel with Spurs - Paul I. Wellman 6613
Another Spring - Loula Grace Erdman 1948
Arizona - Clarence Budington Kelland 3387
Armored Giants: A Novel of the Civil War - F. van Wyck Mason 4145
Arouse and Beware - MacKinlay Kantor 3360
Artillery of Time - Chard Powers Smith 5919
Ask My Brother - Constance Wagner 6518
An Autumn in Araby - Carola Salisbury 5565
The Band Plays Dixie - Morris Markey 4089
Banished Children of Eve - Peter Quinn 5227
Banner at Shenandoah - Bruce Catton 963
The Barefoot Brigade - Douglas C. Jones 3274
Bates House - Clarence Benadum 437
Battle Flag - Bernard Cornwell 1333
The Bayou Road - Mignon G. Eberhart 1832
Beckoning Ridge - Emerson Waldman 6527
The Belchamber Scandal - Frances Murray 4533
Belgrave Square - Rachel Summerson 6117
Beloved Enemy - Al Lacy 3579
Beyond Surrender - Marian Sims 5860
Beyond the Shadowlands - Georgina Fleming 2126
Big Ember - Edward Havill 2778
The Big Lonesome - Will Bryant 737
Blood Kin - Barbara Anne Pauley 4845
Blood Line - Alanna Knight 3515
Blood Red Roses - Elizabeth Boatwright Coker 1163
The Bloody Ground - Bernard Cornwell 1334
The Blue and the Gray - John Leekley 3713
Blue Hurricane - F. van Wyck Mason 4146
Border Line - Robert J. Conley 1238
Borrasca - Octavus Roy Cohen 1160
Bound Girl - Everett Webber 6591
The Branch-Bearers - Glen Petrie 4978
Bread and Circus - Morris Renek 5303
The Breast of the Dove - Herbert Gorman 2491
Bride of a Thousand Cedars - Bruce Lancaster 3637
The Bride of Texas - Josef Skvorecky 5880
The Bright Sword - Eleanor Perenyi 4911
A Bright Tragic Thing - L.D. Clark 1091
The Buffalo Soldiers - John Prebble 5165
Bugle in the Wilderness - John Burress 805
Bugles Blow No More - Clifford Dowdey 1704
Burton and Speke - William Harrison 2751
By Antietam Creek - Don Robertson 5398
By Dim and Flashing Lamps - Alan Le May 3689
By the Dim Lamps - Nathan Schachner 5630
By Valour and Arms - James H. Street 6076
The Cactus and the Crown - Catherine Gavin 2318
Caddie Woodlawn - Carol Brink 692
Cadmus Henry - Walter D. Edmonds 1872
Cain's Daughters - Doris Shannon 5776
Caleb Pettengill U.S.N. - George Fielding Eliot 1912
California Caballero - William Colt MacDonald 3981
Captain Little Ax - James H. Street 6077
Captain Rebel - Frank Yerby 6910
Cargo of Brides - Helen Rucker 5522
Carriage Trade - Robert Thomsen 6271
Carrington - Michael Whitney Straight 6074
Castle Malindine - Hilary Ford 2163
The Catherine - Robert S. MacDonald 3980
The Cavalryman - Harold Sinclair 5861
Cease Firing - Mary Johnston 3230

Chapultepec - Norman Zollinger 6965
Charlotte Morel - Maria Lodi 3829
Charlotte Morel: The Dream - Maria Lodi 3830
Chase Royal - Donald Seaman 5712
Cherokee Dawn - Genell Dellin 1596
The Chester A. Arthur Conspiracy - William Wiegand 6740
Christmas for Tad: A Story of Mary and Abraham Lincoln - Helen Topping Miller 4386
Christmas with Robert E. Lee - Helen Topping Miller 4387
A City Not Forsaken - Lynn Morris 4480
City of the Flags - Clark McMeekin 4290
A Clouded Star - Anne Parrish 4819
Colorado! - Dana Fuller Ross 5471
Comanche Moon - Catherine Anderson 137
Company of Cowards - Jack Schaefer 5634
Company Q - Richard O'Connor 4684
Confederates - Thomas Keneally 3412
The Conquest of Don Pedro - Harvey Fergusson 2066
Conspiracy of Knaves - Dee Brown 711
Copperhead - Bernard Cornwell 1335
Copperhead Moon - Herbert Stover 6067
The Copperheads - William James Blech 544
Cordelia - Winston Graham 2523
Cordelia Chantrell - Meade Minnigerode 4413
The Cortlandts of Washington Square - Janet Fairbank 2001
The Cosgrove Report - G.J.A. O'Toole 4765
The Cotton Road - Frank Feuille 2077
The Court Martial of Robert E. Lee - Douglas Savage 5617
A Court of Owls - Richard Adicks 37
Covent Garden - Claire Rayner 5262
The Crater - Richard Slotkin 5908
The Crisis - Winston Churchill 1079
The Crossed Sabres - Gilbert Morris 4458
The Crowded Hill - Le Roy MacLeod 4008
Cry of the Hawk - Terry C. Johnston 3248
The Crystal Dove - Mollie Hardwick 2692
The Cup, the Blade or the Gun - Mignon G. Eberhart 1833
The Cup Trembling - Karl Brown 723
Dakota! - Dana Fuller Ross 5472
Dances with Wolves - Michael Blake 537
The Dark Command - William R. Burnett 793
Dark Thicket - Elmer Kelton 3402
The Day They Kidnapped Queen Victoria - H.K. Fleming 2127
Death at Rainy Mountain - Mardi Oakley Medawar 4321
Death Wore a Diadem - Iona McGregor 4277
Defiant Hearts - Janelle Taylor 6185
The Devil Gun - William Syers 6148
Diamond Head - Houston Branch 647
The Diary of Emily Dickinson: A Novel - Jamie Fuller 2255
The Dice of God - Hoffman Birney 507
Dinner at Belmont - Alfred Leland Crabb 1398
The Dixie Widow - Gilbert Morris 4459
Dodging Red Cloud - Richard S. Wheeler 6657
Down From the Mountain - Louis Charbonneau 997
The Dram Tree - Hamilton Cochran 1140
A Dream of Kings - Davis Grubb 2604
Drury Randall - Mary Johnston 3232
Dual Destiny - Karen Lynn 3939
Echoes From the Past - Marjorie McEvoy 4268
The Eden Passion - Marilyn Harris 2730
Eight April Days - Scott Hart 2759
Elkhorn Tavern - Douglas C. Jones 3278
Ellen Bray - Jane Julian 3319
Embers of the Heart - Rosanne Bittner 512
The Empire Builders - William Stuart Long 3871
Except for Me and Thee - Jessamyn West 6628
Exit with Drums - Joseph A. Daley 1457
The Extraordinary Adventures of Secret Agent Shipov in Pursuit of Count Leo Tolstoy in the Year 1862 - Bulat Okudzhava 4712

The Fairbrothers - Clark McMeekin 4291
The Falling Hills - Perry Lentz 3720
Family Fortune - Mignon G. Eberhart 1834
The Far Side of Home - Maggie Davis 1536
Farewell, My General - Shirley Seifert 5726
Fata Morgana - William Kotzwinkle 3549
Father Abraham - Irving A. Bacheller 258
The Fathers - Allen Tate 6171
Faye's Folly - Elizabeth Corbett 1322
The Fifth Conspiracy - Ted Jones 3296
Fire on the Wind - David Garth 2304
First the Blade - May Miller 4400
Flashman and the Dragon - George MacDonald Fraser 2206
Flight to Canada - Ishmael Reed 5285
Flowers for Lilian - Anna Gilbert 2405
Fool's Coach - Richard S. Wheeler 6659
For Love and Honor - Antonia Van-Loon 6423
For Us the Living - Antonia Van-Loon 6424
The Foragers - Ben Haas 2630
Forever Free - Honore Morrow 4487
The Fortune Road - James McCague 4217
Fragments of the Ark - Louise Meriwether 4341
Freedom - William Safire 5561
Freedom Road - Howard Fast 2031
The Friendly Persuasion - Jessamyn West 6629
Full of Thy Riches - Elizabeth Ferrell 2070 ·
Gai-Jin: A Novel of Japan - James Clavell 1100
The Gallant Mrs. Stonewall - Harnett T. Kane 3353
Gentlemen From England - Maude Hart Lovelace 3905
Gentlemen, Hush! - Jere Hungerford Wheelwright 6668
Gettysburg - Stephen Longstreet 3887
Gettysburg: Crisis of Command - Harry Albright 65
The Ghost Raider - Ray Hogan 2978
The Giant Joshua - Maurine Whipple 6673
The Gilded Rooster - Richard Emery Roberts 5391
The Glass Dove - Sally Carrighar 943
Glendraco - Laura Black 521
Glory Enough for All: The Battle of the Crater - Duane Philip Schultz 5673
Go-Ahead Rider - Robert J. Conley 1243
God Is an Englishman - R.F. Delderfield 1587
Gods and Generals - Jeff Shaara 5765
Gold - Clarence Budington Kelland 3388
The Golden Circle - John Edward Ames 125
The Golden Circle - Constance Robertson 5396
The Golden Fool - David Divine 1649
Gone to Texas - Forrest Carter 945
Gone to Texas - John Williams Thomason 6247
Gone with the Wind - Margaret Mitchell 4415
The Goodnight Trail - Ralph Compton 1227
Grant's War - Ted Jones 3297
The Grasshopper King - Elizabeth Boatwright Coker 1165
Gray Canaan - David Garth 2305
The Gray Captain - Jere Hungerford Wheelwright 6669
Gray Victory - Robert Skimin 5877
The Great Betrayal - Dorothy Gardiner 2284
Great Day in the Morning - Robert Hardy Andrews 149
Green Rose of Furley - Helen C. Barney 334
Griffin's Way - Frank Yerby 6922
Guns of Chickamauga - Richard O'Connor 4685
The Guns of the South - Harry N. Turtledove 6367
The Hallelujah Train - Bill Gulick 2614
The Hammer of God - Alan Scholefield 5655
The Hand of a Woman - Diana Brown 719
Hard Road to Gettysburg - Ted Jones 3298
Harpoon - C.W. Nicol 4612
Harry Idaho - Hugh Pendexter 4894
The Haversham Legacy - Daoma Winston 6827
A Heart Divided - Al Lacy 3580
Heartland - Robert Douglas Mead 4316
Heaven and Hell - John Jakes 3147
The Heroine's Sister - Frances Murray 4536
High Hearts - Rita Mae Brown 728

Hiwassee: A Novel of the Civil War - Charles F. Price 5176
Ho, the Fair Wind - I.A.R. Wylie 6889
Home to Tennessee - Alfred Leland Crabb 1400
The Horse Soldiers - Harold Sinclair 5862
House Divided - Ben Ames Williams 6765
The House in Ruins - Robert S. Weekley 6595
A Hundred Hills - Howard Breslin 667
The Hungry Goblin: A Victorian Detective Novel - John Dickson Carr 911
I Am Lidian - Naomi Lane Babson 253
I Swear by Apollo - Agatha Young 6939
If I Never Get Back - Darryl Brock 700
An Important Family - Dorothy Eden 1855
In a Dark Garden - Frank G. Slaughter 5891
Intrigue in Baltimore - Janet Whitney 6715
Iron Land - Dorothy Ogley 4697
Iron Ships, Iron Men - Christopher Nicole 4616
Ironclads: Man-of-War - Larry D. Names 4554
Jenny and Barnum: A Novel of Love - Roderick Thorp 6276
Jim Mundy: A Novel of the American Civil War - Robert H. Fowler 2192
Johnny Shiloh - James A. Rhodes 5308
A Journey to Matecumbe - Robert Lewis Taylor 6188
Journey to Shiloh - Will Henry 2843
Joy From Ashes - Al Lacy 3581
Jubilee - John Brick 672
Jubilee Jim and the Wizard of Wall Street - Donald Porter 5112
The Judges of the Secret Court - David Stacton 5972
Kansas Blue - Dylan Harson 2758
The Kays - Margaret Deland 1583
The Keeper of the House - Harry Harrison Kroll 3558
Kentucky Pride - Gene Markey 4087
Killdeer Mountain - Dee Brown 713
The Killer Angels - Michael Shaara 5766
Kingdom Coming - Roark Bradford 622
The Ladies of St. Hedwig's - E.M. Almedingen 117
The Land Is Bright - James Arthur Kjelgaard 3508
A Lantern in Her Hand - Bess Streeter Aldrich 69
The Last Boat out of Cincinnati - Don Tracy 6309
The Last Confederate - Gilbert Morris 4466
The Last Full Measure - Honore Morrow 4488
The Last Plantation - Don Wright 6879
The Last Stand: A Novel about George Armstrong Custer and the Indians of the Plains - Edwin P. Hoyt 3061
The Lattimer Legend - Ann Hebson 2813
The Laughing Stranger - Vina Delmar 1601
The Lawless - John Jakes 3149
Libbie - Judy Alter 121
The Lieutenant's Lady - Bess Streeter Aldrich 70
The Light Infantry Ball - Hamilton Basso 375
Lights Along the Shore - Diane Austell 241
Lincoln: A Novel - Gore Vidal 6490
The Lincoln Diddle - Barbara Steward 6015
Lodging at the Saint Cloud - Alfred Leland Crabb 1403
Lone Star Lady - Jill Gregory 2579
Long Day at Shiloh - Don Bannister 294
The Long Night - Andrew Lytle 3945
Long Remember - MacKinlay Kantor 3362
The Long Roll - Mary Johnston 3236
Long Storm - Ernest Haycox 2790
Long Winter Gone - Terry C. Johnston 3252
Look Away - Harold Coyle 1395
Look Away! - George Nauman Shuster 5841
Look Away, Beulah Land - Lonnie Coleman 1204
Look Away, Look Away - Leslie Turner White 6685
Look Back to Glory - Herbert Ravenel Sass 5607
Lorena - Frank G. Slaughter 5892
The Lost Giants - Alan Scholefield 5657
Lost Wallowa - Bill Gulick 2616
Love and War - John Jakes 3150
Loving Heart - Elsie Singmaster 5869
Madeleine - Catherine Gavin 2323

The Magnificent Savages - Fred Mustard Stewart 6024
Major Stepton's War - Matthew Vaughan 6445
The Mallen Streak - Catherine Cookson 1282
Marching On - James Boyd 612
A Marriage of Convenience - Tim Jeal 3172
Maximilian's Gold - Jane Barry 359
McKensie's Hundred: A Tale of the Old Dominion - Frank Yerby 6924
Me and Gallagher - Jack Farris 2023
The Medicine Whip - Max Hennessy 2835
Melissa Starke - Annulet Andrews 145
Mignon - James M. Cain 845
Mirage - Helen Topping Miller 4390
The Misadventures of Bethany Price - Marian Cockrell 1147
Mockingbird Sang at Chickamauga - Alfred Leland Crabb 1404
Montana! - Dana Fuller Ross 5479
Montana Woman - Rosanne Bittner 513
The Moon-Eyed Appaloosa - Bill Gulick 2617
Morning at Jalna - Mazo de la Roche 1560
Mosby's Last Ride - Ray Hogan 2979
Muddy Banks - Ruby C. Tolliver 6291
Murder, I Presume - Gillian Linscott 3807
My Lady Hoyden - Jane Sheridan 5812
Nebraska Coast - Clyde Brion Davis 1516
Nevada! - Dana Fuller Ross 5481
Night March - Bruce Lancaster 3641
Night Raider - Ray Hogan 2980
No Bugles Blow - Bruce Lancaster 3642
No Surrender - Emma Gelders Sterne 5999
No Tears for Christmas - Helen Topping Miller 4391
None Shall Look Back - Caroline Gordon 2478
North Against the Sioux - Kenneth Ulyatt 6376
North of 36 - Emerson Hough 3042
On a Lonesome Porch - Ovid Williams Pierce 4997
On Jordan's Stormy Banks - Adelaide C. Rowell 5518
On the Midnight Tide - Don Tracy 6310
One Wore Blue - Heather Graham 2517
Oscar and Lucinda - Peter Carey 894
Our Valiant Few - F. van Wyck Mason 4155
Paiute - Sessions S. Wheeler 6666
Passengers to Mexico: The Last Invasion of Mexico - Blair Niles 4627
The Passionate Rebel - Frank G. Slaughter 5894
Peter Ashley - DuBose Heyward 2911
Polsinney Harbour - Mary E. Pearce 4863
The Post of Honor - David Coxe Cooke 1266
Praise at Morning - Mildred Masterson McNeilly 4310
Preacher on Horseback - Cecile Hulse Matschat 4186
Prisoner of Twilight - Don Robertson 5400
A Promise Unbroken - Al Lacy 3582
Proud New Flags - F. van Wyck Mason 4156
The Proud Retreat - Clifford Dowdey 1706
Proving Ground: A Novel of Civil War Days in the North - Leone Lowden 3919
The Pumpkin Rollers - Elmer Kelton 3406
A Question of Honour - Clifford Dowdey 1707
The Quicksilver Pool - Phyllis A. Whitney 6716
The Quiet Shore - Walter Havighurst 2775
The Raiders - William Edward Wilson 6819
The Raiders: A Novel of the Civil War at Sea - Willard Wallace 6541
Ravenburn - Laura Black 522
Rebel - Bernard Cornwell 1336
Rebel in Blue - Herman Toepperwein 6289
Rebel Run - Louis Zara 6952
Rebellion Road - Helen Topping Miller 4392
Rebels of the Heavenly Kingdom - Katherine Paterson 4828
The Red Badge of Courage - Stephen Crane 1414
Red Cloud's Revenge - Terry C. Johnston 3255
Red Lanterns on St. Michael's - Thornwell Jacobs 3139

Red Runs the River - Lewis B. Patten   4831
The Revenge of Dracula - Peter Tremayne   6335
The Revolt of Sarah Perkins - Marian Cockrell   1148
The Richmond Raid - John Brick   674
Ride of the Panther - Kerry Newcomb   4591
The Rising of the Moon - Peter Berresford Ellis   1926
The River and the Wilderness - Don Robertson   5401
The Robber Baroness - William Kendall
   Clarke   1097
Rogue's Kingdom - John Brick   676
Roll, Shenandoah - Bruce Lancaster   3644
Run Me a River - Janice Holt Giles   2415
The Running Thread - Drayton Mayrant   4215
Sail the Dark Tide - Davenport Steward   6017
Salisbury Plain - Henry C. Branson   650
Samuel Drummond - Thomas Alexander Boyd   614
Scandal at High Chimneys: A Victorian Melodrama -
   John Dickson Carr   915
Scarlet Cockerel - Garald Lagard   3584
The Scarlet Guidon - Ray Grant Toepfer   6287
The Scarlet Patch - Bruce Lancaster   3645
Sea Change - Alison McLeay   4287
Sea to Shining Sea - Michael Phillips   4990
Season of the Jew - Maurice Shadbolt   5768
The Second Face of Valor - Ray Grant Toepfer   6288
Secret Service Operator 13 - Robert W.
   Chambers   982
Seek Out and Destroy - James David Horan   3031
The Senator's Lady - Shirley Seifert   5733
Sergeant Verity and the Blood Royal - Francis
   Selwyn   5744
Sergeant Verity Presents His Compliments - Francis
   Selwyn   5746
The Settlers - Vilhelm Moberg   4424
The Seventh Girl: A Romantic Tale of Civil War Texas
   - Tom Pendleton   4900
Seward's Folly - Edison Marshall   4111
Shadow of the Mountains - Lynn Morris   4481
Shadow on the Valley - Kirk Mitchell   4414
Shadowed Memories - Al Lacy   3583
Sherman's March - Cynthia Bass   373
Shiloh - Shelby Foote   2153
Shining Mountains - Steve Frazee   2214
Shod with Flame - Helen Topping Miller   4393
Sing One Song - Helen Topping Miller   4394
The Sinking of the Sarah Diamond - William Dale
   Jennings   3213
Sioux Dawn - Terry C. Johnston   3258
Sioux Splendor - Rosanne Bittner   515
Slaughter - Elmer Kelton   3407
The Smiling Rebel - Harnett T. Kane   3357
So Red the Rose - Stark Young   6944
So Shall They Reap - John Bennett   444
Sojourn of a Stranger - Walter Sullivan   6115
Song of Years - Bess Streeter Aldrich   72
Sons of Fire - Max McCoy   4227
Sons of Fortune - Malcolm Macdonald   3973
Soul of Abe Lincoln - Bernie Babcock   251
The Southern Blade - Nelson Wolford   6844
A Southern Woman - Elena Yates Eulo   1983
Spanish Gold - Kevin D. Randle   5252
Spoon - John Christgau   1074
The Spur - Ardyth Kennelly   3425
A Spy for Napoleon - Baroness Emma Orczy   4746
The Stalkers - Terry C. Johnston   3259
The Standing Hills - Caroline Stickland   6038
The Stars of the South - Julian Green   2568
*The Stonewall Brigade: A Novel of the American Civil
   War* - Frank G. Slaughter   5902
Storm Haven - Frank G. Slaughter   5903
Storm Signals - Joseph C. Lincoln   3785
Strange Company - Robert J. Conley   1251
Stranger in Savannah - Eugenia Price   5187
The Stubborn Heart - Frank G. Slaughter   5904
A Sudden, Fearful Death - Anne Perry   4938
The Sun Shines West - Nathan Schachner   5632
Supper at the Maxwell House - Alfred Leland
   Crabb   1407
Sweet Songbird - Teresa Crane   1418

Swords of Steel - Elsie Singmaster   5870
Talons of Eagles - William W. Johnstone   3268
Tap Roots - James H. Street   6080
Tell Me a Tale: A Novel of the Old South - James
   McEachin   4266
Tenants of the Earth - Sandra Paretti   4793
Tennessee Smith - James E. Hitt   2957
They Came to a Valley - Bill Gulick   2618
Thin Moon and Cold Mist - Kathleen O'Neal
   Gear   2330
This Dark Monarchy - Francis W. Leary   3698
Three Days - Stephen Longstreet   3891
The Three Days - Don Robertson   5402
Three Roads to Valhalla - Catherine Pomeroy
   Stewart   6022
Thunder on the Chesapeake - David Divine   1650
Thunder on the Plains - Rosanne Bittner   517
Time of Drums - John Ehle   1897
Timothy Larkin - Jane Hutchens   3089
The Titans - John Jakes   3154
To Appomattox: Nine April Days, 1865 - Burke
   Davis   1512
To the Swift - Anne Hawkins   2783
Trade Wind - M.M. Kaye   3378
Traveller - Richard Adams   27
Trouble Shooter - Ernest Haycox   2791
Troubled Spring - John Brick   678
Trumpets Sound No More - F. van Wyck
   Mason   4163
Twilight of the Dawn - Elizabeth Nell Dubus   1752
The Twisted Tendril - Alice Glasgow   2427
The Two Medicine River - Richard S. Wheeler   6663
Tyrone of Kentucky - Clark McMeekin   4294
The Unconquered - Ben Ames Williams   6768
The Uncrowned King - Baroness Emma Orczy   4747
The Union Belle - Gilbert Morris   4473
The Unterrified - Constance Robertson   5397
Until the End - Harold Coyle   1396
Unto This Hour - Tom Wicker   6733
Untold Glory - Cothburn O'Neal   4739
The Unvanquished - William Faulkner   2050
*Unvexed to the Sea: A Novel of the Vicksburg
   Campaign* - Gerry Morrison   4484
The Unwritten Chronicles of Robert E. Lee - Lamar
   Herrin   2864
The Valiant Virginians - James Warner Bellah   427
A Very Small Remnant - Michael Whitney
   Straight   6075
The Vixens - Frank Yerby   6929
Wagons to Tucson - Ed Newsom   4604
The Walk into Morning - Mildred Barger
   Herschler   2867
Walk Like a Man - Donald Honig   3024
The Warriors - John Jakes   3155
Washington! - Dana Fuller Ross   5491
The Way to Fort Pillow - James Sherburne   5807
The Web of Days - Edna Lee   3708
Weep No More - Janet Stevenson   6006
West of Appomattox - Harley Duncan   1785
Western Union - Zane Grey   2589
What Law There Was - Al Dempsey   1609
When the Emperor Dies - Mason McCann
   Smith   5926
When the Music Changed - Marie R. Reno   5305
When the War Is Over - Stephen Becker   408
Where My Love Sleeps - Clifford Dowdey   1710
Where the Willows Weep - Patricia Shaw   5781
While Angels Dance - Ralph W. Cotton   1372
While the Music Plays - Diane Austell   242
Whistling Cat - Robert W. Chambers   984
The White Rajah - Nicholas Monsarrat   4433
Wild Cat - Laura Black   524
Wild Is the River - Louis Bromfield   704
Wilderness: A Tale of the Civil War - Robert Penn
   Warren   6573
The Wilderness Brigade - Phyllis Gordon
   Demarest   1605
Willowwood - Mollie Hardwick   2699
The Wings of Morning - Karen Harper   2714

Wings of the Falcon - Barbara Michaels   4361
Winter of the Heart - Linda J. LaRosa   3665
Winter Rain - Terry C. Johnston   3262
With Malice Toward None - Honore Morrow   4492
The Woman Who Loved John Wilkes Booth - Pamela
   Redford Russell   5533
*Woman with a Sword: The Biographical Novel of
   Anna Ella Carroll of Maryland* - Hollister
   Noble   4632
The Wounded Yankee - Gilbert Morris   4475
Wychwood - Nicole St. John   5564
The Yankee Girl - Ellen Argo   186
Yankee Stranger - Elswyth Thane   6217
Years of Peace - Le Roy MacLeod   4009
Yedo - Lynn Guest   2609
You Rolling River - Archie Binns   503
Young Vargas Lewis - Robert Brainard Pearsall   4874

1870s

1876: A Novel - Gore Vidal   6484
The Abductors - Stuart Cloete   1121
*Aces and Eights: A Novel of the Legend of Wild Bill
   Hickok* - Loren D. Estleman   1967
Aide to Glory - Louis Devon   1635
Another Country - Karel Schoeman   5646
Anything for Billy - Larry McMurtry   4295
Arizona! - Dana Fuller Ross   5466
Beneath the Blue Mountain - Richard S.
   Wheeler   6656
Billy the Kid: The Legend of El Chivato - Elizabeth
   Fackler   1994
Bitter Creek - Al Cody   1150
Black Sun - Terry C. Johnston   3242
Blood Song - Terry C. Johnston   3243
Born of the Sun - John H. Culp   1440
Borrasca - Octavus Roy Cohen   1160
Bread and Circus - Morris Renek   5303
Breakfast at the Hermitage - Alfred Leland
   Crabb   1397
Breakheart Pass - Alistair MacLean   3999
Bridge to Brooklyn - Albert E. Idell   3099
The Bright Feathers - John H. Culp   1441
Bugles in the Afternoon - Ernest Haycox   2788
Bush War! - William Moore   4447
Call Home the Heart - Jessica Stirling   6040
The Camp Grant Massacre - Elliott Arnold   191
Candle of the Wicked - Manly Wade Wellman   6612
Captain McRae: A Novel of the Northwest Frontier -
   William Heuman   2872
Cast a Long Shadow - Mary E. Pearce   4861
Celebration! - Dana Fuller Ross   5470
Centennial Summer - Albert E. Idell   3100
Cesar and Augusta - Ronald Harwood   2771
The Changeling - Philippa Carr   918
Charing Cross - Claire Rayner   5260
Charlotte Morel: The Siege - Maria Lodi   3831
Chief of Scouts - Don Bendell   439
The Chieftain: A Story of the Nez Perce People -
   Robert Payne   4852
Clively Close: Dead as Dead Can Be - Ann
   Crowleigh   1434
A Cold Day in Hell - Terry C. Johnston   3247
Colorado Ambush - Jess McCriede   4230
The Court-Martial of George Armstrong Custer -
   Douglas C. Jones   3276
The Cowboys - William Dale Jennings   3211
Crazy Fox Remembers - Don Preston   5174
The Crossed Sabres - Gilbert Morris   4458
The Crown and the Crucible - Michael Phillips   4987
Custer Passed Our Way - Fred S. Kaufman   3370
The Daybreakers - Louis L'Amour   3619
Deadly Beloved - Alanna Knight   3517
Deadwood - Pete Dexter   1638
The Demon Lover - Victoria Holt   3013
Devil's Backbone - Terry C. Johnston   3250
The Dice of God - Hoffman Birney   507
Dr. Gully's Story - Elizabeth Jenkins   3190
Dream Catcher - Terry C. Johnston   3251

The Dreaming: A Novel of Australia - Barbara Wood 6848
Drums of Change: The Story of Running Fawn - Janette Oke 4707
Dubu: A Novel of New Guinean Conquest - Maslyn Williams 6789
Eden Rising - Marilyn Harris 2731
Elizabeth, By Name - Will Cook 1265
Ellen Bray - Jane Julian 3319
Enter Second Murderer - Alanna Knight 3518
Enter the Lion: A Posthumous Memoir of Mycroft Holmes - Michael P. Hodel 2961
Fair is the Rose - Meagan MacKinney 3997
Fair Wind to Java - Garland Roark 5354
The Fairbrothers - Clark McMeekin 4291
Falkenhorst - Mark Rascovich 5254
The Far Canyon - Elmer Kelton 3404
The Far Down - Elizabeth Corbett 1321
The Fast Men - Tom McNab 4302
First the Blade - May Miller 4400
Flashman and the Redskins - George MacDonald Fraser 2208
The Fleet Rabble: A Novel of the Nez Perce War - Frank Borden Hanes 2675
For Time and All Eternity - Paul Bailey 268
The Four Hundred - Stephen Sheppard 5804
Freedom Road - Howard Fast 2031
From Where the Sun Now Stands - Will Henry 2841
The Gambling Man - Catherine Cookson 1276
The Garfield Honor - Frank Yerby 6918
The Gathering Storm - W.E. Davis 1540
Gentlemen From England - Maude Hart Lovelace 3905
Giants in the Earth - O.E. Rolvaag 5434
Gold - Clarence Budington Kelland 3388
Gold Is Where You Find It - Clements Ripley 5345
Golden Horizons - William Corcoran 1324
The Golden Valley - Daoma Winston 6826
Gone with the Wind - Margaret Mitchell 4415
The Great Steamboat Race - John Brunner 736
The Greek Treasure - Irving Stone 6056
The Green Land - Zola Helen Ross 5504
Griffin's Way - Frank Yerby 6922
The Hand of a Woman - Diana Brown 719
Heaven and Hell - John Jakes 3147
A House Behind the Mint - Laurie Huffman 3072
A House Divided - Michael Phillips 4988
I Swear by Apollo - Agatha Young 6939
Illinois! - Dana Fuller Ross 5475
The Invention of Truth - Marta Morazzoni 4449
Isobelle - Mary Lide 3775
Judgment in July - Richard Fisher 2105
Kentucky! - Dana Fuller Ross 5477
Killing Cousins - Alanna Knight 3520
King's Royal - John Quigley 5224
The Lady and Doc Holliday - Preston Lewis 3761
The Last Days of Horse-Shy Halloran - Bill Pronzini 5203
The Last Frontier - Howard Fast 2036
The Last Stand: A Novel about George Armstrong Custer and the Indians of the Plains - Edwin P. Hoyt 3061
The Lawless - John Jakes 3149
Libbie - Judy Alter 121
The Limner - Paul Darcy Boles 564
Liveliest Town in the West - Bill Gulick 2615
Log Jam - Leslie Turner White 6684
Lone Star Lady - Jill Gregory 2579
Lonely on the Mountain - Louis L'Amour 3621
Look Away, Beulah Land - Lonnie Coleman 1204
Lords of the Plains - Max Crawford 1420
Lost Wallowa - Bill Gulick 2616
The Lotus and the Wind - John Masters 4175
Louisiana! - Dana Fuller Ross 5478
Madeleine - Catherine Gavin 2323
The Magnificent Failure - Giles A. Lutz 3928
The Mallen Girl - Catherine Cookson 1280
The Man From Broken Hills - Louis L'Amour 3622
Man on Two Ponies - Don Worcester 6872

Marching to Valhalla: A Novel of Custer's Last Days - Michael Blake 538
A Mighty Afternoon - Charles K. Mills 4407
Miss Martha Mary Crawford - Catherine Marchant 4081
Miss Morissa: Doctor of the Gold Trail - Mari Sandoz 5592
Molokai - Oswald Andrew Bushnell 815
Montana Road - Harry Sinclair Drago 1717
The Moon Stallion - Jim Berry 484
The Mudlark - Theodore Bonnet 573
Mustang Man - Louis L'Amour 3623
My Lady Hoyden - Jane Sheridan 5812
My Sister's Keeper - Beverly Butler 817
No Roof but Heaven - Jeanne Williams 6782
No Survivors - Will Henry 2846
North to Yesterday - Robert Flynn 2145
The Odyssey of Thaddeus Baxter - Robert P. Lund 3926
Oklahoma! - Dana Fuller Ross 5482
One More River to Cross - Will Henry 2847
One of the Raymonds - Jean Rikhoff 5332
The Passion of Letty Fox - Diana Saunders 5610
Peter Doyle - John Vernon 6457
Pistols for Hire - Nelson Coral Nye 4652
The Place of Devils - Lucinda Baker 275
The Powder River - Winfred Blevins 546
Preacher on Horseback - Cecile Hulse Matschat 4186
The Pride of Hannah Wade - Janet Dailey 1455
Quitting Time - Robert J. Conley 1249
Railroad West - Cornelia Meigs 4327
Ravenscroft - Dorothy Eden 1860
Reap the Whirlwind - Terry C. Johnston 3254
Red Fox of the Kinapoo - William Rush 5526
The Restless Land - John H. Culp 1444
Richard Lamb - Richard S. Wheeler 6662
Ride the Dark Trail - Louis L'Amour 3624
The Road - John Ehle 1896
A Road We Do Not Know: A Novel of Custer at the Little Bighorn - Frederick J. Chiaventone 1057
Rough Diamond - Robert L. Fish 2098
The Sackett Brand - Louis L'Amour 3627
Sand in the Wind - Kathleen O'Neal Gear 2329
Sandoval: A Romance of Bad Manners - Thomas Beer 414
Savage Thunder - Johanna Lindsey 3795
The Scandalous Mrs. Blackford - Harriet Kane 3358
Scarlet Women - J.D. Christilian 1077
Scarlett - Alexandra Ripley 5342
The Scout - Harry Combs 1224
Sea Change - Alison McLeay 4287
Sea Jade - Phyllis A. Whitney 6717
The Seafarers - William Stuart Long 3877
Seize the Sky - Terry C. Johnston 3256
The Seventh Winter - Hal Borland 583
A Shadow of Eagles - Jane Barry 360
The Shadow Riders - Terry C. Johnston 3257
The Shadowed Spring - Carola Salisbury 5571
Shaggy Legion - Hal George Evarts 1986
Shoot! - George Bowering 604
Silver Linings - Shirley Davies-Owens 1508
The Sky-Liners - Louis L'Amour 3629
The Snowblind Moon - John Byrne Cooke 1267
Song of the Meadowlark - John A. Sanford 5594
The Sons of Grady Rourke - Douglas Savage 5618
A Spy for Napoleon - Baroness Emma Orczy 4746
The Staked Plain - Frank Xavier Tolbert 6290
The Stars in Their Courses - Harry Brown 722
Stormswift - Madeleine Brent 662
Stuyvesant Square - Margaret Lewerth 3743
Sunflower - Jill Marie Landis 3653
Sweet Songbird - Teresa Crane 1418
The Sweetwater - Jean Rikhoff 5333
The Sword of General Englund - Donald Honig 3023
Talons of Eagles - William W. Johnstone 3268
Tassels on Her Boots - Arthur Cheney Train 6313
Tennessee! - Dana Fuller Ross 5489

Thief of My Heart - Rexanne Becnel 410
This Willing Passion - Patricia Cloud 1132
Three Rivers - Carla J. Mills 4406
Thunder in the Dawn - Earl Murray 4532
Tide-Rode - Adelyn Bushnell 813
Tie My Bones to Her Back - Robert F. Jones 3294
Time for Outrage - Amelia Bean 397
A Time in the Sun - Jane Barry 361
Timothy Baines - John H. Culp 1445
To Love a Stranger - Barbara Paul 4839
Treasure Mountain - Louis L'Amour 3631
The Trial of Mary Todd Lincoln - James A. Rhodes 5309
Trumpet on the Land - Terry C. Johnston 3260
The Tune That They Play - William Clive 1120
Twice upon a Time - Allen Appel 172
The Unconquered - Ben Ames Williams 6768
The Unforgiven - Alan Le May 3692
The Valiant - Sigman Byrd 839
The Valiant Gunman - Gilbert Morris 4474
Vardy - John Harris 2721
The Veil of Illusion - Rebecca Ryman 5545
The Velvet Horn - Andrew Lytle 3946
The Vesey Inheritance - Gwendoline Butler 822
The Vixens - Frank Yerby 6929
The Waterworks - E.L. Doctorow 1659
The Whales in Lake Tanganyika - Lennart Hagerfors 2636
While Angels Dance - Ralph W. Cotton 1372
A Whisper on the Wind - Madeline Baker 276
Winter of the Heart - Linda J. LaRosa 3665
Winter Rain - Terry C. Johnston 3262
The Winter War - William Wister Haines 2640
Wisconsin! - Dana Fuller Ross 5493
Wizards' Country - Daphne Rooke 5438
Wobble to Death - Peter Lovesey 3918
The Wolfling: A Documentary Novel of the 1870s - Sterling North 4648
Woman of Justice - Georgia Di Donato 1639
The Women of Eden - Marilyn Harris 2734
Yellowhorse - Dee Brown 715
Zeke and Ned - Larry McMurtry 4301

1880s
The Abductors - Stuart Cloete 1121
Abracadaver - Peter Lovesey 3906
The Actor - Robert J. Conley 1236
The Admiral's Lady - Mary Ann Gibbs 2395
Adobe Walls: A Novel of the Last Apache Rising - William R. Burnett 791
The Adventure of the Stalwart Companions - H. Paul Jeffers 3177
The Adventures of Jeremiah Dimon: The Novel of Old East Hampton - Everett Rattray 5255
Affairs of Love - Nicola Thorne 6272
American Eden - Marilyn Harris 2728
The Americans - John Jakes 3143
The Ancestors Cry Out - Eugenia Lovett West 6627
Anno-Dracula - Kim Newman 4595
Apache Devil - Edgar Rice Burroughs 806
Apaches - Oakley Hall 2650
The Archduke - Michael Arnold 194
The Assassination of Jesse James by the Coward Robert Ford - Ron Hansen 2680
The Authentic Death of Hendry Jones - Charles Neider 4562
The Bad Lands - Oakley Hall 2651
Belle Starr - Speer Morgan 4453
Bertie and the Tinman - Peter Lovesey 3909
Billy the Kid: The Legend of El Chivato - Elizabeth Fackler 1994
The Black Swan - Philippa Carr 917
Blessed McGill - Edwin Shrake 5834
Blood & Dreams - Leslie Waller 6543
Bloody Season - Loren D. Estleman 1968
Bluegate Fields - Anne Perry 4921
Brave General - Herbert Gorman 2490
Bridge to Brooklyn - Albert E. Idell 3099
Broncho Apache - Paul I. Wellman 6614

Buffalo Coat - Carol Brink   691
Buffalo Girls - Larry McMurtry   4296
The Cage - Michael Weston   6650
Callander Square - Anne Perry   4923
Captain Boycott, a Romantic Novel - Philip
   Rooney   5440
Cardington Crescent - Anne Perry   4924
A Case of Spirits - Peter Lovesey   3910
Castle Barebane - Joan Aiken   43
The Cater Street Hangman - Anne Perry   4925
Catherine Carter - Pamela Hansford Johnson   3227
Chase the Wind - Janelle Taylor   6184
Children of the Dust - Carlile Clancy   1084
Chiricahua - Will Henry   2839
A Circle of Trees - Dana Faralla   2012
City of Widows - Loren D. Estleman   1969
Colfax - Robert J. Conley   1239
Come Spring - Charlotte Hinger   2954
The Coming of Rain - Richard Marius   4084
The Cowboy and the Cossack - Claire Huffaker   3071
Creole Dusk - Walter Adolphe Roberts   5392
Dance Back the Buffalo - Milton Lott   3899
The Day the Cowboys Quit - Elmer Kelton   3403
Death in the Devil's Acre - Anne Perry   4927
The Demise of Billy the Kid - Preston Lewis   3760
Desperadoes - Ron Hansen   2681
The Detective Wore Silk Drawers - Peter
   Lovesey   3911
The Devil's Card - Mary Maher   4030
Dr. Gully's Story - Elizabeth Jenkins   3190
Dr. Jekyll and Mr. Holmes - Loren D.
   Estleman   1970
The Dollar Gold Piece - Virginia Swain   6134
Domina - Barbara Wood   6847
Doubting Castle - Rebecca Kavaler   3373
The Dreaming: A Novel of Australia - Barbara
   Wood   6848
Drums of Change: The Story of Running Fawn -
   Janette Oke   4707
Drums of Khartoum - Chloe Gartner   2307
Duel in the Sun - Niven Busch   812
Dutch Uncle - Marilyn Durham   1815
The Edge of Time - Loula Grace Erdman   1949
Electricity: A Novel - Victoria Glendinning   2431
Faces in the Crowd - William Marshall   4117
Fair Wind to Java - Garland Roark   5354
The Feud - Amelia Bean   396
The Fine and Handsome Captain - Frances
   Lynch   3933
A Fistful of Stars - Sarah Lockwood   3828
For Time and All Eternity - Paul Bailey   268
Free Land - Rose Lane   3660
Freedom or Death - Nikos Kazantzakis   3383
From Time to Time - Jack Finney   2092
The Garfield Honor - Frank Yerby   6918
The Gaynor Women - Virginia Coffman   1153
Gentlemen in England - A.N. Wilson   6795
Geronimo: An American Legend - Robert J.
   Conley   1242
The Ghost and Mrs. Jeffries - Emily Brightwell   681
Good Morning, Irene - Carole Nelson Douglas   1698
The Great Blizzard - Albert E. Idell   3101
Great Dream From Heaven - John Rolfe
   Gardiner   2286
Hard on the Road - Barbara Moore   4440
Harry: A Novel of Australia - Robert Wales   6530
The High Rocks - Loren D. Estleman   1973
Highgate Rise - Anne Perry   4931
The Hill of Doves - Stuart Cloete   1123
Home Mountain - Jeanne Williams   6777
Honor Thy Father - Robert A. Roripaugh   5460
The Hospital - Agatha Young   6938
A House Behind the Mint - Laurie Huffman   3072
A House Divided - Michael Phillips   4988
Hunt for Heaven - Elsie Barber   298
The Inspector and Mrs. Jeffries - Emily
   Brightwell   682
Irene at Large - Carole Nelson Douglas   1700
Irene's Last Waltz - Carole Nelson Douglas   1701

Jack the Ripper - Richard Gordon   2484
Johnnie Cross - Terence de Vere White   6704
Judith Duchesne - Lynda Sargent   5605
The Justicer - Thomas Fall   2010
Katherine - Antonia Van-Loon   6425
Killing Time - Robert J. Conley   1244
Lady of No Man's Land - Jeanne Williams   6780
The Last Encounter - Robin Maugham   4196
The Last Hero - Peter Forbath   2154
The Last Hunt - Milton Lott   3900
The Last Ride - Tom Eidson   1899
Lily - Cindy Bonner   571
The List of Seven - Mark Frost   2237
Lonesome Dove - Larry McMurtry   4298
Longleaf - Rose Brock   701
Looking After Lily - Cindy Bonner   572
Lord of the Plains - Alfred Silver   5852
The Lorimer Line - Anne Melville   4332
The Love Child - Catherine Cookson   1279
Mad Hatter's Holiday - Peter Lovesey   3914
The Magnificent Failure - Giles A. Lutz   3928
The Man Who Loved Cat Dancing - Marilyn
   Durham   1817
Manifest Destiny - Brian Garfield   2290
The Mating Dance - Rona Randall   5250
Megan - Kathleen Magill   4028
The Michaelmas Girls - John Barry   362
Mrs. Jeffries and the Missing Alibi - Emily
   Brightwell   683
Mrs. Jeffries Dusts for Clues - Emily Brightwell   684
Mrs. Jeffries on the Ball - Emily Brightwell   685
Mrs. Jeffries on the Trail - Emily Brightwell   686
Mrs. Jeffries Plays the Cook - Emily Brightwell   687
Mrs. Jeffries Takes Stock - Emily Brightwell   689
Murdock's Law - Loren D. Estleman   1975
Ned Christie's War - Robert J. Conley   1247
Never Call It Loving - Dorothy Eden   1859
Oh! Where Are Bloody Mary's Earrings? - Robert
   Player   5079
Oklahoma Pride - Dana Fuller Ross   5483
On a Far Wide Shore - Malcolm Macdonald   3970
One More River to Cross - Will Henry   2847
Oregon Legacy - Dana Fuller Ross   5485
The Ox-Bow Incident - Walter Van Tilburg
   Clark   1096
Paragon Walk - Anne Perry   4932
Parnell and the Englishwoman - Hugh Leonard   3721
Path of the Sun - Al Dempsey   1608
Peter Doyle - John Vernon   6457
Red Mountain - David Lavender   3677
*Refinements of Love: A Novel about Clover and Henry
   Adams* - Sarah Booth Conroy   1259
Resurrection Row - Anne Perry   4934
Roses From the South - Perceval Reniers   5304
Rough Diamond - Robert L. Fish   2098
Rutland Place - Anne Perry   4935
Sage of Canudos - Lucien Marchal   4080
St. Agnes' Stand - Tom Eidson   1900
Saint Johnson - William R. Burnett   796
Sapphira and the Slave Girl - Willa Cather   958
Saratoga Trunk - Edna Ferber   2062
The Scandalous Mrs. Blackford - Harriet Kane   3358
The Scout - Harry Combs   1224
The Sea Scape - Mary Lide   3778
The Seafarers - William Stuart Long   3877
Seven Rivers West - Edward Hoagland   2959
Sherlock Holmes and the Case of Sabina Hall - L.B.
   Greenwood   2576
Sherlock Holmes and the Case of the Raleigh Legacy -
   L.B. Greenwood   2577
Sherlock Holmes Meets Annie Oakley - Stanley
   Shaw   5782
Sherlock in Love - Sena Jeter Naslund   4557
Silence in Hanover Close - Anne Perry   4936
Silver Linings - Shirley Davies-Owens   1508
The Silver Mountain - Dan Cushman   1453
Sing for a Penny - Clifford Dowdey   1708
Sioux City - John Hyatt Downing   1714
The Six Messiahs - Mark Frost   2238

Solitudes - R.G. Vliet   6507
Somewhere Within This House - Jean Francis
   Webb   6587
Song of Wovoka - Earl Murray   4531
Stamping Ground - Loren D. Estleman   1977
Still Is the Summer Night - August Derleth   1619
Storm Tide - Allan R. Bosworth   590
The Story of Pat Garrett and Billy the Kid - David
   Everitt   1987
Sweet Adelaide - Julian Symons   6152
Swing, Swing Together - Peter Lovesey   3915
Tascosa Gun: The Story of Jim East - Gene
   Shelton   5803
Tessa d'Arblay - Malcolm Macdonald   3974
These Thousand Hills - A.B. Guthrie Jr.   2627
The Tick of Death - Peter Lovesey   3916
Time and Again - Jack Finney   2093
Tombstone Showdown - Leslie Scott   5681
Too Long at the Dance - Mike Blakely   539
Tournament of the Shadows - Nicholas Carnac   901
Tracker - David Wagoner   6521
Traitors Gate - Anne Perry   4939
Travail and Triumph - Michael Phillips   4991
*The Trial of Elizabeth Cree: A Novel of the Limehouse
   Murders* - Peter Ackroyd   21
True Grit - Charles Portis   5139
The True Memoirs of Charley Blankenship - Benjamin
   Capps   890
An Untamed Land - Lauraine Snelling   5936
Warhorse - John Cunningham   1451
Warlock - Oakley Hall   2653
Waxwork - Peter Lovesey   3917
When Nietzsche Wept: A Novel of Obsession - Irvin D.
   Yalom   6892
The White Land - William Dieter   1643
The Whitechapel Horrors - Edward B. Hanna   2678
Wilde West - Walter Satterthwait   5609
Winter Grass - Richard S. Wheeler   6665
The Wizard's Daughter - Barbara Michaels   4362
A Woman Called Fancy - Frank Yerby   6931
A Woman Scorned - Malcolm Macdonald   3978
The Women of Whitechapel and Jack the Ripper - Paul
   West   6638
The Wonderful Country - Tom Lea   3695
Wyatt Earp - Matt Braun   653

1890s
Affairs of Love - Nicola Thorne   6272
The Alienist - Caleb Carr   907
All or Nothing - Stephen Longstreet   3881
America, America - Elia Kazan   3380
American Eden - Marilyn Harris   2728
The Americans - John Jakes   3143
*The Angel of the Opera: Sherlock Holmes Meets the
   Phantom of the Opera* - Sam Siciliano   5842
Arrest Sitting Bull - Douglas C. Jones   3273
Ashworth Hall - Anne Perry   4915
*The Assassination of Jesse James by the Coward
   Robert Ford* - Ron Hansen   2680
The Athelsons - Jocelyn Kettle   3476
Aunt Bel - Guy McCrone   4231
The Balloonist - Macdonald Harris   2724
The Barrier - Robin Maugham   4195
Belgrave Square - Anne Perry   4919
Bertie and the Crime of Passion - Peter
   Lovesey   3907
Bertie and the Seven Bodies - Peter Lovesey   3908
Bethlehem Road - Anne Perry   4920
Beware, Beware the Bight of Benin - Philip
   McCutchan   4241
The Big Stick - Lawrence Alexander   82
Billy Sunday - Rod Jones   3295
Black-Eyed Susan - Deborah Camp   871
The Blackheath Poisonings - Julian Symons   6150
The Blue Dragon - Diana Brown   716
Blue Russell - Will Bryant   738
Buffalo Coat - Carol Brink   691
By Command of the Viceroy - Duncan MacNeil   4010
California Glory - Dana Fuller Ross   5468

The Canary Trainer - Nicholas Meyer 4348

The Capricorn Stone - Madeleine Brent 659

A Captive Freedom - Emma Drummond 1724

Carolina Courage - Dana Fuller Ross 5469

The Case of the Revolutionist's Daughter: Sherlock Holmes Meets Karl Marx - Lewis S. Feuer 2076

Castle Heritage - Elisabeth Barr 337

Charge of Cowardice - Duncan MacNeil 4011

Chicago Girls - Edith Freund 2229

The City of Gold - Francis Brett Young 6940

Count Vronsky's Daughter - Carola Salisbury 5567

Counterfeit of Murder - Ray Harrison 2738

The Covenant - Brigid Knight 3521

A Creek Called Wounded Knee - Douglas C. Jones 3277

Crimson Creek: A Novel of the Early West - Robert McCraig 4228

Cruel in the Shadow - Lorn MacIntyre 3986

The Cup of Strength - Charlotte Paul 4840

The Curse of the Pharaohs - Elizabeth Peters 4948

Dance Back the Buffalo - Milton Lott 3899

The Dark Pasture - Jessica Stirling 6042

The Daughter: A Novel Based on the Life of Eleanor Marx - Judith Chernaik 1012

The Day the Sun Died - Dale Van Every 6408

Days of the Gold - Irwin R. Blacker 526

Dear Laura - Jean Stubbs 6094

Death at Daisy's Folly - Robin Paige 4775

Death at Gallows Green - Robin Paige 4776

Death of a Dancing Lady - Ray Harrison 2739

Death on the Cliff Walk - Mary Kruger 3562

Death on the Mississippi - Peter J. Heck 2815

Deathwatch - Ray Harrison 2740

The Deeds of the Disturber - Elizabeth Peters 4949

The Detling Secret - Julian Symons 6151

The Disappearance of Edwin Drood - Peter Rowland 5521

Dolphin Summer - Carola Salisbury 5569

Domina - Barbara Wood 6847

Dragonmede - Rona Randall 5246

The Dream Seekers - Grace Mark 4085

Drums Along the Khyber - Duncan MacNeil 4013

The Duchess of Duke Street - Mollie Hardwick 2693

Dvorak in Love - Josef Skvorecky 5881

Electricity: A Novel - Victoria Glendinning 2431

The Emigrants - Johan Bojer 561

Empire: A Novel - Gore Vidal 6487

Ever After - Elswyth Thane 6216

The Far Journey - Loula Grace Erdman 1950

Farriers' Lane - Anne Perry 4930

Fenwick Travers and the Years of Empire - Raymond M. Saunders 5614

The Final Adversary - Gilbert Morris 4460

The First to Land - Douglas E. Reeman 5288

The Flight of the Eagle - Per Olof Sundman 6119

Fools' Gold - Richard Wiley 6755

For God and Glory - Tim Jeal 3171

Forbidden City - Anthony Esler 1962

Funny Papers - Tom De Haven 1559

The Gates of Kunara - Duncan MacNeil 4014

The Girl From Storyville: A Victorian Novel - Frank Yerby 6919

Glittering Hill - Clyde Francis Murphy 4520

The God of Mirrors - Robert Reilly 5293

The Golden Nineties - Lisa Mason 4166

The Goldseekers - William R. Burnett 794

A Good Day to Die - Thomas Wakefield Blackburn 525

Good Night, Mr. Holmes - Carole Nelson Douglas 1699

The Great Sky and the Silence - James S. Rand 5245

The Guns of Arrest - Philip McCutchan 4242

The Gypsy From Cadiz - Tamsin Hamilton 2670

Halfhyde and the Chain Gang - Philip McCutchan 4244

Halfhyde and the Flag Captain - Philip McCutchan 4245

Halfhyde and the Fleet Review - Philip McCutchan 4246

Halfhyde for the Queen - Philip McCutchan 4247

Halfhyde Goes to War - Philip McCutchan 4248

Halfhyde on Zanatu - Philip McCutchan 4251

Halfhyde to the Narrows - Philip McCutchan 4253

Halfhyde's Island - Philip McCutchan 4254

The Hampton Heritage - Julie Ellis 1920

Harvest of Death - Ray Harrison 2741

The Harvey Girls - Samuel Hopkins Adams 31

The Head Waters - Archie Binns 500

A Heritage of Shadows - Madeleine Brent 660

Herma - Macdonald Harris 2726

Herzl the King - Norman Kotker 3547

The Hider - Loren D. Estleman 1972

The Hippopotamus Pool - Elizabeth Peters 4950

The Hired Man - Melvyn Bragg 639

Homecoming - Dana Fuller Ross 5474

Homeland - John Jakes 3148

Honor Thy Father - Robert A. Roripaugh 5460

The House on Curtin Street - Millie J. Ragosta 5242

The House on Mulberry Street - Maan Meyers 4354

Hunt for Heaven - Elsie Barber 298

I, Roberta - Elizabeth Gray Vining 6501

Imperial Kelly - Peter Bowen 600

An Innocent Woman - Malcolm Macdonald 3967

Jekyll, Alias Hyde - Donald Thomas 6240

Jewelled Path - Rosalind Laker 3597

The Jewelled Spur - Gilbert Morris 4465

Journey - James A. Michener 4371

The Jump-Off Creek - Molly Gloss 2435

Katherine - Antonia Van-Loon 6425

Kenya - John Halkin 2645

Kimberley - Colin Burke 784

Kings Row - Henry Bellamann 428

The Labyrinth - Thomas William Duncan 1787

The Lady - Conrad Richter 5321

Lady of Mallow - Dorothy Eden 1856

The Last Camel Died at Noon - Elizabeth Peters 4951

The Legacy of Ladysmith - John Kenny Crane 1413

Lieutenant of the Line - Duncan MacNeil 4015

Lion in the Valley - Elizabeth Peters 4952

Lizzie - Evan Hunter 3083

Lizzie Borden - Elizabeth Engstrom 1944

Lord of the Vampires: The Diaries of the Family Dracul - Jeanne Kalogridis 3328

Louisa Elliott - Ann Victoria Roberts 5370

Lovers - Suzanne Goodwin 2476

Mackenna's Gold - Will Henry 2845

The Marigold Field - Diane Pearson 4876

Masterpiece of Murder - Mary Kruger 3563

Maura's Dream - Joel Gross 2602

Men of Men - Wilbur Smith 5927

Mingo Dabney - James H. Street 6078

Minna's Story: The Secret Love of Doctor Sigmund Freud - Kathleen Daniels 1463

The Mortal Gods - Maurice Dolbier 1688

A Most Romantic City - Mary Ann Gibbs 2396

Mount's Mistake - Lew McCreary 4229

The Mummy Case - Elizabeth Peters 4953

Murder Makes an Entree - Amy Myers 4540

The Name of Hero - Richard Seltzer 5742

The Nationalists - William Stuart Long 3876

No Honeymoon for Death - Mary Kruger 3564

Officers and Ladies - Richard O'Connor 4686

Oklahoma Run - Alberta Constant 1260

Omensetter's Luck - William H. Gass 2317

Outlaw Lover - Lindsey Hanks 2676

Outward Bound - Philip McCutchan 4256

Owen Glen - Ben Ames Williams 6766

Pacific Destiny - Dana Fuller Ross 5487

Panama - Eric Zencey 6959

Parnell and the Englishwoman - Hugh Leonard 3721

Patently Murder - Ray Harrison 2742

Peder Victorious - O.E. Rolvaag 5435

A Peep into the 20th Century - Christopher Davis 1515

Pentecost Alley - Anne Perry 4933

Proud Mary - Iris Gower 2501

Queen's Royal - John Quigley 5225

A Question of Honour - Emma Drummond 1726

Rags of Glory - Stuart Cloete 1126

The Red Daniel - Duncan MacNeil 4017

The Red Peony - Yutang Lin 3783

Remember Santiago - Douglas C. Jones 3280

The Restless Frontier - Duncan MacNeil 4018

The Return of Moriarty - John E. Gardner 2287

The Ripper's Apprentice - Donald Thomas 6242

A River Town - Thomas Keneally 3415

The Roar of the Thunder - Wilbur Smith 5929

The Rough Rider - Gilbert Morris 4468

Run of the Stars - Dora Aydelotte 247

Sadhu on the Mountain Peak - Duncan MacNeil 4019

San Juan Hill - Will Henry 2848

Sarsen Place - Gwendoline Butler 821

Sarton Kell - Kate Mallory 4043

The Sea Scape - Mary Lide 3778

The Search for Temperance Moon - Douglas C. Jones 3282 .

A Season for Death - Ray Harrison 2743

The Seven-Per-Cent Solution - Nicholas Meyer 4349

Sherlock Holmes and the Mysterious Friend of Oscar Wilde - Russell A. Brown 731

Sherlock Holmes and the Red Demon - Larry Millett 4404

Sherlock Holmes and the Thistle of Scotland - L.B. Greenwood 2578

Sherlock Holmes vs. Dracula - Loren D. Estleman 1976

Siege in the Sun - Mary Paradise 4788

Sierra Triumph - Dana Fuller Ross 5488

The Silver Mountain - Dan Cushman 1453

Sing for a Penny - Clifford Dowdey 1708

The Single Star - Walter Adolphe Roberts 5394

The Snake, the Crocodile, and the Dog - Elizabeth Peters 4954

Song of Wovoka - Earl Murray 4531

Speak Softly - Lawrence Alexander 83

Sphere of Death - Ray Harrison 2744

The Steps of the Sun - Joanna Trollope 6350

The Story of the Sundance Kid - David Everitt 1988

Storyville - Lois Battle 377

The Strand - Claire Rayner 5269

The Stranglers - Loren D. Estleman 1978

Street of the Madwoman - Isabel Ortega 4756

Streets of Laredo - Larry McMurtry 4300

The Strenuous Life - Lawrence Alexander 84

Subaltern's Choice - Duncan MacNeil 4020

Sudden Country - Loren D. Estleman 1979

The Summer of Jack London - Andrew J. Fenady 2058

The Summer of the Royal Visit - Isabel Colegate 1199

Summoned to Darkness - Anne-Marie Sheridan 5809

Sunset - Christopher Nicole 4623

Tacey Cromwell - Conrad Richter 5324

Tamzen - Jane Gilmore Rushing 5530

Tara Kane - George Markstein 4091

Telluride - Susan Clark Schofield 5648

Tenderloin - Samuel Hopkins Adams 33

Their Fathers' God - O.E. Rolvaag 5436

Time After Time - Karl Alexander 80

The Time of Murder at Mayerling - Ann Dukthas 1778

The Time of the Dragon - Dorothy Eden 1863

Tincture of Death - Ray Harrison 2745

Tomorrow We Reap - James H. Street 6081

Tomorrow's Dream - Peggy Hanchar 2674

Too Long at the Dance - Mike Blakely 539

The Train at Bundarbar - Duncan MacNeil 4021

The Trevarton Inheritance - Malcolm Macdonald 3976

The True Memoirs of Charley Blankenship - Benjamin Capps 890

Trumpets Calling - Dora Aydelotte 248

Voyage: A Novel of 1896 - Sterling Hayden 2798

Welcome to Hard Times - E.L. Doctorow 1660

The West End Horror - Nicholas Meyer 4350

When the Lion Feeds - Wilbur Smith 5931
Where Is My Wandering Boy Tonight? - David Wagoner 6522
The White Dawn - James Houston 3053
White Eagle, Dark Skies - Jean Karsavina 3368
The White Man's Road - Benjamin Capps 891
Why Kill Arthur Potter? - Ray Harrison 2746
Wind of Destiny - Christopher Nicole 4624
Winding Stairs - Douglas C. Jones 3287
The Winter Wolf: Wyatt Earp in Alaska - Richard Parry 4820
Wolf in the Fold - Duncan MacNeil 4022
A Woman of Quality - Jan Westcott 6649
The Year of the Spaniard - Henry Castor 956
Yellow: A Novel - Daniel Lynch 3932
The Yukon Queen - Gilbert Morris 4476

20th CENTURY

Absalom, Absalom! - William Faulkner 2049
Across the Bitter Sea - Eilis Dillon 1646
The Adelita - Oakley Hall 2649
Adversary in the House - Irving Stone 6053
Alice and Edith: A Biographical Novel of the Two Wives of Theodóre Roosevelt - Dorothy Clarke Wilson 6798
All for Love: Baby Doe and Silver Dollar - John Vernon 6456
The American - Howard Fast 2026
The American Cowboy - Will James 3163
And the Stars Shall Fall - True Bowen 603
The Angel with the Trumpet - Ernst Lothar 3898
Angels Falling - Janice Elliott 1915
Angle of Repose - Wallace Stegner 5989
Anna, Ann, Annie - Thomas Trebitsch Parker 4808
Anthony Trant - John Hyatt Downing 1713
Apple Tree Lean Down - Mary E. Pearce 4860
April Rising - Susan Sallis 5574
The Architecture of the Arkansas Ozarks - Donald Harington 2708
The Artist - Norman Garbo 2281
As the Crow Flies - Jeffrey Archer 183
Asya - Michael Ignatieff 3103
The Autobiography of Miss Jane Pittman - Ernest J. Gaines 2270
The Ballad of Typhoid Mary - Jurg Federspiel 2057
The Bank - Stephen Longstreet 3882
Beauty for Ashes - Timothy R. Wilson 6816
The Beckoning Waters - Robert Carse 944
Before My Time - Niccolo Tucci 6358
Before the Glory Ended - Ursula Zilinsky 6963
The Bellamy Saga - John Pearson 4878
Benton's Row - Frank Yerby 6908
Bertie, Albert Edward, Prince of Wales - Tyler Whittle 6720
Between Earth and Sky - Karen Osborn 4758
Between Two Worlds - Monique Raphel High 2913
Bide Me Fair - Harvey Howells 3060
Birdsong - Sebastian Faulks 2051
Biscayne - Barry Jay Kaplan 3365
Bittersweet - Leslie Li 3769
The Black Candle - Catherine Cookson 1273
Blaize - Anne Melville 4331
The Blood Countess - Andrei Codrescu 1149
Blood on the Snow - John Elliott 1916
Blood Red Rose - Maxwell Grant 2538
The Blood Seed - Andrew Ward 6561
Blue Camellia - Frances Parkinson Keyes 3477
Blunted Lance - Max Hennessy 2829
The Book Class - Louis Auchincloss 228
Born with the Century - William Kinsolving 3501
The Bourlotas Fortune - Nicholas Gage 2268
The Boyds of Black River - Walter D. Edmonds 1871
Brave Kingdom - Frances Murray 4534
Bride of Ae - Pamela Hill 2928
Bridey's Mountain - Yvonne Adamson 34
Brothers Three - John Oskison 4764

Brules - Harry Combs 1223
Buller's Guns - Richard Hough 3048
The Burning Man - Stephen Longstreet 3883
Bygones - Frank Wilkinson 6762
Calamity Jane of Deadwood Gulch - Ethel Hueston 3068
California Gold - John Jakes 3145
The Call - John Hersey 2869
The Candlesticks and the Cross - Ruth Freeman Solomon 5940
Captains and the Kings - Taylor Caldwell 851
Cashmere - Nicola Thorne 6273
Castle Garden - Bill Albert 63
Century in Scarlet - Lajos Zilahy 6962
Ceremony of the Innocent - Taylor Caldwell 852
The Chandler Heritage - Ben Haas 2629
Cherokee Rose: A Novel of America's First Cowgirl - Judy Alter 119
Chikara! - Robert Skimin 5876
China Saga - C.Y. Lee 3706
Christopher Strange - Ruth Eleanor McKee 4281
Cimarron - Edna Ferber 2061
Clair De Lune: A Novel about Claude Debussy - Pierre La Mure 3575
Coming through Slaughter - Michael Ondaatje 4736
Contessa - Helene Mansfield 4076
Crazy Snake - Robert J. Conley 1240
The Crown Prince - John Barchilon 300
The Crusader - Noel B. Gerson 2364
Csardas - Diane Pearson 4875
Dancing at the Rascal Fair - Ivan Doig 1682
Dark Rider - Louis Zara 6950
Daughter of Time - Nelia Gardner White 6695
Daughters of the New World - Susan Richards Shreve 5835
Day Is Coming - William Cameron 869
Dear Lily - Malcolm W. Greenough Jr. 2575
The Death of Artemio Cruz - Carlos Fuentes 2246
The Death of Che Guevara - Jay Cantor 886
Deep in My Heart: A Story Based on the Life of Sigmund Romberg - Elliott Arnold 192
Devil's Yard - Ivo Andric 152
Diamond Six - William Fielding Smith 5932
Diamond Wedding - Wilbur Daniel Steele 5986
Doctor Zhivago - Boris Pasternak 4824
Dorothy and Agatha - Gaylord Larsen 3667
The Dream Seekers - Stephen Longstreet 3884
The Dukes: A Novel - Malcolm Ross 5503
Dynasty - Robert S. Elegant 1902
The Earth Abideth - George Dell 1595
The Earth and All It Holds - V.J. Banis 287
Eden and Honor - Marilyn Harris 2729
Edward and Mrs. Simpson - A.C.H. Smith 5916
Eleanora Duse - Jean Stubbs 6095
Elena - Judith Egan 1893
Elgar on the Journey to Hanley - Keith Alldritt 92
Elizabeth and Alexandra - Antony Lambton 3616
The Emperor Franz Joseph - Ottokar Janetschek 3164
The Enduring Years - Claire Rayner 5263
Esau - Meir Shalev 5770
Ethel: The Fictional Autobiography - Tema Nason 4558
An Excess of Love - Cathy Cash Spellman 5959
Eye of the Hurricane - Fergus Reid Buckley 757
The Eye of the Lion: A Novel Based on the Life of Mata Hari - Lael Tucker Wertenbaker 6626
The Fall River Line - Daoma Winston 6824
Family - J. California Cooper 1297
The Family of Women - Richard Peck 4883
The Far Side of the Hill - Nancy Livingston 3811
Farewell to My Concubine - Lilian Lee 3709
A Father and His Fate - Ivy Compton-Burnett 1228
Felding Castle - Edith De Born 1552
The Fifth Horseman - Jose Antonio Villarreal 6496
Forbidden City - Muriel Molland Jernigan 3215
Forefathers - Nancy Cato 960
Fort Worth - Leonard Sanders 5588
Fortune Is a Woman - Elizabeth Adler 39

Fortune's Legacy - Jack Rowe 5515
The Free Frenchman - Piers Paul Read 5277
From a Far Land - Robert S. Elegant 1903
From the Terrace - John O'Hara 4703
Galveston - Suzanne Morris 4482
Generations of Winter - Vassily Aksyonov 61
Gentlemen of Adventure - Ernest K. Gann 2278
The Ginger Tree - Oswald Wynd 6890
Glorious Morning - Julie Ellis 1919
The Glory - Herman Wouk 6873
Gold of Their Bodies: A Novel about Gauguin - Charles Orson Gorham 2488
The Golden Honeycomb - Kamala Markandaya 4086
The Golden Lady - Dorothy Gardiner 2283
Goldeneye - Malcolm Macdonald 3965
Gone the Dreams and the Dancing - Douglas C. Jones 3279
A Grand Passion - Mary Mackey 3991
The Grandmothers - Glenway Westcott 6640
Green City in the Sun - Barbara Wood 6849
Hanover Place - Michael M. Thomas 6245
Hardacre - C.L. Skelton 5872
The Heart of O. Henry - Dale Kramer 3550
The Heart of the Continent - Nancy Cato 961
Heirs of the Motherland - Judith Pella 4893
High Heroic - Constantine FitzGibbon 2118
The Holder of the World - Bharati Mukherjee 4510
The Hope - Herman Wouk 6874
A Horseman Riding By - R.F. Delderfield 1588
Horses of War - Duff Hart-Davis 2760
The House of Cray - Pamela Hill 2936
The House of Five Talents - Louis Auchincloss 231
The House That Tai Ming Built - Virginia Lee 3711
Hubble Time - Tom Bezzi 490
Hungry Hill - Daphne Du Maurier 1746
I Give You Oscar Wilde - Desmond Hall 2647
I Take This Land - Richard Powell 5147
I, Victoria - Cynthia Harrod-Eagles 2755
The Immigrants - Howard Fast 2034
Imperial Woman - Pearl S. Buck 755
Impressionist: A Novel of Mary Cassatt - Joan King 3486
In Those Days - Harvey Fergusson 2068
Inherit the Sun - Maxwell Grant 2539
The Jealous House - Clarence Budington Kelland 3390
Jelly Roll Morton's Last Night at the Jungle Inn: An Imaginary Memoir - Samuel Charters 1002
Johanna: A Novel of the Van Gogh Family - Claire Cooperstein 1317
Joseph - Mervyn Jones 3292
Journey into Fire - Patricia Wright 6882
Kagami - Elizabeth Kata 3369
Kelly Blue - Peter Bowen 601
Kid Curry: The Life and Times of Harvey Logan and the Wild Bunch - F. Bruce Lamb 3606
Kilcaraig - Annabel Carothers 904
Kingdom of Shadows - Barbara Erskine 1954
Ladies Whose Bright Eyes - Ford Madox Ford 2162
Lady of Hay - Barbara Erskine 1955
The Land Was Ours: A Novel of the Great Plains - Charles W. Bailey 266
The Last Valley - A.B. Guthrie Jr. 2626
Leah's Journey - Gloria Goldreich 2460
Lenin: The Novel - Alan Brien 679
The Leopard - Giuseppe di Lampedusa 3634
Light on the Mountain - Leonard Sanders 5589
Lillie - David Butler 818
The Lion of Pescara - George MacBeth 3958
The Lion's Way - Lewis Orde 4750
Live From the Devil - Wyatt Blassingame 542
The Living Reed - Pearl S. Buck 756
London's Child - Philip Boast 560
The Long Afternoon - Ursula Zilinsky 6964
The Longest Winter - Julie Harris 2722
Lord Richard's Passion - Mervyn Jones 3293
Lotus Land - Monica Highland 2917
Lucinda Brayford - Martin Boyd 613
Malkeh and Her Children - Marjorie Edelson 1853

The Mallen Lot - Catherine Cookson 1281
The Maltese Angel - Catherine Cookson 1283
Mamaw - Susan Dodd 1663
Mamigon - Jack Hashian 2772
A Man and His Mountain: The Life of Paul Cezanne - Hugh McLeave 4285
Man of Montmartre: A Novel Based on the Life of Maurice Utrillo - Stephen Longstreet 3888
Manchu Empress - Bluebell Matilda Hunter 3081
Mandalay - Alexandra Jones 3269
Max - Howard Fast 2038
Members of the Tribe - Richard Kluger 3511
Metello - Vasco Pratolini 5163
Miami: A Saga - Evelyn Wilde Mayerson 4204
Michael Torey - Janet Mathewson 4183
Miss Bishop - Bess Streeter Aldrich 71
Modigliani: Prince of Montparnasse - Tadeusz Wittlin 6834
Molly - Teresa Crane 1417
The Moneyman - Judith Liederman 3781
Monte Walsh - Jack Schaefer 5635
Mortal Hunger: A Novel Based on the Life of Lafcadio Hearn - Harry E. Wedeck 6594
Moulin Rouge: A Novel Based on Henri de Toulouse-Lautrec - Pierre La Mure 3576
The Mountain of Immoderate Desires - Leslie Wilson 6811
Mr. Vertigo - Paul Auster 244
Mussolini - Alan Gelb 2348
Mysteries of Winterthurn - Joyce Carol Oates 4659
Naked Came I: A Novel of Rodin - David Weiss 6607
The Nazarene - Sholem Asch 200
A Nest of Simple Folk - Sean O'Faolain 4692
Never Victorious, Never Defeated - Taylor Caldwell 860
The New Confessions - William Boyd 617
New Day - Victor Stafford Reid 5291
Night Shall Overtake Us - Kate Saunders 5611
No Resting Place - William Humphrey 3079
Nothing New under the Sun - Riccardo Bacchelli 255
Of Lizards and Angels: A Saga of Sioux Land - Frederick F. Manfred 4058
The Old Enchantment - Sarah Neilan 4565
Oldest Living Confederate Widow Tells All - Allan Gurganus 2621
Once a Gentleman - Donald James 3157
The Only Sin - Julie Ellis 1923
Ourselves to Know - John O'Hara 4704
Out of This Furnace - Thomas Bell 425
Outlaw - Warren Kiefer 3482
Pacific Cavalcade - Virginia Coffman 1157
Paloverde - Jacqueline Briskin 693
Paradise Falls - Don Robertson 5399
Passage West - Dallas Miller 4382
The Passionate Journey - Irving Stone 6061
The Passions of the Mind - Irving Stone 6062
Pearl - Anne Leaton 3701
Peking: A Novel of China's Revolt - Anthony Grey 2587
Penhally - Caroline Gordon 2479
The People of Juvik - Olav Dunn 1798
Polonaise - Piers Paul Read 5278
Portrait in Brownstone - Louis Auchincloss 232
Power - Howard Fast 2041
The Power of Black - M.B. Longman 3880
Prairie - Anna Lee Waldo 6528
Princess Sophia - Edison Marshall 4110
The Prison Notebooks of Ricardo Flores Magon - Douglas Day 1545
Privileged Children - Frances Vernon 6455
A Prologue to Love - Taylor Caldwell 862
Rabbit Boss - Thomas Sanchez 5581
The Rainbird - Sara Lidman 3780
Raj - Gita Mehta 4325
The Rector of Justin - Louis Auchincloss 233
The Red Monarch: Scenes From the Life of Stalin - Yuri Krotkov 3561
Redemption - Leon Uris 6393

Regards From the Dead Princess: A Novel of a Life - Kenize Mourad 4505
The Regiment - Christopher Nicole 4620
The Regiment - C.L. Skelton 5874
Remnants of Glory - Teresa Miller 4403
Return of the Stranger - Reay Tannahill 6158
The Revolutionist: A Novel of Russia - Robert Littell 3810
Ride the Wind - Lucia St. Clair Robson 5416
The Ring Master - David Gurr 2622
River of Dreams - Gay Courter 1390
The Running Iron - Rachel Ann Fish 2097
The Saga of Henry Starr - Robert J. Conley 1250
Saigon - Anthony Grey 2588
The Saint of Montparnasse: A Novel Based on the Life of Constantin Brancusi - Peter Neagoe 4560
The Salamanca Drum - Dorothy Eden 1861
Sam Chance - Benjamin Capps 888
San Antone - V.J. Banis 288
Sarah - Joel Gross 2603
Saturday City - Jan Webster 6593
The Sea of Grass - Conrad Richter 5323
The Seadon Fortune - Leonard St. Clair 5563
Seasons - Anna Dillon 1645
The Seasons of Heroes - Paxton Davis 1539
Seattle Green - Jane Adams 26
The Secret Annie Oakley - Marcy Moran Heidish 2819
The Secret Years - Judith Lennox-Smith 3718
Serenissima: A Novel of Venice - Erica Jong 3300
Serpent and Staff - Frank Yerby 6927
Shanghai - Christopher New 4588
Show Boat - Edna Ferber 2063
The Smiths - Janet Fairbank 2002
Snow-Water - Dorothy Gardiner 2285
A Soldier of the Great War - Mark Helprin 2823
Speak to Me of Love - Dorothy Eden 1862
The Spirit and the Flesh: A Novel Inspired by the Life of Isadora Duncan - David Weiss 6610
Spring Came on Forever - Bess Streeter Aldrich 73
Spring Moon: A Novel of China - Bette Bao Lord 3897
Stand We at Last - Zoe Fairbairns 1999
Steamboat Gothic - Frances Parkinson Keyes 3481
Stones From the River - Ursula Hegi 2816
The Store - Michael Pearson 4879
Storming Heaven - Denise Giardina 2394
A Story of Deep Delight - Thomas McNamee 4305
Sunshine and Shadow - Antonia Van-Loon 6426
The Taverners' Place - Joanna Trollope 6351
The Tenants of Time - Thomas Flanagan 2120
Testimony of Two Men - Taylor Caldwell 863
Theirs Was the Kingdom - R.F. Delderfield 1590
Theory of War - Joan Brady 637
These Latter Days - Laura Kalpakian 3330
Thine Is the Glory - Samuel A. Schreiner Jr. 5672
This Old Bill - Loren D. Estleman 1980
Thousand Years of Gold - Ruthanne Lum McCunn 4239
Threescore and Ten - Walter Allen 105
Time in Its Flight - Susan Fromberg Schaeffer 5636
The Tin Drum - Gunther Grass 2540
To Seize the Passing Dream - Ted Berkman 479
To Serve Them All My Days - R.F. Delderfield 1591
To the End of Her Days - Malcolm Macdonald 3975
Tolbecken - Samuel Shellabarger 5798
Tom Mix Died for Your Sins - Darryl Ponicsan 5090
TR - Noel B. Gerson 2385
Tregaran - Mary Lide 3779
Trinity - Leon Uris 6394
Triptych - Dora Landey 3652
True Women - Janice Woods Windle 6820
Trumpets of Silver - Norma Harris 2735
Under the Fifth Sun: A Novel of Pancho Villa - Earl Shorris 5832
Union Square - Meredith Tax 6176
Unto the Soul - Aharon Appelfeld 181
Utrillo's Mother - Sarah Baylis 391
El Vago - Laurence Gonzales 2474

Vanessa - Hugh Walpole 6548
A Vein of Riches - John Knowles 3526
The Very Best People - Elizabeth Villars 6499
Victoria Victorious - Jean Plaidy 5073
The View From Coyaba - Peter Abrahams 11
Wallis: The Novel - Anne Edwards 1883
Washington, D.C. - Gore Vidal 6493
Watch for Me on the Mountain - Forrest Carter 947
The Ways of Women - Elaine Crowley 1436
West to Eden - Gloria Goldreich 2461
Westfield - Roderick Thorp 6277
What the Heart Keeps - Rosalind Laker 3605
Whirlwind in Petticoats - Beril Becker 406
The White Hotel - D.M. Thomas 6237
White Poppy - Margaret Gaan 2261
The Widow of Windsor - Jean Plaidy 5076
The Widow of Windsor - Tyler Whittle 6723
Wild Earth's Nobility - Frank Waters 6578
Wild Times - Brian Garfield 2291
The Wind Brings Up the Rain - Eric Malpass 4051
Wings of the Morning - David Beaty 402
A Woman by Design - Frances Kennett 3426
A Woman's Age - Rachel Billington 499
Women in the Wind - Margaret Ritter 5350
The World as I Found It - Bruce Duffy 1755
Yellowstone Kelly - Peter Bowen 602

1900s

1901 - Robert Conroy 1258
Alexa - Anne Melville 4330
All or Nothing - Stephen Longstreet 3881
Amanda/Miranda - Richard Peck 4882
The Anatolian - Elia Kazan 3381
Anna's Book - Barbara Vine 6500
Arrogance - Joanna Scott 5679
The Asking Price - Jessica Stirling 6039
The Athelsons - Jocelyn Kettle 3476
The Blind Bend - Lorn MacIntyre 3985
Buller's Dreadnought - Richard Hough 3047
Bully! - Mark Schorr 5670
The Calling of Emily Evans - Janette Oke 4706
Captain Wonder - Donald Thomas 6238
A Captive Freedom - Emma Drummond 1724
The Celebrant - Eric Rolfe Greenberg 2572
The Chant of Jimmie Blacksmith - Thomas Keneally 3411
Check-Out Time - Kate Kingsbury 3491
Chelsea Reach - Claire Rayner 5261
The Cinderpath - Catherine Cookson 1275
The Clock Tower - Jeanne Montague 4435
Cold Sassy Tree - Olive Ann Burns 797
Cottonwoods Grow Tall - Margaret Bell Houston 3055
Court of Honor - Maria Fagyas 1996
Courting Emma Howe - Margaret A. Robinson 5410
Crime Without Passion - Richard Grayson 2556
Cruel in the Shadow - Lorn MacIntyre 3986
Dance of the Assassins - Maria Fagyas 1997
The Dawning of Deliverance - Judith Pella 4892
Death En Voyage - Richard Grayson 2557
Death Off Stage - Richard Grayson 2558
Death on the Cards - Richard Grayson 2559
The Devil's Lieutenant - Maria Fagyas 1998
Diamond Head - Marian J.A. Jackson 3135
Do Not Disturb - Kate Kingsbury 3492
The Duchess of Duke Street - Mollie Hardwick 2693
The Eagle at the Gate - Rona Randall 5248
The Eagles of Malice - Alan Scholefield 5652
Eat, Drink, and Be Buried - Kate Kingsbury 3493
The Edge of the Storm - Agustin Yanez 6893
Edward - Tyler Whittle 6721
Ellis Island - Fred Mustard Stewart 6023
Emily - Cynthia Harrod-Eagles 2753
Empire: A Novel - Gore Vidal 6487
Encore - Monique Raphel High 2915
The Fabulous Concubine - Hsin-Hai Chang 987
A Falcon for a Queen - Catherine Gaskin 2314
Fenwick Travers and the Forbidden Kingdom - Raymond M. Saunders 5612

Fenwick Travers and the Panama Canal - Raymond M. Saunders 5613
Fenwick Travers and the Years of Empire - Raymond M. Saunders 5614
The Final Adversary - Gilbert Morris 4460
Fire and Fog - Dianne Day 1543
The First to Land - Douglas E. Reeman 5288
The Fixer - Bernard Malamud 4038
Floodtide - Suzanne Goodwin 2475
Foreign Devils - Irvin Faust 2053
The Fountain Overflows - Rebecca West 6639
The Four Winds of Heaven - Monique Raphel High 2916
A Georgian Love Story - Ernest Raymond 5258
The Girl From Storyville: A Victorian Novel - Frank Yerby 6919
The Glendower Conspiracy - Lloyd Biggle Jr. 494
Glowstone - Macdonald Harris 2725
The Golden Crucible - Jean Stubbs 6096
Goldfield - Richard S. Wheeler 6660
The Good Old Boys - Elmer Kelton 3405
The Good Provider - Jessica Stirling 6043
Grandmother and the Priests - Taylor Caldwell 857
Grounds for Murder - Kate Kingsbury 3494
Halfhyde and the Admiral - Philip McCutchan 4243
The Halfhyde Line - Philip McCutchan 4249
Halfhyde Ordered South - Philip McCutchan 4252
Henry James' Midnight Song - Carol de Chellis Hill 2920
Heritage - Lewis Orde 4749
Herma - Macdonald Harris 2726
Herzl the King - Norman Kotker 3547
The Hippopotamus Pool - Elizabeth Peters 4950
The Hired Man - Melvyn Bragg 639
Home Station - Jeanne Williams 6778
Homeland - John Jakes 3148
Honey in the Horn - Harold Lenoir Davis 1523
The Idol Hunter - Barry Unsworth 6386
The Imperial Agent - T.N. Murari 4518
The Imperialists - William Stuart Long 3875
Invading Tibet - Mark Frutkin 2239
The Jade Alliance - Elizabeth Darrell 1497
Jewels - Robert Perrin 4917
Justice, My Brother - James Keene 3386
Kernow & Daughter - Malcolm Macdonald 3968
Kimberley - Colin Burke 784
The King Edward Plot - Robert Lee Hall 2658
Kings Row - Henry Bellamann 428
The Ladies of Hanover Square - Rona Randall 5249
The Last Testament of Oscar Wilde - Peter Ackroyd 19
The Last Waltz - Nancy Zaroulis 6955
The Legacy of Ladysmith - John Kenny Crane 1413
Lenin in Zurich - Alexander Solzhenitsyn 5943
Light - Eva Figes 2083
Lord of the Far Island - Victoria Holt 3016
The Lormes of Castle Rising - Fanny Cradock 1409
Love and Honor - Leslie Arlen 189
Love at Sunset - Jane Sheridan 5811
Lovers - Suzanne Goodwin 2476
The Mamur Zapt and the Donkey-Vous - Michael Pearce 4866
The Mamur Zapt and the Girl in the Nile - Michael Pearce 4867
The Mamur Zapt and the Men Behind - Michael Pearce 4868
The Mamur Zapt and the Night of the Dog - Michael Pearce 4869
The Mamur Zapt and the Return of the Carpet - Michael Pearce 4870
The Mamur Zapt and the Spoils of Egypt - Michael Pearce 4871
The Man Who Loved Mata Hari - Dan Sherman 5813
Marblehead - Joan Thompson 6267
Mariette in Ecstasy - Ron Hansen 2682
The Marigold Field - Diane Pearson 4876
The Master of Oakwindsor - Douglas Kent Hall 2648

Meadowsweet - Gwendoline Butler 820
The Midnight Gun - Berkely Mather 4180
The Midwife - Gay Courter 1388
The Mighty and Their Fall - Ivy Compton-Burnett 1230
The Millionaire's Daughter - Dorothy Eden 1858
Mills of the Gods - Daoma Winston 6828
Mister St. John - Loren D. Estleman 1974
The Monterant Affair - Richard Grayson 2560
The Montmarte Murders - Richard Grayson 2561
Moonraker's Bride - Madeleine Brent 661
Mr. American - George MacDonald Fraser 2211
The Murder at Impasse Louvaine - Richard Grayson 2562
The Name of Hero - Richard Seltzer 5742
The Nationalists - William Stuart Long 3876
Pancho And Black Jack - Fred Bean 398
Petersburg - Emily Hanlon 2677
The Petersburg-Cannes Express - Hans Koning 3538
Pomeroy - Gordon Williams 6770
Poor Boy and a Long Way Home - James Sherburne 5806
Proud Mary - Iris Gower 2501
The Quallsford Inheritance - Lloyd Biggle Jr. 495
The Rage of the Vulture - Barry Unsworth 6388
Rags of Glory - Stuart Cloete 1126
Ragtime - E.L. Doctorow 1658
The Revenge of the Hound - Michael Hardwick 2688
Rivington Street - Meredith Tax 6175
The Road to Wellville - T. Coraghessan Boyle 618
Room with a Clue - Kate Kingsbury 3495
Seance for a Vampire - Fred Saberhagen 5557
The Second Mate - Philip McCutchan 4257
Service for Two - Kate Kingsbury 3496
Shadows over Castle Rising - Fanny Cradock 1410
The Shakespeare Girl - Mollie Hardwick 2698
The Shootist - Glendon Swarthout 6145
Silver Fruit - Patricia Campbell 876
Sister Beneath the Sheet - Gillian Linscott 3808
Spring at The Winged Horse - Ted Willis 6794
Stage Fright - Gillian Linscott 3809
The Story of the Sundance Kid - David Everitt 1988
The Strange Files of Fremont Jones - Dianne Day 1544
The Summer of the Bashinskeys - Diane Pearson 4877
The Sunken Treasure - Marian J.A. Jackson 3136
Temple Bells - Marjorie McEvoy 4271
The Terrible Teague Bunch - Gary Jennings 3197
That Callahan Spunk! - Francis Ames 124
This Sweet and Bitter Earth - Alexander Cordell 1326
Tigerlilies - Judith Glover 2439
The Time of the Dragon - Dorothy Eden 1863
The Truest Pleasure - Robert Morgan 4452
Twilight of the Dragon - Peter Bourne 596
Upstairs Downstairs - John Hawkesworth 2782
Walnut Grove - Jane Gilmore Rushing 5531
Waltzing in Ragtime - Eileen Charbonneau 996
The Welcome Light - Jessica Stirling 6050
When the Owl Cries - Paul Bartlett 367
White Eagle, Dark Skies - Jean Karsavina 3368
The Winter Wolf: Wyatt Earp in Alaska - Richard Parry 4820
The Wishing Tree - Sandra Paretti 4794
A Woman Possessed - Malcolm Macdonald 3977
The Young Men of Paris - Stephen Longstreet 3893
Young Men See Visions - Mary Mian 4357

1910s
1915: A Novel - Roger McDonald 4264
Afterward - Catherine M. Rae 5234
The Alpha Raid - Alan Scholefield 5651
The American Heiress - Dorothy Eden 1854
The Anatolian - Elia Kazan 3381
Arrogance - Joanna Scott 5679
The Ashes of Smyrna - Richard Reinhardt 5294
Attack the Lusitania! - Raymond Hitchcock 2956
August 1914 - Alexander Solzhenitsyn 5942

The Beano - Rony Robinson 5411
The Beekeeper's Apprentice, or, On the Segregation of the Queen - Laurie R. King 3487
Behold the Fire - Michael Blankfort 541
Beloved Soldiers - C.L. Skelton 5871
Beyond the Aegean - Elia Kazan 3382
The Birthday Boys - Beryl Bainbridge 269
Bisbee '17 - Robert Houston 3056
Blood and Sable - Carol J. Kane 3350
Blood Winter - William Patrick 4830
The Bloody Red Baron - Kim Newman 4596
The Blue Max - Jack D. Hunter 3085
Blue Moon - Parris Afton Bonds 569
Blue Ruin: A Novel of the 1919 World Series - Brendan Boyd 610
The Bright Blue Sky - Max Hennessy 2830
The Buckingham Palace Connection - Ted Willis 6792
Buller's Dreadnought - Richard Hough 3047
Buller's Victory - Richard Hough 3049
Burden of Desire - Robert MacNeil 4023
Bury Him Among Kings - Elleston Trevor 6341
By the Green of the Spring - John Masters 4171
A Cadenza for Caruso - Barbara Paul 4834
Camelot Country - Marjorie McEvoy 4267
The Casket Crew - Arch Whitehouse 6709
A Castle in Bavaria - Prince Thibaut d'Orleans 1693
The Celebrant - Eric Rolfe Greenberg 2572
A Certain Splendour - Carola Salisbury 5566
The Challenging Heights - Max Hennessy 2831
Chariots of Fire - W.J. Weatherby 6586
Chihuahua 1916 - Otis Carney 903
The Choiring of the Trees - Donald Harington 2709
The Cinderpath - Catherine Cookson 1275
A Clear Road to Archangel - Geoffrey Rose 5461
A Company of Swans - Eva Ibbotson 3095
Conqueror of the Clouds - William F. Hallstead 2664
Contessa - Richard Oliver Collin 1209
The Cowboy Conspiracy - Larry D. Names 4553
The Crimson Wind - Max Hennessy 2832
Crown Witness - Gillian Linscott 3803
Curse of Magira - David Bee 413
Dead Man's Sweetheart - Gillian Linscott 3804
Death of a Schoolboy - Hans Koning 3537
The Devil in Harbour - Catherine Gavin 2319
The Devil's Spy - Michael Hastings 2773
Devoted Friends - Joe Poyer 5161
Dreaming of Samarkand - Martin Booth 576
An Easy Day for a Lady - Gillian Linscott 3805
The Edge of the Storm - Agustin Yanez 6893
Eleanor: A Novel - Rhoda Lerman 3724
The Eleventh Year - Monique Raphel High 2914
Ellis Island - Fred Mustard Stewart 6023
Emily - Cynthia Harrod-Eagles 2753
The Emperor's Coloured Coat - John Biggins 491
Encore - Monique Raphel High 2915
The End of the Hunt - Thomas Flanagan 2119
The End of the World News - Anthony Burgess 777
An Error of Judgment - Stanley Wolpert 6845
Escape From Sonora - Will Bryant 739
Every Man for Himself - Beryl Bainbridge 270
The Eye in the Door - Pat Barker 307
The Faraway Drums - Jon Cleary 1104
Fifteen Flags - Richard Lynden Hardman 2686
Filaree: A Novel of an American Life - Marguerite Noble 4633
Fire in the Ice - Alan Scholefield 5653
The Fires of Fu Manchu - Cay Van Ash 6399
The First Casualty - William Powell 5149
Flight From Bucharest - R.T. Stevens 6000
Flight From Fifth Avenue - Catherine M. Rae 5235
Floodtide - Suzanne Goodwin 2475
The Four Winds of Heaven - Monique Raphel High 2916
The Friends of Pancho Villa - James Carlos Blake 535
From Time to Time - Jack Finney 2092
The Gathering Wolves - Elizabeth Darrell 1496

The Ghost Road - Pat Barker 308

The Ghosts of Africa - William Stevenson 6013

Give Me the Daggers - Catherine Gavin 2321

Give Us This Day - R.F. Delderfield 1586

God Save the Tsar - Susanna Hoe 2976

Gone the Rainbow, Gone the Dove - Joan Bagnel 264

Goshawk Squadron - Derek Robinson 5403

Gossip From the Forest - Thomas Keneally 3413

Grant's War - Ted Jones 3297

The Green Leaves of Summer - Ted Willis 6793

Grishin - Hans Herlin 2859

Halfhyde on the Amazon - Philip McCutchan 4250

The Ham Reporter - Robert J. Randisi 5251

The Hampton Women - Julie Ellis 1921

Hanging on the Wire - Gillian Linscott 3806

The Hard to Catch Mercy - William Baldwin 281

Heart of War - John Masters 4174

Heaven's Gold - Giles Tippette 6282

Hollywood: A Novel of America in the 1920s - Gore Vidal 6488

Hoopla - Harry Stein 5990

The Hours of Light - Janet Tanner 6160

The House on Bitterness Street - Elizabeth Borton de Trevino 6340

How Young They Die - Stuart Cloete 1124

Hyde Place - Virginia Coffman 1154

An Ice-Cream War - William Boyd 616

Imperial Winds - Priscilla Napier 4555

In My Father's House - Bodie Thoene 6222

In Pale Battalions - Robert Goddard 2444

In the Company of Eagles - Ernest K. Gann 2279

It's Me Again - Donald Jack 3126

John and Anzia: An American Romance - Norma Rosen 5462

Karl and Rosa - Alfred Doblin 1653

Keeping Secrets - Suzanne Morris 4483

The Killing Frost - Thomas Hayden 2799

Killing Mister Watson - Peter Mathiessen 4185

The Kingdom Carver - E.G. Perrault 4916

The King's Commissar - Duncan Kyle 3570

The Ladies of Hanover Square - Rona Randall 5249

The Ladies of Missalonghi - Colleen McCullough 4237

The Land of Our Dreams - Nancy Livingston 3812

Landru - Rene Masson 4170

The Last Farewell - Philip McCutchan 4255

Last Go Round - Ken Kesey 3473

Last Reveille - David Morrell 4456

The Last Station - Jay Parini 4801

The Last Summer of Innocence - Linda Sole 5938

The Last Summer of Mata Hari - Edward Huebsch 3067

The Last Victory - T.N. Murari 4519

Leaving Cold Sassy - Olive Ann Burns 798

The Legacy of Tregaran - Mary Lide 3776

Lenin in Zurich - Alexander Solzhenitsyn 5943

The Leopard and the Cliff - Wallace Breem 655

The Lion at Sea - Max Hennessy 2834

Lion in the Evening - Alan Scholefield 5656

Look to the River - William A. Owens 4771

The Lormes of Castle Rising - Fanny Cradock 1409

Love and Honor - Leslie Arlen 189

Love at Sunset - Jane Sheridan 5811

Lusitania - David Butler 819

Madensky Square - Eva Ibbotson 3096

The Magic Ship - Sandra Paretti 4791

Maiden Voyage - Cynthia Bass 372

The Man From St. Petersburg - Ken Follett 2148

The Man Who Loved Mata Hari - Dan Sherman 5813

Me Too - Donald Jack 3128

Melbury Square - Dorothy Eden 1857

The Men That God Made Mad: A Novel about Ireland's Easter Rising - W.A. Ballinger 286

The Midwife's Advice - Gay Courter 1389

Morning's Gate - Ann Victoria Roberts 5371

The Moth - Catherine Cookson 1284

Mr. American - George MacDonald Fraser 2211

A Mule for the Marquesa - Frank O'Rourke 4753

The Mummy; or Ramses the Damned - Anne Rice 5315

Murder at Ebbets Field - Troy Soos 5947

Murder at Fenway Park - Troy Soos 5948

Murder at Wrigley Field - Troy Soos 5949

My Own Ground - Hugh Nissenson 4628

No Man's Land - William Fairchild 2004

Not of War Only - Norman Zollinger 6966

Now, God Be Thanked - John Masters 4177

The Old Colts - Glendon Swarthout 6144

The Old Gringo - Carlos Fuentes 2247

One Night in Newport - Elizabeth Villars 6498

Over There - Thomas Fleming 2130

Over There - Robert Vaughan 6449

The Passing Bells - Phillip Rock 5421

A People Betrayed - Alfred Doblin 1654

The Petrograd Consignment - Owen Sela 5739

Playboy Squadron - Arch Whitehouse 6710

Poor Boy and a Long Way Home - James Sherburne 5806

Prima Donna at Large - Barbara Paul 4838

Pursuit of Bliss - Betty Palmer Nelson 4577

The Race: A Novel of Polar Exploration - Kare Holt 3008

Ragtime - E.L. Doctorow 1658

The Rainbow Runner - John Cunningham 1450

Rasputin's Revenge - John T. Lescroart 3725

The Ravi Lancers - John Masters 4178

Rebels: The Irish Rising of 1916 - Peter DeRosa 1622

Regeneration - Pat Barker 309

Remember This Time - Gloria Kurian Broder 703

A Rendezvous in Haiti - Stephen Becker 407

The Return of Henry Starr - Richard Slotkin 5909

The Rising of the Moon - William Martin 4140

Rivington Street - Meredith Tax 6175

Sabrina - Madeleine Polland 5086

A Sailor of Austria - John Biggins 492

Saints and Scholars - Terrence Eagleton 1821

Sarah Cobb - Catherine M. Rae 5236

The Scapegoat - Mary Lee Settle 5758

The Scorching Wind - Walter Macken 3988

Searching for the Emperor - Roberto Pazzi 4858

The Secret of Saramount - Lillian Cheatham 1011

Sergeant Gringo - Jack Cummings 1449

Seven Days to Petrograd - Tom Hyman 3094

The Seventh Bullet - Daniel D. Victor 6483

Shadow Catcher - Charles Fergus 2064

The Shadow of the Moth: A Novel of Espionage with Virginia Woolf - Ellen Hawkes 2779

Shadows over Castle Rising - Fanny Cradock 1410

The Shakespeare Girl - Mollie Hardwick 2698

The Shooting Party - Isabel Colegate 1197

Shout at the Devil - Wilbur Smith 5930

Silver Fruit - Patricia Campbell 876

The Sky and Tomorrow - Thomas William Duncan 1788

The Snow Mountain - Catherine Gavin 2324

Son of Holmes - John T. Lescroart 3726

South of the Border - John Byrne Cooke 1268

Spinners' Wharf - Iris Gower 2502

Spy's Honour - Gavin Lyall 3929

Squadron Forty-Four - Arch Whitehouse 6711

Squadron Shilling - Arch Whitehouse 6712

Statues in a Garden - Isabel Colegate 1198

Strange Meeting - Susan Hill 2952

The Summer Day Is Done - R.T. Stevens 6001

The Summer of the Bashinskeys - Diane Pearson 4877

Tempting Fate - Chelsea Quinn Yarbro 6906

Ten Years Beyond Baker Street - Cay Van Ash 6400

That's Me in the Middle - Donald Jack 3129

This Sweet and Bitter Earth - Alexander Cordell 1326

Three Cheers for Me - Donald Jack 3131

Thy Tears Might Cease - Michael Farrell 2018

Tigerlilies - Judith Glover 2439

Time After Time - Allen Appel 171

A Time for Silence - Philippa Carr 930

The Tin Lizzie Troup - Glendon Swarthout 6146

To the Honor of the Fleet - Robert H. Pilpel 5002

A Token of Jewels - Diane Cory 1353

Tom Mix and Pancho Villa - Clifford Irving 3113

Troubles - J.G. Farrell 2017

The Two-Headed Eagle - John Biggins 493

"Utmost Fish!" - Hugh Wray McCann 4219

Verge of Glory - Frederick Wight 6747

Victim of the Aurora - Thomas Keneally 3417

Wandering Star - Steven Yount 6945

War Comes to Castle Rising - Fanny Cradock 1411

War Story: A Novel - Derek Robinson 5404

The War Train: A Novel of 1916 - Brown Meggs 4324

When the Legends Die - Hal Borland 584

While Paris Danced - Patricia Wright 6886

White Nights, Red Dawn - Frederick Nolan 4634

The White Rhino Hotel - Bartle Bull 765

Wind of Change at Castle Rising - Fanny Cradock 1412

Winds of Blame - Jane Gilmore Rushing 5532

The Wingless Bird - Catherine Cookson 1292

Wings for the Chariots - Arch Whitehouse 6713

The Wishing Tree - Sandra Paretti 4794

The Women at Pine Creek - Allis McKay 4279

Words by Heart - Ouida Sebestyen 5713

Young Adolf - Beryl Bainbridge 272

The Young Men of Paris - Stephen Longstreet 3893

Young Mrs. Cavendish and the Kaiser's Men - K.K. Beck 405

Zoya - Danielle Steel 5985

1920s

Agatha - Kathleen Tynan 6374

The Alfred Hitchcock Murder Case - George Baxt 382

The Ashes of Smyrna - Richard Reinhardt 5294

The Aviator - Ernest K. Gann 2277

Behold the Fire - Michael Blankfort 541

Beyond the Aegean - Elia Kazan 3382

Black Gold - Anita Richmond Bunkley 771

The Blood Order - Jack D. Hunter 3084

The Bridge of a Hundred Dragons - Emma Drummond 1723

A Castle in Bavaria - Prince Thibaut d'Orleans 1693

The Challenging Heights - Max Hennessy 2831

Chariots of Fire - W.J. Weatherby 6586

A Chorus of Detectives - Barbara Paul 4835

Contessa - Richard Oliver Collin 1209

The Dangerous Years - Max Hennessy 2833

Dead-Stick - L.J. Washburn 6574

Death in a Deck Chair - K.K. Beck 403

The Devil in Velvet - John Dickson Carr 909

Devoted Friends - Joe Poyer 5161

Dog Heavies - L.J. Washburn 6575

The Dorothy Parker Murder Case - George Baxt 384

The Dream Lover - Mark Upton 6392

Eleanor: A Novel - Rhoda Lerman 3724

The Eleventh Year - Monique Raphel High 2914

The End of the Hunt - Thomas Flanagan 2119

Fallen Skies - Philippa Gregory 2581

The False Inspector Dew - Peter Lovesey 3912

Fiddler's Ferry - Iris Gower 2499

Fifteen Flags - Richard Lynden Hardman 2686

Fire in the Ice - Alan Scholefield 5653

Flickers - Phillip Rock 5419

The Friends of Pancho Villa - James Carlos Blake 535

Gerontius - James Hamilton-Paterson 2672

The Ghosts of Elkhorn - Kerry Newcomb 4589

The Golden Sabre - Jon Cleary 1105

Gone the Rainbow, Gone the Dove - Joan Bagnel 264

Grand Days - Frank Moorhouse 4448

The Grass Kingdom - Jory Sherman 5818

The Green Leaves of Summer - Ted Willis 6793

Hammett: A Novel - Joseph N. Gores 2487

High Road to China - Jon Cleary   1106

Hollywood: A Novel of America in the 1920s - Gore Vidal   6488

Homeward Bound - Elizabeth Walter   6557

Honour and Obey - Malcolm Macdonald   3966

The Hours of Light - Janet Tanner   6160

The House of Eliott - Jean Marsh   4100

The House of Memory: A Novel of Shanghai - Nicholas R. Clifford   1117

The House of War - Catherine Gavin   2322

In Pale Battalions - Robert Goddard   2444

In the Blue Light of African Dreams - Paul Watkins   6580

In the Shadow of the Nile - Sara Hylton   3093

It's Me Again - Donald Jack   3126

Keystone - Peter Lovesey   3913

The Land Endures - Mary E. Pearce   4862

Legs - William Kennedy   3422

A Letter of Mary - Laurie R. King   3488

Little Sister - Margaret Gaan   2259

Loving Little Egypt - Thomas McMahon   4288

Magic Flutes - Eva Ibbotson   3097

Mark - Lonnie Coleman   1205

Me So Far - Donald Jack   3127

Me Too - Donald Jack   3128

The Midwife's Advice - Gay Courter   1389

Miss Lizzie - Walter Satterthwait   5608

A Monstrous Regiment of Women - Laurie R. King   3489

Morgan's Woman - Iris Gower   2500

My Beloved Son - Catherine Cookson   1285

Nevermore - William Hjortsberg   2958

No Man's Land - William Fairchild   2004

No Price Too High - Madeleine Polland   5085

One Last Glimpse - James Aldridge   74

Our Father's House - Stephen Longstreet   3890

The Passing Bells - Phillip Rock   5421

The Passion of Sacco and Vanzetti: A New England Legend - Howard Fast   2040

Peril under the Palms - K.K. Beck   404

Pretty Boy Floyd - Larry McMurtry   4299

A Princess in Berlin - Arthur R.G. Solmssen   5939

The Promise of Light - Paul Watkins   6581

A Revolutionary Woman - Sheila Fugard   2248

Say to This Mountain - Bodie Thoene   6226

The Scorching Wind - Walter Macken   3988

Sherlock in Love - Sena Jeter Naslund   4557

Some Far Elusive Dawn - Emma Drummond   1727

The Talking Pictures Murder Case - George Baxt   388

Tempting Fate - Chelsea Quinn Yarbro   6906

That Vanderbilt Woman - Philip Van Rensselaer   6427

This One's on Me - Donald Jack   3130

A Thousand Shall Fall - Bodie Thoene   6227

Thy Tears Might Cease - Michael Farrell   2018

Time and Chance - Anna Wibberley   6728

The Unplowed Sky - Jeanne Williams   6783

The Warlord - Malcolm Bosse   589

The Wedding Guest - Anna Gilbert   2407

Weedy Rough - Douglas C. Jones   3286

While the Music Lasts - Suzanne Goodwin   2477

Whiskey River - Loren D. Estleman   1981

The White Rhino Hotel - Bartle Bull   765

Wind of Change at Castle Rising - Fanny Cradock   1412

The Wingless Bird - Catherine Cookson   1292

1930s

The Age of Wonders - Aharon Appelfeld   173

The Alfred Hitchcock Murder Case - George Baxt   382

And the Desert Shall Bloom - Phyllis Barber   299

Back to Battle - Max Hennessy   2828

Badenheim 1939 - Aharon Appelfeld   174

Bayou City Secrets - Deborah Powell   5146

The Bette Davis Murder Case - George Baxt   383

Billy Bathgate - E.L. Doctorow   1656

The Black Mask Murderers - William F. Nolan   4635

The Blood Order - Jack D. Hunter   3084

Born of War - Thomas Taylor   6192

Byron: A Novel - Sigrid Combuchen   1225

The Caravaggio Shawl - Samuel M. Steward   6019

The Career of Magda V. - Joseph Machlis   3982

The Crossing - Cormac McCarthy   4221

The Cup of Wrath - Mary Glazener   2429

Dance on a Sinking Ship - Michael Kilian   3483

Danzig Passage - Bodie Thoene   6221

The Dark City - Max Allan Collins   1211

Death Squad London - Jack Gerson   2360

Desperadoes - Ron Hansen   2681

Destiny Express - Howard A. Rodman   5423

Dillinger - Harry Patterson   4832

A Distant Thunder - Teresa de Luca   1561

Eagles at War - Walter J. Boyne   620

Eating Pavlova - D.M. Thomas   6235

English Creek - Ivan Doig   1683

English Music - Peter Ackroyd   18

Exit Sherlock Holmes - Robert Lee Hall   2657

A Few Good Men - William Overgard   4768

A First Class Murder - Elliott Roosevelt   5442

Flanagan's Run - Tom McNab   4303

A Future Arrived - Phillip Rock   5420

La Guerra: A Spanish Saga - Stephen D. Frances   2199

The Hallelujah Flight - Jack Lynn   3937

The Healer - Aharon Appelfeld   176

The Horse Hunters - Robert Newton Peck   4887

The Hyde Park Murder - Elliott Roosevelt   5443

Jerusalem Interlude - Bodie Thoene   6223

Joy in Mudville - Gordon McAlpine   4216

Katerina - Aharon Appelfeld   177

The Last Innocent Hour - Margot Abbott   8

Legs - William Kennedy   3422

The Longest Road - Jeanne Williams   6781

Loon Lake - E.L. Doctorow   1657

Lovelock - James McNeish   4311

Mad Dog - Jack Kelly   3401

The Mae West Murder Case - George Baxt   386

The Man Who Missed the Party - Harold Adams   25

Mark - Lonnie Coleman   1205

The Marrying Kind - Jessica Stirling   6046

Munich Signature - Bodie Thoene   6224

Murder and the First Lady - Elliott Roosevelt   5444

Murder at San Simeon - Robert Lee Hall   2660

Murder by the Numbers - Max Allan Collins   1212

Murder in the Executive Mansion - Elliott Roosevelt   5449

Murder in the Oval Office - Elliott Roosevelt   5450

Murder in the Red Room - Elliott Roosevelt   5451

Murder in the Rose Garden - Elliott Roosevelt   5452

Murder in the West Wing - Elliott Roosevelt   5453

Murder Is Murder Is Murder - Samuel M. Steward   6020

The Murder of Lawrence of Arabia - Matthew Eden   1865

My Beloved Son - Catherine Cookson   1285

New Deal for Death - Elliott Roosevelt   5454

The Noel Coward Murder Case - George Baxt   387

The Normandie Affair - Elizabeth Villars   6497

Once More the Hawks - Max Hennessy   2836

Organized Crime - Nicholas Von Hoffman   6511

The Pale Criminal - Philip Kerr   3471

The Penny Wedding - Jessica Stirling   6047

Perchance to Dream - Robert B. Parker   4807

Piccadilly - Claire Rayner   5267

The Plot to Kill Wallis Simpson: A Work of Faction - Graham Fisher   2104

Prague Counterpoint - Bodie Thoene   6225

The President's Man - Elliott Roosevelt   5455

Pretty Boy Floyd - Larry McMurtry   4299

The Retreat - Aharon Appelfeld   178

Rommel and the Rebel - Lawrence Wells   6622

Saint Mudd - Steve Thayer   6218

Say to This Mountain - Bodie Thoene   6226

Schindler's List - Thomas Keneally   3416

Scotch on the Rocks - Howard Browne   733

Second Generation - Howard Fast   2043

Secret Dreams - Keith Korman   3541

Seedtime and Harvest - Mary E. Pearce   4864

Shanghai Tango: A Novel of China - William Overgard   4769

The Skeleton in the Grass - Robert Barnard   320

Stolen Away - Max Allan Collins   1213

The Stuff of Heroes - Miguel Delibes   1592

The Tent of Orange Mist - Paul West   6636

That Vanderbilt Woman - Philip Van Rensselaer   6427

To the Land of the Cattails - Aharon Appelfeld   179

Tomorrow Is Another Day - Stuart M. Kaminsky   3348

Torsos - John Peyton Cooke   1270

True Crime - Max Allan Collins   1214

True Detective - Max Allan Collins   1215

Vienna Prelude - Bodie Thoene   6228

Walter Winchell: A Novel - Michael Herr   2863

Warsaw Requiem - Bodie Thoene   6229

Wartime Lies - Louis Begley   416

Weedy Rough - Douglas C. Jones   3286

While England Sleeps - David Leavitt   3702

While the Music Lasts - Suzanne Goodwin   2477

Whiskey River - Loren D. Estleman   1981

The White Dove - Rosie Thomas   6246

The William Powell and Myrna Loy Murder Case - George Baxt   390

The Winds of War - Herman Wouk   6876

The Wisdom of Stones - Greg Matthews   4192

World's Fair - E.L. Doctorow   1661

1940s

Artemesia - Anna Banti   295

Back to Battle - Max Hennessy   2828

Beginning the World Again - Roberta Silman   5851

Born of War - Thomas Taylor   6192

Bullet for a Star - Stuart M. Kaminsky   3331

Buried Caesars - Stuart M. Kaminsky   3332

The Career of Magda V. - Joseph Machlis   3982

Carnal Hours - Max Allan Collins   1210

Catch a Falling Star - Stuart M. Kaminsky   3333

The Cup of Wrath - Mary Glazener   2429

Dancing in the Dark - Stuart M. Kaminsky   3334

The Day of the Scorpion - Paul Scott   5682

The Devil Met a Lady - Stuart M. Kaminsky   3335

A Distant Thunder - Teresa de Luca   1561

A Division of the Spoils - Paul Scott   5683

Down for the Count - Stuart M. Kaminsky   3336

Eagles at War - Walter J. Boyne   620

The Establishment - Howard Fast   2030

Eva - Ib Melchior   4329

The Exile of Celine - Tom Clark   1095

The Fala Factor - Stuart M. Kaminsky   3337

A Family Matter - James Roosevelt   5458

Fielder's Choice - Rick Norman   4646

For Every Sin - Aharon Appelfeld   175

A Future Arrived - Phillip Rock   5420

A Gathering of Saints - Christopher Hyde   3092

The Greta Garbo Murder Case - George Baxt   385

The Hangman's Crusade - James Barwick   370

He Done Her Wrong - Stuart M. Kaminsky   3338

High Midnight - Stuart M. Kaminsky   3339

Hitler Has Won - Frederic Mullally   4511

The Howard Hughes Affair - Stuart M. Kaminsky   3340

The Iron Curtain - Robert Vaughan   6447

The Jewel in the Crown - Paul Scott   5684

Katerina - Aharon Appelfeld   177

The King - Donald Barthelme   365

The Last Innocent Hour - Margot Abbott   8

Last Man to Die - Michael Dobbs   1652

The Longest Road - Jeanne Williams   6781

Lovelock - James McNeish   4311

Luciano's Luck - Jack Higgins   2912

The Man on the Train - W.J. Chaput   995

The Man Who Shot Lewis Vance - Stuart M. Kaminsky   3341

Masters of Illusion: A Novel of the Connecticut Circus Fire - Mary-Ann Tirone Smith   5925

The Melting Clock - Stuart M. Kaminsky   3342
Murder at the Palace - Elliott Roosevelt   5445
Murder in the Blue Room - Elliott Roosevelt   5446
Murder in the Chateau - Elliott Roosevelt   5447
Murder in the East Room - Elliott Roosevelt   5448
Murder on the Yellow Brick Road - Stuart M.
   Kaminsky   3343
Never Cross a Vampire - Stuart M. Kaminsky   3344
Nine Hours to Rama - Stanley Wolpert   6846
The Normandie Affair - Elizabeth Villars   6497
Once More the Hawks - Max Hennessy   2836
The Only Thing to Fear - David Poyer   5160
Outlander - Diana Gabaldon   2264
Poor Butterfly - Stuart M. Kaminsky   3345
Rommel and the Rebel - Lawrence Wells   6622
A Royal Murder - Elliott Roosevelt   5456
Schindler's List - Thomas Keneally   3416
Second Generation - Howard Fast   2043
Seedtime and Harvest - Mary E. Pearce   4864
Shadow of the Wolf - James Barwick   371
Smart Moves - Stuart M. Kaminsky   3346
Stallion Gate - Martin Cruz Smith   5924
Think Fast, Mr. Peters - Stuart M. Kaminsky   3347
Till the End of Time - Allen Appel   170
Tomorrow Is Another Day - Stuart M.
   Kaminsky   3348
The Towers of Silence - Paul Scott   5685
Tzili: The Story of a Life - Aharon Appelfeld   180
The Veracruz Blues - Mark Winegardner   6821
The Very Rich Hours of Count von Stauffenberg - Paul
   West   6637
Walter Winchell: A Novel - Michael Herr   2863
War and Remembrance - Herman Wouk   6875
Wartime Lies - Louis Begley   416
The White House Pantry Murder - Elliott
   Roosevelt   5457
The Winds of War - Herman Wouk   6876
Winter Fire - William R. Trotter   6352

The Wisdom of Stones - Greg Matthews   4192
The Year of Our War - Gloria Goldreich   2462
You Bet Your Life - Stuart M. Kaminsky   3349

1950s
Cold War - Robert Vaughan   6446
The Daughter of Time - Josephine Tey   6209
The Establishment - Howard Fast   2030
The Exile of Celine - Tom Clark   1095
The Lattimer Legend - Ann Hebson   2813
Papa and Fidel - Karl Alexander   79
The Tallulah Bankhead Murder Case - George
   Baxt   389
A Whisper on the Wind - Madeline Baker   276

1960s
Curse of Magira - David Bee   413
Dragonfly in Amber - Diana Gabaldon   2262
Flying into Love - D.M. Thomas   6236
For the Love of Robert E. Lee - M.A. Harper   2715
Green Darkness - Anya Seton   5751
The Immortals - Michael Korda   3540
The Legacy - Howard Fast   2037
Libra - Don DeLillo   1593
Papa and Fidel - Karl Alexander   79
Voyager - Diana Gabaldon   2265

1970s
The Buckingham Palace Connection - Ted
   Willis   6792
The Executioner's Song - Norman Mailer   4036
Foreign Devils - Irvin Faust   2053
Gentleman Traitor - Alan Williams   6763
The Immigrant's Daughter - Howard Fast   2035
Memories of the Ford Administration - John
   Updike   6391
Patriot's Dream - Barbara Michaels   4360
Time After Time - Karl Alexander   80
Twice upon a Time - Allen Appel   172

1980s
Called Away - Perdita Buchan   753
The Centurion - Jan de Hartog   2762
The House of Memory: A Novel of Shanghai -
   Nicholas R. Clifford   1117
The Immigrant's Daughter - Howard Fast   2035
The King's Commissar - Duncan Kyle   3570
A Knight in Shining Armor - Jude Deveraux   1631
Ride with Me, Mariah Montana - Ivan Doig   1684
Till the End of Time - Allen Appel   170

1990s
Anna's Book - Barbara Vine   6500
Bay of Arrows - Jay Parini   4800
Di and I - Peter Lefcourt   3714
Live From Golgotha - Gore Vidal   6491
Miss Nobody - Caroline Ross   5465
Morning's Gate - Ann Victoria Roberts   5371
Riding Shotgun - Rita Mae Brown   729

21st CENTURY

Arc d'X - Steve Erickson   1953

2020s
Frankenstein Unbound - Brian Aldiss   68

25th CENTURY

The Golden Nineties - Lisa Mason   4166

26th CENTURY

The Lincoln Hunters - Wilson Tucker   6359

INDETERMINATE

The Queen and I - Sue Townsend   6306

Geographic Index

This index provides access to all featured books by their geographic settings, including oceans, continents, and countries, both contemporary and historic. The American Colonies, Canada, North America, and the United States are subdivided by region, state, or province. Locations are further broken down by city or region. Book titles are listed alphabetically, and include author names and entry numbers.

AFGHANISTAN

The Far Pavilions - M.M. Kaye 3376
Horses of Heaven - Gillian Bradshaw 630
Irene at Large - Carole Nelson Douglas 1700
The Lotus and the Wind - John Masters 4175
Stormswift - Madeleine Brent 662

Kabul
Beyond All Frontiers - Emma Drummond 1722
Flashman - George MacDonald Fraser 2204

Kawarja
The Gates of Kunara - Duncan MacNeil 4014

AFRICA

The African - Harold Courlander 1386
Agotime, Her Legend - Judith Gleason 2430
American Captain - Edison Marshall 4101
Anthony Adverse - Hervey Allen 98
Badge of Glory - Douglas E. Reeman 5287
Burton and Speke - William Harrison 2751
The Captive - Victoria Holt 3011
The Dragon of the Ishtar Gate - L. Sprague De Camp 1555
Drum - Kyle Onstott 4744
Fairoaks - Frank Yerby 6915
The Final Adversary - Gilbert Morris 4460
For God and Glory - Tim Jeal 3171
For My Great Folly - Thomas B. Costain 1365
Freedom, Farewell - Phyllis Bentley 461
The Ghosts of Africa - William Stevenson 6013
The Golden Wind - C.L. Grace 2507
The Great Sky and the Silence - James S. Rand 5245
Harvest of the Sun - E.V. Thompson 6265
Isle of Woman - Piers Anthony 167
Leo Africanus - Amin Maalouf 3947
Lydia Bailey - Kenneth Roberts 5387
Murfy's Men - Gerald Green 2565
Once More the Hawks - Max Hennessy 2836
The Pope's Rhinoceros - Lawrence Norfolk 4642
Queen Victoria's Bomb - Ronald Clark 1094
The Restless Flame - Louis De Wohl 1573
Rommel and the Rebel - Lawrence Wells 6622
Savage Prodigal - Konrad Bercovici 474
Shout at the Devil - Wilbur Smith 5930
Slave - William Malliol 4041
The Slave Ship - Mary Johnston 3240
Soldier of the Queen - Max Hennessy 2837
The Taverners' Place - Joanna Trollope 6351
Three's Company - Alfred Duggan 1774

Trail and Triumph: A Novel about Maimonides - Lester M. Morrison 4485
The Viceroy of Ouidah - Bruce C. Chatwin 1009
The View From Coyaba - Peter Abrahams 11
The Wanderer - Mika Waltari 6556
The Whales in Lake Tanganyika - Lennart Hagerfors 2636
Yellowstone Kelly - Peter Bowen 602

Barbary Coast
Baton Sinister - Carl J. Spinatelli 5967
The Glittering Strand - Judith Lennox-Smith 3716
Isobelle - Mary Lide 3775
The Pyrates - George MacDonald Fraser 2212
The Salem Frigate - John Edward Jennings 3205
The Sea and the Sand - Christopher Nicole 4621
Yankee Pasha - Edison Marshall 4115

Congo
Lord of the Kongo - Peter Forbath 2155

Congo River
The Last Hero - Peter Forbath 2154

Gold Coast
The Sun Is My Undoing - Marguerite Steen 5988

Hippo
Son of Tears - Henry W. Coray 1320

Isandhlwana
The Tune That They Play - William Clive 1120

Kalahari Desert
The Eagles of Malice - Alan Scholefield 5652

Lake Tanganyika
"Utmost Fish!" - Hugh Wray McCann 4219

Niger River
Water Music - T. Coraghessan Boyle 619

Numidia
The First Man in Rome - Colleen McCullough 4234

Sahara Desert
Isobelle - Mary Lide 3775

Segu
The Children of Segu - Maryse Conde 1232

Tripoli
Harp of a Thousand Strings - Harold Lenoir Davis 1522
The Sea Panther: A Novel about the Commander of the U.S.S. Constitution - Philip Vail 6397
Written in Sand - Josephine Case 950

Zululand
Great Elephant - Alan Scholefield 5654
Wizards' Country - Daphne Rooke 5438

ALBANIA

Scutari
Bedford Row - Claire Rayner 5259

ALGERIA

The Death and Life of Miguel De Cervantes - Stephen Marlowe 4094
Under Two Flags - Ouida 4767

Algiers
The Black Cockade - Victor Suthren 6127
The Free Frenchman - Piers Paul Read 5277

AMERICAN COLONIES

Bear His Mild Yoke - Ethel White 6675
The Bellerose Bargain - Robyn Carr 934
The Doom Trail - Arthur Douglas Smith 5917
The Firelands - Karen Harper 2712
Gallant Captain - Pearl Frye 2242
Give Me Your Golden Hand - Evelyn Eaton 1825
His Was the Fire - Showell Styles 6104
In the Days of Poor Richard - Irving A. Bacheller 259
Inherit the Earth - Margaret Shaw 5778
The King's Messenger - Samuel Edwards 1887
Lord Johnnie - Leslie Turner White 6687
The Master of Chaos - Irving A. Bacheller 262
Mistress Devon - Virginia Coffman 1156
Moonfeather - Judith E. French 2223
Northwest Passage - Kenneth Roberts 5388
Old Glory - Christopher Nicole 4618
A Pirate's Pleasure - Heather Graham 2518
Renown - Frank Olney Hough 3045
Salute to Adventurers - John Buchan 752
Treason - Robert Gessner 2389
Tristram Bent - Henry Barnard Safford 5560
Two Crowns for America - Katherine Kurtz 3568

Carolinas
Always a River - Drayton Mayrant 4211
Deepwater: A Novel of the Carolinas - Pamela Jekel 3185
Love's Tender Fury - Jennifer Wilde 6749
Rogue's Holiday - Hamilton Cochran 1141

Connecticut Valley
Three Sides of Agiochook - Eric Kelly   3400
White Indian - Donald Clayton Porter   5134

Goldsboro
Angelique and the Demon - Sergeanne Golon   2466

New Amsterdam
Blessed Is the Land - Louis Zara   6949
The Drowning Room - Michael Kenneth Pye   5212
The Dutchman - Maan Meyers   4351

CONNECTICUT

The Winthrop Woman - Anya Seton   5754
Yankee Trader - Stanley Morton   4496

New Haven
Until the Winds - Jean Clark   1089

Saybrook
*Valley in Arms: A Novel of the Settlement of
   Connecticut* - Earl Schenck Miers   4376

Wetherfield
*Valley in Arms: A Novel of the Settlement of
   Connecticut* - Earl Schenck Miers   4376

Wish-ton-Wish
The Wept of Wish-Ton-Wish - James Fenimore
   Cooper   1312

DELAWARE

Land of the Beautiful River - Helmer
   Linderholm   3788
The Rival Shores - Arthur Beverly-Giddings   487
The Silver Saber - Carter A. Vaughan   6441

Wilmington
Yankee Rogue - Dana Fuller Ross   5496

GEORGIA

Flight of the Crow - Paul Clayton   1103
The Holy Lover - Marie Oemler   4690
MacLyon - Lolah Burford   773
*Ram: Being the Tale of One Ramillies Anstruther -
   Winchombe Taylor   6193
Take Her, Mr. Wesley - John W. Drakeford   1719

St. Simons Island
Dark Sails - Helen Topping Miller   4388

Savannah
Rascal's Heaven - F. van Wyck Mason   4157
Summer Thunder - Willie Snow Ethridge   1982
Trumpet in the Sky - Helen Topping Miller   4397

MARYLAND

Margaret Brent, Adventurer - Dorothy Grant   2533
Mary's Land - Lucia St. Clair Robson   5415
The Power and the Passion - Christina
   Nicholson   4609
Richard Carvel - Winston Churchill   1081
The Rival Shores - Arthur Beverly-Giddings   487

Chesapeake Bay
The Sot-Weed Factor - John Barth   364

MASSACHUSETTS

Always a River - Drayton Mayrant   4211
Ashes in the Wilderness - William Greenough
   Schofield   5649
Cardigan - Robert W. Chambers   976
Israel Potter - Herman Melville   4334
The King's Iron - Robert Newton Peck   4888
The Mists of Manittoo - Lois Swann   6135
Song of a Strange Child - Gilbert Morris   4470

Stately Timber - Rupert Hughes   3075
Torn Covenants - Lois Swann   6136
The Warrior's Path - Louis L'Amour   3633
White Rising - Zane Kotker   3548

Boston
Arthur Dimmesdale - Charles R. Larson   3671
The Bastard - John Jakes   3144
Be My Love - Harriet Hinsdale   2955
The Braintree Mission - Nicholas E. Wyckoff   6887
A Candle in the Wilderness - Irving A.
   Bacheller   256
Concord Bridge - Howard Horne   3035
Covenant of Grace - Jane Gilmore Rushing   5527
For Love of Two Eagles - Barbara Riefe   5328
Freedom's Dues - Robert H. Abel   9
The Gentle Rebel - Gilbert Morris   4461
Gilman of the Redford - William Stearns Davis   1541
The Greater Hunger - Barbara Dodge Borland   581
Guns for Rebellion - F. van Wyck Mason   4151
Hester - Christopher Bigsby   496
The Highwayman - Noel B. Gerson   2372
Hope Leslie; or, Early Times in Massachusetts -
   Catharine Maria Sedgewick   5714
The Indentured Heart - Gilbert Morris   4464
The Invincibles - Carter A. Vaughan   6436
The Latter Adventures of Tom Jones - Bob
   Coleman   1200
Lionel Lincoln; or, The Leaguer of Boston - James
   Fenimore Cooper   1303
Log Cabin Noble - F. van Wyck Mason   4153
The Long Naked Descent into Boston - William
   Eastlake   1823
The Maddest Idea - James L. Nelson   4580
Patriot's Progress - Joseph G.E. Hopkins   3027
Pearl - Christopher Bigsby   497
Rebel Guns - Adam Rutledge   5539
The Road to Bunker Hill - Shirley Barker   316
The Rogue and the Witch - John Edward
   Newton   4605
The Sachem - Donald Clayton Porter   5124
The Scarlet Letter - Nathaniel Hawthorne   2786
Seneca - Donald Clayton Porter   5127
Sergeant Lamb's America - Robert Graves   2552
The Silver Oar - Howard Breslin   669
Silver Shoals - Hamilton Cochran   1142
Sons of Liberty - Adam Rutledge   5540
Sound of the Trumpet - Gilbert Morris   4471
Three Harbors - F. van Wyck Mason   4162
A Toast to the King - Elizabeth Coatsworth   1139
Uncharted Ways - Caroline Snedeker   5935
Valiant Libertine - John Gordon Bryson   748
*Valley in Arms: A Novel of the Settlement of
   Connecticut* - Earl Schenck Miers   4376
The Willing Maid - C.T. Ritchie   5349
The Winthrop Woman - Anya Seton   5754
Witnesses - Marcy Moran Heidish   2820
The Yankee Brig - Carter A. Vaughan   6443
Yankee Doodle Dandy - Noel B. Gerson   2387
Young Titan - F. van Wyck Mason   4165

Canaan
Paradise - Esther Forbes   2158

Cape Cod
The Land Is Bright - Noel B. Gerson   2376
Tomorrow the New Moon - Shirley Barker   319

Concord
April Morning - Howard Fast   2027
Concord Bridge - Howard Horne   3035
Patriot's Progress - Joseph G.E. Hopkins   3027

Deerfield
The Cold Journey - Grace Zaring Stone   6052

Gruel
*Look to Your Geese: A Novel of the Deflowering of
   New England* - Jacquin Sanders   5584

Haverhill
Gallant Warrior - Helen R. Mann   4063

Lexington
April Morning - Howard Fast   2027
The Gentle Rebel - Gilbert Morris   4461
Lionel Lincoln; or, The Leaguer of Boston - James
   Fenimore Cooper   1303

Marshfield
Harvest of Dreams - Jaroldeen Edwards   1884

Martha's Vineyard
Tomorrow the New Moon - Shirley Barker   319

Merry Mount
The Disturber - L.S. Davidson Jr.   1505

Nantucket
Nantucket Rebel - Edouard A. Stackpole   5970
Nantucket Woman - Diana Gaines   2269

Newburyport
The Road to Bunker Hill - Shirley Barker   316

Northampton
Freedom's Dues - Robert H. Abel   9
The Indentured Heart - Gilbert Morris   4464
To Fame Unknown - Clifford Lindsey Alderman   67

Plymouth
The Bondswoman - Caryl Ledner   3705
The Captive Bride - Gilbert Morris   4457
Daughter of Satan - Jean Plaidy   5011
The Disturber - L.S. Davidson Jr.   1505
The Honorable Imposter - Gilbert Morris   4463
The Land Is Bright - Noel B. Gerson   2376
Legacy - Robert Vaughan   6448
O Western Wind - John Anthony Devon   1634
Pilgrims: A Novel of the Mayflower - Gerard
   Mac   3955
The Plymouth Adventure - Ernest Gebler   2342
Thanksgiving - Terry Coleman   1207
The Wickedest Pilgrim - Donald Barr Chidsey   1067

Salem
Blossom Like the Rose - Norah Lofts   3836
The Captive Bride - Gilbert Morris   4457
Come Home at Even - Le Grand Cannon   884
A Dangerous Innocence - Victoria Lincoln   3787
The Devil and the Mathers - Edward E. Elliott   1914
Gallows Hill - Frances Winwar   6831
The Greater Hunger - Barbara Dodge Borland   581
I Seek a City - Gilbert Rees   5289
I, Tituba, Black Witch of Salem - Maryse
   Conde   1233
In Adam's Fall - Constance Dodge   1666
A Mirror for Witches - Esther Forbes   2157
The Navigator: The Story of Nathaniel Bowditch -
   Alfred Stanford   5979
Peace, My Daughters - Shirley Barker   314
Road to Lendor - Esther Hammon   1966
The Rogue and the Witch - John Edward
   Newton   4605

Springfield
Hope Leslie; or, Early Times in Massachusetts -
   Catharine Maria Sedgewick   5714
Renno - Donald Clayton Porter   5123
White Indian - Donald Clayton Porter   5134

Stockbridge
The Measure of the Years - Alice Mary Colver   1218
The Prospering - Elizabeth Speare   5954
There Is a Season - Alice Mary Colver   1219

Wendham
Patriot's Progress - Joseph G.E. Hopkins   3027

NEW ENGLAND

The Bride of the Wilderness - Charles McCarry   4220
Love Not a Rebel - Heather Graham   2516

Milton in America - Peter Ackroyd 20
The Renegade - Donald Clayton Porter 5122
War Chief - Donald Clayton Porter 5130
The Wilderness - Carter A. Vaughan 6442
Young Titan - F. van Wyck Mason 4165

NEW HAMPSHIRE

The Governor's Lady - Thomas H. Raddall 5228
Look to the Mountain - Le Grand Cannon 885
Next to Valour - John Edward Jennings 3202
The Strange Death of Mistress Coffin - Robert J.
    Begiebing 415
That Bennington Mob - Henry Barnard Safford 5558

Boon Island
Boon Island - Kenneth Roberts 5384

Portsmouth
Boon Island - Kenneth Roberts 5384
The Last Gentleman - Shirley Barker 312
Rivers Parting - Shirley Barker 315

NEW JERSEY

Liberty Tavern - Thomas Fleming 2129
Seneca - Donald Clayton Porter 5127

Monmouth
The Drums of Monmouth - Emma Gelders
    Sterne 5998

Morristown
Let My Name Stand Fair - Shirley Seifert 5727

Trenton
The Unvanquished - Howard Fast 2046

NEW YORK

Ambush - Donald Clayton Porter 5113
Bloodbrothers - Robert E. Wall 6535
The Bright Battalions - Howard Breslin 664
Brother Owl - Al Hine 2953
Cardigan - Robert W. Chambers 976
Drums Against Frontenac - Harvey Chalmers 972
The Drums of Monmouth - Emma Gelders
    Sterne 5998
For Love of Two Eagles - Barbara Riefe 5328
Ghost Fox - James Houston 3051
The Governor's Daughter - Denton Whitson 6718
In the Hands of the Senecas - Walter D.
    Edmonds 1876
The Interpreter - Robert Moss 4499
The King's Iron - Robert Newton Peck 4888
Lily of the Mohawks - Jack Casey 952
Mohawk Woman - Barbara Riefe 5329
Night of Decision: A Novel of Colonial New York -
    Dorothy Grant 2534
Red Cloak Flying - Margaret Widdemer 6737
Reluctant Rebel - Frederic F. Van de Water 6403
Renno - Donald Clayton Porter 5123
Seneca - Donald Clayton Porter 5127
Spanish Bayonet - Stephen Vincent Benet 441
That Bennington Mob - Henry Barnard Safford 5558
Thunder in the East - Mike Roarke 5362
War Cry - Donald Clayton Porter 5132
War in the Golden Weather - Stephen
    Longstreet 3892
War Paint and Rouge - Robert W. Chambers 983
West to the Setting Sun - Harvey Chalmers 973
Wilderness Empire - Allen W. Eckert 1847
The Wilderness War - Allen W. Eckert 1848
The Woman Who Fell From the Sky - Barbara
    Riefe 5330

Albany
Buckskin Baronet - Margaret Widdemer 6734
Catherwood - Marly Youmans 6937
Eagle Fur - Robert Newton Peck 4884

Fort Ticonderoga
Fawn - Robert Newton Peck 4885
The Gentle Rebel - Gilbert Morris 4461
The Green Mountain Boys - Daniel Pierce
    Thompson 6249
Hang for Treason - Robert Newton Peck 4886
Rebel Guns - Adam Rutledge 5539
Song of a Strange Child - Gilbert Morris 4470

Hudson River
Forever Possess - Alexandra Phillips 4982

Hudson River Valley
The Marriage Bed - Jean Clark 1088
The Perilous Night - Burke Boyce 609

Lake George
His Majesty's Highlanders - Leslie Turner
    White 6683
The Last of the Mohicans - James Fenimore
    Cooper 1302

Lake Otsego
The Deerslayer - James Fenimore Cooper 1299

Long Island Sound
The Water Witch - James Fenimore Cooper 1311

Mohawk Valley
The Conqueror - John William Tebbel 6194
Drums Along the Mohawk - Walter D.
    Edmonds 1874
Eden's Gate - Karen Harper 2711
Fire Along the Sky: A Novel of America - Robert
    Moss 4497
The Firekeeper - Robert Moss 4498
The King's Rebel - James David Horan 3030
Lady of the Mohawks - Margaret Widdemer 6736
White Indian - Donald Clayton Porter 5134

New York
Anna Zenger: Mother of Freedom - Kent
    Cooper 1316
Brother to the Enemy - Bart Spicer 5964
A Candle in the Wilderness - Irving A.
    Bacheller 256
The Day Before Thunder - Bart Spicer 5965
The Dutchman's Dilemma - Maan Meyers 4352
The Imposter - Noel B. Gerson 2375
The Legion of the Lost - Donald Barr Chidsey 1062
The Master of Ballantrae: A Winter's Tale - Robert
    Louis Stevenson 6011
Richard Pryne: A Novel of the American Revolution -
    Cyril Harris 2718
The Savage City - Jean Paradise 4787
Scoundrels' Brigade - Carter A. Vaughan 6439
Seasons of Fear - Philip McFarland 4272
Thanksgiving - Terry Coleman 1207
The Unvanquished - Howard Fast 2046
The Water Witch - James Fenimore Cooper 1311

Onondagas
Savage Gentleman - Noel B. Gerson 2381

Oswego
The Golden Wildcat - Margaret Widdemer 6735
The Pathfinder; or, The Inland Sea - James Fenimore
    Cooper 1305

Schenectady
Savage Gentleman - Noel B. Gerson 2381

Staten Island
Three Fields to Cross - Francis Tysen Nutt 4651

Thousand Islands
The Pathfinder; or, The Inland Sea - James Fenimore
    Cooper 1305

Ticonderoga
Guns for Rebellion - F. van Wyck Mason 4151
Sergeant Lamb's America - Robert Graves 2552
The White Cockade - Vincent O'Brien 4683

NORTH CAROLINA

Carolina Corsair - Don Tracy 6307
The Dark Stranger - Constance Dodge 1664
Horseshoe Robinson, a Tale of the Tory Ascendancy -
    John P. Kennedy 3418
Meggy MacIntosh - Elizabeth Janet Gray 2555
Roanoke Warrior - Carter A. Vaughan 6438
Scarlet Cockerel - Clifford Sublette 6110
The Scotswoman - Inglis Fletcher 2140
The Wind in the Forest - Inglis Fletcher 2143

Albemarle County
Bennett's Welcome - Inglis Fletcher 2132

Cape Fear
Drums of Autumn - Diana Gabaldon 2263
Lusty Wind for Carolina - Inglis Fletcher 2134
Weathercock - Constance Dodge 1668

Edenton
Cormorant's Brood - Inglis Fletcher 2133

Queen Anne's Town
Men of Albemarle - Inglis Fletcher 2135

Roanoke Island
Croatan - Mary Johnston 3231
The Lost Colony - Edison Marshall 4108
Roanoke Hundred - Inglis Fletcher 2138
Roanoke Renegade - Don Tracy 6311

NORTHEAST

The Warrior's Path - Louis L'Amour 3633

PENNSYLVANIA

*Boone: A Novel Based on the Life and Times of Daniel
    Boone* - Cameron Judd 3311
The First Rebel - Neil Harmon Swanson 6137
The Forest and the Fort - Hervey Allen 100
Free Man - Conrad Richter 5320
Gennie the Huguenot Woman - Bette M. Ross 5464
A High Wind Rising - Elsie Singmaster 5867
The Interpreter - Robert Moss 4499
Jason McGee - Robert H. Fowler 2190
Land for My Sons - Maribelle Cormack 1331
The Light in the Forest - Conrad Richter 5322
The Long Sun - Janice Lucas 3920
One Red Rose Forever - Mildred A. Jordan 3305
The Peaceable Kingdom - Jan de Hartog 2763
The Redemptioner - Isaac Rusling Pennypacker 4910
The Silent Drum - Neil Harmon Swanson 6141
Song of the Susquehanna - Herbert Stover 6071
Toward the Morning - Hervey Allen 101
The Unconquered - Neil Harmon Swanson 6142
The Woodsman - Don Wright 6880

Allegheny Mountains
O Beulah Land - Mary Lee Settle 5756

Bedford
Bedford Village - Hervey Allen 99

Fort Pitt
The Judas Tree - Neil Harmon Swanson 6139
Strife Before Dawn - Mary Schumann 5675

Juniata Valley
Juniata Valley - Virginia C. Cassel 954

Philadelphia
Abigail - Mary Louise Aswell 221
Charming Sally - Maude Hart Lovelace 3903
The Devil and Ben Franklin - Theodore
    Mathieson 4184
Edge of Greatness - Winthrop Neilson 4575
Nantucket Woman - Diana Gaines 2269
The Seneca Hostage - Carter A. Vaughan 6440

Pittsburgh
Fortress Fury - Carter A. Vaughan 6435

RHODE ISLAND

Ashes in the Wilderness - William Greenough
 Schofield 5649
Ask No Quarter - George Tracy Marsh 4099
Captain Adam - Donald Barr Chidsey 1058
I Seek a City - Gilbert Rees 5289
Proud Heritage - Ilse Bishcoff 510
Scoundrels' Brigade - Carter A. Vaughan 6439

Block Island
Let My Name Stand Fair - Shirley Seifert 5727

Newport
Strange Wives - Shirley Barker 317

SOUTH CAROLINA

The Changeling - Alison Macleod 4000
The Fires of July - Sharon Salvato 5576
Hilton Head - Josephine Pinckney 5003
Horseshoe Robinson, a Tale of the Tory Ascendancy -
 John P. Kennedy 3418
The Swamp Fox, Francis Marion - Noel B.
 Gerson 2383
The Yemassee - William Gilmore Simms 5855

Beaufort
Nobody's Angel - Karen Robards 5363

Charleston
Anne Bonny - Chloe Gartner 2306
The Big Drum - Elizabeth Boatwright Coker 1162
Dark Possession - Alice Alison Lide 3771
The Double Man - Elinor Pryor 5205
The Fallon Blood - Reagan O'Neal 4741
The Forest Lord - Noel B. Gerson 2368
Let My Name Stand Fair - Shirley Seifert 5727
There Is a Season - Alice Mary Colver 1219
Three Harbors - F. van Wyck Mason 4162
Wind From the Main - Anne Osborne 4759

VERMONT

The Green Mountain Boys - Daniel Pierce
 Thompson 6249
Hang for Treason - Robert Newton Peck 4886
Wings of the Morning - Frederic F. Van de
 Water 6404

Bennington
Reluctant Rebel - Frederic F. Van de Water 6403
That Bennington Mob - Henry Barnard Safford 5558

VIRGINIA

Ambush - Donald Clayton Porter 5113
Audrey - Mary Johnston 3229
Charming Sally - Maude Hart Lovelace 3903
Christopher Humble - Charles Burnet Judah 3310
Devil Water - Anya Seton 5749
Erskine Dale, Pioneer - John Fox 2195
Follow the River - James Alexander Thom 6231
Gentleman Ranker - John Edward Jennings 3200
Give Me Liberty: The Story of an Innocent Man - John
 Erskine 1956
The Golden Feather - Theda Kenyon 3462
Man Cannot Tell - Philip Lightfoot Scruggs 5711
Morning of a Hero - Burke Boyce 608
Never No More: The Story of Rebecca Boone - Shirley
 Seifert 5730
Now Face to Face - Karleen Koen 3530
A Place Called Freedom - Ken Follett 2150
Prince Charlie's Bluff - Donald Thomas 6241
Prisoners of Hope: A Tale of Colonial Virginia - Mary
 Johnston 3238
The Rival Shores - Arthur Beverly-Giddings 487

Sackett's Land - Louis L'Amour 3628
The Slave Ship - Mary Johnston 3240
Sound of the Trumpet - Gilbert Morris 4471
Stately Timber - Rupert Hughes 3075
Tavern in the Town - Cecile Hulse Matschat 4187
To Have and to Hold - Mary Johnston 3241
War Chief - Donald Clayton Porter 5130
War Cry - Donald Clayton Porter 5132
War in the Golden Weather - Stephen
 Longstreet 3892
Wilderness Adventure - Elizabeth Page 4774
The Young Man From Mount Vernon - Arthur
 Stanwood Pier 4995

Henrico County
The Bright Face of Danger - Clifford Sublette 6108

James River
Bennett's Welcome - Inglis Fletcher 2132
Storm Against the Wind - Helen Hull Jacobs 3138
To the Far Blue Mountains - Louis L'Amour 3630

Jamestown
Daughter of Eve - Noel B. Gerson 2366
A Durable Fire - Virginia Bernhard 480
*Forest Cavalier: A Romance of America's First
 Frontier and of Bacon's Rebellion* - Roy Catesby
 Flannagan 2122
The King's Passenger - Nathan Schachner 5631
The Land Beyond the Tempest - Drayton
 Mayrant 4213
Lovestorm - Judith E. French 2222
Pocahontas - Susan Donnell 1691
Pocahontas; or, The Nonparell of Virginia - David
 Garnett 2297
Powhatan's Daughter - John Clarke Bowman 605
The Sea 'Venture - F. van Wyck Mason 4159
Soldier in Paradise - Burton Wohl 6835

Mount Vernon
The Indentured Heart - Gilbert Morris 4464

Norfolk
Three Harbors - F. van Wyck Mason 4162

Shenandoah Valley
The Great Valley - Mary Johnston 3234

Williamsburg
Gamble's Hundred - Clifford Dowdey 1705
Turn of the Dice - Janet Edmonds 1870
The Virginia Comedians - John Esten Cooke 1269

Yorktown
Sarah Camberwell Tring - Janet Edmonds 1869

ANCIENT CIVILIZATION

Carthage
The Arrows of Hercules - L. Sprague De Camp 1553
The Coin of Carthage - Bryher 740
Count Belisarius - Robert Graves 2544
Dido, Queen of Hearts - Gertrude Atherton 223
Hannibal - Ross Leckie 3704
Hannibal of Carthage - Mary Dolan 1686
*The Purple Quest: A Novel of Seafaring Adventure in
 the Ancient World* - Frank G. Slaughter 5896
Salammbo - Gustave Flaubert 2123
Son of Tears - Henry W. Coray 1320

Kush
Moses, Prince of Egypt - Howard Fast 2039

Moab
Ruth - Irving Fineman 2089

Syracuse
The Arrows of Hercules - L. Sprague De Camp 1553
The Mask of Apollo - Mary Renault 5300

Troy
The Firebrand - Marion Zimmer Bradley 624

Fires in the Sky - Phillip Parotti 4816
The Goddess - Miranda Seymour 5763
The Greek Generals Talk: Memoirs of the Trojan War
 - Phillip Parotti 4817
The Invaders - Peter Danielson 1469
Paris of Troy - George Baker 273
The Promised Land - Peter Danielson 1471
Scandal in Troy - Eva Hemmer Hansen 2679
The Shattered Horse - S.P. Somtow 5945
The Trojan - Noel B. Gerson 2386
The Trojan Generals Talk: Memoirs of the Greek War
 - Phillip Parotti 4818
Troy - Richard Matturro 4194
Whom the Gods Would Destroy - Richard
 Powell 5148

ANGOLA

Lord of Darkness - Robert Silverberg 5854

ANTARCTICA

The Birthday Boys - Beryl Bainbridge 269
The Race: A Novel of Polar Exploration - Kare
 Holt 3008
Victim of the Aurora - Thomas Keneally 3417

ANTIGUA-BARBUDA

Caribee - Christopher Nicole 4614
The Devil's Own - Christopher Nicole 4615
Honor This Day - Alexander Kent 3432
Ramage's Mutiny - Dudley Pope 5106

ARABIA

The Big Fisherman - Lloyd C. Douglas 1702
Blood and Sand - Rosemary Sutcliff 6121
The Gospel of Corax - Paul Park 4802
The Voice of Allah - Edwin P. Hoyt 3062

ARCTIC

The Balloonist - Macdonald Harris 2724
Call of the Arctic - Robert Steelman 5987
The Flight of the Eagle - Per Olof Sundman 6119
North-West by South - Nancy Cato 962
The Rifles - William T. Vollmann 6510
The Undiscovered Country - Jay Walz 6560

ARGENTINA

The Color of Blood - E. Ralph Rundell 5524
Don Gaucho - Alyce Pollock 5088

Buenos Aires
Young Vargas Lewis - Robert Brainard Pearsall 4874

Patagonia
The Moon Stallion - Jim Berry 484

ASIA

Caravan to China - Frank Stanley Stuart 6085
Caravan to Kanadu: A Novel of Marco Polo - Edison
 Marshall 4103
The Challenging Heights - Max Hennessy 2831
Children of the Ice - Charlotte Prentiss 5166
The Corn King and the Spring Queen - Naomi
 Mitchison 4419
Flashman at the Charge - George MacDonald
 Fraser 2209
Master of the World - Cothburn O'Neal 4738
Orlok - Don Dandrea 1461
People of the Wolf - W. Michael Gear 2341
A Private Revenge - Richard Woodman 6863

The Seeking - Robert S. Elegant   1906
Sons of the Steppe: The Story of How the Conqueror Genghis Khan Was Overcome - Hans Baumann   380
Throne of the World - Louis De Wohl   1575
Until the Sun Falls - Cecelia Holland   2998
The Walking Drum - Louis L'Amour   3632
The White Rajah - Nicholas Monsarrat   4433
The Year of the Horsetails - R.F. Tapsell   6162

Bactria
Horses of Heaven - Gillian Bradshaw   630

The Silk Road
Empire of the Eagle - Andre Norton   4649

ASIA MINOR

Alexander of Macedon: The Journey to World's End - Harold Lamb   3607
Captain Vinegar's Commission - Philip Glazebrook   2428
The Death of the Gods - Dmitri Merezhkovski   4338
The Hittite - Noel B. Gerson   2373
The Idol Hunter - Barry Unsworth   6386
The Lady for Ransom - Alfred Duggan   1768
The Long Ships - Frans Gunnar Bengtsson   442
Shards of Empire - Susan Schwartz   5677
The Soothsayer - Laurene Chinn   1069
Their Most Serene Majesties - Ange Vlachos   6505

Mysia
Fires in the Sky - Phillip Parotti   4816

Trebizond
The Burnished Blade - Lawrence Schoonover   5661

AT SEA

1492 - Mary Johnston   3228
Abigail - Joan Druett   1721
Admiral Hornblower in the West Indies - C.S. Forester   2169
The Adventures of Long John Silver - Denis Judd   3317
Agotime, Her Legend - Judith Gleason   2430
An Air of Glory - Sarah Neilan   4563
Angelique in Love - Sergeanne Golon   2470
Annie's Captain - Kathryn Hulme   3077
Apprentice to the Sea - Philip McCutchan   4240
The Argonauts - Yvonne Schoell   5645
Armada - Charles Gidley   2404
Attack the Lusitania! - Raymond Hitchcock   2956
An Autumn in Araby - Carola Salisbury   5565
Back to Battle - Max Hennessy   2828
Before the Wind - Lloyd M. Moxon   4506
Beware, Beware the Bight of Benin - Philip McCutchan   4241
Blind Journey - Bruce Lancaster   3636
Brendan - Frederick Buechner   762
Broadsides - Robert Welter Daly   1459
Buller's Dreadnought - Richard Hough   3047
Buller's Guns - Richard Hough   3048
Buller's Victory - Richard Hough   3049
Caleb Pettengill U.S.N. - George Fielding Eliot   1912
Captain Caution - Kenneth Roberts   5385
Captain of the Sands - Keith Dewhurst   1636
Captain Paul - Edward Ellsberg   1930
Carolina Corsair - Don Tracy   6307
Charco Harbour - Godfrey Blunden   554
Clear for Action! - Noel B. Gerson   2362
Close Quarters - William Golding   2453
Columbus: A Romance - Rafael Sabatini   5549
The Commodore - Patrick O'Brian   4661
Commodore Hornblower - C.S. Forester   2172
The Dangerous Years - Max Hennessy   2833
Darken Ship - Nicholas Monsarrat   4431
Dead Reckoning - C. Northcote Parkinson   4809
Departure - Janet Stevenson   6004

The Edge of Piracy - Donald Barr Chidsey   1060
Fire Down Below - William Golding   2454
The Fireship - C. Northcote Parkinson   4811
Five Black Ships: A Novel of Discoverers - Napoleon Baccino Ponce de Leon   5089
Fleet Surgeon to Pharaoh - Sheldon Jacobson   3140
For King and Company - Ellis K. Meacham   4314
For Love of a Pirate - Anthony Esler   1961
For My Great Folly - Thomas B. Costain   1365
The Fortress - Catherine Gavin   2320
The Fortune of War - Patrick O'Brian   4664
Fourth King - Norbert Coulehan   1373
The Frigate Captain - Showell Styles   6103
Gallant Captain - Pearl Frye   2242
A Game for Empires - Pearl Frye   2243
The Golden Ocean - Patrick O'Brian   4665
Governor Ramage, R.N. - Dudley Pope   5096
Halfhyde and the Fleet Review - Philip McCutchan   4246
Halfhyde for the Queen - Philip McCutchan   4247
Halfhyde to the Narrows - Philip McCutchan   4253
The Harp and the Shadow - Alejo Carpentier   905
Hate - Arthur Douglas Smith   5918
He Brings Great News - Clemence Dane   1462
Her Majesty's Captain - Derek Wilson   6797
A High Wind in Jamaica - Richard Hughes   3074
H.M.S. Cockerel - Dewey Lambdin   3611
Hornblower During the Crisis - C.S. Forester   2177
The Ionian Mission - Patrick O'Brian   4667
Iron Ships, Iron Men - Christopher Nicole   4616
Jemmy Button - Benjamin Subercaseaux   6107
Jewel of the Sea - Ellen Argo   185
Jewel of the Sea - Susan Wiggs   6743
The King's Coat - Dewey Lambdin   3612
The Lady and the Deep Blue Sea - Garland Roark   5356
The Last Mutiny: The Further Adventures of Captain Bligh - Bill Collett   1208
The Legion of the Lost - Donald Barr Chidsey   1062
The Life and Times of Horatio Hornblower - C. Northcote Parkinson   4813
The Lion at Sea - Max Hennessy   2834
The Long Fight - D.A. Rayner   5270
The Maddest Idea - James L. Nelson   4580
The Magnificent Savages - Fred Mustard Stewart   6024
Magnus the Magnificent - Leslie Turner White   6688
Manila Galleon - F. van Wyck Mason   4154
Matthew Early - Alexander Laing   3589
The Mauritius Command - Patrick O'Brian   4670
Men Against the Sea - Charles Nordhoff   4638
The Men That God Forgot - Richard Butler   829
Mister Christian - William Kinsolving   3502
Murfy's Men - Gerald Green   2565
The Nelson Touch - Paul Lewis   3759
The New England Story - Henry Beetle Hough   3046
North to Thule: An Imagined Narrative of the Famous ''Lost'' Voyage of Pytheas of Massalla in the Fourth Century B.C. - John Frye   2241
Old Glory - Christopher Nicole   4618
Paradise - Dikkon Eberhart   1831
Post Captain - Patrick O'Brian   4672
The Raiders: A Novel of the Civil War at Sea - Willard Wallace   6541
Rainbow in the Royals - Garland Roark   5357
Ramage's Prize - Dudley Pope   5107
The Red Rover - James Fenimore Cooper   1309
Restless Voyage - Stanley David Porteus   5138
The Reverse of the Medal - Patrick O'Brian   4673
The Revolutionary - Lawrence Schoonover   5667
Rites of Passage - William Golding   2456
Rogue's Holiday - Hamilton Cochran   1141
Running Proud - Nicholas Monsarrat   4432
The Sable Lion - Jan Van Dorp   6405
Sacred Hunter - Barry Unsworth   6389
A Sailor of Austria - John Biggins   492
The Saintly Buccaneer - Gilbert Morris   4469
The Sea and the Sand - Christopher Nicole   4621
The Sea Eagles - John Edward Jennings   3206

Sea Jade - Phyllis A. Whitney   6717
Sea of Darkness - Roland Huntford   3086
The Sea Officer - Showell Styles   6105
The Sea Stands Watch - Helen Parker Mudgett   4507
The Sleeping Sword: A Biographical Novel - Pearl Frye   2244
So Near So Far - C. Northcote Parkinson   4814
Spirit Knife - Donald Clayton Porter   5128
The Sunken Treasure - Marian J.A. Jackson   3136
The Surgeon's Mate - Patrick O'Brian   4674
That Skipper From Stonington - Theda Kenyon   3464
The Thirteen Gun Salute - Patrick O'Brian   4675
To the Ends of the Earth - Michael Talbot   6155
The Triton Brig - Dudley Pope   5110
The Truelove - Patrick O'Brian   4677
The Voyage of the Destiny - Robert Nye   4657
Wind of Destiny - Christopher Nicole   4624
The Wine-Dark Sea - Patrick O'Brian   4679
Wolfshead - Jere Hungerford Wheelwright   6672
The Yellow Admiral - Patrick O'Brian   4680

Achates
Success to the Brave - Alexander Kent   3441

Adamant
Mutiny Run - Frank Eccles   1836

Adroit
First Lieutenant - Kenneth Maynard   4208

Alacrity
The Gun Ketch - Dewey Lambdin   3610

Amistad
Amistad: The Thunder of Freedom - David Pesci   4944
Echo of Lions - Barbara Chase-Riboud   1004

Antigone
1805 - Richard Woodman   6857
Baltic Mission - Richard Woodman   6859
Decision at Trafalgar - Richard Woodman   6861

Apollo
The Forest Lord - Noel B. Gerson   2368

Argo
Hercules, My Shipmate - Robert Graves   2545

Argus
Jonathan Dearborn: A Novel of the War of 1812 - Willard Wallace   6540

Atalanta
Voyage: A Novel of 1896 - Sterling Hayden   2798

Athena
Royal Yankee - Victor Suthren   6132

Atropos
Hornblower and the Atropos - C.S. Forester   2175

Avenger
Clear for Action! - Simon White   6699
The English Captain - Simon White   6700

Aysgarth Falls
Outward Bound - Philip McCutchan   4256

Banshee
The Dram Tree - Hamilton Cochran   1140

Beagle
The Origin - Irving Stone   6060

Bedford Lass
Storm Tide - Allan R. Bosworth   590

Benbow
The Inshore Squadron - Alexander Kent   3434

Black Duchess
The Black Duchess - Alanna Knight   3514

Bonhomme Richard
Clear for Action: A Novel about John Paul Jones - Clements Ripley 5344
Don't Tread on Me - Walter Karig 3366
Drums - James Boyd 611
Sailor Named Jones - Harvey Haislip 2643

Bounty
Adams of the Bounty - Erle Wilson 6807
H.M.S. Bounty - Alexander McKee 4280
Mr. Christian! - Stanley Miller 4402
Mutiny on the Bounty - Charles Nordhoff 4639

Calypso
Ramage and the Rebels - Dudley Pope 5100
Ramage and the Saracens - Dudley Pope 5101
Ramage at Trafalgar - Dudley Pope 5102
The Ramage Touch - Dudley Pope 5103
Ramage's Mutiny - Dudley Pope 5106
Ramage's Signal - Dudley Pope 5108
Ramage's Trial - Dudley Pope 5109

Catherine
The Catherine - Robert S. MacDonald 3980

Charles Beauchamp
The Closest Possible Union - Joanna Scott 5680

Constitution
The Sea Panther: A Novel about the Commander of the U.S.S. Constitution - Philip Vail 6397

Crystal Star
The Crystal Star - Ellen Argo 184
The Yankee Girl - Ellen Argo 186

Dauphine
Pawn in Frankincense - Dorothy Dunnett 1804

Delaware
The Captain From Connecticut - C.S. Forester 2171

Desire
Captain for Elizabeth - Jan Westcott 6643

Desperate
The French Admiral - Dewey Lambdin 3609

Destiny
Stand into Danger - Alexander Kent 3440

Diana
The Golden Galleon - Victor Suthren 6129

Dido
Ramage and the Dido - Dudley Pope 5098

Dolphin
Dolphin Summer - Carola Salisbury 5569

Echo
The Black Cockade - Victor Suthren 6127
In Perilous Seas - Victor Suthren 6130
A King's Ransom - Victor Suthren 6131

Essex
The Jonah Man - Henry Carlisle 895
The Salem Frigate - John Edward Jennings 3205

Euryalus
The Flag Captain - Alexander Kent 3430

Flying Star
Masts to Spear the Stars - Stephen Longstreet 3889

Gladiator
Harpoon in Eden - F. van Wyck Mason 4152

Glen Halladake
Halfhyde and the Chain Gang - Philip McCutchan 4244

Globe
Captain Marooner - Louis B. Davidson 1504

Gorgon
Richard Bolitho—Midshipman - Alexander Kent 3437

Halcyon
Halfhyde and the Flag Captain - Philip McCutchan 4245

Happy Parrot
The Happy Parrot - Robert W. Chambers 977

Helicon
Colors Aloft! - Alexander Kent 3427

Heron
Lamb in Command - Kenneth Maynard 4209

Hotspur
Hornblower and the Hotspur - C.S. Forester 2176

Huntress
Hazard of Huntress - Vivian Stuart 6087
Victory at Sebastopol - Vivian Stuart 6091

Hyperion
Enemy in Sight! - Alexander Kent 3429
Form Line of Battle! - Alexander Kent 3431

Indefatigable
Mr. Midshipman Hornblower - C.S. Forester 2180

Indomitable
Billy Budd - Herman Melville 4333

Irenia
Death in a Deck Chair - K.K. Beck 403

Jester
A King's Commander - Dewey Lambdin 3613

Judea
By Force of Arms - James L. Nelson 4579

Juno
Ramage's Diamond - Dudley Pope 5105

Karachi
Homeward Bound - Elizabeth Walter 6557

Kestrel
The Flight of the Kestrel - Margaret Abbey 3

Laurentia
The Last Farewell - Philip McCutchan 4255

Lee
Seek Out and Destroy - James David Horan 3031

Leopard
Desolation Island - Patrick O'Brian 4662

Lively Lady
The Lively Lady - Kenneth Roberts 5386

Lusitania
Lusitania - David Butler 819

Lydia
Beat to Quarters - C.S. Forester 2170

Lysander
Signal—Close Action! - Alexander Kent 3438

Mauretania
The False Inspector Dew - Peter Lovesey 3912

Mayflower
The Honorable Imposter - Gilbert Morris 4463
The Land Is Bright - Noel B. Gerson 2376
Pilgrims: A Novel of the Mayflower - Gerard Mac 3955
The Plymouth Adventure - Ernest Gebler 2342
The Wickedest Pilgrim - Donald Barr Chidsey 1067

Melusine
Arctic Treachery - Richard Woodman 6858

Meridian
Halfhyde Ordered South - Philip McCutchan 4252

La Mouette
Frenchman's Creek - Daphne Du Maurier 1744

Neptune's Car
Voyage: A Novel of 1896 - Sterling Hayden 2798

New York
No Honeymoon for Death - Mary Kruger 3564

Normandie
A First Class Murder - Elliott Roosevelt 5442
The Normandie Affair - Elizabeth Villars 6497

Ocean Mistress
The Ocean Mistress - Peter French 2225

Orvega
The Second Mate - Philip McCutchan 4257

Osprey
The Fallon Pride - Reagan O'Neal 4742

Ouzel
The Golden Coast - Philip Rooney 5441

Pallas
Captain Monsoon - Victor Suthren 6128

Patrician
In Distant Waters - Richard Woodman 6862
A Private Revenge - Richard Woodman 6863

Pegasus
Soldier of the Sea - Robert Welter Daly 1460

Phalarope
To Glory We Steer - Alexander Kent 3442

Pinta
The Velvet Doublet - James H. Street 6082

Primrose
Golden Admiral - F. van Wyck Mason 4150

Prince Consort
The Guns of Arrest - Philip McCutchan 4242

Princess
Sea Road to Yorktown - Harvey Haislip 2644

Queen's Own
On the Midnight Tide - Don Tracy 6310

Rapid
The East Indiaman - Ellis K. Meacham 4313
On the Company's Service - Ellis K. Meacham 4315

Regenerate
Mutiny - Frank Tilsley 6280

Renown
Lieutenant Hornblower - C.S. Forester 2178

Resolution
The Last Voyage: Captain Cook's Lost Diary - Hammond Innes 3108
The Return of Lono: A Novel of Captain Cook's Last Voyage - Oswald Andrew Bushnell 816

Santa Maria
Mercedes of Castile - James Fenimore Cooper 1304

Sarah Diamond
The Sinking of the Sarah Diamond - William Dale Jennings 3213

Sea Venture
The Land Beyond the Tempest - Drayton Mayrant 4213

Seal
The Last of the Vikings - Johan Bojer 563

The Shark
Letter of Marque - Andrew Hepburn 2849

Shrike
The King's Commission - Dewey Lambdin   3614

Silenos
Wyvern - A.A. Attanasio   227

Somers
Voyage to the First of December - Henry Carlisle   897

Sophie
Master and Commander - Patrick O'Brian   4669

Sophronia
Tide-Rode - Adelyn Bushnell   813

Southern Cross
The Southern Cross - Peter French   2226

Sparrow
Sloop of War - Alexander Kent   3439

Speranza
Speranza - Sven Delblanc   1584

Sturdy
Lieutenant Lamb - Kenneth Maynard   4210

Styx
A Tradition of Victory - Alexander Kent   3443

Surprise
The Far Side of the World - Patrick O'Brian   4663
H.M.S. Surprise - Patrick O'Brian   4666
The Letter of Marque - Patrick O'Brian   4668
Treason's Harbour - Patrick O'Brian   4676

Susan Constant
Soldiers of Fortune - Peter Bourne   595

Sutherland
Ship of the Line - C.S. Forester   2182

Taronga Park
Halfhyde and the Admiral - Philip McCutchan   4243
The Halfhyde Line - Philip McCutchan   4249
Halfhyde on the Amazon - Philip McCutchan   4250

Telesto
The King's Privateer - Dewey Lambdin   3615

Tempest
Passage to Mutiny - Alexander Kent   3436

Titanic
Every Man for Himself - Beryl Bainbridge   270
From Time to Time - Jack Finney   2092
Maiden Voyage - Cynthia Bass   372
Over There - Robert Vaughan   6449

Trojan
Brave Captains - Vivian Stuart   6086
Hazard's Command - Vivian Stuart   6088
In Gallant Company - Alexander Kent   3433
The Valiant Sailors - Vivian Stuart   6090

Undine
Command a King's Ship - Alexander Kent   3428

Venture
Beauvallet - Georgette Heyer   2876

Viceroy
Halfhyde's Island - Philip McCutchan   4254

Victrix
The Running of the Tide - Esther Forbes   2160

Virago
The Bomb Vessel - Richard Woodman   6860

Vixen
The Prize Master - Harvey Haislip   2642

Wager
The Unknown Shore - Patrick O'Brian   4678

The Wanderer
Sail the Dark Tide - Davenport Steward   6017

Wayward Girl
The Sea Beggars - Cecelia Holland   2996

Western Star
Benjamin Blake - Edison Marshall   4102

Wilhelmina
Dance on a Sinking Ship - Michael Kilian   3483

William Scoresby Sr.
The Greenlander - Mark Adlard   38

AUSTRALIA

1915: A Novel - Roger McDonald   4264
Beyond the Blue Mountains - Jean Plaidy   5006
Charco Harbour - Godfrey Blunden   554
The Colonists - William Stuart Long   3870
Dream Time - Parris Afton Bonds   570
The Explorers - William Stuart Long   3872
The Feather and the Stone - Patricia Shaw   5780
Fortune, Smile Once More - Mary Floyd Williams   6788
The Gallant - William Stuart Long   3873
The Gold Seekers - William Stuart Long   3874
Harry: A Novel of Australia - Robert Wales   6530
I Know My Love - Catherine Gaskin   2315
The Imperialists - William Stuart Long   3875
Midsummer's Eve - Philippa Carr   924
Morning's Gate - Ann Victoria Roberts   5371
My Love Must Wait: The Story of Matthew Flinders - Ernestine Hill   2922
The Nationalists - William Stuart Long   3876
The Only Sin - Julie Ellis   1923
Oscar and Lucinda - Peter Carey   894
The Pagoda Tree - Berkely Mather   4181
The Pool of St. Branok - Philippa Carr   926
The Quade Inheritance - Barbara Ker Wilson   3469
The Seafarers - William Stuart Long   3877
The Settlers - William Stuart Long   3878
Stand We at Last - Zoe Fairbairns   1999
Storm of Time - Eleanor Dark   1494
Voss - Patrick White   6698

Blue Mountains
The Ladies of Missalonghi - Colleen McCullough   4237

Botany Bay
Botany Bay - Charles Nordhoff   4637
To the Ends of the Earth - Michael Talbot   6155
A Wilful Woman - Michael Talbot   6156

Breelong
The Chant of Jimmie Blacksmith - Thomas Keneally   3411

Darwin
The Wisdom of Stones - Greg Matthews   4192

Kempsey
A River Town - Thomas Keneally   3415

Melbourne
The Dreaming: A Novel of Australia - Barbara Wood   6848

New South Wales
And the Wild Birds Sing - Lola Irish   3112
The Chant of Jimmie Blacksmith - Thomas Keneally   3411
The Emancipist: An Unforgettable Epic of Australia - Veronica Geoghegan Sweeney   6147
The Last Mutiny: The Further Adventures of Captain Bligh - Bill Collett   1208
The Nutmeg of Consolation - Patrick O'Brian   4671
The Playmaker - Thomas Keneally   3414
Sara Dane - Catherine Gaskin   2316
The Vines of Yarrabee - Dorothy Eden   1864

Outback
Inherit the Sun - Maxwell Grant   2539

Queensland
Cry of the Rain Bird - Patricia Shaw   5779
The Heart of the Continent - Nancy Cato   961
Where the Willows Weep - Patricia Shaw   5781

Sarah's Island
The Men That God Forgot - Richard Butler   829

Sydney
The Adventurers - William Stuart Long   3869
Antipodes Jane: A Novel of Jane Austen in Australia - Barbara Ker Wilson   3468
Passage to Mutiny - Alexander Kent   3436
Southern Cross - Terry Coleman   1206
The Timeless Land - Eleanor Dark   1495
The Traitors - William Stuart Long   3879

Tasmania
The Emancipist: An Unforgettable Epic of Australia - Veronica Geoghegan Sweeney   6147
Forefathers - Nancy Cato   960
North-West by South - Nancy Cato   962
Pageant - G.B. Lancaster   3650
Swandowne - Daniel Farson   2024
Wild Orchid - Isabel Dick   1640

AUSTRIA

The Age of Wonders - Aharon Appelfeld   173
Badenheim 1939 - Aharon Appelfeld   174
The Battle of Wagram - Gilles Lapouge   3664
A Chance for Glory - Constance Wright   6877
Danzig Passage - Bodie Thoene   6221
The Emperor Franz Joseph - Ottokar Janetschek   3164
The Emperor's Coloured Coat - John Biggins   491
Evermore - Barbara Steward   6014
Far Flies the Eagle - Evelyn Anthony   162
Felding Castle - Edith De Born   1552
The Gentle Fury: A Novel of Margaret of Austria - Paul Lewis   3758
The Golden Knight - George Challis   971
Imperial Waltz - William M. Abrahams   13
Munich Signature - Bodie Thoene   6224
Napoleon and His Son - Pierre Nezelof   4607
Reigning Passions - Kathrin Perutz   4940
The Retreat - Aharon Appelfeld   178
Sacred and Profane: A Novel of the Life and Times of Mozart - David Weiss   6609
Sweet Marie-Antoinette - Lozania Prole   5198
Tempting Fate - Chelsea Quinn Yarbro   6906
The Thousand Fires - Anne Powers   5155
The Time of Murder at Mayerling - Ann Dukthas   1778
To the Land of the Cattails - Aharon Appelfeld   179

Carinthian Mountains
Castle of Eagles - Constance Heaven   2804
The Healer - Aharon Appelfeld   176

Innsbruck
The Flight - Ruth Walgreen Stephan   5994

Salzburg
The Assassination of Mozart - David Weiss   6604

Tyrol
The Ugly Duchess - Lion Feuchtwanger   2075

Vienna
The Angel with the Trumpet - Ernst Lothar   3898
Anna, Ann, Annie - Thomas Trebitsch Parker   4808
The Archduke - Michael Arnold   194
Arrogance - Joanna Scott   5679
The Assassination of Mozart - David Weiss   6604
Before the Glory Ended - Ursula Zilinsky   6963
The Brocken - Pamela Hill   2929
The Cannaways - Graham Shelby   5789

The Career of Magda V. - Joseph Machlis   3982
Cassy - Elizabeth Lyle   3930
A Castle in Bavaria - Prince Thibaut d'Orleans   1693
Castle of Eagles - Constance Heaven   2804
The Castle of the Winds - Jeanne Montague   4434
Consuelo - George Sand   5582
The Crown Prince - John Barchilon   300
The Cry and the Covenant - Morton Thompson   6269
Deep in My Heart: A Story Based on the Life of Sigmund Romberg - Elliott Arnold   192
The Devil's Lieutenant - Maria Fagyas   1998
Edward, Edward - Lolah Burford   772
The End of the World News - Anthony Burgess   777
Eroica: A Novel about Beethoven - Carl von Pidoll   4994
Fata Morgana - William Kotzwinkle   3549
Feast of the Jesters - Manuel Komroff   3533
For They Shall Inherit - Malcolm Macdonald   3964
The Golden Quill: A Novel Based on the Life of Mozart - Bernard Grun   2605
The Healer - Aharon Appelfeld   176
The Healers - Henry Denker   1610
Henry James' Midnight Song - Carol de Chellis Hill   2920
Herzl the King - Norman Kotker   3547
Jenny and Barnum: A Novel of Love - Roderick Thorp   6276
Letty - Clare Darcy   1491
Lustre in the Sky - R.G. Waldeck   6525
Madensky Square - Eva Ibbotson   3096
Magic Flutes - Eva Ibbotson   3097
The Man Who Thought He Was Messiah - Curt Leviant   3735
Minna's Story: The Secret Love of Doctor Sigmund Freud - Kathleen Daniels   1463
Monday's Child - Mollie Hardwick   2697
Music for God - Theresa Weiser   6603
Nephew to the Emperor: A Novel Based on the Life of Beethoven - Jacques Brenner   658
The Passions of the Mind - Irving Stone   6062
The Queen's Confession - Victoria Holt   3019
Rakossy - Cecelia Holland   2995
Red Plush: The Story of the Moorhouse Family - Guy McCrone   4232
Serpent and Staff - Frank Yerby   6927
The Seven-Per-Cent Solution - Nicholas Meyer   4349
The Strange Case of Madamoiselle P. - Patrick Ireland   3109
Theirs Was the Kingdom - R.F. Delderfield   1590
Vienna Prelude - Bodie Thoene   6228
When Nietzsche Wept: A Novel of Obsession - Irvin D. Yalom   6892
The White Hotel - D.M. Thomas   6237
Winter of the Heart - Linda J. LaRosa   3665
The World as I Found It - Bruce Duffy   1755

BABYLON

Alexander in Babylon - Jakob Wassermann   6576
The Assyrian - Nicholas Guild   2610
Babylon - Anthony Esler   1959
The Babylonians - Nathaniel Norsen Weinreb   6600
The Fabulist - John Vornholt   6512
Funeral Games - Mary Renault   5297
Persian Conqueror - George Sidney Hellman   2822
The Prophet - Sholem Asch   201
Prophets and Warriors - Peter Danielson   1473

BAHAMAS

Carnal Hours - Max Allan Collins   1210
The Gun Ketch - Dewey Lambdin   3610
Pilgrims in Paradise - Frank G. Slaughter   5895
A Royal Murder - Elliott Roosevelt   5456
Silver Shoals - Hamilton Cochran   1142
Stars on the Sea - F. van Wyck Mason   4161
Wind From the Carolinas - Robert Wilder   6751

Nassau
Lusty Wind for Carolina - Inglis Fletcher   2134
Sail the Dark Tide - Davenport Steward   6017

BALKAN PENINSULA

The Wanderer - Mika Waltari   6556

BARBADOS

The Big Drum - Elizabeth Boatwright Coker   1162
Buccaneer - Dudley Pope   5093
Caribbean - James A. Michener   4365
Caribbee - Thomas Hoover   3025
Hilton Head - Josephine Pinckney   5003
I, Tituba, Black Witch of Salem - Maryse Conde   1233
Jeremiah Martin: A Revolutionary War Novel - Robert H. Fowler   2191
The Ravishers - Elizabeth Richards   5318
Road to Lendor - Esther Hammon   1966
The Spoils of Eden - Robert H. Fowler   2193
Stately Timber - Rupert Hughes   3075

BAVARIA

Wilderness: A Tale of the Civil War - Robert Penn Warren   6573

Durkheim
The Heidenmauer - James Fenimore Cooper   1301

BELGIUM

Fortune's Legacy - Jack Rowe   5515
The Horn and the Roses: A Novel Based on the Life of Peter Paul Rubens - Ira Jan Wallach   6542
Masquerade for the King - Marina Oliver   4729
Midsummer Moon - Karen Lynn   3940
A Time for Silence - Philippa Carr   930
The Twisted Sword - Winston Graham   2531
Waterloo - Frederic E. Smith   5920
Why Waterloo? - Alan Patrick Herbert   2850

Antwerp
Bruegel, or, The Workshop of Dreams - Claude Henri Rocquet   5422
An Epic Joy: A Novel Based on the Life of Rubens - Donald Braider   642
Lover of Life - Zsolt de Harsanyi   2756
Prophecies - Helena Soister   5937
The Sea Beggars - Cecelia Holland   2996

Bruges
Niccolo Rising - Dorothy Dunnett   1803
The Quickenberry Tree - Annette Motley   4502
The Spring of the Ram - Dorothy Dunnett   1809

Brussels
Allegra - Clare Darcy   1483
The Charlatan - Carter A. Vaughan   6433
Dark Quartet: The Story of the Brontes - Lynne Reid Banks   290
The Girl From Paris - Joan Aiken   47
An Infamous Army - Georgette Heyer   2892
The Queen of Hearts - Joan Rees   5290
Vanity Fair - William Makepeace Thackeray   6213
Waterloo - Bernard Cornwell   1350

Flanders
How Young They Die - Stuart Cloete   1124
The Mohawk Ladder - Noel B. Gerson   2377

Fontenoy
A Day of Battle - Vincent Sheean   5787

Liege
Quentin Durward - Sir Walter Scott   5705

Waterloo
The Charterhouse of Parma - Stendhal   5993
Eliza Stanhope - Joanna Trollope   6347
Feather Castles - Patricia Veryan   6462
An Infamous Army - Georgette Heyer   2892
The Limits of Glory: A Novel of Waterloo - James McDonough   4265
Waterloo - Bernard Cornwell   1350
Waterloo - Manuel Komroff   3536

Ypres
No Man's Land - William Fairchild   2004

BENIN

Beware, Beware the Bight of Benin - Philip McCutchan   4241

BERMUDA

Armored Giants: A Novel of the Civil War - F. van Wyck Mason   4145
Bride of a Thousand Cedars - Bruce Lancaster   3637
The Dram Tree - Hamilton Cochran   1140
Log Cabin Noble - F. van Wyck Mason   4153
The Maddest Idea - James L. Nelson   4580
My Love, My Enemy - Jan Cox Speas   5958
The Sea 'Venture - F. van Wyck Mason   4159
Surprise - Brian Burland   785

Hamilton
On the Midnight Tide - Don Tracy   6310

BOHEMIA

Consuelo - George Sand   5582
The Ugly Duchess - Lion Feuchtwanger   2075

Prague
Irene's Last Waltz - Carole Nelson Douglas   1701

BOLIVIA

The Death of Che Guevara - Jay Cantor   886
The Story of the Sundance Kid - David Everitt   1988

BOSNIA-HERCEGOVINA

Sarajevo
Death of a Schoolboy - Hans Koning   3537
The First Casualty - William Powell   5149

Travik
Bosnian Chronicle - Ivo Andric   150

Visegrad
The Bridge on the Drina - Ivo Andric   151

BRAZIL

Agotime, Her Legend - Judith Gleason   2430
The Braganza Pursuit - Sarah Neilan   4564
Brazil - Errol Lincoln Uys   6395
Halfhyde on the Amazon - Philip McCutchan   4250
The Incredible Brazilian: The Native - Zulfikar Ghose   2392
Sage of Canudos - Lucien Marchal   4080
The Sinking of the Sarah Diamond - William Dale Jennings   3213
Time and the Wind - Erico Verissimo   6451
The Viceroy of Ouidah - Bruce C. Chatwin   1009

Amazon River
Look Away, Look Away - Leslie Turner White   6685

Manaus
A Company of Swans - Eva Ibbotson   3095
Gerontius - James Hamilton-Paterson   2672

Rio de Janeiro
River of Dreams - Gay Courter   1390

BULGARIA

Rhodope Mountains
Time of Parting - Anton Donchev   1690

BURMA

Born of War - Thomas Taylor   6192

Mandalay
Mandalay - Alexandra Jones   3269

BYZANTINE EMPIRE

Against the Fall of Night - Michael Arnold   193
The Lives of Rachel - Joel Gross   2601
The Long Ships - Frans Gunnar Bengtsson   442
The Spring of the Ram - Dorothy Dunnett   1809
The Unholy Pilgrim - R.F. Tapsell   6161
Wine of Satan - Laverne Gay   2327

Byzantium
The Belt of Gold - Cecelia Holland   2984
Byzantium - Stephen R. Lawhead   3680
A Flame in Byzantium - Chelsea Quinn Yarbro   6899
The Iron Crown - Clare Barroll   354
Queen of Swords - Judith Tarr   6169
Silver Leopard - F. van Wyck Mason   4160
The Vandal - Richard O'Connor   4687

Constantinople
Basilissa: A Tale of the Empress Theodora - John
   Masefield   4142
The Bearkeeper's Daughter - Gillian Bradshaw   628
Byzantium - Michael Ennis   1945
Count Belisarius - Robert Graves   2544
Count Robert of Paris - Sir Walter Scott   5695
The Dark Angel - Mika Waltari   6551
The Death of the Gods - Dmitri Merezhkovski   4338
The Eagle's Daughter - Judith Tarr   6165
The Female: A Novel of Another Time - Paul I.
   Wellman   6617
The Fool of Venus - George William Cronyn   1428
Imperial Purple - Gillian Bradshaw   631
The Lady for Ransom - Alfred Duggan   1768
Lord Geoffrey's Fancy - Alfred Duggan   1771
The Seven Hills of Paradise - Rosemary
   Simpson   5859
Shards of Empire - Susan Schwartz   5677
Their Most Serene Majesties - Ange Vlachos   6505
Theodora - Samuel Edwards   1891
Theodora and the Emperor - Harold Lamb   3608
To Love Again - Bertrice Small   5913
The Walking Drum - Louis L'Amour   3632

CAMBODIA

The Golden Exile - Lawrence Schoonover   5664
When God Slept - Peter Bourne   597

CANADA

Birthright - Robert E. Wall   6533
Black Robe - Brian Moore   4441
Blackrobe - Charles Corcoran   1323
Born with the Century - William Kinsolving   3501
A Bride for Donnigan - Janette Oke   4705
The Bride of the Wilderness - Charles McCarry   4220
Cajun - Elizabeth Nell Dubus   1751
Daniel Du Luth - Everett McNeil   4307
The Doom Trail - Arthur Douglas Smith   5917
Fathers and Crows - William T. Vollmann   6508
The Fur Masters - Alan Sullivan   6113
Ghost Fox - James Houston   3051

Goldeneye - Malcolm Macdonald   3965
Greenyards - Joan Lingard   3796
The Half Breed - Maurice Constantin-Weyer   1261
Jim Mundy: A Novel of the American Civil War -
   Robert H. Fowler   2192
The Kidnapped Surgeon - Alexander Knox   3527
The Life and Times of Captain N. - Douglas
   Glover   2436
The Magnificent Failure - Giles A. Lutz   3928
Me Too - Donald Jack   3128
Mission to Mackinac - Myron David Orr   4755
Mohawk Woman - Barbara Riefe   5329
Morning at Jalna - Mazo de la Roche   1560
The Plains of Abraham - James Oliver
   Curwood   1452
The Power and the Glory - Gilbert Parker   4805
Quietly My Captain Waits - Evelyn Eaton   1829
The Rebel Loyalist - Charles William Gordon   2480
The Rifles - William T. Vollmann   6510
The Rising of the Moon - Peter Berresford Ellis   1926
Sapphira and the Slave Girl - Willa Cather   958
This Widowed Land - Kathleen O'Neal Gear   2331
Three Came to Ville Marie - Alan Sullivan   6114
Three Cheers for Me - Donald Jack   3131
Tomorrow's Dream - Peggy Hanchar   2674
Too Long a Stranger - Janette Oke   4710
War Paint and Rouge - Robert W. Chambers   983
Web of Destiny - Muriel Elwood   1939
The White Cockade - Vincent O'Brien   4683
Wolves Against the Moon - Julia Cooley
   Altrocchi   123

Hudson Bay
River and Empty Sea - Louis Vaczek   6396
Running West - James Houston   3052
The White Dawn - James Houston   3053

Pacific Coast
Eagle Song - James Houston   3050

St. Lawrence River
Angelique and the Ghosts - Sergeanne Golon   2467

Talbot Settlement
Paradise - Sarah Neilan   4566

ALBERTA

Drums of Change: The Story of Running Fawn -
   Janette Oke   4707
They Called Her Mrs. Doc - Janette Oke   4709

BRITISH COLUMBIA

Vancouver
Friendly Cove - Irving Brant   651
The Kingdom Carver - E.G. Perrault   4916

Victoria
Shoot! - George Bowering   604

MANITOBA

The Strange Brigade - John Edward Jennings   3209

NEWFOUNDLAND

Passage Home - Alison McLeay   4286

NORTHWEST TERRITORIES

Lord of the Plains - Alfred Silver   5852

NOVA SCOTIA

An Air of Glory - Sarah Neilan   4563
The Governor's Lady - Thomas H. Raddall   5228
His Majesty's Yankees - Thomas H. Raddall   5230
Inherit the Earth - Margaret Shaw   5778

Pride's Fancy - Thomas H. Raddall   5231
Roger Sudden - Thomas H. Raddall   5232
The Willing Maid - C.T. Ritchie   5349

Cape Breton Island
A King's Ransom - Victor Suthren   6131
Loving Little Egypt - Thomas McMahon   4288
Young Titan - F. van Wyck Mason   4165

Halifax
Burden of Desire - Robert MacNeil   4023
Grand Parade - G.B. Lancaster   3649
Hangman's Beach - Thomas H. Raddall   5229

Louisbourg
The Highwayman - Noel B. Gerson   2372
Restless Are the Sails - Evelyn Eaton   1830

Port Royal
Savage Gentleman - Noel B. Gerson   2381

ONTARIO

The Old Enchantment - Sarah Neilan   4565
Visions of a Heart - Emily Carmichael   899

Toronto
Bright to the Wanderer - Bruce Lancaster   3638
What the Heart Keeps - Rosalind Laker   3605

PACIFIC NORTHWEST

The Kingdom Carver - E.G. Perrault   4916

PRAIRIE PROVINCES

The Calling of Emily Evans - Janette Oke   4706

PRINCE EDWARD ISLAND

They Were Dreamers - James F. Murphy Jr.   4525

QUEBEC

The Cold Journey - Grace Zaring Stone   6052
His Majesty's Highlanders - Leslie Turner
   White   6683
The King's Messenger - Samuel Edwards   1887
River and Empty Sea - Louis Vaczek   6396
La Salle - John Vernon   6458
*The Twisted Saber: A Biographical Novel of Benedict
   Arnold* - Philip Vail   6398
Valiant Libertine - John Gordon Bryson   748
The Woman Who Fell From the Sky - Barbara
   Riefe   5330
Yankee Rogue - Dana Fuller Ross   5496

Montreal
The Bright Battalions - Howard Breslin   664
Deeper the Heritage - Muriel Elwood   1936
The Gentleman From Chicago - John Cashman   953
Heritage of the River - Muriel Elwood   1937
My Pride, My Folly - Suzanne Butler   830
They Called Her Mrs. Doc - Janette Oke   4709

Quebec
Ambush - Donald Clayton Porter   5113
Arundel - Kenneth Roberts   5383
Bloodbrothers - Robert E. Wall   6535
Drums Against Frontenac - Harvey Chalmers   972
Heritage of the River - Muriel Elwood   1937
Lord Vanity - Samuel Shellabarger   5796
Rabble in Arms - Kenneth Roberts   5390
The Renegade - Donald Clayton Porter   5122
The Sachem - Donald Clayton Porter   5124
Shadows on the Rock - Willa Cather   959
The Silver Saber - Carter A. Vaughan   6441
Tomahawk - Donald Clayton Porter   5129
Ward of the Sun King - Mildred Allen Butler   826

St. Francis
Northwest Passage - Kenneth Roberts   5388

ROCKY MOUNTAINS

Julia's Last Hope - Janette Oke   4708
Pemmican - Vardis Fisher   2111

WEST

A Woman Named Damaris - Janette Oke   4711

YUKON TERRITORY

Days of the Gold - Irwin R. Blacker   526
Fire in the Sky - J.A. Shears   5785
Pacific Destiny - Dana Fuller Ross   5487
Tara Kane - George Markstein   4091
The Yukon Queen - Gilbert Morris   4476

Klondike River Valley
Journey - James A. Michener   4371

CARIBBEAN

Caribbean - James A. Michener   4365
Cup of Gold - John Steinbeck   5991
Fairoaks - Frank Yerby   6915
The Golden Hawk - Frank Yerby   6921
Kingdom of Gold - Susan Wiggs   6744
Long Pennant - Oliver La Farge   3573
Windward Passage - Hamilton Cochran   1143

CENTRAL AMERICA

Journey to the Sky: A Novel about the True Adventures of Two Men in Search of the Lost Maya Kingdom - Jamake Highwater   2918
Tatham Mound - Piers Anthony   169

Tikal
Tikal: A Novel about the Maya - Daniel Peters   4947

CEYLON

The Spring of the Tiger - Victoria Holt   3021
The Winds of Sinhala - Colin De Silva   1562

CHILE

Friday - Michel Tournier   6305
The Halfhyde Line - Philip McCutchan   4249
The Men That God Forgot - Richard Butler   829
No Price Too High - Madeleine Polland   5085
O'Higgins and Don Bernardo - Edna Deu Pree Nelson   4578
Retreat From the Dolphin - Darwin Le Ora Teilhet   6198
Taste of Glory - Carleton Beals   394

Tierra del Fuego
Jemmy Button - Benjamin Subercaseaux   6107

Valdivia
Sharpe's Devil - Bernard Cornwell   1340

Valparaiso
Halfhyde and the Admiral - Philip McCutchan   4243
The Unknown Shore - Patrick O'Brian   4678

CHINA

The Big Chariot - Charmian Clift   1118
Bittersweet - Leslie Li   3769
Blood Red Rose - Maxwell Grant   2538
Bronze Mirror - Jeanne Larsen   3668
The Call - John Hersey   2869

Caravan to China - Frank Stanley Stuart   6085
Caravan to Kanadu: A Novel of Marco Polo - Edison Marshall   4103
China Saga - C.Y. Lee   3706
The Chinese Emperor - Jean Levi   3733
The Court of the Lion - Eleanor Cooney   1294
Creation - Gore Vidal   6486
The Dangerous Years - Max Hennessy   2833
Deception - Eleanor Cooney   1295
The Dream of Confucius - Jean Levi   3734
Dynasty - Robert S. Elegant   1902
The Emperor's Pearl - Robert van Gulik   6414
Empire of Heaven - Linda Ching Sledge   5907
Empress - Evelyn McCune   4238
The Enchantress - Suyin Han   2673
The Examination - Malcolm Bosse   587
Fenwick Travers and the Years of Empire - Raymond M. Saunders   5614
The First to Land - Douglas E. Reeman   5288
Forbidden City - Muriel Molland Jernigan   3215
Foreign Devils - Irvin Faust   2053
The Good Earth - Pearl S. Buck   754
Green Dragon, White Tiger - Annette Motley   4501
The Haunted Monastery - Robert van Gulik   6415
Hawaii - James A. Michener   4370
High Road to China - Jon Cleary   1106
Hong Kong - Mona Gardner   2288
A House in Peiking - Robert Payne   4853
The House That Tai Ming Built - Virginia Lee   3711
Imperial Woman - Pearl S. Buck   755
Invisible Cities - Italo Calvino   867
The Jade Stalk - Jonathan Fast   2048
The Journeyer - Gary Jennings   3194
The Lacquer Screen - Robert van Gulik   6416
Lady Jane - Leslie O'Grady   4699
Lady Wu - Yutang Lin   3782
The Lost Legion - H. Warner Munn   4516
Louisiana! - Dana Fuller Ross   5478
The Magnificent Savages - Fred Mustard Stewart   6024
Manchu - Robert S. Elegant   1904
Manchu Empress - Bluebell Matilda Hunter   3081
Messer Marco Polo - Donn Byrne   840
Ming: A Novel of Seventeeth Century China - Robert B. Oxnam   4772
The Monkey and the Tiger - Robert van Gulik   6417
Moonraker's Bride - Madeleine Brent   661
Necklace and Calabash - Robert van Gulik   6419
Once More the Hawks - Max Hennessy   2836
Path of the Eclipse - Chelsea Quinn Yarbro   6905
The Phantom of the Temple - Robert van Gulik   6420
A Private Revenge - Richard Woodman   6863
Rebels of the Heavenly Kingdom - Katherine Paterson   4828
The Red Pavilion - Robert van Gulik   6421
The Red Peony - Yutang Lin   3783
Ruler of the Sky: A Novel of Genghis Khan - Pamela Sargent   5606
The Sea Stands Watch - Helen Parker Mudgett   4507
The Second Son of Heaven: A Novel of Nineteenth-Century China - C.Y. Lee   3707
Shike: Time of Dragons - Robert Shea   5784
Silk Road - Jeanne Larsen   3670
Sons of the Steppe: The Story of How the Conqueror Genghis Khan Was Overcome - Hans Baumann   380
Tall Ships to Cathay - Helen Augur   240
Tarnished Angel - Phyllis Leonard   3723
Thousand Years of Gold - Ruthanne Lum McCunn   4239
Wallis: The Novel - Anne Edwards   1883
White Poppy - Margaret Gaan   2261
The Willow Pattern - Robert van Gulik   6422
Winter Cherry - Keith West   6632

Canton
The East Indiaman - Ellis K. Meacham   4313
In Still and Stormy Waters - Reay Tannahill   6157
An Insular Position - Timothy Mo   4421

Mandarin Gold - James Leasor   3700
Manila Galleon - F. van Wyck Mason   4154
Masts to Spear the Stars - Stephen Longstreet   3889
Murder in Canton - Robert van Gulik   6418
Red Barbarian - Margaret Gaan   2260
The Southern Cross - Peter French   2226
Trade Imperial - Alan Lloyd   3814

Hunan
The Warlord - Malcolm Bosse   589

Kinsai
The Black Rose - Thomas B. Costain   1363

Kweichow
Jade - Pat Barr   344

Manchuria
Blood on the Snow - John Elliott   1916
The Dawning of Deliverance - Judith Pella   4892
The Name of Hero - Richard Seltzer   5742

Nanking
The Bridge of a Hundred Dragons - Emma Drummond   1723
Flashman and the Dragon - George MacDonald Fraser   2206
The Tent of Orange Mist - Paul West   6636

Pei-Chow
The Chinese Nail Murders - Robert van Gulik   6413

Peking
The Fabulous Concubine - Hsin-Hai Chang   987
Farewell to My Concubine - Lilian Lee   3709
Flashman and the Dragon - George MacDonald Fraser   2206
Forbidden City - Anthony Esler   1962
The Ginger Tree - Oswald Wynd   6890
Jade - Pat Barr   344
Manchu Palaces - Jeanne Larsen   3669
Mandarin - Robert S. Elegant   1905
Peking: A Novel of China's Revolt - Anthony Grey   2587
Spring Moon: A Novel of China - Bette Bao Lord   3897
The Time of the Dragon - Dorothy Eden   1863
Tournament of the Shadows - Nicholas Carnac   901
Twilight of the Dragon - Peter Bourne   596

Shanghai
The Bridge of a Hundred Dragons - Emma Drummond   1723
Flashman and the Dragon - George MacDonald Fraser   2206
From a Far Land - Robert S. Elegant   1903
The House of Memory: A Novel of Shanghai - Nicholas R. Clifford   1117
Jade - Pat Barr   344
Little Sister - Margaret Gaan   2259
Mandarin - Robert S. Elegant   1905
The Noel Coward Murder Case - George Baxt   387
Shanghai - Christopher New   4588
Shanghai Tango: A Novel of China - William Overgard   4769
The Warlord - Malcolm Bosse   589

Shu Province
Go Ask the River - Evelyn Eaton   1826

Soochow
The Fabulous Concubine - Hsin-Hai Chang   987
Spring Moon: A Novel of China - Bette Bao Lord   3897

Yangtze River
Harpoon - C.W. Nicol   4612
The Midnight Gun - Berkely Mather   4180

COLOMBIA

Cartagena
Drumbeat - Dudley Pope 5094
The Golden Hawk - Frank Yerby 6921

COSTA RICA

The Black Sheep's Daughter - Carola Dunn 1791

CUBA

Dark Rider - Louis Zara 6950
The Death of Che Guevara - Jay Cantor 886
Drum - Kyle Onstott 4744
Fenwick Travers and the Years of Empire - Raymond M. Saunders 5614
Imperial Kelly - Peter Bowen 600
The Indian Chronicles - Jose Barreiro 349
Outlaw - Warren Kiefer 3482
Pacific Destiny - Dana Fuller Ross 5487
The Rough Rider - Gilbert Morris 4468
San Juan Hill - Will Henry 2848
The Single Star - Walter Adolphe Roberts 5394
The Sun Is My Undoing - Marguerite Steen 5988
Wind of Destiny - Christopher Nicole 4624
The Year of the Spaniard - Henry Castor 956
Yellow: A Novel - Daniel Lynch 3932

Havana
Amistad: The Thunder of Freedom - David Pesci 4944
Captain Rebel - Frank Yerby 6910
Floodtide - Frank Yerby 6916
For Love of a Pirate - Anthony Esler 1961
Mingo Dabney - James H. Street 6078
Papa and Fidel - Karl Alexander 79

San Juan
Ever After - Elswyth Thane 6216

Santiago
Remember Santiago - Douglas C. Jones 3280

CYPRUS

Antichrist: A Novel of the Emperor Frederick II - Cecelia Holland 2982
Besieger of Cities - Alfred Duggan 1761
Crusader's Torch - Chelsea Quinn Yarbro 6897
Dara, the Cypriot - Louis Paul 4842
Marcus - Laurene Chinn 1068
Race of Scorpions - Dorothy Dunnett 1806
To Lie with Lions - Dorothy Dunnett 1810
Tomorrow's Fire - Jay Williams 6775

CZECHOSLOVAKIA

Dvorak in Love - Josef Skvorecky 5881
The Hangman's Crusade - James Barwick 370
Mozart on the Way to Prague - Eduard Friedrich Morike 4454

Prague
Kepler: A Novel - John Banville 297
Prague Counterpoint - Bodie Thoene 6225
The Sword of the Golem - Abraham Rothberg 5509

DAHOMEY

The Dahomean - Frank Yerby 6911
Flash for Freedom - George MacDonald Fraser 2203

DENMARK

The Exile of Celine - Tom Clark 1095
Flight of the Swan - Margaret Ann Hubbard 3063

Kingdom Come - Virginia Sorensen 5950
The Lost Queen - Norah Lofts 3850
Paradise Reclaimed - Halldor Laxness 3686
Raven's Wind - Victor Canning 883
The Seducer - Henrik Stangerup 5980
The Tower of Beowulf - Parke Godwin 2450
The Viking - Edison Marshall 4113
White Man - Peter Freuchen 2228

Copenhagen
A Balance of Dangers - Anthony Forrest 2184
The Fall of the King - Johannes Vilhelm Jensen 3214
Louisa Brancusi - Darrell Husted 3088
The Queen's Physician - Edgar Maas 3952

Isle of Fyn
By Love Enslaved - Phoebe Conn 1255

Jutland
The Green Man - Henry Treece 6330

DOMINICAN REPUBLIC

Bay of Arrows - Jay Parini 4800
Cradle of the Sun - John Clagett 1083
The White Cockade - Henry Farrand Griffin 2592

EARTH

The Inheritors - William Golding 2455
Shame of Man - Piers Anthony 168

Green Valley
The Last Mammoth - Margaret Allan 89

EGYPT

Abraham and Sarah: The Long Journey - Roberta Kells Dorr 1694
Akhnaton, King of Egypt - Dmitri Merezhkovski 4337
All the Trumpets Sounded: A Novel Based on the Life of Moses - W.G. Hardy 2701
Alone Atop the Mountain - Samuel Sandmel 5591
The Altar and the Crown - Marian Niven 4631
Ancient Evenings - Norman Mailer 4035
An Autumn in Araby - Carola Salisbury 5565
The Blood Star - Nicholas Guild 2611
Blunted Lance - Max Hennessy 2829
The Bronze God of Rhodes - L. Sprague De Camp 1554
Brumaire - Mark Logan 3864
Caesar - Allan Massie 4168
Charioteer: A Story of Old Egypt in the Days of Joseph - Gertrude Eberle 1835
Child of the Morning - Pauline Gedge 2343
Cleopatra - H. Rider Haggard 2637
The Conqueror: A Novel of Alexander the Great - Edison Marshall 4104
The Corn King and the Spring Queen - Naomi Mitchison 4419
The Curse of the King - Victoria Holt 3012
Departed Glory - Peter Danielson 1466
The Egyptian - Mika Waltari 6552
The Exodus - Konrad Bercovici 473
The Exodus - Peter Danielson 1467
The Fabulist - John Vornholt 6512
Fleet Surgeon to Pharaoh - Sheldon Jacobson 3140
Forty Centuries Look Down - Frederick Britten Austin 245
Freedom's Banner - Teresa Crane 1415
A God Against the Gods - Allen Drury 1738
The Goddess Queen: A Novel Based on the Life of Nefertiti - Nicole Vidal 6494
A Goddess to a God - John Lloyd Balderston 278
The Golden Balance - Arthur Dana Hall 2646
The Golden Lyre - Noel B. Gerson 2371
The Golden Pharaoh - Peter Danielson 1468

Hagar - Cothburn O'Neal 4737
Her-Bak: The Living Face of Ancient Egypt - Isha Schwaller de Lubicz 5676
The Hippopotamus Pool - Elizabeth Peters 4950
Joseph of Egypt - Thomas Mann 4065
Joseph the Provider - Thomas Mann 4066
King and Goddess - Judith Tarr 6166
King of the Two Lands: The Pharaoh Akhenaten - Jacquetta Hawkes 2780
King Tut's Private Eye - Lee Levin 3739
Lady of the Reeds - Pauline Gedge 2345
The Lion in Egypt - Peter Danielson 1470
Lion in the Valley - Elizabeth Peters 4952
Lord of the Two Lands - Judith Tarr 6167
Lot's Wife - Marie Ley-Piscator 3767
The Miracle Hater - Shulamith Hareven 2704
Mirage - Pauline Gedge 2346
Mirage - Ruth McKenney 4283
Moses - Sholem Asch 199
Moses, Prince of Egypt - Howard Fast 2039
The Mummy Case - Elizabeth Peters 4953
Murder at the God's Gate - Lynda S. Robinson 5408
Napoleon Must Die - Quinn Fawcett 2054
Napoleon Symphony - Anthony Burgess 780
On a Balcony - David Stacton 5973
On Eagles' Wings - Arthur E. Southon 5951
Paris of Troy - George Baker 273
Pharaoh - Eloise Jarvis McGraw 4276
Pillar of Fire - Judith Tarr 6168
Prince of Egypt - Dorothy Clarke Wilson 6805
The Prophecy - Peter Danielson 1472
Purple Pirate - Talbot Mundy 4514
The Regiment - C.L. Skelton 5874
Return to Thebes - Allen Drury 1739
The River and the Stone: Moses' Early Years in Egypt - Kathleen Jenks 3192
River God - Wilbur Smith 5928
Saint Francis - Nikos Kazantzakis 3385
The Scapegoat: A Life of Moses - Joan Lawrence 3684
The Shining King - Peter Danielson 1476
The Snake, the Crocodile, and the Dog - Elizabeth Peters 4954
Sword of Glory - Peter Danielson 1477
Table in the Wilderness - Norton S. Parker 4806
Tables of the Law - Thomas Mann 4067
That Egyptian Woman - Noel B. Gerson 2384
The Twelfth Physician - Willa Gibbs 2403
The Twelfth Transforming - Pauline Gedge 2347
Vengeance of the Lion - Peter Danielson 1480
Winged Pharaoh - Joan Grant 2536

Alexandria
The Alexandrian - Martha Rofheart 5425
The Beacon of Alexandria - Gillian Bradshaw 627
Behold the Man - N. Richard Nash 4556
The Clock Tower - Jeanne Montague 4435
Dogheaded Death - Ray Faraday Nelson 4581
Dominic - Kathleen Robinson 5405
The Galileans - Frank G. Slaughter 5888
Hypatia - Charles Kingsley 3498
In the Shadow of the Nile - Sara Hylton 3093
Josephus - Lion Feuchtwanger 2072
Origen: A Historical Novel - Theodore Vrettos 6515
Palaces of Desire - Kate Alexander 81
Son of Judah - Dan Levin 3738
Soul Flame - Barbara Wood 6850
The Sword and the Promise - Benjamin Siegel 5845
The Temple of the Muses - John Maddox Roberts 5382
Throne of Isis - Judith Tarr 6170

Cairo
Behold the Fire - Michael Blankfort 541
Blood and Sand - Rosemary Sutcliff 6121
The Doctor From Cordova: A Biographical Novel about the Great Philosopher Maimonides - Herbert Le Porrier 3693

Dreams of Empire - Jeanne Mackin 3994
The Fires of Fu Manchu - Cay Van Ash 6399
The Mamur Zapt and the Donkey-Vous - Michael Pearce 4866
The Mamur Zapt and the Girl in the Nile - Michael Pearce 4867
The Mamur Zapt and the Men Behind - Michael Pearce 4868
The Mamur Zapt and the Night of the Dog - Michael Pearce 4869
The Mamur Zapt and the Return of the Carpet - Michael Pearce 4870
The Mamur Zapt and the Spoils of Egypt - Michael Pearce 4871
The Mummy; or Ramses the Damned - Anne Rice 5315
The Second Sister - Leslie O'Grady 4701
Zayni Barakat - Gamal Ahitani 42

Luxor
The Curse of the Pharaohs - Elizabeth Peters 4948

Nile Valley
Murder at the Feast of Rejoicing - Lynda S. Robinson 5407

Sinai Peninsula
Hagar - Lois T. Henderson 2824

Suez Canal
Madeleine - Catherine Gavin 2323

Thebes
Death Comes as the End - Agatha Christie 1076
Murder in the Place of Anubis - Lynda S. Robinson 5409
Out of the House of Life - Chelsea Quinn Yarbro 6903

EL SALVADOR

San Salvador
The Immigrant's Daughter - Howard Fast 2035

ENGLAND

The Abandoned Woman - Richard Condon 1235
Absolute Elizabeth - Joanna Dessau 1624
Admiral Hornblower in the West Indies - C.S. Forester 2169
The Admiral's Lady - Mary Ann Gibbs 2395
The Adulteress - Philippa Carr 916
Affairs of Love - Nicola Thorne 6272
The Affairs of Nicholas Culpepper - Mabel L. Tyrrel 6375
An Air of Glory - Sarah Neilan 4563
Albert's Victoria - Tyler Whittle 6719
Alexa - Anne Melville 4330
Alexander the Glorious - Jane Oliver 4719
All the Queen's Men - Evelyn Anthony 157
Angels Falling - Janice Elliott 1915
Ann of Cambray - Mary Lide 3772
Anne of the Thousand Days - Edward Fenton 2059
Apple Tree Lean Down - Mary E. Pearce 4860
Artemia - Pamela Hill 2927
Arthur - Stephen R. Lawhead 3679
Arthur Rex: A Legendary Novel - Thomas Berger 477
Artorius Rex - John Gloag 2432
Ashworth Hall - Anne Perry 4918
Ask Me No Questions - Patricia Veryan 6459
The Athelsons - Jocelyn Kettle 3476
Aurora Rose - Anne Worboys 6870
The Autobiography of Henry VIII - Margaret George 2355
Avalon - Anya Seton 5748
Back to Battle - Max Hennessy 2828
The Banishment - Marion Chesney 1018
Banners of Gold - Pamela Kaufman 3371
The Barons of Runnymede - Pamela Bennetts 445

The Bastard - John Jakes 3144
The Bastard King - Jean Plaidy 5004
The Battle-Ax of God - Le Roy MacLeod 4007
The Battle of the Queens - Jean Plaidy 5005
Bear His Mild Yoke - Ethel White 6675
Beau Blackstone - Richard Falkirk 2005
Beauty's Daughter - Mollie Hardwick 2689
Beauvallet - Georgette Heyer 2876
Before the Wind - Lloyd M. Moxon 4506
The Belchamber Scandal - Frances Murray 4533
Belinda Goes to Bath - Marion Chesney 1020
Beloved Enemy: The Passions of Eleanor of Aquitaine - Ellen Jones 3288
Beloved Exile - Parke Godwin 2446
Beloved Lady - Barbara Jefferis 3174
Below the Salt - Thomas B. Costain 1362
Benjamin Blake - Edison Marshall 4102
Bertie and the Tinman - Peter Lovesey 3909
Beyond the Shadowlands - Georgina Fleming 2126
The Bishop's Tale - Margaret Frazer 2215
The Bisley Boy - Christopher Hunt 3080
The Black Arrow - Robert Louis Stevenson 6008
The Black Candle - Catherine Cookson 1273
The Black Sheep's Daughter - Carola Dunn 1791
The Blacksmith's Daughter - Joanna Dessau 1625
Blackstone's Fancy - Richard Falkirk 2008
The Blade of Castlemayne - Anthony Esler 1960
Blaize - Anne Melville 4331
The Blanket of the Dark - John Buchan 749
The Blood of Roses - Marsha Canham 879
Blood of the Boar - Margaret Abbey 2
Blood Royal - Mollie Hardwick 2690
Blossom Like the Rose - Norah Lofts 3836
The Blue Dragon - Diana Brown 716
The Blue Falcon - Robyn Carr 935
The Blue Heaven Bends Over All - Jane Oliver 4720
Bodin, 1349: An Epic Novel of Christians and Jews in the Plague Years - Roberta Kalechofsky 3322
The Bomb Vessel - Richard Woodman 6860
Bond of Blood - Roberta Gellis 2349
Bond of Honour - Catherine Todd 6284
Born to Be King - Constance Gluyas 2440
The Boy's Tale - Margaret Frazer 2216
The Braeswood Tapestry - Robyn Carr 936
Brazen Whispers - Jane Feather 2055
The Breath of Kings - Gene Farrington 2019
The Briar Rose - Linda Neale 4561
The Bride - Julie Garwood 2311
Bride of Glory - Bradda Field 2078
Bride of the Spear - Kathleen Herbert 2851
Bride of the Unicorn - Kasey Michaels 4363
Brief Gaudy Hour - Margaret Campbell Barnes 322
The Bright Blue Sky - Max Hennessy 2830
The Brittle Glass - Norah Lofts 3837
The Broken Sword - Rhoda S. Edwards 1885
The Brothers of Gwynedd - Edith Pargeter 4796
Brumaire - Mark Logan 3864
Buccaneer Surgeon - C.V. Terry 6205
The Buckingham Palace Connection - Ted Willis 6792
Buckskin Baronet - Margaret Widdemer 6734
Buller's Dreadnought - Richard Hough 3047
Buller's Guns - Richard Hough 3048
The Buried Self: A Background to the Poems of Matthew Arnold - Isobel MacDonald 3961
Burning Gold - Robert Hardy Andrews 148
Bury Him Among Kings - Elleston Trevor 6341
By the Green of the Spring - John Masters 4171
Byron: A Novel - Sigrid Combuchen 1225
Caesar of the Narrow Seas - John Gloag 2433
Call Lady Purbeck - Hilda Lewis 3745
Cambridge - Caryl Phillips 4983
Campion Towers - John Beatty 401
Candle in the Window - Christina Dodd 1662
Candleshine No More - Jane Oliver 4721
Canis the Warrior - James Sinclair 5864
Captain Bashful - Donald Barr Chidsey 1059
Captain Caution - Kenneth Roberts 5385
Captain of the Sands - Keith Dewhurst 1636

Captain Vinegar's Commission - Philip Glazebrook 2428
The Captive - Victoria Holt 3011
The Captive of Kensington Palace - Jean Plaidy 5007
The Captive Princess - Maxine Shore 5831
The Captive Queen of Scots - Jean Plaidy 5008
The Caretaker Wife - Barbara Whitehead 6706
Caroline the Queen - Jean Plaidy 5009
The Case of the Revolutionist's Daughter: Sherlock Holmes Meets Karl Marx - Lewis S. Feuer 2076
Cast a Long Shadow - Mary E. Pearce 4861
The Castle of Fratta - Ippolito Nievo 4625
Catherine - Hilda Lewis 3746
Cato's War - Guy Wheeler 6655
The Centurion - Jan de Hartog 2762
Chain of Destiny - Nigel Tranter 6314
Champion - L. Christian Balling 285
Chariots of Fire - W.J. Weatherby 6586
Charles the King - Evelyn Anthony 160
Chase the Heart - Maggie Osborne 4760
Check-Out Time - Kate Kingsbury 3491
Cherished Enemy - Patricia Veryan 6460
The Chessboard Queen - Sharan Newman 4597
Child of the Northern Spring - Persia Woolley 6867
Christopher Humble - Charles Burnet Judah 3310
The Cinderpath - Catherine Cookson 1275
Circle in the Water - Susan Wiggs 6742
Circle of Gold - Karen Harper 2710
A Civil Contract - Georgette Heyer 2880
Claudius the God - Robert Graves 2543
Clear for Action: A Novel about John Paul Jones - Clements Ripley 5344
Cloak of Folly - Burke Boyce 606
The Coat I Wore - Lucile Finlay 2090
Come Rack! Come Rope! - Robert Hugh Benson 458
The Coming of the King - Nikolai Tolstoy 6296
Command of the King - Mary Lide 3773
Commodore Hornblower - C.S. Forester 2172
The Concubine - Norah Lofts 3839
The Conqueror's Wife - Noel B. Gerson 2363
The Conquest - Jude Deveraux 1630
Conscience of the King - Alfred Duggan 1763
Consort for Victoria - William Vaughan Wilkins 6757
The Constant Star - Dorothy Norris Foote 2151
The Corner That Held Them - Sylvia Townsend Warner 6568
Countess Carrots - Molly Costain Haycraft 2792
The Courts of Illusion - Rosemary Hawley Jarman 3165
The Courts of Love - Jean Plaidy 5010
Cousin Kate - Georgette Heyer 2884
The Crimson Chalice - Victor Canning 882
Crippled Splendour - Evan John 3219
The Cross and the Sword - Evangeline Walton 6558
Crouchback - Carola Oman 4732
The Crow Goddess - Patricia Finney 2094
Crown in Candlelight - Rosemary Hawley Jarman 3166
A Crown in Darkness: A Novel about Lady Jane Grey - Margaret Mullally 4512
Crown of Roses - Valerie Anand 127
Crown Without Sceptre - William Vaughan Wilkins 6758
The Crows of War - Steven Rayson 5276
The Crystal Cave - Mary Stewart 6029
The Cunning of the Dove - Alfred Duggan 1765
The Curse of the King - Victoria Holt 3012
The Curse of the Pharaohs - Elizabeth Peters 4948
Cutlass Empire - F. van Wyck Mason 4148
Daishi-San: A Novel - Robert P. Lund 3925
Damaris - Jane Sheridan 5810
Daneclere - Pamela Hill 2931
A Dangerous Fortune - Ken Follett 2147
The Dark Island - Henry Treece 6326
The Dark Stranger - Dorothy Charques 999
Dark Torrent of Glencoe - Edward Grierson 2590
Daughter of Marignac - Constance Heaven 2805

Daughter of Time - Nelia Gardner White   6695
Daughters of England - Philippa Carr   919
Day Is Coming - William Cameron   869
The Day They Kidnapped Queen Victoria - H.K. Fleming   2127
The De Montfort Legacy - Pamela Bennetts   447
Dead Man's Sweetheart - Gillian Linscott   3804
Dean's Watch - Elizabeth Goudge   2494
Dear Laura - Jean Stubbs   6094
Death and the Chapman - Kate Sedley   5715
Death at Daisy's Folly - Robin Paige   4775
The Death of a King - P.C. Doherty   1672
Deborah - Colette Davenat   1498
Deborah Goes to Dover - Marion Chesney   1023
The Dedicated Villain - Patricia Veryan   6461
The Deer Cry - William Greenough Schofield   5650
Defy Not the Heart - Johanna Lindsey   3794
The Demon Lover - Victoria Holt   3013
The Desirable Duchess - Marion Chesney   1025
Desire and Deceive - Cordia Byers   832
Devil Child - Jo Germany   2359
The Devil Is Loose - Graham Shelby   5790
The Devil on Horseback - Victoria Holt   3014
The Diary of William Harvey: The Imaginary Journal of the Physician Who Revolutionized Medicine - Jean Hamburger   2667
The Disappearance of Edwin Drood - Peter Rowland   5521
A Distant Thunder - Teresa de Luca   1561
Dizzy's Woman - George MacBeth   3957
Do Not Disturb - Kate Kingsbury   3492
Dr. Gully's Story - Elizabeth Jenkins   3190
Dr. Johnson's Dear Mistress - Winifred Carter   948
Doctor Mirabilis - James Blish   550
Dorothy and Agatha - Gaylord Larsen   3667
Double Masquerade - Karen Lynn   3938
Doubting Castle - Rebecca Kavaler   3373
The Dragon and the Rose - Roberta Gellis   2350
A Dragon for Edward - Pamela Bennetts   450
The Dragon Waiting: A Masque of History - John M. Ford   2165
Dreaming of Samarkand - Martin Booth   576
The Duchess of Vidal - Dawn Lindsey   3793
The Duke of War - Walter O'Meara   4734
The Dukes: A Novel - Malcolm Ross   5503
Dynasty of Death - Taylor Caldwell   854
The Eagle and the Raven - Pauline Gedge   2344
Eagles at War - Walter J. Boyne   620
The Eagles Depart - John Gloag   2434
The Earth Goddess - Richard Herley   2856
Earth Song - Catherine Coulter   1374
Eat, Drink, and Be Buried - Kate Kingsbury   3493
Echoes From the Past - Marjorie McEvoy   4268
Edward - Tyler Whittle   6721
Edward and Mrs. Simpson - A.C.H. Smith   5916
Eleanor the Queen - Norah Lofts   3842
Electricity: A Novel - Victoria Glendinning   2431
Elegant Witch - Robert Neill   4568
Elizabeth and the Prince of Spain - Margaret Irwin   3117
Elizabeth, Captive Princess - Margaret Irwin   3118
Elizabeth: Queen & Woman - Helen Thorpe   6279
Elizabeth, the Woman - Amanda Mae Ellis   1917
Eliza's Daughter - Joan Aiken   44
The Elusive Crown - Hebe Elsna   1931
Emerald Fire - Laurie Grant   2537
Emily - Cynthia Harrod-Eagles   2753
Emily Goes to Exeter - Marion Chesney   1027
Emma - F.W. Kenyon   3448
Emma Watson - Joan Aiken   45
The Emperor Arthur - Godfrey Turton   6368
Epitaph for Three Women - Jean Plaidy   5012
Estella - Alanna Knight   3519
The Everlasting Covenant - Robyn Carr   939
Every Man for Himself - Beryl Bainbridge   270
Exiled - Helene Holt   3007
The Fair - Robert Nathan   4559
The Falcon and the Flower - Virginia Henley   2826
The Fallen Angels - Susannah Kells   3397

Falls the Shadow - Sharon Kay Penman   4903
Falstaff - Robert Nye   4653
Farewell the Tranquil - R.F. Delderfield   1585
The Fatal Crown - Ellen Jones   3289
A Father and His Fate - Ivy Compton-Burnett   1228
Feast in the Morning - Hugh Preston   5175
Feather Castles - Patricia Veryan   6462
Feversham - Diane Davidson   1503
The Fifth Queen - Ford Madox Ford   2161
Fire and Morning - Francis W. Leary   3696
Fire over England - A.E.W. Mason   4143
Firelord - Parke Godwin   2447
A Firework for Oliver - John Sanders   5587
First Knight - Elizabeth Chadwick   966
The First Rebellion - Marion Chesney   1030
Flambard's Confession - Marilyn Durham   1816
The Flame in the Dark - Basil Bonallack   568
Flame of Fire - Jane Oliver   4722
Fleur - Cynthia Harrod-Eagles   2754
The Flight of the Kestrel - Margaret Abbey   3
The Flint Anchor - Sylvia Townsend Warner   6569
The Flint Lord - Richard Herley   2857
Floodtide - Suzanne Goodwin   2475
Flowers for Lilian - Anna Gilbert   2405
Flying Colours - C.S. Forester   2173
The Follies of the King - Jean Plaidy   5014
Follow the Drum - James Leasor   3699
The Folly - Marion Chesney   1031
Fonthill - Aubrey Menen   4335
For God and Glory - Tim Jeal   3171
The Forest House - Marion Zimmer Bradley   625
The Fortress - Hugh Walpole   6544
Fortune Made His Sword - Martha Rofheart   5426
The Fortune of War - Patrick O'Brian   4664
Fortune's Wheel - Rhoda S. Edwards   1886
The Foster Brothers - Edward Frankland   2202
The Fourth Queen - Isabel Paterson   4827
The Free Fishers - John Buchan   750
The Frigate Captain - Showell Styles   6103
The Frog Earl - Carola Dunn   1792
A Future Arrived - Phillip Rock   5420
A Game for Empires - Pearl Frye   2243
Gay Crusader - Cleone Knox   3528
Gay Lord Robert - Jean Plaidy   5015
The Gentle Conqueror - Mary Ellen Gronau   2597
The Gentle Falcon - Hilda Lewis   3747
The Gentle Knight - Philip Lindsay   3791
Gentlemen—The Regiment! - Hugh Talbot   6154
Gilded Spurs - Grace Ingram   3105
The Girl - Catherine Cookson   1277
The Girl From Paris - Joan Aiken   47
Give Me Your Golden Hand - Evelyn Eaton   1825
The Glory and the Dream - F.W. Kenyon   3450
Goddess of the Green Room - Jean Plaidy   5016
The Gods Are Not Mocked - Anna Taylor   6177
The Golden Days - Robert Neill   4569
The Golden Exile - Lawrence Schoonover   5664
The Golden Fleece - Norah Lofts   3843
The Golden Hand - Edith Simon   5856
The Golden Harlot - Jeanne Wilson   6808
The Golden Lady - Dorothy Gardiner   2283
The Golden Strangers - Henry Treece   6328
The Golden Years: A Novel Based on the Life and Loves of Percy Bysshe Shelley - F.W. Kenyon   3451
The Golden Yoke: A Novel of the War of the Roses - Olive Eckerson   1837
Goldeneye - Malcolm Macdonald   3965
The Goldsmith's Wife - Jean Plaidy   5017
Good King Harry - Denise Giardina   2393
Grandmother and the Priests - Taylor Caldwell   857
The Great Captains - Henry Treece   6329
The Greater Hunger - Barbara Dodge Borland   581
Green Darkness - Anya Seton   5751
The Green Madonna - C.E. L'Ami   3617
The Green Man - Henry Treece   6330
Grounds for Murder - Kate Kingsbury   3494
Guillotine - Mark Logan   3865
Guinevere - Sharan Newman   4600

Guinevere Evermore - Sharan Newman   4601
Guinevere: The Legend in Autumn - Persia Woolley   6868
Gwendolen - Clare Darcy   1489
Had We Never Loved - Patricia Veryan   6463
The Hammer and the Cross - Harry Harrison   2736
Hammer of the Scots - Jean Plaidy   5018
Hardacre - C.L. Skelton   5872
Harkfast: The Making of the King - Hugh C. Rae   5238
Harlot Queen - Hilda Lewis   3748
Harold Was My King - Hilda Lewis   3749
Harp into Battle - Cecil Maiden   4031
Harry of Monmouth - A.M. Maughan   4199
Hawk of May - Gillian Bradshaw   629
Hawthorn Hill - Doris Shannon   5777
He Brings Great News - Clemence Dane   1462
A Health Unto His Majesty - Jean Plaidy   5019
The Heart Is a Traitor - Margaret Abbey   4
Heart of a Queen - Josephine Delves-Broughton   1603
The Heart of the Lion - Jean Plaidy   5020
Heart of War - John Masters   4174
The Heatherton Heritage - Pamela Hill   2934
The Heir of Allington - Philippa Wiat   6727
The Heiress Bride - Catherine Coulter   1375
Henry VIII and His Six Wives - Maureen Peters   4975
Henry Lunt and the Ranger - Tom McNamara   4304
Her Majesty's Captain - Derek Wilson   6797
Her Royal Destiny - Carol Maxwell Eady   1820
Here Be Dragons - Sharon Kay Penman   4904
Here Comes the King - Philip Lindsay   3792
Here Lies Our Sovereign Lord - Jean Plaidy   5021
The Heretic - Alison Macleod   4002
Hereward the Wake - Charles Kingsley   3497
A Heritage and Its History - Ivy Compton-Burnett   1229
A Heritage of Shadows - Madeleine Brent   660
High Heroic - Constantine FitzGibbon   2118
Highland Belle - Patricia Grasso   2541
His Majesty's Highwayman - Donald Barr Chidsey   1061
The Hollow Hills - Mary Stewart   6030
The Homecoming - Norah Lofts   3844
The Honorable Imposter - Gilbert Morris   4463
Hornblower and the Atropos - C.S. Forester   2175
Horses of War - Duff Hart-Davis   2760
The Hounds of God - Rafael Sabatini   5551
The House at Old Vine - Norah Lofts   3845
I Am Mary Tudor - Hilda Lewis   3750
I, Elizabeth - Rosalind Miles   4378
I, John Mordaunt - Virgil Scott   5687
I Remember Love - Mollie Hardwick   2694
I Seek a City - Gilbert Rees   5289
I, Victoria - Cynthia Harrod-Eagles   2755
The Idylls of the Queen - Phyllis Ann Karr   3367
The Imagination of the Heart - Judith Glover   2437
Immortal Queen - Elizabeth Byrd   834
Imperial Courtesan - F.W. Kenyon   3452
The Imperial Governor - George Shipway   5828
An Important Family - Dorothy Eden   1855
In a Dark Wood Wandering - Hella S. Haasse   2631
In Pale Battalions - Robert Goddard   2444
In Pursuit of the Green Lion - Judith Merkle Riley   5334
In the Days of Poor Richard - Irving A. Bacheller   259
In the House of the King - Louis Zara   6951
In the Shadow of Midnight - Marsha Canham   880
In the Shadow of the Crown - Jean Plaidy   5022
In the Shadow of the Oak King - Courtway Jones   3271
In Winter's Shadow - Gillian Bradshaw   632
The Infinite Woman - Edison Marshall   4107
The Interpreter - Robert Moss   4499
The Intrigue - Marion Chesney   1034
The Iron King - Maurice Druon   1732
The Iron Roads - Forbes Bramble   644

Israel Potter - Herman Melville 4334

It's Me Again - Donald Jack 3126

The Ivy Crown: A Biographical Novel of Queen Katherine Parr - Mary M. Luke 3923

James and Joan - Anne Fremantle 2221

James, by the Grace of God - Hugh Williamson Ross 5499

Jemmy Button - Benjamin Subercaseaux 6107

Jewel of the Sea - Susan Wiggs 6743

John Howard Payne, Skywalker - Maude Barragan 348

John Milton - Edmund Fuller 2249

Journey to Enchantment - Patricia Veryan 6464

Judith Paris - Hugh Walpole 6545

Katharine: The Virgin Widow - Jean Plaidy 5025

Katherine - Anya Seton 5752

Katherine Christian - Hugh Walpole 6546

Katheryn, the Wanton Queen - Maureen Peters 4976

Kathryn: In the Court of Six Queens - Anne Merton Abbey 1

Kean: The Imaginary Memoirs of an Actor - Julius Berstl 485

The Keys of England - William Victor Cooke 1271

Kezzy - Patricia Burns 799

The Killing of Richard the Third - Robert Farrington 2020

The King - Donald Barthelme 365

The King Breaker - Elizabeth Linington 3797

The King James Version - Stanley N. Stewart 6035

The King Liveth - Jeffrey Farnol 2013

King of the Wood - Valerie Anand 131

Kingdom of Gold - Susan Wiggs 6744

Kingdom of Summer - Gillian Bradshaw 633

The Kingmaking - Helen Hollick 3000

The King's Achievement - Robert Hugh Benson 459

King's Agent - Justus Kent Clark 1090

The King's Bastard - Hebe Elsna 1932

The King's Daughters - Molly Costain Haycraft 2793

King's Fool - Margaret Campbell Barnes 325

The King's Good Servant - Olive White 6696

The King's Grey Mare - Rosemary Hawley Jarman 3167

King's Man - C.M. Edmondston 1880

The King's Messenger - Samuel Edwards 1887

King's Minion - Rafael Sabatini 5552

The King's Pleasure - Norah Lofts 3847

The King's Pleasure - Jean Plaidy 5026

The King's Rogue - Max Peacock 4859

The King's Secret Matter - Jean Plaidy 5027

Knave of Hearts - Philippa Carr 920

The Knight - George Shipway 5829

The Knight and the Dove - Lori Wick 6732

A Knight in Shining Armor - Jude Deveraux 1631

Knights - Linda Lael Miller 4399

Knight's Acre - Norah Lofts 3848

Knight's Honor - Roberta Gellis 2351

Ladies Whose Bright Eyes - Ford Madox Ford 2162

The Lady Cicely - Sandra Wilson 6813

Lady Defiant - Suzanne Robinson 5412

Lady Gallant - Suzanne Robinson 5413

Lady Hellfire - Suzanne Robinson 5414

The Lady in the Tower - Jean Plaidy 5028

Lady in Waiting - Rosemary Sutcliff 6123

Lady Jane - Norma Lee Clark 1092

Lady of Hay - Barbara Erskine 1955

A Lady of Repute - Janice James 3158

Lady Rich - Elizabeth Boatwright Coker 1166

The Lady Royal - Molly Costain Haycraft 2794

The Land Endures - Mary E. Pearce 4862

The Last Englishman: The Story of Hereward the Wake - Hebe Weenolsen 6596

Last Man to Die - Michael Dobbs 1652

The Last Pendragon - Robert Rice 5316

Late Harvest - Olive White 6697

Leaves From the Valley - Joanna Trollope 6348

Legacy - Susan Kay 3374

Lempriere's Dictionary - Lawrence Norfolk 4641

Leopards and Lilies - Alfred Duggan 1769

Less Fortunate than Fair - Sandra Wilson 6814

Let the King Beware! - Honore Morrow 4489

Letty - Helen Ashton 218

Lillibullero - Robert Neill 4571

The Lily and the Leopard - Susan Wiggs 6745

The Lily and the Leopards - Alice Harwood 2765

The Lily and the Lion - Maurice Druon 1733

Limmerston Hall - Hester W. Chapman 991

The Lion and the Cross - Joan Lesley Hamilton 2669

The Lion and the Leopard - Mary Ellen Johnson 3226

The Lion and the Rose - Jane Oliver 4724

The Lion at Sea - Max Hennessy 2834

The Lion of England - Margaret Butler 824

The Lion of England - Eve Trevaskis 6336

The Lion of Justice - Jean Plaidy 5031

Lion Rampant - Bernard Shrimsley 5836

Lionheart!: A Novel of Richard I, King of England - Martha Rofheart 5428

The Little Emperors - Alfred Duggan 1770

The Little Victoria - Lozania Prole 5196

The Living Wood - Louis De Wohl 1571

Logic of the Heart - Patricia Veryan 6466

A London Season - Anthea Bell 420

The Lonely Furrow - Norah Lofts 3849

The Long Afternoon - Ursula Zilinsky 6964

The Long Shadow - Anna Gilbert 2406

Lord Iverbrook's Heir - Carola Dunn 1795

Lord of the Ladies - Joanna Dessau 1626

Lord Richard's Passion - Mervyn Jones 3293

The Lords of Lancaster - Pamela Bennetts 452

The Lormes of Castle Rising - Fanny Cradock 1409

The Lost Colony - Edison Marshall 4108

Lost Love Found - Bertrice Small 5910

The Lost Queen - Norah Lofts 3850

Louisa Elliott - Ann Victoria Roberts 5370

Love Alters Not - Patricia Veryan 6467

Love at Sunset - Jane Sheridan 5811

The Love Child - Philippa Carr 923

A Love Divine - Alexandra Ripley 5340

Lovers All Untrue - Norah Lofts 3851

Lovers Meeting - Mollie Hardwick 2695

Love's Duet - Patricia Veryan 6468

Love's Labour's Won - Edward Fisher 2101

Loving Emma - Nigel Foxell 2197

Loving Sands, Deadly Sands - Charlotte Keppel 3465

Luciano's Luck - Jack Higgins 2912

Lucinda Brayford - Martin Boyd 613

Madselin - Norah Lofts 3853

The Magnificent Savages - Fred Mustard Stewart 6024

Magnus the Magnificent - Leslie Turner White 6688

Malefice - Leslie Wilson 6810

The Mallen Girl - Catherine Cookson 1280

The Mallen Lot - Catherine Cookson 1281

The Mallen Streak - Catherine Cookson 1282

The Man on a Donkey - H.F.M. Prescott 5170

The Man on the White Horse - Warwick Deeping 1577

Marianne - Juliette Benzoni 466

Marjorie of Scotland - Pamela Hill 2939

Marlborough's Unfair Lady - Lozania Prole 5197

The Marriage of Meggotta - Edith Pargeter 4799

Marry in Haste - Jane Aiken Hodge 2967

Marsanne - Virginia Coffman 1155

The Marsh King - C. Walter Hodges 2975

Martin Valliant - Warwick Deeping 1578

Mary, Queen of Scotland and the Isles - Margaret George 2356

Masque of Enchantment - Charlene Cross 1432

Masque of Sapphire - Deana James 3156

Master-At-Arms - Rafael Sabatini 5553

The Master of Gray Trilogy - Nigel Tranter 6316

The Master of Oakwindsor - Douglas Kent Hall 2648

Meadowsweet - Gwendoline Butler 820

The Melancholy Virgin - Annabel Laine 3587

Memoirs of a Victorian Gentleman: William Makepeace Thackeray - Margaret Forster 2189

The Memoirs of Lord Byron - Robert Nye 4655

Men Like Shadows - Dorothy Charques 1000

Men Were Deceivers Ever - Patricia Veryan 6470

Merchant of the Ruby - Alice Harwood 2766

The Merchant Prince - Henry Christopher Bailey 267

Merlin - Stephen R. Lawhead 3681

The Merrymaid - Mollie Hardwick 2696

The Michaelmas Tree - Helen Ashfield 209

Midnight Moon - Jeanne Montague 4436

Midsummer Masque - Jill Tattersall 6174

Midsummer Moon - Karen Lynn 3940

Midwinter - John Buchan 751

The Mighty and Their Fall - Ivy Compton-Burnett 1230

Mine Is the Kingdom - Jane Oliver 4726

The Miracle at St. Bruno's - Philippa Carr 925

Miss Hartwell's Dilemma - Carola Dunn 1796

The Missolonghi Manuscript - Frederic Prokosch 5194

Mistaken Virtues - Joanna Trollope 6349

Mister Christian - William Kinsolving 3502

Mistress Anne - Carolly Erickson 1952

Mistress of Willowvale - Patricia Veryan 6471

The Mists of Avalon - Marion Zimmer Bradley 626

Moonfeather - Judith E. French 2223

Moonraker's Bride - Madeleine Brent 661

Morality Play - Barry Unsworth 6387

Mortal Love: A Novel of Eleanor of Aquitaine - Linda Hutchins 3090

Mother and Son - Ivy Compton-Burnett 1231

The Mountain of Immoderate Desires - Leslie Wilson 6811

Mr. Christian! - Stanley Miller 4402

Mr. Oddity, Samuel Johnson - Charles Norman 4643

Mrs. Betsy, or Widowed and Wed - Francis Marton 4141

The Murder in the Tower - Jean Plaidy 5035

Murder Most Royal - Jean Plaidy 5036

The Murder of Lawrence of Arabia - Matthew Eden 1865

The Muscovite - Alison Macleod 4004

The Mutual Friend - Frederick Busch 811

My Beloved Son - Catherine Cookson 1285

My Dear Lover England - Pamela Bennetts 453

My Gallant Enemy - Rexanne Becnel 409

My Grand Enemy - Jean Stubbs 6098

My Lady Glamis - Pamela Hill 2940

My Lady Hoyden - Jane Sheridan 5812

My Lady Innkeeper - Barbara Metzger 4346

My Life for My Sheep - Alfred Duggan 1772

My Lord Brother the Lionheart - Molly Costain Haycraft 2795

My Lord Essex - Olive Eckerson 1838

My Lord Foxe - Constance Gluyas 2443

My Lord John - Georgette Heyer 2895

My Lord of Canterbury - Godfrey Turton 6369

My Lord the Fox - Robert York 6932

My Love Must Wait: The Story of Matthew Flinders - Ernestine Hill 2922

My Sister, My Love - Lucille Iremonger 3111

Myself as Witness - James Goldman 2458

Myself My Enemy - Jean Plaidy 5037

The Nelson Touch - Paul Lewis 3759

Nethergate - Norah Lofts 3854

A Night in Cold Harbor - Margaret Kennedy 3420

Night Shall Overtake Us - Kate Saunders 5611

Night Storm - Catherine Coulter 1378

No Bed for Bacon - Caryl Brahms 640

No Man's Land - William Fairchild 2004

No Price Too High - Madeleine Polland 5085

No Wall So High - Anne Powers 5152

The Noblest Frailty - Patricia Veryan 6474

The Norman Pretender - Valerie Anand 132

The Novice's Tale - Margaret Frazer 2217

Now, God Be Thanked - John Masters 4177

Officer and Gentleman - Josephine Delves-Broughton 1604
The Olympians - Guy Bolton 566
On the Night of the Seventh Moon - Victoria Holt 3018
The Once and Future King - T.H. White 6705
The Origin - Irving Stone 6060
Oscar and Lucinda - Peter Carey 894
Out of the Dark - Norah Lofts 3856
Out on Any Limb - John Myers 4545
The Outlaw's Tale - Margaret Frazer 2218
The Pagan King - Edison Marshall 4109
Painting the Darkness - Robert Goddard 2445
The Paladin - George Shipway 5830
Passage to Pontefract - Jean Plaidy 5038
The Passionate Enemies - Jean Plaidy 5039
The Pearl Pagoda - Susannah Broome 707
The Pendragon - Catherine Christian 1075
Pendragon - Stephen R. Lawhead 3682
Pendragon's Banner - Helen Hollick 3001
Penelope Goes to Portsmouth - Marion Chesney 1043
The Phoenix Rising - Jean Evans 1984
The Physician - Noah Gordon 2482
Physician Extraordinary: A Novel of the Life and Times of William Harvey - David Weiss 6608
Piccadilly - Claire Rayner 5267
The Pilgrim Prince - Gladys H. Barr 343
The Pillars of the Earth - Ken Follett 2149
The Pilot - James Fenimore Cooper 1306
The Pirate and the Pagan - Virginia Henley 2827
A Place of Ravens - Pamela Hill 2942
The Plantagenet Prelude - Jean Plaidy 5041
Playing the Game - Ian Buruma 810
Playing the Jack - Mary Brown 726
The Pleasures of Love - Jean Plaidy 5042
The Plot to Kill Wallis Simpson: A Work of Faction - Graham Fisher 2104
Pocahontas; or, The Nonpareil of Virginia - David Garnett 2297
Pomp and Circumstance - Fred Mustard Stewart 6025
The Portingale - Alison Macleod 4005
Powhatan's Daughter - John Clarke Bowman 605
Practice to Deceive - Patricia Veryan 6475
The Predators - F.A. Parker 4804
Presumption: An Entertainment - Julia Barrett 350
The Pride of Lions - Marsha Canham 881
The Prime Minister's Wife - Doris Leslie 3727
A Prince, a Piper, and a Rose - John Scalzo 5628
The Prince and the Pilgrim - Mary Stewart 6032
The Prince of Darkness - Jean Plaidy 5044
The Prince Regent's Silver Bell - Gladys McGorian 4275
Princess in Amber - Evelyn Wilde Mayerson 4205
Princess of Fire - Shannon Drake 1718
Prisoner of the Queen - Alison Macleod 4006
Prisons - Mary Lee Settle 5757
The Private Life of Florence Nightingale - Richard Gordon 2485
The Proprietor - Ann Schlee 5638
Proud Heritage - Ilse Bishcoff 510
The Proud Servant: The Story of Montrose - Margaret Irwin 3120
The Queen and Lord M - Jean Plaidy 5046
The Queen and the Gypsy - Constance Heaven 2810
Queen Anne Boleyn - Francis Hackett 2634
The Queen From Provence - Jean Plaidy 5047
Queen in Waiting - Jean Plaidy 5048
Queen of the Summer Stars - Persia Woolley 6869
Queen of This Realm: The Story of Queen Elizabeth I - Jean Plaidy 5050
Queen Victoria's Bomb - Ronald Clark 1094
The Queen's Favourites - Jean Plaidy 5051
The Queen's Grace - Jan Westcott 6646
The Queen's Husband - Samuel Edwards 1889
The Queen's Husband - Jean Plaidy 5052
The Queen's Knight - Marvin Borowsky 585
Queen's Play - Dorothy Dunnett 1805

The Queen's Secret - Jean Plaidy 5053
The Queen's Sister - Sandra Wilson 6815
The Queen's Ward - Hebe Elsna 1933
A Quest for Love - Jacquetta Hawkes 2781
A Question of Honour - Emma Drummond 1726
The Quickenberry Tree - Annette Motley 4502
The Quiet Gentleman - Georgette Heyer 2897
Quiet Lady - Norman Collins 1216
The Rag Nymph - Catherine Cookson 1287
Rags of Glory - Stuart Cloete 1126
The Raiders: A Novel of the Civil War at Sea - Willard Wallace 6541
The Railway King - Margaret Mayhew 4207
The Rain Maiden - Jill M. Phillips 4985
The Rake - Karen Lynn 3941
Ralegh's Fair Bess: The Story of Bess Throckmorton - Judy Turner 6365
Ram: Being the Tale of One Ramillies Anstruther - Winchombe Taylor 6193
Ramage and the Guillotine - Dudley Pope 5099
Ramage at Trafalgar - Dudley Pope 5102
The Rationalist - Warwick Collins 1217
Ravenshoe - Henry Kingsley 3500
Ravished - Amanda Quick 5216
Rebel Heiress - Robert Neill 4573
Reckless - Amanda Quick 5217
Reckless Angel - Jane Feather 2056
The Reckoning - Sharon Kay Penman 4906
The Red-Haired Brat - Joanna Dessau 1627
Red Lion and Gold Dragon - Rosemary Sprague 5969
Red Queen, White Queen - Henry Treece 6332
Red Rose of Anjou - Jean Plaidy 5054
Redemption - Leon Uris 6393
Refuge in Avalon - Marguerite Steedman 5984
The Regent's Daughter - Jean Plaidy 5055
Reluctant Cavalier - Donald Barr Chidsey 1064
The Reluctant Heiress - Annabel Laine 3588
The Reluctant Queen - Molly Costain Haycraft 2796
The Reluctant Queen: The Story of Anne of York - Jean Plaidy 5056
Rendezvous - Amanda Quick 5218
Restoration: A Novel of Seventeenth-Century England - Rose Tremain 6333
The Return of the Gypsy - Philippa Carr 927
Return of the Stranger - Reay Tannahill 6158
The Revolt of the Eaglets - Jean Plaidy 5057
The Rich Are with You Always - Malcolm Macdonald 3971
Richard III: The Last Plantagenet - Tyler Whittle 6722
Richard Bolitho—Midshipman - Alexander Kent 3437
Ride East! Ride West!: A Romance of the Hundred Years' War - Anne Powers 5154
Ride Home Tomorrow - Evan John 3221
Rider on a White Horse - Rosemary Sutcliff 6124
The Ring Master - David Gurr 2622
Rivers of Gold - Janet Edmonds 1868
The Road to Avalon - Joan Wolf 6842
Roanoke Hundred - Inglis Fletcher 2138
Robin and the King - Parke Godwin 2448
The Robsart Affair - Jennette Letton 3729
Rogue's Holiday - Hamilton Cochran 1141
The Roman - Mika Waltari 6554
Roman Go Home! - Adam Fergusson 2065
Room with a Clue - Kate Kingsbury 3495
The Rose at Harvest End - Eleanor Fairburn 2003
The Rose Crossing - Nicholas Jose 3306
The Rose Without a Thorn - Jean Plaidy 5058
Rosehaven - Catherine Coulter 1380
Royal Flush: The Story of Minette - Margaret Irwin 3121
Royal Nonesuch: A Tudor Tapestry - Beatrice White 6674
The Royal Pawn - Antonia Ridge 5327
A Royal Quest - Mary Lide 3777
Royal Road to Fotheringay - Jean Plaidy 5059
Royal William - Doris Leslie 3728

Sacred and Profane: A Novel of the Life and Times of Mozart - David Weiss 6609
St. Thomas's Eve - Jean Plaidy 5060
Saraband for Two Sisters - Philippa Carr 928
Satan's Fire - P.C. Doherty 1677
The Saxon Tapestry - Sile Rice 5317
Scandal - Amanda Quick 5219
Scapegoat for a Stuart - Kate Kirby 3504
The Scottish Marriage - Karen Lynn 3942
The Sea Beggars - Cecelia Holland 2996
The Sea Officer - Showell Styles 6105
The Secret Memoirs of Lord Byron - Christopher Nicole 4622
Secret Song - Catherine Coulter 1381
The Secret Years - Judith Lennox-Smith 3718
Seduction - Amanda Quick 5220
Seedtime and Harvest - Mary E. Pearce 4864
Seek Out and Destroy - James David Horan 3031
The Serpent Garden - Judith Merkle Riley 5336
The Serpent's Tooth - Diana L. Paxson 4846
The Servant's Tale - Margaret Frazer 2219
Service for Two - Kate Kingsbury 3496
The Seven Ages - Eva Figes 2084
Seven Men of Gascony - R.F. Delderfield 1589
Seven Tempest - William Vaughan Wilkins 6761
Seventeen of Leyden - John James 3160
The Severed Crown - Jane Lane 3657
Shadow in the Sun: A Novel of Elizabeth I, the Virgin Queen - F.W. Kenyon 3460
The Shadow of the Earth - Lee Wichelns 6731
The Shadow of the Pomegranate - Jean Plaidy 5062
Shadow of the Wolf - James Barwick 371
Shadows and Images - Meriol Trevor 6344
Shadows on the Stones - Moyra Caldecott 847
Shadows over Castle Rising - Fanny Cradock 1410
Sharpe's Regiment - Bernard Cornwell 1345
The She-Wolf - Pamela Bennetts 456
The She-Wolf of France - Maurice Druon 1736
The Sherbrooke Bride - Catherine Coulter 1382
Sherlock Holmes and the Case of Sabina Hall - L.B. Greenwood 2576
Sherlock in Love - Sena Jeter Naslund 4557
Shield of Honor - Alice Walworth Graham 2511
Shield of Three Lions - Pamela Kaufman 3372
Signals of Distress - Jim Crace 1408
The Silent Woman - Edward Marston 4128
Silver Cross - Mary Johnston 3239
A Silver Mirror - Roberta Gellis 2353
The Silver Saber - Carter A. Vaughan 6441
Simon the Coldheart - Georgette Heyer 2901
The Singing Sword - Jack Whyte 6725
The Sinner of Saint Ambrose - Robert Raynolds 5275
Sir Rogue - Leslie Turner White 6691
Sir William - David Stacton 5977
Sister to Jane: The Story of Lady Katharine Grey - Beatrice May 4202
The Sixth Wife - Jean Plaidy 5063
The Skystone: The Forging of Arthur's Britain - Jack Whyte 6726
The Smile of the Stranger - Joan Aiken 53
Snared Nightingale - Geoffrey Trease 6324
So Merciful a Queen, So Cruel a Woman - Alice Harwood 2769
So Perish the Roses - Neil Bell 423
Soldier in Paradise - Burton Wohl 6835
Some Brief Folly - Patricia Veryan 6478
The Son of York - Margaret Abbey 5
The Song of the Siren - Philippa Carr 929
The Sound of Coaches - Leon Garfield 2295
Sound of the Trumpet - Gilbert Morris 4471
A Space of the Heart - Patricia Wright 6884
The Spanish Bridegroom - Jean Plaidy 5064
A Sparkle From the Coal - Prudence Andrew 144
The Spitfire - Bertrice Small 5912
Sprig Muslin - Georgette Heyer 2903
The Spring of the Tiger - Victoria Holt 3021
Squadron Shilling - Arch Whitehouse 6712
Stacey's Flyer - Patricia Burns 800

Stage of Fools - Charles Andrew Brady 635
A Stake in the Kingdom - Nigel Tranter 6321
The Stanbroke Girls - Fiona Hill 2925
Stand We at Last - Zoe Fairbairns 1999
The Star of Lancaster - Jean Plaidy 5065
The Stone Arrow - Richard Herley 2858
Stormswift - Madeleine Brent 662
Strange Meeting - Susan Hill 2952
Stranger at Wildings - Madeleine Brent 663
The Stranger Prince - Margaret Irwin 3122
The Stress of Her Regard - Tim Powers 5157
The Strong Room - Jere Hungerford Wheelwright 6671
The Summer Queen - Alice Walworth Graham 2512
The Sun in Splendour - Jean Plaidy 5066
The Sun Is God - Michael Noonan 4636
The Sunne in Splendour - Sharon Kay Penman 4907
The Surgeon's Mate - Patrick O'Brian 4674
Surrender - Amanda Quick 5221
The Sutburys - Pamela Hill 2944
The Swan and the Rose - Francis W. Leary 3697
The Swan of Usk - Helen Ashton 220
Swandowne - Daniel Farson 2024
The Swedish Nightingale: Jenny Lind - Elizabeth Kyle 3571
Sweet Adelaide - Julian Symons 6152
Sweet Lass of Richmond Hill - Jean Plaidy 5067
Sweet's Folly - Fiona Hill 2926
Sword at Sunset - Rosemary Sutcliff 6125
Swords in the North - Paul Lewis Anderson 138
The Swords of December - Robert York 6933
Take Heed of Loving Me: A Novel about John Donne - Elizabeth Gray Vining 6502
Taliesin - Stephen R. Lawhead 3683
The Tall One - Barbara Jefferis 3175
The Tall Stones - Moyra Caldecott 848
The Taming - Jude Deveraux 1633
Taste of Glory Carleton Beals 394
The Taverners' Place - Joanna Trollope 6351
The Tempestuous Petticoat - Mary Ann Gibbs 2397
The Temple of the Sun - Moyra Caldecott 849
The Ten-Day Queen - Lozania Prole 5199
Ten Years Beyond Baker Street - Cay Van Ash 6400
Thanksgiving - Terry Coleman 1207
That Spanish Woman - F.W. Kenyon 3461
That Sweet and Savage Land - Emma Drummond 1728
Theo and Matilda - Rachel Billington 498
These Old Shades - Georgette Heyer 2906
They Seek a Country - Francis Brett Young 6941
The Third George - Jean Plaidy 5068
This Bright Sword - Donald Barr Chidsey 1066
The Thistle and the Rose - Jean Plaidy 5069
The Thorn of Arimathea - Frank G. Slaughter 5905
Three Cheers for Me - Donald Jack 3131
The Three Crowns - Jean Plaidy 5070
The Three Musketeers - Alexandre Dumas 1782
Tigerlilies - Judith Glover 2439
Till the Day Goes Down - Judith Lennox-Smith 3719
Time and Chance - Gwen Davenport 1501
Time's Fool - Patricia Veryan 6479
To Keep This Oath - Hebe Weenolsen 6597
To Love a Queen - Lawrence Schoonover 5669
To Love Again - Bertrice Small 5913
To Serve Them All My Days - R.F. Delderfield 1591
To Spit Against the Wind - Benjamin H. Levin 3737
A Token of Jewels - Diane Cory 1353
The Toll-Gate - Georgette Heyer 2907
Tomorrow's Fire - Jay Williams 6775
Too Near the Throne - Molly Costain Haycraft 2797
The Tower and the Dream - Jan Westcott 6647
The Town House - Norah Lofts 3861
Trade Imperial - Alan Lloyd 3814
A Trail of Blood - Jeremy Potter 5143
The Traitors of Bosworth - Robert Farrington 2021
Treasure Island - Robert Louis Stevenson 6012
The Tree of Knowledge - Eva Figes 2085
Tricolour - Mark Logan 3866

Tros of Samothrace - Talbot Mundy 4515
Troy Chimneys - Margaret Kennedy 3421
Trumpet at the Gate - Jan Widgery 6739
Tudor Agent - Robert Farrington 2022
The Tudor Rose - Margaret Campbell Barnes 329
Tudor Underground - Denis Meadows 4320
The Tune That They Play - William Clive 1120
Two Corinthians - Carola Dunn 1797
Two Loves Have I - Clara Longworth de Chambrun 985
Two Ravens - Cecelia Holland 2997
The Tynedale Daughters - Norma Lee Clark 1093
The Tyrant - Patricia Veryan 6480
Uneasy Lies the Head - Jean Plaidy 5071
An Unequal Marriage; or Pride and Prejudice Twenty Years Later - Emma Tennant 6202
Unicorn Rampant - Nigel Tranter 6323
The Unknown Ajax - Georgette Heyer 2908
An Unknown Welshman - Jean Stubbs 6100
Until the Colors Fade - Tim Jeal 3173
Up She Rises - David Garnett 2298
Venetia - Georgette Heyer 2909
Version and Diversion - Judith Terry 6207
Vice Avenged: A Moral Tale - Lolah Burford 774
Victoria in the Wings - Jean Plaidy 5072
Victoria Victorious - Jean Plaidy 5073
The Viking - Edison Marshall 4113
The Villains: A Haunting Tale of the Marshes - Charlotte Keppel 3467
A Vision of Light - Judith Merkle Riley 5337
Voices in a Haunted Room - Philippa Carr 931
Vollands - Pamela Hill 2947
The Vow on the Heron - Jean Plaidy 5074
Vows of the Peacock - Alice Walworth Graham 2513
The Wagered Widow - Patricia Veryan 6481
Walk with Peril - Dorothy V.S. Jackson 3132
Wallis: The Novel - Anne Edwards 1883
The Wandering Arm - Sharan Newman 4603
The Wandering Prince - Jean Plaidy 5075
War Comes to Castle Rising - Fanny Cradock 1411
War Story: A Novel - Derek Robinson 5404
Ward of the Sun King - Mildred Allen Butler 826
Warrior Queen - James Sinclair 5865
The Warwick Heiress - Margaret Abbey 6
Waverley - Sir Walter Scott 5709
The Way to the Lantern - Audrey Erskine Lindop 3790
We Speak No Treason - Rosemary Hawley Jarman 3168
We Stood for Freedom - Iris Morley 4455
The Weeping Ash - Joan Aiken 54
When Christ and His Saints Slept - Sharon Kay Penman 4908
When God Slept - Peter Bourne 597
While the Music Lasts - Suzanne Goodwin 2477
The White Boar - Marian Palmer 4780
The White Company - Sir Arthur Conan Doyle 1716
The White Cutter - David Pownall 5158
The White Dove - Rosie Thomas 6246
The White Queen - Frederic Fallon 2011
The White Queen - Lesley J. Nickell 4611
The White Rajah - Nicholas Monsarrat 4433
The White Raven - Diana L. Paxson 4847
The White Rose - Jan Westcott 6648
The White Witch - Elizabeth Goudge 2496
Who Was Then the Gentleman - Charles E. Israel 3125
The Whyte Harte - P.C. Doherty 1681
Wide Sargasso Sea - Jean Rhys 5312
The Widow of Windsor - Jean Plaidy 5076
The Widow of Windsor - Tyler Whittle 6723
Wife to Great Buckingham - Hilda Lewis 3751
Wife to Henry V - Hilda Lewis 3752
Wife to the Bastard - Hilda Lewis 3753
Wild Jasmine - Bertrice Small 5914
Will You Love Me in September? - Philippa Carr 932
William's Wife - Jean Plaidy 5077
The Wind Brings Up the Rain - Eric Malpass 4051

The Wind From Hastings - Morgan Llywelyn 3825
The Wind From the Sea - Constance Heaven 2812
Wind of Change at Castle Rising - Fanny Cradock 1412
Windover - Jane Aiken Hodge 2974
The Wingless Bird - Catherine Cookson 1292
The Wings of Morning - Karen Harper 2714
Wings of the Falcon - Barbara Michaels 4361
Wings of the Morning - David Beaty 402
The Wings of the Morning - Thomas Tryon 6356
The Winter King - Bernard Cornwell 1351
The Winter Rose - Millie J. Ragosta 5243
The Winthrop Woman - Anya Seton 5754
The Wise Virgin - Hebe Elsna 1934
Witch of the North - Courtway Jones 3272
Witness to Treason - Millie J. Ragosta 5244
The Wizard's Daughter - Barbara Michaels 4362
The Wolf at the Door - Graham Shelby 5793
The Wolf of Masada - John Fredman 2220
Wolf's Embrace - Gail Link 3801
Wolfshead - Jere Hungerford Wheelwright 6672
Wolves of the Dawn - William Sarabande 5604
A Woman by Design - Frances Kennett 3426
The Wrong Plantagenet - Marian Palmer 4781
The Yellow Admiral - Patrick O'Brian 4680
The Young and Lonely King - Jane Lane 3659
Young Bess - Margaret Irwin 3123
The Young Elizabeth - Jennette Letton 3730
Young Pitt - A.M. Maughan 4200
The Young Victoria - Tyler Whittle 6724
Yvonne Goes to York - Marion Chesney 1054

Ashby
Ivanhoe - Sir Walter Scott 5699

Ashdon
Women of Ashdon - Valerie Anand 135

Banbury
The Moon in the Water - Pamela Belle 433

Bath
Allegra - Clare Darcy 1483
Antipodes Jane: A Novel of Jane Austen in Australia - Barbara Ker Wilson 3468
Bath Tangle - Georgette Heyer 2875
The Black Moth - Georgette Heyer 2877
Black Sheep - Georgette Heyer 2878
A Falling Star - Pamela Belle 431
The Foundling - Georgette Heyer 2888
Freedom's Banner - Teresa Crane 1415
Georgina - Clare Darcy 1488
Jane and the Unpleasantness at Scargrave Manor - Stephanie Barron 356
Lady of Quality - Georgette Heyer 2893
Last of Britain - Meriol Trevor 6343
Lord Vanity - Samuel Shellabarger 5796
Monsieur Beaucaire - Booth Tarkington 6163
Murder by the Waters - Robert Lee Hall 2661
Parson Austen's Daughter - Helen Ashton 219
The Regiment - Christopher Nicole 4620
The Summer of the Royal Visit - Isabel Colegate 1199
Teverton Hall - Jane Gillespie 2421
Treason's Gift - Pamela Belle 434
Wintercombe - Pamela Belle 435

Bidminster
The Wedding Guest - Anna Gilbert 2407

Birmingham
The Peculiar People - Jan de Hartog 2764
The Shakespeare Girl - Mollie Hardwick 2698

Blastburn
Midnight Is a Place - Joan Aiken 52

Bodmin
Jamaica Inn - Daphne Du Maurier 1747

Brentborough
Red Adam's Lady - Grace Ingram 3106

Bridgewater
Captain Blood - Rafael Sabatini   5546

Brighton
Beatrice Goes to Brighton - Marion Chesney   1019
Blackstone and the Scourge of Europe - Richard Falkirk   2007
Claire - Elizabeth Lyle   3931
Elyza - Clare Darcy   1486
Footman in Powder - Helen Ashton   216
A Love So Wild - Deborah Chester   1056
Mad Hatter's Holiday - Peter Lovesey   3914
Regency Buck - Georgette Heyer   2898
Regency Rogue - Helen Ashfield   212
Regency Royal - Michael Hardwick   2687
Sanguinet's Crown - Patricia Veryan   6476
The Sugar Pavilion - Rosalind Laker   3600
Warwyck's Woman - Rosalind Laker   3604

Bristol
The Cannaway Concern - Graham Shelby   5788
Chatterton - Peter Ackroyd   17
The Clock Tower - Jeanne Montague   4435
The Fine and Handsome Captain - Frances Lynch   3933
The Lorimer Line - Anne Melville   4332
A New Creature - Prudence Andrew   141
Pilgrims in Paradise - Frank G. Slaughter   5895
A Respectable Trade - Philippa Gregory   2584
The Sun Is My Undoing - Marguerite Steen   5988
Warm Wind, West Wind - Anne Irwin Matthew   4188
The Weaver's Tale - Kate Sedley   5719

Bristol Channel
The Maid of Sker - R.D. Blackmore   529

Broadstairs
Murder Makes an Entree - Amy Myers   4540

Buckinghamshire
Bertie and the Seven Bodies - Peter Lovesey   3908

Bury St. Edmonds
A Calf for Venus - Norah Lofts   3838

Cambridge
A Company of Swans - Eva Ibbotson   3095
Liza Bowe - Shirley Barker   313
Mermaid Tavern - George William Cronyn   1429
Once a Gentleman - Donald James   3157
The Shadow Flies - Rose Macaulay   3956
Sporting with Amaryllis - Paul West   6635
To Be a King - Robert DeMaria   1607
An Unholy Alliance - Susanna Gregory   2586
The World as I Found It - Bruce Duffy   1755

Cambridgeshire
The Last Summer of Innocence - Linda Sole   5938
Rake's Ransom - Barbara Metzger   4347

Camelot
A Connecticut Yankee in King Arthur's Court - Mark Twain   6371
The Last Enchantment - Mary Stewart   6031
The Wicked Day - Mary Stewart   6033

Canterbury
The Book of Shadows - C.L. Grace   2505
The Eye of God - C.L. Grace   2506
The Lion of Christ - Margaret Butler   823
The Lion of Justice - Margaret Butler   825
The Merchant of Death - C.L. Grace   2508
The Right Line of Cedric - Alfred Duggan   1773
A Shrine of Murders - C.L. Grace   2509
Thomas: A Novel of the Life, Passions, and Miracles of Becket - Shelley Mydans   4538
To Be a King - Robert DeMaria   1607
The White Rose Murders - Michael Clynes   1137

Canterton
The Time of the Hunter's Moon - Victoria Holt   3022

Carlisle
A Famine of Horses - P.F. Chisholm   1071
A Season of Knives - P.F. Chisholm   1072

Castlewood
Henry Esmond - William Makepeace Thackeray   6212

Channel Coast
Hangman's Cliff - Robert Neill   4570

Chartley
My Enemy the Queen - Victoria Holt   3017

Chelmsford
Familiar Spirits - Leonard Tourney   6298
Frobisher's Savage - Leonard Tourney   6299
Low Treason - Leonard Tourney   6301
The Players' Boy Is Dead - Leonard Tourney   6303
Witness of Bones - Leonard Tourney   6304

Cheltenham
The Hedge of Thorns - Helen Ashton   217

Cheshire
The Country Gentleman - Fiona Hill   2924

Chester
The Long Day Closes - Beatrice Tunstall   6360

Colby
The Time of the Hunter's Moon - Victoria Holt   3022

Colne
The Mills of Colne - Robert Neill   4572

Cornwall
The Angry Tide - Winston Graham   2521
Armada - Charles Gidley   2404
Ben Retallick - E.V. Thompson   6263
The Black Moon - Winston Graham   2522
The Black Swan - Philippa Carr   917
The Cage - Michael Weston   6650
Camelot Country - Marjorie McEvoy   4267
Castle Dor - Sir Arthur Thomas Quiller-Couch   5226
Castle Heritage - Elisabeth Barr   337
The Changeling - Philippa Carr   918
Chase the Wind - E.V. Thompson   6264
Dark Inheritance - Carola Salisbury   5568
Deborah and the Siege of Paris - Colette Davenat   1500
Demelza - Winston Graham   2524
Ellen Bray - Jane Julian   3319
Emerald - Helen Ashfield   206
The Faithful Lovers - Valerie Anand   129
The Far-Off Rhapsody - Anne-Marie Sheridan   5808
The Fortunate Marriage - Meriol Trevor   6342
The Four Swans - Winston Graham   2525
Frenchman's Creek - Daphne Du Maurier   1744
The Grove of Eagles - Winston Graham   2526
Heir to Polventon - Marjorie Watson   6583
An Innocent Woman - Malcolm Macdonald   3967
Jamaica Inn - Daphne Du Maurier   1747
Kernow & Daughter - Malcolm Macdonald   3968
The King's General - Daphne Du Maurier   1748
The Land Beyond the Tempest - Drayton Mayrant   4213
The Last Gamble - Winston Graham   2527
The Legacy of Tregaran - Mary Lide   3776
Lilith - Jean Plaidy   5030
Lord of the Far Island - Victoria Holt   3016
Midshipman Bolitho and the Avenger - Alexander Kent   3435
Midsummer's Eve - Philippa Carr   924
The Miller's Dance - Winston Graham   2528
The Nightingale Legacy - Catherine Coulter   1379
A Notorious Woman - Malcolm Macdonald   3969
O Western Wind - John Anthony Devon   1634
On a Far Wide Shore - Malcolm Macdonald   3970
Polonaise - Piers Paul Read   5278
Polsinney Harbour - Mary E. Pearce   4863
The Pool of St. Branok - Philippa Carr   926

The Pride of the Trevallions - Carola Salisbury   5570
Put Off Thy Shoes - Ethel Lillian Voynich   6513
The Renegade: A Novel of Cornwall, 1783-1787 - Winston Graham   2529
Ruan - Bryher   746
The Sea Scape - Mary Lide   3778
The Sea Treasure - Elisabeth Barr   338
The Shadowed Spring - Carola Salisbury   5571
A Shadow's Bliss - Patricia Veryan   6477
The Stranger From the Sea - Winston Graham   2530
To the End of Her Days - Malcolm Macdonald   3975
A Tradition of Victory - Alexander Kent   3443
Tregaran - Mary Lide   3779
The Trevarton Inheritance - Malcolm Macdonald   3976
The Valiant Lady - Brigid Knight   3523
Venture Once More - Winston Graham   2532
The Winter Bride - Carola Salisbury   5572
A Woman Possessed - Malcolm Macdonald   3977

Cotswolds
The Unsuitable Miss Pelham - June Drummond   1730

Coventry
Brother Cadfael's Penance - Ellis Peters   4955
The Consuming Flame: The Story of George Eliot - F.W. Kenyon   3446
Lady Godiva and Master Tom - Raoul Cohen Faure   2052

Cumberland
Griffith Gaunt - Charles Reade   5280
Hand of Glory - Glen Petrie   4980
The Hired Man - Melvyn Bragg   639
Norah - Pamela Hill   2941
Red Gauntlet - Sir Walter Scott   5706
Rogue Herries - Hugh Walpole   6547
Vanessa - Hugh Walpole   6548

Cumbria
Marianne - Glen Petrie   4981

Darlington
The Far Side of the Hill - Nancy Livingston   3811
The Land of Our Dreams - Nancy Livingston   3812

Dartmoor
The Artist's Daughter - Leslie O'Grady   4698
The Lively Lady - Kenneth Roberts   5386
Lord Raven's Widow - Leslie O'Grady   4700
Topaz - Helen Ashfield   215

Derbyshire
Old Saxon Blood - Leonard Tourney   6302
Pemberley, or Pride and Prejudice Continued - Emma Tennant   6201
Peveril of the Peak - Sir Walter Scott   5703

Devon
Eden and Honor - Marilyn Harris   2729
The Eden Passion - Marilyn Harris   2730
Eden Rising - Marilyn Harris   2731
The Price of Blood - Doris Sutcliffe Adams   24
The Prince of Eden - Marilyn Harris   2732
The Scarlet Cloak - Jean Plaidy   5061
This Other Eden - Marilyn Harris   2733
The Time of the Hunter's Moon - Victoria Holt   3022
The Wanton Fires - Meriol Trevor   6345
Westward Ho! - Charles Kingsley   3499
Wild Swan - Celeste De Blasis   1550
The Women of Eden - Marilyn Harris   2734

Devonshire
The Artist's Daughter - Leslie O'Grady   4698
Hellbane - Anthony Esler   1963
A Horseman Riding By - R.F. Delderfield   1588
The Third Sister - Julia Barrett   351

Dorset
The Darkening Leaf - Caroline Stickland   6036
The Darkness of Corn - Caroline Stickland   6037

Deception - Amanda Quick 5214
Harvest of Death - Ray Harrison 2741
The Standing Hills - Caroline Stickland 6038
The Trial of Jenny Sykes - Hebe Weenolsen 6598
The Trumpet Major - Thomas Hardy 2700

Dover
The Real David Copperfield - Robert Graves 2551

Dungesey
The Morning Gift - Diana Norman 4645

Durham
The Maltese Angel - Catherine Cookson 1283

East Anglia
The Adversary - Jan Widgery 6738
The Floral Companion - Anthea Bell 419
Lord of Ravensley - Constance Heaven 2809
Stephen and the Sleeping Saints - Pamela
  Bennetts 457

Easthampton
Claudine's Daughter - Rosalind Laker 3594

Ely
The Disputed Crown - Valerie Anand 128

Epping Forest
Three Years to Play - Colin MacInnes 3983

Essex
Death at Gallows Green - Robin Paige 4776
Judith - Brian Cleeve 1108
Sara - Brian Cleeve 1110
Teverton Hall - Jane Gillespie 2421

Exeter
This January Tale - Bryher 747

Exmoor
Lorna Doone - R.D. Blackmore 528

Fens
Beauty for Ashes - Timothy R. Wilson 6816
Master of Morholm - Timothy R. Wilson 6817

Finchale
Godric - Frederick Buechner 763

Gildenford
Gildenford - Valerie Anand 130
The Proud Villeins - Valerie Anand 133

Glastonbury
The Grail Murders - Michael Clynes 1135

Gloucester
April Rising - Susan Sallis 5574

Gloucestershire
The Constant Star - Prudence Andrew 139
Cressida - Clare Darcy 1485
Ordeal by Silence - Prudence Andrew 142
A Question of Choice - Prudence Andrew 143
Richard Whittington, London's Mayor - Gwynedd
  Sudworth 6112
The Two Farms - Mary E. Pearce 4865

Greenwich
Anne Boleyn - Evelyn Anthony 158
Boon Island - Kenneth Roberts 5384

Guernsey
Castaway - Frances Murray 4535
Devil to Pay - C. Northcote Parkinson 4810

Hampshire
Borrowed Plumes - Roseleen Milne 4409
The Commodore - Patrick O'Brian 4661
Cousin Susannah - Hazel Hucker 3066
Eliza Stanhope - Joanna Trollope 6347
Jane Fairfax - Joan Aiken 50
Mansfield Revisited - Joan Aiken 51
Ride the Blue Riband - Rosalind Laker 3598

Harrogate
Agatha - Kathleen Tynan 6374

Hastings
The Conqueror - Georgette Heyer 2881
The Firedrake - Cecelia Holland 2988
The Fourteenth of October - Bryher 742
The Golden Warrior: The Story of Harold and William
  - Hope Muntz 4517
Harold, the Last of the Saxon Kings - Edward Bulwer-
  Lytton 767

Haworth
Bronte - Glyn Hughes 3073
Dark Quartet: The Story of the Brontes - Lynne Reid
  Banks 290
In the Shadow of the Brontes - Louise Brindley 690
Path to the Silent Country - Lynne Reid Banks 291
These Were the Brontes - Dorothy Helen
  Cornish 1332
Wild Decembers: A Biographical Portrait of the
  Brontes - Hilda Crystal White 6681

Hayslope
Adam Bede - George Eliot 1908

Henley
Lavender Lady - Carola Dunn 1794
Swing, Swing Together - Peter Lovesey 3915

Herefordshire
The Dragons of Archenfield - Edward Marston 4119

Hertfordshire
Charity Girl - Georgette Heyer 2879
Fitzempress' Law - Diana Norman 4644
Jane and the Unpleasantness at Scargrave Manor -
  Stephanie Barron 356
The Parfit Knight - Juliet Blyth 555

Highbury
A Visit to Highbury - Joan Austen-Leigh 243

Hillbridge
The Hours of Light - Janet Tanner 6160

Hopeworth
Daphne - Marion Chesney 1022
Deirdre and Desire - Marion Chesney 1024
Diana the Huntress - Marion Chesney 1026
Frederica in Fashion - Marion Chesney 1032
Minerva - Marion Chesney 1037
The Taming of Annabelle - Marion Chesney 1052

Hungerford
My Lady Greensleeves - Constance Beresford-
  Howe 476

Huntingdonshire
The Hireling - Alison Macleod 4003

Isle of Man
Black Body - H.C. Turk 6361

Jersey
Lillie - David Butler 818

Kenilworth
The Apothecary Rose - Candace M. Robb 5364
Kenilworth - Sir Walter Scott 5700
My Enemy the Queen - Victoria Holt 3017

Kent
Blake's Reach - Catherine Gaskin 2313
Corner the Moon - Shirley Barker 310
The Detling Secret - Julian Symons 6151
The Eagle at the Gate - Rona Randall 5248
Eugenia - Clare Darcy 1487
Familiar Acts - June Barraclough 345
An Ice-Cream War - William Boyd 616
The Judas Kiss - Victoria Holt 3015
The Last Mutiny: The Further Adventures of Captain
  Bligh - Bill Collett 1208

The Life and Times of Horatio Hornblower - C.
  Northcote Parkinson 4813
The Marigold Field - Diane Pearson 4876
Not by Any Single Man - Brigid Knight 3522
The Summer of the Bashinskeys - Diane
  Pearson 4877
A Tapestry of Murders - C.L. Grace 2510

Knaresborough
Eugene Aram - Edward Bulwer-Lytton 766

Lake District
Angel - Carola Dunn 1790
So Near So Far - C. Northcote Parkinson 4814
Tish - Cissie Miller 4381

Lancashire
By Our Beginnings - Jean Stubbs 6092
Come Home at Even - Le Grand Cannon 884
Crompton Way - Thomas Thompson 6270
Devil's Fire, Love's Revenge - Barbara Paul 4836
An Imperfect Joy - Jean Stubbs 6099
Ladysmead: A Novel in the Jane Austen Tradition -
  Jane Gillespie 2420
A Leaf in the Wind - Marie Joseph 3307
Maggie Craig - Marie Joseph 3308
The Northern Correspondent - Jean Stubbs 6099
The Peaceable Kingdom - Jan de Hartog 2763
Ruby - Helen Ashfield 213
Sapphire - Helen Ashfield 214
Traitor's Moon - Robert Neill 4574
The Vivian Inheritance - Jean Stubbs 6101

Leeds
Dark Winds - Virginia Coffman 1152

Leicester
The King's Bed - Margaret Campbell Barnes 324

Leicestershire
The Witch and the Priest - Hilda Lewis 3754

Liverpool
Captain Rebel - Frank Yerby 6910
The Guernseyman - C. Northcote Parkinson 4812
Halfhyde on the Amazon - Philip McCutchan 4250
Passage Home - Alison McLeay 4286
Sacred Hunter - Barry Unsworth 6389
Sea Change - Alison McLeay 4287
A World Too Wide - Susan Moore 4445
Young Adolf - Beryl Bainbridge 272

London
The Abductors - Stuart Cloete 1121
Abigail - Malcolm Macdonald 3962
Abracadaver - Peter Lovesey 3906
The Absorbing Fire: The Byron Legend - F.W.
  Kenyon 3445
The Adventuress - Marion Chesney 1014
Alethea - Pamela Belle 429
The Alfred Hitchcock Murder Case - George
  Baxt 382
All the Living: A Novel of One Year in the Life of
  William Shakespeare - Henrietta Buckmaster 758
The American Heiress - Dorothy Eden 1854
An Ancient Evil - C.L. Grace 2504
Angel of Death - P.C. Doherty 1670
Angelica - Samuel A. Schreiner Jr. 5671
The Angry Tide - Winston Graham 2521
Animating Maria - Marion Chesney 1015
Anna, Ann, Annie - Thomas Trebitsch Parker 4808
Anna's Book - Barbara Vine 6500
Anne Boleyn - Evelyn Anthony 158
Anno-Dracula - Kim Newman 4595
April Lady - Georgette Heyer 2873
Arabella - Georgette Heyer 2874
Arctic Treachery - Richard Woodman 6858
The Ardent Years - Janet Stevenson 6003
The Artist's Daughter - Leslie O'Grady 4698
As the Crow Flies - Jeffrey Archer 183
The Asherwood Protegee - Mary A. Garratt 2299

At the Sign of the Golden Pineapple - Marion Chesney 1016
Attack the Lusitania! - Raymond Hitchcock 2956
Autumn Lace - Eileen Jackson 3133
The Autumn Rose - Fiona Hill 2923
Back in Society - Marion Chesney 1017
Ballenrose - Mallory Burgess 783
Barnaby Rudge: A Tale of the Riots of Eighty - Charles Dickens 1641
The Baroness of Bow Street - Gail Clark 1085
Barry Lyndon - William Makepeace Thackeray 6210
The Bartholomew Fair Murders - Leonard Tourney 6297
Beau Barron's Lady - Helen Ashfield 204
Bedford Row - Claire Rayner 5259
Behold the Fire - Michael Blankfort 541
Belgrave Square - Anne Perry 4919
Belgrave Square - Rachel Summerson 6117
The Bellamy Saga - John Pearson 4878
The Bellerose Bargain - Robyn Carr 934
Benjamin Franklin and a Case of Artful Murder - Robert Lee Hall 2654
Benjamin Franklin and a Case of Christmas Murder - Robert Lee Hall 2655
Benjamin Franklin Takes the Case - Robert Lee Hall 2656
The Best House in Stratford - Edward Fisher 2100
Bethlehem Road - Anne Perry 4920
The Bette Davis Murder Case - George Baxt 383
Beyond Desire: A Novel Based on the Life of Felix and Cecille Mendelssohn - Pierre La Mure 3574
Beyond the Blue Mountains - Jean Plaidy 5006
The Big Drum - Elizabeth Boatwright Coker 1162
Black Body - H.C. Turk 6361
The Black Moth - Georgette Heyer 2877
The Black Rose - Thomas B. Costain 1363
The Black Swan - Philippa Carr 917
Black William - Robert Neill 4567
The Blackheath Poisonings - Julian Symons 6150
Blackstone - Richard Falkirk 2006
Blind Justice - Bruce Alexander 76
Bluegate Fields - Anne Perry 4921
The Bluestocking - June Drummond 1729
The Bonnet Laird's Daughter - Barbara Annandale 154
The Book of Shadows - C.L. Grace 2505
Borrowed Plumes - Roseleen Milne 4409
Botany Bay - Charles Nordhoff 4637
The Bourlotas Fortune - Nicholas Gage 2268
The Bracegirdle - Burris Atkins Jenkins 3189
The Braganza Pursuit - Sarah Neilan 4564
The Braintree Mission - Nicholas E. Wyckoff 6887
The Branch-Bearers - Glen Petrie 4978
Braveheart - Randall Wallace 6538
The Bride of the Wilderness - Charles McCarry 4220
Bright Captivity - Eugenia Price 5180
Brimstone Club - F. van Wyck Mason 4147
The Brocken - Pamela Hill 2929
A Broken Vessel - Kate Ross 5500
A Brood of Vipers - Michael Clynes 1133
Brother Owl - Al Hine 2953
Buffalo Girls - Larry McMurtry 4296
Burton and Speke - William Harrison 2751
Bush War! - William Moore 4447
Cain and His Brother - Anne Perry 4922
Callander Square - Anne Perry 4923
The Capricorn Stone - Madeleine Brent 659
Captain Adam - Donald Barr Chidsey 1058
Captain Bolton's Corpse - J.G. Jeffreys 3178
Captain Fantom - Charles Underhill 6377
Captain for Elizabeth - Jan Westcott 6643
Captain Ironhand - Rosamond Marshall 4116
Captain Justice - Anthony Forrest 2185
Captain Nash and the Honour of England - Ragan Butler 827
Captain Nash and the Wroth Inheritance - Ragan Butler 828
Captain Wonder - Donald Thomas 6238
A Captive Freedom - Emma Drummond 1724

Cardigan Square - Alexandra Manners 4070
Cardington Crescent - Anne Perry 4924
Caroline and Julia - Clare Darcy 1484
A Case of Spirits - Peter Lovesey 3910
Cashmere - Nicola Thorne 6273
The Casket Crew - Arch Whitehouse 6709
Cassy - Elizabeth Lyle 3930
Castle Barebane - Joan Aiken 43
Castle Heritage - Elisabeth Barr 337
The Castle of the Winds - Jeanne Montague 4434
The Cater Street Hangman - Anne Perry 4925
Catherine Carter - Pamela Hansford Johnson 3227
A Certain Splendour - Carola Salisbury 5566
The Changeling - Philippa Carr 918
Charing Cross - Claire Rayner 5260
Charity Girl - Georgette Heyer 2879
The Charlatan - Carter A. Vaughan 6433
Charles - Victoria Lincoln 3786
Charlie Is My Darling - Mollie Hardwick 2691
Chase Royal - Donald Seaman 5712
Chatterton - Peter Ackroyd 17
Chelsea - Nancy Fitzgerald 2114
Chelsea Reach - Claire Rayner 5261
Chelynne - Robyn Carr 938
Circle of Pearls - Rosalind Laker 3593
Clara Reeve - Leonie Hargrave 2705
The Cleopatra Boy - Eric Malpass 4048
Clively Close: Dead as Dead Can Be - Ann Crowleigh 1434
Cock of the Walk - Roy Lewis 3762
Colonel Sandhurst to the Rescue - Marion Chesney 1021
Come Be My Love - Diana Brown 717
The Conqueror - Georgette Heyer 2881
The Consuming Flame: The Story of George Eliot - F.W. Kenyon 3446
The Convenient Marriage - Georgette Heyer 2882
Coronation Summer - Angela Thirkell 6220
Cotillion - Georgette Heyer 2883
Count Manifred - Miranda Seymour 5761
Counterfeit of Murder - Ray Harrison 2738
The Countess - March Cost 1360
The Country Gentleman - Fiona Hill 2924
Court of Shadows - Cynthia Morgan 4450
Covent Garden - Claire Rayner 5262
Cracksman on Velvet - Francis Selwyn 5743
Cressida - Clare Darcy 1485
The Cross of Frankenstein - Robert J. Myers 4548
Crown Witness - Gillian Linscott 3803
A Crowning Mercy - Susannah Kells 3396
Crystal - Helen Ashfield 205
The Crystal Dove - Mollie Hardwick 2692
Cut to the Quick - Kate Ross 5501
The Dance of Death - Jeremy Potter 5142
Dangerous - Amanda Quick 5213
A Dangerous Mourning - Anne Perry 4926
Daphne - Marion Chesney 1022
The Daughter: A Novel Based on the Life of Eleanor Marx - Judith Chernaik 1012
Daughter of Eve - Noel B. Gerson 2366
The Daughter of Time - Josephine Tey 6209
The Day Before Thunder - Bart Spicer 5965
The Days of the Butterfly - Norah Lofts 3841
A Dead Man in Deptford - Anthony Burgess 776
Dear Mrs. Boswell - Marie Muir 4508
Death in the Devil's Acre - Anne Perry 4927
Death of a Dancing Lady - Ray Harrison 2739
Death of the Fox - George Garrett 2300
Death Squad London - Jack Gerson 2360
Deathwatch - Ray Harrison 2740
Deborah and the Many Faces of Love - Colette Davenat 1499
Deborah and the Siege of Paris - Colette Davenat 1500
Deception - Amanda Quick 5214
The Dedicated - Willa Gibbs 2399
The Deeds of the Disturber - Elizabeth Peters 4949
Defend and Betray - Anne Perry 4928
Deirdre and Desire - Marion Chesney 1024

The Detective and Mr. Dickens - William J. Palmer 4782
The Detective Wore Silk Drawers - Peter Lovesey 3911
The Detling Secret - Julian Symons 6151
The Devil in Harbour - Catherine Gavin 2319
The Devil in Velvet - John Dickson Carr 909
Devil Water - Anya Seton 5749
Devil's Cub - Georgette Heyer 2885
Di and I - Peter Lefcourt 3714
Diana the Huntress - Marion Chesney 1026
Disraeli in Love - Maurice Edelman 1851
Disraeli Rising - Maurice Edelman 1852
The Disturber - L.S. Davidson Jr. 1505
Dr. Jekyll and Mr. Holmes - Loren D. Estleman 1970
Domina - Barbara Wood 6847
The Doom Trail - Arthur Douglas Smith 5917
The Double Man - Elinor Pryor 5205
Dragonmede - Rona Randall 5246
Dreams of Gold - Lewis Orde 4748
The Drummer Was the First to Die - Liza Pennywitt Taylor 6186
Drums - James Boyd 611
The Drums of April - Charles Mergendahl 4340
Dual Destiny - Karen Lynn 3939
The Duchess of Duke Street - Mollie Hardwick 2693
The Duke's Mistress: The Story of Mary Ann Clarke - F.W. Kenyon 3447
Dulcie Bligh - Gail Clark 1086
A Durable Fire - Virginia Bernhard 480
Eagles Where I Walk - Stephen Longstreet 3885
East Indiaman - Frank Pollard 5087
Eating Pavlova - D.M. Thomas 6235
Eden and Honor - Marilyn Harris 2729
The Eden Passion - Marilyn Harris 2730
Eden Rising - Marilyn Harris 2731
Edward, Edward - Lolah Burford 772
Eliza Stanhope - Joanna Trollope 6347
Elyza - Clare Darcy 1486
Emerald - Helen Ashfield 206
The Emerald Necklace - Diana Brown 718
The End of the Hunt - Thomas Flanagan 2119
The Enduring Years - Claire Rayner 5263
English Music - Peter Ackroyd 18
The English Wife - Charity Blackstock 530
Enlightening Delilah - Marion Chesney 1028
Enter the Lion: A Posthumous Memoir of Mycroft Holmes - Michael P. Hodel 2961
Entered From the Sun - George Garrett 2301
Envoy From Elizabeth - Pamela Bennetts 451
Escapade - Jane Aiken Hodge 2962
Eugenia - Clare Darcy 1487
The Eve of Saint Hyacinth - Kate Sedley 5716
Ever After - Elswyth Thane 6216
Evil Mark - Graham Miles 4377
Exit Lady Masham - Louis Auchincloss 230
Exit Sherlock Holmes - Robert Lee Hall 2657
The Eye in the Door - Pat Barker 307
Falconer's Judgement - Ian Morson 4494
The Face of a Stranger - Anne Perry 4929
False Colours - Georgette Heyer 2886
The False Inspector Dew - Peter Lovesey 3912
Familiar Acts - June Barraclough 345
The Family of Women - Richard Peck 4883
Fanny: Being the True History of the Adventures of Fanny Hackabout-Jones - Erica Jong 3299
Faro's Daughter - Georgette Heyer 2887
Farriers' Lane - Anne Perry 4930
A Fatal Assignation - Alice Chetwynd Ley 3764
The Fate of Princes - P.C. Doherty 1673
Finessing Clarissa - Marion Chesney 1029
Fire, Burn! - John Dickson Carr 910
Fire in the Heart - Henrietta Buckmaster 761
Fire in the Ice - Alan Scholefield 5653
The Firedrake's Eye - Patricia Finney 2095
The Fireflower - Edith Layton 3687
First Night - Jane Aiken Hodge 2963

The Five-Minute Marriage - Joan Aiken 46
Flash for Freedom - George MacDonald Fraser 2203
Flashman - George MacDonald Fraser 2204
Flashman at the Charge - George MacDonald Fraser 2209
Flashman's Lady - George MacDonald Fraser 2210
Fleeting Fancy - Rosemary Edghill 1866
The Flight of the Eagle - Donald Thomas 6239
The Floral Companion - Anthea Bell 419
Footman in Powder - Helen Ashton 216
For Love of a Pirate - Anthony Esler 1961
For My Great Folly - Thomas B. Costain 1365
Forever Amber - Kathleen Winsor 6822
The Fortunate Marriage - Meriol Trevor 6342
The Fortunes of Nigel - Sir Walter Scott 5696
The Foundling - Georgette Heyer 2888
The Fountain Overflows - Rebecca West 6639
The Four Hundred - Stephen Sheppard 5804
Frederica - Georgette Heyer 2889
Frederica in Fashion - Marion Chesney 1032
The Free Frenchman - Piers Paul Read 5277
French Slippers - Deborah Chester 1055
Friday's Child - Georgette Heyer 2890
From Fields of Gold - Alexandra Ripley 5339
The Gallows Murder - Michael Clynes 1134
A Gathering of Saints - Christopher Hyde 3092
The Gentleman From America - Paul Benton 464
The Gentleman From Chicago - John Cashman 953
Gentleman of Stratford - John Brophy 708
Gentleman Ranker - John Edward Jennings 3200
Gentlemen in England - A.N. Wilson 6795
A Georgian Love Story - Ernest Raymond 5258
The Ghost and Mrs. Jeffries - Emily Brightwell 681
The Ghost Road - Pat Barker 308
Gilded Splendour - Rosalind Laker 3595
The Girl Who Was Never Queen: A Biographical Novel of Princess Charlotte of Wales - Mary Main 4037
Give Me the Daggers - Catherine Gavin 2321
Give Us This Day - R.F. Delderfield 1586
Glendower Country - Martha Rofheart 5427
Glorious Morning - Julie Ellis 1919
God Is an Englishman - R.F. Delderfield 1587
The God of Mirrors - Robert Reilly 5293
Golden Admiral - F. van Wyck Mason 4150
The Golden Feather - Theda Kenyon 3462
The Golden Veil - Paddy Kitchen 3507
The Golden Warrior: The Story of Harold and William - Hope Muntz 4517
Good Night, Mr. Holmes - Carole Nelson Douglas 1699
The Governor's Lady - Thomas H. Raddall 5228
Gower Street - Claire Rayner 5264
The Grail Murders - Michael Clynes 1135
The Grand Sophy - Georgette Heyer 2891
The Great Train Robbery - Michael Crichton 1426
The Green Leaves of Summer - Ted Willis 6793
The Green Salamander - Pamela Hill 2933
Greygallows - Barbara Michaels 4359
Harvest of Death - Ray Harrison 2741
The Haymarket - Claire Rayner 5265
The Heart of Midlothian - Sir Walter Scott 5698
Henry Esmond - William Makepeace Thackeray 6212
Her Grace's Passion - Marion Chesney 1033
Heritage - Lewis Orde 4749
High Road to China - Jon Cleary 1106
A High Wind in Jamaica - Richard Hughes 3074
Highgate Rise - Anne Perry 4931
The Highwayman and Mr. Dickens - William J. Palmer 4783
The Hireling - Alison Macleod 4003
Honour and Obey - Malcolm Macdonald 3966
The Hooded Falcon - Prudence Andrew 140
The House of Cards - Leon Garfield 2292
The House of Cray - Pamela Hill 2936
The House of Eliott - Jean Marsh 4100
A House of Women - Eric Malpass 4049
How Do I Love Thee - Lucille Iremonger 3110

How Young They Die - Stuart Cloete 1124
The Hoydens and Mr. Dickens - William J. Palmer 4784
The Hungry Goblin: A Victorian Detective Novel - John Dickson Carr 911
I Give You Oscar Wilde - Desmond Hall 2647
I, James McNeill Whistler - Lawrence Williams 6787
I, Madame Tussaud - Sylvia Martin 4135
In the Wilderness - Sigrid Undset 6381
Indigo - Nicholas Carnac 900
The Inspector and Mrs. Jeffries - Emily Brightwell 682
The Ionian Mission - Patrick O'Brian 4667
Irene at Large - Carole Nelson Douglas 1700
Isabel the Fair - Margaret Campbell Barnes 323
It Began in Vauxhall Gardens - Jean Plaidy 5023
Jack Sheppard - William Harrison Ainsworth 56
Jack the Ripper - Richard Gordon 2484
Jarrett's Jade - Frank Yerby 6923
Jekyll, Alias Hyde - Donald Thomas 6240
Jennie about to Be - Elisabeth Ogilvie 4694
Jenny and Barnum: A Novel of Love - Roderick Thorp 6276
Jewelled Path - Rosalind Laker 3597
Jewels - Robert Perrin 4917
John Inglesant - John Henry Shorthouse 5833
John Ruskin's Wife - Eva McDonald 4259
Johnnie Cross - Terence de Vere White 6704
The Journal of Colonel De Lancey - James Warner Bellah 426
Judith - Brian Cleeve 1108
Julie - Jane Kesner Morris 4479
Kate - Brian Cleeve 1109
Kilcaraig - Annabel Carothers 904
A Kind of Justice - Benjamin Siegel 5844
Kindred Spirits - June Barraclough 347
The King Edward Plot - Robert Lee Hall 2658
The King's Brat - Constance Gluyas 2441
The King's Coat - Dewey Lambdin 3612
The King's Commissar - Duncan Kyle 3570
The King's Privateer - Dewey Lambdin 3615
Knaves Templar - Leonard Tourney 6300
The Ladies of Hanover Square - Rona Randall 5249
Lady Fortescue Steps Out - Marion Chesney 1035
The Lady From Yorktown - Eva McDonald 4260
A Lady in Doubt - Annabel Wynne 6891
Lady of Mallow - Dorothy Eden 1856
Lady on the Coin - Margaret Campbell Barnes 326
Lady Pamela - Clare Darcy 1490
Lady's Maid - Margaret Forster 2188
Lament for a Lost Lover - Philippa Carr 921
Lancet - Garet Rogers 5431
The Last of the Barons - Edward Bulwer-Lytton 769
The Last Testament of Oscar Wilde - Peter Ackroyd 19
The Latter Adventures of Tom Jones - Bob Coleman 1200
The Laughing Hangman - Edward Marston 4120
Lavender Lady - Carola Dunn 1794
Letty - Clare Darcy 1491
Lilith - Jean Plaidy 5030
Lillie - David Butler 818
The Lion of Christ - Margaret Butler 823
The Lion of Justice - Margaret Butler 825
The Lion's Way - Lewis Orde 4750
The List of Seven - Mark Frost 2237
Liza Bowe - Shirley Barker 313
The Lodestar - Pamela Belle 432
London's Child - Philip Boast 560
Lord Fancy - Leslie Turner White 6686
Lord Hornblower - C.S. Forester 2179
Lord Johnnie - Leslie Turner White 6687
Lord Libertine - Anthony Esler 1964
Lord of the Dead: The Secret History of Byron - Tom Holland 2999
Lord of the Far Island - Victoria Holt 3016
Lord Raven's Widow - Leslie O'Grady 4700
Lord Rivington's Lady - Eileen Jackson 3134

The Lorimer Line - Anne Melville 4332
The Lost Garden - Jane Aiken Hodge 2966
Louisa Brancusi - Darrell Husted 3088
The Love Knot - Catherine Darby 1482
A Love So Wild - Deborah Chester 1056
The Lovely Lynchs - Magdalen King-Hall 3490
Lovers - Suzanne Goodwin 2476
Love's Children - Judith Chernaik 1013
Love's Tender Fury - Jennifer Wilde 6749
Low Treason - Leonard Tourney 6301
Lucy - Hester W. Chapman 992
Lust for Life - Irving Stone 6059
Lydia, or Love in Town - Clare Darcy 1492
The Mad Courtesan - Edward Marston 4122
Madame Geneva - Jane Lane 3655
The Man From St. Petersburg - Ken Follett 2148
The Marigold Field - Diane Pearson 4876
The Marquis and Miss Jones - Helen Ashfield 208
A Marriage of Convenience - Tim Jeal 3172
Married Past Redemption - Patricia Veryan 6469
Marrying Harriet - Marion Chesney 1036
Mary Anne - Daphne Du Maurier 1749
Mary Reilly - Valerie Martin 4136
Masquerade of Vengeance - Alice Chetwynd Ley 3765
The Masqueraders - Georgette Heyer 2894
Masques of Gold - Roberta Gellis 2352
Master of Bengal: A Novel of Robert Clive of India - Norman Partington 4821
Master of Morholm - Timothy R. Wilson 6817
The Masters of Bow Street - John Creasy 1423
The Mating Dance - Rona Randall 5250
Mayfair - Nancy Fitzgerald 2115
Melbury Square - Dorothy Eden 1857
Mermaid Tavern - George William Cronyn 1429
The Merry Devils - Edward Marston 4123
The Michaelmas Girls - John Barry 362
Midsummer's Eve - Philippa Carr 924
The Millionaire's Daughter - Dorothy Eden 1858
Minerva - Marion Chesney 1037
The Miser of Mayfair - Marion Chesney 1038
Miss Davenport's Christmas - Marion Chesney 1039
Miss Fiona's Fancy - Marion Chesney 1040
Miss Nobody - Caroline Ross 5465
Miss Philadelphia Smith - Paula Allardyce 91
Miss Tonks Turns to Crime - Marion Chesney 1041
Mistress - Amanda Quick 5215
Mistress of Darkness - Christopher Nicole 4617
Mistress of the Boards - Richard Sumner 6118
Molly - Teresa Crane 1417
Monday's Child - Mollie Hardwick 2697
Monsieur Janvier - Elizabeth Linington 3799
A Monstrous Regiment of Women - Laurie R. King 3489
The Mortal Gods - Maurice Dolbier 1688
A Most Extraordinary Pair - Jean Detre 1628
Most Secret - John Dickson Carr 912
Mr. American - George MacDonald Fraser 2211
Mr. Pepys of Seething Lane - Cecil Abernethy 10
Mrs. Budley Falls From Grace - Marion Chesney 1042
Mrs. Jeffries and the Missing Alibi - Emily Brightwell 683
Mrs. Jeffries Dusts for Clues - Emily Brightwell 684
Mrs. Jeffries on the Ball - Emily Brightwell 685
Mrs. Jeffries on the Trail - Emily Brightwell 686
Mrs. Jeffries Plays the Cook - Emily Brightwell 687
Mrs. Jeffries Stands Corrected - Emily Brightwell 688
Mrs. Jeffries Takes Stock - Emily Brightwell 689
Mrs. Shakespeare: The Complete Works - Robert Nye 4656
The Mudlark - Theodore Bonnet 573
The Mummy; or Ramses the Damned - Anne Rice 5315
Murder at Drury Lane - Robert Lee Hall 2659
Murder at the Palace - Elliott Roosevelt 5445
Murder, I Presume - Gillian Linscott 3807
Murder in Grub Street - Bruce Alexander 77

The Murder of Sir Edmund Godfrey - John Dickson Carr 913
My Enemy the Queen - Victoria Holt 3017
My Lady Benbrook - Constance Gluyas 2442
My Lady Greensleeves - Constance Beresford-Howe 476
My Lady of Cleves - Margaret Campbell Barnes 328
My Name Is Clary Brown - Charlotte Keppel 3466
Myself, Christopher Wren - David Weiss 6606
Nanette - Patricia Veryan 6472
Nantucket Woman - Diana Gaines 2269
Neighboring Lives - Thomas M. Disch 1648
Never Call It Loving - Dorothy Eden 1859
Never Doubt I Love - Patricia Veryan 6473
Nicholas Cooke: Actor, Soldier, Physician, Priest - Stephanie Cowell 1393
The Night of the Ripper - Robert Bloch 551
Night Shadow - Catherine Coulter 1377
The Nightingale Gallery - Paul Harding 2684
The Nine Giants - Edward Marston 4124
The Ninth Statue - Roseleen Milne 4410
No Honeymoon for Death - Mary Kruger 3564
Nobody's Angel - Karen Robards 5363
The Nonsuch Lure - Mary M. Luke 3924
Nothing Like the Sun - Anthony Burgess 781
Now Face to Face - Karleen Koen 3530
Oh! Where Are Bloody Mary's Earrings? - Robert Player 5079
The Old Enchantment - Sarah Neilan 4565
Old St. Paul's - William Harrison Ainsworth 57
Old Saxon Blood - Leonard Tourney 6302
The Only Sin - Julie Ellis 1923
Opal - Helen Ashfield 210
Orlando - Virginia Woolf 6866
Our Jo, or The Chronicle of a Coming Man - Kenneth M. Cameron 868
Paddington Green - Claire Rayner 5266
Palais-Royale - Richard Sennett 5747
The Pandora Secret - Anthony Forrest 2186
The Paper Mistress - Dorothea Malm 4045
Paragon Walk - Anne Perry 4932
The Parfit Knight - Juliet Blyth 555
Parnell and the Englishwoman - Hugh Leonard 3721
The Passing Bells - Phillip Rock 5421
Patently Murder - Ray Harrison 2742
Path to the Silent Country - Lynne Reid Banks 291
The Peacock and the Pearl - Jennifer Lang 3661
Pearl - Helen Ashfield 211
Pearl - Christopher Bigsby 497
Peg Woffington - Charles Reade 5281
Pendragon: Late of Prince Albert's Own - Robert Trevelyan 6337
Pendragon. . .The Montenegran Plot - Robert Trevelyan 6338
Pentecost Alley - Anne Perry 4933
Perdita's Prince - Jean Plaidy 5040
Perfecting Fiona - Marion Chesney 1044
Peter Ibbetson - George Du Maurier 1750
Peveril of the Peak - Sir Walter Scott 5703
The Physician of London - Stephanie Cowell 1394
Pilgrims: A Novel of the Mayflower - Gerard Mac 3955
A Place Called Freedom - Ken Follett 2150
Plain Jane - Marion Chesney 1045
Playboy Squadron - Arch Whitehouse 6710
The Player's Boy - Bryher 744
The Pleasure Garden - Leon Garfield 2293
Pocahontas - Susan Donnell 1691
The Poisoned Chalice - Michael Clynes 1136
Pomeroy - Gordon Williams 6770
The Pool of St. Branok - Philippa Carr 926
Poor Richard's Game - G.J.A. O'Toole 4766
The Power and the Passion - Christina Nicholson 4609
The Prince and the Pauper - Mark Twain 6373
The Prince and the Quakeress - Jean Plaidy 5043
The Prince of Darkness - P.C. Doherty 1675
The Prince of Eden - Marilyn Harris 2732

Privileged Children - Frances Vernon 6455
The Proud Man - Elizabeth Linington 3800
Purple Passage: A Novel about a Lady Both Famous and Fantastic - Emily Hahn 2638
The Quade Inheritance - Barbara Ker Wilson 3469
The Quality of Mercy - Faye Kellerman 3391
The Quallsford Inheritance - Lloyd Biggle Jr. 495
The Queen and I - Sue Townsend 6306
The Queen's Head - Edward Marston 4125
The Queen's Man - Sharon Kay Penman 4905
Queen's Royal - John Quigley 5225
A Question of Choice - Prudence Andrew 143
Quicksilver Lady - Barbara Whitehead 6707
The Quincunx - Charles Palliser 4778
Rainbird's Revenge - Marion Chesney 1046
Rake's Progress - Marion Chesney 1047
Rake's Ransom - Barbara Metzger 4347
The Ravens of Blackwater - Edward Marston 4126
Ravenscroft - Dorothy Eden 1860
The Real David Copperfield - Robert Graves 2551
Rebel Heiress - Jane Aiken Hodge 2969
Red Slayer: Being the Second of the Sorrowful Mysteries of Brother Athelstan - Paul Harding 2685
Refining Felicity - Marion Chesney 1048
Regency Buck - Georgette Heyer 2898
Regency Rogue - Helen Ashfield 212
Regency Royal - Michael Hardwick 2687
Regent Square - Forbes Bramble 645
The Renegade - Donald Clayton Porter 5122
A Reputation Dies - Alice Chetwynd Ley 3766
Resurrection Row - Anne Perry 4934
The Return of Moriarty - John E. Gardner 2287
The Revenge of Dracula - Peter Tremayne 6335
The Revenge of the Hound - Michael Hardwick 2688
The Reverse of the Medal - Patrick O'Brian 4673
Richard Carvel - Winston Churchill 1081
Richard Whittington, London's Mayor - Gwynedd Sudworth 6112
Riddle Me a Murder - Duane Crowley 1435
Ride with Me - Thomas B. Costain 1369
The Ringed Castle - Dorothy Dunnett 1807
Riot at Gravesend: A Novel of Wat Tyler's Rebellion - William Howard Woods 6864
The Ripper's Apprentice - Donald Thomas 6242
Rivers Parting - Shirley Barker 315
The Road and the Star - Berkely Mather 4182
Road to Lendor - Esther Hammon 1966
The Roaring Boy - Edward Marston 4127
The Robber Baroness - William Kendall Clarke 1097
The Romance of Charles Dickens - Ursula Bloom 553
Royal Flash - George MacDonald Fraser 2213
Royal Sword at Agincourt - Pamela Bennetts 455
The Ruthless Yeomen - Valerie Anand 134
Rutland Place - Anne Perry 4935
The Sachem - Donald Clayton Porter 5124
Sackett's Land - Louis L'Amour 3628
St. John's Wood - Nancy Fitzgerald 2116
The Sandalwood Fan - Diana Brown 720
Sapphire - Helen Ashfield 214
Sara - Brian Cleeve 1110
Sarah Camberwell Tring - Janet Edmonds 1869
Satan in St. Mary's - P.C. Doherty 1676
The Savage Brood - Martha Rofheart 5430
The Scalpel and the Sword - Dell Shannon 5774
Scandal at High Chimneys: A Victorian Melodrama - John Dickson Carr 915
The Scandalous Lady Wright - Marion Chesney 1049
The Scandalous Marriage - Marion Chesney 1050
The Scarlet Pimpernel - Baroness Emma Orczy 4745
The Scottish Chiefs - Jane Porter 5135
Scoundrels' Brigade - Carter A. Vaughan 6439
The Sea 'Venture - F. van Wyck Mason 4159
Seance for a Vampire - Fred Saberhagen 5557
A Season of Death - Ray Harrison 2743
The Second Sister - Leslie O'Grady 4701

Sergeant Verity Presents His Compliments - Francis Selwyn 5746
The Seven-Per-Cent Solution - Nicholas Meyer 4349
The Shadow of the Moth: A Novel of Espionage with Virginia Woolf - Ellen Hawkes 2779
The Shakespeare Girl - Mollie Hardwick 2698
Sharpe's Revenge - Bernard Cornwell 1346
Sherlock Holmes and the Case of the Raleigh Legacy - L.B. Greenwood 2577
Sherlock Holmes and the Mysterious Friend of Oscar Wilde - Russell A. Brown 731
Sherlock Holmes and the Thistle of Scotland - L.B. Greenwood 2578
Sherlock Holmes Meets Annie Oakley - Stanley Shaw 5782
Sherlock Holmes vs. Dracula - Loren D. Estleman 1976
Silence in Hanover Close - Anne Perry 4936
The Silver Highways - Malcolm Macdonald 3972
Silver Linings - Shirley Davies-Owens 1508
Silver Shoals - Hamilton Cochran 1142
The Silver Touch - Rosalind Laker 3599
Sir Philip's Folly - Marion Chesney 1051
Sisters & Lovers - Nicola Thorne 6274
The Sleep of Life - Richard Gordon 2486
The Slicing Edge of Death - Judith Cook 1263
So Much as Beauty Does - Muriel Elwood 1938
Soho Square - Claire Rayner 5268
Something Gleamed - Theda Kenyon 3463
Sons of Fortune - Malcolm Macdonald 3973
The Spanish Bride - Georgette Heyer 2902
Speak to Me of Love - Dorothy Eden 1862
Sphere of Death - Ray Harrison 2744
The Spoils of Eden - Robert H. Fowler 2193
Sporting with Amaryllis - Paul West 6635
Spring at The Winged Horse - Ted Willis 6794
Spy in Chancery - P.C. Doherty 1680
Spy's Honour - Gavin Lyall 3929
Stage Fright - Gillian Linscott 3809
Starrbelow - China Thompson 6248
Statues in a Garden - Isabel Colegate 1198
The Storm Witch - Elisabeth Barr 339
The Storms of Fate - Patricia Wright 6885
The Strand - Claire Rayner 5269
The Strange Case of Deacon Brodie - Forbes Bramble 646
Strange Devices of the Sun and Moon - Lisa Goldstein 2463
Stranger at the Wedding - Frances Lynch 3934
The Stranger From the Sea - Winston Graham 2530
Stranger in Two Worlds - Hugh Clevely 1111
The Street of Kings - Charles Dexter 1637
The Street Sparrows - Rose Ayers 249
The Succession: A Novel of Elizabeth and James - George Garrett 2302
A Sudden, Fearful Death - Anne Perry 4938
The Sunne in Splendour - Sharon Kay Penman 4907
Sweet Songbird - Teresa Crane 1418
Sweet Will - Eric Malpass 4050
The Sword of Truth - Gilbert Morris 4472
Sylvester; or, The Wicked Uncle - Georgette Heyer 2904
A Tale of Two Cities - Charles Dickens 1642
The Taming of Annabelle - Marion Chesney 1052
Tansy Taniard - Myrtle Strode-Jackson 6084
The Tenants of Time - Thomas Flanagan 2120
Tessa d'Arblay - Malcolm Macdonald 3974
Thaddeus of Warsaw - Jane Porter 5136
That's Me in the Middle - Donald Jack 3129
Theirs Was the Kingdom - R.F. Delderfield 1590
The Thieftaker - J.G. Jeffreys 3180
This One's on Me - Donald Jack 3130
This Other Eden - Marilyn Harris 2733
The Thistlewood Plot - J.G. Jeffreys 3181
Thomas: A Novel of the Life, Passions, and Miracles of Becket - Shelley Mydans 4538
Those Who Love - Irving Stone 6064
Three Years to Play - Colin MacInnes 3983
Through a Glass Darkly - Karleen Koen 3531

Thunder on St. Paul's Day - Jane Lane 3658
The Tick of Death - Peter Lovesey 3916
Time After Time - Karl Alexander 80
A Time for Silence - Philippa Carr 930
Tincture of Death - Ray Harrison 2745
To Be a King - Robert DeMaria 1607
To Seize the Passing Dream - Ted Berkman 479
To the Ends of the Earth - Michael Talbot 6155
To the Honor of the Fleet - Robert H. Pilpel 5002
The Tontine - Thomas B. Costain 1371
Too Late! Too Late! The Maiden Cried - Joan Fleming 2128
Topaz - Helen Ashfield 215
The Tower of London - William Harrison Ainsworth 58
Traitors Gate - Anne Perry 4939
Traitor's Moon - Robert Neill 4574
Treason's Gift - Pamela Belle 434
Tree of Gold - Rosalind Laker 3602
The Trial of Elizabeth Cree: A Novel of the Limehouse Murders - Peter Ackroyd 21
The Trip to Jerusalem - Edward Marston 4129
The Triton Brig - Dudley Pope 5110
The Troubadour's Romance - Robyn Carr 940
Trumpeter, Sound! - D.L. Murray 4528
Trust and Treason - Margaret Birkhead 506
Two of a Kind: An English Trifle - Rosemary Edghill 1867
Under Two Flags - Ouida 4767
The Unsuitable Miss Pelham - June Drummond 1730
Upstairs Downstairs - John Hawkesworth 2782
The Upstart - Edison Marshall 4112
''Utmost Fish!'' - Hugh Wray McCann 4219
Vanessa - Hugh Walpole 6548
Vanity Fair - William Makepeace Thackeray 6213
The Vast Memory of Love - Malcolm Bosse 588
The Vesey Inheritance - Gwendoline Butler 822
Victoire - Clare Darcy 1493
Victoria and Albert - Evelyn Anthony 166
Vindication - Frances Sherwood 5824
The Virginians - William Makepeace Thackeray 6214
A Visit to Highbury - Joan Austen-Leigh 243
The Wanton Fires - Meriol Trevor 6345
Warm Wind, West Wind - Anne Irwin Matthew 4188
Warsaw Requiem - Bodie Thoene 6229
Warwyck's Woman - Rosalind Laker 3604
Water Music - T. Coraghessan Boyle 619
Watery Grave - Bruce Alexander 78
Watson's Apology - Beryl Bainbridge 271
Waxwork - Peter Lovesey 3917
The West End Horror - Nicholas Meyer 4350
What the Heart Keeps - Rosalind Laker 3605
When the Emperor Dies - Mason McCann Smith 5926
While England Sleeps - David Leavitt 3702
The White Rose Murders - Michael Clynes 1137
The Whitechapel Horrors - Edward B. Hanna 2678
Whom the Gods Love - Kate Ross 5502
Why Kill Arthur Potter? - Ray Harrison 2746
The Wicked Godmother - Marion Chesney 1053
A Wicked Way to Die - J.G. Jeffreys 3182
Wide Is the Water - Jane Aiken Hodge 2973
Wife to Mr. Milton - Robert Graves 2553
The Wildcliffe Bird - Constance Heaven 2811
Wilford's Daughter - Alexandra Manners 4071
Will Shakespeare: The Untold Story - John Mortimer 4495
Willowwood - Mollie Hardwick 2699
Willowwood - Elizabeth Savage 5619
With All My Heart - Margaret Campbell Barnes 330
Within the Hollow Crown - Margaret Campbell Barnes 331
Wobble to Death - Peter Lovesey 3918
Wolf in the Fold - Duncan MacNeil 4022
A Woman of Quality - Jan Westcott 6649
A Woman Scorned - Malcolm Macdonald 3978
Women of Ashdon - Valerie Anand 135

The Women of Eden - Marilyn Harris 2734
The Women of Whitechapel and Jack the Ripper - Paul West 6638
A World Too Wide - Susan Moore 4445
Yankee - Dana Fuller Ross 5495
Yankee Rogue - Dana Fuller Ross 5496
You, My Brother - Philip Burton 809

Ludlow
The Virgin in the Ice - Ellis Peters 4974

Lyme Regis
The French Lieutenant's Woman - John Fowles 2194
Jane and the Man of the Cloth - Stephanie Barron 355

Maldon
The Ravens of Blackwater - Edward Marston 4126

Mallow
Lady of Mallow - Dorothy Eden 1856

Manchester
Cordelia - Winston Graham 2523
Threescore and Ten - Walter Allen 105

Marlow
Love's Children - Judith Chernaik 1013

Maudesbury
The Peacock and the Pearl - Jennifer Lang 3661

Middleditch
My Name Is Clary Brown - Charlotte Keppel 3466

Middlemarch
Middlemarch - George Eliot 1909

Midlands
Adam Bede - George Eliot 1908
For They Shall Inherit - Malcolm Macdonald 3964
The World From Rough Stones - Malcolm Macdonald 3979

Minsham
Pargeters - Norah Lofts 3857

New Forest
Death of the Red King - Pamela Bennetts 448
The Pangersbourne Murders - J.G. Jeffreys 3179

Norfolk
Annie - Gloria Jahoda 3141
The French Woman - Barbara Paul 4837
If This Be Magic - Ellen Marsh 4098
The King Edward Plot - Robert Lee Hall 2658
The Lost Garden - Jane Aiken Hodge 2966
Mr. American - George MacDonald Fraser 2211
The Native Air - Sarah Woodhouse 6854
Pearl - Christopher Bigsby 497
The Proud Villeins - Valerie Anand 133
The Song of a Dark Angel - P.C. Doherty 1679
While Paris Danced - Patricia Wright 6886

North Country
The Wildcliffe Bird - Constance Heaven 2811

Northfield
The Ruthless Yeomen - Valerie Anand 134

Northumberland
The Bannaman Legacy - Catherine Cookson 1272
The Black Velvet Gown - Catherine Cookson 1274
Black William - Robert Neill 4567
Devil Water - Anya Seton 5749
Edward, Edward - Lolah Burford 772
If I Were You - Joan Aiken 49
The Love Child - Catherine Cookson 1279
Miss Martha Mary Crawford - Catherine Marchant 4081
The Moth - Catherine Cookson 1284
The Old Enchantment - Sarah Neilan 4565
The Parson's Daughter - Catherine Cookson 1286
Rob Roy - Sir Walter Scott 5707

The Slow Awakening - Catherine Marchant 4082
A Woman's Age - Rachel Billington 499

Northumbria
The Lodestar - Pamela Belle 432
The Proud Villeins - Valerie Anand 133
Queen of the Lightning - Kathleen Herbert 2852
The Vision of Stephen: An Elegy - Lolah Burford 775

Norwich
Hester - Christopher Bigsby 496
The Real David Copperfield - Robert Graves 2551
A Season of Mists - Sarah Woodhouse 6856

Nottingham
Count Manifred - Miranda Seymour 5761
Rivers Parting - Shirley Barker 315
The Sheriff of Nottingham - Richard Kluger 3512
Sherwood - Parke Godwin 2449

Nottinghamshire
The Good Yeomen - Jay Williams 6771
Lady of the Forest - Jennifer Roberson 5368
Locksley - Nicholas Chase 1003

Over Stowey
Walford's Oak - Jill M. Phillips 4986

Oxford
The Age of Miracles - Catherine MacCoun 3960
An Ancient Evil - C.L. Grace 2504
The Black Rose - Thomas B. Costain 1363
Captain Fantom - Charles Underhill 6377
Edmund Campion - Evelyn Waugh 6585
Falconer's Crusade - Ian Morson 4493
Falconer's Judgement - Ian Morson 4494
Kenilworth - Sir Walter Scott 5700
Lovelock - James McNeish 4311
Neighboring Lives - Thomas M. Disch 1648
The Physician of London - Stephanie Cowell 1394
Sarsen Place - Gwendoline Butler 821
The Steps of the Sun - Joanna Trollope 6350
Towers in the Mist - Elizabeth Goudge 2495
Warm Wind, West Wind - Anne Irwin Matthew 4188
Wife to Mr. Milton - Robert Graves 2553

Oxfordshire
Garnet - Helen Ashfield 207
The Moon in the Water - Pamela Belle 433
The Prince of Darkness - P.C. Doherty 1675
The Shooting Party - Isabel Colegate 1197
The Skeleton in the Grass - Robert Barnard 320

Plymouth
Daughter of Satan - Jean Plaidy 5011
The Lion Triumphant - Philippa Carr 922
The Plymouth Cloak - Kate Sedley 5718
The Witch From the Sea - Philippa Carr 933

Portsmouth
Fallen Skies - Philippa Gregory 2581
The Fireship - C. Northcote Parkinson 4811
Halfhyde and the Chain Gang - Philip McCutchan 4244
Halfhyde and the Fleet Review - Philip McCutchan 4246
Micah Clarke - Sir Arthur Conan Doyle 1715
Mutiny - Frank Tilsley 6280
The Pandora Secret - Anthony Forrest 2186
Ship of the Line - C.S. Forester 2182

Raveloe
Silas Marner - George Eliot 1911

Ravenskeer
Lady of the Forest - Jennifer Roberson 5368

Roehampton
The Thieftaker - J.G. Jeffreys 3180

Rotherwood
Ivanhoe - Sir Walter Scott 5699

Rye
Denis Duval - William Makepeace Thackeray   6211
The Haunting of Lamb House - Joan Aiken   48

Salisbury
The Spire - William Golding   2457

Salsford
The Eye in the Door - Pat Barker   307

Sarum
Sarum: The Novel of England - Edward Rutherfurd   5536

Scarborough
The Beano - Rony Robinson   5411

Scilly
Ruan - Bryher   746

Sherwood Forest
Lady of the Forest - Jennifer Roberson   5368
The Sheriff of Nottingham - Richard Kluger   3512

Shrewsbury
The Bloody Field - Edith Pargeter   4795
Brother Cadfael's Penance - Ellis Peters   4955
The Confessions of Brother Halvin - Ellis Peters   4956
Dead Man's Ransom - Ellis Peters   4957
The Devil's Novice - Ellis Peters   4958
An Excellent Mystery - Ellis Peters   4959
The Heaven Tree Trilogy - Edith Pargeter   4797
The Heretic's Apprentice - Ellis Peters   4960
The Hermit of Eyton Forest - Ellis Peters   4961
The Holy Thief - Ellis Peters   4962
The Leper of St. Giles - Ellis Peters   4963
Monk's Hood - Ellis Peters   4964
A Morbid Taste for Bones - Ellis Peters   4965
One Corpse Too Many - Ellis Peters   4966
The Pilgrim of Hate - Ellis Peters   4967
The Potter's Field - Ellis Peters   4968
The Raven in the Foregate - Ellis Peters   4969
The Rose Rent - Ellis Peters   4970
St. Peter's Fair - Ellis Peters   4971
The Summer of the Danes - Ellis Peters   4973
The Virgin in the Ice - Ellis Peters   4974

Shropshire
Precious Bane - Mary Webb   6590
The Prince of Eden - Marilyn Harris   2732
The Serpent Amongst the Lilies - P.C. Doherty   1678

Somerset
Double Wedding Ring - Patricia Wendorf   6624
The Latter Adventures of Tom Jones - Bob Coleman   1200
The Quade Inheritance - Barbara Ker Wilson   3469
The Salamanca Drum - Dorothy Eden   1861
This Dark Monarchy - Francis W. Leary   3698
Walford's Oak - Jill M. Phillips   4986

Southampton
I Came to the Highlands: A Novel of Suspense - Velda Johnston   3263
The Plymouth Adventure - Ernest Gebler   2342

Stafford
The Earl - Cecelia Holland   2987

Staffordshire
The Drayton Legacy - Rona Randall   5247

Steventon
Parson Austen's Daughter - Helen Ashton   219

Stonehenge
Pillar of the Sky - Cecelia Holland   2994

Stratford-on-Avon
The Best House in Stratford - Edward Fisher   2100
The Cleopatra Boy - Eric Malpass   4048
Gentleman of Stratford - John Brophy   708
A House of Women - Eric Malpass   4049

Nothing Like the Sun - Anthony Burgess   781
Shakespeare & Son - Edward Fisher   2102
The Shakespeare Girl - Mollie Hardwick   2698
Shakespeare's Dog - Leon Rooke   5439
Sweet Will - Eric Malpass   4050
Will Shakespeare: The Untold Story - John Mortimer   4495
You, My Brother - Philip Burton   809

Suffolk
Afternoon of a Autocrat - Norah Lofts   3834
An Autumn in Araby - Carola Salisbury   5565
Bless This House - Norah Lofts   3835
The Chains of Fate - Pamela Belle   430
The Hawthorne Legacy - Teresa Crane   1416
The Moon in the Water - Pamela Belle   433
The Ninth Statue - Roseleen Milne   4410
The Old Priory - Norah Lofts   3855
The Peacock's Feather - Sarah Woodhouse   6855
Sweet Songbird - Teresa Crane   1418
A Wayside Tavern - Norah Lofts   3862
Wild Dog Running - Alan Scholefield   5658

Surrey
The Cherished Wives - Valerie Anand   126
The Nonsuch Lure - Mary M. Luke   3924
Watson's Apology - Beryl Bainbridge   271

Sussex
The Blood Endures - Robert Inman   3107
Bride of Ae - Pamela Hill   2928
Circle of Pearls - Rosalind Laker   3593
The Disputed Crown - Valerie Anand   128
Exit Sherlock Holmes - Robert Lee Hall   2657
The Favored Child - Philippa Gregory   2582
I Am England - Patricia Wright   6881
Knight with Armour - Alfred Duggan   1767
Lanterns - Patricia Veryan   6465
A Letter of Mary - Laurie R. King   3488
Meridon - Philippa Gregory   2583
The Near and Distant Place - Patricia Wright   6883
Post Captain - Patrick O'Brian   4672
Purple Passage: A Novel about a Lady Both Famous and Fantastic - Emily Hahn   2638
The Reluctant Widow - Georgette Heyer   2899
The Stallion Man - Judith Glover   2438
Superstition Corner - Sheila Kaye-Smith   3379
The Talisman Ring - Georgette Heyer   2905
Trust and Treason - Margaret Birkhead   506
Two of a Kind: An English Trifle - Rosemary Edghill   1867
Wideacre - Philippa Gregory   2585

Sussex Downs
The Beekeeper's Apprentice, or, On the Segregation of the Queen - Laurie R. King   3487

Taunton
Micah Clarke - Sir Arthur Conan Doyle   1715

Tewkesbury
The Last of the Barons - Edward Bulwer-Lytton   769

Totnes
The Holy Innocents - Kate Sedley   5717

Tutbury
The Earl - Cecelia Holland   2987

Tyneside
The Gambling Man - Catherine Cookson   1276
The Harrogate Secret - Catherine Cookson   1278
Tilly - Catherine Cookson   1288
Tilly Alone - Catherine Cookson   1289
Tilly Wed - Catherine Cookson   1290
The Whip - Catherine Cookson   1291

Ulverton
Ulverton - Adam Thorpe   6278

Warwickshire
The Nunnery - Dorothy Charques   1001
Put Off Thy Shoes - Ethel Lillian Voynich   6513

Wessex
The Edge of Light - Joan Wolf   6839
The Price of Blood - Doris Sutcliffe Adams   24
Raven's Wind - Victor Canning   883

Whitby
Absolution by Murder - Peter Tremayne   6334
Sherlock Holmes vs. Dracula - Loren D. Estleman   1976

Wigan
Rose - Martin Cruz Smith   5923

Wight
Amanda/Miranda - Richard Peck   4882
Mary of Carisbrooke - Margaret Campbell Barnes   327

Wiltshire
Black Angels - C.T. Ritchie   5348
The Cannaway Concern - Graham Shelby   5788
The Cannaways - Graham Shelby   5789
Come Be My Love - Diana Brown   717
Fanny: Being the True History of the Adventures of Fanny Hackabout-Jones - Erica Jong   3299
Lady Pamela - Clare Darcy   1490
The Millionaire's Daughter - Dorothy Eden   1858
Paths of Fortune - Susan Moore   4444
The Wolves of Savernake - Edward Marston   4130

Winchester
Born of the Sun - Joan Wolf   6837
Death of the Red King - Pamela Bennetts   448
Gildenford - Valerie Anand   130
Parson Austen's Daughter - Helen Ashton   219
The Queen's Man - Sharon Kay Penman   4905
The Right Line of Cedric - Alfred Duggan   1773

Windsor
Anne Boleyn - Evelyn Anthony   158
By Right of Arms - Robyn Carr   937
The King's Bishop - Candace M. Robb   5365
Sherlock Holmes Meets Annie Oakley - Stanley Shaw   5782
The Vesey Inheritance - Gwendoline Butler   822
Victoria and Albert - Evelyn Anthony   166
Windsor Castle - William Harrison Ainsworth   59

Wisbech
Bed in Hell - Elfrida Vipont   6504

Wolverhampton
Elgar on the Journey to Hanley - Keith Alldritt   92

Woodstock
Woodstock; or, The Cavalier - Sir Walter Scott   5710

Worcester
Bennett's Welcome - Inglis Fletcher   2132
Royal Escape - Georgette Heyer   2900

Worchestershire
The Valiant and the Daunted - Roy Clews   1115

Wrackham
The Lords of Loone - John James   3159

Wychwood
Wychwood - Nicole St. John   5564

Yarmouth
Guns Forever Echo - Kenneth M. Ellis   1925

York
The Apothecary Rose - Candace M. Robb   5364
The Disputed Crown - Valerie Anand   128
Eugene Aram - Edward Bulwer-Lytton   766
The King's Bishop - Candace M. Robb   5365
The King's Persons - Joanne Greenberg   2573
The Lady Chapel - Candace M. Robb   5366
Masquerade of Vengeance - Alice Chetwynd Ley   3765
Morning's Gate - Ann Victoria Roberts   5371
The Trip to Jerusalem - Edward Marston   4129

Yorkshire
Arabella - Georgette Heyer 2874
The Castle of the Winds - Jeanne Montague 4434
Crossing the River - Caryl Phillips 4984
Dark Winds - Virginia Coffman 1152
The Emerald Necklace - Diana Brown 718
The Fourteenth of October - Bryher 742
Gilded Splendour - Rosalind Laker 3595
Greygallows - Barbara Michaels 4359
H.—: The Story of Heathcliff's Journey Back to Wuthering Heights - Lin Haire-Sargeant 2641
The Heart of the Rose - June Barraclough 346
The Lions of the North - Edward Marston 4121
The Nonesuch - Georgette Heyer 2896
The Nun's Tale - Candace M. Robb 5367
The Physician of London - Stephanie Cowell 1394
The Power and the Glory - Phyllis Bentley 462
Ramillies - Barbara Whitehead 6708
Regency Buck - Georgette Heyer 2898
The Rookery: A Novel of the Victorian Underworld - Hugh C. Rae 5239
The Silver Highways - Malcolm Macdonald 3972
Sons of Fortune - Malcolm Macdonald 3973
Sylvia's Lovers - Elizabeth Gaskell 2312
Vindication - Frances Sherwood 5824
Willowwood - Mollie Hardwick 2699

ESTONIA

The Czar's Madman - Jaan Kross 3560

ETHIOPIA

The Hammer of God - Alan Scholefield 5655
The Name of Hero - Richard Seltzer 5742

Magdala
When the Emperor Dies - Mason McCann Smith 5926

Massawa
When the Emperor Dies - Mason McCann Smith 5926

EUROPE

The Abyss - Marguerite Yourcenar 6946
The Adventurer - Mika Waltari 6550
Against This Rock - Louis Zara 6948
The Alchymist's Journal - Evan S. Connell 1256
The Amazing Mrs. Bonaparte - Harnett T. Kane 3351
The Angel: A Novel Based on the Life of Alexander I of Russia - William James Blech 543
The Anthem - Noel B. Gerson 2361
Anthony Adverse - Hervey Allen 98
An Army of Children - Evan H. Rhodes 5306
Attila's Treasure - Stephan Grundy 2606
Being Met Together - William Vaughan Wilkins 6756
La Belle - Elizabeth Boatwright Coker 1161
Belmarch: A Legend of the First Crusade - Christopher Davis 1514
Bodin, 1349: An Epic Novel of Christians and Jews in the Plague Years - Roberta Kalechofsky 3322
The Book of Abraham - Marek Halter 2665
The Castrato - Lawrence Goldman 2459
Century in Scarlet - Lajos Zilahy 6962
Charles O'Malley - Charles James Lever 3731
The Clan of the Cave Bear - Jean M. Auel 236
The Cloister and the Hearth - Charles Reade 5279
The Courts of Illusion - Rosemary Hawley Jarman 3165
Cross, Sword, and Arrow - Gladys H. Barr 340
Dance of the Tiger: A Novel of the Ice Age - Bjorn Kurten 3566
Daughters of the New World - Susan Richards Shreve 5835

The Death of Attila - Cecelia Holland 2986
The Descent of the Idol - Jaroslav Durych 1818
Draw Near to Battle - Jere Hungerford Wheelwright 6667
The Eagle and the Rock - Frances Winwar 6830
Eaters of the Dead - Michael Crichton 1425
Edward and Mrs. Simpson - A.C.H. Smith 5916
Emperor's Ladies - Noel B. Gerson 2367
For Every Sin - Aharon Appelfeld 175
A Generation of Leaves - Robert S. Bloom 552
Gentleman Traitor - Alan Williams 6763
Gentlemen of Adventure - Ernest K. Gann 2278
The Harp and the Shadow - Alejo Carpentier 905
Henry and Clara - Thomas Mallon 4042
Henry Esmond - William Makepeace Thackeray 6212
High Road to China - Jon Cleary 1106
The Horse Goddess - Morgan Llywelyn 3820
Hungarian Rhapsody: The Life of Franz Liszt - Jean Rousselot 5511
Imperial Venus: A Novel of Napoleon's Favorite Sister - Edgar Maas 3949
Katerina - Aharon Appelfeld 177
The Last Valley - J.B. Pick 4992
Legs - William Kennedy 3422
Lizzie - Evan Hunter 3083
The Lute Player - Norah Lofts 3852
Madame Casanova - Gaby von Schonthan 5659
Magnificent Enemies - Edgar Maas 3951
The Mammoth Hunters - Jean M. Auel 237
Master of the World - Cothburn O'Neal 4738
Napoleon Symphony - Anthony Burgess 780
The New Confessions - William Boyd 617
The Olympians - Guy Bolton 566
Once More the Hawks - Max Hennessy 2836
The Only Thing to Fear - David Poyer 5160
Over There - Robert Vaughan 6449
Pacific Cavalcade - Virginia Coffman 1157
Peter Doyle - John Vernon 6457
The Petersburg-Cannes Express - Hans Koning 3538
The Plains of Passage - Jean M. Auel 238
The Proud Canaries - David Johnson 3222
The Rake and the Rebel - Ira J. Morris 4478
Rhinegold - Stephan Grundy 2607
The Samurai - Shusaku Endo 1941
The Saracen Blade - Frank Yerby 6926
A Search for a King: A 12th-Century Legend - Gore Vidal 6492
Seven Men of Gascony - R.F. Delderfield 1589
Shield of Three Lions - Pamela Kaufman 3372
Shiva: An Adventure of the Ice Age - J.H. Brennan 657
Sign of the Pagan - Don Tracy 6312
Signorina - Henry Myers 4542
Singletusk - Bjorn Kurten 3567
Spangle - Gary Jennings 3196
The Spirit and the Flesh: A Novel Inspired by the Life of Isadora Duncan - David Weiss 6610
Tell Your Sons: A Novel of the Napoleonic Era - Willa Gibbs 2402
This Old Bill - Loren D. Estleman 1980
Tom Burke of Ours - Charles James Lever 3732
The Trumpet of God - David Duncan 1784
Tzili: The Story of a Life - Aharon Appelfeld 180
The Uncrowned King - Baroness Emma Orczy 4747
The Unicorn Hunt - Dorothy Dunnett 1811
Until the Sun Falls - Cecelia Holland 2998
The Valley of Horses - Jean M. Auel 239
The Walking Drum - Louis L'Amour 3632
War and Remembrance - Herman Wouk 6875
The Winds of War - Herman Wouk 6876
Wings of the Morning - David Beaty 402
The Wolf and the Raven - Diana L. Paxson 4848
Woman Astride - Nora Purtscher-Wydenbruch 5209
World and Paradise - Edgar Maas 3953
The Year the Horses Came - Mary Mackey 3993

Central Siberia
The Animal Wife - Elizabeth Marshall Thomas 6243

Reindeer Moon - Elizabeth Marshall Thomas 6244

Danube River
Byzantium - Michael Ennis 1945

Rhine River
Lord of the River - Bernard Clavel 1099
Rhine Journey - Ann Schlee 5639

FIJI

Long Pig - Russell Foreman 2168

FINLAND

The Fortress - Catherine Gavin 2320
Give Me the Daggers - Catherine Gavin 2321
Passion and the Sword - Harald Hornborg 3034
The Snow Mountain - Catherine Gavin 2324
Winter Fire - William R. Trotter 6352

FLANDERS

Deborah and the Many Faces of Love - Colette Davenat 1499
The Firedrake - Cecelia Holland 2988
Hereward the Wake - Charles Kingsley 3497
The Legend of Tyl Ulenspiegel - Charles Theodore Henri De Coster 1558
The Prisoner of Tordesillas - Lawrence Schoonover 5665
The Rain Maiden - Jill M. Phillips 4985
The Traitors of Bosworth - Robert Farrington 2021
Wife to the Bastard - Hilda Lewis 3753

FRANCE

All My Sins: A Novel of the Life and Loves of Ninon de Lenclos - Norbert Estey 1965
All the Golden Gifts - Iola Fuller 2251
All the King's Ladies - Janice Law 3678
All This, and Heaven Too - Rachel Field 2080
Alone Among Men - Marjorie Coryn 1355
Asylum for the Queen - Mildred A. Jordan 3303
Banners of Gold - Pamela Kaufman 3371
The Barons of Runnymede - Pamela Bennetts 445
The Bastard - Brigitte Von Tessin 6208
The Battle of the Queens - Jean Plaidy 5005
Beauty's Daughter - Mollie Hardwick 2689
La Belle Sorel - Jacques Carton 949
Beloved Enemy: The Passions of Eleanor of Aquitaine - Ellen Jones 3288
Beloved Soldiers - C.L. Skelton 5871
Below the Salt - Thomas B. Costain 1362
Benton's Row - Frank Yerby 6908
The Big Family - Vina Delmar 1600
The Black Consul - Anatolii Vinogradov 6503
Blaize - Anne Melville 4331
Blind Journey - Bruce Lancaster 3636
Blood Royal - Mollie Hardwick 2690
The Bloody Red Baron - Kim Newman 4596
The Blue Max - Jack D. Hunter 3085
Blunted Lance - Max Hennessy 2829
Brave General - Herbert Gorman 2490
Braveheart - Randall Wallace 6538
Brazen Whispers - Jane Feather 2055
Bride of the Unicorn - Kasey Michaels 4363
Brief Gaudy Hour - Margaret Campbell Barnes 322
The Bright Blue Sky - Max Hennessy 2830
Brumaire - Mark Logan 3864
The Buried Self: A Background to the Poems of Matthew Arnold - Isobel MacDonald 3961
Bury Him Among Kings - Elleston Trevor 6341
By Right of Arms - Robyn Carr 937
By the Green of the Spring - John Masters 4171
Call Lady Purbeck - Hilda Lewis 3745
Candleshine No More - Jane Oliver 4721
Captain Bashful - Donald Barr Chidsey 1059

Captain Caution - Kenneth Roberts 5385

Catriona - Robert Louis Stevenson 6009

Champion - L. Christian Balling 285

The Chancellor - Lawrence Schoonover 5662

The Chandler Heritage - Ben Haas 2629

The Charterhouse of Parma - Stendhal 5993

Chase the Heart - Maggie Osborne 4760

Cinq-Mars - Alfred Victor de Vigny 6495

Cities of the Flesh - Zoe Oldenbourg 4713

Courtesan - Diane Haeger 2635

The Courts of Love - Jean Plaidy 5010

The Courts of Love: A Romance of Medieval France - Peter Bourne 592

Crippled Splendour - Evan John 3219

The Crown and the Shadow: The Story of Francoise d'Aubigne, Marquise de Maintenon - Pamela Hill 2930

Crown in Candlelight - Rosemary Hawley Jarman 3166

Crown of Roses - Valerie Anand 127

Damned Shall Be Desire: The Passionate Life of Guy de Maupassant - Stephen Coulter 1384

Daughter of Time - Nelia Gardner White 6695

A Day of Battle - Vincent Sheean 5787

Death at the French Creek - Raymond C. Borel 580

The Dedicated - Willa Gibbs 2399

Deep Are the Valleys - Hannah Closs 1129

Devil to Pay - C. Northcote Parkinson 4810

The Devil's Door - Sharan Newman 4599

The Devil's Marchioness - William Fifield 2082

Devoted - Alice Borchardt 578

Doctor Mirabilis - James Blish 550

The Dragon Waiting: A Masque of History - John M. Ford 2165

The Dreamer of the Vine - Liz Greene 2574

The Earth and All It Holds - V.J. Banis 287

Eleanor the Queen - Norah Lofts 3842

Eleanora Duse - Jean Stubbs 6095

The Emperor's Duchess - R.G. Waldeck 6524

Emperor's Ladies - Noel B. Gerson 2367

The Emperor's Lady: A Novel Based on the Life of the Empress Josephine - F.W. Kenyon 3449

Epitaph for Three Women - Jean Plaidy 5012

Eugenie - Hester W. Chapman 989

Evergreen Gallant - Jean Plaidy 5013

Evermore - Barbara Steward 6014

The Exile of Celine - Tom Clark 1095

The Eye of the Lion: A Novel Based on the Life of Mata Hari - Lael Tucker Wertenbaker 6626

The Faith and the Flame - June Dimmit Houston 3054

Falkenhorst - Mark Rascovich 5254

The Fallen Angels - Susannah Kells 3397

The Fallon Pride - Reagan O'Neal 4742

Falls the Shadow - Sharon Kay Penman 4903

Falstaff - Robert Nye 4653

Farewell the Tranquil - R.F. Delderfield 1585

The Fatal Crown - Ellen Jones 3289

The Fatal Friendship: Marie Antoinette, Count Fersen and the Flight to Varennes - Stanley Loomis 3895

The Favourite - Francoise Mallet-Joris 4040

Feast in the Morning - Hugh Preston 5175

The Fifth Queen - Ford Madox Ford 2161

Fire and Morning - Francis W. Leary 3696

The First Gentleman of America: A Comedy of Conquest - James Branch Cabell 841

Floodtide - Suzanne Goodwin 2475

Flying Colours - C.S. Forester 2173

Fortune Made His Sword - Martha Rofheart 5426

Fortune's Wheel - Rhoda S. Edwards 1886

The Free Frenchman - Piers Paul Read 5277

French Dragoon - Roger Rudigoz 5523

The Gamester - Rafael Sabatini 5550

The Gaudy Empire - Alfred Neumann 4584

Gennie the Huguenot Woman - Bette M. Ross 5464

The Ghost Road - Pat Barker 308

The Glory and the Dream - Katharine Dunlap 1789

God's Man: A Novel on the Life of John Calvin - Duncan Norton-Taylor 4650

Gold of Their Bodies: A Novel about Gauguin - Charles Orson Gorham 2488

The Golden Porcupine - Muriel Ray Bolton 567

The Golden Veil - Paddy Kitchen 3507

Golden Venus - David Mynders Smythe 5933

The Golden Yoke: A Novel of the War of the Roses - Olive Eckerson 1837

Good-Bye My Son - Marjorie Coryn 1356

Good King Harry - Denise Giardina 2393

Goshawk Squadron - Derek Robinson 5403

Guillotine - Mark Logan 3865

The Harp and the Blade - John Myers 4543

Harry of Monmouth - A.M. Maughan 4199

Hawthorn Hill - Doris Shannon 5777

Heart of War - John Masters 4174

The Heirs of the Kingdom - Zoe Oldenbourg 4716

Henry, King of France - Heinrich Mann 4061

Here Be Dragons - Sharon Kay Penman 4904

Here Lies Margot - Pamela Hill 2935

High Are the Mountains - Hannah Closs 1130

High Towers - Thomas B. Costain 1366

Holy Week - Louis Aragon 182

Hornblower and the Hotspur - C.S. Forester 2176

The Hours of Light - Janet Tanner 6160

How Young They Die - Stuart Cloete 1124

I Thee Wed - Gilbert Wolf Gabriel 2267

Immortal Queen - Elizabeth Byrd 834

Imperial Courtesan - F.W. Kenyon 3452

Impressionist: A Novel of Mary Cassatt - Joan King 3486

In a Dark Wood Wandering - Hella S. Haasse 2631

In My Father's House - Bodie Thoene 6222

In Pale Battalions - Robert Goddard 2444

In Pursuit of the Green Lion - Judith Merkle Riley 5334

In the Company of Eagles - Ernest K. Gann 2279

In the Days of Poor Richard - Irving A. Bacheller 259

In the Falcon's Claw: A Novel of the Year 1000 - Chet Raymo 5257

In the Shadow of Midnight - Marsha Canham 880

The Incorruptible - Helma De Bois 1551

The Infidels - Chloe Gartner 2308

The Infinite Woman - Edison Marshall 4107

The Iron King - Maurice Druon 1732

Israel Potter - Herman Melville 4334

It Began in Vauxhall Gardens - Jean Plaidy 5023

The Italian Garden - Judith Lennox-Smith 3717

The Italian Woman - Jean Plaidy 5024

It's Me Again - Donald Jack 3126

Joanna the Pope - Daniel Panger 4785

Katherine - Anya Seton 5752

King's Agent - Justus Kent Clark 1090

The King's Cavalier - Samuel Shellabarger 5795

The King's Grey Mare - Rosemary Hawley Jarman 3167

King's Man - C.M. Edmondston 1880

The King's Way - Francoise Chandernagor 986

The Lady and the Arsenic - Marjorie Bowen 598

A Lady at Bay - Edgar Maas 3950

The Lady in the Tower - Jean Plaidy 5028

Lady of Paris - William Vaughan Wilkins 6760

The Lady Royal - Molly Costain Haycraft 2794

Lament for a Lost Lover - Philippa Carr 921

Landru - Rene Masson 4170

The Last of the Barons - Edward Bulwer-Lytton 769

The Last Summer of Innocence - Linda Sole 5938

The Last Summer of Mata Hari - Edward Huebsch 3067

The Last Victory - T.N. Murari 4519

Leopards and Lilies - Alfred Duggan 1769

The Letter of Marque - Patrick O'Brian 4668

The Lighthouse at the End of the World - Stephen Marlowe 4095

The Lily and the Leopard - Susan Wiggs 6745

The Lily and the Lion - Maurice Druon 1733

The Lion of England - Margaret Butler 824

The Lion of Pescara - George MacBeth 3958

Lionheart!: A Novel of Richard I, King of England - Martha Rofheart 5428

The Long Afternoon - Ursula Zilinsky 6964

Lord Hornblower - C.S. Forester 2179

Louis the Well-Beloved - Jean Plaidy 5032

Louisiana Purchase - A.E. Hotchner 3039

Love at Sunset - Jane Sheridan 5811

The Love of Fingin O'Lea - Theodora McCormick Du Bois 1743

The Lure of the Falcon - Juliette Benzoni 465

Lust for Life - Irving Stone 6059

Madame Serpent - Jean Plaidy 5033

The Mallen Lot - Catherine Cookson 1281

A Man and His Mountain: The Life of Paul Cezanne - Hugh McLeave 4285

The Man Who Killed the King - Dennis Wheatley 6654

Marie Antoinette - F.W. Kenyon 3453

The Marriage of Josephine - Marjorie Coryn 1358

Marsanne - Virginia Coffman 1155

Mary, Queen of Scotland and the Isles - Margaret George 2356

Masquerade for the King - Marina Oliver 4729

Master-At-Arms - Rafael Sabatini 5553

The Master of Ballantrae: A Winter's Tale - Robert Louis Stevenson 6011

The Master of Geneva: A Novel Based on the Life of John Calvin - Gladys H. Barr 341

The Master Painter - Edwin Mullins 4513

Mermaid Tavern - George William Cronyn 1429

Mirabeau, Lover and Stateman - Pierre Nezelof 4606

Mistress of Fortune - Sheila Lancaster 3651

Mistress of the Eagles - Elona Malterre 4052

The Moneyman - Thomas B. Costain 1368

Monsieur Moliere - Michael O'Shaughnessy 4762

Morning's Gate - Ann Victoria Roberts 5371

Mortal Love: A Novel of Eleanor of Aquitaine - Linda Hutchins 3090

Most Secret - John Dickson Carr 912

Mr. Midshipman Hornblower - C.S. Forester 2180

Murder in the Chateau - Elliott Roosevelt 5447

Murder Is Murder Is Murder - Samuel M. Steward 6020

My Brother Napoleon: The Confessions of Caroline Bonaparte - F.W. Kenyon 3455

My Lady Hoyden - Jane Sheridan 5812

My Life for My Sheep - Alfred Duggan 1772

Myself My Enemy - Jean Plaidy 5037

Naked Came I: A Novel of Rodin - David Weiss 6607

Napoleon and His Son - Pierre Nezelof 4607

The Native Air - Sarah Woodhouse 6854

The Negotiators - Francis Walder 6526

Niagara - Robert Lewis Taylor 6189

Our Lives Have Just Begun - Henry Myers 4541

Over There - Thomas Fleming 2130

The Palace of Wisdom - Bob Marshall-Andrews 4118

The Passing Bells - Phillip Rock 5421

Personal Recollections of Joan of Arc - Mark Twain 6372

Peter Abelard: A Novel - Helen Waddell 6517

Playboy Squadron - Arch Whitehouse 6710

The Plot to Kill Wallis Simpson: A Work of Faction - Graham Fisher 2104

The Poisoned Crown - Maurice Druon 1734

Post Captain - Patrick O'Brian 4672

The Power and the Glory - Gilbert Parker 4805

The Prince of Darkness - Jean Plaidy 5044

The Prisoner of Tordesillas - Lawrence Schoonover 5665

The Queen From Provence - Jean Plaidy 5047

Queen Margot - Alexandre Dumas 1780

The Queen's Necklace - Alexandre Dumas 1781

Queen's Play - Dorothy Dunnett 1805

The Queen's Secret - Jean Plaidy 5053

Rachel - Anne Powers 5153

The Rain Maiden - Jill M. Phillips 4985

Ramage and the Guillotine - Dudley Pope 5099
Ramage's Devil - Dudley Pope 5104
The Reindeer Hunters - Joan Wolf 6841
The Reluctant Queen - Molly Costain Haycraft 2796
The Revolt of the Eaglets - Jean Plaidy 5057
The Rich Are with You Always - Malcolm Macdonald 3971
Ride East! Ride West!: A Romance of the Hundred Years' War - Anne Powers 5154
The Riven Heart - Genevieve Gennari 2354
The Road to Glory - Frederick Britten Austin 246
The Romance of Leonardo Da Vinci - Dmitri Merezhkovski 4339
A Rose for Virtue - Norah Lofts 3858
Royal Flush: The Story of Minette - Margaret Irwin 3121
The Royal Pawn - Antonia Ridge 5327
A Royal Quest - Mary Lide 3777
Royal Road to Fotheringay - Jean Plaidy 5059
The Royal Succession - Maurice Druon 1735
Savage Prodigal - Konrad Bercovici 474
Scarlet Cockerel - Clifford Sublette 6110
The Secret Wife - Alice Acland 22
The Serpent Garden - Judith Merkle Riley 5336
The Severed Crown - Jane Lane 3657
The Shadow of the Sun - Sylvia Pell 4891
Sharpe's Regiment - Bernard Cornwell 1345
The She-Wolf - Pamela Bennetts 456
The She-Wolf of France - Maurice Druon 1736
The Shepherd's Crook - Paul Frischauer 2234
Ship of the Line - C.S. Forester 2182
The Siege - Jay Williams 6773
The Silent Tarn - Hannah Closs 1131
A Silver Mirror - Roberta Gellis 2353
The Silver Plume - Arthur Meeker 4323
So Brief a Spring - Claude Manceron 4054
So Great a Man - David Pilgrim 5000
Soldier of the Sea - Robert Welter Daly 1460
Sophie - Geoffrey Wagner 6519
Sorrow by Day - Marjorie Coryn 1359
The Spider King - Lawrence Schoonover 5668
A Spy for Napoleon - Baroness Emma Orczy 4746
Squadron Shilling - Arch Whitehouse 6712
A Stake in the Kingdom - Nigel Tranter 6321
The Star of Lancaster - Jean Plaidy 5065
Storm Winds - Iris Johansen 3217
Strange Meeting - Susan Hill 2952
Strong as Death - Sharan Newman 4602
The Sugar Pavilion - Rosalind Laker 3600
Sweet Marie-Antoinette - Lozania Prole 5198
The Sword and the Flame - Pamela Hill 2945
The Swords of December - Robert York 6933
Tempting Fate - Chelsea Quinn Yarbro 6906
That Spanish Woman - F.W. Kenyon 3461
That's Me in the Middle - Donald Jack 3129
This Splendid Earth - V.J. Banis 289
Thomas: A Novel of the Life, Passions, and Miracles of Becket - Shelley Mydans 4538
The Thousand Fires - Anne Powers 5155
Three Came to Ville Marie - Alan Sullivan 6114
Three Cheers for Me - Donald Jack 3131
Through the Green Valley - Barbara Gowdy 2498
Till the Day Goes Down - Judith Lennox-Smith 3719
A Time for Silence - Philippa Carr 930
To Dance with Kings - Rosalind Laker 3601
To Seize a Dream - Virginia Davis Hersch 2866
To Spit Against the Wind - Benjamin H. Levin 3737
To the End of the World - Helen Constance White 6680
Tolbecken - Samuel Shellabarger 5798
Tom Burke of Ours - Charles James Lever 3732
Tricolour - Mark Logan 3866
The Twelfth Physician - Willa Gibbs 2403
The Twisted Sword - Winston Graham 2531
Under the Winter Moon - Teresa Brooke 705
The Unhurrying Chase - H.F.M. Prescott 5172
Utrillo's Mother - Sarah Baylis 391
Vagabond Prophet - Allene Symons 6149

La Vendee - Anthony Trollope 6346
Vincent: A Novel Based on the Life of Van Gogh - Joost Poldermans 5082
The Voice and the Light - Edwin Fadiman 1995
The Vow on the Heron - Jean Plaidy 5074
A Walk with Love and Death - Hans Koning 3539
Walk with Peril - Dorothy V.S. Jackson 3132
The Wandering Prince - Jean Plaidy 5075
War Story: A Novel - Derek Robinson 5404
Waterloo - Manuel Komroff 3536
Waterloo - Frederic E. Smith 5920
When Christ and His Saints Slept - Sharon Kay Penman 4908
The White Cockade - Charles James Louis Gilson 2423
The White Queen - Lesley J. Nickell 4611
Why Kill Arthur Potter? - Ray Harrison 2746
Why Waterloo? - Alan Patrick Herbert 2850
Wife to Great Buckingham - Hilda Lewis 3751
Wife to Henry V - Hilda Lewis 3752
Wine of Life - Charles Orson Gorham 2489
The Wine Widow - Tessa Barclay 301
Wolfshead - Jere Hungerford Wheelwright 6672
The Young and Lonely King - Jane Lane 3659
Young Henry of Navarre - Heinrich Mann 4062

Agincourt
The Whyte Harte - P.C. Doherty 1681

Alencon
The Lacemaker - Janine Montupet 4438

Amiens
Birdsong - Sebastian Faulks 2051
The Invention of Truth - Marta Morazzoni 4449
Squadron Forty-Four - Arch Whitehouse 6711

Angers
The Lost Lands - Peter Vansittart 6430

Angouleme
The Still Storm - Francoise Sagan 5562

Aquitaine
Don Pedro's Captain - Pamela Bennetts 449
The Peacock and the Pearl - Jennifer Lang 3661

Arles
My Beautiful White Roses - Michael Lechner 3703

Arras
Mass for Arras - Andrzej Szczypiorski 6153

Auvergne
The Bastard - John Jakes 3144

Avignon
The Image of Our Lord - Edward Burman 790
Lay Siege to Heaven: A Novel of Saint Catherine of Siena - Louis De Wohl 1570
The Year of the Death - Reuben R. Merliss 4343

Bay of Biscay
Sharpe's Siege - Bernard Cornwell 1348

Biarritz
Sister Beneath the Sheet - Gillian Linscott 3808

Bordeaux
The Chateau - Stephen Coulter 1383
Don Pedro's Captain - Pamela Bennetts 449
The Four Rivers of Paradise - Helen Constance White 6678
The Last Portrait of the Duchess of Alba - Antonio Larreta 3666
Palaces of Desire - Kate Alexander 81
Sharpe's Revenge - Bernard Cornwell 1346
Sharpe's Siege - Bernard Cornwell 1348
The White Company - Sir Arthur Conan Doyle 1716

Boulogne
Captain Cut-Throat - John Dickson Carr 908
Captain Justice - Anthony Forrest 2185
So Near So Far - C. Northcote Parkinson 4814

Brest
As Runs the Glass - Evan John David 1502
Mutiny Run - Frank Eccles 1836
Sailor Named Jones - Harvey Haislip 2643

Brittany
The Angel of the Opera: Sherlock Holmes Meets the Phantom of the Opera - Sam Siciliano 5842
The Gentle Conqueror - Mary Ellen Gronau 2597
In Winter's Shadow - Gillian Bradshaw 632
The Lords of Vaumartin - Cecelia Holland 2992
Marianne and the Privateer - Juliette Benzoni 470
One Last Glimpse - James Aldridge 74

Burgundy
Quentin Durward - Sir Walter Scott 5705
The White Boar - Marian Palmer 4780
The Wrong Plantagenet - Marian Palmer 4781

Calais
My Lady of Cleves - Margaret Campbell Barnes 328

Cambrai
Wings for the Chariots - Arch Whitehouse 6713

Cassel
The Casket Crew - Arch Whitehouse 6709

Centeville
The Demon Lover - Victoria Holt 3013

Chamonix
An Easy Day for a Lady - Gillian Linscott 3805

Champagne
The Cornerstone - Zoe Oldenbourg 4714

Channel Coast
1805 - Richard Woodman 6857

Chantalon
Beguiled - Alice Borchardt 577

Cherigny
The Glass-Blowers - Daphne Du Maurier 1745

Compeigne
Gossip From the Forest - Thomas Keneally 3413

Corsica
Imperial Venus: A Novel of Napoleon's Favorite Sister - Edgar Maas 3949
In What Torn Ship - Evelyn Eaton 1828

Cozar Island
Form Line of Battle! - Alexander Kent 3431

Dijon
Devil's Cub - Georgette Heyer 2885

Dordogne
The Emerald Necklace - Diana Brown 718

Garonne
The Year of the Death - Reuben R. Merliss 4343

Giverny
Light - Eva Figes 2083

Jura Mountains
The Porcelain Dove - Delia Sherman 5815

La Rochelle
Angelique in Revolt - Sergeanne Golon 2471
The Three Musketeers - Alexandre Dumas 1782

Lille
The Heart Is a Traitor - Margaret Abbey 4
The Mohawk Ladder - Noel B. Gerson 2377

Lisieux
Love Is My Vocation: An Imaginative Study of St. Therese of Lisieux - Tom Clarkson 1098

Loire Valley
Lady Defiant - Suzanne Robinson 5412

Lorraine
The Lost Flight - H.F.M. Prescott 5169

Lourdes
The Song of Bernadette - Franz Werfel 6625

Lyon
Checkmate - Dorothy Dunnett 1799
Tree of Gold - Rosalind Laker 3602

Marignac
Daughter of Marignac - Constance Heaven 2805

Marseilles
Angelique in Barbary - Sergeanne Golon 2469
Desiree - Annemarie Selinko 5741
The Glittering Strand - Judith Lennox-Smith 3716

Mont Blanc
An Easy Day for a Lady - Gillian Linscott 3805

Montpellier
The Spanish Doctor - Matt Cohen 1159

Nancy
Anne of Geierstein - Sir Walter Scott 5689

Nantes
Scaramouche - Rafael Sabatini 5554
The White Cockade - Henry Farrand Griffin 2592

Nevers
Lamia: A Witch - Georgia Elizabeth Taylor 6183

Normandy
The Bastard King - Jean Plaidy 5004
Bond of Honour - Catherine Todd 6284
The Breath of Kings - Gene Farrington 2019
The Conqueror - Georgette Heyer 2881
The Conqueror's Wife - Noel B. Gerson 2363
Count Bohemond - Alfred Duggan 1764
The Devil Is Loose - Graham Shelby 5790
The Firedrake - Cecelia Holland 2988
Fortune's Knave: The Making of William the Conqueror - Mary Lide 3774
The Fourteenth of October - Bryher 742
God's Equal - Alain Absire 14
The Golden Warrior: The Story of Harold and William - Hope Muntz 4517
Harold, the Last of the Saxon Kings - Edward Bulwer-Lytton 767
Harold Was My King - Hilda Lewis 3749
Heroic Dust - Theodora Dehon 1581
The Lion of Justice - Jean Plaidy 5031
The Norman Pretender - Valerie Anand 132
The Paladin - George Shipway 5830
Ride Home Tomorrow - Evan John 3221
Royal Sword at Agincourt - Pamela Bennetts 455
Simon the Coldheart - Georgette Heyer 2901
Son of Dust - H.F.M. Prescott 5171
The Strangled Queen - Maurice Druon 1737
Wife to the Bastard - Hilda Lewis 3753

Orleans
An Army of Angels: A Novel of Joan of Arc - Pamela Marcantel 4079
The Serpent Amongst the Lilies - P.C. Doherty 1678

Paris
The Abductors - Stuart Cloete 1121
Adrienne - Barbara Levy 3742
Affairs of Love - Nicola Thorne 6272
The Angel of the Opera: Sherlock Holmes Meets the Phantom of the Opera - Sam Siciliano 5842
Angelique - Sergeanne Golon 2465
Angelique and the King - Sergeanne Golon 2468
Antonietta - John Hersey 2868
Arc d'X - Steve Erickson 1953
The Arm and the Darkness - Taylor Caldwell 850
Asya - Michael Ignatieff 3103
At the Sign of the Reine Pedauque - Anatole France 2198
The Balloonist - Macdonald Harris 2724

Baneful Sorceries, or The Countess Bewitched - Joan Sanders 5585
Banners of Silk - Rosalind Laker 3592
Before My Time - Niccolo Tucci 6358
Before the Glory Ended - Ursula Zilinsky 6963
Bertie and the Crime of Passion - Peter Lovesey 3907
Beyond Desire: A Novel Based on the Life of Felix and Cecille Mendelssohn - Pierre La Mure 3574
The Blood Endures - Robert Inman 3107
The Bonnet Laird's Daughter - Barbara Annandale 154
A Bride for New Orleans - Edward Francis Murphy 4522
The Brotherhood of the Red Poppy - Henri Troyat 6353
The Burning Man - Stephen Longstreet 3883
Bygones - Frank Wilkinson 6762
The Canary Trainer - Nicholas Meyer 4348
A Candle for D'Artagnan - Chelsea Quinn Yarbro 6895
The Cannaways - Graham Shelby 5789
The Capricorn Stone - Madeleine Brent 659
Captain Cut-Throat - John Dickson Carr 908
The Caravaggio Shawl - Samuel M. Steward 6019
The Cardinal and the Queen - Evelyn Anthony 159
A Case of Curiosities - Allen Kurzweil 3569
Cassy - Elizabeth Lyle 3930
Cesar and Augusta - Ronald Harwood 2771
Chariots of Fire - W.J. Weatherby 6586
The Charlatan - Carter A. Vaughan 6433
Charlie Is My Darling - Mollie Hardwick 2691
Charlotte Morel - Maria Lodi 3829
Charlotte Morel: The Dream - Maria Lodi 3830
Charlotte Morel: The Siege - Maria Lodi 3831
The Chess Player: A Novel of New Orleans and Paris - Frances Parkinson Keyes 3478
Citizen Tom Paine - Howard Fast 2028
City of Darkness, City of Light - Marge Piercy 4998
Clair De Lune: A Novel about Claude Debussy - Pierre La Mure 3575
Clear for Action: A Novel about John Paul Jones - Clements Ripley 5344
Colossus: A Novel about Goya and a World Gone Mad - Stephen Marlowe 4093
Concert Grand - Howard Breslin 665
Contessa - Helene Mansfield 4076
Cosette: The Sequel to Les Miserables - Laura Kalpakian 3329
Count Vronsky's Daughter - Carola Salisbury 5567
The Countess - March Cost 1360
Court of Shadows - Cynthia Morgan 4450
Crime Without Passion - Richard Grayson 2556
The Crown Prince - John Barchilon 300
Dance on a Sinking Ship - Michael Kilian 3483
Daughter of Marignac - Constance Heaven 2805
Death Comes as Epiphany - Sharan Newman 4598
Death En Voyage - Richard Grayson 2557
The Death of Napoleon - Simon Leys 3768
Death Off Stage - Richard Grayson 2558
Death on the Cards - Richard Grayson 2559
Deborah and the Siege of Paris - Colette Davenat 1500
The Demon Lover - Victoria Holt 3013
Depths of Glory - Irving Stone 6055
Desiree - Annemarie Selinko 5741
The Devil on Horseback - Victoria Holt 3014
Devil's Cub - Georgette Heyer 2885
The Devil's Laughter - Frank Yerby 6913
Disraeli Rising - Maurice Edelman 1852
Dr. Guillotine: The Eccentric Exploits of an Early Scientist - Herbert Lom 3867
Dragonfly in Amber - Diana Gabaldon 2262
Eden Rising - Marilyn Harris 2731
The Eleventh Year - Monique Raphel High 2914
Encore - Monique Raphel High 2915
The Far-Off Rhapsody - Anne-Marie Sheridan 5808
Fata Morgana - William Kotzwinkle 3549
Fear No More - Hester W. Chapman 990

First Night - Jane Aiken Hodge 2963
Flames of Empire - Peter Bourne 594
Fortune's Knave: The Making of William the Conqueror - Mary Lide 3774
Forty Centuries Look Down - Frederick Britten Austin 245
The Four Hundred - Stephen Sheppard 5804
The Four Winds of Heaven - Monique Raphel High 2916
The French Bride - Evelyn Anthony 163
The Frenchwoman - Jeanne Mackin 3995
The Gentleman From America - Polan Banks 293
The Gentleman From America - Paul Benton 464
The Ghost of Monsieur Scarron - Janet Lewis 3755
The Girl From Paris - Joan Aiken 47
The Glass-Blowers - Daphne Du Maurier 1745
Glowstone - Macdonald Harris 2725
The God of Mirrors - Robert Reilly 5293
The Gods Are Thirsty - Tanith Lee 3710
Good Morning, Irene - Carole Nelson Douglas 1698
A Great Lord - Paul Frischauer 2233
The Gypsy From Cadiz - Tamsin Hamilton 2670
Harp of a Thousand Strings - Harold Lenoir Davis 1522
The Hastening Wind - Edward Grierson 2591
Hawk of Detroit - Arthur Pound 5145
A Heritage of Shadows - Madeleine Brent 660
Herma - Macdonald Harris 2726
Hester - Brian Cleeve 1107
Hotel Transylvania - Chelsea Quinn Yarbro 6900
The Hunchback of Notre Dame - Victor Hugo 3076
I Am Vidocq - Vincent McConnor 4225
I Give You Oscar Wilde - Desmond Hall 2647
I, James McNeill Whistler - Lawrence Williams 6787
I, Madame Tussaud - Sylvia Martin 4135
I, Rachel - March Cost 1361
The Image of Our Lord - Edward Burman 790
In the Blue Light of African Dreams - Paul Watkins 6580
The Incorruptible - Marjorie Coryn 1357
An Innocent Woman - Malcolm Macdonald 3967
Irene at Large - Carole Nelson Douglas 1700
Irene's Last Waltz - Carole Nelson Douglas 1701
The Ironmaster - Anne Powers 5150
Jefferson: A Novel - Max Byrd 838
Jewelled Path - Rosalind Laker 3597
Johanna: A Novel of the Van Gogh Family - Claire Cooperstein 1317
Judith Paris - Hugh Walpole 6545
King of Paris - Guy Endore 1942
Kingkill - Thomas Gavin 2325
King's Masque - Evan John 3220
Knave of Hearts - Philippa Carr 920
Lady on the Coin - Margaret Campbell Barnes 326
Last Love of Camille - Frances Winwar 6832
The Last Testament of Oscar Wilde - Peter Ackroyd 19
The Lawless - John Jakes 3149
The Lonely Strangers - Charity Blackstock 531
The Longest Night - Ada Cook Lewis 3744
Lord Libertine - Anthony Esler 1964
The Lords of Vaumartin - Cecelia Holland 2992
The Lovely Lynchs - Magdalen King-Hall 3490
Lovers - Suzanne Goodwin 2476
Madeleine - Catherine Gavin 2323
Maid of Honour: A Novel Set in the Court of Mary, Queen of Scots - Elizabeth Byrd 836
Man of Montmartre: A Novel Based on the Life of Maurice Utrillo - Stephen Longstreet 3888
The Man Who Loved Mata Hari - Dan Sherman 5813
Marianne - Juliette Benzoni 466
Marianne and the Masked Prince - Juliette Benzoni 469
Marianne and the Privateer - Juliette Benzoni 470
The Marquis - Joan Sanders 5586
The Marquis and Miss Jones - Helen Ashfield 208
The Masked Man - P.C. Doherty 1674

The Master of Oakwindsor - Douglas Kent Hall 2648
McKensie's Hundred: A Tale of the Old Dominion - Frank Yerby 6924
The Midnight Gardener: A Novel about Baudelaire - Max White 6694
Mirage - Ruth McKenney 4283
Modigliani: Prince of Montparnasse - Tadeusz Wittlin 6834
Monday's Child - Mollie Hardwick 2697
Monsieur Janvier - Elizabeth Linington 3799
Monsieur Yankee - Leslie Turner White 6689
The Monterant Affair - Richard Grayson 2560
The Montmarte Murders - Richard Grayson 2561
Moulin Rouge: A Novel Based on Henri de Toulouse-Lautrec - Pierre La Mure 3576
The Murder at Impasse Louvaine - Richard Grayson 2562
Napoleon Symphony - Anthony Burgess 780
Notorious Eliza - Basil Beyea 489
Oliver Wiswell - Kenneth Roberts 5389
One Last Glimpse - James Aldridge 74
The Oracle Glass - Judith Merkle Riley 5335
Painted Lady: Eliza Jumel, Her Life and Times - Leonard Falkner 2009
Palaces of Desire - Kate Alexander 81
Palais-Royale - Richard Sennett 5747
Panama - Eric Zencey 6959
The Passion of Letty Fox - Diana Saunders 5610
The Passionate Journey - Irving Stone 6061
Passionate Rebel: The Story of Hector Berlioz - F.W. Kenyon 3457
The Passions of the Mind - Irving Stone 6062
Perfume: The Story of a Murderer - Patrick Suskind 6120
Peter Ibbetson - George Du Maurier 1750
Phantom - Susan Kay 3375
A Place of Greater Safety - Hilary Mantel 4077
The Poisoned Chalice - Michael Clynes 1136
Polonaise - Jane Aiken Hodge 2968
Polonaise - Piers Paul Read 5278
Poor Richard's Game - G.J.A. O'Toole 4766
The Porcelain Dove - Delia Sherman 5815
Portrait in Brownstone - Louis Auchincloss 232
The Prince Lost to Time - Ann Dukthas 1776
The Prisoners of September - Leon Garfield 2294
The Private Adventures of Captain Shaw - Edith Shay 5783
Les Quarant Cinq - Alexandre Dumas 1779
Queen Jezebel - Jean Plaidy 5049
The Queen's Confession - Victoria Holt 3019
The Questing Heart: A Romantic Novel about George Sand - F.W. Kenyon 3458
Quiet Lady - Norman Collins 1216
A Rage Against Heaven - Fred Mustard Stewart 6026
Rasero - Francisco Rebolledo 5282
The Raven and the Rose - Susan Wiggs 6746
The River Devils - Carter A. Vaughan 6437
Rogue's Legacy: A Novel about Francois Villon - Babette Deutsch 1629
The Rose and the Sword - Sandra Paretti 4792
The Rose of Malmaison: The Turbulent Life of the Beautiful Josephine - Gaby von Schonthan 5660
The Sage and the Olive - Florence Whitfield Barton 369
The Saint of Montparnasse: A Novel Based on the Life of Constantin Brancusi - Peter Neagoe 4560
Sally Hemings - Barbara Chase-Riboud 1006
Sarah - Joel Gross 2603
The Scandalous Mrs. Blackford - Harriet Kane 3358
Scaramouche - Rafael Sabatini 5554
Scaramouche the King-Maker - Rafael Sabatini 5555
The Scarlet Cloak - Jean Plaidy 5061
The Scarlet Pimpernel - Baroness Emma Orczy 4745
Second Generation - Howard Fast 2043
The Secret Life of Laszlo, Count Dracula - Roderick Anscombe 156
The Seducer - Henrik Stangerup 5980

Seed of Mischief - Willa Gibbs 2401
The Serpent Amongst the Lilies - P.C. Doherty 1678
Set All Afire: A Novel of St. Francis Xavier - Louis De Wohl 1574
The Shadowed Spring - Carola Salisbury 5571
Simplicissimus the Vagabond - J.J.C. Grimmelshausen 2594
A Singular Conspiracy - Barry Perowne 4915
So Much as Beauty Does - Muriel Elwood 1938
The Song of the Siren - Philippa Carr 929
Spy in Chancery - P.C. Doherty 1680
Stealing Heaven: The Love Story of Heloise and Abelard - Marion Meade 4317
The Strangled Queen - Maurice Druon 1737
Sweet Songbird - Teresa Crane 1418
A Tale of the Wind: A Novel of Nineteenth-Century France - Kay Nolte Smith 5922
A Tale of Two Cities - Charles Dickens 1642
Tallien: A Brief Romance - Frederic Tuten 6370
Tansy Taniard - Myrtle Strode-Jackson 6084
These Old Shades - Georgette Heyer 2906
This Dark Monarchy - Francis W. Leary 3698
Those Who Love - Irving Stone 6064
The Three Musketeers - Alexandre Dumas 1782
Through a Glass Darkly - Karleen Koen 3531
Tide of Empire - Bates Baldwin 279
A Time for the Death of a King - Ann Dukthas 1777
A Time for Titans - Vina Delmar 1602
To Seize the Passing Dream - Ted Berkman 479
Tomahawk - Donald Clayton Porter 5129
Twenty Years After - Alexandre Dumas 1783
Vale of Tyranny - Suzanne Butler 831
Vardy - John Harris 2721
Verge of Glory - Frederick Wight 6747
Veronique - Virginia Coffman 1158
Vindication - Frances Sherwood 5824
Voltaire! Voltaire! - Guy Endore 1943
The Wandering Arm - Sharan Newman 4603
The Way to the Lantern - Audrey Erskine Lindop 3790
While Paris Danced - Patricia Wright 6886
The White Rose Murders - Michael Clynes 1137
Wild Geese - Eilis Dillon 1647
The Wind From the Sea - Constance Heaven 2812
Winter of the Heart - Linda J. LaRosa 3665
The Winthrop Covenant - Louis Auchincloss 235
A World Too Wide - Susan Moore 4445
Yankee - Dana Fuller Ross 5495
The Year of the French - Thomas Flanagan 2121
The Young Men of Paris - Stephen Longstreet 3893
Zoya - Danielle Steel 5985

Poitiers
The Queen's War: A Novel of Eleanor of Aquitaine - Jeanne Mackin 3996
The Troubadour's Romance - Robyn Carr 940

Poitou
Angelique - Sergeanne Golon 2465
Angelique in Revolt - Sergeanne Golon 2471

Provencal
Sybille - Marion Meade 4318

Provence
Bernadin, My Love - Leonard Rossiter 5506
A Booke of Days: A Journal of the Crusade by Roger, Duke of Lunel - Stephen J. Rivele 5351
The Fool of Venus - George William Cronyn 1428
The Horseman on the Roof - Jean Giono 2424
The Stones of the Abbey - Fernand Pouillon 5144

Pyrenees
The Golden Chain - Jean Gamo 2275
The Horsemasters - Joan Wolf 6840

Rennes
Scaramouche - Rafael Sabatini 5554

Rheims
Come Rack! Come Rope! - Robert Hugh Benson 458

Rouen
An Army of Angels: A Novel of Joan of Arc - Pamela Marcantel 4079
The Breath of Kings - Gene Farrington 2019
The Burnished Blade - Lawrence Schoonover 5661
Fortune's Knave: The Making of William the Conqueror - Mary Lide 3774

St. Tropez
The Montmarte Murders - Richard Grayson 2561

Toulon
Admiral of Fear - Victor Suthren 6126
H.M.S. Cockerel - Dewey Lambdin 3611

Toulouse
Angelique - Sergeanne Golon 2465
Destiny of Fire - Zoe Oldenbourg 4715
Sharpe's Revenge - Bernard Cornwell 1346
The Spanish Bride - Georgette Heyer 2902
Sybille - Marion Meade 4318

Tourney
A Case of Curiosities - Allen Kurzweil 3569

Tours
Vardy - John Harris 2721

Valence
Son of Holmes - John T. Lescroart 3726

Vendee
Hester - Brian Cleeve 1107

Verdun
Captain Justice - Anthony Forrest 2185

Versailles
Angelique and the King - Sergeanne Golon 2468
The Cat and the King - Louis Auchincloss 229
Fear No More - Hester W. Chapman 990
The French Bride - Evelyn Anthony 163
The Ghost of Monsieur Scarron - Janet Lewis 3755
The Gilded Torch - Iola Fuller 2252
If This Be Magic - Ellen Marsh 4098
The Queen's Confession - Victoria Holt 3019
Royal Merry-Go-Round - F.W. Kenyon 3459
Ward of the Sun King - Mildred Allen Butler 826

Vezere
Daughter of the Red Deer - Joan Wolf 6838

Western Front
The Cinderpath - Catherine Cookson 1275

FRENCH GUINEA

Cayenne
Ramage's Devil - Dudley Pope 5104

FRENCH POLYNESIA

Bora Bora
Hawaii - James A. Michener 4370

Marquesas Islands
Gold of Their Bodies: A Novel about Gauguin - Charles Orson Gorham 2488
The Golden Galleon - Victor Suthren 6129

Tahiti
Adams of the Bounty - Erle Wilson 6807
Gold of Their Bodies: A Novel about Gauguin - Charles Orson Gorham 2488
H.M.S. Bounty - Alexander McKee 4280
Mutiny on the Bounty - Charles Nordhoff 4639

GAUL

Caesar - Mirko Jelusich 3188
Caesar - Allan Massie 4168
The Captive Princess - Maxine Shore 5831

The Conquered - Naomi Mitchison 4418
Constantine: The Miracle of the Flaming Cross -
   Frank G. Slaughter 5883
The Dark Island - Henry Treece 6326
Darkness and the Dawn - Thomas B. Costain 1364
Dominic - Kathleen Robinson 5405
Druids - Morgan Llywelyn 3817
The First Man in Rome - Colleen McCullough 4234
Freedom, Farewell - Phyllis Bentley 461
Gaul Is Divided - Esther Fisher Brown 721
I Loved Tiberius - Elisabeth Dored 1692
The Scarlet Beast - Francis Gerard 2357
The Thorn of Arimathea - Frank G. Slaughter 5905
Three's Company - Alfred Duggan 1774
Tros of Samothrace - Talbot Mundy 4515
Women in the Wall - Julia O'Faolain 4691

GERMANY

Arizona! - Dana Fuller Ross 5466
Banners of Gold - Pamela Kaufman 3371
Barry Lyndon - William Makepeace Thackeray 6210
The Blood Order - Jack D. Hunter 3084
The Bloody Red Baron - Kim Newman 4596
The Centurion - Jan de Hartog 2762
Conscience of the King - Alfred Duggan 1763
Court of Honor - Maria Fagyas 1996
Danzig Passage - Bodie Thoene 6221
The Days of the King - Bruno Frank 2200
The Death of Attila - Cecelia Holland 2986
The Devil's Cross - Walter O'Meara 4733
Doctor Copernicus - John Banville 296
Eagle in the Snow - Wallace Breem 654
Eagles at War - Walter J. Boyne 620
The Eagle's Daughter - Judith Tarr 6165
Elizabeth and Alexandra - Antony Lambton 3616
Elizabeth's Greetings - Rosemary Haughton 2774
Eroica: A Novel about Beethoven - Carl von
   Pidoll 4994
Eva - Ib Melchior 4329
The Exile of Celine - Tom Clark 1095
*The Eye of the Lion: A Novel Based on the Life of
   Mata Hari* - Lael Tucker Wertenbaker 6626
Falkenhorst - Mark Rascovich 5254
Faust - Robert Nye 4654
A Finger to Her Lips - Evelyn Berckman 472
The Great Infidel - Joseph Jay Deiss 1582
The Hangman's Crusade - James Barwick 370
Hitler Has Won - Frederic Mullally 4511
Illinois! - Dana Fuller Ross 5475
The Incorruptible - Helma De Bois 1551
The Iron Hand of Mars - Lindsey Davis 1528
Jerusalem Interlude - Bodie Thoene 6223
Joanna the Pope - Daniel Panger 4785
The Journal of Hildegard of Bingen - Barbara
   Lachman 3578
Kentucky! - Dana Fuller Ross 5477
Kepler: A Novel - John Banville 297
Last Man to Die - Michael Dobbs 1652
The Light Bearer - Donna Gillespie 2419
The Little Victoria - Lozania Prole 5196
The Lost Eagles - Ralph Graves 2542
Love at Sunset - Jane Sheridan 5811
Lusitania - David Butler 819
Magic Fire: Scenes around Richard Wagner - Bertita
   Harding 2683
Monk in Armour - Gladys H. Barr 342
Munich Signature - Bodie Thoene 6224
My Lady of Cleves - Margaret Campbell Barnes 328
No Place on Earth - Christa Wolf 6836
Once a Gentleman - Donald James 3157
People of the Book - David Stacton 5974
Piccadilly - Claire Rayner 5267
Pilgermann - Russell Hoban 2960
Power - Lion Feuchtwanger 2074
Queen of the Reformation - Charles Ludwig 3922
Rebel Princess - Evelyn Anthony 164
The Ring Master - David Gurr 2622

The Rogue From Padua - Jay Williams 6772
Royal Flash - George MacDonald Fraser 2213
*Sacred and Profane: A Novel of the Life and Times of
   Mozart* - David Weiss 6609
Secret for a Nightingale - Victoria Holt 3020
Spring Symphony - Eleanor Painter 4777
A Stolen Tongue - Sheri Holman 3002
The Swedish Cavalier - Leo Perutz 4943
Tempting Fate - Chelsea Quinn Yarbro 6906
The Three Legions - Gregory Solon 5941
Tiberius: The Memoirs of the Emperor - Allan
   Massie 4169
The Tin Drum - Gunther Grass 2540
The Twelve Pictures - Edith Simon 5857
Vanity Fair - William Makepeace Thackeray 6213
The Very Rich Hours of Count von Stauffenberg - Paul
   West 6637
Votan - John James 3162
Wisconsin! - Dana Fuller Ross 5493
Young Catherine - E.M. Almedingen 118

Bavaria
A Castle in Bavaria - Prince Thibaut d'Orleans 1693
The Judas Kiss - Victoria Holt 3015

Berlin
Arc d'X - Steve Erickson 1953
Before My Time - Niccolo Tucci 6358
*Beyond Desire: A Novel Based on the Life of Felix
   and Cecille Mendelssohn* - Pierre La Mure 3574
Blood Winter - William Patrick 4830
The Books of Rachel - Joel Gross 2600
Captain Wonder - Donald Thomas 6238
The Career of Magda V. - Joseph Machlis 3982
A Castle in Bavaria - Prince Thibaut d'Orleans 1693
The Crown Prince - John Barchilon 300
The Cup of Wrath - Mary Glazener 2429
Destiny Express - Howard A. Rodman 5423
The Fabulous Concubine - Hsin-Hai Chang 987
A Future Arrived - Phillip Rock 5420
Karl and Rosa - Alfred Doblin 1653
The Last Innocent Hour - Margot Abbott 8
Lovelock - James McNeish 4311
Meadowsweet - Gwendoline Butler 820
The Pale Criminal - Philip Kerr 3471
A People Betrayed - Alfred Doblin 1654
The Petrograd Consignment - Owen Sela 5739
A Princess in Berlin - Arthur R.G. Solmssen 5939
Second Generation - Howard Fast 2043
Seven Days to Petrograd - Tom Hyman 3094
The Wishing Tree - Sandra Paretti 4794

Black Forest
On the Night of the Seventh Moon - Victoria
   Holt 3018

Bugdorf
Stones From the River - Ursula Hegi 2816

Celle
The Princess of Celle - Jean Plaidy 5045

Coblentz
Scaramouche the King-Maker - Rafael Sabatini 5555

Cologne
The Godforgotten - Gladys Schmitt 5642
Simplicissimus the Vagabond - J.J.C.
   Grimmelshausen 2594

Dux
A Night with Casanova - Wolf Mankowitz 4060

East Prussia
August 1914 - Alexander Solzhenitsyn 5942

Friedberg
Meadowsweet - Gwendoline Butler 820

Hamburg
The Ship's Clock - Catherine M. Rae 5237

Hamm
Scaramouche the King-Maker - Rafael Sabatini 5555

Hanau
Simplicissimus the Vagabond - J.J.C.
   Grimmelshausen 2594

Hanover
The Princess of Celle - Jean Plaidy 5045
Queen in Waiting - Jean Plaidy 5048

Hartz Mountains
The Brocken - Pamela Hill 2929

Hessia
The Drums of Winter - Sandra Paretti 4790

Kiel
Spy's Honour - Gavin Lyall 3929

Marienbad
The Only Sin - Julie Ellis 1923

Munich
The Alfred Hitchcock Murder Case - George
   Baxt 382
The Countess - March Cost 1360
The Ugly Duchess - Lion Feuchtwanger 2075

Munster
The Siege - Peter Vansittart 6431

Nuremberg
Written in the Stars: A Novel about Albrecht Durer -
   Frances Hope Fisher 2103

St. Cyprian Island
The Godforgotten - Gladys Schmitt 5642

Saxony
Better in the Dark - Chelsea Quinn Yarbro 6894
Captain Fantom - Charles Underhill 6377

West Prussia
While Paris Danced - Patricia Wright 6886

Westphalia
Anne of Geierstein - Sir Walter Scott 5689

Wittenberg
Flame of Fire - Jane Oliver 4722

GIBRALTAR

1805 - Richard Woodman 6857
Honor This Day - Alexander Kent 3432
The Rock: A Novel about Gibraltar - John
   Masters 4179

GREECE

Alexander of Macedon: The Journey to World's End -
   Harold Lamb 3607
Alexander the God - Maurice Druon 1731
Alexander the God - Robert Payne 4849
Anabasis: A Journey to the Interior - Ellen
   Gilchrist 2408
Banners Against the Wind - John Edward
   Jennings 3198
The Bourlotas Fortune - Nicholas Gage 2268
The Bull From the Sea - Mary Renault 5295
Byron: A Novel - Sigrid Combuchen 1225
A Choice of Murder - Peter Vansittart 6429
Count Bohemond - Alfred Duggan 1764
Creation - Gore Vidal 6486
The Etruscan - Mika Waltari 6553
The Fabulist - John Vornholt 6512
The Goddess - Miranda Seymour 5763
The Greek Treasure - Irving Stone 6056
The Ionian Mission - Patrick O'Brian 4667
Lord Geoffrey's Fancy - Alfred Duggan 1771
Lord of the Dead: The Secret History of Byron - Tom
   Holland 2999

Lord of the Ladies - Joanna Dessau 1626
Marianne and the Rebels - Juliette Benzoni 471
Medea - Miranda Seymour 5764
Mortal Hunger: A Novel Based on the Life of Lafcadio Hearn - Harry E. Wedeck 6594
My Sister, My Love - Lucille Iremonger 3111
Prophets and Warriors - Peter Danielson 1473
The Secret Memoirs of Lord Byron - Christopher Nicole 4622
The Shining - Stephen Marlowe 4097
Soldier of the Mist - Gene Wolfe 6843
The Soothsayer - Laurene Chinn 1069
A Stolen Tongue - Sheri Holman 3002
Three Ships and Three Kings - Georgia Sallaska 5573
The Torch - Wilder Penfield 4902
Winter Quarters - Alfred Duggan 1775
Years of the City - George Rippey Stewart 6028

Athens
Achilles His Armour - Peter Green 2569
Alcibiades, Beloved of Gods - Vincenz Brun 735
The Ashes of Smyrna - Richard Reinhardt 5294
Besieger of Cities - Alfred Duggan 1761
Dear and Glorious Physician - Taylor Caldwell 853
An Elephant for Aristotle - L. Sprague De Camp 1556
The Escape of Socrates - Robert Pick 4993
Farewell Great King: A Novel of Ancient Greece - Jill Paton Walsh 4829
The Flowers of Adonis - Rosemary Sutcliff 6122
Glory and the Lightning - Taylor Caldwell 856
Goat Song: A Novel of Ancient Greece - Frank Yerby 6920
Goatsong - Tom Holt 3009
The Immortal Marriage - Gertrude Atherton 225
Julian - Gore Vidal 6489
The King Must Die - Mary Renault 5298
The Last Athenian - Viktor Rydberg 5543
The Last of the Wine - Mary Renault 5299
Lord Elgin's Lady - Theodore Vrettos 6514
The Magnificent Traitor: A Novel of Alcibiades and the Golden Age of Pericles - Lynn Poole 5092
The Mask of Apollo - Mary Renault 5300
The Maze Maker - Michael Ayrton 250
Nicanor of Athens: The Autobiography of an Unknown Citizen - Owen Francis Grazebrook 2563
Pericles the Athenian - Rex Warner 6566
The Pirate From Rome - John V.D. Southworth 5952
The Praise Singer - Mary Renault 5302
The Private and Public Life of Socrates - Rene Kraus 3552
The Robe - Lloyd C. Douglas 1703
Throne of Isis - Judith Tarr 6170
The Walled Orchard - Tom Holt 3010

Brynos
Woman of Andros - Thornton Wilder 6754

Colchis
Jason - Henry Treece 6331

Corinth
The Eagle King - Henry Treece 6327
God's Warrior - Frank G. Slaughter 5889
Jason - Henry Treece 6331

Crete
Angelique in Barbary - Sergeanne Golon 2469
Color From a Light Within: A Novel Based on the Life of El Greco - Donald Braider 641
The Egyptian - Mika Waltari 6552
Freedom or Death - Nikos Kazantzakis 3383
The Lily and the Bull - Moyra Caldecott 846
The Maze Maker - Michael Ayrton 250
The Shepherd Kings - Peter Danielson 1475
The Taverners' Place - Joanna Trollope 6351

Ithaca
Return to Ithaca - Eyvind Johnson 3224

Knossos
A Quest for Love - Jacquetta Hawkes 2781

Lemnos
Jason - Henry Treece 6331

Lesbos
The Laughter of Aphrodite - Peter Green 2570
My Name Is Sappho - Martha Rofheart 5429
The Other Sappho - Ellen Frye 2240

Missolonghi
The Missolonghi Manuscript - Frederic Prokosch 5194

Mycenae
Amber Princess - Henry Treece 6325

Pyrrha
My Name Is Sappho - Martha Rofheart 5429

Rhodes
The Bronze God of Rhodes - L. Sprague De Camp 1554
The Shadow of God - Aileen Crawley 1422
Tiberius: The Memoirs of the Emperor - Allan Massie 4169

Samos
The Praise Singer - Mary Renault 5302

Scyros
Fires in the Sky - Phillip Parotti 4816

Sparta
The Corn King and the Spring Queen - Naomi Mitchison 4419
The Flowers of Adonis - Rosemary Sutcliff 6122
Goat Song: A Novel of Ancient Greece - Frank Yerby 6920
The Other Sappho - Ellen Frye 2240
The Private Life of Helen of Troy - John Erskine 1957

Thebes
The Eagle King - Henry Treece 6327
Earth Giant - Edison Marshall 4106

Thrace
The Beacon of Alexandria - Gillian Bradshaw 627

GREENLAND

Arctic Treachery - Richard Woodman 6858
Frobisher's Savage - Leonard Tourney 6299
The Greenlander - Mark Adlard 38
The Greenlanders - Jane Smiley 5915
Gudrid's Saga - Constance Irwin 3115
The Ice Shirt - William T. Vollmann 6509
A Viking's Daughter - John Andrews 147
West with the Vikings - Edison Marshall 4114
White Man - Peter Freuchen 2228

GUYANA

Cayenne
The Twelfth Physician - Willa Gibbs 2403

Demerara
Ratoon - Christopher Nicole 4619

HAITI

All Souls' Rising - Madison Smartt Bell 422
The Black Consul - Anatolii Vinogradov 6503
Black Triumvirate: A Novel of Haiti - Benjamin H. Levin 3736
Caribbean - James A. Michener 4365
The Corsair: A Biographical Novel of Jean Lafitte, Hero of the Battle of New Orleans - Madeleine Fabiola Kent 3444
Drums at Dusk - Arna Bontemps 575

Drums of Destiny - Peter Bourne 593
Imperial Venus: A Novel of Napoleon's Favorite Sister - Edgar Maas 3949
Kingdom of This World - Alejo Carpentier 906
Lydia Bailey - Kenneth Roberts 5387
Mercedes of Castile - James Fenimore Cooper 1304
A Rendezvous in Haiti - Stephen Becker 407
Tide of Empire - Bates Baldwin 279
A Time for Titans - Vina Delmar 1602

HONG KONG

The Bridge of a Hundred Dragons - Emma Drummond 1723
The Crystal Star - Ellen Argo 184
Dynasty - Robert S. Elegant 1902
Empire of Heaven - Linda Ching Sledge 5907
Farewell to My Concubine - Lilian Lee 3709
Flowers in the Blood - Gay Courter 1387
Fortune Is a Woman - Elizabeth Adler 39
Gai-Jin: A Novel of Japan - James Clavell 1100
Halfhyde's Island - Philip McCutchan 4254
Hong Kong - Mona Gardner 2288
An Insular Position - Timothy Mo 4421
The Jade Alliance - Elizabeth Darrell 1497
The Midnight Gun - Berkely Mather 4180
The Mountain of Immoderate Desires - Leslie Wilson 6811
The Ocean Mistress - Peter French 2225
The Pagoda Tree - Berkely Mather 4181
Tai-Pan - James Clavell 1102

HUNGARY

The Blood Countess - Andrei Codrescu 1149
The Cry and the Covenant - Morton Thompson 6269
Csardas - Diane Pearson 4875
Fata Morgana - William Kotzwinkle 3549
Rakossy - Cecelia Holland 2995
The Secret Life of Laszlo, Count Dracula - Roderick Anscombe 156
Stranger at Wildings - Madeleine Brent 663

Budapest
Before the Glory Ended - Ursula Zilinsky 6963

ICELAND

Fire in the Ice - Dorothy James Roberts 5375
The Ice Shirt - William T. Vollmann 6509
Paradise Reclaimed - Halldor Laxness 3686
Two Ravens - Cecelia Holland 2997
A Viking's Daughter - John Andrews 147
West with the Vikings - Edison Marshall 4114

Reykjavik
This One's on Me - Donald Jack 3130

IN THE AIR

The Hallelujah Flight - Jack Lynn 3937

INDIA

Afternoon of a Autocrat - Norah Lofts 3834
The Barrier - Robin Maugham 4195
Blood Royal - Robert Payne 4850
The Blood Seed - Andrew Ward 6561
Coromandel! - John Masters 4172
Creation - Gore Vidal 6486
Dando on Delhi Ridge - William Clive 1119
The Dark Dancer - Frederic Prokosch 5193
The Deceivers - John Masters 4173
The Devil's Wind: Nana Saheb's Story - Manohar Malgonkar 4039
The Drummer Was the First to Die - Liza Pennywitt Taylor 6186

An Elephant for Aristotle - L. Sprague De Camp 1556
The Far Pavilions - M.M. Kaye 3376
Flashman - George MacDonald Fraser 2204
Flashman and the Mountain of Light - George MacDonald Fraser 2207
Follow the Drum - James Leasor 3699
For King and Company - Ellis K. Meacham 4314
Forget the Glory - Emma Drummond 1725
Free Lance - George Shipway 5827
The Gallant - William Stuart Long 3873
Golden Fire - Jonathan Fast 2047
The Gospel of Corax - Paul Park 4802
Guy Mannering - Sir Walter Scott 5697
The Holder of the World - Bharati Mukherjee 4510
The Imperial Agent - T.N. Murari 4518
The Infinite Woman - Edison Marshall 4107
Lady of the Lotus - William E. Barrett 353
The Last Victory - T.N. Murari 4519
Lords of the Dance - Robin Lloyd-Jones 3815
The Lotus and the Wind - John Masters 4175
The Maclarens - C.L. Skelton 5873
Master of Bengal: A Novel of Robert Clive of India - Norman Partington 4821
Me So Far - Donald Jack 3127
The Moghul - Thomas Hoover 3026
The Near and the Far - Leopold Hamilton Myers 4547
Nine Hours to Rama - Stanley Wolpert 6846
The Pagoda Tree - Berkely Mather 4181
Path of the Eclipse - Chelsea Quinn Yarbro 6905
Playing the Game - Ian Buruma 810
Pomp and Circumstance - Fred Mustard Stewart 6025
Ram: Being the Tale of One Ramillies Anstruther - Winchombe Taylor 6193
The Ravi Lancers - John Masters 4178
Regards From the Dead Princess: A Novel of a Life - Kenize Mourad 4505
Secret for a Nightingale - Victoria Holt 3020
Sergeant Verity and the Imperial Diamond - Francis Selwyn 5745
Set All Afire: A Novel of St. Francis Xavier - Louis De Wohl 1574
The Shalimar - Betty Hale Hyatt 3091
Star of Randevi - Marjorie McEvoy 4270
That Sweet and Savage Land - Emma Drummond 1728
The Weeping Ash - Joan Aiken 54
Wild Jasmine - Bertrice Small 5914
The Yellow Robe: A Novel of the Life of Buddha - Robert Payne 4856
Yeshua: The Gospel of St. Thomas - Alan Decker McNarie 4306
The Young Emperor - Robert Payne 4857

Amritsar
An Error of Judgment - Stanley Wolpert 6845

Balmer
Raj - Gita Mehta 4325

Bengal
Indigo - Nicholas Carnac 900
Nightrunners of Bengal - John Masters 4176

Bombay
A Division of the Spoils - Paul Scott 5683
H.M.S. Surprise - Patrick O'Brian 4666
Homeward Bound - Elizabeth Walter 6557
The War Chest - Porter Hill 2950

Calcutta
The Day of the Scorpion - Paul Scott 5682
The East Indiaman - Ellis K. Meacham 4313
Flashman and the Angel of the Lord - George MacDonald Fraser 2205
Flowers in the Blood - Gay Courter 1387
Indigo - Nicholas Carnac 900
Mistaken Virtues - Joanna Trollope 6349

Olivia and Jai - Rebecca Ryman 5544
On the Company's Service - Ellis K. Meacham 4315
Tournament of the Shadows - Nicholas Carnac 901
The Veil of Illusion - Rebecca Ryman 5545

Cawnpore
Massacre at Cawnpore - Vivian Stuart 6089

Chandifur
The Sleeping Tiger - Marjorie McEvoy 4269

Darjeeling
Flowers in the Blood - Gay Courter 1387

Delhi
The Faraway Drums - Jon Cleary 1104
Shadow of the Moon - M.M. Kaye 3377

Devapur
The Golden Honeycomb - Kamala Markandaya 4086

Goa
Goa - Kara Dalkey 1458
The Road and the Star - Berkely Mather 4182
So Far From Malabar - Joy DeWeese Wehen 6599

Hindu Kush
Subaltern's Choice - Duncan MacNeil 4020

Kashmir
The Mullah From Kashmir - Duncan MacNeil 4016

Khyber Pass
By Command of the Viceroy - Duncan MacNeil 4010
Drums Along the Khyber - Duncan MacNeil 4013
The Gates of Kunara - Duncan MacNeil 4014
Sadhu on the Mountain Peak - Duncan MacNeil 4019

Krishnapur
The Siege of Krishnapur - J.G. Farrell 2016

Lahore
An Error of Judgment - Stanley Wolpert 6845

Lucknow
Silk and Steel - Stephen Alter 122
Zemindar - Valerie Fitzgerald 2117

Lunjore
Shadow of the Moon - M.M. Kaye 3377

Madras
Command a King's Ship - Alexander Kent 3428

Malabar Coast
So Far From Malabar - Joy DeWeese Wehen 6599

Mayapore
The Jewel in the Crown - Paul Scott 5684

Meerpore
Beyond All Frontiers - Emma Drummond 1722

Mirat
The Day of the Scorpion - Paul Scott 5682
A Division of the Spoils - Paul Scott 5683

North-West Frontier
Charge of Cowardice - Duncan MacNeil 4011
Drums Along the Khyber - Duncan MacNeil 4013
The Gates of Kunara - Duncan MacNeil 4014
The Leopard and the Cliff - Wallace Breem 655
Lieutenant of the Line - Duncan MacNeil 4015

Oudh
Zemindar - Valerie Fitzgerald 2117

Pankot
The Day of the Scorpion - Paul Scott 5682
A Division of the Spoils - Paul Scott 5683
The Towers of Silence - Paul Scott 5685

Patna
The Train at Bundarbar - Duncan MacNeil 4021

Peshawar
Cunningham's Revenge - Duncan MacNeil 4012
The Mullah From Kashmir - Duncan MacNeil 4016
Sadhu on the Mountain Peak - Duncan MacNeil 4019
Wolf in the Fold - Duncan MacNeil 4022

Punjab
Bayonets in the Sun - William Moore 4446

Ranpur
The Towers of Silence - Paul Scott 5685

Simla
The Faraway Drums - Jon Cleary 1104
Lieutenant of the Line - Duncan MacNeil 4015

Sirpur
Raj - Gita Mehta 4325

Waziristan
The Restless Frontier - Duncan MacNeil 4018

INDIAN OCEAN

Captain Monsoon - Victor Suthren 6128
The Deadly Lady of Madagascar - C.V. Terry 6206
The Rose Crossing - Nicholas Jose 3306
The War Chest - Porter Hill 2950

INDONESIA

Fair Wind to Java - Garland Roark 5354

Banda Islands
Silver Nutmeg - Norah Lofts 3860

Java
The Pepper Tree - John Edward Jennings 3203

Moluccas
Scent of Cloves - Norah Lofts 3859

IRELAND

Across the Bitter Sea - Eilis Dillon 1646
Angel of the Delta - Edward Francis Murphy 4521
Attack the Lusitania! - Raymond Hitchcock 2956
Bard: The Odyssey of the Irish - Morgan Llywelyn 3816
Barry Lyndon - William Makepeace Thackeray 6210
The Big Wind - Beatrice Coogan 1262
Brendan - Frederick Buechner 762
By the Green of the Spring - John Masters 4171
Byzantium - Stephen R. Lawhead 3680
Captain Boycott, a Romantic Novel - Philip Rooney 5440
Captain Lightfoot - William R. Burnett 792
Captive of Rome - Theodora McCormick Du Bois 1740
Castle Malindine - Hilary Ford 2163
The Changeling - Alison Macleod 4000
The Crow Goddess - Patricia Finney 2094
The Deer Cry - William Greenough Schofield 5650
Druid's Enchantment - Millie J. Ragosta 5240
The Emancipist: An Unforgettable Epic of Australia - Veronica Geoghegan Sweeney 6147
The Emerald Crown - Theodora McCormick Du Bois 1741
The End of the Hunt - Thomas Flanagan 2119
An Excess of Love - Cathy Cash Spellman 5959
Falstaff - Robert Nye 4653
Famine - Liam O'Flaherty 4693
The Famished Land - Elizabeth Byrd 833
Finn Mac Cool - Morgan Llywelyn 3818
Fire Queen - Deborah Grabien 2503
The Fireship - C. Northcote Parkinson 4811
The Gallowglass - Howard Breslin 666
The Golden Ocean - Patrick O'Brian 4665

Gone the Rainbow, Gone the Dove - Joan
  Bagnel 264
The Halfhyde Line - Philip McCutchan 4249
Heart of War - John Masters 4174
Henry Lunt and the Ranger - Tom McNamara 4304
High Heroic - Constantine FitzGibbon 2118
Hungry Hill - Daphne Du Maurier 1746
In the Falcon's Claw: A Novel of the Year 1000 -
  Chet Raymo 5257
Isle of Glory - Jane Oliver 4723
John Inglesant - John Henry Shorthouse 5833
The Killing Frost - Thomas Hayden 2799
The Kings in Winter - Cecelia Holland 2991
Lady of Conquest - Teresa Medeiros 4322
The Last Prince of Ireland - Morgan Llywelyn 3821
The Lion and the Cross - Joan Lesley
  Hamilton 2669
The Lion of Ireland - Morgan Llywelyn 3822
Lord of Hawkfell Island - Catherine Coulter 1376
The Love of Fingin O'Lea - Theodora McCormick Du
  Bois 1743
A Marriage of Convenience - Tim Jeal 3172
Mistress of the Eagles - Elona Malterre 4052
Never Call It Loving - Dorothy Eden 1859
Nicholas Cooke: Actor, Soldier, Physician, Priest -
  Stephanie Cowell 1393
Night Shall Overtake Us - Kate Saunders 5611
Now, God Be Thanked - John Masters 4177
O'Houlihan's Jest - Rohan O'Grady 4702
Passionate Warriors - Mary Ellen Gronau · 2598
Pride of Lions - Morgan Llywelyn 3823
The Promise of Light - Paul Watkins 6581
The Ravishers - Elizabeth Richards 5318
Redemption - Leon Uris 6393
Return of the Stranger - Dorothy James
  Roberts 5377
The Rich Are with You Always - Malcolm
  Macdonald 3971
*Ride East! Ride West!: A Romance of the Hundred
  Years' War* - Anne Powers 5154
The Rising of the Moon - Peter Berresford Ellis 1926
Ruan - Bryher 746
Saints and Scholars - Terrence Eagleton 1821
The Saxon Tapestry - Sile Rice 5317
The Scorching Wind - Walter Macken 3988
Seasons - Anna Dillon 1645
Seek the Fair Land - Walter Macken 3989
A Shadow of Gulls - Patricia Finney 2096
Sons of Thunder - Barbara Fitz Vroman 6516
Stranger in Two Worlds - Hugh Clevely 1111
Talleyman - John James 3161
They Were Dreamers - James F. Murphy Jr. 4525
This Land Fulfilled - Charles Andrew Brady 636
This Willing Passion - Patricia Cloud 1132
Through the Green Valley - Barbara Gowdy 2498
Thy Tears Might Cease - Michael Farrell 2018
Trinity - Leon Uris 6394
Troubles - J.G. Farrell 2017
The Tune That They Play - William Clive 1120
The Viking's Woman - Heather Graham 2520
Westward Ho! - Charles Kingsley 3499
The White Cutter - David Pownall 5158
The White Raven - Diana L. Paxson 4847
Wild Geese - Eilis Dillon 1647
Wild Jasmine - Bertrice Small 5914
The Wind in His Fists - John Edward Jennings 3210
Within the Hollow Crown - Margaret Campbell
  Barnes 331
A Woman's Age - Rachel Billington 499

Aran Islands
The Dispossessed - Dell Shannon 5773

Belfast
From Time to Time - Jack Finney 2092

Clare
The Silent People - Walter Macken 3990
The Silver Highways - Malcolm Macdonald 3972

Connacht
Cashelmara - Susan Howatch 3058
The Dispossessed - Dell Shannon 5773
Grania: She-King of the Irish Seas - Morgan
  Llywelyn 3819

Cork
A Nest of Simple Folk - Sean O'Faolain 4692
Time and Chance - Anna Wibberley 6728

County Cork
Sabrina - Madeleine Polland 5086

Dublin
All Desires Known - Malcolm Macdonald 3963
All Their Kingdoms - Madeleine Polland 5084
Captain Wonder - Donald Thomas 6238
Charles O'Malley - Charles James Lever 3731
Gerait's Daughter - Millie J. Ragosta 5241
Give Us This Day - R.F. Delderfield 1586
The Golden Coast - Philip Rooney 5441
Heiress of Ardara - Margaret Evans Porter 5137
The House by the Churchyard - Joseph Sheridan Le
  Fanu 3688
The Irish Boy: A Romantic Biography - Naomi
  Jacob 3137
Jewels - Robert Perrin 4917
The Lovely Lynchs - Magdalen King-Hall 3490
*The Men That God Made Mad: A Novel about
  Ireland's Easter Rising* - W.A. Ballinger 286
A Nest of Simple Folk - Sean O'Faolain 4692
Parnell and the Englishwoman - Hugh Leonard 3721
Passage West - Dallas Miller 4382
The Proud Man - Elizabeth Linington 3800
Rebels: The Irish Rising of 1916 - Peter
  DeRosa 1622
The Scalpel and the Sword - Dell Shannon 5774
Sergeant Lamb's America - Robert Graves 2552
The Tenants of Time - Thomas Flanagan 2120
That's Me in the Middle - Donald Jack 3129
A Time for the Death of a King - Ann Dukthas 1777
Tom Burke of Ours - Charles James Lever 3732
Violent Friends - Winston Clewes 1113
The Ways of Women - Elaine Crowley 1436
A Woman Scorned - Malcolm Macdonald 3978
The Year of the French - Thomas Flanagan 2121

Galway
All Their Kingdoms - Madeleine Polland 5084
Charles O'Malley - Charles James Lever 3731
The Rising of the Moon - William Martin 4140
The Silent People - Walter Macken 3990

Kerry
Georgina - Clare Darcy 1488
Maura's Dream - Joel Gross 2602

Kilpeder
The Tenants of Time - Thomas Flanagan 2120

Limerick
A Nest of Simple Folk - Sean O'Faolain 4692

Mayo
The Hedge of Thorns - Helen Ashton 217
The Year of the French - Thomas Flanagan 2121

Meath
Scarlett - Alexandra Ripley 5342

Ulster
Deirdre - James Stephens 5996
The Proud Man - Elizabeth Linington 3800
Red Branch - Morgan Llywelyn 3824

ISRAEL

According to Mary: A Novel of the Magdalene - Willa
  Gibbs 2398
According to Thomas - Gladys Malvern 4053
After Goliath - R.V. Cassill 955
Bathsheba - Roberta Kells Dorr 1695

Bathsheba - Torgny Lindgren 3789
Behold the Man - Toyohiko Kagawa 3321
The Brother - Dorothy Clarke Wilson 6799
The Centurion - Leonard Wibberley 6729
A Certain Woman: The Story of Mary Magdalene -
  Victor MacClure 3959
*The Curse of Jezebel: A Novel of the Biblical Queen of
  Evil* - Frank G. Slaughter 5884
Daughter of Jairus - Paul Hervey Fox 2196
David and Bathsheba - Ari Ibn-Sahav 3098
David of Jerusalem - Louis De Wohl 1564
David the King - Gladys Schmitt 5641
David's Stranger - Moshe Shamir 5771
The Death of Kings - Peter Danielson 1465
The Eighth Veil - Ellis Kadison 3320
The Emperor's Physician - Jacob Randolph
  Perkins 4914
Esau - Meir Shalev 5770
The Galileans - Frank G. Slaughter 5888
Giant Killer - Elmer Holmes Davis 1518
The Glory - Herman Wouk 6873
The Good Tidings - William Sidney 5843
The Gospel According to Gamaliel - Gerald
  Heard 2801
The Herdsman - Dorothy Clarke Wilson 6801
Hidden Victory: A Novel of Jesus - Herbert Francis
  Smith 5921
The Hope - Herman Wouk 6874
Husband of Delilah - Eric Linklater 3802
I, Nathanael, Knew Jesus - William Gilbert Van Tassel
  Sutpen 6133
If I Forget Thee - Robert S. Deropp 1621
If I Forget Thee - Brenda Lesley Segal 5720
The Illusionist - Anita Mason 4144
The Invaders - Peter Danielson 1469
Jacob: An Autobiography - Irving Fineman 2088
Jezebel - Dorothy Clarke Wilson 6802
Josephus and the Emperor - Lion
  Feuchtwanger 2073
King David - Gwyn Jenkins 3191
King Jesus - Robert Graves 2549
The King of Flesh and Blood - Moshe Shamir 5772
King of Kings: A Novel of the Life of David - Malachi
  Martin 4134
The Kingdom of the Wicked - Anthony Burgess 778
The Knifeman: A Novel of Judas Iscariot - William
  Rayner 5271
The Last Temptation of Christ - Nikos
  Kazantzakis 3384
Lazarus - Alain Absire 15
Leah's Journey - Gloria Goldreich 2460
The Legacy - Howard Fast 2037
The Letters of Nicodemus - Jan Dobraczynski 1655
The Life of Jesus: An Apocryphal Novel - Toby
  Olson 4731
The Lord Jesus - Robert Payne 4854
Love and Wisdom: A Novel about Solomon - Richard
  G. Hubler 3064
Martha, Martha - Patricia McGerr 4274
Mary of Magdala - Anne C. Williman 6791
Mary of Nazareth - Esther Kellner 3394
The Master - Max Brod 702
The Moon under Her Feet - Ceysta Kinstler 3503
No King but Caesar - Anne Powers 5151
The Painted Queen - Olga Hesky 2871
Prince of Israel - Elias Gilner 2422
The Promised Land - Peter Danielson 1471
The Prophet and the King - Shirley Watkins 6582
Refuge in Avalon - Marguerite Steedman 5984
Rizpah - Charles E. Israel 3124
Road From Olivet - Edward Francis Murphy 4523
Salome, Princess of Galilee - Henry Denker 1611
The Salt of the Earth - Carlo Monterosso 4437
The Scarlet Lily - Edward Francis Murphy 4524
The Sea Peoples - Peter Danielson 1474
The Shining King - Peter Danielson 1476
Simon Bar Cochba: Rebellion in Judea - Merton
  Finch 2086

The Sins of Herod: A Novel of Rome and the Early Church - Frank G. Slaughter 5900
The Soldier and the Sage: A Novel about Akiba - Richard G. Hubler 3065
Solomon and Sheba - Jay Williams 6774
Solomon's Song - Roberta Kells Dorr 1697
Son of Judah - Dan Levin 3738
The Song of Ruth: A Love Story of the Old Testament - Frank G. Slaughter 5901
The Sorceress - Nathaniel Norsen Weinreb 6602
The Sword and the Promise - Benjamin Siegel 5845
Tamar - Ann Chamberlin 975
Triumph of the Lion - Peter Danielson 1478
The Trojan - Noel B. Gerson 2386
Two Thieves - Manuel Komroff 3535
The Valley of God - Irene Steinman Patai 4825
The Valley of Vision: A Novel of King Solomon and His Time - Vardis Fisher 2113
Vengeance of the Lion - Peter Danielson 1480
The Way - J.M. Hartley 2761
Who Came by Night - Roland Nicholas 4608
The Wolf of Masada - John Fredman 2220
Yeshua: The Gospel of St. Thomas - Alan Decker McNarie 4306

Bethlehem
How Far to Bethlehem? - Norah Lofts 3846
Mary - Sholem Asch 198
Ruth - Irving Fineman 2089
The Unanointed - Laurene Chinn 1070

Galilee
Two From Galilee: A Love Story - Marjorie Holmes 3005

Jerusalem
Agrippa's Daughter - Howard Fast 2025
The Apostle - Sholem Asch 197
The Babylonians - Nathaniel Norsen Weinreb 6600
Barabbas - Par Lagerkvist 3585
Barabbas: A Dream of the World's Tragedy - Marie Corelli 1327
Barabbas: A Novel of the Time of Jesus - Emery Bekessy 417
Behold the Man - N. Richard Nash 4556
Behold Your King - Florence M. Bauer 379
Ben Hur: A Tale of the Christ - Lew Wallace 6536
The Big Fisherman - Lloyd C. Douglas 1702
The Bond and the Free - Charles Dunscomb 1813
The Bride of Pilate - Esther Kellner 3393
Brothers of Vengeance - LeGette Blythe 556
Dara, the Cypriot - Louis Paul 4842
David at Olivet - Wallace Hamilton 2671
David: Warrior and King - Frank G. Slaughter 5885
Dear and Glorious Physician - Taylor Caldwell 853
First the Blade - Drayton Mayrant 4212
Fisher of Men: A Novel of Simon Peter - Kurt Frieberger 2231
The Gifts: A Story of the Boyhood of Jesus - Dorothy Clarke Wilson 6800
The Glorious Folly: A Novel of the Time of St. Paul - Louis De Wohl 1565
The Gospel According to Pontius Pilate - James R. Mills 4408
Great Lion of God - Taylor Caldwell 858
He Came From Galilee - Daniel A. Poling 5083
Hear Me, Pilate! - LeGette Blythe 557
I, Judas - Taylor Caldwell 859
The Island of the Innocent: A Novel of Greek and Jew in the Time of the Maccabees - Vardis Fisher 2108
Josephus - Lion Feuchtwanger 2072
Justus - Arthur L. Lapham 3663
The King David Report - Stefan Heym 2910
The Lance of Longinus - Hubertus Loewenstein 3833
The Last Days - William Rayner 5272
Live From Golgotha - Gore Vidal 6491
The Lives of Rachel - Joel Gross 2601
The Magdalene Gospel - Mary Ellen Ashcroft 203
Man Before the Morning - Cecil Maiden 4032

Man of Nazareth - Anthony Burgess 779
Man on Fire: A Novel on the Life of St. Paul - LeGette Blythe 558
Marcus - Laurene Chinn 1068
Mary - Sholem Asch 198
Merari - Gloria Howe Bremkamp 656
The Messiah - Marjorie Holmes 3003
The Nazarene - Sholem Asch 200
Pontius Pilate: A Biographical Novel - Paul L. Maier 4034
Pontius Pilate Reflects - Werner Koch 3529
The Queen of Sheba - Roberta Kells Dorr 1696
The Robber: A Tale of the Time of the Herods - Bertram Brooker 706
The Robe - Lloyd C. Douglas 1703
The Same Scourge - John Goldthorpe 2464
The Secret of the Kingdom - Mika Waltari 6555
The Silver Chalice - Thomas B. Costain 1370
Solomon and Sheba - Faye Levine 3740
Solomon and the Queen of Sheba - Czenzi Ormonde 4751
A Tear for Judas - LeGette Blythe 559
The Tenth Measure - Brenda Lesley Segal 5721
The Tentmaker - Julius Berstl 486
The Testament of Theophilus - Leonard Wibberley 6730
The Thorn of Arimathea - Frank G. Slaughter 5905
A Time for Judas - Morley Callaghan 866
Two From Galilee: A Love Story - Marjorie Holmes 3005
The Unanointed - Laurene Chinn 1070
Upon This Rock: A Novel of Simon Peter, Prince of Apostles - Frank G. Slaughter 5906
The Voices of Masada - David Kossoff 3545
The Word and the Sword - Theo Lang 3662

Makor
The Source - James A. Michener 4374

Masada
The Antagonists - Ernest K. Gann 2276
The Tenth Measure - Brenda Lesley Segal 5721
The Voices of Masada - David Kossoff 3545

Nazareth
The Brother - Chayym Zeldis 6958
The Gifts: A Story of the Boyhood of Jesus - Dorothy Clarke Wilson 6800
He Came From Galilee - Daniel A. Poling 5083
Man of Nazareth - Anthony Burgess 779
Mary - Sholem Asch 198
The Messiah - Marjorie Holmes 3003
The Shepherd - Robert Payne 4855
Three From Galilee: The Young Man From Nazareth - Marjorie Holmes 3004
Two From Galilee: A Love Story - Marjorie Holmes 3005

ITALY

The Absorbing Fire: The Byron Legend - F.W. Kenyon 3445
Angelica - Samuel A. Schreiner Jr. 5671
Ardent Flame - Frances Winwar 6829
Axe for an Abbot - Elizabeth Eyre 1989
The Bait and the Trap - George Challis 970
Baton Sinister - Carl J. Spinatelli 5967
Bianca - Mabel Conquist 1257
The Blacksmith's Daughter - Joanna Dessau 1625
Blessed Are the Meek: A Novel about St. Francis of Assisi - Zofja Kossak-Szczucka 3542
The Blood Star - Nicholas Guild 2611
Borgia Testament - Nigel Balchin 277
Bravo for the Bride - Elizabeth Eyre 1990
Byron: A Novel - Sigrid Combuchen 1225
Caravan to Kanadu: A Novel of Marco Polo - Edison Marshall 4103
A Cardinal of the Medici - Susan Hicks Beach 393
Carnival of Saints - George Herman 2860

The Castle of Fratta - Ippolito Nievo 4625
Chivalry - Rafael Sabatini 5548
Color From a Light Within: A Novel Based on the Life of El Greco - Donald Braider 641
Condottiere - Jan Westcott 6644
Contessa - Richard Oliver Collin 1209
Count Manifred - Miranda Seymour 5761
Crown Without Sceptre - William Vaughan Wilkins 6758
Curtains for the Cardinal - Elizabeth Eyre 1991
Darkness and the Dawn - Thomas B. Costain 1364
Daughter of Shadows - Miranda Seymour 5762
Death of the Duchess - Elizabeth Eyre 1992
The Devil's Cross - Walter O'Meara 4733
Doctor Copernicus - John Banville 296
Doctor Mirabilis - James Blish 550
The Dragon Waiting: A Masque of History - John M. Ford 2165
Eleanora Duse - Jean Stubbs 6095
An Epic Joy: A Novel Based on the Life of Rubens - Donald Braider 642
The Etruscan - Mika Waltari 6553
Eva - Ib Melchior 4329
Faust - Robert Nye 4654
A Fiddle, a Sword, and a Lady - Albert Spalding 5953
Flight From Bucharest - R.T. Stevens 6000
The Glittering Strand - Judith Lennox-Smith 3716
The Golden Years: A Novel Based on the Life and Loves of Percy Bysshe Shelley - F.W. Kenyon 3451
The Great Infidel - Joseph Jay Deiss 1582
Great Maria - Cecelia Holland 2989
Hitler Has Won - Frederic Mullally 4511
The House of Cray - Pamela Hill 2936
How Do I Love Thee - Lucille Iremonger 3110
The Image of Our Lord - Edward Burman 790
Ippolita - Alberto Denti di Pirajno 1612
The Irish Boy: A Romantic Biography - Naomi Jacob 3137
John Inglesant - John Henry Shorthouse 5833
Lady's Maid - Margaret Forster 2188
Lest Darkness Fall - L. Sprague De Camp 1557
Life as Carola - Joan Grant 2535
Light on Lucrezia - Jean Plaidy 5029
The Lily and the Lion - Maurice Druon 1733
The Lion of Pescara - George MacBeth 3958
Lord Byron's Doctor - Paul West 6634
Lord of the Ladies - Joanna Dessau 1626
The Love of Fingin O'Lea - Theodora McCormick Du Bois 1743
Lover of Life - Zsolt de Harsanyi 2756
Madonna of the Seven Hills - Jean Plaidy 5034
The Magic Bow - Manuel Komroff 3534
The Master of Oakwindsor - Douglas Kent Hall 2648
The Memoirs of Christopher Columbus - Stephen Marlowe 4096
The Memoirs of Lord Byron - Robert Nye 4655
The Memory Cathedral: A Secret History of Leonardo Da Vinci - Jack Dann 1481
The Mercenary - Charles Durbin 1814
The Missolonghi Manuscript - Frederic Prokosch 5194
Modigliani: Prince of Montparnasse - Tadeusz Wittlin 6834
Mussolini - Alan Gelb 2348
My Brother Napoleon: The Confessions of Caroline Bonaparte - F.W. Kenyon 3455
My Sister, My Love - Lucille Iremonger 3111
The Naked Sword: The Story of Lucretia Borgia - F.W. Kenyon 3456
The Name of the Rose - Umberto Eco 1850
Niccolo Rising - Dorothy Dunnett 1803
Not Built with Hands - Helen Constance White 6679
Our Lives Have Just Begun - Henry Myers 4541
A Passion in the Blood - Genevieve Davis 1519
Passionate Rebel: The Story of Hector Berlioz - F.W. Kenyon 3457

The Patriot - Antonio Fogazzaro   2146
Prisoner of the Queen - Alison Macleod   4006
Queen Anne Boleyn - Francis Hackett   2634
The Quiet Light - Louis De Wohl   1572
Ramage - Dudley Pope   5097
Road From Olivet - Edward Francis Murphy   4523
The Road to Glory - Frederick Britten Austin   246
The Rose and the Sword - Sandra Paretti   4792
The Scarlet City - Hella S. Haasse   2632
Snared Nightingale - Geoffrey Trease   6324
A Soldier of the Great War - Mark Helprin   2823
The Star-Gazer - Zsolt de Harsanyi   2757
Stranger at the Wedding - Frances Lynch   3934
The Straw Man - Jean Giono   2425
The Sword of Il Grande - Will Creed   1424
Teresa, or Her Demon Lover - Austin K. Gray   2554
Then and Now - William Somerset Maugham   4198
Titian - Dario Cecchi   965
Triptych - Dora Landey   3652
The Two-Headed Eagle - John Biggins   493
The Viking - Edison Marshall   4113
Vittoria - Robert Merle   4342
Web of Lucifer: A Novel of the Borgia Fury - Maurice Samuel   5580
The Wind Dancer - Iris Johansen   3218
Wine of Satan - Laverne Gay   2327
Wings of the Falcon - Barbara Michaels   4361
The Wrong Horse - Jean Bassan   374

Amalfi
A Dancer in Darkness - David Stacton   5971

Assisi
Bird of Fire: A Tale of Francis of Assisi - Helen Constance White   6676
The Joyful Beggar: A Novel of St. Francis of Assisi - Louis De Wohl   1568
My Beautiful White Roses - Michael Lechner   3703
The Perfect Joy of St. Francis - Felix Timmermans   6281
Saint Francis - Nikos Kazantzakis   3385
Sing to the Sun - Lucille Borden   579

Castello
The Woman in the Cloak - Pamela Hill   2949

Cremora
Antonietta - John Hersey   2868

Elba
Why Waterloo? - Alan Patrick Herbert   2850

Ferrara
The Flame of the Borgias - Jean Briggs   680
The Mill on the Po - Riccardo Bacchelli   254
Prince of Foxes - Samuel Shellabarger   5797
Private Renaissance - Maria Bellonci   436

Florence
The Agony and the Ecstasy - Irving Stone   6054
Artemesia - Anna Banti   295
A Brood of Vipers - Michael Clynes   1133
Captain of the Medici - John J. Pugh   5206
Familiar Acts - June Barraclough   345
The Florentine - Sandra Shulman   5840
The Florentine - Carl J. Spinatelli   5968
The Hand of Michelangelo - Sidney Alexander   85
The Hawthorne Legacy - Teresa Crane   1416
The Medici Emerald - Martin Woodhouse   6851
The Medici Guns - Martin Woodhouse   6852
The Medici Hawks - Martin Woodhouse   6853
Metello - Vasco Pratolini   5163
Michelangelo the Florentine - Sidney Alexander   86
Mona Lisa: The Woman in the Portrait - Sara Mayfield   4206
Mortal Pageant - Johan Fabricius   1993
The Palace - Chelsea Quinn Yarbro   6904
The Palace of Wisdom - Bob Marshall-Andrews   4118
The Private Life of Mona Lisa - Pierre La Mure   3577

The Queen of Hearts - Joan Rees   5290
The Romance of Leonardo Da Vinci - Dmitri Merezhkovski   4339
Romola - George Eliot   1910
The Savage Brood - Martha Rofheart   5430
The Smile of the Stranger - Joan Aiken   53
The Spring of the Ram - Dorothy Dunnett   1809
The Time Returns - Alexandra Ripley   5343
The Wanderer: A Novel of Dante and Beatrice - Nathan Schachner   5633

Genoa
Race of Scorpions - Dorothy Dunnett   1806

Imola
The Borgia Prince - Pamela Bennetts   446

Lombardy
The Betrothed - Alessandro Manzoni   4078
The Unspeakables: A Tale of Lombardy - Laverne Gay   2326
The Valley of Decision - Edith Wharton   6653

Lucca
Marianne and the Masked Prince - Juliette Benzoni   469

Mantua
Private Renaissance - Maria Bellonci   436
The Tears of the Madonna - George Herman   2862

Milan
The Betrothed - Alessandro Manzoni   4078
The Bride of Sforza - Miranda Seymour   5760
A Comedy of Murders - George Herman   2861
Duchess of Milan - Michael Ennis   1946
The Lady in the Mask - Anne Green   2564
Leonardo's Judas - Leo Perutz   4941
The Romance of Leonardo Da Vinci - Dmitri Merezhkovski   4339
The Rose of Malmaison: The Turbulent Life of the Beautiful Josephine - Gaby von Schonthan   5660
The Tears of the Madonna - George Herman   2862

Montevalenti
The Sins of the Lion - Annette Motley   4503

Naples
Artemesia - Anna Banti   295
Bride of Glory - Bradda Field   2078
Clara Reeve - Leonie Hargrave   2705
Clear for Action! - Simon White   6699
Cry to Heaven - Anne Rice   5313
The Dark Fire - Linda Murray   4537
Duchess of Milan - Michael Ennis   1946
Emma - F.W. Kenyon   3448
The English Captain - Simon White   6700
The Flight of the Eagle - Donald Thomas   6239
H.M.S. Cockerel - Dewey Lambdin   3611
Loving Emma - Nigel Foxell   2197
The Nelson Touch - Paul Lewis   3759
Ramage and the Saracens - Dudley Pope   5101
Shadow of a Lady - Jane Aiken Hodge   2971
The Sleeping Sword: A Biographical Novel - Pearl Frye   2244
The Volcano Lover - Susan Sontag   5946

Otranto
The Medici Hawks - Martin Woodhouse   6853

Padua
Divine Mistress - Frank G. Slaughter   5886
Physician Extraordinary: A Novel of the Life and Times of William Harvey - David Weiss   6608

Paestum
Gate to the Sea - Bryher   743

Parma
The Charterhouse of Parma - Stendhal   5993

Po River Valley
Nothing New under the Sun - Riccardo Bacchelli   255

Ravenna
Citadel of God: A Novel of Saint Benedict - Louis De Wohl   1563
Threshold of Fire - Hella S. Haasse   2633

Rimini
Concordia - Frances Fleetwood   2124

Rome
The Agony and the Ecstasy - Irving Stone   6054
Artemesia - Anna Banti   295
Before My Time - Niccolo Tucci   6358
Below the Salt - Thomas B. Costain   1362
A Candle for D'Artagnan - Chelsea Quinn Yarbro   6895
Caravaggio - Robert Payne   4851
The Chancellor - Lawrence Schoonover   5662
Citadel of God: A Novel of Saint Benedict - Louis De Wohl   1563
City of God: A Novel of the Borgias - Cecelia Holland   2985 .
Clair De Lune: A Novel about Claude Debussy - Pierre La Mure   3575
Count Belisarius - Robert Graves   2544
Crown of Grass - Charles Andrew Brady   634
The Dark Fire - Linda Murray   4537
The Eagle's Daughter - Judith Tarr   6165
Edmund Campion - Evelyn Waugh   6585
The Florentine - Carl J. Spinatelli   5968
The Garden of Persephone - Cesar J. Rotondi   5510
The Golden Thread - Louis De Wohl   1566
The Goliath Head - Charles J. Calitri   865
The Greek of Toledo: A Romantic Narrative of El Greco - Elizabeth Borton   586
Gregory the Great - Gerhart Ellert   1913
The Hand of Michelangelo - Sidney Alexander   85
Joanna the Pope - Daniel Panger   4785
Leo Africanus - Amin Maalouf   3947
The Lost Flight - H.F.M. Prescott   5169
A Man Called Cervantes - Bruno Frank   2201
The Medici Emerald - Martin Woodhouse   6851
The Medici Hawks - Martin Woodhouse   6853
Michelangelo the Florentine - Sidney Alexander   86
Middlemarch - George Eliot   1909
Mona Lisa: The Woman in the Portrait - Sara Mayfield   4206
My Crown, My Love - Ruth Walgreen Stephan   5995
Nicodemus: The Roman Years of Michelangelo Buonarroti, 1534-1564 - Sidney Alexander   87
Phantom - Susan Kay   3375
Pope Joan - Donna Woolfolk Cross   1433
The Pope's Rhinoceros - Lawrence Norfolk   4642
Prince of Foxes - Samuel Shellabarger   5797
Private Renaissance - Maria Bellonci   436
The Remarkable Young Man - Cecil Roberts   5373
Rienzi, or The Last of the Tribunes - Edward Bulwer-Lytton   770
The Right Line of Cedric - Alfred Duggan   1773
Saint Francis - Nikos Kazantzakis   3385
The Stress of Her Regard - Tim Powers   5157
A Tale for Midnight - Frederic Prokosch   5195
Threshold of Fire - Hella S. Haasse   2633
Tudor Underground - Denis Meadows   4320
The Unspeakables: A Tale of Lombardy - Laverne Gay   2326
The World, the Flesh, and the Devil - Reay Tannahill   6159

San Severo
The Borgia Prince - Pamela Bennetts   446
Silver Leopard - F. van Wyck Mason   4160

Sicily
Antichrist: A Novel of the Emperor Frederick II - Cecelia Holland   2982
The Council of Europe - Leonardo Sciascia   5678
The Emperor, the Sages and Death - Rachel Berdach   475
Escapade - Jane Aiken Hodge   2962
The Garden of Persephone - Cesar J. Rotondi   5510

Homer's Daughter - Robert Graves 2546
The Laughter of Aphrodite - Peter Green 2570
The Leopard - Giuseppe di Lampedusa 3634
Lord Elgin's Lady - Theodore Vrettos 6514
Luciano's Luck - Jack Higgins 2912
The Praise Singer - Mary Renault 5302
The Saracen Blade - Frank Yerby 6926
Sir William - David Stacton 5977

Siena
Lay Siege to Heaven: A Novel of Saint Catherine of Siena - Louis De Wohl 1570
The Saint - Fritz von Unruh 6385

Tuscany
Caressa - Linda Lang Bartell 363
City of God: A Novel of the Borgias - Cecelia Holland 2985
A Quest for Love - Jacquetta Hawkes 2781
The Rebels - Alfred Neumann 4585

Venice
The Betrothed - Alessandro Manzoni 4078
The Books of Rachel - Joel Gross 2600
The Bravo - James Fenimore Cooper 1298
City of Light - Alison Macleod 4001
Columbus: A Romance - Rafael Sabatini 5549
Consuelo - George Sand 5582
Dark Inheritance - Carola Salisbury 5568
The Dark Palazzo - Virginia Coffman 1151
Divine Mistress - Frank G. Slaughter 5886
Duchess of Milan - Michael Ennis 1946
First Night - Jane Aiken Hodge 2963
The Flame of the Borgias - Jean Briggs 680
The Greek of Toledo: A Romantic Narrative of El Greco - Elizabeth Borton 586
The Heroine's Sister - Frances Murray 4536
High Carnival - John J. Pugh 5207
The Hireling - Alison Macleod 4003
The Italian Garden - Judith Lennox-Smith 3717
The Journeyer - Gary Jennings 3194
A Kind of Justice - Benjamin Siegel 5844
Lord of the Dead: The Secret History of Byron - Tom Holland 2999
Lord Vanity - Samuel Shellabarger 5796
A Mapmaker's Dream - James Cowan 1391
Marianne and the Rebels - Juliette Benzoni 471
The Medici Emerald - Martin Woodhouse 6851
Messer Marco Polo - Donn Byrne 840
A Most Romantic City - Mary Ann Gibbs 2396
Pandora's Galley - Macdonald Harris 2727
The Paper Mistress - Dorothea Malm 4045
Prince of Foxes - Samuel Shellabarger 5797
Race of Scorpions - Dorothy Dunnett 1806
Scales of Gold - Dorothy Dunnett 1808
Serenissima: A Novel of Venice - Erica Jong 3300
Simple Prayers - Michael Golding 2452
Sofia - Ann Chamberlin 974
The Stress of Her Regard - Tim Powers 5157
Summoned to Darkness - Anne-Marie Sheridan 5809
The Tears of the Madonna - George Herman 2862
To Lie with Lions - Dorothy Dunnett 1810
The Venetian - David Weiss 6611
The Venetian Mask - Rosalind Laker 3603
Venetian Masque - Rafael Sabatini 5556
Written in the Stars: A Novel about Albrecht Durer - Frances Hope Fisher 2103

JAMAICA

Alexa - Anne Melville 4330
The Ancestors Cry Out - Eugenia Lovett West 6627
Black Angels - C.T. Ritchie 5348
Black Dawn - Christopher Nicole 4613
Buccaneer - Dudley Pope 5093
Caribbee - Thomas Hoover 3025
Creole Dusk - Walter Adolphe Roberts 5392
First Lieutenant - Kenneth Maynard 4208
Galleon - Dudley Pope 5095

The Golden Harlot - Jeanne Wilson 6808
The Golden Hawk - Frank Yerby 6921
A High Wind in Jamaica - Richard Hughes 3074
Lamb in Command - Kenneth Maynard 4209
The Lorimer Line - Anne Melville 4332
Manitou - Donald Clayton Porter 5120
New Day - Victor Stafford Reid 5291
The Pride of the Trevallions - Carola Salisbury 5570
Ramage's Prize - Dudley Pope 5107
Rivers of Glory - F. van Wyck Mason 4158
Sunset - Christopher Nicole 4623
The View From Coyaba - Peter Abrahams 11
Weep in the Sun - Jeanne Wilson 6809
Wide Sargasso Sea - Jean Rhys 5312

Kingston
The Tontine - Thomas B. Costain 1371

Port Royal
The Imposter - Noel B. Gerson 2375

JAPAN

The Barbarian - Willard Price 5191
The Big Family - Vina Delmar 1600
Bronze Christ - Yoshiro Nagaya 4551
Daishi-San: A Novel - Robert P. Lund 3925
The Exile Way - Ann Woodward 6865
Harpoon - C.W. Nicol 4612
The House of Kanze - Nobuko Albery 64
Kagami - Elizabeth Kata 3369
Mortal Hunger: A Novel Based on the Life of Lafcadio Hearn - Harry E. Wedeck 6594
Musashi: An Epic Novel of the Samurai Era - Eiji Yoshikawa 6935
The Needle-Watcher - Richard Blaker 540
The Ronin - William Dale Jennings 3212
The Running of the Tide - Esther Forbes 2160
Sakuran: A Novel of Medieval Japan - Edward Tolosko 6292
The Samurai - Shusaku Endo 1941
Segaki - David Stacton 5975
Set All Afire: A Novel of St. Francis Xavier - Louis De Wohl 1574
Shike: Time of Dragons - Robert Shea 5784
Shogun - James Clavell 1101
The Signore: Shogun of the Warring States - Kunio Tsuji 6357
The Sword of Hachiman - Lynn Guest 2608
Taiko - Eiji Yoshikawa 6936
The Tokaido Road: A Novel of Feudal Japan - Lucia St. Clair Robson 5417
Venture in the East - Bruce Lancaster 3648
The Vermilion Bridge - Shelley Mydans 4539

Edo
Bundori - Laura Joh Rowland 5519
Shin Ju - Laura Joh Rowland 5520

Hiroshima
Chikara! - Robert Skimin 5876

Kyoto
The Heike Story - Eiji Yoshikawa 6934

Tokyo
The Ginger Tree - Oswald Wynd 6890

Yedo
Gai-Jin: A Novel of Japan - James Clavell 1100
Yedo - Lynn Guest 2609

Yokohama
Gai-Jin: A Novel of Japan - James Clavell 1100

KENYA

Kenya - John Halkin 2645
Lion in the Evening - Alan Scholefield 5656
The White Rhino Hotel - Bartle Bull 765

Nairobi
Green City in the Sun - Barbara Wood 6849
An Ice-Cream War - William Boyd 616
Once a Gentleman - Donald James 3157

KOREA

Cold War - Robert Vaughan 6446
How Far to Bethlehem? - Norah Lofts 3846
The Living Reed - Pearl S. Buck 756
Manchu - Robert S. Elegant 1904

Seoul
The Blue Dragon - Diana Brown 716

LEBANON

Beirut
Dreaming of Samarkand - Martin Booth 576
Regards From the Dead Princess: A Novel of a Life - Kenize Mourad 4505

Tyre
Crusader's Torch - Chelsea Quinn Yarbro 6897
Imperial Purple - Gillian Bradshaw 631
Jezebel - Dorothy Clarke Wilson 6802
Lot's Wife - Marie Ley-Piscator 3767
The Purple Quest: A Novel of Seafaring Adventure in the Ancient World - Frank G. Slaughter 5896

LIBERIA

Crossing the River - Caryl Phillips 4984

LIBYA

Tripoli
The Disorderly Knights - Dorothy Dunnett 1800

LITHUANIA

The Deluge - Henryk Sienkiewicz 5846

MACAO

An Insular Position - Timothy Mo 4421
The King's Privateer - Dewey Lambdin 3615
The Pearl Pagoda - Susannah Broome 707
Trade Imperial - Alan Lloyd 3814
The Wings of the Morning - Thomas Tryon 6356

MACEDONIA

The Conqueror: A Novel of Alexander the Great - Edison Marshall 4104
Fire From Heaven - Mary Renault 5296
Funeral Games - Mary Renault 5297
The Golden Lyre - Noel B. Gerson 2371
Lord of the Two Lands - Judith Tarr 6167
The Shining - Stephen Marlowe 4097
The Soothsayer - Laurene Chinn 1069
Star of Macedon - Karl V. Eiker 1901

Thessalonika
Live From Golgotha - Gore Vidal 6491

MADAGASCAR

Dead Reckoning - C. Northcote Parkinson 4809
The Deadly Lady of Madagascar - C.V. Terry 6206
Flashman's Lady - George MacDonald Fraser 2210
The Legion of the Lost - Donald Barr Chidsey 1062
The War Chest - Porter Hill 2950

MALAYSIA

Sarawak
Flashman's Lady - George MacDonald Fraser   2210

MALI

Segu
Segu - Maryse Conde   1234

Timbuktu
Scales of Gold - Dorothy Dunnett   1808

MALTA

American Captain - Edison Marshall   4101
A Certain Splendour - Carola Salisbury   5566
The Disorderly Knights - Dorothy Dunnett   1800
Treason's Harbour - Patrick O'Brian   4676

Valletta
The Dark Fire - Linda Murray   4537
Touch and Go - C. Northcote Parkinson   4815

MARTINIQUE

The Emperor's Lady: A Novel Based on the Life of the Empress Josephine - F.W. Kenyon   3449
In Perilous Seas - Victor Suthren   6130
Mistress of Fortune - Sheila Lancaster   3651
Ramage and the Dido - Dudley Pope   5098
Ramage's Diamond - Dudley Pope   5105
Stronghold - Donald Barr Chidsey   1065
Sultana - Michael, Prince of Greece   4358

MAURITIUS

Captain Monsoon - Victor Suthren   6128
Dead Reckoning - C. Northcote Parkinson   4809
The Mauritius Command - Patrick O'Brian   4670

MEDITERRANEAN

The Captive - Victoria Holt   3011
Dara, the Cypriot - Louis Paul   4842
Drumbeat - Dudley Pope   5094
I, Paul - Rex Miller   4401
Purple Pirate - Talbot Mundy   4514
Ramage - Dudley Pope   5097
Ramage and the Saracens - Dudley Pope   5101
Ramage's Signal - Dudley Pope   5108
Return to Ithaca - Eyvind Johnson   3224
Three Ships and Three Kings - Georgia Sallaska   5573
Touch and Go - C. Northcote Parkinson   4815
The Unholy Pilgrim - R.F. Tapsell   6161
The Voyage Home - Ernst Schnabel   5644
The Wind in His Fists - John Edward Jennings   3210

Garamus
Judas - Igal Mossinsohn   4500

MESOPOTAMIA

The Last Warrior Queen - Mary Mackey   3992
Sword of Glory - Peter Danielson   1477

Nineveh
The Assyrian - Nicholas Guild   2610
The Blood Star - Nicholas Guild   2611

Sumer
Gilgamesh the King - Robert Silverberg   5853

Ur
Abram, Son of Terah - Florence M. Bauer   378
The Covenant: A Novel of the Life of Abraham the Prophet - Zofja Kossak-Szczucka   3543

No Other Gods - Wilder Penfield   4901
The Promise - Esther Kellner   3395

MEXICO

The Adelita - Oakley Hall   2649
Among the Innocent - Elizabeth Borton de Trevino   6339
Angel with Spurs - Paul I. Wellman   6613
Anything for Billy - Larry McMurtry   4295
The Authentic Death of Hendry Jones - Charles Neider   4562
Aztec - Gary Jennings   3193
Beyond the Blue Sierra - Honore Morrow   4486
Blue Moon - Parris Afton Bonds   569
The Breast of the Dove - Herbert Gorman   2491
The Cactus and the Crown - Catherine Gavin   2318
The Campaign - Carlos Fuentes   2245
Captain Grant - Shirley Seifert   5724
Captain Jack - Gene Shelton   5800
Chapultepec - Norman Zollinger   6965
The Children of the Sun - Oakley Hall   2652
The Coil of the Serpent - Dexter Allen   94
Copilli, Aztec Prince - Miguel Aleman Velasco   75
Cortez and Marina - Edison Marshall   4105
The Crimson Wind - Max Hennessy   2832
The Crossing - Cormac McCarthy   4221
The Death of Artemio Cruz - Carlos Fuentes   2246
Death of the Fifth Sun - Robert Somerlott   5944
Dillinger - Harry Patterson   4832
Doniphan's Ride - Les Savage Jr.   5620
Drumm's War - Bill Bragg   638
Dust on the King's Highway - Helen Constance White   6677
The Eagle and the Raven - James A. Michener   4369
Eagle on the Sun - Julia Davis   1527
The Fair God - Lew Wallace   6537
The Fifth Horseman - Jose Antonio Villarreal   6496
Flames of Empire - Peter Bourne   594
The Friends of Pancho Villa - James Carlos Blake   535
Geronimo: An American Legend - Robert J. Conley   1242
Gods on Horseback - Samuel G. Baggett   263
The Golden Eagle - Noel B. Gerson   2370
The Golden Princess - Alexander Baron   335
The Grasshopper King - Elizabeth Boatwright Coker   1165
The Great White Gods - Eduard Stucken   6102
The Hands of Cantu - Tom Lea   3694
The Heart of Jade - Salvador de Madariaga   4024
A Heritage of Shadows - Madeleine Brent   660
The Jaguar and the Golden Stag - Dexter Allen   95
Lonesome Dove - Larry McMurtry   4298
The Luck of Huemac: A Novel about the Aztecs - Daniel Peters   4946
The Marburg Chronicles - Alfred Coppel   1319
Maximilian's Gold - Jane Barry   359
Mexico - James A. Michener   4372
A Mule for the Marquesa - Frank O'Rourke   4753
Not of War Only - Norman Zollinger   6966
The Old Gringo - Carlos Fuentes   2247
Outlaw - Warren Kiefer   3482
Pancho And Black Jack - Fred Bean   398
Passengers to Mexico: The Last Invasion of Mexico - Blair Niles   4627
The Prison Notebooks of Ricardo Flores Magon - Douglas Day   1545
A Rage Against Heaven - Fred Mustard Stewart   6026
The Rainbow Runner - John Cunningham   1450
Republic: A Novel of Texas - E.V. Thompson   6266
Ride the Red Earth - Paul I. Wellman   6620
The Roads to Guadalupe - Robert Lewis Taylor   6190
The Samurai - Shusaku Endo   1941
Sergeant Gringo - Jack Cummings   1449

The Seven Cities of Gold - Virginia Davis Hersch   2865
Streets of Laredo - Larry McMurtry   4300
The Sun, He Dies: A Novel about the End of the Aztec World - Jamake Highwater   2919
Takers of the City - Hoffman Reynolds Hays   2800
They Are Coming: The Conquest of Mexico - Jose Lopez Portillo y Pacheco   3896
The Tin Lizzie Troup - Glendon Swarthout   6146
Tom Mix and Pancho Villa - Clifford Irving   3113
Trumpets Sound No More - F. van Wyck Mason   4163
Under the Fifth Sun: A Novel of Pancho Villa - Earl Shorris   5832
El Vago - Laurence Gonzales   2474
Valley of Eagles - Dexter Allen   96
The Vengeance Trail of Josey Wales - Forrest Carter   946
The Veracruz Blues - Mark Winegardner   6821
Walks in the Sun - Don Coldsmith   1194
West of Appomattox - Harley Duncan   1785
When the Owl Cries - Paul Bartlett   367
The Wine of San Lorenzo - Herbert Gorman   2493

Chihuahua
Chihuahua 1916 - Otis Carney   903
Last Reveille - David Morrell   4456

Delgado
South of the Border - John Byrne Cooke   1268

Dolores
The Cry of Dolores - Herbert Gorman   2492

Guadalajara District
The Edge of the Storm - Agustin Yanez   6893

Mexico City
Gone to Texas - Don Worcester   6871
The House on Bitterness Street - Elizabeth Borton de Trevino   6340
The Road to Glory - Darwin Le Ora Teilhct   6199
Roses for Mexico - Ethel Cook Eliot   1907
Street of the Madwoman - Isabel Ortega   4756

Sierra Madre
Escape From Sonora - Will Bryant   739

Skeleton Canyon
Geronimo - Bill Dugan   1758

Tenochtitlan
Captain From Castile - Samuel Shellabarger   5794
The Jaguar Princess - Clare Bell   421

Vera Cruz
Star in the Rigging: A Novel of the Texas Navy - Garland Roark   5358

Yucatan
Cradle of the Sun - John Clagett   1083
Father of Waters - Donald Clayton Porter   5118
A Signal Victory - David Stacton   5976

MIDDLE EAST

Abraham and Sarah: The Long Journey - Roberta Kells Dorr   1694
Alamut - Judith Tarr   6164
And Abram Journeyed - Harry Simonhoff   5858
And Walk on Love: A Novel Based on the Life of the Apostle Paul - Henrietta Buckmaster   759
An Army of Children - Evan H. Rhodes   5306
Besieger of Cities - Alfred Duggan   1761
The Book of Abraham - Marek Halter   2665
Captain Vinegar's Commission - Philip Glazebrook   2428
The Challenging Heights - Max Hennessy   2831
Count Bohemond - Alfred Duggan   1764
An Elephant for Aristotle - L. Sprague De Camp   1556
The Golden Thread - Louis De Wohl   1566

Hagar - Cothburn O'Neal   4737
The Heirs of the Kingdom - Zoe Oldenbourg   4716
How Far to Bethlehem? - Norah Lofts   3846
I, Paul - Rex Miller   4401
Jacob - Jean Cabries   844
The Living Wood - Louis De Wohl   1571
Lord of the Two Lands - Judith Tarr   6167
The Lost Legion - H. Warner Munn   4516
Man on Fire: A Novel on the Life of St. Paul -
   LeGette Blythe   558
On Eagles' Wings - Arthur E. Southon   5951
The Promise - Esther Kellner   3395
*The Road to Bithynia: A Novel of Luke, the Beloved
   Physician* - Frank G. Slaughter   5897
Saint Paul: A Historical Novel of His Life - Leon
   Poirier   5081
The Son of Laughter - Frederick Buechner   764
The Tales of Jacob - Thomas Mann   4068
Trail and Triumph: A Novel about Maimonides -
   Lester M. Morrison   4485
The Unicorn Hunt - Dorothy Dunnett   1811
The Vandal - Richard O'Connor   4687
The Wanderer - Mika Waltari   6556
The Weeping Ash - Joan Aiken   54
Winter Quarters - Alfred Duggan   1775
Young Joseph - Thomas Mann   4069

Ephesus
The Beacon of Alexandria - Gillian Bradshaw   627

Tarsus
Great Lion of God - Taylor Caldwell   858
The Tentmaker - Julius Berstl   486

MONACO

Monte Carlo
Jewelled Path - Rosalind Laker   3597
That Vanderbilt Woman - Philip Van
   Rensselaer   6427
Why Kill Arthur Potter? - Ray Harrison   2746

MONGOLIA

Ruler of the Sky: A Novel of Genghis Khan - Pamela
   Sargent   5606
*Sons of the Steppe: The Story of How the Conqueror
   Genghis Khan Was Overcome* - Hans
   Baumann   380

Gobi Desert
*The Earth Is the Lord's: A Tale of the Rise of Genghis
   Khan* - Taylor Caldwell   855

MOROCCO

Captain Ironhand - Rosamond Marshall   4116
In the Blue Light of African Dreams - Paul
   Watkins   6580
Midnight Moon - Jeanne Montague   4436

Meknes
Angelique in Barbary - Sergeanne Golon   2469

Tangier
The Gypsy From Cadiz - Tamsin Hamilton   2670

NAMIBIA

The Eagles of Malice - Alan Scholefield   5652

NEPAL

Kathmandu
By Command of the Viceroy - Duncan MacNeil   4010

NETHERLANDS

Bruegel, or, The Workshop of Dreams - Claude Henri
   Rocquet   5422
Captain General - John P. Stevenson   6007
Catriona - Robert Louis Stevenson   6009
Countess Carrots - Molly Costain Haycraft   2792
*The Eye of the Lion: A Novel Based on the Life of
   Mata Hari* - Lael Tucker Wertenbaker   6626
The Gentle Fury: A Novel of Margaret of Austria -
   Paul Lewis   3758
Here Lies Margot - Pamela Hill   2935
Johanna: A Novel of the Van Gogh Family - Claire
   Cooperstein   1317
The King's Daughters - Molly Costain
   Haycraft   2793
The Legend of Tyl Ulenspiegel - Charles Theodore
   Henri De Coster   1558
Lust for Life - Irving Stone   6059
Mary of Carisbrooke - Margaret Campbell
   Barnes   327
The Master Painter - Edwin Mullins   4513
The Mohawk Ladder - Noel B. Gerson   2377
Old Mortality - Sir Walter Scott   5702
The Queen's Husband - Samuel Edwards   1889
Reckless Angel - Jane Feather   2056
A Rose for Virtue - Norah Lofts   3858
The Three Crowns - Jean Plaidy   5070
The Tides of Dawn - Emma Louise Mally   4044
The Valiant Lady - Brigid Knight   3523
Vincent: A Novel Based on the Life of Van Gogh -
   Joost Poldermans   5082
William's Wife - Jean Plaidy   5077

Amsterdam
*Children of the Vampire: The Diaries of the Family
   Dracul* - Jeanne Kalogridis   3326
The Drowning Room - Michael Kenneth Pye   5212
The Golden Tulip - Rosalind Laker   3596
I, Rembrandt - David Weiss   6605
Rembrandt - Gladys Schmitt   5643
Scent of Cloves - Norah Lofts   3859
Treason's Gift - Pamela Belle   434
West to Eden - Gloria Goldreich   2461
A Woman of Quality - Jan Westcott   6649

Delft
The Golden Tulip - Rosalind Laker   3596

The Hague
The Bride - Margaret Irwin   3116
The Stranger Prince - Margaret Irwin   3122

Leyden
Rembrandt - Gladys Schmitt   5643

Ostend
The Sable Lion - Jan Van Dorp   6405

Rotterdam
The Cloister and the Hearth - Charles Reade   5279

NEW ZEALAND

Abigail - Joan Druett   1721
Aurora Rose - Anne Worboys   6870
Brave Kingdom - Frances Murray   4534
Daughter of Time - Nelia Gardner White   6695
The Empire Builders - William Stuart Long   3871
Greenstone - Yvonne Kalman   3324
Harpoon in Eden - F. van Wyck Mason   4152
An Important Family - Dorothy Eden   1855
Mists of Heaven - Yvonne Kalman   3325
Monday's Warriors - Maurice Shadbolt   5767
The Piano - Jane Campion   878
Redemption - Leon Uris   6393
Season of the Jew - Maurice Shadbolt   5768

Christchurch
After the Rainbow - Yvonne Kalman   3323

NICARAGUA

A Few Good Men - William Overgard   4768
The Journal of Colonel De Lancey - James Warner
   Bellah   426
The Lion's Skin - Darwin Le Ora Teilhet   6197
The Nation Thief - Robert Houston   3057
The Notorious Angel - Patricia Maxwell   4201

NIGERIA

Umuofia
Things Fall Apart - Chinua Achebe   16

NORTH AMERICA

Anthony Adverse - Hervey Allen   98
Avalon - Anya Seton   5748
Beyond the Sea of Ice - William Sarabande   5595
Blackrobe - Robert E. Wall   6534
The Children of the First Man - James Alexander
   Thom   6230
Children of the Ice - Charlotte Prentiss   5166
The Children of the Sun - Oakley Hall   2652
Daniel Du Luth - Everett McNeil   4307
Dawn Land - Joseph Bruchac III   734
The Dogs of Paradise - Abel Posse   5141
Face of the Rising Sun - William Sarabande   5598
*The First Gentleman of America: A Comedy of
   Conquest* - James Branch Cabell   841
The Golden Eagle - John Edward Jennings   3201
Gudrid's Saga - Constance Irwin   3115
High Towers - Thomas B. Costain   1366
The Ice Shirt - William T. Vollmann   6509
Isle of Woman - Piers Anthony   167
The Mammoth Stone - Margaret Allan   90
Paradise - Dikkon Eberhart   1831
People of the Earth - W. Michael Gear   2334
People of the Lightning - W. Michael Gear   2337
The Power and the Glory - Gilbert Parker   4805
Runestone - Don Coldsmith   1186
The Sacred Stones - William Sarabande   5600
Shadow of the Watching Star - William
   Sarabande   5601
Tatham Mound - Piers Anthony   169
This Land Fulfilled - Charles Andrew Brady   636
Walkers of the Wind - William Sarabande   5603
West with the Vikings - Edison Marshall   4114

Columbia River
Children of the Dawn - Patricia Rowe   5516

Mississippi Valley
People of the River - W. Michael Gear   2338
Thunder in the Wilderness - Charles Granville
   Hamilton   2668

Missouri River
Fort De Chastaigne - Don Coldsmith   1177

New France
The Gilded Torch - Iola Fuller   2252
Touched with Fire - John William Tebbel   6195

Rio Grande Valley
The Deer Dancers - Amanda Cockrell   1146

Sierra Nevada Mountains
People of the Sea - W. Michael Gear   2339

Vinland
A Viking's Daughter - John Andrews   147

Wabenaki Territory
Black Angels - C.T. Ritchie   5348

Western Plains
The Prairie - James Fenimore Cooper   1308

ALASKA

Brother Wind - Sue Harrison   2748
Forbidden Land - William Sarabande   5599

Aleutian Islands

Mother Earth, Father Sky - Sue Harrison   2749
My Sister, the Moon - Sue Harrison   2750

Bering Strait

Corridor of Storms - William Sarabande   5596
People of the Wolf - W. Michael Gear   2341

EAST

People of the Lakes - W. Michael Gear   2336

GREAT LAKES

People of the Lakes - W. Michael Gear   2336

GREAT PLAINS

Bearer of the Pipe - Don Coldsmith   1169
Bride of the Morning Star - Don Coldsmith   1170
Buffalo Medicine - Don Coldsmith   1171
Child of the Dead - Don Coldsmith   1172
Daughter of the Eagle - Don Coldsmith   1173
The Edge of the World - William Sarabande   5597
The Elk-Dog Heritage - Don Coldsmith   1174
The Flower in the Mountains - Don Coldsmith   1175
Follow the Wind - Don Coldsmith   1176
Fort De Chastaigne - Don Coldsmith   1177
Man of the Shadows - Don Coldsmith   1178
Medicine Knife - Don Coldsmith   1179
Moon of Thunder - Don Coldsmith   1180
Pale Star - Don Coldsmith   1181
Quest for the White Bull - Don Coldsmith   1182
Return of the Spanish - Don Coldsmith   1183
Return to the River - Don Coldsmith   1184
River of Swans - Don Coldsmith   1185
The Sacred Hills - Don Coldsmith   1187
Song of the Rock - Don Coldsmith   1189
Thunder in the Sky - William Sarabande   5602
Thunderstick - Don Coldsmith   1190
Track of the Bear - Don Coldsmith   1191
Trail of the Spanish Bit - Don Coldsmith   1193
Walks in the Sun - Don Coldsmith   1194
World of Silence - Don Coldsmith   1195

MISSISSIPPI RIVER

The Gilded Torch - Iola Fuller   2252
River of Swans - Don Coldsmith   1185
River out of Eden - Shirley Seifert   5732
Wilderness Adventure - Elizabeth Page   4774

Mississippi River

Blackrobe - Charles Corcoran   1323

PACIFIC NORTHWEST

Beyond the Shining Mountains - Doris Shannon   5775
Columbia - Pamela Jekel   3184
Friendly Cove - Irving Brant   651
I, James Lewis - Gilbert Wolf Gabriel   2266
Keepers of the Misty Time - Patricia Rowe   5517
The White Cockade - Henry Farrand Griffin   2592

ROCKY MOUNTAINS

People of the Fire - W. Michael Gear   2335
Rio Grande - Jory Sherman   5821
Trapper's Moon - Jory Sherman   5823
World of Silence - Don Coldsmith   1195

SOUTHEAST

The Dark Way - Robert J. Conley   1241
The Way of the Priests - Robert J. Conley   1253
The White Path - Robert J. Conley   1254

SOUTHWEST

Children of the Sun - Charlotte Prentiss   5167
Follow the Wind - Don Coldsmith   1176
Jubal Sackett - Louis L'Amour   3620
Let the Drum Speak: A Novel of Ancient America - Linda Lay Shuler   5837
People of the Mesa - Charlotte Prentiss   5168
People of the Silence - W. Michael Gear   2340
Ride the Red Earth - Paul I. Wellman   6620
The Rose and the Flame - Jonreed Lauritzen   3676
The Seven Cities of Gold - Virginia Davis Hersch   2865
She Who Remembers - Linda Lay Shuler   5838
Voice of the Eagle - Linda Lay Shuler   5839

WEST COAST

In Distant Waters - Richard Woodman   6862

NORWAY

Arne - Bjornstjerne Bjornson   518
The Bridal Wreath - Sigrid Undset   6379
Byzantium - Michael Ennis   1945
The Cross - Sigrid Undset   6380
The Cross and the Sword - Evangeline Walton   6558
Dina's Book - Herbjorg Wassmo   6577
The Emigrants - Johan Bojer   561
The Great Hunger - Johan Bojer   562
The Iron Crown - Clare Barroll   354
The Last of the Vikings - Johan Bojer   563
Lindeman's Daughters - Synnove Christensen   1073
The Mistress of Husaby - Sigrid Undset   6382
The People of Juvik - Olav Dunn   1798
Sea of Darkness - Roland Huntford   3086
This Land Fulfilled - Charles Andrew Brady   636
To Love a Stranger - Barbara Paul   4839

Bergen

The Axe - Sigrid Undset   6378

Hestviken

In the Wilderness - Sigrid Undset   6381
The Snake Pit - Sigrid Undset   6383
The Son Avenger - Sigrid Undset   6384

Oslo

The Axe - Sigrid Undset   6378
The Snake Pit - Sigrid Undset   6383
The Son Avenger - Sigrid Undset   6384

OTTOMAN EMPIRE

Acre

Sylvia's Lovers - Elizabeth Gaskell   2312

Belgrade

The Scimitar - Samuel Edwards   1890

Constantinople

The Bride of Suleiman - Aileen Crawley   1421
Devil's Yard - Ivo Andric   152
The Gentle Infidel - Lawrence Schoonover   5663
God Save the Tsar - Susanna Hoe   2976
Hazard's Command - Vivian Stuart   6088
Leo Africanus - Amin Maalouf   3947
Lord Elgin's Lady - Theodore Vrettos   6514
Lost Love Found - Bertrice Small   5910
Marianne and the Lords of the East - Juliette Benzoni   468
Marianne and the Rebels - Juliette Benzoni   471
Pawn in Frankincense - Dorothy Dunnett   1804

The Rage of the Vulture - Barry Unsworth   6388
Regards From the Dead Princess: A Novel of a Life - Kenize Mourad   4505
The Scimitar - Samuel Edwards   1890
The Shadow of God - Aileen Crawley   1422
Sofia - Ann Chamberlin   974
Sultana - Michael, Prince of Greece   4358
Valide: A Novel of the Harem - Barbara Chase-Riboud   1007
Yankee - Dana Fuller Ross   5495
Yankee Pasha - Edison Marshall   4115

PACIFIC ISLANDS

Mangareva

The Witch of Manga Reva - Garland Roark   5359

Pitcairn Island

Adams of the Bounty - Erle Wilson   6807
Pitcairn's Island - Charles Nordhoff   4640

Zanatu

Halfhyde on Zanatu - Philip McCutchan   4251

PACIFIC OCEAN

Benjamin Blake - Edison Marshall   4102
Bring Larks and Heroes - Thomas Keneally   3410
Diamond Head - Houston Branch   647
The Island of the Day Before - Umberto Eco   1849
Mister Christian - William Kinsolving   3502

PALESTINE

As a Driven Leaf - Milton Steinberg   5992
The Battle-Ax of God - Le Roy MacLeod   4007
Behold the Fire - Michael Blankfort   541
Beloved Enemy: The Passions of Eleanor of Aquitaine - Ellen Jones   3288
Blessed Are the Meek: A Novel about St. Francis of Assisi - Zofja Kossak-Szczucka   3542
The Blue Falcon - Robyn Carr   935
A Booke of Days: A Journal of the Crusade by Roger, Duke of Lunel - Stephen J. Rivele   5351
Born of War - Thomas Taylor   6192
Champion - L. Christian Balling   285
The Cornerstone - Zoe Oldenbourg   4714
Cross, Sword, and Arrow - Gladys H. Barr   340
The Devil's Spy - Michael Hastings   2773
Eleanor the Queen - Norah Lofts   3842
The Establishment - Howard Fast   2030
The Fool of Venus - George William Cronyn   1428
Gay Crusader - Cleone Knox   3528
The Heart of the Lion - Jean Plaidy   5020
The Infidels - Chloe Gartner   2308
The Iron Curtain - Robert Vaughan   6447
King's Man - C.M. Edmondston   1880
The Kings of Vain Intent - Graham Shelby   5791
Knight with Armour - Alfred Duggan   1767
The Knights of Dark Renown - Graham Shelby   5792
Lionheart!: A Novel of Richard I, King of England - Martha Rofheart   5428
A Love Divine - Alexandra Ripley   5340
The Lute Player - Norah Lofts   3852
The Man Who Thought He Was Messiah - Curt Leviant   3735
Men Like Shadows - Dorothy Charques   1000
Moses - Sholem Asch   199
My Lord Brother the Lionheart - Molly Costain Haycraft   2795
No Man's Son - Doris Sutcliffe Adams   23
Pilgermann - Russell Hoban   2960
Prophets and Warriors - Peter Danielson   1473
Richard and the Knights of God - Pamela Bennetts   454
Ride Home Tomorrow - Evan John   3221
The Saracen Blade - Frank Yerby   6926
Shield of Three Lions - Pamela Kaufman   3372

Sir Pagan - Henry John Colyton 1222
A Stolen Tongue - Sheri Holman 3002
The Talisman - Sir Walter Scott 5708
The Trumpet and the Sword - Peter Danielson 1479
Trumpets of Silver - Norma Harris 2735

Bethel
Judith - Stella Wilchek 6748

Canaan
Children of the Lion - Peter Danielson 1464
No Other Gods - Wilder Penfield 4901
The Shepherd Kings - Peter Danielson 1475

Jericho
Scarlet Cord: A Novel of the Woman of Jericho - Frank G. Slaughter 5899

Jerusalem
Alamut - Judith Tarr 6164
Antichrist: A Novel of the Emperor Frederick II - Cecelia Holland 2982
The Heirs of the Kingdom - Zoe Oldenbourg 4716
Jerusalem - Cecelia Holland 2990
Jerusalem Interlude - Bodie Thoene 6223
The Leper King - Zofja Kossak-Szczucka 3544
The Lost Flight - H.F.M. Prescott 5169
Queen of Swords - Judith Tarr 6169
Silver Leopard - F. van Wyck Mason 4160
Tomorrow's Fire - Jay Williams 6775
Under the Winter Moon - Teresa Brooke 705

Latin Kingdom of Jerusalem
The True Cross - Carlo Scarfoglio 5629

Samaria
A Woman of Samaria - James W. Ingles 3104

Sodom
Lot's Wife - Marie Ley-Piscator 3767

PANAMA

Balboa: Conquistador - Omar V. Garrison 2303
Beat to Quarters - C.S. Forester 2170
Bride of the Conqueror - Hartzell Spence 5961
Burning Gold - Robert Hardy Andrews 148
Creole Dusk - Walter Adolphe Roberts 5392
Cup of Gold - John Steinbeck 5991
Cutlass Empire - F. van Wyck Mason 4148
Don Pedro and the Devil - Edgar Maas 3948
Dream West - David Nevin 4587
Fenwick Travers and the Panama Canal - Raymond M. Saunders 5613
Forty Pounds of Gold - Philip D. Stong 6066
The Golden Eagle - John Edward Jennings 3201
Jessie: A Novel Based on the Life of Jessie Benton Fremont - Judy Alter 120
Windward Passage - Hamilton Cochran 1143

Panama City
The Devil's Own - Christopher Nicole 4615

PAPUA NEW GUINEA

Dubu: A Novel of New Guinean Conquest - Maslyn Williams 6789
The Imperialists - William Stuart Long 3875

PARAGUAY

I, the Supreme - Augusto Antonio Roa Bastos 5353
Young Vargas Lewis - Robert Brainard Pearsall 4874

PERSIA

Alexander of Macedon: The Journey to World's End - Harold Lamb 3607
Alexander the God - Maurice Druon 1731
Alexander the God - Robert Payne 4849

The Carmelite - Elgin Groseclose 2599
The Conqueror: A Novel of Alexander the Great - Edison Marshall 4104
The Dragon of the Ishtar Gate - L. Sprague De Camp 1555
Esther - Nathaniel Norsen Weinreb 6601
Esther: The Star and the Sceptre - Gina Andrews 146
The Flowers of Adonis - Rosemary Sutcliff 6122
Glory and the Lightning - Taylor Caldwell 856
The Golden Lyre - Noel B. Gerson 2371
The Journeyer - Gary Jennings 3194
Julian - Gore Vidal 6489
Orlok - Don Dandrea 1461
The Persian Boy - Mary Renault 5301
Persian Conqueror - George Sidney Hellman 2822
The Physician - Noah Gordon 2482
Ruler of the Sky: A Novel of Genghis Khan - Pamela Sargent 5606
The Shining - Stephen Marlowe 4097
So Great a Queen: The Story of Esther, Queen of Persia - Paul Frischauer 2235
Star of Macedon - Karl V. Eiker 1901

Bagdhad
Eaters of the Dead - Michael Crichton 1425
The Tyrant of Bagdhad - Glenn Pierce 4996

Tehran
Cry of the Peacock - Gina Barkhordar Nahai 4552
On the Company's Service - Ellis K. Meacham 4315
Phantom - Susan Kay 3375

PERU

Bride of the Conqueror - Hartzell Spence 5961
The Bridge of San Luis Rey - Thornton Wilder 6752
Daimon - Abel Posse 5140
Don Pedro and the Devil - Edgar Maas 3948
The Golden Eagle - John Edward Jennings 3201
I, the King - Howard Clewes 1112
The Last Princess - Charles O. Locke 3826
Mansions of Darkness - Chelsea Quinn Yarbro 6902
O'Higgins and Don Bernardo - Edna Deu Pree Nelson 4578
The Sword and the Sun: The Story of the Spanish Civil Wars in Peru - Gerald Green 2566
Taste of Glory - Carleton Beals 394
The Wine-Dark Sea - Patrick O'Brian 4679

Cuzco
The Incas - Daniel Peters 4945

Lima
Manuela, La Caballeresa Del Sol - Demetrio Aguilera Malta 41
Storm to the South - Thelma Strabel 6073

Machu Picchu
The Incas - Daniel Peters 4945

PHILIPPINES

Fenwick Travers and the Forbidden Kingdom - Raymond M. Saunders 5612
Imperial Kelly - Peter Bowen 600
Pacific Destiny - Dana Fuller Ross 5487
Season for War - P.F. Kluge 3510
The Year of the Spaniard - Henry Castor 956

Manila
Homecoming - Dana Fuller Ross 5474
Officers and Ladies - Richard O'Connor 4686

POLAND

The Deluge - Henryk Sienkiewicz 5846
Fire in the Steppe - Henryk Sienkiewicz 5847
Glorious Morning - Julie Ellis 1919

God Save the Tsar - Susanna Hoe 2976
A Great Lord - Paul Frischauer 2233
Poland - James A. Michener 4373
Polonaise - Piers Paul Read 5278
Salvation - Sholem Asch 202
The Slave - Isaac Bashevis Singer 5866
The Swedish Cavalier - Leo Perutz 4943
Taras Bulba - Nikolai V. Gogol 2451
The Teutonic Knights - Henryk Sienkiewicz 5849
The Tin Drum - Gunther Grass 2540
Valentina - Evelyn Anthony 165
With Fire and Sword - Henryk Sienkiewicz 5850

Cracow
Schindler's List - Thomas Keneally 3416

Danzig
Warsaw Requiem - Bodie Thoene 6229

Warsaw
Ashes - Stefan Zeromski 6960
The Career of Magda V. - Joseph Machlis 3982
The Nazarene - Sholem Asch 200
Polonaise - Jane Aiken Hodge 2968
Thaddeus of Warsaw - Jane Porter 5136
Warsaw Requiem - Bodie Thoene 6229
Wartime Lies - Louis Begley 416
White Eagle, Dark Skies - Jean Karsavina 3368

PORTUGAL

Drums of War - Roy Clews 1114
Eliza's Daughter - Joan Aiken 44
Hate - Arthur Douglas Smith 5918
Lieutenant Lamb - Kenneth Maynard 4210
The Mapmaker: A Novel of the Days of Prince Henry, the Navigator - Frank G. Slaughter 5893
Marry in Haste - Jane Aiken Hodge 2967
The Pleasures of Love - Jean Plaidy 5042
The Portingale - Alison Macleod 4005
Rifleman Dodd - C.S. Forester 2181
Sea of Darkness - Roland Huntford 3086
Sharpe's Battle - Bernard Cornwell 1338
The Stranger From the Sea - Winston Graham 2530
Time of the Unicorn - Barbara Jefferis 3176

Almeida
Sharpe's Gold - Bernard Cornwell 1343

Lisbon
Armada - Charles Gidley 2404
Lisbon - Valerie Sherwood 5825

Oporto
Whispering - Jane Aiken Hodge 2972
The Wine Princes - Margaret Mackay 3987

PRUSSIA

The Deluge - Henryk Sienkiewicz 5846

PUERTO RICO

The Year of the Spaniard - Henry Castor 956

REUNION

The Mauritius Command - Patrick O'Brian 4670

RHODESIA

On Trial for My Country - Stanlake Samkange 5578

ROMAN EMPIRE

And Walk on Love: A Novel Based on the Life of the Apostle Paul - Henrietta Buckmaster 759
The Apostle - Sholem Asch 197

Arena: A Novel of Spartacus and Crassus - Maurice Ghnassia 2391
As Sure as the Dawn - Francine Rivers 5352
Behold, We Live - Charles Dunscomb 1812
Caesar - Mirko Jelusich 3188
Claudius the God - Robert Graves 2543
The Coin of Carthage - Bryher 740
Constantine: The Miracle of the Flaming Cross - Frank G. Slaughter 5883
The Death of Virgil - Hermann Broch 699
The Gladiators - Arthur Koestler 3532
Great Lion of God - Taylor Caldwell 858
Hannibal - Ross Leckie 3704
Hannibal of Carthage - Mary Dolan 1686
I, Claudius - Robert Graves 2547
The Key - Benita Kane Jaro 3169
The Kingdom of the Wicked - Anthony Burgess 778
Roman Shadows - Ron Burns 804
Throne of the World - Louis De Wohl 1575

Bay of Naples
Arms of Nemesis - Steven Saylor 5623
Shadows in Bronze - Lindsey Davis 1531

Byzantium
Imperial Renegade - Louis De Wohl 1567

Capri
The Word and the Sword - Theo Lang 3662

Capua
Spartacus - Howard Fast 2044

Constantinople
Sign of the Pagan - Don Tracy 6312

Etruria
Catalina's Riddle - Steven Saylor 5624

Milan
The Converts: A Historical Novel - Rex Warner 6564
The Restless Flame - Louis De Wohl 1573

Pompeii
The Last Days of Pompeii - Edward Bulwer-Lytton 768

Ravenna
Bury Me in Ravenna - Agnes Carr Vaughan 6432

Rome
Agrippa's Daughter - Howard Fast 2025
The Alexandrian - Martha Rofheart 5425
Augustus - Allan Massie 4167
Augustus - John Williams 6785
Barabbas - Par Lagerkvist 3585
Ben Hur: A Tale of the Christ - Lew Wallace 6536
Between Eternities - Robert H. Pilpel 5001
Beware of Caesar - Vincent Sheean 5786
Blood of the Martyrs - Naomi Mitchison 4417
Bloody Poet - Deszo Kosztolanyi 3546
The Bride of Pilate - Esther Kellner 3393
Brothers of Vengeance - LeGette Blythe 556
Caesar - Allan Massie 4168
Caesar's Women - Colleen McCullough 4233
Captive of Rome - Theodora McCormick Du Bois 1740
The Captive Princess - Maxine Shore 5831
Catalina's Riddle - Steven Saylor 5624
The Catiline Conspiracy - John Maddox Roberts 5379
Chantefable - Eldorous L. Dayton 1546
Children of the Wolf - Alfred Duggan 1762
The City of Libertines - W.G. Hardy 2702
Clodia - Robert DeMaria 1606
Confessors of the Name - Gladys Schmitt 5640
The Conquered - Naomi Mitchison 4418
The Conspiracy - John Hersey 2870
The Converts: A Historical Novel - Rex Warner 6564
Dear and Glorious Physician - Taylor Caldwell 853

The Death of the Gods - Dmitri Merezhkovski 4338
Death on the Appian Way - Kenneth Benton 463
Dominic - Kathleen Robinson 5405
The Eagle and the Crown - Hubertus Loewenstein 3832
The Eagle and the Raven - Pauline Gedge 2344
The Eighth Veil - Ellis Kadison 3320
Epicurus My Master - Max Radin 5233
The Equinox: A Novel of Rome in the Time of Commodus - Carol Saylor 5622
Family Favorites - Alfred Duggan 1766
Farewell, Catullus - Pierson Dixon 1651
The Fates Are Laughing - William Crozier 1439
A Fig in Winter - Willa Gibbs 2400
The First Man in Rome - Colleen McCullough 4234
First the Blade - Drayton Mayrant 4212
Fisher of Men: A Novel of Simon Peter - Kurt Frieberger 2231
A Flame in Byzantium - Chelsea Quinn Yarbro 6899
The Flames of Rome - Paul L. Maier 4033
Fortune's Favorite - Colleen McCullough 4235
The Four Rivers of Paradise - Helen Constance White 6678
Fourth King - Norbert Coulehan 1373
Freedom, Farewell - Phyllis Bentley 461
The Gift of Rome - John Wagner 6520
The Gladiator - Thames Ross Williamson 6790
The Glorious Folly: A Novel of the Time of St. Paul - Louis De Wohl 1565
A Goddess to a God - John Lloyd Balderston 278
The Gods Are Not Mocked - Anna Taylor 6177
God's Warrior - Frank G. Slaughter 5889
Gold for the Caesars - Florence A. Seward 5759
Golden Peacock - Gertrude Atherton 224
The Grass Crown - Colleen McCullough 4236
Hadrian's Memoirs - Marguerite Yourcenar 6947
Hear Me, Pilate! - LeGette Blythe 557
Heaven's Only Daughter - Kathleen Robinson 5406
Hortensius, Friend of Nero - Edith Pargeter 4798
Hypatia - Charles Kingsley 3498
I Am a Barbarian - Edgar Rice Burroughs 807
I Loved Tiberius - Elisabeth Dored 1692
I, Paul - Rex Miller 4401
The Ides of March - Thornton Wilder 6753
The Illusionist - Anita Mason 4144
Imperial Caesar - Rex Warner 6565
The Imperial Governor - George Shipway 5828
The Iron Hand of Mars - Lindsey Davis 1528
The Jew of Rome - Lion Feuchtwanger 2071
Josephus - Lion Feuchtwanger 2072
Josephus and the Emperor - Lion Feuchtwanger 2073
Julian - Gore Vidal 6489
Last Act in Palmyra - Lindsey Davis 1529
The Last Romans - Teodor Jeske-Choinski 3216
The Light Bearer - Donna Gillespie 2419
The Lives of Rachel - Joel Gross 2601
The Living Wood - Louis De Wohl 1571
The Lost Eagles - Ralph Graves 2542
The Lost Legion - H. Warner Munn 4516
A Love Divine - Alexandra Ripley 5340
Man on Fire: A Novel on the Life of St. Paul - LeGette Blythe 558
Marcus - Laurene Chinn 1068
Marius the Epicurean - Walter Pater 4826
A Murder on the Appian Way - Steven Saylor 5625
Nero - Mary Teresa Ronalds 5437
No King but Caesar - Anne Powers 5151
Octavia: A Tale of Ancient Rome - Seymour Van Santvoord 6428
A Pillar of Iron - Taylor Caldwell 861
The Pirate From Home - John V.D. Southworth 5952
Pontius Pilate: A Biographical Novel - Paul L. Maier 4034
Pontius Pilate Reflects - Werner Koch 3529
Poseidon's Gold - Lindsey Davis 1530
Prepare Them for Caesar - Mary Louise Mabie 3954

Prince of Israel - Elias Gilner 2422
Queen of the East - Alexander Baron 336
Quo Vadis - Henryk Sienkiewicz 5848
The Restless Flame - Louis De Wohl 1573
The Robe - Lloyd C. Douglas 1703
The Roman - Mika Waltari 6554
Roman Blood - Steven Saylor 5626
Roman Nights - Ron Burns 803
The Sacrilege - John Maddox Roberts 5380
Saint Paul: A Historical Novel of His Life - Leon Poirier 5081
Scorpus the Moor - Leslie Turner White 6690
The Second Crucifixion - Maurice Samuel 5579
Shadows in Bronze - Lindsey Davis 1531
The Side of the Moon - Amanda Prantera 5162
The Silver Chalice - Thomas B. Costain 1370
The Silver Pigs - Lindsey Davis 1532
The Sinner of Saint Ambrose - Robert Raynolds 5275
The Sins of Herod: A Novel of Rome and the Early Church - Frank G. Slaughter 5900
Son of Judah - Dan Levin 3738
Son of Tears - Henry W. Coray 1320
Soul Flame - Barbara Wood 6850
Spartacus - Howard Fast 2044
SPQR - John Maddox Roberts 5381
Street of the Sandalmakers: A Tale of Rome in the Time of Marcus Aurelius - Nis Peterson 4977
The Sword and the Promise - Benjamin Siegel 5845
Sword of Pleasure: Being the Memoirs of the Most Illustrious Lucius Cornelius Sulla - Peter Green 2571
Swords in the North - Paul Lewis Anderson 138
The Testament of Theophilus - Leonard Wibberley 6730
That Egyptian Woman - Noel B. Gerson 2384
Three's Company - Alfred Duggan 1774
Tiberius: The Memoirs of the Emperor - Allan Massie 4169
Time to Depart - Lindsey Davis 1533
The Triumph - Ernest K. Gann 2280
Tros of Samothrace - Talbot Mundy 4515
Turn Back the River - W.G. Hardy 2703
Upon This Rock: A Novel of Simon Peter, Prince of Apostles - Frank G. Slaughter 5906
Upon This Rock: The Life of St. Peter - Walter F. Murphy 4526
Venus in Copper - Lindsey Davis 1534
The Venus Throw - Steven Saylor 5627
Winter Quarters - Alfred Duggan 1775
The Wolf of Masada - John Fredman 2220
The Word and the Sword - Theo Lang 3662
The Young Caesar - Rex Warner 6567

ROMANIA

The Saint of Montparnasse: A Novel Based on the Life of Constantin Brancusi - Peter Neagoe 4560

Bucharest
Flight From Bucharest - R.T. Stevens 6000
The Fortune Hunter - Ira J. Morris 4477

Tomi
God Was Born in Exile - Vintila Horia 3033
An Imaginary Life - David Malouf 4047
The Last World: A Novel with an Ovidian Repertory - Christoph Ransmayr 5253

RUSSIA

And the Stars Shall Fall - True Bowen 603
The Angel: A Novel Based on the Life of Alexander I of Russia - William James Blech 543
The Artist - Norman Garbo 2281
Asya - Michael Ignatieff 3103
Between Two Worlds - Monique Raphel High 2913
Blaize - Anne Melville 4331

Blood on the Snow - John Elliott 1916
The Brotherhood of the Red Poppy - Henri Troyat 6353
The Candlesticks and the Cross - Ruth Freeman Solomon 5940
The Captain's Daughter - Alexander Pushkin 5210
The Challenging Heights - Max Hennessy 2831
Clair De Lune: A Novel about Claude Debussy - Pierre La Mure 3575
A Clear Road to Archangel - Geoffrey Rose 5461
The Dangerous Years - Max Hennessy 2833
Devil Child - Jo Germany 2359
The Devil Inside: A Novel of Dostoevsky's Life - Stephen Coulter 1385
The Dream Seekers - Stephen Longstreet 3884
Eaters of the Dead - Michael Crichton 1425
Elena - Judith Egan 1893
The Emperor Story: A Historical Romance - George Sava 5615
The Extraordinary Adventures of Secret Agent Shipov in Pursuit of Count Leo Tolstoy in the Year 1862 - Bulat Okudzhava 4712
Far Flies the Eagle - Evelyn Anthony 162
The Gathering Wolves - Elizabeth Darrell 1496
Gentleman Traitor - Alan Williams 6763
God Save the Tsar - Susanna Hoe 2976
Grishin - Hans Herlin 2859
Heritage - Lewis Orde 4749
Horses of War - Duff Hart-Davis 2760
It's Me Again - Donald Jack 3126
Jesters - David Markish 4090
Joseph - Mervyn Jones 3292
Karl and Rosa - Alfred Doblin 1653
Katrina - Jeramie Price 5190
The King's Commissar - Duncan Kyle 3570
Leah's Journey - Gloria Goldreich 2460
Love and Honor - Leslie Arlen 189
Marianne and the Lords of the East - Juliette Benzoni 468
Me Too - Donald Jack 3128
The Midwife - Gay Courter 1388
The Muscovite - Alison Macleod 4004
The Name of Hero - Richard Seltzer 5742
Napoleon and the Cossacks - Peter N. Krassnoff 3551
Orlok - Don Dandrea 1461
Pathetic Symphony: A Novel about Tchaikovsky - Klaus Mann 4064
Peter the Great - Alexey Tolstoy 6293
Prince of Outlaws - Alexey Tolstoy 6294
The Rake and the Rebel - Ira J. Morris 4478
Rebel Princess - Evelyn Anthony 164
Remember This Time - Gloria Kurian Broder 703
The Revolutionary - Lawrence Schoonover 5667
Ride with Me - Thomas B. Costain 1369
Rivington Street - Meredith Tax 6175
Russka: The Novel of Russia - Edward Rutherfurd 5535
Seven Men of Gascony - R.F. Delderfield 1589
Sir Rogue - Leslie Turner White 6691
Soldier of the Queen - Max Hennessy 2837
The Summer Day Is Done - R.T. Stevens 6001
Sweet Ransom - Linda Madl 4026
Taras Bulba - Nikolai V. Gogol 2451
The Thousand Fires - Anne Powers 5155
Time After Time - Allen Appel 171
To the Land of the Cattails - Aharon Appelfeld 179
Tsar's Woman - Pamela Hill 2946
Until the Sun Falls - Cecelia Holland 2998
Up She Rises - David Garnett 2298
Valentina - Evelyn Anthony 165
The White Hotel - D.M. Thomas 6237
Young Catherine - E.M. Almedingen 118
Zoya - Danielle Steel 5985

Astapovo
The Last Station - Jay Parini 4801

Balaclava
Brave Captains - Vivian Stuart 6086

Caucasus
Heir to Kuragin - Constance Heaven 2807

Crimea
Badge of Glory - Douglas E. Reeman 5287
The Eden Passion - Marilyn Harris 2730
Flashman at the Charge - George MacDonald Fraser 2209
Fleur - Cynthia Harrod-Eagles 2754
Forget the Glory - Emma Drummond 1725
Gentlemen—The Regiment! - Hugh Talbot 6154
Leaves From the Valley - Joanna Trollope 6348
Officer and Gentleman - Josephine Delves-Broughton 1604
The Passionate Pilgrim - Charles Terrot 6204
Pendragon: Late of Prince Albert's Own - Robert Trevelyan 6337
The Private Life of Florence Nightingale - Richard Gordon 2485
Ravenshoe - Henry Kingsley 3500
Secret for a Nightingale - Victoria Holt 3020
Sisters & Lovers - Nicola Thorne 6274
Trumpeter, Sound! - D.L. Murray 4528
Until the Colors Fade - Tim Jeal 3173
Valide: A Novel of the Harem - Barbara Chase-Riboud 1007

Eastern Front
Doctor Zhivago - Boris Pasternak 4824

Katyk
Heirs of the Motherland - Judith Pella 4893

Kiev
The Fixer - Bernard Malamud 4038
The Four Winds of Heaven - Monique Raphel High 2916
The Spanish Doctor - Matt Cohen 1159

Moscow
Anna - Cynthia Harrod-Eagles 2752
Darker Jewels - Chelsea Quinn Yarbro 6898
Devoted Friends - Joe Poyer 5161
Doctor Zhivago - Boris Pasternak 4824
Elizabeth and Alexandra - Antony Lambton 3616
The Fortune Hunter - Ira J. Morris 4477
Great Black Russian - John Oliver Killens 3484
Imperial Winds - Priscilla Napier 4555
Katya - Lucy Cores 1328
Lenin: The Novel - Alan Brien 679
Malkeh and Her Children - Marjorie Edelson 1853
Marianne and the Crown of Fire - Juliette Benzoni 467
The Ringed Castle - Dorothy Dunnett 1807
The Summer of the Bashinskeys - Diane Pearson 4877
War and Peace - Leo Tolstoy 6295
White Nights, Red Dawn - Frederick Nolan 4634
The Year of December - Lucy Cores 1329

Odessa
Hazard of Huntress - Vivian Stuart 6087
Trumpets of Silver - Norma Harris 2735

Petrograd
Blood and Sable - Carol J. Kane 3350
The Devil in Harbour - Catherine Gavin 2319
Devoted Friends - Joe Poyer 5161
The Petrograd Consignment - Owen Sela 5739

St. Petersburg
Anna - Cynthia Harrod-Eagles 2752
The Astrov Legacy - Constance Heaven 2802
City of Golden Cages - Jo Germany 2358
Contessa - Helene Mansfield 4076
Count Vronsky's Daughter - Carola Salisbury 5567
The Crown and the Crucible - Michael Phillips 4987
The Dawning of Deliverance - Judith Pella 4892
The Eleventh Year - Monique Raphel High 2914

Elizabeth and Alexandra - Antony Lambton 3616
Emily - Cynthia Harrod-Eagles 2753
Encore - Monique Raphel High 2915
Fleur - Cynthia Harrod-Eagles 2754
The Fortress - Catherine Gavin 2320
The Four Winds of Heaven - Monique Raphel High 2916
The Fourth King - Glen Petrie 4979
The Gentleman From America - Paul Benton 464
A Grand Passion - Mary Mackey 3991
Great Black Russian - John Oliver Killens 3484
Heir to Kuragin - Constance Heaven 2807
Heirs of the Motherland - Judith Pella 4893
A House Divided - Michael Phillips 4988
The House of Kuragin - Constance Heaven 2808
The Incorruptible - Helma De Bois 1551
Katya - Lucy Cores 1328
The Ladies of St. Hedwig's - E.M. Almedingen 117
Lady in the Briars - Carola Dunn 1793
Lenin: The Novel - Alan Brien 679
Malkeh and Her Children - Marjorie Edelson 1853
Petersburg - Emily Hanlon 2677
The Petersburg-Cannes Express - Hans Koning 3538
Polonaise - Jane Aiken Hodge 2968
The Power and the Passion - Christina Nicholson 4609
Praise at Morning - Mildred Masterson McNeilly 4310
Rasputin's Revenge - John T. Lescroart 3725
The Scandalous Mrs. Blackford - Harriet Kane 3358
Seance for a Vampire - Fred Saberhagen 5557
Seven Days to Petrograd - Tom Hyman 3094
The Shadowed Spring - Carola Salisbury 5571
The Snow Mountain - Catherine Gavin 2324
A Space of the Heart - Patricia Wright 6884
The Summer of the Bashinskeys - Diane Pearson 4877
A Token of Jewels - Diane Cory 1353
Tournament of the Shadows - Nicholas Carnac 901
Travail and Triumph - Michael Phillips 4991
Triptych - Dora Landey 3652
Valide: A Novel of the Harem - Barbara Chase-Riboud 1007
War and Peace - Leo Tolstoy 6295
White Nights, Red Dawn - Frederick Nolan 4634

Sebastopol
The Valiant Sailors - Vivian Stuart 6090
Victory at Sebastopol - Vivian Stuart 6091

Siberia
The Buckingham Palace Connection - Ted Willis 6792
The Cowboy and the Cossack - Claire Huffaker 3071
Doctor Zhivago - Boris Pasternak 4824
Fifteen Flags - Richard Lynden Hardman 2686
Fire in the Ice - Alan Scholefield 5653
The Golden Sabre - Jon Cleary 1105
Searching for the Emperor - Roberto Pazzi 4858
The Snow Mountain - Catherine Gavin 2324
Travail and Triumph - Michael Phillips 4991

Tiflis
The Golden Sabre - Jon Cleary 1105

Tilsit
Baltic Mission - Richard Woodman 6859

Yalta
A Family Matter - James Roosevelt 5458

ST. HELENA

Blackstone and the Scourge of Europe - Richard Falkirk 2007
The Last Love - Thomas B. Costain 1367
Sharpe's Devil - Bernard Cornwell 1340

ST. KITTS AND NEVIS

Caribee - Christopher Nicole 4614

ST. LUCIA

The African - Harold Courlander 1386

SCOTLAND

Albany - Laura Black 519
Alexander the Glorious - Jane Oliver 4719
All the Queen's Men - Evelyn Anthony 157
The Antiquary - Sir Walter Scott 5690
Bide Me Fair - Harvey Howells 3060
The Black Dwarf - Sir Walter Scott 5692
The Blue Heaven Bends Over All - Jane Oliver 4720
The Border Lord - Jan Westcott 6641
Born to Be King - Constance Gluyas 2440
Brave Kingdom - Frances Murray 4534
Braveheart - Randall Wallace 6538
The Bride - Julie Garwood 2311
The Bride - Margaret Irwin 3116
The Bride of Lammermoor - Sir Walter Scott 5693
Bride of the MacHugh - Jan Cox Speas 5956
Bright Captivity - Eugenia Price 5180
Candleshine No More - Jane Oliver 4721
Captain Lightfoot - William R. Burnett 792
The Captive Queen of Scots - Jean Plaidy 5008
The Case of Kitty Ogilvie - Jean Stubbs 6093
Catriona - Robert Louis Stevenson 6009
Chain of Destiny - Nigel Tranter 6314
The Chains of Fate - Pamela Belle 430
Charlie Is My Darling - Mollie Hardwick 2691
Child of the Mist - Kathleen Morgan 4451
Clandara - Evelyn Anthony 161
Colliers Row - Jan Webster 6592
Commander of the Mists - D.L. Murray 4527
Creature Comforts - Jessica Stirling 6041
Crest of the Broken Wave - James Barke 302
Crippled Splendour - Evan John 3219
Dancing at the Rascal Fair - Ivan Doig 1682
Daneclere - Pamela Hill 2931
The Dark Rose - Maurice Walsh 6549
The Dark Stranger - Constance Dodge 1664
The Disorderly Knights - Dorothy Dunnett 1800
Dragonfly in Amber - Diana Gabaldon 2262
Drums of Destiny - Peter Bourne 593
Falcon: The Autobiography of His Grace James IV, King of Scots - A.J. Stewart 6021
Falls of Gard - Laura Black 520
The Far Side of the Hill - Nancy Livingston 3811
Fire Opal - Pamela Hill 2932
The Flight of the Heron - Dorothy Kathleen Broster 710
Foes - Mary Johnston 3233
The Follies of the King - Jean Plaidy 5014
Fool of God: A Novel Based on the Life of Alexander Campbell - Louis Cochran 1144
The Foster Brothers - Edward Frankland 2202
The Free Fishers - John Buchan 750
The Game of Kings - Dorothy Dunnett 1801
The Gay Galliard - Margaret Irwin 3119
Graham of Claverhouse - Constance Dodge 1665
Grandmother and the Priests - Taylor Caldwell 857
The Green Salamander - Pamela Hill 2933
Had We Never Loved - Patricia Veryan 6463
Hammer of the Scots - Jean Plaidy 5018
Hearts of Gold - Jessica Stirling 6044
The Heiress Bride - Catherine Coulter 1375
The Hepburn - Jan Westcott 6645
Hereward the Wake - Charles Kingsley 3497
Highland Belle - Patricia Grasso 2541
In Still and Stormy Waters - Reay Tannahill 6157
Isle of Glory - Jane Oliver 4723
James and Joan - Anne Fremantle 2221
James, by the Grace of God - Nigel Tranter 6315
Kidnapped - Robert Louis Stevenson 6010

King Hereafter - Dorothy Dunnett 1802
King in Hell: A Novel of Bothwell and Mary, Queen of Scots - Beverly Balin 282
Kingdom of Shadows - Barbara Erskine 1954
King's Royal - John Quigley 5224
The King's Vixen - Pamela Hill 2937
Lady of Monkton - Elizabeth Byrd 835
Lady of Moray - Bonnie Copeland 1318
Lady of the Glen - Jennifer Roberson 5369
The Legacy of Ladysmith - John Kenny Crane 1413
Legacy of the Wolf - Jean Raynes 5274
The Lion and the Rose - Jane Oliver 4724
The Lion Is Come - Jane Oliver 4725
The Maclarens - C.L. Skelton 5873
Madeleine - Pamela Elizabeth West 6633
The Malvie Inheritance - Pamela Hill 2938
Marjorie of Scotland - Pamela Hill 2939
Mary of Scotland - F.W. Kenyon 3454
Mary, Queen of Scotland and the Isles - Margaret George 2356
The Master of Ballantrae: A Winter's Tale - Robert Louis Stevenson 6011
The Master of Gray Trilogy - Nigel Tranter 6316
Merchant of the Ruby - Alice Harwood 2766
Mine Is the Kingdom - Jane Oliver 4726
Miss Fiona's Fancy - Marion Chesney 1040
Miss Nobody - Caroline Ross 5465
Mistress of The Highlands - Chloe Gartner 2309
Monsieur Janvier - Elizabeth Linington 3799
My Lady Glamis - Pamela Hill 2940
My Lord John - Georgette Heyer 2895
The New Confessions - William Boyd 617
No Smoke Without Fire - Alice Harwood 2767
The Noblest Frailty - Patricia Veryan 6474
Outlander - Diana Gabaldon 2264
Parcel of Rogues - Jane Lane 3656
The Pointless Knife - Constance Dodge 1667
A Prince, a Piper, and a Rose - John Scalzo 5628
The Proud Servant: The Story of Montrose - Margaret Irwin 3120
The Queen From Provence - Jean Plaidy 5047
Queen's Caprice - Marjorie Bowen 599
The Queen's Grace - Jan Westcott 6646
Queen's Play - Dorothy Dunnett 1805
Queen's Royal - John Quigley 5225
Ravenburn - Laura Black 522
The Regiment - C.L. Skelton 5874
Reluctant Cavalier - Donald Barr Chidsey 1064
The Revolutionary - Lawrence Schoonover 5667
The Ringed Castle - Dorothy Dunnett 1807
The Riven Realm - Nigel Tranter 6317
Robert the Bruce: The Path of the Hero King - Nigel Tranter 6318
Robert the Bruce: The Price of the King's Peace - Nigel Tranter 6319
Robert the Bruce: The Steps to the Empty Throne - Nigel Tranter 6320
Royal Road to Fotheringay - Jean Plaidy 5059
Salute to Adventurers - John Buchan 752
The Scottish Chiefs - Jane Porter 5135
Seats of the Mighty: A Novel of James Stuart, Brother of Mary, Queen of Scots - Alice Harwood 2768
Sing Morning Star - Jane Oliver 4727
Song in the Green Thorn Tree - James Barke 303
The Spitfire - Bertrice Small 5912
A Stake in the Kingdom - Nigel Tranter 6321
Stranger's Forest - Pamela Hill 2943
The Stuart Legacy - Robert Kerr 3472
The Succession: A Novel of Elizabeth and James - George Garrett 2302
Sunset at Noon - Jane Oliver 4728
The Sword and the Flame - Pamela Hill 2945
The Thistle and the Rose - Jean Plaidy 5069
Till the Day Goes Down - Judith Lennox-Smith 3719
A Time for the Death of a King - Ann Dukthas 1777
To the Honor of the Fleet - Robert H. Pilpel 5002
Torbeg - Grace Campbell 873
Treasures on Earth - Jessica Stirling 6049

True Thomas - Nigel Tranter 6322
Unicorn Rampant - Nigel Tranter 6323
Up She Rises - David Garnett 2298
Voyager - Diana Gabaldon 2265
Well of the Silent Harp - James Barke 304
The Whyte Harte - P.C. Doherty 1681
The Widow of Windsor - Jean Plaidy 5076
The Wind That Shakes the Barley - James Barke 305
The Winter Servant - M.H. Davis 1537
The Woman from The Glen - Chloe Gartner 2310

Aberdeen
The Absorbing Fire: The Byron Legend - F.W. Kenyon 3445

Blacklaw
Call Home the Heart - Jessica Stirling 6040
The Dark Pasture - Jessica Stirling 6042

Carlisle
Rogue Herries - Hugh Walpole 6547

Cumbria
Queen of the Lightning - Kathleen Herbert 2852

Douglas
Castle Dangerous - Sir Walter Scott 5694

Dumfries
Guy Mannering - Sir Walter Scott 5697
Red Gauntlet - Sir Walter Scott 5706

Dumfrieshire
The Bonnet Laird's Daughter - Barbara Annandale 154

Edinburgh
Blood Line - Alanna Knight 3515
Castle Barebane - Joan Aiken 43
The Crown in Darkness - P.C. Doherty 1671
The Dark Pasture - Jessica Stirling 6042
Deadly Beloved - Alanna Knight 3517
Dear Mrs. Boswell - Marie Muir 4508
Death Wore a Diadem - Iona McGregor 4277
Enter Second Murderer - Alanna Knight 3518
Glendraco - Laura Black 521
Greenyards - Joan Lingard 3796
The Heart of Midlothian - Sir Walter Scott 5698
The Heatherton Heritage - Pamela Hill 2934
Immortal Queen - Elizabeth Byrd 834
Maid of Honour: A Novel Set in the Court of Mary, Queen of Scots - Elizabeth Byrd 836
Meggy MacIntosh - Elizabeth Janet Gray 2555
Red Gauntlet - Sir Walter Scott 5706
Regeneration - Pat Barker 309
The Sins of the Wolf - Anne Perry 4937
The Strange Case of Deacon Brodie - Forbes Bramble 646
Swear by Apollo - Shirley Barker 318
To Lie with Lions - Dorothy Dunnett 1810
The Unicorn Hunt - Dorothy Dunnett 1811
Waverley - Sir Walter Scott 5709
The White Queen - Frederic Fallon 2011
The Witches - Jay Williams 6776
Wonder of All the Gay World - James Barke 306
The World, the Flesh, and the Devil - Reay Tannahill 6159

Glasgow
The Asking Price - Jessica Stirling 6039
Aunt Bel - Guy McCrone 4231
Glendraco - Laura Black 521
The Good Provider - Jessica Stirling 6043
In a Dark Garden - Frank G. Slaughter 5891
Lantern for the Dark - Jessica Stirling 6045
The Marrying Kind - Jessica Stirling 6046
Old Mortality - Sir Walter Scott 5702
The Penny Wedding - Jessica Stirling 6047
Red Plush: The Story of the Moorhouse Family - Guy McCrone 4232
Rob Roy - Sir Walter Scott 5707
Saturday City - Jan Webster 6593

The Welcome Light - Jessica Stirling   6050

Gretna Green
The Scottish Marriage - Karen Lynn   3942

Hawkstone
Masque of Enchantment - Charlene Cross   1432

Hebrides
The Iron Crown - Clare Barroll   354
Sanguinet's Crown - Patricia Veryan   6476
The Scotswoman - Inglis Fletcher   2140
Swear by Apollo - Shirley Barker   318
Two Ravens - Cecelia Holland   2997

Highlands
The Alien Light - Iain Crichton Smith   1427
Beloved Soldiers - C.L. Skelton   5871
The Blind Bend - Lorn MacIntyre   3985
Butcher's Broom - Neil Gunn   2620
Castle of Foxes - Alanna Knight   3516
Chase Royal - Donald Seaman   5712
Cruel in the Shadow - Lorn MacIntyre   3986
The Dark Mile - Dorothy Kathleen Broster   709
Dark Torrent of Glencoe - Edward Grierson   2590
A Falcon for a Queen - Catherine Gaskin   2314
The Fires of Glenlochy - Constance Heaven   2806
Glendraco - Laura Black   521
Greenyards - Joan Lingard   3796
Halfhyde for the Queen - Philip McCutchan   4247
The Highland Hawk - Leslie Turner White   6682
Highlands Rebel - Sally Watson   6584
I Came to the Highlands: A Novel of Suspense - Velda Johnston   3263
The Island Harp - Jeanne Williams   6779
Jarrett's Jade - Frank Yerby   6923
Jennie about to Be - Elisabeth Ogilvie   4694
MacLyon - Lolah Burford   773
My Lord Monleigh - Jan Cox Speas   5957
A Place Called Freedom - Ken Follett   2150
Rob Roy - Sir Walter Scott   5707
Strathgallant - Laura Black   523
Waverley - Sir Walter Scott   5709
Whitton's Folly - Pamela Hill   2948
Wild Cat - Laura Black   524
Witness to Treason - Millie J. Ragosta   5244

Inverness
The English Wife - Charity Blackstock   530
Journey to Enchantment - Patricia Veryan   6464

Ladybrook
Shadows on the Shore - Jessica Stirling   6048

Lochleven
The Abbot - Sir Walter Scott   5688

Mull
Kilcaraig - Annabel Carothers   904

Orkney Islands
The Black Duchess - Alanna Knight   3514
Hawk of May - Gillian Bradshaw   629
Killing Cousins - Alanna Knight   3520
The Pirate - Sir Walter Scott   5704
Princess of the Veil - Helen Mittermeyer   4420
The Wicked Day - Mary Stewart   6033

St. Kilde
The Wings of Morning - Karen Harper   2714

Scapa Flow
The Devil in Harbour - Catherine Gavin   2319

Scottish Borders
Cashmere - Nicola Thorne   6273

Shetland Islands
The Pirate - Sir Walter Scott   5704

Sutherland
The English Wife - Charity Blackstock   530

Tweed
The Monastery - Sir Walter Scott   5701

SERBIA

Belgrade
Dance of the Assassins - Maria Fagyas   1997

SINGAPORE

The Eleventh Year - Monique Raphel High   2914
Some Far Elusive Dawn - Emma Drummond   1727
The Wisdom of Stones - Greg Matthews   4192

SOLOMON ISLANDS

Islands of Unwisdom - Robert Graves   2548

SOUTH AFRICA

Articles of Faith - Ronald Harwood   2770
Blunted Lance - Max Hennessy   2829
The City of Gold - Francis Brett Young   6940
The Covenant - Brigid Knight   3521
The Covenant - James A. Michener   4368
Earthshaker - Robert Wilson Krepps   3553
The Echoing Cliffs - Hjalmar P. Thesen   6219
The Fiercest Heart - Stuart Cloete   1122
Floodtide - Suzanne Goodwin   2475
For They Shall Inherit - Malcolm Macdonald   3964
The Golden Fool - David Divine   1649
The Guns of Arrest - Philip McCutchan   4242
Halfhyde Goes to War - Philip McCutchan   4248
Imperial Kelly - Peter Bowen   600
Jewels - Robert Perrin   4917
King of the Bastards - Sarah Gertrude Millin   4405
The Marigold Field - Diane Pearson   4876
The Mask - Stuart Cloete   1125
Men of Men - Wilbur Smith   5927
The Midnight Gun - Berkely Mather   4180
The Nationalists - William Stuart Long   3876
Rags of Glory - Stuart Cloete   1126
The Regiment - Christopher Nicole   4620
The Regiment - C.L. Skelton   5874
The Roar of the Thunder - Wilbur Smith   5929
Rough Diamond - Robert L. Fish   2098
The Steps of the Sun - Joanna Trollope   6350
They Seek a Country - Francis Brett Young   6941
The Turning Wheels - Stuart Cloete   1127
Watch for the Dawn - Stuart Cloete   1128
Westward the Sun - Brigid Knight   3524
When the Lion Feeds - Wilbur Smith   5931
Wild Conquest - Peter Abrahams   12
Wild Dog Running - Alan Scholefield   5658

Bloemfontein
Another Country - Karel Schoeman   5646

Cape of Good Hope
Fire in the Ice - Alan Scholefield   5653

Capetown
The Road and the Star - Berkely Mather   4182

Karroo District
A Revolutionary Woman - Sheila Fugard   2248

Kimberley
A Captive Freedom - Emma Drummond   1724
Kimberley - Colin Burke   784
The Red Daniel - Duncan MacNeil   4017

Ladysmith
The Legacy of Ladysmith - John Kenny Crane   1413

Mafeking
Siege in the Sun - Mary Paradise   4788

Transvaal
The Hill of Doves - Stuart Cloete   1123

Zululand
Bush War! - William Moore   4447

SOUTH AMERICA

Call the New World - John Edward Jennings   3199
The Campaign - Carlos Fuentes   2245
Jewel of the Sea - Susan Wiggs   6743
The Splendor Stays: An Historic Novel Based on the Lives of the Seven Hart Sisters of Saybrook - Marguerite Allis   114
Vain Shadow - Hartzell Spence   5962

Amazon River
A Crossbowman's Story of the First Exploration of the Amazon - George Millar   4379

Rio Plata
Young Vargas Lewis - Robert Brainard Pearsall   4874

SPAIN

1492 - Newton Frolich   2236
1492 - Mary Johnston   3228
1492: The Life and Times of Juan Cabezon of Castile - Homero Aridjis   187
Among the Innocent - Elizabeth Borton de Trevino   6339
Back to Battle - Max Hennessy   2828
Bard: The Odyssey of the Irish - Morgan Llywelyn   3816
Beauvallet - Georgette Heyer   2876
Bold Encounter: A Novel Based on the Life of St. John of the Cross - Peter-Thomas Rohrbach   5433
The Books of Rachel - Joel Gross   2600
Buccaneer Surgeon - C.V. Terry   6205
The Burning Man - Stephen Longstreet   3883
Catalina - William Somerset Maugham   4197
Colossus: A Novel about Goya and a World Gone Mad - Stephen Marlowe   4093
Columbus: A Romance - Rafael Sabatini   5549
Contessa - Helene Mansfield   4076
Cortez and Marina - Edison Marshall   4105
Court of Shadows - Cynthia Morgan   4450
Cradle of the Sun - John Clagett   1083
Crown of Aloes - Norah Lofts   3840
The Death and Life of Miguel De Cervantes - Stephen Marlowe   4094
A Distant Thunder - Teresa de Luca   1561
Divine Mistress - Frank G. Slaughter   5886
The Dogs of Paradise - Abel Posse   5141
Don Pedro and the Devil - Edgar Maas   3948
Drums of War - Roy Clews   1114
Eagle of the Gredos - Claude Jack Osgood   4761
Envoy From Elizabeth - Pamela Bennetts   451
An Epic Joy: A Novel Based on the Life of Rubens - Donald Braider   642
Eugenie - Hester W. Chapman   989
Ferdinand and Isabella - Hermann Kesten   3474
Fire over England - A.E.W. Mason   4143
The First Gentleman of America: A Comedy of Conquest - James Branch Cabell   841
For One Sweet Grape - Kate O'Brien   4681
Fortune's Favorite - Colleen McCullough   4235
The Gentle Fury: A Novel of Margaret of Austria - Paul Lewis   3758
Gold for the Caesars - Florence A. Seward   5759
Golden Admiral - F. van Wyck Mason   4150
The Golden Thread - Louis De Wohl   1566
La Guerra: A Spanish Saga - Stephen D. Frances   2199
The Gun - C.S. Forester   2174
The Heart of Jade - Salvador de Madariaga   4024
Here Lies Margot - Pamela Hill   2935
His Was the Fire - Showell Styles   6104
The Hounds of God - Rafael Sabatini   5551
I Loved Tiberius - Elisabeth Dored   1692
I, the King - Howard Clewes   1112

I, the King - Hermann Kesten 3475
I, the King - Frances Parkinson Keyes 3479
In the House of the King - Louis Zara 6951
The Infidel - Georgia Elizabeth Taylor 6182
The Inquisitors - Jerzy Andrzejewski 153
Katharine: The Virgin Widow - Jean Plaidy 5025
Katherine - Anya Seton 5752
A Kind of Justice - Benjamin Siegel 5844
The King's Pleasure - Norah Lofts 3847
Knight's Acre - Norah Lofts 3848
The Last Crusader - Louis De Wohl 1569
The Lion Triumphant - Philippa Carr 922
The Long Ships - Frans Gunnar Bengtsson 442
The Lord of the Last Days: Visions of the Year 1000 -
  Homero Aridjis 188
The Man Who Killed the King - Dennis
  Wheatley 6654
The Memoirs of Christopher Columbus - Stephen
  Marlowe 4096
Mercedes of Castile - James Fenimore Cooper 1304
Mexico - James A. Michener 4372
My Master Columbus - Cedric Belfrage 418
The Naked Maja - Noel B. Gerson 2378
The Prisoner of Tordesillas - Lawrence
  Schoonover 5665
The Quality of Mercy - Faye Kellerman 3391
*The Queen's Cross: A Biographical Romance of
  Queen Isabella of Spain* - Lawrence
  Schoonover 5666
Reluctant Cavalier - Donald Barr Chidsey 1064
Ride with Me - Thomas B. Costain 1369
The Scarlet Beast - Francis Gerard 2357
Sea of Lentils - Antonio Benitez-Rojo 443
The Shadow of the Pomegranate - Jean Plaidy 5062
Sharpe's Battle - Bernard Cornwell 1338
Sharpe's Regiment - Bernard Cornwell 1345
So Great a Man - David Pilgrim 5000
The Spanish Bride - Georgette Heyer 2902
The Spanish Bridegroom - Jean Plaidy 5064
The Stuff of Heroes - Miguel Delibes 1592
Swords Against Carthage - Friedrich Donauer 1689
Swords of Anjou - Mario Pei 4890
The Three-Cornered Hat - Pedro Antonio de
  Alarcon 62
Tree of Gold - Rosalind Laker 3602
The Velvet Doublet - James H. Street 6082
While England Sleeps - David Leavitt 3702
The White Dove - Rosie Thomas 6246
The Wind in His Fists - John Edward Jennings 3210
The Young and Lonely King - Jane Lane 3659

Adrados
Sharpe's Enemy - Bernard Cornwell 1342

Algeciras
Touch and Go - C. Northcote Parkinson 4815

Andalusia
The Scarlet Cloak - Jean Plaidy 5061

Avila
The Spanish Bride - Walter O'Meara 4735

Badajoz
Sharpe's Company - Bernard Cornwell 1339

La Bisbal
The Marquis of Bolibar - Leo Perutz 4942

Cadiz
The Gypsy From Cadiz - Tamsin Hamilton 2670
Her Majesty's Captain - Derek Wilson 6797
Ramage at Trafalgar - Dudley Pope 5102

Cordoba
*The Doctor From Cordova: A Biographical Novel
  about the Great Philosopher Maimonides* - Herbert
  Le Porrier 3693
Trail and Triumph: A Novel about Maimonides -
  Lester M. Morrison 4485

Galicia
Sharpe's Rifles - Bernard Cornwell 1347

Granada
Master of Castile - Samuel Edwards 1888
The Year of the Death - Reuben R. Merliss 4343

Jaen
Captain From Castille - Samuel Shellabarger 5794

Leon
Devil to Pay - C. Northcote Parkinson 4810

Madrid
The Adventures of Don Juan - Richard Gardner 2289
In the Blazing Light - Max White 6693
The Last Portrait of the Duchess of Alba - Antonio
  Larreta 3666
The Monk - Matthew Gregory Lewis 3756
Poison - Kathryn Harrison 2737
Rage in Silence: A Novel Based on the Life of Goya -
  Donald Braider 643

Minorca
The Black Cockade - Victor Suthren 6127
Master and Commander - Patrick O'Brian 4669

Najera
Don Pedro's Captain - Pamela Bennetts 449

Navarre
The Lute Player - Norah Lofts 3852

Pyrenees
The White Company - Sir Arthur Conan Doyle 1716

Salamanca
Sharpe's Sword - Bernard Cornwell 1349

Santanilla
The Marburg Chronicles - Alfred Coppel 1319

Santiago de Compostela
Strong as Death - Sharan Newman 4602

Saragossa
Ashes - Stefan Zeromski 6960
Saragossa - Benito Perez Galdos 4912

Segovia
Torquemada - Howard Fast 2045

Seville
Castle of Doves - Constance Heaven 2803
Five Black Ships: A Novel of Discoverers - Napoleon
  Baccino Ponce de Leon 5089
A Man Called Cervantes - Bruno Frank 2201
The Marranos - Liliane Webb 6588
Torquemada - Howard Fast 2045

Talavera
Sharpe's Eagle - Bernard Cornwell 1341

Toledo
*Color From a Light Within: A Novel Based on the Life
  of El Greco* - Donald Braider 641
*The Greek of Toledo: A Romantic Narrative of El
  Greco* - Elizabeth Borton 586
Master of Castile - Samuel Edwards 1888
The Spanish Doctor - Matt Cohen 1159

Torremolinos
Halfhyde for the Queen - Philip McCutchan 4247

Valladolid
Captain From Castille - Samuel Shellabarger 5794

Vitoria
Sharpe's Honour - Bernard Cornwell 1344

SUDAN

The Last Hero - Peter Forbath 2154
The Nationalists - William Stuart Long 3876

Khartoum
Drums of Khartoum - Chloe Gartner 2307
The Last Encounter - Robin Maugham 4196

Nubian Desert
The Last Camel Died at Noon - Elizabeth
  Peters 4951

SURINAME

*Purple Passage: A Novel about a Lady Both Famous
  and Fantastic* - Emily Hahn 2638

SWEDEN

The Emigrants - Vilhelm Moberg 4422
The Flight - Ruth Walgreen Stephan 5994
My Crown, My Love - Ruth Walgreen Stephan 5995
People of the Book - David Stacton 5974
The Rainbird - Sara Lidman 3780
The Red Marten - Peter William Nisser 4630
The Story of Gosta Berling - Selma Lagerlof 3586
The Swedish Cavalier - Leo Perutz 4943
The Swedish Nightingale: Jenny Lind - Elizabeth
  Kyle 3571
The Trees of the Folkungs - Verner Von
  Heidenstam 2817

Stockholm
Desiree - Annemarie Selinko 5741
The Flight of the Eagle - Per Olof Sundman 6119
King's Masque - Evan John 3220

SWITZERLAND

Anne of Geierstein - Sir Walter Scott 5689
Dreaming of Samarkand - Martin Booth 576
The Enchantress - Suyin Han 2673
Frankenstein Unbound - Brian Aldiss 68
I, Madame Tussaud - Sylvia Martin 4135
Lenin: The Novel - Alan Brien 679
Lord Byron's Doctor - Paul West 6634
The Memoirs of Elizabeth Frankenstein - Theodore
  Roszak 5508
The Memoirs of Lord Byron - Robert Nye 4655
Niccolo Rising - Dorothy Dunnett 1803
The Raven and the Rose - Susan Wiggs 6746
Roman Wall - Bryher 745
The Secret Memoirs of Lord Byron - Christopher
  Nicole 4622
The Valley of Decision - Edith Wharton 6653

Berne
The Headsman; or, The Abbaye des Vignerons - James
  Fenimore Cooper 1300

Geneva
City of Light - Alison Macleod 4001
The Dawning of Deliverance - Judith Pella 4892
God's Man: A Novel on the Life of John Calvin -
  Duncan Norton-Taylor 4650
*The Golden Years: A Novel Based on the Life and
  Loves of Percy Bysshe Shelley* - F.W.
  Kenyon 3451
Grand Days - Frank Moorhouse 4448
Love's Children - Judith Chernaik 1013
*The Master of Geneva: A Novel Based on the Life of
  John Calvin* - Gladys H. Barr 341
Voltaire! Voltaire! - Guy Endore 1943

Lake Geneva
Gothic Romance - Emmanuel Carrere 942
Haunted Summer - Anne Edwards 1881
A Single Summer with Lord B. - Derek
  Marlowe 4092

Lausanne
The Colors of Vaud - Bryher 741

Vaud

The Colors of Vaud - Bryher 741

Zurich

Give Me the Daggers - Catherine Gavin 2321
Lenin in Zurich - Alexander Solzhenitsyn 5943
The Passions of the Mind - Irving Stone 6062
The Petrograd Consignment - Owen Sela 5739
Secret Dreams - Keith Korman 3541
Seven Days to Petrograd - Tom Hyman 3094

SYRIA

The Golden Exile - Lawrence Schoonover 5664
Last Act in Palmyra - Lindsey Davis 1529
The Memory Cathedral: A Secret History of Leonardo Da Vinci - Jack Dann 1481

Antioch

Antioch Actress: A Novel of Pagan Against Christian - Jacob Randolph Perkins 4913
Ben Hur: A Tale of the Christ - Lew Wallace 6536
The Glorious Folly: A Novel of the Time of St. Paul - Louis De Wohl 1565
The Leopard Unleashed - Elizabeth Chadwick 967
The Roman - Mika Waltari 6554
The Silver Chalice - Thomas B. Costain 1370
The Sins of Herod: A Novel of Rome and the Early Church - Frank G. Slaughter 5900
Soul Flame - Barbara Wood 6850
Throne of Isis - Judith Tarr 6170
Wine of Satan - Laverne Gay 2327

Damascus

Glory and the Lightning - Taylor Caldwell 856
God's Warrior - Frank G. Slaughter 5889
The Tentmaker - Julius Berstl 486

Palmyra

Queen of the East - Alexander Baron 336

TANZANIA

Curse of Magira - David Bee 413

Dar-Es-Salaam

An Ice-Cream War - William Boyd 616

Lake Tanganyika

The Alpha Raid - Alan Scholefield 5651

THAILAND

The Enchantress - Suyin Han 2673
Temple Bells - Marjorie McEvoy 4271

TIBET

Path of the Eclipse - Chelsea Quinn Yarbro 6905

Lhasa

Invading Tibet - Mark Frutkin 2239

TONGA

The Truelove - Patrick O'Brian 4677

TRANSYLVANIA

Children of the Vampire: The Diaries of the Family Dracul - Jeanne Kalogridis 3326
Covenant with the Vampire: The Diaries of the Family Dracul - Jeanne Kalogridis 3327
Lord of the Vampires: The Diaries of the Family Dracul - Jeanne Kalogridis 3328

TURKEY

Elena - Judith Egan 1893
The Greek Treasure - Irving Stone 6056
The House of War - Catherine Gavin 2322
Woman Astride - Nora Purtscher-Wydenbruch 5209

Anatolia

America, America - Elia Kazan 3380
Beyond the Aegean - Elia Kazan 3382
Mamigon - Jack Hashian 2772

Ankara

The Ashes of Smyrna - Richard Reinhardt 5294

Constantinople

Orlando - Virginia Woolf 6866

Dardanelles

Buller's Victory - Richard Hough 3049

Gallipoli

1915: A Novel - Roger McDonald 4264
The Passing Bells - Phillip Rock 5421

Istanbul

Fire Opal - Pamela Hill 2932

Smyrna

The Ashes of Smyrna - Richard Reinhardt 5294
Beyond the Aegean - Elia Kazan 3382

UKRAINE

With Fire and Sword - Henryk Sienkiewicz 5850

Kharkov

A Space of the Heart - Patricia Wright 6884

UNION OF SOVIET SOCIALIST REPUBLICS

The Red Monarch: Scenes From the Life of Stalin - Yuri Krotkov 3561

Leningrad

Journey into Fire - Patricia Wright 6882
The Revolutionist: A Novel of Russia - Robert Littell 3810

Moscow

Generations of Winter - Vassily Aksyonov 61
Journey into Fire - Patricia Wright 6882
The Revolutionist: A Novel of Russia - Robert Littell 3810

UNITED STATES

1812 - David Nevin 4586
Aide to Glory - Louis Devon 1635
The Anthem - Noel B. Gerson 2361
The Ballad of Typhoid Mary - Jurg Federspiel 2057
The Bank - Stephen Longstreet 3882
Bates House - Clarence Benadum 437
Burr - Gore Vidal 6485
Call of the Arctic - Robert Steelman 5987
Call the New World - John Edward Jennings 3199
Century in Scarlet - Lajos Zilahy 6962
The Chieftain: A Story of the Nez Perce People - Robert Payne 4852
A Clouded Star - Anne Parrish 4819
Cold War - Robert Vaughan 6446
The Conqueror: Being the True and Romantic Story of Alexander Hamilton - Gertrude Atherton 222
Conqueror of the Clouds - William F. Hallstead 2664
The Cross of Frankenstein - Robert J. Myers 4548
Crossing over Jordan - Linda Beatrice Brown 725
Crossing the River - Caryl Phillips 4984
Damaris - Jane Sheridan 5810

Daughters of the New World - Susan Richards Shreve 5835
Deep in My Heart: A Story Based on the Life of Sigmund Romberg - Elliott Arnold 192
Doniphan's Ride - Les Savage Jr. 5620
The Drums of Morning - Philip Van Doren Stern 5997
Eagles at War - Walter J. Boyne 620
Eleanora Duse - Jean Stubbs 6095
The Exquisite Siren - Edwin Haines 2639
Flanagan's Run - Tom McNab 4303
Fool of God: A Novel Based on the Life of Alexander Campbell - Louis Cochran 1144
Free Enterprise - Michelle Cliff 1116
The Gallery of His Dreams - Kristine Kathryn Rusch 5525
Gentlemen of Adventure - Ernest K. Gann 2278
The Glory - Herman Wouk 6873
The Hallelujah Flight - Jack Lynn 3937
Haym Solomon, Son of Liberty - Howard Fast 2032
The Hope - Herman Wouk 6874
I Give You Oscar Wilde - Desmond Hall 2647
The Immortals - Michael Korda 3540
Impressionist: A Novel of Mary Cassatt - Joan King 3486
In My Father's House - Bodie Thoene 6222
Jackson: A Novel - Max Byrd 837
Jelly Roll Morton's Last Night at the Jungle Inn: An Imaginary Memoir - Samuel Charters 1002
Jenny and Barnum: A Novel of Love - Roderick Thorp 6276
John and Anzia: An American Romance - Norma Rosen 5462
John Howard Payne, Skywalker - Maude Barragan 348
Joshua Moore, American - George Frederick Hummel 3078
Kean: The Imaginary Memoirs of an Actor - Julius Berstl 485
Levi Coffin and the Underground Railroad - Charles Ludwig 3921
Lydia Bailey - Kenneth Roberts 5387
A Man Called Grant - Helen Todd 6285
Masque of Sapphire - Deana James 3156
Mexico - James A. Michener 4372
Mortal Hunger: A Novel Based on the Life of Lafcadio Hearn - Harry E. Wedeck 6594
The Mutual Friend - Frederick Busch 811
My Lady Hoyden - Jane Sheridan 5812
The New Confessions - William Boyd 617
On Jordan's Stormy Banks - Adelaide C. Rowell 5518
Over There - Thomas Fleming 2130
A People Betrayed - Alfred Doblin 1654
The Prescott Chronicles - Albert Fried 2232
The Rebel Loyalist - Charles William Gordon 2480
The Red Badge of Courage - Stephen Crane 1414
The Sea and the Sand - Christopher Nicole 4621
The Sea Panther: A Novel about the Commander of the U.S.S. Constitution - Philip Vail 6397
Sergeant Verity and the Blood Royal - Francis Selwyn 5744
Soldier of the Queen - Max Hennessy 2837
The Spirit and the Flesh: A Novel Inspired by the Life of Isadora Duncan - David Weiss 6610
A Star Pointed North - Edmund Fuller 2250
The Swedish Nightingale: Jenny Lind - Elizabeth Kyle 3571
To Spit Against the Wind - Benjamin H. Levin 3737
Trumpets of Silver - Norma Harris 2735
The Twisted Saber: A Biographical Novel of Benedict Arnold - Philip Vail 6398
The Twisted Tendril - Alice Glasgow 2427
Ulysses: A Biographical Novel - Robert Skimin 5878
The View From Coyaba - Peter Abrahams 11
Wallis: The Novel - Anne Edwards 1883
War and Remembrance - Herman Wouk 6875
The Warriors - John Jakes 3155
Where Glory Waits - Gertrude Crownfield 1437

Whistling Cat - Robert W. Chambers　984
Wild Geese - Eilis Dillon　1647
Wilderness: A Tale of the Civil War - Robert Penn Warren　6573
Wind of Destiny - Christopher Nicole　4624
The Winds of War - Herman Wouk　6876
Wings of the Morning - David Beaty　402
The Yankee Rascals - Carter A. Vaughan　6444
Yellowstone Kelly - Peter Bowen　602

Bozeman Trail
Dodging Red Cloud - Richard S. Wheeler　6657
Sioux Dawn - Terry C. Johnston　3258

California Trail
The Ungodly: A Novel of the Donner Party - Richard Rhodes　5311

Carolinas
Phantom Fortress - Bruce Lancaster　3643
The Ragged Ones - Burke Davis　1511
Rogue's March - Maristan Chapman　993

Chesapeake Bay
Chesapeake - James A. Michener　4367

Chisholm Trail
Trail's End - Fred Bean　400

Dakota Territory
Bugles in the Afternoon - Ernest Haycox　2788
The Cowboys - William Dale Jennings　3211
The Crossed Sabres - Gilbert Morris　4458
Custer Passed Our Way - Fred S. Kaufman　3370
Dakota! - Dana Fuller Ross　5472
The Emigrants - Johan Bojer　561
Giants in the Earth - O.E. Rolvaag　5434
Killdeer Mountain - Dee Brown　713
Libbie - Judy Alter　121
The Lieutenant's Lady - Bess Streeter Aldrich　70
Lonely on the Mountain - Louis L'Amour　3621
Manifest Destiny - Brian Garfield　2290
Marching to Valhalla: A Novel of Custer's Last Days - Michael Blake　538
A Mighty Afternoon - Charles K. Mills　4407
Montana Road - Harry Sinclair Drago　1717
No Survivors - Will Henry　2846
Oregon Legacy - Dana Fuller Ross　5485
Peder Victorious - O.E. Rolvaag　5435
A Road We Do Not Know: A Novel of Custer at the Little Bighorn - Frederick J. Chiaventone　1057
Stamping Ground - Loren D. Estleman　1977
The Sword of General Englund - Donald Honig　3023
Their Fathers' God - O.E. Rolvaag　5436
TR - Noel B. Gerson　2385
Welcome to Hard Times - E.L. Doctorow　1660

Detroit River
Fire Along the Sky: A Novel of America - Robert Moss　4497

Fort Reno
Wagons to Tucson - Ed Newsom　4604

Gulf Coast
Beauty Beast - MacKinlay Kantor　3361

Mississippi Valley
The Medicine Horn - Jory Sherman　5820

Missouri River
Beyond the Stars - David William Ross　5497
Captain McRae: A Novel of the Northwest Frontier - William Heuman　2872
Forward the Nation - Donald Culross Peattie　4880
Indian Hater - Glenn R. Vernam　6452
Kings of the Missouri - Hugh Pendexter　4895
Lord Grizzly - Frederick F. Manfred　4056
River of Sky - Karen Harper　2713
The River Witch - Margerie McIntyre　4278
Sacajawea of the Shoshones - Della F. Emmons　1940

Natchez Trace
Love's Tender Fury - Jennifer Wilde　6749

Northwest Territory
Alice of Old Vincennes - Maurice Thompson　6268
The Big Knives - Bruce Lancaster　3635
Black Forest - Meade Minnigerode　4411
Buckskin Cavalier - John Clagett　1082
The Conquerors - Allen W. Eckert　1839
The Forbidden Ground - Neil Harmon Swanson　6138
The Frontiersmen - Allen W. Eckert　1841
Hatchet in the Sky - Margaret Cooper Gay　2328
Long Knife - James Alexander Thom　6233
The Phantom Emperor - Neil Harmon Swanson　6140
The Red Road: A Romance of Braddock's Defeat - Hugh Pendexter　4898
Strife Before Dawn - Mary Schumann　5675
War in the Golden Weather - Stephen Longstreet　3892
Westward the Tide - Harold Sinclair　5863
Wilderness Empire - Allen W. Eckert　1847
The Young Man From Mount Vernon - Arthur Stanwood Pier　4995

Ohio River
Bride of the River - Laura B. Harris　2723
Child of the Snapping Turtle, Mike Fink - Julian Lee Rayford　5256
The Delectable Country - Leland Dewitt Baldwin　280
Follow the River - James Alexander Thom　6231
Passage to Natchez - Cameron Judd　3316
Pull Down to New Orleans - Zachary Ball　283
The Raiders - William Edward Wilson　6819
Reckon with the River - Clark McMeekin　4292
Scarlet Feather - Dale Van Every　6409

Ohio Valley
Bridal Journey - Dale Van Every　6406
From Sea to Shining Sea - James Alexander Thom　6232
Red Morning - Ruby Frazier Frey　2230
The Rock Cried Out - Edward Stanley　5981
The Seneca Hostage - Carter A. Vaughan　6440
Shadow of the Moon - Douglas C. Jones　3284
Silent Drums - Mike Roarke　5361
That Dark and Bloody River - Allen W. Eckert　1845
The Voyagers - Dale Van Every　6412
War Cry - Donald Clayton Porter　5132

Oregon Trail
The Argonauts - Yvonne Schoell　5645
Chant of the Hawk - John Harris　2720
Covered Wagon - Emerson Hough　3041
The Far Country - Marthedith Furnas　2258
Grim Journey - Hoffman Birney　509
Heroine of the Prairies: A Romance of the Oregon Trail - Sheba Hargreaves　2707
The Land Is Bright - Archie Binns　501
The Lost Wagon - James Arthur Kjelgaard　3509
Mountains Ahead - Martha Ferguson McKeown　4284
My Father's World - Michael Phillips　4989
Northwest Passage - David Thompson　6258
On to Oregon! - Honore Morrow　4490
Oregon Bride - Rosanne Bittner　514
The Overland Trail - Wendi Lee　3712
The Pilgrimage - Ann B. Ross　5463
The Pioneers - Courtney Ryley Cooper　1296
The Reluctant Bridegroom - Gilbert Morris　4467
The Sweetwater - Jean Rikhoff　5333
Tamsen - David Galloway　2273
The Taste of Time - Ferol Egan　1892
The Vision Is Fulfilled - Kay L. McDonald　4262
The Way West - A.B. Guthrie Jr.　2628
Wheels West - Homer Croy　1438
Whole Hog - David Wagoner　6523
Wilderness Passage - Forrester Blake　534

Siouxland
Of Lizards and Angels: A Saga of Sioux Land - Frederick F. Manfred　4058

Tennessee River Valley
Darker Grows the Valley - Harry Harrison Kroll　3556

Winterthurn City
Mysteries of Winterthurn - Joyce Carol Oates　4659

ALABAMA

The Forge - Thomas S. Stribling　6083
Foundation Stone - Lella Warren　6571
Horseshoe Bend - Bruce Palmer　4779
The Long Night - Andrew Lytle　3945
No Bugles Blow - Bruce Lancaster　3642
No Surrender - Emma Gelders Sterne　5999
Oh, Promised Land - James H. Street　6079
Rebellion Road - Helen Topping Miller　4392
The Running Iron - Rachel Ann Fish　2097
So Shall They Reap - John Bennett　444

Florence
Home to Tennessee - Alfred Leland Crabb　1400

Litte Tallasee
Alabama Empire - Welbourn Kelley　3392

Mobile
American Eden - Marilyn Harris　2728
Eden and Honor - Marilyn Harris　2729
A Heart Divided - Al Lacy　3580
Iron Ships, Iron Men - Christopher Nicole　4616
The Passionate Rebel - Frank G. Slaughter　5894

Montgomery
Mark - Lonnie Coleman　1205
Some Lose Their Way - Eloise S. Liddon　3770
Southern Discomfort - Rita Mae Brown　730

ALASKA

Alaska - James A. Michener　4364
Ashana - E.P. Roesch　5424
Days of the Gold - Irwin R. Blacker　526
Fire in the Sky - J.A. Shears　5785
Fools' Gold - Richard Wiley　6755
The Goldseekers - William R. Burnett　794
The Great Alone - Janet Dailey　1454
Heaven Is Too High - Mildred Masterson McNeilly　4309
The Law of Larion - Peter Freuchen　2227
The Longest Winter - Julie Harris　2722
A Man's Reach - Charles Morrow Wilson　6796
Princess Sophia - Edison Marshall　4110
Rivers of Gold - Janet Edmonds　1868
Tomorrow's Dream - Peggy Hanchar　2674
The Winter Wolf: Wyatt Earp in Alaska - Richard Parry　4820

New Archangel
The Sea Runners - Ivan Doig　1685

Pea Ridge
Strange Company - Robert J. Conley　1251

Sitka
Seward's Folly - Edison Marshall　4111
The World in His Arms - Rex Beach　392

Skagway
Tara Kane - George Markstein　4091

ARIZONA

Adobe Walls: A Novel of the Last Apache Rising - William R. Burnett　791
Arizona! - Dana Fuller Ross　5466
Beneath the Blue Mountain - Richard S. Wheeler　6656

Billy the Kid: The Legend of El Chivato - Elizabeth Fackler 1994
Blood Brother - Elliott Arnold 190
Chiricahua - Will Henry 2839
Confessions of Johnny Ringo - Geoff Aggeler 40
Defiant Hearts - Janelle Taylor 6185
Dutch Uncle - Marilyn Durham 1815
Escape From Sonora - Will Bryant 739
The Feud - Amelia Bean 396
Filaree: A Novel of an American Life - Marguerite Noble 4633
The Gallows Land - Bill Pronzini 5201
Geronimo - Bill Dugan 1758
Geronimo: An American Legend - Robert J. Conley 1242
Home Mountain - Jeanne Williams 6777
Jessie: A Novel Based on the Life of Jessie Benton Fremont - Judy Alter 120
Mackenna's Gold - Will Henry 2845
Pearl - Anne Leaton 3701
The Post of Honor - David Coxe Cooke 1266
San Juan Hill - Will Henry 2848
The Six Messiahs - Mark Frost 2238
Tacey Cromwell - Conrad Richter 5324
A Time in the Sun - Jane Barry 361
Wagons to Tucson - Ed Newsom 4604
Young Mrs. Cavendish and the Kaiser's Men - K.K. Beck 405

Bisbee
Bisbee '17 - Robert Houston 3056

Camp Grant
The Camp Grant Massacre - Elliott Arnold 191

Casa Grande
The Gila River - Gary McCarthy 4223

Fort Delivery
Distant Trumpet - Paul Horgan 3032

Harqua Hala
The Cowboy Conspiracy - Larry D. Names 4553

Phoenix
I, Jack Swilling - John Myers 4544
West to Eden - Gloria Goldreich 2461

Tombstone
Bloody Season - Loren D. Estleman 1968
Doc Holliday's Woman - Jane Candia Coleman 1201
Fallen Angel - Deborah Camp 872
Saint Johnson - William R. Burnett 796
Tombstone Showdown - Leslie Scott 5681
Wyatt Earp - Matt Braun 653
Wyatt Earp - Dan Gordon 2481

Tucson
The Adelita - Oakley Hall 2649
Arizona - Clarence Budington Kelland 3387
The Camp Grant Massacre - Elliott Arnold 191
Chase the Wind - Janelle Taylor 6184
Dual Destiny - Karen Lynn 3939
The Place of Devils - Lucinda Baker 275

ARKANSAS

Black Jack Davy - John Oskison 4763
Fielder's Choice - Rick Norman 4646
The Impudent Rifle - Richard Pearce 4872
Johnny Osage - Janice Holt Giles 2412
Remember Santiago - Douglas C. Jones 3280
The Saga of Henry Starr - Robert J. Conley 1250
Say to This Mountain - Bodie Thoene 6226
A Thousand Shall Fall - Bodie Thoene 6227
Voyage to Santa Fe - Janice Holt Giles 2418
Walk in My Soul - Lucia St. Clair Robson 5418

Elkhorn Tavern
Elkhorn Tavern - Douglas C. Jones 3278

Fort Gibson
Savanna - Janice Holt Giles 2416

Fort Smith
Belle Starr - Speer Morgan 4453
Ned Christie's War - Robert J. Conley 1247
Pearl - Anne Leaton 3701
The Search for Temperance Moon - Douglas C. Jones 3282
True Grit - Charles Portis 5139
Winding Stairs - Douglas C. Jones 3287
Woman of Justice - Georgia Di Donato 1639

Gourdville
Come Winter - Douglas C. Jones 3275

Ozarks
The Choiring of the Trees - Donald Harington 2709
Shadow of the Mountains - Lynn Morris 4481
This Savage Race - Douglas C. Jones 3285

Point of Rocks
This Savage Race - Douglas C. Jones 3285

Stay More
The Architecture of the Arkansas Ozarks - Donald Harington 2708

Weedy Rough
Weedy Rough - Douglas C. Jones 3286

CALIFORNIA

Adios! - Lanier Bartlett 366
The Adventure of "Horse" Barnsby - Philip D. Stong 6065
Ammahabas - Bill Hotchkiss 3036
The Argonauts - Yvonne Schoell 5645
The Authentic Death of Hendry Jones - Charles Neider 4562
Between Two Worlds - Monique Raphel High 2913
Bound for the Promised Land - Richard Marius 4083
The Buckskin Girl: A Novel of the California Trail in the Mid-Nineteenth Century - Gwen Moffat 4426
California! - Dana Fuller Ross 5467
California Caballero - William Colt MacDonald 3981
The Californian - Todhunter Ballard 284
Captain Grant - Shirley Seifert 5724
Captain Sutter's Gold - Jonreed Lauritzen 3673
Carmen of the Rancho - Frank H. Spearman 5955
The Cross and the Sword - Jonreed Lauritzen 3674
The Dream Ends in Fury - Samuel Anthony Peeples 4889
Dream West - David Nevin 4587
Dust on the King's Highway - Helen Constance White 6677
Eagles Fly West - Edward Maddin Ainsworth 55
East of the Giants - George Rippey Stewart 6027
Escape From Sonora - Will Bryant 739
Filaree: A Novel of an American Life - Marguerite Noble 4633
Firewind - Bill Pronzini 5200
Folded Hills - Stewart Edward White 6701
Forty Pounds of Gold - Philip D. Stong 6066
Gold Is Where You Find It - Clements Ripley 5345
Golden Shore - George Shaftel 5769
Gringo Gold - Dane Coolidge 1293
Immortal Wife - Irving Stone 6057
In Distant Waters - Richard Woodman 6862
Jessie: A Novel Based on the Life of Jessie Benton Fremont - Judy Alter 120
The Longest Road - Jeanne Williams 6781
The Lost Giants - Alan Scholefield 5657
The Lost Years: A Biographical Fiction - Oscar Lewis 3757
Malkeh and Her Children - Marjorie Edelson 1853
Night Wind - Roberta Jean Mountjoy 4504
No Road Too Long - Hildegarde Hawthorne 2785
Oh Glittering Promise - Anne Fisher 2099
Old Misery - Hugh Pendexter 4896

Pacific Cavalcade - Virginia Coffman 1157
Pinto and Sons - Leslie Epstein 1947
Poor Boy and a Long Way Home - James Sherburne 5806
The Proud Breed - Celeste De Blasis 1547
Ranchero - Stewart Edward White 6703
Samuel Brannan and the Golden Fleece - Reva Scott 5686
Savages and Saints - Cora Older 4717
The Sky and Tomorrow - Thomas William Duncan 1788
Soldier in Buckskin - Ray Hogan 2981
Storm to the South - Thelma Strabel 6073
The Taste of Time - Ferol Egan 1892
These Latter Days - Laura Kalpakian 3330
This Land I Hold - Virginia Myers 4550
This Promised Land - Robert Easton 1824
This Splendid Earth - V.J. Banis 289
Tide of Empire - Peter S. Kyne 3572

Bodie
The Gathering Storm - W.E. Davis 1540

Fort Ross
The Russian River - Gary McCarthy 4224

Hollywood
The Black Mask Murderers - William F. Nolan 4635
Bullet for a Star - Stuart M. Kaminsky 3331
Buried Caesars - Stuart M. Kaminsky 3332
Dancing in the Dark - Stuart M. Kaminsky 3334
Dead-Stick - L.J. Washburn 6574
Desperadoes - Ron Hansen 2681
The Devil Met a Lady - Stuart M. Kaminsky 3335
Dog Heavies - L.J. Washburn 6575
The Dream Lover - Mark Upton 6392
Flickers - Phillip Rock 5419
A Grand Passion - Mary Mackey 3991
The Greta Garbo Murder Case - George Baxt 385
He Done Her Wrong - Stuart M. Kaminsky 3338
High Midnight - Stuart M. Kaminsky 3339
Hollywood: A Novel of America in the 1920s - Gore Vidal 6488
Keystone - Peter Lovesey 3913
The Mae West Murder Case - George Baxt 386
Max - Howard Fast 2038
Murder at San Simeon - Robert Lee Hall 2660
Murder on the Yellow Brick Road - Stuart M. Kaminsky 3343
Never Cross a Vampire - Stuart M. Kaminsky 3344
New Deal for Death - Elliott Roosevelt 5454
Passage West - Dallas Miller 4382
The Talking Pictures Murder Case - George Baxt 388
Think Fast, Mr. Peters - Stuart M. Kaminsky 3347
Tom Mix Died for Your Sins - Darryl Ponicsan 5090
Tomorrow Is Another Day - Stuart M. Kaminsky 3348
The William Powell and Myrna Loy Murder Case - George Baxt 390

Lake Tahoe
Rabbit Boss - Thomas Sanchez 5581

Los Angeles
Against the Tide - Muriel Elwood 1935
Arc d'X - Steve Erickson 1953
California Gold - John Jakes 3145
Down for the Count - Stuart M. Kaminsky 3336
The Earth and All It Holds - V.J. Banis 287
The Fala Factor - Stuart M. Kaminsky 3337
Hill of the Hawk - Scott O'Dell 4689
The Howard Hughes Affair - Stuart M. Kaminsky 3340
Hubble Time - Tom Bezzi 490
The Immigrants - Howard Fast 2034
Jubilee Trail - Gwen Bristow 698
Keystone - Peter Lovesey 3913
Lotus Land - Monica Highland 2917

The Man Who Shot Lewis Vance - Stuart M. Kaminsky 3341
The Melting Clock - Stuart M. Kaminsky 3342
Our Father's House - Stephen Longstreet 3890
Paloverde - Jacqueline Briskin 693
Perchance to Dream - Robert B. Parker 4807
The Rainbow Runner - John Cunningham 1450
Tomorrow Is Another Day - Stuart M. Kaminsky 3348

Malibu
The Californios - Louis L'Amour 3618

Mirador
Catch a Falling Star - Stuart M. Kaminsky 3333

Monterey
The Bear Flag: A Novel of the Birth of California - Cecelia Holland 2983

Rancho Cucamonga
Di and I - Peter Lefcourt 3714

Riverside
California Gold - John Jakes 3145

Russian River
The Russian River - Gary McCarthy 4224
To Fell the Giants - Bill Hotchkiss 3038

Sacramento
My Father's World - Michael Phillips 4989
Sea to Shining Sea - Michael Phillips 4990
The Treasure of Pleasant Valley - Frank Yerby 6928

San Diego
Nine Days of Father Serra - Isabelle Gibson Ziegler 6961

San Francisco
Alexa - Anne Melville 4330
All or Nothing - Stephen Longstreet 3881
Annie's Captain - Kathryn Hulme 3077
Calico Palace - Gwen Bristow 694
California Glory - Dana Fuller Ross 5468
California Gold - John Jakes 3145
Cannibal Eliot and the Lost Histories of San Francisco - Hilton Obenzinger 4660
Certain People of Importance - Kathleen Norris 4647
Christopher Strange - Ruth Eleanor McKee 4281
A City for St. Francis - Evelyn Wells 6621
Dakota! - Dana Fuller Ross 5472
Devilseed - Frank Yerby 6914
Domina - Barbara Wood 6847
The Earth and All It Holds - V.J. Banis 287
The Establishment - Howard Fast 2030
The Family of Women - Richard Peck 4883
Fire and Fog - Dianne Day 1543
Fortune Is a Woman - Elizabeth Adler 39
Fortune, Smile Once More - Mary Floyd Williams 6788
The Furies - John Jakes 3146
The Further Adventures of Huckleberry Finn - Greg Matthews 4189
The Golden Circle - John Edward Ames 125
The Golden Crucible - Jean Stubbs 6096
Golden Destiny - June Wyndham Davies 1506
The Golden Nineties - Lisa Mason 4166
Hammett: A Novel - Joseph N. Gores 2487
Herma - Macdonald Harris 2726
A House Behind the Mint - Laurie Huffman 3072
The House That Tai Ming Built - Virginia Lee 3711
Hyde Place - Virginia Coffman 1154
The Immigrants - Howard Fast 2034
The Immigrant's Daughter - Howard Fast 2035
John Barry - Donald F. Bedford 412
The Legacy - Howard Fast 2037
Lights Along the Shore - Diane Austell 241
The Marburg Chronicles - Alfred Coppel 1319
Our Father's House - Stephen Longstreet 3890
Pacific Street - Cecelia Holland 2993

The Passion of Letty Fox - Diana Saunders 5610
Pastora - Joanna Barnes 321
Poor Butterfly - Stuart M. Kaminsky 3345
Rainbow in the Royals - Garland Roark 5357
Rush to Destroy - L. Jay Martin 4133
The Savage Brood - Martha Rofheart 5430
Sea to Shining Sea - Michael Phillips 4990
The Seadon Fortune - Leonard St. Clair 5563
Second Generation - Howard Fast 2043
Sierra Triumph - Dana Fuller Ross 5488
The Strange Files of Fremont Jones - Dianne Day 1544
The Summer of Jack London - Andrew J. Fenady 2058
Tarnished Angel - Phyllis Leonard 3723
Time After Time - Karl Alexander 80
The Treasure of Pleasant Valley - Frank Yerby 6928
Vigilante - Richard Summers 6116
Voyage: A Novel of 1896 - Sterling Hayden 2798
Waltzing in Ragtime - Eileen Charbonneau 996
The World in His Arms - Rex Beach 392
The Yankee Girl - Ellen Argo 186
Yankee Woman - Frederic Baume 381
Young Mrs. Cavendish and the Kaiser's Men - K.K. Beck 405

San Joaquin Valley
Chikara! - Robert Skimin 5876
First the Blade - May Miller 4400

San Jose
The Road to Glory - Darwin Le Ora Teilhet 6199

San Simeon
Murder at San Simeon - Robert Lee Hall 2660

Santa Ana
Herma - Macdonald Harris 2726

Santa Barbara
Ghost Woman - Lawrence Thornton 6275
El Lazo - L. Jay Martin 4132

Sierra Nevada Mountains
Dakota! - Dana Fuller Ross 5472
Golden Destiny - June Wyndham Davies 1506
The Mothers - Vardis Fisher 2109
Rabbit Boss - Thomas Sanchez 5581
The Seadon Fortune - Leonard St. Clair 5563
Tamsen - David Galloway 2273
The Ungodly: A Novel of the Donner Party - Richard Rhodes 5311
Wheels West - Homer Croy 1438
Winter Harvest - Norah Lofts 3863

Sonoma
The Bear Flag: A Novel of the Birth of California - Cecelia Holland 2983

Sonoma Valley
A Season of Swans - Celeste De Blasis 1548

Sutter's Fort
The American River - Gary McCarthy 4222
The Bear Flag: A Novel of the Birth of California - Cecelia Holland 2983

Tule Bend
The Hangings - Bill Pronzini 5202

COLORADO

Butcher's Crossing - John Williams 6786
Centennial - James A. Michener 4366
The Golden Lady - Dorothy Gardiner 2283
The Goodnight Trail - Ralph Compton 1227
Great Day in the Morning - Robert Hardy Andrews 149
The Hallelujah Train - Bill Gulick 2614
Kid Curry: The Life and Times of Harvey Logan and the Wild Bunch - F. Bruce Lamb 3606
The Lost Giants - Alan Scholefield 5657

Paint the Wind - Cathy Cash Spellman 5960
Peter Doyle - John Vernon 6457
The Place of Dead Roads - William S. Burroughs 808
Power in the Blood - Greg Matthews 4191
Pride's Castle - Frank Yerby 6925
Rawhider - Gene Shelton 5802
Red Mountain - David Lavender 3677
The Revolt of Sarah Perkins - Marian Cockrell 1148
The Scout - Harry Combs 1224
The Seventh Winter - Hal Borland 583
Shining Mountains - Steve Frazee 2214
Six-Horse Hitch - Janice Holt Giles 2417
Thin Moon and Cold Mist - Kathleen O'Neal Gear 2330
Too Long at the Dance - Mike Blakely 539
Tracker - David Wagoner 6521
When the Legends Die - Hal Borland 584
Wild Earth's Nobility - Frank Waters 6578
Wilde West - Walter Satterthwait 5609

Arkansas River
The Arkansas River - Jory Sherman 5816

Bartorville
Snow-Water - Dorothy Gardiner 2285

Bent's Fort
Apache Blood - David Thompson 6250

Bright Prairie
The Misadventures of Bethany Price - Marian Cockrell 1147

Charity
Charity, Colorado - Chelsea Quinn Yarbro 6896
The Law in Charity - Chelsea Quinn Yarbro 6901

Denver
All for Love: Baby Doe and Silver Dollar - John Vernon 6456
The Amulet - Hal Borland 582
Colorado! - Dana Fuller Ross 5471
Colorado Ambush - Jess McCriede 4230
Diamond Wedding - Wilbur Daniel Steele 5986
Theory of War - Joan Brady 637
Thief of My Heart - Rexanne Becnel 410

Elkhorn
The Ghosts of Elkhorn - Kerry Newcomb 4589

Fort Lyon
The Great Betrayal - Dorothy Gardiner 2284

Leadville
All for Love: Baby Doe and Silver Dollar - John Vernon 6456

Pullman
Quitting Time - Robert J. Conley 1249

Rocky Mountains
The Aviator - Ernest K. Gann 2277
Forty Guns West - William W. Johnstone 3267

Sand Creek
A Very Small Remnant - Michael Whitney Straight 6075

Sky Valley
Horne's Law - Jory Sherman 5819

Telluride
Bridey's Mountain - Yvonne Adamson 34
Telluride - Susan Clark Schofield 5648

Trinidad
One More River to Cross - Will Henry 2847

CONNECTICUT

All in Good Time - Marguerite Allis 106
American Beauty - Edna Ferber 2060

Amistad: The Thunder of Freedom - David Pesci 4944
Charity Strong - Marguerite Allis 109
Clouds of Destiny - Lou Ellen Davis 1535
Crossings - Earl Rovit 5512
The Culper Spy Ring - Lynn Groh 2596
Echo of Lions - Barbara Chase-Riboud 1004
Law of the Land - Marguerite Allis 111
Michael Torey - Janet Mathewson 4183
Now We Are Free - Marguerite Allis 112
The Secret Road - Bruce Lancaster 3646
Stronghold - Donald Barr Chidsey 1065
Tenants of the Earth - Sandra Paretti 4793
Water over the Dam - Marguerite Allis 116
Whittling Boy: The Story of Eli Whitney - Roger Burlingame 789

Danbury
1901 - Robert Conroy 1258

Hartford
Jonathan Dearborn: A Novel of the War of 1812 - Willard Wallace 6540
Masters of Illusion: A Novel of the Connecticut Circus Fire - Mary-Ann Tirone Smith 5925
The Sleep of Life - Richard Gordon 2486

Housatonic Valley
Patience and Sarah - Isabel Miller 4398

Middletown
The Bridge - Marguerite Allis 108

New Haven
The Bridge - Marguerite Allis 108
East by Day - Blair Niles 4626

Pequot Landing
In the Fire of Spring - Thomas Tryon 6355
The Wings of the Morning - Thomas Tryon 6356

Renborough
The Woman Question - Dorothea Malm 4046

Ridgefield
The Hessian - Howard Fast 2033

Saybrook
The Splendor Stays: An Historic Novel Based on the Lives of the Seven Hart Sisters of Saybrook - Marguerite Allis 114

Stonington
That Skipper From Stonington - Theda Kenyon 3464

Waterbury
The Mill on Mad River - Howard Clark 1087

DELAWARE

Brandywine River Valley
Brandywine - Jack Rowe 5513
Dominion - Jack Rowe 5514
Fortune's Legacy - Jack Rowe 5515

Dunstable
Tolbecken - Samuel Shellabarger 5798

DISTRICT OF COLUMBIA

Washington
54-40 or Fight - Emerson Hough 3040
1876: A Novel - Gore Vidal 6484
Alice and Edith: A Biographical Novel of the Two Wives of Theodore Roosevelt - Dorothy Clarke Wilson 6798
The Alienist - Caleb Carr 907
American Falls - John Calvin Batchelor 376
Beloved Enemy - Al Lacy 3579
The Bloody Ground - Bernard Cornwell 1334
Bride of Fortune - Harnett T. Kane 3352
The Bridge - Marguerite Allis 108

The Buckstones - Paul I. Wellman 6615
Bully! - Mark Schorr 5670
Ceremony of the Innocent - Taylor Caldwell 852
The Chester A. Arthur Conspiracy - William Wiegand 6740
Christmas for Tad: A Story of Mary and Abraham Lincoln - Helen Topping Miller 4386
Clear for Action! - Noel B. Gerson 2362
The Cosgrove Report - G.J.A. O'Toole 4765
A Court of Owls - Richard Adicks 37
The Cup Trembling - Karl Brown 723
A Daughter of Liberty - Allan Cole 1196
Dim the Flaring Lamps - Jan Jordan 3301
The Dixie Widow - Gilbert Morris 4459
Dolley - Rita Mae Brown 727
Dream West - David Nevin 4587
Echo of Lions - Barbara Chase-Riboud 1004
Eleanor: A Novel - Rhoda Lerman 3724
Empire: A Novel - Gore Vidal 6487
The Establishment - Howard Fast 2030
A Family Matter - James Roosevelt 5458
The Fathers - Allen Tate 6171
The Fifth Conspiracy - Ted Jones 3296
Flying into Love - D.M. Thomas 6236
Forever Free - Honore Morrow 4487
Freedom - William Safire 5561
Freedom Road - Howard Fast 2031
From the Terrace - John O'Hara 4703
The Gorgeous Hussy - Samuel Hopkins Adams 30
Gray Canaan - David Garth 2305
The Hampton Women - Julie Ellis 1921
The Haversham Legacy - Daoma Winston 6827
Hawk's Journey - Donald Clayton Porter 5119
Henry and Clara - Thomas Mallon 4042
Here Comes a Candle - Jane Aiken Hodge 2964
Hollywood: A Novel of America in the 1920s - Gore Vidal 6488
Home to Kentucky: A Novel of Henry Clay - Alfred Leland Crabb 1399
Homecoming - Dana Fuller Ross 5474
The Hyde Park Murder - Elliott Roosevelt 5443
I Speak for Thaddeus Stevens - Elsie Singmaster 5868
Immortal Wife - Irving Stone 6057
Ironclads: Man-of-War - Larry D. Names 4554
The Judges of the Secret Court - David Stacton 5972
The Last Full Measure - Honore Morrow 4488
Lights Along the Shore - Diane Austell 241
Lincoln: A Novel - Gore Vidal 6490
The Lincoln Diddle - Barbara Steward 6015
The Lost Years: A Biographical Fiction - Oscar Lewis 3757
Love Is Eternal - Irving Stone 6058
Luise - Dawn Stewart Field 2079
Magnificent Destiny - Paul I. Wellman 6619
Many a Voyage - Loula Grace Erdman 1951
Memories of the Ford Administration - John Updike 6391
Mr. Lincoln's Wife - Anne Colver 1221
Murder and the First Lady - Elliott Roosevelt 5444
Murder in the Blue Room - Elliott Roosevelt 5446
Murder in the East Room - Elliott Roosevelt 5448
Murder in the Executive Mansion - Elliott Roosevelt 5449
Murder in the Oval Office - Elliott Roosevelt 5450
Murder in the Red Room - Elliott Roosevelt 5451
Murder in the Rose Garden - Elliott Roosevelt 5452
Murder in the West Wing - Elliott Roosevelt 5453
My Dear Cousin - Peggy Hoffmann 2977
My Love, My Enemy - Jan Cox Speas 5958
My Theodosia - Anya Seton 5753
Old Hickory - Noel B. Gerson 2379
One Smart Indian - Robert J. Seidman 5722
The Only Thing to Fear - David Poyer 5160
The Passionate Rebel - Frank G. Slaughter 5894
Powderkeg - Richard Vetterli 6482
The President's Lady - Irving Stone 6063
Promises to Keep - Jocelyn Stirling 6051

Queen Dolley: The Life and Times of Dolley Madison - Dorothy Clarke Wilson 6806
Refinements of Love: A Novel about Clover and Henry Adams - Sarah Booth Conroy 1259
The Road to Baltimore - Robert S. Harper 2716
Rogue's Kingdom - John Brick 676
A Royal Murder - Elliott Roosevelt 5456
Sam Houston - Noel B. Gerson 2380
The Senator's Lady - Shirley Seifert 5733
Sioux Splendor - Rosanne Bittner 515
The Slender Reed - Noel B. Gerson 2382
Soul of Abe Lincoln - Bernie Babcock 251
The Spoils of War - Thomas Fleming 2131
The Spur - Ardyth Kennelly 3425
The Stonewall Brigade: A Novel of the American Civil War - Frank G. Slaughter 5902
Storm Center: A Novel about Andy Johnson - Joseph Walker McSpadden 4312
The Three Lives of Elizabeth - Shirley Seifert 5735
Tide of Empire - Bates Baldwin 279
A Time for Titans - Vina Delmar 1602
The Titans - John Jakes 3154
To the Honor of the Fleet - Robert H. Pilpel 5002
TR - Noel B. Gerson 2385
The Very Best People - Elizabeth Villars 6499
Walt Whitman's Secret - Ben Aronin 196
Washington, D.C. - Gore Vidal 6493
Watchfires - Louis Auchincloss 234
The Way to Fort Pillow - James Sherburne 5807
While Rivers Flow - Glen H. Fleischmann 2125
While the Music Plays - Diane Austell 242
The White House Pantry Murder - Elliott Roosevelt 5457
With Malice Toward None - Honore Morrow 4492
The Woman Who Loved John Wilkes Booth - Pamela Redford Russell 5533
Woman with a Sword: The Biographical Novel of Anna Ella Carroll of Maryland - Hollister Noble 4632
The Yankee From Tennessee - Noel B. Gerson 2388

EAST COAST
The Limner - Paul Darcy Boles 564

FLORIDA
At the Moon's Inn - Andrew Lytle 3944
Bright Feather - Robert Wilder 6750
A Court of Owls - Richard Adicks 37
Di and I - Peter Lefcourt 3714
Don Juan McQueen - Eugenia Price 5181
The Flames of Time - Baynard Kendrick 3409
Golden Isle - Frank G. Slaughter 5890
The Great Tide - Rubylea Hall 2662
The Horse Hunters - Robert Newton Peck 4887
I Take This Land - Richard Powell 5147
Juan Ortiz: Gentleman of Seville - Mary Bethell Alfriend 88
The Land Where the Sun Dies - Henry Carlisle 896
Live From the Devil - Wyatt Blassingame 542
On Stranger Tides - Tim Powers 5156
Runaway - Heather Graham 2519
Say These Names (Remember Them) - Betty Sue Cummings 1448
Seminole - Donald Clayton Porter 5126
Spanish Bayonet - Stephen Vincent Benet 441
Storm Haven - Frank G. Slaughter 5903
The Wings of Morning - Karen Harper 2714

Everglades
Killing Mister Watson - Peter Mathiessen 4185

Florida Keys
A Journey to Matecumbe - Robert Lewis Taylor 6188

Jacksonville

Three Roads to Valhalla - Catherine Pomeroy Stewart 6022

Miami

Biscayne - Barry Jay Kaplan 3365
Miami: A Saga - Evelyn Wilde Mayerson 4204
Sacred Hunter - Barry Unsworth 6389
True Detective - Max Allan Collins 1215

Pensacola

Flight From Avatchez - Frank G. Slaughter 5887

St. Augustine

Maria - Eugenia Price 5184
Rascal's Heaven - F. van Wyck Mason 4157
River in the Wind - Edith Pope 5111
Sea of Lentils - Antonio Benitez-Rojo 443
Seminole - Theodore Pratt 5164

St. John's River

Margaret's Story - Eugenia Price 5183

GEORGIA

The African - Harold Courlander 1386
All God's Children - Alston Anderson 136
And Tell of Time - Laura Krey 3554
Cain's Daughters - Doris Shannon 5776
Creek Mary's Blood - Dee Brown 712
Deep River - Henrietta Buckmaster 760
Flight From Avatchez - Frank G. Slaughter 5887
Freedom's Banner - Teresa Crane 1415
Give Us This Valley - Tom Ham 2666
Gone with the Wind - Margaret Mitchell 4415
Hiwassee: A Novel of the Civil War - Charles F. Price 5176
Jubilee - Margaret Walker 6531
Lamb in His Bosom - Caroline Miller 4380
Lorena - Frank G. Slaughter 5892
The Magnolias - Julie Ellis 1922
Melissa Starke - Annulet Andrews 145
No Resting Place - William Humphrey 3079
Oh, Promised Land - James H. Street 6079
The Proud and the Free - Janet Dailey 1456
Rainbow Road - Davenport Steward 6016
Sherman's March - Cynthia Bass 373
The Slave Stealer - Boyd Upchurch 6390
Trail of Tears - Williams Forrest 2187
Trail of Tears - Frances Patton Statham 5983
While Rivers Flow - Glen H. Fleischmann 2125

Atlanta

Company Q - Richard O'Connor 4684
Dreams of Gold - Lewis Orde 4748
The Far Side of Home - Maggie Davis 1536
Gone with the Wind - Margaret Mitchell 4415
The Hampton Heritage - Julie Ellis 1920
The Hampton Women - Julie Ellis 1921
The Warriors - John Jakes 3155

Augusta

The Far Side of Home - Maggie Davis 1536
The Sounds of Chariots: A Novel of John Sevier and the State of Franklin - Helen Topping Miller 4396
A Woman Called Fancy - Frank Yerby 6931

Cold Sassy

Cold Sassy Tree - Olive Ann Burns 797
Leaving Cold Sassy - Olive Ann Burns 798

Jonesboro

The Far Side of Home - Maggie Davis 1536

Luxor

Exit with Drums - Joseph A. Daley 1457

Marietta

Beauty From Ashes - Eugenia Price 5177

St. Simons Island

Beauty From Ashes - Eugenia Price 5177

The Beloved Invader - Eugenia Price 5179
Bright Captivity - Eugenia Price 5180
Lighthouse - Eugenia Price 5182
New Moon Rising - Eugenia Price 5185
Where Shadows Go - Eugenia Price 5189

Savannah

The Band Plays Dixie - Morris Markey 4089
Before Darkness Falls - Eugenia Price 5178
Beulah Land - Lonnie Coleman 1202
The Bride of Texas - Josef Skvorecky 5880
The Distant Lands - Julian Green 2567
Don Juan McQueen - Eugenia Price 5181
Jarrett's Jade - Frank Yerby 6923
Judas Flowering - Jane Aiken Hodge 2965
The Legacy of Beulah Land - Lonnie Coleman 1203
Look Away, Beulah Land - Lonnie Coleman 1204
Look to the Rose - Shirley Seifert 5728
Members of the Tribe - Richard Kluger 3511
Our Valiant Few - F. van Wyck Mason 4155
Rivers of Glory - F. van Wyck Mason 4158
Savage Oaks - Julie Ellis 1924
Savannah - Eugenia Price 5186
Savannah Purchase - Jane Aiken Hodge 2970
Scarlett - Alexandra Ripley 5342
The Stars of the South - Julian Green 2568
Stranger in Savannah - Eugenia Price 5187
To See Your Face Again - Eugenia Price 5188
A Woman Called Fancy - Frank Yerby 6931

Savannah River

Sangaree - Frank G. Slaughter 5898

Sea Islands

Fire in the Heart - Henrietta Buckmaster 761
The Web of Days - Edna Lee 3708

Sumter County

Andersonville - MacKinlay Kantor 3359

Warm Springs

The Only Thing to Fear - David Poyer 5160

GREAT LAKES

The Beckoning Waters - Robert Carse 944
Gateway to Empire - Allen W. Eckert 1842
Wolves Against the Moon - Julia Cooley Altrocchi 123

Lake Erie

The Court Martial of Commodore Perry - James A. Rhodes 5307
D'ri and I - Irving A. Bacheller 257
Fire Along the Sky: A Novel of America - Robert Moss 4497
The Fleet in the Forest - Carl Daniel Lane 3654
My Blood and My Treasure - Mary Schumann 5674
The Quiet Shore - Walter Havighurst 2775

Lake Michigan

The Strangers on the Island - Brand Whitlock 6714

GREAT PLAINS

The Amulet - Hal Borland 582
And One Rode West - Heather Graham 2514
Bound for the Promised Land - Richard Marius 4083
Buffalo Palace - Terry C. Johnston 3245
Buffalo Woman - Dorothy M. Johnson 3223
Dance on the Wind - Terry C. Johnston 3249
The Daybreakers - Louis L'Amour 3619
The Gates of the Mountains - Will Henry 2842
Harp of a Thousand Strings - Harold Lenoir Davis 1522
The Last Hunt - Milton Lott 3900
The Last Warpath - Will Henry 2844
The Morning River - W. Michael Gear 2333
Path of the Sun - Al Dempsey 1608
Shaman - Noah Gordon 2483
Song of the Cheyenne - Jory Sherman 5822

Stone Song: A Novel of the Life of Crazy Horse - Winfred Blevins 548
Thunder on the Plains - Rosanne Bittner 517
Tie My Bones to Her Back - Robert F. Jones 3294
Woman Chief - Benjamin Capps 892

HAWAII

Captain Sutter's Gold - Jonreed Lauritzen 3673
Carolina Courage - Dana Fuller Ross 5469
Diamond Head - Houston Branch 647
Empire of Heaven - Linda Ching Sledge 5907
Hawaii - James A. Michener 4370
The Last Voyage: Captain Cook's Lost Diary - Hammond Innes 3108
Lord of the Isles - Donald Barr Chidsey 1063
The Lord's Anointed - Ruth Eleanor McKee 4282
No Brighter Glory - Armstrong Sperry 5963
Pacific Cavalcade - Virginia Coffman 1157
Restless Voyage - Stanley David Porteus 5138
The Return of Lono: A Novel of Captain Cook's Last Voyage - Oswald Andrew Bushnell 816
Tarnished Angel - Phyllis Leonard 3723
The White King - Samuel Bertram Harrison 2747

Honolulu

Peril under the Palms - K.K. Beck 404
Somewhere Within This House - Jean Francis Webb 6587

Molokai

Molokai - Oswald Andrew Bushnell 815

Oahu

Diamond Head - Marian J.A. Jackson 3135
Ka'a'awa: A Novel about Hawaii in the 1850s - Oswald Andrew Bushnell 814

IDAHO

The Big Lonesome - Will Bryant 737
Buffalo Coat - Carol Brink 691
The Fleet Rabble: A Novel of the Nez Perce War - Frank Borden Hanes 2675
From Where the Sun Now Stands - Will Henry 2841
Harry Idaho - Hugh Pendexter 4894
The Moon-Eyed Appaloosa - Bill Gulick 2617
Song of the Meadowlark - John A. Sanford 5594
These Latter Days - Laura Kalpakian 3330
They Came to a Valley - Bill Gulick 2618
Thousand Years of Gold - Ruthanne Lum McCunn 4239

Fort Bonneville

Hawken Fury - David Thompson 6254

Idaho City

Megan - Kathleen Magill 4028

ILLINOIS

The American - Louis Dodge 1669
And Never Yield - Elinor Pryor 5204
Bitter Creek - Al Cody 1150
Broncho Apache - Paul I. Wellman 6614
Comes an Echo on the Breeze - Edward J. Ryan 5542
The Corinthians - Nicholas E. Wyckoff 6888
Faye's Folly - Elizabeth Corbett 1322
For Us the Living - Bruce Lancaster 3639
Hope of Earth - Jane Gilmore Rushing 5528
Intrigue in Baltimore - Janet Whitney 6715
Lincoln's Mothers: A Story of Nancy and Sally Lincoln - Dorothy Clarke Wilson 6804
A Man for the Ages - Irving A. Bacheller 261
Michael Beam - Richard Hallet 2663
The Soul of Ann Rutledge - Bernie Babcock 252
Thunder on the River - Charlton Laird 3590
Trail-Makers of the Middle Border - Hamlin Garland 2296

The Trial of Mary Todd Lincoln - James A. Rhodes 5309
Twilight of Empire - Allen W. Eckert 1846

Bloomington
The Lincoln Hunters - Wilson Tucker 6359

Chicago
Adversary in the House - Irving Stone 6053
The American - Howard Fast 2026
Blue Ruin: A Novel of the 1919 World Series - Brendan Boyd 610
The Bride of Texas - Josef Skvorecky 5880
California Glory - Dana Fuller Ross 5468
Chicago Girls - Edith Freund 2229
Conspiracy of Knaves - Dee Brown 711
The Devil's Card - Mary Maher 4030
The Dream Seekers - Grace Mark 4085
The Financier - Theodore Dreiser 1720
Gateway to Empire - Allen W. Eckert 1842
The Gentleman From Chicago - John Cashman 953
Goldeneye - Malcolm Macdonald 3965
Homeland - John Jakes 3148
Hoopla - Harry Stein 5990
Hunt for Heaven - Elsie Barber 298
Illinois! - Dana Fuller Ross 5475
Joy in Mudville - Gordon McAlpine 4216
Julie - Jane Kesner Morris 4479
Mad Dog - Jack Kelly 3401
Mr. Vertigo - Paul Auster 244
Murder at Wrigley Field - Troy Soos 5949
Organized Crime - Nicholas Von Hoffman 6511
The President's Man - Elliott Roosevelt 5455
The Senator's Lady - Shirley Seifert 5733
Show Boat - Edna Ferber 2063
The Six Messiahs - Mark Frost 2238
The Smiths - Janet Fairbank 2002
Southern Discomfort - Rita Mae Brown 730
Stranger in Two Worlds - Hugh Clevely 1111
Those the Sun Has Loved - Rose Jourdain 3309
True Crime - Max Allan Collins 1214
True Detective - Max Allan Collins 1215
You Bet Your Life - Stuart M. Kaminsky 3349

Galena
The Bright Land - Janet Fairbank 2000
Captain Grant - Shirley Seifert 5724
Grant's War - Ted Jones 3297

Nauvoo
The Devil's Rainbow - J.C. Furnas 2257
The Everlasting Fire - Jonreed Lauritzen 3675
Salt Lake City - A.R. Reife 5292

New Era
Remembrance Rock - Carl Sandburg 5583

Pomax
Power - Howard Fast 2041

Sangamon River
Steamboat on the River - Darwin Le Ora Teilhet 6200

Springfield
The American - Howard Fast 2026
The Crisis - Winston Churchill 1079
The Father - Katharine Holland Brown 724
Hoffman's Row - Walter Carnahan 902
Love Is Eternal - Irving Stone 6058
Mr. Lincoln's Wife - Anne Colver 1221

Vincennes
The Big Knives - Bruce Lancaster 3635

INDIAN TERRITORY
Desperadoes - Ron Hansen 2681
Strange Company - Robert J. Conley 1251
Timothy Baines - John H. Culp 1445
True Grit - Charles Portis 5139

Fort Sill
The Buffalo Soldiers - John Prebble 5165

INDIANA
Abe Lincoln of Pigeon Creek - William Edward Wilson 6818
Adversary in the House - Irving Stone 6053
The Beckoning Road - Caroline Snedeker 5934
Dillinger - Harry Patterson 4832
Except for Me and Thee - Jessamyn West 6628
For Us the Living - Bruce Lancaster 3639
The Friendly Persuasion - Jessamyn West 6629
The Horn and the Forest - Jamie Lee Cooper 1313
The Inner Voice - Nina Wilcox Putnam 5211
Judith Lankester - Marjorie Allee 93
The Massacre at Fall Creek - Jessamyn West 6631
Proving Ground: A Novel of Civil War Days in the North - Leone Lowden 3919
The Salt and the Savor - Howard William Troyer 6354
So Free We Seem - Helen Todd 6286
Song of Metamoris: A Story That Remains of a People Who Passed This Way - Milford E. Anness 155

Kirtland
The Devil's Rainbow - J.C. Furnas 2257

Lafayette
Viola Gwyn - George Barr McCutcheon 4258

Pendle Hill
The Peculiar People - Jan de Hartog 2764

Raintree County
Raintree County - Ross Lockridge Jr. 3827

Wabash Valley
The Crowded Hill - Le Roy MacLeod 4008
Years of Peace - Le Roy MacLeod 4009

IOWA
The Actor - Robert J. Conley 1236
Border Line - Robert J. Conley 1238
Country People - Ruth Suckow 6111
The Everlasting Fire - Jonreed Lauritzen 3675
Forty Pounds of Gold - Philip D. Stong 6066
The Hawkeye - Herbert Quick 5222
A Lantern in Her Hand - Bess Streeter Aldrich 69
The Sky and Tomorrow - Thomas William Duncan 1788
Song of Years - Bess Streeter Aldrich 72
Spirit Lake - MacKinlay Kantor 3363
Sunflower - Jill Marie Landis 3653
Vandemark's Folly - Herbert Quick 5223

Litchfield
The Labyrinth - Thomas William Duncan 1787

Riddle
Colfax - Robert J. Conley 1239
Killing Time - Robert J. Conley 1244

Sioux City
Anthony Trant - John Hyatt Downing 1713
Sioux City - John Hyatt Downing 1714

Spilville
Dvorak in Love - Josef Skvorecky 5881

KANSAS
Band of Angels - Robert Penn Warren 6572
The Bloody Benders - Robert H. Adelman 35
Bound Girl - Everett Webber 6591
The Bright Feathers - John H. Culp 1441
Butcher's Crossing - John Williams 6786
By Dim and Flashing Lamps - Alan Le May 3689
Candle of the Wicked - Manly Wade Wellman 6612
Cimarron - Edna Ferber 2061

Come Spring - Charlotte Hinger 2954
The Dark Command - William R. Burnett 793
Eli's Road - Lucas Webb 6589
Free Soil - Margaret Lynn 3943
God's Angry Man - Leonard Ehrlich 1898
Golden Horizons - William Corcoran 1324
Heart of the Country - Greg Matthews 4190
The History of Rome Hanks - Joseph Stanley Pennell 4909
The Inner Voice - Nina Wilcox Putnam 5211
Journey by the River - John Prescott 5173
The Justicer - Thomas Fall 2010
Kansas Blue - Dylan Harson 2758
Lady of No Man's Land - Jeanne Williams 6780
The Last Frontier - Howard Fast 2036
The Lawless - John Jakes 3149
Libbie - Judy Alter 121
The Longest Road - Jeanne Williams 6781
Many a Voyage - Loula Grace Erdman 1951
Pillar of Cloud - Jackson Burgess 782
Raising Holy Hell - Bruce Olds 4718
Red Runs the River - Lewis B. Patten 4831
Roman - Douglas C. Jones 3281
Sassafras - Jack Matthews 4193
Scotch on the Rocks - Howard Browne 733
The Senator's Lady - Shirley Seifert 5733
The Sun Shines West - Nathan Schachner 5632
The Surveyor - Truman Nelson 4583
The Trail to Ogallala - Benjamin Capps 889
The Unplowed Sky - Jeanne Williams 6783
Western: A Saga of the Great Plains - Frank Yerby 6930
While Angels Dance - Ralph W. Cotton 1372
Wind Like a Bugle - Leonard Nathan 3722

Abilene
Born of the Sun - John H. Culp 1440
Embers of the Heart - Rosanne Bittner 512
Trail's End - Fred Bean 400

Bountiful
Home Station - Jeanne Williams 6778

Coffeyville
Desperadoes - Ron Hansen 2681

Dodge City
Doc Holliday's Woman - Jane Candia Coleman 1201
The Old Colts - Glendon Swarthout 6144
Wyatt Earp - Dan Gordon 2481

Fort Dodge
Long Winter Gone - Terry C. Johnston 3252

Fort Leavenworth
Farewell, My General - Shirley Seifert 5726

Hays
Brules - Harry Combs 1223

Lawrence
Free Soil - Marguerite Allis 110
McKay's Bees - Thomas McMahon 4289
Sons of Fire - Max McCoy 4227

Leavenworth
Little Big Man - Thomas Berger 478

Mason-Dixon
No Roof but Heaven - Jeanne Williams 6782

Saline River
Heartland - Robert Douglas Mead 4316

Smoky Hill River
The Smoky Hill - Don Coldsmith 1188

Sweetbriar
Theory of War - Joan Brady 637

Wichita
Heartland - Robert Douglas Mead 4316
The Passionate Journey - Irving Stone 6061

KENTUCKY

Arizona! - Dana Fuller Ross   5466
Band of Angels - Robert Penn Warren   6572
Becky Landers, Frontier Warrior - Constance
   Skinner   5879
The Believers - Janice Holt Giles   2409
The Big Sky - A.B. Guthrie Jr.   2624
*Boone: A Novel Based on the Life and Times of Daniel
   Boone* - Cameron Judd   3311
The Border Captains - Jason Manning   4072
Buckskin Cavalier - John Clagett   1082
The Captive Witch - Dale Van Every   6407
The Captives - Don Wright   6878
Cherokee - Donald Clayton Porter   5115
Circle of Gold - Karen Harper   2710
Conspiracy of Knaves - Dee Brown   711
The Crossing - Winston Churchill   1080
Dan'l Boone Kissed Me - Felix Holt   3006
Dark Hills to Westward - Harry M. Caudill   964
Darktown Strutters - Wesley Brown   732
Enslaved - Ron Burns   801
Erskine Dale, Pioneer - John Fox   2195
Eyes of Eagles - William W. Johnstone   3266
The Fields - Conrad Richter   5319
Flintlock - Jason Manning   4073
For Us the Living - Bruce Lancaster   3639
Gone to Texas - Jason Manning   4074
Hannah Fowler - Janice Holt Giles   2411
Home to Kentucky: A Novel of Henry Clay - Alfred
   Leland Crabb   1399
John Bonwell - Charles K. Pulse   5208
A Journey to Matecumbe - Robert Lewis
   Taylor   6188
The Kentuckians - Janice Holt Giles   2413
Kentucky! - Dana Fuller Ross   5477
Kentucky Home - Betty Layman Receveur   5283
Kentucky Pride - Gene Markey   4087
*The Kentucky Trace: A Novel of the American
   Revolution* - Harriette Simpson Arnow   195
The Land Beyond the Mountains - Janice Holt
   Giles   2414
Love Is Eternal - Irving Stone   6058
The Matrix - Maria Thompson Daviess   1509
The Medicine Horn - Jory Sherman   5820
Morning Time - Charles Kendall O'Neill   4743
Never No More: The Story of Rebecca Boone - Shirley
   Seifert   5730
Nick of the Woods; or, The Jibbenainosay - Robert
   Montgomery Bird   505
None Shall Look Back - Caroline Gordon   2478
Panther in the Sky - James Alexander Thom   6234
Raccoon John Smith - Louis Cochran   1145
Reckon with the River - Clark McMeekin   4292
Riders of the Long Road - Stephen E. Bransford   649
The Seekers - John Jakes   3153
Show Me a Land - Clark McMeekin   4293
Sing One Song - Helen Topping Miller   4394
A Story of Deep Delight - Thomas McNamee   4305
Tennessee Smith - James E. Hitt   2957
That Far Paradise - Gene Markey   4088
They Had a Glory - Davenport Steward   6018
The Three Lives of Elizabeth - Shirley Seifert   5735
The Twilighters - Noel M. Loomis   3894
Tyrone of Kentucky - Clark McMeekin   4294
Viola Gwyn - George Barr McCutcheon   4258
The Way to Fort Pillow - James Sherburne   5807
When the War Is Over - Stephen Becker   408
Wild Horizon - F. van Wyck Mason   4164

Berea
Hacey Miller - James Sherburne   5805

Boonesborough
The Court Martial of Daniel Boone - Allen W.
   Eckert   1840
Kentucky Stand - Jere Hungerford Wheelwright   6670
Oh, Kentucky! - Betty Layman Receveur   5284

Bowling Green
Peace at Bowling Green - Alfred Leland Crabb   1405

Green River
Run Me a River - Janice Holt Giles   2415

Harrodsburg
The Great Meadow - Elizabeth Madox Roberts   5378

Lexington
Hacey Miller - James Sherburne   5805
In the Season of the Wild Rose - Clara Rising   5347

Louisburg
The Invincibles - Carter A. Vaughan   6436

Louisville
City of the Flags - Clark McMeekin   4290
The Fairbrothers - Clark McMeekin   4291
Mr. Audubon's Lucy - Lucy Kennedy   3419
Scarlet Feather - Dale Van Every   6409

LOUISIANA

Atala - Francois Rene de Chateaubriand   1008
The Autobiography of Miss Jane Pittman - Ernest J.
   Gaines   2270
Benton's Row - Frank Yerby   6908
Blue Camellia - Frances Parkinson Keyes   3477
The Coat I Wore - Lucile Finlay   2090
Deep Summer - Gwen Bristow   696
The Handsome Road - Gwen Bristow   697
Hard on the Road - Barbara Moore   4440
High Towers - Thomas B. Costain   1366
The Horse Soldiers - Harold Sinclair   5862
The Iron Mistress - Paul I. Wellman   6618
Kingdom Coming - Roark Bradford   622
Masque of Jade - Emma Merritt   4344
Song of the Bayou - Elinor Lynley   3936
Steamboat Gothic - Frances Parkinson Keyes   3481
Tempered Blade - Monte Barrett   352
The Terrible Teague Bunch - Gary Jennings   3197
Thief of My Heart - Rexanne Becnel   410
Twilight of the Dawn - Elizabeth Nell Dubus   1752

Mississippi Delta
Bayou - Pamela Jekel   3183

New Orleans
All God's Children - Alston Anderson   136
Allegheny Captive - Caroline Bourne   591
An American, Sir - Corwin Root   5459
Angel of the Delta - Edward Francis Murphy   4521
Bagatelle - Maurice Denuziere   1613
Band of Angels - Robert Penn Warren   6572
Bayou - Pamela Jekel   3183
The Bayou Road - Mignon G. Eberhart   1832
Beloved - Vina Delmar   1599
The Big Family - Vina Delmar   1600
Black Ivory - Polan Banks   292
Blood & Dreams - Leslie Waller   6543
A Bride for New Orleans - Edward Francis
   Murphy   4522
By the Dim Lamps - Nathan Schachner   5630
Cajun - Elizabeth Nell Dubus   1751
Captain Rebel - Frank Yerby   6910
The Catherine - Robert S. MacDonald   3980
The Chess Player: A Novel of New Orleans and Paris
   - Frances Parkinson Keyes   3478
Clear for Action! - Noel B. Gerson   2362
Cockades: A Romance - Meade Minnigerode   4412
Coming through Slaughter - Michael Ondaatje   4736
Concert Grand - Howard Breslin   665
A Connecticut Yankee in Criminal Court - Peter J.
   Heck   2814
*The Corsair: A Biographical Novel of Jean Lafitte,
   Hero of the Battle of New Orleans* - Madeleine
   Fabiola Kent   3444
Creole Dusk - Walter Adolphe Roberts   5392
Crescent City - Belva Plain   5078

La Dame De Sainte Hermine - Grace King   3485
Dear Lily - Malcolm W. Greenough Jr.   2575
Dreams of Gold - Lewis Orde   4748
Drum - Kyle Onstott   4744
Eden - Julie Ellis   1918
Elixir of Life - A.E. Cowdrey   1392
Fairoaks - Frank Yerby   6915
The Fallon Pride - Reagan O'Neal   4742
Father of Waters - Donald Clayton Porter   5118
The Feast of All Saints - Anne Rice   5314
Flames of Empire - Peter Bourne   594
Flash for Freedom - George MacDonald Fraser   2203
Floodtide - Frank Yerby   6916
The Foxes of Harrow - Frank Yerby   6917
The Girl From Storyville: A Victorian Novel - Frank
   Yerby   6919
The Golden Circle - John Edward Ames   125
The Grandissimes - George W. Cable   842
The Great Steamboat Race - John Brunner   736
Hearts of Hickory - John Trotwood Moore   4442
Iron Ships, Iron Men - Christopher Nicole   4616
Longleaf - Rose Brock   701
Louisiana! - Dana Fuller Ross   5478
Louisiana Purchase - A.E. Hotchner   3039
Madame Castel's Lodger - Frances Parkinson
   Keyes   3480
Magnificent Destiny - Paul I. Wellman   6619
Marcel Armand - Sallie Bell   424
Mignon - James M. Cain   845
Mississippi Belle - Clements Ripley   5346
Mr. Audubon's Lucy - Lucy Kennedy   3419
New Orleans Legacy - Alexandra Ripley   5341
*New Orleans Woman: A Biographical Novel of Myra
   Clark Gaines* - Harnett T. Kane   3355
The Notorious Angel - Patricia Maxwell   4201
On the Long Tide - Laura Krey   3555
Papa La-Bas - John Dickson Carr   914
The Passionate Rebel - Frank G. Slaughter   5894
Pathway to the Stars - Harnett T. Kane   3356
Pelican Coast - Alan Le May   3690
*Perilous Journey: A Tale of the Mississippi River and
   the Natchez Trace* - Clifford Sublette   6109
Proud New Flags - F. van Wyck Mason   4156
Raintree County - Ross Lockridge Jr.   3827
The Rake and the Hussy - Robert W. Chambers   981
The River Devils - Carter A. Vaughan   6437
Royal Street - Walter Adolphe Roberts   5393
Runaway - Heather Graham   2519
Saratoga Trunk - Edna Ferber   2062
Savage Oaks - Julie Ellis   1924
Sea Change - Alison McLeay   4287
Serpent and Staff - Frank Yerby   6927
Show Boat - Edna Ferber   2063
Star in the Rigging: A Novel of the Texas Navy -
   Garland Roark   5358
Storyville - Lois Battle   377
The Stuart Women - Matt Braun   652
Tennessee Hazard - Maristan Chapman   994
This Willing Passion - Patricia Cloud   1132
Treasure Mountain - Louis L'Amour   3631
The Unconquered - Ben Ames Williams   6768
The Vixens - Frank Yerby   6929
Voodoo Dreams: A Novel of Marie Laveau - Jewell
   Parker Rhodes   5310
The Voyagers - Dale Van Every   6412
The Walk into Morning - Mildred Barger
   Herschler   2867
Walt Whitman's Secret - Ben Aronin   196
Wild Is the River - Louis Bromfield   704

Shreveport
And Wait for the Night - John William
   Corrington   1352

MAINE

American Captain - Edison Marshall   4101
As Runs the Glass - Evan John David   1502
Come Spring - Ben Ames Williams   6764

The Countess Angelique - Sergeanne Golon 2472
Dear Lily - Malcolm W. Greenough Jr. 2575
A Fair Wind Home - Ruth Moore 4443
Hearts and Bones - Margaret Lawrence 3685
Here I Stay - Elizabeth Coatsworth 1138
The Highwayman - Noel B. Gerson 2372
Indian Brother - Hubert Coryell 1354
Jonathan Dearborn: A Novel of the War of 1812 -
  Willard Wallace 6540
Log Cabin Noble - F. van Wyck Mason 4153
No Other Place - John Gould 2497
The Temptation of Angelique - Sergeanne
  Golon 2473
Time out of Mind - Rachel Field 2081
Tomorrow the Harvest - Viola Paradise 4789
Trail-Makers of the Middle Border - Hamlin
  Garland 2296
The World of Jennie G. - Elisabeth Ogilvie 4696

Abenaki Country
Arundel - Kenneth Roberts 5383

Arundel
Arundel - Kenneth Roberts 5383

Bagaduce
East to Bagaduce - Willard Wallace 6539

Bar Harbor
The House of Five Talents - Louis Auchincloss 231
The Magic Ship - Sandra Paretti 4791

Goldsboro
Angelique in Love - Sergeanne Golon 2470

Penobscot County
Blue Hurricane - F. van Wyck Mason 4146

Tranquility
Tide-Rode - Adelyn Bushnell 813

Whittier
Jennie Glenroy - Elisabeth Ogilvie 4695

MARYLAND

Action at Aquila - Hervey Allen 97
The Bloody Ground - Bernard Cornwell 1334
By Antietam Creek - Don Robertson 5398
Heart in Pilgrimage - Evelyn Eaton 1827
Kentucky Stand - Jere Hungerford Wheelwright 6670
Sassafras - Jack Matthews 4193
Scarlet Ribbons - Judith E. French 2224
A Season of Swans - Celeste De Blasis 1548
Swan's Chance - Celeste De Blasis 1549
Wild Swan - Celeste De Blasis 1550
A Woman Called Moses - Marcy Moran
  Heidish 2821
*Woman with a Sword: The Biographical Novel of
  Anna Ella Carroll of Maryland* - Hollister
  Noble 4632

Annapolis
Annapolis - William Martin 4137
Freedom's Way - Theodora McCormick Du
  Bois 1742
My Love, My Enemy - Jan Cox Speas 5958

Baltimore
The Amazing Mrs. Bonaparte - Harnett T.
  Kane 3351
Green Rose of Furley - Helen C. Barney 334
Intrigue in Baltimore - Janet Whitney 6715
The Lighthouse at the End of the World - Stephen
  Marlowe 4095
Miracles - Marcy Moran Heidish 2818
My Dear Cousin - Peggy Hoffmann 2977
*My Savage Muse: The Story of My Life: Edgar Allan
  Poe, an Imaginative Work* - Bernhardt J.
  Hurwood 3087
Proud New Flags - F. van Wyck Mason 4156
The Raven - Chancellor Williams 6769

The Sea Eagles - John Edward Jennings 3206
Very Young Mrs. Poe - Cothburn O'Neal 4740

Chesapeake Bay
Night Storm - Catherine Coulter 1378

Eastern Shore
Crimson Is the Eastern Shore - Don Tracy 6308

Sharpsburg
And One Wore Gray - Heather Graham 2515

MASSACHUSETTS

Banners Against the Wind - John Edward
  Jennings 3198
For Love and Honor - Antonia Van-Loon 6423
The General's Lady - Esther Forbes 2156
If a Lion Could Talk - Mildred Walker 6532
Katherine - Antonia Van-Loon 6425
Major Stepton's War - Matthew Vaughan 6445
Massachusetts: A Novel - Nancy Zaroulis 6956
Miss Lizzie - Walter Satterthwait 5608
The Sprig of Hemlock: A Novel about Shays' Rebellion
  - Robert Muir 4509
Those Who Love - Irving Stone 6064
Whittling Boy: The Story of Eli Whitney - Roger
  Burlingame 789

Amherst
Come Slowly Eden: A Novel about Emily Dickinson -
  Laura Benet 440
The Diary of Emily Dickinson: A Novel - Jamie
  Fuller 2255
The Hesitant Heart - Anne Edwards 1882
I Never Came to You in White - Judith Farr 2014

Beverly
The Pepper Tree - John Edward Jennings 3203

Boston
Affairs of Love - Nicola Thorne 6272
*Alice and Edith: A Biographical Novel of the Two
  Wives of Theodore Roosevelt* - Dorothy Clarke
  Wilson 6798
An American, Sir - Corwin Root 5459
The Americans - John Jakes 3143
Back Bay - William Martin 4138
Birthright - Robert E. Wall 6533
The Brahmins - Eileen Lottman 3901
Bride of Liberty - Frank Yerby 6909
Cannon's Call - Adam Rutledge 5537
The Centurion - Jan de Hartog 2762
China Saga - C.Y. Lee 3706
Death of a Dancing Lady - Ray Harrison 2739
Diana Stair - Floyd Dell 1594
The Dream Seekers - Stephen Longstreet 3884
The Drums of April - Charles Mergendahl 4340
Eagle in the Sky - F. van Wyck Mason 4149
Fair Wind to Java - Garland Roark 5354
Hacey Miller - James Sherburne 5805
Here Comes a Candle - Jane Aiken Hodge 2964
The Holder of the World - Bharati Mukherjee 4510
I Swear by Apollo - Agatha Young 6939
Jeremiah Martin: A Revolutionary War Novel - Robert
  H. Fowler 2191
The Lady and the Deep Blue Sea - Garland
  Roark 5356
The Last Waltz - Nancy Zaroulis 6955
Mamigon - Jack Hashian 2772
Marblehead - Joan Thompson 6267
McKay's Bees - Thomas McMahon 4289
Murder at Fenway Park - Troy Soos 5948
My Pride, My Folly - Suzanne Butler 830
Oliver Wiswell - Kenneth Roberts 5389
*The Passion of Sacco and Vanzetti: A New England
  Legend* - Howard Fast 2040
Pinto and Sons - Leslie Epstein 1947
Portrait of a Scoundrel - Nathaniel Benchley 438
Portrait of Emma - Lillian Cheatham 1010
Proceed, Sergeant Lamb - Robert Graves 2550

A Prologue to Love - Taylor Caldwell 862
Promises to Keep - Jocelyn Stirling 6051
Rainbow in the Royals - Garland Roark 5357
The Rebels - John Jakes 3152
The Regulators - William Degenhard 1580
Return to Treasure Island - Denis Judd 3318
The Rising of the Moon - William Martin 4140
Rivers of Glory - F. van Wyck Mason 4158
The Seekers - John Jakes 3153
Shaman - Noah Gordon 2483
The Sin of the Prophet - Truman Nelson 4582
The Sleep of Life - Richard Gordon 2486
Success to the Brave - Alexander Kent 3441
They Were Dreamers - James F. Murphy Jr. 4525
Time in Its Flight - Susan Fromberg Schaeffer 5636
Trumpet to Arms - Bruce Lancaster 3647
Wagons West - Leslie Turner White 6692
The Winthrop Covenant - Louis Auchincloss 235

Cape Cod
Cape Cod - William Martin 4139
Jewel of the Sea - Ellen Argo 185
The New Hope - Joseph C. Lincoln 3784
The Private Adventures of Captain Shaw - Edith
  Shay 5783
Storm Signals - Joseph C. Lincoln 3785
This Is the House - Deborah Hill 2921
The Yankee Girl - Ellen Argo 186

Concord
Listen for the Voices - Anne Colver 1220
Trumpet to Arms - Bruce Lancaster 3647

Fall River
Avery's Knot - Mary Cable 843
The Fall River Line - Daoma Winston 6824
Lizzie - Evan Hunter 3083
Mills of the Gods - Daoma Winston 6828
*The Tragedy at Tinkerton: An Historical Novel of
  Murder* - Raymond Paul 4844

Holyoke
The Delusson Family - Jacques Ducharme 1753

Lowell
Call the Darkness Light - Nancy Zaroulis 6954
Emmeline - Judith Rossner 5507

Marblehead
Marblehead - Joan Thompson 6267

Martha's Vineyard
Antonietta - John Hersey 2868
Don't Tread on Me - Walter Karig 3366
Ho, the Fair Wind - I.A.R. Wylie 6889

Nantucket
The Beckoning Road - Caroline Snedeker 5934
Captain Paul - Edward Ellsberg 1930
Harpoon in Eden - F. van Wyck Mason 4152
The Jonah Man - Henry Carlisle 895
Masts to Spear the Stars - Stephen Longstreet 3889
Thread of Scarlet - Ben Ames Williams 6767

New Bedford
Abigail - Joan Druett 1721
Diamond Head - Houston Branch 647
Lizzie - Evan Hunter 3083
Lizzie Borden - Elizabeth Engstrom 1944
The Robber Baroness - William Kendall
  Clarke 1097
Storm Tide - Allan R. Bosworth 590
Those the Sun Has Loved - Rose Jourdain 3309

Oldtown
Oldtown Folks - Harriet Beecher Stowe 6072

Plymouth
Remembrance Rock - Carl Sandburg 5583

Salem
Java Head - Joseph Hergesheimer 2854
The Running of the Tide - Esther Forbes 2160

The Salem Frigate - John Edward Jennings 3205
Tall Ships to Cathay - Helen Augur 240
Yankee Pasha - Edison Marshall 4115

Wendover
Young Men See Visions - Mary Mian 4357

Worcester
The Regulators - William Degenhard 1580

MICHIGAN

Born Strangers - Helen Topping Miller 4384
The Captives - Don Wright 6878
Comes an Echo on the Breeze - Edward J.
  Ryan 5542
Gabriel's Search - Della Lutes 3927
The Long Night - Andrew Lytle 3945
Mad Dog - Jack Kelly 3401
Panther in the Sky - James Alexander Thom 6234
Preacher on Horseback - Cecile Hulse
  Matschat 4186

Battle Creek
The Road to Wellville - T. Coraghessan Boyle 618

Detroit
The Forbidden Ground - Neil Harmon
  Swanson 6138
Fortress Fury - Carter A. Vaughan 6435
Hatchet in the Sky - Margaret Cooper Gay 2328
Hawk of Detroit - Arthur Pound 5145
The Loon Feather - Iola Fuller 2253
My Blood and My Treasure - Mary Schumann 5674
Powder Mission - Herbert Stover 6070
Silent Drums - Mike Roarke 5361
Trumpet in the Wilderness - Robert S. Harper 2717
Whiskey River - Loren D. Estleman 1981

Mackinac
The Loon Feather - Iola Fuller 2253

Mackinac Island
Black Feather - Harold Titus 6283
Bright Journey - August Derleth 1614
The Citadel of the Lakes - Myron David Orr 4754
Mission to Mackinac - Myron David Orr 4755

Michilimackinac
Visions of a Heart - Emily Carmichael 899

Monroe
Libbie - Judy Alter 121

Saginaw Valley
Log Jam - Leslie Turner White 6684

Upper Peninsula
Fire on the Wind - David Garth 2304

MIDWEST

The Able McLaughlins - Margaret Wilson 6812
*The Assassination of Jesse James by the Coward
  Robert Ford* - Ron Hansen 2680
Beulah Land - Harold Lenoir Davis 1520
Children of God - Vardis Fisher 2106
Creek Mary's Blood - Dee Brown 712
Darktown Strutters - Wesley Brown 732
The Far Down - Elizabeth Corbett 1321
The Great Hunger - Johan Bojer 562
Kings Row - Henry Bellamann 428
Miss Bishop - Bess Streeter Aldrich 71
Mr. Vertigo - Paul Auster 244
Orphan Train - James Magnuson 4029
The Plums Hang High - Gertrude E. Finney 2091
Strange Adventure of Jonathan Drew - Christopher
  Ward 6562
The Warriors - John Jakes 3155

MINNESOTA

Big Ember - Edward Havill 2778
The Black Angels - Maude Hart Lovelace 3902
A Circle of Trees - Dana Faralla 2012
Gentlemen From England - Maude Hart
  Lovelace 3905
Giants in the Earth - O.E. Rolvaag 5434
The God-Seeker - Sinclair Lewis 3763
Iron Land - Dorothy Ogley 4697
Last Letter Home - Vilhelm Moberg 4423
The Manly-Hearted Woman - Frederick F.
  Manfred 4057
The Settlers - Vilhelm Moberg 4424
Sherlock Holmes and the Red Demon - Larry
  Millett 4404
Spoon - John Christgau 1074
Swift Rivers - Cornelia Meigs 4328
Unto a Good Land - Vilhelm Moberg 4425

Fort Snelling
Early Candlelight - Maude Hart Lovelace 3904

Minneapolis
The Land Was Ours: A Novel of the Great Plains -
  Charles W. Bailey 266

St. Paul
Saint Mudd - Steve Thayer 6218

MISSISSIPPI

Cease Firing - Mary Johnston 3230
The Cup, the Blade or the Gun - Mignon G.
  Eberhart 1833
Daughter of Strangers - Elizabeth Boatwright
  Coker 1164
Double Moscadine - Frances Gaither 2271
Heaven Trees - Stark Young 6943
The Horse Soldiers - Harold Sinclair 5862
The Keeper of the House - Harry Harrison
  Kroll 3558
Mingo Dabney - James H. Street 6078
The Mississippi Run - Paul Darcy Boles 565
No Bugles Blow - Bruce Lancaster 3642
Powder Mission - Herbert Stover 6070
The Red Cock Crows - Frances Gaither 2272
Rommel and the Rebel - Lawrence Wells 6622
Tomorrow We Reap - James H. Street 6081
The Unvanquished - William Faulkner 2050

Cold Forks
The House in Ruins - Robert S. Weekley 6595

Jefferson
Absalom, Absalom! - William Faulkner 2049

Jones County
Tap Roots - James H. Street 6080

Jordan County
Jordan County: A Landscape in Narrative - Shelby
  Foote 2152

Natchez
Beulah Land - Harold Lenoir Davis 1520
Bride of Fortune - Harnett T. Kane 3352
By Valour and Arms - James H. Street 6076
The Coat I Wore - Lucile Finlay 2090
*A Darkness at Ingraham's Crest: A Tale of the
  Slaveholding South* - Frank Yerby 6912
Flight From Avatchez - Frank G. Slaughter 5887
Floodtide - Frank Yerby 6916
Natchez: A Novel of the Deep South - Pamela
  Jekel 3186
Oh, Promised Land - James H. Street 6079
The Proud Way - Shirley Seifert 5731
So Red the Rose - Stark Young 6944

Natchez Trace
Flintlock - Jason Manning 4073

*Perilous Journey: A Tale of the Mississippi River and
  the Natchez Trace* - Clifford Sublette 6109
The Robber Bridegroom - Eudora Welty 6623
Rogues' Company: A Novel of John Murrell - Harry
  Harrison Kroll 3559
Sow the Seeds of Hemp - Gary Jennings 3195
The Twilighters - Noel M. Loomis 3894

Vicksburg
And Wait for the Night - John William
  Corrington 1352
The Blue and the Gray - John Leekley 3713
By Valour and Arms - James H. Street 6076
Grant's War - Ted Jones 3297
Griffin's Way - Frank Yerby 6922
A Hundred Hills - Howard Breslin 667
In a Dark Garden - Frank G. Slaughter 5891
*Unvexed to the Sea: A Novel of the Vicksburg
  Campaign* - Gerry Morrison 4484

Yazoo River
The Wild Yazoo - John Myers 4546

MISSISSIPPI RIVER

Allegheny Captive - Caroline Bourne 591
Benjy Boone - Maurice Dolbier 1687
Blue Hurricane - F. van Wyck Mason 4146
By Valour and Arms - James H. Street 6076
Child of the Snapping Turtle, Mike Fink - Julian Lee
  Rayford 5256
Dance on the Wind - Terry C. Johnston 3249
Death on the Mississippi - Peter J. Heck 2815
An Embarrassment of Riches - James Howard
  Kunstler 3565
Fevre Dream - George R.R. Martin 4131
The Great Steamboat Race - John Brunner 736
A Journey to Matecumbe - Robert Lewis
  Taylor 6188
Passage to Natchez - Cameron Judd 3316
*Perilous Journey: A Tale of the Mississippi River and
  the Natchez Trace* - Clifford Sublette 6109
Pull Down to New Orleans - Zachary Ball 283
The River Devils - Carter A. Vaughan 6437
The River Witch - Margerie McIntyre 4278
The Robber Bridegroom - Eudora Welty 6623
La Salle - John Vernon 6458
The Shining Trail - Iola Fuller 2254
Show Boat - Edna Ferber 2063
Steamboat Gothic - Frances Parkinson Keyes 3481
Swift Rivers - Cornelia Meigs 4328
This Land Is Ours - Louis Zara 6953
Touched with Fire - John William Tebbel 6195
The Treasure of the Chisos - John H. Culp 1446
Twilight of Empire - Allen W. Eckert 1846
The Voyagers - Dale Van Every 6412
War Drums - Donald Clayton Porter 5133
West of the River - Charlton Laird 3591

MISSOURI

The Amulet - Hal Borland 582
And Never Yield - Elinor Pryor 5204
Another Spring - Loula Grace Erdman 1948
Belle Starr - Deborah Camp 870
The Big Sky - A.B. Guthrie Jr. 2624
Bound Girl - Everett Webber 6591
Bugle in the Wilderness - John Burress 805
By Dim and Flashing Lamps - Alan Le May 3689
Confessions of Johnny Ringo - Geoff Aggeler 40
The Corinthians - Nicholas E. Wyckoff 6888
The Cowboys - William Dale Jennings 3211
Cry of the Hawk - Terry C. Johnston 3248
Death of a Legend - Will Henry 2840
Enslaved - Ron Burns 801
The Far Journey - Loula Grace Erdman 1950
First the Blade - May Miller 4400
The Further Adventures of Huckleberry Finn - Greg
  Matthews 4189

Gone to Texas - Forrest Carter   945
The Holy Warrior - Gilbert Morris   4462
If a Lion Could Talk - Mildred Walker   6532
Journey by the River - John Prescott   5173
Killdeer Mountain - Dee Brown   713
King of the Mountain - David Thompson   6255
Mamaw - Susan Dodd   1663
Maximilian's Gold - Jane Barry   359
No Resting Place - William Humphrey   3079
Passage Home - Alison McLeay   4286
So Free We Seem - Helen Todd   6286
The Three Lives of Elizabeth - Shirley Seifert   5735
Timothy Larkin - Jane Hutchens   3089
The Trembling Earth - Dale Van Every   6411
Vision of the Eagle - Kay L. McDonald   4263
Wagons West - Leslie Turner White   6692
The Wayfarer - Shirley Seifert   5738
While Angels Dance - Ralph W. Cotton   1372
The White Slave - Fanny Howe   3059

Chanta Creek
Ride of the Panther - Kerry Newcomb   4591

Independence
Fairacres - Gladys Waters   6579
Independence! - Dana Fuller Ross   5476
Nebraska! - Dana Fuller Ross   5480
The Turquoise Trail - Shirley Seifert   5736
The Vision Is Fulfilled - Kay L. McDonald   4262

Kansas City
The Assassination of Jesse James by the Coward Robert Ford - Ron Hansen   2680
The Dollar Gold Piece - Virginia Swain   6134
The Long Trail North - Robert J. Conley   1245
Pretty Boy Floyd - Larry McMurtry   4299

New Madrid
Fury in the Earth: A Novel of the New Madrid Earthquake - Harry Harrison Kroll   3557

St. Joseph
The Assassination of Jesse James by the Coward Robert Ford - Ron Hansen   2680

St. Louis
Bighorn Legacy - W. Michael Gear   2332
Black-Eyed Susan - Deborah Camp   871
Blue Hurricane - F. van Wyck Mason   4146
Blue Russell - Will Bryant   738
Buffalo Palace - Terry C. Johnston   3245
Colfax - Robert J. Conley   1239
The Crisis - Winston Churchill   1079
Dance on the Wind - Terry C. Johnston   3249
Distant Trails - Bill Gulick   2612
Drumm's War - Bill Bragg   638
Eagles of Destiny - Jory Sherman   5817
Farewell the Stranger - Saliee O'Brien   4682
Fielder's Choice - Rick Norman   4646
Heart of the Country - Greg Matthews   4190
High Country - Jason Manning   4075
The Iron Curtain - Robert Vaughan   6447
Kings of the Missouri - Hugh Pendexter   4895
Louisiana Purchase - A.E. Hotchner   3039
The Man of the Storm - Ethel Hueston   3069
The Medicine Horn - Jory Sherman   5820
The Medicine Man - Shirley Seifert   5729
The Morning River - W. Michael Gear   2333
Mr. Vertigo - Paul Auster   244
Murder at Fenway Park - Troy Soos   5948
The Mysterious Death of Meriwether Lewis - Ron Burns   802
One-Eyed Dream - Terry C. Johnston   3253
Over There - Robert Vaughan   6449
Plume Rouge: A Novel of the Pathfinders - John Upton Terrell   6203
Pretty Boy Floyd - Larry McMurtry   4299
Quitting Time - Robert J. Conley   1249
River of Sky - Karen Harper   2713
Rivers West - Louis L'Amour   3626
Roman - Douglas C. Jones   3281

Swift Rivers - Cornelia Meigs   4328
This Savage Race - Douglas C. Jones   3285
Those Who Go Against the Current - Shirley Seifert   5734
The Two Medicine River - Richard S. Wheeler   6663
Waters of the Wilderness - Shirley Seifert   5737

MONTANA

The Big Lonesome - Will Bryant   737
Black Sun - Terry C. Johnston   3242
Blood Song - Terry C. Johnston   3243
A Cold Day in Hell - Terry C. Johnston   3247
The Dice of God - Hoffman Birney   507
Eli's Road - Lucas Webb   6589
The Fleet Rabble: A Novel of the Nez Perce War - Frank Borden Hanes   2675
From Where the Sun Now Stands - Will Henry   2841
High Freedom - Earl Murray   4530
The High Rocks - Loren D. Estleman   1973
I Am Lidian - Naomi Lane Babson   253
In the Season of the Sun - Kerry Newcomb   4590
Lonesome Dove - Larry McMurtry   4298
Montana Hitch - Richard S. Wheeler   6661
Montana Woman - Rosanne Bittner   513
Richard Lamb - Richard S. Wheeler   6662
Ride with Me, Mariah Montana - Ivan Doig   1684
A Roaring in the Wind - Robert Lewis Taylor   6191
Sand in the Wind - Kathleen O'Neal Gear   2329
A Shadow of Eagles - Jane Barry   360
The Silver Mountain - Dan Cushman   1453
Sitting Bull - Bill Dugan   1760
Song of the Meadowlark - John A. Sanford   5594
That Callahan Spunk! - Francis Ames   124
These Thousand Hills - A.B. Guthrie Jr.   2627
This Land Is Mine - Frances Casey Kerns   3470
Thunder in the Dawn - Earl Murray   4532
Trumpet on the Land - Terry C. Johnston   3260
Wanderers Eastward, Wanderers West - Kathleen Winsor   6823
Warhorse - John Cunningham   1451
Where the River Runs - Richard S. Wheeler   6664
The White Land - William Dieter   1643
Winter Grass - Richard S. Wheeler   6665
The Winter War - William Wister Haines   2640
The Wounded Yankee - Gilbert Morris   4475
The Yellowstone - Winfred Blevins   549

Arfive
Arfive - A.B. Guthrie Jr.   2623
The Last Valley - A.B. Guthrie Jr.   2626

Bannack
What Law There Was - Al Dempsey   1609

Breen
Murdock's Law - Loren D. Estleman   1975

Butte
Glittering Hill - Clyde Francis Murphy   4520

English Creek
Dancing at the Rascal Fair - Ivan Doig   1682
English Creek - Ivan Doig   1683

Fort C.F. Smith
Red Cloud's Revenge - Terry C. Johnston   3255

Fort Shaw
Montana! - Dana Fuller Ross   5479

Helena
The Last Days of Horse-Shy Halloran - Bill Pronzini   5203
The Stranglers - Loren D. Estleman   1978

Little Bighorn River
Chief of Scouts - Don Bendell   439
Custer Passed Our Way - Fred S. Kaufman   3370
The Last Stand: A Novel about George Armstrong Custer and the Indians of the Plains - Edwin P. Hoyt   3061

A Road We Do Not Know: A Novel of Custer at the Little Bighorn - Frederick J. Chiaventone   1057
Seize the Sky - Terry C. Johnston   3256

Medicine Lodge
Crimson Creek: A Novel of the Early West - Robert McCraig   4228

Powder River
The Powder River - Winfred Blevins   546

Rocky Mountains
The Far Tribes - Richard S. Wheeler   6658

Rosebud River
Reap the Whirlwind - Terry C. Johnston   3254

Three Forks
High Country - Jason Manning   4075
The High Missouri - Winfred Blevins   545

Virginia City
Me and Gallagher - Jack Farris   2023

Yellowstone River
Lord Grizzly - Frederick F. Manfred   4056

NEBRASKA

The Homesman - Glendon Swarthout   6143
The Land Was Ours: A Novel of the Great Plains - Charles W. Bailey   266
A Lantern in Her Hand - Bess Streeter Aldrich   69
The Last Frontier - Howard Fast   2036
Megan - Kathleen Magill   4028
Nebraska! - Dana Fuller Ross   5480
Nebraska Coast - Clyde Brion Davis   1516
Rawhider - Gene Shelton   5802
Sand in the Wind - Kathleen O'Neal Gear   2329
Son of the Gamblin' Man: The Youth of an Artist - Mari Sandoz   5593
Spring Came on Forever - Bess Streeter Aldrich   73
The Trail to Ogallala - Benjamin Capps   889
The Union Belle - Gilbert Morris   4473

Beecher's Island
The Stalkers - Terry C. Johnston   3259

Fort Abraham Lincoln
Seize the Sky - Terry C. Johnston   3256

Great Plains
One Smart Indian - Robert J. Seidman   5722

Lincoln
The War Train: A Novel of 1916 - Brown Meggs   4324

North Platte River
Miss Morissa: Doctor of the Gold Trail - Mari Sandoz   5592

Ogalalla
Warhorse - John Cunningham   1451

Omaha
The Fortune Road - James McCague   4217
The Jewelled Spur - Gilbert Morris   4465
The Lieutenant's Lady - Bess Streeter Aldrich   70

Republican River
Cry of the Hawk - Terry C. Johnston   3248

NEVADA

Goldfield - Richard S. Wheeler   6660
The Ox-Bow Incident - Walter Van Tilburg Clark   1096
Paiute - Sessions S. Wheeler   6666

Hoover Dam
And the Desert Shall Bloom - Phyllis Barber   299

Virginia City
Birthright - Phillip Finch 2087
Borrasca - Octavus Roy Cohen 1160
City of Illusion - Vardis Fisher 2107
The Family of Women - Richard Peck 4883
Nevada! - Dana Fuller Ross 5481
Oregon Legacy - Dana Fuller Ross 5485
Sister Wives - Cleo Jones 3270

NEW ENGLAND

Big River, Big Man - Thomas William Duncan 1786
Conjuror's Journal - Frances L. Shine 5826
Faith and Honor - Robin Maderich 4025
The Hospital - Agatha Young 6938
Morning Time - Charles Kendall O'Neill 4743
The New England Story - Henry Beetle Hough 3046
Rainbow on the Road - Esther Forbes 2159
The Rector of Justin - Louis Auchincloss 233
Sea Jade - Phyllis A. Whitney 6717
The Sea Stands Watch - Helen Parker Mudgett 4507
Strange Adventure of Jonathan Drew - Christopher Ward 6562
Wide Is the Water - Jane Aiken Hodge 2973

NEW HAMPSHIRE

Boy with a Pack - Stephen Warren Meader 4319
Hue and Cry - Elizabeth Yates 6907
Judith Duchesne - Lynda Sargent 5605
Memories of the Ford Administration - John Updike 6391
The Nancy Flyer - Ernest Poole 5091
The Pilgrim Soul - Anne Miller Downes 1711

Portsmouth
The Shadow and the Glory - John Edward Jennings 3207

NEW JERSEY

Dark Rider - Louis Zara 6950
I, Roberta - Elizabeth Gray Vining 6501
Janice Meredith - Paul Leicester Ford 2166
The Laughing Stranger - Vina Delmar 1601
Look Away - Harold Coyle 1395
Man From Mt. Vernon - Burke Boyce 607
Morning in America - Willard Wiener 6741
The Proud and the Free - Howard Fast 2042
The Shadow and the Glory - John Edward Jennings 3207
The Spy: A Tale of the Neutral Ground - James Fenimore Cooper 1310
Stolen Away - Max Allan Collins 1213
The Tontine - Thomas B. Costain 1371
Tory Tavern - Henry Barnard Safford 5559
Trumpets at Dawn - Cyril Harris 2719

Bordentown
Rogers' Folly - Albert E. Idell 3102

Camden
Dawn's Early Light - Elswyth Thane 6215

Hoboken
The Tragedy at Tinkerton: An Historical Novel of Murder - Raymond Paul 4844

Monmouth
Conceived in Liberty - Howard Fast 2029
Farewell to Valley Forge - David Taylor 6178
Monmouth - Charles Bracelen Flood 2144
The Strong Men - John Brick 677

Morristown
Retreat and Recall - Joseph G.E. Hopkins 3029
The Traitor - Dan Sherman 5814

New Brunswick
Until the End - Harold Coyle 1396

Newark
The Secret Annie Oakley - Marcy Moran Heidish 2819

Patterson
Sam Patch: Ballad of a Jumping Man - William Getz 2390

Princeton
A Rage Against Heaven - Fred Mustard Stewart 6026
Tolbecken - Samuel Shellabarger 5798

Trenton
The Drums of Winter - Sandra Paretti 4790
Fire and the Hammer - Shirley Barker 311

NEW MEXICO

Apaches - Oakley Hall 2650
Between Earth and Sky - Karen Osborn 4758
Big River, Big Man - Thomas William Duncan 1786
Blood Brother - Elliott Arnold 190
City of Widows - Loren D. Estleman 1969
Company of Cowards - Jack Schaefer 5634
The Conquest of Don Pedro - Harvey Fergusson 2066
The Devil Gun - William Syers 6148
Drumm's War - Bill Bragg 638
The Franciscan - Forrester Blake 532
The Golden Valley - Daoma Winston 6826
Grant of Kingdom - Harvey Fergusson 2067
Kid Curry: The Life and Times of Harvey Logan and the Wild Bunch - F. Bruce Lamb 3606
The Lady - Conrad Richter 5321
Lords of the Plains - Max Crawford 1420
Many a Voyage - Loula Grace Erdman 1951
Mustang Man - Louis L'Amour 3623
Night Wind's Woman - Shirl Henke 2825
Pancho And Black Jack - Fred Bean 398
The Pride of Hannah Wade - Janet Dailey 1455
St. Agnes' Stand - Tom Eidson 1900
The Searchers - Alan Le May 3691
Season of Yellow Leaf - Douglas C. Jones 3283
Sergeant Gringo - Jack Cummings 1449
The Sky-Liners - Louis L'Amour 3629
The Southern Blade - Nelson Wolford 6844
The Spanish Bride - Walter O'Meara 4735
Tascosa Gun: The Story of Jim East - Gene Shelton 5803
Too Long at the Dance - Mike Blakely 539
El Vago - Laurence Gonzales 2474
The Valley - Clifford Irving 3114

Albuquerque
Albuquerque - Sara Orwig 4757

Arredondo
Dutch Uncle - Marilyn Durham 1815

Columbus
Chihuahua 1916 - Otis Carney 903
Last Reveille - David Morrell 4456

Fort Sumner
The Demise of Billy the Kid - Preston Lewis 3760

Lincoln County
Billy the Kid - Edwin Corle 1330
Billy the Kid: The Legend of El Chivato - Elizabeth Fackler 1994
The Demise of Billy the Kid - Preston Lewis 3760
Pistols for Hire - Nelson Coral Nye 4652
The Sons of Grady Rourke - Douglas Savage 5618
The Story of Pat Garrett and Billy the Kid - David Everitt 1987
Time for Outrage - Amelia Bean 397

Los Alamos
Beginning the World Again - Roberta Silman 5851
A Family Matter - James Roosevelt 5458
Stallion Gate - Martin Cruz Smith 5924

Pecos River
The Pecos River - Fred Bean 399

Sangre de Cristo Mountains
Bighorn Legacy - W. Michael Gear 2332

Santa Fe
Apache Autumn - Robert Skimin 5875
Daughter of Fortune - Carla Kelly 3398
Dead Man's Walk - Larry McMurtry 4297
Death Comes for the Archbishop - Willa Cather 957
Eagle in the Sun - Hoffman Birney 508
Eagles of Destiny - Jory Sherman 5817
The Great Adventure - Janice Holt Giles 2410
Jornada - Robert L. Duffus 1754
Jubilee Trail - Gwen Bristow 698
Medicine Knife - Don Coldsmith 1179
Oh, Valley Green - John H. Culp 1443
Rio Grande - Jory Sherman 5821
The Royal City - Les Savage Jr. 5621
The Scout - Harry Combs 1224
Shadows in the Dusk - John Edward Jennings 3208
Taos - Irwin R. Blacker 527
Trail from Taos - Don Coldsmith 1192
The Turquoise Trail - Shirley Seifert 5736
Voyage to Santa Fe - Janice Holt Giles 2418
War Eagles - Frank Burleson 788
The Wind Leaves No Shadow - Ruth Laughlin 3672

Santa Fe Trail
Apache Blood - David Thompson 6250

Silver City
Billy the Kid: The Legend of El Chivato - Elizabeth Fackler 1994

Staked Plains
The Goodnight Trail - Ralph Compton 1227

Taos
The Arkansas River - Jory Sherman 5816
Far Mountains - Frank O'Rourke 4752
Homecoming - Dana Fuller Ross 5474
One-Eyed Dream - Terry C. Johnston 3253
Taos - Irwin R. Blacker 527

NEW YORK

Alexander Hamilton's Wife - Alice Curtis Desmond 1623
The Arch of Stars - Clifford Lindsey Alderman 66
Artillery of Time - Chard Powers Smith 5919
The Boyds of Black River - Walter D. Edmonds 1871
Eagle in the Sky - F. van Wyck Mason 4149
Eagle of Niagara: The Story of David Harper and His Indian Captivity - John Brick 671
Eagles Where I Walk - Stephen Longstreet 3885
Erie Water - Walter D. Edmonds 1875
The Final Adversary - Gilbert Morris 4460
From the Terrace - John O'Hara 4703
A Generation of Leaves - Robert S. Bloom 552
Henry and Clara - Thomas Mallon 4042
Hidden Children - Robert W. Chambers 978
If I Never Get Back - Darryl Brock 700
I'll Storm Hell - Noel B. Gerson 2374
The Iron Chain - Jim DeFelice 1579
The Ironmaster - Anne Powers 5150
Jubilee - John Brick 672
Katherine - Antonia Van-Loon 6425
Law of the Land - Marguerite Allis 111
The Life and Times of Captain N. - Douglas Glover 2436
Light in the Clearing - Irving A. Bacheller 260
Little Red Foot - Robert W. Chambers 979
The Lure of the Falcon - Juliette Benzoni 465
Man From Mt. Vernon - Burke Boyce 607
Mariette in Ecstasy - Ron Hansen 2682
Mars' Butterfly - Henry Pleasants 5080
Mistress Nancy - Barbara Bentley 460
Morning in America - Willard Wiener 6741

Mount's Mistake - Lew McCreary 4229
Mr. Arnold - Francis Lynde 3935
Nebraska Coast - Clyde Brion Davis 1516
No Brighter Glory - Armstrong Sperry 5963
One Small Candle - Mary Linehan MacKinnon 3998
Orphan Train - James Magnuson 4029
A Peep into the 20th Century - Christopher Davis 1515
Peter Doyle - John Vernon 6457
The Raid - John Brick 673
The Rising of the Moon - Peter Berresford Ellis 1926
River's Run - Jane Ludlow Abbot 7
The Shadow in the Glass - August Derleth 1618
Storm Before Sunrise - June Wyndham Davies 1507
The Sunshine Patriot: A Novel of Benedict Arnold - Norman Partington 4822
The Unterrified - Constance Robertson 5397
Vandemark's Folly - Herbert Quick 5223
The Wide House - Taylor Caldwell 864

Adirondacks
Buttes Landing - Jean Rikhoff 5331
Loon Lake - E.L. Doctorow 1657
One of the Raymonds - Jean Rikhoff 5332
Shadows on the Long House - Mike Roarke 5360

Albany
Bright to the Wanderer - Bruce Lancaster 3638
Quinn's Book - William Kennedy 3423
Rome Haul - Walter D. Edmonds 1877

Bedford
Lucifer Land - Mildred B. Davis 1538

Brooklyn
Beecher: A Novel - Dan McCall 4218
The Great Blizzard - Albert E. Idell 3101
The Year of Our War - Gloria Goldreich 2462

Catskill Mountains
The Golden Season - Oriana Akinson 60

Coney Island
Murder at Ebbets Field - Troy Soos 5947

East Hampton
The Adventures of Jeremiah Dimon: The Novel of Old East Hampton - Everett Rattray 5255

Elmira
The Blue and the Gray - John Leekley 3713

Erie Canal
Banner by the Wayside - Samuel Hopkins Adams 28
Benjy Boone - Maurice Dolbier 1687
Chad Hanna - Walter D. Edmonds 1873
Rome Haul - Walter D. Edmonds 1877
The Wedding Journey - Walter D. Edmonds 1878

Fair Haven
Eye of the Hurricane - Fergus Reid Buckley 757

Genesee Valley
Genesee Fever - Carl Lamson Carmer 898
O Genesee - Janet O'Daniel 4688

Great South Bay
Eye of the Hurricane - Fergus Reid Buckley 757

Hudson River
Crum Elbow Folks - Percy Raymond Barnes 332

Hudson River Valley
Dragonwyck - Anya Seton 5750
The Moreland Legacy - Diana Haviland 2777
Scarborough House - Sharon Salvato 5577
Shad Run - Howard Breslin 668
Troubled Spring - John Brick 678

Hyde Park
The Hyde Park Murder - Elliott Roosevelt 5443

Lake Champlain
Rabble in Arms - Kenneth Roberts 5390

Sarton Kell - Kate Mallory 4043

Long Island
1901 - Robert Conroy 1258
The Big Stick - Lawrence Alexander 82
The Culper Spy Ring - Lynn Groh 2596
Independence! - Dana Fuller Ross 5476
The Secret Road - Bruce Lancaster 3646
Speak Softly - Lawrence Alexander 83
Tory Tavern - Henry Barnard Safford 5559
Trumpet to Arms - Bruce Lancaster 3647
Walk Like a Man - Donald Honig 3024

Madison County
Rogue's Kingdom - John Brick 676

Mohawk Valley
Preacher on Horseback - Cecile Hulse Matschat 4186

New Rochelle
Ragtime - E.L. Doctorow 1658

New York
1876: A Novel - Gore Vidal 6484
1901 - Robert Conroy 1258
The Adventure of the Stalwart Companions - H. Paul Jeffers 3177
Afterward - Catherine M. Rae 5234
Ain't Goin' to Glory - David Delman 1597
Alabama Empire - Welbourn Kelley 3392
Alice and Edith: A Biographical Novel of the Two Wives of Theodore Roosevelt - Dorothy Clarke Wilson 6798
The Alienist - Caleb Carr 907
All This, and Heaven Too - Rachel Field 2080
America, America - Elia Kazan 3380
American Falls - John Calvin Batchelor 376
The American Heiress - Dorothy Eden 1854
The Americans - John Jakes 3143
The Anatolian - Elia Kazan 3381
Anna, Ann, Annie - Thomas Trebitsch Parker 4808
Armored Giants: A Novel of the Civil War - F. van Wyck Mason 4145
The Artist - Norman Garbo 2281
Banished Children of Eve - Peter Quinn 5227
La Belle - Elizabeth Boatwright Coker 1161
The Big Freeze - Bellamy Partridge 4823
The Big Stick - Lawrence Alexander 82
Billy Bathgate - E.L. Doctorow 1656
Black Plume: The Supressed Memoirs of Edgar Allan Poe - David Madsen 4027
The Blood Countess - Andrei Codrescu 1149
The Bluestocking - David Delman 1598
The Book Class - Louis Auchincloss 228
Born with the Century - William Kinsolving 3501
The Bourlotas Fortune - Nicholas Gage 2268
Bread and Circus - Morris Renek 5303
Bride of Liberty - Frank Yerby 6909
Bridge to Brooklyn - Albert E. Idell 3099
Bridle the Wind - Julia Davis 1525
Bully! - Mark Schorr 5670
Bygones - Frank Wilkinson 6762
A Cadenza for Caruso - Barbara Paul 4834
Carolina Courage - Dana Fuller Ross 5469
Casey - Ramona Stewart 6034
Castle Barebane - Joan Aiken 43
Castle Garden - Bill Albert 63
The Celebrant - Eric Rolfe Greenberg 2572
Celebration! - Dana Fuller Ross 5470
Centennial Summer - Albert E. Idell 3100
Ceremony of the Innocent - Taylor Caldwell 852
Certain Harvest: A Novel of the Time of Peter Cooper - Ruth Adams Knight 3525
Charity Strong - Marguerite Allis 109
The Chester A. Arthur Conspiracy - William Wiegand 6740
Chicago Girls - Edith Freund 2229
A Chorus of Detectives - Barbara Paul 4835
A City Not Forsaken - Lynn Morris 4480

Coasts of Folly - Joel Williams 6784
The Copperheads - William James Blech 544
The Cortlandts of Washington Square - Janet Fairbank 2001
The Cosgrove Report - G.J.A. O'Toole 4765
The Court-Martial of George Armstrong Custer - Douglas C. Jones 3276
The Crusader - Noel B. Gerson 2364
The Culper Spy Ring - Lynn Groh 2596
Dark Rider - Louis Zara 6950
Darktown Strutters - Wesley Brown 732
The Deadly Lady of Madagascar - C.V. Terry 6206
Death on the Mississippi - Peter J. Heck 2815
Domina - Barbara Wood 6847
The Dorothy Parker Murder Case - George Baxt 384
The Dream Seekers - Stephen Longstreet 3884
Dvorak in Love - Josef Skvorecky 5881
Eagles Fly West - Edward Maddin Ainsworth 55
Ellis Island - Fred Mustard Stewart 6023
Empire: A Novel - Gore Vidal 6487
The End of the World News - Anthony Burgess 777
Ethel: The Fictional Autobiography - Tema Nason 4558
Expedition! - Dana Fuller Ross 5473
Faces in the Crowd - William Marshall 4117
Fenwick Travers and the Panama Canal - Raymond M. Saunders 5613
The Fever Called Living - Barbara Moore 4439
Flight From Fifth Avenue - Catherine M. Rae 5235
For Us the Living - Antonia Van-Loon 6424
Foreign Devils - Irvin Faust 2053
The Four Hundred - Stephen Sheppard 5804
From Time to Time - Jack Finney 2092
Funny Papers - Tom De Haven 1559
The Furies - John Jakes 3146
Glorious Morning - Julie Ellis 1919
Gold - Clarence Budington Kelland 3388
A Grand Passion - Mary Mackey 3991
The Great Blizzard - Albert E. Idell 3101
The Guernseyman - C. Northcote Parkinson 4812
The Ham Reporter - Robert J. Randisi 5251
The Hand of a Woman - Diana Brown 719
Hanover Place - Michael M. Thomas 6245
Hard Money - Clarence Budington Kelland 3389
The Healers - Henry Denker 1610
Heart in Pilgrimage - Evelyn Eaton 1827
The Heart of O. Henry - Dale Kramer 3550
The High Constable - Maan Meyers 4353
Hoopla - Harry Stein 5990
The House of Five Talents - Louis Auchincloss 231
The House on Mulberry Street - Maan Meyers 4354
The Hyde Park Murder - Elliott Roosevelt 5443
I, James Lewis - Gilbert Wolf Gabriel 2266
I Swear by Apollo - Agatha Young 6939
In a Dark Garden - Frank G. Slaughter 5891
The Jealous House - Clarence Budington Kelland 3390
Jubilee Jim and the Wizard of Wall Street - Donald Porter 5112
Jubilee Trail - Gwen Bristow 698
The Kingsbridge Plot - Maan Meyers 4355
The Last Mystery of Edgar Allan Poe - Manny Meyers 4356
The Lawless - John Jakes 3149
Leah's Journey - Gloria Goldreich 2460
Legs - William Kennedy 3422
The Lion's Way - Lewis Orde 4750
The Long Watch - Elizabeth Linington 3798
Loon Lake - E.L. Doctorow 1657
Lovelock - James McNeish 4311
Lusitania - David Butler 819
Masterpiece of Murder - Mary Kruger 3563
Maura's Dream - Joel Gross 2602
Max - Howard Fast 2038
McKensie's Hundred: A Tale of the Old Dominion - Frank Yerby 6924
Men of No Property - Dorothy Davis 1517
The Midwife - Gay Courter 1388

The Midwife's Advice - Gay Courter 1389
The Millionaire's Daughter - Dorothy Eden 1858
Miracles - Marcy Moran Heidish 2818
The Moneyman - Judith Liederman 3781
The Moreland Legacy - Diana Haviland 2777
Murder at Ebbets Field - Troy Soos 5947
Murder at Fenway Park - Troy Soos 5948
My Own Ground - Hugh Nissenson 4628
My Savage Muse: The Story of My Life: Edgar Allan Poe, an Imaginative Work - Bernhardt J. Hurwood 3087
My Theodosia - Anya Seton 5753
Nevermore - William Hjortsberg 2958
Niagara - Robert Lewis Taylor 6189
No Honeymoon for Death - Mary Kruger 3564
The Noel Coward Murder Case - George Baxt 387
Notorious Eliza - Basil Beyea 489
The Ocean Mistress - Peter French 2225
The Old Colts - Glendon Swarthout 6144
The Old Maid - Edith Wharton 6652
Oliver Wiswell - Kenneth Roberts 5389
One Smart Indian - Robert J. Seidman 5722
Our Father's House - Stephen Longstreet 3890
Paint the Wind - Cathy Cash Spellman 5960
Painted Lady: Eliza Jumel, Her Life and Times - Leonard Falkner 2009
Painted Minx - Robert W. Chambers 980
Papa and Fidel - Karl Alexander 79
The Paper Mistress - Dorothea Malm 4045
Passage West - Dallas Miller 4382
The Passion of Sacco and Vanzetti: A New England Legend - Howard Fast 2040
The Passionate Journey - Irving Stone 6061
Portrait in Brownstone - Louis Auchincloss 232
Praise at Morning - Mildred Masterson McNeilly 4310
The President's Man - Elliott Roosevelt 5455
Pride's Castle - Frank Yerby 6925
Prima Donna at Large - Barbara Paul 4838
Proceed, Sergeant Lamb - Robert Graves 2550
Ragtime - E.L. Doctorow 1658
The Raiders: A Novel of the Civil War at Sea - Willard Wallace 6541
Raintree County - Ross Lockridge Jr. 3827
The Raven - Chancellor Williams 6769
The Rebel and the Turncoat - Malcolm Decker 1576
The Reluctant Bridegroom - Gilbert Morris 4467
Retreat and Recall - Joseph G.E. Hopkins 3029
River to the West: A Novel of the Astor Adventure - John Edward Jennings 3204
Rivington Street - Meredith Tax 6175
The Robber Baroness - William Kendall Clarke 1097
Rommel and the Rebel - Lawrence Wells 6622
Roses From the South - Perceval Reniers 5304
The Rough Rider - Gilbert Morris 4468
Sandoval: A Romance of Bad Manners - Thomas Beer 414
Sarah Cobb - Catherine M. Rae 5236
Scarborough House - Sharon Salvato 5577
Scarlet Women - J.D. Christilian 1077
The Secret Road - Bruce Lancaster 3646
Secret Service Operator 13 - Robert W. Chambers 982
The Seventh Bullet - Daniel D. Victor 6483
The Ship's Clock - Catherine M. Rae 5237
A Singular Conspiracy - Barry Perowne 4915
The Six Messiahs - Mark Frost 2238
Sloop of War - Alexander Kent 3439
Smart Moves - Stuart M. Kaminsky 3346
Something Gleamed - Theda Kenyon 3463
Sons of Fortune - Malcolm Macdonald 3973
The Southern Cross - Peter French 2226
Speak Softly - Lawrence Alexander 83
The Splendor Stays: An Historic Novel Based on the Lives of the Seven Hart Sisters of Saybrook - Marguerite Allis 114
The Spoils of War - Thomas Fleming 2131
Stars and Stripes - Adam Rutledge 5541

The Strenuous Life - Lawrence Alexander 84
Stuyvesant Square - Margaret Lewerth 3743
Sunshine and Shadow - Antonia Van-Loon 6426
The Tallulah Bankhead Murder Case - George Baxt 389
Tassels on Her Boots - Arthur Cheney Train 6313
Tenants of the Earth - Sandra Paretti 4793
Tenderloin - Samuel Hopkins Adams 33
That Vanderbilt Woman - Philip Van Rensselaer 6427
This Willing Passion - Patricia Cloud 1132
The Thomas Street Horror - Raymond Paul 4843
A Thousand Shall Fall - Bodie Thoene 6227
Thunder on the Chesapeake - David Divine 1650
Till the End of Time - Allen Appel 170
Time After Time - Allen Appel 171
Time and Again - Jack Finney 2093
Time in Its Flight - Susan Fromberg Schaeffer 5636
The Titans - John Jakes 3154
TR - Noel B. Gerson 3150
The Tragedy at Tinkerton: An Historical Novel of Murder - Raymond Paul 4844
The Tree of Liberty - Elizabeth Page 4773
Triptych - Dora Landey 3652
Trumpets at Dawn - Cyril Harris 2719
Twice upon a Time - Allen Appel 172
Union Square - Meredith Tax 6176
Very Young Mrs. Poe - Cothburn O'Neal 4740
A Voice in the Streets - John William Tebbel 6196
Voyage to the First of December - Henry Carlisle 897
Walt Whitman's Secret - Ben Aronin 196
Walter Winchell: A Novel - Michael Herr 2863
Wanderers Eastward, Wanderers West - Kathleen Winsor 6823
Watchfires - Louis Auchincloss 234
The Waterworks - E.L. Doctorow 1659
Westfield - Roderick Thorp 6277
When the Music Changed - Marie R. Reno 5305
Whirlwind in Petticoats - Beril Becker 406
Wild Times - Brian Garfield 2291
The Winthrop Covenant - Louis Auchincloss 235
A Woman by Design - Frances Kennett 3426
World's Fair - E.L. Doctorow 1661
Yellow: A Novel - Daniel Lynch 3932
Young Ames - Walter D. Edmonds 1879
Zoya - Danielle Steel 5985

Niagara Falls
American Falls - John Calvin Batchelor 376
Niagara - Robert Lewis Taylor 6189
Sam Patch: Ballad of a Jumping Man - William Getz 2390

Otsego County
The Pioneers; or, The Sources of the Susquehanna - James Fenimore Cooper 1307

Palmyra
Canal Town - Samuel Hopkins Adams 29
Children of God - Vardis Fisher 2106

Poughkeepsie
Shad Run - Howard Breslin 668

Rome
Rome Haul - Walter D. Edmonds 1877

Sag Harbor
The Silver Dolphin - Velda Johnston 3264

Saratoga
Guns of Burgoyne - Bruce Lancaster 3640
Quinn's Book - William Kennedy 3423
Rabble in Arms - Kenneth Roberts 5390
The Rifleman - John Brick 675
Roses From the South - Perceval Reniers 5304

Saratoga Springs
Notorious Eliza - Basil Beyea 489
Saratoga Trunk - Edna Ferber 2062
A Season of Swans - Celeste De Blasis 1548

Schoharie
The Rifleman - John Brick 675

Seneca County
The Rifleman - John Brick 675

Seneca Falls
Blackwater Spirits - Miriam Grace Monfredo 4427
North Star Conspiracy - Miriam Grace Monfredo 4428
Seneca Falls Inheritance - Miriam Grace Monfredo 4429
Through a Gold Eagle - Miriam Grace Monfredo 4430

Staten Island
The Quicksilver Pool - Phyllis A. Whitney 6716

Syracuse
The Call - John Hersey 2869
Fire Bell in the Night - Constance Robertson 5395

Tappan
Major Andre - Anthony Bailey 265

Tarrytown
Storm the Last Rampart - David Taylor 6180

Templeton
The Pioneers; or, The Sources of the Susquehanna - James Fenimore Cooper 1307

Troy
Sunrise to Sunset - Samuel Hopkins Adams 32

West Point
North and South - John Jakes 3151

Westchester County
If Not Victory - Frank Olney Hough 3043
The Neutral Ground - Frank Olney Hough 3044
The Spy: A Tale of the Neutral Ground - James Fenimore Cooper 1310
Thomas Forty - Edward Stanley 5982

Woodstock
The Year of Our War - Gloria Goldreich 2462

NORTH CAROLINA

Beulah Land - Harold Lenoir Davis 1520
By Reason of Strength - Gerald White Johnson 3225
Carolina Courage - Dana Fuller Ross 5469
The Carolinians - Jane Barry 357
The Chandler Heritage - Ben Haas 2629
The Crossing - Winston Churchill 1080
Drums - James Boyd 611
From Fields of Gold - Alexandra Ripley 5339
Gallows Way - Daoma Winston 6825
The Inner Voice - Nina Wilcox Putnam 5211
Jim Mundy: A Novel of the American Civil War - Robert H. Fowler 2192
The Journey of August King - John Ehle 1894
The Land Breakers - John Ehle 1895
The Long March - Jane Barry 358
A Man's Reach - Charles Morrow Wilson 6796
Marching On - James Boyd 612
Mountain Windsong - Robert J. Conley 1246
On a Lonesome Porch - Ovid Williams Pierce 4997
One of the Raymonds - Jean Rikhoff 5332
Outpost! - Dana Fuller Ross 5486
Pushing the Bear: A Novel of the Trail of Tears - Diane Glancy 2426
The Road - John Ehle 1896
Tell Me a Tale: A Novel of the Old South - James McEachin 4266
Time of Drums - John Ehle 1897
The Truest Pleasure - Robert Morgan 4452
Young Hickory - Stanley Young 6942

Albemarle County
Raleigh's Eden - Inglis Fletcher 2137
Toil of the Brave - Inglis Fletcher 2141

Bentonville
The Bride of Texas - Josef Skvorecky   5880

Cape Fear
The Stubborn Heart - Frank G. Slaughter   5904

Edenton
Queen's Gift - Inglis Fletcher   2136
Wicked Lady - Inglis Fletcher   2142

Hillsborough
Queen's Gift - Inglis Fletcher   2136

Hiwassee River
Hiwassee: A Novel of the Civil War - Charles F. Price   5176

Perquimans District
Rogue's Harbor - Inglis Fletcher   2139

Smokey Mountains
The Tall Woman - Wilma Dykeman   1819

Wilkes County
The Wilderness Brigade - Phyllis Gordon Demarest   1605

Wilmington
The Dram Tree - Hamilton Cochran   1140
On the Midnight Tide - Don Tracy   6310

NORTH DAKOTA

The Dice of God - Hoffman Birney   507
Song of Wovoka - Earl Murray   4531

Badlands
The Cavalryman - Harold Sinclair   5861

Fargo
Oklahoma! - Dana Fuller Ross   5482

Red River Valley
An Untamed Land - Lauraine Snelling   5936

Standing Rock
Arrest Sitting Bull - Douglas C. Jones   3273

NORTHEAST

Spirit Knife - Donald Clayton Porter   5128

OHIO

All Ye People - Merle Estes Colby   1167
The Bounty Lands - William Donohue Ellis   1927
Boy with a Pack - Stephen Warren Meader   4319
Buckskin Baronet - Margaret Widdemer   6734
The Captives - Don Wright   6878
The Dark Command - William R. Burnett   793
The Fields - Conrad Richter   5319
Forty Guns West - William W. Johnstone   3267
Fruit in His Season - Helen C. Barney   333
The Golden Circle - Constance Robertson   5396
The Heart of O. Henry - Dale Kramer   3550
In the Season of the Wild Rose - Clara Rising   5347
The Ironmaster - Anne Powers   5150
John Bonwell - Charles K. Pulse   5208
Johnny Logan: Shawnee Spy - Allen W. Eckert   1843
Johnny Shiloh - James A. Rhodes   5308
Jonathan Blair, Bounty Lands Lawyer - William Donohue Ellis   1929
The Light in the Forest - Conrad Richter   5322
Morning of a Hero - Burke Boyce   608
Mount's Mistake - Lew McCreary   4229
New Road - Merle Estes Colby   1168
Now We Are Free - Marguerite Allis   112
Owen Glen - Ben Ames Williams   6766
Panther in the Sky - James Alexander Thom   6234
The Quiet Shore - Walter Havighurst   2775
Samuel Drummond - Thomas Alexander Boyd   614
Sassafras - Jack Matthews   4193

The Secret Annie Oakley - Marcy Moran Heidish   2819
Shadow of the Long Knives - Thomas Alexander Boyd   615
The Thing about Clarissa - Roberta St. Clair Cook   1264
The Trees - Conrad Richter   5326
Trumpet in the Wilderness - Robert S. Harper   2717
Waters of the Wilderness - Shirley Seifert   5737
West Goes the Road - Tim Pridgen   5192
The Woodsman - Don Wright   6880

Americus
The Town - Conrad Richter   5325

Cincinnati
Brave Pursuit - Marguerite Allis   107
Conspiracy of Knaves - Dee Brown   711
Follow the River - Albert Mayer   4203
Free Soil - Marguerite Allis   110
The Last Boat out of Cincinnati - Don Tracy   6309
Leafy Rivers - Jessamyn West   6630
The Rising Storm - Marguerite Allis   113
The Slave Stealer - Boyd Upchurch   6390
Steamboat on the River - Darwin Le Ora Teilhet   6200
When the War Is Over - Stephen Becker   408

Cleveland
The Dark City - Max Allan Collins   1211
Murder by the Numbers - Max Allan Collins   1212
To Keep Us Free - Marguerite Allis   115
Torsos - John Peyton Cooke   1270

Fairfield County
The Earth Abideth - George Dell   1595

Gallipolis
The Wild Ohio - Bart Spicer   5966

Gilean
Omensetter's Luck - William H. Gass   2317

Jericho
The Glass Dove - Sally Carrighar   943

Marietta
To Keep Us Free - Marguerite Allis   115

Maumee Valley
Sachem's Son - Donald Clayton Porter   5125

Mesopotamia
The Brooks Legend - William Donohue Ellis   1928

Ohio River
An Embarrassment of Riches - James Howard Kunstler   3565

Ohio Valley
Father and Son - Donald Clayton Porter   5117
Follow the River - Albert Mayer   4203
Red Stick - Donald Clayton Porter   5121
War Clouds - Donald Clayton Porter   5131
Westward! - Dana Fuller Ross   5492

Paradise Falls
Paradise Falls - Don Robertson   5399

Richland County
The Tree of Life - Hugh Nissenson   4629

OKLAHOMA

Back to Malachi - Robert J. Conley   1237
Belle Starr - Deborah Camp   870
The Bright Feathers - John H. Culp   1441
Brothers Three - John Oskison   4764
Cherokee Dawn - Genell Dellin   1596
Cherokee Rose: A Novel of America's First Cowgirl - Judy Alter   119
Children of the Dust - Carlile Clancy   1084
Cimarron - Edna Ferber   2061

Crazy Snake - Robert J. Conley   1240
Home Station - Jeanne Williams   6778
Johnny Osage - Janice Holt Giles   2412
Light on the Mountain - Leonard Sanders   5589
The Longest Road - Jeanne Williams   6781
Oklahoma! - Dana Fuller Ross   5482
Oklahoma Run - Alberta Constant   1260
Pushing the Bear: A Novel of the Trail of Tears - Diane Glancy   2426
Remnants of Glory - Teresa Miller   4403
The Return of Henry Starr - Richard Slotkin   5909
Run of the Stars - Dora Aydelotte   247
The Saga of Henry Starr - Robert J. Conley   1250
Scotch on the Rocks - Howard Browne   733
Tom Mix Died for Your Sins - Darryl Ponicsan   5090
Trumpets Calling - Dora Aydelotte   248
Women in the Wind - Margaret Ritter   5350

Camp Supply
The Shadow Riders - Terry C. Johnston   3257

Cherokee Nation
Belle Starr - Speer Morgan   4453
Give Me the Wind - Jan Jordan   3302
Mountain Windsong - Robert J. Conley   1246
Ned Christie's War - Robert J. Conley   1247
Nickajack - Robert J. Conley   1248
The Proud and the Free - Janet Dailey   1456
To Make a Killing - Robert J. Conley   1252
Walk in My Soul - Lucia St. Clair Robson   5418
Zeke and Ned - Larry McMurtry   4301

Cherokee Strip
Justice, My Brother - James Keene   3386

Cheyenne Reservation
The Powder River - Winfred Blevins   546

Fort Sill
Geronimo - Bill Dugan   1758
Gone the Dreams and the Dancing - Douglas C. Jones   3279
The Strenuous Life - Lawrence Alexander   84

Guthrie
Oklahoma Pride - Dana Fuller Ross   5483

Indian Nations
The Search for Temperance Moon - Douglas C. Jones   3282
Winding Stairs - Douglas C. Jones   3287

Oklahoma City
Pretty Boy Floyd - Larry McMurtry   4299

Tahlequah
Go-Ahead Rider - Robert J. Conley   1243

Tulsa
Black-Eyed Susan - Deborah Camp   871

Washita River
Long Winter Gone - Terry C. Johnston   3252

OREGON

Across the Shining Mountains - Christian McCord   4226
The Adventurers - Ernest Haycox   2787
The Brightwood Expedition - Kay L. McDonald   4261
Doctor in Buckskin - T.D. Allen   103
Each Bright River - Mildred Masterson McNeilly   4308
The Earthbreakers - Ernest Haycox   2789
The Hider - Loren D. Estleman   1972
Honey in the Horn - Harold Lenoir Davis   1523
The Jump-Off Creek - Molly Gloss   2435
Moontrap - Don Berry   481
No Road Too Long - Hildegarde Hawthorne   2785
Oregon! - Dana Fuller Ross   5484
Pioneer Breed - Glenn R. Vernam   6453

Poor Boy and a Long Way Home - James Sherburne 5806
The Quiet Life of Mrs. General Lane - Victoria Case 951
The Second Kiss - Gayle Rogers 5432
These Thousand Hills - A.B. Guthrie Jr. 2627
To Build a Ship - Don Berry 482
To Heaven on Horseback - Paul F. Cranston 1419
Trask - Don Berry 483
The Valiant - Sigman Byrd 839
We Must March: A Novel of the Winning of Oregon - Honore Morrow 4491

Astoria
Scalpdancers - Kerry Newcomb 4592
The Sea Runners - Ivan Doig 1685
You Rolling River - Archie Binns 503

Clarke's Landing
Distant Music - Harold Lenoir Davis 1521

Columbia River
Departure - Janet Stevenson 6004

Jacksonville
Sweetwater Fever - Robert H. Adelman 36

Oregon City
The Reluctant Bridegroom - Gilbert Morris 4467

Pendleton
Last Go Round - Ken Kesey 3473

Portland
California Glory - Dana Fuller Ross 5468
Departure - Janet Stevenson 6004
Long Storm - Ernest Haycox 2790
Treasure in Hell's Canyon - Bill Gulick 2619

Snake River
The Snake River - Winfred Blevins 547
Treasure in Hell's Canyon - Bill Gulick 2619

Tule Lake
Devil's Backbone - Terry C. Johnston 3250

Wallowa Valley
Song of the Meadowlark - John A. Sanford 5594

Willamette Valley
The Cabin at the Trail's End - Sheba Hargreaves 2706
The Vision Is Fulfilled - Kay L. McDonald 4262

OZARKS
Zeke and Ned - Larry McMurtry 4301

PACIFIC NORTHWEST
Bright Journey - August Derleth 1614
Call the Beast Thy Brother - William Oliver Turner 6366
Distant Trails - Bill Gulick 2612
Doctor in Buckskin - T.D. Allen 103
Down From the Mountain - Louis Charbonneau 997
Fair Land, Fair Land - A.B. Guthrie Jr. 2625
Forward the Nation - Donald Culross Peattie 4880
Fur Brigade - Hal George Evarts 1985
The Gates of the Mountains - Will Henry 2842
Gathering Storm - Bill Gulick 2613
The Great Adventure - Janice Holt Giles 2410
The Green Land - Zola Helen Ross 5504
Hawk's Journey - Donald Clayton Porter 5119
The Head Waters - Archie Binns 500
Lost Wallowa - Bill Gulick 2616
No Brighter Glory - Armstrong Sperry 5963
Plume Rouge: A Novel of the Pathfinders - John Upton Terrell 6203
Red Fox of the Kinapoo - William Rush 5526
River to the West: A Novel of the Astor Adventure - John Edward Jennings 3204

Sacajawea of the Shoshones - Della F. Emmons 1940
Six-Horse Hitch - Janice Holt Giles 2417
Star of the West - Ethel Hueston 3070
Trail: The Story of the Lewis and Clark Expedition - Louis Charbonneau 998
Troubled Border - T.D. Allen 104
Vision of the Eagle - Kay L. McDonald 4263

Elkhorn Creek
Scalpdancers - Kerry Newcomb 4592

PENNSYLVANIA
Action at Aquila - Hervey Allen 97
Asylum for the Queen - Mildred A. Jordan 3303
Bridge to Brooklyn - Albert E. Idell 3099
Ceremony of the Innocent - Taylor Caldwell 852
Copperhead Moon - Herbert Stover 6067
The Day Must Dawn - Agnes Sligh Turnbull 6362
Dynasty of Death - Taylor Caldwell 854
The Eagle and the Wind - Herbert Stover 6068
Ellis Island - Fred Mustard Stewart 6023
Fabulous Valley - Cornelia Stratton Parker 4803
The Frenchwoman - Jeanne Mackin 3995
From the Terrace - John O'Hara 4703
Give Us This Valley - Tom Ham 2666
Hunt for Heaven - Elsie Barber 298
I Thee Wed - Gilbert Wolf Gabriel 2267
I'll Storm Hell - Noel B. Gerson 2374
The Kays - Margaret Deland 1583
Look Away - Harold Coyle 1395
Love and War - John Jakes 3150
The Lure of the Falcon - Juliette Benzoni 465
Mistress of the Forge - David Taylor 6179
Morning Time - Charles Kendall O'Neill 4743
Mr. Audubon's Lucy - Lucy Kennedy 3419
Never Victorious, Never Defeated - Taylor Caldwell 860
Now We Are Free - Marguerite Allis 112
Power - Howard Fast 2041
Pride's Castle - Frank Yerby 6925
The Proud and the Free - Howard Fast 2042
The Richlands - Agnes Sligh Turnbull 6364
Rogue's Kingdom - John Brick 676
The Scarlet Patch - Bruce Lancaster 3645
Shadow of the Moon - Douglas C. Jones 3284
Testimony of Two Men - Taylor Caldwell 863
The Three Black Pennys - Joseph Hergesheimer 2855
Traveller - Richard Adams 27
The Trees - Conrad Richter 5326
West Goes the Road - Tim Pridgen 5192

Allegheny Mountains
Allegheny Captive - Caroline Bourne 591

Bellefonte
The House on Curtin Street - Millie J. Ragosta 5242

Bethlehem
The Price of Liberty - Joseph G.E. Hopkins 3028

Bloodsmoor Valley
A Bloodsmoor Romance - Joyce Carol Oates 4658

Braddock
Out of This Furnace - Thomas Bell 425

Bucks County
Fire and the Hammer - Shirley Barker 311

Chambersburg
Roll, Shenandoah - Bruce Lancaster 3644

Delaware Water Gap
The Hawks of Hawk-Hollow - Robert Montgomery Bird 504

Erie
The Fleet in the Forest - Carl Daniel Lane 3654

Fort Pitt
Buckskin Cavalier - John Clagett 1082
The King's Orchard - Agnes Sligh Turnbull 6363

Gettysburg
The Barefoot Brigade - Douglas C. Jones 3274
Carriage Trade - Robert Thomsen 6271
The Dixie Widow - Gilbert Morris 4459
For Us the Living - Antonia Van-Loon 6424
Gettysburg - Stephen Longstreet 3887
Gettysburg: Crisis of Command - Harry Albright 65
Hard Road to Gettysburg - Ted Jones 3298
I Speak for Thaddeus Stevens - Elsie Singmaster 5868
Jubilee - John Brick 672
The Killer Angels - Michael Shaara 5766
Long Remember - MacKinlay Kantor 3362
Loving Heart - Elsie Singmaster 5869
The President's Daughter - Barbara Chase-Riboud 1005
The Scarlet Guidon - Ray Grant Toepfer 6287
The Stonewall Brigade: A Novel of the American Civil War - Frank G. Slaughter 5902
Swords of Steel - Elsie Singmaster 5870
Three Days - Stephen Longstreet 3891
The Three Days - Don Robertson 5402

Lyons
Ourselves to Know - John O'Hara 4704

Philadelphia
Alabama Empire - Welbourn Kelley 3392
The Ardent Years - Janet Stevenson 6003
Benjy Boone - Maurice Dolbier 1687
Bygones - Frank Wilkinson 6762
Captain Barney - Jan Westcott 6642
Captains and the Kings - Taylor Caldwell 851
Centennial Summer - Albert E. Idell 3100
Citizen Tom Paine - Howard Fast 2028
A Daughter of Liberty - Allan Cole 1196
Dear Lily - Malcolm W. Greenough Jr. 2575
Dim the Flaring Lamps - Jan Jordan 3301
Echo of the Flute - Mildred A. Jordan 3304
Enough Good Men - Charles Mercer 4336
Farewell to Valley Forge - David Taylor 6178
The Financier - Theodore Dreiser 1720
Fire and the Hammer - Shirley Barker 311
Hearts of Fire - Christina Savage 5616
Heaven and Hell - John Jakes 3147
Hugh Wynne, Free Quaker - Silas Weir Mitchell 4416
Jeremiah Martin: A Revolutionary War Novel - Robert H. Fowler 2191
Kentucky Home - Betty Layman Receveur 5283
Monmouth - Charles Bracelen Flood 2144
The Peculiar People - Jan de Hartog 2764
Portrait of a Scoundrel - Nathaniel Benchley 438
Powder Mission - Herbert Stover 6070
The President's Daughter - Barbara Chase-Riboud 1005
The Quality of Mercy - Anne Miller Downes 1712
Queen Dolley: The Life and Times of Dolley Madison - Dorothy Clarke Wilson 6806
The Rebel and the Turncoat - Malcolm Decker 1576
Redcoat - Bernard Cornwell 1337
Remembrance Rock - Carl Sandburg 5583
Rogers' Folly - Albert E. Idell 3102
Sisters and Brothers - Janet Stevenson 6005
Stars and Stripes - Adam Rutledge 5541
Storm the Last Rampart - David Taylor 6180
Tidewater Dynasty: A Biographical Novel of the Lees of Stratford Hall - Carey Roberts 5372
The Traitor - Dan Sherman 5814
The Tree of Liberty - Elizabeth Page 4773
Twice upon a Time - Allen Appel 172
The Undiscovered Country - Jay Walz 6560
The Very Best People - Elizabeth Villars 6499
Wide Is the Water - Jane Aiken Hodge 2973
Woman's Own - Robyn Carr 941

Pittsburgh
The Delectable Country - Leland Dewitt
   Baldwin   280
Michael Torey - Janet Mathewson   4183
The Rebels - John Jakes   3152
Rivers West - Louis L'Amour   3626
Thine Is the Glory - Samuel A. Schreiner Jr.   5672

Springtown
Sword of Vengeance - Kerry Newcomb   4593

Susquehanna Valley
Men in Buckskin - Herbert Stover   6069
This Land Is Ours - Louis Zara   6953

Valley Forge
Bride of Liberty - Frank Yerby   6909
Conceived in Liberty - Howard Fast   2029
A Daughter of Liberty - Allan Cole   1196
Farewell to Valley Forge - David Taylor   6178
Monmouth - Charles Bracelen Flood   2144
Return to Treasure Island - Denis Judd   3318
The Saintly Buccaneer - Gilbert Morris   4469
The Strong Men - John Brick   677
Valley Forge - MacKinlay Kantor   3364

RHODE ISLAND

The Catherine - Robert S. MacDonald   3980
Murfy's Men - Gerald Green   2565

Newport
The Americans - John Jakes   3143
Death on the Cliff Walk - Mary Kruger   3562
Dragon Cove - Carter A. Vaughan   6434
The House of Five Talents - Louis Auchincloss   231
The Last Waltz - Nancy Zaroulis   6955
Matthew Early - Alexander Laing   3589
North and South - John Jakes   3151
One Night in Newport - Elizabeth Villars   6498
The Red Rover - James Fenimore Cooper   1309
Stars on the Sea - F. van Wyck Mason   4161
That Vanderbilt Woman - Philip Van
   Rensselaer   6427

Providence
The Golden Mistress - Basil Beyea   488

ROCKY MOUNTAINS

Ammahabas - Bill Hotchkiss   3036
Blackfoot Massacre - David Thompson   6251
Blood Fury - David Thompson   6252
Blood Truce - David Thompson   6253
Borderlords - Terry C. Johnston   3244
Breakheart Pass - Alistair MacLean   3999
Buffalo Palace - Terry C. Johnston   3245
Carry the Wind - Terry C. Johnston   3246
Forward the Nation - Donald Culross Peattie   4880
The Great Adventure - Janice Holt Giles   2410
The High Missouri - Winfred Blevins   545
King of the Mountain - David Thompson   6255
The Long Rifle - Stewart Edward White   6702
Lure of the Wind - David Thompson   6256
Mountain Devil - David Thompson   6257
Mountain Laurel - Jude Deveraux   1632
Mountain Man - Vardis Fisher   2110
One-Eyed Dream - Terry C. Johnston   3253
Outpost! - Dana Fuller Ross   5486
Sacajawea of the Shoshones - Della F.
   Emmons   1940
The Shining Mountains - Dale Van Every   6410
Star of the West - Ethel Hueston   3070
Sweet Mountain Magic - Rosanne Bittner   516
Tenderfoot - David Thompson   6259
Tomahawk Revenge - David Thompson   6260
Trapper's Blood - David Thompson   6261
The Two Medicine River - Richard S. Wheeler   6663
We Must March: A Novel of the Winning of Oregon -
   Honore Morrow   4491

Winterkill - David Thompson   6262

SOUTH

The Barefoot Brigade - Douglas C. Jones   3274
Family - J. California Cooper   1297
Father Abraham - Irving A. Bacheller   258
Jubilee - John Brick   672
The Live Goat - Cecil Dawkins   1542
Oldest Living Confederate Widow Tells All - Allan
   Gurganus   2621
The Proud Retreat - Clifford Dowdey   1706
Spangle - Gary Jennings   3196

SOUTH CAROLINA

Battle Lanterns - Merrit Parmalee Allen   102
Beyond Surrender - Marian Sims   5860
Cato's War - Guy Wheeler   6655
Daughter of Strangers - Elizabeth Boatwright
   Coker   1164
Dawn's Early Light - Elswyth Thane   6215
The Drums of December - Sharon Salvato   5575
For the Love of Robert E. Lee - M.A. Harper   2715
Foundation Stone - Lella Warren   6571
Freedom Road - Howard Fast   2031
The Hard to Catch Mercy - William Baldwin   281
Kings Mountain - Florette Henri   2838
The Light Infantry Ball - Hamilton Basso   375
The Long March - Jane Barry   358
Look Back to Glory - Herbert Ravenel Sass   5607
North and South - John Jakes   3151
Othneil Jones - John Adams Leland   3715
The Power of Black - M.B. Longman   3880
Sycamore Men - David Taylor   6181
A Woman Called Fancy - Frank Yerby   6931

Charleston
Beloved - Vina Delmar   1599
The Carolinian - Rafael Sabatini   5547
Celia Garth - Gwen Bristow   695
Charleston - Alexandra Ripley   5338
Cordelia Chantrell - Meade Minnigerode   4413
The Crossing - Winston Churchill   1080
A Few Painted Feathers - Stephen Longstreet   3886
Fragments of the Ark - Louise Meriwether   4341
The Guernseyman - C. Northcote Parkinson   4812
Heaven and Hell - John Jakes   3147
Ironclads: Man-of-War - Larry D. Names   4554
Love and War - John Jakes   3150
Madame Castel's Lodger - Frances Parkinson
   Keyes   3480
The Magnolias - Julie Ellis   1922
The Moreland Legacy - Diana Haviland   2777
Our Valiant Few - F. van Wyck Mason   4155
Peter Ashley - DuBose Heyward   2911
Red Lanterns on St. Michael's - Thornwell
   Jacobs   3139
The Running Thread - Drayton Mayrant   4215
Scarlett - Alexandra Ripley   5342
The Secret of Saramount - Lillian Cheatham   1011
Sisters and Brothers - Janet Stevenson   6005
Slow Dies the Thunder - Helen Topping Miller   4395
The Stars of the South - Julian Green   2568
Stars on the Sea - F. van Wyck Mason   4161
Those the Sun Has Loved - Rose Jourdain   3309
The Tides of Malvern - Francis Griswold   2595
Up Country: A Story of the Vanguard - Donald
   Culross Peattie   4881
The Woman of Catawba - Hilda Stahl   5978
Wychwood - Nicole St. John   5564

Columbia
La Belle - Elizabeth Boatwright Coker   1161

Hilton Head Island
Blood Red Roses - Elizabeth Boatwright Coker   1163

Santee
The Red Doe - Drayton Mayrant   4214

Sea Islands
Fragments of the Ark - Louise Meriwether   4341

SOUTH DAKOTA

Arrest Sitting Bull - Douglas C. Jones   3273
Dance Back the Buffalo - Milton Lott   3899
The Day the Sun Died - Dale Van Every   6408
Free Land - Rose Lane   3660
The Land Was Ours: A Novel of the Great Plains -
   Charles W. Bailey   266
The Long Trail North - Robert J. Conley   1245
Lord Grizzly - Frederick F. Manfred   4056
Man on Two Ponies - Don Worcester   6872
Sioux Splendor - Rosanne Bittner   515
Song of Wovoka - Earl Murray   4531
Whisper of the Wolf - Terry C. Johnston   3261
A Whisper on the Wind - Madeline Baker   276

Badlands
The Bad Lands - Oakley Hall   2651

Black Hills
Crazy Horse - Bill Dugan   1757
Lakota - G. Clifton Wisler   6833
*The Last Stand: A Novel about George Armstrong
   Custer and the Indians of the Plains* - Edwin P.
   Hoyt   3061
Sudden Country - Loren D. Estleman   1979

Corden
The Man Who Missed the Party - Harold Adams   25

Deadwood
*Aces and Eights: A Novel of the Legend of Wild Bill
   Hickok* - Loren D. Estleman   1967
Calamity Jane of Deadwood Gulch - Ethel
   Hueston   3068
Deadwood - Pete Dexter   1638
Judgment in July - Richard Fisher   2105

Rapid City
Path of the Sun - Al Dempsey   1608
Twice upon a Time - Allen Appel   172

Wounded Knee
A Creek Called Wounded Knee - Douglas C.
   Jones   3277
A Good Day to Die - Thomas Wakefield
   Blackburn   525

SOUTHEAST

Give Me the Wind - Jan Jordan   3302
A Sorrow in Our Heart - Allen W. Eckert   1844

SOUTHWEST

The American Cowboy - Will James   3163
Angel with Spurs - Paul I. Wellman   6613
Anything for Billy - Larry McMurtry   4295
Apache - Will Comfort   1226
Apache - Donald Clayton Porter   5114
Apache Devil - Edgar Rice Burroughs   806
Arizona Ecstasy - Rosanne Bittner   511
Black Jack Davy - John Oskison   4763
Blessed McGill - Edwin Shrake   5834
Broncho Apache - Paul I. Wellman   6614
Brules - Harry Combs   1223
The Crossing - Cormac McCarthy   4221
Death Comes for the Archbishop - Willa Cather   957
Desert Hawks - Frank Burleson   786
Far Mountains - Frank O'Rourke   4752
I, Jack Swilling - John Myers   4544
In Those Days - Harvey Fergusson   2068
Johnny Christmas - Forrester Blake   533
Jornada - Robert L. Duffus   1754
The Last Ride - Tom Eidson   1899
Lonesome Dove - Larry McMurtry   4298
Mi Amigo - William R. Burnett   795

Outlaw - Warren Kiefer 3482
Ride the Wind - Lucia St. Clair Robson 5416
The Sackett Brand - Louis L'Amour 3627
Savage Frontier - Frank Burleson 787
The Sea of Grass - Conrad Richter 5323
Season for War - P.F. Kluge 3510
Streets of Laredo - Larry McMurtry 4300
Valley of the Shadow - Charles Marquis
    Warren 6570
War Eagles - Frank Burleson 788
The War Train: A Novel of 1916 - Brown
    Meggs 4324
Watch for Me on the Mountain - Forrest Carter 947
The White Man's Road - Benjamin Capps 891
Wolf Song - Harvey Fergusson 2069
Words by Heart - Ouida Sebestyen 5713
Yankee Rover - Christopher Ward 6563

Sandrock

The Harvey Girls - Samuel Hopkins Adams 31

Warlock

Warlock - Oakley Hall 2653

TENNESSEE

After the Glory - Helen Topping Miller 4383
All the Brave Rifles - Clarke Venable 6450
As Long as the Rivers Run - Sam J. Slate 5882
The Border Men - Cameron Judd 3312
The Bright Sword - Eleanor Perenyi 4911
The Buckstones - Paul I. Wellman 6615
Captain Little Ax - James H. Street 6077
The Cavalier of Tennessee - Meredith
    Nicholson 4610
Choctaw - Donald Clayton Porter 5116
*Crockett of Tennessee: A Novel Based on the Life and
    Times of David Crockett* - Cameron Judd 3314
The Cumberland Rifles - Noel B. Gerson 2365
The Daybreakers - Louis L'Amour 3619
Father of Waters - Donald Clayton Porter 5118
The Fifth Conspiracy - Ted Jones 3296
Forest of the Night - Madison Jones 3291
Freedom - William Safire 5561
*Fury in the Earth: A Novel of the New Madrid
    Earthquake* - Harry Harrison Kroll 3557
Hearts of Hickory - John Trotwood Moore 4442
*Her Christmas at the Hermitage: A Tale about Rachel
    and Andrew Jackson* - Helen Topping Miller 4389
The History of Rome Hanks - Joseph Stanley
    Pennell 4909
The Horse Soldiers - Harold Sinclair 5862
Johnny Shiloh - James A. Rhodes 5308
Journey to Shiloh - Will Henry 2843
The Land Where the Sun Dies - Henry Carlisle 896
The Long Night - Andrew Lytle 3945
Longleaf - Rose Brock 701
The Mysterious Death of Meriwether Lewis - Ron
    Burns 802
No Tears for Christmas - Helen Topping
    Miller 4391
None Shall Look Back - Caroline Gordon 2478
Old Hickory - Noel B. Gerson 2379
On the Long Tide - Laura Krey 3555
Othniel Jones - John Adams Leland 3715
The Overmountain Men - Cameron Judd 3315
Penhally - Caroline Gordon 2479
The President's Lady - Irving Stone 6063
Pursuit of Bliss - Betty Palmer Nelson 4577
The Quality of Mercy - Anne Miller Downes 1712
The Raider - Jesse Hill Ford 2164
The Raven's Bride - Elizabeth Crook 1431
Rebel Run - Louis Zara 6952
Red Belts - Hugh Pendexter 4897
Ride the River - Louis L'Amour 3625
Rogue's March - Maristan Chapman 993
Sam Houston - Noel B. Gerson 2378
The Sam Houston Story - Dean Owen 4770
Seminole - Donald Clayton Porter 5126

Shadowed Memories - Al Lacy 3583
Shod with Flame - Helen Topping Miller 4393
The Slender Reed - Noel B. Gerson 2382
Sojourn of a Stranger - Walter Sullivan 6115
*The Sounds of Chariots: A Novel of John Sevier and
    the State of Franklin* - Helen Topping Miller 4396
A Southern Woman - Elena Yates Eulo 1983
Storm Center: A Novel about Andy Johnson - Joseph
    Walker McSpadden 4312
A Story of Deep Delight - Thomas McNamee 4305
Talons of Eagles - William C. Johnstone 3268
Tennessee Hazard - Maristan Chapman 994
Tidewater - Clifford Dowdey 1709
War Drums - Donald Clayton Porter 5133
Wave High the Banner - Dee Brown 714
While Rivers Flow - Glen H. Fleischmann 2125
Wild Horizon - F. van Wyck Mason 4164
The Yankee From Tennessee - Noel B. Gerson 2388
Young Hickory - Stanley Young 6942

Bourbonville

The Coming of Rain - Richard Marius 4084

Chattanooga

Guns of Chickamauga - Richard O'Connor 4685
Mockingbird Sang at Chickamauga - Alfred Leland
    Crabb 1404
Reunion at Chattanooga - Alfred Leland Crabb 1406

Clinch River Valley

Delilah's Mountain - Gloria Jahoda 3142

Coal Creek

Great Dream From Heaven - John Rolfe
    Gardiner 2286

Cumberlands

The Velvet Horn - Andrew Lytle 3946

Fort Pillow

The Falling Hills - Perry Lentz 3720
The Way to Fort Pillow - James Sherburne 5807

Franklin

The Canebrake Men - Cameron Judd 3313

Gallatin

The Last Plantation - Don Wright 6879

Hiwassee River

Walk in My Soul - Lucia St. Clair Robson 5418

Memphis

The Hand of a Woman - Diana Brown 719
Mississippi Belle - Clements Ripley 5346
Tennessee! - Dana Fuller Ross 5489
Untold Glory - Cothburn O'Neal 4739

Nashville

Bend Your Heads All - Rowena Rutherford
    Farrar 2015
Blood Kin - Barbara Anne Pauley 4845
Breakfast at the Hermitage - Alfred Leland
    Crabb 1397
Dinner at Belmont - Alfred Leland Crabb 1398
Home to Tennessee - Alfred Leland Crabb 1400
Home to the Hermitage - Alfred Leland Crabb 1401
Journey to Nashville - Alfred Leland Crabb 1402
Lodging at the Saint Cloud - Alfred Leland
    Crabb 1403
Night March - Bruce Lancaster 3641
No Bugles Blow - Bruce Lancaster 3642
Supper at the Maxwell House - Alfred Leland
    Crabb 1407

Phinizy County

Three-Headed Angel - Roark Bradford 623

Pittsburg Landing

Long Day at Shiloh - Don Bannister 294
Shiloh - Shelby Foote 2153

Spencer County

Private Knowledge - Betty Palmer Nelson 4576

TEXAS

The Adelita - Oakley Hall 2649
All the Brave Rifles - Clarke Venable 6450
And Tell of Time - Laura Krey 3554
Belle Starr - Deborah Camp 870
Black Gold - Anita Richmond Bunkley 771
Blue Moon - Parris Afton Bonds 569
Born of the Sun - John H. Culp 1440
The Bright Feathers - John H. Culp 1441
The Brothers of Uterica - Benjamin Capps 887
*The Bugles Are Silent: A Novel of the Texas
    Revolution* - John R. Knaggs 3513
By the King's Command - Shirley Seifert 5723
Captain Jack - Gene Shelton 5800
Colfax - Robert J. Conley 1239
Comanche Moon - Catherine Anderson 137
The Comancheros - Paul I. Wellman 6616
Confessions of Johnny Ringo - Geoff Aggeler 40
Cottonwoods Grow Tall - Margaret Bell
    Houston 3055
*Crockett of Tennessee: A Novel Based on the Life and
    Times of David Crockett* - Cameron Judd 3314
Dark Thicket - Elmer Kelton 3402
Dead Man's Walk - Larry McMurtry 4297
Death at the French Creek - Raymond C. Borel 580
Death of a Legend - Will Henry 2840
The Devil Gun - William Syers 6148
Diamond Six - William Fielding Smith 5932
Divine Average - Elithe Hamilton Kirkland 3505
Duel in the Sun - Niven Busch 812
The Eagle and the Raven - James A. Michener 4369
Elizabeth, By Name - Will Cook 1265
*Empire of Bones: A Novel of Sam Houston and the
    Texas Revolution* - Jeff Long 3868
Eye of the Hawk - David William Ross 5498
The Far Journey - Loula Grace Erdman 1950
The Garfield Honor - Frank Yerby 6918
Gone to Texas - Jason Manning 4074
The Good Old Boys - Elmer Kelton 3405
The Goodnight Trail - Ralph Compton 1227
The Heart of O. Henry - Dale Kramer 3550
Hellfire Jackson - Garland Roark 5355
The Iron Mistress - Paul I. Wellman 6618
Killing Time - Robert J. Conley 1244
Lady of No Man's Land - Jeanne Williams 6780
Lily - Cindy Bonner 571
The Live Goat - Cecil Dawkins 1542
Lone Star Lady - Jill Gregory 2579
The Long Trail North - Robert J. Conley 1245
Looking After Lily - Cindy Bonner 572
Lords of the Plains - Max Crawford 1420
Love Is a Wild Assault - Elithe Hamilton
    Kirkland 3506
Magnificent Destiny - Paul I. Wellman 6619
Mary Dove - Jane Gilmore Rushing 5529
Maximilian's Gold - Jane Barry 359
Mirage - Helen Topping Miller 4390
No Resting Place - William Humphrey 3079
North of 36 - Emerson Hough 3042
North to Yesterday - Robert Flynn 2145
The Odyssey of Thaddeus Baxter - Robert P.
    Lund 3926
On the Long Tide - Laura Krey 3555
Pancho And Black Jack - Fred Bean 398
Pearl - Anne Leaton 3701
The Pistoleer - James Carlos Blake 536
The Power of Black - M.B. Longman 3880
Promised Lands - Elizabeth Crook 1430
The Pumpkin Rollers - Elmer Kelton 3406
Quanah Parker - Bill Dugan 1759
The Rainbow Promise - Lisa Gregory 2580
Rawhider - Gene Shelton 5802
Refugio, They Named You Wrong - Susan Clark
    Schofield 5647
Republic: A Novel of Texas - E.V. Thompson 6266
The Restless Land - John H. Culp 1444
The Road to San Jacinto - James F. Davis 1524

The Road to San Jacinto - Leonard L. Foreman 2167
Rockspring - R.G. Vliet 6506
The Running Iron - Rachel Ann Fish 2097
La Salle - John Vernon 6458
Sam Chance - Benjamin Capps 888
Sam Houston - Noel B. Gerson 2380
The Sam Houston Story - Dean Owen 4770
Scotch on the Rocks - Howard Browne 733
The Searchers - Alan Le May 3691
Season of Yellow Leaf - Douglas C. Jones 3283
The Seventh Girl: A Romantic Tale of Civil War Texas - Tom Pendleton 4900
A Shadow of Eagles - Jane Barry 360
Slaughter - Elmer Kelton 3407
Solitudes - R.G. Vliet 6507
Spanish Gold - Kevin D. Randle 5252
The Staked Plain - Frank Xavier Tolbert 6290
Star in the Rigging: A Novel of the Texas Navy - Garland Roark 5358
Strange Company - Robert J. Conley 1251
Tamzen - Jane Gilmore Rushing 5530
Tempered Blade - Monte Barrett 352
Tennessee Smith - James E. Hitt 2957
The Terrible Teague Bunch - Gary Jennings 3197
Texas - James A. Michener 4375
Texas! - Dana Fuller Ross 5490
Tilly Wed - Catherine Cookson 1290
Timothy Baines - John H. Culp 1445
The Trail to Ogallala - Benjamin Capps 889
Trail's End - Fred Bean 400
The Treasure of the Chisos - John H. Culp 1446
True Women - Janice Woods Windle 6820
The Union Belle - Gilbert Morris 4473
The Vengeance Trail of Josey Wales - Forrest Carter 946
Walnut Grove - Jane Gilmore Rushing 5531
Wave High the Banner - Dee Brown 714
A Whistle in the Wind - John H. Culp 1447
The Wolf and the Buffalo - Elmer Kelton 3408
A Woman of Texas - R.T. Stevens 6002
A Woman of the People - Benjamin Capps 893

Adobe Walls
The Shadow Riders - Terry C. Johnston 3257

Baronsville
The Grass Kingdom - Jory Sherman 5818

Brazos River
Brazos Dreamer - Gene Shelton 5799
Thunder Before Seven - Anna Brand 648

Brownsville
The Cotton Road - Frank Feuille 2077

Dallas
American Eden - Marilyn Harris 2728
Destiny in Dallas - Shirley Seifert 5725
Flying into Love - D.M. Thomas 6236
Libra - Don DeLillo 1593

El Paso
Last Gun: The Legend of John Selman - Gene Shelton 5801
The Shootist - Glendon Swarthout 6145

Fort Griffin
The Lady and Doc Holliday - Preston Lewis 3761

Fort Worth
Dog Heavies - L.J. Washburn 6575
Fort Worth - Leonard Sanders 5588
One More River to Cross - Will Henry 2847

Fredericksburg
Rebel in Blue - Herman Toepperwein 6289

Gainesville
A Bright Tragic Thing - L.D. Clark 1091

Galveston
Death of a Dancing Lady - Ray Harrison 2739

Galveston - Suzanne Morris 4482
West to Eden - Gloria Goldreich 2461

Glenn Springs
The Tin Lizzie Troup - Glendon Swarthout 6146

Gonzales
The Men of Gonzales - John H. Culp 1442

Greenfields
Winds of Blame - Jane Gilmore Rushing 5532

High Plains
Wandering Star - Steven Yount 6945

Houston
Bayou City Secrets - Deborah Powell 5146
Galveston - Suzanne Morris 4482

Nacogdoches
Star of the Wilderness - Karle Wilson Baker 274

Odessa
When the Legends Die - Hal Borland 584

Palo Duro Canyon
Winter Rain - Terry C. Johnston 3262

Panhandle
The Day the Cowboys Quit - Elmer Kelton 3403
The Edge of Time - Loula Grace Erdman 1949
Sudden Country - Loren D. Estleman 1979
The Unforgiven - Alan Le May 3692

Piedras
The Far Canyon - Elmer Kelton 3404

Preston
Border Line - Robert J. Conley 1238

Puerto
The Wonderful Country - Tom Lea 3695

Red River
Look to the River - William A. Owens 4771
The Restless Border - Richard Pearce 4873

Rio Grande
Gone to Texas - John Williams Thomason 6247
The Stuart Women - Matt Braun 652

Sabine Pass
Muddy Banks - Ruby C. Tolliver 6291

San Antonio
Eyes of Eagles - William W. Johnstone 3266
The Furies - John Jakes 3146
Gone to Texas - Don Worcester 6871
Heaven's Gold - Giles Tippette 6282
Keeping Secrets - Suzanne Morris 4483
San Antone - V.J. Banis 288
Sons of Texas - Tom Early 1822
Star of Empire: A Novel of Old San Antonio - Leonard Sanders 5590
Warriors of the Night - Kerry Newcomb 4594
West of Appomattox - Harley Duncan 1785

Santa Rita
Shadows in the Dusk - John Edward Jennings 3208

Tascosa
Tascosa Gun: The Story of Jim East - Gene Shelton 5803

UTAH

Blue Russell - Will Bryant 738
Children of God - Vardis Fisher 2106
Dream Catcher - Terry C. Johnston 3251
The Executioner's Song - Norman Mailer 4036
The Fancher Train - Amelia Bean 395
For Time and All Eternity - Paul Bailey 268
The Giant Joshua - Maurine Whipple 6673
No Road Too Long - Hildegarde Hawthorne 2785

The Odyssey of Thaddeus Baxter - Robert P. Lund 3926
Paradise Reclaimed - Halldor Laxness 3686
Powderkeg - Richard Vetterli 6482
The Predators - F.A. Parker 4804
The Proselyte - Susan Ertz 1958
Six-Horse Hitch - Janice Holt Giles 2417
The Story of the Sundance Kid - David Everitt 1988
The Union Belle - Gilbert Morris 4473
Wilderness Passage - Forrester Blake 534
Wives of the Wind - Marjorie Jarrett 3170

Salt Lake City
Good Morning, Young Lady - Ardyth Kennelly 3424
Salt Lake City - A.R. Reife 5292
Sister Wives - Cleo Jones 3270

VERMONT

All Ye People - Merle Estes Colby 1167
The Arch of Stars - Clifford Lindsey Alderman 66
Call of the Mountains - Cornelia Meigs 4326
Called Away - Perdita Buchan 753
Catch a Falling Star - Frederic F. Van de Water 6401
Day of Battle - Frederic F. Van de Water 6402
D'ri and I - Irving A. Bacheller 257
The Man on the Train - W.J. Chaput 995

Bennington
The Shadow and the Glory - John Edward Jennings 3207

Coniston
Coniston - Winston Churchill 1078

Stratton
Tamarack Tree - Howard Breslin 670

VIRGINIA

All God's Children - Alston Anderson 136
And One Rode West - Heather Graham 2514
And One Wore Gray - Heather Graham 2515
Ask My Brother - Constance Wagner 6518
Balisand - Joseph Hergesheimer 2853
Battle Flag - Bernard Cornwell 1333
Being Met Together - William Vaughan Wilkins 6756
Beloved Enemy - Al Lacy 3579
The Bizarre Sisters - Jay Walz 6559
The Bloody Ground - Bernard Cornwell 1334
The Blue and the Gray - John Leekley 3713
Bridle the Wind - Julia Davis 1525
Cadmus Henry - Walter D. Edmonds 1872
Captains and the Kings - Taylor Caldwell 851
Cato's War - Guy Wheeler 6655
Cease Firing - Mary Johnston 3230
Cloud on the Land - Julia Davis 1526
Company of Cowards - Jack Schaefer 5634
Confederates - Thomas Keneally 3412
Copperhead - Bernard Cornwell 1335
A Court of Owls - Richard Adicks 37
The Crisis - Winston Churchill 1079
Crockett of Tennessee: A Novel Based on the Life and Times of David Crockett - Cameron Judd 3314
Dark Hills to Westward - Harry M. Caudill 964
Dim the Flaring Lamps - Jan Jordan 3301
The Distant Lands - Julian Green 2567
A Dream of Kings - Davis Grubb 2604
Drury Randall - Mary Johnston 3232
Eagle on the Sun - Julia Davis 1527
Eight April Days - Scott Hart 2759
Enslaved - Ron Burns 801
Exit with Drums - Joseph A. Daley 1457
Family Fortune - Mignon G. Eberhart 1834
Farewell, My General - Shirley Seifert 5726
The Fathers - Allen Tate 6171
The Fever Called Living - Barbara Moore 4439
A Few Painted Feathers - Stephen Longstreet 3886

Flight to Canada - Ishmael Reed 5285
For the Love of Robert E. Lee - M.A. Harper 2715
The Foragers - Ben Haas 2630
Freedom - William Safire 5561
From Fields of Gold - Alexandra Ripley 5339
From Sea to Shining Sea - James Alexander Thom 6232
Fruit in His Season - Helen C. Barney 333
The Gallant Mrs. Stonewall - Harnett T. Kane 3353
The Gaynor Women - Virginia Coffman 1153
A Generation of Leaves - Robert S. Bloom 552
Gentlemen, Hush! - Jere Hungerford Wheelwright 6668
Gettysburg: Crisis of Command - Harry Albright 65
The Ghost Raider - Ray Hogan 2978
Give Me Liberty - Noel B. Gerson 2369
Gods and Generals - Jeff Shaara 5765
God's Angry Man - Leonard Ehrlich 1898
The Gray Captain - Jere Hungerford Wheelwright 6669
The Great Meadow - Elizabeth Madox Roberts 5378
The Guns of the South - Harry N. Turtledove 6367
Hard Road to Gettysburg - Ted Jones 3298
High Hearts - Rita Mae Brown 728
Home to Kentucky: A Novel of Henry Clay - Alfred Leland Crabb 1399
House Divided - Ben Ames Williams 6765
The Hunting Shirt - Mary Johnston 3235
I Swear by Apollo - Agatha Young 6939
Janice Meredith - Paul Leicester Ford 2166
Jim Mundy: A Novel of the American Civil War - Robert H. Fowler 2192
Journey Proud - Thomasine McGehee 4273
Know Nothing - Mary Lee Settle 5755
Lady Washington - Dorothy Clarke Wilson 6803
The Last Confederate - Gilbert Morris 4466
The Lattimer Legend - Ann Hebson 2813
Let the Spring Come - Henry Schindall 5637
The Long March - Jane Barry 358
The Long Roll - Mary Johnston 3236
Look Away - Harold Coyle 1395
Major Stepton's War - Matthew Vaughan 6445
Miss Delicia Allen - Mary Johnston 3237
Mistress Nancy - Barbara Bentley 460
Mosby's Last Ride - Ray Hogan 2979
My Thomas: A Novel of Martha Jefferson's Life - Roberta Grimes 2593
Night Raider - Ray Hogan 2980
North Star Conspiracy - Miriam Grace Monfredo 4428
Ol' Prophet Nat - Daniel Panger 4786
Old Miss - Thomas Campbell 877
Pomp and Circumstance - Fred Mustard Stewart 6025
A Promise Unbroken - Al Lacy 3582
The Rebels - John Jakes 3152
Riding Shotgun - Rita Mae Brown 729
The River and the Wilderness - Don Robertson 5401
Salisbury Plain - Henry C. Branson 650
Sapphira and the Slave Girl - Willa Cather 958
Scarlet Cockerel - Garald Lagard 3584
The Scarlet Guidon - Ray Grant Toepfer 6287
The Scarlet Patch - Bruce Lancaster 3645
The Seasons of Heroes - Paxton Davis 1539
Secret Service Operator 13 - Robert W. Chambers 982
The Seekers - John Jakes 3153
Show Me a Land - Clark McMeekin 4293
The Slave of Frankenstein - Robert J. Myers 4549
The Smiling Rebel - Harnett T. Kane 3357
Stars and Stripes - Adam Rutledge 5541
The Stonewall Brigade: A Novel of the American Civil War - Frank G. Slaughter 5902
Storm the Last Rampart - David Taylor 6180
Talons of Eagles - William W. Johnstone 3268
That Far Paradise - Gene Markey 4088
Thin Moon and Cold Mist - Kathleen O'Neal Gear 2330
Tidewater - Clifford Dowdey 1709

Time of Drums - John Ehle 1897
To Appomattox: Nine April Days, 1865 - Burke Davis 1512
Traveller - Richard Adams 27
Trumpets Sound No More - F. van Wyck Mason 4163
Until the End - Harold Coyle 1396
Unto This Hour - Tom Wicker 6733
The Unwritten Chronicles of Robert E. Lee - Lamar Herrin 2864
The Valiant Virginians - James Warner Bellah 427
A Virginia Scout - Hugh Pendexter 4899
The Virginians - William Makepeace Thackeray 6214
Walk Like a Man - Donald Honig 3024

Albermarle County
Blood Red Roses - Elizabeth Boatwright Coker 1163

Alexandria
Luise - Dawn Stewart Field 2079

Appalachia
The Chisholms - Evan Hunter 3082

Arlington
The Lady of Arlington - Harnett T. Kane 3354

Belle Isle
Arouse and Beware - MacKinlay Kantor 3360

Blue Ridge Mountains
Beckoning Ridge - Emerson Waldman 6527
The Land Is Bright - James Arthur Kjelgaard 3508

Charlottesville
Jefferson: A Novel - Max Byrd 838

Chesapeake Bay
Caleb Pettengill U.S.N. - George Fielding Eliot 1912
Thunder on the Chesapeake - David Divine 1650

Fredericksburg
The Band Plays Dixie - Morris Markey 4089
Joy From Ashes - Al Lacy 3581

Harpers Ferry
Flashman and the Angel of the Lord - George MacDonald Fraser 2205
One Wore Blue - Heather Graham 2517
Raising Holy Hell - Bruce Olds 4718

James River
A Question of Honour - Clifford Dowdey 1707

Lexington
Christmas with Robert E. Lee - Helen Topping Miller 4387

Manassas
Madame Castel's Lodger - Frances Parkinson Keyes 3480
Rebel - Bernard Cornwell 1336

Monticello
The President's Daughter - Barbara Chase-Riboud 1005
Sally Hemings - Barbara Chase-Riboud 1006

Mount Vernon
Christmas at Mount Vernon - Helen Topping Miller 4385
Man From Mt. Vernon - Burke Boyce 607

Norfolk
Armored Giants: A Novel of the Civil War - F. van Wyck Mason 4145
Proud New Flags - F. van Wyck Mason 4156

Petersburg
The Crater - Richard Slotkin 5908
Glory Enough for All: The Battle of the Crater - Duane Philip Schultz 5673
Where My Love Sleeps - Clifford Dowdey 1710

Portsmouth
Thunder on the Chesapeake - David Divine 1650

Prince Edward County
The World Turned Upside Down - William Rayner 5273

Prince William County
The Stars of the South - Julian Green 2568

Richmond
The Band Plays Dixie - Morris Markey 4089
Beloved - Vina Delmar 1599
Black Thunder - Arna Bontemps 574
Bride of Fortune - Harnett T. Kane 3352
The Bright Sword - Eleanor Perenyi 4911
Bugles Blow No More - Clifford Dowdey 1704
The Court Martial of Robert E. Lee - Douglas Savage 5617
Defiant Hearts - Janelle Taylor 6185
The Fifth Conspiracy - Ted Jones 3296
Gray Canaan - David Garth 2305
Gray Victory - Robert Skimin 5877
The Lady of Arlington - Harnett T. Kane 3354
The Light Infantry Ball - Hamilton Basso 375
Love and War - John Jakes 3150
McKensie's Hundred: A Tale of the Old Dominion - Frank Yerby 6924
My Savage Muse: The Story of My Life: Edgar Allan Poe, an Imaginative Work - Bernhardt J. Hurwood 3087
My Theodosia - Anya Seton 5753
Night March - Bruce Lancaster 3641
Prisoner of Twilight - Don Robertson 5400
The Proud Retreat - Clifford Dowdey 1706
The Raven - Chancellor Williams 6769
Rebel - Bernard Cornwell 1336
The Richmond Raid - John Brick 674
Sing for a Penny - Clifford Dowdey 1708
The Titans - John Jakes 3154
Very Young Mrs. Poe - Cothburn O'Neal 4740
Weep No More - Janet Stevenson 6006
Where My Love Sleeps - Clifford Dowdey 1710
While the Music Plays - Diane Austell 242
Yankee Stranger - Elswyth Thane 6217

Shenandoah Valley
Action at Aquila - Hervey Allen 97
Banner at Shenandoah - Bruce Catton 963
Beckoning Ridge - Emerson Waldman 6527
Roll, Shenandoah - Bruce Lancaster 3644
The Second Face of Valor - Ray Grant Toepfer 6288
Shadow on the Valley - Kirk Mitchell 4414

Southampton
The Confessions of Nat Turner - William Styron 6106

Tidewater
Tidewater Dynasty: A Biographical Novel of the Lees of Stratford Hall - Carey Roberts 5372

Williamsburg
Dawn's Early Light - Elswyth Thane 6215
Ever After - Elswyth Thane 6216
Patriot's Dream - Barbara Michaels 4360
The Tree of Liberty - Elizabeth Page 4773
Yankee Stranger - Elswyth Thane 6217

Yorktown
Blind Journey - Bruce Lancaster 3636
The French Admiral - Dewey Lambdin 3609
King's Masque - Evan John 3220
The Lady From Yorktown - Eva McDonald 4260
Proceed, Sergeant Lamb - Robert Graves 2550
The Proud and the Free - Howard Fast 2042
Sea Road to Yorktown - Harvey Haislip 2644
Yorktown - Burke Davis 1513

WASHINGTON

All the Brave Rifles - Clarke Venable 6450
Cargo of Brides - Helen Rucker 5522
Chief Joseph - Bill Dugan 1756
Mighty Mountain - Archie Binns 502
Poor Boy and a Long Way Home - James Sherburne 5806
Washington! - Dana Fuller Ross 5491

Bellingham Bay
The Living - Annie Dillard 1644

Columbia River Valley
The Women at Pine Creek - Allis McKay 4279

North Falls
Courting Emma Howe - Margaret A. Robinson 5410

Port Garry
Silver Fruit - Patricia Campbell 876

Port Townsend
Cedarhaven - Patricia Campbell 874

Puget Sound
The Glorious Three - June Wetherell 6651
The Royal Ann Tree - Patricia Campbell 875

Seattle
The Goldseekers - William R. Burnett 794
The Living - Annie Dillard 1644
Seattle Green - Jane Adams 26

Snoqualmie Valley
The Cup of Strength - Charlotte Paul 4840
Gold Mountain - Charlotte Paul 4841

Walla Walla
The Moon-Eyed Appaloosa - Bill Gulick 2617

Yakima Valley
A Land to Tame - Zola Helen Ross 5505

WEST

The American - Louis Dodge 1669
American Eden - Marilyn Harris 2728
Angle of Repose - Wallace Stegner 5989
The Big Sky - A.B. Guthrie Jr. 2624
Bitter Creek - Al Cody 1150
The Buckskin Girl: A Novel of the California Trail in the Mid-Nineteenth Century - Gwen Moffat 4426
Buffalo Girls - Larry McMurtry 4296
Burton and Speke - William Harrison 2751
Castle Garden - Bill Albert 63
The Chisholms - Evan Hunter 3082
Cloud on the Land - Julia Davis 1526
Conquering Horse - Frederick F. Manfred 4055
Crazy Fox Remembers - Don Preston 5174
Creek Mary's Blood - Dee Brown 712
Dances with Wolves - Michael Blake 537
Death at Rainy Mountain - Mardi Oakley Medawar 4321
The Fast Men - Tom McNab 4302
Flashman and the Redskins - George MacDonald Fraser 2208
Follow the Free Wind - Leigh Brackett 621
Fool's Coach - Richard S. Wheeler 6659
From Sea to Shining Sea - James Alexander Thom 6232
The Further Adventures of Huckleberry Finn - Greg Matthews 4189
A Good Day to Die - Del Barton 368
Gunman - Loren D. Estleman 1971
Hanta Yo - Ruth Beebe Hill 2951
Hard on the Road - Barbara Moore 4440
Heaven and Hell - John Jakes 3147
The Holy Warrior - Gilbert Morris 4462
Kelly Blue - Peter Bowen 601
Little Big Man - Thomas Berger 478
Loving Belle Star - Robert Taylor 6187

The Man From Broken Hills - Louis L'Amour 3622
The Medicine Calf - Bill Hotchkiss 3037
Monte Walsh - Jack Schaefer 5635
The No-Return Trail - Sonia Levitin 3741
Power in the Blood - Greg Matthews 4191
Prairie - Anna Lee Waldo 6528
Railroad West - Cornelia Meigs 4327
Rapaho - Jamie Lee Cooper 1314
Ride the Dark Trail - Louis L'Amour 3624
Sacajawea - Anna Lee Waldo 6529
Seven Rivers West - Edward Hoagland 2959
Shadow Catcher - Charles Fergus 2064
Shaggy Legion - Hal George Evarts 1986
The Shining Mountains - Dale Van Every 6410
Soldier in Buckskin - Ray Hogan 2981
The Stars in Their Courses - Harry Brown 722
Tale of Valor - Vardis Fisher 2112
This Old Bill - Loren D. Estleman 1980
To the Swift - Anne Hawkins 2783
Trail: The Story of the Lewis and Clark Expedition - Louis Charbonneau 998
The True Memoirs of Charley Blankenship - Benjamin Capps 890
Western Union - Zane Grey 2589
Wild Times - Brian Garfield 2291
Yellowhorse - Dee Brown 715

Sante Fe Trail
Oh, Valley Green - John H. Culp 1443

Yellowstone River
Expedition! - Dana Fuller Ross 5473
Westward! - Dana Fuller Ross 5492

WEST VIRGINIA

Full of Thy Riches - Elizabeth Ferrell 2070
Loving Little Egypt - Thomas McMahon 4288
Power - Howard Fast 2041
The Scapegoat - Mary Lee Settle 5758
A Vein of Riches - John Knowles 3526

Justice County
Storming Heaven - Denise Giardina 2394

Wheeling
The Road to Baltimore - Robert S. Harper 2716

White Sulphur Springs
Roses From the South - Perceval Reniers 5304

WISCONSIN

Big River, Big Man - Thomas William Duncan 1786
Billy Sunday - Rod Jones 3295
Caddie Woodlawn - Carol Brink 692
Double Wedding Ring - Patricia Wendorf 6624
Elegant Journey - John Selby 5740
A Fistful of Stars - Sarah Lockwood 3828
The Grandmothers - Glenway Westcott 6640
The Hills Stand Watch - August Derleth 1615
The House on the Mound - August Derleth 1616
Look Away! - George Nauman Shuster 5841
Michael Beam - Richard Hallet 2663
Richard Walden's Wife - Eleanor Kelly 3399
The Shadow in the Glass - August Derleth 1618
Trail-Makers of the Middle Border - Hamlin Garland 2296
Wind over Wisconsin - August Derleth 1620
Winds of Spring - Walter Havighurst 2776
The Wolfling: A Documentary Novel of the 1870s - Sterling North 4648

Milwaukee
A Token of Jewels - Diane Cory 1353
Wisconsin! - Dana Fuller Ross 5493

Peshtigo
My Sister's Keeper - Beverly Butler 817

Prairie du Chien
There Was a Season: A Biographical Novel of Jefferson Davis - Theodore Olsen 4730

Sac Prairie
Restless Is the River - August Derleth 1617
Still Is the Summer Night - August Derleth 1619

Sheboygan
She Rode a Yellow Stallion - Walter Reed 5286

WYOMING

Black Sun - Terry C. Johnston 3242
Blood Song - Terry C. Johnston 3243
Blue Russell - Will Bryant 738
Carrington - Michael Whitney Straight 6074
A Cold Day in Hell - Terry C. Johnston 3247
The Cowboys - William Dale Jennings 3211
Fair is the Rose - Meagan MacKinney 3997
The Fleet Rabble: A Novel of the Nez Perce War - Frank Borden Hanes 2675
The Gilded Rooster - Richard Emery Roberts 5391
The Jewelled Spur - Gilbert Morris 4465
Lakota - G. Clifton Wisler 6833
The Man Who Loved Cat Dancing - Marilyn Durham 1817
The Medicine Whip - Max Hennessy 2835
North Against the Sioux - Kenneth Ulyatt 6376
The Odyssey of Thaddeus Baxter - Robert P. Lund 3926
Riders of Judgment - Frederick F. Manfred 4059
The Running Iron - Rachel Ann Fish 2097
Savage Thunder - Johanna Lindsey 3795
The Scout - Harry Combs 1224
Sitting Bull - Bill Dugan 1760
The Story of the Sundance Kid - David Everitt 1988
The Talking Rifle - Glenn R. Vernam 6454
Thunder in the Dawn - Earl Murray 4532
Trumpet on the Land - Terry C. Johnston 3260
The Valiant Gunman - Gilbert Morris 4474
Where Is My Wandering Boy Tonight? - David Wagoner 6522
Wyoming! - Dana Fuller Ross 5494
The Yellowstone - Winfred Blevins 549

Big Horn Mountains
The Legend of Ben Tree - Paul Hawkins 2784
Winter Rain - Terry C. Johnston 3262

Cheyenne
The Fortune Road - James McCague 4217
Mister St. John - Loren D. Estleman 1974
Theory of War - Joan Brady 637
Trouble Shooter - Ernest Haycox 2791

Collins
Outlaw Lover - Lindsey Hanks 2676

Dustville
Liveliest Town in the West - Bill Gulick 2615

Fort Laramie
John Crews - Arthur Chapman 988
Journey by the River - John Prescott 5173
Wagons West - Leslie Turner White 6692

Fort Phil Kearney
Red Cloud's Revenge - Terry C. Johnston 3255

Jamesville
Three Rivers - Carla J. Mills 4406

Laramie
Calamity Jane of Deadwood Gulch - Ethel Hueston 3068
The Fortune Road - James McCague 4217

Oregon Trail
Blood on the Divide - William W. Johnstone 3265

Platte Bridge
Cry of the Hawk - Terry C. Johnston 3248

Powder River
The Snowblind Moon - John Byrne Cooke   1267

Sweetwater Valley
Honor Thy Father - Robert A. Roripaugh   5460

Ten Smoke River
The Grassman - Len Fulton   2256

Wind River
Free Flows the River - Earl Murray   4529

Yellowstone River
Free Flows the River - Earl Murray   4529
Wilderness - Roger Zelazny   6957

URUGUAY

Halfhyde and the Flag Captain - Philip McCutchan   4245

UZBEKISTAN

Samarkand
Master of the World - Cothburn O'Neal   4738

VENEZUELA

Coasts of Folly - Joel Williams   6784
Ramage's Mutiny - Dudley Pope   5106
The Red Lances - Arturo Uslar Pietri   4999

Caracas
Manuela, La Caballeresa Del Sol - Demetrio Aguilera Malta   41
Westward Ho! - Charles Kingsley   3499

VIETNAM

Saigon
Saigon - Anthony Grey   2588

WALES

Ann of Cambray - Mary Lide   3772
Autumn Lace - Eileen Jackson   3133
The Betrothed - Sir Walter Scott   5691
Bond of Blood - Roberta Gellis   2349
The Brothers of Gwynedd - Edith Pargeter   4796
Canis the Warrior - James Sinclair   5864
The Children of the First Man - James Alexander Thom   6230
Crown in Candlelight - Rosemary Hawley Jarman   3166
The Crystal Cave - Mary Stewart   6029
Cup of Gold - John Steinbeck   5991
Dark at Noon - Jill Tattersall   6173
The De Montfort Legacy - Pamela Bennetts   447
A Dragon for Edward - Pamela Bennetts   450
Falls the Shadow - Sharon Kay Penman   4903
Fortune Made His Sword - Martha Rofheart   5426
The Foster Brothers - Edward Frankland   2202
The Fox-Red Hills - Cynthia S. Roberts   5374
The Glendower Conspiracy - Lloyd Biggle Jr.   494
Glendower Country - Martha Rofheart   5427
Good King Harry - Denise Giardina   2393

Hammer of the Scots - Jean Plaidy   5018
Hanging on the Wire - Gillian Linscott   3806
Harp into Battle - Cecil Maiden   4031
Harry of Monmouth - A.M. Maughan   4199
Here Be Dragons - Sharon Kay Penman   4904
The Hollow Hills - Mary Stewart   6030
The Hooded Falcon - Prudence Andrew   140
How Green Was My Valley - Richard Llewellyn   3813
In the Shadow of Midnight - Marsha Canham   880
A King Reluctant - William Vaughan Wilkins   6759
Kingdom of the Grail - A.A. Attanasio   226
Kinsmen of the Grail - Dorothy James Roberts   5376
Lady of Hay - Barbara Erskine   1955
The Last Enchantment - Mary Stewart   6031
Lord of Misrule - Gareth Jones   3290
The Maid of Sker - R.D. Blackmore   529
A Moment in Time - Bertrice Small   5911
A Morbid Taste for Bones - Ellis Peters   4965
Owen Glendower - John Cowper Powys   5159
Proud Mary - Iris Gower   2501
The Rape of the Fair Country - Alexander Cordell   1325
The Reckoning - Sharon Kay Penman   4906
The Road to Avalon - Joan Wolf   6842
A Royal Quest - Mary Lide   3777
Sara - Brian Cleeve   1110
Simon the Coldheart - Georgette Heyer   2901
The Summer of the Danes - Ellis Peters   4973
The Swan of Usk - Helen Ashton   220
Ten Years Beyond Baker Street - Cay Van Ash   6400
This Sweet and Bitter Earth - Alexander Cordell   1326
Through the Green Valley - Barbara Gowdy   2498
An Unknown Welshman - Jean Stubbs   6100
Vale of Tyranny - Suzanne Butler   831
When Christ and His Saints Slept - Sharon Kay Penman   4908
The Wind From Hastings - Morgan Llywelyn   3825

Neath
Spy in Chancery - P.C. Doherty   1680

Radnor Forest
Where Magic Dwells - Rexanne Becnel   411

Swansea
Fiddler's Ferry - Iris Gower   2499
Morgan's Woman - Iris Gower   2500
Spinners' Wharf - Iris Gower   2502

Welsh Marches
The Briar Rose - Linda Neale   4561
The Heaven Tree Trilogy - Edith Pargeter   4797
The Leopard Unleashed - Elizabeth Chadwick   967
The Running Vixen Elizabeth Chadwick   968
The Wild Hunt - Elizabeth Chadwick   969

WEST INDIES

The Adventures of Long John Silver - Denis Judd   3317
Anne Bonny - Chloe Gartner   2306
Buccaneer Surgeon - C.V. Terry   6205
Cambridge - Caryl Phillips   4983
Captain Adam - Donald Barr Chidsey   1058
Captain Blood - Rafael Sabatini   5546

The Captain From Connecticut - C.S. Forester   2171
Caribbee - Thomas Hoover   3025
The Changeling - Alison Macleod   4000
The Cross and the Sword - Manuel de Jesus Galvan   2274
Cutlass Empire - F. van Wyck Mason   4148
Damnation Reef - Jill Tattersall   6172
Die the Long Day - Orlando Patterson   4833
The Edge of Piracy - Donald Barr Chidsey   1060
Fanny: Being the True History of the Adventures of Fanny Hackabout-Jones - Erica Jong   3299
First Lieutenant - Kenneth Maynard   4208
Governor Ramage, R.N. - Dudley Pope   5096
The Harp and the Shadow - Alejo Carpentier   905
I, John Mordaunt - Virgil Scott   5687
The King's Coat - Dewey Lambdin   3612
The King's Commission - Dewey Lambdin   3614
The Memoirs of Christopher Columbus - Stephen Marlowe   4096
Mistress of Darkness - Christopher Nicole   4617
My Master Columbus - Cedric Belfrage   418
On Stranger Tides - Tim Powers   5156
Pride's Fancy - Thomas H. Raddall   5231
The Privateer - Gordon Daviot   1510
The Pyrates - George MacDonald Fraser   2212
Ramage and the Rebels - Dudley Pope   5100
Ramage's Prize - Dudley Pope   5107
Ramage's Trial - Dudley Pope   5109
Return to Treasure Island - Denis Judd   3318
Sea of Lentils - Antonio Benitez-Rojo   443
Sea Road to Yorktown - Harvey Haislip   2644
Sea Star: The Private Life of Anne Bonny, Pirate - Pamela Jekel   3187
Seventeen of Leyden - John James   3160
Surprise - Brian Burland   785
Treasure Island - Robert Louis Stevenson   6012
The Triton Brig - Dudley Pope   5110
Voyager - Diana Gabaldon   2265
War Chief - Donald Clayton Porter   5130
Westward to Laughter - Colin MacInnes   3984
Wind From the Main - Anne Osborne   4759

Grand Turk
Eagle in the Sky - F. van Wyck Mason   4149

Hispaniola
The Devil's Own - Christopher Nicole   4615
To the Indies - C.S. Forester   2183

Stacia
Captain Barney - Jan Westcott   6642

Tortuga
Burning Gold - Robert Hardy Andrews   148

YUGOSLAVIA

Belgrade
Flight From Bucharest - R.T. Stevens   6000

ZANZIBAR

Trade Wind - M.M. Kaye   3378

ZIMBABWE

The Covenant - James A. Michener   4368

Subject Index

This index lists subjects that are covered in the featured titles. These include such things as historical events (e.g. the Jacobite Rebellion, World War I), story types (e.g. Mystery, Sea Story), major time periods (e.g. the Middle Ages, the Victorian Period), and social concerns (e.g. the Labor Movement, Racial Conflict). Beneath each subject heading, titles are arranged alphabetically, with author names and entry numbers.

Abolition Movement

Diana Stair - Floyd Dell 1594
Fire Bell in the Night - Constance Robertson 5395
The Inner Voice - Nina Wilcox Putnam 5211
Matthew Early - Alexander Laing 3589
The Sun Shines West - Nathan Schachner 5632

Aborigines

The Chant of Jimmie Blacksmith - Thomas Keneally 3411
The Dreaming: A Novel of Australia - Barbara Wood 6848
Where the Willows Weep - Patricia Shaw 5781

Adolescence

Unto the Soul - Aharon Appelfeld 181

Adventure

The Golden Sabre - Jon Cleary 1105
High Road to China - Jon Cleary 1106
Lord of the Isles - Donald Barr Chidsey 1063

Afghan War

Beyond All Frontiers - Emma Drummond 1722
Flashman - George MacDonald Fraser 2204
The Leopard and the Cliff - Wallace Breem 655
Stormswift - Madeleine Brent 662

Afrikaaners

The Covenant - Brigid Knight 3521
The Fiercest Heart - Stuart Cloete 1122
The Great Sky and the Silence - James S. Rand 5245
King of the Bastards - Sarah Gertrude Millin 4405
The Mask - Stuart Cloete 1125
The Turning Wheels - Stuart Cloete 1127
Watch for the Dawn - Stuart Cloete 1128

Agincourt, Battle of

Falstaff - Robert Nye 4653
Fortune Made His Sword - Martha Rofheart 5426
Good King Harry - Denise Giardina 2393
Harry of Monmouth - A.M. Maughan 4199
The Lily and the Leopard - Susan Wiggs 6745
Royal Sword at Agincourt - Pamela Bennetts 455
The Star of Lancaster - Jean Plaidy 5065

Walk with Peril - Dorothy V.S. Jackson 3132
Wife to Henry V - Hilda Lewis 3752

Alamance, Battle of

Weathercock - Constance Dodge 1668

Alamo, Battle of the

All the Brave Rifles - Clarke Venable 6450
The Bugles Are Silent: A Novel of the Texas Revolution - John R. Knaggs 3513
Crockett of Tennessee: A Novel Based on the Life and Times of David Crockett - Cameron Judd 3314
Empire of Bones: A Novel of Sam Houston and the Texas Revolution - Jeff Long 3868
The Furies - John Jakes 3146
The Iron Mistress - Paul I. Wellman 6618
The Men of Gonzales - John H. Culp 1442
The Road to San Jacinto - Leonard L. Foreman 2167
Tempered Blade - Monte Barrett 352
Wave High the Banner - Dee Brown 714

Albigensian Crusade

Bernadin, My Love - Leonard Rossiter 5506
Cities of the Flesh - Zoe Oldenbourg 4713
Deep Are the Valleys - Hannah Closs 1129
Destiny of Fire - Zoe Oldenbourg 4715
High Are the Mountains - Hannah Closs 1130
The Siege - Jay Williams 6773
The Silent Tarn - Hannah Closs 1131
Sybille - Marion Meade 4318

Alchemy

The Alchemist's Journal - Evan S. Connell 1256

Alien and Sedition Acts

Mistress of the Forge - David Taylor 6179

Alternate History

1901 - Robert Conroy 1258
Anno-Dracula - Kim Newman 4595
The Court-Martial of George Armstrong Custer - Douglas C. Jones 3276
Daimon - Abel Posse 5140
The Death of Napoleon - Simon Leys 3768

Eva - Ib Melchior 4329
God Save the Tsar - Susanna Hoe 2976
Hitler Has Won - Frederic Mullally 4511
A King Reluctant - William Vaughan Wilkins 6759
The Lost Years: A Biographical Fiction - Oscar Lewis 3757
Sea of Darkness - Roland Huntford 3086

American Colonies

Abigail - Mary Louise Aswell 221
Alexander Hamilton's Wife - Alice Curtis Desmond 1623
Always a River - Drayton Mayrant 4211
Ambush - Donald Clayton Porter 5113
American Beauty - Edna Ferber 2060
Angelique and the Demon - Sergeanne Golon 2466
Angelique in Love - Sergeanne Golon 2470
Anna Zenger: Mother of Freedom - Kent Cooper 1316
Arthur Dimmesdale - Charles R. Larson 3671
Ashes in the Wilderness - William Greenough Schofield 5649
Ask No Quarter - George Tracy Marsh 4099
Audrey - Mary Johnston 3229
Be My Love - Harriet Hinsdale 2955
Bear His Mild Yoke - Ethel White 6675
Bedford Village - Hervey Allen 99
Bend Your Heads All - Rowena Rutherford Farrar 2015
Bennett's Welcome - Inglis Fletcher 2132
The Big Drum - Elizabeth Boatwright Coker 1162
Black Angels - C.T. Ritchie 5348
Black Forest - Meade Minnigerode 4411
Blackrobe - Robert E. Wall 6534
Blessed Is the Land - Louis Zara 6949
Bloodbrothers - Robert E. Wall 6535
Blossom Like the Rose - Norah Lofts 3836
The Bondswoman - Caryl Ledner 3705
Boone: A Novel Based on the Life and Times of Daniel Boone - Cameron Judd 3311
The Braintree Mission - Nicholas E. Wyckoff 6887
Bridal Journey - Dale Van Every 6406
The Bride of the Wilderness - Charles McCarry 4220
The Bright Battalions - Howard Breslin 664
The Bright Face of Danger - Clifford Sublette 6108
Buckskin Baronet - Margaret Widdemer 6734
A Candle in the Wilderness - Irving A. Bacheller 256
Cape Cod - William Martin 4139
Captain Adam - Donald Barr Chidsey 1058
The Captive Bride - Gilbert Morris 4457
The Captive Witch - Dale Van Every 6407

Cardigan - Robert W. Chambers   976
Carolina Corsair - Don Tracy   6307
Catherwood - Marly Youmans   6937
The Changeling - Alison Macleod   4000
Charming Sally - Maude Hart Lovelace   3903
Cherokee - Donald Clayton Porter   5115
Chesapeake - James A. Michener   4367
Christopher Humble - Charles Burnet Judah   3310
The Cold Journey - Grace Zaring Stone   6052
Come Home at Even - Le Grand Cannon   884
Come Spring - Ben Ames Williams   6764
The Conqueror - John William Tebbel   6194
Cormorant's Brood - Inglis Fletcher   2133
The Countess Angelique - Sergeanne Golon   2472
Covenant of Grace - Jane Gilmore Rushing   5527
Croatan - Mary Johnston   3231
A Dangerous Innocence - Victoria Lincoln   3787
Dark Possession - Alice Alison Lide   3771
Dark Sails - Helen Topping Miller   4388
The Dark Stranger - Constance Dodge   1664
Daughter of Eve - Noel B. Gerson   2366
Daughter of Satan - Jean Plaidy   5011
Dawn's Early Light - Elswyth Thane   6215
The Day Before Thunder - Bart Spicer   5965
Deepwater: A Novel of the Carolinas - Pamela
   Jekel   3185
The Devil and Ben Franklin - Theodore
   Mathieson   4184
The Devil and the Mathers - Edward E. Elliott   1914
Devil Water - Anya Seton   5749
The Disturber - L.S. Davidson Jr.   1505
Don't Tread on Me - Walter Karig   3366
The Doom Trail - Arthur Douglas Smith   5917
The Drowning Room - Michael Kenneth Pye   5212
Drums of Autumn - Diana Gabaldon   2263
The Drums of December - Sharon Salvato   5575
A Durable Fire - Virginia Bernhard   480
The Dutchman - Maan Meyers   4351
The Dutchman's Dilemma - Maan Meyers   4352
The Eagle and the Wind - Herbert Stover   6068
Eagle Fur - Robert Newton Peck   4884
Echo of the Flute - Mildred A. Jordan   3304
Eden's Gate - Karen Harper   2711
Edge of Greatness - Winthrop Neilson   4575
Enough Good Men - Charles Mercer   4336
Erskine Dale, Pioneer - John Fox   2195
A Fair Wind Home - Ruth Moore   4443
Fire and the Hammer - Shirley Barker   311
The Firekeeper - Robert Moss   4498
The Fires of July - Sharon Salvato   5576
The First Rebel - Neil Harmon Swanson   6137
Flight From Avatchez - Frank G. Slaughter   5887
Follow the River - James Alexander Thom   6231
For Love of Two Eagles - Barbara Riefe   5328
The Forest and the Fort - Hervey Allen   100
*Forest Cavalier: A Romance of America's First
   Frontier and of Bacon's Rebellion* - Roy Catesby
   Flannagan   2122
The Forest Lord - Noel B. Gerson   2368
Forever Possess - Alexandra Phillips   4982
Fortress Fury - Carter A. Vaughan   6435
Free Man - Conrad Richter   5320
Freedom's Dues - Robert H. Abel   9
Freedom's Way - Theodora McCormick Du
   Bois   1742
Gallant Warrior - Helen R. Mann   4063
Gallows Hill - Frances Winwar   6831
Gamble's Hundred - Clifford Dowdey   1705
Gentleman Ranker - John Edward Jennings   3200
Gilman of the Redford - William Stearns Davis   1541
Give Me Liberty - Noel B. Gerson   2369
Give Me Liberty: The Story of an Innocent Man - John
   Erskine   1956
Give Me Your Golden Hand - Evelyn Eaton   1825
The Golden Feather - Theda Kenyon   3462
The Golden Wildcat - Margaret Widdemer   6735
The Governor's Daughter - Denton Whitson   6718
The Great Valley - Mary Johnston   3234
The Greater Hunger - Barbara Dodge Borland   581

The Green Mountain Boys - Daniel Pierce
   Thompson   6249
Hannah Fowler - Janice Holt Giles   2411
Harvest of Dreams - Jaroldeen Edwards   1884
Hester - Christopher Bigsby   496
A High Wind Rising - Elsie Singmaster   5867
The Highwayman - Noel B. Gerson   2372
Hilton Head - Josephine Pinckney   5003
The Holder of the World - Bharati Mukherjee   4510
The Holy Lover - Marie Oemler   4690
The Honorable Imposter - Gilbert Morris   4463
Hope Leslie; or, Early Times in Massachusetts -
   Catharine Maria Sedgwick   5714
Horseshoe Robinson, a Tale of the Tory Ascendancy -
   John P. Kennedy   3418
The Hunting Shirt - Mary Johnston   3235
I Seek a City - Gilbert Rees   5289
I, Tituba, Black Witch of Salem - Maryse
   Conde   1233
If Not Victory - Frank Olney Hough   3043
In Adam's Fall - Constance Dodge   1666
In the Days of Poor Richard - Irving A.
   Bacheller   259
The Indentured Heart - Gilbert Morris   4464
Indian Brother - Hubert Coryell   1354
Inherit the Earth - Margaret Shaw   5778
The Invincibles - Carter A. Vaughan   6436
Jason McGee - Robert H. Fowler   2190
Jeremiah Martin: A Revolutionary War Novel - Robert
   H. Fowler   2191
Judas Flowering - Jane Aiken Hodge   2965
The Judas Tree - Neil Harmon Swanson   6139
Juniata Valley - Virginia C. Cassel   954
The Kentuckians - Janice Holt Giles   2413
The King's Messenger - Samuel Edwards   1887
The King's Passenger - Nathan Schachner   5631
The Kingsbridge Plot - Maan Meyers   4355
Lady of the Mohawks - Margaret Widdemer   6736
Lady Washington - Dorothy Clarke Wilson   6803
The Land Beyond the Tempest - Drayton
   Mayrant   4213
The Land Breakers - John Ehle   1895
The Land Is Bright - Noel B. Gerson   2376
Land of the Beautiful River - Helmer
   Linderholm   3788
The Last Gentleman - Shirley Barker   312
The Latter Adventures of Tom Jones - Bob
   Coleman   1200
Legacy - Robert Vaughan   6448
Let the Spring Come - Henry Schindall   5637
Liberty Tavern - Thomas Fleming   2129
The Light in the Forest - Conrad Richter   5322
Lily of the Mohawks - Jack Casey   952
Log Cabin Noble - F. van Wyck Mason   4153
The Long Watch - Elizabeth Linington   3798
Look to the Mountain - Le Grand Cannon   885
*Look to Your Geese: A Novel of the Deflowering of
   New England* - Jacquin Sanders   5718
Lord Johnnie - Leslie Turner White   6687
The Lost Colony - Edison Marshall   4108
Love's Tender Fury - Jennifer Wilde   6749
Lovestorm - Judith E. French   2222
Lusty Wind for Carolina - Inglis Fletcher   2134
MacLyon - Lolah Burford   773
Man Cannot Tell - Philip Lightfoot Scruggs   5711
Margaret Brent, Adventurer - Dorothy Grant   2533
The Marriage Bed - Jean Clark   1088
Mary's Land - Lucia St. Clair Robson   5415
Massachusetts: A Novel - Nancy Zaroulis   6956
The Measure of the Years - Alice Mary Colver   1218
Meggy MacIntosh - Elizabeth Janet Gray   2555
Men of Albemarle - Inglis Fletcher   2135
Milton in America - Peter Ackroyd   20
A Mirror for Witches - Esther Forbes   2157
Mistress Devon - Virginia Coffman   1156
The Mists of Manittoo - Lois Swann   6135
Mohawk Woman - Barbara Riefe   5329
Moonfeather - Judith E. French   2223
Morning of a Hero - Burke Boyce   608

My Thomas: A Novel of Martha Jefferson's Life -
   Roberta Grimes   2593
Nantucket Woman - Diana Gaines   2269
The Navigator: The Story of Nathaniel Bowditch -
   Alfred Stanford   5979
Next to Valour - John Edward Jennings   3202
Night of Decision: A Novel of Colonial New York -
   Dorothy Grant   2534
No Other Place - John Gould   2497
Nobody's Angel - Karen Robards   5363
Northwest Passage - Kenneth Roberts   5388
Now Face to Face - Karleen Koen   3530
O Beulah Land - Mary Lee Settle   5756
O Western Wind - John Anthony Devon   1634
Oh, Kentucky! - Betty Layman Receveur   5284
One Red Rose Forever - Mildred A. Jordan   3305
The Overmountain Men - Cameron Judd   3315
Paradise - Esther Forbes   2158
Peace, My Daughters - Shirley Barker   314
Pearl - Christopher Bigsby   497
The Perilous Night - Burke Boyce   609
Pilgrims: A Novel of the Mayflower - Gerard
   Mac   3955
A Pirate's Pleasure - Heather Graham   2518
A Place Called Freedom - Ken Follett   2150
The Plymouth Adventure - Ernest Gebler   2342
Pocahontas - Susan Donnell   1691
Pocahontas; or, The Nonpareil of Virginia - David
   Garnett   2297
The Power and the Passion - Christina
   Nicholson   4609
Powhatan's Daughter - John Clarke Bowman   605
Prisoners of Hope: A Tale of Colonial Virginia - Mary
   Johnston   3238
Proceed, Sergeant Lamb - Robert Graves   2550
The Prospering - Elizabeth Speare   5954
Raleigh's Eden - Inglis Fletcher   2137
Ram: Being the Tale of One Ramillies Anstruther -
   Winchombe Taylor   6193
Rascal's Heaven - F. van Wyck Mason   4157
The Rebel and the Turncoat - Malcolm Decker   1576
Red Cloak Flying - Margaret Widdemer   6737
Red Morning - Ruby Frazier Frey   2230
Redcoat - Bernard Cornwell   1337
The Redemptioner - Isaac Rusling Pennypacker   4910
Remembrance Rock - Carl Sandburg   5583
The Renegade - Donald Clayton Porter   5122
Renno - Donald Clayton Porter   5123
Riding Shotgun - Rita Mae Brown   729
The Rival Shores - Arthur Beverly-Giddings   487
River out of Eden - Shirley Seifert   5732
Rivers Parting - Shirley Barker   315
The Road to Bunker Hill - Shirley Barker   316
Road to Lendor - Esther Hammon   1966
Roanoke Renegade - Don Tracy   6311
Roanoke Warrior - Carter A. Vaughan   6438
Roger Sudden - Thomas H. Raddall   5232
The Rogue and the Witch - John Edward
   Newton   4605
Rogue's Harbor - Inglis Fletcher   2139
The Sachem - Donald Clayton Porter   5124
Sackett's Land - Louis L'Amour   3628
Salute to Adventurers - John Buchan   752
Sarah Camberwell Tring - Janet Edmonds   1869
The Savage City - Jean Paradise   4787
Savage Gentleman - Noel B. Gerson   2381
Scarlet Cockerel - Clifford Sublette   6110
Scarlet Feather - Dale Van Every   6409
The Scarlet Letter - Nathaniel Hawthorne   2786
Scarlet Ribbons - Judith E. French   2224
The Scotswoman - Inglis Fletcher   2140
Scoundrels' Brigade - Carter A. Vaughan   6439
The Sea 'Venture - F. van Wyck Mason   4159
Seasons of Fear - Philip McFarland   4272
Seneca - Donald Clayton Porter   5127
The Seneca Hostage - Carter A. Vaughan   6440
Shadow of the Moon - Douglas C. Jones   3284
The Silent Drum - Neil Harmon Swanson   6141
Silent Drums - Mike Roarke   5361

The Silver Oar - Howard Breslin 669
The Silver Saber - Carter A. Vaughan 6441
Silver Shoals - Hamilton Cochran 1142
The Slave Ship - Mary Johnston 3240
Soldier in Paradise - Burton Wohl 6835
Soldiers of Fortune - Peter Bourne 595
Song of the Susquehanna - Herbert Stover 6071
Sons of Liberty - Adam Rutledge 5540
The Sot-Weed Factor - John Barth 364
Sound of the Trumpet - Gilbert Morris 4471
The Sounds of Chariots: A Novel of John Sevier and the State of Franklin - Helen Topping Miller 4396
Stately Timber - Rupert Hughes 3075
Storm Against the Wind - Helen Hull Jacobs 3138
The Strange Death of Mistress Coffin - Robert J. Begiebing 415
Summer Thunder - Willie Snow Ethridge 1982
Take Her, Mr. Wesley - John W. Drakeford 1719
Tavern in the Town - Cecile Hulse Matschat 4187
The Temptation of Angelique - Sergeanne Golon 2473
Thanksgiving - Terry Coleman 1207
That Dark and Bloody River - Allen W. Eckert 1845
There Is a Season - Alice Mary Colver 1219
Three Fields to Cross - Francis Tysen Nutt 4651
Three Sides of Agiochook - Eric Kelly 3400
Thunder in the East - Mike Roarke 5362
Tidewater Dynasty: A Biographical Novel of the Lees of Stratford Hall - Carey Roberts 5372
To Fame Unknown - Clifford Lindsey Alderman 67
To Have and to Hold - Mary Johnston 3241
To the Far Blue Mountains - Louis L'Amour 3630
A Toast to the King - Elizabeth Coatsworth 1139
Toil of the Brave - Inglis Fletcher 2141
Tomahawk - Donald Clayton Porter 5129
Tomorrow the New Moon - Shirley Barker 319
Torn Covenants - Lois Swann 6136
Toward the Morning - Hervey Allen 101
The Tree of Liberty - Elizabeth Page 4773
Tristram Bent - Henry Barnard Safford 5560
Turn of the Dice - Janet Edmonds 1870
Uncharted Ways - Caroline Snedeker 5935
The Unconquered - Neil Harmon Swanson 6142
Until the Winds - Jean Clark 1089
The Unvanquished - Howard Fast 2046
Up Country: A Story of the Vanguard - Donald Culross Peattie 4881
Valley in Arms: A Novel of the Settlement of Connecticut - Earl Schenck Miers 4376
The Virginia Comedians - John Esten Cooke 1269
The Voyagers - Dale Van Every 6412
War Chief - Donald Clayton Porter 5130
War Cry - Donald Clayton Porter 5132
War in the Golden Weather - Stephen Longstreet 3892
War Paint and Rouge - Robert W. Chambers 983
The Warrior's Path - Louis L'Amour 3633
The Water Witch - James Fenimore Cooper 1311
Waters of the Wilderness - Shirley Seifert 5737
Weathercock - Constance Dodge 1668
The Wept of Wish-Ton-Wish - James Fenimore Cooper 1312
White Indian - Donald Clayton Porter 5134
White Rising - Zane Kotker 3548
Wicked Lady - Inglis Fletcher 2142
The Wickedest Pilgrim - Donald Barr Chidsey 1067
The Wilderness - Carter A. Vaughan 6442
Wilderness Adventure - Elizabeth Page 4774
The Willing Maid - C.T. Ritchie 5349
Wind From the Main - Anne Osborne 4759
The Wind in the Forest - Inglis Fletcher 2143
The Winthrop Woman - Anya Seton 5754
Witnesses - Marcy Moran Heidish 2820
The Woman Who Fell From the Sky - Barbara Riefe 5330
The Yankee Brig - Carter A. Vaughan 6443
Yankee Doodle Dandy - Noel B. Gerson 2387
Yankee Rogue - Dana Fuller Ross 5496
Yankee Trader - Stanley Morton 4496

The Yemassee - William Gilmore Simms 5855
Yorktown - Burke Davis 1513
The Young Man From Mount Vernon - Arthur Stanwood Pier 4995

American Revolution

Alice of Old Vincennes - Maurice Thompson 6268
April Morning - Howard Fast 2027
The Arch of Stars - Clifford Lindsey Alderman 66
Arundel - Kenneth Roberts 5383
The Bastard - John Jakes 3144
Battle Lanterns - Merrit Parmalee Allen 102
Bend Your Heads All - Rowena Rutherford Farrar 2015
The Big Family - Vina Delmar 1600
The Big Knives - Bruce Lancaster 3635
Birthright - Robert E. Wall 6533
Black Forest - Meade Minnigerode 4411
Blind Journey - Bruce Lancaster 3636
The Bonnet Laird's Daughter - Barbara Annandale 154
The Border Men - Cameron Judd 3312
The Brahmins - Eileen Lottman 3901
The Braintree Mission - Nicholas E. Wyckoff 6887
Bridal Journey - Dale Van Every 6406
Bride of Liberty - Frank Yerby 6909
Brother Owl - Al Hine 2953
Brother to the Enemy - Bart Spicer 5964
Burr - Gore Vidal 6485
By Force of Arms - James L. Nelson 4579
Cannon's Call - Adam Rutledge 5537
Captain Barney - Jan Westcott 6642
Captain Paul - Edward Ellsberg 1930
The Captive Witch - Dale Van Every 6407
The Captives - Don Wright 6878
Cardigan - Robert W. Chambers 976
The Carolinian - Rafael Sabatini 5547
The Carolinians - Jane Barry 357
Catch a Falling Star - Frederic F. Van de Water 6401
Cato's War - Guy Wheeler 6655
Celia Garth - Gwen Bristow 695
Cherokee - Donald Clayton Porter 5115
Chesapeake - James A. Michener 4367
Choctaw - Donald Clayton Porter 5116
Christmas at Mount Vernon - Helen Topping Miller 4385
Citizen Tom Paine - Howard Fast 2028
Clear for Action: A Novel about John Paul Jones - Clements Ripley 5344
Clouds of Destiny - Lou Ellen Davis 1535
The Coat I Wore - Lucile Finlay 2090
Come Spring - Ben Ames Williams 6764
Conceived in Liberty - Howard Fast 2029
Concord Bridge - Howard Horne 3035
The Conqueror: Being the True and Romantic Story of Alexander Hamilton - Gertrude Atherton 222
The Court Martial of Daniel Boone - Allen W. Eckert 1840
The Crossing - Winston Churchill 1080
The Culper Spy Ring - Lynn Groh 2596
The Dark Stranger - Constance Dodge 1664
A Daughter of Liberty - Allan Cole 1196
Dawn's Early Light - Elswyth Thane 6215
The Day Before Thunder - Bart Spicer 5965
The Day Must Dawn - Agnes Sligh Turnbull 6362
Day of Battle - Frederic F. Van de Water 6402
Delilah's Mountain - Gloria Jahoda 3142
Don't Tread on Me - Walter Karig 3366
Dragon Cove - Carter A. Vaughan 6434
Drums - James Boyd 611
Drums Along the Mohawk - Walter D. Edmonds 1874
The Drums of April - Charles Mergendahl 4340
The Drums of December - Sharon Salvato 5575
The Drums of Monmouth - Emma Gelders Sterne 5998

The Drums of Winter - Sandra Paretti 4790
The Eagle and the Wind - Herbert Stover 6068
Eagle in the Sky - F. van Wyck Mason 4149
Eagle of Niagara: The Story of David Harper and His Indian Captivity - John Brick 671
Eagles Where I Walk - Stephen Longstreet 3885
East to Bagaduce - Willard Wallace 6539
Echo of the Flute - Mildred A. Jordan 3304
The Edge of Piracy - Donald Barr Chidsey 1060
Enough Good Men - Charles Mercer 4336
Erskine Dale, Pioneer - John Fox 2195
The Exquisite Siren - Edwin Haines 2639
Faith and Honor - Robin Maderich 4025
The Fallon Blood - Reagan O'Neal 4741
Farewell to Valley Forge - David Taylor 6178
A Few Painted Feathers - Stephen Longstreet 3886
Fire and the Hammer - Shirley Barker 311
The Firelands - Karen Harper 2712
The Fires of July - Sharon Salvato 5576
Flight From Avatchez - Frank G. Slaughter 5887
Flintlock - Jason Manning 4073
The Forbidden Ground - Neil Harmon Swanson 6138
Fortress Fury - Carter A. Vaughan 6435
Free Man - Conrad Richter 5320
Freedom's Dues - Robert H. Abel 9
Freedom's Way - Theodora McCormick Du Bois 1742
The French Admiral - Dewey Lambdin 3609
From Sea to Shining Sea - James Alexander Thom 6232
Gallant Captain - Pearl Frye 2242
The General's Lady - Esther Forbes 2156
The Gentle Rebel - Gilbert Morris 4461
Gilman of the Redford - William Stearns Davis 1541
Give Me Liberty - Noel B. Gerson 2369
Give Me Liberty: The Story of an Innocent Man - John Erskine 1956
Give Me Your Golden Hand - Evelyn Eaton 1825
The Governor's Lady - Thomas H. Raddall 5228
The Great Meadow - Elizabeth Madox Roberts 5378
The Green Mountain Boys - Daniel Pierce Thompson 6249
The Guernseyman - C. Northcote Parkinson 4812
Guns for Rebellion - F. van Wyck Mason 4151
Guns of Burgoyne - Bruce Lancaster 3640
Hang for Treason - Robert Newton Peck 4886
Harvest of Dreams - Jaroldeen Edwards 1884
The Hawks of Hawk-Hollow - Robert Montgomery Bird 504
Haym Solomon, Son of Liberty - Howard Fast 2032
Hearts of Fire - Christina Savage 5616
Henry Lunt and the Ranger - Tom McNamara 4304
The Hessian - Howard Fast 2033
Hidden Children - Robert W. Chambers 978
His Majesty's Yankees - Thomas H. Raddall 5230
His Was the Fire - Showell Styles 6104
Horseshoe Robinson, a Tale of the Tory Ascendancy - John P. Kennedy 3418
Hugh Wynne, Free Quaker - Silas Weir Mitchell 4416
If Not Victory - Frank Olney Hough 3043
I'll Storm Hell - Noel B. Gerson 2374
In Gallant Company - Alexander Kent 3433
In the Days of Poor Richard - Irving A. Bacheller 259
Inherit the Earth - Margaret Shaw 5778
The Iron Chain - Jim DeFelice 1579
Israel Potter - Herman Melville 4334
Janice Meredith - Paul Leicester Ford 2166
Jarrett's Jade - Frank Yerby 6923
Jefferson: A Novel - Max Byrd 838
Jeremiah Martin: A Revolutionary War Novel - Robert H. Fowler 2191
Joshua Moore, American - George Frederick Hummel 3078
Judas Flowering - Jane Aiken Hodge 2965
The Kentuckians - Janice Holt Giles 2413
Kentucky Stand - Jere Hungerford Wheelwright 6670

The Kentucky Trace: A Novel of the American
  Revolution - Harriette Simpson Arnow 195
The King's Coat - Dewey Lambdin 3612
The King's Commission - Dewey Lambdin 3614
The King's Iron - Robert Newton Peck 4888
King's Masque - Evan John 3220
Kings Mountain - Florette Henri 2838
The King's Orchard - Agnes Sligh Turnbull 6363
The King's Rebel - James David Horan 3030
The Kingsbridge Plot - Maan Meyers 4355
The Lady From Yorktown - Eva McDonald 4260
Lady Washington - Dorothy Clarke Wilson 6803
Land for My Sons - Maribelle Cormack 1331
The Last Gentleman - Shirley Barker 312
The Latter Adventures of Tom Jones - Bob
  Coleman 1200
Let My Name Stand Fair - Shirley Seifert 5727
Let the King Beware! - Honore Morrow 4489
Let the Spring Come - Henry Schindall 5637
Liberty Tavern - Thomas Fleming 2129
Life and Liberty - Adam Rutledge 5538
The Life and Times of Captain N. - Douglas
  Glover 2436
Lionel Lincoln; or, The Leaguer of Boston - James
  Fenimore Cooper 1303
Little Red Foot - Robert W. Chambers 979
Long Knife - James Alexander Thom 6233
The Long March - Jane Barry 358
The Long Naked Descent into Boston - William
  Eastlake 1823
The Long Watch - Elizabeth Linington 3798
Look to the Mountain - Le Grand Cannon 885
Love Not a Rebel - Heather Graham 2516
Lucifer Land - Mildred B. Davis 1538
The Lure of the Falcon - Juliette Benzoni 465
The Maddest Idea - James L. Nelson 4580
Major Andre - Anthony Bailey 265
Man From Mt. Vernon - Burke Boyce 607
Maria - Eugenia Price 5184
Mars' Butterfly - Henry Pleasants 5080
Massachusetts: A Novel - Nancy Zaroulis 6956
The Master of Chaos - Irving A. Bacheller 262
The Measure of the Years - Alice Mary Colver 1218
Men in Buckskin - Herbert Stover 6069
Monmouth - Charles Bracelen Flood 2144
Morning in America - Willard Wiener 6741
Mr. Arnold - Francis Lynde 3935
Murfy's Men - Gerald Green 2565
My Thomas: A Novel of Martha Jefferson's Life -
  Roberta Grimes 2593
Nantucket Rebel - Edouard A. Stackpole 5970
The Neutral Ground - Frank Olney Hough 3044
Old Glory - Christopher Nicole 4618
Old Hickory - Noel B. Gerson 2379
Oliver Wiswell - Kenneth Roberts 5389
Othniel Jones - John Adams Leland 3715
Painted Minx - Robert W. Chambers 980
Patriot's Dream - Barbara Michaels 4360
Patriot's Progress - Joseph G.E. Hopkins 3027
The Perilous Night - Burke Boyce 609
Phantom Fortress - Bruce Lancaster 3643
The Pilot - James Fenimore Cooper 1306
Poor Richard's Game - G.J.A. O'Toole 4766
Portrait of a Scoundrel - Nathaniel Benchley 438
Powder Mission - Herbert Stover 6070
The Prescott Chronicles - Albert Fried 2232
The Price of Liberty - Joseph G.E. Hopkins 3028
The Prize Master - Harvey Haislip 2642
Proceed, Sergeant Lamb - Robert Graves 2550
The Proud and the Free - Howard Fast 2042
Proud Heritage - Ilse Bischoff 510
Rabble in Arms - Kenneth Roberts 5390
The Ragged Ones - Burke Davis 1511
The Raid - John Brick 673
Raleigh's Eden - Inglis Fletcher 2137
The Rebel and the Turncoat - Malcolm Decker 1576
Rebel Guns - Adam Rutledge 5539
The Rebel Loyalist - Charles William Gordon 2480
The Rebels - John Jakes 3152

The Red Doe - Drayton Mayrant 4214
The Red Rover - James Fenimore Cooper 1309
Redcoat - Bernard Cornwell 1337
The Redemptioner - Isaac Rusling Pennypacker 4910
Reluctant Rebel - Frederic F. Van de Water 6403
Remembrance Rock - Carl Sandburg 5583
Renown - Frank Olney Hough 3045
Retreat and Recall - Joseph G.E. Hopkins 3029
Return to Treasure Island - Denis Judd 3318
The Revolutionary - Lawrence Schoonover 5667
Richard Carvel - Winston Churchill 1081
Richard Pryne: A Novel of the American Revolution -
  Cyril Harris 2718
The Rifleman - John Brick 675
The Rival Shores - Arthur Beverly-Giddings 487
Rivers of Glory - F. van Wyck Mason 4158
The Road to Bunker Hill - Shirley Barker 316
Rogue's March - Maristan Chapman 993
Sailor Named Jones - Harvey Haislip 2643
The Saintly Buccaneer - Gilbert Morris 4469
Sally Hemings - Barbara Chase-Riboud 1006
Scarlet Feather - Dale Van Every 6409
Scarlet Ribbons - Judith E. French 2224
The Scotswoman - Inglis Fletcher 2140
Scoundrels' Brigade - Carter A. Vaughan 6439
The Sea Eagles - John Edward Jennings 3206
Sea Road to Yorktown - Harvey Haislip 2644
The Secret Road - Bruce Lancaster 3646
Seneca - Donald Clayton Porter 5127
Sergeant Lamb's America - Robert Graves 2552
The Shadow and the Glory - John Edward
  Jennings 3207
Shadow of the Long Knives - Thomas Alexander
  Boyd 615
Shadows on the Long House - Mike Roarke 5360
Sloop of War - Alexander Kent 3439
Slow Dies the Thunder - Helen Topping Miller 4395
Something Gleamed - Theda Kenyon 3463
Song of a Strange Child - Gilbert Morris 4470
Sons of Liberty - Adam Rutledge 5540
Sound of the Trumpet - Gilbert Morris 4471
The Sounds of Chariots: A Novel of John Sevier and
  the State of Franklin - Helen Topping Miller 4396
Spanish Bayonet - Stephen Vincent Benet 441
The Spy: A Tale of the Neutral Ground - James
  Fenimore Cooper 1310
Stars and Stripes - Adam Rutledge 5541
Stars on the Sea - F. van Wyck Mason 4161
Storm the Last Rampart - David Taylor 6180
Strange Wives - Shirley Barker 317
Strife Before Dawn - Mary Schumann 5675
The Strong Men - John Brick 677
The Sunshine Patriot: A Novel of Benedict Arnold -
  Norman Partington 4822
The Swamp Fox, Francis Marion - Noel B.
  Gerson 2383
Sycamore Men - David Taylor 6181
That Bennington Mob - Henry Barnard Safford 5558
The Third George - Jean Plaidy 5068
This Land Is Ours - Louis Zara 6953
Thomas Forty - Edward Stanley 5982
Those the Sun Has Loved - Rose Jourdain 3309
Those Who Love - Irving Stone 6064
Three Fields to Cross - Francis Tysen Nutt 4651
Three Harbors - F. van Wyck Mason 4162
Three Sides of Agiochook - Eric Kelly 3400
Tidewater Dynasty: A Biographical Novel of the Lees
  of Stratford Hall - Carey Roberts 5372
To Glory We Steer - Alexander Kent 3442
To Spit Against the Wind - Benjamin H. Levin 3737
A Toast to the King - Elizabeth Coatsworth 1139
Toil of the Brave - Inglis Fletcher 2141
Tory Tavern - Henry Barnard Safford 5559
The Traitor - Dan Sherman 5814
Treason - Robert Gessner 2389
The Tree of Liberty - Elizabeth Page 4773
Trumpet in the Sky - Helen Topping Miller 4397
Trumpet to Arms - Bruce Lancaster 3647
Trumpets at Dawn - Cyril Harris 2719

The Twisted Saber: A Biographical Novel of Benedict
  Arnold - Philip Vail 6398
Two Crowns for America - Katherine Kurtz 3568
The Unvanquished - Howard Fast 2046
Up Country: A Story of the Vanguard - Donald
  Culross Peattie 4881
Valiant Libertine - John Gordon Bryson 748
Valley Forge - MacKinlay Kantor 3364
The Virginians - William Makepeace
  Thackeray 6214
The Voyagers - Dale Van Every 6412
Weathercock - Constance Dodge 1668
West to the Setting Sun - Harvey Chalmers 973
Westward the Tide - Harold Sinclair 5863
Wicked Lady - Inglis Fletcher 2142
Wide Is the Water - Jane Aiken Hodge 2973
Wild Geese - Eilis Dillon 1647
Wild Horizon - F. van Wyck Mason 4164
The Wilderness War - Allen W. Eckert 1848
Wind From the Carolinas - Robert Wilder 6751
Wings of the Morning - Frederic F. Van de
  Water 6404
The World Turned Upside Down - William
  Rayner 5273
Yankee Doodle Dandy - Noel B. Gerson 2387
The Yankee Rascals - Carter A. Vaughan 6444
Yorktown - Burke Davis 1513

American West

Aces and Eights: A Novel of the Legend of Wild Bill
  Hickok - Loren D. Estleman 1967
Across the Shining Mountains - Christian
  McCord 4226
The Actor - Robert J. Conley 1236
Adios! - Lanier Bartlett 366
Adobe Walls: A Novel of the Last Apache Rising -
  William R. Burnett 791
The Adventurers - Ernest Haycox 2787
Against the Tide - Muriel Elwood 1935
Albuquerque - Sara Orwig 4757
All for Love: Baby Doe and Silver Dollar - John
  Vernon 6456
The American - Louis Dodge 1669
The American Cowboy - Will James 3163
The American River - Gary McCarthy 4222
The Amulet - Hal Borland 582
And One Rode West - Heather Graham 2514
Angle of Repose - Wallace Stegner 5989
Anything for Billy - Larry McMurtry 4295
Apache - Will Comfort 1226
Apache - Donald Clayton Porter 5114
Apache Autumn - Robert Skimin 5875
Apache Blood - David Thompson 6250
Apache Devil - Edgar Rice Burroughs 806
Apaches - Oakley Hall 2650
Arfive - A.B. Guthrie Jr. 2623
The Argonauts - Yvonne Schoell 5645
Arizona - Clarence Budington Kelland 3387
Arizona! - Dana Fuller Ross 5466
Arizona Ecstasy - Rosanne Bittner 511
The Arkansas River - Jory Sherman 5816
Arrest Sitting Bull - Douglas C. Jones 3273
The Assassination of Jesse James by the Coward
  Robert Ford - Ron Hansen 2680
The Authentic Death of Hendry Jones - Charles
  Neider 4562
Back to Malachi - Robert J. Conley 1237
The Bad Lands - Oakley Hall 2651
The Bear Flag: A Novel of the Birth of California -
  Cecelia Holland 2983
Belle Starr - Deborah Camp 870
Belle Starr - Speer Morgan 4453
Beneath the Blue Mountain - Richard S.
  Wheeler 6656
Between Earth and Sky - Karen Osborn 4758
Beulah Land - Harold Lenoir Davis 1520
Beyond the Stars - David William Ross 5497

The Big Lonesome - Will Bryant 737
The Big Sky - A.B. Guthrie Jr. 2624
Bighorn Legacy - W. Michael Gear 2332
Billy the Kid - Edwin Corle 1330
Billy the Kid: The Legend of El Chivato - Elizabeth Fackler 1994
Birthright - Phillip Finch 2087
Bisbee '17 - Robert Houston 3056
Bitter Creek - Al Cody 1150
Black-Eyed Susan - Deborah Camp 871
Black Feather - Harold Titus 6283
Black Sun - Terry C. Johnston 3242
Blackfoot Massacre - David Thompson 6251
Blessed McGill - Edwin Shrake 5834
Blood Brother - Elliott Arnold 190
The Blood Endures - Robert Inman 3107
Blood Fury - David Thompson 6252
Blood on the Divide - William W. Johnstone 3265
Blood Song - Terry C. Johnston 3243
Blood Truce - David Thompson 6253
The Bloody Benders - Robert H. Adelman 35
Bloody Season - Loren D. Estleman 1968
Blue Russell - Will Bryant 738
Border Line - Robert J. Conley 1238
Borderlords - Terry C. Johnston 3244
Born of the Sun - John H. Culp 1440
Borrasca - Octavus Roy Cohen 1160
Bound for the Promised Land - Richard Marius 4083
Brazos Dreamer - Gene Shelton 5799
Breakheart Pass - Alistair MacLean 3999
The Bright Feathers - John H. Culp 1441
A Bright Tragic Thing - L.D. Clark 1091
Broncho Apache - Paul I. Wellman 6614
The Brothers of Uterica - Benjamin Capps 887
Brules - Harry Combs 1223
The Buckskin Girl: A Novel of the California Trail in the Mid-Nineteenth Century - Gwen Moffat 4426
Buffalo Coat - Carol Brink 691
Buffalo Girls - Larry McMurtry 4296
Buffalo Palace - Terry C. Johnston 3245
The Buffalo Soldiers - John Prebble 5165
Buffalo Woman - Dorothy M. Johnson 3223
The Bugles Are Silent: A Novel of the Texas Revolution - John R. Knaggs 3513
Bugles in the Afternoon - Ernest Haycox 2788
Butcher's Crossing - John Williams 6786
By the King's Command - Shirley Seifert 5723
The Cabin at the Trail's End - Sheba Hargreaves 2706
Calamity Jane of Deadwood Gulch - Ethel Hueston 3068
Calico Palace - Gwen Bristow 694
California! - Dana Fuller Ross 5467
California Caballero - William Colt MacDonald 3981
California Gold - John Jakes 3145
The Californios - Louis L'Amour 3618
Call the Beast Thy Brother - William Oliver Turner 6366
The Camp Grant Massacre - Elliott Arnold 191
Cannibal Eliot and the Lost Histories of San Francisco - Hilton Obenzinger 4660
Captain Jack - Gene Shelton 5800
Captain McRae: A Novel of the Northwest Frontier - William Heuman 2872
Captain Sutter's Gold - Jonreed Lauritzen 3673
Cargo of Brides - Helen Rucker 5522
Carrington - Michael Whitney Straight 6074
Carry the Wind - Terry C. Johnston 3246
Castle Garden - Bill Albert 63
The Cavalryman - Harold Sinclair 5861
Cedarhaven - Patricia Campbell 874
Centennial - James A. Michener 4366
Certain People of Importance - Kathleen Norris 4647
Chant of the Hawk - John Harris 2720
Charity, Colorado - Chelsea Quinn Yarbro 6896
Chase the Wind - Janelle Taylor 6184
Cherokee Dawn - Genell Dellin 1596

Cherokee Rose: A Novel of America's First Cowgirl - Judy Alter 119
Chief Joseph - Bill Dugan 1756
The Chieftain: A Story of the Nez Perce People - Robert Payne 4852
Chihuahua 1916 - Otis Carney 903
Children of the Dust - Carlile Clancy 1084
Chiricahua - Will Henry 2839
The Chisholms - Evan Hunter 3082
Christopher Strange - Ruth Eleanor McKee 4281
Cimarron - Edna Ferber 2061
City of Illusion - Vardis Fisher 2107
City of Widows - Loren D. Estleman 1969
A Cold Day in Hell - Terry C. Johnston 3247
Colfax - Robert J. Conley 1239
Colorado! - Dana Fuller Ross 5471
Colorado Ambush - Jess McCriede 4230
Columbia - Pamela Jekel 3184
Comanche Moon - Catherine Anderson 137
The Comancheros - Paul I. Wellman 6616
Come Spring - Charlotte Hinger 2954
Company of Cowards - Jack Schaefer 5634
Confessions of Johnny Ringo - Geoff Aggeler 40
The Conquest of Don Pedro - Harvey Fergusson 2066
Cottonwoods Grow Tall - Margaret Bell Houston 3055
Covered Wagon - Emerson Hough 3041
The Cowboy Conspiracy - Larry D. Names 4553
The Cowboys - William Dale Jennings 3211
Crazy Fox Remembers - Don Preston 5174
Crazy Snake - Robert J. Conley 1240
Crimson Creek: A Novel of the Early West - Robert McCraig 4228
The Cross and the Sword - Jonreed Lauritzen 3674
The Crossed Sabres - Gilbert Morris 4458
The Crossing - Cormac McCarthy 4221
Cry of the Hawk - Terry C. Johnston 3248
The Cup of Strength - Charlotte Paul 4840
Custer Passed Our Way - Fred S. Kaufman 3370
Dakota! - Dana Fuller Ross 5472
Dance Back the Buffalo - Milton Lott 3899
Dances with Wolves - Michael Blake 537
Dark Thicket - Elmer Kelton 3402
Daughter of Fortune - Carla Kelly 3398
The Day the Cowboys Quit - Elmer Kelton 3403
The Daybreakers - Louis L'Amour 3619
Dead Man's Walk - Larry McMurtry 4297
Deadwood - Pete Dexter 1638
Death at Rainy Mountain - Mardi Oakley Medawar 4321
Death at the French Creek - Raymond C. Borel 580
Death Comes for the Archbishop - Willa Cather 957
Death of a Legend - Will Henry 2840
The Demise of Billy the Kid - Preston Lewis 3760
Desert Hawks - Frank Burleson 786
Desperadoes - Ron Hansen 2681
Destiny in Dallas - Shirley Seifert 5725
The Devil Gun - William Syers 6148
Devil's Backbone - Terry C. Johnston 3250
Devilseed - Frank Yerby 6914
Diamond Six - William Fielding Smith 5932
Diamond Wedding - Wilbur Daniel Steele 5986
The Dice of God - Hoffman Birney 507
Distant Music - Harold Lenoir Davis 1521
Distant Trails - Bill Gulick 2612
Distant Trumpet - Paul Horgan 3032
Divine Average - Elithe Hamilton Kirkland 3505
Doc Holliday's Woman - Jane Candia Coleman 1201
Dodging Red Cloud - Richard S. Wheeler 6657
Doniphan's Ride - Les Savage Jr. 5620
Down From the Mountain - Louis Charbonneau 997
Dream Catcher - Terry C. Johnston 3251
The Dream Ends in Fury - Samuel Anthony Peeples 4889
Dream West - David Nevin 4587
Drumm's War - Bill Bragg 638
Duel in the Sun - Niven Busch 812
Dutch Uncle - Marilyn Durham 1815

Each Bright River - Mildred Masterson McNeilly 4308
The Eagle and the Raven - James A. Michener 4369
Eagles Fly West - Edward Maddin Ainsworth 55
Eagles of Destiny - Jory Sherman 5817
The Earthbreakers - Ernest Haycox 2789
East of the Giants - George Rippey Stewart 6027
The Edge of Time - Loula Grace Erdman 1949
Eli's Road - Lucas Webb 6589
Elizabeth, By Name - Will Cook 1265
Embers of the Heart - Rosanne Bittner 512
Escape From Sonora - Will Bryant 739
Eye of the Hawk - David William Ross 5498
Eyes of Eagles - William W. Johnstone 3266
Fair is the Rose - Meagan MacKinney 3997
Fair Land, Fair Land - A.B. Guthrie Jr. 2625
Fallen Angel - Deborah Camp 872
The Fancher Train - Amelia Bean 395
The Far Canyon - Elmer Kelton 3404
The Far Country - Marthedith Furnas 2258
The Far Journey - L'oula Grace Erdman 1950
Far Mountains - Frank O'Rourke 4752
The Far Tribes - Richard S. Wheeler 6658
The Fast Men - Tom McNab 4302
The Feud - Amelia Bean 396
Filaree: A Novel of an American Life - Marguerite Noble 4633
Firewind - Bill Pronzini 5200
Flashman and the Redskins - George MacDonald Fraser 2208
The Fleet Rabble: A Novel of the Nez Perce War - Frank Borden Hanes 2675
Folded Hills - Stewart Edward White 6701
Follow the Free Wind - Leigh Brackett 621
Fool's Coach - Richard S. Wheeler 6659
For Time and All Eternity - Paul Bailey 268
Fort Worth - Leonard Sanders 5588
The Fortune Road - James McCague 4217
Fortune, Smile Once More - Mary Floyd Williams 6788
Forty Guns West - William W. Johnstone 3267
The Franciscan - Forrester Blake 532
Free Flows the River - Earl Murray 4529
Free Land - Rose Lane 3660
From Where the Sun Now Stands - Will Henry 2841
Fur Brigade - Hal George Evarts 1985
The Further Adventures of Huckleberry Finn - Greg Matthews 4189
The Gallows Land - Bill Pronzini 5201
The Gates of the Mountains - Will Henry 2842
The Gathering Storm - W.E. Davis 1540
Gathering Storm - Bill Gulick 2613
Geronimo - Bill Dugan 1758
Geronimo: An American Legend - Robert J. Conley 1242
Ghost Woman - Lawrence Thornton 6275
The Ghosts of Elkhorn - Kerry Newcomb 4589
The Giant Joshua - Maurine Whipple 6673
Giants in the Earth - O.E. Rolvaag 5434
The Gila River - Gary McCarthy 4223
The Gilded Rooster - Richard Emery Roberts 5391
Glittering Hill - Clyde Francis Murphy 4520
The Glorious Three - June Wetherell 6651
Go-Ahead Rider - Robert J. Conley 1243
Gold Is Where You Find It - Clements Ripley 5345
Gold Mountain - Charlotte Paul 4841
Golden Destiny - June Wyndham Davies 1506
The Golden Lady - Dorothy Gardiner 2283
Golden Shore - George Shaftel 5769
The Golden Valley - Daoma Winston 6826
Goldfield - Richard S. Wheeler 6660
Gone the Dreams and the Dancing - Douglas C. Jones 3279
Gone to Texas - Forrest Carter 945
Gone to Texas - Jason Manning 4074
Gone to Texas - John Williams Thomason 6247
Gone to Texas - Don Worcester 6871
A Good Day to Die - Del Barton 368

A Good Day to Die - Thomas Wakefield Blackburn 525
Good Morning, Young Lady - Ardyth Kennelly 3424
The Good Old Boys - Elmer Kelton 3405
The Goodnight Trail - Ralph Compton 1227
Grant of Kingdom - Harvey Fergusson 2067
The Grass Kingdom - Jory Sherman 5818
The Grassman - Len Fulton 2256
The Great Adventure - Janice Holt Giles 2410
The Great Betrayal - Dorothy Gardiner 2284
Great Day in the Morning - Robert Hardy Andrews 149
The Green Land - Zola Helen Ross 5504
Grim Journey - Hoffman Birney 509
Gunman - Loren D. Estleman 1971
The Hallelujah Train - Bill Gulick 2614
The Hangings - Bill Pronzini 5202
Hard on the Road - Barbara Moore 4440
Harry Idaho - Hugh Pendexter 4894
The Harvey Girls - Samuel Hopkins Adams 31
Hawken Fury - David Thompson 6254
The Head Waters - Archie Binns 500
Heart of the Country - Greg Matthews 4190
Heartland - Robert Douglas Mead 4316
Heroine of the Prairies: A Romance of the Oregon Trail - Sheba Hargreaves 2707
The Hider - Loren D. Estleman 1972
High Country - Jason Manning 4075
High Freedom - Earl Murray 4530
The High Missouri - Winfred Blevins 545
The High Rocks - Loren D. Estleman 1973
Hill of the Hawk - Scott O'Dell 4689
The Holy Warrior - Gilbert Morris 4462
Home Mountain - Jeanne Williams 6777
The Homesman - Glendon Swarthout 6143
Honey in the Horn - Harold Lenoir Davis 1523
Honor Thy Father - Robert A. Roripaugh 5460
Horne's Law - Jory Sherman 5819
A House Behind the Mint - Laurie Huffman 3072
I Am Lidian - Naomi Lane Babson 253
I, Jack Swilling - John Myers 4544
Immortal Wife - Irving Stone 6057
In the Season of the Sun - Kerry Newcomb 4590
In Those Days - Harvey Fergusson 2068
Independence! - Dana Fuller Ross 5476
Indian Hater - Glenn R. Vernam 6452
Jessie: A Novel Based on the Life of Jessie Benton Fremont - Judy Alter 120
The Jewelled Spur - Gilbert Morris 4465
John Barry - Donald F. Bedford 412
John Crews - Arthur Chapman 988
Johnny Christmas - Forrester Blake 533
Jornada - Robert L. Duffus 1754
Journey by the River - John Prescott 5173
Jubal Sackett - Louis L'Amour 3620
Jubilee Trail - Gwen Bristow 698
Judgment in July - Richard Hunt 2105
The Jump-Off Creek - Molly Gloss 2435
Justice, My Brother - James Keene 3386
The Justicer - Thomas Fall 2010
Kansas Blue - Dylan Harson 2758
Kelly Blue - Peter Bowen 601
Kid Curry: The Life and Times of Harvey Logan and the Wild Bunch - F. Bruce Lamb 3606
Killdeer Mountain - Dee Brown 713
Killing Time - Robert J. Conley 1244
King of the Mountain - David Thompson 6255
The Lady - Conrad Richter 5321
The Lady and Doc Holliday - Preston Lewis 3761
Lady of No Man's Land - Jeanne Williams 6780
Lakota - G. Clifton Wisler 6833
The Land Is Bright - Archie Binns 501
A Land to Tame - Zola Helen Ross 5505
The Last Days of Horse-Shy Halloran - Bill Pronzini 5203
The Last Frontier - Howard Fast 2036
Last Go Round - Ken Kesey 3473
Last Gun: The Legend of John Selman - Gene Shelton 5801

The Last Hunt - Milton Lott 3900
Last Reveille - David Morrell 4456
The Last Ride - Tom Eidson 1899
The Last Stand: A Novel about George Armstrong Custer and the Indians of the Plains - Edwin P. Hoyt 3061
The Last Valley - A.B. Guthrie Jr. 2626
The Last Warpath - Will Henry 2844
The Law in Charity - Chelsea Quinn Yarbro 6901
The Lawless - John Jakes 3149
El Lazo - L. Jay Martin 4132
The Legend of Ben Tree - Paul Hawkins 2784
The Lieutenant's Lady - Bess Streeter Aldrich 70
Light on the Mountain - Leonard Sanders 5589
Lights Along the Shore - Diane Austell 241
Lily - Cindy Bonner 571
Little Big Man - Thomas Berger 478
Liveliest Town in the West - Bill Gulick 2615
The Living - Annie Dillard 1644
Lone Star Lady - Jill Gregory 2579
Lonely on the Mountain - Louis L'Amour 3621
Lonesome Dove - Larry McMurtry 4298
The Long Rifle - Stewart Edward White 6702
Long Storm - Ernest Haycox 2790
The Long Trail North - Robert J. Conley 1245
Long Winter Gone - Terry C. Johnston 3252
Looking After Lily - Cindy Bonner 572
Lord Grizzly - Frederick F. Manfred 4056
Lords of the Plains - Max Crawford 1420
The Lost Giants - Alan Scholefield 5657
The Lost Wagon - James Arthur Kjelgaard 3509
Lost Wallowa - Bill Gulick 2616
Lotus Land - Monica Highland 2917
Loving Belle Star - Robert Taylor 6187
Lure of the Wind - David Thompson 6256
Mackenna's Gold - Will Henry 2845
The Man From Broken Hills - Louis L'Amour 3622
Man on Two Ponies - Don Worcester 6872
The Man Who Loved Cat Dancing - Marilyn Durham 1817
Manifest Destiny - Brian Garfield 2290
Marching to Valhalla: A Novel of Custer's Last Days - Michael Blake 538
Mary Dove - Jane Gilmore Rushing 5529
Me and Gallagher - Jack Farris 2023
The Medicine Horn - Jory Sherman 5820
The Medicine Man - Shirley Seifert 5729
The Medicine Whip - Max Hennessy 2835
Megan - Kathleen Magill 4028
Mi Amigo - William R. Burnett 795
Mighty Mountain - Archie Binns 502
Mirage - Helen Topping Miller 4390
The Misadventures of Bethany Price - Marian Cockrell 1147
Miss Morissa: Doctor of the Gold Trail - Mari Sandoz 5592
Mister St. John - Loren D. Estleman 1974
Montana! - Dana Fuller Ross 5479
Montana Hitch - Richard S. Wheeler 6661
Montana Road - Harry Sinclair Drago 1717
Montana Woman - Rosanne Bittner 513
Monte Walsh - Jack Schaefer 5635
The Moon-Eyed Appaloosa - Bill Gulick 2617
The Morning River - W. Michael Gear 2333
The Mothers - Vardis Fisher 2109
Mountain Devil - David Thompson 6257
Mountain Laurel - Jude Deveraux 1632
Mountain Man - Vardis Fisher 2110
Mountains Ahead - Martha Ferguson McKeown 4284
Murdock's Law - Loren D. Estleman 1975
Mustang Man - Louis L'Amour 3623
Nebraska! - Dana Fuller Ross 5480
Ned Christie's War - Robert J. Conley 1247
Nevada! - Dana Fuller Ross 5481
Nickajack - Robert J. Conley 1248
Night Wind - Roberta Jean Mountjoy 4504
No Brighter Glory - Armstrong Sperry 5963
The No-Return Trail - Sonia Levitin 3741

No Road Too Long - Hildegarde Hawthorne 2785
No Roof but Heaven - Jeanne Williams 6782
No Survivors - Will Henry 2846
North Against the Sioux - Kenneth Ulyatt 6376
North of 36 - Emerson Hough 3042
North to Yesterday - Robert Flynn 2145
Northwest Passage - David Thompson 6258
The Odyssey of Thaddeus Baxter - Robert P. Lund 3926
Oh Glittering Promise - Anne Fisher 2099
Oh, Valley Green - John H. Culp 1443
Oklahoma! - Dana Fuller Ross 5482
Oklahoma Pride - Dana Fuller Ross 5483
The Old Colts - Glendon Swarthout 6144
On to Oregon! - Honore Morrow 4490
One-Eyed Dream - Terry C. Johnston 3253
One More River to Cross - Will Henry 2847
One Smart Indian - Robert J. Seidman 5722
Oregon! - Dana Fuller Ross 5484
Oregon Bride - Rosanne Bittner 514
Outlaw - Warren Kiefer 3482
Outlaw Lover - Lindsey Hanks 2676
The Overland Trail - Wendi Lee 3712
The Ox-Bow Incident - Walter Van Tilburg Clark 1096
Paint the Wind - Cathy Cash Spellman 5960
Paiute - Sessions S. Wheeler 6666
Paradise Reclaimed - Halldor Laxness 3686
Passage Home - Alison McLeay 4286
Pastora - Joanna Barnes 321
Path of the Sun - Al Dempsey 1608
Pearl - Anne Leaton 3701
The Pecos River - Fred Bean 399
Peder Victorious - O.E. Rolvaag 5435
The Pilgrimage - Ann B. Ross 5463
Pillar of Cloud - Jackson Burgess 782
Pioneer Breed - Glenn R. Vernam 6453
The Pioneers - Courtney Ryley Cooper 1296
The Pistoleer - James Carlos Blake 536
Pistols for Hire - Nelson Coral Nye 4652
The Place of Dead Roads - William S. Burroughs 808
The Place of Devils - Lucinda Baker 275
The Post of Honor - David Coxe Cooke 1266
The Powder River - Winfred Blevins 546
Powderkeg - Richard Vetterli 6482
Power in the Blood - Greg Matthews 4191
Prairie - Anna Lee Waldo 6528
The Predators - F.A. Parker 4804
The Pride of Hannah Wade - Janet Dailey 1455
Promised Lands - Elizabeth Crook 1430
The Proselyte - Susan Ertz 1958
The Proud Breed - Celeste De Blasis 1547
The Pumpkin Rollers - Elmer Kelton 3406
Quanah Parker - Bill Dugan 1759
The Quiet Life of Mrs. General Lane - Victoria Case 951
Quitting Time - Robert J. Conley 1249
Rabbit Boss - Thomas Sanchez 5581
Railroad West - Cornelia Meigs 4327
The Rainbow Promise - Lisa Gregory 2580
The Rainbow Runner - John Cunningham 1450
Ranchero - Stewart Edward White 6703
Rapaho - Jamie Lee Cooper 1314
Rawhider - Gene Shelton 5802
Reap the Whirlwind - Terry C. Johnston 3254
Red Cloud's Revenge - Terry C. Johnston 3255
Red Fox of the Kinapoo - William Rush 5526
Red Runs the River - Lewis B. Patten 4831
Refugio, They Named You Wrong - Susan Clark Schofield 5647
The Reluctant Bridegroom - Gilbert Morris 4467
Remnants of Glory - Teresa Miller 4403
Republic: A Novel of Texas - E.V. Thompson 6266
The Restless Land - John H. Culp 1444
The Return of Henry Starr - Richard Slotkin 5909
The Revolt of Sarah Perkins - Marian Cockrell 1148
Richard Lamb - Richard S. Wheeler 6662
Ride of the Panther - Kerry Newcomb 4591

Ride the Dark Trail - Louis L'Amour 3624
Ride the Wind - Lucia St. Clair Robson 5416
Riders of Judgment - Frederick F. Manfred 4059
Rio Grande - Jory Sherman 5821
River of Sky - Karen Harper 2713
Rivers West - Louis L'Amour 3626
The Road to Glory - Darwin Le Ora Teilhet 6199
A Roaring in the Wind - Robert Lewis Taylor 6191
Rockspring - R.G. Vliet 6506
Roman - Douglas C. Jones 3281
Run of the Stars - Dora Aydelotte 247
The Running Iron - Rachel Ann Fish 2097
Rush to Destroy - L. Jay Martin 4133
The Russian River - Gary McCarthy 4224
Sacajawea - Anna Lee Waldo 6529
The Sackett Brand - Louis L'Amour 3627
The Saga of Henry Starr - Robert J. Conley 1250
St. Agnes' Stand - Tom Eidson 1900
Saint Johnson - William R. Burnett 796
Salt Lake City - A.R. Reife 5292
Sam Chance - Benjamin Capps 888
San Antone - V.J. Banis 288
Sand in the Wind - Kathleen O'Neal Gear 2329
Savage Frontier - Frank Burleson 787
Savage Thunder - Johanna Lindsey 3795
Savages and Saints - Cora Older 4717
Savanna - Janice Holt Giles 2416
Scalpdancers - Kerry Newcomb 4592
The Scout - Harry Combs 1224
The Sea of Grass - Conrad Richter 5323
Sea to Shining Sea - Michael Phillips 4990
The Search for Temperance Moon - Douglas C. Jones 3282
The Searchers - Alan Le May 3691
Season for War - P.F. Kluge 3510
Season of Yellow Leaf - Douglas C. Jones 3283
The Second Kiss - Gayle Rogers 5432
The Secret Annie Oakley - Marcy Moran Heidish 2819
Seven Rivers West - Edward Hoagland 2959
The Seventh Girl: A Romantic Tale of Civil War Texas - Tom Pendleton 4900
The Seventh Winter - Hal Borland 583
Shadow Catcher - Charles Fergus 2064
A Shadow of Eagles - Jane Barry 360
The Shadow Riders - Terry C. Johnston 3257
Shadows in the Dusk - John Edward Jennings 3208
Shaggy Legion - Hal George Evarts 1986
Shaman - Noah Gordon 2483
Shining Mountains - Steve Frazee 2214
The Shining Mountains - Dale Van Every 6410
The Shootist - Glendon Swarthout 6145
Sierra Triumph - Dana Fuller Ross 5488
Silver Fruit - Patricia Campbell 876
The Silver Mountain - Dan Cushman 1453
Sioux Dawn - Terry C. Johnston 3258
Sioux Splendor - Rosanne Bittner 515
Sister Wives - Cleo Jones 3270
Sitting Bull - Bill Dugan 1760
Six-Horse Hitch - Janice Holt Giles 2417
The Six Messiahs - Mark Frost 2238
The Sky-Liners - Louis L'Amour 3629
Slaughter - Elmer Kelton 3407
The Smoky Hill - Don Coldsmith 1188
The Snake River - Winfred Blevins 547
Snow-Water - Dorothy Gardiner 2285
The Snowblind Moon - John Byrne Cooke 1267
Soldier in Buckskin - Ray Hogan 2981
Solitudes - R.G. Vliet 6507
Son of the Gamblin' Man: The Youth of an Artist - Mari Sandoz 5593
Song of the Cheyenne - Jory Sherman 5822
Song of the Meadowlark - John A. Sanford 5594
Song of Wovoka - Earl Murray 4531
The Sons of Grady Rourke - Douglas Savage 5618
Sons of Texas - Tom Early 1822
South of the Border - John Byrne Cooke 1268
The Southern Blade - Nelson Wolford 6844
Spanish Gold - Kevin D. Randle 5252

The Staked Plain - Frank Xavier Tolbert 6290
The Stalkers - Terry C. Johnston 3259
Stamping Ground - Loren D. Estleman 1977
Star of Empire: A Novel of Old San Antonio - Leonard Sanders 5590
Star of the West - Ethel Hueston 3070
The Stars in Their Courses - Harry Brown 722
Stone Song: A Novel of the Life of Crazy Horse - Winfred Blevins 548
The Story of Pat Garrett and Billy the Kid - David Everitt 1987
The Story of the Sundance Kid - David Everitt 1988
Strange Company - Robert J. Conley 1251
The Stranglers - Loren D. Estleman 1978
Streets of Laredo - Larry McMurtry 4300
Sudden Country - Loren D. Estleman 1979
Sunflower - Jill Marie Landis 3653
Sweet Mountain Magic - Rosanne Bittner 516
Sweetwater Fever - Robert H. Adelman 36
The Sword of General Englund - Donald Honig 3023
Tacey Cromwell - Conrad Richter 5324
Tale of Valor - Vardis Fisher 2112
The Talking Rifle - Glenn R. Vernam 6454
Tamsen - David Galloway 2273
Tamzen - Jane Gilmore Rushing 5530
Tascosa Gun: The Story of Jim East - Gene Shelton 5803
The Taste of Time - Ferol Egan 1892
Telluride - Susan Clark Schofield 5648
Tenderfoot - David Thompson 6259
The Terrible Teague Bunch - Gary Jennings 3197
Texas - James A. Michener 4375
Texas! - Dana Fuller Ross 5490
That Callahan Spunk! - Francis Ames 124
Their Fathers' God - O.E. Rolvaag 5436
These Latter Days - Laura Kalpakian 3330
These Thousand Hills - A.B. Guthrie Jr. 2627
They Came to a Valley - Bill Gulick 2618
Thin Moon and Cold Mist - Kathleen O'Neal Gear 2330
This Land I Hold - Virginia Myers 4550
This Land Is Mine - Frances Casey Kerns 3470
This Old Bill - Loren D. Estleman 1980
This Promised Land - Robert Easton 1824
Thousand Years of Gold - Ruthanne Lum McCunn 4239
Three Rivers - Carla J. Mills 4406
Thunder on the Plains - Rosanne Bittner 517
Tide of Empire - Peter S. Kyne 3572
Tie My Bones to Her Back - Robert F. Jones 3294
Tilly Wed - Catherine Cookson 1290
Time for Outrage - Amelia Bean 397
A Time in the Sun - Jane Barry 361
Timothy Baines - John H. Culp 1445
To Fell the Giants - Bill Hotchkiss 3038
To Heaven on Horseback - Paul F. Cranston 1419
To Make a Killing - Robert J. Conley 1252
To the Swift - Anne Hawkins 2783
Tom Mix Died for Your Sins - Darryl Ponicsan 5090
Tomahawk Revenge - David Thompson 6260
Tombstone Showdown - Leslie Scott 5681
Tomorrow's Dream - Peggy Hanchar 2674
Too Long at the Dance - Mike Blakely 539
Tracker - David Wagoner 6521
The Trail to Ogallala - Benjamin Capps 889
Trail's End - Fred Bean 400
Trapper's Blood - David Thompson 6261
Trapper's Moon - Jory Sherman 5823
Treasure in Hell's Canyon - Bill Gulick 2619
The Treasure of Pleasant Valley - Frank Yerby 6928
The Treasure of the Chisos - John H. Culp 1446
Trouble Shooter - Ernest Haycox 2791
Troubled Border - T.D. Allen 104
True Grit - Charles Portis 5139
The True Memoirs of Charley Blankenship - Benjamin Capps 890
True Women - Janice Woods Windle 6820
Trumpet on the Land - Terry C. Johnston 3260

The Turquoise Trail - Shirley Seifert 5736
The Two Medicine River - Richard S. Wheeler 6663
The Unforgiven - Alan Le May 3692
The Ungodly: A Novel of the Donner Party - Richard Rhodes 5311
The Union Belle - Gilbert Morris 4473
The Valiant - Sigman Byrd 839
The Valiant Gunman - Gilbert Morris 4474
The Valley - Clifford Irving 3114
Valley of the Shadow - Charles Marquis Warren 6570
The Vengeance Trail of Josey Wales - Forrest Carter 946
A Very Small Remnant - Michael Whitney Straight 6075
Vigilante - Richard Summers 6116
The Vision Is Fulfilled - Kay L. McDonald 4262
Voyage to Santa Fe - Janice Holt Giles 2418
Wagons to Tucson - Ed Newsom 4604
Wagons West - Leslie Turner White 6692
Walnut Grove - Jane Gilmore Rushing 5531
Waltzing in Ragtime - Eileen Charbonneau 996
Wanderers Eastward, Wanderers West - Kathleen Winsor 6823
Wandering Star - Steven Yount 6945
War Eagles - Frank Burleson 788
Warhorse - John Cunningham 1451
Warlock - Oakley Hall 2653
Warriors of the Night - Kerry Newcomb 4594
Washington! - Dana Fuller Ross 5491
Watch for Me on the Mountain - Forrest Carter 947
The Way West - A.B. Guthrie Jr. 2628
We Must March: A Novel of the Winning of Oregon - Honore Morrow 4491
Welcome to Hard Times - E.L. Doctorow 1660
West of Appomattox - Harley Duncan 1785
West to Eden - Gloria Goldreich 2461
Western: A Saga of the Great Plains - Frank Yerby 6930
Western Union - Zane Grey 2589
What Law There Was - Al Dempsey 1609
Wheels West - Homer Croy 1438
When the Legends Die - Hal Borland 584
Where Is My Wandering Boy Tonight? - David Wagoner 6522
Where the River Runs - Richard S. Wheeler 6664
Whisper of the Wolf - Terry C. Johnston 3261
A Whisper on the Wind - Madeline Baker 276
A Whistle in the Wind - John H. Culp 1447
The White Land - William Dieter 1643
Whole Hog - David Wagoner 6523
Wild Earth's Nobility - Frank Waters 6578
Wild Times - Brian Garfield 2291
Wilde West - Walter Satterthwait 5609
Wilderness - Roger Zelazny 6957
Wilderness Passage - Forrester Blake 534
Winding Stairs - Douglas C. Jones 3287
Winds of Blame - Jane Gilmore Rushing 5532
Winter Grass - Richard S. Wheeler 6665
Winter Harvest - Norah Lofts 3863
Winter Rain - Terry C. Johnston 3262
The Winter War - William Wister Haines 2640
Winterkill - David Thompson 6262
Wives of the Wind - Marjorie Jarrett 3170
The Wolf and the Buffalo - Elmer Kelton 3408
Wolf Song - Harvey Fergusson 2069
Woman Chief - Benjamin Capps 892
Woman of Justice - Georgia Di Donato 1639
A Woman of Texas - R.T. Stevens 6002
A Woman of the People - Benjamin Capps 893
Women in the Wind - Margaret Ritter 5350
The Wonderful Country - Tom Lea 3695
The World in His Arms - Rex Beach 392
The Wounded Yankee - Gilbert Morris 4475
Wyatt Earp - Matt Braun 653
Wyatt Earp - Dan Gordon 2481
Wyoming! - Dana Fuller Ross 5494
Yankee Woman - Frederic Baume 381
Yellowhorse - Dee Brown 715

The Yellowstone - Winfred Blevins 549
Yellowstone Kelly - Peter Bowen 602
You Rolling River - Archie Binns 503
Zeke and Ned - Larry McMurtry 4301

Anabaptists

The Siege - Peter Vansittart 6431

Ancient Egypt

Abraham and Sarah: The Long Journey - Roberta Kells Dorr 1694
Akhnaton, King of Egypt - Dmitri Merezhkovski 4337
The Alexandrian - Martha Rofheart 5425
All the Trumpets Sounded: A Novel Based on the Life of Moses - W.G. Hardy 2701
Alone Atop the Mountain - Samuel Sandmel 5591
The Altar and the Crown - Marian Niven 4631
Ancient Evenings - Norman Mailer 4035
Charioteer: A Story of Old Egypt in the Days of Joseph - Gertrude Eberle 1835
Child of the Morning - Pauline Gedge 2343
Cleopatra - H. Rider Haggard 2637
Death Comes as the End - Agatha Christie 1076
Departed Glory - Peter Danielson 1466
Dreams of Empire - Jeanne Mackin 3994
The Egyptian - Mika Waltari 6552
The Exodus - Konrad Bercovici 473
The Exodus - Peter Danielson 1467
Fleet Surgeon to Pharaoh - Sheldon Jacobson 3140
A God Against the Gods - Allen Drury 1738
The Goddess Queen: A Novel Based on the Life of Nefertiti - Nicole Vidal 6494
The Golden Balance - Arthur Dana Hall 2646
The Golden Pharaoh - Peter Danielson 1468
Hagar - Cothburn O'Neal 4737
Her-Bak: The Living Face of Ancient Egypt - Isha Schwaller de Lubicz 5676
Joseph of Egypt - Thomas Mann 4065
Joseph the Provider - Thomas Mann 4066
King and Goddess - Judith Tarr 6166
King of the Two Lands: The Pharaoh Akhenaten - Jacquetta Hawkes 2780
King Tut's Private Eye - Lee Levin 3739
Lady of the Reeds - Pauline Gedge 2345
The Lion in Egypt - Peter Danielson 1470
Lord of the Two Lands - Judith Tarr 6167
Mirage - Pauline Gedge 2346
Moses - Sholem Asch 199
The Mummy; or Ramses the Damned - Anne Rice 5315
Murder at the Feast of Rejoicing - Lynda S. Robinson 5407
Murder at the God's Gate - Lynda S. Robinson 5408
Murder in the Place of Anubis - Lynda S. Robinson 5409
On a Balcony - David Stacton 5973
Out of the House of Life - Chelsea Quinn Yarbro 6903
Pharaoh - Eloise Jarvis McGraw 4276
Pillar of Fire - Judith Tarr 6168
Prince of Egypt - Dorothy Clarke Wilson 6805
The Prophecy - Peter Danielson 1472
Return to Thebes - Allen Drury 1739
The River and the Stone: Moses' Early Years in Egypt - Kathleen Jenks 3192
River God - Wilbur Smith 5928
The Shining King - Peter Danielson 1476
Sword of Glory - Peter Danielson 1477
Tables of the Law - Thomas Mann 4067
The Temple of the Muses - John Maddox Roberts 5382
The Twelfth Transforming - Pauline Gedge 2347
Vengeance of the Lion - Peter Danielson 1480
Winged Pharaoh - Joan Grant 2536

Ancient Greece

Achilles His Armour - Peter Green 2569
Alcibiades, Beloved of Gods - Vincenz Brun 735
Alexander of Macedon: The Journey to World's End - Harold Lamb 3607
Alexander the God - Robert Payne 4849
Amber Princess - Henry Treece 6325
Anabasis: A Journey to the Interior - Ellen Gilchrist 2408
Besieger of Cities - Alfred Duggan 1761
The Bull From the Sea - Mary Renault 5295
A Choice of Murder - Peter Vansittart 6429
The Corn King and the Spring Queen - Naomi Mitchison 4419
Creation - Gore Vidal 6486
The Eagle King - Henry Treece 6327
Earth Giant - Edison Marshall 4106
An Elephant for Aristotle - L. Sprague De Camp 1556
The Escape of Socrates - Robert Pick 4993
Farewell Great King: A Novel of Ancient Greece - Jill Paton Walsh 4829
The Flowers of Adonis - Rosemary Sutcliff 6122
Gate to the Sea - Bryher 743
Glory and the Lightning - Taylor Caldwell 856
Goat Song: A Novel of Ancient Greece - Frank Yerby 6920
Goatsong - Tom Holt 3009
The Goddess - Miranda Seymour 5763
The Golden Wind - C.L. Grace 2507
Horses of Heaven - Gillian Bradshaw 630
The Immortal Marriage - Gertrude Atherton 225
The Invaders - Peter Danielson 1469
Jason - Henry Treece 6331
The King Must Die - Mary Renault 5298
The Last of the Wine - Mary Renault 5299
The Laughter of Aphrodite - Peter Green 2570
The Magnificent Traitor: A Novel of Alcibiades and the Golden Age of Pericles - Lynn Poole 5092
The Mask of Apollo - Mary Renault 5300
Medea - Miranda Seymour 5764
My Name Is Sappho - Martha Rofheart 5429
Nicanor of Athens: The Autobiography of an Unknown Citizen - Owen Francis Grazebrook 2563
North to Thule: An Imagined Narrative of the Famous "Lost" Voyage of Pytheas of Massalla in the Fourth Century B.C. - John Frye 2241
The Other Sappho - Ellen Frye 2240
Paris of Troy - George Baker 273
Pericles the Athenian - Rex Warner 6566
The Praise Singer - Mary Renault 5302
The Private and Public Life of Socrates - Rene Kraus 3552
The Private Life of Helen of Troy - John Erskine 1957
The Promised Land - Peter Danielson 1471
Return to Ithaca - Eyvind Johnson 3224
Scandal in Troy - Eva Hemmer Hansen 2679
The Shining - Stephen Marlowe 4097
Soldier of the Mist - Gene Wolfe 6843
Three Ships and Three Kings - Georgia Sallaska 5573
The Torch - Wilder Penfield 4902
The Trojan - Noel B. Gerson 2386
Troy - Richard Matturro 4194
The Voyage Home - Ernst Schnabel 5644
The Walled Orchard - Tom Holt 3010
Years of the City - George Rippey Stewart 6028

Ancient India

Lady of the Lotus - William E. Barrett 353

Ancient Israel

After Goliath - R.V. Cassill 955
Bathsheba - Roberta Kells Dorr 1695
Bathsheba - Torgny Lindgren 3789

Dara, the Cypriot - Louis Paul 4842
David and Bathsheba - Ari Ibn-Sahav 3098
David of Jerusalem - Louis De Wohl 1564
David the King - Gladys Schmitt 5641
David's Stranger - Moshe Shamir 5771
Esther - Nathaniel Norsen Weinreb 6601
Esther: The Star and the Sceptre - Gina Andrews 146
Giant Killer - Elmer Holmes Davis 1518
The Herdsman - Dorothy Clarke Wilson 6801
The Invaders - Peter Danielson 1469
The Island of the Innocent: A Novel of Greek and Jew in the Time of the Maccabees - Vardis Fisher 2108
Jacob: An Autobiography - Irving Fineman 2088
King David - Gwyn Jenkins 3191
The King David Report - Stefan Heym 2910
The King of Flesh and Blood - Moshe Shamir 5772
King of Kings: A Novel of the Life of David - Malachi Martin 4134
The Painted Queen - Olga Hesky 2871
The Promised Land - Peter Danielson 1471
The Queen of Sheba - Roberta Kells Dorr 1696
Rizpah - Charles E. Israel 3124
Ruth - Irving Fineman 2089
Scarlet Cord: A Novel of the Woman of Jericho - Frank G. Slaughter 5899
Solomon and Sheba - Jay Williams 6774
Solomon's Song - Roberta Kells Dorr 1697
The Sorceress - Nathaniel Norsen Weinreb 6602
The Source - James A. Michener 4374
The Unanointed - Laurene Chinn 1070
The Valley of God - Irene Steinman Patai 4825

Anglo-Saxon Period

Avalon - Anya Seton 5748
Born of the Sun - Joan Wolf 6837
The Breath of Kings - Gene Farrington 2019
Conscience of the King - Alfred Duggan 1763
The Cunning of the Dove - Alfred Duggan 1765
The Edge of Light - Joan Wolf 6839
The Fair - Robert Nathan 4559
The Flame in the Dark - Basil Bonallack 568
Gildenford - Valerie Anand 130
Harold, the Last of the Saxon Kings - Edward Bulwer-Lytton 767
The King Liveth - Jeffrey Farnol 2013
The Last Englishman: The Story of Hereward the Wake - Hebe Weenolsen 6596
The Last Pendragon - Robert Rice 5316
The Marsh King - C. Walter Hodges 2975
The Norman Pretender - Valerie Anand 132
The Proud Villeins - Valerie Anand 133
Raven's Wind - Victor Canning 883
The Right Line of Cedric - Alfred Duggan 1773
The Saxon Tapestry - Sile Rice 5317
This January Tale - Bryher 747
To Love Again - Bertrice Small 5913

Animals

The Animal Wife - Elizabeth Marshall Thomas 6243
Reindeer Moon - Elizabeth Marshall Thomas 6244
Sam Patch: Ballad of a Jumping Man - William Getz 2390
Traveller - Richard Adams 27
The Wolfling: A Documentary Novel of the 1870s - Sterling North 4648

Antebellum South

Absalom, Absalom! - William Faulkner 2049
The African - Harold Courlander 1386
The Ardent Years - Janet Stevenson 6003
Bagatelle - Maurice Denuziere 1613
Balisand - Joseph Hergesheimer 2853
Band of Angels - Robert Penn Warren 6572

Bayou - Pamela Jekel 3183
Beauty Beast - MacKinlay Kantor 3361
Beauty From Ashes - Eugenia Price 5177
Before Darkness Falls - Eugenia Price 5178
Benton's Row - Frank Yerby 6908
Beulah Land - Lonnie Coleman 1202
Black Thunder - Arna Bontemps 574
Bride of the River - Laura B. Harris 2723
Bridle the Wind - Julia Davis 1525
Bright Captivity - Eugenia Price 5180
By Reason of Strength - Gerald White Johnson 3225
The Chess Player: A Novel of New Orleans and Paris - Frances Parkinson Keyes 3478
Cloud on the Land - Julia Davis 1526
A Clouded Star - Anne Parrish 4819
Cordelia Chantrell - Meade Minnigerode 4413
A Darkness at Ingraham's Crest: A Tale of the Slaveholding South - Frank Yerby 6912
Daughter of Strangers - Elizabeth Boatwright Coker 1164
Deep River - Henrietta Buckmaster 760
Deep Summer - Gwen Bristow 696
Dinner at Belmont - Alfred Leland Crabb 1398
The Distant Lands - Julian Green 2567
Don Juan McQueen - Eugenia Price 5181
Double Moscadine - Frances Gaither 2271
Dreams of Gold - Lewis Orde 4748
Drum - Kyle Onstott 4744
Eagle on the Sun - Julia Davis 1527
East by Day - Blair Niles 4626
Eden - Julie Ellis 1918
Elegant Journey - John Selby 5740
Elixir of Life - A.E. Cowdrey 1392
Fairoaks - Frank Yerby 6915
Family - J. California Cooper 1297
Father Abraham - Irving A. Bacheller 258
The Feast of All Saints - Anne Rice 5314
Fevre Dream - George R.R. Martin 4131
Fire in the Heart - Henrietta Buckmaster 761
Floodtide - Frank Yerby 6916
The Forge - Thomas S. Stribling 6083
Foundation Stone - Lella Warren 6571
The Foxes of Harrow - Frank Yerby 6917
Freedom's Banner - Teresa Crane 1415
Gallows Way - Daoma Winston 6825
Golden Isle - Frank G. Slaughter 5890
Gone with the Wind - Margaret Mitchell 4415
The Grandissimes - George W. Cable 842
The Great Tide - Rubylea Hall 2662
Hacey Miller - James Sherburne 5805
The Handsome Road - Gwen Bristow 697
Heaven Trees - Stark Young 6943
Her Christmas at the Hermitage: A Tale about Rachel and Andrew Jackson - Helen Topping Miller 4389
In the Season of the Wild Rose - Clara Rising 5347
Iron Ships, Iron Men - Christopher Nicole 4616
The Journey of August King - John Ehle 1894
Journey Proud - Thomasine McGehee 4273
The Keeper of the House - Harry Harrison Kroll 3558
Know Nothing - Mary Lee Settle 5755
Lamb in His Bosom - Caroline Miller 4380
The Light Infantry Ball - Hamilton Basso 375
Lighthouse - Eugenia Price 5182
The Live Goat - Cecil Dawkins 1542
Look Back to Glory - Herbert Ravenel Sass 5607
Look to the Rose - Shirley Seifert 5728
Madame Castel's Lodger - Frances Parkinson Keyes 3480
The Magnolias - Julie Ellis 1922
Margaret's Story - Eugenia Price 5183
Maria - Eugenia Price 5184
Miss Delicia Allen - Mary Johnston 3237
Mississippi Belle - Clements Ripley 5346
Natchez: A Novel of the Deep South - Pamela Jekel 3186
New Moon Rising - Eugenia Price 5185
New Orleans Legacy - Alexandra Ripley 5341

New Orleans Woman: A Biographical Novel of Myra Clark Gaines - Harnett T. Kane 3355
North and South - John Jakes 3151
Ol' Prophet Nat - Daniel Panger 4786
Old Miss - Thomas Campbell 877
Papa La-Bas - John Dickson Carr 914
Pathway to the Stars - Harnett T. Kane 3356
Peace at Bowling Green - Alfred Leland Crabb 1405
Penhally - Caroline Gordon 2479
Peter Ashley - DuBose Heyward 2911
Pomp and Circumstance - Fred Mustard Stewart 6025
Private Knowledge - Betty Palmer Nelson 4576
The Proud and the Free - Janet Dailey 1456
The Proud Way - Shirley Seifert 5731
Pull Down to New Orleans - Zachary Ball 283
The Raider - Jesse Hill Ford 2164
Raising Holy Hell - Bruce Olds 4718
The Red Cock Crows - Frances Gaither 2272
Royal Street - Walter Adolphe Roberts 5393
The Running Thread - Drayton Mayrant 4215
Sangaree - Frank G. Slaughter 5898
Sapphira and the Slave Girl - Willa Cather 958
Savage Oaks - Julie Ellis 1924
Savannah - Eugenia Price 5186
Savannah Purchase - Jane Aiken Hodge 2970
Show Me a Land - Clark McMeekin 4293
Sisters and Brothers - Janet Stevenson 6005
The Slave Stealer - Boyd Upchurch 6390
Some Lose Their Way - Eloise S. Liddon 3770
Song of the Bayou - Elinor Lynley 3936
Southern Discomfort - Rita Mae Brown 730
Sow the Seeds of Hemp - Gary Jennings 3195
The Stars of the South - Julian Green 2568
A Story of Deep Delight - Thomas McNamee 4305
Stranger in Savannah - Eugenia Price 5187
The Stuart Women - Matt Braun 652
Three-Headed Angel - Roark Bradford 623
The Tides of Malvern - Francis Griswold 2595
To See Your Face Again - Eugenia Price 5188
Twilight of the Dawn - Elizabeth Nell Dubus 1752
Where Shadows Go - Eugenia Price 5189
The Wild Yazoo - John Myers 4546
The Woman of Catawba - Hilda Stahl 5978

Anti-Semitism

The Age of Wonders - Aharon Appelfeld 173
Bodin, 1349: An Epic Novel of Christians and Jews in the Plague Years - Roberta Kalechofsky 3322
Farriers' Lane - Anne Perry 4930
The Fixer - Bernard Malamud 4038
The Healer - Aharon Appelfeld 176
Members of the Tribe - Richard Kluger 3511
The Retreat - Aharon Appelfeld 178
The Second Crucifixion - Maurice Samuel 5579

Antietam, Battle of

The Bloody Ground - Bernard Cornwell 1334
By Antietam Creek - Don Robertson 5398
Confederates - Thomas Keneally 3412
Freedom - William Safire 5561
Oldest Living Confederate Widow Tells All - Allan Gurganus 2621
The River and the Wilderness - Don Robertson 5401
The Scarlet Patch - Bruce Lancaster 3645
The Stonewall Brigade: A Novel of the American Civil War - Frank G. Slaughter 5902

Archaeology

The Curse of the King - Victoria Holt 3012
The Curse of the Pharaohs - Elizabeth Peters 4948
The Deeds of the Disturber - Elizabeth Peters 4949
The Greek Treasure - Irving Stone 6056
The Hippopotamus Pool - Elizabeth Peters 4950

The Last Camel Died at Noon - Elizabeth Peters 4951
Lion in the Valley - Elizabeth Peters 4952
The Mummy Case - Elizabeth Peters 4953
The Snake, the Crocodile, and the Dog - Elizabeth Peters 4954

Architecture

The House on Curtin Street - Millie J. Ragosta 5242
Myself, Christopher Wren - David Weiss 6606
Palais-Royale - Richard Sennett 5747
The Pillars of the Earth - Ken Follett 2149
The Stones of the Abbey - Fernand Pouillon 5144
The White Cutter - David Pownall 5158

Armenian Massacre

Mamigon - Jack Hashian 2772

Arthurian Legends

Arthur - Stephen R. Lawhead 3679
Arthur Rex: A Legendary Novel - Thomas Berger 477
Artorius Rex - John Gloag 2432
Beloved Exile - Parke Godwin 2446
The Chessboard Queen - Sharan Newman 4597
Child of the Northern Spring - Persia Woolley 6867
The Coming of the King - Nikolai Tolstoy 6296
A Connecticut Yankee in King Arthur's Court - Mark Twain 6371
The Crimson Chalice - Victor Canning 882
The Crystal Cave - Mary Stewart 6029
The Duke of War - Walter O'Meara 4734
The Emperor Arthur - Godfrey Turton 6368
Firelord - Parke Godwin 2447
First Knight - Elizabeth Chadwick 966
The Great Captains - Henry Treece 6329
The Green Man - Henry Treece 6330
Guinevere - Sharan Newman 4600
Guinevere Evermore - Sharan Newman 4601
Guinevere: The Legend in Autumn - Persia Woolley 6868
Hawk of May - Gillian Bradshaw 629
The Hollow Hills - Mary Stewart 6030
The Idylls of the Queen - Phyllis Ann Karr 3367
In the Shadow of the Oak King - Courtway Jones 3271
In Winter's Shadow - Gillian Bradshaw 632
The King - Donald Barthelme 365
Kingdom of Summer - Gillian Bradshaw 633
The Kingmaking - Helen Hollick 3000
Kinsmen of the Grail - Dorothy James Roberts 5376
The Last Enchantment - Mary Stewart 6031
The Last Pendragon - Robert Rice 5316
Merlin - Stephen R. Lawhead 3681
The Mists of Avalon - Marion Zimmer Bradley 626
The Once and Future King - T.H. White 6705
The Pagan King - Edison Marshall 4109
The Pendragon - Catherine Christian 1075
Pendragon - Stephen R. Lawhead 3682
Pendragon's Banner - Helen Hollick 3001
The Prince and the Pilgrim - Mary Stewart 6032
Queen of the Summer Stars - Persia Woolley 6869
The Queen's Knight - Marvin Borowsky 585
The Road to Avalon - Joan Wolf 6842
Salisbury Plain - Henry C. Branson 650
The Singing Sword - Jack Whyte 6725
The Skystone: The Forging of Arthur's Britain - Jack Whyte 6726
Sword at Sunset - Rosemary Sutcliff 6125
Taliesin - Stephen R. Lawhead 3683
The Wicked Day - Mary Stewart 6033
The Winter King - Bernard Cornwell 1351
Witch of the North - Courtway Jones 3272

Artistic Life

The Agony and the Ecstasy - Irving Stone 6054
Alethea - Pamela Belle 429
Angelica - Samuel A. Schreiner Jr. 5671
Arrogance - Joanna Scott 5679
Artemesia - Anna Banti 295
The Artist - Norman Garbo 2281
The Artist's Daughter - Leslie O'Grady 4698
Benjamin Franklin and a Case of Artful Murder -
   Robert Lee Hall 2654
The Branch-Bearers - Glen Petrie 4978
Bruegel, or, The Workshop of Dreams - Claude Henri
   Rocquet 5422
The Burning Man - Stephen Longstreet 3883
Caravaggio - Robert Payne 4851
Chelsea - Nancy Fitzgerald 2114
*Color From a Light Within: A Novel Based on the Life
   of El Greco* - Donald Braider 641
*Colossus: A Novel about Goya and a World Gone
   Mad* - Stephen Marlowe 4093
A Comedy of Murders - George Herman 2861
The Dance of Death - Jeremy Potter 5142
The Dark Fire - Linda Murray 4537
The Days of the Butterfly - Norah Lofts 3841
Depths of Glory - Irving Stone 6055
An Epic Joy: A Novel Based on the Life of Rubens -
   Donald Braider 642
The Florentine - Sandra Shulman 5840
The Florentine - Carl J. Spinatelli 5968
Funny Papers - Tom De Haven 1559
Gold of Their Bodies: A Novel about Gauguin -
   Charles Orson Gorham 2488
The Golden Tulip - Rosalind Laker 3596
The Golden Veil - Paddy Kitchen 3507
The Goliath Head - Charles J. Calitri 865
*The Greek of Toledo: A Romantic Narrative of El
   Greco* - Elizabeth Borton 586
The Hand of Michelangelo - Sidney Alexander 85
The Heaven Tree Trilogy - Edith Pargeter 4797
*The Horn and the Roses: A Novel Based on the Life of
   Peter Paul Rubens* - Ira Jan Wallach 6542
The House of Cray - Pamela Hill 2936
I, James McNeill Whistler - Lawrence
   Williams 6787
I, Rembrandt - David Weiss 6605
Impressionist: A Novel of Mary Cassatt - Joan
   King 3486
In the Blazing Light - Max White 6693
The Invention of Truth - Marta Morazzoni 4449
The Italian Garden - Judith Lennox-Smith 3717
Johanna: A Novel of the Van Gogh Family - Claire
   Cooperstein 1317
John Ruskin's Wife - Eva McDonald 4259
The Last Portrait of the Duchess of Alba - Antonio
   Larreta 3666
Leonardo's Judas - Leo Perutz 4941
Light - Eva Figes 2083
Lover of Life - Zsolt de Harsanyi 2756
Lust for Life - Irving Stone 6059
A Man and His Mountain: The Life of Paul Cezanne -
   Hugh McLeave 4285
*Man of Montmartre: A Novel Based on the Life of
   Maurice Utrillo* - Stephen Longstreet 3888
The Master of Oakwindsor - Douglas Kent
   Hall 2648
The Master Painter - Edwin Mullins 4513
Melbury Square - Dorothy Eden 1857
The Melting Clock - Stuart M. Kaminsky 3342
*The Memory Cathedral: A Secret History of Leonardo
   Da Vinci* - Jack Dann 1481
Michelangelo the Florentine - Sidney Alexander 86
Modigliani: Prince of Montparnasse - Tadeusz
   Wittlin 6834
Mona Lisa: The Woman in the Portrait - Sara
   Mayfield 4206
The Montmarte Murders - Richard Grayson 2561
*Moulin Rouge: A Novel Based on Henri de Toulouse-
   Lautrec* - Pierre La Mure 3576

Mr. Audubon's Lucy - Lucy Kennedy 3419
My Lady of Cleves - Margaret Campbell Barnes 328
Naked Came I: A Novel of Rodin - David
   Weiss 6607
The Naked Maja - Noel B. Gerson 2378
*Nicodemus: The Roman Years of Michelangelo
   Buonarroti, 1534-1564* - Sidney Alexander 87
The Passionate Journey - Irving Stone 6061
The Private Life of Mona Lisa - Pierre La
   Mure 3577
Privileged Children - Frances Vernon 6455
Proud Heritage - Ilse Bishcoff 510
Rage in Silence: A Novel Based on the Life of Goya -
   Donald Braider 643
The Remarkable Young Man - Cecil Roberts 5373
Rembrandt - Gladys Schmitt 5643
The Romance of Leonardo Da Vinci - Dmitri
   Merezhkovski 4339
*The Saint of Montparnasse: A Novel Based on the Life
   of Constantin Brancusi* - Peter Neagoe 4560
The Serpent Garden - Judith Merkle Riley 5336
Son of the Gamblin' Man: The Youth of an Artist -
   Mari Sandoz 5593
The Sun Is God - Michael Noonan 4636
*A Tale of the Wind: A Novel of Nineteenth-Century
   France* - Kay Nolte Smith 5922
The Time Returns - Alexandra Ripley 5343
Titian - Dario Cecchi 965
To Seize a Dream - Virginia Davis Hersch 2866
To Seize the Passing Dream - Ted Berkman 479
Triptych - Dora Landey 3652
Utrillo's Mother - Sarah Baylis 391
The Venetian - David Weiss 6611
Verge of Glory - Frederick Wight 6747
Vincent: A Novel Based on the Life of Van Gogh -
   Joost Poldermans 5082
Willowwood - Elizabeth Savage 5619
Written in the Stars: A Novel about Albrecht Durer -
   Frances Hope Fisher 2103
The Young Men of Paris - Stephen Longstreet 3893

Assassination

Death of a Schoolboy - Hans Koning 3537
The Faraway Drums - Jon Cleary 1104
Flying into Love - D.M. Thomas 6236
Henry and Clara - Thomas Mallon 4042
The Ides of March - Thornton Wilder 6753
The Judges of the Secret Court - David Stacton 5972
The Last Full Measure - Honore Morrow 4488
Libra - Don DeLillo 1593
The Lincoln Diddle - Barbara Steward 6015
Nine Hours to Rama - Stanley Wolpert 6846
The Plot to Kill Wallis Simpson: A Work of Faction -
   Graham Fisher 2104
The President's Man - Elliott Roosevelt 5455
Three's Company - Alfred Duggan 1774
The Twisted Tendril - Alice Glasgow 2427
The Very Rich Hours of Count von Stauffenberg - Paul
   West 6637
The Woman Who Loved John Wilkes Booth - Pamela
   Redford Russell 5533

Assyrian Empire

The Assyrian - Nicholas Guild 2610
The Blood Star - Nicholas Guild 2611
*The Curse of Jezebel: A Novel of the Biblical Queen of
   Evil* - Frank G. Slaughter 5884

Atlanta, Battle of

Company Q - Richard O'Connor 4684
The Far Side of Home - Maggie Davis 1536
Jubilee - John Brick 672

Austerlitz, Battle of

The Thousand Fires - Anne Powers 5155

Austro-Hungarian Empire

The Archduke - Michael Arnold 194
Csardas - Diane Pearson 4875
The Devil's Lieutenant - Maria Fagyas 1998
The Emperor's Coloured Coat - John Biggins 491
Felding Castle - Edith De Born 1552
The First Casualty - William Powell 5149

Aviation

The Aviator - Ernest K. Gann 2277
The Balloonist - Macdonald Harris 2724
The Blood Order - Jack D. Hunter 3084
The Blue Max - Jack D. Hunter 3085
The Bright Blue Sky - Max Hennessy 2830
The Casket Crew - Arch Whitehouse 6709
The Challenging Heights - Max Hennessy 2831
Conqueror of the Clouds - William F.
   Hallstead 2664
Eagles at War - Walter J. Boyne 620
The Fine and Handsome Captain - Frances
   Lynch 3933
The Flight of the Eagle - Per Olof Sundman 6119
Gentlemen of Adventure - Ernest K. Gann 2278
Goshawk Squadron - Derek Robinson 5403
The Hallelujah Flight - Jack Lynn 3937
The Heart of the Continent - Nancy Cato 961
Herma - Macdonald Harris 2726
High Road to China - Jon Cleary 1106
Honour and Obey - Malcolm Macdonald 3966
In the Blue Light of African Dreams - Paul
   Watkins 6580
In the Company of Eagles - Ernest K. Gann 2279
It's Me Again - Donald Jack 3126
London's Child - Philip Boast 560
The Longest Winter - Julie Harris 2722
Me So Far - Donald Jack 3127
Once a Gentleman - Donald James 3157
Once More the Hawks - Max Hennessy 2836
Paloverde - Jacqueline Briskin 693
Playboy Squadron - Arch Whitehouse 6710
The Sky and Tomorrow - Thomas William
   Duncan 1788
Squadron Forty-Four - Arch Whitehouse 6711
Squadron Shilling - Arch Whitehouse 6712
That's Me in the Middle - Donald Jack 3129
Three Cheers for Me - Donald Jack 3131
The Two-Headed Eagle - John Biggins 493
War Story: A Novel - Derek Robinson 5404
Wings for the Chariots - Arch Whitehouse 6713
Wings of the Morning - David Beaty 402

Aztec Empire

Aztec - Gary Jennings 3193
Captain From Castile - Samuel Shellabarger 5794
The Coil of the Serpent - Dexter Allen 94
Copilli, Aztec Prince - Miguel Aleman Velasco 75
Cortez and Marina - Edison Marshall 4105
Death of the Fifth Sun - Robert Somerlott 5944
The Fair God - Lew Wallace 6537
Gods on Horseback - Samuel G. Baggett 263
The Golden Princess - Alexander Baron 335
The Great White Gods - Eduard Stucken 6102
The Heart of Jade - Salvador de Madariaga 4024
The Jaguar and the Golden Stag - Dexter Allen 95
The Jaguar Princess - Clare Bell 421
The Luck of Huemac: A Novel about the Aztecs -
   Daniel Peters 4946
Mexico - James A. Michener 4372
*The Sun, He Dies: A Novel about the End of the Aztec
   World* - Jamake Highwater 2919

They Are Coming: The Conquest of Mexico - Jose Lopez Portillo y Pacheco 3896
Valley of Eagles - Dexter Allen 96

Babylonian Empire

Babylon - Anthony Esler 1959
The Babylonians - Nathaniel Norsen Weinreb 6600
Judith - Stella Wilchek 6748

Bacon's Rebellion

The Bright Face of Danger - Clifford Sublette 6108
Forest Cavalier: A Romance of America's First Frontier and of Bacon's Rebellion - Roy Catesby Flannagan 2122
The King's Passenger - Nathan Schachner 5631
Man Cannot Tell - Philip Lightfoot Scruggs 5711

Balaclava, Battle of

Brave Captains - Vivian Stuart 6086
Trumpeter, Sound! - D.L. Murray 4528

Balloons

Cadmus Henry - Walter D. Edmonds 1872
Tish - Cissie Miller 4381

Bannockburn, Battle of

Robert the Bruce: The Path of the Hero King - Nigel Tranter 6318

Barbarians

Caesar of the Narrow Seas - John Gloag 2433
Count Belisarius - Robert Graves 2544
The Death of Attila - Cecelia Holland 2986
Eagle in the Snow - Wallace Breem 654
Gate to the Sea - Bryher 743
The Iron Hand of Mars - Lindsey Davis 1528
The Lost Eagles - Ralph Graves 2542
Roman Wall - Bryher 745
The Sinner of Saint Ambrose - Robert Raynolds 5275
Throne of the World - Louis De Wohl 1575

Barons' War

Below the Salt - Thomas B. Costain 1362
The De Montfort Legacy - Pamela Bennetts 447
Falconer's Crusade - Ian Morson 4493
The Keys of England - William Victor Cooke 1271
The Queen From Provence - Jean Plaidy 5047
Shield of Honor - Alice Walworth Graham 2511
The Wolf at the Door - Graham Shelby 5793

Baseball

Blue Ruin: A Novel of the 1919 World Series - Brendan Boyd 610
The Celebrant - Eric Rolfe Greenberg 2572
Fielder's Choice - Rick Norman 4646
The Great Blizzard - Albert E. Idell 3101
Hoopla - Harry Stein 5990
If I Never Get Back - Darryl Brock 700
Joy in Mudville - Gordon McAlpine 4216
Mr. Vertigo - Paul Auster 244
Murder at Ebbets Field - Troy Soos 5947
Murder at Fenway Park - Troy Soos 5948
Murder at Wrigley Field - Troy Soos 5949
The Veracruz Blues - Mark Winegardner 6821

Battle of Agincourt

Falstaff - Robert Nye 4653

Fortune Made His Sword - Martha Rofheart 5426
Good King Harry - Denise Giardina 2393
Harry of Monmouth - A.M. Maughan 4199
The Lily and the Leopard - Susan Wiggs 6745
Royal Sword at Agincourt - Pamela Bennetts 455
The Star of Lancaster - Jean Plaidy 5065
Walk with Peril - Dorothy V.S. Jackson 3132
Wife to Henry V - Hilda Lewis 3752

Battle of Alamance

Weathercock - Constance Dodge 1668

Battle of Antietam

The Bloody Ground - Bernard Cornwell 1334
By Antietam Creek - Don Robertson 5398
Confederates - Thomas Keneally 3412
Freedom - William Safire 5561
Oldest Living Confederate Widow Tells All - Allan Gurganus 2621
The River and the Wilderness - Don Robertson 5401
The Scarlet Patch - Bruce Lancaster 3645
The Stonewall Brigade: A Novel of the American Civil War - Frank G. Slaughter 5902

Battle of Atlanta

Company Q - Richard O'Connor 4684
The Far Side of Home - Maggie Davis 1536
Jubilee - John Brick 672

Battle of Austerlitz

The Thousand Fires - Anne Powers 5155

Battle of Balaclava

Brave Captains - Vivian Stuart 6086
Trumpeter, Sound! - D.L. Murray 4528

Battle of Bannockburn

Robert the Bruce: The Path of the Hero King - Nigel Tranter 6318

Battle of Bennington

Day of Battle - Frederic F. Van de Water 6402
The Shadow and the Glory - John Edward Jennings 3207
That Bennington Mob - Henry Barnard Safford 5558

Battle of Blair Mountain

Storming Heaven - Denise Giardina 2394

Battle of Bloody Marsh

Dark Sails - Helen Topping Miller 4388

Battle of Bull Run

Battle Flag - Bernard Cornwell 1333
Beloved Enemy - Al Lacy 3579
Gray Canaan - David Garth 2305
The Passionate Rebel - Frank G. Slaughter 5894
Rebel - Bernard Cornwell 1336

Battle of Bunker Hill

The Drums of April - Charles Mergendahl 4340
The Gentle Rebel - Gilbert Morris 4461
Guns for Rebellion - F. van Wyck Mason 4151
Israel Potter - Herman Melville 4334

Lionel Lincoln; or, The Leaguer of Boston - James Fenimore Cooper 1303
Oliver Wiswell - Kenneth Roberts 5389
The Road to Bunker Hill - Shirley Barker 316
The Shadow and the Glory - John Edward Jennings 3207
Song of a Strange Child - Gilbert Morris 4470
Three Harbors - F. van Wyck Mason 4162

Battle of Cambrai

Wings for the Chariots - Arch Whitehouse 6713

Battle of Chancellorsville

Gods and Generals - Jeff Shaara 5765
Time of Drums - John Ehle 1897

Battle of Chickamauga

Captain Little Ax - James H. Street 6077
The Fifth Conspiracy - Ted Jones 3296
Guns of Chickamauga - Richard O'Connor 4685
Hiwassee: A Novel of the Civil War - Charles F. Price 5176
In a Dark Garden - Frank G. Slaughter 5891
Mockingbird Sang at Chickamauga - Alfred Leland Crabb 1404
None Shall Look Back - Caroline Gordon 2478

Battle of Concord

April Morning - Howard Fast 2027
Concord Bridge - Howard Horne 3035
Patriot's Progress - Joseph G.E. Hopkins 3027
Trumpet to Arms - Bruce Lancaster 3647

Battle of Copenhagen

A Balance of Dangers - Anthony Forrest 2184
The Bomb Vessel - Richard Woodman 6860
The Inshore Squadron - Alexander Kent 3434

Battle of Corinth

Journey to Shiloh - Will Henry 2843

Battle of Cowpens

The Carolinians - Jane Barry 357
The Fallon Blood - Reagan O'Neal 4741
The Long March - Jane Barry 358
The Ragged Ones - Burke Davis 1511

Battle of Crecy

The Lady Royal - Molly Costain Haycraft 2794
Ride East! Ride West!: A Romance of the Hundred Years' War - Anne Powers 5154
The Vow on the Heron - Jean Plaidy 5074

Battle of Culloden

Born to Be King - Constance Gluyas 2440
Candleshine No More - Jane Oliver 4721
The Flight of the Heron - Dorothy Kathleen Broster 710
Highlands Rebel - Sally Watson 6584
The Woman from The Glen - Chloe Gartner 2310

Battle of Eylau

Draw Near to Battle - Jere Hungerford Wheelwright 6667

Battle of Flodden

Falcon: The Autobiography of His Grace James IV, King of Scots - A.J. Stewart 6021

Battle of Fontenoy

A Day of Battle - Vincent Sheean 5787
Pope Joan - Donna Woolfolk Cross 1433

Battle of Fort Duquesne

Juniata Valley - Virginia C. Cassel 954

Battle of Fort Pillow

The Falling Hills - Perry Lentz 3720

Battle of Franklin

The Bright Sword - Eleanor Perenyi 4911
Night March - Bruce Lancaster 3641

Battle of Fredericksburg

Gods and Generals - Jeff Shaara 5765
Joy From Ashes - Al Lacy 3581
The River and the Wilderness - Don Robertson 5401

Battle of Gallipoli

1915: A Novel - Roger McDonald 4264
Redemption - Leon Uris 6393

Battle of Gettysburg

The Barefoot Brigade - Douglas C. Jones 3274
Carriage Trade - Robert Thomsen 6271
Copperhead Moon - Herbert Stover 6067
The Court Martial of Robert E. Lee - Douglas Savage 5617
A Court of Owls - Richard Adicks 37
For Us the Living - Antonia Van-Loon 6424
Gettysburg - Stephen Longstreet 3887
Gettysburg: Crisis of Command - Harry Albright 65
Gray Victory - Robert Skimin 5877
Hard Road to Gettysburg - Ted Jones 3298
The History of Rome Hanks - Joseph Stanley Pennell 4909
House Divided - Ben Ames Williams 6765
Jubilee - John Brick 672
The Killer Angels - Michael Shaara 5766
Long Remember - MacKinlay Kantor 3362
Look Away - Harold Coyle 1395
Loving Heart - Elsie Singmaster 5869
The President's Daughter - Barbara Chase-Riboud 1005
The Scarlet Guidon - Ray Grant Toepfer 6287
The Scarlet Patch - Bruce Lancaster 3645
Spanish Gold - Kevin D. Randle 5252
The Stonewall Brigade: A Novel of the American Civil War - Frank G. Slaughter 5902
Swords of Steel - Elsie Singmaster 5870
Three Days - Stephen Longstreet 3891
The Three Days - Don Robertson 5402
Time of Drums - John Ehle 1897

Battle of Glorieta

The Devil Gun - William Syers 6148

Battle of Hastings

The Bastard King - Jean Plaidy 5004
The Conqueror's Wife - Noel B. Gerson 2363
The Firedrake - Cecelia Holland 2988
The Fourteenth of October - Bryher 742

The Golden Warrior: The Story of Harold and William - Hope Muntz 4517
Harold Was My King - Hilda Lewis 3749
Red Lion and Gold Dragon - Rosemary Sprague 5969
The Wind From Hastings - Morgan Llywelyn 3825

Battle of Horseshoe Bend

Horseshoe Bend - Bruce Palmer 4779

Battle of Jutland

Buller's Victory - Richard Hough 3049
The Devil in Harbour - Catherine Gavin 2319
The Lion at Sea - Max Hennessy 2834
To the Honor of the Fleet - Robert H. Pilpel 5002

Battle of Kennesaw Mountain

The Far Side of Home - Maggie Davis 1536

Battle of Kings Mountain

The Border Men - Cameron Judd 3312
The Carolinians - Jane Barry 357
The Fallon Blood - Reagan O'Neal 4741
Kings Mountain - Florette Henri 2838
Rogue's March - Maristan Chapman 993
Slow Dies the Thunder - Helen Topping Miller 4395
Toil of the Brave - Inglis Fletcher 2141
Wild Horizon - F. van Wyck Mason 4164

Battle of Lake Erie

The Court Martial of Commodore Perry - James A. Rhodes 5307
D'ri and I - Irving A. Bacheller 257
The Fleet in the Forest - Carl Daniel Lane 3654
My Blood and My Treasure - Mary Schumann 5674
Trumpet in the Wilderness - Robert S. Harper 2717

Battle of Lepanto

The Last Crusader - Louis De Wohl 1569
A Man Called Cervantes - Bruno Frank 2201
The Wind in His Fists - John Edward Jennings 3210

Battle of Lexington

April Morning - Howard Fast 2027
Bride of Liberty - Frank Yerby 6909
Concord Bridge - Howard Horne 3035
Lionel Lincoln; or, The Leaguer of Boston - James Fenimore Cooper 1303
Patriot's Progress - Joseph G.E. Hopkins 3027

Battle of Long Island

Oliver Wiswell - Kenneth Roberts 5389

Battle of Malazgirt

Shards of Empire - Susan Schwartz 5677

Battle of Manzikent

The Lady for Ransom - Alfred Duggan 1768

Battle of Missionary Ridge

Banner at Shenandoah - Bruce Catton 963

Battle of Mobile Bay

A Heart Divided - Al Lacy 3580

Battle of Monmouth

The Drums of Monmouth - Emma Gelders Sterne 5998
Farewell to Valley Forge - David Taylor 6178
Monmouth - Charles Bracelen Flood 2144
Morning in America - Willard Wiener 6741

Battle of Nashville

The Bright Sword - Eleanor Perenyi 4911

Battle of New Orleans

1812 - David Nevin 4586
Black Ivory - Polan Banks 292
Hearts of Hickory - John Trotwood Moore 4442
The Rake and the Hussy - Robert W. Chambers 981

Battle of Pea Ridge

Elkhorn Tavern - Douglas C. Jones 3278

Battle of Petersburg

Where My Love Sleeps - Clifford Dowdey 1710

Battle of Quebec

Lord Vanity - Samuel Shellabarger 5796
Web of Destiny - Muriel Elwood 1939
The White Cockade - Vincent O'Brien 4683
Yankee Rogue - Dana Fuller Ross 5496

Battle of Rhode Island

Murfy's Men - Gerald Green 2565

Battle of Rich Mountain

A Promise Unbroken - Al Lacy 3582

Battle of Salamis

Farewell Great King: A Novel of Ancient Greece - Jill Paton Walsh 4829

Battle of San Jacinto

The Eagle and the Raven - James A. Michener 4369
Empire of Bones: A Novel of Sam Houston and the Texas Revolution - Jeff Long 3868
The Sam Houston Story - Dean Owen 4770
Thunder Before Seven - Anna Brand 648

Battle of San Juan Hill

Ever After - Elswyth Thane 6216
Remember Santiago - Douglas C. Jones 3280
The Rough Rider - Gilbert Morris 4468
San Juan Hill - Will Henry 2848

Battle of Saratoga

Guns of Burgoyne - Bruce Lancaster 3640
Rabble in Arms - Kenneth Roberts 5390
The Rifleman - John Brick 675
The Twisted Saber: A Biographical Novel of Benedict Arnold - Philip Vail 6398

Battle of Sebastopol

Victory at Sebastopol - Vivian Stuart 6091

Battle of Second Bull Run/Manassas

Unto This Hour - Tom Wicker 6733

Battle of Sekigahara

Musashi: An Epic Novel of the Samurai Era - Eiji Yoshikawa 6935

Battle of Shiloh

Captain Little Ax - James H. Street 6077
Grant's War - Ted Jones 3297
The History of Rome Hanks - Joseph Stanley Pennell 4909
In the Season of the Wild Rose - Clara Rising 5347
Johnny Shiloh - James A. Rhodes 5308
Journey to Shiloh - Will Henry 2843
Long Day at Shiloh - Don Bannister 294
The Long Night - Andrew Lytle 3945
Proving Ground: A Novel of Civil War Days in the North - Leone Lowden 3919
Shadowed Memories - Al Lacy 3583
Shiloh - Shelby Foote 2153

Battle of Shrewsbury

Falstaff - Robert Nye 4653

Battle of Tannenberg

August 1914 - Alexander Solzhenitsyn 5942

Battle of the Alamo

All the Brave Rifles - Clarke Venable 6450
The Bugles Are Silent: A Novel of the Texas Revolution - John R. Knaggs 3513
Crockett of Tennessee: A Novel Based on the Life and Times of David Crockett - Cameron Judd 3314
Empire of Bones: A Novel of Sam Houston and the Texas Revolution - Jeff Long 3868
The Furies - John Jakes 3146
The Iron Mistress - Paul I. Wellman 6618
The Men of Gonzales - John H. Culp 1442
The Road to San Jacinto - Leonard L. Foreman 2167
Tempered Blade - Monte Barrett 352
Wave High the Banner - Dee Brown 714

Battle of the Crater

The Crater - Richard Slotkin 5908
Glory Enough for All: The Battle of the Crater - Duane Philip Schultz 5673

Battle of the Frigidus

The Last Romans - Teodor Jeske-Choinski 3216

Battle of the Little Bighorn

Bugles in the Afternoon - Ernest Haycox 2788
Chief of Scouts - Don Bendell 439
The Court-Martial of George Armstrong Custer - Douglas C. Jones 3276
The Crossed Sabres - Gilbert Morris 4458
Custer Passed Our Way - Fred S. Kaufman 3370
Flashman and the Redskins - George MacDonald Fraser 2208
The Last Stand: A Novel about George Armstrong Custer and the Indians of the Plains - Edwin P. Hoyt 3061
A Mighty Afternoon - Charles K. Mills 4407
Montana Road - Harry Sinclair Drago 1717
No Survivors - Will Henry 2846

A Road We Do Not Know: A Novel of Custer at the Little Bighorn - Frederick J. Chiaventone 1057
The Scout - Harry Combs 1224
Seize the Sky - Terry C. Johnston 3256
Trumpet on the Land - Terry C. Johnston 3260

Battle of the *Monitor* vs. the *Merrimac*

Armored Giants: A Novel of the Civil War - F. van Wyck Mason 4145
Thunder on the Chesapeake - David Divine 1650

Battle of the Nile

A Game for Empires - Pearl Frye 2243
Mirage - Ruth McKenney 4283

Battle of the Pyramids

Mirage - Ruth McKenney 4283

Battle of the Rosebud

Crazy Horse - Bill Dugan 1757
Thunder in the Dawn - Earl Murray 4532

Battle of the Somme

War Story: A Novel - Derek Robinson 5404

Battle of the Wilderness

Thin Moon and Cold Mist - Kathleen O'Neal Gear 2330

Battle of Ticonderoga

Day of Battle - Frederic F. Van de Water 6402
Rebel Guns - Adam Rutledge 5539
Reluctant Rebel - Frederic F. Van de Water 6403

Battle of Tippecanoe

The Horn and the Forest - Jamie Lee Cooper 1313

Battle of Trafalgar

1805 - Richard Woodman 6857
Darken Ship - Nicholas Monsarrat 4431
Decision at Trafalgar - Richard Woodman 6861
He Brings Great News - Clemence Dane 1462
Ramage at Trafalgar - Dudley Pope 5102
The Scalpel and the Sword - Dell Shannon 5774

Battle of Trent

The Drums of Winter - Sandra Paretti 4790

Battle of Trenton

Trumpets at Dawn - Cyril Harris 2719

Battle of Ulandi

Bush War! - William Moore 4447

Battle of Vincennes

The Big Knives - Bruce Lancaster 3635

Battle of Wagram

The Battle of Wagram - Gilles Lapouge 3664

Battle of Waterloo

Allegra - Clare Darcy 1483
The Charterhouse of Parma - Stendhal 5993
Eliza Stanhope - Joanna Trollope 6347
Feather Castles - Patricia Veryan 6462
The Flight of the Eagle - Donald Thomas 6239
An Infamous Army - Georgette Heyer 2892
The Limits of Glory: A Novel of Waterloo - James McDonough 4265
Midsummer Moon - Karen Lynn 3940
The Spanish Bride - Georgette Heyer 2902
The Thousand Fires - Anne Powers 5155
The Twisted Sword - Winston Graham 2531
Vanity Fair - William Makepeace Thackeray 6213
Waterloo - Bernard Cornwell 1350
Waterloo - Manuel Komroff 3536
Waterloo - Frederic E. Smith 5920
Why Waterloo? - Alan Patrick Herbert 2850

Battle of Wounded Knee

A Creek Called Wounded Knee - Douglas C. Jones 3277
Dance Back the Buffalo - Milton Lott 3899
The Day the Sun Died - Dale Van Every 6408
A Good Day to Die - Thomas Wakefield Blackburn 525
Song of Wovoka - Earl Murray 4531

Battle of Yorktown

Blind Journey - Bruce Lancaster 3636
Cato's War - Guy Wheeler 6655
Dawn's Early Light - Elswyth Thane 6215
A Few Painted Feathers - Stephen Longstreet 3886
The Lady From Yorktown - Eva McDonald 4260
The Proud and the Free - Howard Fast 2042
Sea Road to Yorktown - Harvey Haislip 2644
Storm the Last Rampart - David Taylor 6180
Yorktown - Burke Davis 1513

Bear Flag Revolt

The Bear Flag: A Novel of the Birth of California - Cecelia Holland 2983

Bennington, Battle of

Day of Battle - Frederic F. Van de Water 6402
The Shadow and the Glory - John Edward Jennings 3207
That Bennington Mob - Henry Barnard Safford 5558

Biblical Story

Abraham and Sarah: The Long Journey - Roberta Kells Dorr 1694
Abram, Son of Terah - Florence M. Bauer 378
According to Mary: A Novel of the Magdalene - Willa Gibbs 2398
According to Thomas - Gladys Malvern 4053
After Goliath - R.V. Cassill 955
All the Trumpets Sounded: A Novel Based on the Life of Moses - W.G. Hardy 2701
Alone Atop the Mountain - Samuel Sandmel 5591
And Abram Journeyed - Harry Simonhoff 5858
The Apostle - Sholem Asch 197
The Babylonians - Nathaniel Norsen Weinreb 6600
Barabbas - Par Lagerkvist 3585
Barabbas: A Dream of the World's Tragedy - Marie Corelli 1327
Barabbas: A Novel of the Time of Jesus - Emery Bekessy 417
Bathsheba - Roberta Kells Dorr 1695
Bathsheba - Torgny Lindgren 3789
Behold the Man - Toyohiko Kagawa 3321
Behold the Man - N. Richard Nash 4556

Behold Your King - Florence M. Bauer 379

The Big Fisherman - Lloyd C. Douglas 1702

The Bond and the Free - Charles Dunscomb 1813

The Bride of Pilate - Esther Kellner 3393

The Brother - Dorothy Clarke Wilson 6799

The Brother - Chayym Zeldis 6958

Brothers of Vengeance - LeGette Blythe 556

The Centurion - Leonard Wibberley 6729

A Certain Woman: The Story of Mary Magdalene - Victor MacClure 3959

Charioteer: A Story of Old Egypt in the Days of Joseph - Gertrude Eberle 1835

Children of the Lion - Peter Danielson 1464

The Covenant: A Novel of the Life of Abraham the Prophet - Zofja Kossak-Szczucka 3543

The Curse of Jezebel: A Novel of the Biblical Queen of Evil - Frank G. Slaughter 5884

Dara, the Cypriot - Louis Paul 4842

Daughter of Jairus - Paul Hervey Fox 2196

David and Bathsheba - Ari Ibn-Sahav 3098

David at Olivet - Wallace Hamilton 2671

David of Jerusalem - Louis De Wohl 1564

David the King - Gladys Schmitt 5641

David: Warrior and King - Frank G. Slaughter 5885

David's Stranger - Moshe Shamir 5771

Dear and Glorious Physician - Taylor Caldwell 853

The Death of Kings - Peter Danielson 1465

Departed Glory - Peter Danielson 1466

The Emperor's Physician - Jacob Randolph Perkins 4914

Esther - Nathaniel Norsen Weinreb 6601

Esther: The Star and the Sceptre - Gina Andrews 146

The Exodus - Konrad Bercovici 473

The Exodus - Peter Danielson 1467

First the Blade - Drayton Mayrant 4212

Fisher of Men: A Novel of Simon Peter - Kurt Frieberger 2231

The Galileans - Frank G. Slaughter 5888

Giant Killer - Elmer Holmes Davis 1518

The Gifts: A Story of the Boyhood of Jesus - Dorothy Clarke Wilson 6800

The Good Tidings - William Sidney 5843

The Gospel According to Gamaliel - Gerald Heard 2801

The Gospel According to Pontius Pilate - James R. Mills 4408

The Gospel of Corax - Paul Park 4802

Great Lion of God - Taylor Caldwell 858

Hagar - Lois T. Henderson 2824

Hagar - Cothburn O'Neal 4737

He Came From Galilee - Daniel A. Poling 5083

Hear Me, Pilate! - LeGette Blythe 557

The Herdsman - Dorothy Clarke Wilson 6801

Hidden Victory: A Novel of Jesus - Herbert Francis Smith 5921

How Far to Bethlehem? - Norah Lofts 3846

Husband of Delilah - Eric Linklater 3802

I, Judas - Taylor Caldwell 859

I, Nathanael, Knew Jesus - William Gilbert Van Tassel Sutpen 6133

I, Paul - Rex Miller 4401

Jacob - Jean Cabries 844

Jacob: An Autobiography - Irving Fineman 2088

Jezebel - Dorothy Clarke Wilson 6802

Joseph of Egypt - Thomas Mann 4065

Joseph the Provider - Thomas Mann 4066

Judas - Igal Mossinsohn 4500

Judith - Stella Wilchek 6748

Justus - Arthur L. Lapham 3663

King David - Gwyn Jenkins 3191

The King David Report - Stefan Heym 2910

King Jesus - Robert Graves 2549

King of Kings: A Novel of the Life of David - Malachi Martin 4134

The Knifeman: A Novel of Judas Iscariot - William Rayner 5271

The Lance of Longinus - Hubertus Loewenstein 3833

The Last Temptation of Christ - Nikos Kazantzakis 3384

Lazarus - Alain Absire 15

The Letters of Nicodemus - Jan Dobraczynski 1655

The Life of Jesus: An Apocryphal Novel - Toby Olson 4731

The Lion in Egypt - Peter Danielson 1470

Live From Golgotha - Gore Vidal 6491

The Lord Jesus - Robert Payne 4854

Lot's Wife - Marie Ley-Piscator 3767

Love and Wisdom: A Novel about Solomon - Richard G. Hubler 3064

A Love Divine - Alexandra Ripley 5340

The Magdalene Gospel - Mary Ellen Ashcroft 203

Man Before the Morning - Cecil Maiden 4032

Man of Nazareth - Anthony Burgess 779

Marcus - Laurene Chinn 1068

Martha, Martha - Patricia McGerr 4274

Mary - Sholem Asch 198

Mary of Magdala - Anne C. Williman 6791

Mary of Nazareth - Esther Kellner 3394

The Master - Max Brod 702

Merari - Gloria Howe Bremkamp 656

The Messiah - Marjorie Holmes 3003

The Miracle Hater - Shulamith Hareven 2704

The Moon under Her Feet - Ceysta Kinstler 3503

Moses - Sholem Asch 199

Moses, Prince of Egypt - Howard Fast 2039

The Nazarene - Sholem Asch 200

No Other Gods - Wilder Penfield 4901

On Eagles' Wings - Arthur E. Southon 5951

The Painted Queen - Olga Hesky 2871

Pillar of Fire - Judith Tarr 6168

Pontius Pilate: A Biographical Novel - Paul L. Maier 4034

Pontius Pilate Reflects - Werner Koch 3529

Prince of Egypt - Dorothy Clarke Wilson 6805

The Promise - Esther Kellner 3395

The Prophet - Sholem Asch 201

The Prophet and the King - Shirley Watkins 6582

Prophets and Warriors - Peter Danielson 1473

The Queen of Sheba - Roberta Kells Dorr 1696

Refuge in Avalon - Marguerite Steedman 5984

The River and the Stone: Moses' Early Years in Egypt - Kathleen Jenks 3192

Rizpah - Charles E. Israel 3124

Road From Olivet - Edward Francis Murphy 4523

The Road to Bithynia: A Novel of Luke, the Beloved Physician - Frank G. Slaughter 5897

The Robber: A Tale of the Time of the Herods - Bertram Brooker 706

The Robe - Lloyd C. Douglas 1703

Ruth - Irving Fineman 2089

Salome, Princess of Galilee - Henry Denker 1611

The Salt of the Earth - Carlo Monterosso 4437

The Same Scourge - John Goldthorpe 2464

The Scapegoat: A Life of Moses - Joan Lawrence 3684

Scarlet Cord: A Novel of the Woman of Jericho - Frank G. Slaughter 5899

The Scarlet Lily - Edward Francis Murphy 4524

The Sea Peoples - Peter Danielson 1474

The Secret of the Kingdom - Mika Waltari 6555

The Shepherd - Robert Payne 4855

The Shepherd Kings - Peter Danielson 1475

The Shining King - Peter Danielson 1476

The Silver Chalice - Thomas B. Costain 1370

So Great a Queen: The Story of Esther, Queen of Persia - Paul Frischauer 2235

Solomon and Sheba - Faye Levine 3740

Solomon and Sheba - Jay Williams 6774

Solomon and the Queen of Sheba - Czenzi Ormonde 4751

Solomon's Song - Roberta Kells Dorr 1697

The Son of Laughter - Frederick Buechner 764

The Song of Ruth: A Love Story of the Old Testament - Frank G. Slaughter 5901

The Soothsayer - Laurene Chinn 1069

The Sorceress - Nathaniel Norsen Weinreb 6602

Table in the Wilderness - Norton S. Parker 4806

Tables of the Law - Thomas Mann 4067

The Tales of Jacob - Thomas Mann 4068

Tamar - Ann Chamberlin 975

A Tear for Judas - LeGette Blythe 559

The Tentmaker - Julius Berstl 486

The Thorn of Arimathea - Frank G. Slaughter 5905

Three From Galilee: The Young Man From Nazareth - Marjorie Holmes 3004

A Time for Judas - Morley Callaghan 866

Triumph of the Lion - Peter Danielson 1478

The Trumpet and the Sword - Peter Danielson 1479

Two From Galilee: A Love Story - Marjorie Holmes 3005

Two Thieves - Manuel Komroff 3535

The Unanointed - Laurene Chinn 1070

Upon This Rock: A Novel of Simon Peter, Prince of Apostles - Frank G. Slaughter 5906

The Valley of God - Irene Steinman Patai 4825

The Valley of Vision: A Novel of King Solomon and His Time - Vardis Fisher 2113

Vengeance of the Lion - Peter Danielson 1480

The Way - J.M. Hartley 2761

Who Came by Night - Roland Nicholas 4608

A Woman of Samaria - James W. Ingles 3104

The Word and the Sword - Theo Lang 3662

Yeshua: The Gospel of St. Thomas - Alan Decker McNarie 4306

Young Joseph - Thomas Mann 4069

Biography, Fictionalized

Abe Lincoln of Pigeon Creek - William Edward Wilson 6818

The Absorbing Fire: The Byron Legend - F.W. Kenyon 3445

Achilles His Armour - Peter Green 2569

Adrienne - Barbara Levy 3742

Adversary in the House - Irving Stone 6053

The Affairs of Nicholas Culpepper - Mabel L. Tyrrel 6375

Against This Rock - Louis Zara 6948

The Agony and the Ecstasy - Irving Stone 6054

Aide to Glory - Louis Devon 1635

Albert's Victoria - Tyler Whittle 6719

Alexander Hamilton's Wife - Alice Curtis Desmond 1623

Alexander of Macedon: The Journey to World's End - Harold Lamb 3607

Alexander the God - Maurice Druon 1731

Alexander the God - Robert Payne 4849

The Alexandrian - Martha Rofheart 5425

Alice and Edith: A Biographical Novel of the Two Wives of Theodore Roosevelt - Dorothy Clarke Wilson 6798

All My Sins: A Novel of the Life and Loves of Ninon de Lenclos - Norbert Estey 1965

All the Living: A Novel of One Year in the Life of William Shakespeare - Henrietta Buckmaster 758

All the Trumpets Sounded: A Novel Based on the Life of Moses - W.G. Hardy 2701

The American - Howard Fast 2026

Ammahabas - Bill Hotchkiss 3036

And Walk on Love: A Novel Based on the Life of the Apostle Paul - Henrietta Buckmaster 759

Angel of the Delta - Edward Francis Murphy 4521

Anna Zenger: Mother of Freedom - Kent Cooper 1316

Anne Bonny - Chloe Gartner 2306

Apache - Will Comfort 1226

An Army of Angels: A Novel of Joan of Arc - Pamela Marcantel 4079

Arrogance - Joanna Scott 5679

Augustus - Allan Massie 4167

Augustus - John Williams 6785

The Autobiography of Henry VIII - Margaret George 2355

Banners Against the Wind - John Edward Jennings 3198

Basilissa: A Tale of the Empress Theodora - John Masefield 4142

Behold the Man - Toyohiko Kagawa 3321

La Belle Sorel - Jacques Carton 949

Beloved - Vina Delmar 1599

The Beloved Invader - Eugenia Price 5179

Bertie, Albert Edward, Prince of Wales - Tyler Whittle 6720

The Best House in Stratford - Edward Fisher 2100

Beyond Desire: A Novel Based on the Life of Felix and Cecille Mendelssohn - Pierre La Mure 3574

Billy the Kid - Edwin Corle 1330

Bird of Fire: A Tale of Francis of Assisi - Helen Constance White 6676

Black Plume: The Supressed Memoirs of Edgar Allan Poe - David Madsen 4027

The Blacksmith's Daughter - Joanna Dessau 1625

The Blue Heaven Bends Over All - Jane Oliver 4720

Bold Encounter: A Novel Based on the Life of St. John of the Cross - Peter-Thomas Rohrbach 5433

Boone: A Novel Based on the Life and Times of Daniel Boone - Cameron Judd 3311

Born of War - Thomas Taylor 6192

Brave General - Herbert Gorman 2490

Brazos Dreamer - Gene Shelton 5799

Bride of Fortune - Harnett T. Kane 3352

Bride of Glory - Bradda Field 2078

Bronte - Glyn Hughes 3073

Brother Owl - Al Hine 2953

Bruegel, or, The Workshop of Dreams - Claude Henri Rocquet 5422

The Buried Self: A Background to the Poems of Matthew Arnold - Isobel MacDonald 3961

The Burning Man - Stephen Longstreet 3883

Byron: A Novel - Sigrid Combuchen 1225

Caesar - Mirko Jelusich 3188

Caesar - Allan Massie 4168

Calamity Jane of Deadwood Gulch - Ethel Hueston 3068

Captain Jack - Gene Shelton 5800

Captain Sutter's Gold - Jonreed Lauritzen 3673

Caravaggio - Robert Payne 4851

The Castrato - Lawrence Goldman 2459

The Cavalier of Tennessee - Meredith Nicholson 4610

Certain Harvest: A Novel of the Time of Peter Cooper - Ruth Adams Knight 3525

Chain of Destiny - Nigel Tranter 6314

Chantefable - Eldorous L. Dayton 1546

Charles - Victoria Lincoln 3786

Chief Joseph - Bill Dugan 1756

Child of the Snapping Turtle, Mike Fink - Julian Lee Rayford 5256

The Chinese Emperor - Jean Levi 3733

Citadel of God: A Novel of Saint Benedict - Louis De Wohl 1563

Citizen Tom Paine - Howard Fast 2028

Clair De Lune: A Novel about Claude Debussy - Pierre La Mure 3575

The Cleopatra Boy - Eric Malpass 4048

Colossus: A Novel about Goya and a World Gone Mad - Stephen Marlowe 4093

Come Slowly Eden: A Novel about Emily Dickinson - Laura Benet 440

Coming through Slaughter - Michael Ondaatje 4736

Concert Grand - Howard Breslin 665

The Concubine - Norah Lofts 3839

The Conqueror - Georgette Heyer 2881

The Conqueror: A Novel of Alexander the Great - Edison Marshall 4104

The Conqueror: Being the True and Romantic Story of Alexander Hamilton - Gertrude Atherton 222

Conscience of the King - Alfred Duggan 1763

The Consuming Flame: The Story of George Eliot - F.W. Kenyon 3446

The Corsair: A Biographical Novel of Jean Lafitte, Hero of the Battle of New Orleans - Madeleine Fabiola Kent 3444

The Countess - March Cost 1360

The Court Martial of Commodore Perry - James A. Rhodes 5307

The Courts of Love - Jean Plaidy 5010

Crazy Horse - Bill Dugan 1757

Crest of the Broken Wave - James Barke 302

Crippled Splendour - Evan John 3219

Crockett of Tennessee: A Novel Based on the Life and Times of David Crockett - Cameron Judd 3314

Crompton Way - Thomas Thompson 6270

The Crown and the Shadow: The Story of Francoise d'Aubigne, Marquise de Maintenon - Pamela Hill 2930

A Crown in Darkness: A Novel about Lady Jane Grey - Margaret Mullally 4512

Crown of Aloes - Norah Lofts 3840

The Crown Prince - John Barchilon 300

The Crusader - Noel B. Gerson 2364

The Cry and the Covenant - Morton Thompson 6269

Cup of Gold - John Steinbeck 5991

Damned Shall Be Desire: The Passionate Life of Guy de Maupassant - Stephen Coulter 1384

The Dark Fire - Linda Murray 4537

Dark Quartet: The Story of the Brontes - Lynne Reid Banks 290

Dark Rider - Louis Zara 6950

Daughter of Time - Nelia Gardner White 6695

David of Jerusalem - Louis De Wohl 1564

David: Warrior and King - Frank G. Slaughter 5885

The Days of the King - Bruno Frank 2200

Dear Mrs. Boswell - Marie Muir 4508

The Death and Life of Miguel De Cervantes - Stephen Marlowe 4094

The Death of Che Guevara - Jay Cantor 886

Deep in My Heart: A Story Based on the Life of Sigmund Romberg - Elliott Arnold 192

The Deer Cry - William Greenough Schofield 5650

Depths of Glory - Irving Stone 6055

The Devil Inside: A Novel of Dostoevsky's Life - Stephen Coulter 1385

Diamond Six - William Fielding Smith 5932

The Diary of Emily Dickinson: A Novel - Jamie Fuller 2255

Dim the Flaring Lamps - Jan Jordan 3301

Disraeli in Love - Maurice Edelman 1851

Disraeli Rising - Maurice Edelman 1852

Dizzy's Woman - George MacBeth 3957

Doc Holliday's Woman - Jane Candia Coleman 1201

Doctor Copernicus - John Banville 296

The Doctor From Cordova: A Biographical Novel about the Great Philosopher Maimonides - Herbert Le Porrier 3693

Dr. Johnson's Dear Mistress - Winifred Carter 948

Doctor Mirabilis - James Blish 550

Dolley - Rita Mae Brown 727

Dream West - David Nevin 4587

The Dreamer of the Vine - Liz Greene 2574

The Drums of Monmouth - Emma Gelders Sterne 5998

Dvorak in Love - Josef Skvorecky 5881

The Eagle and the Rock - Frances Winwar 6830

The Earth Is the Lord's: A Tale of the Rise of Genghis Khan - Taylor Caldwell 855

Edmund Campion - Evelyn Waugh 6585

Edward - Tyler Whittle 6721

Edward and Mrs. Simpson - A.C.H. Smith 5916

Eleanor: A Novel - Rhoda Lerman 3724

Eleanora Duse - Jean Stubbs 6095

Elizabeth, the Woman - Amanda Mae Ellis 1917

Elizabeth's Greetings - Rosemary Haughton 2774

The Emperor Franz Joseph - Ottokar Janetschek 3164

The Emperor's Lady: A Novel Based on the Life of the Empress Josephine - F.W. Kenyon 3449

An Epic Joy: A Novel Based on the Life of Rubens - Donald Braider 642

Eroica: A Novel about Beethoven - Carl von Pidoll 4994

Ethel: The Fictional Autobiography - Tema Nason 4558

Eugenie - Hester W. Chapman 989

Falcon: The Autobiography of His Grace James IV, King of Scots - A.J. Stewart 6021

Ferdinand and Isabella - Hermann Kesten 3474

The Fever Called Living - Barbara Moore 4439

A Fiddle, a Sword, and a Lady - Albert Spalding 5953

Fisher of Men: A Novel of Simon Peter - Kurt Frieberger 2231

Flame of Fire - Jane Oliver 4722

The Flight - Ruth Walgreen Stephan 5994

Flight of the Swan - Margaret Ann Hubbard 3063

The Florentine - Carl J. Spinatelli 5968

Follow the Free Wind - Leigh Brackett 621

Fool of God: A Novel Based on the Life of Alexander Campbell - Louis Cochran 1144

For the Love of Robert E. Lee - M.A. Harper 2715

Freedom, Farewell - Phyllis Bentley 461

Gallant Captain - Pearl Frye 2242

The Gallant Mrs. Stonewall - Harnett T. Kane 3353

Gallant Warrior - Helen R. Mann 4063

The Gentle Fury: A Novel of Margaret of Austria - Paul Lewis 3758

The Gentleman From America - Polan Banks 293

Gentleman of Stratford - John Brophy 708

Geronimo - Bill Dugan 1758

Geronimo: An American Legend - Robert J. Conley 1242

Gilded Splendour - Rosalind Laker 3595

The Girl Who Was Never Queen: A Biographical Novel of Princess Charlotte of Wales - Mary Main 4103

Give Me Liberty - Noel B. Gerson 2369

Give Me the Wind - Jan Jordan 3302

The Glorious Folly: A Novel of the Time of St. Paul - Louis De Wohl 1565

God's Angry Man - Leonard Ehrlich 1898

God's Man: A Novel on the Life of John Calvin - Duncan Norton-Taylor 4650

God's Warrior - Frank G. Slaughter 5889

Gold of Their Bodies: A Novel about Gauguin - Charles Orson Gorham 2488

The Golden Eagle - John Edward Jennings 3201

The Golden Mistress - Basil Beyea 488

The Golden Quill: A Novel Based on the Life of Mozart - Bernard Grun 2605

The Golden Thread - Louis De Wohl 1566

The Golden Veil - Paddy Kitchen 3507

Golden Venus - David Mynders Smythe 5933

The Golden Years: A Novel Based on the Life and Loves of Percy Bysshe Shelley - F.W. Kenyon 3451

The Goliath Head - Charles J. Calitri 865

Good-Bye My Son - Marjorie Coryn 1356

The Governor's Lady - Thomas H. Raddall 5228

Great Black Russian - John Oliver Killens 3484

The Great Infidel - Joseph Jay Deiss 1582

Great Lion of God - Taylor Caldwell 858

The Greek of Toledo: A Romantic Narrative of El Greco - Elizabeth Borton 586

The Greek Treasure - Irving Stone 6056

Gregory the Great - Gerhart Ellert 1913

The Hand of Michelangelo - Sidney Alexander 85

Hannibal - Ross Leckie 3704

Haym Solomon, Son of Liberty - Howard Fast 2032

Heart in Pilgrimage - Evelyn Eaton 1827

Heart of a Queen - Josephine Delves-Broughton 1603

The Heart of O. Henry - Dale Kramer 3550

Henry, King of France - Heinrich Mann 4061

Her Royal Destiny - Carol Maxwell Eady 1820

The Herdsman - Dorothy Clarke Wilson 6801

Here Lies Margot - Pamela Hill 2935

Herzl the King - Norman Kotker 3547

The Hesitant Heart - Anne Edwards 1882

High Heroic - Constantine FitzGibbon 2118
His Was the Fire - Showell Styles 6104
Hoffman's Row - Walter Carnahan 902
The Holy Lover - Marie Oemler 4690
Home to Kentucky: A Novel of Henry Clay - Alfred Leland Crabb 1399
Home to the Hermitage - Alfred Leland Crabb 1401
The Horn and the Roses: A Novel Based on the Life of Peter Paul Rubens - Ira Jan Wallach 6542
A House of Women - Eric Malpass 4049
How Do I Love Thee - Lucille Iremonger 3110
Hubble Time - Tom Bezzi 490
Hungarian Rhapsody: The Life of Franz Liszt - Jean Rousselot 5511
I Am Mary Tudor - Hilda Lewis 3750
I, Elizabeth - Rosalind Miles 4378
* *I Give You Oscar Wilde* - Desmond Hall 2647
I, Jack Swilling - John Myers 4544
I, James McNeill Whistler - Lawrence Williams 6787
I, Madame Tussaud - Sylvia Martin 4135
I Never Came to You in White - Judith Farr 2014
I, Paul - Rex Miller 4401
I, Rachel - March Cost 1361
I, Rembrandt - David Weiss 6605
I Seek a City - Gilbert Rees 5289
I Speak for Thaddeus Stevens - Elsie Singmaster 5868
I, the King - Hermann Kesten 3475
I, the King - Frances Parkinson Keyes 3479
I, the Supreme - Augusto Antonio Roa Bastos 5353
I, Victoria - Cynthia Harrod-Eagles 2755
I'll Storm Hell - Noel B. Gerson 2374
Immortal Queen - Elizabeth Byrd 834
Immortal Wife - Irving Stone 6057
Imperial Caesar - Rex Warner 6565
Imperial Venus: A Novel of Napoleon's Favorite Sister - Edgar Maas 3949
Impressionist: A Novel of Mary Cassatt - Joan King 3486
In the Blazing Light - Max White 6693
In the House of the King - Louis Zara 6951
In the Shadow of the Crown - Jean Plaidy 5022
The Irish Boy: A Romantic Biography - Naomi Jacob 3137
The Iron Mistress - Paul I. Wellman 6618
The Ivy Crown: A Biographical Novel of Queen Katherine Parr - Mary M. Luke 3923
Jackson: A Novel - Max Byrd 837
Jelly Roll Morton's Last Night at the Jungle Inn: An Imaginary Memoir - Samuel Charters 1002
Jessie: A Novel Based on the Life of Jessie Benton Fremont - Judy Alter 120
Johanna: A Novel of the Van Gogh Family - Claire Cooperstein 1317
John and Anzia: An American Romance - Norma Rosen 5462
John Howard Payne, Skywalker - Maude Barragan 348
John Milton - Edmund Fuller 2249
Johnny Logan: Shawnee Spy - Allen W. Eckert 1843
Joseph - Mervyn Jones 3292
The Joyful Beggar: A Novel of St. Francis of Assisi - Louis De Wohl 1568
Katherine - Anya Seton 5752
Kean: The Imaginary Memoirs of an Actor - Julius Berstl 485
Kepler: A Novel - John Banville 297
King of Kings: A Novel of the Life of David - Malachi Martin 4134
King of Paris - Guy Endore 1942
The King's Good Servant - Olive White 6696
The King's Orchard - Agnes Sligh Turnbull 6363
The King's Pleasure - Norah Lofts 3847
The King's Way - Francoise Chandernagor 986
The Lady and the Arsenic - Marjorie Bowen 598
The Lady in the Tower - Jean Plaidy 5028
The Lady of Arlington - Harnett T. Kane 3354
Lady of the Lotus - William E. Barrett 353

Lady Washington - Dorothy Clarke Wilson 6803
The Last Englishman: The Story of Hereward the Wake - Hebe Weenolsen 6596
The Last Station - Jay Parini 4801
The Laughter of Aphrodite - Peter Green 2570
Lay Siege to Heaven: A Novel of Saint Catherine of Siena - Louis De Wohl 1570
Lenin: The Novel - Alan Brien 679
Leo Africanus - Amin Maalouf 3947
Letty - Helen Ashton 218
Levi Coffin and the Underground Railroad - Charles Ludwig 3921
Lillie - David Butler 818
Lincoln's Mothers: A Story of Nancy and Sally Lincoln - Dorothy Clarke Wilson 6804
The Lion of Pescara - George MacBeth 3958
Louis the Well-Beloved - Jean Plaidy 5032
Love Is a Wild Assault - Elithe Hamilton Kirkland 3506
Love Is Eternal - Irving Stone 6058
Love Is My Vocation: An Imaginative Study of St. Therese of Lisieux - Tom Clarkson 1098
Lover of Life - Zsolt de Harsanyi 2756
Love's Labour's Won - Edward Fisher 2101
Lust for Life - Irving Stone 6059
The Magic Bow - Manuel Komroff 3534
Magic Fire: Scenes around Richard Wagner - Bertita Harding 2683
Mamaw - Susan Dodd 1663
A Man and His Mountain: The Life of Paul Cezanne - Hugh McLeave 4285
A Man Called Cervantes - Bruno Frank 2201
A Man Called Grant - Helen Todd 6285
A Man for the Ages - Irving A. Bacheller 261
Man From Mt. Vernon - Burke Boyce 607
Man of Montmartre: A Novel Based on the Life of Maurice Utrillo - Stephen Longstreet 3888
Man of Nazareth - Anthony Burgess 779
Man on Fire: A Novel on the Life of St. Paul - LeGette Blythe 558
Manchu Empress - Bluebell Matilda Hunter 3081
Manifest Destiny - Brian Garfield 2290
A Man's Reach - Charles Morrow Wilson 6796
Many a Voyage - Loula Grace Erdman 1951
Marie Antoinette - F.W. Kenyon 3453
Mary, Queen of Scotland and the Isles - Margaret George 2356
Master of Bengal: A Novel of Robert Clive of India - Norman Partington 4821
The Master of Geneva: A Novel Based on the Life of John Calvin - Gladys H. Barr 341
Master of the World - Cothburn O'Neal 4738
The Medicine Calf - Bill Hotchkiss 3037
The Medicine Man - Shirley Seifert 5729
Memoirs of a Victorian Gentleman: William Makepeace Thackeray - Margaret Forster 2189
The Memoirs of Lord Byron - Robert Nye 4655
Michelangelo the Florentine - Sidney Alexander 86
The Midnight Gardener: A Novel about Baudelaire - Max White 6694
Minna's Story: The Secret Love of Doctor Sigmund Freud - Kathleen Daniels 1463
Mirabeau, Lover and Stateman - Pierre Nezelof 4606
Miracles - Marcy Moran Heidish 2818
The Missolonghi Manuscript - Frederic Prokosch 5194
Mistress Anne - Carolly Erickson 1952
Mistress of Fortune - Sheila Lancaster 3651
Modigliani: Prince of Montparnasse - Tadeusz Wittlin 6834
Mona Lisa: The Woman in the Portrait - Sara Mayfield 4206
Monk in Armour - Gladys H. Barr 342
Monsieur Moliere - Michael O'Shaughnessy 4762
Morning of a Hero - Burke Boyce 608
Mortal Hunger: A Novel Based on the Life of Lafcadio Hearn - Harry E. Wedeck 6594

Mortal Love: A Novel of Eleanor of Aquitaine - Linda Hutchins 3090
Moulin Rouge: A Novel Based on Henri de Toulouse-Lautrec - Pierre La Mure 3576
Mozart on the Way to Prague - Eduard Friedrich Morike 4454
Mr. Audubon's Lucy - Lucy Kennedy 3419
Mr. Lincoln's Wife - Anne Colver 1221
Mr. Oddity, Samuel Johnson - Charles Norman 4643
Mr. Pepys of Seething Lane - Cecil Abernethy 10
Music for God - Theresa Weiser 6603
Mussolini - Alan Gelb 2348
The Mutual Friend - Frederick Busch 811
My Crown, My Love - Ruth Walgreen Stephan 5995
My Life for My Sheep - Alfred Duggan 1772
My Lord of Canterbury - Godfrey Turton 6369
My Love Must Wait: The Story of Matthew Flinders - Ernestine Hill 2922
My Savage Muse: The Story of My Life: Edgar Allan Poe, an Imaginative Work - Bernhardt J. Hurwood 3087
My Thomas: A Novel of Martha Jefferson's Life - Roberta Grimes 2593
Myself, Christopher Wren - David Weiss 6606
Myself My Enemy - Jean Plaidy 5037
Naked Came I: A Novel of Rodin - David Weiss 6607
The Naked Maja - Noel B. Gerson 2378
Napoleon and His Son - Pierre Nezelof 4607
The Navigator: The Story of Nathaniel Bowditch - Alfred Stanford 5979
The Nelson Touch - Paul Lewis 3759
Nephew to the Emperor: A Novel Based on the Life of Beethoven - Jacques Brenner 658
Nero - Mary Teresa Ronalds 5437
New Orleans Woman: A Biographical Novel of Myra Clark Gaines - Harnett T. Kane 3355
Nicodemus: The Roman Years of Michelangelo Buonarroti, 1534-1564 - Sidney Alexander 87
North-West by South - Nancy Cato 962
Nothing Like the Sun - Anthony Burgess 781
Notorious Eliza - Basil Beyea 489
Old Hickory - Noel B. Gerson 2379
On Eagles' Wings - Arthur E. Southon 5951
One Red Rose Forever - Mildred A. Jordan 3305
Origen: A Historical Novel - Theodore Vrettos 6515
The Origin - Irving Stone 6060
Painted Lady: Eliza Jumel, Her Life and Times - Leonard Falkner 2009
Panther in the Sky - James Alexander Thom 6234
Parson Austen's Daughter - Helen Ashton 219
The Passionate Journey - Irving Stone 6061
Passionate Rebel: The Story of Hector Berlioz - F.W. Kenyon 3457
The Passions of the Mind - Irving Stone 6062
Path to the Silent Country - Lynne Reid Banks 291
Pathetic Symphony: A Novel about Tchaikovsky - Klaus Mann 4064
Pathway to the Stars - Harnett T. Kane 3356
The Perfect Joy of St. Francis - Felix Timmermans 6281
Pericles the Athenian - Rex Warner 6566
Personal Recollections of Joan of Arc - Mark Twain 6372
The Pilgrim Prince - Gladys H. Barr 343
The Pistoleer - James Carlos Blake 536
The Pleasures of Love - Jean Plaidy 5042
Pontius Pilate: A Biographical Novel - Paul L. Maier 4034
The Portingale - Alison Macleod 4005
Prairie - Anna Lee Waldo 6528
Prepare Them for Caesar - Mary Louise Mabie 3954
The Prison Notebooks of Ricardo Flores Magon - Douglas Day 1545
The Private and Public Life of Socrates - Rene Kraus 3552
The Proud Servant: The Story of Montrose - Margaret Irwin 3120

Quanah Parker - Bill Dugan 1759

Queen Anne Boleyn - Francis Hackett 2634

Queen Dolley: The Life and Times of Dolley Madison - Dorothy Clarke Wilson 6806

The Queen of Hearts - Joan Rees 5290

Queen of the Reformation - Charles Ludwig 3922

Queen of This Realm: The Story of Queen Elizabeth I - Jean Plaidy 5050

The Queen's Cross: A Biographical Romance of Queen Isabella of Spain - Lawrence Schoonover 5666

The Queen's Secret - Jean Plaidy 5053

The Questing Heart: A Romantic Novel about George Sand - F.W. Kenyon 3458

The Quiet Life of Mrs. General Lane - Victoria Case 951

The Quiet Light - Louis De Wohl 1572

Quietly My Captain Waits - Evelyn Eaton 1829

Rachel - Anne Powers 5153

Rage in Silence: A Novel Based on the Life of Goya - Donald Braider 643

Raising Holy Hell - Bruce Olds 4718

The Raven - Chancellor Williams 6769

Rawhider - Gene Shelton 5802

Rebel Princess - Evelyn Anthony 164

The Red-Haired Brat - Joanna Dessau 1627

The Red Monarch: Scenes From the Life of Stalin - Yuri Krotkov 3561

Reigning Passions - Kathrin Perutz 4940

The Reluctant Queen: The Story of Anne of York - Jean Plaidy 5056

Rembrandt - Gladys Schmitt 5643

Renown - Frank Olney Hough 3045

The Restless Flame - Louis De Wohl 1573

The Return of Henry Starr - Richard Slotkin 5909

The Revolutionary - Lawrence Schoonover 5667

Richard Whittington, London's Mayor - Gwynedd Sudworth 6112

Road to Lendor - Esther Hammon 1966

Rogues' Company: A Novel of John Murrell - Harry Harrison Kroll 3559

Rogue's Legacy: A Novel about Francois Villon - Babette Deutsch 1629

The Romance of Charles Dickens - Ursula Bloom 553

The Romance of Leonardo Da Vinci - Dmitri Merezhkovski 4339

A Rose for Virtue - Norah Lofts 3858

The Rose of Malmaison: The Turbulent Life of the Beautiful Josephine - Gaby von Schonthan 5660

The Rose Without a Thorn - Jean Plaidy 5058

Royal William - Doris Leslie 3728

Ruler of the Sky: A Novel of Genghis Khan - Pamela Sargent 5606

Sacajawea of the Shoshones - Della F. Emmons 1940

Sacred and Profane: A Novel of the Life and Times of Mozart - David Weiss 6609

The Saga of Henry Starr - Robert J. Conley 1250

The Sage and the Olive - Florence Whitfield Barton 369

The Saint - Fritz von Unruh 6385

The Saint of Montparnasse: A Novel Based on the Life of Constantin Brancusi - Peter Neagoe 4560

Saint Paul: A Historical Novel of His Life - Leon Poirier 5081

Sam Houston - Noel B. Gerson 2380

The Sam Houston Story - Dean Owen 4770

Samuel Brannan and the Golden Fleece - Reva Scott 5686

Sarah - Joel Gross 2603

Savage Prodigal - Konrad Bercovici 474

The Scapegoat: A Life of Moses - Joan Lawrence 3684

The Secret Memoirs of Lord Byron - Christopher Nicole 4622

The Seducer - Henrik Stangerup 5980

The Senator's Lady - Shirley Seifert 5733

Set All Afire: A Novel of St. Francis Xavier - Louis De Wohl 1574

The Shadow in the Glass - August Derleth 1618

Shadow in the Sun: A Novel of Elizabeth I, the Virgin Queen - F.W. Kenyon 3460

The Shadow of the Earth - Lee Wichelns 6731

Shakespeare & Son - Edward Fisher 2102

Signorina - Henry Myers 4542

Sitting Bull - Bill Dugan 1760

The Sleeping Sword: A Biographical Novel - Pearl Frye 2244

The Slender Reed - Noel B. Gerson 2382

So Perish the Roses - Neil Bell 423

Soldier in Buckskin - Ray Hogan 2981

Soldier in Paradise - Burton Wohl 6835

Son of Tears - Henry W. Coray 1320

Song in the Green Thorn Tree - James Barke 303

Sophie - Geoffrey Wagner 6519

A Sorrow in Our Heart - Allen W. Eckert 1844

The Soul of Ann Rutledge - Bernie Babcock 252

Spring Symphony - Eleanor Painter 4777

The Star-Gazer - Zsolt de Harsanyi 2757

A Star Pointed North - Edmund Fuller 2250

Stone Song: A Novel of the Life of Crazy Horse - Winfred Blevins 548

Storm Center: A Novel about Andy Johnson - Joseph Walker McSpadden 4312

The Summer of Jack London - Andrew J. Fenady 2058

The Sun Is God - Michael Noonan 4636

The Swamp Fox, Francis Marion - Noel B. Gerson 2383

The Swan of Usk - Helen Ashton 220

The Swedish Nightingale: Jenny Lind - Elizabeth Kyle 3571

Sweet Marie-Antoinette - Lozania Prole 5198

Sweet Will - Eric Malpass 4050

Sword of Pleasure: Being the Memoirs of the Most Illustrious Lucius Cornelius Sulla - Peter Green 2571

Tables of the Law - Thomas Mann 4067

Take Her, Mr. Wesley - John W. Drakeford 1719

Taste of Glory - Carleton Beals 394

Tempered Blade - Monte Barrett 352

Teresa, or Her Demon Lover - Austin K. Gray 2554

That Skipper From Stonington - Theda Kenyon 3464

That Spanish Woman - F.W. Kenyon 3461

That Vanderbilt Woman - Philip Van Rensselaer 6427

There Was a Season: A Biographical Novel of Jefferson Davis - Theodore Olsen 4730

Those Who Love - Irving Stone 6064

Thousand Years of Gold - Ruthanne Lum McCunn 4239

Tiberius: The Memoirs of the Emperor - Allan Massie 4169

Tidewater Dynasty: A Biographical Novel of the Lees of Stratford Hall - Carey Roberts 5372

Titian - Dario Cecchi 965

To Heaven on Horseback - Paul F. Cranston 1419

To Seize a Dream - Virginia Davis Hersch 2866

To Seize the Passing Dream - Ted Berkman 479

To Spit Against the Wind - Benjamin H. Levin 3737

TR - Noel B. Gerson 2385

Trail-Makers of the Middle Border - Hamlin Garland 2296

Treason - Robert Gessner 2389

Troubled Border - T.D. Allen 104

The Twisted Saber: A Biographical Novel of Benedict Arnold - Philip Vail 6398

The Twisted Tendril - Alice Glasgow 2427

Two Loves Have I - Clara Longworth de Chambrun 985

Ulysses: A Biographical Novel - Robert Skimin 5878

Under the Fifth Sun: A Novel of Pancho Villa - Earl Shorris 5832

Untold Glory - Cothburn O'Neal 4739

Upon This Rock: The Life of St. Peter - Walter F. Murphy 4526

Utrillo's Mother - Sarah Baylis 391

Vain Shadow - Hartzell Spence 5962

The Venetian - David Weiss 6611

Verge of Glory - Frederick Wight 6747

Very Young Mrs. Poe - Cothburn O'Neal 4740

Vincent: A Novel Based on the Life of Van Gogh - Joost Poldermans 5082

Violent Friends - Winston Clewes 1113

The Voice and the Light - Edwin Fadiman 1995

The Voice of Allah - Edwin P. Hoyt 3062

Voltaire! Voltaire! - Guy Endore 1943

Wallis: The Novel - Anne Edwards 1883

Walt Whitman's Secret - Ben Aronin 196

Walter Winchell: A Novel - Michael Herr 2863

Watch for Me on the Mountain - Forrest Carter 947

Wave High the Banner - Dee Brown 714

The Wayfarer - Shirley Seifert 5738

Well of the Silent Harp - James Barke 304

West to the Setting Sun - Harvey Chalmers 973

Where Glory Waits - Gertrude Crownfield 1437

Whirlwind in Petticoats - Beril Becker 406

Whittling Boy: The Story of Eli Whitney - Roger Burlingame 789

The Widow of Windsor - Tyler Whittle 6723

Wild Decembers: A Biographical Portrait of the Brontes - Hilda Crystal White 6681

William's Wife - Jean Plaidy 5077

The Wind That Shakes the Barley - James Barke 305

Wine of Life - Charles Orson Gorham 2489

With All My Heart - Margaret Campbell Barnes 330

With Malice Toward None - Honore Morrow 4492

The Woman in the Cloak - Pamela Hill 2949

Woman with a Sword: The Biographical Novel of Anna Ella Carroll of Maryland - Hollister Noble 4632

Wonder of All the Gay World - James Barke 306

The World as I Found It - Bruce Duffy 1755

Wyatt Earp - Matt Braun 653

Wyatt Earp - Dan Gordon 2481

Yankee Doodle Dandy - Noel B. Gerson 2387

The Yankee From Tennessee - Noel B. Gerson 2388

The Yellow Robe: A Novel of the Life of Buddha - Robert Payne 4856

Young Adolf - Beryl Bainbridge 272

The Young and Lonely King - Jane Lane 3659

The Young Caesar - Rex Warner 6567

Young Catherine - E.M. Almedingen 118

Young Henry of Navarre - Heinrich Mann 4062

Young Hickory - Stanley Young 6942

The Young Man From Mount Vernon - Arthur Stanwood Pier 4995

The Young Men of Paris - Stephen Longstreet 3893

The Young Victoria - Tyler Whittle 6724

Black Hawk War

Comes an Echo on the Breeze - Edward J. Ryan 5542

For Us the Living - Bruce Lancaster 3639

Michael Beam - Richard Hallet 2663

The Shining Trail - Iola Fuller 2254

There Was a Season: A Biographical Novel of Jefferson Davis - Theodore Olsen 4730

Thunder on the River - Charlton Laird 3590

Twilight of Empire - Allen W. Eckert 1846

Wind over Wisconsin - August Derleth 1620

Black Sox Scandal

Hoopla - Harry Stein 5990

Blair Mountain, Battle of

Storming Heaven - Denise Giardina 2394

Bloody Marsh, Battle of

Dark Sails - Helen Topping Miller 4388

Boer War

Blunted Lance - Max Hennessy 2829
A Captive Freedom - Emma Drummond 1724
The City of Gold - Francis Brett Young 6940
The Covenant - Brigid Knight 3521
The Covenant - James A. Michener 4368
Cruel in the Shadow - Lorn MacIntyre 3986
Eden and Honor - Marilyn Harris 2729
Floodtide - Suzanne Goodwin 2475
Halfhyde and the Chain Gang - Philip McCutchan 4244
Halfhyde Goes to War - Philip McCutchan 4248
Imperial Kelly - Peter Bowen 600
Kimberley - Colin Burke 784
The Legacy of Ladysmith - John Kenny Crane 1413
Lord Richard's Passion - Mervyn Jones 3293
The Marigold Field - Diane Pearson 4876
The Midnight Gun - Berkely Mather 4180
Molly - Teresa Crane 1417
The Nationalists - William Stuart Long 3876
Rags of Glory - Stuart Cloete 1126
The Red Daniel - Duncan MacNeil 4017
The Regiment - Christopher Nicole 4620
The Regiment - C.L. Skelton 5874
The Roar of the Thunder - Wilbur Smith 5929
Siege in the Sun - Mary Paradise 4788
The Steps of the Sun - Joanna Trollope 6350

Boers

A Revolutionary Woman - Sheila Fugard 2248
Westward the Sun - Brigid Knight 3524
Wild Conquest - Peter Abrahams 12

Boxer Rebellion

China Saga - C.Y. Lee 3706
The Fabulous Concubine - Hsin-Hai Chang 987
Fenwick Travers and the Years of Empire - Raymond M. Saunders 5614
The First to Land - Douglas E. Reeman 5288
Forbidden City - Anthony Esler 1962
Forbidden City - Muriel Molland Jernigan 3215
Foreign Devils - Irvin Faust 2053
Imperial Woman - Pearl S. Buck 755
The Midnight Gun - Berkely Mather 4180
Moonraker's Bride - Madeleine Brent 661
The Name of Hero - Richard Seltzer 5742
The Time of the Dragon - Dorothy Eden 1863
Twilight of the Dragon - Peter Bourne 596
White Poppy - Margaret Gaan 2261

Boxing

Blackstone's Fancy - Richard Falkirk 2008
Deborah Goes to Dover - Marion Chesney 1023
Down for the Count - Stuart M. Kaminsky 3336
The Ham Reporter - Robert J. Randisi 5251
Heritage - Lewis Orde 4749
Lord Fancy - Leslie Turner White 6686
Warwyck's Woman - Rosalind Laker 3604

Bridge Building

The Bridge of a Hundred Dragons - Emma Drummond 1723
The Bridge on the Drina - Ivo Andric 151
Bridge to Brooklyn - Albert E. Idell 3099
The Gathering Wolves - Elizabeth Darrell 1496

British Colonies

And the Wild Birds Sing - Lola Irish 3112
The Barrier - Robin Maugham 4195
The Covenant - Brigid Knight 3521
The Fiercest Heart - Stuart Cloete 1122
The Imposter - Noel B. Gerson 2375

The Last Victory - T.N. Murari 4519
The Leopard and the Cliff - Wallace Breem 655
Master of Bengal: A Novel of Robert Clive of India - Norman Partington 4821
The Pagoda Tree - Berkely Mather 4181
Raj - Gita Mehta 4325
The Roar of the Thunder - Wilbur Smith 5929
Season of the Jew - Maurice Shadbolt 5768
The Sleeping Tiger - Marjorie McEvoy 4269
Some Far Elusive Dawn - Emma Drummond 1727
The Spring of the Tiger - Victoria Holt 3021
Star of Randevi - Marjorie McEvoy 4270
That Sweet and Savage Land - Emma Drummond 1728
The Turning Wheels - Stuart Cloete 1127
The War Chest - Porter Hill 2950
The White Rhino Hotel - Bartle Bull 765

British Raj

The Barrier - Robin Maugham 4195
Bayonets in the Sun - William Moore 4446
Beyond All Frontiers - Emma Drummond 1722
The Blood Seed - Andrew Ward 6561
Charge of Cowardice - Duncan MacNeil 4011
Cunningham's Revenge - Duncan MacNeil 4012
Dando on Delhi Ridge - William Clive 1119
The Day of the Scorpion - Paul Scott 5682
The Devil's Wind: Nana Saheb's Story - Manohar Malgonkar 4039
A Division of the Spoils - Paul Scott 5683
Drums Along the Khyber - Duncan MacNeil 4013
An Error of Judgment - Stanley Wolpert 6845
The Far Pavilions - M.M. Kaye 3376
The Faraway Drums - Jon Cleary 1104
Flashman and the Mountain of Light - George MacDonald Fraser 2207
Flowers in the Blood - Gay Courter 1387
Follow the Drum - James Leasor 3699
Free Lance - George Shipway 5827
The Gates of Kunara - Duncan MacNeil 4014
The Golden Honeycomb - Kamala Markandaya 4086
Indigo - Nicholas Carnac 900
The Jewel in the Crown - Paul Scott 5684
Lieutenant of the Line - Duncan MacNeil 4015
The Lotus and the Wind - John Masters 4175
Massacre at Cawnpore - Vivian Stuart 6089
Master of Bengal: A Novel of Robert Clive of India - Norman Partington 4821
Mistaken Virtues - Joanna Trollope 6349
The Mullah From Kashmir - Duncan MacNeil 4016
Nightrunners of Bengal - John Masters 4176
Olivia and Jai - Rebecca Ryman 5544
Playing the Game - Ian Buruma 810
Raj - Gita Mehta 4325
The Ravi Lancers - John Masters 4178
The Restless Frontier - Duncan MacNeil 4018
Sadhu on the Mountain Peak - Duncan MacNeil 4019
Shadow of the Moon - M.M. Kaye 3377
The Shalimar - Betty Hale Hyatt 3091
The Siege of Krishnapur - J.G. Farrell 2016
The Sleeping Tiger - Marjorie McEvoy 4269
Star of Randevi - Marjorie McEvoy 4270
Subaltern's Choice - Duncan MacNeil 4020
The Towers of Silence - Paul Scott 5685
The Train at Bundarbar - Duncan MacNeil 4021
The Veil of Illusion - Rebecca Ryman 5545
Wolf in the Fold - Duncan MacNeil 4022
Zemindar - Valerie Fitzgerald 2117

Bronze Age

The Horse Goddess - Morgan Llywelyn 3820
Shadows on the Stones - Moyra Caldecott 847
The Tall Stones - Moyra Caldecott 848
The Temple of the Sun - Moyra Caldecott 849

Bull Run, Battle of

Battle Flag - Bernard Cornwell 1333
Beloved Enemy - Al Lacy 3579
Gray Canaan - David Garth 2305
The Passionate Rebel - Frank G. Slaughter 5894
Rebel - Bernard Cornwell 1336

Bunker Hill, Battle of

The Drums of April - Charles Mergendahl 4340
The Gentle Rebel - Gilbert Morris 4461
Guns for Rebellion - F. van Wyck Mason 4151
Israel Potter - Herman Melville 4334
Lionel Lincoln; or, The Leaguer of Boston - James Fenimore Cooper 1303
Oliver Wiswell - Kenneth Roberts 5389
The Road to Bunker Hill - Shirley Barker 316
The Shadow and the Glory - John Edward Jennings 3207
Song of a Strange Child - Gilbert Morris 4470
Three Harbors - F. van Wyck Mason 4162

Business Building

1876: A Novel - Gore Vidal 6484
All in Good Time - Marguerite Allis 106
Anthony Trant - John Hyatt Downing 1713
Arizona - Clarence Budington Kelland 3387
As the Crow Flies - Jeffrey Archer 183
At the Sign of the Golden Pineapple - Marion Chesney 1016
Back in Society - Marion Chesney 1017
The Bank - Stephen Longstreet 3882
The Beckoning Waters - Robert Carse 944
Big River, Big Man - Thomas William Duncan 1786
Biscayne - Barry Jay Kaplan 3365
Blood & Dreams - Leslie Waller 6543
Born with the Century - William Kinsolving 3501
The Bourlotas Fortune - Nicholas Gage 2268
Brandywine - Jack Rowe 5513
The Bridge - Marguerite Allis 108
The Cannaways - Graham Shelby 5789
Cashmere - Nicola Thorne 6273
The Chandler Heritage - Ben Haas 2629
The Chateau - Stephen Coulter 1383
Colonel Sandhurst to the Rescue - Marion Chesney 1021
The Crystal Star - Ellen Argo 184
A Dangerous Fortune - Ken Follett 2147
The Dollar Gold Piece - Virginia Swain 6134
Dominion - Jack Rowe 5514
The Dream Seekers - Stephen Longstreet 3884
Dream Time - Parris Afton Bonds 570
The Duchess of Duke Street - Mollie Hardwick 2693
Dynasty - Robert S. Elegant 1902
Dynasty of Death - Taylor Caldwell 854
The Earth and All It Holds - V.J. Banis 287
Emerald - Helen Ashfield 206
Fabulous Valley - Cornelia Stratton Parker 4803
The Financier - Theodore Dreiser 1720
Floodtide - Frank Yerby 6916
For They Shall Inherit - Malcolm Macdonald 3964
Fortune Is a Woman - Elizabeth Adler 39
Fortune's Legacy - Jack Rowe 5515
From Fields of Gold - Alexandra Ripley 5339
Full of Thy Riches - Elizabeth Ferrell 2070
Gai-Jin: A Novel of Japan - James Clavell 1100
The Garfield Honor - Frank Yerby 6918
Gold - Clarence Budington Kelland 3388
Goldeneye - Malcolm Macdonald 3965
The Hampton Heritage - Julie Ellis 1920
Hanover Place - Michael M. Thomas 6245
Hard Money - Clarence Budington Kelland 3389
Harvest of the Sun - E.V. Thompson 6265
Honour and Obey - Malcolm Macdonald 3966
The House of Cray - Pamela Hill 2936
The House of Eliott - Jean Marsh 4100
The House That Tai Ming Built - Virginia Lee 3711

The Ironmaster - Anne Powers 5150
The Jealous House - Clarence Budington Kelland 3390
Jewel of the Sea - Ellen Argo 185
Jewelled Path - Rosalind Laker 3597
Jubilee Jim and the Wizard of Wall Street - Donald Porter 5112
Kernow & Daughter - Malcolm Macdonald 3968
King's Royal - John Quigley 5224
Lady Fortescue Steps Out - Marion Chesney 1035
The Land of Our Dreams - Nancy Livingston 3812
The Lorimer Line - Anne Melville 4332
Magnificent Enemies - Edgar Maas 3951
Mandarin - Robert S. Elegant 1905
Max - Howard Fast 2038
The Merchant Prince - Henry Christopher Bailey 267
Michael Torey - Janet Mathewson 4183
The Midnight Gun - Berkely Mather 4180
The Mill on Mad River - Howard Clark 1087
Mills of the Gods - Daoma Winston 6828
Miss Tonks Turns to Crime - Marion Chesney 1041
Molly - Teresa Crane 1417
The Moneyman - Judith Liederman 3781
Mrs. Budley Falls From Grace - Marion Chesney 1042
Niccolo Rising - Dorothy Dunnett 1803
One Night in Newport - Elizabeth Villars 6498
The Only Sin - Julie Ellis 1923
Our Father's House - Stephen Longstreet 3890
The Pagoda Tree - Berkely Mather 4181
Paradise Falls - Don Robertson 5399
Portrait in Brownstone - Louis Auchincloss 232
Portrait of a Scoundrel - Nathaniel Benchley 438
The Power of Black - M.B. Longman 3880
Pride's Castle - Frank Yerby 6925
A Prologue to Love - Taylor Caldwell 862
Queen's Royal - John Quigley 5225
The Quiet Shore - Walter Havighurst 2775
Race of Scorpions - Dorothy Dunnett 1806
A Respectable Trade - Philippa Gregory 2584
The Rich Are with You Always - Malcolm Macdonald 3971
The Road to Wellville - T. Coraghessan Boyle 618
The Robber Baroness - William Kendall Clarke 1097
San Antone - V.J. Banis 288
Saratoga Trunk - Edna Ferber 2062
Scales of Gold - Dorothy Dunnett 1808
Scarborough House - Sharon Salvato 5577
The Seadon Fortune - Leonard St. Clair 5563
The Ship's Clock - Catherine M. Rae 5237
The Silver Mountain - Dan Cushman 1453
Silver Nutmeg - Norah Lofts 3860
The Silver Touch - Rosalind Laker 3599
Sing for a Penny - Clifford Dowdey 1708
Sir Philip's Folly - Marion Chesney 1051
Sons of Fortune - Malcolm Macdonald 3973
Speak to Me of Love - Dorothy Eden 1862
The Spring of the Ram - Dorothy Dunnett 1809
Stacey's Flyer - Patricia Burns 800
The Store - Michael Pearson 4879
The Stuart Women - Matt Braun 652
The Sugar Pavilion - Rosalind Laker 3600
Tai-Pan - James Clavell 1102
Theirs Was the Kingdom - R.F. Delderfield 1590
Thine Is the Glory - Samuel A. Schreiner Jr. 5672
This Splendid Earth - V.J. Banis 289
The Three Black Pennys - Joseph Hergesheimer 2855
The Unconquered - Ben Ames Williams 6768
The Unicorn Hunt - Dorothy Dunnett 1811
Wanderers Eastward, Wanderers West - Kathleen Winsor 6823
The Wine Princes - Margaret Mackay 3987
The Wine Widow - Tessa Barclay 301
Wisconsin! - Dana Fuller Ross 5493
The Wishing Tree - Sandra Paretti 4794

The World From Rough Stones - Malcolm Macdonald 3979
The Yankee Girl - Ellen Argo 186
Young Ames - Walter D. Edmonds 1879

Byzantine Empire

Against the Fall of Night - Michael Arnold 193
Basilissa: A Tale of the Empress Theodora - John Masefield 4142
The Bearkeeper's Daughter - Gillian Bradshaw 628
The Belt of Gold - Cecelia Holland 2984
Byzantium - Michael Ennis 1945
Byzantium - Stephen R. Lawhead 3680
The Dark Angel - Mika Waltari 6551
The Eagle's Daughter - Judith Tarr 6165
The Female: A Novel of Another Time - Paul I. Wellman 6617
A Flame in Byzantium - Chelsea Quinn Yarbro 6899
Imperial Purple - Gillian Bradshaw 631
The Iron Crown - Clare Barroll 354
The Lady for Ransom - Alfred Duggan 1768
The Long Ships - Frans Gunnar Bengtsson 442
The Seven Hills of Paradise - Rosemary Simpson 5859
Shards of Empire - Susan Schwartz 5677
The Spring of the Ram - Dorothy Dunnett 1809
Their Most Serene Majesties - Ange Vlachos 6505
Theodora - Samuel Edwards 1891
Theodora and the Emperor - Harold Lamb 3608
The Unholy Pilgrim - R.F. Tapsell 6161
The Vandal - Richard O'Connor 4687
The Walking Drum - Louis L'Amour 3632
Wine of Satan - Laverne Gay 2327

Cambrai, Battle of

Wings for the Chariots - Arch Whitehouse 6713

Canal Building

Banner by the Wayside - Samuel Hopkins Adams 28
Canal Town - Samuel Hopkins Adams 29
Creole Dusk - Walter Adolphe Roberts 5392
The Drayton Legacy - Rona Randall 5247
Erie Water - Walter D. Edmonds 1875
Fenwick Travers and the Panama Canal - Raymond M. Saunders 5613
Madeleine - Catherine Gavin 2323
Paths of Fortune - Susan Moore 4444
Rome Haul - Walter D. Edmonds 1877
The Silver Highways - Malcolm Macdonald 3972
Water over the Dam - Marguerite Allis 116

Carbonari Uprising

The Rebels - Alfred Neumann 4585

Carthaginian Empire

Hannibal of Carthage - Mary Dolan 1686

Cattle Drives

Born of the Sun - John H. Culp 1440
The Cowboy and the Cossack - Claire Huffaker 3071
The Cowboys - William Dale Jennings 3211
The Far Canyon - Elmer Kelton 3404
The Goodnight Trail - Ralph Compton 1227
Lonely on the Mountain - Louis L'Amour 3621
Lonesome Dove - Larry McMurtry 4298
North of 36 - Emerson Hough 3042
North to Yesterday - Robert Flynn 2145
The Pumpkin Rollers - Elmer Kelton 3406
The Restless Land - John H. Culp 1444
A Shadow of Eagles - Jane Barry 360
Storm Haven - Frank G. Slaughter 5903

These Thousand Hills - A.B. Guthrie Jr. 2627
Too Long at the Dance - Mike Blakely 539
The Trail to Ogallala - Benjamin Capps 889
Trail's End - Fred Bean 400

Celtic Britain

Bride of the Spear - Kathleen Herbert 2851
Canis the Warrior - James Sinclair 5864
The Crows of War - Steven Rayson 5276
The Dark Island - Henry Treece 6326
The Eagle and the Raven - Pauline Gedge 2344
The Gods Are Not Mocked - Anna Taylor 6177
Harkfast: The Making of the King - Hugh C. Rae 5238
Queen of the Lightning - Kathleen Herbert 2852
The Serpent's Tooth - Diana L. Paxson 4846
Warrior Queen - James Sinclair 5865

Celtic Ireland

Deirdre - James Stephens 5996
Druid's Enchantment - Millie J. Ragosta 5240
The Emerald Crown - Theodora McCormick Du Bois 1741
The Gallowglass - Howard Breslin 666
The Kings in Winter - Cecelia Holland 2991

Chancellorsville, Battle of

Gods and Generals - Jeff Shaara 5765
Time of Drums - John Ehle 1897

Chartist Revolt

The Mills of Colne - Robert Neill 4572
The Rape of the Fair Country - Alexander Cordell 1325
The Wildcliffe Bird - Constance Heaven 2811

Chess

The Chess Player: A Novel of New Orleans and Paris - Frances Parkinson Keyes 3478
Kingkill - Thomas Gavin 2325

Chicago World's Fair

Chicago Girls - Edith Freund 2229
The Dream Seekers - Grace Mark 4085

Chickamauga, Battle of

Captain Little Ax - James H. Street 6077
The Fifth Conspiracy - Ted Jones 3296
Guns of Chickamauga - Richard O'Connor 4685
Hiwassee: A Novel of the Civil War - Charles F. Price 5176
In a Dark Garden - Frank G. Slaughter 5891
Mockingbird Sang at Chickamauga - Alfred Leland Crabb 1404
None Shall Look Back - Caroline Gordon 2478

Childhood

The Cinderpath - Catherine Cookson 1275
A Dream of Kings - Davis Grubb 2604
English Music - Peter Ackroyd 18
Familiar Acts - June Barraclough 345
The Harrogate Secret - Catherine Cookson 1278
A High Wind in Jamaica - Richard Hughes 3074
London's Child - Philip Boast 560
Midnight Is a Place - Joan Aiken 52
My Beloved Son - Catherine Cookson 1285
The Rag Nymph - Catherine Cookson 1287
Wartime Lies - Louis Begley 416

Children's Crusade

An Army of Children - Evan H. Rhodes 5306
Cross, Sword, and Arrow - Gladys H. Barr 340
The Devil's Cross - Walter O'Meara 4733
Our Lives Have Just Begun - Henry Myers 4541
The Trumpet of God - David Duncan 1784

Chinese Empire

The Big Chariot - Charmian Clift 1118
The Black Rose - Thomas B. Costain 1363
Bronze Mirror - Jeanne Larsen 3668
The Call - John Hersey 2869
Caravan to China - Frank Stanley Stuart 6085
Caravan to Kanadu: A Novel of Marco Polo - Edison Marshall 4103
The Chinese Emperor - Jean Levi 3733
The Chinese Nail Murders - Robert van Gulik 6413
The Court of the Lion - Eleanor Cooney 1294
Creation - Gore Vidal 6486
Deception - Eleanor Cooney 1295
The Dream of Confucius - Jean Levi 3734
The Emperor's Pearl - Robert van Gulik 6414
Empire of Heaven - Linda Ching Sledge 5907
Empress - Evelyn McCune 4238
The Enchantress - Suyin Han 2673
The Examination - Malcolm Bosse 587
The Fabulous Concubine - Hsin-Hai Chang 987
Flashman and the Dragon - George MacDonald Fraser 2206
Forbidden City - Anthony Esler 1962
Forbidden City - Muriel Molland Jernigan 3215
The Ginger Tree - Oswald Wynd 6890
Go Ask the River - Evelyn Eaton 1826
The Good Earth - Pearl S. Buck 754
Green Dragon, White Tiger - Annette Motley 4501
The Haunted Monastery - Robert van Gulik 6415
Hong Kong - Mona Gardner 2288
A House in Peiking - Robert Payne 4853
Imperial Woman - Pearl S. Buck 755
An Insular Position - Timothy Mo 4421
Invisible Cities - Italo Calvino 867
Jade - Pat Barr 344
The Jade Stalk - Jonathan Fast 2048
The Lacquer Screen - Robert van Gulik 6416
Lady Jane - Leslie O'Grady 4699
Lady Wu - Yutang Lin 3782
Louisiana! - Dana Fuller Ross 5478
Manchu - Robert S. Elegant 1904
Manchu Empress - Bluebell Matilda Hunter 3081
Manchu Palaces - Jeanne Larsen 3669
Mandarin - Robert S. Elegant 1905
Mandarin Gold - James Leasor 3700
Ming: A Novel of Seventeeth Century China - Robert B. Oxnam 4772
The Monkey and the Tiger - Robert van Gulik 6417
Murder in Canton - Robert van Gulik 6418
The Name of Hero - Richard Seltzer 5742
Necklace and Calabash - Robert van Gulik 6419
The Pearl Pagoda - Susannah Broome 707
The Phantom of the Temple - Robert van Gulik 6420
A Private Revenge - Richard Woodman 6863
Rebels of the Heavenly Kingdom - Katherine Paterson 4828
Red Barbarian - Margaret Gaan 2260
The Red Pavilion - Robert van Gulik 6421
The Red Peony - Yutang Lin 3783
Ruler of the Sky: A Novel of Genghis Khan - Pamela Sargent 5606
The Second Son of Heaven: A Novel of Nineteenth-Century China - C.Y. Lee 3707
Shanghai Tango: A Novel of China - William Overgard 4769
Shike: Time of Dragons - Robert Shea 5784
Silk Road - Jeanne Larsen 3670
Sons of the Steppe: The Story of How the Conqueror Genghis Khan Was Overcome - Hans Baumann 380

Spring Moon: A Novel of China - Bette Bao Lord 3897
Tall Ships to Cathay - Helen Augur 240
The Time of the Dragon - Dorothy Eden 1863
Trade Imperial - Alan Lloyd 3814
White Poppy - Margaret Gaan 2261
The Willow Pattern - Robert van Gulik 6422
Winter Cherry - Keith West 6632

Chinese Revolution

The Bridge of a Hundred Dragons - Emma Drummond 1723
Dynasty - Robert S. Elegant 1902
From a Far Land - Robert S. Elegant 1903
The House of Memory: A Novel of Shanghai - Nicholas R. Clifford 1117
Little Sister - Margaret Gaan 2259
Spring Moon: A Novel of China - Bette Bao Lord 3897
The Warlord - Malcolm Bosse 589

Chouan Revolt

Heroic Dust - Theodora Dehon 1581
Master-At-Arms - Rafael Sabatini 5553

Christianity

And Walk on Love: A Novel Based on the Life of the Apostle Paul - Henrietta Buckmaster 759
Antioch Actress: A Novel of Pagan Against Christian - Jacob Randolph Perkins 4913
The Apostle - Sholem Asch 197
As Sure as the Dawn - Francine Rivers 5352
The Beacon of Alexandria - Gillian Bradshaw 627
Behold, We Live - Charles Dunscomb 1812
Ben Hur: A Tale of the Christ - Lew Wallace 6536
The Big Fisherman - Lloyd C. Douglas 1702
Blood of the Martyrs - Naomi Mitchison 4417
The Bond and the Free - Charles Dunscomb 1813
Bronze Christ - Yoshiro Nagaya 4551
The Captive Princess - Maxine Shore 5831
Confessors of the Name - Gladys Schmitt 5640
Constantine: The Miracle of the Flaming Cross - Frank G. Slaughter 5883
Count Belisarius - Robert Graves 2544
Dear and Glorious Physician - Taylor Caldwell 853
Death Comes for the Archbishop - Willa Cather 957
The Death of the Gods - Dmitri Merezhkovski 4338
The Eagle and the Crown - Hubertus Loewenstein 3832
The Eighth Veil - Ellis Kadison 3320
The Equinox: A Novel of Rome in the Time of Commodus - Carol Saylor 5622
The Fates Are Laughing - William Crozier 1439
A Fig in Winter - Willa Gibbs 2400
First the Blade - Drayton Mayrant 4212
Fisher of Men: A Novel of Simon Peter - Kurt Frieberger 2231
The Flames of Rome - Paul L. Maier 4033
The Four Rivers of Paradise - Helen Constance White 6678
The Gladiator - Thames Ross Williamson 6790
The Glorious Folly: A Novel of the Time of St. Paul - Louis De Wohl 1565
God's Warrior - Frank G. Slaughter 5889
Hypatia - Charles Kingsley 3498
I, Nathanael, Knew Jesus - William Gilbert Van Tassel Sutpen 6133
I, Paul - Rex Miller 4401
The Illusionist - Anita Mason 4144
Imperial Renegade - Louis De Wohl 1567
Judas - Igal Mossinsohn 4500
Julian - Gore Vidal 6489
King Jesus - Robert Graves 2549
The Kingdom of the Wicked - Anthony Burgess 778
The Last Athenian - Viktor Rydberg 5543

The Last Romans - Teodor Jeske-Choinski 3216
The Lion and the Cross - Joan Lesley Hamilton 2669
The Living Wood - Louis De Wohl 1571
Man on Fire: A Novel on the Life of St. Paul - LeGette Blythe 558
The Man on the White Horse - Warwick Deeping 1577
Marcus - Laurene Chinn 1068
Octavia: A Tale of Ancient Rome - Seymour Van Santvoord 6428
The Price of Blood - Doris Sutcliffe Adams 24
Quo Vadis - Henryk Sienkiewicz 5848
The Road to Bithynia: A Novel of Luke, the Beloved Physician - Frank G. Slaughter 5897
The Robe - Lloyd C. Douglas 1703
The Roman - Mika Waltari 6554
Saint Paul: A Historical Novel of His Life - Leon Poirier 5081
The Samurai - Shusaku Endo 1941
Scorpus the Moor - Leslie Turner White 6690
The Silver Chalice - Thomas B. Costain 1370
The Sinner of Saint Ambrose - Robert Raynolds 5275
The Sins of Herod: A Novel of Rome and the Early Church - Frank G. Slaughter 5900
The Soothsayer - Laurene Chinn 1069
Street of the Sandalmakers: A Tale of Rome in the Time of Marcus Aurelius - Nis Peterson 4977
The Testament of Theophilus - Leonard Wibberley 6730
The Thorn of Arimathea - Frank G. Slaughter 5905
Upon This Rock: A Novel of Simon Peter, Prince of Apostles - Frank G. Slaughter 5906
Upon This Rock: The Life of St. Peter - Walter F. Murphy 4526
Yeshua: The Gospel of St. Thomas - Alan Decker McNarie 4306

Christmas

Christmas at Mount Vernon - Helen Topping Miller 4385
Christmas for Tad: A Story of Mary and Abraham Lincoln - Helen Topping Miller 4386
Christmas with Robert E. Lee - Helen Topping Miller 4387
Her Christmas at the Hermitage: A Tale about Rachel and Andrew Jackson - Helen Topping Miller 4389
No Tears for Christmas - Helen Topping Miller 4391

Circus Life

Catch a Falling Star - Stuart M. Kaminsky 3333
Chad Hanna - Walter D. Edmonds 1873
Jenny and Barnum: A Novel of Love - Roderick Thorp 6276
Masters of Illusion: A Novel of the Connecticut Circus Fire - Mary-Ann Tirone Smith 5925
Spangle - Gary Jennings 3196
Stranger at Wildings - Madeleine Brent 663

Civil Rights Movement

The Iron Curtain - Robert Vaughan 6447

Civil War—China

Blood Red Rose - Maxwell Grant 2538
Peking: A Novel of China's Revolt - Anthony Grey 2587

Civil War—Cuba

Yellow: A Novel - Daniel Lynch 3932

Civil War—England

Bennett's Welcome - Inglis Fletcher 2132
The Bride - Margaret Irwin 3116
The Bride of Lammermoor - Sir Walter Scott 5693
Campion Towers - John Beatty 401
Captain Fantom - Charles Underhill 6377
The Chains of Fate - Pamela Belle 430
Charles the King - Evelyn Anthony 160
Circle of Pearls - Rosalind Laker 3593
A Crowning Mercy - Susannah Kells 3396
Daneclere - Pamela Hill 2931
The Dark Stranger - Dorothy Charques 999
The Diary of William Harvey: The Imaginary Journal of the Physician Who Revolutionized Medicine - Jean Hamburger 2667
The Dispossessed - Dell Shannon 5773
The Faithful Lovers - Valerie Anand 129
A Firework for Oliver - John Sanders 5587
The Highland Hawk - Leslie Turner White 6682
The House at Old Vine - Norah Lofts 3845
I, John Mordaunt - Virgil Scott 5687
John Inglesant - John Henry Shorthouse 5833
John Milton - Edmund Fuller 2249
Katherine Christian - Hugh Walpole 6546
The King Breaker - Elizabeth Linington 3797
The King's General - Daphne Du Maurier 1748
Lament for a Lost Lover - Philippa Carr 921
Malefice - Leslie Wilson 6810
Mary of Carisbrooke - Margaret Campbell Barnes 327
Mistress of The Highlands - Chloe Gartner 2309
The Moon in the Water - Pamela Belle 433
My Lord Foxe - Constance Gluyas 2443
My Lord Monleigh - Jan Cox Speas 5957
Myself My Enemy - Jean Plaidy 5037
The Near and Distant Place - Patricia Wright 6883
Pargeters - Norah Lofts 3857
The Physician of London - Stephanie Cowell 1394
The Pilgrim Prince - Gladys H. Barr 343
A Place of Ravens - Pamela Hill 2942
The Power and the Glory - Phyllis Bentley 462
Prisons - Mary Lee Settle 5757
The Proud Servant: The Story of Montrose - Margaret Irwin 3120
The Quickenberry Tree - Annette Motley 4502
Rebel Heiress - Robert Neill 4573
Reckless Angel - Jane Feather 2056
Rider on a White Horse - Rosemary Sutcliff 6124
The Road and the Star - Berkely Mather 4182
The Rose Crossing - Nicholas Jose 3306
Royal Escape - Georgette Heyer 2900
Saraband for Two Sisters - Philippa Carr 928
Scent of Cloves - Norah Lofts 3859
Seek the Fair Land - Walter Macken 3989
The Severed Crown - Jane Lane 3657
The Stranger Prince - Margaret Irwin 3122
Twenty Years After - Alexandre Dumas 1783
Ulverton - Adam Thorpe 6278
The White Witch - Elizabeth Goudge 2496
Wife to Mr. Milton - Robert Graves 2553
Wintercombe - Pamela Belle 435
Woman Astride - Nora Purtscher-Wydenbruch 5209
Woodstock; or, The Cavalier - Sir Walter Scott 5710

Civil War—Ireland

The End of the Hunt - Thomas Flanagan 2119
An Excess of Love - Cathy Cash Spellman 5959
High Heroic - Constantine FitzGibbon 2118
The Scorching Wind - Walter Macken 3988
Thy Tears Might Cease - Michael Farrell 2018
Time and Chance - Anna Wibberley 6728
The Ways of Women - Elaine Crowley 1436

Civil War—Russia

Fifteen Flags - Richard Lynden Hardman 2686
The Gathering Wolves - Elizabeth Darrell 1496

Civil War—Spain

Back to Battle - Max Hennessy 2828
Contessa - Helene Mansfield 4076
A Distant Thunder - Teresa de Luca 1561
La Guerra: A Spanish Saga - Stephen D. Frances 2199
The Skeleton in the Grass - Robert Barnard 320
The Stuff of Heroes - Miguel Delibes 1592
While England Sleeps - David Leavitt 3702
The White Dove - Rosie Thomas 6246

Civil War—U.S.

Absalom, Absalom! - William Faulkner 2049
Action at Aquila - Hervey Allen 97
Aide to Glory - Louis Devon 1635
Ain't Goin' to Glory - David Delman 1597
All God's Children - Alston Anderson 136
American Falls - John Calvin Batchelor 376
The Amulet - Hal Borland 582
And One Wore Gray - Heather Graham 2515
And Wait for the Night - John William Corrington 1352
Andersonville - MacKinlay Kantor 3359
Angel of the Delta - Edward Francis Murphy 4521
Angel with Spurs - Paul I. Wellman 6613
Another Spring - Loula Grace Erdman 1948
Arizona - Clarence Budington Kelland 3387
Armored Giants: A Novel of the Civil War - F. van Wyck Mason 4145
Arouse and Beware - MacKinlay Kantor 3360
Artillery of Time - Chard Powers Smith 5919
Ask My Brother - Constance Wagner 6518
The Autobiography of Miss Jane Pittman - Ernest J. Gaines 2270
Bagatelle - Maurice Denuziere 1613
Band of Angels - Robert Penn Warren 6572
The Band Plays Dixie - Morris Markey 4089
Banished Children of Eve - Peter Quinn 5227
The Bank - Stephen Longstreet 3882
Banner at Shenandoah - Bruce Catton 963
The Barefoot Brigade - Douglas C. Jones 3274
Bates House - Clarence Benadum 437
Battle Flag - Bernard Cornwell 1333
Bayou - Pamela Jekel 3183
The Bayou Road - Mignon G. Eberhart 1832
Beauty From Ashes - Eugenia Price 5177
Beckoning Ridge - Emerson Waldman 6527
La Belle - Elizabeth Boatwright Coker 1161
Belle Starr - Deborah Camp 870
Beloved - Vina Delmar 1599
Beloved Enemy - Al Lacy 3579
The Big Family - Vina Delmar 1600
Big River, Big Man - Thomas William Duncan 1786
Blood Brother - Elliott Arnold 190
Blood Kin - Barbara Anne Pauley 4845
Blood Red Roses - Elizabeth Boatwright Coker 1163
The Bloody Ground - Bernard Cornwell 1334
The Blue and the Gray - John Leekley 3713
Blue Hurricane - F. van Wyck Mason 4146
Bound Girl - Everett Webber 6591
Bride of a Thousand Cedars - Bruce Lancaster 3637
Bride of Fortune - Harnett T. Kane 3352
The Bride of Texas - Josef Skvorecky 5880
The Bridge - Marguerite Allis 108
The Bright Land - Janet Fairbank 2000
The Bright Sword - Eleanor Perenyi 4911
A Bright Tragic Thing - L.D. Clark 1091
Bugle in the Wilderness - John Burress 805
Bugles Blow No More - Clifford Dowdey 1704
By Antietam Creek - Don Robertson 5398
By Dim and Flashing Lamps - Alan Le May 3689
By Reason of Strength - Gerald White Johnson 3225
By the Dim Lamps - Nathan Schachner 5630
By Valour and Arms - James H. Street 6076
Cadmus Henry - Walter D. Edmonds 1872
Cain's Daughters - Doris Shannon 5776
Caleb Pettengill U.S.N. - George Fielding Eliot 1912

Captain Grant - Shirley Seifert 5724
Captain Little Ax - James H. Street 6077
Captain Rebel - Frank Yerby 6910
Carriage Trade - Robert Thomsen 6271
Casey - Ramona Stewart 6034
The Catherine - Robert S. MacDonald 3980
Cease Firing - Mary Johnston 3230
Charleston - Alexandra Ripley 5338
Cherokee Dawn - Genell Dellin 1596
The Chess Player: A Novel of New Orleans and Paris - Frances Parkinson Keyes 3478
The Chester A. Arthur Conspiracy - William Wiegand 6740
Christmas for Tad: A Story of Mary and Abraham Lincoln - Helen Topping Miller 4386
Christmas with Robert E. Lee - Helen Topping Miller 4387
City of the Flags - Clark McMeekin 4290
Clear for Action! - Noel B. Gerson 2362
Colorado! - Dana Fuller Ross 5471
Company of Cowards - Jack Schaefer 5634
Company Q - Richard O'Connor 4684
Concert Grand - Howard Breslin 665
Confederates - Thomas Keneally 3412
Confessions of Johnny Ringo - Geoff Aggeler 40
Conspiracy of Knaves - Dee Brown 711
Copperhead - Bernard Cornwell 1335
Copperhead Moon - Herbert Stover 6067
The Copperheads - William James Blech 544
Cordelia Chantrell - Meade Minnigerode 4413
The Cortlandts of Washington Square - Janet Fairbank 2001
The Cosgrove Report - G.J.A. O'Toole 4765
The Cotton Road - Frank Feuille 2077
The Court Martial of Robert E. Lee - Douglas Savage 5617
A Court of Owls - Richard Adicks 37
The Crater - Richard Slotkin 5908
Crazy Snake - Robert J. Conley 1240
Crescent City - Belva Plain 5078
The Crisis - Winston Churchill 1079
Cry of the Hawk - Terry C. Johnston 3248
The Cup, the Blade or the Gun - Mignon G. Eberhart 1833
The Cup Trembling - Karl Brown 723
The Dark Command - William R. Burnett 793
Dark Thicket - Elmer Kelton 3402
Darktown Strutters - Wesley Brown 732
Daughter of Strangers - Elizabeth Boatwright Coker 1164
Dear Lily - Malcolm W. Greenough Jr. 2575
Defiant Hearts - Janelle Taylor 6185
The Devil Gun - William Syers 6148
Diamond Head - Houston Branch 647
Dim the Flaring Lamps - Jan Jordan 3301
Dinner at Belmont - Alfred Leland Crabb 1398
The Dixie Widow - Gilbert Morris 4459
Dominion - Jack Rowe 5514
Double Wedding Ring - Patricia Wendorf 6624
The Dram Tree - Hamilton Cochran 1140
A Dream of Kings - Davis Grubb 2604
Dream West - David Nevin 4587
Dreams of Gold - Lewis Orde 4748
The Drums of Morning - Philip Van Doren Stern 5997
Drury Randall - Mary Johnston 3232
Eight April Days - Scott Hart 2759
Elkhorn Tavern - Douglas C. Jones 3278
Embers of the Heart - Rosanne Bittner 512
Except for Me and Thee - Jessamyn West 6628
Exit with Drums - Joseph A. Daley 1457
Fairoaks - Frank Yerby 6915
The Falling Hills - Perry Lentz 3720
Family Fortune - Mignon G. Eberhart 1834
The Far Side of Home - Maggie Davis 1536
Farewell, My General - Shirley Seifert 5726
Father Abraham - Irving A. Bacheller 258
The Fathers - Allen Tate 6171
Faye's Folly - Elizabeth Corbett 1322

The Fifth Conspiracy - Ted Jones 3296
First the Blade - May Miller 4400
Flames of Empire - Peter Bourne 594
Flight to Canada - Ishmael Reed 5285
For Love and Honor - Antonia Van-Loon 6423
For the Love of Robert E. Lee - M.A. Harper 2715
For Us the Living - Antonia Van-Loon 6424
The Foragers - Ben Haas 2630
Forever Free - Honore Morrow 4487
The Forge - Thomas S. Stribling 6083
Foundation Stone - Lella Warren 6571
The Foxes of Harrow - Frank Yerby 6917
Fragments of the Ark - Louise Meriwether 4341
Freedom - William Safire 5561
Freedom's Banner - Teresa Crane 1415
The Friendly Persuasion - Jessamyn West 6629
Full of Thy Riches - Elizabeth Ferrell 2070
The Gallant Mrs. Stonewall - Harnett T. Kane 3353
The Gallery of His Dreams - Kristine Kathryn
  Rusch 5525
Gentlemen, Hush! - Jere Hungerford
  Wheelwright 6668
Gettysburg - Stephen Longstreet 3887
Gettysburg: Crisis of Command - Harry Albright 65
The Ghost Raider - Ray Hogan 2978
The Glass Dove - Sally Carrighar 943
Glory Enough for All: The Battle of the Crater -
  Duane Philip Schultz 5673
Gods and Generals - Jeff Shaara 5765
The Golden Circle - John Edward Ames 125
The Golden Circle - Constance Robertson 5396
Gone with the Wind - Margaret Mitchell 4415
Grant's War - Ted Jones 3297
Gray Canaan - David Garth 2305
The Gray Captain - Jere Hungerford
  Wheelwright 6669
Gray Victory - Robert Skimin 5877
Great Day in the Morning - Robert Hardy
  Andrews 149
Green Rose of Furley - Helen C. Barney 334
Griffin's Way - Frank Yerby 6922
Guns of Chickamauga - Richard O'Connor 4685
The Guns of the South - Harry N. Turtledove 6367
The Hand of a Woman - Diana Brown 719
The Handsome Road - Gwen Bristow 697
Hard Road to Gettysburg - Ted Jones 3298
The Haversham Legacy - Daoma Winston 6827
The Healers - Henry Denker 1610
A Heart Divided - Al Lacy 3580
Heaven and Hell - John Jakes 3147
Henry and Clara - Thomas Mallon 4042
High Hearts - Rita Mae Brown 728
The History of Rome Hanks - Joseph Stanley
  Pennell 4909
Hiwassee: A Novel of the Civil War - Charles F.
  Price 5176
Ho, the Fair Wind - I.A.R. Wylie 6889
Home to Tennessee - Alfred Leland Crabb 1400
The Horse Soldiers - Harold Sinclair 5862
House Divided - Ben Ames Williams 6765
A Hundred Hills - Howard Breslin 667
I Speak for Thaddeus Stevens - Elsie
  Singmaster 5868
I Swear by Apollo - Agatha Young 6939
In a Dark Garden - Frank G. Slaughter 5891
In the Season of the Wild Rose - Clara Rising 5347
Intrigue in Baltimore - Janet Whitney 6715
Iron Ships, Iron Men - Christopher Nicole 4616
Ironclads: Man-of-War - Larry D. Names 4554
Jim Mundy: A Novel of the American Civil War -
  Robert H. Fowler 2192
John Bonwell - Charles K. Pulse 5208
Johnny Shiloh - James A. Rhodes 5308
Jordan County: A Landscape in Narrative - Shelby
  Foote 2152
Journey Proud - Thomasine McGehee 4273
Journey to Shiloh - Will Henry 2843
Joy From Ashes - Al Lacy 3581
Jubilee - John Brick 672

Jubilee - Margaret Walker 6531
The Judges of the Secret Court - David Stacton 5972
The Kays - Margaret Deland 1583
The Keeper of the House - Harry Harrison
  Kroll 3558
Kelly Blue - Peter Bowen 601
The Killer Angels - Michael Shaara 5766
Kingdom Coming - Roark Bradford 622
Know Nothing - Mary Lee Settle 5755
The Lady of Arlington - Harnett T. Kane 3354
Lamb in His Bosom - Caroline Miller 4380
The Land Is Bright - James Arthur Kjelgaard 3508
The Last Boat out of Cincinnati - Don Tracy 6309
The Last Confederate - Gilbert Morris 4466
The Last Full Measure - Honore Morrow 4488
Last Letter Home - Vilhelm Moberg 4423
The Last Plantation - Don Wright 6879
The Lattimer Legend - Ann Hebson 2813
The Laughing Stranger - Vina Delmar 1601
The Light Infantry Ball - Hamilton Basso 375
Lights Along the Shore - Diane Austell 241
Lincoln: A Novel - Gore Vidal 6490
The Lincoln Diddle - Barbara Steward 6015
Lodging at the Saint Cloud - Alfred Leland
  Crabb 1403
Long Day at Shiloh - Don Bannister 294
The Long Night - Andrew Lytle 3945
Long Remember - MacKinlay Kantor 3362
The Long Roll - Mary Johnston 3236
Long Storm - Ernest Haycox 2790
Look Away - Harold Coyle 1395
Look Away! - George Nauman Shuster 5841
Look Away, Beulah Land - Lonnie Coleman 1204
Look Away, Look Away - Leslie Turner White 6685
Look Back to Glory - Herbert Ravenel Sass 5607
Look to the Rose - Shirley Seifert 5728
Lorena - Frank G. Slaughter 5892
Love and War - John Jakes 3150
Love Is Eternal - Irving Stone 6058
Loving Heart - Elsie Singmaster 5869
Madame Castel's Lodger - Frances Parkinson
  Keyes 3480
Major Stepton's War - Matthew Vaughan 6445
Mamaw - Susan Dodd 1663
A Man Called Grant - Helen Todd 6285
Many a Voyage - Loula Grace Erdman 1951
The Marburg Chronicles - Alfred Coppel 1319
Marching On - James Boyd 612
Margaret's Story - Eugenia Price 5183
Maximilian's Gold - Jane Barry 359
McKensie's Hundred: A Tale of the Old Dominion -
  Frank Yerby 6924
Mignon - James M. Cain 845
Miss Delicia Allen - Mary Johnston 3237
Mockingbird Sang at Chickamauga - Alfred Leland
  Crabb 1404
Morning at Jalna - Mazo de la Roche 1560
Mosby's Last Ride - Ray Hogan 2979
Mr. Lincoln's Wife - Anne Colver 1221
Muddy Banks - Ruby C. Tolliver 6291
My Lady Hoyden - Jane Sheridan 5812
The Nancy Flyer - Ernest Poole 5091
Natchez: A Novel of the Deep South - Pamela
  Jekel 3186
Nevada! - Dana Fuller Ross 5481
New Moon Rising - Eugenia Price 5185
Night March - Bruce Lancaster 3641
Night Raider - Ray Hogan 2980
No Bugles Blow - Bruce Lancaster 3642
No Surrender - Emma Gelders Sterne 5999
No Tears for Christmas - Helen Topping
  Miller 4391
None Shall Look Back - Caroline Gordon 2478
North and South - John Jakes 3151
Old Miss - Thomas Campbell 877
Oldest Living Confederate Widow Tells All - Allan
  Gurganus 2621
On Jordan's Stormy Banks - Adelaide C.
  Rowell 5518

On the Midnight Tide - Don Tracy 6310
One Smart Indian - Robert J. Seidman 5722
One Wore Blue - Heather Graham 2517
Our Valiant Few - F. van Wyck Mason 4155
Paint the Wind - Cathy Cash Spellman 5960
The Passionate Rebel - Frank G. Slaughter 5894
Pastora - Joanna Barnes 321
Peace at Bowling Green - Alfred Leland Crabb 1405
Penhally - Caroline Gordon 2479
Peter Ashley - DuBose Heyward 2911
Pomp and Circumstance - Fred Mustard
  Stewart 6025
Praise at Morning - Mildred Masterson
  McNeilly 4310
The Prescott Chronicles - Albert Fried 2232
The President's Daughter - Barbara Chase-
  Riboud 1005
Prisoner of Twilight - Don Robertson 5400
A Promise Unbroken - Al Lacy 3582
Proud New Flags - F. van Wyck Mason 4156
The Proud Retreat - Clifford Dowdey 1706
*Proving Ground: A Novel of Civil War Days in the
  North* - Leone Lowden 3919
The Quicksilver Pool - Phyllis A. Whitney 6716
Quinn's Book - William Kennedy 3423
A Rage Against Heaven - Fred Mustard
  Stewart 6026
The Raider - Jesse Hill Ford 2164
The Raiders - William Edward Wilson 6819
The Raiders: A Novel of the Civil War at Sea -
  Willard Wallace 6541
Raintree County - Ross Lockridge Jr. 3827
Rebel - Bernard Cornwell 1336
Rebel in Blue - Herman Toepperwein 6289
Rebel Run - Louis Zara 6952
The Red Badge of Courage - Stephen Crane 1414
Red Lanterns on St. Michael's - Thornwell
  Jacobs 3139
Remembrance Rock - Carl Sandburg 5583
Richard Walden's Wife - Eleanor Kelly 3399
The Richmond Raid - John Brick 674
Ride of the Panther - Kerry Newcomb 4591
The River and the Wilderness - Don Robertson 5401
The Robber Baroness - William Kendall
  Clarke 1097
Rogue's Kingdom - John Brick 676
Roll, Shenandoah - Bruce Lancaster 3644
Rommel and the Rebel - Lawrence Wells 6622
Run Me a River - Janice Holt Giles 2415
The Running Thread - Drayton Mayrant 4215
Sail the Dark Tide - Davenport Steward 6017
Salisbury Plain - Henry C. Branson 650
Sam Houston - Noel B. Gerson 2380
Samuel Drummond - Thomas Alexander Boyd 614
Scarlet Cockerel - Garald Lagard 3584
The Scarlet Guidon - Ray Grant Toepfer 6287
The Scarlet Patch - Bruce Lancaster 3645
Sea Change - Alison McLeay 4287
Sea to Shining Sea - Michael Phillips 4990
The Seasons of Heroes - Paxton Davis 1539
The Second Face of Valor - Ray Grant Toepfer 6288
Secret Service Operator 13 - Robert W.
  Chambers 982
Seek Out and Destroy - James David Horan 3031
The Senator's Lady - Shirley Seifert 5733
The Seventh Girl: A Romantic Tale of Civil War Texas
  - Tom Pendleton 4900
Shadow on the Valley - Kirk Mitchell 4414
Shadowed Memories - Al Lacy 3583
Sherman's March - Cynthia Bass 373
Shiloh - Shelby Foote 2153
Shod with Flame - Helen Topping Miller 4393
Show Me a Land - Clark McMeekin 4293
Sing One Song - Helen Topping Miller 4394
The Sinking of the Sarah Diamond - William Dale
  Jennings 3213
The Smiling Rebel - Harnett T. Kane 3357
So Red the Rose - Stark Young 6944
So Shall They Reap - John Bennett 444

Sojourn of a Stranger - Walter Sullivan   6115
Soldier of the Queen - Max Hennessy   2837
Song of Years - Bess Streeter Aldrich   72
Sons of Fire - Max McCoy   4227
Soul of Abe Lincoln - Bernie Babcock   251
The Southern Blade - Nelson Wolford   6844
A Southern Woman - Elena Yates Eulo   1983
Spanish Gold - Kevin D. Randle   5252
The Spur - Ardyth Kennelly   3425
A Star Pointed North - Edmund Fuller   2250
The Stars of the South - Julian Green   2568
The Stonewall Brigade: A Novel of the American Civil War - Frank G. Slaughter   5902
Storm Haven - Frank G. Slaughter   5903
Storm Signals - Joseph C. Lincoln   3785
A Story of Deep Delight - Thomas McNamee   4305
Strange Company - Robert J. Conley   1251
Stranger in Savannah - Eugenia Price   5187
Swan's Chance - Celeste De Blasis   1549
Swords of Steel - Elsie Singmaster   5870
The Tall Woman - Wilma Dykeman   1819
Talons of Eagles - William W. Johnstone   3268
Tap Roots - James H. Street   6080
Texas - James A. Michener   4375
Thin Moon and Cold Mist - Kathleen O'Neal Gear   2330
Those the Sun Has Loved - Rose Jourdain   3309
Three Days - Stephen Longstreet   3891
The Three Days - Don Robertson   5402
Three-Headed Angel - Roark Bradford   623
Thunder on the Chesapeake - David Divine · 1650
The Tides of Malvern - Francis Griswold   2595
Time of Drums - John Ehle   1897
Timothy Larkin - Jane Hutchens   3089
The Titans - John Jakes   3154
To Appomattox: Nine April Days, 1865 - Burke Davis   1512
Trail-Makers of the Middle Border - Hamlin Garland   2296
Traveller - Richard Adams   27
Troubled Spring - John Brick   678
Trumpets Sound No More - F. van Wyck Mason   4163
Twilight of the Dawn - Elizabeth Nell Dubus   1752
The Twisted Tendril - Alice Glasgow   2427
Ulysses: A Biographical Novel - Robert Skimin   5878
The Unterrified - Constance Robertson   5397
Until the End - Harold Coyle   1396
Unto This Hour - Tom Wicker   6733
Untold Glory - Cothburn O'Neal   4739
The Unvanquished - William Faulkner   2050
Unvexed to the Sea: A Novel of the Vicksburg Campaign - Gerry Morrison   4484
The Unwritten Chronicles of Robert E. Lee - Lamar Herrin   2864
The Valiant Virginians - James Warner Bellah   427
A Voice in the Streets - John William Tebbel   6196
Wagons to Tucson - Ed Newsom   4604
The Walk into Morning - Mildred Barger Herschler   2867
Walk Like a Man - Donald Honig   3024
Walt Whitman's Secret - Ben Aronin   196
The Warriors - John Jakes   3155
Watchfires - Louis Auchincloss   234
The Way to Fort Pillow - James Sherburne   5807
The Wayfarer - Shirley Seifert   5738
Weep No More - Janet Stevenson   6006
West of Appomattox - Harley Duncan   1785
When the Music Changed - Marie R. Reno   5305
When the War Is Over - Stephen Becker   408
Where My Love Sleeps - Clifford Dowdey   1710
While Angels Dance - Ralph W. Cotton   1372
While the Music Plays - Diane Austell   242
Whistling Cat - Robert W. Chambers   984
Wild Is the River - Louis Bromfield   704
Wilderness: A Tale of the Civil War - Robert Penn Warren   6573
The Wilderness Brigade - Phyllis Gordon Demarest   1605

Wind From the Carolinas - Robert Wilder   6751
The Wings of Morning - Karen Harper   2714
With Malice Toward None - Honore Morrow   4492
A Woman Called Moses - Marcy Moran Heidish   2821
The Woman Who Loved John Wilkes Booth - Pamela Redford Russell   5533
Woman with a Sword: The Biographical Novel of Anna Ella Carroll of Maryland - Hollister Noble   4632
The Wounded Yankee - Gilbert Morris   4475
Wychwood - Nicole St. John   5564
The Yankee From Tennessee - Noel B. Gerson   2388
Yankee Stranger - Elswyth Thane   6217

Class Conflict

The Black Candle - Catherine Cookson   1273
The Black Velvet Gown - Catherine Cookson   1274
Tilly - Catherine Cookson   1288
Tilly Alone - Catherine Cookson   1289

Clipper Ships

Annie's Captain - Kathryn Hulme   3077
The Crystal Star - Ellen Argo   184
Java Head - Joseph Hergesheimer   2854
Jewel of the Sea - Ellen Argo   185
The Lady and the Deep Blue Sea - Garland Roark   5356
Masts to Spear the Stars - Stephen Longstreet   3889
Rainbow in the Royals - Garland Roark   5357
Sea Jade - Phyllis A. Whitney   6717
The Seafarers - William Stuart Long   3877
Tall Ships to Cathay - Helen Augur   240
The Yankee Girl - Ellen Argo   186

Cold War

Ethel: The Fictional Autobiography - Tema Nason   4558

College Life

Miss Bishop - Bess Streeter Aldrich   71

Comic Strips

Funny Papers - Tom De Haven   1559

Coming of Age

The Crossing - Cormac McCarthy   4221
The Dahomean - Frank Yerby   6911
The Golden Season - Oriana Akinson   60
Grand Days - Frank Moorhouse   4448
The Greenlander - Mark Adlard   38
The Hooded Falcon - Prudence Andrew   140
Manchu Palaces - Jeanne Larsen   3669
Marblehead - Joan Thompson   6267
Mark - Lonnie Coleman   1205
Mists of Heaven - Yvonne Kalman   3325
Passage Home - Alison McLeay   4286
Paths of Fortune - Susan Moore   4444
The Pumpkin Rollers - Elmer Kelton   3406
The Sweetwater - Jean Rikhoff   5333
The Unvanquished - William Faulkner   2050
Walk Like a Man - Donald Honig   3024
The War Train: A Novel of 1916 - Brown Meggs   4324

Communism

The Establishment - Howard Fast   2030

Concord, Battle of

April Morning - Howard Fast   2027
Concord Bridge - Howard Horne   3035
Patriot's Progress - Joseph G.E. Hopkins   3027
Trumpet to Arms - Bruce Lancaster   3647

Confederate States of America

Gray Victory - Robert Skimin   5877
The Light Infantry Ball - Hamilton Basso   375

Congress of Vienna

Feast of the Jesters - Manuel Komroff   3533
Lustre in the Sky - R.G. Waldeck   6525
The Rake and the Rebel - Ira J. Morris   4478

Copenhagen, Battle of

A Balance of Dangers - Anthony Forrest   2184
The Bomb Vessel - Richard Woodman   6860
The Inshore Squadron - Alexander Kent   3434

Copperhead Movement

The Golden Circle - Constance Robertson   5396
The Unterrified - Constance Robertson   5397

Corinth, Battle of

Journey to Shiloh - Will Henry   2843

Cossacks

The Captain's Daughter - Alexander Pushkin   5210
Sweet Ransom - Linda Madl   4026
Taras Bulba - Nikolai V. Gogol   2451
With Fire and Sword - Henryk Sienkiewicz   5850

Covenanters

The Dark Rose - Maurice Walsh   6549
Mistress of The Highlands - Chloe Gartner   2309
Old Mortality - Sir Walter Scott   5702

Cowpens, Battle of

The Carolinians - Jane Barry   357
The Fallon Blood - Reagan O'Neal   4741
The Long March - Jane Barry   358
The Ragged Ones - Burke Davis   1511

Crater, Battle of the

The Crater - Richard Slotkin   5908
Glory Enough for All: The Battle of the Crater - Duane Philip Schultz   5673

Crecy, Battle of

The Lady Royal - Molly Costain Haycraft   2794
Ride East! Ride West!: A Romance of the Hundred Years' War - Anne Powers   5154
The Vow on the Heron - Jean Plaidy   5074

Crime and Criminals

Aces and Eights: A Novel of the Legend of Wild Bill Hickok - Loren D. Estleman   1967
Adam Bede - George Eliot   1908
Adios! - Lanier Bartlett   366
All This, and Heaven Too - Rachel Field   2080
Anything for Billy - Larry McMurtry   4295
The Assassination of Jesse James by the Coward Robert Ford - Ron Hansen   2680

The Authentic Death of Hendry Jones - Charles Neider 4562
Avery's Knot - Mary Cable 843
The Axe - Sigrid Undset 6378
Belle Starr - Deborah Camp 870
Belle Starr - Speer Morgan 4453
Billy Bathgate - E.L. Doctorow 1656
Billy the Kid: The Legend of El Chivato - Elizabeth Fackler 1994
The Bizarre Sisters - Jay Walz 6559
The Black Moth - Georgette Heyer 2877
Blake's Reach - Catherine Gaskin 2313
Blind Justice - Bruce Alexander 76
The Blood Countess - Andrei Codrescu 1149
The Bloody Benders - Robert H. Adelman 35
Bloody Season - Loren D. Estleman 1968
Blue Ruin: A Novel of the 1919 World Series - Brendan Boyd 610
Blue Russell - Will Bryant 738
Bring Larks and Heroes - Thomas Keneally 3410
Broncho Apache - Paul I. Wellman 6614
Brules - Harry Combs 1223
The Buckstones - Paul I. Wellman 6615
A Calf for Venus - Norah Lofts 3838
California Caballero - William Colt MacDonald 3981
Candle of the Wicked - Manly Wade Wellman 6612
Captain Lightfoot - William R. Burnett 792
The Case of Kitty Ogilvie - Jean Stubbs 6093
Castle Barebane - Joan Aiken 43
Catriona - Robert Louis Stevenson 6009
The Choiring of the Trees - Donald Harington 2709
City of Widows - Loren D. Estleman 1969
Come Winter - Douglas C. Jones 3275
Confessions of Johnny Ringo - Geoff Aggeler 40
The Council of Europe - Leonardo Sciascia 5678
The Dark City - Max Allan Collins 1211
The Day They Kidnapped Queen Victoria - H.K. Fleming 2127
Death of a Legend - Will Henry 2840
The Demise of Billy the Kid - Preston Lewis 3760
Denis Duval - William Makepeace Thackeray 6211
Desperadoes - Ron Hansen 2681
The Devil's Marchioness - William Fifield 2082
Dillinger - Harry Patterson 4832
The Dream Ends in Fury - Samuel Anthony Peeples 4889
Entered From the Sun - George Garrett 2301
Escape From Sonora - Will Bryant 739
Eugene Aram - Edward Bulwer-Lytton 766
Evil Mark - Graham Miles 4377
The Executioner's Song - Norman Mailer 4036
Fair is the Rose - Meagan MacKinney 3997
Fanny: Being the True History of the Adventures of Fanny Hackabout-Jones - Erica Jong 3299
Fata Morgana - William Kotzwinkle 3549
Fortune, Smile Once More - Mary Floyd Williams 6788
The Fortunes of Nigel - Sir Walter Scott 5696
The Four Hundred - Stephen Sheppard 5804
The Gallows Land - Bill Pronzini 5201
The Gentleman From Chicago - John Cashman 953
The Ghosts of Elkhorn - Kerry Newcomb 4589
Gone to Texas - Forrest Carter 945
Good Morning, Young Lady - Ardyth Kennelly 3424
The Good Provider - Jessica Stirling 6043
The Great Train Robbery - Michael Crichton 1426
Griffith Gaunt - Charles Reade 5280
Gringo Gold - Dane Coolidge 1293
Gunman - Loren D. Estleman 1971
Guy Mannering - Sir Walter Scott 5697
The Ham Reporter - Robert J. Randisi 5251
Hand of Glory - Glen Petrie 4980
Hangman's Cliff - Robert Neill 4570
Hard on the Road - Barbara Moore 4440
The Headsman; or, The Abbaye des Vignerons - James Fenimore Cooper 1300
The Heart of Midlothian - Sir Walter Scott 5698
Heaven's Gold - Giles Tippette 6282

Hereward the Wake - Charles Kingsley 3497
High Road to China - Jon Cleary 1106
His Majesty's Highwayman - Donald Barr Chidsey 1061
A House Behind the Mint - Laurie Huffman 3072
The House by the Churchyard - Joseph Sheridan Le Fanu 3688
Hue and Cry - Elizabeth Yates 6907
I Am Vidocq - Vincent McConnor 4225
Jack Sheppard - William Harrison Ainsworth 56
Jewels - Robert Perrin 4917
Kate - Brian Cleeve 1109
Kid Curry: The Life and Times of Harvey Logan and the Wild Bunch - F. Bruce Lamb 3606
Killing Mister Watson - Peter Mathiessen 4185
Killing Time - Robert J. Conley 1244
The King's Rogue - Max Peacock 4859
The Lady and the Arsenic - Marjorie Bowen 598
A Lady at Bay - Edgar Maas 3950
Landru - Rene Masson 4170
The Last Days of Horse-Shy Halloran - Bill Pronzini 5203
Last Gun: The Legend of John Selman - Gene Shelton 5801
The Law in Charity - Chelsea Quinn Yarbro 6901
Legs - William Kennedy 3422
Libra - Don DeLillo 1593
Lily - Cindy Bonner 571
The Live Goat - Cecil Dawkins 1542
The Living - Annie Dillard 1644
Lizzie - Evan Hunter 3083
Lizzie Borden - Elizabeth Engstrom 1944
Locksley - Nicholas Chase 1003
The Long Night - Andrew Lytle 3945
Looking After Lily - Cindy Bonner 572
Lord Johnnie - Leslie Turner White 6687
Lorna Doone - R.D. Blackmore 528
Loving Belle Star - Robert Taylor 6187
Luciano's Luck - Jack Higgins 2912
Mad Dog - Jack Kelly 3401
Mamaw - Susan Dodd 1663
Marianne - Glen Petrie 4981
The Masked Man - P.C. Doherty 1674
The Masters of Bow Street - John Creasy 1423
Me and Gallagher - Jack Farris 2023
The Men That God Forgot - Richard Butler 829
The Michaelmas Girls - John Barry 362
Mister St. John - Loren D. Estleman 1974
Mistress - Amanda Quick 5215
Mr. American - George MacDonald Fraser 2211
Murder by the Numbers - Max Allan Collins 1212
Murder in the Red Room - Elliott Roosevelt 5451
The Murder in the Tower - Jean Plaidy 5035
Murder in the West Wing - Elliott Roosevelt 5453
Murdock's Law - Loren D. Estleman 1975
My Grand Enemy - Jean Stubbs 6098
Mysteries of Winterthurn - Joyce Carol Oates 4659
The Old Colts - Glendon Swarthout 6144
Organized Crime - Nicholas Von Hoffman 6511
Ourselves to Know - John O'Hara 4704
Out of the Dark - Norah Lofts 3856
Outlaw Lover - Lindsey Hanks 2676
Outpost! - Dana Fuller Ross 5486
The Ox-Bow Incident - Walter Van Tilburg Clark 1096
The Passion of Sacco and Vanzetti: A New England Legend - Howard Fast 2040
Pearl - Anne Leaton 3701
A Peep into the 20th Century - Christopher Davis 1515
Pelican Coast - Alan Le May 3690
Perfume: The Story of a Murderer - Patrick Suskind 6120
Peter Ibbetson - George Du Maurier 1750
The Pistoleer - James Carlos Blake 536
A Place Called Freedom - Ken Follett 2150
The Playmaker - Thomas Keneally 3414
The Pleasure Garden - Leon Garfield 2293
Power in the Blood - Greg Matthews 4191

The President's Man - Elliott Roosevelt 5455
Pretty Boy Floyd - Larry McMurtry 4299
Proud Mary - Iris Gower 2501
Ragtime - E.L. Doctorow 1658
Ravenscroft - Dorothy Eden 1860
Rawhider - Gene Shelton 5802
Refugio, They Named You Wrong - Susan Clark Schofield 5647
The Return of Henry Starr - Richard Slotkin 5909
Rob Roy - Sir Walter Scott 5707
The Robber Bridegroom - Eudora Welty 6623
Robin and the King - Parke Godwin 2448
Rockspring - R.G. Vliet 6506
Rogues' Company: A Novel of John Murrell - Harry Harrison Kroll 3559
Rogue's Kingdom - John Brick 676
Romola - George Eliot 1910
The Rookery: A Novel of the Victorian Underworld - Hugh C. Rae 5239
The Saga of Henry Starr - Robert J. Conley 1250
Saint Johnson - William R. Burnett 796
Saint Mudd - Steve Thayer 6218
Sara Dane - Catherine Gaskin 2316
Scotch on the Rocks - Howard Browne 733
The Search for Temperance Moon - Douglas C. Jones 3282
Shadow on the Valley - Kirk Mitchell 4414
Shanghai Tango: A Novel of China - William Overgard 4769
Sherwood - Parke Godwin 2449
Shoot! - George Bowering 604
The Shootist - Glendon Swarthout 6145
Silas Marner - George Eliot 1911
The Snake Pit - Sigrid Undset 6383
The Sons of Grady Rourke - Douglas Savage 5618
South of the Border - John Byrne Cooke 1268
Sow the Seeds of Hemp - Gary Jennings 3195
Stolen Away - Max Allan Collins 1213
The Story of Pat Garrett and Billy the Kid - David Everitt 1987
The Story of the Sundance Kid - David Everitt 1988
The Strange Case of Deacon Brodie - Forbes Bramble 646
The Stranglers - Loren D. Estleman 1978
The Street of Kings - Charles Dexter 1637
The Street Sparrows - Rose Ayers 249
Streets of Laredo - Larry McMurtry 4300
Sunrise to Sunset - Samuel Hopkins Adams 32
Swandowne - Daniel Farson 2024
The Swedish Cavalier - Leo Perutz 4943
Sweet Adelaide - Julian Symons 6152
A Tale for Midnight - Frederic Prokosch 5195
The Talisman Ring - Georgette Heyer 2905
Tascosa Gun: The Story of Jim East - Gene Shelton 5803
Ten Years Beyond Baker Street - Cay Van Ash 6400
Tenderloin - Samuel Hopkins Adams 33
The Terrible Teague Bunch - Gary Jennings 3197
Tessa d'Arblay - Malcolm Macdonald 3974
Testimony of Two Men - Taylor Caldwell 863
This Dark Monarchy - Francis W. Leary 3698
Time After Time - Karl Alexander 80
To the Ends of the Earth - Michael Talbot 6155
Tombstone Showdown - Leslie Scott 5681
Tracker - David Wagoner 6521
The Tragedy at Tinkerton: An Historical Novel of Murder - Raymond Paul 4844
The Trial of Elizabeth Cree: A Novel of the Limehouse Murders - Peter Ackroyd 21
True Crime - Max Allan Collins 1214
True Detective - Max Allan Collins 1215
True Grit - Charles Portis 5139
The Twilighters - Noel M. Loomis 3894
The Vast Memory of Love - Malcolm Bosse 588
The Vengeance Trail of Josey Wales - Forrest Carter 946
Watson's Apology - Beryl Bainbridge 271
Weedy Rough - Douglas C. Jones 3286
Welcome to Hard Times - E.L. Doctorow 1660

While Angels Dance - Ralph W. Cotton 1372
Whiskey River - Loren D. Estleman 1981
The Whitechapel Horrors - Edward B. Hanna 2678
Wilford's Daughter - Alexandra Manners 4071
Winding Stairs - Douglas C. Jones 3287
Winds of Blame - Jane Gilmore Rushing 5532
A Woman Called Fancy - Frank Yerby 6931
Woman of Justice - Georgia Di Donato 1639
The Women of Whitechapel and Jack the Ripper - Paul West 6638
Wyatt Earp - Matt Braun 653
You Bet Your Life - Stuart M. Kaminsky 3349

Crimean War

Artemia - Pamela Hill 2927
Badge of Glory - Douglas E. Reeman 5287
Bedford Row - Claire Rayner 5259
Brave Captains - Vivian Stuart 6086
Burton and Speke - William Harrison 2751
Century in Scarlet - Lajos Zilahy 6962
The Eden Passion - Marilyn Harris 2730
Flashman at the Charge - George MacDonald Fraser 2209
Fleur - Cynthia Harrod-Eagles 2754
Forget the Glory - Emma Drummond 1725
The Fortress - Catherine Gavin 2320
The Gallant - William Stuart Long 3873
Gentlemen—The Regiment! - Hugh Talbot 6154
Hazard of Huntress - Vivian Stuart 6087
Hazard's Command - Vivian Stuart 6088
Leaves From the Valley - Joanna Trollope 6348
Officer and Gentleman - Josephine Delves-Broughton 1604
The Passionate Pilgrim - Charles Terrot 6204
Pendragon: Late of Prince Albert's Own - Robert Trevelyan 6337
The Private Life of Florence Nightingale - Richard Gordon 2485
The Queen's Husband - Jean Plaidy 5052
Ravenshoe - Henry Kingsley 3500
Secret for a Nightingale - Victoria Holt 3020
Sisters & Lovers - Nicola Thorne 6274
Soldier of the Queen - Max Hennessy 2837
A Space of the Heart - Patricia Wright 6884
Trumpeter, Sound! - D.L. Murray 4528
Until the Colors Fade - Tim Jeal 3173
The Valiant Sailors - Vivian Stuart 6090
Victoria Victorious - Jean Plaidy 5073
Victory at Sebastopol - Vivian Stuart 6091

Crusades

Against the Fall of Night - Michael Arnold 193
Alamut - Judith Tarr 6164
Antichrist: A Novel of the Emperor Frederick II - Cecelia Holland 2982
An Army of Children - Evan H. Rhodes 5306
The Battle-Ax of God - Le Roy MacLeod 4007
Belmarch: A Legend of the First Crusade - Christopher Davis 1514
The Betrothed - Sir Walter Scott 5691
Blessed Are the Meek: A Novel about St. Francis of Assisi - Zofja Kossak-Szczucka 3542
The Blue Falcon - Robyn Carr 935
A Booke of Days: A Journal of the Crusade by Roger, Duke of Lunel - Stephen J. Rivele 5351
Champion - L. Christian Balling 285
Count Bohemond - Alfred Duggan 1764
Count Robert of Paris - Sir Walter Scott 5695
Cross, Sword, and Arrow - Gladys H. Barr 340
The Devil's Cross - Walter O'Meara 4733
Eleanor the Queen - Norah Lofts 3842
Emerald Fire - Laurie Grant 2537
The Fool of Venus - George William Cronyn 1428
Gay Crusader - Cleone Knox 3528
The Heart of the Lion - Jean Plaidy 5020
The Heirs of the Kingdom - Zoe Oldenbourg 4716

The Homecoming - Norah Lofts 3844
The Infidels - Chloe Gartner 2308
Jerusalem - Cecelia Holland 2990
King's Man - C.M. Edmondston 1880
The Kings of Vain Intent - Graham Shelby 5791
Knight with Armour - Alfred Duggan 1767
Knight's Acre - Norah Lofts 3848
The Knights of Dark Renown - Graham Shelby 5792
The Leopard Unleashed - Elizabeth Chadwick 967
The Leper King - Zofja Kossak-Szczucka 3544
Lionheart!: A Novel of Richard I, King of England - Martha Rofheart 5428
Lord Geoffrey's Fancy - Alfred Duggan 1771
The Lost Flight - H.F.M. Prescott 5169
The Lute Player - Norah Lofts 3852
Men Like Shadows - Dorothy Charques 1000
My Lord Brother the Lionheart - Molly Costain Haycraft 2795
No Man's Son - Doris Sutcliffe Adams 23
Our Lives Have Just Begun - Henry Myers 4541
Pilgermann - Russell Hoban 2960
Queen of Swords - Judith Tarr 6169
Richard and the Knights of God - Pamela Bennetts 454
Ride Home Tomorrow - Evan John 3221
The Saracen Blade - Frank Yerby 6926
The Seven Hills of Paradise - Rosemary Simpson 5859
Shield of Three Lions - Pamela Kaufman 3372
Silver Leopard - F. van Wyck Mason 4160
Sir Pagan - Henry John Colyton 1222
The Talisman - Sir Walter Scott 5708
Tomorrow's Fire - Jay Williams 6775
Trail and Triumph: A Novel about Maimonides - Lester M. Morrison 4485
The True Cross - Carlo Scarfoglio 5629
The Trumpet of God - David Duncan 1784
Under the Winter Moon - Teresa Brooke 705
The Unholy Pilgrim - R.F. Tapsell 6161
Wine of Satan - Laverne Gay 2327

Culloden, Battle of

Born to Be King - Constance Gluyas 2440
Candleshine No More - Jane Oliver 4721
The Flight of the Heron - Dorothy Kathleen Broster 710
Highlands Rebel - Sally Watson 6584
The Woman from The Glen - Chloe Gartner 2310

Dance

Death Off Stage - Richard Grayson 2558
Encore - Monique Raphel High 2915
A Grand Passion - Mary Mackey 3991
The Infinite Woman - Edison Marshall 4107
Louisa Brancusi - Darrell Husted 3088

Dark Ages

Absolution by Murder - Peter Tremayne 6334
The Adversary - Jan Widgery 6738
Arthur - Stephen R. Lawhead 3679
Arthur Rex: A Legendary Novel - Thomas Berger 477
Attila's Treasure - Stephan Grundy 2606
Beloved Exile - Parke Godwin 2446
Better in the Dark - Chelsea Quinn Yarbro 6894
Born of the Sun - Joan Wolf 6837
Brendan - Frederick Buechner 762
Bride of the Spear - Kathleen Herbert 2851
By Love Enslaved - Phoebe Conn 1255
Byzantium - Stephen R. Lawhead 3680
The Chessboard Queen - Sharan Newman 4597
Child of the Northern Spring - Persia Woolley 6867
The Coming of the King - Nikolai Tolstoy 6296
Conscience of the King - Alfred Duggan 1763
The Crimson Chalice - Victor Canning 882

The Cross and the Sword - Evangeline Walton 6558
The Crow Goddess - Patricia Finney 2094
The Crystal Cave - Mary Stewart 6029
Darkness and the Dawn - Thomas B. Costain 1364
The Deer Cry - William Greenough Schofield 5650
Devoted - Alice Borchardt 578
Druid's Enchantment - Millie J. Ragosta 5240
The Duke of War - Walter O'Meara 4734
The Eagle's Daughter - Judith Tarr 6165
Eaters of the Dead - Michael Crichton 1425
The Edge of Light - Joan Wolf 6839
The Emerald Crown - Theodora McCormick Du Bois 1741
The Emperor Arthur - Godfrey Turton 6368
The Fair - Robert Nathan 4559
Fire Queen - Deborah Grabien 2503
Firelord - Parke Godwin 2447
First Knight - Elizabeth Chadwick 966
The Flame in the Dark - Basil Bonallack 568
The Gentle Conqueror - Mary Ellen Gronau 2597
The Great Captains - Henry Treece 6329
The Green Man - Henry Treece 6330
Guinevere - Sharan Newman 4600
Guinevere Evermore - Sharan Newman 4601
Guinevere: The Legend in Autumn - Persia Woolley 6868
The Hammer and the Cross - Harry Harrison 2736
Harkfast: The Making of the King - Hugh C. Rae 5238
The Harp and the Blade - John Myers 4543
Hawk of May - Gillian Bradshaw 629
The Hollow Hills - Mary Stewart 6030
The Idylls of the Queen - Phyllis Ann Karr 3367
In the Shadow of the Oak King - Courtway Jones 3271
In Winter's Shadow - Gillian Bradshaw 632
Isle of Glory - Jane Oliver 4723
Kingdom of Summer - Gillian Bradshaw 633
The Kingmaking - Helen Hollick 3000
Lady of Conquest - Teresa Medeiros 4322
The Last Enchantment - Mary Stewart 6031
Last of Britain - Meriol Trevor 6343
The Last Pendragon - Robert Rice 5316
Lest Darkness Fall - L. Sprague De Camp 1557
The Lion and the Cross - Joan Lesley Hamilton 2669
The Long Ships - Frans Gunnar Bengtsson 442
Lord of Hawkfell Island - Catherine Coulter 1376
The Marsh King - C. Walter Hodges 2975
Merlin - Stephen R. Lawhead 3681
The Mists of Avalon - Marion Zimmer Bradley 626
The Once and Future King - T.H. White 6705
The Pagan King - Edison Marshall 4109
Paradise - Dikkon Eberhart 1831
Passionate Warriors - Mary Ellen Gronau 2598
The Pendragon - Catherine Christian 1075
Pendragon - Stephen R. Lawhead 3682
Pendragon's Banner - Helen Hollick 3001
Pope Joan - Donna Woolfolk Cross 1433
The Price of Blood - Doris Sutcliffe Adams 24
The Prince and the Pilgrim - Mary Stewart 6032
Queen of the Lightning - Kathleen Herbert 2852
Queen of the Summer Stars - Persia Woolley 6869
The Queen's Knight - Marvin Borowsky 585
Raven's Wind - Victor Canning 883
Return of the Stranger - Dorothy James Roberts 5377
The Road to Avalon - Joan Wolf 6842
Ruan - Bryher 746
A Shadow of Gulls - Patricia Finney 2096
The Singing Sword - Jack Whyte 6725
The Skystone: The Forging of Arthur's Britain - Jack Whyte 6726
Sword at Sunset - Rosemary Sutcliff 6125
Taliesin - Stephen R. Lawhead 3683
Theo and Matilda - Rachel Billington 498
To Love Again - Bertrice Small 5913
The Tower of Beowulf - Parke Godwin 2450
The Twelve Pictures - Edith Simon 5857

The Tyrant of Bagdhad - Glenn Pierce   4996
The Unspeakables: A Tale of Lombardy - Laverne
   Gay   2326
The Viking - Edison Marshall   4113
The Viking's Woman - Heather Graham   2520
The Vision of Stephen: An Elegy - Lolah
   Burford   775
The White Raven - Diana L. Paxson   4847
The Wicked Day - Mary Stewart   6033
The Winter King - Bernard Cornwell   1351
The Winter Servant - M.H. Davis   1537
Witch of the North - Courtway Jones   3272
The Wolf and the Raven - Diana L. Paxson   4848
Women in the Wall - Julia O'Faolain   4691
The Year of the Horsetails - R.F. Tapsell   6162

Decembrist Uprising

The Astrov Legacy - Constance Heaven   2802
The Year of December - Lucy Cores   1329

Depression Era

And the Desert Shall Bloom - Phyllis Barber   299
Billy Bathgate - E.L. Doctorow   1656
The Dark City - Max Allan Collins   1211
Flanagan's Run - Tom McNab   4303
Joy in Mudville - Gordon McAlpine   4216
The Land Endures - Mary E. Pearce   4862
Leah's Journey - Gloria Goldreich   2460
The Longest Road - Jeanne Williams   6781
Loon Lake - E.L. Doctorow   1657
Mad Dog - Jack Kelly   3401
Mark - Lonnie Coleman   1205
The Marrying Kind - Jessica Stirling   6046
Mr. Vertigo - Paul Auster   244
Murder by the Numbers - Max Allan Collins   1212
Murder in the Oval Office - Elliott Roosevelt   5450
Murder in the Red Room - Elliott Roosevelt   5451
Murder in the Rose Garden - Elliott Roosevelt   5452
Murder in the West Wing - Elliott Roosevelt   5453
New Deal for Death - Elliott Roosevelt   5454
Pacific Cavalcade - Virginia Coffman   1157
The Penny Wedding - Jessica Stirling   6047
Pretty Boy Floyd - Larry McMurtry   4299
Say to This Mountain - Bodie Thoene   6226
Scotch on the Rocks - Howard Browne   733
Second Generation - Howard Fast   2043
Stolen Away - Max Allan Collins   1213
Torsos - John Peyton Cooke   1270
True Crime - Max Allan Collins   1214
True Detective - Max Allan Collins   1215
The Unplowed Sky - Jeanne Williams   6783
The Very Best People - Elizabeth Villars   6499
Weedy Rough - Douglas C. Jones   3286
While the Music Lasts - Suzanne Goodwin   2477
World's Fair - E.L. Doctorow   1661

Diplomacy

54-40 or Fight - Emerson Hough   3040
1901 - Robert Conroy   1258
The Garden of Persephone - Cesar J. Rotondi   5510
Grand Days - Frank Moorhouse   4448
Let the King Beware! - Honore Morrow   4489
Lustre in the Sky - R.G. Waldeck   6525
The Negotiators - Francis Walder   6526
Praise at Morning - Mildred Masterson
   McNeilly   4310
A Time for Titans - Vina Delmar   1602
When the Emperor Dies - Mason McCann
   Smith   5926

Disasters

The Bridge of San Luis Rey - Thornton Wilder   6752

Disasters—Natural

Admiral Hornblower in the West Indies - C.S.
   Forester   2169
Eye of the Hurricane - Fergus Reid Buckley   757
Famine - Liam O'Flaherty   4693
The Famished Land - Elizabeth Byrd   833
Fortune Is a Woman - Elizabeth Adler   39
*Fury in the Earth: A Novel of the New Madrid
   Earthquake* - Harry Harrison Kroll   3557
The Great Blizzard - Albert E. Idell   3101
The Great Tide - Rubylea Hall   2662
The Hedge of Thorns - Helen Ashton   217
Hyde Place - Virginia Coffman   1154
I Take This Land - Richard Powell   5147
Kagami - Elizabeth Kata   3369
The Last Days of Pompeii - Edward Bulwer-
   Lytton   768
Lisbon - Valerie Sherwood   5825
Passage to Natchez - Cameron Judd   3316
The Seafarers - William Stuart Long   3877
West to Eden - Gloria Goldreich   2461

Dogs

Shakespeare's Dog - Leon Rooke   5439
Trail: The Story of the Lewis and Clark Expedition -
   Louis Charbonneau   998

Donner Party

The American River - Gary McCarthy   4222
Grim Journey - Hoffman Birney   509
The Mothers - Vardis Fisher   2109
Tamsen - David Galloway   2273
The Ungodly: A Novel of the Donner Party - Richard
   Rhodes   5311
Wheels West - Homer Croy   1438
Winter Harvest - Norah Lofts   3863

Draft Riots

Ain't Goin' to Glory - David Delman   1597
Banished Children of Eve - Peter Quinn   5227
Bread and Circus - Morris Renek   5303
Casey - Ramona Stewart   6034
The Copperheads - William James Blech   544
For Us the Living - Antonia Van-Loon   6424
Quinn's Book - William Kennedy   3423
The Raiders: A Novel of the Civil War at Sea -
   Willard Wallace   6541
Secret Service Operator 13 - Robert W.
   Chambers   982
A Voice in the Streets - John William Tebbel   6196

Druids

Druids - Morgan Llywelyn   3817
Druid's Enchantment - Millie J. Ragosta   5240
The Eagle and the Raven - Pauline Gedge   2344
The Forest House - Marion Zimmer Bradley   625
The Gods Are Not Mocked - Anna Taylor   6177
Harkfast: The Making of the King - Hugh C.
   Rae   5238
Refuge in Avalon - Marguerite Steedman   5984
Ruan - Bryher   746

Dutch Colonies

Scent of Cloves - Norah Lofts   3859
Silver Nutmeg - Norah Lofts   3860
Tristram Bent - Henry Barnard Safford   5560

Earthquakes

Alexa - Anne Melville   4330
All or Nothing - Stephen Longstreet   3881
California Gold - John Jakes   3145

Cannibal Eliot and the Lost Histories of San Francisco
   - Hilton Obenzinger   4660
Enslaved - Ron Burns   801
The Family of Women - Richard Peck   4883
Fire and Fog - Dianne Day   1543
Fortune Is a Woman - Elizabeth Adler   39
*Fury in the Earth: A Novel of the New Madrid
   Earthquake* - Harry Harrison Kroll   3557
The Ginger Tree - Oswald Wynd   6890
The Golden Crucible - Jean Stubbs   6096
Hyde Place - Virginia Coffman   1154
The Immigrants - Howard Fast   2034
Lisbon - Valerie Sherwood   5825
Passage to Natchez - Cameron Judd   3316
The Trembling Earth - Dale Van Every   6411
Vision of the Eagle - Kay L. McDonald   4263
Waltzing in Ragtime - Eileen Charbonneau   996

East/West Relations

The Barbarian - Willard Price   5191
The Blue Dragon - Diana Brown   716
Dynasty - Robert S. Elegant   1902
The Enchantress - Suyin Han   2673
Gai-Jin: A Novel of Japan - James Clavell   1100
The Ginger Tree - Oswald Wynd   6890
Hong Kong - Mona Gardner   2288
An Insular Position - Timothy Mo   4421
Invading Tibet - Mark Frutkin   2239
Jade - Pat Barr   344
The Jade Alliance - Elizabeth Darrell   1497
Java Head - Joseph Hergesheimer   2854
The Journeyer - Gary Jennings   3194
Little Sister - Margaret Gaan   2259
Manchu - Robert S. Elegant   1904
Mandarin - Robert S. Elegant   1905
Mandarin Gold - James Leasor   3700
The Needle-Watcher - Richard Blaker   540
Red Barbarian - Margaret Gaan   2260
The Samurai - Shusaku Endo   1941
*The Second Son of Heaven: A Novel of Nineteenth-
   Century China* - C.Y. Lee   3707
Shogun - James Clavell   1101
The Signore: Shogun of the Warring States - Kunio
   Tsuji   6357
Tai-Pan - James Clavell   1102
Twilight of the Dragon - Peter Bourne   596
Venture in the East - Bruce Lancaster   3648
When God Slept - Peter Bourne   597
Yedo - Lynn Guest   2609

Easter Rising

Across the Bitter Sea - Eilis Dillon   1646
An Excess of Love - Cathy Cash Spellman   5959
Heart of War - John Masters   4174
The Killing Frost - Thomas Hayden   2799
*The Men That God Made Mad: A Novel about
   Ireland's Easter Rising* - W.A. Ballinger   286
Passage West - Dallas Miller   4382
Rebels: The Irish Rising of 1916 - Peter
   DeRosa   1622
The Rising of the Moon - William Martin   4140
Saints and Scholars - Terrence Eagleton   1821
The Scorching Wind - Walter Macken   3988
Seasons - Anna Dillon   1645
Thy Tears Might Cease - Michael Farrell   2018
Trinity - Leon Uris   6394

Education

Brave Pursuit - Marguerite Allis   107
Miss Bishop - Bess Streeter Aldrich   71
The Rector of Justin - Louis Auchincloss   233
The Revolt of Sarah Perkins - Marian Cockrell   1148
To Serve Them All My Days - R.F. Delderfield   1591

Edwardian Period

Amanda/Miranda - Richard Peck 4882
Anna's Book - Barbara Vine 6500
The Asking Price - Jessica Stirling 6039
The Bellamy Saga - John Pearson 4878
The Blind Bend - Lorn MacIntyre 3985
Captain Wonder - Donald Thomas 6238
Check-Out Time - Kate Kingsbury 3491
Chelsea Reach - Claire Rayner 5261
The Cinderpath - Catherine Cookson 1275
Do Not Disturb - Kate Kingsbury 3492
The Duchess of Duke Street - Mollie Hardwick 2693
The Eagle at the Gate - Rona Randall 5248
Eat, Drink, and Be Buried - Kate Kingsbury 3493
Edward - Tyler Whittle 6721
The Glendower Conspiracy - Lloyd Biggle Jr. 494
The Good Provider - Jessica Stirling 6043
Grounds for Murder - Kate Kingsbury 3494
The Halfhyde Line - Philip McCutchan 4249
Halfhyde Ordered South - Philip McCutchan 4252
Kernow & Daughter - Malcolm Macdonald 3968
The King Edward Plot - Robert Lee Hall 2658
The Ladies of Hanover Square - Rona Randall 5249
The Long Afternoon - Ursula Zilinsky 6964
Lord of the Far Island - Victoria Holt 3016
The Lormes of Castle Rising - Fanny Cradock 1409
Love at Sunset - Jane Sheridan 5811
Lovers - Suzanne Goodwin 2476
The Mamur Zapt and the Donkey-Vous - Michael Pearce 4866
The Mamur Zapt and the Girl in the Nile - Michael Pearce 4867
The Mamur Zapt and the Men Behind - Michael Pearce 4868
The Mamur Zapt and the Night of the Dog - Michael Pearce 4869
The Mamur Zapt and the Return of the Carpet - Michael Pearce 4870
The Mamur Zapt and the Spoils of Egypt - Michael Pearce 4871
Mr. American - George MacDonald Fraser 2211
The Old Enchantment - Sarah Neilan 4565
Pomeroy - Gordon Williams 6770
Proud Mary - Iris Gower 2501
The Revenge of the Hound - Michael Hardwick 2688
Room with a Clue - Kate Kingsbury 3495
Seance for a Vampire - Fred Saberhagen 5557
Service for Two - Kate Kingsbury 3496
Shadows over Castle Rising - Fanny Cradock 1410
The Shakespeare Girl - Mollie Hardwick 2698
Spring at The Winged Horse - Ted Willis 6794
The Store - Michael Pearson 4879
The Summer of the Bashinskeys - Diane Pearson 4877
Upstairs Downstairs - John Hawkesworth 2782
Vanessa - Hugh Walpole 6548
The Welcome Light - Jessica Stirling 6050

Elizabethan Period

The Abbot - Sir Walter Scott 5688
Absolute Elizabeth - Joanna Dessau 1624
All the Living: A Novel of One Year in the Life of William Shakespeare - Henrietta Buckmaster 758
All the Queen's Men - Evelyn Anthony 157
Armada - Charles Gidley 2404
The Bartholomew Fair Murders - Leonard Tourney 6297
Beauvallet - Georgette Heyer 2876
The Best House in Stratford - Edward Fisher 2100
The Bisley Boy - Christopher Hunt 3080
The Black Duchess - Alanna Knight 3514
The Blade of Castlemayne - Anthony Esler 1960
Bless This House - Norah Lofts 3835
The Border Lord - Jan Westcott 6641
Buccaneer Surgeon - C.V. Terry 6205
Captain Bashful - Donald Barr Chidsey 1059
Captain for Elizabeth - Jan Westcott 6643

The Captive Queen of Scots - Jean Plaidy 5008
Chase the Heart - Maggie Osborne 4760
The Cleopatra Boy - Eric Malpass 4048
Cloak of Folly - Burke Boyce 606
Come Rack! Come Rope! - Robert Hugh Benson 458
The Constant Star - Dorothy Norris Foote 2151
Court of Shadows - Cynthia Morgan 4450
Daishi-San: A Novel - Robert P. Lund 3925
A Dead Man in Deptford - Anthony Burgess 776
Death of the Fox - George Garrett 2300
Deborah - Colette Davenat 1498
Deborah and the Many Faces of Love - Colette Davenat 1499
Deborah and the Siege of Paris - Colette Davenat 1500
Edmund Campion - Evelyn Waugh 6585
Elizabeth and the Prince of Spain - Margaret Irwin 3117
Elizabeth: Queen & Woman - Helen Thorpe 6279
Elizabeth, the Woman - Amanda Mae Ellis 1917
Entered From the Sun - George Garrett 2301
Envoy From Elizabeth - Pamela Bennetts 451
Familiar Spirits - Leonard Tourney 6298
A Famine of Horses - P.F. Chisholm 1071
Fire over England - A.E.W. Mason 4143
The Firedrake's Eye - Patricia Finney 2095
The Flight of the Kestrel - Margaret Abbey 3
For Love of a Pirate - Anthony Esler 1961
The Fourth Queen - Isabel Paterson 4827
Frobisher's Savage - Leonard Tourney 6299
Gay Lord Robert - Jean Plaidy 5015
Gentleman of Stratford - John Brophy 708
Goa - Kara Dalkey 1458
Golden Admiral - F. van Wyck Mason 4150
Grania: She-King of the Irish Seas - Morgan Llywelyn 3819
The Grove of Eagles - Winston Graham 2526
Heart of a Queen - Josephine Delves-Broughton 1603
Her Majesty's Captain - Derek Wilson 6797
The Hounds of God - Rafael Sabatini 5551
A House of Women - Eric Malpass 4049
I, Elizabeth - Rosalind Miles 4378
Immortal Queen - Elizabeth Byrd 834
Kenilworth - Sir Walter Scott 5700
A Kind of Justice - Benjamin Siegel 5844
Kingdom of Gold - Susan Wiggs 6744
Knaves Templar - Leonard Tourney 6300
Lady Defiant - Suzanne Robinson 5412
Lady Gallant - Suzanne Robinson 5413
Lady in Waiting - Rosemary Sutcliff 6123
Lady Rich - Elizabeth Boatwright Coker 1166
The Last Prince of Ireland - Morgan Llywelyn 3821
Late Harvest - Olive White 6697
The Laughing Hangman - Edward Marston 4120
Legacy - Susan Kay 3374
The Lion and the Rose - Jane Oliver 4724
The Lion Triumphant - Philippa Carr 922
Liza Bowe - Shirley Barker 313
Lord of Darkness - Robert Silverberg 5854
Lost Love Found - Bertrice Small 5910
Love's Labour's Won - Edward Fisher 2101
Low Treason - Leonard Tourney 6301
The Mad Courtesan - Edward Marston 4122
Magnus the Magnificent - Leslie Turner White 6688
Maid of Honour: A Novel Set in the Court of Mary, Queen of Scots - Elizabeth Byrd 836
Mary of Scotland - F.W. Kenyon 3454
Mary, Queen of Scotland and the Isles - Margaret George 2356
The Master of Gray Trilogy - Nigel Tranter 6316
Mermaid Tavern - George William Cronyn 1429
The Merry Devils - Edward Marston 4123
The Monastery - Sir Walter Scott 5701
Mrs. Shakespeare: The Complete Works - Robert Nye 4656
The Muscovite - Alison Macleod 4004
My Dear Lover England - Pamela Bennetts 453
My Enemy the Queen - Victoria Holt 3017

My Lady Greensleeves - Constance Beresford-Howe 476
My Lord Essex - Olive Eckerson 1838
My Lord the Fox - Robert York 6932
The Needle-Watcher - Richard Blaker 540
Nicholas Cooke: Actor, Soldier, Physician, Priest - Stephanie Cowell 1393
The Nine Giants - Edward Marston 4124
No Bed for Bacon - Caryl Brahms 640
No Smoke Without Fire - Alice Harwood 2767
No Wall So High - Anne Powers 5152
Nothing Like the Sun - Anthony Burgess 781
The Old Priory - Norah Lofts 3855
Old Saxon Blood - Leonard Tourney 6302
Out on Any Limb - John Myers 4545
The Players' Boy Is Dead - Leonard Tourney 6303
Prisoner of the Queen - Alison Macleod 4006
The Proud Man - Elizabeth Linington 3800
The Quality of Mercy - Faye Kellerman 3391
The Queen and the Gypsy - Constance Heaven 2810
Queen of This Realm: The Story of Queen Elizabeth I - Jean Plaidy 5050
The Queen's Head - Edward Marston 4125
The Queen's Ward - Hebe Elsna 1933
Ralegh's Fair Bess: The Story of Bess Throckmorton - Judy Turner 6365
Reluctant Cavalier - Donald Barr Chidsey 1064
Roanoke Hundred - Inglis Fletcher 2138
Roanoke Renegade - Don Tracy 6311
The Roaring Boy - Edward Marston 4127
The Robsart Affair - Jennette Letton 3729
Royal Road to Fotheringay - Jean Plaidy 5059
Sackett's Land - Louis L'Amour 3628
The Scarlet Cloak - Jean Plaidy 5061
A Season of Knives - P.F. Chisholm 1072
Shadow in the Sun: A Novel of Elizabeth I, the Virgin Queen - F.W. Kenyon 3460
The Shadow of the Earth - Lee Wichelns 6731
Shakespeare & Son - Edward Fisher 2102
Shakespeare's Dog - Leon Rooke 5439
The Silent Woman - Edward Marston 4128
Sir Rogue - Leslie Turner White 6691
The Slicing Edge of Death - Judith Cook 1263
So Merciful a Queen, So Cruel a Woman - Alice Harwood 2769
Strange Devices of the Sun and Moon - Lisa Goldstein 2463
The Succession: A Novel of Elizabeth and James - George Garrett 2302
Superstition Corner - Sheila Kaye-Smith 3379
Sweet Will - Eric Malpass 4050
Take Heed of Loving Me: A Novel about John Donne - Elizabeth Gray Vining 6502
Tansy Taniard - Myrtle Strode-Jackson 6084
Three Years to Play - Colin MacInnes 3983
Till the Day Goes Down - Judith Lennox-Smith 3719
To Be a King - Robert DeMaria 1607
To Love a Queen - Lawrence Schoonover 5669
Too Near the Throne - Molly Costain Haycraft 2797
The Tower and the Dream - Jan Westcott 6647
The Tower of London - William Harrison Ainsworth 58
Towers in the Mist - Elizabeth Goudge 2495
The Trip to Jerusalem - Edward Marston 4129
Trust and Treason - Margaret Birkhead 506
Tudor Underground - Denis Meadows 4320
Two Loves Have I - Clara Longworth de Chambrun 985
The Valiant Lady - Brigid Knight 3523
Westward Ho! - Charles Kingsley 3499
The White Queen - Frederic Fallon 2011
Will Shakespeare: The Untold Story - John Mortimer 4495
The Witch From the Sea - Philippa Carr 933
Witness of Bones - Leonard Tourney 6304
Wolfshead - Jere Hungerford Wheelwright 6672
Women of Ashdon - Valerie Anand 135
You, My Brother - Philip Burton 809

English Colonies

The Adventurers - William Stuart Long 3869
After the Rainbow - Yvonne Kalman 3323
Aurora Rose - Anne Worboys 6870
By Command of the Viceroy - Duncan MacNeil 4010
Caribbee - Thomas Hoover 3025
Charge of Cowardice - Duncan MacNeil 4011
The Colonists - William Stuart Long 3870
The Deceivers - John Masters 4173
The Devil's Wind: Nana Saheb's Story - Manohar
 Malgonkar 4039
Drums Along the Khyber - Duncan MacNeil 4013
Drums of Khartoum - Chloe Gartner 2307
Dubu: A Novel of New Guinean Conquest - Maslyn
 Williams 6789
The Empire Builders - William Stuart Long 3871
The Explorers - William Stuart Long 3872
The Far Pavilions - M.M. Kaye 3376
For God and Glory - Tim Jeal 3171
The Gates of Kunara - Duncan MacNeil 4014
Grand Parade - G.B. Lancaster 3649
Greenstone - Yvonne Kalman 3324
The Jade Alliance - Elizabeth Darrell 1497
Lieutenant of the Line - Duncan MacNeil 4015
Mandalay - Alexandra Jones 3269
Mistaken Virtues - Joanna Trollope 6349
Mists of Heaven - Yvonne Kalman 3325
The Mountain of Immoderate Desires - Leslie
 Wilson 6811
New Day - Victor Stafford Reid 5291
Olivia and Jai - Rebecca Ryman 5544
On Trial for My Country - Stanlake Samkange 5578
Pomp and Circumstance - Fred Mustard
 Stewart 6025
The Ravishers - Elizabeth Richards 5318
The Restless Frontier - Duncan MacNeil 4018
Running West - James Houston 3052
Sadhu on the Mountain Peak - Duncan
 MacNeil 4019
Sara Dane - Catherine Gaskin 2316
The Settlers - William Stuart Long 3878
Shadow of the Moon - M.M. Kaye 3377
The Spoils of Eden - Robert H. Fowler 2193
Subaltern's Choice - Duncan MacNeil 4020
Things Fall Apart - Chinua Achebe 16
Trade Imperial - Alan Lloyd 3814
The Train at Bundarbar - Duncan MacNeil 4021
The Traitors - William Stuart Long 3879
The Veil of Illusion - Rebecca Ryman 5545
Watch for the Dawn - Stuart Cloete 1128
Wizards' Country - Daphne Rooke 5438
Wolf in the Fold - Duncan MacNeil 4022

Enlightenment Period

Rasero - Francisco Rebolledo 5282

Erie Canal

Chad Hanna - Walter D. Edmonds 1873
Erie Water - Walter D. Edmonds 1875
Rome Haul - Walter D. Edmonds 1877
Scarborough House - Sharon Salvato 5577
Vandemark's Folly - Herbert Quick 5223
The Wedding Journey - Walter D. Edmonds 1878

Espionage

American Falls - John Calvin Batchelor 376
Arizona! - Dana Fuller Ross 5466
A Balance of Dangers - Anthony Forrest 2184
Baltic Mission - Richard Woodman 6859
Behold the Fire - Michael Blankfort 541
Beloved Enemy - Al Lacy 3579
The Blood of Roses - Marsha Canham 879
Blood Winter - William Patrick 4830
The Bravo - James Fenimore Cooper 1298

Bride of the Unicorn - Kasey Michaels 4363
Brother to the Enemy - Bart Spicer 5964
Captain Justice - Anthony Forrest 2185
Captain Wonder - Donald Thomas 6238
Celia Garth - Gwen Bristow 695
The Charlatan - Carter A. Vaughan 6433
Chase Royal - Donald Seaman 5712
A Clear Road to Archangel - Geoffrey Rose 5461
Cockades: A Romance - Meade Minnigerode 4412
Company Q - Richard O'Connor 4684
Conspiracy of Knaves - Dee Brown 711
Copperhead Moon - Herbert Stover 6067
Cormorant's Brood - Inglis Fletcher 2133
Court of Shadows - Cynthia Morgan 4450
The Culper Spy Ring - Lynn Groh 2596
Dance on a Sinking Ship - Michael Kilian 3483
A Dancer in Darkness - David Stacton 5971
A Dead Man in Deptford - Anthony Burgess 776
Deborah - Colette Davenat 1498
Deborah and the Many Faces of Love - Colette
 Davenat 1499
Deborah and the Siege of Paris - Colette
 Davenat 1500
Defiant Hearts - Janelle Taylor 6185
The Devil in Harbour - Catherine Gavin 2319
The Devil Met a Lady - Stuart M. Kaminsky 3335
The Devil's Spy - Michael Hastings 2773
The Dixie Widow - Gilbert Morris 4459
Dragon Cove - Carter A. Vaughan 6434
The Drums of April - Charles Mergendahl 4340
Envoy From Elizabeth - Pamela Bennetts 451
Ethel: The Fictional Autobiography - Tema
 Nason 4558
*The Extraordinary Adventures of Secret Agent Shipov
 in Pursuit of Count Leo Tolstoy in the Year 1862* -
 Bulat Okudzhava 4712
*The Eye of the Lion: A Novel Based on the Life of
 Mata Hari* - Lael Tucker Wertenbaker 6626
Faith and Honor - Robin Maderich 4025
Farewell the Tranquil - R.F. Delderfield 1585
Farewell to Valley Forge - David Taylor 6178
Fenwick Travers and the Panama Canal - Raymond
 M. Saunders 5613
The Fifth Conspiracy - Ted Jones 3296
Fire over England - A.E.W. Mason 4143
The Firedrake's Eye - Patricia Finney 2095
A Firework for Oliver - John Sanders 5587
Flashman and the Mountain of Light - George
 MacDonald Fraser 2207
Fortress Fury - Carter A. Vaughan 6435
The Free Fishers - John Buchan 750
Gentleman Traitor - Alan Williams 6763
The Gilded Torch - Iola Fuller 2252
The Golden Circle - Constance Robertson 5396
The Golden Eagle - Noel B. Gerson 2370
Gray Canaan - David Garth 2305
Hard Road to Gettysburg - Ted Jones 3298
The Hastening Wind - Edward Grierson 2591
Henry Lunt and the Ranger - Tom McNamara 4304
High Carnival - John J. Pugh 5207
Home to Tennessee - Alfred Leland Crabb 1400
Hugh Wynne, Free Quaker - Silas Weir
 Mitchell 4416
The Idol Hunter - Barry Unsworth 6386
Illinois! - Dana Fuller Ross 5475
The Imperial Agent - T.N. Murari 4518
In a Dark Garden - Frank G. Slaughter 5891
Irene at Large - Carole Nelson Douglas 1700
The Iron Chain - Jim DeFelice 1579
Ironclads: Man-of-War - Larry D. Names 4554
Johnny Logan: Shawnee Spy - Allen W. Eckert 1843
Keeping Secrets - Suzanne Morris 4483
Kentucky! - Dana Fuller Ross 5477
The Killing of Richard the Third - Robert
 Farrington 2020
The King Breaker - Elizabeth Linington 3797
Lady Gallant - Suzanne Robinson 5413
Last Man to Die - Michael Dobbs 1652

The Last Summer of Mata Hari - Edward
 Huebsch 3067
Life and Liberty - Adam Rutledge 5538
Lion Rampant - Bernard Shrimsley 5836
Lodging at the Saint Cloud - Alfred Leland
 Crabb 1403
Look Away! - George Nauman Shuster 5841
Major Andre - Anthony Bailey 265
The Man From St. Petersburg - Ken Follett 2148
The Man on the Train - W.J. Chaput 995
The Man Who Killed the King - Dennis
 Wheatley 6654
The Man Who Loved Mata Hari - Dan
 Sherman 5813
Manchu - Robert S. Elegant 1904
Marianne - Juliette Benzoni 466
Mars' Butterfly - Henry Pleasants 5080
Mockingbird Sang at Chickamauga - Alfred Leland
 Crabb 1404
The Mohawk Ladder - Noel B. Gerson 2377
Mr. Arnold - Francis Lynde 3935
Murder in the Executive Mansion - Elliott
 Roosevelt 5449
My Lord the Fox - Robert York 6932
My Love, My Enemy - Jan Cox Speas 5958
A Nest of Simple Folk - Sean O'Faolain 4692
No Bugles Blow - Bruce Lancaster 3642
Oh, Valley Green - John H. Culp 1443
On Jordan's Stormy Banks - Adelaide C.
 Rowell 5518
Once More the Hawks - Max Hennessy 2836
The Palace of Wisdom - Bob Marshall-
 Andrews 4118
The Pandora Secret - Anthony Forrest 2186
Pandora's Galley - Macdonald Harris 2727
The Passionate Rebel - Frank G. Slaughter 5894
Pendragon: Late of Prince Albert's Own - Robert
 Trevelyan 6337
Pendragon. . .The Montenegran Plot - Robert
 Trevelyan 6338
The Petersburg-Cannes Express - Hans Koning 3538
The Poisoned Chalice - Michael Clynes 1136
Pomeroy - Gordon Williams 6770
Poor Richard's Game - G.J.A. O'Toole 4766
The Pride of Lions - Marsha Canham 881
*Purple Passage: A Novel about a Lady Both Famous
 and Fantastic* - Emily Hahn 2638
The Rebel and the Turncoat - Malcolm Decker 1576
Rebel Guns - Adam Rutledge 5539
Rebel in Blue - Herman Toepperwein 6289
Rebel Run - Louis Zara 6952
The Red Daniel - Duncan MacNeil 4017
Retreat and Recall - Joseph G.E. Hopkins 3029
The Revolutionist: A Novel of Russia - Robert
 Littell 3810
Richard Pryne: A Novel of the American Revolution -
 Cyril Harris 2718
Scoundrels' Brigade - Carter A. Vaughan 6439
The Secret Road - Bruce Lancaster 3646
Secret Service Operator 13 - Robert W.
 Chambers 982
Seek Out and Destroy - James David Horan 3031
Seven Days to Petrograd - Tom Hyman 3094
Seventeen of Leyden - John James 3160
*The Shadow of the Moth: A Novel of Espionage with
 Virginia Woolf* - Ellen Hawkes 2779
Shadow of the Wolf - James Barwick 371
Shanghai Tango: A Novel of China - William
 Overgard 4769
The Slicing Edge of Death - Judith Cook 1263
The Smiling Rebel - Harnett T. Kane 3357
The Spy: A Tale of the Neutral Ground - James
 Fenimore Cooper 1310
A Spy for Napoleon - Baroness Emma Orczy 4746
Spy in Chancery - P.C. Doherty 1680
Spy's Honour - Gavin Lyall 3929
Squadron Shilling - Arch Whitehouse 6712
Stallion Gate - Martin Cruz Smith 5924
Storm the Last Rampart - David Taylor 6180

Three Fields to Cross - Francis Tysen Nutt 4651
To Be a King - Robert DeMaria 1607
Tory Tavern - Henry Barnard Safford 5559
Tournament of the Shadows - Nicholas Carnac 901
The Traitor - Dan Sherman 5814
The Traitors of Bosworth - Robert Farrington 2021
Tristram Bent - Henry Barnard Safford 5560
Tudor Agent - Robert Farrington 2022
The Unterrified - Constance Robertson 5397
Untold Glory - Cothburn O'Neal 4739
Valentina - Evelyn Anthony 165
Weep No More - Janet Stevenson 6006
While the Music Plays - Diane Austell 242
The White Witch - Elizabeth Goudge 2496
Wicked Lady - Inglis Fletcher 2142
The Wilderness - Carter A. Vaughan 6442
The Witches - Jay Williams 6776
Yankee - Dana Fuller Ross 5495
The Yankee Rascals - Carter A. Vaughan 6444
Young Mrs. Cavendish and the Kaiser's Men - K.K. Beck 405

Etruscan Civilization

The Etruscan - Mika Waltari 6553

Exploration

1492 - Newton Frolich 2236
1492 - Mary Johnston 3228
Alaska - James A. Michener 4364
At the Moon's Inn - Andrew Lytle 3944
Avalon - Anya Seton 5748
Balboa: Conquistador - Omar V. Garrison 2303
Bard: The Odyssey of the Irish - Morgan Llywelyn 3816
Bay of Arrows - Jay Parini 4800
Beyond the Blue Sierra - Honore Morrow 4486
Blackrobe - Charles Corcoran 1323
Brendan - Frederick Buechner 762
Burton and Speke - William Harrison 2751
Call of the Arctic - Robert Steelman 5987
Caravan to Kanadu: A Novel of Marco Polo - Edison Marshall 4103
Charco Harbour - Godfrey Blunden 554
The Children of the First Man - James Alexander Thom 6230
The Children of the Sun - Oakley Hall 2652
A City for St. Francis - Evelyn Wells 6621
Columbus: A Romance - Rafael Sabatini 5549
A Crossbowman's Story of the First Exploration of the Amazon - George Millar 4379
Daimon - Abel Posse 5140
Daniel Du Luth - Everett McNeil 4307
The Dogs of Paradise - Abel Posse 5141
An Embarrassment of Riches - James Howard Kunstler 3565
The Fair God - Lew Wallace 6537
Fathers and Crows - William T. Vollmann 6508
Five Black Ships: A Novel of Discoverers - Napoleon Baccino Ponce de Leon 5089
Fort De Chastaigne - Don Coldsmith 1177
Forward the Nation - Donald Culross Peattie 4880
Frobisher's Savage - Leonard Tourney 6299
The Gates of the Mountains - Will Henry 2842
The Gila River - Gary McCarthy 4223
The Gilded Torch - Iola Fuller 2252
Gods on Horseback - Samuel G. Baggett 263
The Golden Eagle - John Edward Jennings 3201
The Golden Princess - Alexander Baron 335
The Golden Wind - C.L. Grace 2507
Gudrid's Saga - Constance Irwin 3115
The Harp and the Shadow - Alejo Carpentier 905
Hawk of Detroit - Arthur Pound 5145
High Towers - Thomas B. Costain 1366
The Ice Shirt - William T. Vollmann 6509
The Indian Chronicles - Jose Barreiro 349
Invisible Cities - Italo Calvino 867

Islands of Unwisdom - Robert Graves 2548
Jemmy Button - Benjamin Subercaseaux 6107
Journey to the Sky: A Novel about the True Adventures of Two Men in Search of the Lost Maya Kingdom - Jamake Highwater 2918
The Journeyer - Gary Jennings 3194
Juan Ortiz: Gentleman of Seville - Mary Bethell Alfriend 88
The Last Hero - Peter Forbath 2154
The Last Voyage: Captain Cook's Lost Diary - Hammond Innes 3108
Lord of the Kongo - Peter Forbath 2155
The Lost Legion - H. Warner Munn 4516
The Mapmaker: A Novel of the Days of Prince Henry, the Navigator - Frank G. Slaughter 5893
A Mapmaker's Dream - James Cowan 1391
The Memoirs of Christopher Columbus - Stephen Marlowe 4096
Mercedes of Castile - James Fenimore Cooper 1304
Murder, I Presume - Gillian Linscott 3807
My Love Must Wait: The Story of Matthew Flinders - Ernestine Hill 2922
My Master Columbus - Cedric Belfrage 418
No Road Too Long - Hildegarde Hawthorne 2785
North-West by South - Nancy Cato 962
Paradise - Dikkon Eberhart 1831
The Power and the Glory - Gilbert Parker 4805
The Race: A Novel of Polar Exploration - Kare Holt 3008
The Return of Lono: A Novel of Captain Cook's Last Voyage - Oswald Andrew Bushnell 816
The Rifles - William T. Vollmann 6510
River of Swans - Don Coldsmith 1185
River to the West: A Novel of the Astor Adventure - John Edward Jennings 3204
Runestone - Don Coldsmith 1186
Running Proud - Nicholas Monsarrat 4432
La Salle - John Vernon 6458
Sea of Darkness - Roland Huntford 3086
Sea of Lentils - Antonio Benitez-Rojo 443
The Seven Cities of Gold - Virginia Davis Hersch 2865
Star of the West - Ethel Hueston 3070
The Sun, He Dies: A Novel about the End of the Aztec World - Jamake Highwater 2919
Tale of Valor - Vardis Fisher 2112
They Are Coming: The Conquest of Mexico - Jose Lopez Portillo y Pacheco 3896
This Land Fulfilled - Charles Andrew Brady 636
To the Indies - C.S. Forester 2183
Touched with Fire - John William Tebbel 6195
Trail: The Story of the Lewis and Clark Expedition - Louis Charbonneau 998
The Undiscovered Country - Jay Walz 6560
Vain Shadow - Hartzell Spence 5962
The Velvet Doublet - James H. Street 6082
A Viking's Daughter - John Andrews 147
Voss - Patrick White 6698
Water Music - T. Coraghessan Boyle 619
West with the Vikings - Edison Marshall 4114
The Whales in Lake Tanganyika - Lennart Hagerfors 2636

Eylau, Battle of

Draw Near to Battle - Jere Hungerford Wheelwright 6667

Family Saga

Abigail - Malcolm Macdonald 3962
Absalom, Absalom! - William Faulkner 2049
The Adulteress - Philippa Carr 916
Alethea - Pamela Belle 429
All or Nothing - Stephen Longstreet 3881
All Their Kingdoms - Madeleine Polland 5084
America, America - Elia Kazan 3380
American Beauty - Edna Ferber 2060

American Eden - Marilyn Harris 2728
The Americans - John Jakes 3143
The Anatolian - Elia Kazan 3381
The Angel with the Trumpet - Ernst Lothar 3898
Angels Falling - Janice Elliott 1915
Angle of Repose - Wallace Stegner 5989
The Angry Tide - Winston Graham 2521
Annapolis - William Martin 4137
Apple Tree Lean Down - Mary E. Pearce 4860
April Rising - Susan Sallis 5574
The Architecture of the Arkansas Ozarks - Donald Harington 2708
Articles of Faith - Ronald Harwood 2770
The Athelsons - Jocelyn Kettle 3476
Aurora Rose - Anne Worboys 6870
The Axe - Sigrid Undset 6378
Back Bay - William Martin 4138
The Bannaman Legacy - Catherine Cookson 1272
The Bastard - John Jakes 3144
Before My Time - Niccolo Tucci 6358
The Bellamy Saga - John Pearson 4878
The Beloved Invader - Eugenia Price 5179
Beloved Soldiers - C.L. Skelton 5871
Benton's Row - Frank Yerby 6908
Beulah Land - Lonnie Coleman 1202
Beyond the Blue Mountains - Jean Plaidy 5006
Bide Me Fair - Harvey Howells 3060
The Big Family - Vina Delmar 1600
Biscayne - Barry Jay Kaplan 3365
The Black Moon - Winston Graham 2522
The Black Swan - Philippa Carr 917
Blaize - Anne Melville 4331
The Blind Bend - Lorn MacIntyre 3985
A Bloodsmoor Romance - Joyce Carol Oates 4658
The Books of Rachel - Joel Gross 2600
Born with the Century - William Kinsolving 3501
The Boyds of Black River - Walter D. Edmonds 1871
The Brahmins - Eileen Lottman 3901
Brave Kingdom - Frances Murray 4534
Brave Pursuit - Marguerite Allis 107
Brazil - Errol Lincoln Uys 6395
The Bridal Wreath - Sigrid Undset 6379
Bridey's Mountain - Yvonne Adamson 34
Bridge to Brooklyn - Albert E. Idell 3099
Bright Captivity - Eugenia Price 5180
Bright to the Wanderer - Bruce Lancaster 3638
Buttes Landing - Jean Rikhoff 5331
By Our Beginnings - Jean Stubbs 6092
By Reason of Strength - Gerald White Johnson 3225
By the Green of the Spring - John Masters 4171
Bygones - Frank Wilkinson 6762
Cajun - Elizabeth Nell Dubus 1751
California Glory - Dana Fuller Ross 5468
The Cannaway Concern - Graham Shelby 5788
The Cannaways - Graham Shelby 5789
Cape Cod - William Martin 4139
Captains and the Kings - Taylor Caldwell 851
The Captive Bride - Gilbert Morris 4457
Carolina Courage - Dana Fuller Ross 5469
Cashelmara - Susan Howatch 3058
Centennial Summer - Albert E. Idell 3100
The Chains of Fate - Pamela Belle 430
The Chandler Heritage - Ben Haas 2629
The Changeling - Philippa Carr 918
Chelsea Reach - Claire Rayner 5261
The Cherished Wives - Valerie Anand 126
Chesapeake - James A. Michener 4367
Chikara! - Robert Skimin 5876
China Saga - C.Y. Lee 3706
Circle of Pearls - Rosalind Laker 3593
Clara Reeve - Leonie Hargrave 2705
Cold Sassy Tree - Olive Ann Burns 797
Colliers Row - Jan Webster 6592
Columbia - Pamela Jekel 3184
Contessa - Richard Oliver Collin 1209
Coromandel! - John Masters 4172
Country People - Ruth Suckow 6111

Covenant with the Vampire: The Diaries of the Family Dracul - Jeanne Kalogridis 3327
Creek Mary's Blood - Dee Brown 712
The Cross - Sigrid Undset 6380
Crossing over Jordan - Linda Beatrice Brown 725
Crossings - Earl Rovit 5512
The Crown and the Crucible - Michael Phillips 4987
Csardas - Diane Pearson 4875
Dancing at the Rascal Fair - Ivan Doig 1682
Daphne - Marion Chesney 1022
Darker Grows the Valley - Harry Harrison Kroll 3556
Daughters of the New World - Susan Richards Shreve 5835
The Dawning of Deliverance - Judith Pella 4892
The Daybreakers - Louis L'Amour 3619
Deepwater: A Novel of the Carolinas - Pamela Jekel 3185
Deirdre and Desire - Marion Chesney 1024
Demelza - Winston Graham 2524
Diana the Huntress - Marion Chesney 1026
Dina's Book - Herbjorg Wassmo 6577
Distant Music - Harold Lenoir Davis 1521
The Dixie Widow - Gilbert Morris 4459
Dreams of Gold - Lewis Orde 4748
The Drums of Winter - Sandra Paretti 4790
The Dukes: A Novel - Malcolm Ross 5503
Dynasty of Death - Taylor Caldwell 854
The Earth and All It Holds - V.J. Banis 287
Eden and Honor - Marilyn Harris 2729
The Eden Passion - Marilyn Harris 2730
Eden Rising - Marilyn Harris 2731
Emily - Cynthia Harrod-Eagles 2753
The Enduring Years - Claire Rayner 5263
English Creek - Ivan Doig 1683
Esau - Meir Shalev 5770
The Establishment - Howard Fast 2030
The Exodus - Peter Danielson 1467
The Faithful Lovers - Valerie Anand 129
The Fall River Line - Daoma Winston 6824
A Falling Star - Pamela Belle 431
The Fallon Pride - Reagan O'Neal 4742
The Far Down - Elizabeth Corbett 1321
The Far Side of the Hill - Nancy Livingston 3811
The Fathers - Allen Tate 6171
The Favored Child - Philippa Gregory 2582
Felding Castle - Edith De Born 1552
The Final Adversary - Gilbert Morris 4460
The Fires of July - Sharon Salvato 5576
Fleur - Cynthia Harrod-Eagles 2754
The Flint Anchor - Sylvia Townsend Warner 6569
Forefathers - Nancy Cato 960
Fort Worth - Leonard Sanders 5588
The Fortress - Hugh Walpole 6544
The Fortunate Marriage - Meriol Trevor 6342
The Fountain Overflows - Rebecca West 6639
The Four Swans - Winston Graham 2525
Frederica in Fashion - Marion Chesney 1032
From the Terrace - John O'Hara 4703
The Furies - John Jakes 3146
Galveston - Suzanne Morris 4482
The Gaynor Women - Virginia Coffman 1153
Generations of Winter - Vassily Aksyonov 61
The Gentle Rebel - Gilbert Morris 4461
Give Us This Day - R.F. Delderfield 1586
The Glass-Blowers - Daphne Du Maurier 1745
God Is an Englishman - R.F. Delderfield 1587
The Golden Pharaoh - Peter Danielson 1468
Goldeneye - Malcolm Macdonald 3965
Gower Street - Claire Rayner 5264
The Grandmothers - Glenway Westcott 6640
The Great Alone - Janet Dailey 1454
The Great Blizzard - Albert E. Idell 3101
Green City in the Sun - Barbara Wood 6849
The Hampton Heritage - Julie Ellis 1920
The Hampton Women - Julie Ellis 1921
Hanover Place - Michael M. Thomas 6245
Hanta Yo - Ruth Beebe Hill 2951
Hardacre - C.L. Skelton 5872

The Haversham Legacy - Daoma Winston 6827
Hawaii - James A. Michener 4370
The Haymarket - Claire Rayner 5265
Heart of War - John Masters 4174
Heaven and Hell - John Jakes 3147
Heirs of the Motherland - Judith Pella 4893
Heritage - Lewis Orde 4749
High Towers - Thomas B. Costain 1366
The Hill of Doves - Stuart Cloete 1123
The Holy Warrior - Gilbert Morris 4462
Homecoming - Dana Fuller Ross 5474
Homeland - John Jakes 3148
The Honorable Imposter - Gilbert Morris 4463
A Horseman Riding By - R.F. Delderfield 1588
The Hours of Light - Janet Tanner 6160
The House at Old Vine - Norah Lofts 3845
A House Divided - Michael Phillips 4988
The House of Cray - Pamela Hill 2936
The House of Five Talents - Louis Auchincloss 231
The House That Tai Ming Built - Virginia Lee 3711
Hungry Hill - Daphne Du Maurier 1746
The Immigrants - Howard Fast 2034
The Immigrant's Daughter - Howard Fast 2035
An Imperfect Joy - Jean Stubbs 6097
In Still and Stormy Waters - Reay Tannahill 6157
In the Fire of Spring - Thomas Tryon 6355
In the Wilderness - Sigrid Undset 6381
The Indentured Heart - Gilbert Morris 4464
Inherit the Sun - Maxwell Grant 2539
The Invaders - Peter Danielson 1469
Jarrett's Jade - Frank Yerby 6923
The Jealous House - Clarence Budington Kelland 3390
Jennie Glenroy - Elisabeth Ogilvie 4695
Jubal Sackett - Louis L'Amour 3620
Judith Paris - Hugh Walpole 6545
Kagami - Elizabeth Kata 3369
Katherine Christian - Hugh Walpole 6546
Kilcaraig - Annabel Carothers 904
The King's General - Daphne Du Maurier 1748
King's Royal - John Quigley 5224
Knave of Hearts - Philippa Carr 920
The Land of Our Dreams - Nancy Livingston 3812
The Last Confederate - Gilbert Morris 4466
The Last Gamble - Winston Graham 2527
The Last Waltz - Nancy Zaroulis 6955
The Lawless - John Jakes 3149
Leaving Cold Sassy - Olive Ann Burns 798
The Legacy - Howard Fast 2037
The Legacy of Beulah Land - Lonnie Coleman 1203
The Legacy of Tregaran - Mary Lide 3776
Lighthouse - Eugenia Price 5182
Lindeman's Daughters - Synnove Christensen 1073
The Lion in Egypt - Peter Danielson 1470
The Lion's Way - Lewis Orde 4750
The Lives of Rachel - Joel Gross 2601
The Living Reed - Pearl S. Buck 756
Lonely on the Mountain - Louis L'Amour 3621
Look Away, Beulah Land - Lonnie Coleman 1204
The Lormes of Castle Rising - Fanny Cradock 1409
Louisiana! - Dana Fuller Ross 5478
Love and Honor - Leslie Arlen 189
Love and War - John Jakes 3150
The Lovely Lynchs - Magdalen King-Hall 3490
Lucinda Brayford - Martin Boyd 613
The Maclarens - C.L. Skelton 5873
The Mallen Girl - Catherine Cookson 1280
The Mallen Lot - Catherine Cookson 1281
The Mallen Streak - Catherine Cookson 1282
The Man From Broken Hills - Louis L'Amour 3622
The Marburg Chronicles - Alfred Coppel 1319
The Marigold Field - Diane Pearson 4876
The Marrying Kind - Jessica Stirling 6046
The Mask - Stuart Cloete 1125
Massachusetts: A Novel - Nancy Zaroulis 6956
Master of Morholm - Timothy R. Wilson 6817
The Masters of Bow Street - John Creasy 1423
McKensie's Hundred: A Tale of the Old Dominion - Frank Yerby 6924

Men of Men - Wilbur Smith 5927
Meridon - Philippa Gregory 2583
Miami: A Saga - Evelyn Wilde Mayerson 4204
The Mighty and Their Fall - Ivy Compton-Burnett 1230
The Miller's Dance - Winston Graham 2528
Minerva - Marion Chesney 1037
The Mistress of Husaby - Sigrid Undset 6382
The Moneyman - Judith Liederman 3781
The Moon in the Water - Pamela Belle 433
Morning at Jalna - Mazo de la Roche 1560
Mustang Man - Louis L'Amour 3623
Natchez: A Novel of the Deep South - Pamela Jekel 3186
Never Victorious, Never Defeated - Taylor Caldwell 860
The New England Story - Henry Beetle Hough 3046
The Northern Correspondent - Jean Stubbs 6099
Now, God Be Thanked - John Masters 4177
Of Lizards and Angels: A Saga of Sioux Land - Frederick F. Manfred 4058
Oklahoma Pride - Dana Fuller Ross 5483
One of the Raymonds - Jean Rikhoff 5332
Oregon Legacy - Dana Fuller Ross 5485
Our Father's House - Stephen Longstreet 3890
Pacific Cavalcade - Virginia Coffman 1157
Pacific Destiny - Dana Fuller Ross 5487
Paddington Green - Claire Rayner 5266
Pageant - G.B. Lancaster 3650
Paloverde - Jacqueline Briskin 693
Paradise - Sarah Neilan 4566
Passage West - Dallas Miller 4382
Penhally - Caroline Gordon 2479
The People of Juvik - Olav Dunn 1798
Piccadilly - Claire Rayner 5267
Polonaise - Piers Paul Read 5278
Portrait in Brownstone - Louis Auchincloss 232
The Power of Black - M.B. Longman 3880
The Prescott Chronicles - Albert Fried 2232
The Prince of Eden - Marilyn Harris 2732
The Promised Land - Peter Danielson 1471
The Prophecy - Peter Danielson 1472
The Proud Breed - Celeste De Blasis 1547
Queen's Royal - John Quigley 5225
A Question of Honour - Emma Drummond 1726
The Quickenberry Tree - Annette Motley 4502
The Quincunx - Charles Palliser 4778
Ravenshoe - Henry Kingsley 3500
The Rebels - John Jakes 3152
Red Plush: The Story of the Moorhouse Family - Guy McCrone 4232
Regent Square - Forbes Bramble 645
The Regiment - C.L. Skelton 5874
The Reluctant Bridegroom - Gilbert Morris 4467
Remnants of Glory - Teresa Miller 4403
The Renegade: A Novel of Cornwall, 1783-1787 - Winston Graham 2529
Return of the Stranger - Reay Tannahill 6158
The Rich Are with You Always - Malcolm Macdonald 3971
Ride the Dark Trail - Louis L'Amour 3624
Ride the River - Louis L'Amour 3625
Ride with Me, Mariah Montana - Ivan Doig 1684
Rogers' Folly - Albert E. Idell 3102
Rogue Herries - Hugh Walpole 6547
The Rough Rider - Gilbert Morris 4468
The Sackett Brand - Louis L'Amour 3627
Sackett's Land - Louis L'Amour 3628
The Saintly Buccaneer - Gilbert Morris 4469
The Salamanca Drum - Dorothy Eden 1861
San Antone - V.J. Banis 288
Sarum: The Novel of England - Edward Rutherfurd 5536
Saturday City - Jan Webster 6593
The Savage Brood - Martha Rofheart 5430
Savannah - Eugenia Price 5186
Scarborough House - Sharon Salvato 5577
Scarlett - Alexandra Ripley 5342
The Sea Peoples - Peter Danielson 1474

The Seadon Fortune - Leonard St. Clair 5563
A Season of Swans - Celeste De Blasis 1548
The Seasons of Heroes - Paxton Davis 1539
Seattle Green - Jane Adams 26
Second Generation - Howard Fast 2043
The Seekers - John Jakes 3153
Segu - Maryse Conde 1234
Serpent and Staff - Frank Yerby 6927
Shadows over Castle Rising - Fanny Cradock 1410
The Ship's Clock - Catherine M. Rae 5237
Sierra Triumph - Dana Fuller Ross 5488
Silver Fruit - Patricia Campbell 876
The Sky-Liners - Louis L'Amour 3629
The Smiths - Janet Fairbank 2002
The Snake Pit - Sigrid Undset 6383
Snow-Water - Dorothy Gardiner 2285
The Son Avenger - Sigrid Undset 6384
Song of a Strange Child - Gilbert Morris 4470
The Song of the Siren - Philippa Carr 929
Sons of Fortune - Malcolm Macdonald 3973
Sound of the Trumpet - Gilbert Morris 4471
The Splendor Stays: An Historic Novel Based on the Lives of the Seven Hart Sisters of Saybrook - Marguerite Allis 114
The Spoils of War - Thomas Fleming 2131
Spring Came on Forever - Bess Streeter Aldrich 73
Spring Moon: A Novel of China - Bette Bao Lord 3897
Stand We at Last - Zoe Fairbairns 1999
The Stars of the South - Julian Green 2568
Steamboat Gothic - Frances Parkinson Keyes 3481
The Strand - Claire Rayner 5269
The Stranger From the Sea - Winston Graham 2530
Stranger in Savannah - Eugenia Price 5187
The Sun Is My Undoing - Marguerite Steen 5988
Swan's Chance - Celeste De Blasis 1549
The Sweetwater - Jean Rikhoff 5333
Sword of Glory - Peter Danielson 1477
The Taming of Annabelle - Marion Chesney 1052
The Taverners' Place - Joanna Trollope 6351
Theirs Was the Kingdom - R.F. Delderfield 1590
These Latter Days - Laura Kalpakian 3330
They Were Dreamers - James F. Murphy Jr. 4525
This Is the House - Deborah Hill 2921
This Other Eden - Marilyn Harris 2733
This Splendid Earth - V.J. Banis 289
Those the Sun Has Loved - Rose Jourdain 3309
The Three Black Pennys - Joseph Hergesheimer 2855
Threescore and Ten - Walter Allen 105
The Tides of Malvern - Francis Griswold 2595
Tilly - Catherine Cookson 1288
Tilly Alone - Catherine Cookson 1289
Tilly Wed - Catherine Cookson 1290
Time and Chance - Gwen Davenport 1501
Time and the Wind - Erico Verissimo 6451
Time in Its Flight - Susan Fromberg Schaeffer 5636
Time out of Mind - Rachel Field 2081
The Tin Drum - Gunther Grass 2540
The Titans - John Jakes 3154
To Fell the Giants - Bill Hotchkiss 3038
To See Your Face Again - Eugenia Price 5188
To Serve Them All My Days - R.F. Delderfield 1591
Tolbecken - Samuel Shellabarger 5798
The Tontine - Thomas B. Costain 1371
The Town House - Norah Lofts 3861
Travail and Triumph - Michael Phillips 4991
Treason's Gift - Pamela Belle 434
Treasure Mountain - Louis L'Amour 3631
The Trees of the Folkungs - Verner Von Heidenstam 2817
Tregaran - Mary Lide 3779
Triptych - Dora Landey 3652
True Women - Janice Woods Windle 6820
Trust and Treason - Margaret Birkhead 506
The Twisted Sword - Winston Graham 2531
Vanessa - Hugh Walpole 6548
Vengeance of the Lion - Peter Danielson 1480
Venture Once More - Winston Graham 2532

The Vivian Inheritance - Jean Stubbs 6101
The Wanton Fires - Meriol Trevor 6345
War Comes to Castle Rising - Fanny Cradock 1411
The Warriors - John Jakes 3155
The Warrior's Path - Louis L'Amour 3633
The Wedding Guest - Anna Gilbert 2407
Westfield - Roderick Thorp 6277
Where Shadows Go - Eugenia Price 5189
Wild Swan - Celeste De Blasis 1550
Will You Love Me in September? - Philippa Carr 932
Wind From the Carolinas - Robert Wilder 6751
Wind of Change at Castle Rising - Fanny Cradock 1412
The Wine Widow - Tessa Barclay 301
The Wings of the Morning - Thomas Tryon 6356
Wintercombe - Pamela Belle 435
The Winthrop Covenant - Louis Auchincloss 235
The Wishing Tree - Sandra Paretti 4794
A Woman's Age - Rachel Billington 499
Woman's Own - Robyn Carr 941
The Women of Eden - Marilyn Harris 2734
The Yukon Queen - Gilbert Morris 4476

Fantasy

Alamut - Judith Tarr 6164
Arc d'X - Steve Erickson 1953
Attila's Treasure - Stephan Grundy 2606
The Bloody Red Baron - Kim Newman 4596
Bronze Mirror - Jeanne Larsen 3668
The Centurion - Jan de Hartog 2762
A Connecticut Yankee in King Arthur's Court - Mark Twain 6371
The Death of Napoleon - Simon Leys 3768
Di and I - Peter Lefcourt 3714
The Dragon Waiting: A Masque of History - John M. Ford 2165
Empire of the Eagle - Andre Norton 4649
The End of the World News - Anthony Burgess 777
Eva - Ib Melchior 4329
The Fabulist - John Vornholt 6512
Family - J. California Cooper 1297
Fire Opal - Pamela Hill 2932
For the Love of Robert E. Lee - M.A. Harper 2715
The Forest House - Marion Zimmer Bradley 625
Frankenstein Unbound - Brian Aldiss 68
Gilgamesh the King - Robert Silverberg 5853
The Golden Nineties - Lisa Mason 4166
The Guns of the South - Harry N. Turtledove 6367
Hercules, My Shipmate - Robert Graves 2545
Homer's Daughter - Robert Graves 2546
The Horse Goddess - Morgan Llywelyn 3820
Horses of Heaven - Gillian Bradshaw 630
Invisible Cities - Italo Calvino 867
Isle of Woman - Piers Anthony 167
The Jaguar Princess - Clare Bell 421
Joy in Mudville - Gordon McAlpine 4216
The King - Donald Barthelme 365
The Lighthouse at the End of the World - Stephen Marlowe 4095
Live From Golgotha - Gore Vidal 6491
The Lost Years: A Biographical Fiction - Oscar Lewis 3757
The Man Who Thought He Was Messiah - Curt Leviant 3735
The Memory Cathedral: A Secret History of Leonardo Da Vinci - Jack Dann 1481
The Nazarene - Sholem Asch 200
A Night with Casanova - Wolf Mankowitz 4060
No Man's Land - William Fairchild 2004
On Stranger Tides - Tim Powers 5156
Orlando - Virginia Woolf 6866
Peter Doyle - John Vernon 6457
Peter Ibbetson - George Du Maurier 1750
The Place of Dead Roads - William S. Burroughs 808
The Queen and I - Sue Townsend 6306
Rhinegold - Stephan Grundy 2607

Serenissima: A Novel of Venice - Erica Jong 3300
Shame of Man - Piers Anthony 168
The Stress of Her Regard - Tim Powers 5157
Two Crowns for America - Katherine Kurtz 3568
The Wolf and the Raven - Diana L. Paxson 4848

Farming

Artillery of Time - Chard Powers Smith 5919
Blue Camellia - Frances Parkinson Keyes 3477
Brothers Three - John Oskison 4764
Caddie Woodlawn - Carol Brink 692
Call of the Mountains - Cornelia Meigs 4326
Country People - Ruth Suckow 6111
The Earth Abideth - George Dell 1595
The Edge of Time - Loula Grace Erdman 1949
The Emigrants - Vilhelm Moberg 4422
Free Land - Rose Lane 3660
Gentlemen From England - Maude Hart Lovelace 3905
Gold Is Where You Find It - Clements Ripley 5345
Golden Horizons - William Corcoran 1324
The Great Hunger - Johan Bojer 562
The Hawkeye - Herbert Quick 5222
Here I Stay - Elizabeth Coatsworth 1138
Last Letter Home - Vilhelm Moberg 4423
The Marriage Bed - Jean Clark 1088
Of Lizards and Angels: A Saga of Sioux Land - Frederick F. Manfred 4058
One Small Candle - Mary Linehan MacKinnon 3998
Patience and Sarah - Isabel Miller 4398
The Perilous Night - Burke Boyce 609
The Plums Hang High - Gertrude E. Finney 2091
Samuel Drummond - Thomas Alexander Boyd 614
The Sea Scape - Mary Lide 3778
The Settlers - Vilhelm Moberg 4424
She Rode a Yellow Stallion - Walter Reed 5286
The Truest Pleasure - Robert Morgan 4452
Trumpets Calling - Dora Aydelotte 248
The Unplowed Sky - Jeanne Williams 6783
An Untamed Land - Lauraine Snelling 5936
Unto a Good Land - Vilhelm Moberg 4425
The Women at Pine Creek - Allis McKay 4279

Fashion Industry

Banners of Silk - Rosalind Laker 3592
Cashmere - Nicola Thorne 6273
The House of Eliott - Jean Marsh 4100
Union Square - Meredith Tax 6176
A Woman by Design - Frances Kennett 3426

Fenians

Chase Royal - Donald Seaman 5712
A Nest of Simple Folk - Sean O'Faolain 4692
The Rising of the Moon - Peter Berresford Ellis 1926
Scarlett - Alexandra Ripley 5342
Stranger in Two Worlds - Hugh Clevely 1111
The Tenants of Time - Thomas Flanagan 2120
Through the Green Valley - Barbara Gowdy 2498

Fetterman Massacre

Carrington - Michael Whitney Straight 6074

Feuds

Arne - Bjornstjerne Bjornson 518
The Braeswood Tapestry - Robyn Carr 936
Clandara - Evelyn Anthony 161
Dark Torrent of Glencoe - Edward Grierson 2590
The New England Story - Henry Beetle Hough 3046
The Pointless Knife - Constance Dodge 1667
The Sutburys - Pamela Hill 2944
Tree of Gold - Rosalind Laker 3602
A Woman Scorned - Malcolm Macdonald 3978

Fires

Afterward - Catherine M. Rae   5234
Firewind - Bill Pronzini   5200
Flight From Fifth Avenue - Catherine M. Rae   5235
Forever Amber - Kathleen Winsor   6822
A Health Unto His Majesty - Jean Plaidy   5019
Illinois! - Dana Fuller Ross   5475
Lament for a Lost Lover - Philippa Carr   921
Masters of Illusion: A Novel of the Connecticut Circus Fire - Mary-Ann Tirone Smith   5925
Mistress of the Boards - Richard Sumner   6118
My Lady Benbrook - Constance Gluyas   2442
My Sister's Keeper - Beverly Butler   817
Old St. Paul's - William Harrison Ainsworth   57
Our Jo, or The Chronicle of a Coming Man - Kenneth M. Cameron   868
Rivers Parting - Shirley Barker   315
Stranger in Two Worlds - Hugh Clevely   1111

Fishing

Ben Retallick - E.V. Thompson   6263
Eye of the Hurricane - Fergus Reid Buckley   757
The Free Fishers - John Buchan   750
The Last of the Vikings - Johan Bojer   563
Shad Run - Howard Breslin   668

Flodden, Battle of

Falcon: The Autobiography of His Grace James IV, King of Scots - A.J. Stewart   6021

Fontenoy, Battle of

A Day of Battle - Vincent Sheean   5787
Pope Joan - Donna Woolfolk Cross   1433

Forgery

Chatterton - Peter Ackroyd   17

Fort Duquesne, Battle of

Juniata Valley - Virginia C. Cassel   954

Fort Pillow, Battle of

The Falling Hills - Perry Lentz   3720

Franco-Prussian War

The Blood Endures - Robert Inman   3107
Cesar and Augusta - Ronald Harwood   2771
Charlotte Morel: The Siege - Maria Lodi   3831
Daughter of Marignac - Constance Heaven   2805
The Demon Lover - Victoria Holt   3013
Falkenhorst - Mark Rascovich   5254
The Far-Off Rhapsody - Anne-Marie Sheridan   5808
Illinois! - Dana Fuller Ross   5475
Madeleine - Catherine Gavin   2323
On the Night of the Seventh Moon - Victoria Holt   3018
Quiet Lady - Norman Collins   1216
A Rage Against Heaven - Fred Mustard Stewart   6026
The Scandalous Mrs. Blackford - Harriet Kane   3358
A Spy for Napoleon - Baroness Emma Orczy   4746
Sweet Songbird - Teresa Crane   1418
Vale of Tyranny - Suzanne Butler   831
Vardy - John Harris   2721
The Wine Widow - Tessa Barclay   301
Winter of the Heart - Linda J. LaRosa   3665
Wisconsin! - Dana Fuller Ross   5493

Franklin, Battle of

The Bright Sword - Eleanor Perenyi   4911
Night March - Bruce Lancaster   3641

Fredericksburg, Battle of

Gods and Generals - Jeff Shaara   5765
Joy From Ashes - Al Lacy   3581
The River and the Wilderness - Don Robertson   5401

Free Soil Movement

Free Soil - Margaret Lynn   3943
The Sun Shines West - Nathan Schachner   5632
Wind Like a Bugle - Leonard Nathan   3722

French and Indian War

Ambush - Donald Clayton Porter   5113
Bloodbrothers - Robert E. Wall   6535
The Bright Battalions - Howard Breslin   664
The Conqueror - John William Tebbel   6194
The Deerslayer - James Fenimore Cooper   1299
The Double Man - Elinor Pryor   5205
Drums Against Frontenac - Harvey Chalmers   972
Eagle Fur - Robert Newton Peck   4884
Eden's Gate - Karen Harper   2711
Edge of Greatness - Winthrop Neilson   4575
Fawn - Robert Newton Peck   4885
Fire Along the Sky: A Novel of America - Robert Moss   4497
The Firekeeper - Robert Moss   4498
The First Rebel - Neil Harmon Swanson   6137
Follow the River - James Alexander Thom   6231
The Forest and the Fort - Hervey Allen   100
Gennie the Huguenot Woman - Bette M. Ross   5464
Gentleman Ranker - John Edward Jennings   3200
Ghost Fox - James Houston   3051
The Golden Wildcat - Margaret Widdemer   6735
The Governor's Daughter - Denton Whitson   6718
The Great Valley - Mary Johnston   3234
Hatchet in the Sky - Margaret Cooper Gay   2328
The Highwayman - Noel B. Gerson   2372
His Majesty's Highlanders - Leslie Turner White   6683
The Indentured Heart - Gilbert Morris   4464
The Interpreter - Robert Moss   4499
The Invincibles - Carter A. Vaughan   6436
Jason McGee - Robert H. Fowler   2190
Juniata Valley - Virginia C. Cassel   954
The Last of the Mohicans - James Fenimore Cooper   1302
Lord Vanity - Samuel Shellabarger   5796
The Marriage Bed - Jean Clark   1088
The Measure of the Years - Alice Mary Colver   1218
Morning of a Hero - Burke Boyce   608
Next to Valour - John Edward Jennings   3202
Northwest Passage - Kenneth Roberts   5388
O Beulah Land - Mary Lee Settle   5756
The Pathfinder; or, The Inland Sea - James Fenimore Cooper   1305
The Plains of Abraham - James Oliver Curwood   1452
Prince Charlie's Bluff - Donald Thomas   6241
Red Morning - Ruby Frazier Frey   2230
The Red Road: A Romance of Braddock's Defeat - Hugh Pendexter   4898
The Renegade - Donald Clayton Porter   5122
Renno - Donald Clayton Porter   5123
Restless Are the Sails - Evelyn Eaton   1830
The Sachem - Donald Clayton Porter   5124
The Silver Saber - Carter A. Vaughan   6441
Song of the Susquehanna - Herbert Stover   6071
Tavern in the Town - Cecile Hulse Matschat   4187
This Land Is Ours - Louis Zara   6953
Thunder in the East - Mike Roarke   5362
To Fame Unknown - Clifford Lindsey Alderman   67

Tomahawk - Donald Clayton Porter   5129
The Virginians - William Makepeace Thackeray   6214
War Cry - Donald Clayton Porter   5132
War in the Golden Weather - Stephen Longstreet   3892
War Paint and Rouge - Robert W. Chambers   983
Web of Destiny - Muriel Elwood   1939
The White Cockade - Vincent O'Brien   4683
The Wilderness - Carter A. Vaughan   6442
Wilderness Empire - Allen W. Eckert   1847
The Willing Maid - C.T. Ritchie   5349
The Woodsman - Don Wright   6880
Yankee Rogue - Dana Fuller Ross   5496
The Young Man From Mount Vernon - Arthur Stanwood Pier   4995
Young Titan - F. van Wyck Mason   4165

French Colonies

All Souls' Rising - Madison Smartt Bell   422
Black Triumvirate: A Novel of Haiti - Benjamin H. Levin   3736
A Bride for New Orleans - Edward Francis Murphy   4522
Caribee - Christopher Nicole   4614
The Children of Segu - Maryse Conde   1232
Hawk of Detroit - Arthur Pound   5145
Louisiana Purchase - A.E. Hotchner   3039
Ride the Red Earth - Paul I. Wellman   6620
Roger Sudden - Thomas H. Raddall   5232
Saigon - Anthony Grey   2588
Shadows on the Rock - Willa Cather   959
This Widowed Land - Kathleen O'Neal Gear   2331

French Foreign Legion

Under Two Flags - Ouida   4767

French Revolution

As Runs the Glass - Evan John David   1502
Asylum for the Queen - Mildred A. Jordan   3303
The Black Consul - Anatolii Vinogradov   6503
The Black Moon - Winston Graham   2522
Blake's Reach - Catherine Gaskin   2313
The Brittle Glass - Norah Lofts   3837
Brumaire - Mark Logan   3864
A Chance for Glory - Constance Wright   6877
Citizen Tom Paine - Howard Fast   2028
City of Darkness, City of Light - Marge Piercy   4998
Claire - Elizabeth Lyle   3931
Cockades: A Romance - Meade Minnigerode   4412
The Colors of Vaud - Bryher   741
The Dark Palazzo - Virginia Coffman   1151
The Devil on Horseback - Victoria Holt   3014
The Devil's Laughter - Frank Yerby   6913
Dr. Guillotine: The Eccentric Exploits of an Early Scientist - Herbert Lom   3867
Drums at Dusk - Arna Bontemps   575
The Eagle and the Rock - Frances Winwar   6830
Enemy in Sight! - Alexander Kent   3429
The Fallen Angels - Susannah Kells   3397
Farewell the Tranquil - R.F. Delderfield   1585
The Fatal Friendship: Marie Antoinette, Count Fersen and the Flight to Varennes - Stanley Loomis   3895
Fear No More - Hester W. Chapman   990
The Flag Captain - Alexander Kent   3430
Form Line of Battle! - Alexander Kent   3431
The Frenchwoman - Jeanne Mackin   3995
The Glass-Blowers - Daphne Du Maurier   1745
The Gods Are Thirsty - Tanith Lee   3710
The Golden Harlot - Jeanne Wilson   6808
Guillotine - Mark Logan   3865
Harp of a Thousand Strings - Harold Lenoir Davis   1522
Hawthorn Hill - Doris Shannon   5777
Heroic Dust - Theodora Dehon   1581

Hester - Brian Cleeve   1107
H.M.S. Cockerel - Dewey Lambdin   3611
I Thee Wed - Gilbert Wolf Gabriel   2267
If This Be Magic - Ellen Marsh   4098
The Incorruptible - Marjorie Coryn   1357
The Incorruptible - Helma De Bois   1551
The Ironmaster - Anne Powers   5150
Kate - Brian Cleeve   1109
A King Reluctant - William Vaughan Wilkins   6759
King's Masque - Evan John   3220
Lady of Paris - William Vaughan Wilkins   6760
Lord Libertine - Anthony Esler   1964
The Man Who Killed the King - Dennis
    Wheatley   6654
Marie Antoinette - F.W. Kenyon   3453
The Marquis and Miss Jones - Helen Ashfield   208
The Marriage of Josephine - Marjorie Coryn   1358
Master-At-Arms - Rafael Sabatini   5553
Mirabeau, Lover and Stateman - Pierre
    Nezelof   4606
Mistress of Fortune - Sheila Lancaster   3651
Monsieur Yankee - Leslie Turner White   6689
Nethergate - Norah Lofts   3854
Palaces of Desire - Kate Alexander   81
A Place of Greater Safety - Hilary Mantel   4077
The Porcelain Dove - Delia Sherman   5815
The Prince Lost to Time - Ann Dukthas   1776
The Prisoners of September - Leon Garfield   2294
The Private Adventures of Captain Shaw - Edith
    Shay   5783
The Queen's Confession - Victoria Holt   3019
Rasero - Francisco Rebolledo   5282
The Riven Heart - Genevieve Gennari   2354
*The Rose of Malmaison: The Turbulent Life of the
    Beautiful Josephine* - Gaby von Schonthan   5660
Scaramouche - Rafael Sabatini   5554
Scaramouche the King-Maker - Rafael Sabatini   5555
The Scarlet Pimpernel - Baroness Emma Orczy   4745
Seed of Mischief - Willa Gibbs   2401
The Smile of the Stranger - Joan Aiken   53
Storm Winds - Iris Johansen   3217
The Sugar Pavilion - Rosalind Laker   3600
Sweet Marie-Antoinette - Lozania Prole   5198
A Tale of Two Cities - Charles Dickens   1642
Tallien: A Brief Romance - Frederic Tuten   6370
This Other Eden - Marilyn Harris   2733
To Dance with Kings - Rosalind Laker   3601
To Spit Against the Wind - Benjamin H. Levin   3737
To the End of the World - Helen Constance
    White   6680
Tricolour - Mark Logan   3866
The Twelfth Physician - Willa Gibbs   2403
The Uncrowned King - Baroness Emma Orczy   4747
La Vendee - Anthony Trollope   6346
Veronique - Virginia Coffman   1158
Vindication - Frances Sherwood   5824
The Way to the Lantern - Audrey Erskine
    Lindop   3790
The White Cockade - Charles James Louis
    Gilson   2423
The White Cockade - Henry Farrand Griffin   2592
The Wild Ohio - Bart Spicer   5966
The Wind From the Sea - Constance Heaven   2812
Windover - Jane Aiken Hodge   2974

Friendship

The Book Class - Louis Auchincloss   228

Frigidus, Battle of the

The Last Romans - Teodor Jeske-Choinski   3216

The Fronde

Twenty Years After - Alexandre Dumas   1783

Frontier—Africa

Another Country - Karel Schoeman   5646
Articles of Faith - Ronald Harwood   2770
Burton and Speke - William Harrison   2751
The City of Gold - Francis Brett Young   6940
The Covenant - James A. Michener   4368
The Fiercest Heart - Stuart Cloete   1122
The Final Adversary - Gilbert Morris   4460
The Great Sky and the Silence - James S. Rand   5245
Harvest of the Sun - E.V. Thompson   6265
The Hill of Doves - Stuart Cloete   1123
Kenya - John Halkin   2645
King of the Bastards - Sarah Gertrude Millin   4405
Lion in the Evening - Alan Scholefield   5656
Lord of the Kongo - Peter Forbath   2155
The Mask - Stuart Cloete   1125
Men of Men - Wilbur Smith   5927
Rough Diamond - Robert L. Fish   2098
They Seek a Country - Francis Brett Young   6941
The Turning Wheels - Stuart Cloete   1127
Watch for the Dawn - Stuart Cloete   1128
Water Music - T. Coraghessan Boyle   619
Westward the Sun - Brigid Knight   3524
The Whales in Lake Tanganyika - Lennart
    Hagerfors   2636
When the Lion Feeds - Wilbur Smith   5931
Wild Conquest - Peter Abrahams   12
Wild Dog Running - Alan Scholefield   5658

Frontier—Alaska

Heaven Is Too High - Mildred Masterson
    McNeilly   4309

Frontier—Australia

The Adventurers - William Stuart Long   3869
And the Wild Birds Sing - Lola Irish   3112
Beyond the Blue Mountains - Jean Plaidy   5006
Botany Bay - Charles Nordhoff   4637
Cry of the Rain Bird - Patricia Shaw   5779
Dream Time - Parris Afton Bonds   570
The Dreaming: A Novel of Australia - Barbara
    Wood   6848
The Emancipist: An Unforgettable Epic of Australia -
    Veronica Geoghegan Sweeney   6147
The Explorers - William Stuart Long   3872
The Feather and the Stone - Patricia Shaw   5780
Forefathers - Nancy Cato   960
The Gallant - William Stuart Long   3873
The Gold Seekers - William Stuart Long   3874
Harry: A Novel of Australia - Robert Wales   6530
The Heart of the Continent - Nancy Cato   961
I Know My Love - Catherine Gaskin   2315
The Imperialists - William Stuart Long   3875
Inherit the Sun - Maxwell Grant   2539
The Ladies of Missalonghi - Colleen
    McCullough   4237
Pageant - G.B. Lancaster   3650
The Playmaker - Thomas Keneally   3414
The Pool of St. Branok - Philippa Carr   926
A River Town - Thomas Keneally   3415
The Settlers - William Stuart Long   3878
Southern Cross - Terry Coleman   1206
Storm of Time - Eleanor Dark   1494
Swandowne - Daniel Farson   2024
The Timeless Land - Eleanor Dark   1495
To the Ends of the Earth - Michael Talbot   6155
The Traitors - William Stuart Long   3879
The Vines of Yarrabee - Dorothy Eden   1864
Voss - Patrick White   6698
Where the Willows Weep - Patricia Shaw   5781
Wild Orchid - Isabel Dick   1640
A Wilful Woman - Michael Talbot   6156
The Wisdom of Stones - Greg Matthews   4192

Frontier—Brazil

Sage of Canudos - Lucien Marchal   4080

Frontier—Canada

Angelique and the Ghosts - Sergeanne Golon   2467
Black Robe - Brian Moore   4441
Blackrobe - Robert E. Wall   6534
Deeper the Heritage - Muriel Elwood   1936
Fire in the Sky - J.A. Shears   5785
The Fur Masters - Alan Sullivan   6113
Ghost Fox - James Houston   3051
Greenyards - Joan Lingard   3796
The Half Breed - Maurice Constantin-Weyer   1261
Heritage of the River - Muriel Elwood   1937
Julia's Last Hope - Janette Oke   4708
The Kidnapped Surgeon - Alexander Knox   3527
The Kingdom Carver - E.G. Perrault   4916
Paradise - Sarah Neilan   4566
Pemmican - Vardis Fisher   2111
Quietly My Captain Waits - Evelyn Eaton   1829
River and Empty Sea - Louis Vaczek   6396
Running West - James Houston   3052
Shadows on the Rock - Willa Cather   959
The Strange Brigade - John Edward Jennings   3209
They Called Her Mrs. Doc - Janette Oke   4709
Three Came to Ville Marie - Alan Sullivan   6114
Too Long a Stranger - Janette Oke   4710
A Woman Named Damaris - Janette Oke   4711

Frontier—New Zealand

Aurora Rose - Anne Worboys   6870
Greenstone - Yvonne Kalman   3324
An Important Family - Dorothy Eden   1855
Mists of Heaven - Yvonne Kalman   3325

Fur Trade

Ashana - E.P. Roesch   5424

Gabriel's Insurrection

Black Thunder - Arna Bontemps   574

Gallic War

The Conquered - Naomi Mitchison   4418
Gaul Is Divided - Esther Fisher Brown   721

Gallipoli, Battle of

1915: A Novel - Roger McDonald   4264
Redemption - Leon Uris   6393

Gambling

Vice Avenged: A Moral Tale - Lolah Burford   774

Gay Nineties

The Big Stick - Lawrence Alexander   82
Speak Softly - Lawrence Alexander   83
The Strenuous Life - Lawrence Alexander   84
Tenderloin - Samuel Hopkins Adams   33

Gempei Wars

The Sword of Hachiman - Lynn Guest   2608

Georgian Period

Adam Bede - George Eliot   1908
The Adulteress - Philippa Carr   916
Angelica - Samuel A. Schreiner Jr.   5671
The Angry Tide - Winston Graham   2521

Antipodes Jane: A Novel of Jane Austen in Australia - Barbara Ker Wilson 3468

Ask Me No Questions - Patricia Veryan 6459

Barnaby Rudge: A Tale of the Riots of Eighty - Charles Dickens 1641

Bed in Hell - Elfrida Vipont 6504

Benjamin Franklin and a Case of Artful Murder - Robert Lee Hall 2654

Benjamin Franklin and a Case of Christmas Murder - Robert Lee Hall 2655

Benjamin Franklin Takes the Case - Robert Lee Hall 2656

The Black Moon - Winston Graham 2522

The Black Moth - Georgette Heyer 2877

Blind Justice - Bruce Alexander 76

The Bonnet Laird's Daughter - Barbara Annandale 154

Brimstone Club - F. van Wyck Mason 4147

By Our Beginnings - Jean Stubbs 6092

Captain Bolton's Corpse - J.G. Jeffreys 3178

Captain Nash and the Honour of England - Ragan Butler 827

The Case of Kitty Ogilvie - Jean Stubbs 6093

Cherished Enemy - Patricia Veryan 6460

The Cherished Wives - Valerie Anand 126

Commander of the Mists - D.L. Murray 4527

The Convenient Marriage - Georgette Heyer 2882

Cousin Susannah - Hazel Hucker 3066

The Dedicated Villain - Patricia Veryan 6461

Demelza - Winston Graham 2524

Devil's Cub - Georgette Heyer 2885

Dr. Johnson's Dear Mistress - Winifred Carter 948

The Drayton Legacy - Rona Randall 5247

East Indiaman - Frank Pollard 5087

Eugene Aram - Edward Bulwer-Lytton 766

The Favored Child - Philippa Gregory 2582

The Flight of the Heron - Dorothy Kathleen Broster 710

Footman in Powder - Helen Ashton 216

The Four Swans - Winston Graham 2525

Freedom's Way - Theodora McCormick Du Bois 1742

Gilded Splendour - Rosalind Laker 3595

Goddess of the Green Room - Jean Plaidy 5016

The Golden Harlot - Jeanne Wilson 6808

Had We Never Loved - Patricia Veryan 6463

Hand of Glory - Glen Petrie 4980

Hangman's Cliff - Robert Neill 4570

Heir to Polventon - Marjorie Watson 6583

Heiress of Ardara - Margaret Evans Porter 5137

His Majesty's Highwayman - Donald Barr Chidsey 1061

I Came to the Highlands: A Novel of Suspense - Velda Johnston 3263

An Imperfect Joy - Jean Stubbs 6097

Jamaica Inn - Daphne Du Maurier 1747

Jane and the Unpleasantness at Scargrave Manor - Stephanie Barron 356

Journey to Enchantment - Patricia Veryan 6464

Judith - Brian Cleeve 1108

Lancet - Garet Rogers 5431

Lantern for the Dark - Jessica Stirling 6045

The Last Gamble - Winston Graham 2527

Lempriere's Dictionary - Lawrence Norfolk 4641

Lord Fancy - Leslie Turner White 6686

Lord Johnnie - Leslie Turner White 6687

Lord Libertine - Anthony Esler 1964

Lord Vanity - Samuel Shellabarger 5796

Love Alters Not - Patricia Veryan 6467

Loving Sands, Deadly Sands - Charlotte Keppel 3465

The Masqueraders - Georgette Heyer 2894

Master of Morholm - Timothy R. Wilson 6817

The Michaelmas Tree - Helen Ashfield 209

Midnight Moon - Jeanne Montague 4436

Midwinter - John Buchan 751

Miss Philadelphia Smith - Paula Allardyce 91

Mistress of Willowvale - Patricia Veryan 6471

Monsieur Janvier - Elizabeth Linington 3799

A Most Extraordinary Pair - Jean Detre 1628

Murder at Drury Lane - Robert Lee Hall 2659

Murder by the Waters - Robert Lee Hall 2661

Murder in Grub Street - Bruce Alexander 77

My Grand Enemy - Jean Stubbs 6098

My Name Is Clary Brown - Charlotte Keppel 3466

The Near and Distant Place - Patricia Wright 6883

Never Doubt I Love - Patricia Veryan 6473

A New Creature - Prudence Andrew 141

The Ninth Statue - Roseleen Milne 4410

Now Face to Face - Karleen Koen 3530

The Peacock's Feather - Sarah Woodhouse 6855

Peg Woffington - Charles Reade 5281

Perdita's Prince - Jean Plaidy 5040

Playing the Jack - Mary Brown 726

The Pleasure Garden - Leon Garfield 2293

Practice to Deceive - Patricia Veryan 6475

A Prince, a Piper, and a Rose - John Scalzo 5628

The Prince and the Quakeress - Jean Plaidy 5043

The Princess of Celle - Jean Plaidy 5045

Put Off Thy Shoes - Ethel Lillian Voynich 6513

Queen in Waiting - Jean Plaidy 5048

The Renegade: A Novel of Cornwall, 1783-1787 - Winston Graham 2529

Ruby - Helen Ashfield 213

A Season of Mists - Sarah Woodhouse 6856

The Seven Ages - Eva Figes 2084

A Shadow's Bliss - Patricia Veryan 6477

The Silver Highways - Malcolm Macdonald 3972

Starbelow - China Thompson 6248

The Sun Is My Undoing - Marguerite Steen 5988

Swear by Apollo - Shirley Barker 318

Sweet Lass of Richmond Hill - Jean Plaidy 5067

The Talisman Ring - Georgette Heyer 2905

The Tempestuous Petticoat - Mary Ann Gibbs 2397

These Old Shades - Georgette Heyer 2906

The Thieftaker - J.G. Jeffreys 3180

The Third George - Jean Plaidy 5068

Time's Fool - Patricia Veryan 6479

The Tyrant - Patricia Veryan 6480

The Unknown Shore - Patrick O'Brian 4678

The Upstart - Edison Marshall 4112

The Vast Memory of Love - Malcolm Bosse 588

Venture Once More - Winston Graham 2532

Vice Avenged: A Moral Tale - Lolah Burford 774

Vindication - Frances Sherwood 5824

The Volcano Lover - Susan Sontag 5946

The Wagered Widow - Patricia Veryan 6481

Walford's Oak - Jill M. Phillips 4986

Watery Grave - Bruce Alexander 78

The Weeping Ash - Joan Aiken 54

A Wicked Way to Die - J.G. Jeffreys 3182

Wideacre - Philippa Gregory 2585

Wild Geese - Eilis Dillon 1647

Windover - Jane Aiken Hodge 2974

The Woman from The Glen - Chloe Gartner 2310

Wonder of All the Gay World - James Barke 306

The Year of the French - Thomas Flanagan 2121

Young Pitt - A.M. Maughan 4200

Gettysburg, Battle of

The Barefoot Brigade - Douglas C. Jones 3274

Carriage Trade - Robert Thomsen 6271

Copperhead Moon - Herbert Stover 6067

The Court Martial of Robert E. Lee - Douglas Savage 5617

A Court of Owls - Richard Adicks 37

For Us the Living - Antonia Van-Loon 6424

Gettysburg - Stephen Longstreet 3887

Gettysburg: Crisis of Command - Harry Albright 65

Gray Victory - Robert Skimin 5877

Hard Road to Gettysburg - Ted Jones 3298

The History of Rome Hanks - Joseph Stanley Pennell 4909

House Divided - Ben Ames Williams 6765

Jubilee - John Brick 672

The Killer Angels - Michael Shaara 5766

Long Remember - MacKinlay Kantor 3362

Look Away - Harold Coyle 1395

Loving Heart - Elsie Singmaster 5869

The President's Daughter - Barbara Chase-Riboud 1005

The Scarlet Guidon - Ray Grant Toepfer 6287

The Scarlet Patch - Bruce Lancaster 3645

Spanish Gold - Kevin O. Randle 5252

The Stonewall Brigade: A Novel of the American Civil War - Frank G. Slaughter 5902

Swords of Steel - Elsie Singmaster 5870

Three Days - Stephen Longstreet 3891

The Three Days - Don Robertson 5402

Time of Drums - John Ehle 1897

Gilded Age

The Adventure of the Stalwart Companions - H. Paul Jeffers 3177

Death on the Cliff Walk - Mary Kruger 3562

No Honeymoon for Death - Mary Kruger 3564

Pride's Castle - Frank Yerby 6925

Time and Again - Jack Finney 2093

Voyage: A Novel of 1896 - Sterling Hayden 2798

Gladiators

Spartacus - Howard Fast 2044

Glencoe Massacre

Dark Torrent of Glencoe - Edward Grierson 2590

Lady of the Glen - Jennifer Roberson 5369

Glorieta, Battle of

The Devil Gun - William Syers 6148

Glorious Revolution

The Glory and the Dream - F.W. Kenyon 3450

James, by the Grace of God - Hugh Williamson Ross 5499

King's Agent - Justus Kent Clark 1090

Lillibullero - Robert Neill 4571

The Queen's Husband - Samuel Edwards 1889

Treason's Gift - Pamela Belle 434

Gold Rush—Africa

When the Lion Feeds - Wilbur Smith 5931

Gold Rush—California

The Adventure of "Horse" Barnsby - Philip D. Stong 6065

The American River - Gary McCarthy 4222

The Argonauts - Yvonne Schoell 5645

Birthright - Phillip Finch 2087

Bound for the Promised Land - Richard Marius 4083

Calico Palace - Gwen Bristow 694

California! - Dana Fuller Ross 5467

The Californian - Todhunter Ballard 284

Cannibal Eliot and the Lost Histories of San Francisco - Hilton Obenzinger 4660

Captain Sutter's Gold - Jonreed Lauritzen 3673

Certain People of Importance - Kathleen Norris 4647

Christopher Strange - Ruth Eleanor McKee 4281

Devilseed - Frank Yerby 6914

The Dream Ends in Fury - Samuel Anthony Peeples 4889

Eagles Fly West - Edward Maddin Ainsworth 55

East of the Giants - George Rippey Stewart 6027

Fortune, Smile Once More - Mary Floyd
    Williams 6788
Forty Pounds of Gold - Philip D. Stong 6066
The Further Adventures of Huckleberry Finn - Greg
    Matthews 4189
Gold Is Where You Find It - Clements Ripley 5345
Golden Destiny - June Wyndham Davies 1506
Gringo Gold - Dane Coolidge 1293
The House That Tai Ming Built - Virginia Lee 3711
John Barry - Donald F. Bedford 412
My Father's World - Michael Phillips 4989
Night Wind - Roberta Jean Mountjoy 4504
Oh Glittering Promise - Anne Fisher 2099
Old Misery - Hugh Pendexter 4896
Pacific Street - Cecelia Holland 2993
Pinto and Sons - Leslie Epstein 1947
Samuel Brannan and the Golden Fleece - Reva
    Scott 5686
Tarnished Angel - Phyllis Leonard 3723
Tide of Empire - Peter S. Kyne 3572
The Treasure of Pleasant Valley - Frank Yerby 6928

Gold Rush—Klondike

Alaska - James A. Michener 4364
Days of the Gold - Irwin R. Blacker 526
Fools' Gold - Richard Wiley 6755
The Goldseekers - William R. Burnett 794
The Great Alone - Janet Dailey 1454
Journey - James A. Michener 4371
Pacific Destiny - Dana Fuller Ross 5487
Princess Sophia - Edison Marshall 4110
Rivers of Gold - Janet Edmonds 1868
The Summer of Jack London - Andrew J.
    Fenady 2058
Tara Kane - George Markstein 4091
Tomorrow's Dream - Peggy Hanchar 2674
The Winter Wolf: Wyatt Earp in Alaska - Richard
    Parry 4820
The Yukon Queen - Gilbert Morris 4476

Gordon Riots

Barnaby Rudge: A Tale of the Riots of Eighty -
    Charles Dickens 1641

Gothic Romance

The Black Dwarf - Sir Walter Scott 5692
Bride of Ae - Pamela Hill 2928
The Brocken - Pamela Hill 2929
The Captive - Victoria Holt 3011
Count Manifred - Miranda Seymour 5761
The Cross of Frankenstein - Robert J. Myers 4548
The Dark Palazzo - Virginia Coffman 1151
Dark Winds - Virginia Coffman 1152
Doubting Castle - Rebecca Kavaler 3373
Dragonmede - Rona Randall 5246
Dragonwyck - Anya Seton 5750
A Falcon for a Queen - Catherine Gaskin 2314
Frankenstein Unbound - Brian Aldiss 68
The Heatherton Heritage - Pamela Hill 2934
Limmerston Hall - Hester W. Chapman 991
Lord Raven's Widow - Leslie O'Grady 4700
Loving Sands, Deadly Sands - Charlotte
    Keppel 3465
Luise - Dawn Stewart Field 2079
The Memoirs of Elizabeth Frankenstein - Theodore
    Roszak 5508
Midsummer Masque - Jill Tattersall 6174
The Monk - Matthew Gregory Lewis 3756
The Secret Life of Laszlo, Count Dracula - Roderick
    Anscombe 156
The Slave of Frankenstein - Robert J. Myers 4549
Somewhere Within This House - Jean Francis
    Webb 6587
This Dark Monarchy - Francis W. Leary 3698

The Villains: A Haunting Tale of the Marshes -
    Charlotte Keppel 3467
The Witch From the Sea - Philippa Carr 933

Governor's Rebellion

The Chant of Jimmie Blacksmith - Thomas
    Keneally 3411

Great Trek

Wild Conquest - Peter Abrahams 12

Greco-Turkish War

The Ashes of Smyrna - Richard Reinhardt 5294
Beyond the Aegean - Elia Kazan 3382

Gunpowder Plot

Scapegoat for a Stuart - Kate Kirby 3504

Gypsies

Beyond the Shadowlands - Georgina Fleming 2126
Grounds for Murder - Kate Kingsbury 3494
Guy Mannering - Sir Walter Scott 5697
The Gypsy From Cadiz - Tamsin Hamilton 2670
The Hunchback of Notre Dame - Victor Hugo 3076
Norah - Pamela Hill 2941
Phantom - Susan Kay 3375
The Return of the Gypsy - Philippa Carr 927
Spangle - Gary Jennings 3196
Topaz - Helen Ashfield 215
Wild Cat - Laura Black 524

Hanseatic League

Magnificent Enemies - Edgar Maas 3951

Hapsburg Empire

The Time of Murder at Mayerling - Ann
    Dukthas 1778

Hastings, Battle of

The Bastard King - Jean Plaidy 5004
The Conqueror's Wife - Noel B. Gerson 2363
The Firedrake - Cecelia Holland 2988
The Fourteenth of October - Bryher 742
The Golden Warrior: The Story of Harold and William
    - Hope Muntz 4517
Harold Was My King - Hilda Lewis 3749
Red Lion and Gold Dragon - Rosemary
    Sprague 5969
The Wind From Hastings - Morgan Llywelyn 3825

Haymarket Riots

Julie - Jane Kesner Morris 4479

Herrero Rising

The Eagles of Malice - Alan Scholefield 5652

Highland Clearances

The Alien Light - Iain Crichton Smith 1427
Butcher's Broom - Neil Gunn 2620
The English Wife - Charity Blackstock 530
The Island Harp - Jeanne Williams 6779

Hittites

The Hittite - Noel B. Gerson 2373

The Trojan - Noel B. Gerson 2386

Holocaust

Badenheim 1939 - Aharon Appelfeld 174
The Book of Abraham - Marek Halter 2665
Danzig Passage - Bodie Thoene 6221
For Every Sin - Aharon Appelfeld 175
The Hangman's Crusade - James Barwick 370
Jerusalem Interlude - Bodie Thoene 6223
Katerina - Aharon Appelfeld 177
Munich Signature - Bodie Thoene 6224
Prague Counterpoint - Bodie Thoene 6225
Schindler's List - Thomas Keneally 3416
Stones From the River - Ursula Hegi 2816
To the Land of the Cattails - Aharon Appelfeld 179
Tzili: The Story of a Life - Aharon Appelfeld 180
Vienna Prelude - Bodie Thoene 6228
War and Remembrance - Herman Wouk 6875
Warsaw Requiem - Bodie Thoene 6229
Wartime Lies - Louis Begley 416
The White Hotel - D.M. Thomas 6237

Holy Roman Empire

Against This Rock - Louis Zara 6948
The Eagle's Daughter - Judith Tarr 6165

Homesteading

Beneath the Blue Mountain - Richard S.
    Wheeler 6656
Big Ember - Edward Havill 2778
The Bounty Lands - William Donohue Ellis 1927
Courting Emma Howe - Margaret A. Robinson 5410
Free Land - Rose Lane 3660
Honey in the Horn - Harold Lenoir Davis 1523
Honor Thy Father - Robert A. Roripaugh 5460
The Jump-Off Creek - Molly Gloss 2435
The Quiet Shore - Walter Havighurst 2775
The Sea of Grass - Conrad Richter 5323
Tamzen - Jane Gilmore Rushing 5530
That Callahan Spunk! - Francis Ames 124
Thousand Years of Gold - Ruthanne Lum
    McCunn 4239

Homosexuality

Bayou City Secrets - Deborah Powell 5146
Court of Honor - Maria Fagyas 1996
David at Olivet - Wallace Hamilton 2671
Death Wore a Diadem - Iona McGregor 4277
Dreaming of Samarkand - Martin Booth 576
Edward, Edward - Lolah Burford 772
The God of Mirrors - Robert Reilly 5293
Harlot Queen - Hilda Lewis 3748
Jewels - Robert Perrin 4917
Lizzie - Evan Hunter 3083
Mark - Lonnie Coleman 1205
The Other Sappho - Ellen Frye 2240
Patience and Sarah - Isabel Miller 4398
The Persian Boy - Mary Renault 5301
Torsos - John Peyton Cooke 1270
While England Sleeps - David Leavitt 3702

Horror

Anno-Dracula - Kim Newman 4595

Horse Racing

Arizona! - Dana Fuller Ross 5466
The Fairbrothers - Clark McMeekin 4291
The Mississippi Run - Paul Darcy Boles 565
The Prince Regent's Silver Bell - Gladys
    McGorian 4275
Ride the Blue Riband - Rosalind Laker 3598

Show Me a Land - Clark McMeekin   4293

Horses

The Boyds of Black River - Walter D. Edmonds   1871
Double Masquerade - Karen Lynn   3938
The Hands of Cantu - Tom Lea   3694
The Horse Hunters - Robert Newton Peck   4887
Horses of War - Duff Hart-Davis   2760
The Mississippi Run - Paul Darcy Boles   565
The Proud Breed - Celeste De Blasis   1547
A Season of Swans - Celeste De Blasis   1548
Wild Swan - Celeste De Blasis   1550

Horseshoe Bend, Battle of

Horseshoe Bend - Bruce Palmer   4779

Hotels

Back in Society - Marion Chesney   1017
Colonel Sandhurst to the Rescue - Marion Chesney   1021
Lady Fortescue Steps Out - Marion Chesney   1035
Miss Tonks Turns to Crime - Marion Chesney   1041
Mrs. Budley Falls From Grace - Marion Chesney   1042
Sir Philip's Folly - Marion Chesney   1051

Huguenots

Angelique in Revolt - Sergeanne Golon   2471
Evergreen Gallant - Jean Plaidy   5013
Gennie the Huguenot Woman - Bette M. Ross   5464
The Longest Night - Ada Cook Lewis   3744
The Negotiators - Francis Walder   6526
Queen Jezebel - Jean Plaidy   5049
Scarlet Cockerel - Clifford Sublette   6110
The Shepherd's Crook - Paul Frischauer   2234
Young Henry of Navarre - Heinrich Mann   4062

Hundred Years War

An Army of Angels: A Novel of Joan of Arc - Pamela Marcantel   4079
The Burnished Blade - Lawrence Schoonover   5661
Epitaph for Three Women - Jean Plaidy   5012
Guns Forever Echo - Kenneth M. Ellis   1925
In a Dark Wood Wandering - Hella S. Haasse   2631
In Pursuit of the Green Lion - Judith Merkle Riley   5334
Personal Recollections of Joan of Arc - Mark Twain   6372
Ride East! Ride West!: A Romance of the Hundred Years' War - Anne Powers   5154
Rogue's Legacy: A Novel about Francois Villon - Babette Deutsch   1629
The Serpent Amongst the Lilies - P.C. Doherty   1678
The Spider King - Lawrence Schoonover   5668
The Voice and the Light - Edwin Fadiman   1995
The Vow on the Heron - Jean Plaidy   5074
A Walk with Love and Death - Hans Koning   3539

Hunting

Diana the Huntress - Marion Chesney   1026
The Shooting Party - Isabel Colegate   1197

Identity—Concealed

The American Heiress - Dorothy Eden   1854
Angel - Carola Dunn   1790
The Bellerose Bargain - Robyn Carr   934
The Bisley Boy - Christopher Hunt   3080
The Blood Endures - Robert Inman   3107
Borrowed Plumes - Roseleen Milne   4409

Cormorant's Brood - Inglis Fletcher   2133
Cousin Susannah - Hazel Hucker   3066
Double Masquerade - Karen Lynn   3938
The False Inspector Dew - Peter Lovesey   3912
The Florentine - Sandra Shulman   5840
The Frog Earl - Carola Dunn   1792
The Headsman; or, The Abbaye des Vignerons - James Fenimore Cooper   1300
A Heritage of Shadows - Madeleine Brent   660
High Hearts - Rita Mae Brown   728
If I Were You - Joan Aiken   49
Joanna the Pope - Daniel Panger   4785
Kingdom of the Grail - A.A. Attanasio   226
A Lady of Repute - Janice James   3158
Longleaf - Rose Brock   701
The Marquis and Miss Jones - Helen Ashfield   208
The Masqueraders - Georgette Heyer   2894
Mississippi Belle - Clements Ripley   5346
Monsieur Janvier - Elizabeth Linington   3799
Painting the Darkness - Robert Goddard   2445
People of the Silence - W. Michael Gear   2340
The Pilgrimage - Ann B. Ross   5463
The Pioneers; or, The Sources of the Susquehanna - James Fenimore Cooper   1307
The Promise of Light - Paul Watkins   6581
Savannah Purchase - Jane Aiken Hodge   2970
Scaramouche - Rafael Sabatini   5554
The Silver Plume - Arthur Meeker   4323
Stranger at the Wedding - Frances Lynch   3934
The Swedish Cavalier - Leo Perutz   4943
These Old Shades - Georgette Heyer   2906
Thief of My Heart - Rexanne Becnel   410
The White Cockade - Charles James Louis Gilson   2423
Woman Astride - Nora Purtscher-Wydenbruch   5209

Immigrants

All or Nothing - Stephen Longstreet   3881
America, America - Elia Kazan   3380
The Anatolian - Elia Kazan   3381
The Ballad of Typhoid Mary - Jurg Federspiel   2057
Banished Children of Eve - Peter Quinn   5227
The Beckoning Waters - Robert Carse   944
Big Ember - Edward Havill   2778
A Bride for Donnigan - Janette Oke   4705
The Bride of Texas - Josef Skvorecky   5880
Call the Darkness Light - Nancy Zaroulis   6954
Casey - Ramona Stewart   6034
The Chisholms - Evan Hunter   3082
A Circle of Trees - Dana Faralla   2012
Dancing at the Rascal Fair - Ivan Doig   1682
Double Wedding Ring - Patricia Wendorf   6624
The Dream Seekers - Stephen Longstreet   3884
The Dream Seekers - Grace Mark   4085
Ellis Island - Fred Mustard Stewart   6023
The Emigrants - Johan Bojer   561
The Emigrants - Vilhelm Moberg   4422
Free Man - Conrad Richter   5320
Giants in the Earth - O.E. Rolvaag   5434
Glittering Hill - Clyde Francis Murphy   4520
The Great Hunger - Johan Bojer   562
Greenyards - Joan Lingard   3796
Heritage - Lewis Orde   4749
Homeland - John Jakes   3148
The Immigrants - Howard Fast   2034
Joshua Moore, American - George Frederick Hummel   3078
Lady of No Man's Land - Jeanne Williams   6780
Last Letter Home - Vilhelm Moberg   4423
Leah's Journey - Gloria Goldreich   2460
The Lost Wagon - James Arthur Kjelgaard   3509
Malkeh and Her Children - Marjorie Edelson   1853
Maura's Dream - Joel Gross   2602
Men of No Property - Dorothy Davis   1517
My Own Ground - Hugh Nissenson   4628
Now We Are Free - Marguerite Allis   112
Out of This Furnace - Thomas Bell   425

Paradise - Sarah Neilan   4566
Paradise Reclaimed - Halldor Laxness   3686
Peder Victorious - O.E. Rolvaag   5435
The Plums Hang High - Gertrude E. Finney   2091
The Quality of Mercy - Anne Miller Downes   1712
Quinn's Book - William Kennedy   3423
Rebel in Blue - Herman Toepperwein   6289
Rivington Street - Meredith Tax   6175
The Settlers - Vilhelm Moberg   4424
Shadow of the Moon - Douglas C. Jones   3284
Storm Before Sunrise - June Wyndham Davies   1507
Sunflower - Jill Marie Landis   3653
Sunshine and Shadow - Antonia Van-Loon   6426
They Were Dreamers - James F. Murphy Jr.   4525
An Untamed Land - Lauraine Snelling   5936
Unto a Good Land - Vilhelm Moberg   4425
What the Heart Keeps - Rosalind Laker   3605

Inca Empire

Don Pedro and the Devil - Edgar Maas   3948
I, the King - Howard Clewes   1112
The Incas - Daniel Peters   4945
The Last Princess - Charles O. Locke   3826
The Sword and the Sun: The Story of the Spanish Civil Wars in Peru - Gerald Green   2566

Independence—California

El Lazo - L. Jay Martin   4132
Rush to Destroy - L. Jay Martin   4133

Independence—Central America

The Nation Thief - Robert Houston   3057

Independence—Corsica

In What Torn Ship - Evelyn Eaton   1828

Independence—Cuba

Papa and Fidel - Karl Alexander   79
The Single Star - Walter Adolphe Roberts   5394

Independence—Greece

Banners Against the Wind - John Edward Jennings   3198
The Bourlotas Fortune - Nicholas Gage   2268
My Sister, My Love - Lucille Iremonger   3111

Independence—Haiti

All Souls' Rising - Madison Smartt Bell   422
The Black Consul - Anatolii Vinogradov   6503
Black Triumvirate: A Novel of Haiti - Benjamin H. Levin   3736
Caribbean - James A. Michener   4365
Drums at Dusk - Arna Bontemps   575
Drums of Destiny - Peter Bourne   593
Kingdom of This World - Alejo Carpentier   906
Lydia Bailey - Kenneth Roberts   5387
Mistress of Darkness - Christopher Nicole   4617
A Rendezvous in Haiti - Stephen Becker   407
A Time for Titans - Vina Delmar   1602

Independence—India

The Blood Seed - Andrew Ward   6561
The Day of the Scorpion - Paul Scott   5682
A Division of the Spoils - Paul Scott   5683
An Error of Judgment - Stanley Wolpert   6845
The Imperial Agent - T.N. Murari   4518
The Jewel in the Crown - Paul Scott   5684
The Last Victory - T.N. Murari   4519
Nine Hours to Rama - Stanley Wolpert   6846

Raj - Gita Mehta 4325
The Towers of Silence - Paul Scott 5685

Independence—Ireland

Across the Bitter Sea - Eilis Dillon 1646
Ashworth Hall - Anne Perry 4918
The Big Wind - Beatrice Coogan 1262
The Black Swan - Philippa Carr 917
Captain Boycott, a Romantic Novel - Philip
  Rooney 5440
Cashelmara - Susan Howatch 3058
The Detling Secret - Julian Symons 6151
The End of the Hunt - Thomas Flanagan 2119
An Excess of Love - Cathy Cash Spellman 5959
Gone the Rainbow, Gone the Dove - Joan
  Bagnel 264
High Heroic - Constantine FitzGibbon 2118
The Killing Frost - Thomas Hayden 2799
*The Men That God Made Mad: A Novel about
  Ireland's Easter Rising* - W.A. Ballinger 286
A Nest of Simple Folk - Sean O'Faolain 4692
Never Call It Loving - Dorothy Eden 1859
O'Houlihan's Jest - Rohan O'Grady 4702
Parnell and the Englishwoman - Hugh Leonard 3721
The Promise of Light - Paul Watkins 6581
The Ravishers - Elizabeth Richards 5318
Rebels: The Irish Rising of 1916 - Peter
  DeRosa 1622
Redemption - Leon Uris 6393
*Ride East! Ride West!: A Romance of the Hundred
  Years' War* - Anne Powers 5154
The Rising of the Moon - Peter Berresford Ellis 1926
The Rising of the Moon - William Martin 4140
Saints and Scholars - Terrence Eagleton 1821
The Scorching Wind - Walter Macken 3988
Seasons - Anna Dillon 1645
Seek the Fair Land - Walter Macken 3989
The Silent People - Walter Macken 3990
Sons of Thunder - Barbara Fitz Vroman 6516
Stranger in Two Worlds - Hugh Clevely 1111
Talleyman - John James 3161
The Tenants of Time - Thomas Flanagan 2120
Through the Green Valley - Barbara Gowdy 2498
Thy Tears Might Cease - Michael Farrell 2018
The Tick of Death - Peter Lovesey 3916
Time and Chance - Anna Wibberley 6728
Trinity - Leon Uris 6394
Troubles - J.G. Farrell 2017
The Ways of Women - Elaine Crowley 1436
Wild Geese - Eilis Dillon 1647
The Year of the French - Thomas Flanagan 2121

Independence—Israel

The Glory - Herman Wouk 6873
The Hope - Herman Wouk 6874
The Iron Curtain - Robert Vaughan 6447

Independence—Italy

The Castle of Fratta - Ippolito Nievo 4625
Ippolita - Alberto Denti di Pirajno 1612
The Leopard - Giuseppe di Lampedusa 3634
The Mill on the Po - Riccardo Bacchelli 254
The Patriot - Antonio Fogazzaro 2146
The Rebels - Alfred Neumann 4585
The Valley of Decision - Edith Wharton 6653

Independence—Korea

The Living Reed - Pearl S. Buck 756

Independence—Mexico

The Breast of the Dove - Herbert Gorman 2491
Chapultepec - Norman Zollinger 6965
The Cry of Dolores - Herbert Gorman 2492

The Grasshopper King - Elizabeth Boatwright
  Coker 1165
Sons of Texas - Tom Early 1822

Independence—Netherlands

Captain General - John P. Stevenson 6007
The Legend of Tyl Ulenspiegel - Charles Theodore
  Henri De Coster 1558
The Queen's Husband - Samuel Edwards 1889
The Tides of Dawn - Emma Louise Mally 4044
The Valiant Lady - Brigid Knight 3523

Independence—Poland

The Deluge - Henryk Sienkiewicz 5846
Fire in the Steppe - Henryk Sienkiewicz 5847
Poland - James A. Michener 4373
Polonaise - Jane Aiken Hodge 2968
The Teutonic Knights - Henryk Sienkiewicz 5849
Thaddeus of Warsaw - Jane Porter 5136
White Eagle, Dark Skies - Jean Karsavina 3368
With Fire and Sword - Henryk Sienkiewicz 5850

Independence—Russia

The Czar's Madman - Jaan Kross 3560

Independence—Scotland

Braveheart - Randall Wallace 6538
Robert the Bruce: The Path of the Hero King - Nigel
  Tranter 6318
Robert the Bruce: The Price of the King's Peace -
  Nigel Tranter 6319
Robert the Bruce: The Steps to the Empty Throne -
  Nigel Tranter 6320

Independence—South America

Call the New World - John Edward Jennings 3199
The Campaign - Carlos Fuentes 2245
Coasts of Folly - Joel Williams 6784
The Color of Blood - E. Ralph Rundell 5524
Don Gaucho - Alyce Pollock 5088
The General in His Labyrinth - Gabriel Garcia
  Marquez 2282
I, the Supreme - Augusto Antonio Roa Bastos 5353
Manuela, La Caballeresa Del Sol - Demetrio Aguilera
  Malta 41
O'Higgins and Don Bernardo - Edna Deu Pree
  Nelson 4578
The Red Lances - Arturo Uslar Pietri 4999
Retreat From the Dolphin - Darwin Le Ora
  Teilhet 6198
Storm to the South - Thelma Strabel 6073
Taste of Glory - Carleton Beals 394
Time and the Wind - Erico Verissimo 6451

Independence—Switzerland

The Colors of Vaud - Bryher 741

Independence—Turkey

The House of War - Catherine Gavin 2322

Independence—Wales

Owen Glendower - John Cowper Powys 5159

Indian Empire

Coromandel! - John Masters 4172
Golden Fire - Jonathan Fast 2047
The Golden Honeycomb - Kamala Markandaya 4086
Lords of the Dance - Robin Lloyd-Jones 3815

The Near and the Far - Leopold Hamilton
  Myers 4547
Silk and Steel - Stephen Alter 122
The Young Emperor - Robert Payne 4857

Indian Mutiny

The Blood Seed - Andrew Ward 6561
Dando on Delhi Ridge - William Clive 1119
The Devil's Wind: Nana Saheb's Story - Manohar
  Malgonkar 4039
Flashman and the Mountain of Light - George
  MacDonald Fraser 2207
Follow the Drum - James Leasor 3699
The Gallant - William Stuart Long 3873
Indigo - Nicholas Carnac 900
Massacre at Cawnpore - Vivian Stuart 6089
Nightrunners of Bengal - John Masters 4176
Olivia and Jai - Rebecca Ryman 5544
Sergeant Verity and the Imperial Diamond - Francis
  Selwyn 5745
Shadow of the Moon - M.M. Kaye 3377
The Siege of Krishnapur - J.G. Farrell 2016
The Sleeping Tiger - Marjorie McEvoy 4269
Zemindar - Valerie Fitzgerald 2117

Indians

Across the Shining Mountains - Christian
  McCord 4226
Adobe Walls: A Novel of the Last Apache Rising -
  William R. Burnett 791
Alabama Empire - Welbourn Kelley 3392
Ambush - Donald Clayton Porter 5113
Ammahabas - Bill Hotchkiss 3036
Angelique and the Demon - Sergeanne Golon 2466
Angelique in Love - Sergeanne Golon 2470
Apache - Will Comfort 1226
Apache - Donald Clayton Porter 5114
Apache Autumn - Robert Skimin 5875
Apache Blood - David Thompson 6250
Apache Devil - Edgar Rice Burroughs 806
Apaches - Oakley Hall 2650
Arizona Ecstasy - Rosanne Bittner 511
Arrest Sitting Bull - Douglas C. Jones 3273
As Long as the Rivers Run - Sam J. Slate 5882
Ashana - E.P. Roesch 5424
Ashes in the Wilderness - William Greenough
  Schofield 5649
Ask No Quarter - George Tracy Marsh 4099
At the Moon's Inn - Andrew Lytle 3944
Atala - Francois Rene de Chateaubriand 1008
Back to Malachi - Robert J. Conley 1237
Bearer of the Pipe - Don Coldsmith 1169
Becky Landers, Frontier Warrior - Constance
  Skinner 5879
Belle Starr - Speer Morgan 4453
Beyond the Stars - David William Ross 5497
The Big Drum - Elizabeth Boatwright Coker 1162
Big Ember - Edward Havill 2778
The Big Lonesome - Will Bryant 737
The Big Sky - A.B. Guthrie Jr. 2624
Bitter Creek - Al Cody 1150
Black Angels - C.T. Ritchie 5348
Black Robe - Brian Moore 4441
Black Sun - Terry C. Johnston 3242
Blackfoot Massacre - David Thompson 6251
Blackrobe - Charles Corcoran 1323
Blackrobe - Robert E. Wall 6534
Blackwater Spirits - Miriam Grace Monfredo 4427
Blood Brother - Elliott Arnold 190
Blood Fury - David Thompson 6252
Blood Song - Terry C. Johnston 3243
Blood Truce - David Thompson 6253
Blossom Like the Rose - Norah Lofts 3836
The Border Captains - Jason Manning 4072
Border Line - Robert J. Conley 1238
The Border Men - Cameron Judd 3312

Borderlords - Terry C. Johnston 3244

Brazos Dreamer - Gene Shelton 5799

Breakheart Pass - Alistair MacLean 3999

Bride of the Morning Star - Don Coldsmith 1170

The Bride of the Wilderness - Charles McCarry 4220

Bright Feather - Robert Wilder 6750

The Brightwood Expedition - Kay L. McDonald 4261

Broncho Apache - Paul I. Wellman 6614

Brother Owl - Al Hine 2953

Brules - Harry Combs 1223

Buckskin Baronet - Margaret Widdemer 6734

Buckskin Cavalier - John Clagett 1082

Buffalo Medicine - Don Coldsmith 1171

Buffalo Palace - Terry C. Johnston 3245

The Buffalo Soldiers - John Prebble 5165

Buffalo Woman - Dorothy M. Johnson 3223

Bugles in the Afternoon - Ernest Haycox 2788

Buttes Landing - Jean Rikhoff 5331

The Cabin at the Trail's End - Sheba Hargreaves 2706

Call the Beast Thy Brother - William Oliver Turner 6366

The Camp Grant Massacre - Elliott Arnold 191

The Canebrake Men - Cameron Judd 3313

Captain McRae: A Novel of the Northwest Frontier - William Heuman 2872

Cardigan - Robert W. Chambers 976

Carmen of the Rancho - Frank H. Spearman 5955

Carrington - Michael Whitney Straight 6074

Carry the Wind - Terry C. Johnston 3246

The Cavalryman - Harold Sinclair 5861

Centennial - James A. Michener 4366

Chant of the Hawk - John Harris 2720

Chase the Wind - Janelle Taylor 6184

Cherokee - Donald Clayton Porter 5115

Cherokee Dawn - Genell Dellin 1596

Chief Joseph - Bill Dugan 1756

Chief of Scouts - Don Bendell 439

The Chieftain: A Story of the Nez Perce People - Robert Payne 4852

Child of the Dead - Don Coldsmith 1172

The Children of the First Man - James Alexander Thom 6230

Chiricahua - Will Henry 2839

Choctaw - Donald Clayton Porter 5116

Cimarron - Edna Ferber 2061

Cloud on the Land - Julia Davis 1526

A Cold Day in Hell - Terry C. Johnston 3247

The Cold Journey - Grace Zaring Stone 6052

Comanche Moon - Catherine Anderson 137

The Comancheros - Paul I. Wellman 6616

Comes an Echo on the Breeze - Edward J. Ryan 5542

Company of Cowards - Jack Schaefer 5634

Conquering Horse - Frederick F. Manfred 4055

The Conqueror - John William Tebbel 6194

The Conquerors - Allen W. Eckert 1839

The Countess Angelique - Sergeanne Golon 2472

The Court Martial of Daniel Boone - Allen W. Eckert 1840

Crazy Horse - Bill Dugan 1757

Crazy Snake - Robert J. Conley 1240

A Creek Called Wounded Knee - Douglas C. Jones 3277

Creek Mary's Blood - Dee Brown 712

Crimson Creek: A Novel of the Early West - Robert McCraig 4228

Croatan - Mary Johnston 3231

The Cross and the Sword - Manuel de Jesus Galvan 2274

The Cross and the Sword - Jonreed Lauritzen 3674

The Crossed Sabres - Gilbert Morris 4458

Custer Passed Our Way - Fred S. Kaufman 3370

Dakota! - Dana Fuller Ross 5472

Dance Back the Buffalo - Milton Lott 3899

Dances with Wolves - Michael Blake 537

Daniel Du Luth - Everett McNeil 4307

Dark Hills to Westward - Harry M. Caudill 964

The Dark Way - Robert J. Conley 1241

Daughter of Eve - Noel B. Gerson 2366

Daughter of Fortune - Carla Kelly 3398

Daughter of the Eagle - Don Coldsmith 1173

Dawn Land - Joseph Bruchac III 734

The Day Must Dawn - Agnes Sligh Turnbull 6362

The Day the Sun Died - Dale Van Every 6408

Dead Man's Walk - Larry McMurtry 4297

Death at Rainy Mountain - Mardi Oakley Medawar 4321

Death at the French Creek - Raymond C. Borel 580

Deeper the Heritage - Muriel Elwood 1936

The Deerslayer - James Fenimore Cooper 1299

Delilah's Mountain - Gloria Jahoda 3142

Desert Hawks - Frank Burleson 786

Devil's Backbone - Terry C. Johnston 3250

The Dice of God - Hoffman Birney 507

Distant Trails - Bill Gulick 2612

Distant Trumpet - Paul Horgan 3032

Doctor in Buckskin - T.D. Allen 103

Dodging Red Cloud - Richard S. Wheeler 6657

The Doom Trail - Arthur Douglas Smith 5917

The Double Man - Elinor Pryor 5205

Down From the Mountain - Louis Charbonneau 997

Dream Catcher - Terry C. Johnston 3251

Drums Along the Mohawk - Walter D. Edmonds 1874

Drums of Change: The Story of Running Fawn - Janette Oke 4707

A Durable Fire - Virginia Bernhard 480

Dust on the King's Highway - Helen Constance White 6677

Eagle of Niagara: The Story of David Harper and His Indian Captivity - John Brick 671

Eagle Song - James Houston 3050

Eagles of Destiny - Jory Sherman 5817

The Elk-Dog Heritage - Don Coldsmith 1174

An Embarrassment of Riches - James Howard Kunstler 3565

Erskine Dale, Pioneer - John Fox 2195

Expedition! - Dana Fuller Ross 5473

Eye of the Hawk - David William Ross 5498

Eyes of Eagles - William W. Johnstone 3266

The Far Tribes - Richard S. Wheeler 6658

Father and Son - Donald Clayton Porter 5117

Father of Waters - Donald Clayton Porter 5118

Fathers and Crows - William T. Vollmann 6508

Fawn - Robert Newton Peck 4885

Fire Along the Sky: A Novel of America - Robert Moss 4497

Fire in the Sky - J.A. Shears 5785

The Firekeeper - Robert Moss 4498

The First Rebel - Neil Harmon Swanson 6137

The Flames of Time - Baynard Kendrick 3409

Flashman and the Redskins - George MacDonald Fraser 2208

The Fleet Rabble: A Novel of the Nez Perce War - Frank Borden Hanes 2675

Flight of the Crow - Paul Clayton 1103

The Flower in the Mountains - Don Coldsmith 1175

Follow the Free Wind - Leigh Brackett 621

Follow the River - Albert Mayer 4203

Follow the River - James Alexander Thom 6231

Follow the Wind - Don Coldsmith 1176

For Love of Two Eagles - Barbara Riefe 5328

For Us the Living - Bruce Lancaster 3639

The Forbidden Ground - Neil Harmon Swanson 6138

The Forest Lord - Noel B. Gerson 2368

Fort De Chastaigne - Don Coldsmith 1177

The Franciscan - Forrester Blake 532

Free Flows the River - Earl Murray 4529

From Where the Sun Now Stands - Will Henry 2841

The Frontiersmen - Allen W. Eckert 1841

Fur Brigade - Hal George Evarts 1985

Gallant Warrior - Helen R. Mann 4063

Gateway to Empire - Allen W. Eckert 1842

Gathering Storm - Bill Gulick 2613

Geronimo - Bill Dugan 1758

Geronimo: An American Legend - Robert J. Conley 1242

Ghost Fox - James Houston 3051

Ghost Woman - Lawrence Thornton 6275

The Gila River - Gary McCarthy 4223

The Gilded Rooster - Richard Emery Roberts 5391

Give Me the Wind - Jan Jordan 3302

Go-Ahead Rider - Robert J. Conley 1243

The God-Seeker - Sinclair Lewis 3763

The Golden Wildcat - Margaret Widdemer 6735

Gone the Dreams and the Dancing - Douglas C. Jones 3279

A Good Day to Die - Del Barton 368

A Good Day to Die - Thomas Wakefield Blackburn 525

The Great Betrayal - Dorothy Gardiner 2284

The Great Meadow - Elizabeth Madox Roberts 5378

The Half Breed - Maurice Constantin-Weyer 1261

The Hallelujah Train - Bill Gulick 2614

The Hands of Cantu - Tom Lea 3694

Hannah Fowler - Janice Holt Giles 2411

Hanta Yo - Ruth Beebe Hill 2951

Hatchet in the Sky - Margaret Cooper Gay 2328

Hawk's Journey - Donald Clayton Porter 5119

Heartland - Robert Douglas Mead 4316

Heritage of the River - Muriel Elwood 1937

Hidden Children - Robert W. Chambers 978

The High Missouri - Winfred Blevins 545

High Towers - Thomas B. Costain 1366

A High Wind Rising - Elsie Singmaster 5867

The Holy Warrior - Gilbert Morris 4462

Hope Leslie; or, Early Times in Massachusetts - Catharine Maria Sedgewick 5714

The Horn and the Forest - Jamie Lee Cooper 1313

Horseshoe Bend - Bruce Palmer 4779

The Hunting Shirt - Mary Johnston 3235

If a Lion Could Talk - Mildred Walker 6532

The Impudent Rifle - Richard Pearce 4872

In the Days of Poor Richard - Irving A. Bacheller 259

In the Hands of the Senecas - Walter D. Edmonds 1876

In the Season of the Sun - Kerry Newcomb 4590

Indian Brother - Hubert Coryell 1354

Indian Hater - Glenn R. Vernam 6452

The Interpreter - Robert Moss 4499

Jason McGee - Robert H. Fowler 2190

John Crews - Arthur Chapman 988

Johnny Logan: Shawnee Spy - Allen W. Eckert 1843

Johnny Osage - Janice Holt Giles 2412

Jordan County: A Landscape in Narrative - Shelby Foote 2152

Journey by the River - John Prescott 5173

Journey to Nashville - Alfred Leland Crabb 1402

The Judas Tree - Neil Harmon Swanson 6139

Judgment in July - Richard Fisher 2105

The Justicer - Thomas Fall 2010

Kelly Blue - Peter Bowen 601

Kentucky Stand - Jere Hungerford Wheelwright 6670

The Kidnapped Surgeon - Alexander Knox 3527

Killdeer Mountain - Dee Brown 713

The King's Rebel - James David Horan 3030

Lady of the Mohawks - Margaret Widdemer 6736

Lakota - G. Clifton Wisler 6833

Land for My Sons - Maribelle Cormack 1331

Land of the Beautiful River - Helmer Linderholm 3788

A Land to Tame - Zola Helen Ross 5505

The Land Where the Sun Dies - Henry Carlisle 896

The Last Frontier - Howard Fast 2036

The Last Hunt - Milton Lott 3900

The Last of the Mohicans - James Fenimore Cooper 1302

The Last Ride - Tom Eidson 1899

The Last Stand: A Novel about George Armstrong Custer and the Indians of the Plains - Edwin P. Hoyt 3061

The Last Warpath - Will Henry 2844

The Law of Larion - Peter Freuchen 2227

The Legend of Ben Tree - Paul Hawkins 2784

Let the Drum Speak: A Novel of Ancient America - Linda Lay Shuler 5837

Libbie - Judy Alter 121

The Lieutenant's Lady - Bess Streeter Aldrich 70

The Life and Times of Captain N. - Douglas Glover 2436

The Light in the Forest - Conrad Richter 5322

Light on the Mountain - Leonard Sanders 5589

Lily of the Mohawks - Jack Casey 952

Little Big Man - Thomas Berger 478

Little Red Foot - Robert W. Chambers 979

Lonesome Dove - Larry McMurtry 4298

Long Knife - James Alexander Thom 6233

The Long Sun - Janice Lucas 3920

The Long Trail North - Robert J. Conley 1245

Long Winter Gone - Terry C. Johnston 3252

Look to Your Geese: A Novel of the Deflowering of New England - Jacquin Sanders 5584

The Loon Feather - Iola Fuller 2253

Lord Grizzly - Frederick F. Manfred 4056

Lord of the Plains - Alfred Silver 5852

Lords of the Plains - Max Crawford 1420

The Lost Colony - Edison Marshall 4108

Lost Wallowa - Bill Gulick 2616

The Lure of the Falcon - Juliette Benzoni 465

Lure of the Wind - David Thompson 6256

Mackenna's Gold - Will Henry 2845

Man of the Shadows - Don Coldsmith 1178

Man on Two Ponies - Don Worcester 6872

The Man Who Loved Cat Dancing - Marilyn Durham 1817

Manitou - Donald Clayton Porter 5120

The Manly-Hearted Woman - Frederick F. Manfred 4057

Marching to Valhalla: A Novel of Custer's Last Days - Michael Blake 538

The Massacre at Fall Creek - Jessamyn West 6631

Maximilian's Gold - Jane Barry 359

The Medicine Calf - Bill Hotchkiss 3037

Medicine Knife - Don Coldsmith 1179

The Medicine Whip - Max Hennessy 2835

Men in Buckskin - Herbert Stover 6069

Mi Amigo - William R. Burnett 795

Michael Beam - Richard Hallet 2663

A Mighty Afternoon - Charles K. Mills 4407

Mighty Mountain - Archie Binns 502

The Mists of Manittoo - Lois Swann 6135

Mohawk Woman - Barbara Riefe 5329

Montana! - Dana Fuller Ross 5479

Montana Road - Harry Sinclair Drago 1717

The Moon-Eyed Appaloosa - Bill Gulick 2617

Moon of Thunder - Don Coldsmith 1180

The Moon Stallion - Jim Berry 484

Moonfeather - Judith E. French 2223

The Morning River - W. Michael Gear 2333

Mountain Man - Vardis Fisher 2110

Mountain Windsong - Robert J. Conley 1246

My Master Columbus - Cedric Belfrage 418

Ned Christie's War - Robert J. Conley 1247

Never No More: The Story of Rebecca Boone - Shirley Seifert 5730

Nick of the Woods; or, The Jibbenainosay - Robert Montgomery Bird 505

Nickajack - Robert J. Conley 1248

Night Wind - Roberta Jean Mountjoy 4504

Night Wind's Woman - Shirl Henke 2825

Nine Days of Father Serra - Isabelle Gibson Ziegler 6961

No Resting Place - William Humphrey 3079

No Survivors - Will Henry 2846

North Against the Sioux - Kenneth Ulyatt 6376

Northwest Passage - Kenneth Roberts 5388

Oh, Kentucky! - Betty Layman Receveur 5284

Oh, Promised Land - James H. Street 6079

Oklahoma! - Dana Fuller Ross 5482

Old Misery - Hugh Pendexter 4896

One Smart Indian - Robert J. Seidman 5722

Outpost! - Dana Fuller Ross 5486

The Overland Trail - Wendi Lee 3712

The Overmountain Men - Cameron Judd 3315

Paint the Wind - Cathy Cash Spellman 5960

Paiute - Sessions S. Wheeler 6666

Pale Star - Don Coldsmith 1181

Panther in the Sky - James Alexander Thom 6234

Paradise - Esther Forbes 2158

The Pathfinder; or, The Inland Sea - James Fenimore Cooper 1305

The Pecos River - Fred Bean 399

The Peculiar People - Jan de Hartog 2764

Pemmican - Vardis Fisher 2111

People of the Lakes - W. Michael Gear 2336

People of the River - W. Michael Gear 2338

People of the Silence - W. Michael Gear 2340

The Pilgrim Soul - Anne Miller Downes 1711

Pinto and Sons - Leslie Epstein 1947

Pioneer Breed - Glenn R. Vernam 6453

Pocahontas - Susan Donnell 1691

Pocahontas; or, The Nonpareil of Virginia - David Garnett 2297

The Post of Honor - David Coxe Cooke 1266

The Powder River - Winfred Blevins 546

Powhatan's Daughter - John Clarke Bowman 605

The Prairie - James Fenimore Cooper 1308

The Pride of Hannah Wade - Janet Dailey 1455

The Prospering - Elizabeth Speare 5954

The Proud and the Free - Janet Dailey 1456

Pushing the Bear: A Novel of the Trail of Tears - Diane Glancy 2426

The Quality of Mercy - Anne Miller Downes 1712

Quanah Parker - Bill Dugan 1759

Quest for the White Bull - Don Coldsmith 1182

Rabbit Boss - Thomas Sanchez 5581

The Raid - John Brick 673

Rainbow Road - Davenport Steward 6016

Rapaho - Jamie Lee Cooper 1314

Rascal's Heaven - F. van Wyck Mason 4157

Reap the Whirlwind - Terry C. Johnston 3254

Red Cloud's Revenge - Terry C. Johnston 3255

Red Fox of the Kinapoo - William Rush 5526

Red Morning - Ruby Frazier Frey 2230

Red Stick - Donald Clayton Porter 5121

The Renegade - Donald Clayton Porter 5122

Renno - Donald Clayton Porter 5123

Republic: A Novel of Texas - E.V. Thompson 6266

The Restless Border - Richard Pearce 4873

The Restless Land - John H. Culp 1444

Return of the Spanish - Don Coldsmith 1183

Return to the River - Don Coldsmith 1184

Richard Lamb - Richard S. Wheeler 6662

Ride the Wind - Lucia St. Clair Robson 5416

The Rifleman - John Brick 675

River in the Wind - Edith Pope 5111

River of Sky - Karen Harper 2713

River of Swans - Don Coldsmith 1185

The Road to Glory - Darwin Le Ora Teilhet 6199

A Road We Do Not Know: A Novel of Custer at the Little Bighorn - Frederick J. Chiaventone 1057

Roanoke Warrior - Carter A. Vaughan 6438

Roger Sudden - Thomas H. Raddall 5232

Roman - Douglas C. Jones 3281

The Rose and the Flame - Jonreed Lauritzen 3676

The Royal City - Les Savage Jr. 5621

Runaway - Heather Graham 2519

Runestone - Don Coldsmith 1186

Sacajawea - Anna Lee Waldo 6529

Sacajawea of the Shoshones - Della F. Emmons 1940

The Sachem - Donald Clayton Porter 5124

Sachem's Son - Donald Clayton Porter 5125

The Sacred Hills - Don Coldsmith 1187

St. Agnes' Stand - Tom Eidson 1900

Sand in the Wind - Kathleen O'Neal Gear 2329

Savage Frontier - Frank Burleson 787

Savage Gentleman - Noel B. Gerson 2381

Savages and Saints - Cora Older 4717

Savanna - Janice Holt Giles 2416

Say These Names (Remember Them) - Betty Sue Cummings 1448

Scalpdancers - Kerry Newcomb 4592

The Scout - Harry Combs 1224

The Search for Temperance Moon - Douglas C. Jones 3282

The Searchers - Alan Le May 3691

Season of Yellow Leaf - Douglas C. Jones 3283

The Second Kiss - Gayle Rogers 5432

The Seekers - John Jakes 3153

Seize the Sky - Terry C. Johnston 3256

Seminole - Donald Clayton Porter 5126

Seminole - Theodore Pratt 5164

Seneca - Donald Clayton Porter 5127

The Seneca Hostage - Carter A. Vaughan 6440

Sergeant Lamb's America - Robert Graves 2552

Seven Rivers West - Edward Hoagland 2959

Shadow Catcher - Charles Fergus 2064

Shadow of a Star - Jamie Lee Cooper 1315

The Shadow Riders - Terry C. Johnston 3257

Shadows in the Dusk - John Edward Jennings 3208

Shadows on the Long House - Mike Roarke 5360

Shaman - Noah Gordon 2483

She Who Remembers - Linda Lay Shuler 5838

The Shining Mountains - Dale Van Every 6410

The Shining Trail - Iola Fuller 2254

The Silent Drum - Neil Harmon Swanson 6141

Silent Drums - Mike Roarke 5361

Sioux Dawn - Terry C. Johnston 3258

Sioux Splendor - Rosanne Bittner 515

Sitting Bull - Bill Dugan 1760

Six-Horse Hitch - Janice Holt Giles 2417

Slaughter - Elmer Kelton 3407

The Smoky Hill - Don Coldsmith 1188

The Snake River - Winfred Blevins 547

The Snowblind Moon - John Byrne Cooke 1267

Some Lose Their Way - Eloise S. Liddon 3770

Song of Metamoris: A Story That Remains of a People Who Passed This Way - Milford E. Anness 155

Song of the Cheyenne - Jory Sherman 5822

Song of the Meadowlark - John A. Sanford 5594

Song of the Rock - Don Coldsmith 1189

Song of Wovoka - Earl Murray 4531

A Sorrow in Our Heart - Allen W. Eckert 1844

Spirit Knife - Donald Clayton Porter 5128

Spirit Lake - MacKinlay Kantor 3363

Spoon - John Christgau 1074

The Staked Plain - Frank Xavier Tolbert 6290

The Stalkers - Terry C. Johnston 3259

Stamping Ground - Loren D. Estleman 1977

Stone Song: A Novel of the Life of Crazy Horse - Winfred Blevins 548

A Story of Deep Delight - Thomas McNamee 4305

Sudden Country - Loren D. Estleman 1979

The Sweetwater - Jean Rikhoff 5333

Takers of the City - Hoffman Reynolds Hays 2800

Taos - Irwin R. Blacker 527

Tatham Mound - Piers Anthony 169

The Temptation of Angelique - Sergeanne Golon 2473

That Bennington Mob - Henry Barnard Safford 5558

That Dark and Bloody River - Allen W. Eckert 1845

They Came to a Valley - Bill Gulick 2618

This Land Is Mine - Frances Casey Kerns 3470

This Promised Land - Robert Easton 1824

This Savage Race - Douglas C. Jones 3285

This Widowed Land - Kathleen O'Neal Gear 2331

Three Came to Ville Marie - Alan Sullivan 6114

Three Sides of Agiochook - Eric Kelly 3400

Thunder in the Dawn - Earl Murray 4532

Thunder in the East - Mike Roarke 5362

Thunder in the Wilderness - Charles Granville Hamilton 2668

Thunder on the River - Charlton Laird 3590

Thunderstick - Don Coldsmith 1190

Tie My Bones to Her Back - Robert F. Jones 3294

Tilly Wed - Catherine Cookson 1290

A Time in the Sun - Jane Barry 361

Timothy Baines - John H. Culp 1445

To Build a Ship - Don Berry   482
To Have and to Hold - Mary Johnston   3241
To Keep Us Free - Marguerite Allis   115
To Make a Killing - Robert J. Conley   1252
To the Far Blue Mountains - Louis L'Amour   3630
Tomahawk - Donald Clayton Porter   5129
Tomahawk Revenge - David Thompson   6260
Torn Covenants - Lois Swann   6136
Track of the Bear - Don Coldsmith   1191
Trail From Taos - Don Coldsmith   1192
Trail of Tears - Williams Forrest   2187
Trail of Tears - Frances Patton Statham   5983
Trail of the Spanish Bit - Don Coldsmith   1193
Trail's End - Fred Bean   400
Trask - Don Berry   483
The Tree of Life - Hugh Nissenson   4629
The Trees - Conrad Richter   5326
Trumpet on the Land - Terry C. Johnston   3260
Twice upon a Time - Allen Appel   172
Twilight of Empire - Allen W. Eckert   1846
The Two Medicine River - Richard S. Wheeler   6663
The Unconquered - Neil Harmon Swanson   6142
The Unforgiven - Alan Le May   3692
The Valiant - Sigman Byrd   839
Valley in Arms: A Novel of the Settlement of Connecticut - Earl Schenck Miers   4376
Valley of the Shadow - Charles Marquis Warren   6570
A Very Small Remnant - Michael Whitney Straight   6075
A Virginia Scout - Hugh Pendexter   4899
The Vision Is Fulfilled - Kay L. McDonald   4262
Vision of the Eagle - Kay L. McDonald   4263
Voice of the Eagle - Linda Lay Shuler   5839
Walk in My Soul - Lucia St. Clair Robson   5418
Walks in the Sun - Don Coldsmith   1194
War Chief - Donald Clayton Porter   5130
War Clouds - Donald Clayton Porter   5131
War Cry - Donald Clayton Porter   5132
War Drums - Donald Clayton Porter   5133
War Eagles - Frank Burleson   788
War in the Golden Weather - Stephen Longstreet   3892
Warriors of the Night - Kerry Newcomb   4594
Watch for Me on the Mountain - Forrest Carter   947
The Way of the Priests - Robert J. Conley   1253
The Wept of Wish-Ton-Wish - James Fenimore Cooper   1312
West Goes the Road - Tim Pridgen   5192
West of the River - Charlton Laird   3591
West to the Setting Sun - Harvey Chalmers   973
Westward! - Dana Fuller Ross   5492
When the Legends Die - Hal Borland   584
Where the River Runs - Richard S. Wheeler   6664
While Rivers Flow - Glen H. Fleischmann   2125
Whisper of the Wolf - Terry C. Johnston   3261
A Whisper on the Wind - Madeline Baker   276
A Whistle in the Wind - John H. Culp   1447
The White Dawn - James Houston   3053
White Indian - Donald Clayton Porter   5134
The White Man's Road - Benjamin Capps   891
The White Path - Robert J. Conley   1254
White Rising - Zane Kotker   3548
Wild Horizon - F. van Wyck Mason   4164
Wilderness - Roger Zelazny   6957
Wilderness Adventure - Elizabeth Page   4774
Wilderness Empire - Allen W. Eckert   1847
Wilderness Passage - Forrester Blake   534
The Wilderness War - Allen W. Eckert   1848
Wind over Wisconsin - August Derleth   1620
Winding Stairs - Douglas C. Jones   3287
Winter Rain - Terry C. Johnston   3262
The Winter War - William Wister Haines   2640
The Wolf and the Buffalo - Elmer Kelton   3408
Woman Chief - Benjamin Capps   892
A Woman of the People - Benjamin Capps   893
The Woman Who Fell From the Sky - Barbara Riefe   5330
Women in the Wind - Margaret Ritter   5350

The Woodsman - Don Wright   6880
World of Silence - Don Coldsmith   1195
Wyoming! - Dana Fuller Ross   5494
Yellowhorse - Dee Brown   715
The Yellowstone - Winfred Blevins   549
Yellowstone Kelly - Peter Bowen   602
The Yemassee - William Gilmore Simms   5855
Young Titan - F. van Wyck Mason   4165
Zeke and Ned - Larry McMurtry   4301

Industrial Revolution

Crompton Way - Thomas Thompson   6270

Inheritance—Disputed

Albany - Laura Black   519
The Ancestors Cry Out - Eugenia Lovett West   6627
The Bastard - Brigitte Von Tessin   6208
The Bride of Lammermoor - Sir Walter Scott   5693
Bridey's Mountain - Yvonne Adamson   34
Captain Nash and the Wroth Inheritance - Ragan Butler   828
Caroline and Julia - Clare Darcy   1484
Castaway - Frances Murray   4535
Castle Heritage - Elisabeth Barr   337
Castle Malindine - Hilary Ford   2163
Clara Reeve - Leonie Hargrave   2705
The Dukes: A Novel - Malcolm Ross   5503
Family Fortune - Mignon G. Eberhart   1834
A Father and His Fate - Ivy Compton-Burnett   1228
The Five-Minute Marriage - Joan Aiken   46
The Girl From Paris - Joan Aiken   47
Guy Mannering - Sir Walter Scott   5697
The Hawthorne Legacy - Teresa Crane   1416
A Heritage and Its History - Ivy Compton-Burnett   1229
In Still and Stormy Waters - Reay Tannahill   6157
Indigo - Nicholas Carnac   900
The Intrigue - Marion Chesney   1034
The Iron Crown - Clare Barroll   354
A Lady in Doubt - Annabel Wynne   6891
Lady of Mallow - Dorothy Eden   1856
Lord Iverbrook's Heir - Carola Dunn   1795
Lord of Misrule - Gareth Jones   3290
The Lords of Vaumartin - Cecelia Holland   2992
The Malvie Inheritance - Pamela Hill   2938
Meridon - Philippa Gregory   2583
Mistaken Virtues - Joanna Trollope   6349
My Beloved Son - Catherine Cookson   1285
Norah - Pamela Hill   2941
On a Far Wide Shore - Malcolm Macdonald   3970
The Pangersbourne Murders - J.G. Jeffreys   3179
The Peacock's Feather - Sarah Woodhouse   6855
The Quade Inheritance - Barbara Ker Wilson   3469
The Quincunx - Charles Palliser   4778
The Rake - Karen Lynn   3941
Ravenshoe - Henry Kingsley   3500
Sarah Camberwell Tring - Janet Edmonds   1869
Snared Nightingale - Geoffrey Trease   6324
The Storm Witch - Elisabeth Barr   339
Stranger's Forest - Pamela Hill   2943
The Stuart Legacy - Robert Kerr   3472
Viola Gwyn - George Barr McCutcheon   4258
Wideacre - Philippa Gregory   2585

Inquisition

1492 - Newton Frolich   2236
1492: The Life and Times of Juan Cabezon de Castile - Homero Aridjis   187
The Adventures of Don Juan - Richard Gardner   2289
Among the Innocent - Elizabeth Borton de Trevino   6339
Captain From Castile - Samuel Shellabarger   5794
Catalina - William Somerset Maugham   4197
Color From a Light Within: A Novel Based on the Life of El Greco - Donald Braider   641

Court of Shadows - Cynthia Morgan   4450
Cradle of the Sun - John Clagett   1083
Crown of Aloes - Norah Lofts   3840
Divine Mistress - Frank G. Slaughter   5886
Don Pedro and the Devil - Edgar Maas   3948
Ferdinand and Isabella - Hermann Kesten   3474
Goa - Kara Dalkey   1458
The Greek of Toledo: A Romantic Narrative of El Greco - Elizabeth Borton   586
The Hounds of God - Rafael Sabatini   5551
The Inquisitors - Jerzy Andrzejewski   153
Mansions of Darkness - Chelsea Quinn Yarbro   6902
The Marranos - Liliane Webb   6588
The Memoirs of Christopher Columbus - Stephen Marlowe   4096
The Monk - Matthew Gregory Lewis   3756
The Palace of Wisdom - Bob Marshall-Andrews   4118
Poison - Kathryn Harrison   2737
The Queen's Cross: A Biographical Romance of Queen Isabella of Spain - Lawrence Schoonover   5666
The Scarlet Cloak - Jean Plaidy   5061
The Spanish Bridegroom - Jean Plaidy   5064
The Spanish Doctor - Matt Cohen   1159
Torquemada - Howard Fast   2045
Vagabond Prophet - Allene Symons   6149
The Velvet Doublet - James H. Street   6082
Westward Ho! - Charles Kingsley   3499

Inventions

A Case of Curiosities - Allen Kurzweil   3569
Crompton Way - Thomas Thompson   6270
Loving Little Egypt - Thomas McMahon   4288
Mount's Mistake - Lew McCreary   4229
A Peep into the 20th Century - Christopher Davis   1515
Whittling Boy: The Story of Eli Whitney - Roger Burlingame   789

Irish Potato Famine

Across the Bitter Sea - Eilis Dillon   1646
The Big Wind - Beatrice Coogan   1262
The Emancipist: An Unforgettable Epic of Australia - Veronica Geoghegan Sweeney   6147
Famine - Liam O'Flaherty   4693
The Famished Land - Elizabeth Byrd   833
The Hedge of Thorns - Helen Ashton   217
The Silent People - Walter Macken   3990
Trinity - Leon Uris   6394

Iron Age

The Serpent's Tooth - Diana L. Paxson   4846

Islam

Cry of the Peacock - Gina Barkhordar Nahai   4552
The Voice of Allah - Edwin P. Hoyt   3062

Jacobean Period

Bride of the MacHugh - Jan Cox Speas   5956
Call Lady Purbeck - Hilda Lewis   3745
For My Great Folly - Thomas B. Costain   1365
The Fortunes of Nigel - Sir Walter Scott   5696
Hellbane - Anthony Esler   1963
Katherine Christian - Hugh Walpole   6546
The King James Version - Stanley N. Stewart   6035
King's Minion - Rafael Sabatini   5552
Lion Rampant - Bernard Shrimsley   5836
Mine Is the Kingdom - Jane Oliver   4726
The Physician of London - Stephanie Cowell   1394
The Player's Boy - Bryher   744
Ralegh's Fair Bess: The Story of Bess Throckmorton - Judy Turner   6365

Scapegoat for a Stuart - Kate Kirby   3504
The Street of Kings - Charles Dexter   1637
Take Heed of Loving Me: A Novel about John Donne - Elizabeth Gray Vining   6502
Unicorn Rampant - Nigel Tranter   6323
The Voyage of the Destiny - Robert Nye   4657
Wife to Great Buckingham - Hilda Lewis   3751
The Young and Lonely King - Jane Lane   3659

Jacobite Rebellion

An Air of Glory - Sarah Neilan   4563
Bed in Hell - Elfrida Vipont   6504
Black William - Robert Neill   4567
The Blood of Roses - Marsha Canham   879
Born to Be King - Constance Gluyas   2440
Candleshine No More - Jane Oliver   4721
Catriona - Robert Louis Stevenson   6009
Charlie Is My Darling - Mollie Hardwick   2691
Cherished Enemy - Patricia Veryan   6460
Clandara - Evelyn Anthony   161
Commander of the Mists - D.L. Murray   4527
Crown Without Sceptre - William Vaughan Wilkins   6758
The Dark Mile - Dorothy Kathleen Broster   709
The Dark Stranger - Constance Dodge   1664
The Dedicated Villain - Patricia Veryan   6461
Devil Water - Anya Seton   5749
Dragonfly in Amber - Diana Gabaldon   2262
The Fires of Glenlochy - Constance Heaven   2806
The Flight of the Heron - Dorothy Kathleen Broster   710
Foes - Mary Johnston   3233
Henry Esmond - William Makepeace Thackeray   6212
Highlands Rebel - Sally Watson   6584
I Came to the Highlands: A Novel of Suspense - Velda Johnston   3263
Journey to Enchantment - Patricia Veryan   6464
Kidnapped - Robert Louis Stevenson   6010
Lady of the Glen - Jennifer Roberson   5369
The Lonely Strangers - Charity Blackstock   531
The Long Day Closes - Beatrice Tunstall   6360
Lord of Misrule - Gareth Jones   3290
Love Alters Not - Patricia Veryan   6467
MacLyon - Lolah Burford   773
Madame Geneva - Jane Lane   3655
The Masqueraders - Georgette Heyer   2894
The Master of Ballantrae: A Winter's Tale - Robert Louis Stevenson   6011
Meggy MacIntosh - Elizabeth Janet Gray   2555
Midwinter - John Buchan   751
Mistress of Willowvale - Patricia Veryan   6471
Monsieur Janvier - Elizabeth Linington   3799
Now Face to Face - Karleen Koen   3530
Outlander - Diana Gabaldon   2264
Practice to Deceive - Patricia Veryan   6475
The Pride of Lions - Marsha Canham   881
A Prince, a Piper, and a Rose - John Scalzo   5628
Prince Charlie's Bluff - Donald Thomas   6241
Queen in Waiting - Jean Plaidy   5048
Red Cloak Flying - Margaret Widdemer   6737
Red Gauntlet - Sir Walter Scott   5706
Rob Roy - Sir Walter Scott   5707
Rogue Herries - Hugh Walpole   6547
The Song of the Siren - Philippa Carr   929
The Stuart Legacy - Robert Kerr   3472
Torbeg - Grace Campbell   873
Two Crowns for America - Katherine Kurtz   3568
The Tyrant - Patricia Veryan   6480
The Wagered Widow - Patricia Veryan   6481
Waverley - Sir Walter Scott   5709
The White Cockade - Vincent O'Brien   4683
Will You Love Me in September? - Philippa Carr   932
The Woman from The Glen - Chloe Gartner   2310

Jacquerie

A Walk with Love and Death - Hans Koning   3539

Jameson Raid

The City of Gold - Francis Brett Young   6940
Westward the Sun - Brigid Knight   3524

Japanese Empire

The Barbarian - Willard Price   5191
Bronze Christ - Yoshiro Nagaya   4551
Bundori - Laura Joh Rowland   5519
Daishi-San: A Novel - Robert P. Lund   3925
The Exile Way - Ann Woodward   6865
Gai-Jin: A Novel of Japan - James Clavell   1100
Harpoon - C.W. Nicol   4612
The Heike Story - Eiji Yoshikawa   6934
Kagami - Elizabeth Kata   3369
Musashi: An Epic Novel of the Samurai Era - Eiji Yoshikawa   6935
The Needle-Watcher - Richard Blaker   540
The Ronin - William Dale Jennings   3212
The Running of the Tide - Esther Forbes   2160
Sakuran: A Novel of Medieval Japan - Edward Tolosko   6292
The Samurai - Shusaku Endo   1941
Segaki - David Stacton   5975
Shike: Time of Dragons - Robert Shea   5784
Shin Ju - Laura Joh Rowland   5520
Shogun - James Clavell   1101
The Signore: Shogun of the Warring States - Kunio Tsuji   6357
The Sword of Hachiman - Lynn Guest   2608
Taiko - Eiji Yoshikawa   6936
The Tokaido Road: A Novel of Feudal Japan - Lucia St. Clair Robson   5417
Venture in the East - Bruce Lancaster   3648
The Vermilion Bridge - Shelley Mydans   4539
Yedo - Lynn Guest   2609

Jewish Revolt

Agrippa's Daughter - Howard Fast   2025
If I Forget Thee - Brenda Lesley Segal   5720
The Last Days - William Rayner   5272
Prince of Israel - Elias Gilner   2422
Simon Bar Cochba: Rebellion in Judea - Merton Finch   2086
The Soldier and the Sage: A Novel about Akiba - Richard G. Hubler   3065
The Sword and the Promise - Benjamin Siegel   5845
The Tenth Measure - Brenda Lesley Segal   5721
The Voices of Masada - David Kossoff   3545
The Wolf of Masada - John Fredman   2220

Jews

1492 - Newton Frolich   2236
1492: The Life and Times of Juan Cabezon of Castile - Homero Aridjis   187
According to Thomas - Gladys Malvern   4053
The Age of Wonders - Aharon Appelfeld   173
Agrippa's Daughter - Howard Fast   2025
The Antagonists - Ernest K. Gann   2276
As a Driven Leaf - Milton Steinberg   5992
Babylon - Anthony Esler   1959
Badenheim 1939 - Aharon Appelfeld   174
Behold the Fire - Michael Blankfort   541
Belmarch: A Legend of the First Crusade - Christopher Davis   1514
Ben Hur: A Tale of the Christ - Lew Wallace   6536
Blessed Is the Land - Louis Zara   6949
The Book of Abraham - Marek Halter   2665
The Books of Rachel - Joel Gross   2600
The Brother - Chayym Zeldis   6958

The Candlesticks and the Cross - Ruth Freeman Solomon   5940
Crescent City - Belva Plain   5078
Cry of the Peacock - Gina Barkhordar Nahai   4552
Danzig Passage - Bodie Thoene   6221
The Devil's Spy - Michael Hastings   2773
The Doctor From Cordova: A Biographical Novel about the Great Philosopher Maimonides - Herbert Le Porrier   3693
The Dream Seekers - Stephen Longstreet   3884
The Dutchman's Dilemma - Maan Meyers   4352
The Eighth Veil - Ellis Kadison   3320
The Emperor, the Sages and Death - Rachel Berdach   475
The Enduring Years - Claire Rayner   5263
Esau - Meir Shalev   5770
Esther: The Star and the Sceptre - Gina Andrews   146
The Fixer - Bernard Malamud   4038
Flowers in the Blood - Gay Courter   1387
For Every Sin - Aharon Appelfeld   175
The Four Winds of Heaven - Monique Raphel High   2916
The Glory - Herman Wouk   6873
The Healer - Aharon Appelfeld   176
Herzl the King - Norman Kotker   3547
The Hope - Herman Wouk   6874
The House on Mulberry Street - Maan Meyers   4354
Hypatia - Charles Kingsley   3498
If I Forget Thee - Robert S. Deropp   1621
The Inquisitors - Jerzy Andrzejewski   153
The Island of the Innocent: A Novel of Greek and Jew in the Time of the Maccabees - Vardis Fisher   2108
Ivanhoe - Sir Walter Scott   5699
Jerusalem Interlude - Bodie Thoene   6223
Jesters - David Markish   4090
The Jew of Rome - Lion Feuchtwanger   2071
Josephus - Lion Feuchtwanger   2072
Josephus and the Emperor - Lion Feuchtwanger   2073
Katerina - Aharon Appelfeld   177
A Kind of Justice - Benjamin Siegel   5844
King Jesus - Robert Graves   2549
The Kingdom of the Wicked - Anthony Burgess   778
The King's Persons - Joanne Greenberg   2573
Leah's Journey - Gloria Goldreich   2460
The Letters of Nicodemus - Jan Dobraczynski   1655
The Lives of Rachel - Joel Gross   2601
Love and Wisdom: A Novel about Solomon - Richard G. Hubler   3064
Malkeh and Her Children - Marjorie Edelson   1853
The Man Who Thought He Was Messiah - Curt Leviant   3735
The Marranos - Liliane Webb   6588
Members of the Tribe - Richard Kluger   3511
The Midwife - Gay Courter   1388
Moses, Prince of Egypt - Howard Fast   2039
Munich Signature - Bodie Thoene   6224
My Beautiful White Roses - Michael Lechner   3703
Persian Conqueror - George Sidney Hellman   2822
Pilgermann - Russell Hoban   2960
Power - Lion Feuchtwanger   2074
Prague Counterpoint - Bodie Thoene   6225
Prince of Israel - Elias Gilner   2422
The Prophet - Sholem Asch   201
The Retreat - Aharon Appelfeld   178
Salvation - Sholem Asch   202
Schindler's List - Thomas Keneally   3416
The Slave - Isaac Bashevis Singer   5866
Son of Judah - Dan Levin   3738
The Source - James A. Michener   4374
Strange Wives - Shirley Barker   317
The Sword of the Golem - Abraham Rothberg   5509
To the Land of the Cattails - Aharon Appelfeld   179
Torquemada - Howard Fast   2045
Trail and Triumph: A Novel about Maimonides - Lester M. Morrison   4485
The Triumph - Ernest K. Gann   2280

Trumpets of Silver - Norma Harris 2735
Two Thieves - Manuel Komroff 3535
Tzili: The Story of a Life - Aharon Appelfeld 180
The Unanointed - Laurene Chinn 1070
Unto the Soul - Aharon Appelfeld 181
Vienna Prelude - Bodie Thoene 6228
The Wandering Arm - Sharan Newman 4603
War and Remembrance - Herman Wouk 6875
Warsaw Requiem - Bodie Thoene 6229
West to Eden - Gloria Goldreich 2461
The Winds of War - Herman Wouk 6876

Johnson County War

Too Long at the Dance - Mike Blakely 539

Journalism

Funny Papers - Tom De Haven 1559
Walter Winchell: A Novel - Michael Herr 2863

Jutland, Battle of

Buller's Victory - Richard Hough 3049
The Devil in Harbour - Catherine Gavin 2319
The Lion at Sea - Max Hennessy 2834
To the Honor of the Fleet - Robert H. Pilpel 5002

Kennesaw Mountain, Battle of

The Far Side of Home - Maggie Davis 1536

Khartoum, Siege of

Drums of Khartoum - Chloe Gartner 2307
The Last Encounter - Robin Maugham 4196

King Philip's War

Ashes in the Wilderness - William Greenough
    Schofield 5649
Legacy - Robert Vaughan 6448
Paradise - Esther Forbes 2158
The Wept of Wish-Ton-Wish - James Fenimore
    Cooper 1312
White Rising - Zane Kotker 3548

Kings Mountain, Battle of

The Border Men - Cameron Judd 3312
The Carolinians - Jane Barry 357
The Fallon Blood - Reagan O'Neal 4741
Kings Mountain - Florette Henri 2838
Rogue's March - Maristan Chapman 993
Slow Dies the Thunder - Helen Topping Miller 4395
Toil of the Brave - Inglis Fletcher 2141
Wild Horizon - F. van Wyck Mason 4164

Korean War

Cold War - Robert Vaughan 6446

Ku Klux Klan

American Eden - Marilyn Harris 2728
And Tell of Time - Laura Krey 3554
Children of the Dust - Carlile Clancy 1084
The Grass Kingdom - Jory Sherman 5818
Griffin's Way - Frank Yerby 6922
A Journey to Matecumbe - Robert Lewis
    Taylor 6188
Lorena - Frank G. Slaughter 5892
The Stubborn Heart - Frank G. Slaughter 5904
Supper at the Maxwell House - Alfred Leland
    Crabb 1407

Labor Movement

Adversary in the House - Irving Stone 6053
The Big Wind - Beatrice Coogan 1262
Bisbee '17 - Robert Houston 3056
California Glory - Dana Fuller Ross 5468
Call Home the Heart - Jessica Stirling 6040
Call the Darkness Light - Nancy Zaroulis 6954
Castle Garden - Bill Albert 63
Chase the Wind - E.V. Thompson 6264
The Day the Cowboys Quit - Elmer Kelton 3403
The Dream Seekers - Grace Mark 4085
Emmeline - Judith Rossner 5507
The God-Seeker - Sinclair Lewis 3763
Great Dream From Heaven - John Rolfe
    Gardiner 2286
How Green Was My Valley - Richard
    Llewellyn 3813
Hunt for Heaven - Elsie Barber 298
Julie - Jane Kesner Morris 4479
Metello - Vasco Pratolini 5163
The Mills of Colne - Robert Neill 4572
Mills of the Gods - Daoma Winston 6828
Out of This Furnace - Thomas Bell 425
Owen Glen - Ben Ames Williams 6766
Passage West - Dallas Miller 4382
Poor Boy and a Long Way Home - James
    Sherburne 5806
Power - Howard Fast 2041
The Rape of the Fair Country - Alexander
    Cordell 1325
Rivington Street - Meredith Tax 6175
The Scapegoat - Mary Lee Settle 5758
Storming Heaven - Denise Giardina 2394
Sunrise to Sunset - Samuel Hopkins Adams 32
This Sweet and Bitter Earth - Alexander
    Cordell 1326
Union Square - Meredith Tax 6176
The Valiant and the Daunted - Roy Clews 1115
A Vein of Riches - John Knowles 3526
Voyage: A Novel of 1896 - Sterling Hayden 2798
The White Dove - Rosie Thomas 6246

Ladysmith, Siege of

The Legacy of Ladysmith - John Kenny Crane 1413

Lake Erie, Battle of

The Court Martial of Commodore Perry - James A.
    Rhodes 5307
D'ri and I - Irving A. Bacheller 257
The Fleet in the Forest - Carl Daniel Lane 3654
My Blood and My Treasure - Mary Schumann 5674
Trumpet in the Wilderness - Robert S. Harper 2717

League of Nations

Grand Days - Frank Moorhouse 4448

Legal Profession

Jonathan Blair, Bounty Lands Lawyer - William
    Donohue Ellis 1929
Knaves Templar - Leonard Tourney 6300
Regent Square - Forbes Bramble 645
Woman of Justice - Georgia Di Donato 1639

Leisler's Rebellion

Forever Possess - Alexandra Phillips 4982

Lepanto, Battle of

The Last Crusader - Louis De Wohl 1569
A Man Called Cervantes - Bruno Frank 2201
The Wind in His Fists - John Edward Jennings 3210

Lewis and Clark Expedition

Distant Trails - Bill Gulick 2612
Forward the Nation - Donald Culross Peattie 4880
From Sea to Shining Sea - James Alexander
    Thom 6232
The Gates of the Mountains - Will Henry 2842
Hawk's Journey - Donald Clayton Porter 5119
The Man of the Storm - Ethel Hueston 3069
Sacajawea - Anna Lee Waldo 6529
Sacajawea of the Shoshones - Della F.
    Emmons 1940
The Shining Mountains - Dale Van Every 6410
Star of the West - Ethel Hueston 3070
Tale of Valor - Vardis Fisher 2112
Those Who Go Against the Current - Shirley
    Seifert 5734
Trail: The Story of the Lewis and Clark Expedition -
    Louis Charbonneau 998
Westward! - Dana Fuller Ross 5492

Lexington, Battle of

April Morning - Howard Fast 2027
Bride of Liberty - Frank Yerby 6909
Concord Bridge - Howard Horne 3035
Lionel Lincoln; or, The Leaguer of Boston - James
    Fenimore Cooper 1303
Patriot's Progress - Joseph G.E. Hopkins 3027

Lincoln County War

Apaches - Oakley Hall 2650
Billy the Kid - Edwin Corle 1330
Billy the Kid: The Legend of El Chivato - Elizabeth
    Fackler 1994
The Demise of Billy the Kid - Preston Lewis 3760
Pistols for Hire - Nelson Coral Nye 4652
The Sons of Grady Rourke - Douglas Savage 5618
Time for Outrage - Amelia Bean 397

Literary Life

The Absorbing Fire: The Byron Legend - F.W.
    Kenyon 3445
Agatha - Kathleen Tynan 6374
All This, and Heaven Too - Rachel Field 2080
The Best House in Stratford - Edward Fisher 2100
*Black Plume: The Supressed Memoirs of Edgar Allan
    Poe* - David Madsen 4027
The Blue Heaven Bends Over All - Jane Oliver 4720
Bronte - Glyn Hughes 3073
*The Buried Self: A Background to the Poems of
    Matthew Arnold* - Isobel MacDonald 3961
Byron: A Novel - Sigrid Combuchen 1225
The Caravaggio Shawl - Samuel M. Steward 6019
Chantefable - Eldorous L. Dayton 1546
Charles - Victoria Lincoln 3786
Chatterton - Peter Ackroyd 17
The City of Libertines - W.G. Hardy 2702
Cloak of Folly - Burke Boyce 606
Clodia - Robert DeMaria 1606
Come Be My Love - Diana Brown 717
Come Slowly Eden: A Novel about Emily Dickinson -
    Laura Benet 440
A Connecticut Yankee in Criminal Court - Peter J.
    Heck 2814
The Consuming Flame: The Story of George Eliot -
    F.W. Kenyon 3446
Count Manifred - Miranda Seymour 5761
Crest of the Broken Wave - James Barke 302
Crown of Grass - Charles Andrew Brady 634
*Damned Shall Be Desire: The Passionate Life of Guy
    de Maupassant* - Stephen Coulter 1384
Dark Quartet: The Story of the Brontes - Lynne Reid
    Banks 290
Dark Rider - Louis Zara 6950

The Daughter: A Novel Based on the Life of Eleanor Marx - Judith Chernaik   1012
Daughter of Time - Nelia Gardner White   6695
Dear Mrs. Boswell - Marie Muir   4508
The Death and Life of Miguel De Cervantes - Stephen Marlowe   4094
The Death of Virgil - Hermann Broch   699
The Detective and Mr. Dickens - William J. Palmer   4782
The Devil Inside: A Novel of Dostoevsky's Life - Stephen Coulter   1385
The Diary of Emily Dickinson: A Novel - Jamie Fuller   2255
Disraeli in Love - Maurice Edelman   1851
Dr. Johnson's Dear Mistress - Winifred Carter   948
Dorothy and Agatha - Gaylord Larsen   3667
The Dorothy Parker Murder Case - George Baxt   384
Dreaming of Samarkand - Martin Booth   576
Entered From the Sun - George Garrett   2301
The Exile of Celine - Tom Clark   1095
Farewell, Catullus - Pierson Dixon   1651
The Fever Called Living - Barbara Moore   4439
Flight of the Swan - Margaret Ann Hubbard   3063
Fonthill - Aubrey Menen   4335
The Fourth King - Glen Petrie   4979
The Girl From Paris - Joan Aiken   47
Go Ask the River - Evelyn Eaton   1826
The God of Mirrors - Robert Reilly   5293
God Was Born in Exile - Vintila Horia   3033
The Golden Years: A Novel Based on the Life and Loves of Percy Bysshe Shelley - F.W. Kenyon   3451
Gothic Romance - Emmanuel Carrere   942
Great Black Russian - John Oliver Killens   3484
H.—: The Story of Heathcliff's Journey Back to Wuthering Heights - Lin Haire-Sargeant   2641
Haunted Summer - Anne Edwards   1881
The Haunting of Lamb House - Joan Aiken   48
The Heart of O. Henry - Dale Kramer   3550
The Hesitant Heart - Anne Edwards   1882
The Highwayman and Mr. Dickens - William J. Palmer   4783
How Do I Love Thee - Lucille Iremonger   3110
The Hoydens and Mr. Dickens - William J. Palmer   4784
I Am Vidocq - Vincent McConnor   4225
I Give You Oscar Wilde - Desmond Hall   2647
I Never Came to You in White - Judith Farr   2014
An Imaginary Life - David Malouf   4047
In the Shadow of the Brontes - Louise Brindley   690
James and Joan - Anne Fremantle   2221
John Howard Payne, Skywalker - Maude Barragan   348
John Ruskin's Wife - Eva McDonald   4259
Johnnie Cross - Terence de Vere White   6704
Kindred Spirits - June Barraclough   347
King of Paris - Guy Endore   1942
Lady's Maid - Margaret Forster   2188
The Last Mystery of Edgar Allan Poe - Manny Meyers   4356
The Last Station - Jay Parini   4801
The Last Testament of Oscar Wilde - Peter Ackroyd   19
The Last World: A Novel with an Ovidian Repertory - Christoph Ransmayr   5253
The Laughter of Aphrodite - Peter Green   2570
Letty - Helen Ashton   218
The Lighthouse at the End of the World - Stephen Marlowe   4095
The Lion of Pescara - George MacBeth   3958
Listen for the Voices - Anne Colver   1220
Lord Byron's Doctor - Paul West   6634
Lord of the Dead: The Secret History of Byron - Tom Holland   2999
Lord of the Ladies - Joanna Dessau   1626
The Love Knot - Catherine Darby   1482
Love's Children - Judith Chernaik   1013
Love's Labour's Won - Edward Fisher   2101

A Man Called Cervantes - Bruno Frank   2201
Memoirs of a Victorian Gentleman: William Makepeace Thackeray - Margaret Forster   2189
The Memoirs of Lord Byron - Robert Nye   4655
Mermaid Tavern - George William Cronyn   1429
The Midnight Gardener: A Novel about Baudelaire - Max White   6694
The Missolonghi Manuscript - Frederic Prokosch   5194
Monsieur Moliere - Michael O'Shaughnessy   4762
Mortal Hunger: A Novel Based on the Life of Lafcadio Hearn - Harry E. Wedeck   6594
A Most Extraordinary Pair - Jean Detre   1628
Mr. Oddity, Samuel Johnson - Charles Norman   4643
Mrs. Shakespeare: The Complete Works - Robert Nye   4656
Murder Is Murder Is Murder - Samuel M. Steward   6020
The Mutual Friend - Frederick Busch   811
My Name Is Sappho - Martha Rofheart   5429
My Savage Muse: The Story of My Life: Edgar Allan Poe, an Imaginative Work - Bernhardt J. Hurwood   3087
My Sister, My Love - Lucille Iremonger   3111
Neighboring Lives - Thomas M. Disch   1648
Nicholas Cooke: Actor, Soldier, Physician, Priest - Stephanie Cowell   1393
No Bed for Bacon - Caryl Brahms   640
No Place on Earth - Christa Wolf   6836
The Noel Coward Murder Case - George Baxt   387
The Olympians - Guy Bolton   566
One Last Glimpse - James Aldridge   74
The Other Sappho - Ellen Frye   2240
Papa and Fidel - Karl Alexander   79
Parson Austen's Daughter - Helen Ashton   219
Path to the Silent Country - Lynne Reid Banks   291
The Pilgrim Prince - Gladys H. Barr   343
The Praise Singer - Mary Renault   5302
Purple Passage: A Novel about a Lady Both Famous and Fantastic - Emily Hahn   2638
The Questing Heart: A Romantic Novel about George Sand - F.W. Kenyon   3458
The Raven - Chancellor Williams   6769
Refinements of Love: A Novel about Clover and Henry Adams - Sarah Booth Conroy   1259
Reigning Passions - Kathrin Perutz   4940
The Remarkable Young Man - Cecil Roberts   5373
The Romance of Charles Dickens - Ursula Bloom   553
Savage Prodigal - Konrad Bercovici   474
The Secret Memoirs of Lord Byron - Christopher Nicole   4622
The Seducer - Henrik Stangerup   5980
The Shadow Flies - Rose Macaulay   3956
The Shadow of the Earth - Lee Wichelns   6731
Shakespeare & Son - Edward Fisher   2102
Shakespeare's Dog - Leon Rooke   5439
Sherlock Holmes and the Mysterious Friend of Oscar Wilde - Russell A. Brown   731
A Single Summer with Lord B. - Derek Marlowe   4092
A Singular Conspiracy - Barry Perowne   4915
So Perish the Roses - Neil Bell   423
Song in the Green Thorn Tree - James Barke   303
The Sot-Weed Factor - John Barth   364
Sporting with Amaryllis - Paul West   6635
The Still Storm - Francoise Sagan   5562
The Stress of Her Regard - Tim Powers   5157
The Swan of Usk - Helen Ashton   220
Take Heed of Loving Me: A Novel about John Donne - Elizabeth Gray Vining   6502
Teresa, or Her Demon Lover - Austin K. Gray   2554
These Were the Brontes - Dorothy Helen Cornish   1332
The Tree of Knowledge - Eva Figes   2085
Twice upon a Time - Allen Appel   172
Two Loves Have I - Clara Longworth de Chambrun   985
Very Young Mrs. Poe - Cothburn O'Neal   4740

Vindication - Frances Sherwood   5824
Violent Friends - Winston Clewes   1113
Voltaire! Voltaire! - Guy Endore   1943
Walt Whitman's Secret - Ben Aronin   196
The Wanderer: A Novel of Dante and Beatrice - Nathan Schachner   5633
Well of the Silent Harp - James Barke   304
Wife to Mr. Milton - Robert Graves   2553
Wild Decembers: A Biographical Portrait of the Brontes - Hilda Crystal White   6681
Wilde West - Walter Satterthwait   5609
The Wind That Shakes the Barley - James Barke   305
Wine of Life - Charles Orson Gorham   2489
Wonder of All the Gay World - James Barke   306

Little Bighorn, Battle of the

Bugles in the Afternoon - Ernest Haycox   2788
Chief of Scouts - Don Bendell   439
The Court-Martial of George Armstrong Custer - Douglas C. Jones   3276
The Crossed Sabres - Gilbert Morris   4458
Custer Passed Our Way - Fred S. Kaufman   3370
Flashman and the Redskins - George MacDonald Fraser   2208
The Last Stand: A Novel about George Armstrong Custer and the Indians of the Plains - Edwin P. Hoyt   3061
A Mighty Afternoon - Charles K. Mills   4407
Montana Road - Harry Sinclair Drago   1717
No Survivors - Will Henry   2846
A Road We Do Not Know: A Novel of Custer at the Little Bighorn - Frederick J. Chiaventone   1057
The Scout - Harry Combs   1224
Seize the Sky - Terry C. Johnston   3256
Trumpet on the Land - Terry C. Johnston   3260

Long Island, Battle of

Oliver Wiswell - Kenneth Roberts   5389

Louisburg, Siege of

Restless Are the Sails - Evelyn Eaton   1830
The Willing Maid - C.T. Ritchie   5349

Louisiana Purchase

Hawk's Journey - Donald Clayton Porter   5119
Louisiana Purchase - A.E. Hotchner   3039
The Man of the Storm - Ethel Hueston   3069
The River Devils - Carter A. Vaughan   6437
Those Who Go Against the Current - Shirley Seifert   5734
A Time for Titans - Vina Delmar   1602

Luddites

An Imperfect Joy - Jean Stubbs   6097
The Valiant and the Daunted - Roy Clews   1115

Lumber Industry

The Cup of Strength - Charlotte Paul   4840
Fire on the Wind - David Garth   2304
A Fistful of Stars - Sarah Lockwood   3828
Log Jam - Leslie Turner White   6684

Macedonian Empire

Alexander in Babylon - Jakob Wassermann   6576
Alexander of Macedon: The Journey to World's End - Harold Lamb   3607
Alexander the God - Maurice Druon   1731
Alexander the God - Robert Payne   4849
The Bronze God of Rhodes - L. Sprague De Camp   1554

The Conqueror: A Novel of Alexander the Great - Edison Marshall 4104
An Elephant for Aristotle - L. Sprague De Camp 1556
Fire From Heaven - Mary Renault 5296
Funeral Games - Mary Renault 5297
The Golden Lyre - Noel B. Gerson 2371
Lord of the Two Lands - Judith Tarr 6167
The Persian Boy - Mary Renault 5301
Star of Macedon - Karl V. Eiker 1901

Mafeking, Siege of

Siege in the Sun - Mary Paradise 4788

Magic

Conjuror's Journal - Frances L. Shine 5826
The Crystal Dove - Mollie Hardwick 2692
Fata Morgana - William Kotzwinkle 3549
The Illusionist - Anita Mason 4144
Mr. Vertigo - Paul Auster 244
Silk Road - Jeanne Larsen 3670

Malazgirt, Battle of

Shards of Empire - Susan Schwartz 5677

Manzikent, Battle of

The Lady for Ransom - Alfred Duggan 1768

Maoris

The Empire Builders - William Stuart Long 3871
Monday's Warriors - Maurice Shadbolt 5767

Masada, Siege of

The Antagonists - Ernest K. Gann 2276
The Last Days - William Rayner 5272
The Tenth Measure - Brenda Lesley Segal 5721
The Voices of Masada - David Kossoff 3545
The Wolf of Masada - John Fredman 2220

Mayan Empire

Cradle of the Sun - John Clagett 1083
Journey to the Sky: A Novel about the True Adventures of Two Men in Search of the Lost Maya Kingdom - Jamake Highwater 2918
A Signal Victory - David Stacton 5976
Tikal: A Novel about the Maya - Daniel Peters 4947

McCarthy Era

The Establishment - Howard Fast 2030

Medical Profession

The Abyss - Marguerite Yourcenar 6946
Affairs of Love - Nicola Thorne 6272
After the Rainbow - Yvonne Kalman 3323
Alabama Empire - Welbourn Kelley 3392
The Babylonians - Nathaniel Norsen Weinreb 6600
The Beacon of Alexandria - Gillian Bradshaw 627
Bedford Row - Claire Rayner 5259
The Book of Shadows - C.L. Grace 2505
The Brooks Legend - William Donohue Ellis 1928
Canal Town - Samuel Hopkins Adams 29
Charing Cross - Claire Rayner 5260
A City Not Forsaken - Lynn Morris 4480
Covent Garden - Claire Rayner 5262
Creole Dusk - Walter Adolphe Roberts 5392
The Cry and the Covenant - Morton Thompson 6269
The Dedicated - Willa Gibbs 2399

The Diary of William Harvey: The Imaginary Journal of the Physician Who Revolutionized Medicine - Jean Hamburger 2667
Divine Mistress - Frank G. Slaughter 5886
Dr. Gully's Story - Elizabeth Jenkins 3190
Domina - Barbara Wood 6847
The Drummer Was the First to Die - Liza Pennywitt Taylor 6186
Dual Destiny - Karen Lynn 3939
Eagle in the Sky - F. van Wyck Mason 4149
Eagles Where I Walk - Stephen Longstreet 3885
Eating Pavlova - D.M. Thomas 6235
The Emperor's Physician - Jacob Randolph Perkins 4914
The Eye in the Door - Pat Barker 307
The Eye of God - C.L. Grace 2506
A Few Painted Feathers - Stephen Longstreet 3886
Fleet Surgeon to Pharaoh - Sheldon Jacobson 3140
The Gentleman From Chicago - John Cashman 953
The Ghost Road - Pat Barker 308
Gower Street - Claire Rayner 5264
Green City in the Sun - Barbara Wood 6849
The Hand of a Woman - Diana Brown 719
Hanging on the Wire - Gillian Linscott 3806
The Haymarket - Claire Rayner 5265
The Healers - Henry Denker 1610
The Heart of the Continent - Nancy Cato 961
Henry James' Midnight Song - Carol de Chellis Hill 2920
Hilton Head - Josephine Pinckney 5003
The Hospital - Agatha Young 6938
I Swear by Apollo - Agatha Young 6939
Jack the Ripper - Richard Gordon 2484
The Kidnapped Surgeon - Alexander Knox 3527
Kings Row - Henry Bellamann 428
Lancet - Garet Rogers 5431
The Love of Fingin O'Lea - Theodora McCormick Du Bois 1743
The Medicine Man - Shirley Seifert 5729
The Merchant of Death - C.L. Grace 2508
Middlemarch - George Eliot 1909
The Midwife - Gay Courter 1388
The Midwife's Advice - Gay Courter 1389
Minna's Story: The Secret Love of Doctor Sigmund Freud - Kathleen Daniels 1463
Miss Morissa: Doctor of the Gold Trail - Mari Sandoz 5592
Molokai - Oswald Andrew Bushnell 815
Paddington Green - Claire Rayner 5266
The Passionate Pilgrim - Charles Terrot 6204
The Passions of the Mind - Irving Stone 6062
The Physician - Noah Gordon 2482
Physician Extraordinary: A Novel of the Life and Times of William Harvey - David Weiss 6608
The Physician of London - Stephanie Cowell 1394
Pinto and Sons - Leslie Epstein 1947
The Price of Liberty - Joseph G.E. Hopkins 3028
The Private Life of Florence Nightingale - Richard Gordon 2485
The Queen's Physician - Edgar Maas 3952
The Rationalist - Warwick Collins 1217
Regeneration - Pat Barker 309
Restoration: A Novel of Seventeenth-Century England - Rose Tremain 6333
The Road to Bithynia: A Novel of Luke, the Beloved Physician - Frank G. Slaughter 5897
The Road to Wellville - T. Coraghessan Boyle 618
Sangaree - Frank G. Slaughter 5898
The Scalpel and the Sword - Dell Shannon 5774
Secret Dreams - Keith Korman 3541
The Secret Life of Laszlo, Count Dracula - Roderick Anscombe 156
Serpent and Staff - Frank Yerby 6927
Shadow of the Mountains - Lynn Morris 4481
Shaman - Noah Gordon 2483
A Shrine of Murders - C.L. Grace 2509
The Sleep of Life - Richard Gordon 2486
Soho Square - Claire Rayner 5268
Soul Flame - Barbara Wood 6850

The Spanish Doctor - Matt Cohen 1159
Storm Before Sunrise - June Wyndham Davies 1507
The Strand - Claire Rayner 5269
The Strange Case of Madamoiselle P. - Patrick Ireland 3109
The Stubborn Heart - Frank G. Slaughter 5904
The Swan of Usk - Helen Ashton 220
Swear by Apollo - Shirley Barker 318
Testimony of Two Men - Taylor Caldwell 863
They Called Her Mrs. Doc - Janette Oke 4709
Time in Its Flight - Susan Fromberg Schaeffer 5636
Timothy Baines - John H. Culp 1445
To Keep This Oath - Hebe Weenolsen 6597
The Torch - Wilder Penfield 4902
The Trial of Jenny Sykes - Hebe Weenolsen 6598
The Twelfth Physician - Willa Gibbs 2403
An Unholy Alliance - Susanna Gregory 2586
A Vision of Light - Judith Merkle Riley 5337
When Nietzsche Wept: A Novel of Obsession - Irvin D. Yalom 6892
The White Hotel - D.M. Thomas 6237
The Year of the Death - Reuben R. Merliss 4343

Mexican Empire

A Rage Against Heaven - Fred Mustard Stewart 6026

Mexican Revolution

The Adelita - Oakley Hall 2649
Blue Moon - Parris Afton Bonds 569
The Cactus and the Crown - Catherine Gavin 2318
Chapultepec - Norman Zollinger 6965
Chihuahua 1916 - Otis Carney 903
The Crimson Wind - Max Hennessy 2832
Escape From Sonora - Will Bryant 739
The Fifth Horseman - Jose Antonio Villarreal 6496
The Friends of Pancho Villa - James Carlos Blake 535
The House on Bitterness Street - Elizabeth Borton de Trevino 6340
Keeping Secrets - Suzanne Morris 4483
Last Reveille - David Morrell 4456
Mexico - James A. Michener 4372
A Mule for the Marquesa - Frank O'Rourke 4753
Not of War Only - Norman Zollinger 6966
The Prison Notebooks of Ricardo Flores Magon - Douglas Day 1545
Sergeant Gringo - Jack Cummings 1449
South of the Border - John Byrne Cooke 1268
The Tin Lizzie Troup - Glendon Swarthout 6146
Tom Mix and Pancho Villa - Clifford Irving 3113
Under the Fifth Sun: A Novel of Pancho Villa - Earl Shorris 5832
El Vago - Laurence Gonzales 2474
The War Train: A Novel of 1916 - Brown Meggs 4324
When the Owl Cries - Paul Bartlett 367

Mexican War

Before Darkness Falls - Eugenia Price 5178
Captain Grant - Shirley Seifert 5724
Captain Jack - Gene Shelton 5800
Carmen of the Rancho - Frank H. Spearman 5955
Divine Average - Elithe Hamilton Kirkland 3505
Dominion - Jack Rowe 5514
Doniphan's Ride - Les Savage Jr. 5620
Drumm's War - Bill Bragg 638
Eagle in the Sun - Hoffman Birney 508
Eagle on the Sun - Julia Davis 1527
Folded Hills - Stewart Edward White 6701
The Golden Eagle - Noel B. Gerson 2370
Hill of the Hawk - Scott O'Dell 4689
Jornada - Robert L. Duffus 1754
Jubilee Trail - Gwen Bristow 698
A Man's Reach - Charles Morrow Wilson 6796

The Quiet Life of Mrs. General Lane - Victoria Case   951
The Roads to Guadalupe - Robert Lewis Taylor   6190
Rush to Destroy - L. Jay Martin   4133
The Slender Reed - Noel B. Gerson   2382
Star of Empire: A Novel of Old San Antonio - Leonard Sanders   5590
The Wine of San Lorenzo - Herbert Gorman   2493

Middle Ages

The Age of Miracles - Catherine MacCoun   3960
Alamut - Judith Tarr   6164
The Alchymist's Journal - Evan S. Connell   1256
Alexander the Glorious - Jane Oliver   4719
An Ancient Evil - C.L. Grace   2504
Angel of Death - P.C. Doherty   1670
Ann of Cambray - Mary Lide   3772
Antichrist: A Novel of the Emperor Frederick II - Cecelia Holland   2982
The Apothecary Rose - Candace M. Robb   5364
Ardent Flame - Frances Winwar   6829
An Army of Angels: A Novel of Joan of Arc - Pamela Marcantel   4079
An Army of Children - Evan H. Rhodes   5306
The Axe - Sigrid Undset   6378
Banners of Gold - Pamela Kaufman   3371
The Barons of Runnymede - Pamela Bennetts   445
The Battle-Ax of God - Le Roy MacLeod   4007
The Battle of the Queens - Jean Plaidy   5005
Beguiled - Alice Borchardt   577
La Belle Sorel - Jacques Carton   949
Belmarch: A Legend of the First Crusade - Christopher Davis   1514
Beloved Enemy: The Passions of Eleanor of Aquitaine - Ellen Jones   3288
Beloved Lady - Barbara Jefferis   3174
Below the Salt - Thomas B. Costain   1362
Bernadin, My Love - Leonard Rossiter   5506
The Betrothed - Sir Walter Scott   5691
Bird of Fire: A Tale of Francis of Assisi - Helen Constance White   6676
The Bishop's Tale - Margaret Frazer   2215
The Black Arrow - Robert Louis Stevenson   6008
The Black Rose - Thomas B. Costain   1363
Blessed Are the Meek: A Novel about St. Francis of Assisi - Zofja Kossak-Szczucka   3542
The Bloody Field - Edith Pargeter   4795
The Blue Falcon - Robyn Carr   935
Bodin, 1349: An Epic Novel of Christians and Jews in the Plague Years - Roberta Kalechofsky   3322
Bond of Blood - Roberta Gellis   2349
Bond of Honour - Catherine Todd   6284
A Booke of Days: A Journal of the Crusade by Roger, Duke of Lunel - Stephen J. Rivele   5351
The Boy's Tale - Margaret Frazer   2216
Braveheart - Randall Wallace   6538
Brazen Whispers - Jane Feather   2055
The Breath of Kings - Gene Farrington   2019
The Briar Rose - Linda Neale   4561
The Bridal Wreath - Sigrid Undset   6379
The Bride - Julie Garwood   2311
Bronze Mirror - Jeanne Larsen   3668
Brother Cadfael's Penance - Ellis Peters   4955
The Brothers of Gwynedd - Edith Pargeter   4796
By Right of Arms - Robyn Carr   937
Candle in the Window - Christina Dodd   1662
Castle Dangerous - Sir Walter Scott   5694
Champion - L. Christian Balling   285
The Children of the First Man - James Alexander Thom   6230
Cities of the Flesh - Zoe Oldenbourg   4713
The Cloister and the Hearth - Charles Reade   5279
Concordia - Frances Fleetwood   2124
The Confessions of Brother Halvin - Ellis Peters   4956

A Connecticut Yankee in King Arthur's Court - Mark Twain   6371
The Conqueror - Georgette Heyer   2881
The Conqueror's Wife - Noel B. Gerson   2363
The Conquest - Jude Deveraux   1630
The Constant Star - Prudence Andrew   139
The Corner That Held Them - Sylvia Townsend Warner   6568
The Cornerstone - Zoe Oldenbourg   4714
Count Bohemond - Alfred Duggan   1764
Count Robert of Paris - Sir Walter Scott   5695
The Courts of Love: A Romance of Medieval France - Peter Bourne   592
The Cross - Sigrid Undset   6380
Cross, Sword, and Arrow - Gladys H. Barr   340
The Crown in Darkness - P.C. Doherty   1671
Crusader's Torch - Chelsea Quinn Yarbro   6897
The De Montfort Legacy - Pamela Bennetts   447
Dead Man's Ransom - Ellis Peters   4957
Death and the Chapman - Kate Sedley   5715
Death Comes as Epiphany - Sharan Newman   4598
The Death of a King - P.C. Doherty   1672
Death of the Red King - Pamela Bennetts   448
Deep Are the Valleys - Hannah Closs   1129
Defy Not the Heart - Johanna Lindsey   3794
Desire and Deceive - Cordia Byers   832
Destiny of Fire - Zoe Oldenbourg   4715
The Devil Is Loose - Graham Shelby   5790
The Devil's Cross - Walter O'Meara   4733
The Devil's Door - Sharan Newman   4599
The Devil's Novice - Ellis Peters   4958
The Disputed Crown - Valerie Anand   128
The Doctor From Cordova: A Biographical Novel about the Great Philosopher Maimonides - Herbert Le Porrier   3693
Doctor Mirabilis - James Blish   550
Don Pedro's Captain - Pamela Bennetts   449
A Dragon for Edward - Pamela Bennetts   450
The Dragons of Archenfield - Edward Marston   4119
Eagle of the Gredos - Claude Jack Osgood   4761
The Earl - Cecelia Holland   2987
Earth Song - Catherine Coulter   1374
Eleanor the Queen - Norah Lofts   3842
Elizabeth's Greetings - Rosemary Haughton   2774
Emerald Fire - Laurie Grant   2537
The Emperor, the Sages and Death - Rachel Berdach   475
The Eve of Saint Hyacinth - Kate Sedley   5716
An Excellent Mystery - Ellis Peters   4959
The Eye of God - C.L. Grace   2506
The Falcon and the Flower - Virginia Henley   2826
Falconer's Crusade - Ian Morson   4493
Falconer's Judgement - Ian Morson   4494
Falls the Shadow - Sharon Kay Penman   4903
Falstaff - Robert Nye   4653
The Fatal Crown - Ellen Jones   3289
Fire in the Ice - Dorothy James Roberts   5375
The Firedrake - Cecelia Holland   2988
Fitzempress' Law - Diana Norman   4644
Flambard's Confession - Marilyn Durham   1816
The Follies of the King - Jean Plaidy   5014
The Fool of Venus - George William Cronyn   1428
Fortune Made His Sword - Martha Rofheart   5426
Fortune's Knave: The Making of William the Conqueror - Mary Lide   3774
The Foster Brothers - Edward Frankland   2202
The Gallowglass - Howard Breslin   666
The Garden of Persephone - Cesar J. Rotondi   5510
Gay Crusader - Cleone Knox   3528
The Gentle Falcon - Hilda Lewis   3747
The Gentle Knight - Philip Lindsay   3791
Gilded Spurs - Grace Ingram   3105
Gildenford - Valerie Anand   130
Glendower Country - Martha Rofheart   5427
The Godforgotten - Gladys Schmitt   5642
Godric - Frederick Buechner   763
God's Equal - Alain Absire   14
The Golden Chain - Jean Gamo   2275
The Golden Exile - Lawrence Schoonover   5664

The Golden Hand - Edith Simon   5856
The Golden Knight - George Challis   971
The Golden Warrior: The Story of Harold and William - Hope Muntz   4517
The Goldsmith's Wife - Jean Plaidy   5017
Good King Harry - Denise Giardina   2393
The Good Yeomen - Jay Williams   6771
The Great Infidel - Joseph Jay Deiss   1582
Great Maria - Cecelia Holland   2989
The Greenlanders - Jane Smiley   5915
Guns Forever Echo - Kenneth M. Ellis   1925
Hammer of the Scots - Jean Plaidy   5018
Harlot Queen - Hilda Lewis   3748
Harold, the Last of the Saxon Kings - Edward Bulwer-Lytton   767
Harold Was My King - Hilda Lewis   3749
Harp into Battle - Cecil Maiden   4031
Harry of Monmouth - A.M. Maughan   4199
The Heart of the Lion - Jean Plaidy   5020
The Heaven Tree Trilogy - Edith Pargeter   4797
The Heirs of the Kingdom - Zoe Oldenbourg   4716
Here Be Dragons - Sharon Kay Penman   4904
The Heretic's Apprentice - Ellis Peters   4960
Hereward the Wake - Charles Kingsley   3497
The Hermit of Eyton Forest - Ellis Peters   4961
High Are the Mountains - Hannah Closs   1130
The Holy Innocents - Kate Sedley   5717
The Holy Thief - Ellis Peters   4962
The Homecoming - Norah Lofts   3844
The Hooded Falcon - Prudence Andrew   140
The Hunchback of Notre Dame - Victor Hugo   3076
I Am England - Patricia Wright   6881
The Image of Our Lord - Edward Burman   790
In Pursuit of the Green Lion - Judith Merkle Riley   5334
In the Falcon's Claw: A Novel of the Year 1000 - Chet Raymo   5257
In the Shadow of Midnight - Marsha Canham   880
In the Wilderness - Sigrid Undset   6381
The Infidel - Georgia Elizabeth Taylor   6182
The Infidels - Chloe Gartner   2308
The Invention of Truth - Marta Morazzoni   4449
The Iron King - Maurice Druon   1732
Isabel the Fair - Margaret Campbell Barnes   323
Ivanhoe - Sir Walter Scott   5699
Jerusalem - Cecelia Holland   2990
Joanna the Pope - Daniel Panger   4785
The Journal of Hildegard of Bingen - Barbara Lachman   3578
The Journeyer - Gary Jennings   3194
The Joyful Beggar: A Novel of St. Francis of Assisi - Louis De Wohl   1568
Katherine - Anya Seton   5752
The Keys of England - William Victor Cooke   1271
King Hereafter - Dorothy Dunnett   1802
King of the Wood - Valerie Anand   131
Kingdom of Shadows - Barbara Erskine   1954
Kingdom of the Grail - A.A. Attanasio   226
The King's Bishop - Candace M. Robb   5365
The King's Daughters - Molly Costain Haycraft   2793
The Kings in Winter - Cecelia Holland   2991
King's Man - C.M. Edmondston   1880
The Kings of Vain Intent - Graham Shelby   5791
The King's Persons - Joanne Greenberg   2573
Kinsmen of the Grail - Dorothy James Roberts   5376
The Knight - George Shipway   5829
Knight with Armour - Alfred Duggan   1767
Knights - Linda Lael Miller   4399
Knight's Acre - Norah Lofts   3848
Knight's Honor - Roberta Gellis   2351
The Knights of Dark Renown - Graham Shelby   5792
Ladies Whose Bright Eyes - Ford Madox Ford   2162
The Lady Chapel - Candace M. Robb   5366
The Lady for Ransom - Alfred Duggan   1768
Lady Godiva and Master Tom - Raoul Cohen Faure   2052
Lady of Hay - Barbara Erskine   1955
Lady of Monkton - Elizabeth Byrd   835

Lady of Moray - Bonnie Copeland 1318

Lady of the Forest - Jennifer Roberson 5368

The Lady Royal - Molly Costain Haycraft 2794

Lay Siege to Heaven: A Novel of Saint Catherine of Siena - Louis De Wohl 1570

The Leopard Unleashed - Elizabeth Chadwick 967

Leopards and Lilies - Alfred Duggan 1769

The Leper King - Zofja Kossak-Szczucka 3544

The Leper of St. Giles - Ellis Peters 4963

The Lily and the Leopard - Susan Wiggs 6745

The Lily and the Lion - Maurice Druon 1733

The Lion and the Leopard - Mary Ellen Johnson 3226

The Lion Is Come - Jane Oliver 4725

The Lion of Christ - Margaret Butler 823

The Lion of England - Margaret Butler 824

The Lion of England - Eve Trevaskis 6336

The Lion of Ireland - Morgan Llywelyn 3822

The Lion of Justice - Margaret Butler 825

The Lion of Justice - Jean Plaidy 5031

Lionheart!: A Novel of Richard I, King of England - Martha Rofheart 5428

The Lions of the North - Edward Marston 4121

Locksley - Nicholas Chase 1003

The Lodestar - Pamela Belle 432

Lord Geoffrey's Fancy - Alfred Duggan 1771

The Lord of the Last Days: Visions of the Year 1000 - Homero Aridjis 188

The Lords of Lancaster - Pamela Bennetts 452

The Lords of Vaumartin - Cecelia Holland 2992

The Lost Flight - H.F.M. Prescott 5169

The Lost Lands - Peter Vansittart 6430

The Love Knot - Catherine Darby 1482

The Love of Fingin O'Lea - Theodora McCormick Du Bois 1743

The Lute Player - Norah Lofts 3852

Madselin - Norah Lofts 3853

Magnificent Enemies - Edgar Maas 3951

Marjorie of Scotland - Pamela Hill 2939

The Marriage of Meggotta - Edith Pargeter 4799

Masques of Gold - Roberta Gellis 2352

Mass for Arras - Andrzej Szczypiorski 6153

The Master Painter - Edwin Mullins 4513

Men Like Shadows - Dorothy Charques 1000

The Mistress of Husaby - Sigrid Undset 6382

Mistress of the Eagles - Elona Malterre 4052

A Moment in Time - Bertrice Small 5911

Monk's Hood - Ellis Peters 4964

Morality Play - Barry Unsworth 6387

A Morbid Taste for Bones - Ellis Peters 4965

The Morning Gift - Diana Norman 4645

Mortal Love: A Novel of Eleanor of Aquitaine - Linda Hutchins 3090

Mortal Pageant - Johan Fabricius 1993

My Beautiful White Roses - Michael Lechner 3703

My Gallant Enemy - Rexanne Becnel 409

My Life for My Sheep - Alfred Duggan 1772

My Lord Brother the Lionheart - Molly Costain Haycraft 2795

My Lord John - Georgette Heyer 2895

Myself as Witness - James Goldman 2458

The Name of the Rose - Umberto Eco 1850

The Nightingale Gallery - Paul Harding 2684

No Man's Son - Doris Sutcliffe Adams 23

The Norman Pretender - Valerie Anand 132

Not Built with Hands - Helen Constance White 6679

The Novice's Tale - Margaret Frazer 2217

The Nun's Tale - Candace M. Robb 5367

One Corpse Too Many - Ellis Peters 4966

Ordeal by Silence - Prudence Andrew 142

Our Lives Have Just Begun - Henry Myers 4541

The Outlaw's Tale - Margaret Frazer 2218

Owen Glendower - John Cowper Powys 5159

The Paladin - George Shipway 5830

Passage to Pontefract - Jean Plaidy 5038

The Passionate Enemies - Jean Plaidy 5039

The Peacock and the Pearl - Jennifer Lang 3661

The Perfect Joy of St. Francis - Felix Timmermans 6281

Peter Abelard: A Novel - Helen Waddell 6517

The Physician - Noah Gordon 2482

Pilgermann - Russell Hoban 2960

The Pilgrim of Hate - Ellis Peters 4967

The Pillars of the Earth - Ken Follett 2149

The Plantagenet Prelude - Jean Plaidy 5041

The Plymouth Cloak - Kate Sedley 5718

The Poisoned Crown - Maurice Druon 1734

Poland - James A. Michener 4373

The Potter's Field - Ellis Peters 4968

Pride of Lions - Morgan Llywelyn 3823

The Prince and the Pauper - Mark Twain 6373

The Prince of Darkness - P.C. Doherty 1675

The Prince of Darkness - Jean Plaidy 5044

Princess of Fire - Shannon Drake 1718

The Proud Villeins - Valerie Anand 133

The Queen From Provence - Jean Plaidy 5047

Queen of Swords - Judith Tarr 6169

The Queen's Man - Sharon Kay Penman 4905

The Queen's Secret - Jean Plaidy 5053

The Queen's War: A Novel of Eleanor of Aquitaine - Jeanne Mackin 3996

Quentin Durward - Sir Walter Scott 5705

The Quiet Light - Louis De Wohl 1572

The Rain Maiden - Jill M. Phillips 4985

The Raven in the Foregate - Ellis Peters 4969

The Ravens of Blackwater - Edward Marston 4126

The Reckoning - Sharon Kay Penman 4906

Red Adam's Lady - Grace Ingram 3106

Red Lion and Gold Dragon - Rosemary Sprague 5969

Red Slayer: Being the Second of the Sorrowful Mysteries of Brother Athelstan - Paul Harding 2685

The Revolt of the Eaglets - Jean Plaidy 5057

Richard and the Knights of God - Pamela Bennetts 454

Richard Whittington, London's Mayor - Gwynedd Sudworth 6112

Riddle Me a Murder - Duane Crowley 1435

Ride Home Tomorrow - Evan John 3221

Rienzi, or The Last of the Tribunes - Edward Bulwer-Lytton 770

Riot at Gravesend: A Novel of Wat Tyler's Rebellion - William Howard Woods 6864

Robert the Bruce: The Path of the Hero King - Nigel Tranter 6318

Robert the Bruce: The Price of the King's Peace - Nigel Tranter 6319

Robert the Bruce: The Steps to the Empty Throne - Nigel Tranter 6320

Robin and the King - Parke Godwin 2448

The Ronin - William Dale Jennings 3212

The Rose Rent - Ellis Peters 4970

Rosehaven - Catherine Coulter 1380

The Royal Pawn - Antonia Ridge 5327

A Royal Quest - Mary Lide 3777

The Royal Succession - Maurice Druon 1735

Royal Sword at Agincourt - Pamela Bennetts 455

The Running Vixen - Elizabeth Chadwick 968

The Ruthless Yeomen - Valerie Anand 134

The Saint - Fritz von Unruh 6385

Saint Francis - Nikos Kazantzakis 3385

St. Peter's Fair - Ellis Peters 4971

The Sanctuary Sparrow - Ellis Peters 4972

The Saracen Blade - Frank Yerby 6926

Satan in St. Mary's - P.C. Doherty 1676

Satan's Fire - P.C. Doherty 1677

The Saxon Tapestry - Sile Rice 5317

The Scottish Chiefs - Jane Porter 5135

A Search for a King: A 12th-Century Legend - Gore Vidal 6492

Secret Song - Catherine Coulter 1381

The Serpent Amongst the Lilies - P.C. Doherty 1678

The Servant's Tale - Margaret Frazer 2219

The Seven Ages - Eva Figes 2084

The Seven Hills of Paradise - Rosemary Simpson 5859

The She-Wolf - Pamela Bennetts 456

The She-Wolf of France - Maurice Druon 1736

The Sheriff of Nottingham - Richard Kluger 3512

Sherwood - Parke Godwin 2449

Shield of Honor - Alice Walworth Graham 2511

Shield of Three Lions - Pamela Kaufman 3372

A Shrine of Murders - C.L. Grace 2509

The Siege - Jay Williams 6773

The Silent Tarn - Hannah Closs 1131

Silver Leopard - F. van Wyck Mason 4160

A Silver Mirror - Roberta Gellis 2353

Simon the Coldheart - Georgette Heyer 2901

Simple Prayers - Michael Golding 2452

Sing Morning Star - Jane Oliver 4727

Sing to the Sun - Lucille Borden 579

Sir Pagan - Henry John Colyton 1222

The Snake Pit - Sigrid Undset 6383

The Son Avenger - Sigrid Undset 6384

Son of Dust - H.F.M. Prescott 5171

The Song of a Dark Angel - P.C. Doherty 1679

Sons of the Steppe: The Story of How the Conqueror Genghis Khan Was Overcome - Hans Baumann 380

A Sparkle From the Coal - Prudence Andrew 144

The Spire - William Golding 2457

Spy in Chancery - P.C. Doherty 1680

Stealing Heaven: The Love Story of Heloise and Abelard - Marion Meade 4317

Stephen and the Sleeping Saints - Pamela Bennetts 457

A Stolen Tongue - Sheri Holman 3002

The Stones of the Abbey - Fernand Pouillon 5144

The Strangled Queen - Maurice Druon 1737

Strong as Death - Sharan Newman 4602

The Summer of the Danes - Ellis Peters 4973

Sunset at Noon - Jane Oliver 4728

Swords of Anjou - Mario Pei 4890

The Swords of December - Robert York 6933

Sybille - Marion Meade 4318

The Talisman - Sir Walter Scott 5708

The Tall One - Barbara Jefferis 3175

The Taming - Jude Deveraux 1633

A Tapestry of Murders - C.L. Grace 2510

The Teutonic Knights - Henryk Sienkiewicz 5849

Their Most Serene Majesties - Ange Vlachos 6505

This Bright Sword - Donald Barr Chidsey 1066

This January Tale - Bryher 747

Thomas: A Novel of the Life, Passions, and Miracles of Becket - Shelley Mydans 4538

Time of the Unicorn - Barbara Jefferis 3176

To Keep This Oath - Hebe Weenolsen 6597

Tomorrow's Fire - Jay Williams 6775

The Town House - Norah Lofts 3861

Trail and Triumph: A Novel about Maimonides - Lester M. Morrison 4485

The Trees of the Folkungs - Verner Von Heidenstam 2817

The Troubadour's Romance - Robyn Carr 940

The True Cross - Carlo Scarfoglio 5629

True Thomas - Nigel Tranter 6322

The Trumpet of God - David Duncan 1784

Two Ravens - Cecelia Holland 2997

The Ugly Duchess - Lion Feuchtwanger 2075

Under the Winter Moon - Teresa Brooke 705

An Unholy Alliance - Susanna Gregory 2586

The Unholy Pilgrim - R.F. Tapsell 6161

The Unhurrying Chase - H.F.M. Prescott 5172

A Viking's Daughter - John Andrews 147

The Virgin in the Ice - Ellis Peters 4974

A Vision of Light - Judith Merkle Riley 5337

Vows of the Peacock - Alice Walworth Graham 2513

A Walk with Love and Death - Hans Koning 3539

Walk with Peril - Dorothy V.S. Jackson 3132

The Walking Drum - Louis L'Amour 3632

The Wanderer: A Novel of Dante and Beatrice - Nathan Schachner 5633

The Wandering Arm - Sharan Newman 4603

The Weaver's Tale - Kate Sedley 5719

When Christ and His Saints Slept - Sharon Kay Penman 4908
When God Slept - Peter Bourne 597
Where Magic Dwells - Rexanne Becnel 411
The White Company - Sir Arthur Conan Doyle 1716
The White Cutter - David Pownall 5158
Who Was Then the Gentleman - Charles E. Israel 3125
The Whyte Harte - P.C. Doherty 1681
Wife to the Bastard - Hilda Lewis 3753
The Wild Hunt - Elizabeth Chadwick 969
Wine of Satan - Laverne Gay 2327
Within the Hollow Crown - Margaret Campbell Barnes 331
Witness to Treason - Millie J. Ragosta 5244
The Wolf at the Door - Graham Shelby 5793
Wolf's Embrace - Gail Link 3801
The Wolves of Savernake - Edward Marston 4130
The Woman in the Cloak - Pamela Hill 2949
The Wrong Horse - Jean Bassan 374
The Year of the Death - Reuben R. Merliss 4343

Military Life

The Arrows of Hercules - L. Sprague De Camp 1553
The Barefoot Brigade - Douglas C. Jones 3274
Battle Flag - Bernard Cornwell 1333
Beloved Soldiers - C.L. Skelton 5871
The Bloody Ground - Bernard Cornwell 1334
Blue Hurricane - F. van Wyck Mason 4146
Blunted Lance - Max Hennessy 2829
Captain Grant - Shirley Seifert 5724
Condottiere - Jan Westcott 6644
Copperhead - Bernard Cornwell 1335
Court of Honor - Maria Fagyas 1996
The Deluge - Henryk Sienkiewicz 5846
The Devil's Lieutenant - Maria Fagyas 1998
Eagle in the Snow - Wallace Breem 654
Farewell, My General - Shirley Seifert 5726
Fenwick Travers and the Years of Empire - Raymond M. Saunders 5614
A Few Good Men - William Overgard 4768
Fire in the Steppe - Henryk Sienkiewicz 5847
Gentlemen—The Regiment! - Hugh Talbot 6154
The Gray Captain - Jere Hungerford Wheelwright 6669
The Gun - C.S. Forester 2174
Invading Tibet - Mark Frutkin 2239
The Killer Angels - Michael Shaara 5766
The Limits of Glory: A Novel of Waterloo - James McDonough 4265
Long Day at Shiloh - Don Bannister 294
Look Away - Harold Coyle 1395
The Mullah From Kashmir - Duncan MacNeil 4016
Officer and Gentleman - Josephine Delves-Broughton 1604
Our Valiant Few - F. van Wyck Mason 4155
The Proud Canaries - David Johnson 3222
Proud New Flags - F. van Wyck Mason 4156
Rags of Glory - Stuart Cloete 1126
Rebel - Bernard Cornwell 1336
Rommel and the Rebel - Lawrence Wells 6622
Salisbury Plain - Henry C. Branson 650
The Scarlet Guidon - Ray Grant Toepfer 6287
The Sea Panther: A Novel about the Commander of the U.S.S. Constitution - Philip Vail 6397
Sergeant Gringo - Jack Cummings 1449
Seven Men of Gascony - R.F. Delderfield 1589
Sherman's March - Cynthia Bass 373
Shiloh - Shelby Foote 2153
The Sword of General Englund - Donald Honig 3023
Talleyman - John James 3161
That's Me in the Middle - Donald Jack 3129
Three Cheers for Me - Donald Jack 3131
The Three Legions - Gregory Solon 5941
The Tin Lizzie Troup - Glendon Swarthout 6146
Trumpet to Arms - Bruce Lancaster 3647

Ulysses: A Biographical Novel - Robert Skimin 5878
The Unwritten Chronicles of Robert E. Lee - Lamar Herrin 2864
The Valiant Virginians - James Warner Bellah 427
Valley Forge - MacKinlay Kantor 3364
Winter Quarters - Alfred Duggan 1775
With Fire and Sword - Henryk Sienkiewicz 5850

Military Life—British Army

Badge of Glory - Douglas E. Reeman 5287
Barry Lyndon - William Makepeace Thackeray 6210
Bayonets in the Sun - William Moore 4446
Bush War! - William Moore 4447
By Command of the Viceroy - Duncan MacNeil 4010
Charge of Cowardice - Duncan MacNeil 4011
Dando on Delhi Ridge - William Clive 1119
Drums Along the Khyber - Duncan MacNeil 4013
Drums of War - Roy Clews 1114
The First to Land - Douglas E. Reeman 5288
Flashman - George MacDonald Fraser 2204
Flashman at the Charge - George MacDonald Fraser 2209
Forget the Glory - Emma Drummond 1725
The Gates of Kunara - Duncan MacNeil 4014
Guns of Burgoyne - Bruce Lancaster 3640
How Young They Die - Stuart Cloete 1124
The Leopard and the Cliff - Wallace Breem 655
Lieutenant of the Line - Duncan MacNeil 4015
The Maclarens - C.L. Skelton 5873
Proceed, Sergeant Lamb - Robert Graves 2550
A Question of Honour - Emma Drummond 1726
The Ravi Lancers - John Masters 4178
The Red Daniel - Duncan MacNeil 4017
Redcoat - Bernard Cornwell 1337
The Regiment - Christopher Nicole 4620
The Restless Frontier - Duncan MacNeil 4018
Rifleman Dodd - C.S. Forester 2181
Sadhu on the Mountain Peak - Duncan MacNeil 4019
The Salamanca Drum - Dorothy Eden 1861
Sergeant Lamb's America - Robert Graves 2552
Sharpe's Battle - Bernard Cornwell 1338
Sharpe's Company - Bernard Cornwell 1339
Sharpe's Eagle - Bernard Cornwell 1341
Sharpe's Enemy - Bernard Cornwell 1342
Sharpe's Gold - Bernard Cornwell 1343
Sharpe's Honour - Bernard Cornwell 1344
Sharpe's Regiment - Bernard Cornwell 1345
Sharpe's Revenge - Bernard Cornwell 1346
Sharpe's Rifles - Bernard Cornwell 1347
Sharpe's Siege - Bernard Cornwell 1348
Sharpe's Sword - Bernard Cornwell 1349
Something Gleamed - Theda Kenyon 3463
Subaltern's Choice - Duncan MacNeil 4020
That Sweet and Savage Land - Emma Drummond 1728
The Train at Bundarbar - Duncan MacNeil 4021
The Tune That They Play - William Clive 1120
Waterloo - Bernard Cornwell 1350
Wolf in the Fold - Duncan MacNeil 4022

Military Life—British Navy

1805 - Richard Woodman 6857
Adams of the Bounty - Erle Wilson 6807
Admiral Hornblower in the West Indies - C.S. Forester 2169
Admiral of Fear - Victor Suthren 6126
Apprentice to the Sea - Philip McCutchan 4240
Beat to Quarters - C.S. Forester 2170
Before the Wind - Lloyd M. Moxon 4506
Beware, Beware the Bight of Benin - Philip McCutchan 4241
Billy Budd - Herman Melville 4333
Broadsides - Robert Welter Daly 1459
Buller's Dreadnought - Richard Hough 3047
Buller's Guns - Richard Hough 3048

Buller's Victory - Richard Hough 3049
Captain Monsoon - Victor Suthren 6128
Clear for Action! - Simon White 6699
Colors Aloft! - Alexander Kent 3427
Command a King's Ship - Alexander Kent 3428
The Commodore - Patrick O'Brian 4661
Commodore Hornblower - C.S. Forester 2172
The Dangerous Years - Max Hennessy 2833
Dead Reckoning - C. Northcote Parkinson 4809
Desolation Island - Patrick O'Brian 4662
Devil to Pay - C. Northcote Parkinson 4810
Drumbeat - Dudley Pope 5094
The East Indiaman - Ellis K. Meacham 4313
Enemy in Sight! - Alexander Kent 3429
The English Captain - Simon White 6700
The Far Side of the World - Patrick O'Brian 4663
The Fireship - C. Northcote Parkinson 4811
First Lieutenant - Kenneth Maynard 4208
The Flag Captain - Alexander Kent 3430
Flying Colours - C.S. Forester 2173
For King and Company - Ellis K. Meacham 4314
Form Line of Battle! - Alexander Kent 3431
The Fortune of War - Patrick O'Brian 4664
The French Admiral - Dewey Lambdin 3609
The Frigate Captain - Showell Styles 6103
The Golden Galleon - Victor Suthren 6129
The Golden Ocean - Patrick O'Brian 4665
Governor Ramage, R.N. - Dudley Pope 5096
The Guernseyman - C. Northcote Parkinson 4812
The Gun Ketch - Dewey Lambdin 3610
The Guns of Arrest - Philip McCutchan 4242
Halfhyde and the Admiral - Philip McCutchan 4243
Halfhyde and the Chain Gang - Philip McCutchan 4244
Halfhyde and the Flag Captain - Philip McCutchan 4245
Halfhyde and the Fleet Review - Philip McCutchan 4246
Halfhyde for the Queen - Philip McCutchan 4247
Halfhyde Goes to War - Philip McCutchan 4248
Halfhyde on Zanatu - Philip McCutchan 4251
Halfhyde Ordered South - Philip McCutchan 4252
Halfhyde to the Narrows - Philip McCutchan 4253
Halfhyde's Island - Philip McCutchan 4254
Hazard of Huntress - Vivian Stuart 6087
Hazard's Command - Vivian Stuart 6088
H.M.S. Bounty - Alexander McKee 4280
H.M.S. Cockerel - Dewey Lambdin 3611
H.M.S. Surprise - Patrick O'Brian 4666
Honor This Day - Alexander Kent 3432
Hornblower and the Atropos - C.S. Forester 2175
Hornblower and the Hotspur - C.S. Forester 2176
Hornblower During the Crisis - C.S. Forester 2177
In Distant Waters - Richard Woodman 6862
In Gallant Company - Alexander Kent 3433
The Inshore Squadron - Alexander Kent 3434
The Ionian Mission - Patrick O'Brian 4667
The King's Coat - Dewey Lambdin 3612
A King's Commander - Dewey Lambdin 3613
The King's Commission - Dewey Lambdin 3614
The King's Privateer - Dewey Lambdin 3615
Lamb in Command - Kenneth Maynard 4209
The Letter of Marque - Patrick O'Brian 4668
Lieutenant Hornblower - C.S. Forester 2178
Lieutenant Lamb - Kenneth Maynard 4210
The Life and Times of Horatio Hornblower - C. Northcote Parkinson 4813
The Lion at Sea - Max Hennessy 2834
The Long Fight - D.A. Rayner 5270
Lord Hornblower - C.S. Forester 2179
Manila Galleon - F. van Wyck Mason 4154
Master and Commander - Patrick O'Brian 4669
The Mauritius Command - Patrick O'Brian 4670
Men Against the Sea - Charles Nordhoff 4638
Midshipman Bolitho and the Avenger - Alexander Kent 3435
Mr. Christian! - Stanley Miller 4402
Mr. Midshipman Hornblower - C.S. Forester 2180
Mutiny - Frank Tilsley 6280

Mutiny on the Bounty - Charles Nordhoff   4639
Mutiny Run - Frank Eccles   1836
The Nutmeg of Consolation - Patrick O'Brian   4671
On the Company's Service - Ellis K. Meacham   4315
Passage to Mutiny - Alexander Kent   3436
Pitcairn's Island - Charles Nordhoff   4640
Post Captain - Patrick O'Brian   4672
A Private Revenge - Richard Woodman   6863
Ramage - Dudley Pope   5097
Ramage and the Dido - Dudley Pope   5098
Ramage and the Guillotine - Dudley Pope   5099
Ramage and the Rebels - Dudley Pope   5100
Ramage and the Saracens - Dudley Pope   5101
The Ramage Touch - Dudley Pope   5103
Ramage's Devil - Dudley Pope   5104
Ramage's Diamond - Dudley Pope   5105
Ramage's Mutiny - Dudley Pope   5106
Ramage's Prize - Dudley Pope   5107
Ramage's Signal - Dudley Pope   5108
Ramage's Trial - Dudley Pope   5109
The Reverse of the Medal - Patrick O'Brian   4673
Richard Bolitho—Midshipman - Alexander
  Kent   3437
Royal Yankee - Victor Suthren   6132
The Sea Officer - Showell Styles   6105
Ship of the Line - C.S. Forester   2182
Signal—Close Action! - Alexander Kent   3438
Sloop of War - Alexander Kent   3439
So Near So Far - C. Northcote Parkinson   4814
Soldier of the Sea - Robert Welter Daly   1460
Stand into Danger - Alexander Kent   3440
Success to the Brave - Alexander Kent   3441
The Surgeon's Mate - Patrick O'Brian   4674
The Thirteen Gun Salute - Patrick O'Brian   4675
To Glory We Steer - Alexander Kent   3442
Touch and Go - C. Northcote Parkinson   4815
A Tradition of Victory - Alexander Kent   3443
Treason's Harbour - Patrick O'Brian   4676
The Triton Brig - Dudley Pope   5110
The Truelove - Patrick O'Brian   4677
The Unknown Shore - Patrick O'Brian   4678
The Valiant Sailors - Vivian Stuart   6090
The War Chest - Porter Hill   2950
The Wine-Dark Sea - Patrick O'Brian   4679

Military Life—Confederate

Jim Mundy: A Novel of the American Civil War -
  Robert H. Fowler   2192

Military Life—U.S. Army

Remember Santiago - Douglas C. Jones   3280
The Strong Men - John Brick   677

Military Life—U.S. Cavalry

Black Sun - Terry C. Johnston   3242
Blood Song - Terry C. Johnston   3243
The Buffalo Soldiers - John Prebble   5165
Chief of Scouts - Don Bendell   439
Chiricahua - Will Henry   2839
A Cold Day in Hell - Terry C. Johnston   3247
A Creek Called Wounded Knee - Douglas C.
  Jones   3277
Devil's Backbone - Terry C. Johnston   3250
The Dice of God - Hoffman Birney   507
Distant Trumpet - Paul Horgan   3032
Drumm's War - Bill Bragg   638
The Horse Soldiers - Harold Sinclair   5862
Libbie - Judy Alter   121
Long Winter Gone - Terry C. Johnston   3252
Lords of the Plains - Max Crawford   1420
Marching to Valhalla: A Novel of Custer's Last Days -
  Michael Blake   538
Mi Amigo - William R. Burnett   795
A Mighty Afternoon - Charles K. Mills   4407
The Moon-Eyed Appaloosa - Bill Gulick   2617

Night March - Bruce Lancaster   3641
Reap the Whirlwind - Terry C. Johnston   3254
Red Cloud's Revenge - Terry C. Johnston   3255
*A Road We Do Not Know: A Novel of Custer at the
  Little Bighorn* - Frederick J. Chiaventone   1057
Season for War - P.F. Kluge   3510
Seize the Sky - Terry C. Johnston   3256
The Shadow Riders - Terry C. Johnston   3257
Sioux Dawn - Terry C. Johnston   3258
The Stalkers - Terry C. Johnston   3259
Valley of the Shadow - Charles Marquis
  Warren   6570
The Wolf and the Buffalo - Elmer Kelton   3408
Yellowhorse - Dee Brown   715

Military Life—U.S. Navy

The Captain From Connecticut - C.S. Forester   2171

Mills and Millwork

Emmeline - Judith Rossner   5507

Mining

The Adventure of ''Horse'' Barnsby - Philip D.
  Stong   6065
Ben Retallick - E.V. Thompson   6263
Birthright - Phillip Finch   2087
Bisbee '17 - Robert Houston   3056
Borrasca - Octavus Roy Cohen   1160
The Cage - Michael Weston   6650
Call Home the Heart - Jessica Stirling   6040
Chase the Wind - E.V. Thompson   6264
City of Illusion - Vardis Fisher   2107
The Dark Pasture - Jessica Stirling   6042
Ellen Bray - Jane Julian   3319
Glittering Hill - Clyde Francis Murphy   4520
The Golden Fool - David Divine   1649
The Golden Lady - Dorothy Gardiner   2283
Goldfield - Richard S. Wheeler   6660
Great Dream From Heaven - John Rolfe
  Gardiner   2286
Hearts of Gold - Jessica Stirling   6044
The Hills Stand Watch - August Derleth   1615
The Hired Man - Melvyn Bragg   639
How Green Was My Valley - Richard
  Llewellyn   3813
Iron Land - Dorothy Ogley   4697
Judgment in July - Richard Fisher   2105
The Last Days of Horse-Shy Halloran - Bill
  Pronzini   5203
Oregon Legacy - Dana Fuller Ross   5485
Owen Glen - Ben Ames Williams   6766
Power - Howard Fast   2041
Red Mountain - David Lavender   3677
Rose - Martin Cruz Smith   5923
The Scapegoat - Mary Lee Settle   5758
Shining Mountains - Steve Frazee   2214
The Silver Mountain - Dan Cushman   1453
Storming Heaven - Denise Giardina   2394
Sweetwater Fever - Robert H. Adelman   36
Tacey Cromwell - Conrad Richter   5324
Telluride - Susan Clark Schofield   5648
This Sweet and Bitter Earth - Alexander
  Cordell   1326
Tregaran - Mary Lide   3779
The Trembling Earth - Dale Van Every   6411
A Vein of Riches - John Knowles   3526
What Law There Was - Al Dempsey   1609
Wild Earth's Nobility - Frank Waters   6578

Minoan Civilization

The Lily and the Bull - Moyra Caldecott   846

Minstrel Shows

Darktown Strutters - Wesley Brown   732

Missionary Ridge, Battle of

Banner at Shenandoah - Bruce Catton   963

Mobile Bay, Battle of

A Heart Divided - Al Lacy   3580

Mogul Empire

Blood Royal - Robert Payne   4850
The Dark Dancer - Frederic Prokosch   5193
The Holder of the World - Bharati Mukherjee   4510
Lords of the Dance - Robin Lloyd-Jones   3815
The Moghul - Thomas Hoover   3026
The Young Emperor - Robert Payne   4857

Mongol Empire

*The Earth Is the Lord's: A Tale of the Rise of Genghis
  Khan* - Taylor Caldwell   855
Master of the World - Cothburn O'Neal   4738
Orlok - Don Dandrea   1461
Path of the Eclipse - Chelsea Quinn Yarbro   6905
Ruler of the Sky: A Novel of Genghis Khan - Pamela
  Sargent   5606
The Seeking - Robert S. Elegant   1906
*Sons of the Steppe: The Story of How the Conqueror
  Genghis Khan Was Overcome* - Hans
  Baumann   380
The Year of the Horsetails - R.F. Tapsell   6162

Mongols

Until the Sun Falls - Cecelia Holland   2998

Monitor vs. the Merrimac, Battle of the

Armored Giants: A Novel of the Civil War - F. van
  Wyck Mason   4145
Thunder on the Chesapeake - David Divine   1650

Monmouth, Battle of

The Drums of Monmouth - Emma Gelders
  Sterne   5998
Farewell to Valley Forge - David Taylor   6178
Monmouth - Charles Bracelen Flood   2144
Morning in America - Willard Wiener   6741

Monmouth's Rebellion

Black Angels - C.T. Ritchie   5348
Captain Blood - Rafael Sabatini   5546
A Falling Star - Pamela Belle   431
The Golden Days - Robert Neill   4569
Here Lies Our Sovereign Lord - Jean Plaidy   5021
Lorna Doone - R.D. Blackmore   528
The Love Child - Philippa Carr   923
Micah Clarke - Sir Arthur Conan Doyle   1715
Seventeen of Leyden - John James   3160
The Three Crowns - Jean Plaidy   5070
We Stood for Freedom - Iris Morley   4455

Mormons

And Never Yield - Elinor Pryor   5204
Children of God - Vardis Fisher   2106
The Corinthians - Nicholas E. Wyckoff   6888
The Devil's Rainbow - J.C. Furnas   2257
The Everlasting Fire - Jonreed Lauritzen   3675
The Fancher Train - Amelia Bean   395
For Time and All Eternity - Paul Bailey   268

The Giant Joshua - Maurine Whipple   6673
Harry Idaho - Hugh Pendexter   4894
John Crews - Arthur Chapman   988
Kingdom Come - Virginia Sorensen   5950
Paradise Reclaimed - Halldor Laxness   3686
Powderkeg - Richard Vetterli   6482
The Predators - F.A. Parker   4804
The Proselyte - Susan Ertz   1958
Salt Lake City - A.R. Reife   5292
Samuel Brannan and the Golden Fleece - Reva
   Scott   5686
Sister Wives - Cleo Jones   3270
The Strangers on the Island - Brand Whitlock   6714
These Latter Days - Laura Kalpakian   3330
Wilderness Passage - Forrester Blake   534
Wives of the Wind - Marjorie Jarrett   3170

Motion Picture Industry

The Alfred Hitchcock Murder Case - George
   Baxt   382
The Bette Davis Murder Case - George Baxt   383
Between Two Worlds - Monique Raphel High   2913
The Black Mask Murderers - William F. Nolan   4635
Bullet for a Star - Stuart M. Kaminsky   3331
California Gold - John Jakes   3145
Dancing in the Dark - Stuart M. Kaminsky   3334
Dead-Stick - L.J. Washburn   6574
Destiny Express - Howard A. Rodman   5423
Dog Heavies - L.J. Washburn   6575
The Dream Lover - Mark Upton   6392
Flickers - Phillip Rock   5419
Glorious Morning - Julie Ellis   1919
A Grand Passion - Mary Mackey   3991
The Greta Garbo Murder Case - George Baxt   385
He Done Her Wrong - Stuart M. Kaminsky   3338
Hollywood: A Novel of America in the 1920s - Gore
   Vidal   6488
Homecoming - Dana Fuller Ross   5474
The Howard Hughes Affair - Stuart M.
   Kaminsky   3340
The Immortals - Michael Korda   3540
Keystone - Peter Lovesey   3913
The Mae West Murder Case - George Baxt   386
The Man Who Shot Lewis Vance - Stuart M.
   Kaminsky   3341
Max - Howard Fast   2038
Murder at San Simeon - Robert Lee Hall   2660
Murder on the Yellow Brick Road - Stuart M.
   Kaminsky   3343
Never Cross a Vampire - Stuart M. Kaminsky   3344
The New Confessions - William Boyd   617
Our Father's House - Stephen Longstreet   3890
Paloverde - Jacqueline Briskin   693
Poor Boy and a Long Way Home - James
   Sherburne   5806
The Savage Brood - Martha Rofheart   5430
The Talking Pictures Murder Case - George
   Baxt   388
Think Fast, Mr. Peters - Stuart M. Kaminsky   3347
Tom Mix Died for Your Sins - Darryl Ponicsan   5090
Tomorrow Is Another Day - Stuart M.
   Kaminsky   3348
What the Heart Keeps - Rosalind Laker   3605
The William Powell and Myrna Loy Murder Case -
   George Baxt   390

Mountaineering

An Easy Day for a Lady - Gillian Linscott   3805

Musical Life

Alexa - Anne Melville   4330
Anna, Ann, Annie - Thomas Trebitsch Parker   4808
Antonietta - John Hersey   2868
The Assassination of Mozart - David Weiss   6604

*Beyond Desire: A Novel Based on the Life of Felix
   and Cecille Mendelssohn* - Pierre La Mure   3574
Brave Kingdom - Frances Murray   4534
The Canary Trainer - Nicholas Meyer   4348
The Career of Magda V. - Joseph Machlis   3982
The Castrato - Lawrence Goldman   2459
Cesar and Augusta - Ronald Harwood   2771
Charity Strong - Marguerite Allis   109
Clair De Lune: A Novel about Claude Debussy -
   Pierre La Mure   3575
Coming through Slaughter - Michael Ondaatje   4736
Concert Grand - Howard Breslin   665
Consuelo - George Sand   5582
The Crown Prince - John Barchilon   300
Cry to Heaven - Anne Rice   5313
*Deep in My Heart: A Story Based on the Life of
   Sigmund Romberg* - Elliott Arnold   192
Dvorak in Love - Josef Skvorecky   5881
Elgar on the Journey to Hanley - Keith Alldritt   92
Eroica: A Novel about Beethoven - Carl von
   Pidoll   4994
A Fiddle, a Sword, and a Lady - Albert
   Spalding   5953
First Night - Jane Aiken Hodge   2963
Gerontius - James Hamilton-Paterson   2672
*The Golden Quill: A Novel Based on the Life of
   Mozart* - Bernard Grun   2605
Hungarian Rhapsody: The Life of Franz Liszt - Jean
   Rousselot   5511
The Irish Boy: A Romantic Biography - Naomi
   Jacob   3137
*Jelly Roll Morton's Last Night at the Jungle Inn: An
   Imaginary Memoir* - Samuel Charters   1002
Last Love of Camille - Frances Winwar   6832
The Magic Bow - Manuel Komroff   3534
Magic Fire: Scenes around Richard Wagner - Bertita
   Harding   2683
Mozart on the Way to Prague - Eduard Friedrich
   Morike   4454
Music for God - Theresa Weiser   6603
*Nephew to the Emperor: A Novel Based on the Life of
   Beethoven* - Jacques Brenner   658
Passionate Rebel: The Story of Hector Berlioz - F.W.
   Kenyon   3457
Pathetic Symphony: A Novel about Tchaikovsky -
   Klaus Mann   4064
Poor Butterfly - Stuart M. Kaminsky   3345
*The Questing Heart: A Romantic Novel about George
   Sand* - F.W. Kenyon   3458
*Sacred and Profane: A Novel of the Life and Times of
   Mozart* - David Weiss   6609
Signorina - Henry Myers   4542
Spring Symphony - Eleanor Painter   4777
The Strange Case of Madamoiselle P. - Patrick
   Ireland   3109
The Swedish Nightingale: Jenny Lind - Elizabeth
   Kyle   3571
The Venetian Mask - Rosalind Laker   3603
Winter Fire - William R. Trotter   6352

Mutiny

Adams of the Bounty - Erle Wilson   6807
Captain Marooner - Louis B. Davidson   1504
H.M.S. Bounty - Alexander McKee   4280
*The Last Mutiny: The Further Adventures of Captain
   Bligh* - Bill Collett   1208
Mr. Christian! - Stanley Miller   4402
Mutiny - Frank Tilsley   6280
Mutiny on the Bounty - Charles Nordhoff   4639
Mutiny Run - Frank Eccles   1836
Voyage to the First of December - Henry
   Carlisle   897

Mycenean Civilization

Whom the Gods Would Destroy - Richard
   Powell   5148

Mystery

Abracadaver - Peter Lovesey   3906
Absolution by Murder - Peter Tremayne   6334
The Adventure of the Stalwart Companions - H. Paul
   Jeffers   3177
Agatha - Kathleen Tynan   6374
The Alfred Hitchcock Murder Case - George
   Baxt   382
The Alienist - Caleb Carr   907
An Ancient Evil - C.L. Grace   2504
Angel of Death - P.C. Doherty   1670
*The Angel of the Opera: Sherlock Holmes Meets the
   Phantom of the Opera* - Sam Siciliano   5842
Anna's Book - Barbara Vine   6500
The Apothecary Rose - Candace M. Robb   5364
April Lady - Georgette Heyer   2873
Arms of Nemesis - Steven Saylor   5623
Ashworth Hall - Anne Perry   4918
Axe for an Abbot - Elizabeth Eyre   1989
Back Bay - William Martin   4138
The Baroness of Bow Street - Gail Clark   1085
The Bartholomew Fair Murders - Leonard
   Tourney   6297
Bayou City Secrets - Deborah Powell   5146
Beau Blackstone - Richard Falkirk   2005
*The Beekeeper's Apprentice, or, On the Segregation of
   the Queen* - Laurie R. King   3487
Belgrave Square - Anne Perry   4919
Benjamin Franklin and a Case of Artful Murder -
   Robert Lee Hall   2654
Benjamin Franklin and a Case of Christmas Murder -
   Robert Lee Hall   2655
Benjamin Franklin Takes the Case - Robert Lee
   Hall   2656
Bertie and the Crime of Passion - Peter
   Lovesey   3907
Bertie and the Seven Bodies - Peter Lovesey   3908
Bertie and the Tinman - Peter Lovesey   3909
Bethlehem Road - Anne Perry   4920
The Bette Davis Murder Case - George Baxt   383
The Big Stick - Lawrence Alexander   82
Billy Sunday - Rod Jones   3295
The Bishop's Tale - Margaret Frazer   2215
The Black Mask Murderers - William F. Nolan   4635
The Blackheath Poisonings - Julian Symons   6150
Blackstone - Richard Falkirk   2006
Blackstone and the Scourge of Europe - Richard
   Falkirk   2007
Blackstone's Fancy - Richard Falkirk   2008
Blackwater Spirits - Miriam Grace Monfredo   4427
Blind Justice - Bruce Alexander   76
Blood Line - Alanna Knight   3515
Bluegate Fields - Anne Perry   4921
The Book of Shadows - C.L. Grace   2505
The Boy's Tale - Margaret Frazer   2216
Bravo for the Bride - Elizabeth Eyre   1990
A Broken Vessel - Kate Ross   5500
A Brood of Vipers - Michael Clynes   1133
Brother Cadfael's Penance - Ellis Peters   4955
Bullet for a Star - Stuart M. Kaminsky   3331
Bully! - Mark Schorr   5670
Bundori - Laura Joh Rowland   5519
Buried Caesars - Stuart M. Kaminsky   3332
A Cadenza for Caruso - Barbara Paul   4834
Cain and His Brother - Anne Perry   4922
Callander Square - Anne Perry   4923
The Canary Trainer - Nicholas Meyer   4348
Captain Bolton's Corpse - J.G. Jeffreys   3178
Captain Cut-Throat - John Dickson Carr   908
Captain Nash and the Honour of England - Ragan
   Butler   827
Captain Nash and the Wroth Inheritance - Ragan
   Butler   828
The Caravaggio Shawl - Samuel M. Steward   6019
Cardington Crescent - Anne Perry   4924
Carnal Hours - Max Allan Collins   1210
A Case of Spirits - Peter Lovesey   3910

The Case of the Revolutionist's Daughter: Sherlock Holmes Meets Karl Marx - Lewis S. Feuer 2076
Castle Barebane - Joan Aiken 43
Catalina's Riddle - Steven Saylor 5624
Catch a Falling Star - Stuart M. Kaminsky 3333
The Cater Street Hangman - Anne Perry 4925
The Catiline Conspiracy - John Maddox Roberts 5379
Charity, Colorado - Chelsea Quinn Yarbro 6896
Chatterton - Peter Ackroyd 17
Check-Out Time - Kate Kingsbury 3491
The Chinese Nail Murders - Robert van Gulik 6413
A Chorus of Detectives - Barbara Paul 4835
Clively Close: Dead as Dead Can Be - Ann Crowleigh 1434
Colfax - Robert J. Conley 1239
A Comedy of Murders - George Herman 2861
The Coming of Rain - Richard Marius 4084
The Confessions of Brother Halvin - Ellis Peters 4956
A Connecticut Yankee in Criminal Court - Peter J. Heck 2814
Counterfeit of Murder - Ray Harrison 2738
The Cowboy Conspiracy - Larry D. Names 4553
Cracksman on Velvet - Francis Selwyn 5743
Crime Without Passion - Richard Grayson 2556
The Crown in Darkness - P.C. Doherty 1671
Crown Witness - Gillian Linscott 3803
The Cup, the Blade or the Gun - Mignon G. Eberhart 1833
Curse of Magira - David Bee 413
The Curse of the Pharaohs - Elizabeth Peters 4948
Curtains for the Cardinal - Elizabeth Eyre 1991
Cut to the Quick - Kate Ross 5501
The Dance of Death - Jeremy Potter 5142
Dancing in the Dark - Stuart M. Kaminsky 3334
Dangerous - Amanda Quick 5213
A Dangerous Mourning - Anne Perry 4926
The Daughter of Time - Josephine Tey 6209
Dead Man's Ransom - Ellis Peters 4957
Dead Man's Sweetheart - Gillian Linscott 3804
Dead-Stick - L.J. Washburn 6574
Deadly Beloved - Alanna Knight 3517
Dear Laura - Jean Stubbs 6094
Death and the Chapman - Kate Sedley 5715
Death at Daisy's Folly - Robin Paige 4775
Death at Gallows Green - Robin Paige 4776
Death at Rainy Mountain - Mardi Oakley Medawar 4321
Death Comes as Epiphany - Sharan Newman 4598
Death Comes as the End - Agatha Christie 1076
Death En Voyage - Richard Grayson 2557
Death in a Deck Chair - K.K. Beck 403
Death in the Devil's Acre - Anne Perry 4927
Death of a Dancing Lady - Ray Harrison 2739
The Death of a King - P.C. Doherty 1672
Death of the Duchess - Elizabeth Eyre 1992
Death of the Red King - Pamela Bennetts 448
Death Off Stage - Richard Grayson 2558
Death on the Cards - Richard Grayson 2559
Death on the Cliff Walk - Mary Kruger 3562
Death on the Mississippi - Peter J. Heck 2815
Death Squad London - Jack Gerson 2360
Death Wore a Diadem - Iona McGregor 4277
Deathwatch - Ray Harrison 2740
Deception - Eleanor Cooney 1295
The Deeds of the Disturber - Elizabeth Peters 4949
Defend and Betray - Anne Perry 4928
The Detective and Mr. Dickens - William J. Palmer 4782
The Detective Wore Silk Drawers - Peter Lovesey 3911
The Detling Secret - Julian Symons 6151
The Devil and Ben Franklin - Theodore Mathieson 4184
The Devil in Velvet - John Dickson Carr 909
The Devil Met a Lady - Stuart M. Kaminsky 3335
The Devil's Card - Mary Maher 4030
The Devil's Door - Sharan Newman 4599

The Devil's Novice - Ellis Peters 4958
Diamond Head - Marian J.A. Jackson 3135
The Disappearance of Edwin Drood - Peter Rowland 5521
Do Not Disturb - Kate Kingsbury 3492
Dr. Jekyll and Mr. Holmes - Loren D. Estleman 1970
Dog Heavies - L.J. Washburn 6575
Dogheaded Death - Ray Faraday Nelson 4581
Dorothy and Agatha - Gaylord Larsen 3667
The Dorothy Parker Murder Case - George Baxt 384
Down for the Count - Stuart M. Kaminsky 3336
The Dragons of Archenfield - Edward Marston 4119
Dulcie Bligh - Gail Clark 1086
The Dutchman - Maan Meyers 4351
The Dutchman's Dilemma - Maan Meyers 4352
An Easy Day for a Lady - Gillian Linscott 3805
Eat, Drink, and Be Buried - Kate Kingsbury 3493
The Emperor's Pearl - Robert van Gulik 6414
Enslaved - Ron Burns 801
Enter Second Murderer - Alanna Knight 3518
Enter the Lion: A Posthumous Memoir of Mycroft Holmes - Michael P. Hodel 2961
The Eve of Saint Hyacinth - Kate Sedley 5716
Evermore - Barbara Steward 6014
An Excellent Mystery - Ellis Peters 4959
The Exile Way - Ann Woodward 6865
Exit Sherlock Holmes - Robert Lee Hall 2657
The Eye of God - C.L. Grace 2506
The Face of a Stranger - Anne Perry 4929
Faces in the Crowd - William Marshall 4117
The Fala Factor - Stuart M. Kaminsky 3337
Falconer's Crusade - Ian Morson 4493
Falconer's Judgement - Ian Morson 4494
The False Inspector Dew - Peter Lovesey 3912
Familiar Acts - June Barraclough 345
Familiar Spirits - Leonard Tourney 6298
A Famine of Horses - P.F. Chisholm 1071
Farriers' Lane - Anne Perry 4930
Fata Morgana - William Kotzwinkle 3549
A Fatal Assignation - Alice Chetwynd Ley 3764
The Fate of Princes - P.C. Doherty 1673
Feversham - Diane Davidson 1503
Fire and Fog - Dianne Day 1543
Fire, Burn! - John Dickson Carr 910
The Fires of Fu Manchu - Cay Van Ash 6399
A First Class Murder - Elliott Roosevelt 5442
Frobisher's Savage - Leonard Tourney 6299
The Gallows Murder - Michael Clynes 1134
A Gathering of Saints - Christopher Hyde 3092
The General's Lady - Esther Forbes 2156
The Gentleman From Chicago - John Cashman 953
The Ghost and Mrs. Jeffries - Emily Brightwell 681
The Glendower Conspiracy - Lloyd Biggle Jr. 494
The Golden Crucible - Jean Stubbs 6096
Good Morning, Irene - Carole Nelson Douglas 1698
Good Night, Mr. Holmes - Carole Nelson Douglas 1699
The Grail Murders - Michael Clynes 1135
The Greta Garbo Murder Case - George Baxt 385
Grounds for Murder - Kate Kingsbury 3494
Halfhyde on the Amazon - Philip McCutchan 4250
Hammett: A Novel - Joseph N. Gores 2487
Hanging on the Wire - Gillian Linscott 3806
The Hangings - Bill Pronzini 5202
Harvest of Death - Ray Harrison 2741
The Haunted Monastery - Robert van Gulik 6415
He Done Her Wrong - Stuart M. Kaminsky 3338
Hearts and Bones - Margaret Lawrence 3685
The Heiress Bride - Catherine Coulter 1375
Henry James' Midnight Song - Carol de Chellis Hill 2920
The Heretic's Apprentice - Ellis Peters 4960
The Hermit of Eyton Forest - Ellis Peters 4961
The High Constable - Maan Meyers 4353
High Midnight - Stuart M. Kaminsky 3339
Highgate Rise - Anne Perry 4931

The Highwayman and Mr. Dickens - William J. Palmer 4783
The Hippopotamus Pool - Elizabeth Peters 4950
The Holy Innocents - Kate Sedley 5717
The Holy Thief - Ellis Peters 4962
The House by the Churchyard - Joseph Sheridan Le Fanu 3688
The House on Mulberry Street - Maan Meyers 4354
The Howard Hughes Affair - Stuart M. Kaminsky 3340
The Hoydens and Mr. Dickens - William J. Palmer 4784
The Hungry Goblin: A Victorian Detective Novel - John Dickson Carr 911
The Hyde Park Murder - Elliott Roosevelt 5443
I Am Vidocq - Vincent McConnor 4225
The Idylls of the Queen - Phyllis Ann Karr 3367
The Inspector and Mrs. Jeffries - Emily Brightwell 682
Irene at Large - Carole Nelson Douglas 1700
Irene's Last Waltz - Carole Nelson Douglas 1701
The Iron Hand of Mars - Lindsey Davis 1528
Jack the Ripper - Richard Gordon 2484
Jane and the Man of the Cloth - Stephanie Barron 355
Jane and the Unpleasantness at Scargrave Manor - Stephanie Barron 356
Jekyll, Alias Hyde - Donald Thomas 6240
Keystone - Peter Lovesey 3913
Killdeer Mountain - Dee Brown 713
Killing Cousins - Alanna Knight 3520
The King Edward Plot - Robert Lee Hall 2658
King Tut's Private Eye - Lee Levin 3739
The King's Bishop - Candace M. Robb 5365
The Kingsbridge Plot - Maan Meyers 4355
Knaves Templar - Leonard Tourney 6300
The Lacquer Screen - Robert van Gulik 6416
A Lady at Bay - Edgar Maas 3950
The Lady Chapel - Candace M. Robb 5366
Lantern for the Dark - Jessica Stirling 6045
Last Act in Palmyra - Lindsey Davis 1529
The Last Camel Died at Noon - Elizabeth Peters 4951
The Last Mystery of Edgar Allan Poe - Manny Meyers 4356
The Laughing Hangman - Edward Marston 4120
The Leper of St. Giles - Ellis Peters 4963
A Letter of Mary - Laurie R. King 3488
The Limner - Paul Darcy Boles 564
Lion in the Valley - Elizabeth Peters 4952
The Lions of the North - Edward Marston 4121
The List of Seven - Mark Frost 2237
Low Treason - Leonard Tourney 6301
The Mad Courtesan - Edward Marston 4122
Mad Hatter's Holiday - Peter Lovesey 3914
The Mae West Murder Case - George Baxt 386
The Mamur Zapt and the Donkey-Vous - Michael Pearce 4866
The Mamur Zapt and the Girl in the Nile - Michael Pearce 4867
The Mamur Zapt and the Men Behind - Michael Pearce 4868
The Mamur Zapt and the Night of the Dog - Michael Pearce 4869
The Mamur Zapt and the Return of the Carpet - Michael Pearce 4870
The Mamur Zapt and the Spoils of Egypt - Michael Pearce 4871
The Man Who Missed the Party - Harold Adams 25
The Man Who Shot Lewis Vance - Stuart M. Kaminsky 3341
The Masked Man - P.C. Doherty 1674
Masquerade of Vengeance - Alice Chetwynd Ley 3765
Masterpiece of Murder - Mary Kruger 3563
Meadowsweet - Gwendoline Butler 820
The Melancholy Virgin - Annabel Laine 3587
The Melting Clock - Stuart M. Kaminsky 3342
The Merchant of Death - C.L. Grace 2508

The Merry Devils - Edward Marston 4123

The Michaelmas Girls - John Barry 362

Midnight Is a Place - Joan Aiken 52

Miss Lizzie - Walter Satterthwait 5608

The Monkey and the Tiger - Robert van Gulik 6417

Monk's Hood - Ellis Peters 4964

A Monstrous Regiment of Women - Laurie R. King 3489

The Monterant Affair - Richard Grayson 2560

The Montmarte Murders - Richard Grayson 2561

Morality Play - Barry Unsworth 6387

A Morbid Taste for Bones - Ellis Peters 4965

Mrs. Jeffries and the Missing Alibi - Emily Brightwell 683

Mrs. Jeffries Dusts for Clues - Emily Brightwell 684

Mrs. Jeffries on the Ball - Emily Brightwell 685

Mrs. Jeffries on the Trail - Emily Brightwell 686

Mrs. Jeffries Plays the Cook - Emily Brightwell 687

Mrs. Jeffries Stands Corrected - Emily Brightwell 688

Mrs. Jeffries Takes Stock - Emily Brightwell 689

The Mummy Case - Elizabeth Peters 4953

Murder and the First Lady - Elliott Roosevelt 5444

Murder at Drury Lane - Robert Lee Hall 2659

Murder at Ebbets Field - Troy Soos 5947

Murder at Fenway Park - Troy Soos 5948

The Murder at Impasse Louvaine - Richard Grayson 2562

Murder at San Simeon - Robert Lee Hall 2660

Murder at the Feast of Rejoicing - Lynda S. Robinson 5407

Murder at the God's Gate - Lynda S. Robinson 5408

Murder at the Palace - Elliott Roosevelt 5445

Murder at Wrigley Field - Troy Soos 5949

Murder by the Numbers - Max Allan Collins 1212

Murder by the Waters - Robert Lee Hall 2661

Murder, I Presume - Gillian Linscott 3807

Murder in Canton - Robert van Gulik 6418

Murder in Grub Street - Bruce Alexander 77

Murder in the Blue Room - Elliott Roosevelt 5446

Murder in the Chateau - Elliott Roosevelt 5447

Murder in the East Room - Elliott Roosevelt 5448

Murder in the Executive Mansion - Elliott Roosevelt 5449

Murder in the Oval Office - Elliott Roosevelt 5450

Murder in the Place of Anubis - Lynda S. Robinson 5409

Murder in the Red Room - Elliott Roosevelt 5451

Murder in the Rose Garden - Elliott Roosevelt 5452

Murder in the West Wing - Elliott Roosevelt 5453

Murder Is Murder Is Murder - Samuel M. Steward 6020

Murder Makes an Entree - Amy Myers 4540

The Murder of Lawrence of Arabia - Matthew Eden 1865

The Murder of Sir Edmund Godfrey - John Dickson Carr 913

A Murder on the Appian Way - Steven Saylor 5625

Murder on the Yellow Brick Road - Stuart M. Kaminsky 3343

Mysteries of Winterthurn - Joyce Carol Oates 4659

The Mysterious Death of Meriwether Lewis - Ron Burns 802

The Name of the Rose - Umberto Eco 1850

Napoleon Must Die - Quinn Fawcett 2054

Necklace and Calabash - Robert van Gulik 6419

Never Cross a Vampire - Stuart M. Kaminsky 3344

Nevermore - William Hjortsberg 2958

New Deal for Death - Elliott Roosevelt 5454

The Night of the Ripper - Robert Bloch 551

The Nightingale Gallery - Paul Harding 2684

The Nine Giants - Edward Marston 4124

No Honeymoon for Death - Mary Kruger 3564

The Noel Coward Murder Case - George Baxt 387

North Star Conspiracy - Miriam Grace Monfredo 4428

The Novice's Tale - Margaret Frazer 2217

The Nun's Tale - Candace M. Robb 5367

Oh! Where Are Bloody Mary's Earrings? - Robert Player 5079

Old Saxon Blood - Leonard Tourney 6302

One Corpse Too Many - Ellis Peters 4966

Out on Any Limb - John Myers 4545

The Outlaw's Tale - Margaret Frazer 2218

The Pale Criminal - Philip Kerr 3471

Panama - Eric Zencey 6959

The Pangersbourne Murders - J.G. Jeffreys 3179

Papa La-Bas - John Dickson Carr 914

Paragon Walk - Anne Perry 4932

Patently Murder - Ray Harrison 2742

Pentecost Alley - Anne Perry 4933

Perchance to Dream - Robert B. Parker 4807

Peril under the Palms - K.K. Beck 404

The Phantom of the Temple - Robert van Gulik 6420

The Pilgrim of Hate - Ellis Peters 4967

Plain Jane - Marion Chesney 1045

The Players' Boy Is Dead - Leonard Tourney 6303

The Plymouth Cloak - Kate Sedley 5718

The Poisoned Chalice - Michael Clynes 1136

Poor Butterfly - Stuart M. Kaminsky 3345

The Porcelain Dove - Delia Sherman 5815

Poseidon's Gold - Lindsey Davis 1530

The Potter's Field - Ellis Peters 4968

The President's Man - Elliott Roosevelt 5455

Prima Donna at Large - Barbara Paul 4838

The Prince Lost to Time - Ann Dukthas 1776

The Prince of Darkness - P.C. Doherty 1675

Prophecies - Helena Soister 5937

The Quality of Mercy - Faye Kellerman 3391

The Quallsford Inheritance - Lloyd Biggle Jr. 495

The Queen and the Gypsy - Constance Heaven 2810

The Queen's Head - Edward Marston 4125

The Queen's Man - Sharon Kay Penman 4905

The Quincunx - Charles Palliser 4778

Quitting Time - Robert J. Conley 1249

Rasputin's Revenge - John T. Lescroart 3725

The Raven in the Foregate - Ellis Peters 4969

The Ravens of Blackwater - Edward Marston 4126

Ravenscroft - Dorothy Eden 1860

The Red Pavilion - Robert van Gulik 6421

Red Slayer: Being the Second of the Sorrowful Mysteries of Brother Athelstan - Paul Harding 2685

Refinements of Love: A Novel about Clover and Henry Adams - Sarah Booth Conroy 1259

Regency Rogue - Helen Ashfield 212

The Reluctant Heiress - Annabel Laine 3588

A Reputation Dies - Alice Chetwynd Ley 3766

Resurrection Row - Anne Perry 4934

The Return of Moriarty - John E. Gardner 2287

The Revenge of the Hound - Michael Hardwick 2688

Riddle Me a Murder - Duane Crowley 1435

The Ripper's Apprentice - Donald Thomas 6242

The Roaring Boy - Edward Marston 4127

Roman Blood - Steven Saylor 5626

Roman Nights - Ron Burns 803

Roman Shadows - Ron Burns 804

Room with a Clue - Kate Kingsbury 3495

Rose - Martin Cruz Smith 5923

The Rose Rent - Ellis Peters 4970

A Royal Murder - Elliott Roosevelt 5456

Rutland Place - Anne Perry 4935

The Sacrilege - John Maddox Roberts 5380

Saint Mudd - Steve Thayer 6218

St. Peter's Fair - Ellis Peters 4971

The Sanctuary Sparrow - Ellis Peters 4972

Sarsen Place - Gwendoline Butler 821

Satan in St. Mary's - P.C. Doherty 1676

Satan's Fire - P.C. Doherty 1677

Scandal at High Chimneys: A Victorian Melodrama - John Dickson Carr 915

The Scandalous Lady Wright - Marion Chesney 1049

Scarlet Women - J.D. Christilian 1077

Scotch on the Rocks - Howard Browne 733

Seance for a Vampire - Fred Saberhagen 5557

A Season for Death - Ray Harrison 2743

A Season of Knives - P.F. Chisholm 1072

Seneca Falls Inheritance - Miriam Grace Monfredo 4429

Sergeant Verity and the Blood Royal - Francis Selwyn 5744

Sergeant Verity and the Imperial Diamond - Francis Selwyn 5745

Sergeant Verity Presents His Compliments - Francis Selwyn 5746

The Serpent Amongst the Lilies - P.C. Doherty 1678

The Servant's Tale - Margaret Frazer 2219

Service for Two - Kate Kingsbury 3496

The Seven-Per-Cent Solution - Nicholas Meyer 4349

The Seventh Bullet - Daniel D. Victor 6483

The Shadow of the Moth: A Novel of Espionage with Virginia Woolf - Ellen Hawkes 2779

Shadows in Bronze - Lindsey Davis 1531

Shadows on the Shore - Jessica Stirling 6048

Sherlock Holmes and the Case of Sabina Hall - L.B. Greenwood 2576

Sherlock Holmes and the Case of the Raleigh Legacy - L.B. Greenwood 2577

Sherlock Holmes and the Mysterious Friend of Oscar Wilde - Russell A. Brown 731

Sherlock Holmes and the Red Demon - Larry Millett 4404

Sherlock Holmes and the Thistle of Scotland - L.B. Greenwood 2578

Sherlock Holmes Meets Annie Oakley - Stanley Shaw 5782

Sherlock Holmes vs. Dracula - Loren D. Estleman 1976

Sherlock in Love - Sena Jeter Naslund 4557

Shin Ju - Laura Joh Rowland 5520

A Shrine of Murders - C.L. Grace 2509

Silence in Hanover Close - Anne Perry 4936

The Silent Woman - Edward Marston 4128

The Silver Pigs - Lindsey Davis 1532

The Sins of the Wolf - Anne Perry 4937

Sister Beneath the Sheet - Gillian Linscott 3808

The Six Messiahs - Mark Frost 2238

The Skeleton in the Grass - Robert Barnard 320

The Slicing Edge of Death - Judith Cook 1263

Smart Moves - Stuart M. Kaminsky 3346

The Snake, the Crocodile, and the Dog - Elizabeth Peters 4954

Son of Holmes - John T. Lescroart 3726

The Song of a Dark Angel - P.C. Doherty 1679

Speak Softly - Lawrence Alexander 83

Sphere of Death - Ray Harrison 2744

SPQR - John Maddox Roberts 5381

Spy in Chancery - P.C. Doherty 1680

Stage Fright - Gillian Linscott 3809

Stolen Away - Max Allan Collins 1213

A Stolen Tongue - Sheri Holman 3002

The Strange Death of Mistress Coffin - Robert J. Begiebing 415

The Strange Files of Fremont Jones - Dianne Day 1544

The Strenuous Life - Lawrence Alexander 84

Strong as Death - Sharan Newman 4602

A Sudden, Fearful Death - Anne Perry 4938

The Summer of the Danes - Ellis Peters 4973

Summoned to Darkness - Anne-Marie Sheridan 5809

The Sunken Treasure - Marian J.A. Jackson 3136

Sweet Adelaide - Julian Symons 6152

Swing, Swing Together - Peter Lovesey 3915

The Sword of General Englund - Donald Honig 3023

The Talking Pictures Murder Case - George Baxt 388

The Tallulah Bankhead Murder Case - George Baxt 389

A Tapestry of Murders - C.L. Grace 2510

The Tears of the Madonna - George Herman 2862

The Temple of the Muses - John Maddox Roberts 5382

Ten Years Beyond Baker Street - Cay Van Ash 6400

Tessa d'Arblay - Malcolm Macdonald 3974

The Thieftaker - J.G. Jeffreys 3180
Think Fast, Mr. Peters - Stuart M. Kaminsky 3347
The Thistlewood Plot - J.G. Jeffreys 3181
The Thomas Street Horror - Raymond Paul 4843
Through a Gold Eagle - Miriam Grace
   Monfredo 4430
The Tick of Death - Peter Lovesey 3916
A Time for the Death of a King - Ann Dukthas 1777
The Time of Murder at Mayerling - Ann
   Dukthas 1778
Time to Depart - Lindsey Davis 1533
Tincture of Death - Ray Harrison 2745
Tomorrow Is Another Day - Stuart M.
   Kaminsky 3348
Torsos - John Peyton Cooke 1270
*The Tragedy at Tinkerton: An Historical Novel of
   Murder* - Raymond Paul 4844
A Trail of Blood - Jeremy Potter 5143
The Traitor - Dan Sherman 5814
Traitors Gate - Anne Perry 4939
The Trip to Jerusalem - Edward Marston 4129
True Crime - Max Allan Collins 1214
True Detective - Max Allan Collins 1215
An Unholy Alliance - Susanna Gregory 2586
Venus in Copper - Lindsey Davis 1534
The Venus Throw - Steven Saylor 5627
The Vesey Inheritance - Gwendoline Butler 822
Victim of the Aurora - Thomas Keneally 3417
The Virgin in the Ice - Ellis Peters 4974
The Wandering Arm - Sharan Newman 4603
Watery Grave - Bruce Alexander 78
Waxwork - Peter Lovesey 3917
The Weaver's Tale - Kate Sedley 5719
The West End Horror - Nicholas Meyer 4350
Whiskey River - Loren D. Estleman 1981
The White House Pantry Murder - Elliott
   Roosevelt 5457
The White Rose Murders - Michael Clynes 1137
The Whitechapel Horrors - Edward B. Hanna 2678
Whom the Gods Love - Kate Ross 5502
Why Kill Arthur Potter? - Ray Harrison 2746
The Whyte Harte - P.C. Doherty 1681
A Wicked Way to Die - J.G. Jeffreys 3182
Wilde West - Walter Satterthwait 5609
The William Powell and Myrna Loy Murder Case -
   George Baxt 390
The Willow Pattern - Robert van Gulik 6422
Witness of Bones - Leonard Tourney 6304
Wobble to Death - Peter Lovesey 3918
The Wolves of Savernake - Edward Marston 4130
A Woman Scorned - Malcolm Macdonald 3978
You Bet Your Life - Stuart M. Kaminsky 3349

Myths and Legends

Amber Princess - Henry Treece 6325
Arthur - Stephen R. Lawhead 3679
Attila's Treasure - Stephan Grundy 2606
Bard: The Odyssey of the Irish - Morgan
   Llywelyn 3816
Beloved Exile - Parke Godwin 2446
Born of the Sun - Joan Wolf 6837
Bride of the Spear - Kathleen Herbert 2851
The Bull From the Sea - Mary Renault 5295
The Chessboard Queen - Sharan Newman 4597
Child of the Northern Spring - Persia Woolley 6867
*Children of the Vampire: The Diaries of the Family
   Dracul* - Jeanne Kalogridis 3326
Children of the Wolf - Alfred Duggan 1762
The Coming of the King - Nikolai Tolstoy 6296
The Crimson Chalice - Victor Canning 882
Deirdre - James Stephens 5996
Dido, Queen of Hearts - Gertrude Atherton 223
The Eagle King - Henry Treece 6327
Earth Giant - Edison Marshall 4106
Faust - Robert Nye 4654
Finn Mac Cool - Morgan Llywelyn 3818
The Firebrand - Marion Zimmer Bradley 624

Firelord - Parke Godwin 2447
First Knight - Elizabeth Chadwick 966
Gilgamesh the King - Robert Silverberg 5853
The Goddess - Miranda Seymour 5763
The Good Yeomen - Jay Williams 6771
The Great Captains - Henry Treece 6329
The Green Man - Henry Treece 6330
Guinevere - Sharan Newman 4600
Guinevere Evermore - Sharan Newman 4601
Guinevere: The Legend in Autumn - Persia
   Woolley 6868
Hawk of May - Gillian Bradshaw 629
Hercules, My Shipmate - Robert Graves 2545
Homer's Daughter - Robert Graves 2546
The Horse Goddess - Morgan Llywelyn 3820
The Ice Shirt - William T. Vollmann 6509
In the Shadow of the Oak King - Courtway
   Jones 3271
In Winter's Shadow - Gillian Bradshaw 632
Jason - Henry Treece 6331
The King Must Die - Mary Renault 5298
Kingdom of Summer - Gillian Bradshaw 633
The Kingmaking - Helen Hollick 3000
Kinsmen of the Grail - Dorothy James Roberts 5376
Lady Godiva and Master Tom - Raoul Cohen
   Faure 2052
Lady of the Forest - Jennifer Roberson 5368
The Lily and the Bull - Moyra Caldecott 846
The Lion and the Cross - Joan Lesley
   Hamilton 2669
Locksley - Nicholas Chase 1003
The Maze Maker - Michael Ayrton 250
Medea - Miranda Seymour 5764
Merlin - Stephen R. Lawhead 3681
The Moon under Her Feet - Ceysta Kinstler 3503
The Once and Future King - T.H. White 6705
The Pagan King - Edison Marshall 4109
Paris of Troy - George Baker 273
The Pendragon - Catherine Christian 1075
Pendragon - Stephen R. Lawhead 3682
Pendragon's Banner - Helen Hollick 3001
The Private Life of Helen of Troy - John
   Erskine 1957
Queen of the Lightning - Kathleen Herbert 2852
Queen of the Summer Stars - Persia Woolley 6869
The Queen's Knight - Marvin Borowsky 585
Red Branch - Morgan Llywelyn 3824
Return of the Stranger - Dorothy James
   Roberts 5377
Return to Ithaca - Eyvind Johnson 3224
Rhinegold - Stephan Grundy 2607
The Ring Master - David Gurr 2622
The Road to Avalon - Joan Wolf 6842
Scandal in Troy - Eva Hemmer Hansen 2679
A Search for a King: A 12th-Century Legend - Gore
   Vidal 6492
A Shadow of Gulls - Patricia Finney 2096
Shadows on the Stones - Moyra Caldecott 847
The Shattered Horse - S.P. Somtow 5945
The Sheriff of Nottingham - Richard Kluger 3512
The Singing Sword - Jack Whyte 6725
Soldier of the Mist - Gene Wolfe 6843
Sporting with Amaryllis - Paul West 6635
Sword at Sunset - Rosemary Sutcliff 6125
Swords of Anjou - Mario Pei 4890
Taliesin - Stephen R. Lawhead 3683
The Tall Stones - Moyra Caldecott 848
The Temple of the Sun - Moyra Caldecott 849
Three Ships and Three Kings - Georgia
   Sallaska 5573
The Tower of Beowulf - Parke Godwin 2450
Troy - Richard Matturro 4194
The Twelve Pictures - Edith Simon 5857
Votan - John James 3162
The Voyage Home - Ernst Schnabel 5644
The White Raven - Diana L. Paxson 4847
The Winter King - Bernard Cornwell 1351
Witch of the North - Courtway Jones 3272
The Wolf and the Raven - Diana L. Paxson 4848

Napoleonic Era

Alone Among Men - Marjorie Coryn 1355
The Amazing Mrs. Bonaparte - Harnett T.
   Kane 3351
Anthony Adverse - Hervey Allen 98
Being Met Together - William Vaughan
   Wilkins 6756
Bosnian Chronicle - Ivo Andric 150
Brumaire - Mark Logan 3864
Captain Cut-Throat - John Dickson Carr 908
Close Quarters - William Golding 2453
The Death of Napoleon - Simon Leys 3768
Desiree - Annemarie Selinko 5741
Dreams of Empire - Jeanne Mackin 3994
The Eagle and the Rock - Frances Winwar 6830
The Emperor's Duchess - R.G. Waldeck 6524
Emperor's Ladies - Noel B. Gerson 2367
*The Emperor's Lady: A Novel Based on the Life of the
   Empress Josephine* - F.W. Kenyon 3449
Feast of the Jesters - Manuel Komroff 3533
Fire Down Below - William Golding 2454
First Night - Jane Aiken Hodge 2963
Good-Bye My Son - Marjorie Coryn 1356
The Hastening Wind - Edward Grierson 2591
Holy Week - Louis Aragon 182
Imperial Venus: A Novel of Napoleon's Favorite Sister
   - Edgar Maas 3949
The Last Love - Thomas B. Costain 1367
Lustre in the Sky - R.G. Waldeck 6525
Madame Casanova - Gaby von Schonthan 5659
Marianne - Juliette Benzoni 466
Marianne and the Lords of the East - Juliette
   Benzoni 468
Marianne and the Masked Prince - Juliette
   Benzoni 469
Marianne and the Privateer - Juliette Benzoni 470
Marianne and the Rebels - Juliette Benzoni 471
The Marriage of Josephine - Marjorie Coryn 1358
Marsanne - Virginia Coffman 1155
*My Brother Napoleon: The Confessions of Caroline
   Bonaparte* - F.W. Kenyon 3455
Napoleon and His Son - Pierre Nezelof 4607
Napoleon Symphony - Anthony Burgess 780
Palaces of Desire - Kate Alexander 81
Pandora's Galley - Macdonald Harris 2727
Rasero - Francisco Rebolledo 5282
The Raven and the Rose - Susan Wiggs 6746
Rites of Passage - William Golding 2456
The Riven Heart - Genevieve Gennari 2354
The Rose and the Sword - Sandra Paretti 4792
A Rose for Virtue - Norah Lofts 3858
*The Rose of Malmaison: The Turbulent Life of the
   Beautiful Josephine* - Gaby von Schonthan 5660
Sir William - David Stacton 5977
So Great a Man - David Pilgrim 5000
So Much as Beauty Does - Muriel Elwood 1938
Tell Your Sons: A Novel of the Napoleonic Era - Willa
   Gibbs 2402
Wild Swan - Celeste De Blasis 1550

Napoleonic Wars

Allegra - Clare Darcy 1483
*The Angel: A Novel Based on the Life of Alexander I
   of Russia* - William James Blech 543
Anna - Cynthia Harrod-Eagles 2752
Arctic Treachery - Richard Woodman 6858
Ashes - Stefan Zeromski 6960
A Balance of Dangers - Anthony Forrest 2184
Baltic Mission - Richard Woodman 6859
The Battle of Wagram - Gilles Lapouge 3664
Beat to Quarters - C.S. Forester 2170
Beauty's Daughter - Mollie Hardwick 2689
Before the Wind - Lloyd M. Moxon 4506
The Blacksmith's Daughter - Joanna Dessau 1625
Blood and Sand - Rosemary Sutcliff 6121
The Bomb Vessel - Richard Woodman 6860
Bride of Glory - Bradda Field 2078

The Brittle Glass - Norah Lofts 3837

Broadsides - Robert Welter Daly 1459

The Brotherhood of the Red Poppy - Henri Troyat 6353

Captain Justice - Anthony Forrest 2185

The Caretaker Wife - Barbara Whitehead 6706

Castaway - Frances Murray 4535

The Castle of Fratta - Ippolito Nievo 4625

Century in Scarlet - Lajos Zilahy 6962

Charles O'Malley - Charles James Lever 3731

The Charterhouse of Parma - Stendhal 5993

Clear for Action! - Simon White 6699

Colors Aloft! - Alexander Kent 3427

Colossus: A Novel about Goya and a World Gone Mad - Stephen Marlowe 4093

The Commodore - Patrick O'Brian 4661

Commodore Hornblower - C.S. Forester 2172

Corner the Moon - Shirley Barker 310

Creature Comforts - Jessica Stirling 6041

Damaris - Jane Sheridan 5810

Dead Reckoning - C. Northcote Parkinson 4809

Death at the French Creek - Raymond C. Borel 580

Decision at Trafalgar - Richard Woodman 6861

The Dedicated - Willa Gibbs 2399

Desiree - Annemarie Selinko 5741

Desolation Island - Patrick O'Brian 4662

Devil to Pay - C. Northcote Parkinson 4810

Draw Near to Battle - Jere Hungerford Wheelwright 6667

Drumbeat - Dudley Pope 5094

Drums of War - Roy Clews 1114

Edward, Edward - Lolah Burford 772

Eliza Stanhope - Joanna Trollope 6347

Emma - F.W. Kenyon 3448

The Emperor Story: A Historical Romance - George Sava 5615

The English Captain - Simon White 6700

Escapade - Jane Aiken Hodge 2962

Far Flies the Eagle - Evelyn Anthony 162

The Fireship - C. Northcote Parkinson 4811

First Lieutenant - Kenneth Maynard 4208

The Flight of the Eagle - Donald Thomas 6239

Flying Colours - C.S. Forester 2173

For King and Company - Ellis K. Meacham 4314

Forty Centuries Look Down - Frederick Britten Austin 245

The Free Fishers - John Buchan 750

French Dragoon - Roger Rudigoz 5523

The French Woman - Barbara Paul 4837

The Frigate Captain - Showell Styles 6103

A Game for Empires - Pearl Frye 2243

A Generation of Leaves - Robert S. Bloom 552

Governor Ramage, R.N. - Dudley Pope 5096

A Great Lord - Paul Frischauer 2233

The Gun - C.S. Forester 2174

Hangman's Beach - Thomas H. Raddall 5229

He Brings Great News - Clemence Dane 1462

His Was the Fire - Showell Styles 6104

H.M.S. Surprise - Patrick O'Brian 4666

Honor This Day - Alexander Kent 3432

Hornblower and the Atropos - C.S. Forester 2175

Hornblower and the Hotspur - C.S. Forester 2176

Hornblower During the Crisis - C.S. Forester 2177

An Infamous Army - Georgette Heyer 2892

The Ionian Mission - Patrick O'Brian 4667

Lamb in Command - Kenneth Maynard 4209

The Last Mutiny: The Further Adventures of Captain Bligh - Bill Collett 1208

The Letter of Marque - Patrick O'Brian 4668

Lieutenant Hornblower - C.S. Forester 2178

Lieutenant Lamb - Kenneth Maynard 4210

The Life and Times of Horatio Hornblower - C. Northcote Parkinson 4813

The Limits of Glory: A Novel of Waterloo - James McDonough 4265

The Long Fight - D.A. Rayner 5270

Lord Hornblower - C.S. Forester 2179

The Lost Garden - Jane Aiken Hodge 2966

Loving Emma - Nigel Foxell 2197

The Maid of Sker - R.D. Blackmore 529

Marianne and the Crown of Fire - Juliette Benzoni 467

The Marquis of Bolibar - Leo Perutz 4942

Marry in Haste - Jane Aiken Hodge 2967

Master and Commander - Patrick O'Brian 4669

The Mauritius Command - Patrick O'Brian 4670

Midsummer Moon - Karen Lynn 3940

The Mill on the Po - Riccardo Bacchelli 254

The Miller's Dance - Winston Graham 2528

Mirage - Ruth McKenney 4283

Mister Christian - William Kinsolving 3502

Napoleon and the Cossacks - Peter N. Krassnoff 3551

Napoleon Must Die - Quinn Fawcett 2054

The Native Air - Sarah Woodhouse 6854

The Nelson Touch - Paul Lewis 3759

Not by Any Single Man - Brigid Knight 3522

The Nutmeg of Consolation - Patrick O'Brian 4671

The Pandora Secret - Anthony Forrest 2186

Polonaise - Jane Aiken Hodge 2968

Post Captain - Patrick O'Brian 4672

The Prince Regent's Silver Bell - Gladys McGorian 4275

The Proud Canaries - David Johnson 3222

Rage in Silence: A Novel Based on the Life of Goya - Donald Braider 643

The Rake and the Rebel - Ira J. Morris 4478

Ramage - Dudley Pope 5097

Ramage and the Dido - Dudley Pope 5098

Ramage and the Guillotine - Dudley Pope 5099

Ramage and the Rebels - Dudley Pope 5100

Ramage and the Saracens - Dudley Pope 5101

Ramage at Trafalgar - Dudley Pope 5102

The Ramage Touch - Dudley Pope 5103

Ramage's Devil - Dudley Pope 5104

Ramage's Diamond - Dudley Pope 5105

Ramage's Mutiny - Dudley Pope 5106

Ramage's Prize - Dudley Pope 5107

Ramage's Signal - Dudley Pope 5108

Ramage's Trial - Dudley Pope 5109

Rebel Heiress - Jane Aiken Hodge 2969

The Return of the Gypsy - Philippa Carr 927

The Reverse of the Medal - Patrick O'Brian 4673

Ride with Me - Thomas B. Costain 1369

Rifleman Dodd - C.S. Forester 2181

The Road to Glory - Frederick Britten Austin 246

The Rock: A Novel about Gibraltar - John Masters 4179

Salvation - Sholem Asch 202

Saragossa - Benito Perez Galdos 4912

The Scalpel and the Sword - Dell Shannon 5774

Seven Men of Gascony - R.F. Delderfield 1589

Shadow of a Lady - Jane Aiken Hodge 2971

Sharpe's Battle - Bernard Cornwell 1338

Sharpe's Company - Bernard Cornwell 1339

Sharpe's Eagle - Bernard Cornwell 1341

Sharpe's Enemy - Bernard Cornwell 1342

Sharpe's Gold - Bernard Cornwell 1343

Sharpe's Honour - Bernard Cornwell 1344

Sharpe's Regiment - Bernard Cornwell 1345

Sharpe's Revenge - Bernard Cornwell 1346

Sharpe's Rifles - Bernard Cornwell 1347

Sharpe's Siege - Bernard Cornwell 1348

Sharpe's Sword - Bernard Cornwell 1349

Ship of the Line - C.S. Forester 2182

Signal—Close Action! - Alexander Kent 3438

The Sleeping Sword: A Biographical Novel - Pearl Frye 2244

So Brief a Spring - Claude Manceron 4054

So Near So Far - C. Northcote Parkinson 4814

The Spanish Bride - Georgette Heyer 2902

The Storm Witch - Elisabeth Barr 339

Success to the Brave - Alexander Kent 3441

Sylvia's Lovers - Elizabeth Gaskell 2312

The Thirteen Gun Salute - Patrick O'Brian 4675

The Thousand Fires - Anne Powers 5155

Tom Burke of Ours - Charles James Lever 3732

Touch and Go - C. Northcote Parkinson 4815

A Tradition of Victory - Alexander Kent 3443

Treason's Harbour - Patrick O'Brian 4676

Tree of Gold - Rosalind Laker 3602

The Triton Brig - Dudley Pope 5110

The Truelove - Patrick O'Brian 4677

The Trumpet Major - Thomas Hardy 2700

The Twisted Sword - Winston Graham 2531

Up She Rises - David Garnett 2298

Valentina - Evelyn Anthony 165

Valide: A Novel of the Harem - Barbara Chase-Riboud 1007

Venetian Masque - Rafael Sabatini 5556

Voices in a Haunted Room - Philippa Carr 931

The Volcano Lover - Susan Sontag 5946

The Wanton Fires - Meriol Trevor 6345

War and Peace - Leo Tolstoy 6295

Waterloo - Bernard Cornwell 1350

Waterloo - Manuel Komroff 3536

Waterloo - Frederic E. Smith 5920

Whispering - Jane Aiken Hodge 2972

Why Waterloo? - Alan Patrick Herbert 2850

The Wine-Dark Sea - Patrick O'Brian 4679

The Wine Princes - Margaret Mackay 3987

The Yellow Admiral - Patrick O'Brian 4680

Nashville, Battle of

The Bright Sword - Eleanor Perenyi 4911

Nazis

The Blood Order - Jack D. Hunter 3084

The Career of Magda V. - Joseph Machlis 3982

A Castle in Bavaria - Prince Thibaut d'Orleans 1693

The Cup of Wrath - Mary Glazener 2429

Destiny Express - Howard A. Rodman 5423

The Last Innocent Hour - Margot Abbott 8

Munich Signature - Bodie Thoene 6224

The Pale Criminal - Philip Kerr 3471

Piccadilly - Claire Rayner 5267

Prague Counterpoint - Bodie Thoene 6225

The Ring Master - David Gurr 2622

Stones From the River - Ursula Hegi 2816

The Very Rich Hours of Count von Stauffenberg - Paul West 6637

Vienna Prelude - Bodie Thoene 6228

The Winds of War - Herman Wouk 6876

New Orleans, Battle of

1812 - David Nevin 4586

Black Ivory - Polan Banks 292

Hearts of Hickory - John Trotwood Moore 4442

The Rake and the Hussy - Robert W. Chambers 981

Nile, Battle of the

A Game for Empires - Pearl Frye 2243

Mirage - Ruth McKenney 4283

Norman Conquest

The Bastard King - Jean Plaidy 5004

The Black Rose - Thomas B. Costain 1363

Bond of Honour - Catherine Todd 6284

The Conqueror - Georgette Heyer 2881

The Conqueror's Wife - Noel B. Gerson 2363

The Disputed Crown - Valerie Anand 128

The Dragons of Archenfield - Edward Marston 4119

The Firedrake - Cecelia Holland 2988

The Fourteenth of October - Bryher 742

The Golden Warrior: The Story of Harold and William - Hope Muntz 4517

Harold, the Last of the Saxon Kings - Edward Bulwer-Lytton 767

Harold Was My King - Hilda Lewis 3749

Hereward the Wake - Charles Kingsley 3497

King of the Wood - Valerie Anand 131

The Last Englishman: The Story of Hereward the Wake - Hebe Weenolsen 6596
The Lion of Justice - Jean Plaidy 5031
Madselin - Norah Lofts 3853
A Moment in Time - Bertrice Small 5911
The Norman Pretender - Valerie Anand 132
Princess of Fire - Shannon Drake 1718
The Ravens of Blackwater - Edward Marston 4126
Red Lion and Gold Dragon - Rosemary Sprague 5969
Robin and the King - Parke Godwin 2448
The Saxon Tapestry - Sile Rice 5317
Sherwood - Parke Godwin 2449
Sing Morning Star - Jane Oliver 4727
This January Tale - Bryher 747
Wife to the Bastard - Hilda Lewis 3753
The Wind From Hastings - Morgan Llywelyn 3825
The Wolves of Savernake - Edward Marston 4130

Northwest Rebellion

Lord of the Plains - Alfred Silver 5852

Occult

The Alchymist's Journal - Evan S. Connell 1256
The List of Seven - Mark Frost 2237

Ocean Liners

Dance on a Sinking Ship - Michael Kilian 3483
Every Man for Himself - Beryl Bainbridge 270
The Fall River Line - Daoma Winston 6824
The False Inspector Dew - Peter Lovesey 3912
A First Class Murder - Elliott Roosevelt 5442
Homeward Bound - Elizabeth Walter 6557
The Last Farewell - Philip McCutchan 4255
Maiden Voyage - Cynthia Bass 372
The Normandie Affair - Elizabeth Villars 6497

Oil Industry

Black Gold - Anita Richmond Bunkley 771
Blood & Dreams - Leslie Waller 6543
Fabulous Valley - Cornelia Stratton Parker 4803
Fort Worth - Leonard Sanders 5588
Full of Thy Riches - Elizabeth Ferrell 2070
The Power of Black - M.B. Longman 3880
A Vein of Riches - John Knowles 3526
Women in the Wind - Margaret Ritter 5350

Oklahoma Land Rush

Children of the Dust - Carlile Clancy 1084

Olympic Games

Chariots of Fire - W.J. Weatherby 6586

Opera

A Cadenza for Caruso - Barbara Paul 4834
A Chorus of Detectives - Barbara Paul 4835
The Lion's Way - Lewis Orde 4750
Prima Donna at Large - Barbara Paul 4838

Opium War

Hong Kong - Mona Gardner 2288
An Insular Position - Timothy Mo 4421
Mandarin Gold - James Leasor 3700
The Pearl Pagoda - Susannah Broome 707
Red Barbarian - Margaret Gaan 2260
Trade Imperial - Alan Lloyd 3814
White Poppy - Margaret Gaan 2261

Ottoman Empire

Blood and Sand - Rosemary Sutcliff 6121
The Bride of Suleiman - Aileen Crawley 1421
The Dark Angel - Mika Waltari 6551
The Gentle Infidel - Lawrence Schoonover 5663
The Idol Hunter - Barry Unsworth 6386
Pawn in Frankincense - Dorothy Dunnett 1804
The Rage of the Vulture - Barry Unsworth 6388
Regards From the Dead Princess: A Novel of a Life - Kenize Mourad 4505
The Scimitar - Samuel Edwards 1890
The Shadow of God - Aileen Crawley 1422
Sofia - Ann Chamberlin 974
Sultana - Michael, Prince of Greece 4358
Time of Parting - Anton Donchev 1690
Valide: A Novel of the Harem - Barbara Chase-Riboud 1007
The Wanderer - Mika Waltari 6556
Yankee - Dana Fuller Ross 5495
Zayni Barakat - Gamal Ahitani 42

Paleontology

Ravished - Amanda Quick 5216

Panama Canal

Creole Dusk - Walter Adolphe Roberts 5392
Fenwick Travers and the Panama Canal - Raymond M. Saunders 5613

Paraguayan War

Young Vargas Lewis - Robert Brainard Pearsall 4874

Paris Commune

The Far-Off Rhapsody - Anne-Marie Sheridan 5808
Quiet Lady - Norman Collins 1216
A Tale of the Wind: A Novel of Nineteenth-Century France - Kay Nolte Smith 5922
Vardy - John Harris 2721

Paris, Siege of

Daughter of Marignac - Constance Heaven 2805
Quiet Lady - Norman Collins 1216
Vardy - John Harris 2721

Pea Ridge, Battle of

Elkhorn Tavern - Douglas C. Jones 3278

Peasants' Revolt

The Constant Star - Prudence Andrew 139
Glendower Country - Martha Rofheart 5427
Katherine - Anya Seton 5752
Passage to Pontefract - Jean Plaidy 5038
The Peacock and the Pearl - Jennifer Lang 3661
Richard Whittington, London's Mayor - Gwynedd Sudworth 6112
Riot at Gravesend: A Novel of Wat Tyler's Rebellion - William Howard Woods 6864
The Ruthless Yeomen - Valerie Anand 134
Who Was Then the Gentleman - Charles E. Israel 3125

Peasants' War

The Rogue From Padua - Jay Williams 6772

Peloponnesian War

Achilles His Armour - Peter Green 2569

Anabasis: A Journey to the Interior - Ellen Gilchrist 2408
The Flowers of Adonis - Rosemary Sutcliff 6122
Goat Song: A Novel of Ancient Greece - Frank Yerby 6920
The Magnificent Traitor: A Novel of Alcibiades and the Golden Age of Pericles - Lynn Poole 5092

Pemmican War

Pemmican - Vardis Fisher 2111

Penal Colonies

Beyond the Blue Mountains - Jean Plaidy 5006
Botany Bay - Charles Nordhoff 4637
Bring Larks and Heroes - Thomas Keneally 3410
The Emancipist: An Unforgettable Epic of Australia - Veronica Geoghegan Sweeney 6147
The Playmaker - Thomas Keneally 3414
The Settlers - William Stuart Long 3878
A Wilful Woman - Michael Talbot 6156

Peninsular Campaign

Cadmus Henry - Walter D. Edmonds 1872
Copperhead - Bernard Cornwell 1335

Peninsular War

Ashes - Stefan Zeromski 6960
Drums of War - Roy Clews 1114
The Emperor's Duchess - R.G. Waldeck 6524
The Gun - C.S. Forester 2174
The Marquis of Bolibar - Leo Perutz 4942
Ride with Me - Thomas B. Costain 1369
Rifleman Dodd - C.S. Forester 2181
Saragossa - Benito Perez Galdos 4912
Sharpe's Battle - Bernard Cornwell 1338
Sharpe's Company - Bernard Cornwell 1339
Sharpe's Eagle - Bernard Cornwell 1341
Sharpe's Enemy - Bernard Cornwell 1342
Sharpe's Gold - Bernard Cornwell 1343
Sharpe's Honour - Bernard Cornwell 1344
Sharpe's Revenge - Bernard Cornwell 1346
Sharpe's Rifles - Bernard Cornwell 1347
Sharpe's Sword - Bernard Cornwell 1349
The Spanish Bride - Georgette Heyer 2902
Whispering - Jane Aiken Hodge 2972
The Wine Princes - Margaret Mackay 3987

Pennamite Wars

Mistress of the Forge - David Taylor 6179

Persian Empire

Creation - Gore Vidal 6486
Persian Conqueror - George Sidney Hellman 2822
So Great a Queen: The Story of Esther, Queen of Persia - Paul Frischauer 2235
The Tyrant of Bagdad - Glenn Pierce 4996

Petersburg, Battle of

Where My Love Sleeps - Clifford Dowdey 1710

Pharaohs

Akhnaton, King of Egypt - Dmitri Merezhkovski 4337
Alone Atop the Mountain - Samuel Sandmel 5591
Ancient Evenings - Norman Mailer 4035
Child of the Morning - Pauline Gedge 2343
The Egyptian - Mika Waltari 6552
The Exodus - Konrad Bercovici 473
A God Against the Gods - Allen Drury 1738

The Goddess Queen: A Novel Based on the Life of Nefertiti - Nicole Vidal 6494
The Golden Balance - Arthur Dana Hall 2646
The Golden Pharaoh - Peter Danielson 1468
Her-Bak: The Living Face of Ancient Egypt - Isha Schwaller de Lubicz 5676
King and Goddess - Judith Tarr 6166
King of the Two Lands: The Pharaoh Akhenaten - Jacquetta Hawkes 2780
King Tut's Private Eye - Lee Levin 3739
Lady of the Reeds - Pauline Gedge 2345
Mirage - Pauline Gedge 2346
Moses - Sholem Asch 199
Moses, Prince of Egypt - Howard Fast 2039
The Mummy; or Ramses the Damned - Anne Rice 5315
Murder at the Feast of Rejoicing - Lynda S. Robinson 5407
Murder at the God's Gate - Lynda S. Robinson 5408
Murder in the Place of Anubis - Lynda S. Robinson 5409
On a Balcony - David Stacton 5973
Pharaoh - Eloise Jarvis McGraw 4276
Pillar of Fire - Judith Tarr 6168
Prince of Egypt - Dorothy Clarke Wilson 6805
The Prophecy - Peter Danielson 1472
Return to Thebes - Allen Drury 1739
The River and the Stone: Moses' Early Years in Egypt - Kathleen Jenks 3192
River God - Wilbur Smith 5928
The Twelfth Transforming - Pauline Gedge 2347
Winged Pharaoh - Joan Grant 2536

Philosophy

Saints and Scholars - Terrence Eagleton 1821
The World as I Found It - Bruce Duffy 1755

Phoenicians

The Purple Quest: A Novel of Seafaring Adventure in the Ancient World - Frank G. Slaughter 5896

Photography

The Gallery of His Dreams - Kristine Kathryn Rusch 5525
Shadow Catcher - Charles Fergus 2064

Picaresque Adventure

The Adventures of Don Juan - Richard Gardner 2289
The Adventures of Jeremiah Dimon: The Novel of Old East Hampton - Everett Rattray 5255
Anthony Adverse - Hervey Allen 98
At the Sign of the Reine Pedauque - Anatole France 2198
Barry Lyndon - William Makepeace Thackeray 6210
Benjy Boone - Maurice Dolbier 1687
The Bright Feathers - John H. Culp 1441
The Buckstones - Paul I. Wellman 6615
Captain Fantom - Charles Underhill 6377
Captain Vinegar's Commission - Philip Glazebrook 2428
Castle Garden - Bill Albert 63
Conjuror's Journal - Frances L. Shine 5826
Crazy Fox Remembers - Don Preston 5174
Dominic - Kathleen Robinson 5405
Edward, Edward - Lolah Burford 772
An Embarrassment of Riches - James Howard Kunstler 3565
Fanny: Being the True History of the Adventures of Fanny Hackabout-Jones - Erica Jong 3299
The Horseman on the Roof - Jean Giono 2424
The Incredible Brazilian: The Native - Zulfikar Ghose 2392

A Journey to Matecumbe - Robert Lewis Taylor 6188
The Latter Adventures of Tom Jones - Bob Coleman 1200
The Legend of Tyl Ulenspiegel - Charles Theodore Henri De Coster 1558
Lempriere's Dictionary - Lawrence Norfolk 4641
Life as Carola - Joan Grant 2535
The Limner - Paul Darcy Boles 564
Look to the River - William A. Owens 4771
Lords of the Dance - Robin Lloyd-Jones 3815
Messer Marco Polo - Donn Byrne 840
The Misadventures of Bethany Price - Marian Cockrell 1147
Most Secret - John Dickson Carr 912
Mount's Mistake - Lew McCreary 4229
The Odyssey of Thaddeus Baxter - Robert P. Lund 3926
Our Jo, or The Chronicle of a Coming Man - Kenneth M. Cameron 868
Outlaw - Warren Kiefer 3482
Peter Doyle - John Vernon 6457
Playing the Jack - Mary Brown 726
Poor Boy and a Long Way Home - James Sherburne 5806
The Pope's Rhinoceros - Lawrence Norfolk 4642
Rainbow on the Road - Esther Forbes 2159
The Roads to Guadalupe - Robert Lewis Taylor 6190
A Roaring in the Wind - Robert Lewis Taylor 6191
Sam Patch: Ballad of a Jumping Man - William Getz 2390
Sassafras - Jack Matthews 4193
Seven Rivers West - Edward Hoagland 2959
Simplicissimus the Vagabond - J.J.C. Grimmelshausen 2594
The Sot-Weed Factor - John Barth 364
Spangle - Gary Jennings 3196
Spoon - John Christgau 1074
Strange Adventure of Jonathan Drew - Christopher Ward 6562
The Straw Man - Jean Giono 2425
This One's on Me - Donald Jack 3130
The Tin Drum - Gunther Grass 2540
Too Late! Too Late! The Maiden Cried - Joan Fleming 2128
The Vast Memory of Love - Malcolm Bosse 588
The Wanderer - Mika Waltari 6556
Yankee Rover - Christopher Ward 6563

Pilgrims

The Bondswoman - Caryl Ledner 3705
Cape Cod - William Martin 4139
Daughter of Satan - Jean Plaidy 5011
The Disturber - L.S. Davidson Jr. 1505
The Honorable Imposter - Gilbert Morris 4463
The Land Is Bright - Noel B. Gerson 2376
Legacy - Robert Vaughan 6448
Pilgrims: A Novel of the Mayflower - Gerard Mac 3955
The Plymouth Adventure - Ernest Gebler 2342
Thanksgiving - Terry Coleman 1207
The Wickedest Pilgrim - Donald Barr Chidsey 1067

Pirates

Abigail - Joan Druett 1721
Admiral Hornblower in the West Indies - C.S. Forester 2169
The Adventures of Long John Silver - Denis Judd 3317
Angelique in Barbary - Sergeanne Golon 2469
Angelique in Love - Sergeanne Golon 2470
Anne Bonny - Chloe Gartner 2306
Ask No Quarter - George Tracy Marsh 4099
Beauvallet - Georgette Heyer 2876
Black Ivory - Polan Banks 292

Buccaneer - Dudley Pope 5093
Buccaneer Surgeon - C.V. Terry 6205
Burning Gold - Robert Hardy Andrews 148
Captain Adam - Donald Barr Chidsey 1058
Captain Blood - Rafael Sabatini 5546
Captain Ironhand - Rosamond Marshall 4116
The Captive - Victoria Holt 3011
Caribbean - James A. Michener 4365
Caribbee - Thomas Hoover 3025
Caribee - Christopher Nicole 4614
Carolina Corsair - Don Tracy 6307
The Changeling - Alison Macleod 4000
The Corsair: A Biographical Novel of Jean Lafitte, Hero of the Battle of New Orleans - Madeleine Fabiola Kent 3444
Cup of Gold - John Steinbeck 5991
Cutlass Empire - F. van Wyck Mason 4148
The Deadly Lady of Madagascar - C.V. Terry 6206
The Devil's Own - Christopher Nicole 4615
Fanny: Being the True History of the Adventures of Fanny Hackabout-Jones - Erica Jong 3299
Flashman's Lady - George MacDonald Fraser 2210
The Flight of the Kestrel - Margaret Abbey 3
For Love of a Pirate - Anthony Esler 1961
For My Great Folly - Thomas B. Costain 1365
Frenchman's Creek - Daphne Du Maurier 1744
Galleon - Dudley Pope 5095
The Glittering Strand - Judith Lennox-Smith 3716
The Golden Coast - Philip Rooney 5441
The Golden Hawk - Frank Yerby 6921
Grania: She-King of the Irish Seas - Morgan Llywelyn 3819
The Gun Ketch - Dewey Lambdin 3610
Harp of a Thousand Strings - Harold Lenoir Davis 1522
A High Wind in Jamaica - Richard Hughes 3074
A King's Ransom - Victor Suthren 6131
The Legion of the Lost - Donald Barr Chidsey 1062
Lusty Wind for Carolina - Inglis Fletcher 2134
Marcel Armand - Sallie Bell 424
On Stranger Tides - Tim Powers 5156
Pelican Coast - Alan Le May 3690
The Pirate - Sir Walter Scott 5704
The Pirate and the Pagan - Virginia Henley 2827
The Pirate From Rome - John V.D. Southworth 5952
A Pirate's Pleasure - Heather Graham 2518
Pride's Fancy - Thomas H. Raddall 5231
The Privateer - Gordon Daviot 1510
The Pyrates - George MacDonald Fraser 2212
The Red Rover - James Fenimore Cooper 1309
Return to Treasure Island - Denis Judd 3318
The Road and the Star - Berkely Mather 4182
Rogue's Harbor - Inglis Fletcher 2139
Rogue's Holiday - Hamilton Cochran 1141
Running Proud - Nicholas Monsarrat 4432
The Sable Lion - Jan Van Dorp 6405
The Savage City - Jean Paradise 4787
The Sea and the Sand - Christopher Nicole 4621
The Sea Beggars - Cecelia Holland 2996
Sea Star: The Private Life of Anne Bonny, Pirate - Pamela Jekel 3187
The Sea Treasure - Elisabeth Barr 338
Seventeen of Leyden - John James 3160
The Silver Oar - Howard Breslin 669
So Far From Malabar - Joy DeWeese Wehen 6599
Sultana - Michael, Prince of Greece 4358
Treasure Island - Robert Louis Stevenson 6012
Voyager - Diana Gabaldon 2265
The Water Witch - James Fenimore Cooper 1311
The White Rajah - Nicholas Monsarrat 4433
Wind From the Main - Anne Osborne 4759
Windward Passage - Hamilton Cochran 1143
Wolfshead - Jere Hungerford Wheelwright 6672
Written in Sand - Josephine Case 950
Wyvern - A.A. Attanasio 227
Yankee Pasha - Edison Marshall 4115

Plague

The Betrothed - Alessandro Manzoni 4078
Bodin, 1349: An Epic Novel of Christians and Jews in the Plague Years - Roberta Kalechofsky 3322
The Cross - Sigrid Undset 6380
Forever Amber - Kathleen Winsor 6822
The Gallows Murder - Michael Clynes 1134
Guns Forever Echo - Kenneth M. Ellis 1925
The Horseman on the Roof - Jean Giono 2424
Mortal Pageant - Johan Fabricius 1993
Old St. Paul's - William Harrison Ainsworth 57
The Year of the Death - Reuben R. Merliss 4343

Polar Exploration

The Birthday Boys - Beryl Bainbridge 269
The Flight of the Eagle - Per Olof Sundman 6119
Victim of the Aurora - Thomas Keneally 3417

Politics

54-40 or Fight - Emerson Hough 3040
1876: A Novel - Gore Vidal 6484
Alice and Edith: A Biographical Novel of the Two Wives of Theodore Roosevelt - Dorothy Clarke Wilson 6798
Alone Among Men - Marjorie Coryn 1355
The American - Howard Fast 2026
Balisand - Joseph Hergesheimer 2853
Beloved - Vina Delmar 1599
The Big Freeze - Bellamy Partridge 4823
The Borgia Prince - Pamela Bennetts 446
Bread and Circus - Morris Renek 5303
Brimstone Club - F. van Wyck Mason 4147
Bully! - Mark Schorr 5670
Burr - Gore Vidal 6485
Caesar's Women - Colleen McCullough 4233
Captains and the Kings - Taylor Caldwell 851
Celebration! - Dana Fuller Ross 5470
Ceremony of the Innocent - Taylor Caldwell 852
The Chester A. Arthur Conspiracy - William Wiegand 6740
Cold War - Robert Vaughan 6446
Coniston - Winston Churchill 1078
The Conqueror: Being the True and Romantic Story of Alexander Hamilton - Gertrude Atherton 222
The Conspiracy - John Hersey 2870
The Cosgrove Report - G.J.A. O'Toole 4765
Dance of the Assassins - Maria Fagyas 1997
Day Is Coming - William Cameron 869
The Devil's Card - Mary Maher 4030
Disraeli in Love - Maurice Edelman 1851
Disraeli Rising - Maurice Edelman 1852
Dolley - Rita Mae Brown 727
Duchess of Milan - Michael Ennis 1946
Echo of Lions - Barbara Chase-Riboud 1004
Empire: A Novel - Gore Vidal 6487
The End of the Hunt - Thomas Flanagan 2119
Exit Lady Masham - Louis Auchincloss 230
A Family Matter - James Roosevelt 5458
The First Casualty - William Powell 5149
The First Man in Rome - Colleen McCullough 4234
Flying into Love - D.M. Thomas 6236
Forever Free - Honore Morrow 4487
Fortune's Favorite - Colleen McCullough 4235
Galveston - Suzanne Morris 4482
The Gorgeous Hussy - Samuel Hopkins Adams 30
Gossip From the Forest - Thomas Keneally 3413
The Grass Crown - Colleen McCullough 4236
Her Christmas at the Hermitage: A Tale about Rachel and Andrew Jackson - Helen Topping Miller 4389
Hollywood: A Novel of America in the 1920s - Gore Vidal 6488
Home to Kentucky: A Novel of Henry Clay - Alfred Leland Crabb 1399
Home to the Hermitage - Alfred Leland Crabb 1401
The Ides of March - Thornton Wilder 6753
Immortal Wife - Irving Stone 6057

The Immortals - Michael Korda 3540
Intrigue in Baltimore - Janet Whitney 6715
The Ironmaster - Anne Powers 5150
Jackson: A Novel - Max Byrd 837
The Jealous House - Clarence Budington Kelland 3390
Jefferson: A Novel - Max Byrd 838
Kentucky! - Dana Fuller Ross 5477
Kentucky Home - Betty Layman Receveur 5283
The Land Was Ours: A Novel of the Great Plains - Charles W. Bailey 266
The Last Gentleman - Shirley Barker 312
Lenin in Zurich - Alexander Solzhenitsyn 5943
Light in the Clearing - Irving A. Bacheller 260
Lincoln: A Novel - Gore Vidal 6490
Magnificent Destiny - Paul I. Wellman 6619
Me Too - Donald Jack 3128
Memories of the Ford Administration - John Updike 6391
Middlemarch - George Eliot 1909
Ming: A Novel of Seventeeth Century China - Robert B. Oxnam 4772
The Moreland Legacy - Diana Haviland 2777
My Theodosia - Anya Seton 5753
Never Call It Loving - Dorothy Eden 1859
New Deal for Death - Elliott Roosevelt 5454
Notorious Eliza - Basil Beyea 489
Parnell and the Englishwoman - Hugh Leonard 3721
Passengers to Mexico: The Last Invasion of Mexico - Blair Niles 4627
A Pillar of Iron - Taylor Caldwell 861
Power - Lion Feuchtwanger 2074
The President's Lady - Irving Stone 6063
The Prime Minister's Wife - Doris Leslie 3727
The Prison Notebooks of Ricardo Flores Magon - Douglas Day 1545
Private Renaissance - Maria Bellonci 436
Queen Dolley: The Life and Times of Dolley Madison - Dorothy Clarke Wilson 6806
Queen's Gift - Inglis Fletcher 2136
The Raven's Bride - Elizabeth Crook 1431
Refinements of Love: A Novel about Clover and Henry Adams - Sarah Booth Conroy 1259
The River Devils - Carter A. Vaughan 6437
The Rock Cried Out - Edward Stanley 5981
Roman Nights - Ron Burns 803
The Sea Stands Watch - Helen Parker Mudgett 4507
The Senator's Lady - Shirley Seifert 5733
Seward's Folly - Edison Marshall 4111
Shad Run - Howard Breslin 668
The Shadow in the Glass - August Derleth 1618
Statues in a Garden - Isabel Colegate 1198
Storm Center: A Novel about Andy Johnson - Joseph Walker McSpadden 4312
Tamarack Tree - Howard Breslin 670
Tassels on Her Boots - Arthur Cheney Train 6313
The Tenants of Time - Thomas Flanagan 2120
Those Who Love - Irving Stone 6064
The Three Lives of Elizabeth - Shirley Seifert 5735
Three's Company - Alfred Duggan 1774
Tide of Empire - Bates Baldwin 279
Tomorrow We Reap - James H. Street 6081
The Unconquered - Ben Ames Williams 6768
The Valley of Decision - Edith Wharton 6653
Washington, D.C. - Gore Vidal 6493
The Wide House - Taylor Caldwell 864
Wings of the Morning - Frederic F. Van de Water 6404
With Malice Toward None - Honore Morrow 4492
The Year of the French - Thomas Flanagan 2121
Young Pitt - A.M. Maughan 4200

Pontiac's Rebellion

Fire Along the Sky: A Novel of America - Robert Moss 4497
The Judas Tree - Neil Harmon Swanson 6139
Silent Drums - Mike Roarke 5361

Strife Before Dawn - Mary Schumann 5675
Thunder in the Wilderness - Charles Granville Hamilton 2668
The Unconquered - Neil Harmon Swanson 6142

Pony Express

To the Swift - Anne Hawkins 2783

Popish Plot

The Golden Days - Robert Neill 4569
The Love Child - Philippa Carr 923
The Murder of Sir Edmund Godfrey - John Dickson Carr 913
Peveril of the Peak - Sir Walter Scott 5703
Thunder on St. Paul's Day - Jane Lane 3658
Traitor's Moon - Robert Neill 4574

Porteous Riot

The Heart of Midlothian - Sir Walter Scott 5698

Portuguese Colonies

Brazil - Errol Lincoln Uys 6395

Prehistory

Alaska - James A. Michener 4364
The Animal Wife - Elizabeth Marshall Thomas 6243
Beyond the Sea of Ice - William Sarabande 5595
Brother Wind - Sue Harrison 2748
Children of the Dawn - Patricia Rowe 5516
Children of the Ice - Charlotte Prentiss 5166
Children of the Sun - Charlotte Prentiss 5167
The Clan of the Cave Bear - Jean M. Auel 236
Columbia - Pamela Jekel 3184
Corridor of Storms - William Sarabande 5596
Dance of the Tiger: A Novel of the Ice Age - Bjorn Kurten 3566
Daughter of the Red Deer - Joan Wolf 6838
Dawn Land - Joseph Bruchac III 734
The Deer Dancers - Amanda Cockrell 1146
The Earth Goddess - Richard Herley 2856
The Edge of the World - William Sarabande 5597
Face of the Rising Sun - William Sarabande 5598
The Flint Lord - Richard Herley 2857
Forbidden Land - William Sarabande 5599
The Golden Strangers - Henry Treece 6328
The Horsemasters - Joan Wolf 6840
The Inheritors - William Golding 2455
Isle of Woman - Piers Anthony 167
Keepers of the Misty Time - Patricia Rowe 5517
The Last Mammoth - Margaret Allan 89
The Last Warrior Queen - Mary Mackey 3992
Let the Drum Speak: A Novel of Ancient America - Linda Lay Shuler 5837
The Mammoth Hunters - Jean M. Auel 237
The Mammoth Stone - Margaret Allan 90
Mother Earth, Father Sky - Sue Harrison 2749
My Sister, the Moon - Sue Harrison 2750
People of the Earth - W. Michael Gear 2334
People of the Fire - W. Michael Gear 2335
People of the Lightning - W. Michael Gear 2337
People of the Mesa - Charlotte Prentiss 5168
People of the Sea - W. Michael Gear 2339
People of the Wolf - W. Michael Gear 2341
Pillar of the Sky - Cecelia Holland 2994
The Plains of Passage - Jean M. Auel 238
The Reindeer Hunters - Joan Wolf 6841
Reindeer Moon - Elizabeth Marshall Thomas 6244
The Rock: A Novel about Gibraltar - John Masters 4179
The Sacred Stones - William Sarabande 5600
Shadow of the Watching Star - William Sarabande 5601
Shadows on the Stones - Moyra Caldecott 847

Shame of Man - Piers Anthony 168
Shiva: An Adventure of the Ice Age - J.H. Brennan 657
Singletusk - Bjorn Kurten 3567
The Stone Arrow - Richard Herley 2858
The Tall Stones - Moyra Caldecott 848
The Temple of the Sun - Moyra Caldecott 849
Thunder in the Sky - William Sarabande 5602
The Valley of Horses - Jean M. Auel 239
Walkers of the Wind - William Sarabande 5603
Wolves of the Dawn - William Sarabande 5604
The Year the Horses Came - Mary Mackey 3993

Prisoners of War

Andersonville - MacKinlay Kantor 3359
Arouse and Beware - MacKinlay Kantor 3360

Prohibition Era

Whiskey River - Loren D. Estleman 1981

Prostitution

The Abductors - Stuart Cloete 1121
Abigail - Malcolm Macdonald 3962
Brimstone Club - F. van Wyck Mason 4147
The Girl From Storyville: A Victorian Novel - Frank Yerby 6919
An Innocent Woman - Malcolm Macdonald 3967
St. John's Wood - Nancy Fitzgerald 2116
Storyville - Lois Battle 377

Protestant Reformation

God's Man: A Novel on the Life of John Calvin - Duncan Norton-Taylor 4650
Queen of the Reformation - Charles Ludwig 3922
The Rogue From Padua - Jay Williams 6772
The Sage and the Olive - Florence Whitfield Barton 369

Psychiatry

The Eye in the Door - Pat Barker 307
The Ghost Road - Pat Barker 308
Regeneration - Pat Barker 309

Psychology

The Alienist - Caleb Carr 907
Henry James' Midnight Song - Carol de Chellis Hill 2920

Pueblo Revolt

Daughter of Fortune - Carla Kelly 3398
The Royal City - Les Savage Jr. 5621
Taos - Irwin R. Blacker 527
Trail From Taos - Don Coldsmith 1192

Punic Wars

The Coin of Carthage - Bryher 740
Hannibal - Ross Leckie 3704
Hannibal of Carthage - Mary Dolan 1686
Salammbo - Gustave Flaubert 2123
The Scarlet Beast - Francis Gerard 2357
Swords Against Carthage - Friedrich Donauer 1689

Puritans

Always a River - Drayton Mayrant 4211
Arthur Dimmesdale - Charles R. Larson 3671
Bear His Mild Yoke - Ethel White 6675
Campion Towers - John Beatty 401

A Candle in the Wilderness - Irving A. Bacheller 256
The Captive Bride - Gilbert Morris 4457
Come Home at Even - Le Grand Cannon 884
Covenant of Grace - Jane Gilmore Rushing 5527
A Crowning Mercy - Susannah Kells 3396
A Dangerous Innocence - Victoria Lincoln 3787
The Devil and the Mathers - Edward E. Elliott 1914
The Disturber - L.S. Davidson Jr. 1505
Exiled - Helene Holt 3007
Gallows Hill - Frances Winwar 6831
Hester - Christopher Bigsby 496
The Holder of the World - Bharati Mukherjee 4510
I Seek a City - Gilbert Rees 5289
I, Tituba, Black Witch of Salem - Maryse Conde 1233
In Adam's Fall - Constance Dodge 1666
Look to Your Geese: A Novel of the Deflowering of New England - Jacquin Sanders 5584
Malefice - Leslie Wilson 6810
Milton in America - Peter Ackroyd 20
O Western Wind - John Anthony Devon 1634
Pilgrims in Paradise - Frank G. Slaughter 5895
The Scarlet Letter - Nathaniel Hawthorne 2786
Stately Timber - Rupert Hughes 3075
Tomorrow the New Moon - Shirley Barker 319
Until the Winds - Jean Clark 1089
The Winthrop Covenant - Louis Auchincloss 235
The Winthrop Woman - Anya Seton 5754
Witnesses - Marcy Moran Heidish 2820

Pyramids, Battle of the

Mirage - Ruth McKenney 4283

Quakers

Abigail - Mary Louise Aswell 221
Bear His Mild Yoke - Ethel White 6675
The Beckoning Road - Caroline Snedeker 5934
Charming Sally - Maude Hart Lovelace 3903
Crum Elbow Folks - Percy Raymond Barnes 332
Except for Me and Thee - Jessamyn West 6628
Fire and the Hammer - Shirley Barker 311
The Friendly Persuasion - Jessamyn West 6629
Fruit in His Season - Helen C. Barney 333
Give Me Your Golden Hand - Evelyn Eaton 1825
Green Rose of Furley - Helen C. Barney 334
Hugh Wynne, Free Quaker - Silas Weir Mitchell 4416
If Not Victory - Frank Olney Hough 3043
The Inner Voice - Nina Wilcox Putnam 5211
Judith Lankester - Marjorie Allee 93
Nantucket Rebel - Edouard A. Stackpole 5970
The Peaceable Kingdom - Jan de Hartog 2763
The Peculiar People - Jan de Hartog 2764
The Prince and the Quakeress - Jean Plaidy 5043
Sisters and Brothers - Janet Stevenson 6005
Uncharted Ways - Caroline Snedeker 5935

Quebec, Battle of

Lord Vanity - Samuel Shellabarger 5796
Web of Destiny - Muriel Elwood 1939
The White Cockade - Vincent O'Brien 4683
Yankee Rogue - Dana Fuller Ross 5496

Queen Anne's War

Deeper the Heritage - Muriel Elwood 1936
Mohawk Woman - Barbara Riefe 5329
Savage Gentleman - Noel B. Gerson 2381

Racial Conflict

Ain't Goin' to Glory - David Delman 1597
The Autobiography of Miss Jane Pittman - Ernest J. Gaines 2270

The Barrier - Robin Maugham 4195
Black Gold - Anita Richmond Bunkley 771
Blackwater Spirits - Miriam Grace Monfredo 4427
Carolina Courage - Dana Fuller Ross 5469
The Chant of Jimmie Blacksmith - Thomas Keneally 3411
Crossing the River - Caryl Phillips 4984
The Falling Hills - Perry Lentz 3720
The Feast of All Saints - Anne Rice 5314
Free Enterprise - Michelle Cliff 1116
The God-Seeker - Sinclair Lewis 3763
The Hallelujah Flight - Jack Lynn 3937
In My Father's House - Bodie Thoene 6222
Mary Dove - Jane Gilmore Rushing 5529
Men of No Property - Dorothy Davis 1517
One More River to Cross - Will Henry 2847
Pacific Street - Cecelia Holland 2993
A Revolutionary Woman - Sheila Fugard 2248
The Savage City - Jean Paradise 4787
Seasons of Fear - Philip McFarland 4272
Sojourn of a Stranger - Walter Sullivan 6115
Surprise - Brian Burland 785
Sweetwater Fever - Robert H. Adelman 36
Takers of the City - Hoffman Reynolds Hays 2800
A Thousand Shall Fall - Bodie Thoene 6227
Three Roads to Valhalla - Catherine Pomeroy Stewart 6022
The View From Coyaba - Peter Abrahams 11
The Wide House - Taylor Caldwell 864
Words by Heart - Ouida Sebestyen 5713

Railroads

Beau Blackstone - Richard Falkirk 2005
Blue Russell - Will Bryant 738
The Bridge - Marguerite Allis 108
Certain Harvest: A Novel of the Time of Peter Cooper - Ruth Adams Knight 3525
Dakota! - Dana Fuller Ross 5472
Fifteen Flags - Richard Lynden Hardman 2686
Fire on the Wind - David Garth 2304
First the Blade - May Miller 4400
The Fortune Road - James McCague 4217
Gold - Clarence Budington Kelland 3388
The Great Train Robbery - Michael Crichton 1426
The Green Land - Zola Helen Ross 5504
The Harvey Girls - Samuel Hopkins Adams 31
Home Station - Jeanne Williams 6778
I Take This Land - Richard Powell 5147
The Iron Roads - Forbes Bramble 644
Jubilee Jim and the Wizard of Wall Street - Donald Porter 5112
Kenya - John Halkin 2645
Kezzy - Patricia Burns 799
Lion in the Evening - Alan Scholefield 5656
Never Victorious, Never Defeated - Taylor Caldwell 860
Path of the Sun - Al Dempsey 1608
The Petersburg-Cannes Express - Hans Koning 3538
Railroad West - Cornelia Meigs 4327
The Railway King - Margaret Mayhew 4207
The Road - John Ehle 1896
Roman - Douglas C. Jones 3281
Sherlock Holmes and the Red Demon - Larry Millett 4404
Tamzen - Jane Gilmore Rushing 5530
Tenants of the Earth - Sandra Paretti 4793
Theory of War - Joan Brady 637
Thunder on the Plains - Rosanne Bittner 517
Trouble Shooter - Ernest Haycox 2791
The Union Belle - Gilbert Morris 4473
The Vivian Inheritance - Jean Stubbs 6101
The War Train: A Novel of 1916 - Brown Meggs 4324
The Warriors - John Jakes 3155
The World From Rough Stones - Malcolm Macdonald 3979

Ranching

The American Cowboy - Will James 3163
The Bad Lands - Oakley Hall 2651
Bitter Creek - Al Cody 1150
Colorado Ambush - Jess McCriede 4230
Cottonwoods Grow Tall - Margaret Bell
   Houston 3055
The Cowboys - William Dale Jennings 3211
The Crossing - Cormac McCarthy 4221
The Day the Cowboys Quit - Elmer Kelton 3403
The Dreaming: A Novel of Australia - Barbara
   Wood 6848
Duel in the Sun - Niven Busch 812
Eye of the Hawk - David William Ross 5498
The Far Canyon - Elmer Kelton 3404
The Feud - Amelia Bean 396
Filaree: A Novel of an American Life - Marguerite
   Noble 4633
The Goodnight Trail - Ralph Compton 1227
The Grass Kingdom - Jory Sherman 5818
The Grassman - Len Fulton 2256
Home Mountain - Jeanne Williams 6777
Honor Thy Father - Robert A. Roripaugh 5460
Horne's Law - Jory Sherman 5819
Inherit the Sun - Maxwell Grant 2539
Justice, My Brother - James Keene 3386
The Lady - Conrad Richter 5321
Lights Along the Shore - Diane Austell 241
Live From the Devil - Wyatt Blassingame 542
Mirage - Helen Topping Miller 4390
Montana! - Dana Fuller Ross 5479
Monte Walsh - Jack Schaefer 5635
Murdock's Law - Loren D. Estleman 1975
Oregon Legacy - Dana Fuller Ross 5485
Riders of Judgment - Frederick F. Manfred 4059
The Running Iron - Rachel Ann Fish 2097
Sam Chance - Benjamin Capps 888
The Sea of Grass - Conrad Richter 5323
The Seventh Winter - Hal Borland 583
A Shadow of Eagles - Jane Barry 360
The Talking Rifle - Glenn R. Vernam 6454
These Thousand Hills - A.B. Guthrie Jr. 2627
Three Rivers - Carla J. Mills 4406
The True Memoirs of Charley Blankenship - Benjamin
   Capps 890
The Valiant Gunman - Gilbert Morris 4474
The Valley - Clifford Irving 3114
Warhorse - John Cunningham 1451
The White Land - William Dieter 1643
Winter Grass - Richard S. Wheeler 6665
The Wisdom of Stones - Greg Matthews 4192

Reconstruction Period

The Able McLaughlins - Margaret Wilson 6812
After the Glory - Helen Topping Miller 4383
All God's Children - Alston Anderson 136
And One Rode West - Heather Graham 2514
And Tell of Time - Laura Krey 3554
And Wait for the Night - John William
   Corrington 1352
Angel of the Delta - Edward Francis Murphy 4521
The Autobiography of Miss Jane Pittman - Ernest J.
   Gaines 2270
The Beloved Invader - Eugenia Price 5179
Beyond Surrender - Marian Sims 5860
Bread and Circus - Morris Renek 5303
Breakfast at the Hermitage - Alfred Leland
   Crabb 1397
By the Dim Lamps - Nathan Schachner 5630
Candle of the Wicked - Manly Wade Wellman 6612
The Chandler Heritage - Ben Haas 2629
Charleston - Alexandra Ripley 5338
The Chester A. Arthur Conspiracy - William
   Wiegand 6740
A City Not Forsaken - Lynn Morris 4480
The Crowded Hill - Le Roy MacLeod 4008
Dear Lily - Malcolm W. Greenough Jr. 2575

The Earth Abideth - George Dell 1595
Elizabeth, By Name - Will Cook 1265
The Fairbrothers - Clark McMeekin 4291
Fire on the Wind - David Garth 2304
The Forge - Thomas S. Stribling 6083
Freedom Road - Howard Fast 2031
From Fields of Gold - Alexandra Ripley 5339
The Garfield Honor - Frank Yerby 6918
Gentlemen, Hush! - Jere Hungerford
   Wheelwright 6668
Gone to Texas - Forrest Carter 945
Gone to Texas - John Williams Thomason 6247
Gone with the Wind - Margaret Mitchell 4415
The Grasshopper King - Elizabeth Boatwright
   Coker 1165
The Great Steamboat Race - John Brunner 736
Griffin's Way - Frank Yerby 6922
The Handsome Road - Gwen Bristow 697
The Haversham Legacy - Daoma Winston 6827
Heaven and Hell - John Jakes 3147
The House in Ruins - Robert S. Weekley 6595
I Speak for Thaddeus Stevens - Elsie
   Singmaster 5868
Journey Proud - Thomasine McGehee 4273
A Journey to Matecumbe - Robert Lewis
   Taylor 6188
Jubilee - Margaret Walker 6531
Kentucky Pride - Gene Markey 4087
The Laughing Stranger - Vina Delmar 1601
The Legacy of Beulah Land - Lonnie Coleman 1203
Look Away, Beulah Land - Lonnie Coleman 1204
Look Away, Look Away - Leslie Turner White 6685
Lorena - Frank G. Slaughter 5892
The Lost Years: A Biographical Fiction - Oscar
   Lewis 3757
Madame Castel's Lodger - Frances Parkinson
   Keyes 3480
Margaret's Story - Eugenia Price 5183
Melissa Starke - Annulet Andrews 145
Miami: A Saga - Evelyn Wilde Mayerson 4204
Mirage - Helen Topping Miller 4390
The Mississippi Run - Paul Darcy Boles 565
North of 36 - Emerson Hough 3042
On a Lonesome Porch - Ovid Williams Pierce 4997
One of the Raymonds - Jean Rikhoff 5332
Paradise Falls - Don Robertson 5399
Preacher on Horseback - Cecile Hulse
   Matschat 4186
A Question of Honour - Clifford Dowdey 1707
The Quiet Shore - Walter Havighurst 2775
Rebellion Road - Helen Topping Miller 4392
Reunion at Chattanooga - Alfred Leland Crabb 1406
Sam Chance - Benjamin Capps 888
Scarlett - Alexandra Ripley 5342
A Season of Swans - Celeste De Blasis 1548
Seward's Folly - Edison Marshall 4111
The Spoils of War - Thomas Fleming 2131
Steamboat Gothic - Frances Parkinson Keyes 3481
Storm Center: A Novel about Andy Johnson - Joseph
   Walker McSpadden 4312
The Stubborn Heart - Frank G. Slaughter 5904
Supper at the Maxwell House - Alfred Leland
   Crabb 1407
The Tall Woman - Wilma Dykeman 1819
Tell Me a Tale: A Novel of the Old South - James
   McEachin 4266
Tennessee! - Dana Fuller Ross 5489
Tennessee Smith - James E. Hitt 2957
Theory of War - Joan Brady 637
Thief of My Heart - Rexanne Becnel 410
Three Roads to Valhalla - Catherine Pomeroy
   Stewart 6022
Trumpets Sound No More - F. van Wyck
   Mason 4163
Tyrone of Kentucky - Clark McMeekin 4294
The Unconquered - Ben Ames Williams 6768
The Velvet Horn - Andrew Lytle 3946
The Vixens - Frank Yerby 6929
The Web of Days - Edna Lee 3708

The Yankee From Tennessee - Noel B. Gerson 2388
Years of Peace - Le Roy MacLeod 4009

Red River Rebellion

The Half Breed - Maurice Constantin-Weyer 1261
The Magnificent Failure - Giles A. Lutz 3928

Regency Period

The Absorbing Fire: The Byron Legend - F.W.
   Kenyon 3445
The Baroness of Bow Street - Gail Clark 1085
Blackstone - Richard Falkirk 2006
A Broken Vessel - Kate Ross 5500
A Calf for Venus - Norah Lofts 3838
Creature Comforts - Jessica Stirling 6041
Cut to the Quick - Kate Ross 5501
Damaris - Jane Sheridan 5810
Damnation Reef - Jill Tattersall 6172
The Duke's Mistress: The Story of Mary Ann Clarke -
   F.W. Kenyon 3447
Dulcie Bligh - Gail Clark 1086
Eliza Stanhope - Joanna Trollope 6347
Emma Watson - Joan Aiken 45
Escapade - Jane Aiken Hodge 2962
A Fatal Assignation - Alice Chetwynd Ley 3764
Fire, Burn! - John Dickson Carr 910
First Night - Jane Aiken Hodge 2963
The Flight of the Eagle - Donald Thomas 6239
Fonthill - Aubrey Menen 4335
The Gentleman From America - Paul Benton 464
*The Girl Who Was Never Queen: A Biographical
   Novel of Princess Charlotte of Wales* - Mary
   Main 4037
The Golden Fleece - Norah Lofts 3843
*The Golden Years: A Novel Based on the Life and
   Loves of Percy Bysshe Shelley* - F.W.
   Kenyon 3451
Haunted Summer - Anne Edwards 1881
Hearts of Gold - Jessica Stirling 6044
Jane and the Man of the Cloth - Stephanie
   Barron 355
Jennie about to Be - Elisabeth Ogilvie 4694
Lord Byron's Doctor - Paul West 6634
Lord Elgin's Lady - Theodore Vrettos 6514
Lord of the Dead: The Secret History of Byron - Tom
   Holland 2999
Lord of the Ladies - Joanna Dessau 1626
Louisa Brancusi - Darrell Husted 3088
Lovers Meeting - Mollie Hardwick 2695
Love's Children - Judith Chernaik 1013
Marry in Haste - Jane Aiken Hodge 2967
Marsanne - Virginia Coffman 1155
Mary Anne - Daphne Du Maurier 1749
Masquerade of Vengeance - Alice Chetwynd
   Ley 3765
The Melancholy Virgin - Annabel Laine 3587
The Memoirs of Lord Byron - Robert Nye 4655
Meridon - Philippa Gregory 2583
Midsummer Masque - Jill Tattersall 6174
The Miller's Dance - Winston Graham 2528
My Sister, My Love - Lucille Iremonger 3111
Nethergate - Norah Lofts 3854
A Night in Cold Harbor - Margaret Kennedy 3420
The Olympians - Guy Bolton 566
The Pangersbourne Murders - J.G. Jeffreys 3179
Regency Royal - Michael Hardwick 2687
The Regent's Daughter - Jean Plaidy 5055
A Reputation Dies - Alice Chetwynd Ley 3766
The Secret Memoirs of Lord Byron - Christopher
   Nicole 4622
Shadows on the Shore - Jessica Stirling 6048
A Single Summer with Lord B. - Derek
   Marlowe 4092
The Stranger From the Sea - Winston Graham 2530
The Stress of Her Regard - Tim Powers 5157
The Sun Is God - Michael Noonan 4636

The Third Sister - Julia Barrett 351
The Thistlewood Plot - J.G. Jeffreys 3181
The Tontine - Thomas B. Costain 1371
Troy Chimneys - Margaret Kennedy 3421
An Unequal Marriage; or Pride and Prejudice Twenty Years Later - Emma Tennant 6202
The Valiant and the Daunted - Roy Clews 1115
Vanity Fair - William Makepeace Thackeray 6213
A Visit to Highbury - Joan Austen-Leigh 243
The Vivian Inheritance - Jean Stubbs 6101
Whom the Gods Love - Kate Ross 5502

Regency Romance

The Adventuress - Marion Chesney 1014
An Air of Glory - Sarah Neilan 4563
Allegra - Clare Darcy 1483
Angel - Carola Dunn 1790
Animating Maria - Marion Chesney 1015
April Lady - Georgette Heyer 2873
Arabella - Georgette Heyer 2874
The Asherwood Protegee - Mary A. Garratt 2299
At the Sign of the Golden Pineapple - Marion Chesney 1016
The Autumn Rose - Fiona Hill 2923
Back in Society - Marion Chesney 1017
The Banishment - Marion Chesney 1018
Bath Tangle - Georgette Heyer 2875
Beatrice Goes to Brighton - Marion Chesney 1019
Beau Barron's Lady - Helen Ashfield 204
Belinda Goes to Bath - Marion Chesney 1020
Black Sheep - Georgette Heyer 2878
The Black Sheep's Daughter - Carola Dunn 1791
The Bluestocking - June Drummond 1729
Borrowed Plumes - Roseleen Milne 4409
The Braganza Pursuit - Sarah Neilan 4564
Bride of the Unicorn - Kasey Michaels 4363
The Caretaker Wife - Barbara Whitehead 6706
Caroline and Julia - Clare Darcy 1484
Cassy - Elizabeth Lyle 3930
The Castle of the Winds - Jeanne Montague 4434
Charity Girl - Georgette Heyer 2879
A Civil Contract - Georgette Heyer 2880
Colonel Sandhurst to the Rescue - Marion Chesney 1021
Come Be My Love - Diana Brown 717
Cotillion - Georgette Heyer 2883
The Country Gentleman - Fiona Hill 2924
Cousin Kate - Georgette Heyer 2884
Cressida - Clare Darcy 1485
Crystal - Helen Ashfield 205
Dangerous - Amanda Quick 5213
Daphne - Marion Chesney 1022
Deborah Goes to Dover - Marion Chesney 1023
Deception - Amanda Quick 5214
Deirdre and Desire - Marion Chesney 1024
The Desirable Duchess - Marion Chesney 1025
Diana the Huntress - Marion Chesney 1026
Double Masquerade - Karen Lynn 3938
The Duchess of Vidal - Dawn Lindsey 3793
The Earl and the Heiress - Barbara Metzger 4345
Eliza's Daughter - Joan Aiken 44
Elyza - Clare Darcy 1486
The Emerald Necklace - Diana Brown 718
Emily Goes to Exeter - Marion Chesney 1027
The English Wife - Charity Blackstock 530
Enlightening Delilah - Marion Chesney 1028
Escapade - Jane Aiken Hodge 2962
Eugenia - Clare Darcy 1487
False Colours - Georgette Heyer 2886
Faro's Daughter - Georgette Heyer 2887
Feather Castles - Patricia Veryan 6462
Finessing Clarissa - Marion Chesney 1029
The First Rebellion - Marion Chesney 1030
The Five-Minute Marriage - Joan Aiken 46
Fleeting Fancy - Rosemary Edghill 1866
The Folly - Marion Chesney 1031
The Fortunate Marriage - Meriol Trevor 6342

The Foundling - Georgette Heyer 2888
Frederica - Georgette Heyer 2889
Frederica in Fashion - Marion Chesney 1032
French Slippers - Deborah Chester 1055
Friday's Child - Georgette Heyer 2890
The Frog Earl - Carola Dunn 1792
Georgina - Clare Darcy 1488
The Grand Sophy - Georgette Heyer 2891
Gwendolen - Clare Darcy 1489
The Hawthorne Legacy - Teresa Crane 1416
The Heiress Bride - Catherine Coulter 1375
Her Grace's Passion - Marion Chesney 1033
If I Were You - Joan Aiken 49
The Intrigue - Marion Chesney 1034
Jane Fairfax - Joan Aiken 50
Lady Fortescue Steps Out - Marion Chesney 1035
Lady in the Briars - Carola Dunn 1793
Lady Jane - Norma Lee Clark 1092
Lady of Quality - Georgette Heyer 2893
Lady Pamela - Clare Darcy 1490
Ladysmead: A Novel in the Jane Austen Tradition - Jane Gillespie 2420
Lanterns - Patricia Veryan 6465
Lavender Lady - Carola Dunn 1794
Letty - Clare Darcy 1491
Logic of the Heart - Patricia Veryan 6466
Lord Iverbrook's Heir - Carola Dunn 1795
Lord Rivington's Lady - Eileen Jackson 3134
The Lost Garden - Jane Aiken Hodge 2966
A Love So Wild - Deborah Chester 1056
Love's Duet - Patricia Veryan 6468
Lydia, or Love in Town - Clare Darcy 1492
Mansfield Revisited - Joan Aiken 51
Married Past Redemption - Patricia Veryan 6469
Marrying Harriet - Marion Chesney 1036
Men Were Deceivers Ever - Patricia Veryan 6470
Midsummer Moon - Karen Lynn 3940
Minerva - Marion Chesney 1037
The Miser of Mayfair - Marion Chesney 1038
Miss Davenport's Christmas - Marion Chesney 1039
Miss Fiona's Fancy - Marion Chesney 1040
Miss Hartwell's Dilemma - Carola Dunn 1796
Miss Tonks Turns to Crime - Marion Chesney 1041
Mistress - Amanda Quick 5215
Mrs. Budley Falls From Grace - Marion Chesney 1042
My Lady Innkeeper - Barbara Metzger 4346
Nanette - Patricia Veryan 6472
Night Shadow - Catherine Coulter 1377
Night Storm - Catherine Coulter 1378
The Nightingale Legacy - Catherine Coulter 1379
The Noblest Frailty - Patricia Veryan 6474
The Nonesuch - Georgette Heyer 2896
The Parfit Knight - Juliet Blyth 555
Paths of Fortune - Susan Moore 4444
Pemberley, or Pride and Prejudice Continued - Emma Tennant 6201
Penelope Goes to Portsmouth - Marion Chesney 1043
Perfecting Fiona - Marion Chesney 1044
Plain Jane - Marion Chesney 1045
Presumption: An Entertainment - Julia Barrett 350
The Prince Regent's Silver Bell - Gladys McGorian 4275
Quicksilver Lady - Barbara Whitehead 6707
The Quiet Gentleman - Georgette Heyer 2897
Rainbird's Revenge - Marion Chesney 1046
The Rake - Karen Lynn 3941
Rake's Progress - Marion Chesney 1047
Rake's Ransom - Barbara Metzger 4347
Ramillies - Barbara Whitehead 6708
Ravished - Amanda Quick 5216
Rebel Heiress - Jane Aiken Hodge 2969
Reckless - Amanda Quick 5217
Refining Felicity - Marion Chesney 1048
Regency Buck - Georgette Heyer 2898
Regency Rogue - Helen Ashfield 212
The Reluctant Heiress - Annabel Laine 3588
The Reluctant Widow - Georgette Heyer 2899

Rendezvous - Amanda Quick 5218
The Return of the Gypsy - Philippa Carr 927
The Sandalwood Fan - Diana Brown 720
Sanguinet's Crown - Patricia Veryan 6476
Sapphire - Helen Ashfield 214
Sara - Brian Cleeve 1110
Scandal - Amanda Quick 5219
The Scandalous Lady Wright - Marion Chesney 1049
The Scandalous Marriage - Marion Chesney 1050
The Scottish Marriage - Karen Lynn 3942
Seduction - Amanda Quick 5220
The Sherbrooke Bride - Catherine Coulter 1382
Sir Philip's Folly - Marion Chesney 1051
Some Brief Folly - Patricia Veryan 6478
Sprig Muslin - Georgette Heyer 2903
The Stanbroke Girls - Fiona Hill 2925
The Sugar Pavilion - Rosalind Laker 3600
Surrender - Amanda Quick 5221
Sweet's Folly - Fiona Hill 2926
Sylvester; or, The Wicked Uncle - Georgette Heyer 2904
The Taming of Annabelle - Marion Chesney 1052
Teverton Hall - Jane Gillespie 2421
Tish - Cissie Miller 4381
The Toll-Gate - Georgette Heyer 2907
Topaz - Helen Ashfield 215
Two Corinthians - Carola Dunn 1797
Two of a Kind: An English Trifle - Rosemary Edghill 1867
The Tynedale Daughters - Norma Lee Clark 1093
The Unknown Ajax - Georgette Heyer 2908
The Unsuitable Miss Pelham - June Drummond 1730
Venetia - Georgette Heyer 2909
Version and Diversion - Judith Terry 6207
Victoire - Clare Darcy 1493
The Wanton Fires - Meriol Trevor 6345
The Wicked Godmother - Marion Chesney 1053
Wilford's Daughter - Alexandra Manners 4071
A World Too Wide - Susan Moore 4445
Yvonne Goes to York - Marion Chesney 1054

Reign of Terror

The Devil's Laughter - Frank Yerby 6913
The Gods Are Thirsty - Tanith Lee 3710
Guillotine - Mark Logan 3865
The Incorruptible - Marjorie Coryn 1357
The Incorruptible - Helma De Bois 1551
Lady of Paris - William Vaughan Wilkins 6760
Monsieur Yankee - Leslie Turner White 6689
A Place of Greater Safety - Hilary Mantel 4077
The Private Adventures of Captain Shaw - Edith Shay 5783
The Riven Heart - Genevieve Gennari 2354
Scaramouche the King-Maker - Rafael Sabatini 5555
The Scarlet Pimpernel - Baroness Emma Orczy 4745
A Tale of Two Cities - Charles Dickens 1642
Tallien: A Brief Romance - Frederic Tuten 6370
To the End of the World - Helen Constance White 6680
The Twelfth Physician - Willa Gibbs 2403
Veronique - Virginia Coffman 1158

Reincarnation

Ancient Evenings - Norman Mailer 4035
Arc d'X - Steve Erickson 1953
Fire Opal - Pamela Hill 2932
Green Darkness - Anya Seton 5751
Isle of Woman - Piers Anthony 167
The Nonsuch Lure - Mary M. Luke 3924
A Quest for Love - Jacquetta Hawkes 2781
Shame of Man - Piers Anthony 168

Religious Conflict

1492: The Life and Times of Juan Cabezon of Castile - Homero Aridjis 187

Absolution by Murder - Peter Tremayne 6334

The Abyss - Marguerite Yourcenar 6946

The Adventurer - Mika Waltari 6550

Akhnaton, King of Egypt - Dmitri Merezhkovski 4337

Among the Innocent - Elizabeth Borton de Trevino 6339

And Never Yield - Elinor Pryor 5204

Angelique in Revolt - Sergeanne Golon 2471

The Anthem - Noel B. Gerson 2361

Antioch Actress: A Novel of Pagan Against Christian - Jacob Randolph Perkins 4913

The Arm and the Darkness - Taylor Caldwell 850

Barnaby Rudge: A Tale of the Riots of Eighty - Charles Dickens 1641

The Bastard - Brigitte Von Tessin 6208

The Believers - Janice Holt Giles 2409

Blessed Is the Land - Louis Zara 6949

Blossom Like the Rose - Norah Lofts 3836

Bronze Christ - Yoshiro Nagaya 4551

Campion Towers - John Beatty 401

Catalina - William Somerset Maugham 4197

Children of God - Vardis Fisher 2106

The Children of Segu - Maryse Conde 1232

Cities of the Flesh - Zoe Oldenbourg 4713

City of Light - Alison Macleod 4001

Cock of the Walk - Roy Lewis 3762

Come Rack! Come Rope! - Robert Hugh Benson 458

The Converts: A Historical Novel - Rex Warner 6564

Covenant of Grace - Jane Gilmore Rushing 5527

Cunningham's Revenge - Duncan MacNeil 4012

The Dark Rose - Maurice Walsh 6549

Daughters of England - Philippa Carr 919

Deep Are the Valleys - Hannah Closs 1129

The Descent of the Idol - Jaroslav Durych 1818

Destiny of Fire - Zoe Oldenbourg 4715

The Devil's Rainbow - J.C. Furnas 2257

Devil's Yard - Ivo Andric 152

The Dispossessed - Dell Shannon 5773

Dogheaded Death - Ray Faraday Nelson 4581

Edmund Campion - Evelyn Waugh 6585

Evergreen Gallant - Jean Plaidy 5013

The Everlasting Fire - Jonreed Lauritzen 3675

Exiled - Helene Holt 3007

The Faith and the Flame - June Dimmit Houston 3054

Falconer's Judgement - Ian Morson 4494

Fathers and Crows - William T. Vollmann 6508

The Garden of Persephone - Cesar J. Rotondi 5510

Gennie the Huguenot Woman - Bette M. Ross 5464

A God Against the Gods - Allen Drury 1738

God's Man: A Novel on the Life of John Calvin - Duncan Norton-Taylor 4650

The Golden Feather - Theda Kenyon 3462

Graham of Claverhouse - Constance Dodge 1665

The Greater Hunger - Barbara Dodge Borland 581

The Green Madonna - C.E. L'Ami 3617

The Heidenmauer - James Fenimore Cooper 1301

The Heretic - Alison Macleod 4002

Herzl the King - Norman Kotker 3547

High Are the Mountains - Hannah Closs 1130

The Image of Our Lord - Edward Burman 790

In My Father's House - Bodie Thoene 6222

In the Falcon's Claw: A Novel of the Year 1000 - Chet Raymo 5257

The Infidel - Georgia Elizabeth Taylor 6182

The Italian Woman - Jean Plaidy 5024

John Inglesant - John Henry Shorthouse 5833

Julian - Gore Vidal 6489

King of the Two Lands: The Pharaoh Akhenaten - Jacquetta Hawkes 2780

The King's Achievement - Robert Hugh Benson 459

The King's Bishop - Candace M. Robb 5365

The King's Good Servant - Olive White 6696

The King's Persons - Joanne Greenberg 2573

The Lacemaker - Janine Montupet 4438

The Last Athenian - Viktor Rydberg 5543

The Last Crusader - Louis De Wohl 1569

Late Harvest - Olive White 6697

The Lion of Christ - Margaret Butler 823

The Lion of Justice - Margaret Butler 825

The Lord of the Last Days: Visions of the Year 1000 - Homero Aridjis 188

The Mamur Zapt and the Night of the Dog - Michael Pearce 4869

The Man on a Donkey - H.F.M. Prescott 5170

Margaret Brent, Adventurer - Dorothy Grant 2533

Mass for Arras - Andrzej Szczypiorski 6153

Milton in America - Peter Ackroyd 20

The Near and the Far - Leopold Hamilton Myers 4547

The Negotiators - Francis Walder 6526

A New Creature - Prudence Andrew 141

Night of Decision: A Novel of Colonial New York - Dorothy Grant 2534

O Western Wind - John Anthony Devon 1634

Old Mortality - Sir Walter Scott 5702

On a Balcony - David Stacton 5973

People of the Book - David Stacton 5974

Peveril of the Peak - Sir Walter Scott 5703

Pilgrims in Paradise - Frank G. Slaughter 5895

The Plantagenet Prelude - Jean Plaidy 5041

Power - Lion Feuchtwanger 2074

Prisoner of the Queen - Alison Macleod 4006

Prophecies - Helena Soister 5937

The Quality of Mercy - Faye Kellerman 3391

Queen of the Reformation - Charles Ludwig 3922

The Quickenberry Tree - Annette Motley 4502

Return to Thebes - Allen Drury 1739

The Rogue and the Witch - John Edward Newton 4605

The Rogue From Padua - Jay Williams 6772

The Sage and the Olive - Florence Whitfield Barton 369

St. Thomas's Eve - Jean Plaidy 5060

Salt Lake City - A.R. Reife 5292

The Second Crucifixion - Maurice Samuel 5579

Segu - Maryse Conde 1234

The Shepherd's Crook - Paul Frischauer 2234

The Siege - Peter Vansittart 6431

The Siege - Jay Williams 6773

The Silent People - Walter Macken 3990

Silk and Steel - Stephen Alter 122

The Spanish Doctor - Matt Cohen 1159

A Sparkle From the Coal - Prudence Andrew 144

The Spoils of Eden - Robert H. Fowler 2193

Stage of Fools - Charles Andrew Brady 635

Superstition Corner - Sheila Kaye-Smith 3379

The Sword of the Golem - Abraham Rothberg 5509

Sybille - Marion Meade 4318

Their Fathers' God - O.E. Rolvaag 5436

Thomas: A Novel of the Life, Passions, and Miracles of Becket - Shelley Mydans 4538

Thunder on St. Paul's Day - Jane Lane 3658

Tomorrow the New Moon - Shirley Barker 319

Traitor's Moon - Robert Neill 4574

Trumpets of Silver - Norma Harris 2735

Tudor Underground - Denis Meadows 4320

Uncharted Ways - Caroline Snedeker 5935

Vagabond Prophet - Allene Symons 6149

The White Cutter - David Pownall 5158

The Wide House - Taylor Caldwell 864

William's Wife - Jean Plaidy 5077

Witnesses - Marcy Moran Heidish 2820

Woodstock; or, The Cavalier - Sir Walter Scott 5710

The World, the Flesh, and the Devil - Reay Tannahill 6159

Religious Life

The Age of Miracles - Catherine MacCoun 3960

And the Desert Shall Bloom - Phyllis Barber 299

And Walk on Love: A Novel Based on the Life of the Apostle Paul - Henrietta Buckmaster 759

Beecher: A Novel - Dan McCall 4218

Bird of Fire: A Tale of Francis of Assisi - Helen Constance White 6676

The Bishop's Tale - Margaret Frazer 2215

Black Robe - Brian Moore 4441

Blessed Are the Meek: A Novel about St. Francis of Assisi - Zofja Kossak-Szczucka 3542

Blessed McGill - Edwin Shrake 5834

Bold Encounter: A Novel Based on the Life of St. John of the Cross - Peter-Thomas Rohrbach 5433

The Boy's Tale - Margaret Frazer 2216

Brendan - Frederick Buechner 762

A Bride for New Orleans - Edward Francis Murphy 4522

Brother Cadfael's Penance - Ellis Peters 4955

Byzantium - Stephen R. Lawhead 3680

The Call - John Hersey 2869

The Calling of Emily Evans - Janette Oke 4706

The Carmelite - Elgin Groseclose 2599

Citadel of God: A Novel of Saint Benedict - Louis De Wohl 1563

The Confessions of Brother Halvin - Ellis Peters 4956

The Corner That Held Them - Sylvia Townsend Warner 6568

Dead Man's Ransom - Ellis Peters 4957

Dean's Watch - Elizabeth Goudge 2494

Death Comes as Epiphany - Sharan Newman 4598

The Devil's Door - Sharan Newman 4599

The Devil's Novice - Ellis Peters 4958

Doctor in Buckskin - T.D. Allen 103

Drums of Change: The Story of Running Fawn - Janette Oke 4707

Dust on the King's Highway - Helen Constance White 6677

An Excellent Mystery - Ellis Peters 4959

The Favourite - Francoise Mallet-Joris 4040

The Final Adversary - Gilbert Morris 4460

Flame of Fire - Jane Oliver 4722

Fool of God: A Novel Based on the Life of Alexander Campbell - Louis Cochran 1144

For God and Glory - Tim Jeal 3171

The Franciscan - Forrester Blake 532

Gate to the Sea - Bryher 743

The Glorious Folly: A Novel of the Time of St. Paul - Louis De Wohl 1565

The Godforgotten - Gladys Schmitt 5642

Godric - Frederick Buechner 763

The Golden Thread - Louis De Wohl 1566

Grandmother and the Priests - Taylor Caldwell 857

Gregory the Great - Gerhart Ellert 1913

Heart in Pilgrimage - Evelyn Eaton 1827

The Heidenmauer - James Fenimore Cooper 1301

Hellfire Jackson - Garland Roark 5355

The Heretic's Apprentice - Ellis Peters 4960

The Hermit of Eyton Forest - Ellis Peters 4961

The Holy Thief - Ellis Peters 4962

Hunt for Heaven - Elsie Barber 298

If a Lion Could Talk - Mildred Walker 6532

The Image of Our Lord - Edward Burman 790

Isle of Glory - Jane Oliver 4723

Joanna the Pope - Daniel Panger 4785

The Journal of Hildegard of Bingen - Barbara Lachman 3578

The Joyful Beggar: A Novel of St. Francis of Assisi - Louis De Wohl 1568

Kingdom Come - Virginia Sorensen 5950

The King's Achievement - Robert Hugh Benson 459

The Ladies of St. Hedwig's - E.M. Almedingen 117

Lady of the Lotus - William E. Barrett 353

Lay Siege to Heaven: A Novel of Saint Catherine of Siena - Louis De Wohl 1570

The Leper of St. Giles - Ellis Peters 4963

Lily of the Mohawks - Jack Casey 952

The Lord's Anointed - Ruth Eleanor McKee 4282

Love Is My Vocation: An Imaginative Study of St. Therese of Lisieux - Tom Clarkson 1098

The Man Who Thought He Was Messiah - Curt Leviant 3735
A Mapmaker's Dream - James Cowan 1391
Mariette in Ecstasy - Ron Hansen 2682
The Master of Geneva: A Novel Based on the Life of John Calvin - Gladys H. Barr 341
The Miracle at St. Bruno's - Philippa Carr 925
Miracles - Marcy Moran Heidish 2818
Molokai - Oswald Andrew Bushnell 815
The Monastery - Sir Walter Scott 5701
Monk in Armour - Gladys H. Barr 342
Monk's Hood - Ellis Peters 4964
A Morbid Taste for Bones - Ellis Peters 4965
My Beautiful White Roses - Michael Lechner 3703
My Life for My Sheep - Alfred Duggan 1772
My Lord of Canterbury - Godfrey Turton 6369
The Name of the Rose - Umberto Eco 1850
The Nightingale Gallery - Paul Harding 2684
Nine Days of Father Serra - Isabelle Gibson Ziegler 6961
The Novice's Tale - Margaret Frazer 2217
The Nunnery - Dorothy Charques 1001
Omensetter's Luck - William H. Gass 2317
One Corpse Too Many - Ellis Peters 4966
Ordeal by Silence - Prudence Andrew 142
Origen: A Historical Novel - Theodore Vrettos 6515
Orphan Train - James Magnuson 4029
Oscar and Lucinda - Peter Carey 894
The Outlaw's Tale - Margaret Frazer 2218
Palais-Royale - Richard Sennett 5747
Passion and the Sword - Harald Hornborg 3034
The Peaceable Kingdom - Jan de Hartog 2763
The Perfect Joy of St. Francis - Felix Timmermans 6281
Personal Recollections of Joan of Arc - Mark Twain 6372
Peter Abelard: A Novel - Helen Waddell 6517
The Pilgrim of Hate - Ellis Peters 4967
The Pillars of the Earth - Ken Follett 2149
Pope Joan - Donna Woolfolk Cross 1433
The Potter's Field - Ellis Peters 4968
Preacher on Horseback - Cecile Hulse Matschat 4186
The Prophet - Sholem Asch 201
A Question of Choice - Prudence Andrew 143
The Quiet Light - Louis De Wohl 1572
Raccoon John Smith - Louis Cochran 1145
The Raven in the Foregate - Ellis Peters 4969
Red Slayer: Being the Second of the Sorrowful Mysteries of Brother Athelstan - Paul Harding 2685
The Restless Flame - Louis De Wohl 1573
Riders of the Long Road - Stephen E. Bransford 649
The Rose Rent - Ellis Peters 4970
Roses for Mexico - Ethel Cook Eliot 1907
The Saint - Fritz von Unruh 6385
Saint Francis - Nikos Kazantzakis 3385
Saint Paul: A Historical Novel of His Life - Leon Poirier 5081
St. Peter's Fair - Ellis Peters 4971
Salvation - Sholem Asch 202
The Sanctuary Sparrow - Ellis Peters 4972
Savages and Saints - Cora Older 4717
Segaki - David Stacton 5975
The Servant's Tale - Margaret Frazer 2219
Set All Afire: A Novel of St. Francis Xavier - Louis De Wohl 1574
Shadows and Images - Meriol Trevor 6344
Silver Cross - Mary Johnston 3239
Sing to the Sun - Lucille Borden 579
The Slave - Isaac Bashevis Singer 5866
Son of Tears - Henry W. Coray 1320
The Song of Bernadette - Franz Werfel 6625
The Spire - William Golding 2457
Stealing Heaven: The Love Story of Heloise and Abelard - Marion Meade 4317
A Stolen Tongue - Sheri Holman 3002
The Stones of the Abbey - Fernand Pouillon 5144
The Summer of the Danes - Ellis Peters 4973

Take Her, Mr. Wesley - John W. Drakeford 1719
This Widowed Land - Kathleen O'Neal Gear 2331
The Virgin in the Ice - Ellis Peters 4974
The Voice and the Light - Edwin Fadiman 1995
The Voice of Allah - Edwin P. Hoyt 3062
The Woman in the Cloak - Pamela Hill 2949
Women in the Wall - Julia O'Faolain 4691
The Yellow Robe: A Novel of the Life of Buddha - Robert Payne 4856

Renaissance

The Agony and the Ecstasy - Irving Stone 6054
Axe for an Abbot - Elizabeth Eyre 1989
The Bait and the Trap - George Challis 970
Baton Sinister - Carl J. Spinatelli 5967
Bianca - Mabel Conquist 1257
The Borgia Prince - Pamela Bennetts 446
Borgia Testament - Nigel Balchin 277
The Bravo - James Fenimore Cooper 1298
Bravo for the Bride - Elizabeth Eyre 1990
The Bride of Sforza - Miranda Seymour 5760
The Burnished Blade - Lawrence Schoonover 5661
Captain of the Medici - John J. Pugh 5206
Caravaggio - Robert Payne 4851
A Cardinal of the Medici - Susan Hicks Beach 393
Caressa - Linda Lang Bartell 363
Carnival of Saints - George Herman 2860
The Chancellor - Lawrence Schoonover 5662
Chivalry - Rafael Sabatini 5548
City of God: A Novel of the Borgias - Cecelia Holland 2985
Color From a Light Within: A Novel Based on the Life of El Greco - Donald Braider 641
A Comedy of Murders - George Herman 2861
Condottiere - Jan Westcott 6644
Curtains for the Cardinal - Elizabeth Eyre 1991
A Dancer in Darkness - David Stacton 5971
Daughter of Shadows - Miranda Seymour 5762
The Death and Life of Miguel De Cervantes - Stephen Marlowe 4094
Death of the Duchess - Elizabeth Eyre 1992
Divine Mistress - Frank G. Slaughter 5886
The Dragon Waiting: A Masque of History - John M. Ford 2165
Duchess of Milan - Michael Ennis 1946
The Flame of the Borgias - Jean Briggs 680
The Florentine - Sandra Shulman 5840
The Florentine - Carl J. Spinatelli 5968
The Glittering Strand - Judith Lennox-Smith 3716
The Hand of Michelangelo - Sidney Alexander 85
High Carnival - John J. Pugh 5207
The Italian Garden - Judith Lennox-Smith 3717
The Lady in the Mask - Anne Green 2564
Leo Africanus - Amin Maalouf 3947
Leonardo's Judas - Leo Perutz 4941
Life as Carola - Joan Grant 2535
Light on Lucrezia - Jean Plaidy 5029
Madonna of the Seven Hills - Jean Plaidy 5034
A Mapmaker's Dream - James Cowan 1391
The Medici Emerald - Martin Woodhouse 6851
The Medici Guns - Martin Woodhouse 6852
The Medici Hawks - Martin Woodhouse 6853
The Memory Cathedral: A Secret History of Leonardo Da Vinci - Jack Dann 1481
The Mercenary - Charles Durbin 1814
Michelangelo the Florentine - Sidney Alexander 86
Mona Lisa: The Woman in the Portrait - Sara Mayfield 4206
The Naked Sword: The Story of Lucretia Borgia - F.W. Kenyon 3456
Niccolo Rising - Dorothy Dunnett 1803
Nicodemus: The Roman Years of Michelangelo Buonarroti, 1534-1564 - Sidney Alexander 87
The Palace - Chelsea Quinn Yarbro 6904
The Palace of Wisdom - Bob Marshall-Andrews 4118
A Passion in the Blood - Genevieve Davis 1519

The Pope's Rhinoceros - Lawrence Norfolk 4642
Prince of Foxes - Samuel Shellabarger 5797
The Private Life of Mona Lisa - Pierre La Mure 3577
Private Renaissance - Maria Bellonci 436
Race of Scorpions - Dorothy Dunnett 1806
The Romance of Leonardo Da Vinci - Dmitri Merezhkovski 4339
Romola - George Eliot 1910
Scales of Gold - Dorothy Dunnett 1808
The Scarlet City - Hella S. Haasse 2632
Serenissima: A Novel of Venice - Erica Jong 3300
The Sins of the Lion - Annette Motley 4503
Snared Nightingale - Geoffrey Trease 6324
The Spider King - Lawrence Schoonover 5668
The Spring of the Ram - Dorothy Dunnett 1809
The Star-Gazer - Zsolt de Harsanyi 2757
The Sword of Il Grande - Will Creed 1424
A Tale for Midnight - Frederic Prokosch 5195
The Tears of the Madonna - George Herman 2862
Then and Now - William Somerset Maugham 4198
The Time Returns - Alexandra Ripley 5343
Titian - Dario Cecchi 965
To Lie with Lions - Dorothy Dunnett 1810
The Unicorn Hunt - Dorothy Dunnett 1811
Vagabond Prophet - Allene Symons 6149
The Venetian - David Weiss 6611
Vittoria - Robert Merle 4342
Web of Lucifer: A Novel of the Borgia Fury - Maurice Samuel 5580
The Wind Dancer - Iris Johansen 3218
Written in the Stars: A Novel about Albrecht Durer - Frances Hope Fisher 2103

Restoration Period

Alethea - Pamela Belle 429
Annie - Gloria Jahoda 3141
The Bellerose Bargain - Robyn Carr 934
The Braeswood Tapestry - Robyn Carr 936
Catherine - Hilda Lewis 3746
Chelynne - Robyn Carr 938
Christopher Humble - Charles Burnet Judah 3310
Countess Carrots - Molly Costain Haycraft 2792
Daughters of England - Philippa Carr 919
The Devil in Velvet - John Dickson Carr 909
The Faithful Lovers - Valerie Anand 129
A Falling Star - Pamela Belle 431
The Fireflower - Edith Layton 3687
Forever Amber - Kathleen Winsor 6822
Frenchman's Creek - Daphne Du Maurier 1744
Graham of Claverhouse - Constance Dodge 1665
A Health Unto His Majesty - Jean Plaidy 5019
Here Lies Our Sovereign Lord - Jean Plaidy 5021
I, John Mordaunt - Virgil Scott 5687
The King's Bastard - Hebe Elsna 1932
The King's Brat - Constance Gluyas 2441
The King's Rogue - Max Peacock 4859
Lady on the Coin - Margaret Campbell Barnes 326
Lament for a Lost Lover - Philippa Carr 921
Lucy - Hester W. Chapman 992
Masquerade for the King - Marina Oliver 4729
Mistress of the Boards - Richard Sumner 6118
Most Secret - John Dickson Carr 912
Mr. Pepys of Seething Lane - Cecil Abernethy 10
The Murder of Sir Edmund Godfrey - John Dickson Carr 913
My Lady Benbrook - Constance Gluyas 2442
Our Jo, or The Chronicle of a Coming Man - Kenneth M. Cameron 868
The Pirate and the Pagan - Virginia Henley 2827
The Pleasures of Love - Jean Plaidy 5042
The Portingale - Alison Macleod 4005
The Power and the Glory - Phyllis Bentley 462
Purple Passage: A Novel about a Lady Both Famous and Fantastic - Emily Hahn 2638
Rebel Heiress - Robert Neill 4573

Restoration: A Novel of Seventeenth-Century England - Rose Tremain 6333
Royal Flush: The Story of Minette - Margaret Irwin 3121
The Storms of Fate - Patricia Wright 6885
The Three Crowns - Jean Plaidy 5070
Traitor's Moon - Robert Neill 4574
Weep in the Sun - Jeanne Wilson 6809
With All My Heart - Margaret Campbell Barnes 330

Revolution—Central America

The Journal of Colonel De Lancey - James Warner Bellah 426
The Lion's Skin - Darwin Le Ora Teilhet 6197
The Notorious Angel - Patricia Maxwell 4201

Revolution—China

Bittersweet - Leslie Li 3769
Blood Red Rose - Maxwell Grant 2538
The Call - John Hersey 2869
China Saga - C.Y. Lee 3706
Farewell to My Concubine - Lilian Lee 3709
Peking: A Novel of China's Revolt - Anthony Grey 2587
Shanghai - Christopher New 4588

Revolution—Cuba

Mingo Dabney - James H. Street 6078

Revolution—Germany

Karl and Rosa - Alfred Doblin 1653
A People Betrayed - Alfred Doblin 1654

Revolution—Greece

Freedom or Death - Nikos Kazantzakis 3383

Revolution—Mexico

The Death of Artemio Cruz - Carlos Fuentes 2246
Desert Hawks - Frank Burleson 786
The Edge of the Storm - Agustin Yanez 6893
The Old Gringo - Carlos Fuentes 2247
Pancho And Black Jack - Fred Bean 398
The Rainbow Runner - John Cunningham 1450

Revolution of 1848

Cosette: The Sequel to Les Miserables - Laura Kalpakian 3329
Royal Flash - George MacDonald Fraser 2213

Revolution—South America

Sharpe's Devil - Bernard Cornwell 1340

Rhode Island, Battle of

Murfy's Men - Gerald Green 2565

Rich Mountain, Battle of

A Promise Unbroken - Al Lacy 3582

Risorgimento

The Castle of Fratta - Ippolito Nievo 4625
Wings of the Falcon - Barbara Michaels 4361

Riverboats

Allegheny Captive - Caroline Bourne 591

Child of the Snapping Turtle, Mike Fink - Julian Lee Rayford 5256
Dance on the Wind - Terry C. Johnston 3249
Death on the Mississippi - Peter J. Heck 2815
Fevre Dream - George R.R. Martin 4131
The Great Steamboat Race - John Brunner 736
Lord of the River - Bernard Clavel 1099
Pull Down to New Orleans - Zachary Ball 283
The River Witch - Margerie McIntyre 4278
Run Me a River - Janice Holt Giles 2415
Sea Change - Alison McLeay 4287
Show Boat - Edna Ferber 2063
Steamboat on the River - Darwin Le Ora Teilhet 6200
The Stuart Women - Matt Braun 652

Rodeos

Last Go Round - Ken Kesey 3473
When the Legends Die - Hal Borland 584

Roman Empire

According to Mary: A Novel of the Magdalene - Willa Gibbs 2398
Agrippa's Daughter - Howard Fast 2025
The Alexandrian - Martha Rofheart 5425
The Antagonists - Ernest K. Gann 2276
Antioch Actress: A Novel of Pagan Against Christian - Jacob Randolph Perkins 4913
Arena: A Novel of Spartacus and Crassus - Maurice Ghnassia 2391
Arms of Nemesis - Steven Saylor 5623
Artorius Rex - John Gloag 2432
As a Driven Leaf - Milton Steinberg 5992
As Sure as the Dawn - Francine Rivers 5352
Augustus - Allan Massie 4167
Augustus - John Williams 6785
Barabbas - Par Lagerkvist 3585
The Beacon of Alexandria - Gillian Bradshaw 627
The Bearkeeper's Daughter - Gillian Bradshaw 628
Behold, We Live - Charles Dunscomb 1812
Ben Hur: A Tale of the Christ - Lew Wallace 6536
Between Eternities - Robert H. Pilpel 5001
Beware of Caesar - Vincent Sheean 5786
Blood of the Martyrs - Naomi Mitchison 4417
Bloody Poet - Deszo Kosztolanyi 3546
The Bond and the Free - Charles Dunscomb 1813
The Book of Abraham - Marek Halter 2665
The Bride of Pilate - Esther Kellner 3393
The Brother - Chayym Zeldis 6958
Brothers of Vengeance - LeGette Blythe 556
Bury Me in Ravenna - Agnes Carr Vaughan 6432
Caesar - Mirko Jelusich 3108
Caesar - Allan Massie 4168
Caesar of the Narrow Seas - John Gloag 2433
Caesar's Women - Colleen McCullough 4233
Canis the Warrior - James Sinclair 5864
Captive of Rome - Theodora McCormick Du Bois 1740
The Captive Princess - Maxine Shore 5831
Caravan to China - Frank Stanley Stuart 6085
Catalina's Riddle - Steven Saylor 5624
The Catiline Conspiracy - John Maddox Roberts 5379
The Centurion - Jan de Hartog 2762
The Centurion - Leonard Wibberley 6729
Chantefable - Eldorous L. Dayton 1546
Children of the Wolf - Alfred Duggan 1762
Citadel of God: A Novel of Saint Benedict - Louis De Wohl 1563
The City of Libertines - W.G. Hardy 2702
Claudius the God - Robert Graves 2543
Clodia - Robert DeMaria 1606
The Coin of Carthage - Bryher 740
Confessors of the Name - Gladys Schmitt 5640
The Conquered - Naomi Mitchison 4418
The Conspiracy - John Hersey 2870

Constantine: The Miracle of the Flaming Cross - Frank G. Slaughter 5883
The Converts: A Historical Novel - Rex Warner 6564
Count Belisarius - Robert Graves 2544
The Crow Goddess - Patricia Finney 2094
The Crows of War - Steven Rayson 5276
The Dark Island - Henry Treece 6326
Darkness and the Dawn - Thomas B. Costain 1364
Dear and Glorious Physician - Taylor Caldwell 853
The Death of Attila - Cecelia Holland 2986
The Death of the Gods - Dmitri Merezhkovski 4338
The Death of Virgil - Hermann Broch 699
Death on the Appian Way - Kenneth Benton 463
Dogheaded Death - Ray Faraday Nelson 4581
Dominic - Kathleen Robinson 5405
Druids - Morgan Llywelyn 3817
The Duke of War - Walter O'Meara 4734
The Eagle and the Crown - Hubertus Loewenstein 3832
The Eagle and the Raven - Pauline Gedge 2344
Eagle in the Snow - Wallace Breem 654
The Eagles Depart - John Gloag 2434
The Eighth Veil - Ellis Kadison 3320
The Emperor Arthur - Godfrey Turton 6368
The Emperor's Physician - Jacob Randolph Perkins 4914
Empire of the Eagle - Andre Norton 4649
Epicurus My Master - Max Radin 5233
The Equinox: A Novel of Rome in the Time of Commodus - Carol Saylor 5622
Family Favorites - Alfred Duggan 1766
Farewell, Catullus - Pierson Dixon 1651
The Fates Are Laughing - William Crozier 1439
A Fig in Winter - Willa Gibbs 2400
The First Man in Rome - Colleen McCullough 4234
First the Blade - Drayton Mayrant 4212
The Flames of Rome - Paul L. Maier 4033
The Forest House - Marion Zimmer Bradley 625
Fortune's Favorite - Colleen McCullough 4235
The Four Rivers of Paradise - Helen Constance White 6678
Fourth King - Norbert Coulehan 1373
Freedom, Farewell - Phyllis Bentley 461
Gaul Is Divided - Esther Fisher Brown 721
The Gift of Rome - John Wagner 6520
The Gladiator - Thames Ross Williamson 6790
The Gladiators - Arthur Koestler 3532
God Was Born in Exile - Vintila Horia 3033
A Goddess to a God - John Lloyd Balderston 278
The Gods Are Not Mocked - Anna Taylor 6177
God's Warrior - Frank G. Slaughter 5889
Gold for the Caesars - Florence A. Seward 5759
Golden Peacock - Gertrude Atherton 224
The Gospel According to Pontius Pilate - James R. Mills 4408
The Gospel of Corax - Paul Park 4802
The Grass Crown - Colleen McCullough 4236
Gregory the Great - Gerhart Ellert 1913
Hadrian's Memoirs - Marguerite Yourcenar 6947
Hannibal - Ross Leckie 3704
Hannibal of Carthage - Mary Dolan 1686
Hear Me, Pilate! - LeGette Blythe 557
Heaven's Only Daughter - Kathleen Robinson 5406
Hortensius, Friend of Nero - Edith Pargeter 4798
Hypatia - Charles Kingsley 3498
I Am a Barbarian - Edgar Rice Burroughs 807
I, Claudius - Robert Graves 2547
I Loved Tiberius - Elisabeth Dored 1692
The Ides of March - Thornton Wilder 6753
If I Forget Thee - Robert S. Deropp 1621
If I Forget Thee - Brenda Lesley Segal 5720
The Illusionist - Anita Mason 4144
An Imaginary Life - David Malouf 4047
Imperial Caesar - Rex Warner 6565
The Imperial Governor - George Shipway 5828
Imperial Renegade - Louis De Wohl 1567
The Iron Hand of Mars - Lindsey Davis 1528
The Jew of Rome - Lion Feuchtwanger 2071

Josephus - Lion Feuchtwanger 2072
Josephus and the Emperor - Lion
    Feuchtwanger 2073
Julian - Gore Vidal 6489
Justus - Arthur L. Lapham 3663
The Key - Benita Kane Jaro 3169
The Kingdom of the Wicked - Anthony Burgess 778
The Lance of Longinus - Hubertus Loewenstein 3833
Last Act in Palmyra - Lindsey Davis 1529
The Last Athenian - Viktor Rydberg 5543
The Last Days - William Rayner 5272
The Last Days of Pompeii - Edward Bulwer-
    Lytton 768
The Last Romans - Teodor Jeske-Choinski 3216
The Last World: A Novel with an Ovidian Repertory -
    Christoph Ransmayr 5253
The Letters of Nicodemus - Jan Dobraczynski 1655
The Light Bearer - Donna Gillespie 2419
The Little Emperors - Alfred Duggan 1770
The Lives of Rachel - Joel Gross 2601
The Living Wood - Louis De Wohl 1571
The Lost Eagles - Ralph Graves 2542
The Lost Legion - H. Warner Munn 4516
A Love Divine - Alexandra Ripley 5340
Man of Nazareth - Anthony Burgess 779
Man on Fire: A Novel on the Life of St. Paul -
    LeGette Blythe 558
The Man on the White Horse - Warwick
    Deeping 1577
Marcus - Laurene Chinn 1068
Marius the Epicurean - Walter Pater 4826
A Murder on the Appian Way - Steven Saylor 5625
Nero - Mary Teresa Ronalds 5437
No King but Caesar - Anne Powers 5151
Octavia: A Tale of Ancient Rome - Seymour Van
    Santvoord 6428
A Pillar of Iron - Taylor Caldwell 861
The Pirate From Rome - John V.D.
    Southworth 5952
Pontius Pilate: A Biographical Novel - Paul L.
    Maier 4034
Pontius Pilate Reflects - Werner Koch 3529
Poseidon's Gold - Lindsey Davis 1530
Prepare Them for Caesar - Mary Louise
    Mabie 3954
Prince of Israel - Elias Gilner 2422
Purple Pirate - Talbot Mundy 4514
Queen of the East - Alexander Baron 336
Quo Vadis - Henryk Sienkiewicz 5848
Red Queen, White Queen - Henry Treece 6332
The Restless Flame - Louis De Wohl 1573
Road From Olivet - Edward Francis Murphy 4523
The Robe - Lloyd C. Douglas 1703
The Rock: A Novel about Gibraltar - John
    Masters 4179
The Roman - Mika Waltari 6554
Roman Blood - Steven Saylor 5626
Roman Go Home! - Adam Fergusson 2065
Roman Nights - Ron Burns 803
Roman Shadows - Ron Burns 804
Roman Wall - Bryher 745
The Sacrilege - John Maddox Roberts 5380
Salammbo - Gustave Flaubert 2123
The Same Scourge - John Goldthorpe 2464
The Scarlet Beast - Francis Gerard 2357
Scorpus the Moor - Leslie Turner White 6690
The Second Crucifixion - Maurice Samuel 5579
The Secret of the Kingdom - Mika Waltari 6555
Shadows in Bronze - Lindsey Davis 1531
The Shepherd - Robert Payne 4855
The Side of the Moon - Amanda Prantera 5162
Sign of the Pagan - Don Tracy 6312
The Silver Pigs - Lindsey Davis 1532
Simon Bar Cochba: Rebellion in Judea - Merton
    Finch 2086
The Sinner of Saint Ambrose - Robert
    Raynolds 5275
*The Sins of Herod: A Novel of Rome and the Early
    Church* - Frank G. Slaughter 5900

The Skystone: The Forging of Arthur's Britain - Jack
    Whyte 6726
The Soldier and the Sage: A Novel about Akiba -
    Richard G. Hubler 3065
Son of Judah - Dan Levin 3738
Son of Tears - Henry W. Coray 1320
Soul Flame - Barbara Wood 6850
The Source - James A. Michener 4374
Spartacus - Howard Fast 2044
SPQR - John Maddox Roberts 5381
*Street of the Sandalmakers: A Tale of Rome in the
    Time of Marcus Aurelius* - Nis Peterson 4977
The Sword and the Promise - Benjamin Siegel 5845
*Sword of Pleasure: Being the Memoirs of the Most
    Illustrious Lucius Cornelius Sulla* - Peter
    Green 2571
Swords Against Carthage - Friedrich Donauer 1689
Swords in the North - Paul Lewis Anderson 138
A Tear for Judas - LeGette Blythe 559
The Temple of the Muses - John Maddox
    Roberts 5382
The Tenth Measure - Brenda Lesley Segal 5721
The Testament of Theophilus - Leonard
    Wibberley 6730
That Egyptian Woman - Noel B. Gerson 2384
Theodora and the Emperor - Harold Lamb 3608
The Thorn of Arimathea - Frank G. Slaughter 5905
The Three Legions - Gregory Solon 5941
Three's Company - Alfred Duggan 1774
Threshold of Fire - Hella S. Haasse 2633
Throne of Isis - Judith Tarr 6170
Throne of the World - Louis De Wohl 1575
Tiberius: The Memoirs of the Emperor - Allan
    Massie 4169
Time to Depart - Lindsey Davis 1533
The Triumph - Ernest K. Gann 2280
Tros of Samothrace - Talbot Mundy 4515
Turn Back the River - W.G. Hardy 2703
Two Thieves - Manuel Komroff 3535
*Upon This Rock: A Novel of Simon Peter, Prince of
    Apostles* - Frank G. Slaughter 5906
Upon This Rock: The Life of St. Peter - Walter F.
    Murphy 4526
Venus in Copper - Lindsey Davis 1534
The Venus Throw - Steven Saylor 5627
The Voices of Masada - David Kossoff 3545
Votan - John James 3162
Warrior Queen - James Sinclair 5865
The Way - J.M. Hartley 2761
A Wayside Tavern - Norah Lofts 3862
Who Came by Night - Roland Nicholas 4608
Winter Quarters - Alfred Duggan 1775
The Wolf of Masada - John Fredman 2220
The Word and the Sword - Theo Lang 3662
The Young Caesar - Rex Warner 6567

Romance

The Admiral's Lady - Mary Ann Gibbs 2395
The Adulteress - Philippa Carr 916
Albany - Laura Black 519
Albuquerque - Sara Orwig 4757
Alexa - Anne Melville 4330
Allegheny Captive - Caroline Bourne 591
And One Wore Gray - Heather Graham 2515
Arizona Ecstasy - Rosanne Bittner 511
Artemia - Pamela Hill 2927
The Artist's Daughter - Leslie O'Grady 4698
Ask Me No Questions - Patricia Veryan 6459
The Astrov Legacy - Constance Heaven 2802
An Autumn in Araby - Carola Salisbury 5565
Autumn Lace - Eileen Jackson 3133
Ballenrose - Mallory Burgess 783
The Bannaman Legacy - Catherine Cookson 1272
Banners of Silk - Rosalind Laker 3592
Belgrave Square - Rachel Summerson 6117
The Bellerose Bargain - Robyn Carr 934
Between Two Worlds - Monique Raphel High 2913

Black-Eyed Susan - Deborah Camp 871
The Black Moth - Georgette Heyer 2877
The Black Velvet Gown - Catherine Cookson 1274
The Blood of Roses - Marsha Canham 879
The Blue Dragon - Diana Brown 716
The Blue Falcon - Robyn Carr 935
The Braeswood Tapestry - Robyn Carr 936
Brazen Whispers - Jane Feather 2055
The Bride - Julie Garwood 2311
By Love Enslaved - Phoebe Conn 1255
By Right of Arms - Robyn Carr 937
Camelot Country - Marjorie McEvoy 4267
Candle in the Window - Christina Dodd 1662
The Capricorn Stone - Madeleine Brent 659
Cardigan Square - Alexandra Manners 4070
Caressa - Linda Lang Bartell 363
Castle Dor - Sir Arthur Thomas Quiller-Couch 5226
Castle Heritage - Elisabeth Barr 337
Castle of Doves - Constance Heaven 2803
Castle of Eagles - Constance Heaven 2804
A Certain Splendour - Carola Salisbury 5566
The Chains of Fate - Pamela Belle 430
The Changeling - Philippa Carr 918
Charleston - Alexandra Ripley 5338
Charlotte Morel - Maria Lodi 3829
Charlotte Morel: The Dream - Maria Lodi 3830
Charlotte Morel: The Siege - Maria Lodi 3831
Chase the Wind - Janelle Taylor 6184
The Chateau - Stephen Coulter 1383
Chelynne - Robyn Carr 938
Child of the Mist - Kathleen Morgan 4451
Circle in the Water - Susan Wiggs 6742
Circle of Gold - Karen Harper 2710
Circle of Pearls - Rosalind Laker 3593
City of Golden Cages - Jo Germany 2358
Claire - Elizabeth Lyle 3931
Claudine's Daughter - Rosalind Laker 3594
The Clock Tower - Jeanne Montague 4435
Comanche Moon - Catherine Anderson 137
A Company of Swans - Eva Ibbotson 3095
The Conquest - Jude Deveraux 1630
Count Vronsky's Daughter - Carola Salisbury 5567
Daneclere - Pamela Hill 2931
Dark Inheritance - Carola Salisbury 5568
Daughter of Marignac - Constance Heaven 2805
Defiant Hearts - Janelle Taylor 6185
Defy Not the Heart - Johanna Lindsey 3794
The Demon Lover - Victoria Holt 3013
Desire and Deceive - Cordia Byers 832
The Devil on Horseback - Victoria Holt 3014
Devil's Cub - Georgette Heyer 2885
Devil's Fire, Love's Revenge - Barbara Paul 4836
A Distant Thunder - Teresa de Luca 1561
Dolphin Summer - Carola Salisbury 5569
Dragonfly in Amber - Diana Gabaldon 2262
The Drayton Legacy - Rona Randall 5247
Dual Destiny - Karen Lynn 3939
Earth Song - Catherine Coulter 1374
Echoes From the Past - Marjorie McEvoy 4268
The Eleventh Year - Monique Raphel High 2914
Emerald - Helen Ashfield 206
Emerald Fire - Laurie Grant 2537
The Everlasting Covenant - Robyn Carr 939
Fair is the Rose - Meagan MacKinney 3997
Faith and Honor - Robin Maderich 4025
The Falcon and the Flower - Virginia Henley 2826
Fallen Angel - Deborah Camp 872
Falls of Gard - Laura Black 520
Family Fortune - Mignon G. Eberhart 1834
Farewell the Stranger - Saliee O'Brien 4682
The Favored Child - Philippa Gregory 2582
The Fine and Handsome Captain - Frances
    Lynch 3933
A Finger to Her Lips - Evelyn Berckman 472
Fire Queen - Deborah Grabien 2503
The Fireflower - Edith Layton 3687
The Fires of Glenlochy - Constance Heaven 2806
Flight From Fifth Avenue - Catherine M. Rae 5235
Floodtide - Suzanne Goodwin 2475

The Floral Companion - Anthea Bell   419
The French Bride - Evelyn Anthony   163
The French Woman - Barbara Paul   4837
Garnet - Helen Ashfield   207
The Gaynor Women - Virginia Coffman   1153
The Gentle Conqueror - Mary Ellen Gronau   2597
A Georgian Love Story - Ernest Raymond   5258
Gerait's Daughter - Millie J. Ragosta   5241
Gilded Splendour - Rosalind Laker   3595
The Girl - Catherine Cookson   1277
Glendraco - Laura Black   521
The Golden Tulip - Rosalind Laker   3596
Greygallows - Barbara Michaels   4359
The Hand of a Woman - Diana Brown   719
Hawthorn Hill - Doris Shannon   5777
The Heart of the Rose - June Barraclough   346
Hearts of Fire - Christina Savage   5616
Heir to Kuragin - Constance Heaven   2807
Heiress of Ardara - Margaret Evans Porter   5137
A Heritage of Shadows - Madeleine Brent   660
Highland Belle - Patricia Grasso   2541
Honour and Obey - Malcolm Macdonald   3966
Horses of War - Duff Hart-Davis   2760
The House of Kuragin - Constance Heaven   2808
Hyde Place - Virginia Coffman   1154
If This Be Magic - Ellen Marsh   4098
The Imagination of the Heart - Judith Glover   2437
In the Shadow of Midnight - Marsha Canham   880
In the Shadow of the Nile - Sara Hylton   3093
An Innocent Woman - Malcolm Macdonald   3967
It Began in Vauxhall Gardens - Jean Plaidy   5023
Jennie about to Be - Elisabeth Ogilvie   4694
Jennie Glenroy - Elisabeth Ogilvie   4695
Jewel of the Sea - Susan Wiggs   6743
Jewelled Path - Rosalind Laker   3597
The Judas Kiss - Victoria Holt   3015
Judith - Brian Cleeve   1108
Katherine - Antonia Van-Loon   6425
Katya - Lucy Cores   1328
Kezzy - Patricia Burns   799
Kindred Spirits - June Barraclough   347
Kingdom of Gold - Susan Wiggs   6744
Kingdom of Shadows - Barbara Erskine   1954
Knave of Hearts - Philippa Carr   920
A Knight in Shining Armor - Jude Deveraux   1631
Knights - Linda Lael Miller   4399
The Ladies of Hanover Square - Rona Randall   5249
Lady Defiant - Suzanne Robinson   5412
Lady Gallant - Suzanne Robinson   5413
Lady Hellfire - Suzanne Robinson   5414
A Lady in Doubt - Annabel Wynne   6891
Lady of Conquest - Teresa Medeiros   4322
Lady of Mallow - Dorothy Eden   1856
Lady of the Forest - Jennifer Roberson   5368
Lady of the Glen - Jennifer Roberson   5369
A Leaf in the Wind - Marie Joseph   3307
Lily - Cindy Bonner   571
The Lily and the Leopard - Susan Wiggs   6745
The Lion Triumphant - Philippa Carr   922
Lisbon - Valerie Sherwood   5825
A London Season - Anthea Bell   420
Lone Star Lady - Jill Gregory   2579
The Lonely Strangers - Charity Blackstock   531
Longleaf - Rose Brock   701
Looking After Lily - Cindy Bonner   572
Lord Libertine - Anthony Esler   1964
Lord of Hawkfell Island - Catherine Coulter   1376
Lord of Ravensley - Constance Heaven   2809
Lord of the Far Island - Victoria Holt   3016
Lord Richard's Passion - Mervyn Jones   3293
The Lorimer Line - Anne Melville   4332
Lost Love Found - Bertrice Small   5910
Louisa Elliott - Ann Victoria Roberts   5370
The Love Child - Philippa Carr   923
The Love Child - Catherine Cookson   1279
Love Not a Rebel - Heather Graham   2516
Lovers - Suzanne Goodwin   2476
Lovers Meeting - Mollie Hardwick   2695
Love's Tender Fury - Jennifer Wilde   6749

Lovestorm - Judith E. French   2222
Madensky Square - Eva Ibbotson   3096
Maggie Craig - Marie Joseph   3308
Magic Flutes - Eva Ibbotson   3097
The Magnolias - Julie Ellis   1922
The Mallen Girl - Catherine Cookson   1280
The Mallen Lot - Catherine Cookson   1281
The Mallen Streak - Catherine Cookson   1282
The Malvie Inheritance - Pamela Hill   2938
Marianne - Juliette Benzoni   466
Marianne and the Lords of the East - Juliette Benzoni   468
Marianne and the Masked Prince - Juliette Benzoni   469
Marianne and the Privateer - Juliette Benzoni   470
Marianne and the Rebels - Juliette Benzoni   471
The Marquis and Miss Jones - Helen Ashfield   208
Marsanne - Virginia Coffman   1155
Masque of Enchantment - Charlene Cross   1432
Masque of Jade - Emma Merritt   4344
Masque of Sapphire - Deana James   3156
Masques of Gold - Roberta Gellis   2352
The Mating Dance - Rona Randall   5250
Mayfair - Nancy Fitzgerald   2115
Meadowsweet - Gwendoline Butler   820
Megan - Kathleen Magill   4028
Melbury Square - Dorothy Eden   1857
The Merrymaid - Mollie Hardwick   2696
The Michaelmas Tree - Helen Ashfield   209
Midnight Moon - Jeanne Montague   4436
Midsummer's Eve - Philippa Carr   924
The Millionaire's Daughter - Dorothy Eden   1858
The Miracle at St. Bruno's - Philippa Carr   925
Miss Martha Mary Crawford - Catherine Marchant   4081
Miss Philadelphia Smith - Paula Allardyce   91
Mistress of the Eagles - Elona Malterre   4052
A Moment in Time - Bertrice Small   5911
Monday's Child - Mollie Hardwick   2697
Montana Woman - Rosanne Bittner   513
The Moon in the Water - Pamela Belle   433
Moonfeather - Judith E. French   2223
Moonraker's Bride - Madeleine Brent   661
The Moreland Legacy - Diana Haviland   2777
Morning's Gate - Ann Victoria Roberts   5371
A Most Romantic City - Mary Ann Gibbs   2396
The Moth - Catherine Cookson   1284
Mountain Laurel - Jude Deveraux   1632
My Gallant Enemy - Rexanne Becnel   409
My Name Is Clary Brown - Charlotte Keppel   3466
My Pride, My Folly - Suzanne Butler   830
Never Doubt I Love - Patricia Veryan   6473
New Orleans Legacy - Alexandra Ripley   5341
Night Wind's Woman - Shirl Henke   2825
No Price Too High - Madeleine Polland   5085
Nobody's Angel - Karen Robards   5363
Norah - Pamela Hill   2941
A Notorious Woman - Malcolm Macdonald   3969
The Old Enchantment - Sarah Neilan   4565
On a Far Wide Shore - Malcolm Macdonald   3970
On the Night of the Seventh Moon - Victoria Holt   3018
One Wore Blue - Heather Graham   2517
The Only Sin - Julie Ellis   1923
Opal - Helen Ashfield   210
Oregon Bride - Rosanne Bittner   514
Outlander - Diana Gabaldon   2264
Outlaw Lover - Lindsey Hanks   2676
The Parson's Daughter - Catherine Cookson   1286
The Passion of Letty Fox - Diana Saunders   5610
Passionate Warriors - Mary Ellen Gronau   2598
Patriot's Dream - Barbara Michaels   4360
Pearl - Helen Ashfield   211
The Pearl Pagoda - Susannah Broome   707
The Pirate and the Pagan - Virginia Henley   2827
A Pirate's Pleasure - Heather Graham   2518
The Place of Devils - Lucinda Baker   275
A Place of Ravens - Pamela Hill   2942
The Pool of St. Branok - Philippa Carr   926

Portrait of Emma - Lillian Cheatham   1010
The Pride of Lions - Marsha Canham   881
The Pride of the Trevallions - Carola Salisbury   5570
Princess of Fire - Shannon Drake   1718
Princess of the Veil - Helen Mittermeyer   4420
The Railway King - Margaret Mayhew   4207
The Rainbow Promise - Lisa Gregory   2580
The Raven and the Rose - Susan Wiggs   6746
Ravenburn - Laura Black   522
A Respectable Trade - Philippa Gregory   2584
Ride the Blue Riband - Rosalind Laker   3598
River of Dreams - Gay Courter   1390
Rosehaven - Catherine Coulter   1380
Ruby - Helen Ashfield   213
The Running Vixen - Elizabeth Chadwick   968
Sabrina - Madeleine Polland   5086
Saraband for Two Sisters - Philippa Carr   928
Sarah Cobb - Catherine M. Rae   5236
Sarton Kell - Kate Mallory   4043
Savage Oaks - Julie Ellis   1924
Savage Thunder - Johanna Lindsey   3795
Scarlet Ribbons - Judith E. French   2224
Sea Change - Alison McLeay   4287
The Sea Treasure - Elisabeth Barr   338
Secret for a Nightingale - Victoria Holt   3020
The Secret of Saramount - Lillian Cheatham   1011
Secret Song - Catherine Coulter   1381
The Shadowed Spring - Carola Salisbury   5571
A Shadow's Bliss - Patricia Veryan   6477
The Shakespeare Girl - Mollie Hardwick   2698
The Silver Highways - Malcolm Macdonald   3972
Silver Linings - Shirley Davies-Owens   1508
A Silver Mirror - Roberta Gellis   2353
The Silver Touch - Rosalind Laker   3599
Sioux Splendor - Rosanne Bittner   515
Song of the Bayou - Elinor Lynley   3936
The Song of the Siren - Philippa Carr   929
The Spitfire - Bertrice Small   5912
The Spring of the Tiger - Victoria Holt   3021
Stacey's Flyer - Patricia Burns   800
The Stallion Man - Judith Glover   2438
Storm Winds - Iris Johansen   3217
The Storm Witch - Elisabeth Barr   339
Stormswift - Madeleine Brent   662
Storyville - Lois Battle   377
Stranger at the Wedding - Frances Lynch   3934
Stranger at Wildings - Madeleine Brent   663
Stranger's Forest - Pamela Hill   2943
Strathgallant - Laura Black   523
Street of the Madwoman - Isabel Ortega   4756
The Sutburys - Pamela Hill   2944
Sweet Mountain Magic - Rosanne Bittner   516
Sweet Ransom - Linda Madl   4026
The Taming - Jude Deveraux   1633
The Tempestuous Petticoat - Mary Ann Gibbs   2397
Temple Bells - Marjorie McEvoy   4271
That Sweet and Savage Land - Emma Drummond   1728
These Old Shades - Georgette Heyer   2906
Thief of My Heart - Rexanne Becnel   410
This Willing Passion - Patricia Cloud   1132
Through a Glass Darkly - Karleen Koen   3531
Thunder on the Plains - Rosanne Bittner   517
Tilly - Catherine Cookson   1288
A Time for Silence - Philippa Carr   930
The Time of the Hunter's Moon - Victoria Holt   3022
To Dance with Kings - Rosalind Laker   3601
To Love a Stranger - Barbara Paul   4839
To Love Again - Bertrice Small   5913
To the End of Her Days - Malcolm Macdonald   3975
A Token of Jewels - Diane Cory   1353
Tomorrow's Dream - Peggy Hanchar   2674
Tree of Gold - Rosalind Laker   3602
The Troubadour's Romance - Robyn Carr   940
Vale of Tyranny - Suzanne Butler   831
The Venetian Mask - Rosalind Laker   3603
Veronique - Virginia Coffman   1158
The Very Best People - Elizabeth Villars   6499
The Viking's Woman - Heather Graham   2520

Visions of a Heart - Emily Carmichael   899
Voices in a Haunted Room - Philippa Carr   931
Vollands - Pamela Hill   2947
Voyager - Diana Gabaldon   2265
Warwyck's Woman - Rosalind Laker   3604
What the Heart Keeps - Rosalind Laker   3605
Where Magic Dwells - Rexanne Becnel   411
While the Music Lasts - Suzanne Goodwin   2477
The Whip - Catherine Cookson   1291
Whitton's Folly - Pamela Hill   2948
Wild Cat - Laura Black   524
Wild Jasmine - Bertrice Small   5914
The Wildcliffe Bird - Constance Heaven   2811
Will You Love Me in September? - Philippa Carr   932
Willowwood - Mollie Hardwick   2699
The Wind Dancer - Iris Johansen   3218
The Wind From the Sea - Constance Heaven   2812
Windover - Jane Aiken Hodge   2974
The Wingless Bird - Catherine Cookson   1292
The Wings of Morning - Karen Harper   2714
Wings of the Falcon - Barbara Michaels   4361
The Winter Bride - Carola Salisbury   5572
Winter of the Heart - Linda J. LaRosa   3665
Wolf's Embrace - Gail Link   3801
Woman of Andros - Thornton Wilder   6754
A Woman of Quality - Jan Westcott   6649
A Woman Possessed - Malcolm Macdonald   3977
A Woman Scorned - Malcolm Macdonald   3978
Woman's Own - Robyn Carr   941
The World of Jennie G. - Elisabeth Ogilvie   4696

Rosebud, Battle of the

Crazy Horse - Bill Dugan   1757
Thunder in the Dawn - Earl Murray   4532

Royalty—Austria

The Archduke - Michael Arnold   194
The Emperor Franz Joseph - Ottokar
  Janetschek   3164
Imperial Waltz - William M. Abrahams   13
The Strange Case of Madamoiselle P. - Patrick
  Ireland   3109

Royalty—Bactria

Horses of Heaven - Gillian Bradshaw   630

Royalty—China

The Chinese Emperor - Jean Levi   3733
The Court of the Lion - Eleanor Cooney   1294
Deception - Eleanor Cooney   1295
The Dream of Confucius - Jean Levi   3734
Empress - Evelyn McCune   4238
Forbidden City - Muriel Molland Jernigan   3215
Green Dragon, White Tiger - Annette Motley   4501
A House in Peiking - Robert Payne   4853
Imperial Woman - Pearl S. Buck   755
The Jade Stalk - Jonathan Fast   2048
Lady Wu - Yutang Lin   3782
Manchu Empress - Bluebell Matilda Hunter   3081
Twilight of the Dragon - Peter Bourne   596

Royalty—Denmark

The Fall of the King - Johannes Vilhelm
  Jensen   3214
The Lost Queen - Norah Lofts   3850
The Queen's Physician - Edgar Maas   3952

Royalty—Egypt

Cleopatra - H. Rider Haggard   2637
Pharaoh - Eloise Jarvis McGraw   4276

Royalty—England

The Abandoned Woman - Richard Condon   1235
Absolute Elizabeth - Joanna Dessau   1624
Albert's Victoria - Tyler Whittle   6719
All the Queen's Men - Evelyn Anthony   157
Angel of Death - P.C. Doherty   1670
Anne Boleyn - Evelyn Anthony   158
Anne of the Thousand Days - Edward Fenton   2059
The Autobiography of Henry VIII - Margaret
  George   2355
Banners of Gold - Pamela Kaufman   3371
The Barons of Runnymede - Pamela Bennetts   445
The Bartholomew Fair Murders - Leonard
  Tourney   6297
The Bastard King - Jean Plaidy   5004
The Battle of the Queens - Jean Plaidy   5005
Beloved Enemy: The Passions of Eleanor of Aquitaine
  - Ellen Jones   3288
Bennett's Welcome - Inglis Fletcher   2132
Bertie, Albert Edward, Prince of Wales - Tyler
  Whittle   6720
Bertie and the Crime of Passion - Peter
  Lovesey   3907
Bertie and the Seven Bodies - Peter Lovesey   3908
Bertie and the Tinman - Peter Lovesey   3909
The Bisley Boy - Christopher Hunt   3080
Blackstone - Richard Falkirk   2006
Blackstone and the Scourge of Europe - Richard
  Falkirk   2007
The Blanket of the Dark - John Buchan   749
Blood of the Boar - Margaret Abbey   2
Blood Royal - Mollie Hardwick   2690
The Bloody Field - Edith Pargeter   4795
The Breath of Kings - Gene Farrington   2019
The Bride - Margaret Irwin   3116
Brief Gaudy Hour - Margaret Campbell Barnes   322
The Broken Sword - Rhoda S. Edwards   1885
A Brood of Vipers - Michael Clynes   1133
The Buckingham Palace Connection - Ted
  Willis   6792
Call Lady Purbeck - Hilda Lewis   3745
The Captive of Kensington Palace - Jean
  Plaidy   5007
Caroline the Queen - Jean Plaidy   5009
Catherine - Hilda Lewis   3746
Champion - L. Christian Balling   285
Charles the King - Evelyn Anthony   160
Chase the Heart - Maggie Osborne   4760
Command of the King - Mary Lide   3773
The Concubine - Norah Lofts   3839
Consort for Victoria - William Vaughan
  Wilkins   6757
Countess Carrots - Molly Costain Haycraft   2792
The Courts of Illusion - Rosemary Hawley
  Jarman   3165
The Courts of Love - Jean Plaidy   5010
The Courts of Love: A Romance of Medieval France -
  Peter Bourne   592
Crippled Splendour - Evan John   3219
Crouchback - Carola Oman   4732
Crown in Candlelight - Rosemary Hawley
  Jarman   3166
A Crown in Darkness: A Novel about Lady Jane Grey
  - Margaret Mullally   4512
Crown of Roses - Valerie Anand   127
The Cunning of the Dove - Alfred Duggan   1765
Dance on a Sinking Ship - Michael Kilian   3483
Dark Torrent of Glencoe - Edward Grierson   2590
The Daughter of Time - Josephine Tey   6209
The De Montfort Legacy - Pamela Bennetts   447
The Death of a King - P.C. Doherty   1672
Death of the Fox - George Garrett   2300
Death of the Red King - Pamela Bennetts   448
The Devil Is Loose - Graham Shelby   5790
Di and I - Peter Lefcourt   3714
The Disputed Crown - Valerie Anand   128
Don Pedro's Captain - Pamela Bennetts   449
The Dragon and the Rose - Roberta Gellis   2350

A Dragon for Edward - Pamela Bennetts   450
The Duke's Mistress: The Story of Mary Ann Clarke -
  F.W. Kenyon   3447
The Earl - Cecelia Holland   2987
Edward - Tyler Whittle   6721
Edward and Mrs. Simpson - A.C.H. Smith   5916
Eleanor the Queen - Norah Lofts   3842
Elizabeth and the Prince of Spain - Margaret
  Irwin   3117
Elizabeth, Captive Princess - Margaret Irwin   3118
Elizabeth: Queen & Woman - Helen Thorpe   6279
Elizabeth, the Woman - Amanda Mae Ellis   1917
The Elusive Crown - Hebe Elsna   1931
Envoy From Elizabeth - Pamela Bennetts   451
Epitaph for Three Women - Jean Plaidy   5012
Exit Lady Masham - Louis Auchincloss   230
Falls the Shadow - Sharon Kay Penman   4903
The Fatal Crown - Ellen Jones   3289
The Fate of Princes - P.C. Doherty   1673
Feast in the Morning - Hugh Preston   5175
The Fifth Queen - Ford Madox Ford   2161
Fire and Morning - Francis W. Leary   3696
Fitzempress' Law - Diana Norman   4644
Flambard's Confession - Marilyn Durham   1816
The Flame in the Dark - Basil Bonallack   568
The Follies of the King - Jean Plaidy   5014
Footman in Powder - Helen Ashton   216
Fortune Made His Sword - Martha Rofheart   5426
Fortune's Wheel - Rhoda S. Edwards   1886
The Fourth Queen - Isabel Paterson   4827
Gay Lord Robert - Jean Plaidy   5015
The Gentle Falcon - Hilda Lewis   3747
Gildenford - Valerie Anand   130
*The Girl Who Was Never Queen: A Biographical
  Novel of Princess Charlotte of Wales* - Mary
  Main   4037
The Glory and the Dream - F.W. Kenyon   3450
Goddess of the Green Room - Jean Plaidy   5016
The Golden Days - Robert Neill   4569
The Golden Knight - George Challis   971
The Golden Yoke: A Novel of the War of the Roses -
  Olive Eckerson   1837
The Goldsmith's Wife - Jean Plaidy   5017
Good King Harry - Denise Giardina   2393
The Green Salamander - Pamela Hill   2933
Hammer of the Scots - Jean Plaidy   5018
Harlot Queen - Hilda Lewis   3748
Harp into Battle - Cecil Maiden   4031
Harry of Monmouth - A.M. Maughan   4199
A Health Unto His Majesty - Jean Plaidy   5019
The Heart Is a Traitor - Margaret Abbey   4
Heart of a Queen - Josephine Delves-
  Broughton   1603
The Heart of the Lion - Jean Plaidy   5020
The Heir of Allington - Philippa Wiat   6727
Henry VIII and His Six Wives - Maureen
  Peters   4975
Her Majesty's Captain - Derek Wilson   6797
Her Royal Destiny - Carol Maxwell Eady   1820
Here Be Dragons - Sharon Kay Penman   4904
Here Comes the King - Philip Lindsay   3792
Here Lies Our Sovereign Lord - Jean Plaidy   5021
The Heretic - Alison Macleod   4002
The Hireling - Alison Macleod   4003
I Am Mary Tudor - Hilda Lewis   3750
I, Elizabeth - Rosalind Miles   4017
I, Victoria - Cynthia Harrod-Eagles   2755
Immortal Queen - Elizabeth Byrd   834
In a Dark Wood Wandering - Hella S. Haasse   2631
In the Shadow of the Crown - Jean Plaidy   5022
Isabel the Fair - Margaret Campbell Barnes   323
*The Ivy Crown: A Biographical Novel of Queen
  Katherine Parr* - Mary M. Luke   3923
James, by the Grace of God - Hugh Williamson
  Ross   5499
Jewels - Robert Perrin   4917
Katharine: The Virgin Widow - Jean Plaidy   5025
Katheryn, the Wanton Queen - Maureen Peters   4976

Kathryn: In the Court of Six Queens - Anne Merton Abbey 1

The Killing of Richard the Third - Robert Farrington 2020

The King Breaker - Elizabeth Linington 3797

The King Edward Plot - Robert Lee Hall 2658

The King James Version - Stanley N. Stewart 6035

The King Liveth - Jeffrey Farnol 2013

King of the Wood - Valerie Anand 131

King's Agent - Justus Kent Clark 1090

The King's Bastard - Hebe Elsna 1932

The King's Bed - Margaret Campbell Barnes 324

The King's Brat - Constance Gluyas 2441

The King's Daughters - Molly Costain Haycraft 2793

King's Fool - Margaret Campbell Barnes 325

The King's Grey Mare - Rosemary Hawley Jarman 3167

King's Man - C.M. Edmondston 1880

The King's Pleasure - Norah Lofts 3847

The King's Pleasure - Jean Plaidy 5026

The King's Secret Matter - Jean Plaidy 5027

Knight's Honor - Roberta Gellis 2351

The Lady Cicely - Sandra Wilson 6813

The Lady in the Tower - Jean Plaidy 5028

Lady in Waiting - Rosemary Sutcliff 6123

Lady on the Coin - Margaret Campbell Barnes 326

Lady Rich - Elizabeth Boatwright Coker 1166

The Lady Royal - Molly Costain Haycraft 2794

The Last of the Barons - Edward Bulwer-Lytton 769

Legacy - Susan Kay 3374

Leopards and Lilies - Alfred Duggan 1769

Less Fortunate than Fair - Sandra Wilson 6814

Let the King Beware! - Honore Morrow 4489

Lillibullero - Robert Neill 4571

Lillie - David Butler 818

The Lily and the Leopards - Alice Harwood 2765

The Lily and the Lion - Maurice Druon 1733

The Lion and the Leopard - Mary Ellen Johnson 3226

The Lion of Christ - Margaret Butler 823

The Lion of England - Margaret Butler 824

The Lion of England - Eve Trevaskis 6336

The Lion of Justice - Margaret Butler 825

The Lion of Justice - Jean Plaidy 5031

Lion Rampant - Bernard Shrimsley 5836

Lionheart!: A Novel of Richard I, King of England - Martha Rofheart 5428

The Little Victoria - Lozania Prole 5196

The Lodestar - Pamela Belle 432

The Lords of Lancaster - Pamela Bennetts 452

The Lost Queen - Norah Lofts 3850

The Lute Player - Norah Lofts 3852

The Man on a Donkey - H.F.M. Prescott 5170

Marlborough's Unfair Lady - Lozania Prole 5197

The Marriage of Meggotta - Edith Pargeter 4799

Mary Anne - Daphne Du Maurier 1749

Mary of Carisbrooke - Margaret Campbell Barnes 327

Masquerade for the King - Marina Oliver 4729

The Master of Gray Trilogy - Nigel Tranter 6316

Merchant of the Ruby - Alice Harwood 2766

Mine Is the Kingdom - Jane Oliver 4726

Miss Nobody - Caroline Ross 5465

Mistress Anne - Carolly Erickson 1952

The Mountain of Immoderate Desires - Leslie Wilson 6811

The Mudlark - Theodore Bonnet 573

Murder at the Palace - Elliott Roosevelt 5445

The Murder in the Tower - Jean Plaidy 5035

Murder Most Royal - Jean Plaidy 5036

My Dear Lover England - Pamela Bennetts 453

My Enemy the Queen - Victoria Holt 3017

My Lady Benbrook - Constance Gluyas 2442

My Lady Glamis - Pamela Hill 2940

My Lady of Cleves - Margaret Campbell Barnes 328

My Lord Brother the Lionheart - Molly Costain Haycraft 2795

My Lord Essex - Olive Eckerson 1838

My Lord Foxe - Constance Gluyas 2443

My Lord John - Georgette Heyer 2895

Myself as Witness - James Goldman 2458

Myself, Christopher Wren - David Weiss 6606

Myself My Enemy - Jean Plaidy 5037

The Ninth Statue - Roseleen Milne 4410

Oh! Where Are Bloody Mary's Earrings? - Robert Player 5079

Old St. Paul's - William Harrison Ainsworth 57

The Paladin - George Shipway 5830

Passage to Pontefract - Jean Plaidy 5038

The Passionate Enemies - Jean Plaidy 5039

The Peacock and the Pearl - Jennifer Lang 3661

Perdita's Prince - Jean Plaidy 5040

The Phoenix Rising - Jean Evans 1984

Physician Extraordinary: A Novel of the Life and Times of William Harvey - David Weiss 6608

The Plantagenet Prelude - Jean Plaidy 5041

The Pleasures of Love - Jean Plaidy 5042

The Plot to Kill Wallis Simpson: A Work of Faction - Graham Fisher 2104

The Portingale - Alison Macleod 4005

The Power and the Passion - Christina Nicholson 4609

The Prince and the Pauper - Mark Twain 6373

The Prince and the Quakeress - Jean Plaidy 5043

The Prince of Darkness - P.C. Doherty 1675

The Prince of Darkness - Jean Plaidy 5044

Princess in Amber - Evelyn Wilde Mayerson 4205

The Princess of Celle - Jean Plaidy 5045

Princess Pamela - Ray Russell 5534

The Proud Man - Elizabeth Linington 3800

The Proud Servant: The Story of Montrose - Margaret Irwin 3120

The Queen and I - Sue Townsend 6306

The Queen and Lord M - Jean Plaidy 5046

The Queen and the Gypsy - Constance Heaven 2810

Queen Anne Boleyn - Francis Hackett 2634

The Queen From Provence - Jean Plaidy 5047

Queen in Waiting - Jean Plaidy 5048

Queen of This Realm: The Story of Queen Elizabeth I - Jean Plaidy 5050

The Queen's Favourites - Jean Plaidy 5051

The Queen's Grace - Jan Westcott 6646

The Queen's Husband - Samuel Edwards 1889

The Queen's Husband - Jean Plaidy 5052

The Queen's Secret - Jean Plaidy 5053

The Queen's Sister - Sandra Wilson 6815

The Queen's War: A Novel of Eleanor of Aquitaine - Jeanne Mackin 3996

The Queen's Ward - Hebe Elsna 1933

The Rain Maiden - Jill M. Phillips 4985

Ralegh's Fair Bess: The Story of Bess Throckmorton - Judy Turner 6365

The Reckoning - Sharon Kay Penman 4906

The Red-Haired Brat - Joanna Dessau 1627

Red Rose of Anjou - Jean Plaidy 5054

Regency Rogue - Helen Ashfield 212

Regency Royal - Michael Hardwick 2687

The Regent's Daughter - Jean Plaidy 5055

The Reluctant Queen - Molly Costain Haycraft 2796

The Reluctant Queen: The Story of Anne of York - Jean Plaidy 5056

Restoration: A Novel of Seventeenth-Century England - Rose Tremain 6333

The Revolt of the Eaglets - Jean Plaidy 5057

Richard III: The Last Plantagenet - Tyler Whittle 6722

Richard and the Knights of God - Pamela Bennetts 454

The Right Line of Cedric - Alfred Duggan 1773

The Ringed Castle - Dorothy Dunnett 1807

Riot at Gravesend: A Novel of Wat Tyler's Rebellion - William Howard Woods 6864

The Robsart Affair - Jennette Letton 3729

The Rose at Harvest End - Eleanor Fairburn 2003

The Rose Without a Thorn - Jean Plaidy 5058

Royal Escape - Georgette Heyer 2900

Royal Flush: The Story of Minette - Margaret Irwin 3121

A Royal Murder - Elliott Roosevelt 5456

Royal Nonesuch: A Tudor Tapestry - Beatrice White 6674

The Royal Pawn - Antonia Ridge 5327

A Royal Quest - Mary Lide 3777

Royal Road to Fotheringay - Jean Plaidy 5059

Royal Sword at Agincourt - Pamela Bennetts 455

Royal William - Doris Leslie 3728

The Ruthless Yeomen - Valerie Anand 134

St. Thomas's Eve - Jean Plaidy 5060

Satan in St. Mary's - P.C. Doherty 1676

Satan's Fire - P.C. Doherty 1677

Scapegoat for a Stuart - Kate Kirby 3504

The Scotswoman - Inglis Fletcher 2140

The Scottish Chiefs - Jane Porter 5135

A Search for a King: A 12th-Century Legend - Gore Vidal 6492

The Severed Crown - Jane Lane 3657

Shadow in the Sun: A Novel of Elizabeth I, the Virgin Queen - F.W. Kenyon 3460

The Shadow of the Pomegranate - Jean Plaidy 5062

The She-Wolf - Pamela Bennetts 456

The She-Wolf of France - Maurice Druon 1736

The Sheriff of Nottingham - Richard Kluger 3512

Shield of Honor - Alice Walworth Graham 2511

Shield of Three Lions - Pamela Kaufman 3372

Simon the Coldheart - Georgette Heyer 2901

Sister to Jane: The Story of Lady Katharine Grey - Beatrice May 4202

The Sixth Wife - Jean Plaidy 5063

So Merciful a Queen, So Cruel a Woman - Alice Harwood 2769

Stage of Fools - Charles Andrew Brady 635

A Stake in the Kingdom - Nigel Tranter 6321

The Star of Lancaster - Jean Plaidy 5065

Stephen and the Sleeping Saints - Pamela Bennetts 457

The Stranger Prince - Margaret Irwin 3122

The Strong Room - Jere Hungerford Wheelwright 6671

The Succession: A Novel of Elizabeth and James - George Garrett 2302

The Summer Queen - Alice Walworth Graham 2512

The Sun in Splendour - Jean Plaidy 5066

The Sunne in Splendour - Sharon Kay Penman 4907

The Swan and the Rose - Francis W. Leary 3697

Sweet Lass of Richmond Hill - Jean Plaidy 5067

The Sword of Truth - Gilbert Morris 4472

The Swords of December - Robert York 6933

Tansy Taniard - Myrtle Strode-Jackson 6084

A Tapestry of Murders - C.L. Grace 2510

The Ten-Day Queen - Lozania Prole 5199

The Third George - Jean Plaidy 5068

This Bright Sword - Donald Barr Chidsey 1066

The Thistle and the Rose - Jean Plaidy 5069

Thomas: A Novel of the Life, Passions, and Miracles of Becket - Shelley Mydans 4538

The Three Crowns - Jean Plaidy 5070

To Love a Queen - Lawrence Schoonover 5669

Too Near the Throne - Molly Costain Haycraft 2797

The Tower and the Dream - Jan Westcott 6647

The Tower of London - William Harrison Ainsworth 58

A Trail of Blood - Jeremy Potter 5143

The Traitors of Bosworth - Robert Farrington 2021

Trumpet at the Gate - Jan Widgery 6739

The Tudor Rose - Margaret Campbell Barnes 329

Uneasy Lies the Head - Jean Plaidy 5071

Unicorn Rampant - Nigel Tranter 6323

An Unknown Welshman - Jean Stubbs 6100

Victoria and Albert - Evelyn Anthony 166

Victoria in the Wings - Jean Plaidy 5072

Victoria Victorious - Jean Plaidy 5073

The Vow on the Heron - Jean Plaidy 5074

Vows of the Peacock - Alice Walworth Graham 2513

Walk with Peril - Dorothy V.S. Jackson 3132

Wallis: The Novel - Anne Edwards 1883
The Wandering Prince - Jean Plaidy 5075
The Warwick Heiress - Margaret Abbey 6
We Speak No Treason - Rosemary Hawley Jarman 3168
When Christ and His Saints Slept - Sharon Kay Penman 4908
The White Boar - Marian Palmer 4780
The White Queen - Lesley J. Nickell 4611
The White Rose - Jan Westcott 6648
The White Rose Murders - Michael Clynes 1137
The Whyte Harte - P.C. Doherty 1681
The Widow of Windsor - Jean Plaidy 5076
The Widow of Windsor - Tyler Whittle 6723
Wife to Great Buckingham - Hilda Lewis 3751
Wife to Henry V - Hilda Lewis 3752
Wife to the Bastard - Hilda Lewis 3753
William's Wife - Jean Plaidy 5077
The Wind From Hastings - Morgan Llywelyn 3825
Windsor Castle - William Harrison Ainsworth 59
The Winter Rose - Millie J. Ragosta 5243
The Wise Virgin - Hebe Elsna 1934
With All My Heart - Margaret Campbell Barnes 330
Within the Hollow Crown - Margaret Campbell Barnes 331
Witness to Treason - Millie J. Ragosta 5244
The Wolf at the Door - Graham Shelby 5793
Women of Ashdon - Valerie Anand 135
The Women of Whitechapel and Jack the Ripper - Paul West 6638
The Wrong Plantagenet - Marian Palmer 4781
The Young and Lonely King - Jane Lane 3659
Young Bess - Margaret Irwin 3123
The Young Elizabeth - Jennette Letton 3730
The Young Victoria - Tyler Whittle 6724

Royalty—France

All the Golden Gifts - Iola Fuller 2251
All the King's Ladies - Janice Law 3678
Angelique - Sergeanne Golon 2465
Angelique and the King - Sergeanne Golon 2468
Angelique in Revolt - Sergeanne Golon 2471
Asylum for the Queen - Mildred A. Jordan 3303
The Battle of the Queens - Jean Plaidy 5005
La Belle Sorel - Jacques Carton 949
Beloved Enemy: The Passions of Eleanor of Aquitaine - Ellen Jones 3288
The Burnished Blade - Lawrence Schoonover 5661
The Cardinal and the Queen - Evelyn Anthony 159
The Cat and the King - Louis Auchincloss 229
The Chancellor - Lawrence Schoonover 5662
Cinq-Mars - Alfred Victor de Vigny 6495
Cockades: A Romance - Meade Minnigerode 4412
Courtesan - Diane Haeger 2635
The Courts of Love - Jean Plaidy 5010
The Crown and the Shadow: The Story of Francoise d'Aubigne, Marquise de Maintenon - Pamela Hill 2930
A Day of Battle - Vincent Sheean 5787
Emperor's Ladies - Noel B. Gerson 2367
The Emperor's Lady: A Novel Based on the Life of the Empress Josephine - F.W. Kenyon 3449
Eugenie - Hester W. Chapman 989
Evergreen Gallant - Jean Plaidy 5013
The Faith and the Flame - June Dimmit Houston 3054
The Fatal Friendship: Marie Antoinette, Count Fersen and the Flight to Varennes - Stanley Loomis 3895
The Favourite - Francoise Mallet-Joris 4040
Fear No More - Hester W. Chapman 990
Flames of Empire - Peter Bourne 594
The French Bride - Evelyn Anthony 163
The Gamester - Rafael Sabatini 5550
The Gaudy Empire - Alfred Neumann 4584
The Gentle Fury: A Novel of Margaret of Austria - Paul Lewis 3758
The Ghost of Monsieur Scarron - Janet Lewis 3755

The Golden Porcupine - Muriel Ray Bolton 567
Golden Venus - David Mynders Smythe 5933
The Golden Yoke: A Novel of the War of the Roses - Olive Eckerson 1837
Henry, King of France - Heinrich Mann 4061
Here Lies Margot - Pamela Hill 2935
Hester - Brian Cleeve 1107
Holy Week - Louis Aragon 182
I Thee Wed - Gilbert Wolf Gabriel 2267
Imperial Courtesan - F.W. Kenyon 3452
In a Dark Wood Wandering - Hella S. Haasse 2631
The Iron King - Maurice Druon 1732
The Italian Woman - Jean Plaidy 5024
A King Reluctant - William Vaughan Wilkins 6759
The King's Cavalier - Samuel Shellabarger 5795
King's Masque - Evan John 3220
The King's Way - Francoise Chandernagor 986
A Lady at Bay - Edgar Maas 3950
The Lily and the Lion - Maurice Druon 1733
The Longest Night - Ada Cook Lewis 3744
Louis the Well-Beloved - Jean Plaidy 5032
Madame Serpent - Jean Plaidy 5033
Madeleine - Catherine Gavin 2323
The Man Who Killed the King - Dennis Wheatley 6654
Marie Antoinette - F.W. Kenyon 3453
The Marquis - Joan Sanders 5586
The Moneyman - Thomas B. Costain 1368
My Brother Napoleon: The Confessions of Caroline Bonaparte - F.W. Kenyon 3455
Napoleon Symphony - Anthony Burgess 780
The Oracle Glass - Judith Merkle Riley 5335
Palaces of Desire - Kate Alexander 81
The Passion of Letty Fox - Diana Saunders 5610
The Poisoned Crown - Maurice Druon 1734
Les Quarant Cinq - Alexandre Dumas 1779
Queen Jezebel - Jean Plaidy 5049
Queen Margot - Alexandre Dumas 1780
The Queen's Confession - Victoria Holt 3019
The Queen's Necklace - Alexandre Dumas 1781
Queen's Play - Dorothy Dunnett 1805
Quentin Durward - Sir Walter Scott 5705
The Rain Maiden - Jill M. Phillips 4985
The Rose and the Sword - Sandra Paretti 4792
A Rose for Virtue - Norah Lofts 3858
Royal Flush: The Story of Minette - Margaret Irwin 3121
Royal Merry-Go-Round - F.W. Kenyon 3459
The Royal Pawn - Antonia Ridge 5327
The Royal Succession - Maurice Druon 1735
The Secret Wife - Alice Acland 22
Seed of Mischief - Willa Gibbs 2401
The Shadow of the Sun - Sylvia Pell 4891
The She-Wolf of France - Maurice Druon 1736
The Shepherd's Crook - Paul Frischauer 2234
So Much as Beauty Does - Muriel Elwood 1938
Sorrow by Day - Marjorie Coryn 1359
The Spider King - Lawrence Schoonover 5668
The Strangled Queen - Maurice Druon 1737
Sweet Marie-Antoinette - Lozania Prole 5198
That Spanish Woman - F.W. Kenyon 3461
The Three Musketeers - Alexandre Dumas 1782
Through a Glass Darkly - Karleen Koen 3531
To Dance with Kings - Rosalind Laker 3601
Twenty Years After - Alexandre Dumas 1783
The Uncrowned King - Baroness Emma Orczy 4747
Ward of the Sun King - Mildred Allen Butler 826
Wife to Great Buckingham - Hilda Lewis 3751
Young Henry of Navarre - Heinrich Mann 4062

Royalty—Germany

A Castle in Bavaria - Prince Thibaut d'Orleans 1693
The Days of the King - Bruno Frank 2200
The Princess of Celle - Jean Plaidy 5045

Royalty—Hawaii

Ka'a'awa: A Novel about Hawaii in the 1850s - Oswald Andrew Bushnell 814
The White King - Samuel Bertram Harrison 2747

Royalty—India

The Dark Dancer - Frederic Prokosch 5193
Golden Fire - Jonathan Fast 2047

Royalty—Ireland

The Emerald Crown - Theodora McCormick Du Bois 1741
The Last Prince of Ireland - Morgan Llywelyn 3821
The Lion of Ireland - Morgan Llywelyn 3822
Pride of Lions - Morgan Llywelyn 3823
The Proud Man - Elizabeth Linington 3800
Red Branch - Morgan Llywelyn 3824

Royalty—Japan

The House of Kanze - Nobuko Albery 64
The Vermilion Bridge - Shelley Mydans 4539

Royalty—Portugal

The Braganza Pursuit - Sarah Neilan 4564

Royalty—Rome

Family Favorites - Alfred Duggan 1766

Royalty—Russia

And the Stars Shall Fall - True Bowen 603
The Angel: A Novel Based on the Life of Alexander I of Russia - William James Blech 543
By Command of the Viceroy - Duncan MacNeil 4010
City of Golden Cages - Jo Germany 2358
Devoted Friends - Joe Poyer 5161
Elizabeth and Alexandra - Antony Lambton 3616
The Emperor Story: A Historical Romance - George Sava 5615
Far Flies the Eagle - Evelyn Anthony 162
The Fourth King - Glen Petrie 4979
God Save the Tsar - Susanna Hoe 2976
Jesters - David Markish 4090
Katrina - Jeramie Price 5190
Peter the Great - Alexey Tolstoy 6293
Petersburg - Emily Hanlon 2677
The Power and the Passion - Christina Nicholson 4609
Prince of Outlaws - Alexey Tolstoy 6294
Rasputin's Revenge - John T. Lescroart 3725
Rebel Princess - Evelyn Anthony 164
The Ringed Castle - Dorothy Dunnett 1807
The Scandalous Mrs. Blackford - Harriet Kane 3358
Searching for the Emperor - Roberto Pazzi 4858
The Snow Mountain - Catherine Gavin 2324
Time After Time - Allen Appel 171
Tsar's Woman - Pamela Hill 2946
White Nights, Red Dawn - Frederick Nolan 4634
The Year of December - Lucy Cores 1329
Young Catherine - E.M. Almedingen 118

Royalty—Scotland

The Abbot - Sir Walter Scott 5688
Alexander the Glorious - Jane Oliver 4719
The Border Lord - Jan Westcott 6641
Braveheart - Randall Wallace 6538
Candleshine No More - Jane Oliver 4721
The Captive Queen of Scots - Jean Plaidy 5008
Chain of Destiny - Nigel Tranter 6314
Checkmate - Dorothy Dunnett 1799

Crippled Splendour - Evan John 3219
The Crown in Darkness - P.C. Doherty 1671
The Disorderly Knights - Dorothy Dunnett 1800
*Falcon: The Autobiography of His Grace James IV,
    King of Scots* - A.J. Stewart 6021
The Game of Kings - Dorothy Dunnett 1801
The Gay Galliard - Margaret Irwin 3119
The Green Salamander - Pamela Hill 2933
The Hepburn - Jan Westcott 6645
James and Joan - Anne Fremantle 2221
James, by the Grace of God - Nigel Tranter 6315
King Hereafter - Dorothy Dunnett 1802
*King in Hell: A Novel of Bothwell and Mary, Queen of
    Scots* - Beverly Balin 282
The King's Vixen - Pamela Hill 2937
Lady of Moray - Bonnie Copeland 1318
The Lion and the Rose - Jane Oliver 4724
The Lion Is Come - Jane Oliver 4725
*Maid of Honour: A Novel Set in the Court of Mary,
    Queen of Scots* - Elizabeth Byrd 836
Marjorie of Scotland - Pamela Hill 2939
Mary of Scotland - F.W. Kenyon 3454
Mary, Queen of Scotland and the Isles - Margaret
    George 2356
The Master of Gray Trilogy - Nigel Tranter 6316
Mine Is the Kingdom - Jane Oliver 4726
My Lady Glamis - Pamela Hill 2940
No Smoke Without Fire - Alice Harwood 2767
Parcel of Rogues - Jane Lane 3656
A Prince, a Piper, and a Rose - John Scalzo 5628
Queen's Caprice - Marjorie Bowen 599
Queen's Play - Dorothy Dunnett 1805
The Riven Realm - Nigel Tranter 6317
Royal Road to Fotheringay - Jean Plaidy 5059
*Seats of the Mighty: A Novel of James Stuart, Brother
    of Mary, Queen of Scots* - Alice Harwood 2768
Sing Morning Star - Jane Oliver 4727
A Stake in the Kingdom - Nigel Tranter 6321
Sunset at Noon - Jane Oliver 4728
The Sword and the Flame - Pamela Hill 2945
The Thistle and the Rose - Jean Plaidy 5069
A Time for the Death of a King - Ann Dukthas 1777
True Thomas - Nigel Tranter 6322
The White Queen - Frederic Fallon 2011
The Witches - Jay Williams 6776
The World, the Flesh, and the Devil - Reay
    Tannahill 6159

Royalty—Spain

The Adventures of Don Juan - Richard Gardner 2289
Captain From Castille - Samuel Shellabarger 5794
Columbus: A Romance - Rafael Sabatini 5549
Crown of Aloes - Norah Lofts 3840
The Dogs of Paradise - Abel Posse 5141
Ferdinand and Isabella - Hermann Kesten 3474
For One Sweet Grape - Kate O'Brien 4681
The Gentle Fury: A Novel of Margaret of Austria -
    Paul Lewis 3758
Here Lies Margot - Pamela Hill 2935
I, the King - Hermann Kesten 3475
I, the King - Frances Parkinson Keyes 3479
In the House of the King - Louis Zara 6951
The Last Crusader - Louis De Wohl 1569
The Last Portrait of the Duchess of Alba - Antonio
    Larreta 3666
Master of Castile - Samuel Edwards 1888
The Memoirs of Christopher Columbus - Stephen
    Marlowe 4096
Poison - Kathryn Harrison 2737
The Prisoner of Tordesillas - Lawrence
    Schoonover 5665
*The Queen's Cross: A Biographical Romance of
    Queen Isabella of Spain* - Lawrence
    Schoonover 5666
The Spanish Bridegroom - Jean Plaidy 5064

Royalty—Sweden

The Flight - Ruth Walgreen Stephan 5994
My Crown, My Love - Ruth Walgreen Stephan 5995
The Trees of the Folkungs - Verner Von
    Heidenstam 2817

Royalty—Wales

The Brothers of Gwynedd - Edith Pargeter 4796

Rum Rebellion

Storm of Time - Eleanor Dark 1494
The Traitors - William Stuart Long 3879

Rural Life—China

The Good Earth - Pearl S. Buck 754

Rural Life—Denmark

Kingdom Come - Virginia Sorensen 5950

Rural Life—England

Afternoon of a Autocrat - Norah Lofts 3834
Apple Tree Lean Down - Mary E. Pearce 4860
Ben Retallick - E.V. Thompson 6263
The Cage - Michael Weston 6650
The Darkness of Corn - Caroline Stickland 6037
Fiddler's Ferry - Iris Gower 2499
The Hired Man - Melvyn Bragg 639
The Land Endures - Mary E. Pearce 4862
The Lords of Loone - John James 3159
The Maltese Angel - Catherine Cookson 1283
Morgan's Woman - Iris Gower 2500
A Notorious Woman - Malcolm Macdonald 3969
Precious Bane - Mary Webb 6590
Seedtime and Harvest - Mary E. Pearce 4864
Silas Marner - George Eliot 1911
Spinners' Wharf - Iris Gower 2502
The Stallion Man - Judith Glover 2438
The Standing Hills - Caroline Stickland 6038
To the End of Her Days - Malcolm Macdonald 3975
The Two Farms - Mary E. Pearce 4865

Rural Life—Ireland

The Dispossessed - Dell Shannon 5773
The Famished Land - Elizabeth Byrd 833
The Hedge of Thorns - Helen Ashton 217
Through the Green Valley - Barbara Gowdy 2498

Rural Life—Italy

Nothing New under the Sun - Riccardo Bacchelli 255
Simple Prayers - Michael Golding 2452

Rural Life—Norway

Arne - Bjornstjerne Bjornson 518
The People of Juvik - Olav Dunn 1798

Rural Life—Scotland

The Alien Light - Iain Crichton Smith 1427
Butcher's Broom - Neil Gunn 2620
Treasures on Earth - Jessica Stirling 6049

Rural Life—Spain

La Guerra: A Spanish Saga - Stephen D.
    Frances 2199
The Three-Cornered Hat - Pedro Antonio de
    Alarcon 62

Rural Life—Sweden

The Emigrants - Vilhelm Moberg 4422
The Rainbird - Sara Lidman 3780
The Red Marten - Peter William Nisser 4630
The Story of Gosta Berling - Selma Lagerlof 3586

Rural Life—U.S.

The Architecture of the Arkansas Ozarks - Donald
    Harington 2708
Blue Camellia - Frances Parkinson Keyes 3477
Brothers Three - John Oskison 4764
Caddie Woodlawn - Carol Brink 692
Call of the Mountains - Cornelia Meigs 4326
Called Away - Perdita Buchan 753
The Choiring of the Trees - Donald Harington 2709
Cold Sassy Tree - Olive Ann Burns 797
Come Winter - Douglas C. Jones 3275
Courting Emma Howe - Margaret A. Robinson 5410
Crum Elbow Folks - Percy Raymond Barnes 332
Dan'l Boone Kissed Me - Felix Holt 3006
Faye's Folly - Elizabeth Corbett 1322
The Hard to Catch Mercy - William Baldwin 281
Hue and Cry - Elizabeth Yates 6907
Judith Duchesne - Lynda Sargent 5605
Kings Row - Henry Bellamann 428
The Labyrinth - Thomas William Duncan 1787
Leaving Cold Sassy - Olive Ann Burns 798
Omensetter's Luck - William H. Gass 2317
Private Knowledge - Betty Palmer Nelson 4576
Pursuit of Bliss - Betty Palmer Nelson 4577
The Richlands - Agnes Sligh Turnbull 6364
The Salt and the Savor - Howard William
    Troyer 6354
Shadow of the Mountains - Lynn Morris 4481
So Red the Rose - Stark Young 6944
Tamarack Tree - Howard Breslin 670
The Truest Pleasure - Robert Morgan 4452
The Velvet Horn - Andrew Lytle 3946
Weedy Rough - Douglas C. Jones 3286
Winds of Blame - Jane Gilmore Rushing 5532
The Wolfling: A Documentary Novel of the 1870s -
    Sterling North 4648
The Women at Pine Creek - Allis McKay 4279
Words by Heart - Ouida Sebestyen 5713

Russian Empire

And the Stars Shall Fall - True Bowen 603
*The Angel: A Novel Based on the Life of Alexander I
    of Russia* - William James Blech 543
Anna - Cynthia Harrod-Eagles 2752
The Astrov Legacy - Constance Heaven 2802
August 1914 - Alexander Solzhenitsyn 5942
Blood and Sable - Carol J. Kane 3350
The Candlesticks and the Cross - Ruth Freeman
    Solomon 5940
The Captain's Daughter - Alexander Pushkin 5210
City of Golden Cages - Jo Germany 2358
Count Vronsky's Daughter - Carola Salisbury 5567
The Cowboy and the Cossack - Claire Huffaker 3071
The Crown and the Crucible - Michael Phillips 4987
The Czar's Madman - Jaan Kross 3560
Darker Jewels - Chelsea Quinn Yarbro 6898
The Dawning of Deliverance - Judith Pella 4892
Devil Child - Jo Germany 2359
The Devil Inside: A Novel of Dostoevsky's Life -
    Stephen Coulter 1385
Devoted Friends - Joe Poyer 5161
Elizabeth and Alexandra - Antony Lambton 3616
Emily - Cynthia Harrod-Eagles 2753
The Emperor Story: A Historical Romance - George
    Sava 5615
*The Extraordinary Adventures of Secret Agent Shipov
    in Pursuit of Count Leo Tolstoy in the Year 1862* -
    Bulat Okudzhava 4712
Far Flies the Eagle - Evelyn Anthony 162
The Fixer - Bernard Malamud 4038

Fleur - Cynthia Harrod-Eagles 2754
The Fortune Hunter - Ira J. Morris 4477
The Fourth King - Glen Petrie 4979
Great Black Russian - John Oliver Killens 3484
Heir to Kuragin - Constance Heaven 2807
Heirs of the Motherland - Judith Pella 4893
A House Divided - Michael Phillips 4988
The House of Kuragin - Constance Heaven 2808
Imperial Winds - Priscilla Napier 4555
The Incorruptible - Helma De Bois 1551
Jesters - David Markish 4090
Katrina - Jeramie Price 5190
Katya - Lucy Cores 1328
The Ladies of St. Hedwig's - E.M. Almedingen 117
Lady in the Briars - Carola Dunn 1793
The Last Station - Jay Parini 4801
Lenin in Zurich - Alexander Solzhenitsyn 5943
Love and Honor - Leslie Arlen 189
The Muscovite - Alison Macleod 4004
The Name of Hero - Richard Seltzer 5742
Napoleon and the Cossacks - Peter N. Krassnoff 3551
Peter the Great - Alexey Tolstoy 6293
The Petersburg-Cannes Express - Hans Koning 3538
Prince of Outlaws - Alexey Tolstoy 6294
Rasputin's Revenge - John T. Lescroart 3725
Rebel Princess - Evelyn Anthony 164
The Revolutionist: A Novel of Russia - Robert Littell 3810
Russka: The Novel of Russia - Edward Rutherfurd 5535
The Scandalous Mrs. Blackford - Harriet Kane 3358
Sir Rogue - Leslie Turner White 6691
A Space of the Heart - Patricia Wright 6884
The Summer Day Is Done - R.T. Stevens 6001
Taras Bulba - Nikolai V. Gogol 2451
Travail and Triumph - Michael Phillips 4991
Tsar's Woman - Pamela Hill 2946
Valentina - Evelyn Anthony 165
White Eagle, Dark Skies - Jean Karsavina 3368
Young Catherine - E.M. Almedingen 118
Zoya - Danielle Steel 5985

Russian Revolution

And the Stars Shall Fall - True Bowen 603
Asya - Michael Ignatieff 3103
Between Two Worlds - Monique Raphel High 2913
Blaize - Anne Melville 4331
Blood and Sable - Carol J. Kane 3350
Blood on the Snow - John Elliott 1916
The Buckingham Palace Connection - Ted Willis 6792
The Challenging Heights - Max Hennessy 2831
A Clear Road to Archangel - Geoffrey Rose 5461
Contessa - Helene Mansfield 4076
Devoted Friends - Joe Poyer 5161
Doctor Zhivago - Boris Pasternak 4824
Elena - Judith Egan 1893
The Eleventh Year - Monique Raphel High 2914
Elizabeth and Alexandra - Antony Lambton 3616
Emily - Cynthia Harrod-Eagles 2753
Fifteen Flags - Richard Lynden Hardman 2686
Fire in the Ice - Alan Scholefield 5653
The Four Winds of Heaven - Monique Raphel High 2916
The Gathering Wolves - Elizabeth Darrell 1496
Give Me the Daggers - Catherine Gavin 2321
God Save the Tsar - Susanna Hoe 2976
The Golden Sabre - Jon Cleary 1105
Grishin - Hans Herlin 2859
Horses of War - Duff Hart-Davis 2760
Imperial Winds - Priscilla Napier 4555
It's Me Again - Donald Jack 3126
Joseph - Mervyn Jones 3292
Journey into Fire - Patricia Wright 6882
The King's Commissar - Duncan Kyle 3570
Lenin in Zurich - Alexander Solzhenitsyn 5943

Lenin: The Novel - Alan Brien 679
Love and Honor - Leslie Arlen 189
Malkeh and Her Children - Marjorie Edelson 1853
Me Too - Donald Jack 3128
Over There - Robert Vaughan 6449
Petersburg - Emily Hanlon 2677
The Petrograd Consignment - Owen Sela 5739
Remember This Time - Gloria Kurian Broder 703
The Revolutionist: A Novel of Russia - Robert Littell 3810
Searching for the Emperor - Roberto Pazzi 4858
Seven Days to Petrograd - Tom Hyman 3094
The Snow Mountain - Catherine Gavin 2324
The Summer Day Is Done - R.T. Stevens 6001
The Summer of the Bashinskeys - Diane Pearson 4877
Sweet Ransom - Linda Madl 4026
Time After Time - Allen Appel 171
Triptych - Dora Landey 3652
White Nights, Red Dawn - Frederick Nolan 4634
Zoya - Danielle Steel 5985

Russo-Japanese War

Blood on the Snow - John Elliott 1916
The Dawning of Deliverance - Judith Pella 4892

St. Bartholomew's Day Massacre

The Italian Woman - Jean Plaidy 5024
The Longest Night - Ada Cook Lewis 3744
Queen Jezebel - Jean Plaidy 5049
Queen Margot - Alexandre Dumas 1780

Salamis, Battle of

Farewell Great King: A Novel of Ancient Greece - Jill Paton Walsh 4829

Samurai

The Ronin - William Dale Jennings 3212
Shogun - James Clavell 1101
The Sword of Hachiman - Lynn Guest 2608
The Tokaido Road: A Novel of Feudal Japan - Lucia St. Clair Robson 5417

San Jacinto, Battle of

The Eagle and the Raven - James A. Michener 4369
Empire of Bones: A Novel of Sam Houston and the Texas Revolution - Jeff Long 3868
The Sam Houston Story - Dean Owen 4770
Thunder Before Seven - Anna Brand 648

San Juan Hill, Battle of

Ever After - Elswyth Thane 6216
Remember Santiago - Douglas C. Jones 3280
The Rough Rider - Gilbert Morris 4468
San Juan Hill - Will Henry 2848

Sand Creek Massacre

The Great Betrayal - Dorothy Gardiner 2284
A Very Small Remnant - Michael Whitney Straight 6075

Saratoga, Battle of

Guns of Burgoyne - Bruce Lancaster 3640
Rabble in Arms - Kenneth Roberts 5390
The Rifleman - John Brick 675
The Twisted Saber: A Biographical Novel of Benedict Arnold - Philip Vail 6398

Science

The Affairs of Nicholas Culpepper - Mabel L. Tyrrel 6375
Beginning the World Again - Roberta Silman 5851
Doctor Copernicus - John Banville 296
Dr. Guillotine: The Eccentric Exploits of an Early Scientist - Herbert Lom 3867
Doctor Mirabilis - James Blish 550
Glowstone - Macdonald Harris 2725
Hubble Time - Tom Bezzi 490
Kepler: A Novel - John Banville 297
Loving Little Egypt - Thomas McMahon 4288
McKay's Bees - Thomas McMahon 4289
The Origin - Irving Stone 6060
Physician Extraordinary: A Novel of the Life and Times of William Harvey - David Weiss 6608
Queen Victoria's Bomb - Ronald Clark 1094
Stallion Gate - Martin Cruz Smith 5924
The Star-Gazer - Zsolt de Harsanyi 2757

Sea Story

1805 - Richard Woodman 6857
Abigail - Joan Druett 1721
Adams of the Bounty - Erle Wilson 6807
Admiral of Fear - Victor Suthren 6126
The Adventures of Jeremiah Dimon: The Novel of Old East Hampton - Everett Rattray 5255
The Adventures of Long John Silver - Denis Judd 3317
American Captain - Edison Marshall 4101
Annapolis - William Martin 4137
Anne Bonny - Chloe Gartner 2306
Annie's Captain - Kathryn Hulme 3077
Apprentice to the Sea - Philip McCutchan 4240
Arctic Treachery - Richard Woodman 6858
Armada - Charles Gidley 2404
Armored Giants: A Novel of the Civil War - F. van Wyck Mason 4145
As Runs the Glass - Evan John David 1502
Attack the Lusitania! - Raymond Hitchcock 2956
Back to Battle - Max Hennessy 2828
Baltic Mission - Richard Woodman 6859
Beat to Quarters - C.S. Forester 2170
Beauvallet - Georgette Heyer 2876
Before the Wind - Lloyd M. Moxon 4506
Benjamin Blake - Edison Marshall 4102
Beware, Beware the Bight of Benin - Philip McCutchan 4241
Billy Budd - Herman Melville 4333
The Black Cockade - Victor Suthren 6127
The Black Duchess - Alanna Knight 3514
Blind Journey - Bruce Lancaster 3636
Blue Hurricane - F. van Wyck Mason 4146
The Bomb Vessel - Richard Woodman 6860
Boon Island - Kenneth Roberts 5384
Botany Bay - Charles Nordhoff 4637
Brave Captains - Vivian Stuart 6086
Bride of a Thousand Cedars - Bruce Lancaster 3637
Broadsides - Robert Welter Daly 1459
Buccaneer - Dudley Pope 5093
Buller's Dreadnought - Richard Hough 3047
Buller's Guns - Richard Hough 3048
Burning Gold - Robert Hardy Andrews 148
By Force of Arms - James L. Nelson 4579
By Valour and Arms - James H. Street 6076
Caleb Pettengill U.S.N. - George Fielding Eliot 1912
Captain Adam - Donald Barr Chidsey 1058
Captain Barney - Jan Westcott 6642
Captain Blood - Rafael Sabatini 5546
Captain Bolton's Corpse - J.G. Jeffreys 3178
Captain Caution - Kenneth Roberts 5385
Captain for Elizabeth - Jan Westcott 6643
The Captain From Connecticut - C.S. Forester 2171
Captain Ironhand - Rosamond Marshall 4116
Captain Marooner - Louis B. Davidson 1504
Captain Monsoon - Victor Suthren 6128
Captain of the Sands - Keith Dewhurst 1636

Captain Paul - Edward Ellsberg 1930
Captain Rebel - Frank Yerby 6910
Castaway - Frances Murray 4535
The Catherine - Robert S. MacDonald 3980
Charco Harbour - Godfrey Blunden 554
Clear for Action! - Noel B. Gerson 2362
Clear for Action! - Simon White 6699
Clear for Action: A Novel about John Paul Jones -
  Clements Ripley 5344
Close Quarters - William Golding 2453
The Closest Possible Union - Joanna Scott 5680
Colors Aloft! - Alexander Kent 3427
Columbus: A Romance - Rafael Sabatini 5549
Command a King's Ship - Alexander Kent 3428
The Commodore - Patrick O'Brian 4661
Commodore Hornblower - C.S. Forester 2172
The Crystal Star - Ellen Argo 184
Cup of Gold - John Steinbeck 5991
Cutlass Empire - F. van Wyck Mason 4148
The Dangerous Years - Max Hennessy 2833
Darken Ship - Nicholas Monsarrat 4431
Dead Reckoning - C. Northcote Parkinson 4809
The Deadly Lady of Madagascar - C.V. Terry 6206
Decision at Trafalgar - Richard Woodman 6861
Departure - Janet Stevenson 6004
Desolation Island - Patrick O'Brian 4662
Devil to Pay - C. Northcote Parkinson 4810
Diamond Head - Houston Branch 647
The Dogs of Paradise - Abel Posse 5141
Don't Tread on Me - Walter Karig 3366
Dragon Cove - Carter A. Vaughan 6434
The Dram Tree - Hamilton Cochran 1140
Drumbeat - Dudley Pope 5094
Drums - James Boyd 611
Eagle in the Sky - F. van Wyck Mason 4149
The East Indiaman - Ellis K. Meacham 4313
East to Bagaduce - Willard Wallace 6539
Echoes From the Past - Marjorie McEvoy 4268
The Edge of Piracy - Donald Barr Chidsey 1060
Enemy in Sight! - Alexander Kent 3429
The English Captain - Simon White 6700
Eye of the Hurricane - Fergus Reid Buckley 757
A Fair Wind Home - Ruth Moore 4443
Fair Wind to Java - Garland Roark 5354
The Far Side of the World - Patrick O'Brian 4663
Fire Down Below - William Golding 2454
The Fireship - C. Northcote Parkinson 4811
First Lieutenant - Kenneth Maynard 4208
Five Black Ships: A Novel of Discoverers - Napoleon
  Baccino Ponce de Leon 5089
The Flag Captain - Alexander Kent 3430
Fleet Surgeon to Pharaoh - Sheldon Jacobson 3140
The Flight of the Kestrel - Margaret Abbey 3
Flying Colours - C.S. Forester 2173
For King and Company - Ellis K. Meacham 4314
For Love of a Pirate - Anthony Esler 1961
For My Great Folly - Thomas B. Costain 1365
The Forest Lord - Noel B. Gerson 2368
Form Line of Battle! - Alexander Kent 3431
The Fortress - Catherine Gavin 2320
The Fortune of War - Patrick O'Brian 4664
Fourth King - Norbert Coulehan 1373
Fragments of the Ark - Louise Meriwether 4341
The French Admiral - Dewey Lambdin 3609
Frenchman's Creek - Daphne Du Maurier 1744
Friendly Cove - Irving Brant 651
The Frigate Captain - Showell Styles 6103
Gallant Captain - Pearl Frye 2242
Galleon - Dudley Pope 5095
A Game for Empires - Pearl Frye 2243
Golden Admiral - F. van Wyck Mason 4150
The Golden Coast - Philip Rooney 5441
The Golden Galleon - Victor Suthren 6129
The Golden Hawk - Frank Yerby 6921
The Golden Ocean - Patrick O'Brian 4665
The Golden Wind - C.L. Grace 2507
Governor Ramage, R.N. - Dudley Pope 5096
The Greenlander - Mark Adlard 38
The Guernseyman - C. Northcote Parkinson 4812

The Gun Ketch - Dewey Lambdin 3610
The Guns of Arrest - Philip McCutchan 4242
Halfhyde and the Admiral - Philip McCutchan 4243
Halfhyde and the Chain Gang - Philip
  McCutchan 4244
Halfhyde and the Flag Captain - Philip
  McCutchan 4245
Halfhyde and the Fleet Review - Philip
  McCutchan 4246
Halfhyde for the Queen - Philip McCutchan 4247
Halfhyde Goes to War - Philip McCutchan 4248
The Halfhyde Line - Philip McCutchan 4249
Halfhyde on the Amazon - Philip McCutchan 4250
Halfhyde on Zanatu - Philip McCutchan 4251
Halfhyde Ordered South - Philip McCutchan 4252
Halfhyde to the Narrows - Philip McCutchan 4253
Halfhyde's Island - Philip McCutchan 4254
The Happy Parrot - Robert W. Chambers 977
Harpoon in Eden - F. van Wyck Mason 4152
Hate - Arthur Douglas Smith 5918
Hazard of Huntress - Vivian Stuart 6087
Hazard's Command - Vivian Stuart 6088
He Brings Great News - Clemence Dane 1462
Henry Lunt and the Ranger - Tom McNamara 4304
Her Majesty's Captain - Derek Wilson 6797
A High Wind in Jamaica - Richard Hughes 3074
H.M.S. Bounty - Alexander McKee 4280
H.M.S. Cockerel - Dewey Lambdin 3611
H.M.S. Surprise - Patrick O'Brian 4666
Honor This Day - Alexander Kent 3432
Hornblower and the Atropos - C.S. Forester 2175
Hornblower and the Hotspur - C.S. Forester 2176
Hornblower During the Crisis - C.S. Forester 2177
In Distant Waters - Richard Woodman 6862
In Gallant Company - Alexander Kent 3433
In Perilous Seas - Victor Suthren 6130
The Inshore Squadron - Alexander Kent 3434
The Ionian Mission - Patrick O'Brian 4667
Iron Ships, Iron Men - Christopher Nicole 4616
The Island of the Day Before - Umberto Eco 1849
Islands of Unwisdom - Robert Graves 2548
Jemmy Button - Benjamin Subercaseaux 6107
Jewel of the Sea - Ellen Argo 185
The Jonah Man - Henry Carlisle 895
Jonathan Dearborn: A Novel of the War of 1812 -
  Willard Wallace 6540
Kingdom of Gold - Susan Wiggs 6744
The King's Coat - Dewey Lambdin 3612
A King's Commander - Dewey Lambdin 3613
The King's Commission - Dewey Lambdin 3614
The King's Privateer - Dewey Lambdin 3615
A King's Ransom - Victor Suthren 6131
The Lady and the Deep Blue Sea - Garland
  Roark 5356
Lamb in Command - Kenneth Maynard 4209
The Land Beyond the Tempest - Drayton
  Mayrant 4213
The Last Farewell - Philip McCutchan 4255
*The Last Mutiny: The Further Adventures of Captain
  Bligh* - Bill Collett 1208
The Last of the Vikings - Johan Bojer 563
The Last Voyage: Captain Cook's Lost Diary -
  Hammond Innes 3108
El Lazo - L. Jay Martin 4132
The Legion of the Lost - Donald Barr Chidsey 1062
Letter of Marque - Andrew Hepburn 2849
The Letter of Marque - Patrick O'Brian 4668
Lieutenant Hornblower - C.S. Forester 2178
Lieutenant Lamb - Kenneth Maynard 4210
The Life and Times of Horatio Hornblower - C.
  Northcote Parkinson 4813
The Lively Lady - Kenneth Roberts 5386
Log Cabin Noble - F. van Wyck Mason 4153
The Long Fight - D.A. Rayner 5270
Long Pennant - Oliver La Farge 3573
Long Pig - Russell Foreman 2168
Lord Hornblower - C.S. Forester 2179
Lord of Darkness - Robert Silverberg 5854
Loving Emma - Nigel Foxell 2197

Lusitania - David Butler 819
The Maddest Idea - James L. Nelson 4580
The Magnificent Savages - Fred Mustard
  Stewart 6024
Magnus the Magnificent - Leslie Turner White 6688
The Maid of Sker - R.D. Blackmore 529
Manila Galleon - F. van Wyck Mason 4154
Manitou - Donald Clayton Porter 5120
Master and Commander - Patrick O'Brian 4669
Masts to Spear the Stars - Stephen Longstreet 3889
Matthew Early - Alexander Laing 3589
The Mauritius Command - Patrick O'Brian 4670
Men Against the Sea - Charles Nordhoff 4638
Mercedes of Castile - James Fenimore Cooper 1304
Mister Christian - William Kinsolving 3502
Mr. Christian! - Stanley Miller 4402
Mr. Midshipman Hornblower - C.S. Forester 2180
Mutiny - Frank Tilsley 6280
Mutiny on the Bounty - Charles Nordhoff 4639
Mutiny Run - Frank Eccles 1836
My Love, My Enemy - Jan Cox Speas 5958
Nantucket Rebel - Edouard A. Stackpole 5970
The Nelson Touch - Paul Lewis 3759
The New Hope - Joseph C. Lincoln 3784
*North to Thule: An Imagined Narrative of the Famous
  ''Lost'' Voyage of Pytheas of Massalla in the
  Fourth Century B.C.* - John Frye 2241
The Nutmeg of Consolation - Patrick O'Brian 4671
The Ocean Mistress - Peter French 2225
Old Glory - Christopher Nicole 4618
On Stranger Tides - Tim Powers 5156
On the Company's Service - Ellis K. Meacham 4315
On the Midnight Tide - Don Tracy 6310
Our Valiant Few - F. van Wyck Mason 4155
Outward Bound - Philip McCutchan 4256
Paradise - Dikkon Eberhart 1831
Passage to Mutiny - Alexander Kent 3436
The Pepper Tree - John Edward Jennings 3203
Pilgrims: A Novel of the Mayflower - Gerard
  Mac 3955
The Pilot - James Fenimore Cooper 1306
Pitcairn's Island - Charles Nordhoff 4640
Post Captain - Patrick O'Brian 4672
Praise at Morning - Mildred Masterson
  McNeilly 4310
Pride's Fancy - Thomas H. Raddall 5231
A Private Revenge - Richard Woodman 6863
The Privateer - Gordon Daviot 1510
The Prize Master - Harvey Haislip 2642
Proud New Flags - F. van Wyck Mason 4156
*The Purple Quest: A Novel of Seafaring Adventure in
  the Ancient World* - Frank G. Slaughter 5896
The Pyrates - George MacDonald Fraser 2212
The Raiders: A Novel of the Civil War at Sea -
  Willard Wallace 6541
Rainbow in the Royals - Garland Roark 5357
Ramage - Dudley Pope 5097
Ramage and the Dido - Dudley Pope 5098
Ramage and the Guillotine - Dudley Pope 5099
Ramage and the Rebels - Dudley Pope 5100
Ramage and the Saracens - Dudley Pope 5101
Ramage at Trafalgar - Dudley Pope 5102
The Ramage Touch - Dudley Pope 5103
Ramage's Devil - Dudley Pope 5104
Ramage's Diamond - Dudley Pope 5105
Ramage's Mutiny - Dudley Pope 5106
Ramage's Prize - Dudley Pope 5107
Ramage's Signal - Dudley Pope 5108
Ramage's Trial - Dudley Pope 5109
The Red Rover - James Fenimore Cooper 1309
Reluctant Cavalier - Donald Barr Chidsey 1064
Restless Voyage - Stanley David Porteus 5138
*The Return of Lono: A Novel of Captain Cook's Last
  Voyage* - Oswald Andrew Bushnell 816
The Reverse of the Medal - Patrick O'Brian 4673
The Revolutionary - Lawrence Schoonover 5667
Richard Bolitho—Midshipman - Alexander
  Kent 3437
Richard Carvel - Winston Churchill 1081

Rites of Passage - William Golding 2456
Rivers of Glory - F. van Wyck Mason 4158
Roanoke Hundred - Inglis Fletcher 2138
Rogue's Holiday - Hamilton Cochran 1141
Royal Yankee - Victor Suthren 6132
Ruan - Bryher 746
The Running of the Tide - Esther Forbes 2160
Running Proud - Nicholas Monsarrat 4432
The Sable Lion - Jan Van Dorp 6405
Sacred Hunter - Barry Unsworth 6389
Sail the Dark Tide - Davenport Steward 6017
Sailor Named Jones - Harvey Haislip 2643
A Sailor of Austria - John Biggins 492
The Saintly Buccaneer - Gilbert Morris 4469
The Salem Frigate - John Edward Jennings 3205
The Sea and the Sand - Christopher Nicole 4621
The Sea Eagles - John Edward Jennings 3206
Sea Jade - Phyllis A. Whitney 6717
Sea of Darkness - Roland Huntford 3086
The Sea Officer - Showell Styles 6105
*The Sea Panther: A Novel about the Commander of
   the U.S.S. Constitution* - Philip Vail 6397
Sea Road to Yorktown - Harvey Haislip 2644
The Sea Stands Watch - Helen Parker Mudgett 4507
The Sea 'Venture - F. van Wyck Mason 4159
The Seafarers - William Stuart Long 3877
The Second Mate - Philip McCutchan 4257
Seek Out and Destroy - James David Horan 3031
Ship of the Line - C.S. Forester 2182
Shout at the Devil - Wilbur Smith 5930
Signal—Close Action! - Alexander Kent 3438
Signals of Distress - Jim Crace 1408
Silver Shoals - Hamilton Cochran 1142
The Sinking of the Sarah Diamond - William Dale
   Jennings 3213
The Slave Ship - Mary Johnston 3240
The Sleeping Sword: A Biographical Novel - Pearl
   Frye 2244
Sloop of War - Alexander Kent 3439
So Near So Far - C. Northcote Parkinson 4814
Soldier of the Sea - Robert Welter Daly 1460
Soldiers of Fortune - Peter Bourne 595
The Southern Cross - Peter French 2226
Speranza - Sven Delblanc 1584
Spirit Knife - Donald Clayton Porter 5128
Stand into Danger - Alexander Kent 3440
Star in the Rigging: A Novel of the Texas Navy -
   Garland Roark 5358
Stars on the Sea - F. van Wyck Mason 4161
Storm Signals - Joseph C. Lincoln 3785
Storm Tide - Allan R. Bosworth 590
Stronghold - Donald Barr Chidsey 1065
Success to the Brave - Alexander Kent 3441
The Summer of Jack London - Andrew J.
   Fenady 2058
The Surgeon's Mate - Patrick O'Brian 4674
Surprise - Brian Burland 785
Tall Ships to Cathay - Helen Augur 240
Tarnished Angel - Phyllis Leonard 3723
The Thirteen Gun Salute - Patrick O'Brian 4675
Thread of Scarlet - Ben Ames Williams 6767
Three Harbors - F. van Wyck Mason 4162
Thunder on the Chesapeake - David Divine 1650
Tide-Rode - Adelyn Bushnell 813
To Glory We Steer - Alexander Kent 3442
To the Honor of the Fleet - Robert H. Pilpel 5002
Touch and Go - C. Northcote Parkinson 4815
A Tradition of Victory - Alexander Kent 3443
Treason's Harbour - Patrick O'Brian 4676
Treasure Island - Robert Louis Stevenson 6012
Tricolour - Mark Logan 3866
The Triton Brig - Dudley Pope 5110
The Truelove - Patrick O'Brian 4677
The Unknown Shore - Patrick O'Brian 4678
''Utmost Fish!'' - Hugh Wray McCann 4219
The Valiant Sailors - Vivian Stuart 6090
The Velvet Doublet - James H. Street 6082
Victory at Sebastopol - Vivian Stuart 6091
Voyage: A Novel of 1896 - Sterling Hayden 2798

The Voyage of the Destiny - Robert Nye 4657
Voyage to the First of December - Henry
   Carlisle 897
The War Chest - Porter Hill 2950
War Clouds - Donald Clayton Porter 5131
The Water Witch - James Fenimore Cooper 1311
West with the Vikings - Edison Marshall 4114
Westward Ho! - Charles Kingsley 3499
Wind From the Main - Anne Osborne 4759
The Wind in His Fists - John Edward Jennings 3210
Wind of Destiny - Christopher Nicole 4624
Windward Passage - Hamilton Cochran 1143
The Wine-Dark Sea - Patrick O'Brian 4679
The Witch of Manga Reva - Garland Roark 5359
Wolfshead - Jere Hungerford Wheelwright 6672
Wyvern - A.A. Attanasio 227
The Yankee Brig - Carter A. Vaughan 6443
The Yankee Girl - Ellen Argo 186
Yankee Woman - Frederic Baume 381
The Yellow Admiral - Patrick O'Brian 4680

Sebastopol, Battle of

Victory at Sebastopol - Vivian Stuart 6091

Second Bull Run/Manassas, Battle of

Unto This Hour - Tom Wicker 6733

Sekigahara, Battle of

Musashi: An Epic Novel of the Samurai Era - Eiji
   Yoshikawa 6935

Seminole Wars

Bright Feather - Robert Wilder 6750
The Land Where the Sun Dies - Henry Carlisle 896
River in the Wind - Edith Pope 5111
Say These Names (Remember Them) - Betty Sue
   Cummings 1448

Servants

The Adventuress - Marion Chesney 1014
Amanda/Miranda - Richard Peck 4882
Annie - Gloria Jahoda 3141
Autumn Lace - Eileen Jackson 3133
The Crown and the Crucible - Michael Phillips 4987
The Duchess of Duke Street - Mollie Hardwick 2693
A Finger to Her Lips - Evelyn Berckman 472
Footman in Powder - Helen Ashton 216
The Heart of the Rose - June Barraclough 346
A House Divided - Michael Phillips 4988
Lady Jane - Norma Lee Clark 1092
Lady's Maid - Margaret Forster 2188
Lilith - Jean Plaidy 5030
A London Season - Anthea Bell 420
The Lormes of Castle Rising - Fanny Cradock 1409
Mary Reilly - Valerie Martin 4136
The Michaelmas Tree - Helen Ashfield 209
The Miser of Mayfair - Marion Chesney 1038
The Passing Bells - Phillip Rock 5421
Plain Jane - Marion Chesney 1045
Rainbird's Revenge - Marion Chesney 1046
Rake's Progress - Marion Chesney 1047
Sarsen Place - Gwendoline Butler 821
The Still Storm - Francoise Sagan 5562
Travail and Triumph - Michael Phillips 4991
Upstairs Downstairs - John Hawkesworth 2782
Version and Diversion - Judith Terry 6207
The Wicked Godmother - Marion Chesney 1053
A Woman of Quality - Jan Westcott 6649

Servile War

Arena: A Novel of Spartacus and Crassus - Maurice
   Ghnassia 2391
Arms of Nemesis - Steven Saylor 5623
Fortune's Favorite - Colleen McCullough 4235
The Gladiators - Arthur Koestler 3532
The Pirate From Rome - John V.D.
   Southworth 5952
Spartacus - Howard Fast 2044

Settlement of the American Frontier

Abe Lincoln of Pigeon Creek - William Edward
   Wilson 6818
Across the Shining Mountains - Christian
   McCord 4226
All Ye People - Merle Estes Colby 1167
Anthony Trant - John Hyatt Downing 1713
Arfive - A.B. Guthrie Jr. 2623
Atala - Francois Rene de Chateaubriand 1008
The Beckoning Road - Caroline Snedeker 5934
Becky Landers, Frontier Warrior - Constance
   Skinner 5879
Bedford Village - Hervey Allen 99
The Believers - Janice Holt Giles 2409
Bend Your Heads All - Rowena Rutherford
   Farrar 2015
Between Earth and Sky - Karen Osborn 4758
Beulah Land - Harold Lenoir Davis 1520
Beyond the Shining Mountains - Doris
   Shannon 5775
The Big Sky - A.B. Guthrie Jr. 2624
Black Forest - Meade Minnigerode 4411
Black Jack Davy - John Oskison 4763
*Boone: A Novel Based on the Life and Times of Daniel
   Boone* - Cameron Judd 3311
The Border Captains - Jason Manning 4072
Born Strangers - Helen Topping Miller 4384
The Bounty Lands - William Donohue Ellis 1927
Boy with a Pack - Stephen Warren Meader 4319
Bridal Journey - Dale Van Every 6406
Bright Journey - August Derleth 1614
The Bright Land - Janet Fairbank 2000
The Brightwood Expedition - Kay L.
   McDonald 4261
The Brooks Legend - William Donohue Ellis 1928
Buttes Landing - Jean Rikhoff 5331
The Cabin at the Trail's End - Sheba
   Hargreaves 2706
The Canebrake Men - Cameron Judd 3313
The Captive Witch - Dale Van Every 6407
The Captives - Don Wright 6878
Cedarhaven - Patricia Campbell 874
Centennial - James A. Michener 4366
Chant of the Hawk - John Harris 2720
Children of God - Vardis Fisher 2106
A Circle of Trees - Dana Faralla 2012
Come Spring - Charlotte Hinger 2954
The Conquerors - Allen W. Eckert 1839
Country People - Ruth Suckow 6111
*Crockett of Tennessee: A Novel Based on the Life and
   Times of David Crockett* - Cameron Judd 3314
The Crossing - Winston Churchill 1080
The Cumberland Rifles - Noel B. Gerson 2365
La Dame De Sainte Hermine - Grace King 3485
Dance on the Wind - Terry C. Johnston 3249
Dancing at the Rascal Fair - Ivan Doig 1682
Dark Hills to Westward - Harry M. Caudill 964
Darker Grows the Valley - Harry Harrison
   Kroll 3556
Daughter of Eve - Noel B. Gerson 2366
Death Comes for the Archbishop - Willa Cather 957
The Deerslayer - James Fenimore Cooper 1299
The Delectable Country - Leland Dewitt
   Baldwin 280
Delilah's Mountain - Gloria Jahoda 3142
Diamond Wedding - Wilbur Daniel Steele 5986
Distant Music - Harold Lenoir Davis 1521

Doctor in Buckskin - T.D. Allen 103
A Durable Fire - Virginia Bernhard 480
Each Bright River - Mildred Masterson McNeilly 4308
Early Candlelight - Maude Hart Lovelace 3904
The Earthbreakers - Ernest Haycox 2789
The Emigrants - Johan Bojer 561
Expedition! - Dana Fuller Ross 5473
Fair Land, Fair Land - A.B. Guthrie Jr. 2625
Fairacres - Gladys Waters 6579
Farewell the Stranger - Saliee O'Brien 4682
The Fields - Conrad Richter 5319
First the Blade - May Miller 4400
A Fistful of Stars - Sarah Lockwood 3828
Follow the River - Albert Mayer 4203
For Us the Living - Bruce Lancaster 3639
The Forest and the Fort - Hervey Allen 100
Forest of the Night - Madison Jones 3291
Free Soil - Marguerite Allis 110
Free Soil - Margaret Lynn 3943
The Frenchwoman - Jeanne Mackin 3995
From Sea to Shining Sea - James Alexander Thom 6232
The Frontiersmen - Allen W. Eckert 1841
Fruit in His Season - Helen C. Barney 333
Gabriel's Search - Della Lutes 3927
Gateway to Empire - Allen W. Eckert 1842
Gentlemen From England - Maude Hart Lovelace 3905
Giants in the Earth - O.E. Rolvaag 5434
Give Us This Valley - Tom Ham 2666
Golden Horizons - William Corcoran 1324
The Golden Season - Oriana Akinson 60
The Grandmothers - Glenway Westcott 6640
The Great Alone - Janet Dailey 1454
The Great Meadow - Elizabeth Madox Roberts 5378
Hannah Fowler - Janice Holt Giles 2411
Harp of a Thousand Strings - Harold Lenoir Davis 1522
Harvest of Dreams - Jaroldeen Edwards 1884
Here I Stay - Elizabeth Coatsworth 1138
High Country - Jason Manning 4075
High Freedom - Earl Murray 4530
A High Wind Rising - Elsie Singmaster 5867
The Hills Stand Watch - August Derleth 1615
The Homesman - Glendon Swarthout 6143
Honey in the Horn - Harold Lenoir Davis 1523
Hope Leslie; or, Early Times in Massachusetts - Catharine Maria Sedgewick 5714
Hope of Earth - Jane Gilmore Rushing 5528
The House on the Mound - August Derleth 1616
I, James Lewis - Gilbert Wolf Gabriel 2266
The Impudent Rifle - Richard Pearce 4872
In the Hands of the Senecas - Walter D. Edmonds 1876
The Interpreter - Robert Moss 4499
Iron Land - Dorothy Ogley 4697
The Jewelled Spur - Gilbert Morris 4465
John Bonwell - Charles K. Pulse 5208
Johnny Osage - Janice Holt Giles 2412
Jonathan Blair, Bounty Lands Lawyer - William Donohue Ellis 1929
Jordan County: A Landscape in Narrative - Shelby Foote 2152
Joshua Moore, American - George Frederick Hummel 3078
Journey to Nashville - Alfred Leland Crabb 1402
Jubal Sackett - Louis L'Amour 3620
Kansas Blue - Dylan Harson 2758
The Kentuckians - Janice Holt Giles 2413
Kentucky Stand - Jere Hungerford Wheelwright 6670
The Kentucky Trace: A Novel of the American Revolution - Harriette Simpson Arnow 195
Kings of the Missouri - Hugh Pendexter 4895
The Land Beyond the Mountains - Janice Holt Giles 2414
The Land Breakers - John Ehle 1895
The Land Is Bright - Noel B. Gerson 2376

Land of the Beautiful River - Helmer Linderholm 3788
A Land to Tame - Zola Helen Ross 5505
A Lantern in Her Hand - Bess Streeter Aldrich 69
The Last Frontier - Howard Fast 2036
The Last of the Mohicans - James Fenimore Cooper 1302
The Last Valley - A.B. Guthrie Jr. 2626
Leafy Rivers - Jessamyn West 6630
Libbie - Judy Alter 121
The Lieutenant's Lady - Bess Streeter Aldrich 70
Lincoln's Mothers: A Story of Nancy and Sally Lincoln - Dorothy Clarke Wilson 6804
The Living - Annie Dillard 1644
Long Knife - James Alexander Thom 6233
The Long Sun - Janice Lucas 3920
Lotus Land - Monica Highland 2917
Louisiana Purchase - A.E. Hotchner 3039
Love Is a Wild Assault - Elithe Hamilton Kirkland 3506
Lusty Wind for Carolina - Inglis Fletcher 2134
A Man's Reach - Charles Morrow Wilson 6796
The Massacre at Fall Creek - Jessamyn West 6631
The Matrix - Maria Thompson Daviess 1509
The Medicine Horn - Jory Sherman 5820
Men of Albemarle - Inglis Fletcher 2135
Miami: A Saga - Evelyn Wilde Mayerson 4204
Michael Beam - Richard Hallet 2663
Mighty Mountain - Archie Binns 502
Mission to Mackinac - Myron David Orr 4755
Moontrap - Don Berry 481
Nebraska Coast - Clyde Brion Davis 1516
Never No More: The Story of Rebecca Boone - Shirley Seifert 5730
New Road - Merle Estes Colby 1168
Nick of the Woods; or, The Jibbenainosay - Robert Montgomery Bird 505
Now We Are Free - Marguerite Allis 112
O Beulah Land - Mary Lee Settle 5756
O Genesee - Janet O'Daniel 4688
Of Lizards and Angels: A Saga of Sioux Land - Frederick F. Manfred 4058
Oh, Kentucky! - Betty Layman Receveur 5284
Oh, Promised Land - James H. Street 6079
Oklahoma Run - Alberta Constant 1260
Outpost! - Dana Fuller Ross 5486
Panther in the Sky - James Alexander Thom 6234
Passage to Natchez - Cameron Judd 3316
The Pathfinder; or, The Inland Sea - James Fenimore Cooper 1305
Peace at Bowling Green - Alfred Leland Crabb 1405
The Peaceable Kingdom - Jan de Hartog 2763
The Pecos River - Fred Bean 399
Peder Victorious - O.E. Rolvaag 5435
Perilous Journey: A Tale of the Mississippi River and the Natchez Trace - Clifford Sublette 6109
The Phantom Emperor - Neil Harmon Swanson 6140
The Pilgrim Soul - Anne Miller Downes 1711
The Pioneers; or, The Sources of the Susquehanna - James Fenimore Cooper 1307
Plume Rouge: A Novel of the Pathfinders - John Upton Terrell 6203
Pocahontas - Susan Donnell 1691
The Prairie - James Fenimore Cooper 1308
The Prospering - Elizabeth Speare 5954
The Quality of Mercy - Anne Miller Downes 1712
Raccoon John Smith - Louis Cochran 1145
The Raid - John Brick 673
The Raider - Jesse Hill Ford 2164
Rainbow Road - Davenport Steward 6016
Rascal's Heaven - F. van Wyck Mason 4157
Reckon with the River - Clark McMeekin 4292
Red Belts - Hugh Pendexter 4897
Red Mountain - David Lavender 3677
Restless Is the River - August Derleth 1617
Ride with Me, Mariah Montana - Ivan Doig 1684
Riders of the Long Road - Stephen E. Bransford 649

River to the West: A Novel of the Astor Adventure - John Edward Jennings 3204
Rivers Parting - Shirley Barker 315
Roanoke Hundred - Inglis Fletcher 2138
The Rock Cried Out - Edward Stanley 5981
The Royal Ann Tree - Patricia Campbell 875
Run of the Stars - Dora Aydelotte 247
The Running Iron - Rachel Ann Fish 2097
The Salt and the Savor - Howard William Troyer 6354
Sassafras - Jack Matthews 4193
Scarlet Feather - Dale Van Every 6409
The Sea Runners - Ivan Doig 1685
The Sea 'Venture - F. van Wyck Mason 4159
Seattle Green - Jane Adams 26
The Settlers - Vilhelm Moberg 4424
Shadow of the Moon - Douglas C. Jones 3284
She Rode a Yellow Stallion - Walter Reed 5286
The Silent Drum - Neil Harmon Swanson 6141
Sioux City - John Hyatt Downing 1714
The Smoky Hill - Don Coldsmith 1188
The Snake River - Winfred Blevins 547
So Free We Seem - Helen Todd 6286
Son of the Gamblin' Man: The Youth of an Artist - Mari Sandoz 5593
Song of Metamoris: A Story That Remains of a People Who Passed This Way - Milford E. Anness 155
Song of Years - Bess Streeter Aldrich 72
The Soul of Ann Rutledge - Bernie Babcock 252
The Sounds of Chariots: A Novel of John Sevier and the State of Franklin - Helen Topping Miller 4396
Spirit Lake - MacKinlay Kantor 3363
Spring Came on Forever - Bess Streeter Aldrich 73
Still Is the Summer Night - August Derleth 1619
Strife Before Dawn - Mary Schumann 5675
The Sun Shines West - Nathan Schachner 5632
Swift Rivers - Cornelia Meigs 4328
Tennessee Hazard - Maristan Chapman 994
Thanksgiving - Terry Coleman 1207
That Dark and Bloody River - Allen W. Eckert 1845
That Far Paradise - Gene Markey 4088
Their Fathers' God - O.E. Rolvaag 5436
They Had a Glory - Davenport Steward 6018
The Thing about Clarissa - Roberta St. Clair Cook 1264
This Savage Race - Douglas C. Jones 3285
Those Who Go Against the Current - Shirley Seifert 5734
The Three Lives of Elizabeth - Shirley Seifert 5735
Tidewater - Clifford Dowdey 1709
To Build a Ship - Don Berry 482
To Keep Us Free - Marguerite Allis 115
To the Far Blue Mountains - Louis L'Amour 3630
Tomorrow the Harvest - Viola Paradise 4789
Toward the Morning - Hervey Allen 101
The Town - Conrad Richter 5325
Trapper's Moon - Jory Sherman 5823
Trask - Don Berry 483
The Tree of Life - Hugh Nissenson 4629
The Trees - Conrad Richter 5326
Trumpets Calling - Dora Aydelotte 248
Twilight of Empire - Allen W. Eckert 1846
The Twilighters - Noel M. Loomis 3894
An Untamed Land - Lauraine Snelling 5936
Unto a Good Land - Vilhelm Moberg 4425
Up Country: A Story of the Vanguard - Donald Culross Peattie 4881
Valley in Arms: A Novel of the Settlement of Connecticut - Earl Schenck Miers 4376
Vandemark's Folly - Herbert Quick 5223
Viola Gwyn - George Barr McCutcheon 4258
The Voyagers - Dale Van Every 6412
Walk in My Soul - Lucia St. Clair Robson 5418
Wanderers Eastward, Wanderers West - Kathleen Winsor 6823
Warlock - Oakley Hall 2653
Washington! - Dana Fuller Ross 5491
Waters of the Wilderness - Shirley Seifert 5737
The Way West - A.B. Guthrie Jr. 2628

We Must March: A Novel of the Winning of Oregon - Honore Morrow 4491
West Goes the Road - Tim Pridgen 5192
West of the River - Charlton Laird 3591
Western: A Saga of the Great Plains - Frank Yerby 6930
Westward! - Dana Fuller Ross 5492
The Wild Ohio - Bart Spicer 5966
The Wild Yazoo - John Myers 4546
Wilderness Empire - Allen W. Eckert 1847
The Wilderness War - Allen W. Eckert 1848
Winds of Spring - Walter Havighurst 2776
The Woodsman - Don Wright 6880
You Rolling River - Archie Binns 503
Young Hickory - Stanley Young 6942
Young Titan - F. van Wyck Mason 4165

Seven Years War

Barry Lyndon - William Makepeace Thackeray 6210

Sexuality

Orlando - Virginia Woolf 6866
Reigning Passions - Kathrin Perutz 4940

Shakers

The Believers - Janice Holt Giles 2409
Circle of Gold - Karen Harper 2710

Shays' Rebellion

The Regulators - William Degenhard 1580
The Sprig of Hemlock: A Novel about Shays' Rebellion - Robert Muir 4509

Shenandoah Valley Campaign

Action at Aquila - Hervey Allen 97
Banner at Shenandoah - Bruce Catton 963
Roll, Shenandoah - Bruce Lancaster 3644
The Second Face of Valor - Ray Grant Toepfer 6288
Shadow on the Valley - Kirk Mitchell 4414

Sherman's March to the Sea

Sherman's March - Cynthia Bass 373

Shiloh, Battle of

Captain Little Ax - James H. Street 6077
Grant's War - Ted Jones 3297
The History of Rome Hanks - Joseph Stanley Pennell 4909
In the Season of the Wild Rose - Clara Rising 5347
Johnny Shiloh - James A. Rhodes 5308
Journey to Shiloh - Will Henry 2843
Long Day at Shiloh - Don Bannister 294
The Long Night - Andrew Lytle 3945
Proving Ground: A Novel of Civil War Days in the North - Leone Lowden 3919
Shadowed Memories - Al Lacy 3583
Shiloh - Shelby Foote 2153

Shipbuilding

Masts to Spear the Stars - Stephen Longstreet 3889
The Running of the Tide - Esther Forbes 2160

Shipwrecks

The American Heiress - Dorothy Eden 1854
Attack the Lusitania! - Raymond Hitchcock 2956
Every Man for Himself - Beryl Bainbridge 270
Friday - Michel Tournier 6305
From Time to Time - Jack Finney 2092

The Hampton Women - Julie Ellis 1921
Lusitania - David Butler 819
Maiden Voyage - Cynthia Bass 372
Over There - Robert Vaughan 6449

Shrewsbury, Battle of

Falstaff - Robert Nye 4653

Siege of Khartoum

Drums of Khartoum - Chloe Gartner 2307
The Last Encounter - Robin Maugham 4196

Siege of Ladysmith

The Legacy of Ladysmith - John Kenny Crane 1413

Siege of Louisburg

Restless Are the Sails - Evelyn Eaton 1830
The Willing Maid - C.T. Ritchie 5349

Siege of Mafeking

Siege in the Sun - Mary Paradise 4788

Siege of Masada

The Antagonists - Ernest K. Gann 2276
The Last Days - William Rayner 5272
The Tenth Measure - Brenda Lesley Segal 5721
The Voices of Masada - David Kossoff 3545
The Wolf of Masada - John Fredman 2220

Siege of Paris

Daughter of Marignac - Constance Heaven 2805
Quiet Lady - Norman Collins 1216
Vardy - John Harris 2721

Siege of Vicksburg

By Valour and Arms - James H. Street 6076
Grant's War - Ted Jones 3297
A Hundred Hills - Howard Breslin 667
No Bugles Blow - Bruce Lancaster 3642
Unvexed to the Sea: A Novel of the Vicksburg Campaign - Gerry Morrison 4484

Sikh War

Bayonets in the Sun - William Moore 4446

Sinhala Empire

The Winds of Sinhala - Colin De Silva 1562

Sino-Japanese Conflict, 1937-1945

The Tent of Orange Mist - Paul West 6636

Sioux War of 1876

Thunder in the Dawn - Earl Murray 4532

Six-Day War

The Hope - Herman Wouk 6874

Slavery

The Abductors - Stuart Cloete 1121
The African - Harold Courlander 1386
Agotime, Her Legend - Judith Gleason 2430

All God's Children - Alston Anderson 136
All Souls' Rising - Madison Smartt Bell 422
American Captain - Edison Marshall 4101
Amistad: The Thunder of Freedom - David Pesci 4944
The Ancestors Cry Out - Eugenia Lovett West 6627
Angelique in Barbary - Sergeanne Golon 2469
Anthony Adverse - Hervey Allen 98
Arc d'X - Steve Erickson 1953
Arena: A Novel of Spartacus and Crassus - Maurice Ghnassia 2391
Band of Angels - Robert Penn Warren 6572
Beauty Beast - MacKinlay Kantor 3361
Beulah Land - Lonnie Coleman 1202
The Big Drum - Elizabeth Boatwright Coker 1162
Black Dawn - Christopher Nicole 4613
Black Thunder - Arna Bontemps 574
Black Triumvirate: A Novel of Haiti - Benjamin H. Levin 3736
The Bondswoman - Caryl Ledner 3705
Bride of the River - Laura B. Harris 2723
Bridle the Wind - Julia Davis 1525
Cambridge - Caryl Phillips 4983
Captain Caution - Kenneth Roberts 5385
Captain of the Sands - Keith Dewhurst 1636
Caribbean - James A. Michener 4365
Caribbee - Thomas Hoover 3025
The Closest Possible Union - Joanna Scott 5680
Cloud on the Land - Julia Davis 1526
A Clouded Star - Anne Parrish 4819
The Confessions of Nat Turner - William Styron 6106
Crossing over Jordan - Linda Beatrice Brown 725
Crossing the River - Caryl Phillips 4984
The Dahomean - Frank Yerby 6911
The Dark Command - William R. Burnett 793
Dark Possession - Alice Alison Lide 3771
Darken Ship - Nicholas Monsarrat 4431
A Darkness at Ingraham's Crest: A Tale of the Slaveholding South - Frank Yerby 6912
Darktown Strutters - Wesley Brown 732
Daughter of Strangers - Elizabeth Boatwright Coker 1164
Deep River - Henrietta Buckmaster 760
The Devil's Own - Christopher Nicole 4615
Die the Long Day - Orlando Patterson 4833
Drum - Kyle Onstott 4744
Drums of Destiny - Peter Bourne 593
The Drums of Morning - Philip Van Doren Stern 5997
Eagle on the Sun - Julia Davis 1527
East by Day - Blair Niles 4626
Echo of Lions - Barbara Chase-Riboud 1004
Eden - Julie Ellis 1918
Elegant Journey - John Selby 5740
Eli's Road - Lucas Webb 6589
Enslaved - Ron Burns 801
Fairacres - Gladys Waters 6579
Fairoaks - Frank Yerby 6915
Family - J. California Cooper 1297
The Father - Katharine Holland Brown 724
Fire Bell in the Night - Constance Robertson 5395
Flash for Freedom - George MacDonald Fraser 2203
Flashman and the Angel of the Lord - George MacDonald Fraser 2205
Flight to Canada - Ishmael Reed 5285
Floodtide - Frank Yerby 6916
Foundation Stone - Lella Warren 6571
The Foxes of Harrow - Frank Yerby 6917
Fragments of the Ark - Louise Meriwether 4341
Free Enterprise - Michelle Cliff 1116
Free Soil - Marguerite Allis 110
Freedom - William Safire 5561
Freedom Road - Howard Fast 2031
Freedom's Banner - Teresa Crane 1415
Freedom's Dues - Robert H. Abel 9
Gallows Way - Daoma Winston 6825
The Glass Dove - Sally Carrighar 943
The Glittering Strand - Judith Lennox-Smith 3716

God's Angry Man - Leonard Ehrlich   1898
The Golden Circle - John Edward Ames   125
Golden Isle - Frank G. Slaughter   5890
Green Rose of Furley - Helen C. Barney   334
Hacey Miller - James Sherburne   5805
The Hawthorne Legacy - Teresa Crane   1416
High Hearts - Rita Mae Brown   728
In the Fire of Spring - Thomas Tryon   6355
The Inner Voice - Nina Wilcox Putnam   5211
Isobelle - Mary Lide   3775
The Journey of August King - John Ehle   1894
Jubilee - Margaret Walker   6531
Kingdom Coming - Roark Bradford   622
Kingdom of This World - Alejo Carpentier   906
Know Nothing - Mary Lee Settle   5755
The Land Where the Sun Dies - Henry Carlisle   896
Levi Coffin and the Underground Railroad - Charles Ludwig   3921
Lord of the Kongo - Peter Forbath   2155
The Magnolias - Julie Ellis   1922
Manitou - Donald Clayton Porter   5120
Many a Voyage - Loula Grace Erdman   1951
Matthew Early - Alexander Laing   3589
McKay's Bees - Thomas McMahon   4289
Mistress of Darkness - Christopher Nicole   4617
The Moreland Legacy - Diana Haviland   2777
Muddy Banks - Ruby C. Tolliver   6291
Murfy's Men - Gerald Green   2565
New Moon Rising - Eugenia Price   5185
North and South - John Jakes   3151
North Star Conspiracy - Miriam Grace Monfredo   4428
Ol' Prophet Nat - Daniel Panger   4786
Oldest Living Confederate Widow Tells All - Allan Gurganus   2621
Pathway to the Stars - Harnett T. Kane   3356
The President's Daughter - Barbara Chase-Riboud   1005
The Proud Villeins - Valerie Anand   133
Raintree County - Ross Lockridge Jr.   3827
Raising Holy Hell - Bruce Olds   4718
Ratoon - Christopher Nicole   4619
The Red Cock Crows - Frances Gaither   2272
A Respectable Trade - Philippa Gregory   2584
The Rising Storm - Marguerite Allis   113
Sacred Hunter - Barry Unsworth   6389
Sally Hemings - Barbara Chase-Riboud   1006
Sapphira and the Slave Girl - Willa Cather   958
Sea of Lentils - Antonio Benitez-Rojo   443
Segu - Maryse Conde   1234
Signals of Distress - Jim Crace   1408
Silver Nutmeg - Norah Lofts   3860
The Sin of the Prophet - Truman Nelson   4582
Sisters and Brothers - Janet Stevenson   6005
Slave - William Malliol   4041
The Slave of Frankenstein - Robert J. Myers   4549
The Slave Ship - Mary Johnston   3240
The Slave Stealer - Boyd Upchurch   6390
So Red the Rose - Stark Young   6944
Sojourn of a Stranger - Walter Sullivan   6115
Sow the Seeds of Hemp - Gary Jennings   3195
Speranza - Sven Delblanc   1584
The Spoils of Eden - Robert H. Fowler   2193
A Star Pointed North - Edmund Fuller   2250
The Sun Is My Undoing - Marguerite Steen   5988
Surprise - Brian Burland   785
The Surveyor - Truman Nelson   4583
Swan's Chance - Celeste De Blasis   1549
Tell Me a Tale: A Novel of the Old South - James McEachin   4266
Theory of War - Joan Brady   637
Trade Wind - M.M. Kaye   3378
Turn of the Dice - Janet Edmonds   1870
Twilight of the Dawn - Elizabeth Nell Dubus   1752
Valide: A Novel of the Harem - Barbara Chase-Riboud   1007
The Viceroy of Ouidah - Bruce C. Chatwin   1009
The Walk into Morning - Mildred Barger Herschler   2867

The Way to Fort Pillow - James Sherburne   5807
Westward to Laughter - Colin MacInnes   3984
Where Shadows Go - Eugenia Price   5189
The White Cockade - Henry Farrand Griffin   2592
The White Slave - Fanny Howe   3059
Wind Like a Bugle - Leonard Nathan   3722
A Woman Called Moses - Marcy Moran Heidish   2821
The World Turned Upside Down - William Rayner   5273

Social Chronicle

The Angel with the Trumpet - Ernst Lothar   3898
Before the Glory Ended - Ursula Zilinsky   6963
The Conquest of Don Pedro - Harvey Fergusson   2066
The Delusson Family - Jacques Ducharme   1753
I Take This Land - Richard Powell   5147
The Land Was Ours: A Novel of the Great Plains - Charles W. Bailey   266
Niagara - Robert Lewis Taylor   6189
The Old Maid - Edith Wharton   6652
Roses From the South - Perceval Reniers   5304
Russka: The Novel of Russia - Edward Rutherfurd   5535
Sandoval: A Romance of Bad Manners - Thomas Beer   414
Sarum: The Novel of England - Edward Rutherfurd   5536
Stuyvesant Square - Margaret Lewerth   3743
Ulverton - Adam Thorpe   6278
A Voice in the Streets - John William Tebbel   6196
Young Men See Visions - Mary Mian   4357

Socialism

Day Is Coming - William Cameron   869
Karl and Rosa - Alfred Doblin   1653
A People Betrayed - Alfred Doblin   1654

Somme, Battle of the

War Story: A Novel - Derek Robinson   5404

Spanish-American War

Empire: A Novel - Gore Vidal   6487
Ever After - Elswyth Thane   6216
Fenwick Travers and the Forbidden Kingdom - Raymond M. Saunders   5612
Fenwick Travers and the Years of Empire - Raymond M. Saunders   5614
Fortune's Legacy - Jack Rowe   5515
The Hampton Heritage - Julie Ellis   1920
Homecoming - Dana Fuller Ross   5474
Imperial Kelly - Peter Bowen   600
Officers and Ladies - Richard O'Connor   4686
Outlaw - Warren Kiefer   3482
Owen Glen - Ben Ames Williams   6766
Pacific Destiny - Dana Fuller Ross   5487
Remember Santiago - Douglas C. Jones   3280
The Rough Rider - Gilbert Morris   4468
San Juan Hill - Will Henry   2848
Season for War - P.F. Kluge   3510
The Single Star - Walter Adolphe Roberts   5394
The Spoils of War - Thomas Fleming   2131
Sunset - Christopher Nicole   4623
TR - Noel B. Gerson   2385
Wind of Destiny - Christopher Nicole   4624
The Year of the Spaniard - Henry Castor   956

Spanish Armada

Armada - Charles Gidley   2404
The Black Duchess - Alanna Knight   3514
Deborah and the Many Faces of Love - Colette Davenat   1499

Fire over England - A.E.W. Mason   4143
Golden Admiral - F. van Wyck Mason   4150
The Lion Triumphant - Philippa Carr   922
No Wall So High - Anne Powers   5152
Reluctant Cavalier - Donald Barr Chidsey   1064
The Scarlet Cloak - Jean Plaidy   5061

Spanish Colonies

Among the Innocent - Elizabeth Borton de Trevino   6339
At the Moon's Inn - Andrew Lytle   3944
Aztec - Gary Jennings   3193
Beyond the Blue Sierra - Honore Morrow   4486
Bride of the Conqueror - Hartzell Spence   5961
The Bridge of San Luis Rey - Thornton Wilder   6752
By the King's Command - Shirley Seifert   5723
The Children of the Sun - Oakley Hall   2652
A City for St. Francis - Evelyn Wells   6621
Cortez and Marina - Edison Marshall   4105
Cradle of the Sun - John Clagett   1083
The Cross and the Sword - Manuel de Jesus Galvan   2274
The Cross and the Sword - Jonreed Lauritzen   3674
Daimon - Abel Posse   5140
Death of the Fifth Sun - Robert Somerlott   5944
Don Juan McQueen - Eugenia Price   5181
Don Pedro and the Devil - Edgar Maas   3948
Dust on the King's Highway - Helen Constance White   6677
The First Gentleman of America: A Comedy of Conquest - James Branch Cabell   841
The Flames of Time - Baynard Kendrick   3409
Flight of the Crow - Paul Clayton   1103
Follow the Wind - Don Coldsmith   1176
The Golden Eagle - John Edward Jennings   3201
The Great White Gods - Eduard Stucken   6102
The Hands of Cantu - Tom Lea   3694
The Heart of Jade - Salvador de Madariaga   4024
Hill of the Hawk - Scott O'Dell   4689
I, the King - Howard Clewes   1112
Islands of Unwisdom - Robert Graves   2548
Jewel of the Sea - Susan Wiggs   6743
The Last Princess - Charles O. Locke   3826
The Luck of Huemac: A Novel about the Aztecs - Daniel Peters   4946
Mansions of Darkness - Chelsea Quinn Yarbro   6902
Maria - Eugenia Price   5184
Medicine Knife - Don Coldsmith   1179
Mexico - James A. Michener   4372
Night Wind's Woman - Shirl Henke   2825
Nine Days of Father Serra - Isabelle Gibson Ziegler   6961
Return of the Spanish - Don Coldsmith   1183
Ride the Red Earth - Paul I. Wellman   6620
Rio Grande - Jory Sherman   5821
The Rose and the Flame - Jonreed Lauritzen   3676
The Royal City - Les Savage Jr.   5621
Sea of Lentils - Antonio Benitez-Rojo   443
Shadow of a Star - Jamie Lee Cooper   1315
Sharpe's Devil - Bernard Cornwell   1340
The Single Star - Walter Adolphe Roberts   5394
Sons of Texas - Tom Early   1822
The Spanish Bride - Walter O'Meara   4735
Summer Thunder - Willie Snow Ethridge   1982
The Sword and the Sun: The Story of the Spanish Civil Wars in Peru - Gerald Green   2566
Sword of Vengeance - Kerry Newcomb   4593
Takers of the City - Hoffman Reynolds Hays   2800
Taos - Irwin R. Blacker   527
Tennessee Hazard - Maristan Chapman   994
They Are Coming: The Conquest of Mexico - Jose Lopez Portillo y Pacheco   3896
This Promised Land - Robert Easton   1824
To the Indies - C.S. Forester   2183
Trail From Taos - Don Coldsmith   1192
Trail of the Spanish Bit - Don Coldsmith   1193
The Wind Leaves No Shadow - Ruth Laughlin   3672

Spanish Conquest

Tatham Mound - Piers Anthony 169

Spiritualism

Billy Sunday - Rod Jones 3295
A Case of Spirits - Peter Lovesey 3910
Nevermore - William Hjortsberg 2958
The Undiscovered Country - Jay Walz 6560
The Wizard's Daughter - Barbara Michaels 4362

Sports

The Celebrant - Eric Rolfe Greenberg 2572
Chariots of Fire - W.J. Weatherby 6586
The Detective Wore Silk Drawers - Peter Lovesey 3911
Down for the Count - Stuart M. Kaminsky 3336
The Fast Men - Tom McNab 4302
Fielder's Choice - Rick Norman 4646
Flanagan's Run - Tom McNab 4303
The Ham Reporter - Robert J. Randisi 5251
Hoopla - Harry Stein 5990
If I Never Get Back - Darryl Brock 700
Lord Fancy - Leslie Turner White 6686
Lovelock - James McNeish 4311
Murder at Ebbets Field - Troy Soos 5947
Murder at Fenway Park - Troy Soos 5948
Playing the Game - Ian Buruma 810
Willowwood - Mollie Hardwick 2699
Wobble to Death - Peter Lovesey 3918

Stagecoaches

Beatrice Goes to Brighton - Marion Chesney 1019
Belinda Goes to Bath - Marion Chesney 1020
The Californian - Todhunter Ballard 284
Deborah Goes to Dover - Marion Chesney 1023
Emily Goes to Exeter - Marion Chesney 1027
Kezzy - Patricia Burns 799
The Nancy Flyer - Ernest Poole 5091
Penelope Goes to Portsmouth - Marion Chesney 1043
The Road to Baltimore - Robert S. Harper 2716
Six-Horse Hitch - Janice Holt Giles 2417
The Sound of Coaches - Leon Garfield 2295
Stacey's Flyer - Patricia Burns 800
Yvonne Goes to York - Marion Chesney 1054

Stalinism

Generations of Winter - Vassily Aksyonov 61

Submarines

A Sailor of Austria - John Biggins 492

Sumerian Civilization

Gilgamesh the King - Robert Silverberg 5853

Supernatural

Better in the Dark - Chelsea Quinn Yarbro 6894
The Black Dwarf - Sir Walter Scott 5692
A Candle for D'Artagnan - Chelsea Quinn Yarbro 6895
Covenant with the Vampire: The Diaries of the Family Dracul - Jeanne Kalogridis 3327
The Cross of Frankenstein - Robert J. Myers 4548
Crusader's Torch - Chelsea Quinn Yarbro 6897
Dangerous - Amanda Quick 5213
Darker Jewels - Chelsea Quinn Yarbro 6898
Devoted - Alice Borchardt 578
Dr. Jekyll and Mr. Holmes - Loren D. Estleman 1970

The Fair - Robert Nathan 4559
A Flame in Byzantium - Chelsea Quinn Yarbro 6899
Gothic Romance - Emmanuel Carrere 942
The Haunting of Lamb House - Joan Aiken 48
Hotel Transylvania - Chelsea Quinn Yarbro 6900
Lord of the Vampires: The Diaries of the Family Dracul - Jeanne Kalogridis 3328
Manchu Palaces - Jeanne Larsen 3669
Mary Reilly - Valerie Martin 4136
The Monastery - Sir Walter Scott 5701
The Mummy; or Ramses the Damned - Anne Rice 5315
Out of the House of Life - Chelsea Quinn Yarbro 6903
The Palace - Chelsea Quinn Yarbro 6904
Path of the Eclipse - Chelsea Quinn Yarbro 6905
Sherlock Holmes vs. Dracula - Loren D. Estleman 1976
Silk Road - Jeanne Larsen 3670
The Slave of Frankenstein - Robert J. Myers 4549
Soldier of the Mist - Gene Wolfe 6843
Tempting Fate - Chelsea Quinn Yarbro 6906
Walford's Oak - Jill M. Phillips 4986

Suspense

An Autumn in Araby - Carola Salisbury 5565
Blood Kin - Barbara Anne Pauley 4845
The Branch-Bearers - Glen Petrie 4978
Castle of Foxes - Alanna Knight 3516
Damnation Reef - Jill Tattersall 6172
Dark at Noon - Jill Tattersall 6173
Dark Inheritance - Carola Salisbury 5568
Devil Child - Jo Germany 2359
Dolphin Summer - Carola Salisbury 5569
The Duchess of Vidal - Dawn Lindsey 3793
The Eagle at the Gate - Rona Randall 5248
Evil Mark - Graham Miles 4377
The Fallen Angels - Susannah Kells 3397
A Finger to Her Lips - Evelyn Berckman 472
Flight From Fifth Avenue - Catherine M. Rae 5235
Flowers for Lilian - Anna Gilbert 2405
The Harrogate Secret - Catherine Cookson 1278
Heir to Polventon - Marjorie Watson 6583
Here Comes a Candle - Jane Aiken Hodge 2964
The House on Curtin Street - Millie J. Ragosta 5242
I Came to the Highlands: A Novel of Suspense - Velda Johnston 3263
I, Roberta - Elizabeth Gray Vining 6501
In Pale Battalions - Robert Goddard 2444
Jamaica Inn - Daphne Du Maurier 1747
Legacy of the Wolf - Jean Raynes 5274
Limmerston Hall - Hester W. Chapman 991
The Long Shadow - Anna Gilbert 2406
Marry in Haste - Jane Aiken Hodge 2967
The Only Thing to Fear - David Poyer 5160
Out of the Dark - Norah Lofts 3856
Portrait of Emma - Lillian Cheatham 1010
The Pride of the Trevallions - Carola Salisbury 5570
The Rationalist - Warwick Collins 1217
Sarton Kell - Kate Mallory 4043
The Second Sister - Leslie O'Grady 4701
The Secret of Saramount - Lillian Cheatham 1011
The Shadowed Spring - Carola Salisbury 5571
The Silver Dolphin - Velda Johnston 3264
Summoned to Darkness - Anne-Marie Sheridan 5809
The Tempestuous Petticoat - Mary Ann Gibbs 2397
The Weeping Ash - Joan Aiken 54
The Winter Bride - Carola Salisbury 5572
Witness to Treason - Millie J. Ragosta 5244
The Wizard's Daughter - Barbara Michaels 4362
Wychwood - Nicole St. John 5564

Taiping Rebellion

Empire of Heaven - Linda Ching Sledge 5907
Flashman and the Dragon - George MacDonald Fraser 2206

The Magnificent Savages - Fred Mustard Stewart 6024
Rebels of the Heavenly Kingdom - Katherine Paterson 4828
The Second Son of Heaven: A Novel of Nineteenth-Century China - C.Y. Lee 3707

Tannenberg, Battle of

August 1914 - Alexander Solzhenitsyn 5942

Texas Revolution

All the Brave Rifles - Clarke Venable 6450
The Bugles Are Silent: A Novel of the Texas Revolution - John R. Knaggs 3513
Dead Man's Walk - Larry McMurtry 4297
Divine Average - Elithe Hamilton Kirkland 3505
The Eagle and the Raven - James A. Michener 4369
Empire of Bones: A Novel of Sam Houston and the Texas Revolution - Jeff Long 3868
Eyes of Eagles - William W. Johnstone 3266
The Furies - John Jakes 3146
Gone to Texas - Jason Manning 4074
Gone to Texas - Don Worcester 6871
Hellfire Jackson - Garland Roark 5355
The Iron Mistress - Paul I. Wellman 6618
Love Is a Wild Assault - Elithe Hamilton Kirkland 3506
Magnificent Destiny - Paul I. Wellman 6619
The Men of Gonzales - John H. Culp 1442
On the Long Tide - Laura Krey 3555
Promised Lands - Elizabeth Crook 1430
Republic: A Novel of Texas - E.V. Thompson 6266
The Restless Border - Richard Pearce 4873
The Road to San Jacinto - James F. Davis 1524
The Road to San Jacinto - Leonard L. Foreman 2167
Sam Houston - Noel B. Gerson 2380
The Sam Houston Story - Dean Owen 4770
The Slender Reed - Noel B. Gerson 2382
Star in the Rigging: A Novel of the Texas Navy - Garland Roark 5358
Star of Empire: A Novel of Old San Antonio - Leonard Sanders 5590
Star of the Wilderness - Karle Wilson Baker 274
Tempered Blade - Monte Barrett 352
Texas - James A. Michener 4375
Texas! - Dana Fuller Ross 5490
Thunder Before Seven - Anna Brand 648
True Women - Janice Woods Windle 6820
Wave High the Banner - Dee Brown 714
The Wine of San Lorenzo - Herbert Gorman 2493

Theatrical Life

Abracadaver - Peter Lovesey 3906
The Actor - Robert J. Conley 1236
Adrienne - Barbara Levy 3742
Affairs of Love - Nicola Thorne 6272
All the Living: A Novel of One Year in the Life of William Shakespeare - Henrietta Buckmaster 758
The Angel of the Opera: Sherlock Holmes Meets the Phantom of the Opera - Sam Siciliano 5842
The Ardent Years - Janet Stevenson 6003
Banner by the Wayside - Samuel Hopkins Adams 28
Bedford Row - Claire Rayner 5259
Benjy Boone - Maurice Dolbier 1687
The Black Angels - Maude Hart Lovelace 3902
The Bluestocking - David Delman 1598
The Bracegirdle - Burris Atkins Jenkins 3189
A Cadenza for Caruso - Barbara Paul 4834
The Capricorn Stone - Madeleine Brent 659
A Captive Freedom - Emma Drummond 1724
Carnival of Saints - George Herman 2860
Caroline and Julia - Clare Darcy 1484
Cassy - Elizabeth Lyle 3930
Catherine Carter - Pamela Hansford Johnson 3227

Charing Cross - Claire Rayner 5260
Charming Sally - Maude Hart Lovelace 3903
Chelsea Reach - Claire Rayner 5261
A Chorus of Detectives - Barbara Paul 4835
The Cleopatra Boy - Eric Malpass 4048
A Company of Swans - Eva Ibbotson 3095
Conjuror's Journal - Frances L. Shine 5826
Consuelo - George Sand 5582
Covent Garden - Claire Rayner 5262
The Crystal Dove - Mollie Hardwick 2692
A Dead Man in Deptford - Anthony Burgess 776
Death Off Stage - Richard Grayson 2558
Dim the Flaring Lamps - Jan Jordan 3301
The Eagle at the Gate - Rona Randall 5248
Eleanora Duse - Jean Stubbs 6095
Encore - Monique Raphel High 2915
English Music - Peter Ackroyd 18
The Eye of the Lion: A Novel Based on the Life of Mata Hari - Lael Tucker Wertenbaker 6626
Farewell to My Concubine - Lilian Lee 3709
Feast of the Jesters - Manuel Komroff 3533
Fire in the Heart - Henrietta Buckmaster 761
Gentleman of Stratford - John Brophy 708
Glorious Morning - Julie Ellis 1919
The Glory and the Dream - Katharine Dunlap 1789
Goddess of the Green Room - Jean Plaidy 5016
The Golden Crucible - Jean Stubbs 6096
Gower Street - Claire Rayner 5264
A Grand Passion - Mary Mackey 3991
The Gypsy From Cadiz - Tamsin Hamilton 2670
The Haymarket - Claire Rayner 5265
Herma - Macdonald Harris 2726
The House of Kanze - Nobuko Albery 64
A House of Women - Eric Malpass 4049
I Am Lidian - Naomi Lane Babson 253
I, Rachel - March Cost 1361
The Infinite Woman - Edison Marshall 4107
Jenny and Barnum: A Novel of Love - Roderick Thorp 6276
The Jewelled Spur - Gilbert Morris 4465
Kate - Brian Cleeve 1109
Kean: The Imaginary Memoirs of an Actor - Julius Berstl 485
Last Act in Palmyra - Lindsey Davis 1529
The Laughing Hangman - Edward Marston 4120
Liza Bowe - Shirley Barker 313
Louisa Brancusi - Darrell Husted 3088
Lovers Meeting - Mollie Hardwick 2695
Lucy - Hester W. Chapman 992
The Mad Courtesan - Edward Marston 4122
Magic Flutes - Eva Ibbotson 3097
The Mask of Apollo - Mary Renault 5300
The Mating Dance - Rona Randall 5250
The Melancholy Virgin - Annabel Laine 3587
The Merry Devils - Edward Marston 4123
Mistress Devon - Virginia Coffman 1156
Mistress of the Boards - Richard Sumner 6118
Monsieur Moliere - Michael O'Shaughnessy 4762
The Monterant Affair - Richard Grayson 2560
Morality Play - Barry Unsworth 6387
The Mortal Gods - Maurice Dolbier 1688
Murder at Drury Lane - Robert Lee Hall 2659
My Name Is Clary Brown - Charlotte Keppel 3466
Nicholas Cooke: Actor, Soldier, Physician, Priest - Stephanie Cowell 1393
The Nine Giants - Edward Marston 4124
Nothing Like the Sun - Anthony Burgess 781
Opal - Helen Ashfield 210
Peg Woffington - Charles Reade 5281
Perdita's Prince - Jean Plaidy 5040
Phantom - Susan Kay 3375
Piccadilly - Claire Rayner 5267
The Player's Boy - Bryher 744
The Players' Boy Is Dead - Leonard Tourney 6303
Playing the Jack - Mary Brown 726
Prima Donna at Large - Barbara Paul 4838
The Queen's Head - Edward Marston 4125
Quitting Time - Robert J. Conley 1249
Rachel - Anne Powers 5153

The Roaring Boy - Edward Marston 4127
Sam Patch: Ballad of a Jumping Man - William Getz 2390
Sarah - Joel Gross 2603
The Savage Brood - Martha Rofheart 5430
Scaramouche - Rafael Sabatini 5554
The Secret Annie Oakley - Marcy Moran Heidish 2819
The Shakespeare Girl - Mollie Hardwick 2698
Show Boat - Edna Ferber 2063
The Silent Woman - Edward Marston 4128
Soho Square - Claire Rayner 5268
Some Lose Their Way - Eloise S. Liddon 3770
The Spirit and the Flesh: A Novel Inspired by the Life of Isadora Duncan - David Weiss 6610
The Spur - Ardyth Kennelly 3425
Stage Fright - Gillian Linscott 3809
Sweet Songbird - Teresa Crane 1418
Sweet Will - Eric Malpass 4050
A Tale of the Wind: A Novel of Nineteenth-Century France - Kay Nolte Smith 5922
The Tallulah Bankhead Murder Case - George Baxt 389
This Old Bill - Loren D. Estleman 1980
This Willing Passion - Patricia Cloud 1132
Three Years to Play - Colin MacInnes 3983
To Be a King - Robert DeMaria 1607
The Trial of Elizabeth Cree: A Novel of the Limehouse Murders - Peter Ackroyd 21
The Trip to Jerusalem - Edward Marston 4129
The Upstart - Edison Marshall 4112
The Way to the Lantern - Audrey Erskine Lindop 3790
The West End Horror - Nicholas Meyer 4350
Will Shakespeare: The Untold Story - John Mortimer 4495
You, My Brother - Philip Burton 809

Thirty Years War

Captain Fantom - Charles Underhill 6377
The Descent of the Idol - Jaroslav Durych 1818
An Epic Joy: A Novel Based on the Life of Rubens - Donald Braider 642
The Island of the Day Before - Umberto Eco 1849
The Last Valley - J.B. Pick 4992
People of the Book - David Stacton 5974
Simplicissimus the Vagabond - J.J.C. Grimmelshausen 2594
The Sword of the Golem - Abraham Rothberg 5509
Woman Astride - Nora Purtscher-Wydenbruch 5209
World and Paradise - Edgar Maas 3953

Ticonderoga, Battle of

Day of Battle - Frederic F. Van de Water 6402
Rebel Guns - Adam Rutledge 5539
Reluctant Rebel - Frederic F. Van de Water 6403

Time Travel

Called Away - Perdita Buchan 753
The Centurion - Jan de Hartog 2762
The Devil in Velvet - John Dickson Carr 909
Dragonfly in Amber - Diana Gabaldon 2262
Drums of Autumn - Diana Gabaldon 2263
Exit Sherlock Holmes - Robert Lee Hall 2657
Fire, Burn! - John Dickson Carr 910
Fitzempress' Law - Diana Norman 4644
Foreign Devils - Irvin Faust 2053
Frankenstein Unbound - Brian Aldiss 68
From Time to Time - Jack Finney 2092
The Golden Nineties - Lisa Mason 4166
If I Never Get Back - Darryl Brock 700
Kingdom of Shadows - Barbara Erskine 1954
A Knight in Shining Armor - Jude Deveraux 1631
Knights - Linda Lael Miller 4399
Ladies Whose Bright Eyes - Ford Madox Ford 2162

Lady of Hay - Barbara Erskine 1955
Lest Darkness Fall - L. Sprague De Camp 1557
The Lincoln Hunters - Wilson Tucker 6359
Outlander - Diana Gabaldon 2264
Patriot's Dream - Barbara Michaels 4360
A Quest for Love - Jacquetta Hawkes 2781
Riding Shotgun - Rita Mae Brown 729
Serenissima: A Novel of Venice - Erica Jong 3300
Till the End of Time - Allen Appel 170
Time After Time - Karl Alexander 80
Time After Time - Allen Appel 171
Time and Again - Jack Finney 2093
Twice upon a Time - Allen Appel 172
The Vision of Stephen: An Elegy - Lolah Burford 775
Voyager - Diana Gabaldon 2265
A Whisper on the Wind - Madeline Baker 276

Tippecanoe, Battle of

The Horn and the Forest - Jamie Lee Cooper 1313

Trafalgar, Battle of

1805 - Richard Woodman 6857
Darken Ship - Nicholas Monsarrat 4431
Decision at Trafalgar - Richard Woodman 6861
He Brings Great News - Clemence Dane 1462
Ramage at Trafalgar - Dudley Pope 5102
The Scalpel and the Sword - Dell Shannon 5774

Trail of Tears

Mountain Windsong - Robert J. Conley 1246
Pushing the Bear: A Novel of the Trail of Tears - Diane Glancy 2426
Trail of Tears - Williams Forrest 2187

Treasure Hunt

Abigail - Joan Druett 1721
Apache - Donald Clayton Porter 5114
Beyond the Stars - David William Ross 5497
Deception - Amanda Quick 5214
Dreams of Empire - Jeanne Mackin 3994
Lady Defiant - Suzanne Robinson 5412
Log Cabin Noble - F. van Wyck Mason 4153
Mackenna's Gold - Will Henry 2845
Maximilian's Gold - Jane Barry 359
Moonraker's Bride - Madeleine Brent 661
Return to Treasure Island - Denis Judd 3318
The Seven Cities of Gold - Virginia Davis Hersch 2865
Silver Shoals - Hamilton Cochran 1142
Sudden Country - Loren D. Estleman 1979
Treasure Island - Robert Louis Stevenson 6012
Treasure Mountain - Louis L'Amour 3631
The Treasure of the Chisos - John H. Culp 1446
Trumpets Sound No More - F. van Wyck Mason 4163

Trent, Battle of

The Drums of Winter - Sandra Paretti 4790

Trenton, Battle of

Trumpets at Dawn - Cyril Harris 2719

Trials

Aces and Eights: A Novel of the Legend of Wild Bill Hickok - Loren D. Estleman 1967
Amistad: The Thunder of Freedom - David Pesci 4944
Anna Zenger: Mother of Freedom - Kent Cooper 1316

Avery's Knot - Mary Cable   843
Beecher: A Novel - Dan McCall   4218
The Bizarre Sisters - Jay Walz   6559
The Bluestocking - David Delman   1598
The Case of Kitty Ogilvie - Jean Stubbs   6093
The Court Martial of Daniel Boone - Allen W. Eckert   1840
The Court-Martial of George Armstrong Custer - Douglas C. Jones   3276
The Court Martial of Robert E. Lee - Douglas Savage   5617
The Dark Pasture - Jessica Stirling   6042
Defend and Betray - Anne Perry   4928
The Devil's Lieutenant - Maria Fagyas   1998
Double Moscadine - Frances Gaither   2271
Echo of Lions - Barbara Chase-Riboud   1004
The Escape of Socrates - Robert Pick   4993
Fire in the Ice - Alan Scholefield   5653
The Gift of Rome - John Wagner   6520
Hellbane - Anthony Esler   1963
The Hessian - Howard Fast   2033
I Give You Oscar Wilde - Desmond Hall   2647
The Judges of the Secret Court - David Stacton   5972
The Justicer - Thomas Fall   2010
Lantern for the Dark - Jessica Stirling   6045
Lizzie - Evan Hunter   3083
Madeleine - Pamela Elizabeth West   6633
A Marriage of Convenience - Tim Jeal   3172
The Massacre at Fall Creek - Jessamyn West   6631
Members of the Tribe - Richard Kluger   3511
Mistress Nancy - Barbara Bentley   460
My Grand Enemy - Jean Stubbs   6098
Nickajack - Robert J. Conley   1248
The Passion of Sacco and Vanzetti: A New England Legend - Howard Fast   2040
The Severed Crown - Jane Lane   3657
The Silver Dolphin - Velda Johnston   3264
The Silver Oar - Howard Breslin   669
A Sudden, Fearful Death - Anne Perry   4938
Sweet Adelaide - Julian Symons   6152
A Tale for Midnight - Frederic Prokosch   5195
This Willing Passion - Patricia Cloud   1132
The Thomas Street Horror - Raymond Paul   4843
The Tragedy at Tinkerton: An Historical Novel of Murder - Raymond Paul   4844
The Trial of Jenny Sykes - Hebe Weenolsen   6598
The Trial of Mary Todd Lincoln - James A. Rhodes   5309
The Venus Throw - Steven Saylor   5627
Voyage to the First of December - Henry Carlisle   897
Watson's Apology - Beryl Bainbridge   271
When the War Is Over - Stephen Becker   408
The Witch and the Priest - Hilda Lewis   3754

Tribal Life—African

The Covenant - James A. Michener   4368
The Dahomean - Frank Yerby   6911
Earthshaker - Robert Wilson Krepps   3553
The Echoing Cliffs - Hjalmar P. Thesen   6219
Great Elephant - Alan Scholefield   5654
The Great Sky and the Silence - James S. Rand   5245
Isobelle - Mary Lide   3775
Lord of Darkness - Robert Silverberg   5854
Slave - William Malliol   4041
Things Fall Apart - Chinua Achebe   16
Wizards' Country - Daphne Rooke   5438

Tribal Life—Aztec

The Sun, He Dies: A Novel about the End of the Aztec World - Jamake Highwater   2919

Tribal Life—Eskimo

The Longest Winter - Julie Harris   2722
The White Dawn - James Houston   3053

White Man - Peter Freuchen   2228

Tribal Life—Germanic

The Light Bearer - Donna Gillespie   2419

Tribal Life—Hawaiian

Ka'a'awa: A Novel about Hawaii in the 1850s - Oswald Andrew Bushnell   814

Tribal Life—Mongol

The Earth Is the Lord's: A Tale of the Rise of Genghis Khan - Taylor Caldwell   855

Tribal Life—Native American

Ammahabas - Bill Hotchkiss   3036
Bearer of the Pipe - Don Coldsmith   1169
Bride of the Morning Star - Don Coldsmith   1170
Buffalo Medicine - Don Coldsmith   1171
Buffalo Woman - Dorothy M. Johnson   3223
Call the Beast Thy Brother - William Oliver Turner   6366
Child of the Dead - Don Coldsmith   1172
Conquering Horse - Frederick F. Manfred   4055
The Dark Way - Robert J. Conley   1241
Daughter of the Eagle - Don Coldsmith   1173
The Double Man - Elinor Pryor   5205
Eagle Song - James Houston   3050
The Elk-Dog Heritage - Don Coldsmith   1174
The Fleet Rabble: A Novel of the Nez Perce War - Frank Borden Hanes   2675
The Flower in the Mountains - Don Coldsmith   1175
Follow the Wind - Don Coldsmith   1176
For Love of Two Eagles - Barbara Riefe   5328
Fort De Chastaigne - Don Coldsmith   1177
From Where the Sun Now Stands - Will Henry   2841
A Good Day to Die - Del Barton   368
Hanta Yo - Ruth Beebe Hill   2951
Lakota - G. Clifton Wisler   6833
The Last Warpath - Will Henry   2844
The Law of Larion - Peter Freuchen   2227
Let the Drum Speak: A Novel of Ancient America - Linda Lay Shuler   5837
The Long Sun - Janice Lucas   3920
The Loon Feather - Iola Fuller   2253
Lord of the Plains - Alfred Silver   5852
Man of the Shadows - Don Coldsmith   1178
The Manly-Hearted Woman - Frederick F. Manfred   4057
The Medicine Calf - Bill Hotchkiss   3037
Medicine Knife - Don Coldsmith   1179
The Mists of Manittoo - Lois Swann   6135
Moon of Thunder - Don Coldsmith   1180
Mountain Windsong - Robert J. Conley   1246
Pale Star - Don Coldsmith   1181
People of the Lakes - W. Michael Gear   2336
People of the River - W. Michael Gear   2338
People of the Silence - W. Michael Gear   2340
Pushing the Bear: A Novel of the Trail of Tears - Diane Glancy   2426
Quest for the White Bull - Don Coldsmith   1182
Return of the Spanish - Don Coldsmith   1183
Return to the River - Don Coldsmith   1184
The Rifles - William T. Vollmann   6510
River of Swans - Don Coldsmith   1185
The Sacred Hills - Don Coldsmith   1187
Season of Yellow Leaf - Douglas C. Jones   3283
The Second Kiss - Gayle Rogers   5432
She Who Remembers - Linda Lay Shuler   5838
Song of the Cheyenne - Jory Sherman   5822
Song of the Meadowlark - John A. Sanford   5594
Song of the Rock - Don Coldsmith   1189
Tatham Mound - Piers Anthony   169
Thunderstick - Don Coldsmith   1190
Torn Covenants - Lois Swann   6136

Track of the Bear - Don Coldsmith   1191
Trail of Tears - Williams Forrest   2187
Trail of the Spanish Bit - Don Coldsmith   1193
Voice of the Eagle - Linda Lay Shuler   5839
Walk in My Soul - Lucia St. Clair Robson   5418
Walks in the Sun - Don Coldsmith   1194
The Way of the Priests - Robert J. Conley   1253
Whisper of the Wolf - Terry C. Johnston   3261
White Indian - Donald Clayton Porter   5134
The White Path - Robert J. Conley   1254
Woman Chief - Benjamin Capps   892
A Woman of the People - Benjamin Capps   893
The Woman Who Fell From the Sky - Barbara Riefe   5330
World of Silence - Don Coldsmith   1195

Tribal Life—New Guinean

Dubu: A Novel of New Guinean Conquest - Maslyn Williams   6789

Tribal Life—Prehistoric

The Animal Wife - Elizabeth Marshall Thomas   6243
Beyond the Sea of Ice - William Sarabande   5595
Brother Wind - Sue Harrison   2748
Children of the Dawn - Patricia Rowe   5516
Children of the Ice - Charlotte Prentiss   5166
Children of the Sun - Charlotte Prentiss   5167
The Clan of the Cave Bear - Jean M. Auel   236
Corridor of Storms - William Sarabande   5596
Dance of the Tiger: A Novel of the Ice Age - Bjorn Kurten   3566
Daughter of the Red Deer - Joan Wolf   6838
Dawn Land - Joseph Bruchac III   734
The Deer Dancers - Amanda Cockrell   1146
The Earth Goddess - Richard Herley   2856
The Edge of the World - William Sarabande   5597
Face of the Rising Sun - William Sarabande   5598
The Flint Lord - Richard Herley   2857
Forbidden Land - William Sarabande   5599
The Golden Strangers - Henry Treece   6328
The Horsemasters - Joan Wolf   6840
The Inheritors - William Golding   2455
Keepers of the Misty Time - Patricia Rowe   5517
The Last Mammoth - Margaret Allan   89
The Last Warrior Queen - Mary Mackey   3992
The Mammoth Hunters - Jean M. Auel   237
The Mammoth Stone - Margaret Allan   90
Mother Earth, Father Sky - Sue Harrison   2749
My Sister, the Moon - Sue Harrison   2750
People of the Earth - W. Michael Gear   2334
People of the Fire - W. Michael Gear   2335
People of the Lightning - W. Michael Gear   2337
People of the Mesa - Charlotte Prentiss   5168
People of the Sea - W. Michael Gear   2339
People of the Wolf - W. Michael Gear   2341
Pillar of the Sky - Cecelia Holland   2994
The Plains of Passage - Jean M. Auel   238
The Reindeer Hunters - Joan Wolf   6841
Reindeer Moon - Elizabeth Marshall Thomas   6244
The Sacred Stones - William Sarabande   5600
Shadow of the Watching Star - William Sarabande   5601
Shiva: An Adventure of the Ice Age - J.H. Brennan   657
Singletusk - Bjorn Kurten   3567
The Stone Arrow - Richard Herley   2858
Thunder in the Sky - William Sarabande   5602
The Valley of Horses - Jean M. Auel   239
Walkers of the Wind - William Sarabande   5603
Wolves of the Dawn - William Sarabande   5604
The Year the Horses Came - Mary Mackey   3993

Tribal Life—South American

The Moon Stallion - Jim Berry   484

Tribal Life—South Pacific

Hawaii - James A. Michener   4370

Tripolitan War

Lydia Bailey - Kenneth Roberts   5387
The Salem Frigate - John Edward Jennings   3205
Written in Sand - Josephine Case   950

Trojan War

The Firebrand - Marion Zimmer Bradley   624
Fires in the Sky - Phillip Parotti   4816
The Goddess - Miranda Seymour   5763
The Greek Generals Talk: Memoirs of the Trojan War - Phillip Parotti   4817
Paris of Troy - George Baker   273
The Private Life of Helen of Troy - John Erskine   1957
Scandal in Troy - Eva Hemmer Hansen   2679
The Shattered Horse - S.P. Somtow   5945
The Trojan Generals Talk: Memoirs of the Greek War - Phillip Parotti   4818
Troy - Richard Matturro   4194
Whom the Gods Would Destroy - Richard Powell   5148

Tudor Period

Anne Boleyn - Evelyn Anthony   158
Anne of the Thousand Days - Edward Fenton   2059
The Autobiography of Henry VIII - Margaret George   2355
The Blanket of the Dark - John Buchan   749
Blood Royal - Mollie Hardwick   2690
Brief Gaudy Hour - Margaret Campbell Barnes   322
A Brood of Vipers - Michael Clynes   1133
Chain of Destiny - Nigel Tranter   6314
Checkmate - Dorothy Dunnett   1799
Child of the Mist - Kathleen Morgan   4451
Circle in the Water - Susan Wiggs   6742
City of Light - Alison Macleod   4001
Command of the King - Mary Lide   3773
The Concubine - Norah Lofts   3839
The Courts of Illusion - Rosemary Hawley Jarman   3165
A Crown in Darkness: A Novel about Lady Jane Grey - Margaret Mullally   4512
The Disorderly Knights - Dorothy Dunnett   1800
The Dragon and the Rose - Roberta Gellis   2350
Elizabeth, Captive Princess - Margaret Irwin   3118
Feast in the Morning - Hugh Preston   5175
Feversham - Diane Davidson   1503
The Fifth Queen - Ford Madox Ford   2161
Flame of Fire - Jane Oliver   4722
The Gallows Murder - Michael Clynes   1134
The Game of Kings - Dorothy Dunnett   1801
Gerait's Daughter - Millie J. Ragosta   5241
The Grail Murders - Michael Clynes   1135
Green Darkness - Anya Seton   5751
The Green Madonna - C.E. L'Ami   3617
The Green Salamander - Pamela Hill   2933
The Heir of Allington - Philippa Wiat   6727
Henry VIII and His Six Wives - Maureen Peters   4975
Her Royal Destiny - Carol Maxwell Eady   1820
Here Comes the King - Philip Lindsay   3792
The Heretic - Alison Macleod   4002
Highland Belle - Patricia Grasso   2541
The Hireling - Alison Macleod   4003
The House at Old Vine - Norah Lofts   3845
I Am England - Patricia Wright   6881
I Am Mary Tudor - Hilda Lewis   3750
I Remember Love - Mollie Hardwick   2694
In the Shadow of the Crown - Jean Plaidy   5022
The Ivy Crown: A Biographical Novel of Queen Katherine Parr - Mary M. Luke   3923

James, by the Grace of God - Nigel Tranter   6315
Katharine: The Virgin Widow - Jean Plaidy   5025
Katheryn, the Wanton Queen - Maureen Peters   4976
Kathryn: In the Court of Six Queens - Anne Merton Abbey   1
The King's Achievement - Robert Hugh Benson   459
King's Fool - Margaret Campbell Barnes   325
The King's Good Servant - Olive White   6696
The King's Pleasure - Norah Lofts   3847
The King's Pleasure - Jean Plaidy   5026
The King's Secret Matter - Jean Plaidy   5027
The Knight and the Dove - Lori Wick   6732
A Knight in Shining Armor - Jude Deveraux   1631
The Lady Cicely - Sandra Wilson   6813
The Lady in the Tower - Jean Plaidy   5028
The Lily and the Leopards - Alice Harwood   2765
The Lonely Furrow - Norah Lofts   3849
The Man on a Donkey - H.F.M. Prescott   5170
The Merrymaid - Mollie Hardwick   2696
The Miracle at St. Bruno's - Philippa Carr   925
Mistress Anne - Carolly Erickson   1952
Murder Most Royal - Jean Plaidy   5036
My Lady Glamis - Pamela Hill   2940
My Lady of Cleves - Margaret Campbell Barnes   328
My Lord of Canterbury - Godfrey Turton   6369
My Lord the Fox - Robert York   6932
The Nonsuch Lure - Mary M. Luke   3924
The Nunnery - Dorothy Charques   1001
Pawn in Frankincense - Dorothy Dunnett   1804
The Poisoned Chalice - Michael Clynes   1136
The Prince and the Pauper - Mark Twain   6373
Queen Anne Boleyn - Francis Hackett   2634
The Queen's Grace - Jan Westcott   6646
Queen's Play - Dorothy Dunnett   1805
The Queen's Sister - Sandra Wilson   6815
The Red-Haired Brat - Joanna Dessau   1627
The Reluctant Queen - Molly Costain Haycraft   2796
The Ringed Castle - Dorothy Dunnett   1807
The Riven Realm - Nigel Tranter   6317
The Rose Without a Thorn - Jean Plaidy   5058
Royal Nonesuch: A Tudor Tapestry - Beatrice White   6674
St. Thomas's Eve - Jean Plaidy   5060
The Serpent Garden - Judith Merkle Riley   5336
The Shadow of the Pomegranate - Jean Plaidy   5062
Silver Cross - Mary Johnston   3239
Sister to Jane: The Story of Lady Katharine Grey - Beatrice May   4202
The Sixth Wife - Jean Plaidy   5063
The Spanish Bridegroom - Jean Plaidy   5064
Stage of Fools - Charles Andrew Brady   635
A Stake in the Kingdom - Nigel Tranter   6321
The Strong Room - Jere Hungerford Wheelwright   6671
The Sword and the Flame - Pamela Hill   2945
The Sword of Truth - Gilbert Morris   4472
The Ten-Day Queen - Lozania Prole   5199
Theo and Matilda - Rachel Billington   498
The Thistle and the Rose - Jean Plaidy   5069
A Trail of Blood - Jeremy Potter   5143
The Traitors of Bosworth - Robert Farrington   2021
Tudor Agent - Robert Farrington   2022
The Tudor Rose - Margaret Campbell Barnes   329
Uneasy Lies the Head - Jean Plaidy   5071
Warm Wind, West Wind - Anne Irwin Matthew   4188
A Wayside Tavern - Norah Lofts   3862
The White Rose Murders - Michael Clynes   1137
Windsor Castle - William Harrison Ainsworth   59
The Wise Virgin - Hebe Elsna   1934
Women of Ashdon - Valerie Anand   135
The Wrong Plantagenet - Marian Palmer   4781
Young Bess - Margaret Irwin   3123
The Young Elizabeth - Jennette Letton   3730

Turk-Magyr Wars

Rakossy - Cecelia Holland   2995

Ulandi, Battle of

Bush War! - William Moore   4447

Underground Railroad

Bride of the River - Laura B. Harris   2723
A Clouded Star - Anne Parrish   4819
The Drums of Morning - Philip Van Doren Stern   5997
Except for Me and Thee - Jessamyn West   6628
Fire Bell in the Night - Constance Robertson   5395
Gallows Way - Daoma Winston   6825
The Glass Dove - Sally Carrighar   943
Hacey Miller - James Sherburne   5805
Levi Coffin and the Underground Railroad - Charles Ludwig   3921
Loving Heart - Elsie Singmaster   5869
A Man for the Ages - Irving A. Bacheller   261
The Nancy Flyer - Ernest Poole   5091
North Star Conspiracy - Miriam Grace Monfredo   4428
The Rising Storm - Marguerite Allis   113
Vandemark's Folly - Herbert Quick   5223
Watchfires - Louis Auchincloss   234
Wind Like a Bugle - Leonard Nathan   3722
A Woman Called Moses - Marcy Moran Heidish   2821

Upper Canada Revolt

Bright to the Wanderer - Bruce Lancaster   3638

Utopian Communities

The Brothers of Uterica - Benjamin Capps   887

Valley Forge

Bride of Liberty - Frank Yerby   6909

Vampires

Anno-Dracula - Kim Newman   4595
Better in the Dark - Chelsea Quinn Yarbro   6894
The Bloody Red Baron - Kim Newman   4596
A Candle for D'Artagnan - Chelsea Quinn Yarbro   6895
Children of the Vampire: The Diaries of the Family Dracul - Jeanne Kalogridis   3326
Covenant with the Vampire: The Diaries of the Family Dracul - Jeanne Kalogridis   3327
Crusader's Torch - Chelsea Quinn Yarbro   6897
Darker Jewels - Chelsea Quinn Yarbro   6898
Fevre Dream - George R.R. Martin   4131
A Flame in Byzantium - Chelsea Quinn Yarbro   6899
Hotel Transylvania - Chelsea Quinn Yarbro   6900
Lord of the Dead: The Secret History of Byron - Tom Holland   2999
Lord of the Vampires: The Diaries of the Family Dracul - Jeanne Kalogridis   3328
Mansions of Darkness - Chelsea Quinn Yarbro   6902
Out of the House of Life - Chelsea Quinn Yarbro   6903
The Palace - Chelsea Quinn Yarbro   6904
Path of the Eclipse - Chelsea Quinn Yarbro   6905
The Revenge of Dracula - Peter Tremayne   6335
Seance for a Vampire - Fred Saberhagen   5557
The Seventh Bullet - Daniel D. Victor   6483
Tempting Fate - Chelsea Quinn Yarbro   6906

Vendee Uprising

The White Cockade - Henry Farrand Griffin   2592

Vicksburg, Siege of

By Valour and Arms - James H. Street   6076
Grant's War - Ted Jones   3297
A Hundred Hills - Howard Breslin   667
No Bugles Blow - Bruce Lancaster   3642
Unvexed to the Sea: A Novel of the Vicksburg Campaign - Gerry Morrison   4484

Victorian Period

The Abductors - Stuart Cloete   1121
Abigail - Malcolm Macdonald   3962
Abracadaver - Peter Lovesey   3906
The Admiral's Lady - Mary Ann Gibbs   2395
Affairs of Love - Nicola Thorne   6272
Albert's Victoria - Tyler Whittle   6719
All Desires Known - Malcolm Macdonald   3963
All Their Kingdoms - Madeleine Polland   5084
The Angel of the Opera: Sherlock Holmes Meets the Phantom of the Opera - Sam Siciliano   5842
Apple Tree Lean Down - Mary E. Pearce   4860
Apprentice to the Sea - Philip McCutchan   4240
Artemia - Pamela Hill   2927
The Artist's Daughter - Leslie O'Grady   4698
Ashworth Hall - Anne Perry   4918
Aunt Bel - Guy McCrone   4231
An Autumn in Araby - Carola Salisbury   5565
Autumn Lace - Eileen Jackson   3133
Badge of Glory - Douglas E. Reeman   5287
Beauty for Ashes - Timothy R. Wilson   6816
The Belchamber Scandal - Frances Murray   4533
Belgrave Square - Anne Perry   4919
Belgrave Square - Rachel Summerson   6117
Bertie, Albert Edward, Prince of Wales - Tyler Whittle   6720
Bertie and the Crime of Passion - Peter Lovesey   3907
Bertie and the Seven Bodies - Peter Lovesey   3908
Bertie and the Tinman - Peter Lovesey   3909
Bethlehem Road - Anne Perry   4920
Beware, Beware the Bight of Benin - Philip McCutchan   4241
Beyond All Frontiers - Emma Drummond   1722
Beyond the Shadowlands - Georgina Fleming   2126
The Black Candle - Catherine Cookson   1273
The Black Swan - Philippa Carr   917
The Blackheath Poisonings - Julian Symons   6150
Bless This House - Norah Lofts   3835
Blood Line - Alanna Knight   3515
Bluegate Fields - Anne Perry   4921
The Branch-Bearers - Glen Petrie   4978
The Brocken - Pamela Hill   2929
Buller's Guns - Richard Hough   3048
The Buried Self: A Background to the Poems of Matthew Arnold - Isobel MacDonald   3961
The Cage - Michael Weston   6650
Cain and His Brother - Anne Perry   4922
Call Home the Heart - Jessica Stirling   6040
Callander Square - Anne Perry   4923
The Capricorn Stone - Madeleine Brent   659
Captain Vinegar's Commission - Philip Glazebrook   2428
The Captive - Victoria Holt   3011
A Captive Freedom - Emma Drummond   1724
Cardington Crescent - Anne Perry   4924
A Case of Spirits - Peter Lovesey   3910
The Case of the Revolutionist's Daughter: Sherlock Holmes Meets Karl Marx - Lewis S. Feuer   2076
Cast a Long Shadow - Mary E. Pearce   4861
Castle Barebane - Joan Aiken   43
Castle Dor - Sir Arthur Thomas Quiller-Couch   5226
Castle Heritage - Elisabeth Barr   337
Castle Malindine - Hilary Ford   2163
Castle of Foxes - Alanna Knight   3516
The Cater Street Hangman - Anne Perry   4925
Catherine Carter - Pamela Hansford Johnson   3227
The Changeling - Philippa Carr   918
Charing Cross - Claire Rayner   5260

Charles - Victoria Lincoln   3786
Chase Royal - Donald Seaman   5712
Chase the Wind - E.V. Thompson   6264
Chelsea - Nancy Fitzgerald   2114
Children of the Vampire: The Diaries of the Family Dracul - Jeanne Kalogridis   3326
Circle of Gold - Karen Harper   2710
Clara Reeve - Leonie Hargrave   2705
Claudine's Daughter - Rosalind Laker   3594
Clively Close: Dead as Dead Can Be - Ann Crowleigh   1434
The Clock Tower - Jeanne Montague   4435
Cock of the Walk - Roy Lewis   3762
Colliers Row - Jan Webster   6592
Consort for Victoria - William Vaughan Wilkins   6757
The Consuming Flame: The Story of George Eliot - F.W. Kenyon   3446
Cordelia - Winston Graham   2523
Coronation Summer - Angela Thirkell   6220
Counterfeit of Murder - Ray Harrison   2738
Covent Garden - Claire Rayner   5262
Cracksman on Velvet - Francis Selwyn   5743
Cruel in the Shadow - Lorn MacIntyre   3986
The Crystal Dove - Mollie Hardwick   2692
Cunningham's Revenge - Duncan MacNeil   4012
The Curse of the King - Victoria Holt   3012
The Curse of the Pharaohs - Elizabeth Peters   4948
The Dance of Death - Jeremy Potter   5142
A Dangerous Fortune - Ken Follett   2147
A Dangerous Mourning - Anne Perry   4926
Dark Inheritance - Carola Salisbury   5568
The Dark Pasture - Jessica Stirling   6042
Dark Quartet: The Story of the Brontes - Lynne Reid Banks   290
Dark Winds - Virginia Coffman   1152
The Darkening Leaf - Caroline Stickland   6036
The Darkness of Corn - Caroline Stickland   6037
The Daughter: A Novel Based on the Life of Eleanor Marx - Judith Chernaik   1012
Day Is Coming - William Cameron   869
The Day They Kidnapped Queen Victoria - H.K. Fleming   2127
Deadly Beloved - Alanna Knight   3517
Dean's Watch - Elizabeth Goudge   2494
Dear Laura - Jean Stubbs   6094
Death at Daisy's Folly - Robin Paige   4775
Death at Gallows Green - Robin Paige   4776
Death in the Devil's Acre - Anne Perry   4927
Death of a Dancing Lady - Ray Harrison   2739
Death Wore a Diadem - Iona McGregor   4277
Deathwatch - Ray Harrison   2740
The Deeds of the Disturber - Elizabeth Peters   4949
Defend and Betray - Anne Perry   4928
The Detective and Mr. Dickens - William J. Palmer   4782
The Detective Wore Silk Drawers - Peter Lovesey   3911
The Detling Secret - Julian Symons   6151
The Disappearance of Edwin Drood - Peter Rowland   5521
Disraeli Rising - Maurice Edelman   1852
Dizzy's Woman - George MacBeth   3957
Dr. Gully's Story - Elizabeth Jenkins   3190
Dr. Jekyll and Mr. Holmes - Loren D. Estleman   1970
Dolphin Summer - Carola Salisbury   5569
Double Wedding Ring - Patricia Wendorf   6624
Doubting Castle - Rebecca Kavaler   3373
Dragonmede - Rona Randall   5246
The Drummer Was the First to Die - Liza Pennywitt Taylor   6186
Dual Destiny - Karen Lynn   3939
The Dukes: A Novel - Malcolm Ross   5503
Echoes From the Past - Marjorie McEvoy   4268
The Eden Passion - Marilyn Harris   2730
Eden Rising - Marilyn Harris   2731
Electricity: A Novel - Victoria Glendinning   2431
Elgar on the Journey to Hanley - Keith Alldritt   92

Ellen Bray - Jane Julian   3319
Enter Second Murderer - Alanna Knight   3518
Enter the Lion: A Posthumous Memoir of Mycroft Holmes - Michael P. Hodel   2961
Estella - Alanna Knight   3519
Evil Mark - Graham Miles   4377
Exit Sherlock Holmes - Robert Lee Hall   2657
The Face of a Stranger - Anne Perry   4929
A Falcon for a Queen - Catherine Gaskin   2314
Familiar Acts - June Barraclough   345
The Family of Women - Richard Peck   4883
The Far-Off Rhapsody - Anne-Marie Sheridan   5808
The Far Side of the Hill - Nancy Livingston   3811
Farriers' Lane - Anne Perry   4930
A Father and His Fate - Ivy Compton-Burnett   1228
The Fine and Handsome Captain - Frances Lynch   3933
Fire in the Heart - Henrietta Buckmaster   761
The First to Land - Douglas E. Reeman   5288
Flash for Freedom - George MacDonald Fraser   2203
Flashman - George MacDonald Fraser   2204
Flashman and the Angel of the Lord - George MacDonald Fraser   2205
Flashman at the Charge - George MacDonald Fraser   2209
Flashman's Lady - George MacDonald Fraser   2210
The Flint Anchor - Sylvia Townsend Warner   6569
Flowers for Lilian - Anna Gilbert   2405
Follow the Drum - James Leasor   3699
For God and Glory - Tim Jeal   3171
For They Shall Inherit - Malcolm Macdonald   3964
Forget the Glory - Emma Drummond   1725
The Four Hundred - Stephen Sheppard   5804
The Fox-Red Hills - Cynthia S. Roberts   5374
The French Lieutenant's Woman - John Fowles   2194
The Gambling Man - Catherine Cookson   1276
Gentlemen in England - A.N. Wilson   6795
Gentlemen—The Regiment! - Hugh Talbot   6154
The Ghost and Mrs. Jeffries - Emily Brightwell   681
The Girl - Catherine Cookson   1277
The Girl From Paris - Joan Aiken   47
Glendraco - Laura Black   521
God Is an Englishman - R.F. Delderfield   1587
The God of Mirrors - Robert Reilly   5293
The Gold Seekers - William Stuart Long   3874
The Golden Veil - Paddy Kitchen   3507
Good Morning, Irene - Carole Nelson Douglas   1698
Good Night, Mr. Holmes - Carole Nelson Douglas   1699
The Great Train Robbery - Michael Crichton   1426
Greenyards - Joan Lingard   3796
Greygallows - Barbara Michaels   4359
The Guns of Arrest - Philip McCutchan   4242
H.—: The Story of Heathcliff's Journey Back to Wuthering Heights - Lin Haire-Sargeant   2641
Halfhyde and the Flag Captain - Philip McCutchan   4245
Halfhyde and the Fleet Review - Philip McCutchan   4246
Halfhyde for the Queen - Philip McCutchan   4247
Halfhyde on Zanatu - Philip McCutchan   4251
Halfhyde to the Narrows - Philip McCutchan   4253
Halfhyde's Island - Philip McCutchan   4254
The Hammer of God - Alan Scholefield   5655
Harvest of Death - Ray Harrison   2741
The Heart of the Rose - June Barraclough   346
A Heritage and Its History - Ivy Compton-Burnett   1229
The Heroine's Sister - Frances Murray   4536
Highgate Rise - Anne Perry   4931
The Highwayman and Mr. Dickens - William J. Palmer   4783
The Hippopotamus Pool - Elizabeth Peters   4950
The House of Cards - Leon Garfield   2292
How Do I Love Thee - Lucille Iremonger   3110
The Hoydens and Mr. Dickens - William J. Palmer   4784
The Hungry Goblin: A Victorian Detective Novel - John Dickson Carr   911

189

I Remember Love - Mollie Hardwick   2694

I, Victoria - Cynthia Harrod-Eagles   2755

The Imagination of the Heart - Judith Glover   2437

Imperial Courtesan - F.W. Kenyon   3452

In Still and Stormy Waters - Reay Tannahill   6157

In the Shadow of the Brontes - Louise Brindley   690

An Innocent Woman - Malcolm Macdonald   3967

The Inspector and Mrs. Jeffries - Emily Brightwell   682

The Invention of Truth - Marta Morazzoni   4449

Irene at Large - Carole Nelson Douglas   1700

Irene's Last Waltz - Carole Nelson Douglas   1701

The Iron Roads - Forbes Bramble   644

It Began in Vauxhall Gardens - Jean Plaidy   5023

Jack the Ripper - Richard Gordon   2484

Jekyll, Alias Hyde - Donald Thomas   6240

John Ruskin's Wife - Eva McDonald   4259

Johnnie Cross - Terence de Vere White   6704

The Judas Kiss - Victoria Holt   3015

Julie - Jane Kesner Morris   4479

Killing Cousins - Alanna Knight   3520

King's Royal - John Quigley   5224

Lady Hellfire - Suzanne Robinson   5414

A Lady in Doubt - Annabel Wynne   6891

A Lady of Repute - Janice James   3158

Lady's Maid - Margaret Forster   2188

The Last Camel Died at Noon - Elizabeth Peters   4951

The Last Hero - Peter Forbath   2154

The Last Testament of Oscar Wilde - Peter Ackroyd   19

A Leaf in the Wind - Marie Joseph   3307

Leaves From the Valley - Joanna Trollope   6348

Legacy of the Wolf - Jean Raynes   5274

Lilith - Jean Plaidy   5030

Lillie - David Butler   818

Limmerston Hall - Hester W. Chapman   991

Lion in the Valley - Elizabeth Peters   4952

The List of Seven - Mark Frost   2237

The Little Victoria - Lozania Prole   5196

The Long Shadow - Anna Gilbert   2406

Lord Raven's Widow - Leslie O'Grady   4700

The Lorimer Line - Anne Melville   4332

Louisa Elliott - Ann Victoria Roberts   5370

The Love Child - Catherine Cookson   1279

Lovers All Untrue - Norah Lofts   3851

The Maclarens - C.L. Skelton   5873

Mad Hatter's Holiday - Peter Lovesey   3914

Madeleine - Pamela Elizabeth West   6633

Maggie Craig - Marie Joseph   3308

The Mallen Girl - Catherine Cookson   1280

The Mallen Streak - Catherine Cookson   1282

The Maltese Angel - Catherine Cookson   1283

Marianne - Glen Petrie   4981

The Marigold Field - Diane Pearson   4876

A Marriage of Convenience - Tim Jeal   3172

Mary Reilly - Valerie Martin   4136

Masque of Enchantment - Charlene Cross   1432

Massacre at Cawnpore - Vivian Stuart   6089

The Mating Dance - Rona Randall   5250

Mayfair - Nancy Fitzgerald   2115

Meadowsweet - Gwendoline Butler   820

Memoirs of a Victorian Gentleman: William Makepeace Thackeray - Margaret Forster   2189

The Michaelmas Girls - John Barry   362

Midnight Is a Place - Joan Aiken   52

Midsummer's Eve - Philippa Carr   924

The Mills of Colne - Robert Neill   4572

Miss Martha Mary Crawford - Catherine Marchant   4081

Monday's Child - Mollie Hardwick   2697

The Mortal Gods - Maurice Dolbier   1688

A Most Romantic City - Mary Ann Gibbs   2396

Mother and Son - Ivy Compton-Burnett   1231

The Mountain of Immoderate Desires - Leslie Wilson   6811

Mrs. Betsy, or Widowed and Wed - Francis Marton   4141

Mrs. Jeffries and the Missing Alibi - Emily Brightwell   683

Mrs. Jeffries Dusts for Clues - Emily Brightwell   684

Mrs. Jeffries on the Ball - Emily Brightwell   685

Mrs. Jeffries on the Trail - Emily Brightwell   686

Mrs. Jeffries Plays the Cook - Emily Brightwell   687

Mrs. Jeffries Stands Corrected - Emily Brightwell   688

Mrs. Jeffries Takes Stock - Emily Brightwell   689

The Mudlark - Theodore Bonnet   573

The Mullah From Kashmir - Duncan MacNeil   4016

The Mummy Case - Elizabeth Peters   4953

Murder, I Presume - Gillian Linscott   3807

Murder Makes an Entree - Amy Myers   4540

The Mutual Friend - Frederick Busch   811

My Lady Hoyden - Jane Sheridan   5812

Neighboring Lives - Thomas M. Disch   1648

Never Call It Loving - Dorothy Eden   1859

The Night of the Ripper - Robert Bloch   551

The Northern Correspondent - Jean Stubbs   6099

Officer and Gentleman - Josephine Delves-Broughton   1604

Oh! Where Are Bloody Mary's Earrings? - Robert Player   5079

On a Far Wide Shore - Malcolm Macdonald   3970

On the Night of the Seventh Moon - Victoria Holt   3018

Opal - Helen Ashfield   210

The Origin - Irving Stone   6060

Oscar and Lucinda - Peter Carey   894

Out of the Dark - Norah Lofts   3856

Outward Bound - Philip McCutchan   4256

Paddington Green - Claire Rayner   5266

The Pagoda Tree - Berkely Mather   4181

Painting the Darkness - Robert Goddard   2445

Palais-Royale - Richard Sennett   5747

The Paper Mistress - Dorothea Malm   4045

Paragon Walk - Anne Perry   4932

Parnell and the Englishwoman - Hugh Leonard   3721

The Parson's Daughter - Catherine Cookson   1286

The Passionate Pilgrim - Charles Terrot   6204

Patently Murder - Ray Harrison   2742

Path to the Silent Country - Lynne Reid Banks   291

Pearl - Helen Ashfield   211

Pendragon: Late of Prince Albert's Own - Robert Trevelyan   6337

Pendragon. . .The Montenegran Plot - Robert Trevelyan   6338

Pentecost Alley - Anne Perry   4933

The Piano - Jane Campion   878

Playing the Game - Ian Buruma   810

Polsinney Harbour - Mary E. Pearce   4863

The Pool of St. Branok - Philippa Carr   926

The Pride of the Trevallions - Carola Salisbury   5570

The Prime Minister's Wife - Doris Leslie   3727

The Prince of Eden - Marilyn Harris   2732

Princess in Amber - Evelyn Wilde Mayerson   4205

Princess Pamela - Ray Russell   5534

The Private Life of Florence Nightingale - Richard Gordon   2485

The Proprietor - Ann Schlee   5638

Proud Mary - Iris Gower   2501

The Quade Inheritance - Barbara Ker Wilson   3469

The Quallsford Inheritance - Lloyd Biggle Jr.   495

The Queen and Lord M - Jean Plaidy   5046

Queen Victoria's Bomb - Ronald Clark   1094

The Queen's Husband - Jean Plaidy   5052

Queen's Royal - John Quigley   5225

A Question of Honour - Emma Drummond   1726

The Rag Nymph - Catherine Cookson   1287

Rags of Glory - Stuart Cloete   1126

The Railway King - Margaret Mayhew   4207

Ravenburn - Laura Black   522

Ravenscroft - Dorothy Eden   1860

Red Plush: The Story of the Moorhouse Family - Guy McCrone   4232

Regent Square - Forbes Bramble   645

The Regiment - Christopher Nicole   4620

The Regiment - C.L. Skelton   5874

Resurrection Row - Anne Perry   4934

The Return of Moriarty - John E. Gardner   2287

Return of the Stranger - Reay Tannahill   6158

The Revenge of Dracula - Peter Tremayne   6335

Rhine Journey - Ann Schlee   5639

The Rich Are with You Always - Malcolm Macdonald   3971

Ride the Blue Riband - Rosalind Laker   3598

The Ripper's Apprentice - Donald Thomas   6242

A River Town - Thomas Keneally   3415

The Romance of Charles Dickens - Ursula Bloom   553

The Rookery: A Novel of the Victorian Underworld - Hugh C. Rae   5239

Rose - Martin Cruz Smith   5923

Royal Flash - George MacDonald Fraser   2213

Rutland Place - Anne Perry   4935

St. John's Wood - Nancy Fitzgerald   2116

Sarsen Place - Gwendoline Butler   821

Saturday City - Jan Webster   6593

Scandal at High Chimneys: A Victorian Melodrama - John Dickson Carr   915

The Sea Scape - Mary Lide   3778

A Season for Death - Ray Harrison   2743

The Second Sister - Leslie O'Grady   4701

Secret for a Nightingale - Victoria Holt   3020

Sergeant Verity and the Blood Royal - Francis Selwyn   5744

Sergeant Verity and the Imperial Diamond - Francis Selwyn   5745

Sergeant Verity Presents His Compliments - Francis Selwyn   5746

The Seven Ages - Eva Figes   2084

The Seven-Per-Cent Solution - Nicholas Meyer   4349

Seven Tempest - William Vaughan Wilkins   6761

The Shadowed Spring - Carola Salisbury   5571

Shadows and Images - Meriol Trevor   6344

Sherlock Holmes and the Case of Sabina Hall - L.B. Greenwood   2576

Sherlock Holmes and the Case of the Raleigh Legacy - L.B. Greenwood   2577

Sherlock Holmes and the Mysterious Friend of Oscar Wilde - Russell A. Brown   731

Sherlock Holmes and the Thistle of Scotland - L.B. Greenwood   2578

Sherlock Holmes Meets Annie Oakley - Stanley Shaw   5782

Sherlock Holmes vs. Dracula - Loren D. Estleman   1976

Sherlock in Love - Sena Jeter Naslund   4557

Silence in Hanover Close - Anne Perry   4936

Silver Linings - Shirley Davies-Owens   1508

The Sins of the Wolf - Anne Perry   4937

Sister Beneath the Sheet - Gillian Linscott   3808

Sisters & Lovers - Nicola Thorne   6274

The Sleep of Life - Richard Gordon   2486

The Slow Awakening - Catherine Marchant   4082

The Snake, the Crocodile, and the Dog - Elizabeth Peters   4954

Soho Square - Claire Rayner   5268

Sons of Fortune - Malcolm Macdonald   3973

Sphere of Death - Ray Harrison   2744

The Stallion Man - Judith Glover   2438

Stand We at Last - Zoe Fairbairns   1999

The Standing Hills - Caroline Stickland   6038

The Steps of the Sun - Joanna Trollope   6350

The Store - Michael Pearson   4879

Stormswift - Madeleine Brent   662

The Strand - Claire Rayner   5269

Stranger at the Wedding - Frances Lynch   3934

Strathgallant - Laura Black   523

The Street Sparrows - Rose Ayers   249

A Sudden, Fearful Death - Anne Perry   4938

The Summer of the Royal Visit - Isabel Colegate   1199

The Sutburys - Pamela Hill   2944

Sweet Songbird - Teresa Crane   1418

Swing, Swing Together - Peter Lovesey   3915

Talleyman - John James   3161

Tessa d'Arblay - Malcolm Macdonald 3974

That Spanish Woman - F.W. Kenyon 3461

Theo and Matilda - Rachel Billington 498

These Were the Brontes - Dorothy Helen Cornish 1332

This Dark Monarchy - Francis W. Leary 3698

The Tick of Death - Peter Lovesey 3916

Time and Chance - Gwen Davenport 1501

Tincture of Death - Ray Harrison 2745

To Love a Stranger - Barbara Paul 4839

To Seize the Passing Dream - Ted Berkman 479

The Tontine - Thomas B. Costain 1371

Too Late! Too Late! The Maiden Cried - Joan Fleming 2128

Tournament of the Shadows - Nicholas Carnac 901

Trade Wind - M.M. Kaye 3378

Traitors Gate - Anne Perry 4939

The Trevarton Inheritance - Malcolm Macdonald 3976

The Trial of Elizabeth Cree: A Novel of the Limehouse Murders - Peter Ackroyd 21

Trumpeter, Sound! - D.L. Murray 4528

The Two Farms - Mary E. Pearce 4865

Until the Colors Fade - Tim Jeal 3173

Vanity Fair - William Makepeace Thackeray 6213

The Veil of Illusion - Rebecca Ryman 5545

The Vesey Inheritance - Gwendoline Butler 822

Victoria and Albert - Evelyn Anthony 166

Victoria Victorious - Jean Plaidy 5073

The Vision of Stephen: An Elegy - Lolah Burford 775

Vollands - Pamela Hill 2947

Watson's Apology - Beryl Bainbridge 271

Waxwork - Peter Lovesey 3917

The West End Horror - Nicholas Meyer 4350

When the Emperor Dies - Mason McCann Smith 5926

Where the Willows Weep - Patricia Shaw 5781

The White Rajah - Nicholas Monsarrat 4433

The Whitechapel Horrors - Edward B. Hanna 2678

Why Kill Arthur Potter? - Ray Harrison 2746

Wide Sargasso Sea - Jean Rhys 5312

The Widow of Windsor - Jean Plaidy 5076

The Widow of Windsor - Tyler Whittle 6723

Wild Cat - Laura Black 524

Wild Decembers: A Biographical Portrait of the Brontes - Hilda Crystal White 6681

Willowwood - Mollie Hardwick 2699

Willowwood - Elizabeth Savage 5619

The Wings of Morning - Karen Harper 2714

The Winter Bride - Carola Salisbury 5572

The Wizard's Daughter - Barbara Michaels 4362

Wobble to Death - Peter Lovesey 3918

A Woman by Design - Frances Kennett 3426

A Woman of Quality - Jan Westcott 6649

The Women of Eden - Marilyn Harris 2734

The Women of Whitechapel and Jack the Ripper - Paul West 6638

The World From Rough Stones - Malcolm Macdonald 3979

The Young Victoria - Tyler Whittle 6724

Zemindar - Valerie Fitzgerald 2117

Vietnam War

Saigon - Anthony Grey 2588

Vigilantes

Me and Gallagher - Jack Farris 2023

The Ox-Bow Incident - Walter Van Tilburg Clark 1096

A Revolutionary Woman - Sheila Fugard 2248

Vigilante - Richard Summers 6116

Vikings

The Adversary - Jan Widgery 6738

Beguiled - Alice Borchardt 577

By Love Enslaved - Phoebe Conn 1255

Byzantium - Michael Ennis 1945

The Cross and the Sword - Evangeline Walton 6558

Devoted - Alice Borchardt 578

Eaters of the Dead - Michael Crichton 1425

The Edge of Light - Joan Wolf 6839

The Foster Brothers - Edward Frankland 2202

The Fourteenth of October - Bryher 742

The Gallowglass - Howard Breslin 666

The Greenlanders - Jane Smiley 5915

Gudrid's Saga - Constance Irwin 3115

The Hammer and the Cross - Harry Harrison 2736

I Am England - Patricia Wright 6881

The Ice Shirt - William T. Vollmann 6509

The Iron Crown - Clare Barroll 354

King Hereafter - Dorothy Dunnett 1802

The Kings in Winter - Cecelia Holland 2991

The Lion of Ireland - Morgan Llywelyn 3822

The Long Ships - Frans Gunnar Bengtsson 442

Lord of Hawkfell Island - Catherine Coulter 1376

The Marsh King - C. Walter Hodges 2975

The Price of Blood - Doris Sutcliffe Adams 24

Princess of the Veil - Helen Mittermeyer 4420

Raven's Wind - Victor Canning 883

Runestone - Don Coldsmith 1186

This Land Fulfilled - Charles Andrew Brady 636

Two Ravens - Cecelia Holland 2997

The Viking - Edison Marshall 4113

A Viking's Daughter - John Andrews 147

The Viking's Woman - Heather Graham 2520

A Wayside Tavern - Norah Lofts 3862

West with the Vikings - Edison Marshall 4114

The Winter Servant - M.H. Davis 1537

Vincennes, Battle of

The Big Knives - Bruce Lancaster 3635

Voodoo

Voodoo Dreams: A Novel of Marie Laveau - Jewell Parker Rhodes 5310

Wagon Trains

The Argonauts - Yvonne Schoell 5645

Blood on the Divide - William W. Johnstone 3265

Bound for the Promised Land - Richard Marius 4083

The Buckskin Girl: A Novel of the California Trail in the Mid-Nineteenth Century - Gwen Moffat 4426

The Cavalryman - Harold Sinclair 5861

Covered Wagon - Emerson Hough 3041

Down From the Mountain - Louis Charbonneau 997

The Fancher Train - Amelia Bean 395

The Far Country - Marthedith Furnas 2258

Grim Journey - Hoffman Birney 509

The Hallelujah Train - Bill Gulick 2614

Heroine of the Prairies: A Romance of the Oregon Trail - Sheba Hargreaves 2707

I Am Lidian - Naomi Lane Babson 253

Independence! - Dana Fuller Ross 5476

Jornada - Robert L. Duffus 1754

Journey by the River - John Prescott 5173

Kansas Blue - Dylan Harson 2758

The Land Is Bright - Archie Binns 501

The Lost Wagon - James Arthur Kjelgaard 3509

The Medicine Whip - Max Hennessy 2835

The Mothers - Vardis Fisher 2109

Mountains Ahead - Martha Ferguson McKeown 4284

My Father's World - Michael Phillips 4989

Nebraska! - Dana Fuller Ross 5480

The No-Return Trail - Sonia Levitin 3741

Northwest Passage - David Thompson 6258

On to Oregon! - Honore Morrow 4490

Oregon! - Dana Fuller Ross 5484

Oregon Bride - Rosanne Bittner 514

The Overland Trail - Wendi Lee 3712

The Pilgrimage - Ann B. Ross 5463

The Pioneers - Courtney Ryley Cooper 1296

The Reluctant Bridegroom - Gilbert Morris 4467

Tamsen - David Galloway 2273

The Taste of Time - Ferol Egan 1892

Texas! - Dana Fuller Ross 5490

The Ungodly: A Novel of the Donner Party - Richard Rhodes 5311

The Vision Is Fulfilled - Kay L. McDonald 4262

Wagons to Tucson - Ed Newsom 4604

Wagons West - Leslie Turner White 6692

The Way West - A.B. Guthrie Jr. 2628

Wheels West - Homer Croy 1438

Winter Harvest - Norah Lofts 3863

Wyoming! - Dana Fuller Ross 5494

Wagram, Battle of

The Battle of Wagram - Gilles Lapouge 3664

Wales—England Conflict

Falls the Shadow - Sharon Kay Penman 4903

Here Be Dragons - Sharon Kay Penman 4904

The Hooded Falcon - Prudence Andrew 140

The Reckoning - Sharon Kay Penman 4906

War of 1812

1812 - David Nevin 4586

An American, Sir - Corwin Root 5459

Bayou - Pamela Jekel 3183

Black Ivory - Polan Banks 292

The Border Captains - Jason Manning 4072

Bright Captivity - Eugenia Price 5180

Bright Journey - August Derleth 1614

The Brooks Legend - William Donohue Ellis 1928

Call the New World - John Edward Jennings 3199

Captain Caution - Kenneth Roberts 5385

The Captain From Connecticut - C.S. Forester 2171

The Citadel of the Lakes - Myron David Orr 4754

Clear for Action! - Noel B. Gerson 2362

The Corsair: A Biographical Novel of Jean Lafitte, Hero of the Battle of New Orleans - Madeleine Fabiola Kent 3444

The Court Martial of Commodore Perry - James A. Rhodes 5307

Crimson Is the Eastern Shore - Don Tracy 6308

A Daughter of Liberty - Allan Cole 1196

Dolley - Rita Mae Brown 727

D'ri and I - Irving A. Bacheller 257

The Fallon Pride - Reagan O'Neal 4742

The Far Side of the World - Patrick O'Brian 4663

The Fleet in the Forest - Carl Daniel Lane 3654

The Fortune of War - Patrick O'Brian 4664

Gateway to Empire - Allen W. Eckert 1842

A Generation of Leaves - Robert S. Bloom 552

Give Me the Wind - Jan Jordan 3302

The Golden Season - Oriana Akinson 60

The Gorgeous Hussy - Samuel Hopkins Adams 30

Grand Parade - G.B. Lancaster 3649

The Happy Parrot - Robert W. Chambers 977

Hate - Arthur Douglas Smith 5918

Hearts of Hickory - John Trotwood Moore 4442

Here Comes a Candle - Jane Aiken Hodge 2964

The Horn and the Forest - Jamie Lee Cooper 1313

Jackson: A Novel - Max Byrd 837

Jonathan Dearborn: A Novel of the War of 1812 - Willard Wallace 6540

Kentucky Home - Betty Layman Receveur 5283

Letter of Marque - Andrew Hepburn 2849

The Lively Lady - Kenneth Roberts 5386

Long Pennant - Oliver La Farge 3573

Luise - Dawn Stewart Field 2079

Magnificent Destiny - Paul I. Wellman 6619

Marcel Armand - Sallie Bell 424

Masque of Jade - Emma Merritt 4344

Masque of Sapphire - Deana James   3156
My Blood and My Treasure - Mary Schumann   5674
My Dear Cousin - Peggy Hoffmann   2977
My Love, My Enemy - Jan Cox Speas   5958
The Mysterious Death of Meriwether Lewis - Ron Burns   802
The New Hope - Joseph C. Lincoln   3784
O Genesee - Janet O'Daniel   4688
Oh, Promised Land - James H. Street   6079
Old Hickory - Noel B. Gerson   2379
The President's Lady - Irving Stone   6063
Promises to Keep - Jocelyn Stirling   6051
Queen Dolley: The Life and Times of Dolley Madison - Dorothy Clarke Wilson   6806
The Rake and the Hussy - Robert W. Chambers   981
River's Run - Jane Ludlow Abbot   7
The Salem Frigate - John Edward Jennings   3205
Savannah - Eugenia Price   5186.
The Sea and the Sand - Christopher Nicole   4621
The Sea Panther: A Novel about the Commander of the U.S.S. Constitution - Philip Vail   6397
The Seekers - John Jakes   3153
A Sorrow in Our Heart - Allen W. Eckert   1844
The Splendor Stays: An Historic Novel Based on the Lives of the Seven Hart Sisters of Saybrook - Marguerite Allis   114
Stronghold - Donald Barr Chidsey   1065
The Surgeon's Mate - Patrick O'Brian   4674
Sword of Vengeance - Kerry Newcomb   4593
That Skipper From Stonington - Theda Kenyon   3464
This Is the House - Deborah Hill   2921
This Land Is Ours - Louis Zara   6953
Thread of Scarlet - Ben Ames Williams   6767
To Keep Us Free - Marguerite Allis   115
Trumpet in the Wilderness - Robert S. Harper   2717
Vision of the Eagle - Kay L. McDonald   4263
Visions of a Heart - Emily Carmichael   899
War Clouds - Donald Clayton Porter   5131
Wolves Against the Moon - Julia Cooley Altrocchi   123

War of the Austrian Succession

A Day of Battle - Vincent Sheean   5787

War of the Roses

Anne of Geierstein - Sir Walter Scott   5689
Beloved Lady - Barbara Jefferis   3174
The Black Arrow - Robert Louis Stevenson   6008
Blood of the Boar - Margaret Abbey   2
The Book of Shadows - C.L. Grace   2505
The Broken Sword - Rhoda S. Edwards   1885
The Courts of Illusion - Rosemary Hawley Jarman   3165
Crouchback - Carola Oman   4732
Crown in Candlelight - Rosemary Hawley Jarman   3166
Crown of Roses - Valerie Anand   127
The Daughter of Time - Josephine Tey   6209
Death and the Chapman - Kate Sedley   5715
The Dragon and the Rose - Roberta Gellis   2350
The Dragon Waiting: A Masque of History - John M. Ford   2165
The Everlasting Covenant - Robyn Carr   939
The Fate of Princes - P.C. Doherty   1673
Fire and Morning - Francis W. Leary   3696
Fortune's Wheel - Rhoda S. Edwards   1886
The Golden Yoke: A Novel of the War of the Roses - Olive Eckerson   1837
The Heart Is a Traitor - Margaret Abbey   4
The Holy Innocents - Kate Sedley   5717
I Remember Love - Mollie Hardwick   2694
The Killing of Richard the Third - Robert Farrington   2020
The King's Bed - Margaret Campbell Barnes   324
The King's Grey Mare - Rosemary Hawley Jarman   3167

The Last of the Barons - Edward Bulwer-Lytton   769
Less Fortunate than Fair - Sandra Wilson   6814
The Lodestar - Pamela Belle   432
The Lords of Lancaster - Pamela Bennetts   452
Martin Valliant - Warwick Deeping   1578
Merchant of the Ruby - Alice Harwood   2766
The Merchant Prince - Henry Christopher Bailey   267
The Plymouth Cloak - Kate Sedley   5718
A Question of Choice - Prudence Andrew   143
Red Rose of Anjou - Jean Plaidy   5054
The Reluctant Queen: The Story of Anne of York - Jean Plaidy   5056
Richard III: The Last Plantagenet - Tyler Whittle   6722
The Rose at Harvest End - Eleanor Fairburn   2003
The Son of York - Margaret Abbey   5
The Spitfire - Bertrice Small   5912
The Star of Lancaster - Jean Plaidy   5065
The Summer Queen - Alice Walworth Graham   2512
The Sun in Splendour - Jean Plaidy   5066
The Sunne in Splendour - Sharon Kay Penman   4907
The Swan and the Rose - Francis W. Leary   3697
Trumpet at the Gate - Jan Widgery   6739
Tudor Agent - Robert Farrington   2022
The Tudor Rose - Margaret Campbell Barnes   329
An Unknown Welshman - Jean Stubbs   6100
The Warwick Heiress - Margaret Abbey   6
We Speak No Treason - Rosemary Hawley Jarman   3168
The White Boar - Marian Palmer   4780
The White Queen - Lesley J. Nickell   4611
The White Rose - Jan Westcott   6648
The Winter Rose - Millie J. Ragosta   5243

War of the Spanish Succession

The Mohawk Ladder - Noel B. Gerson   2377
Ram: Being the Tale of One Ramillies Anstruther - Winchombe Taylor   6193
The Sable Lion - Jan Van Dorp   6405

Wars of Montrose

The Dark Rose - Maurice Walsh   6549

Waterloo, Battle of

Allegra - Clare Darcy   1483
The Charterhouse of Parma - Stendhal   5993
Eliza Stanhope - Joanna Trollope   6347
Feather Castles - Patricia Veryan   6462
The Flight of the Eagle - Donald Thomas   6239
An Infamous Army - Georgette Heyer   2892
The Limits of Glory: A Novel of Waterloo - James McDonough   4265
Midsummer Moon - Karen Lynn   3940
The Spanish Bride - Georgette Heyer   2902
The Thousand Fires - Anne Powers   5155
The Twisted Sword - Winston Graham   2531
Vanity Fair - William Makepeace Thackeray   6213
Waterloo - Bernard Cornwell   1350
Waterloo - Manuel Komroff   3536
Waterloo - Frederic E. Smith   5920
Why Waterloo? - Alan Patrick Herbert   2850

Whaling

Arctic Treachery - Richard Woodman   6858
Captain Marooner - Louis B. Davidson   1504
Diamond Head - Houston Branch   647
The Greenlander - Mark Adlard   38
Harpoon - C.W. Nicol   4612
Harpoon in Eden - F. van Wyck Mason   4152
The Jonah Man - Henry Carlisle   895
Nantucket Woman - Diana Gaines   2269
The New England Story - Henry Beetle Hough   3046
The Silver Dolphin - Velda Johnston   3264

Spirit Knife - Donald Clayton Porter   5128
Storm Tide - Allan R. Bosworth   590
That Skipper From Stonington - Theda Kenyon   3464
The White Dawn - James Houston   3053

Whiskey Rebellion

The Delectable Country - Leland Dewitt Baldwin   280
Genesee Fever - Carl Lamson Carmer   898

Wiemar Republic

A Princess in Berlin - Arthur R.G. Solmssen   5939

Wild West Show

Buffalo Girls - Larry McMurtry   4296

Wilderness, Battle of the

Thin Moon and Cold Mist - Kathleen O'Neal Gear   2330

Wilkinson Plot

Morning Time - Charles Kendall O'Neill   4743
West Goes the Road - Tim Pridgen   5192

Witchcraft and Sorcery

The Age of Miracles - Catherine MacCoun   3960
All the King's Ladies - Janice Law   3678
Always a River - Drayton Mayrant   4211
Baneful Sorceries, or The Countess Bewitched - Joan Sanders   5585
Bard: The Odyssey of the Irish - Morgan Llywelyn   3816
Beguiled - Alice Borchardt   577
Black Body - H.C. Turk   6361
Child of the Mist - Kathleen Morgan   4451
The Corn King and the Spring Queen - Naomi Mitchison   4419
Corner the Moon - Shirley Barker   310
Crown in Candlelight - Rosemary Hawley Jarman   3166
The Crystal Cave - Mary Stewart   6029
A Dangerous Innocence - Victoria Lincoln   3787
Dark Possession - Alice Alison Lide   3771
The Dark Stranger - Dorothy Charques   999
Daughter of Satan - Jean Plaidy   5011
The Devil and the Mathers - Edward E. Elliott   1914
The Dragon of the Ishtar Gate - L. Sprague De Camp   1555
Druids - Morgan Llywelyn   3817
Elegant Witch - Robert Neill   4568
Empire of the Eagle - Andre Norton   4649
The Falcon and the Flower - Virginia Henley   2826
Familiar Spirits - Leonard Tourney   6298
Faust - Robert Nye   4654
Gallows Hill - Frances Winwar   6831
Gilded Spurs - Grace Ingram   3105
Hellbane - Anthony Esler   1963
The Hollow Hills - Mary Stewart   6030
The Hunchback of Notre Dame - Victor Hugo   3076
I, Tituba, Black Witch of Salem - Maryse Conde   1233
In Adam's Fall - Constance Dodge   1666
In Pursuit of the Green Lion - Judith Merkle Riley   5334
Lady of Monkton - Elizabeth Byrd   835
Lamia: A Witch - Georgia Elizabeth Taylor   6183
The Last Enchantment - Mary Stewart   6031
The Last of the Barons - Edward Bulwer-Lytton   769
Malefice - Leslie Wilson   6810
Mass for Arras - Andrzej Szczypiorski   6153
Medea - Miranda Seymour   5764

The Memoirs of Elizabeth Frankenstein - Theodore Roszak 5508
A Mirror for Witches - Esther Forbes 2157
The Mists of Avalon - Marion Zimmer Bradley 626
The Moon under Her Feet - Ceysta Kinstler 3503
The Murder in the Tower - Jean Plaidy 5035
The Oracle Glass - Judith Merkle Riley 5335
Papa La-Bas - John Dickson Carr 914
Peace, My Daughters - Shirley Barker 314
Portrait of Emma - Lillian Cheatham 1010
The Prince and the Pilgrim - Mary Stewart 6032
Prophecies - Helena Soister 5937
Road to Lendor - Esther Hammon 1966
The Rogue and the Witch - John Edward Newton 4605
The Rose at Harvest End - Eleanor Fairburn 2003
Stately Timber - Rupert Hughes 3075
The Strange Death of Mistress Coffin - Robert J. Begiebing 415
Strange Devices of the Sun and Moon - Lisa Goldstein 2463
Swear by Apollo - Shirley Barker 318
Time of the Unicorn - Barbara Jefferis 3176
A Vision of Light - Judith Merkle Riley 5337
Voodoo Dreams: A Novel of Marie Laveau - Jewell Parker Rhodes 5310
Where Magic Dwells - Rexanne Becnel 411
Whitton's Folly - Pamela Hill 2948
The Wicked Day - Mary Stewart 6033
The Witch and the Priest - Hilda Lewis 3754
The Witch of Manga Reva - Garland Roark 5359

Women's Rights

Artemesia - Anna Banti 295
Beecher: A Novel - Dan McCall 4218
Brave Pursuit - Marguerite Allis 107
Chicago Girls - Edith Freund 2229
Crown Witness - Gillian Linscott 3803
The Crusader - Noel B. Gerson 2364
Dead Man's Sweetheart - Gillian Linscott 3804
Diana Stair - Floyd Dell 1594
An Easy Day for a Lady - Gillian Linscott 3805
Glory and the Lightning - Taylor Caldwell 856
A Lady of Repute - Janice James 3158
Law of the Land - Marguerite Allis 111
Maura's Dream - Joel Gross 2602
The Midwife's Advice - Gay Courter 1389
The Misadventures of Bethany Price - Marian Cockrell 1147
Night Shall Overtake Us - Kate Saunders 5611
The Revolt of Sarah Perkins - Marian Cockrell 1148
Rivington Street - Meredith Tax 6175
Scarlet Women - J.D. Christilian 1077
Seneca Falls Inheritance - Miriam Grace Monfredo 4429
Sierra Triumph - Dana Fuller Ross 5488
Sister Beneath the Sheet - Gillian Linscott 3808
Stand We at Last - Zoe Fairbairns 1999
The Tree of Knowledge - Eva Figes 2085
Watchfires - Louis Auchincloss 234
Whirlwind in Petticoats - Beril Becker 406
The Woman Question - Dorothea Malm 4046

Wonders of the World

The Bronze God of Rhodes - L. Sprague De Camp 1554

World War I

1915: A Novel - Roger McDonald 4264
The Alpha Raid - Alan Scholefield 5651
The American Heiress - Dorothy Eden 1854
April Rising - Susan Sallis 5574
As the Crow Flies - Jeffrey Archer 183
Attack the Lusitania! - Raymond Hitchcock 2956
August 1914 - Alexander Solzhenitsyn 5942

The Beano - Rony Robinson 5411
Beauty for Ashes - Timothy R. Wilson 6816
The Beekeeper's Apprentice, or, On the Segregation of the Queen - Laurie R. King 3487
Behold the Fire - Michael Blankfort 541
The Bellamy Saga - John Pearson 4878
Beloved Soldiers - C.L. Skelton 5871
Benton's Row - Frank Yerby 6908
Birdsong - Sebastian Faulks 2051
Blaize - Anne Melville 4331
Blood Winter - William Patrick 4830
The Bloody Red Baron - Kim Newman 4596
The Blue Max - Jack D. Hunter 3085
Blunted Lance - Max Hennessy 2829
The Bridge on the Drina - Ivo Andric 151
The Bright Blue Sky - Max Hennessy 2830
Buller's Dreadnought - Richard Hough 3047
Buller's Victory - Richard Hough 3049
Burden of Desire - Robert MacNeil 4023
The Burning Man - Stephen Longstreet 3883
Bury Him Among Kings - Elleston Trevor 6341
By the Green of the Spring - John Masters 4171
Bygones - Frank Wilkinson 6762
The Casket Crew - Arch Whitehouse 6709
A Castle in Bavaria - Prince Thibaut d'Orleans 1693
Ceremony of the Innocent - Taylor Caldwell 852
A Certain Splendour - Carola Salisbury 5566
The Cinderpath - Catherine Cookson 1275
A Clear Road to Archangel - Geoffrey Rose 5461
Contessa - Richard Oliver Collin 1209
The Crown Prince - John Barchilon 300
Csardas - Diane Pearson 4875
Curse of Magira - David Bee 413
Daughters of the New World - Susan Richards Shreve 5835
Death of a Schoolboy - Hans Koning 3537
The Devil in Harbour - Catherine Gavin 2319
The Devil's Spy - Michael Hastings 2773
Doctor Zhivago - Boris Pasternak 4824
The Earth and All It Holds - V.J. Banis 287
Eden and Honor - Marilyn Harris 2729
Elena - Judith Egan 1893
The Eleventh Year - Monique Raphel High 2914
The Emperor Franz Joseph - Ottokar Janetschek 3164
The Emperor's Coloured Coat - John Biggins 491
Encore - Monique Raphel High 2915
The Eye in the Door - Pat Barker 307
The Eye of the Lion: A Novel Based on the Life of Mata Hari - Lael Tucker Wertenbaker 6626
Fallen Skies - Philippa Gregory 2581
The Family of Women - Richard Peck 4883
The Fires of Fu Manchu - Cay Van Ash 6399
The First Casualty - William Powell 5149
Flight From Bucharest - R.T. Stevens 6000
Floodtide - Suzanne Goodwin 2475
The Four Winds of Heaven - Monique Raphel High 2916
Gentlemen of Adventure - Ernest K. Gann 2278
The Ghost Road - Pat Barker 308
The Ghosts of Africa - William Stevenson 6013
Give Me the Daggers - Catherine Gavin 2321
Give Us This Day - R.F. Delderfield 1586
Glorious Morning - Julie Ellis 1919
The Golden Honeycomb - Kamala Markandaya 4086
Goshawk Squadron - Derek Robinson 5403
Gossip From the Forest - Thomas Keneally 3413
The Green Leaves of Summer - Ted Willis 6793
The Hampton Women - Julie Ellis 1921
Hanging on the Wire - Gillian Linscott 3806
Heart of War - John Masters 4174
Heaven's Gold - Giles Tippette 6282
Hollywood: A Novel of America in the 1920s - Gore Vidal 6488
A Horseman Riding By - R.F. Delderfield 1588
The Hours of Light - Janet Tanner 6160
How Young They Die - Stuart Cloete 1124
An Ice-Cream War - William Boyd 616
Imperial Winds - Priscilla Napier 4555

In My Father's House - Bodie Thoene 6222
In Pale Battalions - Robert Goddard 2444
In the Company of Eagles - Ernest K. Gann 2279
It's Me Again - Donald Jack 3126
Karl and Rosa - Alfred Doblin 1653
Keeping Secrets - Suzanne Morris 4483
The Ladies of Hanover Square - Rona Randall 5249
The Land of Our Dreams - Nancy Livingston 3812
Landru - Rene Masson 4170
The Last Farewell - Philip McCutchan 4255
The Last Summer of Innocence - Linda Sole 5938
The Last Summer of Mata Hari - Edward Huebsch 3067
The Last Victory - T.N. Murari 4519
The Legacy of Tregaran - Mary Lide 3776
The Lion at Sea - Max Hennessy 2834
Lion in the Evening - Alan Scholefield 5656
London's Child - Philip Boast 560
The Long Afternoon - Ursula Zilinsky 6964
Lord Richard's Passion - Mervyn Jones 3293
Lusitania - David Butler 819
The Magic Ship - Sandra Paretti 4791
The Mallen Lot - Catherine Cookson 1281
Mamigon - Jack Hashian 2772
The Man From St. Petersburg - Ken Follett 2148
The Man Who Loved Mata Hari - Dan Sherman 5813
The Men That God Made Mad: A Novel about Ireland's Easter Rising - W.A. Ballinger 286
Molly - Teresa Crane 1417
Morning's Gate - Ann Victoria Roberts 5371
The Moth - Catherine Cookson 1284
Murder at Wrigley Field - Troy Soos 5949
The New Confessions - William Boyd 617
Night Shall Overtake Us - Kate Saunders 5611
No Man's Land - William Fairchild 2004
Nothing New under the Sun - Riccardo Bacchelli 255
Now, God Be Thanked - John Masters 4177
The Old Enchantment - Sarah Neilan 4565
Once a Gentleman - Donald James 3157
Over There - Thomas Fleming 2130
Over There - Robert Vaughan 6449
Pancho And Black Jack - Fred Bean 398
The Passing Bells - Phillip Rock 5421
A People Betrayed - Alfred Doblin 1654
The Petrograd Consignment - Owen Sela 5739
Playboy Squadron - Arch Whitehouse 6710
Privileged Children - Frances Vernon 6455
Pursuit of Bliss - Betty Palmer Nelson 4577
The Ravi Lancers - John Masters 4178
Rebels: The Irish Rising of 1916 - Peter DeRosa 1622
Redemption - Leon Uris 6393
Regeneration - Pat Barker 309
Remember This Time - Gloria Kurian Broder 703
A Rendezvous in Haiti - Stephen Becker 407
The Rising of the Moon - William Martin 4140
Sabrina - Madeleine Polland 5086
A Sailor of Austria - John Biggins 492
The Salamanca Drum - Dorothy Eden 1861
The Secret Years - Judith Lennox-Smith 3718
Seven Days to Petrograd - Tom Hyman 3094
The Shadow of the Moth: A Novel of Espionage with Virginia Woolf - Ellen Hawkes 2779
Shadows over Castle Rising - Fanny Cradock 1410
The Shooting Party - Isabel Colegate 1197
Shout at the Devil - Wilbur Smith 5930
The Sky and Tomorrow - Thomas William Duncan 1788
The Snow Mountain - Catherine Gavin 2324
A Soldier of the Great War - Mark Helprin 2823
Some Far Elusive Dawn - Emma Drummond 1727
Son of Holmes - John T. Lescroart 3726
Spinners' Wharf - Iris Gower 2502
Squadron Forty-Four - Arch Whitehouse 6711
Squadron Shilling - Arch Whitehouse 6712
Statues in a Garden - Isabel Colegate 1198
Strange Meeting - Susan Hill 2952
The Summer Day Is Done - R.T. Stevens 6001

The Summer of the Bashinskeys - Diane Pearson 4877
Sunshine and Shadow - Antonia Van-Loon 6426
That's Me in the Middle - Donald Jack 3129
Three Cheers for Me - Donald Jack 3131
Tigerlilies - Judith Glover 2439
A Time for Silence - Philippa Carr 930
To the Honor of the Fleet - Robert H. Pilpel 5002
A Token of Jewels - Diane Cory 1353
Tolbecken - Samuel Shellabarger 5798
TR - Noel B. Gerson 2385
The Two-Headed Eagle - John Biggins 493
"Utmost Fish!" - Hugh Wray McCann 4219
Verge of Glory - Frederick Wight 6747
War Comes to Castle Rising - Fanny Cradock 1411
War Story: A Novel - Derek Robinson 5404
The Ways of Women - Elaine Crowley 1436
The Wedding Guest - Anna Gilbert 2407
While Paris Danced - Patricia Wright 6886
White Nights, Red Dawn - Frederick Nolan 4634
The Wind Brings Up the Rain - Eric Malpass 4051
The Wingless Bird - Catherine Cookson 1292
Wings for the Chariots - Arch Whitehouse 6713
Wings of the Morning - David Beaty 402
The Wishing Tree - Sandra Paretti 4794
The World as I Found It - Bruce Duffy 1755
The Young Men of Paris - Stephen Longstreet 3893
Young Mrs. Cavendish and the Kaiser's Men - K.K. Beck 405

World War II

Anna, Ann, Annie - Thomas Trebitsch Parker 4808
Artemesia - Anna Banti 295
Back to Battle - Max Hennessy 2828
Badenheim 1939 - Aharon Appelfeld 174
Beginning the World Again - Roberta Silman 5851
Bide Me Fair - Harvey Howells 3060
Bittersweet - Leslie Li 3769
Born of War - Thomas Taylor 6192
Buried Caesars - Stuart M. Kaminsky 3332
The Career of Magda V. - Joseph Machlis 3982
Carnal Hours - Max Allan Collins 1210
Chikara! - Robert Skimin 5876
Contessa - Helene Mansfield 4076
The Cup of Wrath - Mary Glazener 2429
Dancing in the Dark - Stuart M. Kaminsky 3334
The Day of the Scorpion - Paul Scott 5682
The Devil Met a Lady - Stuart M. Kaminsky 3335
Eagles at War - Walter J. Boyne 620
Eva - Ib Melchior 4329
The Exile of Celine - Tom Clark 1095
The Fala Factor - Stuart M. Kaminsky 3337
A Family Matter - James Roosevelt 5458
Farewell to My Concubine - Lilian Lee 3709
Fielder's Choice - Rick Norman 4646

For Every Sin - Aharon Appelfeld 175
The Free Frenchman - Piers Paul Read 5277
From the Terrace - John O'Hara 4703
A Future Arrived - Phillip Rock 5420
A Gathering of Saints - Christopher Hyde 3092
Generations of Winter - Vassily Aksyonov 61
Gentlemen of Adventure - Ernest K. Gann 2278
Goldeneye - Malcolm Macdonald 3965
The Greta Garbo Murder Case - George Baxt 385
The Hangman's Crusade - James Barwick 370
He Done Her Wrong - Stuart M. Kaminsky 3338
High Midnight - Stuart M. Kaminsky 3339
Hitler Has Won - Frederic Mullally 4511
A Horseman Riding By - R.F. Delderfield 1588
The Iron Curtain - Robert Vaughan 6447
The Jewel in the Crown - Paul Scott 5684
Joseph - Mervyn Jones 3292
Journey into Fire - Patricia Wright 6882
The King - Donald Barthelme 365
The Last Innocent Hour - Margot Abbott 8
Last Man to Die - Michael Dobbs 1652
The Lion's Way - Lewis Orde 4750
The Living Reed - Pearl S. Buck 756
The Longest Road - Jeanne Williams 6781
Luciano's Luck - Jack Higgins 2912
The Man on the Train - W.J. Chaput 995
The Marrying Kind - Jessica Stirling 6046
The Melting Clock - Stuart M. Kaminsky 3342
Murder and the First Lady - Elliott Roosevelt 5444
Murder at the Palace - Elliott Roosevelt 5445
Murder in the Blue Room - Elliott Roosevelt 5446
Murder in the Chateau - Elliott Roosevelt 5447
Murder in the East Room - Elliott Roosevelt 5448
Mussolini - Alan Gelb 2348
Once More the Hawks - Max Hennessy 2836
The Only Thing to Fear - David Poyer 5160
Pacific Cavalcade - Virginia Coffman 1157
Poland - James A. Michener 4373
Polonaise - Piers Paul Read 5278
Poor Butterfly - Stuart M. Kaminsky 3345
Regards From the Dead Princess: A Novel of a Life - Kenize Mourad 4505
Rommel and the Rebel - Lawrence Wells 6622
A Royal Murder - Elliott Roosevelt 5456
Schindler's List - Thomas Keneally 3416
Second Generation - Howard Fast 2043
Seedtime and Harvest - Mary E. Pearce 4864
Shadow of the Wolf - James Barwick 371
Shanghai - Christopher New 4588
Smart Moves - Stuart M. Kaminsky 3346
Stallion Gate - Martin Cruz Smith 5924
Stones From the River - Ursula Hegi 2816
Till the End of Time - Allen Appel 170
The Tin Drum - Gunther Grass 2540
To the End of Her Days - Malcolm Macdonald 3975
The Towers of Silence - Paul Scott 5685

Tregaran - Mary Lide 3779
Tzili: The Story of a Life - Aharon Appelfeld 180
The Very Rich Hours of Count von Stauffenberg - Paul West 6637
War and Remembrance - Herman Wouk 6875
Warsaw Requiem - Bodie Thoene 6229
Wartime Lies - Louis Begley 416
The White Hotel - D.M. Thomas 6237
The White House Pantry Murder - Elliott Roosevelt 5457
The Wind Brings Up the Rain - Eric Malpass 4051
The Winds of War - Herman Wouk 6876
Wings of the Morning - David Beaty 402
Winter Fire - William R. Trotter 6352
The Wisdom of Stones - Greg Matthews 4192
The Year of Our War - Gloria Goldreich 2462

Wounded Knee, Battle of

A Creek Called Wounded Knee - Douglas C. Jones 3277
Dance Back the Buffalo - Milton Lott 3899
The Day the Sun Died - Dale Van Every 6408
A Good Day to Die - Thomas Wakefield Blackburn 525
Song of Wovoka - Earl Murray 4531

Yom Kippur War

The Glory - Herman Wouk 6873

Yorktown, Battle of

Blind Journey - Bruce Lancaster 3636
Cato's War - Guy Wheeler 6655
Dawn's Early Light - Elswyth Thane 6215
A Few Painted Feathers - Stephen Longstreet 3886
The Lady From Yorktown - Eva McDonald 4260
The Proud and the Free - Howard Fast 2042
Sea Road to Yorktown - Harvey Haislip 2644
Storm the Last Rampart - David Taylor 6180
Yorktown - Burke Davis 1513

Zulu Empire

Great Elephant - Alan Scholefield 5654

Zulu War

Bush War! - William Moore 4447
Soldier of the Queen - Max Hennessy 2837
The Tune That They Play - William Clive 1120
When the Lion Feeds - Wilbur Smith 5931
Yellowstone Kelly - Peter Bowen 602

Fictional Character Name Index

This index alphabetically lists the major fictional characters in each featured title. (Note: Historical characters are listed in a separate index.) Each fictional character name is followed by a description of the character. There may be multiple entries for a character if the descriptions differ between books. Citations also provide titles, author names, and entry numbers. For characters appearing in more than one book, titles are listed in alphabetical order.

A

Abbabba, Hadi Guwah (Adventurer)
Slave - William Malliol 4041

Abberline, Frederick (Detective—Police)
The Night of the Ripper - Robert Bloch 551

Abbot, Jim (Veteran)
The Marrying Kind - Jessica Stirling 6046

Abbott, Jim (Teacher)
The Penny Wedding - Jessica Stirling 6047

Abbott, Lady Letitia (Noblewoman)
Tish - Cissie Miller 4381

Abel, Aaron (Businessman)
The Moneyman - Judith Liederman 3781

Abel, Jennie (Young Woman)
The Moneyman - Judith Liederman 3781

Abercrombie, Estella (Actress)
Affairs of Love - Nicola Thorne 6272

Abercrombie, Lindsey (Doctor)
Affairs of Love - Nicola Thorne 6272

Abh Allah (Warrior)
The Lord of the Last Days: Visions of the Year 1000 - Homero Aridjis 188

Abidaga (Businessman)
The Bridge on the Drina - Ivo Andric 151

Abimelech (Warrior)
Prophets and Warriors - Peter Danielson 1473

Abraham (Writer)
The Book of Abraham - Marek Halter 2665

Abram (Young Man)
The King's Persons - Joanne Greenberg 2573

Abrois, Noe (Doctor)
The Year of the Death - Reuben R. Merliss 4343

Acco (Military Personnel)
Winter Quarters - Alfred Duggan 1775

Acconciaiuoco, Guido (Knight)
The True Cross - Carlo Scarfoglio 5629

Achates (Warrior)
Paris of Troy - George Baker 273

Achilles (Warrior)
The Greek Generals Talk: Memoirs of the Trojan War - Phillip Parotti 4817
The Invaders - Peter Danielson 1469
Troy - Richard Matturro 4194

Whom the Gods Would Destroy - Richard Powell 5148

Acklen, Adelicia (Southern Belle)
Dinner at Belmont - Alfred Leland Crabb 1398
Lodging at the Saint Cloud - Alfred Leland Crabb 1403

Acklen, Joseph (Gentleman)
Dinner at Belmont - Alfred Leland Crabb 1398

Acock, Sir John (Gentleman)
The Nunnery - Dorothy Charques 1001

Acominatus, Nicetas (Government Official)
Against the Fall of Night - Michael Arnold 193

Acox, Hamilton (Lawyer; Military Personnel)
The Falling Hills - Perry Lentz 3720

Acton, Richard (Diplomat)
Look Back to Glory - Herbert Ravenel Sass 5607

Adair, Abigail (Widow(er))
The Wings of Morning - Karen Harper 2714

Adair, Arthur (Military Personnel)
The Swan and the Rose - Francis W. Leary 3697

Adair, Daisy (Gentlewoman)
Meadowsweet - Gwendoline Butler 820

Adair, Damien (Doctor)
Secret for a Nightingale - Victoria Holt 3020

Adair, Trelawney (Gentlewoman)
Meadowsweet - Gwendoline Butler 820

Adam, Thomas (Farmer)
The Constant Star - Prudence Andrew 139

Adams, Cameron (Lawyer)
Lantern for the Dark - Jessica Stirling 6045

Adams, Cort (Journalist)
When the Music Changed - Marie R. Reno 5305

Adams, Joel (Farmer; Religious)
Hope of Earth - Jane Gilmore Rushing 5528

Adams, Joel (Settler)
Come Spring - Ben Ames Williams 6764

Adams, John (Sailor)
East Indiaman - Frank Pollard 5087

Adams, Kevin (Pioneer)
The Argonauts - Yvonne Schoell 5645

Adams, Laura (Spy)
Defiant Hearts - Janelle Taylor 6185

Adams, Sam (Editor)
Wandering Star - Steven Yount 6945

Adare, Edward (Nobleman)
Opal - Helen Ashfield 210

Adderly, Mark (Political Figure; Rake)
The Angry Tide - Winston Graham 2521

Addison, Margaret (Frontierswoman; Gentlewoman)
For Love of Two Eagles - Barbara Riefe 5328
The Woman Who Fell From the Sky - Barbara Riefe 5330

Adelaid, Lady (Gentlewoman)
Red Lion and Gold Dragon - Rosemary Sprague 5969

Adelita (Revolutionary)
The Adelita - Oakley Hall 2649

Adi, Lady (Gentlewoman)
The Exile Way - Ann Woodward 6865

Adi (Religious)
Bundori - Laura Joh Rowland 5519

Adiawano (Indian; Royalty)
Savage Gentleman - Noel B. Gerson 2381

Adler, Irene (Singer)
The Canary Trainer - Nicholas Meyer 4348
Good Morning, Irene - Carole Nelson Douglas 1698
Good Night, Mr. Holmes - Carole Nelson Douglas 1699
Irene at Large - Carole Nelson Douglas 1700
Irene's Last Waltz - Carole Nelson Douglas 1701

Adler, Seth (Lawyer)
Members of the Tribe - Richard Kluger 3511

Adriance, Dan (Journalist)
Tenderloin - Samuel Hopkins Adams 33

Adrianna (Gentlewoman)
The Venetian Mask - Rosalind Laker 3603

Adverse, Anthony (Adventurer; Bastard Son)
Anthony Adverse - Hervey Allen 98

Aegeus (Ruler)
Medea - Miranda Seymour 5764

Aelredson, Edward (Nobleman)
Sherwood - Parke Godwin 2449

Aelredson, Edward (Outlaw; Nobleman)
Robin and the King - Parke Godwin 2448

Aeneas (Wanderer)
Dido, Queen of Hearts - Gertrude Atherton 223

Aeneas (Warrior)
Whom the Gods Would Destroy - Richard Powell 5148

Aeshia (Young Woman)
The Gentle Infidel - Lawrence Schoonover 5663

Aethon (Adventurer)
Homer's Daughter - Robert Graves 2546

Agamemnon (Leader; Ruler)
Whom the Gods Would Destroy - Richard
Powell 5148

Agamemnon (Ruler)
Amber Princess - Henry Treece 6325
The Greek Generals Talk: Memoirs of the Trojan War
- Phillip Parotti 4817
Scandal in Troy - Eva Hemmer Hansen 2679

Agar, Robert (Thief)
The Great Train Robbery - Michael Crichton 1426

Agnew, Peter (Settler)
The Sea 'Venture - F. van Wyck Mason 4159

Aguila, Ramon del (Knight)
Eagle of the Gredos - Claude Jack Osgood 4761

Ah-Wen-Ga (Indian; Fiance(e))
Tomahawk - Donald Clayton Porter 5129

Ahbleza (Indian)
Hanta Yo - Ruth Beebe Hill 2951

Ahearn, Kate (Young Woman)
They Were Dreamers - James F. Murphy Jr. 4525

Ahgavni (Spouse)
Mamigon - Jack Hashian 2772

Ahrens, Kurt (Military Personnel)
Guns of Burgoyne - Bruce Lancaster 3640

Ahuna (Young Woman; Artisan)
Children of the Lion - Peter Danielson 1464

Aidan (Royalty)
Alamut - Judith Tarr 6164

Ailerman (Religious)
In the Falcon's Claw: A Novel of the Year 1000 -
Chet Raymo 5257

Ailroth, Father (Religious)
The Raven in the Foregate - Ellis Peters 4969

Aimesley, Dorothy (Young Woman)
Power - Howard Fast 2041

Ainsworth, Jeremy (Military Personnel)
Midsummer Moon - Karen Lynn 3940

Ainvar (Religious)
Druids - Morgan Llywelyn 3817

Airmid (Young Woman)
The Crows of War - Steven Rayson 5276

Akbal Balam (Artist)
Tikal: A Novel about the Maya - Daniel Peters 4947

Akeham, Henry (Teacher; Heir)
Ramillies - Barbara Whitehead 6708

Alane (Prehistoric Human; Young Woman)
The Reindeer Hunters - Joan Wolf 6841

Alard, Catharine (Gentlewoman)
Superstition Corner - Sheila Kaye-Smith 3379

Alaric of Anion (Nobleman)
Princess of Fire - Shannon Drake 1718

Alastair, Dominic (Nobleman)
Devil's Cub - Georgette Heyer 2885

Alastair, Justin (Nobleman)
Devil's Cub - Georgette Heyer 2885
These Old Shades - Georgette Heyer 2906

Alastair, Leonie (Noblewoman)
Devil's Cub - Georgette Heyer 2885

Alavedo, Olivio Fonseca (Saloon Keeper/Owner)
The White Rhino Hotel - Bartle Bull 765

Alba (Witch; Ward)
Black Body - H.C. Turk 6361

Albany, Leondra (Gentlewoman; Heiress)
Albany - Laura Black 519

Albertino (Businessman)
Simple Prayers - Michael Golding 2452

Albine, Salathiel (Frontiersman)
Bedford Village - Hervey Allen 99
The Forest and the Fort - Hervey Allen 100
Toward the Morning - Hervey Allen 101

Albrecht, Father (Religious)
The Godforgotten - Gladys Schmitt 5642

Albriton, Charles (Religious)
Cherished Enemy - Patricia Veryan 6460

Albriton, Rosamond (Gentlewoman)
Cherished Enemy - Patricia Veryan 6460

Alcock, J.D. (Teacher)
To Serve Them All My Days - R.F. Delderfield 1591

Alden, Susanna (Teacher)
No Roof but Heaven - Jeanne Williams 6782

Alderley, Barbara (Gentlewoman)
Through a Glass Darkly - Karleen Koen 3531

Aldrich, Job (Farmer)
Wings of the Morning - Frederic F. Van de
Water 6404

Aldulf (Sorcerer)
Hawk of May - Gillian Bradshaw 629

Aletta (Settler)
Watch for the Dawn - Stuart Cloete 1128

Alexander (Royalty)
The Prince and the Pilgrim - Mary Stewart 6032

Alexander, Karl (Nobleman)
Power - Lion Feuchtwanger 2074

Alexander, Keith (Young Man)
Tap Roots - James H. Street 6080

Alexander, Tom Christopher (Orphan)
A Dream of Kings - Davis Grubb 2604

Alexandra (Royalty)
Valentina - Evelyn Anthony 165

Alexandrovski, Nikolai (Nobleman)
Tarnished Angel - Phyllis Leonard 3723

Alexias (Young Man)
The Last of the Wine - Mary Renault 5299

Alfonso (Artisan)
The Lord of the Last Days: Visions of the Year 1000 -
Homero Aridjis 188

Alice (Wanderer)
The Prince and the Pilgrim - Mary Stewart 6032

Alicock, Jeremy (Farmer)
Soldiers of Fortune - Peter Bourne 595

Aliena (Noblewoman)
The Pillars of the Earth - Ken Follett 2149

Aligorko (Religious)
Time of Parting - Anton Donchev 1690

Alin (Young Woman; Prehistoric Human)
Daughter of the Red Deer - Joan Wolf 6838

Aline (Young Woman)
One Corpse Too Many - Ellis Peters 4966

Alix of Wanthwaite (Gentlewoman; Adventurer)
Banners of Gold - Pamela Kaufman 3371

Alix of Wanthwaite (Orphan; Heiress—
Dispossessed)
Shield of Three Lions - Pamela Kaufman 3372

Allard, Fontaine (Landowner)
None Shall Look Back - Caroline Gordon 2478

Allard, Ned (Military Personnel)
None Shall Look Back - Caroline Gordon 2478

Allen, Buford (Rancher)
Warhorse - John Cunningham 1451

Allen, Delicia (Southern Belle)
Miss Delicia Allen - Mary Johnston 3237

Allen, Lindsey (Young Woman)
And Never Yield - Elinor Pryor 5204

Allen, Minga (Gentlewoman)
Rivers of Glory - F. van Wyck Mason 4158

Allesandro, Dante de (Nobleman)
Caressa - Linda Lang Bartell 363

Alleyn, Philobeth (Young Woman)
The Darkening Leaf - Caroline Stickland 6036

Allingham, Julian (Nobleman)
Cassy - Elizabeth Lyle 3930

Allington, Ruth (Widow(er); Artist)
Ask Me No Questions - Patricia Veryan 6459

Allison, Anthony (Military Personnel; Spy)
Toil of the Brave - Inglis Fletcher 2141

Allison, Georgiana (Young Woman)
The Wanton Fires - Meriol Trevor 6345

Allister, Gregory (Military Personnel)
For Us the Living - Antonia Van-Loon 6424

Allson, Captain (Sea Captain)
The Hard to Catch Mercy - William Baldwin 281

Allson, Colonel (Veteran)
The Hard to Catch Mercy - William Baldwin 281

Allyn, Hebron (Farmer)
Ho, the Fair Wind - I.A.R. Wylie 6889

Alorge, Marie (Convict)
La Dame De Sainte Hermine - Grace King 3485

Alt, Hans (Artisan)
The Angel with the Trumpet - Ernst Lothar 3898

Altondale, Toby (Gentleman)
The Long Afternoon - Ursula Zilinsky 6964

Altoviti, Carlo (Patriot)
The Castle of Fratta - Ippolito Nievo 4625

Alvarado, Don Julian (Landowner)
Beat to Quarters - C.S. Forester 2170

Alvarez, Rodrigo (Sailor; Carpenter)
Friendly Cove - Irving Brant 651

Alwin, Deborah (Young Woman; Captive)
White Indian - Donald Clayton Porter 5134

Alwyn, Chid (Worker)
The Fleet in the Forest - Carl Daniel Lane 3654

Alypius (Gentleman)
The Converts: A Historical Novel - Rex
Warner 6564

Alys (Witch)
Hellbane - Anthony Esler 1963

Alysin, Garth (Sailor)
The Keys of England - William Victor Cooke 1271

Amalia (Young Woman; Orphan)
Unto the Soul - Aharon Appelfeld 181

Amaurey, Hugo (Gentleman; Adventurer)
Free Lance - George Shipway 5827

Amberley, Lord (Nobleman; Rake)
The Parfit Knight - Juliet Blyth 555

Amberly, Roger (Nobleman)
The Bastard - John Jakes 3144

Ambiala (Lover)
The Seeking - Robert S. Elegant 1906

Ambrosio (Religious)
The Monk - Matthew Gregory Lewis 3756

Ambrosius (Nobleman)
The Great Captains - Henry Treece 6329

Amelia (Noblewoman)
A Dancer in Darkness - David Stacton   5971

Amergin (Religious)
The Gods Are Not Mocked - Anna Taylor   6177

Ames, Caroline (Businesswoman)
A Prologue to Love - Taylor Caldwell   862

Ames, Joel (Settler)
Valley in Arms: A Novel of the Settlement of Connecticut - Earl Schenck Miers   4376

Ames, John (Businessman)
A Prologue to Love - Taylor Caldwell   862
Young Ames - Walter D. Edmonds   1879

Amesley, Nellanor (Gentlewoman; Widow(er))
Chase the Heart - Maggie Osborne   4760

Amiel, Benjamin (Adventurer)
Beyond the Stars - David William Ross   5497

Amigigh (Indian; Prehistoric Human)
My Sister, the Moon - Sue Harrison   2750

Amleth (Royalty)
The Green Man - Henry Treece   6330

Amlie, Horace (Doctor)
Canal Town - Samuel Hopkins Adams   29

Ammidon, Gerrit (Sea Captain)
Java Head - Joseph Hergesheimer   2854

Amory, Tristram (Diplomat)
Let the King Beware! - Honore Morrow   4489

Anacrites (Spy)
Last Act in Palmyra - Lindsey Davis   1529

Ancaeus (Sailor)
Hercules, My Shipmate - Robert Graves   2545

Ancrum, Davin (Military Personnel)
The Valiant Virginians - James Warner Bellah   427

Anderson, Bear (Mountain Man)
The High Rocks - Loren D. Estleman   1973

Anderson, Doreen (Heiress)
Three Rivers - Carla J. Mills   4406

Anderson, Eric (Miner)
Princess Sophia - Edison Marshall   4110

Anderson, Jane (Widow(er))
In a Dark Garden - Frank G. Slaughter   5891

Anderson, John (Adventurer)
The Lion's Skin - Darwin Le Ora Teilhet   6197

Anderson, Paul (Engineer)
The Gathering Wolves - Elizabeth Darrell   1496

Anderson, Robert (Military Personnel)
Ironclads: Man-of-War - Larry D. Names   4554

Anderson, Sarah Kent (Young Woman)
Chapultepec - Norman Zollinger   6965

Anderson, Wil (Rancher)
The Cowboys - William Dale Jennings   3211

Andigones (Philosopher)
Judas - Igal Mossinsohn   4500

Andiora (Indian; Shaman)
This Widowed Land - Kathleen O'Neal Gear   2331

Andrasta (Slave)
The Wolf of Masada - John Fredman   2220

Andreas (Doctor)
Soul Flame - Barbara Wood   6850

Andreas, Jean Marc (Banker)
Storm Winds - Iris Johansen   3217

Andreas, Lionello (Nobleman; Mercenary)
The Wind Dancer - Iris Johansen   3218

Andreda, Dona Maria (Noblewoman)
Buccaneer Surgeon - C.V. Terry   6205

Andresson, Simon (Landowner)
The Mistress of Husaby - Sigrid Undset   6382

Andrew, Drurie (Orphan; Actress)
Banner by the Wayside - Samuel Hopkins Adams   28

Andrewes, Hester (Spouse)
Kenya - John Halkin   2645

Andrewes, John (Engineer)
Kenya - John Halkin   2645

Andrews, Clayton (Military Personnel)
Zoya - Danielle Steel   5985

Andrews, James (Military Personnel; Spy)
Rebel Run - Louis Zara   6952

Andrews, Murray (Widow(er))
City of the Flags - Clark McMeekin   4290

Andrews, Will (Student—College)
Butcher's Crossing - John Williams   6786

Andru (Warrior)
Taras Bulba - Nikolai V. Gogol   2451

Angel, Johnny (Cowboy)
Apaches - Oakley Hall   2650

Angel, Roger (Entertainer)
The Black Angels - Maude Hart Lovelace   3902

Angelelli, Rosa (Immigrant)
Storming Heaven - Denise Giardina   2394

Angelica (Young Woman)
The Gentle Infidel - Lawrence Schoonover   5663

Angelos, John (Heir)
The Dark Angel - Mika Waltari   6551

Anicah, Sparrow (Servant)
Mary's Land - Lucia St. Clair Robson   5415

Anichis (Slave)
The Trojan - Noel B. Gerson   2386

Anicius, Marcus (Nobleman)
Threshold of Fire - Hella S. Haasse   2633

Anjuli (Royalty)
The Far Pavilions - M.M. Kaye   3376

Ann (Dancer)
Shame of Man - Piers Anthony   168

Ann of Cambray (Gentlewoman)
Ann of Cambray - Mary Lide   3772

Anna (Revolutionary; Teacher)
The Petersburg-Cannes Express - Hans Koning   3538

Anna (Slave)
The Walk into Morning - Mildred Barger Herschler   2867

Annas (Leader)
Belmarch: A Legend of the First Crusade - Christopher Davis   1514

Anne (Spouse)
The Barrier - Robin Maugham   4195

Anne Elizabeth (Artisan)
The Invention of Truth - Marta Morazzoni   4449

Anne Louise of Limburg (Noblewoman)
Seven Tempest - William Vaughan Wilkins   6761

Anne of Geierstein (Noblewoman)
Anne of Geierstein - Sir Walter Scott   5689

Anne of Meziere, Lady (Noblewoman)
Under the Winter Moon - Teresa Brooke   705

Anne of Nanteuil (Religious)
The Seven Hills of Paradise - Rosemary Simpson   5859

Annie (Servant; Prostitute)
Abigail - Malcolm Macdonald   3962

Anoud (Spouse)
Blood and Sand - Rosemary Sutcliff   6121

Ansculfson, Aelfred (Fugitive; Adventurer)
Red Lion and Gold Dragon - Rosemary Sprague   5969

Ansell, Luke (Military Personnel)
Celia Garth - Gwen Bristow   695

Anselm (Religious)
The Spire - William Golding   2457

Anstruther, Ramillies (Adventurer)
Ram: Being the Tale of One Ramillies Anstruther - Winchombe Taylor   6193

Antelope (Doctor)
Bitter Creek - Al Cody   1150

Antelope (Indian)
Let the Drum Speak: A Novel of Ancient America - Linda Lay Shuler   5837

Anthony the Turk (Sailor)
The Drowning Room - Michael Kenneth Pye   5212

Antigone (Royalty)
The Eagle King - Henry Treece   6327

Antiphus (Military Personnel)
The Trojan Generals Talk: Memoirs of the Greek War - Phillip Parotti   4818

Antipov, Pavel (Revolutionary; Government Official)
Doctor Zhivago - Boris Pasternak   4824

Antonia (Young Woman)
The Monk - Matthew Gregory Lewis   3756

Antrobus, Miles (Military Personnel)
The War Train: A Novel of 1916 - Brown Meggs   4324

Anysworth, Lillian (Young Woman)
The Drummer Was the First to Die - Liza Pennywitt Taylor   6186

ap-Maddox, Ivor (Spy)
The King Breaker - Elizabeth Linington   3797

ap Owen, Morgan (Bastard Daughter)
Fortune Made His Sword - Martha Rofheart   5426

Apeyahola (Indian)
Harp of a Thousand Strings - Harold Lenoir Davis   1522

Apfegrun, Otto (Young Man)
The Battle of Wagram - Gilles Lapouge   3664

Apieta, Anna (Noblewoman)
The Lute Player - Norah Lofts   3852

Apollonovitch, Sergei (Military Personnel)
Asya - Michael Ignatieff   3103

Appelbaux, Elizabeth (Noblewoman)
Louisa Brancusi - Darrell Husted   3088

Applegarth, Ingram (Young Man)
Out on Any Limb - John Myers   4545

Applegate, Luke (Artist; Wanderer)
The Limner - Paul Darcy Boles   564

Appleton, Adam (Military Personnel)
The Governor's Daughter - Denton Whitson   6718

Appleton, Ellen (Gentlewoman)
Rainbow in the Royals - Garland Roark   5357

Appleton, Margaret (Young Woman)
Hangman's Cliff - Robert Neill   4570

Appleton, Captain William (Landowner)
Hangman's Cliff - Robert Neill   4570

Aragon, Clint (Farmer)
Run of the Stars - Dora Aydelotte   247

Aramis (Military Personnel)
The Three Musketeers - Alexandre Dumas   1782

Aramis (Veteran; Nobleman)
Twenty Years After - Alexandre Dumas   1783

Arbaces (Guardian)
The Last Days of Pompeii - Edward Bulwer-Lytton   768

Arbor, Louise (Socialite)
Young Mrs. Cavendish and the Kaiser's Men - K.K.
   Beck   405

Arbuckle, Maude (Prospector)
Goldfield - Richard S. Wheeler   6660

Archdale, Mary (Gentlewoman)
Lieutenant of the Line - Duncan MacNeil   4015
Sadhu on the Mountain Peak - Duncan
   MacNeil   4019

Archer, Ann (Spouse)
A Dangerous Innocence - Victoria Lincoln   3787

Archer, Brendan (Military Personnel)
Troubles - J.G. Farrell   2017

Archer, Cyril (Gentleman)
Daphne - Marion Chesney   1022

Archer, Frank (Military Personnel; Spy)
Company Q - Richard O'Connor   4684

Archer, Lucie (Spouse)
The Lady Chapel - Candace M. Robb   5366

Archer, Nicholas (Military Personnel)
The Courts of Illusion - Rosemary Hawley
   Jarman   3165

Archer, Owen (Military Personnel; Detective—
   Amateur)
The Apothecary Rose - Candace M. Robb   5364
The Lady Chapel - Candace M. Robb   5366

Archer, Owen (Veteran; Detective—Amateur)
The King's Bishop - Candace M. Robb   5365
The Nun's Tale - Candace M. Robb   5367

Archias (Outcast)
Gate to the Sea - Bryher   743

Archias (Young Man)
Years of the City - George Rippey Stewart   6028

Archibald, Allan (Socialite; Student)
Organized Crime - Nicholas Von Hoffman   6511

Archibald, Philippa (Gentlewoman)
While England Sleeps - David Leavitt   3702

Ardenly, Alec (Nobleman)
Tish - Cissie Miller   4381

Ardleigh, Kathryn (Writer)
Death at Daisy's Folly - Robin Paige   4775
Death at Gallows Green - Robin Paige   4776

Argentine, Giles (Doctor; Gentleman)
The Fate of Princes - P.C. Doherty   1673

Ariadne (Royalty)
The King Must Die - Mary Renault   5298

Aricia (Royalty)
The Eagle and the Raven - Pauline Gedge   2344

Arik-Buka (Warrior)
*Sons of the Steppe: The Story of How the Conqueror
   Genghis Khan Was Overcome* - Hans
   Baumann   380

Arinna (Spouse)
The Hittite - Noel B. Gerson   2373

Aristander (Religious)
Alexander the God - Maurice Druon   1731

Ariston (Warrior; Captive)
Goat Song: A Novel of Ancient Greece - Frank
   Yerby   6920

Ark, Henry (Military Personnel)
The Red Rover - James Fenimore Cooper   1309

Armagh, Bernadette (Spouse)
Captains and the Kings - Taylor Caldwell   851

Armagh, Joseph (Immigrant; Financier)
Captains and the Kings - Taylor Caldwell   851

Armagh, Rory (Gentleman)
Captains and the Kings - Taylor Caldwell   851

Armand, Marcel (Pirate)
Marcel Armand - Sallie Bell   424

Armando (Adventurer)
Jewel of the Sea - Susan Wiggs   6743

Armbrecht, Kurt (Veteran; Writer)
Hitler Has Won - Frederic Mullally   4511

Armes, Artillery (Orphan)
The Flames of Time - Baynard Kendrick   3409

Arminius (Adventurer)
The Rogue From Padua - Jay Williams   6772

Armitage, Annabelle (Gentlewoman)
The Taming of Annabelle - Marion Chesney   1052

Armitage, Charles (Religious)
Diana the Huntress - Marion Chesney   1026
Frederica in Fashion - Marion Chesney   1032
Minerva - Marion Chesney   1037
The Taming of Annabelle - Marion Chesney   1052

Armitage, Daphne (Gentlewoman)
Daphne - Marion Chesney   1022

Armitage, Deirdre (Gentlewoman)
Deirdre and Desire - Marion Chesney   1024

Armitage, Diana (Gentlewoman)
Diana the Huntress - Marion Chesney   1026

Armitage, Frederica (Gentlewoman)
Frederica in Fashion - Marion Chesney   1032

Armitage, Hugh (Military Personnel)
The Four Swans - Winston Graham   2525

Armitage, Jonathan (Outcast)
A Shadow's Bliss - Patricia Veryan   6477

Armitage, Minerva (Gentlewoman)
Minerva - Marion Chesney   1037

Armitage, Susan (Governess)
Black-Eyed Susan - Deborah Camp   871

Armourer, Guy (Bastard Son)
Gilded Spurs - Grace Ingram   3105

Armstrong, Amanda (Heroine)
Woman's Own - Robyn Carr   941

Armstrong, Emily (Heroine)
Woman's Own - Robyn Carr   941

Armstrong, Grace (Gentlewoman)
The Black Dwarf - Sir Walter Scott   5692

Armstrong, Jonathan (Gentleman)
The Distant Lands - Julian Green   2567

Armstrong, Lilly (Heroine)
Woman's Own - Robyn Carr   941

Armstrong, Merrin (Spouse)
The Dark Pasture - Jessica Stirling   6042

Armstrong, Noelle (Heiress)
The Earl and the Heiress - Barbara Metzger   4345

Armstrong, Tom (Farmer)
The Dark Pasture - Jessica Stirling   6042

Arnall, Hoke (Military Personnel)
Unto This Hour - Tom Wicker   6733

Arnaud, Claudine (Gentlewoman)
All Souls' Rising - Madison Smartt Bell   422

Arne (Worker)
Arne - Bjornstjerne Bjornson   518

Arnold, Althea (Young Woman)
The Firelands - Karen Harper   2712

Arnst, Sol (Journalist)
Crimson Creek: A Novel of the Early West - Robert
   McCraig   4228

Arnvid (Young Man)
The Foster Brothers - Edward Frankland   2202

Arothgar (Ruler)
The Tower of Beowulf - Parke Godwin   2450

Arouet, Lucien (Nobleman)
French Slippers - Deborah Chester   1055

Arran, Nathan ben (Doctor)
Glendower Country - Martha Rofheart   5427

Arrowe, Quinton (Military Personnel)
Officer and Gentleman - Josephine Delves-
   Broughton   1604

Arrowe, Thomas (Military Personnel)
Officer and Gentleman - Josephine Delves-
   Broughton   1604

Arrowsmith, Francis (Mercenary; Adventurer)
Manchu - Robert S. Elegant   1904

Arroya, Tomas (Military Personnel)
The Old Gringo - Carlos Fuentes   2247

Arthur, Sir (Knight)
Guinevere - Sharan Newman   4600

Arthur (Ruler)
Arthur - Stephen R. Lawhead   3679
Arthur Rex: A Legendary Novel - Thomas
   Berger   477
The Chessboard Queen - Sharan Newman   4597
Child of the Northern Spring - Persia Woolley   6867
The Coming of the King - Nikolai Tolstoy   6296
A Connecticut Yankee in King Arthur's Court - Mark
   Twain   6371
The Emperor Arthur - Godfrey Turton   6368
Firelord - Parke Godwin   2447
First Knight - Elizabeth Chadwick   966
The Green Man - Henry Treece   6330
Guinevere Evermore - Sharan Newman   4601
Guinevere: The Legend in Autumn - Persia
   Woolley   6868
Hawk of May - Gillian Bradshaw   629
In the Shadow of the Oak King - Courtway
   Jones   3271
In Winter's Shadow - Gillian Bradshaw   632
The King - Donald Barthelme   365
Kingdom of Summer - Gillian Bradshaw   633
Kinsmen of the Grail - Dorothy James Roberts   5376
The Last Enchantment - Mary Stewart   6031
The Last Pendragon - Robert Rice   5316
The Mists of Avalon - Marion Zimmer Bradley   626
The Once and Future King - T.H. White   6705
The Pagan King - Edison Marshall   4109
The Pendragon - Catherine Christian   1075
Pendragon - Stephen R. Lawhead   3682
Pendragon's Banner - Helen Hollick   3001
Queen of the Summer Stars - Persia Woolley   6869
The Queen's Knight - Marvin Borowsky   585
The Road to Avalon - Joan Wolf   6842
The Wicked Day - Mary Stewart   6033
The Winter King - Bernard Cornwell   1351
Witch of the North - Courtway Jones   3272

Arthur (Warrior)
The Duke of War - Walter O'Meara   4734
The Kingmaking - Helen Hollick   3000

Arthur (Warrior; Ruler)
The Crimson Chalice - Victor Canning   882

Arthur (Young Man)
The Hollow Hills - Mary Stewart   6030

Artorius (Military Personnel)
Artorius Rex - John Gloag   2432

Artos the Bear (Warrior)
The Great Captains - Henry Treece   6329
Sword at Sunset - Rosemary Sutcliff   6125

Arundel, Christopher (Nobleman; Rake)
Lord Libertine - Anthony Esler   1964

Asa (Indian; Young Woman)
The Pecos River - Fred Bean   399

Asano, Lady (Noblewoman)
The Tokaido Road: A Novel of Feudal Japan - Lucia
   St. Clair Robson   5417

Asgeirsdottir, Margaret (Young Woman)
The Greenlanders - Jane Smiley 5915

Asgeirsson, Gunnar (Young Man)
The Greenlanders - Jane Smiley 5915

Ashan (Prehistoric Human; Chieftain)
Children of the Dawn - Patricia Rowe 5516
Keepers of the Misty Time - Patricia Rowe 5517

Ashana (Indian)
Ashana - E.P. Roesch 5424

Ashbrooke, Catherine (Gentlewoman)
The Blood of Roses - Marsha Canham 879
The Pride of Lions - Marsha Canham 881

Ashburn, Emily (Pioneer)
The Glorious Three - June Wetherell 6651

Ashburne, Tom (Nobleman)
Lost Love Found - Bertrice Small 5910

Ashburnham, Jack (Military Personnel)
The Severed Crown - Jane Lane 3657

Ashby, Henrietta (Young Woman)
Reckless Angel - Jane Feather 2056

Ashe, Homer (Landowner)
The Power of Black - M.B. Longman 3880

Ashe, Jay-Wade (Artist)
The Power of Black - M.B. Longman 3880

Asher, Faith Mary (Spy; Widow(er))
Faith and Honor - Robin Maderich 4025

Ashford, Alissa (Imposter; Governess)
Masque of Enchantment - Charlene Cross 1432

Ashington, Sarah (Heiress; Plantation Owner)
The Spring of the Tiger - Victoria Holt 3021

Ashland, Roger (Landowner)
By Dim and Flashing Lamps - Alan Le May 3689

Ashleigh, Delia (Actress)
The Ladies of Hanover Square - Rona Randall 5249

Ashleigh, Gilliard (Gentleman; Veteran)
A Question of Honour - Emma Drummond 1726

Ashleigh, Valentine (Gentleman)
A Question of Honour - Emma Drummond 1726

Ashleigh, Vere (Gentleman)
A Question of Honour - Emma Drummond 1726

Ashley, Elizabeth (Gentlewoman)
Guns of Chickamauga - Richard O'Connor 4685

Ashley, Julia (Orphan)
Scent of Cloves - Norah Lofts 3859

Ashley, Peter (Gentleman)
Peter Ashley - DuBose Heyward 2911

Ashted, Billy (Artisan)
Threescore and Ten - Walter Allen 105

Ashted, Rose Thompson (Spouse)
Threescore and Ten - Walter Allen 105

Ashton, Lord (Nobleman)
Deborah Goes to Dover - Marion Chesney 1023

Ashton, Charles (Nobleman)
Double Masquerade - Karen Lynn 3938

Ashton, Emma (Orphan)
Portrait of Emma - Lillian Cheatham 1010

Ashton, Lucy (Gentlewoman)
The Bride of Lammermoor - Sir Walter Scott 5693

Ashton, Robert (Sailor)
Three Harbors - F. van Wyck Mason 4162

Ashton, William (Nobleman; Lawyer)
The Bride of Lammermoor - Sir Walter Scott 5693

Ashur, Tiglath (Royalty)
The Assyrian - Nicholas Guild 2610

Ashur, Tiglath (Royalty; Outcast)
The Blood Star - Nicholas Guild 2611

Ashville, Felice (Traitor)
Royal Sword at Agincourt - Pamela Bennetts 455

Ashwood, Harry (Veteran)
Gentlemen, Hush! - Jere Hungerford
  Wheelwright 6668

Ashworth, Cecilia (Gentlewoman)
A Lady of Repute - Janice James 3158

Ashworth, Emily (Gentlewoman)
Paragon Walk - Anne Perry 4932

Askwani (Indian)
Beulah Land - Harold Lenoir Davis 1520

Aslalfetch (Young Woman)
The Name of Hero - Richard Seltzer 5742

Aspar, Flavius (Military Personnel)
To Love Again - Bertrice Small 5913

Aspasia (Royalty; Widow(er))
The Eagle's Daughter - Judith Tarr 6165

Aspern, Mark (Military Personnel)
Tournament of the Shadows - Nicholas Carnac 901

Aspinal, Samantha (Young Woman)
The Magnificent Savages - Fred Mustard
  Stewart 6024

Aspley, Meriet (Religious)
The Devil's Novice - Ellis Peters 4958

Astley, Andrew de (Knight)
Shield of Honor - Alice Walworth Graham 2511

Astrid (Young Woman)
The Foster Brothers - Edward Frankland 2202

Astrov, Leonid (Royalty)
The Astrov Legacy - Constance Heaven 2802

Astyanax (Ruler)
The Shattered Horse - S.P. Somtow 5945

Atala (Indian; Young Woman)
Atala - Francois Rene de Chateaubriand 1008

Atarho (Indian; Warrior)
Father of Waters - Donald Clayton Porter 5118

Atawulf (Warrior)
Heaven's Only Daughter - Kathleen Robinson 5406

Athanasios (Religious)
The Beacon of Alexandria - Gillian Bradshaw 627

Athelson, Athel (Heir)
The Athelsons - Jocelyn Kettle 3476

Athelson, Justine (Young Woman)
The Athelsons - Jocelyn Kettle 3476

Athelstan, Brother (Religious; Clerk)
The Nightingale Gallery - Paul Harding 2684
*Red Slayer: Being the Second of the Sorrowful
  Mysteries of Brother Athelstan* - Paul
  Harding 2685

Athenais (Captive)
The Man Who Killed the King - Dennis
  Wheatley 6654

Atherstone, Francis (Nobleman)
Bride of Ae - Pamela Hill 2928

Atherton (Rake; Gentleman)
Miss Philadelphia Smith - Paula Allardyce 91

Atherton, Emily (Young Woman; Journalist)
The Normandie Affair - Elizabeth Villars 6497

Atherton-Moore, Edward (Gentleman)
Winter of the Heart - Linda J. LaRosa 3665

Athos (Military Personnel)
The Three Musketeers - Alexandre Dumas 1782

Athos (Veteran)
Twenty Years After - Alexandre Dumas 1783

Atlaw (Chieftain; Prehistoric Human)
Daughter of the Red Deer - Joan Wolf 6838

Atretes (Warrior; Gladiator)
As Sure as the Dawn - Francine Rivers 5352

Attaroa (Chieftain; Prehistoric Human)
The Plains of Passage - Jean M. Auel 238

Attiba (Slave)
Caribbee - Thomas Hoover 3025

Attucks, Adeline (Madam)
Heart of the Country - Greg Matthews 4190

Aubery, Jean-Benoit (Pirate)
Frenchman's Creek - Daphne Du Maurier 1744

Aubrey, Claire (Musician)
The Fountain Overflows - Rebecca West 6639

Aubrey, Cordelia (Musician)
The Fountain Overflows - Rebecca West 6639

Aubrey, Jack (Military Personnel)
The Commodore - Patrick O'Brian 4661
Desolation Island - Patrick O'Brian 4662
The Far Side of the World - Patrick O'Brian 4663
The Fortune of War - Patrick O'Brian 4664
H.M.S. Surprise - Patrick O'Brian 4666
The Ionian Mission - Patrick O'Brian 4667
The Letter of Marque - Patrick O'Brian 4668
Master and Commander - Patrick O'Brian 4669
The Mauritius Command - Patrick O'Brian 4670
The Nutmeg of Consolation - Patrick O'Brian 4671
Post Captain - Patrick O'Brian 4672
The Reverse of the Medal - Patrick O'Brian 4673
The Surgeon's Mate - Patrick O'Brian 4674
The Thirteen Gun Salute - Patrick O'Brian 4675
Treason's Harbour - Patrick O'Brian 4676
The Truelove - Patrick O'Brian 4677
The Wine-Dark Sea - Patrick O'Brian 4679

Aubrey, Jack (Military Personnel; Landowner)
The Yellow Admiral - Patrick O'Brian 4680

Aubrey, Piers (Journalist)
The Fountain Overflows - Rebecca West 6639

Aubrey, Robin (Spy)
Fire over England - A.E.W. Mason 4143

Aubrey, Sophie (Spouse)
The Commodore - Patrick O'Brian 4661
The Mauritius Command - Patrick O'Brian 4670
The Yellow Admiral - Patrick O'Brian 4680

Aubrey of Epping (Actor)
Three Years to Play - Colin MacInnes 3983

Auburn, Autumn (Entertainer)
Spangle - Gary Jennings 3196

Auclair, Cecile (Heroine)
Shadows on the Rock - Willa Cather 959

Auclair, Euclide (Pharmacist)
Shadows on the Rock - Willa Cather 959

Audley, Charles (Military Personnel)
An Infamous Army - Georgette Heyer 2892

Audley, Isabelle (Orphan)
Castaway - Frances Murray 4535

Audley, Julian (Nobleman; Guardian)
Regency Buck - Georgette Heyer 2898

Audley, Kathryn (Gentlewoman)
Bennett's Welcome - Inglis Fletcher 2132

Audrey, Robin (Religious)
Come Rack! Come Rope! - Robert Hugh Benson 458

Audubon, Lord (Nobleman)
The Shadowed Spring - Carola Salisbury 5571

Audunsson, Olav (Knight; Nobleman)
The Axe - Sigrid Undset 6378
In the Wilderness - Sigrid Undset 6381
The Snake Pit - Sigrid Undset 6383
The Son Avenger - Sigrid Undset 6384

Augusta of Berkeley (Gentlewoman)
Castle Dangerous - Sir Walter Scott 5694

Augustine (Military Personnel)
Silk and Steel - Stephen Alter 122

Aulirios, Niklos (Servant)
A Candle for D'Artagnan - Chelsea Quinn
  Yarbro 6895
Crusader's Torch - Chelsea Quinn Yarbro 6897
A Flame in Byzantium - Chelsea Quinn Yarbro 6899

Aumarle, John (Nobleman)
The Strong Room - Jere Hungerford
  Wheelwright 6671

Aumarle, John (Pirate)
Wolfshead - Jere Hungerford Wheelwright 6672

Aumeric of Montjoie (Knight)
The Siege - Jay Williams 6773

Aumont, Nicole (Lawyer)
Winter Grass - Richard S. Wheeler 6665

Aupick, General (Military Personnel)
A Singular Conspiracy - Barry Perowne 4915

Auria (Slave)
Anabasis: A Journey to the Interior - Ellen
  Gilchrist 2408

Auriane (Warrior; Religious)
The Light Bearer - Donna Gillespie 2419

Ausonia, Fausta (Young Woman)
The Last Romans - Teodor Jeske-Choinski 3216

Austell, Lucius (Nobleman)
The Quiet Gentleman - Georgette Heyer 2897

Austin, Harry (Military Personnel)
Fifteen Flags - Richard Lynden Hardman 2686

Austin, Jack (Journalist)
A Distant Thunder - Teresa de Luca 1561

Austin, Melissa (Captive)
California! - Dana Fuller Ross 5467

Austin, Melody (Young Woman)
Hue and Cry - Elizabeth Yates 6907

Avenel, Mary (Orphan)
The Monastery - Sir Walter Scott 5701

Avery, Benjamin (Sea Captain)
The Pyrates - George MacDonald Fraser 2212

Avery, Charity (Widow(er); Spy)
Monmouth - Charles Bracelen Flood 2144

Avinga (Eskimo)
The White Dawn - James Houston 3053

Avington, Jack (Nobleman)
Albany - Laura Black 519

Ayla (Prehistoric Human)
The Clan of the Cave Bear - Jean M. Auel 236
The Mammoth Hunters - Jean M. Auel 237
The Plains of Passage - Jean M. Auel 238
The Valley of Horses - Jean M. Auel 239

Aylsham, Alyne (Foundling)
Lord of Ravensley - Constance Heaven 2809

Aylsham, Oliver (Gentleman)
Lord of Ravensley - Constance Heaven 2809

Aynsworth, Christopher (Nobleman)
Mistress of Willowvale - Patricia Veryan 6471

Ayres, Judith (Fiance(e))
The Trembling Earth - Dale Van Every 6411

Ayrton, Christy (Trader)
Silver Nutmeg - Norah Lofts 3860

Ayrton, Matthew (Artist)
Lovers - Suzanne Goodwin 2476

Ayscough, Adam (Religious)
Dean's Watch - Elizabeth Goudge 2494

Aysgarth, Annie (Businesswoman)
Fortune Is a Woman - Elizabeth Adler 39

Azael (Angel)
The Fair - Robert Nathan 4559

Azaire, Isabelle (Gentlewoman)
Birdsong - Sebastian Faulks 2051

B

Babcock, Lord (Nobleman)
Lady Pamela - Clare Darcy 1490

Babcock, Ned (Animal Trainer)
The Bartholomew Fair Murders - Leonard
  Tourney 6297

Babtista, Anton (Military Personnel)
Sea of Lentils - Antonio Benitez-Rojo 443

Bad Belly/Still Water (Prehistoric Human)
People of the Earth - W. Michael Gear 2334

Bad Man From Bodie (Outlaw)
Welcome to Hard Times - E.L. Doctorow 1660

Bade, Jonathan (Lawyer)
The Tontine - Thomas B. Costain 1371

Baffo, Sofia (Gentlewoman; Captive)
Sofia - Ann Chamberlin 974

Bagley (Military Personnel)
The Alpha Raid - Alan Scholefield 5651

Baglione, Camilla (Noblewoman)
Prince of Foxes - Samuel Shellabarger 5797

Bagnall, Clive (Rancher)
The Wisdom of Stones - Greg Matthews 4192

Bahadur, Victor (Royalty)
Raj - Gita Mehta 4325

Bailey, Lydia (Gentlewoman)
Lydia Bailey - Kenneth Roberts 5387

Bailey, Scon (Sea Captain)
Storm Tide - Allan R. Bosworth 590

Bainbridge, Rose (Settler)
The Cabin at the Trail's End - Sheba
  Hargreaves 2706

Baines (Landowner)
The Piano - Jane Campion 878

Baines, Timothy (Servant)
Timothy Baines - John H. Culp 1445

Bak-Isis (Royalty)
The River and the Stone: Moses' Early Years in Egypt
  - Kathleen Jenks 3192

Baker, Annie Saunders (Widow(er); Refugee)
Sherman's March - Cynthia Bass 373

Baker, Ben (Rancher)
Filaree: A Novel of an American Life - Marguerite
  Noble 4633

Baker, Boniface (Settler)
The Peaceable Kingdom - Jan de Hartog 2763

Baker, Melissa (Spouse; Cook)
Filaree: A Novel of an American Life - Marguerite
  Noble 4633

Balam Xoc (Rebel)
Tikal: A Novel about the Maya - Daniel Peters 4947

Balater, George Eustace (Nobleman; Businessman)
The Bad Lands - Oakley Hall 2651

Balbinius, Pius (Organized Crime Figure)
Time to Depart - Lindsey Davis 1533

Baldwin, Maggie (Young Woman)
The Last Ride - Tom Eidson 1899

Bale, Daniel (Farmer)
Long Remember - MacKinlay Kantor 3362

Bale, Morganna (Loyalist; Spouse)
The General's Lady - Esther Forbes 2156

Bale, Richard (Plantation Owner)
Balisand - Joseph Hergesheimer 2853

Bales, Ezekiel (Military Personnel)
The King's Coat - Dewey Lambdin 3612

Balfour, Alex (Historian; Time Traveller)
Till the End of Time - Allen Appel 170
Time After Time - Allen Appel 171
Twice upon a Time - Allen Appel 172

Balfour, David (Gentleman)
Catriona - Robert Louis Stevenson 6009

Balfour, David (Heir—Dispossessed; Orphan)
Kidnapped - Robert Louis Stevenson 6010

Balfour, Ebenezer (Kidnapper)
Kidnapped - Robert Louis Stevenson 6010

Balfour, John (Fanatic)
Old Mortality - Sir Walter Scott 5702

Balfrey, Francis (Gentleman)
Killing Cousins - Alanna Knight 3520

Ballantyne, Zouga (Settler; Businessman)
Men of Men - Wilbur Smith 5927

Ballard, Christopher (Surveyor)
Gamble's Hundred - Clifford Dowdey 1705

Ballard, Jean (Mountain Man)
Grant of Kingdom - Harvey Fergusson 2067

Ballard, John (Mine Owner)
The Silver Mountain - Dan Cushman 1453

Ballasteros, Winter de (Gentlewoman)
Shadow of the Moon - M.M. Kaye 3377

Ballenrose (Gentleman)
Ballenrose - Mallory Burgess 783

Ballinger, Augusta (Noblewoman)
Rendezvous - Amanda Quick 5218

Ballinger, Max (Businessman)
The Normandie Affair - Elizabeth Villars 6497

Balliol, Roussel de (Knight)
The Lady for Ransom - Alfred Duggan 1768

Ballou, Ohio (Actress)
The Great Blizzard - Albert E. Idell 3101

Balor (Wanderer; Prehistoric Human)
Wolves of the Dawn - William Sarabande 5604

Balthazar (Biblical Figure; Scholar)
How Far to Bethlehem? - Norah Lofts 3846

Balthazar (Nobleman; Biblical Figure)
Ben Hur: A Tale of the Christ - Lew Wallace 6536

Balthazar (Parent)
The Headsman; or, The Abbaye des Vignerons - James
  Fenimore Cooper 1300

Balthazar (Religious; Biblical Figure)
The Way - J.M. Hartley 2761

Balz, Guillaume (Religious; Architect)
The Stones of the Abbey - Fernand Pouillon 5144

Balzane, Captain (Military Personnel)
The Breast of the Dove - Herbert Gorman 2491

Ban-Ya (Prehistoric Human)
The Edge of the World - William Sarabande 5597

Banastre, Hortensia (Gentlewoman)
Southern Discomfort - Rita Mae Brown 730

Bancroft, Marianna (Young Woman)
Cargo of Brides - Helen Rucker 5522

Bancroft, Mercy (Young Woman)
The Gold Seekers - William Stuart Long 3874

Bandfield, Frank (Military Personnel; Pilot)
Eagles at War - Walter J. Boyne 620

Bandy, Bartholemew (Military Personnel; Pilot)
It's Me Again - Donald Jack 3126
Me So Far - Donald Jack 3127
That's Me in the Middle - Donald Jack 3129
Three Cheers for Me - Donald Jack 3131

Bandy, Bartholomew (Adventurer)
This One's on Me - Donald Jack 3130

Bandy, Bartholomew (Adventurer; Political Figure)
Me Too - Donald Jack 3128

Bandylegs, Captain Bob (Indian)
Here I Stay - Elizabeth Coatsworth 1138

Bangs, Jonathon (Sailor)
The New Hope - Joseph C. Lincoln 3784

Banicek, Tom (Immigrant; Miner)
Ellis Island - Fred Mustard Stewart 6023

Bank, James (Doctor)
The Rainbow Promise - Lisa Gregory 2580

Banks, Bethel (Widow(er))
Muddy Banks - Ruby C. Tolliver 6291

Banks, Boy "Muddy" (Slave)
Muddy Banks - Ruby C. Tolliver 6291

Banks, Rafe (Frontiersman)
As Long as the Rivers Run - Sam J. Slate 5882

Banner, Gabriel (Nobleman; Writer)
Reckless - Amanda Quick 5217

Banner, Libbie (Teenager)
Northwest Passage - David Thompson 6258

Banner, Simon (Wagonmaster)
Northwest Passage - David Thompson 6258

Banning, Mark (Adventurer)
The Blue Dragon - Diana Brown 716

Bannock, Bart (Horse Trainer)
Kimberley - Colin Burke 784

Bannon, James (Military Personnel)
Until the End - Harold Coyle 1396

Bannon, James (Student—College; Military Personnel)
Look Away - Harold Coyle 1395

Bannon, Kevin (Military Personnel)
Until the End - Harold Coyle 1396

Bannon, Kevin (Student—College; Military Personnel)
Look Away - Harold Coyle 1395

Bannon, Millie (Worker)
Thy Tears Might Cease - Michael Farrell 2018

Bantham, Jane (Writer)
Kindred Spirits - June Barraclough 347

Barak, Bel (Gentleman)
The Golden Crucible - Jean Stubbs 6096

Barak, Zev (Military Personnel)
The Hope - Herman Wouk 6874

Barak, Zev (Military Personnel; Diplomat)
The Glory - Herman Wouk 6873

Barakat, Zayni (Government Official)
Zayni Barakat - Gamal Ahitani 42

Baranov, Walter (Dentist; Imposter)
The False Inspector Dew - Peter Lovesey 3912

Barber, Nicholas (Religious)
Morality Play - Barry Unsworth 6387

Barbour, Caroline (Captive)
A Rendezvous in Haiti - Stephen Becker 407

Barbour, Joseph (Businessman)
Dynasty of Death - Taylor Caldwell 854

Barbour, Martin (Businessman)
Dynasty of Death - Taylor Caldwell 854

Barclay, Adair (Immigrant)
Dancing at the Rascal Fair - Ivan Doig 1682

Barclay, Frances (Waiter/Waitress)
Niagara - Robert Lewis Taylor 6189

Barclay, Rob (Immigrant)
Dancing at the Rascal Fair - Ivan Doig 1682

Bardagne, Nicholas de (Diplomat)
Angelique and the Ghosts - Sergeanne Golon 2467

Bardiya (Warrior)
The Year of the Horsetails - R.F. Tapsell 6162

Barfoot, Captain (Military Personnel; Detective—Amateur)
Entered From the Sun - George Garrett 2301

Barham, Jack (Nobleman)
Two of a Kind: An English Trifle - Rosemary Edghill 1867

Baring, Eliot (Engineer)
Honour and Obey - Malcolm Macdonald 3966

Barinthus (Sailor)
Paradise - Dikkon Eberhart 1831

Barker, Jack (Political Figure)
The Queen and I - Sue Townsend 6306

Barker, John (Convict)
The Men That God Forgot - Richard Butler 829

Barlow, Arabella (Gentlewoman)
Law of the Land - Marguerite Allis 111

Barlow, Ben (Worker)
Law of the Land - Marguerite Allis 111

Barlow, Prentiss (Military Personnel)
Arouse and Beware - MacKinlay Kantor 3360

Barnabas (Revolutionary)
Shadows in Bronze - Lindsey Davis 1531

Barnabas, Robert (Smuggler)
Judith - Brian Cleeve 1108

Barnard, John (Gentleman; Businessman)
The Flint Anchor - Sylvia Townsend Warner 6569

Barnard, Julia (Spouse)
The Flint Anchor - Sylvia Townsend Warner 6569

Barnard, Sir Ralph (Gentleman)
King's Agent - Justus Kent Clark 1090

Barnes, Jefferson (Military Personnel)
Jubilee - John Brick 672

Barnes, Kate (Spouse)
Jubilee - John Brick 672

Barnes, Kirsty (Orphan)
The Asking Price - Jessica Stirling 6039
The Good Provider - Jessica Stirling 6043
The Welcome Light - Jessica Stirling 6050

Barnet, Barney (Adventurer)
Rough Diamond - Robert L. Fish 2098

Barney, Joshua (Military Personnel)
Captain Barney - Jan Westcott 6642

Barney, Joshua (Sailor)
The Sea Eagles - John Edward Jennings 3206

Barnsby, Horace "Horse" (Teenager)
The Adventure of "Horse" Barnsby - Philip D. Stong 6065

Barnstable, Richard (Sea Captain; Military Personnel)
The Pilot - James Fenimore Cooper 1306

Baron, Charles (Gentleman; Rake)
Beau Barron's Lady - Helen Ashfield 204

Baron, Matt (Rancher)
The Grass Kingdom - Jory Sherman 5818

Baronsheath, Felicity (Gentlewoman)
Refining Felicity - Marion Chesney 1048

Barraclough, Ira (Sailor)
Masts to Spear the Stars - Stephen Longstreet 3889

Barrasford, Ivo (Nobleman)
Bath Tangle - Georgette Heyer 2875

Barratt, Jonathan (Young Man)
Riders of the Long Road - Stephen E. Bransford 649

Barre, Michael (Convict)
Tavern in the Town - Cecile Hulse Matschat 4187

Barrett, Evelyn (Young Woman)
The House of War - Catherine Gavin 2322

Barrett, Justin (Plantation Owner)
The Golden Harlot - Jeanne Wilson 6808

Barrett, Topaze (Foundling)
The Golden Harlot - Jeanne Wilson 6808

Barrie, Billy (Military Personnel)
The Sword of General Englund - Donald Honig 3023

Barringer, Lelia (Southern Belle)
Roses From the South - Perceval Reniers 5304

Barrington, Nathanial (Military Personnel)
Desert Hawks - Frank Burleson 786
Savage Frontier - Frank Burleson 787
War Eagles - Frank Burleson 788

Barrington, Ruby (Worker)
Stand We at Last - Zoe Fairbairns 1999

Barrington, Timothy (Gentleman)
The Love Child - Catherine Cookson 1279

Barrow, Elspeth (Gentlewoman)
Foes - Mary Johnston 3233

Barrow, Tobias (Doctor)
The Unknown Shore - Patrick O'Brian 4678

Barry, Alan (Surveyor)
Rebel in Blue - Herman Toepperwein 6289

Barry, Jannion (Spouse)
The Covenant - Brigid Knight 3521

Barry, John (Businessman)
John Barry - Donald F. Bedford 412

Barry, Redmond (Adventurer; Rake)
Barry Lyndon - William Makepeace Thackeray 6210

Barry, Stephen (Landowner)
The Covenant - Brigid Knight 3521

Bartel, Adrienne (Young Woman)
The Renegade - Donald Clayton Porter 5122

Bartholomew, Matthew (Doctor)
An Unholy Alliance - Susanna Gregory 2586

Bartleet, Abigail (Young Woman)
The Valiant and the Daunted - Roy Clews 1115

Barton, Conway (Government Official)
Shadow of the Moon - M.M. Kaye 3377

Barton, David (Military Personnel)
Strange Meeting - Susan Hill 2952

Barton, Joe (Worker)
Maggie Craig - Marie Joseph 3308

Barton, Josh (Gentleman)
Claudine's Daughter - Rosalind Laker 3594

Barton, Judith (Young Woman)
The Pioneers - Courtney Ryley Cooper 1296

Barzor (Outlaw)
Two Thieves - Manuel Komroff 3535

Bas-Thornton, Emily (Child; Captive)
A High Wind in Jamaica - Richard Hughes 3074

Bascom, Rob (Plantation Owner)
Iron Ships, Iron Men - Christopher Nicole 4616

Bascombe, Henrietta (Heiress; Businesswoman)
At the Sign of the Golden Pineapple - Marion Chesney 1016

Bashford, Hendon (Student—College)
The Steps of the Sun - Joanna Trollope 6350

Bashinskey, Galina (Young Woman)
The Summer of the Bashinskeys - Diane
  Pearson 4877

Basia (Heroine)
Fire in the Steppe - Henryk Sienkiewicz 5847

Basil of Antioch (Artisan; Slave)
The Silver Chalice - Thomas B. Costain 1370

Basket, Fuegia (Indian)
Jemmy Button - Benjamin Subercaseaux 6107

Bass, Jethro (Political Figure)
Coniston - Winston Churchill 1078

Bass, Sam (Military Personnel)
Chase Royal - Donald Seaman 5712

Bass, Scratch (Mountain Man)
Borderlords - Terry C. Johnston 3244
One-Eyed Dream - Terry C. Johnston 3253

Bass, Titus (Mountain Man)
Buffalo Palace - Terry C. Johnston 3245
Carry the Wind - Terry C. Johnston 3246

Bass, Titus (Teenager)
Dance on the Wind - Terry C. Johnston 3249

Bassinghorn, Henry (Military Personnel)
The Guns of Arrest - Philip McCutchan 4242
Halfhyde's Island - Philip McCutchan 4254

Bast, Michael (Adventurer; Bastard Son)
The Adventurer - Mika Waltari 6550

Batara, David (Revolutionary)
The View From Coyaba - Peter Abrahams 11

Batchelor, Barbara (Religious; Teacher)
The Towers of Silence - Paul Scott 5685

Batchelor, Clyde (Landowner)
Steamboat Gothic - Frances Parkinson Keyes 3481

Bateman, John (Artisan)
The Silver Touch - Rosalind Laker 3599

Bateman, Warren (Military Personnel)
The Ravi Lancers - John Masters 4178

Bates, Rachel (Gentlewoman)
The Stallion Man - Judith Glover 2438

Bathory-Kereshtur, Drake (Young Man)
The Blood Countess - Andrei Codrescu 1149

Bathurst, Roger Fitzroy (Young Man)
Intrigue in Baltimore - Janet Whitney 6715

Batz, Baron Jean de (Nobleman; Revolutionary)
Scaramouche the King-Maker - Rafael Sabatini 5555

Baude, Simon de (Knight)
Time of the Unicorn - Barbara Jefferis 3176

Bauer, Harry (Spy)
Seven Days to Petrograd - Tom Hyman 3094

Bawajira (Ruler)
The Golden Honeycomb - Kamala Markandaya 4086

Bawn, Molly (Young Woman)
O'Houlihan's Jest - Rohan O'Grady 4702

Baxter, August (Sailor; Fisherman)
Eye of the Hurricane - Fergus Reid Buckley 757

Baxter, David (Sea Captain)
The Crystal Star - Ellen Argo 184
Jewel of the Sea - Ellen Argo 185
The Yankee Girl - Ellen Argo 186

Baxter, Goldie (Orphan; Pioneer)
The Argonauts - Yvonne Schoell 5645

Baxter, Thad (Wanderer)
The Odyssey of Thaddeus Baxter - Robert P.
  Lund 3926

Bay, Maurice (Plantation Owner)
The Running Thread - Drayton Mayrant 4215

Baylen, Fate (Cowboy; Military Personnel)
San Juan Hill - Will Henry 2848

Baynes, Barton (Young Man)
Light in the Clearing - Irving A. Bacheller 260

Beale, Ned (Military Personnel)
Rush to Destroy - L. Jay Martin 4133

Beals, Dan (Sailor)
Look Away, Look Away - Leslie Turner White 6685

Beam, Michael (Frontiersman)
Michael Beam - Richard Hallet 2663

Bear Paws (Indian; Warrior)
Bride of the Morning Star - Don Coldsmith 1170

Bear Talker (Indian)
Dawn Land - Joseph Bruchac III 734

Beard, Andrew (Young Man)
Spanish Bayonet - Stephen Vincent Benet 441

Beard, Califa (Heiress)
To Fell the Giants - Bill Hotchkiss 3038

Beard, William (Frontiersman)
To Fell the Giants - Bill Hotchkiss 3038

Beaton, David (Settler)
Free Land - Rose Lane 3660

Beaton, Mary (Gentlewoman)
The Stuart Legacy - Robert Kerr 3472

Beatriz (Dancer; Gypsy)
Columbus: A Romance - Rafael Sabatini 5549

Beatty, Haywood (Young Man)
Looking After Lily - Cindy Bonner 572

Beatty, Marion (Young Man)
Lily - Cindy Bonner 571

Beaucaire, Victor M. (Nobleman)
Monsieur Beaucaire - Booth Tarkington 6163

Beauchamp, Guy (Nobleman)
Melbury Square - Dorothy Eden 1857

Beauchamp, Philippa de (Noblewoman)
Earth Song - Catherine Coulter 1374

Beaufort (Religious)
The Bishop's Tale - Margaret Frazer 2215

Beaufort, Jason (Gentleman)
Marianne and the Crown of Fire - Juliette
  Benzoni 467

Beaufort, Jason (Sea Captain)
Marianne - Juliette Benzoni 466
Marianne and the Lords of the East - Juliette
  Benzoni 468
Marianne and the Privateer - Juliette Benzoni 470
Marianne and the Rebels - Juliette Benzoni 471

Beaufort, Victor (Prospector)
Black Gold - Anita Richmond Bunkley 771

Beauleigh, Diana (Gentlewoman)
The Black Moth - Georgette Heyer 2877

Beauman, Lucy (Gentlewoman)
The King's Commission - Dewey Lambdin 3614

Beaumanoir, Charles de (Military Personnel)
Castaway - Frances Murray 4535

Beaumaris, Guy (Nobleman)
Midnight Moon - Jeanne Montague 4436

Beaumaris, Lallage (Spouse)
Midnight Moon - Jeanne Montague 4436

Beaumaris, Robert (Gentleman)
Arabella - Georgette Heyer 2874

Beaumont, Anthony (Gentleman)
The Tynedale Daughters - Norma Lee Clark 1093

Beaumont, Beth (Gentlewoman)
Apache - Donald Clayton Porter 5114

Beaumont, Sir Charles (Gentleman)
The Son of York - Margaret Abbey 5

Beaumont, Dorothy (Gentlewoman)
Charlie Is My Darling - Mollie Hardwick 2691

Beaumont, Francis (Military Personnel)
Eliza Stanhope - Joanna Trollope 6347

Beaumont, Simon (Nobleman)
The Hooded Falcon - Prudence Andrew 140

Beauregard, Charles (Adventurer)
Anno-Dracula - Kim Newman 4595

Beauty Beast (Slave)
Beauty Beast - MacKinlay Kantor 3361

Beauvaise, Jane (Indian)
Women in the Wind - Margaret Ritter 5350

Beauvallet, Nicholas (Pirate; Sea Captain)
Beauvallet - Georgette Heyer 2876

Becca (Sorceress)
The Gods Are Not Mocked - Anna Taylor 6177

Beche, Edmund (Government Official)
The Death of a King - P.C. Doherty 1672

Beck, Morgan (Adventurer; Frontiersman)
The American River - Gary McCarthy 4222

Becker, Claire (Young Woman)
Galveston - Suzanne Morris 4482

Becker, Frank (Outlaw)
Dutch Uncle - Marilyn Durham 1815

Becker, Friedrich (Veteran; Teacher)
Karl and Rosa - Alfred Doblin 1653
A People Betrayed - Alfred Doblin 1654

Becket, David (Military Personnel)
The Firedrake's Eye - Patricia Finney 2095

Becket, Eleanora (Noblewoman; Spy)
Lady Gallant - Suzanne Robinson 5413

Becket, Jonathon (Orphan; Patriot)
Redcoat - Bernard Cornwell 1337

Beckford, Will (Businessman)
A New Creature - Prudence Andrew 141

Beckwith, Hollis (Detective—Police)
The Last Mystery of Edgar Allan Poe - Manny
  Meyers 4356

Beckwith, Sam (Young Man)
The Coming of Rain - Richard Marius 4084

Becque, Thomas (Journalist)
Charlotte Morel - Maria Lodi 3829
Charlotte Morel: The Dream - Maria Lodi 3830
Charlotte Morel: The Siege - Maria Lodi 3831

Bede, Adam (Carpenter)
Adam Bede - George Eliot 1908

Bedford, Charles (Stock Broker)
Banished Children of Eve - Peter Quinn 5227

Bedford, Duncan (Military Personnel)
So Red the Rose - Stark Young 6944

Bedford, Katherine (Gentlewoman)
Caribbee - Thomas Hoover 3025

Bedford, Malcolm (Plantation Owner)
So Red the Rose - Stark Young 6944

Bedham, Cassie (Young Woman)
Lucifer Land - Mildred B. Davis 1538

Bedivere (Knight)
Beloved Exile - Parke Godwin 2446
The Pendragon - Catherine Christian 1075

Bedloe, Tom (Military Personnel)
Wild Is the River - Louis Bromfield 704

Bedwyr (Knight)
In Winter's Shadow - Gillian Bradshaw 632
The Last Pendragon - Robert Rice 5316
Sword at Sunset - Rosemary Sutcliff 6125

Beehunter (Lawman; Indian)
To Make a Killing - Robert J. Conley   1252

Beeljie (Slave)
Fairoaks - Frank Yerby   6915

Beguildy, Jancis (Fiance(e))
Precious Bane - Mary Webb   6590

Behaim, Joachim (Businessman)
Leonardo's Judas - Leo Perutz   4941

Behan, Billy (Hero)
Billy Bathgate - E.L. Doctorow   1656

Beladar (Doctor; Companion)
The Babylonians - Nathaniel Norsen Weinreb   6600

Belchamber, Amelia (Governess)
The Belchamber Scandal - Frances Murray   4533

Belden, Joshua (Heir; Gambler)
Birthright - Phillip Finch   2087

Belfort, Lord (Nobleman)
Dual Destiny - Karen Lynn   3939

Belinda (Foundling)
The Foundling - Georgette Heyer   2888

Belknap, Thomas (Spy; Religious)
The Fate of Princes - P.C. Doherty   1673

Bell, Jane (Spouse; Captive)
Red Morning - Ruby Frazier Frey   2230

Bell, Ramon (Military Personnel)
D'ri and I - Irving A. Bacheller   257

Bellac, Charles de (Diplomat)
The Hastening Wind - Edward Grierson   2591

Bellamy, James (Military Personnel; Gentleman)
The Bellamy Saga - John Pearson   4878

Bellamy, Lady Marjorie (Noblewoman)
The Bellamy Saga - John Pearson   4878
Upstairs Downstairs - John Hawkesworth   2782

Bellamy, Richard (Gentleman; Political Figure)
The Bellamy Saga - John Pearson   4878
Upstairs Downstairs - John Hawkesworth   2782

Bellarmi, Lucia (Young Woman)
Divine Mistress - Frank G. Slaughter   5886

Bellebelle (Prostitute)
Beloved Enemy: The Passions of Eleanor of Aquitaine - Ellen Jones   3288

Bellefleur, Lilian (Gentlewoman)
Flowers for Lilian - Anna Gilbert   2405

Belleme, Robert de (Nobleman)
The Wild Hunt - Elizabeth Chadwick   969

Bellerophon (Hero)
Three Ships and Three Kings - Georgia Sallaska   5573

Bellnap, Martha (Spouse)
Troubled Spring - John Brick   678

Bellnap, Robert (Businessman)
Troubled Spring - John Brick   678

Bellnap, Samuel (Veteran)
Troubled Spring - John Brick   678

Belmanoir, Tracy (Nobleman; Rake)
The Black Moth - Georgette Heyer   2877

Belmarch (Military Personnel)
Belmarch: A Legend of the First Crusade - Christopher Davis   1514

Belmont, Eleanor (Gentlewoman)
The Prince of Darkness - P.C. Doherty   1675

Belnatan (Sea Captain)
Fleet Surgeon to Pharaoh - Sheldon Jacobson   3140

Belstone, Kit (Nobleman)
Deborah - Colette Davenat   1498

Belton, Clinton (Political Figure; Military Personnel)
The History of Rome Hanks - Joseph Stanley Pennell   4909

Belville, Henry (Military Personnel)
Gwendolen - Clare Darcy   1489

Bemford, Lord (Rake; Adventurer)
The Road and the Star - Berkely Mather   4182

Ben (Orphan; Worker)
The Rag Nymph - Catherine Cookson   1287

Ben (Slave)
Tell Me a Tale: A Novel of the Old South - James McEachin   4266

ben Abdiel, Asa (Doctor)
Fleet Surgeon to Pharaoh - Sheldon Jacobson   3140

Ben-Hadad (Artisan)
The Lion in Egypt - Peter Danielson   1470

Ben Hur, Judah (Royalty; Slave)
Ben Hur: A Tale of the Christ - Lew Wallace   6536

ben Kition, Dara (Wanderer)
Dara, the Cypriot - Louis Paul   4842

Benchly, Roger (Steward)
Evil Mark - Graham Miles   4377

Bendelbinder, Aaron (Immigrant)
The Dream Seekers - Stephen Longstreet   3884

Bending Reed (Indian)
Lord Grizzly - Frederick F. Manfred   4056

Benedetto, Diana (Young Woman)
1915: A Novel - Roger McDonald   4264

Benedict, Adam (Financier)
Home Station - Jeanne Williams   6778

Benedict, Alice (Gentlewoman)
Statues in a Garden - Isabel Colegate   1198

Benet, Skinner (Trader)
Eagle Fur - Robert Newton Peck   4884

Benfras (Minstrel)
Harp into Battle - Cecil Maiden   4031

Benkei (Religious)
The Sword of Hachiman - Lynn Guest   2608

Bennet, F.W. (Businessman)
Loon Lake - E.L. Doctorow   1657

Bennett, Clay (Military Personnel)
Angel with Spurs - Paul I. Wellman   6613

Bennett, Elizabeth (Spouse)
An Unequal Marriage; or Pride and Prejudice Twenty Years Later - Emma Tennant   6202

Bennett, Gill (Trader)
Hong Kong - Mona Gardner   2288

Bennett, Timothy (Military Personnel)
Stars on the Sea - F. van Wyck Mason   4161

Benno (Servant)
Axe for an Abbot - Elizabeth Eyre   1989
Bravo for the Bride - Elizabeth Eyre   1990
Curtains for the Cardinal - Elizabeth Eyre   1991
Death of the Duchess - Elizabeth Eyre   1992

Benoit (Knight)
The Queen's War: A Novel of Eleanor of Aquitaine - Jeanne Mackin   3996

Bensham, Benjamin (Military Personnel)
The Mallen Lot - Catherine Cookson   1281

Bensham, Daniel (Gentleman)
The Mallen Girl - Catherine Cookson   1280

Bensham, Katie (Gentlewoman)
The Mallen Lot - Catherine Cookson   1281

Bent, Jerry (Rancher)
She Rode a Yellow Stallion - Walter Reed   5286

Bent, Tristram (Adventurer; Spy)
Tristram Bent - Henry Barnard Safford   5560

Benteen, Dick (Veteran; Scout)
Wagons to Tucson - Ed Newsom   4604

Benton, Andrew (Frontiersman; Military Personnel)
This Land Is Ours - Louis Zara   6953

Benton, Harry (Military Personnel)
Molly - Teresa Crane   1417

Benton, Joseph Bonaparte (Adventurer)
Peter Doyle - John Vernon   6457

Benton, Roland (Military Personnel)
Benton's Row - Frank Yerby   6908

Benton, Sarah (Young Woman)
Benton's Row - Frank Yerby   6908

Benton, Scot (Teenager)
The Bright Feathers - John H. Culp   1441

Benton, Tom (Plantation Owner)
Benton's Row - Frank Yerby   6908

Bentwood, Simon (Gentleman)
Tilly Alone - Catherine Cookson   1289

Beothainn (Chieftain)
The Crows of War - Steven Rayson   5276

Beowulf (Warrior; Chieftain)
The Coming of the King - Nikolai Tolstoy   6296
The Green Man - Henry Treece   6330
The Tower of Beowulf - Parke Godwin   2450

Berdeyev, Kolya (Musician)
Journey into Fire - Patricia Wright   6882

Berdeyev, Nicolai (Military Personnel)
A Space of the Heart - Patricia Wright   6884

Berenger, Eveline (Gentlewoman)
The Betrothed - Sir Walter Scott   5691

Beresford, Alex (Businessman)
Some Far Elusive Dawn - Emma Drummond   1727

Beresford, Lydia (Young Woman)
Some Far Elusive Dawn - Emma Drummond   1727

Berg, Dirk Van der (Young Man)
The Hill of Doves - Stuart Cloete   1123

Berg, Noah (Murderer)
Members of the Tribe - Richard Kluger   3511

Berg, Simon Van der (Trader)
The Mask - Stuart Cloete   1125

Bergeron, Maximilien (Revolutionary)
The Riven Heart - Genevieve Gennari   2354

Bergheim, Max von (Nobleman)
Letty - Clare Darcy   1491

Beric (Young Man)
Blood of the Martyrs - Naomi Mitchison   4417

Beringar, Hugh (Government Official)
Dead Man's Ransom - Ellis Peters   4957
One Corpse Too Many - Ellis Peters   4966
The Raven in the Foregate - Ellis Peters   4969
The Virgin in the Ice - Ellis Peters   4974

Berkeley, Belle (Actress)
Why Kill Arthur Potter? - Ray Harrison   2746

Berliner, Ruby Levy (Designer)
Union Square - Meredith Tax   6176

Berling, Elizabeth (Heroine)
The Story of Gosta Berling - Selma Lagerlof   3586

Berling, Gosta (Religious)
The Story of Gosta Berling - Selma Lagerlof   3586

Bermejo, Juan Rodrigo (Sailor)
The Velvet Doublet - James H. Street   6082

Bernadin (Minstrel)
Bernadin, My Love - Leonard Rossiter   5506

Bernardino (Outlaw)
Rockspring - R.G. Vliet   6506

Bernardo (Companion)
The Pope's Rhinoceros - Lawrence Norfolk 4642

Bernay, Michael de (Servant; Slave)
When God Slept - Peter Bourne 597

Bernay, Odilon de (Religious)
God's Equal - Alain Absire 14

Berne, Gabriel (Businessman)
Angelique in Love - Sergeanne Golon 2470
Angelique in Revolt - Sergeanne Golon 2471

Bernstein, Baroness Beatrix (Noblewoman)
The Virginians - William Makepeace Thackeray 6214

Berrien, Angelica (Southern Belle)
Blood Red Roses - Elizabeth Boatwright Coker 1163

Berrien, Angelica (Spouse)
The Grasshopper King - Elizabeth Boatwright Coker 1165

Berrien, Beau (Gentleman)
The Grasshopper King - Elizabeth Boatwright Coker 1165

Berrien, Beau (Plantation Owner; Military Personnel)
Blood Red Roses - Elizabeth Boatwright Coker 1163

Berry, Edith Campbell (Diplomat)
Grand Days - Frank Moorhouse 4448

Berry, Syke (Lawyer)
Double Moscadine - Frances Gaither 2271

Berthois, Nicole (Farmer; Spouse)
The Wine Widow - Tessa Barclay 301

Bertomy, Haidee (Spy)
The Wilderness - Carter A. Vaughan 6442

Bertram, Edmund (Gentleman)
Mansfield Revisited - Joan Aiken 51

Bertram, Fanny (Gentlewoman)
Mansfield Revisited - Joan Aiken 51

Bertram, Julia (Gentlewoman)
Version and Diversion - Judith Terry 6207

Bertrand, Cyril (Young Man)
The Uncrowned King - Baroness Emma Orczy 4747

Bessas (Adventurer)
The Dragon of the Ishtar Gate - L. Sprague De Camp 1555

Best, Lydia (Young Woman)
The Peculiar People - Jan de Hartog 2764

Betchley, Eugene (Gentleman)
The Legacy of Beulah Land - Lonnie Coleman 1203

Bethune, James (Journalist)
The Long Watch - Elizabeth Linington 3798

Betram, Harry (Heir—Dispossessed; Gentleman)
Guy Mannering - Sir Walter Scott 5697

Bevan, Hywel (Religious)
Lord of Misrule - Gareth Jones 3290

Beventini, Tobias (Doctor)
Race of Scorpions - Dorothy Dunnett 1806

Beverley, Isabella (Gentlewoman)
The Banishment - Marion Chesney 1018

Beverley, Jessica (Gentlewoman)
The Intrigue - Marion Chesney 1034

Beverley, Rachel (Gentlewoman)
The Folly - Marion Chesney 1031

Bevis, Leoline (Artist)
Willowwood - Mollie Hardwick 2699

Bewley, Lord (Nobleman)
Colonel Sandhurst to the Rescue - Marion Chesney 1021

Beynon, Nerys (Young Woman)
Fiddler's Ferry - Iris Gower 2499

Bezuhov, Pierre (Bastard Son; Gentleman)
War and Peace - Leo Tolstoy 6295

Bezvidenhout, Frederik (Settler)
Watch for the Dawn - Stuart Cloete 1128

Bezy, Marianne de (Noblewoman)
In Perilous Seas - Victor Suthren 6130

Bias (Doctor)
The Sword and the Promise - Benjamin Siegel 5845

Bibbs, Pamela (Southern Belle)
A Darkness at Ingraham's Crest: A Tale of the Slaveholding South - Frank Yerby 6912

Bibikov, Caroline (Spouse)
Devil Child - Jo Germany 2359

Bibikov, Sergei (Nobleman)
Devil Child - Jo Germany 2359

Bickley, Charles (Settler)
Delilah's Mountain - Gloria Jahoda 3142

Bickley, Francis (Gentleman)
Annie - Gloria Jahoda 3141

Biddlescomb, Isaac (Sea Captain)
By Force of Arms - James L. Nelson 4579
The Maddest Idea - James L. Nelson 4580

Big Turtle (Indian)
The Forest and the Fort - Hervey Allen 100

Biggs, Hazel (Waiter/Waitress)
The Harvey Girls - Samuel Hopkins Adams 31

Bigod, Lady Barbara (Noblewoman; Bastard Daughter)
A Silver Mirror - Roberta Gellis 2353

El Bilbanto (Rebel)
The Gun - C.S. Forester 2174

Bilby, Jared (Sea Captain)
A Mirror for Witches - Esther Forbes 2157

Bill (Cowboy)
The American Cowboy - Will James 3163

Billinghurst, Surprise (Sailor)
Surprise - Brian Burland 785

Billings, Wichita (Young Woman)
Apache Devil - Edgar Rice Burroughs 806

Billingsley, Lettie (Southern Belle)
The Last Plantation - Don Wright 6879

Billips, Priscilla Ann (Young Woman; Settler)
The Long Sun - Janice Lucas 3920

Bingham, Captain Teddie (Military Personnel)
The Towers of Silence - Paul Scott 5685

Bion (Military Personnel)
Years of the City - George Rippey Stewart 6028

Biraygue, Pe de (Servant)
The Golden Chain - Jean Gamo 2275

Birch, Harvey (Peddler; Spy)
The Spy: A Tale of the Neutral Ground - James Fenimore Cooper 1310

Bird, Evelyn (Gentlewoman)
Audrey - Mary Johnston 3229

Birdson, Joe (Indian)
Rabbit Boss - Thomas Sanchez 5581

Birdwell, Eliza (Farmer)
Except for Me and Thee - Jessamyn West 6628

Birdwell, Eliza (Farmer; Religious)
The Friendly Persuasion - Jessamyn West 6629

Birdwell, Jess (Farmer)
Except for Me and Thee - Jessamyn West 6628
The Friendly Persuasion - Jessamyn West 6629

Birdwell, Josh (Military Personnel)
The Friendly Persuasion - Jessamyn West 6629

Bishop, Colonel (Plantation Owner; Government Official)
Captain Blood - Rafael Sabatini 5546

Bishop, Arabella (Gentlewoman)
Captain Blood - Rafael Sabatini 5546

Bishop, Bridget (Widow(er))
Gallows Hill - Frances Winwar 6831

Bishop, Carrie (Nurse)
Storming Heaven - Denise Giardina 2394

Bishop, Edward (Gentleman; Businessman)
Trade Imperial - Alan Lloyd 3814

Bishop, Ella (Teacher)
Miss Bishop - Bess Streeter Aldrich 71

Bishop, Joel (Gentleman)
Trade Imperial - Alan Lloyd 3814

Bishop, Joshua (Trader)
Trade Imperial - Alan Lloyd 3814

Bishop, Mary (Young Woman)
Gallows Hill - Frances Winwar 6831

Bishop, Tamsen (Young Woman)
The Hills Stand Watch - August Derleth 1615

Bittersweet (Spouse)
Bittersweet - Leslie Li 3769

Bjarni (Adventurer)
Two Ravens - Cecelia Holland 2997

Bjorgulfson, Laurans (Knight; Landowner)
The Bridal Wreath - Sigrid Undset 6379

Bjorklund, Ingeborg (Immigrant)
An Untamed Land - Lauraine Snelling 5936

Bjorklund, Ronald (Immigrant)
An Untamed Land - Lauraine Snelling 5936

Black, Andrew (Police Officer; Military Personnel)
The Eagles of Malice - Alan Scholefield 5652

Black, Charlie (Indian)
Back to Malachi - Robert J. Conley 1237

Black, Christopher (Political Figure; Revolutionary)
The End of the Hunt - Thomas Flanagan 2119

Black, Gideon (Teacher; Pioneer)
The Land Is Bright - Archie Binns 501

Black, James Fraser (Convict)
Great Elephant - Alan Scholefield 5654

Black, Morris (Detective—Police)
A Gathering of Saints - Christopher Hyde 3092

Black, Robbie (Young Man)
Great Elephant - Alan Scholefield 5654

Black Bull, Thomas (Indian)
When the Legends Die - Hal Borland 584

Black Dog (Pirate)
Return to Treasure Island - Denis Judd 3318

Black Eunuch (Slave)
Valide: A Novel of the Harem - Barbara Chase-Riboud 1007

Black Skull (Indian; Warrior)
People of the Lakes - W. Michael Gear 2336

Blackford, James (Military Personnel)
The World Turned Upside Down - William Rayner 5273

Blacksmith, Gilda (Heroine)
The Chant of Jimmie Blacksmith - Thomas Keneally 3411

Blacksmith, Jimmie (Worker)
The Chant of Jimmie Blacksmith - Thomas Keneally 3411

Blackstone, Edmund (Detective—Police)
Beau Blackstone - Richard Falkirk 2005
Blackstone - Richard Falkirk 2006

Blackstone and the Scourge of Europe - Richard
Falkirk 2007
Blackstone's Fancy - Richard Falkirk 2008

Blackstone, Henrietta (Actress)
The River and the Wilderness - Don Robertson 5401

Blackthorne, Harlan A. (Judge)
The Stranglers - Loren D. Estleman 1978

Blackthorne, John (Sailor)
Shogun - James Clavell 1101

Blackwater, Major (Nobleman; Military Personnel)
Trumpeter, Sound! - D.L. Murray 4528

Blackwood, Alexander (Gentleman)
Sweet's Folly - Fiona Hill 2926

Blackwood, Charles (Widow(er))
The Folly - Marion Chesney 1031

Blackwood, David (Military Personnel)
The First to Land - Douglas E. Reeman 5288

Blackwood, Emily (Gentlewoman; Artist)
Sweet's Folly - Fiona Hill 2926

Blackwood, Philip (Military Personnel)
Badge of Glory - Douglas E. Reeman 5287

Blackwood, Pryor Deyhle (Widow(er); Time
Traveller)
Riding Shotgun - Rita Mae Brown 729

Blagden, Robin (Diplomat)
Drums Against Frontenac - Harvey Chalmers· 972

Blair, Charles (Doctor)
Drums of Khartoum - Chloe Gartner 2307

Blair, Jonathan (Adventurer)
Rose - Martin Cruz Smith 5923

Blair, Jonathan (Lawyer)
Jonathan Blair, Bounty Lands Lawyer - William
Donohue Ellis 1929

Blair, Susan (Spouse)
The Quality of Mercy - Anne Miller Downes 1712

Blair, Todd (Teenager)
A Bright Tragic Thing - L.D. Clark 1091

Blaise, Malvina (Noblewoman)
Castle Heritage - Elisabeth Barr 337

Blaisedell, Clay (Lawman; Gunfighter)
Warlock - Oakley Hall 2653

Blake, Benjamin (Bastard Son; Sailor)
Benjamin Blake - Edison Marshall 4102

Blake, Beth (Young Woman)
Washington! - Dana Fuller Ross 5491

Blake, Cathy Van Ayl (Spouse)
Texas! - Dana Fuller Ross 5490

Blake, Frank (Prospector)
Pacific Destiny - Dana Fuller Ross 5487

Blake, Frank (Teenager)
Sierra Triumph - Dana Fuller Ross 5488

Blake, Giletta (Spy)
Three Fields to Cross - Francis Tysen Nutt 4651

Blake, Henry (Government Official)
Carolina Courage - Dana Fuller Ross 5469

Blake, Henry (Military Personnel)
Celebration! - Dana Fuller Ross 5470
Oklahoma! - Dana Fuller Ross 5482

Blake, Henry (Military Personnel; Spy)
Arizona! - Dana Fuller Ross 5466
Homecoming - Dana Fuller Ross 5474
Illinois! - Dana Fuller Ross 5475
Kentucky! - Dana Fuller Ross 5477
Wisconsin! - Dana Fuller Ross 5493

Blake, John (Veteran)
Three Fields to Cross - Francis Tysen Nutt 4651

Blake, Leland (Military Personnel)
Colorado! - Dana Fuller Ross 5471
Nevada! - Dana Fuller Ross 5481
Oregon! - Dana Fuller Ross 5484
Texas! - Dana Fuller Ross 5490

Blake, Marah (Fiance(e))
Bridal Journey - Dale Van Every 6406

Blake, Norris (Journalist)
Foreign Devils - Irvin Faust 2053

Blake, Peter (Teenager)
Oklahoma Pride - Dana Fuller Ross 5483

Blake, Rainer (Gentleman)
In Still and Stormy Waters - Reay Tannahill 6157

Blake, Rebecca (Orphan)
Circle of Gold - Karen Harper 2710

Blake, Simon (Artist)
The Big Drum - Elizabeth Boatwright Coker 1162

Blake, Thomas (Adventurer)
Blood Red Rose - Maxwell Grant 2538

Blakely, Dixon (Military Personnel)
Sycamore Men - David Taylor 6181

Blakely, Morgan (Nobleman; Spy)
Bride of the Unicorn - Kasey Michaels 4363

Blakeney, Marguerite (Gentlewoman)
The Scarlet Pimpernel - Baroness Emma Orczy 4745

Blakeney, Sir Percy (Nobleman; Adventurer)
The Scarlet Pimpernel - Baroness Emma Orczy 4745

Blakeslee, E. Rucker (Veteran; Store Owner)
Cold Sassy Tree - Olive Ann Burns 797

Blakeslee, Love Simpson (Spouse)
Cold Sassy Tree - Olive Ann Burns 797

Blakeslee, Will Tweedy (Teenager)
Cold Sassy Tree - Olive Ann Burns 797

Blakeslee, Will Tweedy (Young Man)
Leaving Cold Sassy - Olive Ann Burns 798

Blamey, Captain Andrew (Sea Captain)
Demelza - Winston Graham 2524

Blanchard, Catherine (Socialite)
Seattle Green - Jane Adams 26

Blanchard, Holly (Young Woman)
Sound of the Trumpet - Gilbert Morris 4471

Blanchard, Marie (Spy)
The Charlatan - Carter A. Vaughan 6433

Blanchard, Natalie (Journalist)
Seattle Green - Jane Adams 26

Blanchard, Nicholas (Military Personnel)
The Wild Ohio - Bart Spicer 5966

Blanche, Lady (Noblewoman)
The Seven Ages - Eva Figes 2084

Blanchfleur, Anne (Gentlewoman)
The Town House - Norah Lofts 3861

Blanford, Clytie (Gentlewoman)
The Spring of the Tiger - Victoria Holt 3021

Blatonikos, Leir (Chieftain)
The Serpent's Tooth - Diana L. Paxson 4846

Blau, Hannah (Nurse; Midwife)
The Midwife - Gay Courter 1388

Blaylock, Nathan (Bastard Son)
The Winter Wolf: Wyatt Earp in Alaska - Richard
Parry 4820

Blaylock, Serena (Artist)
The Bluestocking - David Delman 1598

Blaze (Blacksmith)
Isle of Woman - Piers Anthony 167

Bleasdale, Sarah (Gentlewoman)
A Leaf in the Wind - Marie Joseph 3307

Blease, Roger (Pirate; Sailor)
For My Great Folly - Thomas B. Costain 1365

Blecourt, Jean Pierre de (Gentleman)
All the Golden Gifts - Iola Fuller 2251

Bleddyn, Morgan (Wanderer)
The High Missouri - Winfred Blevins 545

Blenkinsop, Sue Ellen (Heiress; Widow(er))
Wind of Change at Castle Rising - Fanny
Cradock 1412

Blevins, Clay (Businessman)
Reunion at Chattanooga - Alfred Leland Crabb 1406

Blevins, Grandma (Businesswoman)
Reunion at Chattanooga - Alfred Leland Crabb 1406

Blevins, Ruth (Young Woman)
Reunion at Chattanooga - Alfred Leland Crabb 1406

Bleymont, Catherine de (Noblewoman)
Captain General - John P. Stevenson 6007

Bligh, Dulcie (Noblewoman)
The Baroness of Bow Street - Gail Clark 1085
Dulcie Bligh - Gail Clark 1086

Blish, Belinda (Gentlewoman)
The Scandalous Marriage - Marion Chesney 1050

Blish, Lucy (Gentlewoman)
The Scandalous Marriage - Marion Chesney 1050

Bliss, John (Religious)
Hunt for Heaven - Elsie Barber 298

Bliss, Malvern Hill (Military Personnel)
Over There - Thomas Fleming 2130

Bliss, Savanna (Spouse)
Deep River - Henrietta Buckmaster 760

Bliss, Simon (Gentleman)
The King Edward Plot - Robert Lee Hall 2658

Bliss, Simon (Landowner; Political Figure)
Deep River - Henrietta Buckmaster 760

Blondelyn (Musician)
Lionheart: A Novel of Richard I, King of England -
Martha Rofheart 5428

Blood, Colonel (Pirate)
The Pyrates - George MacDonald Fraser 2212

Blood, Kate (Young Woman)
Blood & Dreams - Leslie Waller 6543

Blood, Peter (Doctor; Pirate)
Captain Blood - Rafael Sabatini 5546

Blood Hawk (Indian; Warrior)
Eye of the Hawk - David William Ross 5498

Bloody Shad (Pirate; Demon)
A Mirror for Witches - Esther Forbes 2157

Bloom, Leopold (Businessman)
Saints and Scholars - Terrence Eagleton 1821

Bloundel, Amabel (Young Woman)
Old St. Paul's - William Harrison Ainsworth 57

Bloundel, Stephen (Store Owner)
Old St. Paul's - William Harrison Ainsworth 57

Blount, Sulien (Religious)
The Potter's Field - Ellis Peters 4968

Blue (Political Figure)
Welcome to Hard Times - E.L. Doctorow 1660

Blue Elk (Indian)
When the Legends Die - Hal Borland 584

Blue Jay (Indian; Explorer)
Walks in the Sun - Don Coldsmith 1194

Blue Paints (Indian)
Moon of Thunder - Don Coldsmith 1180

Blue Wing (Indian)
River of Sky - Karen Harper 2713

Bluett, Rodney (Gentleman; Military Personnel)
The Maid of Sker - R.D. Blackmore 529

Blum, Naomi (Gentlewoman)
The Northern Correspondent - Jean Stubbs 6099

Blundell, Roper (Actor)
The Merry Devils - Edward Marston 4123

Blunt, Richard (Artist)
The Merchant of Death - C.L. Grace 2508

Blythe, Annie (Young Woman)
Kingdom of Gold - Susan Wiggs 6744

Blythe, Lally (Young Woman)
The Secret Years - Judith Lennox-Smith 3718

Blythe, Nicholas (Military Personnel)
The Secret Years - Judith Lennox-Smith 3718

Bobrov, Boris (Landowner)
Russka: The Novel of Russia - Edward Rutherfurd 5535

Boccetta (Businessman)
Leonardo's Judas - Leo Perutz 4941

Bodeen, Ladd (Teenager)
The Horse Hunters - Robert Newton Peck 4887

Bodine, Captain (Veteran)
Shanghai Tango: A Novel of China - William Overgard 4769

Boggs, Enoch Angus (Adventurer)
Shield of Three Lions - Pamela Kaufman 3372

Bogoljubov, Vassily (Royalty)
The Power and the Passion - Christina Nicholson 4609

Bogun (Military Personnel)
With Fire and Sword - Henryk Sienkiewicz 5850

Boisdesert, Louis-Auguste de (Gentleman)
Heroic Dust - Theodora Dehon 1581

Boissart, Marguerite (Twin; Captive)
Heritage of the River - Muriel Elwood 1937

Boissart, Paul (Twin; Trapper)
Heritage of the River - Muriel Elwood 1937

Boite (Nobleman)
Lady of Moray - Bonnie Copeland 1318

Bok, Yakov (Worker; Murderer)
The Fixer - Bernard Malamud 4038

Bold Talent (Scholar; Writer)
Spring Moon: A Novel of China - Bette Bao Lord 3897

Bolderman, Martyn (Shipowner; Young Man)
The Sinking of the Sarah Diamond - William Dale Jennings 3213

Bolitho, Belinda (Spouse)
Success to the Brave - Alexander Kent 3441

Bolitho, Richard (Military Personnel)
Colors Aloft! - Alexander Kent 3427
Command a King's Ship - Alexander Kent 3428
Enemy in Sight! - Alexander Kent 3429
The Flag Captain - Alexander Kent 3430
Form Line of Battle! - Alexander Kent 3431
Honor This Day - Alexander Kent 3432
In Gallant Company - Alexander Kent 3433
The Inshore Squadron - Alexander Kent 3434
Midshipman Bolitho and the Avenger - Alexander Kent 3435
Passage to Mutiny - Alexander Kent 3436
Richard Bolitho—Midshipman - Alexander Kent 3437
Signal—Close Action! - Alexander Kent 3438
Sloop of War - Alexander Kent 3439
Stand into Danger - Alexander Kent 3440
Success to the Brave - Alexander Kent 3441
To Glory We Steer - Alexander Kent 3442
A Tradition of Victory - Alexander Kent 3443

Bolivar, Hogshead (Frontiersman)
Fury in the Earth: A Novel of the New Madrid Earthquake - Harry Harrison Kroll 3557

Bolkonsky, Andrey (Royalty)
War and Peace - Leo Tolstoy 6295

Boll, Captain (Sea Captain; Adventurer)
Fair Wind to Java - Garland Roark 5354

Boller, Melissa (Young Woman)
The Fancher Train - Amelia Bean 395

Bolton, Francis (Gentleman)
Jeremiah Martin: A Revolutionary War Novel - Robert H. Fowler 2191

Bolton, Isaac (Sea Captain)
Captain Bolton's Corpse - J.G. Jeffreys 3178

Bolton, Richard (Plantation Owner)
The Spoils of Eden - Robert H. Fowler 2193

Bonchurch, William (Gentleman)
The Woman Question - Dorothea Malm 4046

Bond, Ezra (Sailor)
The Edge of Piracy - Donald Barr Chidsey 1060

Bond, Hamish (Plantation Owner)
Band of Angels - Robert Penn Warren 6572

Bondenland, Joe (Time Traveller)
Frankenstein Unbound - Brian Aldiss 68

Bondone, Enrico (Art Dealer)
The House of Cray - Pamela Hill 2936

Bone, Bartle (Mountain Man)
Buffalo Girls - Larry McMurtry 4296

Bone, Esmond (Military Personnel)
Attack the Lusitania! - Raymond Hitchcock 2956

Bone, Isaac (Mountain Man)
A Dream of Kings - Davis Grubb 2604

Bonel (Courtier)
Banners of Gold - Pamela Kaufman 3371

Bonel, Mistress (Gentlewoman)
Monk's Hood - Ellis Peters 4964

Bonel, Gervase (Gentleman)
Monk's Hood - Ellis Peters 4964

Bones, Billy (Outlaw)
Anything for Billy - Larry McMurtry 4295

Bones, Billy (Pirate)
The Adventures of Long John Silver - Denis Judd 3317

Boneu, Antonio (Military Personnel)
This Promised Land - Robert Easton 1824

Bonning, George (Plantation Owner)
Ratoon - Christopher Nicole 4619

Bonnington, Beatrice (Businesswoman)
Speak to Me of Love - Dorothy Eden 1862

Bonnyfeather (Businessman)
Anthony Adverse - Hervey Allen 98

Bontine, Randall (Laird)
Hearts of Gold - Jessica Stirling 6044

Bonville, Cicely (Gentlewoman)
The Summer Queen - Alice Walworth Graham 2512

Bonwell, John (Settler)
John Bonwell - Charles K. Pulse 5208

Booker, Major (Military Personnel)
The Crater - Richard Slotkin 5908

Booker, Abel (Military Personnel)
Hang for Treason - Robert Newton Peck 4886

Books, John Bernard (Gunfighter)
The Shootist - Glendon Swarthout 6145

Boone, Benjy (Actor)
Benjy Boone - Maurice Dolbier 1687

Boone, Crassus Cornelius (Actor)
Benjy Boone - Maurice Dolbier 1687

Boone, Jonathan (Sailor)
The Barbarian - Willard Price 5191

Boone, Ray (Widow(er); Wanderer)
The Gallows Land - Bill Pronzini 5201

Booth, Sir Adam (Knight)
The Winter Rose - Millie J. Ragosta 5243

Booth, Gabe (Mountain Man)
The Smoky Hill - Don Coldsmith 1188

Booth, Howard (Businessman; Political Figure)
Damaris - Jane Sheridan 5810

Booth, Jesse (Military Personnel)
The Smoky Hill - Don Coldsmith 1188

Booth, Lemuel (Prospector)
The Smoky Hill - Don Coldsmith 1188

Boothby, Dora (Gentlewoman)
Creole Dusk - Walter Adolphe Roberts 5392

Borelli, Augustina (Young Woman)
Rogers' Folly - Albert E. Idell 3102

Born, Bertran de (Young Man)
Cross, Sword, and Arrow - Gladys H. Barr 340

Born Swimming (Indian)
Fathers and Crows - William T. Vollmann 6508

Born Underwater (Indian; Shaman)
Fathers and Crows - William T. Vollmann 6508

Borodin, Ilona (Gentlewoman)
Love and Honor - Leslie Arlen 189

Borowska, Wanda (Young Woman; Revolutionary)
White Eagle, Dark Skies - Jean Karsavina 3368

Borselen, Gelis van (Gentlewoman)
Scales of Gold - Dorothy Dunnett 1808
To Lie with Lions - Dorothy Dunnett 1810

Borst, Delia (Captive)
In the Hands of the Senecas - Walter D. Edmonds 1876

Borst, Gertje (Settler)
Valley in Arms: A Novel of the Settlement of Connecticut - Earl Schenck Miers 4376

Boruchowicz, Lazar (Young Man)
Heritage - Lewis Orde 4749

Boruchowicz, Leah (Young Woman)
Heritage - Lewis Orde 4749

Boruchowicz, Shmuel (Sports Figure)
Heritage - Lewis Orde 4749

Boscage, Rupert de (Nobleman)
Tansy Taniard - Myrtle Strode-Jackson 6084

Bosola (Spy)
A Dancer in Darkness - David Stacton 5971

Bossereau, Jean (Leader)
The Brothers of Uterica - Benjamin Capps 887

Boston, Lewis (Gentleman)
The Prisoners of September - Leon Garfield 2294

Boswell, Clementine (Actress)
The Mating Dance - Rona Randall 5250

Boswell, Jon (Doctor)
The House on Curtin Street - Millie J. Ragosta 5242

Boteler, Adam (Adventurer)
The Heaven Tree Trilogy - Edith Pargeter 4797

Botsford, Brian (Writer)
While England Sleeps - David Leavitt 3702

Bottomley, Cameron (Gentleman)
The Light Infantry Ball - Hamilton Basso 375

Bottomley, John (Gentleman; Plantation Owner)
The Light Infantry Ball - Hamilton Basso 375

Boudreau, Paul (Trader)
West of the River - Charlton Laird   3591

Boudreaux (Worker)
The Terrible Teague Bunch - Gary Jennings   3197

Bourke, Austin (Veteran; Wagonmaster)
Kansas Blue - Dylan Harson   2758

Bourlotas, Kosmas (Shipowner)
The Bourlotas Fortune - Nicholas Gage   2268

Bourne, Jason (Businessman)
Dark Winds - Virginia Coffman   1152

Bowden, Ash (Businessman)
Lady of No Man's Land - Jeanne Williams   6780

Bowden, Kate (Widow(er))
Mountain Man - Vardis Fisher   2110

Bowe, Liza (Saloon Hostess)
Liza Bowe - Shirley Barker   313

Bowen, Susan (Pioneer)
The Sun Shines West - Nathan Schachner   5632

Bower, Chuck (Military Personnel)
Wings for the Chariots - Arch Whitehouse   6713

Bowers, Eilley (Young Woman)
City of Illusion - Vardis Fisher   2107

Bowie, Henry (Scout)
Carmen of the Rancho - Frank H. Spearman   5955

Bowles, Anthony (Archaeologist)
The Idol Hunter - Barry Unsworth   6386

Bowman, Mark (Orphan; Homosexual)
Mark - Lonnie Coleman   1205

Bowman, Ralph (Artist)
The Whip - Catherine Cookson   1291

Bowman, Toby (Spy)
A Few Painted Feathers - Stephen Longstreet   3886

Boyce, Alfred (Heir)
The Dukes: A Novel - Malcolm Ross   5503

Boyd, Doone (Young Man)
The Boyds of Black River - Walter D.
  Edmonds   1871

Boyd, Harriet (Spouse)
Bide Me Fair - Harvey Howells   3060

Boyd, Hiram (Miner; Banker)
Calico Palace - Gwen Bristow   694

Boyd, Ledyard (Gentleman)
The Boyds of Black River - Walter D.
  Edmonds   1871

Boyd, Robert (Gentleman)
Bide Me Fair - Harvey Howells   3060

Boyd, Salathiel (Sailor; Pirate)
The Wickedest Pilgrim - Donald Barr Chidsey   1067

Boyd, Willie (Military Personnel; Actor)
Bide Me Fair - Harvey Howells   3060

Boyle, Hannah (Bastard Daughter)
The Girl - Catherine Cookson   1277

Boyle, Kenny (Sailor)
The Sea Eagles - John Edward Jennings   3206

Boyle, Michael (Railroad Worker)
The Warriors - John Jakes   3155

Braaf (Thief)
The Sea Runners - Ivan Doig   1685

Bracciolini, Vittorio (Actor)
Carnival of Saints - George Herman   2860

Brace, Hugh (Pioneer)
For Us the Living - Bruce Lancaster   3639

Bracegirdle, Anne (Actress)
The Bracegirdle - Burris Atkins Jenkins   3189

Bracewell, Nicholas (Manager)
The Laughing Hangman - Edward Marston   4120

The Mad Courtesan - Edward Marston   4122
The Merry Devils - Edward Marston   4123
The Nine Giants - Edward Marston   4124
The Queen's Head - Edward Marston   4125
The Roaring Boy - Edward Marston   4127
The Silent Woman - Edward Marston   4128
The Trip to Jerusalem - Edward Marston   4129

Bracken, Harriat (Spouse)
Wild Orchid - Isabel Dick   1640

Bracken of Hawkings Crest, Lord (Nobleman)
The Knight and the Dove - Lori Wick   6732

Brackley, Daniel (Nobleman)
The Black Arrow - Robert Louis Stevenson   6008

Braddee, David (Sailor; Religious)
The Delectable Country - Leland Dewitt
  Baldwin   280

Braddon, Eleanor (Young Woman)
Night Shall Overtake Us - Kate Saunders   5611

Braden, Whip (Frontiersman)
The Medicine Whip - Max Hennessy   2835

Bradford, Dake (Patriot)
Song of a Strange Child - Gilbert Morris   4470

Bradford, Daniel (Servant)
Sound of the Trumpet - Gilbert Morris   4471

Bradford, Fiona (Young Woman)
The Dedicated Villain - Patricia Veryan   6461

Bradford, Jonathan (Young Man)
The Drums of Morning - Philip Van Doren
  Stern   5997

Bradford, Roark (Military Personnel)
The Wilderness Brigade - Phyllis Gordon
  Demarest   1605

Bradley, Garnet (Store Owner)
Garnet - Helen Ashfield   207

Bradley, Ma (Criminal)
The Slow Awakening - Catherine Marchant   4082

Bradley, Page (Young Woman)
My Love, My Enemy - Jan Cox Speas   5958

Bradley, Robert (Carpenter)
The Moth - Catherine Cookson   1284

Bradley, Roger (Settler)
The Quiet Shore - Walter Havighurst   2775

Bradwardine, Rose (Noblewoman)
Waverley - Sir Walter Scott   5709

Brady, Martin (Gunfighter)
The Wonderful Country - Tom Lea   3695

Brady, Sam (Cowboy)
Blue Moon - Parris Afton Bonds   569

Brag, Branton (Murderer)
Bighorn Legacy - W. Michael Gear   2332

Bragelonne, Raoul de (Nobleman)
Twenty Years After - Alexandre Dumas   1783

Bragg, Joseph (Police Officer)
Counterfeit of Murder - Ray Harrison   2738
Death of a Dancing Lady - Ray Harrison   2739
Deathwatch - Ray Harrison   2740
Harvest of Death - Ray Harrison   2741
Patently Murder - Ray Harrison   2742
A Season for Death - Ray Harrison   2743
Sphere of Death - Ray Harrison   2744
Tincture of Death - Ray Harrison   2745
Why Kill Arthur Potter? - Ray Harrison   2746

Braide, Simon (Engineer; Spy)
Men in Buckskin - Herbert Stover   6069

Braithwaite, Henry (Abolitionist)
Echo of Lions - Barbara Chase-Riboud   1004

Braithwaite, Vivian (Abolitionist)
Echo of Lions - Barbara Chase-Riboud   1004

Branch, Anne (Gentlewoman)
Man Cannot Tell - Philip Lightfoot Scruggs   5711

Brancusi, Louisa (Dancer)
Louisa Brancusi - Darrell Husted   3088

Brand (Knight)
The Disputed Crown - Valerie Anand   128

Brand (Servant)
Gildenford - Valerie Anand   130

Brand (Warrior)
The Hammer and the Cross - Harry Harrison   2736

Brandon (Military Personnel)
The Eye of God - C.L. Grace   2506

Brandon (Nobleman)
Moonfeather - Judith E. French   2223

Brandon, Henry (Gentleman)
My Lady Greensleeves - Constance Beresford-
  Howe   476

Brandon, Kitty (Actress; Convict)
To the Ends of the Earth - Michael Talbot   6155
A Wilful Woman - Michael Talbot   6156

Brandon, Luke (Scientist)
Colorado! - Dana Fuller Ross   5471

Brandon, Margaretta (Widow(er))
The Merrymaid - Mollie Hardwick   2696

Brandon, Romilly (Gentleman)
A Night in Cold Harbor - Margaret Kennedy   3420

Brandt, Kirstina (Spouse)
My Pride, My Folly - Suzanne Butler   830

Brandt, Margaret (Young Woman)
The Cloister and the Hearth - Charles Reade   5279

Brandt, Naftali (Writer; Farmer)
Behold the Fire - Michael Blankfort   541

Brandt, Roger (Military Personnel; Loyalist)
The Rebel Loyalist - Charles William Gordon   2480

Bransom, Penelope (Widow(er))
The Sandalwood Fan - Diana Brown   720

Brantley, Court (Businessman)
A Woman Called Fancy - Frank Yerby   6931

Branwen (Servant)
The White Raven - Diana L. Paxson   4847

Brassova, Annastatia (Socialite)
A Token of Jewels - Diane Cory   1353

Brautigan, John (Police Officer)
Ain't Goin' to Glory - David Delman   1597

Brave Man (Prehistoric Human; Chieftain)
People of the Earth - W. Michael Gear   2334

Bravo, Ruben (Trader)
Strange Wives - Shirley Barker   317

Brawne, Cathie (Young Woman)
The Dollar Gold Piece - Virginia Swain   6134

Braxton, Isaac (Journalist)
The Long Naked Descent into Boston - William
  Eastlake   1823

Braxton, Jared (Gentleman)
Masque of Enchantment - Charlene Cross   1432

Braxton, Richard (Young Man)
Mistress of the Forge - David Taylor   6179

Bray, Ellen (Young Woman)
Ellen Bray - Jane Julian   3319

Bray, John (Settler)
All Ye People - Merle Estes Colby   1167

Bray, Julian (Gentlewoman)
The Lodestar - Pamela Belle   432

Bray, Nell (Suffragette; Detective—Amateur)
Crown Witness - Gillian Linscott   3803
Dead Man's Sweetheart - Gillian Linscott   3804

An Easy Day for a Lady - Gillian Linscott   3805
Hanging on the Wire - Gillian Linscott   3806
Sister Beneath the Sheet - Gillian Linscott   3808
Stage Fright - Gillian Linscott   3809

Braybon, General (Landowner)
The Near and Distant Place - Patricia Wright   6883

Brayford, Arthur (Nobleman)
Lucinda Brayford - Martin Boyd   613

Brayford, Hugo (Gentleman)
Lucinda Brayford - Martin Boyd   613

Brayford, Lucinda (Gentlewoman)
Lucinda Brayford - Martin Boyd   613

Breault, Blaise de (Fugitive)
Scarlet Cockerel - Clifford Sublette   6110

Brecht, Elisha (Outlaw)
The Border Men - Cameron Judd   3312

Breckenridge, Hunter (Trapper)
Fur Brigade - Hal George Evarts   1985

Breda, Anna von (Gentlewoman)
The Valiant Lady - Brigid Knight   3523

Breed, Navarro (Government Official)
Chase the Wind - Janelle Taylor   6184

Breen, Caty (Captive)
In the Hands of the Senecas - Walter D.
   Edmonds   1876

Brendan (Slave)
By Love Enslaved - Phoebe Conn   1255

Brendan, Alicia (Young Woman)
The Hedge of Thorns - Helen Ashton   217

Brenhilda (Gentlewoman)
Count Robert of Paris - Sir Walter Scott   5695

Brennan, Alice (Captive)
Beyond the Shadowlands - Georgina Fleming   2126

Brennan, Mary (Convict)
The Playmaker - Thomas Keneally   3414

Brent, Margaret (Plantation Owner)
Mary's Land - Lucia St. Clair Robson   5415

Brent, Tara (Fugitive)
Runaway - Heather Graham   2519

Brenthaven, Evangelina (Gentlewoman)
Angel - Carola Dunn   1790

Brentwood, Sam (Wagonmaster)
Independence! - Dana Fuller Ross   5476

Brereton, John (Military Personnel; Patriot)
Janice Meredith - Paul Leicester Ford   2166

Brese, Magdalen de (Noblewoman)
Brazen Whispers - Jane Feather   2055

Breslain, Esther (Immigrant; Photographer)
The House on Mulberry Street - Maan Meyers   4354

Bret, Gervaise (Lawyer)
The Dragons of Archenfield - Edward Marston   4119
The Lions of the North - Edward Marston   4121
The Ravens of Blackwater - Edward Marston   4126
The Wolves of Savernake - Edward Marston   4130

Brett, Charlotte (Gentlewoman)
Lamb in Command - Kenneth Maynard   4209

Brett, Jeremy (Sea Captain; Gentleman)
Brimstone Club - F. van Wyck Mason   4147

Brett, Luke (Military Personnel)
The Gun - C.S. Forester   2174

Brevaux, Antoine de (Military Personnel)
Deeper the Heritage - Muriel Elwood   1936

Brevoort, Geraldine (Gentlewoman)
Portrait in Brownstone - Louis Auchincloss   232

Brewster (Military Personnel)
Mutiny Run - Frank Eccles   1836

Brewster, Jonathan (Sea Captain)
The White Cockade - Henry Farrand Griffin   2592

Brewster, Philip (Student—College)
Three Sides of Agiochook - Eric Kelly   3400

Brewton, Hal (Doctor)
The Sea of Grass - Conrad Richter   5323

Brewton, Colonel Jim (Rancher)
The Sea of Grass - Conrad Richter   5323

Briallen (Gentlewoman)
The Briar Rose - Linda Neale   4561

Briavel, Lord Gavin (Nobleman)
Heiress of Ardara - Margaret Evans Porter   5137

Brice, Stephen (Lawyer; Military Personnel)
The Crisis - Winston Churchill   1079

Brice, Thomas (Military Personnel)
The Gray Captain - Jere Hungerford
   Wheelwright   6669

Bridgenorth, Alice (Gentlewoman)
Peveril of the Peak - Sir Walter Scott   5703

Brien, Louise (Fugitive)
Wild Geese - Eilis Dillon   1647

Brien, Robert (Fugitive; Military Personnel)
Wild Geese - Eilis Dillon   1647

Briggs, George (Frontiersman)
The Homesman - Glendon Swarthout   6143

Briggs, Nelly (Worker; Actress)
Lovers - Suzanne Goodwin   2476

Brighde (Royalty)
Swords in the North - Paul Lewis Anderson   138

Bright, Amanda (Spouse)
Departure - Janet Stevenson   6004

Bright, Cecilia (Gentlewoman)
Murder, I Presume - Gillian Linscott   3807

Bright, Iphigenia (Spinster; Teacher)
Mistress - Amanda Quick   5215

Bright, Jonathan (Sea Captain)
Departure - Janet Stevenson   6004

Brightwood, Joshua (Pioneer; Settler)
The Brightwood Expedition - Kay L.
   McDonald   4261

Brightwood, Marlette (Pioneer)
The Vision Is Fulfilled - Kay L. McDonald   4262

Brightwood, Marlette (Pioneer; Settler)
The Brightwood Expedition - Kay L.
   McDonald   4261

Brigmore, Anna (Governess)
The Mallen Girl - Catherine Cookson   1280
The Mallen Streak - Catherine Cookson   1282

Brinton, Clarissa (Young Woman)
The Golden Feather - Theda Kenyon   3462

Briscoll, Nan (Convict; Businesswoman)
Dream Time - Parris Afton Bonds   570

Brisker (Child)
The Pleasure Garden - Leon Garfield   2293

Brisson, Philippe (Adventurer)
Touched with Fire - John William Tebbel   6195

Bristed, Georgia (Socialite)
The Book Class - Louis Auchincloss   228

Bristol, Saul (Settler)
Ka'a'awa: A Novel about Hawaii in the 1850s -
   Oswald Andrew Bushnell   814

Britannicus, Caius (Military Personnel)
The Skystone: The Forging of Arthur's Britain - Jack
   Whyte   6726

Britewell, Jennifer (Gentlewoman; Teacher)
A Shadow's Bliss - Patricia Veryan   6477

Britsky, Max (Businessman)
Max - Howard Fast   2038

Brittanicus (Slave)
I Am a Barbarian - Edgar Rice Burroughs   807

Brittany, Morgan (Southern Belle)
Floodtide - Frank Yerby   6916

Briwerr, William de (Knight)
Lord Geoffrey's Fancy - Alfred Duggan   1771

Brixham, Anne (Gentlewoman)
The Golden Galleon - Victor Suthren   6129
Royal Yankee - Victor Suthren   6132

Broadbent, Jim (Gentleman)
Monday's Child - Mollie Hardwick   2697

Broadhurst, Hester (Gentlewoman)
Hester - Brian Cleeve   1107

Broadwinder, Jenny (Spouse)
The Lady and the Deep Blue Sea - Garland
   Roark   5356

Broadwinder, Philip (Sea Captain)
The Lady and the Deep Blue Sea - Garland
   Roark   5356

Brock, Tyler (Businessman; Trader)
Tai-Pan - James Clavell   1102

Brodkin, Ivan (Farmer)
Peter the Great - Alexey Tolstoy   6293

Brodrick, Copper John (Landowner)
Hungry Hill - Daphne Du Maurier   1746

Brodrick, Henry (Gentleman)
Hungry Hill - Daphne Du Maurier   1746

Brody, Jake (Immigrant; Orphan)
My Own Ground - Hugh Nissenson   4628

Brogmar, Augustin (Nobleman)
Restless Is the River - August Derleth   1617

Brome, Christopher (Nobleman)
Lydia, or Love in Town - Clare Darcy   1492

Brond, Black (Scout)
The Red Road: A Romance of Braddock's Defeat -
   Hugh Pendexter   4898

Bronowsky, Count Dimitri (Government Official)
The Day of the Scorpion - Paul Scott   5682

Brook, Marisa Estrada (Young Woman)
The House on Bitterness Street - Elizabeth Borton de
   Trevino   6340

Brook, Roger (Spy)
The Man Who Killed the King - Dennis
   Wheatley   6654

Brooke, Dorothea (Gentlewoman)
Middlemarch - George Eliot   1909

Brooke, Joshua (Rake)
The Rake and the Hussy - Robert W. Chambers   981

Brooke, Margaret (Young Woman)
Rogue's March - Maristan Chapman   993

Brooke, Peter (Adventurer)
Call the New World - John Edward Jennings   3199

Brooke-Hardinge, Anthony (Gentleman)
Murder at the Palace - Elliott Roosevelt   5445

Brookes, Nina (Gentlewoman)
A Notorious Woman - Malcolm Macdonald   3969

Brooks, Saul (Doctor)
The Brooks Legend - William Donohue Ellis   1928

Brooks, Winsome (Settler)
Rascal's Heaven - F. van Wyck Mason   4157

Broome, Arthur (Religious)
The Year of the French - Thomas Flanagan   2121

Broome, Francia (Young Woman)
The Mississippi Run - Paul Darcy Boles   565

Broome, Jenny (Settler)
The Traitors - William Stuart Long   3879

Broome, Jenny (Young Woman)
The Gallant - William Stuart Long   3873

Broome, Johnny (Journalist)
The Empire Builders - William Stuart Long   3871
The Gallant - William Stuart Long   3873
The Seafarers - William Stuart Long   3877

Broome, Justin (Adventurer)
The Explorers - William Stuart Long   3872

Broome, Kitty (Spouse)
The Empire Builders - William Stuart Long   3871
The Seafarers - William Stuart Long   3877

Broome, Minerva (Gentlewoman)
Cousin Kate - Georgette Heyer   2884

Broome, Philip (Gentleman)
Cousin Kate - Georgette Heyer   2884

Broome, Tom (Jockey)
The Mississippi Run - Paul Darcy Boles   565

Broome, Torquil (Mentally Ill Person)
Cousin Kate - Georgette Heyer   2884

Brotherton, William (Gentleman)
Charing Cross - Claire Rayner   5260

Brough, Joanna de (Gentlewoman)
The Faith and the Flame - June Dimmit
  Houston   3054

Broughton, Abigail (Gentlewoman; Servant)
Turn of the Dice - Janet Edmonds   1870

Broughton, Lucius (Military Personnel)
The Flag Captain - Alexander Kent   3430

Brown, Arnold (Steward)
Cambridge - Caryl Phillips   4983

Brown, Caesar (Frontiersman)
West Goes the Road - Tim Pridgen   5192

Brown, Clary (Actress)
My Name Is Clary Brown - Charlotte Keppel   3466

Brown, Emma (Spouse)
I Know My Love - Catherine Gaskin   2315

Brown, Harriet (Gentlewoman)
Marrying Harriet - Marion Chesney   1036

Brown, Harriet (Servant)
The American Heiress - Dorothy Eden   1854

Brown, Harriet (Young Woman)
Whispering - Jane Aiken Hodge   2972

Brown, Humility (Settler)
Daughter of Satan - Jean Plaidy   5011

Brown, Jacob (Religious)
The View From Coyaba - Peter Abrahams   11

Brown, Jamie (Convict)
Forefathers - Nancy Cato   960

Brown, Jared (Religious)
The Trembling Earth - Dale Van Every   6411

Brown, Jeremiah H. (Sea Captain)
Star in the Rigging: A Novel of the Texas Navy -
  Garland Roark   5358

Brown, Martin (Miner)
The Trembling Earth - Dale Van Every   6411

Brown, Stacey (Young Woman)
Stacey's Flyer - Patricia Burns   800

Brown, Styler (Journalist)
The Misadventures of Bethany Price - Marian
  Cockrell   1147

Brown, Tracy (Young Woman)
The Medicine Whip - Max Hennessy   2835

Browne, Isabel (Prostitute)
Clouds of Destiny - Lou Ellen Davis   1535

Browne, Lucy (Actress; Foundling)
Lucy - Hester W. Chapman   992

Browne, Richard (Detective—Amateur)
The Strange Death of Mistress Coffin - Robert J.
  Begiebing   415

Browne-Huntley, Lady Summer (Gentlewoman)
The Shalimar - Betty Hale Hyatt   3091

Brownell, Buck (Military Personnel)
Beloved Enemy - Al Lacy   3579

Browning, Caroline (Spouse)
Savannah - Eugenia Price   5186

Browning, Jonathon (Gentleman)
Before Darkness Falls - Eugenia Price   5178

Browning, Jonathon (Military Personnel)
Stranger in Savannah - Eugenia Price   5187

Browning, Mark (Gentleman)
Savannah - Eugenia Price   5186

Browning, Mark (Landowner)
Stranger in Savannah - Eugenia Price   5187

Browning, Natalie (Southern Belle)
To See Your Face Again - Eugenia Price   5188

Bruce, Donald (Military Personnel)
The Regiment - C.L. Skelton   5874

Bruce, Gordon (Military Personnel)
Beloved Soldiers - C.L. Skelton   5871

Bruce, James (Engineer)
Madeleine - Catherine Gavin   2323

Bruce, Naomi (Bastard Daughter)
Beloved Soldiers - C.L. Skelton   5871
The Regiment - C.L. Skelton   5874

Bruce, Willie (Military Personnel)
The Maclarens - C.L. Skelton   5873

Bruin (Animal)
Sam Patch: Ballad of a Jumping Man - William
  Getz   2390

Brules, Cat (Cowboy; Outlaw)
Brules - Harry Combs   1223

Brules, Cat (Frontiersman)
The Scout - Harry Combs   1224

Brules, Melisande (Spouse)
The Scout - Harry Combs   1224

Brun (Chieftain; Prehistoric Human)
The Clan of the Cave Bear - Jean M. Auel   236

Brunahild (Royalty; Warrior)
The Wolf and the Raven - Diana L. Paxson   4848

Brunhilde (Maiden)
The Twelve Pictures - Edith Simon   5857

Brunne, Guy de (Nobleman)
The Golden Exile - Lawrence Schoonover   5664

Bruno (Hero)
The Age of Wonders - Aharon Appelfeld   173

Bruno (Orphan; Religious)
The Miracle at St. Bruno's - Philippa Carr   925

Brusilov, Nadja (Young Woman)
The Jade Alliance - Elizabeth Darrell   1497

Bruyere, Christine de (Gentlewoman)
The Thousand Fires - Anne Powers   5155

Bruyere, Geoffrey de (Nobleman; Knight)
Lord Geoffrey's Fancy - Alfred Duggan   1771

Bryant, Claire (Gentlewoman)
While the Music Lasts - Suzanne Goodwin   2477

Bryant, Evangeline (Young Woman)
Promises to Keep - Jocelyn Stirling   6051

Bryant, Isobel (Artist)
While the Music Lasts - Suzanne Goodwin   2477

Bryant, Julie (Socialite)
While the Music Lasts - Suzanne Goodwin   2477

Bryant, Toby (Pilot)
Gentlemen of Adventure - Ernest K. Gann   2278

Bryant, Vivien (Gentlewoman)
While the Music Lasts - Suzanne Goodwin   2477

Bryce, Asa (Military Personnel)
The Horse Soldiers - Harold Sinclair   5862

Bryn, Ivor (Entertainer)
Lovers Meeting - Mollie Hardwick   2695

Bryson, Alistair (Journalist)
Our Valiant Few - F. van Wyck Mason   4155

Bryson, India (Gentlewoman)
Our Valiant Few - F. van Wyck Mason   4155

Bryson, Raphael (Sea Captain; Blockade Runner)
Our Valiant Few - F. van Wyck Mason   4155

Buchan, Lewis (Gentleman)
The Fathers - Allen Tate   6171

Buchanan (Laird; Teacher)
Rogue's Harbor - Inglis Fletcher   2139

Buchanan, Devlin (Doctor)
A City Not Forsaken - Lynn Morris   4480

Buchanan, Euphemia (Gentlewoman)
Some Brief Folly - Patricia Veryan   6478

Buchanan, Murdoch (Military Personnel;
  Frontiersman)
Rebel Guns - Adam Rutledge   5539

Buck, Henry (Indian; Companion)
Sassafras - Jack Matthews   4193

Buckerel, Dick (Worker)
Liza Bowe - Shirley Barker   313

Buckhart, Ezekiel (Outlaw)
The Flames of Time - Baynard Kendrick   3409

Buckmaster, Jim (Frontiersman)
Big River, Big Man - Thomas William Duncan   1786

Buckstone, Bion B. (Veteran; Convict)
The Buckstones - Paul I. Wellman   6615

Buckstone, Prudence (Young Woman)
The Buckstones - Paul I. Wellman   6615

Buckwell, Kathleen (Young Woman)
Crimson Creek: A Novel of the Early West - Robert
  McCraig   4228

Budd, Billy (Military Personnel)
Billy Budd - Herman Melville   4333

Budge, Mary (Widow(er))
Sir Philip's Folly - Marion Chesney   1051

Budley, Eliza (Widow(er))
Mrs. Budley Falls From Grace - Marion
  Chesney   1042

Buell, Thomas (Loyalist; Military Personnel)
Oliver Wiswell - Kenneth Roberts   5389

Buffalo Hump (Indian; Chieftain)
Dead Man's Walk - Larry McMurtry   4297

Buffalo Jake (Mountain Man)
The Amulet - Hal Borland   582

Buford, Evelyn (Gentlewoman)
Storm Against the Wind - Helen Hull Jacobs   3138

Buk, Janko (Farmer)
Poland - James A. Michener   4373

Bukowski, Szymon (Government Official)
Poland - James A. Michener   4373

Bulain, Jeems (Orphan)
The Plains of Abraham - James Oliver
  Curwood   1452

Bulba, Taras (Warrior)
Taras Bulba - Nikolai V. Gogol   2451

Buller, Archibald (Military Personnel)
Buller's Dreadnought - Richard Hough   3047
Buller's Guns - Richard Hough   3048
Buller's Victory - Richard Hough   3049

Buller, Richard (Military Personnel)
Buller's Victory - Richard Hough   3049

Bullinger, Frank (Journalist)
The Veracruz Blues - Mark Winegardner   6821

Bullington, Viscount (Heir; Nobleman)
Barry Lyndon - William Makepeace Thackeray   6210

Bumpass, Ephephtha (Heroine)
Confederates - Thomas Keneally   3412

Bumpass, Usaph (Military Personnel)
Confederates - Thomas Keneally   3412

Bumppo, Natty (Frontiersman; Guide)
The Deerslayer - James Fenimore Cooper   1299
The Last of the Mohicans - James Fenimore
   Cooper   1302
The Pathfinder; or, The Inland Sea - James Fenimore
   Cooper   1305
The Prairie - James Fenimore Cooper   1308

Bumppo, Natty (Frontiersman; Hunter)
The Pioneers; or, The Sources of the Susquehanna -
   James Fenimore Cooper   1307

Bundy, Andrew (Young Man)
A Kind of Justice - Benjamin Siegel   5844

Bungey, Friar (Religious; Astrologer)
The Last of the Barons - Edward Bulwer-Lytton   769

Buoncorso, Riccardo Del (Adventurer)
High Carnival - John J. Pugh   5207

Burchard, Sela (Teacher)
Run of the Stars - Dora Aydelotte   247

Burdock, Judith (Gentlewoman)
The Regulators - William Degenhard   1580

Burdon, Ellis (Military Personnel)
Playboy Squadron - Arch Whitehouse   6710

Burenin, Anna Yevnovna (Servant)
The Crown and the Crucible - Michael Phillips   4987
A House Divided - Michael Phillips   4988
Travail and Triumph - Michael Phillips   4991

Burenin, Paul (Revolutionary)
A House Divided - Michael Phillips   4988

Burgess, Elizabeth (Orphan; Madam)
Birthright - Phillip Finch   2087

Burgey, Joanna (Young Woman)
The Peacock and the Pearl - Jennifer Lang   3661

Burgh, Falcon de (Knight)
The Falcon and the Flower - Virginia Henley   2826

Burgoyne, Margery (Gentlewoman)
I Remember Love - Mollie Hardwick   2694

Burk, Nicholas (Military Personnel)
Monmouth - Charles Bracelen Flood   2144

Burke, Elizabeth (Captive)
The Great Valley - Mary Johnston   3234

Burke, Hailey (Settler; Prospector)
The Treasure of Pleasant Valley - Frank Yerby   6928

Burke, James (Military Personnel)
While Rivers Flow - Glen H. Fleischmann   2125

Burke, John (Religious)
Blackfoot Massacre - David Thompson   6251

Burke, Myles (Revolutionary; Veteran)
The Killing Frost - Thomas Hayden   2799

Burke, Thad (Scientist)
Sassafras - Jack Matthews   4193

Burke, Tom (Gentleman; Mercenary)
Tom Burke of Ours - Charles James Lever   3732

Burling, Susan (Spouse)
Angle of Repose - Wallace Stegner   5989

Burlingame, Henry (Teacher)
The Sot-Weed Factor - John Barth   364

Burlington, Edward (Gentleman)
In the Shadow of the Nile - Sara Hylton   3093

Burnaby, Sir Harry (Gentleman)
Lillibullero - Robert Neill   4571

Burnaby, Sir Harry (Gentleman; Political Figure)
The Golden Days - Robert Neill   4569

Burnaby, John (Gentleman)
Lillibullero - Robert Neill   4571

Burnaby, Nicholas (Lawyer)
Lillibullero - Robert Neill   4571

Burnet, Clemency (Gentlewoman)
Shadows and Images - Meriol Trevor   6344

Burnett, Andy (Frontiersman)
The Long Rifle - Stewart Edward White   6702
Ranchero - Stewart Edward White   6703

Burnett, Andy (Frontiersman; Rancher)
Folded Hills - Stewart Edward White   6701

Burnett, Carmel (Spouse)
Folded Hills - Stewart Edward White   6701

Burnett, Rice (Settler)
The Earthbreakers - Ernest Haycox   2789

Burney, Josiah (Heir—Dispossessed)
The Forest Lord - Noel B. Gerson   2368

Burnham, Matt (Blacksmith)
Lord Fancy - Leslie Turner White   6686

Burnham, Peter (Doctor)
Eagle in the Sky - F. van Wyck Mason   4149

Burnie, Davey (Teenager; Orphan)
A Journey to Matecumbe - Robert Lewis
   Taylor   6188

Burnie, Jim (Veteran)
A Journey to Matecumbe - Robert Lewis
   Taylor   6188

Burns, Molly (Servant)
The Indentured Heart - Gilbert Morris   4464

Burns, Tommy Jo (Frontierswoman; Entertainer)
Cherokee Rose: A Novel of America's First Cowgirl -
   Judy Alter   119

Burnside, Alex (Businessman)
The Penny Wedding - Jessica Stirling   6047

Burnside, Alison (Student)
The Marrying Kind - Jessica Stirling   6046

Burnside, Alison (Teenager; Student)
The Penny Wedding - Jessica Stirling   6047

Burritt, Adam (Explorer)
Call of the Arctic - Robert Steelman   5987

Burrows, John (Pirate)
For Love of a Pirate - Anthony Esler   1961

Burton, Amanda (Teenager)
Miss Lizzie - Walter Satterthwait   5608

Burton, Cal (Political Figure)
Sea to Shining Sea - Michael Phillips   4990

Burton, Thad (Orphan; Indian)
Rascal's Heaven - F. van Wyck Mason   4157

Bush, Ishmael (Kidnapper)
The Prairie - James Fenimore Cooper   1308

Bush, William (Military Personnel)
Beat to Quarters - C.S. Forester   2170
Commodore Hornblower - C.S. Forester   2172
Flying Colours - C.S. Forester   2173
Hornblower and the Hotspur - C.S. Forester   2176
Lieutenant Hornblower - C.S. Forester   2178

The Life and Times of Horatio Hornblower - C.
   Northcote Parkinson   4813
Lord Hornblower - C.S. Forester   2179
Ship of the Line - C.S. Forester   2182

Busson, Michel (Revolutionary)
The Glass-Blowers - Daphne Du Maurier   1745

Busson, Robert (Revolutionary)
The Glass-Blowers - Daphne Du Maurier   1745

Bustos, Baltasar (Student; Revolutionary)
The Campaign - Carlos Fuentes   2245

Butler, Aileen (Gentlewoman)
The Financier - Theodore Dreiser   1720

Butler, Arthur (Military Personnel)
Horseshoe Robinson, a Tale of the Tory Ascendancy -
   John P. Kennedy   3418

Butler, Edward (Political Figure; Businessman)
The Financier - Theodore Dreiser   1720

Butler, Fanny Kemble (Actress; Abolitionist)
Where Shadows Go - Eugenia Price   5189

Butler, James (Sea Captain)
The Power and the Passion - Christina
   Nicholson   4609

Butler, Jeremy (Sports Figure)
Catch a Falling Star - Stuart M. Kaminsky   3333
Down for the Count - Stuart M. Kaminsky   3336
The Fala Factor - Stuart M. Kaminsky   3337
Poor Butterfly - Stuart M. Kaminsky   3345

Butler, John (Captive)
The Light in the Forest - Conrad Richter   5322

Butler, Melissa (Spouse)
Look to the Mountain - Le Grand Cannon   885

Butler, Neal (Sailor; Actor)
Boon Island - Kenneth Roberts   5384

Butler, Rhett (Adventurer; Blockade Runner)
Gone with the Wind - Margaret Mitchell   4415

Butler, Rhett (Businessman)
Scarlett - Alexandra Ripley   5342

Butler, Smedley D. (Military Personnel)
A Few Good Men - William Overgard   4768

Butter, Amaziah (Spy; Military Personnel)
American Falls - John Calvin Batchelor   376

Butterfield, Elizabeth (Young Woman)
A Rage Against Heaven - Fred Mustard
   Stewart   6026

Butterworth, Jack (Frontiersman)
The Hider - Loren D. Estleman   1972

Buttes, Cobus (Military Personnel; Farmer)
Buttes Landing - Jean Rikhoff   5331

Buttes, Emily Guthrie (Spouse)
Buttes Landing - Jean Rikhoff   5331

Buttes, Guthrie (Farmer)
Buttes Landing - Jean Rikhoff   5331

Buttes, John (Farmer; Prospector)
The Sweetwater - Jean Rikhoff   5333

Buttes, Mason Raymond (Orphan)
One of the Raymonds - Jean Rikhoff   5332
The Sweetwater - Jean Rikhoff   5333

Buttes, Odder (Settler)
Buttes Landing - Jean Rikhoff   5331

Button, Jemmy (Indian)
Jemmy Button - Benjamin Subercaseaux   6107

Button, Susannah (Young Woman)
Dark Inheritance - Carola Salisbury   5568

Byam, Roger (Military Personnel)
Mutiny on the Bounty - Charles Nordhoff   4639

Byam, Sholto (Nobleman)
Belgrave Square - Anne Perry   4919

Byford, Kate (Gentlewoman; Governess)
Paths of Fortune - Susan Moore 4444

Byford, Sophy (Gentlewoman)
Paths of Fortune - Susan Moore 4444

Byrd, Tracker (Indian)
Tracker - David Wagoner 6521

Byrn, Lane (Military Personnel; Doctor)
Scarlet Cockerel - Garald Lagard 3584

Byrne, Anne (Nurse)
The Cortlandts of Washington Square - Janet
   Fairbank 2001

Byrne, Garrett (Military Personnel)
The Buffalo Soldiers - John Prebble 5165

Byrnes, Thomas (Detective—Police)
Time and Again - Jack Finney 2093

Byron, Jack (Military Personnel)
The Unknown Shore - Patrick O'Brian 4678

Bzik, Jan (Farmer)
The Slave - Isaac Bashevis Singer 5866

Bzik, Wanda (Young Woman)
The Slave - Isaac Bashevis Singer 5866

C

Caballito (Indian; Chieftain)
Apaches - Oakley Hall 2650

Cabell, Matt (Engineer)
The Golden Sabre - Jon Cleary 1105

Cabeza, Ramon (Military Personnel)
Follow the Wind - Don Coldsmith 1176

Cabezon, Juan (Orphan)
1492: The Life and Times of Juan Cabezon of Castile -
   Homero Aridjis 187

Cabot, Colin (Military Personnel)
The Master of Chaos - Irving A. Bacheller 262

Cabot, Electra (Gentlewoman)
Keeping Secrets - Suzanne Morris 4483

Cabot, Wentworth (Secretary)
A Connecticut Yankee in Criminal Court - Peter J.
   Heck 2814
Death on the Mississippi - Peter J. Heck 2815

Cade, Lucy (Orphan; Businesswoman)
Pastora - Joanna Barnes 321

Cadejac, Arsen de (Gentlewoman)
Destiny of Fire - Zoe Oldenbourg 4715

Cadfael, Brother (Religious; Detective—Amateur)
Brother Cadfael's Penance - Ellis Peters 4955
The Confessions of Brother Halvin - Ellis
   Peters 4956
Dead Man's Ransom - Ellis Peters 4957
The Devil's Novice - Ellis Peters 4958
An Excellent Mystery - Ellis Peters 4959
The Heretic's Apprentice - Ellis Peters 4960
The Hermit of Eyton Forest - Ellis Peters 4961
The Holy Thief - Ellis Peters 4962
The Leper of St. Giles - Ellis Peters 4963
Monk's Hood - Ellis Peters 4964
A Morbid Taste for Bones - Ellis Peters 4965
One Corpse Too Many - Ellis Peters 4966
The Pilgrim of Hate - Ellis Peters 4967
The Potter's Field - Ellis Peters 4968
The Raven in the Foregate - Ellis Peters 4969
The Rose Rent - Ellis Peters 4970
St. Peter's Fair - Ellis Peters 4971
The Sanctuary Sparrow - Ellis Peters 4972
The Summer of the Danes - Ellis Peters 4973
The Virgin in the Ice - Ellis Peters 4974

Cadiere, Aicart de la (Knight)
Destiny of Fire - Zoe Oldenbourg 4715

Cadman, Emma (Young Woman)
Silver Linings - Shirley Davies-Owens 1508

Cadogan, Kitty (Heiress)
The Gallant - William Stuart Long 3873

Cadorson, Annora (Gentlewoman)
Midsummer's Eve - Philippa Carr 924

Cadwallader, Owen (Government Official)
The Mamur Zapt and the Spoils of Egypt - Michael
   Pearce 4871

Cadwell, Christopher (Trapper)
Jason McGee - Robert H. Fowler 2190

Caelius (Gentleman)
The Key - Benita Kane Jaro 3169

Caffrey, Laird (Military Personnel)
The Land Where the Sun Dies - Henry Carlisle 896

Cain, Macaulay (Veteran; Outlaw)
Fair is the Rose - Meagan MacKinney 3997

Cain, Nathan (Sea Captain)
Pride's Fancy - Thomas H. Raddall 5231

Caine, Matthew (Mountain Man)
Rio Grande - Jory Sherman 5821

Caithris, David (Laird)
Hatchet in the Sky - Margaret Cooper Gay 2328

Caius Porteus (Government Official)
Sarum: The Novel of England - Edward
   Rutherfurd 5536

Calash, Gentleman Joe (Outlaw)
Rome Haul - Walter D. Edmonds 1877

Calderon, Juan (Military Personnel)
*The Bugles Are Silent: A Novel of the Texas
   Revolution* - John R. Knaggs 3513

Caldwell, Duke (Landowner)
Dan'l Boone Kissed Me - Felix Holt 3006

Caldwell, Ward (Veteran)
On a Lonesome Porch - Ovid Williams Pierce 4997

Caleb (Invalid)
Molokai - Oswald Andrew Bushnell 815

Calendar, Miles (Military Personnel; Scout)
Last Reveille - David Morrell 4456

Call, Woodrow F. (Gunfighter; Rancher)
Lonesome Dove - Larry McMurtry 4298

Call, Woodrow F. (Lawman)
Dead Man's Walk - Larry McMurtry 4297
Streets of Laredo - Larry McMurtry 4300

Callant, John (Servant)
The Boyds of Black River - Walter D.
   Edmonds 1871

Callaway, Mike (Military Personnel; Frontiersman)
Slow Dies the Thunder - Helen Topping Miller 4395

Calling Bird (Indian; Captive)
Bride of the Morning Star - Don Coldsmith 1170

Calling Crow (Indian)
Flight of the Crow - Paul Clayton 1103

Calling Owl (Indian)
Red Stick - Donald Clayton Porter 5121

Calloway, Bart (Sea Captain)
Summer Thunder - Willie Snow Ethridge 1982

Calloway, Hewey (Cowboy)
The Good Old Boys - Elmer Kelton 3405

Calvalcanti, Inacio (Religious)
Brazil - Errol Lincoln Uys 6395

Calvalcanti, Nicolau (Landowner)
Brazil - Errol Lincoln Uys 6395

Calverleigh, Miles (Gentleman; Rake)
Black Sheep - Georgette Heyer 2878

Calverleigh, Stacy (Gentleman)
Black Sheep - Georgette Heyer 2878

Calverley, Paul (Religious)
Prisoner of the Queen - Alison Macleod 4006

Calverly, Brandon (Plantation Owner)
Up Country: A Story of the Vanguard - Donald
   Culross Peattie 4881

Calvert, Clay (Outlaw)
Honey in the Horn - Harold Lenoir Davis 1523

Calvert, Leander (Prospector)
The American - Louis Dodge 1669

Calverton, Cressida (Gentlewoman)
Cressida - Clare Darcy 1485

Cambara, Licurgo (Landowner)
Time and the Wind - Erico Verissimo 6451

Cambara, Captain Rôdrigo (Adventurer)
Time and the Wind - Erico Verissimo 6451

Camboys, Hugh (Businessman)
The Merchant Prince - Henry Christopher
   Bailey 267

Cambridge (Slave)
Cambridge - Caryl Phillips 4983

Cambridge, Phillip (Nobleman)
Glorious Morning - Julie Ellis 1919

Cambrin, Ma'am (Settler)
Reckon with the River - Clark McMeekin 4292

Cameron, Alexander (Spy)
The Blood of Roses - Marsha Canham 879
The Pride of Lions - Marsha Canham 881

Cameron, Bethany (Settler)
The Edge of Time - Loula Grace Erdman 1949

Cameron, Caroline (Young Woman)
Wind From the Carolinas - Robert Wilder 6751

Cameron, Christa (Young Woman)
And One Rode West - Heather Graham 2514

Cameron, Clarissa (Young Woman)
The Thing about Clarissa - Roberta St. Clair
   Cook 1264

Cameron, Daniel (Military Personnel)
And One Wore Gray - Heather Graham 2515

Cameron, Donnie (Military Personnel)
Beloved Soldiers - C.L. Skelton 5871

Cameron, Eric (Patriot)
Love Not a Rebel - Heather Graham 2516

Cameron, Ewen (Laird)
The Flight of the Heron - Dorothy Kathleen
   Broster 710

Cameron, Garnet (Young Woman)
Jubilee Trail - Gwen Bristow 698

Cameron, Jesse (Doctor; Military Personnel)
One Wore Blue - Heather Graham 2517

Cameron, Justin (Lawyer)
The Strange Files of Fremont Jones - Dianne
   Day 1544

Cameron, Lauren (Young Woman)
Highlands Rebel - Sally Watson 6584

Cameron, Lynn (Gentleman)
Buckskin Cavalier - John Clagett 1082

Cameron, Martin (Orphan; Teenager)
The Restless Land - John H. Culp 1444

Cameron, Roc "Silver Hawk" (Pirate)
A Pirate's Pleasure - Heather Graham 2518

Cameron, Ronald (Plantation Owner)
Wind From the Carolinas - Robert Wilder 6751

Cameron, Wade (Settler)
The Edge of Time - Loula Grace Erdman 1949

Cameron, Wayne (Frontiersman)
Western Union - Zane Grey 2589

Camillina, Sosia (Young Woman)
The Silver Pigs - Lindsey Davis 1532

Camillus (Military Personnel)
Winter Quarters - Alfred Duggan 1775

Campbell, Angus (Trader)
The Fur Masters - Alan Sullivan 6113

Campbell, Catriona (Young Woman)
Lady of the Glen - Jennifer Roberson 5369

Campbell, Colin (Judge; Landowner)
The Land Is Bright - James Arthur Kjelgaard 3508

Campbell, Dylan (Wanderer; Trapper)
The High Missouri - Winfred Blevins 545

Campbell, Gavin (Gentleman)
A Falcon for a Queen - Catherine Gaskin 2314

Campbell, Jamil (Military Personnel)
Dark Torrent of Glencoe - Edward Grierson 2590

Campbell, John (Landowner)
New Day - Victor Stafford Reid 5291

Campbell, Neil (Young Man)
The Fur Masters - Alan Sullivan 6113

Campbell, Niall (Laird)
Child of the Mist - Kathleen Morgan 4451

Campbell, Olivia (Young Woman)
The Dark Mile - Dorothy Kathleen Broster 709

Campbell, Whitney (Military Personnel)
Buller's Dreadnought - Richard Hough 3047

Campbell-Bannerman, Madeleine (Gentlewoman)
The Stuart Legacy - Robert Kerr 3472

Campden, Clarissa (Gentlewoman)
Clear for Action! - Simon White 6699

Campion, Anne (Gentlewoman)
Corner the Moon - Shirley Barker 310

Campion, Ward (Businessman)
I Take This Land - Richard Powell 5147

Campos, Presentacion (Overseer)
The Red Lances - Arturo Uslar Pietri 4999

Candidianus, Lucius (Nobleman)
Last of Britain - Meriol Trevor 6343

Candish, Lilian (Young Woman)
Angels Falling - Janice Elliott 1915

Candler, Edmund (Journalist)
Invading Tibet - Mark Frutkin 2239

Canfield, Billy (Pilot)
Over There - Robert Vaughan 6449

Canfield, Jefferson (Convict)
Say to This Mountain - Bodie Thoene 6226

Canfield, Jefferson (Military Personnel)
In My Father's House - Bodie Thoene 6222

Canillejas, Dona Eloisa (Noblewoman)
Bride of the Conqueror - Hartzell Spence 5961

Cannaway, Byrdd (Artisan; Businessman)
The Cannaways - Graham Shelby 5789

Cannaway, Charlotte (Young Woman)
The Cannaway Concern - Graham Shelby 5788

Cannon, Gabrielle (Southern Belle)
Twilight of the Dawn - Elizabeth Nell Dubus 1752

Cannon, Jonathan (Teacher)
Forest of the Night - Madison Jones 3291

Cannon, Tom (Gentleman)
Twilight of the Dawn - Elizabeth Nell Dubus 1752

Cantillon, Rosamund (Young Woman)
Red Cloak Flying - Margaret Widdemer 6737

Cantrell, Edward (Veteran; Military Personnel)
Gone to Texas - John Williams Thomason 6247

Cantril, Maynard (Artisan)
A Fair Wind Home - Ruth Moore 4443

Cantu, Don Vito (Landowner)
The Hands of Cantu - Tom Lea 3694

Canty, Tom (Streetperson)
The Prince and the Pauper - Mark Twain 6373

Canynges, Crede (Young Woman)
Warm Wind, West Wind - Anne Irwin Matthew 4188

Cape, Hannah (Young Woman)
The Massacre at Fall Creek - Jessamyn West 6631

Cape, Markham (Businessman)
The Big Knives - Bruce Lancaster 3635

Capello, Rachele (Singer)
Creole Dusk - Walter Adolphe Roberts 5392

Capers, Lett (Bastard Son)
The Keeper of the House - Harry Harrison Kroll 3558

Caprice, Mary (Servant)
Christopher Humble - Charles Burnet Judah 3310

Captain Rex (Indian)
Rabbit Boss - Thomas Sanchez 5581

Captain S. (Spy)
A Clear Road to Archangel - Geoffrey Rose 5461

Caradoc (Royalty)
The Eagle and the Raven - Pauline Gedge 2344

Carboy, Samuel (Businessman)
The Tontine - Thomas B. Costain 1371

Carbury, Jessica (Fiance(e))
Promises to Keep - Jocelyn Stirling 6051

Cardenas, Barbara (Gentlewoman)
The Royal City - Les Savage Jr. 5621

Cardenas, Carlota de (Captive; Spouse)
Apache Autumn - Robert Skimin 5875

Cardess, John (Military Personnel)
War Paint and Rouge - Robert W. Chambers 983

Cardew, Cornelius (Gentleman)
The Shooting Party - Isabel Colegate 1197

Cardiff, Hugh (Frontiersman; Entertainer)
Wild Times - Brian Garfield 2291

Cardigan, Michael (Bodyguard)
Cardigan - Robert W. Chambers 976

Care, Maggie (Young Woman)
Polsinney Harbour - Mary E. Pearce 4863

Carew, Alexander (Military Personnel)
The Killing Frost - Thomas Hayden 2799

Carew, Charity (Secretary)
The Winter Bride - Carola Salisbury 5572

Carew, Sir Charles (Gentleman)
Prisoners of Hope: A Tale of Colonial Virginia - Mary Johnston 3238

Carew, Evan (Sea Captain)
Kingdom of Gold - Susan Wiggs 6744

Carewe, Maitland (Diplomat)
The Dark Palazzo - Virginia Coffman 1151

Carewe, Rachel (Gentlewoman)
The Dark Palazzo - Virginia Coffman 1151

Carey, Sir Andrew (Gentleman; Loyalist)
The Carolinian - Rafael Sabatini 5547

Carey, Clementina (Spouse)
Up She Rises - David Garnett 2298

Carey, Daniel (Printer; Historian)
A Generation of Leaves - Robert S. Bloom 552

Carey, Eleanore (Gentlewoman)
The Crystal Dove - Mollie Hardwick 2692

Carey, Sir Robert (Nobleman; Government Official)
A Famine of Horses - P.F. Chisholm 1071
A Season of Knives - P.F. Chisholm 1072

Carey, Robert (Veteran; Landowner)
Rebel Heiress - Robert Neill 4573

Cargill, Robert (Carpenter)
Come Home at Even - Le Grand Cannon 884

Carleton, Lord Bruce (Nobleman)
Forever Amber - Kathleen Winsor 6822

Carleton, Lucilla (Heiress)
Lady of Quality - Georgette Heyer 2893

Carleton, Ned (Criminal)
The Vast Memory of Love - Malcolm Bosse 588

Carleton, Oliver (Guardian)
Lady of Quality - Georgette Heyer 2893

Carlile, John (Young Man)
Walnut Grove - Jane Gilmore Rushing 5531

Carlington, Aurora (Young Woman)
Night Shall Overtake Us - Kate Saunders 5611

Carlisle, Hunkpapa Jack (Military Personnel; Indian)
Fifteen Flags - Richard Lynden Hardman 2686

Carlisle, Mary (Noblewoman)
Monsieur Beaucaire - Booth Tarkington 6163

Carlos (Explorer)
The Seven Cities of Gold - Virginia Davis Hersch 2865

Carlow, Fanny (Widow(er); Noblewoman)
Bath Tangle - Georgette Heyer 2875

Carlow, Lady Serena (Noblewoman)
Bath Tangle - Georgette Heyer 2875

Carlow, Vincent (Gentleman)
Claire - Elizabeth Lyle 3931

Carlton, Lord Guy (Nobleman; Rake)
Rake's Progress - Marion Chesney 1047

Carlton, Roger (Gentleman)
The Wizard's Daughter - Barbara Michaels 4362

Carlyon, Alexandria (Gentlewoman)
Defend and Betray - Anne Perry 4928

Carlyon, Anne (Spouse)
Inherit the Sun - Maxwell Grant 2539

Carlyon, Beth Brennan (Teacher)
Inherit the Sun - Maxwell Grant 2539

Carlyon, Edward (Nobleman)
The Reluctant Widow - Georgette Heyer 2899

Carlyon, John (Rancher)
Inherit the Sun - Maxwell Grant 2539

Carlyon, Thaddeus (Military Personnel)
Defend and Betray - Anne Perry 4928

Carnavon, Francis (Businessman)
A Fair Wind Home - Ruth Moore 4443

Carne, David (Doctor)
To the End of Her Days - Malcolm Macdonald 3975

Carne, Demelza (Servant)
The Renegade: A Novel of Cornwall, 1783-1787 - Winston Graham 2529

Carne, Drake (Blacksmith)
The Angry Tide - Winston Graham 2521
The Black Moon - Winston Graham 2522
The Four Swans - Winston Graham 2525

Carnmore, Alexander (Nobleman)
Wild Cat - Laura Black 524

Carola (Bastard Daughter; Entertainer)
Life as Carola - Joan Grant 2535

Carpenter, Benjamin (Student—College; Recluse)
A Sparkle From the Coal - Prudence Andrew 144

Carpenter, Brett (Military Personnel; Veteran)
The Laughing Stranger - Vina Delmar   1601

Carpenter, Elizabeth (Spouse)
The Laughing Stranger - Vina Delmar   1601

Carpenter, Harry (Prospector)
Journey - James A. Michener   4371

Carpenter, Hollis (Journalist; Lesbian)
Bayou City Secrets - Deborah Powell   5146

Carr, Rosie (Orphan)
Spring at The Winged Horse - Ted Willis   6794

Carr, Rosie (Widow(er))
The Green Leaves of Summer - Ted Willis   6793

Carradine, Brent (Writer)
The Daughter of Time - Josephine Tey   6209

Carramadino, Blasco (Adventurer)
The Scarlet Cloak - Jean Plaidy   5061

Carramadino, Domingo (Adventurer)
The Scarlet Cloak - Jean Plaidy   5061

Carrasquez, Dolores (Gentlewoman)
A Distant Thunder - Teresa de Luca   1561

Carrick, Alec (Sea Captain; Nobleman)
Night Storm - Catherine Coulter   1378

Carrick, Hugh (Nobleman)
Lord Iverbrook's Heir - Carola Dunn   1795

Carrick, Johnathan (Slave)
Theory of War - Joan Brady   637

Carrick, Peter (Orphan; Child)
Lord Iverbrook's Heir - Carola Dunn   1795

Carrick, Sebastian (Actor)
The Mad Courtesan - Edward Marston   4122

Carrill, Catherine (Gentlewoman)
Thunder on St. Paul's Day - Jane Lane   3658

Carrill, Charles (Student)
Thunder on St. Paul's Day - Jane Lane   3658

Carrington, Amelia (Gentlewoman; Collector)
The Time of the Dragon - Dorothy Eden   1863

Carrington, Ashley (Nobleman)
Charity Girl - Georgette Heyer   2879

Carrington, Gincie (Abolitionist)
Swan's Chance - Celeste De Blasis   1549

Carrington, Gincie (Landowner)
A Season of Swans - Celeste De Blasis   1548

Carrington, Nathaniel (Gentleman; Collector)
The Time of the Dragon - Dorothy Eden   1863

Carrington, Philip (Gentleman)
Lord of the Far Island - Victoria Holt   3016

Carrington, St. John (Military Personnel)
Wild Swan - Celeste De Blasis   1550

Carrington, Sarah (Loyalist)
Clouds of Destiny - Lou Ellen Davis   1535

Carrington, Stephen (Adventurer)
The Stranger From the Sea - Winston Graham   2530

Carrington, Stephen (Businessman)
The Miller's Dance - Winston Graham   2528

Carrisdowne, Rupert (Nobleman)
At the Sign of the Golden Pineapple - Marion Chesney   1016

Carroll, Caithlin (Young Woman)
Time and Chance - Anna Wibberley   6728

Carroll, Christine (Murderer)
This Dark Monarchy - Francis W. Leary   3698

Carroll, Daniel (Military Personnel)
Lorena - Frank G. Slaughter   5892

Carroll, Davy (Rebel)
Time and Chance - Anna Wibberley   6728

Carrolton, Sue (Young Woman)
Shaggy Legion - Hal George Evarts   1986

Carroway, Pete (Refugee)
Another Spring - Loula Grace Erdman   1948

Carruthers, Lady (Noblewoman)
Sir Philip's Folly - Marion Chesney   1051

Carruthers, Meredith (Gentleman)
The Tyrant - Patricia Veryan   6480

Carsons, Kim (Adventurer; Writer)
The Place of Dead Roads - William S. Burroughs   808

Carstares, John (Highwayman; Nobleman)
The Black Moth - Georgette Heyer   2877

Cart, Denna (Young Woman)
Timothy Baines - John H. Culp   1445

Carter, Barry (Gentleman)
Tassels on Her Boots - Arthur Cheney Train   6313

Carter, Catherine (Actress)
Catherine Carter - Pamela Hansford Johnson   3227

Carter, Lady Harriet (Widow(er); Gentlewoman)
The Stranger From the Sea - Winston Graham   2530

Carter, Harry (Military Personnel)
Luciano's Luck - Jack Higgins   2912

Carter, Magnus (Sea Captain; Privateer)
Magnus the Magnificent - Leslie Turner White   6688

Carteret, Charlessie (Young Woman)
Michael Beam - Richard Hallet   2663

Carteret, Delphie (Heiress—Dispossessed)
The Five-Minute Marriage - Joan Aiken   46

Cartier, Jean (Frontiersman)
Return to the River - Don Coldsmith   1184

Cartier, Jean "Woodchuck" (Frontiersman)
The Flower in the Mountains - Don Coldsmith   1175

Cartier, Paul (Revolutionary)
Coasts of Folly - Joel Williams   6784

Carton, Sydney (Lawyer)
A Tale of Two Cities - Charles Dickens   1642

Cartwright, Bohannon (Sailor)
Run Me a River - Janice Holt Giles   2415

Cartwright, Cassius (Military Personnel)
The Land Beyond the Mountains - Janice Holt Giles   2414

Cartwright, Emily (Gentlewoman)
Cambridge - Caryl Phillips   4983

Cartwright, George (Shipowner)
The Lady and the Deep Blue Sea - Garland Roark   5356

Cartwright, Lucy (Orphan; Heiress)
Greygallows - Barbara Michaels   4359

Cartwright, Pearl (Young Woman)
Pearl - Helen Ashfield   211

Carty, Judith (Heroine)
A Woman Scorned - Malcolm Macdonald   3978

Carvel, Richard (Gentleman; Military Personnel)
Richard Carvel - Winston Churchill   1081

Carvel, Virginia (Southern Belle)
The Crisis - Winston Churchill   1079

Carver, Cean (Settler)
Lamb in His Bosom - Caroline Miller   4380

Carver, Elizabeth (Gentlewoman)
The Fallon Blood - Reagan O'Neal   4741

Carver, Lonzo (Settler)
Lamb in His Bosom - Caroline Miller   4380

Carver, Thomas (Businessman)
The Fallon Blood - Reagan O'Neal   4741

Cary, Edward (Military Personnel)
Cease Firing - Mary Johnston   3230

Casanova, Felicine Elisa Maria (Adventurer)
Madame Casanova - Gaby von Schonthan   5659

Casaubon, Edward (Religious; Scholar)
Middlemarch - George Eliot   1909

Cascamond, Michel (Military Personnel)
Hangman's Beach - Thomas H. Raddall   5229

Casebolt, Tom (Rancher)
The Grass Kingdom - Jory Sherman   5818

Casey, Dan (Political Figure)
Casey - Ramona Stewart   6034

Casey, Peadar (Revolutionary)
The Men That God Made Mad: A Novel about Ireland's Easter Rising - W.A. Ballinger   286

Caspar, Freddy (Doctor)
Covent Garden - Claire Rayner   5262

Casper (Businessman)
Whole Hog - David Wagoner   6523

Cass, Dunstan (Gentleman; Criminal)
Silas Marner - George Eliot   1911

Cass, Eppie (Orphan; Heir—Lost)
Silas Marner - George Eliot   1911

Cassandra (Royalty)
Whom the Gods Would Destroy - Richard Powell   5148

Cassidy, Brooke (Socialite)
Death on the Cliff Walk - Mary Kruger   3562

Cassidy, Brooke (Socialite; Spouse)
No Honeymoon for Death - Mary Kruger   3564

Cassidy, Patrick (Immigrant)
Passage West - Dallas Miller   4382

Casson-Perceval, Edwin (Nobleman)
The Ring Master - David Gurr   2622

Casson-Perceval, Edwina (Singer)
The Ring Master - David Gurr   2622

Casta, Carmen de (Child)
The Place of Devils - Lucinda Baker   275

Casta, Raphael de (Rancher)
The Place of Devils - Lucinda Baker   275

Castameto, Mariposa (Captive)
California Caballero - William Colt MacDonald   3981

Castelar, Don Alfonso (Nobleman)
In Perilous Seas - Victor Suthren   6130

Castelmarten, Lucian (Nobleman)
Dark at Noon - Jill Tattersall   6173

Castetter, Alf J. (Military Personnel)
The Three Days - Don Robertson   5402

Castleman, Caroline (Seamstress; Governess)
The Michaelmas Tree - Helen Ashfield   209

Castlemayne, Walter (Gentleman)
The Blade of Castlemayne - Anthony Esler   1960

Casvellyn, Colum (Adventurer)
The Witch From the Sea - Philippa Carr   933

Catalina (Handicapped)
Catalina - William Somerset Maugham   4197

Catalina (Ward; Gentlewoman)
Envoy From Elizabeth - Pamela Bennetts   451

Catchstraw (Prehistoric Human)
People of the Sea - W. Michael Gear   2339

Cate, Christopher (Landowner; Gentleman)
By the Green of the Spring - John Masters   4171
Heart of War - John Masters   4174

Cateret, Quentin (Gentleman)
The Belchamber Scandal - Frances Murray   4533

Cathcart, Colin (Writer)
Johnnie Cross - Terence de Vere White   6704

Catherine (Femme Fatale)
At the Sign of the Reine Pedauque - Anatole
   France   2198

Catherwood, Lyle (Young Man)
A Vein of Riches - John Knowles   3526

Catlett, Johnny (Young Man)
Know Nothing - Mary Lee Settle   5755

Catlett, Melinda (Young Woman)
Know Nothing - Mary Lee Settle   5755

Catlett, Roan (Military Personnel)
The Valiant Virginians - James Warner Bellah   427

Catlin, Bartholomew (Businessman)
Prophecies - Helena Soister   5937

Cato, Philip (Military Personnel)
Cato's War - Guy Wheeler   6655

El Catolico (Revolutionary; Military Personnel)
Sharpe's Gold - Bernard Cornwell   1343

Catto, Marius (Military Personnel)
When the War Is Over - Stephen Becker   408

Catton, Bram (Outlaw)
Bighorn Legacy - W. Michael Gear   2332

Catton, Gideon (Farmer; Settler)
Salt Lake City - A.R. Reife   5292

Catton, Jeremiel (Religious)
Bighorn Legacy - W. Michael Gear   2332

Cauder, Janie (Widow(er))
The Wide House - Taylor Caldwell   864

Caudill, Boone (Mountain Man)
The Big Sky - A.B. Guthrie Jr.   2624
Fair Land, Fair Land - A.B. Guthrie Jr.   2625

Caulfield, Antoinette (Heiress)
Peril under the Palms - K.K. Beck   404

Caussinade, Gildas (Writer)
The Still Storm - Francoise Sagan   5562

Cavanaugh, Kate (Prostitute)
Storyville - Lois Battle   377

Cavanaugh, Kit (Sailor)
The Catherine - Robert S. MacDonald   3980

Cavanaugh, Thomas (Military Personnel)
''Utmost Fish!'' - Hugh Wray McCann   4219

Cavazza, Gaetano (Artist)
The Italian Garden - Judith Lennox-Smith   3717

Cavendish, Maude Teasdale (Journalist)
Young Mrs. Cavendish and the Kaiser's Men - K.K.
   Beck   405

Cavendish, Lord Randal (Nobleman)
My Dear Lover England - Pamela Bennetts   453

Cavendish, Richard (Businessman)
Mills of the Gods - Daoma Winston   6828

Cavill, Bartle (Adventurer)
Daughter of Satan - Jean Plaidy   5011

Cavitty, James (Artist)
Benjamin Franklin and a Case of Artful Murder -
   Robert Lee Hall   2654

Cayle, Barry (Journalist)
Gentleman Traitor - Alan Williams   6763

Caylew, Templeton (Businessman)
The Hand of a Woman - Diana Brown   719

Caynnes, Lord Adrian (Nobleman)
The Wanton Fires - Meriol Trevor   6345

Cearbhall (Knight)
The Kings in Winter - Cecelia Holland   2991

Cecil, Bertie (Gentleman; Military Personnel)
Under Two Flags - Ouida   4767

Cecil, Robert (Government Official)
Knaves Templar - Leonard Tourney   6300

Cecilia (Orphan)
The Mill on the Po - Riccardo Bacchelli   254

Cecilia (Young Woman)
In the Wilderness - Sigrid Undset   6381
The Son Avenger - Sigrid Undset   6384

Cecily (Religious)
The Corner That Held Them - Sylvia Townsend
   Warner   6568

Cedonius (Slave)
Behold, We Live - Charles Dunscomb   1812

Celer, Lucius (Sports Figure)
Between Eternities - Robert H. Pilpel   5001

Celisma (Slave)
Bayou - Pamela Jekel   3183

Cellini, Marco (Businessman)
Lamia: A Witch - Georgia Elizabeth Taylor   6183

Censorinus (Veteran)
Poseidon's Gold - Lindsey Davis   1530

Centeville, Baron Rollo de (Nobleman)
The Demon Lover - Victoria Holt   3013

Cera (Religious; Young Woman)
Pride of Lions - Morgan Llywelyn   3823

Cerdic (Religious)
A Wayside Tavern - Norah Lofts   3862

Cerulis, John (Nobleman)
The Belt of Gold - Cecelia Holland   2984

Cethlinn (Religious; Prehistoric Human)
Wolves of the Dawn - William Sarabande   5604

Cha-Kwena (Prehistoric Human; Shaman)
Shadow of the Watching Star - William
   Sarabande   5601
Thunder in the Sky - William Sarabande   5602
The Edge of the World - William Sarabande   5597

Chaco (Indian)
Arizona Ecstasy - Rosanne Bittner   511

Chactas (Indian)
Atala - Francois Rene de Chateaubriand   1008

Chadmore, Julian (Gentleman)
Paiute - Sessions S. Wheeler   6666

Chafin (Trader; Captive)
A Whistle in the Wind - John H. Culp   1447

Chagak (Prehistoric Human; Indian)
Mother Earth, Father Sky - Sue Harrison   2749

Chain, John (Trader)
Eagle in the Sun - Hottman Birney   508

Challoner, Edwin (Heir)
A Heritage and Its History - Ivy Compton-
   Burnett   1229

Challoner, Frances (Gentlewoman)
Old Saxon Blood - Leonard Tourney   6302

Challoner, Hamish (Gentleman)
A Heritage and Its History - Ivy Compton-
   Burnett   1229

Challoner, James (Sea Captain)
Captain Ironhand - Rosamond Marshall   4116

Challoner, Mary (Gentlewoman)
Devil's Cub - Georgette Heyer   2885

Challoner, Simon (Heir)
A Heritage and Its History - Ivy Compton-
   Burnett   1229

Chalmers, Natasha (Gentlewoman)
A Certain Splendour - Carola Salisbury   5566

Chalmers, Richard (Settler)
Gentlemen From England - Maude Hart
   Lovelace   3905

Chalmers, Rufus (Gentleman)
The Branch-Bearers - Glen Petrie   4978

Chalmers, Stephanie (Widow(er))
Echoes From the Past - Marjorie McEvoy   4268

Chaloner, Simon (Gentleman)
The Roaring Boy - Edward Marston   4127

Chamay, Paul (Military Personnel; Pilot)
In the Company of Eagles - Ernest K. Gann   2279

Chamberlain, Brice (Lawyer)
The Sea of Grass - Conrad Richter   5323

Chambers, Alexandra (Noblewoman)
The Sherbrooke Bride - Catherine Coulter   1382

Chambon, Anne du (Young Woman)
Restless Are the Sails - Evelyn Eaton   1830

Chambord, India de (Young Woman)
No Brighter Glory - Armstrong Sperry   5963

Champelle, Hank (Teenager)
The Last Boat out of Cincinnati - Don Tracy   6309

Champeney, Reina de (Noblewoman)
Defy Not the Heart - Johanna Lindsey   3794

Champion, John (Military Personnel; Spy)
Brother to the Enemy - Bart Spicer   5964

Champlittle, Sophie de (Widow(er))
The Brotherhood of the Red Poppy - Henri
   Troyat   6353

Chance, Bridie (Orphan; Actress)
The Capricorn Stone - Madeleine Brent   659

Chance, James Macklin "Mack" (Adventurer)
California Gold - John Jakes   3145

Chance, Jeff (Guardian)
Family Fortune - Mignon G. Eberhart   1834

Chance, Lucinda (Heiress)
Family Fortune - Mignon G. Eberhart   1834

Chance, Sam (Veteran; Rancher)
Sam Chance - Benjamin Capps   888

Chandagnac, John (Accountant; Pirate)
On Stranger Tides - Tim Powers   5156

Chandler, Sir Brian (Gentleman)
Ask Me No Questions - Patricia Veryan   6459

Chandler, Gordon (Heir)
Ask Me No Questions - Patricia Veryan   6459

Chandler, Harper (Cowboy)
The Seventh Girl: A Romantic Tale of Civil War Texas
   - Tom Pendleton   4900

Chandler, Heath (Military Personnel)
The Chandler Heritage - Ben Haas   2629

Chandler, Laura (Spy; Widow(er))
While the Music Plays - Diane Austell   242

Chandler, Lloyd (Businessman)
The Chandler Heritage - Ben Haas   2629

Chandler, Quentin (Fugitive)
Practice to Deceive - Patricia Veryan   6475

Chandler, Thomas (Religious)
Miracles - Marcy Moran Heidish   2818

Chandler, Troy (Cowboy)
The Seventh Girl: A Romantic Tale of Civil War Texas
   - Tom Pendleton   4900

Chandon, Claire (Servant)
Eden's Gate - Karen Harper   2711

Chaney, Tom (Outlaw; Murderer)
True Grit - Charles Portis   5139

Channing, Barbara (Young Woman)
Matthew Early - Alexander Laing   3589

Channing, Dickson (Veteran)
Mirage - Helen Topping Miller   4390

Channing, Jeb (Rancher)
Mirage - Helen Topping Miller 4390

Channing, Victoria (Young Woman)
Mirage - Helen Topping Miller 4390

Chantal (Entertainer)
Stranger at Wildings - Madeleine Brent 663

Chantra (Orphan; Royalty)
Temple Bells - Marjorie McEvoy 4271

Chantrell, Cordelia (Southern Belle)
Cordelia Chantrell - Meade Minnigerode 4413

Chap (Slave; Teenager)
The Walk into Morning - Mildred Barger
   Herschler 2867

Chapin, Matthew (Doctor)
The Hospital - Agatha Young 6938
I Swear by Apollo - Agatha Young 6939

Chapman, Dick (Settler)
Cormorant's Brood - Inglis Fletcher 2133

Chapman, Graham (Businessman)
Come Spring - Charlotte Hinger 2954

Chapman, Philip (Military Personnel)
Lords of the Plains - Max Crawford 1420

Chappell, Alastair (Military Personnel)
Gentlemen—The Regiment! - Hugh Talbot 6154

Chappelle, Constance (Young Woman)
Walk with Peril - Dorothy V.S. Jackson 3132

Chappelle, Lewis (Businessman)
Walk with Peril - Dorothy V.S. Jackson 3132

Charboneau, Marie (Innkeeper; Actress)
The Bastard - John Jakes 3144

Charboneau, Phillipe (Bastard Son; Heir—
   Dispossessed)
The Bastard - John Jakes 3144

Charbonneau, Julia (Young Woman)
Time and Again - Jack Finney 2093

Chard, Steve (Military Personnel)
The Medicine Whip - Max Hennessy 2835

Charetty, Catherine de (Young Woman)
The Spring of the Ram - Dorothy Dunnett 1809

Charetty, Marian de (Widow(er); Businesswoman)
Niccolo Rising - Dorothy Dunnett 1803
The Spring of the Ram - Dorothy Dunnett 1809

Charing, Kitty (Heiress)
Cotillion - Georgette Heyer 2883

Charis (Doctor)
The Beacon of Alexandria - Gillian Bradshaw 627

Charis (Royalty)
Taliesin - Stephen R. Lawhead 3683

Charles (Nobleman)
Falls of Gard - Laura Black 520

Charles, Holly (Young Woman)
Gray Canaan - David Garth 2305

Charron, Pierre (Trader)
Shadows on the Rock - Willa Cather 959

Chartley, Richard (Gentleman)
The Wildcliffe Bird - Constance Heaven 2811

Chartley, Sybil (Gentlewoman)
The Wildcliffe Bird - Constance Heaven 2811

Chase, David (Writer)
Jackson: A Novel - Max Byrd 837

Chase, Gideon (Journalist)
An Insular Position - Timothy Mo 4421

Chase, Kathryn (Gentlewoman)
Kathryn: In the Court of Six Queens - Anne Merton
   Abbey 1

Chase, Miranda (Young Woman)
When the Music Changed - Marie R. Reno 5305

Chaske (Indian; Warrior)
The Shining Trail - Iola Fuller 2254

Chastain, Marcy (Southern Belle)
The Bayou Road - Mignon G. Eberhart 1832

Chatfield, Geneva (Spouse; Military Personnel)
High Hearts - Rita Mae Brown 728

Chatfield, Mary (Gentlewoman)
Young Men See Visions - Mary Mian 4357

Chatrois, Jacqueline Crois de (Gentlewoman)
The Tides of Dawn - Emma Louise Mally 4044

Chatto, Tom (Military Personnel)
Apprentice to the Sea - Philip McCutchan 4240
The Second Mate - Philip McCutchan 4257

Chavelin (Diplomat)
The Scarlet Pimpernel - Baroness Emma Orczy 4745

Chavez, Pearl (Young Woman)
Duel in the Sun - Niven Busch 812

Chawleigh, Jenny (Heiress)
A Civil Contract - Georgette Heyer 2880

Chekote, Ridge (Indian)
Cherokee Dawn - Genell Dellin 1596

Chen, Gordon (Businessman; Trader)
Tai-Pan - James Clavell 1102

Chen Kai Tsu (Immigrant)
Golden Destiny - June Wyndham Davies 1506

Chen Li (Doctor)
Forbidden City - Anthony Esler 1962

Chenevix, Kitty (Gentlewoman)
Cressida - Clare Darcy 1485

Cheng Wei (Nobleman)
The Big Chariot - Charmian Clift 1118

Cheng Yuan (Nobleman)
The Big Chariot - Charmian Clift 1118

Cheoh, Joe (Indian; Lawyer)
Carolina Courage - Dana Fuller Ross 5469

Chernik, Hannah (Young Woman)
The Dream Seekers - Grace Mark 4085

Chernik, Josef (Criminal)
The Dream Seekers - Grace Mark 4085

Chernov, Danilo (Nobleman)
Heaven Is Too High - Mildred Masterson
   McNeilly 4309

Cherrill, Philip (Landowner)
Tidewater - Clifford Dowdey 1709

Chesney, Jenny (Nurse)
Hanging on the Wire - Gillian Linscott 3806

Chesney, Nalambigi (Indian; Spouse)
Shadow of the Moon - Douglas C. Jones 3284

Chesney, Old Sergeant Bobby (Immigrant; Settler)
Shadow of the Moon - Douglas C. Jones 3284

Chesnieres, Germaine de (Gentlewoman)
Master-At-Arms - Rafael Sabatini 5553

Chesnut, Ross (Frontiersman)
The Vision Is Fulfilled - Kay L. McDonald 4262

Chester, Elizabeth (Gentlewoman; Spouse)
Knight's Honor - Roberta Gellis 2351

Chester, Sir John (Nobleman)
Barnaby Rudge: A Tale of the Riots of Eighty -
   Charles Dickens 1641

Chestnut, Ross (Frontiersman; Guide)
The Brightwood Expedition - Kay L.
   McDonald 4261

Cheston, James (Young Man)
Kentucky Stand - Jere Hungerford Wheelwright 6670

Chetwynd-Dunleigh, Lucinda (Gentlewoman)
Over There - Robert Vaughan 6449

Chevalier, Christine (Gentlewoman)
Young Ames - Walter D. Edmonds 1879

Chevalier, Louise (Gentlewoman)
Treason's Gift - Pamela Belle 434

Chevereuil, Claude de (Noblewoman)
Monsieur Janvier - Elizabeth Linington 3799

Chevillon, Denise (Southern Belle)
The Moreland Legacy - Diana Haviland 2777

Cheviot, John (Detective—Police; Time Traveller)
Fire, Burn! - John Dickson Carr 910

Chiao Tai (Assistant)
The Lacquer Screen - Robert van Gulik 6416
Murder in Canton - Robert van Gulik 6418
The Willow Pattern - Robert van Gulik 6422

Chichley, Frederic (Gentleman)
The Paper Mistress - Dorothea Malm 4045

Chilcott, Topaz (Gypsy)
Topaz - Helen Ashfield 215

Childe, Barbara (Noblewoman; Widow(er))
An Infamous Army - Georgette Heyer 2892

Childers, Duncan (Doctor)
Serpent and Staff - Frank Yerby 6927

Childs, Marian (Gentlewoman)
The Last Waltz - Nancy Zaroulis 6955

Chillingworth, Roger (Doctor)
Arthur Dimmesdale - Charles R. Larson 3671
Hester - Christopher Bigsby 496
The Scarlet Letter - Nathaniel Hawthorne 2786

Chimalman (Sorcerer)
The Luck of Huemac: A Novel about the Aztecs -
   Daniel Peters 4946

Chimes, Queenie (Actress)
Bertie and the Seven Bodies - Peter Lovesey 3908

Chinese Sonya (Orphan)
The Name of Hero - Richard Seltzer 5742

Ching, Joshua (Financier)
Wanderers Eastward, Wanderers West - Kathleen
   Winsor 6823

Chingachgook (Indian)
The Deerslayer - James Fenimore Cooper 1299
The Last of the Mohicans - James Fenimore
   Cooper 1302
The Pathfinder; or, The Inland Sea - James Fenimore
   Cooper 1305

Chinnery, Thomas (Adventurer)
Goa - Kara Dalkey 1458

Chirke, Nicholas (Lawyer)
A Tapestry of Murders - C.L. Grace 2510

Chisahahoma (Indian)
Jordan County: A Landscape in Narrative - Shelby
   Foote 2152

Chisholm, Hadley (Settler)
The Chisholms - Evan Hunter 3082

Chisholm, Julian (Doctor)
In a Dark Garden - Frank G. Slaughter 5891

Chisholm, Julian (Doctor; Plantation Owner)
The Stubborn Heart - Frank G. Slaughter 5904

Chisholm, Miverva (Spouse)
The Chisholms - Evan Hunter 3082

Chism, Nail (Convict)
The Choiring of the Trees - Donald Harington 2709

Chiswick, Caroly (Young Woman)
The French Admiral - Dewey Lambdin 3609

Chodorov, Kala (Young Woman)
Remember This Time - Gloria Kurian Broder 703

Cholmondeley, Cuthbert (Knight)
The Tower of London - William Harrison
    Ainsworth 58

Chomac (Indian)
Let the Drum Speak: A Novel of Ancient America -
    Linda Lay Shuler 5837

Chomina (Indian)
Black Robe - Brian Moore 4441

Choundas, Guillaume (Military Personnel)
A King's Commander - Dewey Lambdin 3613

Christian, Katherine (Gentlewoman)
Katherine Christian - Hugh Walpole 6546

Christmas, Anne (Abolitionist)
Free Enterprise - Michelle Cliff 1116

Christmas, Johnny (Mountain Man)
Johnny Christmas - Forrester Blake 533
Wilderness Passage - Forrester Blake 534

Chrysanteus (Philosopher)
The Last Athenian - Viktor Rydberg 5543

Chrysaphos (Servant)
Imperial Purple - Gillian Bradshaw 631

Chrysis (Teacher; Philosopher)
Woman of Andros - Thornton Wilder 6754

Chung Lin (Immigrant)
Sweetwater Fever - Robert H. Adelman 36

Church, Christopher (Servant)
The Long Day Closes - Beatrice Tunstall 6360

Church, Jonathan (Young Man)
Prisons - Mary Lee Settle 5757

Churchill, Frank (Gentleman)
Jane Fairfax - Joan Aiken 50

Chynoweth, Morwenna (Gentlewoman)
The Black Moon - Winston Graham 2522

Cicely (Young Woman)
The Tower of London - William Harrison
    Ainsworth 58

Cigarette (Entertainer)
Under Two Flags - Ouida 4767

Cimber, Lucius (Young Man)
If I Forget Thee - Robert S. Deropp 1621

Circe (Sorceress)
The Voyage Home - Ernst Schnabel 5644

Ciriaco (Indian)
The Cry of Dolores - Herbert Gorman 2492

Civilis, Julius (Leader)
The Iron Hand of Mars - Lindsey Davis 1528

Claffey, Ira (Landowner)
Andersonville - MacKinlay Kantor 3359

Claggart (Military Personnel)
Billy Budd - Herman Melville 4333

Claiborne, Colin (Gentleman)
McKensie's Hundred: A Tale of the Old Dominion -
    Frank Yerby 6924

Claiborne, Margaret (Gentlewoman; Musician)
River of Dreams - Gay Courter 1390

Claibourne, Leigh (Nobleman; Rake)
Rake's Ransom - Barbara Metzger 4347

Clampton, Mary (Convict)
A Love So Wild - Deborah Chester 1056

Clancy, Jack (Journalist)
Death in a Deck Chair - K.K. Beck 403
Peril under the Palms - K.K. Beck 404

Clanreydon, Lord (Nobleman)
Castle Barebane - Joan Aiken 43

Clare, Lady Ariel de (Noblewoman)
In the Shadow of Midnight - Marsha Canham 880

Clare, Charles (Settler)
Paradise - Sarah Neilan 4566

Clare, Edward (Nobleman)
Greygallows - Barbara Michaels 4359

Clare, Edward (Ward)
Edward, Edward - Lolah Burford 772

Clare, Hannah (Teacher)
Ramillies - Barbara Whitehead 6708

Clare, Jocellin (Gentlewoman)
The Bluestocking - June Drummond 1729

Clare, Quality (Young Woman)
Paradise - Sarah Neilan 4566

Clare, Rose (Settler)
Paradise - Sarah Neilan 4566

Clarence, Mrs. (Gentlewoman)
Yvonne Goes to York - Marion Chesney 1054

Clark, Cassandra (Gentlewoman)
The Second Sister - Leslie O'Grady 4701

Clark, Christopher (Doctor)
Storm Haven - Frank G. Slaughter 5903

Clark, Jonathan (Outlaw; Sea Captain)
The World in His Arms - Rex Beach 392

Clark, Oliver (Military Personnel)
Arouse and Beware - MacKinlay Kantor 3360

Clarke, Clara (Young Woman)
The Revenge of Dracula - Peter Tremayne 6335

Clarke, Mary (Widow(er))
Forget the Glory - Emma Drummond 1725

Clarke, Micah (Fisherman)
Micah Clarke - Sir Arthur Conan Doyle 1715

Clarkson, Matthew (Military Personnel)
Treason - Robert Gessner 2389

Clarkson, Penninah (Young Woman)
The Power and the Glory - Phyllis Bentley 462

Classicus, Cornelius (Government Official)
Gold for the Caesars - Florence A. Seward 5759

Claudia, Lady (Captive)
The Gentle Conqueror - Mary Ellen Gronau 2597

Claudia (Gentlewoman; Spouse)
Hear Me, Pilate! - LeGette Blythe 557
Man on Fire: A Novel on the Life of St. Paul -
    LeGette Blythe 558

Claudia (Noblewoman; Orphan)
A Walk with Love and Death - Hans Koning 3539

Claudia (Spouse)
The Bride of Pilate - Esther Kellner 3393

Claus, Jeffry (Artisan; Servant)
The Eagle and the Wind - Herbert Stover 6068

Clavering, Lance (Military Personnel)
Will You Love Me in September? - Philippa Carr 932

Clavier, Clay (Political Figure)
Those the Sun Has Loved - Rose Jourdain 3309

Clavier, Isabella (Young Woman)
Those the Sun Has Loved - Rose Jourdain 3309

Clavier, Jacques (Military Personnel; Shipowner)
Those the Sun Has Loved - Rose Jourdain 3309

Clay, George (Plantation Owner)
Heaven Trees - Stark Young 6943

Clay, Jubal (Military Personnel; Expatriate)
Mexico - James A. Michener 4372

Clay, Maggie (Orphan; Rancher)
Lone Star Lady - Jill Gregory 2579

Clay, Margaret (Southern Belle)
Trumpet in the Sky - Helen Topping Miller 4397

Clay, Norman (Journalist)
Mexico - James A. Michener 4372

Clayborn, Lance (Settler; Hunter)
*Forest Cavalier: A Romance of America's First
    Frontier and of Bacon's Rebellion* - Roy Catesby
    Flannagan 2122

Clayburn, Henry (Gentleman)
The Raiders - William Edward Wilson 6819

Clayton, Colonel (Military Personnel)
No Survivors - Will Henry 2846

Clayton, Alfred (Historian; Professor)
Memories of the Ford Administration - John
    Updike 6391

Clayton, Clark (Prospector)
Forty Pounds of Gold - Philip D. Stong 6066

Clayton, John (Writer)
Murder in Grub Street - Bruce Alexander 77

Cleander (Servant)
*The Equinox: A Novel of Rome in the Time of
    Commodus* - Carol Saylor 5622

Cleave, Linden (Southern Belle)
Thunder on the Chesapeake - David Divine 1650

Cleave, Richard (Military Personnel)
The Long Roll - Mary Johnston 3236

Clemence, Celia (Spouse)
Restoration: A Novel of Seventeenth-Century England -
    Rose Tremain 6333

Clemence, Peter (Political Figure)
The Devil's Novice - Ellis Peters 4958

Clemence of Saxe-Salsa (Noblewoman)
The Battle of Wagram - Gilles Lapouge 3664

Clemens, Atta Olivia (Noblewoman; Vampire)
A Candle for D'Artagnan - Chelsea Quinn
    Yarbro 6895
Crusader's Torch - Chelsea Quinn Yarbro 6897
Darker Jewels - Chelsea Quinn Yarbro 6898
A Flame in Byzantium - Chelsea Quinn Yarbro 6899
The Palace - Chelsea Quinn Yarbro 6904

Clement, Alvey (Student)
If I Were You - Joan Aiken 49

Clement, Juliette de (Student; Gentlewoman)
Storm Winds - Iris Johansen 3217

Clement, Keith (Military Personnel)
Wings for the Chariots - Arch Whitehouse 6713

Clements, Hannah (Saloon Hostess; Spy)
Storm the Last Rampart - David Taylor 6180

Clements, Joseph (Jockey; Horse Trainer)
Horses of War - Duff Hart-Davis 2760

Clemmens, Jeremiah (Military Personnel)
Grant's War - Ted Jones 3297

Cleo (Young Woman)
The Road to San Jacinto - Leonard L.
    Foreman 2167

Clerc, Lorelei Du (Young Woman)
The Raven and the Rose - Susan Wiggs 6746

Clervaux, Nicole de (Noblewoman; Ward)
Palaces of Desire - Kate Alexander 81

Cleveden, Charles (Nobleman)
Miss Fiona's Fancy - Marion Chesney 1040

Cleveland, Clement (Pirate)
The Pirate - Sir Walter Scott 5704

Clewellyn, John T. (Military Personnel)
Prisoner of Twilight - Don Robertson 5400

Clifford, Guy (Gentleman)
At the Sign of the Golden Pineapple - Marion
    Chesney 1016

Clifford, Jo (Time Traveller; Journalist)
Lady of Hay - Barbara Erskine 1955

Clifford, Yolande de (Gentlewoman)
I Remember Love - Mollie Hardwick 2694

Clifford, Zoe (Artist)
Morning's Gate - Ann Victoria Roberts 5371

Clinch, Josiah (Farmer)
Darker Grows the Valley - Harry Harrison
    Kroll 3556

Clinch, Rachel (Pioneer)
Darker Grows the Valley - Harry Harrison
    Kroll 3556

Clint (Convict)
Escape From Sonora - Will Bryant 739

Clinton, Isabella (Teenager)
The Gentle Falcon - Hilda Lewis 3747

Clinton, Jim (Scout)
The Devil Gun - William Syers 6148

Clivedon, Peter (Military Personnel)
Men Were Deceivers Ever - Patricia Veryan 6470

Clively, Miranda (Spinster)
Clively Close: Dead as Dead Can Be - Ann
    Crowleigh 1434

Clively-Murdoch, Clare (Widow(er))
Clively Close: Dead as Dead Can Be - Ann
    Crowleigh 1434

Clodagh (Young Woman)
Time of the Unicorn - Barbara Jefferis 3176

Clora (Slave; Spirit)
Family - J. California Cooper 1297

Clothier, Mary (Gentlewoman)
The Quincunx - Charles Palliser 4778

Cloud, Adam (Young Man)
Bound for the Promised Land - Richard Marius 4083

Cloud, Marcus Valerius (Nobleman)
Mistress - Amanda Quick 5215

Cloud, Rondall (Labor Organizer)
Storming Heaven - Denise Giardina 2394

Clover (Young Woman)
Called Away - Perdita Buchan 753

Clytemnestra (Royalty)
Amber Princess - Henry Treece 6325
Scandal in Troy - Eva Hemmer Hansen 2679

Coale, Susan (Young Woman)
Green Rose of Furley - Helen C. Barney 334

Coates, Eben (Religious)
Show Me a Land - Clark McMeekin 4293

Coates, Rafael (Religious)
The Marranos - Liliane Webb 6588

Coatl (Slave; Chieftain)
Captain From Castile - Samuel Shellabarger 5794

Cobb, Charis (Spouse)
An Ice-Cream War - William Boyd 616

Cobb, Felix (Military Personnel)
An Ice-Cream War - William Boyd 616

Cobb, Gabriel (Military Personnel)
An Ice-Cream War - William Boyd 616

Cobb, Henry (Gentleman)
Sarah Cobb - Catherine M. Rae 5236

Cobbold, Charley (Thief)
The Rookery: A Novel of the Victorian Underworld -
    Hugh C. Rae 5239

Cobbold, Gabby (Farmer)
Ulverton - Adam Thorpe 6278

Cobden, Joe (Frontiersman; Hunter)
Heart of the Country - Greg Matthews 4190

Coberley, Brandon (Southern Belle)
The Laughing Stranger - Vina Delmar 1601

Cochran, Coll (Farmer)
Treasures on Earth - Jessica Stirling 6049

Cochrane, Charnisay (Young Woman)
Grand Parade - G.B. Lancaster 3649

Cochrane, Joanna (Frontierswoman)
The Forest Lord - Noel B. Gerson 2368

Cockfoster, Mark (Pilot)
The Sky and Tomorrow - Thomas William
    Duncan 1788

Cockley, Thomas (Religious)
Ladysmead: A Novel in the Jane Austen Tradition -
    Jane Gillespie 2420

Cody, Clara (Young Woman)
My Sister's Keeper - Beverly Butler 817

Cody, Ellery (Worker)
My Sister's Keeper - Beverly Butler 817

Coe, Abbott (Servant)
Eagle Fur - Robert Newton Peck 4884

Coen, Emma (Companion)
West to Eden - Gloria Goldreich 2461

Coffee Soldier (Indian)
Nickajack - Robert J. Conley 1248

Coffield, Victoria Manning (Spouse)
A Heart Divided - Al Lacy 3580

Coffin, Damaris (Young Woman)
Thread of Scarlet - Ben Ames Williams 6767

Coffin, Kathrin (Settler)
The Strange Death of Mistress Coffin - Robert J.
    Begiebing 415

Coffman, Israel (Religious)
The Border Men - Cameron Judd 3312

Coffyn, Dencey (Settler)
The Beckoning Road - Caroline Snedeker 5934

Coffyn, Hubert (Sailor)
Golden Admiral - F. van Wyck Mason 4150

Cogburn, Rooster (Lawman)
True Grit - Charles Portis 5139

Cohen, Bernie (Adventurer)
The Establishment - Howard Fast 2030

Cohen, Rachel (Young Woman)
The Books of Rachel - Joel Gross 2600

Cohran, Caline (Southern Belle)
The Great Tide - Rubylea Hall 2662

Coit, Shubael (Sea Captain)
The Pepper Tree - John Edward Jennings 3203

Coit, Simon (Prospector)
Days of the Gold - Irwin R. Blacker 526

Colbert, Henry (Businessman)
Sapphira and the Slave Girl - Willa Cather 958

Colbert, Sapphira (Gentlewoman)
Sapphira and the Slave Girl - Willa Cather 958

Colby (Indian)
Children of the Dust - Carlile Clancy 1084

Colden, Emma (Feminist)
Jackson: A Novel - Max Byrd 837

Cole, Doc (Adventurer; Sports Figure)
Flanagan's Run - Tom McNab 4303

Cole, Josiah (Trader)
A Respectable Trade - Philippa Gregory 2584

Cole, Rob J. (Doctor)
The Physician - Noah Gordon 2482
Shaman - Noah Gordon 2483

Cole, Sarah (Spouse)
Shaman - Noah Gordon 2483

Cole, Weaver (Businessman)
Supper at the Maxwell House - Alfred Leland
    Crabb 1407

Colebrook, Lucas (Nobleman)
Surrender - Amanda Quick 5221

Coleman, Aphra (Actress)
The Eagle at the Gate - Rona Randall 5248

Coleman, Breck (Frontiersman)
Shaggy Legion - Hal George Evarts 1986

Coleman, Charles (Actor; Manager)
The Eagle at the Gate - Rona Randall 5248

Coleman, Gretel (Young Woman)
Telluride - Susan Clark Schofield 5648

Coleman, Stuart (Gentleman)
The Wide House - Taylor Caldwell 864

Coleman, Zachary "Cole" (Gunfighter)
Telluride - Susan Clark Schofield 5648

Colfax, Clarence (Gentleman; Military Personnel)
The Crisis - Winston Churchill 1079

Colfax, Oliver (Outlaw; Gunfighter)
Colfax - Robert J. Conley 1239
Killing Time - Robert J. Conley 1244
Quitting Time - Robert J. Conley 1249

Colin (Engineer)
McKay's Bees - Thomas McMahon 4289

Colland, Harriet (Gentlewoman)
The Blackheath Poisonings - Julian Symons 6150

College (Outcast)
Theory of War - Joan Brady 637

Colley, Robert (Religious)
Rites of Passage - William Golding 2456

Colling, Daniel (Military Personnel)
The Glass Dove - Sally Carrighar 943

Collingsworth, Benton (Teacher)
Arfive - A.B. Guthrie Jr. 2623
The Last Valley - A.B. Guthrie Jr. 2626

Collingsworth, Richard (Diplomat)
The Ginger Tree - Oswald Wynd 6890

Collingwood, James (Gentleman)
My Pride, My Folly - Suzanne Butler 830

Collingwood, Stephen (Religious)
The Summer of the Royal Visit - Isabel
    Colegate 1199

Collins, Leslie (Frontiersman; Surveyor)
*The Kentucky Trace: A Novel of the American
    Revolution* - Harriette Simpson Arnow 195

Collins, Martin (Settler)
Jornada - Robert L. Duffus 1754

Collins, Rita (Gentlewoman)
You Rolling River - Archie Binns 503

Collins, Venetia (Young Woman)
Street of the Madwoman - Isabel Ortega 4756

Collins, William (Religious)
Teverton Hall - Jane Gillespie 2421

Collison, Kate (Artist)
The Demon Lover - Victoria Holt 3013

Colmer, Amelia (Spouse)
Murder in the Oval Office - Elliott Roosevelt 5450

Colmer, Winstead (Political Figure)
Murder in the Oval Office - Elliott Roosevelt 5450

Colmore, Ellie (Gentlewoman)
Lord Richard's Passion - Mervyn Jones 3293

Colt, Chris (Frontiersman; Scout)
Chief of Scouts - Don Bendell 439

Colter, Joshua (Frontiersman)
The Border Men - Cameron Judd 3312
The Overmountain Men - Cameron Judd 3315

Colvin, Adam (Landowner; Businessman)
Echoes From the Past - Marjorie McEvoy 4268

Combardi, Rosaria (Farmer)
Contessa - Richard Oliver Collin   1209

Comfort, Mary (Young Woman)
Hang for Treason - Robert Newton Peck   4886

Comfrey, Sylvester (Nobleman)
Minerva - Marion Chesney   1037

Comstock, George (Sailor)
Captain Marooner - Louis B. Davidson   1504

Comstock, Sam (Sailor)
Captain Marooner - Louis B. Davidson   1504

Comyn, Charlotte (Gentlewoman)
Escapade - Jane Aiken Hodge   2962

Comyn, Jenny (Young Woman)
Pageant - G.B. Lancaster   3650

Comyn, Mab (Pioneer)
Pageant - G.B. Lancaster   3650

Conachur, Mac Nessa (Ruler)
Deirdre - James Stephens   5996

Conal, Logan (Sailor)
The Feather and the Stone - Patricia Shaw   5780

Conklin, Abigail (Pioneer)
Between Earth and Sky - Karen Osborn   4758

Conklin, Jim (Military Personnel)
The Red Badge of Courage - Stephen Crane   1414

Conn (Ruler; Warrior)
Lady of Conquest - Teresa Medeiros   4322

Connal (Chieftain; Warrior)
Fire Queen - Deborah Grabien   2503

Connelly, Ian (Nobleman; Servant)
Nobody's Angel - Karen Robards   5363

Connington, Drummond (Gentleman)
The Tempestuous Petticoat - Mary Ann Gibbs   2397

Connolly, Morgan (Revolutionary)
Across the Bitter Sea - Eilis Dillon   1646

Connor, Michael (Military Personnel)
Forbidden City - Anthony Esler   1962

Connor, Rory (Businessman; Gambler)
The Gambling Man - Catherine Cookson   1276

Conquy, Judah (Shipowner)
The Rock: A Novel about Gibraltar - John Masters   4179

Conrad (Nobleman)
The Talisman - Sir Walter Scott   5708

Consett, Amy (Gypsy)
Had We Never Loved - Patricia Veryan   6463

Consett, Helena (Gentlewoman)
Bride of Ae - Pamela Hill   2928

Consuelo (Singer)
Consuelo - George Sand   5582

Conte, Sieur Louis de (Secretary)
Personal Recollections of Joan of Arc - Mark Twain   6372

Conti, Clelia (Gentlewoman)
The Charterhouse of Parma - Stendhal   5993

Conway, Agnes (Worker)
The Wingless Bird - Catherine Cookson   1292

Conway, Clara (Spouse)
That Callahan Spunk! - Francis Ames   124

Conway, Jessie (Student)
The Wingless Bird - Catherine Cookson   1292

Conway, John (Settler)
That Callahan Spunk! - Francis Ames   124

Conway, Tom (Young Man)
That Callahan Spunk! - Francis Ames   124

Conybeare, Julian (Young Woman)
The Shadow Flies - Rose Macaulay   3956

Conyers, Joscelyn (Knight)
I Remember Love - Mollie Hardwick   2694

Cooke, Anna (Gentlewoman; Twin)
The Sot-Weed Factor - John Barth   364

Cooke, Flora (Young Woman)
Farewell, My General - Shirley Seifert   5726

Cooke, Mary (Servant)
Amanda/Miranda - Richard Peck   4882

Cooke, Nicholas (Actor; Military Personnel)
Nicholas Cooke: Actor, Soldier, Physician, Priest - Stephanie Cowell   1393

Cooke, Nicholas (Doctor; Religious)
The Physician of London - Stephanie Cowell   1394

Coombes, Jane (Servant)
Lady Jane - Norma Lee Clark   1092

Coombs, Eulalie (Landowner; Southern Belle)
Miami: A Saga - Evelyn Wilde Mayerson   4204

Cooney (Thief)
The Rookery: A Novel of the Victorian Underworld - Hugh C. Rae   5239

Cooper, Adam (Patriot; Military Personnel)
April Morning - Howard Fast   2027

Cooper, Andy (Outlaw)
The Feud - Amelia Bean   396

Cooper, David (Frontiersman)
The Kentuckians - Janice Holt Giles   2413

Cooper, Deborah (Young Woman)
Gabriel's Search - Della Lutes   3927

Cooper, Eve (Young Woman)
Yorktown - Burke Davis   1513

Cooper, Garvin (Settler)
Pillar of Cloud - Jackson Burgess   782

Cooper, Iris (Detective—Amateur)
Death in a Deck Chair - K.K. Beck   403
Peril under the Palms - K.K. Beck   404

Cooper, Jed (Mountain Man)
The Gilded Rooster - Richard Emery Roberts   5391

Cooper, Moses (Patriot; Military Personnel)
April Morning - Howard Fast   2027

Cooper, Rachel (Worker)
The Standing Hills - Caroline Stickland   6038

Cooper, Richard (Settler)
The Believers - Janice Holt Giles   2409

Cooper, Robert (Government Official)
Trust and Treason - Margaret Birkhead   506

Coopersand, Louise Danielle (Settler)
Kansas Blue - Dylan Harson   2758

Copilli (Royalty)
Copilli, Aztec Prince - Miguel Aleman Velasco   75

Copley, Suzanna (Nurse)
An Autumn in Araby - Carola Salisbury   5565

Copp, Dolly (Settler)
The Pilgrim Soul - Anne Miller Downes   1711

Copp, Hayes (Settler)
The Pilgrim Soul - Anne Miller Downes   1711

Coppen, Hetty (Gentlewoman)
Familiar Acts - June Barraclough   345

Copperfield, David (Writer)
The Real David Copperfield - Robert Graves   2551

Corax (Slave)
The Gospel of Corax - Paul Park   4802

Corbeau, Jeanne (Young Woman)
Song of a Strange Child - Gilbert Morris   4470

Corbera, Don Fabrizio (Royalty)
The Leopard - Giuseppe di Lampedusa   3634

Corbett, Hugh (Government Official; Detective—Amateur)
Angel of Death - P.C. Doherty   1670
The Crown in Darkness - P.C. Doherty   1671
The Prince of Darkness - P.C. Doherty   1675
Satan in St. Mary's - P.C. Doherty   1676
Satan's Fire - P.C. Doherty   1677
The Song of a Dark Angel - P.C. Doherty   1679
Spy in Chancery - P.C. Doherty   1680

Corbett of Colchester (Nobleman)
My Gallant Enemy - Rexanne Becnel   409

Corbney, Conan de (Knight)
The Blue Falcon - Robyn Carr   935

Corbney, Udele de (Gentlewoman)
The Blue Falcon - Robyn Carr   935

Corcoran, Dermot (Journalist)
Seasons - Anna Dillon   1645

Cordera de Tosta, Anabel (Outlaw)
Warriors of the Night - Kerry Newcomb   4594

Cordoba, Luis (Military Personnel)
The Furies - John Jakes   3146

Cordor, Davy (Journalist)
The Thomas Street Horror - Raymond Paul   4843

Cordova, Isabella (Landowner)
A Woman of Texas - R.T. Stevens   6002

Cordova, Don Pedro (Nobleman; Adventurer)
Don Pedro and the Devil - Edgar Maas   3948

Corelli, Wordlaw (Artist)
A Story of Deep Delight - Thomas McNamee   4305

Corey, Nancy (Gentlewoman)
For Time and All Eternity - Paul Bailey   268

Corimer, Charles Alexander (Nobleman)
Seasons of Fear - Philip McFarland   4272

Corlaer, Adam (Young Man)
Reluctant Rebel - Frederic F. Van de Water   6403

Corleone, Maria (Young Woman)
The Rebels - Alfred Neumann   4585

Corley, Dinah (Young Woman)
The Running Thread - Drayton Mayrant   4215

Corley, Thomas (Military Personnel)
Thin Moon and Cold Mist - Kathleen O'Neal Gear   2330

Cormac (Warrior)
Finn Mac Cool - Morgan Llywelyn   3818

Corn Flower (Indian; Captive)
The Way of the Priests - Robert J. Conley   1253

Corn-Sucker (Indian)
Spirit Lake - MacKinlay Kantor   3363

Cornelius (Military Personnel)
Marius the Epicurean - Walter Pater   4826

Cornish, Harry (Artisan)
The Storms of Fate - Patricia Wright   6885

Cornish, Colonel Jack (Landowner)
Golden Destiny - June Wyndham Davies   1506

Cornsilk (Indian)
People of the Silence - W. Michael Gear   2340

Cornwall, Charlotte (Teacher)
Out of the Dark - Norah Lofts   3856

Cornwallace, Judith (Noblewoman)
The Woodsman - Don Wright   6880

Coronel, Dona Consuelo (Gentlewoman)
Grant of Kingdom - Harvey Fergusson   2067

Corper, Julie (Gentlewoman)
Julie - Jane Kesner Morris   4479

Correnes, Victor de (Courtier; Spy)
The Gilded Torch - Iola Fuller   2252

Corrough, Sibilla (Gentlewoman)
Mayfair - Nancy Fitzgerald 2115

Corrough, Sophia (Gentlewoman)
Mayfair - Nancy Fitzgerald 2115

Corry, Basil (Store Owner)
Crystal - Helen Ashfield 205

Cortland, Lalia (Governess)
The Place of Devils - Lucinda Baker 275

Cortlandt, David (Doctor; Military Personnel)
Eagles Where I Walk - Stephen Longstreet 3885
A Few Painted Feathers - Stephen Longstreet 3886

Cortlandt, Roxanne (Spouse)
Eagles Where I Walk - Stephen Longstreet 3885
A Few Painted Feathers - Stephen Longstreet 3886

Cortlandt, Will (Artist; Military Personnel)
War in the Golden Weather - Stephen Longstreet 3892

Coryat, Thomas (Doctor)
Lords of the Dance - Robin Lloyd-Jones 3815

Corydon, Rupert Flood (Military Personnel)
Floodtide - Suzanne Goodwin 2475

Cosette (Revolutionary; Orphan)
Cosette: The Sequel to Les Miserables - Laura Kalpakian 3329

Cosgrove, Nicholas (Detective—Private)
The Cosgrove Report - G.J.A. O'Toole 4765

Costello (Detective—Private)
Escape From Sonora - Will Bryant 739

Costello, Peter Jack (Cowboy)
Refugio, They Named You Wrong - Susan Clark Schofield 5647

Cosway, Antoinette Bertha (Spouse)
Wide Sargasso Sea - Jean Rhys 5312

Cothburn, Ramsey (Gentleman)
Star of Empire: A Novel of Old San Antonio - Leonard Sanders 5590

Cotta, Maximus (Gentleman)
The Last World: A Novel with an Ovidian Repertory - Christoph Ransmayr 5253

Cottar, Dickie (Bastard Son)
A Night in Cold Harbor - Margaret Kennedy 3420

Cottier, Louise (Gentlewoman)
Proud New Flags - F. van Wyck Mason 4156

Cottrell, Sally (Young Woman)
Bride of a Thousand Cedars - Bruce Lancaster 3637

Coult, James (Businessman)
The Day Before Thunder - Bart Spicer 5965

Couper, Anne (Gentlewoman)
Bright Captivity - Eugenia Price 5180

Courteney, Sean (Adventurer)
The Roar of the Thunder - Wilbur Smith 5929
When the Lion Feeds - Wilbur Smith 5931

Courtine, Anne-Marie (Gentlewoman)
All the Golden Gifts - Iola Fuller 2251

Courtland, Charles (Religious)
Palais-Royale - Richard Sennett 5747

Courtland, Frederick (Architect)
Palais-Royale - Richard Sennett 5747

Courtney, Miranda (Seamstress; Servant)
Autumn Lace - Eileen Jackson 3133

Courville-Boissart, Elise de (Young Woman)
Deeper the Heritage - Muriel Elwood 1936

Courville-Boissart, Philippe (Military Personnel)
Web of Destiny - Muriel Elwood 1939

Couville, Nigel (Gentleman)
Satan in St. Mary's - P.C. Doherty 1676

Coventry (Veteran; Servant)
Fallen Skies - Philippa Gregory 2581

Coventry, Daniel (Actor)
The Sound of Coaches - Leon Garfield 2295

Covington, Siobonna (Young Woman)
Sons of Thunder - Barbara Fitz Vroman 6516

Cowbone, Joe (Indian)
The White Man's Road - Benjamin Capps 891

Cowen, Jim (Spouse)
The Cup of Strength - Charlotte Paul 4840

Cowen, Merrie (Spouse)
The Cup of Strength - Charlotte Paul 4840

Cowper, Christabel (Religious)
The Man on a Donkey - H.F.M. Prescott 5170

Cowper, Francis (Businessman)
Yankee Trader - Stanley Morton 4496

Cowperwood, Frank A. (Businessman)
The Financier - Theodore Dreiser 1720

Cox-Neville, Alexandra (Gentlewoman; Writer)
Come Be My Love - Diana Brown 717

Coyote (Indian; Warrior)
The Elk-Dog Heritage - Don Coldsmith 1174
Trail of the Spanish Bit - Don Coldsmith 1193

Crabb, Jack (Frontiersman; Gunfighter)
Little Big Man - Thomas Berger 478

Crabb, Joe (Convict; Veteran)
To the Ends of the Earth - Michael Talbot 6155

Crabtree, Ella (Spouse)
Certain People of Importance - Kathleen Norris 4647

Crabtree, Robert (Settler)
Certain People of Importance - Kathleen Norris 4647

Craddock, Jeremy (Gentleman)
Whispering - Jane Aiken Hodge 2972

Craddock, Paul (Veteran)
A Horseman Riding By - R.F. Delderfield 1588

Cradock, Paul (Lawyer)
The Legacy of Tregaran - Mary Lide 3776

Craig, Kate (Widow(er))
River of Sky - Karen Harper 2713

Craig, Maggie (Young Woman)
Maggie Craig - Marie Joseph 3308

Craig, Mary (Spy)
The Long March - Jane Barry 358

Craigie, Andrew (Journalist)
The Shakespeare Girl - Mollie Hardwick 2698

Craigvalloch, Ian (Fugitive)
Red Cloak Flying - Margaret Widdemer 6737

Crandall, Lew (Young Man)
A Rage Against Heaven - Fred Mustard Stewart 6026

Crane, Beulah (Farmer)
The Regulators - William Degenhard 1580

Crane, Edwina (Religious)
The Jewel in the Crown - Paul Scott 5684

Crane, John (Frontiersman)
Gathering Storm - Bill Gulick 2613
Lost Wallowa - Bill Gulick 2616

Crane, John (Young Man)
Distant Trails - Bill Gulick 2612

Crane, Matt (Frontiersman)
Distant Trails - Bill Gulick 2612

Cranford, Dimity (Gentlewoman)
Love Alters Not - Patricia Veryan 6467

Cranford, Peregrine (Military Personnel)
Never Doubt I Love - Patricia Veryan 6473

Cranleigh, Rosetta (Gentlewoman)
The Captive - Victoria Holt 3011

Cranmere, Francis (Nobleman)
Marianne - Juliette Benzoni 466
Marianne and the Masked Prince - Juliette Benzoni 469

Cranston, John (Gentleman; Government Official)
The Nightingale Gallery - Paul Harding 2684
Red Slayer: Being the Second of the Sorrowful Mysteries of Brother Athelstan - Paul Harding 2685

Crassus, Publius (Military Personnel)
Winter Quarters - Alfred Duggan 1775

Cravat, Yancey (Frontiersman; Journalist)
Cimarron - Edna Ferber 2061

Craven, Oliver (Entertainer)
The Far-Off Rhapsody - Anne-Marie Sheridan 5808

Craven, Taylor (Widow(er))
The Woman of Catawba - Hilda Stahl 5978

Crawford, Captain (Military Personnel)
Mutiny - Frank Tilsley 6280

Crawford, Bill (Teenager; Peddler)
Boy with a Pack - Stephen Warren Meader 4319

Crawford, Francis (Adventurer)
Checkmate - Dorothy Dunnett 1799
The Disorderly Knights - Dorothy Dunnett 1800
The Game of Kings - Dorothy Dunnett 1801
Pawn in Frankincense - Dorothy Dunnett 1804
Queen's Play - Dorothy Dunnett 1805
The Ringed Castle - Dorothy Dunnett 1807

Crawford, Sir James (Military Personnel)
Until the Colors Fade - Tim Jeal 3173

Crawford, Martha Mary (Heroine)
Miss Martha Mary Crawford - Catherine Marchant 4081

Crawford, Melancthon (Settler)
Harp of a Thousand Strings - Harold Lenoir Davis 1522

Crawford, Michael (Doctor)
The Stress of Her Regard - Tim Powers 5157

Crawford, Richard (Nobleman)
The Game of Kings - Dorothy Dunnett 1801
Queen's Play - Dorothy Dunnett 1805

Cray, Marcus (Businessman)
The House of Cray - Pamela Hill 2936

Crayford, Thomas (Nobleman)
Beau Barron's Lady - Helen Ashfield 204

Crazy Fox (Indian)
Crazy Fox Remembers - Don Preston 5174

Crazy Walking (Indian; Young Man)
Dance Back the Buffalo - Milton Lott 3899

Creamer, Eddie (Companion)
Rainbow on the Road - Esther Forbes 2159

Credi, Frederico Sforzi (Gentleman)
The Palace of Wisdom - Bob Marshall-Andrews 4118

Cree, Elizabeth (Actress)
The Trial of Elizabeth Cree: A Novel of the Limehouse Murders - Peter Ackroyd 21

Cree, Captain Joe (Landowner)
The Velvet Horn - Andrew Lytle 3946

Cree, Lucius (Young Man)
The Velvet Horn - Andrew Lytle 3946

Cree Medicine (Indian; Captive)
The High Missouri - Winfred Blevins 545

Creek Mary (Indian)
Creek Mary's Blood - Dee Brown 712

Creekmore, Harry (Adventurer)
Bound for the Promised Land - Richard Marius 4083

Creel, Sugar Jim (Outlaw)
The Stranglers - Loren D. Estleman 1978

Creighton, Colonel (Military Personnel)
The Imperial Agent - T.N. Murari 4518
The Last Victory - T.N. Murari 4519

Creighton, Clifford (Businessman)
Lotus Land - Monica Highland 2917

Cresap, Bill (Veteran)
Mignon - James M. Cain 845

Crespi (Leader)
The Wrong Horse - Jean Bassan 374

Cresswell, Joe (Gentleman)
Midsummer's Eve - Philippa Carr 924

Creston, Peronneau (Plantation Owner)
Red Lanterns on St. Michael's - Thornwell
  Jacobs 3139

Creticus, Metellus (Diplomat)
The Temple of the Muses - John Maddox
  Roberts 5382

Crews, John (Trapper)
John Crews - Arthur Chapman 988

Cribb, Sergeant (Police Officer)
Abracadaver - Peter Lovesey 3906
A Case of Spirits - Peter Lovesey 3910
The Detective Wore Silk Drawers - Peter
  Lovesey 3911
Mad Hatter's Holiday - Peter Lovesey 3914
Swing, Swing Together - Peter Lovesey 3915
The Tick of Death - Peter Lovesey 3916
Waxwork - Peter Lovesey 3917
Wobble to Death - Peter Lovesey 3918

Cribb, Joe (Military Personnel; Convict)
A Wilful Woman - Michael Talbot 6156

Crick, Harley (Settler)
Sister Wives - Cleo Jones 3270

Cridilla (Royalty)
The Serpent's Tooth - Diana L. Paxson 4846

Crillon (Military Personnel)
Les Quarant Cinq - Alexandre Dumas 1779

Crispin, Anna (Spouse)
Heir to Kuragin - Constance Heaven 2807

Crispin, Bartley (Military Personnel; Pilot)
Squadron Shilling - Arch Whitehouse 6712

Crispin, Gustave (Scientist)
The Balloonist - Macdonald Harris 2724

Crittenden, Elizabeth (Spouse)
Action at Aquila - Hervey Allen 97

Crivelli, Margo (Artist)
The Bank - Stephen Longstreet 3882

Croasdale, Leonie (Young Woman; Heiress)
Hand of Glory - Glen Petrie 4980

Crocker, Catherine (Captive)
The Man Who Loved Cat Dancing - Marilyn
  Durham 1817

Crocker, Elizabeth Allen (Young Woman)
A Southern Woman - Elena Yates Eulo 1983

Crockett, Hume (Military Personnel; Spy)
Home to Tennessee - Alfred Leland Crabb 1400
Lodging at the Saint Cloud - Alfred Leland
  Crabb 1403
Mockingbird Sang at Chickamauga - Alfred Leland
  Crabb 1404

Croft, Art (Rancher)
The Ox-Bow Incident - Walter Van Tilburg
  Clark 1096

Croft, Helena (Gentlewoman)
Stand We at Last - Zoe Fairbairns 1999

Croft, Michael (Detective—Private)
The Cosgrove Report - G.J.A. O'Toole 4765

Croft, Ralph (Outlaw; Detective—Amateur)
The Masked Man - P.C. Doherty 1674

Croft, Sarah (Gentlewoman)
Stand We at Last - Zoe Fairbairns 1999

Cromer, Miriam (Murderer)
Waxwork - Peter Lovesey 3917

Cromwell, Tacey (Young Woman)
Tacey Cromwell - Conrad Richter 5324

Crook, Annie (Model)
The Women of Whitechapel and Jack the Ripper - Paul
  West 6638

Crooked Fingers (Indian)
Birthright - Phillip Finch 2087

Cropotkin, Countess (Noblewoman)
Fire in the Ice - Alan Scholefield 5653

Crosbie, Duncan (Military Personnel)
The Wild Ohio - Bart Spicer 5966

Crosby, Mariana (Young Woman)
The Castle of the Winds - Jeanne Montague 4434

Crossley, Stephen (Writer)
Cordelia - Winston Graham 2523

Croston, Kate (Widow(er))
Here Comes a Candle - Jane Aiken Hodge 2964

Crow, Angus McCready (Police Officer)
The Return of Moriarty - John E. Gardner 2287

Crow, Jim (Dancer)
Darktown Strutters - Wesley Brown 732

Crow Feather (Indian; Warrior)
The Far Canyon - Elmer Kelton 3404
Slaughter - Elmer Kelton 3407

Crowbetter, Athene (Spinster)
The Brocken - Pamela Hill 2929

Crowbetter, Nicholas (Banker)
The Brocken - Pamela Hill 2929

Crowe, Thomas (Military Personnel)
Sergeant Verity and the Blood Royal - Francis
  Selwyn 5744

Crown, Joseph (Businessman; Veteran)
Homeland - John Jakes 3148

Crown, Paul (Immigrant)
Homeland - John Jakes 3148

Crowninshield, Philippe (Military Personnel)
And Wait for the Night - John William
  Corrington 1352

Crozat, Edmund (Gentleman)
Blood & Dreams - Leslie Waller 6543

Crozier, Laura (Spouse)
Dear Laura - Jean Stubbs 6094

Crozier, Theodore (Gentleman)
Dear Laura - Jean Stubbs 6094

Cruickshank, Will (Nobleman)
Greenyards - Joan Lingard 3796

Crusoe, Robinson (Castaway)
Friday - Michel Tournier 6305

Cruz, Artemio (Financier; Revolutionary)
The Death of Artemio Cruz - Carlos Fuentes 2246

Cruz, Catalina (Spouse)
The Death of Artemio Cruz - Carlos Fuentes 2246

Cuan (Outlaw)
The Silent People - Walter Macken 3990

Cuchulain (Warrior)
Red Branch - Morgan Llywelyn 3824

Cuddesdon, Jasper (Nobleman)
Turn of the Dice - Janet Edmonds 1870

Cuddington, Chloe (Gentlewoman)
The Nonsuch Lure - Mary M. Luke 3924

Cuddy, Mary Bee (Frontierswoman)
The Homesman - Glendon Swarthout 6143

Cudjo (Slave)
Chesapeake - James A. Michener 4367

Cuheno, Rachel (Young Woman)
The Books of Rachel - Joel Gross 2600

Culhane, Lexy (Journalist)
A Season of Swans - Celeste De Blasis 1548

Culhane, Travis (Landowner)
A Season of Swans - Celeste De Blasis 1548

Culhaney, Margaret (Young Woman)
Gone the Rainbow, Gone the Dove - Joan
  Bagnel 264

Cullen, Arthur (Worker)
Day Is Coming - William Cameron 869

Cullen, Rose Mary O'Driscoll (Widow(er))
Grandmother and the Priests - Taylor Caldwell 857

Culpepper, India (Young Woman)
Full of Thy Riches - Elizabeth Ferrell 2070

Culver, Robert (Businessman)
Fair Wind to Java - Garland Roark 5354

Cumanus, Sergius (Doctor)
The Emperor's Physician - Jacob Randolph
  Perkins 4914

Cummings, Amory (Businessman)
Silver Fruit - Patricia Campbell 876

Cummings, Dee (Businesswoman)
Silver Fruit - Patricia Campbell 876

Cummings, Jack (Military Personnel)
A Certain Splendour - Carola Salisbury 5566

Cunningham, Alison (Loyalist)
Patriot's Progress - Joseph G.E. Hopkins 3027

Cunningham, Maude (Companion)
Diamond Head - Marian J.A. Jackson 3135
The Sunken Treasure - Marian J.A. Jackson 3136

Cunningham, Sarah (Spouse)
Sarah Cobb - Catherine M. Rae 5236

Curle, Jody (Gypsy)
Norah - Pamela Hill 2941

Curle, Norah (Heiress)
Norah - Pamela Hill 2941

Curley, Brent (Cowboy)
The Talking Rifle - Glenn R. Vernam 6454

Curnet, Buck (Military Personnel)
Journey to Shiloh - Will Henry 2843

Curnow, Giles (Gentleman)
A Woman Possessed - Malcolm Macdonald 3977

Currain, Cinda (Southern Belle)
House Divided - Ben Ames Williams 6765

Currain, Lucy (Young Woman)
The Unconquered - Ben Ames Williams 6768

Currain, Travis (Military Personnel)
House Divided - Ben Ames Williams 6765

Currain, Travis (Veteran)
The Unconquered - Ben Ames Williams 6768

Currito (Guide)
Shadows in the Dusk - John Edward Jennings 3208

Curry, Jeff (Young Man)
The Hider - Loren D. Estleman 1972

Curry, Kid (Outlaw)
Mr. American - George MacDonald Fraser 2211

Curtis, Abigail (Young Woman)
Marblehead - Joan Thompson 6267

Curtis, Madison (Farmer)
Hiwassee: A Novel of the Civil War - Charles F. Price 5176

Curtis, Sarah (Spouse)
Hiwassee: A Novel of the Civil War - Charles F. Price 5176

Curtwright, Alain (Gentleman)
Devilseed - Frank Yerby 6914

Cusak, Marcus (Editor)
Castle Barebane - Joan Aiken 43

Cusi Huaman (Warrior)
The Incas - Daniel Peters 4945

Cuthred (Recluse)
The Hermit of Eyton Forest - Ellis Peters 4961

Cutler, Captain (Military Personnel)
Lieutenant Lamb - Kenneth Maynard 4210

Cutler, Jocelyn (Young Woman)
The Braeswood Tapestry - Robyn Carr 936

Cutter, Jake (Military Personnel)
The Pride of Hannah Wade - Janet Dailey 1455

Cutter, Vardy (Bastard Daughter)
Vardy - John Harris 2721

Cutterfield, Annie Bee (Young Woman)
Pursuit of Bliss - Betty Palmer Nelson 4577

D

da Burgos, Jorges (Religious)
The Name of the Rose - Umberto Eco 1850

da Melck, Adso (Religious)
The Name of the Rose - Umberto Eco 1850

Da Silva, Francisco (Trader)
The Viceroy of Ouidah - Bruce C. Chatwin 1009

da Silva, Miriam (Heiress)
The Strand - Claire Rayner 5269

Daae, Christine (Singer)
Phantom - Susan Kay 3375

Dabney, Big Sans (Businessman)
Tomorrow We Reap - James H. Street 6081

Dabney, Hoab (Plantation Owner)
Tap Roots - James H. Street 6080

Dabney, Mingo (Adventurer)
Mingo Dabney - James H. Street 6078

Dabney, Mingo (Businessman)
Tomorrow We Reap - James H. Street 6081

Dabney, Morna (Young Woman)
Tap Roots - James H. Street 6080

Dacre, Verney (Criminal)
Cracksman on Velvet - Francis Selwyn 5743
Sergeant Verity and the Blood Royal - Francis Selwyn 5744

Daedalus (Artisan)
The Maze Maker - Michael Ayrton 250

d'Agrigente, Emma (Widow(er); Royalty)
1876: A Novel - Gore Vidal 6484

Dagshaw, Anna (Young Woman)
The Love Child - Catherine Cookson 1279

Dagshaw, Maria (Gentlewoman)
The Love Child - Catherine Cookson 1279

Dahlberg, Chris (Teenager)
Swift Rivers - Cornelia Meigs 4328

Daigle, Axford (Bastard Son)
Give Me Your Golden Hand - Evelyn Eaton 1825

Dain (Young Man)
The Road to San Jacinto - Leonard L. Foreman 2167

d'Aire, Thalia (Young Woman)
The Longest Night - Ada Cook Lewis 3744

Daisy (Entertainer; Saloon Hostess)
Pacific Street - Cecelia Holland 2993

D'Aix, Sir Alphonse (Nobleman; Bastard Son)
A Silver Mirror - Roberta Gellis 2353

D'Alais, Guy (Nobleman)
The Shepherd's Crook - Paul Frischauer 2234

Dale, Erskine (Frontiersman)
Erskine Dale, Pioneer - John Fox 2195

Dale, Sally (Orphan)
The Man of the Storm - Ethel Hueston 3069

Daley, Jamie (Revolutionary)
Gone the Rainbow, Gone the Dove - Joan Bagnel 264

Dalgarvo (Nobleman)
The Fortunes of Nigel - Sir Walter Scott 5696

Dalgleish, Jenny (Young Woman)
Night Shall Overtake Us - Kate Saunders 5611

Dallas, Madeleine (Bastard Daughter)
Not by Any Single Man - Brigid Knight 3522

Dallet, Susanna (Artist; Widow(er))
The Serpent Garden - Judith Merkle Riley 5336

Dallow, Corinna (Gentlewoman)
Teverton Hall - Jane Gillespie 2421

Dallow, George (Gentleman)
Teverton Hall - Jane Gillespie 2421

d'Almada, Zena (Gentlewoman)
Hong Kong - Mona Gardner 2288

Dalsgaard, Hanne (Young Woman)
Kingdom Come - Virginia Sorensen 5950

Dalton, Bradford (Heir)
Scarborough House - Sharon Salvato 5577

Dalton, Layne (Military Personnel)
Joy From Ashes - Al Lacy 3581

Dalton, Melody (Spouse)
Joy From Ashes - Al Lacy 3581

Dalton, Tyler (Fugitive)
Outlaw Lover - Lindsey Hanks 2676

Dalven, Carlin (Nobleman)
Lady Pamela - Clare Darcy 1490

Daly, Barney (Veteran)
The Ways of Women - Elaine Crowley 1436

Dalyrymple, Jim (Young Man)
Perilous Journey: A Tale of the Mississippi River and the Natchez Trace - Clifford Sublette 6109

Damao, Bonita (Young Woman)
The Deadly Lady of Madagascar - C.V. Terry 6206

Damerel, Jasper (Nobleman; Rake)
Venetia - Georgette Heyer 2909

Damian (Nobleman)
The Betrothed - Sir Walter Scott 5691

Damianus (Secretary)
Gregory the Great - Gerhart Ellert 1913

Damon (Young Man)
O Western Wind - John Anthony Devon 1634

Damon, Camille (Nobleman)
Love's Duet - Patricia Veryan 6468

Damon, Kate (Gentlewoman)
Scandal at High Chimneys: A Victorian Melodrama - John Dickson Carr 915

Damon, Victor (Gentleman)
Scandal at High Chimneys: A Victorian Melodrama - John Dickson Carr 915

Dana (Landowner)
By Love Enslaved - Phoebe Conn 1255

Danbury, Lady Eleanor (Noblewoman)
Room with a Clue - Kate Kingsbury 3495

Danby, April (Actress; Singer)
Albuquerque - Sara Orwig 4757

Dance, John (Organized Crime Figure)
Whiskey River - Loren D. Estleman 1981

Dancing Rabbit (Indian)
The White Path - Robert J. Conley 1254

D'Ancours, Diane (Spy)
The Mohawk Ladder - Noel B. Gerson 2377

Dando, Joseph (Military Personnel)
Dando on Delhi Ridge - William Clive 1119

Dandridge, Clarence (Plantation Owner)
Bagatelle - Maurice Denuziere 1613

Dane, Jared (Murderer)
Come Winter - Douglas C. Jones 3275

Dane, Sara (Convict)
Sara Dane - Catherine Gaskin 2316

Danement, Petula (Gentlewoman)
Shadows over Castle Rising - Fanny Cradock 1410

Danford, Owen (Veteran)
Dark Thicket - Elmer Kelton 3402

Danforth, Abigail (Detective—Private)
Diamond Head - Marian J.A. Jackson 3135
The Sunken Treasure - Marian J.A. Jackson 3136

Dangerfield, Faith (Gentlewoman)
A Certain Splendour - Carola Salisbury 5566

Dangerfield, Paul (Murderer)
The House by the Churchyard - Joseph Sheridan Le Fanu 3688

Daniels, Eugene (Labor Leader)
Great Dream From Heaven - John Rolfe Gardiner 2286

Daniels, Kitty (Orphan; Singer)
Sweet Songbird - Teresa Crane 1418

Daniels, Matt (Thief)
Sweet Songbird - Teresa Crane 1418

Daniels, Shep (Cowboy)
By Dim and Flashing Lamps - Alan Le May 3689

Danin, Vassily (Spy)
Tournament of the Shadows - Nicholas Carnac 901

D'Antoni, Ursula (Southern Belle)
The Golden Circle - John Edward Ames 125

Dantry, Charles (Nobleman)
Diana the Huntress - Marion Chesney 1026

Danver, George (Nobleman; Twin)
Double Masquerade - Karen Lynn 3938

Danver, Georginna (Noblewoman; Twin)
Double Masquerade - Karen Lynn 3938

Danver, Marietta (Servant)
Love's Tender Fury - Jennifer Wilde 6749

Danvers, Clinton (Military Personnel; Nobleman)
A Marriage of Convenience - Tim Jeal 3172

Danvers, Esmond (Gentleman)
A Marriage of Convenience - Tim Jeal 3172

Danville, John (Nobleman)
Lady in the Briars - Carola Dunn 1793

Danville, Teresa (Gentlewoman)
The Black Sheep's Daughter - Carola Dunn   1791

d'Arblay, Tessa (Gentlewoman)
Tessa d'Arblay - Malcolm Macdonald   3974

d'Arbonne, Madeleine (Gentlewoman)
Madeleine - Catherine Gavin   2323

Darby, Quint (Young Man)
River's Run - Jane Ludlow Abbot   7

D'Arcy, Ann (Gentlewoman)
A Prince, a Piper, and a Rose - John Scalzo   5628

Darcy, Cavin (Veteran)
And Tell of Time - Laura Krey   3554

D'Arcy, Dermod (Young Man)
Tide of Empire - Peter S. Kyne   3572

Darcy, Elizabeth (Gentlewoman)
Pemberley, or Pride and Prejudice Continued - Emma Tennant   6201
Presumption: An Entertainment - Julia Barrett   350

Darcy, Fitzwilliam (Gentleman)
Pemberley, or Pride and Prejudice Continued - Emma Tennant   6201
An Unequal Marriage; or Pride and Prejudice Twenty Years Later - Emma Tennant   6202

Darcy, Georgiana (Gentlewoman)
Pemberley, or Pride and Prejudice Continued - Emma Tennant   6201
Presumption: An Entertainment - Julia Barrett   350

Darcy, Thomas (Nobleman)
The Man on a Donkey - H.F.M. Prescott   5170

Dare, Cain (Indian)
Lovestorm - Judith E. French   2222

Dare, Jeannie (Young Woman)
The Land Is Bright - James Arthur Kjelgaard   3508

Dark Hand (Indian; Bounty Hunter)
Forty Guns West - William W. Johnstone   3267

Dark Mairi (Healer)
Butcher's Broom - Neil Gunn   2620

Darling, Miles (Young Man)
Croatan - Mary Johnston   3231

Darling, Tristram (Journalist)
The Private Life of Florence Nightingale - Richard Gordon   2485

Darnay, Charles (Nobleman)
A Tale of Two Cities - Charles Dickens   1642

Darnley, Fanny (Gentlewoman)
Coronation Summer - Angela Thirkell   6220

Darracott, Anthea (Gentlewoman)
The Unknown Ajax - Georgette Heyer   2908

Darracott, Hugh (Heir; Military Personnel)
The Unknown Ajax - Georgette Heyer   2908

Darragh, Roxanne (Patriot)
Sons of Liberty - Adam Rutledge   5540

Darragh, Roxanne (Patriot; Spy)
Rebel Guns - Adam Rutledge   5539

Darrell, Thames (Gentleman; Heir—Dispossessed)
Jack Sheppard - William Harrison Ainsworth   56

Dart, Joan (Plantation Owner)
Ratoon - Christopher Nicole   4619

D'Artagnan (Military Personnel)
The Three Musketeers - Alexandre Dumas   1782
Twenty Years After - Alexandre Dumas   1783

D'Artagnan, Charles (Military Personnel)
A Candle for D'Artagnan - Chelsea Quinn Yarbro   6895

d'Arthus, Morel (Businessman)
The Lacemaker - Janine Montupet   4438

Dash, Hannibal (Professor; Scientist)
Goldfield - Richard S. Wheeler   6660

Dashkova, Sophia (Noblewoman)
Death Off Stage - Richard Grayson   2558

Dashwood, Elinor (Gentlewoman)
Eliza's Daughter - Joan Aiken   44

Dashwood, Margaret (Gentlewoman)
The Third Sister - Julia Barrett   351

Dashwood, Marianne (Gentlewoman)
Eliza's Daughter - Joan Aiken   44

Dasius (Trader)
The Coin of Carthage - Bryher   740

d'Asselnat, Marianne (Noblewoman)
Marianne and the Lords of the East - Juliette Benzoni   468
Marianne and the Privateer - Juliette Benzoni   470
Marianne and the Rebels - Juliette Benzoni   471

d'Asselnat, Marianne (Noblewoman; Singer)
Marianne and the Masked Prince - Juliette Benzoni   469

d'Asselnat, Marianne (Orphan; Noblewoman)
Marianne - Juliette Benzoni   466

d'Asselnat, Marianne (Royalty)
Marianne and the Crown of Fire - Juliette Benzoni   467

d'Astarac, Sybille (Entertainer; Writer)
Sybille - Marion Meade   4318

D'Astrarac (Philosopher)
At the Sign of the Reine Pedauque - Anatole France   2198

Daunbey, Benjamin (Gentleman)
A Brood of Vipers - Michael Clynes   1133
The Gallows Murder - Michael Clynes   1134
The Grail Murders - Michael Clynes   1135
The Poisoned Chalice - Michael Clynes   1136
The White Rose Murders - Michael Clynes   1137

Dauntry, Vernon (Nobleman)
Frederica - Georgette Heyer   2889

Dave (Businessman)
World's Fair - E.L. Doctorow   1661

Davelle, Victoria (Young Woman)
Mills of the Gods - Daoma Winston   6828

Davenport, Amanda (Gentlewoman; Orphan)
Miss Davenport's Christmas - Marion Chesney   1039

Davenport, Gillian (Gentlewoman; Orphan)
Miss Davenport's Christmas - Marion Chesney   1039

Daventry, Julia (Widow(er); Actress)
Caroline and Julia - Clare Darcy   1484

Davey, Francis (Religious)
Jamaica Inn - Daphne Du Maurier   1747

David, William (Child)
The Kentucky Trace: A Novel of the American Revolution - Harriette Simpson Arnow   195

Davies, Toby (Miner)
This Sweet and Bitter Earth - Alexander Cordell   1326

DaVille, M. Jean (Diplomat)
Bosnian Chronicle - Ivo Andric   150

Davis, Aaron (Hunter; Frontiersman)
Journey by the River - John Prescott   5173

Davis, Benjamin (Gentleman)
Look Away, Beulah Land - Lonnie Coleman   1204

d'Avnay, Paul (Military Personnel)
Tell Your Sons: A Novel of the Napoleonic Era - Willa Gibbs   2402

Dawe, Gilbert (Religious)
The Man on a Donkey - H.F.M. Prescott   5170

Dawes, David (Teenager)
Black Jack Davy - John Oskison   4763

Dawkins, Scrape (Teenager)
The Bright Feathers - John H. Culp   1441

Dawson, Angel (Gentlewoman; Spouse)
My Lady Benbrook - Constance Gluyas   2442

Dawson, Angel (Streetperson)
The King's Brat - Constance Gluyas   2441

Dawson, Anthony (Settler; Spy)
Cormorant's Brood - Inglis Fletcher   2133

Dawson, Nicholas (Diplomat; Spy)
City of God: A Novel of the Borgias - Cecelia Holland   2985

Dawson, Pride (Businessman)
Pride's Castle - Frank Yerby   6925

Dawson, Spicy (Young Woman)
The Labyrinth - Thomas William Duncan   1787

Dawson, William (Military Personnel)
The Long Fight - D.A. Rayner   5270

Day, Eden (Southern Belle)
Yankee Stranger - Elswyth Thane   6217

Day, James Burden (Political Figure)
Hollywood: A Novel of America in the 1920s - Gore Vidal   6488
Washington, D.C. - Gore Vidal   6493

Day, Julian (Teacher)
Dawn's Early Light - Elswyth Thane   6215

De Aix, Ralph (Knight)
King of the Wood - Valerie Anand   131

de Barberie, Alinda (Heiress; Fiance(e))
The Water Witch - James Fenimore Cooper   1311

De Bernard, Anne (Gentlewoman)
The French Bride - Evelyn Anthony   163

de Brealte, Falkes (Knight)
Leopards and Lilies - Alfred Duggan   1769

De Bretagne, Olivier (Knight)
Brother Cadfael's Penance - Ellis Peters   4955

De Brussac, Anne (Gentlewoman)
This Splendid Earth - V.J. Banis   289

De Brussac, Claude (Businessman)
This Splendid Earth - V.J. Banis   289

De Brussac, Philip (Heir—Dispossessed)
This Splendid Earth - V.J. Banis   289

De Brussac, Philip (Heir—Dispossessed; Businessman)
The Earth and All It Holds - V.J. Banis   287

de Bunez, Catherine (Gentlewoman)
Rakossy - Cecelia Holland   2995

de Charny, Count (Military Personnel)
The Queen's Necklace - Alexandre Dumas   1781

De Chartes, Anne (Young Woman)
Touched with Fire - John William Tebbel   6195

De Chavel, Colonel (Military Personnel)
Valentina - Evelyn Anthony   165

De Clairpont, Ivon (Knight; Slave)
The Proud Villeins - Valerie Anand   133

de Harcourt, Raoul (Nobleman; Knight)
The Conqueror - Georgette Heyer   2881

De Hartog, Sianna (Nurse)
The Nationalists - William Stuart Long   3876

De Jeneau, Antoine (Ward; Heir)
The Sugar Pavilion - Rosalind Laker   3600

De la Barca, Tamar (Gentlewoman)
For Love of a Pirate - Anthony Esler   1961

De La Ferte, Comte (Nobleman)
The Girl From Paris - Joan Aiken   47

De la Motte, Chevalier (Nobleman; Smuggler)
Denis Duval - William Makepeace Thackeray 6211

de la Rosa, Domingo (Rancher)
Promised Lands - Elizabeth Crook 1430

de la Tour d'Azur Gervais, Marquis (Nobleman)
Scaramouche - Rafael Sabatini 5554

De Lacy, Hugo (Nobleman)
The Betrothed - Sir Walter Scott 5691

de Lalliere, Blaise (Military Personnel)
The King's Cavalier - Samuel Shellabarger 5795

De Lancey, Christopher (Military Personnel;
    Mercenary)
The Journal of Colonel De Lancey - James Warner
    Bellah 426

De Lancey, George (Gentleman)
The Adventurers - William Stuart Long 3869

de Long, Laurel (Spouse)
The Valley - Clifford Irving 3114

De Malassise (Diplomat)
The Negotiators - Francis Walder 6526

de Montemayor, Marquesa (Noblewoman)
The Bridge of San Luis Rey - Thornton Wilder 6752

de Montreal, Walter (Mercenary)
Rienzi, or The Last of the Tribunes - Edward Bulwer-
    Lytton 770

de Rada y Sylva, Dominica (Noblewoman)
Beauvallet - Georgette Heyer 2876

de Redvers, Count (Nobleman)
Leopards and Lilies - Alfred Duggan 1769

De Rhetoree, Germaine (Writer)
The Girl From Paris - Joan Aiken 47

de Saint-Vire, Henri (Nobleman)
These Old Shades - Georgette Heyer 2906

De Salis, Edward (Widow(er); Landowner)
Cashelmara - Susan Howatch 3058

De Salis, Patrick (Young Man)
Cashelmara - Susan Howatch 3058

De Salis, Sarah (Spouse)
Cashelmara - Susan Howatch 3058

de Silva, Diego (Landowner; Government Official)
Captain From Castile - Samuel Shellabarger 5794

De Soto, Don Guzman (Military Personnel)
Westward Ho! - Charles Kingsley 3499

De Talmond, Prince (Royalty)
Hester - Brian Cleeve 1107

de Vargas, Pedro (Gentleman; Military Personnel)
Captain From Castile - Samuel Shellabarger 5794

de Vauban, Eustacie (Gentlewoman)
The Talisman Ring - Georgette Heyer 2905

De Vaumartin, Everard (Orphan; Knight)
The Lords of Vaumartin - Cecelia Holland 2992

De Vere, Arthur (Nobleman)
Anne of Geierstein - Sir Walter Scott 5689

de Villanegas, Matilda (Witch)
The Monk - Matthew Gregory Lewis 3756

De Vitale, Louise (Gentlewoman)
The French Bride - Evelyn Anthony 163

De Walton, John (Knight; Nobleman)
Castle Dangerous - Sir Walter Scott 5694

de Willading, Adelheid (Noblewoman)
The Headsman; or, The Abbaye des Vignerons - James
    Fenimore Cooper 1300

de Winter, Milady (Spy)
The Three Musketeers - Alexandre Dumas 1782

Deaderick, Elly (Patriot)
Slow Dies the Thunder - Helen Topping Miller 4395

Deakin, John (Outlaw)
Breakheart Pass - Alistair MacLean 3999

Deakins, Jim (Mountain Man)
The Big Sky - A.B. Guthrie Jr. 2624

Deal, Abbie (Frontierswoman)
A Lantern in Her Hand - Bess Streeter Aldrich 69

Dean, John (Sea Captain)
Boon Island - Kenneth Roberts 5384

Dean, Rachel (Widow(er))
Passage Home - Alison McLeay 4286

Dean, Sara (Young Woman)
Scoundrels' Brigade - Carter A. Vaughan 6439

Deane, Amelie (Young Woman)
Paloverde - Jacqueline Briskin 693

Deane, John (Teenager; Military Personnel)
Swords of Steel - Elsie Singmaster 5870

Deans, Effie (Prisoner)
The Heart of Midlothian - Sir Walter Scott 5698

Deans, Jeanie (Heroine)
The Heart of Midlothian - Sir Walter Scott 5698

Dearborn, Jonathan (Lawyer; Military Personnel)
Jonathan Dearborn: A Novel of the War of 1812 -
    Willard Wallace 6540

Dearborn, Tom (Military Personnel)
East to Bagaduce - Willard Wallace 6539

DeBoer, Marinus (Sea Captain)
The Sable Lion - Jan Van Dorp 6405

Deborah (Gentlewoman)
The Silver Chalice - Thomas B. Costain 1370

Decimus (Outlaw; Pirate)
The Bride of Pilate - Esther Kellner 3393

Decimus, Versus Camillus (Political Figure)
The Silver Pigs - Lindsey Davis 1532

Decker, Gabriel (Mercenary; Adventurer)
Earthshaker - Robert Wilson Krepps 3553

Dee, Christmas (Nobleman)
Regency Rogue - Helen Ashfield 212

Deems, Molly (Young Woman)
This Is the House - Deborah Hill 2921

Deer Shadow (Prehistoric Human; Shaman)
The Deer Dancers - Amanda Cockrell 1146

Deesohay (Indian; Chieftain)
Valley of the Shadow - Charles Marquis
    Warren 6570

Degnan, Linus (Military Personnel)
A Time in the Sun - Jane Barry 361

d'Egremont (Nobleman)
Damaris - Jane Sheridan 5810

Deirdre (Ward)
Deirdre - James Stephens 5996

Deirdre (Young Woman)
Red Branch - Morgan Llywelyn 3824

Dekker, Leon (Activist)
Julie - Jane Kesner Morris 4479

del Vecchio, Cecco (Blacksmith)
Rienzi, or The Last of the Tribunes - Edward Bulwer-
    Lytton 770

Delacourt, Geoffrey (Military Personnel)
Journey to Enchantment - Patricia Veryan 6464

Delacourt, William (Military Personnel)
That Sweet and Savage Land - Emma
    Drummond 1728

Delacroix, Lily (Lesbian)
Bayou City Secrets - Deborah Powell 5146

Delaford, Laura (Spouse)
The Standing Hills - Caroline Stickland 6038

Delaford, Samuel (Gentleman)
The Standing Hills - Caroline Stickland 6038

Delahanty, Mick (Wanderer; Writer)
O'Houlihan's Jest - Rohan O'Grady 4702

Delahousse, Juliette (Young Woman)
The French Woman - Barbara Paul 4837

Delahunty, Sibell (Settler)
The Feather and the Stone - Patricia Shaw 5780

Delamaine, James (Gentleman)
Daughter of Marignac - Constance Heaven 2805

Delanay, Mary (Settler; Young Woman)
Dark Sails - Helen Topping Miller 4388

Delancey, Clytie (Young Woman)
The Governor's Daughter - Denton Whitson 6718

Delancey, Fiona (Spouse)
Dead Reckoning - C. Northcote Parkinson 4809

Delancey, Richard (Military Personnel)
Dead Reckoning - C. Northcote Parkinson 4809
Devil to Pay - C. Northcote Parkinson 4810
The Fireship - C. Northcote Parkinson 4811
The Guernseyman - C. Northcote Parkinson 4812
So Near So Far - C. Northcote Parkinson 4814
Touch and Go - C. Northcote Parkinson 4815

Delaney, Edward (Gentleman)
The Far Journey - Loula Grace Erdman 1950

Delaney, Robert (Revolutionary; Political Figure)
The Tenants of Time - Thomas Flanagan 2120

Delange, Theophile (Artist; Heir)
The Montmarte Murders - Richard Grayson 2561

Delchard, Ralph (Military Personnel)
The Dragons of Archenfield - Edward Marston 4119
The Lions of the North - Edward Marston 4121
The Ravens of Blackwater - Edward Marston 4126
The Wolves of Savernake - Edward Marston 4130

Delcourt, Sophie (Refugee; Businesswoman)
The Sugar Pavilion - Rosalind Laker 3600

Delfino, Pancito (Outlaw)
Adios! - Lanier Bartlett 366

Delibe, Charles August (Nobleman)
The Devil on Horseback - Victoria Holt 3014

Delibe, Margot (Gentlewoman)
The Devil on Horseback - Victoria Holt 3014

Delin (Military Personnel; Political Figure)
Bittersweet - Leslie Li 3769

Delisle, Yvonne (Young Woman)
A Bride for New Orleans - Edward Francis
    Murphy 4522

Dell, Sara (Actress)
Lovers Meeting - Mollie Hardwick 2695

DeLong, Lily (Young Woman)
Lily - Cindy Bonner 571
Looking After Lily - Cindy Bonner 572

Delorme, Julie (Young Woman)
By Dim and Flashing Lamps - Alan Le May 3689

Delusson, Cecile (Spouse)
The Delusson Family - Jacques Ducharme 1753

Delusson, Jean Baptiste (Settler)
The Delusson Family - Jacques Ducharme 1753

Demarest, Adelaide (Gentlewoman)
Sarsen Place - Gwendoline Butler 821

Demaury, Giles (Gentleman)
Summoned to Darkness - Anne-Marie Sheridan 5809

Demaury, Meg (Young Woman)
Summoned to Darkness - Anne-Marie Sheridan 5809

DeMayne, Rowan (Military Personnel)
Forget the Glory - Emma Drummond 1725

Demere, John Fraser (Military Personnel)
Beauty From Ashes - Eugenia Price 5177

Demetrias (Artisan)
Imperial Purple - Gillian Bradshaw 631

Demetrius (Slave)
The Robe - Lloyd C. Douglas 1703

Demetrius (Trader)
Roman Wall - Bryher 745

Deming, Mark (Religious)
Young Men See Visions - Mary Mian 4357

Dennetry, Sophia (Young Woman)
Drums of War - Roy Clews 1114

Dennison, Flora (Gentlewoman)
Tigerlilies - Judith Glover 2439

Denny, Mark (Doctor)
No Brighter Glory - Armstrong Sperry 5963

Dent, Abner (Rancher)
Montana Hitch - Richard S. Wheeler 6661

Dent, Eve (Spouse)
Montana Hitch - Richard S. Wheeler 6661

Denton, Eric (Gentleman)
Black Body - H.C. Turk 6361

Denton, John (Government Official; Trader)
Shanghai - Christopher New 4588

Denver, Annabelinda (Student)
A Time for Silence - Philippa Carr 930

Denys (Knight)
The Cloister and the Hearth - Charles Reade 5279

Denys, Paul (Young Man)
River and Empty Sea - Louis Vaczek 6396

Derker, Tom (Sailor)
Captain of the Sands - Keith Dewhurst 1636

Derker, William (Sea Captain)
Captain of the Sands - Keith Dewhurst 1636

Dermot (Ruler)
The Love of Fingin O'Lea - Theodora McCormick Du
  Bois 1743

Dernent, Claire (Spouse)
A Horseman Riding By - R.F. Delderfield 1588

Derriman, Festus (Farmer)
The Trumpet Major - Thomas Hardy 2700

Derwent, Marina (Young Woman)
Damnation Reef - Jill Tattersall 6172

Derwent-Jones, Caroline (Young Woman)
The Nightingale Legacy - Catherine Coulter 1379

Desautels, Diron (Nobleman)
Drums at Dusk - Arna Bontemps 575

Deschaumes, Constance (Young Woman)
The Riven Heart - Genevieve Gennari 2354

D'Escoville, Ralf (Knight)
I Am England - Patricia Wright 6881

Desire, Harry (Nobleman)
Deirdre and Desire - Marion Chesney 1024

Desmond, Arthur (Gentleman)
Traitors Gate - Anne Perry 4939

Desmond, Lizzie (Young Woman)
Pomp and Circumstance - Fred Mustard
  Stewart 6025

Desportes, John (Military Personnel; Scout)
Mi Amigo - William R. Burnett 795

d'Este, Gervase (Young Man)
The Longest Night - Ada Cook Lewis 3744

D'Estivet, Captain (Military Personnel)
The Masked Man - P.C. Doherty 1674

Detling, Sir Arthur (Gentleman)
The Detling Secret - Julian Symons 6151

Detling, Dolly (Gentlewoman)
The Detling Secret - Julian Symons 6151

Devalon, Henri (Landowner)
Forever Possess - Alexandra Phillips 4982

Devane, Barbara (Widow(er); Landowner)
Now Face to Face - Karleen Koen 3530

Devant, James (Smuggler)
Clouds of Destiny - Lou Ellen Davis 1535

Devaux, Nicolas (Gentleman; Military Personnel)
Tree of Gold - Rosalind Laker 3602

Devenham, Godfrey (Gentleman)
The Malvie Inheritance - Pamela Hill 2938

Devenish, Alain (Fiance(e))
The Noblest Frailty - Patricia Veryan 6474

Devenish, John (Nobleman)
An Important Family - Dorothy Eden 1855

Devera, Camille (Young Woman)
Keeping Secrets - Suzanne Morris 4483

Deveraux, Captain Edward (Adventurer)
The Fine and Handsome Captain - Frances
  Lynch 3933

Devereaux, Caroline (Gentlewoman; Orphan)
Caroline and Julia - Clare Darcy 1484

Devereaux, Clarissa (Gentlewoman)
Love at Sunset - Jane Sheridan 5811

Devereaux, Juliette (Gentlewoman)
Two of a Kind: An English Trifle - Rosemary
  Edghill 1867

Devereaux, Neville (Gentleman)
Caroline and Julia - Clare Darcy 1484

Deverell, Fancy (Young Woman)
Paint the Wind - Cathy Cash Spellman 5960

Devereux, Brigitte (Bride; Noblewoman)
Highland Belle - Patricia Grasso 2541

Devereux, Malcolm (Gentleman)
The Blade of Castlemayne - Anthony Esler 1960

Deveril, Adam (Nobleman)
A Civil Contract - Georgette Heyer 2880

Deveron, Andra (Sorceress)
Swear by Apollo - Shirley Barker 318

Deveron, Ellen (Young Woman)
Swear by Apollo - Shirley Barker 318

Devers, Harry (Heir)
The Intrigue - Marion Chesney 1034

Devers, Walt (Businessman)
Log Jam - Leslie Turner White 6684

Devigne, Sophia (Young Woman)
Starrbelow - China Thompson 6248

Devize, Elizabeth (Orphan)
The Dark Stranger - Dorothy Charques 999

Devlin, Brooke (Socialite)
Masterpiece of Murder - Mary Kruger 3563

Devlin, Gavin (Veteran)
The Rising of the Moon - Peter Berresford Ellis 1926

Devlin, John-Joe (Veteran)
The Rising of the Moon - Peter Berresford Ellis 1926

Devlin, Lisette (Young Woman)
Wanderers Eastward, Wanderers West - Kathleen
  Winsor 6823

Devlin, Matt (Detective—Police)
Death on the Cliff Walk - Mary Kruger 3562
Masterpiece of Murder - Mary Kruger 3563
No Honeymoon for Death - Mary Kruger 3564

Devlin, Mike (Manager)
Cry of the Rain Bird - Patricia Shaw 5779

Devlin, Sean (Mountain Man)
High Country - Jason Manning 4075

Devoe, Lucius (Doctor)
Eagle in the Sky - F. van Wyck Mason 4149

Dewar, Ellen (Young Woman)
Hangman's Beach - Thomas H. Raddall 5229

Dewar, Hamish (Military Personnel)
Subaltern's Choice - Duncan MacNeil 4020

deWitt, Aaron (Businessman)
Never Victorious, Never Defeated - Taylor
  Caldwell 860

deWitt, Rufus (Businessman)
Never Victorious, Never Defeated - Taylor
  Caldwell 860

deWitt, Stephen (Businessman)
Never Victorious, Never Defeated - Taylor
  Caldwell 860

DeWolfe, Angus (Lawyer)
The Justicer - Thomas Fall 2010

Dexter, David (Military Personnel; Spy)
Armored Giants: A Novel of the Civil War - F. van
  Wyck Mason 4145

Dexter, Kate (Teacher)
Remnants of Glory - Teresa Miller 4403

Deyo, Gina (Young Woman)
The Golden Circle - Constance Robertson 5396

Dhruvadeva (Royalty)
Golden Fire - Jonathan Fast 2047

Di Blasi, Francesco (Revolutionary)
The Council of Europe - Leonardo Sciascia 5678

Di Castelloni, Lucy (Widow(er); Gentlewoman)
Claudine's Daughter - Rosalind Laker 3594

di Donati, Pietro (Knight)
The Saracen Blade - Frank Yerby 6926

Di Marco, Beltrame (Prisoner; Gentleman)
The Borgia Prince - Pamela Bennetts 446

Di Marco, Bianca (Prisoner; Gentlewoman)
The Borgia Prince - Pamela Bennetts 446

Di-Peachy (Slave)
High Hearts - Rita Mae Brown 728

Diamond, Jack (Dancer)
Darktown Strutters - Wesley Brown 732

Diamond, Laura (Worker)
Monday's Child - Mollie Hardwick 2697

Diarcy, Lady Valerie (Noblewoman)
Fire Along the Sky: A Novel of America - Robert
  Moss 4497

Dickinson, Benoni (Landowner; Businessman)
Water over the Dam - Marguerite Allis 116

Dickinson, Deborah (Gentlewoman)
Water over the Dam - Marguerite Allis 116

Dickinson, Edna (Spouse)
Time in Its Flight - Susan Fromberg Schaeffer 5636

Dickoe, Peter (Military Personnel)
Soldier of the Sea - Robert Welter Daly 1460

Dickson, Hazel (Journalist)
The Talking Pictures Murder Case - George
  Baxt 388

Didier, Auguste (Cook; Detective—Amateur)
Murder Makes an Entree - Amy Myers 4540

Dido (Ruler)
Dido, Queen of Hearts - Gertrude Atherton 223

Dietric (Warrior)
The Death of Attila - Cecelia Holland 2986

Dieudonne, Genevieve (Vampire)
Anno-Dracula - Kim Newman 4595

Digby, Fred (Gentleman)
Kindred Spirits - June Barraclough   347

Digging Owl (Indian; Shaman)
Quest for the White Bull - Don Coldsmith   1182

Digweed, Barney (Criminal)
The Quincunx - Charles Palliser   4778

Dikeston, H.G. (Military Personnel)
The King's Commissar - Duncan Kyle   3570

Dillard, Branch (Cowboy)
California Caballero - William Colt
   MacDonald   3981

Dillon, James (Military Personnel)
Master and Commander - Patrick O'Brian   4669

Dimmesdale, Arthur (Religious)
Arthur Dimmesdale - Charles R. Larson   3671
Hester - Christopher Bigsby   496
The Scarlet Letter - Nathaniel Hawthorne   2786

Dimon, Jeremiah (Teenager)
*The Adventures of Jeremiah Dimon: The Novel of Old
   East Hampton* - Everett Rattray   5255

Dineas, Daniel Bar (Revolutionary)
The Eighth Veil - Ellis Kadison   3320

Dingwall, Henry (Sailor)
Captain of the Sands - Keith Dewhurst   1636

Dinkle, Stanley (Military Personnel)
The Tin Lizzie Troup - Glendon Swarthout   6146

Dinsdale, Henry (Doctor)
The Seven Ages - Eva Figes   2084

Dio of Alexandria (Diplomat)
The Venus Throw - Steven Saylor   5627

Diomedes (Military Personnel)
The Greek Generals Talk: Memoirs of the Trojan War
   - Phillip Parotti   4817

Diplock, Cecil (Gentleman)
The Bright Blue Sky - Max Hennessy   2830
Once More the Hawks - Max Hennessy   2836

Dipper (Servant)
A Broken Vessel - Kate Ross   5500
Cut to the Quick - Kate Ross   5501

Disbrow, Packy (Thief; Handicapped)
Blue Russell - Will Bryant   738

Disley, Pete (Police Officer)
Curse of Magira - David Bee   413

Divine, Gladys (Actress)
The Dream Lover - Mark Upton   6392

Dixon, Kathy (Young Woman)
The Master of Oakwindsor - Douglas Kent
   Hall   2648

Dixon, Tempe (Military Personnel)
A Hundred Hills - Howard Breslin   667

Djamic (Nobleman)
Devil's Yard - Ivo Andric   152

Dmitreyevna, Anna (Spouse)
Journey into Fire - Patricia Wright   6882

Doaks, Charity (Pioneer)
Darker Grows the Valley - Harry Harrison
   Kroll   3556

Doane, Isabel (Young Woman)
Winds of Blame - Jane Gilmore Rushing   5532

Doane, Joanna (Young Woman)
Winds of Blame - Jane Gilmore Rushing   5532

Doban (Prehistoric Human; Child)
Shiva: An Adventure of the Ice Age - J.H.
   Brennan   657

Dobrejcak, Dobie (Labor Organizer)
Out of This Furnace - Thomas Bell   425

Dobrejcak, Mary (Spouse)
Out of This Furnace - Thomas Bell   425

Dobrejcak, Mike (Worker)
Out of This Furnace - Thomas Bell   425

Dobson, Julia Turner (Widow(er))
The Rainbow Promise - Lisa Gregory   2580

Doctor (Doctor)
Before My Time - Niccolo Tucci   6358

Dodd, Matthew (Military Personnel)
Rifleman Dodd - C.S. Forester   2181

Dodge, Jonas (Sea Captain)
Long Pennant - Oliver La Farge   3573

Doheny, Susie (Heroine)
Peder Victorious - O.E. Rolvaag   5435

Doherty, John "Thunderbolt" (Highwayman)
Captain Lightfoot - William R. Burnett   792

Doireann (Young Woman)
The Winter Servant - M.H. Davis   1537

Dole, Isaiah (Sea Captain)
The New Hope - Joseph C. Lincoln   3784

Doll (Orphan; Witch)
A Mirror for Witches - Esther Forbes   2157

Doll, Hannah (Young Woman)
The Man on the Train - W.J. Chaput   995

Dolliver, Eben (Military Personnel; Prisoner)
Andersonville - MacKinlay Kantor   3359

Dolly, Mr. (Businessman)
The House of Cards - Leon Garfield   2292

Dominguez, Cayetana (Young Woman)
A Shadow of Eagles - Jane Barry   360

Dominguez, Ramon (Rancher)
A Shadow of Eagles - Jane Barry   360

Dominic (Patriot)
The Scorching Wind - Walter Macken   3988

Dominic Dio (Orphan; Entertainer)
Dominic - Kathleen Robinson   5405

Domitillia (Royalty)
The Triumph - Ernest K. Gann   2280

Domitius, Annaeus (Political Figure)
The Last Athenian - Viktor Rydberg   5543

Donahoe, Cathlin (Spouse)
The Seadon Fortune - Leonard St. Clair   5563

Donaldson, Simon (Gentleman)
Albany - Laura Black   519

Donegan, Samantha (Spouse)
Trumpet on the Land - Terry C. Johnston   3260

Donegan, Seamus (Military Personnel)
Blood Song - Terry C. Johnston   3243
A Cold Day in Hell - Terry C. Johnston   3247
Devil's Backbone - Terry C. Johnston   3250
The Shadow Riders - Terry C. Johnston   3257
Trumpet on the Land - Terry C. Johnston   3260

Donegan, Seamus (Military Personnel; Scout)
Reap the Whirlwind - Terry C. Johnston   3254
Red Cloud's Revenge - Terry C. Johnston   3255
Sioux Dawn - Terry C. Johnston   3258
The Stalkers - Terry C. Johnston   3259

Donegan, Seamus (Scout; Veteran)
Black Sun - Terry C. Johnston   3242

Donellan, Aurora (Heiress)
Heiress of Ardara - Margaret Evans Porter   5137

Doniphan, Alexander (Military Personnel)
Doniphan's Ride - Les Savage Jr.   5620

Donnelly, John Samson (Businessman)
Elixir of Life - A.E. Cowdrey   1392

Donnithorne, Arthur (Gentleman; Military
   Personnel)
Adam Bede - George Eliot   1908

Donovan, Andrew (Sea Captain)
Allegheny Captive - Caroline Bourne   591

Donovan, Earl P. (Businessman)
Flickers - Phillip Rock   5419

Donovan, Sean (Revolutionary)
Chase Royal - Donald Seaman   5712

Donsky, Saul (Spy)
The Devil's Spy - Michael Hastings   2773

Doon, Annabel (Heiress)
The Malvie Inheritance - Pamela Hill   2938

Doon, Morven (Heir—Dispossessed)
The Malvie Inheritance - Pamela Hill   2938

Doone, Carver (Outlaw)
Lorna Doone - R.D. Blackmore   528

Doone, Ligun (Fugitive)
Journey to Enchantment - Patricia Veryan   6464

Doone, Lorna (Captive; Ward)
Lorna Doone - R.D. Blackmore   528

Dorfrichter, Peter (Military Personnel)
The Devil's Lieutenant - Maria Fagyas   1998

Doria, Marco (Bastard Son; Adventurer)
Baton Sinister - Carl J. Spinatelli   5967

Dorie, Lidian (Actress; Pioneer)
I Am Lidian - Naomi Lane Babson   253

Dorio (Military Personnel)
The Same Scourge - John Goldthorpe   2464

Dorman, Benbow (Young Man)
The Wind Brings Up the Rain - Eric Malpass   4051

Dorman, Corunna (Young Woman)
Captain Caution - Kenneth Roberts   5385

Dorman, Nell (Widow(er))
The Wind Brings Up the Rain - Eric Malpass   4051

Dorn, Mahlon (Outlaw; Religious)
Fire and the Hammer - Shirley Barker   311

Dornay, Charles (Nobleman)
The Melancholy Virgin - Annabel Laine   3587
The Reluctant Heiress - Annabel Laine   3588

Dorring, Sophy (Spinster; Gentlewoman)
Seduction - Amanda Quick   5220

Douay, Paul (Young Man)
Daniel Du Luth - Everett McNeil   4307

Doucain, Veach (Military Personnel)
Kentucky Pride - Gene Markey   4087

Doucet, Olivia (Young Woman)
Bayou - Pamela Jekel   3183

Dougherty, Levi (Cowboy)
The Cowboy and the Cossack - Claire Huffaker   3071

Doughty, Frank (Military Personnel)
The Copperheads - William James Blech   544

Douglas, Catriona (Gentlewoman)
Wild Cat - Laura Black   524

Douglas, John (Landowner)
Indigo - Nicholas Carnac   900

Douglas, Jonet (Gentlewoman)
My Lady Glamis - Pamela Hill   2940

Douglas, Maddy (Settler)
Seattle Green - Jane Adams   26

Douglas, Malcolm (Young Man)
Borrasca - Octavus Roy Cohen   1160

Douglas, Matthew (Military Personnel)
Sand in the Wind - Kathleen O'Neal Gear   2329

Douglas, Richard (Sea Captain)
The Deadly Lady of Madagascar - C.V. Terry   6206

Douglas, Roger (Gentleman)
Lady of Monkton - Elizabeth Byrd 835

Douglass, Ruth (Spouse)
These Latter Days - Laura Kalpakian 3330

Douglass, Samuel (Farmer)
These Latter Days - Laura Kalpakian 3330

Dousmann, Jenny (Young Woman)
Tie My Bones to Her Back - Robert F. Jones 3294

Dousmann, Otto (Young Man)
Tie My Bones to Her Back - Robert F. Jones 3294

Dove, Mary (Young Woman)
Mary Dove - Jane Gilmore Rushing 5529

Dow, Caleb (Sea Captain)
Tide-Rode - Adelyn Bushnell 813

Dow, Delight (Spouse)
Tide-Rode - Adelyn Bushnell 813

Dow, John (Young Man)
Tide-Rode - Adelyn Bushnell 813

Dow, Margaret (Traveller)
The Lost Giants - Alan Scholefield 5657

Dowland, Elizabeth (Spouse)
Torn Covenants - Lois Swann 6136

Dowland, Elizabeth (Young Woman)
The Mists of Manittoo - Lois Swann 6135

Dowling, Sarah (Lesbian)
Patience and Sarah - Isabel Miller 4398

Downing, Hetty (Young Woman)
The Greater Hunger - Barbara Dodge Borland 581

Downing, Samuel (Scientist)
The Greater Hunger - Barbara Dodge Borland 581

Doyle, Cormac (Pirate; Convict)
The Silver Oar - Howard Breslin 669

Doyle, Peter (Young Man)
Peter Doyle - John Vernon 6457

Draco (Military Personnel)
First the Blade - Drayton Mayrant 4212

Draco, Lord (Nobleman)
Glendraco - Laura Black 521

Dracula (Military Personnel; Vampire)
The Bloody Red Baron - Kim Newman 4596

Dracula (Vampire)
The Revenge of Dracula - Peter Tremayne 6335
Seance for a Vampire - Fred Saberhagen 5557
Sherlock Holmes vs. Dracula - Loren D.
  Estleman 1976

Drake, Deborah (Young Woman)
River to the West: A Novel of the Astor Adventure -
  John Edward Jennings 3204

Drake, Sarah (Young Woman)
Sons of Fire - Max McCoy 4227

Drake, Susan (Southern Belle)
Captain Rebel - Frank Yerby 6910

Drake, Susanna (Southern Belle)
Raintree County - Ross Lockridge Jr. 3827

Drakelon, Dominic (Gentleman)
The Moon in the Water - Pamela Belle 433

Drakelon, Kit (Gentleman)
Alethea - Pamela Belle 429

Draper, Ellen (Young Woman)
Lovers All Untrue - Norah Lofts 3851

Draper, Kiffen (Pilot)
Gentlemen of Adventure - Ernest K. Gann 2278

Draper, Marion (Young Woman)
Lovers All Untrue - Norah Lofts 3851

Draskovich (Government Official)
The Petersburg-Cannes Express - Hans Koning 3538

Drayton, Annabel (Captive)
John Crews - Arthur Chapman 988

Drayton, Lady Flora (Gentlewoman)
Fire, Burn! - John Dickson Carr 910

Drayton, Joseph (Artisan)
The Drayton Legacy - Rona Randall 5247

Drayton, Lady Sophia (Gentlewoman)
Love's Duet - Patricia Veryan 6468

Drayton, Thorn (Heiress)
Vale of Tyranny - Suzanne Butler 831

Drelincourt, Marcus (Nobleman)
The Convenient Marriage - Georgette Heyer 2882

Dremont, Jeanne (Worker)
To Dance with Kings - Rosalind Laker 3601

Dremont, Marguerite (Gentlewoman)
To Dance with Kings - Rosalind Laker 3601

Drew, Hosea (Sea Captain)
The Great Steamboat Race - John Brunner 736

Drew, Jonathan (Peddler; Wanderer)
Strange Adventure of Jonathan Drew - Christopher
  Ward 6562
Yankee Rover - Christopher Ward 6563

Driant, Pierre (Trapper)
The Great Adventure - Janice Holt Giles 2410

Driggs, Bill (Hunter)
The Bad Lands - Oakley Hall 2651

Drinkwater, Edward (Gentleman)
The Bomb Vessel - Richard Woodman 6860

Drinkwater, Nathaniel (Military Personnel)
1805 - Richard Woodman 6857
Arctic Treachery - Richard Woodman 6858
Baltic Mission - Richard Woodman 6859
The Bomb Vessel - Richard Woodman 6860
Decision at Trafalgar - Richard Woodman 6861
In Distant Waters - Richard Woodman 6862
A Private Revenge - Richard Woodman 6863

Drogue, John (Military Personnel)
Little Red Foot - Robert W. Chambers 979

Drosis (Young Woman)
Son of Judah - Dan Levin 3738

Drum (Slave)
Drum - Kyle Onstott 4744

Drum, Betina (Teacher)
Blood on the Divide - William W. Johnstone 3265

Drum, Ned (Guide)
Pillar of Cloud - Jackson Burgess 782

Drumm, Andrew (Military Personnel)
Drumm's War - Bill Bragg 638

Drummle, Bentley (Gentleman)
Estella - Alanna Knight 3519

Drummond, Amelia (Gentlewoman; Widow(er))
Bertie and the Seven Bodies - Peter Lovesey 3908

Drummond, Blanche (Gentlewoman)
Leaves From the Valley - Joanna Trollope 6348

Drummond, Catriona (Heroine)
Catriona - Robert Louis Stevenson 6009

Drummond, Cristina (Gentlewoman)
Glendraco - Laura Black 521

Drummond, Sir Daniel (Gentleman; Widow(er))
Reckless Angel - Jane Feather 2056

Drummond, Edgar (Military Personnel)
Leaves From the Valley - Joanna Trollope 6348

Drummond, Elizabeth (Young Woman)
Born to Be King - Constance Gluyas 2440

Drummond, Ninian (Artist)
The World, the Flesh, and the Devil - Reay
  Tannahill 6159

Drummond, Samuel (Farmer)
Samuel Drummond - Thomas Alexander Boyd 614

Drummond, Sarah (Gentlewoman)
Leaves From the Valley - Joanna Trollope 6348

Drummond, Yolande (Young Woman)
The Noblest Frailty - Patricia Veryan 6474

Drumson (Slave)
Drum - Kyle Onstott 4744

Drury, Joanna (Heiress)
The Dreaming: A Novel of Australia - Barbara
  Wood 6848

Drussard, Justine (Actress; Prostitute)
Fallen Angel - Deborah Camp 872

Drusus (Military Personnel)
A Flame in Byzantium - Chelsea Quinn Yarbro 6899

Drusus, Cailin (Captive; Fugitive)
To Love Again - Bertrice Small 5913

du Fourchet, Adele (Noblewoman)
The Porcelain Dove - Delia Sherman 5815

du Levassoux, Comte (Nobleman)
Hawthorn Hill - Doris Shannon 5777

Du Pres, Andre (Military Personnel; Explorer)
River of Swans - Don Coldsmith 1185

Dualta (Patriot)
The Scorching Wind - Walter Macken 3988

Dualta (Patriot; Farmer)
The Silent People - Walter Macken 3990

Duatha (Warrior)
Red Queen, White Queen - Henry Treece 6332

Dubelsky, Kolya (Young Man)
Imperial Winds - Priscilla Napier 4555

Dubelsky, Misha (Young Man)
Imperial Winds - Priscilla Napier 4555

DuBois, Baptiste (Frontiersman)
Fort De Chastaigne - Don Coldsmith 1177

Dubois, Dulcie (Southern Belle)
The Dram Tree - Hamilton Cochran 1140

Duc de Malvoeux (Nobleman)
The Porcelain Dove - Delia Sherman 5815

Ducas, Leo (Nobleman)
Shards of Empire - Susan Schwartz 5677

Duchesne, Judith (Young Woman)
Judith Duchesne - Lynda Sargent 5605

Duclos, Mireille (Heroine)
Devilseed - Frank Yerby 6914

Duclos, Paul (Trader)
Thunder in the Wilderness - Charles Granville
  Hamilton 2668

Ducos, Pierre (Military Personnel)
Sharpe's Siege - Bernard Cornwell 1348

Ducos, Pierre (Spy)
Sharpe's Honour - Bernard Cornwell 1344

Dudley, Mark (Gentleman)
Law of the Land - Marguerite Allis 111

Duffey, Adam (Doctor)
Long Remember - MacKinlay Kantor 3362

Dugald, Davy (Servant; Military Personnel)
The Highland Hawk - Leslie Turner White 6682

Dugan, Clayton (Lawman; Orphan)
Power in the Blood - Greg Matthews 4191

Dugan, Drew (Outlaw)
Power in the Blood - Greg Matthews 4191

Dugan, Zoe (Orphan)
Power in the Blood - Greg Matthews 4191

DuGay, Delia (Young Woman)
Early Candlelight - Maude Hart Lovelace 3904

Dukay, Albert (Nobleman; Twin)
Century in Scarlet - Lajos Zilahy 6962

Dukay, Antal (Nobleman; Twin)
Century in Scarlet - Lajos Zilahy 6962

Duke of Ferrant (Nobleman)
The Desirable Duchess - Marion Chesney 1025

Duke of Pelham (Nobleman)
Rainbird's Revenge - Marion Chesney 1046

Duke of Pembury (Nobleman)
Frederica in Fashion - Marion Chesney 1032

Duke of Salisbury (Nobleman)
Vice Avenged: A Moral Tale - Lolah Burford 774

Dulaine, Clio (Young Woman)
Saratoga Trunk - Edna Ferber 2062

Dull Knife (Indian)
The Last Frontier - Howard Fast 2036

Dumaresq, Henry Vere (Military Personnel)
Stand into Danger - Alexander Kent 3440

Dunavant, Grady (Settler)
Hill of the Hawk - Scott O'Dell 4689

Dunbar, Douglas (Businessman)
Queen's Royal - John Quigley 5225

Dunbar, John (Military Personnel)
Dances with Wolves - Michael Blake 537

Dunbar, Margaret (Businesswoman; Model)
Cashmere - Nicola Thorne 6273

Dunbar, Munro (Veteran)
They Had a Glory - Davenport Steward 6018

Dunboyne, Kit (Military Personnel)
Seek Out and Destroy - James David Horan 3031

Duncan, Katherine (Teacher)
Gold Mountain - Charlotte Paul 4841

Duncan, Leila (Actress)
A Captive Freedom - Emma Drummond 1724

Duncannon, Georgina (Nurse)
Morning's Gate - Ann Victoria Roberts 5371

Duncannon, Robert (Gentleman)
Louisa Elliott - Ann Victoria Roberts 5370

Dunellen, Nathaniel (Musician)
Remnants of Glory - Teresa Miller 4403

Dungillis, Sir John (Landowner)
Castle Malindine - Hilary Ford 2163

Dunham, Mabel (Young Woman)
The Pathfinder; or, The Inland Sea - James Fenimore Cooper 1305

Dunhill, Jonathan (Journalist; Businessman)
Freedom's Dues - Robert H. Abel 9

Dunhill, Lydia (Heroine)
Freedom's Dues - Robert H. Abel 9

Dunkaldir, Kevin (Singer)
Dominic - Kathleen Robinson 5405

Dunn, Magnus (Mine Owner)
Glittering Hill - Clyde Francis Murphy 4520

Dunn, Matt (Military Personnel)
Sergeant Gringo - Jack Cummings 1449

Dunn, Nicholas (Laird)
Mistress of The Highlands - Chloe Gartner 2309

Dunn, Sandy (Laird)
Mistress of The Highlands - Chloe Gartner 2309

Dunncastle, Matilda (Gentlewoman)
The Salamanca Drum - Dorothy Eden 1861

Dunne, Jimmy (Thief)
Banished Children of Eve - Peter Quinn 5227

Dunne, Vincent (Immigrant)
Men of No Property - Dorothy Davis 1517

Dunsche, Otto (Military Personnel)
The Career of Magda V. - Joseph Machlis 3982

Dunwoodie, Major Peyton (Patriot; Military Personnel)
The Spy: A Tale of the Neutral Ground - James Fenimore Cooper 1310

Dupin, Auguste C. (Detective—Police)
The Lighthouse at the End of the World - Stephen Marlowe 4095

Duppan, Jack (Highwayman)
The Highwayman - Noel B. Gerson 2372

Dupre, Blacky (Settler)
Wagons West - Leslie Turner White 6692

Dupre, Marc (Religious)
This Widowed Land - Kathleen O'Neal Gear 2331

Dupre, Merry (Young Woman)
Wagons West - Leslie Turner White 6692

Dupree, Suzanne (Orphan; Heiress)
Savage Oaks - Julie Ellis 1924

Dupres, Darcy (Gentleman)
The Argonauts - Yvonne Schoell 5645

Dupuy-Preaux, Sophie de (Noblewoman)
Death at the French Creek - Raymond C. Borel 580

Durand, Blake (Military Personnel)
The Walk into Morning - Mildred Barger Herschler 2867

Durant, Adrian (Young Man)
Westward the Sun - Brigid Knight 3524

Durant, Charlotte (Young Woman)
Westward the Sun - Brigid Knight 3524

Durant, Luke (Outlaw)
Beyond the Shadowlands - Georgina Fleming 2126

Duratius (Military Personnel)
Family Favorites - Alfred Duggan 1766

Duriez, Bea (Young Woman)
The Enchantress - Suyin Han 2673

Duriez, Colin (Young Man)
The Enchantress - Suyin Han 2673

Durkin, William (Journalist)
The Killing Frost - Thomas Hayden 2799

Duroc, Paul (Government Official)
Murder in the West Wing - Elliott Roosevelt 5453

Durrie, Henry (Gentleman)
The Master of Ballantrae: A Winter's Tale - Robert Louis Stevenson 6011

Durrie, James (Gentleman)
The Master of Ballantrae: A Winter's Tale - Robert Louis Stevenson 6011

Durris, Edward (Heir; Nobleman)
Castle of Foxes - Alanna Knight 3516

Durris, Tanya (Widow(er))
Castle of Foxes - Alanna Knight 3516

Durward, Quentin (Military Personnel)
Quentin Durward - Sir Walter Scott 5705

Duryea, Micah (Military Personnel)
Unto This Hour - Tom Wicker 6733

Dutton, John (Plantation Owner)
Jubilee - Margaret Walker 6531

Duval, Annette (Governess)
The Quade Inheritance - Barbara Ker Wilson 3469

Duval, Denis (Hero)
Denis Duval - William Makepeace Thackeray 6211

Duval, Sophie (Young Woman)
The Glass-Blowers - Daphne Du Maurier 1745

Duvall, Cheney (Doctor)
A City Not Forsaken - Lynn Morris 4480
Shadow of the Mountains - Lynn Morris 4481

Duvall, Rita (Entertainer)
The Reluctant Bridegroom - Gilbert Morris 4467

Duvallier, Rene (Adventurer)
The Gypsy From Cadiz - Tamsin Hamilton 2670

Duvernay, Victoire (Gentlewoman)
Victoire - Clare Darcy 1493

Duvet, Berthe (Servant; Orphan)
The Porcelain Dove - Delia Sherman 5815

Dwyer, Rick (Journalist)
While Paris Danced - Patricia Wright 6886

Dye, Danny (Young Man)
The Fortune Road - James McCague 4217

Dye, Nancy (Young Woman)
The Fortune Road - James McCague 4217

Dymas (Military Personnel)
Fires in the Sky - Phillip Parotti 4816

Dynever, Cecil (Heroine)
Lionel Lincoln; or, The Leaguer of Boston - James Fenimore Cooper 1303

Dynham, Sir Miles (Gentleman)
The Wanton Fires - Meriol Trevor 6345

Dynham, Sir Rowland (Gentleman)
The Fortunate Marriage - Meriol Trevor 6342

Dysart, Martha (Captive)
In the Hands of the Senecas - Walter D. Edmonds 1876

Dyson, Edwin (Military Personnel)
The Tune That They Play - William Clive 1120

E

Eadulf, Brother (Religious)
Absolution by Murder - Peter Tremayne 6334

Eadwin (Nobleman)
The Adversary - Jan Widgery 6738

Eagle (Indian; Warrior)
Man of the Shadows - Don Coldsmith 1178

Eagle, Sam (Cowboy)
Chihuahua 1916 - Otis Carney 903

Eagle Woman (Indian; Warrior)
Daughter of the Eagle - Don Coldsmith 1173

Earl of Monkshood (Nobleman)
The Millionaire's Daughter - Dorothy Eden 1858

Earl of Oxford (Nobleman)
Anne of Geierstein - Sir Walter Scott 5689

Earle, Belinda (Gentlewoman)
Belinda Goes to Bath - Marion Chesney 1020

Early, Gordon (Military Personnel)
Strange Company - Robert J. Conley 1251

Early, Matthew (Sea Captain)
Matthew Early - Alexander Laing 3589

Earnshaw, Catherine (Gentlewoman)
H.—: The Story of Heathcliff's Journey Back to Wuthering Heights - Lin Haire-Sargeant 2641

Eastbrook, Ann (Detective—Amateur)
Anna's Book - Barbara Vine 6500

Easter, Buddy (Teenager)
Joy in Mudville - Gordon McAlpine 4216

Easterbrook, Chance (Journalist)
A Good Day to Die - Thomas Wakefield Blackburn 525

Easterwood, Tom (Military Personnel)
Yellowhorse - Dee Brown 715

Eastman, Walter (Journalist)
An Insular Position - Timothy Mo 4421

Eastmere, Arch (Gunfighter)
The Stars in Their Courses - Harry Brown   722

Easton, Hannah (Young Woman)
The Holder of the World - Bharati Mukherjee   4510

Easton, Warwick (Actor; Detective—Amateur)
Keystone - Peter Lovesey   3913

Eaton, James (Immigrant)
The Quality of Mercy - Anne Miller Downes   1712

Eaton, Raymond Alfred (Businessman)
From the Terrace - John O'Hara   4703

Eaton, Samuel (Businessman)
From the Terrace - John O'Hara   4703

Eber (Slave)
Abram, Son of Terah - Florence M. Bauer   378

Ecuyer, Captain (Military Personnel)
Bedford Village - Hervey Allen   99

Eden, Edward (Bastard Son; Heir)
The Prince of Eden - Marilyn Harris   2732

Eden, Elizabeth (Convict)
Eden Rising - Marilyn Harris   2731

Eden, Geoffrey (Military Personnel)
Eden and Honor - Marilyn Harris   2729

Eden, Harriet (Gentlewoman)
The Eden Passion - Marilyn Harris   2730

Eden, John (Gentleman)
Eden and Honor - Marilyn Harris   2729
Eden Rising - Marilyn Harris   2731
The Women of Eden - Marilyn Harris   2734

Eden, John (Heir)
The Eden Passion - Marilyn Harris   2730
The Prince of Eden - Marilyn Harris   2732

Eden, Mary (Gentlewoman)
The Women of Eden - Marilyn Harris   2734

Eden, Michael (Heir; Plantation Owner)
Eden - Julie Ellis   1918

Eden, Thomas (Nobleman)
This Other Eden - Marilyn Harris   2733

Edgar (Servant)
The Cunning of the Dove - Alfred Duggan   1765

Edgar of Marwell (Nobleman)
The Conqueror - Georgette Heyer   2881

Edge, Zachary (Veteran)
Spangle - Gary Jennings   3196

Edmundson, Edmund (Knight)
Harold Was My King - Hilda Lewis   3749

Edohi (Indian; Warrior)
The Dark Way - Robert J. Conley   1241
The Way of the Priests - Robert J. Conley   1253
The White Path - Robert J. Conley   1254

Edred (Warrior)
I Am England - Patricia Wright   6881

Edricson, Alleyne (Military Personnel)
The White Company - Sir Arthur Conan Doyle   1716

Edward of Kent (Knight)
The Flame in the Dark - Basil Bonallack   568

Edwards, Amos (Cowboy)
The Searchers - Alan Le May   3691

Edwards, Ballard (Artist; Veteran)
A Question of Honour - Clifford Dowdey   1707

Edwards, Harriet (Feminist)
The Brothers of Uterica - Benjamin Capps   887

Edwards, Madeleine (Spouse)
A Question of Honour - Clifford Dowdey   1707

Edwards, Oliver (Imposter; Heir—Lost)
The Pioneers; or, The Sources of the Susquehanna -
   James Fenimore Cooper   1307

Effingham, Champ (Gentleman)
The Virginia Comedians - John Esten Cooke   1269

Ehrler, Caspar (Military Personnel)
The Petrograd Consignment - Owen Sela   5739

Eilan (Young Woman; Religious)
The Forest House - Marion Zimmer Bradley   625

Eirik (Heir)
In the Wilderness - Sigrid Undset   6381
The Son Avenger - Sigrid Undset   6384

Eirik (Spirit)
*The Angel of the Opera: Sherlock Holmes Meets the
   Phantom of the Opera* - Sam Siciliano   5842

Eisenstadt, Franz (Nobleman)
Winter of the Heart - Linda J. LaRosa   3665

Eisenstadt, Jullienne (Noblewoman; Spouse)
Winter of the Heart - Linda J. LaRosa   3665

Eisner, Letty (Young Woman)
The Limner - Paul Darcy Boles   564

Ekridge, Russell (Military Personnel)
The Southern Blade - Nelson Wolford   6844

El-i-chi (Indian; Guide)
War Drums - Donald Clayton Porter   5133

El-i-chi (Indian; Shaman)
Sachem's Son - Donald Clayton Porter   5125

El Tigre (Scout)
The Rose and the Flame - Jonreed Lauritzen   3676

Elaine (Captive)
The Golden Exile - Lawrence Schoonover   5664

Elave (Servant)
The Heretic's Apprentice - Ellis Peters   4960

Eldred (Knight)
This January Tale - Bryher   747

Eldridge, Cyril (Spy)
Stars and Stripes - Adam Rutledge   5541

Eldridge, Mark (Pioneer; Captive)
Thunder on the River - Charlton Laird   3590

Eldridge, Mary Ann (Captive)
Juniata Valley - Virginia C. Cassel   954

Eleanor (Gentlewoman; Fiance(e))
The Leopard Unleashed - Elizabeth Chadwick   967

Eleanor (Young Woman)
The Unholy Pilgrim - R.F. Tapsell   6161

Eleazar, Simon ben (Gladiator; Military Personnel)
The Wolf of Masada - John Fredman   2220

Electra (Royalty)
Amber Princess - Henry Treece   6325

Elena (Gentlewoman)
The Venetian Mask - Rosalind Laker   3603

Elfreda (Young Woman)
This January Tale - Bryher   747

Elholm (Military Personnel)
The Cumberland Rifles - Noel B. Gerson   2365

Eli (Worker)
Tracker - David Wagoner   6521

Eliason, Gerard (Artist)
The Cloister and the Hearth - Charles Reade   5279

Eliazar (Businessman; Scholar)
The Wandering Arm - Sharan Newman   4603

Elidan (Royalty)
Kingdom of Summer - Gillian Bradshaw   633

Elie (Heroine)
Butcher's Broom - Neil Gunn   2620

Elijah, Eliezar Ben (Gentleman)
Threshold of Fire - Hella S. Haasse   2633

Elin (Young Woman)
Beguiled - Alice Borchardt   577

Devoted - Alice Borchardt   578

Eliot, Cannibal (Sailor; Adventurer)
Cannibal Eliot and the Lost Histories of San Francisco
   - Hilton Obenzinger   4660

Eliott, Beatrice (Businesswoman; Seamstress)
The House of Eliott - Jean Marsh   4100

Eliott, Evangeline (Businesswoman; Seamstress)
The House of Eliott - Jean Marsh   4100

Elissa (Royalty)
*The Purple Quest: A Novel of Seafaring Adventure in
   the Ancient World* - Frank G. Slaughter   5896

Elkins, Harrell (Doctor)
Andersonville - MacKinlay Kantor   3359

Ellard, Chandra (Gentlewoman)
The Blue Falcon - Robyn Carr   935

Ellershaw, Jack (Gardener)
Willowwood - Mollie Hardwick   2699

Ellery, Francis (Publisher)
Ride with Me - Thomas B. Costain   1369

Elliot, Bronwen (Young Woman; Abuse Victim)
The Valiant and the Daunted - Roy Clews   1115

Elliot, Will (Cowboy)
The Goodnight Trail - Ralph Compton   1227

Elliott, Caroline (Widow(er); Artist)
The Floral Companion - Anthea Bell   419

Elliott, Edward (Gentleman)
Louisa Elliott - Ann Victoria Roberts   5370

Elliott, Fiona (Gentlewoman)
The Train at Bundarbar - Duncan MacNeil   4021

Elliott, Liam (Military Personnel)
Morning's Gate - Ann Victoria Roberts   5371

Elliott, Louisa (Bastard Daughter)
Louisa Elliott - Ann Victoria Roberts   5370

Elliott, Steven (Sea Captain)
Morning's Gate - Ann Victoria Roberts   5371

Ellis, Geoffrey (Gentleman)
Guns Forever Echo - Kenneth M. Ellis   1925

Ellis, Guinevere (Young Woman)
The Sea Scape - Mary Lide   3778

Ellis, Mary (Captive; Actress)
Yankee - Dana Fuller Ross   5495

Ellis, Nathan (Settler)
A Fair Wind Home - Ruth Moore   4443

Ellis, Peter (Veteran; Artist)
A Princess in Berlin - Arthur R.G. Solmssen   5939

Ellis, Roswell (Military Personnel)
The Long Night - Andrew Lytle   3945

Ellison, Caroline (Gentlewoman)
Rutland Place - Anne Perry   4935

Ellison, Charlotte (Gentlewoman)
The Cater Street Hangman - Anne Perry   4925

Ellison, Emily (Gentlewoman)
The Cater Street Hangman - Anne Perry   4925

Elmet, Laetitia (Gentlewoman)
Ramillies - Barbara Whitehead   6708

Elphinstone, Charles (Historian)
The Smile of the Stranger - Joan Aiken   53

Elshender the Recluse (Outcast)
The Black Dwarf - Sir Walter Scott   5692

Eluric, Brother (Religious)
The Rose Rent - Ellis Peters   4970

Ember (Parent; Leader)
Isle of Woman - Piers Anthony   167

Embree, Philip (Adventurer)
The Warlord - Malcolm Bosse   589

Emerson, Radcliffe (Archaeologist)
The Curse of the Pharaohs - Elizabeth Peters 4948
The Deeds of the Disturber - Elizabeth Peters 4949
The Hippopotamus Pool - Elizabeth Peters 4950
The Last Camel Died at Noon - Elizabeth
    Peters 4951
Lion in the Valley - Elizabeth Peters 4952
The Mummy Case - Elizabeth Peters 4953
The Snake, the Crocodile, and the Dog - Elizabeth
    Peters 4954

Emerson, Ramses (Child)
Lion in the Valley - Elizabeth Peters 4952

Emerton, Lucy (Young Woman)
Count Manifred - Miranda Seymour 5761

Emery, Racewell (Military Personnel)
Gray Canaan - David Garth 2305

Emich of Leiningen-Hartenburg, Count (Nobleman)
The Heidenmauer - James Fenimore Cooper 1301

Emine (Young Woman)
Freedom or Death - Nikos Kazantzakis 3383

Emmet, Joel (Farmer)
I Take This Land - Richard Powell 5147

Emory, Elizabeth (Suffragette)
Sierra Triumph - Dana Fuller Ross 5488

Endicott, Brand (Sea Captain)
The Fortress - Catherine Gavin 2320

Endicott, Jack (Gentleman)
The President's Man - Elliott Roosevelt 5455

Endicott, Jack "Blackjack" (Banker)
New Deal for Death - Elliott Roosevelt 5454

Enfield, Clovis (Young Woman)
Crossings - Earl Rovit 5512

Enfield, Elizabeth (Spouse)
Crossings - Earl Rovit 5512

Enfield, Mayhew (Religious)
Crossings - Earl Rovit 5512

Enfield, Prentiss (Young Man)
Crossings - Earl Rovit 5512

Enfield, Tyson (Young Man)
The Very Best People - Elizabeth Villars 6499

England, Kirby (Businessman; Guardian)
The Railway King - Margaret Mayhew 4207

England, Nicholas (Businessman)
The Mills of Colne - Robert Neill 4572

Englund, Alfred (Military Personnel)
The Sword of General Englund - Donald
    Honig 3023

Enoch (Rebel)
The Brother - Chayym Zeldis 6958

Enriquillo (Indian)
The Cross and the Sword - Manuel de Jesus
    Galvan 2274

Enys, Dwight (Doctor)
Demelza - Winston Graham 2524
The Last Gamble - Winston Graham 2527
Venture Once More - Winston Graham 2532

Epona (Young Woman)
The Horse Goddess - Morgan Llywelyn 3820

Epron, Captain (Military Personnel)
The Long Fight - D.A. Rayner 5270

Erbin (Sailor)
Ruan - Bryher 746

Erdman, Lisa (Young Woman)
The White Hotel - D.M. Thomas 6237

Erec (Revolutionary)
Kingdom of the Grail - A.A. Attanasio 226

Eri (Artisan)
The Death of Kings - Peter Danielson 1465

Eri (Slave; Warrior)
Departed Glory - Peter Danielson 1466

Eric (Bastard Son; Warrior)
The Iron Crown - Clare Barroll 354

Eric of Dubhlain (Royalty; Warrior)
The Viking's Woman - Heather Graham 2520

Eric of Normandy, Count (Nobleman; Diplomat)
The Tyrant of Bagdhad - Glenn Pierce 4996

Erickson, Guri (Immigrant; Settler)
Big Ember - Edward Havill 2778

Ericson, Magnus (Sailor)
The Island Harp - Jeanne Williams 6779

Erif Der (Sorceress)
The Corn King and the Spring Queen - Naomi
    Mitchison 4419

Erik (Handicapped)
Phantom - Susan Kay 3375

Ermenegilda (Gentlewoman)
Simple Prayers - Michael Golding 2452

Erskine, Oliver (Gentleman)
Zemindar - Valerie Fitzgerald 2117

Erzberger, Matthias (Diplomat)
Gossip From the Forest - Thomas Keneally 3413

Escalona, Lorenzo de (Religious)
The Franciscan - Forrester Blake 532

Escaridge, Elizabeth (Gentlewoman)
The Distant Lands - Julian Green 2567

Esharhamat (Royalty)
The Assyrian - Nicholas Guild 2610

Eshkal (Wanderer)
The Miracle Hater - Shulamith Hareven 2704

Esmeralda (Gypsy; Dancer)
The Hunchback of Notre Dame - Victor Hugo 3076

Esmikan (Royalty)
Sofia - Ann Chamberlin 974

Esmond, Beatrix (Gentlewoman; Femme Fatale)
Henry Esmond - William Makepeace
    Thackeray 6212

Esmond, Henry (Military Personnel; Gentleman)
Henry Esmond - William Makepeace
    Thackeray 6212

Esmond, Rachel (Gentlewoman)
Henry Esmond - William Makepeace
    Thackeray 6212

Espinosa, Maria (Orphan)
Daughter of Fortune - Carla Kelly 3398

Esther the Soothsayer (Psychic)
Cry of the Peacock - Gina Barkhordar Nahai 4552

Estrada, Carmen (Young Woman)
Carmen of the Rancho - Frank H. Spearman 5955

Estrada, Magdalena (Young Woman)
This Land I Hold - Virginia Myers 4550

Etain (Young Woman)
Return of the Stranger - Dorothy James
    Roberts 5377

Etcher (Thief)
Arc d'X - Steve Erickson 1953

Ethan (Historian; Writer)
The King David Report - Stefan Heym 2910

Ethnea (Royalty; Captive)
Captive of Rome - Theodora McCormick Du
    Bois 1740

Eugenio, Don (Nobleman)
The Three-Cornered Hat - Pedro Antonio de
    Alarcon 62

Eupolis (Farmer; Writer)
Goatsong - Tom Holt 3009

The Walled Orchard - Tom Holt 3010

Eurgain (Spouse)
The Eagle and the Raven - Pauline Gedge 2344

Eusopus, Israel (Military Personnel)
Morning in America - Willard Wiener 6741

Evandale (Nobleman)
Old Mortality - Sir Walter Scott 5702

Evans, Angela (Young Woman)
Afterward - Catherine M. Rae 5234

Evans, Emily (Religious)
The Calling of Emily Evans - Janette Oke 4706

Evans, Evan (Captive)
The Cold Journey - Grace Zaring Stone 6052

Evans, Gwyneth (Young Woman)
Bygones - Frank Wilkinson 6762

Evans, Lat (Cowboy)
These Thousand Hills - A.B. Guthrie Jr. 2627

Evans, Lije (Settler)
The Way West - A.B. Guthrie Jr. 2628

Evans, Lincoln (Lawman)
The Hangings - Bill Pronzini 5202

Evans, Maria (Midwife; Spouse)
Maria - Eugenia Price 5184

Evans, Maud (Young Woman)
Afterward - Catherine M. Rae 5234

Evans, Molly (Young Woman)
His Majesty's Highwayman - Donald Barr
    Chidsey 1061

Evans, Wilberforce (Spy)
Chase Royal - Donald Seaman 5712

Evans, William Hughes (Diplomat)
Devoted Friends - Joe Poyer 5161

Everard, Markham (Military Personnel)
Woodstock; or, The Cavalier - Sir Walter Scott 5710

Everden, Blaise (Military Personnel)
Corner the Moon - Shirley Barker 310

Everden, Mary (Spouse)
Corner the Moon - Shirley Barker 310

Evereaux, Richard (Nobleman)
A Prince, a Piper, and a Rose - John Scalzo 5628

Eversleigh, Carlotta (Gentlewoman)
The Song of the Siren - Philippa Carr 929

Eversleigh, Damaris (Gentlewoman)
The Song of the Siren - Philippa Carr 929

Eversleigh, Edwin (Heir)
Lament for a Lost Lover - Philippa Carr 921

Eversleigh, Priscilla (Gentlewoman)
The Love Child - Philippa Carr 923

Eves, Fancy (Gentlewoman)
Consort for Victoria - William Vaughan
    Wilkins 6757

Evesden, Sir Godfrey (Gentleman)
An Ancient Evil - C.L. Grace 2504

Evesham, Roger (Spouse)
A Dangerous Innocence - Victoria Lincoln 3787

Evgeneiva, Xenya (Noblewoman)
Darker Jewels - Chelsea Quinn Yarbro 6898

Ewell, Francine (Gentlewoman)
The Judas Kiss - Victoria Holt 3015

Ewell, Pippa (Gentlewoman)
The Judas Kiss - Victoria Holt 3015

Ewing, Mort (Rancher)
Arfive - A.B. Guthrie Jr. 2623
The Last Valley - A.B. Guthrie Jr. 2626

Exforth, James (Sea Captain; Smuggler)
The Ravishers - Elizabeth Richards 5318

Eye (Government Official)
King Tut's Private Eye - Lee Levin 3739

Eynesby, Lionel (Gentleman)
Crown of Roses - Valerie Anand 127

Eyring, Myra (Young Woman)
The Everlasting Fire - Jonreed Lauritzen 3675

Eyring, Nathan (Judge)
The Everlasting Fire - Jonreed Lauritzen 3675

Eyring, Rafael (Young Man)
The Everlasting Fire - Jonreed Lauritzen 3675

F

Fabatus, Marcus (Military Personnel)
Captive of Rome - Theodora McCormick Du
Bois 1740

Faber, Walter (Sea Captain)
Time of the Unicorn - Barbara Jefferis 3176

Fabian, Adam (Revolutionary; Businessman)
White Eagle, Dark Skies - Jean Karsavina 3368

Fabius (Spy)
Dead Reckoning - C. Northcote Parkinson 4809

Fabrizio, Del Dongo (Military Personnel;
Adventurer)
The Charterhouse of Parma - Stendhal 5993

Fahnee (Indian; Healer)
Crazy Snake - Robert J. Conley 1240

Fairbanks, Walter (Lawyer)
California Gold - John Jakes 3145

Fairbourn, Francesca (Orphan)
Wings of the Falcon - Barbara Michaels 4361

Fairbrass, Frederick (Businessman)
Benjamin Franklin and a Case of Christmas Murder -
Robert Lee Hall 2655

Fairbrother, Jenny (Widow(er))
The Fairbrothers - Clark McMeekin 4291

Fairbrother, Tolley (Veteran)
The Fairbrothers - Clark McMeekin 4291

Fairchild, Dexter (Lawyer)
Watchfires - Louis Auchincloss 234

Fairchild, Helen (Young Woman; Settler)
O Genesee - Janet O'Daniel 4688

Fairchild, Nathan (Settler)
Harvest of Dreams - Jaroldeen Edwards 1884

Fairchild, Pepper (Teenager)
Hard on the Road - Barbara Moore 4440

Fairchild, Rosalie (Spouse)
Watchfires - Louis Auchincloss 234

Fairchild, Talmadge (Captive)
Harvest of Dreams - Jaroldeen Edwards 1884

Fairfax, David (Nobleman)
Lavender Lady - Carola Dunn 1794

Fairfax, Ingrid (Teenager; Healer)
The Age of Miracles - Catherine MacCoun 3960

Fairfax, Jane (Gentlewoman)
Jane Fairfax - Joan Aiken 50

Fairfield, Robert (Knight)
Walk with Peril - Dorothy V.S. Jackson 3132

Fairford, Alan (Lawyer)
Red Gauntlet - Sir Walter Scott 5706

Fairservice, Andrew (Servant)
Rob Roy - Sir Walter Scott 5707

Fairweather, Alice (Gentlewoman)
The Colonists - William Stuart Long 3870

Fairweather, George (Military Personnel)
Season of the Jew - Maurice Shadbolt 5768

Falco, Marcus Didius (Detective—Private)
The Iron Hand of Mars - Lindsey Davis 1528
Last Act in Palmyra - Lindsey Davis 1529
Poseidon's Gold - Lindsey Davis 1530
Shadows in Bronze - Lindsey Davis 1531
The Silver Pigs - Lindsey Davis 1532
Time to Depart - Lindsey Davis 1533
Venus in Copper - Lindsey Davis 1534

Falcon, Robert (Gentleman)
Moonraker's Bride - Madeleine Brent 661

Falconer, Alexandra Thaine (Landowner)
Swan's Chance - Celeste De Blasis 1549

Falconer, Henry (Hero)
The Hawks of Hawk-Hollow - Robert Montgomery
Bird 504

Falconer, Jim (Captive)
Indian Hater - Glenn R. Vernam 6452

Falconer, Rane (Landowner)
Swan's Chance - Celeste De Blasis 1549

Falconer, Rane (Young Man)
Wild Swan - Celeste De Blasis 1550

Falconer, William (Teacher; Philosopher)
Falconer's Crusade - Ian Morson 4493
Falconer's Judgement - Ian Morson 4494

Falconeri, Tancredi (Royalty; Ward)
The Leopard - Giuseppe di Lampedusa 3634

Faldene, Petronel (Gentlewoman)
Crown of Roses - Valerie Anand 127

Faljan (Gladiator)
The Gladiator - Thames Ross Williamson 6790

Falke, Egidius Maximillian (Doctor)
Out of the House of Life - Chelsea Quinn
Yarbro 6903

Falkenhorst, Albrecht von (Gentleman; Military
Personnel)
Falkenhorst - Mark Rascovich 5254

Falkenhorst, Gustaf von (Military Personnel)
Falkenhorst - Mark Rascovich 5254

Falkenhorst, Tessa von (Gentlewoman; Spouse)
Falkenhorst - Mark Rascovich 5254

Falkland, Barbara (Widow(er))
Whom the Gods Love - Kate Ross 5502

Falkland, William (Nobleman)
Palaces of Desire - Kate Alexander 81

Falks, Guy (Plantation Owner)
Fairoaks - Frank Yerby 6915

Fallon, Maud (Young Woman)
Quinn's Book - William Kennedy 3423

Fallon, Michael (Servant; Landowner)
The Fallon Blood - Reagan O'Neal 4741

Fallon, Peter (Student)
Back Bay - William Martin 4138

Fallon, Robert (Sea Captain; Bastard Son)
The Fallon Pride - Reagan O'Neal 4742

Falstaff, Jack (Knight)
Falstaff - Robert Nye 4653

Famin, Nikholai (Outlaw; Leader)
Sweet Ransom - Linda Madl 4026

Fancot, Amabel (Noblewoman; Parent)
False Colours - Georgette Heyer 2886

Fancot, Christopher "Kit" (Twin; Diplomat)
False Colours - Georgette Heyer 2886

Fancot, Evelyn (Nobleman; Twin)
False Colours - Georgette Heyer 2886

Fanning, Tyler (Military Personnel)
Long Remember - MacKinlay Kantor 3362

Fanshawe, Sir Anthony (Nobleman)
The Masqueraders - Georgette Heyer 2894

Fanshawe, Damaris (Child-Care Giver; Doctor)
The Hand of a Woman - Diana Brown 719

Fantom, Carlo (Adventurer)
Captain Fantom - Charles Underhill 6377

Fara (Royalty)
The Big Fisherman - Lloyd C. Douglas 1702

Farag, Ahmed Hassan (Royalty)
In the Shadow of the Nile - Sara Hylton 3093

Faraji, Osman (Servant)
Angelique in Barbary - Sergeanne Golon 2469

Farden, Henry (Cowboy)
A Mule for the Marquesa - Frank O'Rourke 4753

Farebrother, Ellen (Young Woman)
The Darkening Leaf - Caroline Stickland 6036

Farebrother, Sir John (Military Personnel)
The Admiral's Lady - Mary Ann Gibbs 2395

Farebrother, Susanna (Gentlewoman)
The Admiral's Lady - Mary Ann Gibbs 2395

Farebrother, Will (Gentleman)
The Admiral's Lady - Mary Ann Gibbs 2395

Faringdon, Emily (Spinster)
Scandal - Amanda Quick 5219

Farland, Catherine (Young Woman)
The Lion Triumphant - Philippa Carr 922

Farland, Damask (Gentlewoman)
The Miracle at St. Bruno's - Philippa Carr 925

Farleigh, Anne (Gentlewoman)
The Blood Endures - Robert Inman 3107

Farmiloe, Maud (Gentlewoman)
Daneclere - Pamela Hill 2931

Farmiloe, Richard (Gentleman)
Daneclere - Pamela Hill 2931

Farne, Guy (Businessman)
Magic Flutes - Eva Ibbotson 3097

Farnol, Clive (Government Official)
The Faraway Drums - Jon Cleary 1104

Faro, Jeremy (Police Officer)
Blood Line - Alanna Knight 3515
Deadly Beloved - Alanna Knight 3517
Enter Second Murderer - Alanna Knight 3518
Killing Cousins - Alanna Knight 3520

Farquharson, Andrew (Adventurer)
Stranger's Forest - Pamela Hill 2943

Farr, Dr. Brockholst (Religious)
Tenderloin - Samuel Hopkins Adams 33

Farr, Jason (Military Personnel)
Promises to Keep - Jocelyn Stirling 6051

Farr, Roland (Gentleman)
Captain Vinegar's Commission - Philip
Glazebrook 2428

Farraline, Mary (Gentlewoman)
The Sins of the Wolf - Anne Perry 4937

Farrands, Doug (Rancher)
The Wisdom of Stones - Greg Matthews 4192

Farrar, Anthony (Military Personnel)
Love Alters Not - Patricia Veryan 6467

Farrell, Christopher (Journalist)
The Hungry Goblin: A Victorian Detective Novel -
John Dickson Carr 911

Farrell, Grant (Military Personnel)
The Notorious Angel - Patricia Maxwell 4201

Farrell, John (Military Personnel)
The Bayou Road - Mignon G. Eberhart   1832

Farrell, Michael (Immigrant)
Dominion - Jack Rowe   5514

Farrier, Charles (Gentleman)
The Wingless Bird - Catherine Cookson   1292

Farrill, David (Young Man)
Give Me Liberty: The Story of an Innocent Man - John Erskine   1956

Farringdon, Kate (Young Woman)
Warwyck's Woman - Rosalind Laker   3604

Farsum, Flick (Cowboy)
Pistols for Hire - Nelson Coral Nye   4652

Faulconer, Adam (Military Personnel)
The Bloody Ground - Bernard Cornwell   1334
Copperhead - Bernard Cornwell   1335

Faulconer, Washington (Landowner; Military Personnel)
Rebel - Bernard Cornwell   1336

Faulconer, William (Military Personnel)
Battle Flag - Bernard Cornwell   1333

Favor, Delia (Young Woman)
Goldfield - Richard S. Wheeler   6660

Favoury, Willa Mae (Teacher)
Arrest Sitting Bull - Douglas C. Jones   3273

Fawkes, Fancy (Dancer)
Trumpeter, Sound! - D.L. Murray   4528

Fawley, Boone (Settler)
This Savage Race - Douglas C. Jones   3285

Fawley, Molly (Settler)
This Savage Race - Douglas C. Jones   3285

Fawley, Noah (Military Personnel; Farmer)
The Barefoot Brigade - Douglas C. Jones   3274

Fawley, Zachery (Military Personnel; Farmer)
The Barefoot Brigade - Douglas C. Jones   3274

Fawn (Indian)
Fawn - Robert Newton Peck   4885
Song of Wovoka - Earl Murray   4531

Fay, Evelyn (Military Personnel)
The Red Doe - Drayton Mayrant   4214

Fay, Molly (Revolutionary)
Stranger in Two Worlds - Hugh Clevely   1111

Fay, Morgan (Young Woman)
Silver Cross - Mary Johnston   3239

Faye, Sheba (Farmer)
Faye's Folly - Elizabeth Corbett   1322

Fayema, Laya (Noblewoman)
The Scimitar - Samuel Edwards   1890

Fayerdon, Beatrice (Spouse)
The Darkness of Corn - Caroline Stickland   6037

Fayerdon, Daniel (Worker)
The Darkness of Corn - Caroline Stickland   6037

Fayerweather, Patience (Loyalist)
The Master of Chaos - Irving A. Bacheller   262

Fearon, Lewis (Nobleman)
Victoire - Clare Darcy   1493

Featherstone, Alexander (Artist)
Spoon - John Christgau   1074

Featherstone, Angela (Fiance(e))
Mandalay - Alexandra Jones   3269

Fedorcenko, Anna (Spouse)
The Dawning of Deliverance - Judith Pella   4892
Heirs of the Motherland - Judith Pella   4893

Fedorcenko, Katrina (Royalty)
The Crown and the Crucible - Michael Phillips   4987
A House Divided - Michael Phillips   4988

Fedorcenko, Sergei (Royalty)
The Dawning of Deliverance - Judith Pella   4892
Heirs of the Motherland - Judith Pella   4893
A House Divided - Michael Phillips   4988
Travail and Triumph - Michael Phillips   4991

Feeney, Noreen (Young Woman)
Brandywine - Jack Rowe   5513

Feldman, Lady Catherine (Gentlewoman)
Artemia - Pamela Hill   2927

Feldstein, Leah (Young Woman)
Jerusalem Interlude - Bodie Thoene   6223
Munich Signature - Bodie Thoene   6224
Prague Counterpoint - Bodie Thoene   6225

Feldstein, Shimon (Young Man)
Jerusalem Interlude - Bodie Thoene   6223

Felix, Caius Sempronius (Government Official)
The Little Emperors - Alfred Duggan   1770

Fell, Thomas (Military Personnel)
Admiral Hornblower in the West Indies - C.S. Forester   2169

Fellowes, Captain (Military Personnel)
Hate - Arthur Douglas Smith   5918

Fenn, Frank (Military Personnel)
Sons of Fire - Max McCoy   4227

Fenn, Zach (Military Personnel)
Sons of Fire - Max McCoy   4227

Fenner, Lady Ermentrude (Noblewoman)
The Novice's Tale - Margaret Frazer   2217

Fenton, Clarissa (Spouse)
Lord of Ravensley - Constance Heaven   2809

Fenton, Nicholas (Professor; Time Traveller)
The Devil in Velvet - John Dickson Carr   909

Fentress, Jeffrey (Settler)
On the Long Tide - Laura Krey   3555

Fenwick, Augustus (Government Official)
An Air of Glory - Sarah Neilan   4563

Fenwick, David (Military Personnel)
Maria - Eugenia Price   5184

Fenwick, Lizzie (Spouse)
The Old Enchantment - Sarah Neilan   4565

Fenwick, Peregrine (Gentleman)
The Old Enchantment - Sarah Neilan   4565

Fenwolf, Morgan (Servant)
Windsor Castle - William Harrison Ainsworth   59

Ferenc, Eva (Young Woman)
Csardas - Diane Pearson   4875

Ferenc, Malie (Young Woman)
Csardas - Diane Pearson   4875

Ferguson, Colonel (Military Personnel)
Kings Mountain - Florette Henri   2838

Ferguson, Amos "Noquisi" (Indian)
No Resting Place - William Humphrey   3079

Ferguson, Brook (Businessman)
Cordelia - Winston Graham   2523

Ferguson, Cordelia (Spouse)
Cordelia - Winston Graham   2523

Ferguson, Ellen (Young Woman)
The Ship's Clock - Catherine M. Rae   5237

Ferguson, James (Scout; Frontiersman)
Next to Valour - John Edward Jennings   3202

Ferguson, John (Businessman)
The Ship's Clock - Catherine M. Rae   5237

Ferguson, Robert (Banker)
The Ship's Clock - Catherine M. Rae   5237

Fergusson, Davy (Teenager; Military Personnel)
The Shadow and the Glory - John Edward Jennings   3207

Fernald, Kate (Young Woman)
Time out of Mind - Rachel Field   2081

Fernley, Alan (Businessman)
What the Heart Keeps - Rosalind Laker   3605

Ferrand, Francis (Gentleman)
The Power and the Glory - Phyllis Bentley   462

Ferrand, Oliver de (Knight)
Sybille - Marion Meade   4318

Ferrand, Paul (Spy)
The Wilderness - Carter A. Vaughan   6442

Ferrier, Angela (Heroine)
Toil of the Brave - Inglis Fletcher   2141

Ferrier, Jonathon (Doctor)
Testimony of Two Men - Taylor Caldwell   863

Ferris, Cotton (Military Personnel)
The Last Plantation - Don Wright   6879

Ferris, Serena (Young Woman)
Gold Is Where You Find It - Clements Ripley   5345

Ferris, Colonel Virginius (Rancher)
Gold Is Where You Find It - Clements Ripley   5345

Ferro, Jane (Southern Belle)
Jim Mundy: A Novel of the American Civil War - Robert H. Fowler   2192

Fervacques, Alde de (Gentlewoman)
Son of Dust - H.F.M. Prescott   5171

Fervacques, Mauger de (Gentleman)
Son of Dust - H.F.M. Prescott   5171

Festus, Marcus Didius (Adventurer)
Poseidon's Gold - Lindsey Davis   1530

Fetchen, James Black (Rancher)
The Sky-Liners - Louis L'Amour   3629

Fettleworth, Francis (Military Personnel)
The Train at Bundarbar - Duncan MacNeil   4021

Feversham (Doctor)
The Hessian - Howard Fast   2033

Fialka, Lisa (Spouse)
Beginning the World Again - Roberta Silman   5851

Fialka, Peter (Scientist)
Beginning the World Again - Roberta Silman   5851

Fiammetta (Captive)
Fire Opal - Pamela Hill   2932

Fiann Sionna (Royalty)
The Emerald Crown - Theodora McCormick Du Bois   1741

Fidelis, Brother (Religious)
An Excellent Mystery - Ellis Peters   4959

Fidelma, Sister (Religious)
Absolution by Murder - Peter Tremayne   6334

Field, Arthur (Gentleman)
Tamzen - Jane Gilmore Rushing   5530

Field, Ashbel (Military Personnel; Explorer)
Now We Are Free - Marguerite Allis   112

Field, Ashbel (Settler)
Brave Pursuit - Marguerite Allis   107
To Keep Us Free - Marguerite Allis   115

Field, Buddy (Young Man)
The Longest Road - Jeanne Williams   6781

Field, Clarissa (Gentlewoman)
Will You Love Me in September? - Philippa Carr   932

Field, Connie (Settler; Feminist)
Brave Pursuit - Marguerite Allis   107

Field, Eve (Southern Belle; Settler)
Free Soil - Marguerite Allis   110

Field, Faith (Settler)
To Keep Us Free - Marguerite Allis   115

Field, Lafayette (Gentleman; Twin)
The Rising Storm - Marguerite Allis   113

Field, Lafayette (Settler)
Free Soil - Marguerite Allis   110

Field, Lancelot (Gentleman; Twin)
The Rising Storm - Marguerite Allis   113

Field, Laurie (Young Woman)
The Longest Road - Jeanne Williams   6781

Fielder, Andrew Jackson (Sports Figure; Military Personnel)
Fielder's Choice - Rick Norman   4646

Fieldfare, Bobbie (Suffragette)
Sister Beneath the Sheet - Gillian Linscott   3808

Fierro, Rodolfo (Revolutionary)
The Friends of Pancho Villa - James Carlos Blake   535

Fifth, Brennis Gehan (Chieftain; Prehistoric Human)
The Flint Lord - Richard Herley   2857

Figaro, Randolph (Gambler)
Fool's Coach - Richard S. Wheeler   6659

Filbyter, Folke (Adventurer; Warrior)
The Trees of the Folkungs - Verner Von Heidenstam   2817

Filmore, Douglas (Gentleman)
The Black Candle - Catherine Cookson   1273

Finbar (Outcast; Artisan)
Paradise - Dikkon Eberhart   1831

Findly, Tom (Military Personnel)
Sing One Song - Helen Topping Miller   4394

Findon, Elinor (Orphan)
The Wedding Guest - Anna Gilbert   2407

Findon, Kelda (Gentlewoman)
The Wedding Guest - Anna Gilbert   2407

Findon, May (Artist)
The Wedding Guest - Anna Gilbert   2407

Fineaux, Philip (Scholar)
Liza Bowe - Shirley Barker   313

Finn, Ben (Rancher)
The Grassman - Len Fulton   2256

Finn, Corinna (Young Woman)
Spy's Honour - Gavin Lyall   3929

Finn, Huckleberry (Adventurer)
The Further Adventures of Huckleberry Finn - Greg Matthews   4189

Finney, Calico Jack (Pirate)
The Gun Ketch - Dewey Lambdin   3610

Finnian (Minstrel)
The Harp and the Blade - John Myers   4543

Fiore, George (Businessman)
Our Father's House - Stephen Longstreet   3890

Fiore, George (Immigrant; Businessman)
All or Nothing - Stephen Longstreet   3881

Firebrace, Jack (Military Personnel; Miner)
Birdsong - Sebastian Faulks   2051

Firethorn, Lawrence (Actor)
The Mad Courtesan - Edward Marston   4122
The Nine Giants - Edward Marston   4124
The Queen's Head - Edward Marston   4125
The Trip to Jerusalem - Edward Marston   4129

Firethorne, Lawrence (Actor)
The Merry Devils - Edward Marston   4123
The Silent Woman - Edward Marston   4128

Firle, Augustine (Gentleman)
Shadows and Images - Meriol Trevor   6344

Fishburn, Claire (Businessman)
The Living - Annie Dillard   1644

Fisher, Caroline (Gentlewoman)
Redcoat - Bernard Cornwell   1337

Fisher, Manesseh (Military Personnel)
Don't Tread on Me - Walter Karig   3366

Fisher, Peter (Engineer)
Electricity: A Novel - Victoria Glendinning   2431

Fiske, Adam (Gentleman)
The Red Cock Crows - Frances Gaither   2272

Fitch, Ned (Young Man)
Stuyvesant Square - Margaret Lewerth   3743

Fitz-Gerold, Margaret (Gentlewoman)
Leopards and Lilies - Alfred Duggan   1769

Fitz Hugh, Ranulf (Knight; Bastard Son)
Defy Not the Heart - Johanna Lindsey   3794

Fitz-Stephen, Pagan de (Bastard Son; Knight)
Sir Pagan - Henry John Colyton   1222

fitz Warren, Guy (Knight)
This Bright Sword - Donald Barr Chidsey   1066

FitzAdeline, Leonia (Gentlewoman)
Stephen and the Sleeping Saints - Pamela Bennetts   457

FitzAilwin, Sir Justin (Knight)
Masques of Gold - Roberta Gellis   2352

Fitzalan, Simon (Knight)
Richard and the Knights of God - Pamela Bennetts   454

Fitzbolton, Robert (Gentleman)
The Hawthorne Legacy - Teresa Crane   1416

Fitzcorbucion, Hamo (Nobleman)
The Ravens of Blackwater - Edward Marston   4126

Fitzgerald, Edward (Military Personnel)
The Maddest Idea - James L. Nelson   4580

Fitzgerald, Gerait (Nobleman)
Gerait's Daughter - Millie J. Ragosta   5241

Fitzgerald, Hugh (Gentleman)
Wolf's Embrace - Gail Link   3801

Fitzgerald, John S. (Mountain Man)
Lord Grizzly - Frederick F. Manfred   4056

Fitzgerald, Magheen (Young Woman)
Gerait's Daughter - Millie J. Ragosta   5241

FitzGerald, Ralf (Knight)
Sherwood - Parke Godwin   2449

Fitzgerald, Roland (Gentleman)
The Black Swan - Philippa Carr   917

FitzGibbon, Beth (Writer)
An Excess of Love - Cathy Cash Spellman   5959

FitzGibbon, Constance (Patriot; Rebel)
An Excess of Love - Cathy Cash Spellman   5959

Fitzhugh, Bernal (Doctor; Sea Captain)
Buccaneer Surgeon - C.V. Terry   6205

Fitzmarc, Enguarrand (Knight)
The Lily and the Leopard - Susan Wiggs   6745

FitzNigel, Julien (Scholar; Diplomat)
The Garden of Persephone - Cesar J. Rotondi   5510

fitzOdo, Roger (Knight)
The Lady for Ransom - Alfred Duggan   1768

Fitzpaine, Pev (Diplomat)
Yedo - Lynn Guest   2609

Fitzpatrick, Viscount (Nobleman)
The Banishment - Marion Chesney   1018

Fitzpercy, Charles (Writer)
Kindred Spirits - June Barraclough   347

FitzRandwulf d'Amboise, Eduard (Knight; Bastard Son)
In the Shadow of Midnight - Marsha Canham   880

FitzRobert, Philip (Nobleman)
Brother Cadfael's Penance - Ellis Peters   4955

Fitzstephen, Blade (Spy)
Lady Defiant - Suzanne Robinson   5412

FitzWarin, Sir Cleve (Knight)
Where Magic Dwells - Rexanne Becnel   411

Fitzwilliam, George (Diplomat)
Reluctant Cavalier - Donald Barr Chidsey   1064

Fitzwilliam, Rannulf (Knight)
Jerusalem - Cecelia Holland   2990

Flael, Lissa de (Widow(er))
Masques of Gold - Roberta Gellis   2352

Flagg, Abby-Delight (Settler)
The Bright Land - Janet Fairbank   2000

Flaherty, Alice (Spouse)
Across the Bitter Sea - Eilis Dillon   1646

Flaherty, Samuel (Landowner)
Across the Bitter Sea - Eilis Dillon   1646

Flaminius, Marcus (Warrior)
The Scarlet Beast - Francis Gerard   2357

Flanagan, Bella (Actress)
Stage Fright - Gillian Linscott   3809

Flanagan, Charles C. (Businessman)
Flanagan's Run - Tom McNab   4303

Flashman, Elsbeth (Gentlewoman)
Flashman at the Charge - George MacDonald Fraser   2209
Flashman's Lady - George MacDonald Fraser   2210

Flashman, Harry (Gentleman; Adventurer)
Flash for Freedom - George MacDonald Fraser   2203
Flashman and the Angel of the Lord - George MacDonald Fraser   2205
Flashman and the Dragon - George MacDonald Fraser   2206
Flashman and the Redskins - George MacDonald Fraser   2208
Flashman's Lady - George MacDonald Fraser   2210

Flashman, Harry (Military Personnel)
Flashman - George MacDonald Fraser   2204
Flashman and the Mountain of Light - George MacDonald Fraser   2207
Flashman at the Charge - George MacDonald Fraser   2209
Royal Flash - George MacDonald Fraser   2213

Flat Warclub (Indian; Warrior)
The Manly-Hearted Woman - Frederick F. Manfred   4057

Flavius, Crispus (Political Figure)
Blood of the Martyrs - Naomi Mitchison   4417

Flavius, Quintus (Nobleman)
No King but Caesar - Anne Powers   5151

Flecke, Saul (Activist)
We Stood for Freedom - Iris Morley   4455

Fleet, Seaborn (Adventurer)
Stately Timber - Rupert Hughes   3075

Fleetwood, Sebastian (Nobleman; Detective—Private)
Dangerous - Amanda Quick   5213

Fleischer, Herman (Government Official)
Shout at the Devil - Wilbur Smith   5930

Fleming, Duncan (Gentleman)
Saturday City - Jan Webster   6593

Fleming, Harry (Nobleman; Spy)
Rendezvous - Amanda Quick   5218

Fleming, Henry (Military Personnel)
The Red Badge of Courage - Stephen Crane   1414

Fleming, Jeannie (Orphan)
The Magnolias - Julie Ellis   1922

Fleming, Jocelyn (Noblewoman; Widow(er))
Savage Thunder - Johanna Lindsey 3795

Fleming, Lloyd (Diplomat)
Grishin - Hans Herlin 2859

Fleming, Mary (Spouse)
Born with the Century - William Kinsolving 3501

Fleming, Samuel (Religious)
The Witch and the Priest - Hilda Lewis 3754

Fleming, Tom (Veteran)
Give Me the Daggers - Catherine Gavin 2321

Flemming, Noah (Adventurer)
The Golden Circle - John Edward Ames 125

Fletcher, Bruce (Military Personnel)
His Majesty's Highlanders - Leslie Turner White 6683

Fletcher, Curt (Pioneer)
Each Bright River - Mildred Masterson McNeilly 4308

Fletcher, Judson (Gentleman)
The Rebels - John Jakes 3152

Fletcher, Ralph (Religious)
The Cage - Michael Weston 6650

Fletcher, William (Settler)
Hope Leslie; or, Early Times in Massachusetts - Catharine Maria Sedgewick 5714

Fletcher, Zack (Prospector)
Wanderers Eastward, Wanderers West - Kathleen Winsor 6823

Flett, David (Military Personnel)
The Devil in Harbour - Catherine Gavin 2319

Flevry, George (Military Personnel)
The Siege of Krishnapur - J.G. Farrell 2016

Flickner, Otto (Military Personnel)
Shiloh - Shelby Foote 2153

Flinders, Mary (Heroine)
The Silver Highways - Malcolm Macdonald 3972

Flint, Hugh (Plantation Owner)
By the Dim Lamps - Nathan Schachner 5630

Flood, Matthew (Trader)
The Sun Is My Undoing - Marguerite Steen 5988

Flood, Wick (Trader)
Montana Road - Harry Sinclair Drago 1717

Florian (Entertainer; Businessman)
Spangle - Gary Jennings 3196

Florian, Charlot (Doctor)
The Twelfth Physician - Willa Gibbs 2403

Flory, John (Gentleman; Military Personnel)
Fire and Morning - Francis W. Leary 3696

Flower, George (Nobleman)
Soldiers of Fortune - Peter Bourne 595

Flowers, Miss (Governess; Companion)
Eugenie - Hester W. Chapman 989

Flowers, Fanny Rosa (Young Woman)
Hungry Hill - Daphne Du Maurier 1746

Flowers, Molly (Young Woman)
Ballenrose - Mallory Burgess 783

Fly Catcher (Indian; Warrior)
People of the River - W. Michael Gear 2338

Flynn, Dinah (Saloon Hostess)
The Stallion Man - Judith Glover 2438

Flynn, Elizabeth Gurley (Labor Organizer)
Bisbee '17 - Robert Houston 3056

Flynn, Jonathan (Veteran)
Sudden Country - Loren D. Estleman 1979

Flynn, Lafe (Plantation Owner)
Gallows Way - Daoma Winston 6825

Fogarty, Tim (Servant)
Journey - James A. Michener 4371

Foley, Max (Landowner)
The Twilighters - Noel M. Loomis 3894

Folger, Tom (Sailor)
Captain Paul - Edward Ellsberg 1930

Folland, Robert (Veteran)
The Lords of Loone - John James 3159

Fomor (Chieftain; Prehistoric Human)
Wolves of the Dawn - William Sarabande 5604

Fong Tai (Government Official)
China Saga - C.Y. Lee 3706

Fong Yun, Brigid (Young Woman)
China Saga - C.Y. Lee 3706

Fonta, Fernando (Plantation Owner)
The Red Lances - Arturo Uslar Pietri 4999

Fontaine, Myra (Young Woman)
The Hunting Shirt - Mary Johnston 3235

Fontclair, Hugh (Nobleman)
Cut to the Quick - Kate Ross 5501

Forbes, Arthur (Organized Crime Figure)
Dancing in the Dark - Stuart M. Kaminsky 3334

Forbes, Cecily (Gentlewoman)
A Most Romantic City - Mary Ann Gibbs 2396

Forbes, Josh (Farmer; Rancher)
Forefathers - Nancy Cato 960

Forbes, Martin (Religious)
Drums of Change: The Story of Running Fawn - Janette Oke 4707

Force, George (Military Personnel)
The Scarlet Patch - Bruce Lancaster 3645

Ford, Case (Pioneer)
The Land Is Bright - Archie Binns 501

Ford, Jeremy (Military Personnel)
The Yankee Rascals - Carter A. Vaughan 6444

Ford, Laurence de (Nobleman)
A Lady of Repute - Janice James 3158

Fordyce, Leonora (Noblewoman)
The Emerald Necklace - Diana Brown 718

Forest, Camilla (Spouse)
Marry in Haste - Jane Aiken Hodge 2967

Forester, Millie (Abandoned Child)
The Rag Nymph - Catherine Cookson 1287

Forge, Fonella (Spouse)
The Running Iron - Rachel Ann Fish 2097

Forge, Robert (Veteran)
The Running Iron - Rachel Ann Fish 2097

Forrest, John (Sailor)
The Return of Lono: A Novel of Captain Cook's Last Voyage - Oswald Andrew Bushnell 816

Forrester, Dallas (Southern Belle)
Wagons to Tucson - Ed Newsom 4604

Forrester, Dominique (Governess)
The Duchess of Vidal - Dawn Lindsey 3793

Forrester, Edit (Orphan)
Nick of the Woods; or, The Jibbenainosay - Robert Montgomery Bird 505

Forrester, Mary (Young Woman)
Hawthorn Hill - Doris Shannon 5777

Forrester, Roland (Military Personnel; Settler)
Nick of the Woods; or, The Jibbenainosay - Robert Montgomery Bird 505

Forster, Arbel (Orphan)
Till the Day Goes Down - Judith Lennox-Smith 3719

Forster, Christie (Orphan)
Till the Day Goes Down - Judith Lennox-Smith 3719

Forster, Polly (Young Woman)
An Air of Glory - Sarah Neilan 4563

Forsyth, Heather (Settler)
Summer Thunder - Willie Snow Ethridge 1982

Forsythe, Margaret (Gentlewoman)
Trumpets Sound No More - F. van Wyck Mason 4163

Fort, Charlie (Lawyer)
The Massacre at Fall Creek - Jessamyn West 6631

Fortenberry, Dienwald de (Nobleman)
Earth Song - Catherine Coulter 1374

Fortescue, Lady (Noblewoman)
Lady Fortescue Steps Out - Marion Chesney 1035
Miss Tonks Turns to Crime - Marion Chesney 1041

Fortescue, James (Gentleman)
The Favored Child - Philippa Gregory 2582

Fortesque, Daria de (Noblewoman; Heiress)
Secret Song - Catherine Coulter 1381

Forth, Willoughby (Explorer)
The Last Camel Died at Noon - Elizabeth Peters 4951

Fortini, Colombia (Prostitute; Actress)
Carnival of Saints - George Herman 2860

Fortune, John (Government Official)
You Rolling River - Archie Binns 503

Fortune, Nathaniel (Heir)
Time out of Mind - Rachel Field 2081

Forty, Thomas (Military Personnel; Printer)
Thomas Forty - Edward Stanley 5982

Foss, Erik (Immigrant)
The Emigrants - Johan Bojer 561

Foster, Augustus John (Diplomat)
My Dear Cousin - Peggy Hoffmann 2977

Foster, Nate (Lawman)
Embers of the Heart - Rosanne Bittner 512

Fouche, Lord (Nobleman)
The Rose and the Sword - Sandra Paretti 4792

Fountain, Walter (Military Personnel)
Shiloh - Shelby Foote 2153

Fountaine, Robert (Landowner)
Lusty Wind for Carolina - Inglis Fletcher 2134

Fournier, Andre (Military Personnel)
Marcel Armand - Sallie Bell 424

Fournier, Jacques (Religious)
The Image of Our Lord - Edward Burman 790

Fournois, Laird (Veteran)
The Vixens - Frank Yerby 6929

Fournois, Sabrina (Spouse)
The Vixens - Frank Yerby 6929

Fowl-Filcher (Criminal)
The Swedish Cavalier - Leo Perutz 4943

Fowler, Hannah Moore (Settler)
Hannah Fowler - Janice Holt Giles 2411

Fowler, Iris (Young Woman)
Born with the Century - William Kinsolving 3501

Fowler, Janice (Spouse)
Voyage to Santa Fe - Janice Holt Giles 2418

Fowler, Jerry (Worker)
Erie Water - Walter D. Edmonds 1875

Fowler, Joe (Mountain Man; Guide)
The Great Adventure - Janice Holt Giles 2410

Fowler, Johnny (Trader)
The Great Adventure - Janice Holt Giles 2410

Voyage to Santa Fe - Janice Holt Giles 2418

Fowler, Rebecca (Spouse)
The Believers - Janice Holt Giles 2409

Fowler, Sam (Time Traveller; Journalist)
If I Never Get Back - Darryl Brock 700

Fowler, Savanna (Widow(er))
Savanna - Janice Holt Giles 2416

Fowler, Starr (Driver)
Six-Horse Hitch - Janice Holt Giles 2417

Fowler, Tice (Frontiersman)
Hannah Fowler - Janice Holt Giles 2411

Fox, John (Government Official)
The Heretic - Alison Macleod 4002

Fox, Letty (Entertainer)
The Passion of Letty Fox - Diana Saunders 5610

Fox, Odalie (Southern Belle)
The Foxes of Harrow - Frank Yerby 6917

Fox, Philip (Engineer)
Railroad West - Cornelia Meigs 4327

Fox, Stephen (Gambler; Plantation Owner)
The Foxes of Harrow - Frank Yerby 6917

Foxe-Donnell, Leo (Patriot)
A Nest of Simple Folk - Sean O'Faolain 4692

Foxefield, Brett (Nobleman)
My Lord Foxe - Constance Gluyas 2443

Foxhill, Tom (Smuggler)
The Sugar Pavilion - Rosalind Laker 3600

Foxley, Charlotte (Gentlewoman)
The Spoils of Eden - Robert H. Fowler 2193

Foyt, L.R. (Cowboy)
The Terrible Teague Bunch - Gary Jennings 3197

Frame, Maria (Captive)
The Second Kiss - Gayle Rogers 5432

Franchet, Pierre (Military Personnel)
The Cactus and the Crown - Catherine Gavin 2318

Frane, Adam (Scout; Frontiersman)
The Captive Witch - Dale Van Every 6407

Frane, Evelyn (Spouse)
Gamble's Hundred - Clifford Dowdey 1705

Frane, Sydney (Plantation Owner)
Gamble's Hundred - Clifford Dowdey 1705

Frankenstein, Elizabeth (Gentlewoman)
The Memoirs of Elizabeth Frankenstein - Theodore Roszak 5508

Frankenstein, Victor (Scientist)
The Cross of Frankenstein - Robert J. Myers 4548
Frankenstein Unbound - Brian Aldiss 68
The Memoirs of Elizabeth Frankenstein - Theodore Roszak 5508
The Slave of Frankenstein - Robert J. Myers 4549

Frankland, Harry (Government Official)
Be My Love - Harriet Hinsdale 2955

Franklin, John (Guide; Veteran)
The Hammer of God - Alan Scholefield 5655

Franklin, Mark (Outlaw)
Mr. American - George MacDonald Fraser 2211

Franklin, Nathaniel (Military Personnel)
Action at Aquila - Hervey Allen 97

Franklin, Toby (Servant)
The Legion of the Lost - Donald Barr Chidsey 1062

Franklyn, Jim (Journalist)
The Hangman's Crusade - James Barwick 370

Frant, Gervais (Nobleman)
The Quiet Gentleman - Georgette Heyer 2897

Frant, Martin (Gentleman)
The Quiet Gentleman - Georgette Heyer 2897

Frant, Theodore (Gentleman; Steward)
The Quiet Gentleman - Georgette Heyer 2897

Fraser, Anne Couper (Spouse)
Where Shadows Go - Eugenia Price 5189

Fraser, Anne Couper (Widow(er))
Beauty From Ashes - Eugenia Price 5177

Fraser, Claire (Time Traveller; Spouse)
Drums of Autumn - Diana Gabaldon 2263

Fraser, James (Engineer)
Paths of Fortune - Susan Moore 4444

Fraser, James (Farmer)
Marching On - James Boyd 612

Fraser, James (Military Personnel)
Dragonfly in Amber - Diana Gabaldon 2262
Outlander - Diana Gabaldon 2264
Voyager - Diana Gabaldon 2265

Fraser, Jamie (Adventurer; Spouse)
Drums of Autumn - Diana Gabaldon 2263

Fraser, John (Gentleman)
Drums - James Boyd 611

Fraser, John (Military Personnel)
Bright Captivity - Eugenia Price 5180

Fraser, John (Plantation Owner)
Where Shadows Go - Eugenia Price 5189

Fraser, John Couper (Gentleman)
Beauty From Ashes - Eugenia Price 5177

Fraser, Katherine (Gentlewoman)
Clandara - Evelyn Anthony 161

Fraser, Katrine (Young Woman)
Mistress of The Highlands - Chloe Gartner 2309

Fraser, Lovat (Military Personnel)
Prince Charlie's Bluff - Donald Thomas 6241

Fraser, Rupert (Gentleman)
Falls of Gard - Laura Black 520

Fraser, Tom (Gentleman)
A World Too Wide - Susan Moore 4445

Frasquita (Spouse)
The Three-Cornered Hat - Pedro Antonio de Alarcon 62

Frater, Simon (Gentleman)
Crown Witness - Gillian Linscott 3803

Frayne, Dylan de (Gentleman)
The Everlasting Covenant - Robyn Carr 939

Frayne, John (Doctor)
Patriot's Progress - Joseph G.E. Hopkins 3027
The Price of Liberty - Joseph G.E. Hopkins 3028

Frayne, John (Spy; Doctor)
Retreat and Recall - Joseph G.E. Hopkins 3029

Frayne, Pamela (Gentlewoman)
Lady Pamela - Clare Darcy 1490

Frazier, Ian (Military Personnel)
"Utmost Fish!" - Hugh Wray McCann 4219

Frazier, John (Trader)
Red Morning - Ruby Frazier Frey 2230

Frazier, Willa (Young Woman)
Galveston - Suzanne Morris 4482

Frederickson, William (Military Personnel)
Sharpe's Revenge - Bernard Cornwell 1346

Free, Henry (Immigrant; Servant)
Free Man - Conrad Richter 5320

Freed, Vesper (Rancher)
The Far Canyon - Elmer Kelton 3404

Freeman, Ernestina (Gentlewoman)
The French Lieutenant's Woman - John Fowles 2194

Freeman, Eve (Actress)
The Family of Women - Richard Peck 4883

Freemantle, Emily (Gentlewoman; Heiress)
Emily Goes to Exeter - Marion Chesney 1027

Freire, Joaquin (Composer)
River of Dreams - Gay Courter 1390

Fremney, Lady Jane (Noblewoman)
Back in Society - Marion Chesney 1017

French, Alexander (Doctor)
The Native Air - Sarah Woodhouse 6854
The Peacock's Feather - Sarah Woodhouse 6855

French, Jared (Young Man)
The Arch of Stars - Clifford Lindsey Alderman 66

Frenshaw, David (Gentleman)
Voices in a Haunted Room - Philippa Carr 931

Frenshaw, Dickson (Gentleman)
Knave of Hearts - Philippa Carr 920
Will You Love Me in September? - Philippa Carr 932

Frenshaw, Jessica (Gentlewoman)
The Return of the Gypsy - Philippa Carr 927

Frenshaw, Jonathan (Gentleman)
Voices in a Haunted Room - Philippa Carr 931

Frevisse, Sister (Religious; Detective—Amateur)
The Bishop's Tale - Margaret Frazer 2215
The Boy's Tale - Margaret Frazer 2216
The Novice's Tale - Margaret Frazer 2217
The Outlaw's Tale - Margaret Frazer 2218
The Servant's Tale - Margaret Frazer 2219

Frey, Meta (Young Woman)
The Heidenmauer - James Fenimore Cooper 1301

Freyling, Clara (Settler)
Of Lizards and Angels: A Saga of Sioux Land - Frederick F. Manfred 4058

Freyling, Tunis (Settler)
Of Lizards and Angels: A Saga of Sioux Land - Frederick F. Manfred 4058

Friday (Indian)
Friday - Michel Tournier 6305

Frinton, Jocelyn (Gentleman)
The Love Child - Philippa Carr 923

Frisbie, Colonel (Military Personnel)
Jordan County: A Landscape in Narrative - Shelby Foote 2152

Frollo, Claude (Religious)
The Hunchback of Notre Dame - Victor Hugo 3076

Frome, Alexander (Nobleman; Diplomat)
The Unsuitable Miss Pelham - June Drummond 1730

Froniga (Gypsy)
The White Witch - Elizabeth Goudge 2496

Frontoni, Jacopo (Spy; Criminal)
The Bravo - James Fenimore Cooper 1298

Frosbie, Ellen (Young Woman)
Ho, the Fair Wind - I.A.R. Wylie 6889

Frost, Angus (Mine Owner)
No Price Too High - Madeleine Polland 5085

Frost, Isabella (Young Woman)
No Price Too High - Madeleine Polland 5085

Frost, Rory (Trader)
Trade Wind - M.M. Kaye 3378

Frowenfeld, Joseph (Pharmacist)
The Grandissimes - George W. Cable 842

Fry, Ansel (Photographer)
Shadow Catcher - Charles Fergus 2064

Frye, Michael (Young Man)
Trumpet at the Gate - Jan Widgery 6739

Fu Manchu, Dr. (Criminal)
The Fires of Fu Manchu - Cay Van Ash 6399
Ten Years Beyond Baker Street - Cay Van Ash 6400

Fuente, Ricardo de la (Gentleman)
Takers of the City - Hoffman Reynolds Hays 2800

Fulbert, Pierre (Religious)
Ordeal by Silence - Prudence Andrew 142

Fuller, Gordon (Military Personnel)
The Invincibles - Carter A. Vaughan 6436

Fuller, Hop (Gypsy)
The Slow Awakening - Catherine Marchant 4082

Fulton, Susanna (Editor)
Nevada! - Dana Fuller Ross 5481

Fultz, Mark (Trader)
The Eagle and the Wind - Herbert Stover 6068

Fulvius (Lawyer)
The Gladiators - Arthur Koestler 3532

Furber, Jethro (Religious)
Omensetter's Luck - William H. Gass 2317

Furfoot, Michael (Adventurer)
The Wanderer - Mika Waltari 6556

Furikake, Lady (Gentlewoman)
Segaki - David Stacton 5975

Furlong, Bryce (Military Personnel)
A Hundred Hills - Howard Breslin 667

Furneau, Caroline (Gentlewoman; Twin)
Stranger at the Wedding - Frances Lynch 3934

Furneau, Katherine (Gentlewoman; Twin)
Stranger at the Wedding - Frances Lynch 3934

Furniss, Hannah (Rancher)
The Garfield Honor - Frank Yerby 6918

Furnival, Adam (Bastard Son)
The Storms of Fate - Patricia Wright 6885

Furnival, James (Judge)
The Masters of Bow Street - John Creasy 1423

Fussholdt, Dr. (Historian)
Badenheim 1939 - Aharon Appelfeld 174

Fuzzy (Animal)
Funny Papers - Tom De Haven 1559

Fyfe, John Adam (Doctor)
Alabama Empire - Welbourn Kelley 3392

G

Gaar, Thorold (Teenager)
Sandoval: A Romance of Bad Manners - Thomas Beer 414

Gabriel, Rabbi (Religious)
Power - Lion Feuchtwanger 2074

Gabriel, Paul (Scientist)
Victim of the Aurora - Thomas Keneally 3417

Gad (Young Man; Orphan)
Unto the Soul - Aharon Appelfeld 181

Gadd, Aaron (Carpenter; Activist)
The God-Seeker - Sinclair Lewis 3763

Gadiani, Gregory (Nobleman)
Heir to Kuragin - Constance Heaven 2807

Gadney, Deborah (Young Woman)
Seventeen of Leyden - John James 3160

Gael, John de (Gentleman)
Kathryn: In the Court of Six Queens - Anne Merton Abbey 1

Gage, Daniel (Bastard Son)
The Near and Distant Place - Patricia Wright 6883

Gagini (Military Personnel)
The Wrong Horse - Jean Bassan 374

Gaillard, Desiree (Southern Belle)
Cease Firing - Mary Johnston 3230

Gaillard, Diantha (Servant)
The Judas Tree - Neil Harmon Swanson 6139

Gaius (Military Personnel)
According to Mary: A Novel of the Magdalene - Willa Gibbs 2398

Gaius (Nobleman; Military Personnel)
Swords in the North - Paul Lewis Anderson 138

Galahad (Knight)
The Winter King - Bernard Cornwell 1351

Galban, Rafaela (Revolutionary)
Mingo Dabney - James H. Street 6078

Galbraith, James (Journalist)
Jade - Pat Barr 344

Galbraith, James (Religious)
Colliers Row - Jan Webster 6592

Gale, Bob (Step-Parent)
The Nancy Flyer - Ernest Poole 5091

Galitzine, Asya (Royalty)
Asya - Michael Ignatieff 3103

Galla Placidia (Royalty)
Heaven's Only Daughter - Kathleen Robinson 5406

Gallagher (Lawman)
Me and Gallagher - Jack Farris 2023

Gallagher, Abigail (Spouse)
Vision of the Eagle - Kay L. McDonald 4263

Gallagher, Con (Revolutionary)
The Killing Frost - Thomas Hayden 2799

Gallagher, Patrick (Artisan)
Brandywine - Jack Rowe 5513

Gallagher, Ross (Frontiersman)
Vision of the Eagle - Kay L. McDonald 4263

Gallant, Paul (Sea Captain)
The Black Cockade - Victor Suthren 6127
In Perilous Seas - Victor Suthren 6130
A King's Ransom - Victor Suthren 6131

Galliard, Inigo (Gentleman)
Daughter of Strangers - Elizabeth Boatwright Coker 1164

Galliard, Jack (Spy)
Secret Service Operator 13 - Robert W. Chambers 982

Gallio, Marcellus (Military Personnel)
The Robe - Lloyd C. Douglas 1703

Gallus (Nobleman)
The Sword and the Promise - Benjamin Siegel 5845

Gallus, Diana (Young Woman)
The Robe - Lloyd C. Douglas 1703

Galmon, Jack (Trader)
Dubu: A Novel of New Guinean Conquest - Maslyn Williams 6789

Galphine, Rike (Farmer)
Show Me a Land - Clark McMeekin 4293

Gamble, Libby (Young Woman)
Tidewater - Clifford Dowdey 1709

Gaminini (Heir; Royalty)
The Winds of Sinhala - Colin De Silva 1562

Gao (Indian)
Red Stick - Donald Clayton Porter 5121

Gao (Indian; Teenager)
Father and Son - Donald Clayton Porter 5117

Gapon, George (Religious)
Blood on the Snow - John Elliott 1916

Garces, Francisco (Religious)
Dust on the King's Highway - Helen Constance White 6677

Garcia, Juan (Adventurer; Military Personnel)
Captain From Castille - Samuel Shellabarger 5794

Garcia, Juan (Military Personnel)
Trail of the Spanish Bit - Don Coldsmith 1193

Garcia, Pedro (Gentleman)
Follow the Wind - Don Coldsmith 1176

Garcia, Tomas (Revolutionary)
A Distant Thunder - Teresa de Luca 1561

Garcia de la Lastra, Gervasio (Military Personnel)
The Stuff of Heroes - Miguel Delibes 1592

Gardiner, Asa B. (Lawyer)
The Court-Martial of George Armstrong Custer - Douglas C. Jones 3276

Gardner, Rowland (Settler)
Spirit Lake - MacKinlay Kantor 3363

Garfield, Roak (Rancher)
The Garfield Honor - Frank Yerby 6918

Garfield, Simon (Nobleman)
Daphne - Marion Chesney 1022

Garland, Andrew (Journalist)
Angels Falling - Janice Elliott 1915

Garland, Anne (Young Woman)
The Trumpet Major - Thomas Hardy 2700

Garland, Francesca (Young Woman)
Night Shall Overtake Us - Kate Saunders 5611

Garland, Lee Oliver (Adventurer)
Outlaw - Warren Kiefer 3482

Garrard, Adrian (Military Personnel)
No Man's Land - William Fairchild 2004

Garrega, Leonor de (Young Woman)
Eagle of the Gredos - Claude Jack Osgood 4761

Garret, Serena (Young Woman)
Galveston - Suzanne Morris 4482

Garrett, J.C. (Trapper; Mountain Man)
The Pilgrimage - Ann B. Ross 5463

Garrett, Paul (Rancher)
Centennial - James A. Michener 4366

Garroch (Prehistoric Human; Chieftain)
The Golden Strangers - Henry Treece 6328

Garth, Celia (Seamstress; Spy)
Celia Garth - Gwen Bristow 695

Garuald, Andrew (Adventurer; Businessman)
Salute to Adventurers - John Buchan 752

Garvey, James (Gentleman)
Married Past Redemption - Patricia Veryan 6469

Garvey, Marietta (Plantation Owner)
Gallows Way - Daoma Winston 6825

Garza, Joey (Outlaw)
Streets of Laredo - Larry McMurtry 4300

Garza, Katie (Outlaw)
Anything for Billy - Larry McMurtry 4295

Gaskell, Obadiah (Religious; Sailor)
The Forest Lord - Noel B. Gerson 2368

Gaspar (Biblical Figure; Warrior)
How Far to Bethlehem? - Norah Lofts 3846

Gates, Jason (Military Personnel)
The Bugles Are Silent: A Novel of the Texas Revolution - John R. Knaggs 3513

Gates, Johnnie (Gentleman)
Mistaken Virtues - Joanna Trollope 6349

Gates, Tamar (Young Woman)
The Land Beyond the Tempest - Drayton Mayrant 4213

Gatewood, Kitty (Young Woman)
Each Bright River - Mildred Masterson McNeilly 4308

Gatewood, Tenny (Teenager; Orphan)
Pioneer Breed - Glenn R. Vernam 6453

Gatling, Tom (Lawman)
The Comancheros - Paul I. Wellman 6616

Gattlin, Jacob (Military Personnel)
Grant's War - Ted Jones 3297

Gaudeans, Captain Richard (Spy; Adventurer)
Captain Wonder - Donald Thomas 6238

Gaunt, Adam (Frontiersman)
Passage Home - Alison McLeay 4286

Gaunt, Adam (Gentleman)
Sea Change - Alison McLeay 4287

Gaunt, Griffith (Gentleman)
Griffith Gaunt - Charles Reade 5280

Gauntry, Crawford (Veteran)
The House in Ruins - Robert S. Weekley 6595

Gautier, Francis (Landowner)
The Chateau - Stephen Coulter 1383

Gautier, Jean-Paul (Police Officer)
Crime Without Passion - Richard Grayson 2556
Death En Voyage - Richard Grayson 2557
Death Off Stage - Richard Grayson 2558
Death on the Cards - Richard Grayson 2559
The Monterant Affair - Richard Grayson 2560
The Montmarte Murders - Richard Grayson 2561
The Murder at Impasse Louvaine - Richard
    Grayson 2562

Gautier, Susannah (Spouse)
The Chateau - Stephen Coulter 1383

Gawaine (Knight)
Guinevere - Sharan Newman 4600

Gawaine, Sir (Knight)
The Idylls of the Queen - Phyllis Ann Karr 3367

Gawin, Sir (Knight)
Kinsmen of the Grail - Dorothy James Roberts 5376

Gayabuc (Indian; Hunter)
Rabbit Boss - Thomas Sanchez 5581

Gaynor, Ellen (Gentlewoman)
The Gaynor Women - Virginia Coffman 1153

Gaynor, Maggilee (Gentlewoman)
The Gaynor Women - Virginia Coffman 1153

Gaynor, Varina Dunmore (Gentlewoman)
The Gaynor Women - Virginia Coffman 1153

Gearhart, Thaddeus (Military Personnel)
The Hallelujah Train - Bill Gulick 2614

Gebhart, M.P. (Director)
Poor Boy and a Long Way Home - James
    Sherburne 5806

Geddes, Neal (Abolitionist)
Wind Like a Bugle - Leonard Nathan 3722

Gefjon, Jaki (Outcast; Adventurer)
Wyvern - A.A. Attanasio 227

Gefroy, Martin (Doctor)
The Italian Garden - Judith Lennox-Smith 3717

Gehlman, Benjamin (Military Personnel)
To the Honor of the Fleet - Robert H. Pilpel 5002

Geladius, Caius (Government Official)
Artorius Rex - John Gloag 2432

Geladius, Marcus (Military Personnel)
The Eagles Depart - John Gloag 2434

Gelbman, Anna (Patriot)
The Iron Curtain - Robert Vaughan 6447

Gemellus (Military Personnel)
Red Queen, White Queen - Henry Treece 6332

Genovese, Christopher (Professor; Writer)
Bay of Arrows - Jay Parini 4800

Genovese, Susan (Spouse)
Bay of Arrows - Jay Parini 4800

Gentian (Gentlewoman)
Destiny of Fire - Zoe Oldenbourg 4715

Gentry, Kitty (Settler)
Oh, Kentucky! - Betty Layman Receveur 5284

Gentry, Kitty (Spouse)
Kentucky Home - Betty Layman Receveur 5283

Gentry, Marin (Young Woman)
Lights Along the Shore - Diane Austell 241

Gentry, Roman (Political Figure)
Kentucky Home - Betty Layman Receveur 5283

Gentry, Roman (Settler)
Oh, Kentucky! - Betty Layman Receveur 5284

Genville, Mary (Young Woman)
The Devil in Velvet - John Dickson Carr 909

George, Johnny (Indian)
The Kingdom Carver - E.G. Perrault 4916

Geraint (Landowner; Warlord)
The Man on the White Horse - Warwick
    Deeping 1577

Gerard, Ann (Gentlewoman)
The Native Air - Sarah Woodhouse 6854

Gerard, Clarissa (Gentlewoman)
The Floral Companion - Anthea Bell 419

Gerard, Sir Harry (Gentleman; Landowner)
A Season of Mists - Sarah Woodhouse 6856

Gerard, William (Gentleman)
The Floral Companion - Anthea Bell 419

Gerardo, Kit (Pirate; Sea Captain)
The Golden Hawk - Frank Yerby 6921

Gerbert (Religious)
The Heretic's Apprentice - Ellis Peters 4960

Geroy, Fulcun (Knight)
Son of Dust - H.F.M. Prescott 5171

Gerrick, Mark (Gentleman)
The Artist's Daughter - Leslie O'Grady 4698

Geyser, John (Artist)
The Blue and the Gray - John Leekley 3713

Geyser, Luke (Military Personnel)
The Blue and the Gray - John Leekley 3713

Ghislaine (Young Woman)
The Courts of Love: A Romance of Medieval France -
    Peter Bourne 592

Ghonkaba (Indian; Chieftain)
Cherokee - Donald Clayton Porter 5115
The Sachem - Donald Clayton Porter 5124
Seneca - Donald Clayton Porter 5127

Ghonkaba (Indian; Warrior)
Ambush - Donald Clayton Porter 5113
War Cry - Donald Clayton Porter 5132

Ghost Shirt (Indian)
Stamping Ground - Loren D. Estleman 1977

Ghostwind (Indian; Shaman)
Thunder in the Dawn - Earl Murray 4532

Gibboney, Bobby (Military Personnel)
The Seasons of Heroes - Paxton Davis 1539

Gibboney, Matthew (Military Personnel)
The Seasons of Heroes - Paxton Davis 1539

Gibboney, William (Government Official)
The Seasons of Heroes - Paxton Davis 1539

Gibbons, Jane (Gentlewoman)
Sharpe's Regiment - Bernard Cornwell 1345

Gibbs, John (Spy; Patriot)
The Iron Chain - Jim DeFelice 1579

Gibson, Amelia (Spouse)
Murder in the East Room - Elliott Roosevelt 5448

Gibson, Mark (Worker)
The Drayton Legacy - Rona Randall 5247

Gibson, Vance (Political Figure)
Murder in the East Room - Elliott Roosevelt 5448

Gibson, Ward (Farmer)
The Maltese Angel - Catherine Cookson 1283

Gifford, Anne (Gentlewoman)
The Everlasting Covenant - Robyn Carr 939

Gifford, Jonathan (Saloon Keeper/Owner)
Liberty Tavern - Thomas Fleming 2129

Gifford, Sarah (Spouse)
Liberty Tavern - Thomas Fleming 2129

Gil, Carter (Cowboy)
The Ox-Bow Incident - Walter Van Tilburg
    Clark 1096

Gilbert, Joseph (Settler)
Old Misery - Hugh Pendexter 4896

Gilbert of Axford (Captive)
Black Angels - C.T. Ritchie 5348

Gilchrist, Alick (Young Man)
Jennie about to Be - Elisabeth Ogilvie 4694
The World of Jennie G. - Elisabeth Ogilvie 4696

Gilchrist, Jennie (Widow(er))
The World of Jennie G. - Elisabeth Ogilvie 4696

Gilchrist, Nigel (Military Personnel; Landowner)
Jennie about to Be - Elisabeth Ogilvie 4694

Gilchrist, Walter (Military Personnel)
1915: A Novel - Roger McDonald 4264

Gilderson, Adam (Innkeeper)
A Wayside Tavern - Norah Lofts 3862

Giles, Lucy (Gentlewoman)
East by Day - Blair Niles 4626

Gill, Peter (Sailor)
The Greenlander - Mark Adlard 38

Gilles, Sir Rafe (Gentleman)
The Dark Stranger - Dorothy Charques 999

Gillespie, Arch (Military Personnel)
Golden Shore - George Shaftel 5769

Gillivray, Vespasian (Military Personnel)
By Valour and Arms - James H. Street 6076

Gillroy, Daniel (Military Personnel)
The Secret Years - Judith Lennox-Smith 3718

Gilman, Roger (Student—College)
Gilman of the Redford - William Stearns Davis 1541

Gilman, Thomas (Clerk)
*Ride East! Ride West!: A Romance of the Hundred
    Years' War* - Anne Powers 5154

Gilmor, Harry (Military Personnel)
Roll, Shenandoah - Bruce Lancaster 3644

Gilmore, Cary (Gentlewoman)
Draw Near to Battle - Jere Hungerford
    Wheelwright 6667

Gilmore, Delia (Fiance(e))
Devil's Fire, Love's Revenge - Barbara Paul 4836

Gilmore, Martha (Servant)
Whom the Gods Love - Kate Ross 5502

Gilmour, Marietta (Young Woman)
The Fires of Glenlochy - Constance Heaven 2806

Gilpin, Sam (Military Personnel)
Redcoat - Bernard Cornwell 1337

Gilson, Charley (Hunter)
The Last Hunt - Milton Lott 3900

Gintult, Prince (Royalty)
Ashes - Stefan Zeromski 6960

Giolitti-Crispi, Lorenzo (Royalty; Police Officer)
Summoned to Darkness - Anne-Marie Sheridan 5809

Giraldus (Religious)
Myself as Witness - James Goldman 2458

Girard, Chase (Spy)
While the Music Plays - Diane Austell 242

Girard, Philippe (Carpenter)
High Towers - Thomas B. Costain 1366

Giraud, Jules (Sidekick)
Rasputin's Revenge - John T. Lescroart 3725

Giron, Irena (Student)
Organized Crime - Nicholas Von Hoffman 6511

Gisbert, Lord (Nobleman)
The Green Madonna - C.E. L'Ami 3617

Gitan (Gypsy)
The Fallen Angels - Susannah Kells 3397

Giuliani, Alessandro (Veteran)
A Soldier of the Great War - Mark Helprin 2823

Glasman, Ronya Von (Young Woman)
The Candlesticks and the Cross - Ruth Freeman Solomon 5940

Glass, Jason (Writer)
The Legacy of Ladysmith - John Kenny Crane 1413

Glaucus (Young Man)
The Last Days of Pompeii - Edward Bulwer-Lytton 768

Glen, Molly (Journalist)
Twice upon a Time - Allen Appel 172

Glen, Owen (Teenager; Labor Leader)
Owen Glen - Ben Ames Williams 6766

Glen, Stephen (Government Official)
Montana Road - Harry Sinclair Drago 1717

Glenalban, Duncan (Nobleman)
Albany - Laura Black 519

Glendenning, Horatio (Fugitive)
Love Alters Not - Patricia Veryan 6467

Glendenning, Horatio (Nobleman)
Had We Never Loved - Patricia Veryan 6463

Glendinning, Edward (Gentleman)
The Monastery - Sir Walter Scott 5701

Glendinning, Edward (Religious)
The Abbot - Sir Walter Scott 5688

Glendinning, Halbert (Gentleman)
The Monastery - Sir Walter Scott 5701

Glendower, Gethin (Landowner)
Autumn Lace - Eileen Jackson 3133

Glendower, Lindsey (Spouse)
Beckoning Ridge - Emerson Waldman 6527

Glendower, Martin (Farmer)
Beckoning Ridge - Emerson Waldman 6527

Glenn, Molly (Journalist)
Till the End of Time - Allen Appel 170

Glenn, Morgan (Military Personnel)
The Firelands - Karen Harper 2712

Glenny, Dave (Settler)
Winter Harvest - Norah Lofts 3863

Glenroy, Alick (Businessman)
Jennie Glenroy - Elisabeth Ogilvie 4695

Glenroy, Jennie (Spouse)
Jennie Glenroy - Elisabeth Ogilvie 4695

Go-Ahead Rider (Indian; Lawman)
Go-Ahead Rider - Robert J. Conley 1243
To Make a Killing - Robert J. Conley 1252

Goddard, Jebediah (Military Personnel)
Governor Ramage, R.N. - Dudley Pope 5096

Goddard, Mary (Teacher)
A Visit to Highbury - Joan Austen-Leigh 243

Godefroi, Richard de (Gentleman)
Sarum: The Novel of England - Edward Rutherfurd 5536

Godenhausen, Hans Gunther von (Military Personnel)
Court of Honor - Maria Fagyas 1996

Godfrey (Actor)
The Queen's War: A Novel of Eleanor of Aquitaine - Jeanne Mackin 3996

Godfrey, Lance (Businessman)
The Cotton Road - Frank Feuille 2077

Godiva, Lady (Noblewoman)
Hereward the Wake - Charles Kingsley 3497

Godolphin, Lizzie (Servant)
In the Shadow of the Brontes - Louise Brindley 690

Godolphin, Mordaunt Fitzmaurice (Landowner)
The Wild Yazoo - John Myers 4546

Godric (Knight)
This January Tale - Bryher 747

Godric, Hester (Gentlewoman)
Lavender Lady - Carola Dunn 1794

Godscale of Cologne (Religious)
Scales of Gold - Dorothy Dunnett 1808

Godwinson, Fallon (Royalty)
Princess of Fire - Shannon Drake 1718

Goedzak, Lamme (Military Personnel)
The Legend of Tyl Ulenspiegel - Charles Theodore Henri De Coster 1558

Goelo, Gilles (Bastard Son; Military Personnel)
The Lure of the Falcon - Juliette Benzoni 465

Goff, Colby William Rollo (Military Personnel)
Blunted Lance - Max Hennessy 2829
Soldier of the Queen - Max Hennessy 2837

Goff, Dabney (Military Personnel)
Blunted Lance - Max Hennessy 2829

Goffett, Thomas (Government Official)
Dubu: A Novel of New Guinean Conquest - Maslyn Williams 6789

Goforth, Billy (Teenager)
Bugle in the Wilderness - John Burress 805

Gold, Riva (Gentlewoman)
Strange Wives - Shirley Barker 317

Gold Beard (Pirate)
The Temptation of Angelique - Sergeanne Golon 2473

Golden Bells (Royalty)
Messer Marco Polo - Donn Byrne 840

Golden Orchard (Young Woman)
The Fabulous Concubine - Hsin-Hai Chang 987

Goldfeder, Aaron (Military Personnel)
Leah's Journey - Gloria Goldreich 2460

Goldfeder, David (Immigrant)
Leah's Journey - Gloria Goldreich 2460

Goldfeder, Leah (Immigrant)
Leah's Journey - Gloria Goldreich 2460

Goldman, Eleanor Kent (Actress)
The Americans - John Jakes 3143

Golem (Warrior)
The Sword of the Golem - Abraham Rothberg 5509

Gomez, Caterina (Young Woman)
Whispering - Jane Aiken Hodge 2972

Gomez, Francisca de (Young Woman)
Against the Tide - Muriel Elwood 1935

Gonzago y Cordoza, Margarita (Noblewoman)
The Sinking of the Sarah Diamond - William Dale Jennings 3213

Gonzalez, Pedro (Outlaw)
Brules - Harry Combs 1223

Gonzalo (Young Man)
Among the Innocent - Elizabeth Borton de Trevino 6339

Goo-Ga-Ro-No (Indian)
Renno - Donald Clayton Porter 5123

Goodacre, Joanna (Young Woman)
The Pride of the Trevallions - Carola Salisbury 5570

Goodchild, Helen (Gentlewoman)
Until the Colors Fade - Tim Jeal 3173

Goodenough, Emily (Gentlewoman)
The Adventuress - Marion Chesney 1014

Goodenough, Sir George (Gentleman)
The Adventuress - Marion Chesney 1014

Goodhill, Mary (Immigrant)
Erie Water - Walter D. Edmonds 1875

Goodwin, Isabel (Gentlewoman)
Beauty for Ashes - Timothy R. Wilson 6816

Gordianus the Finder (Detective—Private)
Arms of Nemesis - Steven Saylor 5623
A Murder on the Appian Way - Steven Saylor 5625
Roman Blood - Steven Saylor 5626
The Venus Throw - Steven Saylor 5627

Gordianus the Finder (Farmer; Detective—Private)
Catalina's Riddle - Steven Saylor 5624

Gordon, Arabella (Gentlewoman)
Falls of Gard - Laura Black 520

Gordon, Clive (Doctor; Loyalist)
Song of a Strange Child - Gilbert Morris 4470

Gordon, Eli (Doctor)
Blood Winter - William Patrick 4830

Gordon, Faith (Young Woman)
Flight From Avatchez - Frank G. Slaughter 5887

Gordon, Rachel Java (Gentlewoman)
The Nationalists - William Stuart Long 3876

Gordon, Temple (Southern Belle; Indian)
The Proud and the Free - Janet Dailey 1456

Gordon, Wayne (Military Personnel; Amnesiac)
Shadowed Memories - Al Lacy 3583

Gore, Bysshe (Nobleman; Rake)
Vice Avenged: A Moral Tale - Lolah Burford 774

Gorion (Young Man)
The Last Days - William Rayner 5272

Gorman, Marcus (Lawyer)
Legs - William Kennedy 3422

Gorsinski, Prince (Military Personnel)
Beware, Beware the Bight of Benin - Philip McCutchan 4241
Halfhyde's Island - Philip McCutchan 4254

Gotha (Shaman; Prehistoric Human)
The Last Mammoth - Margaret Allan 89

Gough, Paddy (Military Personnel)
Bayonets in the Sun - William Moore 4446

Gowd, Skinner (Mountain Man; Scout)
Diamond Wedding - Wilbur Daniel Steele 5986

Gower, Colby (Frontiersman; Military Personnel)
Bridal Journey - Dale Van Every 6406

Goyah (Indian; Warrior)
The Pecos River - Fred Bean 399

Gracchus (Political Figure)
Spartacus - Howard Fast 2044

Gradov, Boris (Doctor)
Generations of Winter - Vassily Aksyonov 61

Gradov, Mary (Musician)
Generations of Winter - Vassily Aksyonov 61

Gradov, Nikita (Military Personnel)
Generations of Winter - Vassily Aksyonov 61

Graeme, Allison (Gentlewoman)
The Master of Ballantrae: A Winter's Tale - Robert Louis Stevenson 6011

Graeme, Roland (Servant; Spy)
The Abbot - Sir Walter Scott 5688

Grafton, Sir Edmund (Nobleman)
A London Season - Anthea Bell 420

Grafton, Janse (Prospector)
The City of Gold - Francis Brett Young 6940

Grafton, Persephone (Ward; Heiress)
A London Season - Anthea Bell 420

Graham, Anthony (Adventurer)
Fire Opal - Pamela Hill 2932

Graham, Gavin (Military Personnel)
Drums of Khartoum - Chloe Gartner 2307

Grail, Edmund (Veteran)
Death at the French Creek - Raymond C. Borel 580

Grailhe, Eloise (Young Woman)
The Comancheros - Paul I. Wellman 6616

Grainger, Lucinda (Actress; Bastard Daughter)
The Mating Dance - Rona Randall 5250

Grainger, Penn (Spy)
No Bugles Blow - Bruce Lancaster 3642

Grainger, Zadok (Sea Captain)
Pull Down to New Orleans - Zachary Ball 283

Grainger, Zoe (Young Woman)
Never Doubt I Love - Patricia Veryan 6473

Grainne (Ruler)
This Land Fulfilled - Charles Andrew Brady 636

Grammy (Slave)
Kingdom Coming - Roark Bradford 622

Gramont, Alain de (Military Personnel)
The Renegade - Donald Clayton Porter 5122
The Sachem - Donald Clayton Porter 5124

Grande, Gano (Mercenary)
The Sword of Il Grande - Will Creed 1424

Grandison, Cathryn (Gentlewoman)
Lady of Monkton - Elizabeth Byrd 835

Grandissime, Honore (Nobleman; Businessman)
The Grandissimes - George W. Cable 842

Grandmother (Heroine; Grandparent)
Little Sister - Margaret Gaan 2259

Grange, Silas (Doctor)
The Rationalist - Warwick Collins 1217

Granger, Henry (Religious)
The Whip - Catherine Cookson 1291

Granger, Zachary (Spy)
The Golden Circle - Constance Robertson 5396

Grant, Alan (Detective—Police)
The Daughter of Time - Josephine Tey 6209

Grant, Angelina (Captive)
A Mule for the Marquesa - Frank O'Rourke 4753

Grant, Augustus (Rancher)
A Mule for the Marquesa - Frank O'Rourke 4753

Grant, Cordelia (Teacher)
The Time of the Hunter's Moon - Victoria Holt 3022

Grant, Finlay Ban (Laird)
Torbeg - Grace Campbell 873

Grant, Fiona (Gentlewoman)
Miss Fiona's Fancy - Marion Chesney 1040

Grant, Jack (Lawman)
Apaches - Oakley Hall 2650

Grant, John (Naturalist)
Here I Stay - Elizabeth Coatsworth 1138

Grant, Mary Elisabeth (Gentlewoman)
MacLyon - Lolah Burford 773

Grant, Penelope (Gentlewoman)
Little Red Foot - Robert W. Chambers 979

Grant, Richard (Gentleman)
Wild Cat - Laura Black 524

Grant, Sapphire (Teacher)
Sapphire - Helen Ashfield 214

Grantham, Deborah (Gambler)
Faro's Daughter - Georgette Heyer 2887

Granville, Alexis de (Nobleman; Rake)
Lady Hellfire - Suzanne Robinson 5414

Granville, Beaumont (Gentleman)
The Love Child - Philippa Carr 923

Granville, Marcus (Landowner)
Damnation Reef - Jill Tattersall 6172

Granville, Simeon St. Leger (Mercenary)
By Valour and Arms - James H. Street 6076

Gratwick, Ward (Patriot)
Blind Journey - Bruce Lancaster 3636

Graves, John (Settler)
Juniata Valley - Virginia C. Cassel 954

Graves, Thomas "Grubber" (Teenager; Orphan)
Me and Gallagher - Jack Farris 2023

Gray, Benjamin (Businessman)
Tarnished Angel - Phyllis Leonard 3723

Gray, Billy (Convict)
Proud Mary - Iris Gower 2501

Gray, Catherine (Young Woman)
Not by Any Single Man - Brigid Knight 3522

Gray, Dick (Military Personnel)
The Horse Soldiers - Harold Sinclair 5862

Gray, Ellen (Widow(er); Gentlewoman)
On a Lonesome Porch - Ovid Williams Pierce 4997

Gray, Frederica (Gentlewoman)
Colonel Sandhurst to the Rescue - Marion Chesney 1021

Gray, Judith (Settler)
Forest of the Night - Madison Jones 3291

Gray, Lucy (Widow(er))
On a Lonesome Porch - Ovid Williams Pierce 4997

Gray, Nancy (Orphan)
The Clock Tower - Jeanne Montague 4435

Gray, Nicholas (Artist)
The Man Who Loved Mata Hari - Dan Sherman 5813

Gray, Rhian (Worker)
Spinners' Wharf - Iris Gower 2502

Gray Fox (Indian; Warrior)
Tomahawk - Donald Clayton Porter 5129

Gray Mouse (Indian; Child)
Child of the Dead - Don Coldsmith 1172

Graylag (Prehistoric Human; Chieftain)
Reindeer Moon - Elizabeth Marshall Thomas 6244

Grayle, David (Teenager)
Sudden Country - Loren D. Estleman 1979

Graylin, Andrew (Gentleman)
The Black Sheep's Daughter - Carola Dunn 1791

Graylin, Teresa (Gentlewoman)
Lady in the Briars - Carola Dunn 1793

Grayson, Champ (Sailor)
On the Midnight Tide - Don Tracy 6310

Grayson, Letitia (Heiress)
The Masqueraders - Georgette Heyer 2894

Green, Lord Hibbard (Nobleman)
A Shadow's Bliss - Patricia Veryan 6477

Green, Perry (Worker)
Charity Strong - Marguerite Allis 109

Greenback, Roddy (Orphan)
The Bannaman Legacy - Catherine Cookson 1272

Greenbourne, Solly (Heir)
A Dangerous Fortune - Ken Follett 2147

Greenfall, Jonathan (Explorer; Frontiersman)
No Road Too Long - Hildegarde Hawthorne 2785

Greenfield, Nancy Ann (Pioneer)
The Land Is Bright - Archie Binns 501

Greenham, Joel (Fiance(e); Gentleman)
The Black Swan - Philippa Carr 917

Greenham, Lucinda (Student)
A Time for Silence - Philippa Carr 930

Greenleaf, Kitty (Teenager)
The Road to Bunker Hill - Shirley Barker 316

Greenleaf, Laura (Young Woman)
Distant Trumpet - Paul Horgan 3032

Greenpearl (Captive; Prostitute)
Silk Road - Jeanne Larsen 3670

Greenway, Damask (Young Woman)
Afternoon of a Autocrat - Norah Lofts 3834

Greenway, Jenny (Nurse)
Serpent and Staff - Frank Yerby 6927

Greenwood, Alice (Captive; Gentlewoman)
Jade - Pat Barr 344

Greenwood, Frank (Gentleman)
Jade - Pat Barr 344

Greenwood, Josiana (Gentlewoman)
The House at Old Vine - Norah Lofts 3845

Greer, Tamzen (Settler)
Tamzen - Jane Gilmore Rushing 5530

Greer, Tom (Teenager)
Wandering Star - Steven Yount 6945

Greetwell, Primula (Gentlewoman)
Fleeting Fancy - Rosemary Edghill 1866

Gregorio (Servant)
The Lady in the Mask - Anne Green 2564

Gregory, Brother (Religious)
A Vision of Light - Judith Merkle Riley 5337

Gregory, Morna (Heroine)
Bridey's Mountain - Yvonne Adamson 34

Gregson, Badger (Thief)
The Rookery: A Novel of the Victorian Underworld - Hugh C. Rae 5239

Gregson, David (Banker)
The Lorimer Line - Anne Melville 4332

Gregson, Sarah (Young Woman)
The Rookery: A Novel of the Victorian Underworld - Hugh C. Rae 5239

Grein, Walter (Scout)
Adobe Walls: A Novel of the Last Apache Rising - William R. Burnett 791

Grendel (Monster)
The Tower of Beowulf - Parke Godwin 2450

Grenier, Yvonne (Gentlewoman)
Yvonne Goes to York - Marion Chesney 1054

Grenouille, Jean-Baptiste (Orphan; Murderer)
Perfume: The Story of a Murderer - Patrick Suskind 6120

Grenville, Lady Caroline (Noblewoman)
Captain Monsoon - Victor Suthren 6128

Greppia, Malatesta (Mercenary)
High Carnival - John J. Pugh 5207

Grevel, Claudia (Gentlewoman)
Midwinter - John Buchan 751

Greville, Anthony (Nobleman)
The Passing Bells - Phillip Rock 5421

Greville, Charles (Military Personnel; Gentleman)
The Passing Bells - Phillip Rock 5421

Grey, Arabella (Noblewoman)
The Spitfire - Bertrice Small 5912

Grey, Katherine (Heiress)
Lady Hellfire - Suzanne Robinson 5414

Grey, Townsend (Gentlewoman)
If This Be Magic - Ellen Marsh 4098

Grey Horse Running (Indian; Warrior)
The Wolf and the Buffalo - Elmer Kelton 3408

Greypaull, Rhoda (Immigrant; Orphan)
Double Wedding Ring - Patricia Wendorf 6624

Griewson, Eliza (Spy)
Pancho And Black Jack - Fred Bean 398

Griffen, Tristram (Student)
The Black Rose - Thomas B. Costain 1363

Griffin, Paris (Plantation Owner)
Griffin's Way - Frank Yerby 6922

Griffith (Businessman)
The White Land - William Dieter 1643

Griffith, Edward (Military Personnel)
The Pilot - James Fenimore Cooper 1306

Griggs, Devora (Young Woman)
Farewell the Stranger - Saliee O'Brien 4682

Grigsby, Robert (Lawman)
Wilde West - Walter Satterthwait 5609

Grijalva, Juan Pablo (Military Personnel)
Cannibal Eliot and the Lost Histories of San Francisco - Hilton Obenzinger 4660

Grimes, Matt (Sailor)
Benjamin Blake - Edison Marshall 4102

Grimes, Sinjin (Sea Captain)
In the Fire of Spring - Thomas Tryon 6355
The Wings of the Morning - Thomas Tryon 6356

Grineff, Peter (Military Personnel)
The Captain's Daughter - Alexander Pushkin 5210

Grishin, Mikhail (Spy)
Grishin - Hans Herlin 2859

Griva, Roberto della (Sailor)
The Island of the Day Before - Umberto Eco 1849

Grobart, Jay (Veteran; Outlaw)
The Man Who Loved Cat Dancing - Marilyn Durham 1817

Gromeko, Antonina "Tonia" (Spouse)
Doctor Zhivago - Boris Pasternak 4824

Gronelu, Jacob (Landowner)
Dina's Book - Herbjorg Wassmo 6577

Groody, Helen (Activist)
The Tontine - Thomas B. Costain 1371

Gross, Alice (Young Woman)
Gettysburg - Stephen Longstreet 3887

Gross Mama Chen (Gentlewoman)
Before My Time - Niccolo Tucci 6358

Grossberg, Sharon (Teenager; Student—High School)
The Year of Our War - Gloria Goldreich 2462

Grove, Matty (Spy)
The Traitor - Dan Sherman 5814

Grove, Peter (Military Personnel)
Song of the Susquehanna - Herbert Stover 6071

Groves, Christopher (Military Personnel)
Gone to Texas - Jason Manning 4074

Groves, Jonathan (Military Personnel)
Flintlock - Jason Manning 4073

Gruffydd (Heir)
Lord of Misrule - Gareth Jones 3290

Gruffydd, Wynne ab (Sorceress)
Where Magic Dwells - Rexanne Becnel 411

Grunewald, Joshua (Businessman)
Echo of the Flute - Mildred A. Jordan 3304

Grunewald, Juditha (Spouse)
Echo of the Flute - Mildred A. Jordan 3304

Grunowski, Valentina (Noblewoman; Spy)
Valentina - Evelyn Anthony 165

Gruoch (Royalty; Spouse)
Lady of Moray - Bonnie Copeland 1318

Guard, Philip (Frontiersman)
Westward the Tide - Harold Sinclair 5863

Guardi, Serafina (Heiress)
The Glittering Strand - Judith Lennox-Smith 3716

Guatamozin (Nobleman)
The Fair God - Lew Wallace 6537

Gudrid (Young Woman)
A Viking's Daughter - John Andrews 147

Guemont, Marc de (Young Man)
The Incorruptible - Helma De Bois 1551

Guenevere (Gentlewoman)
The Duke of War - Walter O'Meara 4734

Guenevere (Royalty)
Beloved Exile - Parke Godwin 2446
Firelord - Parke Godwin 2447
The Idylls of the Queen - Phyllis Ann Karr 3367
The Once and Future King - T.H. White 6705

Guere, Jeffrey de (Rake)
The Stanbroke Girls - Fiona Hill 2925

Guerrero (Sailor)
A Signal Victory - David Stacton 5976

Guerrero, Estrella (Young Woman)
The Franciscan - Forrester Blake 532

Guerrero, Josepha (Young Woman)
Tide of Empire - Peter S. Kyne 3572

Guerro, Gasto (Revolutionary)
The Rebels - Alfred Neumann 4585

Guest, Marie (Actress; Loyalist)
Painted Minx - Robert W. Chambers 980

Guidmar (Young Woman)
Among the Innocent - Elizabeth Borton de Trevino 6339

Guidron, Lord (Religious; Prehistoric Human)
The Temple of the Sun - Moyra Caldecott 849

Guilame, Gabriel (Military Personnel; Artist)
Seven Men of Gascony - R.F. Delderfield 1589

Guiletta (Singer)
Fairoaks - Frank Yerby 6915

Guilfoyle, Anne (Gentlewoman)
The Country Gentleman - Fiona Hill 2924

Guillet, Andre (Gentleman)
Monsieur Yankee - Leslie Turner White 6689

Guinevere (Royalty)
Arthur Rex: A Legendary Novel - Thomas Berger 477
The Chessboard Queen - Sharan Newman 4597
Child of the Northern Spring - Persia Woolley 6867
The Emperor Arthur - Godfrey Turton 6368
First Knight - Elizabeth Chadwick 966
Guinevere Evermore - Sharan Newman 4601
Guinevere: The Legend in Autumn - Persia Woolley 6868
The King - Donald Barthelme 365
The Last Enchantment - Mary Stewart 6031

The Pendragon - Catherine Christian 1075
Queen of the Summer Stars - Persia Woolley 6869
The Queen's Knight - Marvin Borowsky 585
The Wicked Day - Mary Stewart 6033
The Winter King - Bernard Cornwell 1351
Witch of the North - Courtway Jones 3272

Guinevere (Young Woman)
Guinevere - Sharan Newman 4600

Guinevra (Orphan)
The Man on the White Horse - Warwick Deeping 1577

Guishar, Larisa "Lara" (Spouse)
Doctor Zhivago - Boris Pasternak 4824

Gullington, Laurence (Gentleman)
The Black Velvet Gown - Catherine Cookson 1274

Gunarduilla (Royalty)
The Serpent's Tooth - Diana L. Paxson 4846

Gundrun (Maiden)
Rhinegold - Stephan Grundy 2607

Gunn, Robert (Doctor; Trader)
Mandarin Gold - James Leasor 3700

Gunnar (Chieftain)
Fire in the Ice - Dorothy James Roberts 5375

Gunnar (Young Man)
The Foster Brothers - Edward Frankland 2202

Gunnarsson, Asgeir (Farmer)
The Greenlanders - Jane Smiley 5915

Gunnor (Slave)
The Proud Villeins - Valerie Anand 133

Gunther, Bernie (Detective—Private)
The Pale Criminal - Philip Kerr 3471

Gunzburg, David de (Nobleman)
The Four Winds of Heaven - Monique Raphel High 2916

Gunzburg, Sonia de (Noblewoman)
The Four Winds of Heaven - Monique Raphel High 2916

Gupta, Candra (Royalty)
Golden Fire - Jonathan Fast 2047

Gupta, Rama (Royalty)
Golden Fire - Jonathan Fast 2047

Guriandio, Adriano (Young Man)
Sing to the Sun - Lucille Borden 579

Gurney, Edwin (Gentleman)
Monk's Hood - Ellis Peters 4964

Gurney, Hester (Ward)
The Railway King - Margaret Mayhew 4207

Guthfrid (Royalty)
Born of the Sun - Joan Wolf 6837

Guthorn (Warrior)
The Marsh King - C. Walter Hodges 2975

Guy of Nissan (Knight)
The Siege - Jay Williams 6773

Guyon (Nobleman)
The Wild Hunt - Elizabeth Chadwick 969

Gwalchmai (Knight)
Hawk of May - Gillian Bradshaw 629
Kingdom of Summer - Gillian Bradshaw 633

Gwanga (Slave)
Freedom's Dues - Robert H. Abel 9

Gwenhwyfar (Gentlewoman)
The Kingmaking - Helen Hollick 3000
The Road to Avalon - Joan Wolf 6842

Gwenhwyfar (Royalty)
The Mists of Avalon - Marion Zimmer Bradley 626
Pendragon's Banner - Helen Hollick 3001

Gwenhwyvar (Royalty)
Arthur - Stephen R. Lawhead 3679

Gwinfreda (Royalty)
Artorius Rex - John Gloag 2432

Gwladys (Royalty)
The Captive Princess - Maxine Shore 5831

Gwyn, Viola (Young Woman)
Viola Gwyn - George Barr McCutcheon 4258

Gwynhwyfar (Royalty)
In Winter's Shadow - Gillian Bradshaw 632

Gwynne, Kenneth (Lawyer)
Viola Gwyn - George Barr McCutcheon 4258

Gwynne, Nora (Actress)
Dance on a Sinking Ship - Michael Kilian 3483

Gyges (Slave)
Star of Macedon - Karl V. Eiker 1901

Gyllenlove, Alexandra (Patriot)
The Fortress - Catherine Gavin 2320

Gys, Hugh de (Knight)
The Devil's Cross - Walter O'Meara 4733

H

Haaberg, Anders (Farmer)
The People of Juvik - Olav Dunn 1798

Haan, Evert (Landowner; Trader)
Silver Nutmeg - Norah Lofts 3860

Habash, Bandy (Herbalist)
A River Town - Thomas Keneally 3415

Hackabout-Jones, Fanny (Outcast; Prostitute)
Fanny: Being the True History of the Adventures of Fanny Hackabout-Jones - Erica Jong 3299

Hadad (Artisan)
The Shepherd Kings - Peter Danielson 1475

Hadley, Ama (Landowner)
A Southern Woman - Elena Yates Eulo 1983

Hadrian (Government Official)
Threshold of Fire - Hella S. Haasse 2633

Hadshire, Matilda (Noblewoman)
Her Grace's Passion - Marion Chesney 1033

Hafner, Bruno (Pilot; Engineer)
Eagles at War - Walter J. Boyne 620

Hagan (Nobleman)
The Belt of Gold - Cecelia Holland 2984

Hagan (Royalty)
Attila's Treasure - Stephan Grundy 2606

Hagen, Peter (Immigrant)
What the Heart Keeps - Rosalind Laker 3605

Haguenier of Linnieres (Knight)
The Cornerstone - Zoe Oldenbourg 4714

Hakeswill, Obadiah (Military Personnel)
Sharpe's Company - Bernard Cornwell 1339
Sharpe's Enemy - Bernard Cornwell 1342

Hakon (Warrior)
Beguiled - Alice Borchardt 577

Halay, Felicite-Anne (Ward)
High Towers - Thomas B. Costain 1366

Halder, Alton (Farmer)
Still Is the Summer Night - August Derleth 1619

Halder, Julie (Spouse)
Still Is the Summer Night - August Derleth 1619

Halder, Ratio (Farmer)
Still Is the Summer Night - August Derleth 1619

Hale, Abner (Settler)
Hawaii - James A. Michener 4370

Hale, Allen (Military Personnel)
Conceived in Liberty - Howard Fast 2029

Hale, Andy (Scout; Rancher)
They Came to a Valley - Bill Gulick 2618

Hale, Ann (Young Woman)
Railroad West - Cornelia Meigs 4327

Hale, Anthony (Military Personnel)
The Band Plays Dixie - Morris Markey 4089

Hale, Elmer (Sailor; Settler)
Mighty Mountain - Archie Binns 502

Hale, Jared (Military Personnel; Servant)
Yankee Rogue - Dana Fuller Ross 5496
The Silver Saber - Carter A. Vaughan 6441

Hale, Kirk (Military Personnel)
The Band Plays Dixie - Morris Markey 4089

Hale, Lisette (Settler; Spouse)
Mighty Mountain - Archie Binns 502

Hale, Malachy (Military Personnel)
The Blue and the Gray - John Leekley 3713

Hale, Oliver (Trader)
Jubilee Trail - Gwen Bristow 698

Hale, Shoshoni (Frontiersman)
Harry Idaho - Hugh Pendexter 4894

Haleevie, Fronah (Young Woman)
Mandarin - Robert S. Elegant 1905

Haleevie, Sal (Businessman)
Mandarin - Robert S. Elegant 1905

Halevi, Avram (Doctor)
The Spanish Doctor - Matt Cohen 1159

Halfhyde, St. Vincent (Military Personnel)
Beware, Beware the Bight of Benin - Philip McCutchan 4241
The Guns of Arrest - Philip McCutchan 4242
Halfhyde and the Chain Gang - Philip McCutchan 4244
Halfhyde and the Flag Captain - Philip McCutchan 4245
Halfhyde and the Fleet Review - Philip McCutchan 4246
Halfhyde for the Queen - Philip McCutchan 4247
Halfhyde Goes to War - Philip McCutchan 4248
Halfhyde on Zanatu - Philip McCutchan 4251
Halfhyde Ordered South - Philip McCutchan 4252
Halfhyde to the Narrows - Philip McCutchan 4253
Halfhyde's Island - Philip McCutchan 4254

Halfhyde, St. Vincent (Sea Captain)
Halfhyde and the Admiral - Philip McCutchan 4243
The Halfhyde Line - Philip McCutchan 4249
Halfhyde on the Amazon - Philip McCutchan 4250
Outward Bound - Philip McCutchan 4256

Halifax, Charlie (Pilot)
In the Blue Light of African Dreams - Paul Watkins 6580

Halifax, Jan (Settler)
Wild Orchid - Isabel Dick 1640

Haliwell, Leonie (Fiance(e))
Mistress of Willowvale - Patricia Veryan 6471

Haliwell, Terence (Government Official)
The King's Messenger - Samuel Edwards 1887

Hall, Charlotte (Parent)
The Hours of Light - Janet Tanner 6160

Hall, Eliza (Teacher)
The Proud and the Free - Janet Dailey 1456

Hall, Jack (Military Personnel)
The Hours of Light - Janet Tanner 6160

Hall, Mason (Military Personnel)
Thunder in the Dawn - Earl Murray 4532

Hall, Ted (Military Personnel)
The Hours of Light - Janet Tanner 6160

Hallam, Beatrice (Actress)
The Virginia Comedians - John Esten Cooke 1269

Hallam, Christopher (Young Man)
The King's Rogue - Max Peacock 4859

Hallam, Dennis (Journalist; Pacifist)
The Skeleton in the Grass - Robert Barnard 320

Hallam, Lesley (Teenager)
Blood Kin - Barbara Anne Pauley 4845

Hallam, Lucus (Detective—Private; Actor)
Dead-Stick - L.J. Washburn 6574
Dog Heavies - L.J. Washburn 6575

Hallard, Marta (Actress)
The Daughter of Time - Josephine Tey 6209

Halleluiah Bob (Indian)
Rabbit Boss - Thomas Sanchez 5581

Hallim, Lizzie (Gentlewoman)
A Place Called Freedom - Ken Follett 2150

Halloran (Military Personnel)
Bring Larks and Heroes - Thomas Keneally 3410

Halloran, Horse-Shy (Outlaw)
The Last Days of Horse-Shy Halloran - Bill Pronzini 5203

Hallows, John (Military Personnel; Heir)
In Pale Battalions - Robert Goddard 2444

Hallows, Leonora (Gentlewoman)
In Pale Battalions - Robert Goddard 2444

Halstad, Theo (Landowner)
Dark Possession - Alice Alison Lide 3771

Halt, Welland (Miner)
The Cage - Michael Weston 6650

Halter, Abraham (Printer)
The Book of Abraham - Marek Halter 2665

Halvin, Brother (Religious)
The Confessions of Brother Halvin - Ellis Peters 4956

Halyi, Istvan (Military Personnel)
Before the Glory Ended - Ursula Zilinsky 6963

Hamilton, Catherine (Heroine)
Goldeneye - Malcolm Macdonald 3965

Hamilton, Fleur (Gentlewoman)
Fleur - Cynthia Harrod-Eagles 2754

Hamilton, Julian (Military Personnel)
The Scimitar - Samuel Edwards 1890

Hamilton, Mary (Young Woman)
The Far Side of the Hill - Nancy Livingston 3811

Hamilton, Melanie (Gentlewoman)
Gone with the Wind - Margaret Mitchell 4415

Hamilton, Richard (Student—College)
The Morning River - W. Michael Gear 2333

Hamlin, Albion (Lawyer)
Lydia Bailey - Kenneth Roberts 5387

Hammett, Cain (Cowboy)
Riders of Judgment - Frederick F. Manfred 4059

Hammond, Annabella (Spouse)
The Far Side of Home - Maggie Davis 1536

Hammond, Charlotte (Orphan)
City of Golden Cages - Jo Germany 2358

Hammond, Clay (Heir)
Bright Feather - Robert Wilder 6750

Hammond, Elizabeth (Gentlewoman)
Trumpet at the Gate - Jan Widgery 6739

Hammond, Helena (Gentlewoman)
Men Were Deceivers Ever - Patricia Veryan 6470

Hammond, Sarah (Spy)
Ironclads: Man-of-War - Larry D. Names 4554

Hampton, Caroline (Businesswoman)
The Hampton Women - Julie Ellis 1921

Hampton, Caroline (Heiress; Orphan)
The Hampton Heritage - Julie Ellis 1920

Hampton, Elizabeth (Teenager)
The Hampton Women - Julie Ellis 1921

Hampton, Eric (Political Figure)
The Hampton Heritage - Julie Ellis 1920

Hampton, Josiah (Businessman)
The Hampton Heritage - Julie Ellis 1920

Hampton, Maureen (Bastard Daughter)
The Hampton Women - Julie Ellis 1921

Hampton, Merit (Young Woman)
Angel with Spurs - Paul I. Wellman 6613

Hampton, Molly (Young Woman)
Private Knowledge - Betty Palmer Nelson 4576

Hampton, Tina (Spouse)
The Hampton Heritage - Julie Ellis 1920

Hanard, Audrey (Orphan; Ward)
Audrey - Mary Johnston 3229

Hanbury, Edwin (Engineer)
The Summer of the Royal Visit - Isabel
  Colegate 1199

Hancock, Leah (Settler)
Deepwater: A Novel of the Carolinas - Pamela
  Jekel 3185

Hand, Carrie (Publisher)
Dutch Uncle - Marilyn Durham 1815

Handy, Nicholas (Bastard Son)
Benjamin Franklin and a Case of Artful Murder -
  Robert Lee Hall 2654
Benjamin Franklin and a Case of Christmas Murder -
  Robert Lee Hall 2655
Benjamin Franklin Takes the Case - Robert Lee
  Hall 2656
Murder at Drury Lane - Robert Lee Hall 2659
Murder by the Waters - Robert Lee Hall 2661

Hanks, Rome (Military Personnel)
The History of Rome Hanks - Joseph Stanley
  Pennell 4909

Hanna, Caroline (Fugitive)
Miami: A Saga - Evelyn Wilde Mayerson 4204

Hanna, Chad (Orphan; Worker)
Chad Hanna - Walter D. Edmonds 1873

Hanna, Giles (Military Personnel)
*The Sounds of Chariots: A Novel of John Sevier and
  the State of Franklin* - Helen Topping Miller 4396

Hannah, Alfred Doolittle (Businessman)
The Hyde Park Murder - Elliott Roosevelt 5443

Hannah, Zach (Mountain Man)
High Country - Jason Manning 4075

Hansa, Beret (Settler)
Giants in the Earth - O.E. Rolvaag 5434

Hansa, Per (Settler)
Giants in the Earth - O.E. Rolvaag 5434

Hanshiro, Tosano (Warrior)
The Tokaido Road: A Novel of Feudal Japan - Lucia
  St. Clair Robson 5417

Hanson, Rolf (Gentleman)
Midsummer's Eve - Philippa Carr 924

Hapgood, Nathaniel (Settler)
Beneath the Blue Mountain - Richard S.
  Wheeler 6656

Haraldsson, Sweyn (Young Man)
The Cross and the Sword - Evangeline Walton 6558

Harbin, Joan (Young Woman)
A Question of Honour - Clifford Dowdey 1707

Harbourne, Grizelda (Young Woman)
The Holy Innocents - Kate Sedley 5717

Harcombe, Clement (Entertainer)
English Music - Peter Ackroyd 18

Harcombe, Timothy (Psychic)
English Music - Peter Ackroyd 18

Hard-Heart (Indian)
The Prairie - James Fenimore Cooper 1308

Hardacre, Mary (Spouse)
Hardacre - C.L. Skelton 5872

Hardacre, Sam (Worker; Businessman)
Hardacre - C.L. Skelton 5872

Hardacre, Shane (Gambler)
Fire Along the Sky: A Novel of America - Robert
  Moss 4497

Hardeman, Chris (Scout)
The Snowblind Moon - John Byrne Cooke 1267

Hardenberg, Claus von (Nobleman)
Once a Gentleman - Donald James 3157

Hardhardt, Frances (Saloon Keeper/Owner)
Pacific Street - Cecelia Holland 2993

Harding, Caroline (Young Woman)
Mistaken Virtues - Joanna Trollope 6349

Harding, Fanny (Heroine)
The Bride of the Wilderness - Charles McCarry 4220

Harding, Rance (Teenager; Orphan)
Pioneer Breed - Glenn R. Vernam 6453

Hardinge, George Nicholas (Military Personnel)
The Long Fight - D.A. Rayner 5270

Hardwick, George (Heir; Gentleman)
Master of Morholm - Timothy R. Wilson 6817

Hardwick, James (Gentleman)
Master of Morholm - Timothy R. Wilson 6817

Hardwick, Mary (Orphan)
Master of Morholm - Timothy R. Wilson 6817

Hardy, Alice (Businesswoman)
A Woman by Design - Frances Kennett 3426

Hardy, Jim (Prospector)
The Goldseekers - William R. Burnett 794

Hardy, Yule (Rancher)
The Bad Lands - Oakley Hall 2651

Hare, Margaret (Young Woman)
In the Days of Poor Richard - Irving A.
  Bacheller 259

Haredale, John (Gentleman)
Barnaby Rudge: A Tale of the Riots of Eighty -
  Charles Dickens 1641

Haredon, Caroline (Convict; Servant)
Beyond the Blue Mountains - Jean Plaidy 5006

Hargrave, Samantha (Doctor)
Domina - Barbara Wood 6847

Hargreave, William (Detective—Police)
The Adventure of the Stalwart Companions - H. Paul
  Jeffers 3177

Harinxma, Martinus (Sea Captain)
The Centurion - Jan de Hartog 2762

Harinxma, Sylvia (Spouse)
The Centurion - Jan de Hartog 2762

Harkana (Indian)
The Moon Stallion - Jim Berry 484

Harker, Tom (Worker)
The Shooting Party - Isabel Colegate 1197

Harkfast (Religious)
Harkfast: The Making of the King - Hugh C.
  Rae 5238

Harkness, Bruce (Settler; Prospector)
The Treasure of Pleasant Valley - Frank Yerby 6928

Harley, Arabella (Young Woman)
Castle Malindine - Hilary Ford 2163

Harley, Ranger (Nobleman)
Emily Goes to Exeter - Marion Chesney 1027

Harlow, George (Nobleman; Heir)
The Heart of the Rose - June Barraclough 346

Harmachis (Religious; Magician)
Cleopatra - H. Rider Haggard 2637

Harman, Perry (Settler)
The Salt and the Savor - Howard William
  Troyer 6354

Harmonia (Religious)
Gate to the Sea - Bryher 743

Harmonie, Gennie (Servant)
Gennie the Huguenot Woman - Bette M. Ross 5464

Harmony, Desire (Outcast; Prostitute)
Stars on the Sea - F. van Wyck Mason 4161

Harp (Detective—Private)
Scarlet Women - J.D. Christilian 1077

Harpcore, Dennison (Landowner; Rake)
The Parson's Daughter - Catherine Cookson 1286

Harper, Allan (Farmer)
Golden Horizons - William Corcoran 1324

Harper, David (Military Personnel; Captive)
*Eagle of Niagara: The Story of David Harper and His
  Indian Captivity* - John Brick 671

Harper, Elizabeth (Spouse)
Ghost Woman - Lawrence Thornton 6275

Harper, Henry (Settler)
Ghost Woman - Lawrence Thornton 6275

Harper, Hume (Banker)
Sing One Song - Helen Topping Miller 4394

Harper, Patrick (Military Personnel)
Sharpe's Company - Bernard Cornwell 1339
Sharpe's Devil - Bernard Cornwell 1340
Sharpe's Eagle - Bernard Cornwell 1341
Sharpe's Enemy - Bernard Cornwell 1342
Sharpe's Gold - Bernard Cornwell 1343
Sharpe's Regiment - Bernard Cornwell 1345
Sharpe's Revenge - Bernard Cornwell 1346
Sharpe's Rifles - Bernard Cornwell 1347
Sharpe's Sword - Bernard Cornwell 1349
Waterloo - Bernard Cornwell 1350

Harper, Thomas (Military Personnel)
Sharpe's Battle - Bernard Cornwell 1338

Harper, William (Young Man)
Sing One Song - Helen Topping Miller 4394

Harrach, Karl Von (Nobleman)
World and Paradise - Edgar Maas 3953

Harrap (Royalty)
The Seeking - Robert S. Elegant 1906

Harrifield, Emma (Abolitionist)
Caleb Pettengill U.S.N. - George Fielding Eliot 1912

Harrigan, John (Spouse)
Julia's Last Hope - Janette Oke 4708

Harrigan, Julia (Spouse)
Julia's Last Hope - Janette Oke 4708

Harrington, Edward Albert (Religious)
Grandmother and the Priests - Taylor Caldwell 857

Harrington, Lee (Young Man)
The History of Rome Hanks - Joseph Stanley
  Pennell 4909

Harrington, Pinckney (Military Personnel)
The History of Rome Hanks - Joseph Stanley
Pennell 4909

Harris (Animal)
The Queen and I - Sue Townsend 6306

Harris, Clayton (Military Personnel; Gentleman)
The Last Plantation - Don Wright 6879

Harris, David (Artist)
The Master of Oakwindsor - Douglas Kent
Hall 2648

Harris, Lady Douglass (Gentlewoman)
Captain Barney - Jan Westcott 6642

Harris, Laura (Gentlewoman)
Kezzy - Patricia Burns 799

Harris, Stacey (Veteran)
Gentlemen, Hush! - Jere Hungerford
Wheelwright 6668

Harrison, Abigail (Young Woman)
Abigail - Mary Louise Aswell 221

Harrison, Donnigan (Farmer)
A Bride for Donnigan - Janette Oke 4705

Harrison, Francie (Heiress—Dispossessed)
Fortune Is a Woman - Elizabeth Adler 39

Harrison, Gabriel (Settler)
The Yemassee - William Gilmore Simms 5855

Harrison, Tinkler (Settler)
The Land Breakers - John Ehle 1895

Harron, Kirby (Businessman)
Sing for a Penny - Clifford Dowdey 1708

Harrow, Dan (Farmer)
Rome Haul - Walter D. Edmonds 1877

Harrow, Dan (Pioneer)
Mountains Ahead - Martha Ferguson
McKeown 4284

Harrow, Harmony (Pioneer)
Mountains Ahead - Martha Ferguson
McKeown 4284

Harsom, Alexandra bat (Gentlewoman)
The Tenth Measure - Brenda Lesley Segal 5721

Hart, Aaron (Heir)
Devil's Fire, Love's Revenge - Barbara Paul 4836

Hart, Amy (Spy)
The Storm Witch - Elisabeth Barr 339

Hart, Euphemia (Gentlewoman)
Plain Jane - Marion Chesney 1045

Hart, Jane (Gentlewoman)
Plain Jane - Marion Chesney 1045

Hart, Matthew (Ranger)
Waltzing in Ragtime - Eileen Charbonneau 996

Hart, Nash (Military Personnel)
High Hearts - Rita Mae Brown 728

Hart, Nathan (Teacher)
Genesee Fever - Carl Lamson Carmer 898

Hart, Worth (Hunter)
One of the Raymonds - Jean Rikhoff 5332

Harte, Jack (Veteran)
The Ways of Women - Elaine Crowley 1436

Harte, Joanna (Rancher)
San Antone - V.J. Banis 288

Harte, Julia (Spouse)
The Ways of Women - Elaine Crowley 1436

Harte, Lewis (Rancher)
San Antone - V.J. Banis 288

Hartford, Meredith (Gentlewoman)
My Lord Foxe - Constance Gluyas 2443

Hartley, Derrick (Businessman)
Portrait in Brownstone - Louis Auchincloss 232

Hartley, Ida Trask (Gentlewoman)
Portrait in Brownstone - Louis Auchincloss 232

Hartnett, Emily (Teacher)
Mamigon - Jack Hashian 2772

Hartwell, Amaryllis (Gentlewoman; Student)
Miss Hartwell's Dilemma - Carola Dunn 1796

Hartwell, Jane (Servant)
Version and Diversion - Judith Terry 6207

Harvard, Carne (Orphan)
The Fox-Red Hills - Cynthia S. Roberts 5374

Harvard, Georgina (Gentlewoman)
Lord Rivington's Lady - Eileen Jackson 3134

Harvard, Mostyn (Orphan)
The Fox-Red Hills - Cynthia S. Roberts 5374

Harvard, Penelope (Gentlewoman)
Lord Rivington's Lady - Eileen Jackson 3134

Harvard, Peregrine (Gentleman)
Lord Rivington's Lady - Eileen Jackson 3134

Harvey, David (Gentleman)
The Long Afternoon - Ursula Zilinsky 6964

Harvie, Dion (Gentleman)
Roanoke Renegade - Don Tracy 6311

Harvill, Clarissa (Convict)
The Truelove - Patrick O'Brian 4677

Harwar, Simon Basil (Sailor)
Voyage: A Novel of 1896 - Sterling Hayden 2798

Harwood, Lord (Nobleman)
Court of Shadows - Cynthia Morgan 4450

Hasan, Abu (Nobleman)
The Infidel - Georgia Elizabeth Taylor 6182

Hascott, Warren (Veteran)
The Regulators - William Degenhard 1580

Hasdai, Gabriela (Young Woman)
The Spanish Doctor - Matt Cohen 1159

Haseman, Karen (Settler; Spouse)
White Man - Peter Freuchen 2228

Haseman, Peter (Convict; Settler)
White Man - Peter Freuchen 2228

Hasford, Catrina (Heroine)
Come Winter - Douglas C. Jones 3275

Hasford, Martin (Military Personnel; Farmer)
The Barefoot Brigade - Douglas C. Jones 3274

Hasford, Ora (Farmer)
Elkhorn Tavern - Douglas C. Jones 3278

Hasford, Roman (Businessman)
Roman - Douglas C. Jones 3281

Hasford, Roman (Farmer)
Elkhorn Tavern - Douglas C. Jones 3278

Hasford, Roman (Political Figure; Businessman)
Come Winter - Douglas C. Jones 3275

Haskell, Fred (Young Man)
Where Is My Wandering Boy Tonight? - David
Wagoner 6522

Haslam, Robert (Religious)
For God and Glory - Tim Jeal 3171

Haslewood, Jenny (Young Woman)
The White Witch - Elizabeth Goudge 2496

Hassler, Josephine (Gentlewoman)
The Murder at Impasse Louvaine - Richard
Grayson 2562

Hastings (Nobleman)
The Viking - Edison Marshall 4113

Hastings, Anthony (Military Personnel)
The Coat I Wore - Lucile Finlay 2090

Hastings, Marilyn (Young Woman)
An American, Sir - Corwin Root 5459

Hastings, Walter (Rancher)
Tamzen - Jane Gilmore Rushing 5530

Hastings of Trent (Heiress)
Rosehaven - Catherine Coulter 1380

Hatcher, Nate (Military Personnel)
Doniphan's Ride - Les Savage Jr. 5620

Hathaway, Bess (Streetperson; Madam)
Beau Barron's Lady - Helen Ashfield 204

Hatton, Glen (Teenager; Con Artist)
Poor Boy and a Long Way Home - James
Sherburne 5806

Havenell, Francis (Young Man)
The Bright Face of Danger - Clifford Sublette 6108

Havering, Clara (Gentlewoman)
Meridon - Philippa Gregory 2583

Haversham, John (Businessman)
The Haversham Legacy - Daoma Winston 6827

Haversham, Miranda (Young Woman)
The Haversham Legacy - Daoma Winston 6827

Haversham, Reed (Veteran)
The Haversham Legacy - Daoma Winston 6827

Haversham, Stuart (Nobleman)
Crystal - Helen Ashfield 205

Havisham, Estella (Young Woman)
Estella - Alanna Knight 3519

Haward, Marmaduke (Young Man)
Audrey - Mary Johnston 3229

Hawk, John (Indian; Warrior)
The Overmountain Men - Cameron Judd 3315

Hawke, Derek (Landowner)
Love's Tender Fury - Jennifer Wilde 6749

Hawke, Lemuel (Frontiersman)
The Medicine Horn - Jory Sherman 5820
Trapper's Moon - Jory Sherman 5823

Hawke, Morgan (Child)
The Medicine Horn - Jory Sherman 5820

Hawke, Morgan (Frontiersman; Teenager)
Trapper's Moon - Jory Sherman 5823

Hawke, Roberta (Spouse)
The Medicine Horn - Jory Sherman 5820

Hawkes, Gideon (Landowner)
The Fireflower - Edith Layton 3687

Hawkes, Robert (Sea Captain)
The Pearl Pagoda - Susannah Broome 707

Hawkhurst, Garret (Rake)
Some Brief Folly - Patricia Veryan 6478

Hawkins, Caleb (Military Personnel)
The Year of the Spaniard - Henry Castor 956

Hawkins, James (Doctor)
The Adventures of Long John Silver - Denis
Judd 3317
Return to Treasure Island - Denis Judd 3318

Hawkins, Jim (Sailor)
Treasure Island - Robert Louis Stevenson 6012

Hawkins, Willard J. (Doctor)
Buffalo Coat - Carol Brink 691

Hawkridge, Sir Waldo (Nobleman; Philanthropist)
The Nonesuch - Georgette Heyer 2896

Hawk's Shadow (Indian; Warrior)
This Land Is Mine - Frances Casey Kerns 3470

Hawksworth, Brian (Military Personnel)
The Moghul - Thomas Hoover 3026

Hawley, Andrew (Military Personnel)
The Settlers - William Stuart Long 3878

Hawley, Andrew (Political Figure)
The Traitors - William Stuart Long 3879

Hawley, Jenny (Settler)
The Explorers - William Stuart Long 3872

Hawley, Theron (Veteran)
Morning Time - Charles Kendall O'Neill 4743

Haworth, Ephraim (Religious)
Jason McGee - Robert H. Fowler 2190

Hawthorne, Cecily (Orphan; Servant)
Chelsea - Nancy Fitzgerald 2114

Hawthorne, Chadwick (Heir; Nobleman)
Chelynne - Robyn Carr 938

Hawthorne, Jennie (Young Woman)
Jennie about to Be - Elisabeth Ogilvie 4694

Hawthorne, Jessica (Gentlewoman)
The Hawthorne Legacy - Teresa Crane 1416

Haybury, Frederick (Gentleman)
Wings of the Morning - David Beaty 402

Hayden, Bob (Military Personnel)
Banner at Shenandoah - Bruce Catton 963

Hayden de Morgan, Pieter (Landowner)
The Great Sky and the Silence - James S. Rand 5245

Hayes, Diana (Gentlewoman)
We Stood for Freedom - Iris Morley 4455

Hayes, Porter (Military Personnel)
The Amulet - Hal Borland 582

Hayman, George (Journalist)
Love and Honor - Leslie Arlen 189

Haynes, Jo (Bastard Son; Adventurer)
Our Jo, or The Chronicle of a Coming Man - Kenneth M. Cameron 868

Haynes, Ruth (Immigrant)
The Cavalryman - Harold Sinclair 5861

Haynow, Anna (Spouse)
The Drums of Winter - Sandra Paretti 4790

Haynow, Claus (Military Personnel)
The Drums of Winter - Sandra Paretti 4790

Haynow, Gottfried (Nobleman)
The Drums of Winter - Sandra Paretti 4790

Hays, Jake (Police Officer)
The High Constable - Maan Meyers 4353

Hazard, George (Military Personnel)
Love and War - John Jakes 3150
North and South - John Jakes 3151

Hazard, George (Veteran)
Heaven and Hell - John Jakes 3147

Hazard, Matthew Carlton (Military Personnel)
Distant Trumpet - Paul Horgan 3032

Hazard, Phillip (Military Personnel)
Brave Captains - Vivian Stuart 6086
Hazard of Huntress - Vivian Stuart 6087
Hazard's Command - Vivian Stuart 6088
The Valiant Sailors - Vivian Stuart 6090
Victory at Sebastopol - Vivian Stuart 6091

Hazard, Rufus (Military Personnel)
My Blood and My Treasure - Mary Schumann 5674

Hazard, Tom (Frontiersman)
Tennessee Hazard - Maristan Chapman 994

Hazlitt, Isaiah (Sea Captain)
The Yankee Brig - Carter A. Vaughan 6443

Hazzard, Hugo (Nobleman)
The American Heiress - Dorothy Eden 1854

Heads Off (Indian; Chieftain)
The Elk-Dog Heritage - Don Coldsmith 1174
Follow the Wind - Don Coldsmith 1176
Moon of Thunder - Don Coldsmith 1180

Healey, Celia (Young Woman)
All Their Kingdoms - Madeleine Polland 5084

Heath, Emma Louise (Orphan; Imposter)
The Pilgrimage - Ann B. Ross 5463

Heath, Jared (Military Personnel)
Company of Cowards - Jack Schaefer 5634

Heath, Jessie (Orphan; Teenager)
The Pilgrimage - Ann B. Ross 5463

Heath, Keziah (Servant)
Kezzy - Patricia Burns 799

Heath, Micah (Military Personnel)
Enough Good Men - Charles Mercer 4336

Heath, Miranda (Orphan)
Sea Jade - Phyllis A. Whitney 6717

Heathcliff (Outcast)
H.—: The Story of Heathcliff's Journey Back to Wuthering Heights - Lin Haire-Sargeant 2641

Heathcote, Frances (Noblewoman)
Garnet - Helen Ashfield 207

Heathcote, Jonathan (Nobleman)
Garnet - Helen Ashfield 207

Heathcote, Mark (Settler)
The Wept of Wish-Ton-Wish - James Fenimore Cooper 1312

Heather (Child)
The Aviator - Ernest K. Gann 2277

Heathers, Robert (Fugitive)
A Candle in the Wilderness - Irving A. Bacheller 256

Heatherton, Robin (Spy)
Thin Moon and Cold Mist - Kathleen O'Neal Gear 2330

Heatherton, William (Religious)
The Heatherton Heritage - Pamela Hill 2934

Hebert, Antoine (Doctor)
All Souls' Rising - Madison Smartt Bell 422

Hebron, Eli (Businessman)
The Dream Lover - Mark Upton 6392

Hebworthy, Daniel (Gentleman)
Flowers for Lilian - Anna Gilbert 2405

Hector (Warrior)
The Trojan Generals Talk: Memoirs of the Greek War - Phillip Parotti 4818
Troy - Richard Matturro 4194
Whom the Gods Would Destroy - Richard Powell 5148

Hedges, Jasper (Adventurer)
The Voyagers - Dale Van Every 6412

Hedrick, Tjaden (Military Personnel)
Gettysburg - Stephen Longstreet 3887

Heggie, Calvin (Trader)
The Kidnapped Surgeon - Alexander Knox 3527

Heidemann, Hauptmann Otto (Military Personnel)
The Blue Max - Jack D. Hunter 3085

Heiden, Boris (Revolutionary)
Give Me the Daggers - Catherine Gavin 2321

Heindrichs, Gwendolyn (Teacher)
The Garfield Honor - Frank Yerby 6918

Helen (Heroine)
Ashes - Stefan Zeromski 6960

Helen of Troy (Noblewoman)
The Firebrand - Marion Zimmer Bradley 624
The Invaders - Peter Danielson 1469
The Promised Land - Peter Danielson 1471
Scandal in Troy - Eva Hemmer Hansen 2679
Troy - Richard Matturro 4194
Whom the Gods Would Destroy - Richard Powell 5148

Helen of Troy (Royalty)
The Goddess - Miranda Seymour 5763
Paris of Troy - George Baker 273
The Private Life of Helen of Troy - John Erskine 1957

Helford, Ruark (Pirate; Nobleman)
The Pirate and the Pagan - Virginia Henley 2827

Heliokleia (Royalty)
Horses of Heaven - Gillian Bradshaw 630

Helios (Servant)
Whom the Gods Would Destroy - Richard Powell 5148

Hellbane, Nicholas (Fanatic)
Hellbane - Anthony Esler 1963

Heller, Nate (Detective—Private)
Carnal Hours - Max Allan Collins 1210
Stolen Away - Max Allan Collins 1213
True Crime - Max Allan Collins 1214

Heller, Nate (Police Officer; Detective—Private)
True Detective - Max Allan Collins 1215

Hellier, Colonel (Military Personnel)
Wintercombe - Pamela Belle 435

Helm, Leonard (Military Personnel)
The Big Knives - Bruce Lancaster 3635

Helphand, Alexander (Doctor)
The Petrograd Consignment - Owen Sela 5739

Hemings, Harriet (Abolitionist; Nurse)
The President's Daughter - Barbara Chase-Riboud 1005

Hencke, Peter (Military Personnel)
Last Man to Die - Michael Dobbs 1652

Hendee, Alma (Gentlewoman)
The Green Mountain Boys - Daniel Pierce Thompson 6249

Henderson, Mattie (Spouse)
Freedom's Banner - Teresa Crane 1415

Henderson, Ral (Young Woman)
Pursuit of Bliss - Betty Palmer Nelson 4577

Henderson, Simon (Spouse)
Private Knowledge - Betty Palmer Nelson 4576

Hendrick, Allen (Plantation Owner)
Sojourn of a Stranger - Walter Sullivan 6115

Hendricks, Colonel John B. (Landowner)
A Woman of Texas - R.T. Stevens 6002

Henley, Susan (Widow(er))
Logic of the Heart - Patricia Veryan 6466

Henna, Jesse (Heroine)
Ben Retallick - E.V. Thompson 6263

Henneker, Victor (Journalist; Writer)
Victim of the Aurora - Thomas Keneally 3417

Henniker, John (Religious)
The Rogue and the Witch - John Edward Newton 4605

Henning, Johannes (Religious)
Articles of Faith - Ronald Harwood 2770

Henri, Father (Religious)
Dubu: A Novel of New Guinean Conquest - Maslyn Williams 6789

Henry, Byron (Military Personnel)
War and Remembrance - Herman Wouk 6875

Henry, Byron (Young Man)
The Winds of War - Herman Wouk 6876

Henry, Cadmus (Military Personnel)
Cadmus Henry - Walter D. Edmonds 1872

Henry, Victor (Military Personnel)
War and Remembrance - Herman Wouk 6875
The Winds of War - Herman Wouk 6876

Henslow, Philip (Prospector)
Journey - James A. Michener 4371

Hepburn, Allan (Spy)
Captain Cut-Throat - John Dickson Carr 908

Hepburn, Philip (Clerk)
Sylvia's Lovers - Elizabeth Gaskell 2312

Her-Bak (Child; Servant)
Her-Bak: The Living Face of Ancient Egypt - Isha
  Schwaller de Lubicz 5676

Heraldsson, Rorik (Warrior)
Lord of Hawkfell Island - Catherine Coulter 1376

Herbert, Clarissa (Teacher; Spinster)
The Shadowed Spring - Carola Salisbury 5571

Herbert, Thomas (Gentleman)
The Severed Crown - Jane Lane 3657

Herbert of Garstang (Artisan)
The White Cutter - David Pownall 5158

Herbertson, Hedric (Architect)
The White Cutter - David Pownall 5158

Hercules (Adventurer)
Earth Giant - Edison Marshall 4106
Hercules, My Shipmate - Robert Graves 2545

Herennius, Favorinus (Nobleman)
Confessors of the Name - Gladys Schmitt 5640

Hereward (Knight)
Count Robert of Paris - Sir Walter Scott 5695

Herger (Warrior)
Eaters of the Dead - Michael Crichton 1425

Herington, Allegra (Gentlewoman)
Allegra - Clare Darcy 1483

Herington, Derek (Military Personnel)
Allegra - Clare Darcy 1483

Herington, Hilary (Gentlewoman)
Allegra - Clare Darcy 1483

Heriot, Miranda (Orphan; Actress)
The Shakespeare Girl - Mollie Hardwick 2698

Herlvin, Brother (Religious)
The Holy Thief - Ellis Peters 4962

Herma (Singer)
Herma - Macdonald Harris 2726

Hermione (Young Woman)
The Private Life of Helen of Troy - John
  Erskine 1957

Herne the Hunter (Demon; Spirit)
Windsor Castle - William Harrison Ainsworth 59

Heron (Prehistoric Human; Shaman)
People of the Wolf - W. Michael Gear 2341

Heron, Alathea (Artist)
Alethea - Pamela Belle 429

Heron, Lady Amanda (Gentlewoman)
My Lady Hoyden - Jane Sheridan 5812

Heron, Christopher (Gentleman; Courtier)
The Lodestar - Pamela Belle 432

Heron, Francis (Gentleman)
The Moon in the Water - Pamela Belle 433

Heron, Francis (Military Personnel)
The Chains of Fate - Pamela Belle 430

Heron, Lisa (Orphan; Musician)
Castle of Eagles - Constance Heaven 2804

Heron, Lucy (Gentlewoman)
The Quickenberry Tree - Annette Motley 4502

Heron, Maeve (Actress; Widow(er))
This Willing Passion - Patricia Cloud 1132

Heron, Sabrina (Young Woman)
Sabrina - Madeleine Polland 5086

Heron, Thomazine (Gentlewoman)
The Chains of Fate - Pamela Belle 430

Heron, Thomazine (Heiress; Orphan)
The Moon in the Water - Pamela Belle 433

Heron of Foix (Student)
A Walk with Love and Death - Hans Koning 3539

Herrick, Beau (Military Personnel)
The Wilderness Brigade - Phyllis Gordon
  Demarest 1605

Herrick, Emmeline (Southern Belle)
The Wilderness Brigade - Phyllis Gordon
  Demarest 1605

Herrick, Thomas (Military Personnel)
Form Line of Battle! - Alexander Kent 3431
Passage to Mutiny - Alexander Kent 3436
Signal—Close Action! - Alexander Kent 3438
To Glory We Steer - Alexander Kent 3442
A Tradition of Victory - Alexander Kent 3443

Herries, Benjamin "Benjie" (Gentleman)
Vanessa - Hugh Walpole 6548

Herries, Ellis (Gentleman)
Vanessa - Hugh Walpole 6548

Herries, Francis (Adventurer)
Rogue Herries - Hugh Walpole 6547

Herries, Nicholas (Landowner)
Katherine Christian - Hugh Walpole 6546

Herries, Walter (Gentleman)
The Fortress - Hugh Walpole 6544

Herries, William (Gentleman)
Judith Paris - Hugh Walpole 6545

Herriot, Kate (Actress)
Kate - Brian Cleeve 1109

Hervey, Jane (Heiress)
An Innocent Woman - Malcolm Macdonald 3967

Hervey, Penitence (Teenager)
Campion Towers - John Beatty 401

Hervey, Winifred (Gentlewoman)
Pandora's Galley - Macdonald Harris 2727

Hesketh, Eleanor (Gentlewoman)
A Woman's Age - Rachel Billington 499

Hesketh, Violet (Gentlewoman)
A Woman's Age - Rachel Billington 499

Hesperian, Gaius (Military Personnel)
Dogheaded Death - Ray Faraday Nelson 4581

Hessenfield, Lord (Nobleman)
The Song of the Siren - Philippa Carr 929

Heulwen (Widow(er))
The Running Vixen - Elizabeth Chadwick 968

Hewitt, Laura (Gentlewoman)
Zemindar - Valerie Fitzgerald 2117

Hewitt, Maggie (Businesswoman)
The Harrogate Secret - Catherine Cookson 1278

Hewitt, Thomas (Young Man)
*Look to Your Geese: A Novel of the Deflowering of
  New England* - Jacquin Sanders 5584

Heydon, William (Fugitive)
A Candle in the Wilderness - Irving A.
  Bacheller 256

Heyets (Indian; Warrior)
From Where the Sun Now Stands - Will Henry 2841

Heywood, Charley (Spy)
Conspiracy of Knaves - Dee Brown 711

Heywood, Thomas (Military Personnel)
Presumption: An Entertainment - Julia Barrett 350

Hickey, Margaret (Immigrant)
Men of No Property - Dorothy Davis 1517

Hickey, Norah (Immigrant)
Men of No Property - Dorothy Davis 1517

Hiero of Marathon (Young Man)
The Shining - Stephen Marlowe 4097

Higganbotham, David (Doctor)
The Spoils of Eden - Robert H. Fowler 2193

Higgins, Elizabeth (Settler)
The Strange Death of Mistress Coffin - Robert J.
  Begiebing 415

Higgins, Gerald (Student)
Ourselves to Know - John O'Hara 4704

Higgins, Porteous (Businessman)
The Halfhyde Line - Philip McCutchan 4249

Highet, Henry (Gentleman)
The Country Gentleman - Fiona Hill 2924

Hilary of Bordeaux (Young Man)
The Four Rivers of Paradise - Helen Constance
  White 6678

Hildreth, Anne (Spouse)
The Lotus and the Wind - John Masters 4175

Hill, Arabella (Gentlewoman)
Quicksilver Lady - Barbara Whitehead 6707

Hill, Caroline (Spouse)
The Caretaker Wife - Barbara Whitehead 6706

Hill, James (Financier)
Path of the Sun - Al Dempsey 1608

Hill, Leah (Gentlewoman)
Savage Gentleman - Noel B. Gerson 2381

Hill, Marion (Military Personnel)
The Strong Men - John Brick 677

Hill, Matt (Military Personnel)
The Strong Men - John Brick 677

Hill, Sir Sigismund (Businessman)
For My Great Folly - Thomas B. Costain 1365

Hill, Sophia (Young Woman)
Princess Sophia - Edison Marshall 4110

Hillaby (Slave; Servant)
The Bondswoman - Caryl Ledner 3705

Hillard, Sheldon (Gentleman)
Storm Against the Wind - Helen Hull Jacobs 3138

Hilliard, John (Military Personnel)
Strange Meeting - Susan Hill 2952

Hillyard, David (Gentleman)
The Eagle at the Gate - Rona Randall 5248

Hilton, Andhra (Spouse; Royalty)
Star of Randevi - Marjorie McEvoy 4270

Hilton, Andhra (Young Woman)
The Sleeping Tiger - Marjorie McEvoy 4269

Hilton, Anthony (Plantation Owner)
Black Dawn - Christopher Nicole 4613

Hilton, Hope (Young Woman)
Tavern in the Town - Cecile Hulse Matschat 4187

Hilton, Jim (Military Personnel)
How Young They Die - Stuart Cloete 1124

Hilton, Kit (Pirate)
The Devil's Own - Christopher Nicole 4615

Hilton, Martha (Captive)
Indian Brother - Hubert Coryell 1354

Hilton, Matt (Young Man)
Mistress of Darkness - Christopher Nicole 4617

Hilton, Meg (Young Woman)
Sunset - Christopher Nicole 4623

Hilton, Richard (Plantation Owner)
Black Dawn - Christopher Nicole 4613

Hilton, Robert (Plantation Owner)
Mistress of Darkness - Christopher Nicole 4617

Hilton, Sam (Captive)
Indian Brother - Hubert Coryell   1354

Hilyard, Geoff (Heir)
Cape Cod - William Martin   4139

Hilyard, Jack (Settler)
Cape Cod - William Martin   4139

Hind, Jason (Sea Captain)
The Witch of Manga Reva - Garland Roark   5359

Hindfoot (Indian; Chieftain)
Look to Your Geese: A Novel of the Deflowering of New England - Jacquin Sanders   5584

Hingham, Judith (Young Woman)
East of the Giants - George Rippey Stewart   6027

Hintermayer, Berchtold (Servant)
The Heidenmauer - James Fenimore Cooper   1301

Hippolita (Ruler)
The Bull From the Sea - Mary Renault   5295

Hippolochus (Hero)
Three Ships and Three Kings - Georgia Sallaska   5573

Hippolytos (Bastard Son)
The Bull From the Sea - Mary Renault   5295

Hiram (Prehistoric Human)
Shiva: An Adventure of the Ice Age - J.H. Brennan   657

Hiram (Warrior)
The Trojan - Noel B. Gerson   2386

Hitchcock, Hugh (Cowboy)
The Day the Cowboys Quit - Elmer Kelton   3403

Hite, Fred (Businessman)
Herma - Macdonald Harris   2726

Hobbs, Maria Zion (Young Woman)
The Fairbrothers - Clark McMeekin   4291

Hodano (Indian; Shaman)
Manitou - Donald Clayton Porter   5120
Spirit Knife - Donald Clayton Porter   5128

Hofman, Camilla (Businesswoman)
The Wishing Tree - Sandra Paretti   4794

Hofman, Fritz (Businessman)
The Wishing Tree - Sandra Paretti   4794

Hojo, Muchaku (Religious)
Segaki - David Stacton   5975

Hojo, Yasumaro (Artist)
Segaki - David Stacton   5975

Holcomb, Amelia (Widow(er))
Too Long at the Dance - Mike Blakely   539

Holcomb, Arthur Jackson Jr. (Young Man)
Where Is My Wandering Boy Tonight? - David Wagoner   6522

Holcomb, Caleb (Cowboy; Musician)
Too Long at the Dance - Mike Blakely   539

Holden, Chris (Frontiersman)
The Unconquered - Neil Harmon Swanson   6142

Holder, Nicholas (Gentleman)
Bennett's Welcome - Inglis Fletcher   2132

Holland, Frank (Revolutionary; Worker)
Beauty for Ashes - Timothy R. Wilson   6816

Holland, James Noel (Nobleman)
Edward, Edward - Lolah Burford   772

Hollander, Jake (Lawman)
Dutch Uncle - Marilyn Durham   1815

Holles, Clemency (Gentlewoman)
A Place of Ravens - Pamela Hill   2942

Hollingshead, Irene (Businesswoman; Madam)
Paradise Falls - Don Robertson   5399

Hollingsworth, Lydia (Gentlewoman)
My Dear Cousin - Peggy Hoffmann   2977

Hollingworth, Daniel (Farmer)
Come Spring - Charlotte Hinger   2954

Hollis, America (Pioneer)
The Overland Trail - Wendi Lee   3712

Hollis, Hero (Young Woman)
Trade Wind - M.M. Kaye   3378

Hollister, Althea (Settler)
The Women at Pine Creek - Allis McKay   4279

Hollister, Corrie Belle (Journalist)
Sea to Shining Sea - Michael Phillips   4990

Hollister, Corrie Belle (Pioneer)
My Father's World - Michael Phillips   4989

Hollister, Mary (Settler)
The Women at Pine Creek - Allis McKay   4279

Holloway, George (Judge)
Warlock - Oakley Hall   2653

Holloway, Jonas (Farmer; Military Personnel)
Day of Battle - Frederic F. Van de Water   6402

Holm, Beret (Farmer)
Their Fathers' God - O.E. Rolvaag   5436

Holm, Beret (Settler)
Peder Victorious - O.E. Rolvaag   5435

Holm, Dina (Young Woman)
Dina's Book - Herbjorg Wassmo   6577

Holm, Peder Victorious (Farmer)
Peder Victorious - O.E. Rolvaag   5435

Holm, Peder Victorious (Farmer; Political Figure)
Their Fathers' God - O.E. Rolvaag   5436

Holm, Peer (Immigrant; Farmer)
The Great Hunger - Johan Bojer   562

Holm, Susie (Farmer)
Their Fathers' God - O.E. Rolvaag   5436

Holmes, David J. (Psychic)
The Wizard's Daughter - Barbara Michaels   4362

Holmes, Mycroft (Detective—Private)
Enter the Lion: A Posthumous Memoir of Mycroft Holmes - Michael P. Hodel   2961

Holmes, Mycroft (Gentleman)
The Whitechapel Horrors - Edward B. Hanna   2678

Holmes, Sherlock (Detective—Private)
The Adventure of the Stalwart Companions - H. Paul Jeffers   3177
The Angel of the Opera: Sherlock Holmes Meets the Phantom of the Opera - Sam Siciliano   5842
The Beekeeper's Apprentice, or, On the Segregation of the Queen - Laurie R. King   3487
The Canary Trainer - Nicholas Meyer   4348
The Case of the Revolutionist's Daughter: Sherlock Holmes Meets Karl Marx - Lewis S. Feuer   2076
The Disappearance of Edwin Drood - Peter Rowland   5521
Dr. Jekyll and Mr. Holmes - Loren D. Estleman   1970
Enter the Lion: A Posthumous Memoir of Mycroft Holmes - Michael P. Hodel   2961
Exit Sherlock Holmes - Robert Lee Hall   2657
The Glendower Conspiracy - Lloyd Biggle Jr.   494
Irene's Last Waltz - Carole Nelson Douglas   1701
A Letter of Mary - Laurie R. King   3488
A Monstrous Regiment of Women - Laurie R. King   3489
The Quallsford Inheritance - Lloyd Biggle Jr.   495
The Return of Moriarty - John E. Gardner   2287
The Revenge of the Hound - Michael Hardwick   2688
Seance for a Vampire - Fred Saberhagen   5557
The Seven-Per-Cent Solution - Nicholas Meyer   4349
The Seventh Bullet - Daniel D. Victor   6483

Sherlock Holmes and the Case of Sabina Hall - L.B. Greenwood   2576
Sherlock Holmes and the Case of the Raleigh Legacy - L.B. Greenwood   2577
Sherlock Holmes and the Mysterious Friend of Oscar Wilde - Russell A. Brown   731
Sherlock Holmes and the Red Demon - Larry Millett   4404
Sherlock Holmes and the Thistle of Scotland - L.B. Greenwood   2578
Sherlock Holmes Meets Annie Oakley - Stanley Shaw   5782
Sherlock Holmes vs. Dracula - Loren D. Estleman   1976
Sherlock in Love - Sena Jeter Naslund   4557
Ten Years Beyond Baker Street - Cay Van Ash   6400
The West End Horror - Nicholas Meyer   4350
The Whitechapel Horrors - Edward B. Hanna   2678

Holmquist, Jake (Labor Organizer)
Poor Boy and a Long Way Home - James Sherburne   5806

Holofernes (Biblical Figure; Military Personnel)
Judith - Stella Wilchek   6748

Holt, Ashton (Businessman)
The Mill on Mad River - Howard Clark   1087

Holt, Benjamin (Miner)
Power - Howard Fast   2041

Holt, Caroline Brandon (Spouse)
Washington! - Dana Fuller Ross   5491

Holt, Cindy (Young Woman)
Louisiana! - Dana Fuller Ross   5478

Holt, Clarissa (Spouse)
Tennessee! - Dana Fuller Ross   5489

Holt, Clay (Frontiersman)
Expedition! - Dana Fuller Ross   5473
Outpost! - Dana Fuller Ross   5486
Westward! - Dana Fuller Ross   5492

Holt, Daisy (Servant; Dancer)
The Days of the Butterfly - Norah Lofts   3841

Holt, Elizabeth (Spouse; Suffragette)
Pacific Destiny - Dana Fuller Ross   5487

Holt, Frank (Adventurer)
Homecoming - Dana Fuller Ross   5474

Holt, Hannah (Young Woman)
Dodging Red Cloud - Richard S. Wheeler   6657

Holt, Jefferson (Frontiersman)
Westward! - Dana Fuller Ross   5492

Holt, Jefferson (Frontiersman; Trapper)
Expedition! - Dana Fuller Ross   5473
Outpost! - Daha Fuller Ross   5486

Holt, Jellis (Servant)
Man Cannot Tell - Philip Lightfoot Scruggs   5711

Holt, Leonard (Apprentice)
Old St. Paul's - William Harrison Ainsworth   57

Holt, Michael (Businessman)
Homecoming - Dana Fuller Ross   5474

Holt, Michael "Whip" (Frontiersman)
California! - Dana Fuller Ross   5467
Independence! - Dana Fuller Ross   5476
Nebraska! - Dana Fuller Ross   5480
Nevada! - Dana Fuller Ross   5481
Oregon! - Dana Fuller Ross   5484
Texas! - Dana Fuller Ross   5490
Wyoming! - Dana Fuller Ross   5494

Holt, Richard (Young Man)
The Redemptioner - Isaac Rusling Pennypacker   4910

Holt, Tim (Journalist)
California Glory - Dana Fuller Ross   5468
Oklahoma Pride - Dana Fuller Ross   5483
Pacific Destiny - Dana Fuller Ross   5487

Sierra Triumph - Dana Fuller Ross 5488

Holt, Tim (Young Man)
Oregon Legacy - Dana Fuller Ross 5485

Holt, Toby (Frontiersman)
Arizona! - Dana Fuller Ross 5466
Celebration! - Dana Fuller Ross 5470
Dakota! - Dana Fuller Ross 5472
Illinois! - Dana Fuller Ross 5475
Kentucky! - Dana Fuller Ross 5477
Montana! - Dana Fuller Ross 5479
Oklahoma! - Dana Fuller Ross 5482
Tennessee! - Dana Fuller Ross 5489
Wisconsin! - Dana Fuller Ross 5493

Holt, Toby (Political Figure)
California Glory - Dana Fuller Ross 5468
Oklahoma Pride - Dana Fuller Ross 5483

Holt, Toby (Rancher)
Oregon Legacy - Dana Fuller Ross 5485

Holt, Toby (Veteran)
Washington! - Dana Fuller Ross 5491

Holt, Toby (Young Man)
Louisiana! - Dana Fuller Ross 5478

Holyoke, Horace (Gentleman)
Oldtown Folks - Harriet Beecher Stowe 6072

Honer, Minta (Settler)
The Living - Annie Dillard 1644

Honeycutt, Charlie "Slim" (Teenager)
The Cowboys - William Dale Jennings 3211

Hoode, Edmund (Writer)
The Roaring Boy - Edward Marston 4127
The Silent Woman - Edward Marston 4128

Hook, Jeremiah (Captive; Child)
Winter Rain - Terry C. Johnston 3262

Hook, Jonah (Veteran)
Cry of the Hawk - Terry C. Johnston 3248
Dream Catcher - Terry C. Johnston 3251
Winter Rain - Terry C. Johnston 3262

Hook, Marcus (Trader)
O Genesee - Janet O'Daniel 4688

Hoong Liang (Assistant)
The Chinese Nail Murders - Robert van Gulik 6413
The Emperor's Pearl - Robert van Gulik 6414
The Phantom of the Temple - Robert van Gulik 6420

Hoosen, Annetje (Spouse)
Forever Possess - Alexandra Phillips 4982

Hope, Randall (Young Man)
Father Abraham - Irving A. Bacheller 258

Hopkins, Mr. (Government Official)
The Siege of Krishnapur - J.G. Farrell 2016

Hopkins, Faith (Young Woman)
Dragon Cove - Carter A. Vaughan 6434

Hopkins, Oscar (Religious)
Oscar and Lucinda - Peter Carey 894

Hordle, John (Military Personnel)
The White Company - Sir Arthur Conan Doyle 1716

Hori (Secretary)
Death Comes as the End - Agatha Christie 1076

Horn, Alfred (Pilot)
Shadow of the Wolf - James Barwick 371

Horn, Damaris (Young Woman)
In Adam's Fall - Constance Dodge 1666

Horn, Joe (Mountain Man)
The Big Lonesome - Will Bryant 737

Hornblower, Barbara (Spouse)
Admiral Hornblower in the West Indies - C.S. Forester 2169
Commodore Hornblower - C.S. Forester 2172
Lord Hornblower - C.S. Forester 2179

Hornblower, Horatio (Military Personnel)
Admiral Hornblower in the West Indies - C.S. Forester 2169
Beat to Quarters - C.S. Forester 2170
Commodore Hornblower - C.S. Forester 2172
Flying Colours - C.S. Forester 2173
Hornblower and the Atropos - C.S. Forester 2175
Hornblower and the Hotspur - C.S. Forester 2176
Hornblower During the Crisis - C.S. Forester 2177
Lieutenant Hornblower - C.S. Forester 2178
The Life and Times of Horatio Hornblower - C. Northcote Parkinson 4813
Lord Hornblower - C.S. Forester 2179
Mr. Midshipman Hornblower - C.S. Forester 2180
Ship of the Line - C.S. Forester 2182

Hornblower, Maria (Spouse)
Hornblower and the Atropos - C.S. Forester 2175
Hornblower and the Hotspur - C.S. Forester 2176
Ship of the Line - C.S. Forester 2182

Hornbrook, Cathie (Foundling)
A Dream of Kings - Davis Grubb 2604

Hornby, Sim (Outlaw)
The Raider - Jesse Hill Ford 2164

Horne, Adam (Military Personnel)
The War Chest - Porter Hill 2950

Horne, Jackson (Rancher; Mountain Man)
Horne's Law - Jory Sherman 5819

Horne, John (Artisan)
Peace, My Daughters - Shirley Barker 314

Horner, Alex (Blacksmith)
Conqueror of the Clouds - William F. Hallstead 2664

Horner, Ben (Pilot)
Conqueror of the Clouds - William F. Hallstead 2664

Hortensius (Gentleman)
Hortensius, Friend of Nero - Edith Pargeter 4798

Horton, William (Servant)
Ravenshoe - Henry Kingsley 3500

Horton, Zack (Heir)
Path of the Sun - Al Dempsey 1608

Hoshi, Hiroshi (Military Personnel)
Chikara! - Robert Skimin 5876

Hoshi, Itoko (Spouse)
Chikara! - Robert Skimin 5876

Hoshi, Sataro (Immigrant)
Chikara! - Robert Skimin 5876

Hoskuldsdaughter, Hallgerda (Heroine)
Fire in the Ice - Dorothy James Roberts 5375

Hotfoot (Indian)
Tatham Mound - Piers Anthony 169

Houldway, Major Richard (Gentleman)
Consort for Victoria - William Vaughan Wilkins 6757

Houseman (Murderer)
Eugene Aram - Edward Bulwer-Lytton 766

Hovey, Matt (Smuggler; Military Personnel)
Blue Hurricane - F. van Wyck Mason 4146

Howard, Colonel (Loyalist; Gentleman)
The Pilot - James Fenimore Cooper 1306

Howard, Ann (Young Woman)
For They Shall Inherit - Malcolm Macdonald 3964

Howard, Arminta (Gentlewoman)
Sapphire - Helen Ashfield 214

Howard, Ashton (Gentleman)
Sapphire - Helen Ashfield 214

Howard, Devon (Seamstress; Actress)
Mistress Devon - Virginia Coffman 1156

Howard, Dulcima (Socialite)
The Ladies of Hanover Square - Rona Randall 5249

Howard, Hannah Maria (Immigrant; Spouse)
The Plums Hang High - Gertrude E. Finney 2091

Howard, Harry (Lawman)
Adios! - Lanier Bartlett 366

Howard, Jane (Young Woman)
Blake's Reach - Catherine Gaskin 2313

Howard, Jethro (Farmer; Immigrant)
The Plums Hang High - Gertrude E. Finney 2091

Howard, John (Military Personnel)
Wilderness Adventure - Elizabeth Page 4774

Howard, Julia (Sailor)
Jewel of the Sea - Ellen Argo 185

Howard, Kirsty (Young Woman)
A Falcon for a Queen - Catherine Gaskin 2314

Howard, Martin (Plantation Owner)
Natchez: A Novel of the Deep South - Pamela Jekel 3186

Howard, Matthew (Frontiersman)
The Tree of Liberty - Elizabeth Page 4773

Howard, Nancy Ann (Young Woman)
The Parson's Daughter - Catherine Cookson 1286

Howard, Peyton (Military Personnel)
The Tree of Liberty - Elizabeth Page 4773

Howard, Ridley (Military Personnel)
Draw Near to Battle - Jere Hungerford Wheelwright 6667

Howard, Sam (Frontiersman)
To Build a Ship - Don Berry 482

Howard, Sara (Secretary)
The Alienist - Caleb Carr 907

Howard, Tearle (Nobleman)
The Conquest - Jude Deveraux 1630

Howarth, Anna (Young Woman)
The Vivian Inheritance - Jean Stubbs 6101

Howarth, Charlotte (Widow(er))
An Imperfect Joy - Jean Stubbs 6097

Howarth, Dick (Farmer)
An Imperfect Joy - Jean Stubbs 6097

Howarth, Lance (Servant; Landowner)
Turn of the Dice - Janet Edmonds 1870

Howarth, Ned (Farmer)
By Our Beginnings - Jean Stubbs 6092

Howarth, William (Businessman)
An Imperfect Joy - Jean Stubbs 6097
The Northern Correspondent - Jean Stubbs 6099
The Vivian Inheritance - Jean Stubbs 6101

Howatt, Tommy (Journalist)
Tenderloin - Samuel Hopkins Adams 33

Howe, Emily (Young Woman)
From a Far Land - Robert S. Elegant 1903

Howe, Emma (Spinster)
Courting Emma Howe - Margaret A. Robinson 5410

Howe, Martina (Gentlewoman; Imposter)
The Marquis and Miss Jones - Helen Ashfield 208

Howe, Tommy (Revolutionary)
From a Far Land - Robert S. Elegant 1903

Howell, Asa (Farmer)
The Perilous Night - Burke Boyce 609

Howell, Pelham (Military Personnel)
Eliza Stanhope - Joanna Trollope 6347

Howell, Tempy Ann (Young Woman)
The Perilous Night - Burke Boyce 609

Howells, Dan (Military Personnel)
The Scarlet Guidon - Ray Grant Toepfer 6287

Howland, Abigail (Loyalist)
The Gentle Rebel - Gilbert Morris 4461

Howland, Robert (Settler)
The Captive Bride - Gilbert Morris 4457

Hoxworth, Rafer (Sea Captain; Businessman)
Hawaii - James A. Michener 4370

Hoyt (Military Personnel)
Squadron Forty-Four - Arch Whitehouse 6711

Huai-i (Sports Figure; Farmer)
The Jade Stalk - Jonathan Fast 2048

Huayna Capac (Chieftain)
The Incas - Daniel Peters 4945

Hubbard, Elvira (Gentlewoman)
All in Good Time - Marguerite Allis 106

Hubbard, Job (Artisan)
All in Good Time - Marguerite Allis 106

Hubbard, Sam (Young Man)
The Nancy Flyer - Ernest Poole 5091

Hubbard, Victoria (Gentlewoman)
Drums of Khartoum - Chloe Gartner 2307

Hubble, Jane (Writer)
Hubble Time - Tom Bezzi 490

Hudson, Angus (Servant)
Upstairs Downstairs - John Hawkesworth 2782

Hudspeth, A.C. (Lawman)
Stamping Ground - Loren D. Estleman 1977

Huemac (Warrior)
The Luck of Huemac: A Novel about the Aztecs -
Daniel Peters 4946

Huff, Cap (Military Personnel)
Rabble in Arms - Kenneth Roberts 5390

Huffam, John (Gentleman)
The Quincunx - Charles Palliser 4778

Hugh (Musician)
Shame of Man - Piers Anthony 168

Hugonin, Yves (Knight)
Brother Cadfael's Penance - Ellis Peters 4955

Hui (Nobleman)
Lady of the Reeds - Pauline Gedge 2345

Hull, Harrison (Military Personnel; Explorer)
Enslaved - Ron Burns 801
The Mysterious Death of Meriwether Lewis - Ron
Burns 802

Humbird, Edward (Nobleman)
The Braintree Mission - Nicholas E. Wyckoff 6887

Humble, Christopher (Adventurer)
Christopher Humble - Charles Burnet Judah 3310

Hume, Julius (Gentleman)
Mother and Son - Ivy Compton-Burnett 1231

Hume, Miranda (Gentlewoman)
Mother and Son - Ivy Compton-Burnett 1231

Hume, Rosebery (Gentleman)
Mother and Son - Ivy Compton-Burnett 1231

Hume, Sam (Teenager)
Sweetwater Fever - Robert H. Adelman 36

Humilis, Brother (Religious)
An Excellent Mystery - Ellis Peters 4959

Hummel, John (Prospector)
Fools' Gold - Richard Wiley 6755

Humphrey, Lionel (Journalist)
Armored Giants: A Novel of the Civil War - F. van
Wyck Mason 4145

Humphreys, Oswald (Military Personnel)
''Utmost Fish!'' - Hugh Wray McCann 4219

Humphries, Claudia (Widow(er))
Independence! - Dana Fuller Ross 5476

Hung (Revolutionary)
Empire of Heaven - Linda Ching Sledge 5907

Hungry Bear (Prehistoric Human; Shaman)
People of the Fire - W. Michael Gear 2335

Hunnyman, Joseph (Actor; Detective—Amateur)
Entered From the Sun - George Garrett 2301

Hunsacker, Mary (Immigrant; Captive)
The Life and Times of Captain N. - Douglas
Glover 2436

Hunt, Louise (Young Woman)
The Post of Honor - David Coxe Cooke 1266

Hunt, Zeke (Pioneer)
Whole Hog - David Wagoner 6523

Hunter, Adam (Activist)
Cardigan Square - Alexandra Manners 4070

Hunter, Andrew (Military Personnel)
Guns for Rebellion - F. van Wyck Mason 4151

Hunter, David (Military Personnel)
No Tears for Christmas - Helen Topping
Miller 4391

Hunter, Herman (Artist)
The Hawks of Hawk-Hollow - Robert Montgomery
Bird 504

Hunter, James (Rancher; Veteran)
Colorado Ambush - Jess McCriede 4230

Hunter, Morgan (Gentleman)
Cardigan Square - Alexandra Manners 4070

Hunter, Teresa (Young Woman)
No Tears for Christmas - Helen Topping
Miller 4391

Hunter of the Wolf (Indian; Warrior)
Comanche Moon - Catherine Anderson 137

Huntington, Beth (Spouse)
Manitou - Donald Clayton Porter 5120
Spirit Knife - Donald Clayton Porter 5128

Huntington, Victoria (Spinster)
Surrender - Amanda Quick 5221

Huntley, Dick (Journalist)
The Devil's Card - Mary Maher 4030

Huntley, Peter (Military Personnel)
Toil of the Brave - Inglis Fletcher 2141

Hurrocks, Thalia (Writer)
St. John's Wood - Nancy Fitzgerald 2116

Hurst, Simon (Servant; Nobleman)
The Frog Earl - Carola Dunn 1792

Hussey, Johnny (Police Officer; Spy)
A Nest of Simple Folk - Sean O'Faolain 4692

Hussey, Sara (Young Woman)
Armada - Charles Gidley 2404

Hutchins, Eliza (Spouse)
The Land Where the Sun Dies - Henry Carlisle 896

Hutchins, John (Government Official)
The Land Where the Sun Dies - Henry Carlisle 896

Hutter, Thomas (Backwoodsman)
The Deerslayer - James Fenimore Cooper 1299

Huw (Sailor)
Grania: She-King of the Irish Seas - Morgan
Llywelyn 3819

Huw (Servant)
The Hooded Falcon - Prudence Andrew 140

Huxleigh, Penelope (Companion)
Good Morning, Irene - Carole Nelson Douglas 1698
Good Night, Mr. Holmes - Carole Nelson
Douglas 1699
Irene at Large - Carole Nelson Douglas 1700
Irene's Last Waltz - Carole Nelson Douglas 1701

Huxtable, Franklin (Scientist)
Queen Victoria's Bomb - Ronald Clark 1094

Hwesuhunu (Slave)
The African - Harold Courlander 1386

Hyatt, Stephen (Sailor)
The Southern Cross - Peter French 2226

Hyde, Benjamin (Military Personnel)
One Smart Indian - Robert J. Seidman 5722

Hyde, Gabriel (Military Personnel)
Mandarin - Robert S. Elegant 1905

Hyde, Merideth (Young Woman)
Hyde Place - Virginia Coffman 1154

Hypsipyle (Ruler)
Jason - Henry Treece 6331

Hywelis (Witch)
Crown in Candlelight - Rosemary Hawley
Jarman 3166

I

Iago (Rebel)
The Briar Rose - Linda Neale 4561

Ibarbo, Antonio (Rancher)
By the King's Command - Shirley Seifert 5723

Ibbetson, Colonel (Gentleman)
Peter Ibbetson - George Du Maurier 1750

Ibbetson, Peter (Gentleman; Murderer)
Peter Ibbetson - George Du Maurier 1750

Ibbott, Katherine (Gentlewoman)
Golden Admiral - F. van Wyck Mason 4150

Ibsen, Lori (Young Woman)
Warsaw Requiem - Bodie Thoene 6229

Icarus (Young Man)
The Maze Maker - Michael Ayrton 250

Ichiro, Sano (Warrior; Detective—Police)
Bundori - Laura Joh Rowland 5519
Shin Ju - Laura Joh Rowland 5520

Idaho, Harriet (Young Woman)
Harry Idaho - Hugh Pendexter 4894

Ide (Religious)
Paradise - Dikkon Eberhart 1831

Ierii (Young Woman)
The Lily and the Bull - Moyra Caldecott 846

Ifort, Gerda von (Spouse)
Foundation Stone - Lella Warren 6571

Ilchee (Indian; Royalty)
Columbia - Pamela Jekel 3184

Ildico (Young Woman)
Darkness and the Dawn - Thomas B. Costain 1364

Imhotep (Religious)
Death Comes as the End - Agatha Christie 1076

Imogen (Royalty)
Roman Go Home! - Adam Fergusson 2065

Inanna (Prehistoric Human; Ruler)
The Last Warrior Queen - Mary Mackey 3992

Inconnu, Simon (Knight)
The Disputed Crown - Valerie Anand 128

Indian John (Slave; Spouse)
I, Tituba, Black Witch of Salem - Maryse
Conde 1233

Ines, Heraclio (Young Man)
The Fifth Horseman - Jose Antonio Villarreal 6496

Ingham, Jane (Orphan; Ward)
The Nunnery - Dorothy Charques 1001

Ingledew, Jacob (Settler)
The Architecture of the Arkansas Ozarks - Donald Harington 2708

Ingledew, Noah (Settler)
The Architecture of the Arkansas Ozarks - Donald Harington 2708

Inglesant, Eustace (Gentleman)
John Inglesant - John Henry Shorthouse 5833

Inglesant, John (Philosopher)
John Inglesant - John Henry Shorthouse 5833

Ingraham, Thomas (Apprentice)
Low Treason - Leonard Tourney 6301

Inman, Dash (Sea Captain)
The Running of the Tide - Esther Forbes 2160

Innis, Nick (Composer)
Brave Kingdom - Frances Murray 4534

Insel, Maria (Companion)
The Country Gentleman - Fiona Hill 2924

Iolanthe (Noblewoman)
The Saracen Blade - Frank Yerby 6926

Iona (Royalty)
Princess of the Veil - Helen Mittermeyer 4420

Ione (Ward)
The Last Days of Pompeii - Edward Bulwer-Lytton 768

Irena of Moldavia (Royalty)
Flight From Bucharest - R.T. Stevens 6000

Iri (Artisan)
The Sea Peoples - Peter Danielson 1474

Iri (Artisan; Wanderer)
The Promised Land - Peter Danielson 1471

Irion (Knight)
The Last Pendragon - Robert Rice 5316

Iron, Shiloh (Nurse)
A City Not Forsaken - Lynn Morris 4480

Iron Shirt (Indian)
Season of Yellow Leaf - Douglas C. Jones 3283

Ironfist, Wulf (Warrior)
To Love Again - Bertrice Small 5913

Ironfoot (Indian; Chieftain)
Beyond the Stars - David William Ross 5497

Irons, Fletcher (Military Personnel; Nobleman)
Faith and Honor - Robin Maderich 4025

Irons, Forest (Spy)
Scarlet Ribbons - Judith E. French 2224

Irons, Jack (Frontiersman)
In the Days of Poor Richard - Irving A. Bacheller 259

Irons, Shiloh (Nurse)
Shadow of the Mountains - Lynn Morris 4481

Irvine, Isabella (Widow(er))
Ravenburn - Laura Black 522

Irvine, Katherine (Heiress; Gentlewoman)
Ravenburn - Laura Black 522

Isaacs, Hannele (Prostitute)
My Own Ground - Hugh Nissenson 4628

Isabel of Northfield (Young Woman)
The Ruthless Yeomen - Valerie Anand 134

Isabelle de Croye (Noblewoman; Heiress)
Quentin Durward - Sir Walter Scott 5705

Isambord, Ranf (Nobleman)
The Heaven Tree Trilogy - Edith Pargeter 4797

Isar (Captive; Prehistoric Human)
Shadows on the Stones - Moyra Caldecott 847

Isca (Prehistoric Human; Royalty)
The Golden Strangers - Henry Treece 6328

Iscariot, Judith (Young Woman)
Barabbas: A Dream of the World's Tragedy - Marie Corelli 1327

Island Woman (Indian; Shaman)
The Firekeeper - Robert Moss 4498
The Interpreter - Robert Moss 4499

Ismail (Doctor)
The Eagle's Daughter - Judith Tarr 6165

Ismene (Shepherd)
Earth Giant - Edison Marshall 4106

Isobel, Bridget (Heroine)
Bridey's Mountain - Yvonne Adamson 34

Isobelle (Captive)
Isobelle - Mary Lide 3775

Isolde (Royalty)
The White Raven - Diana L. Paxson 4847

Itaz (Royalty)
Horses of Heaven - Gillian Bradshaw 630

Itchakoma (Indian; Royalty)
Jubal Sackett - Louis L'Amour 3620

Ivanov, Oleg (Revolutionary)
Blood and Sable - Carol J. Kane 3350

Ivanovna, Maria (Young Woman)
The Captain's Daughter - Alexander Pushkin 5210

Ivanushka (Landowner)
Russka: The Novel of Russia - Edward Rutherfurd 5535

Ivar (Warrior)
The Hammer and the Cross - Harry Harrison 2736

Ives, John (Trader; Rancher)
Jubilee Trail - Gwen Bristow 698

Iveta (Royalty)
The Leper of St. Giles - Ellis Peters 4963

Ivory, Florence (Suffragette)
Bethlehem Road - Anne Perry 4920

Ixcawatzin (Warrior; Religious)
The Heart of Jade - Salvador de Madariaga 4024

Iza (Healer; Prehistoric Human)
The Clan of the Cave Bear - Jean M. Auel 236

Izquierdo, Conchita (Revolutionary)
Floodtide - Frank Yerby 6916

Izzard, Betony (Teacher)
The Land Endures - Mary E. Pearce 4862

J

Ja-Gonh (Indian; Warrior)
Tomahawk - Donald Clayton Porter 5129
War Cry - Donald Clayton Porter 5132

Jabalwan (Teacher)
Wyvern - A.A. Attanasio 227

Jack (Entertainer)
Playing the Jack - Mary Brown 726

Jack, Mansel (Businessman)
Spinners' Wharf - Iris Gower 2502

Jackson, Gideon (Slave; Political Figure)
Freedom Road - Howard Fast 2031

Jackson, Horatio (Religious)
Hellfire Jackson - Garland Roark 5355

Jackson, John (Doctor)
Wagons West - Leslie Turner White 6692

Jackson, Marietta (Young Woman)
The Ancestors Cry Out - Eugenia Lovett West 6627

Jackson, Rebekah (Young Woman)
The Reluctant Bridegroom - Gilbert Morris 4467

Jackson, Sally (Military Personnel)
The Last Innocent Hour - Margot Abbott 8

Jackson, Sheldon (Religious)
Alaska - James A. Michener 4364

Jackson, Travis (Veteran; Pilot)
Cold War - Robert Vaughan 6446
The Iron Curtain - Robert Vaughan 6447

Jacob (Scholar; Slave)
The Slave - Isaac Bashevis Singer 5866

Jacobson, Allan (Lawyer)
The Court-Martial of George Armstrong Custer - Douglas C. Jones 3276

Jacova (Spouse; Indian)
The Gila River - Gary McCarthy 4223

Jacques (Artisan)
The Heirs of the Kingdom - Zoe Oldenbourg 4716

Jago, Henry (Police Officer; Sports Figure)
The Detective Wore Silk Drawers - Peter Lovesey 3911

Jahn, Trudy (Young Woman)
Chicago Girls - Edith Freund 2229

Jake, Romany (Gypsy)
The Return of the Gypsy - Philippa Carr 927

James, Harriet (Cook)
Lady Fortescue Steps Out - Marion Chesney 1035

James, Jeremiah (Military Personnel)
Chapultepec - Norman Zollinger 6965

James, Mary (Young Woman)
My Sister's Keeper - Beverly Butler 817

Jameson, Isaac (Frontiersman)
Jordan County: A Landscape in Narrative - Shelby Foote 2152

Jamie (Foundling; Streetperson)
The Street Sparrows - Rose Ayers 249

Jamison, Jamie (Noblewoman)
The Bride - Julie Garwood 2311

Jan (Gentleman)
Mass for Arras - Andrzej Szczypiorski 6153

Jankyn, Matthew (Spy; Military Personnel)
The Whyte Harte - P.C. Doherty 1681

Jankyn, Matthew (Thief; Spy)
The Serpent Amongst the Lilies - P.C. Doherty 1678

Jansen, Anna (Spouse)
Wild Conquest - Peter Abrahams 12

Jansen, Kaspar (Landowner)
Wild Conquest - Peter Abrahams 12

January, Isabel (Gentlewoman)
The Last Waltz - Nancy Zaroulis 6955

Jara (Young Woman)
If I Forget Thee - Brenda Lesley Segal 5720

Jardine, Alexander (Laird)
Foes - Mary Johnston 3233

Jardine, Camille (Young Woman)
Wychwood - Nicole St. John 5564

Jardine, Maida (Gentlewoman)
Flight From Fifth Avenue - Catherine M. Rae 5235

Jardine, Margaret (Spouse)
Ain't Goin' to Glory - David Delman 1597

Jardine, Nell (Young Woman)
Wychwood - Nicole St. John 5564

Jardine, Stephen (Journalist)
Ain't Goin' to Glory - David Delman 1597

Jared (Young Man)
Called Away - Perdita Buchan 753

Jarret, James (Laird)
Jarrett's Jade - Frank Yerby 6923

Jarret, Jarl (Patriot; Military Personnel)
Jarrett's Jade - Frank Yerby 6923

Jarvis, Berk (Farmer; Military Personnel)
The Great Meadow - Elizabeth Madox Roberts 5378

Jarvis, Diony (Farmer)
The Great Meadow - Elizabeth Madox Roberts 5378

Jarvis, Molly (Servant)
The Vines of Yarrabee - Dorothy Eden 1864

Jasmine (Bastard Daughter)
The Falcon and the Flower - Virginia Henley 2826

Jasmine (Gentlewoman)
To Dance with Kings - Rosalind Laker 3601

Jason (Adventurer)
Jason - Henry Treece 6331
Medea - Miranda Seymour 5764

Jason (Sea Captain)
Hercules, My Shipmate - Robert Graves 2545

Jasper, John (Gentleman)
The Disappearance of Edwin Drood - Peter Rowland 5521

Jassa (Religious)
A Quest for Love - Jacquetta Hawkes 2781

Jastrow, Aaron (Scholar)
War and Remembrance - Herman Wouk 6875
The Winds of War - Herman Wouk 6876

Jastrow, Natalie (Spouse)
War and Remembrance - Herman Wouk 6875

Jastrow, Natalie (Young Woman)
The Winds of War - Herman Wouk 6876

Jayarajadevi (Royalty)
When God Slept - Peter Bourne 597

Jayson, Robert (Settler)
In Those Days - Harvey Fergusson 2068

Jebeau, Arthur (Lawyer; Widow(er))
My Beloved Son - Catherine Cookson 1285

Jebeau, Ellen (Gentlewoman; Widow(er))
My Beloved Son - Catherine Cookson 1285

Jebeau, Joseph (Military Personnel)
My Beloved Son - Catherine Cookson 1285

Jebu (Religious)
Shike: Time of Dragons - Robert Shea 5784

Jed (Teenager; Peddler)
Look to the River - William A. Owens 4771

Jefferson, Adam (Military Personnel)
Molly - Teresa Crane 1417

Jeffreys, Anne (Settler)
Western: A Saga of the Great Plains - Frank Yerby 6930

Jeffries, Mrs. (Housekeeper)
The Ghost and Mrs. Jeffries - Emily Brightwell 681
The Inspector and Mrs. Jeffries - Emily Brightwell 682
Mrs. Jeffries and the Missing Alibi - Emily Brightwell 683
Mrs. Jeffries Dusts for Clues - Emily Brightwell 684
Mrs. Jeffries on the Trail - Emily Brightwell 686
Mrs. Jeffries Plays the Cook - Emily Brightwell 687
Mrs. Jeffries Stands Corrected - Emily Brightwell 688
Mrs. Jeffries Takes Stock - Emily Brightwell 689

Jekyll, Henry (Doctor)
The Highwayman and Mr. Dickens - William J. Palmer 4783

Jekyll, Henry (Doctor; Murderer)
Dr. Jekyll and Mr. Holmes - Loren D. Estleman 1970
Jekyll, Alias Hyde - Donald Thomas 6240
Mary Reilly - Valerie Martin 4136

Jenkins, Marianne (Gentlewoman; Murderer)
Marianne - Glen Petrie 4981

Jenkins, Mary (Young Woman)
Proud Mary - Iris Gower 2501

Jenny (Servant)
The Sound of Coaches - Leon Garfield 2295

Jensie (Teenager; Captive)
Rockspring - R.G. Vliet 6506

Jenson, Alfred (Worker)
And the Desert Shall Bloom - Phyllis Barber 299

Jenson, Esther (Spouse)
And the Desert Shall Bloom - Phyllis Barber 299

Jericho, Lucas (Military Personnel; Pirate)
Hearts of Fire - Christina Savage 5616

Jermyn, Amanda (Photographer)
Daughters of the New World - Susan Richards Shreve 5835

Jermyn, Anna (Immigrant)
Daughters of the New World - Susan Richards Shreve 5835

Jermyn, Sir Aubrey (Gentleman; Rake)
A Fatal Assignation - Alice Chetwynd Ley 3764

Jerningham, Amelia (Gentlewoman; Pilot)
Wings of the Morning - David Beaty 402

Jerrold, Araminta (Gentlewoman)
Canal Town - Samuel Hopkins Adams 29

Jervis, Clemency (Heiress)
The American Heiress - Dorothy Eden 1854

Jessop, Ivor (Nobleman)
The Baroness of Bow Street - Gail Clark 1085

Jesu-Maria (Doctor)
To Keep This Oath - Hebe Weenolsen 6597

Jewel, Margaret (Teacher)
The Snake River - Winfred Blevins 547

Jewitt, John (Sailor; Artisan)
Eagle Song - James Houston 3050

Jhadel (Prehistoric Human; Shaman)
Face of the Rising Sun - William Sarabande 5598

Jim (Adventurer; Slave)
The Further Adventures of Huckleberry Finn - Greg Matthews 4189

Jim (Child; Worker)
The Two Farms - Mary E. Pearce 4865

Jin-See (Businessman)
White Poppy - Margaret Gaan 2261

Jinsuke (Sailor; Spy)
Harpoon - C.W. Nicol 4612

Jo-Gonh (Indian; Warrior)
Renno - Donald Clayton Porter 5123

Joan of Hawkingham (Noblewoman)
Emerald Fire - Laurie Grant 2537

Jocelin (Religious)
The Spire - William Golding 2457

Jocelyn (Maiden)
The Queen's Knight - Marvin Borowsky 585

Jocelyn, Hugh (Adventurer)
Ask No Quarter - George Tracy Marsh 4099

Jochanan (Student)
The Nazarene - Sholem Asch 200

Jocita (Indian; Warrior)
War Eagles - Frank Burleson 788

Jode, Don (Frontiersman)
Shadows in the Dusk - John Edward Jennings 3208

Joel (Indian; Chieftain)
The Valiant - Sigman Byrd 839

John (Courtier)
The Bearkeeper's Daughter - Gillian Bradshaw 628

John (Magician)
Voodoo Dreams: A Novel of Marie Laveau - Jewell Parker Rhodes 5310

John of Oversley (Knight)
Men Like Shadows - Dorothy Charques 1000

Johns, Alenn (Young Woman)
Plume Rouge: A Novel of the Pathfinders - John Upton Terrell 6203

Johnson, Emily (Fiance(e); Captive)
Seminole - Donald Clayton Porter 5126

Johnson, Emily (Gentlewoman)
Choctaw - Donald Clayton Porter 5116

Johnson, Emily (Spouse)
War Drums - Donald Clayton Porter 5133

Johnson, Jubal (Journalist)
Trumpet in the Wilderness - Robert S. Harper 2717

Johnson, Toussaint (Police Officer)
Murder by the Numbers - Max Allan Collins 1212

Johnson, Wayt (Lawman)
Saint Johnson - William R. Burnett 796

Johnson, Will (Cowboy)
Pancho And Black Jack - Fred Bean 398

Jonathan (Teenager)
An Army of Children - Evan H. Rhodes 5306

Jonathan of Cyrene (Young Man)
Behold Your King - Florence M. Bauer 379

Jondalar (Lover; Prehistoric Human)
The Mammoth Hunters - Jean M. Auel 237
The Plains of Passage - Jean M. Auel 238

Jondalar (Prehistoric Human)
The Valley of Horses - Jean M. Auel 239

Jones, Amelia (Young Woman)
The Latter Adventures of Tom Jones - Bob Coleman 1200

Jones, Amity (Young Woman)
Rivers of Gold - Janet Edmonds 1868

Jones, Big Sam (Trader)
Goldfield - Richard S. Wheeler 6660

Jones, Caroline Fremont (Secretary)
The Strange Files of Fremont Jones - Dianne Day 1544

Jones, Charlie (Gentleman)
The Distant Lands - Julian Green 2567
The Stars of the South - Julian Green 2568

Jones, Edward Porter (Detective—Private)
The Glendower Conspiracy - Lloyd Biggle Jr. 494
The Quallsford Inheritance - Lloyd Biggle Jr. 495

Jones, Elizabeth (Widow(er))
The Stars of the South - Julian Green 2568

Jones, Esther (Gentlewoman)
Rake's Progress - Marion Chesney 1047

Jones, Fremont (Businesswoman)
Fire and Fog - Dianne Day 1543

Jones, Garwood B. (Political Figure)
Raintree County - Ross Lockridge Jr. 3827

Jones, Habakkuk (Sailor)
Stronghold - Donald Barr Chidsey 1065

Jones, Hacksem (Gentleman)
The Latter Adventures of Tom Jones - Bob Coleman 1200

Jones, Hendry (Gunfighter; Murderer)
The Authentic Death of Hendry Jones - Charles Neider 4562

Jones, Megan (Young Woman)
The Pearl Pagoda - Susannah Broome 707

Jones, Nathaniel "Flintlock" (Frontiersman)
The Border Captains - Jason Manning 4072
Flintlock - Jason Manning 4073
Gone to Texas - Jason Manning 4074

Jones, Orpheus (Writer)
The Pleasure Garden - Leon Garfield 2293

Jones, Othnell (Military Personnel)
Othneil Jones - John Adams Leland 3715

Jones, Red (Cowboy)
Mary Dove - Jane Gilmore Rushing 5529

Jones, Rowlandson (Art Dealer)
The Dance of Death - Jeremy Potter 5142

Jones, Samuel (Frontiersman)
The Last Ride - Tom Eidson 1899

Jones, Tom (Landowner)
The Latter Adventures of Tom Jones - Bob
   Coleman 1200

Jons, Coleman (Military Personnel)
Copperhead Moon - Herbert Stover 6067

Jonsen (Pirate; Sea Captain)
A High Wind in Jamaica - Richard Hughes 3074

Jordan, Bethia (Settler)
The Kentuckians - Janice Holt Giles 2413

Jordan, Betsy (Widow(er); Housekeeper)
Mrs. Betsy, or Widowed and Wed - Francis
   Marton 4141

Jordan, Caleb (Military Personnel)
Scarlet Feather - Dale Van Every 6409

Jordan, Duncan (Frontiersman)
Scarlet Feather - Dale Van Every 6409

Jordan, Felicia (Widow(er))
The Brooks Legend - William Donohue Ellis 1928

Jordan, Jenny (Young Woman)
Beloved Enemy - Al Lacy 3579

Jordan, Revell (Military Personnel)
Thunder on the Chesapeake - David Divine 1650

Jordan, Sumner (Child)
Maiden Voyage - Cynthia Bass 372

Josefina (Actress; Dancer)
The Spanish Bride - Walter O'Meara 4735

Joseph, Brother (Religious)
A Question of Choice - Prudence Andrew 143

Joshua (Religious)
The Last Days - William Rayner 5272

Josselyn, Daniel (Veteran)
Hearts and Bones - Margaret Lawrence 3685

Joubert (Military Personnel)
Colors Aloft! - Alexander Kent 3427

Jourdain, Nicholas (Widow(er); Plantation Owner)
Song of the Bayou - Elinor Lynley 3936

Jovian, June (Actress)
The Mortal Gods - Maurice Dolbier 1688

Jovian, Robert (Actor; Businessman)
The Mortal Gods - Maurice Dolbier 1688

Joy, Miss (Madam)
Carriage Trade - Robert Thomsen 6271

Juan (Spy)
Captain General - John P. Stevenson 6007

Juana-Maria, Lady (Noblewoman)
The Golden Chain - Jean Gamo 2275

Judd, Ajax (Gentleman)
The Banishment - Marion Chesney 1018

Judith (Biblical Figure; Widow(er))
Judith - Stella Wilchek 6748

Judith (Dancer)
*The Island of the Innocent: A Novel of Greek and Jew
   in the Time of the Maccabees* - Vardis
   Fisher 2108

Judith of Ravenstow (Gentlewoman)
The Wild Hunt - Elizabeth Chadwick 969

Juggins, Robert (Trader)
The Doom Trail - Arthur Douglas Smith 5917

Jujiro (Royalty)
Sakuran: A Novel of Medieval Japan - Edward
   Tolosko 6292

Julian, Gregory (Nobleman)
The Sinner of Saint Ambrose - Robert
   Raynolds 5275

Julianus, Marcus (Political Figure)
The Light Bearer - Donna Gillespie 2419

Julienne (Seamstress)
The Frenchwoman - Jeanne Mackin 3995

Julius (Military Personnel)
The Rock: A Novel about Gibraltar - John
   Masters 4179

Jumelle, Justine (Young Woman)
The Alpha Raid - Alan Scholefield 5651

Jupiter, Mona (Young Woman)
Organized Crime - Nicholas Von Hoffman 6511

Jurer, Nancy (Prostitute)
Winter Harvest - Norah Lofts 3863

Justice, Hunt (Architect)
Breakfast at the Hermitage - Alfred Leland
   Crabb 1397

Justice, John Valcourt (Military Personnel; Spy)
A Balance of Dangers - Anthony Forrest 2184
Captain Justice - Anthony Forrest 2185
The Pandora Secret - Anthony Forrest 2186

Justin, Philip (Gentleman)
Marsanne - Virginia Coffman 1155

Justina, Helena (Noblewoman)
The Iron Hand of Mars - Lindsey Davis 1528
Last Act in Palmyra - Lindsey Davis 1529
Shadows in Bronze - Lindsey Davis 1531
Time to Depart - Lindsey Davis 1533

Justus (Military Personnel)
Justus - Arthur L. Lapham 3663

Justus (Slave)
Raven's Wind - Victor Canning 883

Juvika, Per Anders (Landowner; Farmer)
The People of Juvik - Olav Dunn 1798

K

Kaatje (Housekeeper)
A Woman of Quality - Jan Westcott 6649

Kade, David (Gentleman)
Fire in the Ice - Alan Scholefield 5653

Kaetter-Henry, August (Farmer)
Country People - Ruth Suckow 6111

Kaetter-Henry, Carl (Farmer)
Country People - Ruth Suckow 6111

Kagan (Chieftain)
The Year of the Horsetails - R.F. Tapsell 6162

Kagg, Jim (Mountain Man)
Buffalo Girls - Larry McMurtry 4296

Kakuktak (Sailor)
The White Dawn - James Houston 3053

Kalinin, Alexei (Businessman)
Petersburg - Emily Hanlon 2677

Kalner, Jacob (Young Man)
Warsaw Requiem - Bodie Thoene 6229

Kaminsky, Sarah (Spouse)
Trumpets of Silver - Norma Harris 2735

Kaminsky, Shmuel (Worker)
Trumpets of Silver - Norma Harris 2735

Kamose (Bastard Son)
The Prophecy - Peter Danielson 1472

Kamose (Bastard Son; Ruler)
Sword of Glory - Peter Danielson 1477

Kane, Rachel (Young Woman)
The Books of Rachel - Joel Gross 2600

Kane, Tara (Young Woman)
Tara Kane - George Markstein 4091

Kaneda (Prospector)
Fools' Gold - Richard Wiley 6755

Kapp, Arthur (Businessman)
The Celebrant - Eric Rolfe Greenberg 2572

Kapp, Eli (Businessman)
The Celebrant - Eric Rolfe Greenberg 2572

Kapp, Jackie (Immigrant; Artisan)
The Celebrant - Eric Rolfe Greenberg 2572

Karaibrahim (Military Personnel)
Time of Parting - Anton Donchev 1690

Karakou, Luka (Hunter)
The Great Alone - Janet Dailey 1454

Karana (Prehistoric Human; Orphan)
Beyond the Sea of Ice - William Sarabande 5595

Karana (Prehistoric Human; Shaman)
Corridor of Storms - William Sarabande 5596
Forbidden Land - William Sarabande 5599

Karella (Sorcerer)
Pillar of the Sky - Cecelia Holland 2994

Karenina, Anna (Heiress)
Count Vronsky's Daughter - Carola Salisbury 5567

Karl-Eberhard (Nobleman)
A Finger to Her Lips - Evelyn Berckman 472

Karlin, Anna (Young Woman; Widow(er))
Quiet Lady - Norman Collins 1216

Karlinsky, David (Artist)
The Artist - Norman Garbo 2281

Karlotte, Anna-Marie Elsbet (Socialite;
   Noblewoman)
The Blood Order - Jack D. Hunter 3084

Karlsson, Nils (Backwoodsman)
The Sea Runners - Ivan Doig 1685

Karnes (Oil Industry Worker)
The Terrible Teague Bunch - Gary Jennings 3197

Kartright, Becky (Young Woman)
Night of Decision: A Novel of Colonial New York -
   Dorothy Grant 2534

Karus, Julius (Military Personnel)
The Crow Goddess - Patricia Finney 2094

Kasakov (Military Personnel)
The Buckingham Palace Connection - Ted
   Willis 6792

Kasane (Companion; Worker)
The Tokaido Road: A Novel of Feudal Japan - Lucia
   St. Clair Robson 5417

Kasim, Ahmed (Secretary)
The Day of the Scorpion - Paul Scott 5682

Kassandra (Royalty)
The Firebrand - Marion Zimmer Bradley 624

Katerina (Servant; Housekeeper)
Katerina - Aharon Appelfeld 177

Katz, Felix (Businessman)
The Healer - Aharon Appelfeld   176

Katz, Helga (Child)
The Healer - Aharon Appelfeld   176

Katz, Henrietta (Heroine)
The Healer - Aharon Appelfeld   176

Kay, Sir (Knight)
The Idylls of the Queen - Phyllis Ann Karr   3367

Kay, Agnes (Gentlewoman)
The Kays - Margaret Deland   1583

Kay, Arthur (Young Man)
The Kays - Margaret Deland   1583

Kazhak (Warrior)
The Horse Goddess - Morgan Llywelyn   3820

Keagh (Doctor)
Druid's Enchantment - Millie J. Ragosta   5240

Kean, Charlotte (Gentlewoman)
The Gambling Man - Catherine Cookson   1276

Keanu (Convict)
Molokai - Oswald Andrew Bushnell   815

Keating, Simon (Young Man)
Stacey's Flyer - Patricia Burns   800

Keele, Christopher (Social Worker)
The Michaelmas Girls - John Barry   362

Keene, Thomas (Settler)
The Tree of Life - Hugh Nissenson   4629

Kehwa, Charley (Indian; Guide)
Trask - Don Berry   483

Keith, Christoph (Veteran)
A Princess in Berlin - Arthur R.G. Solmssen   5939

Kellar, Melville (Doctor)
Deadly Beloved - Alanna Knight   3517

Kellaway, Ellen (Orphan)
Lord of the Far Island - Victoria Holt   3016

Kelleway, Henry (Lawyer)
The Iron Roads - Forbes Bramble   644
Regent Square - Forbes Bramble   645

Kelleway, John (Adventurer)
Regent Square - Forbes Bramble   645

Kelleway, Thomas (Lawyer)
Regent Square - Forbes Bramble   645

Kelleway, William (Artist)
Regent Square - Forbes Bramble   645

Kellner, Jakob (Religious)
Peking: A Novel of China's Revolt - Anthony Grey   2587

Kelly, Anna (Businesswoman)
Embers of the Heart - Rosanne Bittner   512

Kelly, Arthur (Historian)
Grant's War - Ted Jones   3297

Kelly, Jim (Worker)
Home Station - Jeanne Williams   6778

Kelly, Justin (Adventurer)
Stranger in Two Worlds - Hugh Clevely   1111

Kelly, Luther "Yellowstone" (Adventurer)
Imperial Kelly - Peter Bowen   600
Kelly Blue - Peter Bowen   601
Yellowstone Kelly - Peter Bowen   602

Kelly, Marie (Prostitute)
The Women of Whitechapel and Jack the Ripper - Paul West   6638

Kelly, Richard (Diplomat)
A Few Good Men - William Overgard   4768

Kelso, Clare (Gentlewoman)
Shadows on the Shore - Jessica Stirling   6048

Kelso, Clare (Servant)
Lantern for the Dark - Jessica Stirling   6045

Kemp, Erasmus (Heir)
Sacred Hunter - Barry Unsworth   6389

Kemp, Hannah (Young Woman)
The Sword of Truth - Gilbert Morris   4472

Kemp, William (Businessman)
Sacred Hunter - Barry Unsworth   6389

Kemper, Frank (Military Personnel)
The Man on the Train - W.J. Chaput   995

Kenbrook, Gloriana (Gentlewoman; Time Traveller)
Knights - Linda Lael Miller   4399

Kendall, Maria (Gentlewoman)
Animating Maria - Marion Chesney   1015

Kendall, Simon (Worker; Engineer)
The Drayton Legacy - Rona Randall   5247

Kendon, Richard (Engineer)
Lion in the Evening - Alan Scholefield   5656

Kendrick, Arnold (Plantation Owner)
Beulah Land - Lonnie Coleman   1202

Kendrick, Deborah (Spouse)
Beulah Land - Lonnie Coleman   1202

Kendrick, Sarah (Plantation Owner)
Look Away, Beulah Land - Lonnie Coleman   1204

Kendrick, Stella (Young Woman)
The Valiant - Sigman Byrd   839

Kengston, Margaret (Gentlewoman)
The Men That God Made Mad: A Novel about Ireland's Easter Rising - W.A. Ballinger   286

Kennard, Alan (Sailor; Businessman)
The Beckoning Waters - Robert Carse   944

Kennedy, Gillian (Military Personnel)
The White Cockade - Vincent O'Brien   4683

Kennedy, Kitty (Gentlewoman)
Beyond the Blue Mountains - Jean Plaidy   5006

Kenner, Hugh (Doctor; Farmer)
Promised Lands - Elizabeth Crook   1430

Kenner, Katie (Young Woman)
Promised Lands - Elizabeth Crook   1430

Kenneth, Sir (Knight)
The Talisman - Sir Walter Scott   5708

Kensal, Aidan (Veteran)
Kentucky Pride - Gene Markey   4087

Kensal, Jared (Veteran)
That Far Paradise - Gene Markey   4088

Kent, Abraham (Military Personnel)
The Seekers - John Jakes   3153

Kent, Amanda (Hotel Owner)
The Furies - John Jakes   3146

Kent, Ann (Spouse)
The Rebels - John Jakes   3152

Kent, Gideon (Journalist; Publisher)
The Americans - John Jakes   3143

Kent, Gideon (Labor Leader; Journalist)
The Lawless - John Jakes   3149

Kent, Gideon (Military Personnel)
The Titans - John Jakes   3154

Kent, Gideon (Military Personnel; Labor Leader)
The Warriors - John Jakes   3155

Kent, Gilbert (Publisher)
The Seekers - John Jakes   3153

Kent, Jared (Journalist)
The Titans - John Jakes   3154

Kent, Jared (Military Personnel)
The Seekers - John Jakes   3153

Kent, Jephtha (Journalist)
The Titans - John Jakes   3154

Kent, Jeremiah (Military Personnel)
The Warriors - John Jakes   3155

Kent, Jeremiah (Murderer; Outlaw)
The Lawless - John Jakes   3149

Kent, Matthew (Artist)
The Lawless - John Jakes   3149

Kent, Philip (Military Personnel)
The Rebels - John Jakes   3152

Kent, Tobias (Doctor)
Sangaree - Frank G. Slaughter   5898

Kent, Toby (Artist)
A Heritage of Shadows - Madeleine Brent   660

Kent, William (Doctor)
The Americans - John Jakes   3143

Kentaro (Nobleman)*
The Ginger Tree - Oswald Wynd   6890

Kentwood, Barbara (Gentlewoman)
The House at Old Vine - Norah Lofts   3845

Kentwood, Elizabeth (Gentlewoman)
The House at Old Vine - Norah Lofts   3845

Kenwood, Katharine (Singer)
The Melancholy Virgin - Annabel Laine   3587

Keokotah (Indian; Warrior)
Jubal Sackett - Louis L'Amour   3620

Kephaolos (Servant)
The Blood Star - Nicholas Guild   2611

Kerbouchard (Knight; Scholar)
The Walking Drum - Louis L'Amour   3632

Kerbow, Ivan (Cowboy)
The Pumpkin Rollers - Elmer Kelton   3406

Kercadiou, Aline de (Noblewoman)
Scaramouche - Rafael Sabatini   5554

Kercadiou, Aline de (Noblewoman; Refugee)
Scaramouche the King-Maker - Rafael Sabatini   5555

Kernow, Barney (Businessman)
Kernow & Daughter - Malcolm Macdonald   3968

Kernow, Jessica (Businesswoman)
Kernow & Daughter - Malcolm Macdonald   3968

Kernunnos (Religious)
The Horse Goddess - Morgan Llywelyn   3820

Kerr, Cindy Holt (Young Woman)
Celebration! - Dana Fuller Ross   5470

Kerr, Daniel (Singer)
The Lion's Way - Lewis Orde   4750

Kerr, Reed (Military Personnel)
Arizona! - Dana Fuller Ross   5466

Kerr, Ringan (Businessman)
The English Wife - Charity Blackstock   530

Kerr, Stephen (Gentleman)
The Braeswood Tapestry - Robyn Carr   936

Kershaw, Julius (Heir)
Dragonmede - Rona Randall   5246

Kestrel (Prehistoric Human; Runaway)
People of the Sea - W. Michael Gear   2339

Kestrel, Julian (Gentleman; Detective—Amateur)
A Broken Vessel - Kate Ross   5500
Cut to the Quick - Kate Ross   5501
Whom the Gods Love - Kate Ross   5502

Kettering, Karl-Heinz (Military Personnel)
The Blue Max - Jack D. Hunter   3085

Kettlestang, Jacob (Businessman; Banker)
The Lords of Loone - John James   3159

Keturah (Captive; Spouse)
The Sea Peoples - Peter Danielson   1474

Key, Jacob (Spy)
Oh, Valley Green - John H. Culp 1443

Keynes, Rowan (Gentleman)
Lisbon - Valerie Sherwood 5825

Khan, Hari (Chieftain)
The Near and the Far - Leopold Hamilton
  Myers 4547

Khana Tule Yasmin (Royalty)
Yankee - Dana Fuller Ross 5495

Khasturba (Prostitute)
Silk and Steel - Stephen Alter 122

Khu-Ren (Religious; Prehistoric Human)
Shadows on the Stones - Moyra Caldecott 847

Khurrem (Slave; Seamstress)
The Bride of Suleiman - Aileen Crawley 1421

Kia (Royalty)
The River and the Stone: Moses' Early Years in Egypt
  - Kathleen Jenks 3192

Kicking Bird (Indian; Warrior)
Dances with Wolves - Michael Blake 537

Kientpoos (Indian; Chieftain)
Devil's Backbone - Terry C. Johnston 3250

Kieq Lan (Young Woman)
Saigon - Anthony Grey 2588

Kiin (Prehistoric Human)
Brother Wind - Sue Harrison 2748
My Sister, the Moon - Sue Harrison 2750

Kilbourne, Dan (Military Personnel; Veteran)
West of Appomattox - Harley Duncan 1785

Kilgour, Kate (Housekeeper)
Colliers Row - Jan Webster 6592

Kilgour, Robert (Nobleman)
The Wind From the Sea - Constance Heaven 2812

Kilgour, Sandia (Young Woman)
Saturday City - Jan Webster 6593

Kilkenny, Coyote (Outlaw; Guide)
In the Season of the Sun - Kerry Newcomb 4590

Killefer, Emaline (Captive)
The Canebrake Men - Cameron Judd 3313

Killefer, Owen (Teenager; Frontiersman)
The Canebrake Men - Cameron Judd 3313

Killegrew, Gervase (Gentleman)
The Hounds of God - Rafael Sabatini 5551

Killick, Cornelius (Military Personnel; Mercenary)
Sharpe's Siege - Bernard Cornwell 1348

Killigrew, Maugan (Young Man)
The Grove of Eagles - Winston Graham 2526

Kilmartin, Brian (Farmer)
Famine - Liam O'Flaherty 4693

Kilpatrick, Brian (Adventurer)
Full of Thy Riches - Elizabeth Ferrell 2070

Kilrain, Buster (Military Personnel)
The Killer Angels - Michael Shaara 5766

Kilvarin, Xavier (Detective—Police)
Mysteries of Winterthurn - Joyce Carol Oates 4659

Kim Il-Han (Gentleman)
The Living Reed - Pearl S. Buck 756

Kim Yul-Chun (Revolutionary)
The Living Reed - Pearl S. Buck 756

Kimball, Armand (Lawyer)
They Came to a Valley - Bill Gulick 2618

Kimball, Jonathan (Military Personnel; Spy)
Farewell to Valley Forge - David Taylor 6178

Kincaid, Alec (Laird)
The Bride - Julie Garwood 2311

Kincaid, Augusta (Young Woman)
The Fall River Line - Daoma Winston 6824

Kincaid, Marcus (Businessman)
The Fall River Line - Daoma Winston 6824

Kincaid, Matt (Rancher)
Firewind - Bill Pronzini 5200

Kincaid, Soledad (Young Woman)
Solitudes - R.G. Vliet 6507

Kincross, Colin (Widow(er); Nobleman)
The Heiress Bride - Catherine Coulter 1375

King, August (Mountain Man)
The Journey of August King - John Ehle 1894

King, Ezekiel (Mountain Man; Trapper)
King of the Mountain - David Thompson 6255

King, Fergus (Saloon Keeper/Owner)
King's Royal - John Quigley 5224

King, Fiona Fraser (Gentlewoman)
Queen's Royal - John Quigley 5225

King, Linda (Farmer)
Three Days - Stephen Longstreet 3891

King, Nathaniel (Mountain Man; Teenager)
Lure of the Wind - David Thompson 6256

King, Nathaniel (Mountain Man; Trapper)
Apache Blood - David Thompson 6250
Blackfoot Massacre - David Thompson 6251
Blood Fury - David Thompson 6252
Blood Truce - David Thompson 6253
Hawken Fury - David Thompson 6254
Mountain Devil - David Thompson 6257
Northwest Passage - David Thompson 6258
Tenderfoot - David Thompson 6259
Tomahawk Revenge - David Thompson 6260
Trapper's Blood - David Thompson 6261
Winterkill - David Thompson 6262

King, Nathaniel (Teenager; Wanderer)
King of the Mountain - David Thompson 6255

King, Ranyard (Spy)
The Unterrified - Constance Robertson 5397

King, Robert (Businessman)
King's Royal - John Quigley 5224
Queen's Royal - John Quigley 5225

King, Rufus (Gambler)
The Treasure of Pleasant Valley - Frank Yerby 6928

King, Sam (Prospector)
Forefathers - Nancy Cato 960

King, Susannah (Gentlewoman)
Southern Cross - Terry Coleman 1206

King, Winona (Indian; Spouse)
Apache Blood - David Thompson 6250
Blood Truce - David Thompson 6253
Hawken Fury - David Thompson 6254
Tenderfoot - David Thompson 6259
Tomahawk Revenge - David Thompson 6260
Trapper's Blood - David Thompson 6261
Winterkill - David Thompson 6262

King, Zach (Child)
Tenderfoot - David Thompson 6259

King Dick (Prisoner)
The Lively Lady - Kenneth Roberts 5386

Kingaby, Sorrel (Bastard Daughter; Heiress)
The Brittle Glass - Norah Lofts 3837

Kingsford, Sir Hugh (Gentleman)
Blood of the Boar - Margaret Abbey 2
The Heart Is a Traitor - Margaret Abbey 4

Kingsley, Adam (Doctor)
Storm Before Sunrise - June Wyndham Davies 1507

Kingston, Thomas (Businessman)
The Store - Michael Pearson 4879

Kinich Kakmoo (Warrior)
Tikal: A Novel about the Maya - Daniel Peters 4947

Kinnersley, Patrick (Gentleman)
The Michaelmas Tree - Helen Ashfield 209

Kinraid, Charley (Sailor)
Sylvia's Lovers - Elizabeth Gaskell 2312

Kinsdale, Skye (Runaway)
A Pirate's Pleasure - Heather Graham 2518

Kinsmere, Roderick (Adventurer)
Most Secret - John Dickson Carr 912

Kipp, Peter (Trader)
The Two Medicine River - Richard S. Wheeler 6663

Kirby, Ambrose (Military Personnel)
Bugles Blow No More - Clifford Dowdey 1704

Kirby, Elizabeth (Southern Belle)
Bugles Blow No More - Clifford Dowdey 1704

Kirby, John (Spy)
The Summer Day Is Done - R.T. Stevens 6001

Kirby, Paul (Military Personnel)
Bugles Blow No More - Clifford Dowdey 1704

Kirk, Egan (Gunfighter; Frontiersman)
Father of Waters - Donald Clayton Porter 5118

Kirk, Morissa (Doctor)
Miss Morissa: Doctor of the Gold Trail - Mari
  Sandoz 5592

Kirk, Stuart (Journalist)
The Day the Sun Died - Dale Van Every 6408

Kirov, Sergei (Nobleman)
Fleur - Cynthia Harrod-Eagles 2754

Kirov, Sergei (Nobleman; Diplomat)
Anna - Cynthia Harrod-Eagles 2752

Kirta (Artisan)
The Shepherd Kings - Peter Danielson 1475

Kirwan, Captain Roderick (Landowner)
The Hedge of Thorns - Helen Ashton 217

Kischessinsky, Feliks (Spy)
The Man From St. Petersburg - Ken Follett 2148

Kishote, Don (Military Personnel)
The Glory - Herman Wouk 6873
The Hope - Herman Wouk 6874

Kittering, Alexandra (Southern Belle)
A Hundred Hills - Howard Breslin 667

Klein, Sanna (Teacher)
Leaving Cold Sassy - Olive Ann Burns 798

Kmita, Andrei (Military Personnel)
The Deluge - Henryk Sienkiewicz 5846

Knight, Charles (Rancher)
Crazy Fox Remembers - Don Preston 5174

Knight, Elzada (Young Woman)
No Other Place - John Gould 2497

Knight, Jabez (Settler)
No Other Place - John Gould 2497

Knight, Jack (Adventurer)
Crazy Fox Remembers - Don Preston 5174

Knight, Nan (Spinster)
Rivers Parting - Shirley Barker 315

Knipperdollink (Leader)
The Siege - Peter Vansittart 6431

Knott, Stephen (Military Personnel)
Thunder on the Chesapeake - David Divine 1650

Knowles, Charles (Military Personnel)
The Yankee Brig - Carter A. Vaughan 6443

Knowles, Ethan (Military Personnel; Patriot)
Bride of Liberty - Frank Yerby 6909

Knowles, Kathy (Loyalist; Fiance(e))
Bride of Liberty - Frank Yerby 6909

Knowles, Polly (Patriot)
Bride of Liberty - Frank Yerby 6909

Knutsson, Colum (Gentleman)
The Slow Awakening - Catherine Marchant 4082

Kokopelli (Indian; Shaman)
She Who Remembers - Linda Lay Shuler 5838

Komarovsky, Victor (Lawyer)
Doctor Zhivago - Boris Pasternak 4824

Konoualchik, Ivan (Mechanic)
In the Blue Light of African Dreams - Paul
    Watkins 6580

Kooti (Leader)
Season of the Jew - Maurice Shadbolt 5768

Kori (Prehistoric Human; Hunter)
The Animal Wife - Elizabeth Marshall Thomas 6243

Kornowski, Krystyna (Young Woman)
Polonaise - Piers Paul Read 5278

Kornowski, Stefan (Young Man)
Polonaise - Piers Paul Read 5278

Kortenaer, Dorande van (Young Woman)
Phantom Fortress - Bruce Lancaster 3643

Korzeniowski, Joe (Hero)
Loon Lake - E.L. Doctorow 1657

Kosar-Eh (Prehistoric Human; Hunter)
Shadow of the Watching Star - William
    Sarabande 5601

Kozlowski, David (Young Man)
The House of Cards - Leon Garfield 2292

Kracha, Djuro (Immigrant)
Out of This Furnace - Thomas Bell 425

Krakar, Janez (Revolutionary)
Pendragon. . .The Montenegran Plot - Robert
    Trevelyan 6338

Kraker, Sarge (Lawman)
Arfive - A.B. Guthrie Jr. 2623

Kraus, Tzili (Heroine)
Tzili: The Story of a Life - Aharon Appelfeld 180

Kreizler, Dr. Lazlo (Psychologist; Detective—
    Amateur)
The Alienist - Caleb Carr 907

Kriemhild (Widow(er))
The Twelve Pictures - Edith Simon 5857

Krona (Prehistoric Human; Warrior)
Sarum: The Novel of England - Edward
    Rutherfurd 5536

Kronkhyte, Abe (Teenager; Military Personnel)
If Not Victory - Frank Olney Hough 3043

Kropotka, Katerina (Streetperson)
The House of Cards - Leon Garfield 2292

Kukutux (Widow(er); Prehistoric Human)
Brother Wind - Sue Harrison 2748

Kumar, Hari (Journalist)
The Day of the Scorpion - Paul Scott 5682
The Jewel in the Crown - Paul Scott 5684

Kuntz, Herbert (Journalist)
The Retreat - Aharon Appelfeld 178

Kunze, Emile (Judge)
The Devil's Lieutenant - Maria Fagyas 1998

Kupper, Sebastian (Military Personnel; Pilot)
In the Company of Eagles - Ernest K. Gann 2279

Kuragin, Andrei (Nobleman)
The House of Kuragin - Constance Heaven 2808

Kuragin, Paul (Military Personnel)
Heir to Kuragin - Constance Heaven 2807

Kuragin, Rilla Weston (Noblewoman)
The Astrov Legacy - Constance Heaven 2802

Kurtsevich, Helena (Royalty)
With Fire and Sword - Henryk Sienkiewicz 5850

Kussov, Boris (Nobleman)
Encore - Monique Raphel High 2915

Kvidal, Morten (Immigrant; Carpenter)
The Emigrants - Johan Bojer 561

Kwani (Indian; Shaman)
Voice of the Eagle - Linda Lay Shuler 5839

Kwani (Indian; Wanderer)
She Who Remembers - Linda Lay Shuler 5838

Kwiknee (Young Woman)
The Echoing Cliffs - Hjalmar P. Thesen 6219

Kybbet, Tom (Gentleman)
Riot at Gravesend: A Novel of Wat Tyler's Rebellion -
    William Howard Woods 6864

Kyle, Jason (Prospector)
Judgment in July - Richard Fisher 2105

Kyra (Psychic)
The Temple of the Sun - Moyra Caldecott 849

Kyra (Psychic; Prehistoric Human)
The Tall Stones - Moyra Caldecott 848

Kyra (Religious)
Shadows on the Stones - Moyra Caldecott 847

Kysen (Companion)
Murder at the God's Gate - Lynda S.
    Robinson 5408

L

La-ena (Indian; Young Woman)
Wyoming! - Dana Fuller Ross 5494

La Fayette, Louise de (Gentlewoman)
The Favourite - Francoise Mallet-Joris 4040

La Jeune, Charlotte (Young Woman; Slave)
Daughter of Strangers - Elizabeth Boatwright
    Coker 1164

La Salle, Claire (Young Woman)
Mission to Mackinac - Myron David Orr 4755

Lacer, Gaius Julius (Slave; Architect)
Gold for the Caesars - Florence A. Seward 5759

Lacey, Adam de (Knight)
The Running Vixen - Elizabeth Chadwick 968

Lacey, Alan de (Military Personnel)
The Thousand Fires - Anne Powers 5155

Lacey, Alice (Gentlewoman)
The Desirable Duchess - Marion Chesney 1025
A Lady in Doubt - Annabel Wynne 6891

Lacey, Beatrice (Gentlewoman)
Wideacre - Philippa Gregory 2585

Lacey, Ben Franklin (Military Personnel)
Strange Company - Robert J. Conley 1251

Lacey, Ben Franklin (Rancher)
Border Line - Robert J. Conley 1238

Lacey, Sir Geoffrey (Gentleman)
A Lady in Doubt - Annabel Wynne 6891

Lacey, Jonathan (Frontiersman)
O Beulah Land - Mary Lee Settle 5756

Lacey, Julia (Gentlewoman)
The Favored Child - Philippa Gregory 2582

Lacey, Lily (Activist)
The Scapegoat - Mary Lee Settle 5758

Lacey, Pedro (Religious)
Savages and Saints - Cora Older 4717

Lacey, Prudence (Imposter)
The Masqueraders - Georgette Heyer 2894

Lacey, Robert de (Knight)
The Briar Rose - Linda Neale 4561

Lacey, Robin (Imposter)
The Masqueraders - Georgette Heyer 2894

Lacey, Sal (Spouse)
O Beulah Land - Mary Lee Settle 5756

Lacey, Stephen de (Nobleman)
Circle in the Water - Susan Wiggs 6742

Lackland, Abel (Doctor)
Gower Street - Claire Rayner 5264
The Haymarket - Claire Rayner 5265
Paddington Green - Claire Rayner 5266

Lackland, Harry (Gentleman)
Piccadilly - Claire Rayner 5267

Lackland, Jonah (Gentleman)
Soho Square - Claire Rayner 5268

Lackland, Jonah (Young Man)
The Haymarket - Claire Rayner 5265

Lackland, Lettice (Young Woman)
Chelsea Reach - Claire Rayner 5261

Lackland, Lewis (Doctor)
The Strand - Claire Rayner 5269

Lackland, Martha (Nurse)
Bedford Row - Claire Rayner 5259

Lackland, Peter (Gentleman)
Piccadilly - Claire Rayner 5267

Lackland, Phoebe (Young Woman)
Soho Square - Claire Rayner 5268

Lackland, Sophie (Orphan; Doctor)
Charing Cross - Claire Rayner 5260

Lacosta, Josefina (Gentlewoman)
Sharpe's Eagle - Bernard Cornwell 1341

Lacy, Frank (Revolutionary)
The End of the Hunt - Thomas Flanagan 2119

Lacy, Sir Fulk de (Knight)
Gay Crusader - Cleone Knox 3528

Lacy, Vivian (Plantation Owner)
Celia Garth - Gwen Bristow 695

Ladanova, Natasha (Dancer)
A Grand Passion - Mary Mackey 3991

Ladd, Elizabeth (Spy)
Farewell to Valley Forge - David Taylor 6178

Ladland, Katie (Young Woman)
For My Great Folly - Thomas B. Costain 1365

Lady (Military Personnel)
Three Days - Stephen Longstreet 3891

Laeghaire of Tralee (Knight)
The Firedrake - Cecelia Holland 2988

Laena (Prehistoric Human)
Children of the Ice - Charlotte Prentiss 5166

Laforgue (Religious)
Black Robe - Brian Moore 4441

Lai Tsin (Businessman)
Fortune Is a Woman - Elizabeth Adler 39

Laiage (Dancer)
Blood of the Martyrs - Naomi Mitchison 4417

Laidley, Hyatt (Knight)
By Right of Arms - Robyn Carr 937

Lainie (Outlaw)
The Ghosts of Elkhorn - Kerry Newcomb 4589

Laird, Dave (Young Man)
The Kingdom Carver - E.G. Perrault 4916

Lake, John (Military Personnel)
Salisbury Plain - Henry C. Branson 650

Lally (Orphan)
Ravenscroft - Dorothy Eden 1860

Lamb, Johnny (Adventurer; Sailor)
Lord of the Isles - Donald Barr Chidsey   1063

Lamb, Matthew (Military Personnel)
First Lieutenant - Kenneth Maynard   4208
Lamb in Command - Kenneth Maynard   4209
Lieutenant Lamb - Kenneth Maynard   4210

Lamb, Richard (Trader)
Richard Lamb - Richard S. Wheeler   6662

Lamb, Toby (Child)
The Haunting of Lamb House - Joan Aiken   48

Lambert, Etienne (Bastard Son)
The Emerald Necklace - Diana Brown   718

Lambert, Louise de (Gentlewoman)
Q'ri and I - Irving A. Bacheller   257

Lambkin, Rudy (Outlaw)
Rainbow on the Road - Esther Forbes   2159

Lambriere, Philippe de (Actor; Adventurer)
The Way to the Lantern - Audrey Erskine Lindop   3790

Lame Beaver (Indian)
Centennial - James A. Michener   4366

Lamia (Witch)
Lamia: A Witch - Georgia Elizabeth Taylor   6183

Lammas, Anthony (Religious)
The Free Fishers - John Buchan   750

Lamming, Lord (Nobleman; Hunter)
The Hammer of God - Alan Scholefield   5655

Lamond, Elsbeth (Gentlewoman)
Bride of the MacHugh - Jan Cox Speas   5956

Lamond, Peter (Military Personnel)
Up She Rises - David Garnett   2298

Lamont, Baptiste (Trader)
The Loon Feather - Iola Fuller   2253

Lamont, Catriona (Gentlewoman)
Kilcaraig - Annabel Carothers   904

Lamont, Grania (Gentlewoman)
Kilcaraig - Annabel Carothers   904

Lamont, Mary (Governess)
Sarsen Place - Gwendoline Butler   821

Lamont, Rorie (Gentleman)
Kilcaraig - Annabel Carothers   904

Lamoreaux, Madeleine (Young Woman)
Touched with Fire - John William Tebbel   6195

Lamott, Cherie (Gentlewoman)
Royal Street - Walter Adolphe Roberts   5393

Lamotte, Lucienne (Gentlewoman)
Captain Justice - Anthony Forrest   2185

Lampassas (Store Owner)
North to Yesterday - Robert Flynn   2145

Lamsaloff, Mischa (Royalty)
The Only Sin - Julie Ellis   1923

Lancelot (Knight)
The Chessboard Queen - Sharan Newman   4597
The Emperor Arthur - Godfrey Turton   6368
Guinevere Evermore - Sharan Newman   4601
Guinevere: The Legend in Autumn - Persia Woolley   6868
The King - Donald Barthelme   365
The Once and Future King - T.H. White   6705
Queen of the Summer Stars - Persia Woolley   6869
The Queen's Knight - Marvin Borowsky   585

Lancelot du Lac (Knight)
First Knight - Elizabeth Chadwick   966

Lancey, Oliver de (Military Personnel)
Concord Bridge - Howard Horne   3035

Lancy, Gerard Paul de (Nobleman)
A Spy for Napoleon - Baroness Emma Orczy   4746

Lancy, Richard (Businessman)
Cast a Long Shadow - Mary E. Pearce   4861

Landacta, Martin de (Religious)
Cannibal Eliot and the Lost Histories of San Francisco - Hilton Obenzinger   4660

Landau, Lilli (Bastard Daughter; Businesswoman)
The Only Sin - Julie Ellis   1923

Landeck, Felix Von (Heir)
The Long Afternoon - Ursula Zilinsky   6964

Landers, Becky (Young Woman)
Becky Landers, Frontier Warrior - Constance Skinner   5879

Landers, Sunny (Gentlewoman; Businesswoman)
Thunder on the Plains - Rosanne Bittner   517

Landerson, Roberto "Blanco" (Young Man; Cowboy)
The Color of Blood - E. Ralph Rundell   5524

Landis, Dolly (Actress)
Most Secret - John Dickson Carr   912

Landis, Leah (Spouse)
Piccadilly - Claire Rayner   5267

Landless, Geoffrey (Convict)
Prisoners of Hope: A Tale of Colonial Virginia - Mary Johnston   3238

Landon (Chieftain)
Pillar of the Sky - Cecelia Holland   2994

Landor, Angelet (Gentlewoman; Twin)
Saraband for Two Sisters - Philippa Carr   928

Landor, Bersaba (Gentlewoman; Twin)
Saraband for Two Sisters - Philippa Carr   928

Landry, Mignon (Young Woman)
Mignon - James M. Cain   845

Lane, Beau (Linguist; Indian)
A Good Day to Die - Thomas Wakefield Blackburn   525

Lane, Corey (Lawman)
Not of War Only - Norman Zollinger   6966

Lane, Jane (Young Woman)
Royal Escape - Georgette Heyer   2900

Laney, Garnet (Young Woman)
For the Love of Robert E. Lee - M.A. Harper   2715

Lang, Richard (Military Personnel)
Follow the Drum - James Leasor   3699

Lang Liu (Businessman)
Necklace and Calabash - Robert van Gulik   6419

Langalieve, Roger (Spy)
Tory Tavern - Henry Barnard Safford   5559

Langdon, Alicia (Young Woman)
Golden Destiny - June Wyndham Davies   1506

Langdon, Burke (Military Personnel)
The Moon-Eyed Appaloosa - Bill Gulick   2617

Langdon, Kat (Gentlewoman)
Court of Shadows - Cynthia Morgan   4450

Lange, Chris de (Young Woman)
The Covenant - Brigid Knight   3521

Langham, Piers (Knight)
The Warwick Heiress - Margaret Abbey   6

Langley, Adam (Sea Captain)
I Know My Love - Catherine Gaskin   2315

Langley, Penelope (Young Woman)
Traitor's Moon - Robert Neill   4574

Langlinais, Claude (Gentleman)
Cajun - Elizabeth Nell Dubus   1751

Langlinais, Mathilde (Spouse)
Cajun - Elizabeth Nell Dubus   1751

Langman, Christopher (Sailor)
Boon Island - Kenneth Roberts   5384

Langmeade, Lucky (Government Official)
Vigilante - Richard Summers   6116

Langrish, Malcolm (Sea Captain)
Pandora's Galley - Macdonald Harris   2727

Langtry, Leda (Editor; Feminist)
The Baroness of Bow Street - Gail Clark   1085

Lankester, Judith (Settler)
Judith Lankester - Marjorie Allee   93

Lansdon, Benedict (Gentleman)
The Pool of St. Branok - Philippa Carr   926

Lansdon, Benedict (Gentleman; Step-Parent)
The Changeling - Philippa Carr   918

Lansdon, Lucie (Orphan; Gentlewoman)
The Black Swan - Philippa Carr   917

Lansdowne, Valerie (Rancher)
The Wisdom of Stones - Greg Matthews   4192

Lansing, Jill (Young Woman)
The Ironmaster - Anne Powers   5150

Lanyon, Aubrey (Scholar; Teenager)
Venetia - Georgette Heyer   2909

Lanyon, Jessica (Widow(er))
To the End of Her Days - Malcolm Macdonald   3975

Lanyon, Venetia (Gentlewoman)
Venetia - Georgette Heyer   2909

Lao Chen (Student)
The Examination - Malcolm Bosse   587

Lao Hong (Young Man)
The Examination - Malcolm Bosse   587

Lao-ke (Indian; Young Woman)
Roanoke Warrior - Carter A. Vaughan   6438

Lapenotiere, John Richards (Military Personnel)
He Brings Great News - Clemence Dane   1462

Larcher, Jean (Businessman)
The Ghost of Monsieur Scarron - Janet Lewis   3755

Lark (Child; Prehistoric Human)
Shadows on the Stones - Moyra Caldecott   847

Larkin, Conor (Young Man)
Trinity - Leon Uris   6394

Larkin, Liam (Rancher)
Redemption - Leon Uris   6393

Larkin, Rory (Revolutionary; Military Personnel)
Redemption - Leon Uris   6393

Larkin, Timothy (Military Personnel; Scout)
Timothy Larkin - Jane Hutchens   3089

Larkins, Molly (Cook)
Rome Haul - Walter D. Edmonds   1877

Larne, Philip (Gentleman)
Deep Summer - Gwen Bristow   696

Larochejaquelin, Henri (Leader)
La Vendee - Anthony Trollope   6346

Laroule, Guy (Adventurer)
Louisiana Purchase - A.E. Hotchner   3039

Larrimer, Linc (Orphan)
Dodging Red Cloud - Richard S. Wheeler   6657

Larrimore, Ed (Rancher)
Home Mountain - Jeanne Williams   6777

Larsen, Hannale (Young Woman)
People of the Book - David Stacton   5974

Larsen, Lars (Young Man)
People of the Book - David Stacton   5974

Larsen, Simon (Gentleman)
The House of Memory: A Novel of Shanghai - Nicholas R. Clifford   1117

Larson, Erik (Gentleman)
River of Dreams - Gay Courter 1390

LaSalle, Charles (Military Personnel)
The Proud Canaries - David Johnson 3222

Lash, Sam (Mountain Man)
Wolf Song - Harvey Fergusson 2069

Lassiter, Lakshmi (Royalty)
The Frog Earl - Carola Dunn 1792

Latham, Reva (Spouse)
Fort Worth - Leonard Sanders 5588

Lathbury, Sara (Widow(er))
Prophecies - Helena Soister 5937

Lathrop, Isaac (Farmer)
Artillery of Time - Chard Powers Smith 5919

Lathrop, John (Farmer)
Artillery of Time - Chard Powers Smith 5919

Latimer, Burke (Young Man)
To See Your Face Again - Eugenia Price 5188

Latimer, Darsie (Nobleman)
Red Gauntlet - Sir Walter Scott 5706

Latimer, Harry (Patriot; Military Personnel)
The Carolinian - Rafael Sabatini 5547

Latimer, Natalie Browning (Southern Belle)
Before Darkness Falls - Eugenia Price 5178

Latour, Jean Marie (Religious)
Death Comes for the Archbishop - Willa Cather 957

Latrec, Blue Rhonda (Prostitute)
Southern Discomfort - Rita Mae Brown 730

Latro (Mercenary; Amnesiac)
Soldier of the Mist - Gene Wolfe 6843

Latterly, Hester (Nurse)
A Dangerous Mourning - Anne Perry 4926
Defend and Betray - Anne Perry 4928
The Face of a Stranger - Anne Perry 4929
The Sins of the Wolf - Anne Perry 4937
A Sudden, Fearful Death - Anne Perry 4938

Lattimer, Kate (Widow(er))
The Lattimer Legend - Ann Hebson 2813

Launcelot (Knight)
Arthur Rex: A Legendary Novel - Thomas
    Berger 477
Beloved Exile - Parke Godwin 2446
Firelord - Parke Godwin 2447
The Pendragon - Catherine Christian 1075
The Winter King - Bernard Cornwell 1351
Witch of the North - Courtway Jones 3272

Launcelot (Warrior)
The Duke of War - Walter O'Meara 4734

Laurelle (Teenager)
An Army of Children - Evan H. Rhodes 5306

Laurence, Alexander (Doctor)
Bedford Row - Claire Rayner 5259

Laurie, Vincent (Doctor)
Blood Line - Alanna Knight 3515
Deadly Beloved - Alanna Knight 3517
Enter Second Murderer - Alanna Knight 3518
Killing Cousins - Alanna Knight 3520

Laurignac, Edmond (Nobleman)
Vale of Tyranny - Suzanne Butler 831

Laury, Ann (Young Woman)
Soul of Abe Lincoln - Bernie Babcock 251

Lausley, Sarah (Governess)
The Skeleton in the Grass - Robert Barnard 320

Laval, Jacques (Adventurer)
The Only Sin - Julie Ellis 1923

Lavalette, Marie (Gentlewoman)
Captain Bolton's Corpse - J.G. Jeffreys 3178

Lavelle, Adrienne (Young Woman)
Ward of the Sun King - Mildred Allen Butler 826

Lavenham, Ludovic (Nobleman; Smuggler)
The Talisman Ring - Georgette Heyer 2905

Lavery, Dennis (Sailor)
Men of No Property - Dorothy Davis 1517

Lavette, Barbara (Writer)
The Establishment - Howard Fast 2030
The Legacy - Howard Fast 2037
Second Generation - Howard Fast 2043

Lavette, Barbara (Writer; Political Figure)
The Immigrant's Daughter - Howard Fast 2035

Lavette, Dan (Businessman)
Second Generation - Howard Fast 2043

Lavette, Dan (Fisherman; Businessman)
The Immigrants - Howard Fast 2034

Lavette, Jean (Socialite)
The Immigrants - Howard Fast 2034

Lavinia (Young Woman)
The Bond and the Free - Charles Dunscomb 1813

Lavransdatter, Kristin (Gentlewoman)
The Bridal Wreath - Sigrid Undset 6379
The Cross - Sigrid Undset 6380
The Mistress of Husaby - Sigrid Undset 6382

Lavrin, Alexandra Sergeivna (Noblewoman;
    Heiress)
The Fortune Hunter - Ira J. Morris 4477

Lavrin, Nicholas (Nobleman)
The Fortune Hunter - Ira J. Morris 4477

Lawe, Matthew (Sailor)
Darken Ship - Nicholas Monsarrat 4431
Running Proud - Nicholas Monsarrat 4432

Lawless (Outlaw)
The Black Arrow - Robert Louis Stevenson 6008

Lawless, Desmond de (Military Personnel;
    Nobleman)
Poor Richard's Game - G.J.A. O'Toole 4766

Lawley, Jemimah (Heiress)
Stormswift - Madeleine Brent 662

Lawley, John (Young Man)
Black William - Robert Neill 4567

Lawley, Molly (Young Woman)
Black William - Robert Neill 4567

Lawrence, Anne (Southern Belle)
Natchez: A Novel of the Deep South - Pamela
    Jekel 3186

Lawrence, Arden (Southern Belle)
Natchez: A Novel of the Deep South - Pamela
    Jekel 3186

Lawrence, Janessa Holt (Doctor)
Carolina Courage - Dana Fuller Ross 5469

Lawson, Henry (Military Personnel)
Season for War - P.F. Kluge 3510

Lawson, John (Military Personnel)
Mutiny Run - Frank Eccles 1836

Lawson, Lucy (Spouse)
Season for War - P.F. Kluge 3510

Lawson, Sanchia (Servant)
Masquerade for the King - Marina Oliver 4729

Lawton, Ben (Outlaw)
Rogue's Kingdom - John Brick 676

Lawton, Dolly (Young Woman)
Brimstone Club - F. van Wyck Mason 4147

Layne, Jeff (Veteran)
Slaughter - Elmer Kelton 3407

Layne, Jeff (Veteran; Rancher)
The Far Canyon - Elmer Kelton 3404

Layton, Phoebe (Noblewoman)
Reckless - Amanda Quick 5217

Layton, Sarah (Military Personnel)
A Division of the Spoils - Paul Scott 5683

Layton, Sarah (Young Woman)
The Day of the Scorpion - Paul Scott 5682

Lazar, Hannah (Seamstress)
The Enduring Years - Claire Rayner 5263

Lazare, Ric (Magician)
Fata Morgana - William Kotzwinkle 3549

Lazarevna, Zeinab "Zica" (Gentlewoman)
Between Two Worlds - Monique Raphel High 2913

Lazaro (Indian; Chieftain)
Apache Autumn - Robert Skimin 5875

Lazender, Lady Campion (Noblewoman)
The Fallen Angels - Susannah Kells 3397

Lazender, Toby (Young Man)
A Crowning Mercy - Susannah Kells 3396

Lazlo (Nobleman; Doctor)
The Secret Life of Laszlo, Count Dracula - Roderick
    Anscombe 156

Le Clerc, Maritza (Noblewoman; Spy)
The Passionate Rebel - Frank G. Slaughter 5894

Le Gros, Herbert (Heir)
The Cornerstone - Zoe Oldenbourg 4714

Le Grys, Nicholas (Heir)
Aurora Rose - Anne Worboys 6870

Le Noir, Justin (Knight)
The Infidels - Chloe Gartner 2308

Le Vendeur, Catherine (Gentlewoman)
The Wandering Arm - Sharan Newman 4603

Le Vendeur, Catherine (Spouse)
Strong as Death - Sharan Newman 4602

Leach (Servant)
Lady Jane - Norma Lee Clark 1092

Leaf, Dorney (Teenager)
Good Morning, Young Lady - Ardyth Kennelly 3424

Leah (Young Woman)
Babylon - Anthony Esler 1959

LeBlanc, Inspector (Detective—Police)
Henry James' Midnight Song - Carol de Chellis
    Hill 2920

Lebrun, Paul (Doctor)
Over There - Thomas Fleming 2130

Leche, Elaine de (Southern Belle)
Wild Is the River - Louis Bromfield 704

Ledbetter, Brian (Veteran)
The Coming of Rain - Richard Marius 4084

Ledbetter, Gideon (Military Personnel)
The Wolf and the Buffalo - Elmer Kelton 3408

Ledesma, Rafael (Military Personnel)
La Guerra: A Spanish Saga - Stephen D.
    Frances 2199

Ledyard, Grant (Military Personnel)
The Secret Road - Bruce Lancaster 3646

Lee, Aisek (Businessman)
Mandarin - Robert S. Elegant 1905

Lee, Alice (Gentlewoman)
Woodstock; or, The Cavalier - Sir Walter Scott 5710

Lee, Aura (Gentlewoman)
Come Spring - Charlotte Hinger 2954

Lee, Henry (Nobleman)
Woodstock; or, The Cavalier - Sir Walter Scott 5710

Lee, Leila (Socialite)
The Book Class - Louis Auchincloss 228

Lee, Mary Ellen (Young Woman)
The Bannaman Legacy - Catherine Cookson 1272

Lee, Sunset (Mountain Man)
Each Bright River - Mildred Masterson
  McNeilly 4308

LeFever, Captain (Military Personnel)
Fort De Chastaigne - Don Coldsmith 1177

LeGrand, St. Clair (Plantation Owner)
The Web of Days - Edna Lee 3708

Leguay, Gay (Young Woman; Seamstress)
I Thee Wed - Gilbert Wolf Gabriel 2267

Leibig, Vane (Gentleman)
London's Child - Philip Boast 560

Leigh, Adam (Plantation Owner)
Golden Isle - Frank G. Slaughter 5890

Leigh, Amanda (Gentlewoman)
Lilith - Jean Plaidy 5030

Leigh, Amyas (Sailor)
Westward Ho! - Charles Kingsley 3499

Leigh, Elyza (Gentlewoman)
Elyza - Clare Darcy 1486

Leigh, Gervas (Religious)
Towers in the Mist - Elizabeth Goudge 2495

Leigh, Tristram (Military Personnel)
Feather Castles - Patricia Veryan 6462

Leighton, Amelia (Young Woman)
One Night in Newport - Elizabeth Villars 6498

Leighton, Royce (Knight)
The Troubadour's Romance - Robyn Carr 940

Leiston, Robert (Military Personnel)
Bayonets in the Sun - William Moore 4446

Leith, Rachel (Gentlewoman)
Sanguinet's Crown - Patricia Veryan 6476

Lemaire, Jacques (Farmer)
The Golden Fool - David Divine 1649

Lempriere, John (Scholar)
Lempriere's Dictionary - Lawrence Norfolk 4641

Len (Farmer)
Fitzempress' Law - Diana Norman 4644

Lenihan, Liam (Farmer)
The Famished Land - Elizabeth Byrd 833

Lenoir, Nicole (Young Woman)
Always a River - Drayton Mayrant 4211

Lenoir, Pierre (Frontiersman)
The Strangers on the Island - Brand Whitlock 6714

Lenton, Edward (Nobleman)
The Abductors - Stuart Cloete 1121

Lenton, Lavinia (Noblewoman)
The Abductors - Stuart Cloete 1121

Leo, Brother (Religious)
Saint Francis - Nikos Kazantzakis 3385

Leominster, Lord Lavenham (Nobleman)
Marry in Haste - Jane Aiken Hodge 2967

Leon of Atrax (Military Personnel)
An Elephant for Aristotle - L. Sprague De
  Camp 1556

Leonard, Elden (Criminal)
Winterkill - David Thompson 6262

Leonard, Sam (Military Personnel)
By Antietam Creek - Don Robertson 5398

Leonard, Selena (Criminal)
Winterkill - David Thompson 6262

Leone, Achille (Gentleman)
Contessa - Richard Oliver Collin 1209

Leonie (Orphan)
The Villains: A Haunting Tale of the Marshes -
  Charlotte Keppel 3467

Leonie (Streetperson; Heiress—Dispossessed)
These Old Shades - Georgette Heyer 2906

Leonora (Survivor; Amnesiac)
The Sea Treasure - Elisabeth Barr 338

Leplastrier, Lucinda (Businesswoman)
Oscar and Lucinda - Peter Carey 894

Lerner, Dan (Conductor)
The Career of Magda V. - Joseph Machlis 3982

Leroux, Captain (Military Personnel)
Sharpe's Sword - Bernard Cornwell 1349

Leschi (Indian)
Mighty Mountain - Archie Binns 502

Lescure, Marie de (Young Woman)
La Vendee - Anthony Trollope 6346

Leslie, Ann (Young Woman)
The King's Rebel - James David Horan 3030

Leslie, Arnett (Military Personnel; Trader)
The Judas Tree - Neil Harmon Swanson 6139

Leslie, Hope (Heroine)
Hope Leslie; or, Early Times in Massachusetts -
  Catharine Maria Sedgewick 5714

Lester, Geoffrey (Gentleman)
The Second Sister - Leslie O'Grady 4701

Lester, Leonie (Spouse)
The Second Sister - Leslie O'Grady 4701

Lester, Madeline (Gentlewoman)
Eugene Aram - Edward Bulwer-Lytton 766

Lethbridge, Robert (Nobleman; Rake)
The Convenient Marriage - Georgette Heyer 2882

Levendeur, Catherine (Scholar; Detective—
  Amateur)
Death Comes as Epiphany - Sharan Newman 4598
The Devil's Door - Sharan Newman 4599

Leverett, Ira (Military Personnel)
Fifteen Flags - Richard Lynden Hardman 2686

Levi (Indian)
They Came to a Valley - Bill Gulick 2618

Levinson-Gore, Laura (Young Woman)
In the Shadow of the Nile - Sara Hylton 3093

Levinson-Gore, Lavinia (Gentlewoman)
In the Shadow of the Nile - Sara Hylton 3093

Levka, Rachel (Activist)
The Rising of the Moon - William Martin 4140

Levy, Abraham (Baker)
Esau - Meir Shalev 5770

Levy, Abraham (Doctor; Convict)
To the Ends of the Earth - Michael Talbot 6155

Levy, Esau (Writer)
Esau - Meir Shalev 5770

Levy, Hannah (Immigrant)
Rivington Street - Meredith Tax 6175
Union Square - Meredith Tax 6176

Levy, Ruby (Businesswoman)
Rivington Street - Meredith Tax 6175

Levy, Sarah (Labor Organizer)
Rivington Street - Meredith Tax 6175

Levy, Sarah (Spouse)
Esau - Meir Shalev 5770

Levy, Zalman (Immigrant)
Miami: A Saga - Evelyn Wilde Mayerson 4204

Lewarne, Linnet (Young Woman)
Castle Dor - Sir Arthur Thomas Quiller-Couch 5226

Lewellyn, David (Servant)
A Place of Ravens - Pamela Hill 2942

Lewin, Isaac (Immigrant)
West to Eden - Gloria Goldreich 2461

Lewis, Amy (Gentlewoman)
The Stanbroke Girls - Fiona Hill 2925

Lewis, Daphne (Captive)
Mister Christian - William Kinsolving 3502

Lewis, John (Military Personnel)
Seasons - Anna Dillon 1645

Lewis, Jonathan (Adventurer; Captive)
The Seneca Hostage - Carter A. Vaughan 6440

Lewis, Michael (Frontiersman)
Sons of Texas - Tom Early 1822

Lewis, Mordecai (Frontiersman)
Sons of Texas - Tom Early 1822

Lewis, Vargas (Engineer; Military Personnel)
Young Vargas Lewis - Robert Brainard Pearsall 4874

Lewrie, Alan (Military Personnel)
The French Admiral - Dewey Lambdin 3609
The Gun Ketch - Dewey Lambdin 3610
H.M.S. Cockerel - Dewey Lambdin 3611
The King's Coat - Dewey Lambdin 3612
A King's Commander - Dewey Lambdin 3613
The King's Commission - Dewey Lambdin 3614
The King's Privateer - Dewey Lambdin 3615

Leyburne, John (Artisan)
Traitor's Moon - Robert Neill 4574

Leyland, Francis (Spy; Nobleman)
The White Witch - Elizabeth Goudge 2496

Leyland, Lydia (Gentlewoman)
Lydia, or Love in Town - Clare Darcy 1492

Leyton, Louisa (Businesswoman; Cook)
The Duchess of Duke Street - Mollie Hardwick 2693

Li, General (Military Personnel)
Empire of Heaven - Linda Ching Sledge 5907

Libanius (Philosopher; Editor)
Julian - Gore Vidal 6489

Libba (Young Woman)
Scorpus the Moor - Leslie Turner White 6690

Libby (Servant)
Mary of Carisbrooke - Margaret Campbell
  Barnes 327

Lichen (Indian; Young Woman)
People of the River - W. Michael Gear 2338

Liddiard, Eugenia (Young Woman)
Eugenia - Clare Darcy 1487

Liddiard, Gerald (Young Man)
Eugenia - Clare Darcy 1487

Liddiard, Richard (Young Man)
Eugenia - Clare Darcy 1487

Liebermann, Meyer (Adventurer)
Castle Garden - Bill Albert 63

Lien (Royalty)
A House in Peiking - Robert Payne 4853

Lightbody, Eleanor (Spouse)
The Road to Wellville - T. Coraghessan Boyle 618

Lightbody, Will (Gentleman)
The Road to Wellville - T. Coraghessan Boyle 618

Lightburn, Rush (Hunter)
I Take This Land - Richard Powell 5147

Liklik (Wanderer; Hunter)
The Echoing Cliffs - Hjalmar P. Thesen 6219

Lilia (Young Woman)
The Lost Legion - H. Warner Munn 4516

Lilianna (Noblewoman; Heiress)
The Lily and the Leopard - Susan Wiggs 6745

Liliwin (Entertainer)
The Sanctuary Sparrow - Ellis Peters 4972

Lilliane of Orrick, Lady (Noblewoman)
My Gallant Enemy - Rexanne Becnel 409

Lilliendahl, David (Doctor)
The Healers - Henry Denker 1610

Lilly, Max Cary de (Veteran; Mercenary)
Vardy - John Harris 2721

Lily (Young Woman)
The Mountain of Immoderate Desires - Leslie
  Wilson 6811

Lin Kwong (Young Woman)
The House That Tai Ming Built - Virginia Lee 3711

Lincoln, Lionel (Military Personnel; Loyalist)
Lionel Lincoln; or, The Leaguer of Boston - James
  Fenimore Cooper 1303

Lindeman, Hans Jacob (Artist)
Lindeman's Daughters - Synnove Christensen 1073

Lindhelm, Elisa (Young Woman)
Prague Counterpoint - Bodie Thoene 6225
Vienna Prelude - Bodie Thoene 6228

Lindley, Andrew (Rake)
The Rake - Karen Lynn 3941

Lindley, Rowan (Nobleman)
Wild Jasmine - Bertrice Small 5914

Lindowska, Rissa (Immigrant; Actress)
Glorious Morning - Julie Ellis 1919

Lindsay, Alasdair (Landowner)
Indigo - Nicholas Carnac 900

Lindsay, Anne (Orphan; Companion)
My Lord Monleigh - Jan Cox Speas 5957

Lindsay, Craig (Heir)
Indigo - Nicholas Carnac 900

Lindsay, Edmund (Jeweler)
Jewelled Path - Rosalind Laker 3597

Lindsay, Gloria (Actress; Widow(er))
The Magic Ship - Sandra Paretti 4791

Lindsay, Hannah (Young Woman)
Brave Kingdom - Frances Murray 4534

Lindsay, Irene (Gentlewoman; Designer)
Jewelled Path - Rosalind Laker 3597

Lindsay, Mildrid (Gentlewoman)
Horseshoe Robinson, a Tale of the Tory Ascendancy -
  John P. Kennedy 3418

Lindsay, Nathan (Farmer)
Call of the Mountains - Cornelia Meigs 4326

Ling, May (Heroine)
The Immigrants - Howard Fast 2034

Ling-ling (Spouse)
Red Barbarian - Margaret Gaan 2260

Lingarde, Richard (Military Personnel; Engineer)
Beyond All Frontiers - Emma Drummond 1722

Lingford, Henry (Gentleman)
The Tempestuous Petticoat - Mary Ann Gibbs 2397

Lingford, Martha (Orphan)
The Tempestuous Petticoat - Mary Ann Gibbs 2397

Linnieres, Ansiau de (Nobleman)
The Cornerstone - Zoe Oldenbourg 4714

Linthorne, Sara (Spouse)
The Earth Abideth - George Dell 1595

Linthorne, Thomas (Farmer)
The Earth Abideth - George Dell 1595

Linton, Edgar (Gentleman)
*H.—: The Story of Heathcliff's Journey Back to
  Wuthering Heights* - Lin Haire-Sargeant 2641

Linton, Emma (Widow(er))
The Last Summer of Innocence - Linda Sole 5938

Linton, Kate (Young Woman)
The Last Summer of Innocence - Linda Sole 5938

Lintott, Inspector (Detective—Police)
Dear Laura - Jean Stubbs 6094
The Golden Crucible - Jean Stubbs 6096

Linwood, Martin (Veteran)
Some Far Elusive Dawn - Emma Drummond 1727

Lirey, Nicholas (Nobleman; Heir—Dispossessed)
The Image of Our Lord - Edward Burman 790

Lisa, Manuel (Settler; Trader)
Those Who Go Against the Current - Shirley
  Seifert 5734

Little, Will (Gentleman)
Willowwood - Elizabeth Savage 5619

Little Bear, Tom (Cowboy)
The Talking Rifle - Glenn R. Vernam 6454

Little Brother (Indian)
*The Kentucky Trace: A Novel of the American
  Revolution* - Harriette Simpson Arnow 195

Little Dancer (Prehistoric Human)
People of the Fire - W. Michael Gear 2335

Little David (Slave)
Wind Like a Bugle - Leonard Nathan 3722

Little Emily (Orphan; Fiance(e))
The Real David Copperfield - Robert Graves 2551

Little Hawk (Indian)
Red Stick - Donald Clayton Porter 5121
Sachem's Son - Donald Clayton Porter 5125

Little Hawk (Indian; Chieftain)
Hawk's Journey - Donald Clayton Porter 5119

Little Hawk (Indian; Warrior)
War Clouds - Donald Clayton Porter 5131

Little Hoop (Indian; Spouse)
The Legend of Ben Tree - Paul Hawkins 2784

Little John (Outlaw)
The Good Yeomen - Jay Williams 6771

Little Runner (Indian)
These Thousand Hills - A.B. Guthrie Jr. 2627

Little Sister (Child)
Little Sister - Margaret Gaan 2259

Little Wolf (Indian)
The Last Frontier - Howard Fast 2036

Little Wound (Handicapped; Indian)
Dance Back the Buffalo - Milton Lott 3899

Livingston, Andrew (Banker; Political Figure)
The Bad Lands - Oakley Hall 2651

Livingston, Charley (Captive)
The Wine of San Lorenzo - Herbert Gorman 2493

Livingston, Tom (Sea Captain)
Dream Time - Parris Afton Bonds 570

Livingston, Whit (Trapper)
Look to the Mountain - Le Grand Cannon 885

Livingstone, Charlotte (Spouse)
Wives of the Wind - Marjorie Jarrett 3170

Livingstone, Harry (Settler)
Wives of the Wind - Marjorie Jarrett 3170

Livingstone, Kolfinna (Spouse)
Wives of the Wind - Marjorie Jarrett 3170

Livingstone, Mellie (Spouse)
Wives of the Wind - Marjorie Jarrett 3170

Livingstone, Sybil (Spouse)
Wives of the Wind - Marjorie Jarrett 3170

Llewellyn, Davy (Sailor; Fisherman)
The Maid of Sker - R.D. Blackmore 529

Llewellyn, Nicholas (Plantation Owner)
Penhally - Caroline Gordon 2479

Llewellyn, Ralph (Plantation Owner)
Penhally - Caroline Gordon 2479

Llewelyn, Gwen (Young Woman)
The White Rhino Hotel - Bartle Bull 765

Lloyd, Martin (Worker)
Morgan's Woman - Iris Gower 2500

Lloyd, Stephen (Revolutionary)
The Single Star - Walter Adolphe Roberts 5394

Loam, Fred (Gentleman)
The Girl - Catherine Cookson 1277

Lobach, Kendall (Banker)
The Great Betrayal - Dorothy Gardiner 2284

Locke, Anne (Immigrant)
Down From the Mountain - Louis Charbonneau 997

Locke, Dan (Frontiersman; Trapper)
Fire in the Sky - J.A. Shears 5785

Locke, Jane (Young Woman)
This Other Eden - Marilyn Harris 2733

Locke, Marianne (Servant)
This Other Eden - Marilyn Harris 2733

Locker, Sarah (Young Woman)
The Price of Liberty - Joseph G.E. Hopkins 3028

Lockhart, David (Religious)
The Asking Price - Jessica Stirling 6039
The Good Provider - Jessica Stirling 6043

Lockhart, Jamie (Outlaw)
The Robber Bridegroom - Eudora Welty 6623

Lockhart, Randall (Gentleman)
Twilight of the Dragon - Peter Bourne 596

Lockhart, Taisie (Orphan; Rancher)
North of 36 - Emerson Hough 3042

Lockley, Sophia (Gentlewoman)
Ladysmead: A Novel in the Jane Austen Tradition -
  Jane Gillespie 2420

Lockwood, Dillon (Heir)
Thief of My Heart - Rexanne Becnel 410

Lockwood, Wayne (Military Personnel; Settler)
Song of Years - Bess Streeter Aldrich 72

Lockyear, Cal (Settler)
The Earthbreakers - Ernest Haycox 2789

Logan, Anthony (Heir—Dispossessed; Adventurer)
The Blood Endures - Robert Inman 3107

Logan, Ben (Engineer)
Crimson Creek: A Novel of the Early West - Robert
  McCraig 4228

Logan, Carey (Gambler)
Black Gold - Anita Richmond Bunkley 771

Logan, Carrie (Spouse)
Star of Empire: A Novel of Old San Antonio - Leonard
  Sanders 5590

Logan, Elizabeth (Gentlewoman)
I Came to the Highlands: A Novel of Suspense - Velda
  Johnston 3263

Logan, Julia Howard (Businesswoman; Sailor)
The Crystal Star - Ellen Argo 184

Logan, Julia Howard (Sea Captain; Businesswoman)
The Yankee Girl - Ellen Argo 186

Logan, Kendra (Young Woman)
Calico Palace - Gwen Bristow 694

Logan, Mary (Gentlewoman)
The Pointless Knife - Constance Dodge 1667

Logan, Stephen (Sea Captain)
The Crystal Star - Ellen Argo 184
The Yankee Girl - Ellen Argo 186

Logan, Tad (Political Figure)
Star of Empire: A Novel of Old San Antonio - Leonard
    Sanders 5590

Lohmann, Ernst (Refugee)
Death Squad London - Jack Gerson 2360

Lok (Prehistoric Human)
The Inheritors - William Golding 2455

Lokenburg, Maximilian (Nobleman)
On the Night of the Seventh Moon - Victoria
    Holt 3018

Lomassou, Bernat (Nobleman)
The Golden Chain - Jean Gamo 2275

Lomax, H.H. (Businessman)
The Demise of Billy the Kid - Preston Lewis 3760

Lombard, Randi (Gentlewoman)
Pacific Cavalcade - Virginia Coffman 1157

Lomont, Nicholas (Lawyer)
The Still Storm - Francoise Sagan 5562

London, Ben (Foundling; Military Personnel)
London's Child - Philip Boast 560

Lone Walker (Indian; Shaman)
Scalpdancers - Kerry Newcomb 4592

Lone Wolf (Indian)
Wolf Song - Harvey Fergusson 2069

Long, Adam (Sea Captain)
Captain Adam - Donald Barr Chidsey 1058

Long Walker (Indian; Warrior)
Daughter of the Eagle - Don Coldsmith 1173

Longacre, Jarrett (Outlaw)
The Pumpkin Rollers - Elmer Kelton 3406

Longbaugh, Lacey (Orphan)
Cherokee Dawn - Genell Dellin 1596

Longbras, Marie (Artisan)
The Heirs of the Kingdom - Zoe Oldenbourg 4716

Longe, Ambrose (Editor)
The Northern Correspondent - Jean Stubbs 6099

Longinus (Military Personnel)
The Centurion - Leonard Wibberley 6729
Hear Me, Pilate! - LeGette Blythe 557
The Lance of Longinus - Hubertus Loewenstein 3833
Man on Fire: A Novel on the Life of St. Paul -
    LeGette Blythe 558
A Tear for Judas - LeGette Blythe 559

Longyan (Young Man; Military Personnel)
Ming: A Novel of Seventeeth Century China - Robert
    B. Oxnam 4772

Lonit (Prehistoric Human)
Beyond the Sea of Ice - William Sarabande 5595
Corridor of Storms - William Sarabande 5596
Forbidden Land - William Sarabande 5599
Walkers of the Wind - William Sarabande 5603

Looks Far (Indian; Shaman)
The Sacred Hills - Don Coldsmith 1187

Loon Cry (Indian)
Fire in the Sky - J.A. Shears 5785

Lopez, Rebecca (Young Woman)
The Quality of Mercy - Faye Kellerman 3391

Lopez y Montenegro, Dona Luisa (Gentlewoman)
Not of War Only - Norman Zollinger 6966

Lord, Lucius (Businessman)
The Bridge - Marguerite Allis 108

Lord, Sarah (Gentlewoman)
The Bridge - Marguerite Allis 108

Lorendana, Juanita (Dancer; Spy)
A Spy for Napoleon - Baroness Emma Orczy 4746

Lorenzo (Artisan)
The Betrothed - Alessandro Manzoni 4078

Lorimer, Alexa (Singer)
Blaize - Anne Melville 4331

Lorimer, Alexa (Singer; Ward)
Alexa - Anne Melville 4330

Lorimer, Andrew (Doctor)
The Cactus and the Crown - Catherine Gavin 2318

Lorimer, Brinsley (Military Personnel)
Blaize - Anne Melville 4331

Lorimer, John Junius (Banker)
The Lorimer Line - Anne Melville 4332

Lorimer, Margaret (Doctor)
Blaize - Anne Melville 4331

Lorimer, Margaret (Gentlewoman)
The Lorimer Line - Anne Melville 4332

Lorimer, Matthew (Artist)
Alexa - Anne Melville 4330

Lorimer, Paul de (Settler)
Three Came to Ville Marie - Alan Sullivan 6114

Lorimer, Sally (Young Woman)
The Cactus and the Crown - Catherine Gavin 2318

Loring, Cassy (Actress; Orphan)
Cassy - Elizabeth Lyle 3930

Loring, Catherine (Heroine)
The Hawks of Hawk-Hollow - Robert Montgomery
    Bird 504

Loring, Nigel (Nobleman; Knight)
The White Company - Sir Arthur Conan Doyle 1716

Lorme, Alicia de (Noblewoman)
The Lormes of Castle Rising - Fanny Cradock 1409
Shadows over Castle Rising - Fanny Cradock 1410

Lorme, Christine (Spouse)
War Comes to Castle Rising - Fanny Cradock 1411

Lorme, Gyles (Nobleman)
War Comes to Castle Rising - Fanny Cradock 1411

Lorme, Henry (Gentleman)
Shadows over Castle Rising - Fanny Cradock 1410
Wind of Change at Castle Rising - Fanny
    Cradock 1412

Lorme, Justin Henry de (Nobleman)
The Lormes of Castle Rising - Fanny Cradock 1409

Lorne, Raurie (Young Woman)
And the Wild Birds Sing - Lola Irish 3112

Lorrenes, Marc de (Frontiersman)
The Gilded Torch - Iola Fuller 2252

Loskiel, Evan (Military Personnel)
Hidden Children - Robert W. Chambers 978

Lospe (Indian; Young Woman)
This Promised Land - Robert Easton 1824

Lostris (Young Woman)
River God - Wilbur Smith 5928

Loth (Ruler)
Bride of the Spear - Kathleen Herbert 2851

Lottie (Gentlewoman)
Knave of Hearts - Philippa Carr 920

Lotus (Indian)
Mountain Man - Vardis Fisher 2110

Lotus (Young Woman)
Manchu Palaces - Jeanne Larsen 3669

Lotus Blossom (Prostitute)
The Good Earth - Pearl S. Buck 754

Louis XIX (Heir)
The Uncrowned King - Baroness Emma Orczy 4747

Louise (Orphan; Seamstress)
Banners of Silk - Rosalind Laker 3592

Louise (Prostitute)
The Age of Wonders - Aharon Appelfeld 173

Loup, Guy (Military Personnel)
Sharpe's Battle - Bernard Cornwell 1338

Lovat, Oswin (Nobleman)
Topaz - Helen Ashfield 215

Loveday, Bob (Sailor)
The Trumpet Major - Thomas Hardy 2700

Loveday, John (Military Personnel)
The Trumpet Major - Thomas Hardy 2700

Lovejoy, Ethan (Settler)
Western: A Saga of the Great Plains - Frank
    Yerby 6930

Lovel (Bastard Son; Heir—Lost)
The Antiquary - Sir Walter Scott 5690

Loveless, Gail (Spy; Actress)
Secret Service Operator 13 - Robert W.
    Chambers 982

Lovell, Amy (Gentlewoman)
The White Dove - Rosie Thomas 6246

Lovell, Charlotte (Gentlewoman)
The Old Maid - Edith Wharton 6652

Lovell, Eleanor (Gentlewoman)
A Space of the Heart - Patricia Wright 6884

Lovell, Grace (Spouse)
A Horseman Riding By - R.F. Delderfield 1588

Lovell, Richard (Gentleman)
The Bracegirdle - Burris Atkins Jenkins 3189

Lovell, Tina (Ward)
The Old Maid - Edith Wharton 6652

Lovell, Tyson (Outlaw)
The Long Night - Andrew Lytle 3945

Lovey (Slave)
Beulah Land - Lonnie Coleman 1202

Lowell, Adam (Widow(er); Diplomat)
Blood and Sable - Carol J. Kane 3350

Lowell, Judith (Teacher)
Johnny Osage - Janice Holt Giles 2412

Lowell, Wolsey (Settler)
Thanksgiving - Terry Coleman 1207

Lowensohn, Gershon (Businessman)
Dreams of Gold - Lewis Orde 4748

Lowrie, Angus (Clerk)
Clear for Action: A Novel about John Paul Jones -
    Clements Ripley 5344

Lu Mei-ling (Revolutionary)
Peking: A Novel of China's Revolt - Anthony
    Grey 2587

Luarca, Francisca de (Young Woman)
Poison - Kathryn Harrison 2737

Lubloff, Arthur (Financier)
Hanover Place - Michael M. Thomas 6245

Lubonski, Count Cyprjan (Nobleman)
Poland - James A. Michener 4373

Luca, Don Antonio (Organized Crime Figure)
Luciano's Luck - Jack Higgins 2912

Lucan (Knight)
The Queen's Knight - Marvin Borowsky 585

Lucas (Teenager)
Midnight Is a Place - Joan Aiken 52

Lucas (Worker)
The Three-Cornered Hat - Pedro Antonio de
    Alarcon 62

Lucas, Amy (Actress)
Covent Garden - Claire Rayner 5262

Lucas, Celia (Young Woman)
The Haymarket - Claire Rayner 5265

Lucas, Claudette (Actress)
The Strand - Claire Rayner 5269

Lucas, Fenton (Actor)
Covent Garden - Claire Rayner 5262

Lucas, Lilith (Actress)
Gower Street - Claire Rayner 5264
The Haymarket - Claire Rayner 5265
Paddington Green - Claire Rayner 5266

Lucat-mael (Religious)
Druid's Enchantment - Millie J. Ragosta 5240

Lucca, Pietro (Military Personnel)
Captain of the Medici - John J. Pugh 5206

Luceiia (Noblewoman)
The Skystone: The Forging of Arthur's Britain - Jack
  Whyte 6726

Luceiia (Spouse)
The Singing Sword - Jack Whyte 6725

Lucero, Don Juan (Gentleman)
The Adventures of Don Juan - Richard Gardner 2289

Lucia (Fiance(e))
The Betrothed - Alessandro Manzoni 4078

Lucie (Actress)
The Queen's War: A Novel of Eleanor of Aquitaine -
  Jeanne Mackin 3996

Lucie (Settler)
Honey in the Horn - Harold Lenoir Davis 1523

Lucie, James (Artist)
Melbury Square - Dorothy Eden 1857

Lucie, Maude (Model)
Melbury Square - Dorothy Eden 1857

Luckett, Sayward (Backwoodswoman)
The Trees - Conrad Richter 5326

Luckett, Worth (Backwoodsman)
The Trees - Conrad Richter 5326

Luckner, Erich (Businessman)
The Warlord - Malcolm Bosse 589

Lucy, Jocelin (Nobleman)
The Leper of St. Giles - Ellis Peters 4963

Ludel, Richard (Nobleman)
The Hermit of Eyton Forest - Ellis Peters 4961

Ludlow, Captain (Sea Captain; Military Personnel)
The Water Witch - James Fenimore Cooper 1311

Ludlow, Sir Gareth (Nobleman)
Sprig Muslin - Georgette Heyer 2903

Ludona (Indian; Warrior)
Ambush - Donald Clayton Porter 5113

Lufton, Miles (Political Figure)
Troy Chimneys - Margaret Kennedy 3421

Luis, Don (Gentleman)
Mercedes of Castile - James Fenimore Cooper 1304

Luis, Don (Nobleman)
Anthony Adverse - Hervey Allen 98
The Golden Hawk - Frank Yerby 6921

Luisa (Young Woman)
The Balloonist - Macdonald Harris 2724

Luken, Charlotte (Businesswoman)
Mistress of the Forge - David Taylor 6179

Lumley, Melloney (Invalid)
Dolphin Summer - Carola Salisbury 5569

Lumley, Oliver (Police Officer)
Jekyll, Alias Hyde - Donald Thomas 6240
The Ripper's Apprentice - Donald Thomas 6242

Lundy, Katherine (Servant)
Seasons - Anna Dillon 1645

Luovitch, Yakov "Yasha" (Young Man)
Between Two Worlds - Monique Raphel High 2913

Lupa, Auguste (Detective—Private)
Rasputin's Revenge - John T. Lescroart 3725
Son of Holmes - John T. Lescroart 3726

Lupton, Timothy (Artist)
Gentlemen in England - A.N. Wilson 6795

Luria, Benny (Military Personnel)
The Glory - Herman Wouk 6873

Luria, Benny (Military Personnel; Pilot)
The Hope - Herman Wouk 6874

Lutero (Indian; Warrior)
The Pride of Hannah Wade - Janet Dailey 1455

Luti (Sorceress)
Prophets and Warriors - Peter Danielson 1473
The Trumpet and the Sword - Peter Danielson 1479

Luton, Bluff (Lawman)
The Actor - Robert J. Conley 1236
Colfax - Robert J. Conley 1239
Killing Time - Robert J. Conley 1244

Luton, Lord Evelyn (Nobleman)
Journey - James A. Michener 4371

Lutonville, Lady Naomi (Gentlewoman)
Time's Fool - Patricia Veryan 6479

Luttrell, Edmund (Religious; Thief)
The Whyte Harte - P.C. Doherty 1681

Luz (Indian)
The Cry of Dolores - Herbert Gorman 2492

Lydgate, Tertius (Doctor)
Middlemarch - George Eliot 1909

Lydiard, Maurice (Gentleman)
Bed in Hell - Elfrida Vipont 6504

Lygia (Royalty)
Quo Vadis - Henryk Sienkiewicz 5848

Lykaina (Slave; Writer)
The Other Sappho - Ellen Frye 2240

Lykos (Slave)
Gate to the Sea - Bryher 743

Lyle, Mark (Young Man)
The Road to San Jacinto - James F. Davis 1524

Lyle, Rena (Young Woman)
Cottonwoods Grow Tall - Margaret Bell
  Houston 3055

Lynch, Dorothea (Young Woman)
The Lovely Lynchs - Magdalen King-Hall 3490

Lynch, Ella (Young Woman)
Young Vargas Lewis - Robert Brainard Pearsall 4874

Lynch, Jenny (Young Woman)
The Lovely Lynchs - Magdalen King-Hall 3490

Lyndale (Nobleman)
Gwendolen - Clare Darcy 1489

Lyndon, Lady Honoria (Gentlewoman)
Barry Lyndon - William Makepeace Thackeray 6210

Lyngate, Adam (Heir)
Midsummer Masque - Jill Tattersall 6174

Lyse, Clementine (Singer)
The Monterant Affair - Richard Grayson 2560

Lysis (Young Man)
The Last of the Wine - Mary Renault 5299

Lyte, Catherwood (Immigrant; Settler)
Catherwood - Marly Youmans 6937

Lytton, Lavender (Companion)
Dulcie Bligh - Gail Clark 1086

M

Ma Joong (Assistant)
The Chinese Nail Murders - Robert van Gulik 6413
The Phantom of the Temple - Robert van Gulik 6420
The Red Pavilion - Robert van Gulik 6421
The Willow Pattern - Robert van Gulik 6422

Mablethorpe, Adrian (Nobleman)
Faro's Daughter - Georgette Heyer 2887

mac Cainnech, Aidan (Religious)
Byzantium - Stephen R. Lawhead 3680

Mac Cool, Finn (Warrior)
Finn Mac Cool - Morgan Llywelyn 3818

Macadam, John (Musician)
Brave Kingdom - Frances Murray 4534

Macalister, Guy (Manager)
Castle of Doves - Constance Heaven 2803

MacAllan, Jennie (Young Woman; Twin)
The Woman from The Glen - Chloe Gartner 2310

MacAllan, Pollux (Young Man; Twin)
The Woman from The Glen - Chloe Gartner 2310

MacAllister, Malcolm (Teacher)
The Strange Brigade - John Edward Jennings 3209

MacAndrew, Joan (Doctor)
Wideacre - Philippa Gregory 2585

MacAndrew, Richard (Gentleman)
The Favored Child - Philippa Gregory 2582

MacArthur, Ian (Laird)
Highland Belle - Patricia Grasso 2541

MaCartney, Jenny (Worker; Servant)
A Leaf in the Wind - Marie Joseph 3307

Macbean, Robert (Prospector)
The Adelita - Oakley Hall 2649

MacBraugh, Jefferson (Sea Captain)
The Sinking of the Sarah Diamond - William Dale
  Jennings 3213

MacCallister, Jamie Ian (Military Personnel)
Talons of Eagles - William W. Johnstone 3268

MacClaine, Jessica (Servant)
The Explorers - William Stuart Long 3872

MacClaren, Andrew (Rancher)
Women in the Wind - Margaret Ritter 5350

MacClaren, Reanna (Spouse)
Women in the Wind - Margaret Ritter 5350

MacCroy, Max (Government Official)
The Passion of Letty Fox - Diana Saunders 5610

MacCullough, Andrew (Frontiersman)
The River Devils - Carter A. Vaughan 6437

MacDermott, Reece (Military Personnel)
Kings Mountain - Florette Henri 2838

MacDonald, Alasdair Og (Young Man)
Lady of the Glen - Jennifer Roberson 5369

MacDonald, Major Angus (Frontiersman)
Trapper's Moon - Jory Sherman 5823

MacDonald, Angus (Gentleman)
A Falcon for a Queen - Catherine Gaskin 2314

MacDonald, Arabella (Fiance(e))
Follow the Drum - James Leasor 3699

Macdonald, Charles (Gentleman)
The French Bride - Evelyn Anthony 163

MacDonald, David (Frontiersman)
Pemmican - Vardis Fisher 2111

Macdonald, Iain (Military Personnel)
The Island Harp - Jeanne Williams 6779

Macdonald, James (Gentleman)
Clandara - Evelyn Anthony 161

Macdonald, J.R.L. (Military Personnel)
Invading Tibet - Mark Frutkin 2239

MacDonald, Laura (Gentlewoman)
Cruel in the Shadow - Lorn MacIntyre 3986

MacDonald, Laurel (Indian; Teacher)
Trail of Tears - Frances Patton Statham 5983

MacDonald, Mary Rose (Spouse)
The Blind Bend - Lorn MacIntyre 3985

MacDonald, Niall (Laird)
The Blind Bend - Lorn MacIntyre 3985

MacDonald, Niall (Military Personnel)
Cruel in the Shadow - Lorn MacIntyre 3986

MacDonald, Robert (Journalist)
The Long Watch - Elizabeth Linington 3798

MacDonnell, Call (Fugitive)
The Lonely Strangers - Charity Blackstock 531

MacDougall, Jack (Settler; Farmer)
Nebraska Coast - Clyde Brion Davis 1516

Maceachern, Darthula (Young Woman)
Commander of the Mists - D.L. Murray 4527

MacFarland, Andrew (Gentleman)
Devilseed - Frank Yerby 6914

MacFarlane, Alix (Nurse)
The Heart of the Continent - Nancy Cato 961

MacFarlane, Barbara (Gentlewoman)
Lord Libertine - Anthony Esler 1964

MacFarlane, Ian (Adventurer; Loyalist)
Valiant Libertine - John Gordon Bryson 748

MacFell, Charlie (Military Personnel)
The Cinderpath - Catherine Cookson 1275

MacFell, Edward (Gentleman)
The Cinderpath - Catherine Cookson 1275

MacGregor, Baril (Trader; Frontiersman)
The Forbidden Ground - Neil Harmon
  Swanson 6138

MacGregor, Kirsten (Orphan; Servant)
The Slow Awakening - Catherine Marchant 4082

MacGregor, Neil Roy (Fugitive)
The Pointless Knife - Constance Dodge 1667

MacHugh, Alexander (Laird)
Bride of the MacHugh - Jan Cox Speas 5956

MacHugh, Ronan (Mercenary)
The Gallowglass - Howard Breslin 666

MacIan, Fiona (Young Woman)
Dark Torrent of Glencoe - Edward Grierson 2590

Maciek (Orphan)
Wartime Lies - Louis Begley 416

MacIntosh, Andrew (Farmer; Abolitionist)
The Glass Dove - Sally Carrighar 943

MacIntosh, Meggy (Teenager)
Meggy MacIntosh - Elizabeth Janet Gray 2555

MacIntosh, Ralph (Military Personnel)
Squadron Shilling - Arch Whitehouse 6712

MacIntosh, Sarah (Young Woman)
The Glass Dove - Sally Carrighar 943

MacIntyre, Abijah (Settler)
The Giant Joshua - Maurine Whipple 6673

MacIntyre, Clory (Young Woman; Orphan)
The Giant Joshua - Maurine Whipple 6673

MacIvor, Fergus (Laird)
Waverley - Sir Walter Scott 5709

Mackaill, Douglas (Military Personnel)
Dark Sails - Helen Topping Miller 4388

Mackay, Callum (Immigrant)
Promised Lands - Elizabeth Crook 1430

Mackay, Eliza (Gentlewoman)
Stranger in Savannah - Eugenia Price 5187

Mackay, George (Military Personnel)
Journey Proud - Thomasine McGehee 4273

MacKay, Kieran (Southern Belle; Widow(er))
One Wore Blue - Heather Graham 2517

Mackay, Philip (Young Man)
Against the Tide - Muriel Elwood 1935

Mackay, Thomas (Plantation Owner)
Journey Proud - Thomasine McGehee 4273

Mackenna, Glen (Prospector)
Mackenna's Gold - Will Henry 2845

Mackensie, Sir Morrell (Doctor)
Jack the Ripper - Richard Gordon 2484

MacKensie, Sandy (Hunter)
The Last Hunt - Milton Lott 3900

Mackenzie, Billy (Military Personnel)
1915: A Novel - Roger McDonald 4264

Mackenzie, Christabel (Student; Lesbian)
Death Wore a Diadem - Iona McGregor 4277

Mackenzie, Mary (Spouse)
The Ginger Tree - Oswald Wynd 6890

MacKenzie, Sage (Mountain Man)
Sweet Mountain Magic - Rosanne Bittner 516

MacKinder, Mary Beth (Widow(er))
Oregon Bride - Rosanne Bittner 514

Mackinder, Murdoch (Military Personnel)
The Regiment - Christopher Nicole 4620

Mackinnon, Sir Alan (Gentleman)
Monsieur Janvier - Elizabeth Linington 3799

Macko (Veteran)
The Teutonic Knights - Henryk Sienkiewicz 5849

Mackworth (Religious)
Ravenshoe - Henry Kingsley 3500

Maclaren, Andrew (Military Personnel)
The Maclarens - C.L. Skelton 5873

MacLaren, Ian (Military Personnel)
The Regiment - C.L. Skelton 5874

Maclay, Andrew (Military Personnel)
Sara Dane - Catherine Gaskin 2316

Maclean, Adam Smith (Doctor)
The Powder River - Winfred Blevins 546

MacLean, Alasdair (Gentleman)
Midwinter - John Buchan 751

MacLean, Alec (Religious)
The Strange Brigade - John Edward Jennings 3209

MacLean, Dugald (Military Personnel)
The Dark Stranger - Constance Dodge 1664

Maclean, Elaine (Spouse; Teacher)
The Powder River - Winfred Blevins 546

MacLean, Jeannie (Young Woman)
The Strange Brigade - John Edward Jennings 3209

MacLean, Lachlan (Laird)
The Dark Stranger - Constance Dodge 1664

Maclean, Robert Burns (Mountain Man; Trader)
The Yellowstone - Winfred Blevins 549

MacLeod, Alastair (Frontiersman)
The Hunting Shirt - Mary Johnston 3235

MacLeod, Angus (Plantation Owner)
Bridle the Wind - Julia Davis 1525
Cloud on the Land - Julia Davis 1526
Eagle on the Sun - Julia Davis 1527

MacLeod, Fiona (Gentlewoman; Heiress)
Perfecting Fiona - Marion Chesney 1044

MacLeod, Junius (Military Personnel)
Eagle on the Sun - Julia Davis 1527

MacLeod, Katie (Teenager; Singer)
Home Mountain - Jeanne Williams 6777

MacLeod, Lucy (Spouse)
Bridle the Wind - Julia Davis 1525
Cloud on the Land - Julia Davis 1526

MacLeod, Mairi (Young Woman)
The Island Harp - Jeanne Williams 6779

MacLeod, Randal (Frontiersman)
River of Sky - Karen Harper 2713

Maclewin, Rod (Military Personnel)
Buller's Dreadnought - Richard Hough 3047
Buller's Guns - Richard Hough 3048

MacLyon, Diarmid (Gentleman)
MacLyon - Lolah Burford 773

MacMahon, Dominick (Young Man)
Seek the Fair Land - Walter Macken 3989

MacMahon, Hugh (Teacher; Revolutionary)
The Tenants of Time - Thomas Flanagan 2120

MacMahon, Lorna (Heroine)
The Power and the Passion - Christina
  Nicholson 4609

Macmillan, Rachel (Bastard Daughter; Heiress)
In Still and Stormy Waters - Reay Tannahill 6157

Macmillan, Sophie (Young Woman)
In Still and Stormy Waters - Reay Tannahill 6157

Macnab, Otto (Lawman)
Texas - James A. Michener 4375

MacNamara, Paul (Rancher; Widow(er))
Where the Willows Weep - Patricia Shaw 5781

MacNamara, Seagan (Nobleman)
Mistress of the Eagles - Elona Malterre 4052

Macpherson, Magnus (Businessman)
Born with the Century - William Kinsolving 3501

Macpherson, Nancy (Young Woman)
Give Me the Daggers - Catherine Gavin 2321

MacPherson, Stewart (Psychologist)
Burden of Desire - Robert MacNeil 4023

MacPhiggan, Alastair (Nobleman)
The Gentleman From America - Paul Benton 464

Macrae, Burgo (Businessman)
Goldeneye - Malcolm Macdonald 3965

Macrae, Dick (Diplomat)
Papa La-Bas - John Dickson Carr 914

MacRomain, Lugh (Bastard Son; Warrior)
The Crow Goddess - Patricia Finney 2094
A Shadow of Gulls - Patricia Finney 2096

MacSualtim, Cuchulain (Warrior)
The Crow Goddess - Patricia Finney 2094
A Shadow of Gulls - Patricia Finney 2096

Macswain, James John (Military Personnel)
Lords of the Plains - Max Crawford 1420

MacVey, Lint (Young Man)
A Fistful of Stars - Sarah Lockwood 3828

MacWain, Fiona (Spouse)
The Silver Dolphin - Velda Johnston 3264

Macy, Abigail (Young Woman)
Diamond Head - Houston Branch 647

Madden, Felicity (Spy)
Valiant Libertine - John Gordon Bryson 748

Maddox, Juan (Military Personnel)
Whistling Cat - Robert W. Chambers 984

Maddox, Minella (Teacher)
The Devil on Horseback - Victoria Holt 3014

Madison, Burton (Gentleman)
Marblehead - Joan Thompson 6267

Madison, Edward (Businessman)
Katherine - Antonia Van-Loon 6425

Madoc of Powys (Royalty)
A Moment in Time - Bertrice Small 5911

Madselin (Widow(er))
Madselin - Norah Lofts 3853

Maeve (Noblewoman)
Deirdre - James Stephens 5996

Maeve (Ruler)
Fire Queen - Deborah Grabien 2503

Maeve (Young Woman)
Isle of Glory - Jane Oliver 4723
Spy in Chancery - P.C. Doherty 1680

Maffeo, Guido (Singer)
Cry to Heaven - Anne Rice 5313

Magali (Orphan; Heiress)
Bernadin, My Love - Leonard Rossiter 5506

Magawisca (Indian)
Hope Leslie; or, Early Times in Massachusetts -
  Catharine Maria Sedgewick 5714

Magnus (Chieftain)
Princess of the Veil - Helen Mittermeyer 4420

Magnusson, K.L. (Military Personnel)
A Few Good Men - William Overgard 4768

Magpie Maggie Hag (Gypsy)
Spangle - Gary Jennings 3196

Magua (Indian)
The Last of the Mohicans - James Fenimore
  Cooper 1302

Maguire, Kelly (Military Personnel)
Back to Battle - Max Hennessy 2828
The Dangerous Years - Max Hennessy 2833
The Lion at Sea - Max Hennessy 2834

Maguire, Rose (Young Woman)
I Know My Love - Catherine Gaskin 2315

Mah-Ree (Prehistoric Human)
The Edge of the World - William Sarabande 5597

Mahan, Patrick (Military Personnel)
1901 - Robert Conroy 1258

Mahmoud (Lawyer)
The Mamur Zapt and the Night of the Dog - Michael
  Pearce 4869

Mahmoud el Zaki (Lawyer)
The Mamur Zapt and the Return of the Carpet -
  Michael Pearce 4870

Mahommed, Jara (Chieftain)
The Gates of Kunara - Duncan MacNeil 4014

Maia (Religious)
The Other Sappho - Ellen Frye 2240

Maid of Sker (Outcast)
The Maid of Sker - R.D. Blackmore 529

Main, Charles (Military Personnel)
Love and War - John Jakes 3150

Main, Charles (Military Personnel; Trader)
Heaven and Hell - John Jakes 3147

Main, Harriet (Actress)
Lament for a Lost Lover - Philippa Carr 921

Main, Madelaine (Widow(er))
Heaven and Hell - John Jakes 3147

Main, Orry (Military Personnel)
Love and War - John Jakes 3150
North and South - John Jakes 3151

Mainwairing, Roger (Landowner)
Men of Albemarle - Inglis Fletcher 2135

Mainwaring, Edward (Military Personnel)
Admiral of Fear - Victor Suthren 6126
Captain Monsoon - Victor Suthren 6128

The Golden Galleon - Victor Suthren 6129
Royal Yankee - Victor Suthren 6132

Maironi, Don Franco (Patriot)
The Patriot - Antonio Fogazzaro 2146

Maitland, Hope (Spouse)
Strife Before Dawn - Mary Schumann 5675

Maitland, Keith (Settler; Frontiersman)
Strife Before Dawn - Mary Schumann 5675

Makcheyeva, Tatiana (Noblewoman)
White Nights, Red Dawn - Frederick Nolan 4634

Makwa-Ikwa (Indian; Shaman)
Shaman - Noah Gordon 2483

Mal (Prehistoric Human; Chieftain)
The Inheritors - William Golding 2455

Malabestia (Nobleman)
The King's Persons - Joanne Greenberg 2573

Malachi (Indian)
Back to Malachi - Robert J. Conley 1237

Malachi, Brother (Religious)
In Pursuit of the Green Lion - Judith Merkle
  Riley 5334

Malatesta, Concordia (Young Woman)
Concordia - Frances Fleetwood 2124

Malbray, Liebaut de (Knight)
God's Equal - Alain Absire 14

Malcolm, Caroline (Gentlewoman)
The Reluctant Heiress - Annabel Laine 3588

Malcolm, Leonora (Dancer)
*The Spirit and the Flesh: A Novel Inspired by the Life
  of Isadora Duncan* - David Weiss 6610

Maldry, Sir Robin (Gentleman)
The Flight of the Kestrel - Margaret Abbey 3

Malencz, Count (Nobleman)
Rakossy - Cecelia Holland 2995

Malfrey, Damaris (Noblewoman)
Damaris - Jane Sheridan 5810

Malitas, Demo (Shipowner)
The Bourlotas Fortune - Nicholas Gage 2268

Maliwal (Prehistoric Human; Hunter)
The Sacred Stones - William Sarabande 5600

Mallandine, Herbert (Military Personnel)
Bush War! - William Moore 4447

Mallary, Dorien (Highwayman; Gentleman)
The Storm Witch - Elisabeth Barr 339

Mallen, Barbara (Gentlewoman)
The Mallen Lot - Catherine Cookson 1281

Mallen, Barbara (Ward; Gentlewoman)
The Mallen Girl - Catherine Cookson 1280

Mallen, Thomas (Gentleman)
The Mallen Streak - Catherine Cookson 1282

Mallett, Graham Reid (Gentleman)
Pawn in Frankincense - Dorothy Dunnett 1804

Mallindine, Eldred (Military Personnel)
Bayonets in the Sun - William Moore 4446

Mallory, Jim (Detective—Police)
The William Powell and Myrna Loy Murder Case -
  George Baxt 390

Mallow, Ambrose (Heir—Dispossessed)
Lady of Mallow - Dorothy Eden 1856

Mallow, Blane (Heir; Gentleman)
Lady of Mallow - Dorothy Eden 1856

Malmedy-Armagnac, Eugenie de (Spy)
Concord Bridge - Howard Horne 3035

Malone, Madge (Young Woman)
The Far Down - Elizabeth Corbett 1321

Malone, Michael (Young Man)
Through the Green Valley - Barbara Gowdy 2498

Malone, Rowan (Young Woman)
Beyond the Shining Mountains - Doris
  Shannon 5775

Malone, Sean (Journalist)
Street of the Madwoman - Isabel Ortega 4756

Malone, Shane (Journalist)
Eagles Fly West - Edward Maddin Ainsworth 55

Malone, Tessie (Young Woman)
The Far Down - Elizabeth Corbett 1321

Malone, Tim (Veteran)
The Far Down - Elizabeth Corbett 1321

Malory, Horace (Banker)
The King's Commissar - Duncan Kyle 3570

Malpass, Hester (Orphan)
The Fine and Handsome Captain - Frances
  Lynch 3933

Maltbie, Harris (Military Personnel)
To the Honor of the Fleet - Robert H. Pilpel 5002

Malton, Sir Richard (Gentleman)
Check-Out Time - Kate Kingsbury 3491

Malvern, Kate (Orphan)
Cousin Kate - Georgette Heyer 2884

Mama Yaya (Spirit; Healer)
I, Tituba, Black Witch of Salem - Maryse
  Conde 1233

Mamigon (Military Personnel)
Mamigon - Jack Hashian 2772

Mamuta, Cynthia (Actress)
Antioch Actress: A Novel of Pagan Against Christian -
  Jacob Randolph Perkins 4913

Man Face (Indian)
The Children of the First Man - James Alexander
  Thom 6230

Manaravak (Prehistoric Human; Twin)
Walkers of the Wind - William Sarabande 5603

Mandelkern, Malkeh (Spouse)
Malkeh and Her Children - Marjorie Edelson 1853

Mandelkern, Yoysef (Tailor)
Malkeh and Her Children - Marjorie Edelson 1853

Mandeville, Angelet (Gentlewoman)
The Pool of St. Branok - Philippa Carr 926

Mandeville, Belinda (Orphan; Gentlewoman)
The Changeling - Philippa Carr 918

Mandeville, Gervaise (Gentleman)
The Pool of St. Branok - Philippa Carr 926

Mandeville, Rebecca (Orphan; Gentlewoman)
The Changeling - Philippa Carr 918

Manentes, Diego (Religious)
The Inquisitors - Jerzy Andrzejewski 153

Manette, Alexander (Doctor; Political Prisoner)
A Tale of Two Cities - Charles Dickens 1642

Manette, Lucie (Gentlewoman; Spouse)
A Tale of Two Cities - Charles Dickens 1642

Mango, Peter (Slave; Sailor)
Fragments of the Ark - Louise Meriwether 4341

Mango, Rain (Spouse)
Fragments of the Ark - Louise Meriwether 4341

Manigault, Forney (Military Personnel)
The Valiant Virginians - James Warner Bellah 427

Manilianus, Marcus Mezentius (Philosopher)
The Secret of the Kingdom - Mika Waltari 6555

Manilianus, Minutus Lausus (Military Personnel;
  Government Official)
The Roman - Mika Waltari 6554

Manlove, James (Military Personnel)
Trumpets Sound No More - F. van Wyck Mason 4163

Manly Heart (Indian)
The Manly-Hearted Woman - Frederick F. Manfred 4057

Mannering, Guy (Military Personnel)
Guy Mannering - Sir Walter Scott 5697

Manners, Daphne (Young Woman)
The Jewel in the Crown - Paul Scott 5684

Manners, Dorothy (Gentlewoman)
Richard Carvel - Winston Churchill 1081

Manners, Marjorie (Gentlewoman)
Come Rack! Come Rope! - Robert Hugh Benson 458

Manning, Andrew (Patriot)
The Drums of December - Sharon Salvato 5575

Manning, Andrew (Young Man)
The Fires of July - Sharon Salvato 5576

Manning, Caro (Nurse; Pilot)
The Heart of the Continent - Nancy Cato 961

Manning, Charles (Military Personnel; Homosexual)
The Eye in the Door - Pat Barker 307

Manning, Elizabeth (Plantation Owner)
The Drums of December - Sharon Salvato 5575

Manning, Elizabeth (Spouse)
The Fires of July - Sharon Salvato 5576

Manning, Gwynne (Spouse)
The Drums of December - Sharon Salvato 5575

Manning, Jim (Rancher)
The Heart of the Continent - Nancy Cato 961

Manning, Joseph (Plantation Owner)
The Fires of July - Sharon Salvato 5576

Manning, Margaret (Southern Belle)
Bates House - Clarence Benadum 437

Manning, Marietta (Noblewoman)
Sons of Thunder - Barbara Fitz Vroman 6516

Manningford, James (Gentleman; Heir)
Cousin Susannah - Hazel Hucker 3066

Mannion, Stephen (Landowner)
Storm of Time - Eleanor Dark 1494

Mannus, Optio (Military Personnel)
Dogheaded Death - Ray Faraday Nelson 4581

Manrique, Alonso (Nobleman)
The Heart of Jade - Salvador de Madariaga 4024

Mantle, Susan (Nurse)
Eden Rising - Marilyn Harris 2731

Manville, Rowena (Orphan; Companion)
Midsummer Masque - Jill Tattersall 6174

Many Berries (Indian)
Free Flows the River - Earl Murray 4529

Many Clouds (Indian)
Bitter Creek - Al Cody 1150

Maples, Sam (Lawman)
Ned Christie's War - Robert J. Conley 1247

Maplethorpe, Ada (Spouse)
The Scottish Marriage - Karen Lynn 3942

Maplethorpe, Vincent (Nobleman)
The Scottish Marriage - Karen Lynn 3942

Mar (Warrior; Prehistoric Human)
Daughter of the Red Deer - Joan Wolf 6838

Mara (Prehistoric Human)
People of the Mesa - Charlotte Prentiss 5168

Mara (Spouse)
Sword of Glory - Peter Danielson 1477

Marbot, Felix (Young Man)
So Great a Man - David Pilgrim 5000

Marburg, Aaron (Military Personnel)
The Marburg Chronicles - Alfred Coppel 1319

Marburg, Micah (Banker)
The Marburg Chronicles - Alfred Coppel 1319

Marcellius, Gaius (Military Personnel)
The Forest House - Marion Zimmer Bradley 625

Marcellus (Writer)
Street of the Sandalmakers: A Tale of Rome in the Time of Marcus Aurelius - Nis Peterson 4977

March, Alex (Lawyer)
Enough Good Men - Charles Mercer 4336

March, Catherine (Spouse)
The Imagination of the Heart - Judith Glover 2437

March, Emily (Gentlewoman)
Cardington Crescent - Anne Perry 4924

March, Hannah (Young Woman)
Beauty for Ashes - Timothy R. Wilson 6816

March, James (Engineer; Pilot)
Wings of the Morning - David Beaty 402

March, Philip (Editor)
Kindred Spirits - June Barraclough 347

Marchena, Jayme De (Sailor)
1492 - Mary Johnston 3228

Marcher, Andre (Adventurer)
Beyond the Stars - David William Ross 5497

Marchmont, Henrietta (Heiress)
Rebel Heiress - Jane Aiken Hodge 2969

Marcia (Young Woman)
The Pirate From Rome - John V.D. Southworth 5952

Marcian (Military Personnel)
Sign of the Pagan - Don Tracy 6312

Marcius (Royalty)
The Eagle and the Crown - Hubertus Loewenstein 3832

Marcum, C.J. (Political Figure)
Storming Heaven - Denise Giardina 2394

Marcus (Military Personnel)
Children of the Wolf - Alfred Duggan 1762

Marcy, Susan (Heiress)
Storm Tide - Allan R. Bosworth 590

Marda (Royalty)
Druid's Enchantment - Millie J. Ragosta 5240

Marden, Ranger (Nobleman)
Miss Davenport's Christmas - Marion Chesney 1039

Mardon, Clint (Businessman)
Saratoga Trunk - Edna Ferber 2062

Marduk (Military Personnel)
The Hittite - Noel B. Gerson 2373

Maretzka, Olga (Spy)
Dance on a Sinking Ship - Michael Kilian 3483

Margaret of Ashbury (Gentlewoman)
A Vision of Light - Judith Merkle Riley 5337

Margaret of Ashbury (Widow(er); Heiress)
In Pursuit of the Green Lion - Judith Merkle Riley 5334

Margaret of Belremy (Noblewoman)
Simon the Coldheart - Georgette Heyer 2901

Margelasse, Flora de (Orphan; Gentlewoman)
The Still Storm - Francoise Sagan 5562

Margery (Child)
The Vision of Stephen: An Elegy - Lolah Burford 775

Margery (Witch)
Strange Devices of the Sun and Moon - Lisa Goldstein 2463

Margit (Heroine)
Arne - Bjornstjerne Bjornson 518

Maria (Heroine)
The Stuart Women - Matt Braun 652

Maria (Noblewoman)
Byzantium - Michael Ennis 1945
Great Maria - Cecelia Holland 2989

Maria (Revolutionary)
The Edge of the Storm - Agustin Yanez 6893

Maria, Dona Ana (Gentlewoman)
In Distant Waters - Richard Woodman 6862

Maria Amalia Elizabeth Theresa (Noblewoman)
Felding Castle - Edith De Born 1552

Mariah, Pete (Teenager)
Walk Like a Man - Donald Honig 3024

Marian (Spouse)
Robin and the King - Parke Godwin 2448

Marian (Young Woman)
Sherwood - Parke Godwin 2449

Marian of Ravenskeep (Gentlewoman)
Lady of the Forest - Jennifer Roberson 5368

Marianne (Young Woman)
Son of Judah - Dan Levin 3738

Marietta (Gentlewoman)
The Venetian Mask - Rosalind Laker 3603

Mariette Baptiste (Religious)
Mariette in Ecstasy - Ron Hansen 2682

Marigny, Alfred de (Gentleman)
Carnal Hours - Max Allan Collins 1210

Marigold, Lady (Noblewoman)
The Knight and the Dove - Lori Wick 6732

Marin, Jean Paul (Gentleman)
The Devil's Laughter - Frank Yerby 6913

Mariot, Lisle (Loyalist; Young Woman)
The Sounds of Chariots: A Novel of John Sevier and the State of Franklin - Helen Topping Miller 4396

Mariquilla (Heroine)
Saragossa - Benito Perez Galdos 4912

Marisco, Jasmine de (Royalty)
Wild Jasmine - Bertrice Small 5914

Marita (Revolutionary)
Storm to the South - Thelma Strabel 6073

Maritole (Indian)
Pushing the Bear: A Novel of the Trail of Tears - Diane Glancy 2426

Marius (Philosopher)
Marius the Epicurean - Walter Pater 4826

Marius the Vandal (Military Personnel)
The Vandal - Richard O'Connor 4687

Mark, Brother (Religious)
A Question of Choice - Prudence Andrew 143
The Summer of the Danes - Ellis Peters 4973

Mark (Ruler)
The White Raven - Diana L. Paxson 4847

Mark, Philip (Government Official; Mercenary)
The Sheriff of Nottingham - Richard Kluger 3512

Markham, Dominic (Nobleman; Military Personnel)
Angel - Carola Dunn 1790

Markham, Elizabeth (Gentlewoman)
Angel - Carola Dunn 1790

Markham, Elizabeth (Spouse)
The Rage of the Vulture - Barry Unsworth 6388

Markham, Elliot (Patriot)
Stars and Stripes - Adam Rutledge 5541

Markham, Elliott (Spy)
Life and Liberty - Adam Rutledge 5538

Markham, Lyndell (Heiress)
My Lady Innkeeper - Barbara Metzger 4346

Markham, Robert (Government Official)
The Rage of the Vulture - Barry Unsworth 6388

Markham, Will (Spy; Frontiersman)
Fortress Fury - Carter A. Vaughan 6435

Markland, Jack (Veteran)
After the Glory - Helen Topping Miller 4383

Markland, Sue (Spouse)
After the Glory - Helen Topping Miller 4383

Markland, William (Veteran)
After the Glory - Helen Topping Miller 4383

Marlow, Phoebe (Gentlewoman; Writer)
Sylvester; or, The Wicked Uncle - Georgette Heyer 2904

Marlow, Tansy (Heiress; Gentlewoman)
Ride the Blue Riband - Rosalind Laker 3598

Marlowe, Jack (Military Personnel)
The Cavalryman - Harold Sinclair 5861
The Horse Soldiers - Harold Sinclair 5862

Marlowe, Philip (Detective—Private)
Perchance to Dream - Robert B. Parker 4807

Marlowe, Thomas (Sailor)
The Glittering Strand - Judith Lennox-Smith 3716

Marmion, Clarence (Gentleman)
The Trip to Jerusalem - Edward Marston 4129

Marner, Silas (Artisan)
Silas Marner - George Eliot 1911

Marquand, Mary (Young Woman)
Golden Shore - George Shaftel 5769

La Marquesa (Prostitute; Widow(er))
Sharpe's Honour - Bernard Cornwell 1344

Marquess of Fenton (Nobleman)
Belinda Goes to Bath - Marion Chesney 1020

Marquess of Porterhouse (Nobleman)
Mrs. Budley Falls From Grace - Marion Chesney 1042

Marquis, Harley (Journalist)
The Crimson Wind - Max Hennessy 2832

Marquis of Bolibar (Nobleman)
The Marquis of Bolibar - Leo Perutz 4942

Marquis of Brabington (Nobleman)
The Taming of Annabelle - Marion Chesney 1052

Marrah (Religious; Prehistoric Human)
The Year the Horses Came - Mary Mackey 3993

Marriott, Charles (Gentleman)
Free Lance - George Shipway 5827

Marriott, Richard (Adventurer; Pirate)
The White Rajah - Nicholas Monsarrat 4433

Mars, Eddie (Criminal)
Perchance to Dream - Robert B. Parker 4807

Marsan, Gilles (Revolutionary)
Veronique - Virginia Coffman 1158

Marsden, Catherine (Journalist)
Counterfeit of Murder - Ray Harrison 2738
Death of a Dancing Lady - Ray Harrison 2739
Deathwatch - Ray Harrison 2740
A Season for Death - Ray Harrison 2743
Sphere of Death - Ray Harrison 2744

Marsden, Lucy (Widow(er))
Oldest Living Confederate Widow Tells All - Allan Gurganus 2621

Marsden, Willie (Veteran)
Oldest Living Confederate Widow Tells All - Allan Gurganus 2621

Marsdon, Celia (Young Woman; Spouse)
Green Darkness - Anya Seton 5751

Marsdon, Stephen (Young Man; Spouse)
Green Darkness - Anya Seton 5751

Marsh, Abner (Sailor)
Fevre Dream - George R.R. Martin 4131

Marsh, Leon (Bastard Son; Heir)
The Legacy of Beulah Land - Lonnie Coleman 1203

Marsh, Margaret (Suffragette)
Chicago Girls - Edith Freund 2229

Marsh, Robert (Innkeeper)
The King's Bed - Margaret Campbell Barnes 324

Marsh, Tansy (Young Woman)
The King's Bed - Margaret Campbell Barnes 324

Marshall, Faith (Young Woman)
Catch a Falling Star - Frederic F. Van de Water 6401

Marshall, James (Detective—Police)
The Masters of Bow Street - John Creasy 1423

Marshall, Michael (Scout)
Land for My Sons - Maribelle Cormack 1331

Marsham, Beatrice (Gentlewoman; Widow(er))
Beatrice Goes to Brighton - Marion Chesney 1019

Marston, Yates (Widow(er))
The Woman of Catawba - Hilda Stahl 5978

Martell, Nathaniel (Gentleman)
The Love Child - Catherine Cookson 1279

Martha (Servant)
The Still Storm - Francoise Sagan 5562

Martin, Beth (Spouse)
Dakota! - Dana Fuller Ross 5472

Martin, Beth (Young Woman)
Montana! - Dana Fuller Ross 5479

Martin, Caleb (Settler)
The Peaceable Kingdom - Jan de Hartog 2763

Martin, Dom (Nobleman)
The Braganza Pursuit - Sarah Neilan 4564

Martin, Gilbert (Farmer; Military Personnel)
Drums Along the Mohawk - Walter D. Edmonds 1874

Martin, Jenny (Young Woman)
The Drums of April - Charles Mergendahl 4340

Martin, Jeremiah (Gentleman)
Jeremiah Martin: A Revolutionary War Novel - Robert H. Fowler 2191

Martin, Jeremiah (Settler)
Song of Years - Bess Streeter Aldrich 72

Martin, Kate (Gentlewoman; Heiress)
The Prince Regent's Silver Bell - Gladys McGorian 4275

Martin, Kid (Orphan; Rancher)
Born of the Sun - John H. Culp 1440

Martin, Lana (Spouse)
Drums Along the Mohawk - Walter D. Edmonds 1874

Martin, Luna (Dancer)
Dancing in the Dark - Stuart M. Kaminsky 3334

Martin, Mark (Settler; Sea Captain)
The Measure of the Years - Alice Mary Colver 1218

Martin, Mary (Young Woman)
There Is a Season - Alice Mary Colver 1219

Martin, Michael (Young Man)
Captain Lightfoot - William R. Burnett 792

Martin, Nina (Gentlewoman)
Homeward Bound - Elizabeth Walter 6557

Martin, Rob (Engineer)
Dakota! - Dana Fuller Ross 5472

Martin, Sable (Companion)
Cardigan Square - Alexandra Manners 4070

Martin, Sarah (Singer)
Paiute - Sessions S. Wheeler 6666

Martin, Suzanne (Settler)
Song of Years - Bess Streeter Aldrich 72

Martin, Thomas (Military Personnel; Spy)
When the War Is Over - Stephen Becker 408

Martin, Tom (Journalist)
The Devil's Card - Mary Maher 4030

Martinez, Anitra (Young Woman)
The Golden Valley - Daoma Winston 6826

Martinez, Jorge (Revolutionary)
Not of War Only - Norman Zollinger 6966

Martinson, James (Political Figure)
Tennessee! - Dana Fuller Ross 5489

Martock, Sergeant (Police Officer)
Sergeant Verity and the Imperial Diamond - Francis Selwyn 5745

Marvayne, Lass (Young Woman)
Fire and the Hammer - Shirley Barker 311

Marvin, Daniel (Sailor)
Captain Caution - Kenneth Roberts 5385

Marvin, Phoebe (Young Woman)
Arundel - Kenneth Roberts 5383

Marvin, Silas (Military Personnel; Explorer)
Now We Are Free - Marguerite Allis 112

Marwick, Bess (Widow(er))
Prophecies - Helena Soister 5937

Marwood, Elizabeth (Nurse; Spouse)
To Serve Them All My Days - R.F. Delderfield 1591

Mary (Spouse)
Before My Time - Niccolo Tucci 6358

Mary, Mary (Young Woman)
The Tall One - Barbara Jefferis 3175

Maryam, Lady (Noblewoman)
The Black Rose - Thomas B. Costain 1363

Masa, Lady (Spouse)
Kagami - Elizabeth Kata 3369

Masau (Prehistoric Human; Hunter)
The Sacred Stones - William Sarabande 5600

Mascharenhas, Leonora (Young Woman)
The Pagoda Tree - Berkely Mather 4181

Masferrer, Cristobal (Rancher)
Daughter of Fortune - Carla Kelly 3398

Masferrer, Diego (Rancher)
Daughter of Fortune - Carla Kelly 3398

Maskey, Laura (Young Woman)
Where the Willows Weep - Patricia Shaw 5781

Mason, Daisy (Teenager; Settler)
Pilgrims: A Novel of the Mayflower - Gerard Mac 3955

Mason, Daisy (Young Woman)
The Maltese Angel - Catherine Cookson 1283

Mason, Deborah (Spy)
Deborah - Colette Davenat 1498

Mason, Deborah (Spy; Noblewoman)
Deborah and the Many Faces of Love - Colette Davenat 1499

Mason, Ella (Young Woman)
Lord Raven's Widow - Leslie O'Grady 4700

Mason, Java Gordon (Spouse)
The Imperialists - William Stuart Long 3875

Mason, Roderick (Gentleman)
Westward the Sun - Brigid Knight 3524

Mason, Roger (Artisan)
The Spire - William Golding 2457

Mason, Samuel (Doctor)
Wild Horizon - F. van Wyck Mason 4164

Mason, Tolo (Prospector)
The Imperialists - William Stuart Long 3875

Mason, Wendy (Young Woman)
His Majesty's Highlanders - Leslie Turner
  White 6683

Massingham, Eugenia (Gentlewoman)
The Vines of Yarrabee - Dorothy Eden 1864

Massingham, Gilbert (Plantation Owner)
The Vines of Yarrabee - Dorothy Eden 1864

Masson, Philippe (Revolutionary)
The Colors of Vaud - Bryher 741

Massy, Raymond (Young Man)
A Bride for New Orleans - Edward Francis
  Murphy 4522

Master, The (Chieftain)
Isobelle - Mary Lide 3775

Master, York (Detective—Private)
Fallen Angel - Deborah Camp 872

Master Jan (Artist)
The Master Painter - Edwin Mullins 4513

Masterman, Katherine (Gentlewoman)
Beyond the Blue Mountains - Jean Plaidy 5006

Masters, Beigh (Young Woman)
The Holder of the World - Bharati Mukherjee 4510

Masters, Joline (Widow(er); Settler)
Montana Woman - Rosanne Bittner 513

Mathes, Donald (Businessman)
White Poppy - Margaret Gaan 2261

Mathewson, Ann (Widow(er))
Lord of the Isles - Donald Barr Chidsey 1063

Mathick, Ann (Heiress; Landowner)
A Season of Mists - Sarah Woodhouse 6856

Mathieson, Roland Farleigh (Gentleman; Rake)
The Dedicated Villain - Patricia Veryan 6461

Mathilde (Healer)
God's Equal - Alain Absire 14

Mathis, Blount (Military Personnel)
Where My Love Sleeps - Clifford Dowdey 1710

Matho (Chieftain)
Salammbo - Gustave Flaubert 2123

Matilda (Royalty)
Theo and Matilda - Rachel Billington 498

Matilda (Spouse; Gentlewoman)
The Lady for Ransom - Alfred Duggan 1768

Matilda, Caroline (Convict; Servant)
Freedom's Way - Theodora McCormick Du
  Bois 1742

Matlock, Craig (Young Man)
Tenants of the Earth - Sandra Paretti 4793

Matlock, John Tyler (Financier)
Tenants of the Earth - Sandra Paretti 4793

Matthias (Fanatic; Leader)
The Siege - Peter Vansittart 6431

Maturin, Stephen (Doctor; Spy)
The Commodore - Patrick O'Brian 4661
Desolation Island - Patrick O'Brian 4662
The Far Side of the World - Patrick O'Brian 4663
The Fortune of War - Patrick O'Brian 4664
H.M.S. Surprise - Patrick O'Brian 4666
The Ionian Mission - Patrick O'Brian 4667
The Letter of Marque - Patrick O'Brian 4668
Master and Commander - Patrick O'Brian 4669
The Mauritius Command - Patrick O'Brian 4670
The Nutmeg of Consolation - Patrick O'Brian 4671

Post Captain - Patrick O'Brian 4672
The Reverse of the Medal - Patrick O'Brian 4673
The Surgeon's Mate - Patrick O'Brian 4674
The Thirteen Gun Salute - Patrick O'Brian 4675
Treason's Harbour - Patrick O'Brian 4676
The Truelove - Patrick O'Brian 4677
The Wine-Dark Sea - Patrick O'Brian 4679
The Yellow Admiral - Patrick O'Brian 4680

Matyeh (Trader)
Shadow of a Star - Jamie Lee Cooper 1315

Matzerath, Oskar (Murderer)
The Tin Drum - Gunther Grass 2540

Mauakes (Ruler)
Horses of Heaven - Gillian Bradshaw 630

Maud (Young Woman)
This Bright Sword - Donald Barr Chidsey 1066

Maudribourg, Ambroisine de (Noblewoman)
Angelique and the Demon - Sergeanne Golon 2466

Maum, Anna (Slave; Servant)
The Hard to Catch Mercy - William Baldwin 281

Maurepas (Scholar; Librarian)
The Masked Man - P.C. Doherty 1674

Maurice, Geraldine (Gentlewoman)
The Vesey Inheritance - Gwendoline Butler 822

Mautravers, Jane (Gentlewoman)
Captain Bashful - Donald Barr Chidsey 1059

Maximus (Military Personnel)
Eagle in the Snow - Wallace Breem 654

Maximus (Sorcerer)
Julian - Gore Vidal 6489

Maxwell, John (Teacher)
Children of the Dust - Carlile Clancy 1084

Maxwell, Rachel (Young Woman)
Children of the Dust - Carlile Clancy 1084

Maya (Prehistoric Human; Shaman)
The Mammoth Stone - Margaret Allan 90

Mayfield, Corinna (Gentlewoman)
Elyza - Clare Darcy 1486

Mayhew, Bartholomew (Settler)
Young Titan - F. van Wyck Mason 4165

Mayhew, Coffin (Outlaw)
The Law in Charity - Chelsea Quinn Yarbro 6901

Mayhew, Megan (Settler)
Young Titan - F. van Wyck Mason 4165

Maynard, Robert (Military Personnel)
Rogue's Holiday - Hamilton Cochran 1141

Maynard, Thomas (Military Personnel)
The Sword of General Englund - Donald
  Honig 3023

Mayne, Ripley (Military Personnel)
Trumpet to Arms - Bruce Lancaster 3647

Mayr, Christian (Military Personnel)
The Last Innocent Hour - Margot Abbott 8

Maywood, Marcus (Indian)
The Justicer - Thomas Fall 2010

McAlister, Mary (Orphan)
New Orleans Legacy - Alexandra Ripley 5341

McAllister (Military Personnel)
A Rendezvous in Haiti - Stephen Becker 407

McAllister, Ariana (Heroine)
Bridey's Mountain - Yvonne Adamson 34

McAllister, Chance (Gambler)
Paint the Wind - Cathy Cash Spellman 5960

McAllister, Hart (Artist)
Paint the Wind - Cathy Cash Spellman 5960

McAllister, Jamie (Frontiersman; Captive)
Eyes of Eagles - William W. Johnstone 3266

McAlpine, Jesse (Spouse)
Star of the Wilderness - Karle Wilson Baker 274

McAlpine, Paul (Settler)
Star of the Wilderness - Karle Wilson Baker 274

McArdle, James (Religious)
The Forest and the Fort - Hervey Allen 100

McAsh, Mack (Miner)
A Place Called Freedom - Ken Follett 2150

McBain, Alexander (Clerk)
An Ancient Evil - C.L. Grace 2504

McBride, Archibald (Plantation Owner)
Tell Me a Tale: A Novel of the Old South - James
  McEachin 4266

McCaleb, Benton (Cowboy; Gunfighter)
The Goodnight Trail - Ralph Compton 1227

McCallum, Peter (Gentleman)
Falls of Gard - Laura Black 520

McCanless, Asa (Rancher)
No Roof but Heaven - Jeanne Williams 6782

McCann, Kevin (Outlaw)
The Dispossessed - Dell Shannon 5773

McCann, Margot (Young Woman)
She Rode a Yellow Stallion - Walter Reed 5286

McCannon, Geordie (Criminal)
The Street Sparrows - Rose Ayers 249

McCarthy, Owen (Writer; Teacher)
The Year of the French - Thomas Flanagan 2121

McCaskill, Angus (Immigrant)
Dancing at the Rascal Fair - Ivan Doig 1682

McCaskill, Beth (Housewife)
English Creek - Ivan Doig 1683

McCaskill, Jick (Rancher)
English Creek - Ivan Doig 1683
Ride with Me, Mariah Montana - Ivan Doig 1684

McCaskill, Mariah (Photographer)
Ride with Me, Mariah Montana - Ivan Doig 1684

McCaskill, Varick (Ranger)
English Creek - Ivan Doig 1683

McCauley, Jeremy (Military Personnel)
And One Rode West - Heather Graham 2514

McClellan, Belle (Gentlewoman)
*Unvexed to the Sea: A Novel of the Vicksburg
  Campaign* - Gerry Morrison 4484

McClellan, Malvina (Gentlewoman)
*Unvexed to the Sea: A Novel of the Vicksburg
  Campaign* - Gerry Morrison 4484

McCloud, Georgia (Slave)
Crossing over Jordan - Linda Beatrice Brown 725

McCloud, Mary (Young Woman)
The Dark Command - William R. Burnett 793

McCloud, Noah (Frontiersman)
Albuquerque - Sara Orwig 4757

McClure, Hardee (Landowner; Widow(er))
Trumpet in the Sky - Helen Topping Miller 4397

McConkey, Fremont (Young Man)
The Hawkeye - Herbert Quick 5222

McConles, Jesse (Rancher)
Duel in the Sun - Niven Busch 812

McConnell, Hugh (Young Man)
The Day Must Dawn - Agnes Sligh Turnbull 6362

McConnell, Rose (Young Woman)
Grandmother and the Priests - Taylor Caldwell 857

McCoy, Luff (Prospector)
City of Illusion - Vardis Fisher 2107

McCrae, Augustus (Gunfighter; Rancher)
Lonesome Dove - Larry McMurtry 4298

McCrae, Augustus (Lawman)
Dead Man's Walk - Larry McMurtry 4297

McCready, Spanish (Veteran)
Candle of the Wicked - Manly Wade Wellman 6612

McCutcheon, Elias (Settler; Military Personnel)
The Raider - Jesse Hill Ford 2164

McDaniel, Sharon (Spy)
No Bugles Blow - Bruce Lancaster 3642

McDermott, Angus (Frontiersman; Scout)
Shadow of the Long Knives - Thomas Alexander
  Boyd 615

McDonagh, Con (Doctor)
The Scalpel and the Sword - Dell Shannon 5774

McDougal, Caleb (Settler)
Columbia - Pamela Jekel 3184

McDougal, Suzanne (Spouse)
Columbia - Pamela Jekel 3184

McElroy, Duncan (Farmer)
The Live Goat - Cecil Dawkins 1542

McEverside, Stella (Widow(er))
Tennessee Smith - James E. Hitt 2957

McFadden, Hugh (Religious)
The Dispossessed - Dell Shannon 5773

McFlaherty, Moira (Farmer)
The Famished Land - Elizabeth Byrd 833

McGann, Harry (Sea Captain)
Old Glory - Christopher Nicole 4618

McGann, Jeremiah (Sea Captain)
Iron Ships, Iron Men - Christopher Nicole 4616

McGann, Joe (Military Personnel)
Wind of Destiny - Christopher Nicole 4624

McGann, Marguerite (Spouse)
Iron Ships, Iron Men - Christopher Nicole 4616

McGann, Toby (Sailor)
The Sea and the Sand - Christopher Nicole 4621

McGee, Gerta (Gentlewoman)
Jeremiah Martin: A Revolutionary War Novel - Robert
  H. Fowler 2191

McGee, Jason (Teenager)
Jason McGee - Robert H. Fowler 2190

McGee, Rossanna (Terrorist)
The Tick of Death - Peter Lovesey 3916

McGehee, Hugh (Plantation Owner)
So Red the Rose - Stark Young 6944

McGill, Bart (Sea Captain)
The Furies - John Jakes 3146

McGill, Cassie (Engineer; Railroad Worker)
The War Train: A Novel of 1916 - Brown
  Meggs 4324

McGinty, Rascal (Cowboy)
The Day the Cowboys Quit - Elmer Kelton 3403

McGook, Ham Esposita (Teenager)
The Bright Feathers - John H. Culp 1441

McGrath, Ada (Young Woman; Handicapped)
The Piano - Jane Campion 878

McGrath, Howard (Gentleman)
The Marrying Kind - Jessica Stirling 6046

McGrath, Steve (Gentleman)
Tilly Alone - Catherine Cookson 1289

McGrath, Stewart (Landowner)
The Piano - Jane Campion 878

McGraw, Ryan (Military Personnel)
A Heart Divided - Al Lacy 3580

McGregor, Anne (Witch)
Child of the Mist - Kathleen Morgan 4451

McGuinness, Rory (Military Personnel)
The Proud Man - Elizabeth Linington 3800

McIlvaine, James (Military Personnel)
Loving Heart - Elsie Singmaster 5869

McIlvane (Journalist)
The Waterworks - E.L. Doctorow 1659

McIntyre, Dorch (Doctor)
Timothy Baines - John H. Culp 1445

McIvor, Pleasant (Military Personnel)
The Long Night - Andrew Lytle 3945

McKay, Gordon (Businessman)
McKay's Bees - Thomas McMahon 4289

McKay, Shaylin (Journalist)
Cold War - Robert Vaughan 6446
The Iron Curtain - Robert Vaughan 6447

McKee, Owen (Military Personnel)
Eagle Fur - Robert Newton Peck 4884

McKenna, Kit (Young Woman)
Captain Ironhand - Rosamond Marshall 4116

McKensie, Kate (Young Woman)
The Seventh Girl: A Romantic Tale of Civil War Texas
  - Tom Pendleton 4900

McKensie, Rosa Ann (Southern Belle; Spy)
McKensie's Hundred: A Tale of the Old Dominion -
  Frank Yerby 6924

McKenzie, Benton (Frontiersman)
Plume Rouge: A Novel of the Pathfinders - John Upton
  Terrell 6203

McKenzie, Dan (Rancher)
Harry: A Novel of Australia - Robert Wales 6530

McKenzie, Ewan (Gentleman)
Silver Linings - Shirley Davies-Owens 1508

McKenzie, Jarrett (Widow(er))
Runaway - Heather Graham 2519

McKenzie, Max (Heir)
Return of the Stranger - Reay Tannahill 6158

McKetch, Dan (Outlaw)
The Flames of Time - Baynard Kendrick 3409

McKie, Davie (Young Man)
The Far Side of the Hill - Nancy Livingston 3811

McKie, Jane (Dancer)
The Land of Our Dreams - Nancy Livingston 3812

McKie, John (Store Owner)
The Far Side of the Hill - Nancy Livingston 3811
The Land of Our Dreams - Nancy Livingston 3812

McKie, Luke (Student)
The Land of Our Dreams - Nancy Livingston 3812

McKillop, Jim (Frontiersman)
The Kingdom Carver - E.G. Perrault 4916

McLaughlin, James (Government Official)
Arrest Sitting Bull - Douglas C. Jones 3273

McLaughlin, Willy (Veteran)
The Able McLaughlins - Margaret Wilson 6812

McLean, Brock (Sea Captain)
Sea Jade - Phyllis A. Whitney 6717

McLean, Trey (Rancher)
The Pumpkin Rollers - Elmer Kelton 3406

McLellan, Herd (Rancher)
The Long Trail North - Robert J. Conley 1245

McLeod, Garth (Farmer)
The Unplowed Sky - Jeanne Williams 6783

McLeod, Hannah (Waiter/Waitress; Teacher)
A Heritage of Shadows - Madeleine Brent 660

McLeod, Johnny (Military Personnel)
The Far Side of Home - Maggie Davis 1536

McLeod, Quentin (Sea Captain)
Biscayne - Barry Jay Kaplan 3365

McMahon, Angus (Warrior)
The Gentle Conqueror - Mary Ellen Gronau 2597

McMahon, Brendan (Immigrant; Farmer)
They Were Dreamers - James F. Murphy Jr. 4525

McMahon, Dorcas (Warrior)
Passionate Warriors - Mary Ellen Gronau 2598

McMahon, Mary (Spouse)
They Were Dreamers - James F. Murphy Jr. 4525

McManus, Philip (Writer)
Julie - Jane Kesner Morris 4479

McMaster, Damon (Military Personnel)
When the Music Changed - Marie R. Reno 5305

McNair, Christie (Young Woman)
The Able McLaughlins - Margaret Wilson 6812

McNair, Shakespeare (Mountain Man; Trapper)
Apache Blood - David Thompson 6250
King of the Mountain - David Thompson 6255
Lure of the Wind - David Thompson 6256
Tomahawk Revenge - David Thompson 6260
Trapper's Blood - David Thompson 6261

McNeil, Amelie (Settler)
First the Blade - May Miller 4400

McNeil, Neil (Warrior)
Passionate Warriors - Mary Ellen Gronau 2598

McPherson, Mary Beth (Gentlewoman)
Look Away - Harold Coyle 1395
Until the End - Harold Coyle 1396

McQueen, Ben (Military Personnel)
Warriors of the Night - Kerry Newcomb 4594

McQueen, Daniel Pacer Wolf (Military Personnel)
Ride of the Panther - Kerry Newcomb 4591

McQueen, Fanny (Dancer)
The Maltese Angel - Catherine Cookson 1283

McQueen, Jesse Redbow (Military Personnel)
Ride of the Panther - Kerry Newcomb 4591

McQueen, Kit (Military Personnel)
Sword of Vengeance - Kerry Newcomb 4593

McQueen, Lydia (Mountain Woman)
The Tall Woman - Wilma Dykeman 1819

McQuirk, Sally (Journalist)
1812 - David Nevin 4586

McRae, Brant (Sea Captain)
Captain McRae: A Novel of the Northwest Frontier -
  William Heuman 2872

McSwasey, Caleb (Businessman)
Big River, Big Man - Thomas William Duncan 1786

McTavish, Prudence (Gentlewoman)
Journey to Enchantment - Patricia Veryan 6464

McVey, Bob (Settler)
Pillar of Cloud - Jackson Burgess 782

Mead, Caroline (Spouse)
The Green Land - Zola Helen Ross 5504

Mead, Raleigh (Doctor)
The Green Land - Zola Helen Ross 5504

Meadows, James Percival (Military Personnel)
Hornblower During the Crisis - C.S. Forester 2177

Meares, John (Sea Captain)
Friendly Cove - Irving Brant 651

Medbeth (Ward)
The Ravishers - Elizabeth Richards 5318

Medea (Murderer; Sorceress)
Medea - Miranda Seymour 5764

Medea (Sorceress)
Jason - Henry Treece 6331
The King Must Die - Mary Renault 5298

Medicine Plant (Indian)
Dawn Land - Joseph Bruchac III   734

Medigo, Andrea del (Artist)
Michelangelo the Florentine - Sidney Alexander   86

Medina, Don Raul (Landowner)
When the Owl Cries - Paul Bartlett   367

Medlar, Hannah (Gentlewoman)
The Long Shadow - Anna Gilbert   2406

Medlar, Zilla (Gentlewoman)
The Long Shadow - Anna Gilbert   2406

Medley, Joshua (Entertainer; Magician)
Conjuror's Journal - Frances L. Shine   5826

Megan, Lady (Noblewoman)
The Knight and the Dove - Lori Wick   6732

Mehuru (Religious; Slave)
A Respectable Trade - Philippa Gregory   2584

Mei Lin (Young Woman)
Rebels of the Heavenly Kingdom - Katherine
   Paterson   4828

Mei Ling (Royalty)
Tournament of the Shadows - Nicholas Carnac   901

Meier, Matthias (Settler)
Spring Came on Forever - Bess Streeter Aldrich   73

Meihua (Young Woman)
Ming: A Novel of Seventeeth Century China - Robert
   B. Oxnam   4772

Meiklejohn, Angus (Sea Captain)
Homeward Bound - Elizabeth Walter   6557

Meinhardt, Maria (Young Woman)
The Copperheads - William James Blech   544

Meion (Young Man)
Anabasis: A Journey to the Interior - Ellen
   Gilchrist   2408

Melaine, Judith de Saint (Noblewoman)
The Lure of the Falcon - Juliette Benzoni   465

Melander (Settler)
The Sea Runners - Ivan Doig   1685

Melchior (Biblical Figure; Scientist)
How Far to Bethlehem? - Norah Lofts   3846

Meleager (Writer)
The Master - Max Brod   702

Melema, Tito (Adventurer; Criminal)
Romola - George Eliot   1910

Melgares, Don Facundo (Military Personnel)
Rio Grande - Jory Sherman   5821

Melinda of Ibelin (Gentlewoman)
The Unholy Pilgrim - R.F. Tapsell   6161

Melisane (Gentlewoman)
In the Falcon's Claw: A Novel of the Year 1000 -
   Chet Raymo   5257

Mellarius (Military Personnel)
The Centurion - Jan de Hartog   2762

Mellish, Dolly (Saloon Hostess; Settler)
The Sea 'Venture - F. van Wyck Mason   4159

Mencius, Nicator (Government Official)
The Big Fisherman - Lloyd C. Douglas   1702

Mendelson, Ruth (Spy)
The Devil's Spy - Michael Hastings   2773

Mendes, Eugene (Gentleman)
Crescent City - Belva Plain   5078

Mendes, Leo (Store Owner)
The Conquest of Don Pedro - Harvey
   Fergusson   2066

Mendes, Magdalena (Spouse)
The Conquest of Don Pedro - Harvey
   Fergusson   2066

Mendoza (Outlaw)
Season of Yellow Leaf - Douglas C. Jones   3283

Mendoza (Religious)
Torquemada - Howard Fast   2045

Mendoza, Mariana (Young Woman)
The Kingsbridge Plot - Maan Meyers   4355

Mendoza, Racquel (Spouse)
The Dutchman's Dilemma - Maan Meyers   4352

Mendoza, Racquel (Spy)
The Dutchman - Maan Meyers   4351

Mendoza y Luna, Don Pedro de (Nobleman)
The Hounds of God - Rafael Sabatini   5551

Menelaus (Ruler)
The Goddess - Miranda Seymour   5763
The Private Life of Helen of Troy - John
   Erskine   1957

Menendez, Coralita (Prostitute)
Proud New Flags - F. van Wyck Mason   4156

Menenhetet (Wanderer; Military Personnel)
Ancient Evenings - Norman Mailer   4035

Menetrier, Jacques (Scholar)
At the Sign of the Reine Pedauque - Anatole
   France   2198

Menkh, Lord (Nobleman)
Her-Bak: The Living Face of Ancient Egypt - Isha
   Schwaller de Lubicz   5676

Menteen, Milo (Trapper)
Mountain Devil - David Thompson   6257

Menteith, Margaret (Heroine)
The Bonnet Laird's Daughter - Barbara
   Annandale   154

Menton, Aubrey (Nobleman)
A Love So Wild - Deborah Chester   1056

Menzies, Roberts (Doctor)
The Legacy of Ladysmith - John Kenny Crane   1413

Mer, Katherine de (Amnesiac; Ward)
Witness to Treason - Millie J. Ragosta   5244

Mera (Healer)
Soul Flame - Barbara Wood   6850

Merac, Jean de (Military Personnel)
The Scarlet Patch - Bruce Lancaster   3645

Merari (Young Woman)
Merari - Gloria Howe Bremkamp   656

Mercedes (Noblewoman)
Mercedes of Castile - James Fenimore Cooper   1304

Mercer, John (Gentleman)
Pargeters - Norah Lofts   3857

Mercer, Penelope (Young Woman)
Pargeters - Norah Lofts   3857

Mercure, Anne (Actress)
Palais-Royale - Richard Sennett   5747

Mercybright, Jack (Farmer)
Apple Tree Lean Down - Mary E. Pearce   4860

Mercybright, Linn (Spouse)
Seedtime and Harvest - Mary E. Pearce   4864

Meredith, Hallie (Housekeeper; Cook)
The Unplowed Sky - Jeanne Williams   6783

Meredith, Janice (Young Woman)
Janice Meredith - Paul Leicester Ford   2166

Meredith, Tyler (Sea Captain; Blockade Runner)
Captain Rebel - Frank Yerby   6910

Mereet (Spouse)
The Golden Pharaoh - Peter Danielson   1468

Meren, Lord (Nobleman; Government Official)
Murder at the Feast of Rejoicing - Lynda S.
   Robinson   5407

Murder at the God's Gate - Lynda S.
   Robinson   5408
Murder in the Place of Anubis - Lynda S.
   Robinson   5409

Merenda, Lorenzo (Nobleman; Landowner)
Castle of Doves - Constance Heaven   2803

Merewether, Caroline (Spouse)
For King and Company - Ellis K. Meacham   4314

Merewether, Percival (Military Personnel)
The East Indiaman - Ellis K. Meacham   4313
For King and Company - Ellis K. Meacham   4314
On the Company's Service - Ellis K. Meacham   4315

Merewyn (Young Woman)
Avalon - Anya Seton   5748

Meriamon (Royalty; Religious)
Lord of the Two Lands - Judith Tarr   6167

Meridon (Heiress)
Meridon - Philippa Gregory   2583

Merion, Giles (Nobleman)
April Lady - Georgette Heyer   2873

Merion, Lady Letitia (Noblewoman)
April Lady - Georgette Heyer   2873

Merion, Nell (Noblewoman)
April Lady - Georgette Heyer   2873

Merivel, Robert (Doctor)
Restoration: A Novel of Seventeenth-Century England -
   Rose Tremain   6333

Merlin (Bastard Son)
The Crystal Cave - Mary Stewart   6029

Merlin (Courtier)
Artorius Rex - John Gloag   2432

Merlin (Sorcerer)
Arthur - Stephen R. Lawhead   3679
The Coming of the King - Nikolai Tolstoy   6296
A Connecticut Yankee in King Arthur's Court - Mark
   Twain   6371
The Crimson Chalice - Victor Canning   882
The Crystal Dove - Mollie Hardwick   2692
The Emperor Arthur - Godfrey Turton   6368
The Hollow Hills - Mary Stewart   6030
The Last Enchantment - Mary Stewart   6031
Merlin - Stephen R. Lawhead   3681
The Pagan King - Edison Marshall   4109
Pendragon - Stephen R. Lawhead   3682
The Road to Avalon - Joan Wolf   6842
The Winter King - Bernard Cornwell   1351

Merlin, Christian (Sea Captain)
Lord of the River - Bernard Clavel   1099

Merlyn, Joss (Innkeeper)
Jamaica Inn - Daphne Du Maurier   1747

Meromic (Warrior; Chieftain)
The Conquered - Naomi Mitchison   4418

Merops (Military Personnel)
The Trojan Generals Talk: Memoirs of the Greek War
   - Phillip Parotti   4818

Merrick, Elijah (Sea Captain)
This Is the House - Deborah Hill   2921

Merrick, James (Military Personnel)
Exit with Drums - Joseph A. Daley   1457

Merrick, Ronald (Government Official)
The Jewel in the Crown - Paul Scott   5684

Merrick, Ronald (Military Personnel)
The Day of the Scorpion - Paul Scott   5682
A Division of the Spoils - Paul Scott   5683
The Towers of Silence - Paul Scott   5685

Merridew, Jack (Servant)
The King Edward Plot - Robert Lee Hall   2658

Merrilies, Meg (Gypsy)
Guy Mannering - Sir Walter Scott   5697

Merrill, Barbara (Gentlewoman)
And the Wild Birds Sing - Lola Irish 3112

Merrill, Colleen (Young Woman)
Sand in the Wind - Kathleen O'Neal Gear 2329

Merritt, Johnny (Military Personnel)
Heart of War - John Masters 4174

Merrivale, Charis (Debutante)
Frederica - Georgette Heyer 2889

Merrivale, Frederica (Gentlewoman)
Frederica - Georgette Heyer 2889

Merryn, Christy (Companion)
The Elusive Crown - Hebe Elsna 1931

Merryweather, Prudence (Detective—Private)
Dangerous - Amanda Quick 5213

Mertoun, Mordaunt (Gentleman)
The Pirate - Sir Walter Scott 5704

Mervyn (Nobleman; Detective—Amateur)
The House by the Churchyard - Joseph Sheridan Le Fanu 3688

Mervyn, Francis (Secretary)
The Melancholy Virgin - Annabel Laine 3587

Merza (Sorceress)
The Soothsayer - Laurene Chinn 1069

Mesler, Mordecai (Banker)
The Sword of the Golem - Abraham Rothberg 5509

Messala (Military Personnel)
Ben Hur: A Tale of the Christ - Lew Wallace 6536

Metamoris (Indian; Chieftain)
Song of Metamoris: A Story That Remains of a People Who Passed This Way - Milford E. Anness 155

Metcalf, Harriet (Gentlewoman; Heiress)
The Wicked Godmother - Marion Chesney 1053

Metcalfe, Palmer (Military Personnel)
Shiloh - Shelby Foote 2153

Metella (Noblewoman)
The Fates Are Laughing - William Crozier 1439

Metellus, Decius Caecilius (Detective—Amateur; Nobleman)
The Temple of the Muses - John Maddox Roberts 5382
The Catiline Conspiracy - John Maddox Roberts 5379
The Sacrilege - John Maddox Roberts 5380
SPQR - John Maddox Roberts 5381

Metzner, Helen (Time Traveller)
From Time to Time - Jack Finney 2092

Meyer, Max (Journalist)
A Thousand Shall Fall - Bodie Thoene 6227

Mgobozi (Warrior)
Great Elephant - Alan Scholefield 5654

Micawber, Wilkins (Gentleman)
The Real David Copperfield - Robert Graves 2551

Micay (Spouse)
The Incas - Daniel Peters 4945

Michael, Brother (Religious)
An Unholy Alliance - Susanna Gregory 2586

Michael (Warrior; Royalty)
The Curse of Jezebel: A Novel of the Biblical Queen of Evil - Frank G. Slaughter 5884

Michaelmas, Charity (Servant; Prostitute)
A World Too Wide - Susan Moore 4445

Michaelmas, Georgiana (Bastard Daughter)
A World Too Wide - Susan Moore 4445

Michaelson, Callie (Young Woman)
And One Wore Gray - Heather Graham 2515

Michales, Captain (Revolutionary)
Freedom or Death - Nikos Kazantzakis 3383

Michefalt, Pierre de (Patriot)
Asylum for the Queen - Mildred A. Jordan 3303

Middleton, Egbert (Young Man)
The Mighty and Their Fall - Ivy Compton-Burnett 1230

Middleton, Lavinia (Young Woman)
The Mighty and Their Fall - Ivy Compton-Burnett 1230

Middleton, Nina (Widow(er))
The Mighty and Their Fall - Ivy Compton-Burnett 1230

Miguel, Don (Cowboy)
Don Gaucho - Alyce Pollock 5088

Milam, Andy (Prospector)
Forty Pounds of Gold - Philip D. Stong 6066

Milam, Jacob "Sun Gift" (Captive)
In the Season of the Sun - Kerry Newcomb 4590

Milam, Tom (Outlaw)
In the Season of the Sun - Kerry Newcomb 4590

Milcroft, Lord (Nobleman)
Claire - Elizabeth Lyle 3931

Mildway, Sarah (Governess; Fiance(e))
Lady of Mallow - Dorothy Eden 1856

Miles, Hendon (Knight)
The Prince and the Pauper - Mark Twain 6373

Miles, Morris (Businessman)
Hanover Place - Michael M. Thomas 6245

Milholme, Denise (Young Woman)
The Prize Master - Harvey Haislip 2642

Miller (Hunter; Frontiersman)
Butcher's Crossing - John Williams 6786

Miller, Buck (Sports Figure)
The Fast Men - Tom McNab 4302

Miller, Hacey (Teacher; Military Personnel)
The Way to Fort Pillow - James Sherburne 5807

Miller, Hacey (Teenager)
Hacey Miller - James Sherburne 5805

Miller, Jason (Businessman)
The Moneyman - Judith Liederman 3781

Miller, Jonas (Military Personnel; Captive)
Roanoke Warrior - Carter A. Vaughan 6438

Miller, Max (Businessman)
Glorious Morning - Julie Ellis 1919

Miller, Rick (Lawman)
California! - Dana Fuller Ross 5467

Millhouser, Hedwig (Spouse)
Ourselves to Know - John O'Hara 4704

Millhouser, Robert (Banker; Landowner)
Ourselves to Know - John O'Hara 4704

Millican, Biddy (Servant)
The Black Velvet Gown - Catherine Cookson 1274

Millican, Maria (Widow(er); Servant)
The Black Velvet Gown - Catherine Cookson 1274

Millinder, Augusta (Gentlewoman)
The House of Five Talents - Louis Auchincloss 231

Millinder, Julius (Gentleman)
The House of Five Talents - Louis Auchincloss 231

Millinder, Oswald (Gentleman)
The House of Five Talents - Louis Auchincloss 231

Milroy, Arnold (Military Personnel)
The General's Lady - Esther Forbes 2156

Mina (Wanderer)
For Every Sin - Aharon Appelfeld 175

Minaleff, Kousma (Military Personnel)
Napoleon and the Cossacks - Peter N. Krassnoff 3551

Minard, Sam (Mountain Man)
Mountain Man - Vardis Fisher 2110

Minck, Sheldon (Dentist)
Bullet for a Star - Stuart M. Kaminsky 3331
Catch a Falling Star - Stuart M. Kaminsky 3333
Down for the Count - Stuart M. Kaminsky 3336
The Fala Factor - Stuart M. Kaminsky 3337
He Done Her Wrong - Stuart M. Kaminsky 3338
The Man Who Shot Lewis Vance - Stuart M. Kaminsky 3341
Smart Moves - Stuart M. Kaminsky 3346
Think Fast, Mr. Peters - Stuart M. Kaminsky 3347

Minerva (Royalty)
Curtains for the Cardinal - Elizabeth Eyre 1991

Ming Sen (Young Woman)
Treasure in Hell's Canyon - Bill Gulick 2619

Minnett, Nicholas (Gentleman)
Brumaire - Mark Logan 3864
Guillotine - Mark Logan 3865
Tricolour - Mark Logan 3866

Minor, Constantine (Journalist)
Whiskey River - Loren D. Estleman 1981

Minos (Ruler)
The King Must Die - Mary Renault 5298
The Maze Maker - Michael Ayrton 250

Minotaur (Pirate)
The Sea Peoples - Peter Danielson 1474

Minter, Monica (Gentlewoman)
Hanging on the Wire - Gillian Linscott 3806

Mirador, Consuelo (Captive)
War Chief - Donald Clayton Porter 5130

Mirana (Royalty; Captive)
Lord of Hawkfell Island - Catherine Coulter 1376

Miranda, Micky (Financier)
A Dangerous Fortune - Ken Follett 2147

Miriam (Gentlewoman)
The Curse of Jezebel: A Novel of the Biblical Queen of Evil - Frank G. Slaughter 5884
Simple Prayers - Michael Golding 2452

Miriam (Outcast)
Bodin, 1349: An Epic Novel of Christians and Jews in the Plague Years - Roberta Kalechofsky 3322

Mironov, Katya (Royalty)
Horses of War - Duff Hart-Davis 2760

Mitana (Indian)
The Russian River - Gary McCarthy 4224

Mitchell, Dennis (Heir)
The Magnolias - Julie Ellis 1922

Mitchell, Parris (Young Man; Student)
Kings Row - Henry Bellamann 428

Mitchell, Sam (Military Personnel)
So Shall They Reap - John Bennett 444

Mitla (Young Woman)
Gods on Horseback - Samuel G. Baggett 263

Mitterer, Joseph Von (Diplomat)
Bosnian Chronicle - Ivo Andric 150

Mixcatl (Royalty)
The Jaguar Princess - Clare Bell 421

Mixtli (Nobleman)
Aztec - Gary Jennings 3193

Modena, Cosimo di (Banker)
The Sword of Il Grande - Will Creed 1424

Modred (Bastard Son)
The Wicked Day - Mary Stewart 6033

Modred (Knight)
The Pagan King - Edison Marshall 4109

Modred (Knight; Royalty)
Guinevere: The Legend in Autumn - Persia
Woolley   6868

Moffatt, Andrew (Young Man)
The Nonsuch Lure - Mary M. Luke   3924

Mohegan, John (Indian)
The Pioneers; or, The Sources of the Susquehanna -
James Fenimore Cooper   1307

Mohini (Young Woman)
The Golden Honeycomb - Kamala Markandaya   4086

Mohun, Edith (Handicapped)
An Ancient Evil - C.L. Grace   2504

Mohun, Lydia (Actress)
Bedford Row - Claire Rayner   5259
Soho Square - Claire Rayner   5268

Moidore, Basil (Gentleman)
A Dangerous Mourning - Anne Perry   4926

Molinero, Emma (Orphan)
The Whip - Catherine Cookson   1291

Molloy, Alice (Artist)
Privileged Children - Frances Vernon   6455

Molloy, Charles (Widow(er))
Passage West - Dallas Miller   4382

Molloy, Molly (Young Woman)
Rogue's Holiday - Hamilton Cochran   1141

Moloquin (Outcast; Chieftain)
Pillar of the Sky - Cecelia Holland   2994

Mompesson, Polly (Young Woman)
The Running of the Tide - Esther Forbes   2160

Mompesson, Ralph (Criminal)
In Pale Battalions - Robert Goddard   2444

Monaseetah (Indian)
Long Winter Gone - Terry C. Johnston   3252
Seize the Sky - Terry C. Johnston   3256
Whisper of the Wolf - Terry C. Johnston   3261

Moncada, Juan de (Military Personnel)
Cradle of the Sun - John Clagett   1083

Moncey, Caroline (Spouse)
Guillotine - Mark Logan   3865

Monckton, May (Young Woman)
Lady Jane - Leslie O'Grady   4699

Monckton, Ules (Journalist; Military Personnel)
The Light Infantry Ball - Hamilton Basso   375

Moncrieff, Christopher (Adventurer)
Born to Be King - Constance Gluyas   2440

Moncrieff, Ian (Nobleman)
If This Be Magic - Ellen Marsh   4098

Monday, Caroline (Heiress—Lost; Noblewoman)
Bride of the Unicorn - Kasey Michaels   4363

Monday, Johnson (Mountain Man)
Moontrap - Don Berry   481

Monday, Viridis (Artist; Journalist)
The Choiring of the Trees - Donald Harington   2709

Mondeloy, Chelynne (Gentlewoman)
Chelynne - Robyn Carr   938

Monforte, Don Camillo (Nobleman)
The Bravo - James Fenimore Cooper   1298

Monington, Richard (Nobleman)
Bennett's Welcome - Inglis Fletcher   2132

Monk, Mary (Prostitute)
The Fireflower - Edith Layton   3687

Monk, Mordecai (Religious)
The Peculiar People - Jan de Hartog   2764

Monk, William (Detective—Police; Amnesiac)
Cain and His Brother - Anne Perry   4922
A Dangerous Mourning - Anne Perry   4926
Defend and Betray - Anne Perry   4928

The Face of a Stranger - Anne Perry   4929
The Sins of the Wolf - Anne Perry   4937
A Sudden, Fearful Death - Anne Perry   4938

Montag, Trudi (Handicapped; Librarian)
Stones From the River - Ursula Hegi   2816

Montagu, Jack (Gentleman)
The Fourth Queen - Isabel Paterson   4827

Montague, Michael (Worker)
Madame Geneva - Jane Lane   3655

Montague, Mignon (Gentlewoman)
The Baroness of Bow Street - Gail Clark   1085

Montalia, Madelaine de (Gentlewoman; Vampire)
Hotel Transylvania - Chelsea Quinn Yarbro   6900
Out of the House of Life - Chelsea Quinn
Yarbro   6903
Tempting Fate - Chelsea Quinn Yarbro   6906

Montanis, Lorenzo (Gentleman)
A Distant Thunder - Teresa de Luca   1561

Montargis, Lise de (Noblewoman)
The Rake and the Rebel - Ira J. Morris   4478

Montauban, Maurice de (Nobleman)
The Anthem - Noel B. Gerson   2361

Montauban, Michel de (Nobleman)
The Anthem - Noel B. Gerson   2361

Montauban, Philippe de (Nobleman)
The Anthem - Noel B. Gerson   2361

Montclair, Valentine (Gentleman)
Logic of the Heart - Patricia Veryan   6466

Monteith, Ringan (Heir)
Monsieur Janvier - Elizabeth Linington   3799

Montelupo, Michael da (Military Personnel)
The Gentle Infidel - Lawrence Schoonover   5663

Monterant, Sophie (Actress)
The Monterant Affair - Richard Grayson   2560

Montero, Lola (Dancer)
The Infinite Woman - Edison Marshall   4107

Montez, Lola (Young Woman)
The Union Belle - Gilbert Morris   4473

Montgeil, Ricord de (Nobleman)
Destiny of Fire - Zoe Oldenbourg   4715

Montgeoffrey, Roger (Nobleman)
Through a Glass Darkly - Karleen Koen   3531

Montgomerie, Sir Edmund de (Knight)
Silver Leopard - F. van Wyck Mason   4160

Montgomery, Catherine (Gentlewoman)
The Far Journey - Loula Grace Erdman   1950

Montgomery, Dougless (Teacher)
A Knight in Shining Armor - Jude Deveraux   1631

Montgomery, Lacie (Teacher; Imposter)
Thief of My Heart - Rexanne Becnel   410

Montgomery, Penelope (Gentlewoman)
Practice to Deceive - Patricia Veryan   6475

Montgomery, Ring (Military Personnel)
Mountain Laurel - Jude Deveraux   1632

Montgomery, Val (Heroine)
Castle Barebane - Joan Aiken   43

Montmorency, Jasper (Nobleman)
Lady Jane - Norma Lee Clark   1092

Montoria, Don Jose de (Gentleman; Patriot)
Saragossa - Benito Perez Galdos   4912

Montorio, Antonio de (Hero)
Saragossa - Benito Perez Galdos   4912

Montour, Esther (Indian)
The King's Rebel - James David Horan   3030

Montressor, Letty (Singer)
Letty - Clare Darcy   1491

Montreuse, Felipe Flores y Lennox (Sea Captain;
Pirate)
The Black Duchess - Alanna Knight   3514

Montrevil, Jean de (Nobleman)
The Severed Crown - Jane Lane   3657

Montrigord, Julietta de (Gentlewoman)
Red Adam's Lady - Grace Ingram   3106

Moodie, James (Businessman)
Creature Comforts - Jessica Stirling   6041

Moolman (Hunter)
Rags of Glory - Stuart Cloete   1126

Moon, Jewel (Madam)
The Search for Temperance Moon - Douglas C.
Jones   3282

Moore, Cristobel (Orphan)
The Trevarton Inheritance - Malcolm
Macdonald   3976

Moore, George (Historian; Writer)
The Year of the French - Thomas Flanagan   2121

Moore, John Schuler (Journalist)
The Alienist - Caleb Carr   907

Moore, Jonas (Frontiersman)
Look to the Mountain - Le Grand Cannon   885

Moore, Joshua (Immigrant)
Joshua Moore, American - George Frederick
Hummel   3078

Moore, Marian (Orphan)
The Trevarton Inheritance - Malcolm
Macdonald   3976

Moore, Megan Byers (Young Woman)
Megan - Kathleen Magill   4028

Moore, Samuel (Settler)
Hannah Fowler - Janice Holt Giles   2411

Moore, Teresa (Orphan)
The Trevarton Inheritance - Malcolm
Macdonald   3976

Moorfield, Lydia (Gentlewoman)
Forget the Glory - Emma Drummond   1725

Moorhouse, Arthur (Businessman)
Aunt Bel - Guy McCrone   4231
Red Plush: The Story of the Moorhouse Family - Guy
McCrone   4232

Moorhouse, Bel (Spouse)
Aunt Bel - Guy McCrone   4231
Red Plush: The Story of the Moorhouse Family - Guy
McCrone   4232

Moram (Ruler)
Ruan - Bryher   746

Morandi, Richard (Gentleman)
Lord Vanity - Samuel Shellabarger   5796

Morane, Henry (Government Official)
The Killing of Richard the Third - Robert
Farrington   2020
The Traitors of Bosworth - Robert Farrington   2021
Tudor Agent - Robert Farrington   2022

Morane, Matilda (Spouse)
The Traitors of Bosworth - Robert Farrington   2021
Tudor Agent - Robert Farrington   2022

Mordal, Kirsten (Orphan; Seamstress)
Lady of No Man's Land - Jeanne Williams   6780

Mordaunt, Bridget (Businesswoman)
The Black Candle - Catherine Cookson   1273

More, Adriana (Actress)
Some Lose Their Way - Eloise S. Liddon   3770

Moreau, Andre-Louis (Lawyer; Revolutionary)
Scaramouche the King-Maker - Rafael Sabatini   5555

Moreau, Andre-Louis (Political Figure; Revolutionary)
Scaramouche - Rafael Sabatini 5554

Morel, Charlotte (Young Woman)
Charlotte Morel - Maria Lodi 3829
Charlotte Morel: The Dream - Maria Lodi 3830
Charlotte Morel: The Siege - Maria Lodi 3831

Morel, Jeanne (Young Woman)
A Tale of the Wind: A Novel of Nineteenth-Century France - Kay Nolte Smith 5922

Moreland, Jason (Trader; Adventurer)
The Moreland Legacy - Diana Haviland 2777

Morelli, Anthony (Gentleman)
I, Roberta - Elizabeth Gray Vining 6501

Morelli, Roberta (Spouse)
I, Roberta - Elizabeth Gray Vining 6501

Morewood, Oliver (Gentleman)
Windover - Jane Aiken Hodge 2974

Morgan (Gentleman)
Every Man for Himself - Beryl Bainbridge 270

Morgan, Lord (Nobleman)
Spy in Chancery - P.C. Doherty 1680

Morgan (Witch)
The Mists of Avalon - Marion Zimmer Bradley 626

Morgan, Beth (Heroine)
How Green Was My Valley - Richard Llewellyn 3813

Morgan, Charles (Prospector)
Oh Glittering Promise - Anne Fisher 2099

Morgan, Corby (Plantation Owner)
Cry of the Rain Bird - Patricia Shaw 5779

Morgan, Daisy (Doctor)
After the Rainbow - Yvonne Kalman 3323

Morgan, Frank (Adventurer; Gypsy)
The Stallion Man - Judith Glover 2438

Morgan, Gwilym (Miner)
How Green Was My Valley - Richard Llewellyn 3813

Morgan, Hank (Mechanic)
A Connecticut Yankee in King Arthur's Court - Mark Twain 6371

Morgan, Huw (Hero)
How Green Was My Valley - Richard Llewellyn 3813

Morgan, Jane (Young Woman)
West of Appomattox - Harley Duncan 1785

Morgan, Jeremy (Privateer; Spy)
Yankee - Dana Fuller Ross 5495

Morgan, Jessie (Spouse)
Cry of the Rain Bird - Patricia Shaw 5779

Morgan, Liverpool (Frontiersman)
Gone the Dreams and the Dancing - Douglas C. Jones 3279

Morgan, Matt (Scout)
The Shining Mountains - Dale Van Every 6410

Morgan, Myles (Heir)
The Sword of Truth - Gilbert Morris 4472

Morgan, Polly (Spy)
The Secret Road - Bruce Lancaster 3646

Morgan, Rhys (Landowner)
After the Rainbow - Yvonne Kalman 3323

Morgan, Robert (Doctor)
Testimony of Two Men - Taylor Caldwell 863

Morgan, Seth (Sea Captain)
Abigail - Joan Druett 1721

Morgan, William (Gentleman)
This Willing Passion - Patricia Cloud 1132

Morgan Le Fay (Gentlewoman)
The Road to Avalon - Joan Wolf 6842

Morgan Le Fay (Sorceress)
The Prince and the Pilgrim - Mary Stewart 6032

Morgan Le Fey (Sorceress)
Witch of the North - Courtway Jones 3272

Morgana (Royalty; Captive)
The Viking - Edison Marshall 4113

Morgause (Witch)
The Last Enchantment - Mary Stewart 6031
The Wicked Day - Mary Stewart 6033

Morgawse (Sorceress)
Hawk of May - Gillian Bradshaw 629

Morgiana (Gentlewoman)
Alamut - Judith Tarr 6164

Moriarty, James (Criminal; Professor)
The Case of the Revolutionist's Daughter: Sherlock Holmes Meets Karl Marx - Lewis S. Feuer 2076
Enter the Lion: A Posthumous Memoir of Mycroft Holmes - Michael P. Hodel 2961
Exit Sherlock Holmes - Robert Lee Hall 2657
The Return of Moriarty - John E. Gardner 2287

Moriss, Sir John (Gentleman)
Masquerade for the King - Marina Oliver 4729

Morlaix, Quentin de (Gentleman)
Master-At-Arms - Rafael Sabatini 5553

Morland, Emma (Gentlewoman)
Murder by the Waters - Robert Lee Hall 2661

Morland, Lesley (Young Woman)
Home Station - Jeanne Williams 6778

Morley, Simon (Artist; Time Traveller)
Time and Again - Jack Finney 2093

Morley, Simon (Time Traveller)
From Time to Time - Jack Finney 2092

Mornay, Guy de (Military Personnel)
All the Golden Gifts - Iola Fuller 2251

Morning Sky (Indian; Spouse)
High Country - Jason Manning 4075

Morning Swan (Indian)
High Freedom - Earl Murray 4530

Morpain, Paul de (Young Man)
Restless Are the Sails - Evelyn Eaton 1830

Morrigan, Johnny (Migrant Worker)
The Longest Road - Jeanne Williams 6781

Morris, Basdel (Frontiersman)
A Virginia Scout - Hugh Pendexter 4899

Morris, Dinah (Religious)
Adam Bede - George Eliot 1908

Morris, Jeremy (Gentleman; Lawyer)
Luise - Dawn Stewart Field 2079

Morrison, Charlotte (Spinster)
Rhine Journey - Ann Schlee 5639

Morrison, Edwin Carter (Journalist)
Season for War - P.F. Kluge 3510

Morrison, Helen (Captive)
A Woman of the People - Benjamin Capps 893

Morrison, Sam (Journalist)
Killdeer Mountain - Dee Brown 713

Morrison, William (Journalist)
Niagara - Robert Lewis Taylor 6189

Morrow, Sloan (Gambler)
The Earth and All It Holds - V.J. Banis 287

Morrow, Tom (Teacher; Frontiersman)
Follow the River - Albert Mayer 4203

Morse, Elkanah (Scientist)
The Far Tribes - Richard S. Wheeler 6658

Morse, Remembrance (Young Woman)
Trumpet to Arms - Bruce Lancaster 3647

Mort (Worker)
The Chant of Jimmie Blacksmith - Thomas Keneally 3411

Morteigne, Adam de (Knight)
The Lost Flight - H.F.M. Prescott 5169

Mortimer, Amelia (Widow(er))
Evil Mark - Graham Miles 4377

Mortimer, Charles (Businessman)
The Blackheath Poisonings - Julian Symons 6150

Mortimer, Charles (Military Personnel; Nobleman)
The Sandalwood Fan - Diana Brown 720

Mortimer, Charlotte (Young Woman)
Electricity: A Novel - Victoria Glendinning 2431

Mortimer, Clive (Heir; Businessman)
For They Shall Inherit - Malcolm Macdonald 3964

Mortimer, Judith (Orphan; Gentlewoman)
Judith - Brian Cleeve 1108

Mortimer, Richard (Nobleman; Revolutionary)
The Prisoners of September - Leon Garfield 2294

Mortimer, Warrin de (Knight)
The Running Vixen - Elizabeth Chadwick 968

Morton, Harriet Jane (Dancer)
A Company of Swans - Eva Ibbotson 3095

Morton, Henry (Gentleman)
Old Mortality - Sir Walter Scott 5702

Morton, James (Police Officer; Gentleman)
Counterfeit of Murder - Ray Harrison 2738
Death of a Dancing Lady - Ray Harrison 2739
Deathwatch - Ray Harrison 2740
Harvest of Death - Ray Harrison 2741
Patently Murder - Ray Harrison 2742
A Season for Death - Ray Harrison 2743
Sphere of Death - Ray Harrison 2744
Tincture of Death - Ray Harrison 2745
Why Kill Arthur Potter? - Ray Harrison 2746

Mortymer, Hywel (Worker)
The Rape of the Fair Country - Alexander Cordell 1325

Mortymer, Iestyn (Worker)
The Rape of the Fair Country - Alexander Cordell 1325

Morville, Drusilla (Gentlewoman)
The Quiet Gentleman - Georgette Heyer 2897

Morwenna, Lady (Noblewoman)
The King Liveth - Jeffrey Farnol 2013

Moscrop, Albert (Gentleman)
Mad Hatter's Holiday - Peter Lovesey 3914

Moser, Anna (Musician)
Anna, Ann, Annie - Thomas Trebitsch Parker 4808

Moses (Slave)
Tell Me a Tale: A Novel of the Old South - James McEachin 4266

Moshesh (Chieftain)
Wild Conquest - Peter Abrahams 12

Mostyn, Alexandra (Artist)
The Bridge of a Hundred Dragons - Emma Drummond 1723

Motte-Valois, Countess de la (Noblewoman)
The Prisoners of September - Leon Garfield 2294

Mounslic (Military Personnel)
Soldiers of Fortune - Peter Bourne 595

Mount, Jay Fielding (Outcast)
Mount's Mistake - Lew McCreary 4229

Mount, Stirling (Naturalist)
River of Sky - Karen Harper 2713

Mountain, Colin (Young Man)
The Secret of Saramount - Lillian Cheatham   1011

Mountain, Joe (Frontiersman; Military Personnel)
Remember Santiago - Douglas C. Jones   3280

Mountain, Sarah (Young Woman)
The Secret of Saramount - Lillian Cheatham   1011

Mourne, Lex (Military Personnel; Farmer)
The Red Doe - Drayton Mayrant   4214

Mourouane, Ahmed Ben (Entertainer)
Scorpus the Moor - Leslie Turner White   6690

Mowbray, Caroline (Gentlewoman)
Sherlock Holmes and the Thistle of Scotland - L.B.
   Greenwood   2578

Mowbray, Ellen (Spouse)
A Father and His Fate - Ivy Compton-Burnett   1228

Mowbray, Malcolm (Gentleman; Heir)
A Father and His Fate - Ivy Compton-Burnett   1228

Mowbray, Miles (Landowner)
A Father and His Fate - Ivy Compton-Burnett   1228

Moynahan, Ellen (Immigrant; Servant)
One Small Candle - Mary Linehan MacKinnon   3998

Moynihan, Gerrard (Gentleman)
Sabrina - Madeleine Polland   5086

Mr. Hooker (Animal)
Shakespeare's Dog - Leon Rooke   5439

Mudd, Grover (Journalist)
Saint Mudd - Steve Thayer   6218

Mudspell, Curt (Peddler; Deity)
Called Away - Perdita Buchan   753

Muir, Evan (Farmer)
The Great Meadow - Elizabeth Madox Roberts   5378

Muirheal (Sorceress)
The Saxon Tapestry - Sile Rice   5317

Muirtagh (Knight)
The Kings in Winter - Cecelia Holland   2991

Mulcahey, Jack (Entertainer)
Banished Children of Eve - Peter Quinn   5227

Muldoon, Ned (Detective—Police)
Faces in the Crowd - William Marshall   4117

Mulkerin, Eileen (Widow(er))
The Californios - Louis L'Amour   3618

Mulkerin, Michael (Religious)
The Californios - Louis L'Amour   3618

Mulkerin, Sean (Sailor)
The Californios - Louis L'Amour   3618

Muller, Jonathan (Young Man)
Patriot's Dream - Barbara Michaels   4360

Mulock, Ranse (Frontiersman)
Distant Music - Harold Lenoir Davis   1521

Muncie, Peter (Frontiersman)
Arizona - Clarence Budington Kelland   3387

Mundy, Jim (Military Personnel)
Jim Mundy: A Novel of the American Civil War -
   Robert H. Fowler   2192

Munro, Alice (Young Woman)
The Last of the Mohicans - James Fenimore
   Cooper   1302

Munro, Alistair (Nobleman)
Beatrice Goes to Brighton - Marion Chesney   1019

Munro, Cora (Young Woman)
The Last of the Mohicans - James Fenimore
   Cooper   1302

Munro, Donald (Young Man)
Greenyards - Joan Lingard   3796

Murdoc (Revolutionary; Patriot)
Seek the Fair Land - Walter Macken   3989

Murdoch, Jill (Young Woman)
The Silver Oar - Howard Breslin   669

Murdock, Page (Lawman)
City of Widows - Loren D. Estleman   1969
The High Rocks - Loren D. Estleman   1973
Murdock's Law - Loren D. Estleman   1975
Stamping Ground - Loren D. Estleman   1977
The Stranglers - Loren D. Estleman   1978

Murdockson, Meg (Witch)
The Heart of Midlothian - Sir Walter Scott   5698

Murfy, Malachi Desmond (Military Personnel)
Murfy's Men - Gerald Green   2565

Murgatroyd, Anna-Marie (Teenager)
Midnight Is a Place - Joan Aiken   52

Murphy, Elisa (Young Woman)
Munich Signature - Bodie Thoene   6224

Murphy, John (Religious)
Sons of Thunder - Barbara Fitz Vroman   6516

Murphy, Luke (Adventurer)
The Gold Seekers - William Stuart Long   3874

Murphy, Rafael (Military Personnel)
Apache Autumn - Robert Skimin   5875

Murray, Bracken (Journalist)
Ever After - Elswyth Thane   6216

Murray, Cabot (Military Personnel)
Yankee Stranger - Elswyth Thane   6217

Murray, Martha (Spouse)
The Day Must Dawn - Agnes Sligh Turnbull   6362

Murray, Sam (Settler)
The Day Must Dawn - Agnes Sligh Turnbull   6362

Murray, Violet (Young Woman)
The Day Must Dawn - Agnes Sligh Turnbull   6362

Murtagh, Caroline (Gentlewoman)
The Silver Saber - Carter A. Vaughan   6441
Yankee Rogue - Dana Fuller Ross   5496

Murtagh, Colum (Government Official)
The Book of Shadows - C.L. Grace   2505

Murtagh, Colum (Military Personnel)
The Eye of God - C.L. Grace   2506
The Merchant of Death - C.L. Grace   2508
A Shrine of Murders - C.L. Grace   2509

Musgrave, Freddie (Worker)
The Harrogate Secret - Catherine Cookson   1278

Musgrave, Noel (Nobleman)
Borrowed Plumes - Roseleen Milne   4409

Musgrove, John (Trader)
Rascal's Heaven - F. van Wyck Mason   4157

Musgrove, Rosamond (Gentlewoman)
The Robber Bridegroom - Eudora Welty   6623

Musick, Adam (Sea Captain)
Long Storm - Ernest Haycox   2790

Musselwhite (Prehistoric Human; Warrior)
People of the Lightning - W. Michael Gear   2337

Musson, Clara (Young Woman)
For God and Glory - Tim Jeal   3171

Myer, Dr. (Doctor)
Carriage Trade - Robert Thomsen   6271

Myran, Kristaver (Sea Captain; Fisherman)
The Last of the Vikings - Johan Bojer   563

Myran, Lars (Fisherman; Sailor)
The Last of the Vikings - Johan Bojer   563

Myrddin (Blacksmith)
In the Shadow of the Oak King - Courtway
   Jones   3271

Myron (Adventurer)
The Dragon of the Ishtar Gate - L. Sprague De
   Camp   1555

N

Nabu (Military Personnel)
Babylon - Anthony Esler   1959

Nails, David (Captive)
Call the Beast Thy Brother - William Oliver
   Turner   6366

Nairn, Alexander (Slave)
Westward to Laughter - Colin MacInnes   3984

Nakoa (Indian; Warrior)
The Second Kiss - Gayle Rogers   5432

Nakwisi (Indian; Captive)
The Double Man - Elinor Pryor   5205

Nalda (Nurse)
Isle of Glory - Jane Oliver   4723

Nanautzin (Government Official)
*The Sun, He Dies: A Novel about the End of the Aztec
   World* - Jamake Highwater   2919

Nanconou, Aurora (Widow(er))
The Grandissimes - George W. Cable   842

Nandou (Actor)
*A Tale of the Wind: A Novel of Nineteenth-Century
   France* - Kay Nolte Smith   5922

Nanette (Orphan)
The Villains: A Haunting Tale of the Marshes -
   Charlotte Keppel   3467

Naomi (Fugitive)
Arouse and Beware - MacKinlay Kantor   3360

Naomi (Young Woman)
Daughter of Jairus - Paul Hervey Fox   2196

Napier, Gavin (Military Personnel)
The Bonnet Laird's Daughter - Barbara
   Annandale   154

Napier, Margaret (Teacher)
Death Wore a Diadem - Iona McGregor   4277

Nardo (Prehistoric Human; Young Man)
The Reindeer Hunters - Joan Wolf   6841

Narni, Francesca de (Gentlewoman)
The Florentine - Sandra Shulman   5840

Narouz (Royalty)
The Mamur Zapt and the Girl in the Nile - Michael
   Pearce   4867

Narra-mattah (Indian)
The Wept of Wish-Ton-Wish - James Fenimore
   Cooper   1312

Narses (Servant)
The Bearkeeper's Daughter - Gillian Bradshaw   628

Nash, Charles "Buck" (Military Personnel)
A Wilful Woman - Michael Talbot   6156

Nash, Captain George (Detective—Private)
Captain Nash and the Honour of England - Ragan
   Butler   827
Captain Nash and the Wroth Inheritance - Ragan
   Butler   828

Nash, Jeston (Outlaw)
While Angels Dance - Ralph W. Cotton   1372

Nash, Richard (Actor)
Lucy - Hester W. Chapman   992

Nason, Richard (Sea Captain; Prisoner)
The Lively Lady - Kenneth Roberts   5386

Nason, Steven (Military Personnel)
Arundel - Kenneth Roberts   5383
Rabble in Arms - Kenneth Roberts   5390

Nateby-Dyce, Thomas (Gentleman)
Too Late! Too Late! The Maiden Cried - Joan
   Fleming   2128

Nausicaa (Noblewoman)
The Voyage Home - Ernst Schnabel 5644

Nausicaa (Royalty)
Homer's Daughter - Robert Graves 2546

Navahk (Prehistoric Human; Shaman)
Corridor of Storms - William Sarabande 5596

Navarro, Julio Diaz (Artist)
The Burning Man - Stephen Longstreet 3883

Neal, William (Artisan)
Proving Ground: A Novel of Civil War Days in the North - Leone Lowden 3919

Neill, Dan (Businessman)
The Scapegoat - Mary Lee Settle 5758

Neilson, Gunnar (Immigrant; Settler)
A Circle of Trees - Dana Faralla 2012

Neilson, Kersti (Immigrant; Settler)
A Circle of Trees - Dana Faralla 2012

Nel (Prehistoric Human)
The Horsemasters - Joan Wolf 6840

Nellis, Hendrick (Loyalist; Military Personnel)
The Life and Times of Captain N. - Douglas Glover 2436

Nellis, Oskar (Young Man)
The Life and Times of Captain N. - Douglas Glover 2436

Nemattanon (Indian; Chieftain)
The First Gentleman of America: A Comedy of Conquest - James Branch Cabell 841

Nemo, Adam (Eskimo; Servant)
Frobisher's Savage - Leonard Tourney 6299

Nesbitt, Horatio (Judge)
Sing One Song - Helen Topping Miller 4394

Nettleby, Randolph (Nobleman)
The Shooting Party - Isabel Colegate 1197

Nettleship, Lionel (Religious)
Gentlemen in England - A.N. Wilson 6795

Nettleship, Maudie (Teenager)
Gentlemen in England - A.N. Wilson 6795

Neville, John (Imposter)
The Bisley Boy - Christopher Hunt 3080

Neville, Liana (Heiress)
The Taming - Jude Deveraux 1633

Nevins, Hal (Military Personnel)
Something Gleamed - Theda Kenyon 3463

Newberry, Catherine (Spouse)
Blood of the Boar - Margaret Abbey 2

Newberry, Catherine (Ward)
The Heart Is a Traitor - Margaret Abbey 4

Newbolt, Mary (Companion)
Death En Voyage - Richard Grayson 2557

Newbury, Captain Jack (Adventurer)
The Gentleman From America - Paul Benton 464

Newcombe, Honoria (Orphan; Ward)
Sweet's Folly - Fiona Hill 2926

Newman, Dr. (Doctor)
Molokai - Oswald Andrew Bushnell 815

Newton, Carlina (Nurse)
Remember Santiago - Douglas C. Jones 3280

Niall Black-Knee (Royalty)
The Emerald Crown - Theodora McCormick Du Bois 1741

Nicanor (Young Man)
Nicanor of Athens: The Autobiography of an Unknown Citizen - Owen Francis Grazebrook 2563

Niccola (Young Woman)
Leonardo's Judas - Leo Perutz 4941

Niccolo (Entertainer)
A Comedy of Murders - George Herman 2861

Nichol, Beasley (Military Personnel; Spy)
Home to Tennessee - Alfred Leland Crabb 1400
Lodging at the Saint Cloud - Alfred Leland Crabb 1403
Mockingbird Sang at Chickamauga - Alfred Leland Crabb 1404

Nicholas (Outlaw)
The Outlaw's Tale - Margaret Frazer 2218

Nicholas, Brother (Religious)
Wandering Star - Steven Yount 6945

Nicholls, Geoffrey (Gentleman)
Falls of Gard - Laura Black 520

Nichols, Constance (Gentlewoman)
The Family of Women - Richard Peck 4883

Nicholson, Craig (Criminal)
The Good Provider - Jessica Stirling 6043

Nicholson, Craig (Police Officer)
The Asking Price - Jessica Stirling 6039
The Welcome Light - Jessica Stirling 6050

Nicholson, Gislane (Bastard Daughter)
Mistress of Darkness - Christopher Nicole 4617

Nickajack (Indian)
Nickajack - Robert J. Conley 1248

Nickerson, Ross (Student—College)
A Roaring in the Wind - Robert Lewis Taylor 6191

Nicola (Young Woman)
The Ruthless Yeomen - Valerie Anand 134

Nicolas (Young Man)
Darkness and the Dawn - Thomas B. Costain 1364

Nicols, Susan (Refugee)
Another Spring - Loula Grace Erdman 1948

Night Hawk (Indian)
Trail of Tears - Frances Patton Statham 5983

Night Wind (Indian)
Night Wind - Roberta Jean Mountjoy 4504

Night Wind (Indian; Warrior)
Night Wind's Woman - Shirl Henke 2825

Nightingale, Frederic North (Nobleman)
The Nightingale Legacy - Catherine Coulter 1379

Nightshade (Indian; Shaman)
People of the River - W. Michael Gear 2338

Nihoa, Hiram (Spy)
Ka'a'awa: A Novel about Hawaii in the 1850s - Oswald Andrew Bushnell 814

Nikeratos (Actor)
The Mask of Apollo - Mary Renault 5300

Nikolayeva, Valentina (Noblewoman)
Contessa - Helene Mansfield 4076

Nikolayevitch, Alexei (Gentleman)
Emily - Cynthia Harrod-Eagles 2753

Nikulausson, Erlend (Knight; Landowner)
The Bridal Wreath - Sigrid Undset 6379
The Cross - Sigrid Undset 6380
The Mistress of Husaby - Sigrid Undset 6382

Nils (Tailor; Musician)
Arne - Bjornstjerne Bjornson 518

Nilson, Anne (Gentlewoman)
Limmerston Hall - Hester W. Chapman 991

Nilsson, Karl Oskar (Farmer)
Last Letter Home - Vilhelm Moberg 4423
The Settlers - Vilhelm Moberg 4424

Nilsson, Karl Oskar (Immigrant)
The Emigrants - Vilhelm Moberg 4422
Unto a Good Land - Vilhelm Moberg 4425

Nilsson, Kristina (Spouse)
Last Letter Home - Vilhelm Moberg 4423
The Settlers - Vilhelm Moberg 4424
Unto a Good Land - Vilhelm Moberg 4425

Nilsson, Kristina (Spouse; Immigrant)
The Emigrants - Vilhelm Moberg 4422

Nilsson, Robert (Immigrant)
The Emigrants - Vilhelm Moberg 4422
Unto a Good Land - Vilhelm Moberg 4425

Nilsson, Robert (Prospector)
The Settlers - Vilhelm Moberg 4424

Nine-Lizard (Writer)
The Jaguar Princess - Clare Bell 421

Niniane (Royalty; Captive)
Born of the Sun - Joan Wolf 6837

Nisbet, Laura (Gentlewoman)
A Woman Possessed - Malcolm Macdonald 3977

Nisha (Prehistoric Human)
Children of the Sun - Charlotte Prentiss 5167

No Ears (Indian)
Buffalo Girls - Larry McMurtry 4296

No Name (Indian; Warrior)
Conquering Horse - Frederick F. Manfred 4055

Noble Popjoy (Indian; Guide)
Shadow of the Moon - Douglas C. Jones 3284

Noble Talent (Military Personnel)
Spring Moon: A Novel of China - Bette Bao Lord 3897

Nofret (Servant)
Pillar of Fire - Judith Tarr 6168

Nolan, Ned (Revolutionary)
The Tenants of Time - Thomas Flanagan 2120

Norcrosse, Del (Military Personnel)
Soul of Abe Lincoln - Bernie Babcock 251

Norland, Deborah (Noblewoman; Spy)
Deborah and the Siege of Paris - Colette Davenat 1500

Norrey, Sir John (Gentleman)
Midwinter - John Buchan 751

Norris, Jacqueline (Settler)
Strife Before Dawn - Mary Schumann 5675

Norris-Newman, Charles "Noggs" (Journalist)
The Tune That They Play - William Clive 1120

North, Frederick (Gentleman)
The Darkening Leaf - Caroline Stickland 6036

North, Mahalia (Young Woman)
Fire Bell in the Night - Constance Robertson 5395

North, Rob (Veteran; Renegade)
Red Cloud's Revenge - Terry C. Johnston 3255

Northrup, Job (Smuggler)
Pelican Coast - Alan Le May 3690

Norton, Geoffrey (Lawyer)
Good Morning, Irene - Carole Nelson Douglas 1698

Norton, George (Banker)
The Land Was Ours: A Novel of the Great Plains - Charles W. Bailey 266

Norton, Godfrey (Lawyer)
Good Night, Mr. Holmes - Carole Nelson Douglas 1700
Irene's Last Waltz - Carole Nelson Douglas 1701

Norton, James (Heir)
Painting the Darkness - Robert Goddard 2445

Norvall, Annie (Widow(er))
The Buffalo Soldiers - John Prebble 5165

Norville, Jean de (Gentlewoman)
The King's Cavalier - Samuel Shellabarger 5795

Norwell, Stephen (Businessman; Loyalist)
Birthright - Robert E. Wall 6533

Norwell, Stephen (Frontiersman)
Bloodbrothers - Robert E. Wall 6535

Norwell, Stephen (Orphan)
Blackrobe - Robert E. Wall 6534

Notaras, Anna (Gentlewoman)
The Dark Angel - Mika Waltari 6551

Novak, Thad (Young Man)
The Last Confederate - Gilbert Morris 4466

Novus, Hortensius (Businessman; Fiance(e))
Venus in Copper - Lindsey Davis 1534

Nowell, Roger (Gentleman)
Elegant Witch - Robert Neill 4568

Nowell-Grey, Brockton (Plantation Owner)
The Ravishers - Elizabeth Richards 5318

Noyes, John (Sea Captain)
The Sea Stands Watch - Helen Parker Mudgett 4507

Noyes, Julia (Spouse)
The Sea Stands Watch - Helen Parker Mudgett 4507

Nuala (Young Woman)
The Gallowglass - Howard Breslin 666

Nugent, Janice (Gentlewoman)
The End of the Hunt - Thomas Flanagan 2119

Nyasanu (Warrior; Chieftain)
The Dahomean - Frank Yerby 6911

Nydia (Peddler; Handicapped)
The Last Days of Pompeii - Edward Bulwer-
Lytton 768

O

O-Lan (Slave)
The Good Earth - Pearl S. Buck 754

Oakes, Sir Harry (Financier)
Carnal Hours - Max Allan Collins 1210

Oakes, Jude (Farmer)
American Beauty - Edna Ferber 2060

Oakes, Orrange (Settler)
American Beauty - Edna Ferber 2060

Oakley, Harriet (Young Woman)
The Golden Fleece - Norah Lofts 3843

Oakley, John (Convict)
They Seek a Country - Francis Brett Young 6941

Oakley, Myrtle (Young Woman)
The Golden Fleece - Norah Lofts 3843

Oakley, Will (Innkeeper)
The Golden Fleece - Norah Lofts 3843

O'Bedlam, Tom (Mentally Ill Person)
The Firedrake's Eye - Patricia Finney 2095

Obenchain, Beal (Murderer)
The Living - Annie Dillard 1644

Oblonova, Natalia (Dancer)
Encore - Monique Raphel High 2915

O'Brady, Bridie (Journalist)
The Faraway Drums - Jon Cleary 1104

Obregon, Juan (Young Man)
Far Mountains - Frank O'Rourke 4752

O'Breslin, Fergal (Chieftain)
The Dispossessed - Dell Shannon 5773

O'Brien, Aidan (Convict; Landowner)
The Emancipist: An Unforgettable Epic of Australia -
Veronica Geoghegan Sweeney 6147

O'Brien, Elayna (Young Woman)
A Whisper on the Wind - Madeline Baker 276

O'Brien, Patrick (Farmer; Rancher)
Lady of No Man's Land - Jeanne Williams 6780

O'Cain, Michael (Sea Captain)
Golden Shore - George Shaftel 5769

O'Carroll, Kathleen (Young Woman)
Tassels on Her Boots - Arthur Cheney Train 6313

O'Carroll, Roderick (Landowner)
The Big Wind - Beatrice Coogan 1262

Oconechee (Indian; Young Woman)
Mountain Windsong - Robert J. Conley 1246

O'Connell, Maura Dooley (Widow(er); Immigrant)
Maura's Dream - Joel Gross 2602

O'Connell, Patrick (Immigrant)
Maura's Dream - Joel Gross 2602

O'Connor, Cathal (Gentleman)
The Quickenberry Tree - Annette Motley 4502

O'Connor, Giles (Gentleman)
Princess Pamela - Ray Russell 5534

O'Connor, Kate (Gentlewoman)
An Important Family - Dorothy Eden 1855

O'Connor, Kevin (Military Personnel; Adventurer)
The Bright Battalions - Howard Breslin 664

O'Connor, Matthew (Young Man)
All Their Kingdoms - Madeleine Polland 5084

O'Connor, Roseen (Gentlewoman; Widow(er))
Tigerlilies - Judith Glover 2439

O'Connor, Tierney (Patriot; Rebel)
An Excess of Love - Cathy Cash Spellman 5959

Oconor, Hugo (Adventurer)
The Road to Glory - Darwin Le Ora Teilhet 6199

O'Corboy, Edward (Military Personnel)
Broadsides - Robert Welter Daly 1459

Ocre, Pietro di (Religious)
The Image of Our Lord - Edward Burman 790

O'Dalaigh, Duvessa (Gentlewoman)
Wolf's Embrace - Gail Link 3801

O'Dare, Cord (Rancher)
Justice, My Brother - James Keene 3386

O'Dare, Danny (Outlaw)
Hue and Cry - Elizabeth Yates 6907

O'Dare, Henry "Smoke" (Cowboy)
Justice, My Brother - James Keene 3386

Odda (Landowner)
The Price of Blood - Doris Sutcliffe Adams 24

O'Dea, Dion (Convict)
Armored Giants: A Novel of the Civil War - F. van
Wyck Mason 4145

Odell, Alonzo (Gentleman)
The Paper Mistress - Dorothea Malm 4045

Odell, Henry (Writer)
Brothers Three - John Oskison 4764

Odell, Roger (Rancher)
Brothers Three - John Oskison 4764

Odell, Timothy (Businessman)
Brothers Three - John Oskison 4764

Odin (Indian; Guide)
Runestone - Don Coldsmith 1186

O'Donnel, Daniel (Artist)
The Hawthorne Legacy - Teresa Crane 1416

O'Donnell, Arrah (Noblewoman; Pirate)
Mistress of the Eagles - Elona Malterre 4052

O'Donnell, Johno (Patriot)
A Nest of Simple Folk - Sean O'Faolain 4692

O'Donohue, Jack (Detective—Private)
The Rainbow Runner - John Cunningham 1450

O'Donovan, Declan (Revolutionary)
*The Men That God Made Mad: A Novel about
Ireland's Easter Rising* - W.A. Ballinger 286

O'Dowd, Molly (Secretary; Businesswoman)
Molly - Teresa Crane 1417

O'Dwyer, Oonagh (Captive)
Pawn in Frankincense - Dorothy Dunnett 1804

Odysseus (Adventurer)
Return to Ithaca - Eyvind Johnson 3224

Odysseus (Wanderer)
The Voyage Home - Ernst Schnabel 5644

Odysseus (Warrior)
Troy - Richard Matturro 4194
Whom the Gods Would Destroy - Richard
Powell 5148

Oedipus (Ruler)
The Eagle King - Henry Treece 6327

Oenone (Young Woman)
Paris of Troy - George Baker 273

O'Flaherty, Flare (Mountain Man)
The Snake River - Winfred Blevins 547

O'Flynn, Flynn Patrick (Adventurer)
Shout at the Devil - Wilbur Smith 5930

Ogden, John (Businessman)
Red Mountain - David Lavender 3677

Ogier (Slave; Adventurer)
The Viking - Edison Marshall 4113

Ogilivie, Ian (Military Personnel)
Drums Along the Khyber - Duncan MacNeil 4013

O'Gilroy, Conall (Sidekick)
Spy's Honour - Gavin Lyall 3929

Ogilvie, Angela (Spouse)
The Restless Frontier - Duncan MacNeil 4018

Ogilvie, Hector (Government Official)
The Restless Frontier - Duncan MacNeil 4018

Ogilvie, Ian (Doctor)
The Kidnapped Surgeon - Alexander Knox 3527

Ogilvie, Ian (Military Personnel)
By Command of the Viceroy - Duncan MacNeil 4010
Charge of Cowardice - Duncan MacNeil 4011

Ogilvie, James (Military Personnel)
By Command of the Viceroy - Duncan MacNeil 4010
Charge of Cowardice - Duncan MacNeil 4011
Cunningham's Revenge - Duncan MacNeil 4012
Drums Along the Khyber - Duncan MacNeil 4013
The Gates of Kunara - Duncan MacNeil 4014
Lieutenant of the Line - Duncan MacNeil 4015
The Mullah From Kashmir - Duncan MacNeil 4016
The Red Daniel - Duncan MacNeil 4017
The Restless Frontier - Duncan MacNeil 4018
Sadhu on the Mountain Peak - Duncan
MacNeil 4019
Subaltern's Choice - Duncan MacNeil 4020
The Train at Bundarbar - Duncan MacNeil 4021
Wolf in the Fold - Duncan MacNeil 4022

Ogilvie, Kitty (Spouse)
The Case of Kitty Ogilvie - Jean Stubbs 6093

Ogilvie, Patrick (Gentleman)
The Case of Kitty Ogilvie - Jean Stubbs 6093

Ogilvie, Thomas (Laird)
The Case of Kitty Ogilvie - Jean Stubbs 6093

Ogloblin, Evgueny (Nobleman)
Napoleon and the Cossacks - Peter N.
Krassnoff 3551

O'Halloran, Tabor (Businessman)
Masque of Sapphire - Deana James 3156

O'Hara, Father Colum (Leader; Religious)
Scarlett - Alexandra Ripley 5342

O'Hara, Kimball (Military Personnel)
The Last Victory - T.N. Murari 4519

O'Hara, Kimball (Spy)
The Imperial Agent - T.N. Murari 4518

O'Hara, Scarlett (Businesswoman; Landowner)
Scarlett - Alexandra Ripley 5342

O'Hara, Scarlett (Southern Belle)
Gone with the Wind - Margaret Mitchell 4415

O'Hare, Lucas (Actor)
Chelsea Reach - Claire Rayner 5261

Ohchenov, Irina (Noblewoman)
Tempting Fate - Chelsea Quinn Yarbro 6906

O'Houlihan, Sean (Royalty)
O'Houlihan's Jest - Rohan O'Grady 4702

Ojarra, Angelica (Young Woman)
The Crimson Wind - Max Hennessy 2832

O'Keefe, Patrick (Adventurer)
Sword of Vengeance - Kerry Newcomb 4593

O'Keefe, Raven (Frontierswoman)
Sword of Vengeance - Kerry Newcomb 4593

Okonkwo (Chieftain)
Things Fall Apart - Chinua Achebe 16

Olafson, Eric (Knight)
The Proud Villeins - Valerie Anand 133

Olbromski, Raphael (Military Personnel)
Ashes - Stefan Zeromski 6960

Old Bear Trap (Military Personnel)
The Mohawk Ladder - Noel B. Gerson 2377

Old Lodge (Indian; Shaman)
Song of the Cheyenne - Jory Sherman 5822

Old Lodge Skins (Indian)
Little Big Man - Thomas Berger 478

Old Man (Indian; Recluse)
Man of the Shadows - Don Coldsmith 1178

Old Misery (Mountain Man)
Old Misery - Hugh Pendexter 4896

Old Pine (Trader)
Eight April Days - Scott Hart 2759

Old White Buffalo (Indian; Shaman)
Buffalo Medicine - Don Coldsmith 1171

Old Woman (Indian)
A Woman of the People - Benjamin Capps 893

Oldbuck, Jonathan (Scholar)
The Antiquary - Sir Walter Scott 5690

Oldsmith, Sebastian (Sailor)
Shout at the Devil - Wilbur Smith 5930

O'Lea, Fingin (Doctor)
The Love of Fingin O'Lea - Theodora McCormick Du Bois 1743

Olenka (Heroine)
The Deluge - Henryk Sienkiewicz 5846

Olepi (Indian)
Hanta Yo - Ruth Beebe Hill 2951

Oleson, Anders (Sea Captain)
Lindeman's Daughters - Synnove Christensen 1073

Oleson, Anne Pernille (Spouse)
Lindeman's Daughters - Synnove Christensen 1073

Olifaunt, Nigel (Nobleman)
The Fortunes of Nigel - Sir Walter Scott 5696

Olin, Darius (Backwoodsman; Military Personnel)
D'ri and I - Irving A. Bacheller 257

Oliphant, John (Spy)
American Falls - John Calvin Batchelor 376

Olivas, Raymondo (Businessman)
To Fell the Giants - Bill Hotchkiss 3038

Oliver, Matthew (Gentleman)
Sea Change - Alison McLeay 4287

Olivera, Don Ignacio (Landowner)
Beneath the Blue Mountain - Richard S. Wheeler 6656

Olivier, Victor (Gentleman)
Royal Street - Walter Adolphe Roberts 5393

Olivier, Yvon (Doctor)
Creole Dusk - Walter Adolphe Roberts 5392

Ollenshaw, Philip (Settler)
Blossom Like the Rose - Norah Lofts 3836

Olmstead, Kate (Frontierswoman)
Eyes of Eagles - William W. Johnstone 3266

Olszak, Orrange (Worker)
American Beauty - Edna Ferber 2060

Olwen (Entertainer; Dancer)
The Leopard Unleashed - Elizabeth Chadwick 967

O'Malley, Charles (Military Personnel)
Charles O'Malley - Charles James Lever 3731

O'Malley, Kathleen (Immigrant; Mail Order Bride)
A Bride for Donnigan - Janette Oke 4705

O'Malley, Katie (Settler)
The Adventurers - William Stuart Long 3869

O'Malley, William Bede (Pilot)
High Road to China - Jon Cleary 1106

Omensetter, Brackett (Farmer)
Omensetter's Luck - William H. Gass 2317

O'Monoghan, Gelina (Warrior)
Lady of Conquest - Teresa Medeiros 4322

O'More, Dennis (Adventurer)
The Wind in His Fists - John Edward Jennings 3210

O'More, Grattan (Mine Owner)
The Silver Mountain - Dan Cushman 1453

Omri, Mary (Dancer)
The Emperor's Physician - Jacob Randolph Perkins 4914

O'Murray, Stewart (Young Man)
A Georgian Love Story - Ernest Raymond 5258

O'Neill, Bucky (Lawman)
San Juan Hill - Will Henry 2848

O'Neill, Carlos (Military Personnel)
The Gun - C.S. Forester 2174

O'Neill, Charlie (Fire Fighter)
Masters of Illusion: A Novel of the Connecticut Circus Fire - Mary-Ann Tirone Smith 5925

O'Neill, Maeve (Young Woman)
The Black Duchess - Alanna Knight 3514

O'Neill, Sharon (Seamstress)
Pride's Castle - Frank Yerby 6925

Onesimus (Government Official)
Brothers of Vengeance - LeGette Blythe 556

Ookumi (Slave)
The African - Harold Courlander 1386

Opalgate, Marcus (Young Man)
Night Wind - Roberta Jean Mountjoy 4504

Opalgate, Richard (Young Man)
Night Wind - Roberta Jean Mountjoy 4504

Opothle (Indian)
Creek Mary's Blood - Dee Brown 712

Oppenheimer, Josef Suss (Courtier)
Power - Lion Feuchtwanger 2074

Ord, Dallas (Abolitionist)
Fire Bell in the Night - Constance Robertson 5395

Ord, Jason (Judge)
Look to Your Geese: A Novel of the Deflowering of New England - Jacquin Sanders 5584

O'Reiley, Colin (Adventurer)
The Treasure of the Chisos - John H. Culp 1446

Orestes (Government Official)
Hypatia - Charles Kingsley 3498

Orestes (Royalty)
Amber Princess - Henry Treece 6325

O'Riley, Kathleen (Prospector)
Tomorrow's Dream - Peggy Hanchar 2674

Orlandini, Giacopo (Gentleman)
Mortal Pageant - Johan Fabricius 1993

Orlando (Gentleman)
Orlando - Virginia Woolf 6866

Orloff, Sacha (Rake; Bastard Son)
The Rake and the Rebel - Ira J. Morris 4478

Orlov, Aleksey (Royalty)
The Man From St. Petersburg - Ken Follett 2148

Orlov, Anna (Musician)
Petersburg - Emily Hanlon 2677

Ormandy, Blaize (Wanderer)
So Free We Seem - Helen Todd 6286

Orme (Young Man)
The Battle-Ax of God - Le Roy MacLeod 4007

Ormerod, Asa (Revolutionary)
The Golden Circle - Constance Robertson 5396

Ormerod, Harry (Trader)
The Doom Trail - Arthur Douglas Smith 5917

Ormerod, Justin (Artist)
An Autumn in Araby - Carola Salisbury 5565

Ormley, Edmund (Nobleman)
Flight From Fifth Avenue - Catherine M. Rae 5235

O'Roarke, Ian (Rancher)
Devil's Backbone - Terry C. Johnston 3250

O'Rourke, Olivia (Spouse)
The Veil of Illusion - Rebecca Ryman 5545

O'Rourke, Olivia (Young Woman)
Olivia and Jai - Rebecca Ryman 5544

O'Rourke, Rocheblave Xavier (Frontiersman; Trader)
River to the West: A Novel of the Astor Adventure - John Edward Jennings 3204

Orozco, Jesus (Military Personnel)
The Bear Flag: A Novel of the Birth of California - Cecelia Holland 2983

Orr, Susan (Widow(er))
Wind Like a Bugle - Leonard Nathan 3722

Orry, Charles (Orphan)
North and South - John Jakes 3151

Orsini, Andrea (Adventurer)
Prince of Foxes - Samuel Shellabarger 5797

Orsini, Orso (Singer)
Familiar Acts - June Barraclough 345

Orso, Giacomo (Young Man)
Web of Lucifer: A Novel of the Borgia Fury - Maurice Samuel 5580

Orsola, Marchesa (Noblewoman)
The Patriot - Antonio Fogazzaro 2146

Ortiz, Magdalena (Young Woman)
Lotus Land - Monica Highland 2917

Orton, Sir Giles (Veteran; Landowner)
Rebel Heiress - Robert Neill 4573

Osage, Johnny Fowler (Trader)
Johnny Osage - Janice Holt Giles 2412

Osbaldistone, Frank (Gentleman)
Rob Roy - Sir Walter Scott 5707

Osbaldistone, Rasleigh (Gentleman)
Rob Roy - Sir Walter Scott 5707

Osborn, Samuel (Teacher)
Tomorrow the New Moon - Shirley Barker 319

Osborne, Constance (Landowner)
Borrowed Plumes - Roseleen Milne 4409

Osborne, George (Gentleman; Military Personnel)
Vanity Fair - William Makepeace Thackeray 6213

Osborne, Richard (Military Personnel)
Mary of Carisbrooke - Margaret Campbell
Barnes 327

Osgood, Jeanne (Young Woman)
The Wilderness - Carter A. Vaughan 6442

Osgood, Mary (Young Woman)
Dynasty - Robert S. Elegant 1902

O'Shea, Brick (Convict)
And the Wild Birds Sing - Lola Irish 3112

O'Shea, Hogan (Prospector)
Tomorrow's Dream - Peggy Hanchar 2674

O'Shea, Timmie (Teenager)
The Cotton Road - Frank Feuille 2077

Osmanagic, Fata (Young Woman)
The Bridge on the Drina - Ivo Andric 151

Osmond, Judith (Archaeologist)
The Curse of the King - Victoria Holt 3012

Osric (Servant)
Red Lion and Gold Dragon - Rosemary
Sprague 5969

Ossian, Maggie (Gentlewoman)
Flowers for Lilian - Anna Gilbert 2405

Ossupov, Zoya (Dancer)
Zoya - Danielle Steel 5985

Ostneige, Gudrun (Widow(er))
Tempting Fate - Chelsea Quinn Yarbro 6906

Oswy (Royalty)
Queen of the Lightning - Kathleen Herbert 2852

Oswy (Ruler)
Absolution by Murder - Peter Tremayne 6334

Otap (Warrior)
Taras Bulba - Nikolai V. Gogol 2451

Otis, Deborah (Spouse)
The Assassination of Mozart - David Weiss 6604

Otis, Jason (Musician; Composer)
The Assassination of Mozart - David Weiss 6604

O'Toole, Frances Melissa (Settler; Spouse)
Toward the Morning - Hervey Allen 101

Otter (Indian; Trader)
People of the Lakes - W. Michael Gear 2336

Otter (Young Woman)
A Shadow of Gulls - Patricia Finney 2096

Otto (Slave; Cook)
Signals of Distress - Jim Crace 1408

Ottoway, Eve (Nurse)
While Paris Danced - Patricia Wright 6886

Otway, Raymond (Actor)
Lovers Meeting - Mollie Hardwick 2695

Outakke (Indian; Chieftain)
The Countess Angelique - Sergeanne Golon 2472

Overbury, Clay (Political Figure)
Washington, D.C. - Gore Vidal 6493

Overman, Adele (Pioneer)
Bend Your Heads All - Rowena Rutherford
Farrar 2015

Overman, Seth (Pioneer)
Bend Your Heads All - Rowena Rutherford
Farrar 2015

Overton, Charles (Gentleman)
The Days of the Butterfly - Norah Lofts 3841

Overton, William (Gentleman)
Speak to Me of Love - Dorothy Eden 1862

Ovinska, Casimir (Royalty)
Polonaise - Jane Aiken Hodge 2968

Ovinska, Isobel (Royalty)
Polonaise - Jane Aiken Hodge 2968

Owen, Mr. (Artist)
The Beano - Rony Robinson 5411

Owen (Religious)
Beguiled - Alice Borchardt 577
Devoted - Alice Borchardt 578

Owen (Royalty)
Bride of the Spear - Kathleen Herbert 2851

Owen, Captain Cadwallader (Government Official)
The Mamur Zapt and the Donkey-Vous - Michael
Pearce 4866
The Mamur Zapt and the Girl in the Nile - Michael
Pearce 4867
The Mamur Zapt and the Men Behind - Michael
Pearce 4868
The Mamur Zapt and the Night of the Dog - Michael
Pearce 4869
The Mamur Zapt and the Return of the Carpet -
Michael Pearce 4870

Owen, Jed (Military Personnel)
Where the River Runs - Richard S. Wheeler 6664

Owen, Kathryn (Young Woman)
The Very Best People - Elizabeth Villars 6499

Owens, Horace (Young Man)
Steamboat on the River - Darwin Le Ora
Teilhet 6200

Owens, Jim (Engineer)
Steamboat on the River - Darwin Le Ora
Teilhet 6200

Owl (Indian)
Buffalo Medicine - Don Coldsmith 1171

Oxley, Freddy (Worker; Businessman)
For They Shall Inherit - Malcolm Macdonald 3964

Ozeroff, Nikolai (Military Personnel)
The Brotherhood of the Red Poppy - Henri
Troyat 6353

P

Pacal Balam (Government Official)
Tikal: A Novel about the Maya - Daniel Peters 4947

Pacey, William (Sea Captain)
The Last Farewell - Philip McCutchan 4255

Packenham (Military Personnel)
The Hessian - Howard Fast 2033

Paddock, Jedediah (Sea Captain)
Harpoon in Eden - F. van Wyck Mason 4152

Paddock, Josiah (Frontiersman)
Carry the Wind - Terry C. Johnston 3246

Paddock, Josiah (Mountain Man)
Borderlords - Terry C. Johnston 3244
One-Eyed Dream - Terry C. Johnston 3253

Paddock, Micajah (Sea Captain)
Harpoon in Eden - F. van Wyck Mason 4152

Paddock, Obediah (Sea Captain)
Harpoon in Eden - F. van Wyck Mason 4152

Pader, Benjamin (Young Man)
Private Knowledge - Betty Palmer Nelson 4576

Padway, Martin (Time Traveller; Archaeologist)
Lest Darkness Fall - L. Sprague De Camp 1557

Paenus (Government Official)
The Conspiracy - John Hersey 2870

Page, Claude (Inventor; Artisan)
A Case of Curiosities - Allen Kurzweil 3569

Page, Dick (Military Personnel; Spy)
Mr. Arnold - Francis Lynde 3935

Page, Jasper (Trader)
Early Candlelight - Maude Hart Lovelace 3904

Page, Leah (Businesswoman)
Path of the Sun - Al Dempsey 1608

Page, Lucy (Spouse)
Steamboat Gothic - Frances Parkinson Keyes 3481

Page, Matt (Lawman)
The Gathering Storm - W.E. Davis 1540

Paget, Anne (Young Woman)
Rebel Heiress - Robert Neill 4573

Paget, Barbara (Young Woman)
Rebel Heiress - Robert Neill 4573

Paget, Carloman (Hero)
The Weeping Ash - Joan Aiken 54

Paget, Ellen (Governess)
The Girl From Paris - Joan Aiken 47

Paget, Emily (Young Woman)
Emily - Cynthia Harrod-Eagles 2753

Paget, Fanny (Heroine)
The Weeping Ash - Joan Aiken 54

Paget, Frances (Young Woman)
The Steps of the Sun - Joanna Trollope 6350

Paget, Juliana (Gentlewoman)
The Smile of the Stranger - Joan Aiken 53

Paget, Matthew (Student—College)
The Steps of the Sun - Joanna Trollope 6350

Paget, Scylla (Heroine)
The Weeping Ash - Joan Aiken 54

Paige, Bennett (Military Personnel; Spy)
Storm the Last Rampart - David Taylor 6180

Painter, Christian (Military Personnel)
Ashes in the Wilderness - William Greenough
Schofield 5649

Paisley, Diccon (Spy)
Lanterns - Patricia Veryan 6465

Palafox, Antonio (Military Personnel)
Mexico - James A. Michener 4372

Palafox, Peter (Military Personnel)
The Golden Ocean - Patrick O'Brian 4665

Pale Star (Indian)
Medicine Knife - Don Coldsmith 1179
Return to the River - Don Coldsmith 1184
River of Swans - Don Coldsmith 1185

Pale Star (Indian; Teenager)
Pale Star - Don Coldsmith 1181

Palfrey, John (Young Man)
Fire Bell in the Night - Constance Robertson 5395

Palfrey, Sabra (Worker)
Call the Darkness Light - Nancy Zaroulis 6954

Pallister, Julia (Gentlewoman)
Circle of Pearls - Rosalind Laker 3593

Palmer, Meg (Actress)
Charming Sally - Maude Hart Lovelace 3903

Paloma (Slave)
Jewel of the Sea - Susan Wiggs 6743

Palomar, Juan (Adventurer)
Among the Innocent - Elizabeth Borton de
    Trevino   6339

Pamphilius (Student)
Woman of Andros - Thornton Wilder   6754

Pancoast, Calvin (Military Personnel)
Green Rose of Furley - Helen C. Barney   334

Pandra (Indian)
The Moon Stallion - Jim Berry   484

Pangersbourne, Amelia (Streetperson; Bastard
    Daughter)
The Pangersbourne Murders - J.G. Jeffreys   3179

Pao An (Captive)
Empire of Heaven - Linda Ching Sledge   5907

Paoul (Orphan; Heir)
The Earth Goddess - Richard Herley   2856

Pappenheim, Dr. (Entertainer)
Badenheim 1939 - Aharon Appelfeld   174

Parbury, Miles (Sea Captain; Handicapped)
The Great Steamboat Race - John Brunner   736

Pardee, Eban (Frontiersman)
Down From the Mountain - Louis Charbonneau   997

Pardee, Gage (Frontiersman)
Down From the Mountain - Louis Charbonneau   997

Pardee, Malachi (Outlaw)
Blood on the Divide - William W. Johnstone   3265

Pardi, Angelo (Military Personnel)
The Horseman on the Roof - Jean Giono   2424
The Straw Man - Jean Giono   2425

Parham, Billy (Teenager; Rancher)
The Crossing - Cormac McCarthy   4221

Parham, Boyd (Child; Rancher)
The Crossing - Cormac McCarthy   4221

Paris (Royalty)
The Firebrand - Marion Zimmer Bradley   624
The Goddess - Miranda Seymour   5763
Paris of Troy - George Baker   273
Scandal in Troy - Eva Hemmer Hansen   2679
Whom the Gods Would Destroy - Richard
    Powell   5148

Paris, George (Smuggler; Gambler)
Judith Paris - Hugh Walpole   6545

Paris, Judith (Gentlewoman)
The Fortress - Hugh Walpole   6544
Judith Paris - Hugh Walpole   6545

Paris, Marie Therese (Indian)
The Two Medicine River - Richard S. Wheeler   6663

Paris, Matthew (Doctor)
Sacred Hunter - Barry Unsworth   6389

Paris, Vanessa (Gentlewoman)
Vanessa - Hugh Walpole   6548

Parker, Banana Mae (Prostitute)
Southern Discomfort - Rita Mae Brown   730

Parks, Elam (Landowner)
Forty Guns West - William W. Johnstone   3267

Parks, Greg (Government Official)
Mission to Mackinac - Myron David Orr   4755

Parks, Wes (Slave)
*A Darkness at Ingraham's Crest: A Tale of the
    Slaveholding South* - Frank Yerby   6912

Parolles, Landry de (Knight)
No Man's Son - Doris Sutcliffe Adams   23

Parolles, Rodriga de (Young Woman)
No Man's Son - Doris Sutcliffe Adams   23

Parr, Muriel (Gentlewoman)
The Black Sheep's Daughter - Carola Dunn   1791

Parr, Rebecca (Young Woman)
Lady in the Briars - Carola Dunn   1793

Parre, Jude (Settler)
Paradise - Esther Forbes   2158

Parrington, Stacey (Nobleman)
St. John's Wood - Nancy Fitzgerald   2116

Parrish, Guy (Landowner)
The Hand of a Woman - Diana Brown   719

Parrish, Rebecca (Widow(er))
The Wagered Widow - Patricia Veryan   6481

Parry, Sir Jonathan (Gentleman)
Feast of the Jesters - Manuel Komroff   3533

Parry, Kwahadi (Indian)
Gone the Dreams and the Dancing - Douglas C.
    Jones   3279

Parry, Morfydd Annon (Captive; Indian)
Season of Yellow Leaf - Douglas C. Jones   3283

Parsons, Ann (Young Woman)
The Yankee Brig - Carter A. Vaughan   6443

Partridge, Joseph (Military Personnel)
Richard Lamb - Richard S. Wheeler   6662

Parvati (Outcast)
The Faithful Lovers - Valerie Anand   129

Parvati (Young Woman)
The Last Victory - T.N. Murari   4519

Pary, Ross (Businessman)
Floodtide - Frank Yerby   6916

Pasay, Gui de (Knight)
Men Like Shadows - Dorothy Charques   1000

Pascali, Basil (Spy)
The Idol Hunter - Barry Unsworth   6386

Pascoe, Harry (Fisherman)
Armada - Charles Gidley   2404

Pascoe, Tristram (Spy)
Armada - Charles Gidley   2404

Pasha, Abdullah (Young Man)
The Ashes of Smyrna - Richard Reinhardt   5294

Pasquelle, Marie (Young Woman)
The Citadel of the Lakes - Myron David Orr   4754

Pasquier, Genevieve (Psychic)
The Oracle Glass - Judith Merkle Riley   5335

Pasquinel (Trapper; Trader)
Centennial - James A. Michener   4366

Pasternak, Sam (Military Personnel)
The Glory - Herman Wouk   6873
The Hope - Herman Wouk   6874

Paston, Margery (Young Woman)
Beloved Lady - Barbara Jefferis   3174

Patch (Entertainer)
We Speak No Treason - Rosemary Hawley
    Jarman   3168

Patche (Trapper; Outlaw)
Shadow of a Star - Jamie Lee Cooper   1315

Pathkiller, Mose (Indian)
Back to Malachi - Robert J. Conley   1237

Patridge, Edgar Allen (Writer)
The Strange Files of Fremont Jones - Dianne
    Day   1544

Patterson, Sergeant (Military Personnel)
Prisoner of Twilight - Don Robertson   5400

Patterson, Anna (Spouse)
Creature Comforts - Jessica Stirling   6041

Patterson, Anna (Young Woman)
Hearts of Gold - Jessica Stirling   6044

Patterson, Elspeth (Orphan)
Treasures on Earth - Jessica Stirling   6049

Patterson, Elspeth (Spouse)
Creature Comforts - Jessica Stirling   6041
Hearts of Gold - Jessica Stirling   6044

Patterson, Gaddy (Wanderer)
Treasures on Earth - Jessica Stirling   6049

Patterson, G.K. (Military Personnel)
Squadron Forty-Four - Arch Whitehouse   6711

Patterson, Morgan (Backwoodsman; Military
    Personnel)
The Captives - Don Wright   6878

Patterson, Morgan (Frontiersman; Military
    Personnel)
The Woodsman - Don Wright   6880

Patterson, Rufus (Military Personnel)
The Three Days - Don Robertson   5402

Patterson, Susan (Heroine)
The Captives - Don Wright   6878

Pauley, Martin (Cowboy)
The Searchers - Alan Le May   3691

Paulinus, Suetonious (Government Official)
The Imperial Governor - George Shipway   5828

Paulus (Veteran)
A Wayside Tavern - Norah Lofts   3862

Paulus, Marcus Lucius (Young Man; Pirate)
The Pirate From Rome - John V.D.
    Southworth   5952

Pavernen, Julia (Young Woman)
From a Far Land - Robert S. Elegant   1903

Paxmore, Edward (Landowner)
Chesapeake - James A. Michener   4367

Paxton, Eugenia (Businesswoman; Imposter)
Night Storm - Catherine Coulter   1378

Paxton, Marcella (Young Woman)
Scarborough House - Sharon Salvato   5577

Paxton, Oliver (Military Personnel; Pilot)
War Story: A Novel - Derek Robinson   5404

Paxton, Rush (Scout)
A Land to Tame - Zola Helen Ross   5505

Paxton, Susanna (Southern Belle)
Song of the Bayou - Elinor Lynley   3936

Pay, Allan Eben (Military Personnel)
Elkhorn Tavern - Douglas C. Jones   3278

Pay, Barton (Businessman)
Weedy Rough - Douglas C. Jones   3286

Pay, Duny Gene (Young Man)
Weedy Rough - Douglas C. Jones   3286

Pay, Eben (Lawyer)
Weedy Rough - Douglas C. Jones   3286
Winding Stairs - Douglas C. Jones   3287

Pay, Eben (Lawyer; Military Personnel)
Remember Santiago - Douglas C. Jones   3280

Payne, Fitzroy (Nobleman)
Jane and the Unpleasantness at Scargrave Manor -
    Stephanie Barron   356

Payne, Isobel (Noblewoman; Widow(er))
Jane and the Unpleasantness at Scargrave Manor -
    Stephanie Barron   356

Payton, Sebastian (Invalid)
Lady Jane - Norma Lee Clark   1092

Pazzi, Ginevra de (Gentlewoman)
The Time Returns - Alexandra Ripley   5343

Pea Eye (Lawman)
Streets of Laredo - Larry McMurtry   4300

Peabody, Amelia (Archaeologist)
The Curse of the Pharaohs - Elizabeth Peters   4948
The Deeds of the Disturber - Elizabeth Peters   4949
The Hippopotamus Pool - Elizabeth Peters   4950

The Last Camel Died at Noon - Elizabeth
    Peters   4951
Lion in the Valley - Elizabeth Peters   4952
The Mummy Case - Elizabeth Peters   4953
The Snake, the Crocodile, and the Dog - Elizabeth
    Peters   4954

Peabody, Asa (Doctor)
Eagle in the Sky - F. van Wyck Mason   4149

Peabody, Isaac (Artisan)
Dean's Watch - Elizabeth Goudge   2494

Peabody, Jeremy (Young Man)
An American, Sir - Corwin Root   5459

Peabody, Joshua (Military Personnel)
The Captain From Connecticut - C.S. Forester   2171

Peabody, Martha (Heiress)
First Night - Jane Aiken Hodge   2963

Peace, Frank (Frontiersman)
Trouble Shooter - Ernest Haycox   2791

Peace, Ginny (Landowner)
The Truest Pleasure - Robert Morgan   4452

Peacock (Heroine)
Cry of the Peacock - Gina Barkhordar Nahai   4552

Pearce, Nathan (Lawman)
Breakheart Pass - Alistair MacLean   3999

Pears, Gilbert Brice (Military Personnel)
In Gallant Company - Alexander Kent   3433

Pearse, Fingal (Military Personnel)
This Willing Passion - Patricia Cloud   1132

Pearson, Willard (Sailor)
You Rolling River - Archie Binns   503

Peat, Flora (Young Woman)
Belgrave Square - Rachel Summerson   6117

Peattie, Joshua (Military Personnel)
The Mohawk Ladder - Noel B. Gerson   2377

Peck, Caleb (Settler)
White Rising - Zane Kotker   3548

Peck, Evaline (Spouse)
The Crowded Hill - Le Roy MacLeod   4008
Years of Peace - Le Roy MacLeod   4009

Peck, Tyler (Spouse)
The Crowded Hill - Le Roy MacLeod   4008
Years of Peace - Le Roy MacLeod   4009

Peel, Crider (Businessman)
Roman - Douglas C. Jones   3281

Peirot, Jocelin (Knight)
The Siege - Jay Williams   6773

Peixoto da Silva Xavier, Gregorio (Adventurer)
The Incredible Brazilian: The Native - Zulfikar
    Ghose   2392

Pelham, Daisy (Governess)
Imperial Winds - Priscilla Napier   4555

Pelham, Sir Harry (Gentleman)
Captain Nash and the Wroth Inheritance - Ragan
    Butler   828

Pelham, Lucilla (Gentlewoman)
The Unsuitable Miss Pelham - June
    Drummond   1730

Pelham-Martin, Commodore (Military Personnel)
Enemy in Sight! - Alexander Kent   3429

Pelham-Martyn, Ashton (Military Personnel)
The Far Pavilions - M.M. Kaye   3376

Pelleas (Bastard Son)
In the Shadow of the Oak King - Courtway
    Jones   3271

Pelleas (Knight)
The Emperor Arthur - Godfrey Turton   6368

Pelon (Indian; Outlaw)
Mackenna's Gold - Will Henry   2845

Pemberton, Martin (Writer)
The Waterworks - E.L. Doctorow   1659

Pembroke, Lord (Nobleman)
Bond of Blood - Roberta Gellis   2349

Pembroke, Leah (Gentlewoman)
Bond of Blood - Roberta Gellis   2349

Pembroke, Ross (Military Personnel)
Phantom Fortress - Bruce Lancaster   3643

Pena, Joe (Military Personnel; Indian)
Stallion Gate - Martin Cruz Smith   5924

Pence, Virgil (Labor Organizer)
A Vein of Riches - John Knowles   3526

Pendellow, Drew (Gentleman; Heir)
Castle Heritage - Elisabeth Barr   337

Pender, Luke (Cowboy)
Time for Outrage - Amelia Bean   397

Pendergass, Garrett (Businessman)
Bedford Village - Hervey Allen   99

Pendlebury, Christian (Gentleman)
The Veil of Illusion - Rebecca Ryman   5545

Pendleton, Irons Saul (Sea Captain)
Voyage: A Novel of 1896 - Sterling Hayden   2798

Pendleton, Nancy (Young Woman)
Sing for a Penny - Clifford Dowdey   1708

Pendragon, John Hawkdale (Military Personnel;
    Spy)
Pendragon: Late of Prince Albert's Own - Robert
    Trevelyan   6337
Pendragon...The Montenegran Plot - Robert
    Trevelyan   6338

Pendragon, Uther (Chieftain)
The Great Captains - Henry Treece   6329

Pendrake, Mrs. (Gentlewoman)
Little Big Man - Thomas Berger   478

Penelope (Servant)
Gold for the Caesars - Florence A. Seward   5759

Penelope (Spouse)
Return to Ithaca - Eyvind Johnson   3224

Penfield (Writer)
Loon Lake - E.L. Doctorow   1657

Penfold, Eden (Governess)
The Golden Sabre - Jon Cleary   1105

Pengallion, Dominic (Gentleman; Landowner)
The Sea Treasure - Elisabeth Barr   338

Pengellen, David (Businessman)
The Hills Stand Watch - August Derleth   1615

Pengrath, Madeline (Herbalist)
Do Not Disturb - Kate Kingsbury   3492

Penhaligon, Jethro Cockerill (Military Personnel)
Clear for Action! - Simon White   6699
The English Captain - Simon White   6700

Peniston, Darthea (Young Woman)
Hugh Wynne, Free Quaker - Silas Weir
    Mitchell   4416

Penistone, Gareth (Heir)
The Five-Minute Marriage - Joan Aiken   46

Penmerry, Morgan (Sea Captain)
Scalpdancers - Kerry Newcomb   4592

Penn, Victoria (Young Woman)
Halfhyde and the Fleet Review - Philip
    McCutchan   4246

Pennam, Kathryn (Gentlewoman)
Windover - Jane Aiken Hodge   2974

Pennant, Robert (Religious)
A Morbid Taste for Bones - Ellis Peters   4965

Pennlyon, Jake (Sea Captain)
The Lion Triumphant - Philippa Carr   922

Pennlyon, Linnet (Gentlewoman)
The Witch From the Sea - Philippa Carr   933

Penny, Dora (Gentlewoman)
Elgar on the Journey to Hanley - Keith Alldritt   92

Penny, Howat (Businessman)
The Three Black Pennys - Joseph
    Hergesheimer   2855

Penny, Howat II (Businessman)
The Three Black Pennys - Joseph
    Hergesheimer   2855

Penny, Jasper (Businessman)
The Three Black Pennys - Joseph
    Hergesheimer   2855

Penny, Nick (Labor Organizer)
The White Dove - Rosie Thomas   6246

Pennyform, Nokomis (Young Woman; Indian)
Too Late! Too Late! The Maiden Cried - Joan
    Fleming   2128

Pennypacker, Zebulon (Businessman)
I Am Vidocq - Vincent McConnor   4225

Penrose, Hal (Gentleman)
A Notorious Woman - Malcolm Macdonald   3969

Penrose, Jon (Businessman)
Here Comes a Candle - Jane Aiken Hodge   2964

Penryhd (Orphan)
The Fair - Robert Nathan   4559

Pentacoste (Noblewoman)
Better in the Dark - Chelsea Quinn Yarbro   6894

Pentecost, Owen (Young Man)
Great Day in the Morning - Robert Hardy
    Andrews   149

Pentecost, Peter (Adventurer; Scholar)
The Blanket of the Dark - John Buchan   749

Pentland, Peter (Explorer)
Murder, I Presume - Gillian Linscott   3807

Penvennan, Caroline (Heiress)
The Last Gamble - Winston Graham   2527
Venture Once More - Winston Graham   2532

Penwardine, Lord (Nobleman)
Stage Fright - Gillian Linscott   3809

Peony (Widow(er))
The Red Peony - Yutang Lin   3783

Pepi (Artisan)
The Invaders - Peter Danielson   1469

Pepper Tom (Cowboy)
The Sweetwater - Jean Rikhoff   5333

Pepperell, Mercy (Young Woman)
The Highwayman - Noel B. Gerson   2372

Perceval, Sir (Knight)
Kinsmen of the Grail - Dorothy James Roberts   5376

Percy, Elizabeth (Heiress)
Countess Carrots - Molly Costain Haycraft   2792

Percy, Ralph (Settler)
To Have and to Hold - Mary Johnston   3241

Perdita (Heroine)
Mysteries of Winterthurn - Joyce Carol Oates   4659

Perdriel, Gilonne (Artisan)
The Lacemaker - Janine Montupet   4438

Peregrine, Rogan (Landowner)
The Taming - Jude Deveraux   1633

Peregrine, Zared (Noblewoman)
The Conquest - Jude Deveraux   1630

Perez, Catana (Saloon Hostess)
Captain From Castile - Samuel Shellabarger   5794

La Perichole (Actress)
The Bridge of San Luis Rey - Thornton Wilder 6752

Peridot, Evangeline (Settler)
Greenstone - Yvonne Kalman 3324

Peridot, Juliette (Young Woman)
Greenstone - Yvonne Kalman 3324

Perkins, Sarah (Teacher)
The Revolt of Sarah Perkins - Marian Cockrell 1148

Perle, Judith (Landowner; Widow(er))
The Rose Rent - Ellis Peters 4970

Perreira, Jolene (Heroine)
The Earth and All It Holds - V.J. Banis 287

Perrell, John (Vagrant)
Escape From Sonora - Will Bryant 739

Perrin, Laurent (Farmer)
The Colors of Vaud - Bryher 741

Perrin, Sophie (Young Woman)
The Colors of Vaud - Bryher 741

Perrivale, Simon (Nobleman; Bastard Son)
The Captive - Victoria Holt 3011

Perron, Guy (Historian; Military Personnel)
A Division of the Spoils - Paul Scott 5683

Perrot, Lady Katherine (Noblewoman)
No Wall So High - Anne Powers 5152

Perry, Althea (Young Woman)
The Anatolian - Elia Kazan 3381

Perry, Culver (Gentleman)
The Bellerose Bargain - Robyn Carr 934

Perry, Elizabeth (Young Woman)
The Willing Maid - C.T. Ritchie 5349

Perry, Geoffrey (Sea Captain)
The Bellerose Bargain - Robyn Carr 934

Perry, Rebecca (Young Woman)
Too Long a Stranger - Janette Oke 4710

Perry, Sarah (Widow(er))
Too Long a Stranger - Janette Oke 4710

Perseus (Hero)
Three Ships and Three Kings - Georgia
  Sallaska 5573

Peta (Indian)
Hanta Yo - Ruth Beebe Hill 2951

Petar, Brother (Religious)
Devil's Yard - Ivo Andric 152

Pete (Knight)
Fitzempress' Law - Diana Norman 4644

Petenera (Young Woman)
The Memoirs of Christopher Columbus - Stephen
  Marlowe 4096

Peter (Religious)
The Last Athenian - Viktor Rydberg 5543

Peter, Brother (Religious)
Lords of the Dance - Robin Lloyd-Jones 3815

Peters, Anne (Governess)
Anna - Cynthia Harrod-Eagles 2752

Peters, George (Actor; Military Personnel)
The River and the Wilderness - Don Robertson 5401

Peters, Toby (Detective—Private)
Bullet for a Star - Stuart M. Kaminsky 3331
Buried Caesars - Stuart M. Kaminsky 3332
Catch a Falling Star - Stuart M. Kaminsky 3333
Dancing in the Dark - Stuart M. Kaminsky 3334
The Devil Met a Lady - Stuart M. Kaminsky 3335
Down for the Count - Stuart M. Kaminsky 3336
The Fala Factor - Stuart M. Kaminsky 3337
He Done Her Wrong - Stuart M. Kaminsky 3338
High Midnight - Stuart M. Kaminsky 3339
The Howard Hughes Affair - Stuart M.
  Kaminsky 3340

The Man Who Shot Lewis Vance - Stuart M.
  Kaminsky 3341
The Melting Clock - Stuart M. Kaminsky 3342
Murder on the Yellow Brick Road - Stuart M.
  Kaminsky 3343
Never Cross a Vampire - Stuart M. Kaminsky 3344
Poor Butterfly - Stuart M. Kaminsky 3345
Smart Moves - Stuart M. Kaminsky 3346
Think Fast, Mr. Peters - Stuart M. Kaminsky 3347
Tomorrow Is Another Day - Stuart M.
  Kaminsky 3348
You Bet Your Life - Stuart M. Kaminsky 3349

Petifer, Maurice (Businessman)
A Woman Possessed - Malcolm Macdonald 3977

Petrie (Doctor)
The Fires of Fu Manchu - Cay Van Ash 6399

Petrovna, Elena (Dancer)
The Devil in Harbour - Catherine Gavin 2319

Petrovna, Natasha (Gentlewoman)
Emily - Cynthia Harrod-Eagles 2753

Petrovna, Sophia (Noblewoman; Widow(er))
Blood on the Snow - John Elliott 1916

Petrovsky, Semyon (Royalty)
The World in His Arms - Rex Beach 392

Petrucci, Scapino (Entertainer)
Carnival of Saints - George Herman 2860

Pettengill, Caleb (Military Personnel)
Caleb Pettengill U.S.N. - George Fielding Eliot 1912

Pettigrew, Scott (Military Personnel)
The Raiders: A Novel of the Civil War at Sea -
  Willard Wallace 6541

Peveral, Luke (Gypsy; Thief)
Sweet Songbird - Teresa Crane 1418

Peverel, Henry (Actor)
Catherine Carter - Pamela Hansford Johnson 3227

Peverel, Jenny (Young Woman)
Polonaise - Jane Aiken Hodge 2968

Peverel, Kit (Adventurer)
Captain Bashful - Donald Barr Chidsey 1059

Peveril, Geoffrey (Nobleman)
Peveril of the Peak - Sir Walter Scott 5703

Peveril, Julian (Gentleman)
Peveril of the Peak - Sir Walter Scott 5703

Peyrac, Angelique de (Noblewoman)
Angelique and the Demon - Sergeanne Golon 2466
Angelique and the Ghosts - Sergeanne Golon 2467
The Countess Angelique - Sergeanne Golon 2472
The Temptation of Angelique - Sergeanne
  Golon 2473

Peyrac, Joffrey de (Nobleman)
Angelique - Sergeanne Golon 2465
Angelique and the Demon - Sergeanne Golon 2466
Angelique and the Ghosts - Sergeanne Golon 2467
The Countess Angelique - Sergeanne Golon 2472
The Temptation of Angelique - Sergeanne
  Golon 2473

Peyton, Caroline (Plantation Owner)
Shod with Flame - Helen Topping Miller 4393

Peyton, Carr (Military Personnel)
Shod with Flame - Helen Topping Miller 4393

Peyton, Jane (Young Woman)
The Tree of Liberty - Elizabeth Page 4773

Peyton, Kate (Gentlewoman)
Griffith Gaunt - Charles Reade 5280

Peyton, Mercedes (Gentlewoman)
Jornada - Robert L. Duffus 1754

Phaedra (Royalty; Spouse)
The Bull From the Sea - Mary Renault 5295

Pharos (Teacher)
Fires in the Sky - Phillip Parotti 4816

Phelan, Edward (Worker; Activist)
While England Sleeps - David Leavitt 3702

Phelps, Amoret (Settler)
Hope of Earth - Jane Gilmore Rushing 5528

Phelps, Stephen (Settler)
Hope of Earth - Jane Gilmore Rushing 5528

Philammon (Religious)
Hypatia - Charles Kingsley 3498

Philemon (Wanderer)
*The Island of the Innocent: A Novel of Greek and Jew
  in the Time of the Maccabees* - Vardis
  Fisher 2108

Philip (Religious)
The Pillars of the Earth - Ken Follett 2149

Philip of Evesham (Servant; Religious)
Ordeal by Silence - Prudence Andrew 142

Phillips, Harry (Military Personnel; Captive)
Flight From Bucharest - R.T. Stevens 6000

Phillips, John (Businessman)
The Mills of Colne - Robert Neill 4572

Phillips, Mercy (Young Woman)
Judas Flowering - Jane Aiken Hodge 2965

Philo of Crete (Servant)
A Time for Judas - Morley Callaghan 866

Philokrates (Teacher)
Anabasis: A Journey to the Interior - Ellen
  Gilchrist 2408

Philon (Doctor)
The Beacon of Alexandria - Gillian Bradshaw 627

Phinney, Desiree (Servant)
Inherit the Earth - Margaret Shaw 5778

Photina (Young Woman)
A Woman of Samaria - James W. Ingles 3104

Photinus (Adventurer)
Votan - John James 3162

Picard, Paul (Detective—Police)
Fata Morgana - William Kotzwinkle 3549

Pickett, Jonathan (Landowner)
The Inner Voice - Nina Wilcox Putnam 5211

Pickford, Ellen (Governess; Prostitute)
The Abductors - Stuart Cloete 1121

Pierce, Edward (Thief)
The Great Train Robbery - Michael Crichton 1426

Pierce, Frederick (Spy; Military Personnel)
Blood Red Roses - Elizabeth Boatwright Coker 1163

Pierce, Louisa (Gentlewoman)
The Fortunate Marriage - Meriol Trevor 6342

Pierneau, Pierre Chalfonte (Frontiersman)
Wind over Wisconsin - August Derleth 1620

Pierre (Artisan; Adventurer)
The Burnished Blade - Lawrence Schoonover 5661

Piete du Plessis, Zwart (Hunter)
The Turning Wheels - Stuart Cloete 1127

Pieteria (Young Woman)
Cross, Sword, and Arrow - Gladys H. Barr 340

Pietranera, Gina (Gentlewoman)
The Charterhouse of Parma - Stendhal 5993

Pigge, Johnny (Young Man)
Paradise - Esther Forbes 2158

Pike, Noah (Wanderer)
Heart of the Country - Greg Matthews 4190

Piksarett (Indian; Chieftain)
Angelique and the Demon - Sergeanne Golon 2466

Pilaster, Augusta (Gentlewoman)
A Dangerous Fortune - Ken Follett 2147

Pilaster, Edward (Gentleman)
A Dangerous Fortune - Ken Follett 2147

Pilee (Sailor)
The White Dawn - James Houston 3053

Pilgermann (Wanderer)
Pilgermann - Russell Hoban 2960

Pilgrim, Laurence (Banker)
The King's Commissar - Duncan Kyle 3570

Pimber, Henry (Landowner)
Omensetter's Luck - William H. Gass 2317

Pinfold (Streetperson)
Funny Papers - Tom De Haven 1559

Pingree, Kitty (Widow(er))
Proud New Flags - F. van Wyck Mason 4156

Pink, Samuel (Bastard Son; Gentleman)
The Mountain of Immoderate Desires - Leslie Wilson 6811

Pinkney, Charlotte (Spouse)
A Visit to Highbury - Joan Austen-Leigh 243

Pinto, Adolph (Doctor; Teacher)
Pinto and Sons - Leslie Epstein 1947

Pio (Actor)
The Bridge of San Luis Rey - Thornton Wilder 6752

Pippin, Harry (Doctor)
Miss Martha Mary Crawford - Catherine Marchant 4081

Pirov, Boris (Nobleman)
The Candlesticks and the Cross - Ruth Freeman Solomon 5940

Pirrip, Philip "Pip" (Young Man)
Estella - Alanna Knight 3519

Pisana (Gentlewoman)
The Castle of Fratta - Ippolito Nievo 4625

Pitborough, Charles (Banker; Widow(er))
A Most Romantic City - Mary Ann Gibbs 2396

Pitcher, Tresham (Young Man)
Captain Vinegar's Commission - Philip Glazebrook 2428

Pitler, Jake (Military Personnel)
Night March - Bruce Lancaster 3641

Pitt, Charlotte (Spouse; Gentlewoman)
Ashworth Hall - Anne Perry 4918
Belgrave Square - Anne Perry 4919
Bethlehem Road - Anne Perry 4920
Bluegate Fields - Anne Perry 4921
Callander Square - Anne Perry 4923
Cardington Crescent - Anne Perry 4924
Death in the Devil's Acre - Anne Perry 4927
Farriers' Lane - Anne Perry 4930
Highgate Rise - Anne Perry 4931
Paragon Walk - Anne Perry 4932
Pentecost Alley - Anne Perry 4933
Resurrection Row - Anne Perry 4934
Rutland Place - Anne Perry 4935
Silence in Hanover Close - Anne Perry 4936
Traitors Gate - Anne Perry 4939

Pitt, Thomas (Detective—Police)
Ashworth Hall - Anne Perry 4918
Pentecost Alley - Anne Perry 4933

Pitt, Thomas (Police Officer)
Belgrave Square - Anne Perry 4919
Bethlehem Road - Anne Perry 4920
Bluegate Fields - Anne Perry 4921
Callander Square - Anne Perry 4923
Cardington Crescent - Anne Perry 4924
The Cater Street Hangman - Anne Perry 4925
Death in the Devil's Acre - Anne Perry 4927
Farriers' Lane - Anne Perry 4930

Highgate Rise - Anne Perry 4931
Paragon Walk - Anne Perry 4932
Resurrection Row - Anne Perry 4934
Rutland Place - Anne Perry 4935
Silence in Hanover Close - Anne Perry 4936
Traitors Gate - Anne Perry 4939

Pittman, Jane (Heroine)
The Autobiography of Miss Jane Pittman - Ernest J. Gaines 2270

Place, James (Farmer)
The Lords of Loone - John James 3159

Platt, Elizabeth (Widow(er))
By Antietam Creek - Don Robertson 5398

Plattner, Sophronia (Young Woman)
The Paper Mistress - Dorothea Malm 4045

Plessis-Belliere, Angelique du (Noblewoman)
Angelique and the King - Sergeanne Golon 2468
Angelique in Barbary - Sergeanne Golon 2469
Angelique in Love - Sergeanne Golon 2470
Angelique in Revolt - Sergeanne Golon 2471

Plessis-Belliere, Honorine du (Gentlewoman)
Angelique in Revolt - Sergeanne Golon 2471

Plessis-Belliere, Philippe du (Government Official)
Angelique - Sergeanne Golon 2465

Plessis-Belliere, Philippe du (Nobleman)
Angelique and the King - Sergeanne Golon 2468

Pleydell, Susanna (Nurse)
Secret for a Nightingale - Victoria Holt 3020

Plummer, Henry (Lawman)
What Law There Was - Al Dempsey 1609

Polack, Charley (Sea Captain)
The Magic Ship - Sandra Paretti 4791

Poldark, Agatha (Gentlewoman)
The Black Moon - Winston Graham 2522

Poldark, Clowance (Fiance(e))
The Miller's Dance - Winston Graham 2528

Poldark, Demelza (Spouse)
The Angry Tide - Winston Graham 2521
The Black Moon - Winston Graham 2522
Demelza - Winston Graham 2524
The Four Swans - Winston Graham 2525
The Last Gamble - Winston Graham 2527
The Miller's Dance - Winston Graham 2528
The Stranger From the Sea - Winston Graham 2530
The Twisted Sword - Winston Graham 2531
Venture Once More - Winston Graham 2532

Poldark, Elizabeth (Spouse)
Demelza - Winston Graham 2524
The Last Gamble - Winston Graham 2527
The Renegade: A Novel of Cornwall, 1783-1787 - Winston Graham 2529
Venture Once More - Winston Graham 2532

Poldark, Francis (Businessman; Gentleman)
Demelza - Winston Graham 2524

Poldark, Francis (Gentleman)
The Last Gamble - Winston Graham 2527
The Renegade: A Novel of Cornwall, 1783-1787 - Winston Graham 2529
Venture Once More - Winston Graham 2532

Poldark, Jeremy (Military Personnel)
The Twisted Sword - Winston Graham 2531

Poldark, Jeremy (Relative)
The Miller's Dance - Winston Graham 2528

Poldark, Ross (Businessman)
The Black Moon - Winston Graham 2522
Demelza - Winston Graham 2524
The Last Gamble - Winston Graham 2527
The Twisted Sword - Winston Graham 2531
Venture Once More - Winston Graham 2532

Poldark, Ross (Businessman; Political Figure)
The Angry Tide - Winston Graham 2521
The Four Swans - Winston Graham 2525
The Miller's Dance - Winston Graham 2528
The Stranger From the Sea - Winston Graham 2530

Poldark, Captain Ross (Veteran; Landowner)
The Renegade: A Novel of Cornwall, 1783-1787 - Winston Graham 2529

Poldark, Verity (Gentlewoman)
Demelza - Winston Graham 2524
The Renegade: A Novel of Cornwall, 1783-1787 - Winston Graham 2529

Poliakov, Sonya (Revolutionary)
Triptych - Dora Landey 3652

Pollard, Cynthia (Spy)
Squadron Shilling - Arch Whitehouse 6712

Polleven, Julian (Gentleman)
The Sea Scape - Mary Lide 3778

Pollock, Oliver (Businessman)
The Big Knives - Bruce Lancaster 3635

Polonsky, Elise Chatham (Noblewoman; Captive)
Sweet Ransom - Linda Madl 4026

Polventon, Ben (Heir)
Heir to Polventon - Marjorie Watson 6583

Polventon, Julie (Spouse)
Heir to Polventon - Marjorie Watson 6583

Polydamas (Military Personnel)
The Trojan Generals Talk: Memoirs of the Greek War - Phillip Parotti 4818

Polyxigis, Captain (Revolutionary)
Freedom or Death - Nikos Kazantzakis 3383

Pomander, Charles (Nobleman)
Peg Woffington - Charles Reade 5281

Pomegranate (Young Woman)
Bronze Mirror - Jeanne Larsen 3668

Pomeroy, Bertram (Nobleman; Heir)
Miss Hartwell's Dilemma - Carola Dunn 1796
Two Corinthians - Carola Dunn 1797

Pomeroy, Ezra (Military Personnel; Explorer)
Now We Are Free - Marguerite Allis 112

Pomeroy, Harriet (Naturalist; Spinster)
Ravished - Amanda Quick 5216

Pomeroy, Joe (Orphan)
The Devil's Rainbow - J.C. Furnas 2257

Pomeroy, John Stockley (Adventurer; Spy)
Pomeroy - Gordon Williams 6770

Pomponia (Teenager)
Golden Peacock - Gertrude Atherton 224

Ponce, Juanillo (Entertainer)
Five Black Ships: A Novel of Discoverers - Napoleon Baccino Ponce de Leon 5089

Pond, Luther (Journalist)
Hoopla - Harry Stein 5990

Pondwader (Prehistoric Human; Teenager)
People of the Lightning - W. Michael Gear 2337

Pontefract, Amelia (Gentlewoman)
The Proprietor - Ann Schlee 5638

Pontifrac, Berry (Young Woman)
Loving Heart - Elsie Singmaster 5869

Pontmercy, Marius (Revolutionary)
Cosette: The Sequel to Les Miserables - Laura Kalpakian 3329

Poor Singer (Indian)
People of the Silence - W. Michael Gear 2340

Popple, Edward (Scientist)
The Rose Crossing - Nicholas Jose 3306

Porpora (Teacher)
Consuelo - George Sand 5582

Porre, Elured (Banker)
Thomas: A Novel of the Life, Passions, and Miracles of Becket - Shelley Mydans 4538

Portagee (Sailor)
The White Dawn - James Houston 3053

Porteous, Flora (Singer)
The Heroine's Sister - Frances Murray 4536

Porteous, Jim (Teenager)
Retreat From the Dolphin - Darwin Le Ora Teilhet 6198

Porteous, Mary (Young Woman; Governess)
The Heroine's Sister - Frances Murray 4536

Porter, Ellen Watson (Spouse)
Ceremony of the Innocent - Taylor Caldwell 852

Porter, James (Convict)
The Men That God Forgot - Richard Butler 829

Porter, Jeremy (Political Figure)
Ceremony of the Innocent - Taylor Caldwell 852

Porter, Thomas (Military Personnel)
Sailor Named Jones - Harvey Haislip 2643

Porthos (Military Personnel)
The Three Musketeers - Alexandre Dumas 1782

Porthos (Veteran)
Twenty Years After - Alexandre Dumas 1783

Posey, George (Gentleman)
The Fathers - Allen Tate 6171

Postlewaite, Jane (Gentlewoman)
The Mamur Zapt and the Night of the Dog - Michael Pearce 4869

Potter, Israel (Military Personnel)
Israel Potter - Herman Melville 4334

Potter, Maggie (Young Woman)
Masters of Illusion: A Novel of the Connecticut Circus Fire - Mary-Ann Tirone Smith 5925

Potter, Thomas (Military Personnel)
The Prize Master - Harvey Haislip 2642
Sea Road to Yorktown - Harvey Haislip 2644

Pourure, Aurelie de (Gentlewoman; Widow(er))
By Right of Arms - Robyn Carr 937

Powell, Tom (Farmer)
The Truest Pleasure - Robert Morgan 4452

Power, Georgina (Heiress)
Georgina - Clare Darcy 1488

Power, Liam (Doctor)
No Price Too High - Madeleine Polland 5085

Powers, Diana (Gentlewoman)
All Desires Known - Malcolm Macdonald 3963

Powers, John (Doctor; Loyalist)
Flight From Avatchez - Frank G. Slaughter 5887

Powers, Lisa (Captive)
Arizona Ecstasy - Rosanne Bittner 511

Powlett-Jones, David (Teacher)
To Serve Them All My Days - R.F. Delderfield 1591

Pownall, Sara (Orphan)
Sara - Brian Cleeve 1110

Poxe, Hieronymous (Editor; Journalist)
The Long Naked Descent into Boston - William Eastlake 1823

Poynder, Loftus (Financier)
Tenants of the Earth - Sandra Paretti 4793

Pratt, Horace Taylor (Businessman)
Back Bay - William Martin 4138

Prawl, David (Settler)
Trumpets Calling - Dora Aydelotte 248

Prawl, Martha (Settler)
Trumpets Calling - Dora Aydelotte 248

Pray, Job (Military Personnel)
Lionel Lincoln; or, The Leaguer of Boston - James Fenimore Cooper 1303

Preacher (Mountain Man)
Blood on the Divide - William W. Johnstone 3265
Forty Guns West - William W. Johnstone 3267

Preaux, Melisande (Gentlewoman)
Men Like Shadows - Dorothy Charques 1000

Preele, Catherine (Spouse; Farmer)
Morgan's Woman - Iris Gower 2500

Preele, David (Veteran; Handicapped)
Morgan's Woman - Iris Gower 2500

Prentice, Andrew (Convict)
The Timeless Land - Eleanor Dark 1495

Prentiss, Patrick (Historian; Writer)
The Tenants of Time - Thomas Flanagan 2120

Prentiss, Patrick (Lawyer)
The End of the Hunt - Thomas Flanagan 2119

Prentiss, Salita (Pioneer)
Heroine of the Prairies: A Romance of the Oregon Trail - Sheba Hargreaves 2707

Prescott, Bartholomew (Political Figure)
The Prescott Chronicles - Albert Fried 2232

Prescott, Francis (Religious; Teacher)
The Rector of Justin - Louis Auchincloss 233

Prescott, Harriet (Spouse)
The Rector of Justin - Louis Auchincloss 233

Prescott, Julian (Political Figure)
The Prescott Chronicles - Albert Fried 2232

Prescott, Matt (Rancher)
Live From the Devil - Wyatt Blassingame 542

Prescott, Samuel (Settler)
The Prescott Chronicles - Albert Fried 2232

Prestcote, Gilbert (Gentleman)
Dead Man's Ransom - Ellis Peters 4957

Presteigne, Lady Harriet (Noblewoman; Fiance(e))
The Foundling - Georgette Heyer 2888

Preston, David (Doctor)
The Stonewall Brigade: A Novel of the American Civil War - Frank G. Slaughter 5902

Preston, Wayne (Veteran)
Fire on the Wind - David Garth 2304

Preswald, Buck (Gentleman)
Mississippi Belle - Clements Ripley 5346

Preswald, Caitlin (Singer; Widow(er))
Mississippi Belle - Clements Ripley 5346

Prevost, Charles (Gentleman)
Marching On - James Boyd 612

Prevost, Etienne (Trader)
Kings of the Missouri - Hugh Pendexter 4895

Prevost, Steward (Southern Belle)
Marching On - James Boyd 612

Priam (Ruler)
Scandal in Troy - Eva Hemmer Hansen 2679
The Trojan Generals Talk: Memoirs of the Greek War - Phillip Parotti 4818

Price, Ben (Sailor)
The Salem Frigate - John Edward Jennings 3205

Price, Bethany (Orphan)
The Misadventures of Bethany Price - Marian Cockrell 1147

Price, Oliver (Military Personnel)
Hiwassee: A Novel of the Civil War - Charles F. Price 5176

Price, Ria (Streetperson; Actress)
London's Child - Philip Boast 560

Price, Richard (Actor)
The Upstart - Edison Marshall 4112

Price, Susan (Gentlewoman)
Mansfield Revisited - Joan Aiken 51

Price, Webb (Military Personnel)
San Antone - V.J. Banis 288

Pride, Isaac (Hunter)
Heartland - Robert Douglas Mead 4316

Prien, Major Ruben (Military Personnel)
Time and Again - Jack Finney 2093

Prien, Major Ruben (Military Personnel; Historian)
From Time to Time - Jack Finney 2092

Prince, Alexander (Military Personnel)
The Restless Border - Richard Pearce 4873

Prince, Henry (Young Man)
The Rebel and the Turncoat - Malcolm Decker 1576

Prince, Johnathan (Businessman)
The Wine Princes - Margaret Mackay 3987

Prince, Peregrine (Businessman)
The Wine Princes - Margaret Mackay 3987

Prinsloo, Lisbet (Young Woman)
They Seek a Country - Francis Brett Young 6941

Prinsloo Willem, Oom (Settler; Farmer)
The Fiercest Heart - Stuart Cloete 1122

Prior, Beth (Actress)
Escapade - Jane Aiken Hodge 2962

Prior, Billy (Military Personnel)
The Eye in the Door - Pat Barker 307
The Ghost Road - Pat Barker 308
Regeneration - Pat Barker 309

Prior, Juliet (Young Woman)
The Wildcliffe Bird - Constance Heaven 2811

Priscus (Philosopher; Editor)
Julian - Gore Vidal 6489

Priscus, Lucius (Military Personnel)
Caesar of the Narrow Seas - John Gloag 2433

Prissac, Raymond de (Nobleman)
The Courts of Love: A Romance of Medieval France - Peter Bourne 592

Pritchard, Anne-Louise (Servant)
The Marigold Field - Diane Pearson 4876

Probus, Marcus (Nobleman)
Roman Go Home! - Adam Fergusson 2065

Prochurus (Government Official)
The Sins of Herod: A Novel of Rome and the Early Church - Frank G. Slaughter 5900

Proctor, Jeremy (Servant; Teenager)
Blind Justice - Bruce Alexander 76
Murder in Grub Street - Bruce Alexander 77
Watery Grave - Bruce Alexander 78

Prohaska, Otto (Military Personnel)
The Emperor's Coloured Coat - John Biggins 491
A Sailor of Austria - John Biggins 492

Prohaska, Otto (Military Personnel; Pilot)
The Two-Headed Eagle - John Biggins 493

Proops, Elias (Veteran)
Chad Hanna - Walter D. Edmonds 1873

Prosser, Emma (Journalist)
Hard on the Road - Barbara Moore 4440

Prouty, Richard (Military Personnel)
Legacy - Robert Vaughan 6448

Pruitt, Jessica (Actress; Time Traveller)
Serenissima: A Novel of Venice - Erica Jong 3300

Pruitt, Lottie (Young Woman)
Chihuahua 1916 - Otis Carney 903

Pruitt, October (Slave)
All God's Children - Alston Anderson 136

Pryde, Carrington (Military Personnel)
Weathercock - Constance Dodge 1668

Pryde, Clotilda (Widow(er))
Weathercock - Constance Dodge 1668

Pryde, Stephen (Gentleman)
Strange Wives - Shirley Barker 317

Pryne, Richard (Spy)
Richard Pryne: A Novel of the American Revolution - Cyril Harris 2718

Prynne, Hester (Spouse)
Hester - Christopher Bigsby 496

Prynne, Hester (Spouse; Outcast)
Arthur Dimmesdale - Charles R. Larson 3671
Pearl - Christopher Bigsby 497
The Scarlet Letter - Nathaniel Hawthorne 2786

Prynne, Pearl (Bastard Daughter)
Pearl - Christopher Bigsby 497

Prysing, Leo (Director)
Pacific Cavalcade - Virginia Coffman 1157

Psin (Ruler)
Until the Sun Falls - Cecelia Holland 2998

Pullen, Toliver (Farmer)
The Live Goat - Cecil Dawkins 1542

Purbeck, Sandy (Teacher)
Always a River - Drayton Mayrant 4211

Purchis, Hart (Plantation Owner)
Judas Flowering - Jane Aiken Hodge 2965

Purchis, Hart (Plantation Owner; Captive)
Wide Is the Water - Jane Aiken Hodge 2973

Purchis, Hyde (Plantation Owner)
Savannah Purchase - Jane Aiken Hodge 2970

Purchis, Josephine (Spouse)
Savannah Purchase - Jane Aiken Hodge 2970

Purchis, Juliet (Young Woman)
Savannah Purchase - Jane Aiken Hodge 2970

Purchis, Mercy (Spouse)
Wide Is the Water - Jane Aiken Hodge 2973

Purdy, Zillah (Settler)
The Proselyte - Susan Ertz 1958

Purvis, Anthony (Adventurer)
Being Met Together - William Vaughan Wilkins 6756

Putbus, Malte Moritz Von (Nobleman)
Speranza - Sven Delblanc 1584

Putnam, John Quincy (Rancher)
Winter Grass - Richard S. Wheeler 6665

Putnam, Lisa (Rancher)
The Snowblind Moon - John Byrne Cooke 1267

Pye, Manfred (Gentleman)
The Crystal Dove - Mollie Hardwick 2692

Pygmalion (Ruler)
The Purple Quest: A Novel of Seafaring Adventure in the Ancient World - Frank G. Slaughter 5896

Pym, Hannah (Housekeeper; Matchmaker)
Beatrice Goes to Brighton - Marion Chesney 1019
Belinda Goes to Bath - Marion Chesney 1020
Deborah Goes to Dover - Marion Chesney 1023
Emily Goes to Exeter - Marion Chesney 1027
Penelope Goes to Portsmouth - Marion Chesney 1043
Yvonne Goes to York - Marion Chesney 1054

Pym, Nicholas (Spy)
A Firework for Oliver - John Sanders 5587

Pyner, Daniel (Heir)
Kezzy - Patricia Burns 799

Q

Quade, Dixie (Nurse)
A Heart Divided - Al Lacy 3580

Quade, Imogene (Heiress)
The Quade Inheritance - Barbara Ker Wilson 3469

Quade, Nicholas (Heir)
The Quade Inheritance - Barbara Ker Wilson 3469

Quaid, Will (Lawman)
Hearts and Bones - Margaret Lawrence 3685

Quain, Maurice (Businessman)
No Wall So High - Anne Powers 5152

Quantrell, Sabrina (Gentlewoman)
The Carolinians - Jane Barry 357

Quarrendon, Neville (Artist; Widow(er))
Limmerston Hall - Hester W. Chapman 991

Quarternight, Sam (Detective—Private)
The Last Days of Horse-Shy Halloran - Bill Pronzini 5203

Quarters, Gwendolen (Gentlewoman)
Gwendolen - Clare Darcy 1489

Quasheba (Slave)
Die the Long Day - Orlando Patterson 4833

Quasia (Indian; Warrior)
The Buffalo Soldiers - John Prebble 5165

Quasimodo (Handicapped)
The Hunchback of Notre Dame - Victor Hugo 3076

Quayle, Kit (Journalist)
One Last Glimpse - James Aldridge 74

Queen, Robert (Hunter; Adventurer)
The Great Sky and the Silence - James S. Rand 5245

Quick, Bill (Sea Captain)
Rainbow in the Royals - Garland Roark 5357

Quick, James (Sea Captain)
Rainbow in the Royals - Garland Roark 5357

Quickskill, Raven (Slave; Fugitive)
Flight to Canada - Ishmael Reed 5285

Quill, Major (Military Personnel)
Yellowhorse - Dee Brown 715

Quill, Celia (Widow(er))
The Rationalist - Warwick Collins 1217

Quill, Kevin (Settler)
Tomorrow the New Moon - Shirley Barker 319

Quimper, Jubal (Settler)
Texas - James A. Michener 4375

Quincy, Justin de (Bastard Son)
The Queen's Man - Sharon Kay Penman 4905

Quinlaw, Sarah (Young Woman)
The Ways of Women - Elaine Crowley 1436

Quinn, Anthony (Military Personnel; Spy)
The Drums of April - Charles Mergendahl 4340

Quinn, Daniel (Orphan)
Quinn's Book - William Kennedy 3423

Quinncannon, Lon (Lawyer)
The Thomas Street Horror - Raymond Paul 4843
The Tragedy at Tinkerton: An Historical Novel of Murder - Raymond Paul 4844

Quinney, Nicholas Dicken (Pilot; Military Personnel)
The Bright Blue Sky - Max Hennessy 2830
The Challenging Heights - Max Hennessy 2831
Once More the Hawks - Max Hennessy 2836

Quintano, Toribio (Indian; Lawman)
The Royal City - Les Savage Jr. 5621

Quintard, Jans (Actor)
Banner by the Wayside - Samuel Hopkins Adams 28

Quintus (Military Personnel)
Empire of the Eagle - Andre Norton 4649

Quintus (Religious)
Upon This Rock: The Life of St. Peter - Walter F. Murphy 4526

Quintus, Julian (Slave)
A Fig in Winter - Willa Gibbs 2400

Quintus, Marcellus (Military Personnel)
If I Forget Thee - Brenda Lesley Segal 5720

Quist, Lancey (Young Woman)
Shad Run - Howard Breslin 668

Quo, Dinah (Servant)
Lady Jane - Leslie O'Grady 4699

R

Raanah (Slave)
Charioteer: A Story of Old Egypt in the Days of Joseph - Gertrude Eberle 1835

Rabbi (Religious)
The Brother - Chayym Zeldis 6958

Rabbit (Indian; Teenager)
Moon of Thunder - Don Coldsmith 1180

Rabi (Heir)
The Golden Honeycomb - Kamala Markandaya 4086

Rachel (Young Woman)
The Rock: A Novel about Gibraltar - John Masters 4179

Rachel of Byzantium (Gentlewoman)
The Lives of Rachel - Joel Gross 2601

Rachel of Judea (Noblewoman)
The Lives of Rachel - Joel Gross 2601

Rachel of Rome (Slave)
The Lives of Rachel - Joel Gross 2601

Rackham, Jacob (Thief)
The Masters of Bow Street - John Creasy 1423

Racon, Gaston de (Nobleman)
The Bastard - Brigitte Von Tessin 6208

Racon, Madeleine de (Spouse)
The Bastard - Brigitte Von Tessin 6208

Racon, Martin de (Bastard Son)
The Bastard - Brigitte Von Tessin 6208

Radburn, Edward (Nobleman)
The Prince Regent's Silver Bell - Gladys McGorian 4275

Radlet, Donald (Gentleman)
The Mallen Streak - Catherine Cookson 1282

Radley, Elinor (Governess)
A London Season - Anthea Bell 420

Radney, Regina (Gentlewoman)
Dark Possession - Alice Alison Lide 3771

Radnor, Bill (Cowboy)
Home Mountain - Jeanne Williams 6777

Radnor, Cain (Knight)
Bond of Blood - Roberta Gellis 2349

Rafe (Warrior)
The Fourteenth of October - Bryher 742

Rafel, Alvero de (Nobleman)
Torquemada - Howard Fast 2045

Raff, Theodore (Journalist)
Liveliest Town in the West - Bill Gulick 2615

Rafferty, Martin (Businessman)
The Ironmaster - Anne Powers 5150

Raford, Quentin (Businessman)
The Unplowed Sky - Jeanne Williams 6783

Railton, Augustus (Nobleman)
Penelope Goes to Portsmouth - Marion Chesney 1043

Rain (Indian)
Thunderstick - Don Coldsmith 1190
Track of the Bear - Don Coldsmith 1191

Rainaut, Valence (Knight)
Crusader's Torch - Chelsea Quinn Yarbro 6897

Rainbird, John (Servant)
The Adventuress - Marion Chesney 1014
The Miser of Mayfair - Marion Chesney 1038
Rainbird's Revenge - Marion Chesney 1046
Rake's Progress - Marion Chesney 1047
The Wicked Godmother - Marion Chesney 1053

Rake (Servant)
Under Two Flags - Ouida 4767

Rakossy, Janos (Nobleman)
Rakossy - Cecelia Holland 2995

Raleigh, Bruce (Gentleman)
Wind From the Carolinas - Robert Wilder 6751

Ralph, Earl of Clarendon (Nobleman)
The Battle-Ax of God - Le Roy MacLeod 4007

Ralston, Delia (Gentlewoman)
The Old Maid - Edith Wharton 6652

Ram, Krishna (Royalty)
The Ravi Lancers - John Masters 4178

Ramage, Nicholas (Military Personnel)
Drumbeat - Dudley Pope 5094
Governor Ramage, R.N. - Dudley Pope 5096
Ramage - Dudley Pope 5097
Ramage and the Dido - Dudley Pope 5098
Ramage and the Guillotine - Dudley Pope 5099
Ramage and the Rebels - Dudley Pope 5100
Ramage and the Saracens - Dudley Pope 5101
Ramage at Trafalgar - Dudley Pope 5102
The Ramage Touch - Dudley Pope 5103
Ramage's Devil - Dudley Pope 5104
Ramage's Diamond - Dudley Pope 5105
Ramage's Mutiny - Dudley Pope 5106
Ramage's Prize - Dudley Pope 5107
Ramage's Signal - Dudley Pope 5108
Ramage's Trial - Dudley Pope 5109
The Triton Brig - Dudley Pope 5110

Rambaud, Lord (Nobleman)
Bernadin, My Love - Leonard Rossiter 5506

Ramelius, Andreas (Student)
Land of the Beautiful River - Helmer Linderholm 3788

Ramirez, Angelica (Prostitute)
Fool's Coach - Richard S. Wheeler 6659

Rampling, Hugh (Government Official)
Tudor Underground - Denis Meadows 4320

Ramsay, Alex (Student—College)
Strathgallant - Laura Black 523

Ramsay, Catherine (Young Woman)
Fortress Fury - Carter A. Vaughan 6435

Ramsay, Colin (Military Personnel)
Strathgallant - Laura Black 523

Ramsay, Gavin (Trader)
The Proud Breed - Celeste De Blasis 1547

Ramsay, Harry (Gentleman)
Strathgallant - Laura Black 523

Ramsay, Jamie (Lawyer)
Strathgallant - Laura Black 523

Ramsay, Margaret (Young Woman)
The Fortunes of Nigel - Sir Walter Scott 5696

Ramsay, Phoebe (Gentlewoman)
The Tyrant - Patricia Veryan 6480

Ramsay, Tessa (Gentlewoman)
The Proud Breed - Celeste De Blasis 1547

Ramsey, Derek (Gentleman)
A Future Arrived - Phillip Rock 5420

Ramsey, Mary (Amnesiac)
Dark at Noon - Jill Tattersall 6173

Randal, Percy (Rancher)
The Stars in Their Courses - Harry Brown 722

Randall, Alex (Military Personnel)
Shadow of the Moon - M.M. Kaye 3377

Randall, Claire (Doctor)
Voyager - Diana Gabaldon 2265

Randall, Claire (Doctor; Widow(er))
Dragonfly in Amber - Diana Gabaldon 2262

Randall, Claire (Nurse)
Outlander - Diana Gabaldon 2264

Randall, Drury (Gentleman)
Drury Randall - Mary Johnston 3232

Randall, Lilly (Singer)
Tarnished Angel - Phyllis Leonard 3723

Randall, Phoebe (Southern Belle)
Ask My Brother - Constance Wagner 6518

Randall, Walt (Prospector)
Treasure in Hell's Canyon - Bill Gulick 2619

Randall, Warren (Military Personnel)
Ask My Brother - Constance Wagner 6518

Randhurst, Jocelyn (Gentlewoman)
The Wise Virgin - Hebe Elsna 1934

Randolph, Bertram (Doctor)
Jack the Ripper - Richard Gordon 2484

Randolph, Bruce (Teacher)
Griffin's Way - Frank Yerby 6922

Randolph, Christy (Companion)
The Tragedy at Tinkerton: An Historical Novel of Murder - Raymond Paul 4844

Randolph, Marny (Saloon Keeper/Owner)
Calico Palace - Gwen Bristow 694

Randolph, Martha (Settler)
Crossing the River - Caryl Phillips 4984

Randolph, Miles (Villain)
Dream Time - Parris Afton Bonds 570

Randolph, Mitchell (Businessman)
The Californian - Todhunter Ballard 284

Randolph, Peter (Young Man)
Let the Spring Come - Henry Schindall 5637

Randsome, Charles (Businessman)
Storyville - Lois Battle 377

Randsome, Julia (Gentlewoman)
Storyville - Lois Battle 377

Ranec (Hunter; Prehistoric Human)
The Mammoth Hunters - Jean M. Auel 237

Ranegonda (Noblewoman)
Better in the Dark - Chelsea Quinn Yarbro 6894

Ranjana (Royalty)
The Sleeping Tiger - Marjorie McEvoy 4269
Star of Randevi - Marjorie McEvoy 4270

Ranklin, Matthew (Military Personnel; Spy)
Spy's Honour - Gavin Lyall 3929

Rannulf (Knight)
The Earl - Cecelia Holland 2987

Ransom, Marianne (Singer)
The Wizard's Daughter - Barbara Michaels 4362

Ransome, Christina (Teacher)
A Revolutionary Woman - Sheila Fugard 2248

Ransome, Kevin (Plantation Owner)
The Magnolias - Julie Ellis 1922

Ransome, Leigh (Adventurer)
The Golden Valley - Daoma Winston 6826

Ransome, Zipporah (Gentlewoman)
The Adulteress - Philippa Carr 916

Rantzau, Irina (Gentlewoman; Revolutionary)
Petersburg - Emily Hanlon 2677

Ranulf (Nobleman)
The King Liveth - Jeffrey Farnol 2013

Ranulf (Servant; Thief)
Angel of Death - P.C. Doherty 1670
The Crown in Darkness - P.C. Doherty 1671
The Prince of Darkness - P.C. Doherty 1675
Satan in St. Mary's - P.C. Doherty 1676

Rao, Balbeer (Wanderer; Servant)
The Blood Seed - Andrew Ward 6561

Rao, Natholi (Widow(er))
The Blood Seed - Andrew Ward 6561

Raoul, Jonathan (Widow(er); Doctor)
The Horn and the Forest - Jamie Lee Cooper 1313

Raoul, Nathan (Young Man)
The Horn and the Forest - Jamie Lee Cooper 1313

Raoul of Sedgemont (Nobleman)
Ann of Cambray - Mary Lide 3772

Raoul the Terrible (Nobleman)
Simon the Coldheart - Georgette Heyer 2901

Rapaho (Trapper; Frontiersman)
Rapaho - Jamie Lee Cooper 1314

Rapalje, Deborah (Waiter/Waitress)
The Harvey Girls - Samuel Hopkins Adams 31

Raphael, Miriam (Immigrant)
Crescent City - Belva Plain 5078

Rasero, Fausto (Nobleman)
Rasero - Francisco Rebolledo 5282

Rash, Matt (Lawman)
One More River to Cross - Will Henry 2847

Rashleigh, Adam (Diplomat)
Republic: A Novel of Texas - E.V. Thompson 6266

Raskonski, Andreas (Nobleman)
A Great Lord - Paul Frischauer 2233

Raspale, Jean (Government Official)
The Death of a King - P.C. Doherty 1672

Rassam (Diplomat)
When the Emperor Dies - Mason McCann Smith 5926

Ratcliffe, David (Doctor)
The Disturber - L.S. Davidson Jr. 1505

Rathbone, Oliver (Lawyer)
Defend and Betray - Anne Perry 4928
The Sins of the Wolf - Anne Perry 4937

Rathel, Lady Amanda (Noblewoman)
Black Body - H.C. Turk 6361

Rattlesnake (Indian; Warrior)
Choctaw - Donald Clayton Porter 5116

Rau, Bull (Businessman)
Log Jam - Leslie Turner White 6684

Raven (Slave)
The Big Drum - Elizabeth Boatwright Coker 1162

Raven, Bella (Orphan)
Ravenscroft - Dorothy Eden 1860

Raven, Guy (Gentleman; Political Figure)
Ravenscroft - Dorothy Eden 1860

Raven, Lucy (Spouse)
All Desires Known - Malcolm Macdonald 3963

Raven, Michael (Doctor)
All Desires Known - Malcolm Macdonald 3963

Raven, Nora (Widow(er))
Lord Raven's Widow - Leslie O'Grady   4700

Raven Heart (Indian)
Alaska - James A. Michener   4364

Raven Hunter (Prehistoric Human; Warrior)
People of the Wolf - W. Michael Gear   2341

Ravenal, Gaylord (Gambler)
Show Boat - Edna Ferber   2063

Ravenal, Kim (Actress)
Show Boat - Edna Ferber   2063

Ravenal, Magnolia (Actress)
Show Boat - Edna Ferber   2063

Ravenburn, Tom (Outcast)
Ravenburn - Laura Black   522

Ravencroft, Brian (Sea Captain)
The Silver Dolphin - Velda Johnston   3264

Ravencroft, Torrance (Gentleman)
The Silver Dolphin - Velda Johnston   3264

Ravenel, Martin (Spy; Adventurer)
Flames of Empire - Peter Bourne   594

Ravenscar, Max (Gentleman)
Faro's Daughter - Georgette Heyer   2887

Ravenshoe, Charles (Gentleman; Heir—Dispossessed)
Ravenshoe - Henry Kingsley   3500

Ravenswood (Heir—Dispossessed; Nobleman)
The Bride of Lammermoor - Sir Walter Scott   5693

Raventhorne, Jai (Bastard Son)
Olivia and Jai - Rebecca Ryman   5544

Raventhorne, Maya (Young Woman)
The Veil of Illusion - Rebecca Ryman   5545

Rawdon, Matt (Doctor)
No Roof but Heaven - Jeanne Williams   6782

Rawley, Charles (Military Personnel; Frontiersman)
Killdeer Mountain - Dee Brown   713

Rawley, Walter Claireborne (Orphan; Magician)
Mr. Vertigo - Paul Auster   244

Rawlings, Jason (Adventurer)
A Woman of Texas - R.T. Stevens   6002

Rawlings, Mark (Military Personnel; Engineer)
The Bridge of a Hundred Dragons - Emma Drummond   1723

Rawlings, Mickey (Sports Figure)
Murder at Ebbets Field - Troy Soos   5947
Murder at Fenway Park - Troy Soos   5948
Murder at Wrigley Field - Troy Soos   5949

Rawlinson, Henrietta (Gentlewoman)
God Is an Englishman - R.F. Delderfield   1587

Raymond, Jules (Actor)
Feast of the Jesters - Manuel Komroff   3533

Rayne, Edmund (Child)
Sylvester; or, The Wicked Uncle - Georgette Heyer   2904

Rayne, Sylvester (Nobleman)
Sylvester; or, The Wicked Uncle - Georgette Heyer   2904

Raza, China Eye (Kidnapper; Outlaw)
A Mule for the Marquesa - Frank O'Rourke   4753

Reade, Clara (Widow(er))
Biscayne - Barry Jay Kaplan   3365

Reade, Dominic (Gentleman)
Ride the Blue Riband - Rosalind Laker   3598

Reardon, Francis (Religious)
Brandywine - Jack Rowe   5513

Reardon, John (Military Personnel)
Valley of the Shadow - Charles Marquis Warren   6570

Rebecca (Young Woman)
If I Forget Thee - Robert S. Deropp   1621
Ivanhoe - Sir Walter Scott   5699

Rebombar, Ripio de (Businessman)
The Adventures of Don Juan - Richard Gardner   2289

Rebough, Jude (Artist)
Rainbow on the Road - Esther Forbes   2159

Red Adam (Nobleman)
Red Adam's Lady - Grace Ingram   3106

Red Bloom (Indian)
Michael Beam - Richard Hallet   2663

Red Feather (Indian)
The Flower in the Mountains - Don Coldsmith   1175
Trail From Taos - Don Coldsmith   1192

Red Fox (Indian)
Red Fox of the Kinapoo - William Rush   5526

Red Hawk (Indian; Warrior)
Thunder in the East - Mike Roarke   5362

Red Horse (Indian; Shaman)
Quest for the White Bull - Don Coldsmith   1182

Red Jade (Slave)
A House in Peiking - Robert Payne   4853

Red Moon (Indian; Guide)
Mountain Devil - David Thompson   6257

Red Orm (Warrior; Adventurer)
The Long Ships - Frans Gunnar Bengtsson   442

Red Rover (Sea Captain; Pirate)
The Red Rover - James Fenimore Cooper   1309

Red Wolf (Indian; Warrior)
Sioux Splendor - Rosanne Bittner   515

Redgauntlet, Sir Edward Hugh (Gentleman; Fanatic)
Red Gauntlet - Sir Walter Scott   5706

Redman, Susannah (Spinster)
Nobody's Angel - Karen Robards   5363

Redmayne, Cleve (Gentleman)
Elyza - Clare Darcy   1486

Redmond, Sir Harry (Gentleman)
Nanette - Patricia Veryan   6472

Redmond, Isabelle (Spouse)
Eye of the Hawk - David William Ross   5498

Redmond, Mitchell (Gentleman)
Sanguinet's Crown - Patricia Veryan   6476

Redmond, Seth (Rancher)
Eye of the Hawk - David William Ross   5498

Redvers, Tracy de (Knight; Courtier)
Royal Sword at Agincourt - Pamela Bennetts   455

Reed, Adrian (Heir)
Shanghai Tango: A Novel of China - William Overgard   4769

Reed, Daniel (Military Personnel)
Cannon's Call - Adam Rutledge   5537
Life and Liberty - Adam Rutledge   5538
Rebel Guns - Adam Rutledge   5539
Stars and Stripes - Adam Rutledge   5541

Reed, Daniel (Student)
Sons of Liberty - Adam Rutledge   5540

Reed, Gabriel (Settler)
Gabriel's Search - Della Lutes   3927

Reed, Jackey (Slave)
Ratoon - Christopher Nicole   4619

Reed, Kate (Journalist; Vampire)
The Bloody Red Baron - Kim Newman   4596

Reed, Kate (Spouse)
The Town House - Norah Lofts   3861

Reed, Martin (Gentleman)
The Town House - Norah Lofts   3861

Reed, Quincy (Military Personnel)
Rebel Guns - Adam Rutledge   5539

Reed, Quincy (Patriot)
Sons of Liberty - Adam Rutledge   5540

Reeshar, Jesse (Mountain Man; Trapper)
Chant of the Hawk - John Harris   2720

Reeve, Clara (Orphan)
Clara Reeve - Leonie Hargrave   2705

Reeves, Clint (Settler)
Montana Woman - Rosanne Bittner   513

Reeves, Deborah (Gentlewoman)
Rainbow Road - Davenport Steward   6016

Regan, Kate (Young Woman)
Westfield - Roderick Thorp   6277

Regret, Paul (Gambler)
The Comancheros - Paul I. Wellman   6616

Reil, Roxana (Young Woman; Captive)
Yankee Pasha - Edison Marshall   4115

Reilly, Cat (Settler; Widow(er))
The Bear Flag: A Novel of the Birth of California - Cecelia Holland   2983

Reilly, Frances (Young Woman)
1915: A Novel - Roger McDonald   4264

Reilly, Martin (Patriot; Orphan)
Thy Tears Might Cease - Michael Farrell   2018

Reilly, Mary (Servant)
Mary Reilly - Valerie Martin   4136

Reinhardt, Dan (Rancher)
Horne's Law - Jory Sherman   5819

Rellison, John (Sailor)
Stronghold - Donald Barr Chidsey   1065

Remizou, Dmitri (Nobleman)
Heirs of the Motherland - Judith Pella   4893

Remizou, Katrina Fedorcenko (Royalty)
Travail and Triumph - Michael Phillips   4991

Remizou, Mariana (Heiress—Lost)
Heirs of the Motherland - Judith Pella   4893

Remizou, Mariana (Noblewoman; Nurse)
The Dawning of Deliverance - Judith Pella   4892

Remus (Twin)
Children of the Wolf - Alfred Duggan   1762

Renard (Knight; Heir)
The Leopard Unleashed - Elizabeth Chadwick   967

Renard, Margot (Young Woman; Noblewoman)
Baneful Sorceries, or The Countess Bewitched - Joan Sanders   5585

Rendell, Maria (Gentlewoman; Spouse)
The Lion and the Leopard - Mary Ellen Johnson   3226

Rendell, Phillip (Knight)
The Lion and the Leopard - Mary Ellen Johnson   3226

Renfro, Spring (Young Woman)
The Good Old Boys - Elmer Kelton   3405

Renisenb (Widow(er))
Death Comes as the End - Agatha Christie   1076

Rennie, Andrew (Doctor)
After the Rainbow - Yvonne Kalman   3323

Rennie, Lisabeth (Settler; Orphan)
Mists of Heaven - Yvonne Kalman   3325

Renno (Indian; Chieftain)
Apache - Donald Clayton Porter   5114
Father and Son - Donald Clayton Porter   5117
Father of Waters - Donald Clayton Porter   5118
Hawk's Journey - Donald Clayton Porter   5119
Manitou - Donald Clayton Porter   5120
Renno - Donald Clayton Porter   5123

Sachem's Son - Donald Clayton Porter 5125
Spirit Knife - Donald Clayton Porter 5128
Tomahawk - Donald Clayton Porter 5129
War Clouds - Donald Clayton Porter 5131
War Cry - Donald Clayton Porter 5132
War Drums - Donald Clayton Porter 5133

Renno (Indian; Warrior)
Choctaw - Donald Clayton Porter 5116
The Renegade - Donald Clayton Porter 5122
The Sachem - Donald Clayton Porter 5124
Seminole - Donald Clayton Porter 5126
War Chief - Donald Clayton Porter 5130
White Indian - Donald Clayton Porter 5134

Rescator (Pirate)
Angelique in Barbary - Sergeanne Golon 2469
Angelique in Love - Sergeanne Golon 2470

Retallick, Ben (Miner)
Ben Retallick - E.V. Thompson 6263

Retallick, Josh (Miner)
Chase the Wind - E.V. Thompson 6264

Retallick, Josh (Trader)
Harvest of the Sun - E.V. Thompson 6265

Retallick, Miriam (Young Woman)
Harvest of the Sun - E.V. Thompson 6265

Rethy, Alexa de (Gentlewoman)
Court of Honor - Maria Fagyas 1996

Rettig, Elizabeth (Young Woman)
Elizabeth, By Name - Will Cook 1265

Revell, Bartholomew (Orphan; Settler)
Massachusetts: A Novel - Nancy Zaroulis 6956

Revell, Ebenezer (Patriot)
Massachusetts: A Novel - Nancy Zaroulis 6956

Revesby, Martin (Writer)
The Winter Bride - Carola Salisbury 5572

Rex (Military Personnel)
An Error of Judgment - Stanley Wolpert 6845

Reynald of Warby (Knight)
Gilded Spurs - Grace Ingram 3105

Reyns, Henry de (Artisan)
The White Cutter - David Pownall 5158

Rhiannon (Noblewoman)
The Viking's Woman - Heather Graham 2520

Rhinn, Comyn (Laird)
Swear by Apollo - Shirley Barker 318

Rhinn, Margery (Gentlewoman)
Swear by Apollo - Shirley Barker 318

Rhoodie, Andries (Inventor)
The Guns of the South - Harry N. Turtledove 6367

Rhun (Traveller)
The Pilgrim of Hate - Ellis Peters 4967

Riada (Young Woman)
Raven's Wind - Victor Canning 883

Rian (Young Woman)
The Earth Goddess - Richard Herley 2856

Riario, Girolamo (Nobleman)
The Medici Hawks - Martin Woodhouse 6853

Riazhin, Pierre (Artist)
Encore - Monique Raphel High 2915

Ribera, Luis (Nobleman)
The Royal City - Les Savage Jr. 5621

Rice, Jack (Actor)
Will Shakespeare: The Untold Story - John Mortimer 4495

Rice, Tom (Entertainer)
Darktown Strutters - Wesley Brown 732

Rich, Don Narciso (Government Official)
To the Indies - C.S. Forester 2183

Richard (Knight)
Great Maria - Cecelia Holland 2989

Richard of Kingsclere (Knight)
Emerald Fire - Laurie Grant 2537

Richard of Rawen (Knight)
Below the Salt - Thomas B. Costain 1362

Richard of Sussex (Nobleman)
The Lion and the Leopard - Mary Ellen Johnson 3226

Richards, Cameron (Military Personnel)
Diamond Head - Houston Branch 647

Richardson, Esther (Spouse)
The Measure of the Years - Alice Mary Colver 1218

Richardson, Jim (Sailor)
The Greenlander - Mark Adlard 38

Richardson, Lesley Aymes (Socialite)
The Eleventh Year - Monique Raphel High 2914

Richardson, Nate (Plantation Owner)
From Fields of Gold - Alexandra Ripley 5339

Richaud, Angelique (Gentlewoman)
Gai-Jin: A Novel of Japan - James Clavell 1100

Richemont, Denise de (Murderer)
Crime Without Passion - Richard Grayson 2556

Richepane, Arsene de (Nobleman)
The Arm and the Darkness - Taylor Caldwell 850

Richepane, Louis (Religious)
The Arm and the Darkness - Taylor Caldwell 850

Richett, Tony (Organized Crime Figure)
The Black Mask Murderers - William F. Nolan 4635

Richmond, Anthony (Architect)
The House on Curtin Street - Millie J. Ragosta 5242

Richmond, Kate (Doctor)
Blood Red Rose - Maxwell Grant 2538

Richmond, Oriel (Gentlewoman; Heiress)
Lady Defiant - Suzanne Robinson 5412

Richtier, Martin Jon (Frontiersman)
Powder Mission - Herbert Stover 6070

Ricky, Melinda Blake (Slave)
The Slave Stealer - Boyd Upchurch 6390

Ridd, John (Adventurer)
Lorna Doone - R.D. Blackmore 528

Riddler, Morris (Farmer)
The Two Farms - Mary E. Pearce 4865

Rider, Alan (Adventurer)
The White Rhino Hotel - Bartle Bull 765

Rider, Kate (Young Woman)
Three Roads to Valhalla - Catherine Pomeroy Stewart 6022

Ridgeley (Military Personnel)
Wintercombe - Pamela Belle 435

Ridgeway, Joel (Young Man)
Charming Sally - Maude Hart Lovelace 3903

Ridley, Betsy (Young Woman)
War Chief - Donald Clayton Porter 5130

Ridley, Gilbert (Trader)
The Lady Chapel - Candace M. Robb 5366

Ridley, Luke (Adventurer)
Till the Day Goes Down - Judith Lennox-Smith 3719

Riebeck, Jean (Spy; Military Personnel)
Before the Glory Ended - Ursula Zilinsky 6963

Riemmelth (Royalty)
Queen of the Lightning - Kathleen Herbert 2852

Riesling, Margrethe (Young Woman; Lover)
Blood Winter - William Patrick 4830

Rigana (Royalty)
The Serpent's Tooth - Diana L. Paxson 4846

Rigey, Luisa (Heroine)
The Patriot - Antonio Fogazzaro 2146

Riggs, Fred (Settler)
Born Strangers - Helen Topping Miller 4384

Riley, Cordellia (Sea Captain)
The River Witch - Margerie McIntyre 4278

Riley, Jim (Pioneer)
The Glorious Three - June Wetherell 6651

Riley, Michael (Sea Captain)
The River Witch - Margerie McIntyre 4278

Rilke, Martin (Gentleman; Journalist)
The Passing Bells - Phillip Rock 5421

Rilke, Martin (Gentleman; Writer)
A Future Arrived - Phillip Rock 5420

Ring, Willard (Judge) ·
The Justicer - Thomas Fall 2010

Ringan, Captain (Steward)
Wilford's Daughter - Alexandra Manners 4071

Ringham, William (Gentleman)
My Name Is Clary Brown - Charlotte Keppel 3466

Ringo (Companion)
The Unvanquished - William Faulkner 2050

Ringrose, Floyd (Leader)
Long Storm - Ernest Haycox 2790

Rinn, Davy (Heir)
Fabulous Valley - Cornelia Stratton Parker 4803

Rinn, Linda (Landowner)
Fabulous Valley - Cornelia Stratton Parker 4803

Rinzi, Philip de (Architect)
All Desires Known - Malcolm Macdonald 3963

Rioches, Elizabeth de (Gentlewoman)
That Sweet and Savage Land - Emma Drummond 1728

Riordan, Ian (Revolutionary)
Gone the Rainbow, Gone the Dove - Joan Bagnel 264

Riordan, Molly (Prostitute)
Welcome to Hard Times - E.L. Doctorow 1660

Rise, Ned (Thief)
Water Music - T. Coraghessan Boyle 619

Rising, April (Young Woman)
April Rising - Susan Sallis 5574

Rising, Florence (Spouse)
April Rising - Susan Sallis 5574

Rising, Will (Tailor)
April Rising - Susan Sallis 5574

Rising Moon (Indian)
Song of the Meadowlark - John A. Sanford 5594

Rising Sun (Prehistoric Human)
The Last Mammoth - Margaret Allan 89

Risle, Matilda de (Heiress)
The Morning Gift - Diana Norman 4645

Ritchie, David (Orphan; Lawyer)
The Crossing - Winston Churchill 1080

Ritter, Caroline (Young Woman)
Rebel in Blue - Herman Toepperwein 6289

Rivenhall, Charles (Gentleman)
The Grand Sophy - Georgette Heyer 2891

River, Christian de (Nobleman; Spy)
Lady Gallant - Suzanne Robinson 5413

Rivera, Rose de (Young Woman)
Dillinger - Harry Patterson 4832

Rivers, Jenny (Criminal)
The Vast Memory of Love - Malcolm Bosse 588

Rivers, Jonathan (Artist)
The Imagination of the Heart - Judith Glover 2437

Rivers, Josh (Guide)
Oregon Bride - Rosanne Bittner 514

Rivers, Leafy (Bride)
Leafy Rivers - Jessamyn West 6630

Rivers, Reno (Settler)
Leafy Rivers - Jessamyn West 6630

Rivington, Alexander (Nobleman)
Lord Rivington's Lady - Eileen Jackson 3134

Rizpah (Slave)
Rizpah - Charles E. Israel 3124

Rizpah (Widow(er))
As Sure as the Dawn - Francine Rivers 5352

Roade, Kieron (Rake; Heir)
Sarah Camberwell Tring - Janet Edmonds 1869

Robbarde, Marc (Rancher)
The White Land - William Dieter 1643

Robbins, Amy (Clerk)
Time After Time - Karl Alexander 80

Robbins, Philip (Settler)
Come Spring - Ben Ames Williams 6764

Robert of Locksley (Knight)
Lady of the Forest - Jennifer Roberson 5368

Robert of Locksley (Outlaw)
Locksley - Nicholas Chase 1003

Robert of Paris (Knight)
Count Robert of Paris - Sir Walter Scott 5695

Roberts, Amelia (Young Woman)
Where the Willows Weep - Patricia Shaw 5781

Roberts, Obadiah (Settler)
Fruit in His Season - Helen C. Barney 333

Roberts, Patience (Spouse)
Fruit in His Season - Helen C. Barney 333

Robertson, Julia (Young Woman)
Burden of Desire - Robert MacNeil 4023

Robin Hood (Outlaw)
Banners of Gold - Pamela Kaufman 3371
The Good Yeomen - Jay Williams 6771
Ivanhoe - Sir Walter Scott 5699
The Sheriff of Nottingham - Richard Kluger 3512

Robiniere, Claire de la (Refugee)
Claire - Elizabeth Lyle 3931

Robinson, Horseshoe (Military Personnel; Blacksmith)
Horseshoe Robinson, a Tale of the Tory Ascendancy - John P. Kennedy 3418

Robinson, John Cedric (Military Personnel)
The Fiercest Heart - Stuart Cloete 1122

Robinson, Launcelot (Pirate)
Fanny: Being the True History of the Adventures of Fanny Hackabout-Jones - Erica Jong 3299

Robinson, Mark (Doctor)
The Night of the Ripper - Robert Bloch 551

Robson, Sylvia (Young Woman)
Sylvia's Lovers - Elizabeth Gaskell 2312

Roc-sur-Besbre, Comte de (Nobleman; Rake)
Baneful Sorceries, or The Countess Bewitched - Joan Sanders 5585

Rochdale, Elinor (Governess)
The Reluctant Widow - Georgette Heyer 2899

Rochdale, Eustacia (Young Woman; Spouse)
Dragonmede - Rona Randall 5246

Roche, Gabrielle (Gentlewoman)
Tree of Gold - Rosalind Laker 3602

Roche, Louis (Veteran)
A Question of Honour - Clifford Dowdey 1707

Roche-Bourbon, Rigaud de la (Military Personnel)
Admiral of Fear - Victor Suthren 6126
Captain Monsoon - Victor Suthren 6128
The Golden Galleon - Victor Suthren 6129
Royal Yankee - Victor Suthren 6132

Rochefort (Explorer)
Angelique in Revolt - Sergeanne Golon 2471

Rochefort (Nobleman)
The Three Musketeers - Alexandre Dumas 1782

Rochelle, Elbee (Gentlewoman)
Marcel Armand - Sallie Bell 424

Rochester, Edward (Gentleman)
Wide Sargasso Sea - Jean Rhys 5312

Rochina, Alysa (Dancer)
A Grand Passion - Mary Mackey 3991

Rodana (Royalty; Teacher)
The Winds of Sinhala - Colin De Silva 1562

Roderick, Lavinia (Gentlewoman)
Balisand - Joseph Hergesheimer 2853

Rodgers, Deborah (Nurse)
Camelot Country - Marjorie McEvoy 4267

Rodrigo, Don (Nobleman)
The Betrothed - Alessandro Manzoni 4078

Rodriguez, Donna Carlotta de (Gentlewoman)
The Flight of the Kestrel - Margaret Abbey 3

Rodriguez, Micaela (Young Woman)
The Edge of the Storm - Agustin Yanez 6893

Roe, Sir Piers (Gentleman)
Gerait's Daughter - Millie J. Ragosta 5241

Roebuck, Thomas (Trapper)
Gennie the Huguenot Woman - Bette M. Ross 5464

Roebury, Wilhelmina (Young Woman)
Black Angels - C.T. Ritchie 5348

Rogacheva, Vera (Gentlewoman)
The Warlord - Malcolm Bosse 589

Roger, Sir (Knight)
Knight with Armour - Alfred Duggan 1767

Roger (Teenager)
An Army of Children - Evan H. Rhodes 5306

Roger, Duke of Lunel (Nobleman)
A Booke of Days: A Journal of the Crusade by Roger, Duke of Lunel - Stephen J. Rivele 5351

Roger the Chapman (Peddler; Detective—Amateur)
Death and the Chapman - Kate Sedley 5715
The Eve of Saint Hyacinth - Kate Sedley 5716
The Holy Innocents - Kate Sedley 5717
The Plymouth Cloak - Kate Sedley 5718
The Weaver's Tale - Kate Sedley 5719

Rogers, Augustina (Spouse)
Bridge to Brooklyn - Albert E. Idell 3099
Centennial Summer - Albert E. Idell 3100
The Great Blizzard - Albert E. Idell 3101

Rogers, Cody (Entertainer)
The Jewelled Spur - Gilbert Morris 4465

Rogers, Hope (Widow(er))
The Valiant Gunman - Gilbert Morris 4474

Rogers, Jesse (Businessman)
Bridge to Brooklyn - Albert E. Idell 3099
Centennial Summer - Albert E. Idell 3100
The Great Blizzard - Albert E. Idell 3101

Rogers, Jesse (Young Man)
Rogers' Folly - Albert E. Idell 3102

Roget, Hadley (Engineer)
Eagles at War - Walter J. Boyne 620

Rogier, Joseph (Businessman)
Wild Earth's Nobility - Frank Waters 6578

Rogue, Johnnie (Outlaw)
Lord Johnnie - Leslie Turner White 6687

Rojas, Estrellita de (Heiress)
Eagles of Destiny - Jory Sherman 5817

Rokesby, Nicholas (Military Personnel; Spy)
Envoy From Elizabeth - Pamela Bennetts 451

Roland (Knight)
Swords of Anjou - Mario Pei 4890

Rolf (Knight)
Madselin - Norah Lofts 3853

Rolland, Therese (Government Official)
Murder in the West Wing - Elliott Roosevelt 5453

Roman (Outlaw)
The Ghosts of Elkhorn - Kerry Newcomb 4589

Roman Nose (Indian)
Roman - Douglas C. Jones 3281

Romanov, Juliana (Royalty; Gypsy)
Circle in the Water - Susan Wiggs 6742

Romby, Lady Beatrice (Noblewoman)
The Autumn Rose - Fiona Hill 2923

Romig, Jonathan (Religious)
Shining Mountains - Steve Frazee 2214

Romilly, Guy (Journalist)
The Sleep of Life - Richard Gordon 2486

Romme Allery, Caroline de la (Noblewoman)
The Rose and the Sword - Sandra Paretti 4792

Romola (Scholar)
Romola - George Eliot 1910

Romulus (Twin)
Children of the Wolf - Alfred Duggan 1762

Ronan (Prehistoric Human)
The Horsemasters - Joan Wolf 6840

Ronan, Nicholas (Nobleman)
Emerald - Helen Ashfield 206

Rongus (Outlaw)
Two Thieves - Manuel Komroff 3535

Ronin (Warrior)
The Ronin - William Dale Jennings 3212

Ronzha (Writer)
The Revolutionist: A Novel of Russia - Robert Littell 3810

Ronzie, Juliet de (Young Woman)
The Charlatan - Carter A. Vaughan 6433

Roop, Cecil (Adventurer)
Seven Rivers West - Edward Hoagland 2959

Roscius, Sextus (Landowner; Farmer)
Roman Blood - Steven Saylor 5626

Rose (Housewife)
World's Fair - E.L. Doctorow 1661

Rose (Orphan; Young Woman)
Miss Nobody - Caroline Ross 5465

Rose, Egbert (Detective—Police)
Murder Makes an Entree - Amy Myers 4540

Rose, Hannah (Young Woman)
Shadowed Memories - Al Lacy 3583

Rose, Olan (Veterinarian)
The War Train: A Novel of 1916 - Brown Meggs 4324

Rosen, Segal (Artist)
Tessa d'Arblay - Malcolm Macdonald 3974

Rosencrantz, Lulu (Organized Crime Figure)
Billy Bathgate - E.L. Doctorow 1656

Rosenzweig, Adam (Military Personnel)
Wilderness: A Tale of the Civil War - Robert Penn Warren 6573

Rosewarne, Johanna (Orphan)
A Notorious Woman - Malcolm Macdonald 3969

Ross, Bernard (Political Figure)
The Detling Secret - Julian Symons 6151

Ross, Catriona (Young Woman)
Greenyards - Joan Lingard 3796

Ross, Edward (Military Personnel)
The Alpha Raid - Alan Scholefield 5651

Ross, Georgiana (Servant)
The Wings of the Morning - Thomas Tryon 6356

Ross, Georgiana (Teacher)
In the Fire of Spring - Thomas Tryon 6355

Ross, Hildebrand (Student)
Sprig Muslin - Georgette Heyer 2903

Ross, Jeff (Rancher)
The Seventh Winter - Hal Borland 583

Ross, Loretta (Spouse)
The Seventh Winter - Hal Borland 583

Ross, Mattie (Teenager)
True Grit - Charles Portis 5139

Ross, Nellie (Journalist; Feminist)
California Gold - John Jakes 3145

Rossendale, John (Nobleman)
Waterloo - Bernard Cornwell 1350

Rossiter, Deverell (Military Personnel)
Cressida - Clare Darcy 1485

Rossiter, Gideon (Gentleman)
Ask Me No Questions - Patricia Veryan 6459

Rossiter, Gideon (Military Personnel)
Time's Fool - Patricia Veryan 6479

Rosslyn, Lord (Nobleman)
Daughters of England - Philippa Carr 919

Rosslyn, Kate (Young Woman)
Daughters of England - Philippa Carr 919

Rossmayne (Nobleman)
Topaz - Helen Ashfield 215

Rostov, Captain (Military Personnel)
The Cowboy and the Cossack - Claire Huffaker 3071

Rostov, Anton (Military Personnel; Frontiersman)
The Russian River - Gary McCarthy 4224

Rostov, Natasha (Gentlewoman)
War and Peace - Leo Tolstoy 6295

Rothwell, Lord (Nobleman)
Defy Not the Heart - Johanna Lindsey 3794

Rothwell, Adrian (Nobleman)
The Marquis and Miss Jones - Helen Ashfield 208

Rotten Belly (Indian; Chieftain)
Carry the Wind - Terry C. Johnston 3246

Rouault, Henri (Gentleman)
Kingkill - Thomas Gavin 2325

Rouault, Louise (Spouse)
Kingkill - Thomas Gavin 2325

Roujay, Bertrand de (Nobleman; Military Personnel)
The Free Frenchman - Piers Paul Read 5277

Rourke, Liam (Young Man)
The Sons of Grady Rourke - Douglas Savage 5618

Rourke, Patrick (Young Man)
The Sons of Grady Rourke - Douglas Savage 5618

Rourke, Sean (Young Man)
The Sons of Grady Rourke - Douglas Savage 5618

Roussillon, Gaspard (Trader)
Alice of Old Vincennes - Maurice Thompson 6268

Rowan, Letitia (Young Woman)
A Calf for Venus - Norah Lofts 3838

Rowan, Lucas (Nobleman)
The Bluestocking - June Drummond 1729

Rowena (Gentlewoman)
Ivanhoe - Sir Walter Scott 5699

Rowhedge, Alice (Gentlewoman)
Bless This House - Norah Lofts 3835

Rowhedge, Tom (Landowner)
Bless This House - Norah Lofts 3835

Rowland, Guy (Military Personnel)
Heart of War - John Masters 4174

Rowland, Harry (Gentleman; Businessman)
Now, God Be Thanked - John Masters 4177

Rowland, Meg (Gentlewoman)
The English Wife - Charity Blackstock 530

Rowland, Quentin (Military Personnel)
By the Green of the Spring - John Masters 4171
Heart of War - John Masters 4174
Now, God Be Thanked - John Masters 4177

Rowland, Richard (Businessman)
By the Green of the Spring - John Masters 4171
Now, God Be Thanked - John Masters 4177

Rowlands, William (Gentleman)
Marianne - Glen Petrie 4981

Rowntree, Burr (Young Man)
Iron Land - Dorothy Ogley 4697

Rowntree, Elizabeth (Student)
Forbidden City - Anthony Esler 1962

Rowntree, Ethan (Young Man)
Iron Land - Dorothy Ogley 4697

Rowse, Justinian (Gentleman)
Camelot Country - Marjorie McEvoy 4267

Roy, Clayton (Young Man)
The Valley - Clifford Irving 3114

Roy, Gavin (Rancher)
The Valley - Clifford Irving 3114

Roy, Guy (Businessman)
Sunrise to Sunset - Samuel Hopkins Adams 32

Royall, Philip (Military Personnel)
The Impudent Rifle - Richard Pearce 4872

Royce, Charlie (Businessman)
The Dream Lover - Mark Upton 6392

Royden, Olin (Young Man)
Catch a Falling Star - Frederic F. Van de Water 6401

Royland, Clare (Landowner; Psychic)
Kingdom of Shadows - Barbara Erskine 1954

Royland, Paul (Spouse)
Kingdom of Shadows - Barbara Erskine 1954

Royville, Alexandrine de (Gentlewoman)
Heroic Dust - Theodora Dehon 1581

Ruan (Adventurer)
Ruan - Bryher 746

Ruan (Orphan)
Harkfast: The Making of the King - Hugh C. Rae 5238

Rubinstein, Jacob (Immigrant)
Ellis Island - Fred Mustard Stewart 6023

Rudd, Jack (Adventurer)
The Age of Miracles - Catherine MacCoun 3960

Rudd, Tierney (Lawyer)
Pacific Street - Cecelia Holland 2993

Rudolstadt, Albert (Nobleman)
Consuelo - George Sand 5582

Rudyard, Adrian (Gentleman)
The Long Shadow - Anna Gilbert 2406

Ruff, Alan (Engineer; Surveyor)
I Thee Wed - Gilbert Wolf Gabriel 2267

Ruffin, Abby (Southern Belle)
A Promise Unbroken - Al Lacy 3582

Rugger, Caressa (Widow(er); Noblewoman)
Caressa - Linda Lang Bartell 363

Ruhama (Indian)
Beulah Land - Harold Lenoir Davis 1520

Rulan (Young Woman)
Empire of Heaven - Linda Ching Sledge 5907

Rullock, Ian (Gentleman)
Foes - Mary Johnston 3233

Rumon (Explorer)
Avalon - Anya Seton 5748

Rumstick, Ezra (Patriot)
By Force of Arms - James L. Nelson 4579

Running Deer (Prehistoric Human)
The Last Mammoth - Margaret Allan 89

Running Deer (Indian; Widow(er))
Child of the Dead - Don Coldsmith 1172

Running Elk (Indian; Teenager)
Man on Two Ponies - Don Worcester 6872

Running Fawn (Indian; Young Woman)
Drums of Change: The Story of Running Fawn - Janette Oke 4707

Runs in Light (Prehistoric Human; Hunter)
People of the Wolf - W. Michael Gear 2341

Runs with the Wind (Indian)
The Long Sun - Janice Lucas 3920

Rush, Ann (Young Woman)
Bring Larks and Heroes - Thomas Keneally 3410

Rush, Neva (Young Woman)
The Silver Mountain - Dan Cushman 1453

Rush-Hodgeborn, Pamela (Secretary)
Murder and the First Lady - Elliott Roosevelt 5444

Russell, Anne (Gentlewoman)
The King's Cavalier - Samuel Shellabarger 5795

Russell, Blue (Orphan)
Blue Russell - Will Bryant 738

Russell, Clay (Outlaw)
Blue Russell - Will Bryant 738

Russell, Eli (Lawman)
Eli's Road - Lucas Webb 6589

Russell, Jason (Lawman)
Charity, Colorado - Chelsea Quinn Yarbro 6896
The Law in Charity - Chelsea Quinn Yarbro 6901

Russell, Mary (Detective—Amateur; Student)
The Beekeeper's Apprentice, or, On the Segregation of the Queen - Laurie R. King 3487

Russell, Mary (Detective—Private; Scholar)
A Letter of Mary - Laurie R. King 3488
A Monstrous Regiment of Women - Laurie R. King 3489

Russell, Samuel Shaw (Diplomat)
The Winthrop Covenant - Louis Auchincloss 235

Ruth (Slave)
Street of the Sandalmakers: A Tale of Rome in the Time of Marcus Aurelius - Nis Peterson 4977

Rutherford, Anthea (Gentlewoman; Detective—Amateur)
A Fatal Assignation - Alice Chetwynd Ley 3764
Masquerade of Vengeance - Alice Chetwynd Ley 3765
A Reputation Dies - Alice Chetwynd Ley 3766

Rutherford, Justin (Gentleman; Detective—Amateur)
A Fatal Assignation - Alice Chetwynd Ley 3764
Masquerade of Vengeance - Alice Chetwynd Ley 3765
A Reputation Dies - Alice Chetwynd Ley 3766

Ruthven, Lord (Nobleman)
Count Manifred - Miranda Seymour 5761

Fictional Character Name Index

Rutland, Mary Marie (Southern Belle)
Bride of the River - Laura B. Harris   2723

Rutledge, Adam (Landowner)
Queen's Gift - Inglis Fletcher   2136
Raleigh's Eden - Inglis Fletcher   2137

Rutledge, Ann (Spouse)
Queen's Gift - Inglis Fletcher   2136

Rutledge, Belle (Actress; Spy)
Conspiracy of Knaves - Dee Brown   711

Rutledge, Samantha (Southern Belle)
Niagara - Robert Lewis Taylor   6189

Rutter, Ada Belle (Frontierswoman)
The Velvet Horn - Andrew Lytle   3946

Ryall, Jeff (Sea Captain; Blockade Runner)
The Dram Tree - Hamilton Cochran   1140

Ryall, Jim (Farmer)
The Richlands - Agnes Sligh Turnbull   6364

Ryall, Peggy (Spouse)
The Richlands - Agnes Sligh Turnbull   6364

Ryan, John Clinton (Sailor)
El Lazo - L. Jay Martin   4132

Ryan, Lola (Dancer)
Shanghai Tango: A Novel of China - William
   Overgard   4769

Ryan, Michael (Worker)
Sunshine and Shadow - Antonia Van-Loon   6426

Ryder, Grizel (Widow(er))
The Lonely Strangers - Charity Blackstock   531

Ryder, Jared (Nobleman; Imposter)
Deception - Amanda Quick   5214

Ryder, Sara (Artist; Worker)
Bride of Ae - Pamela Hill   2928

Ryder, Sebastian (Gentleman)
A Heritage of Shadows - Madeleine Brent   660

Ryegate, Harriet (Spouse)
If a Lion Could Talk - Mildred Walker   6532

Ryegate, Mark (Religious)
If a Lion Could Talk - Mildred Walker   6532

Ryselius, Martin (Religious)
Passion and the Sword - Harald Hornborg   3034

S

Sabine, Nicholas (Adventurer)
Moonraker's Bride - Madeleine Brent   661

Sabiston, Ingrid (Gentlewoman)
The Devil in Harbour - Catherine Gavin   2319

Sabres, Joscelin de (Knight)
The Courts of Love: A Romance of Medieval France -
   Peter Bourne   592

Sackett, Abigail (Settler)
To the Far Blue Mountains - Louis L'Amour   3630

Sackett, Barnabas (Fugitive; Settler)
Sackett's Land - Louis L'Amour   3628
To the Far Blue Mountains - Louis L'Amour   3630

Sackett, Echo (Young Woman)
Ride the River - Louis L'Amour   3625

Sackett, Flagon (Frontiersman)
The Sky-Liners - Louis L'Amour   3629

Sackett, Galloway (Frontiersman)
The Sky-Liners - Louis L'Amour   3629

Sackett, Jubal (Frontiersman)
Jubal Sackett - Louis L'Amour   3620

Sackett, Kin-Ring (Young Man)
The Warrior's Path - Louis L'Amour   3633

Sackett, Logan (Outlaw)
Ride the Dark Trail - Louis L'Amour   3624

Sackett, Nolan (Fugitive)
Mustang Man - Louis L'Amour   3623

Sackett, Orin (Frontiersman)
Lonely on the Mountain - Louis L'Amour   3621
Treasure Mountain - Louis L'Amour   3631

Sackett, Orin (Frontiersman; Lawman)
The Daybreakers - Louis L'Amour   3619

Sackett, Tell (Frontiersman)
Lonely on the Mountain - Louis L'Amour   3621
The Sackett Brand - Louis L'Amour   3627

Sackett, Tyrel (Frontiersman)
Lonely on the Mountain - Louis L'Amour   3621

Sackett, Tyrel (Frontiersman; Gunfighter)
The Daybreakers - Louis L'Amour   3619

Sackett, Yance (Young Man)
The Warrior's Path - Louis L'Amour   3633

Sackville, Bruce (Gentleman)
Pearl - Helen Ashfield   211

Sackville, James (Gentleman)
Pearl - Helen Ashfield   211

Sadayori (Nobleman)
Harpoon - C.W. Nicol   4612

Sade, Giles de (Nobleman)
Lamia: A Witch - Georgia Elizabeth Taylor   6183

Sadoc (Writer)
The Kingdom of the Wicked - Anthony Burgess   778

Safford, Joel (Settler; Military Personnel)
That Bennington Mob - Henry Barnard Safford   5558

Sager, John (Teenager)
On to Oregon! - Honore Morrow   4490

Saguenary, Richard (Nobleman)
A King Reluctant - William Vaughan Wilkins   6759

Sahak (Slave)
Barabbas - Par Lagerkvist   3585

St. Agnes, Sister (Religious)
St. Agnes' Stand - Tom Eidson   1900

St. Barbe, Alexander (Gentleman)
A Falling Star - Pamela Belle   431

St. Barbe, Alexander (Gentleman; Rake)
Treason's Gift - Pamela Belle   434

St. Barbe, Charles (Gentleman)
A Falling Star - Pamela Belle   431
Treason's Gift - Pamela Belle   434

St. Barbe, Silence (Gentlewoman)
A Falling Star - Pamela Belle   431
Wintercombe - Pamela Belle   435

Saint-Brevin, Valmont (Gentleman)
New Orleans Legacy - Alexandra Ripley   5341

St. Catherine, Summer (Noblewoman)
The Pirate and the Pagan - Virginia Henley   2827

Saint-Christophe, Philippe de (Military Personnel)
The Bride of the Wilderness - Charles McCarry   4220

St. Clair, Glory (Prostitute)
The Great Alone - Janet Dailey   1454

St. Clair, Isabella (Young Woman)
The Storm Witch - Elisabeth Barr   339

St. Clare, Amber (Adventurer; Bastard Daughter)
Forever Amber - Kathleen Winsor   6822

St. Clare, Aubrey (Gentleman)
Secret for a Nightingale - Victoria Holt   3020

St. Clare, Richard (Nobleman; Highwayman)
Desire and Deceive - Cordia Byers   832

St. Columb, Dona (Noblewoman)
Frenchman's Creek - Daphne Du Maurier   1744

St. Cyr, Alex (Gentleman)
Twilight of the Dawn - Elizabeth Nell Dubus   1752

Saint-Germain, Comte de (Nobleman; Vampire)
Better in the Dark - Chelsea Quinn Yarbro   6894
Darker Jewels - Chelsea Quinn Yarbro   6898
Hotel Transylvania - Chelsea Quinn Yarbro   6900
Mansions of Darkness - Chelsea Quinn Yarbro   6902
Out of the House of Life - Chelsea Quinn
   Yarbro   6903
The Palace - Chelsea Quinn Yarbro   6904
Path of the Eclipse - Chelsea Quinn Yarbro   6905
Tempting Fate - Chelsea Quinn Yarbro   6906

Saint-Germain, Alain (Writer)
Vagabond Prophet - Allene Symons   6149

St. Giles, Nicole (Gentlewoman)
The Demon Lover - Victoria Holt   3013

St. Gregory, Dane (Nobleman)
Knights - Linda Lael Miller   4399

St. John, Irons (Lawman)
Mister St. John - Loren D. Estleman   1974

St. John, John (Military Personnel)
Before the Wind - Lloyd M. Moxon   4506

St. Jules, Christopher (Landowner; Gentleman)
The Castle of the Winds - Jeanne Montague   4434

Saint-Juste, Jules (Nobleman)
The Scandalous Lady Wright - Marion
   Chesney   1049

Ste. Marie, Marcel (Young Man)
The Feast of All Saints - Anne Rice   5314

St. Martin, Melisande (Orphan)
It Began in Vauxhall Gardens - Jean Plaidy   5023

Ste. Maxence, Guernes de Pont (Nobleman)
This Bright Sword - Donald Barr Chidsey   1066

St. Michael, Valentine (Widow(er); Noblewoman)
Lost Love Found - Bertrice Small   5910

St. Quentyn, Katherine (Gentlewoman)
Gentlemen—The Regiment! - Hugh Talbot   6154

St. Romer, Anthony (Nobleman)
Regency Rogue - Helen Ashfield   212

Saint-Victor, Remi (Scientist)
Mirage - Ruth McKenney   4283

St. Vrain, Jouette (Gentlewoman)
The Stuart Women - Matt Braun   652

Sal (Ward)
Fitzempress' Law - Diana Norman   4644

Salamanca, Ofelia (Noblewoman)
The Campaign - Carlos Fuentes   2245

Salammbo (Noblewoman; Religious)
Salammbo - Gustave Flaubert   2123

Salani, Metello (Worker)
Metello - Vasco Pratolini   5163

Salas y Montalva, Lucia (Gentlewoman)
Coasts of Folly - Joel Williams   6784

Salazar, Lola (Young Woman)
Wolf Song - Harvey Fergusson   2069

Salen, Edwin (Gentleman)
Flowers in the Blood - Gay Courter   1387

Salisbury, Cressida (Gentlewoman)
Vice Avenged: A Moral Tale - Lolah Burford   774

Salisbury, Samantha (Doctor)
Dual Destiny - Karen Lynn   3939

Salle, Gabrielle de (Gentlewoman)
Ride with Me - Thomas B. Costain   1369

Salling, Lisel (Captive)
Wilderness Adventure - Elizabeth Page   4774

Sally (Prostitute)
Badenheim 1939 - Aharon Appelfeld   174

Salmon (Doctor)
Scarlet Cord: A Novel of the Woman of Jericho - Frank G. Slaughter 5899

Salter, Carolina (Spouse)
The Ocean Mistress - Peter French 2225

Salter, George (Businessman)
Double Wedding Ring - Patricia Wendorf 6624

Salter, Sarah (Spouse)
The Cup, the Blade or the Gun - Mignon G. Eberhart 1833

Salter, Simon (Sea Captain)
The Ocean Mistress - Peter French 2225

Salterne, Rose (Gentlewoman)
Westward Ho! - Charles Kingsley 3499

Saltmarch, Henry (Gentleman)
The Players' Boy Is Dead - Leonard Tourney 6303

Saltwood, Nicholas (Settler)
The Covenant - James A. Michener 4368

Salvador, Felix (Magician)
The Golden Crucible - Jean Stubbs 6096

Salvestro (Mercenary)
The Pope's Rhinoceros - Lawrence Norfolk 4642

Sam (Foundling)
The Sound of Coaches - Leon Garfield 2295

Samiq (Hunter; Prehistoric Human)
Brother Wind - Sue Harrison 2748

Samson (Slave)
The View From Coyaba - Peter Abrahams 11

Sance, Angelique de (Noblewoman)
Angelique - Sergeanne Golon 2465

Sancerre, Isabelle de (Gentlewoman)
Papa La-Bas - John Dickson Carr 914

Sancerre, Margot de (Young Woman)
Papa La-Bas - John Dickson Carr 914

Sanchia (Thief; Slave)
The Wind Dancer - Iris Johansen 3218

Sancreed, Lorna (Widow(er))
To the End of Her Days - Malcolm Macdonald 3975

Sandeman, Charles (Military Personnel)
The Leopard and the Cliff - Wallace Breem 655

Sanderlin, Claiborne (Wanderer)
Solitudes - R.G. Vliet 6507

Sanderson, Lydia (Frontierswoman)
The Jump-Off Creek - Molly Gloss 2435

Sandhurst, Colonel (Military Personnel)
Lady Fortescue Steps Out - Marion Chesney 1035
Miss Tonks Turns to Crime - Marion Chesney 1041

Sandhurst, Colonel (Military Personnel; Businessman)
Colonel Sandhurst to the Rescue - Marion Chesney 1021

Sandor, Janos (Religious)
Preacher on Horseback - Cecile Hulse Matschat 4186

Sandor, Rica (Spouse)
Preacher on Horseback - Cecile Hulse Matschat 4186

Sandoval, Christian Cody de (Adventurer)
Sandoval: A Romance of Bad Manners - Thomas Beer 414

Sands, John (Actor)
The Player's Boy - Bryher 744

Sanducci, Roberto (Religious)
A Dancer in Darkness - David Stacton 5971

Sanford, Blaise (Businessman)
Hollywood: A Novel of America in the 1920s - Gore Vidal 6488

Sanford, Blaise (Businessman; Publisher)
Empire: A Novel - Gore Vidal 6487
Washington, D.C. - Gore Vidal 6493

Sanford, Caroline (Businesswoman; Actress)
Hollywood: A Novel of America in the 1920s - Gore Vidal 6488

Sanford, Caroline (Young Woman)
Empire: A Novel - Gore Vidal 6487

Sanguinet, Claude (Gentleman)
Feather Castles - Patricia Veryan 6462
Sanguinet's Crown - Patricia Veryan 6476

Sanguinet, Nanette (Gentlewoman)
Nanette - Patricia Veryan 6472

Sannazaro, Niccolo (Heir)
Snared Nightingale - Geoffrey Trease 6324

Santana, Adriana (Gentlewoman)
The Marburg Chronicles - Alfred Coppel 1319

Santana, Miguel (Explorer)
The Gila River - Gary McCarthy 4223

Santana, Vitorio (Indian; Warrior)
The Gila River - Gary McCarthy 4223

Sant'Anna, Corrado (Nobleman)
Marianne and the Lords of the East - Juliette Benzoni 468
Marianne and the Masked Prince - Juliette Benzoni 469
Marianne and the Rebels - Juliette Benzoni 471

Santhonax, Edouard (Military Personnel)
1805 - Richard Woodman 6857
Baltic Mission - Richard Woodman 6859
Decision at Trafalgar - Richard Woodman 6861

Santorelli, Marco (Immigrant)
Ellis Island - Fred Mustard Stewart 6023

Santos, Fray Xavier (Religious)
Ghost Woman - Lawrence Thornton 6275

Sanutee (Indian; Chieftain)
The Yemassee - William Gilmore Simms 5855

Sarafian, Fernand (Businessman)
The Anatolian - Elia Kazan 3381

Saragosa, Elizandra (Military Personnel)
Sons of Texas - Tom Early 1822

Sarak (Eskimo; Hunter)
The White Dawn - James Houston 3053

Sarge (Servant)
Invading Tibet - Mark Frutkin 2239

Sarita, Lola (Gypsy; Dancer)
The Gypsy From Cadiz - Tamsin Hamilton 2670

Sarn, Gideon (Farmer)
Precious Bane - Mary Webb 6590

Sarn, Prudence (Fiance(e))
Precious Bane - Mary Webb 6590

Sarton, Christopher (Heir)
Sarton Kell - Kate Mallory 4043

Sarton, Olivia (Spouse)
Sarton Kell - Kate Mallory 4043

Sartoris, Bayard (Young Man)
The Unvanquished - William Faulkner 2050

Sartoris, Colonel John (Military Personnel)
The Unvanquished - William Faulkner 2050

Sarum, Cristabel (Noblewoman)
First Night - Jane Aiken Hodge 2963

Sassoon, Dinah (Young Woman)
Flowers in the Blood - Gay Courter 1387

Satterleigh, Sharisse (Heiress)
The Rake - Karen Lynn 3941

Saudners, Elias (Businessman)
The Catherine - Robert S. MacDonald 3980

Saudners, William (Businessman; Sea Captain)
The Catherine - Robert S. MacDonald 3980

Saunders, Connie (Actress)
Tessa d'Arblay - Malcolm Macdonald 3974

Sauny, Gideon (Young Man)
Seminole - Theodore Pratt 5164

Saura of Roget (Noblewoman; Handicapped)
Candle in the Window - Christina Dodd 1662

Sauvigny, Guy de (Refugee; Smuggler)
The Wind From the Sea - Constance Heaven 2812

Sauvigny, Isabelle de (Refugee)
The Wind From the Sea - Constance Heaven 2812

Savage, Edward (Actor)
The Savage Brood - Martha Rofheart 5430

Savage, Jardine Henry (Gentleman)
The Peacock's Feather - Sarah Woodhouse 6855

Savage, Jason (Adventurer)
Coromandel! - John Masters 4172

Savage, Joseph Peace (Actor)
The Savage Brood - Martha Rofheart 5430

Savage, Justin (Bastard Son; Adventurer)
The Magnificent Savages - Fred Mustard Stewart 6024

Savage, Keith (Heir; Plantation Owner)
Savage Oaks - Julie Ellis 1924

Savage, Miranda (Actress)
The Savage Brood - Martha Rofheart 5430

Savage, Orne (Military Personnel)
The Carolinians - Jane Barry 357

Savage, Phillip (Gentleman)
Savage Oaks - Julie Ellis 1924

Savage, Robin (Military Personnel)
The Lotus and the Wind - John Masters 4175

Savage, Rodney (Military Personnel)
Nightrunners of Bengal - John Masters 4176

Savage, Samantha (Journalist)
Outlaw Lover - Lindsey Hanks 2676

Savage, Thane (Outlaw)
The Long Trail North - Robert J. Conley 1245

Savage, Tom (Adventurer)
His Majesty's Highwayman - Donald Barr Chidsey 1061

Savage, William (Government Official)
The Deceivers - John Masters 4173

Savarin-Decker, Claire (Widow(er))
Glowstone - Macdonald Harris 2725

Savarin-Decker, Hermine (Young Woman)
Glowstone - Macdonald Harris 2725

Savenay, Henri de (Nobleman; Revolutionary)
The White Cockade - Charles James Louis Gilson 2423

Savigny, Annabelle de (Young Woman)
Nethergate - Norah Lofts 3854

Savigny, Isabella de (Noblewoman; Refugee)
Nethergate - Norah Lofts 3854

Sawby (Servant)
The Lormes of Castle Rising - Fanny Cradock 1409
Wind of Change at Castle Rising - Fanny Cradock 1412

Sawling, Dorrit C. (Military Personnel)
The Southern Blade - Nelson Wolford 6844

Sawtrey, Honor (Widow(er))
Daneclere - Pamela Hill 2931

Sawyer, Melissa (Young Woman)
Tomorrow the Harvest - Viola Paradise 4789

Fictional Character Name Index

Saxon, Decimus (Military Personnel)
Micah Clarke - Sir Arthur Conan Doyle 1715

Saxon, Frankie-Julia (Southern Belle)
The Legacy of Beulah Land - Lonnie Coleman 1203

Saxton, Glen Ellen (Spouse)
Tyrone of Kentucky - Clark McMeekin 4294

Scacerini, Dosolina (Spouse)
The Mill on the Po - Riccardo Bacchelli 254

Scacerini, Lazzaro (Worker)
The Mill on the Po - Riccardo Bacchelli 254

Scacerni, Cecilia (Businesswoman)
Nothing New under the Sun - Riccardo Bacchelli 255

Scacerni, Giovanni (Worker)
Nothing New under the Sun - Riccardo Bacchelli 255

Scacerni, Giuseppe (Mentally Ill Person)
Nothing New under the Sun - Riccardo Bacchelli 255

Scald Ibiz (Teenager; Prostitute)
The Tent of Orange Mist - Paul West 6636

Scalley, Ora (Cowboy)
Chihuahua 1916 - Otis Carney 903

Scarisbrooke, Richard (Government Official)
The Fate of Princes - P.C. Doherty 1673

Scarlett, Nancy (Servant)
The Heretic - Alison Macleod 4002

Scarlock, Joan (Settler)
Rivers Parting - Shirley Barker 315

Scarlock, John (Settler)
Rivers Parting - Shirley Barker 315

Scarlock, Will (Settler)
Rivers Parting - Shirley Barker 315

Scarrat, Robert (Criminal)
The Vast Memory of Love - Malcolm Bosse 588

Scarron, Father (Religious)
A Rendezvous in Haiti - Stephen Becker 407

Scawen, Vosper (Lawyer)
An Innocent Woman - Malcolm Macdonald 3967

Scelfton, Felise (Heiress)
The Troubadour's Romance - Robyn Carr 940

Schantz, Anna Sabilla (Settler; Frontierswoman)
A High Wind Rising - Elsie Singmaster 5867

Schantz, Johann Sebastian (Frontiersman)
A High Wind Rising - Elsie Singmaster 5867

Schecter, Leonard (Writer)
Di and I - Peter Lefcourt 3714

Schiller, Oscar (Lawman)
The Search for Temperance Moon - Douglas C.
 Jones 3282
Winding Stairs - Douglas C. Jones 3287

Schilling, Andreas (Detective—Police)
Blood Winter - William Patrick 4830

Schlesinger, Erich (Musician)
The Career of Magda V. - Joseph Machlis 3982

Schloss, Lotte (Heroine)
The Retreat - Aharon Appelfeld 178

Schlumberger, William (Handicapped)
Kingkill - Thomas Gavin 2325

Schroeder, Tonia (Young Woman)
Captain Wonder - Donald Thomas 6238

Schuyler, Charlie (Journalist)
Burr - Gore Vidal 6485
Lincoln: A Novel - Gore Vidal 6490

Schuyler, Charlie (Writer)
1876: A Novel - Gore Vidal 6484

Schuyler, Richard (Gentleman)
When the Music Changed - Marie R. Reno 5305

Scolvessen, Jon (Sea Captain; Explorer)
Sea of Darkness - Roland Huntford 3086

Scot, Micheal (Servant)
Lady of Monkton - Elizabeth Byrd 835

Scott, Mrs. (Widow(er))
The Alien Light - Iain Crichton Smith 1427

Scott, Adam (Heir)
Circle of Gold - Karen Harper 2710

Scott, Billy (Cowboy)
The Trail to Ogallala - Benjamin Capps 889

Scott, Brigid (Young Woman)
Buckskin Baronet - Margaret Widdemer 6734

Scott, Charlotte (Gentlewoman)
Beyond All Frontiers - Emma Drummond 1722

Scott, Darcy (Sports Figure)
Lord Fancy - Leslie Turner White 6686

Scott, David (Convict; Sea Captain)
The Slave Ship - Mary Johnston 3240

Scott, Ellen (Young Woman)
A House Behind the Mint - Laurie Huffman 3072

Scott, Frances (Gentlewoman)
A Respectable Trade - Philippa Gregory 2584

Scott, George (Young Man)
A House Behind the Mint - Laurie Huffman 3072

Scott, Joel (Military Personnel)
For Time and All Eternity - Paul Bailey 268

Scott, Jonathan (Lawyer)
Greygallows - Barbara Michaels 4359

Scott, Jordan (Indian; Frontiersman)
Visions of a Heart - Emily Carmichael 899

Scott, Margaret Lorimer (Guardian)
Alexa - Anne Melville 4330

Scott, Quincy (Military Personnel)
The Amulet - Hal Borland 582

Scott-Hobey, Sir Raymond (Sea Captain)
On the Midnight Tide - Don Tracy 6310

Scott-Paget, Lieutenant (Military Personnel)
Mutiny - Frank Tilsley 6280

Scrimshaw, Aristotle (Businessman)
Fool's Coach - Richard S. Wheeler 6659

Scrope, Harriet (Writer)
Chatterton - Peter Ackroyd 17

Seabright, Terry (Southern Belle)
Caleb Pettengill U.S.N. - George Fielding Eliot 1912

Seabrook, Linda (Young Woman)
Blossom Like the Rose - Norah Lofts 3836

Seabury, Lord (Nobleman)
The Autumn Rose - Fiona Hill 2923

Seabury, Jonathan (Military Personnel)
The Falling Hills - Perry Lentz 3720

Seadon, Ross (Heir)
The Seadon Fortune - Leonard St. Clair 5563

Seadon, Val (Prospector)
The Seadon Fortune - Leonard St. Clair 5563

Seagrave, Nigel (Explorer)
The Hungry Goblin: A Victorian Detective Novel -
 John Dickson Carr 911

Seagraves, Brice (Actor)
The Actor - Robert J. Conley 1236

Seaman (Animal)
Trail: The Story of the Lewis and Clark Expedition -
 Louis Charbonneau 998

Sears, Tobias (Military Personnel)
Band of Angels - Robert Penn Warren 6572

Sebastian, Father (Religious)
Apache - Donald Clayton Porter 5114

Sebastian (Religious)
Seek the Fair Land - Walter Macken 3989

Secombe, Oliver (Rancher)
Centennial - James A. Michener 4366

Seconnet, Denys de (Knight)
Under the Winter Moon - Teresa Brooke 705

Sedgemont, Hue (Heir)
A Royal Quest - Mary Lide 3777

Sedgemont, Olwen (Heir)
A Royal Quest - Mary Lide 3777

Sedgemont, Robert (Heir; Knight)
A Royal Quest - Mary Lide 3777

Sedgwick, Ellen (Fiance(e); Governess)
Somewhere Within This House - Jean Francis
 Webb 6587

Sedley, Amelia (Gentlewoman; Widow(er))
Vanity Fair - William Makepeace Thackeray 6213

See-Ho-Kee (Indian)
Say These Names (Remember Them) - Betty Sue
 Cummings 1448

Seelye, Alma "Cricket" (Waiter/Waitress)
The Harvey Girls - Samuel Hopkins Adams 31

Segalla, Nicholas (Immortal; Scholar)
The Prince Lost to Time - Ann Dukthas 1776
A Time for the Death of a King - Ann Dukthas 1777
The Time of Murder at Mayerling - Ann
 Dukthas 1778

Segle (Prehistoric Human)
The Stone Arrow - Richard Herley 2858

Sekeeta (Royalty; Heiress)
Winged Pharaoh - Joan Grant 2536

Sekloong, Charles (Businessman)
Dynasty - Robert S. Elegant 1902

Sekloong, Jonathan (Bastard Son; Trader)
Dynasty - Robert S. Elegant 1902

Selanova, Marina (Noblewoman)
The World in His Arms - Rex Beach 392

Selby, Lorena (Southern Belle; Plantation Owner)
Lorena - Frank G. Slaughter 5892

Selden, Deborah (Young Woman)
Captain Adam - Donald Barr Chidsey 1058

Selene (Orphan; Healer)
Soul Flame - Barbara Wood 6850

Selkirk (Doctor)
The White Rose Murders - Michael Clynes 1137

Selkirk, James (Knight)
The Crown in Darkness - P.C. Doherty 1671

Selkirk, Jeannie (Spouse)
The Great Valley - Mary Johnston 3234

Selkirk, John (Religious)
The Great Valley - Mary Johnston 3234

Selkirk, Olivia (Accountant; Teacher)
Legacy of the Wolf - Jean Raynes 5274

Senmut (Young Man)
The Golden Balance - Arthur Dana Hall 2646

Sentell, Edward Malcolm (Military Personnel)
And Wait for the Night - John William
 Corrington 1352

Sergeant, John (Religious)
The Prospering - Elizabeth Speare 5954

Serra, Emil (Activist)
La Guerra: A Spanish Saga - Stephen D.
 Frances 2199

Serrano, Francisco (Farmer)
The Arkansas River - Jory Sherman 5816

Servais, Guy de (Nobleman)
Brazen Whispers - Jane Feather 2055

Servetus, Antonio (Teacher)
Divine Mistress - Frank G. Slaughter   5886

Sesostris, Lord (Nobleman)
The Altar and the Crown - Marian Niven   4631

Sessions, Albert (Judge)
The Lady - Conrad Richter   5321

Sessions, Elena (Spouse)
The Lady - Conrad Richter   5321

Sessions, Gregory (Businessman)
Dynasty of Death - Taylor Caldwell   854

Sessions, John (Rancher)
Red Runs the River - Lewis B. Patten   4831

Seth (Artisan)
The Exodus - Peter Danielson   1467
Sword of Glory - Peter Danielson   1477

Seton, John (Young Man)
The Dark Command - William R. Burnett   793

Setran, Odin (Carpenter)
The People of Juvik - Olav Dunn   1798

Sevendor, David (Plantation Owner)
Cain's Daughters - Doris Shannon   5776

Sevendor, Jemima (Spouse)
Cain's Daughters - Doris Shannon   5776

Severance, Stuart (Rancher)
Lights Along the Shore - Diane Austell   241

Severance, Vail (Rancher)
Lights Along the Shore - Diane Austell   241

Severin, Daniel (Mercenary)
The Raven and the Rose - Susan Wiggs   6746

Severin of Langthorne (Nobleman)
Rosehaven - Catherine Coulter   1380

Severn, Lord (Nobleman; Rake)
Fleeting Fancy - Rosemary Edghill   1866

Severus (Military Personnel)
The Way - J.M. Hartley   2761

Severus (Young Man)
The Lost Eagles - Ralph Graves   2542

Severus, Livinius (Lawyer; Detective—Private)
Roman Nights - Ron Burns   803

Severus, Livinius (Political Figure)
Roman Shadows - Ron Burns   804

Sevier, John (Military Personnel)
Wild Horizon - F. van Wyck Mason   4164

Sewall, William (Naturalist)
McKay's Bees - Thomas McMahon   4289

Sewell, Celina (Prostitute)
Sweetwater Fever - Robert H. Adelman   36

Sewell, Jasper (Doctor)
Alethea - Pamela Belle   429

Seyawa (Young Woman)
Long Pig - Russell Foreman   2168

Seymour, Samuel (Military Personnel)
Proud New Flags - F. van Wyck Mason   4156

Seymour, Sylvia (Southern Belle)
Proud New Flags - F. van Wyck Mason   4156

Shackleton, Eve (Young Woman)
The Legion of the Lost - Donald Barr Chidsey   1062

Shad (Cowboy)
The Cowboy and the Cossack - Claire Huffaker   3071

Shadbolt, Humphrey (Doctor)
A Calf for Venus - Norah Lofts   3838

Shafter, Kern (Military Personnel)
Bugles in the Afternoon - Ernest Haycox   2788

Shakespeare, Edward (Actor)
You, My Brother - Philip Burton   809

Shalach (Businessman)
Serenissima: A Novel of Venice - Erica Jong   3300

Shallop, Sidney (Plantation Owner)
Beauty Beast - MacKinlay Kantor   3361

Shallot, Guenvere (Prostitute)
St. John's Wood - Nancy Fitzgerald   2116

Shallot, Roger (Gentleman)
The White Rose Murders - Michael Clynes   1137

Shallot, Roger (Servant)
A Brood of Vipers - Michael Clynes   1133
The Gallows Murder - Michael Clynes   1134
The Grail Murders - Michael Clynes   1135
The Poisoned Chalice - Michael Clynes   1136

Shamala (Royalty)
The Carmelite - Elgin Groseclose   2599

Shan-Teh Tang (Military Personnel; Warlord)
The Warlord - Malcolm Bosse   589

Shannon, Diana (Servant)
A Daughter of Liberty - Allan Cole   1196

Shannon, Emmett (Military Personnel)
A Daughter of Liberty - Allan Cole   1196

Shannon, Mark (Bastard Son; Widow(er))
Georgina - Clare Darcy   1488

Shannon, Nora (Immigrant)
Passage West - Dallas Miller   4382

Shannon, Opal (Thief; Actress)
Opal - Helen Ashfield   210

Shannon, Slone (Military Personnel)
The Nationalists - William Stuart Long   3876

Sharp, Becky (Adventurer)
Vanity Fair - William Makepeace Thackeray   6213

Sharp, Jeff (Veteran)
Seward's Folly - Edison Marshall   4111

Sharp, John (Orphan; Teacher)
The Living - Annie Dillard   1644

Sharpe, Clement (Knight)
The Bishop's Tale - Margaret Frazer   2215

Sharpe, Richard (Military Personnel)
Sharpe's Battle - Bernard Cornwell   1338
Sharpe's Company - Bernard Cornwell   1339
Sharpe's Devil - Bernard Cornwell   1340
Sharpe's Eagle - Bernard Cornwell   1341
Sharpe's Enemy - Bernard Cornwell   1342
Sharpe's Gold - Bernard Cornwell   1343
Sharpe's Honour - Bernard Cornwell   1344
Sharpe's Regiment - Bernard Cornwell   1345
Sharpe's Revenge - Bernard Cornwell   1346
Sharpe's Rifles - Bernard Cornwell   1347
Sharpe's Siege - Bernard Cornwell   1348
Sharpe's Sword - Bernard Cornwell   1349
Waterloo - Bernard Cornwell   1350

Sharpentier, Quint (Sea Captain)
El Lazo - L. Jay Martin   4132

Shattuck, Phineas (Military Personnel)
Dark Thicket - Elmer Kelton   3402

Shattuck, Star (Young Woman)
Storm to the South - Thelma Strabel   6073

Shattuck, Tobin (Prospector)
The Big Lonesome - Will Bryant   737

Shaw, Dr. (Doctor)
Highgate Rise - Anne Perry   4931

Shaw, Clinton (Gentleman)
The Spring of the Tiger - Victoria Holt   3021

Shaw, Harriet (Student)
Swing, Swing Together - Peter Lovesey   3915

Shaw, Jeremy (Military Personnel)
Day of Battle - Frederic F. Van de Water   6402

Shaw, John (Sailor)
The Whales in Lake Tanganyika - Lennart Hagerfors   2636

Shaw, John Robert (Pilot)
The Longest Winter - Julie Harris   2722

Shaw, Jon (Sailor)
The Pepper Tree - John Edward Jennings   3203

Shaw, Lisa (Orphan; Immigrant)
What the Heart Keeps - Rosalind Laker   3605

Shaw, Peggy (Entertainer)
Murder at Fenway Park - Troy Soos   5948

Shaw, Philander (Sea Captain)
The Private Adventures of Captain Shaw - Edith Shay   5783

Shaw, Robert (Businessman)
The Mills of Colne - Robert Neill   4572

Shaw, Rodney (Trader)
Black Feather - Harold Titus   6283

Shaw, Unwin (Pioneer)
The Far Country - Marthedith Furnas   2258

Shawnessy, John Wickliff (Teacher)
Raintree County - Ross Lockridge Jr.   3827

Shea, Kitty (Spouse)
A River Town - Thomas Keneally   3415

Shea, Michael (Sailor)
My Pride, My Folly - Suzanne Butler   830

Shea, Tom (Store Owner)
A River Town - Thomas Keneally   3415

Sheck (Prehistoric Human; Warrior)
Dance of the Tiger: A Novel of the Ice Age - Bjorn Kurten   3566

Shedwell, Chris (Outlaw)
Murdock's Law - Loren D. Estleman   1975

Shef (Blacksmith)
The Hammer and the Cross - Harry Harrison   2736

Sheffield, Aurora (Gentlewoman)
In the Fire of Spring - Thomas Tryon   6355

Shelby (Frontiersman)
Maximilian's Gold - Jane Barry   359

Shelby, Blaine (Military Personnel)
The Roads to Guadalupe - Robert Lewis Taylor   6190

Shelby, Sam (Teenager; Military Personnel)
The Roads to Guadalupe - Robert Lewis Taylor   6190

Sheldon, Gilbert (Landowner)
The Tides of Malvern - Francis Griswold   2595

Sheldon, Huldah (Religious)
Crum Elbow Folks - Percy Raymond Barnes   332

Sheldon, Nell (Orphan)
The Clock Tower - Jeanne Montague   4435

Sheldon, Whipple (Spy)
No Bugles Blow - Bruce Lancaster   3642

Shelmadine, Linda (Spouse)
Afternoon of a Autocrat - Norah Lofts   3834

Shelmadine, Sir Richard (Gentleman; Landowner)
Afternoon of a Autocrat - Norah Lofts   3834

Shelton, Dick (Ward; Orphan)
The Black Arrow - Robert Louis Stevenson   6008

Shen, Sun Lung (Revolutionary)
Blood Red Rose - Maxwell Grant   2538

Shen Wen-Ching (Scholar; Diplomat)
The Fabulous Concubine - Hsin-Hai Chang   987

Shenstone, Lady (Gentlewoman)
Benjamin Franklin and a Case of Artful Murder - Robert Lee Hall   2654

Shepard, Caroline (Young Woman)
The Predators - F.A. Parker   4804

Shepherd, Beth (Nurse)
For Love and Honor - Antonia Van-Loon   6423

Shepherd, Beth (Teacher; Nurse)
For Us the Living - Antonia Van-Loon   6424

Sheramy, Ann (Young Woman)
The Handsome Road - Gwen Bristow   697

Sheramy, Judith (Settler)
Deep Summer - Gwen Bristow   696

Sherborne, Ramsey (Nobleman)
Circle of Gold - Karen Harper   2710

Sherbrooke, Douglas (Nobleman)
The Sherbrooke Bride - Catherine Coulter   1382

Sherbrooke, Joan "Sinjin" (Heiress)
The Heiress Bride - Catherine Coulter   1375

Sheremetiev, Nikolai (Military Personnel)
Devoted Friends - Joe Poyer   5161

Sheridan, Alexander (Military Personnel)
Massacre at Cawnpore - Vivian Stuart   6089

Sheridan, Allegra (Settler; Spouse)
Oklahoma Run - Alberta Constant   1260

Sheridan, Bushrod (Settler)
Oklahoma Run - Alberta Constant   1260

Sheridan, Sir Charles (Gentleman; Scientist)
Death at Daisy's Folly - Robin Paige   4775
Death at Gallows Green - Robin Paige   4776

Sheridan, Devin (Artist)
Chelsea - Nancy Fitzgerald   2114

Sheridan, Emmy (Spouse)
Massacre at Cawnpore - Vivian Stuart   6089

Sheridan, Kate (Dancer)
Flanagan's Run - Tom McNab   4303

Sheridan, Lainey (Young Woman)
Oklahoma Run - Alberta Constant   1260

Sheridan, Mark (Settler)
The Adventurers - Ernest Haycox   2787

Sheridan, Rich (Sailor)
The Golden Coast - Philip Rooney   5441

Sheriden, Ben (Young Man)
The Promise of Light - Paul Watkins   6581

Sheringham, Anthony "Sherry" (Nobleman)
Friday's Child - Georgette Heyer   2890

Sherley, Sir Robert (Diplomat)
The Carmelite - Elgin Groseclose   2599

Sherman, Abigail (Adventurer)
Abigail - Joan Druett   1721

Sherman, Joseph (Military Personnel; Journalist)
Saigon - Anthony Grey   2588

Sherman, Ruth (Teacher)
Rogue's Kingdom - John Brick   676

Sherwood, Anson (Socialite)
The Normandie Affair - Elizabeth Villars   6497

Sherwood, Charissa (Heiress)
Allegheny Captive - Caroline Bourne   591

Sherwood, Felicity (Young Woman)
Reluctant Rebel - Frederic F. Van de Water   6403

Sherwood, Harry (Adventurer)
Freedom's Banner - Teresa Crane   1415

Sherwood, Johnny (Gentleman; Military Personnel)
Freedom's Banner - Teresa Crane   1415

Sherwood, Jonathon (Sea Captain)
Dragon Cove - Carter A. Vaughan   6434

Shield, Sir Tristram (Nobleman)
The Talisman Ring - Georgette Heyer   2905

Shields, Harriet (Nurse)
Until the End - Harold Coyle   1396

Shields, Harriet (Young Woman)
Look Away - Harold Coyle   1395

Shiers, William (Gentleman)
The Men That God Forgot - Richard Butler   829

Shinann (Young Woman; Minstrel)
Bard: The Odyssey of the Irish - Morgan Llywelyn   3816

Shining Moon (Indian; Spouse)
Expedition! - Dana Fuller Ross   5473
Outpost! - Dana Fuller Ross   5486
Westward! - Dana Fuller Ross   5492

Shipman, Albert (Gentleman)
Listen for the Voices - Anne Colver   1220

Shipman, Laura (Spouse)
Listen for the Voices - Anne Colver   1220

Shipman, Lettiele (Slave)
The Tree of Life - Hugh Nissenson   4629

Shipov (Spy)
The Extraordinary Adventures of Secret Agent Shipov in Pursuit of Count Leo Tolstoy in the Year 1862 - Bulat Okudzhava   4712

Shiva (Prehistoric Human; Orphan)
Shiva: An Adventure of the Ice Age - J.H. Brennan   657

Shizuka (Dancer)
The Sword of Hachiman - Lynn Guest   2608

Shobai (Artisan)
The Golden Pharaoh - Peter Danielson   1468
The Lion in Egypt - Peter Danielson   1470
Vengeance of the Lion - Peter Danielson   1480

Shokotee (Indian; Chieftain)
The Raider - Jesse Hill Ford   2164

Shonti (Religious)
Shadow of a Star - Jamie Lee Cooper   1315

Shortland, Gail (Nurse)
The Scarlet Patch - Bruce Lancaster   3645

Shoshana (Young Woman)
The Master - Max Brod   702

Shoz-Dijiji (Indian; Warrior)
Apache Devil - Edgar Rice Burroughs   806

Shuganan (Prehistoric Human; Indian)
Mother Earth, Father Sky - Sue Harrison   2749

Shy Fawn (Indian)
This Land Is Mine - Frances Casey Kerns   3470

Siam (Indian)
Eagle Song - James Houston   3050

Sibindi (Warrior)
The Tune That They Play - William Clive   1120

Sibli (Entertainer)
Glendower Country - Martha Rofheart   5427

Sidirov, Anya (Royalty)
Blood and Sable - Carol J. Kane   3350

Sidmouth, Geoffrey (Religious)
Jane and the Man of the Cloth - Stephanie Barron   355

Siegfried (Warrior)
The Twelve Pictures - Edith Simon   5857

Siena, Colombo De (Nobleman; Mercenary)
Chivalry - Rafael Sabatini   5548

Sigfrid (Mythical Creature; Warrior)
The Wolf and the Raven - Diana L. Paxson   4848

Sigifrith (Warrior)
Rhinegold - Stephan Grundy   2607

Sigismondo (Mercenary; Detective—Amateur)
Axe for an Abbot - Elizabeth Eyre   1989

Bravo for the Bride - Elizabeth Eyre   1990
Curtains for the Cardinal - Elizabeth Eyre   1991
Death of the Duchess - Elizabeth Eyre   1992

Sigismund (Young Man)
The Headsman; or, The Abbaye des Vignerons - James Fenimore Cooper   1300

Signy (Royalty)
The Iron Crown - Clare Barroll   354

Sigourney, Corbet (Student—College)
The Willing Maid - C.T. Ritchie   5349

Sigward (Knight)
The Morning Gift - Diana Norman   4645

Silana, Marcella (Young Woman)
The Second Crucifixion - Maurice Samuel   5579

Silkweb Empress (Ruler)
Bronze Mirror - Jeanne Larsen   3668

Sills, Lena (Child)
Words by Heart - Ouida Sebestyen   5713

Silva, Amador Flores da (Prospector)
Brazil - Errol Lincoln Uys   6395

Silver, Long John (Pirate)
The Adventures of Long John Silver - Denis Judd   3317
Return to Treasure Island - Denis Judd   3318

Silver, Long John (Pirate; Cook)
Treasure Island - Robert Louis Stevenson   6012

Silver Fox (Indian; Young Man)
Drums of Change: The Story of Running Fawn - Janette Oke   4707

Silver Knife (Murderer)
Anno-Dracula - Kim Newman   4595

Silverdale, Henrietta (Gentlewoman)
Charity Girl - Georgette Heyer   2879

Silverthorn, Alex (Immigrant; Businessman)
The Dream Seekers - Stephen Longstreet   3884

Sima (Indian; Teenager)
The Snake River - Winfred Blevins   547

Simmonds, Theresa (Actress)
A Marriage of Convenience - Tim Jeal   3172

Simo (Trader)
Woman of Andros - Thornton Wilder   6754

Simon of Cyrene (Adventurer)
Caravan to China - Frank Stanley Stuart   6085

Simon of Monleigh (Nobleman)
My Lord Monleigh - Jan Cox Speas   5957

Simon the Coldheart (Knight)
Simon the Coldheart - Georgette Heyer   2901

Simonetta (Gentlewoman)
The Lady in the Mask - Anne Green   2564

Simons, Andrew (Gentleman)
The Woman of Catawba - Hilda Stahl   5978

Simplicissimus (Farmer; Courtier)
Simplicissimus the Vagabond - J.J.C. Grimmelshausen   2594

Simpson, Loretta (Handicapped)
Comanche Moon - Catherine Anderson   137

Sims, Rafael (Military Personnel)
Ironclads: Man-of-War - Larry D. Names   4554

Sinan (Knight)
Alamut - Judith Tarr   6164

Sinclair, Cecily (Hotel Owner; Detective—Amateur)
Check-Out Time - Kate Kingsbury   3491
Do Not Disturb - Kate Kingsbury   3492
Eat, Drink, and Be Buried - Kate Kingsbury   3493
Grounds for Murder - Kate Kingsbury   3494
Room with a Clue - Kate Kingsbury   3495
Service for Two - Kate Kingsbury   3496

Sinclair, Clarissa (Spouse)
Montana! - Dana Fuller Ross 5479

Sinclair, Curtis (Gentleman)
Morning at Jalna - Mazo de la Roche 1560

Sinclair, Fiona (Actress)
So Near So Far - C. Northcote Parkinson 4814

Sinclair, Fiona (Gentlewoman; Ward)
The Miser of Mayfair - Marion Chesney 1038

Sinclair, Francis (Nobleman)
Legacy of the Wolf - Jean Raynes 5274

Sinclair, Julian (Nobleman; Widow(er))
Seduction - Amanda Quick 5220

Sinclair, Mary (Doctor)
The Healers - Henry Denker 1610

Sinclair, Matt (Gentleman)
Creature Comforts - Jessica Stirling 6041

Sinclair, Matthew (Fiance(e); Government Official)
Mandalay - Alexandra Jones 3269

Sinclair, Perdita (Heiress; Orphan)
Strathgallant - Laura Black 523

Sinclair, Roderick (Gentleman)
The Miser of Mayfair - Marion Chesney 1038

Singer, Jacob (Detective—Police)
The Dorothy Parker Murder Case - George Baxt 384
The Tallulah Bankhead Murder Case - George Baxt 389

Singer, Rachel (Young Woman)
Behold the Fire - Michael Blankfort 541

Singh, Jai (Ruler)
Raj - Gita Mehta 4325

Singh, Jaya (Royalty)
Raj - Gita Mehta 4325

Singing Brook (Indian; Spouse)
Mohawk Woman - Barbara Riefe 5329

Singing Wolf (Indian)
Thunderstick - Don Coldsmith 1190

Singing Wolf (Indian; Shaman)
Track of the Bear - Don Coldsmith 1191

Sinuhe (Doctor)
The Egyptian - Mika Waltari 6552

Sinyosoglou, Taomna (Young Woman)
America, America - Elia Kazan 3380

Sippy, Ben (Writer)
Anything for Billy - Larry McMurtry 4295

Sissingen, Klaus von (Sea Captain)
Magnificent Enemies - Edgar Maas 3951

Sitting Bear (Indian; Warrior)
Blood Fury - David Thompson 6252

Skaret, Kal (Immigrant; Farmer)
The Emigrants - Johan Bojer 561

Skelton, Jack (Artist)
The Days of the Butterfly - Norah Lofts 3841

Skiles, Ella (Spouse)
Peace at Bowling Green - Alfred Leland Crabb 1405

Skiles, Jacob (Settler)
Peace at Bowling Green - Alfred Leland Crabb 1405

Skiles, Rumsey (Landowner)
Peace at Bowling Green - Alfred Leland Crabb 1405

Skimmer of the Seas (Sea Captain; Pirate)
The Water Witch - James Fenimore Cooper 1311

Skinner, Miss (Gentlewoman)
The Mamur Zapt and the Spoils of Egypt - Michael Pearce 4871

Skinner, Caroline (Gentlewoman)
Liberty Tavern - Thomas Fleming 2129

Skinner, Joseph (Worker)
The Black Candle - Catherine Cookson 1273

Skshetuski, Pan Yan (Military Personnel)
With Fire and Sword - Henryk Sienkiewicz 5850

Sky-Eyes (Frontiersman)
The Flower in the Mountains - Don Coldsmith 1175
Medicine Knife - Don Coldsmith 1179

Sky-Eyes (Military Personnel; Frontiersman)
Return to the River - Don Coldsmith 1184

Sky Toucher (Indian; Spouse)
Mohawk Woman - Barbara Riefe 5329

Skye, Barnaby (Mountain Man)
The Far Tribes - Richard S. Wheeler 6658

Skylark, Jed (Journalist)
The Fortune Road - James McCague 4217

Slade, Captain (Military Personnel)
First Lieutenant - Kenneth Maynard 4208

Slade, Alice (Witch)
Malefice - Leslie Wilson 6810

Slade, Lurman (Sea Captain)
Captain Caution - Kenneth Roberts 5385

Slate, Lingston (Military Personnel)
The Devil Gun - William Syers 6148

Slater, Oliver (Sailor)
Long Pig - Russell Foreman 2168

Slaughter, Nathan (Trapper)
Nick of the Woods; or, The Jibbenainosay - Robert Montgomery Bird 505

Slocum, Martin (Farmer; Military Personnel)
The River and the Wilderness - Don Robertson 5401

Slover, Betsey (Teenager)
Scarlet Feather - Dale Van Every 6409

Slythe, Dorcas (Young Woman)
A Crowning Mercy - Susannah Kells 3396

Smale, Rebecca (Orphan)
The Clock Tower - Jeanne Montague 4435

Smart, Colonel Wiley (Trader)
Dodging Red Cloud - Richard S. Wheeler 6657

Smirnoff, Vladimir (Nobleman)
White Nights, Red Dawn - Frederick Nolan 4634

Smith, Adelaide (Orphan; Governess)
The Braganza Pursuit - Sarah Neilan 4564

Smith, Amanda (Gentlewoman; Runaway)
Sprig Muslin - Georgette Heyer 2903

Smith, Ann (Spouse)
The Smiths - Janet Fairbank 2002

Smith, Aymer (Businessman)
Signals of Distress - Jim Crace 1408

Smith, Buck (Leader)
Trail's End - Fred Bean 400

Smith, Bud (Teenager)
Mi Amigo - William R. Burnett 795

Smith, Calhoun (Young Man)
The Post of Honor - David Coxe Cooke 1266

Smith, Charlie (Teenager)
The Cowboys - William Dale Jennings 3211

Smith, Grace (Gentlewoman)
Return of the Stranger - Reay Tannahill 6158

Smith, Gypsy (Gunfighter; Lawman)
Children of the Dust - Carlile Clancy 1084

Smith, Honoria (Explorer; Traveller)
The Rake and the Rebel - Ira J. Morris 4478

Smith, Jed (Scout)
The Fancher Train - Amelia Bean 395

Smith, Jefferson (Businessman)
Tara Kane - George Markstein 4091

Smith, John (Frontiersman)
The Ladies of Missalonghi - Colleen McCullough 4237

Smith, John (Pilot)
The Near and Distant Place - Patricia Wright 6883

Smith, Laramie (Cowboy)
Three Rivers - Carla J. Mills 4406

Smith, Matthew (Artist; Writer)
The Millionaire's Daughter - Dorothy Eden 1858

Smith, Meg (Foundling; Streetperson)
The Street Sparrows - Rose Ayers 249

Smith, Moses (Criminal)
Sweet Songbird - Teresa Crane 1418

Smith, Nayland (Gentleman)
The Fires of Fu Manchu - Cay Van Ash 6399

Smith, Peter (Businessman)
The Smiths - Janet Fairbank 2002

Smith, Philadelphia (Heroine)
Miss Philadelphia Smith - Paula Allardyce 91

Smith, Raccoon John (Religious)
Raccoon John Smith - Louis Cochran 1145

Smith, Samuel (Doctor)
They Called Her Mrs. Doc - Janette Oke 4709

Smith, Tennessee (Veteran)
Tennessee Smith - James E. Hitt 2957

Smith, Theolic "Fireball" (Sports Figure)
The Veracruz Blues - Mark Winegardner 6821

Smithson, Charles (Gentleman)
The French Lieutenant's Woman - John Fowles 2194

Smollett, Arthur (Settler)
Courting Emma Howe - Margaret A. Robinson 5410

Snape, Rose (Young Woman)
Aurora Rose - Anne Worboys 6870

Sneferu (Military Personnel)
Children of the Lion - Peter Danielson 1464

Snow, Benjamin (Sea Captain)
Storm Signals - Joseph C. Lincoln 3785

Snow, Hester (Governess)
The Web of Days - Edna Lee 3708

Snow, Robert (Convict; Servant)
Pageant - G.B. Lancaster 3650

Soames, Horatio (Military Personnel)
Wolf in the Fold - Duncan MacNeil 4022

Sobieski, Thaddeus (Patriot; Military Personnel)
Thaddeus of Warsaw - Jane Porter 5136

Sohrakoff, Sergei (Adventurer)
The Bear Flag: A Novel of the Birth of California - Cecelia Holland 2983

Sokolovici, Mehmed Pasha (Ruler)
The Bridge on the Drina - Ivo Andric 151

Sokolow, Hannah Blau (Nurse; Midwife)
The Midwife's Advice - Gay Courter 1389

Solassier, Claude (Military Personnel)
French Dragoon - Roger Rudigoz 5523

Soledad (Indian)
Ghost Woman - Lawrence Thornton 6275

Soloman the Man (Musician)
Cry of the Peacock - Gina Barkhordar Nahai 4552

Solomon, Leonora (Young Woman)
Dreams of Gold - Lewis Orde 4748

Solomon, Nathan (Immigrant)
Dreams of Gold - Lewis Orde 4748

Somers, Martin (Military Personnel)
The Dark Rose - Maurice Walsh 6549

Somers, Richard (Nobleman)
Lord Richard's Passion - Mervyn Jones 3293

Somerset, Larla (Widow(er))
Midsummer Moon - Karen Lynn 3940

Somerset, Lady Leanna (Gentlewoman)
Lord Johnnie - Leslie Turner White 6687

Somerset, Pembroke (Military Personnel)
Thaddeus of Warsaw - Jane Porter 5136

Somervell (Nobleman)
Honor This Day - Alexander Kent 3432

Somerville, George (Businessman)
Honour and Obey - Malcolm Macdonald 3966

Somerville, Julia (Businesswoman)
Honour and Obey - Malcolm Macdonald 3966

Somerville, Philippa (Gentlewoman)
Checkmate - Dorothy Dunnett 1799
The Ringed Castle - Dorothy Dunnett 1807

Sommersett, Elizabeth (Noblewoman)
Lovestorm - Judith E. French 2222

Sommerville, Philip (Nobleman)
Back in Society - Marion Chesney 1017
Mrs. Budley Falls From Grace - Marion Chesney 1042
Sir Philip's Folly - Marion Chesney 1051

Sommerville, Robert (Professor)
The Intrigue - Marion Chesney 1034

Sompayac, Philippe (Gentleman; Doctor)
The Girl From Storyville: A Victorian Novel - Frank Yerby 6919

Sonseeahray (Indian)
Blood Brother - Elliott Arnold 190

Soo, Marta (Gentlewoman)
Manchu - Robert S. Elegant 1904

Sopwith, Mark (Gentleman)
Tilly - Catherine Cookson 1288

Sopwith, Matthew (Gentleman)
Tilly Wed - Catherine Cookson 1290

Sopwith, Tilly (Heroine)
Tilly Alone - Catherine Cookson 1289

Sorensen, Jan Carl (Naturalist; Pioneer)
Winds of Spring - Walter Havighurst 2776

Sorensen, Margretta (Spouse)
Winds of Spring - Walter Havighurst 2776

Sorrel, Hetty (Criminal)
Adam Bede - George Eliot 1908

Sorrel, Jannie (Dancer)
Lovers Meeting - Mollie Hardwick 2695

Sorrell, William (Publisher)
Ladies Whose Bright Eyes - Ford Madox Ford 2162

Sosepsis (Indian; Warrior)
Indian Brother - Hubert Coryell 1354

Sosylos (Slave)
Hannibal of Carthage - Mary Dolan 1686

South Wind (Indian; Young Woman)
World of Silence - Don Coldsmith 1195

Southampton, James (Military Personnel)
The Captives - Don Wright 6878

Southey, William (Gentleman)
Evil Mark - Graham Miles 4377

Southfarer, Niall (Sailor; Prisoner)
The Price of Blood - Doris Sutcliffe Adams 24

Southgate, John (Settler; Immigrant)
Wild Dog Running - Alan Scholefield 5658

Southwick, Silence (Businesswoman; Widow(er))
Portrait of Emma - Lillian Cheatham 1010

Southwind (Indian)
Song of the Rock - Don Coldsmith 1189

Spangler, Sir Guy (Gentleman)
Sir Rogue - Leslie Turner White 6691

Spangler, Warren (Journalist)
The Year of the Spaniard - Henry Castor 956

Spargo, Peter (Military Personnel)
Yorktown - Burke Davis 1513

Sparks, Jack (Detective—Private)
The Six Messiahs - Mark Frost 2238

Sparks, Jim (Government Official)
The List of Seven - Mark Frost 2237

Speaks-Not (Indian; Handicapped)
World of Silence - Don Coldsmith 1195

Spector, Sarah Levy (Labor Organizer)
Union Square - Meredith Tax 6176

Speed, Billy Joe (Sports Figure)
The Fast Men - Tom McNab 4302

Speigner, Max (Military Personnel; Linguist)
Rommel and the Rebel - Lawrence Wells 6622

Spence, Frances O'Riordan (Settler)
The Settlers - William Stuart Long 3878

Spencer, C. Jamieson (Journalist)
Dance on a Sinking Ship - Michael Kilian 3483

Spencer, Caledonia (Young Woman)
Sister Wives - Cleo Jones 3270

Spencer, Caroline (Gentlewoman)
Castle Heritage - Elisabeth Barr 337

Spencer, Christabel (Socialite; Noblewoman)
The Millionaire's Daughter - Dorothy Eden 1858

Spencer, Connie (Young Woman)
Sister Wives - Cleo Jones 3270

Spencer, Hugh (Servant; Military Personnel)
Scoundrels' Brigade - Carter A. Vaughan 6439

Spencer, Susan (Servant)
The Woodsman - Don Wright 6880

Spenser, Dorcas (Young Woman)
Something Gleamed - Theda Kenyon 3463

Sperling, Arabella (Gentlewoman)
The Storms of Fate - Patricia Wright 6885

Spiggy (Worker)
The Queen and I - Sue Townsend 6306

Spilsbury, Harriet (Sea Captain)
Yankee Woman - Frederic Baume 381

Spitama, Cyrus (Diplomat)
Creation - Gore Vidal 6486

Spoon (Indian; Guide)
Spoon - John Christgau 1074

Spotted Calf (Indian; Chieftain)
Warriors of the Night - Kerry Newcomb 4594

Spotted Wolf (Indian)
Yellowhorse - Dee Brown 715

Sprague, Fitz (Journalist)
Ever After - Elswyth Thane 6216

Sprague, Lucy (Young Woman)
In a Dark Garden - Frank G. Slaughter 5891

Sprague, Melissa (Young Woman)
Wings of the Morning - Frederic F. Van de Water 6404

Sprat (Orphan)
Playing the Jack - Mary Brown 726

Spring Moon (Young Woman)
Spring Moon: A Novel of China - Bette Bao Lord 3897

Spurlock, Clay (Oil Industry Worker)
Fort Worth - Leonard Sanders 5588

Spurlock, Travis (Lawyer; Political Figure)
Fort Worth - Leonard Sanders 5588

Spurlock, Vern (Military Personnel)
Fort Worth - Leonard Sanders 5588

Squire, The (Smuggler)
Kate - Brian Cleeve 1109

Stacey, Ajax (Young Man)
The Golden Feather - Theda Kenyon 3462

Stacey, Gerald (Young Man)
The Golden Feather - Theda Kenyon 3462

Stacey, Gilbert (Actor)
Charing Cross - Claire Rayner 5260

Stacey, Sedley (Religious)
Cousin Susannah - Hazel Hucker 3066

Stachel, Bruno (Military Personnel; Pilot)
The Blood Order - Jack D. Hunter 3084
The Blue Max - Jack D. Hunter 3085

Stacy, Louise (Gentlewoman)
Silver Fruit - Patricia Campbell 876

Stafford, Bard (Businessman; Adventurer)
The Midnight Gun - Berkely Mather 4180

Stafford, Charles (Settler)
Mists of Heaven - Yvonne Kalman 3325

Stafford, Emily (Immigrant)
The Brahmins - Eileen Lottman 3901

Stafford, Gwynne (Spouse)
Mists of Heaven - Yvonne Kalman 3325

Stafford, Jack (Journalist)
Annapolis - William Martin 4137

Stafford, James (Military Personnel)
Annapolis - William Martin 4137

Stafford, John (Abolitionist)
The Father - Katharine Holland Brown 724

Stafford, Kate (Gentlewoman)
The Brahmins - Eileen Lottman 3901

Stafford, Linnie (Settler)
The Lieutenant's Lady - Bess Streeter Aldrich 70

Stafford, Maury (Military Personnel)
The Long Roll - Mary Johnston 3236

Stafford, Melissa (Young Woman)
Montana Road - Harry Sinclair Drago 1717

Stafford, Neil (Convict; Highwayman)
The Pagoda Tree - Berkely Mather 4181

Stafford, Nicholas (Nobleman)
A Knight in Shining Armor - Jude Deveraux 1631

Stafford, Norman (Military Personnel)
The Lieutenant's Lady - Bess Streeter Aldrich 70

Stafford, Ross (Businessman)
The Midnight Gun - Berkely Mather 4180

Stafford, Ross (Orphan)
The Pagoda Tree - Berkely Mather 4181

Stafford, Samuel (Judge)
Farriers' Lane - Anne Perry 4930

Stafford, Sarah (Patriot)
The Brahmins - Eileen Lottman 3901

Stahl, Egron (Farmer)
The Rainbird - Sara Lidman 3780

Stahl, Freddie (Military Personnel)
The Moon-Eyed Appaloosa - Bill Gulick 2617

Stahl, Hanna (Spouse)
The Rainbird - Sara Lidman 3780

Stahl, Linda (Young Woman)
The Rainbird - Sara Lidman 3780

Stair, Diana (Widow(er); Abolitionist)
Diana Stair - Floyd Dell 1594

Stalker, Andrew (Lawyer)
The Dark Pasture - Jessica Stirling 6042

Stalker, Andrew (Student)
Call Home the Heart - Jessica Stirling 6040

Stalker, Merrin (Young Woman)
Call Home the Heart - Jessica Stirling 6040

Stanbroke, Lady Elizabeth (Noblewoman)
The Stanbroke Girls - Fiona Hill 2925

Stanbroke, Lady Isabella (Noblewoman)
The Stanbroke Girls - Fiona Hill 2925

Standen, Freddy (Gentleman)
Cotillion - Georgette Heyer 2883

Standing Elk (Indian)
Arrest Sitting Bull - Douglas C. Jones 3273

Standing-in-the-Doorway (Indian; Shaman)
The Dark Way - Robert J. Conley 1241
The Way of the Priests - Robert J. Conley 1253

Standish, Francesca (Southern Belle)
From Fields of Gold - Alexandra Ripley 5339

Standish, Sarah (Actress)
Daughters of England - Philippa Carr 919

Stands with a Fist (Indian; Young Woman)
Dances with Wolves - Michael Blake 537

Stangeway, Evelyn (Gentlewoman)
Twilight of the Dragon - Peter Bourne 596

Stanhope, Abigail (Spouse)
The Bondswoman - Caryl Ledner 3705

Stanhope, Burke (Gentleman)
American Eden - Marilyn Harris 2728
The Women of Eden - Marilyn Harris 2734

Stanhope, Eliza (Gentlewoman)
Eliza Stanhope - Joanna Trollope 6347

Stanhope, Eve (Actress)
American Eden - Marilyn Harris 2728
Eden and Honor - Marilyn Harris 2729

Stanhope, Mary Eden (Gentlewoman)
American Eden - Marilyn Harris 2728

Stanhope, Quentin (Military Personnel)
Irene at Large - Carole Nelson Douglas 1700

Stanhope, Robert (Farmer)
The Bondswoman - Caryl Ledner 3705

Stanton, Andrew (Government Official)
The Jade Alliance - Elizabeth Darrell 1497

Stanton, Dick (Sailor; Convict)
Swandowne - Daniel Farson 2024

Stanton, Jethro (Military Personnel)
Drums of War - Roy Clews 1114

Stanton, Jethro (Worker)
The Valiant and the Daunted - Roy Clews 1115

Stanton, Peter (Labor Organizer; Worker)
The Valiant and the Daunted - Roy Clews 1115

Stanton, Sarah (Spouse)
Drums of War - Roy Clews 1114

Stanton-Lacy, Sophia (Gentlewoman)
The Grand Sophy - Georgette Heyer 2891

Staple, John (Military Personnel)
The Toll-Gate - Georgette Heyer 2907

Staples, Peter (Young Man)
The Highwayman - Noel B. Gerson 2372

Stapleton, Cynthia Legrand (Spouse)
The Spoils of War - Thomas Fleming 2131

Stapleton, Jonathan (Veteran; Businessman)
The Spoils of War - Thomas Fleming 2131

Stapleton, Rawdon (Businessman; Military Personnel)
The Spoils of War - Thomas Fleming 2131

Star Shell (Indian)
People of the Lakes - W. Michael Gear 2336

Starbuck, Elial (Religious)
Battle Flag - Bernard Cornwell 1333

Starbuck, Jason (Frontiersman; Adventurer)
Yankee Pasha - Edison Marshall 4115

Starbuck, Nate (Military Personnel)
Battle Flag - Bernard Cornwell 1333
The Bloody Ground - Bernard Cornwell 1334
Copperhead - Bernard Cornwell 1335
Rebel - Bernard Cornwell 1336

Starbuck, Stephen (Sailor)
Nantucket Rebel - Edouard A. Stackpole 5970

Stark, Beau (Young Man)
The Road to Baltimore - Robert S. Harper 2716

Stark, Sarah (Young Woman)
The Pumpkin Rollers - Elmer Kelton 3406

Starke, Jake (Mountain Man)
Maximilian's Gold - Jane Barry 359

Starke, Melissa (Young Woman)
Melissa Starke - Annulet Andrews 145

Starkweather, Belle (Gentlewoman)
Cedarhaven - Patricia Campbell 874

Starkweather, Darrie (Gentlewoman)
Cedarhaven - Patricia Campbell 874

Starkweather, Genia (Gentlewoman)
Cedarhaven - Patricia Campbell 874

Starkweather, Howard Harrison (Financier)
The Bank - Stephen Longstreet 3882

Starkweather, Tyler (Financier; Heir)
The Bank - Stephen Longstreet 3882

Starmont, Giles (Gentleman)
The Long Day Closes - Beatrice Tunstall 6360

Starr, Amantha (Slave; Orphan)
Band of Angels - Robert Penn Warren 6572

Starr, Charlotte (Young Woman)
Castle of Doves - Constance Heaven 2803

Starr, Ellery (Veteran; Journalist)
Roll, Shenandoah - Bruce Lancaster 3644

Starr, Mirabell (Gypsy; Actress)
Rogue Herries - Hugh Walpole 6547

Starr, Padraic (Patriot; Revolutionary)
The Rising of the Moon - William Martin 4140

Staunton, Will (Sea Captain; Adventurer)
The Quickenberry Tree - Annette Motley 4502

Stavan (Warrior; Prehistoric Human)
The Year the Horses Came - Mary Mackey 3993

Stavely, Cressida (Gentlewoman)
False Colours - Georgette Heyer 2886

Stavenham, John (Military Personnel)
That Sweet and Savage Land - Emma Drummond 1728

Staverton, Georgina (Gentlewoman)
The Sandalwood Fan - Diana Brown 720

Steane, Cherry (Ward)
Charity Girl - Georgette Heyer 2879

Stedman, Kirk (Military Personnel)
Night March - Bruce Lancaster 3641

Steed, Edmund (Settler)
Chesapeake - James A. Michener 4367

Steel, Matthew (Sea Captain)
Praise at Morning - Mildred Masterson McNeilly 4310

Steele, Bluford "Blue" (Actor)
The Actor - Robert J. Conley 1236

Steele, Bluford "Blue" (Lawman)
Killing Time - Robert J. Conley 1244

Steele, John (Doctor)
Time in Its Flight - Susan Fromberg Schaeffer 5636

Steele, Mandrake (Slave)
A Promise Unbroken - Al Lacy 3582

Steele, Web (Military Personnel)
A Promise Unbroken - Al Lacy 3582

Steele, Will (Gentleman)
Chase the Heart - Maggie Osborne 4760

Steinfinnsdatter, Ingunn (Fiance(e))
The Axe - Sigrid Undset 6378

Steinfinnsdatter, Ingunn (Noblewoman)
The Snake Pit - Sigrid Undset 6383

Steinsson, Steiner (Farmer; Immigrant)
Paradise Reclaimed - Halldor Laxness 3686

Stenhouse, Helen (Spouse)
Whitton's Folly - Pamela Hill 2948

Stenrood, Gilbert (Doctor)
Bright to the Wanderer - Bruce Lancaster 3638

Stephen (Royalty)
The Vision of Stephen: An Elegy - Lolah Burford 775

Stephenson, Leslie John (Murderer; Doctor)
Time After Time - Karl Alexander 80

Steppleton, Charlotte (Southern Belle)
Old Miss - Thomas Campbell 877

Sterling, Amanda (Noblewoman; Spy)
Love Not a Rebel - Heather Graham 2516

Sterling, Will (Settler)
A Durable Fire - Virginia Bernhard 480

Stern, Delphi (Artist)
Triptych - Dora Landey 3652

Sternes, Jeremy (Publisher)
The Dedicated - Willa Gibbs 2399

Sternwood, Carmen (Young Woman)
Perchance to Dream - Robert B. Parker 4807

Stevens, Emily (Young Woman)
For Love and Honor - Antonia Van-Loon 6423

Stevens, Melisande (Orphan; Immigrant)
Storm Before Sunrise - June Wyndham Davies 1507

Stevens, Morrison (Military Personnel)
And Wait for the Night - John William Corrington 1352

Stevens, Serena (Orphan)
The Yukon Queen - Gilbert Morris 4476

Stevens, Timothy Duncan (Editor)
A Voice in the Streets - John William Tebbel 6196

Stevenson, Abigail (Gentlewoman)
Abigail - Malcolm Macdonald 3962

Stevenson, Boy (Gentleman)
Sons of Fortune - Malcolm Macdonald 3973

Stevenson, Caspar (Gentleman)
Sons of Fortune - Malcolm Macdonald 3973

Stevenson, Emma (Spouse)
Kimberley - Colin Burke 784

Stevenson, Geoffrey (Military Personnel)
Kimberley - Colin Burke 784

Stevenson, John (Businessman)
The Rich Are with You Always - Malcolm Macdonald 3971
The World From Rough Stones - Malcolm Macdonald 3979

Stevenson, Nora (Businesswoman)
The Rich Are with You Always - Malcolm Macdonald 3971

Stevenson, Nora (Worker; Businesswoman)
The World From Rough Stones - Malcolm Macdonald 3979

Steward, Benjamin (Time Traveller)
The Lincoln Hunters - Wilson Tucker 6359

Stewart, Beth (Orphan; Artist)
To Love a Stranger - Barbara Paul 4839

Stewart, Christian (Gentleman)
The Game of Kings - Dorothy Dunnett 1801

Stewart, Duncan (Doctor)
Drums of Destiny - Peter Bourne 593

Stewart, Ebenezer (Military Personnel)
The Peculiar People - Jan de Hartog 2764

Stewart, Eleanor (Servant; Lesbian)
Death Wore a Diadem - Iona McGregor 4277

Stewart, Eugene (Explorer)
Victim of the Aurora - Thomas Keneally 3417

Stewart, Henry (Journalist)
The Bluestocking - David Delman 1598

Stewart, Ian (Young Man)
The Dark Mile - Dorothy Kathleen Broster 709

Stewart, Jamie Lynne (Young Woman)
The Eleventh Year - Monique Raphel High 2914

Stewart, Ling (Hunter; Mountain Man)
The Land Is Bright - James Arthur Kjelgaard 3508

Stewart, Marie Jamesina Sibella (Gentlewoman)
The Black Duchess - Alanna Knight 3514

Stewart, Minerva (Architect)
The House on Curtin Street - Millie J. Ragosta 5242

Stewart, Moonfeather Leah (Indian; Noblewoman)
Moonfeather - Judith E. French 2223

Stewart, Scott Shallenberger (Businessman)
Thine Is the Glory - Samuel A. Schreiner Jr. 5672

Stewart, Tavis (Nobleman)
The Spitfire - Bertrice Small 5912

Stewart, Tom (Veteran)
Gentlemen, Hush! - Jere Hungerford
    Wheelwright 6668

Stieger, Karl (Mercenary)
Blackrobe - Robert E. Wall 6534
Bloodbrothers - Robert E. Wall 6535

Stiles, W.H. (Political Figure)
Before Darkness Falls - Eugenia Price 5178

Stillman, Anna (Captive)
A Time in the Sun - Jane Barry 361

Stock, Joan (Spouse; Detective—Amateur)
The Bartholomew Fair Murders - Leonard
    Tourney 6297
Familiar Spirits - Leonard Tourney 6298
Frobisher's Savage - Leonard Tourney 6299
Knaves Templar - Leonard Tourney 6300
Low Treason - Leonard Tourney 6301
Old Saxon Blood - Leonard Tourney 6302
The Players' Boy Is Dead - Leonard Tourney 6303
Witness of Bones - Leonard Tourney 6304

Stock, Matthew (Businessman; Government
    Official)
The Bartholomew Fair Murders - Leonard
    Tourney 6297
Familiar Spirits - Leonard Tourney 6298
Frobisher's Savage - Leonard Tourney 6299
Knaves Templar - Leonard Tourney 6300
Low Treason - Leonard Tourney 6301
Old Saxon Blood - Leonard Tourney 6302
The Players' Boy Is Dead - Leonard Tourney 6303
Witness of Bones - Leonard Tourney 6304

Stockdale, Lynn (Young Woman)
Night March - Bruce Lancaster 3641

Stockton, Edward (Sailor)
Letter of Marque - Andrew Hepburn 2849

Stockwell, Gordon (Businessman)
Sunrise to Sunset - Samuel Hopkins Adams 32

Stoddard, Roxanne Darragh (Young Woman)
Stars and Stripes - Adam Rutledge 5541

Stokes, Annabelle (Gentlewoman)
Jubilee Jim and the Wizard of Wall Street - Donald
    Porter 5112

Stokes, Sally (Prostitute; Thief)
A Broken Vessel - Kate Ross 5500

Stokes, Timothy (Entertainer)
Peter Doyle - John Vernon 6457

Stoltz, Amelia (Settler)
Spring Came on Forever - Bess Streeter Aldrich 73

Stone (Artisan)
Isle of Woman - Piers Anthony 167

Stone, Caleb (Sea Captain)
The Great Alone - Janet Dailey 1454

Stone, David (Lawyer)
Bates House - Clarence Benadum 437

Stone, Jeremy (Artisan; Imposter)
The Imposter - Noel B. Gerson 2375

Stone, Michael (Doctor)
Golden Isle - Frank G. Slaughter 5890

Stonecipher, Jacob (Mountain Man)
The Arkansas River - Jory Sherman 5816

Stonecutter (Indian)
The Children of the First Man - James Alexander
    Thom 6230

Stonecypher, Elizabeth (Settler)
Give Us This Valley - Tom Ham 2666

Stonecypher, George Washington (Settler)
Give Us This Valley - Tom Ham 2666

Stonefield, Caleb (Gentleman)
Cain and His Brother - Anne Perry 4922

Stonefield, Genevieve (Gentlewoman)
Cain and His Brother - Anne Perry 4922

Stopford, Anthony (Prospector)
The Golden Fool - David Divine 1649

Storey, Frederick Seaton (Hunter)
Lion in the Evening - Alan Scholefield 5656

Storey, Margaret (Young Woman)
Lion in the Evening - Alan Scholefield 5656

Storm, Arthur (Sailor)
The Greenlander - Mark Adlard 38

Storm, Caleb (Frontiersman; Indian)
Sunflower - Jill Marie Landis 3653

Storm, Jayce (Military Personnel)
Defiant Hearts - Janelle Taylor 6185

Storm, Valerie (Southern Belle)
Storm Haven - Frank G. Slaughter 5903

Stornaway, Nell (Heroine)
The Toll-Gate - Georgette Heyer 2907

Story, John (Engineer)
The Buckingham Palace Connection - Ted
    Willis 6792

Stowe, Augustus (Gentleman; Landowner)
Swandowne - Daniel Farson 2024

Stowe, Poland (Gentleman)
Swandowne - Daniel Farson 2024

Stowe, Sarah (Gentlewoman)
Swandowne - Daniel Farson 2024

Stowell, Captain (Military Personnel)
The Gray Captain - Jere Hungerford
    Wheelwright 6669

Strake, Eric (Sea Captain)
The Happy Parrot - Robert W. Chambers 977

Strand, Charity (Gentlewoman)
Sanguinet's Crown - Patricia Veryan 6476

Strand, Justin (Gentleman)
Married Past Redemption - Patricia Veryan 6469

Strand, Rachel (Fiance(e))
Feather Castles - Patricia Veryan 6462

Strang, Davy (Young Man)
His Majesty's Yankees - Thomas H. Raddall 5230

Strange, Christopher (Lawyer; Political Figure)
Christopher Strange - Ruth Eleanor McKee 4281

Stratford, Julie (Young Woman)
The Mummy; or Ramses the Damned - Anne
    Rice 5315

Stratford, Sir Philip (Nobleman)
Street of the Madwoman - Isabel Ortega 4756

Strathy, Lady Dorothy (Noblewoman)
Death En Voyage - Richard Grayson 2557

Straton (Sea Captain)
*The Purple Quest: A Novel of Seafaring Adventure in
    the Ancient World* - Frank G. Slaughter 5896

Stratton, Sebastian (Nobleman)
Ruby - Helen Ashfield 213

Straun, Tess (Businesswoman; Trader)
Gai-Jin: A Novel of Japan - James Clavell 1100

Strauss, Rudi (Outcast; Wanderer)
To the Land of the Cattails - Aharon Appelfeld 179

Strauss, Toni (Outcast; Wanderer)
To the Land of the Cattails - Aharon Appelfeld 179

Stretton, Maud (Gentlewoman)
Murder, I Presume - Gillian Linscott 3807

Strickland, Clive (Lawyer; Writer)
Scandal at High Chimneys: A Victorian Melodrama -
    John Dickson Carr 915

Strickland, Thomas (Artist)
Until the Colors Fade - Tim Jeal 3173

Striecher, Paul (Spy)
The Man on the Train - W.J. Chaput 995

Striker, Frederick (Rake)
Shadows on the Shore - Jessica Stirling 6048

Strong, Charity (Gentlewoman)
Charity Strong - Marguerite Allis 109

Strong, Leon Marshall (Military Personnel)
The Three Days - Don Robertson 5402

Strong, Mama (Settler; Widow(er))
White Rising - Zane Kotker 3548

Strong Bow (Indian; Guide)
Return of the Spanish - Don Coldsmith 1183

Stroud, George (Mountain Man; Trapper)
Chant of the Hawk - John Harris 2720

Strozzi, Clarice (Model)
Divine Mistress - Frank G. Slaughter 5886

Struan, Dirk (Businessman; Trader)
Tai-Pan - James Clavell 1102

Struan, Malcolm (Businessman; Trader)
Gai-Jin: A Novel of Japan - James Clavell 1100

Stryker, Nick (Adventurer)
Glittering Hill - Clyde Francis Murphy 4520

Stuart, Charles (Fugitive)
The White Cockade - Henry Farrand Griffin 2592

Stuart, Charles (Gentleman)
The Street Sparrows - Rose Ayers 249

Stuart, Cullen (Police Officer)
North Star Conspiracy - Miriam Grace
    Monfredo 4428
Seneca Falls Inheritance - Miriam Grace
    Monfredo 4429

Stuart, Francis (Gentlewoman)
Lady on the Coin - Margaret Campbell Barnes 326

Stuart, James (Military Personnel)
Temple Bells - Marjorie McEvoy 4271

Stuart, Jamie (Patriot; Military Personnel)
The Proud and the Free - Howard Fast 2042

Stuart, Jane (Young Woman)
Bed in Hell - Elfrida Vipont 6504

Stuart, Margot (Gentlewoman)
Let the King Beware! - Honore Morrow 4489

Stuart, Tom (Shipowner)
The Stuart Women - Matt Braun 652

Stuart, the Blade (Indian)
The Proud and the Free - Janet Dailey 1456

Sturrock, Jeremy (Detective—Police)
Captain Bolton's Corpse - J.G. Jeffreys 3178
The Pangersbourne Murders - J.G. Jeffreys 3179
The Thieftaker - J.G. Jeffreys 3180
The Thistlewood Plot - J.G. Jeffreys 3181
A Wicked Way to Die - J.G. Jeffreys 3182

Su-Mei (Young Woman)
Shanghai - Christopher New 4588

Sudden, Roger (Adventurer)
Roger Sudden - Thomas H. Raddall 5232

Sueer, Abbe (Religious)
Death Comes as Epiphany - Sharan Newman 4598

Sullivan, Luke (Doctor)
Katherine - Antonia Van-Loon 6425
Sunshine and Shadow - Antonia Van-Loon 6426

Sullivan, Matt (Engineer)
The Silver Highways - Malcolm Macdonald 3972

Sullivan, Tracy (Young Woman)
Sunshine and Shadow - Antonia Van-Loon 6426

Summerbee, Kate (Young Woman)
Sea Change - Alison McLeay 4287

Summerfield, Pamela (Gentlewoman)
Princess Pamela - Ray Russell 5534

Summerfield, Phoebe (Gentlewoman)
Princess Pamela - Ray Russell 5534

Summers, Dick (Frontiersman; Guide)
The Way West - A.B. Guthrie Jr. 2628

Summers, Dick (Mountain Man)
The Big Sky - A.B. Guthrie Jr. 2624

Summers, Dick (Mountain Man; Guide)
Fair Land, Fair Land - A.B. Guthrie Jr. 2625

Summers, Gail (Nurse)
The Rough Rider - Gilbert Morris 4468

Summers, Harry (Gentleman)
Sara - Brian Cleeve 1110

Sun Horse (Indian; Chieftain)
The Snowblind Moon - John Byrne Cooke 1267

Sun Runner (Indian; Warrior)
Song of the Cheyenne - Jory Sherman 5822

Sunchaser (Prehistoric Human; Shaman)
People of the Sea - W. Michael Gear 2339

Sunday (Indian)
Pemmican - Vardis Fisher 2111

Sunday, Billy (Orphan; Teenager)
Billy Sunday - Rod Jones 3295

Sundown, Jacques (Indian; Lawman)
Blackwater Spirits - Miriam Grace Monfredo 4427

Sung Wing On (Worker)
Lotus Land - Monica Highland 2917

Sunil (Servant)
The Barrier - Robin Maugham 4195

Sunu (Warrior)
The Shining King - Peter Danielson 1476
Triumph of the Lion - Peter Danielson 1478

Surriage, Agnes (Ward)
Be My Love - Harriet Hinsdale 2955

Susannah (Frontierswoman; Fiance(e))
Where the River Runs - Richard S. Wheeler 6664

Sutbury, Felix (Nobleman)
The Sutburys - Pamela Hill 2944

Sutbury, Guy (Gentleman)
The Sutburys - Pamela Hill 2944

Sutcliffe, Miriam (Gentlewoman; Fugitive)
Visions of a Heart - Emily Carmichael 899

Sutherland, Clay (Gambler)
Masque of Jade - Emma Merritt 4344

Sutherland, Jenny (Gentlewoman)
Rainbird's Revenge - Marion Chesney 1046

Sutherland, Joseph (Military Personnel)
A Token of Jewels - Diane Cory 1353

Sutpen, Thomas (Plantation Owner)
Absalom, Absalom! - William Faulkner 2049

Sutton (Prospector; Entertainer)
Seven Rivers West - Edward Hoagland 2959

Sutton, Brandon (Businessman)
Proud Mary - Iris Gower 2501

Sutton, Claire (Gentlewoman)
Two Corinthians - Carola Dunn 1797

Sutton, John (Farmer)
The Two Farms - Mary E. Pearce 4865

Sutton, Martyn (Settler)
The Lost Colony - Edison Marshall 4108

Sutton, Paul (Doctor)
Pilgrims in Paradise - Frank G. Slaughter 5895

Sutton, Silas (Leader; Zealot)
Pilgrims in Paradise - Frank G. Slaughter 5895

Svenson (Sailor)
Runestone - Don Coldsmith 1186

Swain, Alfred (Detective—Police)
Jekyll, Alias Hyde - Donald Thomas 6240
The Ripper's Apprentice - Donald Thomas 6242

Swain, David (Sailor)
Thread of Scarlet - Ben Ames Williams 6767

Swann, Adam (Businessman)
God Is an Englishman - R.F. Delderfield 1587
Theirs Was the Kingdom - R.F. Delderfield 1590

Swann, Adam (Veteran; Businessman)
Give Us This Day - R.F. Delderfield 1586

Swann, Alexander (Military Personnel)
Give Us This Day - R.F. Delderfield 1586

Swann, George (Businessman)
Theirs Was the Kingdom - R.F. Delderfield 1590

Swann, Giles (Businessman)
Give Us This Day - R.F. Delderfield 1586

Swann, Henrietta (Spouse)
Theirs Was the Kingdom - R.F. Delderfield 1590

Swanson, Nat (Fugitive)
St. Agnes' Stand - Tom Eidson 1900

Swanton, Julia (Orphan)
French Slippers - Deborah Chester 1055

Swardovsky, Alexander (Military Personnel)
The Gathering Wolves - Elizabeth Darrell 1496

Sweete, Shadrach (Mountain Man)
Cry of the Hawk - Terry C. Johnston 3248

Swenk, Vannie (Young Woman)
The Golden Lady - Dorothy Gardiner 2283

Swift (Prehistoric Human; Hunter)
The Animal Wife - Elizabeth Marshall Thomas 6243
Reindeer Moon - Elizabeth Marshall Thomas 6244

Swille, Arthur (Plantation Owner)
Flight to Canada - Ishmael Reed 5285

Swinbrooke, Kathryn (Detective—Amateur; Scientist)
The Book of Shadows - C.L. Grace 2505
The Eye of God - C.L. Grace 2506
The Merchant of Death - C.L. Grace 2508
A Shrine of Murders - C.L. Grace 2509

Sybil (Gentlewoman)
King of the Wood - Valerie Anand 131

Sybilla-Marie (Royalty)
A Finger to Her Lips - Evelyn Berckman 472

Sykes, Jenny (Young Woman)
The Trial of Jenny Sykes - Hebe Weenolsen 6598

Symon, Thomas (Student—College)
Falconer's Crusade - Ian Morson 4493

Syon, Anne de (Young Woman)
The Winter Rose - Millie J. Ragosta 5243

T

Ta-Na (Indian; Teenager)
Father and Son - Donald Clayton Porter 5117

Tacara-Mi (Royalty)
The Last Princess - Charles O. Locke 3826

Tacios (Young Man)
The Last Princess - Charles O. Locke 3826

Tacs (Military Personnel)
The Death of Attila - Cecelia Holland 2986

Tada Shom (Doctor)
Yedo - Lynn Guest 2609

Tadlock (Settler)
The Way West - A.B. Guthrie Jr. 2628

Tagart (Warrior; Prehistoric Human)
The Flint Lord - Richard Herley 2857
The Stone Arrow - Richard Herley 2858

Taggart, Jenny (Settler; Farmer)
The Settlers - William Stuart Long 3878

Tagiwara, Yusa (Artist)
Bronze Christ - Yoshiro Nagaya 4551

Tai Ming Kwong (Immigrant; Businessman)
The House That Tai Ming Built - Virginia Lee 3711

Taita (Slave)
River God - Wilbur Smith 5928

Talasi (Indian)
Creek Mary's Blood - Dee Brown 712

Talbot, Aubrey (Gentleman)
Bury Him Among Kings - Elleston Trevor 6341

Talbot, Edmund (Gentleman)
Close Quarters - William Golding 2453
Fire Down Below - William Golding 2454
Rites of Passage - William Golding 2456

Talbot, Holly (Spy)
Dragon Cove - Carter A. Vaughan 6434

Talbot, Victor (Military Personnel)
Bury Him Among Kings - Elleston Trevor 6341

Talbot-Harrow, Judith (Businesswoman)
Masque of Sapphire - Deana James 3156

Talbot-Harrow, Laura (Debutante; Gentlewoman)
Masque of Jade - Emma Merritt 4344

Talbott, Ike (Cowboy)
Filaree: A Novel of an American Life - Marguerite Noble 4633

Talbott, Miriam (Young Woman)
Panama - Eric Zencey 6959

Talburt, Wyck (Sea Captain; Blockade Runner)
Sail the Dark Tide - Davenport Steward 6017

Talcott, Aurora (Young Woman)
The Wings of the Morning - Thomas Tryon 6356

Talcott, Ray (Young Man)
Bitter Creek - Al Cody 1150

Taliafero, Vivian (Socialite)
Murder in the Rose Garden - Elliott Roosevelt 5452

Taliesin (Minstrel)
Taliesin - Stephen R. Lawhead 3683

Taliesin (Royalty)
A Royal Quest - Mary Lide 3777

Tall Bird (Indian)
Distant Trails - Bill Gulick 2612
Gathering Storm - Bill Gulick 2613
Lost Wallowa - Bill Gulick 2616

Tall Bull (Indian; Chieftain)
Eyes of Eagles - William W. Johnstone 3266

Tall Bull (Indian; Warrior)
Bride of the Morning Star - Don Coldsmith 1170

Tall One (Indian)
Trail of the Spanish Bit - Don Coldsmith 1193

Tallack, Brice (Fisherman)
Polsinney Harbour - Mary E. Pearce 4863

Tallack, Gus (Fisherman)
Polsinney Harbour - Mary E. Pearce 4863

Tallant, Arabella (Gentlewoman)
Arabella - Georgette Heyer 2874

Tallant, Hugh (Convict)
Botany Bay - Charles Nordhoff 4637

Tallboys, Godfrey (Knight)
The Homecoming - Norah Lofts 3844
Knight's Acre - Norah Lofts 3848

Tallboys, Henry (Landowner)
The Lonely Furrow - Norah Lofts 3849

Tallboys, Sybilla (Spouse)
The Homecoming - Norah Lofts 3844
Knight's Acre - Norah Lofts 3848

Tallentire, John (Worker)
The Hired Man - Melvyn Bragg 639

Talleyman, Thomas (Military Personnel)
Talleyman - John James 3161

Tallien, Jean-Lambert (Revolutionary)
Harp of a Thousand Strings - Harold Lenoir
   Davis 1522

Talmadge, Ambrose (Gentleman)
Somewhere Within This House - Jean Francis
   Webb 6587

Talmadge, Nicholas (Gentleman)
A Place of Ravens - Pamela Hill 2942

Talon, Emily (Rancher)
Ride the Dark Trail - Louis L'Amour 3624

Talon, Jean (Frontiersman)
Rivers West - Louis L'Amour 3626

Talon, Milo (Outlaw)
The Man From Broken Hills - Louis L'Amour 3622

Talus (Warrior)
Prophets and Warriors - Peter Danielson 1473

Talvace, Harry (Artist)
The Heaven Tree Trilogy - Edith Pargeter 4797

Talvas (Nobleman; Landowner)
The Lost Lands - Peter Vansittart 6430

Tamar (Noblewoman; Heiress)
Tamar - Ann Chamberlin 975

Tamar (Witch)
Daughter of Satan - Jean Plaidy 5011

Tamasrajasi (Royalty; Religious)
Path of the Eclipse - Chelsea Quinn Yarbro 6905

Tamboura (Slave)
Drum - Kyle Onstott 4744

Tana (Young Woman)
The Homecoming - Norah Lofts 3844

Tancred of Varville (Knight)
The Unholy Pilgrim - R.F. Tapsell 6161

Tania (Gentlewoman)
Wartime Lies - Louis Begley 416

Tania (Royalty)
The Death of Kings - Peter Danielson 1465

Taniard, Tansy (Young Woman)
Tansy Taniard - Myrtle Strode-Jackson 6084

Taniko, Lady (Noblewoman)
Shike: Time of Dragons - Robert Shea 5784

Taniu (Royalty)
Bride of the Spear - Kathleen Herbert 2851

Tanner, George (Indian; Lawman)
Go-Ahead Rider - Robert J. Conley 1243
To Make a Killing - Robert J. Conley 1252

Tanner, Tom (Military Personnel)
The Second Face of Valor - Ray Grant Toepfer 6288

Tante, Maria (Settler; Farmer)
The Fiercest Heart - Stuart Cloete 1122

Tanus (Military Personnel)
River God - Wilbur Smith 5928

Tao Gan (Assistant)
The Haunted Monastery - Robert van Gulik 6415
The Monkey and the Tiger - Robert van Gulik 6417
Murder in Canton - Robert van Gulik 6418

Tapp, Quinton (Journalist)
A Creek Called Wounded Knee - Douglas C.
   Jones 3277

Tarakandu, Larissa (Spouse)
The Great Alone - Janet Dailey 1454

Tarconti, Andrea (Nobleman; Twin)
Wings of the Falcon - Barbara Michaels 4361

Tarconti, Stefano (Nobleman; Twin)
Wings of the Falcon - Barbara Michaels 4361

Tarleton, Alice (Young Woman)
Alice of Old Vincennes - Maurice Thompson 6268

Tarlton, Peter (Businessman)
Luise - Dawn Stewart Field 2079

Tarranti, Sandra (Spy)
Eagle in the Sun - Hoffman Birney 508

Tarrik (Chieftain)
The Corn King and the Spring Queen - Naomi
   Mitchison 4419

Tate, Ben (Journalist)
The Last Valley - A.B. Guthrie Jr. 2626

Tateh (Artist)
Ragtime - E.L. Doctorow 1658

Taverner, Catherine (Gentlewoman)
The Taverners' Place - Joanna Trollope 6351

Taverner, Judith (Heiress; Ward)
Regency Buck - Georgette Heyer 2898

Taverner, Sir Peregrine (Nobleman; Ward)
Regency Buck - Georgette Heyer 2898

Taverner, Stephen (Adventurer)
The Young Emperor - Robert Payne 4857

Taverner, Stephen (Gentleman)
Blood Royal - Robert Payne 4850

Taverner, Tom (Heir; Landowner)
The Taverners' Place - Joanna Trollope 6351

Taverney, Andree de (Courtier)
The Queen's Necklace - Alexandre Dumas 1781

Taverney, Philippe de (Courtier)
The Queen's Necklace - Alexandre Dumas 1781

Tavington, Nicholas (Nobleman)
The King's Brat - Constance Gluyas 2441
My Lady Benbrook - Constance Gluyas 2442

Tay-Bodal (Indian; Shaman)
Death at Rainy Mountain - Mardi Oakley
   Medawar 4321

Tayloe, William Dudley (Doctor)
Monsieur Yankee - Leslie Turner White 6689

Taylor, Angela (Young Woman)
Lovers All Untrue - Norah Lofts 3851

Taylor, Clay (Young Man)
Walk Like a Man - Donald Honig 3024

Taylor, Jeff (Teenager)
Walk Like a Man - Donald Honig 3024

Tchula Homa (Indian; Chieftain)
A Story of Deep Delight - Thomas McNamee 4305

Teal Eye (Indian)
The Big Sky - A.B. Guthrie Jr. 2624
Fair Land, Fair Land - A.B. Guthrie Jr. 2625

Tebb, Primrose (Heiress)
Stranger's Forest - Pamela Hill 2943

Tecante (Indian; Warrior)
Lakota - G. Clifton Wisler 6833

Tecolote (Indian; Warrior)
Eagles of Destiny - Jory Sherman 5817

Tedelli, Bianca (Gentlewoman; Spouse)
Bianca - Mabel Conquist 1257

Tedelli, Vittorino (Gentleman)
Bianca - Mabel Conquist 1257

Tedric (Knight)
The Blue Falcon - Robyn Carr 935

Teeto Hoonod (Indian)
Song of the Meadowlark - John A. Sanford 5594

Telfair, Helen (Gentlewoman)
Shadow of a Lady - Jane Aiken Hodge 2971

Telford, Beatrice (Gentlewoman)
Put Off Thy Shoes - Ethel Lillian Voynich 6513

Tempest, Abigail (Heiress)
The Traitors - William Stuart Long 3879

Tempest, Elizabeth (Young Woman)
The Gold Seekers - William Stuart Long 3874

Tempest, Rick (Settler)
The Adventurers - William Stuart Long 3869

Tempest, Seven (Heir)
Seven Tempest - William Vaughan Wilkins 6761

Tempkins, Giuseppe (Clerk)
The Braintree Mission - Nicholas E. Wyckoff 6887

Temple, Davina (Gentlewoman)
Regency Rogue - Helen Ashfield 212

Temple, Elizabeth (Gentlewoman)
The Pioneers; or, The Sources of the Susquehanna -
   James Fenimore Cooper 1307

Temple, Marmaduke (Judge; Landowner)
The Pioneers; or, The Sources of the Susquehanna -
   James Fenimore Cooper 1307

Temple, Sadie (Young Woman)
Crossing over Jordan - Linda Beatrice Brown 725

Temple, Story (Young Woman)
Crossing over Jordan - Linda Beatrice Brown 725

Templeton, Cedric (Military Personnel;
   Businessman)
Young Vargas Lewis - Robert Brainard Pearsall 4874

Templeton, Range (Rancher)
Divine Average - Elithe Hamilton Kirkland 3505

T'en Chih-Yu (Warlord)
Path of the Eclipse - Chelsea Quinn Yarbro 6905

Tenatos (Young Man)
The Altar and the Crown - Marian Niven 4631

Teneius, Rufus (Military Personnel)
The Soldier and the Sage: A Novel about Akiba - Richard G. Hubler 3065

Teotl (Outlaw; Revolutionary)
Gods on Horseback - Samuel G. Baggett 263

Teotochi, Mira (Servant)
The Dark Palazzo - Virginia Coffman 1151

Tepes, Vlad (Nobleman)
Anno-Dracula - Kim Newman 4595

Terentius, Titus (Sea Captain)
Fourth King - Norbert Coulehan 1373

Terra, Ana (Pioneer)
Time and the Wind - Erico Verissimo 6451

Terraine, Dana (Southern Belle)
Show Me a Land - Clark McMeekin 4293

Tesseyman, Anne (Servant)
The Heart of the Rose - June Barraclough 346

Teti (Artisan)
The Prophecy - Peter Danielson 1472

Tetley (Rancher)
The Ox-Bow Incident - Walter Van Tilburg Clark 1096

Tewkbury, Jonathan (Rancher)
The Feud - Amelia Bean 396

Tewke, Beth (Young Woman)
Apple Tree Lean Down - Mary E. Pearce 4860

Tewkes, Harry (Highwayman)
His Majesty's Highwayman - Donald Barr Chidsey 1061

Texas Chile (Military Personnel)
Gettysburg - Stephen Longstreet 3887

Thackeray, Edward (Police Officer)
Abracadaver - Peter Lovesey 3906
A Case of Spirits - Peter Lovesey 3910
The Detective Wore Silk Drawers - Peter Lovesey 3911
Mad Hatter's Holiday - Peter Lovesey 3914
Swing, Swing Together - Peter Lovesey 3915
The Tick of Death - Peter Lovesey 3916
Waxwork - Peter Lovesey 3917
Wobble to Death - Peter Lovesey 3918

Thackeray, William (Religious)
Chase the Wind - E.V. Thompson 6264
Harvest of the Sun - E.V. Thompson 6265

Thaine, Alexandra (Young Woman)
Wild Swan - Celeste De Blasis 1550

Thaler, Ben (Frontiersman)
To Build a Ship - Don Berry 482

Thane, Sarah (Gentlewoman)
The Talisman Ring - Georgette Heyer 2905

Tharon (Indian; Chieftain)
People of the River - W. Michael Gear 2338

Thatcher, Bird (Heiress—Lost)
Longleaf - Rose Brock 701

Thatcher, Jason (Sailor)
Jewel of the Sea - Ellen Argo 185

Thatcher, Lorna (Widow(er))
Longleaf - Rose Brock 701

Thaw, James (Landowner)
The Ancestors Cry Out - Eugenia Lovett West 6627

Thayer, Silence (Young Woman)
Wings of the Morning - Frederic F. Van de Water 6404

Theale, Lady Hester (Noblewoman)
Sprig Muslin - Georgette Heyer 2903

Theo (Religious)
Theo and Matilda - Rachel Billington 498

Theo (Wanderer)
For Every Sin - Aharon Appelfeld 175

Theodore (Religious)
Theo and Matilda - Rachel Billington 498

Theophilus (Slave; Businessman)
The Testament of Theophilus - Leonard Wibberley 6730

Theresa-Maria of Pfaffenstein (Royalty)
Magic Flutes - Eva Ibbotson 3097

Theros, Anna (Gentlewoman)
A Woman of Quality - Jan Westcott 6649

Theros, Edward (Gentleman)
A Woman of Quality - Jan Westcott 6649

Therriot, Andre (Adventurer)
River out of Eden - Shirley Seifert 5732

Theseus (Royalty)
The King Must Die - Mary Renault 5298

Theseus (Ruler)
The Bull From the Sea - Mary Renault 5295

Theudelinda (Royalty)
The Unspeakables: A Tale of Lombardy - Laverne Gay 2326

Theus, Pauline (Noblewoman)
The Horseman on the Roof - Jean Giono 2424

Thicke, Hoxie (Prospector)
The Goldseekers - William R. Burnett 794

Thierry of Anjou (Knight)
Swords of Anjou - Mario Pei 4890

Third Princess (Royalty)
Necklace and Calabash - Robert van Gulik 6419

Thoegersen, Mikkel (Student; Companion)
The Fall of the King - Johannes Vilhelm Jensen 3214

Thomas, Brother (Religious; Detective—Amateur)
A Trail of Blood - Jeremy Potter 5143

Thomas, Cottie (Young Woman)
Tyrone of Kentucky - Clark McMeekin 4294

Thomas, Donna (Gentlewoman)
The Asherwood Protegee - Mary A. Garratt 2299

Thomas, Julia (Plantation Owner)
No Surrender - Emma Gelders Sterne 5999

Thomas, Mark (Religious)
Song of Wovoka - Earl Murray 4531

Thomasine, Sister (Religious)
The Novice's Tale - Margaret Frazer 2217
The Servant's Tale - Margaret Frazer 2219

Thomna (Heroine)
Beyond the Aegean - Elia Kazan 3382

Thompson, Delbert (Businessman)
Miss Bishop - Bess Streeter Aldrich 71

Thompson, George (Political Figure)
Threescore and Ten - Walter Allen 105

Thompson, Jethro (Mountain Man)
Free Flows the River - Earl Murray 4529

Thompson, John (Sailor; Artisan)
Eagle Song - James Houston 3050

Thompson, Richard (Settler)
Articles of Faith - Ronald Harwood 2770

Thompson, Tally Ho (Highwayman)
The Highwayman and Mr. Dickens - William J. Palmer 4783

Thompson, Thane (Mountain Man)
Free Flows the River - Earl Murray 4529
High Freedom - Earl Murray 4530

Thonolan (Prehistoric Human)
The Valley of Horses - Jean M. Auel 239

Thorman, Agnes (Young Woman)
The Moth - Catherine Cookson 1284

Thorman, Millie (Child)
The Moth - Catherine Cookson 1284

Thorne, Adam (Nobleman)
Pomp and Circumstance - Fred Mustard Stewart 6025

Thorne, Robin (Trader)
Warm Wind, West Wind - Anne Irwin Matthew 4188

Thorne, Thomasine (Young Woman)
The Secret Years - Judith Lennox-Smith 3718

Thornton, Anne (Gentlewoman)
The Girl - Catherine Cookson 1277

Thornton, Arabella (Gentlewoman)
The Rich Are with You Always - Malcolm Macdonald 3971

Thornton, Henry (Gentleman)
Louisa Brancusi - Darrell Husted 3088

Thornton, John (Gentleman)
Escapade - Jane Aiken Hodge 2962

Thornton, Simon (Military Personnel)
The Fifth Conspiracy - Ted Jones 3296
Hard Road to Gettysburg - Ted Jones 3298

Thornton, Walter (Businessman)
The Rich Are with You Always - Malcolm Macdonald 3971

Thornton, Walter (Engineer)
The World From Rough Stones - Malcolm Macdonald 3979

Thornwood, Alan (Entertainer)
The Merrymaid - Mollie Hardwick 2696

Thorpe, Ben (Farmer; Convict)
To the Ends of the Earth - Michael Talbot 6155

Thorpe, Caroline (Gentlewoman)
The Lost Garden - Jane Aiken Hodge 2966

Thorpe, Jake (Sea Captain)
Tarnished Angel - Phyllis Leonard 3723

Thorpe, John (Businessman)
The Power and the Glory - Phyllis Bentley 462

Thorsson, Nils (Sea Captain)
Runestone - Don Coldsmith 1186

Thorsten (Warrior)
The Winter Servant - M.H. Davis 1537

Thrand (Religious)
This Land Fulfilled - Charles Andrew Brady 636

Thrasymedes (Military Personnel)
The Greek Generals Talk: Memoirs of the Trojan War - Phillip Parotti 4817

Threadgold, Beverley (Gentlewoman)
The Queen and I - Sue Townsend 6306

Three Owls (Indian; Warrior)
Pale Star - Don Coldsmith 1181

Thu (Young Woman)
Lady of the Reeds - Pauline Gedge 2345

Thunder, Colt (Guide; Indian)
Savage Thunder - Johanna Lindsey 3795

Thunzi (Warrior)
Wizards' Country - Daphne Rooke 5438

Thursday, Tessa (Foundling; Actress)
The Far-Off Rhapsody - Anne-Marie Sheridan 5808

Thurston, Dame Louise (Religious)
The Ladies of St. Hedwig's - E.M. Almedingen 117

Thyloss (Young Man)
The Lily and the Bull - Moyra Caldecott 846

Ti Noel (Slave)
Kingdom of This World - Alejo Carpentier 906

Ti-Sar (Royalty)
Lot's Wife - Marie Ley-Piscator 3767

Tibbles, Georgina (Gentlewoman)
East Indiaman - Frank Pollard 5087

Ticquet, Jean (Military Personnel)
Seven Men of Gascony - R.F. Delderfield 1589

Tidmarsh, Miss (Worker)
The Beano - Rony Robinson 5411

Tidwell, Jasper (Military Personnel)
Prisoner of Twilight - Don Robertson 5400

Tiepolo, Violetta (Heiress)
The Bravo - James Fenimore Cooper 1298

Tigellinus (Military Personnel)
The Conspiracy - John Hersey 2870

Tiger (Prehistoric Human)
Singletusk - Bjorn Kurten 3567

Tiger (Prehistoric Human; Warrior)
Dance of the Tiger: A Novel of the Ice Age - Bjorn Kurten 3566

Tigernan (Adventurer)
Grania: She-King of the Irish Seas - Morgan Llywelyn 3819

Tighe, Clay (Lawman)
Grant of Kingdom - Harvey Fergusson 2067

Til, Alexander (Revolutionary)
The Revolutionist: A Novel of Russia - Robert Littell 3810

Tilaki (Slave)
When God Slept - Peter Bourne 597

Tilden, Alicia (Saloon Hostess)
The Bellerose Bargain - Robyn Carr 934

Till, Nancy (Slave)
Sapphira and the Slave Girl - Willa Cather 958

Tilla, Mona (Royalty; Captive)
The Sins of the Lion - Annette Motley 4503

Tillman, Task (Landowner)
Crimson Is the Eastern Shore - Don Tracy 6308

Tillman, Virgil (Detective—Police)
Faces in the Crowd - William Marshall 4117

Tilney, Fiona (Handicapped)
Fire Opal - Pamela Hill 2932

Tilt, Rodney Ajax (Military Personnel)
Trumpets Sound No More - F. van Wyck Mason 4163

Tilverton, Barnaby (Gentleman)
A Most Romantic City - Mary Ann Gibbs 2396

Tipton, Lucius (Doctor)
These Latter Days - Laura Kalpakian 3330

Tipton, Omar (Military Personnel)
By Antietam Creek - Don Robertson 5398

Tirwell, Robert (Spouse)
Old Miss - Thomas Campbell 877

Tisdall, Tom (Doctor)
The Salem Frigate - John Edward Jennings 3205

Titus, Phoebe (Young Woman; Baker)
Arizona - Clarence Budington Kelland 3387

Tizzo (Young Man)
The Bait and the Trap - George Challis 970

Tlingit, Tom (Prospector)
Days of the Gold - Irwin R. Blacker 526

To-Sha-Be (Indian; Captive)
Ambush - Donald Clayton Porter 5113

Toby, Violet (Gentlewoman)
The Queen and I - Sue Townsend 6306

Toda, Lady Mariko (Noblewoman)
Shogun - James Clavell 1101

Todd, Daniel (Military Personnel)
Look Away, Beulah Land - Lonnie Coleman 1204

Todd, Gawin (Plantation Owner)
Balisand - Joseph Hergesheimer 2853

Todd, Jennifer (Abuse Victim; Murderer)
The Gallows Land - Bill Pronzini 5201

Todd, John James (Military Personnel; Director)
The New Confessions - William Boyd 617

Todd, Mavis (Southern Belle)
West of Appomattox - Harley Duncan 1785

Todd, Titus (Clerk; Landowner)
Water over the Dam - Marguerite Allis 116

Todhunter, Inspector (Detective—Police)
The Guns of Arrest - Philip McCutchan 4242
Halfhyde on the Amazon - Philip McCutchan 4250

Toit, Lena du (Young Woman)
The Hill of Doves - Stuart Cloete 1123

Toke (Warrior; Adventurer)
The Long Ships - Frans Gunnar Bengtsson 442

Tolbecken, Jared (Student; Military Personnel)
Tolbecken - Samuel Shellabarger 5798

Tolbecken, Rufus (Judge)
Tolbecken - Samuel Shellabarger 5798

Tolcheff, Andrew (Revolutionary)
The Petersburg-Cannes Express - Hans Koning 3538

Tolchin, Count Gregory (Nobleman; Revolutionary)
Triptych - Dora Landey 3652

Tollemache, Charles Auguste (Military Personnel)
The Flight of the Eagle - Donald Thomas 6239

Toller, John (Doctor)
The Trial of Jenny Sykes - Hebe Weenolsen 6598

Tollington, Hilary (Gentleman)
The Fortunate Marriage - Meriol Trevor 6342

Tolliver, Nathan (Rancher)
The Predators - F.A. Parker 4804

Tolonqua (Indian; Spouse)
Voice of the Eagle - Linda Lay Shuler 5839

Tolworthy, Arabella (Gentlewoman; Widow(er))
Lament for a Lost Lover - Philippa Carr 921

Tolworthy, Richard (Gentleman)
Saraband for Two Sisters - Philippa Carr 928

Tom (Animal)
Traveller - Richard Adams 27

Tom (Artisan)
The Pillars of the Earth - Ken Follett 2149

Tom (Military Personnel)
The Barrier - Robin Maugham 4195

Tom (Teenager)
The Closest Possible Union - Joanna Scott 5680

Tombul (Warrior)
Isle of Glory - Jane Oliver 4723

Tonks, Miss (Gentlewoman; Spinster)
Back in Society - Marion Chesney 1017
Miss Tonks Turns to Crime - Marion Chesney 1041

Tonneman, John (Doctor; Government Official)
The High Constable - Maan Meyers 4353
The Kingsbridge Plot - Maan Meyers 4355

Tonneman, John "Dutch" (Detective—Police)
The House on Mulberry Street - Maan Meyers 4354

Tonneman, Marianna (Spouse)
The High Constable - Maan Meyers 4353

Tonneman, Pieter (Businessman)
The Dutchman's Dilemma - Maan Meyers 4352

Tonneman, Pieter (Lawman; Widow(er))
The Dutchman - Maan Meyers 4351

Tonteur, Toinette (Orphan)
The Plains of Abraham - James Oliver Curwood 1452

Toole, Milly (Servant)
Beyond the Shadowlands - Georgina Fleming 2126

Topouzoglou, Stavros (Businessman; Immigrant)
Beyond the Aegean - Elia Kazan 3382

Topouzoglou, Stavros (Immigrant)
America, America - Elia Kazan 3380
The Anatolian - Elia Kazan 3381

Tor (Prehistoric Human; Hunter)
Children of the Dawn - Patricia Rowe 5516
Keepers of the Misty Time - Patricia Rowe 5517

Toranaga, Lord Yoshi (Nobleman; Warlord)
Shogun - James Clavell 1101

Toresson, Steinfinn (Nobleman)
The Axe - Sigrid Undset 6378

Torey, Michael (Businessman)
Michael Torey - Janet Mathewson 4183

Torfrida (Noblewoman)
Hereward the Wake - Charles Kingsley 3497

Toribio (Orphan)
The Hands of Cantu - Tom Lea 3694

Torka (Prehistoric Human; Hunter)
Beyond the Sea of Ice - William Sarabande 5595
Corridor of Storms - William Sarabande 5596
Forbidden Land - William Sarabande 5599
Walkers of the Wind - William Sarabande 5603

Torkelsen, Rolfe (Immigrant; Lawyer)
Big River, Big Man - Thomas William Duncan 1786

Tornefeld, Christian von (Fugitive)
The Swedish Cavalier - Leo Perutz 4943

Torreon, Inez (Gentlewoman)
Doniphan's Ride - Les Savage Jr. 5620

Torridon, Charles (Nobleman)
Her Grace's Passion - Marion Chesney 1033

Torridon, Christopher (Religious)
The King's Achievement - Robert Hugh Benson 459

Torridon, Ralph (Gentleman)
The King's Achievement - Robert Hugh Benson 459

Torrigiani, Bruno di (Nobleman)
Stranger at the Wedding - Frances Lynch 3934

Torry, Damaris (Settler)
Legacy - Robert Vaughan 6448

Toshabe (Indian)
Seneca - Donald Clayton Porter 5127

Toshack, Annys (Gentlewoman)
The Bright Blue Sky - Max Hennessy 2830

Toshack, Zoe (Pilot)
Once More the Hawks - Max Hennessy 2836

Tostig (Knight)
Below the Salt - Thomas B. Costain 1362

Tottenham, Lord (Nobleman)
The Silver Highways - Malcolm Macdonald 3972

Toupelik, Cyril (Military Personnel)
The Bride of Texas - Josef Skvorecky 5880

Toupelik, Linda (Bride)
The Bride of Texas - Josef Skvorecky 5880

Tour d'Auvergne, Michel de la (Religious)
To the End of the World - Helen Constance White 6680

Tourney, Roland de (Knight)
Secret Song - Catherine Coulter 1381

Tourville, Charles de (Gentleman)
Knave of Hearts - Philippa Carr 920

Tourville, Claudine de (Gentlewoman)
Voices in a Haunted Room - Philippa Carr 931

Tourville, Richard (Nobleman)
Rivers West - Louis L'Amour 3626

Toussaint, Paul (Young Man)
So Brief a Spring - Claude Manceron 4054

Tower, Alwyn (Hero)
The Grandmothers - Glenway Westcott 6640

Tower, Emma (Spouse)
The Lost Wagon - James Arthur Kjelgaard 3509

Tower, Henry (Settler)
The Grandmothers - Glenway Westcott 6640

Tower, Joe (Farmer)
The Lost Wagon - James Arthur Kjelgaard 3509

Tower, Mary (Gentlewoman)
Men of Albemarle - Inglis Fletcher 2135

Tower, Rose (Settler)
The Grandmothers - Glenway Westcott 6640

Towne, Langdon (Artist; Military Personnel)
Northwest Passage - Kenneth Roberts 5388

Townsend, Charles (Military Personnel)
Trumpets at Dawn - Cyril Harris 2719

Townsend, Grahame (Military Personnel)
The Casket Crew - Arch Whitehouse 6709

Townsend, Robert (Spy)
The Secret Road - Bruce Lancaster 3646

Townsend, Sally Rose (Teenager)
The Road to Bunker Hill - Shirley Barker 316

Tozer, Bradley (Businessman)
High Road to China - Jon Cleary 1106

Tozer, Eve (Heiress)
High Road to China - Jon Cleary 1106

Trace, Austin (Landowner)
Firewind - Bill Pronzini 5200

Trace, Sereno (Plantation Owner)
Elegant Journey - John Selby 5740

Tracy, Tom (Political Figure)
The Rising of the Moon - William Martin 4140

Tradd, Elizabeth (Southern Belle)
Charleston - Alexandra Ripley 5338

Trader (Indian)
Tatham Mound - Piers Anthony 169

Trago, Miriam (Heroine)
Chase the Wind - E.V. Thompson 6264

Traherne, Ada (Student)
Doubting Castle - Rebecca Kavaler 3373

Traherne, Arabella (Gentlewoman)
The Blade of Castlemayne - Anthony Esler 1960

Traherne, Simon (Nobleman)
Scandal - Amanda Quick 5219

Traill, Virginia (Guardian)
A King Reluctant - William Vaughan Wilkins 6759

Trainor, Newt (Outlaw)
Border Line - Robert J. Conley 1238

Tramont, Philippe de (Nobleman; Writer)
The Wine Widow - Tessa Barclay 301

Traner, Abel (Adventurer)
The Voyagers - Dale Van Every 6412

Trant, Anthony (Businessman)
Anthony Trant - John Hyatt Downing 1713

Trant, Anthony (Young Man)
Sioux City - John Hyatt Downing 1714

Trant, Helena (Young Woman)
On the Night of the Seventh Moon - Victoria Holt 3018

Traore, Dousika (Nobleman)
Segu - Maryse Conde 1234

Traore, Tiekoro (Young Man)
The Children of Segu - Maryse Conde 1232

Trask, Eldridge (Mountain Man; Settler)
Trask - Don Berry 483

Trasper, Doll (Entertainer)
Rivers Parting - Shirley Barker 315

Traveller (Animal)
Traveller - Richard Adams 27

Travers, Sir Edward (Archaeologist)
The Curse of the King - Victoria Holt 3012

Travers, Fenwick (Military Personnel)
Fenwick Travers and the Forbidden Kingdom - Raymond M. Saunders 5612
Fenwick Travers and the Panama Canal - Raymond M. Saunders 5613
Fenwick Travers and the Years of Empire - Raymond M. Saunders 5614

Travers, Polly (Political Figure)
The Book Class - Louis Auchincloss 228

Travers, Ruby (Heiress)
Ruby - Helen Ashfield 213

Travers, Tybalt (Archaeologist)
The Curse of the King - Victoria Holt 3012

Travis, Colt (Frontiersman)
Thunder on the Plains - Rosanne Bittner 517

Travis, David (Veteran)
Spanish Gold - Kevin D. Randle 5252

Treadup, David (Religious)
The Call - John Hersey 2869

Treadup, Emily (Spouse)
The Call - John Hersey 2869

Treadway, Lady Maisie (Noblewoman)
Captain Adam - Donald Barr Chidsey 1058

Tree, Ben (Mountain Man)
The Legend of Ben Tree - Paul Hawkins 2784

Treffrey, Deirdra (Governess)
Cormorant's Brood - Inglis Fletcher 2133

Trefor, Will (Settler)
Pilgrims: A Novel of the Mayflower - Gerard Mac 3955

Trefusis, Christina (Young Woman)
Women of Ashdon - Valerie Anand 135

Tregan, Caroline (Orphan)
Bagatelle - Maurice Denuziere 1613

Tregaran, Alice (Young Woman)
The Legacy of Tregaran - Mary Lide 3776

Tregaran, John (Young Man)
The Legacy of Tregaran - Mary Lide 3776

Tregaran, Joycelyn (Heiress)
Tregaran - Mary Lide 3779

Tregaran, Philip (Miner)
Tregaran - Mary Lide 3779

Tregarthan, Lord (Nobleman)
Plain Jane - Marion Chesney 1045

Tregellan, Emily (Seamstress; Servant)
Emerald - Helen Ashfield 206

Trelawney, Squire (Gentleman)
Treasure Island - Robert Louis Stevenson 6012

Trelawney, Cornwallis (Gentleman)
Kernow & Daughter - Malcolm Macdonald 3968

Trelawney, Sapphira (Young Woman)
O Western Wind - John Anthony Devon 1634

Trelcar, Davy (Smuggler)
Farewell the Tranquil - R.F. Delderfield 1585

Treleaven, Steven (Heir)
Camelot Country - Marjorie McEvoy 4267

Treloar, Edith (Spouse)
Look Away! - George Nauman Shuster 5841

Treloar, Robert (Lawyer; Spy)
Look Away! - George Nauman Shuster 5841

Tremaine, Lily (Governess)
Night Shadow - Catherine Coulter 1377

Tremaine, Robert (Adventurer; Heir—Lost)
The Masqueraders - Georgette Heyer 2894

Tremayne, James (Government Official)
The Buckingham Palace Connection - Ted Willis 6792

Tremont, Noel (Gentlewoman)
Stuyvesant Square - Margaret Lewerth 3743

Tremor, Sir William (Gentleman)
Deborah and the Siege of Paris - Colette Davenat 1500

Tremorney, Lilith (Servant)
Lilith - Jean Plaidy 5030

Trench, Benedict (Nobleman)
Dulcie Bligh - Gail Clark 1086

Trenchard, Constance (Spouse)
Painting the Darkness - Robert Goddard 2445

Trenchard, William (Businessman)
Painting the Darkness - Robert Goddard 2445

Trent, Ancilla (Governess)
The Nonesuch - Georgette Heyer 2896

Trent, Daniel (Journalist)
The Dawning of Deliverance - Judith Pella 4892

Trent, Ethan (Patriot)
Eden's Gate - Karen Harper 2711

Trent, Robbie (Child)
The Wolfling: A Documentary Novel of the 1870s - Sterling North 4648

Trent, Stephen (Gentleman; Military Personnel)
Gentleman Ranker - John Edward Jennings 3200

Trentham, Guy (Military Personnel)
As the Crow Flies - Jeffrey Archer 183

Treschi, Tonio (Singer)
Cry to Heaven - Anne Rice 5313

Trescorre (Government Official)
The Valley of Decision - Edith Wharton 6653

Tresize, Arthur (Sailor)
The Old Priory - Norah Lofts 3855

Tresize, Lettice (Young Woman)
The Old Priory - Norah Lofts 3855

Tressilian, Edmund (Gentleman)
Kenilworth - Sir Walter Scott 5700

Trestane, Amoyot (Sailor)
Castle Dor - Sir Arthur Thomas Quiller-Couch 5226

Trevaine, Jacelyn (Young Woman)
Rake's Ransom - Barbara Metzger 4347

Trevallion, Benedict (Gentleman)
The Pride of the Trevallions - Carola Salisbury 5570

Trevanion, Lady Margaret (Noblewoman)
The Hounds of God - Rafael Sabatini 5551

Trevelyan, Laura (Gentlewoman)
Voss - Patrick White 6698

Trevenna, Morag (Ward)
The Queen's Ward - Hebe Elsna 1933

Trevenning, Caroline (Gentlewoman)
It Began in Vauxhall Gardens - Jean Plaidy 5023

Trevenning, Charles (Gentleman)
It Began in Vauxhall Gardens - Jean Plaidy 5023

Treverton, Deborah (Doctor)
Green City in the Sun - Barbara Wood 6849

Treverton, Grace (Doctor)
Green City in the Sun - Barbara Wood 6849

Trevor, Anne (Fiance(e))
Pilgrims in Paradise - Frank G. Slaughter 5895

Trevor, Candace (Nurse)
Griffin's Way - Frank Yerby 6922

Trevor, Hannah (Midwife)
Hearts and Bones - Margaret Lawrence 3685

Trevor, Jocelyn (Nobleman)
My Love, My Enemy - Jan Cox Speas 5958

Trewella, Annabel (Companion; Orphan)
Dolphin Summer - Carola Salisbury 5569

Trey, Tatiana (Dancer)
A Grand Passion - Mary Mackey 3991

Tribble, Amy (Spinster)
Animating Maria - Marion Chesney 1015
Enlightening Delilah - Marion Chesney 1028
Finessing Clarissa - Marion Chesney 1029
Marrying Harriet - Marion Chesney 1036
Perfecting Fiona - Marion Chesney 1044
Refining Felicity - Marion Chesney 1048

Tribble, Effy (Spinster)
Animating Maria - Marion Chesney 1015
Enlightening Delilah - Marion Chesney 1028
Finessing Clarissa - Marion Chesney 1029
Marrying Harriet - Marion Chesney 1036
Perfecting Fiona - Marion Chesney 1044
Refining Felicity - Marion Chesney 1048

Trigonis, Christos (Businessman)
The Ashes of Smyrna - Richard Reinhardt 5294

Trigonis, Eleni (Young Woman)
The Ashes of Smyrna - Richard Reinhardt 5294

Tring, Sarah Camberwell (Businesswoman; Widow(er))
Sarah Camberwell Tring - Janet Edmonds 1869

Tripp, Preston (Military Personnel)
Whisper of the Wolf - Terry C. Johnston 3261

Tristan (Knight)
The White Raven - Diana L. Paxson 4847

Tristram of Maudesbury (Knight)
The Peacock and the Pearl - Jennifer Lang 3661

Troil, Ulla (Mentally Ill Person)
The Pirate - Sir Walter Scott 5704

Trollope, Henry (Military Personnel)
The Fireship - C. Northcote Parkinson 4811

Tromba, Marcello (Gentleman)
Lord Vanity - Samuel Shellabarger 5796

Tros (Warrior)
The Trojan - Noel B. Gerson 2386

Tros of Samothrace (Military Personnel)
Purple Pirate - Talbot Mundy 4514
Tros of Samothrace - Talbot Mundy 4515

Trotter, Augustus (Servant)
The Duchess of Duke Street - Mollie Hardwick 2693

Trotter, Susannah (Governess)
Cousin Susannah - Hazel Hucker 3066

Trotter, Tilly (Young Woman)
Tilly - Catherine Cookson 1288
Tilly Wed - Catherine Cookson 1290

Trowbridge, Little Ax (Military Personnel; Teenager)
Captain Little Ax - James H. Street 6077

Trowbridge, Natalie (Gentlewoman)
The Marquis and Miss Jones - Helen Ashfield 208

Trowbridge, Robert (Young Man)
The Neutral Ground - Frank Olney Hough 3044

Troy, Elizabeth (Widow(er); Nurse)
On a Far Wide Shore - Malcolm Macdonald 3970

Troy, Morwenna (Businesswoman)
On a Far Wide Shore - Malcolm Macdonald 3970

Trudeau, Young Bone (Slave)
Shadow of the Moon - Douglas C. Jones 3284

Truman, Ellen (Settler)
Free Soil - Margaret Lynn 3943

Truman, John (Settler)
Free Soil - Margaret Lynn 3943

Trumbull, Nathaniel (Religious)
The Greater Hunger - Barbara Dodge Borland 581

Trumper, Charlie (Businessman)
As the Crow Flies - Jeffrey Archer 183

Truscott, Charlie (Farmer)
Seedtime and Harvest - Mary E. Pearce 4864

Truscott, John (Military Personnel)
Conspiracy of Knaves - Dee Brown 711

Truslow, Thomas (Military Personnel)
Copperhead - Bernard Cornwell 1335

Tryon, Cassie (Young Woman; Heiress)
Hearts of Fire - Christina Savage 5616

Tryon, Glynis (Librarian; Feminist)
Blackwater Spirits - Miriam Grace Monfredo 4427
North Star Conspiracy - Miriam Grace Monfredo 4428
Seneca Falls Inheritance - Miriam Grace Monfredo 4429
Through a Gold Eagle - Miriam Grace Monfredo 4430

Tryon, Katie (Saloon Hostess)
Three Harbors - F. van Wyck Mason 4162

Tryon, Richard (Loyalist; Spy)
Hearts of Fire - Christina Savage 5616

Tsani (Indian; Chieftain)
The Double Man - Elinor Pryor 5205

Tsepesh, Arkady (Gentleman)
Covenant with the Vampire: The Diaries of the Family Dracul - Jeanne Kalogridis 3327

Tsepesh, Arkady (Vampire)
Children of the Vampire: The Diaries of the Family Dracul - Jeanne Kalogridis 3326

Tsepesh, Mary Windham (Gentlewoman)
Covenant with the Vampire: The Diaries of the Family Dracul - Jeanne Kalogridis 3327

Tsepesh, Prince Vlad (Royalty; Vampire)
Children of the Vampire: The Diaries of the Family Dracul - Jeanne Kalogridis 3326
Covenant with the Vampire: The Diaries of the Family Dracul - Jeanne Kalogridis 3327
Lord of the Vampires: The Diaries of the Family Dracul - Jeanne Kalogridis 3328

Tuck, Friar (Religious; Outlaw)
The Good Yeomen - Jay Williams 6771

Tucker, Abel (Farmer)
The Sprig of Hemlock: A Novel about Shays' Rebellion - Robert Muir 4509

Tucker, Adam (Military Personnel)
Exit with Drums - Joseph A. Daley 1457

Tucker, Birch (Military Personnel)
In My Father's House - Bodie Thoene 6222

Tucker, Birch (Veteran)
A Thousand Shall Fall - Bodie Thoene 6227

Tucker, Enoch (Young Man)
The Sprig of Hemlock: A Novel about Shays' Rebellion - Robert Muir 4509

Tucker, Isiah (Farmer)
The Sprig of Hemlock: A Novel about Shays' Rebellion - Robert Muir 4509

Tucker, Richard (Bastard Son; Privateer)
The Savage City - Jean Paradise 4787

Tudor, Dodpher (Bastard Son)
As Runs the Glass - Evan John David 1502

Tudor, Jared (Young Man)
As Runs the Glass - Evan John David 1502

Tufnell, Simon (Clerk)
Marianne - Glen Petrie 4981

Tumbling Hawk (Indian)
One Smart Indian - Robert J. Seidman 5722

Tunstall, Paul (Gentleman; Landowner)
A Leaf in the Wind - Marie Joseph 3307

Tupac, Acanna (Noblewoman)
Mansions of Darkness - Chelsea Quinn Yarbro 6902

Tupper, Jenny (Farmer)
Strange Wives - Shirley Barker 317

Turms, Lars (Warrior; Pirate)
The Etruscan - Mika Waltari 6553

Turnblow, Faye (Young Woman)
The Last Days of Horse-Shy Halloran - Bill Pronzini 5203

Turnbull, John (Military Personnel)
Rags of Glory - Stuart Cloete 1126

Turndale, Thomas (Military Personnel)
The Canebrake Men - Cameron Judd 3313

Turner, Drake (Businessman)
Lord Raven's Widow - Leslie O'Grady 4700

Turner, Fanny (Prostitute)
The Girl From Storyville: A Victorian Novel - Frank Yerby 6919

Turner, Nathan (Sea Captain)
Yankee Trader - Stanley Morton 4496

Turner, Sarah (Innkeeper)
Scarlet Ribbons - Judith E. French 2224

Turning Hawk (Indian; Warrior)
Dance Back the Buffalo - Milton Lott 3899

Tusser, Ursula (Witch; Spirit)
Familiar Spirits - Leonard Tourney 6298

Tussy, Eleanor (Relative)
The Case of the Revolutionist's Daughter: Sherlock Holmes Meets Karl Marx - Lewis S. Feuer 2076

Tuthill, Frederick C. (Military Personnel)
The Dice of God - Hoffman Birney 507

Tutilo, Brother (Religious)
The Holy Thief - Ellis Peters 4962

Twainborough, Eric (Journalist)
Over There - Robert Vaughan 6449

Tweedman, Gavin (Military Personnel)
Attack the Lusitania! - Raymond Hitchcock 2956

Tweng, Thomas (Knight; Government Official)
The Death of a King - P.C. Doherty 1672

Twillow, Philly (Servant)
Enough Good Men - Charles Mercer 4336

Two Eagles (Indian; Warrior)
For Love of Two Eagles - Barbara Riefe 5328
Mohawk Woman - Barbara Riefe 5329
The Woman Who Fell From the Sky - Barbara Riefe 5330

Two Heads (Indian)
The Dark Way - Robert J. Conley 1241

Two Robes (Indian; Warrior)
Song of Wovoka - Earl Murray 4531

Two Shields (Indian)
Tie My Bones to Her Back - Robert F. Jones 3294

Two Sleep (Indian; Warrior)
Dream Catcher - Terry C. Johnston 3251

Tyacke, Will (Businessman)
Meridon - Philippa Gregory 2583

Tyler, Blazely (Revolutionary)
Thunder Before Seven - Anna Brand 648

Tyler, Clardy (Frontiersman)
Passage to Natchez - Cameron Judd 3316

Tyler, Lora (Spouse)
The Quicksilver Pool - Phyllis A. Whitney 6716

Tyler, Robert (Businessman)
Murder at Fenway Park - Troy Soos 5948

Tyler, Thias (Outlaw)
Passage to Natchez - Cameron Judd 3316

Tyler, Tina (Shipowner)
The Dram Tree - Hamilton Cochran 1140

Tyler, Wade (Military Personnel)
The Quicksilver Pool - Phyllis A. Whitney 6716

Tyndale, Craig (Gentleman)
The Noblest Frailty - Patricia Veryan 6474

Tyne, Harry (Gambler; Gentleman)
Letty - Clare Darcy 1491

Tynedale, Geoffrey (Military Personnel)
Red Cloak Flying - Margaret Widdemer 6737

Tynedale, Julian (Nobleman)
Buckskin Baronet - Margaret Widdemer 6734

Tynedale, Kitty (Gentlewoman)
The Tynedale Daughters - Norma Lee Clark 1093

Tynedale, Millie (Gentlewoman)
The Tynedale Daughters - Norma Lee Clark 1093

Tynedale, Norrie (Gentlewoman)
The Tynedale Daughters - Norma Lee Clark 1093

Tyrone, David (Veteran)
Tyrone of Kentucky - Clark McMeekin 4294

Tyrrell, Charles (Nobleman)
The Duchess of Duke Street - Mollie Hardwick 2693

Tyrrell, Ira (Young Man)
Honor Thy Father - Robert A. Roripaugh 5460

Tyrrell, Mart (Young Man)
Honor Thy Father - Robert A. Roripaugh 5460

Tyrrell, Martin (Rancher)
Honor Thy Father - Robert A. Roripaugh 5460

Tyson, Charlie (Businessman)
Red Barbarian - Margaret Gaan 2260

U

Ulenspiegel, Tyl (Wanderer; Military Personnel)
The Legend of Tyl Ulenspiegel - Charles Theodore Henri De Coster 1558

Ulf (Servant)
The Cross - Sigrid Undset 6380

Ulf (Warrior)
The Iron Crown - Clare Barroll 354

Ulric (Teenager)
The Trumpet of God - David Duncan 1784

Ulysses (Warrior)
Scandal in Troy - Eva Hemmer Hansen 2679

Umak (Prehistoric Human; Twin)
Walkers of the Wind - William Sarabande 5603

Umegawa (Prostitute)
Yedo - Lynn Guest 2609

Uncas (Indian)
The Last of the Mohicans - James Fenimore Cooper 1302

Underdown, Philip (Gentleman; Government Official)
The Plymouth Cloak - Kate Sedley 5718

Underwood, Ike (Banker; Publisher)
Paradise Falls - Don Robertson 5399

U'nkomo (Warrior)
Bush War! - William Moore 4447

Unnamed Character (Pilot)
The Aviator - Ernest K. Gann 2277

Upford, Charlotte (Young Woman)
The Lion at Sea - Max Hennessy 2834

Upjohn, Corrie May (Young Woman)
The Handsome Road - Gwen Bristow 697

Upshall, Glory (Young Woman)
The Rogue and the Witch - John Edward Newton 4605

Uremay (Rancher)
A Shadow of Eagles - Jane Barry 360

Usher, Jubilee (Renegade)
Cry of the Hawk - Terry C. Johnston 3248
Dream Catcher - Terry C. Johnston 3251

Ute Killer (Indian; Warrior)
A Woman of the People - Benjamin Capps 893

Uther (Ruler)
Merlin - Stephen R. Lawhead 3681

Utrecht, Simon Vann (Businessman; Sea Captain)
Magnificent Enemies - Edgar Maas 3951

V

Vaeringer, Andrea (Knight)
Ride Home Tomorrow - Evan John 3221

El Vago (Revolutionary)
El Vago - Laurence Gonzales 2474

Vail, Ben (Sea Captain)
Jonathan Dearborn: A Novel of the War of 1812 - Willard Wallace 6540

Vaillant, Joseph (Religious)
Death Comes for the Archbishop - Willa Cather 957

Valaise, Ailena (Noblewoman)
Kingdom of the Grail - A.A. Attanasio 226

Valaise, Guy (Nobleman)
Kingdom of the Grail - A.A. Attanasio 226

Valden, Jimmie (Landowner)
The Forge - Thomas S. Stribling 6083

Valderocas, Isabel (Gentlewoman)
The Marranos - Liliane Webb 6588

Valdez, Orlena (Gentlewoman)
Night Wind's Woman - Shirl Henke 2825

Vale, Matthew (Gentleman)
A Lady in Doubt - Annabel Wynne 6891

Valence, Lily (Spouse; Singer)
Fallen Skies - Philippa Gregory 2581

Valency, Jacquette (Entertainer)
The Merrymaid - Mollie Hardwick 2696

Valenti, Leone da (Royalty)
The Sins of the Lion - Annette Motley 4503

Valentin, Dr. (Doctor)
The Brothers of Uterica - Benjamin Capps 887

Valerius (Military Personnel)
Roman Wall - Bryher 745

Valerius, Lucius (Military Personnel)
The Gods Are Not Mocked - Anna Taylor 6177

Valerius, Manlius (Young Man)
The Equinox: A Novel of Rome in the Time of Commodus - Carol Saylor 5622

Valjean, Jean (Criminal; Fugitive)
Cosette: The Sequel to Les Miserables - Laura Kalpakian 3329

Valli (Dancer; Slave)
So Far From Malabar - Joy DeWeese Wehen 6599

Valliant, Martin (Religious; Knight)
Martin Valliant - Warwick Deeping 1578

Vallon, Louise du (Young Woman)
Daughter of Marignac - Constance Heaven 2805

Vallon, Pierre du (Artist)
Daughter of Marignac - Constance Heaven 2805

Valmy, Nick (Sea Captain)
Tide of Empire - Bates Baldwin 279

Valsecca, Odo (Nobleman; Political Figure)
The Valley of Decision - Edith Wharton 6653

Van Alen, Christal (Gentlewoman)
Fair is the Rose - Meagan MacKinney 3997

Van Ayl, Cathy (Spouse)
Colorado! - Dana Fuller Ross 5471
Oregon! - Dana Fuller Ross 5484

Van Ayl, Cathy (Widow(er))
Nebraska! - Dana Fuller Ross 5480
Wyoming! - Dana Fuller Ross 5494

Van Ayl, Cathy (Young Woman)
Independence! - Dana Fuller Ross 5476

Van Baden, Nicolaus (Gentleman)
The Marriage Bed - Jean Clark 1088

Van Buren, Adeline (Heiress)
Hawken Fury - David Thompson 6254

Van Buren, Frederic (Frontiersman)
The Silent Drum - Neil Harmon Swanson 6141

Van Buren, Joseph (Settler)
The Colonists - William Stuart Long 3870

Van Buren, Matthew (Military Personnel)
The Imperialists - William Stuart Long 3875

Van Buren, Roxana (Journalist; Detective—Private)
Blue Moon - Parris Afton Bonds 569

Van Cleef, Hanneke (Young Woman)
The Sea Beggars - Cecelia Holland 2996

Van Cleef, Jan (Sailor; Pirate)
The Sea Beggars - Cecelia Holland 2996

Van der Berg, Boetie (Military Personnel)
Rags of Glory - Stuart Cloete 1126

Van der Berg, Hendrik (Settler)
The Turning Wheels - Stuart Cloete 1127

Van der Berg, Kaspar (Settler)
Watch for the Dawn - Stuart Cloete 1128

Van Der Kleve, Oliver (Banker)
The Imagination of the Heart - Judith Glover 2437

Van der Meer, Adriana (Gentlewoman)
The Hyde Park Murder - Elliott Roosevelt 5443

Van Deventer, Ludolf (Businessman)
The Golden Tulip - Rosalind Laker 3596

Van Doorn, Willem (Settler)
The Covenant - James A. Michener 4368

Van Dyck, Margaretta (Young Woman)
The Marriage Bed - Jean Clark 1088

Van Fleet, Bartholomew (Financier)
Saratoga Trunk - Edna Ferber 2062

Van Goens, Annabet (Young Woman)
Silver Nutmeg - Norah Lofts 3860

Van Helsing, Abraham (Scientist; Vampire Hunter)
Children of the Vampire: The Diaries of the Family Dracul - Jeanne Kalogridis 3326
Lord of the Vampires: The Diaries of the Family Dracul - Jeanne Kalogridis 3328

Van Horn, Anneke (Banker)
Gold - Clarence Budington Kelland 3388

Van Horn, Jan (Banker)
Hard Money - Clarence Budington Kelland 3389

Van Horn, Jan (Businessman)
The Jealous House - Clarence Budington Kelland 3390

Van Lindsay, Lisette (Gentlewoman)
Married Past Redemption - Patricia Veryan 6469

Van Meeteren, Analisa (Frontierswoman; Seamstress)
Sunflower - Jill Marie Landis 3653

Van Nest, Samuel (Financier)
One Night in Newport - Elizabeth Villars 6498

Van Os, Trudi (Young Woman)
Venture in the East - Bruce Lancaster 3648

Van Reenen, Sannie (Settler)
The Turning Wheels - Stuart Cloete 1127

Van Rensselaer, Jurgen (Financier)
The Copperheads - William James Blech 544

Van Ryn, Nicholas (Gentleman)
Dragonwyck - Anya Seton 5750

Van Schaick, Charles (Photographer)
Billy Sunday - Rod Jones 3295

Van Vliet, 3vee (Heir)
Paloverde - Jacqueline Briskin 693

Van Vliet, Bud (Heir)
Paloverde - Jacqueline Briskin 693

Van Welcker, Count (Nobleman)
The Smile of the Stranger - Joan Aiken 53

Van Zandt, Dirk (Young Man)
Shad Run - Howard Breslin 668

Van Zyl, Joachim (Young Man)
The Great Sky and the Silence - James S. Rand 5245

Vance, Lee (Con Artist)
Scotch on the Rocks - Howard Browne 733

Vance, Logan (Journalist; Publisher)
Black-Eyed Susan - Deborah Camp 871

Vandemark, Jacobus (Farmer)
Vandemark's Folly - Herbert Quick 5223

vander Poele, Claes (Ward; Apprentice)
Niccolo Rising - Dorothy Dunnett 1803

vander Poele, Nicholas (Adventurer; Businessman)
Race of Scorpions - Dorothy Dunnett 1806
Scales of Gold - Dorothy Dunnett 1808
The Spring of the Ram - Dorothy Dunnett 1809
The Unicorn Hunt - Dorothy Dunnett 1811

vander Poele, Nicholas (Banker)
To Lie with Lions - Dorothy Dunnett 1810

Vanderhoff, Julie (Gentlewoman)
Homeland - John Jakes 3148

Vandermark, Fred (Sailor)
The Magic Ship - Sandra Paretti 4791

Vandervent, Paul (Gentleman)
The Blackheath Poisonings - Julian Symons 6150

Vane, Harry (Businessman)
Peg Woffington - Charles Reade 5281

Vane, Louise (Orphan)
The Royal Ann Tree - Patricia Campbell 875

Vane, Richard (Fugitive; Servant)
Weep in the Sun - Jeanne Wilson 6809

Vanneau, Marie (Spouse)
The Heatherton Heritage - Pamela Hill 2934

Varden, Gabriel (Repairman)
Barnaby Rudge: A Tale of the Riots of Eighty - Charles Dickens 1641

Varenne, Alexandre de (Nobleman)
The Eleventh Year - Monique Raphel High 2914

Vargas, Manuel de (Military Personnel)
The Franciscan - Forrester Blake 532

Varinia (Slave)
Spartacus - Howard Fast 2044

Varney, Richard (Servant)
Kenilworth - Sir Walter Scott 5700

Varro, Manlius (Military Personnel)
The Lost Legion - H. Warner Munn 4516

Varrus, Caius Publius (Military Personnel)
The Skystone: The Forging of Arthur's Britain - Jack Whyte 6726

Varrus, Caius Publius (Warrior)
The Singing Sword - Jack Whyte 6725

Varus, Quintillus (Military Personnel)
The Three Legions - Gregory Solon 5941

Vassilchikova, Sonya (Gentlewoman)
The Name of Hero - Richard Seltzer 5742

Vassilovich, Michael (Military Personnel)
Dance of the Assassins - Maria Fagyas 1997

Vaudemont, Latisse de (Captive)
Richard and the Knights of God - Pamela Bennetts 454

Vaudraye, Marsanne de (Heiress; Gentlewoman)
Marsanne - Virginia Coffman 1155

Vaudraye, Veronique de (Gentlewoman)
Veronique - Virginia Coffman 1158

Vaughan, Francis (Military Personnel)
For God and Glory - Tim Jeal 3171

Vaughan, Maria (Religious)
Luciano's Luck - Jack Higgins 2912

Vaughan, Penry (Religious)
The Fox-Red Hills - Cynthia S. Roberts 5374

Vaughan, Rhys (Gentleman)
Vale of Tyranny - Suzanne Butler 831

Vaughan, Tom (Servant; Spy)
City of Light - Alison Macleod 4001
The Hireling - Alison Macleod 4003

Vaughn, Plumbridge (Gentleman)
Michael Torey - Janet Mathewson 4183

Vaughn, Warren (Frontiersman)
To Build a Ship - Don Berry 482

Vayle, Charlotte (Spouse)
Lisbon - Valerie Sherwood 5825

Veasey-Hunter, Vivian (Military Personnel)
A Captive Freedom - Emma Drummond 1724

Veena (Nurse)
Temple Bells - Marjorie McEvoy 4271

Vega, Isabel de la (Fugitive)
1492: The Life and Times of Juan Cabezon of Castile - Homero Aridjis 187

Velasco (Religious)
The Samurai - Shusaku Endo 1941

Velasquez, Rodrigo (Religious)
The Spanish Doctor - Matt Cohen 1159

Velasquez, Tomas (Heir)
All or Nothing - Stephen Longstreet 3881

Vella, Abbot Giuseppe (Criminal)
The Council of Europe - Leonardo Sciascia 5678

Venable, Sabra (Frontierswoman; Political Figure)
Cimarron - Edna Ferber 2061

Venado (Amnesiac)
Sweet Mountain Magic - Rosanne Bittner 516

The Venetian (Nobleman)
Time of Parting - Anton Donchev 1690

Venetis, Jason (Shipowner)
The Bourlotas Fortune - Nicholas Gage 2268

Veniero, Giorgio (Sailor)
Sofia - Ann Chamberlin 974

Venire, Maritza (Dancer)
Lord Vanity - Samuel Shellabarger 5796

Verdier, Marguerite (Artist)
Dreams of Empire - Jeanne Mackin 3994

Vere, Cornelia de (Gentlewoman; Loyalist)
The Lady From Yorktown - Eva McDonald 4260

Vere, Isabella (Gentlewoman)
The Black Dwarf - Sir Walter Scott 5692

Vere, Starry (Military Personnel)
Billy Budd - Herman Melville 4333

Verendrye, Louise de La (Indian; Young Woman)
My Blood and My Treasure - Mary Schumann 5674

Veres-Vorne, Nathan de (Trader; Sea Captain)
Mandalay - Alexandra Jones 3269

Veria (Gentlewoman)
Roman Wall - Bryher 745

Verity, Sergeant William (Police Officer)
Cracksman on Velvet - Francis Selwyn 5743
Sergeant Verity and the Blood Royal - Francis Selwyn 5744
Sergeant Verity and the Imperial Diamond - Francis Selwyn 5745
Sergeant Verity Presents His Compliments - Francis Selwyn 5746

Verne, Martin (Vagrant; Amnesiac)
Stranger at Wildings - Madeleine Brent 663

Verne, Philippa de (Gentlewoman; Heiress—Dispossessed)
Command of the King - Mary Lide 3773

Vernet, Lucien (Military Personnel)
Napoleon Must Die - Quinn Fawcett 2054

Vernet, Michel (Gentleman)
Hester - Brian Cleeve 1107

Vernet, Victoire (Spouse)
Napoleon Must Die - Quinn Fawcett 2054

Verney, Patricia (Gentlewoman)
Prisoners of Hope: A Tale of Colonial Virginia - Mary Johnston 3238

Verney, Romain (Nobleman)
A Company of Swans - Eva Ibbotson 3095

Vernold, Emma (Young Woman)
St. Peter's Fair - Ellis Peters 4971

Vernon, Rosalind (Gentlewoman; Handicapped)
The Parfit Knight - Juliet Blyth 555

Verringer, Jason (Nobleman; Widow(er))
The Time of the Hunter's Moon - Victoria Holt 3022

Versluis (Gentleman)
Another Country - Karel Schoeman 5646

Verve, Adam de (Bastard Son)
The World, the Flesh, and the Devil - Reay Tannahill 6159

Verwien, Henry (Doctor)
The Angel of the Opera: Sherlock Holmes Meets the Phantom of the Opera - Sam Siciliano 5842

Vesey, Errol (Gentlewoman)
The Vesey Inheritance - Gwendoline Butler 822

Vespasian (Government Official)
The Brother - Chayym Zeldis 6958

Vestry, Caroline (Young Woman)
Sisters & Lovers - Nicola Thorne 6274

Vestry, Emily (Young Woman)
Sisters & Lovers - Nicola Thorne 6274

Vestry, Jane (Young Woman)
Sisters & Lovers - Nicola Thorne 6274

Vetch, Silas (Government Official)
Black Angels - C.T. Ritchie 5348

Vevian, Clarissa (Gentlewoman)
Finessing Clarissa - Marion Chesney 1029

Veyde (Prehistoric Human; Leader)
Dance of the Tiger: A Novel of the Ice Age - Bjorn Kurten 3566

Vezenobres, Isabeau (Young Woman)
The Shepherd's Crook - Paul Frischauer 2234

Vicker, Charlotte (Settler; Immigrant)
Wild Dog Running - Alan Scholefield 5658

Vickers, Mars (Military Personnel)
High Hearts - Rita Mae Brown 728

Vickers, Steve (Frontiersman)
Rainbow Road - Davenport Steward 6016

Vicotte, Jules (Settler)
Three Came to Ville Marie - Alan Sullivan 6114

Victor, Robert (Doctor)
Cherished Enemy - Patricia Veryan 6460

Victorevitch, Kyril "Gredka" (Young Man)
Between Two Worlds - Monique Raphel High 2913

Vidal, Justin (Nobleman)
The Duchess of Vidal - Dawn Lindsey 3793

Vignon, Claire de (Prostitute)
The Blood Endures - Robert Inman 3107

Vigon, Benito (Military Personnel)
La Guerra: A Spanish Saga - Stephen D. Frances 2199

Vilers, Gilbert de (Religious)
In Pursuit of the Green Lion - Judith Merkle Riley 5334

Villaricca, Solomon (Peddler)
The Slave Stealer - Boyd Upchurch 6390

Villars, Eleanora (Young Woman)
The Notorious Angel - Patricia Maxwell 4201

Villars, Trevelyan de (Gentleman)
The Wagered Widow - Patricia Veryan 6481

Villasur, Don Pedro de (Military Personnel)
Return of the Spanish - Don Coldsmith 1183

Villebois, Anne de (Gentlewoman)
The Captain From Connecticut - C.S. Forester 2171

Villefont, Jeanne de (Noblewoman)
Seed of Mischief - Willa Gibbs 2401

Villerand, Marian (Gentlewoman)
Rebellion Road - Helen Topping Miller 4392

Villiers, Diana (Gentlewoman)
The Fortune of War - Patrick O'Brian 4664
H.M.S. Surprise - Patrick O'Brian 4666
The Ionian Mission - Patrick O'Brian 4667
The Letter of Marque - Patrick O'Brian 4668
Post Captain - Patrick O'Brian 4672
The Surgeon's Mate - Patrick O'Brian 4674

Villiers de Melville, Marc-Antoine (Adventurer)
Venetian Masque - Rafael Sabatini 5556

Villon, Herbert (Detective—Police)
The Talking Pictures Murder Case - George Baxt 388
The William Powell and Myrna Loy Murder Case - George Baxt 390

Vincent, Adam (Military Personnel)
The Empire Builders - William Stuart Long 3871

Vincenzus, Diana (Gentlewoman)
No King but Caesar - Anne Powers 5151

Vinicius (Nobleman)
Quo Vadis - Henryk Sienkiewicz 5848

Vinodius (Government Official)
Roman Wall - Bryher 745

Vinolas (Spy)
The Witches - Jay Williams 6776

Vint, Mercy (Maiden)
Griffith Gaunt - Charles Reade 5280

Vinton, Celia (Gentlewoman)
The Scimitar - Samuel Edwards 1890

Visconti, Bianca (Noblewoman)
The Medici Emerald - Martin Woodhouse 6851
The Medici Guns - Martin Woodhouse 6852
The Medici Hawks - Martin Woodhouse 6853

Visconti, Niles (Gentleman)
Clara Reeve - Leonie Hargrave 2705

Visconti, Zaide (Noblewoman)
Clara Reeve - Leonie Hargrave 2705

Visser, Francesca (Artist)
The Golden Tulip - Rosalind Laker 3596

Vivaldi, Orazio (Philosopher)
The Valley of Decision - Edith Wharton 6653

Vivar, Blas (Nobleman)
Sharpe's Rifles - Bernard Cornwell 1347

Vivar, Blas (Nobleman; Government Official)
Sharpe's Devil - Bernard Cornwell 1340

Vivian, Hal (Engineer)
The Vivian Inheritance - Jean Stubbs 6101

Vladomsky, Pan (Scholar)
The Nazarene - Sholem Asch 200

Vlassevna, Laisha (Orphan; Ward)
Tempting Fate - Chelsea Quinn Yarbro 6906

Vogel (Wanderer)
The Last Valley - J.B. Pick 4992

Vold, Mourly (Scientist)
Loving Little Egypt - Thomas McMahon 4288

Voldi (Nobleman)
The Big Fisherman - Lloyd C. Douglas 1702

Volkman, Magda (Singer)
The Career of Magda V. - Joseph Machlis 3982

Volkov, Boris (Military Personnel)
Blood on the Snow - John Elliott 1916

Volland, Anna (Widow(er))
Vollands - Pamela Hill 2947

Volland, Hubert (Landowner; Gentleman)
Vollands - Pamela Hill 2947

Volland, James (Landowner; Gentleman)
Vollands - Pamela Hill 2947

Vollar, Nettie (Gentlewoman)
Java Head - Joseph Hergesheimer 2854

Volodyovski, Pan (Military Personnel)
Fire in the Steppe - Henryk Sienkiewicz 5847

Volterra, Gianna di (Noblewoman)
Drumbeat - Dudley Pope 5094
Ramage - Dudley Pope 5097

Volusianus, Quintus (Doctor)
The Thorn of Arimathea - Frank G. Slaughter 5905

Volynski, Grisha (Royalty)
The Year of December - Lucy Cores 1329

Von Bock, Eeva (Spouse)
The Czar's Madman - Jaan Kross 3560

Von Bock, Timotheus (Veteran)
The Czar's Madman - Jaan Kross 3560

Von Doring, Luise (Noblewoman)
Luise - Dawn Stewart Field 2079

Von Falkenburg, Julian (Nobleman)
Castle of Eagles - Constance Heaven 2804

Von Friedberg, Frederick (Royalty)
Meadowsweet - Gwendoline Butler 820

von Grueber, Ippolita (Gentlewoman)
Ippolita - Alberto Denti di Pirajno 1612

Von Hulsen, Cecilie (Noblewoman)
Draw Near to Battle - Jere Hungerford Wheelwright 6667

Von Kobis, Hugo (Military Personnel; Diplomat)
While Paris Danced - Patricia Wright 6886

Von Poellnitz, Baron (Nobleman)
Wicked Lady - Inglis Fletcher 2142

Von Reichmanstaal, Melanie (Noblewoman)
The Brocken - Pamela Hill 2929

Von Thieleman, Manfred (Police Officer)
Curse of Magira - David Bee 413

Von Zweig, Roger (Military Personnel)
Something Gleamed - Theda Kenyon 3463

Vorontzou, Katya (Bastard Daughter)
Katya - Lucy Cores 1328

Vorontzou, Lisa (Gentlewoman)
Katya - Lucy Cores 1328

Vorotyntsev, Colonel (Military Personnel)
August 1914 - Alexander Solzhenitsyn 5942

Vosmar, Simon (Plantation Owner)
Scent of Cloves - Norah Lofts 3859

Voss, Johann Ulrich (Explorer)
Voss - Patrick White 6698

Vouvray, Claudine de (Noblewoman)
The Sword and the Flame - Pamela Hill 2945

Voyle, Simon (Gentleman; Ward)
Familiar Acts - June Barraclough 345

Vredenburg, Stella (Young Woman)
Floodtide - Suzanne Goodwin 2475

W

Wachera, Mama (Healer)
Green City in the Sun - Barbara Wood 6849

Wade, Caffey (Gentleman)
Tidewater - Clifford Dowdey 1709

Wade, Caroline (Widow(er); Businesswoman)
Hard Road to Gettysburg - Ted Jones 3298

Wade, Charlie (Cowboy)
The Day the Cowboys Quit - Elmer Kelton 3403

Wade, Duncan (Veteran)
Rebellion Road - Helen Topping Miller 4392

Wade, Hannah (Spouse; Captive)
The Pride of Hannah Wade - Janet Dailey 1455

Wade, Nathaniel (Sailor)
Manila Galleon - F. van Wyck Mason 4154

Wade, Samuel (Military Personnel)
The Fifth Conspiracy - Ted Jones 3296
Hard Road to Gettysburg - Ted Jones 3298

Wade, Stephen (Military Personnel)
The Pride of Hannah Wade - Janet Dailey 1455

Wagenen, Gerrit van (Businessman)
The Tides of Dawn - Emma Louise Mally 4044

Wagenet, Haille (Young Woman)
To the Swift - Anne Hawkins 2783

Wagenet, Sierra Dave (Frontiersman)
To the Swift - Anne Hawkins 2783

Waggett, Janie (Servant)
The Gambling Man - Catherine Cookson 1276

Wagner, Christopher (Servant)
Faust - Robert Nye 4654

Waguli (Indian; Warrior)
Mountain Windsong - Robert J. Conley 1246

Wainwright, Clementina (Model)
The Branch-Bearers - Glen Petrie 4978

Wainwright, Ellen (Spouse)
Cast a Long Shadow - Mary E. Pearce 4861

Wakefield, Luke (Sailor; Businessman)
The Fall River Line - Daoma Winston 6824

Wakefield, Robert (Nobleman)
The Sword of Truth - Gilbert Morris 4472

Wakeford, Davina (Gentlewoman)
The Bluestocking - June Drummond 1729

Wakemani, David (Engineer)
The Big Freeze - Bellamy Partridge 4823

Wakesfield, Megan (Noblewoman; Highwayman)
Desire and Deceive - Cordia Byers 832

Wakwa Manunnappu (Indian; Warrior)
The Mists of Manittoo - Lois Swann 6135
Torn Covenants - Lois Swann 6136

Walden (Nobleman)
The Man From St. Petersburg - Ken Follett 2148

Walden, Aurora (Spouse)
Richard Walden's Wife - Eleanor Kelly 3399

Walden, Jenny (Teenager)
Buffalo Coat - Carol Brink 691

Walden, Richard (Settler)
Richard Walden's Wife - Eleanor Kelly 3399

Waldstein, Bobby von (Nobleman)
A Princess in Berlin - Arthur R.G. Solmssen 5939

Waldstein, Lili von (Noblewoman)
A Princess in Berlin - Arthur R.G. Solmssen 5939

Wales, Josey (Outlaw)
Gone to Texas - Forrest Carter 945
The Vengeance Trail of Josey Wales - Forrest Carter 946

Wales, Marshall (Military Personnel)
The Foragers - Ben Haas 2630

Walford, Gabe (Frontiersman; Scout)
Liveliest Town in the West - Bill Gulick 2615

Walford, Harry (Worker)
Harry: A Novel of Australia - Robert Wales 6530

Walford, John (Murderer; Spirit)
Walford's Oak - Jill M. Phillips 4986

Walker, Boyd (Military Personnel)
Maximilian's Gold - Jane Barry 359

Walker, Coalhouse (Revolutionary)
Ragtime - E.L. Doctorow 1658

Walker, Dhu (Indian; Military Personnel)
Strange Company - Robert J. Conley 1251

Walker, Dhu (Indian; Rancher)
Border Line - Robert J. Conley 1238
The Long Trail North - Robert J. Conley 1245

Walker, Elizabeth (Nurse)
The Passionate Pilgrim - Charles Terrot 6204

Walker, Lillis (Young Woman)
The Weaver's Tale - Kate Sedley 5719

Walker, Margaret (Widow(er))
The Weaver's Tale - Kate Sedley 5719

Walker, Matthew (Historian)
The House of Memory: A Novel of Shanghai - Nicholas R. Clifford 1117

Walker, Nancy (Young Woman)
Web of Destiny - Muriel Elwood 1939

Walker, Samuel (Explorer)
An Embarrassment of Riches - James Howard Kunstler 3565

Walker, William (Scientist; Explorer)
An Embarrassment of Riches - James Howard Kunstler 3565

Walks in the Sun (Indian; Explorer)
Walks in the Sun - Don Coldsmith 1194

Wallace, Andrew (Leader)
Two Crowns for America - Katherine Kurtz 3568

Wallace, Buck (Adventurer)
The Pecos River - Fred Bean 399

Wallace, Finn (Prospector)
Fools' Gold - Richard Wiley 6755

Wallace, Simon (Military Personnel)
Two Crowns for America - Katherine Kurtz 3568

Wallich, Peter (Young Man)
Danzig Passage - Bodie Thoene 6221
Warsaw Requiem - Bodie Thoene 6229

Walmer, Augustus (Gentleman)
The Proprietor - Ann Schlee 5638

Walsh, Monte (Cowboy)
Monte Walsh - Jack Schaefer 5635

Walter (Religious)
The Corner That Held Them - Sylvia Townsend Warner 6568

Walter of Gurnie (Student; Bastard Son)
The Black Rose - Thomas B. Costain 1363

Walters, Margaret (Housekeeper)
Loving Sands, Deadly Sands - Charlotte Keppel 3465

Walton, Lucie (Spouse)
The Nun's Tale - Candace M. Robb 5367

Walton, Robert (Explorer)
The Memoirs of Elizabeth Frankenstein - Theodore Roszak 5508

Wandering Jew (Wanderer)
A Night with Casanova - Wolf Mankowitz 4060

Wang, Abraham (Detective—Police)
The Noel Coward Murder Case - George Baxt 387

Wang Lee (Revolutionary)
Rebels of the Heavenly Kingdom - Katherine Paterson 4828

Wang Lung (Farmer)
The Good Earth - Pearl S. Buck 754

Wantage, Hero (Orphan)
Friday's Child - Georgette Heyer 2890

War, Perceval de (Gentleman)
Deborah and the Siege of Paris - Colette Davenat 1500

Warakan (Prehistoric Human; Wanderer)
Face of the Rising Sun - William Sarabande 5598

Warburton, Anne (Gentlewoman)
The Dedicated - Willa Gibbs 2399

Warby, Gerald (Gentleman)
The Desirable Duchess - Marion Chesney 1025

Ward, Barnabas (Businessman)
Log Jam - Leslie Turner White 6684

Ward, Hagar (Pioneer; Widow(er))
New Road - Merle Estes Colby 1168

Ward, Jewel May (Gentlewoman)
Sycamore Men - David Taylor 6181

Ward, Lantry (Military Personnel)
Rogue's March - Maristan Chapman 993

Ward, Martin (Settler)
New Road - Merle Estes Colby 1168

Ward, Oliver (Engineer)
Angle of Repose - Wallace Stegner 5989

Ward, Sir Peter (Gentleman)
The Wagered Widow - Patricia Veryan 6481

Ward, Sue (Doctor)
The Hospital - Agatha Young 6938

Ward, Winthrop (Businessman)
The Winthrop Covenant - Louis Auchincloss 235

Ward, Woody (Military Personnel)
Eva - Ib Melchior 4329

Warden, Denis (Veteran)
Beyond Surrender - Marian Sims 5860

Warden, Isaac (Gentleman)
This Is the House - Deborah Hill 2921

Warden, Polly (Nurse)
Over There - Thomas Fleming 2130

Wardour, Isabella (Gentlewoman)
The Antiquary - Sir Walter Scott 5690

Wardshire, Lucifer (Nobleman)
The Scandalous Marriage - Marion Chesney 1050

Wardyke (Sorcerer; Prehistoric Human)
The Tall Stones - Moyra Caldecott 848
The Temple of the Sun - Moyra Caldecott 849

Ware, Cynthia (Heroine)
Coniston - Winston Churchill 1078

Ware, Delia (Spouse)
The Sun Shines West - Nathan Schachner 5632

Ware, Freedom (Young Woman)
The Golden Season - Oriana Akinson 60

Ware, Gillespie Vernon (Nobleman)
The Foundling - Georgette Heyer 2888

Ware, Jonathan (Settler; Professor)
The Sun Shines West - Nathan Schachner 5632

Ware, Randall (Blacksmith)
Jubilee - Margaret Walker 6531

Ware, Vyry (Slave)
Jubilee - Margaret Walker 6531

Waring, Lucy (Orphan)
Moonraker's Bride - Madeleine Brent 661

Warleggan, Elizabeth (Spouse)
The Angry Tide - Winston Graham 2521
The Black Moon - Winston Graham 2522
The Four Swans - Winston Graham 2525

Warleggan, George (Businessman)
The Black Moon - Winston Graham 2522
Demelza - Winston Graham 2524
The Four Swans - Winston Graham 2525
The Last Gamble - Winston Graham 2527
Venture Once More - Winston Graham 2532

Warleggan, George (Businessman; Political Figure)
The Angry Tide - Winston Graham 2521
The Miller's Dance - Winston Graham 2528
The Stranger From the Sea - Winston Graham 2530

Warne, Annie (Orphan; Servant)
Annie - Gloria Jahoda 3141

Warne, Ellis (Doctor)
Say to This Mountain - Bodie Thoene 6226

Warne, Ellis (Military Personnel)
In My Father's House - Bodie Thoene 6222

Warne, Ewen (Settler; Frontiersman)
Beulah Land - Harold Lenoir Davis 1520

Warner, Adam (Philosopher; Inventor)
The Last of the Barons - Edward Bulwer-Lytton 769

Warner, Edward (Adventurer; Settler)
Caribee - Christopher Nicole 4614

Warner, Jerd (Widow(er))
Farewell the Stranger - Saliee O'Brien 4682

Warner, Marguerite (Plantation Owner)
The Devil's Own - Christopher Nicole 4615

Warner, Sibyll (Young Woman)
The Last of the Barons - Edward Bulwer-Lytton 769

Warner, Stephen (Farmer)
The Marriage Bed - Jean Clark 1088

Warner, Tom (Adventurer; Settler)
Caribee - Christopher Nicole 4614 ·

Warren, Andrew (Military Personnel)
Rivers of Glory - F. van Wyck Mason 4158

Warren, Cordy (Settler)
Winter Harvest - Norah Lofts 3863

Warren, Esek (Settler)
To Fame Unknown - Clifford Lindsey Alderman 67

Warren, Hannah (Gentlewoman)
The Double Man - Elinor Pryor 5205

Warrick, John (Prospector)
Forty Pounds of Gold - Philip D. Stong 6066

Warriner, Douglas (Military Personnel)
Officers and Ladies - Richard O'Connor 4686

Warriner, Philip (Military Personnel)
Officers and Ladies - Richard O'Connor 4686

Warrington, Charles (Settler; Patriot)
The Green Mountain Boys - Daniel Pierce
  Thompson 6249

Warrington, George (Military Personnel)
The Virginians - William Makepeace
  Thackeray 6214

Warrington, Harry (Gentleman)
The Virginians - William Makepeace
  Thackeray 6214

Warrington, Howland (Businessman)
Hanover Place - Michael M. Thomas 6245

Warrington, Marietta (Gentlewoman)
Lanterns - Patricia Veryan 6465

Warwyck, Daniel (Sports Figure; Heir)
Warwyck's Woman - Rosalind Laker 3604

Warwyck, Richard (Gentleman)
Claudine's Daughter - Rosalind Laker 3594

Washakie (Indian; Chieftain)
The Man Who Loved Cat Dancing - Marilyn
  Durham 1817

Wasum, Otis (Murderer)
Hard on the Road - Barbara Moore 4440

Waters, Charles (Gentleman)
The Virginia Comedians - John Esten Cooke 1269

Watkins, Sam (Convict)
Fortune, Smile Once More - Mary Floyd
  Williams 6788

Watkiss, Admiral (Military Personnel)
Halfhyde and the Fleet Review - Philip
  McCutchan 4246

Watkiss, Captain (Military Personnel)
Halfhyde Ordered South - Philip McCutchan 4252
Halfhyde to the Narrows - Philip McCutchan 4253

Watley, Sam (Frontiersman; Trapper)
Shadows on the Long House - Mike Roarke 5360
Silent Drums - Mike Roarke 5361
Thunder in the East - Mike Roarke 5362

Watley, Thad (Frontiersman; Trapper)
Shadows on the Long House - Mike Roarke 5360
Silent Drums - Mike Roarke 5361
Thunder in the East - Mike Roarke 5362

Watson, E. J. (Plantation Owner)
Killing Mister Watson - Peter Mathiessen 4185

Watson, Emma (Young Woman)
Emma Watson - Joan Aiken 45

Watson, John H. (Doctor)
*The Beekeeper's Apprentice, or, On the Segregation of
  the Queen* - Laurie R. King 3487
The Canary Trainer - Nicholas Meyer 4348
*The Case of the Revolutionist's Daughter: Sherlock
  Holmes Meets Karl Marx* - Lewis S. Feuer 2076
Dr. Jekyll and Mr. Holmes - Loren D.
  Estleman 1970
Irene's Last Waltz - Carole Nelson Douglas 1701
The Quallsford Inheritance - Lloyd Biggle Jr. 495
The Revenge of the Hound - Michael Hardwick 2688
Seance for a Vampire - Fred Saberhagen 5557
The Seven-Per-Cent Solution - Nicholas Meyer 4349
The Seventh Bullet - Daniel D. Victor 6483
Sherlock Holmes and the Case of Sabina Hall - L.B.
  Greenwood 2576
*Sherlock Holmes and the Case of the Raleigh Legacy -
  L.B. Greenwood 2577
Sherlock Holmes and the Thistle of Scotland - L.B.
  Greenwood 2578
Sherlock Holmes vs. Dracula - Loren D.
  Estleman 1976
Sherlock in Love - Sena Jeter Naslund 4557
The West End Horror - Nicholas Meyer 4350
The Whitechapel Horrors - Edward B. Hanna 2678

Watson, John H. (Doctor; Sidekick)
The Disappearance of Edwin Drood - Peter
  Rowland 5521
*Sherlock Holmes and the Mysterious Friend of Oscar
  Wilde* - Russell A. Brown 731
Sherlock Holmes and the Red Demon - Larry
  Millett 4404
Sherlock Holmes Meets Annie Oakley - Stanley
  Shaw 5782

Watson, John H. (Doctor; Writer)
Exit Sherlock Holmes - Robert Lee Hall 2657

Watts, Deliverance (Young Woman)
Stronghold - Donald Barr Chidsey 1065

Waverley, Edward (Military Personnel)
Waverley - Sir Walter Scott 5709

Waverly, Fanny (Gentlewoman)
The First Rebellion - Marion Chesney 1030

Wayburn, Raney (Young Woman)
A Georgian Love Story - Ernest Raymond 5258

Wayfish, Ike (Entertainer)
Chad Hanna - Walter D. Edmonds 1873

Wayman, Gwen (Spouse)
The Land Endures - Mary E. Pearce 4862

Wayman, Stephen (Lawyer; Farmer)
The Land Endures - Mary E. Pearce 4862

Wayne, Matthew (Military Personnel; Journalist)
Guns of Chickamauga - Richard O'Connor 4685

Wayte, Cecilia (Religious)
The Nunnery - Dorothy Charques 1001

Weatherby, Clint (Sports Figure)
The Great Blizzard - Albert E. Idell 3101

Weatherby, Mark (Teacher)
Windover - Jane Aiken Hodge 2974

Weaver (Government Official; Gentleman)
Death and the Chapman - Kate Sedley 5715

Weaver, Alice (Worker)
The Pilgrim of Hate - Ellis Peters 4967

Weaver, Harry (Bastard Son)
Scapegoat for a Stuart - Kate Kirby 3504

Webb (Mountain Man)
Moontrap - Don Berry 481

Webb, Becky (Worker)
Sunrise to Sunset - Samuel Hopkins Adams 32

Webb, Joshua (Banker)
The Salamanca Drum - Dorothy Eden 1861

Weber, Susanna (Store Owner)
Madensky Square - Eva Ibbotson 3096

Webley (Military Personnel)
Silk and Steel - Stephen Alter 122

Webster, Alma (Gentlewoman)
The False Inspeator Dew - Peter Lovesey 3912

Webster, Richard (Religious)
The Standing Hills - Caroline Stickland 6038

Wedderlie, Edgar (Nobleman)
Strong as Death - Sharan Newman 4602

Weddle, Clorinda (Spouse)
The Corinthians - Nicholas E. Wyckoff 6888

Weddle, Simon (Young Man)
The Corinthians - Nicholas E. Wyckoff 6888

Wedlock, Ben (Outlaw)
Sudden Country - Loren D. Estleman 1979

Weed, Frederick (Businessman)
Trinity - Leon Uris 6394

Weems, Josiah (Religious)
The Blood Seed - Andrew Ward 6561

Weigel, Jake (Businessman)
Anna, Ann, Annie - Thomas Trebitsch Parker 4808

Weill, Victor (Gentleman)
Vardy - John Harris 2721

Weir, Helen (Young Woman)
*The Buckskin Girl: A Novel of the California Trail in
  the Mid-Nineteenth Century* - Gwen Moffat 4426

Weitz, Joseph (Businessman)
Bayou - Pamela Jekel 3183

Welby, Richard (Military Personnel)
The Caretaker Wife - Barbara Whitehead 6706

Welldone, Kate (Heroine)
Sergeant Lamb's America - Robert Graves 2552

Welles, Nathan (Religious)
And Never Yield - Elinor Pryor 5204

Wellesley, Lady Barbara (Noblewoman)
Flying Colours - C.S. Forester 2173
The Life and Times of Horatio Hornblower - C.
  Northcote Parkinson 4813

Wellington, Thance (Businessman)
The President's Daughter - Barbara Chase-
  Riboud 1005

Wells, Charlotte (Gentlewoman)
Weep in the Sun - Jeanne Wilson 6809

Wells, Constance (Spouse)
The Head Waters - Archie Binns 500

Wells, C.P. (Businessman)
Paradise Falls - Don Robertson 5399

Wells, Cynthia Ann (Captive; Gentlewoman)
Sioux Splendor - Rosanne Bittner 515

Wells, Miranda (Young Woman)
Dragonwyck - Anya Seton 5750

Wells, Sarah (Captive)
Ghost Fox - James Houston 3051

Wells, Tom (Pioneer)
The Head Waters - Archie Binns 500

Wells, Colonel Walter (Plantation Owner)
Weep in the Sun - Jeanne Wilson 6809

Welsford, Upton (Government Official)
The Revenge of Dracula - Peter Tremayne   6335

Wen Chin (Government Official)
Twilight of the Dragon - Peter Bourne   596

Wendell, Charlotte (Young Woman)
New Deal for Death - Elliott Roosevelt   5454

Wendover, Abigail (Gentlewoman)
Black Sheep - Georgette Heyer   2878

Wendover, Fanny (Heiress)
Black Sheep - Georgette Heyer   2878

Wentwater, Guy (Gentleman)
Deirdre and Desire - Marion Chesney   1024

Wentworth, Cecilly (Gentlewoman)
Dark Winds - Virginia Coffman   1152

Wentworth, Darius (Heir)
Come Be My Love - Diana Brown   717

Wentworth, Lilian de (Gentlewoman; Invalid)
Willowwood - Mollie Hardwick   2699

Wentworth, Peter (Religious)
Burden of Desire - Robert MacNeil   4023

Wentworth, Thomas (Landowner)
The Physician of London - Stephanie Cowell   1394

Wessel, Simon (Farmer)
The Red Marten - Peter William Nisser   4630

West, Alison (Young Woman)
The Second Face of Valor - Ray Grant Toepfer   6288

West, Morgan (Shipowner; Sea Captain)
The Wings of Morning - Karen Harper   2714

Westbrook, Gideon (Nobleman)
Ravished - Amanda Quick   5216

Westbrook, Hugh (Rancher)
The Dreaming: A Novel of Australia - Barbara Wood   6848

Westburn, Maud (Young Woman)
The Maclarens - C.L. Skelton   5873

Westcott, Trent (Gentleman)
The Braeswood Tapestry - Robyn Carr   936

Western, Deborah (Noblewoman)
Deborah Goes to Dover - Marion Chesney   1023

Westfall, Blake (Young Man)
This Land Is Mine - Frances Casey Kerns   3470

Westfield, Michael (Orphan)
Westfield - Roderick Thorp   6277

Westfield, Thomas (Political Figure)
Westfield - Roderick Thorp   6277

Westing, Tom (Sailor)
Lisbon - Valerie Sherwood   5825

Westlake, Gillian (Young Woman)
Roll, Shenandoah - Bruce Lancaster   3644

Westmoreland, Ed (Trader)
Six-Horse Hitch - Janice Holt Giles   2417

Westmoreland, Olivia (Gentlewoman)
The Highland Hawk - Leslie Turner White   6682

Weston, Aylmer (Political Figure)
Statues in a Garden - Isabel Colegate   1198

Weston, Edmund (Gentleman)
Statues in a Garden - Isabel Colegate   1198

Weston, James (Gentleman)
Women of Ashdon - Valerie Anand   135

Weston, Rilla (Governess; Companion)
The House of Kuragin - Constance Heaven   2808

Weston, Sophie (Young Woman)
The Astrov Legacy - Constance Heaven   2802

Westruther, Jack (Gentleman)
Cotillion - Georgette Heyer   2883

Westwood, Major Ambrose (Diplomat)
Grand Days - Frank Moorhouse   4448

Wharton, Captain Henry (Loyalist; Military Personnel)
The Spy: A Tale of the Neutral Ground - James Fenimore Cooper   1310

Wheatley, Lena (Settler)
The Family of Women - Richard Peck   4883

Wheaton, Elias (Military Personnel)
The Charlatan - Carter A. Vaughan   6433

Wheaton, Francis (Settler)
Thanksgiving - Terry Coleman   1207

Wheeler (Outcast)
The Mudlark - Theodore Bonnet   573

Wheeler (Veteran)
The Terrible Teague Bunch - Gary Jennings   3197

Wheeler, Chancey (Writer)
The Town - Conrad Richter   5325

Wheeler, F. Morrison (Businessman)
Biscayne - Barry Jay Kaplan   3365

Wheeler, Portius (Lawyer)
The Town - Conrad Richter   5325

Wheeler, Portius (Lawyer; Backwoodsman)
The Fields - Conrad Richter   5319
The Trees - Conrad Richter   5326

Wheeler, Sayward (Backwoodswoman)
The Fields - Conrad Richter   5319
The Town - Conrad Richter   5325

Wheeler, Tom (Journalist)
Siege in the Sun - Mary Paradise   4788

Whetstone, Thomas (Plantation Owner; Pirate)
Galleon - Dudley Pope   5095

Whetstone, Yarborough (Plantation Owner)
Foundation Stone - Lella Warren   6571

Whidden, Phoebe (Gentlewoman)
Blue Hurricane - F. van Wyck Mason   4146

Whipple, Abiezar (Shipowner)
The Pepper Tree - John Edward Jennings   3203

Whipple, Ben (Military Personnel; Murderer)
Seminole - Donald Clayton Porter   5126

Whipple, Dora (Spy; Widow(er))
Confederates - Thomas Keneally   3412

Whipple, Jessie (Young Woman; Spouse)
The Pepper Tree - John Edward Jennings   3203

Whipple, John (Religious)
Hawaii - James A. Michener   4370

Whirlwind (Indian)
Buffalo Woman - Dorothy M. Johnson   3223

Whisten, Benjamin Biddle (Gentleman; Heir)
Bygones - Frank Wilkinson   6762

Whistlecraft, Judith (Young Woman)
Blossom Like the Rose - Norah Lofts   3836

Whitaker, Margery (Young Woman)
Elegant Witch - Robert Neill   4568

Whitaker, Otis (Political Figure)
While Rivers Flow - Glen H. Fleischmann   2125

Whitaker, Rene Jo (Spouse)
While Rivers Flow - Glen H. Fleischmann   2125

Whitby, Mary (Teacher; Feminist)
The Woman Question - Dorothea Malm   4046

Whitby, Phoebe (Young Woman)
The Woman Question - Dorothea Malm   4046

Whitcombe, Lionel (Businessman)
Ruby - Helen Ashfield   213

White, Blanco (Rancher)
Glowstone - Macdonald Harris   2725

White, Brant (Gunfighter; Gambler)
Saint Johnson - William R. Burnett   796

White, Jim (Cowboy)
Bully! - Mark Schorr   5670

White, Juan (Teenager)
The Men of Gonzales - John H. Culp   1442

White, Patience (Lesbian)
Patience and Sarah - Isabel Miller   4398

White, Perry Poer (Young Man)
Red Lanterns on St. Michael's - Thornwell Jacobs   3139

White, Polly (Servant)
The Silver Saber - Carter A. Vaughan   6441

White Antelope (Indian)
The Scout - Harry Combs   1224

White Ash (Psychic; Prehistoric Human)
People of the Earth - W. Michael Gear   2334

White Bird (Indian; Warrior)
The Fleet Rabble: A Novel of the Nez Perce War - Frank Borden Hanes   2675

White Buffalo (Indian; Shaman)
Scalpdancers - Kerry Newcomb   4592

White Feathers (Indian)
Thunderstick - Don Coldsmith   1190

White Fox (Indian)
Song of the Rock - Don Coldsmith   1189

White Fox (Indian; Shaman)
Fort De Chastaigne - Don Coldsmith   1177

White Hand (Indian; Chieftain)
Breakheart Pass - Alistair MacLean   3999

White Horn (Indian)
Distant Trumpet - Paul Horgan   3032

White River (Frontiersman)
Beyond the Stars - David William Ross   5497

Whitebear (Indian; Chieftain)
The Shadow Riders - Terry C. Johnston   3257

Whitehall, Amanda (Gentlewoman)
Amanda/Miranda - Richard Peck   4882

Whiteman, Nicholas J. (Military Personnel)
Sherman's March - Cynthia Bass   373

Whiteoak, Adeline (Spouse)
Morning at Jalna - Mazo de la Roche   1560

Whiteoak, Philip (Landowner)
Morning at Jalna - Mazo de la Roche   1560

Whitespear (Prehistoric Human)
Singletusk - Bjorn Kurten   3567

Whitey (Cowboy)
These Thousand Hills - A.B. Guthrie Jr.   2627

Whitfield, Matilda (Gentlewoman)
Theo and Matilda - Rachel Billington   498

Whiting, Richard (Gentleman; Landowner)
Three-Headed Angel - Roark Bradford   623

Whitman, Homer (Sailor)
American Captain - Edison Marshall   4101

Whitman, Jonathan (Worker)
The Marigold Field - Diane Pearson   4876

Whitman, Rebecca (Servant)
Bound Girl - Everett Webber   6591

Whitmead, George (Businessman)
The Cherished Wives - Valerie Anand   126

Whitmead, Lucy-Anne (Spouse)
The Cherished Wives - Valerie Anand   126

Whitmead, Ninian (Landowner)
The Faithful Lovers - Valerie Anand   129

Whitmead, Susannah (Young Woman)
Women of Ashdon - Valerie Anand   135

Whittaker, Olana (Journalist)
Waltzing in Ragtime - Eileen Charbonneau 996

Whitton, Edmund (Heir)
Whitton's Folly - Pamela Hill 2948

Whitton, Selena (Gentlewoman)
Lord Iverbrook's Heir - Carola Dunn 1795

Whitworth, Morwenna (Spouse)
The Angry Tide - Winston Graham 2521
The Four Swans - Winston Graham 2525

Whitworth, Osborne (Religious)
The Angry Tide - Winston Graham 2521
The Four Swans - Winston Graham 2525

Whyte, Catherine (Settler)
By Reason of Strength - Gerald White Johnson 3225

Whytting, Sir John (Loyalist)
The Rival Shores - Arthur Beverly-Giddings 487

Wickersham, Victoria (Spouse)
Eden - Julie Ellis 1918

Wickett, Hugo (Editor)
The Labyrinth - Thomas William Duncan 1787

Wickham, Belle (Widow(er); Spy)
The Dixie Widow - Gilbert Morris 4459

Wicks, James (Military Personnel)
Wild Is the River - Louis Bromfield 704

Widdrington, Lady Elizabeth (Noblewoman)
A Famine of Horses - P.F. Chisholm 1071
A Season of Knives - P.F. Chisholm 1072

Widowson, Alfred (Religious)
The Golden Hand - Edith Simon 5856

Widowson, Edwin (Gentleman)
The Golden Hand - Edith Simon 5856

Wigmore, Frederick (Actor)
The King Edward Plot - Robert Lee Hall 2658

Wilberforce, Oliver (Doctor)
Jack the Ripper - Richard Gordon 2484

Wilcox, Bella (Spouse)
The Wedding Journey - Walter D. Edmonds 1878

Wilcox, Carl (Hotel Worker)
The Man Who Missed the Party - Harold Adams 25

Wilcox, Roger (Young Man)
The Wedding Journey - Walter D. Edmonds 1878

Wild O'Brien (Adventurer)
Thanksgiving - Terry Coleman 1207

Wild Rose (Indian)
Brules - Harry Combs 1223

Wilde, Dorcas (Gentlewoman)
By Our Beginnings - Jean Stubbs 6092

Wilde, Janice (Young Woman)
Patriot's Dream - Barbara Michaels 4360

Wilde, Sam (Trapper)
The Predators - F.A. Parker 4804

Wilder, Leela (Orphan; Spouse)
Black Gold - Anita Richmond Bunkley 771

Wilder, Marigold (Religious)
The Blue Dragon - Diana Brown 716

Wilder, T.J. (Farmer)
Black Gold - Anita Richmond Bunkley 771

Wilford, Emma (Young Woman)
Wilford's Daughter - Alexandra Manners 4071

Wilfred of Ivanhoe (Knight)
Ivanhoe - Sir Walter Scott 5699

Wilkes, Ashley (Gentleman; Plantation Owner)
Gone with the Wind - Margaret Mitchell 4415

Wilkins, Penelope (Gentlewoman)
Penelope Goes to Portsmouth - Marion
  Chesney 1043

Wilkinson, Esther (Prostitute)
An Innocent Woman - Malcolm Macdonald 3967

Will (Musician)
Jewel of the Sea - Susan Wiggs 6743

Will (Worker)
*Bodin, 1349: An Epic Novel of Christians and Jews in
  the Plague Years* - Roberta Kalechofsky 3322

Will, Silas (Religious)
Riders of the Long Road - Stephen E. Bransford 649

Willard, Abigail (Loyalist; Orphan)
A Toast to the King - Elizabeth Coatsworth 1139

Willard, Eli (Trader)
The Architecture of the Arkansas Ozarks - Donald
  Harington 2708

Willard, Georgianna (Loyalist; Orphan)
A Toast to the King - Elizabeth Coatsworth 1139

Willard, Judith (Loyalist; Orphan)
A Toast to the King - Elizabeth Coatsworth 1139

Willard, Simon (Military Personnel)
Savage Gentleman - Noel B. Gerson 2381

Willett, Dorcas (Young Woman)
Tomorrow the Harvest - Viola Paradise 4789

Willetti, Tom (Spy)
The Drums of April - Charles Mergendahl 4340

William, William (Sailor)
The Glittering Strand - Judith Lennox-Smith 3716

William Long-Arm (Knight)
When God Slept - Peter Bourne 597

William of Baskerville (Religious; Scholar)
The Name of the Rose - Umberto Eco 1850

William of Colchester (Gentleman)
The Swords of December - Robert York 6933

William of Miraval (Nobleman; Handicapped)
Candle in the Window - Christina Dodd 1662

William of Sens (Artisan)
The Pillars of the Earth - Ken Follett 2149

Williams, Cary (Companion)
Three Rivers - Carla J. Mills 4406

Williams, Constancy (Young Woman)
The Lord's Anointed - Ruth Eleanor McKee 4282

Williams, Eliza (Governess)
Eliza's Daughter - Joan Aiken 44

Williams, Elizabeth (Young Woman)
The Prospering - Elizabeth Speare 5954

Williams, Ephraim (Settler)
The Prospering - Elizabeth Speare 5954

Williams, Hugh (Military Personnel)
Unto This Hour - Tom Wicker 6733

Williams, Nash (Religious)
Crossing the River - Caryl Phillips 4984

Williamsburg (Slave)
The Journey of August King - John Ehle 1894

Williamson, Fancy (Heroine)
A Woman Called Fancy - Frank Yerby 6931

Willinck, Susan (Prostitute)
Flash for Freedom - George MacDonald Fraser 2203

Willoughby, Edwin (Gentleman)
The Summer of the Bashinskeys - Diane
  Pearson 4877

Willoughby, Lizzie (Young Woman; Nurse)
Siege in the Sun - Mary Paradise 4788

Willoughby, Nathan (Businessman)
Rogue's Harbor - Inglis Fletcher 2139

Willoughby, Robert (Settler)
The Colonists - William Stuart Long 3870

Willoughby, Robin (Sailor)
Rogue's Harbor - Inglis Fletcher 2139

Willoughby, Sophie (Gentlewoman)
The Summer of the Bashinskeys - Diane
  Pearson 4877

Willoughby, Tom (Judge)
The Siege of Krishnapur - J.G. Farrell 2016

Wilmot, Ann (Captive)
The Southern Blade - Nelson Wolford 6844

Wilner, Saul (Peddler)
Behold the Fire - Michael Blankfort 541

Wilson (Military Personnel)
The Red Badge of Courage - Stephen Crane 1414

Wilson, Francis (Settler)
Juniata Valley - Virginia C. Cassel 954

Wilson, Katherine (Young Woman)
Katherine - Antonia Van-Loon 6425

Wilson, Kent (Doctor)
For Love and Honor - Antonia Van-Loon 6423

Wilson, Kent (Military Personnel; Doctor)
For Us the Living - Antonia Van-Loon 6424

Wilson, Samuel (Sea Captain)
The Southern Cross - Peter French 2226

Wilton, Lucie (Young Woman)
The Apothecary Rose - Candace M. Robb 5364

Wilton, Nicholas (Apothecary)
The Apothecary Rose - Candace M. Robb 5364

Wilty, Cotton (Military Personnel)
The King's Iron - Robert Newton Peck 4888

Win, Philip (Tailor)
The Hooded Falcon - Prudence Andrew 140

Wind, Bethany (Government Official)
Chase the Wind - Janelle Taylor 6184

Wind Caller (Prehistoric Human)
The Deer Dancers - Amanda Cockrell 1146

Wind River Kid (Gambler; Recluse)
The Ghosts of Elkhorn - Kerry Newcomb 4589

Windham, Keith (Military Personnel)
The Flight of the Heron - Dorothy Kathleen
  Broster 710

Windrow, Oliver (Settler; Artisan)
Remembrance Rock - Carl Sandburg 5583

Windsor, Ainsley (Young Woman)
Harvest of Dreams - Jaroldeen Edwards 1884

Winfield, Delilah (Settler)
Delilah's Mountain - Gloria Jahoda 3142

Winfred (Nobleman)
The Last Romans - Teodor Jeske-Choinski 3216

Wingate, Ann (Frontierswoman)
So Free We Seem - Helen Todd 6286

Wingate, Molly (Pioneer)
Covered Wagon - Emerson Hough 3041

Wingfield, Olympia (Spinster)
Deception - Amanda Quick 5214

Winkowski, Agnes (Businesswoman)
The Rag Nymph - Catherine Cookson 1287

Winship, Bart (Diplomat)
Storm to the South - Thelma Strabel 6073

Winship, Louisa (Student)
If I Were You - Joan Aiken 49

Winshore, Ordway (Printer)
Remembrance Rock - Carl Sandburg 5583

Winslow, Aaron (Military Personnel)
The Rough Rider - Gilbert Morris 4468

Winslow, Adam (Farmer)
The Indentured Heart - Gilbert Morris 4464

Winslow, Barney (Sports Figure)
The Final Adversary - Gilbert Morris 4460

Winslow, Brent (Settler; Farmer)
Blue Camellia - Frances Parkinson Keyes 3477

Winslow, Cassidy (Young Man)
The Yukon Queen - Gilbert Morris 4476

Winslow, Christmas (Frontiersman)
The Holy Warrior - Gilbert Morris 4462

Winslow, Dan (Rancher)
The Valiant Gunman - Gilbert Morris 4474

Winslow, Davis (Military Personnel)
The Dixie Widow - Gilbert Morris 4459

Winslow, Diana (Noblewoman; Pilot)
Once a Gentleman - Donald James 3157

Winslow, Gilbert (Religious; Settler)
The Honorable Imposter - Gilbert Morris 4463

Winslow, Gilbert (Settler)
The Captive Bride - Gilbert Morris 4457

Winslow, Harriet (Young Woman)
The Old Gringo - Carlos Fuentes 2247

Winslow, Knox (Trader)
The Holy Warrior - Gilbert Morris 4462

Winslow, Laurie (Entertainer)
The Jewelled Spur - Gilbert Morris 4465

Winslow, Lavinia (Young Woman)
Blue Camellia - Frances Parkinson Keyes 3477

Winslow, Margaret (Settler; Orphan)
Here I Stay - Elizabeth Coatsworth 1138

Winslow, Mark (Gunfighter)
The Union Belle - Gilbert Morris 4473

Winslow, Mary (Spouse)
Blue Camellia - Frances Parkinson Keyes 3477

Winslow, Nathan (Military Personnel; Patriot)
The Gentle Rebel - Gilbert Morris 4461
The Saintly Buccaneer - Gilbert Morris 4469

Winslow, Paul (Loyalist)
The Saintly Buccaneer - Gilbert Morris 4469

Winslow, Rachel (Spouse)
The Captive Bride - Gilbert Morris 4457

Winslow, Rebekah (Spouse)
The Last Confederate - Gilbert Morris 4466

Winslow, Sky (Frontiersman)
The Reluctant Bridegroom - Gilbert Morris 4467

Winslow, Sky (Plantation Owner)
The Last Confederate - Gilbert Morris 4466

Winslow, Thomas (Veteran; Government Official)
The Crossed Sabres - Gilbert Morris 4458

Winslow, Whitfield (Military Personnel)
The Dixie Widow - Gilbert Morris 4459

Winslow, Zack (Veteran)
The Wounded Yankee - Gilbert Morris 4475

Winster, Jonathan (Farmer)
Peace, My Daughters - Shirley Barker 314

Winster, Remember (Spouse)
Peace, My Daughters - Shirley Barker 314

Winston, Cassandra Dell (Young Woman)
They Called Her Mrs. Doc - Janette Oke 4709

Winston, Hugh (Adventurer; Pirate)
Caribbee - Thomas Hoover 3025

Winter, Avys (Gentlewoman)
My Lady Greensleeves - Constance Beresford-
Howe 476

Winter, Piers (Gentleman)
My Lady Greensleeves - Constance Beresford-
Howe 476

Winter, Stephen (Veteran)
Fallen Skies - Philippa Gregory 2581

Winter Cherry (Young Woman)
Winter Cherry - Keith West 6632

Winter Swan (Indian)
The Great Alone - Janet Dailey 1454

Winterbourne, Daniel (Nobleman)
Miss Hartwell's Dilemma - Carola Dunn 1796

Winterbourne, George (Gentleman)
Two Corinthians - Carola Dunn 1797

Duke of Winterset (Nobleman)
Monsieur Beaucaire - Booth Tarkington 6163

Wintersill, Brook Henry (Gentleman)
The Cannaway Concern - Graham Shelby 5788

Winthrop, Edwin (Military Personnel)
The Bloody Red Baron - Kim Newman 4596

Winthrop, John (Indian)
The Day the Sun Died - Dale Van Every 6408

Winthrop, Knight (Nobleman; Rake)
Night Shadow - Catherine Coulter 1377

Winton, Leslie (Teacher)
Mills of the Gods - Daoma Winston 6828

Wintour, Gillian (Gentlewoman)
Opal - Helen Ashfield 210

Winwold, Omri (Farmer)
Remembrance Rock - Carl Sandburg 5583

Winwood, Horatia (Noblewoman)
The Convenient Marriage - Georgette Heyer 2882

Wise Coyote (Royalty; Architect)
The Jaguar Princess - Clare Bell 421

Wiswell, Oliver (Loyalist; Military Personnel)
Oliver Wiswell - Kenneth Roberts 5389

Withers, Damaris (Young Woman; Abuse Victim)
A Woman Named Damaris - Janette Oke 4711

Witherspoon, Mrs. (Housekeeper)
Mrs. Jeffries on the Ball - Emily Brightwell 685

Witherspoon, Gerald (Detective—Police)
The Ghost and Mrs. Jeffries - Emily Brightwell 681
The Inspector and Mrs. Jeffries - Emily
Brightwell 682
Mrs. Jeffries and the Missing Alibi - Emily
Brightwell 683
Mrs. Jeffries Dusts for Clues - Emily Brightwell 684
Mrs. Jeffries on the Ball - Emily Brightwell 685
Mrs. Jeffries on the Trail - Emily Brightwell 686
Mrs. Jeffries Plays the Cook - Emily Brightwell 687
Mrs. Jeffries Stands Corrected - Emily
Brightwell 688
Mrs. Jeffries Takes Stock - Emily Brightwell 689

Wivenhoe, Artemia (Companion)
Artemia - Pamela Hill 2927

Woburn, Nora (Spouse)
The Artist's Daughter - Leslie O'Grady 4698

Woburn, Oliver (Gentleman)
The Artist's Daughter - Leslie O'Grady 4698

Wogan, Mrs. (Spy; Convict)
Desolation Island - Patrick O'Brian 4662

Wolders, Alex (Adventurer)
Lady Jane - Leslie O'Grady 4699

Wolf (Prehistoric Human; Warrior)
The Mammoth Stone - Margaret Allan 90

Wolf, Michael (Time Traveller; Indian)
A Whisper on the Wind - Madeline Baker 276

Wolf of Foix (Bastard Son)
Deep Are the Valleys - Hannah Closs 1129
High Are the Mountains - Hannah Closs 1130
The Silent Tarn - Hannah Closs 1131

Wolf Pup (Indian; Healer)
Bearer of the Pipe - Don Coldsmith 1169

Wolfe, Lauren (Actress)
The Only Thing to Fear - David Poyer 5160

Wolfe, Simon (Doctor; Military Personnel)
Shadow on the Valley - Kirk Mitchell 4414

Wolf's Head (Indian; Shaman)
The Sacred Hills - Don Coldsmith 1187

Wolsey, Hester (Companion; Housekeeper)
Mother and Son - Ivy Compton-Burnett 1231

Wood, Ann (Businesswoman)
Strange Devices of the Sun and Moon - Lisa
Goldstein 2463

Wood, Lorena (Prostitute)
Lonesome Dove - Larry McMurtry 4298

Wood, Owen (Carpenter)
Jack Sheppard - William Harrison Ainsworth 56

Wood-Lacy, Jennifer (Young Woman)
A Future Arrived - Phillip Rock 5420

Wood-Lacy, Victoria (Young Woman)
A Future Arrived - Phillip Rock 5420

Woodbridge, Dawn (Captive)
Buckskin Cavalier - John Clagett 1082

Woodbridge, Jonathan (Veteran; Settler)
The Bounty Lands - William Donohue Ellis 1927

Woodbury, Randall (Doctor; Widow(er))
Swear by Apollo - Shirley Barker 318

Woodbyne, Laurie (Gentleman)
Beyond the Shining Mountains - Doris
Shannon 5775

Woodcarver, Thomas (Landowner)
The Ruthless Yeomen - Valerie Anand 134

Woodcott, Anthony (Spy)
My Lord the Fox - Robert York 6932

Woodfall, Cecily (Gentlewoman)
Trust and Treason - Margaret Birkhead 506

Woodfall, Thomas (Gentleman)
Trust and Treason - Margaret Birkhead 506

Woodfoot (Cowboy)
The Last Hunt - Milton Lott 3900

Woodhouse, Emma (Gentlewoman)
Jane Fairfax - Joan Aiken 50

Woodlawn, Caddie (Teenager)
Caddie Woodlawn - Carol Brink 692

Woodleigh, Isabella (Gentlewoman)
Gilded Splendour - Rosalind Laker 3595

Woodley, Adam (Artisan)
Pargeters - Norah Lofts 3857

Woodley, Cato (Sea Captain)
The Great Steamboat Race - John Brunner 736

Woodling, Alexandra (Southern Belle)
Oklahoma! - Dana Fuller Ross 5482

Woodrofe, Mark (Bastard Son)
Trumpeter, Sound! - D.L. Murray 4528

Woodruff, Isabelle Chadwick (Gentlewoman)
The Dream Seekers - Grace Mark 4085

Woodruff, Sarah (Young Woman)
The French Lieutenant's Woman - John Fowles 2194

Woods, Dan (Journalist)
The Land Was Ours: A Novel of the Great Plains -
Charles W. Bailey 266

Woods, Grace (Spouse)
The Land Was Ours: A Novel of the Great Plains -
Charles W. Bailey 266

Woodson, Sylvester (Servant; Slave)
A Story of Deep Delight - Thomas McNamee 4305

Woodville, Loren (Scientist)
Joy in Mudville - Gordon McAlpine 4216

Woodward, Wyeth (Military Personnel)
By Valour and Arms - James H. Street 6076

Woollatt, Margaret (Servant)
The Son of York - Margaret Abbey 5

Woolley, Stanley (Military Personnel)
Goshawk Squadron - Derek Robinson 5403

Wormset, Richard Oliver (Doctor; Spy)
Seventeen of Leyden - John James 3160

Worth, Anthony (Plantation Owner; Political Figure)
Crimson Is the Eastern Shore - Don Tracy 6308

Worth, Gracellen (Young Woman)
Crimson Is the Eastern Shore - Don Tracy 6308

Worth, Maddie (Singer)
Mountain Laurel - Jude Deveraux 1632

Worth, Patience (Spouse)
To Have and to Hold - Mary Johnston 3241

Wounded Bear (Indian; Shaman)
Sand in the Wind - Kathleen O'Neal Gear 2329

Wouwere, Nicholas von (Doctor; Occultist)
Prophecies - Helena Soister 5937

Wraxall, Delilah (Gentlewoman)
Enlightening Delilah - Marion Chesney 1028

Wraysford, Stephen (Businessman; Military Personnel)
Birdsong - Sebastian Faulks 2051

Wreckage, Georgie (Artist)
Funny Papers - Tom De Haven 1559

Wrenthe, Justin (Nobleman)
The Earl and the Heiress - Barbara Metzger 4345

Wrexham, Lord Redvers (Nobleman)
Caroline and Julia - Clare Darcy 1484

Wright, Sir Benjamin (Nobleman)
The Scandalous Lady Wright - Marion Chesney 1049

Wright, Emma (Noblewoman)
The Scandalous Lady Wright - Marion Chesney 1049

Wright, Jedediah (Farmer; Widow(er))
The Taste of Time - Ferol Egan 1892

Wright, Jonathan (Sailor; Fisherman)
Eye of the Hurricane - Fergus Reid Buckley 757

Wright, Missy (Gentlewoman)
The Ladies of Missalonghi - Colleen McCullough 4237

Wright, Mooney (Settler)
The Land Breakers - John Ehle 1895

Wright, Owen (Military Personnel)
Time of Drums - John Ehle 1897

Wright, Riley (Journalist)
Ride with Me, Mariah Montana - Ivan Doig 1684

Wright, Stella (Young Woman)
Flight From Avatchez - Frank G. Slaughter 5887

Wright, Weatherby (Engineer; Railroad Worker)
The Road - John Ehle 1896

Wroth, Oliver (Gentleman)
Captain Nash and the Wroth Inheritance - Ragan Butler 828

Wrox Hampden, Maria (Gentlewoman)
Time and Chance - Gwen Davenport 1501

Wulf (Captive; Warrior)
The Fourteenth of October - Bryher 742

Wulfhild (Young Woman)
The Disputed Crown - Valerie Anand 128

Wulfric (Blacksmith)
The Adversary - Jan Widgery 6738

Wulfrunt (Witch)
Gilded Spurs - Grace Ingram 3105

Wunderlich, Jacob (Scientist)
Beginning the World Again - Roberta Silman 5851

Wyatt, Henry (Sailor)
Golden Admiral - F. van Wyck Mason 4150

Wyatt, Horatio (Businessman; Loyalist)
Trumpets at Dawn - Cyril Harris 2719

Wyatt, Jeffrey (Servant; Military Personnel)
Savage Gentleman - Noel B. Gerson 2381

Wyatt, Jem (Servant)
Footman in Powder - Helen Ashton 216

Wyatt, Jonathan (Spy)
The Golden Eagle - Noel B. Gerson 2370

Wyatt, Sam (Military Personnel)
Trumpets at Dawn - Cyril Harris 2719

Wychwood, Annis (Gentlewoman)
Lady of Quality - Georgette Heyer 2893

Wychwood, Charles (Writer)
Chatterton - Peter Ackroyd 17

Wydawski (Nobleman)
Salvation - Sholem Asch 202

Wyeth, Trevor (Blockade Runner)
Bride of a Thousand Cedars - Bruce Lancaster 3637

Wyllys, Mrs. (Governess)
The Red Rover - James Fenimore Cooper 1309

Wyman, Phyllida (Young Woman)
The Rival Shores - Arthur Beverly-Giddings 487

Wyngarde, Lady Damaris (Noblewoman)
My Dear Lover England - Pamela Bennetts 453

Wynne, Hugh (Military Personnel; Spy)
Hugh Wynne, Free Quaker - Silas Weir Mitchell 4416

Wynne, Jeremy (Convict; Servant)
The King's Passenger - Nathan Schachner 5631

Wynne of Gwernach (Noblewoman)
A Moment in Time - Bertrice Small 5911

Wynter, Richard (Military Personnel)
The Fires of Glenlochy - Constance Heaven 2806

Wyse, Francis (Worker)
I Am England - Patricia Wright 6881

Wythe, Lady Caroline (Noblewoman)
The Autumn Rose - Fiona Hill 2923

X

Xanthus (Professor)
The Fabulist - John Vornholt 6512

Xiao Pouzi (Actor)
Farewell to My Concubine - Lilian Lee 3709

Xiao Shitou (Actor)
Farewell to My Concubine - Lilian Lee 3709

Xuchitl (Royalty)
The Heart of Jade - Salvador de Madariaga 4024

Y

Yamamoto, Kenichi (Scholar)
Kagami - Elizabeth Kata 3369

Yamamoto, Renzo (Diplomat)
Kagami - Elizabeth Kata 3369

Yanagisawa (Government Official)
Bundori - Laura Joh Rowland 5519

Yanan (Prehistoric Human; Teenager)
Reindeer Moon - Elizabeth Marshall Thomas 6244

Yancey, Don (Frontiersman)
Shadows in the Dusk - John Edward Jennings 3208

Yardley, George (Military Personnel)
A Durable Fire - Virginia Bernhard 480

Yardley, Temperance (Settler)
A Durable Fire - Virginia Bernhard 480

Yarico (Young Woman)
Caribee - Christopher Nicole 4614

Yates, Theophilius (Young Woman)
A Land to Tame - Zola Helen Ross 5505

Yayael (Servant; Indian)
My Master Columbus - Cedric Belfrage 418

Yealm, Anna (Widow(er))
Brumaire - Mark Logan 3864
Guillotine - Mark Logan 3865

Yechiel, Reb (Religious)
Salvation - Sholem Asch 202

Yechiel, Rivke (Worker)
Salvation - Sholem Asch 202

Yehudah, Ben (Military Personnel)
Son of Judah - Dan Levin 3738

Yehudi (Magician; Teacher)
Mr. Vertigo - Paul Auster 244

Yellan, Mary (Young Woman)
Jamaica Inn - Daphne Du Maurier 1747

Yellow Bird (Indian; Child)
Seize the Sky - Terry C. Johnston 3256

Yellow Bird (Indian; Shaman)
Whisper of the Wolf - Terry C. Johnston 3261

Yellow Emperor (Ruler)
Bronze Mirror - Jeanne Larsen 3668

Ygerma (Royalty)
Sword at Sunset - Rosemary Sutcliff 6125

Yin-Kwa (Businessman)
White Poppy - Margaret Gaan 2261

York, Jeremiah (Trader)
Eagles of Destiny - Jory Sherman 5817

York, Joshua (Gentleman; Vampire)
Fevre Dream - George R.R. Martin 4131

York, Meg (Young Woman)
The Devil in Velvet - John Dickson Carr 909

York, Veronica (Widow(er); Gentlewoman)
Silence in Hanover Close - Anne Perry 4936

Yorke, Aurelia (Spouse)
Galleon - Dudley Pope 5095

Yorke, Crystal (Streetperson)
Crystal - Helen Ashfield 205

Yorke, Deborah (Young Woman)
The Ladies of Hanover Square - Rona Randall 5249

Yorke, Ned (Plantation Owner; Pirate)
Buccaneer - Dudley Pope 5093
Galleon - Dudley Pope 5095

Yorke, Sara (Young Woman)
Passengers to Mexico: The Last Invasion of Mexico - Blair Niles 4627

Yorkless, Barney (Farmer)
The Whip - Catherine Cookson 1291

Yoshi (Nobleman; Warlord)
Gai-Jin: A Novel of Japan - James Clavell 1100

Young, Dirk (Young Man)
Venture in the East - Bruce Lancaster 3648

Young, Lauren (Spouse)
Heaven's Gold - Giles Tippette 6282

Young, Lawrence (Gentleman)
I Give You Oscar Wilde - Desmond Hall 2647

Young, Martin (Religious)
The Pleasure Garden - Leon Garfield 2293

Young, Wilson (Outlaw; Gunfighter)
Heaven's Gold - Giles Tippette 6282

Young Hunter (Indian; Warrior)
Dawn Land - Joseph Bruchac III 734

Younger, Bas (Landowner)
Three-Headed Angel - Roark Bradford 623

Younger, Pearl (Young Woman)
Pearl - Anne Leaton 3701

Youngman, Charles (Fugitive; Outlaw)
Scent of Cloves - Norah Lofts 3859

Ypsilanti, Prince (Royalty; Military Personnel)
Searching for the Emperor - Roberto Pazzi 4858

Ysuna (Prehistoric Human; Religious)
The Sacred Stones - William Sarabande 5600

Yuen, Taou (Bride)
Java Head - Joseph Hergesheimer 2854

Yusupova, Lili (Royalty)
The Revolutionist: A Novel of Russia - Robert
   Littell 3810

Yves of Rifaucon (Heir; Mercenary)
The Unhurrying Chase - H.F.M. Prescott 5172

Z

Zachary, Ben (Settler)
The Unforgiven - Alan Le May 3692

Zachary, Cassius (Settler)
The Unforgiven - Alan Le May 3692

Zachary, Rachel (Settler)
The Unforgiven - Alan Le May 3692

Zafortezas, Sebastian (Sea Captain)
Spanish Bayonet - Stephen Vincent Benet 441

Zagloba, Pan (Military Personnel)
Fire in the Steppe - Henryk Sienkiewicz 5847

Zakir (Artisan)
Children of the Lion - Peter Danielson 1464

Zalmunnah (Chieftain)
The Trumpet and the Sword - Peter Danielson 1479

Zapalova, Lyudmilla (Dancer)
The Gathering Wolves - Elizabeth Darrell 1496

Zbyszko (Young Man)
The Teutonic Knights - Henryk Sienkiewicz 5849

Zeb (Slave; Servant)
A Journey to Matecumbe - Robert Lewis
   Taylor 6188

Zelter, Rebekka (Widow(er))
Shadow on the Valley - Kirk Mitchell 4414

Zendt, Levi (Settler)
Centennial - James A. Michener 4366

Zeno (Philosopher; Doctor)
The Abyss - Marguerite Yourcenar 6946

Zenobia (Slave)
The Saracen Blade - Frank Yerby 6926

Zhdanko, Trofim (Government Official)
Alaska - James A. Michener 4364

Zhivago, Yurii Andreievich (Doctor; Writer)
Doctor Zhivago - Boris Pasternak 4824

Zhu Wong (Prisoner; Time Traveller)
The Golden Nineties - Lisa Mason 4166

Zia (Gentlewoman)
The Hittite - Noel B. Gerson 2373

Ziani, Vittoria (Young Woman)
Sing to the Sun - Lucille Borden 579

Ziegler, Erich (Military Personnel; Conductor)
Winter Fire - William R. Trotter 6352

Zinn, Constance Philippa (Young Woman)
A Bloodsmoor Romance - Joyce Carol Oates 4658

Zinn, Deirdre (Young Woman)
A Bloodsmoor Romance - Joyce Carol Oates 4658

Zinn, Malvinia (Actress)
A Bloodsmoor Romance - Joyce Carol Oates 4658

Zonas (Trader)
The Coin of Carthage - Bryher 740

Zopyros (Engineer)
The Arrows of Hercules - L. Sprague De Camp 1553

Zotica, Severina (Fiance(e))
Venus in Copper - Lindsey Davis 1534

Zubaran, Luz de (Young Woman)
Hill of the Hawk - Scott O'Dell 4689

Zubaran, Don Saturnino (Landowner)
Hill of the Hawk - Scott O'Dell 4689

Zulian, Joanna (Orphan; Artist)
The Italian Garden - Judith Lennox-Smith 3717

Zulietta (Lover)
Pandora's Galley - Macdonald Harris 2727

Historical Character Name Index

This index alphabetically lists the major historical figures who appear in the featured titles. (Note: Fictional characters are listed in a separate index.) Some characters are cross-indexed under names by which they are otherwise known, including nicknames, variant spellings, titles of nobility, and regnal names. Citations also provide an alphabetical list of books in which the character is featured, author names, and entry numbers.

A

Aaron
The Exodus - Peter Danielson   1467
Moses - Sholem Asch   199
The River and the Stone: Moses' Early Years in Egypt - Kathleen Jenks   3192
The Scapegoat: A Life of Moses - Joan Lawrence   3684

Abdulhamid I (Ottoman Sultan)
Valide: A Novel of the Harem - Barbara Chase-Riboud   1007

Abe No, Hime
The Vermilion Bridge - Shelley Mydans   4539

Abelard, Peter
Death Comes as Epiphany - Sharan Newman   4598
Peter Abelard: A Novel - Helen Waddell   6517
Stealing Heaven: The Love Story of Heloise and Abelard - Marion Meade   4317
Strong as Death - Sharan Newman   4602

Abner
Rizpah - Charles E. Israel   3124

Abraham
Abraham and Sarah: The Long Journey - Roberta Kells Dorr   1694
Abram, Son of Terah - Florence M. Bauer   378
And Abram Journeyed - Harry Simonhoff   5858
Children of the Lion - Peter Danielson   1464
The Covenant: A Novel of the Life of Abraham the Prophet - Zofja Kossak-Szczucka   3543
Hagar - Lois T. Henderson   2824
Hagar - Cothburn O'Neal   4737
Lot's Wife - Marie Ley-Piscator   3767
No Other Gods - Wilder Penfield   4901
The Promise - Esther Kellner   3395
The Son of Laughter - Frederick Buechner   764

Abrahams, Harold
Chariots of Fire - W.J. Weatherby   6586

Abram
Abram, Son of Terah - Florence M. Bauer   378
No Other Gods - Wilder Penfield   4901

Absalom
After Goliath - R.V. Cassill   955
Bathsheba - Roberta Kells Dorr   1695
Bathsheba - Torgny Lindgren   3789
David at Olivet - Wallace Hamilton   2671
David the King - Gladys Schmitt   5641
David: Warrior and King - Frank G. Slaughter   5885

Tamar - Ann Chamberlin   975
The Unanointed - Laurene Chinn   1070

Abuyah, Elisha ben
As a Driven Leaf - Milton Steinberg   5992

Adams, Abigail
The Braintree Mission - Nicholas E. Wyckoff   6887
Jefferson: A Novel - Max Byrd   838
Sally Hemings - Barbara Chase-Riboud   1006
Seneca - Donald Clayton Porter   5127
Those Who Love - Irving Stone   6064
Yankee Doodle Dandy - Noel B. Gerson   2387

Adams, Enoch
The New England Story - Henry Beetle Hough   3046

Adams, Henry
Empire: A Novel - Gore Vidal   6487
Hollywood: A Novel of America in the 1920s - Gore Vidal   6488
Panama - Eric Zencey   6959
The Raiders: A Novel of the Civil War at Sea - Willard Wallace   6541
Refinements of Love: A Novel about Clover and Henry Adams - Sarah Booth Conroy   1259

Adams, John
Adams of the Bounty - Erle Wilson   6807
The Braintree Mission - Nicholas E. Wyckoff   6887
Clear for Action: A Novel about John Paul Jones - Clements Ripley   5344
Freedom's Dues - Robert H. Abel   9
Jefferson: A Novel - Max Byrd   838
The Long Naked Descent into Boston - William Eastlake   1823
Man From Mt. Vernon - Burke Boyce   607
Portrait of a Scoundrel - Nathaniel Benchley   438
The Rebels - John Jakes   3152
The River Devils - Carter A. Vaughan   6437
Sally Hemings - Barbara Chase-Riboud   1006
Seneca - Donald Clayton Porter   5127
Those Who Love - Irving Stone   6064
Tidewater Dynasty: A Biographical Novel of the Lees of Stratford Hall - Carey Roberts   5372
The Tree of Liberty - Elizabeth Page   4773
The Unvanquished - Howard Fast   2046
Yankee Doodle Dandy - Noel B. Gerson   2387

Adams, John Quincy
Amistad: The Thunder of Freedom - David Pesci   4944
Echo of Lions - Barbara Chase-Riboud   1004
Sally Hemings - Barbara Chase-Riboud   1006

Adams, Louisa
Echo of Lions - Barbara Chase-Riboud   1004

Adams, Marian "Clover"
Refinements of Love: A Novel about Clover and Henry Adams - Sarah Booth Conroy   1259

Adams, Samuel
The Bastard - John Jakes   3144
Buckskin Baronet - Margaret Widdemer   6734
The Drums of April - Charles Mergendahl   4340
Freedom's Dues - Robert H. Abel   9
The Gentle Rebel - Gilbert Morris   4461
Gilman of the Redford - William Stearns Davis   1541
The Long Naked Descent into Boston - William Eastlake   1823
Massachusetts: A Novel - Nancy Zaroulis   6956
Seneca - Donald Clayton Porter   5127
Sons of Liberty - Adam Rutledge   5540
Sound of the Trumpet - Gilbert Morris   4471
Those Who Love - Irving Stone   6064
Yankee Doodle Dandy - Noel B. Gerson   2387

Adams, William
Daishi-San: A Novel - Robert P. Lund   3925
The Needle-Watcher - Richard Blaker   540

Addams, Jane
The Dream Seekers - Grace Mark   4085

Addison, Joseph
Henry Esmond - William Makepeace Thackeray   6212

Adler, Alfred
The Passions of the Mind - Irving Stone   6062

Aesop
The Fabulist - John Vornholt   6512
My Name Is Sappho - Martha Rofheart   5429
Persian Conqueror - George Sidney Hellman   2822

Aetius
Darkness and the Dawn - Thomas B. Costain   1364

Affonso I (Lord of the Congo)
Lord of the Kongo - Peter Forbath   2155

Agassiz, Louis
McKay's Bees - Thomas McMahon   4289

Agotime
Agotime, Her Legend - Judith Gleason   2430

Agreda, Maria de
I, the King - Frances Parkinson Keyes   3479

Agrippina
Nero - Mary Teresa Ronalds   5437

Aguirre, Lope de
Daimon - Abel Posse   5140

Ahab
The Curse of Jezebel: A Novel of the Biblical Queen of Evil - Frank G. Slaughter 5884
Dara, the Cypriot - Louis Paul 4842
Jezebel - Dorothy Clarke Wilson 6802
The Painted Queen - Olga Hesky 2871

Ahasuerus
So Great a Queen: The Story of Esther, Queen of Persia - Paul Frischauer 2235

Ahmad, Muhammad
Drums of Khartoum - Chloe Gartner 2307

Akbar (Emperor of India)
The Near and the Far - Leopold Hamilton Myers 4547

Akhenaton (Pharaoh of Egypt)
Akhnaton, King of Egypt - Dmitri Merezhkovski 4337
The Egyptian - Mika Waltari 6552
A God Against the Gods - Allen Drury 1738
The Goddess Queen: A Novel Based on the Life of Nefertiti - Nicole Vidal 6494
King of the Two Lands: The Pharaoh Akhenaten - Jacquetta Hawkes 2780
Murder in the Place of Anubis - Lynda S. Robinson 5409
On a Balcony - David Stacton 5973
Pillar of Fire - Judith Tarr 6168
Return to Thebes - Allen Drury 1739
The Twelfth Transforming - Pauline Gedge 2347

Akiba ben Joseph
If I Forget Thee - Brenda Lesley Segal 5720
Prince of Israel - Elias Gilner 2422
The Soldier and the Sage: A Novel about Akiba - Richard G. Hubler 3065
The Source - James A. Michener 4374

Alaric I (King of the Visigoths)
Bury Me in Ravenna - Agnes Carr Vaughan 6432
Captive of Rome - Theodora McCormick Du Bois 1740
The Last Romans - Teodor Jeske-Choinski 3216
The Sinner of Saint Ambrose - Robert Raynolds 5275

Alba, Duchess of
Colossus: A Novel about Goya and a World Gone Mad - Stephen Marlowe 4093
In the Blazing Light - Max White 6693
The Last Portrait of the Duchess of Alba - Antonio Larreta 3666
The Naked Maja - Noel B. Gerson 2378
Rage in Silence: A Novel Based on the Life of Goya - Donald Braider 643

Alba, Duke of
Captain General - John P. Stevenson 6007
The Sea Beggars - Cecelia Holland 2996

Albert Edward, Duke of Clarence
The Whitechapel Horrors - Edward B. Hanna 2678
The Women of Whitechapel and Jack the Ripper - Paul West 6638

Albert of Saxe-Coburg-Gotha
Albert's Victoria - Tyler Whittle 6719
Bertie, Albert Edward, Prince of Wales - Tyler Whittle 6720
The Captive of Kensington Palace - Jean Plaidy 5007
Castle of Foxes - Alanna Knight 3516
Consort for Victoria - William Vaughan Wilkins 6757
Flashman at the Charge - George MacDonald Fraser 2209
The Iron Roads - Forbes Bramble 644
The Prime Minister's Wife - Doris Leslie 3727
The Queen and Lord M - Jean Plaidy 5046
Queen Victoria's Bomb - Ronald Clark 1094
The Queen's Husband - Jean Plaidy 5052
Seven Tempest - William Vaughan Wilkins 6761

Swandowne - Daniel Farson 2024
Victoria and Albert - Evelyn Anthony 166
Victoria Victorious - Jean Plaidy 5073
The Young Victoria - Tyler Whittle 6724

Albertus Magnus
Doctor Mirabilis - James Blish 550

Alcibiades
Achilles His Armour - Peter Green 2569
Alcibiades, Beloved of Gods - Vincenz Brun 735
The Flowers of Adonis - Rosemary Sutcliff 6122
Goat Song: A Novel of Ancient Greece - Frank Yerby 6920
The Immortal Marriage - Gertrude Atherton 225
The Last of the Wine - Mary Renault 5299
The Magnificent Traitor: A Novel of Alcibiades and the Golden Age of Pericles - Lynn Poole 5092
The Shining - Stephen Marlowe 4097

Alcock, John
Crown of Roses - Valerie Anand 127

Alcott, Louisa May
Love and War - John Jakes 3150

Alcudia, Duke of
The Last Portrait of the Duchess of Alba - Antonio Larreta 3666

Alden, John
The Honorable Imposter - Gilbert Morris 4463
The Land Is Bright - Noel B. Gerson 2376
Legacy - Robert Vaughan 6448
Pilgrims: A Novel of the Mayflower - Gerard Mac 3955
The Plymouth Adventure - Ernest Gebler 2342
The Wickedest Pilgrim - Donald Barr Chidsey 1067

Aldith
The Norman Pretender - Valerie Anand 132

Aleaumes
The Seven Hills of Paradise - Rosemary Simpson 5859

Alexander I (Czar of Russia)
The Angel: A Novel Based on the Life of Alexander I of Russia - William James Blech 543
Anna - Cynthia Harrod-Eagles 2752
Baltic Mission - Richard Woodman 6859
The Emperor Story: A Historical Romance - George Sava 5615
Far Flies the Eagle - Evelyn Anthony 162
Feast of the Jesters - Manuel Komroff 3533
The Gentleman From America - Paul Benton 464
Great Black Russian - John Oliver Killens 3484
Lustre in the Sky - R.G. Waldeck 6525
Madame Casanova - Gaby von Schonthan 5659
Napoleon and the Cossacks - Peter N. Krassnoff 3551
Napoleon Symphony - Anthony Burgess 780
Polonaise - Jane Aiken Hodge 2968
So Great a Man - David Pilgrim 5000

Alexander II (Czar of Russia)
The Crown and the Crucible - Michael Phillips 4987

Alexander III (Czar of Russia)
Travail and Triumph - Michael Phillips 4991

Alexander III (King of Scotland)
Alexander the Glorious - Jane Oliver 4719
True Thomas - Nigel Tranter 6322

Alexander III (Pope)
My Life for My Sheep - Alfred Duggan 1772

Alexander VI (Pope)
Carnival of Saints - George Herman 2860
City of God: A Novel of the Borgias - Cecelia Holland 2985
Daughter of Shadows - Miranda Seymour 5762
The Dogs of Paradise - Abel Posse 5141
Light on Lucrezia - Jean Plaidy 5029
Madonna of the Seven Hills - Jean Plaidy 5034

The Memoirs of Christopher Columbus - Stephen Marlowe 4096
Michelangelo the Florentine - Sidney Alexander 86
Mona Lisa: The Woman in the Portrait - Sara Mayfield 4206
The Naked Sword: The Story of Lucretia Borgia - F.W. Kenyon 3456
A Passion in the Blood - Genevieve Davis 1519
The Scarlet City - Hella S. Haasse 2632

Alexander VII (Pope)
My Crown, My Love - Ruth Walgreen Stephan 5995

Alexander Jannaeus
The King of Flesh and Blood - Moshe Shamir 5772

Alexander of Serbia
Dance of the Assassins - Maria Fagyas 1997

Alexander the Great
Alexander in Babylon - Jakob Wassermann 6576
Alexander of Macedon: The Journey to World's End - Harold Lamb 3607
Alexander the God - Maurice Druon 1731
Alexander the God - Robert Payne 4849
The Conqueror: A Novel of Alexander the Great - Edison Marshall 4104
An Elephant for Aristotle - L. Sprague De Camp 1556
Fire From Heaven - Mary Renault 5296
Funeral Games - Mary Renault 5297
The Golden Lyre - Noel B. Gerson 2371
Lord of the Two Lands - Judith Tarr 6167
The Persian Boy - Mary Renault 5301
Star of Macedon - Karl V. Eiker 1901

Alexandra Feodorovna
And the Stars Shall Fall - True Bowen 603
The Dawning of Deliverance - Judith Pella 4892
Devoted Friends - Joe Poyer 5161
Elizabeth and Alexandra - Antony Lambton 3616
God Save the Tsar - Susanna Hoe 2976
Heirs of the Motherland - Judith Pella 4893
Love and Honor - Leslie Arlen 189
Rasputin's Revenge - John T. Lescroart 3725
Searching for the Emperor - Roberto Pazzi 4858
The Summer Day Is Done - R.T. Stevens 6001
Time After Time - Allen Appel 171

Alexandra of Denmark
Bertie, Albert Edward, Prince of Wales - Tyler Whittle 6720
Bertie and the Seven Bodies - Peter Lovesey 3908
Edward - Tyler Whittle 6721
The Second Sister - Leslie O'Grady 4701
The Widow of Windsor - Jean Plaidy 5076

Alexandrina Victoria
Blackstone - Richard Falkirk 2006

Alexius I Comnenus (Byzantine Emperor)
Count Robert of Paris - Sir Walter Scott 5695
The Lady for Ransom - Alfred Duggan 1768
Wine of Satan - Laverne Gay 2327

Alfieri, Vittorio
Crown Without Sceptre - William Vaughan Wilkins 6758
The Queen of Hearts - Joan Rees 5290

Alfred Atheling
Gildenford - Valerie Anand 130
The Proud Villeins - Valerie Anand 133

Alfred the Great (King of Wessex)
The Edge of Light - Joan Wolf 6839
The Flame in the Dark - Basil Bonallack 568
The King Liveth - Jeffrey Farnol 2013
The Marsh King - C. Walter Hodges 2975
The Price of Blood - Doris Sutcliffe Adams 24
Raven's Wind - Victor Canning 883
The Right Line of Cedric - Alfred Duggan 1773

Alfrida
Avalon - Anya Seton 5748

Alkaios
My Name Is Sappho - Martha Rofheart 5429

Allen, Eliza
The Raven's Bride - Elizabeth Crook 1431

Allen, Ethan
The Arch of Stars - Clifford Lindsey Alderman 66
Catch a Falling Star - Frederic F. Van de
    Water 6401
The Green Mountain Boys - Daniel Pierce
    Thompson 6249
Guns for Rebellion - F. van Wyck Mason 4151
Hang for Treason - Robert Newton Peck 4886
Israel Potter - Herman Melville 4334
Rebel Guns - Adam Rutledge 5539
Reluctant Rebel - Frederic F. Van de Water 6403
That Bennington Mob - Henry Barnard Safford 5558

Allen, Ira
The Arch of Stars - Clifford Lindsey Alderman 66
Catch a Falling Star - Frederic F. Van de
    Water 6401

Allen, Thomas C.
The Hallelujah Flight - Jack Lynn 3937

Allenby, Edmund Henry Hynman
Behold the Fire - Michael Blankfort 541
The Devil's Spy - Michael Hastings 2773

Alleyn, Edward
Sweet Will - Eric Malpass 4050

Alleyne, Richard
Nothing Like the Sun - Anthony Burgess 781

Almagro, Diego de
Don Pedro and the Devil - Edgar Maas 3948
*The Sword and the Sun: The Story of the Spanish Civil
    Wars in Peru* - Gerald Green 2566

Alston, Theodosia Burr
My Theodosia - Anya Seton 5753

Altgeld, John Peter
The American - Howard Fast 2026

Alvarez de Toledo, Fernando
Captain General - John P. Stevenson 6007
The Sea Beggars - Cecelia Holland 2996

Ambrose
The Restless Flame - Louis De Wohl 1573
The Sinner of Saint Ambrose - Robert
    Raynolds 5275

Amenhotep III (Pharaoh of Egypt)
The Twelfth Transforming - Pauline Gedge 2347

Amenhotep IV (Pharaoh of Egypt)
*The Goddess Queen: A Novel Based on the Life of
    Nefertiti* - Nicole Vidal 6494

Amergin
Bard: The Odyssey of the Irish - Morgan
    Llywelyn 3816

Amnon
Tamar - Ann Chamberlin 975

Amos
The Herdsman - Dorothy Clarke Wilson 6801

Amun
Child of the Morning - Pauline Gedge 2343

Amundsen, Roald
The Race: A Novel of Polar Exploration - Kare
    Holt 3008

An Lu-Shan
The Court of the Lion - Eleanor Cooney 1294

Anaxagoras
Glory and the Lightning - Taylor Caldwell 856
Pericles the Athenian - Rex Warner 6566

Andersen, Hans Christian
Flight of the Swan - Margaret Ann Hubbard 3063
The Swedish Nightingale: Jenny Lind - Elizabeth
    Kyle 3571

Andrassy, Julius
Imperial Waltz - William M. Abrahams 13

Andre, John
Eagles Where I Walk - Stephen Longstreet 3885
The Exquisite Siren - Edwin Haines 2639
Hugh Wynne, Free Quaker - Silas Weir
    Mitchell 4416
Major Andre - Anthony Bailey 265
Mars' Butterfly - Henry Pleasants 5080
The Secret Road - Bruce Lancaster 3646
Storm the Last Rampart - David Taylor 6180
The Sunshine Patriot: A Novel of Benedict Arnold -
    Norman Partington 4822
Trumpets at Dawn - Cyril Harris 2719
*The Twisted Saber: A Biographical Novel of Benedict
    Arnold* - Philip Vail 6398

Andree, Salomon August
The Flight of the Eagle - Per Olof Sundman 6119

Andrew, Duke of York
Di and I - Peter Lefcourt 3714

Andronicus I Comnenus (Eastern Roman Emperor)
Against the Fall of Night - Michael Arnold 193
Their Most Serene Majesties - Ange Vlachos 6505
The Walking Drum - Louis L'Amour 3632

Andros, Edward
The Silver Oar - Howard Breslin 669

Anna Comnena
Count Robert of Paris - Sir Walter Scott 5695

Anna O.
When Nietzsche Wept: A Novel of Obsession - Irvin D.
    Yalom 6892

Anne (Queen of England)
The Elusive Crown - Hebe Elsna 1931
Exit Lady Masham - Louis Auchincloss 230
The Glory and the Dream - F.W. Kenyon 3450
Marlborough's Unfair Lady - Lozania Prole 5197
The Power and the Passion - Christina
    Nicholson 4609
The Queen's Favourites - Jean Plaidy 5051
The Queen's Husband - Samuel Edwards 1889
The Sachem - Donald Clayton Porter 5124

Anne of Austria
The Cardinal and the Queen - Evelyn Anthony 159
Cinq-Mars - Alfred Victor de Vigny 6495
The Three Musketeers - Alexandre Dumas 1782
Twenty Years After - Alexandre Dumas 1783
Wife to Great Buckingham - Hilda Lewis 3751

Anne of Bohemia
The Lords of Lancaster - Pamela Bennetts 452
Passage to Pontefract - Jean Plaidy 5038
Within the Hollow Crown - Margaret Campbell
    Barnes 331

Anne of Cleves
The Autobiography of Henry VIII - Margaret
    George 2355
The Fifth Queen - Ford Madox Ford 2161
Henry VIII and His Six Wives - Maureen
    Peters 4975
Kathryn: In the Court of Six Queens - Anne Merton
    Abbey 1
King's Fool - Margaret Campbell Barnes 325
My Lady of Cleves - Margaret Campbell Barnes 328
The Rose Without a Thorn - Jean Plaidy 5058
The Wise Virgin - Hebe Elsna 1934

Anne of Denmark
Daughter of Eve - Noel B. Gerson 2366
For My Great Folly - Thomas B. Costain 1365
Mine Is the Kingdom - Jane Oliver 4726
The Murder in the Tower - Jean Plaidy 5035
Powhatan's Daughter - John Clarke Bowman 605
Unicorn Rampant - Nigel Tranter 6323

Anne of Warwick
The Swan and the Rose - Francis W. Leary 3697

Annianus
Dogheaded Death - Ray Faraday Nelson 4581

Anson, George
The Golden Ocean - Patrick O'Brian 4665
Manila Galleon - F. van Wyck Mason 4154

Anthony, Susan B.
Beecher: A Novel - Dan McCall 4218
Woman of Justice - Georgia Di Donato 1639
The Woman Question - Dorothea Malm 4046

Antigonus I (King of Macedonia)
The Bronze God of Rhodes - L. Sprague De
    Camp 1554
Funeral Games - Mary Renault 5297

Antipatros
Funeral Games - Mary Renault 5297

Antony, Marc
The Alexandrian - Martha Rofheart 5425
Augustus - Allan Massie 4167
Augustus - John Williams 6785
Caesar - Allan Massie 4168
The Ides of March - Thornton Wilder 6753
The Pirate From Rome - John V.D.
    Southworth 5952
That Egyptian Woman - Noel B. Gerson 2384
Three's Company - Alfred Duggan 1774
Throne of Isis - Judith Tarr 6170

Anza, Juan Bautista de
Beyond the Blue Sierra - Honore Morrow 4486
A City for St. Francis - Evelyn Wells 6621
The Cross and the Sword - Jonreed Lauritzen 3674
Dust on the King's Highway - Helen Constance
    White 6677

Apollinaire, Guillaume
The Burning Man - Stephen Longstreet 3883
The Young Men of Paris - Stephen Longstreet 3893

Appleseed, Johnny
Reckon with the River - Clark McMeekin 4292
The Tree of Life - Hugh Nissenson 4629

Aquinas, Thomas
The Quiet Light - Louis De Wohl 1572

Aram, Eugene
Eugene Aram - Edward Bulwer-Lytton 766

Arbogast
The Last Romans - Teodor Jeske-Choinski 3216

Arbuckle, Roscoe "Fatty"
Keystone - Peter Lovesey 3913

Arden, Alice
Feversham - Diane Davidson 1503

Aretino, Pietro
The Scarlet City - Hella S. Haasse 2632

Arias de Avila, Pedro
The Golden Eagle - John Edward Jennings 3201

Aristides
Farewell Great King: A Novel of Ancient Greece - Jill
    Paton Walsh 4829

Aristophanes
Alcibiades, Beloved of Gods - Vincenz Brun 735
Goat Song: A Novel of Ancient Greece - Frank
    Yerby 6920
Goatsong - Tom Holt 3009

Aristotle
The Conqueror: A Novel of Alexander the Great -
    Edison Marshall 4104
An Elephant for Aristotle - L. Sprague De
    Camp 1556
Fire From Heaven - Mary Renault 5296

Arlosoroff, Chaim
Union Square - Meredith Tax 6176

Armour, Jean
Wonder of All the Gay World - James Barke 306

Armstrong, Archie
For My Great Folly - Thomas B. Costain 1365

Armstrong, John
Dolley - Rita Mae Brown 727

Armstrong-Jones, Margaret
The Queen and I - Sue Townsend 6306

Arnold, Benedict
Arundel - Kenneth Roberts 5383
Brother to the Enemy - Bart Spicer 5964
Eagle in the Sky - F. van Wyck Mason 4149
Eagles Where I Walk - Stephen Longstreet 3885
The Exquisite Siren - Edwin Haines 2639
Fawn - Robert Newton Peck 4885
The Firelands - Karen Harper 2712
The Green Mountain Boys - Daniel Pierce
    Thompson 6249
Guns for Rebellion - F. van Wyck Mason 4151
Hugh Wynne, Free Quaker - Silas Weir
    Mitchell 4416
I'll Storm Hell - Noel B. Gerson 2374
The Long Naked Descent into Boston - William
    Eastlake 1823
The Lure of the Falcon - Juliette Benzoni 465
Major Andre - Anthony Bailey 265
Man From Mt. Vernon - Burke Boyce 607
Mars' Butterfly - Henry Pleasants 5080
Mr. Arnold - Francis Lynde 3935
Oliver Wiswell - Kenneth Roberts 5389
Proceed, Sergeant Lamb - Robert Graves 2550
Rabble in Arms - Kenneth Roberts 5390
Renown - Frank Olney Hough 3045
The Rifleman - John Brick 675
The Secret Road - Bruce Lancaster 3646
Sergeant Lamb's America - Robert Graves 2552
Storm the Last Rampart - David Taylor 6180
The Sunshine Patriot: A Novel of Benedict Arnold -
    Norman Partington 4822
Treason - Robert Gessner 2389
*The Twisted Saber: A Biographical Novel of Benedict
    Arnold* - Philip Vail 6398

Arnold, Margaret Shippen
The Exquisite Siren - Edwin Haines 2639
Mars' Butterfly - Henry Pleasants 5080

Arnold, Matthew
*The Buried Self: A Background to the Poems of
    Matthew Arnold* - Isobel MacDonald 3961

Arouet, Francois Marie
Adrienne - Barbara Levy 3742
The Anthem - Noel B. Gerson 2361
A Day of Battle - Vincent Sheean 5787
The Enchantress - Suyin Han 2673
Rasero - Francisco Rebolledo 5282
Voltaire! Voltaire! - Guy Endore 1943

Artaxerxes I (King of Persia)
Farewell Great King: A Novel of Ancient Greece - Jill
    Paton Walsh 4829

Arthur, Chester Alan
The Chester A. Arthur Conspiracy - William
    Wiegand 6740

Arthur, Prince of Wales
Katharine: The Virgin Widow - Jean Plaidy 5025
The Prince of Darkness - Jean Plaidy 5044

Artois, Count of
The Iron King - Maurice Druon 1732
The Lily and the Lion - Maurice Druon 1733
The Poisoned Crown - Maurice Druon 1734
The Royal Succession - Maurice Druon 1735
The Strangled Queen - Maurice Druon 1737
The Vow on the Heron - Jean Plaidy 5074

Ascham, Roger
Elizabeth, Captive Princess - Margaret Irwin 3118

Ashbery, Francis
Riders of the Long Road - Stephen E. Bransford 649

Ashikaga Yoshimitsu
The House of Kanze - Nobuko Albery 64

Ashley, William
The Three Lives of Elizabeth - Shirley Seifert 5735

Aske, Robert
A Trail of Blood - Jeremy Potter 5143

Askew, Anne
The Heretic - Alison Macleod 4002

Aspasia
Alcibiades, Beloved of Gods - Vincenz Brun 735
Glory and the Lightning - Taylor Caldwell 856
The Immortal Marriage - Gertrude Atherton 225

Astaire, Fred
Dancing in the Dark - Stuart M. Kaminsky 3334

Astley, Thomas
Vows of the Peacock - Alice Walworth
    Graham 2513

Astor, John Jacob
Bright Journey - August Derleth 1614
No Brighter Glory - Armstrong Sperry 5963
River to the West: A Novel of the Astor Adventure -
    John Edward Jennings 3204

Ataturk, Kemal
The Ashes of Smyrna - Richard Reinhardt 5294
High Road to China - Jon Cleary 1106
The House of War - Catherine Gavin 2322

Ataulf (King of the Visigoths)
Bury Me in Ravenna - Agnes Carr Vaughan 6432
Captive of Rome - Theodora McCormick Du
    Bois 1740

Atherton, Beatrice
The King's Achievement - Robert Hugh Benson 459

Atticus, Titus Pomponius
Epicurus My Master - Max Radin 5233

Attila the Hun
Attila's Treasure - Stephan Grundy 2606
Darkness and the Dawn - Thomas B. Costain 1364
The Death of Attila - Cecelia Holland 2986
Sign of the Pagan - Don Tracy 6312
Throne of the World - Louis De Wohl 1575
The Twelve Pictures - Edith Simon 5857

d'Aubigne, Francoise
The Anthem - Noel B. Gerson 2361
The Cat and the King - Louis Auchincloss 229
*The Crown and the Shadow: The Story of Francoise
    d'Aubigne, Marquise de Maintenon* - Pamela
    Hill 2930
The Gilded Torch - Iola Fuller 2252
The King's Way - Francoise Chandernagor 986
The Secret Wife - Alice Acland 22
Ward of the Sun King - Mildred Allen Butler 826

Aubrey
Atala - Francois Rene de Chateaubriand 1008

Audubon, John James
The Iron Mistress - Paul I. Wellman 6618
Mr. Audubon's Lucy - Lucy Kennedy 3419
The Mysterious Death of Meriwether Lewis - Ron
    Burns 802

Audubon, Lucy Blackwell
Mr. Audubon's Lucy - Lucy Kennedy 3419

Augustine
The Converts: A Historical Novel - Rex
    Warner 6564
The Four Rivers of Paradise - Helen Constance
    White 6678
The Restless Flame - Louis De Wohl 1573
Son of Tears - Henry W. Coray 1320

Augustus (Roman Emperor)
The Alexandrian - Martha Rofheart 5425
Augustus - Allan Massie 4167
Augustus - John Williams 6785

Golden Peacock - Gertrude Atherton 224
I, Claudius - Robert Graves 2547
I Loved Tiberius - Elisabeth Dored 1692
Roman Shadows - Ron Burns 804
Three's Company - Alfred Duggan 1774
Throne of Isis - Judith Tarr 6170
Tiberius: The Memoirs of the Emperor - Allan
    Massie 4169

Augustus II (King of Poland)
The Power and the Passion - Christina
    Nicholson 4609

Aurelian (Roman Emperor)
Queen of the East - Alexander Baron 336

Austen, Jane
Antipodes Jane: A Novel of Jane Austen in Australia -
    Barbara Ker Wilson 3468
Jane and the Man of the Cloth - Stephanie
    Barron 355
Jane and the Unpleasantness at Scargrave Manor -
    Stephanie Barron 356
Parson Austen's Daughter - Helen Ashton 219

Austin, Stephen F.
Hellfire Jackson - Garland Roark 5355
On the Long Tide - Laura Krey 3555
Sam Houston - Noel B. Gerson 2380
Texas - James A. Michener 4375

Authari
The Unspeakables: A Tale of Lombardy - Laverne
    Gay 2326

Aveling, Edward
*The Daughter: A Novel Based on the Life of Eleanor
    Marx* - Judith Chernaik 1012

Avery, Ephraim
Avery's Knot - Mary Cable 843
*The Tragedy at Tinkerton: An Historical Novel of
    Murder* - Raymond Paul 4844

Avicenna
The Physician - Noah Gordon 2482

Avril, Jane
*Moulin Rouge: A Novel Based on Henri de Toulouse-
    Lautrec* - Pierre La Mure 3576

Axayacatl (Aztec Emperor)
Copilli, Aztec Prince - Miguel Aleman Velasco 75

B

Bach, Johann Sebastian
*Sacred and Profane: A Novel of the Life and Times of
    Mozart* - David Weiss 6609

Bacon, Sir Francis
Death of the Fox - George Garrett 2300
*The Diary of William Harvey: The Imaginary Journal
    of the Physician Who Revolutionized Medicine* -
    Jean Hamburger 2667
For My Great Folly - Thomas B. Costain 1365
Gay Lord Robert - Jean Plaidy 5015
My Lord Essex - Olive Eckerson 1838
No Bed for Bacon - Caryl Brahms 640
*Physician Extraordinary: A Novel of the Life and
    Times of William Harvey* - David Weiss 6608
Unicorn Rampant - Nigel Tranter 6323

Bacon, Nathaniel
*Forest Cavalier: A Romance of America's First
    Frontier and of Bacon's Rebellion* - Roy Catesby
    Flannagan 2122
The King's Passenger - Nathan Schachner 5631
Man Cannot Tell - Philip Lightfoot Scruggs 5711

Bacon, Roger
The Black Rose - Thomas B. Costain 1363
Doctor Mirabilis - James Blish 550

Baglioni, Giampaolo
The Mercenary - Charles Durbin 1814

Bagoas
The Persian Boy - Mary Renault 5301

Bailly, Joseph
Wolves Against the Moon - Julia Cooley
    Altrocchi 123

Bainbridge, William
*The Sea Panther: A Novel about the Commander of
    the U.S.S. Constitution* - Philip Vail 6397

Baird, George Alexander
Bertie and the Tinman - Peter Lovesey 3909

Baker, Jim
Kings of the Missouri - Hugh Pendexter 4895

Baker, Josephine
A First Class Murder - Elliott Roosevelt 5442

Bakhtin, Nikolai
Saints and Scholars - Terrence Eagleton 1821

Balboa, Vasco Nunez de
Balboa: Conquistador - Omar V. Garrison 2303

Balcombe, Betsy
The Last Love - Thomas B. Costain 1367

Baldwin, Stanley
Edward and Mrs. Simpson - A.C.H. Smith 5916

Baldwin I (King of Jerusalem)
Sir Pagan - Henry John Colyton 1222

Baldwin II (King of Jerusalem)
Queen of Swords - Judith Tarr 6169

Baldwin IV (King of Jerusalem)
Alamut - Judith Tarr 6164
Jerusalem - Cecelia Holland 2990
The Leper King - Zofja Kossak-Szczucka 3544

Baldwin V (Count of Flanders)
The Firedrake - Cecelia Holland 2988
*Fortune's Knave: The Making of William the
    Conqueror* - Mary Lide 3774
Wife to the Bastard - Hilda Lewis 3753

Ball, John
The Peacock and the Pearl - Jennifer Lang 3661
Riot at Gravesend: A Novel of Wat Tyler's Rebellion -
    William Howard Woods 6864
Who Was Then the Gentleman - Charles E.
    Israel 3125

Balue, Cardinal Jean
Quentin Durward - Sir Walter Scott 5705

Balzac, Honore de
I Am Vidocq - Vincent McConnor 4225
Wine of Life - Charles Orson Gorham 2489

Bandy, Francis
My Grand Enemy - Jean Stubbs 6098

Bandy, Mary
My Grand Enemy - Jean Stubbs 6098

Bankhead, Tallulah
The Tallulah Bankhead Murder Case - George
    Baxt 389

Banning, James Herman
The Hallelujah Flight - Jack Lynn 3937

Bar Jonah, Simon
The Apostle - Sholem Asch 197

Barabbas
Barabbas - Par Lagerkvist 3585
Barabbas: A Dream of the World's Tragedy - Marie
    Corelli 1327
Barabbas: A Novel of the Time of Jesus - Emery
    Bekessy 417
Behold Your King - Florence M. Bauer 379
Brothers of Vengeance - LeGette Blythe 556
The Eighth Veil - Ellis Kadison 3320
The Gospel of Corax - Paul Park 4802

The Robber: A Tale of the Time of the Herods -
    Bertram Brooker 706

Barak
The Sorceress - Nathaniel Norsen Weinreb 6602

Baranov, Aleksandr
Alaska - James A. Michener 4364
Ashana - E.P. Roesch 5424
Heaven Is Too High - Mildred Masterson
    McNeilly 4309

Barcelo, Dona Tules
The Wind Leaves No Shadow - Ruth Laughlin 3672

Bari, Duke of
The Bride of Sforza - Miranda Seymour 5760
Duchess of Milan - Michael Ennis 1946

Barker, Arthur "Doc"
Saint Mudd - Steve Thayer 6218

Barker, Kate "Ma"
Saint Mudd - Steve Thayer 6218
True Crime - Max Allan Collins 1214

Barlow, Joel
To Spit Against the Wind - Benjamin H. Levin 3737

Barnum, Phineas T.
Concert Grand - Howard Breslin 665
The Fast Men - Tom McNab 4302
Jenny and Barnum: A Novel of Love - Roderick
    Thorp 6276
Rogers' Folly - Albert E. Idell 3102

Baron Burghley
Legacy - Susan Kay 3374
My Lord Essex - Olive Eckerson 1838
My Lord the Fox - Robert York 6932
The Proud Man - Elizabeth Linington 3800
*Shadow in the Sun: A Novel of Elizabeth I, the Virgin
    Queen* - F.W. Kenyon 3460
To Love a Queen - Lawrence Schoonover 5669

Baron Raglan
Flashman at the Charge - George MacDonald
    Fraser 2209
Hazard's Command - Vivian Stuart 6088

Barras, Paul
The Incorruptible - Marjorie Coryn 1357
Lady of Paris - William Vaughan Wilkins 6760
Mistress of Fortune - Sheila Lancaster 3651
Seed of Mischief - Willa Gibbs 2401

Barreto, Ysabel
Islands of Unwisdom - Robert Graves 2548

Barrett, Elizabeth
Lady's Maid - Margaret Forster 2188

Barry, Jeanne du
The French Bride - Evelyn Anthony 163
Golden Venus - David Mynders Smythe 5933
Royal Merry-Go-Round - F.W. Kenyon 3459

Bart, Charles E.
A House Behind the Mint - Laurie Huffman 3072

Bartholomew
I, Nathanael, Knew Jesus - William Gilbert Van Tassel
    Sutpen 6133

Bartlett, Adelaide Blanche
Sweet Adelaide - Julian Symons 6152

Bartlett, Thomas Edwin
Sweet Adelaide - Julian Symons 6152

Barton, Clara
The Bridge - Marguerite Allis 108
Homeland - John Jakes 3148
Remember Santiago - Douglas C. Jones 3280
The Titans - John Jakes 3154

Bartor, Daniel
Snow-Water - Dorothy Gardiner 2285

Bartram, John
Song of the Susquehanna - Herbert Stover 6071

Bateman, Hester
The Silver Touch - Rosalind Laker 3599

Bathory, Elizabeth
The Blood Countess - Andrei Codrescu 1149

Bathory, Istvan
Darker Jewels - Chelsea Quinn Yarbro 6898

Bathsheba
After Goliath - R.V. Cassill 955
Bathsheba - Roberta Kells Dorr 1695
Bathsheba - Torgny Lindgren 3789
David and Bathsheba - Ari Ibn-Sahav 3098
David at Olivet - Wallace Hamilton 2671
David of Jerusalem - Louis De Wohl 1564
David the King - Gladys Schmitt 5641
David: Warrior and King - Frank G. Slaughter 5885
David's Stranger - Moshe Shamir 5771
King David - Gwyn Jenkins 3191
King of Kings: A Novel of the Life of David - Malachi
    Martin 4134
Solomon and Sheba - Faye Levine 3740
Triumph of the Lion - Peter Danielson 1478
The Unanointed - Laurene Chinn 1070
*The Valley of Vision: A Novel of King Solomon and
    His Time* - Vardis Fisher 2113

Battell, Andrew
Lord of Darkness - Robert Silverberg 5854

Batu Khan
Poland - James A. Michener 4373
Until the Sun Falls - Cecelia Holland 2998

Baudelaire, Charles Pierre
The Midnight Gardener: A Novel about Baudelaire -
    Max White 6694
A Singular Conspiracy - Barry Perowne 4915

Baudin, Nicholas
Southern Cross - Terry Coleman 1206

Baudouin IV (King of Jerusalem)
Jerusalem - Cecelia Holland 2990

Bazaine, Francoise-Achille
Chapultepec - Norman Zollinger 6965

Beall, John Yates
Dim the Flaring Lamps - Jan Jordan 3301

Bean, Ellis
Gone to Texas - Don Worcester 6871

Bean, Roy
Streets of Laredo - Larry McMurtry 4300

Beardsley, Aubrey
To Seize the Passing Dream - Ted Berkman 479

Beaton, David
James, by the Grace of God - Nigel Tranter 6315
The Riven Realm - Nigel Tranter 6317
A Stake in the Kingdom - Nigel Tranter 6321

Beatrice (Princess of England)
Princess in Amber - Evelyn Wilde Mayerson 4205
The Widow of Windsor - Tyler Whittle 6723

Beauchamp, Elizabeth de
Vows of the Peacock - Alice Walworth
    Graham 2513

Beauchamp, Guy de
Vows of the Peacock - Alice Walworth
    Graham 2513

Beaufort, Duc de
Twenty Years After - Alexandre Dumas 1783

Beaufort, Henry
Epitaph for Three Women - Jean Plaidy 5012
Micah Clarke - Sir Arthur Conan Doyle 1715
The Serpent Amongst the Lilies - P.C. Doherty 1678

Beaufort, Joan
James and Joan - Anne Fremantle 2221

Beaufort, Margaret
Women of Ashdon - Valerie Anand 135

Beauharnais, Hortense de
A Rose for Virtue - Norah Lofts 3858

Beaumarchais, Pierre Augustin Caron de
Poor Richard's Game - G.J.A. O'Toole 4766

Beaumont, Francis
The Player's Boy - Bryher 744

Beauregard, Pierre Gustave Toutant
Beloved Enemy - Al Lacy 3579
The Chess Player: A Novel of New Orleans and Paris - Frances Parkinson Keyes 3478
Madame Castel's Lodger - Frances Parkinson Keyes 3480
The Passionate Rebel - Frank G. Slaughter 5894
Pomp and Circumstance - Fred Mustard Stewart 6025
A Promise Unbroken - Al Lacy 3582
Shadowed Memories - Al Lacy 3583

Becket, Thomas
Beloved Enemy: The Passions of Eleanor of Aquitaine - Ellen Jones 3288
The Courts of Love - Jean Plaidy 5010
The Lion of Christ - Margaret Butler 823
The Lion of England - Margaret Butler 824
The Lion of Justice - Margaret Butler 825
My Life for My Sheep - Alfred Duggan 1772
The Pillars of the Earth - Ken Follett 2149
The Plantagenet Prelude - Jean Plaidy 5041
The Swords of December - Robert York 6933
Thomas: A Novel of the Life, Passions, and Miracles of Becket - Shelley Mydans 4538

Beckford, William
Fonthill - Aubrey Menen 4335

Beckwourth, Jim
Ammahabas - Bill Hotchkiss 3036
Follow the Free Wind - Leigh Brackett 621
The Medicine Calf - Bill Hotchkiss 3037

Beecher, Henry Ward
Beecher: A Novel - Dan McCall 4218

Beethoven, Karl
Nephew to the Emperor: A Novel Based on the Life of Beethoven - Jacques Brenner 658

Beethoven, Ludwig van
The Assassination of Mozart - David Weiss 6604
Eroica: A Novel about Beethoven - Carl von Pidoll 4994
The Man Who Thought He Was Messiah - Curt Leviant 3735
Nephew to the Emperor: A Novel Based on the Life of Beethoven - Jacques Brenner 658

Beg, Yakub
Flashman at the Charge - George MacDonald Fraser 2209

Begin, Menachem
The Glory - Herman Wouk 6873

Behn, Aphra
The Portingale - Alison Macleod 4005
Purple Passage: A Novel about a Lady Both Famous and Fantastic - Emily Hahn 2638

Belasco, David
A Cadenza for Caruso - Barbara Paul 4834

Belisarius
Count Belisarius - Robert Graves 2544
A Flame in Byzantium - Chelsea Quinn Yarbro 6899
The Vandal - Richard O'Connor 4687

Bell, Alexander Graham
Loving Little Egypt - Thomas McMahon 4288

Bell, Clive
The Shadow of the Moth: A Novel of Espionage with Virginia Woolf - Ellen Hawkes 2779

Bell, Vanessa
The Shadow of the Moth: A Novel of Espionage with Virginia Woolf - Ellen Hawkes 2779

Bellini, Giovanni
Written in the Stars: A Novel about Albrecht Durer - Frances Hope Fisher 2103

Bellini, Vincenzo
Signorina - Henry Myers 4542

Belmont, Alva
Rivington Street - Meredith Tax 6175

Belshazzar
Babylon - Anthony Esler 1959

Bembo, Pietro
The Flame of the Borgias - Jean Briggs 680

Bemis, Polly
Thousand Years of Gold - Ruthanne Lum McCunn 4239

Ben Gurion, David
The Hope - Herman Wouk 6874

ben Yair, Eleazar
The Antagonists - Ernest K. Gann 2276
The Tenth Measure - Brenda Lesley Segal 5721
The Voices of Masada - David Kossoff 3545

Benaron, Jacob Chalif
The Emperor, the Sages and Death - Rachel Berdach 475

Benchley, Robert
The Dorothy Parker Murder Case - George Baxt 384

Bender, Kate
The Bloody Benders - Robert H. Adelman 35

Benedict
Citadel of God: A Novel of Saint Benedict - Louis De Wohl 1563

Benilong
The Timeless Land - Eleanor Dark 1495

Benjamin, Judah P.
Beloved - Vina Delmar 1599
The Big Family - Vina Delmar 1600
The Chess Player: A Novel of New Orleans and Paris - Frances Parkinson Keyes 3478
The Court Martial of Robert E. Lee - Douglas Savage 5617
Gray Victory - Robert Skimin 5877
Papa La-Bas - John Dickson Carr 914
The Proud Retreat - Clifford Dowdey 1706
While the Music Plays - Diane Austell 242

Bennett, James Gordon
Ain't Goin' to Glory - David Delman 1597
Niagara - Robert Lewis Taylor 6189

Benny, Jack
A First Class Murder - Elliott Roosevelt 5442

Benson, E.F.
The Haunting of Lamb House - Joan Aiken 48

Bent, Kimball
Monday's Warriors - Maurice Shadbolt 5767

Benteen, Frederick
A Mighty Afternoon - Charles K. Mills 4407
A Road We Do Not Know: A Novel of Custer at the Little Bighorn - Frederick J. Chiaventone 1057

Bentley, E.C.
Dorothy and Agatha - Gaylord Larsen 3667

Benton, Thomas Hart
The Buckstones - Paul I. Wellman 6615
Dream West - David Nevin 4587
Immortal Wife - Irving Stone 6057
Jessie: A Novel Based on the Life of Jessie Benton Fremont - Judy Alter 120
Sam Houston - Noel B. Gerson 2380

Berengaria of Navarre
The Devil Is Loose - Graham Shelby 5790
The Heart of the Lion - Jean Plaidy 5020
The Kings of Vain Intent - Graham Shelby 5791

Lionheart!: A Novel of Richard I, King of England - Martha Rofheart 5428
The Lute Player - Norah Lofts 3852
My Lord Brother the Lionheart - Molly Costain Haycraft 2795
The Revolt of the Eaglets - Jean Plaidy 5057
The Talisman - Sir Walter Scott 5708

Berenice Basagrippa
Agrippa's Daughter - Howard Fast 2025

Beria, Lavrenty
Generations of Winter - Vassily Aksyonov 61

Bering, Vitus
Alaska - James A. Michener 4364

Berlioz, Louis Hector
Antonietta - John Hersey 2868
Hungarian Rhapsody: The Life of Franz Liszt - Jean Rousselot 5511
Passionate Rebel: The Story of Hector Berlioz - F.W. Kenyon 3457

Bernadette Soubirous
The Song of Bernadette - Franz Werfel 6625

Bernadotte, Jean-Baptiste
Desiree - Annemarie Selinko 5741

Bernard of Clairvaux
The Garden of Persephone - Cesar J. Rotondi 5510

Bernay, Martha
The Passions of the Mind - Irving Stone 6062

Bernay, Minna
Minna's Story: The Secret Love of Doctor Sigmund Freud - Kathleen Daniels 1463

Bernhardt, Sarah
Bertie and the Crime of Passion - Peter Lovesey 3907
Eleanora Duse - Jean Stubbs 6095
The God of Mirrors - Robert Reilly 5293
Good Morning, Irene - Carole Nelson Douglas 1698
Irene at Large - Carole Nelson Douglas 1700
Loving Little Egypt - Thomas McMahon 4288
Sarah - Joel Gross 2603

Bernini, Giovanni Lorenzo
Myself, Christopher Wren - David Weiss 6606

Berthier, Louis-Alexander
Holy Week - Louis Aragon 182

Berwick, James FitzJames
King's Agent - Justus Kent Clark 1090

Bethune, Mary McLeod
Murder in the Rose Garden - Elliott Roosevelt 5452

Beuckelson, Jan
The Siege - Peter Vansittart 6431

Bianco, Andrea
The Mapmaker: A Novel of the Days of Prince Henry, the Navigator - Frank G. Slaughter 5893

Bibulus, Marcus
Caesar's Women - Colleen McCullough 4233

Bidwell, Austin Biron
The Four Hundred - Stephen Sheppard 5804

Bidwell, George
The Four Hundred - Stephen Sheppard 5804

Bidwell, John
The Bear Flag: A Novel of the Birth of California - Cecelia Holland 2983

Bierce, Ambrose
The Old Gringo - Carlos Fuentes 2247
Yellow: A Novel - Daniel Lynch 3932

Big Foot
A Creek Called Wounded Knee - Douglas C. Jones 3277

Billingsley, Sherman
Walter Winchell: A Novel - Michael Herr 2863

Billy the Kid
Billy the Kid - Edwin Corle 1330
Billy the Kid: The Legend of El Chivato - Elizabeth Fackler 1994
The Demise of Billy the Kid - Preston Lewis 3760
Pistols for Hire - Nelson Coral Nye 4652
The Sons of Grady Rourke - Douglas Savage 5618
The Story of Pat Garrett and Billy the Kid - David Everitt 1987
Tascosa Gun: The Story of Jim East - Gene Shelton 5803
Time for Outrage - Amelia Bean 397

Bird, Henry
The Captives - Don Wright 6878

Birkenhead, Earl of
High Heroic - Constantine FitzGibbon 2118

Bismarck, Otto von
Falkenhorst - Mark Rascovich 5254
Quiet Lady - Norman Collins 1216
Royal Flash - George MacDonald Fraser 2213

Black Bart
A House Behind the Mint - Laurie Huffman 3072

Black Douglas
Castle Dangerous - Sir Walter Scott 5694

Black Hawk
Shaman - Noah Gordon 2483
The Shining Trail - Iola Fuller 2254
Thunder on the River - Charlton Laird 3590
Twilight of Empire - Allen W. Eckert 1846
Wind over Wisconsin - August Derleth 1620

Black Kettle
The Last Warpath - Will Henry 2844

The Black Prince
By Right of Arms - Robyn Carr 937
Don Pedro's Captain - Pamela Bennetts 449
The Lady Royal - Molly Costain Haycraft 2794
The Lords of Vaumartin - Cecelia Holland 2992
Passage to Pontefract - Jean Plaidy 5038
The Vow on the Heron - Jean Plaidy 5074
The White Company - Sir Arthur Conan Doyle 1716

Blackbeard
Carolina Corsair - Don Tracy 6307
Lusty Wind for Carolina - Inglis Fletcher 2134
On Stranger Tides - Tim Powers 5156
Rogue's Holiday - Hamilton Cochran 1141
Wind From the Main - Anne Osborne 4759

Blackford, Harriet
The Scandalous Mrs. Blackford - Harriet Kane 3358

Blackstone, William
The Disturber - L.S. Davidson Jr. 1505

Blackwell, Elizabeth
Domina - Barbara Wood 6847

Blackwell, Emily
Domina - Barbara Wood 6847

Blake, William
Vindication - Frances Sherwood 5824

Blanche de Castille
The Battle of the Queens - Jean Plaidy 5005

Blankenship, Charley
The True Memoirs of Charley Blankenship - Benjamin Capps 890

Blennerhasset, Harman
The Rock Cried Out - Edward Stanley 5981

Blennerhasset, Margaret
The Rock Cried Out - Edward Stanley 5981

Bligh, William
Adams of the Bounty - Erle Wilson 6807
Alaska - James A. Michener 4364
The Explorers - William Stuart Long 3872
H.M.S. Bounty - Alexander McKee 4280
The Last Mutiny: The Further Adventures of Captain Bligh - Bill Collett 1208
Men Against the Sea - Charles Nordhoff 4638
Mister Christian - William Kinsolving 3502
Mr. Christian! - Stanley Miller 4402
Mutiny on the Bounty - Charles Nordhoff 4639
The Return of Lono: A Novel of Captain Cook's Last Voyage - Oswald Andrew Bushnell 816
Sara Dane - Catherine Gaskin 2316
The Settlers - William Stuart Long 3878
Southern Cross - Terry Coleman 1206
Storm of Time - Eleanor Dark 1494
The Traitors - William Stuart Long 3879

Bliss, Tasker
Pancho And Black Jack - Fred Bean 398

Blondel de Nesle
The Golden Knight - George Challis 971
The Lute Player - Norah Lofts 3852
A Search for a King: A 12th-Century Legend - Gore Vidal 6492

Blondin
Niagara - Robert Lewis Taylor 6189

Blood, Thomas
The King's Rogue - Max Peacock 4859
Peveril of the Peak - Sir Walter Scott 5703

Blount, Elizabeth
The Shadow of the Pomegranate - Jean Plaidy 5062

Bloy, Leon
The Harp and the Shadow - Alejo Carpentier 905

Blucher, Gebhard Leberecht von
The Limits of Glory: A Novel of Waterloo - James McDonough 4265

Blue Duck
Belle Starr - Speer Morgan 4453

Blue Feather, Peter
A Few Painted Feathers - Stephen Longstreet 3886

Boadicea
The Eagle and the Raven - Pauline Gedge 2344
Red Queen, White Queen - Henry Treece 6332
Warrior Queen - James Sinclair 5865

Boas, Franz
The Alienist - Caleb Carr 907

Boaz
Ruth - Irving Fineman 2089
The Song of Ruth: A Love Story of the Old Testament - Frank G. Slaughter 5901

Boehm, Joseph Edgar
Bertie and the Tinman - Peter Lovesey 3909

Boethius
Citadel of God: A Novel of Saint Benedict - Louis De Wohl 1563

Boguslav
The Deluge - Henryk Sienkiewicz 5846

Bohemond (Bohemond I)
Count Bohemond - Alfred Duggan 1764

Bohemond I (Prince of Antioch)
A Booke of Days: A Journal of the Crusade by Roger, Duke of Lunel - Stephen J. Rivele 5351
Count Bohemond - Alfred Duggan 1764
Wine of Satan - Laverne Gay 2327

Bohemund (Duke of Otranto)
Silver Leopard - F. van Wyck Mason 4160

Bolden, Buddy
Coming through Slaughter - Michael Ondaatje 4736

Boles, Annie
Annie's Captain - Kathryn Hulme 3077

Boleyn, Anne
Anne Boleyn - Evelyn Anthony 158
Anne of the Thousand Days - Edward Fenton 2059
The Autobiography of Henry VIII - Margaret George 2355
Blood Royal - Mollie Hardwick 2690
Brief Gaudy Hour - Margaret Campbell Barnes 322
The Concubine - Norah Lofts 3839
The Heir of Allington - Philippa Wiat 6727
Henry VIII and His Six Wives - Maureen Peters 4975
In the Shadow of the Crown - Jean Plaidy 5022
Kathryn: In the Court of Six Queens - Anne Merton Abbey 1
King's Fool - Margaret Campbell Barnes 325
The King's Pleasure - Jean Plaidy 5026
The King's Secret Matter - Jean Plaidy 5027
The Lady in the Tower - Jean Plaidy 5028
The Man on a Donkey - H.F.M. Prescott 5170
Mistress Anne - Carolly Erickson 1952
Murder Most Royal - Jean Plaidy 5036
My Lord of Canterbury - Godfrey Turton 6369
Queen Anne Boleyn - Francis Hackett 2634
The Sword of Truth - Gilbert Morris 4472
Windsor Castle - William Harrison Ainsworth 59

Boleyn, Mary
Blood Royal - Mollie Hardwick 2690

Boleyn, Thomas
Blood Royal - Mollie Hardwick 2690

Bolingbroke, Henry
The Gentle Falcon - Hilda Lewis 3747
The Lords of Lancaster - Pamela Bennetts 452
Passage to Pontefract - Jean Plaidy 5038
The Peacock and the Pearl - Jennifer Lang 3661
Trumpet at the Gate - Jan Widgery 6739
Within the Hollow Crown - Margaret Campbell Barnes 331

Bolivar, Simon
The General in His Labyrinth - Gabriel Garcia Marquez 2282
Manuela, La Caballeresa Del Sol - Demetrio Aguilera Malta 41
The Splendor Stays: An Historic Novel Based on the Lives of the Seven Hart Sisters of Saybrook - Marguerite Allis 114

Bollman, Justus Erich
A Chance for Glory - Constance Wright 6877

Bonaparte, Carlo
Good-Bye My Son - Marjorie Coryn 1356
In What Torn Ship - Evelyn Eaton 1828

Bonaparte, Caroline
My Brother Napoleon: The Confessions of Caroline Bonaparte - F.W. Kenyon 3455

Bonaparte, Jerome
The Amazing Mrs. Bonaparte - Harnett T. Kane 3351
My Dear Cousin - Peggy Hoffmann 2977
Tide of Empire - Bates Baldwin 279

Bonaparte, Joseph
The Eagle and the Rock - Frances Winwar 6830
Sharpe's Honour - Bernard Cornwell 1344
The Tontine - Thomas B. Costain 1371

Bonaparte, Louis
A Rose for Virtue - Norah Lofts 3858

Bonaparte, Louis Napoleon
The Big Family - Vina Delmar 1600
Rachel - Anne Powers 5153
The Tontine - Thomas B. Costain 1371

Bonaparte, Maria Letizia
Good-Bye My Son - Marjorie Coryn 1356
In What Torn Ship - Evelyn Eaton 1828

Bonaparte, Napoleon
Alone Among Men - Marjorie Coryn 1355
The Amazing Mrs. Bonaparte - Harnett T. Kane 3351
Anna - Cynthia Harrod-Eagles 2752

The Anthem - Noel B. Gerson   2361
Anthony Adverse - Hervey Allen   98
Baltic Mission - Richard Woodman   6859
Being Met Together - William Vaughan
   Wilkins   6756
The Black Consul - Anatolii Vinogradov   6503
Blackstone and the Scourge of Europe - Richard
   Falkirk   2007
Brumaire - Mark Logan   3864
Captain Cut-Throat - John Dickson Carr   908
The Castle of Fratta - Ippolito Nievo   4625
Charles O'Malley - Charles James Lever   3731
Citizen Tom Paine - Howard Fast   2028
*Colossus: A Novel about Goya and a World Gone
   Mad* - Stephen Marlowe   4093
Death at the French Creek - Raymond C. Borel   580
The Death of Napoleon - Simon Leys   3768
The Dedicated - Willa Gibbs   2399
Desiree - Annemarie Selinko   5741
Draw Near to Battle - Jere Hungerford
   Wheelwright   6667
Dreams of Empire - Jeanne Mackin   3994
The Eagle and the Rock - Frances Winwar   6830
Emperor's Ladies - Noel B. Gerson   2367
*The Emperor's Lady: A Novel Based on the Life of the
   Empress Josephine* - F.W. Kenyon   3449
Far Flies the Eagle - Evelyn Anthony   162
The Flight of the Eagle - Donald Thomas   6239
Forty Centuries Look Down - Frederick Britten
   Austin   245
Good-Bye My Son - Marjorie Coryn   1356
A Great Lord - Paul Frischauer   2233
Guillotine - Mark Logan   3865
The Hastening Wind - Edward Grierson   2591
Hester - Brian Cleeve   1107
H.M.S. Cockerel - Dewey Lambdin   3611
Holy Week - Louis Aragon   182
Imperial Venus: A Novel of Napoleon's Favorite Sister
   - Edgar Maas   3949
The Last Love - Thomas B. Costain   1367
The Limits of Glory: A Novel of Waterloo - James
   McDonough   4265
Madame Casanova - Gaby von Schonthan   5659
The Man Who Killed the King - Dennis
   Wheatley   6654
Marianne - Juliette Benzoni   466
Marianne and the Crown of Fire - Juliette
   Benzoni   467
Marianne and the Masked Prince - Juliette
   Benzoni   469
Marianne and the Privateer - Juliette Benzoni   470
Marianne and the Rebels - Juliette Benzoni   471
The Marriage of Josephine - Marjorie Coryn   1358
Mirage - Ruth McKenney   4283
Mistress of Fortune - Sheila Lancaster   3651
*My Brother Napoleon: The Confessions of Caroline
   Bonaparte* - F.W. Kenyon   3455
Napoleon and His Son - Pierre Nezelof   4607
Napoleon and the Cossacks - Peter N.
   Krassnoff   3551
Napoleon Must Die - Quinn Fawcett   2054
Napoleon Symphony - Anthony Burgess   780
Notorious Eliza - Basil Beyea   489
Palaces of Desire - Kate Alexander   81
The Prince Lost to Time - Ann Dukthas   1776
The Raven and the Rose - Susan Wiggs   6746
The River Devils - Carter A. Vaughan   6437
The Road to Glory - Frederick Britten Austin   246
The Rose and the Sword - Sandra Paretti   4792
A Rose for Virtue - Norah Lofts   3858
*The Rose of Malmaison: The Turbulent Life of the
   Beautiful Josephine* - Gaby von Schonthan   5660
Seed of Mischief - Willa Gibbs   2401
Seven Men of Gascony - R.F. Delderfield   1589
Sharpe's Devil - Bernard Cornwell   1340
So Brief a Spring - Claude Manceron   4054
So Great a Man - David Pilgrim   5000
Tallien: A Brief Romance - Frederic Tuten   6370

Tell Your Sons: A Novel of the Napoleonic Era - Willa
   Gibbs   2402
The Thousand Fires - Anne Powers   5155
Tide of Empire - Bates Baldwin   279
A Time for Titans - Vina Delmar   1602
To Spit Against the Wind - Benjamin H. Levin   3737
Tom Burke of Ours - Charles James Lever   3732
The Twelfth Physician - Willa Gibbs   2403
Valentina - Evelyn Anthony   165
Valide: A Novel of the Harem - Barbara Chase-
   Riboud   1007
War and Peace - Leo Tolstoy   6295
Waterloo - Manuel Komroff   3536
Waterloo - Frederic E. Smith   5920
Why Waterloo? - Alan Patrick Herbert   2850

Bonaparte, Pauline
Black Triumvirate: A Novel of Haiti - Benjamin H.
   Levin   3736
Imperial Venus: A Novel of Napoleon's Favorite Sister
   - Edgar Maas   3949

Bonhoeffer, Dietrich
The Cup of Wrath - Mary Glazener   2429

Bonnet, Stede
Wind From the Main - Anne Osborne   4759

Bonneville, Benjamin
The Great Adventure - Janice Holt Giles   2410

Bonney, William
Billy the Kid - Edwin Corle   1330
Billy the Kid: The Legend of El Chivato - Elizabeth
   Fackler   1994
The Demise of Billy the Kid - Preston Lewis   3760
Pistols for Hire - Nelson Coral Nye   4652
The Sons of Grady Rourke - Douglas Savage   5618
The Story of Pat Garrett and Billy the Kid - David
   Everitt   1987
Tascosa Gun: The Story of Jim East - Gene
   Shelton   5803
Time for Outrage - Amelia Bean   397

Bonnie Prince Charlie
Born to Be King - Constance Gluyas   2440
Candleshine No More - Jane Oliver   4721
Charlie Is My Darling - Mollie Hardwick   2691
Clandara - Evelyn Anthony   161
Commander of the Mists - D.L. Murray   4527
Crown Without Sceptre - William Vaughan
   Wilkins   6758
The Dark Mile - Dorothy Kathleen Broster   709
The Flight of the Heron - Dorothy Kathleen
   Broster   710
Highlands Rebel - Sally Watson   6584
I Came to the Highlands: A Novel of Suspense - Velda
   Johnston   3263
The Long Day Closes - Beatrice Tunstall   6360
Louis the Well-Beloved - Jean Plaidy   5032
A Prince, a Piper, and a Rose - John Scalzo   5628
Prince Charlie's Bluff - Donald Thomas   6241
The Queen of Hearts - Joan Rees   5290
Red Gauntlet - Sir Walter Scott   5706
The Scotswoman - Inglis Fletcher   2140
Waverley - Sir Walter Scott   5709
The Woman from The Glen - Chloe Gartner   2310

Bonny, Anne
Anne Bonny - Chloe Gartner   2306
The Changeling - Alison Macleod   4000
*Fanny: Being the True History of the Adventures of
   Fanny Hackabout-Jones* - Erica Jong   3299
Lusty Wind for Carolina - Inglis Fletcher   2134
The Pyrates - George MacDonald Fraser   2212
Sea Star: The Private Life of Anne Bonny, Pirate -
   Pamela Jekel   3187
Wind From the Main - Anne Osborne   4759

Boone, Daniel
Becky Landers, Frontier Warrior - Constance
   Skinner   5879
Black Forest - Meade Minnigerode   4411

*Boone: A Novel Based on the Life and Times of Daniel
   Boone* - Cameron Judd   3311
Buckskin Cavalier - John Clagett   1082
Cherokee - Donald Clayton Porter   5115
The Court Martial of Daniel Boone - Allen W.
   Eckert   1840
The Crossing - Winston Churchill   1080
Flintlock - Jason Manning   4073
The Frontiersmen - Allen W. Eckert   1841
The Kentuckians - Janice Holt Giles   2413
Kentucky Stand - Jere Hungerford Wheelwright   6670
The Long Rifle - Stewart Edward White   6702
Never No More: The Story of Rebecca Boone - Shirley
   Seifert   5730
Oh, Kentucky! - Betty Layman Receveur   5284
Panther in the Sky - James Alexander Thom   6234
That Dark and Bloody River - Allen W. Eckert   1845
Thunder on the River - Charlton Laird   3590
Vision of the Eagle - Kay L. McDonald   4263
Wilderness Empire - Allen W. Eckert   1847

Boone, Rebecca
Never No More: The Story of Rebecca Boone - Shirley
   Seifert   5730

Booth, Edwin
The Chester A. Arthur Conspiracy - William
   Wiegand   6740
The Fast Men - Tom McNab   4302
The Judges of the Secret Court - David Stacton   5972
The Spur - Ardyth Kennelly   3425

Booth, John Wilkes
The Chester A. Arthur Conspiracy - William
   Wiegand   6740
The Cosgrove Report - G.J.A. O'Toole   4765
A Court of Owls - Richard Adicks   37
Dim the Flaring Lamps - Jan Jordan   3301
The Judges of the Secret Court - David Stacton   5972
The Last Full Measure - Honore Morrow   4488
Lincoln: A Novel - Gore Vidal   6490
The Spur - Ardyth Kennelly   3425
The Titans - John Jakes   3154
The Twisted Tendril - Alice Glasgow   2427
The Woman Who Loved John Wilkes Booth - Pamela
   Redford Russell   5533

Boozer, Marie
La Belle - Elizabeth Boatwright Coker   1161

Boquet, Henry
The Conquerors - Allen W. Eckert   1839

Borden, Lizzie
Lizzie - Evan Hunter   3083
Lizzie Borden - Elizabeth Engstrom   1944
Miss Lizzie - Walter Satterthwait   5608

Borghese, Maria Paolina
Imperial Venus: A Novel of Napoleon's Favorite Sister
   - Edgar Maas   3949

Borgia, Cesare
The Bait and the Trap - George Challis   970
The Borgia Prince - Pamela Bennetts   446
Borgia Testament - Nigel Balchin   277
Carnival of Saints - George Herman   2860
City of God: A Novel of the Borgias - Cecelia
   Holland   2985
Daughter of Shadows - Miranda Seymour   5762
Light on Lucrezia - Jean Plaidy   5029
Madonna of the Seven Hills - Jean Plaidy   5034
Michelangelo the Florentine - Sidney Alexander   86
Mona Lisa: The Woman in the Portrait - Sara
   Mayfield   4206
The Naked Sword: The Story of Lucretia Borgia -
   F.W. Kenyon   3456
A Passion in the Blood - Genevieve Davis   1519
Prince of Foxes - Samuel Shellabarger   5797
The Romance of Leonardo Da Vinci - Dmitri
   Merezhkovski   4339
The Scarlet City - Hella S. Haasse   2632
Then and Now - William Somerset Maugham   4198

Web of Lucifer: A Novel of the Borgia Fury - Maurice
   Samuel 5580

Borgia, Giovanni
The Scarlet City - Hella S. Haasse 2632

Borgia, Lucrezia
Carnival of Saints - George Herman 2860
City of God: A Novel of the Borgias - Cecelia
   Holland 2985
Daughter of Shadows - Miranda Seymour 5762
The Flame of the Borgias - Jean Briggs 680
Light on Lucretia - Jean Plaidy 5029
Madonna of the Seven Hills - Jean Plaidy 5034
Michelangelo the Florentine - Sidney Alexander 86
The Naked Sword: The Story of Lucretia Borgia -
   F.W. Kenyon 3456
A Passion in the Blood - Genevieve Davis 1519
Private Renaissance - Maria Bellonci 436
The Scarlet City - Hella S. Haasse 2632

Borgia, Rodrigo
Carnival of Saints - George Herman 2860
City of God: A Novel of the Borgias - Cecelia
   Holland 2985
Daughter of Shadows - Miranda Seymour 5762
The Dogs of Paradise - Abel Posse 5141
Light on Lucretia - Jean Plaidy 5029
Madonna of the Seven Hills - Jean Plaidy 5034
The Medici Guns - Martin Woodhouse 6852
The Memoirs of Christopher Columbus - Stephen
   Marlowe 4096
Michelangelo the Florentine - Sidney Alexander 86
Mona Lisa: The Woman in the Portrait - Sara
   Mayfield 4206
The Naked Sword: The Story of Lucretia Borgia -
   F.W. Kenyon 3456
A Passion in the Blood - Genevieve Davis 1519
The Scarlet City - Hella S. Haasse 2632

Bormann, Martin
The Blood Order - Jack D. Hunter 3084
Eva - Ib Melchior 4329

Boswell, James
Blind Justice - Bruce Alexander 76
The Bonnet Laird's Daughter - Barbara
   Annandale 154
Dear Mrs. Boswell - Marie Muir 4508

Boswell, Margaret
Dear Mrs. Boswell - Marie Muir 4508

Botha, Louis
The Legacy of Ladysmith - John Kenny Crane 1413
Rags of Glory - Stuart Cloete 1126
The Red Daniel - Duncan MacNeil 4017

Bothwell, Earl of (Francis Hepburn)
The Border Lord - Jan Westcott 6641

Bothwell, Earl of (James Hepburn)
A Famine of Horses - P.F. Chisholm 1071
The Gay Galliard - Margaret Irwin 3119
Immortal Queen - Elizabeth Byrd 834
*King in Hell: A Novel of Bothwell and Mary, Queen of
   Scots* - Beverly Balin 282
The Lion and the Rose - Jane Oliver 4724
*Maid of Honour: A Novel Set in the Court of Mary,
   Queen of Scots* - Elizabeth Byrd 836
Mary of Scotland - F.W. Kenyon 3454
Mary, Queen of Scotland and the Isles - Margaret
   George 2356
No Smoke Without Fire - Alice Harwood 2767
Parcel of Rogues - Jane Lane 3656
Royal Road to Fotheringay - Jean Plaidy 5059
A Time for the Death of a King - Ann Dukthas 1777
The White Queen - Frederic Fallon 2011

Botticelli, Sandro
The Florentine - Sandra Shulman 5840
Michelangelo the Florentine - Sidney Alexander 86
Mona Lisa: The Woman in the Portrait - Sara
   Mayfield 4206
The Palace - Chelsea Quinn Yarbro 6904

The Time Returns - Alexandra Ripley 5343

Boucher, Francois
Rasero - Francisco Rebolledo 5282

Boudicca
The Eagle and the Raven - Pauline Gedge 2344
Red Queen, White Queen - Henry Treece 6332
Warrior Queen - James Sinclair 5865

Boulanger, Georges Ernest Jean Marie
Brave General - Herbert Gorman 2490

Bourbon, Antoine de
The Italian Woman - Jean Plaidy 5024

Bourbon, Charles Ferdinand de
So Much as Beauty Does - Muriel Elwood 1938

Bourbon, Francois de Vendome de
Twenty Years After - Alexandre Dumas 1783

Bourbon, Louis I de
The Faith and the Flame - June Dimmit
   Houston 3054

Bourbon, Louise de
Sorrow by Day - Marjorie Coryn 1359

Bourbon, Marie Louise de
Poison - Kathryn Harrison 2737

Bowditch, Nathaniel
The Navigator: The Story of Nathaniel Bowditch -
   Alfred Stanford 5979

Bowers, Henry Robertson
The Birthday Boys - Beryl Bainbridge 269

Bowie, Jim
*The Bugles Are Silent: A Novel of the Texas
   Revolution* - John R. Knaggs 3513
The Furies - John Jakes 3146
The Iron Mistress - Paul I. Wellman 6618
The Road to San Jacinto - James F. Davis 1524
Tempered Blade - Monte Barrett 352
Texas - James A. Michener 4375

Bowles, William Augustus
Alabama Empire - Welbourn Kelley 3392

Boycott, Charles Cunningham
Captain Boycott, a Romantic Novel - Philip
   Rooney 5440

Boyd, Belle
The Smiling Rebel - Harnett T. Kane 3357

Braddock, Edward
Black Forest - Meade Minnigerode 4411
Gentleman Ranker - John Edward Jennings 3200
The Indentured Heart - Gilbert Morris 4464
Morning of a Hero - Burke Boyce 608
Red Morning - Ruby Frazier Frey 2230
The Red Road: A Romance of Braddock's Defeat -
   Hugh Pendexter 4898
War in the Golden Weather - Stephen
   Longstreet 3892
Wilderness Empire - Allen W. Eckert 1847
The Woodsman - Don Wright 6880

Bradford, William
Cape Cod - William Martin 4139
The Honorable Imposter - Gilbert Morris 4463
The Land Is Bright - Noel B. Gerson 2376
O Western Wind - John Anthony Devon 1634
Pilgrims: A Novel of the Mayflower - Gerard
   Mac 3955
The Plymouth Adventure - Ernest Gebler 2342
Thanksgiving - Terry Coleman 1207

Bradse, Matilda
Lady of Hay - Barbara Erskine 1955

Bradstreet, John
Drums Against Frontenac - Harvey Chalmers 972

Brady, James "Diamond Jim"
Fenwick Travers and the Panama Canal - Raymond
   M. Saunders 5613

Brady, Julia
The Gallery of His Dreams - Kristine Kathryn
   Rusch 5525

Brady, Matthew B.
The Gallery of His Dreams - Kristine Kathryn
   Rusch 5525

Brady, William
The Sons of Grady Rourke - Douglas Savage 5618

Bragg, Braxton
In the Season of the Wild Rose - Clara Rising 5347
Journey to Shiloh - Will Henry 2843

Brahe, Tycho
Kepler: A Novel - John Banville 297

Bramante, Donato
The Agony and the Ecstasy - Irving Stone 6054

Brancusi, Constantin
*The Saint of Montparnasse: A Novel Based on the Life
   of Constantin Brancusi* - Peter Neagoe 4560

Brandeis, Louis
The Hyde Park Murder - Elliott Roosevelt 5443

Brandon, Charles
The Reluctant Queen - Molly Costain Haycraft 2796
Royal Nonesuch: A Tudor Tapestry - Beatrice
   White 6674

Brannan, Samuel
Samuel Brannan and the Golden Fleece - Reva
   Scott 5686

Brant, Joseph
Bridal Journey - Dale Van Every 6406
Brother Owl - Al Hine 2953
Buckskin Baronet - Margaret Widdemer 6734
*Eagle of Niagara: The Story of David Harper and His
   Indian Captivity* - John Brick 671
The King's Rebel - James David Horan 3030
The Raid - John Brick 673
Reckon with the River - Clark McMeekin 4292
Three Sides of Agiochook - Eric Kelly 3400
West to the Setting Sun - Harvey Chalmers 973
The Wilderness War - Allen W. Eckert 1848

Brant, Molly
Blackrobe - Robert E. Wall 6534
Bloodbrothers - Robert E. Wall 6535
Lady of the Mohawks - Margaret Widdemer 6736

Braun, Eva
Eva - Ib Melchior 4329
Last Man to Die - Michael Dobbs 1652

Brebeuf, Jean de
Fathers and Crows - William T. Vollmann 6508
This Widowed Land - Kathleen O'Neal Gear 2331

Brecht, Bertold
The Howard Hughes Affair - Stuart M.
   Kaminsky 3340

Breck, Alan
Catriona - Robert Louis Stevenson 6009
Kidnapped - Robert Louis Stevenson 6010

Breckenridge, John Cabell
Freedom - William Safire 5561

Breen, Pat
The Ungodly: A Novel of the Donner Party - Richard
   Rhodes 5311

Brendan the Navigator
Brendan - Frederick Buechner 762
Paradise - Dikkon Eberhart 1831

Brent, Margaret
Margaret Brent, Adventurer - Dorothy Grant 2533

Brett, Peircy
Manila Galleon - F. van Wyck Mason 4154

Breuer, Josef
When Nietzsche Wept: A Novel of Obsession - Irvin D.
   Yalom 6892

Brian Boru
The Gallowglass - Howard Breslin 666
The Kings in Winter - Cecelia Holland 2991
The Lion of Ireland - Morgan Llywelyn 3822

Bridger, Jim
Across the Shining Mountains - Christian
   McCord 4226
The Great Adventure - Janice Holt Giles 2410
Kelly Blue - Peter Bowen 601
Kings of the Missouri - Hugh Pendexter 4895
Lord Grizzly - Frederick F. Manfred 4056
Red Cloud's Revenge - Terry C. Johnston 3255

Briennius, Nicephorus
Count Robert of Paris - Sir Walter Scott 5695

Brillon, Cunegonde
The Gentleman From America - Polan Banks 293

Brinvilliers, Marie Madeleine
The Devil's Marchioness - William Fifield 2082
A Lady at Bay - Edgar Maas 3950

Brocius, Curly Bill
Tombstone Showdown - Leslie Scott 5681

Broderick, David
Vigilante - Richard Summers 6116

Brodie, William
The Strange Case of Deacon Brodie - Forbes
   Bramble 646

Bronte, Anne
Bronte - Glyn Hughes 3073
Dark Quartet: The Story of the Brontes - Lynne Reid
   Banks 290
In the Shadow of the Brontes - Louise Brindley 690
These Were the Brontes - Dorothy Helen
   Cornish 1332
*Wild Decembers: A Biographical Portrait of the
   Brontes* - Hilda Crystal White 6681

Bronte, Branwell
Bronte - Glyn Hughes 3073
Dark Quartet: The Story of the Brontes - Lynne Reid
   Banks 290
*Wild Decembers: A Biographical Portrait of the
   Brontes* - Hilda Crystal White 6681

Bronte, Charlotte
Bronte - Glyn Hughes 3073
Dark Quartet: The Story of the Brontes - Lynne Reid
   Banks 290
*H.—: The Story of Heathcliff's Journey Back to
   Wuthering Heights* - Lin Haire-Sargeant 2641
In the Shadow of the Brontes - Louise Brindley 690
Path to the Silent Country - Lynne Reid Banks 291
These Were the Brontes - Dorothy Helen
   Cornish 1332
*Wild Decembers: A Biographical Portrait of the
   Brontes* - Hilda Crystal White 6681

Bronte, Emily
Bronte - Glyn Hughes 3073
Dark Quartet: The Story of the Brontes - Lynne Reid
   Banks 290
In the Shadow of the Brontes - Louise Brindley 690
These Were the Brontes - Dorothy Helen
   Cornish 1332
*Wild Decembers: A Biographical Portrait of the
   Brontes* - Hilda Crystal White 6681

Bronte, Patrick
Bronte - Glyn Hughes 3073
Dark Quartet: The Story of the Brontes - Lynne Reid
   Banks 290
Path to the Silent Country - Lynne Reid Banks 291
*Wild Decembers: A Biographical Portrait of the
   Brontes* - Hilda Crystal White 6681

Brooke, James
Flashman's Lady - George MacDonald Fraser 2210

Broschi, Carlo
The Castrato - Lawrence Goldman 2459

Brown, Amy
So Much as Beauty Does - Muriel Elwood 1938

Brown, John (American Abolitionist)
The Drums of Morning - Philip Van Doren
   Stern 5997
Flashman and the Angel of the Lord - George
   MacDonald Fraser 2205
Free Soil - Marguerite Allis 110
Free Soil - Margaret Lynn 3943
God's Angry Man - Leonard Ehrlich 1898
House Divided - Ben Ames Williams 6765
McKay's Bees - Thomas McMahon 4289
Raising Holy Hell - Bruce Olds 4718
The Slave of Frankenstein - Robert J. Myers 4549
The Surveyor - Truman Nelson 4583
Through a Gold Eagle - Miriam Grace
   Monfredo 4430

Brown, John (Servant of Queen Victoria)
The Widow of Windsor - Jean Plaidy 5076
The Widow of Windsor - Tyler Whittle 6723

Brown, Salmon
Gray Victory - Robert Skimin 5877

Browning, Elizabeth Barrett
How Do I Love Thee - Lucille Iremonger 3110
Lady's Maid - Margaret Forster 2188

Browning, Robert
How Do I Love Thee - Lucille Iremonger 3110
Lady's Maid - Margaret Forster 2188
Neighboring Lives - Thomas M. Disch 1648

Bruce, James
Flashman and the Dragon - George MacDonald
   Fraser 2206

Bruce, Marjorie
Marjorie of Scotland - Pamela Hill 2939

Bruce, Thomas
Dreams of Empire - Jeanne Mackin 3994
Lord Elgin's Lady - Theodore Vrettos 6514

Bruce, Victor
By Command of the Viceroy - Duncan MacNeil 4010
Charge of Cowardice - Duncan MacNeil 4011

Bruckner, Anton
Music for God - Theresa Weiser 6603

Brudenell, James Thomas
Flashman - George MacDonald Fraser 2204
Flashman at the Charge - George MacDonald
   Fraser 2209
Pendragon: Late of Prince Albert's Own - Robert
   Trevelyan 6337

Brueghel, Pieter
Bruegel, or, The Workshop of Dreams - Claude Henri
   Rocquet 5422

Brummell, Beau
Beau Barron's Lady - Helen Ashfield 204
Brumaire - Mark Logan 3864
Edward, Edward - Lolah Burford 772
Guillotine - Mark Logan 3865
Rebel Heiress - Jane Aiken Hodge 2969
Regency Buck - Georgette Heyer 2898

Brummell, George Bryan
Beau Barron's Lady - Helen Ashfield 204
Brumaire - Mark Logan 3864
Edward, Edward - Lolah Burford 772
Guillotine - Mark Logan 3865
Rebel Heiress - Jane Aiken Hodge 2969
Regency Buck - Georgette Heyer 2898

Brutus, Marcus Junius
Augustus - Allan Massie 4167
Caesar - Allan Massie 4168
Freedom, Farewell - Phyllis Bentley 461
The Ides of March - Thornton Wilder 6753

Bryan, William Jennings
The American - Howard Fast 2026

Empire: A Novel - Gore Vidal 6487
The Land Was Ours: A Novel of the Great Plains -
   Charles W. Bailey 266
Lusitania - David Butler 819

Bryant, William Cullen
1876: A Novel - Gore Vidal 6484
All This, and Heaven Too - Rachel Field 2080
The Furies - John Jakes 3146

Buade, Louis de
The Gilded Torch - Iola Fuller 2252
Heritage of the River - Muriel Elwood 1937
The King's Messenger - Samuel Edwards 1887
The Power and the Glory - Gilbert Parker 4805
Shadows on the Rock - Willa Cather 959

Buchanan, James
Action at Aquila - Hervey Allen 97
The Big Family - Vina Delmar 1600
Colorado! - Dana Fuller Ross 5471
Ironclads: Man-of-War - Larry D. Names 4554
Memories of the Ford Administration - John
   Updike 6391
Powderkeg - Richard Vetterli 6482
Sister Wives - Cleo Jones 3270

Buckingham, Duke of (1454?-1483)
Crown of Roses - Valerie Anand 127
The Fate of Princes - P.C. Doherty 1673

Buckingham, Duke of (1478-1521)
The Grail Murders - Michael Clynes 1135

Buckingham, Duke of (1592-1628)
Call Lady Purbeck - Hilda Lewis 3745
The Cardinal and the Queen - Evelyn Anthony 159
Myself My Enemy - Jean Plaidy 5037
The Three Musketeers - Alexandre Dumas 1782
To Love a Queen - Lawrence Schoonover 5669
Unicorn Rampant - Nigel Tranter 6323
Wife to Great Buckingham - Hilda Lewis 3751
The Young and Lonely King - Jane Lane 3659

Buckingham, Duke of (1628-1687)
Ballenrose - Mallory Burgess 783
Charles the King - Evelyn Anthony 160
A Health Unto His Majesty - Jean Plaidy 5019
Here Lies Our Sovereign Lord - Jean Plaidy 5021
The King Breaker - Elizabeth Linington 3797
The King's General - Daphne Du Maurier 1748
My Lord Foxe - Constance Gluyas 2443
Our Jo, or The Chronicle of a Coming Man - Kenneth
   M. Cameron 868
Peveril of the Peak - Sir Walter Scott 5703
Royal Escape - Georgette Heyer 2900

Buddha
Lady of the Lotus - William E. Barrett 353
The Yellow Robe: A Novel of the Life of Buddha -
   Robert Payne 4856

Buffalo Bill Cody
*Aces and Eights: A Novel of the Legend of Wild Bill
   Hickok* - Loren D. Estleman 1967
The Big Stick - Lawrence Alexander 82
Black Sun - Terry C. Johnston 3242
Buffalo Girls - Larry McMurtry 4296
Castle Garden - Bill Albert 63
Crazy Fox Remembers - Don Preston 5174
The Dream Seekers - Grace Mark 4085
A Good Day to Die - Thomas Wakefield
   Blackburn 525
Homeland - John Jakes 3148
The Jewelled Spur - Gilbert Morris 4465
Kelly Blue - Peter Bowen 601
Last Go Round - Ken Kesey 3473
The Secret Annie Oakley - Marcy Moran
   Heidish 2819
Shaggy Legion - Hal George Evarts 1986
This Old Bill - Loren D. Estleman 1980
Trumpet on the Land - Terry C. Johnston 3260
Wild Times - Brian Garfield 2291
Yellowstone Kelly - Peter Bowen 602

Buford, John
Gettysburg: Crisis of Command - Harry Albright 65
The Killer Angels - Michael Shaara 5766

Bulatovich, Alexander K.
The Name of Hero - Richard Seltzer 5742

Buller, Redvers Henry
The Covenant - James A. Michener 4368
The Red Daniel - Duncan MacNeil 4017

Bulwer-Lytton, Edward
The Prime Minister's Wife - Doris Leslie 3727

Buntline, Ned
Buffalo Girls - Larry McMurtry 4296
This Old Bill - Loren D. Estleman 1980

Bunyan, John
The Pilgrim Prince - Gladys H. Barr 343

Buonarotti, Michelangelo
The Agony and the Ecstasy - Irving Stone 6054
The Hand of Michelangelo - Sidney Alexander 85
Michelangelo the Florentine - Sidney Alexander 86
Mona Lisa: The Woman in the Portrait - Sara Mayfield 4206
Nicodemus: The Roman Years of Michelangelo Buonarroti, 1534-1564 - Sidney Alexander 87
The Scarlet City - Hella S. Haasse 2632
The Time Returns - Alexandra Ripley 5343
The Venetian - David Weiss 6611

Burbage, Richard
The Best House in Stratford - Edward Fisher 2100
The Cleopatra Boy - Eric Malpass 4048
Nothing Like the Sun - Anthony Burgess 781
Sweet Will - Eric Malpass 4050

Burden, Jane
Willowwood - Elizabeth Savage 5619

Burdett-Coutts, Angela
The Hoydens and Mr. Dickens - William J. Palmer 4784

Burgh, Elizabeth de
Robert the Bruce: The Path of the Hero King - Nigel Tranter 6318
Robert the Bruce: The Price of the King's Peace - Nigel Tranter 6319
Robert the Bruce: The Steps to the Empty Throne - Nigel Tranter 6320

Burgh, Hubert de
The Marriage of Meggotta - Edith Pargeter 4799

Burgh, Hugh de
The Battle of the Queens - Jean Plaidy 5005

Burgh, Meggotta de
The Marriage of Meggotta - Edith Pargeter 4799

Burghley, Baron
Legacy - Susan Kay 3374
My Lord Essex - Olive Eckerson 1838
My Lord the Fox - Robert York 6932
The Proud Man - Elizabeth Linington 3800
Shadow in the Sun: A Novel of Elizabeth I, the Virgin Queen - F.W. Kenyon 3460
To Love a Queen - Lawrence Schoonover 5669

Burgoyne, John
The Drums of April - Charles Mergendahl 4340
Guns of Burgoyne - Bruce Lancaster 3640
Jeremiah Martin: A Revolutionary War Novel - Robert H. Fowler 2191
The Long Naked Descent into Boston - William Eastlake 1823
Sergeant Lamb's America - Robert Graves 2552
Valiant Libertine - John Gordon Bryson 748

Burk, Martha Jane Cannary
Buffalo Girls - Larry McMurtry 4296
Calamity Jane of Deadwood Gulch - Ethel Hueston 3068
Crazy Fox Remembers - Don Preston 5174
Deadwood - Pete Dexter 1638

The Lawless - John Jakes 3149
Little Big Man - Thomas Berger 478

Burke, Edmund
Let the King Beware! - Honore Morrow 4489

Burney, Fanny
The Bonnet Laird's Daughter - Barbara Annandale 154
Sweet Lass of Richmond Hill - Jean Plaidy 5067
The Third George - Jean Plaidy 5068

Burns, Anthony
The Sin of the Prophet - Truman Nelson 4582

Burns, Robert
Crest of the Broken Wave - James Barke 302
Song in the Green Thorn Tree - James Barke 303
Well of the Silent Harp - James Barke 304
The Wind That Shakes the Barley - James Barke 305
Wonder of All the Gay World - James Barke 306

Burns, William
The Wind That Shakes the Barley - James Barke 305

Burnside, Ambrose E.
The Crater - Richard Slotkin 5908
Glory Enough for All: The Battle of the Crater - Duane Philip Schultz 5673
Joy From Ashes - Al Lacy 3581

Burr, Aaron
Anthony Adverse - Hervey Allen 98
Burr - Gore Vidal 6485
The Conqueror: Being the True and Romantic Story of Alexander Hamilton - Gertrude Atherton 222
The Fallon Pride - Reagan O'Neal 4742
Flintlock - Jason Manning 4073
Hawk's Journey - Donald Clayton Porter 5119
The High Constable - Maan Meyers 4353
Jackson: A Novel - Max Byrd 837
Kentucky Home - Betty Layman Receveur 5283
My Theodosia - Anya Seton 5753
Notorious Eliza - Basil Beyea 489
Painted Lady: Eliza Jumel, Her Life and Times - Leonard Falkner 2009
Reckon with the River - Clark McMeekin 4292
The Rock Cried Out - Edward Stanley 5981
Shadow of the Moon - Douglas C. Jones 3284
The Unvanquished - Howard Fast 2046
West Goes the Road - Tim Pridgen 5192

Burton, Sir Richard Francis
Burton and Speke - William Harrison 2751
The Highwayman and Mr. Dickens - William J. Palmer 4783

Bush, Sally
Lincoln's Mothers: A Story of Nancy and Sally Lincoln - Dorothy Clarke Wilson 6804

Bushnell, David
The Kingsbridge Plot - Maan Meyers 4355

Butler, Benjamin
Angel of the Delta - Edward Francis Murphy 4521
Captain Rebel - Frank Yerby 6910

Butler, Frank
The Secret Annie Oakley - Marcy Moran Heidish 2819

Butler, Pierce
The Ardent Years - Janet Stevenson 6003
Fire in the Heart - Henrietta Buckmaster 761

Buys, Coenraad de
King of the Bastards - Sarah Gertrude Millin 4405

Byrd, William
Devil Water - Anya Seton 5749

Byron, George Gordon
The Absorbing Fire: The Byron Legend - F.W. Kenyon 3445
The Blue Heaven Bends Over All - Jane Oliver 4720
Byron: A Novel - Sigrid Combuchen 1225
Count Manifred - Miranda Seymour 5761

Frankenstein Unbound - Brian Aldiss 68
The Golden Years: A Novel Based on the Life and Loves of Percy Bysshe Shelley - F.W. Kenyon 3451
Haunted Summer - Anne Edwards 1881
Lord Byron's Doctor - Paul West 6634
Lord of the Dead: The Secret History of Byron - Tom Holland 2999
Lord of the Ladies - Joanna Dessau 1626
Love's Children - Judith Chernaik 1013
The Memoirs of Lord Byron - Robert Nye 4655
The Missolonghi Manuscript - Frederic Prokosch 5194
My Sister, My Love - Lucille Iremonger 3111
The Secret Memoirs of Lord Byron - Christopher Nicole 4622
A Single Summer with Lord B. - Derek Marlowe 4092
The Stress of Her Regard - Tim Powers 5157
Teresa, or Her Demon Lover - Austin K. Gray 2554

Byron, Lord
The Absorbing Fire: The Byron Legend - F.W. Kenyon 3445
The Blue Heaven Bends Over All - Jane Oliver 4720
Byron: A Novel - Sigrid Combuchen 1225
Count Manifred - Miranda Seymour 5761
Frankenstein Unbound - Brian Aldiss 68
The Golden Years: A Novel Based on the Life and Loves of Percy Bysshe Shelley - F.W. Kenyon 3451
Haunted Summer - Anne Edwards 1881
Lord Byron's Doctor - Paul West 6634
Lord of the Dead: The Secret History of Byron - Tom Holland 2999
Lord of the Ladies - Joanna Dessau 1626
Love's Children - Judith Chernaik 1013
The Memoirs of Lord Byron - Robert Nye 4655
The Missolonghi Manuscript - Frederic Prokosch 5194
My Sister, My Love - Lucille Iremonger 3111
The Secret Memoirs of Lord Byron - Christopher Nicole 4622
A Single Summer with Lord B. - Derek Marlowe 4092
The Stress of Her Regard - Tim Powers 5157
Teresa, or Her Demon Lover - Austin K. Gray 2554

C

Cabarrus, Jeanne Marie Therese de
Lady of Paris - William Vaughan Wilkins 6760

Cabeza de Vaca, Alvar Nunez
The Children of the Sun - Oakley Hall 2652
Texas - James A. Michener 4375

Cable, George Washington
A Connecticut Yankee in Criminal Court - Peter J. Heck 2814

Cadillac, Antoine de La Mothe
Hawk of Detroit - Arthur Pound 5145

Caelius, Marcus
Death on the Appian Way - Kenneth Benton 463

Caesar, Gaius Julius
The City of Libertines - W.G. Hardy 2702
Three's Company - Alfred Duggan 1774

Cagliostro, Count Alessandro
The Queen's Necklace - Alexandre Dumas 1781

Cahan, Abraham
Rivington Street - Meredith Tax 6175

Caillot, Blanchette
The Gentleman From America - Polan Banks 293

Calamity Jane
Buffalo Girls - Larry McMurtry 4296

Calamity Jane of Deadwood Gulch - Ethel
    Hueston   3068
Crazy Fox Remembers - Don Preston   5174
Deadwood - Pete Dexter   1638
The Lawless - John Jakes   3149
Little Big Man - Thomas Berger   478

Calderon, Inez
I, the King - Frances Parkinson Keyes   3479

Calhoun, John C.
54-40 or Fight - Emerson Hough   3040
Dolley - Rita Mae Brown   727
Magnificent Destiny - Paul I. Wellman   6619
The Massacre at Fall Creek - Jessamyn West   6631
North and South - John Jakes   3151

Caligula (Roman Emperor)
Brothers of Vengeance - LeGette Blythe   556
I Am a Barbarian - Edgar Rice Burroughs   807
I, Claudius - Robert Graves   2547
The Kingdom of the Wicked - Anthony Burgess   778
The Lost Legion - H. Warner Munn   4516
Man on Fire: A Novel on the Life of St. Paul -
    LeGette Blythe   558
No King but Caesar - Anne Powers   5151
Octavia: A Tale of Ancient Rome - Seymour Van
    Santvoord   6428
Pontius Pilate: A Biographical Novel - Paul L.
    Maier   4034
The Robe - Lloyd C. Douglas   1703
*The Sins of Herod: A Novel of Rome and the Early
    Church* - Frank G. Slaughter   5900
The Testament of Theophilus - Leonard
    Wibberley   6730
The Thorn of Arimathea - Frank G. Slaughter   5905
Tiberius: The Memoirs of the Emperor - Allan
    Massie   4169
The Word and the Sword - Theo Lang   3662

Calvin, John
City of Light - Alison Macleod   4001
God's Man: A Novel on the Life of John Calvin -
    Duncan Norton-Taylor   4650
*The Master of Geneva: A Novel Based on the Life of
    John Calvin* - Gladys H. Barr   341

Cambyses II (King of Persia)
The Prophet - Sholem Asch   201

Cameron, Gavin
The World, the Flesh, and the Devil - Reay
    Tannahill   6159

Cameron, Simon
Heaven and Hell - John Jakes   3147

Campbell, Alexander
*Fool of God: A Novel Based on the Life of Alexander
    Campbell* - Louis Cochran   1144

Campbell, Archibald
Restless Voyage - Stanley David Porteus   5138

Campbell, Colin
Kidnapped - Robert Louis Stevenson   6010

Campbell, Thomas
*Fool of God: A Novel Based on the Life of Alexander
    Campbell* - Louis Cochran   1144

Campion, Edmund
All the Queen's Men - Evelyn Anthony   157
Come Rack! Come Rope! - Robert Hugh Benson   458
Edmund Campion - Evelyn Waugh   6585
Late Harvest - Olive White   6697
Tudor Underground - Denis Meadows   4320

Campion, Edward
English Music - Peter Ackroyd   18

Canis
Canis the Warrior - James Sinclair   5864
Warrior Queen - James Sinclair   5865

Canning, George
The Stranger From the Sea - Winston Graham   2530

Canonchet
The Wept of Wish-Ton-Wish - James Fenimore
    Cooper   1312

Canute (King of England and Denmark)
King Hereafter - Dorothy Dunnett   1802

Capone, Al
Flanagan's Run - Tom McNab   4303
Joy in Mudville - Gordon McAlpine   4216
Organized Crime - Nicholas Von Hoffman   6511
The President's Man - Elliott Roosevelt   5455
True Detective - Max Allan Collins   1215
You Bet Your Life - Stuart M. Kaminsky   3349

Caradoc
The Captive Princess - Maxine Shore   5831
The Dark Island - Henry Treece   6326

Carausius, Marcus Aurelius
Caesar of the Narrow Seas - John Gloag   2433

Caravaggio, Michelangelo da
Caravaggio - Robert Payne   4851
The Dark Fire - Linda Murray   4537
An Epic Joy: A Novel Based on the Life of Rubens -
    Donald Braider   642
The Goliath Head - Charles J. Calitri   865

Cardigan, Earl of
Flashman - George MacDonald Fraser   2204
Flashman at the Charge - George MacDonald
    Fraser   2209
Pendragon: Late of Prince Albert's Own - Robert
    Trevelyan   6337

Cardinal Richelieu
The Anthem - Noel B. Gerson   2361
The Arm and the Darkness - Taylor Caldwell   850
A Candle for D'Artagnan - Chelsea Quinn
    Yarbro   6895
The Cardinal and the Queen - Evelyn Anthony   159
Cinq-Mars - Alfred Victor de Vigny   6495
An Epic Joy: A Novel Based on the Life of Rubens -
    Donald Braider   642
The Favourite - Francoise Mallet-Joris   4040
Louis the Well-Beloved - Jean Plaidy   5032
Louisiana Purchase - A.E. Hotchner   3039
The Three Musketeers - Alexandre Dumas   1782
Wife to Great Buckingham - Hilda Lewis   3751
World and Paradise - Edgar Maas   3953
The Young and Lonely King - Jane Lane   3659

Carey, Robert
The Succession: A Novel of Elizabeth and James -
    George Garrett   2302

Carhampton, Robert
The King's Rebel - James David Horan   3030

Carlos II (King of Spain)
Poison - Kathryn Harrison   2737

Carlos de Austria, Don (Prince of Spain)
The Spanish Bridegroom - Jean Plaidy   5064

Carlota (Empress of Mexico)
The Breast of the Dove - Herbert Gorman   2491
The Cactus and the Crown - Catherine Gavin   2318
Chapultepec - Norman Zollinger   6965
Flames of Empire - Peter Bourne   594
The Grasshopper King - Elizabeth Boatwright
    Coker   1165
Passengers to Mexico: The Last Invasion of Mexico -
    Blair Niles   4627

Carlyle, Jane
Neighboring Lives - Thomas M. Disch   1648

Carlyle, Thomas
Caribbean - James A. Michener   4365
Cock of the Walk - Roy Lewis   3762
The Consuming Flame: The Story of George Eliot -
    F.W. Kenyon   3446
Neighboring Lives - Thomas M. Disch   1648

Carnegie, Andrew
The Americans - John Jakes   3143

The Robber Baroness - William Kendall
    Clarke   1097
Thine Is the Glory - Samuel A. Schreiner Jr.   5672

Caroline-Matilda (Queen of Denmark)
The Lost Queen - Norah Lofts   3850
The Queen's Physician - Edgar Maas   3952

Caroline of Ansbach
Caroline the Queen - Jean Plaidy   5009
The Heart of Midlothian - Sir Walter Scott   5698
Queen in Waiting - Jean Plaidy   5048

Caroline of Brunswick
The Abandoned Woman - Richard Condon   1235
Brumaire - Mark Logan   3864
The Flight of the Eagle - Donald Thomas   6239
Footman in Powder - Helen Ashton   216
Regency Royal - Michael Hardwick   2687
The Regent's Daughter - Jean Plaidy   5055

Caron, Francois
Venture in the East - Bruce Lancaster   3648

Carr, Robert
The King James Version - Stanley N. Stewart   6035
King's Minion - Rafael Sabatini   5552
Lion Rampant - Bernard Shrimsley   5836
The Murder in the Tower - Jean Plaidy   5035
The Street of Kings - Charles Dexter   1637

Carrington, Henry Beebee
Carrington - Michael Whitney Straight   6074
North Against the Sioux - Kenneth Ulyatt   6376

Carroll, Anna Ella
*Woman with a Sword: The Biographical Novel of
    Anna Ella Carroll of Maryland* - Hollister
    Noble   4632

Carroll, Lewis
Neighboring Lives - Thomas M. Disch   1648

Carson, Kit
The Bear Flag: A Novel of the Birth of California -
    Cecelia Holland   2983
Death Comes for the Archbishop - Willa Cather   957
Dream West - David Nevin   4587
Heartland - Robert Douglas Mead   4316
Hill of the Hawk - Scott O'Dell   4689
Immortal Wife - Irving Stone   6057
Kelly Blue - Peter Bowen   601
The Pioneers - Courtney Ryley Cooper   1296
Soldier in Buckskin - Ray Hogan   2981
Wolf Song - Harvey Fergusson   2069

Caruso, Enrico
A Cadenza for Caruso - Barbara Paul   4834
A Chorus of Detectives - Barbara Paul   4835
Herma - Macdonald Harris   2726
Prima Donna at Large - Barbara Paul   4838

Carver, John
Massachusetts: A Novel - Nancy Zaroulis   6956
Pilgrims: A Novel of the Mayflower - Gerard
    Mac   3955

Casanova, Giovanni Jacopo
A Night with Casanova - Wolf Mankowitz   4060

Casement, Roger
Rebels: The Irish Rising of 1916 - Peter
    DeRosa   1622

Casewent, John
Thunder on the Plains - Rosanne Bittner   517

Cass, Lewis
Twilight of Empire - Allen W. Eckert   1846

Cassatt, Mary
Depths of Glory - Irving Stone   6055
Impressionist: A Novel of Mary Cassatt - Joan
    King   3486

Cassidy, Butch
Good Morning, Young Lady - Ardyth Kennelly   3424
*Kid Curry: The Life and Times of Harvey Logan and
    the Wild Bunch* - F. Bruce Lamb   3606

Outlaw Lover - Lindsey Hanks 2676
South of the Border - John Byrne Cooke 1268
The Story of the Sundance Kid - David Everitt 1988

Cassius Longinus, Gaius
Augustus - Allan Massie 4167

Castillo, Alonso del
The Children of the Sun - Oakley Hall 2652

Castlemaine, Countess of
Catherine - Hilda Lewis 3746
Forever Amber - Kathleen Winsor 6822
A Health Unto His Majesty - Jean Plaidy 5019
The King's Brat - Constance Gluyas 2441
Lady on the Coin - Margaret Campbell Barnes 326
My Lady Benbrook - Constance Gluyas 2442
Our Jo, or The Chronicle of a Coming Man - Kenneth
  M. Cameron 868

Castlereagh, Viscount
Brumaire - Mark Logan 3864
Guillotine - Mark Logan 3865
The Sea Officer - Showell Styles 6105

Castro, Fidel
Caribbean - James A. Michener 4365
Papa and Fidel - Karl Alexander 79

Catherine, Grand Duchess of Russia
Far Flies the Eagle - Evelyn Anthony 162

Catherine I (Czarina of Russia)
Katrina - Jeramie Price 5190
Peter the Great - Alexey Tolstoy 6293
Tsar's Woman - Pamela Hill 2946

Catherine II (Czarina of Russia)
The Captain's Daughter - Alexander Pushkin 5210
The Incorruptible - Helma De Bois 1551
Rebel Princess - Evelyn Anthony 164
The Revolutionary - Lawrence Schoonover 5667
Russka: The Novel of Russia - Edward
  Rutherfurd 5535
Valide: A Novel of the Harem - Barbara Chase-
  Riboud 1007
Young Catherine - E.M. Almedingen 118

Catherine of Aragon
Anne Boleyn - Evelyn Anthony 158
Anne of the Thousand Days - Edward Fenton 2059
The Autobiography of Henry VIII - Margaret
  George 2355
The Concubine - Norah Lofts 3839
Henry VIII and His Six Wives - Maureen
  Peters 4975
The Hireling - Alison Macleod 4003
I Am Mary Tudor - Hilda Lewis 3750
In the Shadow of the Crown - Jean Plaidy 5022
Katharine: The Virgin Widow - Jean Plaidy 5025
Kathryn: In the Court of Six Queens - Anne Merton
  Abbey 1
King's Fool - Margaret Campbell Barnes 325
The King's Pleasure - Norah Lofts 3847
The King's Pleasure - Jean Plaidy 5026
The King's Secret Matter - Jean Plaidy 5027
The Lady in the Tower - Jean Plaidy 5028
The Man on a Donkey - H.F.M. Prescott 5170
Mistress Anne - Carolly Erickson 1952
Queen Anne Boleyn - Francis Hackett 2634
The Reluctant Queen - Molly Costain Haycraft 2796
The Shadow of the Pomegranate - Jean Plaidy 5062
The Sword of Truth - Gilbert Morris 4472
Uneasy Lies the Head - Jean Plaidy 5071
The White Rose Murders - Michael Clynes 1137

Catherine of Braganza
Catherine - Hilda Lewis 3746
A Health Unto His Majesty - Jean Plaidy 5019
The King's Bastard - Hebe Elsna 1932
The King's Brat - Constance Gluyas 2441
The Pleasures of Love - Jean Plaidy 5042
The Portingale - Alison Macleod 4005
With All My Heart - Margaret Campbell Barnes 330

Catherine of Siena
*Lay Siege to Heaven: A Novel of Saint Catherine of
  Siena* - Louis De Wohl 1570
The Saint - Fritz von Unruh 6385

Catherine of Valois
Crown in Candlelight - Rosemary Hawley
  Jarman 3166
Epitaph for Three Women - Jean Plaidy 5012
Fortune Made His Sword - Martha Rofheart 5426
Good King Harry - Denise Giardina 2393
Harry of Monmouth - A.M. Maughan 4199
The Queen's Secret - Jean Plaidy 5053
The Royal Pawn - Antonia Ridge 5327
The Star of Lancaster - Jean Plaidy 5065
Wife to Henry V - Hilda Lewis 3752

Catherine the Great
The Captain's Daughter - Alexander Pushkin 5210
The Incorruptible - Helma De Bois 1551
Rebel Princess - Evelyn Anthony 164
The Revolutionary - Lawrence Schoonover 5667
Russka: The Novel of Russia - Edward
  Rutherfurd 5535
Valide: A Novel of the Harem - Barbara Chase-
  Riboud 1007
Young Catherine - E.M. Almedingen 118

Catherwood, Frederick
*Journey to the Sky: A Novel about the True Adventures
  of Two Men in Search of the Lost Maya Kingdom* -
  Jamake Highwater 2918

Catilina, Lucius Sergius
Catalina's Riddle - Steven Saylor 5624
The Catiline Conspiracy - John Maddox
  Roberts 5379
A Pillar of Iron - Taylor Caldwell 861
Turn Back the River - W.G. Hardy 2703
The Young Caesar - Rex Warner 6567

Catiline
Catalina's Riddle - Steven Saylor 5624
The Catiline Conspiracy - John Maddox
  Roberts 5379
A Pillar of Iron - Taylor Caldwell 861
Turn Back the River - W.G. Hardy 2703
The Young Caesar - Rex Warner 6567

Catlin, George
The Children of the First Man - James Alexander
  Thom 6230

Cato, Marcus Porcius
Caesar's Women - Colleen McCullough 4233
Freedom, Farewell - Phyllis Bentley 461

Cato the Younger
Caesar's Women - Colleen McCullough 4233
Freedom, Farewell - Phyllis Bentley 461

Catullus, Gaius Valerius
Chantefable - Eldorous L. Dayton 1546
The City of Libertines - W.G. Hardy 2702
Clodia - Robert DeMaria 1606
Farewell, Catullus - Pierson Dixon 1651
The Gods Are Not Mocked - Anna Taylor 6177
The Ides of March - Thornton Wilder 6753
The Key - Benita Kane Jaro 3169
The Venus Throw - Steven Saylor 5627

Caumont La Force, Antonin-Nompar de
Sorrow by Day - Marjorie Coryn 1359

Cavarly, John
Annie's Captain - Kathryn Hulme 3077

Cavendish, Thomas
Captain for Elizabeth - Jan Westcott 6643

Cayetana, Maria
*Colossus: A Novel about Goya and a World Gone
  Mad* - Stephen Marlowe 4093
In the Blazing Light - Max White 6693
The Last Portrait of the Duchess of Alba - Antonio
  Larreta 3666

The Naked Maja - Noel B. Gerson 2378
Rage in Silence: A Novel Based on the Life of Goya -
  Donald Braider 643

Ce Malinalli
Death of the Fifth Sun - Robert Somerlott 5944

Cea
Canis the Warrior - James Sinclair 5864

Ceawlin
Born of the Sun - Joan Wolf 6837

Cecil, Robert
All the Queen's Men - Evelyn Anthony 157
The Bartholomew Fair Murders - Leonard
  Tourney 6297
Death of the Fox - George Garrett 2300
Deborah and the Many Faces of Love - Colette
  Davenat 1499
Deborah and the Siege of Paris - Colette
  Davenat 1500
For Love of a Pirate - Anthony Esler 1961
Gay Lord Robert - Jean Plaidy 5015
I, Elizabeth - Rosalind Miles 4378
Lady Rich - Elizabeth Boatwright Coker 1166
Low Treason - Leonard Tourney 6301
My Lord Essex - Olive Eckerson 1838
Old Saxon Blood - Leonard Tourney 6302
Scapegoat for a Stuart - Kate Kirby 3504
*Shadow in the Sun: A Novel of Elizabeth I, the Virgin
  Queen* - F.W. Kenyon 3460
So Merciful a Queen, So Cruel a Woman - Alice
  Harwood 2769
The Succession: A Novel of Elizabeth and James -
  George Garrett 2302
Trust and Treason - Margaret Birkhead 506
Witness of Bones - Leonard Tourney 6304

Cecil, William
Elizabeth: Queen & Woman - Helen Thorpe 6279
For Love of a Pirate - Anthony Esler 1961
Legacy - Susan Kay 3374
My Lord Essex - Olive Eckerson 1838
My Lord the Fox - Robert York 6932
The Proud Man - Elizabeth Linington 3800
The Robsart Affair - Jennette Letton 3729
*Shadow in the Sun: A Novel of Elizabeth I, the Virgin
  Queen* - F.W. Kenyon 3460
To Love a Queen - Lawrence Schoonover 5669
The Young Elizabeth - Jennette Letton 3730

Cecily of York
The Dragon Waiting: A Masque of History - John M.
  Ford 2165

Celine, Louis-Ferdinand
The Exile of Celine - Tom Clark 1095

Cellini, Benvenuto
The Chancellor - Lawrence Schoonover 5662
The Florentine - Carl J. Spinatelli 5968

Cenci, Beatrice
A Tale for Midnight - Frederic Prokosch 5195

Cenci, Francesco
A Tale for Midnight - Frederic Prokosch 5195

Cenci, Lucrezia
A Tale for Midnight - Frederic Prokosch 5195

Cerdic
Conscience of the King - Alfred Duggan 1763

Cermak, Anton
Organized Crime - Nicholas Von Hoffman 6511
True Detective - Max Allan Collins 1215

Cervantes, Miguel de
The Death and Life of Miguel De Cervantes - Stephen
  Marlowe 4094
A Man Called Cervantes - Bruno Frank 2201

Cetewayo
Bush War! - William Moore 4447
Yellowstone Kelly - Peter Bowen 602

Cezanne, Paul
Depths of Glory - Irving Stone 6055
The Lawless - John Jakes 3149
Lust for Life - Irving Stone 6059
A Man and His Mountain: The Life of Paul Cezanne - Hugh McLeave 4285
Vincent: A Novel Based on the Life of Van Gogh - Joost Poldermans 5082

Chabot, Francois
Scaramouche the King-Maker - Rafael Sabatini 5555

Chagall, Marc
The Young Men of Paris - Stephen Longstreet 3893

Chaka
The Covenant - James A. Michener 4368
Great Elephant - Alan Scholefield 5654

Chamberlain, Joseph
Rags of Glory - Stuart Cloete 1126
The Tenants of Time - Thomas Flanagan 2120

Chamberlain, Joshua Lawrence
The Dixie Widow - Gilbert Morris 4459
Gods and Generals - Jeff Shaara 5765
The Killer Angels - Michael Shaara 5766

Champlain, Samuel de
Fathers and Crows - William T. Vollmann 6508

Chandler, Raymond
Murder on the Yellow Brick Road - Stuart M. Kaminsky 3343

Chaplin, Charlie
The Man Who Shot Lewis Vance - Stuart M. Kaminsky 3341
Max - Howard Fast 2038
Murder at San Simeon - Robert Lee Hall 2660
Murder in the East Room - Elliott Roosevelt 5448

Chapman, John
Reckon with the River - Clark McMeekin 4292
The Tree of Life - Hugh Nissenson 4629

Charbonneau, Jean Baptiste
Sacajawea - Anna Lee Waldo 6529

Charbonneau, Toussaint
Forward the Nation - Donald Culross Peattie 4880

Charcot, Jean-Martin
Affairs of Love - Nicola Thorne 6272
The Secret Life of Laszlo, Count Dracula - Roderick Anscombe 156

Chares
The Bronze God of Rhodes - L. Sprague De Camp 1554

Charles (Charles I)
The Fortunes of Nigel - Sir Walter Scott 5696
Unicorn Rampant - Nigel Tranter 6323

Charles (Charles II)
Campion Towers - John Beatty 401
Myself My Enemy - Jean Plaidy 5037
Woodstock; or, The Cavalier - Sir Walter Scott 5710

Charles (Charles IV)
The Royal Succession - Maurice Druon 1735

Charles, Duc de Bourbon
The Chancellor - Lawrence Schoonover 5662
The King's Cavalier - Samuel Shellabarger 5795

Charles, Duke of Burgundy
Anne of Geierstein - Sir Walter Scott 5689
Quentin Durward - Sir Walter Scott 5705
To Lie with Lions - Dorothy Dunnett 1810

Charles, Prince of Wales (1948-)
Di and I - Peter Lefcourt 3714
Miss Nobody - Caroline Ross 5465
The Queen and I - Sue Townsend 6306

Charles, Prince of Wales (Charles II)
Royal Escape - Georgette Heyer 2900

Charles I (King of England)
Call Lady Purbeck - Hilda Lewis 3745
Charles the King - Evelyn Anthony 160
The Fortunes of Nigel - Sir Walter Scott 5696
The Golden Feather - Theda Kenyon 3462
John Inglesant - John Henry Shorthouse 5833
Katherine Christian - Hugh Walpole 6546
The King Breaker - Elizabeth Linington 3797
Mary of Carisbrooke - Margaret Campbell Barnes 327
My Lord Foxe - Constance Gluyas 2443
Myself, Christopher Wren - David Weiss 6606
Myself My Enemy - Jean Plaidy 5037
The Phoenix Rising - Jean Evans 1984
Physician Extraordinary: A Novel of the Life and Times of William Harvey - David Weiss 6608
Powhatan's Daughter - John Clarke Bowman 605
The Proud Servant: The Story of Montrose - Margaret Irwin 3120
The Quickenberry Tree - Annette Motley 4502
The Severed Crown - Jane Lane 3657
The Stranger Prince - Margaret Irwin 3122
Thanksgiving - Terry Coleman 1207
Twenty Years After - Alexandre Dumas 1783
Unicorn Rampant - Nigel Tranter 6323
The White Witch - Elizabeth Goudge 2496
Wife to Great Buckingham - Hilda Lewis 3751
Wife to Mr. Milton - Robert Graves 2553
The Young and Lonely King - Jane Lane 3659

Charles I (King of Spain)
Against This Rock - Louis Zara 6948
Captain From Castile - Samuel Shellabarger 5794
An Epic Joy: A Novel Based on the Life of Rubens - Donald Braider 642
The Prisoner of Tordesillas - Lawrence Schoonover 5665

Charles II (King of England)
The Bellerose Bargain - Robyn Carr 934
Bennett's Welcome - Inglis Fletcher 2132
The Braeswood Tapestry - Robyn Carr 936
The Bride - Margaret Irwin 3116
Campion Towers - John Beatty 401
Catherine - Hilda Lewis 3746
Chelynne - Robyn Carr 938
Countess Carrots - Molly Costain Haycraft 2792
Cutlass Empire - F. van Wyck Mason 4148
The Devil in Velvet - John Dickson Carr 909
Forever Amber - Kathleen Winsor 6822
The Golden Days - Robert Neill 4569
A Health Unto His Majesty - Jean Plaidy 5019
Here Lies Our Sovereign Lord - Jean Plaidy 5021
I, John Mordaunt - Virgil Scott 5687
The King's Bastard - Hebe Elsna 1932
The King's Brat - Constance Gluyas 2441
The King's General - Daphne Du Maurier 1748
The King's Rogue - Max Peacock 4859
Lady on the Coin - Margaret Campbell Barnes 326
Lucy - Hester W. Chapman 992
Mary of Carisbrooke - Margaret Campbell Barnes 327
Masquerade for the King - Marina Oliver 4729
Mistress of the Boards - Richard Sumner 6118
Most Secret - John Dickson Carr 912
The Murder of Sir Edmund Godfrey - John Dickson Carr 913
My Lady Benbrook - Constance Gluyas 2442
Myself, Christopher Wren - David Weiss 6606
Myself My Enemy - Jean Plaidy 5037
Old St. Paul's - William Harrison Ainsworth 57
Our Jo, or The Chronicle of a Coming Man - Kenneth M. Cameron 868
Peveril of the Peak - Sir Walter Scott 5703
The Phoenix Rising - Jean Evans 1984
The Pleasures of Love - Jean Plaidy 5042
The Portingale - Alison Macleod 4005
Restoration: A Novel of Seventeenth-Century England - Rose Tremain 6333
Royal Escape - Georgette Heyer 2900

Royal Flush: The Story of Minette - Margaret Irwin 3121
The Spoils of Eden - Robert H. Fowler 2193
The Three Crowns - Jean Plaidy 5070
Traitor's Moon - Robert Neill 4574
The Wandering Prince - Jean Plaidy 5075
With All My Heart - Margaret Campbell Barnes 330
Woodstock; or, The Cavalier - Sir Walter Scott 5710

Charles IV (King of France)
The Royal Succession - Maurice Druon 1735
The She-Wolf - Pamela Bennetts 456
The She-Wolf of France - Maurice Druon 1736

Charles IV (King of Spain)
The Naked Maja - Noel B. Gerson 2378
Rage in Silence: A Novel Based on the Life of Goya - Donald Braider 643

Charles V (Holy Roman Emperor)
Against This Rock - Louis Zara 6948
Captain From Castile - Samuel Shellabarger 5794
In the House of the King - Louis Zara 6951
The Last Crusader - Louis De Wohl 1569
The Prisoner of Tordesillas - Lawrence Schoonover 5665

Charles V (King of Spain)
I, the King - Howard Clewes 1112

Charles VI (King of France)
The Gentle Falcon - Hilda Lewis 3747
In a Dark Wood Wandering - Hella S. Haasse 2631
The Queen's Secret - Jean Plaidy 5053
The Royal Pawn - Antonia Ridge 5327
Royal Sword at Agincourt - Pamela Bennetts 455
The Spider King - Lawrence Schoonover 5668
Wife to Henry V - Hilda Lewis 3752

Charles VII (King of France)
An Army of Angels: A Novel of Joan of Arc - Pamela Marcantel 4079
La Belle Sorel - Jacques Carton 949
The Burnished Blade - Lawrence Schoonover 5661
The Moneyman - Thomas B. Costain 1368
Personal Recollections of Joan of Arc - Mark Twain 6372
The Queen's Secret - Jean Plaidy 5053

Charles VIII (King of France)
The Bride of Sforza - Miranda Seymour 5760
Duchess of Milan - Michael Ennis 1946
The Gentle Fury: A Novel of Margaret of Austria - Paul Lewis 3758
Here Lies Margot - Pamela Hill 2935
The Private Life of Mona Lisa - Pierre La Mure 3577
Romola - George Eliot 1910

Charles IX (King of France)
The Longest Night - Ada Cook Lewis 3744
Queen Margot - Alexandre Dumas 1780

Charles X (King of France)
Holy Week - Louis Aragon 182

Charles XII (King of Sweden)
Peter the Great - Alexey Tolstoy 6293

Charles XIV John (King of Sweden)
Desiree - Annemarie Selinko 5741

Charles of Valois
The Poisoned Crown - Maurice Druon 1734
The Strangled Queen - Maurice Druon 1737

Charles Philippe (Charles X)
Holy Week - Louis Aragon 182

Charlie, Bonnie Prince
Born to Be King - Constance Gluyas 2440
Candleshine No More - Jane Oliver 4721
Charlie Is My Darling - Mollie Hardwick 2691
Clandara - Evelyn Anthony 161
Commander of the Mists - D.L. Murray 4527
Crown Without Sceptre - William Vaughan Wilkins 6758

The Dark Mile - Dorothy Kathleen Broster   709
The Flight of the Heron - Dorothy Kathleen Broster   710
Highlands Rebel - Sally Watson   6584
I Came to the Highlands: A Novel of Suspense - Velda Johnston   3263
The Long Day Closes - Beatrice Tunstall   6360
Louis the Well-Beloved - Jean Plaidy   5032
A Prince, a Piper, and a Rose - John Scalzo   5628
Prince Charlie's Bluff - Donald Thomas   6241
The Queen of Hearts - Joan Rees   5290
Red Gauntlet - Sir Walter Scott   5706
The Scotswoman - Inglis Fletcher   2140
Waverley - Sir Walter Scott   5709
The Woman from The Glen - Chloe Gartner   2310

Charlotte, Princess of Wales
The Girl Who Was Never Queen: A Biographical Novel of Princess Charlotte of Wales - Mary Main   4037
The Regent's Daughter - Jean Plaidy   5055

Charlotte of Mecklenburg-Strelitz
The Bonnet Laird's Daughter - Barbara Annandale   154
Goddess of the Green Room - Jean Plaidy   5016
Guillotine - Mark Logan   3865
Let the King Beware! - Honore Morrow   4489
Regency Royal - Michael Hardwick   2687
Sweet Lass of Richmond Hill - Jean Plaidy   5067
The Third George - Jean Plaidy   5068

Chase, Salmon P.
The Dixie Widow - Gilbert Morris   4459
Freedom - William Safire   5561
Lincoln: A Novel - Gore Vidal   6490
Nevada! - Dana Fuller Ross   5481

Chateaubriand, Francois Rene de
Crown of Grass - Charles Andrew Brady   634

Chatterton, Thomas
Chatterton - Peter Ackroyd   17

Chatto
Chiricahua - Will Henry   2839

Chaucer, Geoffrey
The Gentle Knight - Philip Lindsay   3791
Glendower Country - Martha Rofheart   5427
Katherine - Anya Seton   5752
The Love Knot - Catherine Darby   1482
The Nun's Tale - Candace M. Robb   5367
Riddle Me a Murder - Duane Crowley   1435
A Tapestry of Murders - C.L. Grace   2510
Within the Hollow Crown - Margaret Campbell Barnes   331

Chenier, Andre
The Black Consul - Anatolii Vinogradov   6503

Cherkkov, Vladimir
The Last Station - Jay Parini   4801

Cheyney, Sir Thomas
Feversham - Diane Davidson   1503

Chiang Kai-Shek
Dynasty - Robert S. Elegant   1902
From a Far Land - Robert S. Elegant   1903
The Warlord - Malcolm Bosse   589

Chief Joseph
Chief Joseph - Bill Dugan   1756
The Chieftain: A Story of the Nez Perce People - Robert Payne   4852
The Fleet Rabble: A Novel of the Nez Perce War - Frank Borden Hanes   2675
From Where the Sun Now Stands - Will Henry   2841
Red Fox of the Kinapoo - William Rush   5526
Song of the Meadowlark - John A. Sanford   5594

Ch'ien Lung (Emperor of China)
A House in Peiking - Robert Payne   4853

Chimay, Princess de
Lady of Paris - William Vaughan Wilkins   6760

Ch'in Shih Huang Ti (Emperor of China)
The Chinese Emperor - Jean Levi   3733

Chippendale, Thomas
Gilded Splendour - Rosalind Laker   3595

Chisholm, Jesse
Heartland - Robert Douglas Mead   4316

Chisum, John
The Sons of Grady Rourke - Douglas Savage   5618

Chitto Harjo
Crazy Snake - Robert J. Conley   1240

Chivington, John Milton
The Last Warpath - Will Henry   2844
A Very Small Remnant - Michael Whitney Straight   6075

Chopin, Frederic
Beyond Desire: A Novel Based on the Life of Felix and Cecille Mendelssohn - Pierre La Mure   3574
Hungarian Rhapsody: The Life of Franz Liszt - Jean Rousselot   5511
The Questing Heart: A Romantic Novel about George Sand - F.W. Kenyon   3458

Chou En-lai
From a Far Land - Robert S. Elegant   1903

Chouteau, Auguste
Savanna - Janice Holt Giles   2416

Christian, Fletcher
Adams of the Bounty - Erle Wilson   6807
H.M.S. Bounty - Alexander McKee   4280
The Last Mutiny: The Further Adventures of Captain Bligh - Bill Collett   1208
Mister Christian - William Kinsolving   3502
Mr. Christian! - Stanley Miller   4402
Mutiny on the Bounty - Charles Nordhoff   4639
Pitcairn's Island - Charles Nordhoff   4640

Christian II (King of Denmark)
The Fall of the King - Johannes Vilhelm Jensen   3214

Christian VII (King of Denmark)
The Lost Queen - Norah Lofts   3850
The Queen's Physician - Edgar Maas   3952

Christie, Agatha
Agatha - Kathleen Tynan   6374
The Bette Davis Murder Case - George Baxt   383
Dorothy and Agatha - Gaylord Larsen   3667

Christie, Ned
Ned Christie's War - Robert J. Conley   1247
Zeke and Ned - Larry McMurtry   4301

Christina (Queen of Sweden)
The Flight - Ruth Walgreen Stephan   5994
My Crown, My Love - Ruth Walgreen Stephan   5995

Christophe, Henri
Black Dawn - Christopher Nicole   4613
Black Triumvirate: A Novel of Haiti - Benjamin H. Levin   3736
Drums of Destiny - Peter Bourne   593
Lydia Bailey - Kenneth Roberts   5387
Mistress of Darkness - Christopher Nicole   4617
A Time for Titans - Vina Delmar   1602

Church, Benjamin
Ashes in the Wilderness - William Greenough Schofield   5649
Savage Gentleman - Noel B. Gerson   2381

Churchill, Jane
The Widow of Windsor - Tyler Whittle   6723

Churchill, John
The Charlatan - Carter A. Vaughan   6433
Exit Lady Masham - Louis Auchincloss   230
The Glory and the Dream - F.W. Kenyon   3450
Marlborough's Unfair Lady - Lozania Prole   5197
The Mohawk Ladder - Noel B. Gerson   2377
The Queen's Favourites - Jean Plaidy   5051

Churchill, Randolph
Lillie - David Butler   818
The Whitechapel Horrors - Edward B. Hanna   2678

Churchill, Sarah
The Elusive Crown - Hebe Elsna   1931
Exit Lady Masham - Louis Auchincloss   230
The Glory and the Dream - F.W. Kenyon   3450
Marlborough's Unfair Lady - Lozania Prole   5197
The Power and the Passion - Christina Nicholson   4609
The Queen's Favourites - Jean Plaidy   5051
The Sachem - Donald Clayton Porter   5124

Churchill, Winston
Attack the Lusitania! - Raymond Hitchcock   2956
Blood Winter - William Patrick   4830
Blunted Lance - Max Hennessy   2829
Buller's Dreadnought - Richard Hough   3047
Buller's Victory - Richard Hough   3049
By the Green of the Spring - John Masters   4171
Edward and Mrs. Simpson - A.C.H. Smith   5916
The End of the Hunt - Thomas Flanagan   2119
A Family Matter - James Roosevelt   5458
The Hangman's Crusade - James Barwick   370
High Heroic - Constantine FitzGibbon   2118
Imperial Kelly - Peter Bowen   600
Lusitania - David Butler   819
The Man From St. Petersburg - Ken Follett   2148
The Man on the Train - W.J. Chaput   995
Mr. American - George MacDonald Fraser   2211
Murder at the Palace - Elliott Roosevelt   5445
The Plot to Kill Wallis Simpson: A Work of Faction - Graham Fisher   2104
Redemption - Leon Uris   6393
The Ring Master - David Gurr   2622
Seven Days to Petrograd - Tom Hyman   3094
That's Me in the Middle - Donald Jack   3129
To the Honor of the Fleet - Robert H. Pilpel   5002
"Utmost Fish!" - Hugh Wray McCann   4219
The White House Pantry Murder - Elliott Roosevelt   5457

Cibber, Colley
Peg Woffington - Charles Reade   5281

Cicero, Marcus Tullius
Augustus - Allan Massie   4167
Caesar - Allan Massie   4168
Caesar's Women - Colleen McCullough   4233
Catalina's Riddle - Steven Saylor   5624
The Catiline Conspiracy - John Maddox Roberts   5379
The City of Libertines - W.G. Hardy   2702
Clodia - Robert DeMaria   1606
Death on the Appian Way - Kenneth Benton   463
Freedom, Farewell - Phyllis Bentley   461
The Gift of Rome - John Wagner   6520
The Grass Crown - Colleen McCullough   4236
The Ides of March - Thornton Wilder   6753
A Murder on the Appian Way - Steven Saylor   5625
A Pillar of Iron - Taylor Caldwell   861
Roman Blood - Steven Saylor   5626
Roman Shadows - Ron Burns   804
Spartacus - Howard Fast   2044
The Venus Throw - Steven Saylor   5627
The Young Caesar - Rex Warner   6567

Cid, El
The Infidel - Georgia Elizabeth Taylor   6182

Cinna, Lucius Cornelius
The Grass Crown - Colleen McCullough   4236

Cinq-Mars, Marquis de
The Cardinal and the Queen - Evelyn Anthony   159
Cinq-Mars - Alfred Victor de Vigny   6495

Cinque, Joseph
Echo of Lions - Barbara Chase-Riboud   1004

Claire, Isabelle de
Champion - L. Christian Balling 285

Clairmont, Claire
The Absorbing Fire: The Byron Legend - F.W.
  Kenyon 3445
Count Manifred - Miranda Seymour 5761
Lord of the Ladies - Joanna Dessau 1626
Love's Children - Judith Chernaik 1013
The Memoirs of Lord Byron - Robert Nye 4655
A Single Summer with Lord B. - Derek
  Marlowe 4092
The Year of December - Lucy Cores 1329

Clairmont, Jane
*The Golden Years: A Novel Based on the Life and
  Loves of Percy Bysshe Shelley* - F.W.
  Kenyon 3451

Clanton, Ike
Wyatt Earp - Matt Braun 653

Clare, Richard de
The Marriage of Meggotta - Edith Pargeter 4799

Clark, Ann Rogers
From Sea to Shining Sea - James Alexander
  Thom 6232

Clark, George Rogers
Alice of Old Vincennes - Maurice Thompson 6268
Becky Landers, Frontier Warrior - Constance
  Skinner 5879
The Big Knives - Bruce Lancaster 3635
Black Forest - Meade Minnigerode 4411
Bridal Journey - Dale Van Every 6406
The Captive Witch - Dale Van Every 6407
The Crossing - Winston Churchill 1080
From Sea to Shining Sea - James Alexander
  Thom 6232
Gateway to Empire - Allen W. Eckert 1842
Give Me Liberty - Noel B. Gerson 2369
The King's Orchard - Agnes Sligh Turnbull 6363
Long Knife - James Alexander Thom 6233
Morning Time - Charles Kendall O'Neill 4743
Oh, Kentucky! - Betty Layman Receveur 5284
Panther in the Sky - James Alexander Thom 6234
The Seekers - John Jakes 3153
That Dark and Bloody River - Allen W. Eckert 1845
This Land Is Ours - Louis Zara 6953
Trail: The Story of the Lewis and Clark Expedition -
  Louis Charbonneau 998
The Voyagers - Dale Van Every 6412
Waters of the Wilderness - Shirley Seifert 5737
Westward the Tide - Harold Sinclair 5863

Clark, John
From Sea to Shining Sea - James Alexander
  Thom 6232

Clark, Myra
*New Orleans Woman: A Biographical Novel of Myra
  Clark Gaines* - Harnett T. Kane 3355

Clark, Ralph
The Playmaker - Thomas Keneally 3414

Clark, William
Bridal Journey - Dale Van Every 6406
Distant Trails - Bill Gulick 2612
An Embarrassment of Riches - James Howard
  Kunstler 3565
Forward the Nation - Donald Culross Peattie 4880
From Sea to Shining Sea - James Alexander
  Thom 6232
The Gates of the Mountains - Will Henry 2842
Sacajawea - Anna Lee Waldo 6529
Sacajawea of the Shoshones - Della F.
  Emmons 1940
The Seekers - John Jakes 3153
The Shining Mountains - Dale Van Every 6410
Star of the West - Ethel Hueston 3070
Tale of Valor - Vardis Fisher 2112
Those Who Go Against the Current - Shirley
  Seifert 5734

Trail: The Story of the Lewis and Clark Expedition -
  Louis Charbonneau 998
Westward! - Dana Fuller Ross 5492

Clarke, Mary Anne
The Duke's Mistress: The Story of Mary Ann Clarke -
  F.W. Kenyon 3447
Mary Anne - Daphne Du Maurier 1749

Clarke, Tom
Rebels: The Irish Rising of 1916 - Peter
  DeRosa 1622

Clary, Desiree
Desiree - Annemarie Selinko 5741

Claudel, Camille
Naked Came I: A Novel of Rodin - David
  Weiss 6607

Claudia Procula
First the Blade - Drayton Mayrant 4212

Claudian
Threshold of Fire - Hella S. Haasse 2633

Claudianus, Claudius
Threshold of Fire - Hella S. Haasse 2633

Claudius I (Roman Emperor)
Brothers of Vengeance - LeGette Blythe 556
Claudius the God - Robert Graves 2543
The Eagle and the Raven - Pauline Gedge 2344
The Eighth Veil - Ellis Kadison 3320
The Flames of Rome - Paul L. Maier 4033
The Glorious Folly: A Novel of the Time of St. Paul -
  Louis De Wohl 1565
I, Claudius - Robert Graves 2547
I Loved Tiberius - Elisabeth Dored 1692
Octavia: A Tale of Ancient Rome - Seymour Van
  Santvoord 6428
Sarum: The Novel of England - Edward
  Rutherfurd 5536
Soul Flame - Barbara Wood 6850

Clay, Cassius Marcellus
Hacey Miller - James Sherburne 5805
The Way to Fort Pillow - James Sherburne 5807

Clay, Henry
1812 - David Nevin 4586
The Border Captains - Jason Manning 4072
Dolley - Rita Mae Brown 727
*Fool of God: A Novel Based on the Life of Alexander
  Campbell* - Louis Cochran 1144
The Gorgeous Hussy - Samuel Hopkins Adams 30
Home to Kentucky: A Novel of Henry Clay - Alfred
  Leland Crabb 1399
Love Is Eternal - Irving Stone 6058
Magnificent Destiny - Paul I. Wellman 6619
The Road to Baltimore - Robert S. Harper 2716

Cleaveland, Moses
Now We Are Free - Marguerite Allis 112

Cleland, John
*Fanny: Being the True History of the Adventures of
  Fanny Hackabout-Jones* - Erica Jong 3299

Clem, John Lincoln
Johnny Shiloh - James A. Rhodes 5308

Clemence of Hungary
The Poisoned Crown - Maurice Druon 1734
The Royal Succession - Maurice Druon 1735

Clemenceau, Georges
Over There - Thomas Fleming 2130

Clemens, Samuel L.
1876: A Novel - Gore Vidal 6484
A Bloodsmoor Romance - Joyce Carol Oates 4658
A Connecticut Yankee in Criminal Court - Peter J.
  Heck 2814
Death on the Mississippi - Peter J. Heck 2815
If I Never Get Back - Darryl Brock 700
The Robber Baroness - William Kendall
  Clarke 1097

Sister Wives - Cleo Jones 3270
Twice upon a Time - Allen Appel 172

Clement VII (Pope)
Anne Boleyn - Evelyn Anthony 158
A Brood of Vipers - Michael Clynes 1133
A Cardinal of the Medici - Susan Hicks Beach 393
The Concubine - Norah Lofts 3839
The Image of Our Lord - Edward Burman 790

Clement VIII (Pope)
The Anthem - Noel B. Gerson 2361
The Carmelite - Elgin Groseclose 2599

Clemm, Virginia
*Black Plume: The Supressed Memoirs of Edgar Allan
  Poe* - David Madsen 4027
The Raven - Chancellor Williams 6769
Very Young Mrs. Poe - Cothburn O'Neal 4740

Cleopatra (Queen of Egypt)
The Alexandrian - Martha Rofheart 5425
Augustus - Allan Massie 4167
Augustus - John Williams 6785
Caesar - Allan Massie 4168
Cleopatra - H. Rider Haggard 2637
A Goddess to a God - John Lloyd Balderston 278
The Ides of March - Thornton Wilder 6753
The Mummy; or Ramses the Damned - Anne
  Rice 5315
Purple Pirate - Talbot Mundy 4514
That Egyptian Woman - Noel B. Gerson 2384
Throne of Isis - Judith Tarr 6170

Cleveland, Grover
The American - Howard Fast 2026
*Refinements of Love: A Novel about Clover and Henry
  Adams* - Sarah Booth Conroy 1259

Cleveland, John
The Shadow Flies - Rose Macaulay 3956

Clifford, Rosamund
The Revolt of the Eaglets - Jean Plaidy 5057

Clinton, George
Wilderness Empire - Allen W. Eckert 1847

Clinton, Henry
Cato's War - Guy Wheeler 6655
Eagles Where I Walk - Stephen Longstreet 3885
Monmouth - Charles Bracelen Flood 2144
Mr. Arnold - Francis Lynde 3935
Oliver Wiswell - Kenneth Roberts 5389
*The Twisted Saber: A Biographical Novel of Benedict
  Arnold* - Philip Vail 6398
Valiant Libertine - John Gordon Bryson 748
Wicked Lady - Inglis Fletcher 2142
Yorktown - Burke Davis 1513

Clive, Robert
Master of Bengal: A Novel of Robert Clive of India -
  Norman Partington 4821

Clodia
Chantefable - Eldorous L. Dayton 1546
The City of Libertines - W.G. Hardy 2702
Clodia - Robert DeMaria 1606
Death on the Appian Way - Kenneth Benton 463
Farewell, Catullus - Pierson Dixon 1651
The Gods Are Not Mocked - Anna Taylor 6177
The Key - Benita Kane Jaro 3169
Turn Back the River - W.G. Hardy 2703
The Venus Throw - Steven Saylor 5627

Clodius Pulcher, Publius
Caesar's Women - Colleen McCullough 4233
The City of Libertines - W.G. Hardy 2702
Clodia - Robert DeMaria 1606
Death on the Appian Way - Kenneth Benton 463
Farewell, Catullus - Pierson Dixon 1651
The Gods Are Not Mocked - Anna Taylor 6177

Cluentius
The Gift of Rome - John Wagner 6520

Cobb, Ty
Hoopla - Harry Stein 5990
Murder at Fenway Park - Troy Soos 5948

Cochise
Apache Autumn - Robert Skimin 5875
Blood Brother - Elliott Arnold 190
Geronimo - Bill Dugan 1758
A Time in the Sun - Jane Barry 361

Cochrane, Lord
The Frigate Captain - Showell Styles 6103
Sharpe's Devil - Bernard Cornwell 1340

Cochrane, Thomas
The Frigate Captain - Showell Styles 6103
Sharpe's Devil - Bernard Cornwell 1340

Cockburn, George
Crimson Is the Eastern Shore - Don Tracy 6308
Dolley - Rita Mae Brown 727

Cockrell, Alexander
Destiny in Dallas - Shirley Seifert 5725

Cockrell, Sarah
Destiny in Dallas - Shirley Seifert 5725

Cody, Buffalo Bill
Aces and Eights: A Novel of the Legend of Wild Bill Hickok - Loren D. Estleman 1967
The Big Stick - Lawrence Alexander 82
Black Sun - Terry C. Johnston 3242
Buffalo Girls - Larry McMurtry 4296
Castle Garden - Bill Albert 63
Crazy Fox Remembers - Don Preston 5174
The Dream Seekers - Grace Mark 4085
A Good Day to Die - Thomas Wakefield Blackburn 525
Homeland - John Jakes 3148
The Jewelled Spur - Gilbert Morris 4465
Kelly Blue - Peter Bowen 601
Last Go Round - Ken Kesey 3473
The Secret Annie Oakley - Marcy Moran Heidish 2819
Shaggy Legion - Hal George Evarts 1986
This Old Bill - Loren D. Estleman 1980
Trumpet on the Land - Terry C. Johnston 3260
Wild Times - Brian Garfield 2291
Yellowstone Kelly - Peter Bowen 602

Cody, William F.
Aces and Eights: A Novel of the Legend of Wild Bill Hickok - Loren D. Estleman 1967
The Big Stick - Lawrence Alexander 82
Black Sun - Terry C. Johnston 3242
Buffalo Girls - Larry McMurtry 4296
Castle Garden - Bill Albert 63
Crazy Fox Remembers - Don Preston 5174
The Dream Seekers - Grace Mark 4085
A Good Day to Die - Thomas Wakefield Blackburn 525
Homeland - John Jakes 3148
The Jewelled Spur - Gilbert Morris 4465
Kelly Blue - Peter Bowen 601
Last Go Round - Ken Kesey 3473
The Secret Annie Oakley - Marcy Moran Heidish 2819
Shaggy Legion - Hal George Evarts 1986
This Old Bill - Loren D. Estleman 1980
Trumpet on the Land - Terry C. Johnston 3260
Wild Times - Brian Garfield 2291
Yellowstone Kelly - Peter Bowen 602

Coeffier-Ruze d'Effiat, Henri
The Cardinal and the Queen - Evelyn Anthony 159
Cinq-Mars - Alfred Victor de Vigny 6495

Coeur, Jacques
The Burnished Blade - Lawrence Schoonover 5661
The Moneyman - Thomas B. Costain 1368

Coffin, Kezia
Nantucket Woman - Diana Gaines 2269

Coffin, Levi
Levi Coffin and the Underground Railroad - Charles Ludwig 3921

Cohn, Roy
Walter Winchell: A Novel - Michael Herr 2863

Coke, Frances
Call Lady Purbeck - Hilda Lewis 3745

Coleridge, Samuel Taylor
Eliza's Daughter - Joan Aiken 44
Mister Christian - William Kinsolving 3502
Walford's Oak - Jill M. Phillips 4986

Coligny, Gaspard de
The Italian Woman - Jean Plaidy 5024
The Longest Night - Ada Cook Lewis 3744
The Negotiators - Francis Walder 6526
Queen Jezebel - Jean Plaidy 5049

Colleoni, Bartolomeo
Condottiere - Jan Westcott 6644

Collins, Michael
The End of the Hunt - Thomas Flanagan 2119
An Excess of Love - Cathy Cash Spellman 5959
High Heroic - Constantine FitzGibbon 2118

Collins, Wilkie
The Detective and Mr. Dickens - William J. Palmer 4782
The Highwayman and Mr. Dickens - William J. Palmer 4783
The Hoydens and Mr. Dickens - William J. Palmer 4784
The Hungry Goblin: A Victorian Detective Novel - John Dickson Carr 911

Colon, Cristobal
The Dogs of Paradise - Abel Posse 5141
My Master Columbus - Cedric Belfrage 418

Colon, Diego
The Indian Chronicles - Jose Barreiro 349

Colonna, Vittoria
The Scarlet City - Hella S. Haasse 2632

Colter, John
The Man of the Storm - Ethel Hueston 3069
Wilderness - Roger Zelazny 6957

Columba
Isle of Glory - Jane Oliver 4723

Columbus, Christopher
1492 - Newton Frolich 2236
1492 - Mary Johnston 3228
Bay of Arrows - Jay Parini 4800
Caribbean - James A. Michener 4365
Columbus: A Romance - Rafael Sabatini 5549
Crown of Aloes - Norah Lofts 3840
The Dogs of Paradise - Abel Posse 5141
The Harp and the Shadow - Alejo Carpentier 905
The Indian Chronicles - Jose Barreiro 349
The Memoirs of Christopher Columbus - Stephen Marlowe 4096
Mercedes of Castile - James Fenimore Cooper 1304
My Master Columbus - Cedric Belfrage 418
The Queen's Cross: A Biographical Romance of Queen Isabella of Spain - Lawrence Schoonover 5666
Sea of Darkness - Roland Huntford 3086
To the Indies - C.S. Forester 2183
Torquemada - Howard Fast 2045
The Velvet Doublet - James H. Street 6082

Comiskey, Charles
Blue Ruin: A Novel of the 1919 World Series - Brendan Boyd 610

Commines, Philippe de
Quentin Durward - Sir Walter Scott 5705

Commodus, Lucius Aelius Aurelius (Roman Emperor)
Between Eternities - Robert H. Pilpel 5001

The Equinox: A Novel of Rome in the Time of Commodus - Carol Saylor 5622
Roman Nights - Ron Burns 803
The Side of the Moon - Amanda Prantera 5162

Comstock, Anthony
The Alienist - Caleb Carr 907

Comte de Frontenac
The Gilded Torch - Iola Fuller 2252
Heritage of the River - Muriel Elwood 1937
The King's Messenger - Samuel Edwards 1887
The Power and the Glory - Gilbert Parker 4805
Shadows on the Rock - Willa Cather 959

Comte de Mirabeau
The Black Consul - Anatolii Vinogradov 6503
King's Masque - Evan John 3220
Mirabeau, Lover and Stateman - Pierre Nezelof 4606

Comyn, John
The Crown in Darkness - P.C. Doherty 1671
Robert the Bruce: The Steps to the Empty Throne - Nigel Tranter 6320

Conchubar
A Shadow of Gulls - Patricia Finney 2096

Conde, Louis de
Angelique - Sergeanne Golon 2465

Conde, Prince de
The Faith and the Flame - June Dimmit Houston 3054

Condorcet, Nicholas
City of Darkness, City of Light - Marge Piercy 4998

Confucius
Creation - Gore Vidal 6486

Congreve, William
The Bracegirdle - Burris Atkins Jenkins 3189

Connolly, James
An Excess of Love - Cathy Cash Spellman 5959
Heart of War - John Masters 4174
The Men That God Made Mad: A Novel about Ireland's Easter Rising - W.A. Ballinger 286
Rebels: The Irish Rising of 1916 - Peter DeRosa 1622
Saints and Scholars - Terrence Eagleton 1821

Connolly, John
Flying into Love - D.M. Thomas 6236

Conor, Mac Nessa
Red Branch - Morgan Llywelyn 3824

Conrad of Montferrat
The Kings of Vain Intent - Graham Shelby 5791

Conroy, Sir John
The Captive of Kensington Palace - Jean Plaidy 5007
The Queen and Lord M - Jean Plaidy 5046
The Young Victoria - Tyler Whittle 6724

Constantine I (King of the Hellenes)
Beyond the Aegean - Elia Kazan 3382

Constantine I (Roman Emperor)
Constantine: The Miracle of the Flaming Cross - Frank G. Slaughter 5883
The Living Wood - Louis De Wohl 1571

Constantine XI Palaeologus (Eastern Roman Emperor)
The Dark Angel - Mika Waltari 6551

Constantius I (Roman Emperor)
The Living Wood - Louis De Wohl 1571

Constantius II (Roman Emperor)
The Death of the Gods - Dmitri Merezhkovski 4338

Constantius III (Roman Emperor)
Bury Me in Ravenna - Agnes Carr Vaughan 6432

Cook, James
Alaska - James A. Michener 4364

Charco Harbour - Godfrey Blunden 554
The Last Voyage: Captain Cook's Lost Diary - Hammond Innes 3108
The Return of Lono: A Novel of Captain Cook's Last Voyage - Oswald Andrew Bushnell 816
Running Proud - Nicholas Monsarrat 4432

Cooke, Ebenezer
The Sot-Weed Factor - John Barth 364

Coolidge, Calvin
The Land Was Ours: A Novel of the Great Plains - Charles W. Bailey 266
The Passion of Sacco and Vanzetti: A New England Legend - Howard Fast 2040

Cooper, Gary
High Midnight - Stuart M. Kaminsky 3339

Cooper, James Fenimore
The Splendor Stays: An Historic Novel Based on the Lives of the Seven Hart Sisters of Saybrook - Marguerite Allis 114

Cooper, Peter
All This, and Heaven Too - Rachel Field 2080
Certain Harvest: A Novel of the Time of Peter Cooper - Ruth Adams Knight 3525

Copernicus, Nicolaus
Doctor Copernicus - John Banville 296

Corday, Charlotte
Dr. Guillotine: The Eccentric Exploits of an Early Scientist - Herbert Lom 3867
A Place of Greater Safety - Hilary Mantel 4077
To Spit Against the Wind - Benjamin H. Levin 3737

Cordell, Augusta
Bread and Circus - Morris Renek 5303

Cornelius the Ciliarch
The Nazarene - Sholem Asch 200

Cornell, Sarah Maria
Avery's Knot - Mary Cable 843
The Tragedy at Tinkerton: An Historical Novel of Murder - Raymond Paul 4844

Cornforth, Fanny
Willowwood - Elizabeth Savage 5619

Cornwallis, Charles
Cato's War - Guy Wheeler 6655
The Drums of December - Sharon Salvato 5575
The Fallon Blood - Reagan O'Neal 4741
A Few Painted Feathers - Stephen Longstreet 3886
Horseshoe Robinson, a Tale of the Tory Ascendancy - John P. Kennedy 3418
The Lady From Yorktown - Eva McDonald 4260
Proceed, Sergeant Lamb - Robert Graves 2550
Raleigh's Eden - Inglis Fletcher 2137
The Savage Brood - Martha Rofheart 5430
The Sea Stands Watch - Helen Parker Mudgett 4507
The Sunshine Patriot: A Novel of Benedict Arnold - Norman Partington 4822
Sycamore Men - David Taylor 6181
Wicked Lady - Inglis Fletcher 2142
The Year of the French - Thomas Flanagan 2121
Yorktown - Burke Davis 1513

Coronado, Francisco Vasquez de
The Seven Cities of Gold - Virginia Davis Hersch 2865
Texas - James A. Michener 4375

Corot, Camille
Depths of Glory - Irving Stone 6055

Cortez, Hernando
Aztec - Gary Jennings 3193
Captain From Castile - Samuel Shellabarger 5794
Cortez and Marina - Edison Marshall 4105
Death of the Fifth Sun - Robert Somerlott 5944
Don Pedro and the Devil - Edgar Maas 3948
The Fair God - Lew Wallace 6537
Gods on Horseback - Samuel G. Baggett 263
The Golden Princess - Alexander Baron 335

The Great White Gods - Eduard Stucken 6102
The Heart of Jade - Salvador de Madariaga 4024
The Sun, He Dies: A Novel about the End of the Aztec World - Jamake Highwater 2919
They Are Coming: The Conquest of Mexico - Jose Lopez Portillo y Pacheco 3896

Cotter, James
The Wayfarer - Shirley Seifert 5738

Cotton, John
A Candle in the Wilderness - Irving A. Bacheller 256
Covenant of Grace - Jane Gilmore Rushing 5527
Uncharted Ways - Caroline Snedeker 5935
Witnesses - Marcy Moran Heidish 2820

Count of Artois
The Iron King - Maurice Druon 1732
The Lily and the Lion - Maurice Druon 1733
The Poisoned Crown - Maurice Druon 1734
The Royal Succession - Maurice Druon 1735
The Strangled Queen - Maurice Druon 1737
The Vow on the Heron - Jean Plaidy 5074

Countess of Castlemaine
Catherine - Hilda Lewis 3746
Forever Amber - Kathleen Winsor 6822
A Health Unto His Majesty - Jean Plaidy 5019
The King's Brat - Constance Gluyas 2441
Lady on the Coin - Margaret Campbell Barnes 326
My Lady Benbrook - Constance Gluyas 2442
Our Jo, or The Chronicle of a Coming Man - Kenneth M. Cameron 868

Countess of Essex
The King James Version - Stanley N. Stewart 6035

Courbet, Gustave
Depths of Glory - Irving Stone 6055

Courtebarbe, Denys de
Tomorrow's Fire - Jay Williams 6775

Couthon, Georges
The Incorruptible - Marjorie Coryn 1357

Coward, Noel
The Noel Coward Murder Case - George Baxt 387

Cowley, Abraham
The Shadow Flies - Rose Macaulay 3956

Cozad, John Jackson
Son of the Gamblin' Man: The Youth of an Artist - Mari Sandoz 5593

Crandall, John Quincy Adams
Aces and Eights: A Novel of the Legend of Wild Bill Hickok - Loren D. Estleman 1967

Crane, Stephen
Dark Rider - Louis Zara 6950
The Rough Rider - Gilbert Morris 4468
The Year of the Spaniard - Henry Castor 956

Cranmer, Thomas
Anne Boleyn - Evelyn Anthony 158
Brief Gaudy Hour - Margaret Campbell Barnes 322
The Concubine - Norah Lofts 3839
The Fifth Queen - Ford Madox Ford 2161
The Heir of Allington - Philippa Wiat 6727
Henry VIII and His Six Wives - Maureen Peters 4975
I, Elizabeth - Rosalind Miles 4378
The King's Good Servant - Olive White 6696
The Man on a Donkey - H.F.M. Prescott 5170
My Lord of Canterbury - Godfrey Turton 6369
Queen Anne Boleyn - Francis Hackett 2634
The Ten-Day Queen - Lozania Prole 5199
The Wise Virgin - Hebe Elsna 1934
Young Bess - Margaret Irwin 3123

Cranstoun, Willy
My Grand Enemy - Jean Stubbs 6098

Crashaw, Richard
The Shadow Flies - Rose Macaulay 3956

Crassus, Marcus Licinius
Arena: A Novel of Spartacus and Crassus - Maurice Ghnassia 2391
Arms of Nemesis - Steven Saylor 5623
The City of Libertines - W.G. Hardy 2702
Fortune's Favorite - Colleen McCullough 4235
Freedom, Farewell - Phyllis Bentley 461
The Gladiators - Arthur Koestler 3532
Spartacus - Howard Fast 2044

Crawford, Isabel
Light on the Mountain - Leonard Sanders 5589

Crazy Horse
Buffalo Woman - Dorothy M. Johnson 3223
Chief of Scouts - Don Bendell 439
Crazy Horse - Bill Dugan 1757
Creek Mary's Blood - Dee Brown 712
Flashman and the Redskins - George MacDonald Fraser 2208
A Good Day to Die - Del Barton 368
Kelly Blue - Peter Bowen 601
Lakota - G. Clifton Wisler 6833
No Survivors - Will Henry 2846
Reap the Whirlwind - Terry C. Johnston 3254
A Road We Do Not Know: A Novel of Custer at the Little Bighorn - Frederick J. Chiaventone 1057
Sitting Bull - Bill Dugan 1760
Stone Song: A Novel of the Life of Crazy Horse - Winfred Blevins 548
Thunder in the Dawn - Earl Murray 4532
The Winter War - William Wister Haines 2640

Crazy Snake
Crazy Snake - Robert J. Conley 1240

Cream, Thomas Neill
The Gentleman From Chicago - John Cashman 953

Cresap, Michael
Song of the Susquehanna - Herbert Stover 6071

Critias
Goat Song: A Novel of Ancient Greece - Frank Yerby 6920

Crittenden, John Jordan
The Three Lives of Elizabeth - Shirley Seifert 5735

Crockett, Davy
All the Brave Rifles - Clarke Venable 6450
As Long as the Rivers Run - Sam J. Slate 5882
The Bugles Are Silent: A Novel of the Texas Revolution - John R. Knaggs 3513
Crockett of Tennessee: A Novel Based on the Life and Times of David Crockett - Cameron Judd 3314
Empire of Bones: A Novel of Sam Houston and the Texas Revolution - Jeff Long 3868
The Furies - John Jakes 3146
Hearts of Hickory - John Trotwood Moore 4442
Horseshoe Bend - Bruce Palmer 4779
Oh, Promised Land - James H. Street 6079
The Road to San Jacinto - James F. Davis 1524
The Road to San Jacinto - Leonard L. Foreman 2167
Texas - James A. Michener 4375
Wave High the Banner - Dee Brown 714

Crockett, Elizabeth
Crockett of Tennessee: A Novel Based on the Life and Times of David Crockett - Cameron Judd 3314

Croesus (King of Lydia)
Persian Conqueror - George Sidney Hellman 2822

Crompton, Samuel
Crompton Way - Thomas Thompson 6270

Cromwell, Oliver
Bennett's Welcome - Inglis Fletcher 2132
Charles the King - Evelyn Anthony 160
The Highland Hawk - Leslie Turner White 6682
Katherine Christian - Hugh Walpole 6546
The King Breaker - Elizabeth Linington 3797
My Lord Foxe - Constance Gluyas 2443
Myself, Christopher Wren - David Weiss 6606

Myself My Enemy - Jean Plaidy   5037
Prisons - Mary Lee Settle   5757
The Severed Crown - Jane Lane   3657
The Stranger Prince - Margaret Irwin   3122
Twenty Years After - Alexandre Dumas   1783
The White Witch - Elizabeth Goudge   2496
Wife to Mr. Milton - Robert Graves   2553
Woodstock; or, The Cavalier - Sir Walter Scott   5710

Cromwell, Thomas
Anne Boleyn - Evelyn Anthony   158
Anne of the Thousand Days - Edward Fenton   2059
The Concubine - Norah Lofts   3839
The Fifth Queen - Ford Madox Ford   2161
Henry VIII and His Six Wives - Maureen
   Peters   4975
The Hireling - Alison Macleod   4003
The King's Achievement - Robert Hugh Benson   459
The King's Good Servant - Olive White   6696
The King's Pleasure - Jean Plaidy   5026
The Man on a Donkey - H.F.M. Prescott   5170
My Lord of Canterbury - Godfrey Turton   6369
The Nunnery - Dorothy Charques   1001
Queen Anne Boleyn - Francis Hackett   2634

Cronje, Piet
The Legacy of Ladysmith - John Kenny Crane   1413

Crook, George C.
Blood Song - Terry C. Johnston   3243
Geronimo - Bill Dugan   1758
Geronimo: An American Legend - Robert J.
   Conley   1242
The Last Warpath - Will Henry   2844
Reap the Whirlwind - Terry C. Johnston   3254
The Scout - Harry Combs   1224
Sitting Bull - Bill Dugan   1760
Thunder in the Dawn - Earl Murray   4532
Trumpet on the Land - Terry C. Johnston   3260
The Winter War - William Wister Haines   2640

Crosby, Bing
Murder in the Oval Office - Elliott Roosevelt   5450

Cross, John Walter
Johnnie Cross - Terence de Vere White   6704

Crozier, Columba
The World, the Flesh, and the Devil - Reay
   Tannahill   6159

Culpepper, Nicholas
The Affairs of Nicholas Culpepper - Mabel L.
   Tyrrel   6375

Culpepper, Thomas
Katheryn, the Wanton Queen - Maureen Peters   4976
The Rose Without a Thorn - Jean Plaidy   5058

Cunobelin
The Dark Island - Henry Treece   6326

Curio, Gaius Scribonius
Roman Shadows - Ron Burns   804

Currie, Jessica
The Raid - John Brick   673

Currie, Tom
The Raid - John Brick   673

Curry, Kid
*Kid Curry: The Life and Times of Harvey Logan and
   the Wild Bunch* - F. Bruce Lamb   3606

Curzon, George Nathaniel
The Imperial Agent - T.N. Murari   4518

Custer, Elizabeth Bacon
The Court-Martial of George Armstrong Custer -
   Douglas C. Jones   3276
*The Last Stand: A Novel about George Armstrong
   Custer and the Indians of the Plains* - Edwin P.
   Hoyt   3061
Libbie - Judy Alter   121
Marching to Valhalla: A Novel of Custer's Last Days -
   Michael Blake   538
Shadow on the Valley - Kirk Mitchell   4414

Custer, George Armstrong
Black Sun - Terry C. Johnston   3242
Bugles in the Afternoon - Ernest Haycox   2788
Chief of Scouts - Don Bendell   439
The Court-Martial of George Armstrong Custer -
   Douglas C. Jones   3276
Crazy Fox Remembers - Don Preston   5174
Crazy Horse - Bill Dugan   1757
The Crossed Sabres - Gilbert Morris   4458
Custer Passed Our Way - Fred S. Kaufman   3370
Flashman and the Redskins - George MacDonald
   Fraser   2208
A Good Day to Die - Del Barton   368
Heaven and Hell - John Jakes   3147
*The Last Stand: A Novel about George Armstrong
   Custer and the Indians of the Plains* - Edwin P.
   Hoyt   3061
The Last Warpath - Will Henry   2844
Libbie - Judy Alter   121
Little Big Man - Thomas Berger   478
Long Winter Gone - Terry C. Johnston   3252
Love and War - John Jakes   3150
Marching to Valhalla: A Novel of Custer's Last Days -
   Michael Blake   538
A Mighty Afternoon - Charles K. Mills   4407
Montana Road - Harry Sinclair Drago   1717
No Survivors - Will Henry   2846
*A Road We Do Not Know: A Novel of Custer at the
   Little Bighorn* - Frederick J. Chiaventone   1057
Roll, Shenandoah - Bruce Lancaster   3644
Roman - Douglas C. Jones   3281
The Scout - Harry Combs   1224
Seize the Sky - Terry C. Johnston   3256
Shadow on the Valley - Kirk Mitchell   4414
Shaggy Legion - Hal George Evarts   1986
This Old Bill - Loren D. Estleman   1980
Twice upon a Time - Allen Appel   172
The Winter War - William Wister Haines   2640

Custer, Tom
A Mighty Afternoon - Charles K. Mills   4407

Custis, Daniel Parke
Lady Washington - Dorothy Clarke Wilson   6803

Custis, Martha
Morning of a Hero - Burke Boyce   608

Cynric
Born of the Sun - Joan Wolf   6837

Cyrus the Great (King of Persia)
Persian Conqueror - George Sidney Hellman   2822
The Prophet - Sholem Asch   201

D

Dabney, Sam
Oh, Promised Land - James H. Street   6079

Dahlgren, Ulrich
Night March - Bruce Lancaster   3641
The Richmond Raid - John Brick   674

Daley, Richard
You Bet Your Life - Stuart M. Kaminsky   3349

Dalhousie, Marquis of
Follow the Drum - James Leasor   3699

Dali, Salvador
The Melting Clock - Stuart M. Kaminsky   3342

Dalton, Emmett
Desperadoes - Ron Hansen   2681

Dalton, Robert
Desperadoes - Ron Hansen   2681

Damien, Father
Molokai - Oswald Andrew Bushnell   815

Dampier, William
Burning Gold - Robert Hardy Andrews   148

Dandridge, Dorothea
Give Me Liberty - Noel B. Gerson   2369

Daniel
Babylon - Anthony Esler   1959
The Prophet - Sholem Asch   201

D'Annunzio, Gabriele
Eleanora Duse - Jean Stubbs   6095
The Lion of Pescara - George MacBeth   3958

Dante Alighieri
The Wanderer: A Novel of Dante and Beatrice -
   Nathan Schachner   5633

Danton, Georges-Jacques
Citizen Tom Paine - Howard Fast   2028
City of Darkness, City of Light - Marge Piercy   4998
The Devil's Laughter - Frank Yerby   6913
The Gods Are Thirsty - Tanith Lee   3710
The Incorruptible - Marjorie Coryn   1357
The Incorruptible - Helma De Bois   1551
A Place of Greater Safety - Hilary Mantel   4077
Scaramouche - Rafael Sabatini   5554
To Spit Against the Wind - Benjamin H. Levin   3737
Veronique - Virginia Coffman   1158
The Way to the Lantern - Audrey Erskine
   Lindop   3790

d'Aragona, Isabella
Duchess of Milan - Michael Ennis   1946

Dare, Virginia
Croatan - Mary Johnston   3231
The Lost Colony - Edison Marshall   4108

Darius (King of Persia)
Alexander the God - Robert Payne   4849
Creation - Gore Vidal   6486
Farewell Great King: A Novel of Ancient Greece - Jill
   Paton Walsh   4829
The Persian Boy - Mary Renault   5301

Darling, Ralph
The Colonists - William Stuart Long   3870

D'Armagnac, Jean
The Spider King - Lawrence Schoonover   5668

Darnley, Lord
The Gay Galliard - Margaret Irwin   3119
The Green Salamander - Pamela Hill   2933
Immortal Queen - Elizabeth Byrd   834
The Lion and the Rose - Jane Oliver   4724
Mary of Scotland - F.W. Kenyon   3454
Mary, Queen of Scotland and the Isles - Margaret
   George   2356
No Smoke Without Fire - Alice Harwood   2767
Parcel of Rogues - Jane Lane   3656
Queen's Caprice - Marjorie Bowen   599
Royal Road to Fotheringay - Jean Plaidy   5059
A Time for the Death of a King - Ann Dukthas   1777
The White Queen - Frederic Fallon   2011

Darrow, Clarence
The American - Howard Fast   2026
California Glory - Dana Fuller Ross   5468
The Dream Seekers - Grace Mark   4085

Dart, Isom
One More River to Cross - Will Henry   2847

Darwin, Charles
Jemmy Button - Benjamin Subercaseaux   6107
The Origin - Irving Stone   6060

Dashwood, Sir Francis
Master of Bengal: A Novel of Robert Clive of India -
   Norman Partington   4821

Daumier, Honore
Depths of Glory - Irving Stone   6055

Davenport, John
Until the Winds - Jean Clark   1089

David (King of Israel)
After Goliath - R.V. Cassill 955
Bathsheba - Roberta Kells Dorr 1695
Bathsheba - Torgny Lindgren 3789
David and Bathsheba - Ari Ibn-Sahav 3098
David at Olivet - Wallace Hamilton 2671
David of Jerusalem - Louis De Wohl 1564
David the King - Gladys Schmitt 5641
David: Warrior and King - Frank G. Slaughter 5885
David's Stranger - Moshe Shamir 5771
The Death of Kings - Peter Danielson 1465
Giant Killer - Elmer Holmes Davis 1518
King David - Gwyn Jenkins 3191
The King David Report - Stefan Heym 2910
King of Kings: A Novel of the Life of David - Malachi Martin 4134
Rizpah - Charles E. Israel 3124
The Shining King - Peter Danielson 1476
Solomon and Sheba - Faye Levine 3740
Solomon and Sheba - Jay Williams 6774
Solomon's Song - Roberta Kells Dorr 1697
The Source - James A. Michener 4374
Tamar - Ann Chamberlin 975
Triumph of the Lion - Peter Danielson 1478
The Trojan - Noel B. Gerson 2386
The Unanointed - Laurene Chinn 1070
The Valley of Vision: A Novel of King Solomon and His Time - Vardis Fisher 2113

David ap Gruffydd (Prince of Wales)
The Brothers of Gwynedd - Edith Pargeter 4796
The Reckoning - Sharon Kay Penman 4906

Davidson, Randall
The Widow of Windsor - Tyler Whittle 6723

Davies, Marion
The Greta Garbo Murder Case - George Baxt 385
Murder at San Simeon - Robert Lee Hall 2660

Davis, Bette
The Bette Davis Murder Case - George Baxt 383
The Devil Met a Lady - Stuart M. Kaminsky 3335

Davis, Jefferson
Alaska - James A. Michener 4364
Beloved - Vina Delmar 1599
Bride of Fortune - Harnett T. Kane 3352
Comes an Echo on the Breeze - Edward J. Ryan 5542
Copperhead - Bernard Cornwell 1335
The Court Martial of Robert E. Lee - Douglas Savage 5617
Dim the Flaring Lamps - Jan Jordan 3301
The Guns of the South - Harry N. Turtledove 6367
The Lady of Arlington - Harnett T. Kane 3354
Love and War - John Jakes 3150
Powderkeg - Richard Vetterli 6482
The Proud Retreat - Clifford Dowdey 1706
The Proud Way - Shirley Seifert 5731
The Smiling Rebel - Harnett T. Kane 3357
There Was a Season: A Biographical Novel of Jefferson Davis - Theodore Olsen 4730
The Titans - John Jakes 3154
Traveller - Richard Adams 27
The Yankee From Tennessee - Noel B. Gerson 2388

Davis, Richard
Yellow: A Novel - Daniel Lynch 3932

Davis, Sam
On Jordan's Stormy Banks - Adelaide C. Rowell 5518

Davis, Varina Howell
Bride of Fortune - Harnett T. Kane 3352
The Lady of Arlington - Harnett T. Kane 3354
The Proud Way - Shirley Seifert 5731
While the Music Plays - Diane Austell 242

Davitt, Michael
The Tenants of Time - Thomas Flanagan 2120

Davout, Louis Nicolas
The Proud Canaries - David Johnson 3222

Dayan, Moshe
The Glory - Herman Wouk 6873
The Hope - Herman Wouk 6874

de Gaulle, Charles
The Free Frenchman - Piers Paul Read 5277

de la Marck, William
Quentin Durward - Sir Walter Scott 5705

De Quincey, Thomas
The Prince of Eden - Marilyn Harris 2732

de Soto, Hernando
At the Moon's Inn - Andrew Lytle 3944
The Golden Eagle - John Edward Jennings 3201
Juan Ortiz: Gentleman of Seville - Mary Bethell Alfriend 88
Tatham Mound - Piers Anthony 169

De Valera, Eamon
The End of the Hunt - Thomas Flanagan 2119
An Excess of Love - Cathy Cash Spellman 5959
Rebels: The Irish Rising of 1916 - Peter DeRosa 1622

de Veuster, Joseph
Molokai - Oswald Andrew Bushnell 815

Dean, Dizzy
Mr. Vertigo - Paul Auster 244

Dean, Jay Hanna
Mr. Vertigo - Paul Auster 244

Deborah
The Invaders - Peter Danielson 1469
The Sorceress - Nathaniel Norsen Weinreb 6602

Debs, Eugene V.
Adversary in the House - Irving Stone 6053
The American - Howard Fast 2026
The Dream Seekers - Grace Mark 4085
Homeland - John Jakes 3148

Debs, Theodore
Adversary in the House - Irving Stone 6053

Debussy, Claude
Clair De Lune: A Novel about Claude Debussy - Pierre La Mure 3575

Dee, Judge
The Chinese Nail Murders - Robert van Gulik 6413
Deception - Eleanor Cooney 1295
The Emperor's Pearl - Robert van Gulik 6414
The Haunted Monastery - Robert van Gulik 6415
The Lacquer Screen - Robert van Gulik 6416
The Monkey and the Tiger - Robert van Gulik 6417
Murder in Canton - Robert van Gulik 6418
Necklace and Calabash - Robert van Gulik 6419
The Phantom of the Temple - Robert van Gulik 6420
The Red Pavilion - Robert van Gulik 6421
The Willow Pattern - Robert van Gulik 6422

Dee Jen-dieh
The Chinese Nail Murders - Robert van Gulik 6413
Deception - Eleanor Cooney 1295
The Emperor's Pearl - Robert van Gulik 6414
The Haunted Monastery - Robert van Gulik 6415
The Lacquer Screen - Robert van Gulik 6416
The Monkey and the Tiger - Robert van Gulik 6417
Murder in Canton - Robert van Gulik 6418
Necklace and Calabash - Robert van Gulik 6419
The Phantom of the Temple - Robert van Gulik 6420
The Red Pavilion - Robert van Gulik 6421
The Willow Pattern - Robert van Gulik 6422

Defoe, Daniel
Burning Gold - Robert Hardy Andrews 148

Degas, Edgar
Depths of Glory - Irving Stone 6055
Moulin Rouge: A Novel Based on Henri de Toulouse-Lautrec - Pierre La Mure 3576
Naked Came I: A Novel of Rodin - David Weiss 6607
To Seize the Passing Dream - Ted Berkman 479

Utrillo's Mother - Sarah Baylis 391

Delacroix, Eugene
To Seize a Dream - Virginia Davis Hersch 2866

Delilah
Husband of Delilah - Eric Linklater 3802

Deluzy-Desportes, Henriette
All This, and Heaven Too - Rachel Field 2080

Demetrius I (King of Macedon)
Besieger of Cities - Alfred Duggan 1761
The Bronze God of Rhodes - L. Sprague De Camp 1554

DeMille, Cecil B.
He Done Her Wrong - Stuart M. Kaminsky 3338
New Deal for Death - Elliott Roosevelt 5454

Demosthenes
Fire From Heaven - Mary Renault 5296

Dena, Lottie
The Lady and Doc Holliday - Preston Lewis 3761

Derham, Francis
Katheryn, the Wanton Queen - Maureen Peters 4976

Dermot
Isle of Glory - Jane Oliver 4723

Desmond, William
The Raid - John Brick 673

Desmoulins, Camille
City of Darkness, City of Light - Marge Piercy 4998
The Devil's Laughter - Frank Yerby 6913
The Gods Are Thirsty - Tanith Lee 3710
The Incorruptible - Marjorie Coryn 1357
A Place of Greater Safety - Hilary Mantel 4077
Scaramouche the King-Maker - Rafael Sabatini 5555
Tricolour - Mark Logan 3866

Dessalines, Jean-Jacques
Black Triumvirate: A Novel of Haiti - Benjamin H. Levin 3736
Drums of Destiny - Peter Bourne 593
Lydia Bailey - Kenneth Roberts 5387
Mistress of Darkness - Christopher Nicole 4617

Destinn, Emmy
A Cadenza for Caruso - Barbara Paul 4834
A Chorus of Detectives - Barbara Paul 4835

Devereux, Penelope
Lady Rich - Elizabeth Boatwright Coker 1166

Devereux, Robert
The Bisley Boy - Christopher Hunt 3080
The Constant Star - Dorothy Norris Foote 2151
A Dead Man in Deptford - Anthony Burgess 776
Death of the Fox - George Garrett 2300
Heart of a Queen - Josephine Delves-Broughton 1603
I, Elizabeth - Rosalind Miles 4378
Legacy - Susan Kay 3374
The Murder in the Tower - Jean Plaidy 5035
My Enemy the Queen - Victoria Holt 3017
My Lord Essex - Olive Eckerson 1838
Nicholas Cooke: Actor, Soldier, Physician, Priest - Stephanie Cowell 1393
Queen of This Realm: The Story of Queen Elizabeth I - Jean Plaidy 5050
Shadow in the Sun: A Novel of Elizabeth I, the Virgin Queen - F.W. Kenyon 3460
The Succession: A Novel of Elizabeth and James - George Garrett 2302
Sweet Will - Eric Malpass 4050
Take Heed of Loving Me: A Novel about John Donne - Elizabeth Gray Vining 6502
Too Near the Throne - Molly Costain Haycraft 2797
Will Shakespeare: The Untold Story - John Mortimer 4495
You, My Brother - Philip Burton 809

Dewey, John
John and Anzia: An American Romance - Norma Rosen   5462

Dewey, Nelson
The Shadow in the Glass - August Derleth   1618

Diaghilev, Serge
Encore - Monique Raphel High   2915

Diamond, Jack
Legs - William Kennedy   3422

Diamond, Legs
Legs - William Kennedy   3422

Diana, Princess of Wales
Di and I - Peter Lefcourt   3714
The Queen and I - Sue Townsend   6306

Diane de Poitiers
Courtesan - Diane Haeger   2635
Madame Serpent - Jean Plaidy   5033

Diaz, Porfirio
Chapultepec - Norman Zollinger   6965

Diaz de Vivar, Rodrigo
The Infidel - Georgia Elizabeth Taylor   6182

Dickens, Charles
Charles - Victoria Lincoln   3786
The Consuming Flame: The Story of George Eliot - F.W. Kenyon   3446
The Detective and Mr. Dickens - William J. Palmer   4782
English Music - Peter Ackroyd   18
The Highwayman and Mr. Dickens - William J. Palmer   4783
The Hoydens and Mr. Dickens - William J. Palmer   4784
The Mutual Friend - Frederick Busch   811
The Romance of Charles Dickens - Ursula Bloom   553

Dickens, Kate
Charles - Victoria Lincoln   3786

Dickinson, Emily
Come Slowly Eden: A Novel about Emily Dickinson - Laura Benet   440
The Diary of Emily Dickinson: A Novel - Jamie Fuller   2255
The Hesitant Heart - Anne Edwards   1882
I Never Came to You in White - Judith Farr   2014
Peter Doyle - John Vernon   6457

Dickinson, James
The Phantom Emperor - Neil Harmon Swanson   6140

Diderot, Denis
Rasero - Francisco Rebolledo   5282

Diego, Juan
Roses for Mexico - Ethel Cook Eliot   1907

Dillinger, John
Dillinger - Harry Patterson   4832
Mad Dog - Jack Kelly   3401
Saint Mudd - Steve Thayer   6218
True Crime - Max Allan Collins   1214

Dinwiddie, Robert
Red Morning - Ruby Frazier Frey   2230

Dio Cassius
The Side of the Moon - Amanda Prantera   5162

Diogenes, Romanus
The Lady for Ransom - Alfred Duggan   1768

Dion
The Mask of Apollo - Mary Renault   5300

Dionysios the Great
The Arrows of Hercules - L. Sprague De Camp   1553

Dionysios the Younger
The Mask of Apollo - Mary Renault   5300

Dispenser, Hugh
The She-Wolf - Pamela Bennetts   456

Disraeli, Benjamin
Bush War! - William Moore   4447
Cock of the Walk - Roy Lewis   3762
The Day They Kidnapped Queen Victoria - H.K. Fleming   2127
Disraeli in Love - Maurice Edelman   1851
Disraeli Rising - Maurice Edelman   1852
Dizzy's Woman - George MacBeth   3957
Enter the Lion: A Posthumous Memoir of Mycroft Holmes - Michael P. Hodel   2961
The Mudlark - Theodore Bonnet   573
Playing the Game - Ian Buruma   810
Pomp and Circumstance - Fred Mustard Stewart   6025
The Prime Minister's Wife - Doris Leslie   3727
Victoria Victorious - Jean Plaidy   5073
The Widow of Windsor - Jean Plaidy   5076
The Widow of Windsor - Tyler Whittle   6723

Dix, Dorothea
The Bridge - Marguerite Allis   108
Love and War - John Jakes   3150

Dixon, Joseph
Shadow Catcher - Charles Fergus   2064

Dobbin, William
Vanity Fair - William Makepeace Thackeray   6213

Dodge, Anna
The Beloved Invader - Eugenia Price   5179

Dodge, Anson
The Beloved Invader - Eugenia Price   5179

Dodge, Ellen
The Beloved Invader - Eugenia Price   5179

Dodge, Grenville
The Union Belle - Gilbert Morris   4473

Doheny, Edward Lawrence
California Gold - John Jakes   3145

Dokyo
The Vermilion Bridge - Shelley Mydans   4539

Dolby, George
The Mutual Friend - Frederick Busch   811

Domitian (Roman Emperor)
Gold for the Caesars - Florence A. Seward   5759
Josephus and the Emperor - Lion Feuchtwanger   2073
The Triumph - Ernest K. Gann   2280

Donelson, John
Journey to Nashville - Alfred Leland Crabb   1402

Dongan, Thomas
Night of Decision: A Novel of Colonial New York - Dorothy Grant   2534

Donne, John
Knaves Templar - Leonard Tourney   6300
Physician Extraordinary: A Novel of the Life and Times of William Harvey - David Weiss   6608
Take Heed of Loving Me: A Novel about John Donne - Elizabeth Gray Vining   6502

Donner, George
The Mothers - Vardis Fisher   2109
Tamsen - David Galloway   2273
The Ungodly: A Novel of the Donner Party - Richard Rhodes   5311
Wheels West - Homer Croy   1438

Donner, Tamsen
The Mothers - Vardis Fisher   2109
Tamsen - David Galloway   2273
Wheels West - Homer Croy   1438

Donough
Pride of Lions - Morgan Llywelyn   3823

Donovan, William J. "Wild Bill"
Murder in the Chateau - Elliott Roosevelt   5447

Dorantes, Andres
The Children of the Sun - Oakley Hall   2652

d'Orleans, Charles
In a Dark Wood Wandering - Hella S. Haasse   2631

Dostoevsky, Feodor Mikhailovich
The Devil Inside: A Novel of Dostoevsky's Life - Stephen Coulter   1385

Doubleday, Abner
Joy in Mudville - Gordon McAlpine   4216

Douglas, Addie Cutts
The Senator's Lady - Shirley Seifert   5733

Douglas, Lord Alfred Bruce
The God of Mirrors - Robert Reilly   5293

Douglas, George
The Captive Queen of Scots - Jean Plaidy   5008

Douglas, James
Castle Dangerous - Sir Walter Scott   5694
Parcel of Rogues - Jane Lane   3656

Douglas, John Sholto
The God of Mirrors - Robert Reilly   5293

Douglas, Margaret
The Green Salamander - Pamela Hill   2933

Douglas, Stephen A.
The Crisis - Winston Churchill   1079
North and South - John Jakes   3151
The Senator's Lady - Shirley Seifert   5733

Douglas, Thomas
The Strange Brigade - John Edward Jennings   3209

Douglas, William
The Captive Queen of Scots - Jean Plaidy   5008
The Lion Is Come - Jane Oliver   4725

Douglass, Frederick
Darktown Strutters - Wesley Brown   732
The Furies - John Jakes   3146
Hacey Miller - James Sherburne   5805
Raising Holy Hell - Bruce Olds   4718
Seneca Falls Inheritance - Miriam Grace Monfredo   4429
A Star Pointed North - Edmund Fuller   2250
Through a Gold Eagle - Miriam Grace Monfredo   4430

Dousman, Hercules
Bright Journey - August Derleth   1614
The House on the Mound - August Derleth   1616

Dousman, Jane
The House on the Mound - August Derleth   1616

Dover, Thomas
Burning Gold - Robert Hardy Andrews   148

Doyle, Arthur Conan
The List of Seven - Mark Frost   2237
Nevermore - William Hjortsberg   2958
The Night of the Ripper - Robert Bloch   551
The Six Messiahs - Mark Frost   2238

Drake, Sir Francis
Beauvallet - Georgette Heyer   2876
The Black Duchess - Alanna Knight   3514
Captain for Elizabeth - Jan Westcott   6643
Caribbean - James A. Michener   4365
Deborah and the Many Faces of Love - Colette Davenat   1499
Envoy From Elizabeth - Pamela Bennetts   451
Golden Admiral - F. van Wyck Mason   4150
The Hounds of God - Rafael Sabatini   5551
Kingdom of Gold - Susan Wiggs   6744
Reluctant Cavalier - Donald Barr Chidsey   1064
Roanoke Hundred - Inglis Fletcher   2138
Westward Ho! - Charles Kingsley   3499

Drayton, Michael
Two Loves Have I - Clara Longworth de
    Chambrun 985

Dreier, Mary
Rivington Street - Meredith Tax 6175

Drew, Daniel
The Bank - Stephen Longstreet 3882

Drummond, Margaret
Sunset at Noon - Jane Oliver 4728

Drummond, William
The Great Adventure - Janice Holt Giles 2410

Dryden, John
The Bracegirdle - Burris Atkins Jenkins 3189
The Golden Days - Robert Neill 4569
The Renegade - Donald Clayton Porter 5122

Du Luth, Daniel
Daniel Du Luth - Everett McNeil 4307

Du Maurier, George
To Seize the Passing Dream - Ted Berkman 479

Du Pont, Alfred I.
Fortune's Legacy - Jack Rowe 5515

Du Pont, Henry
Dominion - Jack Rowe 5514

Du Pont, Lammot
Dominion - Jack Rowe 5514

Du Pont de Nemours, Pierre Samuel
Brandywine - Jack Rowe 5513

Dubuc, Aimee
Sultana - Michael, Prince of Greece 4358

Duc de Beaufort
Twenty Years After - Alexandre Dumas 1783

Duc de Berry
So Much as Beauty Does - Muriel Elwood 1938

Duc de Lauzun
Sorrow by Day - Marjorie Coryn 1359

Duc de Saint-Simon
The Cat and the King - Louis Auchincloss 229

Duchess of Alba
*Colossus: A Novel about Goya and a World Gone
    Mad* - Stephen Marlowe 4093
In the Blazing Light - Max White 6693
The Last Portrait of the Duchess of Alba - Antonio
    Larreta 3666
The Naked Maja - Noel B. Gerson 2378
Rage in Silence: A Novel Based on the Life of Goya -
    Donald Braider 643

Duchess of Marlborough
The Elusive Crown - Hebe Elsna 1931
Exit Lady Masham - Louis Auchincloss 230
The Glory and the Dream - F.W. Kenyon 3450
Marlborough's Unfair Lady - Lozania Prole 5197
The Power and the Passion - Christina
    Nicholson 4609
The Queen's Favourites - Jean Plaidy 5051
The Sachem - Donald Clayton Porter 5124

Duchess of Montrose
Bertie and the Tinman - Peter Lovesey 3909

Dudley, Lord Guilford
The Tower of London - William Harrison
    Ainsworth 58

Dudley, John
Feast in the Morning - Hugh Preston 5175

Dudley, Joseph
Savage Gentleman - Noel B. Gerson 2381

Dudley, Robert (Duke of Northumberland)
A Crown in Darkness: A Novel about Lady Jane Grey
    - Margaret Mullally 4512
Her Majesty's Captain - Derek Wilson 6797

Dudley, Robert (Earl of Leicester)
All the Queen's Men - Evelyn Anthony 157
The Bisley Boy - Christopher Hunt 3080
Elizabeth: Queen & Woman - Helen Thorpe 6279
Gay Lord Robert - Jean Plaidy 5015
The Green Salamander - Pamela Hill 2933
Heart of a Queen - Josephine Delves-
    Broughton 1603
Kenilworth - Sir Walter Scott 5700
Lady Rich - Elizabeth Boatwright Coker 1166
Legacy - Susan Kay 3374
My Dear Lover England - Pamela Bennetts 453
My Enemy the Queen - Victoria Holt 3017
My Lord Essex - Olive Eckerson 1838
My Lord the Fox - Robert York 6932
The Queen and the Gypsy - Constance Heaven 2810
Queen of This Realm: The Story of Queen Elizabeth I -
    Jean Plaidy 5050
The Queen's Ward - Hebe Elsna 1933
The Red-Haired Brat - Joanna Dessau 1627
The Robsart Affair - Jennette Letton 3729
*Shadow in the Sun: A Novel of Elizabeth I, the Virgin
    Queen* - F.W. Kenyon 3460
So Merciful a Queen, So Cruel a Woman - Alice
    Harwood 2769
Sweet Will - Eric Malpass 4050

Duke of Alba
Captain General - John P. Stevenson 6007
The Sea Beggars - Cecelia Holland 2996

Duke of Alcudia
The Last Portrait of the Duchess of Alba - Antonio
    Larreta 3666

Duke of Bari
The Bride of Sforza - Miranda Seymour 5760
Duchess of Milan - Michael Ennis 1946

Duke of Buckingham (1454?-1483)
Crown of Roses - Valerie Anand 127
The Fate of Princes - P.C. Doherty 1673

Duke of Buckingham (1478-1521)
The Grail Murders - Michael Clynes 1135

Duke of Buckingham (1592-1628)
Call Lady Purbeck - Hilda Lewis 3745
The Cardinal and the Queen - Evelyn Anthony 159
Myself My Enemy - Jean Plaidy 5037
The Three Musketeers - Alexandre Dumas 1782
To Love a Queen - Lawrence Schoonover 5669
Unicorn Rampant - Nigel Tranter 6323
Wife to Great Buckingham - Hilda Lewis 3751
The Young and Lonely King - Jane Lane 3659

Duke of Buckingham (1628-1687)
Ballenrose - Mallory Burgess 783
Charles the King - Evelyn Anthony 160
A Health Unto His Majesty - Jean Plaidy 5019
Here Lies Our Sovereign Lord - Jean Plaidy 5021
The King Breaker - Elizabeth Linington 3797
The King's General - Daphne Du Maurier 1748
My Lord Foxe - Constance Gluyas 2443
Our Jo, or The Chronicle of a Coming Man - Kenneth
    M. Cameron 868
Peveril of the Peak - Sir Walter Scott 5703
Royal Escape - Georgette Heyer 2900

Duke of Marlborough
The Charlatan - Carter A. Vaughan 6433
Exit Lady Masham - Louis Auchincloss 230
The Glory and the Dream - F.W. Kenyon 3450
Marlborough's Unfair Lady - Lozania Prole 5197
The Mohawk Ladder - Noel B. Gerson 2377
The Queen's Favourites - Jean Plaidy 5051
The Queen's Husband - Samuel Edwards 1889
The Renegade - Donald Clayton Porter 5122
The Sachem - Donald Clayton Porter 5124

Duke of Milan
A Comedy of Murders - George Herman 2861
The Lady in the Mask - Anne Green 2564

Duke of Monmouth
A Falling Star - Pamela Belle 431
The King's Bastard - Hebe Elsna 1932
Micah Clarke - Sir Arthur Conan Doyle 1715
The Three Crowns - Jean Plaidy 5070

Duke of Wellington
The Amazing Mrs. Bonaparte - Harnett T.
    Kane 3351
The Asherwood Protegee - Mary A. Garratt 2299
A Balance of Dangers - Anthony Forrest 2184
*Colossus: A Novel about Goya and a World Gone
    Mad* - Stephen Marlowe 4093
Flashman - George MacDonald Fraser 2204
The Flight of the Eagle - Donald Thomas 6239
The Gentleman From America - Paul Benton 464
An Infamous Army - Georgette Heyer 2892
The Life and Times of Horatio Hornblower - C.
    Northcote Parkinson 4813
The Limits of Glory: A Novel of Waterloo - James
    McDonough 4265
The Masters of Bow Street - John Creasy 1423
Rage in Silence: A Novel Based on the Life of Goya -
    Donald Braider 643
Rifleman Dodd - C.S. Forester 2181
Sharpe's Battle - Bernard Cornwell 1338
Sharpe's Company - Bernard Cornwell 1339
Sharpe's Eagle - Bernard Cornwell 1341
Sharpe's Gold - Bernard Cornwell 1343
Sharpe's Honour - Bernard Cornwell 1344
Sharpe's Sword - Bernard Cornwell 1349
The Spanish Bride - Georgette Heyer 2902
Vanity Fair - William Makepeace Thackeray 6213
Waterloo - Bernard Cornwell 1350
Waterloo - Manuel Komroff 3536
Waterloo - Frederic E. Smith 5920
Whispering - Jane Aiken Hodge 2972
The Young Victoria - Tyler Whittle 6724

Dull Knife
The Last Warpath - Will Henry 2844

Dulles, John Foster
A Family Matter - James Roosevelt 5458

Dumas, fils, Alexandre
The Blood Endures - Robert Inman 3107
King of Paris - Guy Endore 1942

Dumas, pere, Alexandre
I Am Vidocq - Vincent McConnor 4225
King of Paris - Guy Endore 1942
Passionate Rebel: The Story of Hector Berlioz - F.W.
    Kenyon 3457
Rachel - Anne Powers 5153

Dumont, Gabriel
Lord of the Plains - Alfred Silver 5852

Dumont, Madeline
Lord of the Plains - Alfred Silver 5852

Duncan, Widow
A Creek Called Wounded Knee - Douglas C.
    Jones 3277

Duncan I (King of Scotland)
King Hereafter - Dorothy Dunnett 1802
Lady of Moray - Bonnie Copeland 1318

Dupin, Aurore
Hungarian Rhapsody: The Life of Franz Liszt - Jean
    Rousselot 5511
*The Questing Heart: A Romantic Novel about George
    Sand* - F.W. Kenyon 3458

Duplessis, Marie
Last Love of Camille - Frances Winwar 6832

Duprat, Antoine
The Chancellor - Lawrence Schoonover 5662

Durant, Dr. Thomas
Thunder on the Plains - Rosanne Bittner 517

Durer, Agnes
Written in the Stars: A Novel about Albrecht Durer -
 Frances Hope Fisher   2103

Durer, Albrecht
Written in the Stars: A Novel about Albrecht Durer -
 Frances Hope Fisher   2103

Duse, Eleanora
Eleanora Duse - Jean Stubbs   6095

Duston, Hannah
Gallant Warrior - Helen R. Mann   4063

Dvorak, Antonin
The Big Stick - Lawrence Alexander   82
Dvorak in Love - Josef Skvorecky   5881
Good Night, Mr. Holmes - Carole Nelson
 Douglas   1699

Dyer, Mary
Bear His Mild Yoke - Ethel White   6675
Uncharted Ways - Caroline Snedeker   5935

E

Eanes, Gil
Lord of the Kongo - Peter Forbath   2155

Earl Mountbatten of Burma
Dance on a Sinking Ship - Michael Kilian   3483

Earl of Birkenhead
High Heroic - Constantine FitzGibbon   2118

Earl of Bothwell (Francis Hepburn)
The Border Lord - Jan Westcott   6641

Earl of Bothwell (James Hepburn)
A Famine of Horses - P.F. Chisholm   1071
The Gay Galliard - Margaret Irwin   3119
Immortal Queen - Elizabeth Byrd   834
*King in Hell: A Novel of Bothwell and Mary, Queen of
 Scots* - Beverly Balin   282
The Lion and the Rose - Jane Oliver   4724
*Maid of Honour: A Novel Set in the Court of Mary,
 Queen of Scots* - Elizabeth Byrd   836
Mary of Scotland - F.W. Kenyon   3454
Mary, Queen of Scotland and the Isles - Margaret
 George   2356
No Smoke Without Fire - Alice Harwood   2767
Parcel of Rogues - Jane Lane   3656
Royal Road to Fotheringay - Jean Plaidy   5059
A Time for the Death of a King - Ann Dukthas   1777
The White Queen - Frederic Fallon   2011

Earl of Cardigan
Flashman - George MacDonald Fraser   2204
Flashman at the Charge - George MacDonald
 Fraser   2209
Pendragon: Late of Prince Albert's Own - Robert
 Trevelyan   6337

Earl of Elgin (1766-1841)
Dreams of Empire - Jeanne Mackin   3994
Lord Elgin's Lady - Theodore Vrettos   6514

Earl of Elgin (1811-1863)
Flashman and the Dragon - George MacDonald
 Fraser   2206

Earl of Elgin (1849-1917)
By Command of the Viceroy - Duncan MacNeil   4010
Charge of Cowardice - Duncan MacNeil   4011

Earl of Essex
The Bisley Boy - Christopher Hunt   3080
The Constant Star - Dorothy Norris Foote   2151
A Dead Man in Deptford - Anthony Burgess   776
Death of the Fox - George Garrett   2300
Heart of a Queen - Josephine Delves-
 Broughton   1603
I, Elizabeth - Rosalind Miles   4378
Legacy - Susan Kay   3374

The Murder in the Tower - Jean Plaidy   5035
My Enemy the Queen - Victoria Holt   3017
My Lord Essex - Olive Eckerson   1838
Nicholas Cooke: Actor, Soldier, Physician, Priest -
 Stephanie Cowell   1393
Queen of This Realm: The Story of Queen Elizabeth I -
 Jean Plaidy   5050
*Shadow in the Sun: A Novel of Elizabeth I, the Virgin
 Queen* - F.W. Kenyon   3460
The Succession: A Novel of Elizabeth and James -
 George Garrett   2302
Sweet Will - Eric Malpass   4050
Take Heed of Loving Me: A Novel about John Donne -
 Elizabeth Gray Vining   6502
Too Near the Throne - Molly Costain Haycraft   2797
Will Shakespeare: The Untold Story - John
 Mortimer   4495
You, My Brother - Philip Burton   809

Earl of Leicester
All the Queen's Men - Evelyn Anthony   157
The Bisley Boy - Christopher Hunt   3080
Elizabeth: Queen & Woman - Helen Thorpe   6279
Gay Lord Robert - Jean Plaidy   5015
The Green Salamander - Pamela Hill   2933
Heart of a Queen - Josephine Delves-
 Broughton   1603
Kenilworth - Sir Walter Scott   5700
Lady Rich - Elizabeth Boatwright Coker   1166
Legacy - Susan Kay   3374
My Dear Lover England - Pamela Bennetts   453
My Enemy the Queen - Victoria Holt   3017
My Lord Essex - Olive Eckerson   1838
My Lord the Fox - Robert York   6932
The Queen and the Gypsy - Constance Heaven   2810
Queen of This Realm: The Story of Queen Elizabeth I -
 Jean Plaidy   5050
The Queen's Ward - Hebe Elsna   1933
The Red-Haired Brat - Joanna Dessau   1627
The Robsart Affair - Jennette Letton   3729
*Shadow in the Sun: A Novel of Elizabeth I, the Virgin
 Queen* - F.W. Kenyon   3460
So Merciful a Queen, So Cruel a Woman - Alice
 Harwood   2769
Sweet Will - Eric Malpass   4050

Earl of Liverpool
The Sea Officer - Showell Styles   6105

Earl of Moray
No Smoke Without Fire - Alice Harwood   2767
*Seats of the Mighty: A Novel of James Stuart, Brother
 of Mary, Queen of Scots* - Alice Harwood   2768

Earl of Morton
Parcel of Rogues - Jane Lane   3656

Earl of Oxford
Cloak of Folly - Burke Boyce   606

Earl of Pembroke
Below the Salt - Thomas B. Costain   1362
The Devil Is Loose - Graham Shelby   5790
The Wolf at the Door - Graham Shelby   5793

Earl of Rochester
Alethea - Pamela Belle   429
Old St. Paul's - William Harrison Ainsworth   57
Royal Escape - Georgette Heyer   2900

Earl of Sandwich
Brimstone Club - F. van Wyck Mason   4147
The Vast Memory of Love - Malcolm Bosse   588

Earl of Selkirk
The Strange Brigade - John Edward Jennings   3209

Earl of Southampton (1573-1624)
The Cleopatra Boy - Eric Malpass   4048
Nicholas Cooke: Actor, Soldier, Physician, Priest -
 Stephanie Cowell   1393
Serenissima: A Novel of Venice - Erica Jong   3300
Sweet Will - Eric Malpass   4050
Will Shakespeare: The Untold Story - John
 Mortimer   4495

Earl of Southampton (1607-1667)
Feast in the Morning - Hugh Preston   5175

Earl of Warwick (Guy de Beauchamp)
Vows of the Peacock - Alice Walworth
 Graham   2513

Earl of Warwick (Richard Neville)
Crouchback - Carola Oman   4732
Crown of Roses - Valerie Anand   127
The Eye of God - C.L. Grace   2506
Fortune's Wheel - Rhoda S. Edwards   1886
The Golden Yoke: A Novel of the War of the Roses -
 Olive Eckerson   1837
I Remember Love - Mollie Hardwick   2694
The Last of the Barons - Edward Bulwer-Lytton   769
A Question of Choice - Prudence Andrew   143
Red Rose of Anjou - Jean Plaidy   5054
The Reluctant Queen: The Story of Anne of York -
 Jean Plaidy   5056
The Rose at Harvest End - Eleanor Fairburn   2003
The Sun in Splendour - Jean Plaidy   5066
The White Queen - Lesley J. Nickell   4611
The White Rose - Jan Westcott   6648

Early, Jubal
Shadow on the Valley - Kirk Mitchell   4414

Earp, Virgil
Wyatt Earp - Dan Gordon   2481

Earp, Wyatt
Bloody Season - Loren D. Estleman   1968
Confessions of Johnny Ringo - Geoff Aggeler   40
The Cowboy Conspiracy - Larry D. Names   4553
Doc Holliday's Woman - Jane Candia Coleman   1201
Little Big Man - Thomas Berger   478
The Old Colts - Glendon Swarthout   6144
Tombstone Showdown - Leslie Scott   5681
Wild Times - Brian Garfield   2291
The Winter Wolf: Wyatt Earp in Alaska - Richard
 Parry   4820
Wyatt Earp - Matt Braun   653
Wyatt Earp - Dan Gordon   2481

East, Jim
Tascosa Gun: The Story of Jim East - Gene
 Shelton   5803

Eaton, Anne
Until the Winds - Jean Clark   1089

Eaton, Peggy
The Gorgeous Hussy - Samuel Hopkins Adams   30

Eaton, Theophilus
Until the Winds - Jean Clark   1089

Eaton, William
Lydia Bailey - Kenneth Roberts   5387
Written in Sand - Josephine Case   950

Ebert, Friedrich
Karl and Rosa - Alfred Doblin   1653
A People Betrayed - Alfred Doblin   1654

Eddy, Mary Baker
Live From Golgotha - Gore Vidal   6491

Eddy, William H.
Grim Journey - Hoffman Birney   509

Edgar (King of England)
Avalon - Anya Seton   5748

Edgeworth, Maria
The Year of the French - Thomas Flanagan   2121

Edison, Thomas Alva
The Big Stick - Lawrence Alexander   82
Homeland - John Jakes   3148
Loving Little Egypt - Thomas McMahon   4288
Mount's Mistake - Lew McCreary   4229
A Peep into the 20th Century - Christopher
 Davis   1515

Edith the Fair
Harold, the Last of the Saxon Kings - Edward Bulwer-
 Lytton   767

Edward (Edward II)
Hammer of the Scots - Jean Plaidy 5018

Edward (Edward III)
The She-Wolf of France - Maurice Druon 1736

Edward, Duke of Kent
The Little Victoria - Lozania Prole 5196

Edward, Duke of Windsor
Carnal Hours - Max Allan Collins 1210
A Royal Murder - Elliott Roosevelt 5456
Wallis: The Novel - Anne Edwards 1883

Edward, Prince of Wales (1474?-1484)
The Swan and the Rose - Francis W. Leary 3697

Edward, Prince of Wales (Edward II)
The Prince of Darkness - P.C. Doherty 1675

Edward, Prince of Wales (Edward VII)
Bertie, Albert Edward, Prince of Wales - Tyler
  Whittle 6720
Bertie and the Crime of Passion - Peter
  Lovesey 3907
Bertie and the Seven Bodies - Peter Lovesey 3908
Bertie and the Tinman - Peter Lovesey 3909
Buffalo Girls - Larry McMurtry 4296
Buller's Guns - Richard Hough 3048
Contessa - Helene Mansfield 4076
Death at Daisy's Folly - Robin Paige 4775
The Duchess of Duke Street - Mollie Hardwick 2693
A Lady of Repute - Janice James 3158
Lillie - David Butler 818
Murder Makes an Entree - Amy Myers 4540
My Lady Hoyden - Jane Sheridan 5812
Oh! Where Are Bloody Mary's Earrings? - Robert
  Player 5079
Princess in Amber - Evelyn Wilde Mayerson 4205
Queen Victoria's Bomb - Ronald Clark 1094
The Queen's Husband - Jean Plaidy 5052
The Return of Moriarty - John E. Gardner 2287
The Robber Baroness - William Kendall
  Clarke 1097
A Season for Death - Ray Harrison 2743
The Second Sister - Leslie O'Grady 4701
Sergeant Verity and the Blood Royal - Francis
  Selwyn 5744
Sherlock Holmes Meets Annie Oakley - Stanley
  Shaw 5782
Victoria Victorious - Jean Plaidy 5073
The Whitechapel Horrors - Edward B. Hanna 2678
The Widow of Windsor - Jean Plaidy 5076
The Widow of Windsor - Tyler Whittle 6723

Edward, Prince of Wales (Edward VIII)
Chariots of Fire - W.J. Weatherby 6586
Dance on a Sinking Ship - Michael Kilian 3483
Edward and Mrs. Simpson - A.C.H. Smith 5916
The White Dove - Rosie Thomas 6246

Edward, the Black Prince
By Right of Arms - Robyn Carr 937
Don Pedro's Captain - Pamela Bennetts 449
The Lady Royal - Molly Costain Haycraft 2794
The Lords of Vaumartin - Cecelia Holland 2992
Passage to Pontefract - Jean Plaidy 5038
The Vow on the Heron - Jean Plaidy 5074
The White Company - Sir Arthur Conan Doyle 1716

Edward I (King of England)
Angel of Death - P.C. Doherty 1670
The Black Rose - Thomas B. Costain 1363
Braveheart - Randall Wallace 6538
The De Montfort Legacy - Pamela Bennetts 447
A Dragon for Edward - Pamela Bennetts 450
Hammer of the Scots - Jean Plaidy 5018
The King's Daughters - Molly Costain
  Haycraft 2793
The Lion of England - Eve Trevaskis 6336
The Prince of Darkness - P.C. Doherty 1675
The Reckoning - Sharon Kay Penman 4906
Robert the Bruce: The Steps to the Empty Throne -
  Nigel Tranter 6320

The Ruthless Yeomen - Valerie Anand 134
Sarum: The Novel of England - Edward
  Rutherfurd 5536
Satan in St. Mary's - P.C. Doherty 1676
Satan's Fire - P.C. Doherty 1677
The Scottish Chiefs - Jane Porter 5135
Spy in Chancery - P.C. Doherty 1680
Witness to Treason - Millie J. Ragosta 5244

Edward II (King of England)
The Follies of the King - Jean Plaidy 5014
Hammer of the Scots - Jean Plaidy 5018
Harlot Queen - Hilda Lewis 3748
Isabel the Fair - Margaret Campbell Barnes 323
The Lion and the Leopard - Mary Ellen
  Johnson 3226
The Prince of Darkness - P.C. Doherty 1675
The She-Wolf - Pamela Bennetts 456
The She-Wolf of France - Maurice Druon 1736
Vows of the Peacock - Alice Walworth
  Graham 2513

Edward III (King of England)
*Bodin, 1349: An Epic Novel of Christians and Jews in
  the Plague Years* - Roberta Kalechofsky 3322
By Right of Arms - Robyn Carr 937
The Death of a King - P.C. Doherty 1672
Harlot Queen - Hilda Lewis 3748
The King's Bishop - Candace M. Robb 5365
The Lady Chapel - Candace M. Robb 5366
The Lady Royal - Molly Costain Haycraft 2794
The Lily and the Lion - Maurice Druon 1733
Passage to Pontefract - Jean Plaidy 5038
The Peacock and the Pearl - Jennifer Lang 3661
The She-Wolf - Pamela Bennetts 456
The She-Wolf of France - Maurice Druon 1736
The Vow on the Heron - Jean Plaidy 5074

Edward IV (King of England)
The Book of Shadows - C.L. Grace 2505
Crown of Roses - Valerie Anand 127
The Dragon and the Rose - Roberta Gellis 2350
The Dragon Waiting: A Masque of History - John M.
  Ford 2165
The Eve of Saint Hyacinth - Kate Sedley 5716
Fortune's Wheel - Rhoda S. Edwards 1886
The Golden Yoke: A Novel of the War of the Roses -
  Olive Eckerson 1837
The Goldsmith's Wife - Jean Plaidy 5017
I Remember Love - Mollie Hardwick 2694
The Killing of Richard the Third - Robert
  Farrington 2020
The King's Grey Mare - Rosemary Hawley
  Jarman 3167
The Last of the Barons - Edward Bulwer-Lytton 769
The Lodestar - Pamela Belle 432
Merchant of the Ruby - Alice Harwood 2766
A Question of Choice - Prudence Andrew 143
Red Rose of Anjou - Jean Plaidy 5054
Richard III: The Last Plantagenet - Tyler
  Whittle 6722
The Rose at Harvest End - Eleanor Fairburn 2003
A Shrine of Murders - C.L. Grace 2509
The Summer Queen - Alice Walworth Graham 2512
The Sun in Splendour - Jean Plaidy 5066
The Sunne in Splendour - Sharon Kay Penman 4907
The Unicorn Hunt - Dorothy Dunnett 1811
The Warwick Heiress - Margaret Abbey 6
The White Queen - Lesley J. Nickell 4611
The White Rose - Jan Westcott 6648
The Winter Rose - Millie J. Ragosta 5243

Edward V (King of England)
Crown of Roses - Valerie Anand 127

Edward VI (King of England)
The Bisley Boy - Christopher Hunt 3080
A Crown in Darkness: A Novel about Lady Jane Grey
  - Margaret Mullally 4512
Feast in the Morning - Hugh Preston 5175
I, Elizabeth - Rosalind Miles 4378

*The Ivy Crown: A Biographical Novel of Queen
  Katherine Parr* - Mary M. Luke 3923
The Lily and the Leopards - Alice Harwood 2765
The Prince and the Pauper - Mark Twain 6373
The Queen's Grace - Jan Westcott 6646
The Red-Haired Brat - Joanna Dessau 1627
The Ten-Day Queen - Lozania Prole 5199

Edward VII (King of England)
Bertie, Albert Edward, Prince of Wales - Tyler
  Whittle 6720
Bertie and the Crime of Passion - Peter
  Lovesey 3907
Bertie and the Seven Bodies - Peter Lovesey 3908
Bertie and the Tinman - Peter Lovesey 3909
Buffalo Girls - Larry McMurtry 4296
Buller's Guns - Richard Hough 3048
Contessa - Helene Mansfield 4076
Death at Daisy's Folly - Robin Paige 4775
The Duchess of Duke Street - Mollie Hardwick 2693
Edward - Tyler Whittle 6721
Jewels - Robert Perrin 4917
The King Edward Plot - Robert Lee Hall 2658
A Lady of Repute - Janice James 3158
Lillie - David Butler 818
Love at Sunset - Jane Sheridan 5811
Mr. American - George MacDonald Fraser 2211
Murder Makes an Entree - Amy Myers 4540
My Lady Hoyden - Jane Sheridan 5812
Oh! Where Are Bloody Mary's Earrings? - Robert
  Player 5079
Princess in Amber - Evelyn Wilde Mayerson 4205
Queen Victoria's Bomb - Ronald Clark 1094
The Queen's Husband - Jean Plaidy 5052
The Return of Moriarty - John E. Gardner 2287
The Revenge of the Hound - Michael Hardwick 2688
The Robber Baroness - William Kendall
  Clarke 1097
A Season for Death - Ray Harrison 2743
The Second Sister - Leslie O'Grady 4701
Sergeant Verity and the Blood Royal - Francis
  Selwyn 5744
Sherlock Holmes Meets Annie Oakley - Stanley
  Shaw 5782
Victoria Victorious - Jean Plaidy 5073
The Whitechapel Horrors - Edward B. Hanna 2678
The Widow of Windsor - Jean Plaidy 5076
The Widow of Windsor - Tyler Whittle 6723

Edward VIII (King of England)
Carnal Hours - Max Allan Collins 1210
Chariots of Fire - W.J. Weatherby 6586
Dance on a Sinking Ship - Michael Kilian 3483
Edward and Mrs. Simpson - A.C.H. Smith 5916
The Plot to Kill Wallis Simpson: A Work of Faction -
  Graham Fisher 2104
A Royal Murder - Elliott Roosevelt 5456
That Vanderbilt Woman - Philip Van
  Rensselaer 6427
Wallis: The Novel - Anne Edwards 1883
The White Dove - Rosie Thomas 6246

Edward Longshanks
Braveheart - Randall Wallace 6538
Hammer of the Scots - Jean Plaidy 5018

Edward the Atheling
The Golden Warrior: The Story of Harold and William
  - Hope Muntz 4517

Edward the Confessor (King of England)
The Breath of Kings - Gene Farrington 2019
The Cunning of the Dove - Alfred Duggan 1765
Gildenford - Valerie Anand 130
The Golden Warrior: The Story of Harold and William
  - Hope Muntz 4517
King Hereafter - Dorothy Dunnett 1802
The Norman Pretender - Valerie Anand 132
The Saxon Tapestry - Sile Rice 5317

Edwards, Jonathan
The Indentured Heart - Gilbert Morris 4464

The Prospering - Elizabeth Speare 5954

Edyth
The Wind From Hastings - Morgan Llywelyn 3825

Einstein, Albert
A Family Matter - James Roosevelt 5458
Loving Little Egypt - Thomas McMahon 4288
Murder in the West Wing - Elliott Roosevelt 5453
Smart Moves - Stuart M. Kaminsky 3346
Till the End of Time - Allen Appel 170

Eiriksdottir, Freydis
The Ice Shirt - William T. Vollmann 6509

Eisenhower, Dwight D.
Luciano's Luck - Jack Higgins 2912
Over There - Robert Vaughan 6449

El Cid
The Infidel - Georgia Elizabeth Taylor 6182

El Greco
Color From a Light Within: A Novel Based on the Life of El Greco - Donald Braider 641
The Greek of Toledo: A Romantic Narrative of El Greco - Elizabeth Borton 586

El-Hadj Omar
The Children of Segu - Maryse Conde 1232

Elagabalus (Roman Emperor)
Family Favorites - Alfred Duggan 1766

Elazar, David
The Glory - Herman Wouk 6873

Elder, Kate
Doc Holliday's Woman - Jane Candia Coleman 1201

Eleanor of Aquitaine
Banners of Gold - Pamela Kaufman 3371
Beloved Enemy: The Passions of Eleanor of Aquitaine - Ellen Jones 3288
Champion - L. Christian Balling 285
The Courts of Love - Jean Plaidy 5010
The Courts of Love: A Romance of Medieval France - Peter Bourne 592
The Devil Is Loose - Graham Shelby 5790
Eleanor the Queen - Norah Lofts 3842
The Heart of the Lion - Jean Plaidy 5020
Here Be Dragons - Sharon Kay Penman 4904
King's Man - C.M. Edmondston 1880
The Lion of Christ - Margaret Butler 823
The Lion of England - Margaret Butler 824
The Lion of Justice - Margaret Butler 825
Lionheart!: A Novel of Richard I, King of England - Martha Rofheart 5428
The Lute Player - Norah Lofts 3852
Mortal Love: A Novel of Eleanor of Aquitaine - Linda Hutchins 3090
The Plantagenet Prelude - Jean Plaidy 5041
The Queen's Man - Sharon Kay Penman 4905
The Queen's War: A Novel of Eleanor of Aquitaine - Jeanne Mackin 3996
The Revolt of the Eaglets - Jean Plaidy 5057
A Royal Quest - Mary Lide 3777
The Swords of December - Robert York 6933
The Troubadour's Romance - Robyn Carr 940
When Christ and His Saints Slept - Sharon Kay Penman 4908
The Wolf at the Door - Graham Shelby 5793

Eleanor of Gloucester
Epitaph for Three Women - Jean Plaidy 5012

Eleanor of Provence
The Queen From Provence - Jean Plaidy 5047

Elesing, Cerdric
Conscience of the King - Alfred Duggan 1763

Elgar, Edward William
Elgar on the Journey to Hanley - Keith Alldritt 92
Gerontius - James Hamilton-Paterson 2672

Elgin, Earl of (1766-1841)
Dreams of Empire - Jeanne Mackin 3994

Lord Elgin's Lady - Theodore Vrettos 6514

Elgin, Earl of (1811-1863)
Flashman and the Dragon - George MacDonald Fraser 2206

Elgin, Earl of (1849-1917)
By Command of the Viceroy - Duncan MacNeil 4010
Charge of Cowardice - Duncan MacNeil 4011

Elijah
The Curse of Jezebel: A Novel of the Biblical Queen of Evil - Frank G. Slaughter 5884
Dara, the Cypriot - Louis Paul 4842
Jezebel - Dorothy Clarke Wilson 6802
The Painted Queen - Olga Hesky 2871

Eliot, George
The Consuming Flame: The Story of George Eliot - F.W. Kenyon 3446
Gentlemen in England - A.N. Wilson 6795
The Hoydens and Mr. Dickens - William J. Palmer 4784
Johnnie Cross - Terence de Vere White 6704

Elisabeth of Valois
The Spanish Bridegroom - Jean Plaidy 5064

Elisha
Merari - Gloria Howe Bremkamp 656

Elizabeth (Elizabeth I)
In the Shadow of the Crown - Jean Plaidy 5022

Elizabeth (Elizabeth II)
Murder at the Palace - Elliott Roosevelt 5445

Elizabeth (Empress of Russia)
Rebel Princess - Evelyn Anthony 164

Elizabeth, Grand Duchess Serge
By Command of the Viceroy - Duncan MacNeil 4010
Elizabeth and Alexandra - Antony Lambton 3616

Elizabeth, the Queen Mother
Miss Nobody - Caroline Ross 5465
The Queen and I - Sue Townsend 6306

Elizabeth I (Queen of England)
Absolute Elizabeth - Joanna Dessau 1624
All the Queen's Men - Evelyn Anthony 157
The Autobiography of Henry VIII - Margaret George 2355
The Bartholomew Fair Murders - Leonard Tourney 6297
Beauvallet - Georgette Heyer 2876
Captain Bashful - Donald Barr Chidsey 1059
Captain for Elizabeth - Jan Westcott 6643
The Captive Queen of Scots - Jean Plaidy 5008
Chase the Heart - Maggie Osborne 4760
Court of Shadows - Cynthia Morgan 4450
A Crown in Darkness: A Novel about Lady Jane Grey - Margaret Mullally 4512
Death of the Fox - George Garrett 2300
Deborah - Colette Davenat 1498
Deborah and the Many Faces of Love - Colette Davenat 1499
Deborah and the Siege of Paris - Colette Davenat 1500
Edmund Campion - Evelyn Waugh 6585
Elizabeth and the Prince of Spain - Margaret Irwin 3117
Elizabeth, Captive Princess - Margaret Irwin 3118
Elizabeth: Queen & Woman - Helen Thorpe 6279
Elizabeth, the Woman - Amanda Mae Ellis 1917
Envoy From Elizabeth - Pamela Bennetts 451
Fire over England - A.E.W. Mason 4143
The Firedrake's Eye - Patricia Finney 2095
The Flight of the Kestrel - Margaret Abbey 3
The Fourth Queen - Isabel Paterson 4827
Gay Lord Robert - Jean Plaidy 5015
Golden Admiral - F. van Wyck Mason 4150
Heart of a Queen - Josephine Delves-Broughton 1603
Her Majesty's Captain - Derek Wilson 6797
The Hounds of God - Rafael Sabatini 5551

I, Elizabeth - Rosalind Miles 4378
Immortal Queen - Elizabeth Byrd 834
In the Shadow of the Crown - Jean Plaidy 5022
The Ivy Crown: A Biographical Novel of Queen Katherine Parr - Mary M. Luke 3923
Kenilworth - Sir Walter Scott 5700
Kingdom of Gold - Susan Wiggs 6744
Lady in Waiting - Rosemary Sutcliff 6123
Lady Rich - Elizabeth Boatwright Coker 1166
Legacy - Susan Kay 3374
The Lily and the Leopards - Alice Harwood 2765
Mary, Queen of Scotland and the Isles - Margaret George 2356
The Master of Gray Trilogy - Nigel Tranter 6316
The Muscovite - Alison Macleod 4004
My Dear Lover England - Pamela Bennetts 453
My Enemy the Queen - Victoria Holt 3017
My Lord Essex - Olive Eckerson 1838
My Lord of Canterbury - Godfrey Turton 6369
My Lord the Fox - Robert York 6932
Oh! Where Are Bloody Mary's Earrings? - Robert Player 5079
Old Saxon Blood - Leonard Tourney 6302
Orlando - Virginia Woolf 6866
Physician Extraordinary: A Novel of the Life and Times of William Harvey - David Weiss 6608
The Prince and the Pauper - Mark Twain 6373
The Proud Man - Elizabeth Linington 3800
The Queen and the Gypsy - Constance Heaven 2810
Queen of This Realm: The Story of Queen Elizabeth I - Jean Plaidy 5050
The Queen's Grace - Jan Westcott 6646
The Queen's Ward - Hebe Elsna 1933
Ralegh's Fair Bess: The Story of Bess Throckmorton - Judy Turner 6365
The Red-Haired Brat - Joanna Dessau 1627
Reluctant Cavalier - Donald Barr Chidsey 1064
Roanoke Hundred - Inglis Fletcher 2138
The Robsart Affair - Jennette Letton 3729
Scapegoat for a Stuart - Kate Kirby 3504
The Scarlet Cloak - Jean Plaidy 5061
Shadow in the Sun: A Novel of Elizabeth I, the Virgin Queen - F.W. Kenyon 3460
The Sixth Wife - Jean Plaidy 5063
So Merciful a Queen, So Cruel a Woman - Alice Harwood 2769
The Spanish Bridegroom - Jean Plaidy 5064
The Strong Room - Jere Hungerford Wheelwright 6671
The Succession: A Novel of Elizabeth and James - George Garrett 2302
Sweet Will - Eric Malpass 4050
Take Heed of Loving Me: A Novel about John Donne - Elizabeth Gray Vining 6502
Tansy Taniard - Myrtle Strode-Jackson 6084
The Ten-Day Queen - Lozania Prole 5199
To Love a Queen - Lawrence Schoonover 5669
Too Near the Throne - Molly Costain Haycraft 2797
The Tower and the Dream - Jan Westcott 6647
The Tower of London - William Harrison Ainsworth 58
Towers in the Mist - Elizabeth Goudge 2495
Trust and Treason - Margaret Birkhead 506
The White Queen - Frederic Fallon 2011
Will Shakespeare: The Untold Story - John Mortimer 4495
Women of Ashdon - Valerie Anand 135
You, My Brother - Philip Burton 809
Young Bess - Margaret Irwin 3123
The Young Elizabeth - Jennette Letton 3730

Elizabeth II (Queen of England)
Di and I - Peter Lefcourt 3714
Miss Nobody - Caroline Ross 5465
Murder at the Palace - Elliott Roosevelt 5445
The Queen and I - Sue Townsend 6306

Elizabeth Fedorovna
By Command of the Viceroy - Duncan MacNeil 4010
Elizabeth and Alexandra - Antony Lambton 3616

Elizabeth of Bavaria
Imperial Waltz - William M. Abrahams　13

Elizabeth of Hungary
Elizabeth's Greetings - Rosemary Haughton　2774

Elizabeth of York
The Broken Sword - Rhoda S. Edwards　1885
The Daughter of Time - Josephine Tey　6209
Fire and Morning - Francis W. Leary　3696
The Queen's Sister - Sandra Wilson　6815
The Traitors of Bosworth - Robert Farrington　2021
Tudor Agent - Robert Farrington　2022
The Tudor Rose - Margaret Campbell Barnes　329
Uneasy Lies the Head - Jean Plaidy　5071
An Unknown Welshman - Jean Stubbs　6100

Elliot, Charles
Mandarin Gold - James Leasor　3700

Ellis, Havelock
The Crusader - Noel B. Gerson　2364
The Daughter: A Novel Based on the Life of Eleanor Marx - Judith Chernaik　1012

Elswyth
The Edge of Light - Joan Wolf　6839

Emerson, Ralph Waldo
The Jonah Man - Henry Carlisle　895
Listen for the Voices - Anne Colver　1220
The Prescott Chronicles - Albert Fried　2232
Walt Whitman's Secret - Ben Aronin　196

Emin Pasha
The Last Hero - Peter Forbath　2154

Emma of Normandy
The Breath of Kings - Gene Farrington　2019
The Cunning of the Dove - Alfred Duggan　1765

Engels, Friedrich
The Case of the Revolutionist's Daughter: Sherlock Holmes Meets Karl Marx - Lewis S. Feuer　2076

Epictetus
The Soldier and the Sage: A Novel about Akiba - Richard G. Hubler　3065

Erasmus, Desiderius
The Cloister and the Hearth - Charles Reade　5279
Flame of Fire - Jane Oliver　4722
Warm Wind, West Wind - Anne Irwin Matthew　4188

Ericsson, John
Armored Giants: A Novel of the Civil War - F. van Wyck Mason　4145
Thunder on the Chesapeake - David Divine　1650

Erik the Red
Gudrid's Saga - Constance Irwin　3115
A Viking's Daughter - John Andrews　147
West with the Vikings - Edison Marshall　4114

Eriksson, Leif
Gudrid's Saga - Constance Irwin　3115
The Ice Shirt - William T. Vollmann　6509
This Land Fulfilled - Charles Andrew Brady　636
A Viking's Daughter - John Andrews　147
West with the Vikings - Edison Marshall　4114

Esarhaddon (King of Assyria)
The Assyrian - Nicholas Guild　2610
The Blood Star - Nicholas Guild　2611

Esau
Jacob - Jean Cabries　844
Jacob: An Autobiography - Irving Fineman　2088
The Shepherd Kings - Peter Danielson　1475

Eschenbach, Wolfram von
Elizabeth's Greetings - Rosemary Haughton　2774

Eskiminzin
The Camp Grant Massacre - Elliott Arnold　191

Essex, Countess of
The King James Version - Stanley N. Stewart　6035

Essex, Earl of
The Bisley Boy - Christopher Hunt　3080
The Constant Star - Dorothy Norris Foote　2151
A Dead Man in Deptford - Anthony Burgess　776
Death of the Fox - George Garrett　2300
Heart of a Queen - Josephine Delves-Broughton　1603
I, Elizabeth - Rosalind Miles　4378
Legacy - Susan Kay　3374
The Murder in the Tower - Jean Plaidy　5035
My Enemy the Queen - Victoria Holt　3017
My Lord Essex - Olive Eckerson　1838
Nicholas Cooke: Actor, Soldier, Physician, Priest - Stephanie Cowell　1393
Queen of This Realm: The Story of Queen Elizabeth I - Jean Plaidy　5050
Shadow in the Sun: A Novel of Elizabeth I, the Virgin Queen - F.W. Kenyon　3460
The Succession: A Novel of Elizabeth and James - George Garrett　2302
Sweet Will - Eric Malpass　4050
Take Heed of Loving Me: A Novel about John Donne - Elizabeth Gray Vining　6502
Too Near the Throne - Molly Costain Haycraft　2797
Will Shakespeare: The Untold Story - John Mortimer　4495
You, My Brother - Philip Burton　809

d'Este, Alfonso
Light on Lucrezia - Jean Plaidy　5029
The Naked Sword: The Story of Lucretia Borgia - F.W. Kenyon　3456

d'Este, Beatrice
The Bride of Sforza - Miranda Seymour　5760
Duchess of Milan - Michael Ennis　1946
The Lady in the Mask - Anne Green　2564

d'Este, Ercole
The Naked Sword: The Story of Lucretia Borgia - F.W. Kenyon　3456

d'Este, Isabella
Light on Lucrezia - Jean Plaidy　5029
Private Renaissance - Maria Bellonci　436

Esther
Esther - Nathaniel Norsen Weinreb　6601
Esther: The Star and the Sceptre - Gina Andrews　146
So Great a Queen: The Story of Esther, Queen of Persia - Paul Frischauer　2235

Estienne, Robert
The Sage and the Olive - Florence Whitfield Barton　369

Ethelred I (King of Wessex)
The Right Line of Cedric - Alfred Duggan　1773

Ethelred II the Unready (King of England)
The Breath of Kings - Gene Farrington　2019

Ethelwulf (King of Wessex)
The Edge of Light - Joan Wolf　6839
The Right Line of Cedric - Alfred Duggan　1773

Etherege, Sir George
Old St. Paul's - William Harrison Ainsworth　57

Eudoxus of Kyzikos
The Golden Wind - C.L. Grace　2507

Eugenie (Empress of France)
Banners of Silk - Rosalind Laker　3592
The Big Family - Vina Delmar　1600
Death Wore a Diadem - Iona McGregor　4277
Eugenie - Hester W. Chapman　989
Madeleine - Catherine Gavin　2323
The Passion of Letty Fox - Diana Saunders　5610
A Spy for Napoleon - Baroness Emma Orczy　4746
That Spanish Woman - F.W. Kenyon　3461

Euripides
Goat Song: A Novel of Ancient Greece - Frank Yerby　6920

Goatsong - Tom Holt　3009
The Shining - Stephen Marlowe　4097

Evans, Edgar
The Birthday Boys - Beryl Bainbridge　269

Evans, Mary Ann
The Consuming Flame: The Story of George Eliot - F.W. Kenyon　3446
Gentlemen in England - A.N. Wilson　6795
The Hoydens and Mr. Dickens - William J. Palmer　4784
Johnnie Cross - Terence de Vere White　6704
The Prime Minister's Wife - Doris Leslie　3727

Exmouth, Viscount
The Sea Officer - Showell Styles　6105

Eyre, Edward John
Caribbean - James A. Michener　4365

F

Fabri, Felix
A Stolen Tongue - Sheri Holman　3002

Fairbanks, Douglas
Hollywood: A Novel of America in the 1920s - Gore Vidal　6488
Max - Howard Fast　2038

Fairfax, Anne
Rider on a White Horse - Rosemary Sutcliff　6124

Fairfax, George William
The Young Man From Mount Vernon - Arthur Stanwood Pier　4995

Fairfax, Sally
Morning of a Hero - Burke Boyce　608
The Young Man From Mount Vernon - Arthur Stanwood Pier　4995

Fairfax, Thomas
Rider on a White Horse - Rosemary Sutcliff　6124

Farinelli
The Castrato - Lawrence Goldman　2459

Farnese, Alessandro
Color From a Light Within: A Novel Based on the Life of El Greco - Donald Braider　641

Farnesse, Giulia
The Naked Sword: The Story of Lucretia Borgia - F.W. Kenyon　3456

Farragut, David
Clear for Action! - Noel B. Gerson　2362
A Heart Divided - Al Lacy　3580

Farrar, Geraldine
A Chorus of Detectives - Barbara Paul　4835
Prima Donna at Large - Barbara Paul　4838

Faulkner, William
Murder in the Executive Mansion - Elliott Roosevelt　5449
Never Cross a Vampire - Stuart M. Kaminsky　3344
Rommel and the Rebel - Lawrence Wells　6622

Faust, John
Faust - Robert Nye　4654

Fawkes, Guy
Scapegoat for a Stuart - Kate Kirby　3504

Felix, Elisa
All This, and Heaven Too - Rachel Field　2080
I, Rachel - March Cost　1361
Rachel - Anne Powers　5153

Fell, Margaret
The Peaceable Kingdom - Jan de Hartog　2763

Ferdinand, Archduke
Rakossy - Cecelia Holland　2995

Ferdinand I (King of Naples)
Duchess of Milan - Michael Ennis 1946

Ferdinand V (King of Spain)
Caribbean - James A. Michener 4365
Columbus: A Romance - Rafael Sabatini 5549
Crown of Aloes - Norah Lofts 3840
The Dogs of Paradise - Abel Posse 5141
Ferdinand and Isabella - Hermann Kesten 3474
The Gentle Fury: A Novel of Margaret of Austria -
   Paul Lewis 3758
Here Lies Margot - Pamela Hill 2935
Katharine: The Virgin Widow - Jean Plaidy 5025
The Memoirs of Christopher Columbus - Stephen
   Marlowe 4096
Mercedes of Castile - James Fenimore Cooper 1304
The Prisoner of Tordesillas - Lawrence
   Schoonover 5665
*The Queen's Cross: A Biographical Romance of
   Queen Isabella of Spain* - Lawrence
   Schoonover 5666
The Shadow of the Pomegranate - Jean Plaidy 5062
Torquemada - Howard Fast 2045

Ferguson, Sarah Margaret
Di and I - Peter Lefcourt 3714

Fermi, Enrico
Beginning the World Again - Roberta Silman 5851
A Family Matter - James Roosevelt 5458

Ferrante of Aragon
Duchess of Milan - Michael Ennis 1946

Fersen, Hans Axel von
*The Fatal Friendship: Marie Antoinette, Count Fersen
   and the Flight to Varennes* - Stanley Loomis 3895
I Thee Wed - Gilbert Wolf Gabriel 2267
King's Masque - Evan John 3220
The Queen's Confession - Victoria Holt 3019

Fetterman, W.J.
Carrington - Michael Whitney Straight 6074

Feucheres, Sophie Dawes
Sophie - Geoffrey Wagner 6519

Field, Henry M.
All This, and Heaven Too - Rachel Field 2080

Field, William
The Detective and Mr. Dickens - William J.
   Palmer 4782
The Highwayman and Mr. Dickens - William J.
   Palmer 4783
The Hoydens and Mr. Dickens - William J.
   Palmer 4784

Fielding, Henry
The Masters of Bow Street - John Creasy 1423
The Vast Memory of Love - Malcolm Bosse 588

Fielding, Sir John
Blind Justice - Bruce Alexander 76
Murder at Drury Lane - Robert Lee Hall 2659
Murder in Grub Street - Bruce Alexander 77
Watery Grave - Bruce Alexander 78

Fink, Mike
Child of the Snapping Turtle, Mike Fink - Julian Lee
   Rayford 5256
Louisiana Purchase - A.E. Hotchner 3039
The Robber Bridegroom - Eudora Welty 6623

Fisher, John
The King's Good Servant - Olive White 6696
The King's Secret Matter - Jean Plaidy 5027
Queen Anne Boleyn - Francis Hackett 2634

Fisher, John Arbuthnot
Buller's Dreadnought - Richard Hough 3047
Buller's Victory - Richard Hough 3049
Flashman and the Dragon - George MacDonald
   Fraser 2206
The Guns of Arrest - Philip McCutchan 4242
To the Honor of the Fleet - Robert H. Pilpel 5002
"Utmost Fish!" - Hugh Wray McCann 4219

Fisk, James
The Bank - Stephen Longstreet 3882
Casey - Ramona Stewart 6034
Jubilee Jim and the Wizard of Wall Street - Donald
   Porter 5112
Tassels on Her Boots - Arthur Cheney Train 6313

Fitz-Roy, Robert
Jemmy Button - Benjamin Subercaseaux 6107

Fitzgerald, F. Scott
One Last Glimpse - James Aldridge 74

Fitzgerald, Zelda
One Last Glimpse - James Aldridge 74

Fitzherbert, Maria Anne
Regency Royal - Michael Hardwick 2687
The Sugar Pavilion - Rosalind Laker 3600
Sweet Lass of Richmond Hill - Jean Plaidy 5067

Fitzpatrick, Tom
Across the Shining Mountains - Christian
   McCord 4226
The Great Adventure - Janice Holt Giles 2410

**Flahaut de la Billarderie, Auguste Charles Joseph
de**
A Rose for Virtue - Norah Lofts 3858

Flambard, Ranulf
Flambard's Confession - Marilyn Durham 1816
Godric - Frederick Buechner 763
The Lion of Justice - Jean Plaidy 5031

Flat Nose
Chiricahua - Will Henry 2839

Flaubert, Gustave
The Girl From Paris - Joan Aiken 47

Flecker, Helle
Dreaming of Samarkand - Martin Booth 576

Flecker, James Elroy
Dreaming of Samarkand - Martin Booth 576

Flegenheimer, Arthur
Billy Bathgate - E.L. Doctorow 1656
The President's Man - Elliott Roosevelt 5455

Fleming, Ian
You Bet Your Life - Stuart M. Kaminsky 3349

Fleming, Lewis
Margaret's Story - Eugenia Price 5183

Fleming, Margaret Seton
Margaret's Story - Eugenia Price 5183

Fletcher, George
Last Go Round - Ken Kesey 3473

Fletcher, John
The Player's Boy - Bryher 744

Fleury, Andre Hercule de
Louis the Well-Beloved - Jean Plaidy 5032

Flinders, Matthew
My Love Must Wait: The Story of Matthew Flinders -
   Ernestine Hill 2922

Flores Magon, Ricardo
The Prison Notebooks of Ricardo Flores Magon -
   Douglas Day 1545

Flower, Joan
The Witch and the Priest - Hilda Lewis 3754

Floyd, Charles Arthur
Pretty Boy Floyd - Larry McMurtry 4299
True Crime - Max Allan Collins 1214

Floyd, Mary
Mary of Carisbrooke - Margaret Campbell
   Barnes 327

Floyd, Pretty Boy
Pretty Boy Floyd - Larry McMurtry 4299
True Crime - Max Allan Collins 1214

Flynn, Errol
Bullet for a Star - Stuart M. Kaminsky 3331

Foch, Ferdinand
Gossip From the Forest - Thomas Keneally 3413

Ford, Gerald R.
Memories of the Ford Administration - John
   Updike 6391

Ford, Henry
Ragtime - E.L. Doctorow 1658

Ford, Robert
*The Assassination of Jesse James by the Coward
   Robert Ford* - Ron Hansen 2680

Forked Path, Hendrick
The Interpreter - Robert Moss 4499

Forrest, Catherine
The Bluestocking - David Delman 1598

Forrest, Edwin
The Bluestocking - David Delman 1598

Forrest, Nathan Bedford
And Wait for the Night - John William
   Corrington 1352
The Falling Hills - Perry Lentz 3720
Home to Tennessee - Alfred Leland Crabb 1400
In the Season of the Wild Rose - Clara Rising 5347
Lodging at the Saint Cloud - Alfred Leland
   Crabb 1403
Mockingbird Sang at Chickamauga - Alfred Leland
   Crabb 1404
None Shall Look Back - Caroline Gordon 2478
Shadowed Memories - Al Lacy 3583
Shiloh - Shelby Foote 2153
A Story of Deep Delight - Thomas McNamee 4305
Supper at the Maxwell House - Alfred Leland
   Crabb 1407
Untold Glory - Cothburn O'Neal 4739

Forsyth, George
The Stalkers - Terry C. Johnston 3259

Foster, Stephen
Banished Children of Eve - Peter Quinn 5227
Walt Whitman's Secret - Ben Aronin 196

Fouche, Joseph
Captain Cut-Throat - John Dickson Carr 908
The Hastening Wind - Edward Grierson 2591
Marianne - Juliette Benzoni 466
Marianne and the Masked Prince - Juliette
   Benzoni 469
So Great a Man - David Pilgrim 5000
The Thousand Fires - Anne Powers 5155

Fox, Charles James
Guillotine - Mark Logan 3865
Perdita's Prince - Jean Plaidy 5040
Regency Royal - Michael Hardwick 2687
Sweet Lass of Richmond Hill - Jean Plaidy 5067
The Third George - Jean Plaidy 5068
Tricolour - Mark Logan 3866
Young Pitt - A.M. Maughan 4200

Fox, George
Bear His Mild Yoke - Ethel White 6675
The Peaceable Kingdom - Jan de Hartog 2763
Richard Carvel - Winston Churchill 1081

Fox, Margaret
The Undiscovered Country - Jay Walz 6560

Francia, Jose Gaspar Rodriguez de
I, the Supreme - Augusto Antonio Roa Bastos 5353

Francis, Peregrine
The Four Hundred - Stephen Sheppard 5804

Francis Joseph I (Emperor of Austria)
The Archduke - Michael Arnold 194

Francis of Assisi
Bird of Fire: A Tale of Francis of Assisi - Helen
   Constance White 6676

Blessed Are the Meek: A Novel about St. Francis of Assisi - Zofja Kossak-Szczucka 3542
The Joyful Beggar: A Novel of St. Francis of Assisi - Louis De Wohl 1568
My Beautiful White Roses - Michael Lechner 3703
The Perfect Joy of St. Francis - Felix Timmermans 6281
Saint Francis - Nikos Kazantzakis 3385
Sing to the Sun - Lucille Borden 579

Franck, Cesar Augustine
Cesar and Augusta - Ronald Harwood 2771

Francois (Francois II)
Queen's Play - Dorothy Dunnett 1805

Francois I (King of France)
Blood Royal - Mollie Hardwick 2690
The Chancellor - Lawrence Schoonover 5662
The King's Cavalier - Samuel Shellabarger 5795

Francois II (King of France)
Mary, Queen of Scotland and the Isles - Margaret George 2356
Queen's Play - Dorothy Dunnett 1805

Frankfurter, Felix
Murder in the East Room - Elliott Roosevelt 5448
Murder in the Oval Office - Elliott Roosevelt 5450
Murder in the Red Room - Elliott Roosevelt 5451
The Passion of Sacco and Vanzetti: A New England Legend - Howard Fast 2040
The Prescott Chronicles - Albert Fried 2232

Franklin, Benjamin
The Bastard - John Jakes 3144
Benjamin Franklin and a Case of Artful Murder - Robert Lee Hall 2654
Benjamin Franklin and a Case of Christmas Murder - Robert Lee Hall 2655
Benjamin Franklin Takes the Case - Robert Lee Hall 2656
Blind Journey - Bruce Lancaster 3636
The Bonnet Laird's Daughter - Barbara Annandale 154
The Braintree Mission - Nicholas E. Wyckoff 6887
Brimstone Club - F. van Wyck Mason 4147
Buckskin Baronet - Margaret Widdemer 6734
Captain Paul - Edward Ellsberg 1930
Citizen Tom Paine - Howard Fast 2028
Clear for Action: A Novel about John Paul Jones - Clements Ripley 5344
The Devil and Ben Franklin - Theodore Mathieson 4184
Edge of Greatness - Winthrop Neilson 4575
The Fallon Blood - Reagan O'Neal 4741
The Firekeeper - Robert Moss 4498
Freedom's Dues - Robert H. Abel 9
The Gentleman From America - Polan Banks 293
The Governor's Daughter - Denton Whitson 6718
A High Wind Rising - Elsie Singmaster 5867
I'll Storm Hell - Noel B. Gerson 2374
In the Days of Poor Richard - Irving A. Bacheller 259
The Indentured Heart - Gilbert Morris 4464
Israel Potter - Herman Melville 4334
Jefferson: A Novel - Max Byrd 838
Jeremiah Martin: A Revolutionary War Novel - Robert H. Fowler 2191
The Latter Adventures of Tom Jones - Bob Coleman 1200
Let the King Beware! - Honore Morrow 4489
The Long Naked Descent into Boston - William Eastlake 1823
Murder at Drury Lane - Robert Lee Hall 2659
Murder by the Waters - Robert Lee Hall 2661
Poor Richard's Game - G.J.A. O'Toole 4766
The Prescott Chronicles - Albert Fried 2232
The Prize Master - Harvey Haislip 2642
The Rebels - John Jakes 3152
Red Morning - Ruby Frazier Frey 2230
The Revolutionary - Lawrence Schoonover 5667

The Seneca Hostage - Carter A. Vaughan 6440
Spirit Knife - Donald Clayton Porter 5128
To Spit Against the Wind - Benjamin H. Levin 3737
Two Crowns for America - Katherine Kurtz 3568

Franklin, Sir John
North-West by South - Nancy Cato 962
The Rifles - William T. Vollmann 6510

Franklin, Temple
The Gentleman From America - Polan Banks 293

Franz Ferdinand (Archduke of Austria)
The Devil's Lieutenant - Maria Fagyas 1998
The First Casualty - William Powell 5149

Franz Josef I (Emperor of Austria)
The Archduke - Michael Arnold 194
The Emperor Franz Joseph - Ottokar Janetschek 3164
Imperial Waltz - William M. Abrahams 13
Poland - James A. Michener 4373
The Time of Murder at Mayerling - Ann Dukthas 1778
Winter of the Heart - Linda J. LaRosa 3665

Frederick (Willem II)
Waterloo - Bernard Cornwell 1350

Frederick II (Holy Roman Emperor)
Antichrist: A Novel of the Emperor Frederick II - Cecelia Holland 2982
Elizabeth's Greetings - Rosemary Haughton 2774
The Emperor, the Sages and Death - Rachel Berdach 475
The Great Infidel - Joseph Jay Deiss 1582
The Joyful Beggar: A Novel of St. Francis of Assisi - Louis De Wohl 1568
The Kings of Vain Intent - Graham Shelby 5791
The Quiet Light - Louis De Wohl 1572
The Saracen Blade - Frank Yerby 6926

Frederick II (King of Prussia)
The Days of the King - Bruno Frank 2200
Rebel Princess - Evelyn Anthony 164

Frederick III (King of Prussia)
The Girl Who Was Never Queen: A Biographical Novel of Princess Charlotte of Wales - Mary Main 4037

Frederick Augustus (Duke of York)
The Duke's Mistress: The Story of Mary Ann Clarke - F.W. Kenyon 3447
Guillotine - Mark Logan 3865
Mary Anne - Daphne Du Maurier 1749
Regency Royal - Michael Hardwick 2687
The Regent's Daughter - Jean Plaidy 5055
Tricolour - Mark Logan 3866

Frederick Barbarossa (Holy Roman Emperor)
The Kings of Vain Intent - Graham Shelby 5791

Frederick Leopold (Archduke)
A Castle in Bavaria - Prince Thibaut d'Orleans 1693

Frederick the Great
The Anthem - Noel B. Gerson 2361
Consuelo - George Sand 5582
The Days of the King - Bruno Frank 2200
Rebel Princess - Evelyn Anthony 164

Fremont, Jessie Benton
Dream West - David Nevin 4587
Immortal Wife - Irving Stone 6057
Jessie: A Novel Based on the Life of Jessie Benton Fremont - Judy Alter 120

Fremont, John C.
The Bear Flag: A Novel of the Birth of California - Cecelia Holland 2983
Dream West - David Nevin 4587
Immortal Wife - Irving Stone 6057
Jessie: A Novel Based on the Life of Jessie Benton Fremont - Judy Alter 120
No Road Too Long - Hildegarde Hawthorne 2785
Rush to Destroy - L. Jay Martin 4133

The Smoky Hill - Don Coldsmith 1188
Soldier in Buckskin - Ray Hogan 2981

Freneau, Philip
The Drums of Monmouth - Emma Gelders Sterne 5998

Freneuse, Louise de
Quietly My Captain Waits - Evelyn Eaton 1829

Freud, Anna
Eating Pavlova - D.M. Thomas 6235

Freud, Sigmund
Affairs of Love - Nicola Thorne 6272
Eating Pavlova - D.M. Thomas 6235
The End of the World News - Anthony Burgess 777
Henry James' Midnight Song - Carol de Chellis Hill 2920
Jack the Ripper - Richard Gordon 2484
Minna's Story: The Secret Love of Doctor Sigmund Freud - Kathleen Daniels 1463
Monday's Child - Mollie Hardwick 2697
The Passions of the Mind - Irving Stone 6062
Ragtime - E.L. Doctorow 1658
Secret Dreams - Keith Korman 3541
The Seven-Per-Cent Solution - Nicholas Meyer 4349
When Nietzsche Wept: A Novel of Obsession - Irvin D. Yalom 6892
The White Hotel - D.M. Thomas 6237

Frick, Henry Clay
Thine Is the Glory - Samuel A. Schreiner Jr. 5672

Frobisher, Martin
Beauvallet - Georgette Heyer 2876
Frobisher's Savage - Leonard Tourney 6299

Frontenac, Comte de
The Gilded Torch - Iola Fuller 2252
Heritage of the River - Muriel Elwood 1937
The King's Messenger - Samuel Edwards 1887
The Power and the Glory - Gilbert Parker 4805
Shadows on the Rock - Willa Cather 959

Fry, Roger
The Shadow of the Moth: A Novel of Espionage with Virginia Woolf - Ellen Hawkes 2779

Fujiwara Nakamaro
The Vermilion Bridge - Shelley Mydans 4539

Fulk (Earl of Stafford)
The Earl - Cecelia Holland 2987

Fulk (King of Jerusalem)
Queen of Swords - Judith Tarr 6169

Fulton, Robert
Being Met Together - William Vaughan Wilkins 6756
The Pandora Secret - Anthony Forrest 2186

Fuseli, Henry
Angelica - Samuel A. Schreiner Jr. 5671
Vindication - Frances Sherwood 5824

G

Gable, Clark
Murder on the Yellow Brick Road - Stuart M. Kaminsky 3343
Tomorrow Is Another Day - Stuart M. Kaminsky 3348

Gabriel
Black Thunder - Arna Bontemps 574

Gadtsung (Emperor of China)
Lady Wu - Yutang Lin 3782

Gage, Thomas
Concord Bridge - Howard Horne 3035
The Gentle Rebel - Gilbert Morris 4461

Jeremiah Martin: A Revolutionary War Novel - Robert
  H. Fowler 2191
The Last Gentleman - Shirley Barker 312
Massachusetts: A Novel - Nancy Zaroulis 6956

Gaines, Myra Clark
*New Orleans Woman: A Biographical Novel of Myra
  Clark Gaines* - Harnett T. Kane 3355

Galbraith, Anne
The Border Lord - Jan Westcott 6641

Galen
Marius the Epicurean - Walter Pater 4826
Roman Nights - Ron Burns 803
The Side of the Moon - Amanda Prantera 5162

Galilei, Galileo
*Physician Extraordinary: A Novel of the Life and
  Times of William Harvey* - David Weiss 6608
The Star-Gazer - Zsolt de Harsanyi 2757

Gall
*A Road We Do Not Know: A Novel of Custer at the
  Little Bighorn* - Frederick J. Chiaventone 1057

Galla Placidia
Bury Me in Ravenna - Agnes Carr Vaughan 6432

Gallatin, Albert
River to the West: A Novel of the Astor Adventure -
  John Edward Jennings 3204

Gallerani, Cecilia
The Bride of Sforza - Miranda Seymour 5760

Galvan, Don Angel
A City for St. Francis - Evelyn Wells 6621

Galvan, Susana
A City for St. Francis - Evelyn Wells 6621

Gamaliel the Elder
The Gospel According to Gamaliel - Gerald
  Heard 2801

Gandhi, Mahatma
The Crusader - Noel B. Gerson 2364
The Last Victory - T.N. Murari 4519
Nine Hours to Rama - Stanley Wolpert 6846

Gandhi, Mohandas K.
The Crusader - Noel B. Gerson 2364
The Last Victory - T.N. Murari 4519
Nine Hours to Rama - Stanley Wolpert 6846

Gapon, Georgi
Petersburg - Emily Hanlon 2677

Garbo, Greta
The Greta Garbo Murder Case - George Baxt 385
Murder in the East Room - Elliott Roosevelt 5448

Garcia y Inigues, Calixto
The Single Star - Walter Adolphe Roberts 5394

Gardiner, Margaret
Imperial Courtesan - F.W. Kenyon 3452

Gardiner, Stephen
The King's Good Servant - Olive White 6696

Gardner, Erle Stanley
Carnal Hours - Max Allan Collins 1210

Garfield, James A.
The Chester A. Arthur Conspiracy - William
  Wiegand 6740
The Spoils of War - Thomas Fleming 2131

Garland, Judy
Murder on the Yellow Brick Road - Stuart M.
  Kaminsky 3343

Garland, Richard
Trail-Makers of the Middle Border - Hamlin
  Garland 2296

Garrett, Pat
Billy the Kid - Edwin Corle 1330
Billy the Kid: The Legend of El Chivato - Elizabeth
  Fackler 1994

City of Widows - Loren D. Estleman 1969
The Demise of Billy the Kid - Preston Lewis 3760
The Story of Pat Garrett and Billy the Kid - David
  Everitt 1987
Tascosa Gun: The Story of Jim East - Gene
  Shelton 5803

Garrick, David
Angelica - Samuel A. Schreiner Jr. 5671
Blind Justice - Bruce Alexander 76
The Bonnet Laird's Daughter - Barbara
  Annandale 154
Dr. Johnson's Dear Mistress - Winifred Carter 948
Murder at Drury Lane - Robert Lee Hall 2659
My Name Is Clary Brown - Charlotte Keppel 3466
The Savage Brood - Martha Rofheart 5430
The Upstart - Edison Marshall 4112

Gasca, Pedro de la
I, the King - Howard Clewes 1112

Gascoyne-Cecil, Robert
By Command of the Viceroy - Duncan MacNeil 4010

Gaskell, Elizabeth
Path to the Silent Country - Lynne Reid Banks 291

Gassendi, Pierre
*The Diary of William Harvey: The Imaginary Journal
  of the Physician Who Revolutionized Medicine* -
  Jean Hamburger 2667

Gates, Horatio
A Few Painted Feathers - Stephen Longstreet 3886
The Long March - Jane Barry 358
Man From Mt. Vernon - Burke Boyce 607
Proceed, Sergeant Lamb - Robert Graves 2550
Rabble in Arms - Kenneth Roberts 5390
Sergeant Lamb's America - Robert Graves 2552
*The Twisted Saber: A Biographical Novel of Benedict
  Arnold* - Philip Vail 6398

Gauguin, Paul
Depths of Glory - Irving Stone 6055
Gold of Their Bodies: A Novel about Gauguin -
  Charles Orson Gorham 2488
Lust for Life - Irving Stone 6059
Vincent: A Novel Based on the Life of Van Gogh -
  Joost Poldermans 5082

Gaveston, Piers
The Follies of the King - Jean Plaidy 5014
Harlot Queen - Hilda Lewis 3748
Isabel the Fair - Margaret Campbell Barnes 323
The Prince of Darkness - P.C. Doherty 1675
The She-Wolf - Pamela Bennetts 456
Vows of the Peacock - Alice Walworth
  Graham 2513

Genghis Khan
*The Earth Is the Lord's: A Tale of the Rise of Genghis
  Khan* - Taylor Caldwell 855
Orlok - Don Dandrea 1461
Poland - James A. Michener 4373
Ruler of the Sky: A Novel of Genghis Khan - Pamela
  Sargent 5606
*Sons of the Steppe: The Story of How the Conqueror
  Genghis Khan Was Overcome* - Hans
  Baumann 380

Gentileschi, Artemisia
Artemisia - Anna Banti 295

Geoffrey of Anjou
Beloved Enemy: The Passions of Eleanor of Aquitaine
  - Ellen Jones 3288
When Christ and His Saints Slept - Sharon Kay
  Penman 4908

Geoffrey of Villehardouin
The Seven Hills of Paradise - Rosemary
  Simpson 5859

George (George II)
Now Face to Face - Karleen Koen 3530

George (George III)
The Prince and the Quakeress - Jean Plaidy 5043

George (George IV)
Brumaire - Mark Logan 3864
Claire - Elizabeth Lyle 3931
The Duke's Mistress: The Story of Mary Ann Clarke -
  F.W. Kenyon 3447
Edward, Edward - Lolah Burford 772
*The Girl Who Was Never Queen: A Biographical
  Novel of Princess Charlotte of Wales* - Mary
  Main 4037
Goddess of the Green Room - Jean Plaidy 5016
Guillotine - Mark Logan 3865
Perdita's Prince - Jean Plaidy 5040
Regency Royal - Michael Hardwick 2687
Sweet Lass of Richmond Hill - Jean Plaidy 5067
The Third George - Jean Plaidy 5068
Tricolour - Mark Logan 3866
Yankee - Dana Fuller Ross 5495

George (George V)*
Buller's Guns - Richard Hough 3048

George, Duke of Clarence
Crown of Roses - Valerie Anand 127
The Dragon Waiting: A Masque of History - John M.
  Ford 2165
The Golden Yoke: A Novel of the War of the Roses -
  Olive Eckerson 1837
Richard III: The Last Plantagenet - Tyler
  Whittle 6722
The Rose at Harvest End - Eleanor Fairburn 2003
The Sun in Splendour - Jean Plaidy 5066

George, Duke of York (George VI)
Edward and Mrs. Simpson - A.C.H. Smith 5916

George, Prince of Wales (George IV)
Footman in Powder - Helen Ashton 216
Lord Fancy - Leslie Turner White 6686
The Scarlet Pimpernel - Baroness Emma Orczy 4745
The Smile of the Stranger - Joan Aiken 53
The Stranger From the Sea - Winston Graham 2530

George, Prince Regent (George IV)
Elyza - Clare Darcy 1486
The Flight of the Eagle - Donald Thomas 6239
Flying Colours - C.S. Forester 2173
A Love So Wild - Deborah Chester 1056
Regency Rogue - Helen Ashfield 212
The Regent's Daughter - Jean Plaidy 5055
Sanguinet's Crown - Patricia Veryan 6476
Sharpe's Regiment - Bernard Cornwell 1345
The Sugar Pavilion - Rosalind Laker 3600
Victoria in the Wings - Jean Plaidy 5072

George I (King of England)
Now Face to Face - Karleen Koen 3530
The Princess of Celle - Jean Plaidy 5045
Queen in Waiting - Jean Plaidy 5048

George II (King of England)
Admiral of Fear - Victor Suthren 6126
Caroline the Queen - Jean Plaidy 5009
Now Face to Face - Karleen Koen 3530
The Prince and the Quakeress - Jean Plaidy 5043
Queen in Waiting - Jean Plaidy 5048

George III (King of England)
The Bonnet Laird's Daughter - Barbara
  Annandale 154
Cato's War - Guy Wheeler 6655
The Duke's Mistress: The Story of Mary Ann Clarke -
  F.W. Kenyon 3447
Footman in Powder - Helen Ashton 216
Guillotine - Mark Logan 3865
The Lady From Yorktown - Eva McDonald 4260
Let the King Beware! - Honore Morrow 4489
Perdita's Prince - Jean Plaidy 5040
The Prince and the Quakeress - Jean Plaidy 5043
Regency Royal - Michael Hardwick 2687
The Regent's Daughter - Jean Plaidy 5055

Sacred and Profane: A Novel of the Life and Times of Mozart - David Weiss 6609
Sweet Lass of Richmond Hill - Jean Plaidy 5067
The Third George - Jean Plaidy 5068
Those Who Love - Irving Stone 6064

George IV (King of England)
The Abandoned Woman - Richard Condon 1235
Blackstone and the Scourge of Europe - Richard Falkirk 2007
Brumaire - Mark Logan 3864
Claire - Elizabeth Lyle 3931
The Duke's Mistress: The Story of Mary Ann Clarke - F.W. Kenyon 3447
Edward, Edward - Lolah Burford 772
Elyza - Clare Darcy 1486
The Flight of the Eagle - Donald Thomas 6239
Flying Colours - C.S. Forester 2173
Footman in Powder - Helen Ashton 216
The Girl Who Was Never Queen: A Biographical Novel of Princess Charlotte of Wales - Mary Main 4037
Goddess of the Green Room - Jean Plaidy 5016
Guillotine - Mark Logan 3865
The Little Victoria - Lozania Prole 5196
Lord Fancy - Leslie Turner White 6686
A Love So Wild - Deborah Chester 1056
Perdita's Prince - Jean Plaidy 5040
Regency Rogue - Helen Ashfield 212
Regency Royal - Michael Hardwick 2687
The Regent's Daughter - Jean Plaidy 5055
Sanguinet's Crown - Patricia Veryan 6476
The Scarlet Pimpernel - Baroness Emma Orczy 4745
Sharpe's Regiment - Bernard Cornwell 1345
The Smile of the Stranger - Joan Aiken 53
The Stranger From the Sea - Winston Graham 2530
The Sugar Pavilion - Rosalind Laker 3600
Sweet Lass of Richmond Hill - Jean Plaidy 5067
The Third George - Jean Plaidy 5068
Tricolour - Mark Logan 3866
Victoria in the Wings - Jean Plaidy 5072
Yankee - Dana Fuller Ross 5495
The Young Victoria - Tyler Whittle 6724

George V (King of England)
Attack the Lusitania! - Raymond Hitchcock 2956
The Buckingham Palace Connection - Ted Willis 6792
Buller's Dreadnought - Richard Hough 3047
Buller's Guns - Richard Hough 3048
Edward and Mrs. Simpson - A.C.H. Smith 5916
The Faraway Drums - Jon Cleary 1104
God Save the Tsar - Susanna Hoe 2976

George VI (King of England)
Edward and Mrs. Simpson - A.C.H. Smith 5916

George Augustus
Queen in Waiting - Jean Plaidy 5048

Gericault, Theodore
Holy Week - Louis Aragon 182

Geronimo
Apache Devil - Edgar Rice Burroughs 806
Chiricahua - Will Henry 2839
City of Widows - Loren D. Estleman 1969
Flashman and the Redskins - George MacDonald Fraser 2208
Geronimo - Bill Dugan 1758
Geronimo: An American Legend - Robert J. Conley 1242
Paint the Wind - Cathy Cash Spellman 5960
The Strenuous Life - Lawrence Alexander 84
Watch for Me on the Mountain - Forrest Carter 947

Ghirlandajo, Domenico
The Agony and the Ecstasy - Irving Stone 6054
The Florentine - Sandra Shulman 5840

Gideon
The Trumpet and the Sword - Peter Danielson 1479

Giguet, Guillemette
The Royal Pawn - Antonia Ridge 5327

Gilgamesh
Gilgamesh the King - Robert Silverberg 5853

Gilmore, Gary
The Executioner's Song - Norman Mailer 4036

Giocondo, Lisa Gherardini
Mona Lisa: The Woman in the Portrait - Sara Mayfield 4206
The Private Life of Mona Lisa - Pierre La Mure 3577
The Romance of Leonardo Da Vinci - Dmitri Merezhkovski 4339

Girty, James
Bridal Journey - Dale Van Every 6406

Girty, Simon
Bridal Journey - Dale Van Every 6406
Buckskin Cavalier - John Clagett 1082
Strife Before Dawn - Mary Schumann 5675
That Dark and Bloody River - Allen W. Eckert 1845
Wilderness Empire - Allen W. Eckert 1847

Gissing, George
The Trial of Elizabeth Cree: A Novel of the Limehouse Murders - Peter Ackroyd 21

Gladstone, William
Cock of the Walk - Roy Lewis 3762
Disraeli Rising - Maurice Edelman 1852
Enter the Lion: A Posthumous Memoir of Mycroft Holmes - Michael P. Hodel 2961
Flash for Freedom - George MacDonald Fraser 2203
Nevada! - Dana Fuller Ross 5481
Never Call It Loving - Dorothy Eden 1859
The Prime Minister's Wife - Doris Leslie 3727
Princess in Amber - Evelyn Wilde Mayerson 4205
Victoria Victorious - Jean Plaidy 5073
When the Emperor Dies - Mason McCann Smith 5926
The Widow of Windsor - Jean Plaidy 5076
The Widow of Windsor - Tyler Whittle 6723

Gladwin, Henry
The Conquerors - Allen W. Eckert 1839
Hatchet in the Sky - Margaret Cooper Gay 2328

Glass, Hugh
Lord Grizzly - Frederick F. Manfred 4056
Wilderness - Roger Zelazny 6957

Glendower, Owen
Glendower Country - Martha Rofheart 5427
Owen Glendower - John Cowper Powys 5159

Glover, John
Trumpet to Arms - Bruce Lancaster 3647

Go-Shirakawa (Emperor of Japan)
The Sword of Hachiman - Lynn Guest 2608

Godfrey, Sir Edmund
The Murder of Sir Edmund Godfrey - John Dickson Carr 913

Godiva, Lady
King Hereafter - Dorothy Dunnett 1802
Lady Godiva and Master Tom - Raoul Cohen Faure 2052

Godoy, Manuel de
The Last Portrait of the Duchess of Alba - Antonio Larreta 3666

Godric
Godric - Frederick Buechner 763

Godse, Natu
Nine Hours to Rama - Stanley Wolpert 6846

Godunov, Boris (Czar of Russia)
Darker Jewels - Chelsea Quinn Yarbro 6898
The Muscovite - Alison Macleod 4004
Prince of Outlaws - Alexey Tolstoy 6294

Godwin (Earl of Wessex)
The Cunning of the Dove - Alfred Duggan 1765
Gildenford - Valerie Anand 130

Godwin, Fanny
Love's Children - Judith Chernaik 1013

Godwin, Mary Wollstonecraft (1759-1797)
A Most Extraordinary Pair - Jean Detre 1628
Vindication - Frances Sherwood 5824

Godwin, Mary Wollstonecraft (1797-1851)
The Absorbing Fire: The Byron Legend - F.W. Kenyon 3445
Frankenstein Unbound - Brian Aldiss 68
The Golden Years: A Novel Based on the Life and Loves of Percy Bysshe Shelley - F.W. Kenyon 3451
My Sister, My Love - Lucille Iremonger 3111
A Single Summer with Lord B. - Derek Marlowe 4092

Godwin, William
A Most Extraordinary Pair - Jean Detre 1628
Vindication - Frances Sherwood 5824

Godwinesson, Harold
The Saxon Tapestry - Sile Rice 5317

Goebbels, Paul Joseph
The Blood Order - Jack D. Hunter 3084
Last Man to Die - Michael Dobbs 1652

Goering, Hermann
The Blood Order - Jack D. Hunter 3084
Jerusalem Interlude - Bodie Thoene 6223

Goethe, Johann Wolfgang von
Angelica - Samuel A. Schreiner Jr. 5671
The Anthem - Noel B. Gerson 2361
Sacred and Profane: A Novel of the Life and Times of Mozart - David Weiss 6609

Gogol, Nikolai
Great Black Russian - John Oliver Killens 3484

Goldman, Emma
The Prison Notebooks of Ricardo Flores Magon - Douglas Day 1545
Ragtime - E.L. Doctorow 1658

Goldoni, Carlo
Lord Vanity - Samuel Shellabarger 5796

Goldsmith, Oliver
Angelica - Samuel A. Schreiner Jr. 5671
Dr. Johnson's Dear Mistress - Winifred Carter 948

Goldwyn, Samuel
New Deal for Death - Elliott Roosevelt 5454
The Talking Pictures Murder Case - George Baxt 388

Gomer
The Valley of God - Irene Steinman Patai 4825

Gomez, Jimena
The Infidel - Georgia Elizabeth Taylor 6182

Gomez, Jose Miguel
The Single Star - Walter Adolphe Roberts 5394

Gompers, Samuel
The American - Howard Fast 2026

Goncourt, Edmond de
The Gypsy From Cadiz - Tamsin Hamilton 2670

Gondomar, Diego
Wife to Great Buckingham - Hilda Lewis 3751

Gonzaga, Francesco
Private Renaissance - Maria Bellonci 436

Goodnight, Charles
The Goodnight Trail - Ralph Compton 1227
Streets of Laredo - Larry McMurtry 4300

Gordon, Catherine
Merchant of the Ruby - Alice Harwood 2766

Gordon, Charles George
Drums of Khartoum - Chloe Gartner 2307
Flashman and the Dragon - George MacDonald Fraser 2206
The Last Encounter - Robin Maugham 4196
The Second Son of Heaven: A Novel of Nineteenth-Century China - C.Y. Lee 3707

Gordon, Eleanor Kinzie
Look to the Rose - Shirley Seifert 5728

Gordon, Lord George
Barnaby Rudge: A Tale of the Riots of Eighty - Charles Dickens 1641

Gordon, Lady Jane
The Hepburn - Jan Westcott 6645

Gordon, William
The Ninth Statue - Roseleen Milne 4410

Gordon, Willy
Look to the Rose - Shirley Seifert 5728

Gorges, Richard
Jewels - Robert Perrin 4917

Gorky, Maxim
Blood on the Snow - John Elliott 1916
Petersburg - Emily Hanlon 2677

Gormlaith
The Lion of Ireland - Morgan Llywelyn 3822
Pride of Lions - Morgan Llywelyn 3823

Gotch, Frank
Last Go Round - Ken Kesey 3473

Gottschalk, Louis Moreau
Concert Grand - Howard Breslin 665

Gould, Deborah
New Moon Rising - Eugenia Price 5185

Gould, Horace
New Moon Rising - Eugenia Price 5185

Gould, James
Lighthouse - Eugenia Price 5182

Gould, Jane Harris
Lighthouse - Eugenia Price 5182

Gould, Jay
The Bank - Stephen Longstreet 3882
Bread and Circus - Morris Renek 5303
Jubilee Jim and the Wizard of Wall Street - Donald Porter 5112
The Spoils of War - Thomas Fleming 2131
The Warriors - John Jakes 3155

Goupil, Pierre
La Salle - John Vernon 6458

Goya y Lucientes, Francisco Jose de
Colossus: A Novel about Goya and a World Gone Mad - Stephen Marlowe 4093
In the Blazing Light - Max White 6693
The Last Portrait of the Duchess of Alba - Antonio Larreta 3666
The Naked Maja - Noel B. Gerson 2378
Rage in Silence: A Novel Based on the Life of Goya - Donald Braider 643
Rasero - Francisco Rebolledo 5282

Grabeau
Amistad: The Thunder of Freedom - David Pesci 4944

Grable, Betty
Dancing in the Dark - Stuart M. Kaminsky 3334
Till the End of Time - Allen Appel 170

Graham, Caroline Agnes
Bertie and the Tinman - Peter Lovesey 3909

Graham, James
The Bride - Margaret Irwin 3116
The Proud Servant: The Story of Montrose - Margaret Irwin 3120

Graham of Claverhouse, John
Graham of Claverhouse - Constance Dodge 1665
Old Mortality - Sir Walter Scott 5702

Grania
Grania: She-King of the Irish Seas - Morgan Llywelyn 3819

Grant, James
Star of the Wilderness - Karle Wilson Baker 274

Grant, Julia Dent
Captain Grant - Shirley Seifert 5724
Ulysses: A Biographical Novel - Robert Skimin 5878

Grant, Ulysses S.
Aide to Glory - Louis Devon 1635
The Bank - Stephen Longstreet 3882
The Blue and the Gray - John Leekley 3713
Captain Grant - Shirley Seifert 5724
The Chester A. Arthur Conspiracy - William Wiegand 6740
A City Not Forsaken - Lynn Morris 4480
Colorado Ambush - Jess McCriede 4230
The Cosgrove Report - G.J.A. O'Toole 4765
The Court-Martial of George Armstrong Custer - Douglas C. Jones 3276
The Crisis - Winston Churchill 1079
Domina - Barbara Wood 6847
Flashman and the Redskins - George MacDonald Fraser 2208
Freedom - William Safire 5561
Freedom Road - Howard Fast 2031
Glory Enough for All: The Battle of the Crater - Duane Philip Schultz 5673
Grant's War - Ted Jones 3297
Gray Victory - Robert Skimin 5877
The Hallelujah Train - Bill Gulick 2614
Henry and Clara - Thomas Mallon 4042
Johnny Shiloh - James A. Rhodes 5308
Jubilee Jim and the Wizard of Wall Street - Donald Porter 5112
Kelly Blue - Peter Bowen 601
The Last Stand: A Novel about George Armstrong Custer and the Indians of the Plains - Edwin P. Hoyt 3061
Lincoln: A Novel - Gore Vidal 6490
Long Day at Shiloh - Don Bannister 294
Louisiana! - Dana Fuller Ross 5478
A Man Called Grant - Helen Todd 6285
Montana! - Dana Fuller Ross 5479
Shadowed Memories - Al Lacy 3583
Shiloh - Shelby Foote 2153
The Spoils of War - Thomas Fleming 2131
To Appomattox: Nine April Days, 1865 - Burke Davis 1512
Ulysses: A Biographical Novel - Robert Skimin 5878
Untold Glory - Cothburn O'Neal 4739
Whistling Cat - Robert W. Chambers 984
Woman of Justice - Georgia Di Donato 1639
Woman with a Sword: The Biographical Novel of Anna Ella Carroll of Maryland - Hollister Noble 4632
The Yankee From Tennessee - Noel B. Gerson 2388

Grasse, Francois Joseph Paul de
The Saintly Buccaneer - Gilbert Morris 4469
Sea Road to Yorktown - Harvey Haislip 2644

Graves, Robert
Regeneration - Pat Barker 309

Graves, William S.
Fifteen Flags - Richard Lynden Hardman 2686

Gray, Effie
John Ruskin's Wife - Eva McDonald 4259

Gray, Patrick
The Master of Gray Trilogy - Nigel Tranter 6316

Greco, El
Color From a Light Within: A Novel Based on the Life of El Greco - Donald Braider 641

The Greek of Toledo: A Romantic Narrative of El Greco - Elizabeth Borton 586

Greeley, Horace
Ain't Goin' to Glory - David Delman 1597
The Furies - John Jakes 3146

Green, Hetty
The Robber Baroness - William Kendall Clarke 1097

Greene, Catherine
Let My Name Stand Fair - Shirley Seifert 5727

Greene, Nathanael
Dawn's Early Light - Elswyth Thane 6215
A Few Painted Feathers - Stephen Longstreet 3886
I'll Storm Hell - Noel B. Gerson 2374
Let My Name Stand Fair - Shirley Seifert 5727
The Long March - Jane Barry 358
Major Andre - Anthony Bailey 265
Man From Mt. Vernon - Burke Boyce 607
Morning in America - Willard Wiener 6741
Murfy's Men - Gerald Green 2565
Phantom Fortress - Bruce Lancaster 3643
The Ragged Ones - Burke Davis 1511
Raleigh's Eden - Inglis Fletcher 2137
Stars on the Sea - F. van Wyck Mason 4161
Storm the Last Rampart - David Taylor 6180
The Swamp Fox, Francis Marion - Noel B. Gerson 2383

Greene, Robert
The Shadow of the Earth - Lee Wichelns 6731

Greenleaf, James
Portrait of a Scoundrel - Nathaniel Benchley 438

Greenough, Malcolm
Dear Lily - Malcolm W. Greenough Jr. 2575

Gregory I (Pope)
Gregory the Great - Gerhart Ellert 1913
The Unspeakables: A Tale of Lombardy - Laverne Gay 2326

Gregory VII (Pope)
Not Built with Hands - Helen Constance White 6679

Gregory XI (Pope)
Lay Siege to Heaven: A Novel of Saint Catherine of Siena - Louis De Wohl 1570

Gregory the Great
Gregory the Great - Gerhart Ellert 1913
The Unspeakables: A Tale of Lombardy - Laverne Gay 2326

Grenville, Sir Richard (16th century)
Roanoke Hundred - Inglis Fletcher 2138

Grenville, Sir Richard (17th century)
The King's General - Daphne Du Maurier 1748

Grey, Sir Edward
Lusitania - David Butler 819
To the Honor of the Fleet - Robert H. Pilpel 5002

Grey, Lady Jane
A Crown in Darkness: A Novel about Lady Jane Grey - Margaret Mullally 4512
Elizabeth, Captive Princess - Margaret Irwin 3118
Feast in the Morning - Hugh Preston 5175
The Lily and the Leopards - Alice Harwood 2765
My Lord of Canterbury - Godfrey Turton 6369
Sister to Jane: The Story of Lady Katharine Grey - Beatrice May 4202
The Sixth Wife - Jean Plaidy 5063
The Ten-Day Queen - Lozania Prole 5199
The Tower of London - William Harrison Ainsworth 58

Grey, John
The King's Grey Mare - Rosemary Hawley Jarman 3167

Grey, Lady Katharine
Sister to Jane: The Story of Lady Katharine Grey - Beatrice May 4202

So Merciful a Queen, So Cruel a Woman - Alice
    Harwood   2769

Grey Wolf
A Good Day to Die - Del Barton   368

Griffith, Arthur
High Heroic - Constantine FitzGibbon   2118
Rebels: The Irish Rising of 1916 - Peter
    DeRosa   1622

Griffith, D.W.
Poor Boy and a Long Way Home - James
    Sherburne   5806

Grimaldi, Joseph
Lovers Meeting - Mollie Hardwick   2695

Grimke, Angelina
Sisters and Brothers - Janet Stevenson   6005

Grimke, Sarah
Sisters and Brothers - Janet Stevenson   6005

Groa
King Hereafter - Dorothy Dunnett   1802

Gros, Antoine
Napoleon Symphony - Anthony Burgess   780

Groves, Leslie R.
Stallion Gate - Martin Cruz Smith   5924

Guevara, Che
The Death of Che Guevara - Jay Cantor   886

Guiccioli, Teresa
Lord of the Ladies - Joanna Dessau   1626
Teresa, or Her Demon Lover - Austin K. Gray   2554

Guillotin, Joseph Ignace
*Dr. Guillotine: The Eccentric Exploits of an Early
    Scientist* - Herbert Lom   3867

Gull, Sir William
The Women of Whitechapel and Jack the Ripper - Paul
    West   6638

Gully, James
Dr. Gully's Story - Elizabeth Jenkins   3190

Gunderode, Karoline von
No Place on Earth - Christa Wolf   6836

Guruji
Nine Hours to Rama - Stanley Wolpert   6846

Gustav III (King of Sweden)
King's Masque - Evan John   3220

Gustavus II Adolphus (King of Sweden)
People of the Book - David Stacton   5974
World and Paradise - Edgar Maas   3953

Guthrie, Woody
Joy in Mudville - Gordon McAlpine   4216

Guyasuta
The King's Orchard - Agnes Sligh Turnbull   6363

Gwynmead, Cadwaladr
The Summer of the Danes - Ellis Peters   4973

Gwynmead, Owain
The Summer of the Danes - Ellis Peters   4973

Gwynne, Nell
Catherine - Hilda Lewis   3746
Christopher Humble - Charles Burnet Judah   3310
Circle of Pearls - Rosalind Laker   3593
Here Lies Our Sovereign Lord - Jean Plaidy   5021
Mistress of the Boards - Richard Sumner   6118
Myself, Christopher Wren - David Weiss   6606
With All My Heart - Margaret Campbell Barnes   330

H

Hadassah
Esther - Nathaniel Norsen Weinreb   6601

Hadjianestis
Beyond the Aegean - Elia Kazan   3382

Hadrian (Roman Emperor)
The Crow Goddess - Patricia Finney   2094
Hadrian's Memoirs - Marguerite Yourcenar   6947
If I Forget Thee - Brenda Lesley Segal   5720
Prince of Israel - Elias Gilner   2422
The Soldier and the Sage: A Novel about Akiba -
    Richard G. Hubler   3065
The Sword and the Promise - Benjamin Siegel   5845

Hafise
The Bride of Suleiman - Aileen Crawley   1421
The Shadow of God - Aileen Crawley   1422

Hagar
Abraham and Sarah: The Long Journey - Roberta
    Kells Dorr   1694
Children of the Lion - Peter Danielson   1464
Hagar - Lois T. Henderson   2824
Hagar - Cothburn O'Neal   4737

Haig, Douglas
Over There - Thomas Fleming   2130
The Red Daniel - Duncan MacNeil   4017

Hale, Nathan
The King's Rebel - James David Horan   3030
The Long Naked Descent into Boston - William
    Eastlake   1823
The Rebel and the Turncoat - Malcolm Decker   1576
The Savage Brood - Martha Rofheart   5430
Sons of Liberty - Adam Rutledge   5540

Halifax, Marquess of
The Bracegirdle - Burris Atkins Jenkins   3189

Hall, Charles Francis
Call of the Arctic - Robert Steelman   5987

Hallandine, Louise
The Bride - Margaret Irwin   3116

Halleck, Fritz-Greene
*The Splendor Stays: An Historic Novel Based on the
    Lives of the Seven Hart Sisters of Saybrook* -
    Marguerite Allis   114

Haman
Esther - Nathaniel Norsen Weinreb   6601
*So Great a Queen: The Story of Esther, Queen of
    Persia* - Paul Frischauer   2235

Hamilcar Barca
Salammbo - Gustave Flaubert   2123

Hamilton, Alexander
Alexander Hamilton's Wife - Alice Curtis
    Desmond   1623
Burr - Gore Vidal   6485
*The Conqueror: Being the True and Romantic Story of
    Alexander Hamilton* - Gertrude Atherton   222
Eagles Where I Walk - Stephen Longstreet   3885
A Few Painted Feathers - Stephen Longstreet   3886
The Ironmaster - Anne Powers   5150
Janice Meredith - Paul Leicester Ford   2166
Kentucky Home - Betty Layman Receveur   5283
Let My Name Stand Fair - Shirley Seifert   5727
The Lure of the Falcon - Juliette Benzoni   465
Mistress of the Forge - David Taylor   6179
Monmouth - Charles Bracelen Flood   2144
Mr. Arnold - Francis Lynde   3935
Murfy's Men - Gerald Green   2565
Notorious Eliza - Basil Beyea   489
Seneca - Donald Clayton Porter   5127
Storm the Last Rampart - David Taylor   6180
The Tree of Liberty - Elizabeth Page   4773
The Unvanquished - Howard Fast   2046
Yankee - Dana Fuller Ross   5495
The Yankee Rascals - Carter A. Vaughan   6444

Hamilton, Andrew
Anna Zenger: Mother of Freedom - Kent
    Cooper   1316

Hamilton, Lady Emma
Angelica - Samuel A. Schreiner Jr.   5671
Beauty's Daughter - Mollie Hardwick   2689
The Blacksmith's Daughter - Joanna Dessau   1625
Bride of Glory - Bradda Field   2078
Brumaire - Mark Logan   3864
Emma - F.W. Kenyon   3448
The English Captain - Simon White   6700
H.M.S. Cockerel - Dewey Lambdin   3611
Lord Elgin's Lady - Theodore Vrettos   6514
Loving Emma - Nigel Foxell   2197
The Nelson Touch - Paul Lewis   3759
Shadow of a Lady - Jane Aiken Hodge   2971
Sir William - David Stacton   5977
The Sleeping Sword: A Biographical Novel - Pearl
    Frye   2244
This Other Eden - Marilyn Harris   2733
The Volcano Lover - Susan Sontag   5946

Hamilton, Henry
The Big Knives - Bruce Lancaster   3635

Hamilton, Mary
Regency Royal - Michael Hardwick   2687

Hamilton, Sir William
The Blacksmith's Daughter - Joanna Dessau   1625
Bride of Glory - Bradda Field   2078
Emma - F.W. Kenyon   3448
The English Captain - Simon White   6700
H.M.S. Cockerel - Dewey Lambdin   3611
Lord Elgin's Lady - Theodore Vrettos   6514
Loving Emma - Nigel Foxell   2197
Shadow of a Lady - Jane Aiken Hodge   2971
Sir William - David Stacton   5977
The Sleeping Sword: A Biographical Novel - Pearl
    Frye   2244
The Volcano Lover - Susan Sontag   5946

Hammett, Dashiell
The Black Mask Murderers - William F. Nolan   4635
Buried Caesars - Stuart M. Kaminsky   3332
Hammett: A Novel - Joseph N. Gores   2487
The William Powell and Myrna Loy Murder Case -
    George Baxt   390

Hampton, Wade
Heaven and Hell - John Jakes   3147

Hancock, John
Back Bay - William Martin   4138
Cardigan - Robert W. Chambers   976
Citizen Tom Paine - Howard Fast   2028
Freedom's Dues - Robert H. Abel   9
The Long Naked Descent into Boston - William
    Eastlake   1823
Portrait of a Scoundrel - Nathaniel Benchley   438
The Unvanquished - Howard Fast   2046
Yankee Doodle Dandy - Noel B. Gerson   2387

Hancock, Winfield Scott
Gods and Generals - Jeff Shaara   5765
The Killer Angels - Michael Shaara   5766
*The Last Stand: A Novel about George Armstrong
    Custer and the Indians of the Plains* - Edwin P.
    Hoyt   3061
Roman - Douglas C. Jones   3281

Hanks, Nancy
Lincoln's Mothers: A Story of Nancy and Sally Lincoln
    - Dorothy Clarke Wilson   6804
The Matrix - Maria Thompson Daviess   1509

Hanna, Mark
The Land Was Ours: A Novel of the Great Plains -
    Charles W. Bailey   266

Hannibal
Hannibal - Ross Leckie   3704
Hannibal of Carthage - Mary Dolan   1686
The Scarlet Beast - Francis Gerard   2357

Harald
The Iron Crown - Clare Barroll   354

Hardee, William Joseph
Untold Glory - Cothburn O'Neal   4739

Hardin, John Wesley
Crazy Fox Remembers - Don Preston   5174
Last Gun: The Legend of John Selman - Gene
   Shelton   5801
The Pistoleer - James Carlos Blake   536
Streets of Laredo - Larry McMurtry   4300

Harding, Warren G.
Hollywood: A Novel of America in the 1920s - Gore
   Vidal   6488

Hariot, Thomas
Nicholas Cooke: Actor, Soldier, Physician, Priest -
   Stephanie Cowell   1393
Roanoke Hundred - Inglis Fletcher   2138

Harley, Robert
Exit Lady Masham - Louis Auchincloss   230
The Queen's Favourites - Jean Plaidy   5051

Harlow, Jean
New Deal for Death - Elliott Roosevelt   5454
The William Powell and Myrna Loy Murder Case -
   George Baxt   390

Harold (Harold II)
The Cunning of the Dove - Alfred Duggan   1765

Harold I (King of England)
Gildenford - Valerie Anand   130
King Hereafter - Dorothy Dunnett   1802

Harold II (King of England)
The Bastard King - Jean Plaidy   5004
The Conqueror - Georgette Heyer   2881
The Conqueror's Wife - Noel B. Gerson   2363
The Cunning of the Dove - Alfred Duggan   1765
The Golden Warrior: The Story of Harold and William
   - Hope Muntz   4517
Harold, the Last of the Saxon Kings - Edward Bulwer-
   Lytton   767
Harold Was My King - Hilda Lewis   3749
The Norman Pretender - Valerie Anand   132
The Saxon Tapestry - Sile Rice   5317
The Wind From Hastings - Morgan Llywelyn   3825

Harold III (King of Norway)
The Iron Crown - Clare Barroll   354

Harold Harefoot
Gildenford - Valerie Anand   130
King Hereafter - Dorothy Dunnett   1802

Harris, Frank
The God of Mirrors - Robert Reilly   5293
The West End Horror - Nicholas Meyer   4350

Harris, Honor
The King's General - Daphne Du Maurier   1748

Harris, Ira
Henry and Clara - Thomas Mallon   4042

Harrison, William Henry
Gateway to Empire - Allen W. Eckert   1842
My Blood and My Treasure - Mary Schumann   5674
Panther in the Sky - James Alexander Thom   6234
Red Stick - Donald Clayton Porter   5121
The Seekers - John Jakes   3153
A Sorrow in Our Heart - Allen W. Eckert   1844
Tamarack Tree - Howard Breslin   670
To Keep Us Free - Marguerite Allis   115
War Clouds - Donald Clayton Porter   5131

Hart, Ann
*The Splendor Stays: An Historic Novel Based on the
   Lives of the Seven Hart Sisters of Saybrook* -
   Marguerite Allis   114

Hart, Elisha
*The Splendor Stays: An Historic Novel Based on the
   Lives of the Seven Hart Sisters of Saybrook* -
   Marguerite Allis   114

Hart, Emily
Beauty's Daughter - Mollie Hardwick   2689

Hart, Jeanette
*The Splendor Stays: An Historic Novel Based on the
   Lives of the Seven Hart Sisters of Saybrook* -
   Marguerite Allis   114

Hart, Mary
*The Splendor Stays: An Historic Novel Based on the
   Lives of the Seven Hart Sisters of Saybrook* -
   Marguerite Allis   114

Hartburg, Aurora
A Castle in Bavaria - Prince Thibaut d'Orleans   1693

Hartburg, Gottfried von
A Castle in Bavaria - Prince Thibaut d'Orleans   1693

Hartburg, Ruprecht
A Castle in Bavaria - Prince Thibaut d'Orleans   1693

Harte, Bret
The Mississippi Run - Paul Darcy Boles   565

Harun al Raschid
The Tyrant of Bagdad - Glenn Pierce   4996

Harvey, William
*The Diary of William Harvey: The Imaginary Journal
   of the Physician Who Revolutionized Medicine* -
   Jean Hamburger   2667
*Physician Extraordinary: A Novel of the Life and
   Times of William Harvey* - David Weiss   6608
The Physician of London - Stephanie Cowell   1394

Haryett, Elizabeth Ann
Imperial Courtesan - F.W. Kenyon   3452

Hasekura, Rokuemon
The Samurai - Shusaku Endo   1941

Hastings, Warren
Master of Bengal: A Novel of Robert Clive of India -
   Norman Partington   4821

Hastings, Lord William
The Last of the Barons - Edward Bulwer-Lytton   769

Hathaway, Anne
The Best House in Stratford - Edward Fisher   2100
The Cleopatra Boy - Eric Malpass   4048
A House of Women - Eric Malpass   4049
Mrs. Shakespeare: The Complete Works - Robert
   Nye   4656
Nothing Like the Sun - Anthony Burgess   781
Shakespeare & Son - Edward Fisher   2102
Sweet Will - Eric Malpass   4050
Two Loves Have I - Clara Longworth de
   Chambrun   985
Will Shakespeare: The Untold Story - John
   Mortimer   4495

Hatshepsut (Queen of Egypt)
Child of the Morning - Pauline Gedge   2343
The Golden Balance - Arthur Dana Hall   2646
King and Goddess - Judith Tarr   6166
Pharaoh - Eloise Jarvis McGraw   4276

Hatton, Christopher
*Shadow in the Sun: A Novel of Elizabeth I, the Virgin
   Queen* - F.W. Kenyon   3460
Trust and Treason - Margaret Birkhead   506

Haughery, Margaret
Angel of the Delta - Edward Francis Murphy   4521

Hawthorne, Nathaniel
Memories of the Ford Administration - John
   Updike   6391

Hay, John
Empire: A Novel - Gore Vidal   6487
*Refinements of Love: A Novel about Clover and Henry
   Adams* - Sarah Booth Conroy   1259

Haydn, Franz Joseph
Consuelo - George Sand   5582
*Sacred and Profane: A Novel of the Life and Times of
   Mozart* - David Weiss   6609

Hayes, Rutherford B.
The Spoils of War - Thomas Fleming   2131

Hays, John Coffee
Captain Jack - Gene Shelton   5800

Haywood, William "Big Bill"
Bisbee '17 - Robert Houston   3056
Castle Garden - Bill Albert   63

Hayworth, Rita
Dancing in the Dark - Stuart M. Kaminsky   3334

Hearn, Lafcadio
The Blue Dragon - Diana Brown   716
*Mortal Hunger: A Novel Based on the Life of Lafcadio
   Hearn* - Harry E. Wedeck   6594

Hearst, William Randolph
The Americans - John Jakes   3143
California Gold - John Jakes   3145
Empire: A Novel - Gore Vidal   6487
Hollywood: A Novel of America in the 1920s - Gore
   Vidal   6488
Loving Little Egypt - Thomas McMahon   4288
Murder at San Simeon - Robert Lee Hall   2660
The Rough Rider - Gilbert Morris   4468
The Seventh Bullet - Daniel D. Victor   6483
The Spoils of War - Thomas Fleming   2131
That Vanderbilt Woman - Philip Van
   Rensselaer   6427
Yellow: A Novel - Daniel Lynch   3932

Hedh
Isle of Glory - Jane Oliver   4723

Heenan, John Carmel
Bread and Circus - Morris Renek   5303

Helena (4th century)
Julian - Gore Vidal   6489

Helena (c. 248-c. 328)
The Living Wood - Louis De Wohl   1571

Heliogabalus (Roman Emperor)
Family Favorites - Alfred Duggan   1766

Hellman, Lillian
The William Powell and Myrna Loy Murder Case -
   George Baxt   390

Heloise
Death Comes as Epiphany - Sharan Newman   4598
The Devil's Door - Sharan Newman   4599
Peter Abelard: A Novel - Helen Waddell   6517
*Stealing Heaven: The Love Story of Heloise and
   Abelard* - Marion Meade   4317

Heminges, John
Nicholas Cooke: Actor, Soldier, Physician, Priest -
   Stephanie Cowell   1393

Hemings, Sally
Arc d'X - Steve Erickson   1953
The President's Daughter - Barbara Chase-
   Riboud   1005
Sally Hemings - Barbara Chase-Riboud   1006

Hemingway, Ernest
High Midnight - Stuart M. Kaminsky   3339
Murder in the Executive Mansion - Elliott
   Roosevelt   5449
One Last Glimpse - James Aldridge   74
Papa and Fidel - Karl Alexander   79
The Veracruz Blues - Mark Winegardner   6821
Walter Winchell: A Novel - Michael Herr   2863

Henderson, Edmund
The Hungry Goblin: A Victorian Detective Novel -
   John Dickson Carr   911

Henri, Robert
Son of the Gamblin' Man: The Youth of an Artist -
   Mari Sandoz   5593

Henri I (King of France)
*Fortune's Knave: The Making of William the
   Conqueror* - Mary Lide   3774

Henri II (King of France)
Courtesan - Diane Haeger   2635

Immortal Queen - Elizabeth Byrd   834
The Italian Woman - Jean Plaidy   5024
Madame Serpent - Jean Plaidy   5033
Queen's Play - Dorothy Dunnett   1805
Royal Road to Fotheringay - Jean Plaidy   5059
Vagabond Prophet - Allene Symons   6149

Henri III (King of France)
Les Quarant Cinq - Alexandre Dumas   1779
Queen Margot - Alexandre Dumas   1780
The Scarlet Cloak - Jean Plaidy   5061

Henri IV (King of France)
The Anthem - Noel B. Gerson   2361
Deborah and the Siege of Paris - Colette
   Davenat   1500
Evergreen Gallant - Jean Plaidy   5013
The Faith and the Flame - June Dimmit
   Houston   3054
Henry, King of France - Heinrich Mann   4061
The Italian Woman - Jean Plaidy   5024
Queen Jezebel - Jean Plaidy   5049
Queen Margot - Alexandre Dumas   1780

Henri de Guise
Queen Jezebel - Jean Plaidy   5049

Henri of Anjou
Queen Margot - Alexandre Dumas   1780

Henri of Navarre
The Anthem - Noel B. Gerson   2361
Deborah and the Siege of Paris - Colette
   Davenat   1500
Evergreen Gallant - Jean Plaidy   5013
The Faith and the Flame - June Dimmit
   Houston   3054
The Italian Woman - Jean Plaidy   5024
Queen Jezebel - Jean Plaidy   5049
Queen Margot - Alexandre Dumas   1780
Young Henry of Navarre - Heinrich Mann   4062

Henrietta Anne of England
The Wandering Prince - Jean Plaidy   5075

Henrietta-Maria
Charles the King - Evelyn Anthony   160
Lady on the Coin - Margaret Campbell Barnes   326
My Lord Foxe - Constance Gluyas   2443
Myself My Enemy - Jean Plaidy   5037
Peveril of the Peak - Sir Walter Scott   5703
Twenty Years After - Alexandre Dumas   1783
Wife to Great Buckingham - Hilda Lewis   3751
The Young and Lonely King - Jane Lane   3659

Henry (Henry I)
The Bastard King - Jean Plaidy   5004
The Paladin - George Shipway   5830

Henry (Henry V)
The Star of Lancaster - Jean Plaidy   5065

Henry (Henry VIII)
Katharine: The Virgin Widow - Jean Plaidy   5025
The Thistle and the Rose - Jean Plaidy   5069
Uneasy Lies the Head - Jean Plaidy   5071

Henry, O.
The Heart of O. Henry - Dale Kramer   3550

Henry, Patrick
Clear for Action: A Novel about John Paul Jones -
   Clements Ripley   5344
Give Me Liberty - Noel B. Gerson   2369
Give Me Liberty: The Story of an Innocent Man - John
   Erskine   1956
Mistress Nancy - Barbara Bentley   460
The Tree of Liberty - Elizabeth Page   4773

Henry I (King of England)
The Bastard King - Jean Plaidy   5004
Death of the Red King - Pamela Bennetts   448
The Fatal Crown - Ellen Jones   3289
The Lion of Justice - Jean Plaidy   5031
The Paladin - George Shipway   5830
The Passionate Enemies - Jean Plaidy   5039

Henry II (Holy Roman Emperor)
Not Built with Hands - Helen Constance White   6679

Henry II (King of England)
Ann of Cambray - Mary Lide   3772
Beloved Enemy: The Passions of Eleanor of Aquitaine
   - Ellen Jones   3288
Champion - L. Christian Balling   285
The Courts of Love - Jean Plaidy   5010
The Courts of Love: A Romance of Medieval France -
   Peter Bourne   592
The Devil Is Loose - Graham Shelby   5790
The Earl - Cecelia Holland   2987
Eleanor the Queen - Norah Lofts   3842
Fitzempress' Law - Diana Norman   4644
King's Man - C.M. Edmondston   1880
Knight's Honor - Roberta Gellis   2351
The Lion of Christ - Margaret Butler   823
The Lion of England - Margaret Butler   824
The Lion of Justice - Margaret Butler   825
Lionheart!: A Novel of Richard I, King of England -
   Martha Rofheart   5428
My Life for My Sheep - Alfred Duggan   1772
Ordeal by Silence - Prudence Andrew   142
The Plantagenet Prelude - Jean Plaidy   5041
The Queen's War: A Novel of Eleanor of Aquitaine -
   Jeanne Mackin   3996
The Rain Maiden - Jill M. Phillips   4985
The Revolt of the Eaglets - Jean Plaidy   5057
A Royal Quest - Mary Lide   3777
The Swords of December - Robert York   6933
Thomas: A Novel of the Life, Passions, and Miracles
   of Becket - Shelley Mydans   4538
To Keep This Oath - Hebe Weenolsen   6597
The Troubadour's Romance - Robyn Carr   940
When Christ and His Saints Slept - Sharon Kay
   Penman   4908

Henry III (King of England)
Alexander the Glorious - Jane Oliver   4719
The Battle of the Queens - Jean Plaidy   5005
The De Montfort Legacy - Pamela Bennetts   447
Doctor Mirabilis - James Blish   550
Falconer's Judgement - Ian Morson   4494
Falls the Shadow - Sharon Kay Penman   4903
The Marriage of Meggotta - Edith Pargeter   4799
The Queen From Provence - Jean Plaidy   5047
Shield of Honor - Alice Walworth Graham   2511
The White Cutter - David Pownall   5158

Henry IV (King of Castile)
The Dogs of Paradise - Abel Posse   5141

Henry IV (King of England)
The Bloody Field - Edith Pargeter   4795
The Gentle Falcon - Hilda Lewis   3747
Glendower Country - Martha Rofheart   5427
Good King Harry - Denise Giardina   2393
Harry of Monmouth - A.M. Maughan   4199
In a Dark Wood Wandering - Hella S. Haasse   2631
The Lords of Lancaster - Pamela Bennetts   452
My Lord John - Georgette Heyer   2895
Passage to Pontefract - Jean Plaidy   5038
The Peacock and the Pearl - Jennifer Lang   3661
Royal Sword at Agincourt - Pamela Bennetts   455
Simon the Coldheart - Georgette Heyer   2901
The Star of Lancaster - Jean Plaidy   5065
Trumpet at the Gate - Jan Widgery   6739
The Whyte Harte - P.C. Doherty   1681
Within the Hollow Crown - Margaret Campbell
   Barnes   331
Young Henry of Navarre - Heinrich Mann   4062

Henry V (King of England)
The Bloody Field - Edith Pargeter   4795
Crippled Splendour - Evan John   3219
Crown in Candlelight - Rosemary Hawley
   Jarman   3166
Falstaff - Robert Nye   4653
Fortune Made His Sword - Martha Rofheart   5426
The Gentle Falcon - Hilda Lewis   3747
Glendower Country - Martha Rofheart   5427

Good King Harry - Denise Giardina   2393
Harry of Monmouth - A.M. Maughan   4199
The Hooded Falcon - Prudence Andrew   140
In a Dark Wood Wandering - Hella S. Haasse   2631
The Lily and the Leopard - Susan Wiggs   6745
My Lord John - Georgette Heyer   2895
The Queen's Secret - Jean Plaidy   5053
The Royal Pawn - Antonia Ridge   5327
Royal Sword at Agincourt - Pamela Bennetts   455
Simon the Coldheart - Georgette Heyer   2901
The Star of Lancaster - Jean Plaidy   5065
Walk with Peril - Dorothy V.S. Jackson   3132
Wife to Henry V - Hilda Lewis   3752

Henry VI (Holy Roman Emperor)
Banners of Gold - Pamela Kaufman   3371

Henry VI (King of England)
Crown in Candlelight - Rosemary Hawley
   Jarman   3166
Epitaph for Three Women - Jean Plaidy   5012
The Last of the Barons - Edward Bulwer-Lytton   769
The Queen's Secret - Jean Plaidy   5053
Red Rose of Anjou - Jean Plaidy   5054
The Royal Pawn - Antonia Ridge   5327
The White Rose - Jan Westcott   6648

Henry VII (Holy Roman Emperor)
The Golden Knight - George Challis   971

Henry VII (King of England)
The Courts of Illusion - Rosemary Hawley
   Jarman   3165
The Dragon and the Rose - Roberta Gellis   2350
Katharine: The Virgin Widow - Jean Plaidy   5025
The King's Grey Mare - Rosemary Hawley
   Jarman   3167
The Lady Cicely - Sandra Wilson   6813
The Lodestar - Pamela Belle   432
Merchant of the Ruby - Alice Harwood   2766
The Queen's Sister - Sandra Wilson   6815
The Thistle and the Rose - Jean Plaidy   5069
The Traitors of Bosworth - Robert Farrington   2021
Tudor Agent - Robert Farrington   2022
The Tudor Rose - Margaret Campbell Barnes   329
Uneasy Lies the Head - Jean Plaidy   5071
An Unknown Welshman - Jean Stubbs   6100
The Wrong Plantagenet - Marian Palmer   4781

Henry VIII (King of England)
Anne Boleyn - Evelyn Anthony   158
Anne of the Thousand Days - Edward Fenton   2059
The Autobiography of Henry VIII - Margaret
   George   2355
The Blanket of the Dark - John Buchan   749
Blood Royal - Mollie Hardwick   2690
Brief Gaudy Hour - Margaret Campbell Barnes   322
A Brood of Vipers - Michael Clynes   1133
Circle in the Water - Susan Wiggs   6742
Command of the King - Mary Lide   3773
The Concubine - Norah Lofts   3839
A Crown in Darkness: A Novel about Lady Jane Grey
   - Margaret Mullally   4512
Feast in the Morning - Hugh Preston   5175
The Fifth Queen - Ford Madox Ford   2161
Flame of Fire - Jane Oliver   4722
The Grail Murders - Michael Clynes   1135
The Green Salamander - Pamela Hill   2933
The Heir of Allington - Philippa Wiat   6727
Henry VIII and His Six Wives - Maureen
   Peters   4975
Her Royal Destiny - Carol Maxwell Eady   1820
Here Comes the King - Philip Lindsay   3792
The Heretic - Alison Macleod   4002
The Hireling - Alison Macleod   4003
I Am Mary Tudor - Hilda Lewis   3750
I, Elizabeth - Rosalind Miles   4378
In the Shadow of the Crown - Jean Plaidy   5022
*The Ivy Crown: A Biographical Novel of Queen
   Katherine Parr* - Mary M. Luke   3923
Katharine: The Virgin Widow - Jean Plaidy   5025
Katheryn, the Wanton Queen - Maureen Peters   4976

Kathryn: In the Court of Six Queens - Anne Merton Abbey   1
The King's Achievement - Robert Hugh Benson   459
King's Fool - Margaret Campbell Barnes   325
The King's Good Servant - Olive White   6696
The King's Pleasure - Norah Lofts   3847
The King's Pleasure - Jean Plaidy   5026
The King's Secret Matter - Jean Plaidy   5027
The Knight and the Dove - Lori Wick   6732
The Lady in the Tower - Jean Plaidy   5028
The Lily and the Leopards - Alice Harwood   2765
The Man on a Donkey - H.F.M. Prescott   5170
Mistress Anne - Carolly Erickson   1952
Murder Most Royal - Jean Plaidy   5036
My Lady Glamis - Pamela Hill   2940
My Lady of Cleves - Margaret Campbell Barnes   328
My Lord of Canterbury - Godfrey Turton   6369
The Poisoned Chalice - Michael Clynes   1136
The Prince and the Pauper - Mark Twain   6373
Queen Anne Boleyn - Francis Hackett   2634
Queen of This Realm: The Story of Queen Elizabeth I - Jean Plaidy   5050
The Queen's Grace - Jan Westcott   6646
The Red-Haired Brat - Joanna Dessau   1627
The Reluctant Queen - Molly Costain Haycraft   2796
The Rose Without a Thorn - Jean Plaidy   5058
Royal Nonesuch: A Tudor Tapestry - Beatrice White   6674
St. Thomas's Eve - Jean Plaidy   5060
The Serpent Garden - Judith Merkle Riley   5336
The Shadow of the Pomegranate - Jean Plaidy   5062
The Sixth Wife - Jean Plaidy   5063
Stage of Fools - Charles Andrew Brady   635
The Sword of Truth - Gilbert Morris   4472
The Thistle and the Rose - Jean Plaidy   5069
The Tudor Rose - Margaret Campbell Barnes   329
Uneasy Lies the Head - Jean Plaidy   5071
The White Rose Murders - Michael Clynes   1137
Windsor Castle - William Harrison Ainsworth   59
The Wise Virgin - Hebe Elsna   1934
Women of Ashdon - Valerie Anand   135

Henry Beauclerc
Death of the Red King - Pamela Bennetts   448

Henry Hotspur
The Bloody Field - Edith Pargeter   4795
Falstaff - Robert Nye   4653
Harry of Monmouth - A.M. Maughan   4199
The Star of Lancaster - Jean Plaidy   5065
The Traitors of Bosworth - Robert Farrington   2021

Henry of Anjou
Knight's Honor - Roberta Gellis   2351

Henry of Battenburg
Princess in Amber - Evelyn Wilde Mayerson   4205

Henry of Monmouth
Harry of Monmouth - A.M. Maughan   4199

Henry of Wales
Di and I - Peter Lefcourt   3714

Henry the Navigator
The Mapmaker: A Novel of the Days of Prince Henry, the Navigator - Frank G. Slaughter   5893

Hepburn, Francis
The Border Lord - Jan Westcott   6641

Hepburn, James
A Famine of Horses - P.F. Chisholm   1071
The Gay Galliard - Margaret Irwin   3119
Immortal Queen - Elizabeth Byrd   834
King in Hell: A Novel of Bothwell and Mary, Queen of Scots - Beverly Balin   282
The Lion and the Rose - Jane Oliver   4724
Maid of Honour: A Novel Set in the Court of Mary, Queen of Scots - Elizabeth Byrd   836
Mary of Scotland - F.W. Kenyon   3454
Mary, Queen of Scotland and the Isles - Margaret George   2356
No Smoke Without Fire - Alice Harwood   2767

Parcel of Rogues - Jane Lane   3656
Royal Road to Fotheringay - Jean Plaidy   5059
A Time for the Death of a King - Ann Dukthas   1777
The White Queen - Frederic Fallon   2011

Hepburn, Patrick
The Hepburn - Jan Westcott   6645

Hephaestion
Alexander in Babylon - Jakob Wassermann   6576
Fire From Heaven - Mary Renault   5296
The Persian Boy - Mary Renault   5301

Herbert, Sidney
Pendragon: Late of Prince Albert's Own - Robert Trevelyan   6337

Hereward the Wake
The Disputed Crown - Valerie Anand   128
Harold Was My King - Hilda Lewis   3749
Hereward the Wake - Charles Kingsley   3497
The Last Englishman: The Story of Hereward the Wake - Hebe Weenolsen   6596
The Saxon Tapestry - Sile Rice   5317

Herleve
Fortune's Knave: The Making of William the Conqueror - Mary Lide   3774

Herod I (King of Judea)
King Jesus - Robert Graves   2549
A Love Divine - Alexandra Ripley   5340
Man of Nazareth - Anthony Burgess   779
The Source - James A. Michener   4374

Herod Agrippa I (King of Judea)
Agrippa's Daughter - Howard Fast   2025
I, Claudius - Robert Graves   2547
The Kingdom of the Wicked - Anthony Burgess   778
Pontius Pilate: A Biographical Novel - Paul L. Maier   4034
The Sins of Herod: A Novel of Rome and the Early Church - Frank G. Slaughter   5900

Herod Agrippa II (King of Judea)
Claudius the God - Robert Graves   2543
The Glorious Folly: A Novel of the Time of St. Paul - Louis De Wohl   1565
Man on Fire: A Novel on the Life of St. Paul - LeGette Blythe   558

Herod Antipas (Tetrarch of Galilee)
The Big Fisherman - Lloyd C. Douglas   1702
Brothers of Vengeance - LeGette Blythe   556
The Eighth Veil - Ellis Kadison   3320
The Good Tidings - William Sidney   5843
Hear Me, Pilate! - LeGette Blythe   557
Justus - Arthur L. Lapham   3663
The Last Temptation of Christ - Nikos Kazantzakis   3384
Pontius Pilate: A Biographical Novel - Paul L. Maier   4034
The Sins of Herod: A Novel of Rome and the Early Church - Frank G. Slaughter   5900

Herod the Great
King Jesus - Robert Graves   2549
A Love Divine - Alexandra Ripley   5340
Man of Nazareth - Anthony Burgess   779
The Source - James A. Michener   4374

Herodias
The Good Tidings - William Sidney   5843

Herold, David
Lincoln: A Novel - Gore Vidal   6490

Herrick, Robert
The Shadow Flies - Rose Macaulay   3956

Herzl, Theodor
Herzl the King - Norman Kotker   3547

Hess, Charles
The Girl Who Was Never Queen: A Biographical Novel of Princess Charlotte of Wales - Mary Main   4037

Hess, Rudolf
Shadow of the Wolf - James Barwick   371

Heydrich, Reinhard
The Hangman's Crusade - James Barwick   370
The Last Innocent Hour - Margot Abbott   8

Hickok, James Butler
Aces and Eights: A Novel of the Legend of Wild Bill Hickok - Loren D. Estleman   1967
Black Sun - Terry C. Johnston   3242
Crazy Fox Remembers - Don Preston   5174
Deadwood - Pete Dexter   1638
Elkhorn Tavern - Douglas C. Jones   3278
Flashman and the Redskins - George MacDonald Fraser   2208
The Lawless - John Jakes   3149
Little Big Man - Thomas Berger   478
The Pistoleer - James Carlos Blake   536
Shaggy Legion - Hal George Evarts   1986
Western: A Saga of the Great Plains - Frank Yerby   6930
Wild Times - Brian Garfield   2291

Hickok, Wild Bill
Aces and Eights: A Novel of the Legend of Wild Bill Hickok - Loren D. Estleman   1967
Black Sun - Terry C. Johnston   3242
Crazy Fox Remembers - Don Preston   5174
Deadwood - Pete Dexter   1638
Elkhorn Tavern - Douglas C. Jones   3278
Flashman and the Redskins - George MacDonald Fraser   2208
The Lawless - John Jakes   3149
Little Big Man - Thomas Berger   478
The Pistoleer - James Carlos Blake   536
Shaggy Legion - Hal George Evarts   1986
Western: A Saga of the Great Plains - Frank Yerby   6930
Wild Times - Brian Garfield   2291

Hidalgo y Costilla, Miguel
The Cry of Dolores - Herbert Gorman   2492

Higginson, Thomas Wentworth
Hacey Miller - James Sherburne   5805
I Never Came to You in White - Judith Farr   2014
The Way to Fort Pillow - James Sherburne   5807

Hikenai
The Lion of England - Margaret Butler   824

Hildegard of Bingen
The Journal of Hildegard of Bingen - Barbara Lachman   3578

Hill, Abigail
The Queen's Favourites - Jean Plaidy   5051

Hill, A.P.
The Court Martial of Robert E. Lee - Douglas Savage   5617
Gettysburg: Crisis of Command - Harry Albright   65

Hill, James J.
The Living - Annie Dillard   1644

Hill, Joe
Tombstone Showdown - Leslie Scott   5681

Hill, John J.
Sherlock Holmes and the Red Demon - Larry Millett   4404

Hillhouse, James
Water over the Dam - Marguerite Allis   116

Himmler, Heinrich
A Family Matter - James Roosevelt   5458

Hines, Henry Thomas
In the Season of the Wild Rose - Clara Rising   5347

Hipparchos
The Praise Singer - Mary Renault   5302

Hippocrates
The Torch - Wilder Penfield   4902

Hiram
Solomon and Sheba - Faye Levine   3740

Hitchcock, Alfred
The Alfred Hitchcock Murder Case - George Baxt   382
Catch a Falling Star - Stuart M. Kaminsky   3333

Hitchcock, Alma
The Alfred Hitchcock Murder Case - George Baxt   382

Hitler, Adolf
The Blood Order - Jack D. Hunter   3084
Eva - Ib Melchior   4329
A Family Matter - James Roosevelt   5458
The Hangman's Crusade - James Barwick   370
Hitler Has Won - Frederic Mullally   4511
Last Man to Die - Michael Dobbs   1652
Mussolini - Alan Gelb   2348
The Ring Master - David Gurr   2622
The Very Rich Hours of Count von Stauffenberg - Paul West   6637
The Winds of War - Herman Wouk   6876
Young Adolf - Beryl Bainbridge   272

Hobhouse, John Cam
Lord of the Dead: The Secret History of Byron - Tom Holland   2999

Hoelun
Ruler of the Sky: A Novel of Genghis Khan - Pamela Sargent   5606

Hoffa, Jimmy
The Immortals - Michael Korda   3540

Hogarth, William
Benjamin Franklin and a Case of Artful Murder - Robert Lee Hall   2654
English Music - Peter Ackroyd   18
Fanny: Being the True History of the Adventures of Fanny Hackabout-Jones - Erica Jong   3299

Hohenstaufen, Henry
Banners of Gold - Pamela Kaufman   3371

Holbein the Younger, Hans
My Lady of Cleves - Margaret Campbell Barnes   328

Holladay, Ben
Six-Horse Hitch - Janice Holt Giles   2417

Holliday, Doc
Anything for Billy - Larry McMurtry   4295
Bloody Season - Loren D. Estleman   1968
Confessions of Johnny Ringo - Geoff Aggeler   40
Doc Holliday's Woman - Jane Candia Coleman   1201
The Lady and Doc Holliday - Preston Lewis   3761
Tombstone Showdown - Leslie Scott   5681
Wilde West - Walter Satterthwait   5609
Wyatt Earp - Matt Braun   653

Holliday, John Henry
Anything for Billy - Larry McMurtry   4295
Bloody Season - Loren D. Estleman   1968
Confessions of Johnny Ringo - Geoff Aggeler   40
Doc Holliday's Woman - Jane Candia Coleman   1201
The Lady and Doc Holliday - Preston Lewis   3761
Tombstone Showdown - Leslie Scott   5681
Wilde West - Walter Satterthwait   5609
Wyatt Earp - Matt Braun   653

Holmes, Augusta
Cesar and Augusta - Ronald Harwood   2771

Holmes, Oliver Wendell
Copperhead - Bernard Cornwell   1335
I Swear by Apollo - Agatha Young   6939
Shaman - Noah Gordon   2483

Honoria
Throne of the World - Louis De Wohl   1575

Honorius (Roman Emperor)
Bury Me in Ravenna - Agnes Carr Vaughan   6432

Captive of Rome - Theodora McCormick Du Bois   1740
Roman Go Home! - Adam Fergusson   2065
Threshold of Fire - Hella S. Haasse   2633

Hood, John Bell
The Bright Sword - Eleanor Perenyi   4911

Hood, Samuel
A King's Commander - Dewey Lambdin   3613

Hooker, Joseph
Unto This Hour - Tom Wicker   6733
When the War Is Over - Stephen Becker   408

Hooker, Richard
Roanoke Hundred - Inglis Fletcher   2138

Hoover, J. Edgar
Dillinger - Harry Patterson   4832
Flying into Love - D.M. Thomas   6236
The Immortals - Michael Korda   3540
Murder and the First Lady - Elliott Roosevelt   5444
Murder in the Executive Mansion - Elliott Roosevelt   5449
Murder in the Oval Office - Elliott Roosevelt   5450
Pretty Boy Floyd - Larry McMurtry   4299
True Crime - Max Allan Collins   1214

Hope, Bob
Murder in the Oval Office - Elliott Roosevelt   5450

Horace
Golden Peacock - Gertrude Atherton   224

Horemheb (Pharaoh of Egypt)
The Egyptian - Mika Waltari   6552
On a Balcony - David Stacton   5973
The Twelfth Transforming - Pauline Gedge   2347

Horsey, Jerome
The Muscovite - Alison Macleod   4004

Hosea
The Valley of God - Irene Steinman Patai   4825

Hotspur, Henry
The Bloody Field - Edith Pargeter   4795
Falstaff - Robert Nye   4653
Harry of Monmouth - A.M. Maughan   4199
The Star of Lancaster - Jean Plaidy   5065
The Traitors of Bosworth - Robert Farrington   2021

Houdini, Harry
Nevermore - William Hjortsberg   2958
One Night in Newport - Elizabeth Villars   6498
Ragtime - E.L. Doctorow   1658
The Sunken Treasure - Marian J.A. Jackson   3136

House, Edward
To the Honor of the Fleet - Robert H. Pilpel   5002

Houston, Sam
All the Brave Rifles - Clarke Venable   6450
The Bugles Are Silent: A Novel of the Texas Revolution - John R. Knaggs   3513
The Comancheros - Paul I. Wellman   6616
The Eagle and the Raven - James A. Michener   4369
Empire of Bones: A Novel of Sam Houston and the Texas Revolution - Jeff Long   3868
The Furies - John Jakes   3146
Hellfire Jackson - Garland Roark   5355
Horseshoe Bend - Bruce Palmer   4779
Jackson: A Novel - Max Byrd   837
Magnificent Destiny - Paul I. Wellman   6619
On the Long Tide - Laura Krey   3555
Promised Lands - Elizabeth Crook   1430
The Raven's Bride - Elizabeth Crook   1431
Republic: A Novel of Texas - E.V. Thompson   6266
The Road to San Jacinto - James F. Davis   1524
Sam Houston - Noel B. Gerson   2380
The Sam Houston Story - Dean Owen   4770
Savanna - Janice Holt Giles   2416
Star of Empire: A Novel of Old San Antonio - Leonard Sanders   5590
Texas - James A. Michener   4375
Texas! - Dana Fuller Ross   5490

True Women - Janice Woods Windle   6820
Walk in My Soul - Lucia St. Clair Robson   5418

Howard, Catherine
The Fifth Queen - Ford Madox Ford   2161
Henry VIII and His Six Wives - Maureen Peters   4975
Here Comes the King - Philip Lindsay   3792
Katheryn, the Wanton Queen - Maureen Peters   4976
Kathryn: In the Court of Six Queens - Anne Merton Abbey   1
King's Fool - Margaret Campbell Barnes   325
Murder Most Royal - Jean Plaidy   5036
The Red-Haired Brat - Joanna Dessau   1627
The Rose Without a Thorn - Jean Plaidy   5058
The Wise Virgin - Hebe Elsna   1934

Howard, Frances
The King James Version - Stanley N. Stewart   6035
King's Minion - Rafael Sabatini   5552
Lion Rampant - Bernard Shrimsley   5836
The Murder in the Tower - Jean Plaidy   5035
The Street of Kings - Charles Dexter   1637

Howard, Harriet
Imperial Courtesan - F.W. Kenyon   3452

Howard, John
The Fate of Princes - P.C. Doherty   1673

Howard, Katherine
The Fifth Queen - Ford Madox Ford   2161
Henry VIII and His Six Wives - Maureen Peters   4975
King's Fool - Margaret Campbell Barnes   325
The Wise Virgin - Hebe Elsna   1934

Howard, Oliver Otis
Blood Brother - Elliott Arnold   190
Chief Joseph - Bill Dugan   1756

Howard, Thomas
The King's Good Servant - Olive White   6696

Howe, Julia Ward
Banners Against the Wind - John Edward Jennings   3198

Howe, Samuel Gridley
Banners Against the Wind - John Edward Jennings   3198

Howe, William
The King's Rebel - James David Horan   3030
Massachusetts: A Novel - Nancy Zaroulis   6956
Monmouth - Charles Bracelen Flood   2144
Oliver Wiswell - Kenneth Roberts   5389
Redcoat - Bernard Cornwell   1337
Three Fields to Cross - Francis Tysen Nutt   4651
Valiant Libertine - John Gordon Bryson   748

Hsien Feng (Emperor of China)
Imperial Woman - Pearl S. Buck   755

Hsu, Paul
Manchu - Robert S. Elegant   1904

Hsuan-tsung (Emperor of China)
The Court of the Lion - Eleanor Cooney   1294

Hubble, Edwin Powell
Hubble Time - Tom Bezzi   490

Hudson, Geoffrey
Peveril of the Peak - Sir Walter Scott   5703

Hudson, George
The Iron Roads - Forbes Bramble   644
The Rich Are with You Always - Malcolm Macdonald   3971

Hudson, Henry
Running Proud - Nicholas Monsarrat   4432

Huger, Francis Kinloch
A Chance for Glory - Constance Wright   6877

Hughes, Charles Evans
Murder in the Red Room - Elliott Roosevelt   5451
Murder in the Rose Garden - Elliott Roosevelt   5452

Hughes, Howard
The Howard Hughes Affair - Stuart M.
  Kaminsky 3340

Hugo, Victor
Naked Came I: A Novel of Rodin - David
  Weiss 6607
Palais-Royale - Richard Sennett 5747

Hull, Isaac
*The Splendor Stays: An Historic Novel Based on the
  Lives of the Seven Hart Sisters of Saybrook* -
  Marguerite Allis 114

Humbert, Jean-Joseph
The Year of the French - Thomas Flanagan 2121

Humphrey, Duke of Gloucester
Epitaph for Three Women - Jean Plaidy 5012
The Royal Pawn - Antonia Ridge 5327

Hung Hsiu-Ch'uan
*The Second Son of Heaven: A Novel of Nineteenth-
  Century China* - C.Y. Lee 3707

Hung Tu
Go Ask the River - Evelyn Eaton 1826

Hunt, Holman
The Golden Veil - Paddy Kitchen 3507

Hunt, Leigh
*The Golden Years: A Novel Based on the Life and
  Loves of Percy Bysshe Shelley* - F.W.
  Kenyon 3451
Love's Children - Judith Chernaik 1013
Neighboring Lives - Thomas M. Disch 1648

Hunter, John
Lancet - Garet Rogers 5431

Hunter, William
Lancet - Garet Rogers 5431

Huntington, Collis Potter
California Gold - John Jakes 3145

Husband, Harmon
The Wind in the Forest - Inglis Fletcher 2143

Hutchinson, Anne
Bear His Mild Yoke - Ethel White 6675
Covenant of Grace - Jane Gilmore Rushing 5527
The Golden Feather - Theda Kenyon 3462
The Winthrop Covenant - Louis Auchincloss 235
The Winthrop Woman - Anya Seton 5754
Witnesses - Marcy Moran Heidish 2820

Huxley, Thomas Henry
The Origin - Irving Stone 6060

Hyde, Edward
The Bride - Margaret Irwin 3116

Hypatia
Hypatia - Charles Kingsley 3498

I

Ibn Fadlan, Ahmad
Eaters of the Dead - Michael Crichton 1425

Ignatius Loyola
The Golden Thread - Louis De Wohl 1566
Set All Afire: A Novel of St. Francis Xavier - Louis De
  Wohl 1574

Ingles, Mary Draper
Follow the River - James Alexander Thom 6231

Innocent III (Pope)
Below the Salt - Thomas B. Costain 1362
*Blessed Are the Meek: A Novel about St. Francis of
  Assisi* - Zofja Kossak-Szczucka 3542
The Joyful Beggar: A Novel of St. Francis of Assisi -
  Louis De Wohl 1568
My Beautiful White Roses - Michael Lechner 3703

Innocent XI (Pope)
The Anthem - Noel B. Gerson 2361
My Crown, My Love - Ruth Walgreen Stephan 5995

Insull, Samuel
Organized Crime - Nicholas Von Hoffman 6511

Iredell, James
Queen's Gift - Inglis Fletcher 2136

Irene (Byzantine Empress)
The Belt of Gold - Cecelia Holland 2984

Irving, Henry
The West End Horror - Nicholas Meyer 4350

Irving, Washington
John Howard Payne, Skywalker - Maude
  Barragan 348
River to the West: A Novel of the Astor Adventure -
  John Edward Jennings 3204

Irwin, Charles Button
Prairie - Anna Lee Waldo 6528

Isaac
Jacob - Jean Cabries 844
Jacob: An Autobiography - Irving Fineman 2088

Isabeau (Queen of France)
In a Dark Wood Wandering - Hella S. Haasse 2631
The Royal Pawn - Antonia Ridge 5327

Isabeau of Bavaria
Wife to Henry V - Hilda Lewis 3752

Isabel (English Princess)
The Lady Royal - Molly Costain Haycraft 2794

Isabel of Bourbon
I, the King - Frances Parkinson Keyes 3479

Isabel of France (1292-1358)
Isabel the Fair - Margaret Campbell Barnes 323

Isabel of Hainault
The Rain Maiden - Jill M. Phillips 4985

Isabel of Portugal
Master of Castile - Samuel Edwards 1888

Isabella (Isabella I)
Columbus: A Romance - Rafael Sabatini 5549
The Prisoner of Tordesillas - Lawrence
  Schoonover 5665

Isabella I (Queen of Spain)
1492 - Newton Frolich 2236
Columbus: A Romance - Rafael Sabatini 5549
Crown of Aloes - Norah Lofts 3840
The Dogs of Paradise - Abel Posse 5141
Ferdinand and Isabella - Hermann Kesten 3474
The Gentle Fury: A Novel of Margaret of Austria -
  Paul Lewis 3758
Here Lies Margot - Pamela Hill 2935
The Memoirs of Christopher Columbus - Stephen
  Marlowe 4096
Mercedes of Castile - James Fenimore Cooper 1304
The Prisoner of Tordesillas - Lawrence
  Schoonover 5665
*The Queen's Cross: A Biographical Romance of
  Queen Isabella of Spain* - Lawrence
  Schoonover 5666
Torquemada - Howard Fast 2045

Isabella of Angouleme
The Barons of Runnymede - Pamela Bennetts 445
The Battle of the Queens - Jean Plaidy 5005
The Prince of Darkness - Jean Plaidy 5044
The Wolf at the Door - Graham Shelby 5793

Isabella of France (1292-1358)
Braveheart - Randall Wallace 6538
The Death of a King - P.C. Doherty 1672
The Follies of the King - Jean Plaidy 5014
Harlot Queen - Hilda Lewis 3748
The Iron King - Maurice Druon 1732
Isabel the Fair - Margaret Campbell Barnes 323
The Lily and the Lion - Maurice Druon 1733

The Lion and the Leopard - Mary Ellen
  Johnson 3226
The She-Wolf - Pamela Bennetts 456
The She-Wolf of France - Maurice Druon 1736
A Tapestry of Murders - C.L. Grace 2510
Vows of the Peacock - Alice Walworth
  Graham 2513

Isabella of France (1389-1409)
The Gentle Falcon - Hilda Lewis 3747
The Lords of Lancaster - Pamela Bennetts 452
Passage to Pontefract - Jean Plaidy 5038
The Star of Lancaster - Jean Plaidy 5065
The Vow on the Heron - Jean Plaidy 5074

Isabelle de Bourbon
The Marranos - Liliane Webb 6588

Isaiah
The Prophet - Sholem Asch 201

Isasaga, Francisco de
*A Crossbowman's Story of the First Exploration of the
  Amazon* - George Millar 4379

Ishmael
Hagar - Cothburn O'Neal 4737

Islavina, Elena
Elena - Judith Egan 1893

Istephan, Reb
The Apostle - Sholem Asch 197

Ivan IV (Czar of Russia)
Darker Jewels - Chelsea Quinn Yarbro 6898
The Muscovite - Alison Macleod 4004
Prince of Outlaws - Alexey Tolstoy 6294
The Ringed Castle - Dorothy Dunnett 1807
Russka: The Novel of Russia - Edward
  Rutherfurd 5535
Sir Rogue - Leslie Turner White 6691

Ivan the Terrible
Darker Jewels - Chelsea Quinn Yarbro 6898
The Muscovite - Alison Macleod 4004
Prince of Outlaws - Alexey Tolstoy 6294
The Ringed Castle - Dorothy Dunnett 1807
Russka: The Novel of Russia - Edward
  Rutherfurd 5535
Sir Rogue - Leslie Turner White 6691

J

Jackson, Andrew
1812 - David Nevin 4586
As Long as the Rivers Run - Sam J. Slate 5882
The Big Family - Vina Delmar 1600
The Buckstones - Paul I. Wellman 6615
Burr - Gore Vidal 6485
The Cavalier of Tennessee - Meredith
  Nicholson 4610
*The Corsair: A Biographical Novel of Jean Lafitte,
  Hero of the Battle of New Orleans* - Madeleine
  Fabiola Kent 3444
Creek Mary's Blood - Dee Brown 712
*Crockett of Tennessee: A Novel Based on the Life and
  Times of David Crockett* - Cameron Judd 3314
The Cumberland Rifles - Noel B. Gerson 2365
The Fallon Pride - Reagan O'Neal 4742
Flintlock - Jason Manning 4073
Give Me the Wind - Jan Jordan 3302
The Gorgeous Hussy - Samuel Hopkins Adams 30
Hearts of Hickory - John Trotwood Moore 4442
*Her Christmas at the Hermitage: A Tale about Rachel
  and Andrew Jackson* - Helen Topping Miller 4389
Home to the Hermitage - Alfred Leland Crabb 1401
Horseshoe Bend - Bruce Palmer 4779
Jackson: A Novel - Max Byrd 837
The Land Where the Sun Dies - Henry Carlisle 896
Magnificent Destiny - Paul I. Wellman 6619

Memories of the Ford Administration - John
   Updike 6391
Mississippi Belle - Clements Ripley 5346
Mr. Audubon's Lucy - Lucy Kennedy 3419
Oh, Promised Land - James H. Street 6079
Old Hickory - Noel B. Gerson 2379
On the Long Tide - Laura Krey 3555
The President's Lady - Irving Stone 6063
The Rake and the Hussy - Robert W. Chambers 981
Sam Houston - Noel B. Gerson 2380
The Sam Houston Story - Dean Owen 4770
The Slender Reed - Noel B. Gerson 2382
A Story of Deep Delight - Thomas McNamee 4305
Texas! - Dana Fuller Ross 5490
Twilight of Empire - Allen W. Eckert 1846
War Drums - Donald Clayton Porter 5133
The Yankee From Tennessee - Noel B. Gerson 2388
Young Ames - Walter D. Edmonds 1879
Young Hickory - Stanley Young 6942

Jackson, Anna Morrison
The Gallant Mrs. Stonewall - Harnett T. Kane 3353

Jackson, Rachel
1812 - David Nevin 4586
The Cavalier of Tennessee - Meredith
   Nicholson 4610
The Gorgeous Hussy - Samuel Hopkins Adams 30
*Her Christmas at the Hermitage: A Tale about Rachel
   and Andrew Jackson* - Helen Topping Miller 4389
Home to the Hermitage - Alfred Leland Crabb 1401
Jackson: A Novel - Max Byrd 837
Magnificent Destiny - Paul I. Wellman 6619
Old Hickory - Noel B. Gerson 2379
The President's Lady - Irving Stone 6063
Young Hickory - Stanley Young 6942

Jackson, Shoeless Joe
Murder at Wrigley Field - Troy Soos 5949

Jackson, Stonewall
Battle Flag - Bernard Cornwell 1333
The Bloody Ground - Bernard Cornwell 1334
Confederates - Thomas Keneally 3412
The Gallant Mrs. Stonewall - Harnett T. Kane 3353
Gettysburg: Crisis of Command - Harry Albright 65
Gods and Generals - Jeff Shaara 5765
Gone to Texas - Jason Manning 4074
Hard Road to Gettysburg - Ted Jones 3298
The Long Roll - Mary Johnston 3236
Look Away - Harold Coyle 1395
Major Stepton's War - Matthew Vaughan 6445
McKensie's Hundred: A Tale of the Old Dominion -
   Frank Yerby 6924
The River and the Wilderness - Don Robertson 5401
The Smiling Rebel - Harnett T. Kane 3357
*The Stonewall Brigade: A Novel of the American Civil
   War* - Frank G. Slaughter 5902
Traveller - Richard Adams 27
Unto This Hour - Tom Wicker 6733
The Unwritten Chronicles of Robert E. Lee - Lamar
   Herrin 2864
The Warriors - John Jakes 3155

Jackson, Thomas Jonathan
Battle Flag - Bernard Cornwell 1333
The Bloody Ground - Bernard Cornwell 1334
Confederates - Thomas Keneally 3412
The Gallant Mrs. Stonewall - Harnett T. Kane 3353
Gettysburg: Crisis of Command - Harry Albright 65
Gods and Generals - Jeff Shaara 5765
Gone to Texas - Jason Manning 4074
Hard Road to Gettysburg - Ted Jones 3298
The Long Roll - Mary Johnston 3236
Look Away - Harold Coyle 1395
Major Stepton's War - Matthew Vaughan 6445
McKensie's Hundred: A Tale of the Old Dominion -
   Frank Yerby 6924
The River and the Wilderness - Don Robertson 5401
The Smiling Rebel - Harnett T. Kane 3357
*The Stonewall Brigade: A Novel of the American Civil
   War* - Frank G. Slaughter 5902

Traveller - Richard Adams 27
Unto This Hour - Tom Wicker 6733
The Unwritten Chronicles of Robert E. Lee - Lamar
   Herrin 2864
The Warriors - John Jakes 3155

Jacob
Jacob - Jean Cabries 844
Jacob: An Autobiography - Irving Fineman 2088
The Shepherd Kings - Peter Danielson 1475
The Son of Laughter - Frederick Buechner 764
The Tales of Jacob - Thomas Mann 4068
Young Joseph - Thomas Mann 4069

Jacqueline of Hainault
The Master Painter - Edwin Mullins 4513

James
The Brother - Dorothy Clarke Wilson 6799
The Centurion - Leonard Wibberley 6729
*The Sins of Herod: A Novel of Rome and the Early
   Church* - Frank G. Slaughter 5900

James (James II)
The Three Crowns - Jean Plaidy 5070

James (James V)
The Thistle and the Rose - Jean Plaidy 5069

James, Frank
*The Assassination of Jesse James by the Coward
   Robert Ford* - Ron Hansen 2680
Death of a Legend - Will Henry 2840
Loving Belle Star - Robert Taylor 6187
Mamaw - Susan Dodd 1663
While Angels Dance - Ralph W. Cotton 1372

James, Henry
Empire: A Novel - Gore Vidal 6487
The Haunting of Lamb House - Joan Aiken 48
Henry James' Midnight Song - Carol de Chellis
   Hill 2920
*Refinements of Love: A Novel about Clover and Henry
   Adams* - Sarah Booth Conroy 1259

James, Jesse
*The Assassination of Jesse James by the Coward
   Robert Ford* - Ron Hansen 2680
Belle Starr - Deborah Camp 870
Bound Girl - Everett Webber 6591
Death of a Legend - Will Henry 2840
Loving Belle Star - Robert Taylor 6187
Mamaw - Susan Dodd 1663
Sons of Fire - Max McCoy 4227
While Angels Dance - Ralph W. Cotton 1372

James, William
The Haunting of Lamb House - Joan Aiken 48

James, Zerelda Cole
Mamaw - Susan Dodd 1663

James I (King of England)
The Border Lord - Jan Westcott 6641
Call Lady Purbeck - Hilda Lewis 3745
The Cleopatra Boy - Eric Malpass 4048
Daughter of Eve - Noel B. Gerson 2366
Death of the Fox - George Garrett 2300
For My Great Folly - Thomas B. Costain 1365
The Fortunes of Nigel - Sir Walter Scott 5696
Katherine Christian - Hugh Walpole 6546
The King James Version - Stanley N. Stewart 6035
Lady in Waiting - Rosemary Sutcliff 6123
Lion Rampant - Bernard Shrimsley 5836
Mary of Scotland - F.W. Kenyon 3454
The Master of Gray Trilogy - Nigel Tranter 6316
Mine Is the Kingdom - Jane Oliver 4726
The Murder in the Tower - Jean Plaidy 5035
No Smoke Without Fire - Alice Harwood 2767
*Physician Extraordinary: A Novel of the Life and
   Times of William Harvey* - David Weiss 6608
Pocahontas - Susan Donnell 1691
Powhatan's Daughter - John Clarke Bowman 605
Ralegh's Fair Bess: The Story of Bess Throckmorton -
   Judy Turner 6365

Scapegoat for a Stuart - Kate Kirby 3504
The Sea 'Venture - F. van Wyck Mason 4159
The Street of Kings - Charles Dexter 1637
The Succession: A Novel of Elizabeth and James -
   George Garrett 2302
Take Heed of Loving Me: A Novel about John Donne -
   Elizabeth Gray Vining 6502
To Love a Queen - Lawrence Schoonover 5669
Unicorn Rampant - Nigel Tranter 6323
Wife to Great Buckingham - Hilda Lewis 3751
The Young and Lonely King - Jane Lane 3659

James I (King of Scotland)
Crippled Splendour - Evan John 3219
James and Joan - Anne Fremantle 2221
The World, the Flesh, and the Devil - Reay
   Tannahill 6159

James II (King of England)
The Elusive Crown - Hebe Elsna 1931
The Golden Days - Robert Neill 4569
James, by the Grace of God - Hugh Williamson
   Ross 5499
King's Agent - Justus Kent Clark 1090
Lillibullero - Robert Neill 4571
Log Cabin Noble - F. van Wyck Mason 4153
Lorna Doone - R.D. Blackmore 528
Silver Shoals - Hamilton Cochran 1142
The Three Crowns - Jean Plaidy 5070
Treason's Gift - Pamela Belle 434
William's Wife - Jean Plaidy 5077

James III (King of Scotland)
To Lie with Lions - Dorothy Dunnett 1810
The Unicorn Hunt - Dorothy Dunnett 1811

James IV (King of Scotland)
Chain of Destiny - Nigel Tranter 6314
*Falcon: The Autobiography of His Grace James IV,
   King of Scots* - A.J. Stewart 6021
The Hepburn - Jan Westcott 6645
The King's Vixen - Pamela Hill 2937
The Riven Realm - Nigel Tranter 6317
Sunset at Noon - Jane Oliver 4728
The Thistle and the Rose - Jean Plaidy 5069

James V (King of Scotland)
James, by the Grace of God - Nigel Tranter 6315
My Lady Glamis - Pamela Hill 2940
The Riven Realm - Nigel Tranter 6317
A Stake in the Kingdom - Nigel Tranter 6321
The Thistle and the Rose - Jean Plaidy 5069

James VI (King of Scotland)
The Border Lord - Jan Westcott 6641
The Master of Gray Trilogy - Nigel Tranter 6316
Mine Is the Kingdom - Jane Oliver 4726
No Smoke Without Fire - Alice Harwood 2767
*Physician Extraordinary: A Novel of the Life and
   Times of William Harvey* - David Weiss 6608
Ralegh's Fair Bess: The Story of Bess Throckmorton -
   Judy Turner 6365
Take Heed of Loving Me: A Novel about John Donne -
   Elizabeth Gray Vining 6502
To Love a Queen - Lawrence Schoonover 5669

Jan II Kazimir (King of Poland)
Poland - James A. Michener 4373

Jan III Sobieski (King of Poland)
Fire in the Steppe - Henryk Sienkiewicz 5847
Poland - James A. Michener 4373

Jan of Leyden
The Siege - Peter Vansittart 6431

Jaramillo, Josefa
Soldier in Buckskin - Ray Hogan 2981

Jardine, William
Mandarin Gold - James Leasor 3700

Jean de Brienne (King of Jerusalem)
*Blessed Are the Meek: A Novel about St. Francis of
   Assisi* - Zofja Kossak-Szczucka 3542

Jeanne of Navarre
The Italian Woman - Jean Plaidy 5024

Jefferson, Martha
My Thomas: A Novel of Martha Jefferson's Life - Roberta Grimes 2593
Sally Hemings - Barbara Chase-Riboud 1006

Jefferson, Thomas
The Amazing Mrs. Bonaparte - Harnett T. Kane 3351
Arc d'X - Steve Erickson 1953
Burr - Gore Vidal 6485
Citizen Tom Paine - Howard Fast 2028
The Conqueror: Being the True and Romantic Story of Alexander Hamilton - Gertrude Atherton 222
Dawn's Early Light - Elswyth Thane 6215
An Embarrassment of Riches - James Howard Kunstler 3565
Enslaved - Ron Burns 801
The Fallon Pride - Reagan O'Neal 4742
Flintlock - Jason Manning 4073
Fool of God: A Novel Based on the Life of Alexander Campbell - Louis Cochran 1144
Give Me Liberty: The Story of an Innocent Man - John Erskine 1956
Hawk's Journey - Donald Clayton Porter 5119
Jackson: A Novel - Max Byrd 837
Jefferson: A Novel - Max Byrd 838
Kentucky Home - Betty Layman Receveur 5283
Kentucky Stand - Jere Hungerford Wheelwright. 6670
Louisiana Purchase - A.E. Hotchner 3039
My Thomas: A Novel of Martha Jefferson's Life - Roberta Grimes 2593
The President's Daughter - Barbara Chase-Riboud 1005
Queen Dolley: The Life and Times of Dolley Madison - Dorothy Clarke Wilson 6806
The River Devils - Carter A. Vaughan 6437
River to the West: A Novel of the Astor Adventure - John Edward Jennings 3204
Sally Hemings - Barbara Chase-Riboud 1006
The Seekers - John Jakes 3153
Stars and Stripes - Adam Rutledge 5541
Those Who Love - Irving Stone 6064
Tide of Empire - Bates Baldwin 279
A Time for Titans - Vina Delmar 1602
To Spit Against the Wind - Benjamin H. Levin 3737
Trail: The Story of the Lewis and Clark Expedition - Louis Charbonneau 998
The Tree of Liberty - Elizabeth Page 4773
Westward! - Dana Fuller Ross 5492

Jeffords, Thomas
Blood Brother - Elliott Arnold 190

Jeffreys, Sir George
Black Angels - C.T. Ritchie 5348

Jeffries, Jim
Hoopla - Harry Stein 5990

Jellicoe, John Rushworth
The Devil in Harbour - Catherine Gavin 2319
To the Honor of the Fleet - Robert H. Pilpel 5002

Jenkinson, Robert Banks
The Sea Officer - Showell Styles 6105

Jenner, Edward
The Dedicated - Willa Gibbs 2399
Princess in Amber - Evelyn Wilde Mayerson 4205

Jeremiah
The Babylonians - Nathaniel Norsen Weinreb 6600
Persian Conqueror - George Sidney Hellman 2822

Jerome
The Converts: A Historical Novel - Rex Warner 6564
The Four Rivers of Paradise - Helen Constance White 6678

Jerome, Jennie
Imperial Kelly - Peter Bowen 600

Jerrold, Douglas
Princess Pamela - Ray Russell 5534

Jesus Christ
According to Mary: A Novel of the Magdalene - Willa Gibbs 2398
According to Thomas - Gladys Malvern 4053
Barabbas - Par Lagerkvist 3585
Barabbas: A Novel of the Time of Jesus - Emery Bekessy 417
Behold the Man - Toyohiko Kagawa 3321
Behold the Man - N. Richard Nash 4556
Behold Your King - Florence M. Bauer 379
Ben Hur: A Tale of the Christ - Lew Wallace 6536
The Big Fisherman - Lloyd C. Douglas 1702
The Brother - Dorothy Clarke Wilson 6799
Brothers of Vengeance - LeGette Blythe 556
The Centurion - Leonard Wibberley 6729
A Certain Woman: The Story of Mary Magdalene - Victor MacClure 3959
Daughter of Jairus - Paul Hervey Fox 2196
The Emperor's Physician - Jacob Randolph Perkins 4914
Fisher of Men: A Novel of Simon Peter - Kurt Frieberger 2231
The Gifts: A Story of the Boyhood of Jesus - Dorothy Clarke Wilson 6800
The Good Tidings - William Sidney 5843
The Gospel According to Gamaliel - Gerald Heard 2801
The Gospel According to Pontius Pilate - James R. Mills 4408
The Gospel of Corax - Paul Park 4802
Great Lion of God - Taylor Caldwell 858
He Came From Galilee - Daniel A. Poling 5083
Hidden Victory: A Novel of Jesus - Herbert Francis Smith 5921
How Far to Bethlehem? - Norah Lofts 3846
I, Judas - Taylor Caldwell 859
I, Nathanael, Knew Jesus - William Gilbert Van Tassel Sutpen 6133
Justus - Arthur L. Lapham 3663
King Jesus - Robert Graves 2549
The Kingdom of the Wicked - Anthony Burgess 778
The Lance of Longinus - Hubertus Loewenstein 3833
The Last Days - William Rayner 5272
The Last Temptation of Christ - Nikos Kazantzakis 3384
Lazarus - Alain Absire 15
The Life of Jesus: An Apocryphal Novel - Toby Olson 4731
Live From Golgotha - Gore Vidal 6491
The Lord Jesus - Robert Payne 4854
A Love Divine - Alexandra Ripley 5340
The Magdalene Gospel - Mary Ellen Ashcroft 203
Man of Nazareth - Anthony Burgess 779
Marcus - Laurene Chinn 1068
Martha, Martha - Patricia McGerr 4274
Mary - Sholem Asch 198
Mary of Magdala - Anne C. Williman 6791
Mary of Nazareth - Esther Kellner 3394
The Master - Max Brod 702
The Messiah - Marjorie Holmes 3003
The Moon under Her Feet - Ceysta Kinstler 3503
The Nazarene - Sholem Asch 200
Pontius Pilate: A Biographical Novel - Paul L. Maier 4034
Refuge in Avalon - Marguerite Steedman 5984
The Salt of the Earth - Carlo Monterosso 4437
The Same Scourge - John Goldthorpe 2464
The Secret of the Kingdom - Mika Waltari 6555
The Shepherd - Robert Payne 4855
A Tear for Judas - LeGette Blythe 559
The Testament of Theophilus - Leonard Wibberley 6730
Three From Galilee: The Young Man From Nazareth - Marjorie Holmes 3004
A Time for Judas - Morley Callaghan 866

Upon This Rock: A Novel of Simon Peter, Prince of Apostles - Frank G. Slaughter 5906
A Woman of Samaria - James W. Ingles 3104
Yeshua: The Gospel of St. Thomas - Alan Decker McNarie 4306

Jezebel
The Curse of Jezebel: A Novel of the Biblical Queen of Evil - Frank G. Slaughter 5884
Dara, the Cypriot - Louis Paul 4842
Jezebel - Dorothy Clarke Wilson 6802
Merari - Gloria Howe Bremkamp 656
The Painted Queen - Olga Hesky 2871

Jimenez de Cisneros, Francisco
The Shadow of the Pomegranate - Jean Plaidy 5062

Joab
After Goliath - R.V. Cassill 955
Giant Killer - Elmer Holmes Davis 1518
The Shining King - Peter Danielson 1476
The Unanointed - Laurene Chinn 1070

Joan (?-1237)
Harp into Battle - Cecil Maiden 4031
Here Be Dragons - Sharon Kay Penman 4904

Joan of Arc
An Army of Angels: A Novel of Joan of Arc - Pamela Marcantel 4079
The Burnished Blade - Lawrence Schoonover 5661
Epitaph for Three Women - Jean Plaidy 5012
In a Dark Wood Wandering - Hella S. Haasse 2631
The Master Painter - Edwin Mullins 4513
Personal Recollections of Joan of Arc - Mark Twain 6372
The Queen's Secret - Jean Plaidy 5053
The Serpent Amongst the Lilies - P.C. Doherty 1678
The Voice and the Light - Edwin Fadiman 1995

Joan of Sicily
My Lord Brother the Lionheart - Molly Costain Haycraft 2795

Johann
The Ugly Duchess - Lion Feuchtwanger 2075

John (King of England)
Banners of Gold - Pamela Kaufman 3371
The Barons of Runnymede - Pamela Bennetts 445
The Battle of the Queens - Jean Plaidy 5005
Champion - L. Christian Balling 285
The Courts of Love - Jean Plaidy 5010
The Devil Is Loose - Graham Shelby 5790
The Falcon and the Flower - Virginia Henley 2826
Harp into Battle - Cecil Maiden 4031
The Heart of the Lion - Jean Plaidy 5020
Here Be Dragons - Sharon Kay Penman 4904
In the Shadow of Midnight - Marsha Canham 880
Ivanhoe - Sir Walter Scott 5699
Lady of Hay - Barbara Erskine 1955
Leopards and Lilies - Alfred Duggan 1769
The Lords of Vaumartin - Cecelia Holland 2992
Myself as Witness - James Goldman 2458
The Prince of Darkness - Jean Plaidy 5044
The Rain Maiden - Jill M. Phillips 4985
The Sheriff of Nottingham - Richard Kluger 3512
This Bright Sword - Donald Barr Chidsey 1066
The Wolf at the Door - Graham Shelby 5793

John (Saint)
The Messiah - Marjorie Holmes 3003
The Sins of Herod: A Novel of Rome and the Early Church - Frank G. Slaughter 5900
Who Came by Night - Roland Nicholas 4608

John, Duke of Bedford
My Lord John - Georgette Heyer 2895

John II (Eastern Roman Emperor)
Their Most Serene Majesties - Ange Vlachos 6505

John VIII (Pope)
Joanna the Pope - Daniel Panger 4785
Pope Joan - Donna Woolfolk Cross 1433

John Lackland
The Devil Is Loose - Graham Shelby 5790

John of Gaunt
Falstaff - Robert Nye 4653
Fortune Made His Sword - Martha Rofheart 5426
The Gentle Falcon - Hilda Lewis 3747
Good King Harry - Denise Giardina 2393
Harry of Monmouth - A.M. Maughan 4199
Katherine - Anya Seton 5752
The Lords of Lancaster - Pamela Bennetts 452
The Love Knot - Catherine Darby 1482
The Nightingale Gallery - Paul Harding 2684
Passage to Pontefract - Jean Plaidy 5038
The Peacock and the Pearl - Jennifer Lang 3661
Riddle Me a Murder - Duane Crowley 1435
The Star of Lancaster - Jean Plaidy 5065
The Vow on the Heron - Jean Plaidy 5074
Who Was Then the Gentleman - Charles E.
  Israel 3125
Within the Hollow Crown - Margaret Campbell
  Barnes 331

John of Gloucester
Less Fortunate than Fair - Sandra Wilson 6814
The Queen's Sister - Sandra Wilson 6815

John of the Cross
*Bold Encounter: A Novel Based on the Life of St. John
  of the Cross* - Peter-Thomas Rohrbach 5433

John the Baptist
Behold the Man - Toyohiko Kagawa 3321
The Big Fisherman - Lloyd C. Douglas 1702
The Centurion - Leonard Wibberley 6729
The Good Tidings - William Sidney 5843
Hidden Victory: A Novel of Jesus - Herbert Francis
  Smith 5921
I, Judas - Taylor Caldwell 859
The Last Temptation of Christ - Nikos
  Kazantzakis 3384
Martha, Martha - Patricia McGerr 4274
The Messiah - Marjorie Holmes 3003
The Salt of the Earth - Carlo Monterosso 4437
The Shepherd - Robert Payne 4855
A Tear for Judas - LeGette Blythe 559
*Upon This Rock: A Novel of Simon Peter, Prince of
  Apostles* - Frank G. Slaughter 5906

Johnson, Andrew
Heaven and Hell - John Jakes 3147
Montana! - Dana Fuller Ross 5479
The Rising of the Moon - Peter Berresford Ellis 1926
Storm Center: A Novel about Andy Johnson - Joseph
  Walker McSpadden 4312
Texas! - Dana Fuller Ross 5490
The Yankee From Tennessee - Noel B. Gerson 2388

Johnson, Ben
Powhatan's Daughter - John Clarke Bowman 605

Johnson, Esther
Violent Friends - Winston Clewes 1113

Johnson, Jack
Hoopla - Harry Stein 5990
Yellowstone Kelly - Peter Bowen 602

Johnson, Lyndon Baines
Murder and the First Lady - Elliott Roosevelt 5444
Murder in the East Room - Elliott Roosevelt 5448
Murder in the Oval Office - Elliott Roosevelt 5450

Johnson, Mary
The Golden Wildcat - Margaret Widdemer 6735

Johnson, Samuel
Angelica - Samuel A. Schreiner Jr. 5671
Blind Justice - Bruce Alexander 76
The Bonnet Laird's Daughter - Barbara
  Annandale 154
Dr. Johnson's Dear Mistress - Winifred Carter 948
Midwinter - John Buchan 751
Mr. Oddity, Samuel Johnson - Charles Norman 4643

Johnson, Walter
Murder at Fenway Park - Troy Soos 5948

Johnson, Sir William
Brother Owl - Al Hine 2953
Cardigan - Robert W. Chambers 976
The Conqueror - John William Tebbel 6194
The Conquerors - Allen W. Eckert 1839
Fire Along the Sky: A Novel of America - Robert
  Moss 4497
The Firekeeper - Robert Moss 4498
The Golden Wildcat - Margaret Widdemer 6735
Lady of the Mohawks - Margaret Widdemer 6736
Red Cloak Flying - Margaret Widdemer 6737
Strife Before Dawn - Mary Schumann 5675
West to the Setting Sun - Harvey Chalmers 973
Wilderness Empire - Allen W. Eckert 1847
The Wilderness War - Allen W. Eckert 1848

Johnston, Albert Sidney
In the Season of the Wild Rose - Clara Rising 5347
Journey to Shiloh - Will Henry 2843
The Long Night - Andrew Lytle 3945
Powderkeg - Richard Vetterli 6482
Shadowed Memories - Al Lacy 3583
Shiloh - Shelby Foote 2153
Ulysses: A Biographical Novel - Robert Skimin 5878

Johnston, George
The Explorers - William Stuart Long 3872

Johnston, Joseph E.
Beloved Enemy - Al Lacy 3579
Cadmus Henry - Walter D. Edmonds 1872
Copperhead - Bernard Cornwell 1335

Johnston, Sam
Queen's Gift - Inglis Fletcher 2136

Jolliet, Louis
Blackrobe - Charles Corcoran 1323

Jolson, Al
From Time to Time - Jack Finney 2092

Jonathan
David at Olivet - Wallace Hamilton 2671
David of Jerusalem - Louis De Wohl 1564
David the King - Gladys Schmitt 5641
The Death of Kings - Peter Danielson 1465
King of Kings: A Novel of the Life of David - Malachi
  Martin 4134

Jones, Ernest
The Passions of the Mind - Irving Stone 6062

Jones, John Paul
The Bonnet Laird's Daughter - Barbara
  Annandale 154
Captain Paul - Edward Ellsberg 1930
Clear for Action: A Novel about John Paul Jones -
  Clements Ripley 5344
Don't Tread on Me - Walter Karig 3366
Drums - James Boyd 611
Gallant Captain - Pearl Frye 2242
Give Me Liberty - Noel B. Gerson 2369
Henry Lunt and the Ranger - Tom McNamara 4304
Israel Potter - Herman Melville 4334
The Pilot - James Fenimore Cooper 1306
Raleigh's Eden - Inglis Fletcher 2137
The Revolutionary - Lawrence Schoonover 5667
Richard Carvel - Winston Churchill 1081
Sailor Named Jones - Harvey Haislip 2643
The Sea Eagles - John Edward Jennings 3206
Stars on the Sea - F. van Wyck Mason 4161

Jones, Mary Harris
Bisbee '17 - Robert Houston 3056
The Scapegoat - Mary Lee Settle 5758

Jones, Mother
Bisbee '17 - Robert Houston 3056
The Scapegoat - Mary Lee Settle 5758

Jonson, Ben
The Best House in Stratford - Edward Fisher 2100

The Cleopatra Boy - Eric Malpass 4048
The Disturber - L.S. Davidson Jr. 1505
Entered From the Sun - George Garrett 2301
Ralegh's Fair Bess: The Story of Bess Throckmorton -
  Judy Turner 6365
Take Heed of Loving Me: A Novel about John Donne -
  Elizabeth Gray Vining 6502
Two Loves Have I - Clara Longworth de
  Chambrun 985
You, My Brother - Philip Burton 809

Jordan, Dorothy
Goddess of the Green Room - Jean Plaidy 5016

Jorum (King of Israel)
Merari - Gloria Howe Bremkamp 656

Joseph (Saint Joseph)
The Gifts: A Story of the Boyhood of Jesus - Dorothy
  Clarke Wilson 6800
Hidden Victory: A Novel of Jesus - Herbert Francis
  Smith 5921
How Far to Bethlehem? - Norah Lofts 3846
King Jesus - Robert Graves 2549
The Last Temptation of Christ - Nikos
  Kazantzakis 3384
The Life of Jesus: An Apocryphal Novel - Toby
  Olson 4731
Man of Nazareth - Anthony Burgess 779
Mary - Sholem Asch 198
The Shepherd - Robert Payne 4855
Three From Galilee: The Young Man From Nazareth -
  Marjorie Holmes 3004
Two From Galilee: A Love Story - Marjorie
  Holmes 3005

Joseph (Son of Jacob)
*Charioteer: A Story of Old Egypt in the Days of
  Joseph* - Gertrude Eberle 1835
The Golden Pharaoh - Peter Danielson 1468
Jacob - Jean Cabries 844
Jacob: An Autobiography - Irving Fineman 2088
Joseph of Egypt - Thomas Mann 4065
Joseph the Provider - Thomas Mann 4066
The Lion in Egypt - Peter Danielson 1470
The Prophecy - Peter Danielson 1472
The Son of Laughter - Frederick Buechner 764
Table in the Wilderness - Norton S. Parker 4806
The Tales of Jacob - Thomas Mann 4068
Vengeance of the Lion - Peter Danielson 1480
Young Joseph - Thomas Mann 4069

Joseph of Arimathea
According to Thomas - Gladys Malvern 4053
Barabbas: A Novel of the Time of Jesus - Emery
  Bekessy 417
Behold Your King - Florence M. Bauer 379
The Captive Princess - Maxine Shore 5831
Great Lion of God - Taylor Caldwell 858
A Love Divine - Alexandra Ripley 5340
Man Before the Morning - Cecil Maiden 4032
Refuge in Avalon - Marguerite Steedman 5984
The Robber: A Tale of the Time of the Herods -
  Bertram Brooker 706
The Silver Chalice - Thomas B. Costain 1370
The Thorn of Arimathea - Frank G. Slaughter 5905

Josephine (Empress of France)
Alone Among Men - Marjorie Coryn 1355
Desiree - Annemarie Selinko 5741
The Eagle and the Rock - Frances Winwar 6830
*The Emperor's Lady: A Novel Based on the Life of the
  Empress Josephine* - F.W. Kenyon 3449
Far Flies the Eagle - Evelyn Anthony 162
Forty Centuries Look Down - Frederick Britten
  Austin 245
The Marriage of Josephine - Marjorie Coryn 1358
Mirage - Ruth McKenney 4283
Mistress of Fortune - Sheila Lancaster 3651
*My Brother Napoleon: The Confessions of Caroline
  Bonaparte* - F.W. Kenyon 3455
Napoleon Symphony - Anthony Burgess 780

The Raven and the Rose - Susan Wiggs 6746
A Rose for Virtue - Norah Lofts 3858
The Rose of Malmaison: The Turbulent Life of the Beautiful Josephine - Gaby von Schonthan 5660
So Great a Man - David Pilgrim 5000
Sultana - Michael, Prince of Greece 4358
Tom Burke of Ours - Charles James Lever 3732

Josephus, Flavius
The Jew of Rome - Lion Feuchtwanger 2071
Josephus - Lion Feuchtwanger 2072
Josephus and the Emperor - Lion Feuchtwanger 2073
The Soldier and the Sage: A Novel about Akiba - Richard G. Hubler 3065
The Source - James A. Michener 4374
The Tenth Measure - Brenda Lesley Segal 5721
The Triumph - Ernest K. Gann 2280
The Voices of Masada - David Kossoff 3545
The Wolf of Masada - John Fredman 2220
The Word and the Sword - Theo Lang 3662

Joshua
The Promised Land - Peter Danielson 1471
Scarlet Cord: A Novel of the Woman of Jericho - Frank G. Slaughter 5899
The Sea Peoples - Peter Danielson 1474

Juan, Prince of the Asturias
Here Lies Margot - Pamela Hill 2935

Juan II (King of Aragon)
The Dogs of Paradise - Abel Posse 5141

Juan II (King of Castile)
Master of Castile - Samuel Edwards 1888

Juan Carlos I (King of Spain)
Di and I - Peter Lefcourt 3714

Juan of Austria
The Last Crusader - Louis De Wohl 1569

Juana I (Queen of Spain)
The Prisoner of Tordesillas - Lawrence Schoonover 5665

Juana the Mad
The Prisoner of Tordesillas - Lawrence Schoonover 5665

Juarez, Benito
Chapultepec - Norman Zollinger 6965
Passengers to Mexico: The Last Invasion of Mexico - Blair Niles 4627

Judas Iscariot
Barabbas: A Dream of the World's Tragedy - Marie Corelli 1327
Behold the Man - N. Richard Nash 4556
A Certain Woman: The Story of Mary Magdalene - Victor MacClure 3959
Daughter of Jairus - Paul Hervey Fox 2196
He Came From Galilee - Daniel A. Poling 5083
I, Judas - Taylor Caldwell 859
Judas - Igal Mossinsohn 4500
The Knifeman: A Novel of Judas Iscariot - William Rayner 5271
The Last Temptation of Christ - Nikos Kazantzakis 3384
Man of Nazareth - Anthony Burgess 779
Martha, Martha - Patricia McGerr 4274
The Moon under Her Feet - Ceysta Kinstler 3503
The Robber: A Tale of the Time of the Herods - Bertram Brooker 706
The Salt of the Earth - Carlo Monterosso 4437
A Tear for Judas - LeGette Blythe 559
A Time for Judas - Morley Callaghan 866
Upon This Rock: A Novel of Simon Peter, Prince of Apostles - Frank G. Slaughter 5906

Judd, Gerrit Parmalee
The White King - Samuel Bertram Harrison 2747

Judge Dee
The Chinese Nail Murders - Robert van Gulik 6413

Deception - Eleanor Cooney 1295
The Emperor's Pearl - Robert van Gulik 6414
The Haunted Monastery - Robert van Gulik 6415
The Lacquer Screen - Robert van Gulik 6416
The Monkey and the Tiger - Robert van Gulik 6417
Murder in Canton - Robert van Gulik 6418
Necklace and Calabash - Robert van Gulik 6419
The Phantom of the Temple - Robert van Gulik 6420
The Red Pavilion - Robert van Gulik 6421
The Willow Pattern - Robert van Gulik 6422

Julia
I Loved Tiberius - Elisabeth Dored 1692

Julian the Apostate (Roman Emperor)
The Death of the Gods - Dmitri Merezhkovski 4338
Imperial Renegade - Louis De Wohl 1567
Julian - Gore Vidal 6489

Julius II (Pope)
The Agony and the Ecstasy - Irving Stone 6054

Julius Caesar
The Alexandrian - Martha Rofheart 5425
Augustus - Allan Massie 4167
Augustus - John Williams 6785
Caesar - Mirko Jelusich 3188
Caesar - Allan Massie 4168
Caesar's Women - Colleen McCullough 4233
The City of Libertines - W.G. Hardy 2702
The First Man in Rome - Colleen McCullough 4234
Fortune's Favorite - Colleen McCullough 4235
Freedom, Farewell - Phyllis Bentley 461
Gaul Is Divided - Esther Fisher Brown 721
A Goddess to a God - John Lloyd Balderston 278
The Gods Are Not Mocked - Anna Taylor 6177
The Grass Crown - Colleen McCullough 4236
The Ides of March - Thornton Wilder 6753
Imperial Caesar - Rex Warner 6565
The Key - Benita Kane Jaro 3169
A Pillar of Iron - Taylor Caldwell 861
The Pirate From Rome - John V.D. Southworth 5952
Prepare Them for Caesar - Mary Louise Mabie 3954
The Sacrilege - John Maddox Roberts 5380
SPQR - John Maddox Roberts 5381
Swords in the North - Paul Lewis Anderson 138
That Egyptian Woman - Noel B. Gerson 2384
Three's Company - Alfred Duggan 1774
Tros of Samothrace - Talbot Mundy 4515
The Young Caesar - Rex Warner 6567

Jumel, Eliza
The Conqueror: Being the True and Romantic Story of Alexander Hamilton - Gertrude Atherton 222
The Golden Mistress - Basil Beyea 488
Notorious Eliza - Basil Beyea 489
Painted Lady: Eliza Jumel, Her Life and Times - Leonard Falkner 2009

Jumel, Stephen
Notorious Eliza - Basil Beyea 489
Painted Lady: Eliza Jumel, Her Life and Times - Leonard Falkner 2009

Jung, Carl
The End of the World News - Anthony Burgess 777
Henry James' Midnight Song - Carol de Chellis Hill 2920
The Passions of the Mind - Irving Stone 6062
Secret Dreams - Keith Korman 3541

Jung Lu
Forbidden City - Muriel Molland Jernigan 3215

Junot, Andoche
The Emperor's Duchess - R.G. Waldeck 6524
Seed of Mischief - Willa Gibbs 2401

Junot, Laure
The Emperor's Duchess - R.G. Waldeck 6524

Justinian I (Eastern Roman Emperor)
Basilissa: A Tale of the Empress Theodora - John Masefield 4142
The Bearkeeper's Daughter - Gillian Bradshaw 628
Count Belisarius - Robert Graves 2544
The Female: A Novel of Another Time - Paul I. Wellman 6617
A Flame in Byzantium - Chelsea Quinn Yarbro 6899
Theodora - Samuel Edwards 1891
Theodora and the Emperor - Harold Lamb 3608
The Vandal - Richard O'Connor 4687

K

Kaahumanu (Queen of Hawaii)
Lord of the Isles - Donald Barr Chidsey 1063

Kahlo, Frida
The Veracruz Blues - Mark Winegardner 6821

Kalakaua (King of Hawaii)
Somewhere Within This House - Jean Francis Webb 6587

Kalb, Johann de
Dawn's Early Light - Elswyth Thane 6215

Kalmykoff, Ivan
Fifteen Flags - Richard Lynden Hardman 2686

Kamehameha I (King of Hawaii)
No Brighter Glory - Armstrong Sperry 5963

Kamehameha III (King of Hawaii)
Ka'a'awa: A Novel about Hawaii in the 1850s - Oswald Andrew Bushnell 814
The White King - Samuel Bertram Harrison 2747

al-Kamil, al-Malik (Sultan of Egypt)
Antichrist: A Novel of the Emperor Frederick II - Cecelia Holland 2982

Kanakoa (Queen of Hawaii)
Hawaii - James A. Michener 4370

Kanami, Kiyotsugu
The House of Kanze - Nobuko Albery 64

Kane, Elisha Kent
The Undiscovered Country - Jay Walz 6560

Kao Li-shih
The Court of the Lion - Eleanor Cooney 1294

Kao Tsung (Emperor of China)
Empress - Evelyn McCune 4238

Karloff, Boris
Never Cross a Vampire - Stuart M. Kaminsky 3344

Karpis, Alvin
Saint Mudd - Steve Thayer 6218
True Crime - Max Allan Collins 1214

Kassandros
Funeral Games - Mary Renault 5297

Katherine of Aragon
King's Fool - Margaret Campbell Barnes 325
Mistress Anne - Carolly Erickson 1952

Kauffman, Angelica
Angelica - Samuel A. Schreiner Jr. 5671

Kaufman, George S.
The Dorothy Parker Murder Case - George Baxt 384

Kean, Edmund
Kean: The Imaginary Memoirs of an Actor - Julius Berstl 485

Kearney, Philip
The Scarlet Patch - Bruce Lancaster 3645

Kearney, Stephen Watts
Hill of the Hawk - Scott O'Dell 4689

Keaton, Buster
The Fala Factor - Stuart M. Kaminsky   3337

Keats, John
The Remarkable Young Man - Cecil Roberts   5373
The Stress of Her Regard - Tim Powers   5157

Keith, Thomas
Blood and Sand - Rosemary Sutcliff   6121

Kellogg, John Harvey
The Road to Wellville - T. Coraghessan Boyle   618

Kelly, Emmett
Catch a Falling Star - Stuart M. Kaminsky   3333

Kelly, Michael
The Irish Boy: A Romantic Biography - Naomi Jacob   3137

Kelly, Paul
The Alienist - Caleb Carr   907

Kelsey, Nancy
The No-Return Trail - Sonia Levitin   3741

Kemal, Mustafa
The Ashes of Smyrna - Richard Reinhardt   5294
High Road to China - Jon Cleary   1106
The House of War - Catherine Gavin   2322

Kemble, Fanny
All This, and Heaven Too - Rachel Field   2080
The Ardent Years - Janet Stevenson   6003
Fire in the Heart - Henrietta Buckmaster   761

Kempe, Will
Nothing Like the Sun - Anthony Burgess   781

Kennedy, Jacqueline
Flying into Love - D.M. Thomas   6236

Kennedy, Janet
The King's Vixen - Pamela Hill   2937

Kennedy, John F.
Cold War - Robert Vaughan   6446
A First Class Murder - Elliott Roosevelt   5442
Flying into Love - D.M. Thomas   6236
The Immortals - Michael Korda   3540
Libra - Don DeLillo   1593
The Only Thing to Fear - David Poyer   5160
Till the End of Time - Allen Appel   170

Kennedy, Joseph P.
The Bank - Stephen Longstreet   3882
The Hyde Park Murder - Elliott Roosevelt   5443

Kennedy, Robert F.
The Immortals - Michael Korda   3540

Kenton, Simon
The Frontiersmen - Allen W. Eckert   1841
Kentucky Stand - Jere Hungerford Wheelwright   6670

Kepler, Johannes
Kepler: A Novel - John Banville   297
World and Paradise - Edgar Maass   3953

Keppel, Alice
Mr. American - George MacDonald Fraser   2211

Kerensky, Alexandr Feodorovich
Lenin: The Novel - Alan Brien   679

Keroualle, Louise de
Here Lies Our Sovereign Lord - Jean Plaidy   5021

Kesselring, Albert
Luciano's Luck - Jack Higgins   2912

Key, Francis Scott
Crimson Is the Eastern Shore - Don Tracy   6308

Khaemwaset
Mirage - Pauline Gedge   2346

Khan, Akbar
Flashman - George MacDonald Fraser   2204

Kidd, Captain William
The Legion of the Lost - Donald Barr Chidsey   1062

Killigrew, John
The Grove of Eagles - Winston Graham   2526

Kilpatrick, Hugh Judson
The Richmond Raid - John Brick   674

King, Bettie Moss
True Women - Janice Woods Windle   6820

King, Euphemia Texas Ashby
True Women - Janice Woods Windle   6820

King, Philip Gidley
Southern Cross - Terry Coleman   1206

King Philip
Legacy - Robert Vaughan   6448
The Wept of Wish-Ton-Wish - James Fenimore Cooper   1312
White Rising - Zane Kotker   3548

Kinzie, John
Gateway to Empire - Allen W. Eckert   1842

Kissinger, Henry
The Glory - Herman Wouk   6873

Kitchener, Horatio Herbert
Blunted Lance - Max Hennessy   2829
Drums of Khartoum - Chloe Gartner   2307
Rags of Glory - Stuart Cloete   1126
The Red Daniel - Duncan MacNeil   4017

Kiwang Hsi
Imperial Woman - Pearl S. Buck   755

Kleist, Heinrich von
No Place on Earth - Christa Wolf   6836

Kleomenes
The Corn King and the Spring Queen - Naomi Mitchison   4419

Knollys, Letitia
My Enemy the Queen - Victoria Holt   3017

Knox, Henry
The Bastard - John Jakes   3144
The King's Iron - Robert Newton Peck   4888
The Rebels - John Jakes   3152

Knox, John
City of Light - Alison Macleod   4001
The Gay Galliard - Margaret Irwin   3119
Mary, Queen of Scotland and the Isles - Margaret George   2356
The White Queen - Frederic Fallon   2011

Koken-Tenno
The Vermilion Bridge - Shelley Mydans   4539

Kokhba, Simon Bar
If I Forget Thee - Brenda Lesley Segal   5720
Prince of Israel - Elias Gilner   2422
Simon Bar Cochba: Rebellion in Judea - Merton Finch   2086
The Soldier and the Sage: A Novel about Akiba - Richard G. Hubler   3065
The Sword and the Promise - Benjamin Siegel   5845

Kolchak, Aleksandr
Fifteen Flags - Richard Lynden Hardman   2686

Konigsmarck, Philip Christopher
The Princess of Celle - Jean Plaidy   5045

Kordetzki
The Deluge - Henryk Sienkiewicz   5846

Kosciuszko, Thaddeus
Thaddeus of Warsaw - Jane Porter   5136

Kritias
The Last of the Wine - Mary Renault   5299

Kruger, Paul
The City of Gold - Francis Brett Young   6940
The Covenant - James A. Michener   4368
The Mask - Stuart Cloete   1125
Rags of Glory - Stuart Cloete   1126
Westward the Sun - Brigid Knight   3524

Krupskaya, Nadezhda Konstantinovna
Lenin in Zurich - Alexander Solzhenitsyn   5943

Kuang-Hsu (Emperor of China)
Twilight of the Dragon - Peter Bourne   596

Kublai Khan
Caravan to Kanadu: A Novel of Marco Polo - Edison Marshall   4103
Invisible Cities - Italo Calvino   867
The Journeyer - Gary Jennings   3194
Messer Marco Polo - Donn Byrne   840
Shike: Time of Dragons - Robert Shea   5784
Sons of the Steppe: The Story of How the Conqueror Genghis Khan Was Overcome - Hans Baumann   380

Kumlien, Thure
The Wolfling: A Documentary Novel of the 1870s - Sterling North   4648

Kutebar, Izzat
Flashman at the Charge - George MacDonald Fraser   2209

Kutuzov, Mikhail Illarionovich
Far Flies the Eagle - Evelyn Anthony   162
The Fortune Hunter - Ira J. Morris   4477
War and Peace - Leo Tolstoy   6295

Kyd, Thomas
A Dead Man in Deptford - Anthony Burgess   776
Liza Bowe - Shirley Barker   313
The Shadow of the Earth - Lee Wichelns   6731
To Be a King - Robert DeMaria   1607

L

La Guardia, Fiorello
The Hyde Park Murder - Elliott Roosevelt   5443
Murder in the West Wing - Elliott Roosevelt   5453

La Salle, Rene-Robert Cavelier de
The Gilded Torch - Iola Fuller   2252
The Power and the Glory - Gilbert Parker   4805
La Salle - John Vernon   6458
Touched with Fire - John William Tebbel   6195

La Valliere, Louise de
The Shadow of the Sun - Sylvia Pell   4891

Laclos, Pierre Choderlos de
A Place of Greater Safety - Hilary Mantel   4077

Lacombe, Claire
City of Darkness, City of Light - Marge Piercy   4998

LaFarge, Marie
The Lady and the Arsenic - Marjorie Bowen   598

Lafayette, Marie Joseph Paul de
The Bastard - John Jakes   3144
A Chance for Glory - Constance Wright   6877
Conceived in Liberty - Howard Fast   2029
Dawn's Early Light - Elswyth Thane   6215
The Drums of Monmouth - Emma Gelders Sterne   5998
The Fallon Blood - Reagan O'Neal   4741
Farewell to Valley Forge - David Taylor   6178
A Few Painted Feathers - Stephen Longstreet   3886
A Generation of Leaves - Robert S. Bloom   552
Hugh Wynne, Free Quaker - Silas Weir Mitchell   4416
I'll Storm Hell - Noel B. Gerson   2374
The Ironmaster - Anne Powers   5150
Jefferson: A Novel - Max Byrd   838
King's Masque - Evan John   3220
The Lure of the Falcon - Juliette Benzoni   465
Man From Mt. Vernon - Burke Boyce   607
Monmouth - Charles Bracelen Flood   2144
Morning in America - Willard Wiener   6741
A Place of Greater Safety - Hilary Mantel   4077
The Rebels - John Jakes   3152

Storm the Last Rampart - David Taylor 6180
The Strong Men - John Brick 677
To Spit Against the Wind - Benjamin H. Levin 3737
The Tree of Liberty - Elizabeth Page 4773
Valley Forge - MacKinlay Kantor 3364
Wicked Lady - Inglis Fletcher 2142
Yankee - Dana Fuller Ross 5495
Yorktown - Burke Davis 1513

Lafayette, Marquis de
The Bastard - John Jakes 3144
A Chance for Glory - Constance Wright 6877
Conceived in Liberty - Howard Fast 2029
Dawn's Early Light - Elswyth Thane 6215
The Drums of Monmouth - Emma Gelders
  Sterne 5998
The Fallon Blood - Reagan O'Neal 4741
Farewell to Valley Forge - David Taylor 6178
A Few Painted Feathers - Stephen Longstreet 3886
A Generation of Leaves - Robert S. Bloom 552
Hugh Wynne, Free Quaker - Silas Weir
  Mitchell 4416
I'll Storm Hell - Noel B. Gerson 2374
The Ironmaster - Anne Powers 5150
Jefferson: A Novel - Max Byrd 838
King's Masque - Evan John 3220
The Lure of the Falcon - Juliette Benzoni 465
Man From Mt. Vernon - Burke Boyce 607
Monmouth - Charles Bracelen Flood 2144
Morning in America - Willard Wiener 6741
A Place of Greater Safety - Hilary Mantel 4077
The Rebels - John Jakes 3152
Storm the Last Rampart - David Taylor 6180
The Strong Men - John Brick 677
To Spit Against the Wind - Benjamin H. Levin 3737
The Tree of Liberty - Elizabeth Page 4773
Valley Forge - MacKinlay Kantor 3364
Wicked Lady - Inglis Fletcher 2142
Yankee - Dana Fuller Ross 5495
Yorktown - Burke Davis 1513

Laffite, Jean
Anthony Adverse - Hervey Allen 98
Black Ivory - Polan Banks 292
*The Corsair: A Biographical Novel of Jean Lafitte,
  Hero of the Battle of New Orleans* - Madeleine
  Fabiola Kent 3444
The Fallon Pride - Reagan O'Neal 4742
Hearts of Hickory - John Trotwood Moore 4442
The Iron Mistress - Paul I. Wellman 6618
Marcel Armand - Sallie Bell 424
Pelican Coast - Alan Le May 3690

Lamar, Mirabeau Buonaparte
Republic: A Novel of Texas - E.V. Thompson 6266
Star of Empire: A Novel of Old San Antonio - Leonard
  Sanders 5590

Lamb, Lady Caroline
The Absorbing Fire: The Byron Legend - F.W.
  Kenyon 3445
Lord of the Ladies - Joanna Dessau 1626
The Memoirs of Lord Byron - Robert Nye 4655
The Secret Memoirs of Lord Byron - Christopher
  Nicole 4622

Lamb, Charles
John Howard Payne, Skywalker - Maude
  Barragan 348
So Perish the Roses - Neil Bell 423

Lamb, Mary Ann
So Perish the Roses - Neil Bell 423

Lamb, Robert
Proceed, Sergeant Lamb - Robert Graves 2550
Sergeant Lamb's America - Robert Graves 2552

Lamb, William
Albert's Victoria - Tyler Whittle 6719
The Queen and Lord M - Jean Plaidy 5046
The Queen's Husband - Jean Plaidy 5052
Victoria and Albert - Evelyn Anthony 166

The Young Victoria - Tyler Whittle 6724

Lancey, Magdalene de
The Limits of Glory: A Novel of Waterloo - James
  McDonough 4265

Landon, Alf
Murder in the East Room - Elliott Roosevelt 5448

Landon, Letitia Elizabeth
Letty - Helen Ashton 218

Landru, Henri Desire
Landru - Rene Masson 4170

Lane, Joseph
The Quiet Life of Mrs. General Lane - Victoria
  Case 951

Lane, Polly
The Quiet Life of Mrs. General Lane - Victoria
  Case 951

Lane, William
Darktown Strutters - Wesley Brown 732

Lang, Fritz
Destiny Express - Howard A. Rodman 5423

Langton, Stephen
The Barons of Runnymede - Pamela Bennetts 445

Langtry, Lillie
Good Night, Mr. Holmes - Carole Nelson
  Douglas 1699
Lillie - David Butler 818

Lannes, Jean
Seven Men of Gascony - R.F. Delderfield 1589

Lansky, Meyer
Carnal Hours - Max Allan Collins 1210
New Deal for Death - Elliott Roosevelt 5454

Lardner, Ring
Blue Ruin: A Novel of the 1919 World Series -
  Brendan Boyd 610
Hoopla - Harry Stein 5990

Larion
The Law of Larion - Peter Freuchen 2227

Larkin, Thomas
The Bear Flag: A Novel of the Birth of California -
  Cecelia Holland 2983

Las Casas, Bartolome de
Don Pedro and the Devil - Edgar Maas 3948
The Harp and the Shadow - Alejo Carpentier 905
The Indian Chronicles - Jose Barreiro 349
Takers of the City - Hoffman Reynolds Hays 2800

Latimer, Hugh
My Lord of Canterbury - Godfrey Turton 6369

Laud, William
Exiled - Helene Holt 3007
The Golden Feather - Theda Kenyon 3462
John Inglesant - John Henry Shorthouse 5833
The Physician of London - Stephanie Cowell 1394

Lauzun, Duc de
Sorrow by Day - Marjorie Coryn 1359

Laval, Honore
The Witch of Manga Reva - Garland Roark 5359

Laveau, Marie
Voodoo Dreams: A Novel of Marie Laveau - Jewell
  Parker Rhodes 5310

Lavoisier, Antoine Laurent
The Black Consul - Anatolii Vinogradov 6503
Rasero - Francisco Rebolledo 5282

Law, John
The Gamester - Rafael Sabatini 5550

Lawba, Spemica
Johnny Logan: Shawnee Spy - Allen W. Eckert 1843

Lawrence, D.H.
Daughter of Time - Nelia Gardner White 6695

Lawrence, T.E.
Behold the Fire - Michael Blankfort 541
The Devil's Spy - Michael Hastings 2773
Dreaming of Samarkand - Martin Booth 576
The Murder of Lawrence of Arabia - Matthew
  Eden 1865

Lawrence of Arabia
Behold the Fire - Michael Blankfort 541
The Devil's Spy - Michael Hastings 2773
Dreaming of Samarkand - Martin Booth 576
The Murder of Lawrence of Arabia - Matthew
  Eden 1865

Lazarus
According to Mary: A Novel of the Magdalene - Willa
  Gibbs 2398
A Certain Woman: The Story of Mary Magdalene -
  Victor MacClure 3959
The Last Temptation of Christ - Nikos
  Kazantzakis 3384
Lazarus - Alain Absire 15
Martha, Martha - Patricia McGerr 4274
The Messiah - Marjorie Holmes 3003

Le Moyne, Charles
High Towers - Thomas B. Costain 1366

Le Moyne, Jean-Baptiste
High Towers - Thomas B. Costain 1366

Le Moyne, Pierre
High Towers - Thomas B. Costain 1366

Leacock, Robert
Voyage to the First of December - Henry
  Carlisle 897

Leah
Jacob - Jean Cabries 844
Persian Conqueror - George Sidney Hellman 2822
The Tales of Jacob - Thomas Mann 4068

Lear, Tobias
Lydia Bailey - Kenneth Roberts 5387

Learmouth, Thomas
True Thomas - Nigel Tranter 6322

LeClerc, Charles
Black Triumvirate: A Novel of Haiti - Benjamin H.
  Levin 3736

LeClerc, Pauline
Black Triumvirate: A Novel of Haiti - Benjamin H.
  Levin 3736

Lecouvreur, Adrienne
Adrienne - Barbara Levy 3742
The Glory and the Dream - Katharine Dunlap 1789

Ledward, Thomas
Men Against the Sea - Charles Nordhoff 4638

Lee, Charles
Conceived in Liberty - Howard Fast 2029
The Drums of Monmouth - Emma Gelders
  Sterne 5998
Enough Good Men - Charles Mercer 4336
Farewell to Valley Forge - David Taylor 6178
I'll Storm Hell - Noel B. Gerson 2374
Janice Meredith - Paul Leicester Ford 2166
Man From Mt. Vernon - Burke Boyce 607
Morning in America - Willard Wiener 6741
Proceed, Sergeant Lamb - Robert Graves 2550
The Unvanquished - Howard Fast 2046

Lee, Francis Lightfoot
*Tidewater Dynasty: A Biographical Novel of the Lees
  of Stratford Hall* - Carey Roberts 5372

Lee, Henry
Brother to the Enemy - Bart Spicer 5964
Let My Name Stand Fair - Shirley Seifert 5727
Phantom Fortress - Bruce Lancaster 3643
The Swamp Fox, Francis Marion - Noel B.
  Gerson 2383

Tidewater Dynasty: A Biographical Novel of the Lees of Stratford Hall - Carey Roberts 5372

Lee, Light-Horse Harry
Brother to the Enemy - Bart Spicer 5964
Let My Name Stand Fair - Shirley Seifert 5727
Phantom Fortress - Bruce Lancaster 3643
The Swamp Fox, Francis Marion - Noel B. Gerson 2383
Tidewater Dynasty: A Biographical Novel of the Lees of Stratford Hall - Carey Roberts 5372

Lee, Mary Custis
Christmas with Robert E. Lee - Helen Topping Miller 4387
The Lady of Arlington - Harnett T. Kane 3354

Lee, Richard Henry
Tidewater Dynasty: A Biographical Novel of the Lees of Stratford Hall - Carey Roberts 5372

Lee, Robert E.
Battle Flag - Bernard Cornwell 1333
The Bloody Ground - Bernard Cornwell 1334
The Blue and the Gray - John Leekley 3713
Cease Firing - Mary Johnston 3230
Christmas with Robert E. Lee - Helen Topping Miller 4387
The Court Martial of Robert E. Lee - Douglas Savage 5617
Eight April Days - Scott Hart 2759
Farewell, My General - Shirley Seifert 5726
The Fifth Conspiracy - Ted Jones 3296
For the Love of Robert E. Lee - M.A. Harper 2715
Gettysburg - Stephen Longstreet 3887
Gettysburg: Crisis of Command - Harry Albright 65
The Ghost Raider - Ray Hogan 2978
Glory Enough for All: The Battle of the Crater - Duane Philip Schultz 5673
Gods and Generals - Jeff Shaara 5765
The Golden Eagle - Noel B. Gerson 2370
Gray Victory - Robert Skimin 5877
The Guns of the South - Harry N. Turtledove 6367
Hard Road to Gettysburg - Ted Jones 3298
House Divided - Ben Ames Williams 6765
Joy From Ashes - Al Lacy 3581
The Killer Angels - Michael Shaara 5766
The Lady of Arlington - Harnett T. Kane 3354
Major Stepton's War - Matthew Vaughan 6445
McKensie's Hundred: A Tale of the Old Dominion - Frank Yerby 6924
North and South - John Jakes 3151
Oldest Living Confederate Widow Tells All - Allan Gurganus 2621
The Stonewall Brigade: A Novel of the American Civil War - Frank G. Slaughter 5902
Three Days - Stephen Longstreet 3891
The Titans - John Jakes 3154
To Appomattox: Nine April Days, 1865 - Burke Davis 1512
Traveller - Richard Adams 27
Ulysses: A Biographical Novel - Robert Skimin 5878
Unto This Hour - Tom Wicker 6733
Untold Glory - Cothburn O'Neal 4739
The Unwritten Chronicles of Robert E. Lee - Lamar Herrin 2864

Leicester, Earl of
All the Queen's Men - Evelyn Anthony 157
The Bisley Boy - Christopher Hunt 3080
Elizabeth: Queen & Woman - Helen Thorpe 6279
Gay Lord Robert - Jean Plaidy 5015
The Green Salamander - Pamela Hill 2933
Heart of a Queen - Josephine Delves-Broughton 1603
Kenilworth - Sir Walter Scott 5700
Lady Rich - Elizabeth Boatwright Coker 1166
Legacy - Susan Kay 3374
My Dear Lover England - Pamela Bennetts 453
My Enemy the Queen - Victoria Holt 3017
My Lord Essex - Olive Eckerson 1838
My Lord the Fox - Robert York 6932

The Queen and the Gypsy - Constance Heaven 2810
Queen of This Realm: The Story of Queen Elizabeth I - Jean Plaidy 5050
The Queen's Ward - Hebe Elsna 1933
The Red-Haired Brat - Joanna Dessau 1627
The Robsart Affair - Jennette Letton 3729
Shadow in the Sun: A Novel of Elizabeth I, the Virgin Queen - F.W. Kenyon 3460
So Merciful a Queen, So Cruel a Woman - Alice Harwood 2769
Sweet Will - Eric Malpass 4050

Leigh, Augusta
The Memoirs of Lord Byron - Robert Nye 4655
My Sister, My Love - Lucille Iremonger 3111

Lenclos, Ninon de
All My Sins: A Novel of the Life and Loves of Ninon de Lenclos - Norbert Estey 1965

Lenin, Vladimir Ilich
Blood on the Snow - John Elliott 1916
The Dawning of Deliverance - Judith Pella 4892
Grishin - Hans Herlin 2859
Joseph - Mervyn Jones 3292
Karl and Rosa - Alfred Doblin 1653
The King's Commissar - Duncan Kyle 3570
Lenin in Zurich - Alexander Solzhenitsyn 5943
Lenin: The Novel - Alan Brien 679
The Petrograd Consignment - Owen Sela 5739
The Revolutionist: A Novel of Russia - Robert Littell 3810
Seven Days to Petrograd - Tom Hyman 3094
Time After Time - Allen Appel 171
White Nights, Red Dawn - Frederick Nolan 4634

Lennox, Sarah
The Ninth Statue - Roseleen Milne 4410

Leno, Dan
The Trial of Elizabeth Cree: A Novel of the Limehouse Murders - Peter Ackroyd 21

Leo I (Pope)
Throne of the World - Louis De Wohl 1575

Leo IV (Pope)
The Right Line of Cedric - Alfred Duggan 1773

Leo X (Pope)
A Cardinal of the Medici - Susan Hicks Beach 393
Leo Africanus - Amin Maalouf 3947
The Pope's Rhinoceros - Lawrence Norfolk 4642

Leo XII (Pope)
Crown of Grass - Charles Andrew Brady 634

Leo Africanus
Leo Africanus - Amin Maalouf 3947

Leofric
Lady Godiva and Master Tom - Raoul Cohen Faure 2052

Leon, Pauline
City of Darkness, City of Light - Marge Piercy 4998

Leonardo da Vinci
The Bride of Sforza - Miranda Seymour 5760
Carnival of Saints - George Herman 2860
A Comedy of Murders - George Herman 2861
Duchess of Milan - Michael Ennis 1946
The Florentine - Sandra Shulman 5840
The Lady in the Mask - Anne Green 2564
Leonardo's Judas - Leo Perutz 4941
The Medici Emerald - Martin Woodhouse 6851
The Medici Guns - Martin Woodhouse 6852
The Medici Hawks - Martin Woodhouse 6853
The Memory Cathedral: A Secret History of Leonardo Da Vinci - Jack Dann 1481
Michelangelo the Florentine - Sidney Alexander 86
Mona Lisa: The Woman in the Portrait - Sara Mayfield 4206
The Private Life of Mona Lisa - Pierre La Mure 3577

The Romance of Leonardo Da Vinci - Dmitri Merezhkovski 4339
The Tears of the Madonna - George Herman 2862

Leopold, Duke of Austria
Banners of Gold - Pamela Kaufman 3371
The Golden Knight - George Challis 971

Leopold I (King of Belgium)
The Girl Who Was Never Queen: A Biographical Novel of Princess Charlotte of Wales - Mary Main 4037
The Regent's Daughter - Jean Plaidy 5055
Seven Tempest - William Vaughan Wilkins 6761

Leopold II (King of Belgium)
The Gypsy From Cadiz - Tamsin Hamilton 2670
Lillie - David Butler 818

Leopold IV (Duke of Austria)
Banners of Gold - Pamela Kaufman 3371
The Golden Knight - George Challis 971

Leopold of Saxe-Coburg
The Girl Who Was Never Queen: A Biographical Novel of Princess Charlotte of Wales - Mary Main 4037
The Regent's Daughter - Jean Plaidy 5055

Lepidus, Marcus Aemilius
Augustus - Allan Massie 4167
Three's Company - Alfred Duggan 1774

Lesseps, Ferdinand Marie de
Madeleine - Catherine Gavin 2323

Lettow-Vorbeck, Paul Emil von
The Ghosts of Africa - William Stevenson 6013

Levy, Ashur
Blessed Is the Land - Louis Zara 6949

Lewes, George Henry
The Consuming Flame: The Story of George Eliot - F.W. Kenyon 3446

Lewis, James
I, James Lewis - Gilbert Wolf Gabriel 2266

Lewis, Matthew Gregory
The Flight of the Eagle - Donald Thomas 6239

Lewis, Meriwether
Distant Trails - Bill Gulick 2612
An Embarrassment of Riches - James Howard Kunstler 3565
Forward the Nation - Donald Culross Peattie 4880
From Sea to Shining Sea - James Alexander Thom 6232
The Gates of the Mountains - Will Henry 2842
My Theodosia - Anya Seton 5753
The Mysterious Death of Meriwether Lewis - Ron Burns 802
Sacajawea - Anna Lee Waldo 6529
Sacajawea of the Shoshones - Della F. Emmons 1940
The Seekers - John Jakes 3153
The Shining Mountains - Dale Van Every 6410
Star of the West - Ethel Hueston 3070
Tale of Valor - Vardis Fisher 2112
Those Who Go Against the Current - Shirley Seifert 5734
Trail: The Story of the Lewis and Clark Expedition - Louis Charbonneau 998
War Clouds - Donald Clayton Porter 5131
Westward! - Dana Fuller Ross 5492

L'Hermite, Tristan
Quentin Durward - Sir Walter Scott 5705

Li Hung Chang
Forbidden City - Muriel Molland Jernigan 3215

Li Lien Ying
Imperial Woman - Pearl S. Buck 755

Liddell, Eric
Chariots of Fire - W.J. Weatherby 6586

Liebknecht, Karl
Karl and Rosa - Alfred Doblin 1653
A People Betrayed - Alfred Doblin 1654

Lightfoot, Hannah
The Prince and the Quakeress - Jean Plaidy 5043

Liliuokalani (Queen of Hawaii)
Carolina Courage - Dana Fuller Ross 5469

Lincoln, Abraham
Abe Lincoln of Pigeon Creek - William Edward
 Wilson 6818
Beloved Enemy - Al Lacy 3579
Captains and the Kings - Taylor Caldwell 851
*Christmas for Tad: A Story of Mary and Abraham
 Lincoln* - Helen Topping Miller 4386
Comes an Echo on the Breeze - Edward J.
 Ryan 5542
The Cosgrove Report - G.J.A. O'Toole 4765
The Crisis - Winston Churchill 1079
Dim the Flaring Lamps - Jan Jordan 3301
The Dixie Widow - Gilbert Morris 4459
Dream West - David Nevin 4587
The Father - Katharine Holland Brown 724
The Fifth Conspiracy - Ted Jones 3296
Flash for Freedom - George MacDonald Fraser 2203
Flight to Canada - Ishmael Reed 5285
For Us the Living - Bruce Lancaster 3639
Forever Free - Honore Morrow 4487
Freedom - William Safire 5561
Give Me the Wind - Jan Jordan 3302
Grant's War - Ted Jones 3297
Gray Victory - Robert Skimin 5877
Green Rose of Furley - Helen C. Barney 334
Hard Road to Gettysburg - Ted Jones 3298
Henry and Clara - Thomas Mallon 4042
Hoffman's Row - Walter Carnahan 902
House Divided - Ben Ames Williams 6765
Immortal Wife - Irving Stone 6057
Intrigue in Baltimore - Janet Whitney 6715
The Last Full Measure - Honore Morrow 4488
Lincoln: A Novel - Gore Vidal 6490
The Lincoln Hunters - Wilson Tucker 6359
Lincoln's Mothers: A Story of Nancy and Sally Lincoln
 - Dorothy Clarke Wilson 6804
The Lost Years: A Biographical Fiction - Oscar
 Lewis 3757
Love and War - John Jakes 3150
Love Is Eternal - Irving Stone 6058
A Man for the Ages - Irving A. Bacheller 261
McKay's Bees - Thomas McMahon 4289
McKensie's Hundred: A Tale of the Old Dominion -
 Frank Yerby 6924
Mr. Lincoln's Wife - Anne Colver 1221
Nevada! - Dana Fuller Ross 5481
Oldest Living Confederate Widow Tells All - Allan
 Gurganus 2621
The President's Daughter - Barbara Chase-
 Riboud 1005
The Senator's Lady - Shirley Seifert 5733
Soul of Abe Lincoln - Bernie Babcock 251
The Soul of Ann Rutledge - Bernie Babcock 252
Spoon - John Christgau 1074
The Spur - Ardyth Kennelly 3425
Steamboat on the River - Darwin Le Ora
 Teilhet 6200
*The Stonewall Brigade: A Novel of the American Civil
 War* - Frank G. Slaughter 5902
Talons of Eagles - William W. Johnstone 3268
*There Was a Season: A Biographical Novel of
 Jefferson Davis* - Theodore Olsen 4730
The Titans - John Jakes 3154
Twilight of Empire - Allen W. Eckert 1846
Ulysses: A Biographical Novel - Robert Skimin 5878
Unto This Hour - Tom Wicker 6733
With Malice Toward None - Honore Morrow 4492
*Woman with a Sword: The Biographical Novel of
 Anna Ella Carroll of Maryland* - Hollister
 Noble 4632

The Yankee From Tennessee - Noel B. Gerson 2388

Lincoln, Mary Todd
*Christmas for Tad: A Story of Mary and Abraham
 Lincoln* - Helen Topping Miller 4386
The Dixie Widow - Gilbert Morris 4459
Forever Free - Honore Morrow 4487
Henry and Clara - Thomas Mallon 4042
Hoffman's Row - Walter Carnahan 902
Lincoln: A Novel - Gore Vidal 6490
Love Is Eternal - Irving Stone 6058
McKensie's Hundred: A Tale of the Old Dominion -
 Frank Yerby 6924
Mr. Lincoln's Wife - Anne Colver 1221
The Trial of Mary Todd Lincoln - James A.
 Rhodes 5309

Lincoln, Robert Todd
The Trial of Mary Todd Lincoln - James A.
 Rhodes 5309

Lincoln, Tad
*Christmas for Tad: A Story of Mary and Abraham
 Lincoln* - Helen Topping Miller 4386

Lincoln, Thomas
Lincoln's Mothers: A Story of Nancy and Sally Lincoln
 - Dorothy Clarke Wilson 6804
The Matrix - Maria Thompson Daviess 1509

Lind, Jenny
Jenny and Barnum: A Novel of Love - Roderick
 Thorp 6276
The Swedish Nightingale: Jenny Lind - Elizabeth
 Kyle 3571

Lindbergh, Charles
Dance on a Sinking Ship - Michael Kilian 3483
A First Class Murder - Elliott Roosevelt 5442
Stolen Away - Max Allan Collins 1213

Lindsay, David
James, by the Grace of God - Nigel Tranter 6315
The Riven Realm - Nigel Tranter 6317

Linley, Elizabeth
Perdita's Prince - Jean Plaidy 5040

Liston, Robert
The Sleep of Life - Richard Gordon 2486

Liszt, Franz
Hungarian Rhapsody: The Life of Franz Liszt - Jean
 Rousselot 5511
Last Love of Camille - Frances Winwar 6832
Passionate Rebel: The Story of Hector Berlioz - F.W.
 Kenyon 3457
*The Questing Heart: A Romantic Novel about George
 Sand* - F.W. Kenyon 3458

Little Wolf
The Powder River - Winfred Blevins 546

Liu Pang (Emperor of China)
The Dream of Confucius - Jean Levi 3734

Liverpool, Earl of
The Sea Officer - Showell Styles 6105

Livia
Augustus - Allan Massie 4167
I, Claudius - Robert Graves 2547
I Loved Tiberius - Elisabeth Dored 1692
Tiberius: The Memoirs of the Emperor - Allan
 Massie 4169

Livingstone, David
The Whales in Lake Tanganyika - Lennart
 Hagerfors 2636

Lloyd, Constance
I Give You Oscar Wilde - Desmond Hall 2647

Lloyd George, David
Blunted Lance - Max Hennessy 2829
The Buckingham Palace Connection - Ted
 Willis 6792
The End of the Hunt - Thomas Flanagan 2119
Give Us This Day - R.F. Delderfield 1586

High Heroic - Constantine FitzGibbon 2118
It's Me Again - Donald Jack 3126
Rags of Glory - Stuart Cloete 1126

Llywelyn ap Gruffydd (Prince of Wales)
The Brothers of Gwynedd - Edith Pargeter 4796
A Dragon for Edward - Pamela Bennetts 450
Falls the Shadow - Sharon Kay Penman 4903
Hammer of the Scots - Jean Plaidy 5018
The Heaven Tree Trilogy - Edith Pargeter 4797
The Reckoning - Sharon Kay Penman 4906
The Wind From Hastings - Morgan Llywelyn 3825

Llywelyn ap Iowerth (Prince of Wales)
Here Be Dragons - Sharon Kay Penman 4904

Llywelyn the Great (Prince of Wales)
Harp into Battle - Cecil Maiden 4031
Here Be Dragons - Sharon Kay Penman 4904

Lobengula (King of the Matabele)
Earthshaker - Robert Wilson Krepps 3553
On Trial for My Country - Stanlake Samkange 5578

Loe, Judith von
Woman Astride - Nora Purtscher-Wydenbruch 5209

Logan, Benjamin
Johnny Logan: Shawnee Spy - Allen W. Eckert 1843

Logan, Harvey
*Kid Curry: The Life and Times of Harvey Logan and
 the Wild Bunch* - F. Bruce Lamb 3606

London, Jack
The Summer of Jack London - Andrew J.
 Fenady 2058

Longabaugh, Harry
Outlaw Lover - Lindsey Hanks 2676
The Story of the Sundance Kid - David Everitt 1988

Longstreet, James
1901 - Robert Conroy 1258
Confederates - Thomas Keneally 3412
The Court Martial of Robert E. Lee - Douglas
 Savage 5617
The Dixie Widow - Gilbert Morris 4459
Gettysburg - Stephen Longstreet 3887
Gettysburg: Crisis of Command - Harry Albright 65
Gods and Generals - Jeff Shaara 5765
Gray Victory - Robert Skimin 5877
House Divided - Ben Ames Williams 6765
Joy From Ashes - Al Lacy 3581
The Killer Angels - Michael Shaara 5766
Mockingbird Sang at Chickamauga - Alfred Leland
 Crabb 1404
Talons of Eagles - William W. Johnstone 3268
Traveller - Richard Adams 27
Ulysses: A Biographical Novel - Robert Skimin 5878
The Unconquered - Ben Ames Williams 6768
Unto This Hour - Tom Wicker 6733

Loper, Richard Fanning
That Skipper From Stonington - Theda Kenyon 3464

Lopez, Francisco
Young Vargas Lewis - Robert Brainard Pearsall 4874

Lord Byron
The Absorbing Fire: The Byron Legend - F.W.
 Kenyon 3445
The Blue Heaven Bends Over All - Jane Oliver 4720
Byron: A Novel - Sigrid Combuchen 1225
Count Manifred - Miranda Seymour 5761
Frankenstein Unbound - Brian Aldiss 68
*The Golden Years: A Novel Based on the Life and
 Loves of Percy Bysshe Shelley* - F.W.
 Kenyon 3451
Haunted Summer - Anne Edwards 1881
Lord Byron's Doctor - Paul West 6634
Lord of the Dead: The Secret History of Byron - Tom
 Holland 2999
Lord of the Ladies - Joanna Dessau 1626
Love's Children - Judith Chernaik 1013
The Memoirs of Lord Byron - Robert Nye 4655

The Missolonghi Manuscript - Frederic Prokosch 5194
My Sister, My Love - Lucille Iremonger 3111
The Secret Memoirs of Lord Byron - Christopher Nicole 4622
A Single Summer with Lord B. - Derek Marlowe 4092
The Stress of Her Regard - Tim Powers 5157
Teresa, or Her Demon Lover - Austin K. Gray 2554

Lord Cochrane
The Frigate Captain - Showell Styles 6103
Sharpe's Devil - Bernard Cornwell 1340

Lord Darnley
The Gay Galliard - Margaret Irwin 3119
The Green Salamander - Pamela Hill 2933
Immortal Queen - Elizabeth Byrd 834
The Lion and the Rose - Jane Oliver 4724
Mary of Scotland - F.W. Kenyon 3454
Mary, Queen of Scotland and the Isles - Margaret George 2356
No Smoke Without Fire - Alice Harwood 2767
Parcel of Rogues - Jane Lane 3656
Queen's Caprice - Marjorie Bowen 599
Royal Road to Fotheringay - Jean Plaidy 5059
A Time for the Death of a King - Ann Dukthas 1777
The White Queen - Frederic Fallon 2011

Lord Nelson
1805 - Richard Woodman 6857
Angelica - Samuel A. Schreiner Jr. 5671
The Blacksmith's Daughter - Joanna Dessau 1625
The Bomb Vessel - Richard Woodman 6860
Bride of Glory - Bradda Field 2078
Brumaire - Mark Logan 3864
Caribbean - James A. Michener 4365
Darken Ship - Nicholas Monsarrat 4431
Decision at Trafalgar - Richard Woodman 6861
Emma - F.W. Kenyon 3448
The English Captain - Simon White 6700
A Game for Empires - Pearl Frye 2243
Guillotine - Mark Logan 3865
A King's Commander - Dewey Lambdin 3613
The King's Commission - Dewey Lambdin 3614
Lord Elgin's Lady - Theodore Vrettos 6514
Loving Emma - Nigel Foxell 2197
Mister Christian - William Kinsolving 3502
The Nelson Touch - Paul Lewis 3759
Ramage - Dudley Pope 5097
Ramage at Trafalgar - Dudley Pope 5102
Return to Treasure Island - Denis Judd 3318
The Scalpel and the Sword - Dell Shannon 5774
The Sea Officer - Showell Styles 6105
Shadow of a Lady - Jane Aiken Hodge 2971
Sir William - David Stacton 5977
The Sleeping Sword: A Biographical Novel - Pearl Frye 2244
This Other Eden - Marilyn Harris 2733
The Volcano Lover - Susan Sontag 5946

Lord North
Let the King Beware! - Honore Morrow 4489
Poor Richard's Game - G.J.A. O'Toole 4766

Lorre, Peter
The Greta Garbo Murder Case - George Baxt 385
Think Fast, Mr. Peters - Stuart M. Kaminsky 3347

Los Dolores de Leon, Juana
The Spanish Bride - Georgette Heyer 2902

Lot
Lot's Wife - Marie Ley-Piscator 3767

Lothropp, John
Exiled - Helene Holt 3007

Louis (Duke of Orleans)
In a Dark Wood Wandering - Hella S. Haasse 2631

Louis (Louis XI)
Niccolo Rising - Dorothy Dunnett 1803

Louis, Comte de Provence
Scaramouche the King-Maker - Rafael Sabatini 5555

Louis, Joe
Down for the Count - Stuart M. Kaminsky 3336

Louis VI (King of France)
Beloved Enemy: The Passions of Eleanor of Aquitaine - Ellen Jones 3288
The Dragon Waiting: A Masque of History - John M. Ford 2165

Louis VII (King of France)
Beloved Enemy: The Passions of Eleanor of Aquitaine - Ellen Jones 3288
The Courts of Love - Jean Plaidy 5010
Eleanor the Queen - Norah Lofts 3842

Louis VIII (King of France)
The Battle of the Queens - Jean Plaidy 5005

Louis IX (King of France)
The Quiet Light - Louis De Wohl 1572

Louis X (King of France)
The Poisoned Crown - Maurice Druon 1734
The Strangled Queen - Maurice Druon 1737

Louis XI (King of France)
Fortune's Wheel - Rhoda S. Edwards 1886
The Golden Yoke: A Novel of the War of the Roses - Olive Eckerson 1837
The Hunchback of Notre Dame - Victor Hugo 3076
Niccolo Rising - Dorothy Dunnett 1803
Quentin Durward - Sir Walter Scott 5705
The Spider King - Lawrence Schoonover 5668
To Lie with Lions - Dorothy Dunnett 1810
The Unicorn Hunt - Dorothy Dunnett 1811
The White Queen - Lesley J. Nickell 4611

Louis XII (King of France)
The Golden Porcupine - Muriel Ray Bolton 567
The Reluctant Queen - Molly Costain Haycraft 2796
A Stake in the Kingdom - Nigel Tranter 6321

Louis XIII (King of France)
The Arm and the Darkness - Taylor Caldwell 850
The Cardinal and the Queen - Evelyn Anthony 159
Cinq-Mars - Alfred Victor de Vigny 6495
The Three Musketeers - Alexandre Dumas 1782

Louis XIV (King of France)
All the Golden Gifts - Iola Fuller 2251
All the King's Ladies - Janice Law 3678
Angelique - Sergeanne Golon 2465
Angelique and the King - Sergeanne Golon 2468
Angelique in Revolt - Sergeanne Golon 2471
The Anthem - Noel B. Gerson 2361
A Candle for D'Artagnan - Chelsea Quinn Yarbro 6895
The Cat and the King - Louis Auchincloss 229
The Crown and the Shadow: The Story of Francoise d'Aubigne, Marquise de Maintenon - Pamela Hill 2930
The Ghost of Monsieur Scarron - Janet Lewis 3755
The Gilded Torch - Iola Fuller 2252
The King's Way - Francoise Chandernagor 986
Louis the Well-Beloved - Jean Plaidy 5032
The Marquis - Joan Sanders 5586
The Oracle Glass - Judith Merkle Riley 5335
Royal Flush: The Story of Minette - Margaret Irwin 3121
The Secret Wife - Alice Acland 22
The Shadow of the Sun - Sylvia Pell 4891
The Shepherd's Crook - Paul Frischauer 2234
Sorrow by Day - Marjorie Coryn 1359
Three Came to Ville Marie - Alan Sullivan 6114
The Wandering Prince - Jean Plaidy 5075
Ward of the Sun King - Mildred Allen Butler 826

Louis XV (King of France)
A Day of Battle - Vincent Sheean 5787
The French Bride - Evelyn Anthony 163
Golden Venus - David Mynders Smythe 5933
Louis the Well-Beloved - Jean Plaidy 5032

Louisiana Purchase - A.E. Hotchner 3039
Royal Merry-Go-Round - F.W. Kenyon 3459
To Dance with Kings - Rosalind Laker 3601
Tomahawk - Donald Clayton Porter 5129

Louis XVI (King of France)
Asylum for the Queen - Mildred A. Jordan 3303
City of Darkness, City of Light - Marge Piercy 4998
The Devil's Laughter - Frank Yerby 6913
Dr. Guillotine: The Eccentric Exploits of an Early Scientist - Herbert Lom 3867
The Fatal Friendship: Marie Antoinette, Count Fersen and the Flight to Varennes - Stanley Loomis 3895
Fear No More - Hester W. Chapman 990
Hester - Brian Cleeve 1107
The Man Who Killed the King - Dennis Wheatley 6654
Marie Antoinette - F.W. Kenyon 3453
Palaces of Desire - Kate Alexander 81
The Queen's Confession - Victoria Holt 3019
Sweet Marie-Antoinette - Lozania Prole 5198
To Dance with Kings - Rosalind Laker 3601
Tricolour - Mark Logan 3866

Louis XVII (King of France)
Cockades: A Romance - Meade Minnigerode 4412
Fear No More - Hester W. Chapman 990
A King Reluctant - William Vaughan Wilkins 6759
The Man Who Killed the King - Dennis Wheatley 6654
The Prince Lost to Time - Ann Dukthas 1776
Seed of Mischief - Willa Gibbs 2401
The Uncrowned King - Baroness Emma Orczy 4747

Louis XVIII (King of France)
Holy Week - Louis Aragon 182
Scaramouche the King-Maker - Rafael Sabatini 5555
Waterloo - Frederic E. Smith 5920

Louis Charles (Dauphin of France)
Fear No More - Hester W. Chapman 990
The Man Who Killed the King - Dennis Wheatley 6654
The Prince Lost to Time - Ann Dukthas 1776

Louis de Valois
A Comedy of Murders - George Herman 2861

Louis Philippe (King of France)
Disraeli Rising - Maurice Edelman 1852

Lovejoy, Owen
The Drums of Morning - Philip Van Doren Stern 5997

Lovell, Francis
The Fate of Princes - P.C. Doherty 1673
The White Boar - Marian Palmer 4780

Lovell, Phillip
The White Boar - Marian Palmer 4780

Lovelock, Jack
Lovelock - James McNeish 4311

Low, Charles Porter
Tall Ships to Cathay - Helen Augur 240

Low, Judah
The Sword of the Golem - Abraham Rothberg 5509

Low, Seth
Tall Ships to Cathay - Helen Augur 240

Low, William Henry
Tall Ships to Cathay - Helen Augur 240

Lowe, Hudson
The Last Love - Thomas B. Costain 1367

Loy, Myrna
The William Powell and Myrna Loy Murder Case - George Baxt 390

Lucan
The Conspiracy - John Hersey 2870

Lucia
Josephus and the Emperor - Lion
   Feuchtwanger 2073

Luciano, Charles "Lucky"
Luciano's Luck - Jack Higgins 2912
The President's Man - Elliott Roosevelt 5455

Ludendorff, Erich
White Nights, Red Dawn - Frederick Nolan 4634

Ludwig II (King of Bavaria)
Sherlock in Love - Sena Jeter Naslund 4557

Lugosi, Bela
The Greta Garbo Murder Case - George Baxt 385
Never Cross a Vampire - Stuart M. Kaminsky 3344

Luke
Dear and Glorious Physician - Taylor Caldwell 853
The Emperor's Physician - Jacob Randolph
   Perkins 4914
*The Road to Bithynia: A Novel of Luke, the Beloved
   Physician* - Frank G. Slaughter 5897
The Silver Chalice - Thomas B. Costain 1370

Luna, Alvaro de
Master of Castile - Samuel Edwards 1888

Lunt, Henry
Henry Lunt and the Ranger - Tom McNamara 4304

Lunyevitza-Mashin, Draga
Dance of the Assassins - Maria Fagyas 1997

Lusignan, James de
Race of Scorpions - Dorothy Dunnett 1806
To Lie with Lions - Dorothy Dunnett 1810

Lusignon, Carlotta de
Race of Scorpions - Dorothy Dunnett 1806

Luther, Katie
Queen of the Reformation - Charles Ludwig 3922

Luther, Martin
The Adventurer - Mika Waltari 6550
Flame of Fire - Jane Oliver 4722
Monk in Armour - Gladys H. Barr 342
Queen of the Reformation - Charles Ludwig 3922

Luxemburg, Rosa
Karl and Rosa - Alfred Doblin 1653
A People Betrayed - Alfred Doblin 1654

Lyell, Charles
The Origin - Irving Stone 6060

Lyon, Emma
Bride of Glory - Bradda Field 2078

M

MacArthur, Douglas
1901 - Robert Conroy 1258
Buried Caesars - Stuart M. Kaminsky 3332

MacArthur, John
The Adventurers - William Stuart Long 3869
The Settlers - William Stuart Long 3878
Storm of Time - Eleanor Dark 1494
The Traitors - William Stuart Long 3879

Macbeth (King of Scotland)
King Hereafter - Dorothy Dunnett 1802
Lady of Moray - Bonnie Copeland 1318

MacDonald, Flora
Meggy MacIntosh - Elizabeth Janet Gray 2555
Raleigh's Eden - Inglis Fletcher 2137
The Scotswoman - Inglis Fletcher 2140

MacDonald, George
The Four Hundred - Stephen Sheppard 5804

MacDonald, Ramsay
The Murder of Lawrence of Arabia - Matthew
   Eden 1865

MacDonnell, James
The Limits of Glory: A Novel of Waterloo - James
   McDonough 4265

MacGregor, Ian
The Imposter - Noel B. Gerson 2375

Machiavelli, Niccolo
The Borgia Prince - Pamela Bennetts 446
Michelangelo the Florentine - Sidney Alexander 86
Mona Lisa: The Woman in the Portrait - Sara
   Mayfield 4206
Romola - George Eliot 1910
The Scarlet City - Hella S. Haasse 2632
Then and Now - William Somerset Maugham 4198
Web of Lucifer: A Novel of the Borgia Fury - Maurice
   Samuel 5580

Mack, Connie
The Celebrant - Eric Rolfe Greenberg 2572

MacKellar, Patrick
The White Cockade - Vincent O'Brien 4683

Mackenzie, Alexander Slidell
The Big Family - Vina Delmar 1600
Voyage to the First of December - Henry
   Carlisle 897

MacKenzie, Colin
The World of Jennie G. - Elisabeth Ogilvie 4696

Mackenzie, William Lyon
Bright to the Wanderer - Bruce Lancaster 3638

MacLaine, Shirley
Live From Golgotha - Gore Vidal 6491

Maclise, Daniel
Disraeli in Love - Maurice Edelman 1851

Macquarie, Lachlan
The Adventurers - William Stuart Long 3869
The Explorers - William Stuart Long 3872

Madame de Maintenon
The Anthem - Noel B. Gerson 2361
The Cat and the King - Louis Auchincloss 229
*The Crown and the Shadow: The Story of Francoise
   d'Aubigne, Marquise de Maintenon* - Pamela
   Hill 2930
The Gilded Torch - Iola Fuller 2252
The King's Way - Francoise Chandernagor 986
The Secret Wife - Alice Acland 22
Ward of the Sun King - Mildred Allen Butler 826

Madame de Pompadour
A Day of Battle - Vincent Sheean 5787
Louis the Well-Beloved - Jean Plaidy 5032
Louisiana Purchase - A.E. Hotchner 3039
Rasero - Francisco Rebolledo 5282
Royal Merry-Go-Round - F.W. Kenyon 3459

Madero, Francisco Indalecio
The Crimson Wind - Max Hennessy 2832
Under the Fifth Sun: A Novel of Pancho Villa - Earl
   Shorris 5832

Madison, Dolley
1812 - David Nevin 4586
Back Bay - William Martin 4138
Burr - Gore Vidal 6485
A Daughter of Liberty - Allan Cole 1196
Dolley - Rita Mae Brown 727
My Dear Cousin - Peggy Hoffmann 2977
My Theodosia - Anya Seton 5753
Queen Dolley: The Life and Times of Dolley Madison
   - Dorothy Clarke Wilson 6806

Madison, James
1812 - David Nevin 4586
Burr - Gore Vidal 6485
*The Conqueror: Being the True and Romantic Story of
   Alexander Hamilton* - Gertrude Atherton 222
Dolley - Rita Mae Brown 727
Hawk's Journey - Donald Clayton Porter 5119
My Dear Cousin - Peggy Hoffmann 2977

Queen Dolley: The Life and Times of Dolley Madison
   - Dorothy Clarke Wilson 6806
Red Stick - Donald Clayton Porter 5121
The River Devils - Carter A. Vaughan 6437
River to the West: A Novel of the Astor Adventure -
   John Edward Jennings 3204
Sally Hemings - Barbara Chase-Riboud 1006
Tide of Empire - Bates Baldwin 279
A Time for Titans - Vina Delmar 1602

Madoc
The Children of the First Man - James Alexander
   Thom 6230

Madog ab Owain Gwynedd
The Children of the First Man - James Alexander
   Thom 6230

Madox, Henry
Katheryn, the Wanton Queen - Maureen Peters 4976

Maelmordha
The Kings in Winter - Cecelia Holland 2991

Maeve
Red Branch - Morgan Llywelyn 3824

Magellan, Ferdinand
Five Black Ships: A Novel of Discoverers - Napoleon
   Baccino Ponce de Leon 5089

Magnus Maximus (Roman Emperor)
The Eagles Depart - John Gloag 2434

Mago
Hannibal of Carthage - Mary Dolan 1686

Magoffin, Samuel
The Turquoise Trail - Shirley Seifert 5736

Magoffin, Susan Shelby
The Turquoise Trail - Shirley Seifert 5736

Mahaut
The Lily and the Lion - Maurice Druon 1733

The Mahdi
Drums of Khartoum - Chloe Gartner 2307

Mahmud II (Ottoman Sultan)
Sultana - Michael, Prince of Greece 4358
Valide: A Novel of the Harem - Barbara Chase-
   Riboud 1007

Maimiti
Pitcairn's Island - Charles Nordhoff 4640

Maimonides, Moses
*The Doctor From Cordova: A Biographical Novel
   about the Great Philosopher Maimonides* - Herbert
   Le Porrier 3693
The Source - James A. Michener 4374
Trail and Triumph: A Novel about Maimonides -
   Lester M. Morrison 4485

Maintenon, Madame de
The Anthem - Noel B. Gerson 2361
The Cat and the King - Louis Auchincloss 229
*The Crown and the Shadow: The Story of Francoise
   d'Aubigne, Marquise de Maintenon* - Pamela
   Hill 2930
The Gilded Torch - Iola Fuller 2252
The King's Way - Francoise Chandernagor 986
The Secret Wife - Alice Acland 22
Ward of the Sun King - Mildred Allen Butler 826

Maitland, William
The White Queen - Frederic Fallon 2011

Malatesta, Giovanni
Concordia - Frances Fleetwood 2124

Malatesta, Paolo
Ardent Flame - Frances Winwar 6829
Concordia - Frances Fleetwood 2124

Malcolm III (King of Scotland)
Sing Morning Star - Jane Oliver 4727

Malibran, Maria Felicita
Signorina - Henry Myers 4542

Malinche
Cortez and Marina - Edison Marshall 4105
Death of the Fifth Sun - Robert Somerlott 5944
The Golden Princess - Alexander Baron 335

Mallon, Mary
The Ballad of Typhoid Mary - Jurg Federspiel 2057

Mallowan, Sir Max
Agatha - Kathleen Tynan 6374

Malvern, Frances
The Proud Retreat - Clifford Dowdey 1706

Mancini, Hortense
Here Lies Our Sovereign Lord - Jean Plaidy 5021

Mandeville, Geoffrey de
The Knight - George Shipway 5829
Stephen and the Sleeping Saints - Pamela
  Bennetts 457

Manet, Edouard
Depths of Glory - Irving Stone 6055
The Lawless - John Jakes 3149

Mangas Coloradas
Apache - Will Comfort 1226
Desert Hawks - Frank Burleson 786
War Eagles - Frank Burleson 788

Mannerheim, Gustaf
Give Me the Daggers - Catherine Gavin 2321

Manners, Catherine
Wife to Great Buckingham - Hilda Lewis 3751

Mansfield, Josie
Jubilee Jim and the Wizard of Wall Street - Donald
  Porter 5112

Mansfield, Katherine
Daughter of Time - Nelia Gardner White 6695

Manuel I (Eastern Roman Emperor)
Their Most Serene Majesties - Ange Vlachos 6505

Mao Tse-tung
Dynasty - Robert S. Elegant 1902
From a Far Land - Robert S. Elegant 1903
High Road to China - Jon Cleary 1106
The Warlord - Malcolm Bosse 589

Marat, Jean-Paul
The Black Consul - Anatolii Vinogradov 6503
The Devil's Laughter - Frank Yerby 6913
*Dr. Guillotine: The Eccentric Exploits of an Early
  Scientist* - Herbert Lom 3867
A Place of Greater Safety - Hilary Mantel 4077
To Spit Against the Wind - Benjamin H. Levin 3737
The Way to the Lantern - Audrey Erskine
  Lindop 3790

Marc Antony
Throne of Isis - Judith Tarr 6170

Marcel, Antonio
Sage of Canudos - Lucien Marchal 4080

Marcus Aurelius (Roman Emperor)
Between Eternities - Robert H. Pilpel 5001
*The Equinox: A Novel of Rome in the Time of
  Commodus* - Carol Saylor 5622
A Fig in Winter - Willa Gibbs 2400
Marius the Epicurean - Walter Pater 4826
Roman Nights - Ron Burns 803

Margaret (Queen of Scotland)
Sing Morning Star - Jane Oliver 4727

Margaret of Anjou
Anne of Geierstein - Sir Walter Scott 5689
The Dragon Waiting: A Masque of History - John M.
  Ford 2165
Red Rose of Anjou - Jean Plaidy 5054
The Swan and the Rose - Francis W. Leary 3697

Margaret of Austria
The Gentle Fury: A Novel of Margaret of Austria -
  Paul Lewis 3758

Margaret of Burgundy
Here Lies Margot - Pamela Hill 2935

Margaret of Metola
The Woman in the Cloak - Pamela Hill 2949

Margaret of Tyrol
The Ugly Duchess - Lion Feuchtwanger 2075

Margaret Rose
Di and I - Peter Lefcourt 3714
Murder at the Palace - Elliott Roosevelt 5445
The Queen and I - Sue Townsend 6306

Margot
Evergreen Gallant - Jean Plaidy 5013
The Italian Woman - Jean Plaidy 5024
Queen Jezebel - Jean Plaidy 5049
Queen Margot - Alexandre Dumas 1780
Young Henry of Navarre - Heinrich Mann 4062

Marguerite de Bourgogne
The Strangled Queen - Maurice Druon 1737

Marguerite de Valois
Evergreen Gallant - Jean Plaidy 5013
The Italian Woman - Jean Plaidy 5024
Queen Jezebel - Jean Plaidy 5049
Queen Margot - Alexandre Dumas 1780
Young Henry of Navarre - Heinrich Mann 4062

Maria de Jesus, Sor
I, the King - Frances Parkinson Keyes 3479

Maria Louisa Victoria, Duchess of Kent
The Captive of Kensington Palace - Jean
  Plaidy 5007
The Little Victoria - Lozania Prole 5196
The Queen and Lord M - Jean Plaidy 5046
The Young Victoria - Tyler Whittle 6724

Maria Theresa
*Sacred and Profane: A Novel of the Life and Times of
  Mozart* - David Weiss 6609
The Shadow of the Sun - Sylvia Pell 4891
The Strange Case of Madamoiselle P. - Patrick
  Ireland 3109

Mariana of Austria
I, the King - Frances Parkinson Keyes 3479

Marie Antoinette
Asylum for the Queen - Mildred A. Jordan 3303
City of Darkness, City of Light - Marge Piercy 4998
The Devil's Laughter - Frank Yerby 6913
*Dr. Guillotine: The Eccentric Exploits of an Early
  Scientist* - Herbert Lom 3867
*The Fatal Friendship: Marie Antoinette, Count Fersen
  and the Flight to Varennes* - Stanley Loomis 3895
Fear No More - Hester W. Chapman 990
The Frenchwoman - Jeanne Mackin 3995
I Thee Wed - Gilbert Wolf Gabriel 2267
King's Masque - Evan John 3220
The Man Who Killed the King - Dennis
  Wheatley 6654
Marie Antoinette - F.W. Kenyon 3453
Palaces of Desire - Kate Alexander 81
The Prince Lost to Time - Ann Dukthas 1776
The Queen's Confession - Victoria Holt 3019
The Queen's Necklace - Alexandre Dumas 1781
Sweet Marie-Antoinette - Lozania Prole 5198
To Dance with Kings - Rosalind Laker 3601
Tricolour - Mark Logan 3866

Marie de Guise
Mary, Queen of Scotland and the Isles - Margaret
  George 2356

Marie Louise of Austria
Emperor's Ladies - Noel B. Gerson 2367
Far Flies the Eagle - Evelyn Anthony 162
*My Brother Napoleon: The Confessions of Caroline
  Bonaparte* - F.W. Kenyon 3455

Marie-Therese (Queen of France)
*The Crown and the Shadow: The Story of Francoise
  d'Aubigne, Marquise de Maintenon* - Pamela
  Hill 2930
The Oracle Glass - Judith Merkle Riley 5335

Marie Therese (Sister Marie Therese)
The Song of Bernadette - Franz Werfel 6625

Marina
Cortez and Marina - Edison Marshall 4105
The Golden Princess - Alexander Baron 335

Marion, Francis
Battle Lanterns - Merrit Parmalee Allen 102
Celia Garth - Gwen Bristow 695
Dawn's Early Light - Elswyth Thane 6215
The Fallon Blood - Reagan O'Neal 4741
A Few Painted Feathers - Stephen Longstreet 3886
The Long March - Jane Barry 358
Othneil Jones - John Adams Leland 3715
Phantom Fortress - Bruce Lancaster 3643
The Red Doe - Drayton Mayrant 4214
The Swamp Fox, Francis Marion - Noel B.
  Gerson 2383
Sycamore Men - David Taylor 6181

Marius, Caius
The First Man in Rome - Colleen McCullough 4234
The Grass Crown - Colleen McCullough 4236
The Young Caesar - Rex Warner 6567

Mark
Dogheaded Death - Ray Faraday Nelson 4581
Marcus - Laurene Chinn 1068

Markievicz, Constance
An Excess of Love - Cathy Cash Spellman 5959
Rebels: The Irish Rising of 1916 - Peter
  DeRosa 1622
Seasons - Anna Dillon 1645

Marlborough, Duchess of
The Elusive Crown - Hebe Elsna 1931
Exit Lady Masham - Louis Auchincloss 230
The Glory and the Dream - F.W. Kenyon 3450
Marlborough's Unfair Lady - Lozania Prole 5197
The Power and the Passion - Christina
  Nicholson 4609
The Queen's Favourites - Jean Plaidy 5051
The Sachem - Donald Clayton Porter 5124

Marlborough, Duke of
The Charlatan - Carter A. Vaughan 6433
Exit Lady Masham - Louis Auchincloss 230
The Glory and the Dream - F.W. Kenyon 3450
Marlborough's Unfair Lady - Lozania Prole 5197
The Mohawk Ladder - Noel B. Gerson 2377
The Queen's Favourites - Jean Plaidy 5051
The Queen's Husband - Samuel Edwards 1889
The Renegade - Donald Clayton Porter 5122
The Sachem - Donald Clayton Porter 5124

Marlowe, Christopher
A Dead Man in Deptford - Anthony Burgess 776
Liza Bowe - Shirley Barker 313
Mermaid Tavern - George William Cronyn 1429
Nicholas Cooke: Actor, Soldier, Physician, Priest -
  Stephanie Cowell 1393
The Shadow of the Earth - Lee Wichelns 6731
The Slicing Edge of Death - Judith Cook 1263
Strange Devices of the Sun and Moon - Lisa
  Goldstein 2463
To Be a King - Robert DeMaria 1607
Will Shakespeare: The Untold Story - John
  Mortimer 4495

Maro, Publius Vergilius
The Death of Virgil - Hermann Broch 699

Marquard, Rube
Murder at Ebbets Field - Troy Soos 5947

Marquess of Halifax
The Bracegirdle - Burris Atkins Jenkins 3189

Marquette, Jacques
Blackrobe - Charles Corcoran 1323

Marquis de Cinq-Mars
The Cardinal and the Queen - Evelyn Anthony 159
Cinq-Mars - Alfred Victor de Vigny 6495

Marquis de Lafayette
The Bastard - John Jakes 3144
A Chance for Glory - Constance Wright 6877
Conceived in Liberty - Howard Fast 2029
Dawn's Early Light - Elswyth Thane 6215
The Drums of Monmouth - Emma Gelders
    Sterne 5998
The Fallon Blood - Reagan O'Neal 4741
Farewell to Valley Forge - David Taylor 6178
A Few Painted Feathers - Stephen Longstreet 3886
A Generation of Leaves - Robert S. Bloom 552
Hugh Wynne, Free Quaker - Silas Weir
    Mitchell 4416
I'll Storm Hell - Noel B. Gerson 2374
The Ironmaster - Anne Powers 5150
Jefferson: A Novel - Max Byrd 838
King's Masque - Evan John 3220
The Lure of the Falcon - Juliette Benzoni 465
Man From Mt. Vernon - Burke Boyce 607
Monmouth - Charles Bracelen Flood 2144
Morning in America - Willard Wiener 6741
A Place of Greater Safety - Hilary Mantel 4077
The Rebels - John Jakes 3152
Storm the Last Rampart - David Taylor 6180
The Strong Men - John Brick 677
To Spit Against the Wind - Benjamin H. Levin 3737
The Tree of Liberty - Elizabeth Page 4773
Valley Forge - MacKinlay Kantor 3364
Wicked Lady - Inglis Fletcher 2142
Yankee - Dana Fuller Ross 5495
Yorktown - Burke Davis 1513

Marquis de Montespan
The Marquis - Joan Sanders 5586

Marquis of Dalhousie
Follow the Drum - James Leasor 3699

Marquis of Montrose
The Bride - Margaret Irwin 3116
The Proud Servant: The Story of Montrose - Margaret
    Irwin 3120

Marquis of Queensberry
The God of Mirrors - Robert Reilly 5293

Marquis of Salisbury
By Command of the Viceroy - Duncan MacNeil 4010

Marquise de Montespan
All the King's Ladies - Janice Law 3678
Angelique and the King - Sergeanne Golon 2468
*The Crown and the Shadow: The Story of Francoise
    d'Aubigne, Marquise de Maintenon* - Pamela
    Hill 2930
The Gilded Torch - Iola Fuller 2252
The Marquis - Joan Sanders 5586
The Oracle Glass - Judith Merkle Riley 5335
The Shadow of the Sun - Sylvia Pell 4891

Marshal, William
The Battle of the Queens - Jean Plaidy 5005
Below the Salt - Thomas B. Costain 1362
Champion - L. Christian Balling 285
The Courts of Love - Jean Plaidy 5010
The Devil Is Loose - Graham Shelby 5790
In the Shadow of Midnight - Marsha Canham 880
King's Man - C.M. Edmondston 1880
The Marriage of Meggotta - Edith Pargeter 4799
The Prince of Darkness - Jean Plaidy 5044
The Wolf at the Door - Graham Shelby 5793

Marshall, John
Mistress Nancy - Barbara Bentley 460

Martha of Bethany
A Certain Woman: The Story of Mary Magdalene -
    Victor MacClure 3959

Martha, Martha - Patricia McGerr 4274

Martineau, Harriet
Path to the Silent Country - Lynne Reid Banks 291
Sisters & Lovers - Nicola Thorne 6274

Marvell, Andrew
The Portingale - Alison Macleod 4005

Marx, Chico
You Bet Your Life - Stuart M. Kaminsky 3349

Marx, Eleanor
*The Daughter: A Novel Based on the Life of Eleanor
    Marx* - Judith Chernaik 1012

Marx, Groucho
You Bet Your Life - Stuart M. Kaminsky 3349

Marx, Karl
Sisters & Lovers - Nicola Thorne 6274
*The Trial of Elizabeth Cree: A Novel of the Limehouse
    Murders* - Peter Ackroyd 21

Mary
According to Mary: A Novel of the Magdalene - Willa
    Gibbs 2398
Behold the Man - N. Richard Nash 4556
The Centurion - Leonard Wibberley 6729
Dear and Glorious Physician - Taylor Caldwell 853
The Gifts: A Story of the Boyhood of Jesus - Dorothy
    Clarke Wilson 6800
The Gospel of Corax - Paul Park 4802
He Came From Galilee - Daniel A. Poling 5083
Hidden Victory: A Novel of Jesus - Herbert Francis
    Smith 5921
How Far to Bethlehem? - Norah Lofts 3846
I, Judas - Taylor Caldwell 859
King Jesus - Robert Graves 2549
The Last Temptation of Christ - Nikos
    Kazantzakis 3384
The Life of Jesus: An Apocryphal Novel - Toby
    Olson 4731
Man Before the Morning - Cecil Maiden 4032
Man of Nazareth - Anthony Burgess 779
Martha, Martha - Patricia McGerr 4274
Mary - Sholem Asch 198
Mary of Nazareth - Esther Kellner 3394
The Messiah - Marjorie Holmes 3003
The Secret of the Kingdom - Mika Waltari 6555
The Shepherd - Robert Payne 4855
Three From Galilee: The Young Man From Nazareth -
    Marjorie Holmes 3004
Two From Galilee: A Love Story - Marjorie
    Holmes 3005

Mary (Mary II)
The Elusive Crown - Hebe Elsna 1931
The Three Crowns - Jean Plaidy 5070

Mary, Queen of Scots
The Abbot - Sir Walter Scott 5688
All the Queen's Men - Evelyn Anthony 157
The Captive Queen of Scots - Jean Plaidy 5008
Checkmate - Dorothy Dunnett 1799
Come Rack! Come Rope! - Robert Hugh Benson 458
The Game of Kings - Dorothy Dunnett 1801
The Gay Galliard - Margaret Irwin 3119
The Green Salamander - Pamela Hill 2933
I, Elizabeth - Rosalind Miles 4378
Immortal Queen - Elizabeth Byrd 834
*King in Hell: A Novel of Bothwell and Mary, Queen of
    Scots* - Beverly Balin 282
The Lion and the Rose - Jane Oliver 4724
Madame Serpent - Jean Plaidy 5033
*Maid of Honour: A Novel Set in the Court of Mary,
    Queen of Scots* - Elizabeth Byrd 836
Mary of Scotland - F.W. Kenyon 3454
Mary, Queen of Scotland and the Isles - Margaret
    George 2356
The Master of Gray Trilogy - Nigel Tranter 6316
Mine Is the Kingdom - Jane Oliver 4726
No Smoke Without Fire - Alice Harwood 2767
Parcel of Rogues - Jane Lane 3656

The Proud Man - Elizabeth Linington 3800
Queen's Caprice - Marjorie Bowen 599
The Queen's Head - Edward Marston 4125
Queen's Play - Dorothy Dunnett 1805
Reluctant Cavalier - Donald Barr Chidsey 1064
Royal Road to Fotheringay - Jean Plaidy 5059
*Seats of the Mighty: A Novel of James Stuart, Brother
    of Mary, Queen of Scots* - Alice Harwood 2768
So Merciful a Queen, So Cruel a Woman - Alice
    Harwood 2769
The Sword and the Flame - Pamela Hill 2945
A Time for the Death of a King - Ann Dukthas 1777
The Tower and the Dream - Jan Westcott 6647
The White Queen - Frederic Fallon 2011

Mary I (Queen of England)
Anne Boleyn - Evelyn Anthony 158
The Autobiography of Henry VIII - Margaret
    George 2355
The Bisley Boy - Christopher Hunt 3080
Brief Gaudy Hour - Margaret Campbell Barnes 322
Command of the King - Mary Lide 3773
A Crown in Darkness: A Novel about Lady Jane Grey
    - Margaret Mullally 4512
Elizabeth and the Prince of Spain - Margaret
    Irwin 3117
Elizabeth, Captive Princess - Margaret Irwin 3118
The Fifth Queen - Ford Madox Ford 2161
Henry VIII and His Six Wives - Maureen
    Peters 4975
I Am Mary Tudor - Hilda Lewis 3750
I, Elizabeth - Rosalind Miles 4378
In the House of the King - Louis Zara 6951
In the Shadow of the Crown - Jean Plaidy 5022
*The Ivy Crown: A Biographical Novel of Queen
    Katherine Parr* - Mary M. Luke 3923
The King's Secret Matter - Jean Plaidy 5027
Legacy - Susan Kay 3374
The Lily and the Leopards - Alice Harwood 2765
The Man on a Donkey - H.F.M. Prescott 5170
My Lord of Canterbury - Godfrey Turton 6369
Oh! Where Are Bloody Mary's Earrings? - Robert
    Player 5079
The Prince and the Pauper - Mark Twain 6373
Queen of This Realm: The Story of Queen Elizabeth I -
    Jean Plaidy 5050
The Queen's Grace - Jan Westcott 6646
The Red-Haired Brat - Joanna Dessau 1627
The Ringed Castle - Dorothy Dunnett 1807
The Serpent Garden - Judith Merkle Riley 5336
*Shadow in the Sun: A Novel of Elizabeth I, the Virgin
    Queen* - F.W. Kenyon 3460
So Merciful a Queen, So Cruel a Woman - Alice
    Harwood 2769
The Spanish Bridegroom - Jean Plaidy 5064
The Strong Room - Jere Hungerford
    Wheelwright 6671
The Ten-Day Queen - Lozania Prole 5199
The Tower of London - William Harrison
    Ainsworth 58
The White Rose Murders - Michael Clynes 1137
Young Bess - Margaret Irwin 3123
The Young Elizabeth - Jennette Letton 3730

Mary II (Queen of England)
The Elusive Crown - Hebe Elsna 1931
The Glory and the Dream - F.W. Kenyon 3450
The Power and the Passion - Christina
    Nicholson 4609
The Queen's Husband - Samuel Edwards 1889
The Renegade - Donald Clayton Porter 5122
The Three Crowns - Jean Plaidy 5070
William's Wife - Jean Plaidy 5077

Mary Magdalene
According to Mary: A Novel of the Magdalene - Willa
    Gibbs 2398
Barabbas: A Novel of the Time of Jesus - Emery
    Bekessy 417
Behold the Man - N. Richard Nash 4556

A Certain Woman: The Story of Mary Magdalene - Victor MacClure 3959
The Galileans - Frank G. Slaughter 5888
I, Judas - Taylor Caldwell 859
The Last Temptation of Christ - Nikos Kazantzakis 3384
The Magdalene Gospel - Mary Ellen Ashcroft 203
Mary of Magdala - Anne C. Williman 6791
The Messiah - Marjorie Holmes 3003
The Moon under Her Feet - Ceysta Kinstler 3503
Road From Olivet - Edward Francis Murphy 4523
The Scarlet Lily - Edward Francis Murphy 4524
The Secret of the Kingdom - Mika Waltari 6555
A Time for Judas - Morley Callaghan 866
Upon This Rock: A Novel of Simon Peter, Prince of Apostles - Frank G. Slaughter 5906

Mary of Guise
The Game of Kings - Dorothy Dunnett 1801
Queen's Play - Dorothy Dunnett 1805
The Sword and the Flame - Pamela Hill 2945

Mary of Teck
Edward and Mrs. Simpson - A.C.H. Smith 5916
Murder at the Palace - Elliott Roosevelt 5445

Masham, Abigail
Exit Lady Masham - Louis Auchincloss 230
The Queen's Favourites - Jean Plaidy 5051

Mashin, Draga
Dance of the Assassins - Maria Fagyas 1997

Maskelyne, Edward
Master of Bengal: A Novel of Robert Clive of India - Norman Partington 4821

Massai
Broncho Apache - Paul I. Wellman 6614

Massasoit
The Plymouth Adventure - Ernest Gebler 2342

Massaswa
Angelique in Love - Sergeanne Golon 2470

Master Juba
Darktown Strutters - Wesley Brown 732

Masterson, William Barclay "Bat"
Bloody Season - Loren D. Estleman 1968
The Ham Reporter - Robert J. Randisi 5251
The Old Colts - Glendon Swarthout 6144

Mata Hari
The Bloody Red Baron - Kim Newman 4596
The Eye of the Lion: A Novel Based on the Life of Mata Hari - Lael Tucker Wertenbaker 6626
The Last Summer of Mata Hari - Edward Huebsch 3067
The Man Who Loved Mata Hari - Dan Sherman 5813

Mather, Cotton
The Devil and the Mathers - Edward E. Elliott 1914
Gallows Hill - Frances Winwar 6831
Peace, My Daughters - Shirley Barker 314
The Prescott Chronicles - Albert Fried 2232
The Silver Oar - Howard Breslin 669

Mather, Increase
The Devil and the Mathers - Edward E. Elliott 1914
The Rogue and the Witch - John Edward Newton 4605

Matheson, James
Mandarin Gold - James Leasor 3700

Mathewson, Christy
The Celebrant - Eric Rolfe Greenberg 2572
Murder at Ebbets Field - Troy Soos 5947

Matilda (Princess of England)
Bond of Blood - Roberta Gellis 2349
The Fatal Crown - Ellen Jones 3289
The Lion of Justice - Jean Plaidy 5031
The Passionate Enemies - Jean Plaidy 5039

Stephen and the Sleeping Saints - Pamela Bennetts 457
When Christ and His Saints Slept - Sharon Kay Penman 4908

Matilda of Flanders
The Bastard King - Jean Plaidy 5004
The Conqueror - Georgette Heyer 2881
The Conqueror's Wife - Noel B. Gerson 2363
The Disputed Crown - Valerie Anand 128
Fortune's Knave: The Making of William the Conqueror - Mary Lide 3774
The Golden Warrior: The Story of Harold and William - Hope Muntz 4517
The Saxon Tapestry - Sile Rice 5317
Sherwood - Parke Godwin 2449
Wife to the Bastard - Hilda Lewis 3753

Matilda of Tuscany
Not Built with Hands - Helen Constance White 6679

Matisse, Henri
The Burning Man - Stephen Longstreet 3883
The Young Men of Paris - Stephen Longstreet 3893

Matthias, Josef ben
The Tenth Measure - Brenda Lesley Segal 5721

Maud (Princess of England)
Bond of Blood - Roberta Gellis 2349
The Fatal Crown - Ellen Jones 3289
The Lion of Justice - Jean Plaidy 5031
The Passionate Enemies - Jean Plaidy 5039
Stephen and the Sleeping Saints - Pamela Bennetts 457
When Christ and His Saints Slept - Sharon Kay Penman 4908

Maupassant, Guy de
Damned Shall Be Desire: The Passionate Life of Guy de Maupassant - Stephen Coulter 1384
The Gypsy From Cadiz - Tamsin Hamilton 2670

Maurice, Comte de Saxe
A Day of Battle - Vincent Sheean 5787
The Glory and the Dream - Katharine Dunlap 1789

Mauro, Fra
A Mapmaker's Dream - James Cowan 1391

Maximilian (Emperor of Mexico)
The Breast of the Dove - Herbert Gorman 2491
The Cactus and the Crown - Catherine Gavin 2318
Chapultepec - Norman Zollinger 6965
Flames of Empire - Peter Bourne 594
The Grasshopper King - Elizabeth Boatwright Coker 1165
Passengers to Mexico: The Last Invasion of Mexico - Blair Niles 4627

Maximilian I (Holy Roman Emperor)
The Gentle Fury: A Novel of Margaret of Austria - Paul Lewis 3758

Mayer, Louis B.
Murder on the Yellow Brick Road - Stuart M. Kaminsky 3343
The Talking Pictures Murder Case - George Baxt 388
The William Powell and Myrna Loy Murder Case - George Baxt 390

Mazarin, Jules
A Candle for D'Artagnan - Chelsea Quinn Yarbro 6895
The Cardinal and the Queen - Evelyn Anthony 159
My Crown, My Love - Ruth Walgreen Stephan 5995
Twenty Years After - Alexandre Dumas 1783

McAllister, Ward
Tassels on Her Boots - Arthur Cheney Train 6313

McCall, Jack
Aces and Eights: A Novel of the Legend of Wild Bill Hickok - Loren D. Estleman 1967

McCarthy, Joseph
Washington, D.C. - Gore Vidal 6493

McClellan, George
Banished Children of Eve - Peter Quinn 5227
Beloved Enemy - Al Lacy 3579
The Bloody Ground - Bernard Cornwell 1334
Copperhead - Bernard Cornwell 1335
Freedom - William Safire 5561
Gods and Generals - Jeff Shaara 5765
Lincoln: A Novel - Gore Vidal 6490
A Promise Unbroken - Al Lacy 3582

McCutcheon, Peter
The White Slave - Fanny Howe 3059

McDermott, Sean
Rebels: The Irish Rising of 1916 - Peter DeRosa 1622

McDonogh, John
Pathway to the Stars - Harnett T. Kane 3356

McGill, Peter Hermano
Blessed McGill - Edwin Shrake 5834

McGraw, John
The Celebrant - Eric Rolfe Greenberg 2572
Murder at Ebbets Field - Troy Soos 5947

McKinley, William
1901 - Robert Conroy 1258
Empire: A Novel - Gore Vidal 6487
Fenwick Travers and the Years of Empire - Raymond M. Saunders 5614
The Land Was Ours: A Novel of the Great Plains - Charles W. Bailey 266

McLaughlin, James
Shadow Catcher - Charles Fergus 2064

McLean, Allan
Shoot! - George Bowering 604

McLean, Archie
Shoot! - George Bowering 604

McLean, Charlie
Shoot! - George Bowering 604

McLeod, Margaretha Geertruida Zelle
The Last Summer of Mata Hari - Edward Huebsch 3067

McLoughlin, John
Troubled Border - T.D. Allen 104
Vision of the Eagle - Kay L. McDonald 4263

McNab, Peter
Hangman's Beach - Thomas H. Raddall 5229

McQueen, Anne
Don Juan McQueen - Eugenia Price 5181

McQueen, John
Don Juan McQueen - Eugenia Price 5181

Meade, George
The Crater - Richard Slotkin 5908
Gettysburg: Crisis of Command - Harry Albright 65
Glory Enough for All: The Battle of the Crater - Duane Philip Schultz 5673
Three Days - Stephen Longstreet 3891

Medici, Catherine de'
A Cardinal of the Medici - Susan Hicks Beach 393
Courtesan - Diane Haeger 2635
Evergreen Gallant - Jean Plaidy 5013
The Faith and the Flame - June Dimmit Houston 3054
Immortal Queen - Elizabeth Byrd 834
The Italian Woman - Jean Plaidy 5024
The Longest Night - Ada Cook Lewis 3744
Madame Serpent - Jean Plaidy 5033
Mary, Queen of Scotland and the Isles - Margaret George 2356
The Negotiators - Francis Walder 6526
Les Quarant Cinq - Alexandre Dumas 1779
Queen Jezebel - Jean Plaidy 5049
Queen Margot - Alexandre Dumas 1780
Queen's Play - Dorothy Dunnett 1805

Medici, Cosimo de'
Niccolo Rising - Dorothy Dunnett 1803
The Spring of the Ram - Dorothy Dunnett 1809

Medici, Cosimo II de'
The Palace of Wisdom - Bob Marshall-Andrews 4118

Medici, Giulio de'
A Brood of Vipers - Michael Clynes 1133

Medici, Ippolito de'
A Cardinal of the Medici - Susan Hicks Beach 393

Medici, Lorenzo de
The Agony and the Ecstasy - Irving Stone 6054
The Florentine - Sandra Shulman 5840
The Medici Emerald - Martin Woodhouse 6851
The Medici Guns - Martin Woodhouse 6852
The Medici Hawks - Martin Woodhouse 6853
The Palace - Chelsea Quinn Yarbro 6904
The Private Life of Mona Lisa - Pierre La Mure 3577
The Time Returns - Alexandra Ripley 5343

Medici, Marie de'
The Cardinal and the Queen - Evelyn Anthony 159
Evergreen Gallant - Jean Plaidy 5013
The Young and Lonely King - Jane Lane 3659

Meinhard
The Ugly Duchess - Lion Feuchtwanger 2075

Meir, Golda
The Glory - Herman Wouk 6873

Melbourne, Viscount
Albert's Victoria - Tyler Whittle 6719
The Queen and Lord M - Jean Plaidy 5046
The Queen's Husband - Jean Plaidy 5052
Victoria and Albert - Evelyn Anthony 166
The Young Victoria - Tyler Whittle 6724

Melisende
Queen of Swords - Judith Tarr 6169

Melville, Herman
The Robber Baroness - William Kendall Clarke 1097
Walt Whitman's Secret - Ben Aronin 196

Mendana de Neira, Don Alvaro de
Islands of Unwisdom - Robert Graves 2548

Mendelssohn, Cecille
Beyond Desire: A Novel Based on the Life of Felix and Cecille Mendelssohn - Pierre La Mure 3574

Mendelssohn, Felix
Beyond Desire: A Novel Based on the Life of Felix and Cecille Mendelssohn - Pierre La Mure 3574

Mendoza, Ana de
For One Sweet Grape - Kate O'Brien 4681

Mendoza, Juan Hurtado de
Master of Castile - Samuel Edwards 1888

Meng Chaio
Go Ask the River - Evelyn Eaton 1826

Menshikov, Aleksandr
Katrina - Jeramie Price 5190

Meredith, George
Chatterton - Peter Ackroyd 17

Merimee, Prosper
The Questing Heart: A Romantic Novel about George Sand - F.W. Kenyon 3458

Merkle, Fred
Murder at Wrigley Field - Troy Soos 5949

Mesmer, Franz Anton
The Queen's Necklace - Alexandre Dumas 1781
The Strange Case of Madamoiselle P. - Patrick Ireland 3109

Messalina, Valeria
Claudius the God - Robert Graves 2543

Messena, Andre
The Proud Canaries - David Johnson 3222

Metacomet
Legacy - Robert Vaughan 6448
The Wept of Wish-Ton-Wish - James Fenimore Cooper 1312
White Rising - Zane Kotker 3548

Metternich, Clemens von
Century in Scarlet - Lajos Zilahy 6962
Far Flies the Eagle - Evelyn Anthony 162
Lustre in the Sky - R.G. Waldeck 6525

Mezze-Morte
Angelique in Barbary - Sergeanne Golon 2469

Micaiah
Jezebel - Dorothy Clarke Wilson 6802

Michelangelo
The Agony and the Ecstasy - Irving Stone 6054
The Hand of Michelangelo - Sidney Alexander 85
Michelangelo the Florentine - Sidney Alexander 86
Mona Lisa: The Woman in the Portrait - Sara Mayfield 4206
Nicodemus: The Roman Years of Michelangelo Buonarroti, 1534-1564 - Sidney Alexander 87
The Scarlet City - Hella S. Haasse 2632
The Time Returns - Alexandra Ripley 5343
The Venetian - David Weiss 6611

Milan, Duke of
A Comedy of Murders - George Herman 2861
The Lady in the Mask - Anne Green 2564

Milbanke, Isabella
The Absorbing Fire: The Byron Legend - F.W. Kenyon 3445

Miles, Nelson Appleton
The Day the Sun Died - Dale Van Every 6408
The Winter War - William Wister Haines 2640
Yellowstone Kelly - Peter Bowen 602

Mill, John Stuart
Caribbean - James A. Michener 4365
Neighboring Lives - Thomas M. Disch 1648

Millais, John Everett
John Ruskin's Wife - Eva McDonald 4259
Lillie - David Butler 818

Millbanke, Annabella
Lord of the Ladies - Joanna Dessau 1626

Miller, John
Gunman - Loren D. Estleman 1971

Milne, A.A.
Dorothy and Agatha - Gaylord Larsen 3667

Milo, Titus
A Murder on the Appian Way - Steven Saylor 5625

Milton, Deborah
The Tree of Knowledge - Eva Figes 2085

Milton, John
John Inglesant - John Henry Shorthouse 5833
John Milton - Edmund Fuller 2249
Milton in America - Peter Ackroyd 20
Myself, Christopher Wren - David Weiss 6606
The Shadow Flies - Rose Macaulay 3956
Sporting with Amaryllis - Paul West 6635
The Tree of Knowledge - Eva Figes 2085
Wife to Mr. Milton - Robert Graves 2553

Minamoto Yoshitshune
The Sword of Hachiman - Lynn Guest 2608

Ming Huang (Emperor of China)
The Court of the Lion - Eleanor Cooney 1294

Mirabeau, Comte de
The Black Consul - Anatolii Vinogradov 6503
King's Masque - Evan John 3220
Mirabeau, Lover and Stateman - Pierre Nezelof 4606

Miranda, Francisco
Coasts of Folly - Joel Williams 6784

Miriam
The Exodus - Peter Danielson 1467
The River and the Stone: Moses' Early Years in Egypt - Kathleen Jenks 3192
The Scapegoat: A Life of Moses - Joan Lawrence 3684

Mithridates VI (King of Pontus)
The Grass Crown - Colleen McCullough 4236

Mix, Tom
Tom Mix and Pancho Villa - Clifford Irving 3113
Tom Mix Died for Your Sins - Darryl Ponicsan 5090

Miyamoto Musashi
Musashi: An Epic Novel of the Samurai Era - Eiji Yoshikawa 6935

Modigliani, Amedeo
Modigliani: Prince of Montparnasse - Tadeusz Wittlin 6834
The Saint of Montparnasse: A Novel Based on the Life of Constantin Brancusi - Peter Neagoe 4560
Verge of Glory - Frederick Wight 6747
The Young Men of Paris - Stephen Longstreet 3893

Mohammed
The Voice of Allah - Edwin P. Hoyt 3062

Molay, Jacques de
The Iron King - Maurice Druon 1732

Moliere
Monsieur Moliere - Michael O'Shaughnessy 4762

Molke, Kuno von
Court of Honor - Maria Fagyas 1996

Moller, Peder Ludwig
The Seducer - Henrik Stangerup 5980

Molotov, Vyacheslav
Murder in the Blue Room - Elliott Roosevelt 5446

Moltke, Helmuth Johannes Ludwig von
Captain Wonder - Donald Thomas 6238
Falkenhorst - Mark Rascovich 5254
White Nights, Red Dawn - Frederick Nolan 4634

Mona Lisa
Mona Lisa: The Woman in the Portrait - Sara Mayfield 4206
The Private Life of Mona Lisa - Pierre La Mure 3577
The Romance of Leonardo Da Vinci - Dmitri Merezhkovski 4339

Moncrieff, Sir James Wellwood
Madeleine - Pamela Elizabeth West 6633

Monet, Claude
Depths of Glory - Irving Stone 6055
Glowstone - Macdonald Harris 2725
Light - Eva Figes 2083
Naked Came I: A Novel of Rodin - David Weiss 6607

Monica
The Converts: A Historical Novel - Rex Warner 6564
The Restless Flame - Louis De Wohl 1573
Son of Tears - Henry W. Coray 1320

Monmouth, Duke of
A Falling Star - Pamela Belle 431
The King's Bastard - Hebe Elsna 1932
Micah Clarke - Sir Arthur Conan Doyle 1715
The Three Crowns - Jean Plaidy 5070

Monmouth, Harry
The Bloody Field - Edith Pargeter 4795
The Gentle Falcon - Hilda Lewis 3747
Glendower Country - Martha Rofheart 5427
The Hooded Falcon - Prudence Andrew 140
Royal Sword at Agincourt - Pamela Bennetts 455

Monroe, James
Citizen Tom Paine - Howard Fast 2028
The Land Where the Sun Dies - Henry Carlisle 896
Louisiana Purchase - A.E. Hotchner 3039
The Massacre at Fall Creek - Jessamyn West 6631
A Time for Titans - Vina Delmar 1602
Trail: The Story of the Lewis and Clark Expedition -
  Louis Charbonneau 998

Monroe, Marilyn
The Immortals - Michael Korda 3540

Montagu, John
Brimstone Club - F. van Wyck Mason 4147
The Vast Memory of Love - Malcolm Bosse 588

Montbrun, Roger de
Cities of the Flesh - Zoe Oldenbourg 4713

Montcalm, Louis Joseph de
Ambush - Donald Clayton Porter 5113
Bloodbrothers - Robert E. Wall 6535
The Bright Battalions - Howard Breslin 664
The Last of the Mohicans - James Fenimore
  Cooper 1302
Web of Destiny - Muriel Elwood 1939

Montespan, Marquis de
The Marquis - Joan Sanders 5586

Montespan, Marquise de
All the King's Ladies - Janice Law 3678
Angelique and the King - Sergeanne Golon 2468
*The Crown and the Shadow: The Story of Francoise
  d'Aubigne, Marquise de Maintenon* - Pamela
  Hill 2930
The Gilded Torch - Iola Fuller 2252
The Marquis - Joan Sanders 5586
The Oracle Glass - Judith Merkle Riley 5335
The Shadow of the Sun - Sylvia Pell 4891

Montez, Lola
Royal Flash - George MacDonald Fraser 2213

Montezuma II (Aztec Emperor)
Aztec - Gary Jennings 3193
Captain From Castille - Samuel Shellabarger 5794
Copilli, Aztec Prince - Miguel Aleman Velasco 75
Cortez and Marina - Edison Marshall 4105
Death of the Fifth Sun - Robert Somerlott 5944
The Fair God - Lew Wallace 6537
The Golden Princess - Alexander Baron 335
The Great White Gods - Eduard Stucken 6102
The Heart of Jade - Salvador de Madariaga 4024
The Luck of Huemac: A Novel about the Aztecs -
  Daniel Peters 4946
*The Sun, He Dies: A Novel about the End of the Aztec
  World* - Jamake Highwater 2919
They Are Coming: The Conquest of Mexico - Jose
  Lopez Portillo y Pacheco 3896

Montfort, Simon de (1165?-1218)
Deep Are the Valleys - Hannah Closs 1129
High Are the Mountains - Hannah Closs 1130
Sybille - Marion Meade 4318

Montfort, Simon de (1208-1265)
The Battle of the Queens - Jean Plaidy 5005
The De Montfort Legacy - Pamela Bennetts 447
Falls the Shadow - Sharon Kay Penman 4903
Leopards and Lilies - Alfred Duggan 1769
The Lion of England - Eve Trevaskis 6336
The Marriage of Meggotta - Edith Pargeter 4799
The Queen From Provence - Jean Plaidy 5047
Shield of Honor - Alice Walworth Graham 2511
The White Cutter - David Pownall 5158

Montmorency, Charlotte de
Evergreen Gallant - Jean Plaidy 5013

Montpensier, Anne de
Angelique - Sergeanne Golon 2465

Montrose, Duchess of
Bertie and the Tinman - Peter Lovesey 3909

Montrose, Marquis of
The Proud Servant: The Story of Montrose - Margaret
  Irwin 3120

Montvoisin, Catherine
The Oracle Glass - Judith Merkle Riley 5335

Moore, Andrew
Destiny in Dallas - Shirley Seifert 5725

Moore, G.E.
The World as I Found It - Bruce Duffy 1755

Moore, Sir John
His Was the Fire - Showell Styles 6104

Moore, Thomas
Come Be My Love - Diana Brown 717

Mor, Malachy
The Gallowglass - Howard Breslin 666

Moray, Earl of
No Smoke Without Fire - Alice Harwood 2767
*Seats of the Mighty: A Novel of James Stuart, Brother
  of Mary, Queen of Scots* - Alice Harwood 2768

Mordaunt, John
I, John Mordaunt - Virgil Scott 5687

Mordecai
Esther - Nathaniel Norsen Weinreb 6601
Esther: The Star and the Sceptre - Gina
  Andrews 146
*So Great a Queen: The Story of Esther, Queen of
  Persia* - Paul Frischauer 2235

More, Anne
Take Heed of Loving Me: A Novel about John Donne -
  Elizabeth Gray Vining 6502

More, Sir Thomas
Anne Boleyn - Evelyn Anthony 158
The Concubine - Norah Lofts 3839
The King's Achievement - Robert Hugh Benson 459
The King's Good Servant - Olive White 6696
The King's Pleasure - Jean Plaidy 5026
The King's Secret Matter - Jean Plaidy 5027
The Man on a Donkey - H.F.M. Prescott 5170
St. Thomas's Eve - Jean Plaidy 5060
Stage of Fools - Charles Andrew Brady 635
Warm Wind, West Wind - Anne Irwin Matthew 4188

Mores, Marquis de
Manifest Destiny - Brian Garfield 2290

Mores, Medora de
Manifest Destiny - Brian Garfield 2290

Morgan, Daniel
A Few Painted Feathers - Stephen Longstreet 3886
The Long March - Jane Barry 358
The Ragged Ones - Burke Davis 1511
The Rifleman - John Brick 675

Morgan, Henry
Caribbean - James A. Michener 4365
Cup of Gold - John Steinbeck 5991
Cutlass Empire - F. van Wyck Mason 4148
The Devil's Own - Christopher Nicole 4615
The Privateer - Gordon Daviot 1510
The Quickenberry Tree - Annette Motley 4502
Running Proud - Nicholas Monsarrat 4432
Windward Passage - Hamilton Cochran 1143

Morgan, John Hunt
The Golden Circle - Constance Robertson 5396
In the Season of the Wild Rose - Clara Rising 5347

Morgan, John Pierpont
The Alienist - Caleb Carr 907
The Bank - Stephen Longstreet 3882
No Honeymoon for Death - Mary Kruger 3564
One Night in Newport - Elizabeth Villars 6498
Ragtime - E.L. Doctorow 1658

Morpain, Pierre de
Restless Are the Sails - Evelyn Eaton 1830

Morphy, Paul
The Chess Player: A Novel of New Orleans and Paris
  - Frances Parkinson Keyes 3478

Morris, Anne Cary
Mistress Nancy - Barbara Bentley 460

Morris, Gouverneur
A Generation of Leaves - Robert S. Bloom 552
King's Masque - Evan John 3220
The Man Who Killed the King - Dennis
  Wheatley 6654
Mistress Nancy - Barbara Bentley 460
Song of the Susquehanna - Herbert Stover 6071

Morris, May
*The Daughter: A Novel Based on the Life of Eleanor
  Marx* - Judith Chernaik 1012

Morris, Robert
Mistress of the Forge - David Taylor 6179
Portrait of a Scoundrel - Nathaniel Benchley 438

Morris, William
Day Is Coming - William Cameron 869
Willowwood - Elizabeth Savage 5619

Morrissey, John
Bread and Circus - Morris Renek 5303

Morse, Samuel
All This, and Heaven Too - Rachel Field 2080

Mortimer, Roger de
The Follies of the King - Jean Plaidy 5014
Harlot Queen - Hilda Lewis 3748
Isabel the Fair - Margaret Campbell Barnes 323
The Lily and the Lion - Maurice Druon 1733
The Lion and the Leopard - Mary Ellen
  Johnson 3226
The She-Wolf - Pamela Bennetts 456
The She-Wolf of France - Maurice Druon 1736
Vows of the Peacock - Alice Walworth
  Graham 2513

Morton, Earl of
Parcel of Rogues - Jane Lane 3656

Morton, Jelly Roll
*Jelly Roll Morton's Last Night at the Jungle Inn: An
  Imaginary Memoir* - Samuel Charters 1002

Morton, Joseph Ferdinand
*Jelly Roll Morton's Last Night at the Jungle Inn: An
  Imaginary Memoir* - Samuel Charters 1002

Morton, Thomas
The Disturber - L.S. Davidson Jr. 1505

Mosby, John Singleton
The Ghost Raider - Ray Hogan 2978
Gray Victory - Robert Skimin 5877
Mosby's Last Ride - Ray Hogan 2979
Night Raider - Ray Hogan 2980
Scarlet Cockerel - Garald Lagard 3584

Moscoso, Luis de
The Golden Eagle - John Edward Jennings 3201

Moses
*All the Trumpets Sounded: A Novel Based on the Life
  of Moses* - W.G. Hardy 2701
Alone Atop the Mountain - Samuel Sandmel 5591
The Exodus - Konrad Bercovici 473
The Exodus - Peter Danielson 1467
The Miracle Hater - Shulamith Hareven 2704
Moses - Sholem Asch 199
Moses, Prince of Egypt - Howard Fast 2039
On Eagles' Wings - Arthur E. Southon 5951
Pillar of Fire - Judith Tarr 6168
Prince of Egypt - Dorothy Clarke Wilson 6805
The River and the Stone: Moses' Early Years in Egypt
  - Kathleen Jenks 3192
The Scapegoat: A Life of Moses - Joan
  Lawrence 3684
Tables of the Law - Thomas Mann 4067

Mosher, Emmeline
Emmeline - Judith Rossner   5507

Moss, Elizabeth
The Three Lives of Elizabeth - Shirley Seifert   5735

Mother Jones
Bisbee '17 - Robert Houston   3056
The Scapegoat - Mary Lee Settle   5758

Mott, Lucretia
Law of the Land - Marguerite Allis   111
Seneca Falls Inheritance - Miriam Grace
   Monfredo   4429
The Woman Question - Dorothea Malm   4046

Motte, Jeanne de la
The Queen's Necklace - Alexandre Dumas   1781

Moultrie, William
The Carolinian - Rafael Sabatini   5547
The Fallon Blood - Reagan O'Neal   4741
The Swamp Fox, Francis Marion - Noel B.
   Gerson   2383

Mountbatten, Louis
Dance on a Sinking Ship - Michael Kilian   3483

Mountbatten of Burma, Earl
Dance on a Sinking Ship - Michael Kilian   3483

Mourard V (Ottoman Sultan)
Regards From the Dead Princess: A Novel of a Life -
   Kenize Mourad   4505

Mozart, Wolfgang Amadeus
Antonietta - John Hersey   2868
*The Golden Quill: A Novel Based on the Life of
   Mozart* - Bernard Grun   2605
The Irish Boy: A Romantic Biography - Naomi
   Jacob   3137
Mozart on the Way to Prague - Eduard Friedrich
   Morike   4454
Rasero - Francisco Rebolledo   5282
*Sacred and Profane: A Novel of the Life and Times of
   Mozart* - David Weiss   6609

Muhammad II (Ottoman Sultan)
The Dark Angel - Mika Waltari   6551
The Medici Hawks - Martin Woodhouse   6853

Muhammad IV (Ottoman Sultan)
Poland - James A. Michener   4373

Muhlenberg, Henry Melchior
A High Wind Rising - Elsie Singmaster   5867

Muir, John
California Gold - John Jakes   3145

Mulai Ismail
Angelique in Barbary - Sergeanne Golon   2469

Mullins, Priscilla
The Wickedest Pilgrim - Donald Barr Chidsey   1067

Mumtaz Mahal
The Dark Dancer - Frederic Prokosch   5193

Mundelein, George
Organized Crime - Nicholas Von Hoffman   6511

Murad V (Ottoman Sultan)
Regards From the Dead Princess: A Novel of a Life -
   Kenize Mourad   4505

Murat, Joachim
Brumaire - Mark Logan   3864
Far Flies the Eagle - Evelyn Anthony   162
Guillotine - Mark Logan   3865
*My Brother Napoleon: The Confessions of Caroline
   Bonaparte* - F.W. Kenyon   3455
The Proud Canaries - David Johnson   3222
*The Questing Heart: A Romantic Novel about George
   Sand* - F.W. Kenyon   3458
Valentina - Evelyn Anthony   165

Murieta, Joaquin
The Dream Ends in Fury - Samuel Anthony
   Peeples   4889

Gringo Gold - Dane Coolidge   1293

Murphy, Timothy
The Rifleman - John Brick   675

Murrah, Thomas
The Imposter - Noel B. Gerson   2375

Murrell, John
Rogues' Company: A Novel of John Murrell - Harry
   Harrison Kroll   3559
Sow the Seeds of Hemp - Gary Jennings   3195

Murry, John Middleton
Daughter of Time - Nelia Gardner White   6695

Musset, Alfred de
Hungarian Rhapsody: The Life of Franz Liszt - Jean
   Rousselot   5511
*The Questing Heart: A Romantic Novel about George
   Sand* - F.W. Kenyon   3458
Rachel - Anne Powers   5153

Mussolini, Benito
Mussolini - Alan Gelb   2348
*The Passion of Sacco and Vanzetti: A New England
   Legend* - Howard Fast   2040

Muwatallis I (King of the Hittites)
The Hittite - Noel B. Gerson   2373

N

Nabors, Lonnie
The Staked Plain - Frank Xavier Tolbert   6290

Nachman of Bratslav
The Man Who Thought He Was Messiah - Curt
   Leviant   3735

Naksh-i-dil
Valide: A Novel of the Harem - Barbara Chase-
   Riboud   1007

Nana Sahib
Sergeant Verity and the Imperial Diamond - Francis
   Selwyn   5745

Nane
A Time in the Sun - Jane Barry   361

Naomi
Ruth - Irving Fineman   2089
The Song of Ruth: A Love Story of the Old Testament
   - Frank G. Slaughter   5901

Napier, Robert Cornelis
Mandarin Gold - James Leasor   3700
When the Emperor Dies - Mason McCann
   Smith   5926

Napoleon I (Emperor of France)
Alone Among Men - Marjorie Coryn   1355
The Amazing Mrs. Bonaparte - Harnett T.
   Kane   3351
Anna - Cynthia Harrod-Eagles   2752
The Anthem - Noel B. Gerson   2361
Anthony Adverse - Hervey Allen   98
Baltic Mission - Richard Woodman   6859
Being Met Together - William Vaughan
   Wilkins   6756
The Black Consul - Anatolii Vinogradov   6503
Blackstone and the Scourge of Europe - Richard
   Falkirk   2007
Brumaire - Mark Logan   3864
Captain Cut-Throat - John Dickson Carr   908
The Castle of Fratta - Ippolito Nievo   4625
Charles O'Malley - Charles James Lever   3731
Citizen Tom Paine - Howard Fast   2028
*Colossus: A Novel about Goya and a World Gone
   Mad* - Stephen Marlowe   4093
Death at the French Creek - Raymond C. Borel   580
The Death of Napoleon - Simon Leys   3768
The Dedicated - Willa Gibbs   2399

Desiree - Annemarie Selinko   5741
Draw Near to Battle - Jere Hungerford
   Wheelwright   6667
Dreams of Empire - Jeanne Mackin   3994
The Eagle and the Rock - Frances Winwar   6830
Emperor's Ladies - Noel B. Gerson   2367
*The Emperor's Lady: A Novel Based on the Life of the
   Empress Josephine* - F.W. Kenyon   3449
Far Flies the Eagle - Evelyn Anthony   162
The Flight of the Eagle - Donald Thomas   6239
Forty Centuries Look Down - Frederick Britten
   Austin   245
Good-Bye My Son - Marjorie Coryn   1356
A Great Lord - Paul Frischauer   2233
Guillotine - Mark Logan   3865
The Hastening Wind - Edward Grierson   2591
Hester - Brian Cleeve   1107
H.M.S. Cockerel - Dewey Lambdin   3611
Holy Week - Louis Aragon   182
Imperial Venus: A Novel of Napoleon's Favorite Sister
   - Edgar Maas   3949
The Last Love - Thomas B. Costain   1367
The Limits of Glory: A Novel of Waterloo - James
   McDonough   4265
Madame Casanova - Gaby von Schonthan   5659
The Man Who Killed the King - Dennis
   Wheatley   6654
Marianne - Juliette Benzoni   466
Marianne and the Crown of Fire - Juliette
   Benzoni   467
Marianne and the Masked Prince - Juliette
   Benzoni   469
Marianne and the Privateer - Juliette Benzoni   470
Marianne and the Rebels - Juliette Benzoni   471
The Marriage of Josephine - Marjorie Coryn   1358
Mirage - Ruth McKenney   4283
Mistress of Fortune - Sheila Lancaster   3651
*My Brother Napoleon: The Confessions of Caroline
   Bonaparte* - F.W. Kenyon   3455
Napoleon and His Son - Pierre Nezelof   4607
Napoleon and the Cossacks - Peter N.
   Krassnoff   3551
Napoleon Must Die - Quinn Fawcett   2054
Napoleon Symphony - Anthony Burgess   780
Notorious Eliza - Basil Beyea   489
Palaces of Desire - Kate Alexander   81
The Prince Lost to Time - Ann Dukthas   1776
The Raven and the Rose - Susan Wiggs   6746
The River Devils - Carter A. Vaughan   6437
The Road to Glory - Frederick Britten Austin   246
The Rose and the Sword - Sandra Paretti   4792
A Rose for Virtue - Norah Lofts   3858
*The Rose of Malmaison: The Turbulent Life of the
   Beautiful Josephine* - Gaby von Schonthan   5660
Seed of Mischief - Willa Gibbs   2401
Seven Men of Gascony - R.F. Delderfield   1589
Sharpe's Devil - Bernard Cornwell   1340   *
So Brief a Spring - Claude Manceron   4054
So Great a Man - David Pilgrim   5000
Tallien: A Brief Romance - Frederic Tuten   6370
Tell Your Sons: A Novel of the Napoleonic Era - Willa
   Gibbs   2402
The Thousand Fires - Anne Powers   5155
Tide of Empire - Bates Baldwin   279
A Time for Titans - Vina Delmar   1602
To Spit Against the Wind - Benjamin H. Levin   3737
Tom Burke of Ours - Charles James Lever   3732
The Twelfth Physician - Willa Gibbs   2403
Valentina - Evelyn Anthony   165
Valide: A Novel of the Harem - Barbara Chase-
   Riboud   1007
War and Peace - Leo Tolstoy   6295
Waterloo - Manuel Komroff   3536
Waterloo - Frederic E. Smith   5920
Why Waterloo? - Alan Patrick Herbert   2850

Napoleon II
Napoleon and His Son - Pierre Nezelof   4607

Napoleon III (Emperor of France)
The Big Family - Vina Delmar 1600
Eugenie - Hester W. Chapman 989
Flames of Empire - Peter Bourne 594
The Gaudy Empire - Alfred Neumann 4584
I, Rachel - March Cost 1361
Imperial Courtesan - F.W. Kenyon 3452
The Passion of Letty Fox - Diana Saunders 5610
Quiet Lady - Norman Collins 1216
Rachel - Anne Powers 5153
A Spy for Napoleon - Baroness Emma Orczy 4746
That Spanish Woman - F.W. Kenyon 3461
The Tontine - Thomas B. Costain 1371

Narbonidus (King of Babylon)
The Prophet - Sholem Asch 201

Nash, Beau
Lord Vanity - Samuel Shellabarger 5796
Monsieur Beaucaire - Booth Tarkington 6163

Nash, Richard
Lord Vanity - Samuel Shellabarger 5796
Monsieur Beaucaire - Booth Tarkington 6163

Nash, Thomas
Liza Bowe - Shirley Barker 313

Nast, Thomas
Bread and Circus - Morris Renek 5303

Nathanael
I, Nathanael, Knew Jesus - William Gilbert Van Tassel Sutpen 6133

Nathoy, Lalu
Thousand Years of Gold - Ruthanne Lum McCunn 4239

Nebuchadnezzar II (King of Babylon)
The Babylonians - Nathaniel Norsen Weinreb 6600
Judith - Stella Wilchek 6748

Nefertiti
Akhnaton, King of Egypt - Dmitri Merezhkovski 4337
A God Against the Gods - Allen Drury 1738
The Goddess Queen: A Novel Based on the Life of Nefertiti - Nicole Vidal 6494
King of the Two Lands: The Pharaoh Akhenaten - Jacquetta Hawkes 2780
King Tut's Private Eye - Lee Levin 3739
On a Balcony - David Stacton 5973
Pillar of Fire - Judith Tarr 6168
Return to Thebes - Allen Drury 1739
The Twelfth Transforming - Pauline Gedge 2347

Nehru, Jawaharlal
The Last Victory - T.N. Murari 4519

Neighbors, Robert Simpson
Brazos Dreamer - Gene Shelton 5799

Nelson, Baby Face
Mad Dog - Jack Kelly 3401

Nelson, George
Mad Dog - Jack Kelly 3401

Nelson, Horatio
1805 - Richard Woodman 6857
Angelica - Samuel A. Schreiner Jr. 5671
The Blacksmith's Daughter - Joanna Dessau 1625
The Bomb Vessel - Richard Woodman 6860
Bride of Glory - Bradda Field 2078
Brumaire - Mark Logan 3864
Caribbean - James A. Michener 4365
Darken Ship - Nicholas Monsarrat 4431
Decision at Trafalgar - Richard Woodman 6861
Emma - F.W. Kenyon 3448
The English Captain - Simon White 6700
A Game for Empires - Pearl Frye 2243
Guillotine - Mark Logan 3865
A King's Commander - Dewey Lambdin 3613
The King's Commission - Dewey Lambdin 3614
Lord Elgin's Lady - Theodore Vrettos 6514
Loving Emma - Nigel Foxell 2197

Mister Christian - William Kinsolving 3502
The Nelson Touch - Paul Lewis 3759
Ramage - Dudley Pope 5097
Ramage at Trafalgar - Dudley Pope 5102
Return to Treasure Island - Denis Judd 3318
The Scalpel and the Sword - Dell Shannon 5774
The Sea Officer - Showell Styles 6105
Shadow of a Lady - Jane Aiken Hodge 2971
Sir William - David Stacton 5977
The Sleeping Sword: A Biographical Novel - Pearl Frye 2244
This Other Eden - Marilyn Harris 2733
The Volcano Lover - Susan Sontag 5946

Nelson, Lord
1805 - Richard Woodman 6857
Angelica - Samuel A. Schreiner Jr. 5671
The Blacksmith's Daughter - Joanna Dessau 1625
The Bomb Vessel - Richard Woodman 6860
Bride of Glory - Bradda Field 2078
Brumaire - Mark Logan 3864
Caribbean - James A. Michener 4365
Darken Ship - Nicholas Monsarrat 4431
Decision at Trafalgar - Richard Woodman 6861
Emma - F.W. Kenyon 3448
The English Captain - Simon White 6700
A Game for Empires - Pearl Frye 2243
Guillotine - Mark Logan 3865
A King's Commander - Dewey Lambdin 3613
The King's Commission - Dewey Lambdin 3614
Lord Elgin's Lady - Theodore Vrettos 6514
Loving Emma - Nigel Foxell 2197
Mister Christian - William Kinsolving 3502
The Nelson Touch - Paul Lewis 3759
Ramage - Dudley Pope 5097
Ramage at Trafalgar - Dudley Pope 5102
Return to Treasure Island - Denis Judd 3318
The Scalpel and the Sword - Dell Shannon 5774
The Sea Officer - Showell Styles 6105
Shadow of a Lady - Jane Aiken Hodge 2971
Sir William - David Stacton 5977
The Sleeping Sword: A Biographical Novel - Pearl Frye 2244
This Other Eden - Marilyn Harris 2733
The Volcano Lover - Susan Sontag 5946

Nepeda, Osep Grigorievich
The Ringed Castle - Dorothy Dunnett 1807

Nero (Roman Emperor)
The Apostle - Sholem Asch 197
Beware of Caesar - Vincent Sheean 5786
Bloody Poet - Deszo Kosztolanyi 3318
Brothers of Vengeance - LeGette Blythe 556
Claudius the God - Robert Graves 2543
The Conspiracy - John Hersey 2870
The Eighth Veil - Ellis Kadison 3320
The Flames of Rome - Paul L. Maier 4033
The Glorious Folly: A Novel of the Time of St. Paul - Louis De Wohl 1565
Hortensius, Friend of Nero - Edith Pargeter 4798
The Illusionist - Anita Mason 4144
The Imperial Governor - George Shipway 5828
Josephus - Lion Feuchtwanger 2072
The Kingdom of the Wicked - Anthony Burgess 778
Man on Fire: A Novel on the Life of St. Paul - LeGette Blythe 558
Nero - Mary Teresa Ronalds 5437
Octavia: A Tale of Ancient Rome - Seymour Van Santvoord 6428
Quo Vadis - Henryk Sienkiewicz 5848
The Roman - Mika Waltari 6554
Scorpus the Moor - Leslie Turner White 6690
The Silver Chalice - Thomas B. Costain 1370
Upon This Rock: A Novel of Simon Peter, Prince of Apostles - Frank G. Slaughter 5906
The Wolf of Masada - John Fredman 2220

Nesbit, Evelyn
Ragtime - E.L. Doctorow 1658

Ness, Eliot
The Dark City - Max Allan Collins 1211
Murder by the Numbers - Max Allan Collins 1212
Torsos - John Peyton Cooke 1270
True Detective - Max Allan Collins 1215

Neville, Anne
The Broken Sword - Rhoda S. Edwards 1885
Crouchback - Carola Oman 4732
Crown of Roses - Valerie Anand 127
The Dragon Waiting: A Masque of History - John M. Ford 2165
Fire and Morning - Francis W. Leary 3696
Fortune's Wheel - Rhoda S. Edwards 1886
The Golden Yoke: A Novel of the War of the Roses - Olive Eckerson 1837
The Reluctant Queen: The Story of Anne of York - Jean Plaidy 5056
Richard III: The Last Plantagenet - Tyler Whittle 6722
The Sunne in Splendour - Sharon Kay Penman 4907
The Swan and the Rose - Francis W. Leary 3697
The Warwick Heiress - Margaret Abbey 6
The White Queen - Lesley J. Nickell 4611

Neville, Cecily
The Daughter of Time - Josephine Tey 6209
The Dragon Waiting: A Masque of History - John M. Ford 2165
The Rose at Harvest End - Eleanor Fairburn 2003

Neville, Richard
Crouchback - Carola Oman 4732
Crown of Roses - Valerie Anand 127
The Eye of God - C.L. Grace 2506
Fortune's Wheel - Rhoda S. Edwards 1886
The Golden Yoke: A Novel of the War of the Roses - Olive Eckerson 1837
I Remember Love - Mollie Hardwick 2694
The Last of the Barons - Edward Bulwer-Lytton 769
A Question of Choice - Prudence Andrew 143
Red Rose of Anjou - Jean Plaidy 5054
The Reluctant Queen: The Story of Anne of York - Jean Plaidy 5056
The Rose at Harvest End - Eleanor Fairburn 2003
The Sun in Splendour - Jean Plaidy 5066
The White Queen - Lesley J. Nickell 4611
The White Rose - Jan Westcott 6648

Newman, John Henry
Shadows and Images - Meriol Trevor 6344

Newton, Isaac
Myself, Christopher Wren - David Weiss 6606

Ney, Michel
The Flight of the Eagle - Donald Thomas 6239
The Limits of Glory: A Novel of Waterloo - James McDonough 4265
Seven Men of Gascony - R.F. Delderfield 1589
The Thousand Fires - Anne Powers 5155
Valentina - Evelyn Anthony 165
Waterloo - Frederic E. Smith 5920

Nezahual
The Coil of the Serpent - Dexter Allen 94
The Jaguar and the Golden Stag - Dexter Allen 95
Valley of Eagles - Dexter Allen 96

Nicholas
An Army of Children - Evan H. Rhodes 5306

Nicholas I (Czar of Russia)
The Fourth King - Glen Petrie 4979

Nicholas II (Czar of Russia)
And the Stars Shall Fall - True Bowen 603
The Dawning of Deliverance - Judith Pella 4892
Devoted Friends - Joe Poyer 5161
Elizabeth and Alexandra - Antony Lambton 3616
Emily - Cynthia Harrod-Eagles 2753
God Save the Tsar - Susanna Hoe 2976
Heirs of the Motherland - Judith Pella 4893
Petersburg - Emily Hanlon 2677
Rasputin's Revenge - John T. Lescroart 3725

Searching for the Emperor - Roberto Pazzi 4858
The Snow Mountain - Catherine Gavin 2324
The Summer Day Is Done - R.T. Stevens 6001
Time After Time - Allen Appel 171
White Nights, Red Dawn - Frederick Nolan 4634

Nicholson, John
Follow the Drum - James Leasor 3699

Nicodemus
The Letters of Nicodemus - Jan Dobraczynski 1655
A Tear for Judas - LeGette Blythe 559
Who Came by Night - Roland Nicholas 4608

Nietzsche, Friedrich
When Nietzsche Wept: A Novel of Obsession - Irvin D.
Yalom 6892

Nightingale, Florence
Bedford Row - Claire Rayner 5259
Cock of the Walk - Roy Lewis 3762
The Hoydens and Mr. Dickens - William J.
Palmer 4784
My Lady Hoyden - Jane Sheridan 5812
The Passionate Pilgrim - Charles Terrot 6204
The Private Life of Florence Nightingale - Richard
Gordon 2485
Secret for a Nightingale - Victoria Holt 3020
Sisters & Lovers - Nicola Thorne 6274
A Sudden, Fearful Death - Anne Perry 4938

Nisbet, Mary
Lord Elgin's Lady - Theodore Vrettos 6514 ·

Nitti, Frank
Organized Crime - Nicholas Von Hoffman 6511
True Crime - Max Allan Collins 1214
True Detective - Max Allan Collins 1215
You Bet Your Life - Stuart M. Kaminsky 3349

Nixon, Richard
The Savage Brood - Martha Rofheart 5430

Noble, John
The Passionate Journey - Irving Stone 6061

Normand, Mabel
Keystone - Peter Lovesey 3913

Norris, William
Neighboring Lives - Thomas M. Disch 1648

North, Frederick
Let the King Beware! - Honore Morrow 4489
Poor Richard's Game - G.J.A. O'Toole 4766

North, Lord
Let the King Beware! - Honore Morrow 4489
Poor Richard's Game - G.J.A. O'Toole 4766

Nostradamus
The Dreamer of the Vine - Liz Greene 2574
Vagabond Prophet - Allene Symons 6149

Nostredame, Michel de
The Dreamer of the Vine - Liz Greene 2574
Vagabond Prophet - Allene Symons 6149

Noyes, Edwin
The Four Hundred - Stephen Sheppard 5804

Numaga
Paiute - Sessions S. Wheeler 6666

O

Oakley, Annie
Buffalo Girls - Larry McMurtry 4296
Crazy Fox Remembers - Don Preston 5174
The Jewelled Spur - Gilbert Morris 4465
The Secret Annie Oakley - Marcy Moran
Heidish 2819
Sherlock Holmes Meets Annie Oakley - Stanley
Shaw 5782

Oates, Lawrence Edward
The Birthday Boys - Beryl Bainbridge 269

Oates, Titus
A Health Unto His Majesty - Jean Plaidy 5019
The Murder of Sir Edmund Godfrey - John Dickson
Carr 913
Our Jo, or The Chronicle of a Coming Man - Kenneth
M. Cameron 868
Peveril of the Peak - Sir Walter Scott 5703
Thunder on St. Paul's Day - Jane Lane 3658
Traitor's Moon - Robert Neill 4574

O'Casey, Sean
An Excess of Love - Cathy Cash Spellman 5959

O'Connell, Daniel
The Big Wind - Beatrice Coogan 1262
Disraeli in Love - Maurice Edelman 1851
The Silent People - Walter Macken 3990

O'Connor, Cormac
The Disorderly Knights - Dorothy Dunnett 1800

Octavia
Octavia: A Tale of Ancient Rome - Seymour Van
Santvoord 6428

Octavian
Throne of Isis - Judith Tarr 6170

Octavianus, Caius Julius Caesar
Three's Company - Alfred Duggan 1774

Octavius, Gaius
The Alexandrian - Martha Rofheart 5425

Oda Nobunaga
The Signore: Shogun of the Warring States - Kunio
Tsuji 6357
Taiko - Eiji Yoshikawa 6936

Oglethorpe, James Edward
Creek Mary's Blood - Dee Brown 712
Dark Sails - Helen Topping Miller 4388
Jarrett's Jade - Frank Yerby 6923
Rascal's Heaven - F. van Wyck Mason 4157
Summer Thunder - Willie Snow Ethridge 1982

O'Hara, James
The King's Orchard - Agnes Sligh Turnbull 6363

O'Higgins, Ambrosio
O'Higgins and Don Bernardo - Edna Deu Pree
Nelson 4578

O'Higgins, Bernardo
O'Higgins and Don Bernardo - Edna Deu Pree
Nelson 4578
Taste of Glory - Carleton Beals 394

The Old Pretender
Now Face to Face - Karleen Koen 3530
The Stuart Legacy - Robert Kerr 3472

Oldcastle, John
The Star of Lancaster - Jean Plaidy 5065
The Whyte Harte - P.C. Doherty 1681

Olga, Grand Duchess of Russia
The Snow Mountain - Catherine Gavin 2324
The Summer Day Is Done - R.T. Stevens 6001

Olive, Isom Prenice "Print"
Rawhider - Gene Shelton 5802

Olympias
Alexander of Macedon: The Journey to World's End -
Harold Lamb 3607
Fire From Heaven - Mary Renault 5296
Funeral Games - Mary Renault 5297

O'Malley, Grace
Grania: She-King of the Irish Seas - Morgan
Llywelyn 3819

O'Neill, Shane
The Proud Man - Elizabeth Linington 3800

Oneta
The Loon Feather - Iola Fuller 2253

Oppenheimer, J. Robert
Beginning the World Again - Roberta Silman 5851
A Family Matter - James Roosevelt 5458
Stallion Gate - Martin Cruz Smith 5924

Orellana, Francisco de
*A Crossbowman's Story of the First Exploration of the
Amazon* - George Millar 4379
Vain Shadow - Hartzell Spence 5962

Origen Adamantius
Origen: A Historical Novel - Theodore Vrettos 6515

d'Orsay, Alfred
Imperial Courtesan - F.W. Kenyon 3452

Orsini, Paolo
Vittoria - Robert Merle 4342

Ortiz, Juan
Juan Ortiz: Gentleman of Seville - Mary Bethell
Alfriend 88

Osceola
Bright Feather - Robert Wilder 6750
The Land Where the Sun Dies - Henry Carlisle 896
River in the Wind - Edith Pope 5111
Runaway - Heather Graham 2519
Seminole - Theodore Pratt 5164

O'Shea, Katherine
Never Call It Loving - Dorothy Eden 1859
Parnell and the Englishwoman - Hugh Leonard 3721

O'Shea, William
Parnell and the Englishwoman - Hugh Leonard 3721

Ostermin, Don Antonio
Taos - Irwin R. Blacker 527

O'Sullivan, Donal Cam
The Last Prince of Ireland - Morgan Llywelyn 3821

Oswald, Lee Harvey
Flying into Love - D.M. Thomas 6236
Libra - Don DeLillo 1593

Otto II (Holy Roman Emperor)
The Eagle's Daughter - Judith Tarr 6165

Otto IV (Holy Roman Emperor)
The Saracen Blade - Frank Yerby 6926

Otto of Brunswick
The Saracen Blade - Frank Yerby 6926

Overbury, Thomas
The Murder in the Tower - Jean Plaidy 5035
The Street of Kings - Charles Dexter 1637

Ovid
God Was Born in Exile - Vintila Horia 3033
An Imaginary Life - David Malouf 4047

Owen, Robert
The Beckoning Road - Caroline Snedeker 5934

Owen, Wilfred
The Ghost Road - Pat Barker 308

Oxenstierna, Axel
People of the Book - David Stacton 5974

Oxford, Earl of
Cloak of Folly - Burke Boyce 606

P

Pa-nayo-tishn
Chiricahua - Will Henry 2839

Paderewski, Ignacy
Poland - James A. Michener 4373

Paganini, Niccolo
The Magic Bow - Manuel Komroff 3534
Passionate Rebel: The Story of Hector Berlioz - F.W.
Kenyon 3457

Page, Richard
A Heart Divided - Al Lacy 3580

Paget, Sir William
Feast in the Morning - Hugh Preston 5175

Paine, Thomas
Citizen Tom Paine - Howard Fast 2028
City of Darkness, City of Light - Marge Piercy 4998
The Long Naked Descent into Boston - William Eastlake 1823
The Rebels - John Jakes 3152
This Other Eden - Marilyn Harris 2733
To Spit Against the Wind - Benjamin H. Levin 3737

Pakenham, Sir Richard
54-40 or Fight - Emerson Hough 3040

Palmerston, Viscount
Albert's Victoria - Tyler Whittle 6719
Follow the Drum - James Leasor 3699
Nevada! - Dana Fuller Ross 5481
The Queen's Husband - Jean Plaidy 5052
Republic: A Novel of Texas - E.V. Thompson 6266
Victoria and Albert - Evelyn Anthony 166
When the Emperor Dies - Mason McCann Smith 5926
The Widow of Windsor - Jean Plaidy 5076

Pankhurst, Emmeline
Sister Beneath the Sheet - Gillian Linscott 3808

Paoli, Pasquale
In What Torn Ship - Evelyn Eaton 1828

Pappentheim, Bertha
When Nietzsche Wept: A Novel of Obsession - Irvin D. Yalom 6892

Paracelsus, Philippus Aureolus
The Adventurer - Mika Waltari 6550
The Alchymist's Journal - Evan S. Connell 1256

Paradies, Maria Theresa von
The Strange Case of Madamoiselle P. - Patrick Ireland 3109

Pardailande Gondrin, Louis-Henri de
The Marquis - Joan Sanders 5586

Park, Mungo
Water Music - T. Coraghessan Boyle 619

Parker, Cynthia Ann
Quanah Parker - Bill Dugan 1759
Ride the Wind - Lucia St. Clair Robson 5416

Parker, Dorothy
The Dorothy Parker Murder Case - George Baxt 384
The Noel Coward Murder Case - George Baxt 387

Parker, Isaac C.
Ned Christie's War - Robert J. Conley 1247
The Search for Temperance Moon - Douglas C. Jones 3282
True Grit - Charles Portis 5139
Winding Stairs - Douglas C. Jones 3287
Woman of Justice - Georgia Di Donato 1639
Zeke and Ned - Larry McMurtry 4301

Parker, Theodore
The Sin of the Prophet - Truman Nelson 4582

Parnell, Charles Stewart
Never Call It Loving - Dorothy Eden 1859
Parnell and the Englishwoman - Hugh Leonard 3721
The Tenants of Time - Thomas Flanagan 2120

Parr, Catherine
The Autobiography of Henry VIII - Margaret George 2355
Henry VIII and His Six Wives - Maureen Peters 4975
Her Royal Destiny - Carol Maxwell Eady 1820
The Heretic - Alison Macleod 4002
The Ivy Crown: A Biographical Novel of Queen Katherine Parr - Mary M. Luke 3923

Kathryn: In the Court of Six Queens - Anne Merton Abbey 1
King's Fool - Margaret Campbell Barnes 325
The Queen's Grace - Jan Westcott 6646
The Red-Haired Brat - Joanna Dessau 1627
The Sixth Wife - Jean Plaidy 5063
The Young Elizabeth - Jennette Letton 3730

Parr, Katherine
The Autobiography of Henry VIII - Margaret George 2355
Henry VIII and His Six Wives - Maureen Peters 4975
Her Royal Destiny - Carol Maxwell Eady 1820
The Heretic - Alison Macleod 4002
The Ivy Crown: A Biographical Novel of Queen Katherine Parr - Mary M. Luke 3923
Kathryn: In the Court of Six Queens - Anne Merton Abbey 1
King's Fool - Margaret Campbell Barnes 325
The Queen's Grace - Jan Westcott 6646
The Red-Haired Brat - Joanna Dessau 1627
The Sixth Wife - Jean Plaidy 5063
The Young Elizabeth - Jennette Letton 3730

Parris, Samuel
Road to Lendor - Esther Hammon 1966

Pasha, Husref Mehmed
Bosnian Chronicle - Ivo Andric 150

Pasha, Jemel
Behold the Fire - Michael Blankfort 541

Pasteur, Louis
The Gypsy From Cadiz - Tamsin Hamilton 2670

Patch, Sam
Sam Patch: Ballad of a Jumping Man - William Getz 2390

Pater, Walter
Gentlemen in England - A.N. Wilson 6795
The God of Mirrors - Robert Reilly 5293

Patrick
Captive of Rome - Theodora McCormick Du Bois 1740
The Deer Cry - William Greenough Schofield 5650
Druid's Enchantment - Millie J. Ragosta 5240
The Lion and the Cross - Joan Lesley Hamilton 2669

Patterson, Elizabeth
The Amazing Mrs. Bonaparte - Harnett T. Kane 3351
My Dear Cousin - Peggy Hoffmann 2977
Tide of Empire - Bates Baldwin 279

Patton, George S.
Pancho And Black Jack - Fred Bean 398
Tom Mix and Pancho Villa - Clifford Irving 3113

Paul
And Walk on Love: A Novel Based on the Life of the Apostle Paul - Henrietta Buckmaster 759
Brothers of Vengeance - LeGette Blythe 556
The Captive Princess - Maxine Shore 5831
The Eighth Veil - Ellis Kadison 3320
The Flames of Rome - Paul L. Maier 4033
The Glorious Folly: A Novel of the Time of St. Paul - Louis De Wohl 1565
God's Warrior - Frank G. Slaughter 5889
The Gospel According to Gamaliel - Gerald Heard 2801
I, Paul - Rex Miller 4401
The Kingdom of the Wicked - Anthony Burgess 778
Man on Fire: A Novel on the Life of St. Paul - LeGette Blythe 558
Marcus - Laurene Chinn 1068
The Road to Bithynia: A Novel of Luke, the Beloved Physician - Frank G. Slaughter 5897
Saint Paul: A Historical Novel of His Life - Leon Poirier 5081
The Silver Chalice - Thomas B. Costain 1370

The Soothsayer - Laurene Chinn 1069
Upon This Rock: A Novel of Simon Peter, Prince of Apostles - Frank G. Slaughter 5906
Upon This Rock: The Life of St. Peter - Walter F. Murphy 4526

Paul III (Pope)
The Venetian - David Weiss 6611

Paul V (Pope)
The Samurai - Shusaku Endo 1941

Paulinus, Suetonius
Canis the Warrior - James Sinclair 5864

Payne, John Howard
John Howard Payne, Skywalker - Maude Barragan 348

Peaches
Chiricahua - Will Henry 2839

Peacock, Thomas Love
Love's Children - Judith Chernaik 1013

Pearse, Patrick Henry
An Excess of Love - Cathy Cash Spellman 5959
High Heroic - Constantine FitzGibbon 2118
Rebels: The Irish Rising of 1916 - Peter DeRosa 1622

Pearson, Lester
That's Me in the Middle - Donald Jack 3129

Pedro the Cruel (King of Castile and Leon)
Don Pedro's Captain - Pamela Bennetts 449

Peel, Robert
Disraeli in Love - Maurice Edelman 1851
Disraeli Rising - Maurice Edelman 1852
Fire, Burn! - John Dickson Carr 910
The Masters of Bow Street - John Creasy 1423
The Queen and Lord M - Jean Plaidy 5046
The Queen's Husband - Jean Plaidy 5052
Victoria and Albert - Evelyn Anthony 166

Pellew, Edward
The Sea Officer - Showell Styles 6105

Pembroke, Earl of
Below the Salt - Thomas B. Costain 1362
The Devil Is Loose - Graham Shelby 5790
The Wolf at the Door - Graham Shelby 5793

Pepperell, William
The Highwayman - Noel B. Gerson 2372

Pepys, Samuel
Mr. Pepys of Seething Lane - Cecil Abernethy 10
The Portingale - Alison Macleod 4005
Thanksgiving - Terry Coleman 1207

Percy, Henry
The Bloody Field - Edith Pargeter 4795
Falstaff - Robert Nye 4653
Harry of Monmouth - A.M. Maughan 4199
The Star of Lancaster - Jean Plaidy 5065
The Traitors of Bosworth - Robert Farrington 2021

Percy, Henry de
Robert the Bruce: The Steps to the Empty Throne - Nigel Tranter 6320

Perdikkas
Funeral Games - Mary Renault 5297

Peretti, Vittoria
Vittoria - Robert Merle 4342

Pericles
Achilles His Armour - Peter Green 2569
Alcibiades, Beloved of Gods - Vincenz Brun 735
Creation - Gore Vidal 6486
Glory and the Lightning - Taylor Caldwell 856
Goatsong - Tom Holt 3009
The Immortal Marriage - Gertrude Atherton 225
The Magnificent Traitor: A Novel of Alcibiades and the Golden Age of Pericles - Lynn Poole 5092
Pericles the Athenian - Rex Warner 6566

The Private and Public Life of Socrates - Rene
Kraus 3552

Perigord, Dorothea de
Lustre in the Sky - R.G. Waldeck 6525

Perot, H. Ross
Di and I - Peter Lefcourt 3714

Perry, Matthew
The Big Family - Vina Delmar 1600

Perry, Oliver Hazard
The Court Martial of Commodore Perry - James A.
Rhodes 5307
D'ri and I - Irving A. Bacheller 257
The Fleet in the Forest - Carl Daniel Lane 3654
My Blood and My Treasure - Mary Schumann 5674

Pershing, John J.
Chihuahua 1916 - Otis Carney 903
Fenwick Travers and the Years of Empire - Raymond
M. Saunders 5614
A Good Day to Die - Thomas Wakefield
Blackburn 525
Over There - Thomas Fleming 2130
Pancho And Black Jack - Fred Bean 398

Persons, Robert
Tudor Underground - Denis Meadows 4320

Peta Nocona
Quanah Parker - Bill Dugan 1759

Peter
The Big Fisherman - Lloyd C. Douglas 1702
The Centurion - Leonard Wibberley 6729
The Eighth Veil - Ellis Kadison 3320
The Flames of Rome - Paul L. Maier 4033
The Gospel According to Gamaliel - Gerald
Heard 2801
Great Lion of God - Taylor Caldwell 858
Hidden Victory: A Novel of Jesus - Herbert Francis
Smith 5921
The Illusionist - Anita Mason 4144
Judas - Igal Mossinsohn 4500
The Kingdom of the Wicked - Anthony Burgess 778
The Knifeman: A Novel of Judas Iscariot - William
Rayner 5271
The Last Days - William Rayner 5272
Man of Nazareth - Anthony Burgess 779
Man on Fire: A Novel on the Life of St. Paul -
LeGette Blythe 558
Marcus - Laurene Chinn 1068
Martha, Martha - Patricia McGerr 4274
The Master - Max Brod 702
The Messiah - Marjorie Holmes 3003
Quo Vadis - Henryk Sienkiewicz 5848
The Robe - Lloyd C. Douglas 1703
Scorpus the Moor - Leslie Turner White 6690
The Silver Chalice - Thomas B. Costain 1370
*The Sins of Herod: A Novel of Rome and the Early
Church* - Frank G. Slaughter 5900
The Thorn of Arimathea - Frank G. Slaughter 5905
*Upon This Rock: A Novel of Simon Peter, Prince of
Apostles* - Frank G. Slaughter 5906
Upon This Rock: The Life of St. Peter - Walter F.
Murphy 4526

Peter I (Czar of Russia)
Alaska - James A. Michener 4364
Jesters - David Markish 4090
Katrina - Jeramie Price 5190
Peter the Great - Alexey Tolstoy 6293
The Power and the Passion - Christina
Nicholson 4609
Russka: The Novel of Russia - Edward
Rutherfurd 5535
Tsar's Woman - Pamela Hill 2946

Peter III (Czar of Russia)
Rebel Princess - Evelyn Anthony 164

Peter the Great
Alaska - James A. Michener 4364

Jesters - David Markish 4090
Katrina - Jeramie Price 5190
Peter the Great - Alexey Tolstoy 6293
The Power and the Passion - Christina
Nicholson 4609
Russka: The Novel of Russia - Edward
Rutherfurd 5535
Tsar's Woman - Pamela Hill 2946

Petion, Alexandre
Drums of Destiny - Peter Bourne 593

Peyramale, Dean
The Song of Bernadette - Franz Werfel 6625

Phaedo
The Last of the Wine - Mary Renault 5299

Phidias
Alcibiades, Beloved of Gods - Vincenz Brun 735
The Immortal Marriage - Gertrude Atherton 225

Philby, Harold "Kim"
Gentleman Traitor - Alan Williams 6763

Philibert of Savoy
The Gentle Fury: A Novel of Margaret of Austria -
Paul Lewis 3758
Here Lies Margot - Pamela Hill 2935

Philip, Duke of Burgundy
The Master Painter - Edwin Mullins 4513

Philip, Duke of Edinburgh
Di and I - Peter Lefcourt 3714
The Queen and I - Sue Townsend 6306

Philip II (King of France)
The Barons of Runnymede - Pamela Bennetts 445
The Devil Is Loose - Graham Shelby 5790
The Heart of the Lion - Jean Plaidy 5020
The Kings of Vain Intent - Graham Shelby 5791
The Lute Player - Norah Lofts 3852
My Life for My Sheep - Alfred Duggan 1772
The Rain Maiden - Jill M. Phillips 4985
The Revolt of the Eaglets - Jean Plaidy 5057
The Saracen Blade - Frank Yerby 6926

Philip II (King of Macedon)
Alexander of Macedon: The Journey to World's End -
Harold Lamb 3607
The Conqueror: A Novel of Alexander the Great -
Edison Marshall 4104
Fire From Heaven - Mary Renault 5296
Star of Macedon - Karl V. Eiker 1901

Philip II (King of Spain)
Beauvallet - Georgette Heyer 2876
The Bisley Boy - Christopher Hunt 3080
*Color From a Light Within: A Novel Based on the Life
of El Greco* - Donald Braider 641
Elizabeth and the Prince of Spain - Margaret
Irwin 3117
Elizabeth, Captive Princess - Margaret Irwin 3118
For One Sweet Grape - Kate O'Brien 4681
The Hounds of God - Rafael Sabatini 5551
I, the King - Hermann Kesten 3475
In the House of the King - Louis Zara 6951
In the Shadow of the Crown - Jean Plaidy 5022
The Last Crusader - Louis De Wohl 1569
Legacy - Susan Kay 3374
The Legend of Tyl Ulenspiegel - Charles Theodore
Henri De Coster 1558
Oh! Where Are Bloody Mary's Earrings? - Robert
Player 5079
The Scarlet Cloak - Jean Plaidy 5061
Sea of Lentils - Antonio Benitez-Rojo 443
*Shadow in the Sun: A Novel of Elizabeth I, the Virgin
Queen* - F.W. Kenyon 3460
The Spanish Bridegroom - Jean Plaidy 5064
The Venetian - David Weiss 6611

Philip III (King of Spain)
The Adventures of Don Juan - Richard Gardner 2289

Philip IV (King of France)
Braveheart - Randall Wallace 6538
The Image of Our Lord - Edward Burman 790
The Iron King - Maurice Druon 1732
The Prince of Darkness - P.C. Doherty 1675
Spy in Chancery - P.C. Doherty 1680

Philip IV (King of Spain)
I, the King - Frances Parkinson Keyes 3479
The Marranos - Liliane Webb 6588

Philip V (King of France)
The Royal Succession - Maurice Druon 1735

Philip VI (King of France)
The Lily and the Lion - Maurice Druon 1733
The Lords of Vaumartin - Cecelia Holland 2992

Philip the Fair
The Image of Our Lord - Edward Burman 790
The Iron King - Maurice Druon 1732

Philip the Handsome
The Prisoner of Tordesillas - Lawrence
Schoonover 5665

Philipon, Manon
City of Darkness, City of Light - Marge Piercy 4998

Philippa of Hainault
The Vow on the Heron - Jean Plaidy 5074

Philippe (Philip V)
The Royal Succession - Maurice Druon 1735

Philippe I, Duc d'Orleans
Angelique - Sergeanne Golon 2465
Royal Flush: The Story of Minette - Margaret
Irwin 3121

Philippe II, Duc d'Orleans
Through a Glass Darkly - Karleen Koen 3531

Phillip, Arthur
Botany Bay - Charles Nordhoff 4637
The Timeless Land - Eleanor Dark 1495

Phillips, Portugee John
North Against the Sioux - Kenneth Ulyatt 6376

Phillips, Wendell
The Sin of the Prophet - Truman Nelson 4582

Phipps, William
Angelique and the Demon - Sergeanne Golon 2466
Log Cabin Noble - F. van Wyck Mason 4153
Silver Shoals - Hamilton Cochran 1142

Picasso, Pablo
The Young Men of Paris - Stephen Longstreet 3893

Pickett, George Edward
Gray Victory - Robert Skimin 5877
The Killer Angels - Michael Shaara 5766

Pickford, Mary
Max - Howard Fast 2038

Pico della Mirandola, Giovanni
The Florentine - Sandra Shulman 5840

Piehue, U.K.
Petersburg - Emily Hanlon 2677

Pike, Zebulon
Rio Grande - Jory Sherman 5821

Pilate, Pontius
Barabbas: A Novel of the Time of Jesus - Emery
Bekessy 417
The Bond and the Free - Charles Dunscomb 1813
The Bride of Pilate - Esther Kellner 3393
Brothers of Vengeance - LeGette Blythe 556
The Centurion - Leonard Wibberley 6729
Dear and Glorious Physician - Taylor Caldwell 853
The Emperor's Physician - Jacob Randolph
Perkins 4914
First the Blade - Drayton Mayrant 4212
The Glorious Folly: A Novel of the Time of St. Paul -
Louis De Wohl 1565

The Gospel According to Pontius Pilate - James R. Mills 4408
The Gospel of Corax - Paul Park 4802
Great Lion of God - Taylor Caldwell 858
He Came From Galilee - Daniel A. Poling 5083
Hear Me, Pilate! - LeGette Blythe 557
I, Judas - Taylor Caldwell 859
The Kingdom of the Wicked - Anthony Burgess 778
The Last Temptation of Christ - Nikos Kazantzakis 3384
Man Before the Morning - Cecil Maiden 4032
Man of Nazareth - Anthony Burgess 779
Man on Fire: A Novel on the Life of St. Paul - LeGette Blythe 558
The Nazarene - Sholem Asch 200
No King but Caesar - Anne Powers 5151
Pontius Pilate: A Biographical Novel - Paul L. Maier 4034
Pontius Pilate Reflects - Werner Koch 3529
The Robe - Lloyd C. Douglas 1703
The Same Scourge - John Goldthorpe 2464
The Secret of the Kingdom - Mika Waltari 6555
A Tear for Judas - LeGette Blythe 559
The Tentmaker - Julius Berstl 486
The Testament of Theophilus - Leonard Wibberley 6730
The Thorn of Arimathea - Frank G. Slaughter 5905
A Time for Judas - Morley Callaghan 866
The Word and the Sword - Theo Lang 3662

Pinkerton, Allan
The Bloody Ground - Bernard Cornwell 1334
The Cosgrove Report - G.J.A. O'Toole 4765
The Four Hundred - Stephen Sheppard 5804
Secret Service Operator 13 - Robert W. Chambers 982
Talons of Eagles - William W. Johnstone 3268
The Titans - John Jakes 3154

Piozzi, Hester Lynch Thrale
Dr. Johnson's Dear Mistress - Winifred Carter 948

Pissarro, Camille
Depths of Glory - Irving Stone 6055
Gold of Their Bodies: A Novel about Gauguin - Charles Orson Gorham 2488
Moulin Rouge: A Novel Based on Henri de Toulouse-Lautrec - Pierre La Mure 3576

Pitcher, Molly
Farewell to Valley Forge - David Taylor 6178

Pitt the Elder, William
The Braintree Mission - Nicholas E. Wyckoff 6887
The Double Man - Elinor Pryor 5205
His Majesty's Highwayman - Donald Barr Chidsey 1061
The Prince and the Quakeress - Jean Plaidy 5043

Pitt the Younger, William
Brumaire - Mark Logan 3864
Guillotine - Mark Logan 3865
Sweet Lass of Richmond Hill - Jean Plaidy 5067
The Third George - Jean Plaidy 5068
Tricolour - Mark Logan 3866
Young Pitt - A.M. Maughan 4200

Pittacus
My Name Is Sappho - Martha Rofheart 5429

Pittakos
My Name Is Sappho - Martha Rofheart 5429

Pius IV (Pope)
The Agony and the Ecstasy - Irving Stone 6054

Pius IX (Pope)
Cock of the Walk - Roy Lewis 3762
The Harp and the Shadow - Alejo Carpentier 905

Pius XII (Pope)
The Hangman's Crusade - James Barwick 370
Hitler Has Won - Frederic Mullally 4511

Pizarro, Francisco
Don Pedro and the Devil - Edgar Maas 3948

The Golden Eagle - John Edward Jennings 3201
The Sword and the Sun: The Story of the Spanish Civil Wars in Peru - Gerald Green 2566

Pizarro, Gonzalo
A Crossbowman's Story of the First Exploration of the Amazon - George Millar 4379
I, the King - Howard Clewes 1112

Pizarro, Hernando
Don Pedro and the Devil - Edgar Maas 3948

Place, Etta
The Story of the Sundance Kid - David Everitt 1988

Plant, Henry B.
I Take This Land - Richard Powell 5147

Plantagenet, Cicely
The Lady Cicely - Sandra Wilson 6813
Less Fortunate than Fair - Sandra Wilson 6814
The Queen's Sister - Sandra Wilson 6815

Plantagenet, Eleanor
The King's Daughters - Molly Costain Haycraft 2793

Plantagenet, Elizabeth
The King's Daughters - Molly Costain Haycraft 2793

Plantagenet, Henry
The Revolt of the Eaglets - Jean Plaidy 5057

Plantagenet, Henry (Henry II)
To Keep This Oath - Hebe Weenolsen 6597

Plantagenet, Joanna
The King's Daughters - Molly Costain Haycraft 2793

Plantagenet, Mary
The King's Daughters - Molly Costain Haycraft 2793

Plantagenet, Meg
The King's Daughters - Molly Costain Haycraft 2793

Plato
The Last of the Wine - Mary Renault 5299
The Mask of Apollo - Mary Renault 5300
The Private and Public Life of Socrates - Rene Kraus 3552

Pleasant, Mary Ellen
Free Enterprise - Michelle Cliff 1116

Pleasants, Henry
Glory Enough for All: The Battle of the Crater - Duane Philip Schultz 5673

Plessis, Armand-Jean Du
The Anthem - Noel B. Gerson 2361
The Arm and the Darkness - Taylor Caldwell 850
A Candle for D'Artagnan - Chelsea Quinn Yarbro 6895
The Cardinal and the Queen - Evelyn Anthony 159
Cinq-Mars - Alfred Victor de Vigny 6495
An Epic Joy: A Novel Based on the Life of Rubens - Donald Braider 642
The Favourite - Francoise Mallet-Joris 4040
Louis the Well-Beloved - Jean Plaidy 5032
Louisiana Purchase - A.E. Hotchner 3039
The Three Musketeers - Alexandre Dumas 1782
Wife to Great Buckingham - Hilda Lewis 3751
World and Paradise - Edgar Maas 3953
The Young and Lonely King - Jane Lane 3659

Plunkett, Joseph
Rebels: The Irish Rising of 1916 - Peter DeRosa 1622

Pocahontas
Daughter of Eve - Noel B. Gerson 2366
A Durable Fire - Virginia Bernhard 480
Pocahontas - Susan Donnell 1691
Pocahontas; or, The Nonparell of Virginia - David Garnett 2297

Powhatan's Daughter - John Clarke Bowman 605
The Sea 'Venture - F. van Wyck Mason 4159
The Sot-Weed Factor - John Barth 364

Poe, Edgar Allan
Black Plume: The Supressed Memoirs of Edgar Allan Poe - David Madsen 4027
The Bloody Red Baron - Kim Newman 4596
Evermore - Barbara Steward 6014
The Fever Called Living - Barbara Moore 4439
The Last Mystery of Edgar Allan Poe - Manny Meyers 4356
The Lighthouse at the End of the World - Stephen Marlowe 4095
The Lincoln Diddle - Barbara Steward 6015
My Savage Muse: The Story of My Life: Edgar Allan Poe, an Imaginative Work - Bernhardt J. Hurwood 3087
The Raven - Chancellor Williams 6769
A Singular Conspiracy - Barry Perowne 4915
Very Young Mrs. Poe - Cothburn O'Neal 4740

Poisson, Jeanne Antoinette
A Day of Battle - Vincent Sheean 5787
Louis the Well-Beloved - Jean Plaidy 5032
Louisiana Purchase - A.E. Hotchner 3039
Rasero - Francisco Rebolledo 5282
Royal Merry-Go-Round - F.W. Kenyon 3459

Pole, Reginald
The Hireling - Alison Macleod 4003

Polidori, John
Haunted Summer - Anne Edwards 1881
Lord Byron's Doctor - Paul West 6634
A Single Summer with Lord B. - Derek Marlowe 4092

Polk, James K.
Magnificent Destiny - Paul I. Wellman 6619
Sam Houston - Noel B. Gerson 2380
The Slender Reed - Noel B. Gerson 2382
Texas! - Dana Fuller Ross 5490
The Yankee From Tennessee - Noel B. Gerson 2388

Polk, Sarah
Breakfast at the Hermitage - Alfred Leland Crabb 1397
Dinner at Belmont - Alfred Leland Crabb 1398
Home to Tennessee - Alfred Leland Crabb 1400
Lodging at the Saint Cloud - Alfred Leland Crabb 1403
Supper at the Maxwell House - Alfred Leland Crabb 1407

Pollard, George
The Jonah Man - Henry Carlisle 895

Pollard, Mary
The Jonah Man - Henry Carlisle 895

Polo, Marco
Caravan to Kanadu: A Novel of Marco Polo - Edison Marshall 4103
Invisible Cities - Italo Calvino 867
The Journeyer - Gary Jennings 3194
Messer Marco Polo - Donn Byrne 840

Pompadour, Madame de
A Day of Battle - Vincent Sheean 5787
Louis the Well-Beloved - Jean Plaidy 5032
Louisiana Purchase - A.E. Hotchner 3039
Rasero - Francisco Rebolledo 5282
Royal Merry-Go-Round - F.W. Kenyon 3459

Pompeia
Caesar's Women - Colleen McCullough 4233
The Sacrilege - John Maddox Roberts 5380

Pompey
Caesar's Women - Colleen McCullough 4233
The City of Libertines - W.G. Hardy 2702
Fortune's Favorite - Colleen McCullough 4235
Freedom, Farewell - Phyllis Bentley 461
The Pirate From Rome - John V.D. Southworth 5952

The Young Caesar - Rex Warner 6567

Ponsonby, Sir Henry
Oh! Where Are Bloody Mary's Earrings? - Robert Player 5079

Ponte, Don Pedro de
Sea of Lentils - Antonio Benitez-Rojo 443

Pontiac
The Conquerors - Allen W. Eckert 1839
Fire Along the Sky: A Novel of America - Robert Moss 4497
Hatchet in the Sky - Margaret Cooper Gay 2328
Silent Drums - Mike Roarke 5361
Strife Before Dawn - Mary Schumann 5675
This Land Is Ours - Louis Zara 6953

Pope
Taos - Irwin R. Blacker 527

Pope, John
Unto This Hour - Tom Wicker 6733

Pope, Thomas
Nicholas Cooke: Actor, Soldier, Physician, Priest - Stephanie Cowell 1393

Poquelin, Jean Baptiste
Monsieur Moliere - Michael O'Shaughnessy 4762

Porteous, John
The Heart of Midlothian - Sir Walter Scott 5698

Porter, David
The Sea Panther: A Novel about the Commander of the U.S.S. Constitution - Philip Vail 6397

Porter, William Sydney
The Heart of O. Henry - Dale Kramer 3550

Portinari, Beatrice
The Wanderer: A Novel of Dante and Beatrice - Nathan Schachner 5633

Portola, Gaspar de
This Promised Land - Robert Easton 1824

Potiphar
Joseph of Egypt - Thomas Mann 4065

Potter, Beatrix
Death at Gallows Green - Robin Paige 4776

Potter, Harriet
Love Is a Wild Assault - Elithe Hamilton Kirkland 3506

Potter, Robert
Love Is a Wild Assault - Elithe Hamilton Kirkland 3506
Star of Empire: A Novel of Old San Antonio - Leonard Sanders 5590

Pougatcheff, Emelyan
The Captain's Daughter - Alexander Pushkin 5210

Pound, Ezra
The King - Donald Barthelme 365

Powell, Lewis
A Court of Owls - Richard Adicks 37

Powell, Marie
Wife to Mr. Milton - Robert Graves 2553

Powell, William
The William Powell and Myrna Loy Murder Case - George Baxt 390

Powhatan
Daughter of Eve - Noel B. Gerson 2366
Pocahontas - Susan Donnell 1691
Powhatan's Daughter - John Clarke Bowman 605

Pretty Boy Floyd
Pretty Boy Floyd - Larry McMurtry 4299

Prince de Conde
The Faith and the Flame - June Dimmit Houston 3054

Princess de Chimay
Lady of Paris - William Vaughan Wilkins 6760

Princip, Gavrilo
Death of a Schoolboy - Hans Koning 3537
The First Casualty - William Powell 5149

Printz, Johan
Land of the Beautiful River - Helmer Linderholm 3788

Proctor, Ezekiel
Zeke and Ned - Larry McMurtry 4301

Procula
Pontius Pilate: A Biographical Novel - Paul L. Maier 4034

Proust, Marcel
Herma - Macdonald Harris 2726
To Seize the Passing Dream - Ted Berkman 479

Ptolemy (Ptolemy I)
The Conqueror: A Novel of Alexander the Great - Edison Marshall 4104
Funeral Games - Mary Renault 5297
The Golden Lyre - Noel B. Gerson 2371

Ptolemy I (King of Egypt)
The Bronze God of Rhodes - L. Sprague De Camp 1554
The Conqueror: A Novel of Alexander the Great - Edison Marshall 4104
Funeral Games - Mary Renault 5297
The Golden Lyre - Noel B. Gerson 2371

Puccini, Giacomo
A Cadenza for Caruso - Barbara Paul 4834

Pulaski, Casimir
Monmouth - Charles Bracelen Flood 2144

Pulcheria
Imperial Purple - Gillian Bradshaw 631
Sign of the Pagan - Don Tracy 6312

Pulitzer, Joseph
The Americans - John Jakes 3143
Ulysses: A Biographical Novel - Robert Skimin 5878
Yellow: A Novel - Daniel Lynch 3932

Pullman, George
The Dream Seekers - Grace Mark 4085

Purbeck, Viscount
Call Lady Purbeck - Hilda Lewis 3745

Purvis, Melvin
Pretty Boy Floyd - Larry McMurtry 4299
True Crime - Max Allan Collins 1214

Pushchin, Ivan
The Year of December - Lucy Cores 1329

Pushkin, Aleksandr Sergeyevich
The Fourth King - Glen Petrie 4979
Great Black Russian - John Oliver Killens 3484

Pushkin, Natalya
The Fourth King - Glen Petrie 4979

Putnam, Rufus
Now We Are Free - Marguerite Allis 112

Pym, John
The Golden Feather - Theda Kenyon 3462

Pynchon, William
Hope Leslie; or, Early Times in Massachusetts - Catharine Maria Sedgewick 5714

Pytheas
North to Thule: An Imagined Narrative of the Famous "Lost" Voyage of Pytheas of Massalla in the Fourth Century B.C. - John Frye 2241

Q

Quanah Parker
Quanah Parker - Bill Dugan 1759
Ride the Wind - Lucia St. Clair Robson 5416

Quantrill, William Clarke
Belle Starr - Deborah Camp 870
Bound Girl - Everett Webber 6591
Confessions of Johnny Ringo - Geoff Aggeler 40
Major Stepton's War - Matthew Vaughan 6445
Sons of Fire - Max McCoy 4227

Queen of Sheba
The Queen of Sheba - Roberta Kells Dorr 1696
Solomon and Sheba - Faye Levine 3740
Solomon and Sheba - Jay Williams 6774
Solomon and the Queen of Sheba - Czenzi Ormonde 4751

Queensberry, Marquis of
The God of Mirrors - Robert Reilly 5293

Quyuk
Until the Sun Falls - Cecelia Holland 2998

R

Rabbah
Bathsheba - Torgny Lindgren 3789

Rabin, Yitzhak
The Hope - Herman Wouk 6874

Rachel
Jacob - Jean Cabries 844
Jacob: An Autobiography - Irving Fineman 2088
The Tales of Jacob - Thomas Mann 4068

Rachel (Elisa Felix)
All This, and Heaven Too - Rachel Field 2080
I, Rachel - March Cost 1361
Rachel - Anne Powers 5153

Racine, Jean
Monsieur Moliere - Michael O'Shaughnessy 4762

Radcliffe, Charles
Devil Water - Anya Seton 5749

Radcliffe, Jenny
Devil Water - Anya Seton 5749

Radegunde
Women in the Wall - Julia O'Faolain 4691

Radziwill, Yanush
The Deluge - Henryk Sienkiewicz 5846

Raft, George
True Detective - Max Allan Collins 1215

Raglan, Baron
Flashman at the Charge - George MacDonald Fraser 2209
Hazard's Command - Vivian Stuart 6088

Rahab
Scarlet Cord: A Novel of the Woman of Jericho - Frank G. Slaughter 5899

Ralegh, Sir Walter
Ralegh's Fair Bess: The Story of Bess Throckmorton - Judy Turner 6365

Raleigh, Sir Walter
Ralegh's Fair Bess: The Story of Bess Throckmorton - Judy Turner 6365
The Bisley Boy - Christopher Hunt 3080
Daughter of Eve - Noel B. Gerson 2366
A Dead Man in Deptford - Anthony Burgess 776
Death of the Fox - George Garrett 2300
The Firedrake's Eye - Patricia Finney 2095
For Love of a Pirate - Anthony Esler 1961
The Grove of Eagles - Winston Graham 2526

Her Majesty's Captain - Derek Wilson   6797
I, Elizabeth - Rosalind Miles   4378
Kenilworth - Sir Walter Scott   5700
Lady in Waiting - Rosemary Sutcliff   6123
The Lost Colony - Edison Marshall   4108
My Lord Essex - Olive Eckerson   1838
*Physician Extraordinary: A Novel of the Life and
   Times of William Harvey* - David Weiss   6608
The Shadow of the Earth - Lee Wichelns   6731
Take Heed of Loving Me: A Novel about John Donne -
   Elizabeth Gray Vining   6502
To Be a King - Robert DeMaria   1607
To Love a Queen - Lawrence Schoonover   5669
Towers in the Mist - Elizabeth Goudge   2495
The Voyage of the Destiny - Robert Nye   4657
Westward Ho! - Charles Kingsley   3499

Ramsay, James
Simplicissimus the Vagabond - J.J.C.
   Grimmelshausen   2594

Ramsay, James Andrew Broun
Follow the Drum - James Leasor   3699

Ramses I (Pharaoh of Egypt)
Pillar of Fire - Judith Tarr   6168

Ramses II (Pharaoh of Egypt)
Ancient Evenings - Norman Mailer   4035
Mirage - Pauline Gedge   2346
Moses - Sholem Asch   199
Moses, Prince of Egypt - Howard Fast   2039
The Mummy; or Ramses the Damned - Anne
   Rice   5315

Ramses III (Pharaoh of Egypt)
Lady of the Reeds - Pauline Gedge   2345

Ranavalona I (Queen of Madagascar)
Flashman's Lady - George MacDonald Fraser   2210

Rand, Sally
Murder in the Oval Office - Elliott Roosevelt   5450
True Crime - Max Allan Collins   1214

Randolph, John
A Generation of Leaves - Robert S. Bloom   552
Mistress Nancy - Barbara Bentley   460
My Dear Cousin - Peggy Hoffmann   2977

Randolph, Judith
The Bizarre Sisters - Jay Walz   6559

Randolph, Nancy
The Bizarre Sisters - Jay Walz   6559
A Generation of Leaves - Robert S. Bloom   552
Mistress Nancy - Barbara Bentley   460

Randolph, Richard
The Bizarre Sisters - Jay Walz   6559

Ranjitsinhji, K.S.
Playing the Game - Ian Buruma   810

Rank, Otto
The Passions of the Mind - Irving Stone   6062

Ranulf de Gernons
Knight's Honor - Roberta Gellis   2351

Raphael
The Flame of the Borgias - Jean Briggs   680

Rasputin, Grigori Efimovich
Devoted Friends - Joe Poyer   5161
Love and Honor - Leslie Arlen   189
Rasputin's Revenge - John T. Lescroart   3725
Seance for a Vampire - Fred Saberhagen   5557
Time After Time - Allen Appel   171
White Nights, Red Dawn - Frederick Nolan   4634

Rathbone, Basil
The Howard Hughes Affair - Stuart M.
   Kaminsky   3340

Rathbone, Clara Harris
Henry and Clara - Thomas Mallon   4042

Rathbone, Henry
Henry and Clara - Thomas Mallon   4042

Ravel, Maurice
The Crown Prince - John Barchilon   300

Rawlins, John Aaron
Aide to Glory - Louis Devon   1635

Rawls, Delcie
The Proud Retreat - Clifford Dowdey   1706

Rayburn, Sam
The Hyde Park Murder - Elliott Roosevelt   5443
The Land Was Ours: A Novel of the Great Plains -
   Charles W. Bailey   266

Raymond VI of Toulouse
Deep Are the Valleys - Hannah Closs   1129
High Are the Mountains - Hannah Closs   1130

Reagan, John
The Proud Retreat - Clifford Dowdey   1706

Red Cloud
Crazy Horse - Bill Dugan   1757
Creek Mary's Blood - Dee Brown   712
The Day the Sun Died - Dale Van Every   6408
Dodging Red Cloud - Richard S. Wheeler   6657
Kelly Blue - Peter Bowen   601
North Against the Sioux - Kenneth Ulyatt   6376
Stone Song: A Novel of the Life of Crazy Horse -
   Winfred Blevins   548

Red Eagle
Horseshoe Bend - Bruce Palmer   4779

Reed, James Frazier
The Mothers - Vardis Fisher   2109
The Ungodly: A Novel of the Donner Party - Richard
   Rhodes   5311
Wheels West - Homer Croy   1438

Reed, Margaret
The Mothers - Vardis Fisher   2109

Rembrandt
The Golden Tulip - Rosalind Laker   3596
I, Rembrandt - David Weiss   6605
Rembrandt - Gladys Schmitt   5643

Remington, Frederic
The Day the Sun Died - Dale Van Every   6408
A Good Day to Die - Thomas Wakefield
   Blackburn   525
Yellow: A Novel - Daniel Lynch   3932

Rene of Provence
Anne of Geierstein - Sir Walter Scott   5689

Reno, Marcus
A Mighty Afternoon - Charles K. Mills   4407

Renoir, Pierre Auguste
Naked Came I: A Novel of Rodin - David
   Weiss   6607

Restell, Caroline
Stuyvesant Square - Margaret Lewerth   3743

Revere, Paul
Back Bay - William Martin   4138
The Bastard - John Jakes   3144
Bride of Liberty - Frank Yerby   6909
The Drums of April - Charles Mergendahl   4340
East to Bagaduce - Willard Wallace   6539
Gilman of the Redford - William Stearns Davis   1541
The Indentured Heart - Gilbert Morris   4464
The Long Naked Descent into Boston - William
   Eastlake   1823
Massachusetts: A Novel - Nancy Zaroulis   6956
The Traitor - Dan Sherman   5814

Reynauld of Chatillon
The Knights of Dark Renown - Graham Shelby   5792

Reynier, Gretje
The Drowning Room - Michael Kenneth Pye   5212

Reynolds, John
Twilight of Empire - Allen W. Eckert   1846

Reynolds, Joseph T.
Blood Song - Terry C. Johnston   3243

Reynolds, Joshua
Angelica - Samuel A. Schreiner Jr.   5671
The Prince and the Quakeress - Jean Plaidy   5043

Reza Shah Pahlavi (Shah of Iran)
Cry of the Peacock - Gina Barkhordar Nahai   4552

Rhodes, Cecil John
The City of Gold - Francis Brett Young   6940
The Covenant - James A. Michener   4368
Men of Men - Wilbur Smith   5927
On Trial for My Country - Stanlake Samkange   5578
Rough Diamond - Robert L. Fish   2098

Ricardo, Florence
Dr. Gully's Story - Elizabeth Jenkins   3190

Rich, Robert
Lady Rich - Elizabeth Boatwright Coker   1166

Richard, Duke of Gloucester
The Black Arrow - Robert Louis Stevenson   6008
Crown of Roses - Valerie Anand   127
Death and the Chapman - Kate Sedley   5715
The Dragon Waiting: A Masque of History - John M.
   Ford   2165
The Eve of Saint Hyacinth - Kate Sedley   5716
Fortune's Wheel - Rhoda S. Edwards   1886
The Golden Yoke: A Novel of the War of the Roses -
   Olive Eckerson   1837
The Goldsmith's Wife - Jean Plaidy   5017
The Heart Is a Traitor - Margaret Abbey   4
The Lodestar - Pamela Belle   432
The Plymouth Cloak - Kate Sedley   5718
The Rose at Harvest End - Eleanor Fairburn   2003
The Son of York - Margaret Abbey   5
The Sun in Splendour - Jean Plaidy   5066
The Sunne in Splendour - Sharon Kay Penman   4907
The Swan and the Rose - Francis W. Leary   3697
The Warwick Heiress - Margaret Abbey   6
The White Rose - Jan Westcott   6648

Richard I (King of England)
Banners of Gold - Pamela Kaufman   3371
The Blue Falcon - Robyn Carr   935
Champion - L. Christian Balling   285
The Courts of Love - Jean Plaidy   5010
The Courts of Love: A Romance of Medieval France -
   Peter Bourne   592
The Devil Is Loose - Graham Shelby   5790
Eleanor the Queen - Norah Lofts   3842
The Golden Knight - George Challis   971
The Heart of the Lion - Jean Plaidy   5020
Ivanhoe - Sir Walter Scott   5699
King's Man - C.M. Edmondston   1880
The Kings of Vain Intent - Graham Shelby   5791
Lionheart!: A Novel of Richard I, King of England -
   Martha Rofheart   5428
The Lute Player - Norah Lofts   3852
Men Like Shadows - Dorothy Charques   1000
My Lord Brother the Lionheart - Molly Costain
   Haycraft   2795
No Man's Son - Doris Sutcliffe Adams   23
The Queen's War: A Novel of Eleanor of Aquitaine -
   Jeanne Mackin   3996
The Rain Maiden - Jill M. Phillips   4985
The Revolt of the Eaglets - Jean Plaidy   5057
Richard and the Knights of God - Pamela
   Bennetts   454
A Royal Quest - Mary Lide   3777
A Search for a King: A 12th-Century Legend - Gore
   Vidal   6492
Shield of Three Lions - Pamela Kaufman   3372
The Talisman - Sir Walter Scott   5708
Tomorrow's Fire - Jay Williams   6775
The Unhurrying Chase - H.F.M. Prescott   5172

Richard II (King of England)
Fortune Made His Sword - Martha Rofheart   5426
The Gentle Falcon - Hilda Lewis   3747

Glendower Country - Martha Rofheart 5427
Good King Harry - Denise Giardina 2393
In a Dark Wood Wandering - Hella S. Haasse 2631
The Lords of Lancaster - Pamela Bennetts 452
My Lord John - Georgette Heyer 2895
Passage to Pontefract - Jean Plaidy 5038
Richard Whittington, London's Mayor - Gwynedd
    Sudworth 6112
Riot at Gravesend: A Novel of Wat Tyler's Rebellion -
    William Howard Woods 6864
The Ruthless Yeomen - Valerie Anand 134
Trumpet at the Gate - Jan Widgery 6739
Who Was Then the Gentleman - Charles E.
    Israel 3125
The Whyte Harte - P.C. Doherty 1681
Within the Hollow Crown - Margaret Campbell
    Barnes 331

Richard III (King of England)
The Black Arrow - Robert Louis Stevenson 6008
Blood of the Boar - Margaret Abbey 2
The Broken Sword - Rhoda S. Edwards 1885
Crouchback - Carola Oman 4732
Crown of Roses - Valerie Anand 127
The Daughter of Time - Josephine Tey 6209
Death and the Chapman - Kate Sedley 5715
The Dragon and the Rose - Roberta Gellis 2350
The Dragon Waiting: A Masque of History - John M.
    Ford 2165
The Eve of Saint Hyacinth - Kate Sedley 5716
The Fate of Princes - P.C. Doherty 1673
Fire and Morning - Francis W. Leary 3696
Fortune's Wheel - Rhoda S. Edwards 1886
The Golden Yoke: A Novel of the War of the Roses -
    Olive Eckerson 1837
The Goldsmith's Wife - Jean Plaidy 5017
The Heart Is a Traitor - Margaret Abbey 4
The Killing of Richard the Third - Robert
    Farrington 2020
The King's Bed - Margaret Campbell Barnes 324
Less Fortunate than Fair - Sandra Wilson 6814
The Lodestar - Pamela Belle 432
Merchant of the Ruby - Alice Harwood 2766
The Plymouth Cloak - Kate Sedley 5718
The Reluctant Queen: The Story of Anne of York -
    Jean Plaidy 5056
Richard III: The Last Plantagenet - Tyler
    Whittle 6722
The Rose at Harvest End - Eleanor Fairburn 2003
The Son of York - Margaret Abbey 5
The Sun in Splendour - Jean Plaidy 5066
The Sunne in Splendour - Sharon Kay Penman 4907
The Swan and the Rose - Francis W. Leary 3697
An Unknown Welshman - Jean Stubbs 6100
The Warwick Heiress - Margaret Abbey 6
We Speak No Treason - Rosemary Hawley
    Jarman 3168
The White Boar - Marian Palmer 4780
The White Queen - Lesley J. Nickell 4611
The White Rose - Jan Westcott 6648

Richard de Guise
Morality Play - Barry Unsworth 6387

Richard the Lionhearted
Banners of Gold - Pamela Kaufman 3371
The Blue Falcon - Robyn Carr 935
Champion - L. Christian Balling 285
The Courts of Love - Jean Plaidy 5010
The Courts of Love: A Romance of Medieval France -
    Peter Bourne 592
The Devil Is Loose - Graham Shelby 5790
The Golden Knight - George Challis 971
The Heart of the Lion - Jean Plaidy 5020
Ivanhoe - Sir Walter Scott 5699
King's Man - C.M. Edmondston 1880
The Kings of Vain Intent - Graham Shelby 5791
Lionheart!: A Novel of Richard I, King of England -
    Martha Rofheart 5428
The Lute Player - Norah Lofts 3852

Men Like Shadows - Dorothy Charques 1000
My Lord Brother the Lionheart - Molly Costain
    Haycraft 2795
No Man's Son - Doris Sutcliffe Adams 23
The Queen's War: A Novel of Eleanor of Aquitaine -
    Jeanne Mackin 3996
The Rain Maiden - Jill M. Phillips 4985
The Revolt of the Eaglets - Jean Plaidy 5057
Richard and the Knights of God - Pamela
    Bennetts 454
A Royal Quest - Mary Lide 3777
A Search for a King: A 12th-Century Legend - Gore
    Vidal 6492
Shield of Three Lions - Pamela Kaufman 3372
The Talisman - Sir Walter Scott 5708
Tomorrow's Fire - Jay Williams 6775
The Unhurrying Chase - H.F.M. Prescott 5172

Richelieu, Cardinal
The Anthem - Noel B. Gerson 2361
The Arm and the Darkness - Taylor Caldwell 850
A Candle for D'Artagnan - Chelsea Quinn
    Yarbro 6895
The Cardinal and the Queen - Evelyn Anthony 159
Cinq-Mars - Alfred Victor de Vigny 6495
An Epic Joy: A Novel Based on the Life of Rubens -
    Donald Braider 642
The Favourite - Francoise Mallet-Joris 4040
Louis the Well-Beloved - Jean Plaidy 5032
Louisiana Purchase - A.E. Hotchner 3039
The Three Musketeers - Alexandre Dumas 1782
Wife to Great Buckingham - Hilda Lewis 3751
World and Paradise - Edgar Maas 3953
The Young and Lonely King - Jane Lane 3659

Richthofen, Manfred von
The Bloody Red Baron - Kim Newman 4596

Ridge, Major
Trail of Tears - Williams Forrest 2187

Ridley, Nicholas
My Lord of Canterbury - Godfrey Turton 6369

Riel, Louis
Drums of Change: The Story of Running Fawn -
    Janette Oke 4707
The Half Breed - Maurice Constantin-Weyer 1261
Lord of the Plains - Alfred Silver 5852
The Magnificent Failure - Giles A. Lutz 3928

Rienzo, Cola di
The Lily and the Lion - Maurice Druon 1733
Rienzi, or The Last of the Tribunes - Edward Bulwer-
    Lytton 770

Rilke, Rainer Maria
Naked Came I: A Novel of Rodin - David
    Weiss 6607

Rimbaud, Arthur
Savage Prodigal - Konrad Bercovici 474

Rimini, Francesca da
Ardent Flame - Frances Winwar 6829
Concordia - Frances Fleetwood 2124

Rimsky-Korsakov, Nicolai Andreyevich
Petersburg - Emily Hanlon 2677

Ringo, Johnny
Bloody Season - Loren D. Estleman 1968
Confessions of Johnny Ringo - Geoff Aggeler 40
Tombstone Showdown - Leslie Scott 5681
Wyatt Earp - Dan Gordon 2481

Riqueti, Honore Gabriel
The Black Consul - Anatolii Vinogradov 6503
King's Masque - Evan John 3220
Mirabeau, Lover and Stateman - Pierre
    Nezelof 4606

Ritz, Baroness Helena von
54-40 or Fight - Emerson Hough 3040

Rivera, Diego
The Veracruz Blues - Mark Winegardner 6821

Rivers, W.H.R.
The Eye in the Door - Pat Barker 307
The Ghost Road - Pat Barker 308
Regeneration - Pat Barker 309

Rivet, Francois
The Gates of the Mountains - Will Henry 2842

Rizzio, David
Parcel of Rogues - Jane Lane 3656

Robert I (King of Scotland)
Braveheart - Randall Wallace 6538
The Crown in Darkness - P.C. Doherty 1671
The Follies of the King - Jean Plaidy 5014
The Lion Is Come - Jane Oliver 4725
Marjorie of Scotland - Pamela Hill 2939
Robert the Bruce: The Path of the Hero King - Nigel
    Tranter 6318
Robert the Bruce: The Price of the King's Peace -
    Nigel Tranter 6319
Robert the Bruce: The Steps to the Empty Throne -
    Nigel Tranter 6320
The Scottish Chiefs - Jane Porter 5135
Witness to Treason - Millie J. Ragosta 5244

Robert I the Magnificent (Duke of Normandy)
The Conqueror - Georgette Heyer 2881

Robert II Curthose (Duke of Normandy)
The Bastard King - Jean Plaidy 5004
The Lion of Justice - Jean Plaidy 5031
The Paladin - George Shipway 5830

Robert Guiscard
Count Bohemond - Alfred Duggan 1764
Wine of Satan - Laverne Gay 2327

Robert of Artois
The Iron King - Maurice Druon 1732
The Lily and the Lion - Maurice Druon 1733
The Poisoned Crown - Maurice Druon 1734
The Royal Succession - Maurice Druon 1735
The Strangled Queen - Maurice Druon 1737
The Vow on the Heron - Jean Plaidy 5074

Robert of Clari
The Seven Hills of Paradise - Rosemary
    Simpson 5859

Robert the Bruce
Braveheart - Randall Wallace 6538
The Crown in Darkness - P.C. Doherty 1671
The Follies of the King - Jean Plaidy 5014
The Lion Is Come - Jane Oliver 4725
Marjorie of Scotland - Pamela Hill 2939
Robert the Bruce: The Path of the Hero King - Nigel
    Tranter 6318
Robert the Bruce: The Price of the King's Peace -
    Nigel Tranter 6319
Robert the Bruce: The Steps to the Empty Throne -
    Nigel Tranter 6320
The Scottish Chiefs - Jane Porter 5135
Witness to Treason - Millie J. Ragosta 5244

Roberts, Oral
Live From Golgotha - Gore Vidal 6491

Robertson, Geordie
The Heart of Midlothian - Sir Walter Scott 5698

Robertson, James
Journey to Nashville - Alfred Leland Crabb 1402
Wild Horizon - F. van Wyck Mason 4164

Robeson, Paul
Smart Moves - Stuart M. Kaminsky 3346

Robespierre, Maximilien Francois de
The Black Consul - Anatolii Vinogradov 6503
City of Darkness, City of Light - Marge Piercy 4998
The Devil's Laughter - Frank Yerby 6913
The Gods Are Thirsty - Tanith Lee 3710
The Incorruptible - Marjorie Coryn 1357
The Incorruptible - Helma De Bois 1551
The Man Who Killed the King - Dennis
    Wheatley 6654

A Place of Greater Safety - Hilary Mantel 4077
Rasero - Francisco Rebolledo 5282
The Rose of Malmaison: The Turbulent Life of the Beautiful Josephine - Gaby von Schonthan 5660
Scaramouche the King-Maker - Rafael Sabatini 5555
Tallien: A Brief Romance - Frederic Tuten 6370
Tricolour - Mark Logan 3866
La Vendee - Anthony Trollope 6346
Veronique - Virginia Coffman 1158

Robinson, Mary
Perdita's Prince - Jean Plaidy 5040
Regency Royal - Michael Hardwick 2687

Robsart, Amy
Gay Lord Robert - Jean Plaidy 5015
Kenilworth - Sir Walter Scott 5700
The Queen and the Gypsy - Constance Heaven 2810
The Robsart Affair - Jennette Letton 3729

Robusti, Jacopo
The Greek of Toledo: A Romantic Narrative of El Greco - Elizabeth Borton 586

Rochechouart de Mortemart, Francoise Athenais
All the King's Ladies - Janice Law 3678
Angelique and the King - Sergeanne Golon 2468
The Crown and the Shadow: The Story of Francoise d'Aubigne, Marquise de Maintenon - Pamela Hill 2930
The Gilded Torch - Iola Fuller 2252
The Marquis - Joan Sanders 5586
The Oracle Glass - Judith Merkle Riley 5335
The Shadow of the Sun - Sylvia Pell 4891

Rochester, Earl of
Alethea - Pamela Belle 429
Old St. Paul's - William Harrison Ainsworth 57
Royal Escape - Georgette Heyer 2900

Rochester, Viscount
The King James Version - Stanley N. Stewart 6035
King's Minion - Rafael Sabatini 5552
Lion Rampant - Bernard Shrimsley 5836
The Murder in the Tower - Jean Plaidy 5035
The Street of Kings - Charles Dexter 1637

Rochford, Jane
The King's Pleasure - Jean Plaidy 5026

Rockefeller, John D.
The Bank - Stephen Longstreet 3882
Full of Thy Riches - Elizabeth Ferrell 2070
The Strenuous Life - Lawrence Alexander 84
Thine Is the Glory - Samuel A. Schreiner Jr. 5672

Rockefeller, Nelson
Murder in the Blue Room - Elliott Roosevelt 5446

Rodin, Auguste
Naked Came I: A Novel of Rodin - David Weiss 6607

Roet, Katherine de
The Love Knot - Catherine Darby 1482

Roet, Philippa de
Katherine - Anya Seton 5752
The Love Knot - Catherine Darby 1482

Roger II (King of Sicily)
The Garden of Persephone - Cesar J. Rotondi 5510

Roger of Hereford
Knight's Honor - Roberta Gellis 2351

Rogers, Robert
Northwest Passage - Kenneth Roberts 5388
Wilderness Empire - Allen W. Eckert 1847

Rogers, Samuel
Come Be My Love - Diana Brown 717

Rogers, Tiana
Walk in My Soul - Lucia St. Clair Robson 5418

Rogers, Will
The President's Man - Elliott Roosevelt 5455

Rogers, Woodes
Lusty Wind for Carolina - Inglis Fletcher 2134

Rohan, Louis de
The Queen's Confession - Victoria Holt 3019
The Queen's Necklace - Alexandre Dumas 1781

Rohan, Tancrede de
The Silver Plume - Arthur Meeker 4323

Rokossovsky, Konstantin
Journey into Fire - Patricia Wright 6882

Rolfe, John
Daughter of Eve - Noel B. Gerson 2366
A Durable Fire - Virginia Bernhard 480
Pocahontas; or, The Nonpareil of Virginia - David Garnett 2297
Powhatan's Daughter - John Clarke Bowman 605
The Sea 'Venture - F. van Wyck Mason 4159

Roman Nose
The Stalkers - Terry C. Johnston 3259

Romberg, Sigmund
Deep in My Heart: A Story Based on the Life of Sigmund Romberg - Elliott Arnold 192

Rommel, Erwin
Murder in the Chateau - Elliott Roosevelt 5447
Rommel and the Rebel - Lawrence Wells 6622

Roosevelt, Alice Lee
Alice and Edith: A Biographical Novel of the Two Wives of Theodore Roosevelt - Dorothy Clarke Wilson 6798

Roosevelt, Edith
Alice and Edith: A Biographical Novel of the Two Wives of Theodore Roosevelt - Dorothy Clarke Wilson 6798
Speak Softly - Lawrence Alexander 83
TR - Noel B. Gerson 2385

Roosevelt, Eleanor
Eleanor: A Novel - Rhoda Lerman 3724
The Fala Factor - Stuart M. Kaminsky 3337
A First Class Murder - Elliott Roosevelt 5442
Hollywood: A Novel of America in the 1920s - Gore Vidal 6488
The Hyde Park Murder - Elliott Roosevelt 5443
Murder and the First Lady - Elliott Roosevelt 5444
Murder at the Palace - Elliott Roosevelt 5445
Murder in the Blue Room - Elliott Roosevelt 5446
Murder in the Chateau - Elliott Roosevelt 5447
Murder in the East Room - Elliott Roosevelt 5448
Murder in the Executive Mansion - Elliott Roosevelt 5449
Murder in the Oval Office - Elliott Roosevelt 5450
Murder in the Red Room - Elliott Roosevelt 5451
Murder in the Rose Garden - Elliott Roosevelt 5452
Murder in the West Wing - Elliott Roosevelt 5453
The Prescott Chronicles - Albert Fried 2232
A Royal Murder - Elliott Roosevelt 5456
The White House Pantry Murder - Elliott Roosevelt 5457

Roosevelt, Franklin Delano
The Bank - Stephen Longstreet 3882
Eleanor: A Novel - Rhoda Lerman 3724
A Family Matter - James Roosevelt 5458
Hitler Has Won - Frederic Mullally 4511
Hollywood: A Novel of America in the 1920s - Gore Vidal 6488
The Hyde Park Murder - Elliott Roosevelt 5443
The Land Was Ours: A Novel of the Great Plains - Charles W. Bailey 266
Luciano's Luck - Jack Higgins 2912
Murder and the First Lady - Elliott Roosevelt 5444
Murder in the Blue Room - Elliott Roosevelt 5446
Murder in the Chateau - Elliott Roosevelt 5447
Murder in the East Room - Elliott Roosevelt 5448
Murder in the Executive Mansion - Elliott Roosevelt 5449
Murder in the Oval Office - Elliott Roosevelt 5450

Murder in the Red Room - Elliott Roosevelt 5451
Murder in the Rose Garden - Elliott Roosevelt 5452
Murder in the West Wing - Elliott Roosevelt 5453
New Deal for Death - Elliott Roosevelt 5454
The Only Thing to Fear - David Poyer 5160
Power - Howard Fast 2041
The Prescott Chronicles - Albert Fried 2232
The President's Man - Elliott Roosevelt 5455
A Royal Murder - Elliott Roosevelt 5456
Speak Softly - Lawrence Alexander 83
Till the End of Time - Allen Appel 170
To the Honor of the Fleet - Robert H. Pilpel 5002
True Detective - Max Allan Collins 1215
War and Remembrance - Herman Wouk 6875
Washington, D.C. - Gore Vidal 6493
The White House Pantry Murder - Elliott Roosevelt 5457
The Winds of War - Herman Wouk 6876

Roosevelt, James
A Family Matter - James Roosevelt 5458

Roosevelt, Theodore
1901 - Robert Conroy 1258
The Adventure of the Stalwart Companions - H. Paul Jeffers 3177
Alice and Edith: A Biographical Novel of the Two Wives of Theodore Roosevelt - Dorothy Clarke Wilson 6798
The Alienist - Caleb Carr 907
The Americans - John Jakes 3143
The Big Stick - Lawrence Alexander 82
Bully! - Mark Schorr 5670
California Gold - John Jakes 3145
Captains and the Kings - Taylor Caldwell 851
Cherokee Rose: A Novel of America's First Cowgirl - Judy Alter 119
Creek Mary's Blood - Dee Brown 712
Empire: A Novel - Gore Vidal 6487
Fenwick Travers and the Panama Canal - Raymond M. Saunders 5613
Fenwick Travers and the Years of Empire - Raymond M. Saunders 5614
Fort Worth - Leonard Sanders 5588
Fortune's Legacy - Jack Rowe 5515
From Time to Time - Jack Finney 2092
Homeland - John Jakes 3148
Imperial Kelly - Peter Bowen 600
The Land Was Ours: A Novel of the Great Plains - Charles W. Bailey 266
Manifest Destiny - Brian Garfield 2290
Masterpiece of Murder - Mary Kruger 3563
Outlaw - Warren Kiefer 3482
Pomeroy - Gordon Williams 6770
The Prescott Chronicles - Albert Fried 2232
Remember Santiago - Douglas C. Jones 3280
The Rough Rider - Gilbert Morris 4468
San Juan Hill - Will Henry 2848
The Seventh Bullet - Daniel D. Victor 6483
The Single Star - Walter Adolphe Roberts 5394
Speak Softly - Lawrence Alexander 83
The Strenuous Life - Lawrence Alexander 84
TR - Noel B. Gerson 2385
Yellowstone Kelly - Peter Bowen 602

Root, Elihu
1901 - Robert Conroy 1258
Empire: A Novel - Gore Vidal 6487
Fenwick Travers and the Panama Canal - Raymond M. Saunders 5613

Rosecrans, William S.
Mockingbird Sang at Chickamauga - Alfred Leland Crabb 1404
A Promise Unbroken - Al Lacy 3582

Rosenberg, Ethel
Ethel: The Fictional Autobiography - Tema Nason 4558

Rosenberg, Julius
Ethel: The Fictional Autobiography - Tema Nason 4558

Ross, Barney
True Detective - Max Allan Collins 1215

Ross, Edward
Many a Voyage - Loula Grace Erdman 1951

Ross, John
As Long as the Rivers Run - Sam J. Slate 5882
Give Me the Wind - Jan Jordan 3302
Trail of Tears - Williams Forrest 2187

Ross, Robert
The Eye in the Door - Pat Barker 307
The God of Mirrors - Robert Reilly 5293

Rossetti, Dante Gabriel
Cock of the Walk - Roy Lewis 3762
The Golden Veil - Paddy Kitchen 3507
The Hoydens and Mr. Dickens - William J. Palmer 4784
I, James McNeill Whistler - Lawrence Williams 6787
To Seize the Passing Dream - Ted Berkman 479
Willowwood - Elizabeth Savage 5619

Rothschild, Nathan
Beyond Desire: A Novel Based on the Life of Felix and Cecille Mendelssohn - Pierre La Mure 3574
The Four Hundred - Stephen Sheppard 5804

Rothstein, Arnold
Blue Ruin: A Novel of the 1919 World Series - Brendan Boyd 610

Rousseau, Henri
Lust for Life - Irving Stone 6059

Rousseau, Jean Jacques
Rasero - Francisco Rebolledo 5282
Voltaire! Voltaire! - Guy Endore 1943

Rouvroy, Louis de
The Cat and the King - Louis Auchincloss 229

Roy, Rob
Rob Roy - Sir Walter Scott 5707

Royall, Anne
The Gorgeous Hussy - Samuel Hopkins Adams 30

Rubens, Peter Paul
An Epic Joy: A Novel Based on the Life of Rubens - Donald Braider 642
The Horn and the Roses: A Novel Based on the Life of Peter Paul Rubens - Ira Jan Wallach 6542
Lover of Life - Zsolt de Harsanyi 2756

Ruby, Jack
Libra - Don DeLillo 1593

Rudolf, Crown Prince of Austria
The Archduke - Michael Arnold 194

Ruminez, Francisco
Master of Castile - Samuel Edwards 1888

Runyon, Damon
The Ham Reporter - Robert J. Randisi 5251
Nevermore - William Hjortsberg 2958
Walter Winchell: A Novel - Michael Herr 2863

Rupert (1619-1682)
The Stranger Prince - Margaret Irwin 3122

Rusk, Thomas Jefferson
Star of Empire: A Novel of Old San Antonio - Leonard Sanders 5590

Ruskin, John
The Golden Veil - Paddy Kitchen 3507
I, James McNeill Whistler - Lawrence Williams 6787
The Invention of Truth - Marta Morazzoni 4449
John Ruskin's Wife - Eva McDonald 4259
Sisters & Lovers - Nicola Thorne 6274
Willowwood - Elizabeth Savage 5619

Russell, Bertrand
The World as I Found It - Bruce Duffy 1755

Russell, Lord John
Cock of the Walk - Roy Lewis 3762
Victoria and Albert - Evelyn Anthony 166
When the Emperor Dies - Mason McCann Smith 5926

Russell, Lillian
The Big Stick - Lawrence Alexander 82
The House on Mulberry Street - Maan Meyers 4354

Ruth
Ruth - Irving Fineman 2089
The Song of Ruth: A Love Story of the Old Testament - Frank G. Slaughter 5901

Ruth, Babe
Joy in Mudville - Gordon McAlpine 4216
The Veracruz Blues - Mark Winegardner 6821

Ruth, George Herman
Joy in Mudville - Gordon McAlpine 4216
The Veracruz Blues - Mark Winegardner 6821

Rutledge, Ann
Comes an Echo on the Breeze - Edward J. Ryan 5542
The Soul of Ann Rutledge - Bernie Babcock 252

S

Sabinus, Flavius
The Flames of Rome - Paul L. Maier 4033

Sabotai
Orlok - Don Dandrea 1461
Until the Sun Falls - Cecelia Holland 2998

Sabreuois, Henri de
Arundel - Kenneth Roberts 5383

Sacajawea
Forward the Nation - Donald Culross Peattie 4880
The Gates of the Mountains - Will Henry 2842
Sacajawea - Anna Lee Waldo 6529
Sacajawea of the Shoshones - Della F. Emmons 1940
Star of the West - Ethel Hueston 3070
Tale of Valor - Vardis Fisher 2112
Trail: The Story of the Lewis and Clark Expedition - Louis Charbonneau 998

Sacco, Nicola
The Passion of Sacco and Vanzetti: A New England Legend - Howard Fast 2040

Sacher-Masoch, Leopold Ritter von
Reigning Passions - Kathrin Perutz 4940

Sackville, Charles
Here Lies Our Sovereign Lord - Jean Plaidy 5021

Sadat, Anwar
The Glory - Herman Wouk 6873

Saenz, Manuela
Manuela, La Caballeresa Del Sol - Demetrio Aguilera Malta 41

Saheb, Nana
The Devil's Wind: Nana Saheb's Story - Manohar Malgonkar 4039

Saint Ambrose
The Restless Flame - Louis De Wohl · 1573
The Sinner of Saint Ambrose - Robert Raynolds 5275

Saint Augustine
The Converts: A Historical Novel - Rex Warner 6564
The Four Rivers of Paradise - Helen Constance White 6678
The Restless Flame - Louis De Wohl 1573

Son of Tears - Henry W. Coray 1320

Saint Bartholomew
I, Nathanael, Knew Jesus - William Gilbert Van Tassel Sutpen 6133

Saint Benedict
Citadel of God: A Novel of Saint Benedict - Louis De Wohl 1563

Saint Bernadette
The Song of Bernadette - Franz Werfel 6625

Saint Bernard
The Garden of Persephone - Cesar J. Rotondi 5510

Saint Brendan
Brendan - Frederick Buechner 762
Paradise - Dikkon Eberhart 1831

St. Castine, Joseph de
The Golden Wildcat - Margaret Widdemer 6735

Saint Catherine of Siena
Lay Siege to Heaven: A Novel of Saint Catherine of Siena - Louis De Wohl 1570
The Saint - Fritz von Unruh 6385

Saint Columba
Isle of Glory - Jane Oliver 4723

St. Denis, Louis Juchereau
Ride the Red Earth - Paul I. Wellman 6620

Saint Elizabeth Ann Seton
Heart in Pilgrimage - Evelyn Eaton 1827
Miracles - Marcy Moran Heidish 2818

Saint Elizabeth of Hungary
Elizabeth's Greetings - Rosemary Haughton 2774

Saint Francis of Assisi
Bird of Fire: A Tale of Francis of Assisi - Helen Constance White 6676
Blessed Are the Meek: A Novel about St. Francis of Assisi - Zofja Kossak-Szczucka 3542
The Joyful Beggar: A Novel of St. Francis of Assisi - Louis De Wohl 1568
My Beautiful White Roses - Michael Lechner 3703
The Perfect Joy of St. Francis - Felix Timmermans 6281
Saint Francis - Nikos Kazantzakis 3385
Sing to the Sun - Lucille Borden 579

Saint Francis Xavier
The Golden Thread - Louis De Wohl 1566
Set All Afire: A Novel of St. Francis Xavier - Louis De Wohl 1574
So Far From Malabar - Joy DeWeese Wehen 6599

Saint Helena
The Living Wood - Louis De Wohl 1571

Saint Ignatius Loyola
The Golden Thread - Louis De Wohl 1566
Set All Afire: A Novel of St. Francis Xavier - Louis De Wohl 1574

Saint Irene
The Belt of Gold - Cecelia Holland 2984

Saint James
The Brother - Dorothy Clarke Wilson 6799
The Centurion - Leonard Wibberley 6729
The Sins of Herod: A Novel of Rome and the Early Church - Frank G. Slaughter 5900

Saint Jean de Brebeuf
Fathers and Crows - William T. Vollmann 6508
This Widowed Land - Kathleen O'Neal Gear 2331

Saint Jerome
The Converts: A Historical Novel - Rex Warner 6564
The Four Rivers of Paradise - Helen Constance White 6678

Saint Joan of Arc
An Army of Angels: A Novel of Joan of Arc - Pamela Marcantel 4079

The Burnished Blade - Lawrence Schoonover   5661
Epitaph for Three Women - Jean Plaidy   5012
In a Dark Wood Wandering - Hella S. Haasse   2631
The Master Painter - Edwin Mullins   4513
Personal Recollections of Joan of Arc - Mark Twain   6372
The Queen's Secret - Jean Plaidy   5053
The Serpent Amongst the Lilies - P.C. Doherty   1678
The Voice and the Light - Edwin Fadiman   1995

Saint John
The Messiah - Marjorie Holmes   3003
The Sins of Herod: A Novel of Rome and the Early Church - Frank G. Slaughter   5900
Who Came by Night - Roland Nicholas   4608

Saint John Fisher
The King's Good Servant - Olive White   6696
The King's Secret Matter - Jean Plaidy   5027
Queen Anne Boleyn - Francis Hackett   2634

Saint John of the Cross
Bold Encounter: A Novel Based on the Life of St. John of the Cross - Peter-Thomas Rohrbach   5433

Saint John the Baptist
Behold the Man - Toyohiko Kagawa   3321
The Big Fisherman - Lloyd C. Douglas   1702
The Centurion - Leonard Wibberley   6729
The Good Tidings - William Sidney   5843
Hidden Victory: A Novel of Jesus - Herbert Francis Smith   5921
I, Judas - Taylor Caldwell   859
The Last Temptation of Christ - Nikos Kazantzakis   3384
Martha, Martha - Patricia McGerr   4274
The Messiah - Marjorie Holmes   3003
The Salt of the Earth - Carlo Monterosso   4437
A Tear for Judas - LeGette Blythe   559
Upon This Rock: A Novel of Simon Peter, Prince of Apostles - Frank G. Slaughter   5906

Saint Joseph
The Gifts: A Story of the Boyhood of Jesus - Dorothy Clarke Wilson   6800
Hidden Victory: A Novel of Jesus - Herbert Francis Smith   5921
How Far to Bethlehem? - Norah Lofts   3846
King Jesus - Robert Graves   2549
The Last Temptation of Christ - Nikos Kazantzakis   3384
The Life of Jesus: An Apocryphal Novel - Toby Olson   4731
Man of Nazareth - Anthony Burgess   779
Mary - Sholem Asch   198
The Shepherd - Robert Payne   4855
Three From Galilee: The Young Man From Nazareth - Marjorie Holmes   3004
Two From Galilee: A Love Story - Marjorie Holmes   3005

Saint-Just, Louis-Antoine-Leon de
A Place of Greater Safety - Hilary Mantel   4077
Scaramouche the King-Maker - Rafael Sabatini   5555

Saint Luke
Dear and Glorious Physician - Taylor Caldwell   853
The Emperor's Physician - Jacob Randolph Perkins   4914
The Road to Bithynia: A Novel of Luke, the Beloved Physician - Frank G. Slaughter   5897
The Silver Chalice - Thomas B. Costain   1370

Saint Mark
Dogheaded Death - Ray Faraday Nelson   4581
Marcus - Laurene Chinn   1068

Saint Mary Magdalene
According to Mary: A Novel of the Magdalene - Willa Gibbs   2398
Barabbas: A Novel of the Time of Jesus - Emery Bekessy   417
Behold the Man - N. Richard Nash   4556

A Certain Woman: The Story of Mary Magdalene - Victor MacClure   3959
The Galileans - Frank G. Slaughter   5888
I, Judas - Taylor Caldwell   859
The Last Temptation of Christ - Nikos Kazantzakis   3384
The Magdalene Gospel - Mary Ellen Ashcroft   203
Mary of Magdala - Anne C. Williman   6791
The Messiah - Marjorie Holmes   3003
The Moon under Her Feet - Ceysta Kinstler   3503
Road From Olivet - Edward Francis Murphy   4523
The Scarlet Lily - Edward Francis Murphy   4524
The Secret of the Kingdom - Mika Waltari   6555
A Time for Judas - Morley Callaghan   866
Upon This Rock: A Novel of Simon Peter, Prince of Apostles - Frank G. Slaughter   5906

Saint Monica
The Converts: A Historical Novel - Rex Warner   6564
The Restless Flame - Louis De Wohl   1573
Son of Tears - Henry W. Coray   1320

Saint Patrick
Captive of Rome - Theodora McCormick Du Bois   1740
The Deer Cry - William Greenough Schofield   5650
Druid's Enchantment - Millie J. Ragosta   5240
The Lion and the Cross - Joan Lesley Hamilton   2669

Saint Paul
And Walk on Love: A Novel Based on the Life of the Apostle Paul - Henrietta Buckmaster   759
The Apostle - Sholem Asch   197
Brothers of Vengeance - LeGette Blythe   556
The Captive Princess - Maxine Shore   5831
The Eighth Veil - Ellis Kadison   3320
The Flames of Rome - Paul L. Maier   4033
The Glorious Folly: A Novel of the Time of St. Paul - Louis De Wohl   1565
God's Warrior - Frank G. Slaughter   5889
The Gospel According to Gamaliel - Gerald Heard   2801
Great Lion of God - Taylor Caldwell   858
I, Paul - Rex Miller   4401
The Kingdom of the Wicked - Anthony Burgess   778
Man on Fire: A Novel on the Life of St. Paul - LeGette Blythe   558
Marcus - Laurene Chinn   1068
The Road to Bithynia: A Novel of Luke, the Beloved Physician - Frank G. Slaughter   5897
Saint Paul: A Historical Novel of His Life - Leon Poirier   5081
The Silver Chalice - Thomas B. Costain   1370
The Soothsayer - Laurene Chinn   1069
The Tentmaker - Julius Berstl   486
Upon This Rock: A Novel of Simon Peter, Prince of Apostles - Frank G. Slaughter   5906
Upon This Rock: The Life of St. Peter - Walter F. Murphy   4526

Saint Peter
The Apostle - Sholem Asch   197
The Big Fisherman - Lloyd C. Douglas   1702
The Centurion - Leonard Wibberley   6729
The Eighth Veil - Ellis Kadison   3320
Fisher of Men: A Novel of Simon Peter - Kurt Frieberger   2231
The Flames of Rome - Paul L. Maier   4033
The Gospel According to Gamaliel - Gerald Heard   2801
Great Lion of God - Taylor Caldwell   858
Hidden Victory: A Novel of Jesus - Herbert Francis Smith   5921
The Illusionist - Anita Mason   4144
Judas - Igal Mossinsohn   4500
The Kingdom of the Wicked - Anthony Burgess   778
The Knifeman: A Novel of Judas Iscariot - William Rayner   5271
The Last Days - William Rayner   5272

Man of Nazareth - Anthony Burgess   779
Man on Fire: A Novel on the Life of St. Paul - LeGette Blythe   558
Marcus - Laurene Chinn   1068
Martha, Martha - Patricia McGerr   4274
The Master - Max Brod   702
The Messiah - Marjorie Holmes   3003
Quo Vadis - Henryk Sienkiewicz   5848
The Robe - Lloyd C. Douglas   1703
Scorpus the Moor - Leslie Turner White   6690
The Silver Chalice - Thomas B. Costain   1370
The Sins of Herod: A Novel of Rome and the Early Church - Frank G. Slaughter   5900
The Thorn of Arimathea - Frank G. Slaughter   5905
Upon This Rock: A Novel of Simon Peter, Prince of Apostles - Frank G. Slaughter   5906
Upon This Rock: The Life of St. Peter - Walter F. Murphy   4526

Saint Radegunde
Women in the Wall - Julia O'Faolain   4691

Saint-Saens, Camille
Cesar and Augusta - Ronald Harwood   2771

Saint-Simon, Duc de
The Cat and the King - Louis Auchincloss   229

Saint Theresa of Avila
Bold Encounter: A Novel Based on the Life of St. John of the Cross - Peter-Thomas Rohrbach   5433

Saint Therese of Lisieux
Love Is My Vocation: An Imaginative Study of St. Therese of Lisieux - Tom Clarkson   1098

Saint Thomas
According to Thomas - Gladys Malvern   4053
Yeshua: The Gospel of St. Thomas - Alan Decker McNarie   4306

Saint Thomas Aquinas
The Quiet Light - Louis De Wohl   1572

Saint Timothy
Live From Golgotha - Gore Vidal   6491
Man on Fire: A Novel on the Life of St. Paul - LeGette Blythe   558
The Soothsayer - Laurene Chinn   1069

Saint Veronica
The Thorn of Arimathea - Frank G. Slaughter   5905

Sala, Maria
Beyond Desire: A Novel Based on the Life of Felix and Cecille Mendelssohn - Pierre La Mure   3574

Saladin
The Heart of the Lion - Jean Plaidy   5020
Jerusalem - Cecelia Holland   2990
The Kings of Vain Intent - Graham Shelby   5791
The Knights of Dark Renown - Graham Shelby   5792
Richard and the Knights of God - Pamela Bennetts   454
The Talisman - Sir Walter Scott   5708
Trail and Triumph: A Novel about Maimonides - Lester M. Morrison   4485

Salisbury, Marquis of
By Command of the Viceroy - Duncan MacNeil   4010

Salome
The Eighth Veil - Ellis Kadison   3320
The Good Tidings - William Sidney   5843
Martha, Martha - Patricia McGerr   4274
The Robe - Lloyd C. Douglas   1703
Salome, Princess of Galilee - Henry Denker   1611

Salome, Lou
When Nietzsche Wept: A Novel of Obsession - Irvin D. Yalom   6892

Saltonstall, Dudley
East to Bagaduce - Willard Wallace   6539

Samson
Husband of Delilah - Eric Linklater   3802

Samsonov, Aleksandr Vasilyevich
August 1914 - Alexander Solzhenitsyn 5942

Samuel
David of Jerusalem - Louis De Wohl 1564
David: Warrior and King - Frank G. Slaughter 5885
Departed Glory - Peter Danielson 1466
King of Kings: A Novel of the Life of David - Malachi Martin 4134
The Prophet and the King - Shirley Watkins 6582
Rizpah - Charles E. Israel 3124

Sand, George
Hungarian Rhapsody: The Life of Franz Liszt - Jean Rousselot 5511
The Questing Heart: A Romantic Novel about George Sand - F.W. Kenyon 3458

Sandino, Augusto Cesar
A Few Good Men - William Overgard 4768

Sandwich, Earl of
Brimstone Club - F. van Wyck Mason 4147
The Vast Memory of Love - Malcolm Bosse 588

Sanger, Margaret
The Crusader - Noel B. Gerson 2364

Santa Anna, Antonio Lopez de
All the Brave Rifles - Clarke Venable 6450
The Bugles Are Silent: A Novel of the Texas Revolution - John R. Knaggs 3513
The Eagle and the Raven - James A. Michener 4369
Empire of Bones: A Novel of Sam Houston and the Texas Revolution - Jeff Long 3868
The Furies - John Jakes 3146
The Road to San Jacinto - Leonard L. Foreman 2167
Sam Houston - Noel B. Gerson 2380
The Sam Houston Story - Dean Owen 4770
Texas - James A. Michener 4375
The Wine of San Lorenzo - Herbert Gorman 2493

Sanzio, Raphael
The Flame of the Borgias - Jean Briggs 680

Sappho
The Laughter of Aphrodite - Peter Green 2570
My Name Is Sappho - Martha Rofheart 5429
The Other Sappho - Ellen Frye 2240

Sarah
Abraham and Sarah: The Long Journey - Roberta Kells Dorr 1694
Hagar - Lois T. Henderson 2824
Hagar - Cothburn O'Neal 4737
The Promise - Esther Kellner 3395

Sargent, John Singer
To Seize the Passing Dream - Ted Berkman 479

Sassia
The Gift of Rome - John Wagner 6520

Sassoon, Siegfried
The Eye in the Door - Pat Barker 307
Regeneration - Pat Barker 309

Saugrain, Antoine
The Medicine Man - Shirley Seifert 5729

Saul (King of Israel)
David at Olivet - Wallace Hamilton 2671
David of Jerusalem - Louis De Wohl 1564
David the King - Gladys Schmitt 5641
David: Warrior and King - Frank G. Slaughter 5885
The Death of Kings - Peter Danielson 1465
Departed Glory - Peter Danielson 1466
King David - Gwyn Jenkins 3191
King of Kings: A Novel of the Life of David - Malachi Martin 4134
The Prophet and the King - Shirley Watkins 6582
Rizpah - Charles E. Israel 3124

Saul of Tarsus
The Apostle - Sholem Asch 197
Great Lion of God - Taylor Caldwell 858
The Tentmaker - Julius Berstl 486

Saumarez, James
Touch and Go - C. Northcote Parkinson 4815

Sauves, Catherine de
Evergreen Gallant - Jean Plaidy 5013

Savile, George
The Bracegirdle - Burris Atkins Jenkins 3189

Savonarola, Girolamo
The Florentine - Sandra Shulman 5840
The Palace - Chelsea Quinn Yarbro 6904
The Private Life of Mona Lisa - Pierre La Mure 3577
Romola - George Eliot 1910

Sayers, Dorothy L.
Dorothy and Agatha - Gaylord Larsen 3667

Scarron, Paul
The Crown and the Shadow: The Story of Francoise d'Aubigne, Marquise de Maintenon - Pamela Hill 2930

Scarrow, Francoise
The Shadow of the Sun - Sylvia Pell 4891

Scheidemann, Philipp
Karl and Rosa - Alfred Doblin 1653

Schiele, Egon
Arrogance - Joanna Scott 5679

Schiller, Friedrich
The Harp and the Shadow - Alejo Carpentier 905

Schindler, Oskar
Schindler's List - Thomas Keneally 3416

Schlieffen, Alfred von
1901 - Robert Conroy 1258

Schliemann, Heinrich
The Greek Treasure - Irving Stone 6056

Schliemann, Sophia
The Greek Treasure - Irving Stone 6056

Schreiner, Olive
The Daughter: A Novel Based on the Life of Eleanor Marx - Judith Chernaik 1012

Schultz, Dutch
Billy Bathgate - E.L. Doctorow 1656
The President's Man - Elliott Roosevelt 5455

Schumann, Clara Wieck
Spring Symphony - Eleanor Painter 4777

Schumann, Robert
Beyond Desire: A Novel Based on the Life of Felix and Cecille Mendelssohn - Pierre La Mure 3574
Spring Symphony - Eleanor Painter 4777

Schuyler, Elizabeth
Alexander Hamilton's Wife - Alice Curtis Desmond 1623

Schwieger, Walther
Lusitania - David Butler 819

Scipio Africanus, Publius Cornelius
The Scarlet Beast - Francis Gerard 2357
Swords Against Carthage - Friedrich Donauer 1689

Scott, James
A Falling Star - Pamela Belle 431
The King's Bastard - Hebe Elsna 1932
Micah Clarke - Sir Arthur Conan Doyle 1715
The Three Crowns - Jean Plaidy 5070

Scott, Robert Falcon
The Birthday Boys - Beryl Bainbridge 269
The Race: A Novel of Polar Exploration - Kare Holt 3008

Scott, Sir Walter
The Blue Heaven Bends Over All - Jane Oliver 4720
Bright Captivity - Eugenia Price 5180

Scott, Winfield
1812 - David Nevin 4586
My Dear Cousin - Peggy Hoffmann 2977

Nevada! - Dana Fuller Ross 5481
Oregon! - Dana Fuller Ross 5484
The Wine of San Lorenzo - Herbert Gorman 2493

Sejanus, Lucius Aelius
Hear Me, Pilate! - LeGette Blythe 557
I, Claudius - Robert Graves 2547
No King but Caesar - Anne Powers 5151
Pontius Pilate: A Biographical Novel - Paul L. Maier 4034
Tiberius: The Memoirs of the Emperor - Allan Massie 4169

Selim III (Ottoman Sultan)
Bosnian Chronicle - Ivo Andric 150
Lord Elgin's Lady - Theodore Vrettos 6514
Sultana - Michael, Prince of Greece 4358

Selkirk, Earl of
The Strange Brigade - John Edward Jennings 3209

Selma
Regards From the Dead Princess: A Novel of a Life - Kenize Mourad 4505

Selman, John
Last Gun: The Legend of John Selman - Gene Shelton 5801

Semenoff, Grigori
Fifteen Flags - Richard Lynden Hardman 2686

Semmelweis, Ignaz Philipp
The Cry and the Covenant - Morton Thompson 6269

Seneca, Lucius Annaeus
Beware of Caesar - Vincent Sheean 5786
The Conspiracy - John Hersey 2870
The Kingdom of the Wicked - Anthony Burgess 778
Nero - Mary Teresa Ronalds 5437

Senenmut
King and Goddess - Judith Tarr 6166

Senmut
Child of the Morning - Pauline Gedge 2343
Pharaoh - Eloise Jarvis McGraw 4276

Sennett, Mack
Keystone - Peter Lovesey 3913

Serebryany, Prince
Prince of Outlaws - Alexey Tolstoy 6294

Serge, Grand Duke of Russia
Elizabeth and Alexandra - Antony Lambton 3616

Serra, Junipero
A City for St. Francis - Evelyn Wells 6621
The Cross and the Sword - Jonreed Lauritzen 3674
Nine Days of Father Serra - Isabelle Gibson Ziegler 6961
The Road to Glory - Darwin Le Ora Teilhet 6199
This Promised Land - Robert Easton 1824

Servilia
Caesar's Women - Colleen McCullough 4233

Seti I (Pharaoh of Egypt)
Return to Thebes - Allen Drury 1739

Seton, Elizabeth Ann
Heart in Pilgrimage - Evelyn Eaton 1827
Miracles - Marcy Moran Heidish 2818

Seton, Mary
Maid of Honour: A Novel Set in the Court of Mary, Queen of Scots - Elizabeth Byrd 836
Mary of Scotland - F.W. Kenyon 3454

Seton, William
Heart in Pilgrimage - Evelyn Eaton 1827

Seurat, Georges
Depths of Glory - Irving Stone 6055
Lust for Life - Irving Stone 6059

Severin, Joseph
The Remarkable Young Man - Cecil Roberts 5373

Severinus, Anicius
Citadel of God: A Novel of Saint Benedict - Louis De Wohl 1563

Sevier, John
The Cumberland Rifles - Noel B. Gerson 2365
Red Belts - Hugh Pendexter 4897
Rogue's March - Maristan Chapman 993
Slow Dies the Thunder - Helen Topping Miller 4395
The Sounds of Chariots: A Novel of John Sevier and the State of Franklin - Helen Topping Miller 4396
Tennessee Hazard - Maristan Chapman 994

Seward, William Henry
Lincoln: A Novel - Gore Vidal 6490
Nevada! - Dana Fuller Ross 5481
Passengers to Mexico: The Last Invasion of Mexico - Blair Niles 4627
Seward's Folly - Edison Marshall 4111
Woman with a Sword: The Biographical Novel of Anna Ella Carroll of Maryland - Hollister Noble 4632

Seymour, Edward
Feast in the Morning - Hugh Preston 5175
The Game of Kings - Dorothy Dunnett 1801

Seymour, Horatio
The Unterrified - Constance Robertson 5397

Seymour, Jane
The Autobiography of Henry VIII - Margaret George 2355
The Heir of Allington - Philippa Wiat 6727
Henry VIII and His Six Wives - Maureen Peters 4975
Kathryn: In the Court of Six Queens - Anne Merton Abbey 1
King's Fool - Margaret Campbell Barnes 325
The Lily and the Leopards - Alice Harwood 2765
The Queen's Grace - Jan Westcott 6646
Shadow in the Sun: A Novel of Elizabeth I, the Virgin Queen - F.W. Kenyon 3460
So Merciful a Queen, So Cruel a Woman - Alice Harwood 2769
Windsor Castle - William Harrison Ainsworth 59
The Wise Virgin - Hebe Elsna 1934

Seymour, Thomas
Her Royal Destiny - Carol Maxwell Eady 1820
The Ivy Crown: A Biographical Novel of Queen Katherine Parr - Mary M. Luke 3923
The Queen's Grace - Jan Westcott 6646
The Sixth Wife - Jean Plaidy 5063
The Young Elizabeth - Jennette Letton 3730

Sforza, Francesco
Condottiere - Jan Westcott 6644

Sforza, Gian Galeazzo
Duchess of Milan - Michael Ennis 1946

Sforza, Giovanni
The Naked Sword: The Story of Lucretia Borgia - F.W. Kenyon 3456

Sforza, Ludovico (Duke of Bari)
The Bride of Sforza - Miranda Seymour 5760
Duchess of Milan - Michael Ennis 1946

Sforza, Ludovico (Duke of Milan)
A Comedy of Murders - George Herman 2861
The Lady in the Mask - Anne Green 2564

Shackleton, Frank
Jewels - Robert Perrin 4917

Shafter, William R.
Remember Santiago - Douglas C. Jones 3280

Shah Jehan (Emperor of India)
Blood Royal - Robert Payne 4850
The Dark Dancer - Frederic Prokosch 5193
The Young Emperor - Robert Payne 4857

Shaka
The Covenant - James A. Michener 4368
Great Elephant - Alan Scholefield 5654

Shakespeare, William
All the Living: A Novel of One Year in the Life of William Shakespeare - Henrietta Buckmaster 758
The Best House in Stratford - Edward Fisher 2100
The Cleopatra Boy - Eric Malpass 4048
A Dead Man in Deptford - Anthony Burgess 776
Entered From the Sun - George Garrett 2301
Gentleman of Stratford - John Brophy 708
A House of Women - Eric Malpass 4049
Liza Bowe - Shirley Barker 313
Love's Labour's Won - Edward Fisher 2101
Mrs. Shakespeare: The Complete Works - Robert Nye 4656
Nicholas Cooke: Actor, Soldier, Physician, Priest - Stephanie Cowell 1393
No Bed for Bacon - Caryl Brahms 640
Nothing Like the Sun - Anthony Burgess 781
Physician Extraordinary: A Novel of the Life and Times of William Harvey - David Weiss 6608
The Quality of Mercy - Faye Kellerman 3391
Serenissima: A Novel of Venice - Erica Jong 3300
Shakespeare & Son - Edward Fisher 2102
Shakespeare's Dog - Leon Rooke 5439
Sweet Will - Eric Malpass 4050
Three Years to Play - Colin MacInnes 3983
To Be a King - Robert DeMaria 1607
Two Loves Have I - Clara Longworth de Chambrun 985
Will Shakespeare: The Untold Story - John Mortimer 4495
You, My Brother - Philip Burton 809

Shankaracharyarau, P.K.
Nine Hours to Rama - Stanley Wolpert 6846

Shatagin, Ivan
Elena - Judith Egan 1893

Shaw, George Bernard
The Daughter: A Novel Based on the Life of Eleanor Marx - Judith Chernaik 1012
The God of Mirrors - Robert Reilly 5293
Naked Came I: A Novel of Rodin - David Weiss 6607
The Night of the Ripper - Robert Bloch 551
Stage Fright - Gillian Linscott 3809
The West End Horror - Nicholas Meyer 4350

Shays, Daniel
The Regulators - William Degenhard 1580
The Sprig of Hemlock: A Novel about Shays' Rebellion - Robert Muir 4509

Sheba, Queen of
The Queen of Sheba - Roberta Kells Dorr 1696
Solomon and Sheba - Faye Levine 3740
Solomon and Sheba - Jay Williams 6774
Solomon and the Queen of Sheba - Czenzi Ormonde 4751

Shelby, Joseph Orville
Angel with Spurs - Paul I. Wellman 6613
West of Appomattox - Harley Duncan 1785

Shelley, Mary Wollstonecraft
The Absorbing Fire: The Byron Legend - F.W. Kenyon 3445
Count Manifred - Miranda Seymour 5761
Frankenstein Unbound - Brian Aldiss 68
The Golden Years: A Novel Based on the Life and Loves of Percy Bysshe Shelley - F.W. Kenyon 3451
Gothic Romance - Emmanuel Carrere 942
Haunted Summer - Anne Edwards 1881
Lord Byron's Doctor - Paul West 6634
Love's Children - Judith Chernaik 1013
My Sister, My Love - Lucille Iremonger 3111
The Olympians - Guy Bolton 566
A Single Summer with Lord B. - Derek Marlowe 4092
The Stress of Her Regard - Tim Powers 5157

Shelley, Percy Bysshe
The Absorbing Fire: The Byron Legend - F.W. Kenyon 3445
Count Manifred - Miranda Seymour 5761
Frankenstein Unbound - Brian Aldiss 68
The Golden Years: A Novel Based on the Life and Loves of Percy Bysshe Shelley - F.W. Kenyon 3451
Gothic Romance - Emmanuel Carrere 942
Haunted Summer - Anne Edwards 1881
Lord Byron's Doctor - Paul West 6634
Lord of the Dead: The Secret History of Byron - Tom Holland 2999
Lord of the Ladies - Joanna Dessau 1626
Love's Children - Judith Chernaik 1013
The Memoirs of Lord Byron - Robert Nye 4655
The Missolonghi Manuscript - Frederic Prokosch 5194
My Sister, My Love - Lucille Iremonger 3111
The Olympians - Guy Bolton 566
A Single Summer with Lord B. - Derek Marlowe 4092
The Stress of Her Regard - Tim Powers 5157

Shepherd, Catherine
Fairacres - Gladys Waters 6579

Shepherd, James
Fairacres - Gladys Waters 6579

Sheppard, Jack
Jack Sheppard - William Harrison Ainsworth 56

Sheridan, Philip H.
Action at Aquila - Hervey Allen 97
Banner at Shenandoah - Bruce Catton 963
Blood Song - Terry C. Johnston 3243
The Court-Martial of George Armstrong Custer - Douglas C. Jones 3276
Elkhorn Tavern - Douglas C. Jones 3278
The Last Stand: A Novel about George Armstrong Custer and the Indians of the Plains - Edwin P. Hoyt 3061
Long Winter Gone - Terry C. Johnston 3252
Roll, Shenandoah - Bruce Lancaster 3644
Roman - Douglas C. Jones 3281
Shadow on the Valley - Kirk Mitchell 4414
Shaggy Legion - Hal George Evarts 1986
Trumpet on the Land - Terry C. Johnston 3260

Sheridan, Richard Brinsley
Goddess of the Green Room - Jean Plaidy 5016
Perdita's Prince - Jean Plaidy 5040
Regency Royal - Michael Hardwick 2687

Sherman, Philip
Grant's War - Ted Jones 3297

Sherman, William Tecumseh
The Bride of Texas - Josef Skvorecky 5880
The Court-Martial of George Armstrong Custer - Douglas C. Jones 3276
The Crisis - Winston Churchill 1079
Grant's War - Ted Jones 3297
Jubilee - John Brick 672
The Last Stand: A Novel about George Armstrong Custer and the Indians of the Plains - Edwin P. Hoyt 3061
The Last Warpath - Will Henry 2844
Long Day at Shiloh - Don Bannister 294
The Shadow Riders - Terry C. Johnston 3257
Sherman's March - Cynthia Bass 373
Shiloh - Shelby Foote 2153
So Red the Rose - Stark Young 6944
Ulysses: A Biographical Novel - Robert Skimin 5878
Untold Glory - Cothburn O'Neal 4739
Woman with a Sword: The Biographical Novel of Anna Ella Carroll of Maryland - Hollister Noble 4632

Shippen, Elizabeth
The Sunshine Patriot: A Novel of Benedict Arnold - Norman Partington 4822

Shirakawa II (Emperor of Japan)
The Sword of Hachiman - Lynn Guest   2608

Shore, Jane
The Goldsmith's Wife - Jean Plaidy   5017
The Sun in Splendour - Jean Plaidy   5066

Short, William
Jefferson: A Novel - Max Byrd   838

Shover, Felicia Lee Cary Thornton
Untold Glory - Cothburn O'Neal   4739

Shrewsbury, Elizabeth
The Tower and the Dream - Jan Westcott   6647

Shulamit
Solomon's Song - Roberta Kells Dorr   1697

Sibelius, Jean
Winter Fire - William R. Trotter   6352

Sibyl (Queen of Jerusalem)
Jerusalem - Cecelia Holland   2990

Sickert, Walter Richard
The Women of Whitechapel and Jack the Ripper - Paul West   6638

Siddal, Elizabeth Eleanor
Cock of the Walk - Roy Lewis   3762
The Golden Veil - Paddy Kitchen   3507
The Hoydens and Mr. Dickens - William J. Palmer   4784
Willowwood - Elizabeth Savage   5619

Siddhartha Gautama
Lady of the Lotus - William E. Barrett   353
The Yellow Robe: A Novel of the Life of Buddha - Robert Payne   4856

Siddons, Sarah
Fire in the Heart - Henrietta Buckmaster   761

Sidney, Sir Philip
The Constant Star - Dorothy Norris Foote   2151
The Firedrake's Eye - Patricia Finney   2095
Lady Rich - Elizabeth Boatwright Coker   1166
The Master of Gray Trilogy - Nigel Tranter   6316
Roanoke Hundred - Inglis Fletcher   2138
Towers in the Mist - Elizabeth Goudge   2495
Trust and Treason - Margaret Birkhead   506

Sieber, Al
Geronimo: An American Legend - Robert J. Conley   1242

Siegel, Benjamin
The Howard Hughes Affair - Stuart M. Kaminsky   3340
New Deal for Death - Elliott Roosevelt   5454

Siegel, Bugsy
The Howard Hughes Affair - Stuart M. Kaminsky   3340
New Deal for Death - Elliott Roosevelt   5454

Signac, Paul
Vincent: A Novel Based on the Life of Van Gogh - Joost Poldermans   5082

Sigurdarson, Haraldr
Byzantium - Michael Ennis   1945

Silva, Flavius
The Antagonists - Ernest K. Gann   2276
The Triumph - Ernest K. Gann   2280

Silverius (Pope)
Count Belisarius - Robert Graves   2544

Simon Magus
The Illusionist - Anita Mason   4144
The Silver Chalice - Thomas B. Costain   1370

Simon Peter
Fisher of Men: A Novel of Simon Peter - Kurt Frieberger   2231

Simonides
The Praise Singer - Mary Renault   5302

Simpson, Wallis Warfield
Carnal Hours - Max Allan Collins   1210
Dance on a Sinking Ship - Michael Kilian   3483
Edward and Mrs. Simpson - A.C.H. Smith   5916
The Plot to Kill Wallis Simpson: A Work of Faction - Graham Fisher   2104
A Royal Murder - Elliott Roosevelt   5456
Wallis: The Novel - Anne Edwards   1883

Singbe-Pieh
Amistad: The Thunder of Freedom - David Pesci   4944

Singing Grass
Soldier in Buckskin - Ray Hogan   2981

Siringo, Charlie
The Cowboy Conspiracy - Larry D. Names   4553
South of the Border - John Byrne Cooke   1268

Sitting Bull
Arrest Sitting Bull - Douglas C. Jones   3273
Buffalo Girls - Larry McMurtry   4296
Creek Mary's Blood - Dee Brown   712
The Day the Sun Died - Dale Van Every   6408
Dodging Red Cloud - Richard S. Wheeler   6657
Drums of Change: The Story of Running Fawn - Janette Oke   4707
A Good Day to Die - Thomas Wakefield Blackburn   525
The Jewelled Spur - Gilbert Morris   4465
The Last Stand: A Novel about George Armstrong Custer and the Indians of the Plains - Edwin P. Hoyt   3061
A Road We Do Not Know: A Novel of Custer at the Little Bighorn - Frederick J. Chiaventone   1057
The Secret Annie Oakley - Marcy Moran Heidish   2819
Sitting Bull - Bill Dugan   1760
Thunder in the Dawn - Earl Murray   4532
The Winter War - William Wister Haines   2640
Yellowstone Kelly - Peter Bowen   602

Sitting Red Cloud
The Last Stand: A Novel about George Armstrong Custer and the Indians of the Plains - Edwin P. Hoyt   3061

Sixtus IV (Pope)
The Medici Emerald - Martin Woodhouse   6851
The Medici Guns - Martin Woodhouse   6852
The Medici Hawks - Martin Woodhouse   6853

Slade, Jack
Six-Horse Hitch - Janice Holt Giles   2417

Slidell, John
The Big Family - Vina Delmar   1600
The Chess Player: A Novel of New Orleans and Paris - Frances Parkinson Keyes   3478

Smeaton, Mark
The King's Pleasure - Jean Plaidy   5026

Smith, Alfred E.
The Immigrants - Howard Fast   2034

Smith, Frederick Edwin
High Heroic - Constantine FitzGibbon   2118

Smith, Harry
The Spanish Bride - Georgette Heyer   2902

Smith, James
The First Rebel - Neil Harmon Swanson   6137

Smith, John
Daughter of Eve - Noel B. Gerson   2366
A Durable Fire - Virginia Bernhard   480
For My Great Folly - Thomas B. Costain   1365
Pocahontas - Susan Donnell   1691
Pocahontas; or, The Nonpareil of Virginia - David Garnett   2297
Powhatan's Daughter - John Clarke Bowman   605
The Sea 'Venture - F. van Wyck Mason   4159
Soldier in Paradise - Burton Wohl   6835
Soldiers of Fortune - Peter Bourne   595

The Sot-Weed Factor - John Barth   364

Smith, Joseph
Children of God - Vardis Fisher   2106
The Devil's Rainbow - J.C. Furnas   2257
The Everlasting Fire - Jonreed Lauritzen   3675

Smith, Juana
The Spanish Bride - Georgette Heyer   2902

Smith, Madeline Hamilton
Madeleine - Pamela Elizabeth West   6633

Smith, Sydney
Come Be My Love - Diana Brown   717

Smith, Temperance
Woman of Justice - Georgia Di Donato   1639

Smith, Wesley
Diamond Six - William Fielding Smith   5932

Smithson, Harriet
Passionate Rebel: The Story of Hector Berlioz - F.W. Kenyon   3457

Snow, John
The Drummer Was the First to Die - Liza Pennywitt Taylor   6186

Socrates
Alcibiades, Beloved of Gods - Vincenz Brun   735
Creation - Gore Vidal   6486
The Escape of Socrates - Robert Pick   4993
Glory and the Lightning - Taylor Caldwell   856
Goat Song: A Novel of Ancient Greece - Frank Yerby   6920
Goatsong - Tom Holt   3009
The Immortal Marriage - Gertrude Atherton   225
The Last of the Wine - Mary Renault   5299
The Magnificent Traitor: A Novel of Alcibiades and the Golden Age of Pericles - Lynn Poole   5092
The Private and Public Life of Socrates - Rene Kraus   3552
The Walled Orchard - Tom Holt   3010

Solomon (King of Israel)
After Goliath - R.V. Cassill   955
Bathsheba - Torgny Lindgren   3789
David at Olivet - Wallace Hamilton   2671
David of Jerusalem - Louis De Wohl   1564
David: Warrior and King - Frank G. Slaughter   5885
King David - Gwyn Jenkins   3191
The King David Report - Stefan Heym   2910
Love and Wisdom: A Novel about Solomon - Richard G. Hubler   3064
The Queen of Sheba - Roberta Kells Dorr   1696
Solomon and Sheba - Faye Levine   3740
Solomon and Sheba - Jay Williams   6774
Solomon and the Queen of Sheba - Czenzi Ormonde   4751
Solomon's Song - Roberta Kells Dorr   1697
The Unanointed - Laurene Chinn   1070
The Valley of Vision: A Novel of King Solomon and His Time - Vardis Fisher   2113

Solomon, Haym
Haym Solomon, Son of Liberty - Howard Fast   2032

Solon
Farewell Great King: A Novel of Ancient Greece - Jill Paton Walsh   4829

Somers, George
The Sea 'Venture - F. van Wyck Mason   4159

Somers, Will
The Autobiography of Henry VIII - Margaret George   2355
King's Fool - Margaret Campbell Barnes   325

Somerset, Fitzroy
Flashman at the Charge - George MacDonald Fraser   2209
Hazard's Command - Vivian Stuart   6088

Sophia Dorothea
The Princess of Celle - Jean Plaidy   5045

Sophocles
Farewell Great King: A Novel of Ancient Greece - Jill Paton Walsh 4829
Glory and the Lightning - Taylor Caldwell 856
Goat Song: A Novel of Ancient Greece - Frank Yerby 6920
Goatsong - Tom Holt 3009
The Immortal Marriage - Gertrude Atherton 225

Sor Maria de Jesus
I, the King - Frances Parkinson Keyes 3479

Sorel, Agnes
La Belle Sorel - Jacques Carton 949
The Moneyman - Thomas B. Costain 1368

Soubirous, Bernadette
The Song of Bernadette - Franz Werfel 6625

Southampton, Earl of (1573-1624)
The Cleopatra Boy - Eric Malpass 4048
Nicholas Cooke: Actor, Soldier, Physician, Priest - Stephanie Cowell 1393
Serenissima: A Novel of Venice - Erica Jong 3300
Sweet Will - Eric Malpass 4050
Will Shakespeare: The Untold Story - John Mortimer 4495

Southampton, Earl of (1607-1667)
Feast in the Morning - Hugh Preston 5175

Spain, Johnathan E. Lee
Last Go Round - Ken Kesey 3473

Spartacus
Arena: A Novel of Spartacus and Crassus - Maurice Ghnassia 2391
Fortune's Favorite - Colleen McCullough 4235
The Gladiators - Arthur Koestler 3532
Spartacus - Howard Fast 2044

Speke, John Hanning
Burton and Speke - William Harrison 2751

Spencer, Herbert
The Consuming Flame: The Story of George Eliot - F.W. Kenyon 3446

Spencer, Philip
Voyage to the First of December - Henry Carlisle 897

Spencer, Tom
Wild Horizon - F. van Wyck Mason 4164

Spinoza, Baruch
I, Rembrandt - David Weiss 6605

Squanto
The Plymouth Adventure - Ernest Gebler 2342

Stael, Anne Louise Germaine de
The Missolonghi Manuscript - Frederic Prokosch 5194

Stafford, Edward
The Grail Murders - Michael Clynes 1135

Stafford, Henry
Crown of Roses - Valerie Anand 127
The Fate of Princes - P.C. Doherty 1673

Stalin, Joseph
Generations of Winter - Vassily Aksyonov 61
Joseph - Mervyn Jones 3292
Lenin: The Novel - Alan Brien 679
The Red Monarch: Scenes From the Life of Stalin - Yuri Krotkov 3561
The Revolutionist: A Novel of Russia - Robert Littell 3810
The Winds of War - Herman Wouk 6876

Standish, Miles
Cape Cod - William Martin 4139
The Disturber - L.S. Davidson Jr. 1505
The Honorable Imposter - Gilbert Morris 4463
The Land Is Bright - Noel B. Gerson 2376
O Western Wind - John Anthony Devon 1634

Pilgrims: A Novel of the Mayflower - Gerard Mac 3955
The Plymouth Adventure - Ernest Gebler 2342
Thanksgiving - Terry Coleman 1207
The Wickedest Pilgrim - Donald Barr Chidsey 1067

Stanford, Leland
California Gold - John Jakes 3145
The Fast Men - Tom McNab 4302

Stanley, Henry Morton
The Last Hero - Peter Forbath 2154
The Whales in Lake Tanganyika - Lennart Hagerfors 2636

Stanley, William
The Killing of Richard the Third - Robert Farrington 2020
The Traitors of Bosworth - Robert Farrington 2021

Stanton, Edward
The Cosgrove Report - G.J.A. O'Toole 4765

Stanton, Edwin
The Dixie Widow - Gilbert Morris 4459
Freedom - William Safire 5561
Heaven and Hell - John Jakes 3147
The Judges of the Secret Court - David Stacton 5972
Love and War - John Jakes 3150
Memories of the Ford Administration - John Updike 6391
Woman with a Sword: The Biographical Novel of Anna Ella Carroll of Maryland - Hollister Noble 4632

Stanton, Elizabeth Cady
The Americans - John Jakes 3143
Law of the Land - Marguerite Allis 111
North Star Conspiracy - Miriam Grace Monfredo 4428
Seneca Falls Inheritance - Miriam Grace Monfredo 4429
Through a Gold Eagle - Miriam Grace Monfredo 4430

Stark, John
The Shadow and the Glory - John Edward Jennings 3207

Starr, Belle
Belle Starr - Deborah Camp 870
Belle Starr - Speer Morgan 4453
The Bright Feathers - John H. Culp 1441
Dim the Flaring Lamps - Jan Jordan 3301
Loving Belle Star - Robert Taylor 6187
Pearl - Anne Leaton 3701

Starr, Henry
The Return of Henry Starr - Richard Slotkin 5909
The Saga of Henry Starr - Robert J. Conley 1250

Stauffenberg, Claus von
The Very Rich Hours of Count von Stauffenberg - Paul West 6637

Steele, Sir Richard
Henry Esmond - William Makepeace Thackeray 6212

Steffens, Lincoln
The Alienist - Caleb Carr 907

Stein, Gertrude
The Burning Man - Stephen Longstreet 3883
The Caravaggio Shawl - Samuel M. Steward 6019
Murder in the Chateau - Elliott Roosevelt 5447
Murder Is Murder Is Murder - Samuel M. Steward 6020

Stengel, Casey
Murder at Ebbets Field - Troy Soos 5947

Stephen (King of England)
Brother Cadfael's Penance - Ellis Peters 4955
The Fatal Crown - Ellen Jones 3289
The Lion of Justice - Jean Plaidy 5031
One Corpse Too Many - Ellis Peters 4966
The Passionate Enemies - Jean Plaidy 5039

To Keep This Oath - Hebe Weenolsen 6597
When Christ and His Saints Slept - Sharon Kay Penman 4908

Stephen of Blois
When Christ and His Saints Slept - Sharon Kay Penman 4908

Stephen of Cloyes
Our Lives Have Just Begun - Henry Myers 4541

Stephens, John Lloyd
Journey to the Sky: A Novel about the True Adventures of Two Men in Search of the Lost Maya Kingdom - Jamake Highwater 2918

Stephenson, George
Beau Blackstone - Richard Falkirk 2005
The Iron Roads - Forbes Bramble 644

Stepton, Gervase
Major Stepton's War - Matthew Vaughan 6445

Steuben, Friedrich von
Conceived in Liberty - Howard Fast 2029
Eagle in the Sky - F. van Wyck Mason 4149
Farewell to Valley Forge - David Taylor 6178
Monmouth - Charles Bracelen Flood 2144
Storm the Last Rampart - David Taylor 6180
The Strong Men - John Brick 677
Valley Forge - MacKinlay Kantor 3364

Stevens, Thaddeus
Heaven and Hell - John Jakes 3147
I Speak for Thaddeus Stevens - Elsie Singmaster 5868

Steward, Robert
The Sea Officer - Showell Styles 6105

Stewart, Henry (Lord Darnley)
The Gay Galliard - Margaret Irwin 3119
The Green Salamander - Pamela Hill 2933
Immortal Queen - Elizabeth Byrd 834
The Lion and the Rose - Jane Oliver 4724
Mary of Scotland - F.W. Kenyon 3454
Mary, Queen of Scotland and the Isles - Margaret George 2356
No Smoke Without Fire - Alice Harwood 2767
Parcel of Rogues - Jane Lane 3656
Queen's Caprice - Marjorie Bowen 599
Royal Road to Fotheringay - Jean Plaidy 5059
A Time for the Death of a King - Ann Dukthas 1777
The White Queen - Frederic Fallon 2011

Stewart, James (1531?-1570)
The White Queen - Frederic Fallon 2011

Stewart, James (James V)
The Riven Realm - Nigel Tranter 6317

Stewart, James (of the Glen)
Catriona - Robert Louis Stevenson 6009

Stewart, John (4th Earl of Atholl)
A Stake in the Kingdom - Nigel Tranter 6321

Stewart, John (Duke of Lennox)
Unicorn Rampant - Nigel Tranter 6323

Stewart, Robert (1340?-1420)
The World, the Flesh, and the Devil - Reay Tannahill 6159

Stewart, Robert (Viscount Castlereagh)
Brumaire - Mark Logan 3864
Guillotine - Mark Logan 3865

Stewart, Virgil
Sow the Seeds of Hemp - Gary Jennings 3195

Stewart, William
Running West - James Houston 3052

Stiegel, Henry William
One Red Rose Forever - Mildred A. Jordan 3305

Stiles, Ezra
Strange Wives - Shirley Barker 317

Stimson, Henry
Murder in the East Room - Elliott Roosevelt 5448

Stockton, Robert Field
The Bear Flag: A Novel of the Birth of California - Cecelia Holland 2983

Stoke, George
Theory of War - Joan Brady 637

Stoker, Bram
Good Morning, Irene - Carole Nelson Douglas 1698
Good Night, Mr. Holmes - Carole Nelson Douglas 1699
The West End Horror - Nicholas Meyer 4350

Stokowski, Leopold
Poor Butterfly - Stuart M. Kaminsky 3345

Stolberg-Gedern, Louise de
The Queen of Hearts - Joan Rees 5290

Stone, Lucy
The Americans - John Jakes 3143
The Lawless - John Jakes 3149
The Woman Question - Dorothea Malm 4046

Storm, Tehana
Lords of the Plains - Max Crawford 1420

Stowe, Frederick William
The Cup Trembling - Karl Brown 723

Stowe, Harriet Beecher
All This, and Heaven Too - Rachel Field 2080
Beecher: A Novel - Dan McCall 4218
The Cup Trembling - Karl Brown 723

Stradivari, Antonio
Antonietta - John Hersey 2868

Strassburg, Gottfried von
Elizabeth's Greetings - Rosemary Haughton 2774

Stravinsky, Igor
Antonietta - John Hersey 2868

Struensee, Johann Frederick
The Lost Queen - Norah Lofts 3850
The Queen's Physician - Edgar Maas 3952

Stuart, Anne
Queen's Gift - Inglis Fletcher 2136
Wicked Lady - Inglis Fletcher 2142

Stuart, Arabella
Too Near the Throne - Molly Costain Haycraft 2797

Stuart, Caroline
The Imposter - Noel B. Gerson 2375

Stuart, Charles (Charles I)
Powhatan's Daughter - John Clarke Bowman 605
Wife to Great Buckingham - Hilda Lewis 3751

Stuart, Charles (Charles II)
The King's General - Daphne Du Maurier 1748
The Phoenix Rising - Jean Evans 1984
The Wandering Prince - Jean Plaidy 5075

Stuart, Charles Edward
Born to Be King - Constance Gluyas 2440
Candleshine No More - Jane Oliver 4721
Charlie Is My Darling - Mollie Hardwick 2691
Clandara - Evelyn Anthony 161
Commander of the Mists - D.L. Murray 4527
Crown Without Sceptre - William Vaughan Wilkins 6758
The Dark Mile - Dorothy Kathleen Broster 709
The Flight of the Heron - Dorothy Kathleen Broster 710
Highlands Rebel - Sally Watson 6584
I Came to the Highlands: A Novel of Suspense - Velda Johnston 3263
The Long Day Closes - Beatrice Tunstall 6360
Louis the Well-Beloved - Jean Plaidy 5032
A Prince, a Piper, and a Rose - John Scalzo 5628
Prince Charlie's Bluff - Donald Thomas 6241
The Queen of Hearts - Joan Rees 5290
Red Gauntlet - Sir Walter Scott 5706

The Scotswoman - Inglis Fletcher 2140
Waverley - Sir Walter Scott 5709
The Woman from The Glen - Chloe Gartner 2310

Stuart, Gilbert
Proud Heritage - Ilse Bishcoff 510

Stuart, Henrietta
Royal Flush: The Story of Minette - Margaret Irwin 3121

Stuart, Henry Frederick
Lion Rampant - Bernard Shrimsley 5836
The Murder in the Tower - Jean Plaidy 5035

Stuart, James (Earl of Moray)
No Smoke Without Fire - Alice Harwood 2767
Seats of the Mighty: A Novel of James Stuart, Brother of Mary, Queen of Scots - Alice Harwood 2768

Stuart, James (James I)
Mary of Scotland - F.W. Kenyon 3454

Stuart, James Ewell Brown
The Court Martial of Robert E. Lee - Douglas Savage 5617
Farewell, My General - Shirley Seifert 5726
Gettysburg - Stephen Longstreet 3887
Gettysburg: Crisis of Command - Harry Albright 65
The Ghost Raider - Ray Hogan 2978
Gods and Generals - Jeff Shaara 5765
God's Angry Man - Leonard Ehrlich 1898
Gray Victory - Robert Skimin 5877
Major Stepton's War - Matthew Vaughan 6445
Secret Service Operator 13 - Robert W. Chambers 982
Soldier of the Queen - Max Hennessy 2837
The Stonewall Brigade: A Novel of the American Civil War - Frank G. Slaughter 5902
The Titans - John Jakes 3154
Traveller - Richard Adams 27

Stuart, James Francis Edward
Now Face to Face - Karleen Koen 3530
The Stuart Legacy - Robert Kerr 3472

Stuart, Jeb
The Court Martial of Robert E. Lee - Douglas Savage 5617
Farewell, My General - Shirley Seifert 5726
Gettysburg - Stephen Longstreet 3887
Gettysburg: Crisis of Command - Harry Albright 65
The Ghost Raider - Ray Hogan 2978
Gods and Generals - Jeff Shaara 5765
God's Angry Man - Leonard Ehrlich 1898
Gray Victory - Robert Skimin 5877
Major Stepton's War - Matthew Vaughan 6445
Secret Service Operator 13 - Robert W. Chambers 982
Soldier of the Queen - Max Hennessy 2837
The Stonewall Brigade: A Novel of the American Civil War - Frank G. Slaughter 5902
The Titans - John Jakes 3154
Traveller - Richard Adams 27

Stuart, Mary (Mary II)
The Queen's Husband - Samuel Edwards 1889

Stuart, Mary (Queen of Scotland)
All the Queen's Men - Evelyn Anthony 157
Madame Serpent - Jean Plaidy 5033
Mine Is the Kingdom - Jane Oliver 4726
A Time for the Death of a King - Ann Dukthas 1777
The Tower and the Dream - Jan Westcott 6647

Stuyvesant, Peter
The Dutchman - Maan Meyers 4351
Thanksgiving - Terry Coleman 1207

Sublette, Milt
Across the Shining Mountains - Christian McCord 4226

Sublette, William
The Great Adventure - Janice Holt Giles 2410

Subotai
Orlok - Don Dandrea 1461
Until the Sun Falls - Cecelia Holland 2998

Suckling, Sir John
The Golden Feather - Theda Kenyon 3462

Suleiman I (Ottoman Sultan)
The Bride of Suleiman - Aileen Crawley 1421
Pawn in Frankincense - Dorothy Dunnett 1804
The Shadow of God - Aileen Crawley 1422

Sulla, Lucius Cornelius
The First Man in Rome - Colleen McCullough 4234
Fortune's Favorite - Colleen McCullough 4235
The Grass Crown - Colleen McCullough 4236
A Pillar of Iron - Taylor Caldwell 861
Roman Blood - Steven Saylor 5626
Sword of Pleasure: Being the Memoirs of the Most Illustrious Lucius Cornelius Sulla - Peter Green 2571

Sullivan, John
Murfy's Men - Gerald Green 2565
The Wilderness War - Allen W. Eckert 1848

Sullivan, John L.
Hoopla - Harry Stein 5990

Sullivan, Joseph
Blue Ruin: A Novel of the 1919 World Series - Brendan Boyd 610

Summer, Charles
With Malice Toward None - Honore Morrow 4492

Sun Yat-Sen
Dynasty - Robert S. Elegant 1902

The Sundance Kid
Outlaw Lover - Lindsey Hanks 2676
The Story of the Sundance Kid - David Everitt 1988

Sundown, Jackson
Last Go Round - Ken Kesey 3473

Surratt, Mary Eugenia
The Woman Who Loved John Wilkes Booth - Pamela Redford Russell 5533

Suslova, Polina
The Devil Inside: A Novel of Dostoevsky's Life - Stephen Coulter 1385

Sutter, John A.
The American River - Gary McCarthy 4222
The Bear Flag: A Novel of the Birth of California - Cecelia Holland 2983
Calico Palace - Gwen Bristow 694
Captain Sutter's Gold - Jonreed Lauritzen 3673

The Swamp Fox
Battle Lanterns - Merrit Parmalee Allen 102
Celia Garth - Gwen Bristow 695
Dawn's Early Light - Elswyth Thane 6215
The Fallon Blood - Reagan O'Neal 4741
A Few Painted Feathers - Stephen Longstreet 3886
The Long March - Jane Barry 358
Othneil Jones - John Adams Leland 3715
Phantom Fortress - Bruce Lancaster 3643
The Red Doe - Drayton Mayrant 4214
The Swamp Fox, Francis Marion - Noel B. Gerson 2383
Sycamore Men - David Taylor 6181

Swift, Jonathan
Exit Lady Masham - Louis Auchincloss 230
Fanny: Being the True History of the Adventures of Fanny Hackabout-Jones - Erica Jong 3299
Henry Esmond - William Makepeace Thackeray 6212
Violent Friends - Winston Clewes 1113

Swilling, Jack
I, Jack Swilling - John Myers 4544

Swinburne, Algernon
To Seize the Passing Dream - Ted Berkman 479

Swynford, Katherine
Katherine - Anya Seton 5752

Sybilla (Queen of Jerusalem)
Jerusalem - Cecelia Holland 2990

Sykes, Christopher
Bertie and the Tinman - Peter Lovesey 3909

Sykes, Henrietta
Disraeli in Love - Maurice Edelman 1851

Sylvester II (Pope)
In the Falcon's Claw: A Novel of the Year 1000 -
  Chet Raymo 5257

Symms, Edward
Orphan Train - James Magnuson 4029

Szilard, Leo
A Family Matter - James Roosevelt 5458

T

Tabor, Elizabeth "Baby Doe"
All for Love: Baby Doe and Silver Dollar - John
  Vernon 6456
Wilde West - Walter Satterthwait 5609

Tabor, Horace
All for Love: Baby Doe and Silver Dollar - John
  Vernon 6456
Wilde West - Walter Satterthwait 5609

Tabor, Silver Dollar
All for Love: Baby Doe and Silver Dollar - John
  Vernon 6456

Taft, William Howard
TR - Noel B. Gerson 2385

T'ai Tsung (Emperor of China)
Empress - Evelyn McCune 4238

Taira Kiyomori
The Heike Story - Eiji Yoshikawa 6934

Tairo Tamako
The Sword of Hachiman - Lynn Guest 2608

Takakura
The Sword of Hachiman - Lynn Guest 2608

Talleyrand-Perigord, Charles Maurice de
Brumaire - Mark Logan 3864
Captain Cut-Throat - John Dickson Carr 908
Draw Near to Battle - Jere Hungerford
  Wheelwright 6667
Far Flies the Eagle - Evelyn Anthony 162
A Generation of Leaves - Robert S. Bloom 552
Guillotine - Mark Logan 3865
Lustre in the Sky - R.G. Waldeck 6525
Madame Casanova - Gaby von Schonthan 5659
The Man Who Killed the King - Dennis
  Wheatley 6654
Marianne - Juliette Benzoni 466
Marianne and the Masked Prince - Juliette
  Benzoni 469
Marianne and the Privateer - Juliette Benzoni 470
Mirage - Ruth McKenney 4283
Napoleon Symphony - Anthony Burgess 780
Polonaise - Jane Aiken Hodge 2968
The River Devils - Carter A. Vaughan 6437
The Rose and the Sword - Sandra Paretti 4792
So Great a Man - David Pilgrim 5000
The Winthrop Covenant - Louis Auchincloss 235

Tallien, Jean Lambert
The Incorruptible - Marjorie Coryn 1357
Lady of Paris - William Vaughan Wilkins 6760
Tallien: A Brief Romance - Frederic Tuten 6370

Tallmadge, Benjamin
The Culper Spy Ring - Lynn Groh 2596
Major Andre - Anthony Bailey 265

Poor Richard's Game - G.J.A. O'Toole 4766
Scoundrels' Brigade - Carter A. Vaughan 6439
The Secret Road - Bruce Lancaster 3646
Stars and Stripes - Adam Rutledge 5541
Tory Tavern - Henry Barnard Safford 5559
The Traitor - Dan Sherman 5814
The Yankee Rascals - Carter A. Vaughan 6444

Tamatoa VI (King of Bora Bora)
Hawaii - James A. Michener 4370

Tamerlane
Master of the World - Cothburn O'Neal 4738

Tancred
Count Bohemond - Alfred Duggan 1764

Tancred (King of Sicily)
The Kings of Vain Intent - Graham Shelby 5791
My Lord Brother the Lionheart - Molly Costain
  Haycraft 2795

Tanguy, Pierre
*Moulin Rouge: A Novel Based on Henri de Toulouse-
  Lautrec* - Pierre La Mure 3576
Vincent: A Novel Based on the Life of Van Gogh -
  Joost Poldermans 5082

Tao Kuang (Emperor of China)
Mandarin Gold - James Leasor 3700

Tarleton, Banastre
Cato's War - Guy Wheeler 6655
The Fallon Blood - Reagan O'Neal 4741
Raleigh's Eden - Inglis Fletcher 2137

Tartini, Giuseppe
A Fiddle, a Sword, and a Lady - Albert
  Spalding 5953

Tatiana, Grand Duchess of Russia
Devoted Friends - Joe Poyer 5161

Taylor, John
Children of God - Vardis Fisher 2106

Taylor, Sarah Knox
*There Was a Season: A Biographical Novel of
  Jefferson Davis* - Theodore Olsen 4730

Taylor, Zachary
Comes an Echo on the Breeze - Edward J.
  Ryan 5542
The Stuart Women - Matt Braun 652
*There Was a Season: A Biographical Novel of
  Jefferson Davis* - Theodore Olsen 4730
Twilight of Empire - Allen W. Eckert 1846

Tchaikovsky, Peter Ilyich
Pathetic Symphony: A Novel about Tchaikovsky -
  Klaus Mann 4064

Teach, Edward
Carolina Corsair - Don Tracy 6307
Lusty Wind for Carolina - Inglis Fletcher 2134
On Stranger Tides - Tim Powers 5156
Rogue's Holiday - Hamilton Cochran 1141
Wind From the Main - Anne Osborne 4759

Tecumseh
The Border Captains - Jason Manning 4072
Creek Mary's Blood - Dee Brown 712
The Frontiersmen - Allen W. Eckert 1841
Gateway to Empire - Allen W. Eckert 1842
Johnny Logan: Shawnee Spy - Allen W. Eckert 1843
The Loon Feather - Iola Fuller 2253
Panther in the Sky - James Alexander Thom 6234
Red Stick - Donald Clayton Porter 5121
Riders of the Long Road - Stephen E. Bransford 649
*Song of Metamoris: A Story That Remains of a People
  Who Passed This Way* - Milford E. Anness 155
A Sorrow in Our Heart - Allen W. Eckert 1844
War Clouds - Donald Clayton Porter 5131

Tekakwitha, Kateri
Lily of the Mohawks - Jack Casey 952

Tellez, Gabriel
The Adventures of Don Juan - Richard Gardner 2289

Temple, Henry John
Albert's Victoria - Tyler Whittle 6719
Follow the Drum - James Leasor 3699
Nevada! - Dana Fuller Ross 5481
The Queen's Husband - Jean Plaidy 5052
Republic: A Novel of Texas - E.V. Thompson 6266
Victoria and Albert - Evelyn Anthony 166
When the Emperor Dies - Mason McCann
  Smith 5926
The Widow of Windsor - Jean Plaidy 5076

Temujin
Ruler of the Sky: A Novel of Genghis Khan - Pamela
  Sargent 5606

Tennyson, Alfred, Lord
Caribbean - James A. Michener 4365
The Day They Kidnapped Queen Victoria - H.K.
  Fleming 2127
The Hedge of Thorns - Helen Ashton 217
Queen Victoria's Bomb - Ronald Clark 1094

Ternan, Ellen
The Detective and Mr. Dickens - William J.
  Palmer 4782
The Hoydens and Mr. Dickens - William J.
  Palmer 4784
The Mutual Friend - Frederick Busch 811

Terry, Alfred H.
A Mighty Afternoon - Charles K. Mills 4407

Terry, Ellen
Affairs of Love - Nicola Thorne 6272
The West End Horror - Nicholas Meyer 4350

Tesla, Nikola
Loving Little Egypt - Thomas McMahon 4288

Thackeray, William Makepeace
*Memoirs of a Victorian Gentleman: William
  Makepeace Thackeray* - Margaret Forster 2189
Path to the Silent Country - Lynne Reid Banks 291

Thaddeus, Juan
The Carmelite - Elgin Groseclose 2599

Thais
The Golden Lyre - Noel B. Gerson 2371

Thaissa
Alexander the God - Robert Payne 4849

Thales
My Name Is Sappho - Martha Rofheart 5429

Thandelthur
Running West - James Houston 3052

Thaw, Henry
Thine Is the Glory - Samuel A. Schreiner Jr. 5672

Thayendanegea
The Wilderness War - Allen W. Eckert 1848

Themistocles
Farewell Great King: A Novel of Ancient Greece - Jill
  Paton Walsh 4829

Theobald
*Thomas: A Novel of the Life, Passions, and Miracles
  of Becket* - Shelley Mydans 4538

Theodora (12th century)
Against the Fall of Night - Michael Arnold 193

Theodora (c. 500-548)
Basilissa: A Tale of the Empress Theodora - John
  Masefield 4142
The Bearkeeper's Daughter - Gillian Bradshaw 628
The Female: A Novel of Another Time - Paul I.
  Wellman 6617
Theodora - Samuel Edwards 1891
Theodora and the Emperor - Harold Lamb 3608

Theodore II (King of Ethiopia)
The Hammer of God - Alan Scholefield 5655
When the Emperor Dies - Mason McCann
  Smith 5926

Theodosius I (Roman Emperor)
The Last Romans - Teodor Jeske-Choinski 3216

Theodosius II (Eastern Roman Emperor)
Bury Me in Ravenna - Agnes Carr Vaughan 6432
Imperial Purple - Gillian Bradshaw 631
Sign of the Pagan - Don Tracy 6312

Theodosius the Great
The Last Romans - Teodor Jeske-Choinski 3216

Theophano
The Eagle's Daughter - Judith Tarr 6165

Theotokopoulos, Domenikos
Color From a Light Within: A Novel Based on the Life of El Greco - Donald Braider 641
The Greek of Toledo: A Romantic Narrative of El Greco - Elizabeth Borton 586

Theresa of Avila
Bold Encounter: A Novel Based on the Life of St. John of the Cross - Peter-Thomas Rohrbach 5433

Therese of Lisieux
Love Is My Vocation: An Imaginative Study of St. Therese of Lisieux - Tom Clarkson 1098

Thierry
The Earl - Cecelia Holland 2987

Thomas
Yeshua: The Gospel of St. Thomas - Alan Decker McNarie 4306

Thomas Aquinas
The Quiet Light - Louis De Wohl 1572

Thomas of Antioch
According to Thomas - Gladys Malvern 4053

Thomas the Rhymer
True Thomas - Nigel Tranter 6322

Thompson, Benjamin
The Countess - March Cost 1360

Thompson, Sarah
The Countess - March Cost 1360

Thorbjornsdottir, Gudrid
Gudrid's Saga - Constance Irwin 3115
The Ice Shirt - William T. Vollmann 6509

Thoreau, Henry David
God's Angry Man - Leonard Ehrlich 1898
Listen for the Voices - Anne Colver 1220
The Prescott Chronicles - Albert Fried 2232
Walt Whitman's Secret - Ben Aronin 196

Thoresby, John
The Apothecary Rose - Candace M. Robb 5364
The Lady Chapel - Candace M. Robb 5366

Thorfinn Karlsefni
Gudrid's Saga - Constance Irwin 3115

Thorvaldsson, Erik
A Viking's Daughter - John Andrews 147

Throckmorton, Bess
Lady in Waiting - Rosemary Sutcliff 6123
Ralegh's Fair Bess: The Story of Bess Throckmorton - Judy Turner 6365

Thumb, Tom
Jenny and Barnum: A Novel of Love - Roderick Thorp 6276

Thurvaldsson, Eirik
Gudrid's Saga - Constance Irwin 3115

Thutmose II (Pharaoh of Egypt)
King and Goddess - Judith Tarr 6166

Thutmose III (Pharaoh of Egypt)
Pharaoh - Eloise Jarvis McGraw 4276

Tiberius (Roman Emperor)
Augustus - John Williams 6785
Brothers of Vengeance - LeGette Blythe 556
Dear and Glorious Physician - Taylor Caldwell 853

The Eagle and the Crown - Hubertus Loewenstein 3832
I, Claudius - Robert Graves 2547
I Loved Tiberius - Elisabeth Dored 1692
The Kingdom of the Wicked - Anthony Burgess 778
Man on Fire: A Novel on the Life of St. Paul - LeGette Blythe 558
No King but Caesar - Anne Powers 5151
The Robe - Lloyd C. Douglas 1703
The Testament of Theophilus - Leonard Wibberley 6730
Tiberius: The Memoirs of the Emperor - Allan Massie 4169
The Word and the Sword - Theo Lang 3662

Tilden, Samuel
1876: A Novel - Gore Vidal 6484

Timoleon
A Choice of Murder - Peter Vansittart 6429

Timothy
Live From Golgotha - Gore Vidal 6491
Man on Fire: A Novel on the Life of St. Paul - LeGette Blythe 558
The Soothsayer - Laurene Chinn 1069

Timur the Great
Master of the World - Cothburn O'Neal 4738

Tintoretto
The Greek of Toledo: A Romantic Narrative of El Greco - Elizabeth Borton 586

Tirel, Walter
Death of the Red King - Pamela Bennetts 448
The Paladin - George Shipway 5830

Tirpitz, Alfred von
1901 - Robert Conroy 1258
Lusitania - David Butler 819

Tirso de Molina
The Adventures of Don Juan - Richard Gardner 2289

Tisquantum
The Plymouth Adventure - Ernest Gebler 2342

Titian
Color From a Light Within: A Novel Based on the Life of El Greco - Donald Braider 641
The Greek of Toledo: A Romantic Narrative of El Greco - Elizabeth Borton 586
Titian - Dario Cecchi 965
The Venetian - David Weiss 6611

Titokowaru
Monday's Warriors - Maurice Shadbolt 5767

Tituba
I, Tituba, Black Witch of Salem - Maryse Conde 1233
Peace, My Daughters - Shirley Barker 314

Titus (Roman Emperor)
Agrippa's Daughter - Howard Fast 2025
The Iron Hand of Mars - Lindsey Davis 1528
The Silver Pigs - Lindsey Davis 1532
The Triumph - Ernest K. Gann 2280
Venus in Copper - Lindsey Davis 1534
The Voices of Masada - David Kossoff 3545

Tiye
The Twelfth Transforming - Pauline Gedge 2347

Toklas, Alice B.
The Caravaggio Shawl - Samuel M. Steward 6019
Murder Is Murder Is Murder - Samuel M. Steward 6020

Tokugama Ieyasu
Daishi-San: A Novel - Robert P. Lund 3925
The Needle-Watcher - Richard Blaker 540
Taiko - Eiji Yoshikawa 6936

Tolstoy, Leo
The Extraordinary Adventures of Secret Agent Shipov in Pursuit of Count Leo Tolstoy in the Year 1862 - Bulat Okudzhava 4712

The Last Station - Jay Parini 4801

Tolstoy, Sofya Andreyevna
The Last Station - Jay Parini 4801

Tone, Theobald Wolfe
The Year of the French - Thomas Flanagan 2121

Torquemada, Tomas de
Crown of Aloes - Norah Lofts 3840
The Dogs of Paradise - Abel Posse 5141
The Inquisitors - Jerzy Andrzejewski 153
The Memoirs of Christopher Columbus - Stephen Marlowe 4096
The Queen's Cross: A Biographical Romance of Queen Isabella of Spain - Lawrence Schoonover 5666
Torquemada - Howard Fast 2045

Toscanelli, Paoli dal Pozzo
Columbus: A Romance - Rafael Sabatini 5549

Toscanini, Arturo
A Cadenza for Caruso - Barbara Paul 4834

Toulouse-Lautrec, Henri de
Bertie and the Crime of Passion - Peter Lovesey 3907
Lust for Life - Irving Stone 6059
Man of Montmartre: A Novel Based on the Life of Maurice Utrillo - Stephen Longstreet 3888
Moulin Rouge: A Novel Based on Henri de Toulouse-Lautrec - Pierre La Mure 3576
To Seize the Passing Dream - Ted Berkman 479
Vincent: A Novel Based on the Life of Van Gogh - Joost Poldermans 5082

Toussaint l'Ouverture, Pierre Dominique
All Souls' Rising - Madison Smartt Bell 422
The Black Consul - Anatolii Vinogradov 6503
Black Triumvirate: A Novel of Haiti - Benjamin H. Levin 3736
Caribbean - James A. Michener 4365
The Corsair: A Biographical Novel of Jean Lafitte, Hero of the Battle of New Orleans - Madeleine Fabiola Kent 3444
Drums at Dusk - Arna Bontemps 575
Drums of Destiny - Peter Bourne 593
Lydia Bailey - Kenneth Roberts 5387
Mistress of Darkness - Christopher Nicole 4617
A Time for Titans - Vina Delmar 1602

Townsend, Robert
The Culper Spy Ring - Lynn Groh 2596

Toyotomi Hideyoshi
Taiko - Eiji Yoshikawa 6936

Trajan (Roman Emperor)
Gold for the Caesars - Florence A. Seward 5759
The Soldier and the Sage: A Novel about Akiba - Richard G. Hubler 3065

Travis, William Barret
The Bugles Are Silent: A Novel of the Texas Revolution - John R. Knaggs 3513
On the Long Tide - Laura Krey 3555

Trevitnick, Richard
The Miller's Dance - Winston Graham 2528

Trollope, Anthony
Gentlemen in England - A.N. Wilson 6795
Princess Pamela - Ray Russell 5534

Trotsky, Leon
Blood on the Snow - John Elliott 1916
The End of the World News - Anthony Burgess 777
Joseph - Mervyn Jones 3292
Karl and Rosa - Alfred Doblin 1653
The King's Commissar - Duncan Kyle 3570
Lenin: The Novel - Alan Brien 679
Petersburg - Emily Hanlon 2677

Troy, William
The Wind in the Forest - Inglis Fletcher 2143

Truman, Harry S
War and Remembrance - Herman Wouk   6875

Truth, Sojourner
The Hallelujah Train - Bill Gulick   2614

Tsu Hsi (Dowager Empress of China)
China Saga - C.Y. Lee   3706

Tubman, Harriet
A Clouded Star - Anne Parrish   4819
Raising Holy Hell - Bruce Olds   4718
A Woman Called Moses - Marcy Moran
    Heidish   2821

Tudor, Edward
The Bisley Boy - Christopher Hunt   3080
A Crown in Darkness: A Novel about Lady Jane Grey
    - Margaret Mullally   4512
The Ivy Crown: A Biographical Novel of Queen
    Katherine Parr - Mary M. Luke   3923
The Lily and the Leopards - Alice Harwood   2765
The Prince and the Pauper - Mark Twain   6373
The Queen's Grace - Jan Westcott   6646
The Red-Haired Brat - Joanna Dessau   1627

Tudor, Elizabeth
The Autobiography of Henry VIII - Margaret
    George   2355
A Crown in Darkness: A Novel about Lady Jane Grey
    - Margaret Mullally   4512
Elizabeth and the Prince of Spain - Margaret
    Irwin   3117
Elizabeth, Captive Princess - Margaret Irwin   3118
I, Elizabeth - Rosalind Miles   4378
The Ivy Crown: A Biographical Novel of Queen
    Katherine Parr - Mary M. Luke   3923
Legacy - Susan Kay   3374
The Lily and the Leopards - Alice Harwood   2765
My Lord of Canterbury - Godfrey Turton   6369
Oh! Where Are Bloody Mary's Earrings? - Robert
    Player   5079
The Prince and the Pauper - Mark Twain   6373
The Queen's Grace - Jan Westcott   6646
The Red-Haired Brat - Joanna Dessau   1627
The Robsart Affair - Jennette Letton   3729
The Sixth Wife - Jean Plaidy   5063
The Spanish Bridegroom - Jean Plaidy   5064
The Strong Room - Jere Hungerford
    Wheelwright   6671
The Ten-Day Queen - Lozania Prole   5199
To Love a Queen - Lawrence Schoonover   5669
The Tower of London - William Harrison
    Ainsworth   58
Young Bess - Margaret Irwin   3123
The Young Elizabeth - Jennette Letton   3730

Tudor, Henry (Henry VII)
The Courts of Illusion - Rosemary Hawley
    Jarman   3165
The Dragon and the Rose - Roberta Gellis   2350
The Lodestar - Pamela Belle   432
Merchant of the Ruby - Alice Harwood   2766
An Unknown Welshman - Jean Stubbs   6100

Tudor, Henry (Henry VIII)
The Tudor Rose - Margaret Campbell Barnes   329

Tudor, Margaret
Chain of Destiny - Nigel Tranter   6314
James, by the Grace of God - Nigel Tranter   6315
Merchant of the Ruby - Alice Harwood   2766
My Lady Glamis - Pamela Hill   2940
The Riven Realm - Nigel Tranter   6317
A Stake in the Kingdom - Nigel Tranter   6321
Sunset at Noon - Jane Oliver   4728
The Thistle and the Rose - Jean Plaidy   5069
The White Rose Murders - Michael Clynes   1137

Tudor, Mary (Mary I)
Anne Boleyn - Evelyn Anthony   158
The Autobiography of Henry VIII - Margaret
    George   2355
The Bisley Boy - Christopher Hunt   3080

Brief Gaudy Hour - Margaret Campbell Barnes   322
Command of the King - Mary Lide   3773
A Crown in Darkness: A Novel about Lady Jane Grey
    - Margaret Mullally   4512
Elizabeth, Captive Princess - Margaret Irwin   3118
The Fifth Queen - Ford Madox Ford   2161
Henry VIII and His Six Wives - Maureen
    Peters   4975
I Am Mary Tudor - Hilda Lewis   3750
I, Elizabeth - Rosalind Miles   4378
The Ivy Crown: A Biographical Novel of Queen
    Katherine Parr - Mary M. Luke   3923
The King's Secret Matter - Jean Plaidy   5027
Legacy - Susan Kay   3374
The Lily and the Leopards - Alice Harwood   2765
The Man on a Donkey - H.F.M. Prescott   5170
My Lord of Canterbury - Godfrey Turton   6369
The Prince and the Pauper - Mark Twain   6373
The Queen's Grace - Jan Westcott   6646
The Red-Haired Brat - Joanna Dessau   1627
The Serpent Garden - Judith Merkle Riley   5336
The Spanish Bridegroom - Jean Plaidy   5064
The Ten-Day Queen - Lozania Prole   5199
The Tower of London - William Harrison
    Ainsworth   58
The White Rose Murders - Michael Clynes   1137
Young Bess - Margaret Irwin   3123
The Young Elizabeth - Jennette Letton   3730

Tudor, Mary (Queen of France)
The Reluctant Queen - Molly Costain Haycraft   2796
Royal Nonesuch: A Tudor Tapestry - Beatrice
    White   6674
A Stake in the Kingdom - Nigel Tranter   6321

Tudor, Owen
Crown in Candlelight - Rosemary Hawley
    Jarman   3166
The Queen's Secret - Jean Plaidy   5053
The Royal Pawn - Antonia Ridge   5327
Wife to Henry V - Hilda Lewis   3752

Tung Chih (Emperor of China)
Imperial Woman - Pearl S. Buck   755

Turner, Ann
For My Great Folly - Thomas B. Costain   1365

Turner, Frederick Jackson
Billy Sunday - Rod Jones   3295

Turner, J.M.W.
The Sun Is God - Michael Noonan   4636

Turner, Nat
The Confessions of Nat Turner - William
    Styron   6106
Ol' Prophet Nat - Daniel Panger   4786

Turner, Will
Lusitania - David Butler   819

Turpin, Dick
The Long Day Closes - Beatrice Tunstall   6360

Tussaud, Marie Grosholtz
I, Madame Tussaud - Sylvia Martin   4135

Tusson Bey
Blood and Sand - Rosemary Sutcliff   6121

Tutankhamen (Pharaoh of Egypt)
King Tut's Private Eye - Lee Levin   3739
Murder at the Feast of Rejoicing - Lynda S.
    Robinson   5407
Murder at the God's Gate - Lynda S.
    Robinson   5408
Murder in the Place of Anubis - Lynda S.
    Robinson   5409
Pillar of Fire - Judith Tarr   6168
Return to Thebes - Allen Drury   1739

Tutmose III (Pharaoh of Egypt)
Pharaoh - Eloise Jarvis McGraw   4276

Twain, Mark
1876: A Novel - Gore Vidal   6484

A Bloodsmoor Romance - Joyce Carol Oates   4658
A Connecticut Yankee in Criminal Court - Peter J.
    Heck   2814
Death on the Mississippi - Peter J. Heck   2815
If I Never Get Back - Darryl Brock   700
The Robber Baroness - William Kendall
    Clarke   1097
Sister Wives - Cleo Jones   3270
Twice upon a Time - Allen Appel   172

Tweed, Boss
The Bank - Stephen Longstreet   3882
Bread and Circus - Morris Renek   5303
Casey - Ramona Stewart   6034
Tassels on Her Boots - Arthur Cheney Train   6313

Tweed, William Marcy
The Bank - Stephen Longstreet   3882
Bread and Circus - Morris Renek   5303
Casey - Ramona Stewart   6034
Tassels on Her Boots - Arthur Cheney Train   6313

Tydier, Owen
Crown in Candlelight - Rosemary Hawley
    Jarman   3166

Tyler, Wat
Glendower Country - Martha Rofheart   5427
Katherine - Anya Seton   5752
Passage to Pontefract - Jean Plaidy   5038
The Peacock and the Pearl - Jennifer Lang   3661
Richard Whittington, London's Mayor - Gwynedd
    Sudworth   6112
Riot at Gravesend: A Novel of Wat Tyler's Rebellion -
    William Howard Woods   6864
The Ruthless Yeomen - Valerie Anand   134
Who Was Then the Gentleman - Charles E.
    Israel   3125
Within the Hollow Crown - Margaret Campbell
    Barnes   331

Tyndale, William
Flame of Fire - Jane Oliver   4722
The Sword of Truth - Gilbert Morris   4472

Tz'u-hsi (Dowager Empress of China)
China Saga - C.Y. Lee   3706
Forbidden City - Muriel Molland Jernigan   3215
Imperial Woman - Pearl S. Buck   755
Louisiana! - Dana Fuller Ross   5478
Manchu Empress - Bluebell Matilda Hunter   3081
Mandarin - Robert S. Elegant   1905
The Time of the Dragon - Dorothy Eden   1863
Twilight of the Dragon - Peter Bourne   596
White Poppy - Margaret Gaan   2261

U

Ulyanov, Vladimir Ilich
Blood on the Snow - John Elliott   1916
The Dawning of Deliverance - Judith Pella   4892
Grishin - Hans Herlin   2859
Joseph - Mervyn Jones   3292
Karl and Rosa - Alfred Doblin   1653
The King's Commissar - Duncan Kyle   3570
Lenin in Zurich - Alexander Solzhenitsyn   5943
Lenin: The Novel - Alan Brien   679
The Petrograd Consignment - Owen Sela   5739
The Revolutionist: A Novel of Russia - Robert
    Littell   3810
Seven Days to Petrograd - Tom Hyman   3094
Time After Time - Allen Appel   171
White Nights, Red Dawn - Frederick Nolan   4634

Urban VIII (Pope)
The Star-Gazer - Zsolt de Harsanyi   2757

Uriah
Bathsheba - Roberta Kells Dorr   1695
David's Stranger - Moshe Shamir   5771

Urswick, Christopher
The Killing of Richard the Third - Robert
  Farrington 2020
Tudor Agent - Robert Farrington 2022

Utrillo, Maurice
*Man of Montmartre: A Novel Based on the Life of
  Maurice Utrillo* - Stephen Longstreet 3888
Utrillo's Mother - Sarah Baylis 391
The Young Men of Paris - Stephen Longstreet 3893

V

Valadon, Suzanne
*Man of Montmartre: A Novel Based on the Life of
  Maurice Utrillo* - Stephen Longstreet 3888
Utrillo's Mother - Sarah Baylis 391

Valdemar (King of Sweden)
The Trees of the Folkungs - Verner Von
  Heidenstam 2817

Valdes, Don Pedro de
Sea of Lentils - Antonio Benitez-Rojo 443

Valentinian III (Roman Emperor)
Bury Me in Ravenna - Agnes Carr Vaughan 6432

Vallandigham, Clement
The Golden Circle - Constance Robertson 5396
The Unterrified - Constance Robertson 5397

Van Buren, Martin
Amistad: The Thunder of Freedom - David
  Pesci 4944
Burr - Gore Vidal 6485
Echo of Lions - Barbara Chase-Riboud 1004
Gone to Texas - Jason Manning 4074
The Land Where the Sun Dies - Henry Carlisle 896
Oregon! - Dana Fuller Ross 5484
The Slender Reed - Noel B. Gerson 2382
The Yankee From Tennessee - Noel B. Gerson 2388

Van Gogh, Theo
Lust for Life - Irving Stone 6059
Vincent: A Novel Based on the Life of Van Gogh -
  Joost Poldermans 5082

Van Gogh, Vincent
Gold of Their Bodies: A Novel about Gauguin -
  Charles Orson Gorham 2488
Lust for Life - Irving Stone 6059
*Moulin Rouge: A Novel Based on Henri de Toulouse-
  Lautrec* - Pierre La Mure 3576
Vincent: A Novel Based on the Life of Van Gogh -
  Joost Poldermans 5082

Van Gogh-Bonger, Johanna
Johanna: A Novel of the Van Gogh Family - Claire
  Cooperstein 1317

Van Keppel, Augustus
Manila Galleon - F. van Wyck Mason 4154

Van Lew, Elizabeth
Weep No More - Janet Stevenson 6006

van Rijn, Rembrandt
The Golden Tulip - Rosalind Laker 3596
I, Rembrandt - David Weiss 6605
Rembrandt - Gladys Schmitt 5643

Vanderbilt, Cornelius
The Bank - Stephen Longstreet 3882
Bread and Circus - Morris Renek 5303
Jubilee Jim and the Wizard of Wall Street - Donald
  Porter 5112

Vanderbilt, Gloria Morgan
That Vanderbilt Woman - Philip Van
  Rensselaer 6427

Vanderbilt, Reginald
That Vanderbilt Woman - Philip Van
  Rensselaer 6427

Vane, Charles
Lusty Wind for Carolina - Inglis Fletcher 2134

Vane, Sir Henry
A Candle in the Wilderness - Irving A.
  Bacheller 256

Vanhomrigh, Esther
Violent Friends - Winston Clewes 1113

Vanzetti, Bartolomeo
*The Passion of Sacco and Vanzetti: A New England
  Legend* - Howard Fast 2040

Varnum, Charles
*A Road We Do Not Know: A Novel of Custer at the
  Little Bighorn* - Frederick J. Chiaventone 1057

Vaughan, Henry
The Swan of Usk - Helen Ashton 220

Vecelli, Tiziano
*Color From a Light Within: A Novel Based on the Life
  of El Greco* - Donald Braider 641
*The Greek of Toledo: A Romantic Narrative of El
  Greco* - Elizabeth Borton 586
Titian - Dario Cecchi 965
The Venetian - David Weiss 6611

Venizelos, Eleutherios
The Ashes of Smyrna - Richard Reinhardt 5294

Vercingetorix
Caesar - Allan Massie 4168
Druids - Morgan Llywelyn 3817
Gaul Is Divided - Esther Fisher Brown 721

Vere, Edward de
Cloak of Folly - Burke Boyce 606

Vere, Robert de
Passage to Pontefract - Jean Plaidy 5038

Verlaine, Paul
Savage Prodigal - Konrad Bercovici 474

Vermeer, Jan
The Golden Tulip - Rosalind Laker 3596

Verne, Jules
The Harp and the Shadow - Alejo Carpentier 905
King of Paris - Guy Endore 1942

Veronica Giuliani
The Thorn of Arimathea - Frank G. Slaughter 5905

Vespasian (Roman Emperor)
The Crows of War - Steven Rayson 5276
The Iron Hand of Mars - Lindsey Davis 1528
The Jew of Rome - Lion Feuchtwanger 2071
Josephus - Lion Feuchtwanger 2072
The Kingdom of the Wicked - Anthony Burgess 778
Last Act in Palmyra - Lindsey Davis 1529
Shadows in Bronze - Lindsey Davis 1531
The Silver Pigs - Lindsey Davis 1532
The Source - James A. Michener 4374
The Tenth Measure - Brenda Lesley Segal 5721
Time to Depart - Lindsey Davis 1533
The Triumph - Ernest K. Gann 2280
The Voices of Masada - David Kossoff 3545
The Wolf of Masada - John Fredman 2220

Vespasianus, Titus Flavius
Agrippa's Daughter - Howard Fast 2025

Vespucci, Amerigo
The Memoirs of Christopher Columbus - Stephen
  Marlowe 4096

Vetsera, Maria
The Archduke - Michael Arnold 194

Vicar, Sir Arthur
Jewels - Robert Perrin 4917

Victoria (Queen of England)
Albert's Victoria - Tyler Whittle 6719
Anno-Dracula - Kim Newman 4595
Bertie, Albert Edward, Prince of Wales - Tyler
  Whittle 6720

Bertie and the Tinman - Peter Lovesey 3909
*Beyond Desire: A Novel Based on the Life of Felix
  and Cecille Mendelssohn* - Pierre La Mure 3574
Blackstone - Richard Falkirk 2006
By Command of the Viceroy - Duncan MacNeil 4010
The Captive of Kensington Palace - Jean
  Plaidy 5007
Castle of Foxes - Alanna Knight 3516
Chase Royal - Donald Seaman 5712
Cock of the Walk - Roy Lewis 3762
Consort for Victoria - William Vaughan
  Wilkins 6757
The Day They Kidnapped Queen Victoria - H.K.
  Fleming 2127
Elizabeth and Alexandra - Antony Lambton 3616
Flashman - George MacDonald Fraser 2204
Follow the Drum - James Leasor 3699
Halfhyde and the Fleet Review - Philip
  McCutchan 4246
Halfhyde for the Queen - Philip McCutchan 4247
I, Victoria - Cynthia Harrod-Eagles 2755
The Iron Roads - Forbes Bramble 644
The List of Seven - Mark Frost 2237
The Little Victoria - Lozania Prole 5196
Oh! Where Are Bloody Mary's Earrings? - Robert
  Player 5079
Pomp and Circumstance - Fred Mustard
  Stewart 6025
The Prime Minister's Wife - Doris Leslie 3727
Princess in Amber - Evelyn Wilde Mayerson 4205
The Queen and Lord M - Jean Plaidy 5046
Queen Victoria's Bomb - Ronald Clark 1094
The Queen's Husband - Jean Plaidy 5052
The Robber Baroness - William Kendall
  Clarke 1097
Sisters & Lovers - Nicola Thorne 6274
Swandowne - Daniel Farson 2024
That Spanish Woman - F.W. Kenyon 3461
This Old Bill - Loren D. Estleman 1980
The Vesey Inheritance - Gwendoline Butler 822
Victoria and Albert - Evelyn Anthony 166
Victoria in the Wings - Jean Plaidy 5072
Victoria Victorious - Jean Plaidy 5073
The Widow of Windsor - Jean Plaidy 5076
The Widow of Windsor - Tyler Whittle 6723
The Young Victoria - Tyler Whittle 6724

Victoria, Duchess of Kent
The Little Victoria - Lozania Prole 5196
The Queen and Lord M - Jean Plaidy 5046
The Young Victoria - Tyler Whittle 6724

Victoria Adelaide Mary Louise
The Queen's Husband - Jean Plaidy 5052

Victorio
A Time in the Sun - Jane Barry 361

Vidal, Peire
The Fool of Venus - George William Cronyn 1428

Vidocq, Francois Eugene
Crown of Grass - Charles Andrew Brady 634
I Am Vidocq - Vincent McConnor 4225

Vignerot du Plessis, Louis-Francois-Armand de
Through a Glass Darkly - Karleen Koen 3531

Villa, Francisco
Blue Moon - Parris Afton Bonds 569
The Crimson Wind - Max Hennessy 2832
The Fifth Horseman - Jose Antonio Villarreal 6496
The Friends of Pancho Villa - James Carlos
  Blake 535
Last Reveille - David Morrell 4456
Not of War Only - Norman Zollinger 6966
The Old Gringo - Carlos Fuentes 2247
Outlaw - Warren Kiefer 3482
Pancho And Black Jack - Fred Bean 398
The Prison Notebooks of Ricardo Flores Magon -
  Douglas Day 1545
Sergeant Gringo - Jack Cummings 1449

Tom Mix and Pancho Villa - Clifford Irving   3113
Under the Fifth Sun: A Novel of Pancho Villa - Earl
    Shorris   5832
El Vago - Laurence Gonzales   2474

Villa, Pancho
Blue Moon - Parris Afton Bonds   569
The Crimson Wind - Max Hennessy   2832
The Fifth Horseman - Jose Antonio Villarreal   6496
The Friends of Pancho Villa - James Carlos
    Blake   535
Last Reveille - David Morrell   4456
Not of War Only - Norman Zollinger   6966
The Old Gringo - Carlos Fuentes   2247
Outlaw - Warren Kiefer   3482
Pancho And Black Jack - Fred Bean   398
The Prison Notebooks of Ricardo Flores Magon -
    Douglas Day   1545
Sergeant Gringo - Jack Cummings   1449
Tom Mix and Pancho Villa - Clifford Irving   3113
Under the Fifth Sun: A Novel of Pancho Villa - Earl
    Shorris   5832
El Vago - Laurence Gonzales   2474

Villeneuve, Pierre de
1805 - Richard Woodman   6857
Decision at Trafalgar - Richard Woodman   6861

Villiers, Barbara
Catherine - Hilda Lewis   3746
Forever Amber - Kathleen Winsor   6822
A Health Unto His Majesty - Jean Plaidy   5019
The King's Brat - Constance Gluyas   2441
Lady on the Coin - Margaret Campbell Barnes   326
My Lady Benbrook - Constance Gluyas   2442
Our Jo, or The Chronicle of a Coming Man - Kenneth
    M. Cameron   868

Villiers, Elizabeth
The Three Crowns - Jean Plaidy   5070

Villiers, George (1592-1628)
Call Lady Purbeck - Hilda Lewis   3745
The Cardinal and the Queen - Evelyn Anthony   159
Myself My Enemy - Jean Plaidy   5037
The Three Musketeers - Alexandre Dumas   1782
To Love a Queen - Lawrence Schoonover   5669
Unicorn Rampant - Nigel Tranter   6323
Wife to Great Buckingham - Hilda Lewis   3751
The Young and Lonely King - Jane Lane   3659

Villiers, George (1628-1687)
Ballenrose - Mallory Burgess   783
Charles the King - Evelyn Anthony   160
A Health Unto His Majesty - Jean Plaidy   5019
Here Lies Our Sovereign Lord - Jean Plaidy   5021
The King Breaker - Elizabeth Linington   3797
The King's General - Daphne Du Maurier   1748
My Lord Foxe - Constance Gluyas   2443
Our Jo, or The Chronicle of a Coming Man - Kenneth
    M. Cameron   868
Peveril of the Peak - Sir Walter Scott   5703
Royal Escape - Georgette Heyer   2900

Villiers, John
Call Lady Purbeck - Hilda Lewis   3745

Villon, Francois
The Dragon Waiting: A Masque of History - John M.
    Ford   2165
Rogue's Legacy: A Novel about Francois Villon -
    Babette Deutsch   1629

Vining, Mary
Where Glory Waits - Gertrude Crownfield   1437

Violett, Lily
Dear Lily - Malcolm W. Greenough Jr.   2575

Virgil
The Death of Virgil - Hermann Broch   699

The Virgin Mary
According to Mary: A Novel of the Magdalene - Willa
    Gibbs   2398
Behold the Man - N. Richard Nash   4556

The Centurion - Leonard Wibberley   6729
Dear and Glorious Physician - Taylor Caldwell   853
The Gifts: A Story of the Boyhood of Jesus - Dorothy
    Clarke Wilson   6800
The Gospel of Corax - Paul Park   4802
He Came From Galilee - Daniel A. Poling   5083
Hidden Victory: A Novel of Jesus - Herbert Francis
    Smith   5921
How Far to Bethlehem? - Norah Lofts   3846
I, Judas - Taylor Caldwell   859
King Jesus - Robert Graves   2549
The Last Temptation of Christ - Nikos
    Kazantzakis   3384
The Life of Jesus: An Apocryphal Novel - Toby
    Olson   4731
Man Before the Morning - Cecil Maiden   4032
Man of Nazareth - Anthony Burgess   779
Martha, Martha - Patricia McGerr   4274
Mary - Sholem Asch   198
Mary of Nazareth - Esther Kellner   3394
The Messiah - Marjorie Holmes   3003
The Secret of the Kingdom - Mika Waltari   6555
The Shepherd - Robert Payne   4855
Three From Galilee: The Young Man From Nazareth -
    Marjorie Holmes   3004
Two From Galilee: A Love Story - Marjorie
    Holmes   3005

Viscount Castlereagh
Brumaire - Mark Logan   3864
Guillotine - Mark Logan   3865
The Sea Officer - Showell Styles   6105

Viscount Exmouth
The Sea Officer - Showell Styles   6105

Viscount Melbourne
Albert's Victoria - Tyler Whittle   6719
The Queen and Lord M - Jean Plaidy   5046
The Queen's Husband - Jean Plaidy   5052
Victoria and Albert - Evelyn Anthony   166
The Young Victoria - Tyler Whittle   6724

Viscount Palmerston
Albert's Victoria - Tyler Whittle   6719
Follow the Drum - James Leasor   3699
Nevada! - Dana Fuller Ross   5481
The Queen's Husband - Jean Plaidy   5052
Republic: A Novel of Texas - E.V. Thompson   6266
Victoria and Albert - Evelyn Anthony   166
When the Emperor Dies - Mason McCann
    Smith   5926
The Widow of Windsor - Jean Plaidy   5076

Viscount Purbeck
Call Lady Purbeck - Hilda Lewis   3745

Viscount Rochester
The King James Version - Stanley N. Stewart   6035
King's Minion - Rafael Sabatini   5552
Lion Rampant - Bernard Shrimsley   5836
The Murder in the Tower - Jean Plaidy   5035
The Street of Kings - Charles Dexter   1637

Visdelou, Humphrey
The Knight - George Shipway   5829

Vishnyevetski, Yeremi
With Fire and Sword - Henryk Sienkiewicz   5850

Vivonne, Victor de
Angelique in Barbary - Sergeanne Golon   2469

Voisin, La
The Oracle Glass - Judith Merkle Riley   5335

Voltaire
Adrienne - Barbara Levy   3742
The Anthem - Noel B. Gerson   2361
A Day of Battle - Vincent Sheean   5787
The Enchantress - Suyin Han   2673
Rasero - Francisco Rebolledo   5282
Voltaire! Voltaire! - Guy Endore   1943

Von Stroheim, Erich
The Greta Garbo Murder Case - George Baxt   385

W

Wade, Benjamin Franklin
*Woman with a Sword: The Biographical Novel of
    Anna Ella Carroll of Maryland* - Hollister
    Noble   4632

Wagner, Cosima
Hungarian Rhapsody: The Life of Franz Liszt - Jean
    Rousselot   5511
Magic Fire: Scenes around Richard Wagner - Bertita
    Harding   2683

Wagner, Honus
The Celebrant - Eric Rolfe Greenberg   2572

Wagner, Richard
*Beyond Desire: A Novel Based on the Life of Felix
    and Cecille Mendelssohn* - Pierre La Mure   3574
Hungarian Rhapsody: The Life of Franz Liszt - Jean
    Rousselot   5511
Magic Fire: Scenes around Richard Wagner - Bertita
    Harding   2683
The Ring Master - David Gurr   2622

Walewska, Marie
So Great a Man - David Pilgrim   5000

Walker, William
Dinner at Belmont - Alfred Leland Crabb   1398
The Journal of Colonel De Lancey - James Warner
    Bellah   426
The Lion's Skin - Darwin Le Ora Teilhet   6197
The Nation Thief - Robert Houston   3057
The Notorious Angel - Patricia Maxwell   4201

Wallace, George D.
A Creek Called Wounded Knee - Douglas C.
    Jones   3277

Wallace, Lew
Billy the Kid - Edwin Corle   1330
City of Widows - Loren D. Estleman   1969

Wallace, William
Braveheart - Randall Wallace   6538
Hammer of the Scots - Jean Plaidy   5018
The Lion Is Come - Jane Oliver   4725
Robert the Bruce: The Steps to the Empty Throne -
    Nigel Tranter   6320
The Scottish Chiefs - Jane Porter   5135

Wallenstein, Albrecht von
The Descent of the Idol - Jaroslav Durych   1818
World and Paradise - Edgar Maas   3953

Wallis, Henry
Chatterton - Peter Ackroyd   17

Walpole, Horace
Richard Carvel - Winston Churchill   1081

Walpole, Hugh
The Haunting of Lamb House - Joan Aiken   48

Walpole, Robert
Caroline the Queen - Jean Plaidy   5009
Now Face to Face - Karleen Koen   3530
Queen in Waiting - Jean Plaidy   5048

Walsingham, Frances
The Constant Star - Dorothy Norris Foote   2151

Walsingham, Sir Francis
All the Queen's Men - Evelyn Anthony   157
Court of Shadows - Cynthia Morgan   4450
Fire over England - A.E.W. Mason   4143
The Firedrake's Eye - Patricia Finney   2095
Gay Lord Robert - Jean Plaidy   5015
I, Elizabeth - Rosalind Miles   4378
Immortal Queen - Elizabeth Byrd   834
Legacy - Susan Kay   3374
The Master of Gray Trilogy - Nigel Tranter   6316
My Lord Essex - Olive Eckerson   1838
Prisoner of the Queen - Alison Macleod   4006
The Proud Man - Elizabeth Linington   3800

Queen of This Realm: The Story of Queen Elizabeth I - Jean Plaidy 5050
Shadow in the Sun: A Novel of Elizabeth I, the Virgin Queen - F.W. Kenyon 3460
The Shadow of the Earth - Lee Wichelns 6731
Tansy Taniard - Myrtle Strode-Jackson 6084
Till the Day Goes Down - Judith Lennox-Smith 3719
To Be a King - Robert DeMaria 1607
Trust and Treason - Margaret Birkhead 506
Tudor Underground - Denis Meadows 4320
Women of Ashdon - Valerie Anand 135

Walter, Lucy
The Wandering Prince - Jean Plaidy 5075

Warbeck, Perkin
Chain of Destiny - Nigel Tranter 6314
The Courts of Illusion - Rosemary Hawley Jarman 3165
Merchant of the Ruby - Alice Harwood 2766
The Tudor Rose - Margaret Campbell Barnes 329
Women of Ashdon - Valerie Anand 135
The Wrong Plantagenet - Marian Palmer 4781

Ward, John
For My Great Folly - Thomas B. Costain 1365

Warner, Jack
The Talking Pictures Murder Case - George Baxt 388

Warren, Charles
Bertie and the Tinman - Peter Lovesey 3909

Warren, Joseph
The Bastard - John Jakes 3144
Concord Bridge - Howard Horne 3035
The Rebels - John Jakes 3152

Warren, Peter
The Highwayman - Noel B. Gerson 2372

Warwick, Earl of (Guy de Beauchamp)
Vows of the Peacock - Alice Walworth Graham 2513

Warwick, Earl of (Richard Neville)
Crouchback - Carola Oman 4732
Crown of Roses - Valerie Anand 127
The Eye of God - C.L. Grace 2506
Fortune's Wheel - Rhoda S. Edwards 1886
The Golden Yoke: A Novel of the War of the Roses - Olive Eckerson 1837
I Remember Love - Mollie Hardwick 2694
The Last of the Barons - Edward Bulwer-Lytton 769
A Question of Choice - Prudence Andrew 143
Red Rose of Anjou - Jean Plaidy 5054
The Reluctant Queen: The Story of Anne of York - Jean Plaidy 5056
The Rose at Harvest End - Eleanor Fairburn 2003
The Sun in Splendour - Jean Plaidy 5066
The White Queen - Lesley J. Nickell 4611
The White Rose - Jan Westcott 6648

Washington, Booker T.
Ragtime - E.L. Doctorow 1658

Washington, George
Alabama Empire - Welbourn Kelley 3392
Ambush - Donald Clayton Porter 5113
Back Bay - William Martin 4138
Black Forest - Meade Minnigerode 4411
Bride of Liberty - Frank Yerby 6909
Burr - Gore Vidal 6485
Cato's War - Guy Wheeler 6655
Cherokee - Donald Clayton Porter 5115
Christmas at Mount Vernon - Helen Topping Miller 4385
Citizen Tom Paine - Howard Fast 2028
Clear for Action: A Novel about John Paul Jones - Clements Ripley 5344
Conceived in Liberty - Howard Fast 2029
The Culper Spy Ring - Lynn Groh 2596
Dawn's Early Light - Elswyth Thane 6215

The Double Man - Elinor Pryor 5205
The Drums of April - Charles Mergendahl 4340
The Drums of Monmouth - Emma Gelders Sterne 5998
Eagles Where I Walk - Stephen Longstreet 3885
A Few Painted Feathers - Stephen Longstreet 3886
The Firekeeper - Robert Moss 4498
The Gentle Rebel - Gilbert Morris 4461
Give Me Liberty: The Story of an Innocent Man - John Erskine 1956
Give Me the Wind - Jan Jordan 3302
The Governor's Daughter - Denton Whitson 6718
Hugh Wynne, Free Quaker - Silas Weir Mitchell 4416
I'll Storm Hell - Noel B. Gerson 2374
The Indentured Heart - Gilbert Morris 4464
The Ironmaster - Anne Powers 5150
Janice Meredith - Paul Leicester Ford 2166
Jarrett's Jade - Frank Yerby 6923
Juniata Valley - Virginia C. Cassel 954
The King's Iron - Robert Newton Peck 4888
The King's Orchard - Agnes Sligh Turnbull 6363
The Kingsbridge Plot - Maan Meyers 4355
Lady Washington - Dorothy Clarke Wilson 6803
Let My Name Stand Fair - Shirley Seifert 5727
The Long Naked Descent into Boston - William Eastlake 1823
The Lure of the Falcon - Juliette Benzoni 465
The Maddest Idea - James L. Nelson 4580
Man From Mt. Vernon - Burke Boyce 607
Manitou - Donald Clayton Porter 5120
The Master of Chaos - Irving A. Bacheller 262
Men in Buckskin - Herbert Stover 6069
Monmouth - Charles Bracelen Flood 2144
Morning in America - Willard Wiener 6741
Morning of a Hero - Burke Boyce 608
The Neutral Ground - Frank Olney Hough 3044
Portrait of a Scoundrel - Nathaniel Benchley 438
Prince Charlie's Bluff - Donald Thomas 6241
Proceed, Sergeant Lamb - Robert Graves 2550
The Rebels - John Jakes 3152
Red Morning - Ruby Frazier Frey 2230
The Red Road: A Romance of Braddock's Defeat - Hugh Pendexter 4898
Retreat and Recall - Joseph G.E. Hopkins 3029
Scoundrels' Brigade - Carter A. Vaughan 6439
The Sea Eagles - John Edward Jennings 3206
The Seekers - John Jakes 3153
Seminole - Donald Clayton Porter 5126
Seneca - Donald Clayton Porter 5127
The Seneca Hostage - Carter A. Vaughan 6440
Sound of the Trumpet - Gilbert Morris 4471
Spirit Knife - Donald Clayton Porter 5128
The Spy: A Tale of the Neutral Ground - James Fenimore Cooper 1310
Stars on the Sea - F. van Wyck Mason 4161
Storm the Last Rampart - David Taylor 6180
Strange Wives - Shirley Barker 317
Strife Before Dawn - Mary Schumann 5675
The Sunshine Patriot: A Novel of Benedict Arnold - Norman Partington 4822
Tavern in the Town - Cecile Hulse Matschat 4187
That Dark and Bloody River - Allen W. Eckert 1845
Those Who Love - Irving Stone 6064
Tidewater Dynasty: A Biographical Novel of the Lees of Stratford Hall - Carey Roberts 5372
To Spit Against the Wind - Benjamin H. Levin 3737
The Traitor - Dan Sherman 5814
The Tree of Liberty - Elizabeth Page 4773
The Twisted Saber: A Biographical Novel of Benedict Arnold - Philip Vail 6398
Two Crowns for America - Katherine Kurtz 3568
The Unvanquished - Howard Fast 2046
Valley Forge - MacKinlay Kantor 3364
War Cry - Donald Clayton Porter 5132
War in the Golden Weather - Stephen Longstreet 3892
Wilderness Empire - Allen W. Eckert 1847

The Woodsman - Don Wright 6880
Yankee Doodle Dandy - Noel B. Gerson 2387
Yorktown - Burke Davis 1513
The Young Man From Mount Vernon - Arthur Stanwood Pier 4995

Washington, Martha
Christmas at Mount Vernon - Helen Topping Miller 4385
Janice Meredith - Paul Leicester Ford 2166
Lady Washington - Dorothy Clarke Wilson 6803
Man From Mt. Vernon - Burke Boyce 607
Morning of a Hero - Burke Boyce 608
Seneca - Donald Clayton Porter 5127
Valley Forge - MacKinlay Kantor 3364

Watson, Anne
Watson's Apology - Beryl Bainbridge 271

Watson, John Selby
Watson's Apology - Beryl Bainbridge 271

Wayne, Anthony
Bride of Liberty - Frank Yerby 6909
Conceived in Liberty - Howard Fast 2029
Enough Good Men - Charles Mercer 4336
I'll Storm Hell - Noel B. Gerson 2374
The Ironmaster - Anne Powers 5150
The King's Orchard - Agnes Sligh Turnbull 6363
Let My Name Stand Fair - Shirley Seifert 5727
Morning in America - Willard Wiener 6741
Panther in the Sky - James Alexander Thom 6234
The Proud and the Free - Howard Fast 2042
The Seekers - John Jakes 3153
The Strong Men - John Brick 677
This Land Is Ours - Louis Zara 6953
Where Glory Waits - Gertrude Crownfield 1437
Yorktown - Burke Davis 1513

Wayne, John
The Man Who Shot Lewis Vance - Stuart M. Kaminsky 3341

Weatherford, William
Horseshoe Bend - Bruce Palmer 4779

Weaver, George "Buck"
Hoopla - Harry Stein 5990

Weber, Rupert
A Peep into the 20th Century - Christopher Davis 1515

Webster, Daniel
Dolley - Rita Mae Brown 727
The Gorgeous Hussy - Samuel Hopkins Adams 30
Tamarack Tree - Howard Breslin 670

Webster, Noah
Portrait of a Scoundrel - Nathaniel Benchley 438

Weiser, Conrad
A High Wind Rising - Elsie Singmaster 5867
The Interpreter - Robert Moss 4499
Song of the Susquehanna - Herbert Stover 6071

Weiss, Erich
The Sunken Treasure - Marian J.A. Jackson 3136

Weissenberg, Catherine
The Firekeeper - Robert Moss 4498

Weitzman, Chaim
Behold the Fire - Michael Blankfort 541

Wellesley, Arthur
The Amazing Mrs. Bonaparte - Harnett T. Kane 3351
The Asherwood Protegee - Mary A. Garratt 2299
A Balance of Dangers - Anthony Forrest 2184
Colossus: A Novel about Goya and a World Gone Mad - Stephen Marlowe 4093
Flashman - George MacDonald Fraser 2204
The Flight of the Eagle - Donald Thomas 6239
The Gentleman From America - Paul Benton 464
An Infamous Army - Georgette Heyer 2892
The Life and Times of Horatio Hornblower - C. Northcote Parkinson 4813

Historical Character Name Index

Wellington, Duke of

The Limits of Glory: A Novel of Waterloo - James McDonough 4265
The Masters of Bow Street - John Creasy 1423
Rage in Silence: A Novel Based on the Life of Goya - Donald Braider 643
Rifleman Dodd - C.S. Forester 2181
Sharpe's Battle - Bernard Cornwell 1338
Sharpe's Company - Bernard Cornwell 1339
Sharpe's Eagle - Bernard Cornwell 1341
Sharpe's Gold - Bernard Cornwell 1343
Sharpe's Honour - Bernard Cornwell 1344
Sharpe's Sword - Bernard Cornwell 1349
The Spanish Bride - Georgette Heyer 2902
Vanity Fair - William Makepeace Thackeray 6213
Waterloo - Bernard Cornwell 1350
Waterloo - Manuel Komroff 3536
Waterloo - Frederic E. Smith 5920
Whispering - Jane Aiken Hodge 2972
The Young Victoria - Tyler Whittle 6724

Wellington, Duke of

The Amazing Mrs. Bonaparte - Harnett T. Kane 3351
The Asherwood Protegee - Mary A. Garratt 2299
A Balance of Dangers - Anthony Forrest 2184
Colossus: A Novel about Goya and a World Gone Mad - Stephen Marlowe 4093
Flashman - George MacDonald Fraser 2204
The Flight of the Eagle - Donald Thomas 6239
The Gentleman From America - Paul Benton 464
An Infamous Army - Georgette Heyer 2892
The Life and Times of Horatio Hornblower - C. Northcote Parkinson 4813
The Limits of Glory: A Novel of Waterloo - James McDonough 4265
The Masters of Bow Street - John Creasy 1423
Rage in Silence: A Novel Based on the Life of Goya - Donald Braider 643
Rifleman Dodd - C.S. Forester 2181
Sharpe's Battle - Bernard Cornwell 1338
Sharpe's Company - Bernard Cornwell 1339
Sharpe's Eagle - Bernard Cornwell 1341
Sharpe's Gold - Bernard Cornwell 1343
Sharpe's Honour - Bernard Cornwell 1344
Sharpe's Sword - Bernard Cornwell 1349
The Spanish Bride - Georgette Heyer 2902
Vanity Fair - William Makepeace Thackeray 6213
Waterloo - Bernard Cornwell 1350
Waterloo - Manuel Komroff 3536
Waterloo - Frederic E. Smith 5920
Whispering - Jane Aiken Hodge 2972
The Young Victoria - Tyler Whittle 6724

Wells, H.G.
Time After Time - Karl Alexander 80

Wells, William
Gateway to Empire - Allen W. Eckert 1842

Wemyss, Admiral
Gossip From the Forest - Thomas Keneally 3413

Wentworth, Frances
The Governor's Lady - Thomas H. Raddall 5228

Wentworth, John
The Governor's Lady - Thomas H. Raddall 5228
Hangman's Beach - Thomas H. Raddall 5229
The Last Gentleman - Shirley Barker 312

Wesley, Charles
Dark Sails - Helen Topping Miller 4388

Wesley, John
Edward, Edward - Lolah Burford 772
The Holy Lover - Marie Oemler 4690
Jarrett's Jade - Frank Yerby 6923
Lord Vanity - Samuel Shellabarger 5796
A New Creature - Prudence Andrew 141
Take Her, Mr. Wesley - John W. Drakeford 1719

West, Mae
He Done Her Wrong - Stuart M. Kaminsky 3338
The Mae West Murder Case - George Baxt 386

Westbrook, Harriet
The Golden Years: A Novel Based on the Life and Loves of Percy Bysshe Shelley - F.W. Kenyon 3451
Love's Children - Judith Chernaik 1013

Westinghouse, George
A Peep into the 20th Century - Christopher Davis 1515

Wet, Christiaan de
Rags of Glory - Stuart Cloete 1126

Wetzel, Lewis
That Dark and Bloody River - Allen W. Eckert 1845

Weyerhaeuser, Frederick
The Living - Annie Dillard 1644

Weygard, Maxime
Gossip From the Forest - Thomas Keneally 3413

Wharton, Edith
The Haunting of Lamb House - Joan Aiken 48
Henry James' Midnight Song - Carol de Chellis Hill 2920

Wheeler, Hary
Bisbee '17 - Robert Houston 3056

Wheeler, Joe
1901 - Robert Conroy 1258

Whelan, Violett
Dear Lily - Malcolm W. Greenough Jr. 2575

Whetstone, Sir Thomas
Buccaneer - Dudley Pope 5093

Whicher, Jonathan
Scandal at High Chimneys: A Victorian Melodrama - John Dickson Carr 915

Whistler, James Abbott McNeill
Chelsea - Nancy Fitzgerald 2114
I, James McNeill Whistler - Lawrence Williams 6787
The Lawless - John Jakes 3149
Lillie - David Butler 818
The Tenants of Time - Thomas Flanagan 2120
To Seize the Passing Dream - Ted Berkman 479

White, John
Roanoke Hundred - Inglis Fletcher 2138

White Rajah
Flashman's Lady - George MacDonald Fraser 2210

Whitman, Emerson
The Camp Grant Massacre - Elliott Arnold 191

Whitman, Marcus
Doctor in Buckskin - T.D. Allen 103
To Heaven on Horseback - Paul F. Cranston 1419
We Must March: A Novel of the Winning of Oregon - Honore Morrow 4491

Whitman, Narcissa
Doctor in Buckskin - T.D. Allen 103
To Heaven on Horseback - Paul F. Cranston 1419
We Must March: A Novel of the Winning of Oregon - Honore Morrow 4491

Whitman, Walt
Peter Doyle - John Vernon 6457
Walt Whitman's Secret - Ben Aronin 196

Whitney, Eli
Whittling Boy: The Story of Eli Whitney - Roger Burlingame 789

Whittington, Richard
Richard Whittington, London's Mayor - Gwynedd Sudworth 6112

Wieck, Friedrich
Spring Symphony - Eleanor Painter 4777

Wild, Jonathan
Jack Sheppard - William Harrison Ainsworth 56

Wild Bill Hickok
Aces and Eights: A Novel of the Legend of Wild Bill Hickok - Loren D. Estleman 1967
Black Sun - Terry C. Johnston 3242
Crazy Fox Remembers - Don Preston 5174
Deadwood - Pete Dexter 1638
Elkhorn Tavern - Douglas C. Jones 3278
Flashman and the Redskins - George MacDonald Fraser 2208
The Lawless - John Jakes 3149
Little Big Man - Thomas Berger 478
The Pistoleer - James Carlos Blake 536
Shaggy Legion - Hal George Evarts 1986
Western: A Saga of the Great Plains - Frank Yerby 6930
Wild Times - Brian Garfield 2291

Wilde, Oscar
All for Love: Baby Doe and Silver Dollar - John Vernon 6456
Chelsea - Nancy Fitzgerald 2114
Day Is Coming - William Cameron 869
Farriers' Lane - Anne Perry 4930
The God of Mirrors - Robert Reilly 5293
Good Night, Mr. Holmes - Carole Nelson Douglas 1699
I Give You Oscar Wilde - Desmond Hall 2647
Irene at Large - Carole Nelson Douglas 1700
The Last Testament of Oscar Wilde - Peter Ackroyd 19
Lillie - David Butler 818
The Night of the Ripper - Robert Bloch 551
Playing the Game - Ian Buruma 810
A Season for Death - Ray Harrison 2743
Sherlock Holmes and the Mysterious Friend of Oscar Wilde - Russell A. Brown 731
To Seize the Passing Dream - Ted Berkman 479
The West End Horror - Nicholas Meyer 4350
Wilde West - Walter Satterthwait 5609

Wiley, Jennie Sellards
Dark Hills to Westward - Harry M. Caudill 964

Wilhelm II (Kaiser of Germany)
1901 - Robert Conroy 1258
Court of Honor - Maria Fagyas 1996
Lusitania - David Butler 819
To the Honor of the Fleet - Robert H. Pilpel 5002

Wilkes, John
Brimstone Club - F. van Wyck Mason 4147
The Vast Memory of Love - Malcolm Bosse 588

Wilkinson, James
The Fallon Pride - Reagan O'Neal 4742
The Land Beyond the Mountains - Janice Holt Giles 2414
The Medicine Man - Shirley Seifert 5729
Morning Time - Charles Kendall O'Neill 4743
Shadow of the Moon - Douglas C. Jones 3284
Tennessee Hazard - Maristan Chapman 994
The Voyagers - Dale Van Every 6412

Willem II (King of the Netherlands)
Waterloo - Bernard Cornwell 1350

William, Duke of Clarence
Goddess of the Green Room - Jean Plaidy 5016
Regency Buck - Georgette Heyer 2898
Victoria in the Wings - Jean Plaidy 5072

William, Duke of Orange
The Sea Beggars - Cecelia Holland 2996

William I (King of England)
The Bastard King - Jean Plaidy 5004
Bond of Honour - Catherine Todd 6284
The Conqueror - Georgette Heyer 2881
The Conqueror's Wife - Noel B. Gerson 2363
The Cunning of the Dove - Alfred Duggan 1765
The Disputed Crown - Valerie Anand 128
The Firedrake - Cecelia Holland 2988
Fortune's Knave: The Making of William the Conqueror - Mary Lide 3774

The Golden Warrior: The Story of Harold and William - Hope Muntz 4517
Harold, the Last of the Saxon Kings - Edward Bulwer-Lytton 767
Harold Was My King - Hilda Lewis 3749
Hereward the Wake - Charles Kingsley 3497
I Am England - Patricia Wright 6881
The Norman Pretender - Valerie Anand 132
Red Lion and Gold Dragon - Rosemary Sprague 5969
Robin and the King - Parke Godwin 2448
The Saxon Tapestry - Sile Rice 5317
Sherwood - Parke Godwin 2449
Son of Dust - H.F.M. Prescott 5171
Wife to the Bastard - Hilda Lewis 3753

William II (King of England)
The Bastard King - Jean Plaidy 5004
Death of the Red King - Pamela Bennetts 448
Flambard's Confession - Marilyn Durham 1816
King of the Wood - Valerie Anand 131
The Lion of Justice - Jean Plaidy 5031
The Paladin - George Shipway 5830
Robin and the King - Parke Godwin 2448

William III (King of England)
The Bracegirdle - Burris Atkins Jenkins 3189
Dark Torrent of Glencoe - Edward Grierson 2590
The Elusive Crown - Hebe Elsna 1931
The Glory and the Dream - F.W. Kenyon 3450
King's Agent - Justus Kent Clark 1090
The Power and the Passion - Christina Nicholson 4609
The Queen's Husband - Samuel Edwards 1889
The Renegade - Donald Clayton Porter 5122
The Three Crowns - Jean Plaidy 5070
Treason's Gift - Pamela Belle 434
William's Wife - Jean Plaidy 5077

William IV (King of England)
The Captive of Kensington Palace - Jean Plaidy 5007
Goddess of the Green Room - Jean Plaidy 5016
Princess Pamela - Ray Russell 5534
Regency Buck - Georgette Heyer 2898
Royal William - Doris Leslie 3728
Victoria in the Wings - Jean Plaidy 5072
The Young Victoria - Tyler Whittle 6724

William of Orange
The Bracegirdle - Burris Atkins Jenkins 3189
The Elusive Crown - Hebe Elsna 1931
The Queen's Husband - Samuel Edwards 1889
The Three Crowns - Jean Plaidy 5070
Treason's Gift - Pamela Belle 434
William's Wife - Jean Plaidy 5077

William of Wales
Di and I - Peter Lefcourt 3714

William Rufus
The Bastard King - Jean Plaidy 5004
Death of the Red King - Pamela Bennetts 448
Flambard's Confession - Marilyn Durham 1816
King of the Wood - Valerie Anand 131
The Lion of Justice - Jean Plaidy 5031
The Paladin - George Shipway 5830
Robin and the King - Parke Godwin 2448

William the Conqueror
The Bastard King - Jean Plaidy 5004
Bond of Honour - Catherine Todd 6284
The Conqueror - Georgette Heyer 2881
The Conqueror's Wife - Noel B. Gerson 2363
The Cunning of the Dove - Alfred Duggan 1765
The Disputed Crown - Valerie Anand 128
The Firedrake - Cecelia Holland 2988
Fortune's Knave: The Making of William the Conqueror - Mary Lide 3774
The Golden Warrior: The Story of Harold and William - Hope Muntz 4517
Harold, the Last of the Saxon Kings - Edward Bulwer-Lytton 767

Harold Was My King - Hilda Lewis 3749
Hereward the Wake - Charles Kingsley 3497
I Am England - Patricia Wright 6881
The Norman Pretender - Valerie Anand 132
Red Lion and Gold Dragon - Rosemary Sprague 5969
Robin and the King - Parke Godwin 2448
The Saxon Tapestry - Sile Rice 5317
Sherwood - Parke Godwin 2449
Son of Dust - H.F.M. Prescott 5171
Wife to the Bastard - Hilda Lewis 3753

Williams, Ephraim
The Firekeeper - Robert Moss 4498

Williams, Roger
Ashes in the Wilderness - William Greenough Schofield 5649
Come Home at Even - Le Grand Cannon 884
The Greater Hunger - Barbara Dodge Borland 581
I Seek a City - Gilbert Rees 5289

Wilmot, John
Alethea - Pamela Belle 429
Old St. Paul's - William Harrison Ainsworth 57
Royal Escape - Georgette Heyer 2900

Wilson, Alexander
The Mysterious Death of Meriwether Lewis - Ron Burns 802

Wilson, Edith
Hollywood: A Novel of America in the 1920s - Gore Vidal 6488

Wilson, Edward
The Birthday Boys - Beryl Bainbridge 269

Wilson, Elizabeth "Lily"
Lady's Maid - Margaret Forster 2188

Wilson, Sir Robert
Ride with Me - Thomas B. Costain 1369

Wilson, Woodrow
Hollywood: A Novel of America in the 1920s - Gore Vidal 6488
Lusitania - David Butler 819
A People Betrayed - Alfred Doblin 1654
Seven Days to Petrograd - Tom Hyman 3094
To the Honor of the Fleet - Robert H. Pilpel 5002
Tolbecken - Samuel Shellabarger 5798

Winchell, Walter
The Old Colts - Glendon Swarthout 6144
Walter Winchell: A Novel - Michael Herr 2863

Winder, John H.
Andersonville - MacKinlay Kantor 3359

Winder, William
Dolley - Rita Mae Brown 727

Wingate, Orde Charles
Born of War - Thomas Taylor 6192

Winthrop, Elizabeth Fones
The Winthrop Woman - Anya Seton 5754

Winthrop, John
A Candle in the Wilderness - Irving A. Bacheller 256
Covenant of Grace - Jane Gilmore Rushing 5527
The Greater Hunger - Barbara Dodge Borland 581
Hope Leslie; or, Early Times in Massachusetts - Catharine Maria Sedgewick 5714
The Prescott Chronicles - Albert Fried 2232
The Winthrop Covenant - Louis Auchincloss 235
The Winthrop Woman - Anya Seton 5754
Witnesses - Marcy Moran Heidish 2820

Wirz, Henry
Andersonville - MacKinlay Kantor 3359

Wiseman, Nicholas
Cock of the Walk - Roy Lewis 3762

Witt, John de
The Queen's Husband - Samuel Edwards 1889

Witte, Sergei
Petersburg - Emily Hanlon 2677

Wittgenstein, Ludwig
Saints and Scholars - Terrence Eagleton 1821
The World as I Found It - Bruce Duffy 1755

Wittgenstein, Paul
The Crown Prince - John Barchilon 300

Woffington, Peg
Peg Woffington - Charles Reade 5281
The Savage Brood - Martha Rofheart 5430

Wolfe, James
His Majesty's Highlanders - Leslie Turner White 6683
Lord Vanity - Samuel Shellabarger 5796
Running Proud - Nicholas Monsarrat 4432
To Fame Unknown - Clifford Lindsey Alderman 67
The Virginians - William Makepeace Thackeray 6214
Web of Destiny - Muriel Elwood 1939
The White Cockade - Vincent O'Brien 4683

Wollstonecraft, Mary
A Most Extraordinary Pair - Jean Detre 1628
Vindication - Frances Sherwood 5824

Wolsey, Thomas
Anne Boleyn - Evelyn Anthony 158
Anne of the Thousand Days - Edward Fenton 2059
The Autobiography of Henry VIII - Margaret George 2355
A Brood of Vipers - Michael Clynes 1133
Command of the King - Mary Lide 3773
The Concubine - Norah Lofts 3839
The Gallows Murder - Michael Clynes 1134
The Grail Murders - Michael Clynes 1135
Henry VIII and His Six Wives - Maureen Peters 4975
The King's Pleasure - Norah Lofts 3847
The King's Secret Matter - Jean Plaidy 5027
The Lady in the Tower - Jean Plaidy 5028
The Man on a Donkey - H.F.M. Prescott 5170
The Poisoned Chalice - Michael Clynes 1136
Queen Anne Boleyn - Francis Hackett 2634
The Reluctant Queen - Molly Costain Haycraft 2796
St. Thomas's Eve - Jean Plaidy 5060
The Serpent Garden - Judith Merkle Riley 5336
The Shadow of the Pomegranate - Jean Plaidy 5062
The Sword of Truth - Gilbert Morris 4472
The White Rose Murders - Michael Clynes 1137
Windsor Castle - William Harrison Ainsworth 59

Woman Chief
Woman Chief - Benjamin Capps 892

Woodhull, Victoria Claflin
Beecher: A Novel - Dan McCall 4218
Scarlet Women - J.D. Christilian 1077
Whirlwind in Petticoats - Beril Becker 406

Woods, Georgia Virginia Lawshe
True Women - Janice Woods Windle 6820

Woodville, Elizabeth
The Book of Shadows - C.L. Grace 2505
The Dragon Waiting: A Masque of History - John M. Ford 2165
The King's Grey Mare - Rosemary Hawley Jarman 3167
The Rose at Harvest End - Eleanor Fairburn 2003
The Summer Queen - Alice Walworth Graham 2512
The Sun in Splendour - Jean Plaidy 5066
The White Rose - Jan Westcott 6648

Woodville, William
The Dedicated - Willa Gibbs 2399

Woodward, Henry
Hilton Head - Josephine Pinckney 5003

Woolcott, Alexander
The Dorothy Parker Murder Case - George Baxt 384

Woolf, Leonard
The Shadow of the Moth: A Novel of Espionage with Virginia Woolf - Ellen Hawkes   2779

Woolf, Virginia
The Shadow of the Moth: A Novel of Espionage with Virginia Woolf - Ellen Hawkes   2779

Wordsworth, Dorothy
Mister Christian - William Kinsolving   3502

Wordsworth, William
Eliza's Daughter - Joan Aiken   44
Mister Christian - William Kinsolving   3502

Worth, Charles
Banners of Silk - Rosalind Laker   3592

Wovoka
The Day the Sun Died - Dale Van Every   6408
Song of Wovoka - Earl Murray   4531

Wren, Christopher
Circle of Pearls - Rosalind Laker   3593
Myself, Christopher Wren - David Weiss   6606

Wright, George
If I Never Get Back - Darryl Brock   700

Wright, Silas
Light in the Clearing - Irving A. Bacheller   260

Wriothesley, Henry
The Cleopatra Boy - Eric Malpass   4048
Nicholas Cooke: Actor, Soldier, Physician, Priest - Stephanie Cowell   1393
Serenissima: A Novel of Venice - Erica Jong   3300
Sweet Will - Eric Malpass   4050
Will Shakespeare: The Untold Story - John Mortimer   4495

Wriothesley, Thomas
Feast in the Morning - Hugh Preston   5175

Wu Chao (Empress of China)
Deception - Eleanor Cooney   1295
Empress - Evelyn McCune   4238
Green Dragon, White Tiger - Annette Motley   4501
The Jade Stalk - Jonathan Fast   2048
Lady Wu - Yutang Lin   3782

Wyatt, Sir Thomas
Blood Royal - Mollie Hardwick   2690
Brief Gaudy Hour - Margaret Campbell Barnes   322
The Heir of Allington - Philippa Wiat   6727
The King's Pleasure - Jean Plaidy   5026
Mistress Anne - Carolly Erickson   1952
Queen Anne Boleyn - Francis Hackett   2634
The Sword of Truth - Gilbert Morris   4472
The Tower of London - William Harrison Ainsworth   58
Windsor Castle - William Harrison Ainsworth   59

Wycliffe, John
The Peacock and the Pearl - Jennifer Lang   3661

Wyeth, Nathaniel J.
Across the Shining Mountains - Christian McCord   4226

Wynkoop, Edward Wanshear
A Very Small Remnant - Michael Whitney Straight   6075

X

Xanthippe
The Private and Public Life of Socrates - Rene Kraus   3552

Xavier, Francis
The Golden Thread - Louis De Wohl   1566
Set All Afire: A Novel of St. Francis Xavier - Louis De Wohl   1574
So Far From Malabar - Joy DeWeese Wehen   6599

Xerxes I (King of Persia)
Creation - Gore Vidal   6486
The Dragon of the Ishtar Gate - L. Sprague De Camp   1555
Esther - Nathaniel Norsen Weinreb   6601
Esther: The Star and the Sceptre - Gina Andrews   146
Farewell Great King: A Novel of Ancient Greece - Jill Paton Walsh   4829

Ximenes de Cisneros, Francisco
The Shadow of the Pomegranate - Jean Plaidy   5062

Y

Yannai
The King of Flesh and Blood - Moshe Shamir   5772

Yasodhara
Lady of the Lotus - William E. Barrett   353

Yeats, William Butler
An Excess of Love - Cathy Cash Spellman   5959
High Heroic - Constantine FitzGibbon   2118

Yell, Archibald
A Man's Reach - Charles Morrow Wilson   6796

Yenehala (Dowager Empress of China)
Mandarin - Robert S. Elegant   1905

Yeshua
Mary - Sholem Asch   198
The Shepherd - Robert Payne   4855

Yezierska, Anzia
John and Anzia: An American Romance - Norma Rosen   5462

Yona
The Shepherd - Robert Payne   4855

Young, Brigham
Children of God - Vardis Fisher   2106
The Devil's Rainbow - J.C. Furnas   2257
Dream Catcher - Terry C. Johnston   3251
The Everlasting Fire - Jonreed Lauritzen   3675
For Time and All Eternity - Paul Bailey   268
The Giant Joshua - Maurine Whipple   6673
Kelly Blue - Peter Bowen   601
Salt Lake City - A.R. Reife   5292
Sister Wives - Cleo Jones   3270

Younger, Cole
Belle Starr - Deborah Camp   870

Confessions of Johnny Ringo - Geoff Aggeler   40
Death of a Legend - Will Henry   2840
Major Stepton's War - Matthew Vaughan   6445
Pearl - Anne Leaton   3701
While Angels Dance - Ralph W. Cotton   1372

Yurensky, Nadya
The Emperor Story: A Historical Romance - George Sava   5615

Z

Zapata, Emiliano
The Crimson Wind - Max Hennessy   2832
Not of War Only - Norman Zollinger   6966
The Prison Notebooks of Ricardo Flores Magon - Douglas Day   1545
Tom Mix and Pancho Villa - Clifford Irving   3113
El Vago - Laurence Gonzales   2474

Zeami, Fujiwaka Motokiyo
The House of Kanze - Nobuko Albery   64

Zenger, Anna
Anna Zenger: Mother of Freedom - Kent Cooper   1316

Zenger, Peter
Anna Zenger: Mother of Freedom - Kent Cooper   1316

Zeno
Glory and the Lightning - Taylor Caldwell   856

Zenobia (Queen of Palmyra)
Queen of the East - Alexander Baron   336

Zeppelin, Count Ferdinand von
McKensie's Hundred: A Tale of the Old Dominion - Frank Yerby   6924

Zhukov, Georgi Konstantinovich
Journey into Fire - Patricia Wright   6882

Zimmerman, Arthur
The Petrograd Consignment - Owen Sela   5739

Zoe
Byzantium - Michael Ennis   1945

Zola, Emile
Lust for Life - Irving Stone   6059
Naked Came I: A Novel of Rodin - David Weiss   6607

Zucchi, Antonio
Angelica - Samuel A. Schreiner Jr.   5671

Zukor, Adolph
The Talking Pictures Murder Case - George Baxt   388

Zumarraga, Juan de
Roses for Mexico - Ethel Cook Eliot   1907

Character Description Index

This index alphabetically lists descriptions of the major fictional and historical characters in the featured books. Descriptions may be occupations (e.g. Farmer, Writer) or may describe the character's persona (e.g. Gentlewoman, Twin). Under each descriptor, character names are listed alphabetically, along with book titles, author names, and entry numbers.

ABANDONED CHILD

Forester, Millie
The Rag Nymph - Catherine Cookson   1287

ABOLITIONIST

Braithwaite, Henry
Echo of Lions - Barbara Chase-Riboud   1004

Braithwaite, Vivian
Echo of Lions - Barbara Chase-Riboud   1004

Brown, John
The Drums of Morning - Philip Van Doren
   Stern   5997
Flashman and the Angel of the Lord - George
   MacDonald Fraser   2205
Free Soil - Marguerite Allis   110
Free Soil - Margaret Lynn   3943
God's Angry Man - Leonard Ehrlich   1898
House Divided - Ben Ames Williams   6765
McKay's Bees - Thomas McMahon   4289
Raising Holy Hell - Bruce Olds   4718
The Slave of Frankenstein - Robert J. Myers   4549
The Surveyor - Truman Nelson   4583
Through a Gold Eagle - Miriam Grace
   Monfredo   4430

Brown, Salmon
Gray Victory - Robert Skimin   5877

Butler, Fanny Kemble
Where Shadows Go - Eugenia Price   5189

Carrington, Gincie
Swan's Chance - Celeste De Blasis   1549

Christmas, Anne
Free Enterprise - Michelle Cliff   1116

Clay, Cassius Marcellus
Hacey Miller - James Sherburne   5805
The Way to Fort Pillow - James Sherburne   5807

Coffin, Levi
Levi Coffin and the Underground Railroad - Charles
   Ludwig   3921

Douglass, Frederick
Darktown Strutters - Wesley Brown   732
The Furies - John Jakes   3146
Hacey Miller - James Sherburne   5805
Raising Holy Hell - Bruce Olds   4718
Seneca Falls Inheritance - Miriam Grace
   Monfredo   4429
A Star Pointed North - Edmund Fuller   2250

Through a Gold Eagle - Miriam Grace
   Monfredo   4430

Geddes, Neal
Wind Like a Bugle - Leonard Nathan   3722

Grimke, Angelina
Sisters and Brothers - Janet Stevenson   6005

Grimke, Sarah
Sisters and Brothers - Janet Stevenson   6005

Harrifield, Emma
Caleb Pettengill U.S.N. - George Fielding Eliot   1912

Hemings, Harriet
The President's Daughter - Barbara Chase-
   Riboud   1005

Higginson, Thomas Wentworth
Hacey Miller - James Sherburne   5805
I Never Came to You in White - Judith Farr   2014
The Way to Fort Pillow - James Sherburne   5807

Lovejoy, Owen
The Drums of Morning - Philip Van Doren
   Stern   5997

MacIntosh, Andrew
The Glass Dove - Sally Carrighar   943

Martineau, Harriet
Path to the Silent Country - Lynne Reid Banks   291

Ord, Dallas
Fire Bell in the Night - Constance Robertson   5395

Parker, Theodore
The Sin of the Prophet - Truman Nelson   4582

Phillips, Wendell
The Sin of the Prophet - Truman Nelson   4582

Pleasant, Mary Ellen
Free Enterprise - Michelle Cliff   1116

Stafford, John
The Father - Katharine Holland Brown   724

Stair, Diana
Diana Stair - Floyd Dell   1594

Stevens, Thaddeus
Heaven and Hell - John Jakes   3147

Truth, Sojourner
The Hallelujah Train - Bill Gulick   2614

Tubman, Harriet
A Clouded Star - Anne Parrish   4819
Raising Holy Hell - Bruce Olds   4718
A Woman Called Moses - Marcy Moran
   Heidish   2821

ABUSE VICTIM

Elliot, Bronwen
The Valiant and the Daunted - Roy Clews   1115

Todd, Jennifer
The Gallows Land - Bill Pronzini   5201

Withers, Damaris
A Woman Named Damaris - Janette Oke   4711

ACCOUNTANT

Chandagnac, John
On Stranger Tides - Tim Powers   5156

Selkirk, Olivia
Legacy of the Wolf - Jean Raynes   5274

ACTIVIST

Arlosoroff, Chaim
Union Square - Meredith Tax   6176

Barton, Clara
The Titans - John Jakes   3154

Bethune, Mary McLeod
Murder in the Rose Garden - Elliott Roosevelt   5452

Debs, Eugene V.
The Dream Seekers - Grace Mark   4085

Dekker, Leon
Julie - Jane Kesner Morris   4479

Flecke, Saul
We Stood for Freedom - Iris Morley   4455

Flores Magon, Ricardo
The Prison Notebooks of Ricardo Flores Magon -
   Douglas Day   1545

Gadd, Aaron
The God-Seeker - Sinclair Lewis   3763

Goldman, Emma
The Prison Notebooks of Ricardo Flores Magon -
   Douglas Day   1545

Groody, Helen
The Tontine - Thomas B. Costain   1371

Haughery, Margaret
Angel of the Delta - Edward Francis Murphy   4521

Howe, Samuel Gridley
Banners Against the Wind - John Edward
   Jennings   3198

Hunter, Adam
Cardigan Square - Alexandra Manners 4070

King, Euphemia Texas Ashby
True Women - Janice Woods Windle 6820

Lacey, Lily
The Scapegoat - Mary Lee Settle 5758

Levka, Rachel
The Rising of the Moon - William Martin 4140

Marx, Eleanor
The Daughter: A Novel Based on the Life of Eleanor Marx - Judith Chernaik 1012

Muir, John
California Gold - John Jakes 3145

Phelan, Edward
While England Sleeps - David Leavitt 3702

Sanger, Margaret
The Crusader - Noel B. Gerson 2364

Serra, Emil
La Guerra: A Spanish Saga - Stephen D. Frances 2199

Woodhull, Victoria Claflin
Beecher: A Novel - Dan McCall 4218

ACTOR

Alleyn, Edward
Sweet Will - Eric Malpass 4050

Alleyne, Richard
Nothing Like the Sun - Anthony Burgess 781

Arbuckle, Roscoe "Fatty"
Keystone - Peter Lovesey 3913

Astaire, Fred
Dancing in the Dark - Stuart M. Kaminsky 3334

Aubrey of Epping
Three Years to Play - Colin MacInnes 3983

Aveling, Edward
The Daughter: A Novel Based on the Life of Eleanor Marx - Judith Chernaik 1012

Blundell, Roper
The Merry Devils - Edward Marston 4123

Boone, Benjy
Benjy Boone - Maurice Dolbier 1687

Boone, Crassus Cornelius
Benjy Boone - Maurice Dolbier 1687

Booth, Edwin
The Chester A. Arthur Conspiracy - William Wiegand 6740
The Fast Men - Tom McNab 4302
The Judges of the Secret Court - David Stacton 5972
The Spur - Ardyth Kennelly 3425

Booth, John Wilkes
The Cosgrove Report - G.J.A. O'Toole 4765
A Court of Owls - Richard Adicks 37
Dim the Flaring Lamps - Jan Jordan 3301
The Judges of the Secret Court - David Stacton 5972
The Spur - Ardyth Kennelly 3425
The Titans - John Jakes 3154
The Twisted Tendril - Alice Glasgow 2427
The Woman Who Loved John Wilkes Booth - Pamela Redford Russell 5533

Boyd, Willie
Bide Me Fair - Harvey Howells 3060

Bracciolini, Vittorio
Carnival of Saints - George Herman 2860

Burbage, Richard
The Best House in Stratford - Edward Fisher 2100
The Cleopatra Boy - Eric Malpass 4048
Nothing Like the Sun - Anthony Burgess 781
Sweet Will - Eric Malpass 4050

Butler, Neal
Boon Island - Kenneth Roberts 5384

Carrick, Sebastian
The Mad Courtesan - Edward Marston 4122

Chaplin, Charlie
The Man Who Shot Lewis Vance - Stuart M. Kaminsky 3341
Max - Howard Fast 2038
Murder at San Simeon - Robert Lee Hall 2660
Murder in the East Room - Elliott Roosevelt 5448

Cibber, Colley
Peg Woffington - Charles Reade 5281

Coleman, Charles
The Eagle at the Gate - Rona Randall 5248

Cooke, Nicholas
Nicholas Cooke: Actor, Soldier, Physician, Priest - Stephanie Cowell 1393

Cooper, Gary
High Midnight - Stuart M. Kaminsky 3339

Coventry, Daniel
The Sound of Coaches - Leon Garfield 2295

Easton, Warwick
Keystone - Peter Lovesey 3913

Fairbanks, Douglas
Hollywood: A Novel of America in the 1920s - Gore Vidal 6488
Max - Howard Fast 2038

Firethorn, Lawrence
The Mad Courtesan - Edward Marston 4122
The Nine Giants - Edward Marston 4124
The Queen's Head - Edward Marston 4125
The Trip to Jerusalem - Edward Marston 4129

Firethorne, Lawrence
The Merry Devils - Edward Marston 4123
The Silent Woman - Edward Marston 4128

Flynn, Errol
Bullet for a Star - Stuart M. Kaminsky 3331

Forrest, Edwin
The Bluestocking - David Delman 1598

Gable, Clark
Murder on the Yellow Brick Road - Stuart M. Kaminsky 3343
Tomorrow Is Another Day - Stuart M. Kaminsky 3348

Garrick, David
Angelica - Samuel A. Schreiner Jr. 5671
Blind Justice - Bruce Alexander 76
The Bonnet Laird's Daughter - Barbara Annandale 154
Dr. Johnson's Dear Mistress - Winifred Carter 948
Murder at Drury Lane - Robert Lee Hall 2659
My Name Is Clary Brown - Charlotte Keppel 3466
The Savage Brood - Martha Rofheart 5430
The Upstart - Edison Marshall 4112

Godfrey
The Queen's War: A Novel of Eleanor of Aquitaine - Jeanne Mackin 3996

Hallam, Lucus
Dead-Stick - L.J. Washburn 6574
Dog Heavies - L.J. Washburn 6575

Heminges, John
Nicholas Cooke: Actor, Soldier, Physician, Priest - Stephanie Cowell 1393

Hunnyman, Joseph
Entered From the Sun - George Garrett 2301

Irving, Henry
The West End Horror - Nicholas Meyer 4350

Jovian, Robert
The Mortal Gods - Maurice Dolbier 1688

Kanami, Kiyotsugu
The House of Kanze - Nobuko Albery 64

Karloff, Boris
Never Cross a Vampire - Stuart M. Kaminsky 3344

Kean, Edmund
Kean: The Imaginary Memoirs of an Actor - Julius Berstl 485

Keaton, Buster
The Fala Factor - Stuart M. Kaminsky 3337

Kempe, Will
Nothing Like the Sun - Anthony Burgess 781

Lambriere, Philippe de
The Way to the Lantern - Audrey Erskine Lindop 3790

Lorre, Peter
The Greta Garbo Murder Case - George Baxt 385
Think Fast, Mr. Peters - Stuart M. Kaminsky 3347

Lucas, Fenton
Covent Garden - Claire Rayner 5262

Lugosi, Bela
The Greta Garbo Murder Case - George Baxt 385
Never Cross a Vampire - Stuart M. Kaminsky 3344

Marx, Chico
You Bet Your Life - Stuart M. Kaminsky 3349

Marx, Groucho
You Bet Your Life - Stuart M. Kaminsky 3349

Mix, Tom
Tom Mix and Pancho Villa - Clifford Irving 3113
Tom Mix Died for Your Sins - Darryl Ponicsan 5090

Nandou
A Tale of the Wind: A Novel of Nineteenth-Century France - Kay Nolte Smith 5922

Nash, Richard
Lucy - Hester W. Chapman 992

Nikeratos
The Mask of Apollo - Mary Renault 5300

O'Hare, Lucas
Chelsea Reach - Claire Rayner 5261

Otway, Raymond
Lovers Meeting - Mollie Hardwick 2695

Payne, John Howard
John Howard Payne, Skywalker - Maude Barragan 348

Peters, George
The River and the Wilderness - Don Robertson 5401

Peverel, Henry
Catherine Carter - Pamela Hansford Johnson 3227

Pio
The Bridge of San Luis Rey - Thornton Wilder 6752

Pope, Thomas
Nicholas Cooke: Actor, Soldier, Physician, Priest - Stephanie Cowell 1393

Powell, William
The William Powell and Myrna Loy Murder Case - George Baxt 390

Price, Richard
The Upstart - Edison Marshall 4112

Quintard, Jans
Banner by the Wayside - Samuel Hopkins Adams 28

Raft, George
True Detective - Max Allan Collins 1215

Rathbone, Basil
The Howard Hughes Affair - Stuart M. Kaminsky 3340

Raymond, Jules
Feast of the Jesters - Manuel Komroff 3533

Rice, Jack
Will Shakespeare: The Untold Story - John
Mortimer   4495

Robeson, Paul
Smart Moves - Stuart M. Kaminsky   3346

Sands, John
The Player's Boy - Bryher   744

Savage, Edward
The Savage Brood - Martha Rofheart   5430

Savage, Joseph Peace
The Savage Brood - Martha Rofheart   5430

Seagraves, Brice
The Actor - Robert J. Conley   1236

Shakespeare, Edward
You, My Brother - Philip Burton   809

Shakespeare, William
The Cleopatra Boy - Eric Malpass   4048
A Dead Man in Deptford - Anthony Burgess   776
Nicholas Cooke: Actor, Soldier, Physician, Priest -
Stephanie Cowell   1393
Nothing Like the Sun - Anthony Burgess   781
The Quality of Mercy - Faye Kellerman   3391
Sweet Will - Eric Malpass   4050
Will Shakespeare: The Untold Story - John
Mortimer   4495
You, My Brother - Philip Burton   809

Stacey, Gilbert
Charing Cross - Claire Rayner   5260

Steele, Bluford "Blue"
The Actor - Robert J. Conley   1236

Von Stroheim, Erich
The Greta Garbo Murder Case - George Baxt   385

Wayne, John
The Man Who Shot Lewis Vance - Stuart M.
Kaminsky   3341

Wigmore, Frederick
The King Edward Plot - Robert Lee Hall   2658

Xiao Pouzi
Farewell to My Concubine - Lilian Lee   3709

Xiao Shitou
Farewell to My Concubine - Lilian Lee   3709

Zeami, Fujiwaka Motokiyo
The House of Kanze - Nobuko Albery   64

ACTRESS

Abercrombie, Estella
Affairs of Love - Nicola Thorne   6272

Andrew, Drurie
Banner by the Wayside - Samuel Hopkins Adams   28

Ashleigh, Delia
The Ladies of Hanover Square - Rona Randall   5249

Avril, Jane
*Moulin Rouge: A Novel Based on Henri de Toulouse-
Lautrec* - Pierre La Mure   3576

Ballou, Ohio
The Great Blizzard - Albert E. Idell   3101

Bankhead, Tallulah
The Tallulah Bankhead Murder Case - George
Baxt   389

Berkeley, Belle
Why Kill Arthur Potter? - Ray Harrison   2746

Bernhardt, Sarah
Bertie and the Crime of Passion - Peter
Lovesey   3907
Eleanora Duse - Jean Stubbs   6095
The God of Mirrors - Robert Reilly   5293
Good Morning, Irene - Carole Nelson Douglas   1698
Irene at Large - Carole Nelson Douglas   1700

Loving Little Egypt - Thomas McMahon   4288
Sarah - Joel Gross   2603

Blackstone, Henrietta
The River and the Wilderness - Don Robertson   5401

Boswell, Clementine
The Mating Dance - Rona Randall   5250

Bracegirdle, Anne
The Bracegirdle - Burris Atkins Jenkins   3189

Brandon, Kitty
To the Ends of the Earth - Michael Talbot   6155
A Wilful Woman - Michael Talbot   6156

Briggs, Nelly
Lovers - Suzanne Goodwin   2476

Brown, Clary
My Name Is Clary Brown - Charlotte Keppel   3466

Browne, Lucy
Lucy - Hester W. Chapman   992

Butler, Fanny Kemble
Where Shadows Go - Eugenia Price   5189

Calderon, Inez
I, the King - Frances Parkinson Keyes   3479

Carter, Catherine
Catherine Carter - Pamela Hansford Johnson   3227

Chance, Bridie
The Capricorn Stone - Madeleine Brent   659

Charboneau, Marie
The Bastard - John Jakes   3144

Chimes, Queenie
Bertie and the Seven Bodies - Peter Lovesey   3908

Coleman, Aphra
The Eagle at the Gate - Rona Randall   5248

Cree, Elizabeth
*The Trial of Elizabeth Cree: A Novel of the Limehouse
Murders* - Peter Ackroyd   21

Danby, April
Albuquerque - Sara Orwig   4757

Daventry, Julia
Caroline and Julia - Clare Darcy   1484

Davies, Marion
The Greta Garbo Murder Case - George Baxt   385
Murder at San Simeon - Robert Lee Hall   2660

Davis, Bette
The Bette Davis Murder Case - George Baxt   383
The Devil Met a Lady - Stuart M. Kaminsky   3335

Dell, Sara
Lovers Meeting - Mollie Hardwick   2695

Divine, Gladys
The Dream Lover - Mark Upton   6392

Dorie, Lidian
I Am Lidian - Naomi Lane Babson   253

Drussard, Justine
Fallen Angel - Deborah Camp   872

Duncan, Leila
A Captive Freedom - Emma Drummond   1724

Duse, Eleanora
Eleanora Duse - Jean Stubbs   6095

Ellis, Mary
Yankee - Dana Fuller Ross   5495

Felix, Elisa
I, Rachel - March Cost   1361
Rachel - Anne Powers   5153

Flanagan, Bella
Stage Fright - Gillian Linscott   3809

Fortini, Colombia
Carnival of Saints - George Herman   2860

Freeman, Eve
The Family of Women - Richard Peck   4883

Garbo, Greta
The Greta Garbo Murder Case - George Baxt   385
Murder in the East Room - Elliott Roosevelt   5448

Garland, Judy
Murder on the Yellow Brick Road - Stuart M.
Kaminsky   3343

Goldman, Eleanor Kent
The Americans - John Jakes   3143

Grable, Betty
Dancing in the Dark - Stuart M. Kaminsky   3334
Till the End of Time - Allen Appel   170

Grainger, Lucinda
The Mating Dance - Rona Randall   5250

Guest, Marie
Painted Minx - Robert W. Chambers   980

Gwynne, Nell
Catherine - Hilda Lewis   3746
Christopher Humble - Charles Burnet Judah   3310
Circle of Pearls - Rosalind Laker   3593
Here Lies Our Sovereign Lord - Jean Plaidy   5021
Mistress of the Boards - Richard Sumner   6118
Myself, Christopher Wren - David Weiss   6606
With All My Heart - Margaret Campbell Barnes   330

Gwynne, Nora
Dance on a Sinking Ship - Michael Kilian   3483

Hallam, Beatrice
The Virginia Comedians - John Esten Cooke   1269

Hallard, Marta
The Daughter of Time - Josephine Tey   6209

Harlow, Jean
New Deal for Death - Elliott Roosevelt   5454
The William Powell and Myrna Loy Murder Case -
George Baxt   390

Hayworth, Rita
Dancing in the Dark - Stuart M. Kaminsky   3334

Heriot, Miranda
The Shakespeare Girl - Mollie Hardwick   2698

Heron, Maeve
This Willing Passion - Patricia Cloud   1132

Herriot, Kate
Kate - Brian Cleeve   1109

Howard, Devon
Mistress Devon - Virginia Coffman   1156

Jordan, Dorothy
Goddess of the Green Room - Jean Plaidy   5016

Josefina
The Spanish Bride - Walter O'Meara   4735

Jovian, June
The Mortal Gods - Maurice Dolbier   1688

Kemble, Fanny
All This, and Heaven Too - Rachel Field   2080
The Ardent Years - Janet Stevenson   6003
Fire in the Heart - Henrietta Buckmaster   761

Landis, Dolly
Most Secret - John Dickson Carr   912

Langtry, Lillie
Good Night, Mr. Holmes - Carole Nelson
Douglas   1699
Lillie - David Butler   818

Lecouvreur, Adrienne
Adrienne - Barbara Levy   3742
The Glory and the Dream - Katharine Dunlap   1789

Lindowska, Rissa
Glorious Morning - Julie Ellis   1919

Lindsay, Gloria
The Magic Ship - Sandra Paretti   4791

Loring, Cassy
Cassy - Elizabeth Lyle   3930

Loveless, Gail
Secret Service Operator 13 - Robert W. Chambers   982

Loy, Myrna
The William Powell and Myrna Loy Murder Case - George Baxt   390

Lucas, Amy
Covent Garden - Claire Rayner   5262

Lucas, Claudette
The Strand - Claire Rayner   5269

Lucas, Lilith
Gower Street - Claire Rayner   5264
The Haymarket - Claire Rayner   5265
Paddington Green - Claire Rayner   5266

Lucie
The Queen's War: A Novel of Eleanor of Aquitaine - Jeanne Mackin   3996

MacLaine, Shirley
Live From Golgotha - Gore Vidal   6491

Main, Harriet
Lament for a Lost Lover - Philippa Carr   921

Mamuta, Cynthia
Antioch Actress: A Novel of Pagan Against Christian - Jacob Randolph Perkins   4913

Mercure, Anne
Palais-Royale - Richard Sennett   5747

Mohun, Lydia
Bedford Row - Claire Rayner   5259
Soho Square - Claire Rayner   5268

Monroe, Marilyn
The Immortals - Michael Korda   3540

Monterant, Sophie
The Monterant Affair - Richard Grayson   2560

More, Adriana
Some Lose Their Way - Eloise S. Liddon   3770

Normand, Mabel
Keystone - Peter Lovesey   3913

Palmer, Meg
Charming Sally - Maude Hart Lovelace   3903

La Perichole
The Bridge of San Luis Rey - Thornton Wilder   6752

Pickford, Mary
Max - Howard Fast   2038

Price, Ria
London's Child - Philip Boast   560

Prior, Beth
Escapade - Jane Aiken Hodge   2962

Pruitt, Jessica
Serenissima: A Novel of Venice - Erica Jong   3300

Rachel
All This, and Heaven Too - Rachel Field   2080

Ravenal, Kim
Show Boat - Edna Ferber   2063

Ravenal, Magnolia
Show Boat - Edna Ferber   2063

Robinson, Mary
Perdita's Prince - Jean Plaidy   5040
Regency Royal - Michael Hardwick   2687

Russell, Lillian
The Big Stick - Lawrence Alexander   82
The House on Mulberry Street - Maan Meyers   4354

Rutledge, Belle
Conspiracy of Knaves - Dee Brown   711

Sanford, Caroline
Hollywood: A Novel of America in the 1920s - Gore Vidal   6488

Saunders, Connie
Tessa d'Arblay - Malcolm Macdonald   3974

Savage, Miranda
The Savage Brood - Martha Rofheart   5430

Shannon, Opal
Opal - Helen Ashfield   210

Siddons, Sarah
Fire in the Heart - Henrietta Buckmaster   761

Simmonds, Theresa
A Marriage of Convenience - Tim Jeal   3172

Sinclair, Fiona
So Near So Far - C. Northcote Parkinson   4814

Smithson, Harriet
Passionate Rebel: The Story of Hector Berlioz - F.W. Kenyon   3457

Standish, Sarah
Daughters of England - Philippa Carr   919

Stanhope, Eve
American Eden - Marilyn Harris   2728
Eden and Honor - Marilyn Harris   2729

Starr, Mirabell
Rogue Herries - Hugh Walpole   6547

Ternan, Ellen
The Detective and Mr. Dickens - William J. Palmer   4782
The Hoydens and Mr. Dickens - William J. Palmer   4784
The Mutual Friend - Frederick Busch   811

Terry, Ellen
Affairs of Love - Nicola Thorne   6272
The West End Horror - Nicholas Meyer   4350

Thursday, Tessa
The Far-Off Rhapsody - Anne-Marie Sheridan   5808

West, Mae
He Done Her Wrong - Stuart M. Kaminsky   3338
The Mae West Murder Case - George Baxt   386

Woffington, Peg
Peg Woffington - Charles Reade   5281
The Savage Brood - Martha Rofheart   5430

Wolfe, Lauren
The Only Thing to Fear - David Poyer   5160

Zinn, Malvinia
A Bloodsmoor Romance - Joyce Carol Oates   4658

ADVENTURER

Abbabba, Hadi Guwah
Slave - William Malliol   4041

Adverse, Anthony
Anthony Adverse - Hervey Allen   98

Aethon
Homer's Daughter - Robert Graves   2546

Alix of Wanthwaite
Banners of Gold - Pamela Kaufman   3371

Amaurey, Hugo
Free Lance - George Shipway   5827

Amiel, Benjamin
Beyond the Stars - David William Ross   5497

Anderson, John
The Lion's Skin - Darwin Le Ora Teilhet   6197

Ansculfson, Aelfred
Red Lion and Gold Dragon - Rosemary Sprague   5969

Anstruther, Ramillies
Ram: Being the Tale of One Ramillies Anstruther - Winchombe Taylor   6193

Armando
Jewel of the Sea - Susan Wiggs   6743

Arminius
The Rogue From Padua - Jay Williams   6772

Arrowsmith, Francis
Manchu - Robert S. Elegant   1904

Bandy, Bartholomew
Me Too - Donald Jack   3128
This One's on Me - Donald Jack   3130

Banning, Mark
The Blue Dragon - Diana Brown   716

Barnet, Barney
Rough Diamond - Robert L. Fish   2098

Barry, Redmond
Barry Lyndon - William Makepeace Thackeray   6210

Bast, Michael
The Adventurer - Mika Waltari   6550

Battell, Andrew
Lord of Darkness - Robert Silverberg   5854

Beauregard, Charles
Anno-Dracula - Kim Newman   4595

Beck, Morgan
The American River - Gary McCarthy   4222

Bemford, Lord
The Road and the Star - Berkely Mather   4182

Bent, Tristram
Tristram Bent - Henry Barnard Safford   5560

Benton, Joseph Bonaparte
Peter Doyle - John Vernon   6457

Bessas
The Dragon of the Ishtar Gate - L. Sprague De Camp   1555

Bjarni
Two Ravens - Cecelia Holland   2997

Blair, Jonathan
Rose - Martin Cruz Smith   5923

Blake, Thomas
Blood Red Rose - Maxwell Grant   2538

Blakeney, Sir Percy
The Scarlet Pimpernel - Baroness Emma Orczy   4745

Boggs, Enoch Angus
Shield of Three Lions - Pamela Kaufman   3372

Boll, Captain
Fair Wind to Java - Garland Roark   5354

Bollman, Justus Erich
A Chance for Glory - Constance Wright   6877

Boteler, Adam
The Heaven Tree Trilogy - Edith Pargeter   4797

Breck, Alan
Catriona - Robert Louis Stevenson   6009
Kidnapped - Robert Louis Stevenson   6010

Brisson, Philippe
Touched with Fire - John William Tebbel   6195

Brooke, James
Flashman's Lady - George MacDonald Fraser   2210

Brooke, Peter
Call the New World - John Edward Jennings   3199

Broome, Justin
The Explorers - William Stuart Long   3872

Buoncorso, Riccardo Del
High Carnival - John J. Pugh   5207

Butler, Rhett
Gone with the Wind - Margaret Mitchell   4415

Cagliostro, Count Alessandro
The Queen's Necklace - Alexandre Dumas 1781

Cambara, Captain Rodrigo
Time and the Wind - Erico Verissimo 6451

Caron, Francois
Venture in the East - Bruce Lancaster 3648

Carramadino, Blasco
The Scarlet Cloak - Jean Plaidy 5061

Carramadino, Domingo
The Scarlet Cloak - Jean Plaidy 5061

Carrington, Stephen
The Stranger From the Sea - Winston Graham 2530

Carsons, Kim
The Place of Dead Roads - William S. Burroughs 808

Casanova, Felicine Elisa Maria
Madame Casanova - Gaby von Schonthan 5659

Casanova, Giovanni Jacopo
A Night with Casanova - Wolf Mankowitz 4060

Casvellyn, Colum
The Witch From the Sea - Philippa Carr 933

Cavill, Bartle
Daughter of Satan - Jean Plaidy 5011

Chance, James Macklin "Mack"
California Gold - John Jakes 3145

Chinnery, Thomas
Goa - Kara Dalkey 1458

Cohen, Bernie
The Establishment - Howard Fast 2030

Cole, Doc
Flanagan's Run - Tom McNab 4303

Cordova, Don Pedro
Don Pedro and the Devil - Edgar Maas 3948

Courteney, Sean
The Roar of the Thunder - Wilbur Smith 5929
When the Lion Feeds - Wilbur Smith 5931

Crawford, Francis
Checkmate - Dorothy Dunnett 1799
The Disorderly Knights - Dorothy Dunnett 1800
The Game of Kings - Dorothy Dunnett 1801
Pawn in Frankincense - Dorothy Dunnett 1804
Queen's Play - Dorothy Dunnett 1805
The Ringed Castle - Dorothy Dunnett 1807

Creekmore, Harry
Bound for the Promised Land - Richard Marius 4083

Dabney, Mingo
Mingo Dabney - James H. Street 6078

Decker, Gabriel
Earthshaker - Robert Wilson Krepps 3553

Deveraux, Captain Edward
The Fine and Handsome Captain - Frances Lynch 3933

Doria, Marco
Baton Sinister - Carl J. Spinatelli 5967

Duvallier, Rene
The Gypsy From Cadiz - Tamsin Hamilton 2670

Eliot, Cannibal
Cannibal Eliot and the Lost Histories of San Francisco - Hilton Obenzinger 4660

Embree, Philip
The Warlord - Malcolm Bosse 589

Fabrizio, Del Dongo
The Charterhouse of Parma - Stendhal 5993

Fantom, Carlo
Captain Fantom - Charles Underhill 6377

Farquharson, Andrew
Stranger's Forest - Pamela Hill 2943

Festus, Marcus Didius
Poseidon's Gold - Lindsey Davis 1530

Filbyter, Folke
The Trees of the Folkungs - Verner Von Heidenstam 2817

Finn, Huckleberry
The Further Adventures of Huckleberry Finn - Greg Matthews 4189

Flashman, Harry
Flash for Freedom - George MacDonald Fraser 2203
Flashman and the Angel of the Lord - George MacDonald Fraser 2205
Flashman and the Dragon - George MacDonald Fraser 2206
Flashman and the Redskins - George MacDonald Fraser 2208
Flashman's Lady - George MacDonald Fraser 2210

Fleet, Seaborn
Stately Timber - Rupert Hughes 3075

Flemming, Noah
The Golden Circle - John Edward Ames 125

Fraser, Jamie
Drums of Autumn - Diana Gabaldon 2263

Furfoot, Michael
The Wanderer - Mika Waltari 6556

Garcia, Juan
Captain From Castille - Samuel Shellabarger 5794

Garland, Lee Oliver
Outlaw - Warren Kiefer 3482

Garuald, Andrew
Salute to Adventurers - John Buchan 752

Gaudeans, Captain Richard
Captain Wonder - Donald Thomas 6238

Gefjon, Jaki
Wyvern - A.A. Attanasio 227

Graham, Anthony
Fire Opal - Pamela Hill 2932

Gray, Patrick
The Master of Gray Trilogy - Nigel Tranter 6316

Haynes, Jo
Our Jo, or The Chronicle of a Coming Man - Kenneth M. Cameron 868

Hedges, Jasper
The Voyagers - Dale Van Every 6412

Hemingway, Ernest
Papa and Fidel - Karl Alexander 79

Hercules
Earth Giant - Edison Marshall 4106
Hercules, My Shipmate - Robert Graves 2545

Herries, Francis
Rogue Herries - Hugh Walpole 6547

Holt, Frank
Homecoming - Dana Fuller Ross 5474

Huger, Francis Kinloch
A Chance for Glory - Constance Wright 6877

Humble, Christopher
Christopher Humble - Charles Burnet Judah 3310

Jason
Jason - Henry Treece 6331
Medea - Miranda Seymour 5764

Jim
The Further Adventures of Huckleberry Finn - Greg Matthews 4189

Jocelyn, Hugh
Ask No Quarter - George Tracy Marsh 4099

Kelleway, John
Regent Square - Forbes Bramble 645

Kelly, Justin
Stranger in Two Worlds - Hugh Clevely 1111

Kelly, Luther "Yellowstone"
Imperial Kelly - Peter Bowen 600
Kelly Blue - Peter Bowen 601
Yellowstone Kelly - Peter Bowen 602

Kilpatrick, Brian
Full of Thy Riches - Elizabeth Ferrell 2070

Kinsmere, Roderick
Most Secret - John Dickson Carr 912

Knight, Jack
Crazy Fox Remembers - Don Preston 5174

Lamb, Johnny
Lord of the Isles - Donald Barr Chidsey 1063

Lambriere, Philippe de
The Way to the Lantern - Audrey Erskine Lindop 3790

Laroule, Guy
Louisiana Purchase - A.E. Hotchner 3039

Laval, Jacques
The Only Sin - Julie Ellis 1923

Lawrence, T.E.
The Murder of Lawrence of Arabia - Matthew Eden 1865

Lewis, Jonathan
The Seneca Hostage - Carter A. Vaughan 6440

Liebermann, Meyer
Castle Garden - Bill Albert 63

Logan, Anthony
The Blood Endures - Robert Inman 3107

MacFarlane, Ian
Valiant Libertine - John Gordon Bryson 748

Marcher, Andre
Beyond the Stars - David William Ross 5497

Marriott, Richard
The White Rajah - Nicholas Monsarrat 4433

Melema, Tito
Romola - George Eliot 1910

Moncrieff, Christopher
Born to Be King - Constance Gluyas 2440

Moreland, Jason
The Moreland Legacy - Diana Haviland 2777

Morgan, Frank
The Stallion Man - Judith Glover 2438

Morton, Thomas
The Disturber - L.S. Davidson Jr. 1505

Motte, Jeanne de la
The Queen's Necklace - Alexandre Dumas 1781

Murphy, Luke
The Gold Seekers - William Stuart Long 3874

Murrell, John
Sow the Seeds of Hemp - Gary Jennings 3195

Myron
The Dragon of the Ishtar Gate - L. Sprague De Camp 1555

Newbury, Captain Jack
The Gentleman From America - Paul Benton 464

O'Connor, Kevin
The Bright Battalions - Howard Breslin 664

Oconor, Hugo
The Road to Glory - Darwin Le Ora Teilhet 6199

Odysseus
Return to Ithaca - Eyvind Johnson 3224

O'Flynn, Flynn Patrick
Shout at the Devil - Wilbur Smith 5930

Ogier
The Viking - Edison Marshall 4113

O'Keefe, Patrick
Sword of Vengeance - Kerry Newcomb 4593

O'More, Dennis
The Wind in His Fists - John Edward Jennings 3210

O'Reiley, Colin
The Treasure of the Chisos - John H. Culp 1446

Orsini, Andrea
Prince of Foxes - Samuel Shellabarger 5797

Palomar, Juan
Among the Innocent - Elizabeth Borton de Trevino 6339

Peixoto da Silva Xavier, Gregorio
The Incredible Brazilian: The Native - Zulfikar Ghose 2392

Pentecost, Peter
The Blanket of the Dark - John Buchan 749

Peverel, Kit
Captain Bashful - Donald Barr Chidsey 1059

Phipps, William
Log Cabin Noble - F. van Wyck Mason 4153

Photinus
Votan - John James 3162

Pierre
The Burnished Blade - Lawrence Schoonover 5661

Pomeroy, John Stockley
Pomeroy - Gordon Williams 6770

Purvis, Anthony
Being Met Together - William Vaughan Wilkins 6756

Queen, Robert
The Great Sky and the Silence - James S. Rand 5245

Ransome, Leigh
The Golden Valley - Daoma Winston 6826

Ravenel, Martin
Flames of Empire - Peter Bourne 594

Rawlings, Jason
A Woman of Texas - R.T. Stevens 6002

Red Orm
The Long Ships - Frans Gunnar Bengtsson 442

Ridd, John
Lorna Doone - R.D. Blackmore 528

Rider, Alan
The White Rhino Hotel - Bartle Bull 765

Ridley, Luke
Till the Day Goes Down - Judith Lennox-Smith 3719

Roop, Cecil
Seven Rivers West - Edward Hoagland 2959

Ruan
Ruan - Bryher 746

Rudd, Jack
The Age of Miracles - Catherine MacCoun 3960

Sabine, Nicholas
Moonraker's Bride - Madeleine Brent 661

St. Clare, Amber
Forever Amber - Kathleen Winsor 6822

Sandoval, Christian Cody de
Sandoval: A Romance of Bad Manners - Thomas Beer 414

Savage, Jason
Coromandel! - John Masters 4172

Savage, Justin
The Magnificent Savages - Fred Mustard Stewart 6024

Savage, Tom
His Majesty's Highwayman - Donald Barr Chidsey 1061

Sharp, Becky
Vanity Fair - William Makepeace Thackeray 6213

Sherman, Abigail
Abigail - Joan Druett 1721

Sherwood, Harry
Freedom's Banner - Teresa Crane 1415

Simon of Cyrene
Caravan to China - Frank Stanley Stuart 6085

Sohrakoff, Sergei
The Bear Flag: A Novel of the Birth of California - Cecelia Holland 2983

Stafford, Bard
The Midnight Gun - Berkely Mather 4180

Starbuck, Jason
Yankee Pasha - Edison Marshall 4115

Staunton, Will
The Quickenberry Tree - Annette Motley 4502

Stryker, Nick
Glittering Hill - Clyde Francis Murphy 4520

Sudden, Roger
Roger Sudden - Thomas H. Raddall 5232

Sutter, John A.
The American River - Gary McCarthy 4222

Swilling, Jack
I, Jack Swilling - John Myers 4544

Taverner, Stephen
The Young Emperor - Robert Payne 4857

Therriot, Andre
River out of Eden - Shirley Seifert 5732

Tigernan
Grania: She-King of the Irish Seas - Morgan Llywelyn 3819

Toke
The Long Ships - Frans Gunnar Bengtsson 442

Traner, Abel
The Voyagers - Dale Van Every 6412

Tremaine, Robert
The Masqueraders - Georgette Heyer 2894

vander Poele, Nicholas
Race of Scorpions - Dorothy Dunnett 1806
Scales of Gold - Dorothy Dunnett 1808
The Spring of the Ram - Dorothy Dunnett 1809
The Unicorn Hunt - Dorothy Dunnett 1811

Villiers de Melville, Marc-Antoine
Venetian Masque - Rafael Sabatini 5556

Walker, William
Dinner at Belmont - Alfred Leland Crabb 1398
The Journal of Colonel De Lancey - James Warner Bellah 426
The Lion's Skin - Darwin Le Ora Teilhet 6197
The Nation Thief - Robert Houston 3057
The Notorious Angel - Patricia Maxwell 4201

Wallace, Buck
The Pecos River - Fred Bean 399

Warner, Edward
Caribee - Christopher Nicole 4614

Warner, Tom
Caribee - Christopher Nicole 4614

Wild O'Brien
Thanksgiving - Terry Coleman 1207

Winston, Hugh
Caribbee - Thomas Hoover 3025

Wolders, Alex
Lady Jane - Leslie O'Grady 4699

AMNESIAC

Gordon, Wayne
Shadowed Memories - Al Lacy 3583

Latro
Soldier of the Mist - Gene Wolfe 6843

Leonora
The Sea Treasure - Elisabeth Barr 338

Mer, Katherine de
Witness to Treason - Millie J. Ragosta 5244

Monk, William
Cain and His Brother - Anne Perry 4922
A Dangerous Mourning - Anne Perry 4926
Defend and Betray - Anne Perry 4928
The Face of a Stranger - Anne Perry 4929
The Sins of the Wolf - Anne Perry 4937
A Sudden, Fearful Death - Anne Perry 4938

Ramsey, Mary
Dark at Noon - Jill Tattersall 6173

Venado
Sweet Mountain Magic - Rosanne Bittner 516

Verne, Martin
Stranger at Wildings - Madeleine Brent 663

ANGEL

Azael
The Fair - Robert Nathan 4559

ANIMAL

Bruin
Sam Patch: Ballad of a Jumping Man - William Getz 2390

Fuzzy
Funny Papers - Tom De Haven 1559

Harris
The Queen and I - Sue Townsend 6306

Mr. Hooker
Shakespeare's Dog - Leon Rooke 5439

Seaman
Trail: The Story of the Lewis and Clark Expedition - Louis Charbonneau 998

Tom
Traveller - Richard Adams 27

Traveller
Traveller - Richard Adams 27

ANIMAL TRAINER

Babcock, Ned
The Bartholomew Fair Murders - Leonard Tourney 6297

ANTHROPOLOGIST

Boas, Franz
The Alienist - Caleb Carr 907

APOTHECARY

Wilton, Nicholas
The Apothecary Rose - Candace M. Robb 5364

APPRENTICE

Holt, Leonard
Old St. Paul's - William Harrison Ainsworth 57

Ingraham, Thomas
Low Treason - Leonard Tourney 6301

vander Poele, Claes
Niccolo Rising - Dorothy Dunnett   1803

ARCHAEOLOGIST

Bowles, Anthony
The Idol Hunter - Barry Unsworth   6386

Catherwood, Frederick
Journey to the Sky: A Novel about the True Adventures of Two Men in Search of the Lost Maya Kingdom - Jamake Highwater   2918

Emerson, Radcliffe
The Curse of the Pharaohs - Elizabeth Peters   4948
The Deeds of the Disturber - Elizabeth Peters   4949
The Hippopotamus Pool - Elizabeth Peters   4950
The Last Camel Died at Noon - Elizabeth Peters   4951
Lion in the Valley - Elizabeth Peters   4952
The Mummy Case - Elizabeth Peters   4953
The Snake, the Crocodile, and the Dog - Elizabeth Peters   4954

Lawrence, T.E.
Dreaming of Samarkand - Martin Booth   576

Mallowan, Sir Max
Agatha - Kathleen Tynan   6374

Osmond, Judith
The Curse of the King - Victoria Holt   3012

Padway, Martin
Lest Darkness Fall - L. Sprague De Camp   1557

Peabody, Amelia
The Curse of the Pharaohs - Elizabeth Peters   4948
The Deeds of the Disturber - Elizabeth Peters   4949
The Hippopotamus Pool - Elizabeth Peters   4950
The Last Camel Died at Noon - Elizabeth Peters   4951
Lion in the Valley - Elizabeth Peters   4952
The Mummy Case - Elizabeth Peters   4953
The Snake, the Crocodile, and the Dog - Elizabeth Peters   4954

Schliemann, Heinrich
The Greek Treasure - Irving Stone   6056

Schliemann, Sophia
The Greek Treasure - Irving Stone   6056

Travers, Sir Edward
The Curse of the King - Victoria Holt   3012

Travers, Tybalt
The Curse of the King - Victoria Holt   3012

ARCHITECT

Balz, Guillaume
The Stones of the Abbey - Fernand Pouillon   5144

Bernini, Giovanni Lorenzo
Myself, Christopher Wren - David Weiss   6606

Bramante, Donato
The Agony and the Ecstasy - Irving Stone   6054

Courtland, Frederick
Palais-Royale - Richard Sennett   5747

Herbertson, Hedric
The White Cutter - David Pownall   5158

Hiram
Solomon and Sheba - Faye Levine   3740

Justice, Hunt
Breakfast at the Hermitage - Alfred Leland Crabb   1397

Lacer, Gaius Julius
Gold for the Caesars - Florence A. Seward   5759

Richmond, Anthony
The House on Curtin Street - Millie J. Ragosta   5242

Rinzi, Philip de
All Desires Known - Malcolm Macdonald   3963

Senenmut
King and Goddess - Judith Tarr   6166

Senmut
Child of the Morning - Pauline Gedge   2343
Pharaoh - Eloise Jarvis McGraw   4276

Stewart, Minerva
The House on Curtin Street - Millie J. Ragosta   5242

Wise Coyote
The Jaguar Princess - Clare Bell   421

Wren, Christopher
Circle of Pearls - Rosalind Laker   3593
Myself, Christopher Wren - David Weiss   6606

ART DEALER

Bondone, Enrico
The House of Cray - Pamela Hill   2936

Jones, Rowlandson
The Dance of Death - Jeremy Potter   5142

ARTISAN

Ahuna
Children of the Lion - Peter Danielson   1464

Alfonso
The Lord of the Last Days: Visions of the Year 1000 - Homero Aridjis   188

Alt, Hans
The Angel with the Trumpet - Ernst Lothar   3898

Anne Elizabeth
The Invention of Truth - Marta Morazzoni   4449

Ashted, Billy
Threescore and Ten - Walter Allen   105

Basil of Antioch
The Silver Chalice - Thomas B. Costain   1370

Bateman, Hester
The Silver Touch - Rosalind Laker   3599

Bateman, John
The Silver Touch - Rosalind Laker   3599

Ben-Hadad
The Lion in Egypt - Peter Danielson   1470

Brodie, William
The Strange Case of Deacon Brodie - Forbes Bramble   646

Cannaway, Byrdd
The Cannaways - Graham Shelby   5789

Cantril, Maynard
A Fair Wind Home - Ruth Moore   4443

Chippendale, Thomas
Gilded Splendour - Rosalind Laker   3595

Claus, Jeffry
The Eagle and the Wind - Herbert Stover   6068

Cornish, Harry
The Storms of Fate - Patricia Wright   6885

Daedalus
The Maze Maker - Michael Ayrton   250

Demetrias
Imperial Purple - Gillian Bradshaw   631

Drayton, Joseph
The Drayton Legacy - Rona Randall   5247

Eri
The Death of Kings - Peter Danielson   1465

Finbar
Paradise - Dikkon Eberhart   1831

Gallagher, Patrick
Brandywine - Jack Rowe   5513

Hadad
The Shepherd Kings - Peter Danielson   1475

Herbert of Garstang
The White Cutter - David Pownall   5158

Horne, John
Peace, My Daughters - Shirley Barker   314

Hubbard, Job
All in Good Time - Marguerite Allis   106

Iri
The Promised Land - Peter Danielson   1471
The Sea Peoples - Peter Danielson   1474

Jacques
The Heirs of the Kingdom - Zoe Oldenbourg   4716

Jewitt, John
Eagle Song - James Houston   3050

Kapp, Jackie
The Celebrant - Eric Rolfe Greenberg   2572

Kirta
The Shepherd Kings - Peter Danielson   1475

Leyburne, John
Traitor's Moon - Robert Neill   4574

Longbras, Marie
The Heirs of the Kingdom - Zoe Oldenbourg   4716

Lorenzo
The Betrothed - Alessandro Manzoni   4078

Marner, Silas
Silas Marner - George Eliot   1911

Mason, Roger
The Spire - William Golding   2457

Morris, William
Day Is Coming - William Cameron   869

Nabors, Lonnie
The Staked Plain - Frank Xavier Tolbert   6290

Neal, William
Proving Ground: A Novel of Civil War Days in the North - Leone Lowden   3919

Page, Claude
A Case of Curiosities - Allen Kurzweil   3569

Peabody, Isaac
Dean's Watch - Elizabeth Goudge   2494

Pepi
The Invaders - Peter Danielson   1469

Perdriel, Gilonne
The Lacemaker - Janine Montupet   4438

Pierre
The Burnished Blade - Lawrence Schoonover   5661

Revere, Paul
The Bastard - John Jakes   3144
Bride of Liberty - Frank Yerby   6909
Gilman of the Redford - William Stearns Davis   1541
The Indentured Heart - Gilbert Morris   4464

Reyns, Henry de
The White Cutter - David Pownall   5158

Seth
The Exodus - Peter Danielson   1467
Sword of Glory - Peter Danielson   1477

Shobai
The Golden Pharaoh - Peter Danielson   1468
The Lion in Egypt - Peter Danielson   1470
Vengeance of the Lion - Peter Danielson   1480

Stone
Isle of Woman - Piers Anthony   167

Stone, Jeremy
The Imposter - Noel B. Gerson   2375

Stradivari, Antonio
Antonietta - John Hersey   2868

Teti
The Prophecy - Peter Danielson   1472

Thompson, John
Eagle Song - James Houston   3050

Tom
The Pillars of the Earth - Ken Follett   2149

William of Sens
The Pillars of the Earth - Ken Follett   2149

Windrow, Oliver
Remembrance Rock - Carl Sandburg   5583

Woodley, Adam
Pargeters - Norah Lofts   3857

Zakir
Children of the Lion - Peter Danielson   1464

ARTIST

Akbal Balam
Tikal: A Novel about the Maya - Daniel Peters   4947

Allington, Ruth
Ask Me No Questions - Patricia Veryan   6459

Applegate, Luke
The Limner - Paul Darcy Boles   564

Ashe, Jay-Wade
The Power of Black - M.B. Longman   3880

Audubon, John James
Mr. Audubon's Lucy - Lucy Kennedy   3419
The Mysterious Death of Meriwether Lewis - Ron Burns   802

Ayrton, Matthew
Lovers - Suzanne Goodwin   2476

Beardsley, Aubrey
To Seize the Passing Dream - Ted Berkman   479

Bell, Vanessa
The Shadow of the Moth: A Novel of Espionage with Virginia Woolf - Ellen Hawkes   2779

Bellini, Giovanni
Written in the Stars: A Novel about Albrecht Durer - Frances Hope Fisher   2103

Bernini, Giovanni Lorenzo
Myself, Christopher Wren - David Weiss   6606

Bevis, Leoline
Willowwood - Mollie Hardwick   2699

Blackwood, Emily
Sweet's Folly - Fiona Hill   2926

Blake, Simon
The Big Drum - Elizabeth Boatwright Coker   1162

Blaylock, Serena
The Bluestocking - David Delman   1598

Blunt, Richard
The Merchant of Death - C.L. Grace   2508

Boehm, Joseph Edgar
Bertie and the Tinman - Peter Lovesey   3909

Botticelli, Sandro
The Florentine - Sandra Shulman   5840
Michelangelo the Florentine - Sidney Alexander   86
Mona Lisa: The Woman in the Portrait - Sara Mayfield   4206
The Palace - Chelsea Quinn Yarbro   6904
The Time Returns - Alexandra Ripley   5343

Boucher, Francois
Rasero - Francisco Rebolledo   5282

Bowman, Ralph
The Whip - Catherine Cookson   1291

Bramante, Donato
The Agony and the Ecstasy - Irving Stone   6054

Brancusi, Constantin
The Saint of Montparnasse: A Novel Based on the Life of Constantin Brancusi - Peter Neagoe   4560

Bronte, Branwell
Bronte - Glyn Hughes   3073
Dark Quartet: The Story of the Brontes - Lynne Reid Banks   290
Wild Decembers: A Biographical Portrait of the Brontes - Hilda Crystal White   6681

Brueghel, Pieter
Bruegel, or, The Workshop of Dreams - Claude Henri Rocquet   5422

Bryant, Isobel
While the Music Lasts - Suzanne Goodwin   2477

Buonarotti, Michelangelo
The Agony and the Ecstasy - Irving Stone   6054
The Hand of Michelangelo - Sidney Alexander   85
Michelangelo the Florentine - Sidney Alexander   86
Mona Lisa: The Woman in the Portrait - Sara Mayfield   4206
Nicodemus: The Roman Years of Michelangelo Buonarroti, 1534-1564 - Sidney Alexander   87
The Scarlet City - Hella S. Haasse   2632
The Time Returns - Alexandra Ripley   5343
The Venetian - David Weiss   6611

Caravaggio, Michelangelo da
Caravaggio - Robert Payne   4851
The Dark Fire - Linda Murray   4537
An Epic Joy: A Novel Based on the Life of Rubens - Donald Braider   642
The Goliath Head - Charles J. Calitri   865

Cassatt, Mary
Depths of Glory - Irving Stone   6055
Impressionist: A Novel of Mary Cassatt - Joan King   3486

Catlin, George
The Children of the First Man - James Alexander Thom   6230

Cavazza, Gaetano
The Italian Garden - Judith Lennox-Smith   3717

Cavitty, James
Benjamin Franklin and a Case of Artful Murder - Robert Lee Hall   2654

Cellini, Benvenuto
The Chancellor - Lawrence Schoonover   5662
The Florentine - Carl J. Spinatelli   5968

Cezanne, Paul
Depths of Glory - Irving Stone   6055
The Lawless - John Jakes   3149
Lust for Life - Irving Stone   6059
A Man and His Mountain: The Life of Paul Cezanne - Hugh McLeave   4285
Vincent: A Novel Based on the Life of Van Gogh - Joost Poldermans   5082

Chagall, Marc
The Young Men of Paris - Stephen Longstreet   3893

Chares
The Bronze God of Rhodes - L. Sprague De Camp   1554

Claudel, Camille
Naked Came I: A Novel of Rodin - David Weiss   6607

Clifford, Zoe
Morning's Gate - Ann Victoria Roberts   5371

Collison, Kate
The Demon Lover - Victoria Holt   3013

Corelli, Wordlaw
A Story of Deep Delight - Thomas McNamee   4305

Corot, Camille
Depths of Glory - Irving Stone   6055

Cortlandt, Will
War in the Golden Weather - Stephen Longstreet   3892

Courbet, Gustave
Depths of Glory - Irving Stone   6055

Crivelli, Margo
The Bank - Stephen Longstreet   3882

Dali, Salvador
The Melting Clock - Stuart M. Kaminsky   3342

Dallet, Susanna
The Serpent Garden - Judith Merkle Riley   5336

Daumier, Honore
Depths of Glory - Irving Stone   6055

Degas, Edgar
Depths of Glory - Irving Stone   6055
Moulin Rouge: A Novel Based on Henri de Toulouse-Lautrec - Pierre La Mure   3576
Naked Came I: A Novel of Rodin - David Weiss   6607
To Seize the Passing Dream - Ted Berkman   479
Utrillo's Mother - Sarah Baylis   391

Delacroix, Eugene
To Seize a Dream - Virginia Davis Hersch   2866

Delange, Theophile
The Montmarte Murders - Richard Grayson   2561

Drummond, Ninian
The World, the Flesh, and the Devil - Reay Tannahill   6159

Du Maurier, George
To Seize the Passing Dream - Ted Berkman   479

Durer, Albrecht
Written in the Stars: A Novel about Albrecht Durer - Frances Hope Fisher   2103

Edwards, Ballard
A Question of Honour - Clifford Dowdey   1707

Eliason, Gerard
The Cloister and the Hearth - Charles Reade   5279

Elliott, Caroline
The Floral Companion - Anthea Bell   419

Ellis, Peter
A Princess in Berlin - Arthur R.G. Solmssen   5939

Featherstone, Alexander
Spoon - John Christgau   1074

Findon, May
The Wedding Guest - Anna Gilbert   2407

Fry, Roger
The Shadow of the Moth: A Novel of Espionage with Virginia Woolf - Ellen Hawkes   2779

Fuseli, Henry
Angelica - Samuel A. Schreiner Jr.   5671
Vindication - Frances Sherwood   5824

Gauguin, Paul
Depths of Glory - Irving Stone   6055
Gold of Their Bodies: A Novel about Gauguin - Charles Orson Gorham   2488
Lust for Life - Irving Stone   6059
Vincent: A Novel Based on the Life of Van Gogh - Joost Poldermans   5082

Gentileschi, Artemisia
Artemesia - Anna Banti   295

Gericault, Theodore
Holy Week - Louis Aragon   182

Geyser, John
The Blue and the Gray - John Leekley   3713

Ghirlandajo, Domenico
The Agony and the Ecstasy - Irving Stone   6054
The Florentine - Sandra Shulman   5840

Goya y Lucientes, Francisco Jose de
Colossus: A Novel about Goya and a World Gone Mad - Stephen Marlowe 4093
In the Blazing Light - Max White 6693
The Last Portrait of the Duchess of Alba - Antonio Larreta 3666
The Naked Maja - Noel B. Gerson 2378
Rage in Silence: A Novel Based on the Life of Goya - Donald Braider 643
Rasero - Francisco Rebolledo 5282

Gray, Nicholas
The Man Who Loved Mata Hari - Dan Sherman 5813

Gros, Antoine
Napoleon Symphony - Anthony Burgess 780

Guilame, Gabriel
Seven Men of Gascony - R.F. Delderfield 1589

Harris, David
The Master of Oakwindsor - Douglas Kent Hall 2648

Henri, Robert
Son of the Gamblin' Man: The Youth of an Artist - Mari Sandoz 5593

Heron, Alathea
Alethea - Pamela Belle 429

Hogarth, William
Benjamin Franklin and a Case of Artful Murder - Robert Lee Hall 2654
English Music - Peter Ackroyd 18
Fanny: Being the True History of the Adventures of Fanny Hackabout-Jones - Erica Jong 3299

Hojo, Yasumaro
Segaki - David Stacton 5975

Holbein the Younger, Hans
My Lady of Cleves - Margaret Campbell Barnes 328

Hunt, Holman
The Golden Veil - Paddy Kitchen 3507

Hunter, Herman
The Hawks of Hawk-Hollow - Robert Montgomery Bird 504

Kahlo, Frida
The Veracruz Blues - Mark Winegardner 6821

Karlinsky, David
The Artist - Norman Garbo 2281

Kauffman, Angelica
Angelica - Samuel A. Schreiner Jr. 5671

Kelleway, William
Regent Square - Forbes Bramble 645

Kent, Matthew
The Lawless - John Jakes 3149

Kent, Toby
A Heritage of Shadows - Madeleine Brent 660

Leonardo da Vinci
The Bride of Sforza - Miranda Seymour 5760
Carnival of Saints - George Herman 2860
A Comedy of Murders - George Herman 2861
Duchess of Milan - Michael Ennis 1946
The Florentine - Sandra Shulman 5840
The Lady in the Mask - Anne Green 2564
Leonardo's Judas - Leo Perutz 4941
The Medici Emerald - Martin Woodhouse 6851
The Medici Guns - Martin Woodhouse 6852
The Medici Hawks - Martin Woodhouse 6853
The Memory Cathedral: A Secret History of Leonardo Da Vinci - Jack Dann 1481
Michelangelo the Florentine - Sidney Alexander 86
Mona Lisa: The Woman in the Portrait - Sara Mayfield 4206
The Private Life of Mona Lisa - Pierre La Mure 3577

The Romance of Leonardo Da Vinci - Dmitri Merezhkovski 4339
The Tears of the Madonna - George Herman 2862

Lindeman, Hans Jacob
Lindeman's Daughters - Synnove Christensen 1073

Lorimer, Matthew
Alexa - Anne Melville 4330

Lucie, James
Melbury Square - Dorothy Eden 1857

Lupton, Timothy
Gentlemen in England - A.N. Wilson 6795

Maclise, Daniel
Disraeli in Love - Maurice Edelman 1851

Manet, Edouard
Depths of Glory - Irving Stone 6055
The Lawless - John Jakes 3149

Master Jan
The Master Painter - Edwin Mullins 4513

Matisse, Henri
The Burning Man - Stephen Longstreet 3883
The Young Men of Paris - Stephen Longstreet 3893

McAllister, Hart
Paint the Wind - Cathy Cash Spellman 5960

Medigo, Andrea del
Michelangelo the Florentine - Sidney Alexander 86

Millais, John Everett
John Ruskin's Wife - Eva McDonald 4259
Lillie - David Butler 818

Modigliani, Amedeo
Modigliani: Prince of Montparnasse - Tadeusz Wittlin 6834
The Saint of Montparnasse: A Novel Based on the Life of Constantin Brancusi - Peter Neagoe 4560
Verge of Glory - Frederick Wight 6747
The Young Men of Paris - Stephen Longstreet 3893

Molloy, Alice
Privileged Children - Frances Vernon 6455

Monday, Viridis
The Choiring of the Trees - Donald Harington 2709

Monet, Claude
Depths of Glory - Irving Stone 6055
Glowstone - Macdonald Harris 2725
Light - Eva Figes 2083
Naked Came I: A Novel of Rodin - David Weiss 6607

Morley, Simon
Time and Again - Jack Finney 2093

Morris, William
Willowwood - Elizabeth Savage 5619

Mostyn, Alexandra
The Bridge of a Hundred Dragons - Emma Drummond 1723

Nast, Thomas
Bread and Circus - Morris Renek 5303

Navarro, Julio Diaz
The Burning Man - Stephen Longstreet 3883

Noble, John
The Passionate Journey - Irving Stone 6061

Norris, William
Neighboring Lives - Thomas M. Disch 1648

O'Donnel, Daniel
The Hawthorne Legacy - Teresa Crane 1416

Ormerod, Justin
An Autumn in Araby - Carola Salisbury 5565

Owen, Mr.
The Beano - Rony Robinson 5411

Phidias
Alcibiades, Beloved of Gods - Vincenz Brun 735

The Immortal Marriage - Gertrude Atherton 225

Picasso, Pablo
The Young Men of Paris - Stephen Longstreet 3893

Pissarro, Camille
Depths of Glory - Irving Stone 6055
Gold of Their Bodies: A Novel about Gauguin - Charles Orson Gorham 2488
Moulin Rouge: A Novel Based on Henri de Toulouse-Lautrec - Pierre La Mure 3576

Quarrendon, Neville
Limmerston Hall - Hester W. Chapman 991

Rebough, Jude
Rainbow on the Road - Esther Forbes 2159

Rembrandt
The Golden Tulip - Rosalind Laker 3596
I, Rembrandt - David Weiss 6605
Rembrandt - Gladys Schmitt 5643

Remington, Frederic
The Day the Sun Died - Dale Van Every 6408
A Good Day to Die - Thomas Wakefield Blackburn 525
Yellow: A Novel - Daniel Lynch 3932

Renoir, Pierre Auguste
Naked Came I: A Novel of Rodin - David Weiss 6607

Reynolds, Joshua
Angelica - Samuel A. Schreiner Jr. 5671
The Prince and the Quakeress - Jean Plaidy 5043

Riazhin, Pierre
Encore - Monique Raphel High 2915

Rivera, Diego
The Veracruz Blues - Mark Winegardner 6821

Rivers, Jonathan
The Imagination of the Heart - Judith Glover 2437

Rodin, Auguste
Naked Came I: A Novel of Rodin - David Weiss 6607

Rosen, Segal
Tessa d'Arblay - Malcolm Macdonald 3974

Rossetti, Dante Gabriel
Cock of the Walk - Roy Lewis 3762
The Golden Veil - Paddy Kitchen 3507
The Hoydens and Mr. Dickens - William J. Palmer 4784
I, James McNeill Whistler - Lawrence Williams 6787
To Seize the Passing Dream - Ted Berkman 479

Rousseau, Henri
Lust for Life - Irving Stone 6059

Rubens, Peter Paul
An Epic Joy: A Novel Based on the Life of Rubens - Donald Braider 481
The Horn and the Roses: A Novel Based on the Life of Peter Paul Rubens - Ira Jan Wallach 6542
Lover of Life - Zsolt de Harsanyi 2756

Ryder, Sara
Bride of Ae - Pamela Hill 2928

Sanzio, Raphael
The Flame of the Borgias - Jean Briggs 680

Sargent, John Singer
To Seize the Passing Dream - Ted Berkman 479

Schiele, Egon
Arrogance - Joanna Scott 5679

Seurat, Georges
Depths of Glory - Irving Stone 6055
Lust for Life - Irving Stone 6059

Severin, Joseph
The Remarkable Young Man - Cecil Roberts 5373

Pitborough, Charles
A Most Romantic City - Mary Ann Gibbs   2396

Porre, Elured
Thomas: A Novel of the Life, Passions, and Miracles of Becket - Shelley Mydans   4538

Rothschild, Nathan
The Four Hundred - Stephen Sheppard   5804

Underwood, Ike
Paradise Falls - Don Robertson   5399

Van Der Kleve, Oliver
The Imagination of the Heart - Judith Glover   2437

Van Horn, Anneke
Gold - Clarence Budington Kelland   3388

Van Horn, Jan
Hard Money - Clarence Budington Kelland   3389

vander Poele, Nicholas
To Lie with Lions - Dorothy Dunnett   1810

Webb, Joshua
The Salamanca Drum - Dorothy Eden   1861

BASTARD DAUGHTER

ap Owen, Morgan
Fortune Made His Sword - Martha Rofheart   5426

Bartlett, Adelaide Blanche
Sweet Adelaide - Julian Symons   6152

Bigod, Lady Barbara
A Silver Mirror - Roberta Gellis   2353

Boyle, Hannah
The Girl - Catherine Cookson   1277

Bruce, Naomi
Beloved Soldiers - C.L. Skelton   5871
The Regiment - C.L. Skelton   5874

Carola
Life as Carola - Joan Grant   2535

Cutter, Vardy
Vardy - John Harris   2721

Dallas, Madeleine
Not by Any Single Man - Brigid Knight   3522

Eiriksdottir, Freydis
The Ice Shirt - William T. Vollmann   6509

Elliott, Louisa
Louisa Elliott - Ann Victoria Roberts   5370

Godwin, Fanny
Love's Children - Judith Chernaik   1013

Grainger, Lucinda
The Mating Dance - Rona Randall   5250

Hampton, Maureen
The Hampton Women - Julie Ellis   1921

Jasmine
The Falcon and the Flower - Virginia Henley   2826

Joan
Harp into Battle - Cecil Maiden   4031
Here Be Dragons - Sharon Kay Penman   4904

Kingaby, Sorrel
The Brittle Glass - Norah Lofts   3837

Landau, Lilli
The Only Sin - Julie Ellis   1923

Macmillan, Rachel
In Still and Stormy Waters - Reay Tannahill   6157

Michaelmas, Georgiana
A World Too Wide - Susan Moore   4445

Nicholson, Gislane
Mistress of Darkness - Christopher Nicole   4617

Pangersbourne, Amelia
The Pangersbourne Murders - J.G. Jeffreys   3179

Prynne, Pearl
Pearl - Christopher Bigsby   497

St. Clare, Amber
Forever Amber - Kathleen Winsor   6822

Vorontzou, Katya
Katya - Lucy Cores   1328

BASTARD SON

Adverse, Anthony
Anthony Adverse - Hervey Allen   98

Armourer, Guy
Gilded Spurs - Grace Ingram   3105

Bast, Michael
The Adventurer - Mika Waltari   6550

Bezuhov, Pierre
War and Peace - Leo Tolstoy   6295

Blake, Benjamin
Benjamin Blake - Edison Marshall   4102

Blaylock, Nathan
The Winter Wolf: Wyatt Earp in Alaska - Richard Parry   4820

Capers, Lett
The Keeper of the House - Harry Harrison Kroll   3558

Charboneau, Phillipe
The Bastard - John Jakes   3144

Cottar, Dickie
A Night in Cold Harbor - Margaret Kennedy   3420

Cynric
Born of the Sun - Joan Wolf   6837

Daigle, Axford
Give Me Your Golden Hand - Evelyn Eaton   1825

D'Aix, Sir Alphonse
A Silver Mirror - Roberta Gellis   2353

Doria, Marco
Baton Sinister - Carl J. Spinatelli   5967

Eden, Edward
The Prince of Eden - Marilyn Harris   2732

Eric
The Iron Crown - Clare Barroll   354

Fallon, Robert
The Fallon Pride - Reagan O'Neal   4742

Fitz Hugh, Ranulf
Defy Not the Heart - Johanna Lindsey   3794

Fitz-Stephen, Pagan de
Sir Pagan - Henry John Colyton   1222

FitzRandwulf d'Amboise, Eduard
In the Shadow of Midnight - Marsha Canham   880

Franklin, Temple
The Gentleman From America - Polan Banks   293

Furnival, Adam
The Storms of Fate - Patricia Wright   6885

Gage, Daniel
The Near and Distant Place - Patricia Wright   6883

Goelo, Gilles
The Lure of the Falcon - Juliette Benzoni   465

Handy, Nicholas
Benjamin Franklin and a Case of Artful Murder - Robert Lee Hall   2654
Benjamin Franklin and a Case of Christmas Murder - Robert Lee Hall   2655
Benjamin Franklin Takes the Case - Robert Lee Hall   2656
Murder at Drury Lane - Robert Lee Hall   2659
Murder by the Waters - Robert Lee Hall   2661

Haynes, Jo
Our Jo, or The Chronicle of a Coming Man - Kenneth M. Cameron   868

Hippolytos
The Bull From the Sea - Mary Renault   5295

John of Gloucester
Less Fortunate than Fair - Sandra Wilson   6814
The Queen's Sister - Sandra Wilson   6815

Kamose
The Prophecy - Peter Danielson   1472
Sword of Glory - Peter Danielson   1477

Lambert, Etienne
The Emerald Necklace - Diana Brown   718

Lovel
The Antiquary - Sir Walter Scott   5690

Lusignan, James de
Race of Scorpions - Dorothy Dunnett   1806

MacRomain, Lugh
The Crow Goddess - Patricia Finney   2094
A Shadow of Gulls - Patricia Finney   2096

Marsh, Leon
The Legacy of Beulah Land - Lonnie Coleman   1203

McCutcheon, Peter
The White Slave - Fanny Howe   3059

Medici, Ippolito de'
A Cardinal of the Medici - Susan Hicks Beach   393

Merlin
The Crystal Cave - Mary Stewart   6029

Modred
The Wicked Day - Mary Stewart   6033

O'Higgins, Bernardo
O'Higgins and Don Bernardo - Edna Deu Pree Nelson   4578

Orloff, Sacha
The Rake and the Rebel - Ira J. Morris   4478

Pelleas
In the Shadow of the Oak King - Courtway Jones   3271

Perrivale, Simon
The Captive - Victoria Holt   3011

Pink, Samuel
The Mountain of Immoderate Desires - Leslie Wilson   6811

Quincy, Justin de
The Queen's Man - Sharon Kay Penman   4905

Racon, Martin de
The Bastard - Brigitte Von Tessin   6208

Raventhorne, Jai
Olivia and Jai - Rebecca Ryman   5544

Savage, Justin
The Magnificent Savages - Fred Mustard Stewart   6024

Scott, James
The King's Bastard - Hebe Elsna   1932

Sekloong, Jonathan
Dynasty - Robert S. Elegant   1902

Shannon, Mark
Georgina - Clare Darcy   1488

Stewart, James
The White Queen - Frederic Fallon   2011

Stuart, James
No Smoke Without Fire - Alice Harwood   2767

Tucker, Richard
The Savage City - Jean Paradise   4787

Tudor, Dodpher
As Runs the Glass - Evan John David   1502

Verve, Adam de
The World, the Flesh, and the Devil - Reay
   Tannahill 6159

Walter of Gurnie
The Black Rose - Thomas B. Costain 1363

Weaver, Harry
Scapegoat for a Stuart - Kate Kirby 3504

Wolf of Foix
Deep Are the Valleys - Hannah Closs 1129
High Are the Mountains - Hannah Closs 1130
The Silent Tarn - Hannah Closs 1131

Woodrofe, Mark
Trumpeter, Sound! - D.L. Murray 4528

BIBLICAL FIGURE

Aaron
The Exodus - Peter Danielson 1467
Moses - Sholem Asch 199
The River and the Stone: Moses' Early Years in Egypt - Kathleen Jenks 3192
The Scapegoat: A Life of Moses - Joan
   Lawrence 3684

Abner
Rizpah - Charles E. Israel 3124

Abraham
Abraham and Sarah: The Long Journey - Roberta
   Kells Dorr 1694
And Abram Journeyed - Harry Simonhoff 5858
Children of the Lion - Peter Danielson 1464
*The Covenant: A Novel of the Life of Abraham the
   Prophet* - Zofja Kossak-Szczucka 3543
Hagar - Lois T. Henderson 2824
Hagar - Cothburn O'Neal 4737
Lot's Wife - Marie Ley-Piscator 3767
The Promise - Esther Kellner 3395
The Son of Laughter - Frederick Buechner 764

Abram
Abram, Son of Terah - Florence M. Bauer 378
No Other Gods - Wilder Penfield 4901

Absalom
After Goliath - R.V. Cassill 955
Bathsheba - Roberta Kells Dorr 1695
Bathsheba - Torgny Lindgren 3789
David at Olivet - Wallace Hamilton 2671
David the King - Gladys Schmitt 5641
David: Warrior and King - Frank G. Slaughter 5885
Tamar - Ann Chamberlin 975
The Unanointed - Laurene Chinn 1070

Ahab
*The Curse of Jezebel: A Novel of the Biblical Queen of
   Evil* - Frank G. Slaughter 5884
Dara, the Cypriot - Louis Paul 4842
The Painted Queen - Olga Hesky 2871

Amnon
Tamar - Ann Chamberlin 975

Balthazar
Ben Hur: A Tale of the Christ - Lew Wallace 6536
How Far to Bethlehem? - Norah Lofts 3846
The Way - J.M. Hartley 2761

Bar Jonah, Simon
The Apostle - Sholem Asch 197

Barabbas
Barabbas - Par Lagerkvist 3585
Barabbas: A Dream of the World's Tragedy - Marie
   Corelli 1327
Barabbas: A Novel of the Time of Jesus - Emery
   Bekessy 417
Behold Your King - Florence M. Bauer 379
Brothers of Vengeance - LeGette Blythe 556
The Gospel of Corax - Paul Park 4802
The Robber: A Tale of the Time of the Herods -
   Bertram Brooker 706

Barak
The Sorceress - Nathaniel Norsen Weinreb 6602

Bartholomew
I, Nathanael, Knew Jesus - William Gilbert Van Tassel
   Sutpen 6133

Bathsheba
After Goliath - R.V. Cassill 955
Bathsheba - Roberta Kells Dorr 1695
Bathsheba - Torgny Lindgren 3789
David and Bathsheba - Ari Ibn-Sahav 3098
David at Olivet - Wallace Hamilton 2671
David of Jerusalem - Louis De Wohl 1564
David the King - Gladys Schmitt 5641
David: Warrior and King - Frank G. Slaughter 5885
David's Stranger - Moshe Shamir 5771
King David - Gwyn Jenkins 3191
King of Kings: A Novel of the Life of David - Malachi
   Martin 4134
Triumph of the Lion - Peter Danielson 1478
The Unanointed - Laurene Chinn 1070
*The Valley of Vision: A Novel of King Solomon and
   His Time* - Vardis Fisher 2113

Boaz
Ruth - Irving Fineman 2089
The Song of Ruth: A Love Story of the Old Testament
   - Frank G. Slaughter 5901

Daniel
Babylon - Anthony Esler 1959
The Prophet - Sholem Asch 201

David
After Goliath - R.V. Cassill 955
Bathsheba - Roberta Kells Dorr 1695
Bathsheba - Torgny Lindgren 3789
David and Bathsheba - Ari Ibn-Sahav 3098
David of Jerusalem - Louis De Wohl 1564
David the King - Gladys Schmitt 5641
David: Warrior and King - Frank G. Slaughter 5885
David's Stranger - Moshe Shamir 5771
The Death of Kings - Peter Danielson 1465
Giant Killer - Elmer Holmes Davis 1518
King David - Gwyn Jenkins 3191
King of Kings: A Novel of the Life of David - Malachi
   Martin 4134
Rizpah - Charles E. Israel 3124
The Shining King - Peter Danielson 1476
Solomon and Sheba - Faye Levine 3740
Solomon and Sheba - Jay Williams 6774
Solomon's Song - Roberta Kells Dorr 1697
The Source - James A. Michener 4374
Tamar - Ann Chamberlin 975
Triumph of the Lion - Peter Danielson 1478
The Unanointed - Laurene Chinn 1070
*The Valley of Vision: A Novel of King Solomon and
   His Time* - Vardis Fisher 2113

Deborah
The Invaders - Peter Danielson 1469
The Sorceress - Nathaniel Norsen Weinreb 6602

Delilah
Husband of Delilah - Eric Linklater 3802

Elijah
*The Curse of Jezebel: A Novel of the Biblical Queen of
   Evil* - Frank G. Slaughter 5884
Dara, the Cypriot - Louis Paul 4842
Jezebel - Dorothy Clarke Wilson 6802

Elisha
Merari - Gloria Howe Bremkamp 656

Esau
Jacob - Jean Cabries 844
Jacob: An Autobiography - Irving Fineman 2088
The Shepherd Kings - Peter Danielson 1475

Esther
Esther: The Star and the Sceptre - Gina
   Andrews 146

*So Great a Queen: The Story of Esther, Queen of
   Persia* - Paul Frischauer 2235

Gaspar
How Far to Bethlehem? - Norah Lofts 3846

Gideon
The Trumpet and the Sword - Peter Danielson 1479

Gomer
The Valley of God - Irene Steinman Patai 4825

Hadassah
Esther - Nathaniel Norsen Weinreb 6601

Hagar
Abraham and Sarah: The Long Journey - Roberta
   Kells Dorr 1694
Children of the Lion - Peter Danielson 1464
Hagar - Lois T. Henderson 2824

Haman
Esther - Nathaniel Norsen Weinreb 6601
*So Great a Queen: The Story of Esther, Queen of
   Persia* - Paul Frischauer 2235

Herod Antipas
Hear Me, Pilate! - LeGette Blythe 557
Justus - Arthur L. Lapham 3663

Herod the Great
A Love Divine - Alexandra Ripley 5340

Hiram
Solomon and Sheba - Faye Levine 3740

Holofernes
Judith - Stella Wilchek 6748

Hosea
The Valley of God - Irene Steinman Patai 4825

Isaac
Jacob - Jean Cabries 844
Jacob: An Autobiography - Irving Fineman 2088

Isaiah
The Prophet - Sholem Asch 201

Ishmael
Hagar - Cothburn O'Neal 4737

Jacob
Jacob - Jean Cabries 844
Jacob: An Autobiography - Irving Fineman 2088
The Shepherd Kings - Peter Danielson 1475
The Son of Laughter - Frederick Buechner 764
The Tales of Jacob - Thomas Mann 4068
Young Joseph - Thomas Mann 4069

James
The Brother - Dorothy Clarke Wilson 6799
The Centurion - Leonard Wibberley 6729
*The Sins of Herod: A Novel of Rome and the Early
   Church* - Frank G. Slaughter 5900

Jeremiah
The Babylonians - Nathaniel Norsen Weinreb 6600
Persian Conqueror - George Sidney Hellman 2822

Jesus Christ
According to Mary: A Novel of the Magdalene - Willa
   Gibbs 2398
According to Thomas - Gladys Malvern 4053
Barabbas - Par Lagerkvist 3585
Barabbas: A Novel of the Time of Jesus - Emery
   Bekessy 417
Behold the Man - Toyohiko Kagawa 3321
Behold the Man - N. Richard Nash 4556
Behold Your King - Florence M. Bauer 379
Ben Hur: A Tale of the Christ - Lew Wallace 6536
The Big Fisherman - Lloyd C. Douglas 1702
The Brother - Dorothy Clarke Wilson 6799
Brothers of Vengeance - LeGette Blythe 556
The Centurion - Leonard Wibberley 6729
A Certain Woman: The Story of Mary Magdalene -
   Victor MacClure 3959
Daughter of Jairus - Paul Hervey Fox 2196

Man Before the Morning - Cecil Maiden   4032
Man of Nazareth - Anthony Burgess   779
Martha, Martha - Patricia McGerr   4274
Mary - Sholem Asch   198
Mary of Nazareth - Esther Kellner   3394
The Messiah - Marjorie Holmes   3003
The Secret of the Kingdom - Mika Waltari   6555
The Shepherd - Robert Payne   4855
Three From Galilee: The Young Man From Nazareth -
   Marjorie Holmes   3004
Two From Galilee: A Love Story - Marjorie
   Holmes   3005

Mary Magdalene
According to Mary: A Novel of the Magdalene - Willa
   Gibbs   2398
Barabbas: A Novel of the Time of Jesus - Emery
   Bekessy   417
Behold the Man - N. Richard Nash   4556
A Certain Woman: The Story of Mary Magdalene -
   Victor MacClure   3959
The Galileans - Frank G. Slaughter   5888
I, Judas - Taylor Caldwell   859
The Last Temptation of Christ - Nikos
   Kazantzakis   3384
The Magdalene Gospel - Mary Ellen Ashcroft   203
Mary of Magdala - Anne C. Williman   6791
The Messiah - Marjorie Holmes   3003
The Moon under Her Feet - Ceysta Kinstler   3503
Road From Olivet - Edward Francis Murphy   4523
The Scarlet Lily - Edward Francis Murphy   4524
The Secret of the Kingdom - Mika Waltari   6555
A Time for Judas - Morley Callaghan   866
*Upon This Rock: A Novel of Simon Peter, Prince of
   Apostles* - Frank G. Slaughter   5906

Melchior
How Far to Bethlehem? - Norah Lofts   3846

Micaiah
Jezebel - Dorothy Clarke Wilson   6802

Miriam
The Exodus - Peter Danielson   1467
The River and the Stone: Moses' Early Years in Egypt
   - Kathleen Jenks   3192
The Scapegoat: A Life of Moses - Joan
   Lawrence   3684

Mordecai
Esther - Nathaniel Norsen Weinreb   6601
Esther: The Star and the Sceptre - Gina
   Andrews   146
*So Great a Queen: The Story of Esther, Queen of
   Persia* - Paul Frischauer   2235

Moses
*All the Trumpets Sounded: A Novel Based on the Life
   of Moses* - W.G. Hardy   2701
Alone Atop the Mountain - Samuel Sandmel   5591
The Exodus - Konrad Bercovici   473
The Exodus - Peter Danielson   1467
The Miracle Hater - Shulamith Hareven   2704
Moses - Sholem Asch   199
Moses, Prince of Egypt - Howard Fast   2039
On Eagles' Wings - Arthur E. Southon   5951
Pillar of Fire - Judith Tarr   6168
Prince of Egypt - Dorothy Clarke Wilson   6805
The River and the Stone: Moses' Early Years in Egypt
   - Kathleen Jenks   3192
The Scapegoat: A Life of Moses - Joan
   Lawrence   3684
Tables of the Law - Thomas Mann   4067

Naomi
Ruth - Irving Fineman   2089
The Song of Ruth: A Love Story of the Old Testament
   - Frank G. Slaughter   5901

Nathanael
I, Nathanael, Knew Jesus - William Gilbert Van Tassel
   Sutpen   6133

Nicodemus
The Letters of Nicodemus - Jan Dobraczynski   1655
A Tear for Judas - LeGette Blythe   559
Who Came by Night - Roland Nicholas   4608

Paul
*And Walk on Love: A Novel Based on the Life of the
   Apostle Paul* - Henrietta Buckmaster   759
Brothers of Vengeance - LeGette Blythe   556
The Captive Princess - Maxine Shore   5831
The Flames of Rome - Paul L. Maier   4033
The Glorious Folly: A Novel of the Time of St. Paul -
   Louis De Wohl   1565
The Gospel According to Gamaliel - Gerald
   Heard   2801
I, Paul - Rex Miller   4401
The Kingdom of the Wicked - Anthony Burgess   778
Man on Fire: A Novel on the Life of St. Paul -
   LeGette Blythe   558
Marcus - Laurene Chinn   1068
*The Road to Bithynia: A Novel of Luke, the Beloved
   Physician* - Frank G. Slaughter   5897
The Silver Chalice - Thomas B. Costain   1370
The Soothsayer - Laurene Chinn   1069
*Upon This Rock: A Novel of Simon Peter, Prince of
   Apostles* - Frank G. Slaughter   5906
Upon This Rock: The Life of St. Peter - Walter F.
   Murphy   4526

Peter
The Big Fisherman - Lloyd C. Douglas   1702
The Centurion - Leonard Wibberley   6729
The Flames of Rome - Paul L. Maier   4033
The Gospel According to Gamaliel - Gerald
   Heard   2801
Great Lion of God - Taylor Caldwell   858
Hidden Victory: A Novel of Jesus - Herbert Francis
   Smith   5921
The Illusionist - Anita Mason   4144
Judas - Igal Mossinsohn   4500
The Kingdom of the Wicked - Anthony Burgess   778
The Knifeman: A Novel of Judas Iscariot - William
   Rayner   5271
The Last Days - William Rayner   5272
Man of Nazareth - Anthony Burgess   779
Man on Fire: A Novel on the Life of St. Paul -
   LeGette Blythe   558
Marcus - Laurene Chinn   1068
Martha, Martha - Patricia McGerr   4274
The Master - Max Brod   702
The Messiah - Marjorie Holmes   3003
Quo Vadis - Henryk Sienkiewicz   5848
The Robe - Lloyd C. Douglas   1703
Scorpus the Moor - Leslie Turner White   6690
The Silver Chalice - Thomas B. Costain   1370
*The Sins of Herod: A Novel of Rome and the Early
   Church* - Frank G. Slaughter   5900
The Thorn of Arimathea - Frank G. Slaughter   5905
*Upon This Rock: A Novel of Simon Peter, Prince of
   Apostles* - Frank G. Slaughter   5906
Upon This Rock: The Life of St. Peter - Walter F.
   Murphy   4526

Pilate, Pontius
Barabbas: A Novel of the Time of Jesus - Emery
   Bekessy   417
The Bond and the Free - Charles Dunscomb   1813
Brothers of Vengeance - LeGette Blythe   556
Dear and Glorious Physician - Taylor Caldwell   853
The Glorious Folly: A Novel of the Time of St. Paul -
   Louis De Wohl   1565
Great Lion of God - Taylor Caldwell   858
Hear Me, Pilate! - LeGette Blythe   557
I, Judas - Taylor Caldwell   859
The Kingdom of the Wicked - Anthony Burgess   778
Man Before the Morning - Cecil Maiden   4032
Man on Fire: A Novel on the Life of St. Paul -
   LeGette Blythe   558
The Nazarene - Sholem Asch   200

Pontius Pilate: A Biographical Novel - Paul L.
   Maier   4034
Pontius Pilate Reflects - Werner Koch   3529
The Same Scourge - John Goldthorpe   2464
A Tear for Judas - LeGette Blythe   559
The Tentmaker - Julius Berstl   486
A Time for Judas - Morley Callaghan   866
The Word and the Sword - Theo Lang   3662

Potiphar
Joseph of Egypt - Thomas Mann   4065

Queen of Sheba
The Queen of Sheba - Roberta Kells Dorr   1696
Solomon and Sheba - Faye Levine   3740
Solomon and Sheba - Jay Williams   6774
Solomon and the Queen of Sheba - Czenzi
   Ormonde   4751

Rabbah
Bathsheba - Torgny Lindgren   3789

Rachel
Jacob - Jean Cabries   844
Jacob: An Autobiography - Irving Fineman   2088
The Tales of Jacob - Thomas Mann   4068

Rahab
Scarlet Cord: A Novel of the Woman of Jericho -
   Frank G. Slaughter   5899

Ruth
Ruth - Irving Fineman   2089
The Song of Ruth: A Love Story of the Old Testament
   - Frank G. Slaughter   5901

Salome
The Good Tidings - William Sidney   5843
Martha, Martha - Patricia McGerr   4274
The Robe - Lloyd C. Douglas   1703
Salome, Princess of Galilee - Henry Denker   1611

Samson
Husband of Delilah - Eric Linklater   3802

Samuel
David of Jerusalem - Louis De Wohl   1564
David: Warrior and King - Frank G. Slaughter   5885
Departed Glory - Peter Danielson   1466
King of Kings: A Novel of the Life of David - Malachi
   Martin   4134
Rizpah - Charles E. Israel   3124

Sarah
Abraham and Sarah: The Long Journey - Roberta
   Kells Dorr   1694
Hagar - Lois T. Henderson   2824
Hagar - Cothburn O'Neal   4737
The Promise - Esther Kellner   3395

Saul
David of Jerusalem - Louis De Wohl   1564
David the King - Gladys Schmitt   5641
David: Warrior and King - Frank G. Slaughter   5885
The Death of Kings - Peter Danielson   1465
Departed Glory - Peter Danielson   1466
King David - Gwyn Jenkins   3191
Rizpah - Charles E. Israel   3124

Saul of Tarsus
The Apostle - Sholem Asch   197
Great Lion of God - Taylor Caldwell   858
The Tentmaker - Julius Berstl   486

Shulamit
Solomon's Song - Roberta Kells Dorr   1697

Simon Peter
Fisher of Men: A Novel of Simon Peter - Kurt
   Frieberger   2231

Solomon
After Goliath - R.V. Cassill   955
Bathsheba - Torgny Lindgren   3789
David at Olivet - Wallace Hamilton   2671
David of Jerusalem - Louis De Wohl   1564
David: Warrior and King - Frank G. Slaughter   5885
King David - Gwyn Jenkins   3191

Love and Wisdom: A Novel about Solomon - Richard
G. Hubler 3064
The Queen of Sheba - Roberta Kells Dorr 1696
Solomon and Sheba - Faye Levine 3740
Solomon and Sheba - Jay Williams 6774
Solomon and the Queen of Sheba - Czenzi
Ormonde 4751
Solomon's Song - Roberta Kells Dorr 1697
The Unanointed - Laurene Chinn 1070
*The Valley of Vision: A Novel of King Solomon and
His Time* - Vardis Fisher 2113

Thomas
Yeshua: The Gospel of St. Thomas - Alan Decker
McNarie 4306

Thomas of Antioch
According to Thomas - Gladys Malvern 4053

Timothy
Man on Fire: A Novel on the Life of St. Paul -
LeGette Blythe 558
The Soothsayer - Laurene Chinn 1069

Uriah
Bathsheba - Roberta Kells Dorr 1695
David's Stranger - Moshe Shamir 5771

Veronica Giuliani
The Thorn of Arimathea - Frank G. Slaughter 5905

Xerxes I
Esther - Nathaniel Norsen Weinreb 6601

Yeshua
Mary - Sholem Asch 198
The Shepherd - Robert Payne 4855

Yona
The Shepherd - Robert Payne 4855

BLACKSMITH

Blaze
Isle of Woman - Piers Anthony 167

Burnham, Matt
Lord Fancy - Leslie Turner White 6686

Carne, Drake
The Angry Tide - Winston Graham 2521
The Black Moon - Winston Graham 2522
The Four Swans - Winston Graham 2525

del Vecchio, Cecco
Rienzi, or The Last of the Tribunes - Edward Bulwer-
Lytton 770

Horner, Alex
Conqueror of the Clouds - William F.
Hallstead 2664

Myrddin
In the Shadow of the Oak King - Courtway
Jones 3271

Robinson, Horseshoe
Horseshoe Robinson, a Tale of the Tory Ascendancy -
John P. Kennedy 3418

Shef
The Hammer and the Cross - Harry Harrison 2736

Ware, Randall
Jubilee - Margaret Walker 6531

Wulfric
The Adversary - Jan Widgery 6738

BLOCKADE RUNNER

Bryson, Raphael
Our Valiant Few - F. van Wyck Mason 4155

Butler, Rhett
Gone with the Wind - Margaret Mitchell 4415

Meredith, Tyler
Captain Rebel - Frank Yerby 6910

Ryall, Jeff
The Dram Tree - Hamilton Cochran 1140

Talburt, Wyck
Sail the Dark Tide - Davenport Steward 6017

Wyeth, Trevor
Bride of a Thousand Cedars - Bruce Lancaster 3637

BODYGUARD

Cardigan, Michael
Cardigan - Robert W. Chambers 976

BOUNTY HUNTER

Dark Hand
Forty Guns West - William W. Johnstone 3267

Wild, Jonathan
Jack Sheppard - William Harrison Ainsworth 56

BRIDE

Devereux, Brigitte
Highland Belle - Patricia Grasso 2541

Rivers, Leafy
Leafy Rivers - Jessamyn West 6630

Toupelik, Linda
The Bride of Texas - Josef Skvorecky 5880

Yuen, Taou
Java Head - Joseph Hergesheimer 2854

BUSINESSMAN

Abel, Aaron
The Moneyman - Judith Liederman 3781

Abidaga
The Bridge on the Drina - Ivo Andric 151

Albertino
Simple Prayers - Michael Golding 2452

Ames, John
A Prologue to Love - Taylor Caldwell 862
Young Ames - Walter D. Edmonds 1879

Astor, John Jacob
No Brighter Glory - Armstrong Sperry 5963

Balater, George Eustace
The Bad Lands - Oakley Hall 2651

Ballantyne, Zouga
Men of Men - Wilbur Smith 5927

Ballinger, Max
The Normandie Affair - Elizabeth Villars 6497

Barbour, Joseph
Dynasty of Death - Taylor Caldwell 854

Barbour, Martin
Dynasty of Death - Taylor Caldwell 854

Barnard, John
The Flint Anchor - Sylvia Townsend Warner 6569

Barnum, Phineas T.
Concert Grand - Howard Breslin 665
Jenny and Barnum: A Novel of Love - Roderick
Thorp 6276

Barry, John
John Barry - Donald F. Bedford 412

Bartlett, Thomas Edwin
Sweet Adelaide - Julian Symons 6152

Beckford, Will
A New Creature - Prudence Andrew 141

Behaim, Joachim
Leonardo's Judas - Leo Perutz 4941

Bellnap, Robert
Troubled Spring - John Brick 678

Bennet, F.W.
Loon Lake - E.L. Doctorow 1657

Beresford, Alex
Some Far Elusive Dawn - Emma Drummond 1727

Berne, Gabriel
Angelique in Love - Sergeanne Golon 2470
Angelique in Revolt - Sergeanne Golon 2471

Billingsley, Sherman
Walter Winchell: A Novel - Michael Herr 2863

Bishop, Edward
Trade Imperial - Alan Lloyd 3814

Blevins, Clay
Reunion at Chattanooga - Alfred Leland Crabb 1406

Bloom, Leopold
Saints and Scholars - Terrence Eagleton 1821

Boccetta
Leonardo's Judas - Leo Perutz 4941

Bonnyfeather
Anthony Adverse - Hervey Allen 98

Booth, Howard
Damaris - Jane Sheridan 5810

Bourne, Jason
Dark Winds - Virginia Coffman 1152

Bowden, Ash
Lady of No Man's Land - Jeanne Williams 6780

Brantley, Court
A Woman Called Fancy - Frank Yerby 6931

Britsky, Max
Max - Howard Fast 2038

Brock, Tyler
Tai-Pan - James Clavell 1102

Burnside, Alex
The Penny Wedding - Jessica Stirling 6047

Butler, Edward
The Financier - Theodore Dreiser 1720

Butler, Rhett
Scarlett - Alexandra Ripley 5342

Camboys, Hugh
The Merchant Prince - Henry Christopher
Bailey 267

Campion, Ward
I Take This Land - Richard Powell 5147

Cannaway, Byrdd
The Cannaways - Graham Shelby 5789

Cape, Markham
The Big Knives - Bruce Lancaster 3635

Carboy, Samuel
The Tontine - Thomas B. Costain 1371

Carnavon, Francis
A Fair Wind Home - Ruth Moore 4443

Carrington, Stephen
The Miller's Dance - Winston Graham 2528

Carver, Thomas
The Fallon Blood - Reagan O'Neal 4741

Casewent, John
Thunder on the Plains - Rosanne Bittner 517

Casper
Whole Hog - David Wagoner 6523

Catlin, Bartholomew
Prophecies - Helena Soister 5937

Cavendish, Richard
Mills of the Gods - Daoma Winston 6828

Caylew, Templeton
The Hand of a Woman - Diana Brown 719

Cellini, Marco
Lamia: A Witch - Georgia Elizabeth Taylor 6183

Chandler, Lloyd
The Chandler Heritage - Ben Haas 2629

Chapman, Graham
Come Spring - Charlotte Hinger 2954

Chappelle, Lewis
Walk with Peril - Dorothy V.S. Jackson 3132

Chen, Gordon
Tai-Pan - James Clavell 1102

Cluentius
The Gift of Rome - John Wagner 6520

Colbert, Henry
Sapphira and the Slave Girl - Willa Cather 958

Cole, Weaver
Supper at the Maxwell House - Alfred Leland
  Crabb 1407

Colvin, Adam
Echoes From the Past - Marjorie McEvoy 4268

Comiskey, Charles
Blue Ruin: A Novel of the 1919 World Series -
  Brendan Boyd 610

Connor, Rory
The Gambling Man - Catherine Cookson 1276

Coult, James
The Day Before Thunder - Bart Spicer 5965

Cowper, Francis
Yankee Trader - Stanley Morton 4496

Cowperwood, Frank A.
The Financier - Theodore Dreiser 1720

Cray, Marcus
The House of Cray - Pamela Hill 2936

Creighton, Clifford
Lotus Land - Monica Highland 2917

Crown, Joseph
Homeland - John Jakes 3148

Culver, Robert
Fair Wind to Java - Garland Roark 5354

Cummings, Amory
Silver Fruit - Patricia Campbell 876

Dabney, Big Sans
Tomorrow We Reap - James H. Street 6081

Dabney, Mingo
Tomorrow We Reap - James H. Street 6081

d'Arthus, Morel
The Lacemaker - Janine Montupet 4438

Dave
World's Fair - E.L. Doctorow 1661

Dawson, Pride
Pride's Castle - Frank Yerby 6925

De Brussac, Claude
This Splendid Earth - V.J. Banis 289

De Brussac, Philip
The Earth and All It Holds - V.J. Banis 287

Devers, Walt
Log Jam - Leslie Turner White 6684

deWitt, Aaron
Never Victorious, Never Defeated - Taylor
  Caldwell 860

deWitt, Rufus
Never Victorious, Never Defeated - Taylor
  Caldwell 860

deWitt, Stephen
Never Victorious, Never Defeated - Taylor
  Caldwell 860

Diaghilev, Serge
Encore - Monique Raphel High 2915

Dickinson, Benoni
Water over the Dam - Marguerite Allis 116

Doheny, Edward Lawrence
California Gold - John Jakes 3145

Dolly, Mr.
The House of Cards - Leon Garfield 2292

Donnelly, John Samson
Elixir of Life - A.E. Cowdrey 1392

Donovan, Earl P.
Flickers - Phillip Rock 5419

Dousman, Hercules
The House on the Mound - August Derleth 1616

Du Pont, Alfred I.
Fortune's Legacy - Jack Rowe 5515

Du Pont de Nemours, Pierre Samuel
Brandywine - Jack Rowe 5513

Du Pont, Henry
Dominion - Jack Rowe 5514

Du Pont, Lammot
Dominion - Jack Rowe 5514

Dunbar, Douglas
Queen's Royal - John Quigley 5225

Dunhill, Jonathan
Freedom's Dues - Robert H. Abel 9

Durant, Dr. Thomas
Thunder on the Plains - Rosanne Bittner 517

Eaton, Raymond Alfred
From the Terrace - John O'Hara 4703

Eaton, Samuel
From the Terrace - John O'Hara 4703

Eliazar
The Wandering Arm - Sharan Newman 4603

England, Kirby
The Railway King - Margaret Mayhew 4207

England, Nicholas
The Mills of Colne - Robert Neill 4572

Fabian, Adam
White Eagle, Dark Skies - Jean Karsavina 3368

Fairbrass, Frederick
Benjamin Franklin and a Case of Christmas Murder -
  Robert Lee Hall 2655

Farne, Guy
Magic Flutes - Eva Ibbotson 3097

Ferguson, Brook
Cordelia - Winston Graham 2523

Ferguson, John
The Ship's Clock - Catherine M. Rae 5237

Fernley, Alan
What the Heart Keeps - Rosalind Laker 3605

Fiore, George
All or Nothing - Stephen Longstreet 3881
Our Father's House - Stephen Longstreet 3890

Fishburn, Claire
The Living - Annie Dillard 1644

Flanagan, Charles C.
Flanagan's Run - Tom McNab 4303

Florian
Spangle - Gary Jennings 3196

Ford, Henry
Ragtime - E.L. Doctorow 1658

Francis, Peregrine
The Four Hundred - Stephen Sheppard 5804

Franklin, Benjamin
Freedom's Dues - Robert H. Abel 9

Garuald, Andrew
Salute to Adventurers - John Buchan 752

Gauguin, Paul
Lust for Life - Irving Stone 6059

Glenroy, Alick
Jennie Glenroy - Elisabeth Ogilvie 4695

Godfrey, Lance
The Cotton Road - Frank Feuille 2077

Goldwyn, Samuel
New Deal for Death - Elliott Roosevelt 5454
The Talking Pictures Murder Case - George
  Baxt 388

Gordon, Willy
Look to the Rose - Shirley Seifert 5728

Grandissime, Honore
The Grandissimes - George W. Cable 842

Gray, Benjamin
Tarnished Angel - Phyllis Leonard 3723

Griffith
The White Land - William Dieter 1643

Grunewald, Joshua
Echo of the Flute - Mildred A. Jordan 3304

Haleevie, Sal
Mandarin - Robert S. Elegant 1905

Hampton, Josiah
The Hampton Heritage - Julie Ellis 1920

Hancock, John
Freedom's Dues - Robert H. Abel 9
Yankee Doodle Dandy - Noel B. Gerson 2387

Hanna, Mark
The Land Was Ours: A Novel of the Great Plains -
  Charles W. Bailey 266

Hannah, Alfred Doolittle
The Hyde Park Murder - Elliott Roosevelt 5443

Hardacre, Sam
Hardacre - C.L. Skelton 5872

Harron, Kirby
Sing for a Penny - Clifford Dowdey 1708

Hartley, Derrick
Portrait in Brownstone - Louis Auchincloss 232

Hasford, Roman
Come Winter - Douglas C. Jones 3275
Roman - Douglas C. Jones 3281

Haversham, John
The Haversham Legacy - Daoma Winston 6827

Hearst, William Randolph
Empire: A Novel - Gore Vidal 6487

Hebron, Eli
The Dream Lover - Mark Upton 6392

Heminges, John
Nicholas Cooke: Actor, Soldier, Physician, Priest -
  Stephanie Cowell 1393

Higgins, Porteous
The Halfhyde Line - Philip McCutchan 4249

Hill, Sir Sigismund
For My Great Folly - Thomas B. Costain 1365

Hite, Fred
Herma - Macdonald Harris 2726

Hofman, Fritz
The Wishing Tree - Sandra Paretti 4794

Holladay, Ben
Six-Horse Hitch - Janice Holt Giles 2417

Holt, Ashton
The Mill on Mad River - Howard Clark 1087

Holt, Michael
Homecoming - Dana Fuller Ross 5474

Howarth, William
An Imperfect Joy - Jean Stubbs 6097
The Northern Correspondent - Jean Stubbs 6099
The Vivian Inheritance - Jean Stubbs 6101

Hoxworth, Rafer
Hawaii - James A. Michener 4370

Hudson, George
The Rich Are with You Always - Malcolm
  Macdonald 3971

Huntington, Collis Potter
California Gold - John Jakes 3145

Jack, Mansel
Spinners' Wharf - Iris Gower 2502

Jin-See
White Poppy - Margaret Gaan 2261

Jovian, Robert
The Mortal Gods - Maurice Dolbier 1688

Jumel, Stephen
Notorious Eliza - Basil Beyea 489
Painted Lady: Eliza Jumel, Her Life and Times -
  Leonard Falkner 2009

Kalinin, Alexei
Petersburg - Emily Hanlon 2677

Kapp, Arthur
The Celebrant - Eric Rolfe Greenberg 2572

Kapp, Eli
The Celebrant - Eric Rolfe Greenberg 2572

Katz, Felix
The Healer - Aharon Appelfeld 176

Kemp, William
Sacred Hunter - Barry Unsworth 6389

Kennard, Alan
The Beckoning Waters - Robert Carse 944

Kernow, Barney
Kernow & Daughter - Malcolm Macdonald 3968

Kerr, Ringan
The English Wife - Charity Blackstock 530

Kettlestang, Jacob
The Lords of Loone - John James 3159

Kincaid, Marcus
The Fall River Line - Daoma Winston 6824

King, Robert
King's Royal - John Quigley 5224
Queen's Royal - John Quigley 5225

Kingston, Thomas
The Store - Michael Pearson 4879

Lai Tsin
Fortune Is a Woman - Elizabeth Adler 39

Lancy, Richard
Cast a Long Shadow - Mary E. Pearce 4861

Lang Liu
Necklace and Calabash - Robert van Gulik 6419

Larcher, Jean
The Ghost of Monsieur Scarron - Janet Lewis 3755

Lavette, Dan
The Immigrants - Howard Fast 2034
Second Generation - Howard Fast 2043

Lee, Aisek
Mandarin - Robert S. Elegant 1905

Lomax, H.H.
The Demise of Billy the Kid - Preston Lewis 3760

Lord, Lucius
The Bridge - Marguerite Allis 108

Low, Seth
Tall Ships to Cathay - Helen Augur 240

Low, William Henry
Tall Ships to Cathay - Helen Augur 240

Lowensohn, Gershon
Dreams of Gold - Lewis Orde 4748

Luckner, Erich
The Warlord - Malcolm Bosse 589

MacKenzie, Colin
The World of Jennie G. - Elisabeth Ogilvie 4696

Macpherson, Magnus
Born with the Century - William Kinsolving 3501

Macrae, Burgo
Goldeneye - Malcolm Macdonald 3965

Madison, Edward
Katherine - Antonia Van-Loon 6425

Mardon, Clint
Saratoga Trunk - Edna Ferber 2062

Mathes, Donald
White Poppy - Margaret Gaan 2261

Mayer, Louis B.
Murder on the Yellow Brick Road - Stuart M.
  Kaminsky 3343
The Talking Pictures Murder Case - George
  Baxt 388
The William Powell and Myrna Loy Murder Case -
  George Baxt 390

McKay, Gordon
McKay's Bees - Thomas McMahon 4289

McLoughlin, John
Troubled Border - T.D. Allen 104

McSwasey, Caleb
Big River, Big Man - Thomas William Duncan 1786

Miles, Morris
Hanover Place - Michael M. Thomas 6245

Miller, Jason
The Moneyman - Judith Liederman 3781

Miller, Max
Glorious Morning - Julie Ellis 1919

Moodie, James
Creature Comforts - Jessica Stirling 6041

Moorhouse, Arthur
Aunt Bel - Guy McCrone 4231
Red Plush: The Story of the Moorhouse Family - Guy
  McCrone 4232

Morgan, John Pierpont
Ragtime - E.L. Doctorow 1658

Mortimer, Charles
The Blackheath Poisonings - Julian Symons 6150

Mortimer, Clive
For They Shall Inherit - Malcolm Macdonald 3964

Neill, Dan
The Scapegoat - Mary Lee Settle 5758

Norwell, Stephen
Birthright - Robert E. Wall 6533

Novus, Hortensius
Venus in Copper - Lindsey Davis 1534

Odell, Timothy
Brothers Three - John Oskison 4764

Ogden, John
Red Mountain - David Lavender 3677

O'Halloran, Tabor
Masque of Sapphire - Deana James 3156

Olivas, Raymondo
To Fell the Giants - Bill Hotchkiss 3038

Oxley, Freddy
For They Shall Inherit - Malcolm Macdonald 3964

Pary, Ross
Floodtide - Frank Yerby 6916

Pay, Barton
Weedy Rough - Douglas C. Jones 3286

Peel, Crider
Roman - Douglas C. Jones 3281

Pendergass, Garrett
Bedford Village - Hervey Allen 99

Pengellen, David
The Hills Stand Watch - August Derleth 1615

Penny, Howat
The Three Black Pennys - Joseph
  Hergesheimer 2855

Penny, Howat II
The Three Black Pennys - Joseph
  Hergesheimer 2855

Penny, Jasper
The Three Black Pennys - Joseph
  Hergesheimer 2855

Pennypacker, Zebulon
I Am Vidocq - Vincent McConnor 4225

Penrose, Jon
Here Comes a Candle - Jane Aiken Hodge 2964

Perot, H. Ross
Di and I - Peter Lefcourt 3714

Petifer, Maurice
A Woman Possessed - Malcolm Macdonald 3977

Phillips, John
The Mills of Colne - Robert Neill 4572

Poldark, Francis
Demelza - Winston Graham 2524

Poldark, Ross
The Angry Tide - Winston Graham 2521
The Black Moon - Winston Graham 2522
Demelza - Winston Graham 2524
The Four Swans - Winston Graham 2525
The Last Gamble - Winston Graham 2527
The Miller's Dance - Winston Graham 2528
The Stranger From the Sea - Winston Graham 2530
The Twisted Sword - Winston Graham 2531
Venture Once More - Winston Graham 2532

Pollock, Oliver
The Big Knives - Bruce Lancaster 3635

Ponte, Don Pedro de
Sea of Lentils - Antonio Benitez-Rojo 443

Pratt, Horace Taylor
Back Bay - William Martin 4138

Prince, Johnathan
The Wine Princes - Margaret Mackay 3987

Prince, Peregrine
The Wine Princes - Margaret Mackay 3987

Quain, Maurice
No Wall So High - Anne Powers 5152

Rafferty, Martin
The Ironmaster - Anne Powers 5150

Raford, Quentin
The Unplowed Sky - Jeanne Williams 6783

Randolph, Mitchell
The Californian - Todhunter Ballard 284

Randsome, Charles
Storyville - Lois Battle 377

Rau, Bull
Log Jam - Leslie Turner White 6684

Rebombar, Ripio de
The Adventures of Don Juan - Richard Gardner 2289

Rhodes, Cecil John
The Covenant - James A. Michener 4368

Rockefeller, John D.
The Strenuous Life - Lawrence Alexander 84

Rogers, Jesse
Bridge to Brooklyn - Albert E. Idell 3099
Centennial Summer - Albert E. Idell 3100

The Great Blizzard - Albert E. Idell   3101

Rogier, Joseph
Wild Earth's Nobility - Frank Waters   6578

Rothschild, Nathan
Beyond Desire: A Novel Based on the Life of Felix and Cecille Mendelsohn - Pierre La Mure   3574

Rowland, Harry
Now, God Be Thanked - John Masters   4177

Rowland, Richard
By the Green of the Spring - John Masters   4171
Now, God Be Thanked - John Masters   4177

Roy, Guy
Sunrise to Sunset - Samuel Hopkins Adams   32

Royce, Charlie
The Dream Lover - Mark Upton   6392

Salter, George
Double Wedding Ring - Patricia Wendorf   6624

Sandhurst, Colonel
Colonel Sandhurst to the Rescue - Marion Chesney   1021

Sanford, Blaise
Empire: A Novel - Gore Vidal   6487
Hollywood: A Novel of America in the 1920s - Gore Vidal   6488
Washington, D.C. - Gore Vidal   6493

Sarafian, Fernand
The Anatolian - Elia Kazan   3381

Saudners, Elias
The Catherine - Robert S. MacDonald   3980

Saudners, William
The Catherine - Robert S. MacDonald   3980

Schindler, Oskar
Schindler's List - Thomas Keneally   3416

Scrimshaw, Aristotle
Fool's Coach - Richard S. Wheeler   6659

Sekloong, Charles
Dynasty - Robert S. Elegant   1902

Sessions, Gregory
Dynasty of Death - Taylor Caldwell   854

Shalach
Serenissima: A Novel of Venice - Erica Jong   3300

Shaw, Robert
The Mills of Colne - Robert Neill   4572

Silverthorn, Alex
The Dream Seekers - Stephen Longstreet   3884

Smith, Aymer
Signals of Distress - Jim Crace   1408

Smith, Jefferson
Tara Kane - George Markstein   4091

Smith, Peter
The Smiths - Janet Fairbank   2002

Somerville, George
Honour and Obey - Malcolm Macdonald   3966

Stafford, Bard
The Midnight Gun - Berkely Mather   4180

Stafford, Ross
The Midnight Gun - Berkely Mather   4180

Stapleton, Jonathan
The Spoils of War - Thomas Fleming   2131

Stapleton, Rawdon
The Spoils of War - Thomas Fleming   2131

Stevenson, John
The Rich Are with You Always - Malcolm Macdonald   3971
The World From Rough Stones - Malcolm Macdonald   3979

Stewart, Scott Shallenberger
Thine Is the Glory - Samuel A. Schreiner Jr.   5672

Stiegel, Henry William
One Red Rose Forever - Mildred A. Jordan   3305

Stock, Matthew
The Bartholomew Fair Murders - Leonard Tourney   6297
Familiar Spirits - Leonard Tourney   6298
Frobisher's Savage - Leonard Tourney   6299
Knaves Templar - Leonard Tourney   6300
Low Treason - Leonard Tourney   6301
Old Saxon Blood - Leonard Tourney   6302
The Players' Boy Is Dead - Leonard Tourney   6303
Witness of Bones - Leonard Tourney   6304

Stockwell, Gordon
Sunrise to Sunset - Samuel Hopkins Adams   32

Struan, Dirk
Tai-Pan - James Clavell   1102

Struan, Malcolm
Gai-Jin: A Novel of Japan - James Clavell   1100

Sutter, John A.
The Bear Flag: A Novel of the Birth of California - Cecelia Holland   2983
Calico Palace - Gwen Bristow   694

Sutton, Brandon
Proud Mary - Iris Gower   2501

Swann, Adam
Give Us This Day - R.F. Delderfield   1586
God Is an Englishman - R.F. Delderfield   1587
Theirs Was the Kingdom - R.F. Delderfield   1590

Swann, George
Theirs Was the Kingdom - R.F. Delderfield   1590

Swann, Giles
Give Us This Day - R.F. Delderfield   1586

Tabor, Horace
Wilde West - Walter Satterthwait   5609

Tai Ming Kwong
The House That Tai Ming Built - Virginia Lee   3711

Tarlton, Peter
Luise - Dawn Stewart Field   2079

Templeton, Cedric
Young Vargas Lewis - Robert Brainard Pearsall   4874

Thaw, Henry
Thine Is the Glory - Samuel A. Schreiner Jr.   5672

Theophilus
The Testament of Theophilus - Leonard Wibberley   6730

Thompson, Delbert
Miss Bishop - Bess Streeter Aldrich   71

Thornton, Walter
The Rich Are with You Always - Malcolm Macdonald   3971

Thorpe, John
The Power and the Glory - Phyllis Bentley   462

Tonneman, Pieter
The Dutchman's Dilemma - Maan Meyers   4352

Topouzoglou, Stavros
Beyond the Aegean - Elia Kazan   3382

Torey, Michael
Michael Torey - Janet Mathewson   4183

Tozer, Bradley
High Road to China - Jon Cleary   1106

Trant, Anthony
Anthony Trant - John Hyatt Downing   1713

Trenchard, William
Painting the Darkness - Robert Goddard   2445

Trigonis, Christos
The Ashes of Smyrna - Richard Reinhardt   5294

Trumper, Charlie
As the Crow Flies - Jeffrey Archer   183

Turner, Drake
Lord Raven's Widow - Leslie O'Grady   4700

Tyacke, Will
Meridon - Philippa Gregory   2583

Tyler, Robert
Murder at Fenway Park - Troy Soos   5948

Tyson, Charlie
Red Barbarian - Margaret Gaan   2260

Utrecht, Simon Vann
Magnificent Enemies - Edgar Maas   3951

Van Deventer, Ludolf
The Golden Tulip - Rosalind Laker   3596

Van Gogh, Theo
Lust for Life - Irving Stone   6059
Vincent: A Novel Based on the Life of Van Gogh - Joost Poldermans   5082

Van Horn, Jan
The Jealous House - Clarence Budington Kelland   3390

vander Poele, Nicholas
Race of Scorpions - Dorothy Dunnett   1806
Scales of Gold - Dorothy Dunnett   1808
The Spring of the Ram - Dorothy Dunnett   1809
The Unicorn Hunt - Dorothy Dunnett   1811

Vane, Harry
Peg Woffington - Charles Reade   5281

Wagenen, Gerrit van
The Tides of Dawn - Emma Louise Mally   4044

Wakefield, Luke
The Fall River Line - Daoma Winston   6824

Ward, Barnabas
Log Jam - Leslie Turner White   6684

Ward, Winthrop
The Winthrop Covenant - Louis Auchincloss   235

Warleggan, George
The Angry Tide - Winston Graham   2521
The Black Moon - Winston Graham   2522
Demelza - Winston Graham   2524
The Four Swans - Winston Graham   2525
The Last Gamble - Winston Graham   2527
The Miller's Dance - Winston Graham   2528
The Stranger From the Sea - Winston Graham   2530
Venture Once More - Winston Graham   2532

Warner, Jack
The Talking Pictures Murder Case - George Baxt   388

Warrington, Howland
Hanover Place - Michael M. Thomas   6245

Weed, Frederick
Trinity - Leon Uris   6394

Weigel, Jake
Anna, Ann, Annie - Thomas Trebitsch Parker   4808

Weitz, Joseph
Bayou - Pamela Jekel   3183

Wellington, Thance
The President's Daughter - Barbara Chase-Riboud   1005

Wells, C.P.
Paradise Falls - Don Robertson   5399

Westinghouse, George
A Peep into the 20th Century - Christopher Davis   1515

Wheeler, F. Morrison
Biscayne - Barry Jay Kaplan   3365

Whitcombe, Lionel
Ruby - Helen Ashfield   213

Whitmead, George
The Cherished Wives - Valerie Anand 126

Whittington, Richard
Richard Whittington, London's Mayor - Gwynedd Sudworth 6112

Willoughby, Nathan
Rogue's Harbor - Inglis Fletcher 2139

Wraysford, Stephen
Birdsong - Sebastian Faulks 2051

Wyatt, Horatio
Trumpets at Dawn - Cyril Harris 2719

Yin-Kwa
White Poppy - Margaret Gaan 2261

Zukor, Adolph
The Talking Pictures Murder Case - George Baxt 388

BUSINESSWOMAN

Ames, Caroline
A Prologue to Love - Taylor Caldwell 862

Aysgarth, Annie
Fortune Is a Woman - Elizabeth Adler 39

Bascombe, Henrietta
At the Sign of the Golden Pineapple - Marion Chesney 1016

Blevins, Grandma
Reunion at Chattanooga - Alfred Leland Crabb 1406

Bonnington, Beatrice
Speak to Me of Love - Dorothy Eden 1862

Briscoll, Nan
Dream Time - Parris Afton Bonds 570

Cade, Lucy
Pastora - Joanna Barnes 321

Charetty, Marian de
Niccolo Rising - Dorothy Dunnett 1803
The Spring of the Ram - Dorothy Dunnett 1809

Coffin, Kezia
Nantucket Woman - Diana Gaines 2269

Cummings, Dee
Silver Fruit - Patricia Campbell 876

Delcourt, Sophie
The Sugar Pavilion - Rosalind Laker 3600

Dunbar, Margaret
Cashmere - Nicola Thorne 6273

Eliott, Beatrice
The House of Eliott - Jean Marsh 4100

Eliott, Evangeline
The House of Eliott - Jean Marsh 4100

Hampton, Caroline
The Hampton Women - Julie Ellis 1921

Hardy, Alice
A Woman by Design - Frances Kennett 3426

Hewitt, Maggie
The Harrogate Secret - Catherine Cookson 1278

Hofman, Camilla
The Wishing Tree - Sandra Paretti 4794

Hollingshead, Irene
Paradise Falls - Don Robertson 5399

Jones, Fremont
Fire and Fog - Dianne Day 1543

Kelly, Anna
Embers of the Heart - Rosanne Bittner 512

Kernow, Jessica
Kernow & Daughter - Malcolm Macdonald 3968

Landau, Lilli
The Only Sin - Julie Ellis 1923

Landers, Sunny
Thunder on the Plains - Rosanne Bittner 517

Leplastrier, Lucinda
Oscar and Lucinda - Peter Carey 894

Levy, Ruby
Rivington Street - Meredith Tax 6175

Leyton, Louisa
The Duchess of Duke Street - Mollie Hardwick 2693

Logan, Julia Howard
The Crystal Star - Ellen Argo 184
The Yankee Girl - Ellen Argo 186

Luken, Charlotte
Mistress of the Forge - David Taylor 6179

Mordaunt, Bridget
The Black Candle - Catherine Cookson 1273

O'Dowd, Molly
Molly - Teresa Crane 1417

O'Hara, Scarlett
Scarlett - Alexandra Ripley 5342

Page, Leah
Path of the Sun - Al Dempsey 1608

Paxton, Eugenia
Night Storm - Catherine Coulter 1378

Sanford, Caroline
Hollywood: A Novel of America in the 1920s - Gore Vidal 6488

Scacerni, Cecilia
Nothing New under the Sun - Riccardo Bacchelli 255

Somerville, Julia
Honour and Obey - Malcolm Macdonald 3966

Southwick, Silence
Portrait of Emma - Lillian Cheatham 1010

Stevenson, Nora
The Rich Are with You Always - Malcolm Macdonald 3971
The World From Rough Stones - Malcolm Macdonald 3979

Straun, Tess
Gai-Jin: A Novel of Japan - James Clavell 1100

Talbot-Harrow, Judith
Masque of Sapphire - Deana James 3156

Tring, Sarah Camberwell
Sarah Camberwell Tring - Janet Edmonds 1869

Troy, Morwenna
On a Far Wide Shore - Malcolm Macdonald 3970

Tussaud, Marie Grosholtz
I, Madame Tussaud - Sylvia Martin 4135

Wade, Caroline
Hard Road to Gettysburg - Ted Jones 3298

Winkowski, Agnes
The Rag Nymph - Catherine Cookson 1287

Wood, Ann
Strange Devices of the Sun and Moon - Lisa Goldstein 2463

CAPTIVE

Alwin, Deborah
White Indian - Donald Clayton Porter 5134

Ariston
Goat Song: A Novel of Ancient Greece - Frank Yerby 6920

Athenais
The Man Who Killed the King - Dennis Wheatley 6654

Austin, Melissa
California! - Dana Fuller Ross 5467

Baffo, Sofia
Sofia - Ann Chamberlin 974

Barbour, Caroline
A Rendezvous in Haiti - Stephen Becker 407

Bas-Thornton, Emily
A High Wind in Jamaica - Richard Hughes 3074

Bell, Jane
Red Morning - Ruby Frazier Frey 2230

Boissart, Marguerite
Heritage of the River - Muriel Elwood 1937

Borst, Delia
In the Hands of the Senecas - Walter D. Edmonds 1876

Breen, Caty
In the Hands of the Senecas - Walter D. Edmonds 1876

Brennan, Alice
Beyond the Shadowlands - Georgina Fleming 2126

Burke, Elizabeth
The Great Valley - Mary Johnston 3234

Butler, John
The Light in the Forest - Conrad Richter 5322

Calling Bird
Bride of the Morning Star - Don Coldsmith 1170

Cardenas, Carlota de
Apache Autumn - Robert Skimin 5875

Castameto, Mariposa
California Caballero - William Colt MacDonald 3981

Chafin
A Whistle in the Wind - John H. Culp 1447

Claudia, Lady
The Gentle Conqueror - Mary Ellen Gronau 2597

Corn Flower
The Way of the Priests - Robert J. Conley 1253

Cree Medicine
The High Missouri - Winfred Blevins 545

Crocker, Catherine
The Man Who Loved Cat Dancing - Marilyn Durham 1817

Doone, Lorna
Lorna Doone - R.D. Blackmore 528

Drayton, Annabel
John Crews - Arthur Chapman 988

Drusus, Cailin
To Love Again - Bertrice Small 5913

Duston, Hannah
Gallant Warrior - Helen R. Mann 4063

Dysart, Martha
In the Hands of the Senecas - Walter D. Edmonds 1876

Elaine
The Golden Exile - Lawrence Schoonover 5664

Eldridge, Mark
Thunder on the River - Charlton Laird 3590

Eldridge, Mary Ann
Juniata Valley - Virginia C. Cassel 954

Ellis, Mary
Yankee - Dana Fuller Ross 5495

Ethnea
Captive of Rome - Theodora McCormick Du Bois 1740

Evans, Evan
The Cold Journey - Grace Zaring Stone 6052

Fairchild, Talmadge
Harvest of Dreams - Jaroldeen Edwards 1884

Falconer, Jim
Indian Hater - Glenn R. Vernam   6452

Fiammetta
Fire Opal - Pamela Hill   2932

Frame, Maria
The Second Kiss - Gayle Rogers   5432

Gilbert of Axford
Black Angels - C.T. Ritchie   5348

Grant, Angelina
A Mule for the Marquesa - Frank O'Rourke   4753

Greenpearl
Silk Road - Jeanne Larsen   3670

Greenwood, Alice
Jade - Pat Barr   344

Harper, David
Eagle of Niagara: The Story of David Harper and His Indian Captivity - John Brick   671

Hilton, Martha
Indian Brother - Hubert Coryell   1354

Hilton, Sam
Indian Brother - Hubert Coryell   1354

Hook, Jeremiah
Winter Rain - Terry C. Johnston   3262

Hunsacker, Mary
The Life and Times of Captain N. - Douglas Glover   2436

Ibn Fadlan, Ahmad
Eaters of the Dead - Michael Crichton   1425

Ingles, Mary Draper
Follow the River - James Alexander Thom   6231

Isar
Shadows on the Stones - Moyra Caldecott   847

Isobelle
Isobelle - Mary Lide   3775

Jensie
Rockspring - R.G. Vliet   6506

Johnson, Emily
Seminole - Donald Clayton Porter   5126

Keturah
The Sea Peoples - Peter Danielson   1474

Killefer, Emaline
The Canebrake Men - Cameron Judd   3313

Lewis, Daphne
Mister Christian - William Kinsolving   3502

Lewis, Jonathan
The Seneca Hostage - Carter A. Vaughan   6440

Livingston, Charley
The Wine of San Lorenzo - Herbert Gorman   2493

McAllister, Jamie
Eyes of Eagles - William W. Johnstone   3266

Milam, Jacob "Sun Gift"
In the Season of the Sun - Kerry Newcomb   4590

Miller, Jonas
Roanoke Warrior - Carter A. Vaughan   6438

Mirador, Consuelo
War Chief - Donald Clayton Porter   5130

Mirana
Lord of Hawkfell Island - Catherine Coulter   1376

Morgana
The Viking - Edison Marshall   4113

Morrison, Helen
A Woman of the People - Benjamin Capps   893

Nails, David
Call the Beast Thy Brother - William Oliver Turner   6366

Nakwisi
The Double Man - Elinor Pryor   5205

Niniane
Born of the Sun - Joan Wolf   6837

O'Dwyer, Oonagh
Pawn in Frankincense - Dorothy Dunnett   1804

Pao An
Empire of Heaven - Linda Ching Sledge   5907

Parker, Cynthia Ann
Quanah Parker - Bill Dugan   1759
Ride the Wind - Lucia St. Clair Robson   5416

Parry, Morfydd Annon
Season of Yellow Leaf - Douglas C. Jones   3283

Patrick
The Lion and the Cross - Joan Lesley Hamilton   2669

Phillips, Harry
Flight From Bucharest - R.T. Stevens   6000

Polonsky, Elise Chatham
Sweet Ransom - Linda Madl   4026

Powers, Lisa
Arizona Ecstasy - Rosanne Bittner   511

Purchis, Hart
Wide Is the Water - Jane Aiken Hodge   2973

Reil, Roxana
Yankee Pasha - Edison Marshall   4115

Salling, Lisel
Wilderness Adventure - Elizabeth Page   4774

Stillman, Anna
A Time in the Sun - Jane Barry   361

Tilla, Mona
The Sins of the Lion - Annette Motley   4503

To-Sha-Be
Ambush - Donald Clayton Porter   5113

Vaudemont, Latisse de
Richard and the Knights of God - Pamela Bennetts   454

Wade, Hannah
The Pride of Hannah Wade - Janet Dailey   1455

Wells, Cynthia Ann
Sioux Splendor - Rosanne Bittner   515

Wells, Sarah
Ghost Fox - James Houston   3051

Wiley, Jennie Sellards
Dark Hills to Westward - Harry M. Caudill   964

Wilmot, Ann
The Southern Blade - Nelson Wolford   6844

Woodbridge, Dawn
Buckskin Cavalier - John Clagett   1082

Wulf
The Fourteenth of October - Bryher   742

CARPENTER

Alvarez, Rodrigo
Friendly Cove - Irving Brant   651

Bede, Adam
Adam Bede - George Eliot   1908

Bradley, Robert
The Moth - Catherine Cookson   1284

Cargill, Robert
Come Home at Even - Le Grand Cannon   884

Gadd, Aaron
The God-Seeker - Sinclair Lewis   3763

Girard, Philippe
High Towers - Thomas B. Costain   1366

Joseph
King Jesus - Robert Graves   2549
Mary - Sholem Asch   198

Kvidal, Morten
The Emigrants - Johan Bojer   561

Setran, Odin
The People of Juvik - Olav Dunn   1798

Wood, Owen
Jack Sheppard - William Harrison Ainsworth   56

CARTOGRAPHER

Bianco, Andrea
The Mapmaker: A Novel of the Days of Prince Henry, the Navigator - Frank G. Slaughter   5893

Goupil, Pierre
La Salle - John Vernon   6458

Mauro, Fra
A Mapmaker's Dream - James Cowan   1391

Toscanelli, Paoli dal Pozzo
Columbus: A Romance - Rafael Sabatini   5549

CASTAWAY

Crusoe, Robinson
Friday - Michel Tournier   6305

CHIEFTAIN

Ashan
Children of the Dawn - Patricia Rowe   5516
Keepers of the Misty Time - Patricia Rowe   5517

Atlaw
Daughter of the Red Deer - Joan Wolf   6838

Attaroa
The Plains of Passage - Jean M. Auel   238

Beckwourth, Jim
Ammahabas - Bill Hotchkiss   3036
Follow the Free Wind - Leigh Brackett   621
The Medicine Calf - Bill Hotchkiss   3037

Benilong
The Timeless Land - Eleanor Dark   1495

Beothainn
The Crows of War - Steven Rayson   5276

Beowulf
The Coming of the King - Nikolai Tolstoy   6296
The Green Man - Henry Treece   6330
The Tower of Beowulf - Parke Godwin   2450

Black Hawk
Shaman - Noah Gordon   2483
The Shining Trail - Iola Fuller   2254
Thunder on the River - Charlton Laird   3590
Twilight of Empire - Allen W. Eckert   1846
Wind over Wisconsin - August Derleth   1620

Black Kettle
The Last Warpath - Will Henry   2844

Blatonikos, Leir
The Serpent's Tooth - Diana L. Paxson   4846

Brant, Joseph
Bridal Journey - Dale Van Every   6406
Brother Owl - Al Hine   2953
Buckskin Baronet - Margaret Widdemer   6734
Eagle of Niagara: The Story of David Harper and His Indian Captivity - John Brick   671
The King's Rebel - James David Horan   3030
Reckon with the River - Clark McMeekin   4292
Three Sides of Agiochook - Eric Kelly   3400
West to the Setting Sun - Harvey Chalmers   973

Brave Man
People of the Earth - W. Michael Gear   2334

Brian Boru
The Gallowglass - Howard Breslin 666

Brun
The Clan of the Cave Bear - Jean M. Auel 236

Buffalo Hump
Dead Man's Walk - Larry McMurtry 4297

Caballito
Apaches - Oakley Hall 2650

Canonchet
The Wept of Wish-Ton-Wish - James Fenimore
   Cooper 1312

Cetewayo
Bush War! - William Moore 4447

Chief Joseph
Chief Joseph - Bill Dugan 1756
The Chieftain: A Story of the Nez Perce People -
   Robert Payne 4852
From Where the Sun Now Stands - Will Henry 2841
Song of the Meadowlark - John A. Sanford 5594

Chitto Harjo
Crazy Snake - Robert J. Conley 1240

Coatl
Captain From Castille - Samuel Shellabarger 5794

Cochise
Apache Autumn - Robert Skimin 5875
Blood Brother - Elliott Arnold 190
A Time in the Sun - Jane Barry 361

Connal
Fire Queen - Deborah Grabien 2503

Crazy Horse
Chief of Scouts - Don Bendell 439
Lakota - G. Clifton Wisler 6833

Deesohay
Valley of the Shadow - Charles Marquis
   Warren 6570

Eskiminzin
The Camp Grant Massacre - Elliott Arnold 191

Fifth, Brennis Gehan
The Flint Lord - Richard Herley 2857

Fomor
Wolves of the Dawn - William Sarabande 5604

Forked Path, Hendrick
The Interpreter - Robert Moss 4499

Garroch
The Golden Strangers - Henry Treece 6328

Geronimo
Apache Devil - Edgar Rice Burroughs 806
Flashman and the Redskins - George MacDonald
   Fraser 2208
Geronimo - Bill Dugan 1758
Geronimo: An American Legend - Robert J.
   Conley 1242
The Strenuous Life - Lawrence Alexander 84
Watch for Me on the Mountain - Forrest Carter 947

Ghonkaba
Cherokee - Donald Clayton Porter 5115
The Sachem - Donald Clayton Porter 5124
Seneca - Donald Clayton Porter 5127

Graylag
Reindeer Moon - Elizabeth Marshall Thomas 6244

Gunnar
Fire in the Ice - Dorothy James Roberts 5375

Guyasuta
The King's Orchard - Agnes Sligh Turnbull 6363

Heads Off
The Elk-Dog Heritage - Don Coldsmith 1174
Follow the Wind - Don Coldsmith 1176
Moon of Thunder - Don Coldsmith 1180

Hindfoot
*Look to Your Geese: A Novel of the Deflowering of
   New England* - Jacquin Sanders 5584

Huayna Capac
The Incas - Daniel Peters 4945

Ironfoot
Beyond the Stars - David William Ross 5497

Joel
The Valiant - Sigman Byrd 839

Kagan
The Year of the Horsetails - R.F. Tapsell 6162

Khan, Hari
The Near and the Far - Leopold Hamilton
   Myers 4547

Kientpoos
Devil's Backbone - Terry C. Johnston 3250

Landon
Pillar of the Sky - Cecelia Holland 2994

Larion
The Law of Larion - Peter Freuchen 2227

Lazaro
Apache Autumn - Robert Skimin 5875

Little Hawk
Hawk's Journey - Donald Clayton Porter 5119

Magnus
Princess of the Veil - Helen Mittermeyer 4420

Mahommed, Jara
The Gates of Kunara - Duncan MacNeil 4014

Mal
The Inheritors - William Golding 2455

Mangas Coloradas
Apache - Will Comfort 1226
Desert Hawks - Frank Burleson 786
War Eagles - Frank Burleson 788

Massasoit
The Plymouth Adventure - Ernest Gebler 2342

Massaswa
Angelique in Love - Sergeanne Golon 2470

Master, The
Isobelle - Mary Lide 3775

Matho
Salammbo - Gustave Flaubert 2123

Meromic
The Conquered - Naomi Mitchison 4418

Metacomet
Legacy - Robert Vaughan 6448
The Wept of Wish-Ton-Wish - James Fenimore
   Cooper 1312
White Rising - Zane Kotker 3548

Metamoris
*Song of Metamoris: A Story That Remains of a People
   Who Passed This Way* - Milford E. Anness 155

Moloquin
Pillar of the Sky - Cecelia Holland 2994

Moshesh
Wild Conquest - Peter Abrahams 12

Nane
A Time in the Sun - Jane Barry 361

Nemattanon
*The First Gentleman of America: A Comedy of
   Conquest* - James Branch Cabell 841

Numaga
Paiute - Sessions S. Wheeler 6666

Nyasanu
The Dahomean - Frank Yerby 6911

O'Breslin, Fergal
The Dispossessed - Dell Shannon 5773

O'Connor, Cormac
The Disorderly Knights - Dorothy Dunnett 1800

Okonkwo
Things Fall Apart - Chinua Achebe 16

O'Malley, Grace
Grania: She-King of the Irish Seas - Morgan
   Llywelyn 3819

Osceola
Bright Feather - Robert Wilder 6750
The Land Where the Sun Dies - Henry Carlisle 896
River in the Wind - Edith Pope 5111
Runaway - Heather Graham 2519
Seminole - Theodore Pratt 5164

Outakke
The Countess Angelique - Sergeanne Golon 2472

Pendragon, Uther
The Great Captains - Henry Treece 6329

Peta Nocona
Quanah Parker - Bill Dugan 1759

Piksarett
Angelique and the Demon - Sergeanne Golon 2466

Pontiac
The Conquerors - Allen W. Eckert 1839
Fire Along the Sky: A Novel of America - Robert
   Moss 4497
Hatchet in the Sky - Margaret Cooper Gay 2328
Silent Drums - Mike Roarke 5361
Strife Before Dawn - Mary Schumann 5675
This Land Is Ours - Louis Zara 6953

Powhatan
Daughter of Eve - Noel B. Gerson 2366
Pocahontas - Susan Donnell 1691
Powhatan's Daughter - John Clarke Bowman 605

Quanah Parker
Quanah Parker - Bill Dugan 1759
Ride the Wind - Lucia St. Clair Robson 5416

Red Cloud
Crazy Horse - Bill Dugan 1757
Creek Mary's Blood - Dee Brown 712
The Day the Sun Died - Dale Van Every 6408
Kelly Blue - Peter Bowen 601
North Against the Sioux - Kenneth Ulyatt 6376
Stone Song: A Novel of the Life of Crazy Horse -
   Winfred Blevins 548

Renno
Apache - Donald Clayton Porter 5114
Father and Son - Donald Clayton Porter 5117
Father of Waters - Donald Clayton Porter 5118
Hawk's Journey - Donald Clayton Porter 5119
Manitou - Donald Clayton Porter 5120
Renno - Donald Clayton Porter 5123
Sachem's Son - Donald Clayton Porter 5125
Spirit Knife - Donald Clayton Porter 5128
Tomahawk - Donald Clayton Porter 5129
War Clouds - Donald Clayton Porter 5131
War Cry - Donald Clayton Porter 5132
War Drums - Donald Clayton Porter 5133

Ridge, Major
Trail of Tears - Williams Forrest 2187

Roman Nose
The Stalkers - Terry C. Johnston 3259

Ross, John
As Long as the Rivers Run - Sam J. Slate 5882
Give Me the Wind - Jan Jordan 3302
Trail of Tears - Williams Forrest 2187

Rotten Belly
Carry the Wind - Terry C. Johnston 3246

Sanutee
The Yemassee - William Gilmore Simms 5855

Shaka
The Covenant - James A. Michener 4368

Shokotee
The Raider - Jesse Hill Ford   2164

Sitting Bull
Arrest Sitting Bull - Douglas C. Jones   3273
Buffalo Girls - Larry McMurtry   4296
Creek Mary's Blood - Dee Brown   712
The Day the Sun Died - Dale Van Every   6408
Dodging Red Cloud - Richard S. Wheeler   6657
Drums of Change: The Story of Running Fawn -
   Janette Oke   4707
A Good Day to Die - Thomas Wakefield
   Blackburn   525
The Jewelled Spur - Gilbert Morris   4465
*The Last Stand: A Novel about George Armstrong
   Custer and the Indians of the Plains* - Edwin P.
   Hoyt   3061
*A Road We Do Not Know: A Novel of Custer at the
   Little Bighorn* - Frederick J. Chiaventone   1057
The Secret Annie Oakley - Marcy Moran
   Heidish   2819
Sitting Bull - Bill Dugan   1760
Thunder in the Dawn - Earl Murray   4532
The Winter War - William Wister Haines   2640
Yellowstone Kelly - Peter Bowen   602

Sitting Red Cloud
*The Last Stand: A Novel about George Armstrong
   Custer and the Indians of the Plains* - Edwin P.
   Hoyt   3061

Spotted Calf
Warriors of the Night - Kerry Newcomb   4594

Storm, Tehana
Lords of the Plains - Max Crawford   1420

Sun Horse
The Snowblind Moon - John Byrne Cooke   1267

Tall Bull
Eyes of Eagles - William W. Johnstone   3266

Tarrik
The Corn King and the Spring Queen - Naomi
   Mitchison   4419

Tchula Homa
A Story of Deep Delight - Thomas McNamee   4305

Tecumseh
The Border Captains - Jason Manning   4072
Creek Mary's Blood - Dee Brown   712
The Frontiersmen - Allen W. Eckert   1841
Gateway to Empire - Allen W. Eckert   1842
Johnny Logan: Shawnee Spy - Allen W. Eckert   1843
The Loon Feather - Iola Fuller   2253
Panther in the Sky - James Alexander Thom   6234
Red Stick - Donald Clayton Porter   5121
Riders of the Long Road - Stephen E. Bransford   649
*Song of Metamoris: A Story That Remains of a People
   Who Passed This Way* - Milford E. Anness   155
A Sorrow in Our Heart - Allen W. Eckert   1844
War Clouds - Donald Clayton Porter   5131

Tharon
People of the River - W. Michael Gear   2338

Thayendanegea
The Wilderness War - Allen W. Eckert   1848

Tsani
The Double Man - Elinor Pryor   5205

Vercingetorix
Caesar - Allan Massie   4168
Gaul Is Divided - Esther Fisher Brown   721

Victorio
A Time in the Sun - Jane Barry   361

Washakie
The Man Who Loved Cat Dancing - Marilyn
   Durham   1817

Weatherford, William
Horseshoe Bend - Bruce Palmer   4779

White Hand
Breakheart Pass - Alistair MacLean   3999

Whitebear
The Shadow Riders - Terry C. Johnston   3257

Zalmunnah
The Trumpet and the Sword - Peter Danielson   1479

CHILD

Bas-Thornton, Emily
A High Wind in Jamaica - Richard Hughes   3074

Brisker
The Pleasure Garden - Leon Garfield   2293

Carrick, Peter
Lord Iverbrook's Heir - Carola Dunn   1795

Casta, Carmen de
The Place of Devils - Lucinda Baker   275

David, William
*The Kentucky Trace: A Novel of the American
   Revolution* - Harriette Simpson Arnow   195

Doban
Shiva: An Adventure of the Ice Age - J.H.
   Brennan   657

Emerson, Ramses
Lion in the Valley - Elizabeth Peters   4952

Gray Mouse
Child of the Dead - Don Coldsmith   1172

Hawke, Morgan
The Medicine Horn - Jory Sherman   5820

Heather
The Aviator - Ernest K. Gann   2277

Her-Bak
Her-Bak: The Living Face of Ancient Egypt - Isha
   Schwaller de Lubicz   5676

Hook, Jeremiah
Winter Rain - Terry C. Johnston   3262

Jim
The Two Farms - Mary E. Pearce   4865

Jordan, Sumner
Maiden Voyage - Cynthia Bass   372

Katz, Helga
The Healer - Aharon Appelfeld   176

King, Zach
Tenderfoot - David Thompson   6259

Lamb, Toby
The Haunting of Lamb House - Joan Aiken   48

Lark
Shadows on the Stones - Moyra Caldecott   847

Lincoln, Tad
*Christmas for Tad: A Story of Mary and Abraham
   Lincoln* - Helen Topping Miller   4386

Little Sister
Little Sister - Margaret Gaan   2259

Margery
The Vision of Stephen: An Elegy - Lolah
   Burford   775

Parham, Boyd
The Crossing - Cormac McCarthy   4221

Rayne, Edmund
Sylvester; or, The Wicked Uncle - Georgette
   Heyer   2904

Sills, Lena
Words by Heart - Ouida Sebestyen   5713

Thorman, Millie
The Moth - Catherine Cookson   1284

Trent, Robbie
The Wolfling: A Documentary Novel of the 1870s -
   Sterling North   4648

Yellow Bird
Seize the Sky - Terry C. Johnston   3256

CHILD-CARE GIVER

Fanshawe, Damaris
The Hand of a Woman - Diana Brown   719

CLERK

Athelstan, Brother
The Nightingale Gallery - Paul Harding   2684
*Red Slayer: Being the Second of the Sorrowful
   Mysteries of Brother Athelstan* - Paul
   Harding   2685

Gilman, Thomas
*Ride East! Ride West!: A Romance of the Hundred
   Years' War* - Anne Powers   5154

Hepburn, Philip
Sylvia's Lovers - Elizabeth Gaskell   2312

Lowrie, Angus
Clear for Action: A Novel about John Paul Jones -
   Clements Ripley   5344

McBain, Alexander
An Ancient Evil - C.L. Grace   2504

Robbins, Amy
Time After Time - Karl Alexander   80

Tempkins, Giuseppe
The Braintree Mission - Nicholas E. Wyckoff   6887

Todd, Titus
Water over the Dam - Marguerite Allis   116

Tufnell, Simon
Marianne - Glen Petrie   4981

COLLECTOR

Carrington, Amelia
The Time of the Dragon - Dorothy Eden   1863

Carrington, Nathaniel
The Time of the Dragon - Dorothy Eden   1863

COMPANION

Bagoas
The Persian Boy - Mary Renault   5301

Beladar
The Babylonians - Nathaniel Norsen Weinreb   6600

Bernardo
The Pope's Rhinoceros - Lawrence Norfolk   4642

Buck, Henry
Sassafras - Jack Matthews   4193

Coen, Emma
West to Eden - Gloria Goldreich   2461

Creamer, Eddie
Rainbow on the Road - Esther Forbes   2159

Cunningham, Maude
Diamond Head - Marian J.A. Jackson   3135
The Sunken Treasure - Marian J.A. Jackson   3136

Dispenser, Hugh
The She-Wolf - Pamela Bennetts   456

Flowers, Miss
Eugenie - Hester W. Chapman   989

Gaveston, Piers
The She-Wolf - Pamela Bennetts   456
Vows of the Peacock - Alice Walworth
   Graham   2513

Hephaestion
Alexander in Babylon - Jakob Wassermann 6576
Fire From Heaven - Mary Renault 5296
The Persian Boy - Mary Renault 5301

Huxleigh, Penelope
Good Morning, Irene - Carole Nelson Douglas 1698
Good Night, Mr. Holmes - Carole Nelson Douglas 1699
Irene at Large - Carole Nelson Douglas 1700
Irene's Last Waltz - Carole Nelson Douglas 1701

Insel, Maria
The Country Gentleman - Fiona Hill 2924

Kasane
The Tokaido Road: A Novel of Feudal Japan - Lucia St. Clair Robson 5417

Kysen
Murder at the God's Gate - Lynda S. Robinson 5408

Lindsay, Anne
My Lord Monleigh - Jan Cox Speas 5957

Lytton, Lavender
Dulcie Bligh - Gail Clark 1086

Manville, Rowena
Midsummer Masque - Jill Tattersall 6174

Martin, Sable
Cardigan Square - Alexandra Manners 4070

Merryn, Christy
The Elusive Crown - Hebe Elsna 1931

Newbolt, Mary
Death En Voyage - Richard Grayson 2557

Polidori, John
Lord Byron's Doctor - Paul West 6634

Randolph, Christy
The Tragedy at Tinkerton: An Historical Novel of Murder - Raymond Paul 4844

Ringo
The Unvanquished - William Faulkner 2050

Sykes, Christopher
Bertie and the Tinman - Peter Lovesey 3909

Thoegersen, Mikkel
The Fall of the King - Johannes Vilhelm Jensen 3214

Trewella, Annabel
Dolphin Summer - Carola Salisbury 5569

Weston, Rilla
The House of Kuragin - Constance Heaven 2808

Williams, Cary
Three Rivers - Carla J. Mills 4406

Wilson, Elizabeth "Lily"
Lady's Maid - Margaret Forster 2188

Wivenhoe, Artemia
Artemia - Pamela Hill 2927

Wolsey, Hester
Mother and Son - Ivy Compton-Burnett 1231

COMPOSER

Bach, Johann Sebastian
Sacred and Profane: A Novel of the Life and Times of Mozart - David Weiss 6609

Beethoven, Ludwig van
The Assassination of Mozart - David Weiss 6604
Eroica: A Novel about Beethoven - Carl von Pidoll 4994
The Man Who Thought He Was Messiah - Curt Leviant 3735
Nephew to the Emperor: A Novel Based on the Life of Beethoven - Jacques Brenner 658

Bellini, Vincenzo
Signorina - Henry Myers 4542

Berlioz, Louis Hector
Antonietta - John Hersey 2868
Hungarian Rhapsody: The Life of Franz Liszt - Jean Rousselot 5511
Passionate Rebel: The Story of Hector Berlioz - F.W. Kenyon 3457

Bruckner, Anton
Music for God - Theresa Weiser 6603

Chopin, Frederic
Beyond Desire: A Novel Based on the Life of Felix and Cecille Mendelssohn - Pierre La Mure 3574
Hungarian Rhapsody: The Life of Franz Liszt - Jean Rousselot 5511
The Questing Heart: A Romantic Novel about George Sand - F.W. Kenyon 3458

Debussy, Claude
Clair De Lune: A Novel about Claude Debussy - Pierre La Mure 3575

Dvorak, Antonin
The Big Stick - Lawrence Alexander 82
Dvorak in Love - Josef Skvorecky 5881
Good Night, Mr. Holmes - Carole Nelson Douglas 1699

Elgar, Edward William
Elgar on the Journey to Hanley - Keith Alldritt 92
Gerontius - James Hamilton-Paterson 2672

Foster, Stephen
Banished Children of Eve - Peter Quinn 5227
Walt Whitman's Secret - Ben Aronin 196

Franck, Cesar Augustine
Cesar and Augusta - Ronald Harwood 2771

Freire, Joaquin
River of Dreams - Gay Courter 1390

Gottschalk, Louis Moreau
Concert Grand - Howard Breslin 665

Haydn, Franz Joseph
Consuelo - George Sand 5582
Sacred and Profane: A Novel of the Life and Times of Mozart - David Weiss 6609

Holmes, Augusta
Cesar and Augusta - Ronald Harwood 2771

Innis, Nick
Brave Kingdom - Frances Murray 4534

Liszt, Franz
Hungarian Rhapsody: The Life of Franz Liszt - Jean Rousselot 5511
Last Love of Camille - Frances Winwar 6832
Passionate Rebel: The Story of Hector Berlioz - F.W. Kenyon 3457
The Questing Heart: A Romantic Novel about George Sand - F.W. Kenyon 3458

Mendelssohn, Felix
Beyond Desire: A Novel Based on the Life of Felix and Cecille Mendelssohn - Pierre La Mure 3574

Mozart, Wolfgang Amadeus
Antonietta - John Hersey 2868
The Golden Quill: A Novel Based on the Life of Mozart - Bernard Grun 2605
The Irish Boy: A Romantic Biography - Naomi Jacob 3137
Mozart on the Way to Prague - Eduard Friedrich Morike 4454
Rasero - Francisco Rebolledo 5282
Sacred and Profane: A Novel of the Life and Times of Mozart - David Weiss 6609

Otis, Jason
The Assassination of Mozart - David Weiss 6604

Paganini, Niccolo
Passionate Rebel: The Story of Hector Berlioz - F.W. Kenyon 3457

Puccini, Giacomo
A Cadenza for Caruso - Barbara Paul 4834

Ravel, Maurice
The Crown Prince - John Barchilon 300

Rimsky-Korsakov, Nicolai Andreyevich
Petersburg - Emily Hanlon 2677

Romberg, Sigmund
Deep in My Heart: A Story Based on the Life of Sigmund Romberg - Elliott Arnold 192

Schumann, Robert
Beyond Desire: A Novel Based on the Life of Felix and Cecille Mendelssohn - Pierre La Mure 3574
Spring Symphony - Eleanor Painter 4777

Sibelius, Jean
Winter Fire - William R. Trotter 6352

Stravinsky, Igor
Antonietta - John Hersey 2868

Tartini, Giuseppe
A Fiddle, a Sword, and a Lady - Albert Spalding 5953

Tchaikovsky, Peter Ilyich
Pathetic Symphony: A Novel about Tchaikovsky - Klaus Mann 4064

Wagner, Richard
Beyond Desire: A Novel Based on the Life of Felix and Cecille Mendelssohn - Pierre La Mure 3574
Hungarian Rhapsody: The Life of Franz Liszt - Jean Rousselot 5511
Magic Fire: Scenes around Richard Wagner - Bertita Harding 2683
The Ring Master - David Gurr 2622

CON ARTIST

Hatton, Glen
Poor Boy and a Long Way Home - James Sherburne 5806

Vance, Lee
Scotch on the Rocks - Howard Browne 733

CONDUCTOR

Lerner, Dan
The Career of Magda V. - Joseph Machlis 3982

Stokowski, Leopold
Poor Butterfly - Stuart M. Kaminsky 3345

Toscanini, Arturo
A Cadenza for Caruso - Barbara Paul 4834

Ziegler, Erich
Winter Fire - William R. Trotter 6352

CONVICT

Alorge, Marie
La Dame De Sainte Hermine - Grace King 3485

Barker, John
The Men That God Forgot - Richard Butler 829

Barre, Michael
Tavern in the Town - Cecile Hulse Matschat 4187

Black, James Fraser
Great Elephant - Alan Scholefield 5654

Brandon, Kitty
To the Ends of the Earth - Michael Talbot 6155
A Wilful Woman - Michael Talbot 6156

Brennan, Mary
The Playmaker - Thomas Keneally 3414

Briscoll, Nan
Dream Time - Parris Afton Bonds   570

Brown, Jamie
Forefathers - Nancy Cato   960

Buckstone, Bion B.
The Buckstones - Paul I. Wellman   6615

Canfield, Jefferson
Say to This Mountain - Bodie Thoene   6226

Chism, Nail
The Choiring of the Trees - Donald Harington   2709

Clampton, Mary
A Love So Wild - Deborah Chester   1056

Clint
Escape From Sonora - Will Bryant   739

Crabb, Joe
To the Ends of the Earth - Michael Talbot   6155

Cribb, Joe
A Wilful Woman - Michael Talbot   6156

Dane, Sara
Sara Dane - Catherine Gaskin   2316

Doyle, Cormac
The Silver Oar - Howard Breslin   669

Eden, Elizabeth
Eden Rising - Marilyn Harris   2731

Gray, Billy
Proud Mary - Iris Gower   2501

Haredon, Caroline
Beyond the Blue Mountains - Jean Plaidy   5006

Harvill, Clarissa
The Truelove - Patrick O'Brian   4677

Haseman, Peter
White Man - Peter Freuchen   2228

Keanu
Molokai - Oswald Andrew Bushnell   815

Landless, Geoffrey
Prisoners of Hope: A Tale of Colonial Virginia - Mary Johnston   3238

Levy, Abraham
To the Ends of the Earth - Michael Talbot   6155

Matilda, Caroline
Freedom's Way - Theodora McCormick Du Bois   1742

Oakley, John
They Seek a Country - Francis Brett Young   6941

O'Brien, Aidan
The Emancipist: An Unforgettable Epic of Australia - Veronica Geoghegan Sweeney   6147

O'Dea, Dion
Armored Giants: A Novel of the Civil War - F. van Wyck Mason   4145

O'Shea, Brick
And the Wild Birds Sing - Lola Irish   3112

Porter, James
The Men That God Forgot - Richard Butler   829

Prentice, Andrew
The Timeless Land - Eleanor Dark   1495

Scott, David
The Slave Ship - Mary Johnston   3240

Snow, Robert
Pageant - G.B. Lancaster   3650

Stafford, Neil
The Pagoda Tree - Berkely Mather   4181

Stanton, Dick
Swandowne - Daniel Farson   2024

Tallant, Hugh
Botany Bay - Charles Nordhoff   4637

Thorpe, Ben
To the Ends of the Earth - Michael Talbot   6155

Watkins, Sam
Fortune, Smile Once More - Mary Floyd Williams   6788

Wogan, Mrs.
Desolation Island - Patrick O'Brian   4662

Wynne, Jeremy
The King's Passenger - Nathan Schachner   5631

COOK

Baker, Melissa
Filaree: A Novel of an American Life - Marguerite Noble   4633

Didier, Auguste
Murder Makes an Entree - Amy Myers   4540

James, Harriet
Lady Fortescue Steps Out - Marion Chesney   1035

Larkins, Molly
Rome Haul - Walter D. Edmonds   1877

Leyton, Louisa
The Duchess of Duke Street - Mollie Hardwick   2693

Mallon, Mary
The Ballad of Typhoid Mary - Jurg Federspiel   2057

Meredith, Hallie
The Unplowed Sky - Jeanne Williams   6783

Otto
Signals of Distress - Jim Crace   1408

Silver, Long John
Treasure Island - Robert Louis Stevenson   6012

COURTIER

Armstrong, Archie
For My Great Folly - Thomas B. Costain   1365

Bacon, Sir Francis
Death of the Fox - George Garrett   2300

Bonel
Banners of Gold - Pamela Kaufman   3371

Bourbon, Francois de Vendome de
Twenty Years After - Alexandre Dumas   1783

Carey, Robert
The Succession: A Novel of Elizabeth and James - George Garrett   2302

Caumont La Force, Antonin-Nompar de
Sorrow by Day - Marjorie Coryn   1359

Cecil, Robert
Death of the Fox - George Garrett   2300
Deborah and the Many Faces of Love - Colette Davenat   1499
Deborah and the Siege of Paris - Colette Davenat   1500
For Love of a Pirate - Anthony Esler   1961
Scapegoat for a Stuart - Kate Kirby   3504
Shadow in the Sun: A Novel of Elizabeth I, the Virgin Queen - F.W. Kenyon   3460
The Succession: A Novel of Elizabeth and James - George Garrett   2302

Cecil, William
For Love of a Pirate - Anthony Esler   1961
Legacy - Susan Kay   3374
My Lord Essex - Olive Eckerson   1838
The Robsart Affair - Jennette Letton   3729
Shadow in the Sun: A Novel of Elizabeth I, the Virgin Queen - F.W. Kenyon   3460
The Young Elizabeth - Jennette Letton   3730

Coeur, Jacques
The Moneyman - Thomas B. Costain   1368

Conde, Louis de
Angelique - Sergeanne Golon   2465

Correnes, Victor de
The Gilded Torch - Iola Fuller   2252

Cromwell, Thomas
The Hireling - Alison Macleod   4003

Devereux, Robert
Death of the Fox - George Garrett   2300
Heart of a Queen - Josephine Delves-Broughton   1603
My Enemy the Queen - Victoria Holt   3017
The Succession: A Novel of Elizabeth and James - George Garrett   2302

Dudley, Robert
All the Queen's Men - Evelyn Anthony   157
Heart of a Queen - Josephine Delves-Broughton   1603
Kenilworth - Sir Walter Scott   5700
My Enemy the Queen - Victoria Holt   3017
My Lord Essex - Olive Eckerson   1838

Gaveston, Piers
Harlot Queen - Hilda Lewis   3748

Haman
Esther - Nathaniel Norsen Weinreb   6601
So Great a Queen: The Story of Esther, Queen of Persia - Paul Frischauer   2235

Herod Agrippa I
I, Claudius - Robert Graves   2547

Herod Agrippa II
Claudius the God - Robert Graves   2543

Heron, Christopher
The Lodestar - Pamela Belle   432

Hill, Abigail
The Queen's Favourites - Jean Plaidy   5051

Hudson, Geoffrey
Peveril of the Peak - Sir Walter Scott   5703

John
The Bearkeeper's Daughter - Gillian Bradshaw   628

Josephus, Flavius
Josephus - Lion Feuchtwanger   2072

Masham, Abigail
Exit Lady Masham - Louis Auchincloss   230

Merlin
Artorius Rex - John Gloag   2432

Montbrun, Roger de
Cities of the Flesh - Zoe Oldenbourg   4713

Oppenheimer, Josef Suss
Power - Lion Feuchtwanger   2074

Ralegh, Sir Walter
Ralegh's Fair Bess: The Story of Bess Throckmorton - Judy Turner   6365

Raleigh, Sir Walter
The Bisley Boy - Christopher Hunt   3080
Daughter of Eve - Noel B. Gerson   2366
A Dead Man in Deptford - Anthony Burgess   776
Death of the Fox - George Garrett   2300
The Firedrake's Eye - Patricia Finney   2095
For Love of a Pirate - Anthony Esler   1961
The Grove of Eagles - Winston Graham   2526
Her Majesty's Captain - Derek Wilson   6797
I, Elizabeth - Rosalind Miles   4378
Kenilworth - Sir Walter Scott   5700
Lady in Waiting - Rosemary Sutcliff   6123
The Lost Colony - Edison Marshall   4108
My Lord Essex - Olive Eckerson   1838
Physician Extraordinary: A Novel of the Life and Times of William Harvey - David Weiss   6608
The Shadow of the Earth - Lee Wichelns   6731
Take Heed of Loving Me: A Novel about John Donne - Elizabeth Gray Vining   6502
To Be a King - Robert DeMaria   1607

To Love a Queen - Lawrence Schoonover 5669
Towers in the Mist - Elizabeth Goudge 2495
The Voyage of the Destiny - Robert Nye 4657
Westward Ho! - Charles Kingsley 3499

Redvers, Tracy de
Royal Sword at Agincourt - Pamela Bennetts 455

Senmut
Pharaoh - Eloise Jarvis McGraw 4276

Sidney, Sir Philip
The Constant Star - Dorothy Norris Foote 2151
The Firedrake's Eye - Patricia Finney 2095
The Master of Gray Trilogy - Nigel Tranter 6316
Towers in the Mist - Elizabeth Goudge 2495

Simplicissimus
Simplicissimus the Vagabond - J.J.C.
 Grimmelshausen 2594

Struensee, Johann Frederick
The Queen's Physician - Edgar Maas 3952

Taverney, Andree de
The Queen's Necklace - Alexandre Dumas 1781

Taverney, Philippe de
The Queen's Necklace - Alexandre Dumas 1781

Villiers, George
Ballenrose - Mallory Burgess 783
Our Jo, or The Chronicle of a Coming Man - Kenneth
 M. Cameron 868
Royal Escape - Georgette Heyer 2900
The Three Musketeers - Alexandre Dumas 1782
The Young and Lonely King - Jane Lane 3659

Wilmot, John
Royal Escape - Georgette Heyer 2900

Wyatt, Sir Thomas
Blood Royal - Mollie Hardwick 2690
The Heir of Allington - Philippa Wiat 6727
Mistress Anne - Carolly Erickson 1952
Queen Anne Boleyn - Francis Hackett 2634
The Sword of Truth - Gilbert Morris 4472

COWBOY

Angel, Johnny
Apaches - Oakley Hall 2650

Baylen, Fate
San Juan Hill - Will Henry 2848

Bill
The American Cowboy - Will James 3163

Blankenship, Charley
The True Memoirs of Charley Blankenship - Benjamin
 Capps 890

Brady, Sam
Blue Moon - Parris Afton Bonds 569

Brules, Cat
Brules - Harry Combs 1223

Calloway, Hewey
The Good Old Boys - Elmer Kelton 3405

Chandler, Harper
The Seventh Girl: A Romantic Tale of Civil War Texas
 - Tom Pendleton 4900

Chandler, Troy
The Seventh Girl: A Romantic Tale of Civil War Texas
 - Tom Pendleton 4900

Costello, Peter Jack
Refugio, They Named You Wrong - Susan Clark
 Schofield 5647

Curley, Brent
The Talking Rifle - Glenn R. Vernam 6454

Daniels, Shep
By Dim and Flashing Lamps - Alan Le May 3689

Dart, Isom
One More River to Cross - Will Henry 2847

Dillard, Branch
California Caballero - William Colt
 MacDonald 3981

Dougherty, Levi
The Cowboy and the Cossack - Claire Huffaker 3071

Eagle, Sam
Chihuahua 1916 - Otis Carney 903

Edwards, Amos
The Searchers - Alan Le May 3691

Elliot, Will
The Goodnight Trail - Ralph Compton 1227

Evans, Lat
These Thousand Hills - A.B. Guthrie Jr. 2627

Farden, Henry
A Mule for the Marquesa - Frank O'Rourke 4753

Farsum, Flick
Pistols for Hire - Nelson Coral Nye 4652

Fletcher, George
Last Go Round - Ken Kesey 3473

Foyt, L.R.
The Terrible Teague Bunch - Gary Jennings 3197

Gil, Carter
The Ox-Bow Incident - Walter Van Tilburg
 Clark 1096

Hammett, Cain
Riders of Judgment - Frederick F. Manfred 4059

Hitchcock, Hugh
The Day the Cowboys Quit - Elmer Kelton 3403

Holcomb, Caleb
Too Long at the Dance - Mike Blakely 539

Johnson, Will
Pancho And Black Jack - Fred Bean 398

Jones, Red
Mary Dove - Jane Gilmore Rushing 5529

Kerbow, Ivan
The Pumpkin Rollers - Elmer Kelton 3406

Landerson, Roberto "Blanco"
The Color of Blood - E. Ralph Rundell 5524

Little Bear, Tom
The Talking Rifle - Glenn R. Vernam 6454

McCaleb, Benton
The Goodnight Trail - Ralph Compton 1227

McGinty, Rascal
The Day the Cowboys Quit - Elmer Kelton 3403

Miguel, Don
Don Gaucho - Alyce Pollock 5088

Mix, Tom
Tom Mix and Pancho Villa - Clifford Irving 3113
Tom Mix Died for Your Sins - Darryl Ponicsan 5090

O'Dare, Henry "Smoke"
Justice, My Brother - James Keene 3386

Pauley, Martin
The Searchers - Alan Le May 3691

Pender, Luke
Time for Outrage - Amelia Bean 397

Pepper Tom
The Sweetwater - Jean Rikhoff 5333

Radnor, Bill
Home Mountain - Jeanne Williams 6777

Scalley, Ora
Chihuahua 1916 - Otis Carney 903

Scott, Billy
The Trail to Ogallala - Benjamin Capps 889

Shad
The Cowboy and the Cossack - Claire Huffaker 3071

Smith, Laramie
Three Rivers - Carla J. Mills 4406

Spain, Johnathan E. Lee
Last Go Round - Ken Kesey 3473

Talbott, Ike
Filaree: A Novel of an American Life - Marguerite
 Noble 4633

Wade, Charlie
The Day the Cowboys Quit - Elmer Kelton 3403

Walsh, Monte
Monte Walsh - Jack Schaefer 5635

White, Jim
Bully! - Mark Schorr 5670

Whitey
These Thousand Hills - A.B. Guthrie Jr. 2627

Woodfoot
The Last Hunt - Milton Lott 3900

CRIMINAL

Barker, Arthur "Doc"
Saint Mudd - Steve Thayer 6218

Barker, Kate "Ma"
Saint Mudd - Steve Thayer 6218
True Crime - Max Allan Collins 1214

Bidwell, Austin Biron
The Four Hundred - Stephen Sheppard 5804

Bidwell, George
The Four Hundred - Stephen Sheppard 5804

Borden, Lizzie
Lizzie - Evan Hunter 3083

Bradley, Ma
The Slow Awakening - Catherine Marchant 4082

Capone, Al
The President's Man - Elliott Roosevelt 5455
True Detective - Max Allan Collins 1215

Carleton, Ned
The Vast Memory of Love - Malcolm Bosse 588

Cass, Dunstan
Silas Marner - George Eliot 1911

Chernik, Josef
The Dream Seekers - Grace Mark 4085

Dacre, Verney
Cracksman on Velvet - Francis Selwyn 5743
Sergeant Verity and the Blood Royal - Francis
 Selwyn 5744

Diamond, Jack
Legs - William Kennedy 3422

Digweed, Barney
The Quincunx - Charles Palliser 4778

Dillinger, John
Saint Mudd - Steve Thayer 6218
True Crime - Max Allan Collins 1214

Flegenheimer, Arthur
The President's Man - Elliott Roosevelt 5455

Floyd, Charles Arthur
Pretty Boy Floyd - Larry McMurtry 4299
True Crime - Max Allan Collins 1214

Fowl-Filcher
The Swedish Cavalier - Leo Perutz 4943

Frontoni, Jacopo
The Bravo - James Fenimore Cooper 1298

Fu Manchu, Dr.
The Fires of Fu Manchu - Cay Van Ash 6399
Ten Years Beyond Baker Street - Cay Van Ash 6400

Karpis, Alvin
Saint Mudd - Steve Thayer 6218
True Crime - Max Allan Collins 1214

Leonard, Elden
Winterkill - David Thompson 6262

Leonard, Selena
Winterkill - David Thompson 6262

Luciano, Charles "Lucky"
The President's Man - Elliott Roosevelt 5455

MacDonald, George
The Four Hundred - Stephen Sheppard 5804

Mars, Eddie
Perchance to Dream - Robert B. Parker 4807

McCannon, Geordie
The Street Sparrows - Rose Ayers 249

Melema, Tito
Romola - George Eliot 1910

Mompesson, Ralph
In Pale Battalions - Robert Goddard 2444

Moriarty, James
*The Case of the Revolutionist's Daughter: Sherlock
    Holmes Meets Karl Marx* - Lewis S. Feuer 2076
*Enter the Lion: A Posthumous Memoir of Mycroft
    Holmes* - Michael P. Hodel 2961
Exit Sherlock Holmes - Robert Lee Hall 2657
The Return of Moriarty - John E. Gardner 2287

Nicholson, Craig
The Good Provider - Jessica Stirling 6043

Nitti, Frank
True Crime - Max Allan Collins 1214
True Detective - Max Allan Collins 1215

Noyes, Edwin
The Four Hundred - Stephen Sheppard 5804

Oswald, Lee Harvey
Libra - Don DeLillo 1593

Restell, Caroline
Stuyvesant Square - Margaret Lewerth 3743

Rivers, Jenny
The Vast Memory of Love - Malcolm Bosse 588

Rothstein, Arnold
Blue Ruin: A Novel of the 1919 World Series -
    Brendan Boyd 610

Scarrat, Robert
The Vast Memory of Love - Malcolm Bosse 588

Sheppard, Jack
Jack Sheppard - William Harrison Ainsworth 56

Smith, Moses
Sweet Songbird - Teresa Crane 1418

Sorrel, Hetty
Adam Bede - George Eliot 1908

Sullivan, Joseph
Blue Ruin: A Novel of the 1919 World Series -
    Brendan Boyd 610

Surratt, Mary Eugenia
The Woman Who Loved John Wilkes Booth - Pamela
    Redford Russell 5533

Valjean, Jean
Cosette: The Sequel to Les Miserables - Laura
    Kalpakian 3329

Vella, Abbot Giuseppe
The Council of Europe - Leonardo Sciascia 5678

Wild, Jonathan
Jack Sheppard - William Harrison Ainsworth 56

DANCER

Ann
Shame of Man - Piers Anthony 168

Astaire, Fred
Dancing in the Dark - Stuart M. Kaminsky 3334

Beatriz
Columbus: A Romance - Rafael Sabatini 5549

Brancusi, Louisa
Louisa Brancusi - Darrell Husted 3088

Crow, Jim
Darktown Strutters - Wesley Brown 732

Diamond, Jack
Darktown Strutters - Wesley Brown 732

Esmeralda
The Hunchback of Notre Dame - Victor Hugo 3076

Fawkes, Fancy
Trumpeter, Sound! - D.L. Murray 4528

Holt, Daisy
The Days of the Butterfly - Norah Lofts 3841

Josefina
The Spanish Bride - Walter O'Meara 4735

Judith
*The Island of the Innocent: A Novel of Greek and Jew
    in the Time of the Maccabees* - Vardis
    Fisher 2108

Ladanova, Natasha
A Grand Passion - Mary Mackey 3991

Laiage
Blood of the Martyrs - Naomi Mitchison 4417

Lorendana, Juanita
A Spy for Napoleon - Baroness Emma Orczy 4746

Malcolm, Leonora
*The Spirit and the Flesh: A Novel Inspired by the Life
    of Isadora Duncan* - David Weiss 6610

Martin, Luna
Dancing in the Dark - Stuart M. Kaminsky 3334

Mata Hari
*The Eye of the Lion: A Novel Based on the Life of
    Mata Hari* - Lael Tucker Wertenbaker 6626
The Man Who Loved Mata Hari - Dan
    Sherman 5813

McKie, Jane
The Land of Our Dreams - Nancy Livingston 3812

McQueen, Fanny
The Maltese Angel - Catherine Cookson 1283

Montero, Lola
The Infinite Woman - Edison Marshall 4107

Montez, Lola
Royal Flash - George MacDonald Fraser 2213

Morton, Harriet Jane
A Company of Swans - Eva Ibbotson 3095

Oblonova, Natalia
Encore - Monique Raphel High 2915

Olwen
The Leopard Unleashed - Elizabeth Chadwick 967

Omri, Mary
The Emperor's Physician - Jacob Randolph
    Perkins 4914

Ossupov, Zoya
Zoya - Danielle Steel 5985

Petrovna, Elena
The Devil in Harbour - Catherine Gavin 2319

Rand, Sally
Murder in the Oval Office - Elliott Roosevelt 5450
True Crime - Max Allan Collins 1214

Rochina, Alysa
A Grand Passion - Mary Mackey 3991

Ryan, Lola
Shanghai Tango: A Novel of China - William
    Overgard 4769

Salome
The Eighth Veil - Ellis Kadison 3320

Sarita, Lola
The Gypsy From Cadiz - Tamsin Hamilton 2670

Sheridan, Kate
Flanagan's Run - Tom McNab 4303

Shizuka
The Sword of Hachiman - Lynn Guest 2608

Sorrel, Jannie
Lovers Meeting - Mollie Hardwick 2695

Trey, Tatiana
A Grand Passion - Mary Mackey 3991

Valli
So Far From Malabar - Joy DeWeese Wehen 6599

Venire, Maritza
Lord Vanity - Samuel Shellabarger 5796

Zapalova, Lyudmilla
The Gathering Wolves - Elizabeth Darrell 1496

DEBUTANTE

Merrivale, Charis
Frederica - Georgette Heyer 2889

Talbot-Harrow, Laura
Masque of Jade - Emma Merritt 4344

DEITY

Mudspell, Curt
Called Away - Perdita Buchan 753

DEMON

Bloody Shad
A Mirror for Witches - Esther Forbes 2157

Herne the Hunter
Windsor Castle - William Harrison Ainsworth 59

DENTIST

Baranov, Walter
The False Inspector Dew - Peter Lovesey 3912

Holliday, Doc
Wyatt Earp - Matt Braun 653

Holliday, John Henry
Confessions of Johnny Ringo - Geoff Aggeler 40

Minck, Sheldon
Bullet for a Star - Stuart M. Kaminsky 3331
Catch a Falling Star - Stuart M. Kaminsky 3333
Down for the Count - Stuart M. Kaminsky 3336
The Fala Factor - Stuart M. Kaminsky 3337
He Done Her Wrong - Stuart M. Kaminsky 3338
The Man Who Shot Lewis Vance - Stuart M.
    Kaminsky 3341
Smart Moves - Stuart M. Kaminsky 3346
Think Fast, Mr. Peters - Stuart M. Kaminsky 3347

DESIGNER

Berliner, Ruby Levy
Union Square - Meredith Tax 6176

Lindsay, Irene
Jewelled Path - Rosalind Laker 3597

Worth, Charles
Banners of Silk - Rosalind Laker 3592

DETECTIVE

Pinkerton, Allan
The Titans - John Jakes 3154

DETECTIVE—AMATEUR

Archer, Owen
The Apothecary Rose - Candace M. Robb 5364
The King's Bishop - Candace M. Robb 5365
The Lady Chapel - Candace M. Robb 5366
The Nun's Tale - Candace M. Robb 5367

Austen, Jane
Jane and the Unpleasantness at Scargrave Manor -
Stephanie Barron 356

Barfoot, Captain
Entered From the Sun - George Garrett 2301

Bray, Nell
Crown Witness - Gillian Linscott 3803
Dead Man's Sweetheart - Gillian Linscott 3804
An Easy Day for a Lady - Gillian Linscott 3805
Hanging on the Wire - Gillian Linscott 3806
Sister Beneath the Sheet - Gillian Linscott 3808
Stage Fright - Gillian Linscott 3809

Browne, Richard
The Strange Death of Mistress Coffin - Robert J.
Begiebing 415

Cadfael, Brother
Brother Cadfael's Penance - Ellis Peters 4955
The Confessions of Brother Halvin - Ellis
Peters 4956
Dead Man's Ransom - Ellis Peters 4957
The Devil's Novice - Ellis Peters 4958
An Excellent Mystery - Ellis Peters 4959
The Heretic's Apprentice - Ellis Peters 4960
The Hermit of Eyton Forest - Ellis Peters 4961
The Holy Thief - Ellis Peters 4962
The Leper of St. Giles - Ellis Peters 4963
Monk's Hood - Ellis Peters 4964
A Morbid Taste for Bones - Ellis Peters 4965
One Corpse Too Many - Ellis Peters 4966
The Pilgrim of Hate - Ellis Peters 4967
The Potter's Field - Ellis Peters 4968
The Raven in the Foregate - Ellis Peters 4969
The Rose Rent - Ellis Peters 4970
St. Peter's Fair - Ellis Peters 4971
The Sanctuary Sparrow - Ellis Peters 4972
The Summer of the Danes - Ellis Peters 4973
The Virgin in the Ice - Ellis Peters 4974

Cooper, Iris
Death in a Deck Chair - K.K. Beck 403
Peril under the Palms - K.K. Beck 404

Corbett, Hugh
Angel of Death - P.C. Doherty 1670
The Crown in Darkness - P.C. Doherty 1671
The Prince of Darkness - P.C. Doherty 1675
Satan in St. Mary's - P.C. Doherty 1676
Satan's Fire - P.C. Doherty 1677
The Song of a Dark Angel - P.C. Doherty 1679
Spy in Chancery - P.C. Doherty 1680

Croft, Ralph
The Masked Man - P.C. Doherty 1674

Didier, Auguste
Murder Makes an Entree - Amy Myers 4540

Eastbrook, Ann
Anna's Book - Barbara Vine 6500

Easton, Warwick
Keystone - Peter Lovesey 3913

Frevisse, Sister
The Bishop's Tale - Margaret Frazer 2215
The Boy's Tale - Margaret Frazer 2216
The Novice's Tale - Margaret Frazer 2217
The Outlaw's Tale - Margaret Frazer 2218
The Servant's Tale - Margaret Frazer 2219

Hunnyman, Joseph
Entered From the Sun - George Garrett 2301

Kestrel, Julian
A Broken Vessel - Kate Ross 5500
Cut to the Quick - Kate Ross 5501
Whom the Gods Love - Kate Ross 5502

Kreizler, Dr. Lazlo
The Alienist - Caleb Carr 907

Levendeur, Catherine
Death Comes as Epiphany - Sharan Newman 4598
The Devil's Door - Sharan Newman 4599

Mervyn
The House by the Churchyard - Joseph Sheridan Le
Fanu 3688

Metellus, Decius Caecilius
The Catiline Conspiracy - John Maddox
Roberts 5379
The Sacrilege - John Maddox Roberts 5380
SPQR - John Maddox Roberts 5381
The Temple of the Muses - John Maddox
Roberts 5382

Roger the Chapman
Death and the Chapman - Kate Sedley 5715
The Eve of Saint Hyacinth - Kate Sedley 5716
The Holy Innocents - Kate Sedley 5717
The Plymouth Cloak - Kate Sedley 5718
The Weaver's Tale - Kate Sedley 5719

Roosevelt, Eleanor
A First Class Murder - Elliott Roosevelt 5442
The Hyde Park Murder - Elliott Roosevelt 5443
Murder and the First Lady - Elliott Roosevelt 5444
Murder at the Palace - Elliott Roosevelt 5445
Murder in the Blue Room - Elliott Roosevelt 5446
Murder in the East Room - Elliott Roosevelt 5448
Murder in the Executive Mansion - Elliott
Roosevelt 5449
Murder in the Oval Office - Elliott Roosevelt 5450
Murder in the Red Room - Elliott Roosevelt 5451
Murder in the Rose Garden - Elliott Roosevelt 5452
Murder in the West Wing - Elliott Roosevelt 5453
A Royal Murder - Elliott Roosevelt 5456
The White House Pantry Murder - Elliott
Roosevelt 5457

Russell, Mary
*The Beekeeper's Apprentice, or, On the Segregation of
the Queen* - Laurie R. King 3487

Rutherford, Anthea
A Fatal Assignation - Alice Chetwynd Ley 3764
Masquerade of Vengeance - Alice Chetwynd
Ley 3765
A Reputation Dies - Alice Chetwynd Ley 3766

Rutherford, Justin
A Fatal Assignation - Alice Chetwynd Ley 3764
Masquerade of Vengeance - Alice Chetwynd
Ley 3765
A Reputation Dies - Alice Chetwynd Ley 3766

Sigismondo
Axe for an Abbot - Elizabeth Eyre 1989
Bravo for the Bride - Elizabeth Eyre 1990
Curtains for the Cardinal - Elizabeth Eyre 1991
Death of the Duchess - Elizabeth Eyre 1992

Sinclair, Cecily
Check-Out Time - Kate Kingsbury 3491
Do Not Disturb - Kate Kingsbury 3492
Eat, Drink, and Be Buried - Kate Kingsbury 3493
Grounds for Murder - Kate Kingsbury 3494
Room with a Clue - Kate Kingsbury 3495
Service for Two - Kate Kingsbury 3496

Stock, Joan
The Bartholomew Fair Murders - Leonard
Tourney 6297
Familiar Spirits - Leonard Tourney 6298
Frobisher's Savage - Leonard Tourney 6299
Knaves Templar - Leonard Tourney 6300
Low Treason - Leonard Tourney 6301
Old Saxon Blood - Leonard Tourney 6302
The Players' Boy Is Dead - Leonard Tourney 6303
Witness of Bones - Leonard Tourney 6304

Swinbrooke, Kathryn
The Book of Shadows - C.L. Grace 2505
The Eye of God - C.L. Grace 2506
The Merchant of Death - C.L. Grace 2508
A Shrine of Murders - C.L. Grace 2509

Thomas, Brother
A Trail of Blood - Jeremy Potter 5143

DETECTIVE—POLICE

Abberline, Frederick
The Night of the Ripper - Robert Bloch 551

Beckwith, Hollis
The Last Mystery of Edgar Allan Poe - Manny
Meyers 4356

Black, Morris
A Gathering of Saints - Christopher Hyde 3092

Blackstone, Edmund
Beau Blackstone - Richard Falkirk 2005
Blackstone - Richard Falkirk 2006
Blackstone and the Scourge of Europe - Richard
Falkirk 2007
Blackstone's Fancy - Richard Falkirk 2008

Byrnes, Thomas
Time and Again - Jack Finney 2093

Cheviot, John
Fire, Burn! - John Dickson Carr 910

Devlin, Matt
Death on the Cliff Walk - Mary Kruger 3562
Masterpiece of Murder - Mary Kruger 3563
No Honeymoon for Death - Mary Kruger 3564

Dupin, Auguste C.
The Lighthouse at the End of the World - Stephen
Marlowe 4095

Field, William
The Detective and Mr. Dickens - William J.
Palmer 4782
The Highwayman and Mr. Dickens - William J.
Palmer 4783
The Hoydens and Mr. Dickens - William J.
Palmer 4784

Grant, Alan
The Daughter of Time - Josephine Tey 6209

Hargreave, William
The Adventure of the Stalwart Companions - H. Paul
Jeffers 3177

Henderson, Edmund
The Hungry Goblin: A Victorian Detective Novel -
John Dickson Carr 911

Ichiro, Sano
Bundori - Laura Joh Rowland 5519
Shin Ju - Laura Joh Rowland 5520

Kilvarin, Xavier
Mysteries of Winterthurn - Joyce Carol Oates 4659

LeBlanc, Inspector
Henry James' Midnight Song - Carol de Chellis
Hill 2920

Lintott, Inspector
Dear Laura - Jean Stubbs 6094
The Golden Crucible - Jean Stubbs 6096

Mallory, Jim
The William Powell and Myrna Loy Murder Case -
George Baxt 390

Marshall, James
The Masters of Bow Street - John Creasy 1423

Monk, William
Cain and His Brother - Anne Perry 4922
A Dangerous Mourning - Anne Perry 4926
Defend and Betray - Anne Perry 4928
The Face of a Stranger - Anne Perry 4929

The Sins of the Wolf - Anne Perry 4937
A Sudden, Fearful Death - Anne Perry 4938

Muldoon, Ned
Faces in the Crowd - William Marshall 4117

Picard, Paul
Fata Morgana - William Kotzwinkle 3549

Pinkerton, Allan
The Four Hundred - Stephen Sheppard 5804

Pitt, Thomas
Ashworth Hall - Anne Perry 4918
Pentecost Alley - Anne Perry 4933

Rose, Egbert
Murder Makes an Entree - Amy Myers 4540

Schilling, Andreas
Blood Winter - William Patrick 4830

Singer, Jacob
The Dorothy Parker Murder Case - George
  Baxt 384
The Tallulah Bankhead Murder Case - George
  Baxt 389

Sturrock, Jeremy
Captain Bolton's Corpse - J.G. Jeffreys 3178
The Pangersbourne Murders - J.G. Jeffreys 3179
The Thieftaker - J.G. Jeffreys 3180
The Thistlewood Plot - J.G. Jeffreys 3181
A Wicked Way to Die - J.G. Jeffreys 3182

Swain, Alfred
Jekyll, Alias Hyde - Donald Thomas 6240
The Ripper's Apprentice - Donald Thomas 6242

Tillman, Virgil
Faces in the Crowd - William Marshall 4117

Todhunter, Inspector
The Guns of Arrest - Philip McCutchan 4242
Halfhyde on the Amazon - Philip McCutchan 4250

Tonneman, John "Dutch"
The House on Mulberry Street - Maan Meyers 4354

Vidocq, Francois Eugene
Crown of Grass - Charles Andrew Brady 634

Villon, Herbert
The Talking Pictures Murder Case - George
  Baxt 388
The William Powell and Myrna Loy Murder Case -
  George Baxt 390

Wang, Abraham
The Noel Coward Murder Case - George Baxt 387

Whicher, Jonathan
Scandal at High Chimneys: A Victorian Melodrama -
  John Dickson Carr 915

Witherspoon, Gerald
The Ghost and Mrs. Jeffries - Emily Brightwell 681
The Inspector and Mrs. Jeffries - Emily
  Brightwell 682
Mrs. Jeffries and the Missing Alibi - Emily
  Brightwell 683
Mrs. Jeffries Dusts for Clues - Emily Brightwell 684
Mrs. Jeffries on the Ball - Emily Brightwell 685
Mrs. Jeffries on the Trail - Emily Brightwell 686
Mrs. Jeffries Plays the Cook - Emily Brightwell 687
Mrs. Jeffries Stands Corrected - Emily
  Brightwell 688
Mrs. Jeffries Takes Stock - Emily Brightwell 689

DETECTIVE—PRIVATE

Cosgrove, Nicholas
The Cosgrove Report - G.J.A. O'Toole 4765

Costello
Escape From Sonora - Will Bryant 739

Croft, Michael
The Cosgrove Report - G.J.A. O'Toole 4765

Danforth, Abigail
Diamond Head - Marian J.A. Jackson 3135
The Sunken Treasure - Marian J.A. Jackson 3136

Falco, Marcus Didius
The Iron Hand of Mars - Lindsey Davis 1528
Last Act in Palmyra - Lindsey Davis 1529
Poseidon's Gold - Lindsey Davis 1530
Shadows in Bronze - Lindsey Davis 1531
The Silver Pigs - Lindsey Davis 1532
Time to Depart - Lindsey Davis 1533
Venus in Copper - Lindsey Davis 1534

Fleetwood, Sebastian
Dangerous - Amanda Quick 5213

Gordianus the Finder
Arms of Nemesis - Steven Saylor 5623
Catalina's Riddle - Steven Saylor 5624
A Murder on the Appian Way - Steven Saylor 5625
Roman Blood - Steven Saylor 5626
The Venus Throw - Steven Saylor 5627

Gunther, Bernie
The Pale Criminal - Philip Kerr 3471

Hallam, Lucus
Dead-Stick - L.J. Washburn 6574
Dog Heavies - L.J. Washburn 6575

Hammett, Dashiell
Hammett: A Novel - Joseph N. Gores 2487

Harp
Scarlet Women - J.D. Christilian 1077

Heller, Nate
Carnal Hours - Max Allan Collins 1210
Stolen Away - Max Allan Collins 1213
True Crime - Max Allan Collins 1214
True Detective - Max Allan Collins 1215

Holmes, Mycroft
*Enter the Lion: A Posthumous Memoir of Mycroft
  Holmes* - Michael P. Hodel 2961

Holmes, Sherlock
The Adventure of the Stalwart Companions - H. Paul
  Jeffers 3177
*The Angel of the Opera: Sherlock Holmes Meets the
  Phantom of the Opera* - Sam Siciliano 5842
*The Beekeeper's Apprentice, or, On the Segregation of
  the Queen* - Laurie R. King 3487
The Canary Trainer - Nicholas Meyer 4348
*The Case of the Revolutionist's Daughter: Sherlock
  Holmes Meets Karl Marx* - Lewis S. Feuer 2076
The Disappearance of Edwin Drood - Peter
  Rowland 5521
Dr. Jekyll and Mr. Holmes - Loren D.
  Estleman 1970
*Enter the Lion: A Posthumous Memoir of Mycroft
  Holmes* - Michael P. Hodel 2961
Exit Sherlock Holmes - Robert Lee Hall 2657
The Glendower Conspiracy - Lloyd Biggle Jr. 494
Irene's Last Waltz - Carole Nelson Douglas 1701
A Letter of Mary - Laurie R. King 3488
A Monstrous Regiment of Women - Laurie R.
  King 3489
The Quallsford Inheritance - Lloyd Biggle Jr. 495
The Return of Moriarty - John E. Gardner 2287
The Revenge of the Hound - Michael Hardwick 2688
Seance for a Vampire - Fred Saberhagen 5557
The Seven-Per-Cent Solution - Nicholas Meyer 4349
The Seventh Bullet - Daniel D. Victor 6483
Sherlock Holmes and the Case of Sabina Hall - L.B.
  Greenwood 2576
Sherlock Holmes and the Case of the Raleigh Legacy -
  L.B. Greenwood 2577
*Sherlock Holmes and the Mysterious Friend of Oscar
  Wilde* - Russell A. Brown 731
Sherlock Holmes and the Red Demon - Larry
  Millett 4404
Sherlock Holmes and the Thistle of Scotland - L.B.
  Greenwood 2578

Sherlock Holmes Meets Annie Oakley - Stanley
  Shaw 5782
Sherlock Holmes vs. Dracula - Loren D.
  Estleman 1976
Sherlock in Love - Sena Jeter Naslund 4557
Ten Years Beyond Baker Street - Cay Van Ash 6400
The West End Horror - Nicholas Meyer 4350
The Whitechapel Horrors - Edward B. Hanna 2678

Jones, Edward Porter
The Glendower Conspiracy - Lloyd Biggle Jr. 494
The Quallsford Inheritance - Lloyd Biggle Jr. 495

Lupa, Auguste
Rasputin's Revenge - John T. Lescroart 3725
Son of Holmes - John T. Lescroart 3726

Marlowe, Philip
Perchance to Dream - Robert B. Parker 4807

Master, York
Fallen Angel - Deborah Camp 872

Merryweather, Prudence
Dangerous - Amanda Quick 5213

Nash, Captain George
Captain Nash and the Honour of England - Ragan
  Butler 827
Captain Nash and the Wroth Inheritance - Ragan
  Butler 828

O'Donohue, Jack
The Rainbow Runner - John Cunningham 1450

Peters, Toby
Bullet for a Star - Stuart M. Kaminsky 3331
Buried Caesars - Stuart M. Kaminsky 3332
Catch a Falling Star - Stuart M. Kaminsky 3333
Dancing in the Dark - Stuart M. Kaminsky 3334
The Devil Met a Lady - Stuart M. Kaminsky 3335
Down for the Count - Stuart M. Kaminsky 3336
The Fala Factor - Stuart M. Kaminsky 3337
He Done Her Wrong - Stuart M. Kaminsky 3338
High Midnight - Stuart M. Kaminsky 3339
The Howard Hughes Affair - Stuart M.
  Kaminsky 3340
The Man Who Shot Lewis Vance - Stuart M.
  Kaminsky 3341
The Melting Clock - Stuart M. Kaminsky 3342
Murder on the Yellow Brick Road - Stuart M.
  Kaminsky 3343
Never Cross a Vampire - Stuart M. Kaminsky 3344
Poor Butterfly - Stuart M. Kaminsky 3345
Smart Moves - Stuart M. Kaminsky 3346
Think Fast, Mr. Peters - Stuart M. Kaminsky 3347
Tomorrow Is Another Day - Stuart M.
  Kaminsky 3348
You Bet Your Life - Stuart M. Kaminsky 3349

Pinkerton, Allan
The Bloody Ground - Bernard Cornwell 1334
The Cosgrove Report - G.J.A. O'Toole 4765
Talons of Eagles - William W. Johnstone 3268

Quarternight, Sam
The Last Days of Horse-Shy Halloran - Bill
  Pronzini 5203

Russell, Mary
A Letter of Mary - Laurie R. King 3488
A Monstrous Regiment of Women - Laurie R.
  King 3489

Severus, Livinius
Roman Nights - Ron Burns 803

Siringo, Charlie
The Cowboy Conspiracy - Larry D. Names 4553

Sparks, Jack
The Six Messiahs - Mark Frost 2238

Van Buren, Roxana
Blue Moon - Parris Afton Bonds 569

DIPLOMAT

Acton, Richard
Look Back to Glory - Herbert Ravenel Sass 5607

Adams, John
Sally Hemings - Barbara Chase-Riboud 1006

Amory, Tristram
Let the King Beware! - Honore Morrow 4489

Barak, Zev
The Glory - Herman Wouk 6873

Bardagne, Nicholas de
Angelique and the Ghosts - Sergeanne Golon 2467

Barlow, Joel
To Spit Against the Wind - Benjamin H. Levin 3737

Bellac, Charles de
The Hastening Wind - Edward Grierson 2591

Berry, Edith Campbell
Grand Days - Frank Moorhouse 4448

Blagden, Robin
Drums Against Frontenac - Harvey Chalmers 972

Borgia, Cesare
Borgia Testament - Nigel Balchin 277
The Scarlet City - Hella S. Haasse 2632
Then and Now - William Somerset Maugham 4198
Web of Lucifer: A Novel of the Borgia Fury - Maurice
    Samuel 5580

Bruce, Thomas
Lord Elgin's Lady - Theodore Vrettos 6514

Carewe, Maitland
The Dark Palazzo - Virginia Coffman 1151

Catherine of Siena
The Saint - Fritz von Unruh 6385

Chateaubriand, Francois Rene de
Crown of Grass - Charles Andrew Brady 634

Chavelin
The Scarlet Pimpernel - Baroness Emma Orczy 4745

Clay, Cassius Marcellus
Hacey Miller - James Sherburne 5805

Collingsworth, Richard
The Ginger Tree - Oswald Wynd 6890

Creticus, Metellus
The Temple of the Muses - John Maddox
    Roberts 5382

DaVille, M. Jean
Bosnian Chronicle - Ivo Andric 150

Dawson, Nicholas
City of God: A Novel of the Borgias - Cecelia
    Holland 2985

De Malassise
The Negotiators - Francis Walder 6526

Dio of Alexandria
The Venus Throw - Steven Saylor 5627

Dulles, John Foster
A Family Matter - James Roosevelt 5458

Eric of Normandy, Count
The Tyrant of Bagdhad - Glenn Pierce 4996

Erzberger, Matthias
Gossip From the Forest - Thomas Keneally 3413

Evans, William Hughes
Devoted Friends - Joe Poyer 5161

Fancot, Christopher "Kit"
False Colours - Georgette Heyer 2886

Fersen, Hans Axel von
I Thee Wed - Gilbert Wolf Gabriel 2267

FitzNigel, Julien
The Garden of Persephone - Cesar J. Rotondi 5510

Fitzpaine, Pev
Yedo - Lynn Guest 2609

Fitzwilliam, George
Reluctant Cavalier - Donald Barr Chidsey 1064

**Flahaut de la Billarderie, Auguste Charles Joseph
de**
A Rose for Virtue - Norah Lofts 3858

Fleming, Lloyd
Grishin - Hans Herlin 2859

Foster, Augustus John
My Dear Cousin - Peggy Hoffmann 2977

Franklin, Benjamin
The Bastard - John Jakes 3144
Blind Journey - Bruce Lancaster 3636
The Bonnet Laird's Daughter - Barbara
    Annandale 154
Captain Paul - Edward Ellsberg 1930
Citizen Tom Paine - Howard Fast 2028
Clear for Action: A Novel about John Paul Jones -
    Clements Ripley 5344
The Fallon Blood - Reagan O'Neal 4741
The Gentleman From America - Polan Banks 293
Israel Potter - Herman Melville 4334
Jeremiah Martin: A Revolutionary War Novel - Robert
    H. Fowler 2191
Murder by the Waters - Robert Lee Hall 2661
Poor Richard's Game - G.J.A. O'Toole 4766
The Rebels - John Jakes 3152
The Revolutionary - Lawrence Schoonover 5667
To Spit Against the Wind - Benjamin H. Levin 3737

Frome, Alexander
The Unsuitable Miss Pelham - June
    Drummond 1730

Gondomar, Diego
Wife to Great Buckingham - Hilda Lewis 3751

Hamilton, Sir William
The Blacksmith's Daughter - Joanna Dessau 1625
Bride of Glory - Bradda Field 2078
Emma - F.W. Kenyon 3448
The English Captain - Simon White 6700
H.M.S. Cockerel - Dewey Lambdin 3611
Lord Elgin's Lady - Theodore Vrettos 6514
Loving Emma - Nigel Foxell 2197
Shadow of a Lady - Jane Aiken Hodge 2971
Sir William - David Stacton 5977
The Sleeping Sword: A Biographical Novel - Pearl
    Frye 2244
The Volcano Lover - Susan Sontag 5946

Hasekura, Rokuemon
The Samurai - Shusaku Endo 1941

Hawthorne, Nathaniel
Memories of the Ford Administration - John
    Updike 6391

Horsey, Jerome
The Muscovite - Alison Macleod 4004

Ibn Fadlan, Ahmad
Eaters of the Dead - Michael Crichton 1425

Jefferson, Thomas
Arc d'X - Steve Erickson 1953
Citizen Tom Paine - Howard Fast 2028
Sally Hemings - Barbara Chase-Riboud 1006
The Seekers - John Jakes 3153

Kelly, Richard
A Few Good Men - William Overgard 4768

Kennedy, Joseph P.
The Bank - Stephen Longstreet 3882

Kirov, Sergei
Anna - Cynthia Harrod-Eagles 2752

Lowell, Adam
Blood and Sable - Carol J. Kane 3350

Machiavelli, Niccolo
The Borgia Prince - Pamela Bennetts 446
The Scarlet City - Hella S. Haasse 2632

Macrae, Dick
Papa La-Bas - John Dickson Carr 914

Madison, James
A Time for Titans - Vina Delmar 1602

Maitland, William
The White Queen - Frederic Fallon 2011

Metternich, Clemens von
Century in Scarlet - Lajos Zilahy 6962
Lustre in the Sky - R.G. Waldeck 6525

Mitterer, Joseph Von
Bosnian Chronicle - Ivo Andric 150

Molotov, Vyacheslav
Murder in the Blue Room - Elliott Roosevelt 5446

Monroe, James
A Time for Titans - Vina Delmar 1602

Morris, Gouverneur
A Generation of Leaves - Robert S. Bloom 552
King's Masque - Evan John 3220
The Man Who Killed the King - Dennis
    Wheatley 6654
Mistress Nancy - Barbara Bentley 460
Song of the Susquehanna - Herbert Stover 6071

Nepeda, Osep Grigorievich
The Ringed Castle - Dorothy Dunnett 1807

Pakenham, Sir Richard
54-40 or Fight - Emerson Hough 3040

Rashleigh, Adam
Republic: A Novel of Texas - E.V. Thompson 6266

Rassam
When the Emperor Dies - Mason McCann
    Smith 5926

Root, Elihu
1901 - Robert Conroy 1258

Rubens, Peter Paul
An Epic Joy: A Novel Based on the Life of Rubens -
    Donald Braider 642
*The Horn and the Roses: A Novel Based on the Life of
    Peter Paul Rubens* - Ira Jan Wallach 6542
Lover of Life - Zsolt de Harsanyi 2756

Russell, Samuel Shaw
The Winthrop Covenant - Louis Auchincloss 235

Seymour, Thomas
The Queen's Grace - Jan Westcott 6646

Shen Wen-Ching
The Fabulous Concubine - Hsin-Hai Chang 987

Sherley, Sir Robert
The Carmelite - Elgin Groseclose 2599

Slidell, John
The Chess Player: A Novel of New Orleans and Paris
    - Frances Parkinson Keyes 3478

Spitama, Cyrus
Creation - Gore Vidal 6486

Talleyrand-Perigord, Charles Maurice de
Brumaire - Mark Logan 3864
Captain Cut-Throat - John Dickson Carr 908
Draw Near to Battle - Jere Hungerford
    Wheelwright 6667
Far Flies the Eagle - Evelyn Anthony 162
A Generation of Leaves - Robert S. Bloom 552
Guillotine - Mark Logan 3865
Lustre in the Sky - R.G. Waldeck 6525
Madame Casanova - Gaby von Schonthan 5659
The Man Who Killed the King - Dennis
    Wheatley 6654
Marianne - Juliette Benzoni 466
Marianne and the Masked Prince - Juliette
    Benzoni 469

Marianne and the Privateer - Juliette Benzoni 470
Mirage - Ruth McKenney 4283
Napoleon Symphony - Anthony Burgess 780
Polonaise - Jane Aiken Hodge 2968
The River Devils - Carter A. Vaughan 6437
The Rose and the Sword - Sandra Paretti 4792
So Great a Man - David Pilgrim 5000
The Winthrop Covenant - Louis Auchincloss 235

Von Kobis, Hugo
While Paris Danced - Patricia Wright 6886

Westwood, Major Ambrose
Grand Days - Frank Moorhouse 4448

Weygard, Maxime
Gossip From the Forest - Thomas Keneally 3413

Winship, Bart
Storm to the South - Thelma Strabel 6073

Yamamoto, Renzo
Kagami - Elizabeth Kata 3369

DIRECTOR

DeMille, Cecil B.
He Done Her Wrong - Stuart M. Kaminsky 3338
New Deal for Death - Elliott Roosevelt 5454

Gebhart, M.P.
Poor Boy and a Long Way Home - James Sherburne 5806

Griffith, D.W.
Poor Boy and a Long Way Home - James Sherburne 5806

Hitchcock, Alfred
The Alfred Hitchcock Murder Case - George Baxt 382
Catch a Falling Star - Stuart M. Kaminsky 3333

Lang, Fritz
Destiny Express - Howard A. Rodman 5423

Prysing, Leo
Pacific Cavalcade - Virginia Coffman 1157

Sennett, Mack
Keystone - Peter Lovesey 3913

Todd, John James
The New Confessions - William Boyd 617

Von Stroheim, Erich
The Greta Garbo Murder Case - George Baxt 385

DOCTOR

Abercrombie, Lindsey
Affairs of Love - Nicola Thorne 6272

Abrois, Noe
The Year of the Death - Reuben R. Merliss 4343

Adair, Damien
Secret for a Nightingale - Victoria Holt 3020

Adler, Alfred
The Passions of the Mind - Irving Stone 6062

Amlie, Horace
Canal Town - Samuel Hopkins Adams 29

Andreas
Soul Flame - Barbara Wood 6850

Antelope
Bitter Creek - Al Cody 1150

Argentine, Giles
The Fate of Princes - P.C. Doherty 1673

Arran, Nathan ben
Glendower Country - Martha Rofheart 5427

Avicenna
The Physician - Noah Gordon 2482

Bank, James
The Rainbow Promise - Lisa Gregory 2580

Barrow, Tobias
The Unknown Shore - Patrick O'Brian 4678

Bartholomew, Matthew
An Unholy Alliance - Susanna Gregory 2586

Beladar
The Babylonians - Nathaniel Norsen Weinreb 6600

ben Abdiel, Asa
Fleet Surgeon to Pharaoh - Sheldon Jacobson 3140

Beventini, Tobias
Race of Scorpions - Dorothy Dunnett 1806

Bias
The Sword and the Promise - Benjamin Siegel 5845

Blackwell, Elizabeth
Domina - Barbara Wood 6847

Blackwell, Emily
Domina - Barbara Wood 6847

Blair, Charles
Drums of Khartoum - Chloe Gartner 2307

Blood, Peter
Captain Blood - Rafael Sabatini 5546

Bollman, Justus Erich
A Chance for Glory - Constance Wright 6877

Boswell, Jon
The House on Curtin Street - Millie J. Ragosta 5242

Breuer, Josef
When Nietzsche Wept: A Novel of Obsession - Irvin D. Yalom 6892

Brewton, Hal
The Sea of Grass - Conrad Richter 5323

Brooks, Saul
The Brooks Legend - William Donohue Ellis 1928

Buchanan, Devlin
A City Not Forsaken - Lynn Morris 4480

Burnham, Peter
Eagle in the Sky - F. van Wyck Mason 4149

Byrn, Lane
Scarlet Cockerel - Garald Lagard 3584

Cameron, Jesse
One Wore Blue - Heather Graham 2517

Carne, David
To the End of Her Days - Malcolm Macdonald 3975

Caspar, Freddy
Covent Garden - Claire Rayner 5262

Chapin, Matthew
The Hospital - Agatha Young 6938
I Swear by Apollo - Agatha Young 6939

Charcot, Jean-Martin
Affairs of Love - Nicola Thorne 6272
The Secret Life of Laszlo, Count Dracula - Roderick Anscombe 156

Charis
The Beacon of Alexandria - Gillian Bradshaw 627

Chen Li
Forbidden City - Anthony Esler 1962

Childers, Duncan
Serpent and Staff - Frank Yerby 6927

Chillingworth, Roger
Arthur Dimmesdale - Charles R. Larson 3671
Hester - Christopher Bigsby 496
The Scarlet Letter - Nathaniel Hawthorne 2786

Chisholm, Julian
In a Dark Garden - Frank G. Slaughter 5891
The Stubborn Heart - Frank G. Slaughter 5904

Clark, Christopher
Storm Haven - Frank G. Slaughter 5903

Cole, Rob J.
The Physician - Noah Gordon 2482
Shaman - Noah Gordon 2483

Cooke, Nicholas
The Physician of London - Stephanie Cowell 1394

Cortlandt, David
Eagles Where I Walk - Stephen Longstreet 3885
A Few Painted Feathers - Stephen Longstreet 3886

Coryat, Thomas
Lords of the Dance - Robin Lloyd-Jones 3815

Crawford, Michael
The Stress of Her Regard - Tim Powers 5157

Cream, Thomas Neill
The Gentleman From Chicago - John Cashman 953

Cumanus, Sergius
The Emperor's Physician - Jacob Randolph Perkins 4914

Denny, Mark
No Brighter Glory - Armstrong Sperry 5963

Devoe, Lucius
Eagle in the Sky - F. van Wyck Mason 4149

Dinsdale, Henry
The Seven Ages - Eva Figes 2084

Doctor
Before My Time - Niccolo Tucci 6358

Dover, Thomas
Burning Gold - Robert Hardy Andrews 148

Doyle, Arthur Conan
The List of Seven - Mark Frost 2237

Duffey, Adam
Long Remember - MacKinlay Kantor 3362

Duvall, Cheney
A City Not Forsaken - Lynn Morris 4480
Shadow of the Mountains - Lynn Morris 4481

Elkins, Harrell
Andersonville - MacKinlay Kantor 3359

Ellis, Havelock
The Crusader - Noel B. Gerson 2364

Enys, Dwight
Demelza - Winston Graham 2524
The Last Gamble - Winston Graham 2527
Venture Once More - Winston Graham 2532

Falke, Egidius Maximillian
Out of the House of Life - Chelsea Quinn Yarbro 6903

Fanshawe, Damaris
The Hand of a Woman - Diana Brown 719

Ferrier, Jonathon
Testimony of Two Men - Taylor Caldwell 863

Feversham
The Hessian - Howard Fast 2033

Fitzhugh, Bernal
Buccaneer Surgeon - C.V. Terry 6205

Florian, Charlot
The Twelfth Physician - Willa Gibbs 2403

Frayne, John
Patriot's Progress - Joseph G.E. Hopkins 3027
The Price of Liberty - Joseph G.E. Hopkins 3028
Retreat and Recall - Joseph G.E. Hopkins 3029

French, Alexander
The Native Air - Sarah Woodhouse 6854
The Peacock's Feather - Sarah Woodhouse 6855

Freud, Anna
Eating Pavlova - D.M. Thomas 6235

Freud, Sigmund
Affairs of Love - Nicola Thorne 6272
Eating Pavlova - D.M. Thomas 6235
The End of the World News - Anthony Burgess 777

Henry James' Midnight Song - Carol de Chellis
  Hill 2920
Jack the Ripper - Richard Gordon 2484
*Minna's Story: The Secret Love of Doctor Sigmund
  Freud* - Kathleen Daniels 1463
Monday's Child - Mollie Hardwick 2697
The Passions of the Mind - Irving Stone 6062
Ragtime - E.L. Doctorow 1658
Secret Dreams - Keith Korman 3541
The Seven-Per-Cent Solution - Nicholas Meyer 4349
When Nietzsche Wept: A Novel of Obsession - Irvin D.
  Yalom 6892
The White Hotel - D.M. Thomas 6237

Fyfe, John Adam
Alabama Empire - Welbourn Kelley 3392

Galen
Marius the Epicurean - Walter Pater 4826
Roman Nights - Ron Burns 803
The Side of the Moon - Amanda Prantera 5162

Gefroy, Martin
The Italian Garden - Judith Lennox-Smith 3717

Gordon, Clive
Song of a Strange Child - Gilbert Morris 4470

Gordon, Eli
Blood Winter - William Patrick 4830

Gradov, Boris
Generations of Winter - Vassily Aksyonov 61

Grange, Silas
The Rationalist - Warwick Collins 1217

Gull, Sir William
The Women of Whitechapel and Jack the Ripper - Paul
  West 6638

Gully, James
Dr. Gully's Story - Elizabeth Jenkins 3190

Gunn, Robert
Mandarin Gold - James Leasor 3700

Halevi, Avram
The Spanish Doctor - Matt Cohen 1159

Hargrave, Samantha
Domina - Barbara Wood 6847

Harvey, William
*The Diary of William Harvey: The Imaginary Journal
  of the Physician Who Revolutionized Medicine* -
  Jean Hamburger 2667
*Physician Extraordinary: A Novel of the Life and
  Times of William Harvey* - David Weiss 6608
The Physician of London - Stephanie Cowell 1394

Hawkins, James
The Adventures of Long John Silver - Denis
  Judd 3317
Return to Treasure Island - Denis Judd 3318

Hawkins, Willard J.
Buffalo Coat - Carol Brink 691

Hebert, Antoine
All Souls' Rising - Madison Smartt Bell 422

Helphand, Alexander
The Petrograd Consignment - Owen Sela 5739

Higganbotham, David
The Spoils of Eden - Robert H. Fowler 2193

Hippocrates
The Torch - Wilder Penfield 4902

Holmes, Oliver Wendell
Shaman - Noah Gordon 2483

Hunter, John
Lancet - Garet Rogers 5431

Hunter, William
Lancet - Garet Rogers 5431

Ismail
The Eagle's Daughter - Judith Tarr 6165

Jackson, John
Wagons West - Leslie Turner White 6692

Jekyll, Henry
Dr. Jekyll and Mr. Holmes - Loren D.
  Estleman 1970
The Highwayman and Mr. Dickens - William J.
  Palmer 4783
Jekyll, Alias Hyde - Donald Thomas 6240
Mary Reilly - Valerie Martin 4136

Jenner, Edward
The Dedicated - Willa Gibbs 2399
Princess in Amber - Evelyn Wilde Mayerson 4205

Jesu-Maria
To Keep This Oath - Hebe Weenolsen 6597

Jones, Ernest
The Passions of the Mind - Irving Stone 6062

Jung, Carl
The End of the World News - Anthony Burgess 777
Henry James' Midnight Song - Carol de Chellis
  Hill 2920
The Passions of the Mind - Irving Stone 6062
Secret Dreams - Keith Korman 3541

Kane, Elisha Kent
The Undiscovered Country - Jay Walz 6560

Keagh
Druid's Enchantment - Millie J. Ragosta 5240

Kellar, Melville
Deadly Beloved - Alanna Knight 3517

Kellogg, John Harvey
The Road to Wellville - T. Coraghessan Boyle 618

Kenner, Hugh
Promised Lands - Elizabeth Crook 1430

Kent, Tobias
Sangaree - Frank G. Slaughter 5898

Kent, William
The Americans - John Jakes 3143

Kingsley, Adam
Storm Before Sunrise - June Wyndham Davies 1507

Kirk, Morissa
Miss Morissa: Doctor of the Gold Trail - Mari
  Sandoz 5592

Lackland, Abel
Gower Street - Claire Rayner 5264
The Haymarket - Claire Rayner 5265
Paddington Green - Claire Rayner 5266

Lackland, Lewis
The Strand - Claire Rayner 5269

Lackland, Sophie
Charing Cross - Claire Rayner 5260

Laurence, Alexander
Bedford Row - Claire Rayner 5259

Laurie, Vincent
Blood Line - Alanna Knight 3515
Deadly Beloved - Alanna Knight 3517
Enter Second Murderer - Alanna Knight 3518
Killing Cousins - Alanna Knight 3520

Lawrence, Janessa Holt
Carolina Courage - Dana Fuller Ross 5469

Lazlo
The Secret Life of Laszlo, Count Dracula - Roderick
  Anscombe 156

Leacock, Robert
Voyage to the First of December - Henry
  Carlisle 897

Lebrun, Paul
Over There - Thomas Fleming 2130

Ledward, Thomas
Men Against the Sea - Charles Nordhoff 4638

Levy, Abraham
To the Ends of the Earth - Michael Talbot 6155

Lilliendahl, David
The Healers - Henry Denker 1610

Liston, Robert
The Sleep of Life - Richard Gordon 2486

Lorimer, Andrew
The Cactus and the Crown - Catherine Gavin 2318

Lorimer, Margaret
Blaize - Anne Melville 4331

Luke
Dear and Glorious Physician - Taylor Caldwell 853
The Emperor's Physician - Jacob Randolph
  Perkins 4914
*The Road to Bithynia: A Novel of Luke, the Beloved
  Physician* - Frank G. Slaughter 5897

Lydgate, Tertius
Middlemarch - George Eliot 1909

MacAndrew, Joan
Wideacre - Philippa Gregory 2585

Mackensie, Sir Morrell
Jack the Ripper - Richard Gordon 2484

Maclean, Adam Smith
The Powder River - Winfred Blevins 546

Maimonides, Moses
*The Doctor From Cordova: A Biographical Novel
  about the Great Philosopher Maimonides* - Herbert
  Le Porrier 3693
Trail and Triumph: A Novel about Maimonides -
  Lester M. Morrison 4485

Manette, Alexander
A Tale of Two Cities - Charles Dickens 1642

Mason, Samuel
Wild Horizon - F. van Wyck Mason 4164

Maturin, Stephen
The Commodore - Patrick O'Brian 4661
Desolation Island - Patrick O'Brian 4662
The Far Side of the World - Patrick O'Brian 4663
The Fortune of War - Patrick O'Brian 4664
H.M.S. Surprise - Patrick O'Brian 4666
The Ionian Mission - Patrick O'Brian 4667
The Letter of Marque - Patrick O'Brian 4668
Master and Commander - Patrick O'Brian 4669
The Mauritius Command - Patrick O'Brian 4670
The Nutmeg of Consolation - Patrick O'Brian 4671
Post Captain - Patrick O'Brian 4672
The Reverse of the Medal - Patrick O'Brian 4673
The Surgeon's Mate - Patrick O'Brian 4674
The Thirteen Gun Salute - Patrick O'Brian 4675
Treason's Harbour - Patrick O'Brian 4676
The Truelove - Patrick O'Brian 4677
The Wine-Dark Sea - Patrick O'Brian 4679
The Yellow Admiral - Patrick O'Brian 4680

McDonagh, Con
The Scalpel and the Sword - Dell Shannon 5774

McIntyre, Dorch
Timothy Baines - John H. Culp 1445

Mead, Raleigh
The Green Land - Zola Helen Ross 5504

Menzies, Roberts
The Legacy of Ladysmith - John Kenny Crane 1413

Merivel, Robert
Restoration: A Novel of Seventeenth-Century England -
  Rose Tremain 6333

Mesmer, Franz Anton
The Queen's Necklace - Alexandre Dumas 1781
The Strange Case of Madamoiselle P. - Patrick
  Ireland 3109

Morgan, Daisy
After the Rainbow - Yvonne Kalman 3323

Morgan, Robert
Testimony of Two Men - Taylor Caldwell 863

Myer, Dr.
Carriage Trade - Robert Thomsen 6271

Newman, Dr.
Molokai - Oswald Andrew Bushnell 815

Nostradamus
The Dreamer of the Vine - Liz Greene 2574

Nostredame, Michel de
Vagabond Prophet - Allene Symons 6149

Ogilvie, Ian
The Kidnapped Surgeon - Alexander Knox 3527

O'Lea, Fingin
The Love of Fingin O'Lea - Theodora McCormick Du
    Bois 1743

Olivier, Yvon
Creole Dusk - Walter Adolphe Roberts 5392

Paracelsus, Philippus Aureolus
The Adventurer - Mika Waltari 6550

Paris, Matthew
Sacred Hunter - Barry Unsworth 6389

Peabody, Asa
Eagle in the Sky - F. van Wyck Mason 4149

Petrie
The Fires of Fu Manchu - Cay Van Ash 6399

Philon
The Beacon of Alexandria - Gillian Bradshaw 627

Pinto, Adolph
Pinto and Sons - Leslie Epstein 1947

Pippin, Harry
Miss Martha Mary Crawford - Catherine
    Marchant 4081

Polidori, John
Haunted Summer - Anne Edwards 1881
Lord Byron's Doctor - Paul West 6634
A Single Summer with Lord B. - Derek
    Marlowe 4092

Power, Liam
No Price Too High - Madeleine Polland 5085

Powers, John
Flight From Avatchez - Frank G. Slaughter 5887

Preston, David
*The Stonewall Brigade: A Novel of the American Civil
    War* - Frank G. Slaughter 5902

Randall, Claire
Dragonfly in Amber - Diana Gabaldon 2262
Voyager - Diana Gabaldon 2265

Randolph, Bertram
Jack the Ripper - Richard Gordon 2484

Rank, Otto
The Passions of the Mind - Irving Stone 6062

Raoul, Jonathan
The Horn and the Forest - Jamie Lee Cooper 1313

Ratcliffe, David
The Disturber - L.S. Davidson Jr. 1505

Raven, Michael
All Desires Known - Malcolm Macdonald 3963

Rawdon, Matt
No Roof but Heaven - Jeanne Williams 6782

Rennie, Andrew
After the Rainbow - Yvonne Kalman 3323

Richmond, Kate
Blood Red Rose - Maxwell Grant 2538

Rivers, W.H.R.
The Ghost Road - Pat Barker 308

Robinson, Mark
The Night of the Ripper - Robert Bloch 551

Salisbury, Samantha
Dual Destiny - Karen Lynn 3939

Salmon
Scarlet Cord: A Novel of the Woman of Jericho -
    Frank G. Slaughter 5899

Saugrain, Antoine
The Medicine Man - Shirley Seifert 5729

Selkirk
The White Rose Murders - Michael Clynes 1137

Semmelweis, Ignaz Philipp
The Cry and the Covenant - Morton Thompson 6269

Sewell, Jasper
Alethea - Pamela Belle 429

Shadbolt, Humphrey
A Calf for Venus - Norah Lofts 3838

Shaw, Dr.
Highgate Rise - Anne Perry 4931

Sinclair, Mary
The Healers - Henry Denker 1610

Sinuhe
The Egyptian - Mika Waltari 6552

Smith, Samuel
They Called Her Mrs. Doc - Janette Oke 4709

Snow, John
The Drummer Was the First to Die - Liza Pennywitt
    Taylor 6186

Sompayac, Philippe
The Girl From Storyville: A Victorian Novel - Frank
    Yerby 6919

Steele, John
Time in Its Flight - Susan Fromberg Schaeffer 5636

Stenrood, Gilbert
Bright to the Wanderer - Bruce Lancaster 3638

Stephenson, Leslie John
Time After Time - Karl Alexander 80

Stewart, Duncan
Drums of Destiny - Peter Bourne 593

Stone, Michael
Golden Isle - Frank G. Slaughter 5890

Struensee, Johann Frederick
The Lost Queen - Norah Lofts 3850
The Queen's Physician - Edgar Maas 3952

Sullivan, Luke
Katherine - Antonia Van-Loon 6425
Sunshine and Shadow - Antonia Van-Loon 6426

Sutton, Paul
Pilgrims in Paradise - Frank G. Slaughter 5895

Tada Shom
Yedo - Lynn Guest 2609

Tayloe, William Dudley
Monsieur Yankee - Leslie Turner White 6689

Tipton, Lucius
These Latter Days - Laura Kalpakian 3330

Tisdall, Tom
The Salem Frigate - John Edward Jennings 3205

Toller, John
The Trial of Jenny Sykes - Hebe Weenolsen 6598

Tonneman, John
The High Constable - Maan Meyers 4353
The Kingsbridge Plot - Maan Meyers 4355

Treverton, Deborah
Green City in the Sun - Barbara Wood 6849

Treverton, Grace
Green City in the Sun - Barbara Wood 6849

Valentin, Dr.
The Brothers of Uterica - Benjamin Capps 887

Vaughan, Henry
The Swan of Usk - Helen Ashton 220

Verwien, Henry
*The Angel of the Opera: Sherlock Holmes Meets the
    Phantom of the Opera* - Sam Siciliano 5842

Victor, Robert
Cherished Enemy - Patricia Veryan 6460

Volusianus, Quintus
The Thorn of Arimathea - Frank G. Slaughter 5905

Ward, Sue
The Hospital - Agatha Young 6938

Warne, Ellis
Say to This Mountain - Bodie Thoene 6226

Warren, Joseph
The Bastard - John Jakes 3144
Concord Bridge - Howard Horne 3035
The Rebels - John Jakes 3152

Watson, John H.
*The Beekeeper's Apprentice, or, On the Segregation of
    the Queen* - Laurie R. King 3487
The Canary Trainer - Nicholas Meyer 4348
*The Case of the Revolutionist's Daughter: Sherlock
    Holmes Meets Karl Marx* - Lewis S. Feuer 2076
The Disappearance of Edwin Drood - Peter
    Rowland 5521
Dr. Jekyll and Mr. Holmes - Loren D.
    Estleman 1970
Exit Sherlock Holmes - Robert Lee Hall 2657
Irene's Last Waltz - Carole Nelson Douglas 1701
The Quallsford Inheritance - Lloyd Biggle Jr. 495
The Revenge of the Hound - Michael Hardwick 2688
Seance for a Vampire - Fred Saberhagen 5557
The Seven-Per-Cent Solution - Nicholas Meyer 4349
The Seventh Bullet - Daniel D. Victor 6483
Sherlock Holmes and the Case of Sabina Hall - L.B.
    Greenwood 2576
Sherlock Holmes and the Case of the Raleigh Legacy -
    L.B. Greenwood 2577
*Sherlock Holmes and the Mysterious Friend of Oscar
    Wilde* - Russell A. Brown 731
Sherlock Holmes and the Red Demon - Larry
    Millett 4404
Sherlock Holmes and the Thistle of Scotland - L.B.
    Greenwood 2578
Sherlock Holmes Meets Annie Oakley - Stanley
    Shaw 5782
Sherlock Holmes vs. Dracula - Loren D.
    Estleman 1976
Sherlock in Love - Sena Jeter Naslund 4557
The West End Horror - Nicholas Meyer 4350
The Whitechapel Horrors - Edward B. Hanna 2678

Whitman, Marcus
Doctor in Buckskin - T.D. Allen 103
To Heaven on Horseback - Paul F. Cranston 1419

Wilberforce, Oliver
Jack the Ripper - Richard Gordon 2484

Wilson, Edward
The Birthday Boys - Beryl Bainbridge 269

Wilson, Kent
For Love and Honor - Antonia Van-Loon 6423
For Us the Living - Antonia Van-Loon 6424

Wolfe, Simon
Shadow on the Valley - Kirk Mitchell 4414

Woodbury, Randall
Swear by Apollo - Shirley Barker 318

Woodville, William
The Dedicated - Willa Gibbs 2399

Woodward, Henry
Hilton Head - Josephine Pinckney 5003

Wormset, Richard Oliver
Seventeen of Leyden - John James 3160

Wouwere, Nicholas von
Prophecies - Helena Soister 5937

Zeno
The Abyss - Marguerite Yourcenar 6946

Zhivago, Yurii Andreievich
Doctor Zhivago - Boris Pasternak 4824

DRIVER

Fowler, Starr
Six-Horse Hitch - Janice Holt Giles 2417

EDITOR

Adams, Sam
Wandering Star - Steven Yount 6945

Bennett, James Gordon
Ain't Goin' to Glory - David Delman 1597

Cahan, Abraham
Rivington Street - Meredith Tax 6175

Cusak, Marcus
Castle Barebane - Joan Aiken 43

Fulton, Susanna
Nevada! - Dana Fuller Ross 5481

Greeley, Horace
Ain't Goin' to Glory - David Delman 1597

Langtry, Leda
The Baroness of Bow Street - Gail Clark 1085

Libanius
Julian - Gore Vidal 6489

Longe, Ambrose
The Northern Correspondent - Jean Stubbs 6099

March, Philip
Kindred Spirits - June Barraclough 347

Murry, John Middleton
Daughter of Time - Nelia Gardner White 6695

Poxe, Hieronymous
The Long Naked Descent into Boston - William Eastlake 1823

Priscus
Julian - Gore Vidal 6489

Stevens, Timothy Duncan
A Voice in the Streets - John William Tebbel 6196

Stone, Lucy
The Woman Question - Dorothea Malm 4046

Wickett, Hugo
The Labyrinth - Thomas William Duncan 1787

ENGINEER

Anderson, Paul
The Gathering Wolves - Elizabeth Darrell 1496

Andrewes, John
Kenya - John Halkin 2645

Baring, Eliot
Honour and Obey - Malcolm Macdonald 3966

Braide, Simon
Men in Buckskin - Herbert Stover 6069

Bruce, James
Madeleine - Catherine Gavin 2323

Bushnell, David
The Kingsbridge Plot - Maan Meyers 4355

Cabell, Matt
The Golden Sabre - Jon Cleary 1105

Colin
McKay's Bees - Thomas McMahon 4289

Dodge, Grenville
The Union Belle - Gilbert Morris 4473

Ericsson, John
Armored Giants: A Novel of the Civil War - F. van Wyck Mason 4145
Thunder on the Chesapeake - David Divine 1650

Fisher, Peter
Electricity: A Novel - Victoria Glendinning 2431

Fox, Philip
Railroad West - Cornelia Meigs 4327

Fraser, James
Paths of Fortune - Susan Moore 4444

Fulton, Robert
Being Met Together - William Vaughan Wilkins 6756
The Pandora Secret - Anthony Forrest 2186

Hafner, Bruno
Eagles at War - Walter J. Boyne 620

Hanbury, Edwin
The Summer of the Royal Visit - Isabel Colegate 1199

Kendall, Simon
The Drayton Legacy - Rona Randall 5247

Kendon, Richard
Lion in the Evening - Alan Scholefield 5656

Lesseps, Ferdinand Marie de
Madeleine - Catherine Gavin 2323

Lewis, Vargas
Young Vargas Lewis - Robert Brainard Pearsall 4874

Lingarde, Richard
Beyond All Frontiers - Emma Drummond 1722

Logan, Ben
Crimson Creek: A Novel of the Early West - Robert McCraig 4228

MacKellar, Patrick
The White Cockade - Vincent O'Brien 4683

March, James
Wings of the Morning - David Beaty 402

Martin, Rob
Dakota! - Dana Fuller Ross 5472

McGill, Cassie
The War Train: A Novel of 1916 - Brown Meggs 4324

Owens, Jim
Steamboat on the River - Darwin Le Ora Teilhet 6200

Rawlings, Mark
The Bridge of a Hundred Dragons - Emma Drummond 1723

Roget, Hadley
Eagles at War - Walter J. Boyne 620

Ruff, Alan
I Thee Wed - Gilbert Wolf Gabriel 2267

Stephenson, George
Beau Blackstone - Richard Falkirk 2005
The Iron Roads - Forbes Bramble 644

Story, John
The Buckingham Palace Connection - Ted Willis 6792

Sullivan, Matt
The Silver Highways - Malcolm Macdonald 3972

Thornton, Walter
The World From Rough Stones - Malcolm Macdonald 3979

Trevitnick, Richard
The Miller's Dance - Winston Graham 2528

Vivian, Hal
The Vivian Inheritance - Jean Stubbs 6101

Wakemani, David
The Big Freeze - Bellamy Partridge 4823

Ward, Oliver
Angle of Repose - Wallace Stegner 5989

Wright, Weatherby
The Road - John Ehle 1896

Zopyros
The Arrows of Hercules - L. Sprague De Camp 1553

ENTERTAINER

Angel, Roger
The Black Angels - Maude Hart Lovelace 3902

Auburn, Autumn
Spangle - Gary Jennings 3196

Baker, Josephine
A First Class Murder - Elliott Roosevelt 5442

Barnum, Phineas T.
Concert Grand - Howard Breslin 665
The Fast Men - Tom McNab 4302
Jenny and Barnum: A Novel of Love - Roderick Thorp 6276
Rogers' Folly - Albert E. Idell 3102

Benny, Jack
A First Class Murder - Elliott Roosevelt 5442

Blondel de Nesle
A Search for a King: A 12th-Century Legend - Gore Vidal 6492

Blondin
Niagara - Robert Lewis Taylor 6189

Bryn, Ivor
Lovers Meeting - Mollie Hardwick 2695

Burk, Martha Jane Cannary
The Lawless - John Jakes 3149

Burns, Tommy Jo
Cherokee Rose: A Novel of America's First Cowgirl - Judy Alter 119

Butler, Frank
The Secret Annie Oakley - Marcy Moran Heidish 2819

Cardiff, Hugh
Wild Times - Brian Garfield 2291

Carola
Life as Carola - Joan Grant 2535

Chantal
Stranger at Wildings - Madeleine Brent 663

Cigarette
Under Two Flags - Ouida 4767

Cody, William F.
The Big Stick - Lawrence Alexander 82
Buffalo Girls - Larry McMurtry 4296
Castle Garden - Bill Albert 63
Crazy Fox Remembers - Don Preston 5174
The Dream Seekers - Grace Mark 4085
Homeland - John Jakes 3148
The Jewelled Spur - Gilbert Morris 4465
Last Go Round - Ken Kesey 3473
The Secret Annie Oakley - Marcy Moran Heidish 2819
This Old Bill - Loren D. Estleman 1980
Wild Times - Brian Garfield 2291
Yellowstone Kelly - Peter Bowen 602

Courtebarbe, Denys de
Tomorrow's Fire - Jay Williams 6775

Coward, Noel
The Noel Coward Murder Case - George Baxt 387

Craven, Oliver
The Far-Off Rhapsody - Anne-Marie Sheridan 5808

Crosby, Bing
Murder in the Oval Office - Elliott Roosevelt 5450

Daisy
Pacific Street - Cecelia Holland 2993

d'Astarac, Sybille
Sybille - Marion Meade 4318

Dominic Dio
Dominic - Kathleen Robinson 5405

Duvall, Rita
The Reluctant Bridegroom - Gilbert Morris 4467

Florian
Spangle - Gary Jennings 3196

Fox, Letty
The Passion of Letty Fox - Diana Saunders 5610

Grimaldi, Joseph
Lovers Meeting - Mollie Hardwick 2695

Harcombe, Clement
English Music - Peter Ackroyd 18

Hope, Bob
Murder in the Oval Office - Elliott Roosevelt 5450

Jack
Playing the Jack - Mary Brown 726

Jolson, Al
From Time to Time - Jack Finney 2092

Kelly, Emmett
Catch a Falling Star - Stuart M. Kaminsky 3333

Lane, William
Darktown Strutters - Wesley Brown 732

Leno, Dan
The Trial of Elizabeth Cree: A Novel of the Limehouse Murders - Peter Ackroyd 21

Liliwin
The Sanctuary Sparrow - Ellis Peters 4972

Medley, Joshua
Conjuror's Journal - Frances L. Shine 5826

Mourouane, Ahmed Ben
Scorpus the Moor - Leslie Turner White 6690

Mulcahey, Jack
Banished Children of Eve - Peter Quinn 5227

Niccolo
A Comedy of Murders - George Herman 2861

Oakley, Annie
Crazy Fox Remembers - Don Preston 5174
The Jewelled Spur - Gilbert Morris 4465
The Secret Annie Oakley - Marcy Moran Heidish 2819
Sherlock Holmes Meets Annie Oakley - Stanley Shaw 5782

Olwen
The Leopard Unleashed - Elizabeth Chadwick 967

Pappenheim, Dr.
Badenheim 1939 - Aharon Appelfeld 174

Patch
We Speak No Treason - Rosemary Hawley Jarman 3168

Patch, Sam
Sam Patch: Ballad of a Jumping Man - William Getz 2390

Petrucci, Scapino
Carnival of Saints - George Herman 2860

Ponce, Juanillo
Five Black Ships: A Novel of Discoverers - Napoleon Baccino Ponce de Leon 5089

Rice, Tom
Darktown Strutters - Wesley Brown 732

Rogers, Cody
The Jewelled Spur - Gilbert Morris 4465

Rogers, Will
The President's Man - Elliott Roosevelt 5455

Shaw, Peggy
Murder at Fenway Park - Troy Soos 5948

Sibli
Glendower Country - Martha Rofheart 5427

Somers, Will
The Autobiography of Henry VIII - Margaret George 2355
King's Fool - Margaret Campbell Barnes 325

Stokes, Timothy
Peter Doyle - John Vernon 6457

Sutton
Seven Rivers West - Edward Hoagland 2959

Thornwood, Alan
The Merrymaid - Mollie Hardwick 2696

Thumb, Tom
Jenny and Barnum: A Novel of Love - Roderick Thorp 6276

Trasper, Doll
Rivers Parting - Shirley Barker 315

Valency, Jacquette
The Merrymaid - Mollie Hardwick 2696

Vidal, Peire
The Fool of Venus - George William Cronyn 1428

Wayfish, Ike
Chad Hanna - Walter D. Edmonds 1873

Winslow, Laurie
The Jewelled Spur - Gilbert Morris 4465

ESKIMO

Avinga
The White Dawn - James Houston 3053

Nemo, Adam
Frobisher's Savage - Leonard Tourney 6299

Sarak
The White Dawn - James Houston 3053

EXPATRIATE

Clay, Jubal
Mexico - James A. Michener 4372

EXPLORER

Aguirre, Lope de
Daimon - Abel Posse 5140

Amundsen, Roald
The Race: A Novel of Polar Exploration - Kare Holt 3008

Andree, Salomon August
The Flight of the Eagle - Per Olof Sundman 6119

Anza, Juan Bautista de
Beyond the Blue Sierra - Honore Morrow 4486
The Cross and the Sword - Jonreed Lauritzen 3674
Dust on the King's Highway - Helen Constance White 6677

Balboa, Vasco Nunez de
Balboa: Conquistador - Omar V. Garrison 2303

Baudin, Nicholas
Southern Cross - Terry Coleman 1206

Bering, Vitus
Alaska - James A. Michener 4364

Blue Jay
Walks in the Sun - Don Coldsmith 1194

Bowers, Henry Robertson
The Birthday Boys - Beryl Bainbridge 269

Brendan the Navigator
Brendan - Frederick Buechner 762
Paradise - Dikkon Eberhart 1831

Burritt, Adam
Call of the Arctic - Robert Steelman 5987

Burton, Sir Richard Francis
Burton and Speke - William Harrison 2751
The Highwayman and Mr. Dickens - William J. Palmer 4783

Cabeza de Vaca, Alvar Nunez
The Children of the Sun - Oakley Hall 2652
Texas - James A. Michener 4375

Cadillac, Antoine de La Mothe
Hawk of Detroit - Arthur Pound 5145

Carlos
The Seven Cities of Gold - Virginia Davis Hersch 2865

Castillo, Alonso del
The Children of the Sun - Oakley Hall 2652

Catherwood, Frederick
Journey to the Sky: A Novel about the True Adventures of Two Men in Search of the Lost Maya Kingdom - Jamake Highwater 2918

Cavendish, Thomas
Captain for Elizabeth - Jan Westcott 6643

Champlain, Samuel de
Fathers and Crows - William T. Vollmann 6508

Clark, George Rogers
Waters of the Wilderness - Shirley Seifert 5737

Clark, William
Distant Trails - Bill Gulick 2612
An Embarrassment of Riches - James Howard Kunstler 3565
Forward the Nation - Donald Culross Peattie 4880
From Sea to Shining Sea - James Alexander Thom 6232
The Gates of the Mountains - Will Henry 2842
Sacajawea - Anna Lee Waldo 6529
Sacajawea of the Shoshones - Della F. Emmons 1940
The Seekers - John Jakes 3153
The Shining Mountains - Dale Van Every 6410
Star of the West - Ethel Hueston 3070
Tale of Valor - Vardis Fisher 2112
Those Who Go Against the Current - Shirley Seifert 5734
Trail: The Story of the Lewis and Clark Expedition - Louis Charbonneau 998
Westward! - Dana Fuller Ross 5492

Cleaveland, Moses
Now We Are Free - Marguerite Allis 112

Colon, Cristobal
The Dogs of Paradise - Abel Posse 5141
My Master Columbus - Cedric Belfrage 418

Colter, John
The Man of the Storm - Ethel Hueston 3069

Columbus, Christopher
1492 - Newton Frolich 2236
1492 - Mary Johnston 3228
Bay of Arrows - Jay Parini 4800
Caribbean - James A. Michener 4365
Columbus: A Romance - Rafael Sabatini 5549
Crown of Aloes - Norah Lofts 3840
The Harp and the Shadow - Alejo Carpentier 905
The Indian Chronicles - Jose Barreiro 349
The Memoirs of Christopher Columbus - Stephen Marlowe 4096
Mercedes of Castile - James Fenimore Cooper 1304
The Queen's Cross: A Biographical Romance of Queen Isabella of Spain - Lawrence Schoonover 5666
Sea of Darkness - Roland Huntford 3086
To the Indies - C.S. Forester 2183

Torquemada - Howard Fast   2045
The Velvet Doublet - James H. Street   6082

Cook, James
Alaska - James A. Michener   4364
Charco Harbour - Godfrey Blunden   554
The Last Voyage: Captain Cook's Lost Diary -
   Hammond Innes   3108
*The Return of Lono: A Novel of Captain Cook's Last
   Voyage* - Oswald Andrew Bushnell   816
Running Proud - Nicholas Monsarrat   4432

Coronado, Francisco Vasquez de
The Seven Cities of Gold - Virginia Davis
   Hersch   2865
Texas - James A. Michener   4375

Cortez, Hernando
Aztec - Gary Jennings   3193
Captain From Castile - Samuel Shellabarger   5794
Cortez and Marina - Edison Marshall   4105
Death of the Fifth Sun - Robert Somerlott   5944
Don Pedro and the Devil - Edgar Maas   3948
The Fair God - Lew Wallace   6537
Gods on Horseback - Samuel G. Baggett   263
The Golden Princess - Alexander Baron   335
The Great White Gods - Eduard Stucken   6102
The Heart of Jade - Salvador de Madariaga   4024
*The Sun, He Dies: A Novel about the End of the Aztec
   World* - Jamake Highwater   2919
They Are Coming: The Conquest of Mexico - Jose
   Lopez Portillo y Pacheco   3896

Dampier, William
Burning Gold - Robert Hardy Andrews   148

de Soto, Hernando
At the Moon's Inn - Andrew Lytle   3944
The Golden Eagle - John Edward Jennings   3201
Juan Ortiz: Gentleman of Seville - Mary Bethell
   Alfriend   88
Tatham Mound - Piers Anthony   169

Dorantes, Andres
The Children of the Sun - Oakley Hall   2652

Drake, Sir Francis
Captain for Elizabeth - Jan Westcott   6643
Roanoke Hundred - Inglis Fletcher   2138
Westward Ho! - Charles Kingsley   3499

Du Luth, Daniel
Daniel Du Luth - Everett McNeil   4307

Du Pres, Andre
River of Swans - Don Coldsmith   1185

Eiriksdottir, Freydis
The Ice Shirt - William T. Vollmann   6509

Emin Pasha
The Last Hero - Peter Forbath   2154

Erik the Red
West with the Vikings - Edison Marshall   4114

Eriksson, Leif
Gudrid's Saga - Constance Irwin   3115
The Ice Shirt - William T. Vollmann   6509
This Land Fulfilled - Charles Andrew Brady   636
A Viking's Daughter - John Andrews   147
West with the Vikings - Edison Marshall   4114

Eudoxus of Kyzikos
The Golden Wind - C.L. Grace   2507

Evans, Edgar
The Birthday Boys - Beryl Bainbridge   269

Field, Ashbel
Now We Are Free - Marguerite Allis   112

Flinders, Matthew
My Love Must Wait: The Story of Matthew Flinders -
   Ernestine Hill   2922

Forth, Willoughby
The Last Camel Died at Noon - Elizabeth
   Peters   4951

Franklin, Sir John
North-West by South - Nancy Cato   962
The Rifles - William T. Vollmann   6510

Fremont, John C.
Dream West - David Nevin   4587
No Road Too Long - Hildegarde Hawthorne   2785
The Smoky Hill - Don Coldsmith   1188

Frobisher, Martin
Beauvallet - Georgette Heyer   2876
Frobisher's Savage - Leonard Tourney   6299

Greenfall, Jonathan
No Road Too Long - Hildegarde Hawthorne   2785

Grenville, Sir Richard
Roanoke Hundred - Inglis Fletcher   2138

Hall, Charles Francis
Call of the Arctic - Robert Steelman   5987

Hudson, Henry
Running Proud - Nicholas Monsarrat   4432

Hull, Harrison
Enslaved - Ron Burns   801
The Mysterious Death of Meriwether Lewis - Ron
   Burns   802

Isasaga, Francisco de
*A Crossbowman's Story of the First Exploration of the
   Amazon* - George Millar   4379

Jolliet, Louis
Blackrobe - Charles Corcoran   1323

Kane, Elisha Kent
The Undiscovered Country - Jay Walz   6560

La Salle, Rene-Robert Cavelier de
The Gilded Torch - Iola Fuller   2252
The Power and the Glory - Gilbert Parker   4805
La Salle - John Vernon   6458
Touched with Fire - John William Tebbel   6195

Le Moyne, Jean-Baptiste
High Towers - Thomas B. Costain   1366

Le Moyne, Pierre
High Towers - Thomas B. Costain   1366

Lewis, Meriwether
Distant Trails - Bill Gulick   2612
An Embarrassment of Riches - James Howard
   Kunstler   3565
Forward the Nation - Donald Culross Peattie   4880
From Sea to Shining Sea - James Alexander
   Thom   6232
The Gates of the Mountains - Will Henry   2842
My Theodosia - Anya Seton   5753
The Mysterious Death of Meriwether Lewis - Ron
   Burns   802
Sacajawea - Anna Lee Waldo   6529
Sacajawea of the Shoshones - Della F.
   Emmons   1940
The Seekers - John Jakes   3153
The Shining Mountains - Dale Van Every   6410
Star of the West - Ethel Hueston   3070
Tale of Valor - Vardis Fisher   2112
Those Who Go Against the Current - Shirley
   Seifert   5734
Trail: The Story of the Lewis and Clark Expedition -
   Louis Charbonneau   998
War Clouds - Donald Clayton Porter   5131
Westward! - Dana Fuller Ross   5492

Livingstone, David
The Whales in Lake Tanganyika - Lennart
   Hagerfors   2636

Madoc
The Children of the First Man - James Alexander
   Thom   6230

Magellan, Ferdinand
Five Black Ships: A Novel of Discoverers - Napoleon
   Baccino Ponce de Leon   5089

Marquette, Jacques
Blackrobe - Charles Corcoran   1323

Marvin, Silas
Now We Are Free - Marguerite Allis   112

Mendana de Neira, Don Alvaro de
Islands of Unwisdom - Robert Graves   2548

Moscoso, Luis de
The Golden Eagle - John Edward Jennings   3201

Oates, Lawrence Edward
The Birthday Boys - Beryl Bainbridge   269

Orellana, Francisco de
*A Crossbowman's Story of the First Exploration of the
   Amazon* - George Millar   4379
Vain Shadow - Hartzell Spence   5962

Ortiz, Juan
Juan Ortiz: Gentleman of Seville - Mary Bethell
   Alfriend   88

Park, Mungo
Water Music - T. Coraghessan Boyle   619

Pentland, Peter
Murder, I Presume - Gillian Linscott   3807

Pike, Zebulon
Rio Grande - Jory Sherman   5821

Pizarro, Francisco
Don Pedro and the Devil - Edgar Maas   3948
The Golden Eagle - John Edward Jennings   3201

Pizarro, Gonzalo
*A Crossbowman's Story of the First Exploration of the
   Amazon* - George Millar   4379
I, the King - Howard Clewes   1112

Pizarro, Hernando
Don Pedro and the Devil - Edgar Maas   3948

Polo, Marco
Caravan to Kanadu: A Novel of Marco Polo - Edison
   Marshall   4103
Invisible Cities - Italo Calvino   867
The Journeyer - Gary Jennings   3194
Messer Marco Polo - Donn Byrne   840

Pomeroy, Ezra
Now We Are Free - Marguerite Allis   112

Raleigh, Sir Walter
The Lost Colony - Edison Marshall   4108
Westward Ho! - Charles Kingsley   3499

Rochefort
Angelique in Revolt - Sergeanne Golon   2471

Rumon
Avalon - Anya Seton   5748

Santana, Miguel
The Gila River - Gary McCarthy   4223

Scolvessen, Jon
Sea of Darkness - Roland Huntford   3086

Scott, Robert Falcon
The Birthday Boys - Beryl Bainbridge   269
The Race: A Novel of Polar Exploration - Kare
   Holt   3008

Seagrave, Nigel
The Hungry Goblin: A Victorian Detective Novel -
   John Dickson Carr   911

Smith, Honoria
The Rake and the Rebel - Ira J. Morris   4478

Smith, John
For My Great Folly - Thomas B. Costain   1365

Speke, John Hanning
Burton and Speke - William Harrison   2751

Stanley, Henry Morton
The Last Hero - Peter Forbath   2154
The Whales in Lake Tanganyika - Lennart
   Hagerfors   2636

Stephens, John Lloyd
Journey to the Sky: A Novel about the True Adventures of Two Men in Search of the Lost Maya Kingdom - Jamake Highwater 2918

Stewart, Eugene
Victim of the Aurora - Thomas Keneally 3417

Thorbjornsdottir, Gudrid
The Ice Shirt - William T. Vollmann 6509

Thorvaldsson, Erik
A Viking's Daughter - John Andrews 147

Thurvaldsson, Eirik
Gudrid's Saga - Constance Irwin 3115

Vespucci, Amerigo
The Memoirs of Christopher Columbus - Stephen Marlowe 4096

Voss, Johann Ulrich
Voss - Patrick White 6698

Walker, Samuel
An Embarrassment of Riches - James Howard Kunstler 3565

Walker, William
An Embarrassment of Riches - James Howard Kunstler 3565

Walks in the Sun
Walks in the Sun - Don Coldsmith 1194

Walton, Robert
The Memoirs of Elizabeth Frankenstein - Theodore Roszak 5508

Wilson, Edward
The Birthday Boys - Beryl Bainbridge 269

FANATIC

Ahmad, Muhammad
Drums of Khartoum - Chloe Gartner 2307

Balfour, John
Old Mortality - Sir Walter Scott 5702

Brown, John
Raising Holy Hell - Bruce Olds 4718

Gordon, Lord George
Barnaby Rudge: A Tale of the Riots of Eighty - Charles Dickens 1641

Hellbane, Nicholas
Hellbane - Anthony Esler 1963

Marcel, Antonio
Sage of Canudos - Lucien Marchal 4080

Matthias
The Siege - Peter Vansittart 6431

Redgauntlet, Sir Edward Hugh
Red Gauntlet - Sir Walter Scott 5706

FARMER

Adam, Thomas
The Constant Star - Prudence Andrew 139

Adams, Joel
Hope of Earth - Jane Gilmore Rushing 5528

Aldrich, Job
Wings of the Morning - Frederic F. Van de Water 6404

Alicock, Jeremy
Soldiers of Fortune - Peter Bourne 595

Allyn, Hebron
Ho, the Fair Wind - I.A.R. Wylie 6889

Aragon, Clint
Run of the Stars - Dora Aydelotte 247

Armstrong, Tom
The Dark Pasture - Jessica Stirling 6042

Bale, Daniel
Long Remember - MacKinlay Kantor 3362

Berthois, Nicole
The Wine Widow - Tessa Barclay 301

Birdwell, Eliza
Except for Me and Thee - Jessamyn West 6628
The Friendly Persuasion - Jessamyn West 6629

Birdwell, Jess
Except for Me and Thee - Jessamyn West 6628
The Friendly Persuasion - Jessamyn West 6629

Brandt, Naftali
Behold the Fire - Michael Blankfort 541

Brodkin, Ivan
Peter the Great - Alexey Tolstoy 6293

Buk, Janko
Poland - James A. Michener 4373

Burns, William
The Wind That Shakes the Barley - James Barke 305

Buttes, Cobus
Buttes Landing - Jean Rikhoff 5331

Buttes, Guthrie
Buttes Landing - Jean Rikhoff 5331

Buttes, John
The Sweetwater - Jean Rikhoff 5333

Bzik, Jan
The Slave - Isaac Bashevis Singer 5866

Catton, Gideon
Salt Lake City - A.R. Reife 5292

Clinch, Josiah
Darker Grows the Valley - Harry Harrison Kroll 3556

Cobbold, Gabby
Ulverton - Adam Thorpe 6278

Cochran, Coll
Treasures on Earth - Jessica Stirling 6049

Combardi, Rosaria
Contessa - Richard Oliver Collin 1209

Crane, Beulah
The Regulators - William Degenhard 1580

Curtis, Madison
Hiwassee: A Novel of the Civil War - Charles F. Price 5176

Derriman, Festus
The Trumpet Major - Thomas Hardy 2700

Douglass, Samuel
These Latter Days - Laura Kalpakian 3330

Drummond, Samuel
Samuel Drummond - Thomas Alexander Boyd 614

Dualta
The Silent People - Walter Macken 3990

Emmet, Joel
I Take This Land - Richard Powell 5147

Eupolis
Goatsong - Tom Holt 3009
The Walled Orchard - Tom Holt 3010

Fawley, Noah
The Barefoot Brigade - Douglas C. Jones 3274

Fawley, Zachery
The Barefoot Brigade - Douglas C. Jones 3274

Faye, Sheba
Faye's Folly - Elizabeth Corbett 1322

Forbes, Josh
Forefathers - Nancy Cato 960

Fraser, James
Marching On - James Boyd 612

Galphine, Rike
Show Me a Land - Clark McMeekin 4293

Gibson, Ward
The Maltese Angel - Catherine Cookson 1283

Glendower, Martin
Beckoning Ridge - Emerson Waldman 6527

Gordianus the Finder
Catalina's Riddle - Steven Saylor 5624

Gunnarsson, Asgeir
The Greenlanders - Jane Smiley 5915

Haaberg, Anders
The People of Juvik - Olav Dunn 1798

Halder, Alton
Still Is the Summer Night - August Derleth 1619

Halder, Ratio
Still Is the Summer Night - August Derleth 1619

Harper, Allan
Golden Horizons - William Corcoran 1324

Harrison, Donnigan
A Bride for Donnigan - Janette Oke 4705

Harrow, Dan
Rome Haul - Walter D. Edmonds 1877

Hasford, Martin
The Barefoot Brigade - Douglas C. Jones 3274

Hasford, Ora
Elkhorn Tavern - Douglas C. Jones 3278

Hasford, Roman
Elkhorn Tavern - Douglas C. Jones 3278

Hollingworth, Daniel
Come Spring - Charlotte Hinger 2954

Holloway, Jonas
Day of Battle - Frederic F. Van de Water 6402

Holm, Beret
Their Fathers' God - O.E. Rolvaag 5436

Holm, Peder Victorious
Peder Victorious - O.E. Rolvaag 5435
Their Fathers' God - O.E. Rolvaag 5436

Holm, Peer
The Great Hunger - Johan Bojer 562

Holm, Susie
Their Fathers' God - O.E. Rolvaag 5436

Howard, Jethro
The Plums Hang High - Gertrude E. Finney 2091

Howarth, Dick
An Imperfect Joy - Jean Stubbs 6097

Howarth, Ned
By Our Beginnings - Jean Stubbs 6092

Howell, Asa
The Perilous Night - Burke Boyce 609

Huai-i
The Jade Stalk - Jonathan Fast 2048

Jarvis, Berk
The Great Meadow - Elizabeth Madox Roberts 5378

Jarvis, Diony
The Great Meadow - Elizabeth Madox Roberts 5378

Juvika, Per Anders
The People of Juvik - Olav Dunn 1798

Kaetter-Henry, August
Country People - Ruth Suckow 6111

Kaetter-Henry, Carl
Country People - Ruth Suckow 6111

Kenner, Hugh
Promised Lands - Elizabeth Crook 1430

Kilmartin, Brian
Famine - Liam O'Flaherty 4693

King, Linda
Three Days - Stephen Longstreet   3891

Lathrop, Isaac
Artillery of Time - Chard Powers Smith   5919

Lathrop, John
Artillery of Time - Chard Powers Smith   5919

Lemaire, Jacques
The Golden Fool - David Divine   1649

Len
Fitzempress' Law - Diana Norman   4644

Lenihan, Liam
The Famished Land - Elizabeth Byrd   833

Lincoln, Thomas
Lincoln's Mothers: A Story of Nancy and Sally Lincoln
  - Dorothy Clarke Wilson   6804

Lindsay, Nathan
Call of the Mountains - Cornelia Meigs   4326

Linthorne, Thomas
The Earth Abideth - George Dell   1595

MacDougall, Jack
Nebraska Coast - Clyde Brion Davis   1516

MacIntosh, Andrew
The Glass Dove - Sally Carrighar   943

Martin, Gilbert
Drums Along the Mohawk - Walter D.
  Edmonds   1874

McElroy, Duncan
The Live Goat - Cecil Dawkins   1542

McFlaherty, Moira
The Famished Land - Elizabeth Byrd   833

McLeod, Garth
The Unplowed Sky - Jeanne Williams   6783

McMahon, Brendan
They Were Dreamers - James F. Murphy Jr.   4525

Mercybright, Jack
Apple Tree Lean Down - Mary E. Pearce   4860

Mourne, Lex
The Red Doe - Drayton Mayrant   4214

Muir, Evan
The Great Meadow - Elizabeth Madox Roberts   5378

Nilsson, Karl Oskar
Last Letter Home - Vilhelm Moberg   4423
The Settlers - Vilhelm Moberg   4424

Oakes, Jude
American Beauty - Edna Ferber   2060

O'Brien, Patrick
Lady of No Man's Land - Jeanne Williams   6780

Omensetter, Brackett
Omensetter's Luck - William H. Gass   2317

Perrin, Laurent
The Colors of Vaud - Bryher   741

Place, James
The Lords of Loone - John James   3159

Powell, Tom
The Truest Pleasure - Robert Morgan   4452

Preele, Catherine
Morgan's Woman - Iris Gower   2500

Prinsloo Willem, Oom
The Fiercest Heart - Stuart Cloete   1122

Pullen, Toliver
The Live Goat - Cecil Dawkins   1542

Riddler, Morris
The Two Farms - Mary E. Pearce   4865

Roscius, Sextus
Roman Blood - Steven Saylor   5626

Ryall, Jim
The Richlands - Agnes Sligh Turnbull   6364

Sarn, Gideon
Precious Bane - Mary Webb   6590

Serrano, Francisco
The Arkansas River - Jory Sherman   5816

Simplicissimus
Simplicissimus the Vagabond - J.J.C.
  Grimmelshausen   2594

Skaret, Kal
The Emigrants - Johan Bojer   561

Slocum, Martin
The River and the Wilderness - Don Robertson   5401

Stahl, Egron
The Rainbird - Sara Lidman   3780

Stanhope, Robert
The Bondswoman - Caryl Ledner   3705

Steinsson, Steiner
Paradise Reclaimed - Halldor Laxness   3686

Sutton, John
The Two Farms - Mary E. Pearce   4865

Taggart, Jenny
The Settlers - William Stuart Long   3878

Tante, Maria
The Fiercest Heart - Stuart Cloete   1122

Thorpe, Ben
To the Ends of the Earth - Michael Talbot   6155

Tower, Joe
The Lost Wagon - James Arthur Kjelgaard   3509

Truscott, Charlie
Seedtime and Harvest - Mary E. Pearce   4864

Tucker, Abel
The Sprig of Hemlock: A Novel about Shays' Rebellion
  - Robert Muir   4509

Tucker, Isiah
The Sprig of Hemlock: A Novel about Shays' Rebellion
  - Robert Muir   4509

Tupper, Jenny
Strange Wives - Shirley Barker   317

Tyler, Wat
Who Was Then the Gentleman - Charles E.
  Israel   3125

Vandemark, Jacobus
Vandemark's Folly - Herbert Quick   5223

Wang Lung
The Good Earth - Pearl S. Buck   754

Warner, Stephen
The Marriage Bed - Jean Clark   1088

Wayman, Stephen
The Land Endures - Mary E. Pearce   4862

Wessel, Simon
The Red Marten - Peter William Nisser   4630

Wilder, T.J.
Black Gold - Anita Richmond Bunkley   771

Winslow, Adam
The Indentured Heart - Gilbert Morris   4464

Winslow, Brent
Blue Camellia - Frances Parkinson Keyes   3477

Winster, Jonathan
Peace, My Daughters - Shirley Barker   314

Winwold, Omri
Remembrance Rock - Carl Sandburg   5583

Wright, Jedediah
The Taste of Time - Ferol Egan   1892

Yorkless, Barney
The Whip - Catherine Cookson   1291

FBI AGENT

Ness, Eliot
The Dark City - Max Allan Collins   1211
Murder by the Numbers - Max Allan Collins   1212

Purvis, Melvin
Pretty Boy Floyd - Larry McMurtry   4299
True Crime - Max Allan Collins   1214

FEMINIST

Anthony, Susan B.
The Woman Question - Dorothea Malm   4046

Colden, Emma
Jackson: A Novel - Max Byrd   837

Edwards, Harriet
The Brothers of Uterica - Benjamin Capps   887

Field, Connie
Brave Pursuit - Marguerite Allis   107

Langtry, Leda
The Baroness of Bow Street - Gail Clark   1085

Mott, Lucretia
Law of the Land - Marguerite Allis   111
Seneca Falls Inheritance - Miriam Grace
  Monfredo   4429
The Woman Question - Dorothea Malm   4046

Pankhurst, Emmeline
Sister Beneath the Sheet - Gillian Linscott   3808

Ross, Nellie
California Gold - John Jakes   3145

Schreiner, Olive
*The Daughter: A Novel Based on the Life of Eleanor
Marx* - Judith Chernaik   1012

Stanton, Elizabeth Cady
The Americans - John Jakes   3143
Law of the Land - Marguerite Allis   111
North Star Conspiracy - Miriam Grace
  Monfredo   4428
Seneca Falls Inheritance - Miriam Grace
  Monfredo   4429
Through a Gold Eagle - Miriam Grace
  Monfredo   4430

Stone, Lucy
The Americans - John Jakes   3143
The Lawless - John Jakes   3149
The Woman Question - Dorothea Malm   4046

Truth, Sojourner
The Hallelujah Train - Bill Gulick   2614

Tryon, Glynis
Blackwater Spirits - Miriam Grace Monfredo   4427
North Star Conspiracy - Miriam Grace
  Monfredo   4428
Seneca Falls Inheritance - Miriam Grace
  Monfredo   4429
Through a Gold Eagle - Miriam Grace
  Monfredo   4430

Whitby, Mary
The Woman Question - Dorothea Malm   4046

Woodhull, Victoria Claflin
Scarlet Women - J.D. Christilian   1077
Whirlwind in Petticoats - Beril Becker   406

FEMME FATALE

Catherine
At the Sign of the Reine Pedauque - Anatole
  France   2198

Esmond, Beatrix
Henry Esmond - William Makepeace
  Thackeray   6212

FIANCE(E)

Ah-Wen-Ga
Tomahawk - Donald Clayton Porter 5129

Ayres, Judith
The Trembling Earth - Dale Van Every 6411

Beguildy, Jancis
Precious Bane - Mary Webb 6590

Blake, Marah
Bridal Journey - Dale Van Every 6406

Carbury, Jessica
Promises to Keep - Jocelyn Stirling 6051

de Barberie, Alinda
The Water Witch - James Fenimore Cooper 1311

Devenish, Alain
The Noblest Frailty - Patricia Veryan 6474

Eleanor
The Leopard Unleashed - Elizabeth Chadwick 967

Featherstone, Angela
Mandalay - Alexandra Jones 3269

Gilmore, Delia
Devil's Fire, Love's Revenge - Barbara Paul 4836

Greenham, Joel
The Black Swan - Philippa Carr 917

Haliwell, Leonie
Mistress of Willowvale - Patricia Veryan 6471

Johnson, Emily
Seminole - Donald Clayton Porter 5126

Knowles, Kathy
Bride of Liberty - Frank Yerby 6909

Little Emily
The Real David Copperfield - Robert Graves 2551

Lucia
The Betrothed - Alessandro Manzoni 4078

MacDonald, Arabella
Follow the Drum - James Leasor 3699

Mildway, Sarah
Lady of Mallow - Dorothy Eden 1856

Novus, Hortensius
Venus in Copper - Lindsey Davis 1534

Poldark, Clowance
The Miller's Dance - Winston Graham 2528

Presteigne, Lady Harriet
The Foundling - Georgette Heyer 2888

Sarn, Prudence
Precious Bane - Mary Webb 6590

Sedgwick, Ellen
Somewhere Within This House - Jean Francis Webb 6587

Sinclair, Matthew
Mandalay - Alexandra Jones 3269

Steinfinnsdatter, Ingunn
The Axe - Sigrid Undset 6378

Strand, Rachel
Feather Castles - Patricia Veryan 6462

Susannah
Where the River Runs - Richard S. Wheeler 6664

Tabor, Elizabeth "Baby Doe"
Wilde West - Walter Satterthwait 5609

Trevor, Anne
Pilgrims in Paradise - Frank G. Slaughter 5895

Zotica, Severina
Venus in Copper - Lindsey Davis 1534

FINANCIER

Armagh, Joseph
Captains and the Kings - Taylor Caldwell 851

Astor, John Jacob
Bright Journey - August Derleth 1614
River to the West: A Novel of the Astor Adventure - John Edward Jennings 3204

Benedict, Adam
Home Station - Jeanne Williams 6778

Brady, James "Diamond Jim"
Fenwick Travers and the Panama Canal - Raymond M. Saunders 5613

Carnegie, Andrew
The Americans - John Jakes 3143
The Robber Baroness - William Kendall Clarke 1097
Thine Is the Glory - Samuel A. Schreiner Jr. 5672

Ching, Joshua
Wanderers Eastward, Wanderers West - Kathleen Winsor 6823

Coeur, Jacques
The Burnished Blade - Lawrence Schoonover 5661
The Moneyman - Thomas B. Costain 1368

Cooper, Peter
All This, and Heaven Too - Rachel Field 2080
Certain Harvest: A Novel of the Time of Peter Cooper - Ruth Adams Knight 3525

Cruz, Artemio
The Death of Artemio Cruz - Carlos Fuentes 2246

Drew, Daniel
The Bank - Stephen Longstreet 3882

Fisk, James
The Bank - Stephen Longstreet 3882
Casey - Ramona Stewart 6034
Jubilee Jim and the Wizard of Wall Street - Donald Porter 5112
Tassels on Her Boots - Arthur Cheney Train 6313

Frick, Henry Clay
Thine Is the Glory - Samuel A. Schreiner Jr. 5672

Gould, Jay
The Bank - Stephen Longstreet 3882
Bread and Circus - Morris Renek 5303
Jubilee Jim and the Wizard of Wall Street - Donald Porter 5112
The Spoils of War - Thomas Fleming 2131
The Warriors - John Jakes 3155

Green, Hetty
The Robber Baroness - William Kendall Clarke 1097

Greenleaf, James
Portrait of a Scoundrel - Nathaniel Benchley 438

Hearst, William Randolph
Hollywood: A Novel of America in the 1920s - Gore Vidal 6488
Loving Little Egypt - Thomas McMahon 4288
The Spoils of War - Thomas Fleming 2131
That Vanderbilt Woman - Philip Van Rensselaer 6427
Yellow: A Novel - Daniel Lynch 3932

Hill, James
Path of the Sun - Al Dempsey 1608

Hill, James J.
The Living - Annie Dillard 1644

Hill, John J.
Sherlock Holmes and the Red Demon - Larry Millett 4404

Hudson, George
The Iron Roads - Forbes Bramble 644

Hughes, Howard
The Howard Hughes Affair - Stuart M. Kaminsky 3340

Insull, Samuel
Organized Crime - Nicholas Von Hoffman 6511

Law, John
The Gamester - Rafael Sabatini 5550

Lubloff, Arthur
Hanover Place - Michael M. Thomas 6245

Matlock, John Tyler
Tenants of the Earth - Sandra Paretti 4793

Medici, Cosimo de'
Niccolo Rising - Dorothy Dunnett 1803
The Spring of the Ram - Dorothy Dunnett 1809

Miranda, Micky
A Dangerous Fortune - Ken Follett 2147

Morgan, John Pierpont
The Alienist - Caleb Carr 907
The Bank - Stephen Longstreet 3882
No Honeymoon for Death - Mary Kruger 3564
One Night in Newport - Elizabeth Villars 6498

Morris, Robert
Mistress of the Forge - David Taylor 6179
Portrait of a Scoundrel - Nathaniel Benchley 438

Oakes, Sir Harry
Carnal Hours - Max Allan Collins 1210

Plant, Henry B.
I Take This Land - Richard Powell 5147

Poynder, Loftus
Tenants of the Earth - Sandra Paretti 4793

Rhodes, Cecil John
Men of Men - Wilbur Smith 5927

Rockefeller, John D.
The Bank - Stephen Longstreet 3882
Full of Thy Riches - Elizabeth Ferrell 2070
The Strenuous Life - Lawrence Alexander 84
Thine Is the Glory - Samuel A. Schreiner Jr. 5672

Rothschild, Nathan
Beyond Desire: A Novel Based on the Life of Felix and Cecille Mendelssohn - Pierre La Mure 3574
The Four Hundred - Stephen Sheppard 5804

Solomon, Haym
Haym Solomon, Son of Liberty - Howard Fast 2032

Stanford, Leland
The Fast Men - Tom McNab 4302

Starkweather, Howard Harrison
The Bank - Stephen Longstreet 3882

Starkweather, Tyler
The Bank - Stephen Longstreet 3882

Van Fleet, Bartholomew
Saratoga Trunk - Edna Ferber 2062

Van Nest, Samuel
One Night in Newport - Elizabeth Villars 6498

Van Rensselaer, Jurgen
The Copperheads - William James Blech 544

Vanderbilt, Cornelius
The Bank - Stephen Longstreet 3882
Bread and Circus - Morris Renek 5303
Jubilee Jim and the Wizard of Wall Street - Donald Porter 5112

Weyerhaeuser, Frederick
The Living - Annie Dillard 1644

FIRE FIGHTER

O'Neill, Charlie
Masters of Illusion: A Novel of the Connecticut Circus Fire - Mary-Ann Tirone Smith 5925

FISHERMAN

Baxter, August
Eye of the Hurricane - Fergus Reid Buckley   757

Clarke, Micah
Micah Clarke - Sir Arthur Conan Doyle   1715

Lavette, Dan
The Immigrants - Howard Fast   2034

Llewellyn, Davy
The Maid of Sker - R.D. Blackmore   529

Myran, Kristaver
The Last of the Vikings - Johan Bojer   563

Myran, Lars
The Last of the Vikings - Johan Bojer   563

Pascoe, Harry
Armada - Charles Gidley   2404

Tallack, Brice
Polsinney Harbour - Mary E. Pearce   4863

Tallack, Gus
Polsinney Harbour - Mary E. Pearce   4863

Wright, Jonathan
Eye of the Hurricane - Fergus Reid Buckley   757

FOUNDLING

Aylsham, Alyne
Lord of Ravensley - Constance Heaven   2809

Barrett, Topaze
The Golden Harlot - Jeanne Wilson   6808

Belinda
The Foundling - Georgette Heyer   2888

Browne, Lucy
Lucy - Hester W. Chapman   992

Hornbrook, Cathie
A Dream of Kings - Davis Grubb   2604

Jamie
The Street Sparrows - Rose Ayers   249

London, Ben
London's Child - Philip Boast   560

Sam
The Sound of Coaches - Leon Garfield   2295

Smith, Meg
The Street Sparrows - Rose Ayers   249

Thursday, Tessa
The Far-Off Rhapsody - Anne-Marie Sheridan   5808

FRONTIERSMAN

Albine, Salathiel
Bedford Village - Hervey Allen   99
The Forest and the Fort - Hervey Allen   100
Toward the Morning - Hervey Allen   101

Appleseed, Johnny
Reckon with the River - Clark McMeekin   4292
The Tree of Life - Hugh Nissenson   4629

Banks, Rafe
As Long as the Rivers Run - Sam J. Slate   5882

Beam, Michael
Michael Beam - Richard Hallet   2663

Bean, Ellis
Gone to Texas - Don Worcester   6871

Beard, William
To Fell the Giants - Bill Hotchkiss   3038

Beck, Morgan
The American River - Gary McCarthy   4222

Benton, Andrew
This Land Is Ours - Louis Zara   6953

Bolivar, Hogshead
Fury in the Earth: A Novel of the New Madrid Earthquake - Harry Harrison Kroll   3557

Boone, Daniel
Becky Landers, Frontier Warrior - Constance Skinner   5879
Black Forest - Meade Minnigerode   4411
Boone: A Novel Based on the Life and Times of Daniel Boone - Cameron Judd   3311
Buckskin Cavalier - John Clagett   1082
Cherokee - Donald Clayton Porter   5115
The Court Martial of Daniel Boone - Allen W. Eckert   1840
The Crossing - Winston Churchill   1080
Flintlock - Jason Manning   4073
The Frontiersmen - Allen W. Eckert   1841
The Kentuckians - Janice Holt Giles   2413
Kentucky Stand - Jere Hungerford Wheelwright   6670
The Long Rifle - Stewart Edward White   6702
Never No More: The Story of Rebecca Boone - Shirley Seifert   5730
Oh, Kentucky! - Betty Layman Receveur   5284
Panther in the Sky - James Alexander Thom   6234
That Dark and Bloody River - Allen W. Eckert   1845
Thunder on the River - Charlton Laird   3590
Vision of the Eagle - Kay L. McDonald   4263
Wilderness Empire - Allen W. Eckert   1847

Bowie, Jim
The Bugles Are Silent: A Novel of the Texas Revolution - John R. Knaggs   3513
The Iron Mistress - Paul I. Wellman   6618
The Road to San Jacinto - James F. Davis   1524
Tempered Blade - Monte Barrett   352
Texas - James A. Michener   4375

Braden, Whip
The Medicine Whip - Max Hennessy   2835

Bridger, Jim
Across the Shining Mountains - Christian McCord   4226
Kelly Blue - Peter Bowen   601
Kings of the Missouri - Hugh Pendexter   4895
Red Cloud's Revenge - Terry C. Johnston   3255

Briggs, George
The Homesman - Glendon Swarthout   6143

Brown, Caesar
West Goes the Road - Tim Pridgen   5192

Brules, Cat
The Scout - Harry Combs   1224

Buchanan, Murdoch
Rebel Guns - Adam Rutledge   5539

Buckmaster, Jim
Big River, Big Man - Thomas William Duncan   1786

Bumppo, Natty
The Deerslayer - James Fenimore Cooper   1299
The Last of the Mohicans - James Fenimore Cooper   1302
The Pathfinder; or, The Inland Sea - James Fenimore Cooper   1305
The Pioneers; or, The Sources of the Susquehanna - James Fenimore Cooper   1307
The Prairie - James Fenimore Cooper   1308

Burnett, Andy
Folded Hills - Stewart Edward White   6701
The Long Rifle - Stewart Edward White   6702
Ranchero - Stewart Edward White   6703

Butterworth, Jack
The Hider - Loren D. Estleman   1972

Callaway, Mike
Slow Dies the Thunder - Helen Topping Miller   4395

Cameron, Wayne
Western Union - Zane Grey   2589

Cardiff, Hugh
Wild Times - Brian Garfield   2291

Carson, Kit
The Bear Flag: A Novel of the Birth of California - Cecelia Holland   2983
Death Comes for the Archbishop - Willa Cather   957
Dream West - David Nevin   4587
Heartland - Robert Douglas Mead   4316
Hill of the Hawk - Scott O'Dell   4689
Immortal Wife - Irving Stone   6057
Kelly Blue - Peter Bowen   601
The Pioneers - Courtney Ryley Cooper   1296
Soldier in Buckskin - Ray Hogan   2981
Wolf Song - Harvey Fergusson   2069

Cartier, Jean
Return to the River - Don Coldsmith   1184

Cartier, Jean "Woodchuck"
The Flower in the Mountains - Don Coldsmith   1175

Charbonneau, Jean Baptiste
Sacajawea - Anna Lee Waldo   6529

Charbonneau, Toussaint
Forward the Nation - Donald Culross Peattie   4880

Chesnut, Ross
The Vision Is Fulfilled - Kay L. McDonald   4262

Chestnut, Ross
The Brightwood Expedition - Kay L. McDonald   4261

Chisholm, Jesse
Heartland - Robert Douglas Mead   4316

Chouteau, Auguste
Savanna - Janice Holt Giles   2416

Clark, George Rogers
Alice of Old Vincennes - Maurice Thompson   6268
The Seekers - John Jakes   3153
This Land Is Ours - Louis Zara   6953
Westward the Tide - Harold Sinclair   5863

Clark, John
From Sea to Shining Sea - James Alexander Thom   6232

Clark, William
Bridal Journey - Dale Van Every   6406

Cobden, Joe
Heart of the Country - Greg Matthews   4190

Cody, William F.
Aces and Eights: A Novel of the Legend of Wild Bill Hickok - Loren D. Estleman   1967
The Big Stick - Lawrence Alexander   82
Black Sun - Terry C. Johnston   3242
Buffalo Girls - Larry McMurtry   4296
Castle Garden - Bill Albert   63
Crazy Fox Remembers - Don Preston   5174
A Good Day to Die - Thomas Wakefield Blackburn   525
Homeland - John Jakes   3148
The Jewelled Spur - Gilbert Morris   4465
Kelly Blue - Peter Bowen   601
Last Go Round - Ken Kesey   3473
The Secret Annie Oakley - Marcy Moran Heidish   2819
Shaggy Legion - Hal George Evarts   1986
This Old Bill - Loren D. Estleman   1980
Trumpet on the Land - Terry C. Johnston   3260
Wild Times - Brian Garfield   2291
Yellowstone Kelly - Peter Bowen   602

Coleman, Breck
Shaggy Legion - Hal George Evarts   1986

Collins, Leslie
The Kentucky Trace: A Novel of the American Revolution - Harriette Simpson Arnow   195

Colt, Chris
Chief of Scouts - Don Bendell   439

Colter, John
The Man of the Storm - Ethel Hueston   3069

Colter, Joshua
The Border Men - Cameron Judd 3312
The Overmountain Men - Cameron Judd 3315

Cooper, David
The Kentuckians - Janice Holt Giles 2413

Crabb, Jack
Little Big Man - Thomas Berger 478

Crane, John
Gathering Storm - Bill Gulick 2613
Lost Wallowa - Bill Gulick 2616

Crane, Matt
Distant Trails - Bill Gulick 2612

Cravat, Yancey
Cimarron - Edna Ferber 2061

Cresap, Michael
Song of the Susquehanna - Herbert Stover 6071

Crockett, Davy
All the Brave Rifles - Clarke Venable 6450
As Long as the Rivers Run - Sam J. Slate 5882
The Bugles Are Silent: A Novel of the Texas Revolution - John R. Knaggs 3513
Crockett of Tennessee: A Novel Based on the Life and Times of David Crockett - Cameron Judd 3314
Empire of Bones: A Novel of Sam Houston and the Texas Revolution - Jeff Long 3868
The Furies - John Jakes 3146
Hearts of Hickory - John Trotwood Moore 4442
Horseshoe Bend - Bruce Palmer 4779
Oh, Promised Land - James H. Street 6079
The Road to San Jacinto - James F. Davis 1524
The Road to San Jacinto - Leonard L. Foreman 2167
Texas - James A. Michener 4375
Wave High the Banner - Dee Brown 714

Currie, Tom
The Raid - John Brick 673

Dabney, Sam
Oh, Promised Land - James H. Street 6079

Dale, Erskine
Erskine Dale, Pioneer - John Fox 2195

Davis, Aaron
Journey by the River - John Prescott 5173

Dickinson, James
The Phantom Emperor - Neil Harmon Swanson 6140

Dousman, Hercules
Bright Journey - August Derleth 1614

DuBois, Baptiste
Fort De Chastaigne - Don Coldsmith 1177

Ferguson, James
Next to Valour - John Edward Jennings 3202

Fink, Mike
Child of the Snapping Turtle, Mike Fink - Julian Lee Rayford 5256
Louisiana Purchase - A.E. Hotchner 3039
The Robber Bridegroom - Eudora Welty 6623

Fitzpatrick, Tom
Across the Shining Mountains - Christian McCord 4226

Fowler, Tice
Hannah Fowler - Janice Holt Giles 2411

Frane, Adam
The Captive Witch - Dale Van Every 6407

Fremont, John C.
Immortal Wife - Irving Stone 6057
Jessie: A Novel Based on the Life of Jessie Benton Fremont - Judy Alter 120
The Smoky Hill - Don Coldsmith 1188
Soldier in Buckskin - Ray Hogan 2981

Gallagher, Ross
Vision of the Eagle - Kay L. McDonald 4263

Gaunt, Adam
Passage Home - Alison McLeay 4286

Girty, James
Bridal Journey - Dale Van Every 6406

Girty, Simon
Bridal Journey - Dale Van Every 6406
Buckskin Cavalier - John Clagett 1082
Strife Before Dawn - Mary Schumann 5675
That Dark and Bloody River - Allen W. Eckert 1845
Wilderness Empire - Allen W. Eckert 1847

Gower, Colby
Bridal Journey - Dale Van Every 6406

Greenfall, Jonathan
No Road Too Long - Hildegarde Hawthorne 2785

Guard, Philip
Westward the Tide - Harold Sinclair 5863

Hale, Shoshoni
Harry Idaho - Hugh Pendexter 4894

Hawke, Lemuel
The Medicine Horn - Jory Sherman 5820
Trapper's Moon - Jory Sherman 5823

Hawke, Morgan
Trapper's Moon - Jory Sherman 5823

Hazard, Tom
Tennessee Hazard - Maristan Chapman 994

Hickok, James Butler
Aces and Eights: A Novel of the Legend of Wild Bill Hickok - Loren D. Estleman 1967
Crazy Fox Remembers - Don Preston 5174
Deadwood - Pete Dexter 1638
Elkhorn Tavern - Douglas C. Jones 3278
Flashman and the Redskins - George MacDonald Fraser 2208
The Lawless - John Jakes 3149
Little Big Man - Thomas Berger 478
Shaggy Legion - Hal George Evarts 1986
Wild Times - Brian Garfield 2291

Holden, Chris
The Unconquered - Neil Harmon Swanson 6142

Holt, Clay
Expedition! - Dana Fuller Ross 5473
Outpost! - Dana Fuller Ross 5486
Westward! - Dana Fuller Ross 5492

Holt, Jefferson
Expedition! - Dana Fuller Ross 5473
Outpost! - Dana Fuller Ross 5486
Westward! - Dana Fuller Ross 5492

Holt, Michael "Whip"
California! - Dana Fuller Ross 5467
Independence! - Dana Fuller Ross 5476
Nebraska! - Dana Fuller Ross 5480
Nevada! - Dana Fuller Ross 5481
Oregon! - Dana Fuller Ross 5484
Texas! - Dana Fuller Ross 5490
Wyoming! - Dana Fuller Ross 5494

Holt, Toby
Arizona! - Dana Fuller Ross 5466
Celebration! - Dana Fuller Ross 5470
Dakota! - Dana Fuller Ross 5472
Illinois! - Dana Fuller Ross 5475
Kentucky! - Dana Fuller Ross 5477
Montana! - Dana Fuller Ross 5479
Oklahoma! - Dana Fuller Ross 5482
Tennessee! - Dana Fuller Ross 5489
Wisconsin! - Dana Fuller Ross 5493

Houston, Sam
Walk in My Soul - Lucia St. Clair Robson 5418

Howard, Matthew
The Tree of Liberty - Elizabeth Page 4773

Howard, Sam
To Build a Ship - Don Berry 482

Husband, Harmon
The Wind in the Forest - Inglis Fletcher 2143

Irons, Jack
In the Days of Poor Richard - Irving A. Bacheller 259

Irwin, Charles Button
Prairie - Anna Lee Waldo 6528

Jameson, Isaac
Jordan County: A Landscape in Narrative - Shelby Foote 2152

Jeffords, Thomas
Blood Brother - Elliott Arnold 190

Jode, Don
Shadows in the Dusk - John Edward Jennings 3208

Jones, Nathaniel "Flintlock"
The Border Captains - Jason Manning 4072
Flintlock - Jason Manning 4073
Gone to Texas - Jason Manning 4074

Jones, Samuel
The Last Ride - Tom Eidson 1899

Jordan, Duncan
Scarlet Feather - Dale Van Every 6409

Kenton, Simon
The Frontiersmen - Allen W. Eckert 1841
Kentucky Stand - Jere Hungerford Wheelwright 6670

Killefer, Owen
The Canebrake Men - Cameron Judd 3313

Kirk, Egan
Father of Waters - Donald Clayton Porter 5118

Lacey, Jonathan
O Beulah Land - Mary Lee Settle 5756

Lenoir, Pierre
The Strangers on the Island - Brand Whitlock 6714

Lewis, James
I, James Lewis - Gilbert Wolf Gabriel 2266

Lewis, Michael
Sons of Texas - Tom Early 1822

Lewis, Mordecai
Sons of Texas - Tom Early 1822

Locke, Dan
Fire in the Sky - J.A. Shears 5785

Lorrenes, Marc de
The Gilded Torch - Iola Fuller 2252

MacCullough, Andrew
The River Devils - Carter A. Vaughan 6437

MacDonald, Major Angus
Trapper's Moon - Jory Sherman 5823

MacDonald, David
Pemmican - Vardis Fisher 2111

MacGregor, Baril
The Forbidden Ground - Neil Harmon Swanson 6138

MacLeod, Alastair
The Hunting Shirt - Mary Johnston 3235

MacLeod, Randal
River of Sky - Karen Harper 2713

Maitland, Keith
Strife Before Dawn - Mary Schumann 5675

Markham, Will
Fortress Fury - Carter A. Vaughan 6435

McAllister, Jamie
Eyes of Eagles - William W. Johnstone 3266

McCloud, Noah
Albuquerque - Sara Orwig 4757

McDermott, Angus
Shadow of the Long Knives - Thomas Alexander Boyd   615

McGill, Peter Hermano
Blessed McGill - Edwin Shrake   5834

McKenzie, Benton
Plume Rouge: A Novel of the Pathfinders - John Upton Terrell   6203

McKillop, Jim
The Kingdom Carver - E.G. Perrault   4916

McLaughlin, James
Shadow Catcher - Charles Fergus   2064

Miller
Butcher's Crossing - John Williams   6786

Moore, Jonas
Look to the Mountain - Le Grand Cannon   885

Morgan, Liverpool
Gone the Dreams and the Dancing - Douglas C. Jones   3279

Morris, Basdel
A Virginia Scout - Hugh Pendexter   4899

Morrow, Tom
Follow the River - Albert Mayer   4203

Mountain, Joe
Remember Santiago - Douglas C. Jones   3280

Mulock, Ranse
Distant Music - Harold Lenoir Davis   1521

Muncie, Peter
Arizona - Clarence Budington Kelland   3387

Norwell, Stephen
Bloodbrothers - Robert E. Wall   6535

O'Rourke, Rocheblave Xavier
River to the West: A Novel of the Astor Adventure - John Edward Jennings   3204

Paddock, Josiah
Carry the Wind - Terry C. Johnston   3246

Pardee, Eban
Down From the Mountain - Louis Charbonneau   997

Pardee, Gage
Down From the Mountain - Louis Charbonneau   997

Patterson, Morgan
The Woodsman - Don Wright   6880

Peace, Frank
Trouble Shooter - Ernest Haycox   2791

Pierneau, Pierre Chalfonte
Wind over Wisconsin - August Derleth   1620

Rapaho
Rapaho - Jamie Lee Cooper   1314

Rawley, Charles
Killdeer Mountain - Dee Brown   713

Richtier, Martin Jon
Powder Mission - Herbert Stover   6070

Rivet, Francois
The Gates of the Mountains - Will Henry   2842

Rogers, Robert
Northwest Passage - Kenneth Roberts   5388
Wilderness Empire - Allen W. Eckert   1847

Rostov, Anton
The Russian River - Gary McCarthy   4224

Sackett, Flagon
The Sky-Liners - Louis L'Amour   3629

Sackett, Galloway
The Sky-Liners - Louis L'Amour   3629

Sackett, Jubal
Jubal Sackett - Louis L'Amour   3620

Sackett, Orin
The Daybreakers - Louis L'Amour   3619
Lonely on the Mountain - Louis L'Amour   3621
Treasure Mountain - Louis L'Amour   3631

Sackett, Tell
Lonely on the Mountain - Louis L'Amour   3621
The Sackett Brand - Louis L'Amour   3627

Sackett, Tyrel
The Daybreakers - Louis L'Amour   3619
Lonely on the Mountain - Louis L'Amour   3621

Schantz, Johann Sebastian
A High Wind Rising - Elsie Singmaster   5867

Scott, Jordan
Visions of a Heart - Emily Carmichael   899

Sevier, John
The Cumberland Rifles - Noel B. Gerson   2365
Red Belts - Hugh Pendexter   4897
Tennessee Hazard - Maristan Chapman   994

Shelby
Maximilian's Gold - Jane Barry   359

Sky-Eyes
The Flower in the Mountains - Don Coldsmith   1175
Medicine Knife - Don Coldsmith   1179
Return to the River - Don Coldsmith   1184

Smith, James
The First Rebel - Neil Harmon Swanson   6137

Smith, John
The Ladies of Missalonghi - Colleen McCullough   4237

Spencer, Tom
Wild Horizon - F. van Wyck Mason   4164

Starbuck, Jason
Yankee Pasha - Edison Marshall   4115

Stewart, William
Running West - James Houston   3052

Storm, Caleb
Sunflower - Jill Marie Landis   3653

Sublette, Milt
Across the Shining Mountains - Christian McCord   4226

Summers, Dick
The Way West - A.B. Guthrie Jr.   2628

Talon, Jean
Rivers West - Louis L'Amour   3626

Thaler, Ben
To Build a Ship - Don Berry   482

Travis, Colt
Thunder on the Plains - Rosanne Bittner   517

Tyler, Clardy
Passage to Natchez - Cameron Judd   3316

Van Buren, Frederic
The Silent Drum - Neil Harmon Swanson   6141

Vaughn, Warren
To Build a Ship - Don Berry   482

Vickers, Steve
Rainbow Road - Davenport Steward   6016

Wagenet, Sierra Dave
To the Swift - Anne Hawkins   2783

Walford, Gabe
Liveliest Town in the West - Bill Gulick   2615

Warne, Ewen
Beulah Land - Harold Lenoir Davis   1520

Watley, Sam
Shadows on the Long House - Mike Roarke   5360
Silent Drums - Mike Roarke   5361
Thunder in the East - Mike Roarke   5362

Watley, Thad
Shadows on the Long House - Mike Roarke   5360

Silent Drums - Mike Roarke   5361
Thunder in the East - Mike Roarke   5362

Weiser, Conrad
A High Wind Rising - Elsie Singmaster   5867
The Interpreter - Robert Moss   4499
Song of the Susquehanna - Herbert Stover   6071

Wetzel, Lewis
That Dark and Bloody River - Allen W. Eckert   1845

White River
Beyond the Stars - David William Ross   5497

Winslow, Christmas
The Holy Warrior - Gilbert Morris   4462

Winslow, Sky
The Reluctant Bridegroom - Gilbert Morris   4467

Wyeth, Nathaniel J.
Across the Shining Mountains - Christian McCord   4226

Yancey, Don
Shadows in the Dusk - John Edward Jennings   3208

FRONTIERSWOMAN

Addison, Margaret
For Love of Two Eagles - Barbara Riefe   5328
The Woman Who Fell From the Sky - Barbara Riefe   5330

Burk, Martha Jane Cannary
Buffalo Girls - Larry McMurtry   4296
Calamity Jane of Deadwood Gulch - Ethel Hueston   3068
Crazy Fox Remembers - Don Preston   5174
Deadwood - Pete Dexter   1638
The Lawless - John Jakes   3149
Little Big Man - Thomas Berger   478

Burns, Tommy Jo
Cherokee Rose: A Novel of America's First Cowgirl - Judy Alter   119

Cochrane, Joanna
The Forest Lord - Noel B. Gerson   2368

Cuddy, Mary Bee
The Homesman - Glendon Swarthout   6143

Deal, Abbie
A Lantern in Her Hand - Bess Streeter Aldrich   69

Elder, Kate
Doc Holliday's Woman - Jane Candia Coleman   1201

James, Zerelda Cole
Mamaw - Susan Dodd   1663

Oakley, Annie
Buffalo Girls - Larry McMurtry   4296
Crazy Fox Remembers - Don Preston   5174
The Secret Annie Oakley - Marcy Moran Heidish   2819
Sherlock Holmes Meets Annie Oakley - Stanley Shaw   5782

O'Keefe, Raven
Sword of Vengeance - Kerry Newcomb   4593

Olmstead, Kate
Eyes of Eagles - William W. Johnstone   3266

Rutter, Ada Belle
The Velvet Horn - Andrew Lytle   3946

Sanderson, Lydia
The Jump-Off Creek - Molly Gloss   2435

Schantz, Anna Sabilla
A High Wind Rising - Elsie Singmaster   5867

Starr, Belle
Belle Starr - Speer Morgan   4453

Susannah
Where the River Runs - Richard S. Wheeler   6664

Van Meeteren, Analisa
Sunflower - Jill Marie Landis 3653

Venable, Sabra
Cimarron - Edna Ferber 2061

Wingate, Ann
So Free We Seem - Helen Todd 6286

FUGITIVE

Ansculfson, Aelfred
Red Lion and Gold Dragon - Rosemary
Sprague 5969

Breault, Blaise de
Scarlet Cockerel - Clifford Sublette 6110

Brent, Tara
Runaway - Heather Graham 2519

Brien, Louise
Wild Geese - Eilis Dillon 1647

Brien, Robert
Wild Geese - Eilis Dillon 1647

Chandler, Quentin
Practice to Deceive - Patricia Veryan 6475

Christian, Fletcher
Mister Christian - William Kinsolving 3502

Craigvalloch, Ian
Red Cloak Flying - Margaret Widdemer 6737

Dalton, Tyler
Outlaw Lover - Lindsey Hanks 2676

Doone, Ligun
Journey to Enchantment - Patricia Veryan 6464

Drusus, Cailin
To Love Again - Bertrice Small 5913

Glendenning, Horatio
Love Alters Not - Patricia Veryan 6467

Hanna, Caroline
Miami: A Saga - Evelyn Wilde Mayerson 4204

Heathers, Robert
A Candle in the Wilderness - Irving A.
Bacheller 256

Heydon, William
A Candle in the Wilderness - Irving A.
Bacheller 256

MacDonnell, Call
The Lonely Strangers - Charity Blackstock 531

MacGregor, Neil Roy
The Pointless Knife - Constance Dodge 1667

Naomi
Arouse and Beware - MacKinlay Kantor 3360

Quickskill, Raven
Flight to Canada - Ishmael Reed 5285

Sackett, Barnabas
Sackett's Land - Louis L'Amour 3628
To the Far Blue Mountains - Louis L'Amour 3630

Sackett, Nolan
Mustang Man - Louis L'Amour 3623

Stuart, Charles
The White Cockade - Henry Farrand Griffin 2592

Sutcliffe, Miriam
Visions of a Heart - Emily Carmichael 899

Swanson, Nat
St. Agnes' Stand - Tom Eidson 1900

Tornefeld, Christian von
The Swedish Cavalier - Leo Perutz 4943

Valjean, Jean
Cosette: The Sequel to Les Miserables - Laura
Kalpakian 3329

Vane, Richard
Weep in the Sun - Jeanne Wilson 6809

Vega, Isabel de la
1492: The Life and Times of Juan Cabezon of Castile -
Homero Aridjis 187

Youngman, Charles
Scent of Cloves - Norah Lofts 3859

GAMBLER

Baird, George Alexander
Bertie and the Tinman - Peter Lovesey 3909

Belden, Joshua
Birthright - Phillip Finch 2087

Connor, Rory
The Gambling Man - Catherine Cookson 1276

Cozad, John Jackson
Son of the Gamblin' Man: The Youth of an Artist -
Mari Sandoz 5593

Dena, Lottie
The Lady and Doc Holliday - Preston Lewis 3761

Figaro, Randolph
Fool's Coach - Richard S. Wheeler 6659

Fox, Stephen
The Foxes of Harrow - Frank Yerby 6917

Grantham, Deborah
Faro's Daughter - Georgette Heyer 2887

Hardacre, Shane
Fire Along the Sky: A Novel of America - Robert
Moss 4497

Holliday, John Henry
Bloody Season - Loren D. Estleman 1968
Confessions of Johnny Ringo - Geoff Aggeler 40
Doc Holliday's Woman - Jane Candia Coleman 1201
The Lady and Doc Holliday - Preston Lewis 3761
Wilde West - Walter Satterthwait 5609

King, Rufus
The Treasure of Pleasant Valley - Frank Yerby 6928

Lardner, Ring
Blue Ruin: A Novel of the 1919 World Series -
Brendan Boyd 610

Logan, Carey
Black Gold - Anita Richmond Bunkley 771

McAllister, Chance
Paint the Wind - Cathy Cash Spellman 5960

Morrow, Sloan
The Earth and All It Holds - V.J. Banis 287

Paris, George
Judith Paris - Hugh Walpole 6545

Ravenal, Gaylord
Show Boat - Edna Ferber 2063

Regret, Paul
The Comancheros - Paul I. Wellman 6616

Rothstein, Arnold
Blue Ruin: A Novel of the 1919 World Series -
Brendan Boyd 610

Sullivan, Joseph
Blue Ruin: A Novel of the 1919 World Series -
Brendan Boyd 610

Sutherland, Clay
Masque of Jade - Emma Merritt 4344

Tyne, Harry
Letty - Clare Darcy 1491

White, Brant
Saint Johnson - William R. Burnett 796

Wind River Kid
The Ghosts of Elkhorn - Kerry Newcomb 4589

GARDENER

Ellershaw, Jack
Willowwood - Mollie Hardwick 2699

GENTLEMAN

Acklen, Joseph
Dinner at Belmont - Alfred Leland Crabb 1398

Acock, Sir John
The Nunnery - Dorothy Charques 1001

Altondale, Toby
The Long Afternoon - Ursula Zilinsky 6964

Alypius
The Converts: A Historical Novel - Rex
Warner 6564

Amaurey, Hugo
Free Lance - George Shipway 5827

Archer, Cyril
Daphne - Marion Chesney 1022

Argentine, Giles
The Fate of Princes - P.C. Doherty 1673

Armagh, Rory
Captains and the Kings - Taylor Caldwell 851

Armstrong, Jonathan
The Distant Lands - Julian Green 2567

Ashleigh, Gilliard
A Question of Honour - Emma Drummond 1726

Ashleigh, Valentine
A Question of Honour - Emma Drummond 1726

Ashleigh, Vere
A Question of Honour - Emma Drummond 1726

Ashley, Peter
Peter Ashley - DuBose Heyward 2911

Astley, Thomas
Vows of the Peacock - Alice Walworth
Graham 2513

Atherton
Miss Philadelphia Smith - Paula Allardyce 91

Atherton-Moore, Edward
Winter of the Heart - Linda J. LaRosa 3665

Augustine
The Converts: A Historical Novel - Rex
Warner 6564

Aylsham, Oliver
Lord of Ravensley - Constance Heaven 2809

Baird, George Alexander
Bertie and the Tinman - Peter Lovesey 3909

Balfour, David
Catriona - Robert Louis Stevenson 6009

Balfrey, Francis
Killing Cousins - Alanna Knight 3520

Ballenrose
Ballenrose - Mallory Burgess 783

Barak, Bel
The Golden Crucible - Jean Stubbs 6096

Barnard, John
The Flint Anchor - Sylvia Townsend Warner 6569

Barnard, Sir Ralph
King's Agent - Justus Kent Clark 1090

Baron, Charles
Beau Barron's Lady - Helen Ashfield 204

Barrington, Timothy
The Love Child - Catherine Cookson 1279

Barton, Josh
Claudine's Daughter - Rosalind Laker 3594

Beaton, David
The Riven Realm - Nigel Tranter 6317

Beaufort, Jason
Marianne and the Crown of Fire - Juliette Benzoni 467

Beaumaris, Robert
Arabella - Georgette Heyer 2874

Beaumont, Anthony
The Tynedale Daughters - Norma Lee Clark 1093

Beaumont, Sir Charles
The Son of York - Margaret Abbey 5

Bellamy, James
The Bellamy Saga - John Pearson 4878

Bellamy, Richard
The Bellamy Saga - John Pearson 4878
Upstairs Downstairs - John Hawkesworth 2782

Bensham, Daniel
The Mallen Girl - Catherine Cookson 1280

Bentwood, Simon
Tilly Alone - Catherine Cookson 1289

Berrien, Beau
The Grasshopper King - Elizabeth Boatwright Coker 1165

Bertram, Edmund
Mansfield Revisited - Joan Aiken 51

Betchley, Eugene
The Legacy of Beulah Land - Lonnie Coleman 1203

Betram, Harry
Guy Mannering - Sir Walter Scott 5697

Bezuhov, Pierre
War and Peace - Leo Tolstoy 6295

Bickley, Francis
Annie - Gloria Jahoda 3141

Bishop, Edward
Trade Imperial - Alan Lloyd 3814

Bishop, Joel
Trade Imperial - Alan Lloyd 3814

Blackwood, Alexander
Sweet's Folly - Fiona Hill 2926

Blake, Rainer
In Still and Stormy Waters - Reay Tannahill 6157

Blecourt, Jean Pierre de
All the Golden Gifts - Iola Fuller 2251

Bliss, Simon
The King Edward Plot - Robert Lee Hall 2658

Bluett, Rodney
The Maid of Sker - R.D. Blackmore 529

Boisdesert, Louis-Auguste de
Heroic Dust - Theodora Dehon 1581

Boleyn, Thomas
Blood Royal - Mollie Hardwick 2690

Bolton, Francis
Jeremiah Martin: A Revolutionary War Novel - Robert H. Fowler 2191

Bonchurch, William
The Woman Question - Dorothea Malm 4046

Bonel, Gervase
Monk's Hood - Ellis Peters 4964

Borgia, Giovanni
The Scarlet City - Hella S. Haasse 2632

Boston, Lewis
The Prisoners of September - Leon Garfield 2294

Bottomley, Cameron
The Light Infantry Ball - Hamilton Basso 375

Bottomley, John
The Light Infantry Ball - Hamilton Basso 375

Boyd, Ledyard
The Boyds of Black River - Walter D. Edmonds 1871

Boyd, Robert
Bide Me Fair - Harvey Howells 3060

Brandon, Henry
My Lady Greensleeves - Constance Beresford-Howe 476

Brandon, Romilly
A Night in Cold Harbor - Margaret Kennedy 3420

Braxton, Jared
Masque of Enchantment - Charlene Cross 1432

Brayford, Hugo
Lucinda Brayford - Martin Boyd 613

Brett, Jeremy
Brimstone Club - F. van Wyck Mason 4147

Broadbent, Jim
Monday's Child - Mollie Hardwick 2697

Brodrick, Henry
Hungry Hill - Daphne Du Maurier 1746

Brooke-Hardinge, Anthony
Murder at the Palace - Elliott Roosevelt 5445

Broome, Philip
Cousin Kate - Georgette Heyer 2884

Brotherton, William
Charing Cross - Claire Rayner 5260

Browning, Jonathon
Before Darkness Falls - Eugenia Price 5178

Browning, Mark
Savannah - Eugenia Price 5186

Brummell, George Bryan
Beau Barron's Lady - Helen Ashfield 204
Brumaire - Mark Logan 3864
Edward, Edward - Lolah Burford 772
Guillotine - Mark Logan 3865
Rebel Heiress - Jane Aiken Hodge 2969
Regency Buck - Georgette Heyer 2898

Buchan, Lewis
The Fathers - Allen Tate 6171

Burke, Tom
Tom Burke of Ours - Charles James Lever 3732

Burlington, Edward
In the Shadow of the Nile - Sara Hylton 3093

Burnaby, Sir Harry
The Golden Days - Robert Neill 4569
Lillibullero - Robert Neill 4571

Burnaby, John
Lillibullero - Robert Neill 4571

Butler, Pierce
The Ardent Years - Janet Stevenson 6003

Caelius
The Key - Benita Kane Jaro 3169

Caelius, Marcus
Death on the Appian Way - Kenneth Benton 463

Calverleigh, Miles
Black Sheep - Georgette Heyer 2878

Calverleigh, Stacy
Black Sheep - Georgette Heyer 2878

Cameron, Lynn
Buckskin Cavalier - John Clagett 1082

Campbell, Gavin
A Falcon for a Queen - Catherine Gaskin 2314

Cannon, Tom
Twilight of the Dawn - Elizabeth Nell Dubus 1752

Cardew, Cornelius
The Shooting Party - Isabel Colegate 1197

Carew, Sir Charles
Prisoners of Hope: A Tale of Colonial Virginia - Mary Johnston 3238

Carey, Sir Andrew
The Carolinian - Rafael Sabatini 5547

Carlow, Vincent
Claire - Elizabeth Lyle 3931

Carlton, Roger
The Wizard's Daughter - Barbara Michaels 4362

Carr, Robert
The Murder in the Tower - Jean Plaidy 5035

Carrington, Nathaniel
The Time of the Dragon - Dorothy Eden 1863

Carrington, Philip
Lord of the Far Island - Victoria Holt 3016

Carruthers, Meredith
The Tyrant - Patricia Veryan 6480

Carter, Barry
Tassels on Her Boots - Arthur Cheney Train 6313

Carvel, Richard
Richard Carvel - Winston Churchill 1081

Cass, Dunstan
Silas Marner - George Eliot 1911

Castlemayne, Walter
The Blade of Castlemayne - Anthony Esler 1960

Cate, Christopher
By the Green of the Spring - John Masters 4171
Heart of War - John Masters 4174

Cateret, Quentin
The Belchamber Scandal - Frances Murray 4533

Cecil, Bertie
Under Two Flags - Ouida 4767

Chadmore, Julian
Paiute - Sessions S. Wheeler 6666

Challoner, Hamish
A Heritage and Its History - Ivy Compton-Burnett 1229

Chalmers, Rufus
The Branch-Bearers - Glen Petrie 4978

Chaloner, Simon
The Roaring Boy - Edward Marston 4127

Chandler, Sir Brian
Ask Me No Questions - Patricia Veryan 6459

Chartley, Richard
The Wildcliffe Bird - Constance Heaven 2811

Cherkkov, Vladimir
The Last Station - Jay Parini 4801

Chichley, Frederic
The Paper Mistress - Dorothea Malm 4045

Churchill, Frank
Jane Fairfax - Joan Aiken 50

Churchill, Randolph
Lillie - David Butler 818

Claiborne, Colin
McKensie's Hundred: A Tale of the Old Dominion - Frank Yerby 6924

Clayburn, Henry
The Raiders - William Edward Wilson 6819

Clifford, Guy
At the Sign of the Golden Pineapple - Marion Chesney 1016

Cobb, Henry
Sarah Cobb - Catherine M. Rae 5236

Coleman, Stuart
The Wide House - Taylor Caldwell 864

Colfax, Clarence
The Crisis - Winston Churchill 1079

Collingwood, James
My Pride, My Folly - Suzanne Butler 830

Connington, Drummond
The Tempestuous Petticoat - Mary Ann Gibbs 2397

Conroy, Sir John
The Captive of Kensington Palace - Jean
   Plaidy 5007
The Queen and Lord M - Jean Plaidy 5046
The Young Victoria - Tyler Whittle 6724

Cothburn, Ramsey
Star of Empire: A Novel of Old San Antonio - Leonard
   Sanders 5590

Cotta, Maximus
The Last World: A Novel with an Ovidian Repertory -
   Christoph Ransmayr 5253

Couville, Nigel
Satan in St. Mary's - P.C. Doherty 1676

Craddock, Jeremy
Whispering - Jane Aiken Hodge 2972

Cranston, John
The Nightingale Gallery - Paul Harding 2684
*Red Slayer: Being the Second of the Sorrowful
   Mysteries of Brother Athelstan* - Paul
   Harding 2685

Cranstoun, Willy
My Grand Enemy - Jean Stubbs 6098

Credi, Frederico Sforzi
The Palace of Wisdom - Bob Marshall-
   Andrews 4118

Cresswell, Joe
Midsummer's Eve - Philippa Carr 924

Crozat, Edmund
Blood & Dreams - Leslie Waller 6543

Crozier, Theodore
Dear Laura - Jean Stubbs 6094

Culpepper, Thomas
Katheryn, the Wanton Queen - Maureen Peters 4976
The Rose Without a Thorn - Jean Plaidy 5058

Curnow, Giles
A Woman Possessed - Malcolm Macdonald 3977

Curtwright, Alain
Devilseed - Frank Yerby 6914

Dallow, George
Teverton Hall - Jane Gillespie 2421

Damon, Victor
Scandal at High Chimneys: A Victorian Melodrama -
   John Dickson Carr 915

Danvers, Esmond
A Marriage of Convenience - Tim Jeal 3172

Darcy, Fitzwilliam
Pemberley, or Pride and Prejudice Continued - Emma
   Tennant 6201
*An Unequal Marriage; or Pride and Prejudice Twenty
   Years Later* - Emma Tennant 6202

Darrell, Thames
Jack Sheppard - William Harrison Ainsworth 56

Daunbey, Benjamin
A Brood of Vipers - Michael Clynes 1133
The Gallows Murder - Michael Clynes 1134
The Grail Murders - Michael Clynes 1135
The Poisoned Chalice - Michael Clynes 1136
The White Rose Murders - Michael Clynes 1137

Davis, Benjamin
Look Away, Beulah Land - Lonnie Coleman 1204

De Lancey, George
The Adventurers - William Stuart Long 3869

de Vargas, Pedro
Captain From Castille - Samuel Shellabarger 5794

Delaford, Samuel
The Standing Hills - Caroline Stickland 6038

Delamaine, James
Daughter of Marignac - Constance Heaven 2805

Delaney, Edward
The Far Journey - Loula Grace Erdman 1950

Demaury, Giles
Summoned to Darkness - Anne-Marie Sheridan 5809

Denton, Eric
Black Body - H.C. Turk 6361

Derham, Francis
Katheryn, the Wanton Queen - Maureen Peters 4976

Desmond, Arthur
Traitors Gate - Anne Perry 4939

Detling, Sir Arthur
The Detling Secret - Julian Symons 6151

Devaux, Nicolas
Tree of Gold - Rosalind Laker 3602

Devenham, Godfrey
The Malvie Inheritance - Pamela Hill 2938

Devereaux, Neville
Caroline and Julia - Clare Darcy 1484

Devereux, Malcolm
The Blade of Castlemayne - Anthony Esler 1960

Di Marco, Beltrame
The Borgia Prince - Pamela Bennetts 446

Digby, Fred
Kindred Spirits - June Barraclough 347

Diplock, Cecil
The Bright Blue Sky - Max Hennessy 2830
Once More the Hawks - Max Hennessy 2836

Donaldson, Simon
Albany - Laura Black 519

Donnithorne, Arthur
Adam Bede - George Eliot 1908

Douglas, Roger
Lady of Monkton - Elizabeth Byrd 835

Drakelon, Dominic
The Moon in the Water - Pamela Belle 433

Drakelon, Kit
Alethea - Pamela Belle 429

Drinkwater, Edward
The Bomb Vessel - Richard Woodman 6860

Drummle, Bentley
Estella - Alanna Knight 3519

Drummond, Sir Daniel
Reckless Angel - Jane Feather 2056

Dudley, Mark
Law of the Land - Marguerite Allis 111

Duncannon, Robert
Louisa Elliott - Ann Victoria Roberts 5370

Dupres, Darcy
The Argonauts - Yvonne Schoell 5645

Durrie, Henry
The Master of Ballantrae: A Winter's Tale - Robert
   Louis Stevenson 6011

Durrie, James
The Master of Ballantrae: A Winter's Tale - Robert
   Louis Stevenson 6011

Dynham, Sir Miles
The Wanton Fires - Meriol Trevor 6345

Dynham, Sir Rowland
The Fortunate Marriage - Meriol Trevor 6342

Eden, John
Eden and Honor - Marilyn Harris 2729
Eden Rising - Marilyn Harris 2731
The Women of Eden - Marilyn Harris 2734

Effingham, Champ
The Virginia Comedians - John Esten Cooke 1269

Elijah, Eliezar Ben
Threshold of Fire - Hella S. Haasse 2633

Elliott, Edward
Louisa Elliott - Ann Victoria Roberts 5370

Ellis, Geoffrey
Guns Forever Echo - Kenneth M. Ellis 1925

Endicott, Jack
The President's Man - Elliott Roosevelt 5455

Erskine, Oliver
Zemindar - Valerie Fitzgerald 2117

Esmond, Henry
Henry Esmond - William Makepeace
   Thackeray 6212

Evesden, Sir Godfrey
An Ancient Evil - C.L. Grace 2504

Eynesby, Lionel
Crown of Roses - Valerie Anand 127

Fairfax, George William
The Young Man From Mount Vernon - Arthur
   Stanwood Pier 4995

Falcon, Robert
Moonraker's Bride - Madeleine Brent 661

Falkenhorst, Albrecht von
Falkenhorst - Mark Rascovich 5254

Farebrother, Will
The Admiral's Lady - Mary Ann Gibbs 2395

Farmiloe, Richard
Daneclere - Pamela Hill 2931

Farr, Roland
Captain Vinegar's Commission - Philip
   Glazebrook 2428

Farrier, Charles
The Wingless Bird - Catherine Cookson 1292

Fenwick, Peregrine
The Old Enchantment - Sarah Neilan 4565

Ferrand, Francis
The Power and the Glory - Phyllis Bentley 462

Fervacques, Mauger de
Son of Dust - H.F.M. Prescott 5171

Field, Arthur
Tamzen - Jane Gilmore Rushing 5530

Field, Lafayette
The Rising Storm - Marguerite Allis 113

Field, Lancelot
The Rising Storm - Marguerite Allis 113

Filmore, Douglas
The Black Candle - Catherine Cookson 1273

Firle, Augustine
Shadows and Images - Meriol Trevor 6344

Fiske, Adam
The Red Cock Crows - Frances Gaither 2272

Fitzbolton, Robert
The Hawthorne Legacy - Teresa Crane 1416

Fitzgerald, Hugh
Wolf's Embrace - Gail Link 3801

Fitzgerald, Roland
The Black Swan - Philippa Carr 917

Flashman, Harry
Flash for Freedom - George MacDonald Fraser 2203
Flashman and the Angel of the Lord - George
   MacDonald Fraser 2205

Flashman and the Dragon - George MacDonald
Fraser 2206

Flashman and the Redskins - George MacDonald
Fraser 2208

Flashman's Lady - George MacDonald Fraser 2210

Fleming, Duncan
Saturday City - Jan Webster 6593

Fletcher, Judson
The Rebels - John Jakes 3152

Flory, John
Fire and Morning - Francis W. Leary 3696

Fortescue, James
The Favored Child - Philippa Gregory 2582

Frant, Martin
The Quiet Gentleman - Georgette Heyer 2897

Frant, Theodore
The Quiet Gentleman - Georgette Heyer 2897

Fraser, John
Drums - James Boyd 611

Fraser, John Couper
Beauty From Ashes - Eugenia Price 5177

Fraser, Rupert
Falls of Gard - Laura Black 520

Fraser, Tom
A World Too Wide - Susan Moore 4445

Frater, Simon
Crown Witness - Gillian Linscott 3803

Frayne, Dylan de
The Everlasting Covenant - Robyn Carr 939

Frenshaw, David
Voices in a Haunted Room - Philippa Carr 931

Frenshaw, Dickson
Knave of Hearts - Philippa Carr 920
Will You Love Me in September? - Philippa Carr 932

Frenshaw, Jonathan
Voices in a Haunted Room - Philippa Carr 931

Frinton, Jocelyn
The Love Child - Philippa Carr 923

Fuente, Ricardo de la
Takers of the City - Hoffman Reynolds Hays 2800

Gael, John de
Kathryn: In the Court of Six Queens - Anne Merton
Abbey 1

Galliard, Inigo
Daughter of Strangers - Elizabeth Boatwright
Coker 1164

Galvan, Don Angel
A City for St. Francis - Evelyn Wells 6621

Garcia, Pedro
Follow the Wind - Don Coldsmith 1176

Garvey, James
Married Past Redemption - Patricia Veryan 6469

Gates, Johnnie
Mistaken Virtues - Joanna Trollope 6349

Gaunt, Adam
Sea Change - Alison McLeay 4287

Gaunt, Griffith
Griffith Gaunt - Charles Reade 5280

Gaveston, Piers
Isabel the Fair - Margaret Campbell Barnes 323
The Prince of Darkness - P.C. Doherty 1675

Gerard, Sir Harry
A Season of Mists - Sarah Woodhouse 6856

Gerard, William
The Floral Companion - Anthea Bell 419

Gerrick, Mark
The Artist's Daughter - Leslie O'Grady 4698

Gilles, Sir Rafe
The Dark Stranger - Dorothy Charques 999

Glendinning, Edward
The Monastery - Sir Walter Scott 5701

Glendinning, Halbert
The Monastery - Sir Walter Scott 5701

Godefroi, Richard de
Sarum: The Novel of England - Edward
Rutherfurd 5536

Goodenough, Sir George
The Adventuress - Marion Chesney 1014

Grant, Richard
Wild Cat - Laura Black 524

Granville, Beaumont
The Love Child - Philippa Carr 923

Graylin, Andrew
The Black Sheep's Daughter - Carola Dunn 1791

Greenham, Joel
The Black Swan - Philippa Carr 917

Greenough, Malcolm
Dear Lily - Malcolm W. Greenough Jr. 2575

Greenwood, Frank
Jade - Pat Barr 344

Greville, Charles
The Passing Bells - Phillip Rock 5421

Grey, John
The King's Grey Mare - Rosemary Hawley
Jarman 3167

Guillet, Andre
Monsieur Yankee - Leslie Turner White 6689

Gullington, Laurence
The Black Velvet Gown - Catherine Cookson 1274

Gurney, Edwin
Monk's Hood - Ellis Peters 4964

Hamilton, Sir William
Shadow of a Lady - Jane Aiken Hodge 2971
Sir William - David Stacton 5977

Hanson, Rolf
Midsummer's Eve - Philippa Carr 924

Hardwick, George
Master of Morholm - Timothy R. Wilson 6817

Hardwick, James
Master of Morholm - Timothy R. Wilson 6817

Haredale, John
Barnaby Rudge: A Tale of the Riots of Eighty -
Charles Dickens 1641

Harley, Robert
The Queen's Favourites - Jean Plaidy 5051

Harris, Clayton
The Last Plantation - Don Wright 6879

Harvard, Peregrine
Lord Rivington's Lady - Eileen Jackson 3134

Harvey, David
The Long Afternoon - Ursula Zilinsky 6964

Harvie, Dion
Roanoke Renegade - Don Tracy 6311

Hatton, Christopher
Trust and Treason - Margaret Birkhead 506

Haybury, Frederick
Wings of the Morning - David Beaty 402

Hebworthy, Daniel
Flowers for Lilian - Anna Gilbert 2405

Herbert, Thomas
The Severed Crown - Jane Lane 3657

Heron, Christopher
The Lodestar - Pamela Belle 432

Heron, Francis
The Moon in the Water - Pamela Belle 433

Herries, Benjamin "Benjie"
Vanessa - Hugh Walpole 6548

Herries, Ellis
Vanessa - Hugh Walpole 6548

Herries, Walter
The Fortress - Hugh Walpole 6544

Herries, William
Judith Paris - Hugh Walpole 6545

Highet, Henry
The Country Gentleman - Fiona Hill 2924

Hillard, Sheldon
Storm Against the Wind - Helen Hull Jacobs 3138

Hillyard, David
The Eagle at the Gate - Rona Randall 5248

Hobhouse, John Cam
Lord of the Dead: The Secret History of Byron - Tom
Holland 2999

Holder, Nicholas
Bennett's Welcome - Inglis Fletcher 2132

Holmes, Mycroft
The Whitechapel Horrors - Edward B. Hanna 2678

Holyoke, Horace
Oldtown Folks - Harriet Beecher Stowe 6072

Hortensius
Hortensius, Friend of Nero - Edith Pargeter 4798

Houldway, Major Richard
Consort for Victoria - William Vaughan
Wilkins 6757

Howard, Colonel
The Pilot - James Fenimore Cooper 1306

Howard, Ashton
Sapphire - Helen Ashfield 214

Huffam, John
The Quincunx - Charles Palliser 4778

Hume, Julius
Mother and Son - Ivy Compton-Burnett 1231

Hume, Rosebery
Mother and Son - Ivy Compton-Burnett 1231

Hunter, Morgan
Cardigan Square - Alexandra Manners 4070

Ibbetson, Colonel
Peter Ibbetson - George Du Maurier 1750

Ibbetson, Peter
Peter Ibbetson - George Du Maurier 1750

Inglesant, Eustace
John Inglesant - John Henry Shorthouse 5833

Jan
Mass for Arras - Andrzej Szczypiorski 6153

Jasper, John
The Disappearance of Edwin Drood - Peter
Rowland 5521

Jermyn, Sir Aubrey
A Fatal Assignation - Alice Chetwynd Ley 3764

Jones, Charlie
The Distant Lands - Julian Green 2567
The Stars of the South - Julian Green 2568

Jones, Hacksem
The Latter Adventures of Tom Jones - Bob
Coleman 1200

Judd, Ajax
The Banishment - Marion Chesney 1018

Justin, Philip
Marsanne - Virginia Coffman 1155

Kade, David
Fire in the Ice - Alan Scholefield 5653

Kerr, Stephen
The Braeswood Tapestry - Robyn Carr 936

Kestrel, Julian
A Broken Vessel - Kate Ross 5500
Cut to the Quick - Kate Ross 5501
Whom the Gods Love - Kate Ross 5502

Keynes, Rowan
Lisbon - Valerie Sherwood 5825

Killegrew, Gervase
The Hounds of God - Rafael Sabatini 5551

Kim Il-Han
The Living Reed - Pearl S. Buck 756

Kingsford, Sir Hugh
Blood of the Boar - Margaret Abbey 2
The Heart Is a Traitor - Margaret Abbey 4

Kinnersley, Patrick
The Michaelmas Tree - Helen Ashfield 209

Knutsson, Colum
The Slow Awakening - Catherine Marchant 4082

Kybbet, Tom
Riot at Gravesend: A Novel of Wat Tyler's Rebellion -
   William Howard Woods 6864

Lacey, Sir Geoffrey
A Lady in Doubt - Annabel Wynne 6891

Lackland, Harry
Piccadilly - Claire Rayner 5267

Lackland, Jonah
Soho Square - Claire Rayner 5268

Lackland, Peter
Piccadilly - Claire Rayner 5267

Lamont, Rorie
Kilcaraig - Annabel Carothers 904

Langlinais, Claude
Cajun - Elizabeth Nell Dubus 1751

Lansdon, Benedict
The Changeling - Philippa Carr 918
The Pool of St. Branok - Philippa Carr 926

Larne, Philip
Deep Summer - Gwen Bristow 696

Larsen, Simon
The House of Memory: A Novel of Shanghai -
   Nicholas R. Clifford 1117

Larson, Erik
River of Dreams - Gay Courter 1390

Leibig, Vane
London's Child - Philip Boast 560

Leone, Achille
Contessa - Richard Oliver Collin 1209

Lester, Geoffrey
The Second Sister - Leslie O'Grady 4701

Lightbody, Will
The Road to Wellville - T. Coraghessan Boyle 618

Lindsay, David
James, by the Grace of God - Nigel Tranter 6315
The Riven Realm - Nigel Tranter 6317

Lingford, Henry
The Tempestuous Petticoat - Mary Ann Gibbs 2397

Linton, Edgar
H.—: The Story of Heathcliff's Journey Back to
   Wuthering Heights - Lin Haire-Sargeant 2641

Little, Will
Willowwood - Elizabeth Savage 5619

Loam, Fred
The Girl - Catherine Cookson 1277

Lockhart, Randall
Twilight of the Dragon - Peter Bourne 596

Lorme, Henry
Shadows over Castle Rising - Fanny Cradock 1410
Wind of Change at Castle Rising - Fanny
   Cradock 1412

Lovell, Francis
The White Boar - Marian Palmer 4780

Lovell, Phillip
The White Boar - Marian Palmer 4780

Lovell, Richard
The Bracegirdle - Burris Atkins Jenkins 3189

Lucero, Don Juan
The Adventures of Don Juan - Richard Gardner 2289

Luis, Don
Mercedes of Castile - James Fenimore Cooper 1304

Lydiard, Maurice
Bed in Hell - Elfrida Vipont 6504

MacAndrew, Richard
The Favored Child - Philippa Gregory 2582

MacDonald, Angus
A Falcon for a Queen - Catherine Gaskin 2314

Macdonald, Charles
The French Bride - Evelyn Anthony 163

Macdonald, James
Clandara - Evelyn Anthony 161

MacFarland, Andrew
Devilseed - Frank Yerby 6914

MacFell, Edward
The Cinderpath - Catherine Cookson 1275

MacGregor, Ian
The Imposter - Noel B. Gerson 2375

Mackinnon, Sir Alan
Monsieur Janvier - Elizabeth Linington 3799

MacLean, Alasdair
Midwinter - John Buchan 751

MacLyon, Diarmid
MacLyon - Lolah Burford 773

Madison, Burton
Marblehead - Joan Thompson 6267

Madox, Henry
Katheryn, the Wanton Queen - Maureen Peters 4976

Malatesta, Paolo
Ardent Flame - Frances Winwar 6829

Maldry, Sir Robin
The Flight of the Kestrel - Margaret Abbey 3

Mallary, Dorien
The Storm Witch - Elisabeth Barr 339

Mallen, Thomas
The Mallen Streak - Catherine Cookson 1282

Mallett, Graham Reid
Pawn in Frankincense - Dorothy Dunnett 1804

Mallow, Blane
Lady of Mallow - Dorothy Eden 1856

Malton, Sir Richard
Check-Out Time - Kate Kingsbury 3491

Mandeville, Gervaise
The Pool of St. Branok - Philippa Carr 926

Manningford, James
Cousin Susannah - Hazel Hucker 3066

Marigny, Alfred de
Carnal Hours - Max Allan Collins 1210

Marin, Jean Paul
The Devil's Laughter - Frank Yerby 6913

Marmion, Clarence
The Trip to Jerusalem - Edward Marston 4129

Marriott, Charles
Free Lance - George Shipway 5827

Martell, Nathaniel
The Love Child - Catherine Cookson 1279

Martin, Jeremiah
Jeremiah Martin: A Revolutionary War Novel - Robert
   H. Fowler 2191

Mason, Roderick
Westward the Sun - Brigid Knight 3524

Mathieson, Roland Farleigh
The Dedicated Villain - Patricia Veryan 6461

McAllister, Ward
Tassels on Her Boots - Arthur Cheney Train 6313

McCallum, Peter
Falls of Gard - Laura Black 520

McGrath, Howard
The Marrying Kind - Jessica Stirling 6046

McGrath, Steve
Tilly Alone - Catherine Cookson 1289

McKenzie, Ewan
Silver Linings - Shirley Davies-Owens 1508

Mendes, Eugene
Crescent City - Belva Plain 5078

Mercer, John
Pargeters - Norah Lofts 3857

Mertoun, Mordaunt
The Pirate - Sir Walter Scott 5704

Micawber, Wilkins
The Real David Copperfield - Robert Graves 2551

Millinder, Julius
The House of Five Talents - Louis Auchincloss 231

Millinder, Oswald
The House of Five Talents - Louis Auchincloss 231

Minnett, Nicholas
Brumaire - Mark Logan 3864
Guillotine - Mark Logan 3865
Tricolour - Mark Logan 3866

Moidore, Basil
A Dangerous Mourning - Anne Perry 4926

Montagu, Jack
The Fourth Queen - Isabel Paterson 4827

Montanis, Lorenzo
A Distant Thunder - Teresa de Luca 1561

Montclair, Valentine
Logic of the Heart - Patricia Veryan 6466

Montoria, Don Jose de
Saragossa - Benito Perez Galdos 4912

Morandi, Richard
Lord Vanity - Samuel Shellabarger 5796

Morelli, Anthony
I, Roberta - Elizabeth Gray Vining 6501

Morewood, Oliver
Windover - Jane Aiken Hodge 2974

Morgan
Every Man for Himself - Beryl Bainbridge 270

Morgan, William
This Willing Passion - Patricia Cloud 1132

Moriss, Sir John
Masquerade for the King - Marina Oliver 4729

Morlaix, Quentin de
Master-At-Arms - Rafael Sabatini 5553

Morris, Jeremy
Luise - Dawn Stewart Field 2079

Morton, Henry
Old Mortality - Sir Walter Scott 5702

Morton, James
Counterfeit of Murder - Ray Harrison 2738
Death of a Dancing Lady - Ray Harrison 2739
Deathwatch - Ray Harrison 2740
Harvest of Death - Ray Harrison 2741
Patently Murder - Ray Harrison 2742
A Season for Death - Ray Harrison 2743
Sphere of Death - Ray Harrison 2744
Tincture of Death - Ray Harrison 2745
Why Kill Arthur Potter? - Ray Harrison 2746

Moscrop, Albert
Mad Hatter's Holiday - Peter Lovesey 3914

Mowbray, Malcolm
A Father and His Fate - Ivy Compton-Burnett 1228

Moynihan, Gerrard
Sabrina - Madeleine Polland 5086

Nash, Beau
Lord Vanity - Samuel Shellabarger 5796

Nash, Richard
Monsieur Beaucaire - Booth Tarkington 6163

Nateby-Dyce, Thomas
Too Late! Too Late! The Maiden Cried - Joan Fleming 2128

Nicholls, Geoffrey
Falls of Gard - Laura Black 520

Nikolayevitch, Alexei
Emily - Cynthia Harrod-Eagles 2753

Norrey, Sir John
Midwinter - John Buchan 751

North, Frederick
The Darkening Leaf - Caroline Stickland 6036

Nowell, Roger
Elegant Witch - Robert Neill 4568

O'Connor, Cathal
The Quickenberry Tree - Annette Motley 4502

O'Connor, Giles
Princess Pamela - Ray Russell 5534

Odell, Alonzo
The Paper Mistress - Dorothea Malm 4045

Ogilvie, Patrick
The Case of Kitty Ogilvie - Jean Stubbs 6093

Oldcastle, John
The Star of Lancaster - Jean Plaidy 5065

Oliver, Matthew
Sea Change - Alison McLeay 4287

Olivier, Victor
Royal Street - Walter Adolphe Roberts 5393

Orlandini, Giacopo
Mortal Pageant - Johan Fabricius 1993

Orlando
Orlando - Virginia Woolf 6866

Osbaldistone, Frank
Rob Roy - Sir Walter Scott 5707

Osbaldistone, Rasleigh
Rob Roy - Sir Walter Scott 5707

Osborne, George
Vanity Fair - William Makepeace Thackeray 6213

Overbury, Thomas
The Murder in the Tower - Jean Plaidy 5035

Overton, Charles
The Days of the Butterfly - Norah Lofts 3841

Overton, William
Speak to Me of Love - Dorothy Eden 1862

Parry, Sir Jonathan
Feast of the Jesters - Manuel Komroff 3533

Pelham, Sir Harry
Captain Nash and the Wroth Inheritance - Ragan Butler 828

Pendellow, Drew
Castle Heritage - Elisabeth Barr 337

Pendlebury, Christian
The Veil of Illusion - Rebecca Ryman 5545

Pengallion, Dominic
The Sea Treasure - Elisabeth Barr 338

Penrose, Hal
A Notorious Woman - Malcolm Macdonald 3969

Perry, Culver
The Bellerose Bargain - Robyn Carr 934

Peveril, Julian
Peveril of the Peak - Sir Walter Scott 5703

Pilaster, Edward
A Dangerous Fortune - Ken Follett 2147

Pink, Samuel
The Mountain of Immoderate Desires - Leslie Wilson 6811

Poldark, Francis
Demelza - Winston Graham 2524
The Last Gamble - Winston Graham 2527
The Renegade: A Novel of Cornwall, 1783-1787 - Winston Graham 2529
Venture Once More - Winston Graham 2532

Polleven, Julian
The Sea Scape - Mary Lide 3778

Posey, George
The Fathers - Allen Tate 6171

Prestcote, Gilbert
Dead Man's Ransom - Ellis Peters 4957

Preswald, Buck
Mississippi Belle - Clements Ripley 5346

Prevost, Charles
Marching On - James Boyd 612

Pryde, Stephen
Strange Wives - Shirley Barker 317

Pye, Manfred
The Crystal Dove - Mollie Hardwick 2692

Radlet, Donald
The Mallen Streak - Catherine Cookson 1282

Ralegh, Sir Walter
Ralegh's Fair Bess: The Story of Bess Throckmorton - Judy Turner 6365

Raleigh, Bruce
Wind From the Carolinas - Robert Wilder 6751

Raleigh, Sir Walter
Daughter of Eve - Noel B. Gerson 2366
A Dead Man in Deptford - Anthony Burgess 776
Lady in Waiting - Rosemary Sutcliff 6123
My Lord Essex - Olive Eckerson 1838
To Be a King - Robert DeMaria 1607
To Love a Queen - Lawrence Schoonover 5669
Towers in the Mist - Elizabeth Goudge 2495

Ramsay, Harry
Strathgallant - Laura Black 523

Ramsey, Derek
A Future Arrived - Phillip Rock 5420

Randall, Drury
Drury Randall - Mary Johnston 3232

Randolph, Richard
The Bizarre Sisters - Jay Walz 6559

Raven, Guy
Ravenscroft - Dorothy Eden 1860

Ravencroft, Torrance
The Silver Dolphin - Velda Johnston 3264

Ravenscar, Max
Faro's Daughter - Georgette Heyer 2887

Ravenshoe, Charles
Ravenshoe - Henry Kingsley 3500

Reade, Dominic
Ride the Blue Riband - Rosalind Laker 3598

Redgauntlet, Sir Edward Hugh
Red Gauntlet - Sir Walter Scott 5706

Redmayne, Cleve
Elyza - Clare Darcy 1486

Redmond, Sir Harry
Nanette - Patricia Veryan 6472

Redmond, Mitchell
Sanguinet's Crown - Patricia Veryan 6476

Reed, Martin
The Town House - Norah Lofts 3861

Rilke, Martin
A Future Arrived - Phillip Rock 5420
The Passing Bells - Phillip Rock 5421

Ringham, William
My Name Is Clary Brown - Charlotte Keppel 3466

Rivenhall, Charles
The Grand Sophy - Georgette Heyer 2891

Rochester, Edward
Wide Sargasso Sea - Jean Rhys 5312

Roe, Sir Piers
Gerait's Daughter - Millie J. Ragosta 5241

Roosevelt, Franklin Delano
Speak Softly - Lawrence Alexander 83

Ross, Robert
The God of Mirrors - Robert Reilly 5293

Rossiter, Gideon
Ask Me No Questions - Patricia Veryan 6459

Rouault, Henri
Kingkill - Thomas Gavin 2325

Rowland, Harry
Now, God Be Thanked - John Masters 4177

Rowlands, William
Marianne - Glen Petrie 4981

Rowse, Justinian
Camelot Country - Marjorie McEvoy 4267

Rudyard, Adrian
The Long Shadow - Anna Gilbert 2406

Rullock, Ian
Foes - Mary Johnston 3233

Rutherford, Justin
A Fatal Assignation - Alice Chetwynd Ley 3764
Masquerade of Vengeance - Alice Chetwynd Ley 3765
A Reputation Dies - Alice Chetwynd Ley 3766

Ryder, Sebastian
A Heritage of Shadows - Madeleine Brent 660

Sackville, Bruce
Pearl - Helen Ashfield 211

Sackville, Charles
Here Lies Our Sovereign Lord - Jean Plaidy 5021

Sackville, James
Pearl - Helen Ashfield 211

St. Barbe, Alexander
A Falling Star - Pamela Belle 431
Treason's Gift - Pamela Belle 434

St. Barbe, Charles
A Falling Star - Pamela Belle 431
Treason's Gift - Pamela Belle 434

Saint-Brevin, Valmont
New Orleans Legacy - Alexandra Ripley 5341

St. Clare, Aubrey
Secret for a Nightingale - Victoria Holt 3020

St. Cyr, Alex
Twilight of the Dawn - Elizabeth Nell Dubus 1752

St. Jules, Christopher
The Castle of the Winds - Jeanne Montague 4434

Salen, Edwin
Flowers in the Blood - Gay Courter 1387

Saltmarch, Henry
The Players' Boy Is Dead - Leonard Tourney 6303

Sanguinet, Claude
Feather Castles - Patricia Veryan 6462
Sanguinet's Crown - Patricia Veryan 6476

Savage, Jardine Henry
The Peacock's Feather - Sarah Woodhouse 6855

Savage, Phillip
Savage Oaks - Julie Ellis 1924

Schuyler, Richard
When the Music Changed - Marie R. Reno 5305

Seton, William
Heart in Pilgrimage - Evelyn Eaton 1827

Seymour, Thomas
Her Royal Destiny - Carol Maxwell Eady 1820
The Sixth Wife - Jean Plaidy 5063

Shackleton, Frank
Jewels - Robert Perrin 4917

Shallot, Roger
The White Rose Murders - Michael Clynes 1137

Shaw, Clinton
The Spring of the Tiger - Victoria Holt 3021

Shelmadine, Sir Richard
Afternoon of a Autocrat - Norah Lofts 3834

Sheridan, Sir Charles
Death at Daisy's Folly - Robin Paige 4775
Death at Gallows Green - Robin Paige 4776

Sherwood, Johnny
Freedom's Banner - Teresa Crane 1415

Shiers, William
The Men That God Forgot - Richard Butler 829

Shipman, Albert
Listen for the Voices - Anne Colver 1220

Sidney, Sir Philip
Lady Rich - Elizabeth Boatwright Coker 1166
Towers in the Mist - Elizabeth Goudge 2495
Trust and Treason - Margaret Birkhead 506

Simons, Andrew
The Woman of Catawba - Hilda Stahl 5978

Sinclair, Curtis
Morning at Jalna - Mazo de la Roche 1560

Sinclair, Matt
Creature Comforts - Jessica Stirling 6041

Sinclair, Roderick
The Miser of Mayfair - Marion Chesney 1038

Smith, Nayland
The Fires of Fu Manchu - Cay Van Ash 6399

Smithson, Charles
The French Lieutenant's Woman - John Fowles 2194

Sompayac, Philippe
The Girl From Storyville: A Victorian Novel - Frank Yerby 6919

Sopwith, Mark
Tilly - Catherine Cookson 1288

Sopwith, Matthew
Tilly Wed - Catherine Cookson 1290

Southey, William
Evil Mark - Graham Miles 4377

Spangler, Sir Guy
Sir Rogue - Leslie Turner White 6691

Standen, Freddy
Cotillion - Georgette Heyer 2883

Stanhope, Burke
American Eden - Marilyn Harris 2728
The Women of Eden - Marilyn Harris 2734

Starmont, Giles
The Long Day Closes - Beatrice Tunstall 6360

Steele, Will
Chase the Heart - Maggie Osborne 4760

Stevenson, Boy
Sons of Fortune - Malcolm Macdonald 3973

Stevenson, Caspar
Sons of Fortune - Malcolm Macdonald 3973

Stewart, Christian
The Game of Kings - Dorothy Dunnett 1801

Stonefield, Caleb
Cain and His Brother - Anne Perry 4922

Stowe, Augustus
Swandowne - Daniel Farson 2024

Stowe, Poland
Swandowne - Daniel Farson 2024

Strand, Justin
Married Past Redemption - Patricia Veryan 6469

Stuart, Charles
The Street Sparrows - Rose Ayers 249

Summers, Harry
Sara - Brian Cleeve 1110

Sutbury, Guy
The Sutburys - Pamela Hill 2944

Sykes, Christopher
Bertie and the Tinman - Peter Lovesey 3909

Talbot, Aubrey
Bury Him Among Kings - Elleston Trevor 6341

Talbot, Edmund
Close Quarters - William Golding 2453
Fire Down Below - William Golding 2454
Rites of Passage - William Golding 2456

Talmadge, Ambrose
Somewhere Within This House - Jean Francis Webb 6587

Talmadge, Nicholas
A Place of Ravens - Pamela Hill 2942

Taverner, Stephen
Blood Royal - Robert Payne 4850

Tedelli, Vittorino
Bianca - Mabel Conquist 1257

Theros, Edward
A Woman of Quality - Jan Westcott 6649

Thornton, Henry
Louisa Brancusi - Darrell Husted 3088

Thornton, John
Escapade - Jane Aiken Hodge 2962

Tilverton, Barnaby
A Most Romantic City - Mary Ann Gibbs 2396

Tollington, Hilary
The Fortunate Marriage - Meriol Trevor 6342

Tolworthy, Richard
Saraband for Two Sisters - Philippa Carr 928

Torridon, Ralph
The King's Achievement - Robert Hugh Benson 459

Tourville, Charles de
Knave of Hearts - Philippa Carr 920

Trelawney, Squire
Treasure Island - Robert Louis Stevenson 6012

Trelawney, Cornwallis
Kernow & Daughter - Malcolm Macdonald 3968

Tremor, Sir William
Deborah and the Siege of Paris - Colette Davenat 1500

Trent, Stephen
Gentleman Ranker - John Edward Jennings 3200

Tressilian, Edmund
Kenilworth - Sir Walter Scott 5700

Trevallion, Benedict
The Pride of the Trevallions - Carola Salisbury 5570

Trevenning, Charles
It Began in Vauxhall Gardens - Jean Plaidy 5023

Tromba, Marcello
Lord Vanity - Samuel Shellabarger 5796

Tsepesh, Arkady
Covenant with the Vampire: The Diaries of the Family Dracul - Jeanne Kalogridis 3327

Tudor, Owen
The Queen's Secret - Jean Plaidy 5053
Wife to Henry V - Hilda Lewis 3752

Tunstall, Paul
A Leaf in the Wind - Marie Joseph 3307

Tyndale, Craig
The Noblest Frailty - Patricia Veryan 6474

Tyne, Harry
Letty - Clare Darcy 1491

Underdown, Philip
The Plymouth Cloak - Kate Sedley 5718

Valdes, Don Pedro de
Sea of Lentils - Antonio Benitez-Rojo 443

Vale, Matthew
A Lady in Doubt - Annabel Wynne 6891

Van Baden, Nicolaus
The Marriage Bed - Jean Clark 1088

Van Ryn, Nicholas
Dragonwyck - Anya Seton 5750

Vanderbilt, Reginald
That Vanderbilt Woman - Philip Van Rensselaer 6427

Vandervent, Paul
The Blackheath Poisonings - Julian Symons 6150

Vaughan, Rhys
Vale of Tyranny - Suzanne Butler 831

Vaughn, Plumbridge
Michael Torey - Janet Mathewson 4183

Vernet, Michel
Hester - Brian Cleeve 1107

Versluis
Another Country - Karel Schoeman 5646

Villars, Trevelyan de
The Wagered Widow - Patricia Veryan 6481

Visconti, Niles
Clara Reeve - Leonie Hargrave 2705

Volland, Hubert
Vollands - Pamela Hill 2947

Volland, James
Vollands - Pamela Hill 2947

Voyle, Simon
Familiar Acts - June Barraclough 345

Wade, Caffey
Tidewater - Clifford Dowdey 1709

Wallace, William
The Scottish Chiefs - Jane Porter 5135

Walmer, Augustus
The Proprietor - Ann Schlee 5638

War, Perceval de
Deborah and the Siege of Paris - Colette Davenat   1500

Warbeck, Perkin
The Courts of Illusion - Rosemary Hawley Jarman   3165
Merchant of the Ruby - Alice Harwood   2766

Warby, Gerald
The Desirable Duchess - Marion Chesney   1025

Ward, Sir Peter
The Wagered Widow - Patricia Veryan   6481

Warden, Isaac
This Is the House - Deborah Hill   2921

Warrington, Harry
The Virginians - William Makepeace Thackeray   6214

Warwyck, Richard
Claudine's Daughter - Rosalind Laker   3594

Waters, Charles
The Virginia Comedians - John Esten Cooke   1269

Weaver
Death and the Chapman - Kate Sedley   5715

Weill, Victor
Vardy - John Harris   2721

Wentwater, Guy
Deirdre and Desire - Marion Chesney   1024

Westcott, Trent
The Braeswood Tapestry - Robyn Carr   936

Weston, Edmund
Statues in a Garden - Isabel Colegate   1198

Weston, James
Women of Ashdon - Valerie Anand   135

Westruther, Jack
Cotillion - Georgette Heyer   2883

Whisten, Benjamin Biddle
Bygones - Frank Wilkinson   6762

Whiting, Richard
Three-Headed Angel - Roark Bradford   623

Widowson, Edwin
The Golden Hand - Edith Simon   5856

Wilkes, Ashley
Gone with the Wind - Margaret Mitchell   4415

William of Colchester
The Swords of December - Robert York   6933

Willoughby, Edwin
The Summer of the Bashinskeys - Diane Pearson   4877

Winter, Piers
My Lady Greensleeves - Constance Beresford-Howe   476

Winterbourne, George
Two Corinthians - Carola Dunn   1797

Wintersill, Brook Henry
The Cannaway Concern - Graham Shelby   5788

Woburn, Oliver
The Artist's Daughter - Leslie O'Grady   4698

Woodbyne, Laurie
Beyond the Shining Mountains - Doris Shannon   5775

Woodfall, Thomas
Trust and Treason - Margaret Birkhead   506

Wroth, Oliver
Captain Nash and the Wroth Inheritance - Ragan Butler   828

Wyatt, Sir Thomas
Brief Gaudy Hour - Margaret Campbell Barnes   322
The King's Pleasure - Jean Plaidy   5026

York, Joshua
Fevre Dream - George R.R. Martin   4131

Young, Lawrence
I Give You Oscar Wilde - Desmond Hall   2647

GENTLEWOMAN

Adair, Daisy
Meadowsweet - Gwendoline Butler   820

Adair, Trelawney
Meadowsweet - Gwendoline Butler   820

Adams, Abigail
Sally Hemings - Barbara Chase-Riboud   1006

Addison, Margaret
For Love of Two Eagles - Barbara Riefe   5328
The Woman Who Fell From the Sky - Barbara Riefe   5330

Adelaid, Lady
Red Lion and Gold Dragon - Rosemary Sprague   5969

Adi, Lady
The Exile Way - Ann Woodward   6865

Adrianna
The Venetian Mask - Rosalind Laker   3603

Alard, Catharine
Superstition Corner - Sheila Kaye-Smith   3379

Albany, Leondra
Albany - Laura Black   519

Albriton, Rosamond
Cherished Enemy - Patricia Veryan   6460

Alderley, Barbara
Through a Glass Darkly - Karleen Koen   3531

Alix of Wanthwaite
Banners of Gold - Pamela Kaufman   3371

Allen, Eliza
The Raven's Bride - Elizabeth Crook   1431

Allen, Minga
Rivers of Glory - F. van Wyck Mason   4158

Alston, Theodosia Burr
My Theodosia - Anya Seton   5753

Amesley, Nellanor
Chase the Heart - Maggie Osborne   4760

Ann of Cambray
Ann of Cambray - Mary Lide   3772

Appleton, Ellen
Rainbow in the Royals - Garland Roark   5357

Archdale, Mary
Lieutenant of the Line - Duncan MacNeil   4015
Sadhu on the Mountain Peak - Duncan MacNeil   4019

Archibald, Philippa
While England Sleeps - David Leavitt   3702

Arden, Alice
Feversham - Diane Davidson   1503

Armitage, Annabelle
The Taming of Annabelle - Marion Chesney   1052

Armitage, Daphne
Daphne - Marion Chesney   1022

Armitage, Deirdre
Deirdre and Desire - Marion Chesney   1024

Armitage, Diana
Diana the Huntress - Marion Chesney   1026

Armitage, Frederica
Frederica in Fashion - Marion Chesney   1032

Armitage, Minerva
Minerva - Marion Chesney   1037

Armstrong, Grace
The Black Dwarf - Sir Walter Scott   5692

Arnaud, Claudine
All Souls' Rising - Madison Smartt Bell   422

Ashbrooke, Catherine
The Blood of Roses - Marsha Canham   879
The Pride of Lions - Marsha Canham   881

Ashley, Elizabeth
Guns of Chickamauga - Richard O'Connor   4685

Ashton, Lucy
The Bride of Lammermoor - Sir Walter Scott   5693

Ashworth, Cecilia
A Lady of Repute - Janice James   3158

Ashworth, Emily
Paragon Walk - Anne Perry   4932

Aspasia
Alcibiades, Beloved of Gods - Vincenz Brun   735
The Immortal Marriage - Gertrude Atherton   225

Atherton, Beatrice
The King's Achievement - Robert Hugh Benson   459

Audley, Kathryn
Bennett's Welcome - Inglis Fletcher   2132

Augusta of Berkeley
Castle Dangerous - Sir Walter Scott   5694

Azaire, Isabelle
Birdsong - Sebastian Faulks   2051

Baffo, Sofia
Sofia - Ann Chamberlin   974

Bailey, Lydia
Lydia Bailey - Kenneth Roberts   5387

Ballasteros, Winter de
Shadow of the Moon - M.M. Kaye   3377

Banastre, Hortensia
Southern Discomfort - Rita Mae Brown   730

Bandy, Mary
My Grand Enemy - Jean Stubbs   6098

Barcelo, Dona Tules
The Wind Leaves No Shadow - Ruth Laughlin   3672

Barlow, Arabella
Law of the Land - Marguerite Allis   111

Baronsheath, Felicity
Refining Felicity - Marion Chesney   1048

Barreto, Ysabel
Islands of Unwisdom - Robert Graves   2548

Barrow, Elspeth
Foes - Mary Johnston   3233

Bates, Rachel
The Stallion Man - Judith Glover   2438

Beaton, Mary
The Stuart Legacy - Robert Kerr   3472

Beauchamp, Elizabeth de
Vows of the Peacock - Alice Walworth Graham   2513

Beauleigh, Diana
The Black Moth - Georgette Heyer   2877

Beauman, Lucy
The King's Commission - Dewey Lambdin   3614

Beaumont, Beth
Apache - Donald Clayton Porter   5114

Beaumont, Dorothy
Charlie Is My Darling - Mollie Hardwick   2691

Bedford, Katherine
Caribbee - Thomas Hoover   3025

Bellefleur, Lilian
Flowers for Lilian - Anna Gilbert   2405

Belmont, Eleanor
The Prince of Darkness - P.C. Doherty 1675

Benedict, Alice
Statues in a Garden - Isabel Colegate 1198

Bensham, Katie
The Mallen Lot - Catherine Cookson 1281

Berenger, Eveline
The Betrothed - Sir Walter Scott 5691

Bernay, Minna
Minna's Story: The Secret Love of Doctor Sigmund Freud - Kathleen Daniels 1463

Bertram, Fanny
Mansfield Revisited - Joan Aiken 51

Bertram, Julia
Version and Diversion - Judith Terry 6207

Beverley, Isabella
The Banishment - Marion Chesney 1018

Beverley, Jessica
The Intrigue - Marion Chesney 1034

Beverley, Rachel
The Folly - Marion Chesney 1031

Bird, Evelyn
Audrey - Mary Johnston 3229

Bishop, Arabella
Captain Blood - Rafael Sabatini 5546

Blackford, Harriet
The Scandalous Mrs. Blackford - Harriet Kane 3358

Blackwood, Emily
Sweet's Folly - Fiona Hill 2926

Blakeney, Marguerite
The Scarlet Pimpernel - Baroness Emma Orczy 4745

Blanchfleur, Anne
The Town House - Norah Lofts 3861

Blanford, Clytie
The Spring of the Tiger - Victoria Holt 3021

Bleasdale, Sarah
A Leaf in the Wind - Marie Joseph 3307

Blish, Belinda
The Scandalous Marriage - Marion Chesney 1050

Blish, Lucy
The Scandalous Marriage - Marion Chesney 1050

Blount, Elizabeth
The Shadow of the Pomegranate - Jean Plaidy 5062

Blum, Naomi
The Northern Correspondent - Jean Stubbs 6099

Boles, Annie
Annie's Captain - Kathryn Hulme 3077

Boleyn, Anne
The King's Secret Matter - Jean Plaidy 5027

Boleyn, Mary
Blood Royal - Mollie Hardwick 2690

Bonel, Mistress
Monk's Hood - Ellis Peters 4964

Bonville, Cicely
The Summer Queen - Alice Walworth Graham 2512

Boothby, Dora
Creole Dusk - Walter Adolphe Roberts 5392

Borghese, Maria Paolina
Imperial Venus: A Novel of Napoleon's Favorite Sister - Edgar Maas 3949

Borodin, Ilona
Love and Honor - Leslie Arlen 189

Borselen, Gelis van
Scales of Gold - Dorothy Dunnett 1808
To Lie with Lions - Dorothy Dunnett 1810

Branch, Anne
Man Cannot Tell - Philip Lightfoot Scruggs 5711

Bray, Julian
The Lodestar - Pamela Belle 432

Brayford, Lucinda
Lucinda Brayford - Martin Boyd 613

Breda, Anna von
The Valiant Lady - Brigid Knight 3523

Brenhilda
Count Robert of Paris - Sir Walter Scott 5695

Brenthaven, Evangelina
Angel - Carola Dunn 1790

Brett, Charlotte
Lamb in Command - Kenneth Maynard 4209

Brevoort, Geraldine
Portrait in Brownstone - Louis Auchincloss 232

Briallen
The Briar Rose - Linda Neale 4561

Bridgenorth, Alice
Peveril of the Peak - Sir Walter Scott 5703

Bright, Cecilia
Murder, I Presume - Gillian Linscott 3807

Brillon, Cunegonde
The Gentleman From America - Polan Banks 293

Britewell, Jennifer
A Shadow's Bliss - Patricia Veryan 6477

Brixham, Anne
The Golden Galleon - Victor Suthren 6129
Royal Yankee - Victor Suthren 6132

Broadhurst, Hester
Hester - Brian Cleeve 1107

Brooke, Dorothea
Middlemarch - George Eliot 1909

Brookes, Nina
A Notorious Woman - Malcolm Macdonald 3969

Broome, Minerva
Cousin Kate - Georgette Heyer 2884

Brough, Joanna de
The Faith and the Flame - June Dimmit Houston 3054

Broughton, Abigail
Turn of the Dice - Janet Edmonds 1870

Brown, Amy
So Much as Beauty Does - Muriel Elwood 1938

Brown, Harriet
Marrying Harriet - Marion Chesney 1036

Browne-Huntley, Lady Summer
The Shalimar - Betty Hale Hyatt 3091

Bruyere, Christine de
The Thousand Fires - Anne Powers 5155

Bryant, Claire
While the Music Lasts - Suzanne Goodwin 2477

Bryant, Vivien
While the Music Lasts - Suzanne Goodwin 2477

Bryson, India
Our Valiant Few - F. van Wyck Mason 4155

Buchanan, Euphemia
Some Brief Folly - Patricia Veryan 6478

Buford, Evelyn
Storm Against the Wind - Helen Hull Jacobs 3138

Burdock, Judith
The Regulators - William Degenhard 1580

Burgh, Meggotta de
The Marriage of Meggotta - Edith Pargeter 4799

Burgoyne, Margery
I Remember Love - Mollie Hardwick 2694

Burnet, Clemency
Shadows and Images - Meriol Trevor 6344

Butler, Aileen
The Financier - Theodore Dreiser 1720

Byford, Kate
Paths of Fortune - Susan Moore 4444

Byford, Sophy
Paths of Fortune - Susan Moore 4444

Cabot, Electra
Keeping Secrets - Suzanne Morris 4483

Cadejac, Arsen de
Destiny of Fire - Zoe Oldenbourg 4715

Cadorson, Annora
Midsummer's Eve - Philippa Carr 924

Caillot, Blanchette
The Gentleman From America - Polan Banks 293

Calverton, Cressida
Cressida - Clare Darcy 1485

Campbell-Bannerman, Madeleine
The Stuart Legacy - Robert Kerr 3472

Campden, Clarissa
Clear for Action! - Simon White 6699

Campion, Anne
Corner the Moon - Shirley Barker 310

Cardenas, Barbara
The Royal City - Les Savage Jr. 5621

Carewe, Rachel
The Dark Palazzo - Virginia Coffman 1151

Carey, Eleanore
The Crystal Dove - Mollie Hardwick 2692

Carlyon, Alexandria
Defend and Betray - Anne Perry 4928

Carrasquez, Dolores
A Distant Thunder - Teresa de Luca 1561

Carrill, Catherine
Thunder on St. Paul's Day - Jane Lane 3658

Carrington, Amelia
The Time of the Dragon - Dorothy Eden 1863

Carter, Lady Harriet
The Stranger From the Sea - Winston Graham 2530

Cartwright, Emily
Cambridge - Caryl Phillips 4983

Carver, Elizabeth
The Fallon Blood - Reagan O'Neal 4741

Catalina
Envoy From Elizabeth - Pamela Bennetts 451

Challoner, Frances
Old Saxon Blood - Leonard Tourney 6302

Challoner, Mary
Devil's Cub - Georgette Heyer 2885

Chalmers, Natasha
A Certain Splendour - Carola Salisbury 5566

Chartley, Sybil
The Wildcliffe Bird - Constance Heaven 2811

Chase, Kathryn
Kathryn: In the Court of Six Queens - Anne Merton Abbey 1

Chatfield, Mary
Young Men See Visions - Mary Mian 4357

Chatrois, Jacqueline Crois de
The Tides of Dawn - Emma Louise Mally 4044

Chenevix, Kitty
Cressida - Clare Darcy 1485

Chesnieres, Germaine de
Master-At-Arms - Rafael Sabatini 5553

Chester, Elizabeth
Knight's Honor - Roberta Gellis   2351

Chetwynd-Dunleigh, Lucinda
Over There - Robert Vaughan   6449

Chevalier, Christine
Young Ames - Walter D. Edmonds   1879

Chevalier, Louise
Treason's Gift - Pamela Belle   434

Childs, Marian
The Last Waltz - Nancy Zaroulis   6955

Christian, Katherine
Katherine Christian - Hugh Walpole   6546

Chynoweth, Morwenna
The Black Moon - Winston Graham   2522

Claiborne, Margaret
River of Dreams - Gay Courter   1390

Clairmont, Claire
The Absorbing Fire: The Byron Legend - F.W.
   Kenyon   3445
Count Manifred - Miranda Seymour   5761
Lord of the Ladies - Joanna Dessau   1626
Love's Children - Judith Chernaik   1013
The Memoirs of Lord Byron - Robert Nye   4655
A Single Summer with Lord B. - Derek
   Marlowe   4092
The Year of December - Lucy Cores   1329

Clairmont, Jane
*The Golden Years: A Novel Based on the Life and
   Loves of Percy Bysshe Shelley* - F.W.
   Kenyon   3451

Clare, Jocellin
The Bluestocking - June Drummond   1729

Clarence, Mrs.
Yvonne Goes to York - Marion Chesney   1054

Clark, Cassandra
The Second Sister - Leslie O'Grady   4701

Clarke, Mary Anne
The Duke's Mistress: The Story of Mary Ann Clarke -
   F.W. Kenyon   3447

Clary, Desiree
Desiree - Annemarie Selinko   5741

Claudia
Hear Me, Pilate! - LeGette Blythe   557
Man on Fire: A Novel on the Life of St. Paul -
   LeGette Blythe   558

Clement, Juliette de
Storm Winds - Iris Johansen   3217

Clifford, Rosamund
The Revolt of the Eaglets - Jean Plaidy   5057

Clifford, Yolande de
I Remember Love - Mollie Hardwick   2694

Clodia
Death on the Appian Way - Kenneth Benton   463
Farewell, Catullus - Pierson Dixon   1651
The Gods Are Not Mocked - Anna Taylor   6177
The Key - Benita Kane Jaro   3169
The Venus Throw - Steven Saylor   5627

Clothier, Mary
The Quincunx - Charles Palliser   4778

Colbert, Sapphira
Sapphira and the Slave Girl - Willa Cather   958

Colland, Harriet
The Blackheath Poisonings - Julian Symons   6150

Collins, Rita
You Rolling River - Archie Binns   503

Colmore, Ellie
Lord Richard's Passion - Mervyn Jones   3293

Comyn, Charlotte
Escapade - Jane Aiken Hodge   2962

Consett, Helena
Bride of Ae - Pamela Hill   2928

Conti, Clelia
The Charterhouse of Parma - Stendhal   5993

Cooke, Anna
The Sot-Weed Factor - John Barth   364

Coppen, Hetty
Familiar Acts - June Barraclough   345

Corbney, Udele de
The Blue Falcon - Robyn Carr   935

Cordell, Augusta
Bread and Circus - Morris Renek   5303

Corey, Nancy
For Time and All Eternity - Paul Bailey   268

Coronel, Dona Consuelo
Grant of Kingdom - Harvey Fergusson   2067

Corper, Julie
Julie - Jane Kesner Morris   4479

Corrough, Sibilla
Mayfair - Nancy Fitzgerald   2115

Corrough, Sophia
Mayfair - Nancy Fitzgerald   2115

Cottier, Louise
Proud New Flags - F. van Wyck Mason   4156

Couper, Anne
Bright Captivity - Eugenia Price   5180

Courtine, Anne-Marie
All the Golden Gifts - Iola Fuller   2251

Cox-Neville, Alexandra
Come Be My Love - Diana Brown   717

Cranford, Dimity
Love Alters Not - Patricia Veryan   6467

Cranleigh, Rosetta
The Captive - Victoria Holt   3011

Croft, Helena
Stand We at Last - Zoe Fairbairns   1999

Croft, Sarah
Stand We at Last - Zoe Fairbairns   1999

Cuddington, Chloe
The Nonsuch Lure - Mary M. Luke   3924

Custer, Elizabeth Bacon
The Court-Martial of George Armstrong Custer -
   Douglas C. Jones   3276
Libbie - Judy Alter   121

Custis, Martha
Morning of a Hero - Burke Boyce   608

Dagshaw, Maria
The Love Child - Catherine Cookson   1279

Dallow, Corinna
Teverton Hall - Jane Gillespie   2421

d'Almada, Zena
Hong Kong - Mona Gardner   2288

Damon, Kate
Scandal at High Chimneys: A Victorian Melodrama -
   John Dickson Carr   915

Danement, Petula
Shadows over Castle Rising - Fanny Cradock   1410

Dangerfield, Faith
A Certain Splendour - Carola Salisbury   5566

Danville, Teresa
The Black Sheep's Daughter - Carola Dunn   1791

d'Arblay, Tessa
Tessa d'Arblay - Malcolm Macdonald   3974

d'Arbonne, Madeleine
Madeleine - Catherine Gavin   2323

D'Arcy, Ann
A Prince, a Piper, and a Rose - John Scalzo   5628

Darcy, Elizabeth
Pemberley, or Pride and Prejudice Continued - Emma
   Tennant   6201
Presumption: An Entertainment - Julia Barrett   350

Darcy, Georgiana
Pemberley, or Pride and Prejudice Continued - Emma
   Tennant   6201
Presumption: An Entertainment - Julia Barrett   350

Darnley, Fanny
Coronation Summer - Angela Thirkell   6220

Darracott, Anthea
The Unknown Ajax - Georgette Heyer   2908

Dashwood, Elinor
Eliza's Daughter - Joan Aiken   44

Dashwood, Margaret
The Third Sister - Julia Barrett   351

Dashwood, Marianne
Eliza's Daughter - Joan Aiken   44

Davenport, Amanda
Miss Davenport's Christmas - Marion Chesney   1039

Davenport, Gillian
Miss Davenport's Christmas - Marion Chesney   1039

Dawson, Angel
My Lady Benbrook - Constance Gluyas   2442

De Bernard, Anne
The French Bride - Evelyn Anthony   163

De Brussac, Anne
This Splendid Earth - V.J. Banis   289

de Bunez, Catherine
Rakossy - Cecelia Holland   2995

De la Barca, Tamar
For Love of a Pirate - Anthony Esler   1961

de Vauban, Eustacie
The Talisman Ring - Georgette Heyer   2905

De Vitale, Louise
The French Bride - Evelyn Anthony   163

Deborah
The Silver Chalice - Thomas B. Costain   1370

Delibe, Margot
The Devil on Horseback - Victoria Holt   3014

Demarest, Adelaide
Sarsen Place - Gwendoline Butler   821

Dennison, Flora
Tigerlilies - Judith Glover   2439

Detling, Dolly
The Detling Secret - Julian Symons   6151

Devereaux, Caroline
Caroline and Julia - Clare Darcy   1484

Devereaux, Clarissa
Love at Sunset - Jane Sheridan   5811

Devereaux, Juliette
Two of a Kind: An English Trifle - Rosemary
   Edghill   1867

Di Castelloni, Lucy
Claudine's Daughter - Rosalind Laker   3594

Di Marco, Bianca
The Borgia Prince - Pamela Bennetts   446

Dickinson, Deborah
Water over the Dam - Marguerite Allis   116

Dorring, Sophy
Seduction - Amanda Quick   5220

Douglas, Catriona
Wild Cat - Laura Black 524

Douglas, Jonet
My Lady Glamis - Pamela Hill 2940

Drayton, Lady Flora
Fire, Burn! - John Dickson Carr 910

Drayton, Lady Sophia
Love's Duet - Patricia Veryan 6468

Dremont, Marguerite
To Dance with Kings - Rosalind Laker 3601

Drummond, Amelia
Bertie and the Seven Bodies - Peter Lovesey 3908

Drummond, Blanche
Leaves From the Valley - Joanna Trollope 6348

Drummond, Cristina
Glendraco - Laura Black 521

Drummond, Margaret
Sunset at Noon - Jane Oliver 4728

Drummond, Sarah
Leaves From the Valley - Joanna Trollope 6348

Dunncastle, Matilda
The Salamanca Drum - Dorothy Eden 1861

Duvernay, Victoire
Victoire - Clare Darcy 1493

Earle, Belinda
Belinda Goes to Bath - Marion Chesney 1020

Earnshaw, Catherine
H.—: The Story of Heathcliff's Journey Back to Wuthering Heights - Lin Haire-Sargeant 2641

Eaton, Anne
Until the Winds - Jean Clark 1089

Eaton, Peggy
The Gorgeous Hussy - Samuel Hopkins Adams 30

Eden, Harriet
The Eden Passion - Marilyn Harris 2730

Eden, Mary
The Women of Eden - Marilyn Harris 2734

Eleanor
The Leopard Unleashed - Elizabeth Chadwick 967

Elena
The Venetian Mask - Rosalind Laker 3603

Ellard, Chandra
The Blue Falcon - Robyn Carr 935

Elliott, Fiona
The Train at Bundarbar - Duncan MacNeil 4021

Ellison, Caroline
Rutland Place - Anne Perry 4935

Ellison, Charlotte
The Cater Street Hangman - Anne Perry 4925

Ellison, Emily
The Cater Street Hangman - Anne Perry 4925

Elmet, Laetitia
Ramillies - Barbara Whitehead 6708

Ermenegilda
Simple Prayers - Michael Golding 2452

Escaridge, Elizabeth
The Distant Lands - Julian Green 2567

Esmond, Beatrix
Henry Esmond - William Makepeace Thackeray 6212

Esmond, Rachel
Henry Esmond - William Makepeace Thackeray 6212

d'Este, Beatrice
The Bride of Sforza - Miranda Seymour 5760
Duchess of Milan - Michael Ennis 1946

The Lady in the Mask - Anne Green 2564

Eversleigh, Carlotta
The Song of the Siren - Philippa Carr 929

Eversleigh, Damaris
The Song of the Siren - Philippa Carr 929

Eversleigh, Priscilla
The Love Child - Philippa Carr 923

Eves, Fancy
Consort for Victoria - William Vaughan Wilkins 6757

Ewell, Francine
The Judas Kiss - Victoria Holt 3015

Ewell, Pippa
The Judas Kiss - Victoria Holt 3015

Fairfax, Jane
Jane Fairfax - Joan Aiken 50

Fairfax, Sally
Morning of a Hero - Burke Boyce 608
The Young Man From Mount Vernon - Arthur Stanwood Pier 4995

Fairweather, Alice
The Colonists - William Stuart Long 3870

Faldene, Petronel
Crown of Roses - Valerie Anand 127

Falkenhorst, Tessa von
Falkenhorst - Mark Rascovich 5254

Farebrother, Susanna
The Admiral's Lady - Mary Ann Gibbs 2395

Farland, Damask
The Miracle at St. Bruno's - Philippa Carr 925

Farleigh, Anne
The Blood Endures - Robert Inman 3107

Farmiloe, Maud
Daneclere - Pamela Hill 2931

Farnesse, Giulia
The Naked Sword: The Story of Lucretia Borgia - F.W. Kenyon 3456

Farraline, Mary
The Sins of the Wolf - Anne Perry 4937

Feldman, Lady Catherine
Artemia - Pamela Hill 2927

Fervacques, Alde de
Son of Dust - H.F.M. Prescott 5171

Field, Clarissa
Will You Love Me in September? - Philippa Carr 932

Findon, Kelda
The Wedding Guest - Anna Gilbert 2407

Fisher, Caroline
Redcoat - Bernard Cornwell 1337

Fitz-Gerold, Margaret
Leopards and Lilies - Alfred Duggan 1769

FitzAdeline, Leonia
Stephen and the Sleeping Saints - Pamela Bennetts 457

Fitzherbert, Maria Anne
Regency Royal - Michael Hardwick 2687
Sweet Lass of Richmond Hill - Jean Plaidy 5067

Flashman, Elsbeth
Flashman at the Charge - George MacDonald Fraser 2209
Flashman's Lady - George MacDonald Fraser 2210

Forbes, Cecily
A Most Romantic City - Mary Ann Gibbs 2396

Forrest, Catherine
The Bluestocking - David Delman 1598

Forsythe, Margaret
Trumpets Sound No More - F. van Wyck Mason 4163

Foxley, Charlotte
The Spoils of Eden - Robert H. Fowler 2193

Frankenstein, Elizabeth
The Memoirs of Elizabeth Frankenstein - Theodore Roszak 5508

Fraser, Katherine
Clandara - Evelyn Anthony 161

Frayne, Pamela
Lady Pamela - Clare Darcy 1490

Freeman, Ernestina
The French Lieutenant's Woman - John Fowles 2194

Freemantle, Emily
Emily Goes to Exeter - Marion Chesney 1027

Freneuse, Louise de
Quietly My Captain Waits - Evelyn Eaton 1829

Frenshaw, Jessica
The Return of the Gypsy - Philippa Carr 927

Furikake, Lady
Segaki - David Stacton 5975

Furneau, Caroline
Stranger at the Wedding - Frances Lynch 3934

Furneau, Katherine
Stranger at the Wedding - Frances Lynch 3934

Galbraith, Anne
The Border Lord - Jan Westcott 6641

Gallerani, Cecilia
The Bride of Sforza - Miranda Seymour 5760

Gaynor, Ellen
The Gaynor Women - Virginia Coffman 1153

Gaynor, Maggilee
The Gaynor Women - Virginia Coffman 1153

Gaynor, Varina Dunmore
The Gaynor Women - Virginia Coffman 1153

Gentian
Destiny of Fire - Zoe Oldenbourg 4715

Gerard, Ann
The Native Air - Sarah Woodhouse 6854

Gerard, Clarissa
The Floral Companion - Anthea Bell 419

Gibbons, Jane
Sharpe's Regiment - Bernard Cornwell 1345

Gifford, Anne
The Everlasting Covenant - Robyn Carr 939

Giles, Lucy
East by Day - Blair Niles 4626

Gilmore, Cary
Draw Near to Battle - Jere Hungerford Wheelwright 6667

Giocondo, Lisa Gherardini
The Private Life of Mona Lisa - Pierre La Mure 3577

Godric, Hester
Lavender Lady - Carola Dunn 1794

Gold, Riva
Strange Wives - Shirley Barker 317

Goodchild, Helen
Until the Colors Fade - Tim Jeal 3173

Goodenough, Emily
The Adventuress - Marion Chesney 1014

Goodwin, Isabel
Beauty for Ashes - Timothy R. Wilson 6816

Gordon, Arabella
Falls of Gard - Laura Black 520

Gordon, Rachel Java
The Nationalists - William Stuart Long 3876

Graeme, Allison
The Master of Ballantrae: A Winter's Tale - Robert Louis Stevenson 6011

Grandison, Cathryn
Lady of Monkton - Elizabeth Byrd 835

Grant, Fiona
Miss Fiona's Fancy - Marion Chesney 1040

Grant, Mary Elisabeth
MacLyon - Lolah Burford 773

Grant, Penelope
Little Red Foot - Robert W. Chambers 979

Gray, Ellen
On a Lonesome Porch - Ovid Williams Pierce 4997

Gray, Frederica
Colonel Sandhurst to the Rescue - Marion Chesney 1021

Graylin, Teresa
Lady in the Briars - Carola Dunn 1793

Greenwood, Alice
Jade - Pat Barr 344

Greenwood, Josiana
The House at Old Vine - Norah Lofts 3845

Greetwell, Primula
Fleeting Fancy - Rosemary Edghill 1866

Grenier, Yvonne
Yvonne Goes to York - Marion Chesney 1054

Grevel, Claudia
Midwinter - John Buchan 751

Grey, Townsend
If This Be Magic - Ellen Marsh 4098

Gross Mama Chen
Before My Time - Niccolo Tucci 6358

Guenevere
The Duke of War - Walter O'Meara 4734

Guiccioli, Teresa
Lord of the Ladies - Joanna Dessau 1626

Guilfoyle, Anne
The Country Gentleman - Fiona Hill 2924

Gwenhwyfar
The Kingmaking - Helen Hollick 3000
The Road to Avalon - Joan Wolf 6842

Hallim, Lizzie
A Place Called Freedom - Ken Follett 2150

Hallows, Leonora
In Pale Battalions - Robert Goddard 2444

Hamilton, Lady Emma
Angelica - Samuel A. Schreiner Jr. 5671
Beauty's Daughter - Mollie Hardwick 2689
Bride of Glory - Bradda Field 2078
Brumaire - Mark Logan 3864
Emma - F.W. Kenyon 3448
The English Captain - Simon White 6700
Lord Elgin's Lady - Theodore Vrettos 6514
Loving Emma - Nigel Foxell 2197
The Nelson Touch - Paul Lewis 3759
Shadow of a Lady - Jane Aiken Hodge 2971
Sir William - David Stacton 5977
The Sleeping Sword: A Biographical Novel - Pearl Frye 2244
This Other Eden - Marilyn Harris 2733
The Volcano Lover - Susan Sontag 5946

Hamilton, Fleur
Fleur - Cynthia Harrod-Eagles 2754

Hamilton, Melanie
Gone with the Wind - Margaret Mitchell 4415

Hammond, Elizabeth
Trumpet at the Gate - Jan Widgery 6739

Hammond, Helena
Men Were Deceivers Ever - Patricia Veryan 6470

Harris, Lady Douglass
Captain Barney - Jan Westcott 6642

Harris, Laura
Kezzy - Patricia Burns 799

Harsom, Alexandra bat
The Tenth Measure - Brenda Lesley Segal 5721

Hart, Ann
The Splendor Stays: An Historic Novel Based on the Lives of the Seven Hart Sisters of Saybrook - Marguerite Allis 114

Hart, Euphemia
Plain Jane - Marion Chesney 1045

Hart, Jane
Plain Jane - Marion Chesney 1045

Hart, Jeanette
The Splendor Stays: An Historic Novel Based on the Lives of the Seven Hart Sisters of Saybrook - Marguerite Allis 114

Hart, Mary
The Splendor Stays: An Historic Novel Based on the Lives of the Seven Hart Sisters of Saybrook - Marguerite Allis 114

Hartford, Meredith
My Lord Foxe - Constance Gluyas 2443

Hartley, Ida Trask
Portrait in Brownstone - Louis Auchincloss 232

Hartwell, Amaryllis
Miss Hartwell's Dilemma - Carola Dunn 1796

Harvard, Georgina
Lord Rivington's Lady - Eileen Jackson 3134

Harvard, Penelope
Lord Rivington's Lady - Eileen Jackson 3134

Haryett, Elizabeth Ann
Imperial Courtesan - F.W. Kenyon 3452

Hassler, Josephine
The Murder at Impasse Louvaine - Richard Grayson 2562

Havering, Clara
Meridon - Philippa Gregory 2583

Hawthorne, Jessica
The Hawthorne Legacy - Teresa Crane 1416

Hayes, Diana
We Stood for Freedom - Iris Morley 4455

Heloise
Peter Abelard: A Novel - Helen Waddell 6517

Hendee, Alma
The Green Mountain Boys - Daniel Pierce Thompson 6249

Herington, Allegra
Allegra - Clare Darcy 1483

Herington, Hilary
Allegra - Clare Darcy 1483

Heron, Lady Amanda
My Lady Hoyden - Jane Sheridan 5812

Heron, Lucy
The Quickenberry Tree - Annette Motley 4502

Heron, Thomazine
The Chains of Fate - Pamela Belle 430

Hervey, Winifred
Pandora's Galley - Macdonald Harris 2727

Hesketh, Eleanor
A Woman's Age - Rachel Billington 499

Hesketh, Violet
A Woman's Age - Rachel Billington 499

Hewitt, Laura
Zemindar - Valerie Fitzgerald 2117

Hill, Abigail
The Queen's Favourites - Jean Plaidy 5051

Hill, Arabella
Quicksilver Lady - Barbara Whitehead 6707

Hill, Leah
Savage Gentleman - Noel B. Gerson 2381

Holles, Clemency
A Place of Ravens - Pamela Hill 2942

Hollingsworth, Lydia
My Dear Cousin - Peggy Hoffmann 2977

Howard, Arminta
Sapphire - Helen Ashfield 214

Howe, Martina
The Marquis and Miss Jones - Helen Ashfield 208

Hubbard, Elvira
All in Good Time - Marguerite Allis 106

Hubbard, Victoria
Drums of Khartoum - Chloe Gartner 2307

Hume, Miranda
Mother and Son - Ivy Compton-Burnett 1231

Ibbott, Katherine
Golden Admiral - F. van Wyck Mason 4150

Irvine, Katherine
Ravenburn - Laura Black 522

Islavina, Elena
Elena - Judith Egan 1893

January, Isabel
The Last Waltz - Nancy Zaroulis 6955

Jaramillo, Josefa
Soldier in Buckskin - Ray Hogan 2981

Jardine, Maida
Flight From Fifth Avenue - Catherine M. Rae 5235

Jasmine
To Dance with Kings - Rosalind Laker 3601

Jebeau, Ellen
My Beloved Son - Catherine Cookson 1285

Jefferson, Martha
My Thomas: A Novel of Martha Jefferson's Life - Roberta Grimes 2593
Sally Hemings - Barbara Chase-Riboud 1006

Jenkins, Marianne
Marianne - Glen Petrie 4981

Jerningham, Amelia
Wings of the Morning - David Beaty 402

Jerome, Jennie
Imperial Kelly - Peter Bowen 600

Jerrold, Araminta
Canal Town - Samuel Hopkins Adams 29

Johnson, Emily
Choctaw - Donald Clayton Porter 5116

Johnson, Esther
Violent Friends - Winston Clewes 1113

Jones, Esther
Rake's Progress - Marion Chesney 1047

Judith of Ravenstow
The Wild Hunt - Elizabeth Chadwick 969

Kay, Agnes
The Kays - Margaret Deland 1583

Kean, Charlotte
The Gambling Man - Catherine Cookson 1276

Kelso, Clare
Shadows on the Shore - Jessica Stirling 6048

Kenbrook, Gloriana
Knights - Linda Lael Miller 4399

Kendall, Maria
Animating Maria - Marion Chesney 1015

Kengston, Margaret
The Men That God Made Mad: A Novel about Ireland's Easter Rising - W.A. Ballinger 286

Kennedy, Janet
The King's Vixen - Pamela Hill 2937

Kennedy, Kitty
Beyond the Blue Mountains - Jean Plaidy 5006

Kentwood, Barbara
The House at Old Vine - Norah Lofts 3845

Kentwood, Elizabeth
The House at Old Vine - Norah Lofts 3845

Keppel, Alice
Mr. American - George MacDonald Fraser 2211

King, Fiona Fraser
Queen's Royal - John Quigley 5225

King, Susannah
Southern Cross - Terry Coleman 1206

La Fayette, Louise de
The Favourite - Francoise Mallet-Joris 4040

Lacey, Alice
The Desirable Duchess - Marion Chesney 1025
A Lady in Doubt - Annabel Wynne 6891

Lacey, Beatrice
Wideacre - Philippa Gregory 2585

Lacey, Julia
The Favored Child - Philippa Gregory 2582

Lacosta, Josefina
Sharpe's Eagle - Bernard Cornwell 1341

Lambert, Louise de
D'ri and I - Irving A. Bacheller 257

Lamond, Elsbeth
Bride of the MacHugh - Jan Cox Speas 5956

Lamont, Catriona
Kilcaraig - Annabel Carothers 904

Lamont, Grania
Kilcaraig - Annabel Carothers 904

Lamott, Cherie
Royal Street - Walter Adolphe Roberts 5393

Lamotte, Lucienne
Captain Justice - Anthony Forrest 2185

Lancey, Magdalene de
The Limits of Glory: A Novel of Waterloo - James McDonough 4265

Landers, Sunny
Thunder on the Plains - Rosanne Bittner 517

Landor, Angelet
Saraband for Two Sisters - Philippa Carr 928

Landor, Bersaba
Saraband for Two Sisters - Philippa Carr 928

Langdon, Kat
Court of Shadows - Cynthia Morgan 4450

Lansdon, Lucie
The Black Swan - Philippa Carr 917

Lanyon, Venetia
Venetia - Georgette Heyer 2909

Lavalette, Marie
Captain Bolton's Corpse - J.G. Jeffreys 3178

Lavransdatter, Kristin
The Bridal Wreath - Sigrid Undset 6379
The Cross - Sigrid Undset 6380
The Mistress of Husaby - Sigrid Undset 6382

Lazarevna, Zeinab "Zica"
Between Two Worlds - Monique Raphel High 2913

Le Vendeur, Catherine
The Wandering Arm - Sharan Newman 4603

Lee, Alice
Woodstock; or, The Cavalier - Sir Walter Scott 5710

Lee, Aura
Come Spring - Charlotte Hinger 2954

Leigh, Amanda
Lilith - Jean Plaidy 5030

Leigh, Augusta
The Memoirs of Lord Byron - Robert Nye 4655
My Sister, My Love - Lucille Iremonger 3111

Leigh, Elyza
Elyza - Clare Darcy 1486

Leith, Rachel
Sanguinet's Crown - Patricia Veryan 6476

Lenclos, Ninon de
All My Sins: A Novel of the Life and Loves of Ninon de Lenclos - Norbert Estey 1965

Lennox, Sarah
The Ninth Statue - Roseleen Milne 4410

Lester, Madeline
Eugene Aram - Edward Bulwer-Lytton 766

Levinson-Gore, Lavinia
In the Shadow of the Nile - Sara Hylton 3093

Lewis, Amy
The Stanbroke Girls - Fiona Hill 2925

Leyland, Lydia
Lydia, or Love in Town - Clare Darcy 1492

Lincoln, Mary Todd
McKensie's Hundred: A Tale of the Old Dominion - Frank Yerby 6924

Lindsay, Irene
Jewelled Path - Rosalind Laker 3597

Lindsay, Mildrid
Horseshoe Robinson, a Tale of the Tory Ascendancy - John P. Kennedy 3418

Lockley, Sophia
Ladysmead: A Novel in the Jane Austen Tradition - Jane Gillespie 2420

Logan, Elizabeth
I Came to the Highlands: A Novel of Suspense - Velda Johnston 3263

Logan, Mary
The Pointless Knife - Constance Dodge 1667

Lombard, Randi
Pacific Cavalcade - Virginia Coffman 1157

Lopez y Montenegro, Dona Luisa
Not of War Only - Norman Zollinger 6966

Lord, Sarah
The Bridge - Marguerite Allis 108

Lorimer, Margaret
The Lorimer Line - Anne Melville 4332

Lottie
Knave of Hearts - Philippa Carr 920

Lovell, Amy
The White Dove - Rosie Thomas 6246

Lovell, Charlotte
The Old Maid - Edith Wharton 6652

Lovell, Eleanor
A Space of the Heart - Patricia Wright 6884

Lutonville, Lady Naomi
Time's Fool - Patricia Veryan 6479

Lyndon, Lady Honoria
Barry Lyndon - William Makepeace Thackeray 6210

MacDonald, Laura
Cruel in the Shadow - Lorn MacIntyre 3986

MacFarlane, Barbara
Lord Libertine - Anthony Esler 1964

Mackay, Eliza
Stranger in Savannah - Eugenia Price 5187

MacLeod, Fiona
Perfecting Fiona - Marion Chesney 1044

Malcolm, Caroline
The Reluctant Heiress - Annabel Laine 3588

Mallen, Barbara
The Mallen Girl - Catherine Cookson 1280
The Mallen Lot - Catherine Cookson 1281

Mancini, Hortense
Here Lies Our Sovereign Lord - Jean Plaidy 5021

Mandeville, Angelet
The Pool of St. Branok - Philippa Carr 926

Mandeville, Belinda
The Changeling - Philippa Carr 918

Mandeville, Rebecca
The Changeling - Philippa Carr 918

Manette, Lucie
A Tale of Two Cities - Charles Dickens 1642

Manners, Dorothy
Richard Carvel - Winston Churchill 1081

Manners, Marjorie
Come Rack! Come Rope! - Robert Hugh Benson 458

Mansfield, Josie
Jubilee Jim and the Wizard of Wall Street - Donald Porter 5112

March, Emily
Cardington Crescent - Anne Perry 4924

Margaret of Ashbury
A Vision of Light - Judith Merkle Riley 5337

Margelasse, Flora de
The Still Storm - Francoise Sagan 5562

Maria, Dona Ana
In Distant Waters - Richard Woodman 6862

Marian of Ravenskeep
Lady of the Forest - Jennifer Roberson 5368

Marietta
The Venetian Mask - Rosalind Laker 3603

Markham, Elizabeth
Angel - Carola Dunn 1790

Markievicz, Constance
An Excess of Love - Cathy Cash Spellman 5959

Marlow, Phoebe
Sylvester; or, The Wicked Uncle - Georgette Heyer 2904

Marlow, Tansy
Ride the Blue Riband - Rosalind Laker 3598

Marsham, Beatrice
Beatrice Goes to Brighton - Marion Chesney 1019

Martin, Kate
The Prince Regent's Silver Bell - Gladys McGorian 4275

Martin, Nina
Homeward Bound - Elizabeth Walter 6557

Massingham, Eugenia
The Vines of Yarrabee - Dorothy Eden 1864

Masterman, Katherine
Beyond the Blue Mountains - Jean Plaidy 5006

Matilda
The Lady for Ransom - Alfred Duggan 1768

Maurice, Geraldine
The Vesey Inheritance - Gwendoline Butler 822

Mautravers, Jane
Captain Bashful - Donald Barr Chidsey 1059

Mayfield, Corinna
Elyza - Clare Darcy 1486

McClellan, Belle
Unvexed to the Sea: A Novel of the Vicksburg Campaign - Gerry Morrison 4484

McClellan, Malvina
Unvexed to the Sea: A Novel of the Vicksburg Campaign - Gerry Morrison 4484

McGee, Gerta
Jeremiah Martin: A Revolutionary War Novel - Robert H. Fowler 2191

McPherson, Mary Beth
Look Away - Harold Coyle 1395
Until the End - Harold Coyle 1396

McTavish, Prudence
Journey to Enchantment - Patricia Veryan 6464

Medlar, Hannah
The Long Shadow - Anna Gilbert 2406

Medlar, Zilla
The Long Shadow - Anna Gilbert 2406

Melinda of Ibelin
The Unholy Pilgrim - R.F. Tapsell 6161

Melisane
In the Falcon's Claw: A Novel of the Year 1000 - Chet Raymo 5257

Mendelssohn, Cecille
Beyond Desire: A Novel Based on the Life of Felix and Cecille Mendelssohn - Pierre La Mure 3574

Merrill, Barbara
And the Wild Birds Sing - Lola Irish 3112

Merrivale, Frederica
Frederica - Georgette Heyer 2889

Metcalf, Harriet
The Wicked Godmother - Marion Chesney 1053

Millinder, Augusta
The House of Five Talents - Louis Auchincloss 231

Milton, Deborah
The Tree of Knowledge - Eva Figes 2085

Minter, Monica
Hanging on the Wire - Gillian Linscott 3806

Miriam
The Curse of Jezebel: A Novel of the Biblical Queen of Evil - Frank G. Slaughter 5884
Simple Prayers - Michael Golding 2452

Mondeloy, Chelynne
Chelynne - Robyn Carr 938

Monica
The Converts: A Historical Novel - Rex Warner 6564
Son of Tears - Henry W. Coray 1320

Montague, Mignon
The Baroness of Bow Street - Gail Clark 1085

Montalia, Madelaine de
Hotel Transylvania - Chelsea Quinn Yarbro 6900
Out of the House of Life - Chelsea Quinn Yarbro 6903
Tempting Fate - Chelsea Quinn Yarbro 6906

Montgomery, Catherine
The Far Journey - Loula Grace Erdman 1950

Montgomery, Penelope
Practice to Deceive - Patricia Veryan 6475

Montmorency, Charlotte de
Evergreen Gallant - Jean Plaidy 5013

Montrigord, Julietta de
Red Adam's Lady - Grace Ingram 3106

Moorfield, Lydia
Forget the Glory - Emma Drummond 1725

More, Anne
Take Heed of Loving Me: A Novel about John Donne - Elizabeth Gray Vining 6502

Morgan Le Fay
The Road to Avalon - Joan Wolf 6842

Morgiana
Alamut - Judith Tarr 6164

Morland, Emma
Murder by the Waters - Robert Lee Hall 2661

Mortimer, Judith
Judith - Brian Cleeve 1108

Morville, Drusilla
The Quiet Gentleman - Georgette Heyer 2897

Mowbray, Caroline
Sherlock Holmes and the Thistle of Scotland - L.B. Greenwood 2578

Murtagh, Caroline
The Silver Saber - Carter A. Vaughan 6441
Yankee Rogue - Dana Fuller Ross 5496

Musgrove, Rosamond
The Robber Bridegroom - Eudora Welty 6623

Narni, Francesca de
The Florentine - Sandra Shulman 5840

Nichols, Constance
The Family of Women - Richard Peck 4883

Nightingale, Florence
Bedford Row - Claire Rayner 5259
The Hoydens and Mr. Dickens - William J. Palmer 4784
My Lady Hoyden - Jane Sheridan 5812
The Passionate Pilgrim - Charles Terrot 6204
The Private Life of Florence Nightingale - Richard Gordon 2485

Nilson, Anne
Limmerston Hall - Hester W. Chapman 991

Nisbet, Laura
A Woman Possessed - Malcolm Macdonald 3977

Nisbet, Mary
Lord Elgin's Lady - Theodore Vrettos 6514

Norville, Jean de
The King's Cavalier - Samuel Shellabarger 5795

Notaras, Anna
The Dark Angel - Mika Waltari 6551

Nugent, Janice
The End of the Hunt - Thomas Flanagan 2119

O'Connor, Kate
An Important Family - Dorothy Eden 1855

O'Connor, Roseen
Tigerlilies - Judith Glover 2439

O'Dalaigh, Duvessa
Wolf's Embrace - Gail Link 3801

O'Shea, Katherine
Never Call It Loving - Dorothy Eden 1859
Parnell and the Englishwoman - Hugh Leonard 3721

Ossian, Maggie
Flowers for Lilian - Anna Gilbert 2405

Paget, Juliana
The Smile of the Stranger - Joan Aiken 53

Pallister, Julia
Circle of Pearls - Rosalind Laker 3593

Paris, Judith
The Fortress - Hugh Walpole 6544
Judith Paris - Hugh Walpole 6545

Paris, Vanessa
Vanessa - Hugh Walpole 6548

Parr, Muriel
The Black Sheep's Daughter - Carola Dunn 1791

Patterson, Elizabeth
My Dear Cousin - Peggy Hoffmann 2977

Pazzi, Ginevra de
The Time Returns - Alexandra Ripley 5343

Pelham, Lucilla
The Unsuitable Miss Pelham - June Drummond 1730

Pembroke, Leah
Bond of Blood - Roberta Gellis 2349

Pendrake, Mrs.
Little Big Man - Thomas Berger 478

Pennam, Kathryn
Windover - Jane Aiken Hodge 2974

Pennlyon, Linnet
The Witch From the Sea - Philippa Carr 933

Penny, Dora
Elgar on the Journey to Hanley - Keith Alldritt 92

Petrovna, Natasha
Emily - Cynthia Harrod-Eagles 2753

Peyton, Kate
Griffith Gaunt - Charles Reade 5280

Peyton, Mercedes
Jornada - Robert L. Duffus 1754

Pierce, Louisa
The Fortunate Marriage - Meriol Trevor 6342

Pietranera, Gina
The Charterhouse of Parma - Stendhal 5993

Pilaster, Augusta
A Dangerous Fortune - Ken Follett 2147

Pisana
The Castle of Fratta - Ippolito Nievo 4625

Pitt, Charlotte
Ashworth Hall - Anne Perry 4918
Belgrave Square - Anne Perry 4919
Bethlehem Road - Anne Perry 4920
Bluegate Fields - Anne Perry 4921
Callander Square - Anne Perry 4923
Cardington Crescent - Anne Perry 4924
Death in the Devil's Acre - Anne Perry 4927
Farriers' Lane - Anne Perry 4930
Highgate Rise - Anne Perry 4931
Paragon Walk - Anne Perry 4932
Pentecost Alley - Anne Perry 4933
Resurrection Row - Anne Perry 4934
Rutland Place - Anne Perry 4935
Silence in Hanover Close - Anne Perry 4936
Traitors Gate - Anne Perry 4939

Plessis-Belliere, Honorine du
Angelique in Revolt - Sergeanne Golon 2471

Poldark, Agatha
The Black Moon - Winston Graham 2522

Poldark, Verity
Demelza - Winston Graham 2524
The Renegade: A Novel of Cornwall, 1783-1787 - Winston Graham 2529

Pompeia
Caesar's Women - Colleen McCullough 4233

Pontefract, Amelia
The Proprietor - Ann Schlee 5638

Portinari, Beatrice
The Wanderer: A Novel of Dante and Beatrice - Nathan Schachner 5633

Postlewaite, Jane
The Mamur Zapt and the Night of the Dog - Michael Pearce 4869

Pourure, Aurelie de
By Right of Arms - Robyn Carr 937

Powell, Marie
Wife to Mr. Milton - Robert Graves 2553

Powers, Diana
All Desires Known - Malcolm Macdonald 3963

Preaux, Melisande
Men Like Shadows - Dorothy Charques 1000

Price, Susan
Mansfield Revisited - Joan Aiken 51

Quantrell, Sabrina
The Carolinians - Jane Barry 357

Quarters, Gwendolen
Gwendolen - Clare Darcy 1489

Rachel of Byzantium
The Lives of Rachel - Joel Gross 2601

Radcliffe, Jenny
Devil Water - Anya Seton 5749

Radney, Regina
Dark Possession - Alice Alison Lide 3771

Ralston, Delia
The Old Maid - Edith Wharton 6652

Ramsay, Phoebe
The Tyrant - Patricia Veryan 6480

Ramsay, Tessa
The Proud Breed - Celeste De Blasis 1547

Randhurst, Jocelyn
The Wise Virgin - Hebe Elsna 1934

Randolph, Nancy
The Bizarre Sisters - Jay Walz 6559
A Generation of Leaves - Robert S. Bloom 552
Mistress Nancy - Barbara Bentley 460

Randsome, Julia
Storyville - Lois Battle 377

Ransome, Zipporah
The Adulteress - Philippa Carr 916

Rantzau, Irina
Petersburg - Emily Hanlon 2677

Rathbone, Clara Harris
Henry and Clara - Thomas Mallon 4042

Rawlinson, Henrietta
God Is an Englishman - R.F. Delderfield 1587

Reeves, Deborah
Rainbow Road - Davenport Steward 6016

Rendell, Maria
The Lion and the Leopard - Mary Ellen Johnson 3226

Rethy, Alexa de
Court of Honor - Maria Fagyas 1996

Rhinn, Margery
Swear by Apollo - Shirley Barker 318

Ricardo, Florence
Dr. Gully's Story - Elizabeth Jenkins 3190

Richaud, Angelique
Gai-Jin: A Novel of Japan - James Clavell 1100

Richmond, Oriel
Lady Defiant - Suzanne Robinson 5412

Rimini, Francesca da
Ardent Flame - Frances Winwar 6829

Rioches, Elizabeth de
That Sweet and Savage Land - Emma Drummond 1728

Robsart, Amy
Kenilworth - Sir Walter Scott 5700
The Queen and the Gypsy - Constance Heaven 2810
The Robsart Affair - Jennette Letton 3729

Roche, Gabrielle
Tree of Gold - Rosalind Laker 3602

Rochechouart de Mortemart, Francoise Athenais
Angelique and the King - Sergeanne Golon 2468

Rochelle, Elbee
Marcel Armand - Sallie Bell 424

Rochford, Jane
The King's Pleasure - Jean Plaidy 5026

Roderick, Lavinia
Balisand - Joseph Hergesheimer 2853

Rodriguez, Donna Carlotta de
The Flight of the Kestrel - Margaret Abbey 3

Roet, Katherine de
The Love Knot - Catherine Darby 1482

Roet, Philippa de
The Love Knot - Catherine Darby 1482

Rogacheva, Vera
The Warlord - Malcolm Bosse 589

Roosevelt, Edith
Speak Softly - Lawrence Alexander 83

Rostov, Natasha
War and Peace - Leo Tolstoy 6295

Rowena
Ivanhoe - Sir Walter Scott 5699

Rowhedge, Alice
Bless This House - Norah Lofts 3835

Rowland, Meg
The English Wife - Charity Blackstock 530

Royville, Alexandrine de
Heroic Dust - Theodora Dehon 1581

Russell, Anne
The King's Cavalier - Samuel Shellabarger 5795

Rutherford, Anthea
A Fatal Assignation - Alice Chetwynd Ley 3764
Masquerade of Vengeance - Alice Chetwynd Ley 3765
A Reputation Dies - Alice Chetwynd Ley 3766

Sabiston, Ingrid
The Devil in Harbour - Catherine Gavin 2319

St. Barbe, Silence
A Falling Star - Pamela Belle 431
Wintercombe - Pamela Belle 435

St. Giles, Nicole
The Demon Lover - Victoria Holt 3013

St. Quentyn, Katherine
Gentlemen—The Regiment! - Hugh Talbot 6154

St. Vrain, Jouette
The Stuart Women - Matt Braun 652

Salas y Montalva, Lucia
Coasts of Folly - Joel Williams 6784

Salisbury, Cressida
Vice Avenged: A Moral Tale - Lolah Burford 774

Salle, Gabrielle de
Ride with Me - Thomas B. Costain 1369

Salterne, Rose
Westward Ho! - Charles Kingsley 3499

Sancerre, Isabelle de
Papa La-Bas - John Dickson Carr 914

Sanguinet, Nanette
Nanette - Patricia Veryan 6472

Santana, Adriana
The Marburg Chronicles - Alfred Coppel 1319

Sassia
The Gift of Rome - John Wagner 6520

Sauves, Catherine de
Evergreen Gallant - Jean Plaidy 5013

Scarrow, Francoise
The Shadow of the Sun - Sylvia Pell 4891

Schuyler, Elizabeth
Alexander Hamilton's Wife - Alice Curtis Desmond 1623

Scott, Charlotte
Beyond All Frontiers - Emma Drummond 1722

Scott, Frances
A Respectable Trade - Philippa Gregory 2584

Sedley, Amelia
Vanity Fair - William Makepeace Thackeray 6213

Servilia
Caesar's Women - Colleen McCullough 4233

Seton, Mary
Maid of Honour: A Novel Set in the Court of Mary, Queen of Scots - Elizabeth Byrd 836
Mary of Scotland - F.W. Kenyon 3454

Seymour, Jane
The Heir of Allington - Philippa Wiat 6727

Sheffield, Aurora
In the Fire of Spring - Thomas Tryon 6355

Shenstone, Lady
Benjamin Franklin and a Case of Artful Murder - Robert Lee Hall 2654

Shore, Jane
The Sun in Splendour - Jean Plaidy 5066

Silverdale, Henrietta
Charity Girl - Georgette Heyer 2879

Simonetta
The Lady in the Mask - Anne Green 2564

Simpson, Wallis Warfield
Dance on a Sinking Ship - Michael Kilian 3483

Sinclair, Fiona
The Miser of Mayfair - Marion Chesney 1038

Skinner, Miss
The Mamur Zapt and the Spoils of Egypt - Michael Pearce 4871

Skinner, Caroline
Liberty Tavern - Thomas Fleming 2129

Smith, Amanda
Sprig Muslin - Georgette Heyer 2903

Smith, Grace
Return of the Stranger - Reay Tannahill 6158

Somerset, Lady Leanna
Lord Johnnie - Leslie Turner White 6687

Somerville, Philippa
Checkmate - Dorothy Dunnett 1799
The Ringed Castle - Dorothy Dunnett 1807

Soo, Marta
Manchu - Robert S. Elegant 1904

Sorel, Agnes
The Moneyman - Thomas B. Costain 1368

Spencer, Caroline
Castle Heritage - Elisabeth Barr 337

Sperling, Arabella
The Storms of Fate - Patricia Wright 6885

Stacy, Louise
Silver Fruit - Patricia Campbell 876

Stafford, Kate
The Brahmins - Eileen Lottman 3901

Stangeway, Evelyn
Twilight of the Dragon - Peter Bourne 596

Stanhope, Eliza
Eliza Stanhope - Joanna Trollope 6347

Stanhope, Mary Eden
American Eden - Marilyn Harris 2728

Stanton-Lacy, Sophia
The Grand Sophy - Georgette Heyer 2891

Starkweather, Belle
Cedarhaven - Patricia Campbell 874

Starkweather, Darrie
Cedarhaven - Patricia Campbell 874

Starkweather, Genia
Cedarhaven - Patricia Campbell 874

Stavely, Cressida
False Colours - Georgette Heyer 2886

Staverton, Georgina
The Sandalwood Fan - Diana Brown 720

Stevenson, Abigail
Abigail - Malcolm Macdonald 3962

Stewart, Marie Jamesina Sibella
The Black Duchess - Alanna Knight 3514

Stokes, Annabelle
Jubilee Jim and the Wizard of Wall Street - Donald
    Porter 5112

Stonefield, Genevieve
Cain and His Brother - Anne Perry 4922

Stowe, Sarah
Swandowne - Daniel Farson 2024

Strand, Charity
Sanguinet's Crown - Patricia Veryan 6476

Stretton, Maud
Murder, I Presume - Gillian Linscott 3807.

Strong, Charity
Charity Strong - Marguerite Allis 109

Stuart, Arabella
Too Near the Throne - Molly Costain Haycraft 2797

Stuart, Francis
Lady on the Coin - Margaret Campbell Barnes 326

Stuart, Margot
Let the King Beware! - Honore Morrow 4489

Summerfield, Pamela
Princess Pamela - Ray Russell 5534

Summerfield, Phoebe
Princess Pamela - Ray Russell 5534

Suslova, Polina
The Devil Inside: A Novel of Dostoevsky's Life -
    Stephen Coulter 1385

Sutcliffe, Miriam
Visions of a Heart - Emily Carmichael 899

Sutherland, Jenny
Rainbird's Revenge - Marion Chesney 1046

Sutton, Claire
Two Corinthians - Carola Dunn 1797

Swynford, Katherine
Katherine - Anya Seton 5752

Sybil
King of the Wood - Valerie Anand 131

Sykes, Henrietta
Disraeli in Love - Maurice Edelman 1851

Tairo Tamako
The Sword of Hachiman - Lynn Guest 2608

Talbot-Harrow, Laura
Masque of Jade - Emma Merritt 4344

Tallant, Arabella
Arabella - Georgette Heyer 2874

Tania
Wartime Lies - Louis Begley 416

Taverner, Catherine
The Taverners' Place - Joanna Trollope 6351

Taylor, Sarah Knox
*There Was a Season: A Biographical Novel of
    Jefferson Davis* - Theodore Olsen 4730

Tedelli, Bianca
Bianca - Mabel Conquist 1257

Telfair, Helen
Shadow of a Lady - Jane Aiken Hodge 2971

Telford, Beatrice
Put Off Thy Shoes - Ethel Lillian Voynich 6513

Temple, Davina
Regency Rogue - Helen Ashfield 212

Temple, Elizabeth
The Pioneers; or, The Sources of the Susquehanna -
    James Fenimore Cooper 1307

Thane, Sarah
The Talisman Ring - Georgette Heyer 2905

Theros, Anna
A Woman of Quality - Jan Westcott 6649

Thomas, Donna
The Asherwood Protegee - Mary A. Garratt 2299

Thornton, Anne
The Girl - Catherine Cookson 1277

Thornton, Arabella
The Rich Are with You Always - Malcolm
    Macdonald 3971

Thorpe, Caroline
The Lost Garden - Jane Aiken Hodge 2966

Threadgold, Beverley
The Queen and I - Sue Townsend 6306

Throckmorton, Bess
Ralegh's Fair Bess: The Story of Bess Throckmorton -
    Judy Turner 6365

Tibbles, Georgina
East Indiaman - Frank Pollard 5087

Toby, Violet
The Queen and I - Sue Townsend 6306

Tolworthy, Arabella
Lament for a Lost Lover - Philippa Carr 921

Tonks, Miss
Back in Society - Marion Chesney 1017
Miss Tonks Turns to Crime - Marion Chesney 1041

Torreon, Inez
Doniphan's Ride - Les Savage Jr. 5620

Toshack, Annys
The Bright Blue Sky - Max Hennessy 2830

Tourville, Claudine de
Voices in a Haunted Room - Philippa Carr 931

Tower, Mary
Men of Albemarle - Inglis Fletcher 2135

Traherne, Arabella
The Blade of Castlemayne - Anthony Esler 1960

Tremont, Noel
Stuyvesant Square - Margaret Lewerth 3743

Trevelyan, Laura
Voss - Patrick White 6698

Trevenning, Caroline
It Began in Vauxhall Gardens - Jean Plaidy 5023

Trowbridge, Natalie
The Marquis and Miss Jones - Helen Ashfield 208

Tsepesh, Mary Windham
*Covenant with the Vampire: The Diaries of the Family
    Dracul* - Jeanne Kalogridis 3327

Tynedale, Kitty
The Tynedale Daughters - Norma Lee Clark 1093

Tynedale, Millie
The Tynedale Daughters - Norma Lee Clark 1093

Tynedale, Norrie
The Tynedale Daughters - Norma Lee Clark 1093

Valderocas, Isabel
The Marranos - Liliane Webb 6588

Valdez, Orlena
Night Wind's Woman - Shirl Henke 2825

Van Alen, Christal
Fair is the Rose - Meagan MacKinney 3997

Van der Meer, Adriana
The Hyde Park Murder - Elliott Roosevelt 5443

Van Gogh-Bonger, Johanna
Johanna: A Novel of the Van Gogh Family - Claire
    Cooperstein 1317

Van Lindsay, Lisette
Married Past Redemption - Patricia Veryan 6469

Vanderhoff, Julie
Homeland - John Jakes 3148

Vanhomrigh, Esther
Violent Friends - Winston Clewes 1113

Vassilchikova, Sonya
The Name of Hero - Richard Seltzer 5742

Vaudraye, Marsanne de
Marsanne - Virginia Coffman 1155

Vaudraye, Veronique de
Veronique - Virginia Coffman 1158

Vere, Cornelia de
The Lady From Yorktown - Eva McDonald 4260

Vere, Isabella
The Black Dwarf - Sir Walter Scott 5692

Veria
Roman Wall - Bryher 745

Verne, Philippa de
Command of the King - Mary Lide 3773

Verney, Patricia
Prisoners of Hope: A Tale of Colonial Virginia - Mary
    Johnston 3238

Vernon, Rosalind
The Parfit Knight - Juliet Blyth 555

Vesey, Errol
The Vesey Inheritance - Gwendoline Butler 822

Vevian, Clarissa
Finessing Clarissa - Marion Chesney 1029

Villebois, Anne de
The Captain From Connecticut - C.S. Forester 2171

Villerand, Marian
Rebellion Road - Helen Topping Miller 4392

Villiers, Barbara
The King's Brat - Constance Gluyas 2441
Lady on the Coin - Margaret Campbell Barnes 326
My Lady Benbrook - Constance Gluyas 2442

Villiers, Diana
The Fortune of War - Patrick O'Brian 4664
H.M.S. Surprise - Patrick O'Brian 4666
The Ionian Mission - Patrick O'Brian 4667
The Letter of Marque - Patrick O'Brian 4668
Post Captain - Patrick O'Brian 4672
The Surgeon's Mate - Patrick O'Brian 4674

Villiers, Elizabeth
The Three Crowns - Jean Plaidy 5070

Vincenzus, Diana
No King but Caesar - Anne Powers 5151

Vining, Mary
Where Glory Waits - Gertrude Crownfield 1437

Vinton, Celia
The Scimitar - Samuel Edwards 1890

Violett, Lily
Dear Lily - Malcolm W. Greenough Jr. 2575

Vollar, Nettie
Java Head - Joseph Hergesheimer 2854

von Grueber, Ippolita
Ippolita - Alberto Denti di Pirajno   1612

Vorontzou, Lisa
Katya - Lucy Cores   1328

Wakeford, Davina
The Bluestocking - June Drummond   1729

Walsingham, Frances
The Constant Star - Dorothy Norris Foote   2151

Walter, Lucy
The Wandering Prince - Jean Plaidy   5075

Warburton, Anne
The Dedicated - Willa Gibbs   2399

Ward, Jewel May
Sycamore Men - David Taylor   6181

Wardour, Isabella
The Antiquary - Sir Walter Scott   5690

Warren, Hannah
The Double Man - Elinor Pryor   5205

Warrington, Marietta
Lanterns - Patricia Veryan   6465

Waverly, Fanny
The First Rebellion - Marion Chesney   1030

Webster, Alma
The False Inspector Dew - Peter Lovesey   3912

Wells, Charlotte
Weep in the Sun - Jeanne Wilson   6809

Wells, Cynthia Ann
Sioux Splendor - Rosanne Bittner   515

Wendover, Abigail
Black Sheep - Georgette Heyer   2878

Wentworth, Cecilly
Dark Winds - Virginia Coffman   1152

Wentworth, Lilian de
Willowwood - Mollie Hardwick   2699

Westbrook, Harriet
Love's Children - Judith Chernaik   1013

Westmoreland, Olivia
The Highland Hawk - Leslie Turner White   6682

Whelan, Violett
Dear Lily - Malcolm W. Greenough Jr.   2575

Whidden, Phoebe
Blue Hurricane - F. van Wyck Mason   4146

Whitehall, Amanda
Amanda/Miranda - Richard Peck   4882

Whitfield, Matilda
Theo and Matilda - Rachel Billington   498

Whitton, Selena
Lord Iverbrook's Heir - Carola Dunn   1795

Wilde, Dorcas
By Our Beginnings - Jean Stubbs   6092

Wilkins, Penelope
Penelope Goes to Portsmouth - Marion
  Chesney   1043

Willoughby, Sophie
The Summer of the Bashinskeys - Diane
  Pearson   4877

Winter, Avys
My Lady Greensleeves - Constance Beresford-
  Howe   476

Wintour, Gillian
Opal - Helen Ashfield   210

Woodfall, Cecily
Trust and Treason - Margaret Birkhead   506

Woodhouse, Emma
Jane Fairfax - Joan Aiken   50

Woodleigh, Isabella
Gilded Splendour - Rosalind Laker   3595

Woodruff, Isabelle Chadwick
The Dream Seekers - Grace Mark   4085

Wraxall, Delilah
Enlightening Delilah - Marion Chesney   1028

Wright, Missy
The Ladies of Missalonghi - Colleen
  McCullough   4237

Wrox Hampden, Maria
Time and Chance - Gwen Davenport   1501

Wychwood, Annis
Lady of Quality - Georgette Heyer   2893

York, Veronica
Silence in Hanover Close - Anne Perry   4936

Zia
The Hittite - Noel B. Gerson   2373

GLADIATOR

Atretes
As Sure as the Dawn - Francine Rivers   5352

Eleazar, Simon ben
The Wolf of Masada - John Fredman   2220

Faljan
The Gladiator - Thames Ross Williamson   6790

Spartacus
The Gladiators - Arthur Koestler   3532

GOVERNESS

Armitage, Susan
Black-Eyed Susan - Deborah Camp   871

Ashford, Alissa
Masque of Enchantment - Charlene Cross   1432

Belchamber, Amelia
The Belchamber Scandal - Frances Murray   4533

Brigmore, Anna
The Mallen Girl - Catherine Cookson   1280
The Mallen Streak - Catherine Cookson   1282

Byford, Kate
Paths of Fortune - Susan Moore   4444

Castleman, Caroline
The Michaelmas Tree - Helen Ashfield   209

Clairmont, Claire
The Year of December - Lucy Cores   1329

Cortland, Lalia
The Place of Devils - Lucinda Baker   275

Deluzy-Desportes, Henriette
All This, and Heaven Too - Rachel Field   2080

Duval, Annette
The Quade Inheritance - Barbara Ker Wilson   3469

Flowers, Miss
Eugenie - Hester W. Chapman   989

Forrester, Dominique
The Duchess of Vidal - Dawn Lindsey   3793

Hamilton, Mary
Regency Royal - Michael Hardwick   2687

Lamont, Mary
Sarsen Place - Gwendoline Butler   821

Lausley, Sarah
The Skeleton in the Grass - Robert Barnard   320

Mildway, Sarah
Lady of Mallow - Dorothy Eden   1856

Paget, Ellen
The Girl From Paris - Joan Aiken   47

Pelham, Daisy
Imperial Winds - Priscilla Napier   4555

Penfold, Eden
The Golden Sabre - Jon Cleary   1105

Peters, Anne
Anna - Cynthia Harrod-Eagles   2752

Pickford, Ellen
The Abductors - Stuart Cloete   1121

Porteous, Mary
The Heroine's Sister - Frances Murray   4536

Radley, Elinor
A London Season - Anthea Bell   420

Rochdale, Elinor
The Reluctant Widow - Georgette Heyer   2899

Scarrow, Francoise
The Shadow of the Sun - Sylvia Pell   4891

Sedgwick, Ellen
Somewhere Within This House - Jean Francis
  Webb   6587

Smith, Adelaide
The Braganza Pursuit - Sarah Neilan   4564

Snow, Hester
The Web of Days - Edna Lee   3708

Treffrey, Deirdra
Cormorant's Brood - Inglis Fletcher   2133

Tremaine, Lily
Night Shadow - Catherine Coulter   1377

Trent, Ancilla
The Nonesuch - Georgette Heyer   2896

Trotter, Susannah
Cousin Susannah - Hazel Hucker   3066

Weston, Rilla
The House of Kuragin - Constance Heaven   2808

Williams, Eliza
Eliza's Daughter - Joan Aiken   44

Wyllys, Mrs.
The Red Rover - James Fenimore Cooper   1309

GOVERNMENT OFFICIAL

Acominatus, Nicetas
Against the Fall of Night - Michael Arnold   193

Antipatros
Funeral Games - Mary Renault   5297

Antipov, Pavel
Doctor Zhivago - Boris Pasternak   4824

Anza, Juan Bautista de
The Cross and the Sword - Jonreed Lauritzen   3674
Dust on the King's Highway - Helen Constance
  White   6677

Arias de Avila, Pedro
The Golden Eagle - John Edward Jennings   3201

Barakat, Zayni
Zayni Barakat - Gamal Ahitani   42

Baranov, Aleksandr
Alaska - James A. Michener   4364

Barton, Clara
Remember Santiago - Douglas C. Jones   3280

Barton, Conway
Shadow of the Moon - M.M. Kaye   3377

Beaton, David
James, by the Grace of God - Nigel Tranter   6315

Beaufort, Henry
The Serpent Amongst the Lilies - P.C. Doherty   1678

Beche, Edmund
The Death of a King - P.C. Doherty   1672

Benjamin, Judah P.
The Chess Player: A Novel of New Orleans and Paris - Frances Parkinson Keyes 3478
While the Music Plays - Diane Austell 242

Beria, Lavrenty
Generations of Winter - Vassily Aksyonov 61

Beringar, Hugh
Dead Man's Ransom - Ellis Peters 4957
One Corpse Too Many - Ellis Peters 4966
The Raven in the Foregate - Ellis Peters 4969
The Virgin in the Ice - Ellis Peters 4974

Bishop, Colonel
Captain Blood - Rafael Sabatini 5546

Blake, Henry
Carolina Courage - Dana Fuller Ross 5469

Bligh, William
Sara Dane - Catherine Gaskin 2316
Southern Cross - Terry Coleman 1206
Storm of Time - Eleanor Dark 1494

Bliss, Tasker
Pancho And Black Jack - Fred Bean 398

Bradford, William
O Western Wind - John Anthony Devon 1634

Breed, Navarro
Chase the Wind - Janelle Taylor 6184

Bronowsky, Count Dimitri
The Day of the Scorpion - Paul Scott 5682

Buade, Louis de
The Gilded Torch - Iola Fuller 2252
Heritage of the River - Muriel Elwood 1937
The King's Messenger - Samuel Edwards 1887
The Power and the Glory - Gilbert Parker 4805

Bukowski, Szymon
Poland - James A. Michener 4373

Cadwallader, Owen
The Mamur Zapt and the Spoils of Egypt - Michael Pearce 4871

Caius Porteus
Sarum: The Novel of England - Edward Rutherfurd 5536

Carey, Sir Robert
A Famine of Horses - P.F. Chisholm 1071
A Season of Knives - P.F. Chisholm 1072

Casement, Roger
Rebels: The Irish Rising of 1916 - Peter DeRosa 1622

Cecil, Robert
All the Queen's Men - Evelyn Anthony 157
The Bartholomew Fair Murders - Leonard Tourney 6297
Deborah and the Siege of Paris - Colette Davenat 1500
For Love of a Pirate - Anthony Esler 1961
Gay Lord Robert - Jean Plaidy 5015
I, Elizabeth - Rosalind Miles 4378
Knaves Templar - Leonard Tourney 6300
Lady Rich - Elizabeth Boatwright Coker 1166
Low Treason - Leonard Tourney 6301
My Lord Essex - Olive Eckerson 1838
Old Saxon Blood - Leonard Tourney 6302
Scapegoat for a Stuart - Kate Kirby 3504
Witness of Bones - Leonard Tourney 6304

Cecil, William
Elizabeth: Queen & Woman - Helen Thorpe 6279
For Love of a Pirate - Anthony Esler 1961
My Lord the Fox - Robert York 6932
The Proud Man - Elizabeth Linington 3800
The Robsart Affair - Jennette Letton 3729
To Love a Queen - Lawrence Schoonover 5669
The Young Elizabeth - Jennette Letton 3730

Champlain, Samuel de
Fathers and Crows - William T. Vollmann 6508

Cheyney, Sir Thomas
Feversham - Diane Davidson 1503

Churchill, Winston
Attack the Lusitania! - Raymond Hitchcock 2956
To the Honor of the Fleet - Robert H. Pilpel 5002

Classicus, Cornelius
Gold for the Caesars - Florence A. Seward 5759

Cooper, Robert
Trust and Treason - Margaret Birkhead 506

Corbett, Hugh
Angel of Death - P.C. Doherty 1670
The Crown in Darkness - P.C. Doherty 1671
The Prince of Darkness - P.C. Doherty 1675
Satan in St. Mary's - P.C. Doherty 1676
Satan's Fire - P.C. Doherty 1677
The Song of a Dark Angel - P.C. Doherty 1679
Spy in Chancery - P.C. Doherty 1680

Cornelius the Ciliarch
The Nazarene - Sholem Asch 200

Cranston, John
The Nightingale Gallery - Paul Harding 2684
Red Slayer: Being the Second of the Sorrowful Mysteries of Brother Athelstan - Paul Harding 2685

Cromwell, Thomas
The Concubine - Norah Lofts 3839
The Fifth Queen - Ford Madox Ford 2161
The King's Achievement - Robert Hugh Benson 459
The Nunnery - Dorothy Charques 1001
Queen Anne Boleyn - Francis Hackett 2634

Dashwood, Sir Francis
Master of Bengal: A Novel of Robert Clive of India - Norman Partington 4821

de Silva, Diego
Captain From Castile - Samuel Shellabarger 5794

Denton, John
Shanghai - Christopher New 4588

Dinwiddie, Robert
Red Morning - Ruby Frazier Frey 2230

Draskovich
The Petersburg-Cannes Express - Hans Koning 3538

Dudley, Joseph
Savage Gentleman - Noel B. Gerson 2381

Duroc, Paul
Murder in the West Wing - Elliott Roosevelt 5453

Eaton, Theophilus
Until the Winds - Jean Clark 1089

Eye
King Tut's Private Eye - Lee Levin 3739

Eyre, Edward John
Caribbean - James A. Michener 4365

Farnol, Clive
The Faraway Drums - Jon Cleary 1104

Felix, Caius Sempronius
The Little Emperors - Alfred Duggan 1770

Fenwick, Augustus
An Air of Glory - Sarah Neilan 4563

Flambard, Ranulf
Flambard's Confession - Marilyn Durham 1816

Fleischer, Herman
Shout at the Devil - Wilbur Smith 5930

Fong Tai
China Saga - C.Y. Lee 3706

Fortune, John
You Rolling River - Archie Binns 503

Fouche, Joseph
Marianne - Juliette Benzoni 466
Marianne and the Masked Prince - Juliette Benzoni 469

Fox, John
The Heretic - Alison Macleod 4002

Frankland, Harry
Be My Love - Harriet Hinsdale 2955

Fujiwara Nakamaro
The Vermilion Bridge - Shelley Mydans 4539

Geladius, Caius
Artorius Rex - John Gloag 2432

Gibboney, William
The Seasons of Heroes - Paxton Davis 1539

Glen, Stephen
Montana Road - Harry Sinclair Drago 1717

Godoy, Manuel de
The Last Portrait of the Duchess of Alba - Antonio Larreta 3666

Goffett, Thomas
Dubu: A Novel of New Guinean Conquest - Maslyn Williams 6789

Grey, Sir Edward
To the Honor of the Fleet - Robert H. Pilpel 5002

Hadrian
Threshold of Fire - Hella S. Haasse 2633

Haliwell, Terence
The King's Messenger - Samuel Edwards 1887

Hamilton, Alexander
Mistress of the Forge - David Taylor 6179

Herbert, Sidney
Pendragon: Late of Prince Albert's Own - Robert Trevelyan 6337

Heydrich, Reinhard
The Hangman's Crusade - James Barwick 370

Hoover, J. Edgar
Dillinger - Harry Patterson 4832
Flying into Love - D.M. Thomas 6236
The Immortals - Michael Korda 3540
Murder and the First Lady - Elliott Roosevelt 5444
Murder in the Executive Mansion - Elliott Roosevelt 5449
Murder in the Oval Office - Elliott Roosevelt 5450
True Crime - Max Allan Collins 1214

Hopkins, Mr.
The Siege of Krishnapur - J.G. Farrell 2016

Hutchins, John
The Land Where the Sun Dies - Henry Carlisle 896

Hyde, Edward
The Bride - Margaret Irwin 3116

Jeffreys, Sir George
Black Angels - C.T. Ritchie 5348

Johnson, Sir William
Brother Owl - Al Hine 2953
Cardigan - Robert W. Chambers 976
The Conqueror - John William Tebbel 6194
The Conquerors - Allen W. Eckert 1839
Fire Along the Sky: A Novel of America - Robert Moss 4497
The Firekeeper - Robert Moss 4498
The Golden Wildcat - Margaret Widdemer 6735
Lady of the Mohawks - Margaret Widdemer 6736
Red Cloak Flying - Margaret Widdemer 6737
Strife Before Dawn - Mary Schumann 5675
West to the Setting Sun - Harvey Chalmers 973
The Wilderness War - Allen W. Eckert 1848

Kennedy, Joseph P.
The Hyde Park Murder - Elliott Roosevelt 5443

Killigrew, John
The Grove of Eagles - Winston Graham 2526

Langmeade, Lucky
Vigilante - Richard Summers   6116

Li Hung Chang
Forbidden City - Muriel Molland Jernigan   3215

Louis, Comte de Provence
Scaramouche the King-Maker - Rafael Sabatini   5555

Lowe, Hudson
The Last Love - Thomas B. Costain   1367

Luna, Alvaro de
Master of Castile - Samuel Edwards   1888

MacCroy, Max
The Passion of Letty Fox - Diana Saunders   5610

Machiavelli, Niccolo
Mona Lisa: The Woman in the Portrait - Sara
  Mayfield   4206

Manilianus, Minutus Lausus
The Roman - Mika Waltari   6554

Mark, Philip
The Sheriff of Nottingham - Richard Kluger   3512

Markham, Robert
The Rage of the Vulture - Barry Unsworth   6388

McLaughlin, James
Arrest Sitting Bull - Douglas C. Jones   3273

McLoughlin, John
Vision of the Eagle - Kay L. McDonald   4263

Mencius, Nicator
The Big Fisherman - Lloyd C. Douglas   1702

Mendoza, Juan Hurtado de
Master of Castile - Samuel Edwards   1888

Meren, Lord
Murder at the Feast of Rejoicing - Lynda S.
  Robinson   5407
Murder at the God's Gate - Lynda S.
  Robinson   5408
Murder in the Place of Anubis - Lynda S.
  Robinson   5409

Merrick, Ronald
The Jewel in the Crown - Paul Scott   5684

Morane, Henry
The Killing of Richard the Third - Robert
  Farrington   2020
The Traitors of Bosworth - Robert Farrington   2021
Tudor Agent - Robert Farrington   2022

More, Sir Thomas
The Concubine - Norah Lofts   3839
The King's Achievement - Robert Hugh Benson   459
The King's Secret Matter - Jean Plaidy   5027
St. Thomas's Eve - Jean Plaidy   5060

Murtagh, Colum
The Book of Shadows - C.L. Grace   2505

Nanautzin
*The Sun, He Dies: A Novel about the End of the Aztec
  World* - Jamake Highwater   2919

Neighbors, Robert Simpson
Brazos Dreamer - Gene Shelton   5799

Ness, Eliot
Torsos - John Peyton Cooke   1270

Ogilvie, Hector
The Restless Frontier - Duncan MacNeil   4018

O'Hara, James
The King's Orchard - Agnes Sligh Turnbull   6363

O'Higgins, Ambrosio
O'Higgins and Don Bernardo - Edna Deu Pree
  Nelson   4578

Onesimus
Brothers of Vengeance - LeGette Blythe   556

Orestes
Hypatia - Charles Kingsley   3498

Ostermin, Don Antonio
Taos - Irwin R. Blacker   527

Owen, Captain Cadwallader
The Mamur Zapt and the Donkey-Vous - Michael
  Pearce   4866
The Mamur Zapt and the Girl in the Nile - Michael
  Pearce   4867
The Mamur Zapt and the Men Behind - Michael
  Pearce   4868
The Mamur Zapt and the Night of the Dog - Michael
  Pearce   4869
The Mamur Zapt and the Return of the Carpet -
  Michael Pearce   4870

Pacal Balam
Tikal: A Novel about the Maya - Daniel Peters   4947

Paenus
The Conspiracy - John Hersey   2870

Parks, Greg
Mission to Mackinac - Myron David Orr   4755

Paulinus, Suetonious
The Imperial Governor - George Shipway   5828

Peel, Robert
Fire, Burn! - John Dickson Carr   910

Pepys, Samuel
Mr. Pepys of Seething Lane - Cecil Abernethy   10

Phillip, Arthur
Botany Bay - Charles Nordhoff   4637
The Timeless Land - Eleanor Dark   1495

Phipps, William
Angelique and the Demon - Sergeanne Golon   2466

Piehue, U.K.
Petersburg - Emily Hanlon   2677

Pilate, Pontius
Barabbas: A Novel of the Time of Jesus - Emery
  Bekessy   417
The Bond and the Free - Charles Dunscomb   1813
The Bride of Pilate - Esther Kellner   3393
Brothers of Vengeance - LeGette Blythe   556
The Centurion - Leonard Wibberley   6729
Dear and Glorious Physician - Taylor Caldwell   853
The Emperor's Physician - Jacob Randolph
  Perkins   4914
First the Blade - Drayton Mayrant   4212
The Glorious Folly: A Novel of the Time of St. Paul -
  Louis De Wohl   1565
The Gospel According to Pontius Pilate - James R.
  Mills   4408
The Gospel of Corax - Paul Park   4802
Great Lion of God - Taylor Caldwell   858
He Came From Galilee - Daniel A. Poling   5083
Hear Me, Pilate! - LeGette Blythe   557
I, Judas - Taylor Caldwell   859
The Kingdom of the Wicked - Anthony Burgess   778
The Last Temptation of Christ - Nikos
  Kazantzakis   3384
Man Before the Morning - Cecil Maiden   4032
Man of Nazareth - Anthony Burgess   779
Man on Fire: A Novel on the Life of St. Paul -
  LeGette Blythe   558
The Nazarene - Sholem Asch   200
No King but Caesar - Anne Powers   5151
Pontius Pilate: A Biographical Novel - Paul L.
  Maier   4034
Pontius Pilate Reflects - Werner Koch   3529
The Robe - Lloyd C. Douglas   1703
The Same Scourge - John Goldthorpe   2464
The Secret of the Kingdom - Mika Waltari   6555
A Tear for Judas - LeGette Blythe   559
The Tentmaker - Julius Berstl   486
The Testament of Theophilus - Leonard
  Wibberley   6730
The Thorn of Arimathea - Frank G. Slaughter   5905
A Time for Judas - Morley Callaghan   866
The Word and the Sword - Theo Lang   3662

Plessis, Armand-Jean Du
The Anthem - Noel B. Gerson   2361
Wife to Great Buckingham - Hilda Lewis   3751

Plessis-Belliere, Philippe du
Angelique - Sergeanne Golon   2465

Ponsonby, Sir Henry
Oh! Where Are Bloody Mary's Earrings? - Robert
  Player   5079

Printz, Johan
Land of the Beautiful River - Helmer
  Linderholm   3788

Prochurus
*The Sins of Herod: A Novel of Rome and the Early
  Church* - Frank G. Slaughter   5900

Rampling, Hugh
Tudor Underground - Denis Meadows   4320

Ramsay, James Andrew Broun
Follow the Drum - James Leasor   3699

Raspale, Jean
The Death of a King - P.C. Doherty   1672

Rhodes, Cecil John
The City of Gold - Francis Brett Young   6940
On Trial for My Country - Stanlake Samkange   5578

Rich, Don Narciso
To the Indies - C.S. Forester   2183

Rockefeller, Nelson
Murder in the Blue Room - Elliott Roosevelt   5446

Rolland, Therese
Murder in the West Wing - Elliott Roosevelt   5453

Roosevelt, Franklin Delano
To the Honor of the Fleet - Robert H. Pilpel   5002

Roosevelt, Theodore
The Big Stick - Lawrence Alexander   82
Speak Softly - Lawrence Alexander   83
The Strenuous Life - Lawrence Alexander   84

Root, Elihu
1901 - Robert Conroy   1258

Savage, William
The Deceivers - John Masters   4173

Scarisbrooke, Richard
The Fate of Princes - P.C. Doherty   1673

Silva, Flavius
The Triumph - Ernest K. Gann   2280

Sinclair, Matthew
Mandalay - Alexandra Jones   3269

Slidell, John
The Chess Player: A Novel of New Orleans and Paris
  - Frances Parkinson Keyes   3478

Sparks, Jim
The List of Seven - Mark Frost   2237

Stanton, Andrew
The Jade Alliance - Elizabeth Darrell   1497

Stanton, Edwin
Heaven and Hell - John Jakes   3147
Love and War - John Jakes   3150

Stock, Matthew
The Bartholomew Fair Murders - Leonard
  Tourney   6297
Familiar Spirits - Leonard Tourney   6298
Frobisher's Savage - Leonard Tourney   6299
Knaves Templar - Leonard Tourney   6300
Low Treason - Leonard Tourney   6301
Old Saxon Blood - Leonard Tourney   6302
The Players' Boy Is Dead - Leonard Tourney   6303
Witness of Bones - Leonard Tourney   6304

Stuyvesant, Peter
The Dutchman - Maan Meyers   4351

Taira Kiyomori
The Heike Story - Eiji Yoshikawa 6934

Talleyrand-Perigord, Charles Maurice de
Captain Cut-Throat - John Dickson Carr 908
Far Flies the Eagle - Evelyn Anthony 162
Marianne - Juliette Benzoni 466
Marianne and the Masked Prince - Juliette Benzoni 469
Marianne and the Privateer - Juliette Benzoni 470
Napoleon Symphony - Anthony Burgess 780
The Rose and the Sword - Sandra Paretti 4792
The Winthrop Covenant - Louis Auchincloss 235

Tonneman, John
The High Constable - Maan Meyers 4353
The Kingsbridge Plot - Maan Meyers 4355

Tremayne, James
The Buckingham Palace Connection - Ted Willis 6792

Trescorre
The Valley of Decision - Edith Wharton 6653

Tweng, Thomas
The Death of a King - P.C. Doherty 1672

Underdown, Philip
The Plymouth Cloak - Kate Sedley 5718

Urswick, Christopher
The Killing of Richard the Third - Robert Farrington 2020
Tudor Agent - Robert Farrington 2022

Vespasian
The Brother - Chayym Zeldis 6958

Vetch, Silas
Black Angels - C.T. Ritchie 5348

Vinodius
Roman Wall - Bryher 745

Vivar, Blas
Sharpe's Devil - Bernard Cornwell 1340

Walsingham, Sir Francis
All the Queen's Men - Evelyn Anthony 157
Court of Shadows - Cynthia Morgan 4450
Fire over England - A.E.W. Mason 4143
The Firedrake's Eye - Patricia Finney 2095
Gay Lord Robert - Jean Plaidy 5015
I, Elizabeth - Rosalind Miles 4378
Immortal Queen - Elizabeth Byrd 834
Legacy - Susan Kay 3374
The Master of Gray Trilogy - Nigel Tranter 6316
My Lord Essex - Olive Eckerson 1838
Prisoner of the Queen - Alison Macleod 4006
The Proud Man - Elizabeth Linington 3800
Queen of This Realm: The Story of Queen Elizabeth I - Jean Plaidy 5050
Shadow in the Sun: A Novel of Elizabeth I, the Virgin Queen - F.W. Kenyon 3460
Tansy Taniard - Myrtle Strode-Jackson 6084
Till the Day Goes Down - Judith Lennox-Smith 3719
To Be a King - Robert DeMaria 1607
Trust and Treason - Margaret Birkhead 506
Tudor Underground - Denis Meadows 4320
Women of Ashdon - Valerie Anand 135

Weaver
Death and the Chapman - Kate Sedley 5715

Weiser, Conrad
The Interpreter - Robert Moss 4499

Welsford, Upton
The Revenge of Dracula - Peter Tremayne 6335

Wen Chin
Twilight of the Dragon - Peter Bourne 596

Wesley, John
The Holy Lover - Marie Oemler 4690

Wind, Bethany
Chase the Wind - Janelle Taylor 6184

Winslow, Thomas
The Crossed Sabres - Gilbert Morris 4458

Winthrop, John
Covenant of Grace - Jane Gilmore Rushing 5527
Witnesses - Marcy Moran Heidish 2820

Wolsey, Thomas
A Brood of Vipers - Michael Clynes 1133
Command of the King - Mary Lide 3773
The Gallows Murder - Michael Clynes 1134
The Grail Murders - Michael Clynes 1135
The King's Secret Matter - Jean Plaidy 5027
The Lady in the Tower - Jean Plaidy 5028
The Poisoned Chalice - Michael Clynes 1136
St. Thomas's Eve - Jean Plaidy 5060
The Shadow of the Pomegranate - Jean Plaidy 5062
The White Rose Murders - Michael Clynes 1137

Wriothesley, Thomas
Feast in the Morning - Hugh Preston 5175

Yanagisawa
Bundori - Laura Joh Rowland 5519

Zhdanko, Trofim
Alaska - James A. Michener 4364

Zimmerman, Arthur
The Petrograd Consignment - Owen Sela 5739

GRANDPARENT

Grandmother
Little Sister - Margaret Gaan 2259

GUARDIAN

Arbaces
The Last Days of Pompeii - Edward Bulwer-Lytton 768

Audley, Julian
Regency Buck - Georgette Heyer 2898

Carleton, Oliver
Lady of Quality - Georgette Heyer 2893

Chance, Jeff
Family Fortune - Mignon G. Eberhart 1834

England, Kirby
The Railway King - Margaret Mayhew 4207

Scott, Margaret Lorimer
Alexa - Anne Melville 4330

Traill, Virginia
A King Reluctant - William Vaughan Wilkins 6759

GUIDE

Bumppo, Natty
The Deerslayer - James Fenimore Cooper 1299
The Last of the Mohicans - James Fenimore Cooper 1302
The Pathfinder; or, The Inland Sea - James Fenimore Cooper 1305
The Prairie - James Fenimore Cooper 1308

Chestnut, Ross
The Brightwood Expedition - Kay L. McDonald 4261

Currito
Shadows in the Dusk - John Edward Jennings 3208

Drum, Ned
Pillar of Cloud - Jackson Burgess 782

El-i-chi
War Drums - Donald Clayton Porter 5133

Fowler, Joe
The Great Adventure - Janice Holt Giles 2410

Franklin, John
The Hammer of God - Alan Scholefield 5655

Kehwa, Charley
Trask - Don Berry 483

Kilkenny, Coyote
In the Season of the Sun - Kerry Newcomb 4590

Marina
Cortez and Marina - Edison Marshall 4105
The Golden Princess - Alexander Baron 335

Noble Popjoy
Shadow of the Moon - Douglas C. Jones 3284

Odin
Runestone - Don Coldsmith 1186

Red Moon
Mountain Devil - David Thompson 6257

Rivers, Josh
Oregon Bride - Rosanne Bittner 514

Sacajawea
Forward the Nation - Donald Culross Peattie 4880
The Gates of the Mountains - Will Henry 2842
Sacajawea - Anna Lee Waldo 6529
Sacajawea of the Shoshones - Della F. Emmons 1940
Star of the West - Ethel Hueston 3070
Tale of Valor - Vardis Fisher 2112
Trail: The Story of the Lewis and Clark Expedition - Louis Charbonneau 998

Spoon
Spoon - John Christgau 1074

Squanto
The Plymouth Adventure - Ernest Gebler 2342

Strong Bow
Return of the Spanish - Don Coldsmith 1183

Summers, Dick
Fair Land, Fair Land - A.B. Guthrie Jr. 2625
The Way West - A.B. Guthrie Jr. 2628

Thunder, Colt
Savage Thunder - Johanna Lindsey 3795

GUNFIGHTER

Blaisedell, Clay
Warlock - Oakley Hall 2653

Bonney, William
The Demise of Billy the Kid - Preston Lewis 3760

Books, John Bernard
The Shootist - Glendon Swarthout 6145

Brady, Martin
The Wonderful Country - Tom Lea 3695

Call, Woodrow F.
Lonesome Dove - Larry McMurtry 4298

Coleman, Zachary "Cole"
Telluride - Susan Clark Schofield 5648

Colfax, Oliver
Colfax - Robert J. Conley 1239
Killing Time - Robert J. Conley 1244
Quitting Time - Robert J. Conley 1249

Crabb, Jack
Little Big Man - Thomas Berger 478

Dart, Isom
One More River to Cross - Will Henry 2847

Eastmere, Arch
The Stars in Their Courses - Harry Brown 722

Hardin, John Wesley
Last Gun: The Legend of John Selman - Gene Shelton 5801
The Pistoleer - James Carlos Blake 536

Hickok, James Butler
Aces and Eights: A Novel of the Legend of Wild Bill Hickok - Loren D. Estleman 1967
Crazy Fox Remembers - Don Preston 5174
Little Big Man - Thomas Berger 478

Holliday, Doc
Tombstone Showdown - Leslie Scott 5681
Wyatt Earp - Matt Braun 653

Holliday, John Henry
Anything for Billy - Larry McMurtry 4295
Bloody Season - Loren D. Estleman 1968
Doc Holliday's Woman - Jane Candia Coleman 1201
The Lady and Doc Holliday - Preston Lewis 3761
Wilde West - Walter Satterthwait 5609

Jones, Hendry
The Authentic Death of Hendry Jones - Charles Neider 4562

Kirk, Egan
Father of Waters - Donald Clayton Porter 5118

McCaleb, Benton
The Goodnight Trail - Ralph Compton 1227

McCrae, Augustus
Lonesome Dove - Larry McMurtry 4298

Olive, Isom Prenice "Print"
Rawhider - Gene Shelton 5802

Sackett, Tyrel
The Daybreakers - Louis L'Amour 3619

Selman, John
Last Gun: The Legend of John Selman - Gene Shelton 5801

Smith, Gypsy
Children of the Dust - Carlile Clancy 1084

White, Brant
Saint Johnson - William R. Burnett 796

Winslow, Mark
The Union Belle - Gilbert Morris 4473

Young, Wilson
Heaven's Gold - Giles Tippette 6282

GYPSY

Beatriz
Columbus: A Romance - Rafael Sabatini 5549

Chilcott, Topaz
Topaz - Helen Ashfield 215

Consett, Amy
Had We Never Loved - Patricia Veryan 6463

Curle, Jody
Norah - Pamela Hill 2941

Esmeralda
The Hunchback of Notre Dame - Victor Hugo 3076

Froniga
The White Witch - Elizabeth Goudge 2496

Fuller, Hop
The Slow Awakening - Catherine Marchant 4082

Gitan
The Fallen Angels - Susannah Kells 3397

Jake, Romany
The Return of the Gypsy - Philippa Carr 927

Magpie Maggie Hag
Spangle - Gary Jennings 3196

Merrilies, Meg
Guy Mannering - Sir Walter Scott 5697

Morgan, Frank
The Stallion Man - Judith Glover 2438

Peveral, Luke
Sweet Songbird - Teresa Crane 1418

Romanov, Juliana
Circle in the Water - Susan Wiggs 6742

Sarita, Lola
The Gypsy From Cadiz - Tamsin Hamilton 2670

Starr, Mirabell
Rogue Herries - Hugh Walpole 6547

HANDICAPPED

Catalina
Catalina - William Somerset Maugham 4197

Disbrow, Packy
Blue Russell - Will Bryant 738

Erik
Phantom - Susan Kay 3375

Fielding, Sir John
Blind Justice - Bruce Alexander 76
Murder in Grub Street - Bruce Alexander 77
Watery Grave - Bruce Alexander 78

Little Wound
Dance Back the Buffalo - Milton Lott 3899

Margaret of Metola
The Woman in the Cloak - Pamela Hill 2949

McGrath, Ada
The Piano - Jane Campion 878

Mohun, Edith
An Ancient Evil - C.L. Grace 2504

Montag, Trudi
Stones From the River - Ursula Hegi 2816

Nydia
The Last Days of Pompeii - Edward Bulwer-Lytton 768

Paradies, Maria Theresa von
The Strange Case of Madamoiselle P. - Patrick Ireland 3109

Parbury, Miles
The Great Steamboat Race - John Brunner 736

Preele, David
Morgan's Woman - Iris Gower 2500

Quasimodo
The Hunchback of Notre Dame - Victor Hugo 3076

Saura of Roget
Candle in the Window - Christina Dodd 1662

Schlumberger, William
Kingkill - Thomas Gavin 2325

Simpson, Loretta
Comanche Moon - Catherine Anderson 137

Speaks-Not
World of Silence - Don Coldsmith 1195

Tilney, Fiona
Fire Opal - Pamela Hill 2932

Vernon, Rosalind
The Parfit Knight - Juliet Blyth 555

William of Miraval
Candle in the Window - Christina Dodd 1662

HEALER

Dark Mairi
Butcher's Broom - Neil Gunn 2620

Fahnee
Crazy Snake - Robert J. Conley 1240

Fairfax, Ingrid
The Age of Miracles - Catherine MacCoun 3960

Iza
The Clan of the Cave Bear - Jean M. Auel 236

Mama Yaya
I, Tituba, Black Witch of Salem - Maryse Conde 1233

Mathilde
God's Equal - Alain Absire 14

Mera
Soul Flame - Barbara Wood 6850

Selene
Soul Flame - Barbara Wood 6850

Wachera, Mama
Green City in the Sun - Barbara Wood 6849

Wolf Pup
Bearer of the Pipe - Don Coldsmith 1169

HEIR

Akeham, Henry
Ramillies - Barbara Whitehead 6708

Angelos, John
The Dark Angel - Mika Waltari 6551

Athelson, Athel
The Athelsons - Jocelyn Kettle 3476

Belden, Joshua
Birthright - Phillip Finch 2087

Boyce, Alfred
The Dukes: A Novel - Malcolm Ross 5503

Bullington, Viscount
Barry Lyndon - William Makepeace Thackeray 6210

Challoner, Edwin
A Heritage and Its History - Ivy Compton-Burnett 1229

Challoner, Simon
A Heritage and Its History - Ivy Compton-Burnett 1229

Chandler, Gordon
Ask Me No Questions - Patricia Veryan 6459

Clare, Richard de
The Marriage of Meggotta - Edith Pargeter 4799

Dalton, Bradford
Scarborough House - Sharon Salvato 5577

Darracott, Hugh
The Unknown Ajax - Georgette Heyer 2908

De Jeneau, Antoine
The Sugar Pavilion - Rosalind Laker 3600

Delange, Theophile
The Montmartre Murders - Richard Grayson 2561

Devers, Harry
The Intrigue - Marion Chesney 1034

Durris, Edward
Castle of Foxes - Alanna Knight 3516

Eden, Edward
The Prince of Eden - Marilyn Harris 2732

Eden, John
The Eden Passion - Marilyn Harris 2730
The Prince of Eden - Marilyn Harris 2732

Eden, Michael
Eden - Julie Ellis 1918

Eirik
In the Wilderness - Sigrid Undset 6381
The Son Avenger - Sigrid Undset 6384

Eversleigh, Edwin
Lament for a Lost Lover - Philippa Carr 921

Fortune, Nathaniel
Time out of Mind - Rachel Field 2081

Gaminini
The Winds of Sinhala - Colin De Silva 1562

Greenbourne, Solly
A Dangerous Fortune - Ken Follett 2147

Gruffydd
Lord of Misrule - Gareth Jones 3290

Hallows, John
In Pale Battalions - Robert Goddard 2444

Hammond, Clay
Bright Feather - Robert Wilder 6750

Hardwick, George
Master of Morholm - Timothy R. Wilson 6817

Harlow, George
The Heart of the Rose - June Barraclough 346

Hart, Aaron
Devil's Fire, Love's Revenge - Barbara Paul 4836

Hawthorne, Chadwick
Chelynne - Robyn Carr 938

Hilyard, Geoff
Cape Cod - William Martin 4139

Horton, Zack
Path of the Sun - Al Dempsey 1608

Kemp, Erasmus
Sacred Hunter - Barry Unsworth 6389

Kershaw, Julius
Dragonmede - Rona Randall 5246

Landeck, Felix Von
The Long Afternoon - Ursula Zilinsky 6964

Le Gros, Herbert
The Cornerstone - Zoe Oldenbourg 4714

Le Grys, Nicholas
Aurora Rose - Anne Worboys 6870

Lindsay, Craig
Indigo - Nicholas Carnac 900

Lockwood, Dillon
Thief of My Heart - Rexanne Becnel 410

Louis
Niccolo Rising - Dorothy Dunnett 1803

Louis XIX
The Uncrowned King - Baroness Emma Orczy 4747

Louis Charles
Fear No More - Hester W. Chapman 990

Lyngate, Adam
Midsummer Masque - Jill Tattersall 6174

Mallow, Blane
Lady of Mallow - Dorothy Eden 1856

Manningford, James
Cousin Susannah - Hazel Hucker 3066

Marsh, Leon
The Legacy of Beulah Land - Lonnie Coleman 1203

McKenzie, Max
Return of the Stranger - Reay Tannahill 6158

Mitchell, Dennis
The Magnolias - Julie Ellis 1922

Monteith, Ringan
Monsieur Janvier - Elizabeth Linington 3799

Morgan, Myles
The Sword of Truth - Gilbert Morris 4472

Mortimer, Clive
For They Shall Inherit - Malcolm Macdonald 3964

Mowbray, Malcolm
A Father and His Fate - Ivy Compton-Burnett 1228

Nero
Claudius the God - Robert Graves 2543

Norton, James
Painting the Darkness - Robert Goddard 2445

Paoul
The Earth Goddess - Richard Herley 2856

Pendellow, Drew
Castle Heritage - Elisabeth Barr 337

Penistone, Gareth
The Five-Minute Marriage - Joan Aiken 46

Polventon, Ben
Heir to Polventon - Marjorie Watson 6583

Pomeroy, Bertram
Miss Hartwell's Dilemma - Carola Dunn 1796
Two Corinthians - Carola Dunn 1797

Pyner, Daniel
Kezzy - Patricia Burns 799

Quade, Nicholas
The Quade Inheritance - Barbara Ker Wilson 3469

Rabi
The Golden Honeycomb - Kamala Markandaya 4086

Reed, Adrian
Shanghai Tango: A Novel of China - William Overgard 4769

Renard
The Leopard Unleashed - Elizabeth Chadwick 967

Rinn, Davy
Fabulous Valley - Cornelia Stratton Parker 4803

Roade, Kieron
Sarah Camberwell Tring - Janet Edmonds 1869

Sannazaro, Niccolo
Snared Nightingale - Geoffrey Trease 6324

Sarton, Christopher
Sarton Kell - Kate Mallory 4043

Savage, Keith
Savage Oaks - Julie Ellis 1924

Scott, Adam
Circle of Gold - Karen Harper 2710

Seadon, Ross
The Seadon Fortune - Leonard St. Clair 5563

Sedgemont, Hue
A Royal Quest - Mary Lide 3777

Sedgemont, Olwen
A Royal Quest - Mary Lide 3777

Sedgemont, Robert
A Royal Quest - Mary Lide 3777

Starkweather, Tyler
The Bank - Stephen Longstreet 3882

Stuart, Charles
The Wandering Prince - Jean Plaidy 5075

Stuart, James Francis Edward
The Stuart Legacy - Robert Kerr 3472

Taverner, Tom
The Taverners' Place - Joanna Trollope 6351

Tempest, Seven
Seven Tempest - William Vaughan Wilkins 6761

Titus
The Iron Hand of Mars - Lindsey Davis 1528
The Silver Pigs - Lindsey Davis 1532
Venus in Copper - Lindsey Davis 1534

Treleaven, Steven
Camelot Country - Marjorie McEvoy 4267

Van Vliet, 3vee
Paloverde - Jacqueline Briskin 693

Van Vliet, Bud
Paloverde - Jacqueline Briskin 693

Velasquez, Tomas
All or Nothing - Stephen Longstreet 3881

Warwyck, Daniel
Warwyck's Woman - Rosalind Laker 3604

Wentworth, Darius
Come Be My Love - Diana Brown 717

Whisten, Benjamin Biddle
Bygones - Frank Wilkinson 6762

Whitton, Edmund
Whitton's Folly - Pamela Hill 2948

Yves of Rifaucon
The Unhurrying Chase - H.F.M. Prescott 5172

HEIR—DISPOSSESSED

Balfour, David
Kidnapped - Robert Louis Stevenson 6010

Betram, Harry
Guy Mannering - Sir Walter Scott 5697

Burney, Josiah
The Forest Lord - Noel B. Gerson 2368

Charboneau, Phillipe
The Bastard - John Jakes 3144

Darrell, Thames
Jack Sheppard - William Harrison Ainsworth 56

De Brussac, Philip
The Earth and All It Holds - V.J. Banis 287
This Splendid Earth - V.J. Banis 289

Doon, Morven
The Malvie Inheritance - Pamela Hill 2938

Lirey, Nicholas
The Image of Our Lord - Edward Burman 790

Logan, Anthony
The Blood Endures - Robert Inman 3107

Mallow, Ambrose
Lady of Mallow - Dorothy Eden 1856

Ravenshoe, Charles
Ravenshoe - Henry Kingsley 3500

Ravenswood
The Bride of Lammermoor - Sir Walter Scott 5693

HEIR—LOST

Cass, Eppie
Silas Marner - George Eliot 1911

Edwards, Oliver
The Pioneers; or, The Sources of the Susquehanna - James Fenimore Cooper 1307

Lovel
The Antiquary - Sir Walter Scott 5690

Tremaine, Robert
The Masqueraders - Georgette Heyer 2894

HEIRESS

Albany, Leondra
Albany - Laura Black 519

Anderson, Doreen
Three Rivers - Carla J. Mills 4406

Armstrong, Noelle
The Earl and the Heiress - Barbara Metzger 4345

Ashington, Sarah
The Spring of the Tiger - Victoria Holt 3021

Bascombe, Henrietta
At the Sign of the Golden Pineapple - Marion Chesney 1016

Beard, Califa
To Fell the Giants - Bill Hotchkiss 3038

Blenkinsop, Sue Ellen
Wind of Change at Castle Rising - Fanny Cradock 1412

Cadogan, Kitty
The Gallant - William Stuart Long 3873

Carleton, Lucilla
Lady of Quality - Georgette Heyer 2893

Cartwright, Lucy
Greygallows - Barbara Michaels 4359

Caulfield, Antoinette
Peril under the Palms - K.K. Beck 404

Chance, Lucinda
Family Fortune - Mignon G. Eberhart 1834

Charing, Kitty
Cotillion - Georgette Heyer 2883

Chawleigh, Jenny
A Civil Contract - Georgette Heyer 2880

Claire, Isabelle de
Champion - L. Christian Balling 285

Croasdale, Leonie
Hand of Glory - Glen Petrie 4980

Curle, Norah
Norah - Pamela Hill 2941

da Silva, Miriam
The Strand - Claire Rayner 5269

de Barberie, Alinda
The Water Witch - James Fenimore Cooper 1311

Donellan, Aurora
Heiress of Ardara - Margaret Evans Porter 5137

Doon, Annabel
The Malvie Inheritance - Pamela Hill 2938

Drayton, Thorn
Vale of Tyranny - Suzanne Butler 831

Drury, Joanna
The Dreaming: A Novel of Australia - Barbara Wood 6848

Dupree, Suzanne
Savage Oaks - Julie Ellis 1924

Fortesque, Daria de
Secret Song - Catherine Coulter 1381

Freemantle, Emily
Emily Goes to Exeter - Marion Chesney 1027

Gaines, Myra Clark
New Orleans Woman: A Biographical Novel of Myra Clark Gaines - Harnett T. Kane 3355

Grafton, Persephone
A London Season - Anthea Bell 420

Grayson, Letitia
The Masqueraders - Georgette Heyer 2894

Grey, Katherine
Lady Hellfire - Suzanne Robinson 5414

Guardi, Serafina
The Glittering Strand - Judith Lennox-Smith 3716

Hampton, Caroline
The Hampton Heritage - Julie Ellis 1920

Hastings of Trent
Rosehaven - Catherine Coulter 1380

Heron, Thomazine
The Moon in the Water - Pamela Belle 433

Hervey, Jane
An Innocent Woman - Malcolm Macdonald 3967

Irvine, Katherine
Ravenburn - Laura Black 522

Isabelle de Croye
Quentin Durward - Sir Walter Scott 5705

Jervis, Clemency
The American Heiress - Dorothy Eden 1854

Karenina, Anna
Count Vronsky's Daughter - Carola Salisbury 5567

Kingaby, Sorrel
The Brittle Glass - Norah Lofts 3837

Lavrin, Alexandra Sergeivna
The Fortune Hunter - Ira J. Morris 4477

Lawley, Jemimah
Stormswift - Madeleine Brent 662

Lilianna
The Lily and the Leopard - Susan Wiggs 6745

MacLeod, Fiona
Perfecting Fiona - Marion Chesney 1044

Macmillan, Rachel
In Still and Stormy Waters - Reay Tannahill 6157

Magali
Bernadin, My Love - Leonard Rossiter 5506

Marchmont, Henrietta
Rebel Heiress - Jane Aiken Hodge 2969

Marcy, Susan
Storm Tide - Allan R. Bosworth 590

Margaret of Ashbury
In Pursuit of the Green Lion - Judith Merkle Riley 5334

Markham, Lyndell
My Lady Innkeeper - Barbara Metzger 4346

Marlow, Tansy
Ride the Blue Riband - Rosalind Laker 3598

Martin, Kate
The Prince Regent's Silver Bell - Gladys McGorian 4275

Mathick, Ann
A Season of Mists - Sarah Woodhouse 6856

Meridon
Meridon - Philippa Gregory 2583

Metcalf, Harriet
The Wicked Godmother - Marion Chesney 1053

Neville, Liana
The Taming - Jude Deveraux 1633

Peabody, Martha
First Night - Jane Aiken Hodge 2963

Penvennan, Caroline
The Last Gamble - Winston Graham 2527
Venture Once More - Winston Graham 2532

Percy, Elizabeth
Countess Carrots - Molly Costain Haycraft 2792

Power, Georgina
Georgina - Clare Darcy 1488

Quade, Imogene
The Quade Inheritance - Barbara Ker Wilson 3469

Richmond, Oriel
Lady Defiant - Suzanne Robinson 5412

Risle, Matilda de
The Morning Gift - Diana Norman 4645

Rojas, Estrellita de
Eagles of Destiny - Jory Sherman 5817

Satterleigh, Sharisse
The Rake - Karen Lynn 3941

Scelfton, Felise
The Troubadour's Romance - Robyn Carr 940

Sekeeta
Winged Pharaoh - Joan Grant 2536

Sherbrooke, Joan "Sinjin"
The Heiress Bride - Catherine Coulter 1375

Sherwood, Charissa
Allegheny Captive - Caroline Bourne 591

Sinclair, Perdita
Strathgallant - Laura Black 523

Tamar
Tamar - Ann Chamberlin 975

Taverner, Judith
Regency Buck - Georgette Heyer 2898

Tebb, Primrose
Stranger's Forest - Pamela Hill 2943

Tempest, Abigail
The Traitors - William Stuart Long 3879

Tiepolo, Violetta
The Bravo - James Fenimore Cooper 1298

Tozer, Eve
High Road to China - Jon Cleary 1106

Travers, Ruby
Ruby - Helen Ashfield 213

Tregaran, Joycelyn
Tregaran - Mary Lide 3779

Tryon, Cassie
Hearts of Fire - Christina Savage 5616

Van Buren, Adeline
Hawken Fury - David Thompson 6254

Vaudraye, Marsanne de
Marsanne - Virginia Coffman 1155

Wendover, Fanny
Black Sheep - Georgette Heyer 2878

HEIRESS—DISPOSSESSED

Alix of Wanthwaite
Shield of Three Lions - Pamela Kaufman 3372

Carteret, Delphie
The Five-Minute Marriage - Joan Aiken 46

Harrison, Francie
Fortune Is a Woman - Elizabeth Adler 39

Leonie
These Old Shades - Georgette Heyer 2906

Verne, Philippa de
Command of the King - Mary Lide 3773

HEIRESS—LOST

Monday, Caroline
Bride of the Unicorn - Kasey Michaels 4363

Remizou, Mariana
Heirs of the Motherland - Judith Pella 4893

Thatcher, Bird
Longleaf - Rose Brock 701

HERBALIST

Culpepper, Nicholas
The Affairs of Nicholas Culpepper - Mabel L. Tyrrel 6375

Habash, Bandy
A River Town - Thomas Keneally 3415

Pengrath, Madeline
Do Not Disturb - Kate Kingsbury 3492

HERO

Behan, Billy
Billy Bathgate - E.L. Doctorow 1656

Bellerophon
Three Ships and Three Kings - Georgia Sallaska 5573

Bruno
The Age of Wonders - Aharon Appelfeld 173

Duval, Denis
Denis Duval - William Makepeace Thackeray 6211

Falconer, Henry
The Hawks of Hawk-Hollow - Robert Montgomery
    Bird   504

Hippolochus
Three Ships and Three Kings - Georgia
    Sallaska   5573

Korzeniowski, Joe
Loon Lake - E.L. Doctorow   1657

Montorio, Antonio de
Saragossa - Benito Perez Galdos   4912

Morgan, Huw
How Green Was My Valley - Richard
    Llewellyn   3813

Paget, Carloman
The Weeping Ash - Joan Aiken   54

Perseus
Three Ships and Three Kings - Georgia
    Sallaska   5573

Tower, Alwyn
The Grandmothers - Glenway Westcott   6640

HEROINE

Armstrong, Amanda
Woman's Own - Robyn Carr   941

Armstrong, Emily
Woman's Own - Robyn Carr   941

Armstrong, Lilly
Woman's Own - Robyn Carr   941

Auclair, Cecile
Shadows on the Rock - Willa Cather   959

Basia
Fire in the Steppe - Henryk Sienkiewicz   5847

Berling, Elizabeth
The Story of Gosta Berling - Selma Lagerlof   3586

Blacksmith, Gilda
The Chant of Jimmie Blacksmith - Thomas
    Keneally   3411

Bumpass, Ephephtha
Confederates - Thomas Keneally   3412

Carty, Judith
A Woman Scorned - Malcolm Macdonald   3978

Crawford, Martha Mary
Miss Martha Mary Crawford - Catherine
    Marchant   4081

Deans, Jeanie
The Heart of Midlothian - Sir Walter Scott   5698

Doheny, Susie
Peder Victorious - O.E. Rolvaag   5435

Drummond, Catriona
Catriona - Robert Louis Stevenson   6009

Duclos, Mireille
Devilseed - Frank Yerby   6914

Dunhill, Lydia
Freedom's Dues - Robert H. Abel   9

Dynever, Cecil
Lionel Lincoln; or, The Leaguer of Boston - James
    Fenimore Cooper   1303

Elie
Butcher's Broom - Neil Gunn   2620

Ferrier, Angela
Toil of the Brave - Inglis Fletcher   2141

Flinders, Mary
The Silver Highways - Malcolm Macdonald   3972

Grandmother
Little Sister - Margaret Gaan   2259

Gregory, Morna
Bridey's Mountain - Yvonne Adamson   34

Hamilton, Catherine
Goldeneye - Malcolm Macdonald   3965

Harding, Fanny
The Bride of the Wilderness - Charles McCarry   4220

Hasford, Catrina
Come Winter - Douglas C. Jones   3275

Helen
Ashes - Stefan Zeromski   6960

Henna, Jesse
Ben Retallick - E.V. Thompson   6263

Hoskuldsdaughter, Hallgerda
Fire in the Ice - Dorothy James Roberts   5375

Isobel, Bridget
Bridey's Mountain - Yvonne Adamson   34

Katz, Henrietta
The Healer - Aharon Appelfeld   176

Kraus, Tzili
Tzili: The Story of a Life - Aharon Appelfeld   180

Leslie, Hope
Hope Leslie; or, Early Times in Massachusetts -
    Catharine Maria Sedgewick   5714

Ling, May
The Immigrants - Howard Fast   2034

Loring, Catherine
The Hawks of Hawk-Hollow - Robert Montgomery
    Bird   504

MacMahon, Lorna
The Power and the Passion - Christina
    Nicholson   4609

Margit
Arne - Bjornstjerne Bjornson   518

Maria
The Stuart Women - Matt Braun   652

Mariquilla
Saragossa - Benito Perez Galdos   4912

McAllister, Ariana
Bridey's Mountain - Yvonne Adamson   34

Menteith, Margaret
The Bonnet Laird's Daughter - Barbara
    Annandale   154

Montgomery, Val
Castle Barebane - Joan Aiken   43

Morgan, Beth
How Green Was My Valley - Richard
    Llewellyn   3813

Olenka
The Deluge - Henryk Sienkiewicz   5846

Paget, Fanny
The Weeping Ash - Joan Aiken   54

Paget, Scylla
The Weeping Ash - Joan Aiken   54

Patterson, Susan
The Captives - Don Wright   6878

Peacock
Cry of the Peacock - Gina Barkhordar Nahai   4552

Perdita
Mysteries of Winterthurn - Joyce Carol Oates   4659

Perreira, Jolene
The Earth and All It Holds - V.J. Banis   287

Pittman, Jane
The Autobiography of Miss Jane Pittman - Ernest J.
    Gaines   2270

Rigey, Luisa
The Patriot - Antonio Fogazzaro   2146

Schloss, Lotte
The Retreat - Aharon Appelfeld   178

Smith, Philadelphia
Miss Philadelphia Smith - Paula Allardyce   91

Sopwith, Tilly
Tilly Alone - Catherine Cookson   1289

Stornaway, Nell
The Toll-Gate - Georgette Heyer   2907

Thomna
Beyond the Aegean - Elia Kazan   3382

Trago, Miriam
Chase the Wind - E.V. Thompson   6264

Ware, Cynthia
Coniston - Winston Churchill   1078

Welldone, Kate
Sergeant Lamb's America - Robert Graves   2552

Williamson, Fancy
A Woman Called Fancy - Frank Yerby   6931

HIGHWAYMAN

Carstares, John
The Black Moth - Georgette Heyer   2877

Doherty, John "Thunderbolt"
Captain Lightfoot - William R. Burnett   792

Duppan, Jack
The Highwayman - Noel B. Gerson   2372

Mallary, Dorien
The Storm Witch - Elisabeth Barr   339

St. Clare, Richard
Desire and Deceive - Cordia Byers   832

Stafford, Neil
The Pagoda Tree - Berkely Mather   4181

Tewkes, Harry
His Majesty's Highwayman - Donald Barr
    Chidsey   1061

Thompson, Tally Ho
The Highwayman and Mr. Dickens - William J.
    Palmer   4783

Turpin, Dick
The Long Day Closes - Beatrice Tunstall   6360

Wakesfield, Megan
Desire and Deceive - Cordia Byers   832

HISTORIAN

Adams, Henry
Panama - Eric Zencey   6959

Balfour, Alex
Till the End of Time - Allen Appel   170
Time After Time - Allen Appel   171
Twice upon a Time - Allen Appel   172

Carey, Daniel
A Generation of Leaves - Robert S. Bloom   552

Clayton, Alfred
Memories of the Ford Administration - John
    Updike   6391

Dio Cassius
The Side of the Moon - Amanda Prantera   5162

Elphinstone, Charles
The Smile of the Stranger - Joan Aiken   53

Ethan
The King David Report - Stefan Heym   2910

Fussholdt, Dr.
Badenheim 1939 - Aharon Appelfeld   174

Josephus, Flavius
The Jew of Rome - Lion Feuchtwanger   2071

Josephus and the Emperor - Lion
  Feuchtwanger 2073
The Soldier and the Sage: A Novel about Akiba -
  Richard G. Hubler 3065
The Source - James A. Michener 4374
The Triumph - Ernest K. Gann 2280
The Voices of Masada - David Kossoff 3545
The Wolf of Masada - John Fredman 2220
The Word and the Sword - Theo Lang 3662

Kelly, Arthur
Grant's War - Ted Jones 3297

Las Casas, Bartolome de
The Indian Chronicles - Jose Barreiro 349

Matthias, Josef ben
The Tenth Measure - Brenda Lesley Segal 5721

Moore, George
The Year of the French - Thomas Flanagan 2121

Perron, Guy
A Division of the Spoils - Paul Scott 5683

Prentiss, Patrick
The Tenants of Time - Thomas Flanagan 2120

Prien, Major Ruben
From Time to Time - Jack Finney 2092

Turner, Frederick Jackson
Billy Sunday - Rod Jones 3295

Walker, Matthew
The House of Memory: A Novel of Shanghai -
  Nicholas R. Clifford 1117

HOMOSEXUAL

Bowman, Mark
Mark - Lonnie Coleman 1205

Edward II
Harlot Queen - Hilda Lewis 3748

Gaveston, Piers
Harlot Queen - Hilda Lewis 3748

Gorges, Richard
Jewels - Robert Perrin 4917

Manning, Charles
The Eye in the Door - Pat Barker 307

Ross, Robert
The Eye in the Door - Pat Barker 307

HORSE TRAINER

Bannock, Bart
Kimberley - Colin Burke 784

Clements, Joseph
Horses of War - Duff Hart-Davis 2760

HOTEL OWNER

Kent, Amanda
The Furies - John Jakes 3146

Sinclair, Cecily
Check-Out Time - Kate Kingsbury 3491
Do Not Disturb - Kate Kingsbury 3492
Eat, Drink, and Be Buried - Kate Kingsbury 3493
Grounds for Murder - Kate Kingsbury 3494
Room with a Clue - Kate Kingsbury 3495
Service for Two - Kate Kingsbury 3496

HOTEL WORKER

Wilcox, Carl
The Man Who Missed the Party - Harold Adams 25

HOUSEKEEPER

Jeffries, Mrs.
The Ghost and Mrs. Jeffries - Emily Brightwell 681
The Inspector and Mrs. Jeffries - Emily
  Brightwell 682
Mrs. Jeffries and the Missing Alibi - Emily
  Brightwell 683
Mrs. Jeffries Dusts for Clues - Emily Brightwell 684
Mrs. Jeffries on the Trail - Emily Brightwell 686
Mrs. Jeffries Plays the Cook - Emily Brightwell 687
Mrs. Jeffries Stands Corrected - Emily
  Brightwell 688
Mrs. Jeffries Takes Stock - Emily Brightwell 689

Jordan, Betsy
Mrs. Betsy, or Widowed and Wed - Francis
  Marton 4141

Kaatje
A Woman of Quality - Jan Westcott 6649

Katerina
Katerina - Aharon Appelfeld 177

Kilgour, Kate
Colliers Row - Jan Webster 6592

Meredith, Hallie
The Unplowed Sky - Jeanne Williams 6783

Pym, Hannah
Beatrice Goes to Brighton - Marion Chesney 1019
Belinda Goes to Bath - Marion Chesney 1020
Deborah Goes to Dover - Marion Chesney 1023
Emily Goes to Exeter - Marion Chesney 1027
Penelope Goes to Portsmouth - Marion
  Chesney 1043
Yvonne Goes to York - Marion Chesney 1054

Walters, Margaret
Loving Sands, Deadly Sands - Charlotte
  Keppel 3465

Witherspoon, Mrs.
Mrs. Jeffries on the Ball - Emily Brightwell 685

Wolsey, Hester
Mother and Son - Ivy Compton-Burnett 1231

HOUSEWIFE

McCaskill, Beth
English Creek - Ivan Doig 1683

Rose
World's Fair - E.L. Doctorow 1661

HUNTER

Baranov, Aleksandr
Ashana - E.P. Roesch 5424

Bumppo, Natty
The Pioneers; or, The Sources of the Susquehanna -
  James Fenimore Cooper 1307

Clayborn, Lance
*Forest Cavalier: A Romance of America's First
  Frontier and of Bacon's Rebellion* - Roy Catesby
  Flannagan 2122

Cobden, Joe
Heart of the Country - Greg Matthews 4190

Davis, Aaron
Journey by the River - John Prescott 5173

Driggs, Bill
The Bad Lands - Oakley Hall 2651

Gayabuc
Rabbit Boss - Thomas Sanchez 5581

Gilson, Charley
The Last Hunt - Milton Lott 3900

Hart, Worth
One of the Raymonds - Jean Rikhoff 5332

Karakou, Luka
The Great Alone - Janet Dailey 1454

Kori
The Animal Wife - Elizabeth Marshall Thomas 6243

Kosar-Eh
Shadow of the Watching Star - William
  Sarabande 5601

Lamming, Lord
The Hammer of God - Alan Scholefield 5655

Lightburn, Rush
I Take This Land - Richard Powell 5147

Liklik
The Echoing Cliffs - Hjalmar P. Thesen 6219

MacKensie, Sandy
The Last Hunt - Milton Lott 3900

Maliwal
The Sacred Stones - William Sarabande 5600

Masau
The Sacred Stones - William Sarabande 5600

Miller
Butcher's Crossing - John Williams 6786

Moolman
Rags of Glory - Stuart Cloete 1126

Piete du Plessis, Zwart
The Turning Wheels - Stuart Cloete 1127

Pride, Isaac
Heartland - Robert Douglas Mead 4316

Queen, Robert
The Great Sky and the Silence - James S. Rand 5245

Ranec
The Mammoth Hunters - Jean M. Auel 237

Runs in Light
People of the Wolf - W. Michael Gear 2341

Samiq
Brother Wind - Sue Harrison 2748

Sarak
The White Dawn - James Houston 3053

Stewart, Ling
The Land Is Bright - James Arthur Kjelgaard 3508

Storey, Frederick Seaton
Lion in the Evening - Alan Scholefield 5656

Swift
The Animal Wife - Elizabeth Marshall Thomas 6243
Reindeer Moon - Elizabeth Marshall Thomas 6244

Tor
Children of the Dawn - Patricia Rowe 5516
Keepers of the Misty Time - Patricia Rowe 5517

Torka
Beyond the Sea of Ice - William Sarabande 5595
Corridor of Storms - William Sarabande 5596
Forbidden Land - William Sarabande 5599
Walkers of the Wind - William Sarabande 5603

IMMIGRANT

Angelelli, Rosa
Storming Heaven - Denise Giardina 2394

Armagh, Joseph
Captains and the Kings - Taylor Caldwell 851

Banicek, Tom
Ellis Island - Fred Mustard Stewart 6023

Barclay, Adair
Dancing at the Rascal Fair - Ivan Doig 1682

Barclay, Rob
Dancing at the Rascal Fair - Ivan Doig 1682

Bendelbinder, Aaron
The Dream Seekers - Stephen Longstreet 3884

Bjorklund, Ingeborg
An Untamed Land - Lauraine Snelling 5936

Bjorklund, Ronald
An Untamed Land - Lauraine Snelling 5936

Breslain, Esther
The House on Mulberry Street - Maan Meyers 4354

Brody, Jake
My Own Ground - Hugh Nissenson 4628

Cassidy, Patrick
Passage West - Dallas Miller 4382

Chen Kai Tsu
Golden Destiny - June Wyndham Davies 1506

Chesney, Old Sergeant Bobby
Shadow of the Moon - Douglas C. Jones 3284

Chung Lin
Sweetwater Fever - Robert H. Adelman 36

Crown, Paul
Homeland - John Jakes 3148

Dunne, Vincent
Men of No Property - Dorothy Davis 1517

Eaton, James
The Quality of Mercy - Anne Miller Downes 1712

Erickson, Guri
Big Ember - Edward Havill 2778

Farrell, Michael
Dominion - Jack Rowe 5514

Fiore, George
All or Nothing - Stephen Longstreet 3881

Foss, Erik
The Emigrants - Johan Bojer 561

Free, Henry
Free Man - Conrad Richter 5320

Goldfeder, David
Leah's Journey - Gloria Goldreich 2460

Goldfeder, Leah
Leah's Journey - Gloria Goldreich 2460

Goodhill, Mary
Erie Water - Walter D. Edmonds 1875

Greypaull, Rhoda
Double Wedding Ring - Patricia Wendorf 6624

Hagen, Peter
What the Heart Keeps - Rosalind Laker 3605

Haynes, Ruth
The Cavalryman - Harold Sinclair 5861

Hickey, Margaret
Men of No Property - Dorothy Davis 1517

Hickey, Norah
Men of No Property - Dorothy Davis 1517

Holm, Peer
The Great Hunger - Johan Bojer 562

Hoshi, Sataro
Chikara! - Robert Skimin 5876

Howard, Hannah Maria
The Plums Hang High - Gertrude E. Finney 2091

Howard, Jethro
The Plums Hang High - Gertrude E. Finney 2091

Hunsacker, Mary
The Life and Times of Captain N. - Douglas Glover 2436

Jermyn, Anna
Daughters of the New World - Susan Richards Shreve 5835

Kapp, Jackie
The Celebrant - Eric Rolfe Greenberg 2572

Kracha, Djuro
Out of This Furnace - Thomas Bell 425

Kvidal, Morten
The Emigrants - Johan Bojer 561

Levy, Hannah
Rivington Street - Meredith Tax 6175
Union Square - Meredith Tax 6176

Levy, Zalman
Miami: A Saga - Evelyn Wilde Mayerson 4204

Lewin, Isaac
West to Eden - Gloria Goldreich 2461

Lindowska, Rissa
Glorious Morning - Julie Ellis 1919

Locke, Anne
Down From the Mountain - Louis Charbonneau 997

Lyte, Catherwood
Catherwood - Marly Youmans 6937

MacDonald, Flora
Meggy MacIntosh - Elizabeth Janet Gray 2555

Mackay, Callum
Promised Lands - Elizabeth Crook 1430

Mallon, Mary
The Ballad of Typhoid Mary - Jurg Federspiel 2057

McCaskill, Angus
Dancing at the Rascal Fair - Ivan Doig 1682

McMahon, Brendan
They Were Dreamers - James F. Murphy Jr. 4525

Moore, Joshua
Joshua Moore, American - George Frederick Hummel 3078

Moynahan, Ellen
One Small Candle - Mary Linehan MacKinnon 3998

Neilson, Gunnar
A Circle of Trees - Dana Faralla 2012

Neilson, Kersti
A Circle of Trees - Dana Faralla 2012

Nilsson, Karl Oskar
The Emigrants - Vilhelm Moberg 4422
Unto a Good Land - Vilhelm Moberg 4425

Nilsson, Kristina
The Emigrants - Vilhelm Moberg 4422

Nilsson, Robert
The Emigrants - Vilhelm Moberg 4422
Unto a Good Land - Vilhelm Moberg 4425

O'Connell, Maura Dooley
Maura's Dream - Joel Gross 2602

O'Connell, Patrick
Maura's Dream - Joel Gross 2602

O'Malley, Kathleen
A Bride for Donnigan - Janette Oke 4705

Raphael, Miriam
Crescent City - Belva Plain 5078

Rubinstein, Jacob
Ellis Island - Fred Mustard Stewart 6023

Santorelli, Marco
Ellis Island - Fred Mustard Stewart 6023

Shannon, Nora
Passage West - Dallas Miller 4382

Shaw, Lisa
What the Heart Keeps - Rosalind Laker 3605

Silverthorn, Alex
The Dream Seekers - Stephen Longstreet 3884

Skaret, Kal
The Emigrants - Johan Bojer 561

Solomon, Nathan
Dreams of Gold - Lewis Orde 4748

Southgate, John
Wild Dog Running - Alan Scholefield 5658

Stafford, Emily
The Brahmins - Eileen Lottman 3901

Steinsson, Steiner
Paradise Reclaimed - Halldor Laxness 3686

Stevens, Melisande
Storm Before Sunrise - June Wyndham Davies 1507

Tai Ming Kwong
The House That Tai Ming Built - Virginia Lee 3711

Topouzoglou, Stavros
America, America - Elia Kazan 3380
The Anatolian - Elia Kazan 3381
Beyond the Aegean - Elia Kazan 3382

Torkelsen, Rolfe
Big River, Big Man - Thomas William Duncan 1786

Vicker, Charlotte ·
Wild Dog Running - Alan Scholefield 5658

IMMORTAL

Segalla, Nicholas
The Prince Lost to Time - Ann Dukthas 1776
A Time for the Death of a King - Ann Dukthas 1777
The Time of Murder at Mayerling - Ann Dukthas 1778

IMPOSTER

Ashford, Alissa
Masque of Enchantment - Charlene Cross 1432

Baranov, Walter
The False Inspector Dew - Peter Lovesey 3912

Edwards, Oliver
The Pioneers; or, The Sources of the Susquehanna - James Fenimore Cooper 1307

Heath, Emma Louise
The Pilgrimage - Ann B. Ross 5463

Howe, Martina
The Marquis and Miss Jones - Helen Ashfield 208

Lacey, Prudence
The Masqueraders - Georgette Heyer 2894

Lacey, Robin
The Masqueraders - Georgette Heyer 2894

Montgomery, Lacie
Thief of My Heart - Rexanne Becnel 410

Neville, John
The Bisley Boy - Christopher Hunt 3080

Paxton, Eugenia
Night Storm - Catherine Coulter 1378

Ryder, Jared
Deception - Amanda Quick 5214

Stone, Jeremy
The Imposter - Noel B. Gerson 2375

Warbeck, Perkin
Chain of Destiny - Nigel Tranter 6314
The Courts of Illusion - Rosemary Hawley Jarman 3165
Merchant of the Ruby - Alice Harwood 2766
The Tudor Rose - Margaret Campbell Barnes 329
Women of Ashdon - Valerie Anand 135
The Wrong Plantagenet - Marian Palmer 4781

INDIAN

Adiawano
Savage Gentleman - Noel B. Gerson 2381

Ah-Wen-Ga
Tomahawk - Donald Clayton Porter 5129

Ahbleza
Hanta Yo - Ruth Beebe Hill 2951

Amigigh
My Sister, the Moon - Sue Harrison 2750

Andiora
This Widowed Land - Kathleen O'Neal Gear 2331

Antelope
Let the Drum Speak: A Novel of Ancient America -
Linda Lay Shuler 5837

Apeyahola
Harp of a Thousand Strings - Harold Lenoir
Davis 1522

Asa
The Pecos River - Fred Bean 399

Ashana
Ashana - E.P. Roesch 5424

Askwani
Beulah Land - Harold Lenoir Davis 1520

Atala
Atala - Francois Rene de Chateaubriand 1008

Atarho
Father of Waters - Donald Clayton Porter 5118

Bandylegs, Captain Bob
Here I Stay - Elizabeth Coatsworth 1138

Basket, Fuegia
Jemmy Button - Benjamin Subercaseaux 6107

Bear Paws
Bride of the Morning Star - Don Coldsmith 1170

Bear Talker
Dawn Land - Joseph Bruchac III 734

Beauvaise, Jane
Women in the Wind - Margaret Ritter 5350

Beckwourth, Jim
Ammahabas - Bill Hotchkiss 3036
Follow the Free Wind - Leigh Brackett 621
The Medicine Calf - Bill Hotchkiss 3037

Beehunter
To Make a Killing - Robert J. Conley 1252

Bending Reed
Lord Grizzly - Frederick F. Manfred 4056

Big Foot
A Creek Called Wounded Knee - Douglas C.
Jones 3277

Big Turtle
The Forest and the Fort - Hervey Allen 100

Birdson, Joe
Rabbit Boss - Thomas Sanchez 5581

Black Bull, Thomas
When the Legends Die - Hal Borland 584

Black, Charlie
Back to Malachi - Robert J. Conley 1237

Black Hawk
Shaman - Noah Gordon 2483
The Shining Trail - Iola Fuller 2254
Thunder on the River - Charlton Laird 3590
Twilight of Empire - Allen W. Eckert 1846
Wind over Wisconsin - August Derleth 1620

Black Kettle
The Last Warpath - Will Henry 2844

Black Skull
People of the Lakes - W. Michael Gear 2336

Blood Hawk
Eye of the Hawk - David William Ross 5498

Blue Duck
Belle Starr - Speer Morgan 4453

Blue Elk
When the Legends Die - Hal Borland 584

Blue Feather, Peter
A Few Painted Feathers - Stephen Longstreet 3886

Blue Jay
Walks in the Sun - Don Coldsmith 1194

Blue Paints
Moon of Thunder - Don Coldsmith 1180

Blue Wing
River of Sky - Karen Harper 2713

Born Swimming
Fathers and Crows - William T. Vollmann 6508

Born Underwater
Fathers and Crows - William T. Vollmann 6508

Brant, Joseph
Bridal Journey - Dale Van Every 6406
Brother Owl - Al Hine 2953
Buckskin Baronet - Margaret Widdemer 6734
*Eagle of Niagara: The Story of David Harper and His
Indian Captivity* - John Brick 671
The King's Rebel - James David Horan 3030
The Raid - John Brick 673
Reckon with the River - Clark McMeekin 4292
Three Sides of Agiochook - Eric Kelly 3400
West to the Setting Sun - Harvey Chalmers 973
The Wilderness War - Allen W. Eckert 1848

Brant, Molly
Blackrobe - Robert E. Wall 6534
Bloodbrothers - Robert E. Wall 6535
Lady of the Mohawks - Margaret Widdemer 6736

Buck, Henry
Sassafras - Jack Matthews 4193

Buffalo Hump
Dead Man's Walk - Larry McMurtry 4297

Burton, Thad
Rascal's Heaven - F. van Wyck Mason 4157

Button, Jemmy
Jemmy Button - Benjamin Subercaseaux 6107

Byrd, Tracker
Tracker - David Wagoner 6521

Caballito
Apaches - Oakley Hall 2650

Calling Bird
Bride of the Morning Star - Don Coldsmith 1170

Calling Crow
Flight of the Crow - Paul Clayton 1103

Calling Owl
Red Stick - Donald Clayton Porter 5121

Canonchet
The Wept of Wish-Ton-Wish - James Fenimore
Cooper 1312

Captain Rex
Rabbit Boss - Thomas Sanchez 5581

Carlisle, Hunkpapa Jack
Fifteen Flags - Richard Lynden Hardman 2686

Chaco
Arizona Ecstasy - Rosanne Bittner 511

Chactas
Atala - Francois Rene de Chateaubriand 1008

Chagak
Mother Earth, Father Sky - Sue Harrison 2749

Chaske
The Shining Trail - Iola Fuller 2254

Chekote, Ridge
Cherokee Dawn - Genell Dellin 1596

Cheoh, Joe
Carolina Courage - Dana Fuller Ross 5469

Chesney, Nalambigi
Shadow of the Moon - Douglas C. Jones 3284

Chief Joseph
Chief Joseph - Bill Dugan 1756
The Chieftain: A Story of the Nez Perce People -
Robert Payne 4852
The Fleet Rabble: A Novel of the Nez Perce War -
Frank Borden Hanes 2675
From Where the Sun Now Stands - Will Henry 2841
Red Fox of the Kinapoo - William Rush 5526
Song of the Meadowlark - John A. Sanford 5594

Chingachgook
The Deerslayer - James Fenimore Cooper 1299
The Last of the Mohicans - James Fenimore
Cooper 1302
The Pathfinder; or, The Inland Sea - James Fenimore
Cooper 1305

Chisahahoma
Jordan County: A Landscape in Narrative - Shelby
Foote 2152

Chitto Harjo
Crazy Snake - Robert J. Conley 1240

Chomac
Let the Drum Speak: A Novel of Ancient America -
Linda Lay Shuler 5837

Chomina
Black Robe - Brian Moore 4441

Christie, Ned
Ned Christie's War - Robert J. Conley 1247
Zeke and Ned - Larry McMurtry 4301

Ciriaco
The Cry of Dolores - Herbert Gorman 2492

Cochise
Apache Autumn - Robert Skimin 5875
Blood Brother - Elliott Arnold 190
Geronimo - Bill Dugan 1758
A Time in the Sun - Jane Barry 361

Coffee Soldier
Nickajack - Robert J. Conley 1248

Colby
Children of the Dust - Carlile Clancy 1084

Colon, Diego
The Indian Chronicles - Jose Barreiro 349

Corn Flower
The Way of the Priests - Robert J. Conley 1253

Corn-Sucker
Spirit Lake - MacKinlay Kantor 3363

Cornsilk
People of the Silence - W. Michael Gear 2340

Cowbone, Joe
The White Man's Road - Benjamin Capps 891

Coyote
The Elk-Dog Heritage - Don Coldsmith 1174
Trail of the Spanish Bit - Don Coldsmith 1193

Crazy Fox
Crazy Fox Remembers - Don Preston 5174

Crazy Horse
Buffalo Woman - Dorothy M. Johnson 3223
Chief of Scouts - Don Bendell 439
Crazy Horse - Bill Dugan 1757
Creek Mary's Blood - Dee Brown 712
Flashman and the Redskins - George MacDonald
Fraser 2208
A Good Day to Die - Del Barton 368
Kelly Blue - Peter Bowen 601
Lakota - G. Clifton Wisler 6833
No Survivors - Will Henry 2846
Reap the Whirlwind - Terry C. Johnston 3254
*A Road We Do Not Know: A Novel of Custer at the
Little Bighorn* - Frederick J. Chiaventone 1057
Sitting Bull - Bill Dugan 1760
Stone Song: A Novel of the Life of Crazy Horse -
Winfred Blevins 548

Thunder in the Dawn - Earl Murray 4532
The Winter War - William Wister Haines 2640

Crazy Walking
Dance Back the Buffalo - Milton Lott 3899

Cree Medicine
The High Missouri - Winfred Blevins 545

Creek Mary
Creek Mary's Blood - Dee Brown 712

Crooked Fingers
Birthright - Phillip Finch 2087

Crow Feather
The Far Canyon - Elmer Kelton 3404
Slaughter - Elmer Kelton 3407

Dancing Rabbit
The White Path - Robert J. Conley 1254

Dare, Cain
Lovestorm - Judith E. French 2222

Dark Hand
Forty Guns West - William W. Johnstone 3267

Deesohay
Valley of the Shadow - Charles Marquis
    Warren 6570

Diego, Juan
Roses for Mexico - Ethel Cook Eliot 1907

Digging Owl
Quest for the White Bull - Don Coldsmith 1182

Dull Knife
The Last Frontier - Howard Fast 2036
The Last Warpath - Will Henry 2844

Dumont, Gabriel
Lord of the Plains - Alfred Silver 5852

Eagle
Man of the Shadows - Don Coldsmith 1178

Eagle Woman
Daughter of the Eagle - Don Coldsmith 1173

Edohi
The Dark Way - Robert J. Conley 1241
The Way of the Priests - Robert J. Conley 1253
The White Path - Robert J. Conley 1254

El-i-chi
Sachem's Son - Donald Clayton Porter 5125
War Drums - Donald Clayton Porter 5133

Enriquillo
The Cross and the Sword - Manuel de Jesus
    Galvan 2274

Eskiminzin
The Camp Grant Massacre - Elliott Arnold 191

Fahnee
Crazy Snake - Robert J. Conley 1240

Fawn
Fawn - Robert Newton Peck 4885
Song of Wovoka - Earl Murray 4531

Ferguson, Amos "Noquisi"
No Resting Place - William Humphrey 3079

Flat Nose
Chiricahua - Will Henry 2839

Flat Warclub
The Manly-Hearted Woman - Frederick F.
    Manfred 4057

Fly Catcher
People of the River - W. Michael Gear 2338

Forked Path, Hendrick
The Interpreter - Robert Moss 4499

Friday
Friday - Michel Tournier 6305

Gall
*A Road We Do Not Know: A Novel of Custer at the
    Little Bighorn* - Frederick J. Chiaventone 1057

Gao
Father and Son - Donald Clayton Porter 5117
Red Stick - Donald Clayton Porter 5121

Gayabuc
Rabbit Boss - Thomas Sanchez 5581

George, Johnny
The Kingdom Carver - E.G. Perrault 4916

Geronimo
Apache Devil - Edgar Rice Burroughs 806
Chiricahua - Will Henry 2839
City of Widows - Loren D. Estleman 1969
Flashman and the Redskins - George MacDonald
    Fraser 2208
Geronimo - Bill Dugan 1758
Geronimo: An American Legend - Robert J.
    Conley 1242
Paint the Wind - Cathy Cash Spellman 5960
The Strenuous Life - Lawrence Alexander 84
Watch for Me on the Mountain - Forrest Carter 947

Ghonkaba
Ambush - Donald Clayton Porter 5113
Cherokee - Donald Clayton Porter 5115
The Sachem - Donald Clayton Porter 5124
Seneca - Donald Clayton Porter 5127
War Cry - Donald Clayton Porter 5132

Ghost Shirt
Stamping Ground - Loren D. Estleman 1977

Ghostwind
Thunder in the Dawn - Earl Murray 4532

Go-Ahead Rider
Go-Ahead Rider - Robert J. Conley 1243
To Make a Killing - Robert J. Conley 1252

Goo-Ga-Ro-No
Renno - Donald Clayton Porter 5123

Gordon, Temple
The Proud and the Free - Janet Dailey 1456

Goyah
The Pecos River - Fred Bean 399

Gray Fox
Tomahawk - Donald Clayton Porter 5129

Gray Mouse
Child of the Dead - Don Coldsmith 1172

Grey Horse Running
The Wolf and the Buffalo - Elmer Kelton 3408

Grey Wolf
A Good Day to Die - Del Barton 368

Guyasuta
The King's Orchard - Agnes Sligh Turnbull 6363

Halleluiah Bob
Rabbit Boss - Thomas Sanchez 5581

Hard-Heart
The Prairie - James Fenimore Cooper 1308

Harkana
The Moon Stallion - Jim Berry 484

Hawk, John
The Overmountain Men - Cameron Judd 3315

Hawk's Shadow
This Land Is Mine - Frances Casey Kerns 3470

Heads Off
The Elk-Dog Heritage - Don Coldsmith 1174
Follow the Wind - Don Coldsmith 1176
Moon of Thunder - Don Coldsmith 1180

Heyets
From Where the Sun Now Stands - Will Henry 2841

Hindfoot
*Look to Your Geese: A Novel of the Deflowering of
    New England* - Jacquin Sanders 5584

Hodano
Manitou - Donald Clayton Porter 5120
Spirit Knife - Donald Clayton Porter 5128

Hotfoot
Tatham Mound - Piers Anthony 169

Hunter of the Wolf
Comanche Moon - Catherine Anderson 137

Ilchee
Columbia - Pamela Jekel 3184

Iron Shirt
Season of Yellow Leaf - Douglas C. Jones 3283

Ironfoot
Beyond the Stars - David William Ross 5497

Island Woman
The Firekeeper - Robert Moss 4498
The Interpreter - Robert Moss 4499

Itchakoma
Jubal Sackett - Louis L'Amour 3620

Ja-Gonh
Tomahawk - Donald Clayton Porter 5129
War Cry - Donald Clayton Porter 5132

Jacova
The Gila River - Gary McCarthy 4223

Jo-Gonh
Renno - Donald Clayton Porter 5123

Jocita
War Eagles - Frank Burleson 788

Joel
The Valiant - Sigman Byrd 839

Kehwa, Charley
Trask - Don Berry 483

Keokotah
Jubal Sackett - Louis L'Amour 3620

Kicking Bird
Dances with Wolves - Michael Blake 537

Kientpoos
Devil's Backbone - Terry C. Johnston 3250

King, Winona
Apache Blood - David Thompson 6250
Blood Truce - David Thompson 6253
Hawken Fury - David Thompson 6254
Tenderfoot - David Thompson 6259
Tomahawk Revenge - David Thompson 6260
Trapper's Blood - David Thompson 6261
Winterkill - David Thompson 6262

Kokopelli
She Who Remembers - Linda Lay Shuler 5838

Kwani
She Who Remembers - Linda Lay Shuler 5838
Voice of the Eagle - Linda Lay Shuler 5839

La-ena
Wyoming! - Dana Fuller Ross 5494

Lame Beaver
Centennial - James A. Michener 4366

Lane, Beau
A Good Day to Die - Thomas Wakefield
    Blackburn 525

Lao-ke
Roanoke Warrior - Carter A. Vaughan 6438

Larion
The Law of Larion - Peter Freuchen 2227

Lawba, Spemica
Johnny Logan: Shawnee Spy - Allen W. Eckert 1843

Lazaro
Apache Autumn - Robert Skimin 5875

Leschi
Mighty Mountain - Archie Binns   502

Levi
They Came to a Valley - Bill Gulick   2618

Lichen
People of the River - W. Michael Gear   2338

Little Brother
The Kentucky Trace: A Novel of the American Revolution - Harriette Simpson Arnow   195

Little Hawk
Hawk's Journey - Donald Clayton Porter   5119
Red Stick - Donald Clayton Porter   5121
Sachem's Son - Donald Clayton Porter   5125
War Clouds - Donald Clayton Porter   5131

Little Hoop
The Legend of Ben Tree - Paul Hawkins   2784

Little Runner
These Thousand Hills - A.B. Guthrie Jr.   2627

Little Wolf
The Last Frontier - Howard Fast   2036
The Powder River - Winfred Blevins   546

Little Wound
Dance Back the Buffalo - Milton Lott   3899

Lone Walker
Scalpdancers - Kerry Newcomb   4592

Lone Wolf
Wolf Song - Harvey Fergusson   2069

Long Walker
Daughter of the Eagle - Don Coldsmith   1173

Looks Far
The Sacred Hills - Don Coldsmith   1187

Loon Cry
Fire in the Sky - J.A. Shears   5785

Lospe
This Promised Land - Robert Easton   1824

Lotus
Mountain Man - Vardis Fisher   2110

Ludona
Ambush - Donald Clayton Porter   5113

Lutero
The Pride of Hannah Wade - Janet Dailey   1455

Luz
The Cry of Dolores - Herbert Gorman   2492

MacDonald, Laurel
Trail of Tears - Frances Patton Statham   5983

Magawisca
Hope Leslie; or, Early Times in Massachusetts - Catharine Maria Sedgewick   5714

Magua
The Last of the Mohicans - James Fenimore Cooper   1302

Makwa-Ikwa
Shaman - Noah Gordon   2483

Malachi
Back to Malachi - Robert J. Conley   1237

Man Face
The Children of the First Man - James Alexander Thom   6230

Mangas Coloradas
Apache - Will Comfort   1226
Desert Hawks - Frank Burleson   786
War Eagles - Frank Burleson   788

Manly Heart
The Manly-Hearted Woman - Frederick F. Manfred   4057

Many Berries
Free Flows the River - Earl Murray   4529

Many Clouds
Bitter Creek - Al Cody   1150

Maritole
Pushing the Bear: A Novel of the Trail of Tears - Diane Glancy   2426

Massai
Broncho Apache - Paul I. Wellman   6614

Massasoit
The Plymouth Adventure - Ernest Gebler   2342

Massaswa
Angelique in Love - Sergeanne Golon   2470

Maywood, Marcus
The Justicer - Thomas Fall   2010

Medicine Plant
Dawn Land - Joseph Bruchac III   734

Metacomet
Legacy - Robert Vaughan   6448
The Wept of Wish-Ton-Wish - James Fenimore Cooper   1312
White Rising - Zane Kotker   3548

Metamoris
Song of Metamoris: A Story That Remains of a People Who Passed This Way - Milford E. Anness   155

Mitana
The Russian River - Gary McCarthy   4224

Mohegan, John
The Pioneers; or, The Sources of the Susquehanna - James Fenimore Cooper   1307

Monaseetah
Long Winter Gone - Terry C. Johnston   3252
Seize the Sky - Terry C. Johnston   3256
Whisper of the Wolf - Terry C. Johnston   3261

Montour, Esther
The King's Rebel - James David Horan   3030

Morning Sky
High Country - Jason Manning   4075

Morning Swan
High Freedom - Earl Murray   4530

Nakoa
The Second Kiss - Gayle Rogers   5432

Nakwisi
The Double Man - Elinor Pryor   5205

Nane
A Time in the Sun - Jane Barry   361

Narra-mattah
The Wept of Wish-Ton-Wish - James Fenimore Cooper   1312

Nemattanon
The First Gentleman of America: A Comedy of Conquest - James Branch Cabell   841

Nickajack
Nickajack - Robert J. Conley   1248

Night Hawk
Trail of Tears - Frances Patton Statham   5983

Night Wind
Night Wind - Roberta Jean Mountjoy   4504
Night Wind's Woman - Shirl Henke   2825

Nightshade
People of the River - W. Michael Gear   2338

No Ears
Buffalo Girls - Larry McMurtry   4296

No Name
Conquering Horse - Frederick F. Manfred   4055

Noble Popjoy
Shadow of the Moon - Douglas C. Jones   3284

Numaga
Paiute - Sessions S. Wheeler   6666

Oconechee
Mountain Windsong - Robert J. Conley   1246

Odin
Runestone - Don Coldsmith   1186

Old Lodge
Song of the Cheyenne - Jory Sherman   5822

Old Lodge Skins
Little Big Man - Thomas Berger   478

Old Man
Man of the Shadows - Don Coldsmith   1178

Old White Buffalo
Buffalo Medicine - Don Coldsmith   1171

Old Woman
A Woman of the People - Benjamin Capps   893

Olepi
Hanta Yo - Ruth Beebe Hill   2951

Oneta
The Loon Feather - Iola Fuller   2253

Opothle
Creek Mary's Blood - Dee Brown   712

Osceola
Bright Feather - Robert Wilder   6750
The Land Where the Sun Dies - Henry Carlisle   896
River in the Wind - Edith Pope   5111
Runaway - Heather Graham   2519
Seminole - Theodore Pratt   5164

Otter
People of the Lakes - W. Michael Gear   2336

Outakke
The Countess Angelique - Sergeanne Golon   2472

Owl
Buffalo Medicine - Don Coldsmith   1171

Pa-nayo-tishn
Chiricahua - Will Henry   2839

Pale Star
Medicine Knife - Don Coldsmith   1179
Pale Star - Don Coldsmith   1181
Return to the River - Don Coldsmith   1184
River of Swans - Don Coldsmith   1185

Pandra
The Moon Stallion - Jim Berry   484

Paris, Marie Therese
The Two Medicine River - Richard S. Wheeler   6663

Parry, Kwahadi
Gone the Dreams and the Dancing - Douglas C. Jones   3279

Parry, Morfydd Annon
Season of Yellow Leaf - Douglas C. Jones   3283

Pathkiller, Mose
Back to Malachi - Robert J. Conley   1237

Pelon
Mackenna's Gold - Will Henry   2845

Pena, Joe
Stallion Gate - Martin Cruz Smith   5924

Pennyform, Nokomis
Too Late! Too Late! The Maiden Cried - Joan Fleming   2128

Peta
Hanta Yo - Ruth Beebe Hill   2951

Peta Nocona
Quanah Parker - Bill Dugan   1759

Piksarett
Angelique and the Demon - Sergeanne Golon   2466

Pocahontas
Daughter of Eve - Noel B. Gerson   2366
A Durable Fire - Virginia Bernhard   480
Pocahontas - Susan Donnell   1691

Pocahontas; or, The Nonparell of Virginia - David Garnett   2297
Powhatan's Daughter - John Clarke Bowman   605
The Sea 'Venture - F. van Wyck Mason   4159
The Sot-Weed Factor - John Barth   364

Pontiac
The Conquerors - Allen W. Eckert   1839
Fire Along the Sky: A Novel of America - Robert Moss   4497
Hatchet in the Sky - Margaret Cooper Gay   2328
Silent Drums - Mike Roarke   5361
Strife Before Dawn - Mary Schumann   5675
This Land Is Ours - Louis Zara   6953

Poor Singer
People of the Silence - W. Michael Gear   2340

Pope
Taos - Irwin R. Blacker   527

Powhatan
Daughter of Eve - Noel B. Gerson   2366
Pocahontas - Susan Donnell   1691
Powhatan's Daughter - John Clarke Bowman   605

Proctor, Ezekiel
Zeke and Ned - Larry McMurtry   4301

Quanah Parker
Quanah Parker - Bill Dugan   1759
Ride the Wind - Lucia St. Clair Robson   5416

Quasia
The Buffalo Soldiers - John Prebble   5165

Quintano, Toribio
The Royal City - Les Savage Jr.   5621

Rabbit
Moon of Thunder - Don Coldsmith   1180

Rain
Thunderstick - Don Coldsmith   1190
Track of the Bear - Don Coldsmith   1191

Rattlesnake
Choctaw - Donald Clayton Porter   5116

Raven Heart
Alaska - James A. Michener   4364

Red Bloom
Michael Beam - Richard Hallet   2663

Red Cloud
Crazy Horse - Bill Dugan   1757
Creek Mary's Blood - Dee Brown   712
The Day the Sun Died - Dale Van Every   6408
Dodging Red Cloud - Richard S. Wheeler   6657
Kelly Blue - Peter Bowen   601
North Against the Sioux - Kenneth Ulyatt   6376
Stone Song: A Novel of the Life of Crazy Horse - Winfred Blevins   548

Red Feather
The Flower in the Mountains - Don Coldsmith   1175
Trail From Taos - Don Coldsmith   1192

Red Fox
Red Fox of the Kinapoo - William Rush   5526

Red Hawk
Thunder in the East - Mike Roarke   5362

Red Horse
Quest for the White Bull - Don Coldsmith   1182

Red Moon
Mountain Devil - David Thompson   6257

Red Wolf
Sioux Splendor - Rosanne Bittner   515

Renno
Apache - Donald Clayton Porter   5114
Choctaw - Donald Clayton Porter   5116
Father and Son - Donald Clayton Porter   5117
Father of Waters - Donald Clayton Porter   5118
Hawk's Journey - Donald Clayton Porter   5119
Manitou - Donald Clayton Porter   5120

The Renegade - Donald Clayton Porter   5122
Renno - Donald Clayton Porter   5123
The Sachem - Donald Clayton Porter   5124
Sachem's Son - Donald Clayton Porter   5125
Seminole - Donald Clayton Porter   5126
Spirit Knife - Donald Clayton Porter   5128
Tomahawk - Donald Clayton Porter   5129
War Chief - Donald Clayton Porter   5130
War Clouds - Donald Clayton Porter   5131
War Cry - Donald Clayton Porter   5132
War Drums - Donald Clayton Porter   5133
White Indian - Donald Clayton Porter   5134

Ridge, Major
Trail of Tears - Williams Forrest   2187

Rising Moon
Song of the Meadowlark - John A. Sanford   5594

Rogers, Tiana
Walk in My Soul - Lucia St. Clair Robson   5418

Roman Nose
Roman - Douglas C. Jones   3281
The Stalkers - Terry C. Johnston   3259

Ross, John
As Long as the Rivers Run - Sam J. Slate   5882
Give Me the Wind - Jan Jordan   3302
Trail of Tears - Williams Forrest   2187

Rotten Belly
Carry the Wind - Terry C. Johnston   3246

Ruhama
Beulah Land - Harold Lenoir Davis   1520

Running Deer
Child of the Dead - Don Coldsmith   1172

Running Elk
Man on Two Ponies - Don Worcester   6872

Running Fawn
Drums of Change: The Story of Running Fawn - Janette Oke   4707

Runs with the Wind
The Long Sun - Janice Lucas   3920

Sacajawea
Forward the Nation - Donald Culross Peattie   4880
The Gates of the Mountains - Will Henry   2842
Sacajawea - Anna Lee Waldo   6529
Sacajawea of the Shoshones - Della F. Emmons   1940
Star of the West - Ethel Hueston   3070
Tale of Valor - Vardis Fisher   2112
Trail: The Story of the Lewis and Clark Expedition - Louis Charbonneau   998

St. Castine, Joseph de
The Golden Wildcat - Margaret Widdemer   6735

Santana, Vitorio
The Gila River - Gary McCarthy   4223

Sanutee
The Yemassee - William Gilmore Simms   5855

Scott, Jordan
Visions of a Heart - Emily Carmichael   899

See-Ho-Kee
Say These Names (Remember Them) - Betty Sue Cummings   1448

Shining Moon
Expedition! - Dana Fuller Ross   5473
Outpost! - Dana Fuller Ross   5486
Westward! - Dana Fuller Ross   5492

Shokotee
The Raider - Jesse Hill Ford   2164

Shoz-Dijiji
Apache Devil - Edgar Rice Burroughs   806

Shuganan
Mother Earth, Father Sky - Sue Harrison   2749

Shy Fawn
This Land Is Mine - Frances Casey Kerns   3470

Siam
Eagle Song - James Houston   3050

Silver Fox
Drums of Change: The Story of Running Fawn - Janette Oke   4707

Sima
The Snake River - Winfred Blevins   547

Singing Brook
Mohawk Woman - Barbara Riefe   5329

Singing Grass
Soldier in Buckskin - Ray Hogan   2981

Singing Wolf
Thunderstick - Don Coldsmith   1190
Track of the Bear - Don Coldsmith   1191

Sitting Bear
Blood Fury - David Thompson   6252

Sitting Bull
Arrest Sitting Bull - Douglas C. Jones   3273
Buffalo Girls - Larry McMurtry   4296
Creek Mary's Blood - Dee Brown   712
The Day the Sun Died - Dale Van Every   6408
Dodging Red Cloud - Richard S. Wheeler   6657
Drums of Change: The Story of Running Fawn - Janette Oke   4707
A Good Day to Die - Thomas Wakefield Blackburn   525
The Jewelled Spur - Gilbert Morris   4465
The Last Stand: A Novel about George Armstrong Custer and the Indians of the Plains - Edwin P. Hoyt   3061
A Road We Do Not Know: A Novel of Custer at the Little Bighorn - Frederick J. Chiaventone   1057
The Secret Annie Oakley - Marcy Moran Heidish   2819
Sitting Bull - Bill Dugan   1760
Thunder in the Dawn - Earl Murray   4532
The Winter War - William Wister Haines   2640
Yellowstone Kelly - Peter Bowen   602

Sitting Red Cloud
The Last Stand: A Novel about George Armstrong Custer and the Indians of the Plains - Edwin P. Hoyt   3061

Sky Toucher
Mohawk Woman - Barbara Riefe   5329

Soledad
Ghost Woman - Lawrence Thornton   6275

Sonseeahray
Blood Brother - Elliott Arnold   190

Sosepsis
Indian Brother - Hubert Coryell   1354

South Wind
World of Silence - Don Coldsmith   1195

Southwind
Song of the Rock - Don Coldsmith   1189

Speaks-Not
World of Silence - Don Coldsmith   1195

Spoon
Spoon - John Christgau   1074

Spotted Calf
Warriors of the Night - Kerry Newcomb   4594

Spotted Wolf
Yellowhorse - Dee Brown   715

Squanto
The Plymouth Adventure - Ernest Gebler   2342

Standing Elk
Arrest Sitting Bull - Douglas C. Jones   3273

Standing-in-the-Doorway
The Dark Way - Robert J. Conley   1241

The Way of the Priests - Robert J. Conley 1253

Stands with a Fist
Dances with Wolves - Michael Blake 537

Star Shell
People of the Lakes - W. Michael Gear 2336

Starr, Henry
The Return of Henry Starr - Richard Slotkin 5909
The Saga of Henry Starr - Robert J. Conley 1250

Stewart, Moonfeather Leah
Moonfeather - Judith E. French 2223

Stonecutter
The Children of the First Man - James Alexander
Thom 6230

Storm, Caleb
Sunflower - Jill Marie Landis 3653

Storm, Tehana
Lords of the Plains - Max Crawford 1420

Strong Bow
Return of the Spanish - Don Coldsmith 1183

Stuart, the Blade
The Proud and the Free - Janet Dailey 1456

Sun Horse
The Snowblind Moon - John Byrne Cooke 1267

Sun Runner
Song of the Cheyenne - Jory Sherman 5822

Sunday
Pemmican - Vardis Fisher 2111

Sundown, Jackson
Last Go Round - Ken Kesey 3473

Sundown, Jacques
Blackwater Spirits - Miriam Grace Monfredo 4427

Ta-Na
Father and Son - Donald Clayton Porter 5117

Talasi
Creek Mary's Blood - Dee Brown 712

Tall Bird
Distant Trails - Bill Gulick 2612
Gathering Storm - Bill Gulick 2613
Lost Wallowa - Bill Gulick 2616

Tall Bull
Bride of the Morning Star - Don Coldsmith 1170
Eyes of Eagles - William W. Johnstone 3266

Tall One
Trail of the Spanish Bit - Don Coldsmith 1193

Tanner, George
Go-Ahead Rider - Robert J. Conley 1243
To Make a Killing - Robert J. Conley 1252

Tay-Bodal
Death at Rainy Mountain - Mardi Oakley
Medawar 4321

Tchula Homa
A Story of Deep Delight - Thomas McNamee 4305

Teal Eye
The Big Sky - A.B. Guthrie Jr. 2624
Fair Land, Fair Land - A.B. Guthrie Jr. 2625

Tecante
Lakota - G. Clifton Wisler 6833

Tecolote
Eagles of Destiny - Jory Sherman 5817

Tecumseh
The Border Captains - Jason Manning 4072
Creek Mary's Blood - Dee Brown 712
The Frontiersmen - Allen W. Eckert 1841
Gateway to Empire - Allen W. Eckert 1842
Johnny Logan: Shawnee Spy - Allen W. Eckert 1843
The Loon Feather - Iola Fuller 2253
Panther in the Sky - James Alexander Thom 6234
Red Stick - Donald Clayton Porter 5121

Riders of the Long Road - Stephen E. Bransford 649
*Song of Metamoris: A Story That Remains of a People
Who Passed This Way* - Milford E. Anness 155
A Sorrow in Our Heart - Allen W. Eckert 1844
War Clouds - Donald Clayton Porter 5131

Teeto Hoonod
Song of the Meadowlark - John A. Sanford 5594

Tekakwitha, Kateri
Lily of the Mohawks - Jack Casey 952

Thandelthur
Running West - James Houston 3052

Tharon
People of the River - W. Michael Gear 2338

Thayendanegea
The Wilderness War - Allen W. Eckert 1848

Three Owls
Pale Star - Don Coldsmith 1181

Thunder, Colt
Savage Thunder - Johanna Lindsey 3795

To-Sha-Be
Ambush - Donald Clayton Porter 5113

Tolonqua
Voice of the Eagle - Linda Lay Shuler 5839

Toshabe
Seneca - Donald Clayton Porter 5127

Trader
Tatham Mound - Piers Anthony 169

Tsani
The Double Man - Elinor Pryor 5205

Tumbling Hawk
One Smart Indian - Robert J. Seidman 5722

Turning Hawk
Dance Back the Buffalo - Milton Lott 3899

Two Eagles
For Love of Two Eagles - Barbara Riefe 5328
Mohawk Woman - Barbara Riefe 5329
The Woman Who Fell From the Sky - Barbara
Riefe 5330

Two Heads
The Dark Way - Robert J. Conley 1241

Two Robes
Song of Wovoka - Earl Murray 4531

Two Shields
Tie My Bones to Her Back - Robert F. Jones 3294

Two Sleep
Dream Catcher - Terry C. Johnston 3251

Uncas
The Last of the Mohicans - James Fenimore
Cooper 1302

Ute Killer
A Woman of the People - Benjamin Capps 893

Verendrye, Louise de La
My Blood and My Treasure - Mary Schumann 5674

Victorio
A Time in the Sun - Jane Barry 361

Waguli
Mountain Windsong - Robert J. Conley 1246

Wakwa Manunnappu
The Mists of Manittoo - Lois Swann 6135
Torn Covenants - Lois Swann 6136

Walker, Dhu
Border Line - Robert J. Conley 1238
The Long Trail North - Robert J. Conley 1245
Strange Company - Robert J. Conley 1251

Walks in the Sun
Walks in the Sun - Don Coldsmith 1194

Washakie
The Man Who Loved Cat Dancing - Marilyn
Durham 1817

Weatherford, William
Horseshoe Bend - Bruce Palmer 4779

Whirlwind
Buffalo Woman - Dorothy M. Johnson 3223

White Antelope
The Scout - Harry Combs 1224

White Bird
The Fleet Rabble: A Novel of the Nez Perce War -
Frank Borden Hanes 2675

White Buffalo
Scalpdancers - Kerry Newcomb 4592

White Feathers
Thunderstick - Don Coldsmith 1190

White Fox
Fort De Chastaigne - Don Coldsmith 1177
Song of the Rock - Don Coldsmith 1189

White Hand
Breakheart Pass - Alistair MacLean 3999

White Horn
Distant Trumpet - Paul Horgan 3032

Whitebear
The Shadow Riders - Terry C. Johnston 3257

Wild Rose
Brules - Harry Combs 1223

Winter Swan
The Great Alone - Janet Dailey 1454

Winthrop, John
The Day the Sun Died - Dale Van Every 6408

Wolf, Michael
A Whisper on the Wind - Madeline Baker 276

Wolf Pup
Bearer of the Pipe - Don Coldsmith 1169

Wolf's Head
The Sacred Hills - Don Coldsmith 1187

Woman Chief
Woman Chief - Benjamin Capps 892

Wounded Bear
Sand in the Wind - Kathleen O'Neal Gear 2329

Wovoka
The Day the Sun Died - Dale Van Every 6408
Song of Wovoka - Earl Murray 4531

Yayael
My Master Columbus - Cedric Belfrage 418

Yellow Bird
Seize the Sky - Terry C. Johnston 3256
Whisper of the Wolf - Terry C. Johnston 3261

Young Hunter
Dawn Land - Joseph Bruchac III 734

INNKEEPER

Charboneau, Marie
The Bastard - John Jakes 3144

Gilderson, Adam
A Wayside Tavern - Norah Lofts 3862

Marsh, Robert
The King's Bed - Margaret Campbell Barnes 324

Merlyn, Joss
Jamaica Inn - Daphne Du Maurier 1747

Oakley, Will
The Golden Fleece - Norah Lofts 3843

Turner, Sarah
Scarlet Ribbons - Judith E. French 2224

INVALID

Caleb
Molokai - Oswald Andrew Bushnell 815

Lumley, Melloney
Dolphin Summer - Carola Salisbury 5569

Payton, Sebastian
Lady Jane - Norma Lee Clark 1092

Wentworth, Lilian de
Willowwood - Mollie Hardwick 2699

INVENTOR

Bell, Alexander Graham
Loving Little Egypt - Thomas McMahon 4288

Bushnell, David
The Kingsbridge Plot - Maan Meyers 4355

Cooper, Peter
All This, and Heaven Too - Rachel Field 2080
Certain Harvest: A Novel of the Time of Peter Cooper - Ruth Adams Knight 3525

Crompton, Samuel
Crompton Way - Thomas Thompson 6270

Edison, Thomas Alva
The Big Stick - Lawrence Alexander 82
Homeland - John Jakes 3148
Loving Little Egypt - Thomas McMahon 4288
Mount's Mistake - Lew McCreary 4229
A Peep into the 20th Century - Christopher Davis 1515

Ericsson, John
Thunder on the Chesapeake - David Divine 1650

Franklin, Benjamin
Benjamin Franklin and a Case of Artful Murder - Robert Lee Hall 2654
Benjamin Franklin and a Case of Christmas Murder - Robert Lee Hall 2655
Benjamin Franklin Takes the Case - Robert Lee Hall 2656
Citizen Tom Paine - Howard Fast 2028
A High Wind Rising - Elsie Singmaster 5867
Jefferson: A Novel - Max Byrd 838
Murder at Drury Lane - Robert Lee Hall 2659

Fulton, Robert
Being Met Together - William Vaughan Wilkins 6756
The Pandora Secret - Anthony Forrest 2186

Guillotin, Joseph Ignace
Dr. Guillotine: The Eccentric Exploits of an Early Scientist - Herbert Lom 3867

Leonardo da Vinci
Carnival of Saints - George Herman 2860
A Comedy of Murders - George Herman 2861
The Memory Cathedral: A Secret History of Leonardo Da Vinci - Jack Dann 1481
Mona Lisa: The Woman in the Portrait - Sara Mayfield 4206
The Romance of Leonardo Da Vinci - Dmitri Merezhkovski 4339

Loper, Richard Fanning
That Skipper From Stonington - Theda Kenyon 3464

Page, Claude
A Case of Curiosities - Allen Kurzweil 3569

Pullman, George
The Dream Seekers - Grace Mark 4085

Rhoodie, Andries
The Guns of the South - Harry N. Turtledove 6367

Tesla, Nikola
Loving Little Egypt - Thomas McMahon 4288

Trevitnick, Richard
The Miller's Dance - Winston Graham 2528

Warner, Adam
The Last of the Barons - Edward Bulwer-Lytton 769

Westinghouse, George
A Peep into the 20th Century - Christopher Davis 1515

Whitney, Eli
Whittling Boy: The Story of Eli Whitney - Roger Burlingame 789

JEWELER

Lindsay, Edmund
Jewelled Path - Rosalind Laker 3597

JOCKEY

Broome, Tom
The Mississippi Run - Paul Darcy Boles 565

Clements, Joseph
Horses of War - Duff Hart-Davis 2760

JOURNALIST

Adams, Cort
When the Music Changed - Marie R. Reno 5305

Adriance, Dan
Tenderloin - Samuel Hopkins Adams 33

Arnst, Sol
Crimson Creek: A Novel of the Early West - Robert McCraig 4228

Atherton, Emily
The Normandie Affair - Elizabeth Villars 6497

Aubrey, Piers
The Fountain Overflows - Rebecca West 6639

Austin, Jack
A Distant Thunder - Teresa de Luca 1561

Becque, Thomas
Charlotte Morel - Maria Lodi 3829
Charlotte Morel: The Dream - Maria Lodi 3830
Charlotte Morel: The Siege - Maria Lodi 3831

Bennett, James Gordon
Ain't Goin' to Glory - David Delman 1597

Bethune, James
The Long Watch - Elizabeth Linington 3798

Bierce, Ambrose
The Old Gringo - Carlos Fuentes 2247

Blake, Norris
Foreign Devils - Irvin Faust 2053

Blanchard, Natalie
Seattle Green - Jane Adams 26

Braxton, Isaac
The Long Naked Descent into Boston - William Eastlake 1823

Broome, Johnny
The Empire Builders - William Stuart Long 3871
The Gallant - William Stuart Long 3873
The Seafarers - William Stuart Long 3877

Brown, Styler
The Misadventures of Bethany Price - Marian Cockrell 1147

Bryant, William Cullen
The Furies - John Jakes 3146

Bryson, Alistair
Our Valiant Few - F. van Wyck Mason 4155

Bullinger, Frank
The Veracruz Blues - Mark Winegardner 6821

Candler, Edmund
Invading Tibet - Mark Frutkin 2239

Carpenter, Hollis
Bayou City Secrets - Deborah Powell 5146

Cavendish, Maude Teasdale
Young Mrs. Cavendish and the Kaiser's Men - K.K. Beck 405

Cayle, Barry
Gentleman Traitor - Alan Williams 6763

Chase, Gideon
An Insular Position - Timothy Mo 4421

Clancy, Jack
Death in a Deck Chair - K.K. Beck 403
Peril under the Palms - K.K. Beck 404

Clay, Norman
Mexico - James A. Michener 4372

Clifford, Jo
Lady of Hay - Barbara Erskine 1955

Corcoran, Dermot
Seasons - Anna Dillon 1645

Cordor, Davy
The Thomas Street Horror - Raymond Paul 4843

Craigie, Andrew
The Shakespeare Girl - Mollie Hardwick 2698

Cravat, Yancey
Cimarron - Edna Ferber 2061

Culhane, Lexy
A Season of Swans - Celeste De Blasis 1548

Darling, Tristram
The Private Life of Florence Nightingale - Richard Gordon 2485

Davis, Richard
Yellow: A Novel - Daniel Lynch 3932

Desmoulins, Camille
Scaramouche the King-Maker - Rafael Sabatini 5555

Dickson, Hazel
The Talking Pictures Murder Case - George Baxt 388

Douglass, Frederick
A Star Pointed North - Edmund Fuller 2250

Duncan, Widow
A Creek Called Wounded Knee - Douglas C. Jones 3277

Dunhill, Jonathan
Freedom's Dues - Robert H. Abel 9

Durkin, William
The Killing Frost - Thomas Hayden 2799

Dwyer, Rick
While Paris Danced - Patricia Wright 6886

Easterbrook, Chance
A Good Day to Die - Thomas Wakefield Blackburn 525

Eastman, Walter
An Insular Position - Timothy Mo 4421

Farrell, Christopher
The Hungry Goblin: A Victorian Detective Novel - John Dickson Carr 911

Fowler, Sam
If I Never Get Back - Darryl Brock 700

Franklyn, Jim
The Hangman's Crusade - James Barwick 370

Galbraith, James
Jade - Pat Barr 344

Garland, Andrew
Angels Falling - Janice Elliott 1915

Glen, Molly
Twice upon a Time - Allen Appel 172

Glenn, Molly
Till the End of Time - Allen Appel 170

Greeley, Horace
Ain't Goin' to Glory - David Delman 1597
The Furies - John Jakes 3146

Griffith, Arthur
Rebels: The Irish Rising of 1916 - Peter
  DeRosa 1622

Hallam, Dennis
The Skeleton in the Grass - Robert Barnard 320

Hayman, George
Love and Honor - Leslie Arlen 189

Hearst, William Randolph
The Americans - John Jakes 3143
California Gold - John Jakes 3145
The Seventh Bullet - Daniel D. Victor 6483

Henneker, Victor
Victim of the Aurora - Thomas Keneally 3417

Hollister, Corrie Belle
Sea to Shining Sea - Michael Phillips 4990

Holt, Tim
California Glory - Dana Fuller Ross 5468
Oklahoma Pride - Dana Fuller Ross 5483
Pacific Destiny - Dana Fuller Ross 5487
Sierra Triumph - Dana Fuller Ross 5488

Howatt, Tommy
Tenderloin - Samuel Hopkins Adams 33

Humphrey, Lionel
Armored Giants: A Novel of the Civil War - F. van
  Wyck Mason 4145

Huntley, Dick
The Devil's Card - Mary Maher 4030

Jardine, Stephen
Ain't Goin' to Glory - David Delman 1597

Johnson, Jubal
Trumpet in the Wilderness - Robert S. Harper 2717

Kent, Gideon
The Americans - John Jakes 3143
The Lawless - John Jakes 3149

Kent, Jared
The Titans - John Jakes 3154

Kent, Jephtha
The Titans - John Jakes 3154

Kirk, Stuart
The Day the Sun Died - Dale Van Every 6408

Kumar, Hari
The Day of the Scorpion - Paul Scott 5682
The Jewel in the Crown - Paul Scott 5684

Kuntz, Herbert
The Retreat - Aharon Appelfeld 178

Lardner, Ring
Hoopla - Harry Stein 5990

MacDonald, Robert
The Long Watch - Elizabeth Linington 3798

Malone, Sean
Street of the Madwoman - Isabel Ortega 4756

Malone, Shane
Eagles Fly West - Edward Maddin Ainsworth 55

Marat, Jean-Paul
A Place of Greater Safety - Hilary Mantel 4077

Marquis, Harley
The Crimson Wind - Max Hennessy 2832

Marsden, Catherine
Counterfeit of Murder - Ray Harrison 2738
Death of a Dancing Lady - Ray Harrison 2739
Deathwatch - Ray Harrison 2740
A Season for Death - Ray Harrison 2743
Sphere of Death - Ray Harrison 2744

Martin, Tom
The Devil's Card - Mary Maher 4030

Masterson, William Barclay "Bat"
The Ham Reporter - Robert J. Randisi 5251

McIlvane
The Waterworks - E.L. Doctorow 1659

McKay, Shaylin
Cold War - Robert Vaughan 6446
The Iron Curtain - Robert Vaughan 6447

McQuirk, Sally
1812 - David Nevin 4586

Meyer, Max
A Thousand Shall Fall - Bodie Thoene 6227

Minor, Constantine
Whiskey River - Loren D. Estleman 1981

Monckton, Ules
The Light Infantry Ball - Hamilton Basso 375

Monday, Viridis
The Choiring of the Trees - Donald Harington 2709

Moore, John Schuler
The Alienist - Caleb Carr 907

Morrison, Edwin Carter
Season for War - P.F. Kluge 3510

Morrison, Sam
Killdeer Mountain - Dee Brown 713

Morrison, William
Niagara - Robert Lewis Taylor 6189

Mudd, Grover
Saint Mudd - Steve Thayer 6218

Murray, Bracken
Ever After - Elswyth Thane 6216

Norris-Newman, Charles "Noggs"
The Tune That They Play - William Clive 1120

O'Brady, Bridie
The Faraway Drums - Jon Cleary 1104

Pond, Luther
Hoopla - Harry Stein 5990

Porter, William Sydney
The Heart of O. Henry - Dale Kramer 3550

Poxe, Hieronymous
The Long Naked Descent into Boston - William
  Eastlake 1823

Prosser, Emma
Hard on the Road - Barbara Moore 4440

Pulitzer, Joseph
The Americans - John Jakes 3143
Ulysses: A Biographical Novel - Robert Skimin 5878

Quayle, Kit
One Last Glimpse - James Aldridge 74

Raff, Theodore
Liveliest Town in the West - Bill Gulick 2615

Reed, Kate
The Bloody Red Baron - Kim Newman 4596

Rilke, Martin
The Passing Bells - Phillip Rock 5421

Romilly, Guy
The Sleep of Life - Richard Gordon 2486

Ross, Nellie
California Gold - John Jakes 3145

Royall, Anne
The Gorgeous Hussy - Samuel Hopkins Adams 30

Runyon, Damon
The Ham Reporter - Robert J. Randisi 5251
Nevermore - William Hjortsberg 2958

Savage, Samantha
Outlaw Lover - Lindsey Hanks 2676

Schuyler, Charlie
Burr - Gore Vidal 6485

Lincoln: A Novel - Gore Vidal 6490

Sherman, Joseph
Saigon - Anthony Grey 2588

Skylark, Jed
The Fortune Road - James McCague 4217

Spangler, Warren
The Year of the Spaniard - Henry Castor 956

Spencer, C. Jamieson
Dance on a Sinking Ship - Michael Kilian 3483

Sprague, Fitz
Ever After - Elswyth Thane 6216

Stafford, Jack
Annapolis - William Martin 4137

Stanley, Henry Morton
The Last Hero - Peter Forbath 2154

Starr, Ellery
Roll, Shenandoah - Bruce Lancaster 3644

Steffens, Lincoln
The Alienist - Caleb Carr 907

Stewart, Henry
The Bluestocking - David Delman 1598

Tapp, Quinton
A Creek Called Wounded Knee - Douglas C.
  Jones 3277

Tate, Ben
The Last Valley - A.B. Guthrie Jr. 2626

Trent, Daniel
The Dawning of Deliverance - Judith Pella 4892

Twainborough, Eric
Over There - Robert Vaughan 6449

Van Buren, Roxana
Blue Moon - Parris Afton Bonds 569

Vance, Logan
Black-Eyed Susan - Deborah Camp 871

Wayne, Matthew
Guns of Chickamauga - Richard O'Connor 4685

Wheeler, Tom
Siege in the Sun - Mary Paradise 4788

Whittaker, Olana
Waltzing in Ragtime - Eileen Charbonneau 996

Winchell, Walter
The Old Colts - Glendon Swarthout 6144
Walter Winchell: A Novel - Michael Herr 2863

Woods, Dan
The Land Was Ours: A Novel of the Great Plains -
  Charles W. Bailey 266

Wright, Riley
Ride with Me, Mariah Montana - Ivan Doig 1684

Zenger, Peter
Anna Zenger: Mother of Freedom - Kent
  Cooper 1316

JUDGE

Altgeld, John Peter
The American - Howard Fast 2026

Bean, Roy
Streets of Laredo - Larry McMurtry 4300

Blackthorne, Harlan A.
The Stranglers - Loren D. Estleman 1978

Brandeis, Louis
The Hyde Park Murder - Elliott Roosevelt 5443

Campbell, Colin
The Land Is Bright - James Arthur Kjelgaard 3508

Dee Jen-dieh
The Chinese Nail Murders - Robert van Gulik 6413
Deception - Eleanor Cooney 1295

The Emperor's Pearl - Robert van Gulik 6414
The Haunted Monastery - Robert van Gulik 6415
The Lacquer Screen - Robert van Gulik 6416
The Monkey and the Tiger - Robert van Gulik 6417
Murder in Canton - Robert van Gulik 6418
Necklace and Calabash - Robert van Gulik 6419
The Phantom of the Temple - Robert van Gulik 6420
The Red Pavilion - Robert van Gulik 6421
The Willow Pattern - Robert van Gulik 6422

Eyring, Nathan
The Everlasting Fire - Jonreed Lauritzen 3675

Fielding, Henry
The Masters of Bow Street - John Creasy 1423
The Vast Memory of Love - Malcolm Bosse 588

Fielding, Sir John
Blind Justice - Bruce Alexander 76
Murder at Drury Lane - Robert Lee Hall 2659
Murder in Grub Street - Bruce Alexander 77
Watery Grave - Bruce Alexander 78

Frankfurter, Felix
Murder in the East Room - Elliott Roosevelt 5448
The Prescott Chronicles - Albert Fried 2232

Furnival, James
The Masters of Bow Street - John Creasy 1423

Godfrey, Sir Edmund
The Murder of Sir Edmund Godfrey - John Dickson Carr 913

Holloway, George
Warlock - Oakley Hall 2653

Holmes, Oliver Wendell
Copperhead - Bernard Cornwell 1335
I Swear by Apollo - Agatha Young 6939

Hughes, Charles Evans
Murder in the Red Room - Elliott Roosevelt 5451
Murder in the Rose Garden - Elliott Roosevelt 5452

Kunze, Emile
The Devil's Lieutenant - Maria Fagyas 1998

Nesbitt, Horatio
Sing One Song - Helen Topping Miller 4394

Ord, Jason
Look to Your Geese: A Novel of the Deflowering of New England - Jacquin Sanders 5584

Parker, Isaac C.
Ned Christie's War - Robert J. Conley 1247
The Search for Temperance Moon - Douglas C. Jones 3282
True Grit - Charles Portis 5139
Winding Stairs - Douglas C. Jones 3287
Woman of Justice - Georgia Di Donato 1639
Zeke and Ned - Larry McMurtry 4301

Pynchon, William
Hope Leslie; or, Early Times in Massachusetts - Catharine Maria Sedgewick 5714

Ring, Willard
The Justicer - Thomas Fall 2010

Samuel
Departed Glory - Peter Danielson 1466

Sessions, Albert
The Lady - Conrad Richter 5321

Smith, Temperance
Woman of Justice - Georgia Di Donato 1639

Stafford, Samuel
Farriers' Lane - Anne Perry 4930

Temple, Marmaduke
The Pioneers; or, The Sources of the Susquehanna - James Fenimore Cooper 1307

Tolbecken, Rufus
Tolbecken - Samuel Shellabarger 5798

Willoughby, Tom
The Siege of Krishnapur - J.G. Farrell 2016

KIDNAPPER

Balfour, Ebenezer
Kidnapped - Robert Louis Stevenson 6010

Bush, Ishmael
The Prairie - James Fenimore Cooper 1308

Raza, China Eye
A Mule for the Marquesa - Frank O'Rourke 4753

KNIGHT

Acconciaiuoco, Guido
The True Cross - Carlo Scarfoglio 5629

Aguila, Ramon del
Eagle of the Gredos - Claude Jack Osgood 4761

Arthur, Sir
Guinevere - Sharan Newman 4600

Astley, Andrew de
Shield of Honor - Alice Walworth Graham 2511

Audunsson, Olav
The Axe - Sigrid Undset 6378
In the Wilderness - Sigrid Undset 6381
The Snake Pit - Sigrid Undset 6383
The Son Avenger - Sigrid Undset 6384

Aumeric of Montjoie
The Siege - Jay Williams 6773

Balliol, Roussel de
The Lady for Ransom - Alfred Duggan 1768

Baude, Simon de
Time of the Unicorn - Barbara Jefferis 3176

Bedivere
Beloved Exile - Parke Godwin 2446
The Pendragon - Catherine Christian 1075

Bedwyr
In Winter's Shadow - Gillian Bradshaw 632
The Last Pendragon - Robert Rice 5316
Sword at Sunset - Rosemary Sutcliff 6125

Benoit
The Queen's War: A Novel of Eleanor of Aquitaine - Jeanne Mackin 3996

Bjorgulfson, Laurans
The Bridal Wreath - Sigrid Undset 6379

Booth, Sir Adam
The Winter Rose - Millie J. Ragosta 5243

Brand
The Disputed Crown - Valerie Anand 128

Briwerr, William de
Lord Geoffrey's Fancy - Alfred Duggan 1771

Bruyere, Geoffrey de
Lord Geoffrey's Fancy - Alfred Duggan 1771

Burgh, Falcon de
The Falcon and the Flower - Virginia Henley 2826

Cadiere, Aicart de la
Destiny of Fire - Zoe Oldenbourg 4715

Cearbhall
The Kings in Winter - Cecelia Holland 2991

Cholmondeley, Cuthbert
The Tower of London - William Harrison Ainsworth 58

Conyers, Joscelyn
I Remember Love - Mollie Hardwick 2694

Corbney, Conan de
The Blue Falcon - Robyn Carr 935

De Aix, Ralph
King of the Wood - Valerie Anand 131

de Brealte, Falkes
Leopards and Lilies - Alfred Duggan 1769

De Bretagne, Olivier
Brother Cadfael's Penance - Ellis Peters 4955

De Clairpont, Ivon
The Proud Villeins - Valerie Anand 133

de Harcourt, Raoul
The Conqueror - Georgette Heyer 2881

De Vaumartin, Everard
The Lords of Vaumartin - Cecelia Holland 2992

De Walton, John
Castle Dangerous - Sir Walter Scott 5694

Denys
The Cloister and the Hearth - Charles Reade 5279

D'Escoville, Ralf
I Am England - Patricia Wright 6881

di Donati, Pietro
The Saracen Blade - Frank Yerby 6926

Diaz de Vivar, Rodrigo
The Infidel - Georgia Elizabeth Taylor 6182

Douglas, James
Castle Dangerous - Sir Walter Scott 5694

Edmundson, Edmund
Harold Was My King - Hilda Lewis 3749

Edward of Kent
The Flame in the Dark - Basil Bonallack 568

Eldred
This January Tale - Bryher 747

Fairfield, Robert
Walk with Peril - Dorothy V.S. Jackson 3132

Falstaff, Jack
Falstaff - Robert Nye 4653

Ferrand, Oliver de
Sybille - Marion Meade 4318

Fitz Hugh, Ranulf
Defy Not the Heart - Johanna Lindsey 3794

Fitz-Stephen, Pagan de
Sir Pagan - Henry John Colyton 1222

fitz Warren, Guy
This Bright Sword - Donald Barr Chidsey 1066

FitzAilwin, Sir Justin
Masques of Gold - Roberta Gellis 2352

Fitzalan, Simon
Richard and the Knights of God - Pamela Bennetts 454

FitzGerald, Ralf
Sherwood - Parke Godwin 2449

Fitzmarc, Enguarrand
The Lily and the Leopard - Susan Wiggs 6745

fitzOdo, Roger
The Lady for Ransom - Alfred Duggan 1768

FitzRandwulf d'Amboise, Eduard
In the Shadow of Midnight - Marsha Canham 880

FitzWarin, Sir Cleve
Where Magic Dwells - Rexanne Becnel 411

Fitzwilliam, Rannulf
Jerusalem - Cecelia Holland 2990

Galahad
The Winter King - Bernard Cornwell 1351

Gawaine
Guinevere - Sharan Newman 4600

Gawaine, Sir
The Idylls of the Queen - Phyllis Ann Karr 3367

Gawin, Sir
Kinsmen of the Grail - Dorothy James Roberts 5376

Geroy, Fulcun
Son of Dust - H.F.M. Prescott 5171

Godric
This January Tale - Bryher 747

Guy of Nissan
The Siege - Jay Williams 6773

Gwalchmai
Hawk of May - Gillian Bradshaw 629
Kingdom of Summer - Gillian Bradshaw 633

Gys, Hugh de
The Devil's Cross - Walter O'Meara 4733

Haguenier of Linnieres
The Cornerstone - Zoe Oldenbourg 4714

Hereward
Count Robert of Paris - Sir Walter Scott 5695

Hugonin, Yves
Brother Cadfael's Penance - Ellis Peters 4955

Inconnu, Simon
The Disputed Crown - Valerie Anand 128

Irion
The Last Pendragon - Robert Rice 5316

John of Oversley
Men Like Shadows - Dorothy Charques 1000

Kay, Sir
The Idylls of the Queen - Phyllis Ann Karr 3367

Kenneth, Sir
The Talisman - Sir Walter Scott 5708

Kerbouchard
The Walking Drum - Louis L'Amour 3632

Lacey, Adam de
The Running Vixen - Elizabeth Chadwick 968

Lacey, Robert de
The Briar Rose - Linda Neale 4561

Lacy, Sir Fulk de
Gay Crusader - Cleone Knox 3528

Laeghaire of Tralee
The Firedrake - Cecelia Holland 2988

Laidley, Hyatt
By Right of Arms - Robyn Carr 937

Lancelot
The Chessboard Queen - Sharan Newman 4597
The Emperor Arthur - Godfrey Turton 6368
Guinevere Evermore - Sharan Newman 4601
Guinevere: The Legend in Autumn - Persia
  Woolley 6868
The King - Donald Barthelme 365
The Once and Future King - T.H. White 6705
Queen of the Summer Stars - Persia Woolley 6869
The Queen's Knight - Marvin Borowsky 585

Lancelot du Lac
First Knight - Elizabeth Chadwick 966

Langham, Piers
The Warwick Heiress - Margaret Abbey 6

Launcelot
Arthur Rex: A Legendary Novel - Thomas
  Berger 477
Beloved Exile - Parke Godwin 2446
Firelord - Parke Godwin 2447
The Pendragon - Catherine Christian 1075
The Winter King - Bernard Cornwell 1351
Witch of the North - Courtway Jones 3272

Le Noir, Justin
The Infidels - Chloe Gartner 2308

Leighton, Royce
The Troubadour's Romance - Robyn Carr 940

Loring, Nigel
The White Company - Sir Arthur Conan Doyle 1716

Lucan
The Queen's Knight - Marvin Borowsky 585

Malbray, Liebaut de
God's Equal - Alain Absire 14

Marshal, William
The Battle of the Queens - Jean Plaidy 5005
Champion - L. Christian Balling 285
The Courts of Love - Jean Plaidy 5010
The Devil Is Loose - Graham Shelby 5790
King's Man - C.M. Edmondston 1880
The Marriage of Meggotta - Edith Pargeter 4799
The Prince of Darkness - Jean Plaidy 5044

Miles, Hendon
The Prince and the Pauper - Mark Twain 6373

Modred
Guinevere: The Legend in Autumn - Persia
  Woolley 6868
The Pagan King - Edison Marshall 4109

Molay, Jacques de
The Iron King - Maurice Druon 1732

Montbrun, Roger de
Cities of the Flesh - Zoe Oldenbourg 4713

Montgomerie, Sir Edmund de
Silver Leopard - F. van Wyck Mason 4160

Morteigne, Adam de
The Lost Flight - H.F.M. Prescott 5169

Mortimer, Warrin de
The Running Vixen - Elizabeth Chadwick 968

Muirtagh
The Kings in Winter - Cecelia Holland 2991

Nikulausson, Erlend
The Bridal Wreath - Sigrid Undset 6379
The Cross - Sigrid Undset 6380
The Mistress of Husaby - Sigrid Undset 6382

Olafson, Eric
The Proud Villeins - Valerie Anand 133

Parolles, Landry de
No Man's Son - Doris Sutcliffe Adams 23

Pasay, Gui de
Men Like Shadows - Dorothy Charques 1000

Peirot, Jocelin
The Siege - Jay Williams 6773

Pelleas
The Emperor Arthur - Godfrey Turton 6368

Perceval, Sir
Kinsmen of the Grail - Dorothy James Roberts 5376

Percy, Henry
Harry of Monmouth - A.M. Maughan 4199
The Star of Lancaster - Jean Plaidy 5065

Pete
Fitzempress' Law - Diana Norman 4644

Radnor, Cain
Bond of Blood - Roberta Gellis 2349

Rainaut, Valence
Crusader's Torch - Chelsea Quinn Yarbro 6897

Rannulf
The Earl - Cecelia Holland 2987

Redvers, Tracy de
Royal Sword at Agincourt - Pamela Bennetts 455

Renard
The Leopard Unleashed - Elizabeth Chadwick 967

Rendell, Phillip
The Lion and the Leopard - Mary Ellen
  Johnson 3226

Reynald of Warby
Gilded Spurs - Grace Ingram 3105

Richard
Great Maria - Cecelia Holland 2989

Richard of Kingsclere
Emerald Fire - Laurie Grant 2537

Richard of Rawen
Below the Salt - Thomas B. Costain 1362

Robert of Clari
The Seven Hills of Paradise - Rosemary
  Simpson 5859

Robert of Locksley
Lady of the Forest - Jennifer Roberson 5368

Robert of Paris
Count Robert of Paris - Sir Walter Scott 5695

Roger, Sir
Knight with Armour - Alfred Duggan 1767

Roland
Swords of Anjou - Mario Pei 4890

Rolf
Madselin - Norah Lofts 3853

Sabres, Joscelin de
The Courts of Love: A Romance of Medieval France -
  Peter Bourne 592

Seconnet, Denys de
Under the Winter Moon - Teresa Brooke 705

Sedgemont, Robert
A Royal Quest - Mary Lide 3777

Selkirk, James
The Crown in Darkness - P.C. Doherty 1671

Sharpe, Clement
The Bishop's Tale - Margaret Frazer 2215

Sigward
The Morning Gift - Diana Norman 4645

Simon the Coldheart
Simon the Coldheart - Georgette Heyer 2901

Sinan
Alamut - Judith Tarr 6164

Tallboys, Godfrey
The Homecoming - Norah Lofts 3844
Knight's Acre - Norah Lofts 3848

Tancred
My Lord Brother the Lionheart - Molly Costain
  Haycraft 2795

Tancred of Varville
The Unholy Pilgrim - R.F. Tapsell 6161

Tedric
The Blue Falcon - Robyn Carr 935

Thierry of Anjou
Swords of Anjou - Mario Pei 4890

Tostig
Below the Salt - Thomas B. Costain 1362

Tourney, Roland de
Secret Song - Catherine Coulter 1381

Tristan
The White Raven - Diana L. Paxson 4847

Tristram of Maudesbury
The Peacock and the Pearl - Jennifer Lang 3661

Tudor, Owen
The Royal Pawn - Antonia Ridge 5327

Tweng, Thomas
The Death of a King - P.C. Doherty 1672

Vaeringer, Andrea
Ride Home Tomorrow - Evan John 3221

Valliant, Martin
Martin Valliant - Warwick Deeping 1578

Visdelou, Humphrey
The Knight - George Shipway 5829

Wallace, William
Braveheart - Randall Wallace 6538

Wilfred of Ivanhoe
Ivanhoe - Sir Walter Scott 5699

William Long-Arm
When God Slept - Peter Bourne   597

LABOR LEADER

Connolly, James
Rebels: The Irish Rising of 1916 - Peter DeRosa   1622

Daniels, Eugene
Great Dream From Heaven - John Rolfe Gardiner   2286

Debs, Eugene V.
Homeland - John Jakes   3148

Glen, Owen
Owen Glen - Ben Ames Williams   6766

Gompers, Samuel
The American - Howard Fast   2026

Jones, Mary Harris
The Scapegoat - Mary Lee Settle   5758

Kent, Gideon
The Lawless - John Jakes   3149
The Warriors - John Jakes   3155

LABOR ORGANIZER

Cloud, Rondall
Storming Heaven - Denise Giardina   2394

Debs, Eugene V.
Adversary in the House - Irving Stone   6053

Debs, Theodore
Adversary in the House - Irving Stone   6053

Dobrejcak, Dobie
Out of This Furnace - Thomas Bell   425

Dreier, Mary
Rivington Street - Meredith Tax   6175

Flynn, Elizabeth Gurley
Bisbee '17 - Robert Houston   3056

Haywood, William "Big Bill"
Bisbee '17 - Robert Houston   3056
Castle Garden - Bill Albert   63

Hoffa, Jimmy
The Immortals - Michael Korda   3540

Holmquist, Jake
Poor Boy and a Long Way Home - James Sherburne   5806

Jones, Mary Harris
Bisbee '17 - Robert Houston   3056

Levy, Sarah
Rivington Street - Meredith Tax   6175

Pence, Virgil
A Vein of Riches - John Knowles   3526

Penny, Nick
The White Dove - Rosie Thomas   6246

Spector, Sarah Levy
Union Square - Meredith Tax   6176

Stanton, Peter
The Valiant and the Daunted - Roy Clews   1115

LAIRD

Bontine, Randall
Hearts of Gold - Jessica Stirling   6044

Buchanan
Rogue's Harbor - Inglis Fletcher   2139

Caithris, David
Hatchet in the Sky - Margaret Cooper Gay   2328

Cameron, Ewen
The Flight of the Heron - Dorothy Kathleen Broster   710

Campbell, Colin
Kidnapped - Robert Louis Stevenson   6010

Campbell, Niall
Child of the Mist - Kathleen Morgan   4451

Dunn, Nicholas
Mistress of The Highlands - Chloe Gartner   2309

Dunn, Sandy
Mistress of The Highlands - Chloe Gartner   2309

Grant, Finlay Ban
Torbeg - Grace Campbell   873

Jardine, Alexander
Foes - Mary Johnston   3233

Jarret, James
Jarrett's Jade - Frank Yerby   6923

Kincaid, Alec
The Bride - Julie Garwood   2311

MacArthur, Ian
Highland Belle - Patricia Grasso   2541

MacDonald, Niall
The Blind Bend - Lorn MacIntyre   3985

MacHugh, Alexander
Bride of the MacHugh - Jan Cox Speas   5956

MacIvor, Fergus
Waverley - Sir Walter Scott   5709

MacLean, Lachlan
The Dark Stranger - Constance Dodge   1664

Ogilvie, Thomas
The Case of Kitty Ogilvie - Jean Stubbs   6093

Rhinn, Comyn
Swear by Apollo - Shirley Barker   318

Stewart, James
Catriona - Robert Louis Stevenson   6009

LANDOWNER

Allard, Fontaine
None Shall Look Back - Caroline Gordon   2478

Alvarado, Don Julian
Beat to Quarters - C.S. Forester   2170

Andresson, Simon
The Mistress of Husaby - Sigrid Undset   6382

Appleton, Captain William
Hangman's Cliff - Robert Neill   4570

Ashe, Homer
The Power of Black - M.B. Longman   3880

Ashland, Roger
By Dim and Flashing Lamps - Alan Le May   3689

Aubrey, Jack
The Yellow Admiral - Patrick O'Brian   4680

Baines
The Piano - Jane Campion   878

Barry, Stephen
The Covenant - Brigid Knight   3521

Batchelor, Clyde
Steamboat Gothic - Frances Parkinson Keyes   3481

Bjorgulfson, Laurans
The Bridal Wreath - Sigrid Undset   6379

Bliss, Simon
Deep River - Henrietta Buckmaster   760

Bobrov, Boris
Russka: The Novel of Russia - Edward Rutherfurd   5535

Braybon, General
The Near and Distant Place - Patricia Wright   6883

Brodrick, Copper John
Hungry Hill - Daphne Du Maurier   1746

Browning, Mark
Stranger in Savannah - Eugenia Price   5187

Caldwell, Duke
Dan'l Boone Kissed Me - Felix Holt   3006

Calvalcanti, Nicolau
Brazil - Errol Lincoln Uys   6395

Cambara, Licurgo
Time and the Wind - Erico Verissimo   6451

Campbell, Colin
The Land Is Bright - James Arthur Kjelgaard   3508

Campbell, John
New Day - Victor Stafford Reid   5291

Cantu, Don Vito
The Hands of Cantu - Tom Lea   3694

Carey, Robert
Rebel Heiress - Robert Neill   4573

Carrington, Gincie
A Season of Swans - Celeste De Blasis   1548

Cate, Christopher
By the Green of the Spring - John Masters   4171
Heart of War - John Masters   4174

Cherrill, Philip
Tidewater - Clifford Dowdey   1709

Claffey, Ira
Andersonville - MacKinlay Kantor   3359

Colvin, Adam
Echoes From the Past - Marjorie McEvoy   4268

Coombs, Eulalie
Miami: A Saga - Evelyn Wilde Mayerson   4204

Cordova, Isabella
A Woman of Texas - R.T. Stevens   6002

Cornish, Colonel Jack
Golden Destiny - June Wyndham Davies   1506

Cree, Captain Joe
The Velvet Horn - Andrew Lytle   3946

Culhane, Travis
A Season of Swans - Celeste De Blasis   1548

Custis, Daniel Parke
Lady Washington - Dorothy Clarke Wilson   6803

Dana
By Love Enslaved - Phoebe Conn   1255

De Salis, Edward
Cashelmara - Susan Howatch   3058

de Silva, Diego
Captain From Castile - Samuel Shellabarger   5794

Devalon, Henri
Forever Possess - Alexandra Phillips   4982

Devane, Barbara
Now Face to Face - Karleen Koen   3530

Dickinson, Benoni
Water over the Dam - Marguerite Allis   116

Douglas, John
Indigo - Nicholas Carnac   900

Dungillis, Sir John
Castle Malindine - Hilary Ford   2163

Falconer, Alexandra Thaine
Swan's Chance - Celeste De Blasis   1549

Falconer, Rane
Swan's Chance - Celeste De Blasis   1549

Fallon, Michael
The Fallon Blood - Reagan O'Neal   4741

Faulconer, Washington
Rebel - Bernard Cornwell 1336

Flaherty, Samuel
Across the Bitter Sea - Eilis Dillon 1646

Foley, Max
The Twilighters - Noel M. Loomis 3894

Fountaine, Robert
Lusty Wind for Carolina - Inglis Fletcher 2134

Gautier, Francis
The Chateau - Stephen Coulter 1383

Geraint
The Man on the White Horse - Warwick
  Deeping 1577

Gerard, Sir Harry
A Season of Mists - Sarah Woodhouse 6856

Gilchrist, Nigel
Jennie about to Be - Elisabeth Ogilvie 4694

Glendower, Gethin
Autumn Lace - Eileen Jackson 3133

Godolphin, Mordaunt Fitzmaurice
The Wild Yazoo - John Myers 4546

Gould, Horace
New Moon Rising - Eugenia Price 5185

Gould, James
Lighthouse - Eugenia Price 5182

Granville, Marcus
Damnation Reef - Jill Tattersall 6172

Gronelu, Jacob
Dina's Book - Herbjorg Wassmo 6577

Haan, Evert
Silver Nutmeg - Norah Lofts 3860

Hadley, Ama
A Southern Woman - Elena Yates Eulo 1983

Halstad, Theo
Dark Possession - Alice Alison Lide 3771

Harpcore, Dennison
The Parson's Daughter - Catherine Cookson 1286

Hawke, Derek
Love's Tender Fury - Jennifer Wilde 6749

Hawkes, Gideon
The Fireflower - Edith Layton 3687

Hayden de Morgan, Pieter
The Great Sky and the Silence - James S. Rand 5245

Hendricks, Colonel John B.
A Woman of Texas - R.T. Stevens 6002

Herries, Nicholas
Katherine Christian - Hugh Walpole 6546

Howarth, Lance
Turn of the Dice - Janet Edmonds 1870

Ivanushka
Russka: The Novel of Russia - Edward
  Rutherfurd 5535

Jansen, Kaspar
Wild Conquest - Peter Abrahams 12

Jones, Tom
The Latter Adventures of Tom Jones - Bob
  Coleman 1200

Juvika, Per Anders
The People of Juvik - Olav Dunn 1798

Kirwan, Captain Roderick
The Hedge of Thorns - Helen Ashton 217

Le Moyne, Charles
High Towers - Thomas B. Costain 1366

Lindsay, Alasdair
Indigo - Nicholas Carnac 900

MacArthur, John
The Adventurers - William Stuart Long 3869
The Settlers - William Stuart Long 3878
The Traitors - William Stuart Long 3879

Mainwairing, Roger
Men of Albemarle - Inglis Fletcher 2135

Mannion, Stephen
Storm of Time - Eleanor Dark 1494

Mathick, Ann
A Season of Mists - Sarah Woodhouse 6856

McClure, Hardee
Trumpet in the Sky - Helen Topping Miller 4397

McDonogh, John
Pathway to the Stars - Harnett T. Kane 3356

McGrath, Stewart
The Piano - Jane Campion 878

McNab, Peter
Hangman's Beach - Thomas H. Raddall 5229

Medina, Don Raul
When the Owl Cries - Paul Bartlett 367

Merenda, Lorenzo
Castle of Doves - Constance Heaven 2803

Millhouser, Robert
Ourselves to Know - John O'Hara 4704

Morgan, Rhys
After the Rainbow - Yvonne Kalman 3323

Mowbray, Miles
A Father and His Fate - Ivy Compton-Burnett 1228

Nikulausson, Erlend
The Bridal Wreath - Sigrid Undset 6379
The Cross - Sigrid Undset 6380
The Mistress of Husaby - Sigrid Undset 6382

O'Brien, Aidan
The Emancipist: An Unforgettable Epic of Australia -
  Veronica Geoghegan Sweeney 6147

O'Carroll, Roderick
The Big Wind - Beatrice Coogan 1262

Odda
The Price of Blood - Doris Sutcliffe Adams 24

O'Hara, Scarlett
Scarlett - Alexandra Ripley 5342

Olivera, Don Ignacio
Beneath the Blue Mountain - Richard S.
  Wheeler 6656

Orton, Sir Giles
Rebel Heiress - Robert Neill 4573

Osborne, Constance
Borrowed Plumes - Roseleen Milne 4409

Parks, Elam
Forty Guns West - William W. Johnstone 3267

Parrish, Guy
The Hand of a Woman - Diana Brown 719

Paxmore, Edward
Chesapeake - James A. Michener 4367

Peace, Ginny
The Truest Pleasure - Robert Morgan 4452

Pengallion, Dominic
The Sea Treasure - Elisabeth Barr 338

Peregrine, Rogan
The Taming - Jude Deveraux 1633

Perle, Judith
The Rose Rent - Ellis Peters 4970

Pickett, Jonathan
The Inner Voice - Nina Wilcox Putnam 5211

Pimber, Henry
Omensetter's Luck - William H. Gass 2317

Poldark, Captain Ross
The Renegade: A Novel of Cornwall, 1783-1787 -
  Winston Graham 2529

Rinn, Linda
Fabulous Valley - Cornelia Stratton Parker 4803

Rolfe, John
Powhatan's Daughter - John Clarke Bowman 605

Roscius, Sextus
Roman Blood - Steven Saylor 5626

Rowhedge, Tom
Bless This House - Norah Lofts 3835

Royland, Clare
Kingdom of Shadows - Barbara Erskine 1954

Rutledge, Adam
Queen's Gift - Inglis Fletcher 2136
Raleigh's Eden - Inglis Fletcher 2137

St. Jules, Christopher
The Castle of the Winds - Jeanne Montague 4434

Sheldon, Gilbert
The Tides of Malvern - Francis Griswold 2595

Shelmadine, Sir Richard
Afternoon of a Autocrat - Norah Lofts 3834

Skiles, Rumsey
Peace at Bowling Green - Alfred Leland Crabb 1405

Stowe, Augustus
Swandowne - Daniel Farson 2024

Tallboys, Henry
The Lonely Furrow - Norah Lofts 3849

Talvas
The Lost Lands - Peter Vansittart 6430

Taverner, Tom
The Taverners' Place - Joanna Trollope 6351

Temple, Marmaduke
The Pioneers; or, The Sources of the Susquehanna -
  James Fenimore Cooper 1307

Thaw, James
The Ancestors Cry Out - Eugenia Lovett West 6627

Tillman, Task
Crimson Is the Eastern Shore - Don Tracy 6308

Todd, Titus
Water over the Dam - Marguerite Allis 116

Trace, Austin
Firewind - Bill Pronzini 5200

Tunstall, Paul
A Leaf in the Wind - Marie Joseph 3307

Valden, Jimmie
The Forge - Thomas S. Stribling 6083

Volland, Hubert
Vollands - Pamela Hill 2947

Volland, James
Vollands - Pamela Hill 2947

Washington, George
Morning of a Hero - Burke Boyce 608

Wentworth, Thomas
The Physician of London - Stephanie Cowell 1394

Whiteoak, Philip
Morning at Jalna - Mazo de la Roche 1560

Whiting, Richard
Three-Headed Angel - Roark Bradford 623

Whitmead, Ninian
The Faithful Lovers - Valerie Anand 129

Woodcarver, Thomas
The Ruthless Yeomen - Valerie Anand 134

Younger, Bas
Three-Headed Angel - Roark Bradford 623

Zubaran, Don Saturnino
Hill of the Hawk - Scott O'Dell   4689

LAWMAN

Beehunter
To Make a Killing - Robert J. Conley   1252

Blaisedell, Clay
Warlock - Oakley Hall   2653

Brady, William
The Sons of Grady Rourke - Douglas Savage   5618

Call, Woodrow F.
Dead Man's Walk - Larry McMurtry   4297
Streets of Laredo - Larry McMurtry   4300

Cogburn, Rooster
True Grit - Charles Portis   5139

Dugan, Clayton
Power in the Blood - Greg Matthews   4191

Earp, Virgil
Wyatt Earp - Dan Gordon   2481

Earp, Wyatt
Bloody Season - Loren D. Estleman   1968
Confessions of Johnny Ringo - Geoff Aggeler   40
The Cowboy Conspiracy - Larry D. Names   4553
Doc Holliday's Woman - Jane Candia Coleman   1201
Little Big Man - Thomas Berger   478
The Old Colts - Glendon Swarthout   6144
Tombstone Showdown - Leslie Scott   5681
Wild Times - Brian Garfield   2291
The Winter Wolf: Wyatt Earp in Alaska - Richard Parry   4820
Wyatt Earp - Matt Braun   653
Wyatt Earp - Dan Gordon   2481

East, Jim
Tascosa Gun: The Story of Jim East - Gene Shelton   5803

Evans, Lincoln
The Hangings - Bill Pronzini   5202

Foster, Nate
Embers of the Heart - Rosanne Bittner   512

Gallagher
Me and Gallagher - Jack Farris   2023

Garrett, Pat
Billy the Kid - Edwin Corle   1330
Billy the Kid: The Legend of El Chivato - Elizabeth Fackler   1994
City of Widows - Loren D. Estleman   1969
The Demise of Billy the Kid - Preston Lewis   3760
The Story of Pat Garrett and Billy the Kid - David Everitt   1987
Tascosa Gun: The Story of Jim East - Gene Shelton   5803

Gatling, Tom
The Comancheros - Paul I. Wellman   6616

Go-Ahead Rider
Go-Ahead Rider - Robert J. Conley   1243
To Make a Killing - Robert J. Conley   1252

Grant, Jack
Apaches - Oakley Hall   2650

Grigsby, Robert
Wilde West - Walter Satterthwait   5609

Hays, John Coffee
Captain Jack - Gene Shelton   5800

Hickok, James Butler
Black Sun - Terry C. Johnston   3242
The Lawless - John Jakes   3149
The Pistoleer - James Carlos Blake   536
Western: A Saga of the Great Plains - Frank Yerby   6930

Hollander, Jake
Dutch Uncle - Marilyn Durham   1815

Hoover, J. Edgar
Pretty Boy Floyd - Larry McMurtry   4299

Howard, Harry
Adios! - Lanier Bartlett   366

Hudspeth, A.C.
Stamping Ground - Loren D. Estleman   1977

Johnson, Wayt
Saint Johnson - William R. Burnett   796

Kraker, Sarge
Arfive - A.B. Guthrie Jr.   2623

Lane, Corey
Not of War Only - Norman Zollinger   6966

Luton, Bluff
The Actor - Robert J. Conley   1236
Colfax - Robert J. Conley   1239
Killing Time - Robert J. Conley   1244

Macnab, Otto
Texas - James A. Michener   4375

Maples, Sam
Ned Christie's War - Robert J. Conley   1247

Masterson, William Barclay "Bat"
Bloody Season - Loren D. Estleman   1968
The Ham Reporter - Robert J. Randisi   5251
The Old Colts - Glendon Swarthout   6144

McCrae, Augustus
Dead Man's Walk - Larry McMurtry   4297

Miller, Rick
California! - Dana Fuller Ross   5467

Moore, Andrew
Destiny in Dallas - Shirley Seifert   5725

Murdock, Page
City of Widows - Loren D. Estleman   1969
The High Rocks - Loren D. Estleman   1973
Murdock's Law - Loren D. Estleman   1975
Stamping Ground - Loren D. Estleman   1977
The Stranglers - Loren D. Estleman   1978

Neighbors, Robert Simpson
Brazos Dreamer - Gene Shelton   5799

O'Neill, Bucky
San Juan Hill - Will Henry   2848

Page, Matt
The Gathering Storm - W.E. Davis   1540

Pea Eye
Streets of Laredo - Larry McMurtry   4300

Pearce, Nathan
Breakheart Pass - Alistair MacLean   3999

Plummer, Henry
What Law There Was - Al Dempsey   1609

Quaid, Will
Hearts and Bones - Margaret Lawrence   3685

Quintano, Toribio
The Royal City - Les Savage Jr.   5621

Rash, Matt
One More River to Cross - Will Henry   2847

Russell, Eli
Eli's Road - Lucas Webb   6589

Russell, Jason
Charity, Colorado - Chelsea Quinn Yarbro   6896
The Law in Charity - Chelsea Quinn Yarbro   6901

Sackett, Orin
The Daybreakers - Louis L'Amour   3619

St. John, Irons
Mister St. John - Loren D. Estleman   1974

Schiller, Oscar
The Search for Temperance Moon - Douglas C. Jones   3282
Winding Stairs - Douglas C. Jones   3287

Selman, John
Last Gun: The Legend of John Selman - Gene Shelton   5801

Siringo, Charlie
South of the Border - John Byrne Cooke   1268

Smith, Gypsy
Children of the Dust - Carlile Clancy   1084

Steele, Bluford "Blue"
Killing Time - Robert J. Conley   1244

Sundown, Jacques
Blackwater Spirits - Miriam Grace Monfredo   4427

Tanner, George
Go-Ahead Rider - Robert J. Conley   1243
To Make a Killing • Robert J. Conley   1252

Tighe, Clay
Grant of Kingdom - Harvey Fergusson   2067

Tonneman, Pieter
The Dutchman - Maan Meyers   4351

Wheeler, Hary
Bisbee '17 - Robert Houston   3056

LAWYER

Acox, Hamilton
The Falling Hills - Perry Lentz   3720

Adams, Cameron
Lantern for the Dark - Jessica Stirling   6045

Adams, John
Those Who Love - Irving Stone   6064

Adams, John Quincy
Echo of Lions - Barbara Chase-Riboud   1004

Adler, Seth
Members of the Tribe - Richard Kluger   3511

Ashton, William
The Bride of Lammermoor - Sir Walter Scott   5693

Aumont, Nicole
Winter Grass - Richard S. Wheeler   6665

Bacon, Sir Francis
The Diary of William Harvey: The Imaginary Journal of the Physician Who Revolutionized Medicine - Jean Hamburger   2667
My Lord Essex - Olive Eckerson   1838
No Bed for Bacon - Caryl Brahms   640
Unicorn Rampant - Nigel Tranter   6323

Bacon, Nathaniel
The King's Passenger - Nathan Schachner   5631

Bade, Jonathan
The Tontine - Thomas B. Costain   1371

Bandy, Francis
My Grand Enemy - Jean Stubbs   6098

Becket, Thomas
The Lion of England - Margaret Butler   824

Berry, Syke
Double Moscadine - Frances Gaither   2271

Blair, Jonathan
Jonathan Blair, Bounty Lands Lawyer - William Donohue Ellis   1929

Bret, Gervaise
The Dragons of Archenfield - Edward Marston   4119
The Lions of the North - Edward Marston   4121
The Ravens of Blackwater - Edward Marston   4126
The Wolves of Savernake - Edward Marston   4130

Brice, Stephen
The Crisis - Winston Churchill   1079

Bryan, William Jennings
The American - Howard Fast   2026
The Land Was Ours: A Novel of the Great Plains -
   Charles W. Bailey   266

Burnaby, Nicholas
Lillibullero - Robert Neill   4571

Cameron, Justin
The Strange Files of Fremont Jones - Dianne
   Day   1544

Carton, Sydney
A Tale of Two Cities - Charles Dickens   1642

Chamberlain, Brice
The Sea of Grass - Conrad Richter   5323

Cheoh, Joe
Carolina Courage - Dana Fuller Ross   5469

Chirke, Nicholas
A Tapestry of Murders - C.L. Grace   2510

Cicero, Marcus Tullius
Augustus - Allan Massie   4167
Caesar - Allan Massie   4168
Caesar's Women - Colleen McCullough   4233
Catalina's Riddle - Steven Saylor   5624
The City of Libertines - W.G. Hardy   2702
Death on the Appian Way - Kenneth Benton   463
Freedom, Farewell - Phyllis Bentley   461
The Gift of Rome - John Wagner   6520
The Grass Crown - Colleen McCullough   4236
A Murder on the Appian Way - Steven Saylor   5625
Roman Blood - Steven Saylor   5626
The Venus Throw - Steven Saylor   5627
The Young Caesar - Rex Warner   6567

Clay, Henry
Home to Kentucky: A Novel of Henry Clay - Alfred
   Leland Crabb   1399

Cohn, Roy
Walter Winchell: A Novel - Michael Herr   2863

Cradock, Paul
The Legacy of Tregaran - Mary Lide   3776

Crandall, John Quincy Adams
*Aces and Eights: A Novel of the Legend of Wild Bill
   Hickok* - Loren D. Estleman   1967

Danton, Georges-Jacques
Scaramouche - Rafael Sabatini   5554

Darrow, Clarence
The American - Howard Fast   2026
California Glory - Dana Fuller Ross   5468
The Dream Seekers - Grace Mark   4085

Dearborn, Jonathan
Jonathan Dearborn: A Novel of the War of 1812 -
   Willard Wallace   6540

DeWolfe, Angus
The Justicer - Thomas Fall   2010

Fairbanks, Walter
California Gold - John Jakes   3145

Fairchild, Dexter
Watchfires - Louis Auchincloss   234

Fairford, Alan
Red Gauntlet - Sir Walter Scott   5706

Fort, Charlie
The Massacre at Fall Creek - Jessamyn West   6631

Frankfurter, Felix
Murder in the Oval Office - Elliott Roosevelt   5450
Murder in the Red Room - Elliott Roosevelt   5451
*The Passion of Sacco and Vanzetti: A New England
   Legend* - Howard Fast   2040
The Prescott Chronicles - Albert Fried   2232

Fulvius
The Gladiators - Arthur Koestler   3532

Gardiner, Asa B.
The Court-Martial of George Armstrong Custer -
   Douglas C. Jones   3276

Gorman, Marcus
Legs - William Kennedy   3422

Gwynne, Kenneth
Viola Gwyn - George Barr McCutcheon   4258

Hamilton, Andrew
Anna Zenger: Mother of Freedom - Kent
   Cooper   1316

Hamlin, Albion
Lydia Bailey - Kenneth Roberts   5387

Henry, Patrick
Clear for Action: A Novel about John Paul Jones -
   Clements Ripley   5344
Give Me Liberty - Noel B. Gerson   2369
Mistress Nancy - Barbara Bentley   460
The Tree of Liberty - Elizabeth Page   4773

Holmes, Oliver Wendell
I Swear by Apollo - Agatha Young   6939

Hyde, Edward
The Bride - Margaret Irwin   3116

Jacobson, Allan
The Court-Martial of George Armstrong Custer -
   Douglas C. Jones   3276

Jebeau, Arthur
My Beloved Son - Catherine Cookson   1285

Kelleway, Henry
The Iron Roads - Forbes Bramble   644
Regent Square - Forbes Bramble   645

Kelleway, Thomas
Regent Square - Forbes Bramble   645

Kimball, Armand
They Came to a Valley - Bill Gulick   2618

Komarovsky, Victor
Doctor Zhivago - Boris Pasternak   4824

Lincoln, Abraham
Flash for Freedom - George MacDonald Fraser   2203
Hoffman's Row - Walter Carnahan   902

Lincoln, Robert Todd
The Trial of Mary Todd Lincoln - James A.
   Rhodes   5309

Lomont, Nicholas
The Still Storm - Francoise Sagan   5562

Mahmoud
The Mamur Zapt and the Night of the Dog - Michael
   Pearce   4869

Mahmoud el Zaki
The Mamur Zapt and the Return of the Carpet -
   Michael Pearce   4870

March, Alex
Enough Good Men - Charles Mercer   4336

Marshall, John
Mistress Nancy - Barbara Bentley   460

Moncrieff, Sir James Wellwood
Madeleine - Pamela Elizabeth West   6633

Mordecai
Esther: The Star and the Sceptre - Gina
   Andrews   146

Moreau, Andre-Louis
Scaramouche the King-Maker - Rafael Sabatini   5555

Morris, Jeremy
Luise - Dawn Stewart Field   2079

Norton, Geoffrey
Good Morning, Irene - Carole Nelson Douglas   1698

Norton, Godfrey
Good Night, Mr. Holmes - Carole Nelson
   Douglas   1699

Irene's Last Waltz - Carole Nelson Douglas   1701

Pay, Eben
Remember Santiago - Douglas C. Jones   3280
Weedy Rough - Douglas C. Jones   3286
Winding Stairs - Douglas C. Jones   3287

Prentiss, Patrick
The End of the Hunt - Thomas Flanagan   2119

Quinncannon, Lon
The Thomas Street Horror - Raymond Paul   4843
*The Tragedy at Tinkerton: An Historical Novel of
   Murder* - Raymond Paul   4844

Ramsay, Jamie
Strathgallant - Laura Black   523

Rathbone, Oliver
Defend and Betray - Anne Perry   4928
The Sins of the Wolf - Anne Perry   4937

Ritchie, David
The Crossing - Winston Churchill   1080

Rudd, Tierney
Pacific Street - Cecelia Holland   2993

Scawen, Vosper
An Innocent Woman - Malcolm Macdonald   3967

Scott, Jonathan
Greygallows - Barbara Michaels   4359

Severus, Livinius
Roman Nights - Ron Burns   803

Spurlock, Travis
Fort Worth - Leonard Sanders   5588

Stalker, Andrew
The Dark Pasture - Jessica Stirling   6042

Stevens, Thaddeus
I Speak for Thaddeus Stevens - Elsie
   Singmaster   5868

Stone, David
Bates House - Clarence Benadum   437

Strange, Christopher
Christopher Strange - Ruth Eleanor McKee   4281

Strickland, Clive
Scandal at High Chimneys: A Victorian Melodrama -
   John Dickson Carr   915

Torkelsen, Rolfe
Big River, Big Man - Thomas William Duncan   1786

Treloar, Robert
Look Away! - George Nauman Shuster   5841

Wayman, Stephen
The Land Endures - Mary E. Pearce   4862

Wheeler, Portius
The Fields - Conrad Richter   5319
The Town - Conrad Richter   5325
The Trees - Conrad Richter   5326

LEADER

Agamemnon
Whom the Gods Would Destroy - Richard
   Powell   5148

Ahmad, Muhammad
Drums of Khartoum - Chloe Gartner   2307

Alden, John
The Honorable Imposter - Gilbert Morris   4463
The Land Is Bright - Noel B. Gerson   2376
Legacy - Robert Vaughan   6448
Pilgrims: A Novel of the Mayflower - Gerard
   Mac   3955
The Wickedest Pilgrim - Donald Barr Chidsey   1067

Allen, Ethan
The Arch of Stars - Clifford Lindsey Alderman   66
Catch a Falling Star - Frederic F. Van de
   Water   6401

Reluctant Rebel - Frederic F. Van de Water 6403

Annas
Belmarch: A Legend of the First Crusade -
  Christopher Davis 1514

Bacon, Nathaniel
*Forest Cavalier: A Romance of America's First
  Frontier and of Bacon's Rebellion* - Roy Catesby
  Flannagan 2122
The King's Passenger - Nathan Schachner 5631
Man Cannot Tell - Philip Lightfoot Scruggs 5711

Baranov, Aleksandr
Heaven Is Too High - Mildred Masterson
  McNeilly 4309

ben Yair, Eleazar
The Antagonists - Ernest K. Gann 2276
The Tenth Measure - Brenda Lesley Segal 5721
The Voices of Masada - David Kossoff 3545

Bohemond I
*A Booke of Days: A Journal of the Crusade by Roger,
  Duke of Lunel* - Stephen J. Rivele 5351
Wine of Satan - Laverne Gay 2327

Bossereau, Jean
The Brothers of Uterica - Benjamin Capps 887

Bourbon, Francois de Vendome de
Twenty Years After - Alexandre Dumas 1783

Bourbon, Louis I de
The Faith and the Flame - June Dimmit
  Houston 3054

Bradford, William
Cape Cod - William Martin 4139
The Honorable Imposter - Gilbert Morris 4463
The Land Is Bright - Noel B. Gerson 2376
Pilgrims: A Novel of the Mayflower - Gerard
  Mac 3955
Thanksgiving - Terry Coleman 1207

Brannan, Samuel
Samuel Brannan and the Golden Fleece - Reva
  Scott 5686

Campbell, Alexander
*Fool of God: A Novel Based on the Life of Alexander
  Campbell* - Louis Cochran 1144

Campbell, Thomas
*Fool of God: A Novel Based on the Life of Alexander
  Campbell* - Louis Cochran 1144

Carver, John
Massachusetts: A Novel - Nancy Zaroulis 6956
Pilgrims: A Novel of the Mayflower - Gerard
  Mac 3955

Christian, Fletcher
Mr. Christian! - Stanley Miller 4402

Civilis, Julius
The Iron Hand of Mars - Lindsey Davis 1528

Coligny, Gaspard de
The Longest Night - Ada Cook Lewis 3744
The Negotiators - Francis Walder 6526

Crespi
The Wrong Horse - Jean Bassan 374

Donner, George
The Ungodly: A Novel of the Donner Party - Richard
  Rhodes 5311

Dumont, Gabriel
Lord of the Plains - Alfred Silver 5852

Ember
Isle of Woman - Piers Anthony 167

Famin, Nikholai
Sweet Ransom - Linda Madl 4026

Fawkes, Guy
Scapegoat for a Stuart - Kate Kirby 3504

Fox, George
Bear His Mild Yoke - Ethel White 6675

Gandhi, Mahatma
The Crusader - Noel B. Gerson 2364

Genghis Khan
Poland - James A. Michener 4373
*Sons of the Steppe: The Story of How the Conqueror
  Genghis Khan Was Overcome* - Hans
  Baumann 380

Herzl, Theodor
Herzl the King - Norman Kotker 3547

Hess, Rudolf
Shadow of the Wolf - James Barwick 371

Himmler, Heinrich
A Family Matter - James Roosevelt 5458

Hitler, Adolf
Eva - Ib Melchior 4329
The Hangman's Crusade - James Barwick 370
Hitler Has Won - Frederic Mullally 4511
Mussolini - Alan Gelb 2348
The Ring Master - David Gurr 2622
The Winds of War - Herman Wouk 6876

Houston, Sam
Magnificent Destiny - Paul I. Wellman 6619

Hutchinson, Anne
Covenant of Grace - Jane Gilmore Rushing 5527
The Golden Feather - Theda Kenyon 3462
Witnesses - Marcy Moran Heidish 2820

Jan of Leyden
The Siege - Peter Vansittart 6431

Knipperdollink
The Siege - Peter Vansittart 6431

Kokhba, Simon Bar
If I Forget Thee - Brenda Lesley Segal 5720
Prince of Israel - Elias Gilner 2422
Simon Bar Cochba: Rebellion in Judea - Merton
  Finch 2086

Kolchak, Aleksandr
Fifteen Flags - Richard Lynden Hardman 2686

Kooti
Season of the Jew - Maurice Shadbolt 5768

Kruger, Paul
The Mask - Stuart Cloete 1125

Larochejaquelin, Henri
La Vendee - Anthony Trollope 6346

Levy, Ashur
Blessed Is the Land - Louis Zara 6949

Luther, Martin
Monk in Armour - Gladys H. Barr 342

MacDonald, Flora
Meggy MacIntosh - Elizabeth Janet Gray 2555

Marcel, Antonio
Sage of Canudos - Lucien Marchal 4080

Matthias
The Siege - Peter Vansittart 6431

Moses
Alone Atop the Mountain - Samuel Sandmel 5591
The Exodus - Konrad Bercovici 473
Moses, Prince of Egypt - Howard Fast 2039
The River and the Stone: Moses' Early Years in Egypt
  - Kathleen Jenks 3192

Mussolini, Benito
Mussolini - Alan Gelb 2348

Nana Sahib
Sergeant Verity and the Imperial Diamond - Francis
  Selwyn 5745

Nicholas
An Army of Children - Evan H. Rhodes 5306

Oates, Titus
A Health Unto His Majesty - Jean Plaidy 5019
Our Jo, or The Chronicle of a Coming Man - Kenneth
  M. Cameron 868
Thunder on St. Paul's Day - Jane Lane 3658
Traitor's Moon - Robert Neill 4574

Oglethorpe, James Edward
Dark Sails - Helen Topping Miller 4388
Summer Thunder - Willie Snow Ethridge 1982

O'Hara, Father Colum
Scarlett - Alexandra Ripley 5342

Owen, Robert
The Beckoning Road - Caroline Snedeker 5934

Riel, Louis
Lord of the Plains - Alfred Silver 5852

Ringrose, Floyd
Long Storm - Ernest Haycox 2790

Shays, Daniel
The Regulators - William Degenhard 1580

Smith, Buck
Trail's End - Fred Bean 400

Smith, John
Daughter of Eve - Noel B. Gerson 2366
A Durable Fire - Virginia Bernhard 480
Soldier in Paradise - Burton Wohl 6835
Soldiers of Fortune - Peter Bourne 595

Smith, Joseph
The Devil's Rainbow - J.C. Furnas 2257
The Everlasting Fire - Jonreed Lauritzen 3675

Spartacus
Arena: A Novel of Spartacus and Crassus - Maurice
  Ghnassia 2391
The Gladiators - Arthur Koestler 3532

Standish, Miles
Cape Cod - William Martin 4139
The Disturber - L.S. Davidson Jr. 1505
The Honorable Imposter - Gilbert Morris 4463
O Western Wind - John Anthony Devon 1634
Pilgrims: A Novel of the Mayflower - Gerard
  Mac 3955
The Wickedest Pilgrim - Donald Barr Chidsey 1067

Stephen of Cloyes
Our Lives Have Just Begun - Henry Myers 4541

Sutton, Silas
Pilgrims in Paradise - Frank G. Slaughter 5895

Taira Kiyomori
The Heike Story - Eiji Yoshikawa 6934

Turner, Nat
Ol' Prophet Nat - Daniel Panger 4786

Vercingetorix
Gaul Is Divided - Esther Fisher Brown 721

Veyde
Dance of the Tiger: A Novel of the Ice Age - Bjorn
  Kurten 3566

Wallace, Andrew
Two Crowns for America - Katherine Kurtz 3568

Weitzman, Chaim
Behold the Fire - Michael Blankfort 541

Winthrop, John
The Prescott Chronicles - Albert Fried 2232

Young, Brigham
The Devil's Rainbow - J.C. Furnas 2257
Dream Catcher - Terry C. Johnston 3251
The Everlasting Fire - Jonreed Lauritzen 3675
Kelly Blue - Peter Bowen 601
Sister Wives - Cleo Jones 3270

LESBIAN

Carpenter, Hollis
Bayou City Secrets - Deborah Powell   5146

Delacroix, Lily
Bayou City Secrets - Deborah Powell   5146

Dowling, Sarah
Patience and Sarah - Isabel Miller   4398

Mackenzie, Christabel
Death Wore a Diadem - Iona McGregor   4277

Stewart, Eleanor
Death Wore a Diadem - Iona McGregor   4277

White, Patience
Patience and Sarah - Isabel Miller   4398

LIBRARIAN

Maurepas
The Masked Man - P.C. Doherty   1674

Montag, Trudi
Stones From the River - Ursula Hegi   2816

Tryon, Glynis
Blackwater Spirits - Miriam Grace Monfredo   4427
North Star Conspiracy - Miriam Grace
   Monfredo   4428
Seneca Falls Inheritance - Miriam Grace
   Monfredo   4429
Through a Gold Eagle - Miriam Grace
   Monfredo   4430

LINGUIST

Ce Malinalli
Death of the Fifth Sun - Robert Somerlott   5944

Colon, Diego
The Indian Chronicles - Jose Barreiro   349

Lane, Beau
A Good Day to Die - Thomas Wakefield
   Blackburn   525

Speigner, Max
Rommel and the Rebel - Lawrence Wells   6622

LOVER

Ambiala
The Seeking - Robert S. Elegant   1906

Aspasia
Glory and the Lightning - Taylor Caldwell   856

Barry, Jeanne du
The French Bride - Evelyn Anthony   163

Clarke, Mary Anne
Mary Anne - Daphne Du Maurier   1749

Fitzherbert, Maria Anne
The Sugar Pavilion - Rosalind Laker   3600

Guiccioli, Teresa
Teresa, or Her Demon Lover - Austin K. Gray   2554

Gwynne, Nell
Catherine - Hilda Lewis   3746
Circle of Pearls - Rosalind Laker   3593
Mistress of the Boards - Richard Sumner   6118

Jondalar
The Mammoth Hunters - Jean M. Auel   237
The Plains of Passage - Jean M. Auel   238

Keppel, Alice
Mr. American - George MacDonald Fraser   2211

La Valliere, Louise de
The Shadow of the Sun - Sylvia Pell   4891

O'Shea, Katherine
Never Call It Loving - Dorothy Eden   1859

Poisson, Jeanne Antoinette
A Day of Battle - Vincent Sheean   5787
Louisiana Purchase - A.E. Hotchner   3039

Riesling, Margrethe
Blood Winter - William Patrick   4830

Rochechouart de Mortemart, Francoise Athenais
All the King's Ladies - Janice Law   3678
Angelique and the King - Sergeanne Golon   2468
The Shadow of the Sun - Sylvia Pell   4891

Saenz, Manuela
Manuela, La Caballeresa Del Sol - Demetrio Aguilera
   Malta   41

Shore, Jane
The Goldsmith's Wife - Jean Plaidy   5017
The Sun in Splendour - Jean Plaidy   5066

Sorel, Agnes
La Belle Sorel - Jacques Carton   949
The Moneyman - Thomas B. Costain   1368

Vetsera, Maria
The Archduke - Michael Arnold   194

Villiers, Barbara
Catherine - Hilda Lewis   3746
The King's Brat - Constance Gluyas   2441
Lady on the Coin - Margaret Campbell Barnes   326
My Lady Benbrook - Constance Gluyas   2442

Walter, Lucy
The Wandering Prince - Jean Plaidy   5075

Zulietta
Pandora's Galley - Macdonald Harris   2727

LOYALIST

Bale, Morganna
The General's Lady - Esther Forbes   2156

Brandt, Roger
The Rebel Loyalist - Charles William Gordon   2480

Brant, Joseph
The Raid - John Brick   673
The Wilderness War - Allen W. Eckert   1848

Buell, Thomas
Oliver Wiswell - Kenneth Roberts   5389

Carey, Sir Andrew
The Carolinian - Rafael Sabatini   5547

Carrington, Sarah
Clouds of Destiny - Lou Ellen Davis   1535

Cunningham, Alison
Patriot's Progress - Joseph G.E. Hopkins   3027

Fayerweather, Patience
The Master of Chaos - Irving A. Bacheller   262

Gordon, Clive
Song of a Strange Child - Gilbert Morris   4470

Guest, Marie
Painted Minx - Robert W. Chambers   980

Howard, Colonel
The Pilot - James Fenimore Cooper   1306

Howland, Abigail
The Gentle Rebel - Gilbert Morris   4461

Knowles, Kathy
Bride of Liberty - Frank Yerby   6909

Lincoln, Lionel
Lionel Lincoln; or, The Leaguer of Boston - James
   Fenimore Cooper   1303

MacFarlane, Ian
Valiant Libertine - John Gordon Bryson   748

Mariot, Lisle
*The Sounds of Chariots: A Novel of John Sevier and
   the State of Franklin* - Helen Topping Miller   4396

Nellis, Hendrick
The Life and Times of Captain N. - Douglas
   Glover   2436

Norwell, Stephen
Birthright - Robert E. Wall   6533

Powers, John
Flight From Avatchez - Frank G. Slaughter   5887

Shippen, Elizabeth
The Sunshine Patriot: A Novel of Benedict Arnold -
   Norman Partington   4822

Tryon, Richard
Hearts of Fire - Christina Savage   5616

Vere, Cornelia de
The Lady From Yorktown - Eva McDonald   4260

Wentworth, John
The Last Gentleman - Shirley Barker   312

Wharton, Captain Henry
The Spy: A Tale of the Neutral Ground - James
   Fenimore Cooper   1310

Whytting, Sir John
The Rival Shores - Arthur Beverly-Giddings   487

Willard, Abigail
A Toast to the King - Elizabeth Coatsworth   1139

Willard, Georgianna
A Toast to the King - Elizabeth Coatsworth   1139

Willard, Judith
A Toast to the King - Elizabeth Coatsworth   1139

Winslow, Paul
The Saintly Buccaneer - Gilbert Morris   4469

Wiswell, Oliver
Oliver Wiswell - Kenneth Roberts   5389

Wyatt, Horatio
Trumpets at Dawn - Cyril Harris   2719

MADAM

Attucks, Adeline
Heart of the Country - Greg Matthews   4190

Burgess, Elizabeth
Birthright - Phillip Finch   2087

Hathaway, Bess
Beau Barron's Lady - Helen Ashfield   204

Hollingshead, Irene
Paradise Falls - Don Robertson   5399

Joy, Miss
Carriage Trade - Robert Thomsen   6271

Moon, Jewel
The Search for Temperance Moon - Douglas C.
   Jones   3282

MAGICIAN

Faust, John
Faust - Robert Nye   4654

Harmachis
Cleopatra - H. Rider Haggard   2637

Houdini, Harry
Nevermore - William Hjortsberg   2958
One Night in Newport - Elizabeth Villars   6498
Ragtime - E.L. Doctorow   1658

John
Voodoo Dreams: A Novel of Marie Laveau - Jewell
   Parker Rhodes   5310

Lazare, Ric
Fata Morgana - William Kotzwinkle   3549

Medley, Joshua
Conjuror's Journal - Frances L. Shine   5826

Rawley, Walter Claireborne
Mr. Vertigo - Paul Auster 244

Salvador, Felix
The Golden Crucible - Jean Stubbs 6096

Simon Magus
The Illusionist - Anita Mason 4144
The Silver Chalice - Thomas B. Costain 1370

Weiss, Erich
The Sunken Treasure - Marian J.A. Jackson 3136

Yehudi
Mr. Vertigo - Paul Auster 244

MAIDEN

Brunhilde
The Twelve Pictures - Edith Simon 5857

Gundrun
Rhinegold - Stephan Grundy 2607

Jocelyn
The Queen's Knight - Marvin Borowsky 585

Vint, Mercy
Griffith Gaunt - Charles Reade 5280

MAIL ORDER BRIDE

O'Malley, Kathleen
A Bride for Donnigan - Janette Oke 4705

MANAGER

Belasco, David
A Cadenza for Caruso - Barbara Paul 4834

Boycott, Charles Cunningham
Captain Boycott, a Romantic Novel - Philip Rooney 5440

Bracewell, Nicholas
The Laughing Hangman - Edward Marston 4120
The Mad Courtesan - Edward Marston 4122
The Merry Devils - Edward Marston 4123
The Nine Giants - Edward Marston 4124
The Queen's Head - Edward Marston 4125
The Roaring Boy - Edward Marston 4127
The Silent Woman - Edward Marston 4128
The Trip to Jerusalem - Edward Marston 4129

Coleman, Charles
The Eagle at the Gate - Rona Randall 5248

Devlin, Mike
Cry of the Rain Bird - Patricia Shaw 5779

Dolby, George
The Mutual Friend - Frederick Busch 811

Garrick, David
My Name Is Clary Brown - Charlotte Keppel 3466
The Savage Brood - Martha Rofheart 5430

Macalister, Guy
Castle of Doves - Constance Heaven 2803

MATCHMAKER

Pym, Hannah
Beatrice Goes to Brighton - Marion Chesney 1019
Belinda Goes to Bath - Marion Chesney 1020
Deborah Goes to Dover - Marion Chesney 1023
Emily Goes to Exeter - Marion Chesney 1027
Penelope Goes to Portsmouth - Marion Chesney 1043
Yvonne Goes to York - Marion Chesney 1054

MECHANIC

Konoualchik, Ivan
In the Blue Light of African Dreams - Paul Watkins 6580

Morgan, Hank
A Connecticut Yankee in King Arthur's Court - Mark Twain 6371

MENTALLY ILL PERSON

Broome, Torquil
Cousin Kate - Georgette Heyer 2884

O'Bedlam, Tom
The Firedrake's Eye - Patricia Finney 2095

Scacerni, Giuseppe
Nothing New under the Sun - Riccardo Bacchelli 255

Troil, Ulla
The Pirate - Sir Walter Scott 5704

MERCENARY

Andreas, Lionello
The Wind Dancer - Iris Johansen 3218

Arrowsmith, Francis
Manchu - Robert S. Elegant 1904

Baglioni, Giampaolo
The Mercenary - Charles Durbin 1814

Burke, Tom
Tom Burke of Ours - Charles James Lever 3732

Colleoni, Bartolomeo
Condottiere - Jan Westcott 6644

De Lancey, Christopher
The Journal of Colonel De Lancey - James Warner Bellah 426

de Montreal, Walter
Rienzi, or The Last of the Tribunes - Edward Bulwer-Lytton 770

Decker, Gabriel
Earthshaker - Robert Wilson Krepps 3553

Grande, Gano
The Sword of Il Grande - Will Creed 1424

Granville, Simeon St. Leger
By Valour and Arms - James H. Street 6076

Greppia, Malatesta
High Carnival - John J. Pugh 5207

Killick, Cornelius
Sharpe's Siege - Bernard Cornwell 1348

Latro
Soldier of the Mist - Gene Wolfe 6843

Lilly, Max Cary de
Vardy - John Harris 2721

MacHugh, Ronan
The Gallowglass - Howard Breslin 666

Mark, Philip
The Sheriff of Nottingham - Richard Kluger 3512

Salvestro
The Pope's Rhinoceros - Lawrence Norfolk 4642

Severin, Daniel
The Raven and the Rose - Susan Wiggs 6746

Siena, Colombo De
Chivalry - Rafael Sabatini 5548

Sigismondo
Axe for an Abbot - Elizabeth Eyre 1989
Bravo for the Bride - Elizabeth Eyre 1990
Curtains for the Cardinal - Elizabeth Eyre 1991
Death of the Duchess - Elizabeth Eyre 1992

Stieger, Karl
Blackrobe - Robert E. Wall 6534
Bloodbrothers - Robert E. Wall 6535

Yves of Rifaucon
The Unhurrying Chase - H.F.M. Prescott 5172

MIDWIFE

Blau, Hannah
The Midwife - Gay Courter 1388

Evans, Maria
Maria - Eugenia Price 5184

Sokolow, Hannah Blau
The Midwife's Advice - Gay Courter 1389

Trevor, Hannah
Hearts and Bones - Margaret Lawrence 3685

MIGRANT WORKER

Morrigan, Johnny
The Longest Road - Jeanne Williams 6781

MILITARY PERSONNEL

Abner
Rizpah - Charles E. Israel 3124

Acco
Winter Quarters - Alfred Duggan 1775

Acox, Hamilton
The Falling Hills - Perry Lentz 3720

Adair, Arthur
The Swan and the Rose - Francis W. Leary 3697

Adams, John
Adams of the Bounty - Erle Wilson 6807

Aetius
Darkness and the Dawn - Thomas B. Costain 1364

Aguirre, Lope de
Daimon - Abel Posse 5140

Ahrens, Kurt
Guns of Burgoyne - Bruce Lancaster 3640

Ainsworth, Jeremy
Midsummer Moon - Karen Lynn 3940

Alcibiades
Achilles His Armour - Peter Green 2569
Alcibiades, Beloved of Gods - Vincenz Brun 735
The Flowers of Adonis - Rosemary Sutcliff 6122
Goat Song: A Novel of Ancient Greece - Frank Yerby 6920
The Immortal Marriage - Gertrude Atherton 225
The Last of the Wine - Mary Renault 5299
The Magnificent Traitor: A Novel of Alcibiades and the Golden Age of Pericles - Lynn Poole 5092
The Shining - Stephen Marlowe 4097

Allard, Ned
None Shall Look Back - Caroline Gordon 2478

Allen, Ethan
The Arch of Stars - Clifford Lindsey Alderman 66
Catch a Falling Star - Frederic F. Van de Water 6401
The Green Mountain Boys - Daniel Pierce Thompson 6249
Guns for Rebellion - F. van Wyck Mason 4151
Hang for Treason - Robert Newton Peck 4886
Israel Potter - Herman Melville 4334
Rebel Guns - Adam Rutledge 5539
That Bennington Mob - Henry Barnard Safford 5558

Allen, Ira
The Arch of Stars - Clifford Lindsey Alderman 66

Allenby, Edmund Henry Hynman
Behold the Fire - Michael Blankfort 541

The Devil's Spy - Michael Hastings 2773

Allison, Anthony
Toil of the Brave - Inglis Fletcher 2141

Allister, Gregory
For Us the Living - Antonia Van-Loon 6424

Almagro, Diego de
Don Pedro and the Devil - Edgar Maas 3948
The Sword and the Sun: The Story of the Spanish Civil Wars in Peru - Gerald Green 2566

Alvarez de Toledo, Fernando
Captain General - John P. Stevenson 6007
The Sea Beggars - Cecelia Holland 2996

An Lu-Shan
The Court of the Lion - Eleanor Cooney 1294

Ancrum, Davin
The Valiant Virginians - James Warner Bellah 427

Anderson, Robert
Ironclads: Man-of-War - Larry D. Names 4554

Andre, John
Eagles Where I Walk - Stephen Longstreet 3885
The Exquisite Siren - Edwin Haines 2639
Hugh Wynne, Free Quaker - Silas Weir Mitchell 4416
Major Andre - Anthony Bailey 265
Mars' Butterfly - Henry Pleasants 5080
The Secret Road - Bruce Lancaster 3646
Storm the Last Rampart - David Taylor 6180
The Sunshine Patriot: A Novel of Benedict Arnold - Norman Partington 4822
Trumpets at Dawn - Cyril Harris 2719
The Twisted Saber: A Biographical Novel of Benedict Arnold - Philip Vail 6398

Andrews, Clayton
Zoya - Danielle Steel 5985

Andrews, James
Rebel Run - Louis Zara 6952

Ansell, Luke
Celia Garth - Gwen Bristow 695

Anson, George
The Golden Ocean - Patrick O'Brian 4665
Manila Galleon - F. van Wyck Mason 4154

Antigonus I
The Bronze God of Rhodes - L. Sprague De Camp 1554
Funeral Games - Mary Renault 5297

Antiphus
The Trojan Generals Talk: Memoirs of the Greek War - Phillip Parotti 4818

Antony, Marc
The Alexandrian - Martha Rofheart 5425
Augustus - Allan Massie 4167
Augustus - John Williams 6785
Caesar - Allan Massie 4168
The Ides of March - Thornton Wilder 6753
The Pirate From Rome - John V.D. Southworth 5952
That Egyptian Woman - Noel B. Gerson 2384
Three's Company - Alfred Duggan 1774
Throne of Isis - Judith Tarr 6170

Antrobus, Miles
The War Train: A Novel of 1916 - Brown Meggs 4324

Anza, Juan Bautista de
A City for St. Francis - Evelyn Wells 6621

Apollonovitch, Sergei
Asya - Michael Ignatieff 3103

Appleton, Adam
The Governor's Daughter - Denton Whitson 6718

Aramis
The Three Musketeers - Alexandre Dumas 1782

Arbogast
The Last Romans - Teodor Jeske-Choinski 3216

Archer, Brendan
Troubles - J.G. Farrell 2017

Archer, Frank
Company Q - Richard O'Connor 4684

Archer, Nicholas
The Courts of Illusion - Rosemary Hawley Jarman 3165

Archer, Owen
The Apothecary Rose - Candace M. Robb 5364
The Lady Chapel - Candace M. Robb 5366

Aristides
Farewell Great King: A Novel of Ancient Greece - Jill Paton Walsh 4829

Ark, Henry
The Red Rover - James Fenimore Cooper 1309

Armitage, Hugh
The Four Swans - Winston Graham 2525

Arnall, Hoke
Unto This Hour - Tom Wicker 6733

Arnold, Benedict
Arundel - Kenneth Roberts 5383
Brother to the Enemy - Bart Spicer 5964
Eagle in the Sky - F. van Wyck Mason 4149
Eagles Where I Walk - Stephen Longstreet 3885
The Exquisite Siren - Edwin Haines 2639
Fawn - Robert Newton Peck 4885
The Firelands - Karen Harper 2712
The Green Mountain Boys - Daniel Pierce Thompson 6249
Guns for Rebellion - F. van Wyck Mason 4151
Hugh Wynne, Free Quaker - Silas Weir Mitchell 4416
I'll Storm Hell - Noel B. Gerson 2374
The Long Naked Descent into Boston - William Eastlake 1823
The Lure of the Falcon - Juliette Benzoni 465
Major Andre - Anthony Bailey 265
Man From Mt. Vernon - Burke Boyce 607
Mars' Butterfly - Henry Pleasants 5080
Mr. Arnold - Francis Lynde 3935
Oliver Wiswell - Kenneth Roberts 5389
Proceed, Sergeant Lamb - Robert Graves 2550
Rabble in Arms - Kenneth Roberts 5390
Renown - Frank Olney Hough 3045
The Rifleman - John Brick 675
The Secret Road - Bruce Lancaster 3646
Sergeant Lamb's America - Robert Graves 2552
Storm the Last Rampart - David Taylor 6180
The Sunshine Patriot: A Novel of Benedict Arnold - Norman Partington 4822
Treason - Robert Gessner 2389
The Twisted Saber: A Biographical Novel of Benedict Arnold - Philip Vail 6398

Arrowe, Quinton
Officer and Gentleman - Josephine Delves-Broughton 1604

Arrowe, Thomas
Officer and Gentleman - Josephine Delves-Broughton 1604

Arroya, Tomas
The Old Gringo - Carlos Fuentes 2247

Artorius
Artorius Rex - John Gloag 2432

Ashburnham, Jack
The Severed Crown - Jane Lane 3657

Aspar, Flavius
To Love Again - Bertrice Small 5913

Aspern, Mark
Tournament of the Shadows - Nicholas Carnac 901

Ataturk, Kemal
The House of War - Catherine Gavin 2322

Athos
The Three Musketeers - Alexandre Dumas 1782

Aubrey, Jack
The Commodore - Patrick O'Brian 4661
Desolation Island - Patrick O'Brian 4662
The Far Side of the World - Patrick O'Brian 4663
The Fortune of War - Patrick O'Brian 4664
H.M.S. Surprise - Patrick O'Brian 4666
The Ionian Mission - Patrick O'Brian 4667
The Letter of Marque - Patrick O'Brian 4668
Master and Commander - Patrick O'Brian 4669
The Mauritius Command - Patrick O'Brian 4670
The Nutmeg of Consolation - Patrick O'Brian 4671
Post Captain - Patrick O'Brian 4672
The Reverse of the Medal - Patrick O'Brian 4673
The Surgeon's Mate - Patrick O'Brian 4674
The Thirteen Gun Salute - Patrick O'Brian 4675
Treason's Harbour - Patrick O'Brian 4676
The Truelove - Patrick O'Brian 4677
The Wine-Dark Sea - Patrick O'Brian 4679
The Yellow Admiral - Patrick O'Brian 4680

Audley, Charles
An Infamous Army - Georgette Heyer 2892

Augustine
Silk and Steel - Stephen Alter 122

Aupick, General
A Singular Conspiracy - Barry Perowne 4915

Austin, Harry
Fifteen Flags - Richard Lynden Hardman 2686

Babtista, Anton
Sea of Lentils - Antonio Benitez-Rojo 443

Bagley
The Alpha Raid - Alan Scholefield 5651

Bainbridge, William
The Sea Panther: A Novel about the Commander of the U.S.S. Constitution - Philip Vail 6397

Bales, Ezekiel
The King's Coat - Dewey Lambdin 3612

Balzane, Captain
The Breast of the Dove - Herbert Gorman 2491

Bandfield, Frank
Eagles at War - Walter J. Boyne 620

Bandy, Bartholemew
It's Me Again - Donald Jack 3126
Me So Far - Donald Jack 3127
That's Me in the Middle - Donald Jack 3129
Three Cheers for Me - Donald Jack 3131

Bannon, James
Look Away - Harold Coyle 1395
Until the End - Harold Coyle 1396

Bannon, Kevin
Look Away - Harold Coyle 1395
Until the End - Harold Coyle 1396

Barak, Zev
The Glory - Herman Wouk 6873
The Hope - Herman Wouk 6874

Barfoot, Captain
Entered From the Sun - George Garrett 2301

Barlow, Prentiss
Arouse and Beware - MacKinlay Kantor 3360

Barnes, Jefferson
Jubilee - John Brick 672

Barney, Joshua
Captain Barney - Jan Westcott 6642

Barnstable, Richard
The Pilot - James Fenimore Cooper 1306

Barrie, Billy
The Sword of General Englund - Donald
   Honig   3023

Barrington, Nathanial
Desert Hawks - Frank Burleson   786
Savage Frontier - Frank Burleson   787
War Eagles - Frank Burleson   788

Barton, David
Strange Meeting - Susan Hill   2952

Bass, Sam
Chase Royal - Donald Seaman   5712

Bassinghorn, Henry
The Guns of Arrest - Philip McCutchan   4242
Halfhyde's Island - Philip McCutchan   4254

Bateman, Warren
The Ravi Lancers - John Masters   4178

Baylen, Fate
San Juan Hill - Will Henry   2848

Bazaine, Francoise-Achille
Chapultepec - Norman Zollinger   6965

Beale, Ned
Rush to Destroy - L. Jay Martin   4133

Beall, John Yates
Dim the Flaring Lamps - Jan Jordan   3301

Beaumanoir, Charles de
Castaway - Frances Murray   4535

Beaumont, Francis
Eliza Stanhope - Joanna Trollope   6347

Beauregard, Pierre Gustave Toutant
Beloved Enemy - Al Lacy   3579
The Chess Player: A Novel of New Orleans and Paris
   - Frances Parkinson Keyes   3478
Madame Castel's Lodger - Frances Parkinson
   Keyes   3480
The Passionate Rebel - Frank G. Slaughter   5894
Pomp and Circumstance - Fred Mustard
   Stewart   6025
A Promise Unbroken - Al Lacy   3582
Shadowed Memories - Al Lacy   3583

Becket, David
The Firedrake's Eye - Patricia Finney   2095

Bedford, Duncan
So Red the Rose - Stark Young   6944

Bedloe, Tom
Wild Is the River - Louis Bromfield   704

Belisarius
Count Belisarius - Robert Graves   2544
A Flame in Byzantium - Chelsea Quinn Yarbro   6899
The Vandal - Richard O'Connor   4687

Bell, Ramon
D'ri and I - Irving A. Bacheller   257

Bellamy, James
The Bellamy Saga - John Pearson   4878

Belmarch
Belmarch: A Legend of the First Crusade -
   Christopher Davis   1514

Belton, Clinton
The History of Rome Hanks - Joseph Stanley
   Pennell   4909

Belville, Henry
Gwendolen - Clare Darcy   1489

Bennett, Clay
Angel with Spurs - Paul I. Wellman   6613

Bennett, Timothy
Stars on the Sea - F. van Wyck Mason   4161

Bensham, Benjamin
The Mallen Lot - Catherine Cookson   1281

Bent, Kimball
Monday's Warriors - Maurice Shadbolt   5767

Benteen, Frederick
A Mighty Afternoon - Charles K. Mills   4407
*A Road We Do Not Know: A Novel of Custer at the
   Little Bighorn* - Frederick J. Chiaventone   1057

Benton, Andrew
This Land Is Ours - Louis Zara   6953

Benton, Harry
Molly - Teresa Crane   1417

Benton, Roland
Benton's Row - Frank Yerby   6908

Berdeyev, Nicolai
A Space of the Heart - Patricia Wright   6884

Bernadotte, Jean-Baptiste
Desiree - Annemarie Selinko   5741

Berrien, Beau
Blood Red Roses - Elizabeth Boatwright Coker   1163

Berthier, Louis-Alexander
Holy Week - Louis Aragon   182

Bingham, Captain Teddie
The Towers of Silence - Paul Scott   5685

Bion
Years of the City - George Rippey Stewart   6028

Bird, Henry
The Captives - Don Wright   6878

Birdwell, Josh
The Friendly Persuasion - Jessamyn West   6629

Black, Andrew
The Eagles of Malice - Alan Scholefield   5652

Blackford, James
The World Turned Upside Down - William
   Rayner   5273

Blackwater, Major
Trumpeter, Sound! - D.L. Murray   4528

Blackwood, David
The First to Land - Douglas E. Reeman   5288

Blackwood, Philip
Badge of Glory - Douglas E. Reeman   5287

Blake, Henry
Arizona! - Dana Fuller Ross   5466
Celebration! - Dana Fuller Ross   5470
Homecoming - Dana Fuller Ross   5474
Illinois! - Dana Fuller Ross   5475
Kentucky! - Dana Fuller Ross   5477
Oklahoma! - Dana Fuller Ross   5482
Wisconsin! - Dana Fuller Ross   5493

Blake, Leland
Colorado! - Dana Fuller Ross   5471
Nevada! - Dana Fuller Ross   5481
Oregon! - Dana Fuller Ross   5484
Texas! - Dana Fuller Ross   5490

Blakely, Dixon
Sycamore Men - David Taylor   6181

Blanchard, Nicholas
The Wild Ohio - Bart Spicer   5966

Bligh, William
Adams of the Bounty - Erle Wilson   6807
Alaska - James A. Michener   4364
The Explorers - William Stuart Long   3872
H.M.S. Bounty - Alexander McKee   4280
*The Last Mutiny: The Further Adventures of Captain
   Bligh* - Bill Collett   1208
Men Against the Sea - Charles Nordhoff   4638
Mister Christian - William Kinsolving   3502
Mr. Christian! - Stanley Miller   4402
Mutiny on the Bounty - Charles Nordhoff   4639
*The Return of Lono: A Novel of Captain Cook's Last
   Voyage* - Oswald Andrew Bushnell   816
The Settlers - William Stuart Long   3878

Southern Cross - Terry Coleman   1206
The Traitors - William Stuart Long   3879

Bliss, Malvern Hill
Over There - Thomas Fleming   2130

Bliss, Tasker
Pancho And Black Jack - Fred Bean   398

Blucher, Gebhard Leberecht von
The Limits of Glory: A Novel of Waterloo - James
   McDonough   4265

Bluett, Rodney
The Maid of Sker - R.D. Blackmore   529

Blythe, Nicholas
The Secret Years - Judith Lennox-Smith   3718

Bogun
With Fire and Sword - Henryk Sienkiewicz   5850

Bolitho, Richard
Colors Aloft! - Alexander Kent   3427
Command a King's Ship - Alexander Kent   3428
Enemy in Sight! - Alexander Kent   3429
The Flag Captain - Alexander Kent   3430
Form Line of Battle! - Alexander Kent   3431
Honor This Day - Alexander Kent   3432
In Gallant Company - Alexander Kent   3433
The Inshore Squadron - Alexander Kent   3434
Midshipman Bolitho and the Avenger - Alexander
   Kent   3435
Passage to Mutiny - Alexander Kent   3436
Richard Bolitho—Midshipman - Alexander
   Kent   3437
Signal—Close Action! - Alexander Kent   3438
Sloop of War - Alexander Kent   3439
Stand into Danger - Alexander Kent   3440
Success to the Brave - Alexander Kent   3441
To Glory We Steer - Alexander Kent   3442
A Tradition of Victory - Alexander Kent   3443

Bolivar, Simon
The General in His Labyrinth - Gabriel Garcia
   Marquez   2282
Manuela, La Caballeresa Del Sol - Demetrio Aguilera
   Malta   41
*The Splendor Stays: An Historic Novel Based on the
   Lives of the Seven Hart Sisters of Saybrook* -
   Marguerite Allis   114

Bonaparte, Louis
A Rose for Virtue - Norah Lofts   3858

Bonaparte, Napoleon
Alone Among Men - Marjorie Coryn   1355
Anna - Cynthia Harrod-Eagles   2752
The Anthem - Noel B. Gerson   2361
Anthony Adverse - Hervey Allen   98
The Black Consul - Anatolii Vinogradov   6503
Captain Cut-Throat - John Dickson Carr   908
The Castle of Fratta - Ippolito Nievo   4625
Charles O'Malley - Charles James Lever   3731
Citizen Tom Paine - Howard Fast   2028
*Colossus: A Novel about Goya and a World Gone
   Mad* - Stephen Marlowe   4093
Death at the French Creek - Raymond C. Borel   580
The Dedicated - Willa Gibbs   2399
Desiree - Annemarie Selinko   5741
Dreams of Empire - Jeanne Mackin   3994
The Eagle and the Rock - Frances Winwar   6830
Emperor's Ladies - Noel B. Gerson   2367
Far Flies the Eagle - Evelyn Anthony   162
The Flight of the Eagle - Donald Thomas   6239
Forty Centuries Look Down - Frederick Britten
   Austin   245
Good-Bye My Son - Marjorie Coryn   1356
Guillotine - Mark Logan   3865
The Hastening Wind - Edward Grierson   2591
Hester - Brian Cleeve   1107
H.M.S. Cockerel - Dewey Lambdin   3611
The Limits of Glory: A Novel of Waterloo - James
   McDonough   4265

The Man Who Killed the King - Dennis
    Wheatley 6654
Marianne - Juliette Benzoni 466
Marianne and the Privateer - Juliette Benzoni 470
Marianne and the Rebels - Juliette Benzoni 471
The Marriage of Josephine - Marjorie Coryn 1358
Mirage - Ruth McKenney 4283
Mistress of Fortune - Sheila Lancaster 3651
Napoleon Must Die - Quinn Fawcett 2054
Notorious Eliza - Basil Beyea 489
Palaces of Desire - Kate Alexander 81
The Prince Lost to Time - Ann Dukthas 1776
The Road to Glory - Frederick Britten Austin 246
*The Rose of Malmaison: The Turbulent Life of the
    Beautiful Josephine* - Gaby von Schonthan 5660
Seed of Mischief - Willa Gibbs 2401
Seven Men of Gascony - R.F. Delderfield 1589
Sharpe's Devil - Bernard Cornwell 1340
Tallien: A Brief Romance - Frederic Tuten 6370
To Spit Against the Wind - Benjamin H. Levin 3737
Tom Burke of Ours - Charles James Lever 3732
The Twelfth Physician - Willa Gibbs 2403
Valentina - Evelyn Anthony 165
Valide: A Novel of the Harem - Barbara Chase-
    Riboud 1007
War and Peace - Leo Tolstoy 6295
Waterloo - Frederic E. Smith 5920

Bone, Esmond
Attack the Lusitania! - Raymond Hitchcock 2956

Boneu, Antonio
This Promised Land - Robert Easton 1824

Bonneville, Benjamin
The Great Adventure - Janice Holt Giles 2410

Booker, Major
The Crater - Richard Slotkin 5908

Booker, Abel
Hang for Treason - Robert Newton Peck 4886

Booth, Jesse
The Smoky Hill - Don Coldsmith 1188

Boquet, Henry
The Conquerors - Allen W. Eckert 1839

Borgia, Cesare
The Bait and the Trap - George Challis 970
The Borgia Prince - Pamela Bennetts 446
Borgia Testament - Nigel Balchin 277
Carnival of Saints - George Herman 2860
Light on Lucrezia - Jean Plaidy 5029
Madonna of the Seven Hills - Jean Plaidy 5034
Mona Lisa: The Woman in the Portrait - Sara
    Mayfield 4206
The Naked Sword: The Story of Lucretia Borgia -
    F.W. Kenyon 3456
A Passion in the Blood - Genevieve Davis 1519
Prince of Foxes - Samuel Shellabarger 5797
The Scarlet City - Hella S. Haasse 2632
Then and Now - William Somerset Maugham 4198
Web of Lucifer: A Novel of the Borgia Fury - Maurice
    Samuel 5580

Botha, Louis
The Legacy of Ladysmith - John Kenny Crane 1413
Rags of Glory - Stuart Cloete 1126
The Red Daniel - Duncan MacNeil 4017

Boulanger, Georges Ernest Jean Marie
Brave General - Herbert Gorman 2490

Bourbon, Louis I de
The Faith and the Flame - June Dimmit
    Houston 3054

Bower, Chuck
Wings for the Chariots - Arch Whitehouse 6713

Bowie, Jim
The Furies - John Jakes 3146

Boyd, Willie
Bide Me Fair - Harvey Howells 3060

Braddock, Edward
Black Forest - Meade Minnigerode 4411
Gentleman Ranker - John Edward Jennings 3200
The Indentured Heart - Gilbert Morris 4464
Morning of a Hero - Burke Boyce 608
Red Morning - Ruby Frazier Frey 2230
The Red Road: A Romance of Braddock's Defeat -
    Hugh Pendexter 4898
War in the Golden Weather - Stephen
    Longstreet 3892
Wilderness Empire - Allen W. Eckert 1847
The Woodsman - Don Wright 6880

Bradford, Roark
The Wilderness Brigade - Phyllis Gordon
    Demarest 1605

Bradstreet, John
Drums Against Frontenac - Harvey Chalmers 972

Bragg, Braxton
In the Season of the Wild Rose - Clara Rising 5347
Journey to Shiloh - Will Henry 2843

Brandon
The Eye of God - C.L. Grace 2506

Brandt, Roger
The Rebel Loyalist - Charles William Gordon 2480

Brereton, John
Janice Meredith - Paul Leicester Ford 2166

Brett, Luke
The Gun - C.S. Forester 2174

Brett, Peircy
Manila Galleon - F. van Wyck Mason 4154

Brevaux, Antoine de
Deeper the Heritage - Muriel Elwood 1936

Brewster
Mutiny Run - Frank Eccles 1836

Brice, Stephen
The Crisis - Winston Churchill 1079

Brice, Thomas
The Gray Captain - Jere Hungerford
    Wheelwright 6669

Brien, Robert
Wild Geese - Eilis Dillon 1647

Britannicus, Caius
The Skystone: The Forging of Arthur's Britain - Jack
    Whyte 6726

Broughton, Lucius
The Flag Captain - Alexander Kent 3430

Brownell, Buck
Beloved Enemy - Al Lacy 3579

Browning, Jonathon
Stranger in Savannah - Eugenia Price 5187

Bruce, Donald
The Regiment - C.L. Skelton 5874

Bruce, Gordon
Beloved Soldiers - C.L. Skelton 5871

Bruce, Willie
The Maclarens - C.L. Skelton 5873

Brudenell, James Thomas
Pendragon: Late of Prince Albert's Own - Robert
    Trevelyan 6337

Bryce, Asa
The Horse Soldiers - Harold Sinclair 5862

Buchanan, Murdoch
Rebel Guns - Adam Rutledge 5539

Budd, Billy
Billy Budd - Herman Melville 4333

Buell, Thomas
Oliver Wiswell - Kenneth Roberts 5389

Buford, John
Gettysburg: Crisis of Command - Harry Albright 65
The Killer Angels - Michael Shaara 5766

Bulatovich, Alexander K.
The Name of Hero - Richard Seltzer 5742

Buller, Archibald
Buller's Dreadnought - Richard Hough 3047
Buller's Guns - Richard Hough 3048
Buller's Victory - Richard Hough 3049

Buller, Redvers Henry
The Covenant - James A. Michener 4368
The Red Daniel - Duncan MacNeil 4017

Buller, Richard
Buller's Victory - Richard Hough 3049

Bumpass, Usaph
Confederates - Thomas Keneally 3412

Burdon, Ellis
Playboy Squadron - Arch Whitehouse 6710

Burgoyne, John
The Drums of April - Charles Mergendahl 4340
Guns of Burgoyne - Bruce Lancaster 3640
Jeremiah Martin: A Revolutionary War Novel - Robert
    H. Fowler 2191
The Long Naked Descent into Boston - William
    Eastlake 1823
Sergeant Lamb's America - Robert Graves 2552
Valiant Libertine - John Gordon Bryson 748

Burk, Nicholas
Monmouth - Charles Bracelen Flood 2144

Burke, James
While Rivers Flow - Glen H. Fleischmann 2125

Burnside, Ambrose E.
The Crater - Richard Slotkin 5908
Glory Enough for All: The Battle of the Crater -
    Duane Philip Schultz 5673
Joy From Ashes - Al Lacy 3581

Burr, Aaron
Flintlock - Jason Manning 4073

Bush, William
Beat to Quarters - C.S. Forester 2170
Commodore Hornblower - C.S. Forester 2172
Flying Colours - C.S. Forester 2173
Hornblower and the Hotspur - C.S. Forester 2176
Lieutenant Hornblower - C.S. Forester 2178
The Life and Times of Horatio Hornblower - C.
    Northcote Parkinson 4813
Lord Hornblower - C.S. Forester 2179
Ship of the Line - C.S. Forester 2182

Butler, Arthur
Horseshoe Robinson, a Tale of the Tory Ascendancy -
    John P. Kennedy 3418

Butler, Benjamin
Angel of the Delta - Edward Francis Murphy 4521
Captain Rebel - Frank Yerby 6910

Butler, Smedley D.
A Few Good Men - William Overgard 4768

Butter, Amaziah
American Falls - John Calvin Batchelor 376

Buttes, Cobus
Buttes Landing - Jean Rikhoff 5331

Byam, Roger
Mutiny on the Bounty - Charles Nordhoff 4639

Byrn, Lane
Scarlet Cockerel - Garald Lagard 3584

Byrne, Garrett
The Buffalo Soldiers - John Prebble 5165

Byron, Jack
The Unknown Shore - Patrick O'Brian 4678

Cabeza, Ramon
Follow the Wind - Don Coldsmith 1176

Cabot, Colin
The Master of Chaos - Irving A. Bacheller 262

Caesar, Gaius Julius
The City of Libertines - W.G. Hardy 2702
Three's Company - Alfred Duggan 1774

Caffrey, Laird
The Land Where the Sun Dies - Henry Carlisle 896

Calderon, Juan
*The Bugles Are Silent: A Novel of the Texas
Revolution* - John R. Knaggs 3513

Calendar, Miles
Last Reveille - David Morrell 4456

Callaway, Mike
Slow Dies the Thunder - Helen Topping Miller 4395

Cameron, Daniel
And One Wore Gray - Heather Graham 2515

Cameron, Donnie
Beloved Soldiers - C.L. Skelton 5871

Cameron, Jesse
One Wore Blue - Heather Graham 2517

Camillus
Winter Quarters - Alfred Duggan 1775

Campbell, Jamil
Dark Torrent of Glencoe - Edward Grierson 2590

Campbell, Whitney
Buller's Dreadnought - Richard Hough 3047

Canfield, Jefferson
In My Father's House - Bodie Thoene 6222

Cantrell, Edward
Gone to Texas - John Williams Thomason 6247

Carausius, Marcus Aurelius
Caesar of the Narrow Seas - John Gloag 2433

Cardess, John
War Paint and Rouge - Robert W. Chambers 983

Carew, Alexander
The Killing Frost - Thomas Hayden 2799

Carhampton, Robert
The King's Rebel - James David Horan 3030

Carlisle, Hunkpapa Jack
Fifteen Flags - Richard Lynden Hardman 2686

Carlyon, Thaddeus
Defend and Betray - Anne Perry 4928

Carpenter, Brett
The Laughing Stranger - Vina Delmar 1601

Carrington, Henry Beebee
Carrington - Michael Whitney Straight 6074
North Against the Sioux - Kenneth Ulyatt 6376

Carrington, St. John
Wild Swan - Celeste De Blasis 1550

Carroll, Daniel
Lorena - Frank G. Slaughter 5892

Carson, Kit
The Bear Flag: A Novel of the Birth of California -
Cecelia Holland 2983

Carter, Harry
Luciano's Luck - Jack Higgins 2912

Cartwright, Cassius
The Land Beyond the Mountains - Janice Holt
Giles 2414

Carvel, Richard
Richard Carvel - Winston Churchill 1081

Cary, Edward
Cease Firing - Mary Johnston 3230

Cascamond, Michel
Hangman's Beach - Thomas H. Raddall 5229

Casewent, John
Thunder on the Plains - Rosanne Bittner 517

Castetter, Alf J.
The Three Days - Don Robertson 5402

Catlett, Roan
The Valiant Virginians - James Warner Bellah 427

Cato, Philip
Cato's War - Guy Wheeler 6655

El Catolico
Sharpe's Gold - Bernard Cornwell 1343

Catto, Marius
When the War Is Over - Stephen Becker 408

Cavanaugh, Thomas
"Utmost Fish!" - Hugh Wray McCann 4219

Cecil, Bertie
Under Two Flags - Ouida 4767

Chamay, Paul
In the Company of Eagles - Ernest K. Gann 2279

Chamberlain, Joshua Lawrence
The Dixie Widow - Gilbert Morris 4459
Gods and Generals - Jeff Shaara 5765
The Killer Angels - Michael Shaara 5766

Champion, John
Brother to the Enemy - Bart Spicer 5964

Chandler, Heath
The Chandler Heritage - Ben Haas 2629

Chapman, Philip
Lords of the Plains - Max Crawford 1420

Chappell, Alastair
Gentlemen—The Regiment! - Hugh Talbot 6154

Chard, Steve
The Medicine Whip - Max Hennessy 2835

Chatfield, Geneva
High Hearts - Rita Mae Brown 728

Chatto, Tom
Apprentice to the Sea - Philip McCutchan 4240
The Second Mate - Philip McCutchan 4257

Chiang Kai-Shek
The Warlord - Malcolm Bosse 589

Chivington, John Milton
The Last Warpath - Will Henry 2844
A Very Small Remnant - Michael Whitney
Straight 6075

Choundas, Guillaume
A King's Commander - Dewey Lambdin 3613

Christian, Fletcher
Adams of the Bounty - Erle Wilson 6807
H.M.S. Bounty - Alexander McKee 4280
*The Last Mutiny: The Further Adventures of Captain
Bligh* - Bill Collett 1208
Mister Christian - William Kinsolving 3502
Mr. Christian! - Stanley Miller 4402
Mutiny on the Bounty - Charles Nordhoff 4639
Pitcairn's Island - Charles Nordhoff 4640

Church, Benjamin
Ashes in the Wilderness - William Greenough
Schofield 5649
Savage Gentleman - Noel B. Gerson 2381

Churchill, John
The Charlatan - Carter A. Vaughan 6433

Cinna, Lucius Cornelius
The Grass Crown - Colleen McCullough 4236

Claggart
Billy Budd - Herman Melville 4333

Clark, George Rogers
Alice of Old Vincennes - Maurice Thompson 6268
Becky Landers, Frontier Warrior - Constance
Skinner 5879

The Big Knives - Bruce Lancaster 3635
Black Forest - Meade Minnigerode 4411
Bridal Journey - Dale Van Every 6406
The Captive Witch - Dale Van Every 6407
The Crossing - Winston Churchill 1080
From Sea to Shining Sea - James Alexander
Thom 6232
Gateway to Empire - Allen W. Eckert 1842
Give Me Liberty - Noel B. Gerson 2369
The King's Orchard - Agnes Sligh Turnbull 6363
Long Knife - James Alexander Thom 6233
Morning Time - Charles Kendall O'Neill 4743
Oh, Kentucky! - Betty Layman Receveur 5284
Panther in the Sky - James Alexander Thom 6234
The Seekers - John Jakes 3153
That Dark and Bloody River - Allen W. Eckert 1845
This Land Is Ours - Louis Zara 6953
Trail: The Story of the Lewis and Clark Expedition -
Louis Charbonneau 998
The Voyagers - Dale Van Every 6412
Waters of the Wilderness - Shirley Seifert 5737
Westward the Tide - Harold Sinclair 5863

Clark, Oliver
Arouse and Beware - MacKinlay Kantor 3360

Clark, Ralph
The Playmaker - Thomas Keneally 3414

Clark, William
From Sea to Shining Sea - James Alexander
Thom 6232
The Gates of the Mountains - Will Henry 2842
The Seekers - John Jakes 3153
Trail: The Story of the Lewis and Clark Expedition -
Louis Charbonneau 998

Clarkson, Matthew
Treason - Robert Gessner 2389

Clavering, Lance
Will You Love Me in September? - Philippa Carr 932

Clavier, Jacques
Those the Sun Has Loved - Rose Jourdain 3309

Clay, Jubal
Mexico - James A. Michener 4372

Clayton, Colonel
No Survivors - Will Henry 2846

Cleave, Richard
The Long Roll - Mary Johnston 3236

Clem, John Lincoln
Johnny Shiloh - James A. Rhodes 5308

Clement, Keith
Wings for the Chariots - Arch Whitehouse 6713

Clemmens, Jeremiah
Grant's War - Ted Jones 3297

Clewellyn, John T.
Prisoner of Twilight - Don Robertson 5400

Clinton, Henry
Cato's War - Guy Wheeler 6655
Eagles Where I Walk - Stephen Longstreet 3885
Monmouth - Charles Bracelen Flood 2144
Mr. Arnold - Francis Lynde 3935
Oliver Wiswell - Kenneth Roberts 5389
*The Twisted Saber: A Biographical Novel of Benedict
Arnold* - Philip Vail 6398
Valiant Libertine - John Gordon Bryson 748
Wicked Lady - Inglis Fletcher 2142
Yorktown - Burke Davis 1513

Clive, Robert
Master of Bengal: A Novel of Robert Clive of India -
Norman Partington 4821

Clivedon, Peter
Men Were Deceivers Ever - Patricia Veryan 6470

Cobb, Felix
An Ice-Cream War - William Boyd 616

Cobb, Gabriel
An Ice-Cream War - William Boyd 616

Cochrane, Thomas
The Frigate Captain - Showell Styles 6103
Sharpe's Devil - Bernard Cornwell 1340

Cockburn, George
Crimson Is the Eastern Shore - Don Tracy 6308
Dolley - Rita Mae Brown 727

Colfax, Clarence
The Crisis - Winston Churchill 1079

Colling, Daniel
The Glass Dove - Sally Carrighar 943

Conde, Louis de
Angelique - Sergeanne Golon 2465

Conklin, Jim
The Red Badge of Courage - Stephen Crane 1414

Connor, Michael
Forbidden City - Anthony Esler 1962

Constantius I
The Living Wood - Louis De Wohl 1571

Cook, James
Alaska - James A. Michener 4364
The Return of Lono: A Novel of Captain Cook's Last Voyage - Oswald Andrew Bushnell 816

Cooke, Nicholas
Nicholas Cooke: Actor, Soldier, Physician, Priest - Stephanie Cowell 1393

Cooper, Adam
April Morning - Howard Fast 2027

Cooper, Moses
April Morning - Howard Fast 2027

Cordoba, Luis
The Furies - John Jakes 3146

Corley, Thomas
Thin Moon and Cold Mist - Kathleen O'Neal Gear 2330

Cornelius
Marius the Epicurean - Walter Pater 4826

Cornwallis, Charles
Cato's War - Guy Wheeler 6655
The Drums of December - Sharon Salvato 5575
The Fallon Blood - Reagan O'Neal 4741
A Few Painted Feathers - Stephen Longstreet 3886
Horseshoe Robinson, a Tale of the Tory Ascendancy - John P. Kennedy 3418
The Lady From Yorktown - Eva McDonald 4260
Proceed, Sergeant Lamb - Robert Graves 2550
Raleigh's Eden - Inglis Fletcher 2137
The Savage Brood - Martha Rofheart 5430
The Sunshine Patriot: A Novel of Benedict Arnold - Norman Partington 4822
Sycamore Men - David Taylor 6181
Wicked Lady - Inglis Fletcher 2142
The Year of the French - Thomas Flanagan 2121
Yorktown - Burke Davis 1513

Cortez, Hernando
Aztec - Gary Jennings 3193
Captain From Castile - Samuel Shellabarger 5794
Cortez and Marina - Edison Marshall 4105
Death of the Fifth Sun - Robert Somerlott 5944
Don Pedro and the Devil - Edgar Maas 3948
The Fair God - Lew Wallace 6537
Gods on Horseback - Samuel G. Baggett 263
The Golden Princess - Alexander Baron 335
The Great White Gods - Eduard Stucken 6102
The Heart of Jade - Salvador de Madariaga 4024
The Sun, He Dies: A Novel about the End of the Aztec World - Jamake Highwater 2919
They Are Coming: The Conquest of Mexico - Jose Lopez Portillo y Pacheco 3896

Cortlandt, David
Eagles Where I Walk - Stephen Longstreet 3885
A Few Painted Feathers - Stephen Longstreet 3886

Cortlandt, Will
War in the Golden Weather - Stephen Longstreet 3892

Corydon, Rupert Flood
Floodtide - Suzanne Goodwin 2475

Courville-Boissart, Philippe
Web of Destiny - Muriel Elwood 1939

Cranford, Peregrine
Never Doubt I Love - Patricia Veryan 6473

Crassus, Marcus Licinius
Arena: A Novel of Spartacus and Crassus - Maurice Ghnassia 2391
Arms of Nemesis - Steven Saylor 5623
Fortune's Favorite - Colleen McCullough 4235
Freedom, Farewell - Phyllis Bentley 461
The Gladiators - Arthur Koestler 3532
Spartacus - Howard Fast 2044

Crassus, Publius
Winter Quarters - Alfred Duggan 1775

Crawford, Captain
Mutiny - Frank Tilsley 6280

Crawford, Sir James
Until the Colors Fade - Tim Jeal 3173

Creighton, Colonel
The Imperial Agent - T.N. Murari 4518
The Last Victory - T.N. Murari 4519

Cresap, Michael
Song of the Susquehanna - Herbert Stover 6071

Cribb, Joe
A Wilful Woman - Michael Talbot 6156

Crillon
Les Quarant Cinq - Alexandre Dumas 1779

Crispin, Bartley
Squadron Shilling - Arch Whitehouse 6712

Crockett, Hume
Home to Tennessee - Alfred Leland Crabb 1400
Lodging at the Saint Cloud - Alfred Leland Crabb 1403
Mockingbird Sang at Chickamauga - Alfred Leland Crabb 1404

Cromwell, Oliver
Charles the King - Evelyn Anthony 160
The Stranger Prince - Margaret Irwin 3122

Cronje, Piet
The Legacy of Ladysmith - John Kenny Crane 1413

Crook, George C.
Blood Song - Terry C. Johnston 3243
Geronimo - Bill Dugan 1758
Geronimo: An American Legend - Robert J. Conley 1242
The Last Warpath - Will Henry 2844
Reap the Whirlwind - Terry C. Johnston 3254
The Scout - Harry Combs 1224
Sitting Bull - Bill Dugan 1760
Thunder in the Dawn - Earl Murray 4532
Trumpet on the Land - Terry C. Johnston 3260
The Winter War - William Wister Haines 2640

Crosbie, Duncan
The Wild Ohio - Bart Spicer 5966

Crowe, Thomas
Sergeant Verity and the Blood Royal - Francis Selwyn 5744

Crowninshield, Philippe
And Wait for the Night - John William Corrington 1352

Cummings, Jack
A Certain Splendour - Carola Salisbury 5566

Curnet, Buck
Journey to Shiloh - Will Henry 2843

Currain, Travis
House Divided - Ben Ames Williams 6765

Custer, George Armstrong
Black Sun - Terry C. Johnston 3242
Bugles in the Afternoon - Ernest Haycox 2788
Chief of Scouts - Don Bendell 439
The Court-Martial of George Armstrong Custer - Douglas C. Jones 3276
Crazy Fox Remembers - Don Preston 5174
Crazy Horse - Bill Dugan 1757
The Crossed Sabres - Gilbert Morris 4458
Custer Passed Our Way - Fred S. Kaufman 3370
Flashman and the Redskins - George MacDonald Fraser 2208
A Good Day to Die - Del Barton 368
Heaven and Hell - John Jakes 3147
The Last Stand: A Novel about George Armstrong Custer and the Indians of the Plains - Edwin P. Hoyt 3061
The Last Warpath - Will Henry 2844
Libbie - Judy Alter 121
Little Big Man - Thomas Berger 478
Long Winter Gone - Terry C. Johnston 3252
Love and War - John Jakes 3150
Marching to Valhalla: A Novel of Custer's Last Days - Michael Blake 538
A Mighty Afternoon - Charles K. Mills 4407
Montana Road - Harry Sinclair Drago 1717
No Survivors - Will Henry 2846
A Road We Do Not Know: A Novel of Custer at the Little Bighorn - Frederick J. Chiaventone 1057
Roll, Shenandoah - Bruce Lancaster 3644
Roman - Douglas C. Jones 3281
The Scout - Harry Combs 1224
Seize the Sky - Terry C. Johnston 3256
Shadow on the Valley - Kirk Mitchell 4414
Shaggy Legion - Hal George Evarts 1986
This Old Bill - Loren D. Estleman 1980
Twice upon a Time - Allen Appel 172
The Winter War - William Wister Haines 2640

Custer, Tom
A Mighty Afternoon - Charles K. Mills 4407

Cutler, Captain
Lieutenant Lamb - Kenneth Maynard 4210

Cutter, Jake
The Pride of Hannah Wade - Janet Dailey 1455

Dahlgren, Ulrich
Night March - Bruce Lancaster 3641
The Richmond Raid - John Brick 674

Dalton, Layne
Joy From Ashes - Al Lacy 3581

Dando, Joseph
Dando on Delhi Ridge - William Clive 1119

Danvers, Clinton
A Marriage of Convenience - Tim Jeal 3172

Darracott, Hugh
The Unknown Ajax - Georgette Heyer 2908

D'Artagnan
The Three Musketeers - Alexandre Dumas 1782
Twenty Years After - Alexandre Dumas 1783

D'Artagnan, Charles
A Candle for D'Artagnan - Chelsea Quinn Yarbro 6895

Davis, Jefferson
Alaska - James A. Michener 4364
Comes an Echo on the Breeze - Edward J. Ryan 5542
There Was a Season: A Biographical Novel of Jefferson Davis - Theodore Olsen 4730

Davis, Sam
On Jordan's Stormy Banks - Adelaide C. Rowell   5518

d'Avnay, Paul
Tell Your Sons: A Novel of the Napoleonic Era - Willa Gibbs   2402

Davout, Louis Nicolas
The Proud Canaries - David Johnson   3222

Dawson, William
The Long Fight - D.A. Rayner   5270

Dayan, Moshe
The Glory - Herman Wouk   6873
The Hope - Herman Wouk   6874

de Charny, Count
The Queen's Necklace - Alexandre Dumas   1781

De Chavel, Colonel
Valentina - Evelyn Anthony   165

de Gaulle, Charles
The Free Frenchman - Piers Paul Read   5277

de Lalliere, Blaise
The King's Cavalier - Samuel Shellabarger   5795

De Lancey, Christopher
The Journal of Colonel De Lancey - James Warner Bellah   426

De Soto, Don Guzman
Westward Ho! - Charles Kingsley   3499

de Soto, Hernando
The Golden Eagle - John Edward Jennings   3201

de Vargas, Pedro
Captain From Castile - Samuel Shellabarger   5794

Deane, John
Swords of Steel - Elsie Singmaster   5870

Dearborn, Jonathan
Jonathan Dearborn: A Novel of the War of 1812 - Willard Wallace   6540

Dearborn, Tom
East to Bagaduce - Willard Wallace   6539

Degnan, Linus
A Time in the Sun - Jane Barry   361

Delacourt, Geoffrey
Journey to Enchantment - Patricia Veryan   6464

Delacourt, William
That Sweet and Savage Land - Emma Drummond   1728

Delancey, Richard
Dead Reckoning - C. Northcote Parkinson   4809
Devil to Pay - C. Northcote Parkinson   4810
The Fireship - C. Northcote Parkinson   4811
The Guernseyman - C. Northcote Parkinson   4812
So Near So Far - C. Northcote Parkinson   4814
Touch and Go - C. Northcote Parkinson   4815

Delchard, Ralph
The Dragons of Archenfield - Edward Marston   4119
The Lions of the North - Edward Marston   4121
The Ravens of Blackwater - Edward Marston   4126
The Wolves of Savernake - Edward Marston   4130

Delin
Bittersweet - Leslie Li   3769

DeMayne, Rowan
Forget the Glory - Emma Drummond   1725

Demere, John Fraser
Beauty From Ashes - Eugenia Price   5177

Desmond, William
The Raid - John Brick   673

Desportes, John
Mi Amigo - William R. Burnett   795

Dessalines, Jean-Jacques
Drums of Destiny - Peter Bourne   593

D'Estivet, Captain
The Masked Man - P.C. Doherty   1674

Devaux, Nicolas
Tree of Gold - Rosalind Laker   3602

Devereux, Robert
Nicholas Cooke: Actor, Soldier, Physician, Priest - Stephanie Cowell   1393

Dewar, Hamish
Subaltern's Choice - Duncan MacNeil   4020

Dexter, David
Armored Giants: A Novel of the Civil War - F. van Wyck Mason   4145

Diaz, Porfirio
Chapultepec - Norman Zollinger   6965

Dickoe, Peter
Soldier of the Sea - Robert Welter Daly   1460

Dikeston, H.G.
The King's Commissar - Duncan Kyle   3570

Dillon, James
Master and Commander - Patrick O'Brian   4669

Dinkle, Stanley
The Tin Lizzie Troup - Glendon Swarthout   6146

Diomedes
The Greek Generals Talk: Memoirs of the Trojan War - Phillip Parotti   4817

Dion
The Mask of Apollo - Mary Renault   5300

Dixon, Tempe
A Hundred Hills - Howard Breslin   667

Dobbin, William
Vanity Fair - William Makepeace Thackeray   6213

Dodd, Matthew
Rifleman Dodd - C.S. Forester   2181

Dolliver, Eben
Andersonville - MacKinlay Kantor   3359

Donegan, Seamus
Blood Song - Terry C. Johnston   3243
A Cold Day in Hell - Terry C. Johnston   3247
Devil's Backbone - Terry C. Johnston   3250
Reap the Whirlwind - Terry C. Johnston   3254
Red Cloud's Revenge - Terry C. Johnston   3255
The Shadow Riders - Terry C. Johnston   3257
Sioux Dawn - Terry C. Johnston   3258
The Stalkers - Terry C. Johnston   3259
Trumpet on the Land - Terry C. Johnston   3260

Doniphan, Alexander
Doniphan's Ride - Les Savage Jr.   5620

Donnithorne, Arthur
Adam Bede - George Eliot   1908

Dorfrichter, Peter
The Devil's Lieutenant - Maria Fagyas   1998

Dorio
The Same Scourge - John Goldthorpe   2464

Doucain, Veach
Kentucky Pride - Gene Markey   4087

Doughty, Frank
The Copperheads - William James Blech   544

Douglas, Matthew
Sand in the Wind - Kathleen O'Neal Gear   2329

Draco
First the Blade - Drayton Mayrant   4212

Dracula
The Bloody Red Baron - Kim Newman   4596

Drake, Sir Francis
Deborah and the Many Faces of Love - Colette Davenat   1499
Envoy From Elizabeth - Pamela Bennetts   451
Golden Admiral - F. van Wyck Mason   4150

Roanoke Hundred - Inglis Fletcher   2138

Drinkwater, Nathaniel
1805 - Richard Woodman   6857
Arctic Treachery - Richard Woodman   6858
Baltic Mission - Richard Woodman   6859
The Bomb Vessel - Richard Woodman   6860
Decision at Trafalgar - Richard Woodman   6861
In Distant Waters - Richard Woodman   6862
A Private Revenge - Richard Woodman   6863

Drogue, John
Little Red Foot - Robert W. Chambers   979

Drumm, Andrew
Drumm's War - Bill Bragg   638

Drummond, Edgar
Leaves From the Valley - Joanna Trollope   6348

Drummond, William
The Great Adventure - Janice Holt Giles   2410

Drusus
A Flame in Byzantium - Chelsea Quinn Yarbro   6899

Du Pres, Andre
River of Swans - Don Coldsmith   1185

Ducos, Pierre
Sharpe's Siege - Bernard Cornwell   1348

Dudley, John
Feast in the Morning - Hugh Preston   5175

Dugald, Davy
The Highland Hawk - Leslie Turner White   6682

Dumaresq, Henry Vere
Stand into Danger - Alexander Kent   3440

Dunbar, John
Dances with Wolves - Michael Blake   537

Dunboyne, Kit
Seek Out and Destroy - James David Horan   3031

Dunn, Matt
Sergeant Gringo - Jack Cummings   1449

Dunsche, Otto
The Career of Magda V. - Joseph Machlis   3982

Dunwoodie, Major Peyton
The Spy: A Tale of the Neutral Ground - James Fenimore Cooper   1310

Durand, Blake
The Walk into Morning - Mildred Barger Herschler   2867

Duratius
Family Favorites - Alfred Duggan   1766

Durward, Quentin
Quentin Durward - Sir Walter Scott   5705

Duryea, Micah
Unto This Hour - Tom Wicker   6733

Dymas
Fires in the Sky - Phillip Parotti   4816

Dyson, Edwin
The Tune That They Play - William Clive   1120

Early, Gordon
Strange Company - Robert J. Conley   1251

Early, Jubal
Shadow on the Valley - Kirk Mitchell   4414

Easterwood, Tom
Yellowhorse - Dee Brown   715

Eaton, William
Lydia Bailey - Kenneth Roberts   5387
Written in Sand - Josephine Case   950

Ecuyer, Captain
Bedford Village - Hervey Allen   99

Eden, Geoffrey
Eden and Honor - Marilyn Harris   2729

Edricson, Alleyne
The White Company - Sir Arthur Conan Doyle   1716

Ehrler, Caspar
The Petrograd Consignment - Owen Sela   5739

Eisenhower, Dwight D.
Luciano's Luck - Jack Higgins   2912
Over There - Robert Vaughan   6449

Ekridge, Russell
The Southern Blade - Nelson Wolford   6844

Elazar, David
The Glory - Herman Wouk   6873

Eleazar, Simon ben
The Wolf of Masada - John Fredman   2220

Elholm
The Cumberland Rifles - Noel B. Gerson   2365

Elliot, Charles
Mandarin Gold - James Leasor   3700

Elliott, Liam
Morning's Gate - Ann Victoria Roberts   5371

Ellis, Roswell
The Long Night - Andrew Lytle   3945

Emery, Racewell
Gray Canaan - David Garth   2305

Englund, Alfred
The Sword of General Englund - Donald Honig   3023

Epron, Captain
The Long Fight - D.A. Rayner   5270

Esmond, Henry
Henry Esmond - William Makepeace Thackeray   6212

Eusopus, Israel
Morning in America - Willard Wiener   6741

Everard, Markham
Woodstock; or, The Cavalier - Sir Walter Scott   5710

Everden, Blaise
Corner the Moon - Shirley Barker   310

Fabatus, Marcus
Captive of Rome - Theodora McCormick Du Bois   1740

Fabrizio, Del Dongo
The Charterhouse of Parma - Stendhal   5993

Fairfax, Thomas
Rider on a White Horse - Rosemary Sutcliff   6124

Fairweather, George
Season of the Jew - Maurice Shadbolt   5768

Falkenhorst, Albrecht von
Falkenhorst - Mark Rascovich   5254

Falkenhorst, Gustaf von
Falkenhorst - Mark Rascovich   5254

Fanning, Tyler
Long Remember - MacKinlay Kantor   3362

Farebrother, Sir John
The Admiral's Lady - Mary Ann Gibbs   2395

Farr, Jason
Promises to Keep - Jocelyn Stirling   6051

Farragut, David
Clear for Action! - Noel B. Gerson   2362
A Heart Divided - Al Lacy   3580

Farrar, Anthony
Love Alters Not - Patricia Veryan   6467

Farrell, Grant
The Notorious Angel - Patricia Maxwell   4201

Farrell, John
The Bayou Road - Mignon G. Eberhart   1832

Faulconer, Adam
The Bloody Ground - Bernard Cornwell   1334
Copperhead - Bernard Cornwell   1335

Faulconer, Washington
Rebel - Bernard Cornwell   1336

Faulconer, William
Battle Flag - Bernard Cornwell   1333

Fawley, Noah
The Barefoot Brigade - Douglas C. Jones   3274

Fawley, Zachery
The Barefoot Brigade - Douglas C. Jones   3274

Fay, Evelyn
The Red Doe - Drayton Mayrant   4214

Fell, Thomas
Admiral Hornblower in the West Indies - C.S. Forester   2169

Fellowes, Captain
Hate - Arthur Douglas Smith   5918

Fenn, Frank
Sons of Fire - Max McCoy   4227

Fenn, Zach
Sons of Fire - Max McCoy   4227

Fenwick, David
Maria - Eugenia Price   5184

Ferguson, Colonel
Kings Mountain - Florette Henri   2838

Fergusson, Davy
The Shadow and the Glory - John Edward Jennings   3207

Ferris, Cotton
The Last Plantation - Don Wright   6879

Fetterman, W.J.
Carrington - Michael Whitney Straight   6074

Fettleworth, Francis
The Train at Bundarbar - Duncan MacNeil   4021

Field, Ashbel
Now We Are Free - Marguerite Allis   112

Fielder, Andrew Jackson
Fielder's Choice - Rick Norman   4646

Findly, Tom
Sing One Song - Helen Topping Miller   4394

Firebrace, Jack
Birdsong - Sebastian Faulks   2051

Fisher, John Arbuthnot
Buller's Dreadnought - Richard Hough   3047
Buller's Victory - Richard Hough   3049
Flashman and the Dragon - George MacDonald Fraser   2206
The Guns of Arrest - Philip McCutchan   4242
To the Honor of the Fleet - Robert H. Pilpel   5002
"Utmost Fish!" - Hugh Wray McCann   4219

Fisher, Manesseh
Don't Tread on Me - Walter Karig   3366

Fitzgerald, Edward
The Maddest Idea - James L. Nelson   4580

Flahaut de la Billarderie, Auguste Charles Joseph de
A Rose for Virtue - Norah Lofts   3858

Flashman, Harry
Flashman - George MacDonald Fraser   2204
Flashman and the Mountain of Light - George MacDonald Fraser   2207
Flashman at the Charge - George MacDonald Fraser   2209
Royal Flash - George MacDonald Fraser   2213

Fleming, Henry
The Red Badge of Courage - Stephen Crane   1414

Fletcher, Bruce
His Majesty's Highlanders - Leslie Turner White   6683

Flett, David
The Devil in Harbour - Catherine Gavin   2319

Flevry, George
The Siege of Krishnapur - J.G. Farrell   2016

Flickner, Otto
Shiloh - Shelby Foote   2153

Flory, John
Fire and Morning - Francis W. Leary   3696

Foch, Ferdinand
Gossip From the Forest - Thomas Keneally   3413

Force, George
The Scarlet Patch - Bruce Lancaster   3645

Ford, Jeremy
The Yankee Rascals - Carter A. Vaughan   6444

Forrest, Nathan Bedford
And Wait for the Night - John William Corrington   1352
The Falling Hills - Perry Lentz   3720
Home to Tennessee - Alfred Leland Crabb   1400
In the Season of the Wild Rose - Clara Rising   5347
Lodging at the Saint Cloud - Alfred Leland Crabb   1403
Mockingbird Sang at Chickamauga - Alfred Leland Crabb   1404
None Shall Look Back - Caroline Gordon   2478
Shadowed Memories - Al Lacy   3583
Shiloh - Shelby Foote   2153
A Story of Deep Delight - Thomas McNamee   4305
Untold Glory - Cothburn O'Neal   4739

Forrester, Roland
Nick of the Woods; or, The Jibbenainosay - Robert Montgomery Bird   505

Forsyth, George
The Stalkers - Terry C. Johnston   3259

Forty, Thomas
Thomas Forty - Edward Stanley   5982

Fountain, Walter
Shiloh - Shelby Foote   2153

Fournier, Andre
Marcel Armand - Sallie Bell   424

Franchet, Pierre
The Cactus and the Crown - Catherine Gavin   2318

Franklin, Nathaniel
Action at Aquila - Hervey Allen   97

Fraser, James
Dragonfly in Amber - Diana Gabaldon   2262
Outlander - Diana Gabaldon   2264
Voyager - Diana Gabaldon   2265

Fraser, John
Bright Captivity - Eugenia Price   5180

Fraser, Lovat
Prince Charlie's Bluff - Donald Thomas   6241

Frazier, Ian
"Utmost Fish!" - Hugh Wray McCann   4219

Frederick
Waterloo - Bernard Cornwell   1350

Frederickson, William
Sharpe's Revenge - Bernard Cornwell   1346

Fremont, John C.
The Bear Flag: A Novel of the Birth of California - Cecelia Holland   2983
Rush to Destroy - L. Jay Martin   4133

Frisbie, Colonel
Jordan County: A Landscape in Narrative - Shelby Foote   2152

Fuller, Gordon
The Invincibles - Carter A. Vaughan 6436

Furlong, Bryce
A Hundred Hills - Howard Breslin 667

Gage, Thomas
Concord Bridge - Howard Horne 3035
The Gentle Rebel - Gilbert Morris 4461
Jeremiah Martin: A Revolutionary War Novel - Robert H. Fowler 2191
The Last Gentleman - Shirley Barker 312
Massachusetts: A Novel - Nancy Zaroulis 6956

Gagini
The Wrong Horse - Jean Bassan 374

Gaius
According to Mary: A Novel of the Magdalene - Willa Gibbs 2398
Swords in the North - Paul Lewis Anderson 138

Gallio, Marcellus
The Robe - Lloyd C. Douglas 1703

Garcia de la Lastra, Gervasio
The Stuff of Heroes - Miguel Delibes 1592

Garcia, Juan
Captain From Castile - Samuel Shellabarger 5794
Trail of the Spanish Bit - Don Coldsmith 1193

Garland, Richard
Trail-Makers of the Middle Border - Hamlin Garland 2296

Garrard, Adrian
No Man's Land - William Fairchild 2004

Gates, Horatio
A Few Painted Feathers - Stephen Longstreet 3886
The Long March - Jane Barry 358
Man From Mt. Vernon - Burke Boyce 607
Proceed, Sergeant Lamb - Robert Graves 2550
Rabble in Arms - Kenneth Roberts 5390
Sergeant Lamb's America - Robert Graves 2552
The Twisted Saber: A Biographical Novel of Benedict Arnold - Philip Vail 6398

Gates, Jason
The Bugles Are Silent: A Novel of the Texas Revolution - John R. Knaggs 3513

Gattlin, Jacob
Grant's War - Ted Jones 3297

Gearhart, Thaddeus
The Hallelujah Train - Bill Gulick 2614

Gehlman, Benjamin
To the Honor of the Fleet - Robert H. Pilpel 5002

Geladius, Marcus
The Eagles Depart - John Gloag 2434

Gemellus
Red Queen, White Queen - Henry Treece 6332

Gericault, Theodore
Holy Week - Louis Aragon 182

Geyser, Luke
The Blue and the Gray - John Leekley 3713

Gibboney, Bobby
The Seasons of Heroes - Paxton Davis 1539

Gibboney, Matthew
The Seasons of Heroes - Paxton Davis 1539

Gilchrist, Nigel
Jennie about to Be - Elisabeth Ogilvie 4694

Gilchrist, Walter
1915: A Novel - Roger McDonald 4264

Gillespie, Arch
Golden Shore - George Shaftel 5769

Gillivray, Vespasian
By Valour and Arms - James H. Street 6076

Gillroy, Daniel
The Secret Years - Judith Lennox-Smith 3718

Gilmor, Harry
Roll, Shenandoah - Bruce Lancaster 3644

Gilpin, Sam
Redcoat - Bernard Cornwell 1337

Gladwin, Henry
The Conquerors - Allen W. Eckert 1839
Hatchet in the Sky - Margaret Cooper Gay 2328

Glenn, Morgan
The Firelands - Karen Harper 2712

Glover, John
Trumpet to Arms - Bruce Lancaster 3647

Goddard, Jebediah
Governor Ramage, R.N. - Dudley Pope 5096

Godenhausen, Hans Gunther von
Court of Honor - Maria Fagyas 1996

Goedzak, Lamme
The Legend of Tyl Ulenspiegel - Charles Theodore Henri De Coster 1558

Goelo, Gilles
The Lure of the Falcon - Juliette Benzoni 465

Goering, Hermann
Jerusalem Interlude - Bodie Thoene 6223

Goff, Colby William Rollo
Blunted Lance - Max Hennessy 2829
Soldier of the Queen - Max Hennessy 2837

Goff, Dabney
Blunted Lance - Max Hennessy 2829

Goldfeder, Aaron
Leah's Journey - Gloria Goldreich 2460

Gordon, Charles George
Drums of Khartoum - Chloe Gartner 2307
Flashman and the Dragon - George MacDonald Fraser 2206
The Last Encounter - Robin Maugham 4196
The Second Son of Heaven: A Novel of Nineteenth-Century China - C.Y. Lee 3707

Gordon, Wayne
Shadowed Memories - Al Lacy 3583

Gorges, Richard
Jewels - Robert Perrin 4917

Gorsinski, Prince
Beware, Beware the Bight of Benin - Philip McCutchan 4241
Halfhyde's Island - Philip McCutchan 4254

Gough, Paddy
Bayonets in the Sun - William Moore 4446

Gower, Colby
Bridal Journey - Dale Van Every 6406

Gradov, Nikita
Generations of Winter - Vassily Aksyonov 61

Graham, Gavin
Drums of Khartoum - Chloe Gartner 2307

Graham of Claverhouse, John
Old Mortality - Sir Walter Scott 5702

Gramont, Alain de
The Renegade - Donald Clayton Porter 5122
The Sachem - Donald Clayton Porter 5124

Grant, Ulysses S.
Aide to Glory - Louis Devon 1635
The Blue and the Gray - John Leekley 3713
Captain Grant - Shirley Seifert 5724
The Chester A. Arthur Conspiracy - William Wiegand 6740
A City Not Forsaken - Lynn Morris 4480
Colorado Ambush - Jess McCriede 4230
The Cosgrove Report - G.J.A. O'Toole 4765
The Court-Martial of George Armstrong Custer - Douglas C. Jones 3276
The Crisis - Winston Churchill 1079
Freedom - William Safire 5561
Freedom Road - Howard Fast 2031
Glory Enough for All: The Battle of the Crater - Duane Philip Schultz 5673
Grant's War - Ted Jones 3297
Gray Victory - Robert Skimin 5877
The Hallelujah Train - Bill Gulick 2614
Johnny Shiloh - James A. Rhodes 5308
The Last Stand: A Novel about George Armstrong Custer and the Indians of the Plains - Edwin P. Hoyt 3061
Lincoln: A Novel - Gore Vidal 6490
Long Day at Shiloh - Don Bannister 294
A Man Called Grant - Helen Todd 6285
Montana! - Dana Fuller Ross 5479
Shadowed Memories - Al Lacy 3583
Shiloh - Shelby Foote 2153
To Appomattox: Nine April Days, 1865 - Burke Davis 1512
Ulysses: A Biographical Novel - Robert Skimin 5878
Untold Glory - Cothburn O'Neal 4739
Whistling Cat - Robert W. Chambers 984
Woman with a Sword: The Biographical Novel of Anna Ella Carroll of Maryland - Hollister Noble 4632
The Yankee From Tennessee - Noel B. Gerson 2388

Grasse, Francois Joseph Paul de
The Saintly Buccaneer - Gilbert Morris 4469
Sea Road to Yorktown - Harvey Haislip 2644

Graves, Robert
Regeneration - Pat Barker 309

Graves, William S.
Fifteen Flags - Richard Lynden Hardman 2686

Gray, Dick
The Horse Soldiers - Harold Sinclair 5862

Greene, Nathanael
Dawn's Early Light - Elswyth Thane 6215
A Few Painted Feathers - Stephen Longstreet 3886
I'll Storm Hell - Noel B. Gerson 2374
Let My Name Stand Fair - Shirley Seifert 5727
The Long March - Jane Barry 358
Major Andre - Anthony Bailey 265
Man From Mt. Vernon - Burke Boyce 607
Morning in America - Willard Wiener 6741
Murfy's Men - Gerald Green 2565
Phantom Fortress - Bruce Lancaster 3643
The Ragged Ones - Burke Davis 1511
Raleigh's Eden - Inglis Fletcher 2137
Stars on the Sea - F. van Wyck Mason 4161
Storm the Last Rampart - David Taylor 6180
The Swamp Fox, Francis Marion - Noel B. Gerson 2383

Grenville, Sir Richard
The King's General - Daphne Du Maurier 1748

Greville, Charles
The Passing Bells - Phillip Rock 5421

Griffith, Edward
The Pilot - James Fenimore Cooper 1306

Grijalva, Juan Pablo
Cannibal Eliot and the Lost Histories of San Francisco - Hilton Obenzinger 4660

Grineff, Peter
The Captain's Daughter - Alexander Pushkin 5210

Grove, Peter
Song of the Susquehanna - Herbert Stover 6071

Groves, Christopher
Gone to Texas - Jason Manning 4074

Groves, Jonathan
Flintlock - Jason Manning 4073

Groves, Leslie R.
Stallion Gate - Martin Cruz Smith   5924

Guilame, Gabriel
Seven Men of Gascony - R.F. Delderfield   1589

Hadjianestis
Beyond the Aegean - Elia Kazan   3382

Haig, Douglas
Over There - Thomas Fleming   2130
The Red Daniel - Duncan MacNeil   4017

Hakeswill, Obadiah
Sharpe's Company - Bernard Cornwell   1339
Sharpe's Enemy - Bernard Cornwell   1342

Hale, Allen
Conceived in Liberty - Howard Fast   2029

Hale, Anthony
The Band Plays Dixie - Morris Markey   4089

Hale, Jared
The Silver Saber - Carter A. Vaughan   6441
Yankee Rogue - Dana Fuller Ross   5496

Hale, Kirk
The Band Plays Dixie - Morris Markey   4089

Hale, Malachy
The Blue and the Gray - John Leekley   3713

Hale, Nathan
The Rebel and the Turncoat - Malcolm Decker   1576

Halfhyde, St. Vincent
Beware, Beware the Bight of Benin - Philip
  McCutchan   4241
The Guns of Arrest - Philip McCutchan   4242
Halfhyde and the Chain Gang - Philip
  McCutchan   4244
Halfhyde and the Flag Captain - Philip
  McCutchan   4245
Halfhyde and the Fleet Review - Philip
  McCutchan   4246
Halfhyde for the Queen - Philip McCutchan   4247
Halfhyde Goes to War - Philip McCutchan   4248
Halfhyde on Zanatu - Philip McCutchan   4251
Halfhyde Ordered South - Philip McCutchan   4252
Halfhyde to the Narrows - Philip McCutchan   4253
Halfhyde's Island - Philip McCutchan   4254

Hall, Jack
The Hours of Light - Janet Tanner   6160

Hall, Mason
Thunder in the Dawn - Earl Murray   4532

Hall, Ted
The Hours of Light - Janet Tanner   6160

Halloran
Bring Larks and Heroes - Thomas Keneally   3410

Hallows, John
In Pale Battalions - Robert Goddard   2444

Halyi, Istvan
Before the Glory Ended - Ursula Zilinsky   6963

Hamilcar Barca
Salammbo - Gustave Flaubert   2123

Hamilton, Alexander
Eagles Where I Walk - Stephen Longstreet   3885
A Few Painted Feathers - Stephen Longstreet   3886
Janice Meredith - Paul Leicester Ford   2166
Let My Name Stand Fair - Shirley Seifert   5727
The Lure of the Falcon - Juliette Benzoni   465
Monmouth - Charles Bracelen Flood   2144
Mr. Arnold - Francis Lynde   3935
Murfy's Men - Gerald Green   2565
Seneca - Donald Clayton Porter   5127
Storm the Last Rampart - David Taylor   6180
The Tree of Liberty - Elizabeth Page   4773
The Yankee Rascals - Carter A. Vaughan   6444

Hamilton, Henry
The Big Knives - Bruce Lancaster   3635

Hamilton, Julian
The Scimitar - Samuel Edwards   1890

Hampton, Wade
Heaven and Hell - John Jakes   3147

Hancock, Winfield Scott
Gods and Generals - Jeff Shaara   5765
The Killer Angels - Michael Shaara   5766
*The Last Stand: A Novel about George Armstrong
  Custer and the Indians of the Plains* - Edwin P.
  Hoyt   3061
Roman - Douglas C. Jones   3281

Hanks, Rome
The History of Rome Hanks - Joseph Stanley
  Pennell   4909

Hanna, Giles
*The Sounds of Chariots: A Novel of John Sevier and
  the State of Franklin* - Helen Topping Miller   4396

Hannibal
Hannibal - Ross Leckie   3704
Hannibal of Carthage - Mary Dolan   1686
The Scarlet Beast - Francis Gerard   2357

Hardee, William Joseph
Untold Glory - Cothburn O'Neal   4739

Hardinge, George Nicholas
The Long Fight - D.A. Rayner   5270

Harper, David
*Eagle of Niagara: The Story of David Harper and His
  Indian Captivity* - John Brick   671

Harper, Patrick
Sharpe's Company - Bernard Cornwell   1339
Sharpe's Devil - Bernard Cornwell   1340
Sharpe's Eagle - Bernard Cornwell   1341
Sharpe's Enemy - Bernard Cornwell   1342
Sharpe's Gold - Bernard Cornwell   1343
Sharpe's Regiment - Bernard Cornwell   1345
Sharpe's Revenge - Bernard Cornwell   1346
Sharpe's Rifles - Bernard Cornwell   1347
Sharpe's Sword - Bernard Cornwell   1349
Waterloo - Bernard Cornwell   1350

Harper, Thomas
Sharpe's Battle - Bernard Cornwell   1338

Harrington, Pinckney
The History of Rome Hanks - Joseph Stanley
  Pennell   4909

Harris, Clayton
The Last Plantation - Don Wright   6879

Harrison, William Henry
Gateway to Empire - Allen W. Eckert   1842
My Blood and My Treasure - Mary Schumann   5674
Panther in the Sky - James Alexander Thom   6234
The Seekers - John Jakes   3153
A Sorrow in Our Heart - Allen W. Eckert   1844
To Keep Us Free - Marguerite Allis   115

Hart, Nash
High Hearts - Rita Mae Brown   728

Hasford, Martin
The Barefoot Brigade - Douglas C. Jones   3274

Hastings, Anthony
The Coat I Wore - Lucile Finlay   2090

Hatcher, Nate
Doniphan's Ride - Les Savage Jr.   5620

Hawkins, Caleb
The Year of the Spaniard - Henry Castor   956

Hawksworth, Brian
The Moghul - Thomas Hoover   3026

Hawley, Andrew
The Settlers - William Stuart Long   3878

Hayden, Bob
Banner at Shenandoah - Bruce Catton   963

Hayes, Porter
The Amulet - Hal Borland   582

Haynow, Claus
The Drums of Winter - Sandra Paretti   4790

Hazard, George
Love and War - John Jakes   3150
North and South - John Jakes   3151

Hazard, Matthew Carlton
Distant Trumpet - Paul Horgan   3032

Hazard, Phillip
Brave Captains - Vivian Stuart   6086
Hazard of Huntress - Vivian Stuart   6087
Hazard's Command - Vivian Stuart   6088
The Valiant Sailors - Vivian Stuart   6090
Victory at Sebastopol - Vivian Stuart   6091

Hazard, Rufus
My Blood and My Treasure - Mary Schumann   5674

Heath, Jared
Company of Cowards - Jack Schaefer   5634

Heath, Micah
Enough Good Men - Charles Mercer   4336

Hedrick, Tjaden
Gettysburg - Stephen Longstreet   3887

Heidemann, Hauptmann Otto
The Blue Max - Jack D. Hunter   3085

Hellier, Colonel
Wintercombe - Pamela Belle   435

Helm, Leonard
The Big Knives - Bruce Lancaster   3635

Hencke, Peter
Last Man to Die - Michael Dobbs   1652

Henry, Byron
War and Remembrance - Herman Wouk   6875

Henry, Cadmus
Cadmus Henry - Walter D. Edmonds   1872

Henry, Victor
War and Remembrance - Herman Wouk   6875
The Winds of War - Herman Wouk   6876

Herington, Derek
Allegra - Clare Darcy   1483

Heron, Francis
The Chains of Fate - Pamela Belle   430

Herrick, Beau
The Wilderness Brigade - Phyllis Gordon
  Demarest   1605

Herrick, Thomas
Form Line of Battle! - Alexander Kent   3431
Passage to Mutiny - Alexander Kent   3436
Signal—Close Action! - Alexander Kent   3438
To Glory We Steer - Alexander Kent   3442
A Tradition of Victory - Alexander Kent   3443

Hesperian, Gaius
Dogheaded Death - Ray Faraday Nelson   4581

Hess, Charles
*The Girl Who Was Never Queen: A Biographical
  Novel of Princess Charlotte of Wales* - Mary
  Main   4037

Heydrich, Reinhard
The Last Innocent Hour - Margot Abbott   8

Heywood, Thomas
Presumption: An Entertainment - Julia Barrett   350

Hickok, James Butler
Elkhorn Tavern - Douglas C. Jones   3278

Hill, A.P.
The Court Martial of Robert E. Lee - Douglas
  Savage   5617
Gettysburg: Crisis of Command - Harry Albright   65

Hill, Marion
The Strong Men - John Brick 677

Hill, Matt
The Strong Men - John Brick 677

Hilliard, John
Strange Meeting - Susan Hill 2952

Hilton, Jim
How Young They Die - Stuart Cloete 1124

Holloway, Jonas
Day of Battle - Frederic F. Van de Water 6402

Holmes, Oliver Wendell
Copperhead - Bernard Cornwell 1335

Holofernes
Judith - Stella Wilchek 6748

Hood, John Bell
The Bright Sword - Eleanor Perenyi 4911

Hood, Samuel
A King's Commander - Dewey Lambdin 3613

Hooker, Joseph
Unto This Hour - Tom Wicker 6733
When the War Is Over - Stephen Becker 408

Hordle, John
The White Company - Sir Arthur Conan Doyle 1716

Horemheb
The Twelfth Transforming - Pauline Gedge 2347

Hornblower, Horatio
Admiral Hornblower in the West Indies - C.S. Forester 2169
Beat to Quarters - C.S. Forester 2170
Commodore Hornblower - C.S. Forester 2172
Flying Colours - C.S. Forester 2173
Hornblower and the Atropos - C.S. Forester 2175
Hornblower and the Hotspur - C.S. Forester 2176
Hornblower During the Crisis - C.S. Forester 2177
Lieutenant Hornblower - C.S. Forester 2178
The Life and Times of Horatio Hornblower - C. Northcote Parkinson 4813
Lord Hornblower - C.S. Forester 2179
Mr. Midshipman Hornblower - C.S. Forester 2180
Ship of the Line - C.S. Forester 2182

Horne, Adam
The War Chest - Porter Hill 2950

Hoshi, Hiroshi
Chikara! - Robert Skimin 5876

House, Edward
To the Honor of the Fleet - Robert H. Pilpel 5002

Houston, Sam
The Bugles Are Silent: A Novel of the Texas Revolution - John R. Knaggs 3513
The Eagle and the Raven - James A. Michener 4369
Empire of Bones: A Novel of Sam Houston and the Texas Revolution - Jeff Long 3868
The Furies - John Jakes 3146
Hellfire Jackson - Garland Roark 5355
Horseshoe Bend - Bruce Palmer 4779
Promised Lands - Elizabeth Crook 1430
Sam Houston - Noel B. Gerson 2380
The Sam Houston Story - Dean Owen 4770

Hovey, Matt
Blue Hurricane - F. van Wyck Mason 4146

Howard, John
Wilderness Adventure - Elizabeth Page 4774

Howard, Oliver Otis
Blood Brother - Elliott Arnold 190
Chief Joseph - Bill Dugan 1756

Howard, Peyton
The Tree of Liberty - Elizabeth Page 4773

Howard, Ridley
Draw Near to Battle - Jere Hungerford Wheelwright 6667

Howe, William
The King's Rebel - James David Horan 3030
Massachusetts: A Novel - Nancy Zaroulis 6956
Monmouth - Charles Bracelen Flood 2144
Oliver Wiswell - Kenneth Roberts 5389
Redcoat - Bernard Cornwell 1337
Three Fields to Cross - Francis Tysen Nutt 4651
Valiant Libertine - John Gordon Bryson 748

Howell, Pelham
Eliza Stanhope - Joanna Trollope 6347

Howells, Dan
The Scarlet Guidon - Ray Grant Toepfer 6287

Hoyt
Squadron Forty-Four - Arch Whitehouse 6711

Huff, Cap
Rabble in Arms - Kenneth Roberts 5390

Hull, Harrison
Enslaved - Ron Burns 801
The Mysterious Death of Meriwether Lewis - Ron Burns 802

Hull, Isaac
The Splendor Stays: An Historic Novel Based on the Lives of the Seven Hart Sisters of Saybrook - Marguerite Allis 114

Humbert, Jean-Joseph
The Year of the French - Thomas Flanagan 2121

Humphreys, Oswald
"Utmost Fish!" - Hugh Wray McCann 4219

Hunter, Andrew
Guns for Rebellion - F. van Wyck Mason 4151

Hunter, David
No Tears for Christmas - Helen Topping Miller 4391

Huntley, Peter
Toil of the Brave - Inglis Fletcher 2141

Hyde, Benjamin
One Smart Indian - Robert J. Seidman 5722

Hyde, Gabriel
Mandarin - Robert S. Elegant 1905

Ignatius Loyola
The Golden Thread - Louis De Wohl 1566

Irons, Fletcher
Faith and Honor - Robin Maderich 4025

Isasaga, Francisco de
A Crossbowman's Story of the First Exploration of the Amazon - George Millar 4379

Jackson, Andrew
1812 - David Nevin 4586
As Long as the Rivers Run - Sam J. Slate 5882
Burr - Gore Vidal 6485
The Corsair: A Biographical Novel of Jean Lafitte, Hero of the Battle of New Orleans - Madeleine Fabiola Kent 3444
Creek Mary's Blood - Dee Brown 712
The Cumberland Rifles - Noel B. Gerson 2365
The Fallon Pride - Reagan O'Neal 4742
Flintlock - Jason Manning 4073
Give Me the Wind - Jan Jordan 3302
Hearts of Hickory - John Trotwood Moore 4442
Her Christmas at the Hermitage: A Tale about Rachel and Andrew Jackson - Helen Topping Miller 4389
Home to the Hermitage - Alfred Leland Crabb 1401
Horseshoe Bend - Bruce Palmer 4779
Jackson: A Novel - Max Byrd 837
The Land Where the Sun Dies - Henry Carlisle 896
Magnificent Destiny - Paul I. Wellman 6619
Oh, Promised Land - James H. Street 6079
Old Hickory - Noel B. Gerson 2379
The President's Lady - Irving Stone 6063
The Rake and the Hussy - Robert W. Chambers 981
Sam Houston - Noel B. Gerson 2380
A Story of Deep Delight - Thomas McNamee 4305

Twilight of Empire - Allen W. Eckert 1846
War Drums - Donald Clayton Porter 5133
Young Hickory - Stanley Young 6942

Jackson, Sally
The Last Innocent Hour - Margot Abbott 8

Jackson, Thomas Jonathan
Battle Flag - Bernard Cornwell 1333
The Bloody Ground - Bernard Cornwell 1334
Confederates - Thomas Keneally 3412
The Gallant Mrs. Stonewall - Harnett T. Kane 3353
Gettysburg: Crisis of Command - Harry Albright 65
Gods and Generals - Jeff Shaara 5765
Hard Road to Gettysburg - Ted Jones 3298
The Long Roll - Mary Johnston 3236
Look Away - Harold Coyle 1395
Major Stepton's War - Matthew Vaughan 6445
McKensie's Hundred: A Tale of the Old Dominion - Frank Yerby 6924
The River and the Wilderness - Don Robertson 5401
The Smiling Rebel - Harnett T. Kane 3357
The Stonewall Brigade: A Novel of the American Civil War - Frank G. Slaughter 5902
Traveller - Richard Adams 27
Unto This Hour - Tom Wicker 6733
The Unwritten Chronicles of Robert E. Lee - Lamar Herrin 2864
The Warriors - John Jakes 3155

James, Jeremiah
Chapultepec - Norman Zollinger 6965

James, Jesse
Bound Girl - Everett Webber 6591
Sons of Fire - Max McCoy 4227

Jankyn, Matthew
The Whyte Harte - P.C. Doherty 1681

Jarret, Jarl
Jarrett's Jade - Frank Yerby 6923

Jarvis, Berk
The Great Meadow - Elizabeth Madox Roberts 5378

Jebeau, Joseph
My Beloved Son - Catherine Cookson 1285

Jefferson, Adam
Molly - Teresa Crane 1417

Jellicoe, John Rushworth
The Devil in Harbour - Catherine Gavin 2319
To the Honor of the Fleet - Robert H. Pilpel 5002

Jericho, Lucas
Hearts of Fire - Christina Savage 5616

Joab
Giant Killer - Elmer Holmes Davis 1518
The Unanointed - Laurene Chinn 1070

Joan of Arc
An Army of Angels: A Novel of Joan of Arc - Pamela Marcantel 4079
The Master Painter - Edwin Mullins 4513

Johnston, Albert Sidney
In the Season of the Wild Rose - Clara Rising 5347
Journey to Shiloh - Will Henry 2843
The Long Night - Andrew Lytle 3945
Powderkeg - Richard Vetterli 6482
Shadowed Memories - Al Lacy 3583
Shiloh - Shelby Foote 2153
Ulysses: A Biographical Novel - Robert Skimin 5878

Johnston, George
The Explorers - William Stuart Long 3872

Johnston, Joseph E.
Beloved Enemy - Al Lacy 3579
Cadmus Henry - Walter D. Edmonds 1872
Copperhead - Bernard Cornwell 1335

Jones, John Paul
The Bonnet Laird's Daughter - Barbara Annandale 154
Captain Paul - Edward Ellsberg 1930

Clear for Action: A Novel about John Paul Jones -
Clements Ripley 5344
Don't Tread on Me - Walter Karig 3366
Drums - James Boyd 611
Henry Lunt and the Ranger - Tom McNamara 4304
Israel Potter - Herman Melville 4334
The Pilot - James Fenimore Cooper 1306
Raleigh's Eden - Inglis Fletcher 2137
The Revolutionary - Lawrence Schoonover 5667
Richard Carvel - Winston Churchill 1081
Sailor Named Jones - Harvey Haislip 2643
The Sea Eagles - John Edward Jennings 3206
Stars on the Sea - F. van Wyck Mason 4161

Jones, Othnell
Othneil Jones - John Adams Leland 3715

Jons, Coleman
Copperhead Moon - Herbert Stover 6067

Jordan, Caleb
Scarlet Feather - Dale Van Every 6409

Jordan, Revell
Thunder on the Chesapeake - David Divine 1650

Josephus, Flavius
Josephus - Lion Feuchtwanger 2072
The Soldier and the Sage: A Novel about Akiba -
Richard G. Hubler 3065
The Triumph - Ernest K. Gann 2280
The Wolf of Masada - John Fredman 2220
The Word and the Sword - Theo Lang 3662

Joubert
Colors Aloft! - Alexander Kent 3427

Julius
The Rock: A Novel about Gibraltar - John
Masters 4179

Julius Caesar
The Alexandrian - Martha Rofheart 5425
Augustus - Allan Massie 4167
Augustus - John Williams 6785
Caesar - Mirko Jelusich 3188
Caesar - Allan Massie 4168
Caesar's Women - Colleen McCullough 4233
The First Man in Rome - Colleen McCullough 4234
Fortune's Favorite - Colleen McCullough 4235
Freedom, Farewell - Phyllis Bentley 461
Gaul Is Divided - Esther Fisher Brown 721
A Goddess to a God - John Lloyd Balderston 278
The Gods Are Not Mocked - Anna Taylor 6177
The Grass Crown - Colleen McCullough 4236
The Ides of March - Thornton Wilder 6753
Imperial Caesar - Rex Warner 6565
The Key - Benita Kane Jaro 3169
A Pillar of Iron - Taylor Caldwell 861
The Pirate From Rome - John V.D.
Southworth 5952
Prepare Them for Caesar - Mary Louise
Mabie 3954
The Sacrilege - John Maddox Roberts 5380
SPQR - John Maddox Roberts 5381
Swords in the North - Paul Lewis Anderson 138
That Egyptian Woman - Noel B. Gerson 2384
Tros of Samothrace - Talbot Mundy 4515
The Young Caesar - Rex Warner 6567

Jung Lu
Forbidden City - Muriel Molland Jernigan 3215

Junot, Andoche
The Emperor's Duchess - R.G. Waldeck 6524
Seed of Mischief - Willa Gibbs 2401

Justice, John Valcourt
A Balance of Dangers - Anthony Forrest 2184
Captain Justice - Anthony Forrest 2185
The Pandora Secret - Anthony Forrest 2186

Justus
Justus - Arthur L. Lapham 3663

Kalb, Johann de
Dawn's Early Light - Elswyth Thane 6215

Kalmykoff, Ivan
Fifteen Flags - Richard Lynden Hardman 2686

Karaibrahim
Time of Parting - Anton Donchev 1690

Karus, Julius
The Crow Goddess - Patricia Finney 2094

Kasakov
The Buckingham Palace Connection - Ted
Willis 6792

Kearney, Philip
The Scarlet Patch - Bruce Lancaster 3645

Kearney, Stephen Watts
Hill of the Hawk - Scott O'Dell 4689

Keith, Thomas
Blood and Sand - Rosemary Sutcliff 6121

Kemal, Mustafa
The Ashes of Smyrna - Richard Reinhardt 5294

Kemper, Frank
The Man on the Train - W.J. Chaput 995

Kennedy, Gillian
The White Cockade - Vincent O'Brien 4683

Kennedy, John F.
The Only Thing to Fear - David Poyer 5160
Till the End of Time - Allen Appel 170

Kent, Abraham
The Seekers - John Jakes 3153

Kent, Gideon
The Titans - John Jakes 3154
The Warriors - John Jakes 3155

Kent, Jared
The Seekers - John Jakes 3153

Kent, Jeremiah
The Warriors - John Jakes 3155

Kent, Philip
The Rebels - John Jakes 3152

Kerr, Reed
Arizona! - Dana Fuller Ross 5466

Kesselring, Albert
Luciano's Luck - Jack Higgins 2912

Kettering, Karl-Heinz
The Blue Max - Jack D. Hunter 3085

Kilbourne, Dan
West of Appomattox - Harley Duncan 1785

Killick, Cornelius
Sharpe's Siege - Bernard Cornwell 1348

Kilpatrick, Hugh Judson
The Richmond Raid - John Brick 674

Kilrain, Buster
The Killer Angels - Michael Shaara 5766

Kimball, Jonathan
Farewell to Valley Forge - David Taylor 6178

Kirby, Ambrose
Bugles Blow No More - Clifford Dowdey 1704

Kirby, Paul
Bugles Blow No More - Clifford Dowdey 1704

Kishote, Don
The Glory - Herman Wouk 6873
The Hope - Herman Wouk 6874

Kitchener, Horatio Herbert
Blunted Lance - Max Hennessy 2829
Drums of Khartoum - Chloe Gartner 2307
Rags of Glory - Stuart Cloete 1126
The Red Daniel - Duncan MacNeil 4017

Kmita, Andrei
The Deluge - Henryk Sienkiewicz 5846

Knott, Stephen
Thunder on the Chesapeake - David Divine 1650

Knowles, Charles
The Yankee Brig - Carter A. Vaughan 6443

Knowles, Ethan
Bride of Liberty - Frank Yerby 6909

Knox, Henry
The Bastard - John Jakes 3144
The King's Iron - Robert Newton Peck 4888
The Rebels - John Jakes 3152

Kolchak, Aleksandr
Fifteen Flags - Richard Lynden Hardman 2686

Kosciuszko, Thaddeus
Thaddeus of Warsaw - Jane Porter 5136

Kronkhyte, Abe
If Not Victory - Frank Olney Hough 3043

Kruger, Paul
Rags of Glory - Stuart Cloete 1126

Kupper, Sebastian
In the Company of Eagles - Ernest K. Gann 2279

Kuragin, Paul
Heir to Kuragin - Constance Heaven 2807

Kutuzov, Mikhail Illarionovich
Far Flies the Eagle - Evelyn Anthony 162
The Fortune Hunter - Ira J. Morris 4477
War and Peace - Leo Tolstoy 6295

Lacey, Alan de
The Thousand Fires - Anne Powers 5155

Lacey, Ben Franklin
Strange Company - Robert J. Conley 1251

Lady
Three Days - Stephen Longstreet 3891

Lafayette, Marie Joseph Paul de
A Chance for Glory - Constance Wright 6877
Conceived in Liberty - Howard Fast 2029
Dawn's Early Light - Elswyth Thane 6215
The Drums of Monmouth - Emma Gelders
Sterne 5998
The Fallon Blood - Reagan O'Neal 4741
Farewell to Valley Forge - David Taylor 6178
A Generation of Leaves - Robert S. Bloom 552
Hugh Wynne, Free Quaker - Silas Weir
Mitchell 4416
I'll Storm Hell - Noel B. Gerson 2374
The Ironmaster - Anne Powers 5150
King's Masque - Evan John 3220
The Lure of the Falcon - Juliette Benzoni 465
Man from Mt. Vernon - Burke Boyce 607
Monmouth - Charles Bracelen Flood 2144
Morning in America - Willard Wiener 6741
A Place of Greater Safety - Hilary Mantel 4077
The Rebels - John Jakes 3152
Storm the Last Rampart - David Taylor 6180
The Strong Men - John Brick 677
To Spit Against the Wind - Benjamin H. Levin 3737
The Tree of Liberty - Elizabeth Page 4773
Valley Forge - MacKinlay Kantor 3364
Wicked Lady - Inglis Fletcher 2142
Yorktown - Burke Davis 1513

Lake, John
Salisbury Plain - Henry C. Branson 650

Lamb, Matthew
First Lieutenant - Kenneth Maynard 4208
Lamb in Command - Kenneth Maynard 4209
Lieutenant Lamb - Kenneth Maynard 4210

Lamb, Robert
Proceed, Sergeant Lamb - Robert Graves 2550
Sergeant Lamb's America - Robert Graves 2552

Lamond, Peter
Up She Rises - David Garnett 2298

Lancey, Oliver de
Concord Bridge - Howard Horne 3035

Lane, Joseph
The Quiet Life of Mrs. General Lane - Victoria
Case 951

Lang, Richard
Follow the Drum - James Leasor 3699

Langdon, Burke
The Moon-Eyed Appaloosa - Bill Gulick 2617

Lannes, Jean
Seven Men of Gascony - R.F. Delderfield 1589

Lapenotiere, John Richards
He Brings Great News - Clemence Dane 1462

Larkin, Rory
Redemption - Leon Uris 6393

Larkin, Timothy
Timothy Larkin - Jane Hutchens 3089

LaSalle, Charles
The Proud Canaries - David Johnson 3222

Latimer, Harry
The Carolinian - Rafael Sabatini 5547

Lawless, Desmond de
Poor Richard's Game - G.J.A. O'Toole 4766

Lawrence, T.E.
Behold the Fire - Michael Blankfort 541
The Devil's Spy - Michael Hastings 2773
Dreaming of Samarkand - Martin Booth 576

Lawson, Henry
Season for War - P.F. Kluge 3510

Lawson, John
Mutiny Run - Frank Eccles 1836

Layton, Sarah
A Division of the Spoils - Paul Scott 5683

Ledbetter, Gideon
The Wolf and the Buffalo - Elmer Kelton 3408

Ledesma, Rafael
La Guerra: A Spanish Saga - Stephen D.
Frances 2199

Ledyard, Grant
The Secret Road - Bruce Lancaster 3646

Lee, Charles
Conceived in Liberty - Howard Fast 2029
The Drums of Monmouth - Emma Gelders
Sterne 5998
Enough Good Men - Charles Mercer 4336
Farewell to Valley Forge - David Taylor 6178
I'll Storm Hell - Noel B. Gerson 2374
Janice Meredith - Paul Leicester Ford 2166
Man From Mt. Vernon - Burke Boyce 607
Morning in America - Willard Wiener 6741
Proceed, Sergeant Lamb - Robert Graves 2550
The Unvanquished - Howard Fast 2046

Lee, Henry
Brother to the Enemy - Bart Spicer 5964
Let My Name Stand Fair - Shirley Seifert 5727
Phantom Fortress - Bruce Lancaster 3643
The Swamp Fox, Francis Marion - Noel B.
Gerson 2383

Lee, Robert E.
Battle Flag - Bernard Cornwell 1333
The Bloody Ground - Bernard Cornwell 1334
The Blue and the Gray - John Leekley 3713
Cease Firing - Mary Johnston 3230
Christmas with Robert E. Lee - Helen Topping
Miller 4387
The Court Martial of Robert E. Lee - Douglas
Savage 5617
Eight April Days - Scott Hart 2759
Farewell, My General - Shirley Seifert 5726
The Fifth Conspiracy - Ted Jones 3296

For the Love of Robert E. Lee - M.A. Harper 2715
Gettysburg - Stephen Longstreet 3887
Gettysburg: Crisis of Command - Harry Albright 65
The Ghost Raider - Ray Hogan 2978
Glory Enough for All: The Battle of the Crater -
Duane Philip Schultz 5673
Gods and Generals - Jeff Shaara 5765
The Golden Eagle - Noel B. Gerson 2370
Gray Victory - Robert Skimin 5877
The Guns of the South - Harry N. Turtledove 6367
Hard Road to Gettysburg - Ted Jones 3298
House Divided - Ben Ames Williams 6765
Joy From Ashes - Al Lacy 3581
The Killer Angels - Michael Shaara 5766
The Lady of Arlington - Harnett T. Kane 3354
Major Stepton's War - Matthew Vaughan 6445
McKensie's Hundred: A Tale of the Old Dominion -
Frank Yerby 6924
North and South - John Jakes 3151
Oldest Living Confederate Widow Tells All - Allan
Gurganus 2621
*The Stonewall Brigade: A Novel of the American Civil
War* - Frank G. Slaughter 5902
Three Days - Stephen Longstreet 3891
The Titans - John Jakes 3154
To Appomattox: Nine April Days, 1865 - Burke
Davis 1512
Traveller - Richard Adams 27
Ulysses: A Biographical Novel - Robert Skimin 5878
Unto This Hour - Tom Wicker 6733
Untold Glory - Cothburn O'Neal 4739
The Unwritten Chronicles of Robert E. Lee - Lamar
Herrin 2864

LeFever, Captain
Fort De Chastaigne - Don Coldsmith 1177

Leigh, Tristram
Feather Castles - Patricia Veryan 6462

Leiston, Robert
Bayonets in the Sun - William Moore 4446

Leon of Atrax
An Elephant for Aristotle - L. Sprague De
Camp 1556

Leonard, Sam
By Antietam Creek - Don Robertson 5398

Lepidus, Marcus Aemilius
Three's Company - Alfred Duggan 1774

Leroux, Captain
Sharpe's Sword - Bernard Cornwell 1349

Leslie, Arnett
The Judas Tree - Neil Harmon Swanson 6139

Lettow-Vorbeck, Paul Emil von
The Ghosts of Africa - William Stevenson 6013

Leverett, Ira
Fifteen Flags - Richard Lynden Hardman 2686

Lewis, John
Seasons - Anna Dillon 1645

Lewis, Meriwether
From Sea to Shining Sea - James Alexander
Thom 6232
The Gates of the Mountains - Will Henry 2842
The Seekers - John Jakes 3153
Trail: The Story of the Lewis and Clark Expedition -
Louis Charbonneau 998

Lewis, Vargas
Young Vargas Lewis - Robert Brainard Pearsall 4874

Lewrie, Alan
The French Admiral - Dewey Lambdin 3609
The Gun Ketch - Dewey Lambdin 3610
H.M.S. Cockerel - Dewey Lambdin 3611
The King's Coat - Dewey Lambdin 3612
A King's Commander - Dewey Lambdin 3613
The King's Commission - Dewey Lambdin 3614
The King's Privateer - Dewey Lambdin 3615

Li, General
Empire of Heaven - Linda Ching Sledge 5907

Lincoln, Abraham
Comes an Echo on the Breeze - Edward J.
Ryan 5542
*There Was a Season: A Biographical Novel of
Jefferson Davis* - Theodore Olsen 4730

Lincoln, Lionel
Lionel Lincoln; or, The Leaguer of Boston - James
Fenimore Cooper 1303

Lingarde, Richard
Beyond All Frontiers - Emma Drummond 1722

Lockwood, Wayne
Song of Years - Bess Streeter Aldrich 72

Logan, Benjamin
Johnny Logan: Shawnee Spy - Allen W. Eckert 1843

London, Ben
London's Child - Philip Boast 560

Longinus
The Centurion - Leonard Wibberley 6729
Hear Me, Pilate! - LeGette Blythe 557
The Lance of Longinus - Hubertus Loewenstein 3833
Man on Fire: A Novel on the Life of St. Paul -
LeGette Blythe 558
A Tear for Judas - LeGette Blythe 559

Longstreet, James
Confederates - Thomas Keneally 3412
The Court Martial of Robert E. Lee - Douglas
Savage 5617
The Dixie Widow - Gilbert Morris 4459
Gettysburg - Stephen Longstreet 3887
Gettysburg: Crisis of Command - Harry Albright 65
Gods and Generals - Jeff Shaara 5765
Gray Victory - Robert Skimin 5877
House Divided - Ben Ames Williams 6765
Joy From Ashes - Al Lacy 3581
The Killer Angels - Michael Shaara 5766
Mockingbird Sang at Chickamauga - Alfred Leland
Crabb 1404
Talons of Eagles - William W. Johnstone 3268
Traveller - Richard Adams 27
Ulysses: A Biographical Novel - Robert Skimin 5878
The Unconquered - Ben Ames Williams 6768
Unto This Hour - Tom Wicker 6733

Longyan
Ming: A Novel of Seventeeth Century China - Robert
B. Oxnam 4772

Lopez, Francisco
Young Vargas Lewis - Robert Brainard Pearsall 4874

Lorimer, Brinsley
Blaize - Anne Melville 4331

Loskiel, Evan
Hidden Children - Robert W. Chambers 978

Loup, Guy
Sharpe's Battle - Bernard Cornwell 1338

Loveday, John
The Trumpet Major - Thomas Hardy 2700

Lucca, Pietro
Captain of the Medici - John J. Pugh 5206

Ludendorff, Erich
White Nights, Red Dawn - Frederick Nolan 4634

Ludlow, Captain
The Water Witch - James Fenimore Cooper 1311

Luria, Benny
The Glory - Herman Wouk 6873
The Hope - Herman Wouk 6874

MacArthur, Douglas
1901 - Robert Conroy 1258
Buried Caesars - Stuart M. Kaminsky 3332

MacArthur, John
Storm of Time - Eleanor Dark 1494

MacCallister, Jamie Ian
Talons of Eagles - William W. Johnstone 3268

MacDermott, Reece
Kings Mountain - Florette Henri 2838

MacDonald, Iain
The Island Harp - Jeanne Williams 6779

Macdonald, J.R.L.
Invading Tibet - Mark Frutkin 2239

MacDonald, Niall
Cruel in the Shadow - Lorn MacIntyre 3986

MacDonnell, James
The Limits of Glory: A Novel of Waterloo - James McDonough 4265

MacFell, Charlie
The Cinderpath - Catherine Cookson 1275

Macintosh, Ralph
Squadron Shilling - Arch Whitehouse 6712

Mackaill, Douglas
Dark Sails - Helen Topping Miller 4388

Mackay, George
Journey Proud - Thomasine McGehee 4273

Mackenzie, Alexander Slidell
The Big Family - Vina Delmar 1600
Voyage to the First of December - Henry Carlisle 897

MacKenzie, Billy
1915: A Novel - Roger McDonald 4264

Mackinder, Murdoch
The Regiment - Christopher Nicole 4620

Maclaren, Andrew
The Maclarens - C.L. Skelton 5873

MacLaren, Ian
The Regiment - C.L. Skelton 5874

Maclay, Andrew
Sara Dane - Catherine Gaskin 2316

MacLean, Dugald
The Dark Stranger - Constance Dodge 1664

MacLeod, Junius
Eagle on the Sun - Julia Davis 1527

Maclewin, Rod
Buller's Dreadnought - Richard Hough 3047
Buller's Guns - Richard Hough 3048

Macswain, James John
Lords of the Plains - Max Crawford 1420

Maddox, Juan
Whistling Cat - Robert W. Chambers 984

Magnusson, K.L.
A Few Good Men - William Overgard 4768

Maguire, Kelly
Back to Battle - Max Hennessy 2828
The Dangerous Years - Max Hennessy 2833
The Lion at Sea - Max Hennessy 2834

Mahan, Patrick
1901 - Robert Conroy 1258

Main, Charles
Heaven and Hell - John Jakes 3147
Love and War - John Jakes 3150

Main, Orry
Love and War - John Jakes 3150
North and South - John Jakes 3151

Mainwaring, Edward
Admiral of Fear - Victor Suthren 6126
Captain Monsoon - Victor Suthren 6128
The Golden Galleon - Victor Suthren 6129
Royal Yankee - Victor Suthren 6132

Mallandine, Herbert
Bush War! - William Moore 4447

Mallindine, Eldred
Bayonets in the Sun - William Moore 4446

Maltbie, Harris
To the Honor of the Fleet - Robert H. Pilpel 5002

Malvern, Frances
The Proud Retreat - Clifford Dowdey 1706

Mamigon
Mamigon - Jack Hashian 2772

Manigault, Forney
The Valiant Virginians - James Warner Bellah 427

Manilianus, Minutus Lausus
The Roman - Mika Waltari 6554

Manlove, James
Trumpets Sound No More - F. van Wyck Mason 4163

Mannerheim, Gustaf
Give Me the Daggers - Catherine Gavin 2321

Mannering, Guy
Guy Mannering - Sir Walter Scott 5697

Manning, Charles
The Eye in the Door - Pat Barker 307

Mannus, Optio
Dogheaded Death - Ray Faraday Nelson 4581

Marburg, Aaron
The Marburg Chronicles - Alfred Coppel 1319

Marcellius, Gaius
The Forest House - Marion Zimmer Bradley 625

Marcian
Sign of the Pagan - Don Tracy 6312

Marcus
Children of the Wolf - Alfred Duggan 1762

Marduk
The Hittite - Noel B. Gerson 2373

Marion, Francis
Battle Lanterns - Merrit Parmalee Allen 102
Celia Garth - Gwen Bristow 695
Dawn's Early Light - Elswyth Thane 6215
The Fallon Blood - Reagan O'Neal 4741
A Few Painted Feathers - Stephen Longstreet 3886
The Long March - Jane Barry 358
Othneil Jones - John Adams Leland 3715
Phantom Fortress - Bruce Lancaster 3643
The Red Doe - Drayton Mayrant 4214
The Swamp Fox, Francis Marion - Noel B. Gerson 2383
Sycamore Men - David Taylor 6181

Marius, Caius
The First Man in Rome - Colleen McCullough 4234
The Grass Crown - Colleen McCullough 4236
The Young Caesar - Rex Warner 6567

Marius the Vandal
The Vandal - Richard O'Connor 4687

Markham, Dominic
Angel - Carola Dunn 1790

Marlowe, Jack
The Cavalryman - Harold Sinclair 5861
The Horse Soldiers - Harold Sinclair 5862

Martin, Gilbert
Drums Along the Mohawk - Walter D. Edmonds 1874

Martin, Thomas
When the War Is Over - Stephen Becker 408

Marvin, Silas
Now We Are Free - Marguerite Allis 112

Maskelyne, Edward
Master of Bengal: A Novel of Robert Clive of India - Norman Partington 4821

Mathis, Blount
Where My Love Sleeps - Clifford Dowdey 1710

Maurice, Comte de Saxe
A Day of Battle - Vincent Sheean 5787
The Glory and the Dream - Katharine Dunlap 1789

Maximus
Eagle in the Snow - Wallace Breem 654

Maynard, Robert
Rogue's Holiday - Hamilton Cochran 1141

Maynard, Thomas
The Sword of General Englund - Donald Honig 3023

Mayne, Ripley
Trumpet to Arms - Bruce Lancaster 3647

Mayr, Christian
The Last Innocent Hour - Margot Abbott 8

McAllister
A Rendezvous in Haiti - Stephen Becker 407

McCauley, Jeremy
And One Rode West - Heather Graham 2514

McClellan, George
Banished Children of Eve - Peter Quinn 5227
Beloved Enemy - Al Lacy 3579
The Bloody Ground - Bernard Cornwell 1334
Copperhead - Bernard Cornwell 1335
Freedom - William Safire 5561
Gods and Generals - Jeff Shaara 5765
Lincoln: A Novel - Gore Vidal 6490
A Promise Unbroken - Al Lacy 3582

McCutcheon, Elias
The Raider - Jesse Hill Ford 2164

McGann, Joe
Wind of Destiny - Christopher Nicole 4624

McGraw, Ryan
A Heart Divided - Al Lacy 3580

McGuinness, Rory
The Proud Man - Elizabeth Linington 3800

McIlvaine, James
Loving Heart - Elsie Singmaster 5869

McIvor, Pleasant
The Long Night - Andrew Lytle 3945

McKee, Owen
Eagle Fur - Robert Newton Peck 4884

McLeod, Johnny
The Far Side of Home - Maggie Davis 1536

McMaster, Damon
When the Music Changed - Marie R. Reno 5305

McQueen, Ben
Warriors of the Night - Kerry Newcomb 4594

McQueen, Daniel Pacer Wolf
Ride of the Panther - Kerry Newcomb 4591

McQueen, Jesse Redbow
Ride of the Panther - Kerry Newcomb 4591

McQueen, Kit
Sword of Vengeance - Kerry Newcomb 4593

Meade, George
The Crater - Richard Slotkin 5908
Gettysburg: Crisis of Command - Harry Albright 65
Glory Enough for All: The Battle of the Crater - Duane Philip Schultz 5673
Three Days - Stephen Longstreet 3891

Meadows, James Percival
Hornblower During the Crisis - C.S. Forester 2177

Melgares, Don Facundo
Rio Grande - Jory Sherman 5821

Mellarius
The Centurion - Jan de Hartog 2762

Mendana de Neira, Don Alvaro de
Islands of Unwisdom - Robert Graves 2548

Menenhetet
Ancient Evenings - Norman Mailer 4035

Menshikov, Aleksandr
Katrina - Jeramie Price 5190

Merac, Jean de
The Scarlet Patch - Bruce Lancaster 3645

Merewether, Percival
The East Indiaman - Ellis K. Meacham 4313
For King and Company - Ellis K. Meacham 4314
On the Company's Service - Ellis K. Meacham 4315

Merops
The Trojan Generals Talk: Memoirs of the Greek War - Phillip Parotti 4818

Merrick, James
Exit with Drums - Joseph A. Daley 1457

Merrick, Ronald
The Day of the Scorpion - Paul Scott 5682
A Division of the Spoils - Paul Scott 5683
The Towers of Silence - Paul Scott 5685

Merritt, Johnny
Heart of War - John Masters 4174

Messala
Ben Hur: A Tale of the Christ - Lew Wallace 6536

Messena, Andre
The Proud Canaries - David Johnson 3222

Metcalfe, Palmer
Shiloh - Shelby Foote 2153

Miles, Nelson Appleton
The Day the Sun Died - Dale Van Every 6408
The Winter War - William Wister Haines 2640
Yellowstone Kelly - Peter Bowen 602

Miller, Hacey
The Way to Fort Pillow - James Sherburne 5807

Miller, Jonas
Roanoke Warrior - Carter A. Vaughan 6438

Milroy, Arnold
The General's Lady - Esther Forbes 2156

Minaleff, Kousma
Napoleon and the Cossacks - Peter N. Krassnoff 3551

Miranda, Francisco
Coasts of Folly - Joel Williams 6784

Mitchell, Sam
So Shall They Reap - John Bennett 444

Molke, Kuno von
Court of Honor - Maria Fagyas 1996

Moltke, Helmuth Johannes Ludwig von
Captain Wonder - Donald Thomas 6238
Falkenhorst - Mark Rascovich 5254
White Nights, Red Dawn - Frederick Nolan 4634

Moncada, Juan de
Cradle of the Sun - John Clagett 1083

Monckton, Ules
The Light Infantry Ball - Hamilton Basso 375

Montcalm, Louis Joseph de
Ambush - Donald Clayton Porter 5113
Bloodbrothers - Robert E. Wall 6535
The Bright Battalions - Howard Breslin 664
The Last of the Mohicans - James Fenimore Cooper 1302
Web of Destiny - Muriel Elwood 1939

Montelupo, Michael da
The Gentle Infidel - Lawrence Schoonover 5663

Montfort, Simon de
Falls the Shadow - Sharon Kay Penman 4903
Leopards and Lilies - Alfred Duggan 1769

Montgomery, Ring
Mountain Laurel - Jude Deveraux 1632

Moore, Sir John
His Was the Fire - Showell Styles 6104

Morgan, Daniel
A Few Painted Feathers - Stephen Longstreet 3886
The Long March - Jane Barry 358
The Ragged Ones - Burke Davis 1511
The Rifleman - John Brick 675

Morgan, John Hunt
The Golden Circle - Constance Robertson 5396
In the Season of the Wild Rose - Clara Rising 5347

Mornay, Guy de
All the Golden Gifts - Iola Fuller 2251

Mortimer, Charles
The Sandalwood Fan - Diana Brown 720

Mosby, John Singleton
The Ghost Raider - Ray Hogan 2978
Gray Victory - Robert Skimin 5877
Mosby's Last Ride - Ray Hogan 2979
Night Raider - Ray Hogan 2980
Scarlet Cockerel - Garald Lagard 3584

Moscoso, Luis de
The Golden Eagle - John Edward Jennings 3201

Moultrie, William
The Carolinian - Rafael Sabatini 5547
The Fallon Blood - Reagan O'Neal 4741
The Swamp Fox, Francis Marion - Noel B. Gerson 2383

Mounslic
Soldiers of Fortune - Peter Bourne 595

Mountain, Joe
Remember Santiago - Douglas C. Jones 3280

Mourne, Lex
The Red Doe - Drayton Mayrant 4214

Mundy, Jim
Jim Mundy: A Novel of the American Civil War - Robert H. Fowler 2192

Murat, Joachim
Brumaire - Mark Logan 3864
Far Flies the Eagle - Evelyn Anthony 162
Guillotine - Mark Logan 3865
My Brother Napoleon: The Confessions of Caroline Bonaparte - F.W. Kenyon 3455
The Proud Canaries - David Johnson 3222
The Questing Heart: A Romantic Novel about George Sand - F.W. Kenyon 3458
Valentina - Evelyn Anthony 165

Murfy, Malachi Desmond
Murfy's Men - Gerald Green 2565

Murphy, Rafael
Apache Autumn - Robert Skimin 5875

Murphy, Timothy
The Rifleman - John Brick 675

Murray, Cabot
Yankee Stranger - Elswyth Thane 6217

Murtagh, Colum
The Eye of God - C.L. Grace 2506
The Merchant of Death - C.L. Grace 2508
A Shrine of Murders - C.L. Grace 2509

Nabu
Babylon - Anthony Esler 1959

Napier, Gavin
The Bonnet Laird's Daughter - Barbara Annandale 154

Napier, Robert Cornelis
Mandarin Gold - James Leasor 3700

When the Emperor Dies - Mason McCann Smith 5926

Napoleon I
Napoleon Symphony - Anthony Burgess 780

Nash, Charles "Buck"
A Wilful Woman - Michael Talbot 6156

Nason, Steven
Arundel - Kenneth Roberts 5383
Rabble in Arms - Kenneth Roberts 5390

Nellis, Hendrick
The Life and Times of Captain N. - Douglas Glover 2436

Nelson, Horatio
1805 - Richard Woodman 6857
Angelica - Samuel A. Schreiner Jr. 5671
The Blacksmith's Daughter - Joanna Dessau 1625
The Bomb Vessel - Richard Woodman 6860
Bride of Glory - Bradda Field 2078
Brumaire - Mark Logan 3864
Caribbean - James A. Michener 4365
Darken Ship - Nicholas Monsarrat 4431
Decision at Trafalgar - Richard Woodman 6861
Emma - F.W. Kenyon 3448
The English Captain - Simon White 6700
A Game for Empires - Pearl Frye 2243
Guillotine - Mark Logan 3865
A King's Commander - Dewey Lambdin 3613
The King's Commission - Dewey Lambdin 3614
Lord Elgin's Lady - Theodore Vrettos 6514
Loving Emma - Nigel Foxell 2197
Mister Christian - William Kinsolving 3502
The Nelson Touch - Paul Lewis 3759
Ramage - Dudley Pope 5097
Ramage at Trafalgar - Dudley Pope 5102
Return to Treasure Island - Denis Judd 3318
The Scalpel and the Sword - Dell Shannon 5774
The Sea Officer - Showell Styles 6105
Shadow of a Lady - Jane Aiken Hodge 2971
Sir William - David Stacton 5977
The Sleeping Sword: A Biographical Novel - Pearl Frye 2244
This Other Eden - Marilyn Harris 2733
The Volcano Lover - Susan Sontag 5946

Nevins, Hal
Something Gleamed - Theda Kenyon 3463

Ney, Michel
The Flight of the Eagle - Donald Thomas 6239
The Limits of Glory: A Novel of Waterloo - James McDonough 4265
Seven Men of Gascony - R.F. Delderfield 1589
The Thousand Fires - Anne Powers 5155
Valentina - Evelyn Anthony 165
Waterloo - Frederic E. Smith 5920

Nichol, Beasley
Home to Tennessee - Alfred Leland Crabb 1400
Lodging at the Saint Cloud - Alfred Leland Crabb 1403
Mockingbird Sang at Chickamauga - Alfred Leland Crabb 1404

Nicholson, John
Follow the Drum - James Leasor 3699

Noble Talent
Spring Moon: A Novel of China - Bette Bao Lord 3897

Norcrosse, Del
Soul of Abe Lincoln - Bernie Babcock 251

O'Connor, Kevin
The Bright Battalions - Howard Breslin 664

O'Corboy, Edward
Broadsides - Robert Welter Daly 1459

Octavian
Throne of Isis - Judith Tarr 6170

Octavianus, Caius Julius Caesar
Three's Company - Alfred Duggan   1774

Octavius, Gaius
The Alexandrian - Martha Rofheart   5425

Ogilivie, Ian
Drums Along the Khyber - Duncan MacNeil   4013

Ogilvie, Ian
By Command of the Viceroy - Duncan MacNeil   4010
Charge of Cowardice - Duncan MacNeil   4011

Ogilvie, James
By Command of the Viceroy - Duncan MacNeil   4010
Charge of Cowardice - Duncan MacNeil   4011
Cunningham's Revenge - Duncan MacNeil   4012
Drums Along the Khyber - Duncan MacNeil   4013
The Gates of Kunara - Duncan MacNeil   4014
Lieutenant of the Line - Duncan MacNeil   4015
The Mullah From Kashmir - Duncan MacNeil   4016
The Red Daniel - Duncan MacNeil   4017
The Restless Frontier - Duncan MacNeil   4018
Sadhu on the Mountain Peak - Duncan
   MacNeil   4019
Subaltern's Choice - Duncan MacNeil   4020
The Train at Bundarbar - Duncan MacNeil   4021
Wolf in the Fold - Duncan MacNeil   4022

Oglethorpe, James Edward
Creek Mary's Blood - Dee Brown   712
Jarrett's Jade - Frank Yerby   6923
Rascal's Heaven - F. van Wyck Mason   4157
Summer Thunder - Willie Snow Ethridge   1982

O'Hara, James
The King's Orchard - Agnes Sligh Turnbull   6363

O'Hara, Kimball
The Last Victory - T.N. Murari   4519

Olbromski, Raphael
Ashes - Stefan Zeromski   6960

Old Bear Trap
The Mohawk Ladder - Noel B. Gerson   2377

Olin, Darius
D'ri and I - Irving A. Bacheller   257

O'Malley, Charles
Charles O'Malley - Charles James Lever   3731

O'Neill, Carlos
The Gun - C.S. Forester   2174

O'Neill, Shane
The Proud Man - Elizabeth Linington   3800

Orellana, Francisco de
*A Crossbowman's Story of the First Exploration of the
   Amazon* - George Millar   4379

Orozco, Jesus
The Bear Flag: A Novel of the Birth of California -
   Cecelia Holland   2983

Osborne, George
Vanity Fair - William Makepeace Thackeray   6213

Osborne, Richard
Mary of Carisbrooke - Margaret Campbell
   Barnes   327

Owen, Jed
Where the River Runs - Richard S. Wheeler   6664

Owen, Wilfred
The Ghost Road - Pat Barker   308

Ozeroff, Nikolai
The Brotherhood of the Red Poppy - Henri
   Troyat   6353

Packenham
The Hessian - Howard Fast   2033

Page, Dick
Mr. Arnold - Francis Lynde   3935

Page, Richard
A Heart Divided - Al Lacy   3580

Paige, Bennett
Storm the Last Rampart - David Taylor   6180

Painter, Christian
Ashes in the Wilderness - William Greenough
   Schofield   5649

Palafox, Antonio
Mexico - James A. Michener   4372

Palafox, Peter
The Golden Ocean - Patrick O'Brian   4665

Pancoast, Calvin
Green Rose of Furley - Helen C. Barney   334

Pardi, Angelo
The Horseman on the Roof - Jean Giono   2424
The Straw Man - Jean Giono   2425

Partridge, Joseph
Richard Lamb - Richard S. Wheeler   6662

Pasha, Jemel
Behold the Fire - Michael Blankfort   541

Pasternak, Sam
The Glory - Herman Wouk   6873
The Hope - Herman Wouk   6874

Patterson, Sergeant
Prisoner of Twilight - Don Robertson   5400

Patterson, G.K.
Squadron Forty-Four - Arch Whitehouse   6711

Patterson, Morgan
The Captives - Don Wright   6878
The Woodsman - Don Wright   6880

Patterson, Rufus
The Three Days - Don Robertson   5402

Patton, George S.
Pancho And Black Jack - Fred Bean   398
Tom Mix and Pancho Villa - Clifford Irving   3113

Paulinus, Suetonius
Canis the Warrior - James Sinclair   5864

Paxton, Oliver
War Story: A Novel - Derek Robinson   5404

Pay, Allan Eben
Elkhorn Tavern - Douglas C. Jones   3278

Pay, Eben
Remember Santiago - Douglas C. Jones   3280

Peabody, Joshua
The Captain From Connecticut - C.S. Forester   2171

Pears, Gilbert Brice
In Gallant Company - Alexander Kent   3433

Pearse, Fingal
This Willing Passion - Patricia Cloud   1132

Peattie, Joshua
The Mohawk Ladder - Noel B. Gerson   2377

Pelham-Martin, Commodore
Enemy in Sight! - Alexander Kent   3429

Pelham-Martyn, Ashton
The Far Pavilions - M.M. Kaye   3376

Pellew, Edward
The Sea Officer - Showell Styles   6105

Pembroke, Ross
Phantom Fortress - Bruce Lancaster   3643

Pena, Joe
Stallion Gate - Martin Cruz Smith   5924

Pendragon, John Hawkdale
Pendragon: Late of Prince Albert's Own - Robert
   Trevelyan   6337
Pendragon. . .The Montenegran Plot - Robert
   Trevelyan   6338

Penhaligon, Jethro Cockerill
Clear for Action! - Simon White   6699
The English Captain - Simon White   6700

Pepperell, William
The Highwayman - Noel B. Gerson   2372

Perdikkas
Funeral Games - Mary Renault   5297

Pericles
Creation - Gore Vidal   6486

Perron, Guy
A Division of the Spoils - Paul Scott   5683

Perry, Matthew
The Big Family - Vina Delmar   1600

Perry, Oliver Hazard
The Court Martial of Commodore Perry - James A.
   Rhodes   5307
D'ri and I - Irving A. Bacheller   257
The Fleet in the Forest - Carl Daniel Lane   3654
My Blood and My Treasure - Mary Schumann   5674

Pershing, John J.
Chihuahua 1916 - Otis Carney   903
Fenwick Travers and the Years of Empire - Raymond
   M. Saunders   5614
A Good Day to Die - Thomas Wakefield
   Blackburn   525
Over There - Thomas Fleming   2130
Pancho And Black Jack - Fred Bean   398

Peters, George
The River and the Wilderness - Don Robertson   5401

Pettengill, Caleb
Caleb Pettengill U.S.N. - George Fielding Eliot   1912

Pettigrew, Scott
The Raiders: A Novel of the Civil War at Sea -
   Willard Wallace   6541

Peyton, Carr
Shod with Flame - Helen Topping Miller   4393

Phillips, Harry
Flight From Bucharest - R.T. Stevens   6000

Pickett, George Edward
Gray Victory - Robert Skimin   5877
The Killer Angels - Michael Shaara   5766

Pierce, Frederick
Blood Red Roses - Elizabeth Boatwright Coker   1163

Pinkerton, Allan
Secret Service Operator 13 - Robert W.
   Chambers   982
The Titans - John Jakes   3154

Pitler, Jake
Night March - Bruce Lancaster   3641

Pittakos
My Name Is Sappho - Martha Rofheart   5429

Pizarro, Francisco
Don Pedro and the Devil - Edgar Maas   3948
The Golden Eagle - John Edward Jennings   3201
*The Sword and the Sun: The Story of the Spanish Civil
   Wars in Peru* - Gerald Green   2566

Pizarro, Gonzalo
I, the King - Howard Clewes   1112

Pizarro, Hernando
Don Pedro and the Devil - Edgar Maas   3948

Pleasants, Henry
Glory Enough for All: The Battle of the Crater -
   Duane Philip Schultz   5673

Poldark, Jeremy
The Twisted Sword - Winston Graham   2531

Polydamas
The Trojan Generals Talk: Memoirs of the Greek War
   - Phillip Parotti   4818

Pomeroy, Ezra
Now We Are Free - Marguerite Allis   112

Pompey
Caesar's Women - Colleen McCullough   4233

The City of Libertines - W.G. Hardy 2702
Fortune's Favorite - Colleen McCullough 4235
Freedom, Farewell - Phyllis Bentley 461
The Pirate From Rome - John V.D. Southworth 5952
The Young Caesar - Rex Warner 6567

Pope, John
Unto This Hour - Tom Wicker 6733

Porteous, John
The Heart of Midlothian - Sir Walter Scott 5698

Porter, David
The Sea Panther: A Novel about the Commander of the U.S.S. Constitution - Philip Vail 6397

Porter, Thomas
Sailor Named Jones - Harvey Haislip 2643

Porthos
The Three Musketeers - Alexandre Dumas 1782

Portola, Gaspar de
This Promised Land - Robert Easton 1824

Potter, Israel
Israel Potter - Herman Melville 4334

Potter, Thomas
The Prize Master - Harvey Haislip 2642
Sea Road to Yorktown - Harvey Haislip 2644

Powell, Lewis
A Court of Owls - Richard Adicks 37

Pray, Job
Lionel Lincoln; or, The Leaguer of Boston - James Fenimore Cooper 1303

Price, Oliver
Hiwassee: A Novel of the Civil War - Charles F. Price 5176

Price, Webb
San Antone - V.J. Banis 288

Prien, Major Ruben
From Time to Time - Jack Finney 2092
Time and Again - Jack Finney 2093

Prince, Alexander
The Restless Border - Richard Pearce 4873

Prior, Billy
The Eye in the Door - Pat Barker 307
The Ghost Road - Pat Barker 308
Regeneration - Pat Barker 309

Priscus, Lucius
Caesar of the Narrow Seas - John Gloag 2433

Prohaska, Otto
The Emperor's Coloured Coat - John Biggins 491
A Sailor of Austria - John Biggins 492
The Two-Headed Eagle - John Biggins 493

Prouty, Richard
Legacy - Robert Vaughan 6448

Pryde, Carrington
Weathercock - Constance Dodge 1668

Ptolemy
The Conqueror: A Novel of Alexander the Great - Edison Marshall 4104
Funeral Games - Mary Renault 5297
The Golden Lyre - Noel B. Gerson 2371

Pulaski, Casimir
Monmouth - Charles Bracelen Flood 2144

Putnam, Rufus
Now We Are Free - Marguerite Allis 112

Quantrill, William Clarke
Belle Starr - Deborah Camp 870
Bound Girl - Everett Webber 6591
Confessions of Johnny Ringo - Geoff Aggeler 40
Major Stepton's War - Matthew Vaughan 6445
Sons of Fire - Max McCoy 4227

Quill, Major
Yellowhorse - Dee Brown 715

Quinn, Anthony
The Drums of April - Charles Mergendahl 4340

Quinney, Nicholas Dicken
The Bright Blue Sky - Max Hennessy 2830
The Challenging Heights - Max Hennessy 2831
Once More the Hawks - Max Hennessy 2836

Quintus
Empire of the Eagle - Andre Norton 4649

Quintus, Marcellus
If I Forget Thee - Brenda Lesley Segal 5720

Ramage, Nicholas
Drumbeat - Dudley Pope 5094
Governor Ramage, R.N. - Dudley Pope 5096
Ramage - Dudley Pope 5097
Ramage and the Dido - Dudley Pope 5098
Ramage and the Guillotine - Dudley Pope 5099
Ramage and the Rebels - Dudley Pope 5100
Ramage and the Saracens - Dudley Pope 5101
Ramage at Trafalgar - Dudley Pope 5102
The Ramage Touch - Dudley Pope 5103
Ramage's Devil - Dudley Pope 5104
Ramage's Diamond - Dudley Pope 5105
Ramage's Mutiny - Dudley Pope 5106
Ramage's Prize - Dudley Pope 5107
Ramage's Signal - Dudley Pope 5108
Ramage's Trial - Dudley Pope 5109
The Triton Brig - Dudley Pope 5110

Ramsay, Colin
Strathgallant - Laura Black 523

Ramsay, James
Simplicissimus the Vagabond - J.J.C. Grimmelshausen 2594

Randall, Alex
Shadow of the Moon - M.M. Kaye 3377

Randall, Warren
Ask My Brother - Constance Wagner 6518

Ranklin, Matthew
Spy's Honour - Gavin Lyall 3929

Rathbone, Henry
Henry and Clara - Thomas Mallon 4042

Rawley, Charles
Killdeer Mountain - Dee Brown 713

Rawlings, Mark
The Bridge of a Hundred Dragons - Emma Drummond 1723

Rawlins, John Aaron
Aide to Glory - Louis Devon 1635

Reagan, John
The Proud Retreat - Clifford Dowdey 1706

Reardon, John
Valley of the Shadow - Charles Marquis Warren 6570

Reed, Daniel
Cannon's Call - Adam Rutledge 5537
Life and Liberty - Adam Rutledge 5538
Rebel Guns - Adam Rutledge 5539
Stars and Stripes - Adam Rutledge 5541

Reed, Quincy
Rebel Guns - Adam Rutledge 5539

Reno, Marcus
A Mighty Afternoon - Charles K. Mills 4407

Revere, Paul
East to Bagaduce - Willard Wallace 6539

Rex
An Error of Judgment - Stanley Wolpert 6845

Reynolds, Joseph T.
Blood Song - Terry C. Johnston 3243

Richards, Cameron
Diamond Head - Houston Branch 647

Richthofen, Manfred von
The Bloody Red Baron - Kim Newman 4596

Ridgeley
Wintercombe - Pamela Belle 435

Riebeck, Jean
Before the Glory Ended - Ursula Zilinsky 6963

Robertson, James
Wild Horizon - F. van Wyck Mason 4164

Robinson, Horseshoe
Horseshoe Robinson, a Tale of the Tory Ascendancy - John P. Kennedy 3418

Robinson, John Cedric
The Fiercest Heart - Stuart Cloete 1122

Roche-Bourbon, Rigaud de la
Admiral of Fear - Victor Suthren 6126
Captain Monsoon - Victor Suthren 6128
The Golden Galleon - Victor Suthren 6129
Royal Yankee - Victor Suthren 6132

Rogers, Robert
Northwest Passage - Kenneth Roberts 5388

Rokesby, Nicholas
Envoy From Elizabeth - Pamela Bennetts 451

Rokossovsky, Konstantin
Journey into Fire - Patricia Wright 6882

Rommel, Erwin
Murder in the Chateau - Elliott Roosevelt 5447
Rommel and the Rebel - Lawrence Wells 6622

Roosevelt, Theodore
Fenwick Travers and the Years of Empire - Raymond M. Saunders 5614
Outlaw - Warren Kiefer 3482
Remember Santiago - Douglas C. Jones 3280
The Rough Rider - Gilbert Morris 4468
San Juan Hill - Will Henry 2848
The Single Star - Walter Adolphe Roberts 5394

Rosecrans, William S.
Mockingbird Sang at Chickamauga - Alfred Leland Crabb 1404
A Promise Unbroken - Al Lacy 3582

Rosenzweig, Adam
Wilderness: A Tale of the Civil War - Robert Penn Warren 6573

Ross, Edward
The Alpha Raid - Alan Scholefield 5651

Rossiter, Deverell
Cressida - Clare Darcy 1485

Rossiter, Gideon
Time's Fool - Patricia Veryan 6479

Rostov, Captain
The Cowboy and the Cossack - Claire Huffaker 3071

Rostov, Anton
The Russian River - Gary McCarthy 4224

Roujay, Bertrand de
The Free Frenchman - Piers Paul Read 5277

Rowland, Guy
Heart of War - John Masters 4174

Rowland, Quentin
By the Green of the Spring - John Masters 4171
Heart of War - John Masters 4174
Now, God Be Thanked - John Masters 4177

Royall, Philip
The Impudent Rifle - Richard Pearce 4872

Sabinus, Flavius
The Flames of Rome - Paul L. Maier 4033

Sabotai
Until the Sun Falls - Cecelia Holland 2998

Safford, Joel
That Bennington Mob - Henry Barnard Safford 5558

Saint-Christophe, Philippe de
The Bride of the Wilderness - Charles McCarry 4220

St. John, John
Before the Wind - Lloyd M. Moxon 4506

Saltonstall, Dudley
East to Bagaduce - Willard Wallace 6539

Samsonov, Aleksandr Vasilyevich
August 1914 - Alexander Solzhenitsyn 5942

Sandeman, Charles
The Leopard and the Cliff - Wallace Breem 655

Sandhurst, Colonel
Colonel Sandhurst to the Rescue - Marion
    Chesney 1021
Lady Fortescue Steps Out - Marion Chesney 1035
Miss Tonks Turns to Crime - Marion Chesney 1041

Santa Anna, Antonio Lopez de
All the Brave Rifles - Clarke Venable 6450
*The Bugles Are Silent: A Novel of the Texas
    Revolution* - John R. Knaggs 3513
The Eagle and the Raven - James A. Michener 4369
*Empire of Bones: A Novel of Sam Houston and the
    Texas Revolution* - Jeff Long 3868
The Furies - John Jakes 3146
The Road to San Jacinto - Leonard L.
    Foreman 2167
Sam Houston - Noel B. Gerson 2380
The Sam Houston Story - Dean Owen 4770
Texas - James A. Michener 4375
The Wine of San Lorenzo - Herbert Gorman 2493

Santhonax, Edouard
1805 - Richard Woodman 6857
Baltic Mission - Richard Woodman 6859
Decision at Trafalgar - Richard Woodman 6861

Saragosa, Elizandra
Sons of Texas - Tom Early 1822

Sartoris, Colonel John
The Unvanquished - William Faulkner 2050

Sassoon, Siegfried
The Eye in the Door - Pat Barker 307
Regeneration - Pat Barker 309

Saumarez, James
Touch and Go - C. Northcote Parkinson 4815

Savage, Orne
The Carolinians - Jane Barry 357

Savage, Robin
The Lotus and the Wind - John Masters 4175

Savage, Rodney
Nightrunners of Bengal - John Masters 4176

Sawling, Dorrit C.
The Southern Blade - Nelson Wolford 6844

Saxon, Decimus
Micah Clarke - Sir Arthur Conan Doyle 1715

Schlieffen, Alfred von
1901 - Robert Conroy 1258

Schwieger, Walther
Lusitania - David Butler 819

Scipio Africanus, Publius Cornelius
The Scarlet Beast - Francis Gerard 2357
Swords Against Carthage - Friedrich Donauer 1689

Scott, James
Micah Clarke - Sir Arthur Conan Doyle 1715

Scott, Joel
For Time and All Eternity - Paul Bailey 268

Scott-Paget, Lieutenant
Mutiny - Frank Tilsley 6280

Scott, Quincy
The Amulet - Hal Borland 582

Scott, Winfield
1812 - David Nevin 4586
My Dear Cousin - Peggy Hoffmann 2977
Nevada! - Dana Fuller Ross 5481
Oregon! - Dana Fuller Ross 5484
The Wine of San Lorenzo - Herbert Gorman 2493

Seabury, Jonathan
The Falling Hills - Perry Lentz 3720

Sears, Tobias
Band of Angels - Robert Penn Warren 6572

Sejanus, Lucius Aelius
I, Claudius - Robert Graves 2547
No King but Caesar - Anne Powers 5151
Pontius Pilate: A Biographical Novel - Paul L.
    Maier 4034
Tiberius: The Memoirs of the Emperor - Allan
    Massie 4169

Semenoff, Grigori
Fifteen Flags - Richard Lynden Hardman 2686

Sentell, Edward Malcolm
And Wait for the Night - John William
    Corrington 1352

Severus
The Way - J.M. Hartley 2761

Sevier, John
Slow Dies the Thunder - Helen Topping Miller 4395
Wild Horizon - F. van Wyck Mason 4164

Seymour, Samuel
Proud New Flags - F. van Wyck Mason 4156

Shafter, Kern
Bugles in the Afternoon - Ernest Haycox 2788

Shafter, William R.
Remember Santiago - Douglas C. Jones 3280

Shan-Teh Tang
The Warlord - Malcolm Bosse 589

Shannon, Emmett
A Daughter of Liberty - Allan Cole 1196

Shannon, Slone
The Nationalists - William Stuart Long 3876

Sharpe, Richard
Sharpe's Battle - Bernard Cornwell 1338
Sharpe's Company - Bernard Cornwell 1339
Sharpe's Devil - Bernard Cornwell 1340
Sharpe's Eagle - Bernard Cornwell 1341
Sharpe's Enemy - Bernard Cornwell 1342
Sharpe's Gold - Bernard Cornwell 1343
Sharpe's Honour - Bernard Cornwell 1344
Sharpe's Regiment - Bernard Cornwell 1345
Sharpe's Revenge - Bernard Cornwell 1346
Sharpe's Rifles - Bernard Cornwell 1347
Sharpe's Siege - Bernard Cornwell 1348
Sharpe's Sword - Bernard Cornwell 1349
Waterloo - Bernard Cornwell 1350

Shatagin, Ivan
Elena - Judith Egan 1893

Shattuck, Phineas
Dark Thicket - Elmer Kelton 3402

Shaw, Jeremy
Day of Battle - Frederic F. Van de Water 6402

Shelby, Blaine
The Roads to Guadalupe - Robert Lewis
    Taylor 6190

Shelby, Joseph Orville
Angel with Spurs - Paul I. Wellman 6613
West of Appomattox - Harley Duncan 1785

Shelby, Sam
The Roads to Guadalupe - Robert Lewis
    Taylor 6190

Sheremetiev, Nikolai
Devoted Friends - Joe Poyer 5161

Sheridan, Alexander
Massacre at Cawnpore - Vivian Stuart 6089

Sheridan, Philip H.
Action at Aquila - Hervey Allen 97
Banner at Shenandoah - Bruce Catton 963
Blood Song - Terry C. Johnston 3243
The Court-Martial of George Armstrong Custer -
    Douglas C. Jones 3276
Elkhorn Tavern - Douglas C. Jones 3278
*The Last Stand: A Novel about George Armstrong
    Custer and the Indians of the Plains* - Edwin P.
    Hoyt 3061
Long Winter Gone - Terry C. Johnston 3252
Roll, Shenandoah - Bruce Lancaster 3644
Roman - Douglas C. Jones 3281
Shadow on the Valley - Kirk Mitchell 4414
Shaggy Legion - Hal George Evarts 1986
Trumpet on the Land - Terry C. Johnston 3260

Sherman, Joseph
Saigon - Anthony Grey 2588

Sherman, Philip
Grant's War - Ted Jones 3297

Sherman, William Tecumseh
The Bride of Texas - Josef Skvorecky 5880
The Court-Martial of George Armstrong Custer -
    Douglas C. Jones 3276
The Crisis - Winston Churchill 1079
Grant's War - Ted Jones 3297
Jubilee - John Brick 672
*The Last Stand: A Novel about George Armstrong
    Custer and the Indians of the Plains* - Edwin P.
    Hoyt 3061
The Last Warpath - Will Henry 2844
Long Day at Shiloh - Don Bannister 294
The Shadow Riders - Terry C. Johnston 3257
Sherman's March - Cynthia Bass 373
Shiloh - Shelby Foote 2153
So Red the Rose - Stark Young 6944
Ulysses: A Biographical Novel - Robert Skimin 5878
Untold Glory - Cothburn O'Neal 4739
*Woman with a Sword: The Biographical Novel of
    Anna Ella Carroll of Maryland* - Hollister
    Noble 4632

Sherwood, Johnny
Freedom's Banner - Teresa Crane 1415

Silva, Flavius
The Antagonists - Ernest K. Gann 2276
The Triumph - Ernest K. Gann 2280

Sims, Rafael
Ironclads: Man-of-War - Larry D. Names 4554

Skshetuski, Pan Yan
With Fire and Sword - Henryk Sienkiewicz 5850

Sky-Eyes
Return to the River - Don Coldsmith 1184

Slade, Captain
First Lieutenant - Kenneth Maynard 4208

Slate, Lingston
The Devil Gun - William Syers 6148

Slocum, Martin
The River and the Wilderness - Don Robertson 5401

Smith, Harry
The Spanish Bride - Georgette Heyer 2902

Smith, John
Soldiers of Fortune - Peter Bourne 595

Sneferu
Children of the Lion - Peter Danielson 1464

Soames, Horatio
Wolf in the Fold - Duncan MacNeil 4022

Sobieski, Thaddeus
Thaddeus of Warsaw - Jane Porter 5136

Solassier, Claude
French Dragoon - Roger Rudigoz 5523

Somers, Martin
The Dark Rose - Maurice Walsh 6549

Somerset, Fitzroy
Flashman at the Charge - George MacDonald
 Fraser 2209
Hazard's Command - Vivian Stuart 6088

Somerset, Pembroke
Thaddeus of Warsaw - Jane Porter 5136

Southampton, James
The Captives - Don Wright 6878

Spargo, Peter
Yorktown - Burke Davis 1513

Speigner, Max
Rommel and the Rebel - Lawrence Wells 6622

Spencer, Hugh
Scoundrels' Brigade - Carter A. Vaughan 6439

Spencer, Philip
Voyage to the First of December - Henry
 Carlisle 897

Spurlock, Vern
Fort Worth - Leonard Sanders 5588

Stachel, Bruno
The Blood Order - Jack D. Hunter 3084
The Blue Max - Jack D. Hunter 3085

Stafford, James
Annapolis - William Martin 4137

Stafford, Maury
The Long Roll - Mary Johnston 3236

Stafford, Norman
The Lieutenant's Lady - Bess Streeter Aldrich 70

Stahl, Freddie
The Moon-Eyed Appaloosa - Bill Gulick 2617

Standish, Miles
The Land Is Bright - Noel B. Gerson 2376
Thanksgiving - Terry Coleman 1207

Stanhope, Quentin
Irene at Large - Carole Nelson Douglas 1700

Stanton, Jethro
Drums of War - Roy Clews 1114

Staple, John
The Toll-Gate - Georgette Heyer 2907

Stapleton, Rawdon
The Spoils of War - Thomas Fleming 2131

Starbuck, Nate
Battle Flag - Bernard Cornwell 1333
The Bloody Ground - Bernard Cornwell 1334
Copperhead - Bernard Cornwell 1335
Rebel - Bernard Cornwell 1336

Stark, John
The Shadow and the Glory - John Edward
 Jennings 3207

Stauffenberg, Claus von
The Very Rich Hours of Count von Stauffenberg - Paul
 West 6637

Stavenham, John
That Sweet and Savage Land - Emma
 Drummond 1728

Stedman, Kirk
Night March - Bruce Lancaster 3641

Steele, Web
A Promise Unbroken - Al Lacy 3582

Stepton, Gervase
Major Stepton's War - Matthew Vaughan 6445

Steuben, Friedrich von
Conceived in Liberty - Howard Fast 2029
Eagle in the Sky - F. van Wyck Mason 4149

Farewell to Valley Forge - David Taylor 6178
Monmouth - Charles Bracelen Flood 2144
Storm the Last Rampart - David Taylor 6180
The Strong Men - John Brick 677
Valley Forge - MacKinlay Kantor 3364

Stevens, Morrison
And Wait for the Night - John William
 Corrington 1352

Stevenson, Geoffrey
Kimberley - Colin Burke 784

Stewart, Ebenezer
The Peculiar People - Jan de Hartog 2764

Stockton, Robert Field
The Bear Flag: A Novel of the Birth of California -
 Cecelia Holland 2983

Storm, Jayce
Defiant Hearts - Janelle Taylor 6185

Stowe, Frederick William
The Cup Trembling - Karl Brown 723

Stowell, Captain
The Gray Captain - Jere Hungerford
 Wheelwright 6669

Strong, Leon Marshall
The Three Days - Don Robertson 5402

Stuart, James
Temple Bells - Marjorie McEvoy 4271

Stuart, James Ewell Brown
The Court Martial of Robert E. Lee - Douglas
 Savage 5617
Farewell, My General - Shirley Seifert 5726
Gettysburg - Stephen Longstreet 3887
Gettysburg: Crisis of Command - Harry Albright 65
The Ghost Raider - Ray Hogan 2978
Gods and Generals - Jeff Shaara 5765
God's Angry Man - Leonard Ehrlich 1898
Gray Victory - Robert Skimin 5877
Major Stepton's War - Matthew Vaughan 6445
Secret Service Operator 13 - Robert W.
 Chambers 982
*The Stonewall Brigade: A Novel of the American Civil
 War* - Frank G. Slaughter 5902
The Titans - John Jakes 3154
Traveller - Richard Adams 27

Stuart, Jamie
The Proud and the Free - Howard Fast 2042

Stuart, Jeb
Soldier of the Queen - Max Hennessy 2837

Subotai
Orlok - Don Dandrea 1461

Sulla, Lucius Cornelius
Fortune's Favorite - Colleen McCullough 4235
The Grass Crown - Colleen McCullough 4236
A Pillar of Iron - Taylor Caldwell 861
Roman Blood - Steven Saylor 5626
*Sword of Pleasure: Being the Memoirs of the Most
 Illustrious Lucius Cornelius Sulla* - Peter
 Green 2571

Sullivan, John
Murfy's Men - Gerald Green 2565
The Wilderness War - Allen W. Eckert 1848

Sutherland, Joseph
A Token of Jewels - Diane Cory 1353

Swann, Alexander
Give Us This Day - R.F. Delderfield 1586

Swardovsky, Alexander
The Gathering Wolves - Elizabeth Darrell 1496

Tacs
The Death of Attila - Cecelia Holland 2986

Talbot, Victor
Bury Him Among Kings - Elleston Trevor 6341

Talleyman, Thomas
Talleyman - John James 3161

Tallmadge, Benjamin
The Culper Spy Ring - Lynn Groh 2596
Major Andre - Anthony Bailey 265
Poor Richard's Game - G.J.A. O'Toole 4766
Scoundrels' Brigade - Carter A. Vaughan 6439
The Secret Road - Bruce Lancaster 3646
Stars and Stripes - Adam Rutledge 5541
Tory Tavern - Henry Barnard Safford 5559
The Traitor - Dan Sherman 5814
The Yankee Rascals - Carter A. Vaughan 6444

Tanner, Tom
The Second Face of Valor - Ray Grant Toepfer 6288

Tanus
River God - Wilbur Smith 5928

Tarleton, Banastre
Cato's War - Guy Wheeler 6655
The Fallon Blood - Reagan O'Neal 4741
Raleigh's Eden - Inglis Fletcher 2137

Taylor, Zachary
Comes an Echo on the Breeze - Edward J.
 Ryan 5542
The Stuart Women - Matt Braun 652
*There Was a Season: A Biographical Novel of
 Jefferson Davis* - Theodore Olsen 4730
Twilight of Empire - Allen W. Eckert 1846

Templeton, Cedric
Young Vargas Lewis - Robert Brainard Pearsall 4874

Teneius, Rufus
The Soldier and the Sage: A Novel about Akiba -
 Richard G. Hubler 3065

Terry, Alfred H.
A Mighty Afternoon - Charles K. Mills 4407

Texas Chile
Gettysburg - Stephen Longstreet 3887

Themistocles
Farewell Great King: A Novel of Ancient Greece - Jill
 Paton Walsh 4829

Thornton, Simon
The Fifth Conspiracy - Ted Jones 3296
Hard Road to Gettysburg - Ted Jones 3298

Thrasymedes
The Greek Generals Talk: Memoirs of the Trojan War
 - Phillip Parotti 4817

Tiberius
Tiberius: The Memoirs of the Emperor - Allan
 Massie 4169

Ticquet, Jean
Seven Men of Gascony - R.F. Delderfield 1589

Tidwell, Jasper
Prisoner of Twilight - Don Robertson 5400

Tigellinus
The Conspiracy - John Hersey 2870

Tilt, Rodney Ajax
Trumpets Sound No More - F. van Wyck
 Mason 4163

Timoleon
A Choice of Murder - Peter Vansittart 6429

Tipton, Omar
By Antietam Creek - Don Robertson 5398

Tirpitz, Alfred von
1901 - Robert Conroy 1258
Lusitania - David Butler 819

Todd, Daniel
Look Away, Beulah Land - Lonnie Coleman 1204

Todd, John James
The New Confessions - William Boyd 617

Tolbecken, Jared
Tolbecken - Samuel Shellabarger 5798

Tollemache, Charles Auguste
The Flight of the Eagle - Donald Thomas 6239

Tom
The Barrier - Robin Maugham 4195

Toupelik, Cyril
The Bride of Texas - Josef Skvorecky 5880

Towne, Langdon
Northwest Passage - Kenneth Roberts 5388

Townsend, Charles
Trumpets at Dawn - Cyril Harris 2719

Townsend, Grahame
The Casket Crew - Arch Whitehouse 6709

Trajan
Gold for the Caesars - Florence A. Seward 5759

Travers, Fenwick
Fenwick Travers and the Forbidden Kingdom - Raymond M. Saunders 5612
Fenwick Travers and the Panama Canal - Raymond M. Saunders 5613
Fenwick Travers and the Years of Empire - Raymond M. Saunders 5614

Travis, William Barret
The Bugles Are Silent: A Novel of the Texas Revolution - John R. Knaggs 3513

Trent, Stephen
Gentleman Ranker - John Edward Jennings 3200

Trentham, Guy
As the Crow Flies - Jeffrey Archer 183

Tripp, Preston
Whisper of the Wolf - Terry C. Johnston 3261

Trollope, Henry
The Fireship - C. Northcote Parkinson 4811

Tros of Samothrace
Purple Pirate - Talbot Mundy 4514
Tros of Samothrace - Talbot Mundy 4515

Trowbridge, Little Ax
Captain Little Ax - James H. Street 6077

Truscott, John
Conspiracy of Knaves - Dee Brown 711

Truslow, Thomas
Copperhead - Bernard Cornwell 1335

Tucker, Adam
Exit with Drums - Joseph A. Daley 1457

Tucker, Birch
In My Father's House - Bodie Thoene 6222

Turnbull, John
Rags of Glory - Stuart Cloete 1126

Turndale, Thomas
The Canebrake Men - Cameron Judd 3313

Tuthill, Frederick C.
The Dice of God - Hoffman Birney 507

Tweedman, Gavin
Attack the Lusitania! - Raymond Hitchcock 2956

Tydier, Owen
Crown in Candlelight - Rosemary Hawley Jarman 3166

Tyler, Wade
The Quicksilver Pool - Phyllis A. Whitney 6716

Tynedale, Geoffrey
Red Cloak Flying - Margaret Widdemer 6737

Ulenspiegel, Tyl
The Legend of Tyl Ulenspiegel - Charles Theodore Henri De Coster 1558

Valdes, Don Pedro de
Sea of Lentils - Antonio Benitez-Rojo 443

Valerius
Roman Wall - Bryher 745

Valerius, Lucius
The Gods Are Not Mocked - Anna Taylor 6177

Van Buren, Matthew
The Imperialists - William Stuart Long 3875

Van der Berg, Boetie
Rags of Glory - Stuart Cloete 1126

Van Keppel, Augustus
Manila Galleon - F. van Wyck Mason 4154

Vargas, Manuel de
The Franciscan - Forrester Blake 532

Varnum, Charles
A Road We Do Not Know: A Novel of Custer at the Little Bighorn - Frederick J. Chiaventonc 1057

Varro, Manlius
The Lost Legion - H. Warner Munn 4516

Varrus, Caius Publius
The Skystone: The Forging of Arthur's Britain - Jack Whyte 6726

Varus, Quintillus
The Three Legions - Gregory Solon 5941

Vassilovich, Michael
Dance of the Assassins - Maria Fagyas 1997

Vaughan, Francis
For God and Glory - Tim Jeal 3171

Veasey-Hunter, Vivian
A Captive Freedom - Emma Drummond 1724

Vere, Starry
Billy Budd - Herman Melville 4333

Vernet, Lucien
Napoleon Must Die - Quinn Fawcett 2054

Vespasian
The Crows of War - Steven Rayson 5276
The Tenth Measure - Brenda Lesley Segal 5721
The Voices of Masada - David Kossoff 3545

Vickers, Mars
High Hearts - Rita Mae Brown 728

Vigon, Benito
La Guerra: A Spanish Saga - Stephen D. Frances 2199

Villa, Pancho
The Old Gringo - Carlos Fuentes 2247

Villasur, Don Pedro de
Return of the Spanish - Don Coldsmith 1183

Villeneuve, Pierre de
1805 - Richard Woodman 6857
Decision at Trafalgar - Richard Woodman 6861

Vincent, Adam
The Empire Builders - William Stuart Long 3871

Vishnyevetski, Yeremi
With Fire and Sword - Henryk Sienkiewicz 5850

Vivonne, Victor de
Angelique in Barbary - Sergeanne Golon 2469

Volkov, Boris
Blood on the Snow - John Elliott 1916

Volodyovski, Pan
Fire in the Steppe - Henryk Sienkiewicz 5847

Von Kobis, Hugo
While Paris Danced - Patricia Wright 6886

Von Zweig, Roger
Something Gleamed - Theda Kenyon 3463

Vorotyntsev, Colonel
August 1914 - Alexander Solzhenitsyn 5942

Wade, Samuel
The Fifth Conspiracy - Ted Jones 3296
Hard Road to Gettysburg - Ted Jones 3298

Wade, Stephen
The Pride of Hannah Wade - Janet Dailey 1455

Wales, Marshall
The Foragers - Ben Haas 2630

Walker, Boyd
Maximilian's Gold - Jane Barry 359

Walker, Dhu
Strange Company - Robert J. Conley 1251

Wallace, George D.
A Creek Called Wounded Knee - Douglas C. Jones 3277

Wallace, Lew
City of Widows - Loren D. Estleman 1969

Wallace, Simon
Two Crowns for America - Katherine Kurtz 3568

Wallenstein, Albrecht von
The Descent of the Idol - Jaroslav Durych 1818
World and Paradise - Edgar Maas 3953

Ward, Lantry
Rogue's March - Maristan Chapman 993

Ward, Woody
Eva - Ib Melchior 4329

Warne, Ellis
In My Father's House - Bodie Thoene 6222

Warren, Andrew
Rivers of Glory - F. van Wyck Mason 4158

Warren, Peter
The Highwayman - Noel B. Gerson 2372

Warriner, Douglas
Officers and Ladies - Richard O'Connor 4686

Warriner, Philip
Officers and Ladies - Richard O'Connor 4686

Warrington, George
The Virginians - William Makepeace Thackeray 6214

Washington, George
Ambush - Donald Clayton Porter 5113
Back Bay - William Martin 4138
Black Forest - Meade Minnigerode 4411
Bride of Liberty - Frank Yerby 6909
Burr - Gore Vidal 6485
Cato's War - Guy Wheeler 6655
Cherokee - Donald Clayton Porter 5115
Christmas at Mount Vernon - Helen Topping Miller 4385
Citizen Tom Paine - Howard Fast 2028
Clear for Action: A Novel about John Paul Jones - Clements Ripley 5344
Conceived in Liberty - Howard Fast 2029
The Culper Spy Ring - Lynn Groh 2596
Dawn's Early Light - Elswyth Thane 6215
The Double Man - Elinor Pryor 5205
The Drums of April - Charles Mergendahl 4340
The Drums of Monmouth - Emma Gelders Sterne 5998
Eagles Where I Walk - Stephen Longstreet 3885
A Few Painted Feathers - Stephen Longstreet 3886
The Firekeeper - Robert Moss 4498
Follow the River - James Alexander Thom 6231
The Gentle Rebel - Gilbert Morris 4461
Give Me Liberty: The Story of an Innocent Man - John Erskine 1956
The Governor's Daughter - Denton Whitson 6718
Hugh Wynne, Free Quaker - Silas Weir Mitchell 4416
I'll Storm Hell - Noel B. Gerson 2374
The Indentured Heart - Gilbert Morris 4464
Janice Meredith - Paul Leicester Ford 2166
Jarrett's Jade - Frank Yerby 6923
Juniata Valley - Virginia C. Cassel 954
The King's Iron - Robert Newton Peck 4888
The King's Orchard - Agnes Sligh Turnbull 6363

The Kingsbridge Plot - Maan Meyers 4355
Lady Washington - Dorothy Clarke Wilson 6803
Let My Name Stand Fair - Shirley Seifert 5727
The Long Naked Descent into Boston - William Eastlake 1823
The Lure of the Falcon - Juliette Benzoni 465
The Maddest Idea - James L. Nelson 4580
Man From Mt. Vernon - Burke Boyce 607
The Master of Chaos - Irving A. Bacheller 262
Men in Buckskin - Herbert Stover 6069
Monmouth - Charles Bracelen Flood 2144
Morning in America - Willard Wiener 6741
Morning of a Hero - Burke Boyce 608
The Neutral Ground - Frank Olney Hough 3044
Prince Charlie's Bluff - Donald Thomas 6241
Proceed, Sergeant Lamb - Robert Graves 2550
The Rebels - John Jakes 3152
Red Morning - Ruby Frazier Frey 2230
The Red Road: A Romance of Braddock's Defeat - Hugh Pendexter 4898
Retreat and Recall - Joseph G.E. Hopkins 3029
Scoundrels' Brigade - Carter A. Vaughan 6439
The Sea Eagles - John Edward Jennings 3206
The Seekers - John Jakes 3153
Seneca - Donald Clayton Porter 5127
The Seneca Hostage - Carter A. Vaughan 6440
Sound of the Trumpet - Gilbert Morris 4471
The Spy: A Tale of the Neutral Ground - James Fenimore Cooper 1310
Stars on the Sea - F. van Wyck Mason 4161
Storm the Last Rampart - David Taylor 6180
Strange Wives - Shirley Barker 317
Strife Before Dawn - Mary Schumann 5675
The Sunshine Patriot: A Novel of Benedict Arnold - Norman Partington 4822
Tavern in the Town - Cecile Hulse Matschat 4187
That Dark and Bloody River - Allen W. Eckert 1845
Those Who Love - Irving Stone 6064
Tidewater Dynasty: A Biographical Novel of the Lees of Stratford Hall - Carey Roberts 5372
To Spit Against the Wind - Benjamin H. Levin 3737
The Traitor - Dan Sherman 5814
The Tree of Liberty - Elizabeth Page 4773
The Twisted Saber: A Biographical Novel of Benedict Arnold - Philip Vail 6398
Two Crowns for America - Katherine Kurtz 3568
The Unvanquished - Howard Fast 2046
Valley Forge - MacKinlay Kantor 3364
War Cry - Donald Clayton Porter 5132
War in the Golden Weather - Stephen Longstreet 3892
Wilderness Empire - Allen W. Eckert 1847
The Woodsman - Don Wright 6880
Yankee Doodle Dandy - Noel B. Gerson 2387
Yorktown - Burke Davis 1513
The Young Man From Mount Vernon - Arthur Stanwood Pier 4995

Watkiss, Admiral
Halfhyde and the Fleet Review - Philip McCutchan 4246

Watkiss, Captain
Halfhyde Ordered South - Philip McCutchan 4252
Halfhyde to the Narrows - Philip McCutchan 4253

Waverley, Edward
Waverley - Sir Walter Scott 5709

Wayne, Anthony
Bride of Liberty - Frank Yerby 6909
Conceived in Liberty - Howard Fast 2029
Enough Good Men - Charles Mercer 4336
I'll Storm Hell - Noel B. Gerson 2374
The Ironmaster - Anne Powers 5150
The King's Orchard - Agnes Sligh Turnbull 6363
Let My Name Stand Fair - Shirley Seifert 5727
Morning in America - Willard Wiener 6741
Panther in the Sky - James Alexander Thom 6234
The Proud and the Free - Howard Fast 2042
The Seekers - John Jakes 3153

The Strong Men - John Brick 677
This Land Is Ours - Louis Zara 6953
Where Glory Waits - Gertrude Crownfield 1437
Yorktown - Burke Davis 1513

Wayne, Matthew
Guns of Chickamauga - Richard O'Connor 4685

Webley
Silk and Steel - Stephen Alter 122

Welby, Richard
The Caretaker Wife - Barbara Whitehead 6706

Wellesley, Arthur
The Amazing Mrs. Bonaparte - Harnett T. Kane 3351
A Balance of Dangers - Anthony Forrest 2184
Colossus: A Novel about Goya and a World Gone Mad - Stephen Marlowe 4093
The Flight of the Eagle - Donald Thomas 6239
An Infamous Army - Georgette Heyer 2892
The Life and Times of Horatio Hornblower - C. Northcote Parkinson 4813
The Limits of Glory: A Novel of Waterloo - James McDonough 4265
The Masters of Bow Street - John Creasy 1423
Rage in Silence: A Novel Based on the Life of Goya - Donald Braider 643
Rifleman Dodd - C.S. Forester 2181
Sharpe's Battle - Bernard Cornwell 1338
Sharpe's Company - Bernard Cornwell 1339
Sharpe's Eagle - Bernard Cornwell 1341
Sharpe's Gold - Bernard Cornwell 1343
Sharpe's Honour - Bernard Cornwell 1344
Sharpe's Sword - Bernard Cornwell 1349
The Spanish Bride - Georgette Heyer 2902
Vanity Fair - William Makepeace Thackeray 6213
Waterloo - Bernard Cornwell 1350
Waterloo - Manuel Komroff 3536
Waterloo - Frederic E. Smith 5920
Whispering - Jane Aiken Hodge 2972
The Young Victoria - Tyler Whittle 6724

Wells, William
Gateway to Empire - Allen W. Eckert 1842

Wemyss, Admiral
Gossip From the Forest - Thomas Keneally 3413

Wet, Christiaan de
Rags of Glory - Stuart Cloete 1126

Wharton, Captain Henry
The Spy: A Tale of the Neutral Ground - James Fenimore Cooper 1310

Wheaton, Elias
The Charlatan - Carter A. Vaughan 6433

Whipple, Ben
Seminole - Donald Clayton Porter 5126

Whiteman, Nicholas J.
Sherman's March - Cynthia Bass 373

Whitman, Emerson
The Camp Grant Massacre - Elliott Arnold 191

Wicks, James
Wild Is the River - Louis Bromfield 704

Wilkinson, James
The Fallon Pride - Reagan O'Neal 4742
The Land Beyond the Mountains - Janice Holt Giles 2414
The Medicine Man - Shirley Seifert 5729
Morning Time - Charles Kendall O'Neill 4743
Shadow of the Moon - Douglas C. Jones 3284
Tennessee Hazard - Maristan Chapman 994
The Voyagers - Dale Van Every 6412

Willard, Simon
Savage Gentleman - Noel B. Gerson 2381

Williams, Ephraim
The Firekeeper - Robert Moss 4498

Williams, Hugh
Unto This Hour - Tom Wicker 6733

Wilson
The Red Badge of Courage - Stephen Crane 1414

Wilson, Kent
For Us the Living - Antonia Van-Loon 6424

Wilson, Sir Robert
Ride with Me - Thomas B. Costain 1369

Wilty, Cotton
The King's Iron - Robert Newton Peck 4888

Winder, John H.
Andersonville - MacKinlay Kantor 3359

Winder, William
Dolley - Rita Mae Brown 727

Windham, Keith
The Flight of the Heron - Dorothy Kathleen Broster 710

Wingate, Orde Charles
Born of War - Thomas Taylor 6192

Winslow, Aaron
The Rough Rider - Gilbert Morris 4468

Winslow, Davis
The Dixie Widow - Gilbert Morris 4459

Winslow, Nathan
The Gentle Rebel - Gilbert Morris 4461
The Saintly Buccaneer - Gilbert Morris 4469

Winslow, Whitfield
The Dixie Widow - Gilbert Morris 4459

Winthrop, Edwin
The Bloody Red Baron - Kim Newman 4596

Wirz, Henry
Andersonville - MacKinlay Kantor 3359

Wiswell, Oliver
Oliver Wiswell - Kenneth Roberts 5389

Wolfe, James
His Majesty's Highlanders - Leslie Turner White 6683
Lord Vanity - Samuel Shellabarger 5796
Running Proud - Nicholas Monsarrat 4432
To Fame Unknown - Clifford Lindsey Alderman 67
The Virginians - William Makepeace Thackeray 6214
Web of Destiny - Muriel Elwood 1939
The White Cockade - Vincent O'Brien 4683

Wolfe, Simon
Shadow on the Valley - Kirk Mitchell 4414

Woodward, Wyeth
By Valour and Arms - James H. Street 6076

Woolley, Stanley
Goshawk Squadron - Derek Robinson 5403

Wraysford, Stephen
Birdsong - Sebastian Faulks 2051

Wright, Owen
Time of Drums - John Ehle 1897

Wyatt, Jeffrey
Savage Gentleman - Noel B. Gerson 2381

Wyatt, Sam
Trumpets at Dawn - Cyril Harris 2719

Wynkoop, Edward Wanshear
A Very Small Remnant - Michael Whitney Straight 6075

Wynne, Hugh
Hugh Wynne, Free Quaker - Silas Weir Mitchell 4416

Wynter, Richard
The Fires of Glenlochy - Constance Heaven 2806

Yardley, George
A Durable Fire - Virginia Bernhard 480

Yehudah, Ben
Son of Judah - Dan Levin 3738

Younger, Cole
Major Stepton's War - Matthew Vaughan 6445

Ypsilanti, Prince
Searching for the Emperor - Roberto Pazzi 4858

Zagloba, Pan
Fire in the Steppe - Henryk Sienkiewicz 5847

Zhukov, Georgi Konstantinovich
Journey into Fire - Patricia Wright 6882

Ziegler, Erich
Winter Fire - William R. Trotter 6352

MINE OWNER

Ballard, John
The Silver Mountain - Dan Cushman 1453

Dunn, Magnus
Glittering Hill - Clyde Francis Murphy 4520

Frost, Angus
No Price Too High - Madeleine Polland 5085

O'More, Grattan
The Silver Mountain - Dan Cushman 1453

Tabor, Horace
All for Love: Baby Doe and Silver Dollar - John
Vernon 6456

MINER

Anderson, Eric
Princess Sophia - Edison Marshall 4110

Banicek, Tom
Ellis Island - Fred Mustard Stewart 6023

Bidwell, John
The Bear Flag: A Novel of the Birth of California -
Cecelia Holland 2983

Boyd, Hiram
Calico Palace - Gwen Bristow 694

Brown, Martin
The Trembling Earth - Dale Van Every 6411

Davies, Toby
This Sweet and Bitter Earth - Alexander
Cordell 1326

Firebrace, Jack
Birdsong - Sebastian Faulks 2051

Halt, Welland
The Cage - Michael Weston 6650

Holt, Benjamin
Power - Howard Fast 2041

McAsh, Mack
A Place Called Freedom - Ken Follett 2150

Morgan, Gwilym
How Green Was My Valley - Richard
Llewellyn 3813

Retallick, Ben
Ben Retallick - E.V. Thompson 6263

Retallick, Josh
Chase the Wind - E.V. Thompson 6264

Tregaran, Philip
Tregaran - Mary Lide 3779

MINSTREL

Amergin
Bard: The Odyssey of the Irish - Morgan
Llywelyn 3816

Benfras
Harp into Battle - Cecil Maiden 4031

Bernadin
Bernadin, My Love - Leonard Rossiter 5506

Blondel de Nesle
The Golden Knight - George Challis 971
The Lute Player - Norah Lofts 3852

Finnian
The Harp and the Blade - John Myers 4543

Shinann
Bard: The Odyssey of the Irish - Morgan
Llywelyn 3816

Taliesin
Taliesin - Stephen R. Lawhead 3683

MODEL

Claudel, Camille
Naked Came I: A Novel of Rodin - David
Weiss 6607

Cornforth, Fanny
Willowwood - Elizabeth Savage 5619

Crook, Annie
The Women of Whitechapel and Jack the Ripper - Paul
West 6638

Dunbar, Margaret
Cashmere - Nicola Thorne 6273

Duplessis, Marie
Last Love of Camille - Frances Winwar 6832

Giocondo, Lisa Gherardini
The Romance of Leonardo Da Vinci - Dmitri
Merezhkovski 4339

Lucie, Maude
Melbury Square - Dorothy Eden 1857

Siddal, Elizabeth Eleanor
Cock of the Walk - Roy Lewis 3762
The Golden Veil - Paddy Kitchen 3507
The Hoydens and Mr. Dickens - William J.
Palmer 4784
Willowwood - Elizabeth Savage 5619

Strozzi, Clarice
Divine Mistress - Frank G. Slaughter 5886

Wainwright, Clementina
The Branch-Bearers - Glen Petrie 4978

MONSTER

Grendel
The Tower of Beowulf - Parke Godwin 2450

MOUNTAIN MAN

Anderson, Bear
The High Rocks - Loren D. Estleman 1973

Ballard, Jean
Grant of Kingdom - Harvey Fergusson 2067

Bass, Scratch
Borderlords - Terry C. Johnston 3244
One-Eyed Dream - Terry C. Johnston 3253

Bass, Titus
Buffalo Palace - Terry C. Johnston 3245
Carry the Wind - Terry C. Johnston 3246

Bone, Bartle
Buffalo Girls - Larry McMurtry 4296

Bone, Isaac
A Dream of Kings - Davis Grubb 2604

Booth, Gabe
The Smoky Hill - Don Coldsmith 1188

Bridger, Jim
Across the Shining Mountains - Christian
McCord 4226

The Great Adventure - Janice Holt Giles 2410
Lord Grizzly - Frederick F. Manfred 4056

Buffalo Jake
The Amulet - Hal Borland 582

Caine, Matthew
Rio Grande - Jory Sherman 5821

Caudill, Boone
The Big Sky - A.B. Guthrie Jr. 2624
Fair Land, Fair Land - A.B. Guthrie Jr. 2625

Christmas, Johnny
Johnny Christmas - Forrester Blake 533
Wilderness Passage - Forrester Blake 534

Colter, John
Wilderness - Roger Zelazny 6957

Cooper, Jed
The Gilded Rooster - Richard Emery Roberts 5391

Deakins, Jim
The Big Sky - A.B. Guthrie Jr. 2624

Devlin, Sean
High Country - Jason Manning 4075

Fitzgerald, John S.
Lord Grizzly - Frederick F. Manfred 4056

Fitzpatrick, Tom
Across the Shining Mountains - Christian
McCord 4226
The Great Adventure - Janice Holt Giles 2410

Fowler, Joe
The Great Adventure - Janice Holt Giles 2410

Garrett, J.C.
The Pilgrimage - Ann B. Ross 5463

Glass, Hugh
Lord Grizzly - Frederick F. Manfred 4056
Wilderness - Roger Zelazny 6957

Gowd, Skinner
Diamond Wedding - Wilbur Daniel Steele 5986

Hannah, Zach
High Country - Jason Manning 4075

Horn, Joe
The Big Lonesome - Will Bryant 737

Horne, Jackson
Horne's Law - Jory Sherman 5819

Kagg, Jim
Buffalo Girls - Larry McMurtry 4296

King, August
The Journey of August King - John Ehle 1894

King, Ezekiel
King of the Mountain - David Thompson 6255

King, Nathaniel
Apache Blood - David Thompson 6250
Blackfoot Massacre - David Thompson 6251
Blood Fury - David Thompson 6252
Blood Truce - David Thompson 6253
Hawken Fury - David Thompson 6254
Lure of the Wind - David Thompson 6256
Mountain Devil - David Thompson 6257
Northwest Passage - David Thompson 6258
Tenderfoot - David Thompson 6259
Tomahawk Revenge - David Thompson 6260
Trapper's Blood - David Thompson 6261
Winterkill - David Thompson 6262

Lash, Sam
Wolf Song - Harvey Fergusson 2069

Lee, Sunset
Each Bright River - Mildred Masterson
McNeilly 4308

MacKenzie, Sage
Sweet Mountain Magic - Rosanne Bittner 516

Maclean, Robert Burns
The Yellowstone - Winfred Blevins 549

McNair, Shakespeare
Apache Blood - David Thompson 6250
King of the Mountain - David Thompson 6255
Lure of the Wind - David Thompson 6256
Tomahawk Revenge - David Thompson 6260
Trapper's Blood - David Thompson 6261

Minard, Sam
Mountain Man - Vardis Fisher 2110

Monday, Johnson
Moontrap - Don Berry 481

O'Flaherty, Flare
The Snake River - Winfred Blevins 547

Old Misery
Old Misery - Hugh Pendexter 4896

Paddock, Josiah
Borderlords - Terry C. Johnston 3244
One-Eyed Dream - Terry C. Johnston 3253

Preacher
Blood on the Divide - William W. Johnstone 3265
Forty Guns West - William W. Johnstone 3267

Reeshar, Jesse
Chant of the Hawk - John Harris 2720

Skye, Barnaby
The Far Tribes - Richard S. Wheeler 6658

Starke, Jake
Maximilian's Gold - Jane Barry 359

Stewart, Ling
The Land Is Bright - James Arthur Kjelgaard 3508

Stonecipher, Jacob
The Arkansas River - Jory Sherman 5816

Stroud, George
Chant of the Hawk - John Harris 2720

Sublette, Milt
Across the Shining Mountains - Christian McCord 4226

Sublette, William
The Great Adventure - Janice Holt Giles 2410

Summers, Dick
The Big Sky - A.B. Guthrie Jr. 2624
Fair Land, Fair Land - A.B. Guthrie Jr. 2625

Sweete, Shadrach
Cry of the Hawk - Terry C. Johnston 3248

Thompson, Jethro
Free Flows the River - Earl Murray 4529

Thompson, Thane
Free Flows the River - Earl Murray 4529
High Freedom - Earl Murray 4530

Trask, Eldridge
Trask - Don Berry 483

Tree, Ben
The Legend of Ben Tree - Paul Hawkins 2784

Webb
Moontrap - Don Berry 481

Wyeth, Nathaniel J.
Across the Shining Mountains - Christian McCord 4226

MOUNTAIN WOMAN

McQueen, Lydia
The Tall Woman - Wilma Dykeman 1819

MURDERER

Aram, Eugene
Eugene Aram - Edward Bulwer-Lytton 766

Berg, Noah
Members of the Tribe - Richard Kluger 3511

Bok, Yakov
The Fixer - Bernard Malamud 4038

Booth, John Wilkes
The Chester A. Arthur Conspiracy - William Wiegand 6740
A Court of Owls - Richard Adicks 37
Dim the Flaring Lamps - Jan Jordan 3301
The Judges of the Secret Court - David Stacton 5972
The Last Full Measure - Honore Morrow 4488
Lincoln: A Novel - Gore Vidal 6490
The Spur - Ardyth Kennelly 3425
The Twisted Tendril - Alice Glasgow 2427
The Woman Who Loved John Wilkes Booth - Pamela Redford Russell 5533

Borden, Lizzie
Lizzie Borden - Elizabeth Engstrom 1944
Miss Lizzie - Walter Satterthwait 5608

Brag, Branton
Bighorn Legacy - W. Michael Gear 2332

Brinvilliers, Marie Madeleine
The Devil's Marchioness - William Fifield 2082

Carroll, Christine
This Dark Monarchy - Francis W. Leary 3698

Cenci, Beatrice
A Tale for Midnight - Frederic Prokosch 5195

Chaney, Tom
True Grit - Charles Portis 5139

Corday, Charlotte
Dr. Guillotine: The Eccentric Exploits of an Early Scientist - Herbert Lom 3867
A Place of Greater Safety - Hilary Mantel 4077

Cromer, Miriam
Waxwork - Peter Lovesey 3917

Dane, Jared
Come Winter - Douglas C. Jones 3275

Dangerfield, Paul
The House by the Churchyard - Joseph Sheridan Le Fanu 3688

Dillinger, John
True Crime - Max Allan Collins 1214

Ford, Robert
The Assassination of Jesse James by the Coward Robert Ford - Ron Hansen 2680

Gilmore, Gary
The Executioner's Song - Norman Mailer 4036

Godse, Natu
Nine Hours to Rama - Stanley Wolpert 6846

Grenouille, Jean-Baptiste
Perfume: The Story of a Murderer - Patrick Suskind 6120

Houseman
Eugene Aram - Edward Bulwer-Lytton 766

Ibbetson, Peter
Peter Ibbetson - George Du Maurier 1750

Jekyll, Henry
Dr. Jekyll and Mr. Holmes - Loren D. Estleman 1970
Jekyll, Alias Hyde - Donald Thomas 6240
Mary Reilly - Valerie Martin 4136

Jenkins, Marianne
Marianne - Glen Petrie 4981

Jones, Hendry
The Authentic Death of Hendry Jones - Charles Neider 4562

Kent, Jeremiah
The Lawless - John Jakes 3149

LaFarge, Marie
The Lady and the Arsenic - Marjorie Bowen 598

Landru, Henri Desire
Landru - Rene Masson 4170

Matzerath, Oskar
The Tin Drum - Gunther Grass 2540

McCall, Jack
Aces and Eights: A Novel of the Legend of Wild Bill Hickok - Loren D. Estleman 1967

Medea
Medea - Miranda Seymour 5764

Obenchain, Beal
The Living - Annie Dillard 1644

Oswald, Lee Harvey
Flying into Love - D.M. Thomas 6236

Princip, Gavrilo
Death of a Schoolboy - Hans Koning 3537
The First Casualty - William Powell 5149

Richemont, Denise de
Crime Without Passion - Richard Grayson 2556

Ruby, Jack
Libra - Don DeLillo 1593

Sacco, Nicola
The Passion of Sacco and Vanzetti: A New England Legend - Howard Fast 2040

Silver Knife
Anno-Dracula - Kim Newman 4595

Smith, Madeline Hamilton
Madeleine - Pamela Elizabeth West 6633

Stephenson, Leslie John
Time After Time - Karl Alexander 80

Todd, Jennifer
The Gallows Land - Bill Pronzini 5201

Turner, Ann
For My Great Folly - Thomas B. Costain 1365

Vanzetti, Bartolomeo
The Passion of Sacco and Vanzetti: A New England Legend - Howard Fast 2040

Walford, John
Walford's Oak - Jill M. Phillips 4986

Wasum, Otis
Hard on the Road - Barbara Moore 4440

Watson, John Selby
Watson's Apology - Beryl Bainbridge 271

Weber, Rupert
A Peep into the 20th Century - Christopher Davis 1515

Whipple, Ben
Seminole - Donald Clayton Porter 5126

MUSICIAN

Aubrey, Claire
The Fountain Overflows - Rebecca West 6639

Aubrey, Cordelia
The Fountain Overflows - Rebecca West 6639

Beethoven, Ludwig van
The Man Who Thought He Was Messiah - Curt Leviant 3735

Berdeyev, Kolya
Journey into Fire - Patricia Wright 6882

Blondelyn
Lionheart!: A Novel of Richard I, King of England - Martha Rofheart 5428

Bolden, Buddy
Coming through Slaughter - Michael Ondaatje 4736

Bruckner, Anton
Music for God - Theresa Weiser   6603

Chopin, Frederic
Beyond Desire: A Novel Based on the Life of Felix and Cecille Mendelssohn - Pierre La Mure   3574
Hungarian Rhapsody: The Life of Franz Liszt - Jean Rousselot   5511
The Questing Heart: A Romantic Novel about George Sand - F.W. Kenyon   3458

Claiborne, Margaret
River of Dreams - Gay Courter   1390

Debussy, Claude
Clair De Lune: A Novel about Claude Debussy - Pierre La Mure   3575

Dunellen, Nathaniel
Remnants of Glory - Teresa Miller   4403

Franck, Cesar Augustine
Cesar and Augusta - Ronald Harwood   2771

Gottschalk, Louis Moreau
Concert Grand - Howard Breslin   665

Gradov, Mary
Generations of Winter - Vassily Aksyonov   61

Heron, Lisa
Castle of Eagles - Constance Heaven   2804

Holcomb, Caleb
Too Long at the Dance - Mike Blakely   539

Holmes, Augusta
Cesar and Augusta - Ronald Harwood   2771

Hugh
Shame of Man - Piers Anthony   168

Liszt, Franz
Hungarian Rhapsody: The Life of Franz Liszt - Jean Rousselot   5511
Last Love of Camille - Frances Winwar   6832
The Questing Heart: A Romantic Novel about George Sand - F.W. Kenyon   3458

Macadam, John
Brave Kingdom - Frances Murray   4534

Mendelssohn, Felix
Beyond Desire: A Novel Based on the Life of Felix and Cecille Mendelssohn - Pierre La Mure   3574

Morton, Joseph Ferdinand
Jelly Roll Morton's Last Night at the Jungle Inn: An Imaginary Memoir - Samuel Charters   1002

Moser, Anna
Anna, Ann, Annie - Thomas Trebitsch Parker   4808

Mozart, Wolfgang Amadeus
The Golden Quill: A Novel Based on the Life of Mozart - Bernard Grun   2605
The Irish Boy: A Romantic Biography - Naomi Jacob   3137
Mozart on the Way to Prague - Eduard Friedrich Morike   4454
Sacred and Profane: A Novel of the Life and Times of Mozart - David Weiss   6609

Nils
Arne - Bjornstjerne Bjornson   518

Orlov, Anna
Petersburg - Emily Hanlon   2677

Otis, Jason
The Assassination of Mozart - David Weiss   6604

Paganini, Niccolo
The Magic Bow - Manuel Komroff   3534
Passionate Rebel: The Story of Hector Berlioz - F.W. Kenyon   3457

Paradies, Maria Theresa von
The Strange Case of Madamoiselle P. - Patrick Ireland   3109

Rizzio, David
Parcel of Rogues - Jane Lane   3656

Saint-Saens, Camille
Cesar and Augusta - Ronald Harwood   2771

Schlesinger, Erich
The Career of Magda V. - Joseph Machlis   3982

Schumann, Robert
Beyond Desire: A Novel Based on the Life of Felix and Cecille Mendelssohn - Pierre La Mure   3574

Smeaton, Mark
The King's Pleasure - Jean Plaidy   5026

Soloman the Man
Cry of the Peacock - Gina Barkhordar Nahai   4552

Tartini, Giuseppe
A Fiddle, a Sword, and a Lady - Albert Spalding   5953

Wieck, Friedrich
Spring Symphony - Eleanor Painter   4777

Will
Jewel of the Sea - Susan Wiggs   6743

Wittgenstein, Paul
The Crown Prince - John Barchilon   300

MYTHICAL CREATURE

Sigfrid
The Wolf and the Raven - Diana L. Paxson   4848

NATURALIST

Audubon, John James
The Mysterious Death of Meriwether Lewis - Ron Burns   802

Grant, John
Here I Stay - Elizabeth Coatsworth   1138

Mount, Stirling
River of Sky - Karen Harper   2713

Pomeroy, Harriet
Ravished - Amanda Quick   5216

Sewall, William
McKay's Bees - Thomas McMahon   4289

Sorensen, Jan Carl
Winds of Spring - Walter Havighurst   2776

Wilson, Alexander
The Mysterious Death of Meriwether Lewis - Ron Burns   802

NOBLEMAN

Adare, Edward
Opal - Helen Ashfield   210

Aelredson, Edward
Robin and the King - Parke Godwin   2448
Sherwood - Parke Godwin   2449

Alaric of Anion
Princess of Fire - Shannon Drake   1718

Alastair, Dominic
Devil's Cub - Georgette Heyer   2885

Alastair, Justin
Devil's Cub - Georgette Heyer   2885
These Old Shades - Georgette Heyer   2906

Alexander, Karl
Power - Lion Feuchtwanger   2074

Alexandrovski, Nikolai
Tarnished Angel - Phyllis Leonard   3723

Allesandro, Dante de
Caressa - Linda Lang Bartell   363

Allingham, Julian
Cassy - Elizabeth Lyle   3930

Alvarez de Toledo, Fernando
Captain General - John P. Stevenson   6007
The Sea Beggars - Cecelia Holland   2996

Amberley, Lord
The Parfit Knight - Juliet Blyth   555

Amberly, Roger
The Bastard - John Jakes   3144

Ambrosius
The Great Captains - Henry Treece   6329

Andrassy, Julius
Imperial Waltz - William M. Abrahams   13

Andreas, Lionello
The Wind Dancer - Iris Johansen   3218

Anicius, Marcus
Threshold of Fire - Hella S. Haasse   2633

Aramis
Twenty Years After - Alexandre Dumas   1783

Ardenly, Alec
Tish - Cissie Miller   4381

Arias de Avila, Pedro
The Golden Eagle - John Edward Jennings   3201

Arouet, Lucien
French Slippers - Deborah Chester   1055

Arundel, Christopher
Lord Libertine - Anthony Esler   1964

Ashburne, Tom
Lost Love Found - Bertrice Small   5910

Ashton, Lord
Deborah Goes to Dover - Marion Chesney   1023

Ashton, Charles
Double Masquerade - Karen Lynn   3938

Ashton, William
The Bride of Lammermoor - Sir Walter Scott   5693

Atherstone, Francis
Bride of Ae - Pamela Hill   2928

Atticus, Titus Pomponius
Epicurus My Master - Max Radin   5233

Audley, Julian
Regency Buck - Georgette Heyer   2898

Audubon, Lord
The Shadowed Spring - Carola Salisbury   5571

Audunsson, Olav
The Axe - Sigrid Undset   6378
In the Wilderness - Sigrid Undset   6381
The Snake Pit - Sigrid Undset   6383
The Son Avenger - Sigrid Undset   6384

Aumarle, John
The Strong Room - Jere Hungerford Wheelwright   6671

Austell, Lucius
The Quiet Gentleman - Georgette Heyer   2897

Avington, Jack
Albany - Laura Black   519

Aynsworth, Christopher
Mistress of Willowvale - Patricia Veryan   6471

Babcock, Lord
Lady Pamela - Clare Darcy   1490

Bacon, Sir Francis
Death of the Fox - George Garrett   2300

Balater, George Eustace
The Bad Lands - Oakley Hall   2651

Baldwin V
Fortune's Knave: The Making of William the Conqueror - Mary Lide   3774
Wife to the Bastard - Hilda Lewis   3753

Balthazar
Ben Hur: A Tale of the Christ - Lew Wallace   6536

Banner, Gabriel
Reckless - Amanda Quick   5217

Barham, Jack
Two of a Kind: An English Trifle - Rosemary Edghill   1867

Barrasford, Ivo
Bath Tangle - Georgette Heyer   2875

Batz, Baron Jean de
Scaramouche the King-Maker - Rafael Sabatini   5555

Beaucaire, Victor M.
Monsieur Beaucaire - Booth Tarkington   6163

Beauchamp, Guy
Melbury Square - Dorothy Eden   1857

Beauchamp, Guy de
Vows of the Peacock - Alice Walworth Graham   2513

Beaufort, Henry
Micah Clarke - Sir Arthur Conan Doyle   1715

Beaumaris, Guy
Midnight Moon - Jeanne Montague   4436

Beaumont, Simon
The Hooded Falcon - Prudence Andrew   140

Belfort, Lord
Dual Destiny - Karen Lynn   3939

Belleme, Robert de
The Wild Hunt - Elizabeth Chadwick   969

Belmanoir, Tracy
The Black Moth - Georgette Heyer   2877

Belstone, Kit
Deborah - Colette Davenat   1498

Bembo, Pietro
The Flame of the Borgias - Jean Briggs   680

Bergheim, Max von
Letty - Clare Darcy   1491

Berwick, James FitzJames
King's Agent - Justus Kent Clark   1090

Bewley, Lord
Colonel Sandhurst to the Rescue - Marion Chesney   1021

Bibikov, Sergei
Devil Child - Jo Germany   2359

Blackwater, Major
Trumpeter, Sound! - D.L. Murray   4528

Blakely, Morgan
Bride of the Unicorn - Kasey Michaels   4363

Blakeney, Sir Percy
The Scarlet Pimpernel - Baroness Emma Orczy   4745

Bohemond
Count Bohemond - Alfred Duggan   1764

Bohemond I
Wine of Satan - Laverne Gay   2327

Bohemund
Silver Leopard - F. van Wyck Mason   4160

Boite
Lady of Moray - Bonnie Copeland   1318

Bolingbroke, Henry
The Gentle Falcon - Hilda Lewis   3747
The Lords of Lancaster - Pamela Bennetts   452
Passage to Pontefract - Jean Plaidy   5038
The Peacock and the Pearl - Jennifer Lang   3661

Bonaparte, Jerome
Tide of Empire - Bates Baldwin   279

Bonaparte, Joseph
The Eagle and the Rock - Frances Winwar   6830

Borgia, Cesare
The Borgia Prince - Pamela Bennetts   446
Carnival of Saints - George Herman   2860
City of God: A Novel of the Borgias - Cecelia Holland   2985
Daughter of Shadows - Miranda Seymour   5762
Light on Lucrezia - Jean Plaidy   5029
Madonna of the Seven Hills - Jean Plaidy   5034
Michelangelo the Florentine - Sidney Alexander   86
Mona Lisa: The Woman in the Portrait - Sara Mayfield   4206
The Naked Sword: The Story of Lucretia Borgia - F.W. Kenyon   3456
The Romance of Leonardo Da Vinci - Dmitri Merezhkovski   4339

Borgia, Rodrigo
Madonna of the Seven Hills - Jean Plaidy   5034
Mona Lisa: The Woman in the Portrait - Sara Mayfield   4206

Boscage, Rupert de
Tansy Taniard - Myrtle Strode-Jackson   6084

Bourbon, Antoine de
The Italian Woman - Jean Plaidy   5024

Bourbon, Charles Ferdinand de
So Much as Beauty Does - Muriel Elwood   1938

Bracken of Hawkings Crest, Lord
The Knight and the Dove - Lori Wick   6732

Brackley, Daniel
The Black Arrow - Robert Louis Stevenson   6008

Bragelonne, Raoul de
Twenty Years After - Alexandre Dumas   1783

Brandon
Moonfeather - Judith E. French   2223

Brandon, Charles
The Reluctant Queen - Molly Costain Haycraft   2796
Royal Nonesuch: A Tudor Tapestry - Beatrice White   6674

Brayford, Arthur
Lucinda Brayford - Martin Boyd   613

Briavel, Lord Gavin
Heiress of Ardara - Margaret Evans Porter   5137

Briennius, Nicephorus
Count Robert of Paris - Sir Walter Scott   5695

Brogmar, Augustin
Restless Is the River - August Derleth   1617

Brome, Christopher
Lydia, or Love in Town - Clare Darcy   1492

Bruce, Thomas
Dreams of Empire - Jeanne Mackin   3994
Lord Elgin's Lady - Theodore Vrettos   6514

Bruce, Victor
By Command of the Viceroy - Duncan MacNeil   4010
Charge of Cowardice - Duncan MacNeil   4011

Brunne, Guy de
The Golden Exile - Lawrence Schoonover   5664

Brutus, Marcus Junius
The Ides of March - Thornton Wilder   6753

Bruyere, Geoffrey de
Lord Geoffrey's Fancy - Alfred Duggan   1771

Buade, Louis de
The Gilded Torch - Iola Fuller   2252
The King's Messenger - Samuel Edwards   1887
Shadows on the Rock - Willa Cather   959

Bullington, Viscount
Barry Lyndon - William Makepeace Thackeray   6210

Burgh, Hubert de
The Marriage of Meggotta - Edith Pargeter   4799

Burgh, Hugh de
The Battle of the Queens - Jean Plaidy   5005

Byam, Sholto
Belgrave Square - Anne Perry   4919

Byrd, William
Devil Water - Anya Seton   5749

Byron, George Gordon
The Absorbing Fire: The Byron Legend - F.W. Kenyon   3445
The Blue Heaven Bends Over All - Jane Oliver   4720
Byron: A Novel - Sigrid Combuchen   1225
Count Manifred - Miranda Seymour   5761
Frankenstein Unbound - Brian Aldiss   68
The Golden Years: A Novel Based on the Life and Loves of Percy Bysshe Shelley - F.W. Kenyon   3451
Lord Byron's Doctor - Paul West   6634
Lord of the Ladies - Joanna Dessau   1626
Love's Children - Judith Chernaik   1013
The Memoirs of Lord Byron - Robert Nye   4655
My Sister, My Love - Lucille Iremonger   3111
The Secret Memoirs of Lord Byron - Christopher Nicole   4622
A Single Summer with Lord B. - Derek Marlowe   4092
Teresa, or Her Demon Lover - Austin K. Gray   2554

Cagliostro, Count Alessandro
The Queen's Necklace - Alexandre Dumas   1781

Cambridge, Phillip
Glorious Morning - Julie Ellis   1919

Candidianus, Lucius
Last of Britain - Meriol Trevor   6343

Carey, Sir Robert
A Famine of Horses - P.F. Chisholm   1071
A Season of Knives - P.F. Chisholm   1072

Carey, Robert
The Succession: A Novel of Elizabeth and James - George Garrett   2302

Carleton, Lord Bruce
Forever Amber - Kathleen Winsor   6822

Carlton, Lord Guy
Rake's Progress - Marion Chesney   1047

Carlyon, Edward
The Reluctant Widow - Georgette Heyer   2899

Carnmore, Alexander
Wild Cat - Laura Black   524

Carr, Robert
The King James Version - Stanley N. Stewart   6035
King's Minion - Rafael Sabatini   5552
Lion Rampant - Bernard Shrimsley   5836
The Street of Kings - Charles Dexter   1637

Carrick, Alec
Night Storm - Catherine Coulter   1378

Carrick, Hugh
Lord Iverbrook's Heir - Carola Dunn   1795

Carrington, Ashley
Charity Girl - Georgette Heyer   2879

Carrisdowne, Rupert
At the Sign of the Golden Pineapple - Marion Chesney   1016

Carstares, John
The Black Moth - Georgette Heyer   2877

Casson-Perceval, Edwin
The Ring Master - David Gurr   2622

Castelar, Don Alfonso
In Perilous Seas - Victor Suthren   6130

Castelmarten, Lucian
Dark at Noon - Jill Tattersall   6173

Catilina, Lucius Sergius
The Catiline Conspiracy - John Maddox Roberts   5379

Caumont La Force, Antonin-Nompar de
Sorrow by Day - Marjorie Coryn 1359

Cavendish, Lord Randal
My Dear Lover England - Pamela Bennetts 453

Caynnes, Lord Adrian
The Wanton Fires - Meriol Trevor 6345

Cecil, Robert
Death of the Fox - George Garrett 2300
Deborah and the Many Faces of Love - Colette
  Davenat 1499
So Merciful a Queen, So Cruel a Woman - Alice
  Harwood 2769
The Succession: A Novel of Elizabeth and James -
  George Garrett 2302
Trust and Treason - Margaret Birkhead 506

Cecil, William
Elizabeth: Queen & Woman - Helen Thorpe 6279
Legacy - Susan Kay 3374
My Lord Essex - Olive Eckerson 1838
The Proud Man - Elizabeth Linington 3800
*Shadow in the Sun: A Novel of Elizabeth I, the Virgin
  Queen* - F.W. Kenyon 3460
To Love a Queen - Lawrence Schoonover 5669

Cenci, Francesco
A Tale for Midnight - Frederic Prokosch 5195

Centeville, Baron Rollo de
The Demon Lover - Victoria Holt 3013

Cerulis, John
The Belt of Gold - Cecelia Holland 2984

Charles
Falls of Gard - Laura Black 520
The Royal Succession - Maurice Druon 1735

Charles, Duc de Bourbon
The Chancellor - Lawrence Schoonover 5662
The King's Cavalier - Samuel Shellabarger 5795

Charles, Duke of Burgundy
Quentin Durward - Sir Walter Scott 5705
To Lie with Lions - Dorothy Dunnett 1810

Charles of Valois
The Poisoned Crown - Maurice Druon 1734
The Strangled Queen - Maurice Druon 1737

Charles Philippe
Holy Week - Louis Aragon 182

Cheng Wei
The Big Chariot - Charmian Clift 1118

Cheng Yuan
The Big Chariot - Charmian Clift 1118

Chernov, Danilo
Heaven Is Too High - Mildred Masterson
  McNeilly 4309

Chester, Sir John
Barnaby Rudge: A Tale of the Riots of Eighty -
  Charles Dickens 1641

Churchill, John
The Charlatan - Carter A. Vaughan 6433
Exit Lady Masham - Louis Auchincloss 230
The Glory and the Dream - F.W. Kenyon 3450
Marlborough's Unfair Lady - Lozania Prole 5197
The Mohawk Ladder - Noel B. Gerson 2377
The Queen's Favourites - Jean Plaidy 5051
The Queen's Husband - Samuel Edwards 1889
The Renegade - Donald Clayton Porter 5122
The Sachem - Donald Clayton Porter 5124

Churchill, Randolph
The Whitechapel Horrors - Edward B. Hanna 2678

Claibourne, Leigh
Rake's Ransom - Barbara Metzger 4347

Clanreydon, Lord
Castle Barebane - Joan Aiken 43

Clare, Edward
Greygallows - Barbara Michaels 4359

Clare, Richard de
The Marriage of Meggotta - Edith Pargeter 4799

Claudius I
I, Claudius - Robert Graves 2547

Cleveden, Charles
Miss Fiona's Fancy - Marion Chesney 1040

Cloud, Marcus Valerius
Mistress - Amanda Quick 5215

Coeffier-Ruze d'Effiat, Henri
The Cardinal and the Queen - Evelyn Anthony 159
Cinq-Mars - Alfred Victor de Vigny 6495

Colebrook, Lucas
Surrender - Amanda Quick 5221

Coligny, Gaspard de
The Negotiators - Francis Walder 6526

Comfrey, Sylvester
Minerva - Marion Chesney 1037

Comyn, John
Robert the Bruce: The Steps to the Empty Throne -
  Nigel Tranter 6320

Connelly, Ian
Nobody's Angel - Karen Robards 5363

Conrad
The Talisman - Sir Walter Scott 5708

Conrad of Montferrat
The Kings of Vain Intent - Graham Shelby 5791

Corbett of Colchester
My Gallant Enemy - Rexanne Becnel 409

Cordova, Don Pedro
Don Pedro and the Devil - Edgar Maas 3948

Corimer, Charles Alexander
Seasons of Fear - Philip McFarland 4272

Cornwallis, Charles
The Year of the French - Thomas Flanagan 2121

Cranmere, Francis
Marianne - Juliette Benzoni 466
Marianne and the Masked Prince - Juliette
  Benzoni 469

Crassus, Marcus Licinius
Arms of Nemesis - Steven Saylor 5623

Crawford, Richard
The Game of Kings - Dorothy Dunnett 1801
Queen's Play - Dorothy Dunnett 1805

Crayford, Thomas
Beau Barron's Lady - Helen Ashfield 204

Cruickshank, Will
Greenyards - Joan Lingard 3796

Cuddesdon, Jasper
Turn of the Dice - Janet Edmonds 1870

D'Aix, Sir Alphonse
A Silver Mirror - Roberta Gellis 2353

D'Alais, Guy
The Shepherd's Crook - Paul Frischauer 2234

Dalgarvo
The Fortunes of Nigel - Sir Walter Scott 5696

Dalven, Carlin
Lady Pamela - Clare Darcy 1490

Damerel, Jasper
Venetia - Georgette Heyer 2909

Damian
The Betrothed - Sir Walter Scott 5691

Damon, Camille
Love's Duet - Patricia Veryan 6468

Dantry, Charles
Diana the Huntress - Marion Chesney 1026

Danver, George
Double Masquerade - Karen Lynn 3938

Danvers, Clinton
A Marriage of Convenience - Tim Jeal 3172

Danville, John
Lady in the Briars - Carola Dunn 1793

Darcy, Thomas
The Man on a Donkey - H.F.M. Prescott 5170

D'Armagnac, Jean
The Spider King - Lawrence Schoonover 5668

Darnay, Charles
A Tale of Two Cities - Charles Dickens 1642

Dauntry, Vernon
Frederica - Georgette Heyer 2889

David ap Gruffydd
The Reckoning - Sharon Kay Penman 4906

de Harcourt, Raoul
The Conqueror - Georgette Heyer 2881

De La Ferte, Comte
The Girl From Paris - Joan Aiken 47

De la Motte, Chevalier
Denis Duval - William Makepeace Thackeray 6211

de la Tour d'Azur Gervais, Marquis
Scaramouche - Rafael Sabatini 5554

De Lacy, Hugo
The Betrothed - Sir Walter Scott 5691

de Redvers, Count
Leopards and Lilies - Alfred Duggan 1769

de Saint-Vire, Henri
These Old Shades - Georgette Heyer 2906

De Vere, Arthur
Anne of Geierstein - Sir Walter Scott 5689

De Walton, John
Castle Dangerous - Sir Walter Scott 5694

Dee, Christmas
Regency Rogue - Helen Ashfield 212

d'Egremont
Damaris - Jane Sheridan 5810

Delibe, Charles August
The Devil on Horseback - Victoria Holt 3014

Desautels, Diron
Drums at Dusk - Arna Bontemps 575

Desire, Harry
Deirdre and Desire - Marion Chesney 1024

Devenish, John
An Important Family - Dorothy Eden 1855

Devereux, Robert
The Bisley Boy - Christopher Hunt 3080
The Constant Star - Dorothy Norris Foote 2151
A Dead Man in Deptford - Anthony Burgess 776
Death of the Fox - George Garrett 2300
Heart of a Queen - Josephine Delves-
  Broughton 1603
I, Elizabeth - Rosalind Miles 4378
Legacy - Susan Kay 3374
The Murder in the Tower - Jean Plaidy 5035
My Enemy the Queen - Victoria Holt 3017
My Lord Essex - Olive Eckerson 1838
Nicholas Cooke: Actor, Soldier, Physician, Priest -
  Stephanie Cowell 1393
Queen of This Realm: The Story of Queen Elizabeth I -
  Jean Plaidy 5050
*Shadow in the Sun: A Novel of Elizabeth I, the Virgin
  Queen* - F.W. Kenyon 3460
The Succession: A Novel of Elizabeth and James -
  George Garrett 2302
Sweet Will - Eric Malpass 4050

Take Heed of Loving Me: A Novel about John Donne - Elizabeth Gray Vining 6502

Too Near the Throne - Molly Costain Haycraft 2797

Will Shakespeare: The Untold Story - John Mortimer 4495

You, My Brother - Philip Burton 809

Deveril, Adam
A Civil Contract - Georgette Heyer 2880

Djamic
Devil's Yard - Ivo Andric 152

d'Orleans, Charles
In a Dark Wood Wandering - Hella S. Haasse 2631

Dornay, Charles
The Melancholy Virgin - Annabel Laine 3587
The Reluctant Heiress - Annabel Laine 3588

Douglas, Lord Alfred Bruce
The God of Mirrors - Robert Reilly 5293

Douglas, George
The Captive Queen of Scots - Jean Plaidy 5008

Douglas, James
Parcel of Rogues - Jane Lane 3656

Douglas, John Sholto
The God of Mirrors - Robert Reilly 5293

Douglas, Thomas
The Strange Brigade - John Edward Jennings 3209

Douglas, William
The Captive Queen of Scots - Jean Plaidy 5008
The Lion Is Come - Jane Oliver 4725

Draco, Lord
Glendraco - Laura Black 521

Drelincourt, Marcus
The Convenient Marriage - Georgette Heyer 2882

du Levassoux, Comte
Hawthorn Hill - Doris Shannon 5777

Duc de Malvoeux
The Porcelain Dove - Delia Sherman 5815

Ducas, Leo
Shards of Empire - Susan Schwartz 5677

Dudley, Lord Guilford
The Tower of London - William Harrison Ainsworth 58

Dudley, John
Feast in the Morning - Hugh Preston 5175

Dudley, Robert
All the Queen's Men - Evelyn Anthony 157
The Bisley Boy - Christopher Hunt 3080
A Crown in Darkness: A Novel about Lady Jane Grey - Margaret Mullally 4512
Elizabeth: Queen & Woman - Helen Thorpe 6279
Gay Lord Robert - Jean Plaidy 5015
The Green Salamander - Pamela Hill 2933
Heart of a Queen - Josephine Delves-Broughton 1603
Her Majesty's Captain - Derek Wilson 6797
Kenilworth - Sir Walter Scott 5700
Lady Rich - Elizabeth Boatwright Coker 1166
Legacy - Susan Kay 3374
My Dear Lover England - Pamela Bennetts 453
My Enemy the Queen - Victoria Holt 3017
My Lord Essex - Olive Eckerson 1838
My Lord the Fox - Robert York 6932
The Queen and the Gypsy - Constance Heaven 2810
Queen of This Realm: The Story of Queen Elizabeth I - Jean Plaidy 5050
The Queen's Ward - Hebe Elsna 1933
The Red-Haired Brat - Joanna Dessau 1627
The Robsart Affair - Jennette Letton 3729
Shadow in the Sun: A Novel of Elizabeth I, the Virgin Queen - F.W. Kenyon 3460
So Merciful a Queen, So Cruel a Woman - Alice Harwood 2769

Sweet Will - Eric Malpass 4050

Dukay, Albert
Century in Scarlet - Lajos Zilahy 6962

Dukay, Antal
Century in Scarlet - Lajos Zilahy 6962

Duke of Ferrant
The Desirable Duchess - Marion Chesney 1025

Duke of Pelham
Rainbird's Revenge - Marion Chesney 1046

Duke of Pembury
Frederica in Fashion - Marion Chesney 1032

Duke of Salisbury
Vice Avenged: A Moral Tale - Lolah Burford 774

Durris, Edward
Castle of Foxes - Alanna Knight 3516

Eadwin
The Adversary - Jan Widgery 6738

Earl of Monkshood
The Millionaire's Daughter - Dorothy Eden 1858

Earl of Oxford
Anne of Geierstein - Sir Walter Scott 5689

Eden, Thomas
This Other Eden - Marilyn Harris 2733

Edgar of Marwell
The Conqueror - Georgette Heyer 2881

Edward the Atheling
The Golden Warrior: The Story of Harold and William - Hope Muntz 4517

Eisenstadt, Franz
Winter of the Heart - Linda J. LaRosa 3665

Emich of Leiningen-Hartenburg, Count
The Heidenmauer - James Fenimore Cooper 1301

Eric of Normandy, Count
The Tyrant of Bagdad - Glenn Pierce 4996

d'Este, Alfonso
Light on Lucrezia - Jean Plaidy 5029
The Naked Sword: The Story of Lucretia Borgia - F.W. Kenyon 3456

d'Este, Ercole
The Naked Sword: The Story of Lucretia Borgia - F.W. Kenyon 3456

Etherege, Sir George
Old St. Paul's - William Harrison Ainsworth 57

Eugenio, Don
The Three-Cornered Hat - Pedro Antonio de Alarcon 62

Evandale
Old Mortality - Sir Walter Scott 5702

Evereaux, Richard
A Prince, a Piper, and a Rose - John Scalzo 5628

Fairfax, David
Lavender Lady - Carola Dunn 1794

Falkland, William
Palaces of Desire - Kate Alexander 81

Fancot, Evelyn
False Colours - Georgette Heyer 2886

Fanshawe, Sir Anthony
The Masqueraders - Georgette Heyer 2894

Fearon, Lewis
Victoire - Clare Darcy 1493

Fersen, Hans Axel von
The Fatal Friendship: Marie Antoinette, Count Fersen and the Flight to Varennes - Stanley Loomis 3895
I Thee Wed - Gilbert Wolf Gabriel 2267
King's Masque - Evan John 3220
The Queen's Confession - Victoria Holt 3019

Fitzcorbucion, Hamo
The Ravens of Blackwater - Edward Marston 4126

Fitzgerald, Gerait
Gerait's Daughter - Millie J. Ragosta 5241

Fitzpatrick, Viscount
The Banishment - Marion Chesney 1018

FitzRobert, Philip
Brother Cadfael's Penance - Ellis Peters 4955

Flambard, Ranulf
The Lion of Justice - Jean Plaidy 5031

Flavius, Quintus
No King but Caesar - Anne Powers 5151

Fleetwood, Sebastian
Dangerous - Amanda Quick 5213

Fleming, Harry
Rendezvous - Amanda Quick 5218

Flower, George
Soldiers of Fortune - Peter Bourne 595

Fontclair, Hugh
Cut to the Quick - Kate Ross 5501

Ford, Laurence de
A Lady of Repute - Janice James 3158

Fortenberry, Dienwald de
Earth Song - Catherine Coulter 1374

Fouche, Lord
The Rose and the Sword - Sandra Paretti 4792

Foxefield, Brett
My Lord Foxe - Constance Gluyas 2443

Frant, Gervais
The Quiet Gentleman - Georgette Heyer 2897

Frome, Alexander
The Unsuitable Miss Pelham - June Drummond 1730

Fulk
The Earl - Cecelia Holland 2987
Queen of Swords - Judith Tarr 6169

Gadiani, Gregory
Heir to Kuragin - Constance Heaven 2807

Gaius
Swords in the North - Paul Lewis Anderson 138

Gallus
The Sword and the Promise - Benjamin Siegel 5845

Garfield, Simon
Daphne - Marion Chesney 1022

Gascoyne-Cecil, Robert
By Command of the Viceroy - Duncan MacNeil 4010

Geoffrey of Anjou
Beloved Enemy: The Passions of Eleanor of Aquitaine - Ellen Jones 3288
When Christ and His Saints Slept - Sharon Kay Penman 4908

Geoffrey of Villehardouin
The Seven Hills of Paradise - Rosemary Simpson 5859

George, Duke of Clarence
Crown of Roses - Valerie Anand 127
The Golden Yoke: A Novel of the War of the Roses - Olive Eckerson 1837
Richard III: The Last Plantagenet - Tyler Whittle 6722
The Rose at Harvest End - Eleanor Fairburn 2003

Gisbert, Lord
The Green Madonna - C.E. L'Ami 3617

Glenalban, Duncan
Albany - Laura Black 519

Glendenning, Horatio
Had We Never Loved - Patricia Veryan 6463

Glendower, Owen
Owen Glendower - John Cowper Powys   5159

Godoy, Manuel de
The Last Portrait of the Duchess of Alba - Antonio
   Larreta   3666

Godunov, Boris
Darker Jewels - Chelsea Quinn Yarbro   6898
The Muscovite - Alison Macleod   4004
Prince of Outlaws - Alexey Tolstoy   6294

Godwin
The Cunning of the Dove - Alfred Duggan   1765
Gildenford - Valerie Anand   130

Gonzaga, Francesco
Private Renaissance - Maria Bellonci   436

Gordon, Lord George
Barnaby Rudge: A Tale of the Riots of Eighty -
   Charles Dickens   1641

Gordon, William
The Ninth Statue - Roseleen Milne   4410

Gore, Bysshe
Vice Avenged: A Moral Tale - Lolah Burford   774

Grafton, Sir Edmund
A London Season - Anthea Bell   420

Graham, James
The Bride - Margaret Irwin   3116
The Proud Servant: The Story of Montrose - Margaret
   Irwin   3120

Graham of Claverhouse, John
Graham of Claverhouse - Constance Dodge   1665
Old Mortality - Sir Walter Scott   5702

Grandissime, Honore
The Grandissimes - George W. Cable   842

Granville, Alexis de
Lady Hellfire - Suzanne Robinson   5414

Gray, Patrick
The Master of Gray Trilogy - Nigel Tranter   6316

Green, Lord Hibbard
A Shadow's Bliss - Patricia Veryan   6477

Grenville, Sir Richard
Roanoke Hundred - Inglis Fletcher   2138

Greville, Anthony
The Passing Bells - Phillip Rock   5421

Guatamozin
The Fair God - Lew Wallace   6537

Gunzburg, David de
The Four Winds of Heaven - Monique Raphel
   High   2916

Guyon
The Wild Hunt - Elizabeth Chadwick   969

Hagan
The Belt of Gold - Cecelia Holland   2984

Hardenberg, Claus von
Once a Gentleman - Donald James   3157

Harley, Ranger
Emily Goes to Exeter - Marion Chesney   1027

Harley, Robert
Exit Lady Masham - Louis Auchincloss   230

Harlow, George
The Heart of the Rose - June Barraclough   346

Harold
The Cunning of the Dove - Alfred Duggan   1765

Harrach, Karl Von
World and Paradise - Edgar Maas   3953

Harwood, Lord
Court of Shadows - Cynthia Morgan   4450

Hasan, Abu
The Infidel - Georgia Elizabeth Taylor   6182

Hastings
The Viking - Edison Marshall   4113

Hastings, Lord William
The Last of the Barons - Edward Bulwer-Lytton   769

Hatton, Christopher
*Shadow in the Sun: A Novel of Elizabeth I, the Virgin
   Queen* - F.W. Kenyon   3460

Haversham, Stuart
Crystal - Helen Ashfield   205

Hawkridge, Sir Waldo
The Nonesuch - Georgette Heyer   2896

Hawthorne, Chadwick
Chelynne - Robyn Carr   938

Haynow, Gottfried
The Drums of Winter - Sandra Paretti   4790

Hazzard, Hugo
The American Heiress - Dorothy Eden   1854

Heathcote, Jonathan
Garnet - Helen Ashfield   207

Helford, Ruark
The Pirate and the Pagan - Virginia Henley   2827

Henri de Guise
Queen Jezebel - Jean Plaidy   5049

Henri of Navarre
Evergreen Gallant - Jean Plaidy   5013
The Faith and the Flame - June Dimmit
   Houston   3054
The Italian Woman - Jean Plaidy   5024
Queen Jezebel - Jean Plaidy   5049
Young Henry of Navarre - Heinrich Mann   4062

Henry Beauclerc
Death of the Red King - Pamela Bennetts   448

Henry of Anjou
Knight's Honor - Roberta Gellis   2351

Hepburn, Francis
The Border Lord - Jan Westcott   6641

Hepburn, James
A Famine of Horses - P.F. Chisholm   1071
The Gay Galliard - Margaret Irwin   3119
Immortal Queen - Elizabeth Byrd   834
*King in Hell: A Novel of Bothwell and Mary, Queen of
   Scots* - Beverly Balin   282
*Maid of Honour: A Novel Set in the Court of Mary,
   Queen of Scots* - Elizabeth Byrd   836
Mary of Scotland - F.W. Kenyon   3454
Mary, Queen of Scotland and the Isles - Margaret
   George   2356
No Smoke Without Fire - Alice Harwood   2767
Parcel of Rogues - Jane Lane   3656
Royal Road to Fotheringay - Jean Plaidy   5059
A Time for the Death of a King - Ann Dukthas   1777
The White Queen - Frederic Fallon   2011

Hepburn, Patrick
The Hepburn - Jan Westcott   6645

Herennius, Favorinus
Confessors of the Name - Gladys Schmitt   5640

Hessenfield, Lord
The Song of the Siren - Philippa Carr   929

Holland, James Noel
Edward, Edward - Lolah Burford   772

Howard, John
The Fate of Princes - P.C. Doherty   1673

Howard, Tearle
The Conquest - Jude Deveraux   1630

Howard, Thomas
The King's Good Servant - Olive White   6696

Hui
Lady of the Reeds - Pauline Gedge   2345

Humbird, Edward
The Braintree Mission - Nicholas E. Wyckoff   6887

Humphrey, Duke of Gloucester
Epitaph for Three Women - Jean Plaidy   5012
The Royal Pawn - Antonia Ridge   5327

Hurst, Simon
The Frog Earl - Carola Dunn   1792

Irons, Fletcher
Faith and Honor - Robin Maderich   4025

Isambord, Ranf
The Heaven Tree Trilogy - Edith Pargeter   4797

Jan III Sobieski
Fire in the Steppe - Henryk Sienkiewicz   5847

Jenkinson, Robert Banks
The Sea Officer - Showell Styles   6105

Jessop, Ivor
The Baroness of Bow Street - Gail Clark   1085

Julian, Gregory
The Sinner of Saint Ambrose - Robert
   Raynolds   5275

Jung Lu
Forbidden City - Muriel Molland Jernigan   3215

Junot, Andoche
The Emperor's Duchess - R.G. Waldeck   6524

Karl-Eberhard
A Finger to Her Lips - Evelyn Berckman   472

Kassandros
Funeral Games - Mary Renault   5297

Kentaro
The Ginger Tree - Oswald Wynd   6890

Kilgour, Robert
The Wind From the Sea - Constance Heaven   2812

Kincross, Colin
The Heiress Bride - Catherine Coulter   1375

Kirov, Sergei
Anna - Cynthia Harrod-Eagles   2752
Fleur - Cynthia Harrod-Eagles   2754

Konigsmarck, Philip Christopher
The Princess of Celle - Jean Plaidy   5045

Kuragin, Andrei
The House of Kuragin - Constance Heaven   2808

Kussov, Boris
Encore - Monique Raphel High   2915

Lacey, Stephen de
Circle in the Water - Susan Wiggs   6742

Lafayette, Marie Joseph Paul de
The Bastard - John Jakes   3144
A Chance for Glory - Constance Wright   6877
Conceived in Liberty - Howard Fast   2029
Dawn's Early Light - Elswyth Thane   6215
The Drums of Monmouth - Emma Gelders
   Sterne   5998
The Fallon Blood - Reagan O'Neal   4741
Farewell to Valley Forge - David Taylor   6178
A Few Painted Feathers - Stephen Longstreet   3886
A Generation of Leaves - Robert S. Bloom   552
Hugh Wynne, Free Quaker - Silas Weir
   Mitchell   4416
I'll Storm Hell - Noel B. Gerson   2374
The Ironmaster - Anne Powers   5150
Jefferson: A Novel - Max Byrd   838
King's Masque - Evan John   3220
The Lure of the Falcon - Juliette Benzoni   465
Man From Mt. Vernon - Burke Boyce   607
Monmouth - Charles Bracelen Flood   2144
Morning in America - Willard Wiener   6741
A Place of Greater Safety - Hilary Mantel   4077
The Rebels - John Jakes   3152
Storm the Last Rampart - David Taylor   6180
The Strong Men - John Brick   677

To Spit Against the Wind - Benjamin H. Levin 3737
The Tree of Liberty - Elizabeth Page 4773
Valley Forge - MacKinlay Kantor 3364
Wicked Lady - Inglis Fletcher 2142
Yankee - Dana Fuller Ross 5495
Yorktown - Burke Davis 1513

Lamb, William
Albert's Victoria - Tyler Whittle 6719
The Queen and Lord M - Jean Plaidy 5046
The Queen's Husband - Jean Plaidy 5052
Victoria and Albert - Evelyn Anthony 166
The Young Victoria - Tyler Whittle 6724

Lamming, Lord
The Hammer of God - Alan Scholefield 5655

Lancy, Gerard Paul de
A Spy for Napoleon - Baroness Emma Orczy 4746

Latimer, Darsie
Red Gauntlet - Sir Walter Scott 5706

Laurignac, Edmond
Vale of Tyranny - Suzanne Butler 831

Lavenham, Ludovic
The Talisman Ring - Georgette Heyer 2905

Lavrin, Nicholas
The Fortune Hunter - Ira J. Morris 4477

Lawless, Desmond de
Poor Richard's Game - G.J.A. O'Toole 4766

Lazlo
The Secret Life of Laszlo, Count Dracula - Roderick Anscombe 156

LeClerc, Charles
Black Triumvirate: A Novel of Haiti - Benjamin H. Levin 3736

Lee, Henry
Woodstock; or, The Cavalier - Sir Walter Scott 5710

Lenton, Edward
The Abductors - Stuart Cloete 1121

Leofric
Lady Godiva and Master Tom - Raoul Cohen Faure 2052

Leominster, Lord Lavenham
Marry in Haste - Jane Aiken Hodge 2967

Leopold IV
The Golden Knight - George Challis 971

Leopold, Duke of Austria
Banners of Gold - Pamela Kaufman 3371

Leopold of Saxe-Coburg
The Girl Who Was Never Queen: A Biographical Novel of Princess Charlotte of Wales - Mary Main 4037

Lethbridge, Robert
The Convenient Marriage - Georgette Heyer 2882

Leyland, Francis
The White Witch - Elizabeth Goudge 2496

Lindley, Rowan
Wild Jasmine - Bertrice Small 5914

Linnieres, Ansiau de
The Cornerstone - Zoe Oldenbourg 4714

Lirey, Nicholas
The Image of Our Lord - Edward Burman 790

Lokenburg, Maximilian
On the Night of the Seventh Moon - Victoria Holt 3018

Lomassou, Bernat
The Golden Chain - Jean Gamo 2275

Loring, Nigel
The White Company - Sir Arthur Conan Doyle 1716

Lorme, Gyles
War Comes to Castle Rising - Fanny Cradock 1411

Lorme, Justin Henry de
The Lormes of Castle Rising - Fanny Cradock 1409

Louis
In a Dark Wood Wandering - Hella S. Haasse 2631

Lovat, Oswin
Topaz - Helen Ashfield 215

Lovell, Francis
The Fate of Princes - P.C. Doherty 1673

Lubonski, Count Cyprjan
Poland - James A. Michener 4373

Lucy, Jocelin
The Leper of St. Giles - Ellis Peters 4963

Ludel, Richard
The Hermit of Eyton Forest - Ellis Peters 4961

Ludlow, Sir Gareth
Sprig Muslin - Georgette Heyer 2903

Luis, Don
Anthony Adverse - Hervey Allen 98
The Golden Hawk - Frank Yerby 6921

Luton, Lord Evelyn
Journey - James A. Michener 4371

Lyndale
Gwendolen - Clare Darcy 1489

Mablethorpe, Adrian
Faro's Daughter - Georgette Heyer 2887

MacNamara, Seagan
Mistress of the Eagles - Elona Malterre 4052

MacPhiggan, Alastair
The Gentleman From America - Paul Benton 464

Malabestia
The King's Persons - Joanne Greenberg 2573

Malatesta, Giovanni
Concordia - Frances Fleetwood 2124

Malatesta, Paolo
Concordia - Frances Fleetwood 2124

Malencz, Count
Rakossy - Cecelia Holland 2995

Mandeville, Geoffrey de
The Knight - George Shipway 5829
Stephen and the Sleeping Saints - Pamela Bennetts 457

Manrique, Alonso
The Heart of Jade - Salvador de Madariaga 4024

Maplethorpe, Vincent
The Scottish Marriage - Karen Lynn 3942

Marden, Ranger
Miss Davenport's Christmas - Marion Chesney 1039

Markham, Dominic
Angel - Carola Dunn 1790

Marquess of Fenton
Belinda Goes to Bath - Marion Chesney 1020

Marquess of Porterhouse
Mrs. Budley Falls From Grace - Marion Chesney 1042

Marquis of Bolibar
The Marquis of Bolibar - Leo Perutz 4942

Marquis of Brabington
The Taming of Annabelle - Marion Chesney 1052

Marshal, William
The Battle of the Queens - Jean Plaidy 5005
Below the Salt - Thomas B. Costain 1362
Champion - L. Christian Balling 285
The Courts of Love - Jean Plaidy 5010
The Devil Is Loose - Graham Shelby 5790
In the Shadow of Midnight - Marsha Canham 880
King's Man - C.M. Edmondston 1880
The Marriage of Meggotta - Edith Pargeter 4799
The Prince of Darkness - Jean Plaidy 5044

The Wolf at the Door - Graham Shelby 5793

Martin, Dom
The Braganza Pursuit - Sarah Neilan 4564

Maurice, Comte de Saxe
The Glory and the Dream - Katharine Dunlap 1789

Medici, Cosimo II de'
The Palace of Wisdom - Bob Marshall-Andrews 4118

Medici, Lorenzo de
The Agony and the Ecstasy - Irving Stone 6054
The Florentine - Sandra Shulman 5840
The Palace - Chelsea Quinn Yarbro 6904
The Private Life of Mona Lisa - Pierre La Mure 3577

Mendoza y Luna, Don Pedro de
The Hounds of God - Rafael Sabatini 5551

Menkh, Lord
Her-Bak: The Living Face of Ancient Egypt - Isha Schwaller de Lubicz 5676

Menton, Aubrey
A Love So Wild - Deborah Chester 1056

Meren, Lord
Murder at the Feast of Rejoicing - Lynda S. Robinson 5407
Murder at the God's Gate - Lynda S. Robinson 5408
Murder in the Place of Anubis - Lynda S. Robinson 5409

Merenda, Lorenzo
Castle of Doves - Constance Heaven 2803

Merion, Giles
April Lady - Georgette Heyer 2873

Mervyn
The House by the Churchyard - Joseph Sheridan Le Fanu 3688

Metellus, Decius Caecilius
The Catiline Conspiracy - John Maddox Roberts 5379
The Sacrilege - John Maddox Roberts 5380
SPQR - John Maddox Roberts 5381
The Temple of the Muses - John Maddox Roberts 5382

Milcroft, Lord
Claire - Elizabeth Lyle 3931

Milo, Titus
A Murder on the Appian Way - Steven Saylor 5625

Mixtli
Aztec - Gary Jennings 3193

Moncrieff, Ian
If This Be Magic - Ellen Marsh 4098

Monforte, Don Camillo
The Bravo - James Fenimore Cooper 1298

Monington, Richard
Bennett's Welcome - Inglis Fletcher 2132

Monmouth, Harry
The Gentle Falcon - Hilda Lewis 3747

Montagu, John
Brimstone Club - F. van Wyck Mason 4147
The Vast Memory of Love - Malcolm Bosse 588

Montauban, Maurice de
The Anthem - Noel B. Gerson 2361

Montauban, Michel de
The Anthem - Noel B. Gerson 2361

Montauban, Philippe de
The Anthem - Noel B. Gerson 2361

Montfort, Simon de
The Battle of the Queens - Jean Plaidy 5005
The De Montfort Legacy - Pamela Bennetts 447
Deep Are the Valleys - Hannah Closs 1129

Falls the Shadow - Sharon Kay Penman 4903
High Are the Mountains - Hannah Closs 1130
Leopards and Lilies - Alfred Duggan 1769
The Lion of England - Eve Trevaskis 6336
The Marriage of Meggotta - Edith Pargeter 4799
The Queen From Provence - Jean Plaidy 5047
Shield of Honor - Alice Walworth Graham 2511
Sybille - Marion Meade 4318
The White Cutter - David Pownall 5158

Montgeil, Ricord de
Destiny of Fire - Zoe Oldenbourg 4715

Montgeoffrey, Roger
Through a Glass Darkly - Karleen Koen 3531

Montmorency, Jasper
Lady Jane - Norma Lee Clark 1092

Montrevil, Jean de
The Severed Crown - Jane Lane 3657

Mordaunt, John
I, John Mordaunt - Virgil Scott 5687

Morgan, Lord
Spy in Chancery - P.C. Doherty 1680

Mortimer, Charles
The Sandalwood Fan - Diana Brown 720

Mortimer, Richard
The Prisoners of September - Leon Garfield 2294

Mortimer, Roger de
The Follies of the King - Jean Plaidy 5014
Harlot Queen - Hilda Lewis 3748
Isabel the Fair - Margaret Campbell Barnes 323
The Lily and the Lion - Maurice Druon 1733
The Lion and the Leopard - Mary Ellen
  Johnson 3226
The She-Wolf - Pamela Bennetts 456
The She-Wolf of France - Maurice Druon 1736
Vows of the Peacock - Alice Walworth
  Graham 2513

Mountbatten, Louis
Dance on a Sinking Ship - Michael Kilian 3483

Munro, Alistair
Beatrice Goes to Brighton - Marion Chesney 1019

Murrah, Thomas
The Imposter - Noel B. Gerson 2375

Musgrave, Noel
Borrowed Plumes - Roseleen Milne 4409

Nettleby, Randolph
The Shooting Party - Isabel Colegate 1197

Neville, Richard
Crouchback - Carola Oman 4732
Crown of Roses - Valerie Anand 127
The Eye of God - C.L. Grace 2506
Fortune's Wheel - Rhoda S. Edwards 1886
The Golden Yoke: A Novel of the War of the Roses -
  Olive Eckerson 1837
I Remember Love - Mollie Hardwick 2694
The Last of the Barons - Edward Bulwer-Lytton 769
A Question of Choice - Prudence Andrew 143
Red Rose of Anjou - Jean Plaidy 5054
The Reluctant Queen: The Story of Anne of York -
  Jean Plaidy 5056
The Rose at Harvest End - Eleanor Fairburn 2003
The Sun in Splendour - Jean Plaidy 5066
The White Queen - Lesley J. Nickell 4611
The White Rose - Jan Westcott 6648

Nightingale, Frederic North
The Nightingale Legacy - Catherine Coulter 1379

Oda Nobunaga
The Signore: Shogun of the Warring States - Kunio
  Tsuji 6357

Ogloblin, Evgueny
Napoleon and the Cossacks - Peter N.
  Krassnoff 3551

Olifaunt, Nigel
The Fortunes of Nigel - Sir Walter Scott 5696

O'Neill, Shane
The Proud Man - Elizabeth Linington 3800

Ormley, Edmund
Flight From Fifth Avenue - Catherine M. Rae 5235

d'Orsay, Alfred
Imperial Courtesan - F.W. Kenyon 3452

Orsini, Paolo
Vittoria - Robert Merle 4342

Paget, Sir William
Feast in the Morning - Hugh Preston 5175

Pardailande Gondrin, Louis-Henri de
The Marquis - Joan Sanders 5586

Parrington, Stacey
St. John's Wood - Nancy Fitzgerald 2116

Payne, Fitzroy
Jane and the Unpleasantness at Scargrave Manor -
  Stephanie Barron 356

Pellew, Edward
The Sea Officer - Showell Styles 6105

Pembroke, Lord
Bond of Blood - Roberta Gellis 2349

Penwardine, Lord
Stage Fright - Gillian Linscott 3809

Percy, Henry
The Bloody Field - Edith Pargeter 4795
Falstaff - Robert Nye 4653
The Traitors of Bosworth - Robert Farrington 2021

Percy, Henry de
Robert the Bruce: The Steps to the Empty Throne -
  Nigel Tranter 6320

Perrivale, Simon
The Captive - Victoria Holt 3011

Peveril, Geoffrey
Peveril of the Peak - Sir Walter Scott 5703

Peyrac, Joffrey de
Angelique - Sergeanne Golon 2465
Angelique and the Demon - Sergeanne Golon 2466
Angelique and the Ghosts - Sergeanne Golon 2467
The Countess Angelique - Sergeanne Golon 2472
The Temptation of Angelique - Sergeanne
  Golon 2473

Philibert of Savoy
The Gentle Fury: A Novel of Margaret of Austria -
  Paul Lewis 3758
Here Lies Margot - Pamela Hill 2935

Philip, Duke of Burgundy
The Master Painter - Edwin Mullins 4513

Philippe
The Royal Succession - Maurice Druon 1735

Pirov, Boris
The Candlesticks and the Cross - Ruth Freeman
  Solomon 5940

Plantagenet, Henry
To Keep This Oath - Hebe Weenolsen 6597

Plessis-Belliere, Philippe du
Angelique and the King - Sergeanne Golon 2468

Pomander, Charles
Peg Woffington - Charles Reade 5281

Pomeroy, Bertram
Miss Hartwell's Dilemma - Carola Dunn 1796
Two Corinthians - Carola Dunn 1797

Prissac, Raymond de
The Courts of Love: A Romance of Medieval France -
  Peter Bourne 592

Probus, Marcus
Roman Go Home! - Adam Fergusson 2065

Putbus, Malte Moritz Von
Speranza - Sven Delblanc 1584

Racon, Gaston de
The Bastard - Brigitte Von Tessin 6208

Radburn, Edward
The Prince Regent's Silver Bell - Gladys
  McGorian 4275

Radcliffe, Charles
Devil Water - Anya Seton 5749

Rafel, Alvero de
Torquemada - Howard Fast 2045

Railton, Augustus
Penelope Goes to Portsmouth - Marion
  Chesney 1043

Rakossy, Janos
Rakossy - Cecelia Holland 2995

Raleigh, Sir Walter
Death of the Fox - George Garrett 2300
Kenilworth - Sir Walter Scott 5700

Ralph, Earl of Clarendon
The Battle-Ax of God - Le Roy MacLeod 4007

Rambaud, Lord
Bernadin, My Love - Leonard Rossiter 5506

Ramsay, James Andrew Broun
Follow the Drum - James Leasor 3699

Ranulf
The King Liveth - Jeffrey Farnol 2013

Ranulf de Gernons
Knight's Honor - Roberta Gellis 2351

Raoul of Sedgemont
Ann of Cambray - Mary Lide 3772

Raoul the Terrible
Simon the Coldheart - Georgette Heyer 2901

Rasero, Fausto
Rasero - Francisco Rebolledo 5282

Raskonski, Andreas
A Great Lord - Paul Frischauer 2233

Ravenswood
The Bride of Lammermoor - Sir Walter Scott 5693

Raymond VI of Toulouse
Deep Are the Valleys - Hannah Closs 1129
High Are the Mountains - Hannah Closs 1130

Rayne, Sylvester
Sylvester; or, The Wicked Uncle - Georgette
  Heyer 2904

Red Adam
Red Adam's Lady - Grace Ingram 3106

Remizou, Dmitri
Heirs of the Motherland - Judith Pella 4893

Rene of Provence
Anne of Geierstein - Sir Walter Scott 5689

Reynauld of Chatillon
The Knights of Dark Renown - Graham Shelby 5792

Riario, Girolamo
The Medici Hawks - Martin Woodhouse 6853

Ribera, Luis
The Royal City - Les Savage Jr. 5621

Rich, Robert
Lady Rich - Elizabeth Boatwright Coker 1166

Richard de Guise
Morality Play - Barry Unsworth 6387

Richard, Duke of Gloucester
The Black Arrow - Robert Louis Stevenson 6008
Crown of Roses - Valerie Anand 127
Death and the Chapman - Kate Sedley 5715
The Eve of Saint Hyacinth - Kate Sedley 5716
Fortune's Wheel - Rhoda S. Edwards 1886

The Goldsmith's Wife - Jean Plaidy 5017
The Plymouth Cloak - Kate Sedley 5718
The Rose at Harvest End - Eleanor Fairburn 2003
The Swan and the Rose - Francis W. Leary 3697
The Warwick Heiress - Margaret Abbey 6
The White Rose - Jan Westcott 6648

Richard of Sussex
The Lion and the Leopard - Mary Ellen
    Johnson 3226

Richepane, Arsene de
The Arm and the Darkness - Taylor Caldwell 850

Rienzo, Cola di
The Lily and the Lion - Maurice Druon 1733

River, Christian de
Lady Gallant - Suzanne Robinson 5413

Rivington, Alexander
Lord Rivington's Lady - Eileen Jackson 3134

Robert I the Magnificent
The Conqueror - Georgette Heyer 2881

Robert Guiscard
Count Bohemond - Alfred Duggan 1764
Wine of Satan - Laverne Gay 2327

Robert of Artois
The Iron King - Maurice Druon 1732
The Lily and the Lion - Maurice Druon 1733
The Poisoned Crown - Maurice Druon 1734
The Royal Succession - Maurice Druon 1735
The Strangled Queen - Maurice Druon 1737
The Vow on the Heron - Jean Plaidy 5074

Robert the Bruce
Braveheart - Randall Wallace 6538
The Crown in Darkness - P.C. Doherty 1671
Witness to Treason - Millie J. Ragosta 5244

Roc-sur-Besbre, Comte de
Baneful Sorceries, or The Countess Bewitched - Joan
    Sanders 5585

Rochefort
The Three Musketeers - Alexandre Dumas 1782

Rodrigo, Don
The Betrothed - Alessandro Manzoni 4078

Roger, Duke of Lunel
A Booke of Days: A Journal of the Crusade by Roger,
    Duke of Lunel - Stephen J. Rivele 5351

Roger of Hereford
Knight's Honor - Roberta Gellis 2351

Rohan, Tancrede de
The Silver Plume - Arthur Meeker 4323

Ronan, Nicholas
Emerald - Helen Ashfield 206

Rossendale, John
Waterloo - Bernard Cornwell 1350

Rosslyn, Lord
Daughters of England - Philippa Carr 919

Rossmayne
Topaz - Helen Ashfield 215

Rothwell, Lord
Defy Not the Heart - Johanna Lindsey 3794

Rothwell, Adrian
The Marquis and Miss Jones - Helen Ashfield 208

Roujay, Bertrand de
The Free Frenchman - Piers Paul Read 5277

Rouvroy, Louis de
The Cat and the King - Louis Auchincloss 229

Rowan, Lucas
The Bluestocking - June Drummond 1729

Rudolstadt, Albert
Consuelo - George Sand 5582

Ruthven, Lord
Count Manifred - Miranda Seymour 5761

Ryder, Jared
Deception - Amanda Quick 5214

Sabreuois, Henri de
Arundel - Kenneth Roberts 5383

Sadayori
Harpoon - C.W. Nicol 4612

Sade, Giles de
Lamia: A Witch - Georgia Elizabeth Taylor 6183

Saguenary, Richard
A King Reluctant - William Vaughan Wilkins 6759

St. Clare, Richard
Desire and Deceive - Cordia Byers 832

St. Denis, Louis Juchereau
Ride the Red Earth - Paul I. Wellman 6620

Saint-Germain, Comte de
Better in the Dark - Chelsea Quinn Yarbro 6894
Darker Jewels - Chelsea Quinn Yarbro 6898
Hotel Transylvania - Chelsea Quinn Yarbro 6900
Mansions of Darkness - Chelsea Quinn Yarbro 6902
Out of the House of Life - Chelsea Quinn
    Yarbro 6903
The Palace - Chelsea Quinn Yarbro 6904
Path of the Eclipse - Chelsea Quinn Yarbro 6905
Tempting Fate - Chelsea Quinn Yarbro 6906

St. Gregory, Dane
Knights - Linda Lael Miller 4399

Saint-Juste, Jules
The Scandalous Lady Wright - Marion
    Chesney 1049

Ste. Maxence, Guernes de Pont
This Bright Sword - Donald Barr Chidsey 1066

St. Romer, Anthony
Regency Rogue - Helen Ashfield 212

Sant'Anna, Corrado
Marianne and the Lords of the East - Juliette
    Benzoni 468
Marianne and the Masked Prince - Juliette
    Benzoni 469
Marianne and the Rebels - Juliette Benzoni 471

Savenay, Henri de
The White Cockade - Charles James Louis
    Gilson 2423

Savile, George
The Bracegirdle - Burris Atkins Jenkins 3189

Scott, James
A Falling Star - Pamela Belle 431
The King's Bastard - Hebe Elsna 1932
Micah Clarke - Sir Arthur Conan Doyle 1715
The Three Crowns - Jean Plaidy 5070

Seabury, Lord
The Autumn Rose - Fiona Hill 2923

Servais, Guy de
Brazen Whispers - Jane Feather 2055

Sesostris, Lord
The Altar and the Crown - Marian Niven 4631

Severin of Langthorne
Rosehaven - Catherine Coulter 1380

Severn, Lord
Fleeting Fancy - Rosemary Edghill 1866

Seymour, Edward
Feast in the Morning - Hugh Preston 5175
The Game of Kings - Dorothy Dunnett 1801

Seymour, Thomas
The Ivy Crown: A Biographical Novel of Queen
    Katherine Parr - Mary M. Luke 3923
The Queen's Grace - Jan Westcott 6646
The Young Elizabeth - Jennette Letton 3730

Sforza, Francesco
Condottiere - Jan Westcott 6644

Sforza, Gian Galeazzo
Duchess of Milan - Michael Ennis 1946

Sforza, Giovanni
The Naked Sword: The Story of Lucretia Borgia -
    F.W. Kenyon 3456

Sforza, Ludovico
The Bride of Sforza - Miranda Seymour 5760
A Comedy of Murders - George Herman 2861
Duchess of Milan - Michael Ennis 1946
The Lady in the Mask - Anne Green 2564

Sherborne, Ramsey
Circle of Gold - Karen Harper 2710

Sherbrooke, Douglas
The Sherbrooke Bride - Catherine Coulter 1382

Sheringham, Anthony "Sherry"
Friday's Child - Georgette Heyer 2890

Shield, Sir Tristram
The Talisman Ring - Georgette Heyer 2905

Sidney, Sir Philip
Roanoke Hundred - Inglis Fletcher 2138

Siena, Colombo De
Chivalry - Rafael Sabatini 5548

Simon of Monleigh
My Lord Monleigh - Jan Cox Speas 5957

Sinclair, Francis
Legacy of the Wolf - Jean Raynes 5274

Sinclair, Julian
Seduction - Amanda Quick 5220

Smirnoff, Vladimir
White Nights, Red Dawn - Frederick Nolan 4634

Smith, Frederick Edwin
High Heroic - Constantine FitzGibbon 2118

Somers, Richard
Lord Richard's Passion - Mervyn Jones 3293

Somerset, Fitzroy
Hazard's Command - Vivian Stuart 6088

Somervell
Honor This Day - Alexander Kent 3432

Sommerville, Philip
Back in Society - Marion Chesney 1017
Mrs. Budley Falls From Grace - Marion
    Chesney 1042
Sir Philip's Folly - Marion Chesney 1051

Stafford, Edward
The Grail Murders - Michael Clynes 1135

Stafford, Henry
Crown of Roses - Valerie Anand 127
The Fate of Princes - P.C. Doherty 1673

Stafford, Nicholas
A Knight in Shining Armor - Jude Deveraux 1631

Stanley, William
The Killing of Richard the Third - Robert
    Farrington 2020
The Traitors of Bosworth - Robert Farrington 2021

Stauffenberg, Claus von
The Very Rich Hours of Count von Stauffenberg - Paul
    West 6637

Stephen
The Fatal Crown - Ellen Jones 3289
The Lion of Justice - Jean Plaidy 5031

Steuben, Friedrich von
Conceived in Liberty - Howard Fast 2029
Eagle in the Sky - F. van Wyck Mason 4149
Monmouth - Charles Bracelen Flood 2144
Valley Forge - MacKinlay Kantor 3364

Steward, Robert
The Sea Officer - Showell Styles 6105

Stewart, Henry
The Gay Galliard - Margaret Irwin 3119
The Green Salamander - Pamela Hill 2933
Immortal Queen - Elizabeth Byrd 834
The Lion and the Rose - Jane Oliver 4724
Mary of Scotland - F.W. Kenyon 3454
Mary, Queen of Scotland and the Isles - Margaret
  George 2356
No Smoke Without Fire - Alice Harwood 2767
Parcel of Rogues - Jane Lane 3656
Queen's Caprice - Marjorie Bowen 599
Royal Road to Fotheringay - Jean Plaidy 5059
A Time for the Death of a King - Ann Dukthas 1777
The White Queen - Frederic Fallon 2011

Stewart, James
The White Queen - Frederic Fallon 2011

Stewart, John
A Stake in the Kingdom - Nigel Tranter 6321
Unicorn Rampant - Nigel Tranter 6323

Stewart, Robert
Brumaire - Mark Logan 3864
Guillotine - Mark Logan 3865
The World, the Flesh, and the Devil - Reay
  Tannahill 6159

Stewart, Tavis
The Spitfire - Bertrice Small 5912

Stratford, Sir Philip
Street of the Madwoman - Isabel Ortega 4756

Stratton, Sebastian
Ruby - Helen Ashfield 213

Stuart, James
No Smoke Without Fire - Alice Harwood 2767
*Seats of the Mighty: A Novel of James Stuart, Brother
  of Mary, Queen of Scots* - Alice Harwood 2768

Sutbury, Felix
The Sutburys - Pamela Hill 2944

Talvas
The Lost Lands - Peter Vansittart 6430

Tancred
Count Bohemond - Alfred Duggan 1764

Tarconti, Andrea
Wings of the Falcon - Barbara Michaels 4361

Tarconti, Stefano
Wings of the Falcon - Barbara Michaels 4361

Taverner, Sir Peregrine
Regency Buck - Georgette Heyer 2898

Tavington, Nicholas
The King's Brat - Constance Gluyas 2441
My Lady Benbrook - Constance Gluyas 2442

Temple, Henry John
Albert's Victoria - Tyler Whittle 6719
Follow the Drum - James Leasor 3699
Nevada! - Dana Fuller Ross 5481
The Queen's Husband - Jean Plaidy 5052
Republic: A Novel of Texas - E.V. Thompson 6266
Victoria and Albert - Evelyn Anthony 166
When the Emperor Dies - Mason McCann
  Smith 5926
The Widow of Windsor - Jean Plaidy 5076

Tepes, Vlad
Anno-Dracula - Kim Newman 4595

Thierry
The Earl - Cecelia Holland 2987

Thompson, Benjamin
The Countess - March Cost 1360

Thorne, Adam
Pomp and Circumstance - Fred Mustard
  Stewart 6025

Tirel, Walter
Death of the Red King - Pamela Bennetts 448
The Paladin - George Shipway 5830

Tolchin, Count Gregory
Triptych - Dora Landey 3652

Tolstoy, Leo
*The Extraordinary Adventures of Secret Agent Shipov
  in Pursuit of Count Leo Tolstoy in the Year 1862* -
  Bulat Okudzhava 4712

Toranaga, Lord Yoshi
Shogun - James Clavell 1101

Toresson, Steinfinn
The Axe - Sigrid Undset 6378

Torridon, Charles
Her Grace's Passion - Marion Chesney 1033

Torrigiani, Bruno di
Stranger at the Wedding - Frances Lynch 3934

Tottenham, Lord
The Silver Highways - Malcolm Macdonald 3972

Tourville, Richard
Rivers West - Louis L'Amour 3626

Traherne, Simon
Scandal - Amanda Quick 5219

Tramont, Philippe de
The Wine Widow - Tessa Barclay 301

Traore, Dousika
Segu - Maryse Conde 1234

Tregarthan, Lord
Plain Jane - Marion Chesney 1045

Trench, Benedict
Dulcie Bligh - Gail Clark 1086

Trevor, Jocelyn
My Love, My Enemy - Jan Cox Speas 5958

Tudor, Henry
The Lodestar - Pamela Belle 432
Merchant of the Ruby - Alice Harwood 2766
An Unknown Welshman - Jean Stubbs 6100

Tusson Bey
Blood and Sand - Rosemary Sutcliff 6121

Tynedale, Julian
Buckskin Baronet - Margaret Widdemer 6734

Tyrrell, Charles
The Duchess of Duke Street - Mollie Hardwick 2693

Valaise, Guy
Kingdom of the Grail - A.A. Attanasio 226

Valsecca, Odo
The Valley of Decision - Edith Wharton 6653

Van Welcker, Count
The Smile of the Stranger - Joan Aiken 53

Varenne, Alexandre de
The Eleventh Year - Monique Raphel High 2914

The Venetian
Time of Parting - Anton Donchev 1690

Vere, Edward de
Cloak of Folly - Burke Boyce 606

Vere, Robert de
Passage to Pontefract - Jean Plaidy 5038

Verney, Romain
A Company of Swans - Eva Ibbotson 3095

Verringer, Jason
The Time of the Hunter's Moon - Victoria Holt 3022

Vicar, Sir Arthur
Jewels - Robert Perrin 4917

Vidal, Justin
The Duchess of Vidal - Dawn Lindsey 3793

Vignerot du Plessis, Louis-Francois-Armand de
Through a Glass Darkly - Karleen Koen 3531

Villiers, George
Ballenrose - Mallory Burgess 783
Call Lady Purbeck - Hilda Lewis 3745
The Cardinal and the Queen - Evelyn Anthony 159
Charles the King - Evelyn Anthony 160
A Health Unto His Majesty - Jean Plaidy 5019
Here Lies Our Sovereign Lord - Jean Plaidy 5021
The King Breaker - Elizabeth Linington 3797
The King's General - Daphne Du Maurier 1748
My Lord Foxe - Constance Gluyas 2443
Myself My Enemy - Jean Plaidy 5037
Our Jo, or The Chronicle of a Coming Man - Kenneth
  M. Cameron 868
Peveril of the Peak - Sir Walter Scott 5703
Royal Escape - Georgette Heyer 2900
The Three Musketeers - Alexandre Dumas 1782
To Love a Queen - Lawrence Schoonover 5669
Unicorn Rampant - Nigel Tranter 6323
Wife to Great Buckingham - Hilda Lewis 3751
The Young and Lonely King - Jane Lane 3659

Villiers, John
Call Lady Purbeck - Hilda Lewis 3745

Vinicius
Quo Vadis - Henryk Sienkiewicz 5848

Vivar, Blas
Sharpe's Devil - Bernard Cornwell 1340
Sharpe's Rifles - Bernard Cornwell 1347

Voldi
The Big Fisherman - Lloyd C. Douglas 1702

Von Falkenburg, Julian
Castle of Eagles - Constance Heaven 2804

Von Poellnitz, Baron
Wicked Lady - Inglis Fletcher 2142

Wakefield, Robert
The Sword of Truth - Gilbert Morris 4472

Walden
The Man From St. Petersburg - Ken Follett 2148

Waldstein, Bobby von
A Princess in Berlin - Arthur R.G. Solmssen 5939

Walpole, Robert
Queen in Waiting - Jean Plaidy 5048

Wardshire, Lucifer
The Scandalous Marriage - Marion Chesney 1050

Ware, Gillespie Vernon
The Foundling - Georgette Heyer 2888

Wedderlie, Edgar
Strong as Death - Sharan Newman 4602

Wellesley, Arthur
The Amazing Mrs. Bonaparte - Harnett T.
  Kane 3351
The Asherwood Protegee - Mary A. Garratt 2299
A Balance of Dangers - Anthony Forrest 2184
The Flight of the Eagle - Donald Thomas 6239
The Gentleman From America - Paul Benton 464
The Life and Times of Horatio Hornblower - C.
  Northcote Parkinson 4813
The Masters of Bow Street - John Creasy 1423
Rage in Silence: A Novel Based on the Life of Goya -
  Donald Braider 643
Rifleman Dodd - C.S. Forester 2181
Sharpe's Battle - Bernard Cornwell 1338
Sharpe's Company - Bernard Cornwell 1339
Sharpe's Eagle - Bernard Cornwell 1341
Sharpe's Gold - Bernard Cornwell 1343
Sharpe's Honour - Bernard Cornwell 1344
Sharpe's Sword - Bernard Cornwell 1349
Waterloo - Bernard Cornwell 1350
Waterloo - Manuel Komroff 3536
Waterloo - Frederic E. Smith 5920
Whispering - Jane Aiken Hodge 2972

NOBLEWOMAN

Westbrook, Gideon
Ravished - Amanda Quick   5216

Whetstone, Sir Thomas
Buccaneer - Dudley Pope   5093

William I
Fortune's Knave: The Making of William the Conqueror - Mary Lide   3774

William, Duke of Orange
The Sea Beggars - Cecelia Holland   2996

William of Miraval
Candle in the Window - Christina Dodd   1662

William of Orange
The Queen's Husband - Samuel Edwards   1889

William the Conqueror
Bond of Honour - Catherine Todd   6284
The Conqueror's Wife - Noel B. Gerson   2363
The Cunning of the Dove - Alfred Duggan   1765
The Golden Warrior: The Story of Harold and William - Hope Muntz   4517
Harold Was My King - Hilda Lewis   3749
The Norman Pretender - Valerie Anand   132
Red Lion and Gold Dragon - Rosemary Sprague   5969
The Saxon Tapestry - Sile Rice   5317
Son of Dust - H.F.M. Prescott   5171
Wife to the Bastard - Hilda Lewis   3753

Wilmot, John
Alethea - Pamela Belle   429
Old St. Paul's - William Harrison Ainsworth   57
Royal Escape - Georgette Heyer   2900

Winfred
The Last Romans - Teodor Jeske-Choinski   3216

Winterbourne, Daniel
Miss Hartwell's Dilemma - Carola Dunn   1796

Duke of Winterset
Monsieur Beaucaire - Booth Tarkington   6163

Winthrop, Knight
Night Shadow - Catherine Coulter   1377

Wrenthe, Justin
The Earl and the Heiress - Barbara Metzger   4345

Wrexham, Lord Redvers
Caroline and Julia - Clare Darcy   1484

Wright, Sir Benjamin
The Scandalous Lady Wright - Marion Chesney   1049

Wriothesley, Henry
The Cleopatra Boy - Eric Malpass   4048
Nicholas Cooke: Actor, Soldier, Physician, Priest - Stephanie Cowell   1393
Serenissima: A Novel of Venice - Erica Jong   3300
Sweet Will - Eric Malpass   4050
Will Shakespeare: The Untold Story - John Mortimer   4495

Wriothesley, Thomas
Feast in the Morning - Hugh Preston   5175

Wyatt, Sir Thomas
The Tower of London - William Harrison Ainsworth   58
Windsor Castle - William Harrison Ainsworth   59

Wydawski
Salvation - Sholem Asch   202

Yoshi
Gai-Jin: A Novel of Japan - James Clavell   1100

Zeppelin, Count Ferdinand von
McKensie's Hundred: A Tale of the Old Dominion - Frank Yerby   6924

Abbott, Lady Letitia
Tish - Cissie Miller   4381

Alastair, Leonie
Devil's Cub - Georgette Heyer   2885

Aliena
The Pillars of the Earth - Ken Follett   2149

Amelia
A Dancer in Darkness - David Stacton   5971

Andreda, Dona Maria
Buccaneer Surgeon - C.V. Terry   6205

Anne Louise of Limburg
Seven Tempest - William Vaughan Wilkins   6761

Anne of Geierstein
Anne of Geierstein - Sir Walter Scott   5689

Anne of Meziere, Lady
Under the Winter Moon - Teresa Brooke   705

Anne of Warwick
The Swan and the Rose - Francis W. Leary   3697

Apieta, Anna
The Lute Player - Norah Lofts   3852

Appelbaux, Elizabeth
Louisa Brancusi - Darrell Husted   3088

Asano, Lady
The Tokaido Road: A Novel of Feudal Japan - Lucia St. Clair Robson   5417

d'Aubigne, Francoise
The Anthem - Noel B. Gerson   2361
The Cat and the King - Louis Auchincloss   229
The Crown and the Shadow: The Story of Francoise d'Aubigne, Marquise de Maintenon - Pamela Hill   2930
The Gilded Torch - Iola Fuller   2252
The Secret Wife - Alice Acland   22

Baglione, Camilla
Prince of Foxes - Samuel Shellabarger   5797

Ballinger, Augusta
Rendezvous - Amanda Quick   5218

Barry, Jeanne du
The French Bride - Evelyn Anthony   163
Golden Venus - David Mynders Smythe   5933
Royal Merry-Go-Round - F.W. Kenyon   3459

Bathory, Elizabeth
The Blood Countess - Andrei Codrescu   1149

Beauchamp, Philippa de
Earth Song - Catherine Coulter   1374

Becket, Eleanora
Lady Gallant - Suzanne Robinson   5413

Bellamy, Lady Marjorie
The Bellamy Saga - John Pearson   4878
Upstairs Downstairs - John Hawkesworth   2782

Bernstein, Baroness Beatrix
The Virginians - William Makepeace Thackeray   6214

Bezy, Marianne de
In Perilous Seas - Victor Suthren   6130

Bigod, Lady Barbara
A Silver Mirror - Roberta Gellis   2353

Blaise, Malvina
Castle Heritage - Elisabeth Barr   337

Blanche, Lady
The Seven Ages - Eva Figes   2084

Bleymont, Catherine de
Captain General - John P. Stevenson   6007

Bligh, Dulcie
The Baroness of Bow Street - Gail Clark   1085
Dulcie Bligh - Gail Clark   1086

Borgia, Lucrezia
Carnival of Saints - George Herman   2860
City of God: A Novel of the Borgias - Cecelia Holland   2985
Daughter of Shadows - Miranda Seymour   5762
The Flame of the Borgias - Jean Briggs   680
Light on Lucrezia - Jean Plaidy   5029
Madonna of the Seven Hills - Jean Plaidy   5034
Michelangelo the Florentine - Sidney Alexander   86
The Naked Sword: The Story of Lucretia Borgia - F.W. Kenyon   3456
A Passion in the Blood - Genevieve Davis   1519
Private Renaissance - Maria Bellonci   436
The Scarlet City - Hella S. Haasse   2632

Bourbon, Louise de
Sorrow by Day - Marjorie Coryn   1359

Bourbon, Marie Louise de
Poison - Kathryn Harrison   2737

Bradse, Matilda
Lady of Hay - Barbara Erskine   1955

Bradwardine, Rose
Waverley - Sir Walter Scott   5709

Brese, Magdalen de
Brazen Whispers - Jane Feather   2055

Brinvilliers, Marie Madeleine
The Devil's Marchioness - William Fifield   2082
A Lady at Bay - Edgar Maas   3950

Burdett-Coutts, Angela
The Hoydens and Mr. Dickens - William J. Palmer   4784

Cabarrus, Jeanne Marie Therese de
Lady of Paris - William Vaughan Wilkins   6760

Canillejas, Dona Eloisa
Bride of the Conqueror - Hartzell Spence   5961

Carlisle, Mary
Monsieur Beaucaire - Booth Tarkington   6163

Carlow, Fanny
Bath Tangle - Georgette Heyer   2875

Carlow, Lady Serena
Bath Tangle - Georgette Heyer   2875

Carruthers, Lady
Sir Philip's Folly - Marion Chesney   1051

Cayetana, Maria
Colossus: A Novel about Goya and a World Gone Mad - Stephen Marlowe   4093
In the Blazing Light - Max White   6693
The Last Portrait of the Duchess of Alba - Antonio Larreta   3666
The Naked Maja - Noel B. Gerson   2378
Rage in Silence: A Novel Based on the Life of Goya - Donald Braider   643

Cecily of York
The Dragon Waiting: A Masque of History - John M. Ford   2165

Cenci, Beatrice
A Tale for Midnight - Frederic Prokosch   5195

Chambers, Alexandra
The Sherbrooke Bride - Catherine Coulter   1382

Champeney, Reina de
Defy Not the Heart - Johanna Lindsey   3794

Chevereuil, Claude de
Monsieur Janvier - Elizabeth Linington   3799

Childe, Barbara
An Infamous Army - Georgette Heyer   2892

Churchill, Jane
The Widow of Windsor - Tyler Whittle   6723

Churchill, Sarah
The Elusive Crown - Hebe Elsna   1931
Exit Lady Masham - Louis Auchincloss   230
The Glory and the Dream - F.W. Kenyon   3450

Marlborough's Unfair Lady - Lozania Prole   5197
The Power and the Passion - Christina
  Nicholson   4609
The Queen's Favourites - Jean Plaidy   5051
The Sachem - Donald Clayton Porter   5124

Claire, Isabelle de
Champion - L. Christian Balling   285

Clare, Lady Ariel de
In the Shadow of Midnight - Marsha Canham   880

Claudia
A Walk with Love and Death - Hans Koning   3539

Clemence of Saxe-Salsa
The Battle of Wagram - Gilles Lapouge   3664

Clemens, Atta Olivia
A Candle for D'Artagnan - Chelsea Quinn
  Yarbro   6895
Crusader's Torch - Chelsea Quinn Yarbro   6897
Darker Jewels - Chelsea Quinn Yarbro   6898
A Flame in Byzantium - Chelsea Quinn Yarbro   6899
The Palace - Chelsea Quinn Yarbro   6904

Clervaux, Nicole de
Palaces of Desire - Kate Alexander   81

Clodia
Chantefable - Eldorous L. Dayton   1546
The City of Libertines - W.G. Hardy   2702
Clodia - Robert DeMaria   1606
Turn Back the River - W.G. Hardy   2703

Colonna, Vittoria
The Scarlet City - Hella S. Haasse   2632

Cornwallace, Judith
The Woodsman - Don Wright   6880

Cropotkin, Countess
Fire in the Ice - Alan Scholefield   5653

Danbury, Lady Eleanor
Room with a Clue - Kate Kingsbury   3495

Danver, Georginna
Double Masquerade - Karen Lynn   3938

d'Aragona, Isabella
Duchess of Milan - Michael Ennis   1946

Dashkova, Sophia
Death Off Stage - Richard Grayson   2558

d'Asselnat, Marianne
Marianne - Juliette Benzoni   466
Marianne and the Lords of the East - Juliette
  Benzoni   468
Marianne and the Masked Prince - Juliette
  Benzoni   469
Marianne and the Privateer - Juliette Benzoni   470
Marianne and the Rebels - Juliette Benzoni   471

de Montemayor, Marquesa
The Bridge of San Luis Rey - Thornton Wilder   6752

de Rada y Sylva, Dominica
Beauvallet - Georgette Heyer   2876

de Willading, Adelheid
The Headsman; or, The Abbaye des Vignerons - James
  Fenimore Cooper   1300

Devereux, Brigitte
Highland Belle - Patricia Grasso   2541

Devereux, Penelope
Lady Rich - Elizabeth Boatwright Coker   1166

Diane de Poitiers
Courtesan - Diane Haeger   2635
Madame Serpent - Jean Plaidy   5033

Diarcy, Lady Valerie
Fire Along the Sky: A Novel of America - Robert
  Moss   4497

Douglas, Margaret
The Green Salamander - Pamela Hill   2933

du Fourchet, Adele
The Porcelain Dove - Delia Sherman   5815

Dupuy-Preaux, Sophie de
Death at the French Creek - Raymond C. Borel   580

Edith the Fair
Harold, the Last of the Saxon Kings - Edward Bulwer-
  Lytton   767

Eisenstadt, Jullienne
Winter of the Heart - Linda J. LaRosa   3665

Eleanor of Gloucester
Epitaph for Three Women - Jean Plaidy   5012

d'Este, Isabella
Light on Lucrezia - Jean Plaidy   5029
Private Renaissance - Maria Bellonci   436

Evgeneiva, Xenya
Darker Jewels - Chelsea Quinn Yarbro   6898

Fancot, Amabel
False Colours - Georgette Heyer   2886

Fayema, Laya
The Scimitar - Samuel Edwards   1890

Fenner, Lady Ermentrude
The Novice's Tale - Margaret Frazer   2217

Feucheres, Sophie Dawes
Sophie - Geoffrey Wagner   6519

Fleming, Jocelyn
Savage Thunder - Johanna Lindsey   3795

Fordyce, Leonora
The Emerald Necklace - Diana Brown   718

Fortescue, Lady
Lady Fortescue Steps Out - Marion Chesney   1035
Miss Tonks Turns to Crime - Marion Chesney   1041

Fortesque, Daria de
Secret Song - Catherine Coulter   1381

Fremney, Lady Jane
Back in Society - Marion Chesney   1017

Gardiner, Margaret
Imperial Courtesan - F.W. Kenyon   3452

Giocondo, Lisa Gherardini
Mona Lisa: The Woman in the Portrait - Sara
  Mayfield   4206

Godiva, Lady
Hereward the Wake - Charles Kingsley   3497
King Hereafter - Dorothy Dunnett   1802
Lady Godiva and Master Tom - Raoul Cohen
  Faure   2052

Gomez, Jimena
The Infidel - Georgia Elizabeth Taylor   6182

Gonzago y Cordoza, Margarita
The Sinking of the Sarah Diamond - William Dale
  Jennings   3213

Gordon, Catherine
Merchant of the Ruby - Alice Harwood   2766

Gordon, Lady Jane
The Hepburn - Jan Westcott   6645

Graham, Caroline Agnes
Bertie and the Tinman - Peter Lovesey   3909

Grenville, Lady Caroline
Captain Monsoon - Victor Suthren   6128

Grey, Arabella
The Spitfire - Bertrice Small   5912

Grey, Lady Jane
Feast in the Morning - Hugh Preston   5175
The Lily and the Leopards - Alice Harwood   2765
Sister to Jane: The Story of Lady Katharine Grey -
  Beatrice May   4202

Grey, Lady Katharine
Sister to Jane: The Story of Lady Katharine Grey -
  Beatrice May   4202

So Merciful a Queen, So Cruel a Woman - Alice
  Harwood   2769

Grunowski, Valentina
Valentina - Evelyn Anthony   165

Guiccioli, Teresa
Teresa, or Her Demon Lover - Austin K. Gray   2554

Gunzburg, Sonia de
The Four Winds of Heaven - Monique Raphel
  High   2916

Hadshire, Matilda
Her Grace's Passion - Marion Chesney   1033

Hallandine, Louise
The Bride - Margaret Irwin   3116

Heathcote, Frances
Garnet - Helen Ashfield   207

Helen of Troy
The Firebrand - Marion Zimmer Bradley   624
The Invaders - Peter Danielson   1469
The Promised Land - Peter Danielson   1471
Scandal in Troy - Eva Hemmer Hansen   2679
Troy - Richard Matturro   4194
Whom the Gods Would Destroy - Richard
  Powell   5148

Howard, Frances
The King James Version - Stanley N. Stewart   6035
King's Minion - Rafael Sabatini   5552
Lion Rampant - Bernard Shrimsley   5836
The Murder in the Tower - Jean Plaidy   5035
The Street of Kings - Charles Dexter   1637

Iolanthe
The Saracen Blade - Frank Yerby   6926

Isabelle de Croye
Quentin Durward - Sir Walter Scott   5705

Jacqueline of Hainault
The Master Painter - Edwin Mullins   4513

Jamison, Jamie
The Bride - Julie Garwood   2311

Jeanne of Navarre
The Italian Woman - Jean Plaidy   5024

Joan of Hawkingham
Emerald Fire - Laurie Grant   2537

Juana-Maria, Lady
The Golden Chain - Jean Gamo   2275

Junot, Laure
The Emperor's Duchess - R.G. Waldeck   6524

Justina, Helena
The Iron Hand of Mars - Lindsey Davis   1528
Last Act in Palmyra - Lindsey Davis   1529
Shadows in Bronze - Lindsey Davis   1531
Time to Depart - Lindsey Davis   1533

Karlotte, Anna-Marie Elsbet
The Blood Order - Jack D. Hunter   3084

Kercadiou, Aline de
Scaramouche - Rafael Sabatini   5554
Scaramouche the King-Maker - Rafael Sabatini   5555

Keroualle, Louise de
Here Lies Our Sovereign Lord - Jean Plaidy   5021

Knollys, Letitia
My Enemy the Queen - Victoria Holt   3017

Kuragin, Rilla Weston
The Astrov Legacy - Constance Heaven   2802

La Valliere, Louise de
The Shadow of the Sun - Sylvia Pell   4891

Lamb, Lady Caroline
The Absorbing Fire: The Byron Legend - F.W.
  Kenyon   3445
Lord of the Ladies - Joanna Dessau   1626
The Memoirs of Lord Byron - Robert Nye   4655

The Secret Memoirs of Lord Byron - Christopher Nicole   4622

Lavrin, Alexandra Sergeivna
The Fortune Hunter - Ira J. Morris   4477

Layton, Phoebe
Reckless - Amanda Quick   5217

Lazender, Lady Campion
The Fallen Angels - Susannah Kells   3397

Le Clerc, Maritza
The Passionate Rebel - Frank G. Slaughter   5894

Lenton, Lavinia
The Abductors - Stuart Cloete   1121

Lilianna
The Lily and the Leopard - Susan Wiggs   6745

Lilliane of Orrick, Lady
My Gallant Enemy - Rexanne Becnel   409

Livia
I, Claudius - Robert Graves   2547

Loe, Judith von
Woman Astride - Nora Purtscher-Wydenbruch   5209

Lorme, Alicia de
The Lormes of Castle Rising - Fanny Cradock   1409
Shadows over Castle Rising - Fanny Cradock   1410

Los Dolores de Leon, Juana
The Spanish Bride - Georgette Heyer   2902

Luceiia
The Skystone: The Forging of Arthur's Britain - Jack Whyte   6726

Maeve
Deirdre - James Stephens   5996

Mahaut
The Lily and the Lion - Maurice Druon   1733

Makcheyeva, Tatiana
White Nights, Red Dawn - Frederick Nolan   4634

Malfrey, Damaris
Damaris - Jane Sheridan   5810

Manners, Catherine
Wife to Great Buckingham - Hilda Lewis   3751

Manning, Marietta
Sons of Thunder - Barbara Fitz Vroman   6516

Margaret of Belremy
Simon the Coldheart - Georgette Heyer   2901

Margaret of Burgundy
Here Lies Margot - Pamela Hill   2935

Margaret of Tyrol
The Ugly Duchess - Lion Feuchtwanger   2075

Maria
Byzantium - Michael Ennis   1945
Great Maria - Cecelia Holland   2989

Maria Amalia Elizabeth Theresa
Felding Castle - Edith De Born   1552

Marigold, Lady
The Knight and the Dove - Lori Wick   6732

Markievicz, Constance
Rebels: The Irish Rising of 1916 - Peter DeRosa   1622
Seasons - Anna Dillon   1645

Maryam, Lady
The Black Rose - Thomas B. Costain   1363

Masham, Abigail
Exit Lady Masham - Louis Auchincloss   230

Mason, Deborah
Deborah and the Many Faces of Love - Colette Davenat   1499

Matilda of Flanders
The Conqueror - Georgette Heyer   2881
The Conqueror's Wife - Noel B. Gerson   2363

Wife to the Bastard - Hilda Lewis   3753

Matilda of Tuscany
Not Built with Hands - Helen Constance White   6679

Maudribourg, Ambroisine de
Angelique and the Demon - Sergeanne Golon   2466

Medici, Catherine de'
A Cardinal of the Medici - Susan Hicks Beach   393

Medici, Marie de'
The Cardinal and the Queen - Evelyn Anthony   159

Megan, Lady
The Knight and the Dove - Lori Wick   6732

Melaine, Judith de Saint
The Lure of the Falcon - Juliette Benzoni   465

Mercedes
Mercedes of Castile - James Fenimore Cooper   1304

Merion, Lady Letitia
April Lady - Georgette Heyer   2873

Merion, Nell
April Lady - Georgette Heyer   2873

Messalina, Valeria
Claudius the God - Robert Graves   2543

Metella
The Fates Are Laughing - William Crozier   1439

Monday, Caroline
Bride of the Unicorn - Kasey Michaels   4363

Monica
The Restless Flame - Louis De Wohl   1573

Montargis, Lise de
The Rake and the Rebel - Ira J. Morris   4478

Montpensier, Anne de
Angelique - Sergeanne Golon   2465

Morwenna, Lady
The King Liveth - Jeffrey Farnol   2013

Motte, Jeanne de la
The Queen's Necklace - Alexandre Dumas   1781

Motte-Valois, Countess de la
The Prisoners of September - Leon Garfield   2294

Nausicaa
The Voyage Home - Ernst Schnabel   5644

Neville, Anne
Crown of Roses - Valerie Anand   127
The Dragon Waiting: A Masque of History - John M. Ford   2165
Fortune's Wheel - Rhoda S. Edwards   1886
The Golden Yoke: A Novel of the War of the Roses - Olive Eckerson   1837
The Sunne in Splendour - Sharon Kay Penman   4907
The Warwick Heiress - Margaret Abbey   6

Neville, Cecily
The Daughter of Time - Josephine Tey   6209
The Rose at Harvest End - Eleanor Fairburn   2003

Nikolayeva, Valentina
Contessa - Helene Mansfield   4076

Norland, Deborah
Deborah and the Siege of Paris - Colette Davenat   1500

O'Donnell, Arrah
Mistress of the Eagles - Elona Malterre   4052

Ohchenov, Irina
Tempting Fate - Chelsea Quinn Yarbro   6906

Orsola, Marchesa
The Patriot - Antonio Fogazzaro   2146

Payne, Isobel
Jane and the Unpleasantness at Scargrave Manor - Stephanie Barron   356

Pentacoste
Better in the Dark - Chelsea Quinn Yarbro   6894

Peregrine, Zared
The Conquest - Jude Deveraux   1630

Peretti, Vittoria
Vittoria - Robert Merle   4342

Perigord, Dorothea de
Lustre in the Sky - R.G. Waldeck   6525

Perrot, Lady Katherine
No Wall So High - Anne Powers   5152

Petrovna, Sophia
Blood on the Snow - John Elliott   1916

Peyrac, Angelique de
Angelique and the Demon - Sergeanne Golon   2466
Angelique and the Ghosts - Sergeanne Golon   2467
The Countess Angelique - Sergeanne Golon   2472
The Temptation of Angelique - Sergeanne Golon   2473

Plessis-Belliere, Angelique du
Angelique and the King - Sergeanne Golon   2468
Angelique in Barbary - Sergeanne Golon   2469
Angelique in Love - Sergeanne Golon   2470
Angelique in Revolt - Sergeanne Golon   2471

Poisson, Jeanne Antoinette
A Day of Battle - Vincent Sheean   5787
Louis the Well-Beloved - Jean Plaidy   5032
Louisiana Purchase - A.E. Hotchner   3039
Rasero - Francisco Rebolledo   5282
Royal Merry-Go-Round - F.W. Kenyon   3459

Polonsky, Elise Chatham
Sweet Ransom - Linda Madl   4026

Presteigne, Lady Harriet
The Foundling - Georgette Heyer   2888

Rachel of Judea
The Lives of Rachel - Joel Gross   2601

Ranegonda
Better in the Dark - Chelsea Quinn Yarbro   6894

Rathel, Lady Amanda
Black Body - H.C. Turk   6361

Remizou, Mariana
The Dawning of Deliverance - Judith Pella   4892

Renard, Margot
Baneful Sorceries, or The Countess Bewitched - Joan Sanders   5585

Rhiannon
The Viking's Woman - Heather Graham   2520

Rimini, Francesca da
Concordia - Frances Fleetwood   2124

Ritz, Baroness Helena von
54-40 or Fight - Emerson Hough   3040

Rochechouart de Mortemart, Francoise Athenais
All the King's Ladies - Janice Law   3678
The Crown and the Shadow: The Story of Francoise d'Aubigne, Marquise de Maintenon - Pamela Hill   2930
The Gilded Torch - Iola Fuller   2252
The Marquis - Joan Sanders   5586
The Oracle Glass - Judith Merkle Riley   5335
The Shadow of the Sun - Sylvia Pell   4891

Romby, Lady Beatrice
The Autumn Rose - Fiona Hill   2923

Romme Allery, Caroline de la
The Rose and the Sword - Sandra Paretti   4792

Rugger, Caressa
Caressa - Linda Lang Bartell   363

St. Catherine, Summer
The Pirate and the Pagan - Virginia Henley   2827

St. Columb, Dona
Frenchman's Creek - Daphne Du Maurier   1744

St. Michael, Valentine
Lost Love Found - Bertrice Small   5910

Salamanca, Ofelia
The Campaign - Carlos Fuentes 2245

Salammbo
Salammbo - Gustave Flaubert 2123

Sance, Angelique de
Angelique - Sergeanne Golon 2465

Sarum, Cristabel
First Night - Jane Aiken Hodge 2963

Saura of Roget
Candle in the Window - Christina Dodd 1662

Savigny, Isabella de
Nethergate - Norah Lofts 3854

Selanova, Marina
The World in His Arms - Rex Beach 392

Seymour, Jane
Windsor Castle - William Harrison Ainsworth 59

Shrewsbury, Elizabeth
The Tower and the Dream - Jan Westcott 6647

Simpson, Wallis Warfield
Carnal Hours - Max Allan Collins 1210
The Plot to Kill Wallis Simpson: A Work of Faction - Graham Fisher 2104
A Royal Murder - Elliott Roosevelt 5456

Sommersett, Elizabeth
Lovestorm - Judith E. French 2222

Spencer, Christabel
The Millionaire's Daughter - Dorothy Eden 1858

Stanbroke, Lady Elizabeth
The Stanbroke Girls - Fiona Hill 2925

Stanbroke, Lady Isabella
The Stanbroke Girls - Fiona Hill 2925

Steinfinnsdatter, Ingunn
The Snake Pit - Sigrid Undset 6383

Sterling, Amanda
Love Not a Rebel - Heather Graham 2516

Stewart, Moonfeather Leah
Moonfeather - Judith E. French 2223

Strathy, Lady Dorothy
Death En Voyage - Richard Grayson 2557

Stuart, Anne
Queen's Gift - Inglis Fletcher 2136
Wicked Lady - Inglis Fletcher 2142

Stuart, Caroline
The Imposter - Noel B. Gerson 2375

Tamar
Tamar - Ann Chamberlin 975

Taniko, Lady
Shike: Time of Dragons - Robert Shea 5784

Theale, Lady Hester
Sprig Muslin - Georgette Heyer 2903

Theus, Pauline
The Horseman on the Roof - Jean Giono 2424

Thompson, Sarah
The Countess - March Cost 1360

Toda, Lady Mariko
Shogun - James Clavell 1101

Torfrida
Hereward the Wake - Charles Kingsley 3497

Treadway, Lady Maisie
Captain Adam - Donald Barr Chidsey 1058

Trevanion, Lady Margaret
The Hounds of God - Rafael Sabatini 5551

Tupac, Acanna
Mansions of Darkness - Chelsea Quinn Yarbro 6902

Valaise, Ailena
Kingdom of the Grail - A.A. Attanasio 226

Vetsera, Maria
The Archduke - Michael Arnold 194

Villefont, Jeanne de
Seed of Mischief - Willa Gibbs 2401

Villiers, Barbara
Catherine - Hilda Lewis 3746
Forever Amber - Kathleen Winsor 6822
A Health Unto His Majesty - Jean Plaidy 5019
Our Jo, or The Chronicle of a Coming Man - Kenneth M. Cameron 868

Visconti, Bianca
The Medici Emerald - Martin Woodhouse 6851
The Medici Guns - Martin Woodhouse 6852
The Medici Hawks - Martin Woodhouse 6853

Visconti, Zaide
Clara Reeve - Leonie Hargrave 2705

Volterra, Gianna di
Drumbeat - Dudley Pope 5094
Ramage - Dudley Pope 5097

Von Doring, Luise
Luise - Dawn Stewart Field 2079

Von Hulsen, Cecilie
Draw Near to Battle - Jere Hungerford Wheelwright 6667

Von Reichmanstaal, Melanie
The Brocken - Pamela Hill 2929

Vouvray, Claudine de
The Sword and the Flame - Pamela Hill 2945

Wakesfield, Megan
Desire and Deceive - Cordia Byers 832

Waldstein, Lili von
A Princess in Berlin - Arthur R.G. Solmssen 5939

Walewska, Marie
So Great a Man - David Pilgrim 5000

Wellesley, Lady Barbara
Flying Colours - C.S. Forester 2173
The Life and Times of Horatio Hornblower - C. Northcote Parkinson 4813

Western, Deborah
Deborah Goes to Dover - Marion Chesney 1023

Widdrington, Lady Elizabeth
A Famine of Horses - P.F. Chisholm 1071
A Season of Knives - P.F. Chisholm 1072

Winslow, Diana
Once a Gentleman - Donald James 3157

Winwood, Horatia
The Convenient Marriage - Georgette Heyer 2882

Woodville, Elizabeth
The White Rose - Jan Westcott 6648

Wright, Emma
The Scandalous Lady Wright - Marion Chesney 1049

Wyngarde, Lady Damaris
My Dear Lover England - Pamela Bennetts 453

Wynne of Gwernach
A Moment in Time - Bertrice Small 5911

Wythe, Lady Caroline
The Autumn Rose - Fiona Hill 2923

Yurensky, Nadya
The Emperor Story: A Historical Romance - George Sava 5615

NURSE

Alcott, Louisa May
Love and War - John Jakes 3150

Barton, Clara
The Bridge - Marguerite Allis 108

Homeland - John Jakes 3148
Remember Santiago - Douglas C. Jones 3280
The Titans - John Jakes 3154

Bishop, Carrie
Storming Heaven - Denise Giardina 2394

Blau, Hannah
The Midwife - Gay Courter 1388

Byrne, Anne
The Cortlandts of Washington Square - Janet Fairbank 2001

Chesney, Jenny
Hanging on the Wire - Gillian Linscott 3806

Copley, Suzanna
An Autumn in Araby - Carola Salisbury 5565

De Hartog, Sianna
The Nationalists - William Stuart Long 3876

Dix, Dorothea
The Bridge - Marguerite Allis 108
Love and War - John Jakes 3150

Duncannon, Georgina
Morning's Gate - Ann Victoria Roberts 5371

Giguet, Guillemette
The Royal Pawn - Antonia Ridge 5327

Greenway, Jenny
Serpent and Staff - Frank Yerby 6927

Hemings, Harriet
The President's Daughter - Barbara Chase-Riboud 1005

Iron, Shiloh
A City Not Forsaken - Lynn Morris 4480

Irons, Shiloh
Shadow of the Mountains - Lynn Morris 4481

Lackland, Martha
Bedford Row - Claire Rayner 5259

Latterly, Hester
A Dangerous Mourning - Anne Perry 4926
Defend and Betray - Anne Perry 4928
The Face of a Stranger - Anne Perry 4929
The Sins of the Wolf - Anne Perry 4937
A Sudden, Fearful Death - Anne Perry 4938

MacFarlane, Alix
The Heart of the Continent - Nancy Cato 961

Manning, Caro
The Heart of the Continent - Nancy Cato 961

Mantle, Susan
Eden Rising - Marilyn Harris 2731

Marwood, Elizabeth
To Serve Them All My Days - R.F. Delderfield 1591

Nalda
Isle of Glory - Jane Oliver 4723

Newton, Carlina
Remember Santiago - Douglas C. Jones 3280

Nightingale, Florence
Bedford Row - Claire Rayner 5259
Cock of the Walk - Roy Lewis 3762
The Hoydens and Mr. Dickens - William J. Palmer 4784
My Lady Hoyden - Jane Sheridan 5812
The Passionate Pilgrim - Charles Terrot 6204
The Private Life of Florence Nightingale - Richard Gordon 2485
Secret for a Nightingale - Victoria Holt 3020
Sisters & Lovers - Nicola Thorne 6274
A Sudden, Fearful Death - Anne Perry 4938

Ottoway, Eve
While Paris Danced - Patricia Wright 6886

Pleydell, Susanna
Secret for a Nightingale - Victoria Holt 3020

Quade, Dixie
A Heart Divided - Al Lacy 3580

Randall, Claire
Outlander - Diana Gabaldon 2264

Remizou, Mariana
The Dawning of Deliverance - Judith Pella 4892

Rodgers, Deborah
Camelot Country - Marjorie McEvoy 4267

Sanger, Margaret
The Crusader - Noel B. Gerson 2364

Shepherd, Beth
For Love and Honor - Antonia Van-Loon 6423
For Us the Living - Antonia Van-Loon 6424

Shields, Harriet
Until the End - Harold Coyle 1396

Shortland, Gail
The Scarlet Patch - Bruce Lancaster 3645

Sokolow, Hannah Blau
The Midwife's Advice - Gay Courter 1389

Summers, Gail
The Rough Rider - Gilbert Morris 4468

Trevor, Candace
Griffin's Way - Frank Yerby 6922

Troy, Elizabeth
On a Far Wide Shore - Malcolm Macdonald 3970

Veena
Temple Bells - Marjorie McEvoy 4271

Walker, Elizabeth
The Passionate Pilgrim - Charles Terrot 6204

Warden, Polly
Over There - Thomas Fleming 2130

Willoughby, Lizzie
Siege in the Sun - Mary Paradise 4788

OCCULTIST

Wouwere, Nicholas von
Prophecies - Helena Soister 5937

OIL INDUSTRY WORKER

Karnes
The Terrible Teague Bunch - Gary Jennings 3197

Spurlock, Clay
Fort Worth - Leonard Sanders 5588

ORGANIZED CRIME FIGURE

Balbinius, Pius
Time to Depart - Lindsey Davis 1533

Billingsley, Sherman
Walter Winchell: A Novel - Michael Herr 2863

Capone, Al
Flanagan's Run - Tom McNab 4303
Joy in Mudville - Gordon McAlpine 4216
Organized Crime - Nicholas Von Hoffman 6511
True Detective - Max Allan Collins 1215
You Bet Your Life - Stuart M. Kaminsky 3349

Dance, John
Whiskey River - Loren D. Estleman 1981

Flegenheimer, Arthur
Billy Bathgate - E.L. Doctorow 1656

Forbes, Arthur
Dancing in the Dark - Stuart M. Kaminsky 3334

Kelly, Paul
The Alienist - Caleb Carr 907

Lansky, Meyer
Carnal Hours - Max Allan Collins 1210

Luca, Don Antonio
Luciano's Luck - Jack Higgins 2912

Luciano, Charles "Lucky"
Luciano's Luck - Jack Higgins 2912

Nitti, Frank
Organized Crime - Nicholas Von Hoffman 6511
True Crime - Max Allan Collins 1214
True Detective - Max Allan Collins 1215
You Bet Your Life - Stuart M. Kaminsky 3349

Richett, Tony
The Black Mask Murderers - William F. Nolan 4635

Rosencrantz, Lulu
Billy Bathgate - E.L. Doctorow 1656

Siegel, Benjamin
The Howard Hughes Affair - Stuart M. Kaminsky 3340
New Deal for Death - Elliott Roosevelt 5454

ORPHAN

Alexander, Tom Christopher
A Dream of Kings - Davis Grubb 2604

Alix of Wanthwaite
Shield of Three Lions - Pamela Kaufman 3372

Amalia
Unto the Soul - Aharon Appelfeld 181

Andrew, Drurie
Banner by the Wayside - Samuel Hopkins Adams 28

Armes, Artillery
The Flames of Time - Baynard Kendrick 3409

Ashley, Julia
Scent of Cloves - Norah Lofts 3859

Ashton, Emma
Portrait of Emma - Lillian Cheatham 1010

Audley, Isabelle
Castaway - Frances Murray 4535

Avenel, Mary
The Monastery - Sir Walter Scott 5701

Balfour, David
Kidnapped - Robert Louis Stevenson 6010

Barnes, Kirsty
The Asking Price - Jessica Stirling 6039
The Good Provider - Jessica Stirling 6043
The Welcome Light - Jessica Stirling 6050

Baxter, Goldie
The Argonauts - Yvonne Schoell 5645

Becket, Jonathon
Redcoat - Bernard Cornwell 1337

Ben
The Rag Nymph - Catherine Cookson 1287

Blake, Rebecca
Circle of Gold - Karen Harper 2710

Bowman, Mark
Mark - Lonnie Coleman 1205

Brody, Jake
My Own Ground - Hugh Nissenson 4628

Bruno
The Miracle at St. Bruno's - Philippa Carr 925

Bulain, Jeems
The Plains of Abraham - James Oliver Curwood 1452

Burgess, Elizabeth
Birthright - Phillip Finch 2087

Burnie, Davey
A Journey to Matecumbe - Robert Lewis Taylor 6188

New Deal for Death - Elliott Roosevelt 5454

Burton, Thad
Rascal's Heaven - F. van Wyck Mason 4157

Buttes, Mason Raymond
One of the Raymonds - Jean Rikhoff 5332
The Sweetwater - Jean Rikhoff 5333

Cabezon, Juan
1492: The Life and Times of Juan Cabezon of Castile - Homero Aridjis 187

Cade, Lucy
Pastora - Joanna Barnes 321

Cameron, Martin
The Restless Land - John H. Culp 1444

Carr, Rosie
Spring at The Winged Horse - Ted Willis 6794

Carrick, Peter
Lord Iverbrook's Heir - Carola Dunn 1795

Cartwright, Lucy
Greygallows - Barbara Michaels 4359

Cass, Eppie
Silas Marner - George Eliot 1911

Cecilia
The Mill on the Po - Riccardo Bacchelli 254

Chance, Bridie
The Capricorn Stone - Madeleine Brent 659

Chantra
Temple Bells - Marjorie McEvoy 4271

Chinese Sonya
The Name of Hero - Richard Seltzer 5742

Claudia
A Walk with Love and Death - Hans Koning 3539

Clay, Maggie
Lone Star Lady - Jill Gregory 2579

Cosette
Cosette: The Sequel to Les Miserables - Laura Kalpakian 3329

Dale, Sally
The Man of the Storm - Ethel Hueston 3069

Daniels, Kitty
Sweet Songbird - Teresa Crane 1418

d'Asselnat, Marianne
Marianne - Juliette Benzoni 466

Davenport, Amanda
Miss Davenport's Christmas - Marion Chesney 1039

Davenport, Gillian
Miss Davenport's Christmas - Marion Chesney 1039

De Vaumartin, Everard
The Lords of Vaumartin - Cecelia Holland 2992

Devereaux, Caroline
Caroline and Julia - Clare Darcy 1484

Devize, Elizabeth
The Dark Stranger - Dorothy Charques 999

Doll
A Mirror for Witches - Esther Forbes 2157

Dominic Dio
Dominic - Kathleen Robinson 5405

Dugan, Clayton
Power in the Blood - Greg Matthews 4191

Dugan, Zoe
Power in the Blood - Greg Matthews 4191

Dupree, Suzanne
Savage Oaks - Julie Ellis 1924

Duvet, Berthe
The Porcelain Dove - Delia Sherman 5815

Elder, Kate
Doc Holliday's Woman - Jane Candia Coleman 1201

Espinosa, Maria
Daughter of Fortune - Carla Kelly 3398

Fairbourn, Francesca
Wings of the Falcon - Barbara Michaels 4361

Findon, Elinor
The Wedding Guest - Anna Gilbert 2407

Fleming, Jeannie
The Magnolias - Julie Ellis 1922

Forrester, Edit
Nick of the Woods; or, The Jibbenainosay - Robert Montgomery Bird 505

Forster, Arbel
Till the Day Goes Down - Judith Lennox-Smith 3719

Forster, Christie
Till the Day Goes Down - Judith Lennox-Smith 3719

Gad
Unto the Soul - Aharon Appelfeld 181

Gatewood, Tenny
Pioneer Breed - Glenn R. Vernam 6453

Graves, Thomas "Grubber"
Me and Gallagher - Jack Farris 2023

Gray, Nancy
The Clock Tower - Jeanne Montague 4435

Greenback, Roddy
The Bannaman Legacy - Catherine Cookson 1272

Grenouille, Jean-Baptiste
Perfume: The Story of a Murderer - Patrick Suskind 6120

Greypaull, Rhoda
Double Wedding Ring - Patricia Wendorf 6624

Guinevra
The Man on the White Horse - Warwick Deeping 1577

Hammond, Charlotte
City of Golden Cages - Jo Germany 2358

Hampton, Caroline
The Hampton Heritage - Julie Ellis 1920

Hanard, Audrey
Audrey - Mary Johnston 3229

Hanna, Chad
Chad Hanna - Walter D. Edmonds 1873

Harding, Rance
Pioneer Breed - Glenn R. Vernam 6453

Hardwick, Mary
Master of Morholm - Timothy R. Wilson 6817

Hart, Emily
Beauty's Daughter - Mollie Hardwick 2689

Harvard, Carne
The Fox-Red Hills - Cynthia S. Roberts 5374

Harvard, Mostyn
The Fox-Red Hills - Cynthia S. Roberts 5374

Hawthorne, Cecily
Chelsea - Nancy Fitzgerald 2114

Heath, Emma Louise
The Pilgrimage - Ann B. Ross 5463

Heath, Jessie
The Pilgrimage - Ann B. Ross 5463

Heath, Miranda
Sea Jade - Phyllis A. Whitney 6717

Heriot, Miranda
The Shakespeare Girl - Mollie Hardwick 2698

Heron, Lisa
Castle of Eagles - Constance Heaven 2804

Heron, Thomazine
The Moon in the Water - Pamela Belle 433

Ingham, Jane
The Nunnery - Dorothy Charques 1001

Karana
Beyond the Sea of Ice - William Sarabande 5595

Kellaway, Ellen
Lord of the Far Island - Victoria Holt 3016

Lackland, Sophie
Charing Cross - Claire Rayner 5260

Lally
Ravenscroft - Dorothy Eden 1860

Lansdon, Lucie
The Black Swan - Philippa Carr 917

Larrimer, Linc
Dodging Red Cloud - Richard S. Wheeler 6657

Leonie
The Villains: A Haunting Tale of the Marshes - Charlotte Keppel 3467

Lindsay, Anne
My Lord Monleigh - Jan Cox Speas 5957

Lingford, Martha
The Tempestuous Petticoat - Mary Ann Gibbs 2397

Little Emily
The Real David Copperfield - Robert Graves 2551

Lockhart, Taisie
North of 36 - Emerson Hough 3042

Longbaugh, Lacey
Cherokee Dawn - Genell Dellin 1596

Loring, Cassy
Cassy - Elizabeth Lyle 3930

Louise
Banners of Silk - Rosalind Laker 3592

MacGregor, Kirsten
The Slow Awakening - Catherine Marchant 4082

Maciek
Wartime Lies - Louis Begley 416

MacIntyre, Clory
The Giant Joshua - Maurine Whipple 6673

Magali
Bernadin, My Love - Leonard Rossiter 5506

Malpass, Hester
The Fine and Handsome Captain - Frances Lynch 3933

Malvern, Kate
Cousin Kate - Georgette Heyer 2884

Mandeville, Belinda
The Changeling - Philippa Carr 918

Mandeville, Rebecca
The Changeling - Philippa Carr 918

Manville, Rowena
Midsummer Masque - Jill Tattersall 6174

Margelasse, Flora de
The Still Storm - Francoise Sagan 5562

Martin, Kid
Born of the Sun - John H. Culp 1440

McAlister, Mary
New Orleans Legacy - Alexandra Ripley 5341

Molinero, Emma
The Whip - Catherine Cookson 1291

Moore, Cristobel
The Trevarton Inheritance - Malcolm Macdonald 3976

Moore, Marian
The Trevarton Inheritance - Malcolm Macdonald 3976

Moore, Teresa
The Trevarton Inheritance - Malcolm Macdonald 3976

Mordal, Kirsten
Lady of No Man's Land - Jeanne Williams 6780

Mortimer, Judith
Judith - Brian Cleeve 1108

Nanette
The Villains: A Haunting Tale of the Marshes - Charlotte Keppel 3467

Newcombe, Honoria
Sweet's Folly - Fiona Hill 2926

Norwell, Stephen
Blackrobe - Robert E. Wall 6534

Orry, Charles
North and South - John Jakes 3151

Paoul
The Earth Goddess - Richard Herley 2856

Patterson, Elspeth
Treasures on Earth - Jessica Stirling 6049

Penryhd
The Fair - Robert Nathan 4559

Pomeroy, Joe
The Devil's Rainbow - J.C. Furnas 2257

Pownall, Sara
Sara - Brian Cleeve 1110

Price, Bethany
The Misadventures of Bethany Price - Marian Cockrell 1147

Quinn, Daniel
Quinn's Book - William Kennedy 3423

Raven, Bella
Ravenscroft - Dorothy Eden 1860

Rawley, Walter Claireborne
Mr. Vertigo - Paul Auster 244

Reeve, Clara
Clara Reeve - Leonie Hargrave 2705

Reilly, Martin
Thy Tears Might Cease - Michael Farrell 2018

Rennie, Lisabeth
Mists of Heaven - Yvonne Kalman 3325

Revell, Bartholomew
Massachusetts: A Novel - Nancy Zaroulis 6956

Ritchie, David
The Crossing - Winston Churchill 1080

Rose
Miss Nobody - Caroline Ross 5465

Rosewarne, Johanna
A Notorious Woman - Malcolm Macdonald 3969

Ruan
Harkfast: The Making of the King - Hugh C. Rae 5238

Russell, Blue
Blue Russell - Will Bryant 738

St. Martin, Melisande
It Began in Vauxhall Gardens - Jean Plaidy 5023

Selene
Soul Flame - Barbara Wood 6850

Sharp, John
The Living - Annie Dillard 1644

Shaw, Lisa
What the Heart Keeps - Rosalind Laker 3605

Sheldon, Nell
The Clock Tower - Jeanne Montague 4435

Shelton, Dick
The Black Arrow - Robert Louis Stevenson 6008

Shiva
Shiva: An Adventure of the Ice Age - J.H. Brennan   657

Sinclair, Perdita
Strathgallant - Laura Black   523

Smale, Rebecca
The Clock Tower - Jeanne Montague   4435

Smith, Adelaide
The Braganza Pursuit - Sarah Neilan   4564

Sprat
Playing the Jack - Mary Brown   726

Stafford, Ross
The Pagoda Tree - Berkely Mather   4181

Starr, Amantha
Band of Angels - Robert Penn Warren   6572

Stevens, Melisande
Storm Before Sunrise - June Wyndham Davies   1507

Stevens, Serena
The Yukon Queen - Gilbert Morris   4476

Stewart, Beth
To Love a Stranger - Barbara Paul   4839

Sunday, Billy
Billy Sunday - Rod Jones   3295

Swanton, Julia
French Slippers - Deborah Chester   1055 ·

Tonteur, Toinette
The Plains of Abraham - James Oliver Curwood   1452

Toribio
The Hands of Cantu - Tom Lea   3694

Tregan, Caroline
Bagatelle - Maurice Denuziere   1613

Trewella, Annabel
Dolphin Summer - Carola Salisbury   5569

Vane, Louise
The Royal Ann Tree - Patricia Campbell   875

Vlassevna, Laisha
Tempting Fate - Chelsea Quinn Yarbro   6906

Wantage, Hero
Friday's Child - Georgette Heyer   2890

Waring, Lucy
Moonraker's Bride - Madeleine Brent   661

Warne, Annie
Annie - Gloria Jahoda   3141

Westfield, Michael
Westfield - Roderick Thorp   6277

Wilder, Leela
Black Gold - Anita Richmond Bunkley   771

Willard, Abigail
A Toast to the King - Elizabeth Coatsworth   1139

Willard, Georgianna
A Toast to the King - Elizabeth Coatsworth   1139

Willard, Judith
A Toast to the King - Elizabeth Coatsworth   1139

Winslow, Margaret
Here I Stay - Elizabeth Coatsworth   1138

Zulian, Joanna
The Italian Garden - Judith Lennox-Smith   3717

OUTCAST

Archias
Gate to the Sea - Bryher   743

Armitage, Jonathan
A Shadow's Bliss - Patricia Veryan   6477

Ashur, Tiglath
The Blood Star - Nicholas Guild   2611

College
Theory of War - Joan Brady   637

Elshender the Recluse
The Black Dwarf - Sir Walter Scott   5692

Finbar
Paradise - Dikkon Eberhart   1831

Gefjon, Jaki
Wyvern - A.A. Attanasio   227

Hackabout-Jones, Fanny
Fanny: Being the True History of the Adventures of Fanny Hackabout-Jones - Erica Jong   3299

Harmony, Desire
Stars on the Sea - F. van Wyck Mason   4161

Heathcliff
H.—: The Story of Heathcliff's Journey Back to Wuthering Heights - Lin Haire-Sargeant   2641

Hereward the Wake
Hereward the Wake - Charles Kingsley   3497

Maid of Sker
The Maid of Sker - R.D. Blackmore   529

Miriam
Bodin, 1349: An Epic Novel of Christians and Jews in the Plague Years - Roberta Kalechofsky   3322

Moloquin
Pillar of the Sky - Cecelia Holland   2994

Mount, Jay Fielding
Mount's Mistake - Lew McCreary   4229

Parvati
The Faithful Lovers - Valerie Anand   129

Prynne, Hester
Arthur Dimmesdale - Charles R. Larson   3671
Pearl - Christopher Bigsby   497
The Scarlet Letter - Nathaniel Hawthorne   2786

Ravenburn, Tom
Ravenburn - Laura Black   522

Strauss, Rudi
To the Land of the Cattails - Aharon Appelfeld   179

Strauss, Toni
To the Land of the Cattails - Aharon Appelfeld   179

Wheeler
The Mudlark - Theodore Bonnet   573

OUTLAW

Aelredson, Edward
Robin and the King - Parke Godwin   2448

Bad Man From Bodie
Welcome to Hard Times - E.L. Doctorow   1660

Barabbas
Barabbas - Par Lagerkvist   3585
Barabbas: A Dream of the World's Tragedy - Marie Corelli   1327
Behold Your King - Florence M. Bauer   379
The Robber: A Tale of the Time of the Herods - Bertram Brooker   706

Bart, Charles E.
A House Behind the Mint - Laurie Huffman   3072

Barzor
Two Thieves - Manuel Komroff   3535

Becker, Frank
Dutch Uncle - Marilyn Durham   1815

Bender, Kate
The Bloody Benders - Robert H. Adelman   35

Bernardino
Rockspring - R.G. Vliet   6506

Blood, Thomas
The King's Rogue - Max Peacock   4859

Blue Duck
Belle Starr - Speer Morgan   4453

Bones, Billy
Anything for Billy - Larry McMurtry   4295

Bonney, William
Billy the Kid - Edwin Corle   1330
Billy the Kid: The Legend of El Chivato - Elizabeth Fackler   1994
The Demise of Billy the Kid - Preston Lewis   3760
Pistols for Hire - Nelson Coral Nye   4652
The Sons of Grady Rourke - Douglas Savage   5618
The Story of Pat Garrett and Billy the Kid - David Everitt   1987
Tascosa Gun: The Story of Jim East - Gene Shelton   5803
Time for Outrage - Amelia Bean   397

Brecht, Elisha
The Border Men - Cameron Judd   3312

Brocius, Curly Bill
Tombstone Showdown - Leslie Scott   5681

Brules, Cat
Brules - Harry Combs   1223

Buckhart, Ezekiel
The Flames of Time - Baynard Kendrick   3409

Cain, Macaulay
Fair is the Rose - Meagan MacKinney   3997

Calash, Gentleman Joe
Rome Haul - Walter D. Edmonds   1877

Calvert, Clay
Honey in the Horn - Harold Lenoir Davis   1523

Cassidy, Butch
Good Morning, Young Lady - Ardyth Kennelly   3424
Kid Curry: The Life and Times of Harvey Logan and the Wild Bunch - F. Bruce Lamb   3606
Outlaw Lover - Lindsey Hanks   2676
South of the Border - John Byrne Cooke   1268
The Story of the Sundance Kid - David Everitt   1988

Catton, Bram
Bighorn Legacy - W. Michael Gear   2332

Chaney, Tom
True Grit - Charles Portis   5139

Christie, Ned
Ned Christie's War - Robert J. Conley   1247

Clanton, Ike
Wyatt Earp - Matt Braun   653

Clark, Jonathan
The World in His Arms - Rex Beach   392

Colfax, Oliver
Colfax - Robert J. Conley   1239
Killing Time - Robert J. Conley   1244
Quitting Time - Robert J. Conley   1249

Cooper, Andy
The Feud - Amelia Bean   396

Cordera de Tosta, Anabel
Warriors of the Night - Kerry Newcomb   4594

Creel, Sugar Jim
The Stranglers - Loren D. Estleman   1978

Croft, Ralph
The Masked Man - P.C. Doherty   1674

Cuan
The Silent People - Walter Macken   3990

Curry, Kid
Mr. American - George MacDonald Fraser   2211

Dalton, Emmett
Desperadoes - Ron Hansen   2681

Dalton, Robert
Desperadoes - Ron Hansen   2681

de la Marck, William
Quentin Durward - Sir Walter Scott   5705

Deakin, John
Breakheart Pass - Alistair MacLean   3999

Decimus
The Bride of Pilate - Esther Kellner   3393

Delfino, Pancito
Adios! - Lanier Bartlett   366

Dillinger, John
Dillinger - Harry Patterson   4832
Mad Dog - Jack Kelly   3401

Doone, Carver
Lorna Doone - R.D. Blackmore   528

Dorn, Mahlon
Fire and the Hammer - Shirley Barker   311

Dugan, Drew
Power in the Blood - Greg Matthews   4191

Durant, Luke
Beyond the Shadowlands - Georgina Fleming   2126

Famin, Nikholai
Sweet Ransom - Linda Madl   4026

Franklin, Mark
Mr. American - George MacDonald Fraser   2211

Garza, Joey
Streets of Laredo - Larry McMurtry   4300

Garza, Katie
Anything for Billy - Larry McMurtry   4295

Gonzalez, Pedro
Brules - Harry Combs   1223

Grobart, Jay
The Man Who Loved Cat Dancing - Marilyn
   Durham   1817

Halloran, Horse-Shy
The Last Days of Horse-Shy Halloran - Bill
   Pronzini   5203

Hardin, John Wesley
Crazy Fox Remembers - Don Preston   5174
Last Gun: The Legend of John Selman - Gene
   Shelton   5801
The Pistoleer - James Carlos Blake   536
Streets of Laredo - Larry McMurtry   4300

Hereward the Wake
The Disputed Crown - Valerie Anand   128
Harold Was My King - Hilda Lewis   3749
Hereward the Wake - Charles Kingsley   3497
*The Last Englishman: The Story of Hereward the
   Wake* - Hebe Weenolsen   6596
The Saxon Tapestry - Sile Rice   5317

Hill, Joe
Tombstone Showdown - Leslie Scott   5681

Hornby, Sim
The Raider - Jesse Hill Ford   2164

James, Frank
*The Assassination of Jesse James by the Coward
   Robert Ford* - Ron Hansen   2680
Death of a Legend - Will Henry   2840
Loving Belle Star - Robert Taylor   6187
Mamaw - Susan Dodd   1663
While Angels Dance - Ralph W. Cotton   1372

James, Jesse
*The Assassination of Jesse James by the Coward
   Robert Ford* - Ron Hansen   2680
Belle Starr - Deborah Camp   870
Death of a Legend - Will Henry   2840
Loving Belle Star - Robert Taylor   6187
Mamaw - Susan Dodd   1663
While Angels Dance - Ralph W. Cotton   1372

Kent, Jeremiah
The Lawless - John Jakes   3149

Kilkenny, Coyote
In the Season of the Sun - Kerry Newcomb   4590

Lainie
The Ghosts of Elkhorn - Kerry Newcomb   4589

Lambkin, Rudy
Rainbow on the Road - Esther Forbes   2159

Lawless
The Black Arrow - Robert Louis Stevenson   6008

Lawton, Ben
Rogue's Kingdom - John Brick   676

Little John
The Good Yeomen - Jay Williams   6771

Lockhart, Jamie
The Robber Bridegroom - Eudora Welty   6623

Logan, Harvey
*Kid Curry: The Life and Times of Harvey Logan and
   the Wild Bunch* - F. Bruce Lamb   3606

Longabaugh, Harry
The Story of the Sundance Kid - David Everitt   1988

Longacre, Jarrett
The Pumpkin Rollers - Elmer Kelton   3406

Lovell, Tyson
The Long Night - Andrew Lytle   3945

Mayhew, Coffin
The Law in Charity - Chelsea Quinn Yarbro   6901

McCann, Kevin
The Dispossessed - Dell Shannon   5773

McKetch, Dan
The Flames of Time - Baynard Kendrick   3409

McLean, Allan
Shoot! - George Bowering   604

McLean, Archie
Shoot! - George Bowering   604

McLean, Charlie
Shoot! - George Bowering   604

Mendoza
Season of Yellow Leaf - Douglas C. Jones   3283

Milam, Tom
In the Season of the Sun - Kerry Newcomb   4590

Miller, John
Gunman - Loren D. Estleman   1971

Murieta, Joaquin
The Dream Ends in Fury - Samuel Anthony
   Peeples   4889
Gringo Gold - Dane Coolidge   1293

Murrell, John
Rogues' Company: A Novel of John Murrell - Harry
   Harrison Kroll   3559
Sow the Seeds of Hemp - Gary Jennings   3195

Nash, Jeston
While Angels Dance - Ralph W. Cotton   1372

Nelson, Baby Face
Mad Dog - Jack Kelly   3401

Nicholas
The Outlaw's Tale - Margaret Frazer   2218

O'Dare, Danny
Hue and Cry - Elizabeth Yates   6907

Pardee, Malachi
Blood on the Divide - William W. Johnstone   3265

Patche
Shadow of a Star - Jamie Lee Cooper   1315

Pelon
Mackenna's Gold - Will Henry   2845

Place, Etta
The Story of the Sundance Kid - David Everitt   1988

Quantrill, William Clarke
Belle Starr - Deborah Camp   870

Raza, China Eye
A Mule for the Marquesa - Frank O'Rourke   4753

Ringo, Johnny
Bloody Season - Loren D. Estleman   1968
Confessions of Johnny Ringo - Geoff Aggeler   40
Tombstone Showdown - Leslie Scott   5681
Wyatt Earp - Dan Gordon   2481

Robert of Locksley
Locksley - Nicholas Chase   1003

Robertson, Geordie
The Heart of Midlothian - Sir Walter Scott   5698

Robin Hood
Banners of Gold - Pamela Kaufman   3371
The Good Yeomen - Jay Williams   6771
Ivanhoe - Sir Walter Scott   5699
The Sheriff of Nottingham - Richard Kluger   3512

Rogue, Johnnie
Lord Johnnie - Leslie Turner White   6687

Roman
The Ghosts of Elkhorn - Kerry Newcomb   4589

Rongus
Two Thieves - Manuel Komroff   3535

Roy, Rob
Rob Roy - Sir Walter Scott   5707

Russell, Clay
Blue Russell - Will Bryant   738

Sackett, Logan
Ride the Dark Trail - Louis L'Amour   3624

Savage, Thane
The Long Trail North - Robert J. Conley   1245

Shedwell, Chris
Murdock's Law - Loren D. Estleman   1975

Slade, Jack
Six-Horse Hitch - Janice Holt Giles   2417

Starr, Belle
Belle Starr - Deborah Camp   870
Belle Starr - Speer Morgan   4453
The Bright Feathers - John H. Culp   1441
Loving Belle Star - Robert Taylor   6187
Pearl - Anne Leaton   3701

Starr, Henry
The Return of Henry Starr - Richard Slotkin   5909
The Saga of Henry Starr - Robert J. Conley   1250

Stewart, Virgil
Sow the Seeds of Hemp - Gary Jennings   3195

The Sundance Kid
Outlaw Lover - Lindsey Hanks   2676

Talon, Milo
The Man From Broken Hills - Louis L'Amour   3622

Teotl
Gods on Horseback - Samuel G. Baggett   263

Trainor, Newt
Border Line - Robert J. Conley   1238

Tuck, Friar
The Good Yeomen - Jay Williams   6771

Tyler, Thias
Passage to Natchez - Cameron Judd   3316

Villa, Francisco
The Crimson Wind - Max Hennessy   2832
Last Reveille - David Morrell   4456
Outlaw - Warren Kiefer   3482
Pancho And Black Jack - Fred Bean   398
Tom Mix and Pancho Villa - Clifford Irving   3113

Under the Fifth Sun: A Novel of Pancho Villa - Earl Shorris 5832

Wales, Josey
Gone to Texas - Forrest Carter 945
The Vengeance Trail of Josey Wales - Forrest Carter 946

Wedlock, Ben
Sudden Country - Loren D. Estleman 1979

Young, Wilson
Heaven's Gold - Giles Tippette 6282

Younger, Cole
Belle Starr - Deborah Camp 870
Confessions of Johnny Ringo - Geoff Aggeler 40
Death of a Legend - Will Henry 2840
Major Stepton's War - Matthew Vaughan 6445
Pearl - Anne Leaton 3701
While Angels Dance - Ralph W. Cotton 1372

Youngman, Charles
Scent of Cloves - Norah Lofts 3859

OVERSEER

Campos, Presentacion
The Red Lances - Arturo Uslar Pietri 4999

PACIFIST

Hallam, Dennis
The Skeleton in the Grass - Robert Barnard 320

PARENT

Balthazar
The Headsman; or, The Abbaye des Vignerons - James Fenimoore Cooper 1300

Bonaparte, Maria Letizia
Good-Bye My Son - Marjorie Coryn 1356

Ember
Isle of Woman - Piers Anthony 167

Fancot, Amabel
False Colours - Georgette Heyer 2886

Hall, Charlotte
The Hours of Light - Janet Tanner 6160

Hoelun
Ruler of the Sky: A Novel of Genghis Khan - Pamela Sargent 5606

PATRIOT

Adams, John
The Unvanquished - Howard Fast 2046

Adams, Samuel
The Bastard - John Jakes 3144
The Drums of April - Charles Mergendahl 4340
Freedom's Dues - Robert H. Abel 9
Gilman of the Redford - William Stearns Davis 1541
The Long Naked Descent into Boston - William Eastlake 1823
Massachusetts: A Novel - Nancy Zaroulis 6956
Seneca - Donald Clayton Porter 5127
Sons of Liberty - Adam Rutledge 5540
Those Who Love - Irving Stone 6064

Allen, Ethan
The Green Mountain Boys - Daniel Pierce Thompson 6249
Hang for Treason - Robert Newton Peck 4886

Altoviti, Carlo
The Castle of Fratta - Ippolito Nievo 4625

Becket, Jonathon
Redcoat - Bernard Cornwell 1337

Bonaparte, Carlo
In What Torn Ship - Evelyn Eaton 1828

Bradford, Dake
Song of a Strange Child - Gilbert Morris 4470

Brereton, John
Janice Meredith - Paul Leicester Ford 2166

Burr, Aaron
The Unvanquished - Howard Fast 2046

Cameron, Eric
Love Not a Rebel - Heather Graham 2516

Collins, Michael
An Excess of Love - Cathy Cash Spellman 5959

Comyn, John
The Crown in Darkness - P.C. Doherty 1671

Connolly, James
An Excess of Love - Cathy Cash Spellman 5959

Cooper, Adam
April Morning - Howard Fast 2027

Cooper, Moses
April Morning - Howard Fast 2027

Darragh, Roxanne
Rebel Guns - Adam Rutledge 5539
Sons of Liberty - Adam Rutledge 5540

De Valera, Eamon
An Excess of Love - Cathy Cash Spellman 5959

Deaderick, Elly
Slow Dies the Thunder - Helen Topping Miller 4395

Dominic
The Scorching Wind - Walter Macken 3988

Dualta
The Scorching Wind - Walter Macken 3988
The Silent People - Walter Macken 3990

Dunwoodie, Major Peyton
The Spy: A Tale of the Neutral Ground - James Fenimore Cooper 1310

FitzGibbon, Constance
An Excess of Love - Cathy Cash Spellman 5959

Foxe-Donnell, Leo
A Nest of Simple Folk - Sean O'Faolain 4692

Franklin, Benjamin
The Bastard - John Jakes 3144
The Rebels - John Jakes 3152

Gelbman, Anna
The Iron Curtain - Robert Vaughan 6447

Gibbs, John
The Iron Chain - Jim DeFelice 1579

Gratwick, Ward
Blind Journey - Bruce Lancaster 3636

Griffith, Arthur
High Heroic - Constantine FitzGibbon 2118

Gyllenlove, Alexandra
The Fortress - Catherine Gavin 2320

Hale, Nathan
The King's Rebel - James David Horan 3030
The Long Naked Descent into Boston - William Eastlake 1823
The Rebel and the Turncoat - Malcolm Decker 1576
The Savage Brood - Martha Rofheart 5430
Sons of Liberty - Adam Rutledge 5540

Hamilton, Alexander
The Unvanquished - Howard Fast 2046

Hancock, John
Back Bay - William Martin 4138
Cardigan - Robert W. Chambers 976
Citizen Tom Paine - Howard Fast 2028
Freedom's Dues - Robert H. Abel 9
The Unvanquished - Howard Fast 2046
Yankee Doodle Dandy - Noel B. Gerson 2387

Henry, Patrick
Clear for Action: A Novel about John Paul Jones - Clements Ripley 5344
Give Me Liberty - Noel B. Gerson 2369
Give Me Liberty: The Story of an Innocent Man - John Erskine 1956
The Tree of Liberty - Elizabeth Page 4773

Jarret, Jarl
Jarrett's Jade - Frank Yerby 6923

Jefferson, Thomas
Citizen Tom Paine - Howard Fast 2028

Knowles, Ethan
Bride of Liberty - Frank Yerby 6909

Knowles, Polly
Bride of Liberty - Frank Yerby 6909

Latimer, Harry
The Carolinian - Rafael Sabatini 5547

Lee, Francis Lightfoot
Tidewater Dynasty: A Biographical Novel of the Lees of Stratford Hall - Carey Roberts 5372

Lee, Richard Henry
Tidewater Dynasty: A Biographical Novel of the Lees of Stratford Hall - Carey Roberts 5372

Maironi, Don Franco
The Patriot - Antonio Fogazzaro 2146

Manning, Andrew
The Drums of December - Sharon Salvato 5575

Markham, Elliot
Stars and Stripes - Adam Rutledge 5541

Markievicz, Constance
An Excess of Love - Cathy Cash Spellman 5959

Michefalt, Pierre de
Asylum for the Queen - Mildred A. Jordan 3303

Montoria, Don Jose de
Saragossa - Benito Perez Galdos 4912

Morris, Robert
Mistress of the Forge - David Taylor 6179

Murdoc
Seek the Fair Land - Walter Macken 3989

O'Connor, Tierney
An Excess of Love - Cathy Cash Spellman 5959

O'Donnell, Johno
A Nest of Simple Folk - Sean O'Faolain 4692

Paine, Thomas
Citizen Tom Paine - Howard Fast 2028
The Long Naked Descent into Boston - William Eastlake 1823
The Rebels - John Jakes 3152
This Other Eden - Marilyn Harris 2733
To Spit Against the Wind - Benjamin H. Levin 3737

Paoli, Pasquale
In What Torn Ship - Evelyn Eaton 1828

Pearse, Patrick Henry
An Excess of Love - Cathy Cash Spellman 5959
High Heroic - Constantine FitzGibbon 2118

Pitcher, Molly
Farewell to Valley Forge - David Taylor 6178

Pulaski, Casimir
Monmouth - Charles Bracelen Flood 2144

Reed, Quincy
Sons of Liberty - Adam Rutledge 5540

Reilly, Martin
Thy Tears Might Cease - Michael Farrell 2018

Revell, Ebenezer
Massachusetts: A Novel - Nancy Zaroulis 6956

Revere, Paul
Back Bay - William Martin 4138
The Bastard - John Jakes 3144

Bride of Liberty - Frank Yerby   6909
The Drums of April - Charles Mergendahl   4340
East to Bagaduce - Willard Wallace   6539
Gilman of the Redford - William Stearns Davis   1541
The Long Naked Descent into Boston - William
 Eastlake   1823
Massachusetts: A Novel - Nancy Zaroulis   6956
The Traitor - Dan Sherman   5814

Robert the Bruce
The Crown in Darkness - P.C. Doherty   1671

Rumstick, Ezra
By Force of Arms - James L. Nelson   4579

Sobieski, Thaddeus
Thaddeus of Warsaw - Jane Porter   5136

Solomon, Haym
Haym Solomon, Son of Liberty - Howard Fast   2032

Stafford, Sarah
The Brahmins - Eileen Lottman   3901

Starr, Padraic
The Rising of the Moon - William Martin   4140

Stuart, Jamie
The Proud and the Free - Howard Fast   2042

Trent, Ethan
Eden's Gate - Karen Harper   2711

Wallace, William
Braveheart - Randall Wallace   6538
Hammer of the Scots - Jean Plaidy   5018
The Lion Is Come - Jane Oliver   4725
Robert the Bruce: The Steps to the Empty Throne -
 Nigel Tranter   6320
The Scottish Chiefs - Jane Porter   5135

Warren, Joseph
The Bastard - John Jakes   3144
The Rebels - John Jakes   3152

Warrington, Charles
The Green Mountain Boys - Daniel Pierce
 Thompson   6249

Winslow, Nathan
The Gentle Rebel - Gilbert Morris   4461
The Saintly Buccaneer - Gilbert Morris   4469

PEDDLER

Birch, Harvey
The Spy: A Tale of the Neutral Ground - James
 Fenimore Cooper   1310

Crawford, Bill
Boy with a Pack - Stephen Warren Meader   4319

Drew, Jonathan
Strange Adventure of Jonathan Drew - Christopher
 Ward   6562
Yankee Rover - Christopher Ward   6563

Jed
Look to the River - William A. Owens   4771

Mudspell, Curt
Called Away - Perdita Buchan   753

Nydia
The Last Days of Pompeii - Edward Bulwer-
 Lytton   768

Roger the Chapman
Death and the Chapman - Kate Sedley   5715
The Eve of Saint Hyacinth - Kate Sedley   5716
The Holy Innocents - Kate Sedley   5717
The Plymouth Cloak - Kate Sedley   5718
The Weaver's Tale - Kate Sedley   5719

Villaricca, Solomon
The Slave Stealer - Boyd Upchurch   6390

Wilner, Saul
Behold the Fire - Michael Blankfort   541

PHARMACIST

Auclair, Euclide
Shadows on the Rock - Willa Cather   959

Frowenfeld, Joseph
The Grandissimes - George W. Cable   842

PHILANTHROPIST

Hawkridge, Sir Waldo
The Nonesuch - Georgette Heyer   2896

PHILOSOPHER

Abelard, Peter
Death Comes as Epiphany - Sharan Newman   4598
Peter Abelard: A Novel - Helen Waddell   6517
*Stealing Heaven: The Love Story of Heloise and
 Abelard* - Marion Meade   4317

Anaxagoras
Glory and the Lightning - Taylor Caldwell   856
Pericles the Athenian - Rex Warner   6566

Andigones
Judas - Igal Mossinsohn   4500

Aristotle
The Conqueror: A Novel of Alexander the Great -
 Edison Marshall   4104
An Elephant for Aristotle - L. Sprague De
 Camp   1556
Fire From Heaven - Mary Renault   5296

Arouet, Francois Marie
Adrienne - Barbara Levy   3742
The Anthem - Noel B. Gerson   2361
A Day of Battle - Vincent Sheean   5787
Rasero - Francisco Rebolledo   5282
Voltaire! Voltaire! - Guy Endore   1943

Augustine
The Restless Flame - Louis De Wohl   1573
Son of Tears - Henry W. Coray   1320

Avicenna
The Physician - Noah Gordon   2482

Bacon, Sir Francis
*The Diary of William Harvey: The Imaginary Journal
 of the Physician Who Revolutionized Medicine* -
 Jean Hamburger   2667
For My Great Folly - Thomas B. Costain   1365
Gay Lord Robert - Jean Plaidy   5015
*Physician Extraordinary: A Novel of the Life and
 Times of William Harvey* - David Weiss   6608

Bacon, Roger
The Black Rose - Thomas B. Costain   1363

Bakhtin, Nikolai
Saints and Scholars - Terrence Eagleton   1821

Calvin, John
*The Master of Geneva: A Novel Based on the Life of
 John Calvin* - Gladys H. Barr   341

Chrysanteus
The Last Athenian - Viktor Rydberg   5543

Chrysis
Woman of Andros - Thornton Wilder   6754

Cicero, Marcus Tullius
The Catiline Conspiracy - John Maddox
 Roberts   5379
Clodia - Robert DeMaria   1606
The Ides of March - Thornton Wilder   6753
A Murder on the Appian Way - Steven Saylor   5625
A Pillar of Iron - Taylor Caldwell   861
Roman Shadows - Ron Burns   804
Spartacus - Howard Fast   2044

Confucius
Creation - Gore Vidal   6486

D'Astrarac
At the Sign of the Reine Pedauque - Anatole
 France   2198

Dewey, John
John and Anzia: An American Romance - Norma
 Rosen   5462

Diderot, Denis
Rasero - Francisco Rebolledo   5282

Dion
The Mask of Apollo - Mary Renault   5300

Emerson, Ralph Waldo
The Jonah Man - Henry Carlisle   895
Walt Whitman's Secret - Ben Aronin   196

Engels, Friedrich
*The Case of the Revolutionist's Daughter: Sherlock
 Holmes Meets Karl Marx* - Lewis S. Feuer   2076

Epictetus
The Soldier and the Sage: A Novel about Akiba -
 Richard G. Hubler   3065

Erasmus, Desiderius
Flame of Fire - Jane Oliver   4722

Falconer, William
Falconer's Crusade - Ian Morson   4493
Falconer's Judgement - Ian Morson   4494

Gassendi, Pierre
*The Diary of William Harvey: The Imaginary Journal
 of the Physician Who Revolutionized Medicine* -
 Jean Hamburger   2667

Hypatia
Hypatia - Charles Kingsley   3498

Inglesant, John
John Inglesant - John Henry Shorthouse   5833

Libanius
Julian - Gore Vidal   6489

Machiavelli, Niccolo
Romola - George Eliot   1910

Maimonides, Moses
*The Doctor From Cordova: A Biographical Novel
 about the Great Philosopher Maimonides* - Herbert
 Le Porrier   3693
The Source - James A. Michener   4374
Trail and Triumph: A Novel about Maimonides -
 Lester M. Morrison   4485

Manilianus, Marcus Mezentius
The Secret of the Kingdom - Mika Waltari   6555

Marius
Marius the Epicurean - Walter Pater   4826

Marx, Karl
Sisters & Lovers - Nicola Thorne   6274
*The Trial of Elizabeth Cree: A Novel of the Limehouse
 Murders* - Peter Ackroyd   21

Mill, John Stuart
Caribbean - James A. Michener   4365
Neighboring Lives - Thomas M. Disch   1648

Moore, G.E.
The World as I Found It - Bruce Duffy   1755

Nietzsche, Friedrich
When Nietzsche Wept: A Novel of Obsession - Irvin D.
 Yalom   6892

Nostradamus
The Dreamer of the Vine - Liz Greene   2574

Origen Adamantius
Origen: A Historical Novel - Theodore Vrettos   6515

Paine, Thomas
To Spit Against the Wind - Benjamin H. Levin   3737

Paracelsus, Philippus Aureolus
The Alchemist's Journal - Evan S. Connell   1256

Phaedo
The Last of the Wine - Mary Renault 5299

Pico della Mirandola, Giovanni
The Florentine - Sandra Shulman 5840

Plato
The Last of the Wine - Mary Renault 5299
The Mask of Apollo - Mary Renault 5300
The Private and Public Life of Socrates - Rene Kraus 3552

Priscus
Julian - Gore Vidal 6489

Rousseau, Jean Jacques
Rasero - Francisco Rebolledo 5282
Voltaire! Voltaire! - Guy Endore 1943

Russell, Bertrand
The World as I Found It - Bruce Duffy 1755

Seneca, Lucius Annaeus
The Kingdom of the Wicked - Anthony Burgess 778

Severinus, Anicius
Citadel of God: A Novel of Saint Benedict - Louis De Wohl 1563

Siddhartha Gautama
Lady of the Lotus - William E. Barrett 353
The Yellow Robe: A Novel of the Life of Buddha - Robert Payne 4856

Socrates
Alcibiades, Beloved of Gods - Vincenz Brun 735
Creation - Gore Vidal 6486
The Escape of Socrates - Robert Pick 4993
Glory and the Lightning - Taylor Caldwell 856
Goat Song: A Novel of Ancient Greece - Frank Yerby 6920
Goatsong - Tom Holt 3009
The Immortal Marriage - Gertrude Atherton 225
The Last of the Wine - Mary Renault 5299
The Magnificent Traitor: A Novel of Alcibiades and the Golden Age of Pericles - Lynn Poole 5092
The Private and Public Life of Socrates - Rene Kraus 3552
The Walled Orchard - Tom Holt 3010

Spinoza, Baruch
I, Rembrandt - David Weiss 6605

Thales
My Name Is Sappho - Martha Rofheart 5429

Thomas Aquinas
The Quiet Light - Louis De Wohl 1572

Thoreau, Henry David
Walt Whitman's Secret - Ben Aronin 196

Vivaldi, Orazio
The Valley of Decision - Edith Wharton 6653

Voltaire
The Enchantress - Suyin Han 2673

Warner, Adam
The Last of the Barons - Edward Bulwer-Lytton 769

Wittgenstein, Ludwig
Saints and Scholars - Terrence Eagleton 1821
The World as I Found It - Bruce Duffy 1755

Zeno
The Abyss - Marguerite Yourcenar 6946
Glory and the Lightning - Taylor Caldwell 856

PHOTOGRAPHER

Brady, Matthew B.
The Gallery of His Dreams - Kristine Kathryn Rusch 5525

Breslain, Esther
The House on Mulberry Street - Maan Meyers 4354

Dixon, Joseph
Shadow Catcher - Charles Fergus 2064

Fry, Ansel
Shadow Catcher - Charles Fergus 2064

Jermyn, Amanda
Daughters of the New World - Susan Richards Shreve 5835

McCaskill, Mariah
Ride with Me, Mariah Montana - Ivan Doig 1684

Van Schaick, Charles
Billy Sunday - Rod Jones 3295

PILOT

Allen, Thomas C.
The Hallelujah Flight - Jack Lynn 3937

Bandfield, Frank
Eagles at War - Walter J. Boyne 620

Bandy, Bartholemew
It's Me Again - Donald Jack 3126
Me So Far - Donald Jack 3127
That's Me in the Middle - Donald Jack 3129
Three Cheers for Me - Donald Jack 3131

Banning, James Herman
The Hallelujah Flight - Jack Lynn 3937

Bryant, Toby
Gentlemen of Adventure - Ernest K. Gann 2278

Canfield, Billy
Over There - Robert Vaughan 6449

Chamay, Paul
In the Company of Eagles - Ernest K. Gann 2279

Cockfoster, Mark
The Sky and Tomorrow - Thomas William Duncan 1788

Crispin, Bartley
Squadron Shilling - Arch Whitehouse 6712

Draper, Kiffen
Gentlemen of Adventure - Ernest K. Gann 2278

Hafner, Bruno
Eagles at War - Walter J. Boyne 620

Halifax, Charlie
In the Blue Light of African Dreams - Paul Watkins 6580

Horn, Alfred
Shadow of the Wolf - James Barwick 371

Horner, Ben
Conqueror of the Clouds - William F. Hallstead 2664

Jackson, Travis
Cold War - Robert Vaughan 6446
The Iron Curtain - Robert Vaughan 6447

Jerningham, Amelia
Wings of the Morning - David Beaty 402

Kupper, Sebastian
In the Company of Eagles - Ernest K. Gann 2279

Lindbergh, Charles
Dance on a Sinking Ship - Michael Kilian 3483
A First Class Murder - Elliott Roosevelt 5442
Stolen Away - Max Allan Collins 1213

Luria, Benny
The Hope - Herman Wouk 6874

Manning, Caro
The Heart of the Continent - Nancy Cato 961

March, James
Wings of the Morning - David Beaty 402

O'Malley, William Bede
High Road to China - Jon Cleary 1106

Paxton, Oliver
War Story: A Novel - Derek Robinson 5404

Prohaska, Otto
The Two-Headed Eagle - John Biggins 493

Quinney, Nicholas Dicken
The Bright Blue Sky - Max Hennessy 2830
The Challenging Heights - Max Hennessy 2831
Once More the Hawks - Max Hennessy 2836

Shaw, John Robert
The Longest Winter - Julie Harris 2722

Smith, John
The Near and Distant Place - Patricia Wright 6883

Stachel, Bruno
The Blood Order - Jack D. Hunter 3084
The Blue Max - Jack D. Hunter 3085

Toshack, Zoe
Once More the Hawks - Max Hennessy 2836

Unnamed Character
The Aviator - Ernest K. Gann 2277

Winslow, Diana
Once a Gentleman - Donald James 3157

PIONEER

Adams, Kevin
The Argonauts - Yvonne Schoell 5645

Ashburn, Emily
The Glorious Three - June Wetherell 6651

Bartor, Daniel
Snow-Water - Dorothy Gardiner 2285

Baxter, Goldie
The Argonauts - Yvonne Schoell 5645

Black, Gideon
The Land Is Bright - Archie Binns 501

Bowen, Susan
The Sun Shines West - Nathan Schachner 5632

Brace, Hugh
For Us the Living - Bruce Lancaster 3639

Brannan, Samuel
Samuel Brannan and the Golden Fleece - Reva Scott 5686

Brightwood, Joshua
The Brightwood Expedition - Kay L. McDonald 4261

Brightwood, Marlette
The Brightwood Expedition - Kay L. McDonald 4261
The Vision Is Fulfilled - Kay L. McDonald 4262

Clinch, Rachel
Darker Grows the Valley - Harry Harrison Kroll 3556

Comyn, Mab
Pageant - G.B. Lancaster 3650

Conklin, Abigail
Between Earth and Sky - Karen Osborn 4758

Doaks, Charity
Darker Grows the Valley - Harry Harrison Kroll 3556

Donner, George
Tamsen - David Galloway 2273
Wheels West - Homer Croy 1438

Donner, Tamsen
Wheels West - Homer Croy 1438

Dorie, Lidian
I Am Lidian - Naomi Lane Babson 253

Duston, Hannah
Gallant Warrior - Helen R. Mann 4063

Eddy, William H.
Grim Journey - Hoffman Birney 509

Eldridge, Mark
Thunder on the River - Charlton Laird   3590

Fletcher, Curt
Each Bright River - Mildred Masterson
   McNeilly   4308

Ford, Case
The Land Is Bright - Archie Binns   501

Greenfield, Nancy Ann
The Land Is Bright - Archie Binns   501

Harrow, Dan
Mountains Ahead - Martha Ferguson
   McKeown   4284

Harrow, Harmony
Mountains Ahead - Martha Ferguson
   McKeown   4284

Hollis, America
The Overland Trail - Wendi Lee   3712

Hollister, Corrie Belle
My Father's World - Michael Phillips   4989

Hunt, Zeke
Whole Hog - David Wagoner   6523

Kelsey, Nancy
The No-Return Trail - Sonia Levitin   3741

Overman, Adele
Bend Your Heads All - Rowena Rutherford
   Farrar   2015

Overman, Seth
Bend Your Heads All - Rowena Rutherford
   Farrar   2015

Potter, Harriet
Love Is a Wild Assault - Elithe Hamilton
   Kirkland   3506

Prentiss, Salita
*Heroine of the Prairies: A Romance of the Oregon
   Trail* - Sheba Hargreaves   2707

Reed, James Frazier
Wheels West - Homer Croy   1438

Riley, Jim
The Glorious Three - June Wetherell   6651

Shaw, Unwin
The Far Country - Marthedith Furnas   2258

Sorensen, Jan Carl
Winds of Spring - Walter Havighurst   2776

Swilling, Jack
I, Jack Swilling - John Myers   4544

Terra, Ana
Time and the Wind - Erico Verissimo   6451

Ward, Hagar
New Road - Merle Estes Colby   1168

Wells, Tom
The Head Waters - Archie Binns   500

Wingate, Molly
Covered Wagon - Emerson Hough   3041

PIRATE

Armand, Marcel
Marcel Armand - Sallie Bell   424

Aubery, Jean-Benoit
Frenchman's Creek - Daphne Du Maurier   1744

Aumarle, John
Wolfshead - Jere Hungerford Wheelwright   6672

Beauvallet, Nicholas
Beauvallet - Georgette Heyer   2876

Black Dog
Return to Treasure Island - Denis Judd   3318

Blackbeard
On Stranger Tides - Tim Powers   5156

Blease, Roger
For My Great Folly - Thomas B. Costain   1365

Blood, Colonel
The Pyrates - George MacDonald Fraser   2212

Blood, Peter
Captain Blood - Rafael Sabatini   5546

Bloody Shad
A Mirror for Witches - Esther Forbes   2157

Bones, Billy
The Adventures of Long John Silver - Denis
   Judd   3317

Bonnet, Stede
Wind From the Main - Anne Osborne   4759

Bonny, Anne
Anne Bonny - Chloe Gartner   2306
The Changeling - Alison Macleod   4000
*Fanny: Being the True History of the Adventures of
   Fanny Hackabout-Jones* - Erica Jong   3299
Lusty Wind for Carolina - Inglis Fletcher   2134
The Pyrates - George MacDonald Fraser   2212
Sea Star: The Private Life of Anne Bonny, Pirate -
   Pamela Jekel   3187
Wind From the Main - Anne Osborne   4759

Boyd, Salathiel
The Wickedest Pilgrim - Donald Barr Chidsey   1067

Burrows, John
For Love of a Pirate - Anthony Esler   1961

Cameron, Roc "Silver Hawk"
A Pirate's Pleasure - Heather Graham   2518

Chandagnac, John
On Stranger Tides - Tim Powers   5156

Cleveland, Clement
The Pirate - Sir Walter Scott   5704

Decimus
The Bride of Pilate - Esther Kellner   3393

Doyle, Cormac
The Silver Oar - Howard Breslin   669

Finney, Calico Jack
The Gun Ketch - Dewey Lambdin   3610

Gerardo, Kit
The Golden Hawk - Frank Yerby   6921

Gold Beard
The Temptation of Angelique - Sergeanne
   Golon   2473

Helford, Ruark
The Pirate and the Pagan - Virginia Henley   2827

Hilton, Kit
The Devil's Own - Christopher Nicole   4615

Jericho, Lucas
Hearts of Fire - Christina Savage   5616

Jonsen
A High Wind in Jamaica - Richard Hughes   3074

Kidd, Captain William
The Legion of the Lost - Donald Barr Chidsey   1062

Laffite, Jean
Anthony Adverse - Hervey Allen   98
Black Ivory - Polan Banks   292
*The Corsair: A Biographical Novel of Jean Lafitte,
   Hero of the Battle of New Orleans* - Madeleine
   Fabiola Kent   3444
The Fallon Pride - Reagan O'Neal   4742
Hearts of Hickory - John Trotwood Moore   4442
The Iron Mistress - Paul I. Wellman   6618
Marcel Armand - Sallie Bell   424
Pelican Coast - Alan Le May   3690

Marriott, Richard
The White Rajah - Nicholas Monsarrat   4433

Mezze-Morte
Angelique in Barbary - Sergeanne Golon   2469

Minotaur
The Sea Peoples - Peter Danielson   1474

Montreuse, Felipe Flores y Lennox
The Black Duchess - Alanna Knight   3514

Morgan, Henry
Caribbean - James A. Michener   4365
Cup of Gold - John Steinbeck   5991
Cutlass Empire - F. van Wyck Mason   4148
The Devil's Own - Christopher Nicole   4615
The Privateer - Gordon Daviot   1510
The Quickenberry Tree - Annette Motley   4502
Running Proud - Nicholas Monsarrat   4432
Windward Passage - Hamilton Cochran   1143

Morpain, Pierre de
Restless Are the Sails - Evelyn Eaton   1830

O'Donnell, Arrah
Mistress of the Eagles - Elona Malterre   4052

O'Malley, Grace
Grania: She-King of the Irish Seas - Morgan
   Llywelyn   3819

Paulus, Marcus Lucius
The Pirate From Rome - John V.D.
   Southworth   5952

Red Rover
The Red Rover - James Fenimore Cooper   1309

Rescator
Angelique in Barbary - Sergeanne Golon   2469
Angelique in Love - Sergeanne Golon   2470

Robinson, Launcelot
*Fanny: Being the True History of the Adventures of
   Fanny Hackabout-Jones* - Erica Jong   3299

Silver, Long John
The Adventures of Long John Silver - Denis
   Judd   3317
Return to Treasure Island - Denis Judd   3318
Treasure Island - Robert Louis Stevenson   6012

Skimmer of the Seas
The Water Witch - James Fenimore Cooper   1311

Teach, Edward
Carolina Corsair - Don Tracy   6307
Lusty Wind for Carolina - Inglis Fletcher   2134
Rogue's Holiday - Hamilton Cochran   1141
Wind From the Main - Anne Osborne   4759

Turms, Lars
The Etruscan - Mika Waltari   6553

Van Cleef, Jan
The Sea Beggars - Cecelia Holland   2996

Vane, Charles
Lusty Wind for Carolina - Inglis Fletcher   2134

Ward, John
For My Great Folly - Thomas B. Costain   1365

Whetstone, Thomas
Galleon - Dudley Pope   5095

Winston, Hugh
Caribbee - Thomas Hoover   3025

Yorke, Ned
Buccaneer - Dudley Pope   5093
Galleon - Dudley Pope   5095

PLANTATION OWNER

Ashington, Sarah
The Spring of the Tiger - Victoria Holt   3021

Bale, Richard
Balisand - Joseph Hergesheimer   2853

Barrett, Justin
The Golden Harlot - Jeanne Wilson   6808

Bascom, Rob
Iron Ships, Iron Men - Christopher Nicole   4616

Bay, Maurice
The Running Thread - Drayton Mayrant   4215

Bedford, Malcolm
So Red the Rose - Stark Young   6944

Benton, Tom
Benton's Row - Frank Yerby   6908

Berrien, Beau
Blood Red Roses - Elizabeth Boatwright Coker   1163

Bishop, Colonel
Captain Blood - Rafael Sabatini   5546

Bolton, Richard
The Spoils of Eden - Robert H. Fowler   2193

Bond, Hamish
Band of Angels - Robert Penn Warren   6572

Bonning, George
Ratoon - Christopher Nicole   4619

Bottomley, John
The Light Infantry Ball - Hamilton Basso   375

Brent, Margaret
Mary's Land - Lucia St. Clair Robson   5415

Butler, Pierce
The Ardent Years - Janet Stevenson   6003
Fire in the Heart - Henrietta Buckmaster   761

Calverly, Brandon
Up Country: A Story of the Vanguard - Donald Culross Peattie   4881

Cameron, Ronald
Wind From the Carolinas - Robert Wilder   6751

Chisholm, Julian
The Stubborn Heart - Frank G. Slaughter   5904

Clay, George
Heaven Trees - Stark Young   6943

Creston, Peronneau
Red Lanterns on St. Michael's - Thornwell Jacobs   3139

Dabney, Hoab
Tap Roots - James H. Street   6080

Dandridge, Clarence
Bagatelle - Maurice Denuziere   1613

Dart, Joan
Ratoon - Christopher Nicole   4619

Dutton, John
Jubilee - Margaret Walker   6531

Eden, Michael
Eden - Julie Ellis   1918

Falks, Guy
Fairoaks - Frank Yerby   6915

Fleming, Lewis
Margaret's Story - Eugenia Price   5183

Fleming, Margaret Seton
Margaret's Story - Eugenia Price   5183

Flint, Hugh
By the Dim Lamps - Nathan Schachner   5630

Flynn, Lafe
Gallows Way - Daoma Winston   6825

Fonta, Fernando
The Red Lances - Arturo Uslar Pietri   4999

Forrest, Nathan Bedford
A Story of Deep Delight - Thomas McNamee   4305

Fox, Stephen
The Foxes of Harrow - Frank Yerby   6917

Frane, Sydney
Gamble's Hundred - Clifford Dowdey   1705

Fraser, John
Where Shadows Go - Eugenia Price   5189

Garvey, Marietta
Gallows Way - Daoma Winston   6825

Griffin, Paris
Griffin's Way - Frank Yerby   6922

Hendrick, Allen
Sojourn of a Stranger - Walter Sullivan   6115

Hilton, Anthony
Black Dawn - Christopher Nicole   4613

Hilton, Richard
Black Dawn - Christopher Nicole   4613

Hilton, Robert
Mistress of Darkness - Christopher Nicole   4617

Howard, Martin
Natchez: A Novel of the Deep South - Pamela Jekel   3186

Jourdain, Nicholas
Song of the Bayou - Elinor Lynley   3936

Jumel, Stephen
Notorious Eliza - Basil Beyea   489

Kendrick, Arnold
Beulah Land - Lonnie Coleman   1202

Kendrick, Sarah
Look Away, Beulah Land - Lonnie Coleman   1204

Lacy, Vivian
Celia Garth - Gwen Bristow   695

LeGrand, St. Clair
The Web of Days - Edna Lee   3708

Leigh, Adam
Golden Isle - Frank G. Slaughter   5890

Llewellyn, Nicholas
Penhally - Caroline Gordon   2479

Llewellyn, Ralph
Penhally - Caroline Gordon   2479

Mackay, Thomas
Journey Proud - Thomasine McGehee   4273

MacLeod, Angus
Bridle the Wind - Julia Davis   1525
Cloud on the Land - Julia Davis   1526
Eagle on the Sun - Julia Davis   1527

Manning, Elizabeth
The Drums of December - Sharon Salvato   5575

Manning, Joseph
The Fires of July - Sharon Salvato   5576

Massingham, Gilbert
The Vines of Yarrabee - Dorothy Eden   1864

McBride, Archibald
Tell Me a Tale: A Novel of the Old South - James McEachin   4266

McGehee, Hugh
So Red the Rose - Stark Young   6944

McQueen, John
Don Juan McQueen - Eugenia Price   5181

Morgan, Corby
Cry of the Rain Bird - Patricia Shaw   5779

Nowell-Grey, Brockton
The Ravishers - Elizabeth Richards   5318

Peyton, Caroline
Shod with Flame - Helen Topping Miller   4393

Purchis, Hart
Judas Flowering - Jane Aiken Hodge   2965
Wide Is the Water - Jane Aiken Hodge   2973

Purchis, Hyde
Savannah Purchase - Jane Aiken Hodge   2970

Ransome, Kevin
The Magnolias - Julie Ellis   1922

Richardson, Nate
From Fields of Gold - Alexandra Ripley   5339

Savage, Keith
Savage Oaks - Julie Ellis   1924

Selby, Lorena
Lorena - Frank G. Slaughter   5892

Sevendor, David
Cain's Daughters - Doris Shannon   5776

Shallop, Sidney
Beauty Beast - MacKinlay Kantor   3361

Sutpen, Thomas
Absalom, Absalom! - William Faulkner   2049

Swille, Arthur
Flight to Canada - Ishmael Reed   5285

Thomas, Julia
No Surrender - Emma Gelders Sterne   5999

Todd, Gawin
Balisand - Joseph Hergesheimer   2853

Trace, Sereno
Elegant Journey - John Selby   5740

Vosmar, Simon
Scent of Cloves - Norah Lofts   3859

Warner, Marguerite
The Devil's Own - Christopher Nicole   4615

Watson, E. J.
Killing Mister Watson - Peter Mathiessen   4185

Wells, Colonel Walter
Weep in the Sun - Jeanne Wilson   6809

Whetstone, Thomas
Galleon - Dudley Pope   5095

Whetstone, Yarborough
Foundation Stone - Lella Warren   6571

Wilkes, Ashley
Gone with the Wind - Margaret Mitchell   4415

Winslow, Sky
The Last Confederate - Gilbert Morris   4466

Worth, Anthony
Crimson Is the Eastern Shore - Don Tracy   6308

Yorke, Ned
Buccaneer - Dudley Pope   5093
Galleon - Dudley Pope   5095

POLICE OFFICER

Black, Andrew
The Eagles of Malice - Alan Scholefield   5652

Bragg, Joseph
Counterfeit of Murder - Ray Harrison   2738
Death of a Dancing Lady - Ray Harrison   2739
Deathwatch - Ray Harrison   2740
Harvest of Death - Ray Harrison   2741
Patently Murder - Ray Harrison   2742
A Season for Death - Ray Harrison   2743
Sphere of Death - Ray Harrison   2744
Tincture of Death - Ray Harrison   2745
Why Kill Arthur Potter? - Ray Harrison   2746

Brautigan, John
Ain't Goin' to Glory - David Delman   1597

Cribb, Sergeant
Abracadaver - Peter Lovesey   3906
A Case of Spirits - Peter Lovesey   3910
The Detective Wore Silk Drawers - Peter Lovesey   3911
Mad Hatter's Holiday - Peter Lovesey   3914
Swing, Swing Together - Peter Lovesey   3915
The Tick of Death - Peter Lovesey   3916
Waxwork - Peter Lovesey   3917

Wobble to Death - Peter Lovesey 3918

Crow, Angus McCready
The Return of Moriarty - John E. Gardner 2287

Disley, Pete
Curse of Magira - David Bee 413

Faro, Jeremy
Blood Line - Alanna Knight 3515
Deadly Beloved - Alanna Knight 3517
Enter Second Murderer - Alanna Knight 3518
Killing Cousins - Alanna Knight 3520

Gautier, Jean-Paul
Crime Without Passion - Richard Grayson 2556
Death En Voyage - Richard Grayson 2557
Death Off Stage - Richard Grayson 2558
Death on the Cards - Richard Grayson 2559
The Monterant Affair - Richard Grayson 2560
The Montmarte Murders - Richard Grayson 2561
The Murder at Impasse Louvaine - Richard Grayson 2562

Giolitti-Crispi, Lorenzo
Summoned to Darkness - Anne-Marie Sheridan 5809

Hays, Jake
The High Constable - Maan Meyers 4353

Heller, Nate
True Detective - Max Allan Collins 1215

Hussey, Johnny
A Nest of Simple Folk - Sean O'Faolain 4692

Jago, Henry
The Detective Wore Silk Drawers - Peter Lovesey 3911

Johnson, Toussaint
Murder by the Numbers - Max Allan Collins 1212

Lumley, Oliver
Jekyll, Alias Hyde - Donald Thomas 6240
The Ripper's Apprentice - Donald Thomas 6242

Martock, Sergeant
Sergeant Verity and the Imperial Diamond - Francis Selwyn 5745

Morton, James
Counterfeit of Murder - Ray Harrison 2738
Death of a Dancing Lady - Ray Harrison 2739
Deathwatch - Ray Harrison 2740
Harvest of Death - Ray Harrison 2741
Patently Murder - Ray Harrison 2742
A Season for Death - Ray Harrison 2743
Sphere of Death - Ray Harrison 2744
Tincture of Death - Ray Harrison 2745
Why Kill Arthur Potter? - Ray Harrison 2746

Ness, Eliot
True Detective - Max Allan Collins 1215

Nicholson, Craig
The Asking Price - Jessica Stirling 6039
The Welcome Light - Jessica Stirling 6050

Pitt, Thomas
Belgrave Square - Anne Perry 4919
Bethlehem Road - Anne Perry 4920
Bluegate Fields - Anne Perry 4921
Callander Square - Anne Perry 4923
Cardington Crescent - Anne Perry 4924
The Cater Street Hangman - Anne Perry 4925
Death in the Devil's Acre - Anne Perry 4927
Farriers' Lane - Anne Perry 4930
Highgate Rise - Anne Perry 4931
Paragon Walk - Anne Perry 4932
Resurrection Row - Anne Perry 4934
Rutland Place - Anne Perry 4935
Silence in Hanover Close - Anne Perry 4936
Traitors Gate - Anne Perry 4939

Stuart, Cullen
North Star Conspiracy - Miriam Grace Monfredo 4428

Seneca Falls Inheritance - Miriam Grace Monfredo 4429

Thackeray, Edward
Abracadaver - Peter Lovesey 3906
A Case of Spirits - Peter Lovesey 3910
The Detective Wore Silk Drawers - Peter Lovesey 3911
Mad Hatter's Holiday - Peter Lovesey 3914
Swing, Swing Together - Peter Lovesey 3915
The Tick of Death - Peter Lovesey 3916
Waxwork - Peter Lovesey 3917
Wobble to Death - Peter Lovesey 3918

Verity, Sergeant William
Cracksman on Velvet - Francis Selwyn 5743
Sergeant Verity and the Blood Royal - Francis Selwyn 5744
Sergeant Verity and the Imperial Diamond - Francis Selwyn 5745
Sergeant Verity Presents His Compliments - Francis Selwyn 5746

Vidocq, Francois Eugene
I Am Vidocq - Vincent McConnor 4225

Von Thieleman, Manfred
Curse of Magira - David Bee 413

Warren, Charles
Bertie and the Tinman - Peter Lovesey 3909

POLITICAL FIGURE

Adams, John
The Braintree Mission - Nicholas E. Wyckoff 6887
Clear for Action: A Novel about John Paul Jones - Clements Ripley 5344
Freedom's Dues - Robert H. Abel 9
Jefferson: A Novel - Max Byrd 838
The Long Naked Descent into Boston - William Eastlake 1823
Man From Mt. Vernon - Burke Boyce 607
Portrait of a Scoundrel - Nathaniel Benchley 438
The Rebels - John Jakes 3152
The River Devils - Carter A. Vaughan 6437
Sally Hemings - Barbara Chase-Riboud 1006
Seneca - Donald Clayton Porter 5127
Those Who Love - Irving Stone 6064
Tidewater Dynasty: A Biographical Novel of the Lees of Stratford Hall - Carey Roberts 5372
The Tree of Liberty - Elizabeth Page 4773
Yankee Doodle Dandy - Noel B. Gerson 2387

Adams, John Quincy
Amistad: The Thunder of Freedom - David Pesci 4944
Echo of Lions - Barbara Chase-Riboud 1004
Sally Hemings - Barbara Chase-Riboud 1006

Adderly, Mark
The Angry Tide - Winston Graham 2521

Alcibiades
Achilles His Armour - Peter Green 2569
Alcibiades, Beloved of Gods - Vincenz Brun 735
The Immortal Marriage - Gertrude Atherton 225
The Magnificent Traitor: A Novel of Alcibiades and the Golden Age of Pericles - Lynn Poole 5092
The Shining - Stephen Marlowe 4097

Allen, Ira
Catch a Falling Star - Frederic F. Van de Water 6401

Altgeld, John Peter
The American - Howard Fast 2026

Andrassy, Julius
Imperial Waltz - William M. Abrahams 13

Andros, Edward
The Silver Oar - Howard Breslin 669

Antony, Marc
That Egyptian Woman - Noel B. Gerson 2384

Three's Company - Alfred Duggan 1774

Aristides
Farewell Great King: A Novel of Ancient Greece - Jill Paton Walsh 4829

Armstrong, John
Dolley - Rita Mae Brown 727

Arthur, Chester Alan
The Chester A. Arthur Conspiracy - William Wiegand 6740

Ashley, William
The Three Lives of Elizabeth - Shirley Seifert 5735

Ataturk, Kemal
The House of War - Catherine Gavin 2322

Austin, Stephen F.
Hellfire Jackson - Garland Roark 5355
On the Long Tide - Laura Krey 3555
Sam Houston - Noel B. Gerson 2380
Texas - James A. Michener 4375

Bacon, Sir Francis
For My Great Folly - Thomas B. Costain 1365
Gay Lord Robert - Jean Plaidy 5015
Unicorn Rampant - Nigel Tranter 6323

Baldwin, Stanley
Edward and Mrs. Simpson - A.C.H. Smith 5916

Balue, Cardinal Jean
Quentin Durward - Sir Walter Scott 5705

Bandy, Bartholomew
Me Too - Donald Jack 3128

Barker, Jack
The Queen and I - Sue Townsend 6306

Bass, Jethro
Coniston - Winston Churchill 1078

Beaton, David
A Stake in the Kingdom - Nigel Tranter 6321

Becket, Thomas
The Plantagenet Prelude - Jean Plaidy 5041

Beg, Yakub
Flashman at the Charge - George MacDonald Fraser 2209

Begin, Menachem
The Glory - Herman Wouk 6873

Bellamy, Richard
The Bellamy Saga - John Pearson 4878
Upstairs Downstairs - John Hawkesworth 2782

Belton, Clinton
The History of Rome Hanks - Joseph Stanley Pennell 4909

Ben Gurion, David
The Hope - Herman Wouk 6874

Benjamin, Judah P.
Beloved - Vina Delmar 1599
The Big Family - Vina Delmar 1600
The Chess Player: A Novel of New Orleans and Paris - Frances Parkinson Keyes 3478
The Court Martial of Robert E. Lee - Douglas Savage 5617
Gray Victory - Robert Skimin 5877
Papa La-Bas - John Dickson Carr 914
The Proud Retreat - Clifford Dowdey 1706
While the Music Plays - Diane Austell 242

Benton, Thomas Hart
The Buckstones - Paul I. Wellman 6615
Dream West - David Nevin 4587
Immortal Wife - Irving Stone 6057
Jessie: A Novel Based on the Life of Jessie Benton Fremont - Judy Alter 120
Sam Houston - Noel B. Gerson 2380

Bibulus, Marcus
Caesar's Women - Colleen McCullough 4233

Bismarck, Otto von
Falkenhorst - Mark Rascovich 5254
Quiet Lady - Norman Collins 1216
Royal Flash - George MacDonald Fraser 2213

Black, Christopher
The End of the Hunt - Thomas Flanagan 2119

Bligh, William
The Explorers - William Stuart Long 3872
The Settlers - William Stuart Long 3878
The Traitors - William Stuart Long 3879

Bliss, Simon
Deep River - Henrietta Buckmaster 760

Blue
Welcome to Hard Times - E.L. Doctorow 1660

Bonaparte, Carlo
Good-Bye My Son - Marjorie Coryn 1356

Bonaparte, Joseph
The Tontine - Thomas B. Costain 1371

Booth, Howard
Damaris - Jane Sheridan 5810

Borgia, Cesare
The Bait and the Trap - George Challis 970
City of God: A Novel of the Borgias - Cecelia
   Holland 2985
A Passion in the Blood - Genevieve Davis 1519
Prince of Foxes - Samuel Shellabarger 5797
The Romance of Leonardo Da Vinci - Dmitri
   Merezhkovski 4339

Bormann, Martin
The Blood Order - Jack D. Hunter 3084
Eva - Ib Melchior 4329

Botha, Louis
The Legacy of Ladysmith - John Kenny Crane 1413
Rags of Glory - Stuart Cloete 1126

Boulanger, Georges Ernest Jean Marie
Brave General - Herbert Gorman 2490

Bowles, William Augustus
Alabama Empire - Welbourn Kelley 3392

Breckenridge, John Cabell
Freedom - William Safire 5561

Broderick, David
Vigilante - Richard Summers 6116

Bruce, James
Flashman and the Dragon - George MacDonald
   Fraser 2206

Bruce, Victor
By Command of the Viceroy - Duncan MacNeil 4010
Charge of Cowardice - Duncan MacNeil 4011

Brudenell, James Thomas
Flashman - George MacDonald Fraser 2204
Flashman at the Charge - George MacDonald
   Fraser 2209

Brutus, Marcus Junius
Augustus - Allan Massie 4167
Caesar - Allan Massie 4168
Freedom, Farewell - Phyllis Bentley 461

Bryan, William Jennings
The American - Howard Fast 2026
Empire: A Novel - Gore Vidal 6487
The Land Was Ours: A Novel of the Great Plains -
   Charles W. Bailey 266
Lusitania - David Butler 819

Buade, Louis de
Shadows on the Rock - Willa Cather 959

Buchanan, James
Action at Aquila - Hervey Allen 97
The Big Family - Vina Delmar 1600
Colorado! - Dana Fuller Ross 5471
Ironclads: Man-of-War - Larry D. Names 4554

Memories of the Ford Administration - John
   Updike 6391
Powderkeg - Richard Vetterli 6482
Sister Wives - Cleo Jones 3270

Burke, Edmund
Let the King Beware! - Honore Morrow 4489

Burnaby, Sir Harry
The Golden Days - Robert Neill 4569

Burr, Aaron
Anthony Adverse - Hervey Allen 98
Burr - Gore Vidal 6485
*The Conqueror: Being the True and Romantic Story of
   Alexander Hamilton* - Gertrude Atherton 222
The Fallon Pride - Reagan O'Neal 4742
Flintlock - Jason Manning 4073
Hawk's Journey - Donald Clayton Porter 5119
The High Constable - Maan Meyers 4353
Jackson: A Novel - Max Byrd 837
Kentucky Home - Betty Layman Receveur 5283
My Theodosia - Anya Seton 5753
Notorious Eliza - Basil Beyea 489
Painted Lady: Eliza Jumel, Her Life and Times -
   Leonard Falkner 2009
Reckon with the River - Clark McMeekin 4292
The Rock Cried Out - Edward Stanley 5981
Shadow of the Moon - Douglas C. Jones 3284
West Goes the Road - Tim Pridgen 5192

Burton, Cal
Sea to Shining Sea - Michael Phillips 4990

Butler, Edward
The Financier - Theodore Dreiser 1720

Caesar, Gaius Julius
The City of Libertines - W.G. Hardy 2702

Calhoun, John C.
54-40 or Fight - Emerson Hough 3040
Dolley - Rita Mae Brown 727
Magnificent Destiny - Paul I. Wellman 6619
The Massacre at Fall Creek - Jessamyn West 6631
North and South - John Jakes 3151

Cameron, Simon
Heaven and Hell - John Jakes 3147

Canning, George
The Stranger From the Sea - Winston Graham 2530

Casey, Dan
Casey - Ramona Stewart 6034

Cass, Lewis
Twilight of Empire - Allen W. Eckert 1846

Cassius Longinus, Gaius
Augustus - Allan Massie 4167

Castro, Fidel
Caribbean - James A. Michener 4365

Catilina, Lucius Sergius
Catalina's Riddle - Steven Saylor 5624
A Pillar of Iron - Taylor Caldwell 861

Catiline
Turn Back the River - W.G. Hardy 2703
The Young Caesar - Rex Warner 6567

Cato, Marcus Porcius
Caesar's Women - Colleen McCullough 4233
Freedom, Farewell - Phyllis Bentley 461

Cermak, Anton
Organized Crime - Nicholas Von Hoffman 6511
True Detective - Max Allan Collins 1215

Chamberlain, Joseph
Rags of Glory - Stuart Cloete 1126
The Tenants of Time - Thomas Flanagan 2120

Chase, Salmon P.
The Dixie Widow - Gilbert Morris 4459
Freedom - William Safire 5561
Lincoln: A Novel - Gore Vidal 6490
Nevada! - Dana Fuller Ross 5481

Chiang Kai-Shek
Dynasty - Robert S. Elegant 1902
From a Far Land - Robert S. Elegant 1903
The Warlord - Malcolm Bosse 589

Chou En-lai
From a Far Land - Robert S. Elegant 1903

Christophe, Henri
Black Triumvirate: A Novel of Haiti - Benjamin H.
   Levin 3736
A Time for Titans - Vina Delmar 1602

Churchill, Winston
Blood Winter - William Patrick 4830
Blunted Lance - Max Hennessy 2829
Buller's Dreadnought - Richard Hough 3047
Buller's Victory - Richard Hough 3049
By the Green of the Spring - John Masters 4171
Edward and Mrs. Simpson - A.C.H. Smith 5916
The End of the Hunt - Thomas Flanagan 2119
A Family Matter - James Roosevelt 5458
The Hangman's Crusade - James Barwick 370
High Heroic - Constantine FitzGibbon 2118
Imperial Kelly - Peter Bowen 600
Lusitania - David Butler 819
The Man From St. Petersburg - Ken Follett 2148
The Man on the Train - W.J. Chaput 995
Mr. American - George MacDonald Fraser 2211
Murder at the Palace - Elliott Roosevelt 5445
The Plot to Kill Wallis Simpson: A Work of Faction -
   Graham Fisher 2104
Redemption - Leon Uris 6393
The Ring Master - David Gurr 2622
Seven Days to Petrograd - Tom Hyman 3094
That's Me in the Middle - Donald Jack 3129
To the Honor of the Fleet - Robert H. Pilpel 5002
"Utmost Fish!" - Hugh Wray McCann 4219
The White House Pantry Murder - Elliott
   Roosevelt 5457

Cicero, Marcus Tullius
Augustus - Allan Massie 4167
Caesar - Allan Massie 4168
Catalina's Riddle - Steven Saylor 5624
The Catiline Conspiracy - John Maddox
   Roberts 5379
The City of Libertines - W.G. Hardy 2702
Clodia - Robert DeMaria 1606
Death on the Appian Way - Kenneth Benton 463
The Grass Crown - Colleen McCullough 4236
The Ides of March - Thornton Wilder 6753
A Pillar of Iron - Taylor Caldwell 861
Roman Shadows - Ron Burns 804
Spartacus - Howard Fast 2044
The Venus Throw - Steven Saylor 5627

Cinna, Lucius Cornelius
The Grass Crown - Colleen McCullough 4236

Clavier, Clay
Those the Sun Has Loved - Rose Jourdain 3309

Clay, Henry
1812 - David Nevin 4586
The Border Captains - Jason Manning 4072
Dolley - Rita Mae Brown 727
*Fool of God: A Novel Based on the Life of Alexander
   Campbell* - Louis Cochran 1144
The Gorgeous Hussy - Samuel Hopkins Adams 30
Home to Kentucky: A Novel of Henry Clay - Alfred
   Leland Crabb 1399
Love Is Eternal - Irving Stone 6058
Magnificent Destiny - Paul I. Wellman 6619
The Road to Baltimore - Robert S. Harper 2716

Clemence, Peter
The Devil's Novice - Ellis Peters 4958

Clemenceau, Georges
Over There - Thomas Fleming 2130

Cleveland, Grover
The American - Howard Fast 2026

Refinements of Love: A Novel about Clover and Henry Adams - Sarah Booth Conroy   1259

Clinton, George
Wilderness Empire - Allen W. Eckert   1847

Clodius Pulcher, Publius
Caesar's Women - Colleen McCullough   4233
The City of Libertines - W.G. Hardy   2702
Clodia - Robert DeMaria   1606
Death on the Appian Way - Kenneth Benton   463
Farewell, Catullus - Pierson Dixon   1651
The Gods Are Not Mocked - Anna Taylor   6177

Cochrane, Thomas
Sharpe's Devil - Bernard Cornwell   1340

Collins, Michael
The End of the Hunt - Thomas Flanagan   2119
An Excess of Love - Cathy Cash Spellman   5959
High Heroic - Constantine FitzGibbon   2118

Colmer, Winstead
Murder in the Oval Office - Elliott Roosevelt   5450

Comstock, Anthony
The Alienist - Caleb Carr   907

Connolly, John
Flying into Love - D.M. Thomas   6236

Coolidge, Calvin
The Land Was Ours: A Novel of the Great Plains - Charles W. Bailey   266
The Passion of Sacco and Vanzetti: A New England Legend - Howard Fast   2040

Cornelius the Ciliarch
The Nazarene - Sholem Asch   200

Cornwallis, Charles
The Sea Stands Watch - Helen Parker Mudgett   4507

Crassus, Marcus Licinius
Arena: A Novel of Spartacus and Crassus - Maurice Ghnassia   2391
The City of Libertines - W.G. Hardy   2702
Freedom, Farewell - Phyllis Bentley   461

Critias
Goat Song: A Novel of Ancient Greece - Frank Yerby   6920

Crittenden, John Jordan
The Three Lives of Elizabeth - Shirley Seifert   5735

Cromwell, Oliver
Bennett's Welcome - Inglis Fletcher   2132
The Highland Hawk - Leslie Turner White   6682
Katherine Christian - Hugh Walpole   6546
The King Breaker - Elizabeth Linington   3797
My Lord Foxe - Constance Gluyas   2443
Myself, Christopher Wren - David Weiss   6606
Myself My Enemy - Jean Plaidy   5037
Prisons - Mary Lee Settle   5757
The Severed Crown - Jane Lane   3657
The Stranger Prince - Margaret Irwin   3122
Twenty Years After - Alexandre Dumas   1783
The White Witch - Elizabeth Goudge   2496
Wife to Mr. Milton - Robert Graves   2553
Woodstock; or, The Cavalier - Sir Walter Scott   5710

Cromwell, Thomas
Anne Boleyn - Evelyn Anthony   158
Anne of the Thousand Days - Edward Fenton   2059
The King's Good Servant - Olive White   6696
The King's Pleasure - Jean Plaidy   5026
The Man on a Donkey - H.F.M. Prescott   5170
My Lord of Canterbury - Godfrey Turton   6369

Curio, Gaius Scribonius
Roman Shadows - Ron Burns   804

Curzon, George Nathaniel
The Imperial Agent - T.N. Murari   4518

Daley, Richard
You Bet Your Life - Stuart M. Kaminsky   3349

Danton, Georges-Jacques
Citizen Tom Paine - Howard Fast   2028
The Devil's Laughter - Frank Yerby   6913
The Incorruptible - Helma De Bois   1551
To Spit Against the Wind - Benjamin H. Levin   3737
Veronique - Virginia Coffman   1158

Darling, Ralph
The Colonists - William Stuart Long   3870

Davis, Jefferson
Alaska - James A. Michener   4364
Beloved - Vina Delmar   1599
Bride of Fortune - Harnett T. Kane   3352
Copperhead - Bernard Cornwell   1335
The Court Martial of Robert E. Lee - Douglas Savage   5617
Dim the Flaring Lamps - Jan Jordan   3301
The Guns of the South - Harry N. Turtledove   6367
The Lady of Arlington - Harnett T. Kane   3354
Love and War - John Jakes   3150
Powderkeg - Richard Vetterli   6482
The Proud Retreat - Clifford Dowdey   1706
The Proud Way - Shirley Seifert   5731
The Smiling Rebel - Harnett T. Kane   3357
There Was a Season: A Biographical Novel of Jefferson Davis - Theodore Olsen   4730
The Titans - John Jakes   3154
Traveller - Richard Adams   27
The Yankee From Tennessee - Noel B. Gerson   2388

Day, James Burden
Hollywood: A Novel of America in the 1920s - Gore Vidal   6488
Washington, D.C. - Gore Vidal   6493

de Gaulle, Charles
The Free Frenchman - Piers Paul Read   5277

De Valera, Eamon
The End of the Hunt - Thomas Flanagan   2119
An Excess of Love - Cathy Cash Spellman   5959

Debs, Eugene V.
Adversary in the House - Irving Stone   6053
The American - Howard Fast   2026

Decimus, Versus Camillus
The Silver Pigs - Lindsey Davis   1532

Delaney, Robert
The Tenants of Time - Thomas Flanagan   2120

Delin
Bittersweet - Leslie Li   3769

Demosthenes
Fire From Heaven - Mary Renault   5296

Desmoulins, Camille
The Devil's Laughter - Frank Yerby   6913
Tricolour - Mark Logan   3866

Dessalines, Jean-Jacques
Black Triumvirate: A Novel of Haiti - Benjamin H. Levin   3736

Dewey, Nelson
The Shadow in the Glass - August Derleth   1618

Dio Cassius
The Side of the Moon - Amanda Prantera   5162

Dionysios the Younger
The Mask of Apollo - Mary Renault   5300

Disraeli, Benjamin
Bush War! - William Moore   4447
Cock of the Walk - Roy Lewis   3762
The Day They Kidnapped Queen Victoria - H.K. Fleming   2127
Disraeli in Love - Maurice Edelman   1851
Disraeli Rising - Maurice Edelman   1852
Dizzy's Woman - George MacBeth   3957
Enter the Lion: A Posthumous Memoir of Mycroft Holmes - Michael P. Hodel   2961
The Mudlark - Theodore Bonnet   573
Playing the Game - Ian Buruma   810

Pomp and Circumstance - Fred Mustard Stewart   6025
The Prime Minister's Wife - Doris Leslie   3727
Victoria Victorious - Jean Plaidy   5073
The Widow of Windsor - Jean Plaidy   5076
The Widow of Windsor - Tyler Whittle   6723

Domitius, Annaeus
The Last Athenian - Viktor Rydberg   5543

Dongan, Thomas
Night of Decision: A Novel of Colonial New York - Dorothy Grant   2534

Donovan, William J. "Wild Bill"
Till the End of Time - Allen Appel   170

Douglas, Stephen A.
The Crisis - Winston Churchill   1079
North and South - John Jakes   3151
The Senator's Lady - Shirley Seifert   5733

Dulles, John Foster
A Family Matter - James Roosevelt   5458

Duprat, Antoine
The Chancellor - Lawrence Schoonover   5662

Eaton, Peggy
The Gorgeous Hussy - Samuel Hopkins Adams   30

Ebert, Friedrich
Karl and Rosa - Alfred Doblin   1653
A People Betrayed - Alfred Doblin   1654

Flavius, Crispus
Blood of the Martyrs - Naomi Mitchison   4417

Fleury, Andre Hercule de
Louis the Well-Beloved - Jean Plaidy   5032

Ford, Gerald R.
Memories of the Ford Administration - John Updike   6391

Fouche, Joseph
Captain Cut-Throat - John Dickson Carr   908
The Hastening Wind - Edward Grierson   2591
So Great a Man - David Pilgrim   5000

Fox, Charles James
Guillotine - Mark Logan   3865
Perdita's Prince - Jean Plaidy   5040
Regency Royal - Michael Hardwick   2687
Sweet Lass of Richmond Hill - Jean Plaidy   5067
The Third George - Jean Plaidy   5068
Tricolour - Mark Logan   3866
Young Pitt - A.M. Maughan   4200

Franklin, Benjamin
Benjamin Franklin and a Case of Artful Murder - Robert Lee Hall   2654
Benjamin Franklin and a Case of Christmas Murder - Robert Lee Hall   2655
Benjamin Franklin Takes the Case - Robert Lee Hall   2656
Blind Journey - Bruce Lancaster   3636
The Bonnet Laird's Daughter - Barbara Annandale   154
The Braintree Mission - Nicholas E. Wyckoff   6887
Brimstone Club - F. van Wyck Mason   4147
Buckskin Baronet - Margaret Widdemer   6734
Captain Paul - Edward Ellsberg   1930
The Devil and Ben Franklin - Theodore Mathieson   4184
Edge of Greatness - Winthrop Neilson   4575
The Fallon Blood - Reagan O'Neal   4741
The Firekeeper - Robert Moss   4498
Freedom's Dues - Robert H. Abel   9
I'll Storm Hell - Noel B. Gerson   2374
In the Days of Poor Richard - Irving A. Bacheller   259
Israel Potter - Herman Melville   4334
Jefferson: A Novel - Max Byrd   838
The Latter Adventures of Tom Jones - Bob Coleman   1200
Let the King Beware! - Honore Morrow   4489

The Long Naked Descent into Boston - William
  Eastlake 1823
Murder at Drury Lane - Robert Lee Hall 2659
The Prescott Chronicles - Albert Fried 2232
The Prize Master - Harvey Haislip 2642
Red Morning - Ruby Frazier Frey 2230
The Seneca Hostage - Carter A. Vaughan 6440
Spirit Knife - Donald Clayton Porter 5128
Two Crowns for America - Katherine Kurtz 3568

Fremont, John C.
Dream West - David Nevin 4587
Immortal Wife - Irving Stone 6057
*Jessie: A Novel Based on the Life of Jessie Benton
  Fremont* - Judy Alter 120
Soldier in Buckskin - Ray Hogan 2981

Gage, Thomas
The Last Gentleman - Shirley Barker 312

Gallatin, Albert
River to the West: A Novel of the Astor Adventure -
  John Edward Jennings 3204

Gandhi, Mohandas K.
The Last Victory - T.N. Murari 4519
Nine Hours to Rama - Stanley Wolpert 6846

Garfield, James A.
The Chester A. Arthur Conspiracy - William
  Wiegand 6740
The Spoils of War - Thomas Fleming 2131

Gascoyne-Cecil, Robert
By Command of the Viceroy - Duncan MacNeil 4010

Gaveston, Piers
The Follies of the King - Jean Plaidy 5014

Gentry, Roman
Kentucky Home - Betty Layman Receveur 5283

Gibson, Vance
Murder in the East Room - Elliott Roosevelt 5448

Gladstone, William
Cock of the Walk - Roy Lewis 3762
Disraeli Rising - Maurice Edelman 1852
*Enter the Lion: A Posthumous Memoir of Mycroft
  Holmes* - Michael P. Hodel 2961
Flash for Freedom - George MacDonald Fraser 2203
Nevada! - Dana Fuller Ross 5481
Never Call It Loving - Dorothy Eden 1859
The Prime Minister's Wife - Doris Leslie 3727
Princess in Amber - Evelyn Wilde Mayerson 4205
Victoria Victorious - Jean Plaidy 5073
When the Emperor Dies - Mason McCann
  Smith 5926
The Widow of Windsor - Jean Plaidy 5076
The Widow of Windsor - Tyler Whittle 6723

Goebbels, Paul Joseph
The Blood Order - Jack D. Hunter 3084
Last Man to Die - Michael Dobbs 1652

Goering, Hermann
The Blood Order - Jack D. Hunter 3084

Gomez, Jose Miguel
The Single Star - Walter Adolphe Roberts 5394

Gracchus
Spartacus - Howard Fast 2044

Grant, James
Star of the Wilderness - Karle Wilson Baker 274

Grant, Ulysses S.
The Bank - Stephen Longstreet 3882
The Chester A. Arthur Conspiracy - William
  Wiegand 6740
Colorado Ambush - Jess McCriede 4230
The Court-Martial of George Armstrong Custer -
  Douglas C. Jones 3276
Domina - Barbara Wood 6847
Flashman and the Redskins - George MacDonald
  Fraser 2208
Freedom Road - Howard Fast 2031

The Hallelujah Train - Bill Gulick 2614
Henry and Clara - Thomas Mallon 4042
Jubilee Jim and the Wizard of Wall Street - Donald
  Porter 5112
Kelly Blue - Peter Bowen 601
Louisiana! - Dana Fuller Ross 5478
A Man Called Grant - Helen Todd 6285
The Spoils of War - Thomas Fleming 2131
Ulysses: A Biographical Novel - Robert Skimin 5878
Woman of Justice - Georgia Di Donato 1639

Greeley, Horace
The Furies - John Jakes 3146

Grey, Sir Edward
Lusitania - David Butler 819
To the Honor of the Fleet - Robert H. Pilpel 5002

Guruji
Nine Hours to Rama - Stanley Wolpert 6846

Hamilton, Alexander
Alexander Hamilton's Wife - Alice Curtis
  Desmond 1623
Burr - Gore Vidal 6485
*The Conqueror: Being the True and Romantic Story of
  Alexander Hamilton* - Gertrude Atherton 222
Eagles Where I Walk - Stephen Longstreet 3885
The Ironmaster - Anne Powers 5150
Kentucky Home - Betty Layman Receveur 5283
Mistress of the Forge - David Taylor 6179
Notorious Eliza - Basil Beyea 489
The Tree of Liberty - Elizabeth Page 4773
Yankee - Dana Fuller Ross 5495

Hampton, Eric
The Hampton Heritage - Julie Ellis 1920

Hancock, John
The Long Naked Descent into Boston - William
  Eastlake 1823
Portrait of a Scoundrel - Nathaniel Benchley 438

Hanna, Mark
The Land Was Ours: A Novel of the Great Plains -
  Charles W. Bailey 266

Harding, Warren G.
Hollywood: A Novel of America in the 1920s - Gore
  Vidal 6488

Harley, Robert
Exit Lady Masham - Louis Auchincloss 230

Harris, Ira
Henry and Clara - Thomas Mallon 4042

Harrison, William Henry
Gateway to Empire - Allen W. Eckert 1842
Panther in the Sky - James Alexander Thom 6234
Red Stick - Donald Clayton Porter 5121
A Sorrow in Our Heart - Allen W. Eckert 1844
Tamarack Tree - Howard Breslin 670
To Keep Us Free - Marguerite Allis 115
War Clouds - Donald Clayton Porter 5131

Hasford, Roman
Come Winter - Douglas C. Jones 3275

Hastings, Warren
Master of Bengal: A Novel of Robert Clive of India -
  Norman Partington 4821

Hatton, Christopher
Trust and Treason - Margaret Birkhead 506

Hawley, Andrew
The Traitors - William Stuart Long 3879

Hay, John
Empire: A Novel - Gore Vidal 6487
*Refinements of Love: A Novel about Clover and Henry
  Adams* - Sarah Booth Conroy 1259

Hayes, Rutherford B.
The Spoils of War - Thomas Fleming 2131

Henry, Patrick
Give Me Liberty: The Story of an Innocent Man - John
  Erskine 1956

L'Hermite, Tristan
Quentin Durward - Sir Walter Scott 5705

Hillhouse, James
Water over the Dam - Marguerite Allis 116

Hipparchos
The Praise Singer - Mary Renault 5302

Hitler, Adolf
The Blood Order - Jack D. Hunter 3084
Eva - Ib Melchior 4329
A Family Matter - James Roosevelt 5458
The Last Innocent Hour - Margot Abbott 8
Last Man to Die - Michael Dobbs 1652
The Ring Master - David Gurr 2622
The Very Rich Hours of Count von Stauffenberg - Paul
  West 6637
The Winds of War - Herman Wouk 6876
Young Adolf - Beryl Bainbridge 272

Holm, Peder Victorious
Their Fathers' God - O.E. Rolvaag 5436

Holt, Toby
California Glory - Dana Fuller Ross 5468
Oklahoma Pride - Dana Fuller Ross 5483

House, Edward
To the Honor of the Fleet - Robert H. Pilpel 5002

Houston, Sam
All the Brave Rifles - Clarke Venable 6450
The Comancheros - Paul I. Wellman 6616
The Eagle and the Raven - James A. Michener 4369
Hellfire Jackson - Garland Roark 5355
Jackson: A Novel - Max Byrd 837
Magnificent Destiny - Paul I. Wellman 6619
On the Long Tide - Laura Krey 3555
Promised Lands - Elizabeth Crook 1430
The Raven's Bride - Elizabeth Crook 1431
Republic: A Novel of Texas - E.V. Thompson 6266
The Road to San Jacinto - James F. Davis 1524
Sam Houston - Noel B. Gerson 2380
The Sam Houston Story - Dean Owen 4770
Savanna - Janice Holt Giles 2416
Star of Empire: A Novel of Old San Antonio - Leonard
  Sanders 5590
Texas - James A. Michener 4375
Texas! - Dana Fuller Ross 5490
True Women - Janice Woods Windle 6820

Hsu, Paul
Manchu - Robert S. Elegant 1904

Iredell, James
Queen's Gift - Inglis Fletcher 2136

Jackson, Andrew
As Long as the Rivers Run - Sam J. Slate 5882
The Big Family - Vina Delmar 1600
The Buckstones - Paul I. Wellman 6615
Burr - Gore Vidal 6485
The Cavalier of Tennessee - Meredith
  Nicholson 4610
Creek Mary's Blood - Dee Brown 712
*Crockett of Tennessee: A Novel Based on the Life and
  Times of David Crockett* - Cameron Judd 3314
Give Me the Wind - Jan Jordan 3302
The Gorgeous Hussy - Samuel Hopkins Adams 30
*Her Christmas at the Hermitage: A Tale about Rachel
  and Andrew Jackson* - Helen Topping Miller 4389
Home to the Hermitage - Alfred Leland Crabb 1401
Jackson: A Novel - Max Byrd 837
The Land Where the Sun Dies - Henry Carlisle 896
Magnificent Destiny - Paul I. Wellman 6619
Memories of the Ford Administration - John
  Updike 6391
Mississippi Belle - Clements Ripley 5346
Mr. Audubon's Lucy - Lucy Kennedy 3419
Old Hickory - Noel B. Gerson 2379

On the Long Tide - Laura Krey 3555
The President's Lady - Irving Stone 6063
Sam Houston - Noel B. Gerson 2380
The Sam Houston Story - Dean Owen 4770
The Slender Reed - Noel B. Gerson 2382
A Story of Deep Delight - Thomas McNamee 4305
Texas! - Dana Fuller Ross 5490
Twilight of Empire - Allen W. Eckert 1846
The Yankee From Tennessee - Noel B. Gerson 2388
Young Ames - Walter D. Edmonds 1879
Young Hickory - Stanley Young 6942

Jackson, Gideon
Freedom Road - Howard Fast 2031

Jackson, Thomas Jonathan
Gone to Texas - Jason Manning 4074

Jefferson, Thomas
The Amazing Mrs. Bonaparte - Harnett T. Kane 3351
Arc d'X - Steve Erickson 1953
Burr - Gore Vidal 6485
The Conqueror: Being the True and Romantic Story of Alexander Hamilton - Gertrude Atherton 222
Dawn's Early Light - Elswyth Thane 6215
An Embarrassment of Riches - James Howard Kunstler 3565
Enslaved - Ron Burns 801
The Fallon Pride - Reagan O'Neal 4742
Flintlock - Jason Manning 4073
Fool of God: A Novel Based on the Life of Alexander Campbell - Louis Cochran 1144
Give Me Liberty: The Story of an Innocent Man - John Erskine 1956
Hawk's Journey - Donald Clayton Porter 5119
Jackson: A Novel - Max Byrd 837
Jefferson: A Novel - Max Byrd 838
Kentucky Home - Betty Layman Receveur 5283
Kentucky Stand - Jere Hungerford Wheelwright 6670
Louisiana Purchase - A.E. Hotchner 3039
My Thomas: A Novel of Martha Jefferson's Life - Roberta Grimes 2593
The President's Daughter - Barbara Chase-Riboud 1005
Queen Dolley: The Life and Times of Dolley Madison - Dorothy Clarke Wilson 6806
The River Devils - Carter A. Vaughan 6437
River to the West: A Novel of the Astor Adventure - John Edward Jennings 3204
Sally Hemings - Barbara Chase-Riboud 1006
The Seekers - John Jakes 3153
Stars and Stripes - Adam Rutledge 5541
Those Who Love - Irving Stone 6064
Tide of Empire - Bates Baldwin 279
A Time for Titans - Vina Delmar 1602
To Spit Against the Wind - Benjamin H. Levin 3737
Trail: The Story of the Lewis and Clark Expedition - Louis Charbonneau 998
The Tree of Liberty - Elizabeth Page 4773
Westward! - Dana Fuller Ross 5492

Jenkinson, Robert Banks
The Sea Officer - Showell Styles 6105

Jesus Christ
King Jesus - Robert Graves 2549

Johnson, Andrew
Heaven and Hell - John Jakes 3147
Montana! - Dana Fuller Ross 5479
The Rising of the Moon - Peter Berresford Ellis 1926
Storm Center: A Novel about Andy Johnson - Joseph Walker McSpadden 4312
Texas! - Dana Fuller Ross 5490
The Yankee From Tennessee - Noel B. Gerson 2388

Johnson, Lyndon Baines
Murder and the First Lady - Elliott Roosevelt 5444
Murder in the East Room - Elliott Roosevelt 5448
Murder in the Oval Office - Elliott Roosevelt 5450

Johnston, Sam
Queen's Gift - Inglis Fletcher 2136

Jones, Garwood B.
Raintree County - Ross Lockridge Jr. 3827

Josephus, Flavius
Josephus and the Emperor - Lion Feuchtwanger 2073

Juarez, Benito
Chapultepec - Norman Zollinger 6965
Passengers to Mexico: The Last Invasion of Mexico - Blair Niles 4627

Judd, Gerrit Parmalee
The White King - Samuel Bertram Harrison 2747

Julianus, Marcus
The Light Bearer - Donna Gillespie 2419

Julius Caesar
Augustus - Allan Massie 4167
Augustus - John Williams 6785
Caesar - Mirko Jelusich 3188
Caesar - Allan Massie 4168
Caesar's Women - Colleen McCullough 4233
The First Man in Rome - Colleen McCullough 4234
Freedom, Farewell - Phyllis Bentley 461
A Goddess to a God - John Lloyd Balderston 278
The Gods Are Not Mocked - Anna Taylor 6177
The Grass Crown - Colleen McCullough 4236
The Ides of March - Thornton Wilder 6753
Imperial Caesar - Rex Warner 6565
The Key - Benita Kane Jaro 3169
A Pillar of Iron - Taylor Caldwell 861
Prepare Them for Caesar - Mary Louise Mabie 3954
The Sacrilege - John Maddox Roberts 5380
SPQR - John Maddox Roberts 5381
That Egyptian Woman - Noel B. Gerson 2384
Tros of Samothrace - Talbot Mundy 4515

Kao Li-shih
The Court of the Lion - Eleanor Cooney 1294

Kemal, Mustafa
High Road to China - Jon Cleary 1106

Kennedy, John F.
Cold War - Robert Vaughan 6446
Flying into Love - D.M. Thomas 6236
The Immortals - Michael Korda 3540
Libra - Don DeLillo 1593

Kennedy, Robert F.
The Immortals - Michael Korda 3540

Kerensky, Alexandr Feodorovich
Lenin: The Novel - Alan Brien 679

King, Philip Gidley
Southern Cross - Terry Coleman 1206

Kissinger, Henry
The Glory - Herman Wouk 6873

Kosciuszko, Thaddeus
Thaddeus of Warsaw - Jane Porter 5136

Kritias
The Last of the Wine - Mary Renault 5299

Kruger, Paul
The City of Gold - Francis Brett Young 6940
The Covenant - James A. Michener 4368
The Mask - Stuart Cloete 1125
Rags of Glory - Stuart Cloete 1126
Westward the Sun - Brigid Knight 3524

La Guardia, Fiorello
The Hyde Park Murder - Elliott Roosevelt 5443
Murder in the West Wing - Elliott Roosevelt 5453

Lafayette, Marie Joseph Paul de
A Few Painted Feathers - Stephen Longstreet 3886

Lamar, Mirabeau Buonaparte
Republic: A Novel of Texas - E.V. Thompson 6266

Star of Empire: A Novel of Old San Antonio - Leonard Sanders 5590

Lamb, William
Albert's Victoria - Tyler Whittle 6719
The Queen and Lord M - Jean Plaidy 5046
The Queen's Husband - Jean Plaidy 5052
Victoria and Albert - Evelyn Anthony 166
The Young Victoria - Tyler Whittle 6724

Landon, Alf
Murder in the East Room - Elliott Roosevelt 5448

Lane, Joseph
The Quiet Life of Mrs. General Lane - Victoria Case 951

Larkin, Thomas
The Bear Flag: A Novel of the Birth of California - Cecelia Holland 2983

Lavette, Barbara
The Immigrant's Daughter - Howard Fast 2035

Lear, Tobias
Lydia Bailey - Kenneth Roberts 5387

Lee, Francis Lightfoot
Tidewater Dynasty: A Biographical Novel of the Lees of Stratford Hall - Carey Roberts 5372

Lee, Henry
Tidewater Dynasty: A Biographical Novel of the Lees of Stratford Hall - Carey Roberts 5372

Lee, Richard Henry
Tidewater Dynasty: A Biographical Novel of the Lees of Stratford Hall - Carey Roberts 5372

Lenin, Vladimir Ilich
Joseph - Mervyn Jones 3292
The King's Commissar - Duncan Kyle 3570
The Revolutionist: A Novel of Russia - Robert Littell 3810
Time After Time - Allen Appel 171
White Nights, Red Dawn - Frederick Nolan 4634

Lepidus, Marcus Aemilius
Augustus - Allan Massie 4167
Three's Company - Alfred Duggan 1774

Lewis, Meriwether
War Clouds - Donald Clayton Porter 5131

Lincoln, Abraham
Abe Lincoln of Pigeon Creek - William Edward Wilson 6818
Beloved Enemy - Al Lacy 3579
Captains and the Kings - Taylor Caldwell 851
Christmas for Tad: A Story of Mary and Abraham Lincoln - Helen Topping Miller 4386
The Cosgrove Report - G.J.A. O'Toole 4765
The Crisis - Winston Churchill 1079
Dim the Flaring Lamps - Jan Jordan 3301
The Dixie Widow - Gilbert Morris 4459
Dream West - David Nevin 4587
The Father - Katharine Holland Brown 724
The Fifth Conspiracy - Ted Jones 3296
Flash for Freedom - George MacDonald Fraser 2203
Flight to Canada - Ishmael Reed 5285
For Us the Living - Bruce Lancaster 3639
Forever Free - Honore Morrow 4487
Freedom - William Safire 5561
Give Me the Wind - Jan Jordan 3302
Grant's War - Ted Jones 3297
Gray Victory - Robert Skimin 5877
Green Rose of Furley - Helen C. Barney 334
Hard Road to Gettysburg - Ted Jones 3298
Henry and Clara - Thomas Mallon 4042
House Divided - Ben Ames Williams 6765
Immortal Wife - Irving Stone 6057
Intrigue in Baltimore - Janet Whitney 6715
The Last Full Measure - Honore Morrow 4488
Lincoln: A Novel - Gore Vidal 6490
The Lincoln Hunters - Wilson Tucker 6359

Lincoln's Mothers: A Story of Nancy and Sally Lincoln - Dorothy Clarke Wilson 6804
The Lost Years: A Biographical Fiction - Oscar Lewis 3757
Love and War - John Jakes 3150
Love Is Eternal - Irving Stone 6058
A Man for the Ages - Irving A. Bacheller 261
McKay's Bees - Thomas McMahon 4289
McKensie's Hundred: A Tale of the Old Dominion - Frank Yerby 6924
Mr. Lincoln's Wife - Anne Colver 1221
Nevada! - Dana Fuller Ross 5481
Oldest Living Confederate Widow Tells All - Allan Gurganus 2621
The President's Daughter - Barbara Chase-Riboud 1005
The Senator's Lady - Shirley Seifert 5733
Soul of Abe Lincoln - Bernie Babcock 251
The Soul of Ann Rutledge - Bernie Babcock 252
Spoon - John Christgau 1074
The Spur - Ardyth Kennelly 3425
Steamboat on the River - Darwin Le Ora Teilhet 6200
The Stonewall Brigade: A Novel of the American Civil War - Frank G. Slaughter 5902
Talons of Eagles - William W. Johnstone 3268
There Was a Season: A Biographical Novel of Jefferson Davis - Theodore Olsen 4730
The Titans - John Jakes 3154
Twilight of Empire - Allen W. Eckert 1846
Ulysses: A Biographical Novel - Robert Skimin 5878
Unto This Hour - Tom Wicker 6733
With Malice Toward None - Honore Morrow 4492
Woman with a Sword: The Biographical Novel of Anna Ella Carroll of Maryland - Hollister Noble 4632
The Yankee From Tennessee - Noel B. Gerson 2388

Livingston, Andrew
The Bad Lands - Oakley Hall 2651

Lloyd George, David
Blunted Lance - Max Hennessy 2829
The Buckingham Palace Connection - Ted Willis 6792
The End of the Hunt - Thomas Flanagan 2119
Give Us This Day - R.F. Delderfield 1586
High Heroic - Constantine FitzGibbon 2118
It's Me Again - Donald Jack 3126
Rags of Glory - Stuart Cloete 1126

Logan, Tad
Star of Empire: A Novel of Old San Antonio - Leonard Sanders 5590

Lopez, Francisco
Young Vargas Lewis - Robert Brainard Pearsall 4874

Lovell, Francis
The Fate of Princes - P.C. Doherty 1673

Lufton, Miles
Troy Chimneys - Margaret Kennedy 3421

MacDonald, Ramsay
The Murder of Lawrence of Arabia - Matthew Eden 1865

Machiavelli, Niccolo
The Borgia Prince - Pamela Bennetts 446
Michelangelo the Florentine - Sidney Alexander 86
Then and Now - William Somerset Maugham 4198
Web of Lucifer: A Novel of the Borgia Fury - Maurice Samuel 5580

Macquarie, Lachlan
The Adventurers - William Stuart Long 3869
The Explorers - William Stuart Long 3872

Madero, Francisco Indalecio
The Crimson Wind - Max Hennessy 2832
Under the Fifth Sun: A Novel of Pancho Villa - Earl Shorris 5832

Madison, Dolley
Back Bay - William Martin 4138
A Daughter of Liberty - Allan Cole 1196
Dolley - Rita Mae Brown 727
My Theodosia - Anya Seton 5753

Madison, James
1812 - David Nevin 4586
Burr - Gore Vidal 6485
The Conqueror: Being the True and Romantic Story of Alexander Hamilton - Gertrude Atherton 222
Dolley - Rita Mae Brown 727
Hawk's Journey - Donald Clayton Porter 5119
My Dear Cousin - Peggy Hoffmann 2977
Queen Dolley: The Life and Times of Dolley Madison - Dorothy Clarke Wilson 6806
Red Stick - Donald Clayton Porter 5121
The River Devils - Carter A. Vaughan 6437
River to the West: A Novel of the Astor Adventure - John Edward Jennings 3204
Sally Hemings - Barbara Chase-Riboud 1006
Tide of Empire - Bates Baldwin 279
A Time for Titans - Vina Delmar 1602

Maitland, William
The White Queen - Frederic Fallon 2011

Mao Tse-tung
Dynasty - Robert S. Elegant 1902
From a Far Land - Robert S. Elegant 1903
High Road to China - Jon Cleary 1106
The Warlord - Malcolm Bosse 589

Marcum, C.J.
Storming Heaven - Denise Giardina 2394

Marius, Caius
The First Man in Rome - Colleen McCullough 4234
The Grass Crown - Colleen McCullough 4236

Martinson, James
Tennessee! - Dana Fuller Ross 5489

Mazarin, Jules
A Candle for D'Artagnan - Chelsea Quinn Yarbro 6895
The Cardinal and the Queen - Evelyn Anthony 159
My Crown, My Love - Ruth Walgreen Stephan 5995
Twenty Years After - Alexandre Dumas 1783

McCarthy, Joseph
Washington, D.C. - Gore Vidal 6493

McKinley, William
1901 - Robert Conroy 1258
Empire: A Novel - Gore Vidal 6487
Fenwick Travers and the Years of Empire - Raymond M. Saunders 5614
The Land Was Ours: A Novel of the Great Plains - Charles W. Bailey 266

Meir, Golda
The Glory - Herman Wouk 6873

Menshikov, Aleksandr
Katrina - Jeramie Price 5190

Metternich, Clemens von
Far Flies the Eagle - Evelyn Anthony 162

Monroe, James
Citizen Tom Paine - Howard Fast 2028
The Land Where the Sun Dies - Henry Carlisle 896
Louisiana Purchase - A.E. Hotchner 3039
The Massacre at Fall Creek - Jessamyn West 6631
A Time for Titans - Vina Delmar 1602
Trail: The Story of the Lewis and Clark Expedition - Louis Charbonneau 998

Montagu, John
Brimstone Club - F. van Wyck Mason 4147

Montfort, Simon de
The Lion of England - Eve Trevaskis 6336

More, Sir Thomas
Anne Boleyn - Evelyn Anthony 158
The King's Good Servant - Olive White 6696

The King's Pleasure - Jean Plaidy 5026
The Man on a Donkey - H.F.M. Prescott 5170
Stage of Fools - Charles Andrew Brady 635

Moreau, Andre-Louis
Scaramouche - Rafael Sabatini 5554

Morris, Gouverneur
A Generation of Leaves - Robert S. Bloom 552
King's Masque - Evan John 3220
Mistress Nancy - Barbara Bentley 460

Mussolini, Benito
The Passion of Sacco and Vanzetti: A New England Legend - Howard Fast 2040

Nehru, Jawaharlal
The Last Victory - T.N. Murari 4519

Neville, Richard
The Last of the Barons - Edward Bulwer-Lytton 769

Nixon, Richard
The Savage Brood - Martha Rofheart 5430

North, Frederick
Let the King Beware! - Honore Morrow 4489
Poor Richard's Game - G.J.A. O'Toole 4766

O'Connell, Daniel
The Big Wind - Beatrice Coogan 1262
Disraeli in Love - Maurice Edelman 1851
The Silent People - Walter Macken 3990

Octavianus, Caius Julius Caesar
Three's Company - Alfred Duggan 1774

Oglethorpe, James Edward
Creek Mary's Blood - Dee Brown 712
Jarrett's Jade - Frank Yerby 6923
Rascal's Heaven - F. van Wyck Mason 4157

O'Shea, William
Parnell and the Englishwoman - Hugh Leonard 3721

Overbury, Clay
Washington, D.C. - Gore Vidal 6493

Oxenstierna, Axel
People of the Book - David Stacton 5974

Paderewski, Ignacy
Poland - James A. Michener 4373

Pakenham, Sir Richard
54-40 or Fight - Emerson Hough 3040

Parnell, Charles Stewart
Never Call It Loving - Dorothy Eden 1859
Parnell and the Englishwoman - Hugh Leonard 3721
The Tenants of Time - Thomas Flanagan 2120

Pearson, Lester
That's Me in the Middle - Donald Jack 3129

Peel, Robert
Disraeli in Love - Maurice Edelman 1851
Disraeli Rising - Maurice Edelman 1852
Fire, Burn! - John Dickson Carr 910
The Masters of Bow Street - John Creasy 1423
The Queen and Lord M - Jean Plaidy 5046
The Queen's Husband - Jean Plaidy 5052
Victoria and Albert - Evelyn Anthony 166

Pericles
Achilles His Armour - Peter Green 2569
Creation - Gore Vidal 6486
Glory and the Lightning - Taylor Caldwell 856
Goatsong - Tom Holt 3009
The Immortal Marriage - Gertrude Atherton 225
The Magnificent Traitor: A Novel of Alcibiades and the Golden Age of Pericles - Lynn Poole 5092
Pericles the Athenian - Rex Warner 6566
The Private and Public Life of Socrates - Rene Kraus 3552

Petion, Alexandre
Drums of Destiny - Peter Bourne 593

Pitt the Elder, William
The Braintree Mission - Nicholas E. Wyckoff 6887

The Double Man - Elinor Pryor   5205
His Majesty's Highwayman - Donald Barr
   Chidsey   1061
The Prince and the Quakeress - Jean Plaidy   5043

Pitt the Younger, William
Brumaire - Mark Logan   3864
Guillotine - Mark Logan   3865
Sweet Lass of Richmond Hill - Jean Plaidy   5067
The Third George - Jean Plaidy   5068
Tricolour - Mark Logan   3866
Young Pitt - A.M. Maughan   4200

Pittakos
My Name Is Sappho - Martha Rofheart   5429

Plessis, Armand-Jean Du
The Arm and the Darkness - Taylor Caldwell   850
A Candle for D'Artagnan - Chelsea Quinn
   Yarbro   6895
The Cardinal and the Queen - Evelyn Anthony   159
Cinq-Mars - Alfred Victor de Vigny   6495
An Epic Joy: A Novel Based on the Life of Rubens -
   Donald Braider   642
Louis the Well-Beloved - Jean Plaidy   5032
Louisiana Purchase - A.E. Hotchner   3039
The Three Musketeers - Alexandre Dumas   1782
World and Paradise - Edgar Maas   3953
The Young and Lonely King - Jane Lane   3659

Poldark, Ross
The Angry Tide - Winston Graham   2521
The Four Swans - Winston Graham   2525
The Miller's Dance - Winston Graham   2528
The Stranger From the Sea - Winston Graham   2530

Polk, James K.
Magnificent Destiny - Paul I. Wellman   6619
Sam Houston - Noel B. Gerson   2380
The Slender Reed - Noel B. Gerson   2382
Texas! - Dana Fuller Ross   5490
The Yankee From Tennessee - Noel B. Gerson   2388

Pompey
Fortune's Favorite - Colleen McCullough   4235
Freedom, Farewell - Phyllis Bentley   461

Porter, Jeremy
Ceremony of the Innocent - Taylor Caldwell   852

Potter, Robert
Love Is a Wild Assault - Elithe Hamilton
   Kirkland   3506
Star of Empire: A Novel of Old San Antonio - Leonard
   Sanders   5590

Prescott, Bartholomew
The Prescott Chronicles - Albert Fried   2232

Prescott, Julian
The Prescott Chronicles - Albert Fried   2232

Pym, John
The Golden Feather - Theda Kenyon   3462

Rabin, Yitzhak
The Hope - Herman Wouk   6874

Randolph, John
A Generation of Leaves - Robert S. Bloom   552
Mistress Nancy - Barbara Bentley   460
My Dear Cousin - Peggy Hoffmann   2977

Raven, Guy
Ravenscroft - Dorothy Eden   1860

Rayburn, Sam
The Hyde Park Murder - Elliott Roosevelt   5443
The Land Was Ours: A Novel of the Great Plains -
   Charles W. Bailey   266

Reynolds, John
Twilight of Empire - Allen W. Eckert   1846

Rhodes, Cecil John
Rough Diamond - Robert L. Fish   2098

Rienzo, Cola di
The Lily and the Lion - Maurice Druon   1733

Rienzi, or The Last of the Tribunes - Edward Bulwer-
   Lytton   770

Riqueti, Honore Gabriel
King's Masque - Evan John   3220
Mirabeau, Lover and Stateman - Pierre
   Nezelof   4606

Robespierre, Maximilien Francois de
The Devil's Laughter - Frank Yerby   6913
The Incorruptible - Helma De Bois   1551
*The Rose of Malmaison: The Turbulent Life of the
   Beautiful Josephine* - Gaby von Schonthan   5660
Tallien: A Brief Romance - Frederic Tuten   6370
Tricolour - Mark Logan   3866
La Vendee - Anthony Trollope   6346
Veronique - Virginia Coffman   1158

Rogers, Woodes
Lusty Wind for Carolina - Inglis Fletcher   2134

Rohan, Louis de
The Queen's Confession - Victoria Holt   3019
The Queen's Necklace - Alexandre Dumas   1781

Roosevelt, Eleanor
Eleanor: A Novel - Rhoda Lerman   3724
Murder in the Chateau - Elliott Roosevelt   5447
The Prescott Chronicles - Albert Fried   2232

Roosevelt, Franklin Delano
The Bank - Stephen Longstreet   3882
Eleanor: A Novel - Rhoda Lerman   3724
A Family Matter - James Roosevelt   5458
Hitler Has Won - Frederic Mullally   4511
Hollywood: A Novel of America in the 1920s - Gore
   Vidal   6488
The Hyde Park Murder - Elliott Roosevelt   5443
The Land Was Ours: A Novel of the Great Plains -
   Charles W. Bailey   266
Luciano's Luck - Jack Higgins   2912
Murder and the First Lady - Elliott Roosevelt   5444
Murder in the Blue Room - Elliott Roosevelt   5446
Murder in the Chateau - Elliott Roosevelt   5447
Murder in the East Room - Elliott Roosevelt   5448
Murder in the Executive Mansion - Elliott
   Roosevelt   5449
Murder in the Oval Office - Elliott Roosevelt   5450
Murder in the Red Room - Elliott Roosevelt   5451
Murder in the Rose Garden - Elliott Roosevelt   5452
Murder in the West Wing - Elliott Roosevelt   5453
New Deal for Death - Elliott Roosevelt   5454
The Only Thing to Fear - David Poyer   5160
Power - Howard Fast   2041
The Prescott Chronicles - Albert Fried   2232
The President's Man - Elliott Roosevelt   5455
A Royal Murder - Elliott Roosevelt   5456
Till the End of Time - Allen Appel   170
To the Honor of the Fleet - Robert H. Pilpel   5002
True Detective - Max Allan Collins   1215
War and Remembrance - Herman Wouk   6875
Washington, D.C. - Gore Vidal   6493
The White House Pantry Murder - Elliott
   Roosevelt   5457
The Winds of War - Herman Wouk   6876

Roosevelt, Theodore
1901 - Robert Conroy   1258
*Alice and Edith: A Biographical Novel of the Two
   Wives of Theodore Roosevelt* - Dorothy Clarke
   Wilson   6798
The Alienist - Caleb Carr   907
The Americans - John Jakes   3143
Bully! - Mark Schorr   5670
California Gold - John Jakes   3145
Captains and the Kings - Taylor Caldwell   851
Cherokee Rose: A Novel of America's First Cowgirl -
   Judy Alter   119
Creek Mary's Blood - Dee Brown   712
Empire: A Novel - Gore Vidal   6487
Fenwick Travers and the Panama Canal - Raymond
   M. Saunders   5613

Fenwick Travers and the Years of Empire - Raymond
   M. Saunders   5614
Fort Worth - Leonard Sanders   5588
Fortune's Legacy - Jack Rowe   5515
From Time to Time - Jack Finney   2092
Homeland - John Jakes   3148
Imperial Kelly - Peter Bowen   600
The Land Was Ours: A Novel of the Great Plains -
   Charles W. Bailey   266
Masterpiece of Murder - Mary Kruger   3563
Pomeroy - Gordon Williams   6770
The Prescott Chronicles - Albert Fried   2232
The Seventh Bullet - Daniel D. Victor   6483
TR - Noel B. Gerson   2385
Yellowstone Kelly - Peter Bowen   602

Root, Elihu
Empire: A Novel - Gore Vidal   6487
Fenwick Travers and the Panama Canal - Raymond
   M. Saunders   5613

Ross, Bernard
The Detling Secret - Julian Symons   6151

Ross, Edward
Many a Voyage - Loula Grace Erdman   1951

Rusk, Thomas Jefferson
Star of Empire: A Novel of Old San Antonio - Leonard
   Sanders   5590

Russell, Lord John
Cock of the Walk - Roy Lewis   3762
Victoria and Albert - Evelyn Anthony   166
When the Emperor Dies - Mason McCann
   Smith   5926

Sadat, Anwar
The Glory - Herman Wouk   6873

Saenz, Manuela
Manuela, La Caballeresa Del Sol - Demetrio Aguilera
   Malta   41

Santa Anna, Antonio Lopez de
The Sam Houston Story - Dean Owen   4770
The Wine of San Lorenzo - Herbert Gorman   2493

Savonarola, Girolamo
The Palace - Chelsea Quinn Yarbro   6904
The Private Life of Mona Lisa - Pierre La
   Mure   3577

Scheidemann, Philipp
Karl and Rosa - Alfred Doblin   1653

Sejanus, Lucius Aelius
Hear Me, Pilate! - LeGette Blythe   557
No King but Caesar - Anne Powers   5151
Pontius Pilate: A Biographical Novel - Paul L.
   Maier   4034

Seneca, Lucius Annaeus
Beware of Caesar - Vincent Sheean   5786

Severus, Livinius
Roman Shadows - Ron Burns   804

Sevier, John
The Cumberland Rifles - Noel B. Gerson   2365
Red Belts - Hugh Pendexter   4897
Rogue's March - Maristan Chapman   993
*The Sounds of Chariots: A Novel of John Sevier and
   the State of Franklin* - Helen Topping Miller   4396
Tennessee Hazard - Maristan Chapman   994

Seward, William Henry
Lincoln: A Novel - Gore Vidal   6490
Nevada! - Dana Fuller Ross   5481
Passengers to Mexico: The Last Invasion of Mexico -
   Blair Niles   4627
Seward's Folly - Edison Marshall   4111
*Woman with a Sword: The Biographical Novel of
   Anna Ella Carroll of Maryland* - Hollister
   Noble   4632

Seymour, Horatio
The Unterrified - Constance Robertson   5397

Sforza, Ludovico
Duchess of Milan - Michael Ennis   1946

Shankaracharyarau, P.K.
Nine Hours to Rama - Stanley Wolpert   6846

Sheridan, Richard Brinsley
Regency Royal - Michael Hardwick   2687

Slidell, John
The Big Family - Vina Delmar   1600

Smith, Alfred E.
The Immigrants - Howard Fast   2034

Smith, Frederick Edwin
High Heroic - Constantine FitzGibbon   2118

Solon
Farewell Great King: A Novel of Ancient Greece - Jill
   Paton Walsh   4829

Spurlock, Travis
Fort Worth - Leonard Sanders   5588

Stalin, Joseph
Generations of Winter - Vassily Aksyonov   61
Joseph - Mervyn Jones   3292
Lenin: The Novel - Alan Brien   679
The Red Monarch: Scenes From the Life of Stalin -
   Yuri Krotkov   3561
The Revolutionist: A Novel of Russia - Robert
   Littell   3810
The Winds of War - Herman Wouk   6876

Stanford, Leland
California Gold - John Jakes   3145

Stanton, Edward
The Cosgrove Report - G.J.A. O'Toole   4765

Stanton, Edwin
The Dixie Widow - Gilbert Morris   4459
Freedom - William Safire   5561
The Judges of the Secret Court - David Stacton   5972
Memories of the Ford Administration - John
   Updike   6391
*Woman with a Sword: The Biographical Novel of
   Anna Ella Carroll of Maryland* - Hollister
   Noble   4632

Stevens, Thaddeus
Heaven and Hell - John Jakes   3147
I Speak for Thaddeus Stevens - Elsie
   Singmaster   5868

Steward, Robert
The Sea Officer - Showell Styles   6105

Stewart, Robert
Brumaire - Mark Logan   3864
Guillotine - Mark Logan   3865

Stiles, W.H.
Before Darkness Falls - Eugenia Price   5178

Stimson, Henry
Murder in the East Room - Elliott Roosevelt   5448

Stoke, George
Theory of War - Joan Brady   637

Strange, Christopher
Christopher Strange - Ruth Eleanor McKee   4281

Struensee, Johann Frederick
The Lost Queen - Norah Lofts   3850

Stuyvesant, Peter
Thanksgiving - Terry Coleman   1207

Sulla, Lucius Cornelius
The First Man in Rome - Colleen McCullough   4234
The Grass Crown - Colleen McCullough   4236
Roman Blood - Steven Saylor   5626
*Sword of Pleasure: Being the Memoirs of the Most
   Illustrious Lucius Cornelius Sulla* - Peter
   Green   2571

Summer, Charles
With Malice Toward None - Honore Morrow   4492

Sun Yat-Sen
Dynasty - Robert S. Elegant   1902

Taft, William Howard
TR - Noel B. Gerson   2385

Talleyrand-Perigord, Charles Maurice de
Brumaire - Mark Logan   3864
Guillotine - Mark Logan   3865
The Man Who Killed the King - Dennis
   Wheatley   6654

Taylor, Zachary
*There Was a Season: A Biographical Novel of
   Jefferson Davis* - Theodore Olsen   4730
Twilight of Empire - Allen W. Eckert   1846

Temple, Henry John
Albert's Victoria - Tyler Whittle   6719
Follow the Drum - James Leasor   3699
Nevada! - Dana Fuller Ross   5481
The Queen's Husband - Jean Plaidy   5052
Republic: A Novel of Texas - E.V. Thompson   6266
Victoria and Albert - Evelyn Anthony   166
When the Emperor Dies - Mason McCann
   Smith   5926
The Widow of Windsor - Jean Plaidy   5076

Themistocles
Farewell Great King: A Novel of Ancient Greece - Jill
   Paton Walsh   4829

Thompson, George
Threescore and Ten - Walter Allen   105

Tilden, Samuel
1876: A Novel - Gore Vidal   6484

Toussaint l'Ouverture, Pierre Dominique
All Souls' Rising - Madison Smartt Bell   422
Black Triumvirate: A Novel of Haiti - Benjamin H.
   Levin   3736
Drums at Dusk - Arna Bontemps   575
Drums of Destiny - Peter Bourne   593
A Time for Titans - Vina Delmar   1602

Tracy, Tom
The Rising of the Moon - William Martin   4140

Travers, Polly
The Book Class - Louis Auchincloss   228

Travis, William Barret
On the Long Tide - Laura Krey   3555

Trotsky, Leon
Joseph - Mervyn Jones   3292
The King's Commissar - Duncan Kyle   3570

Troy, William
The Wind in the Forest - Inglis Fletcher   2143

Truman, Harry S
War and Remembrance - Herman Wouk   6875

Tweed, William Marcy
The Bank - Stephen Longstreet   3882
Bread and Circus - Morris Renek   5303
Casey - Ramona Stewart   6034
Tassels on Her Boots - Arthur Cheney Train   6313

Ulyanov, Vladimir Ilich
Lenin: The Novel - Alan Brien   679
The Petrograd Consignment - Owen Sela   5739

Vallandigham, Clement
The Golden Circle - Constance Robertson   5396
The Unterrified - Constance Robertson   5397

Valsecca, Odo
The Valley of Decision - Edith Wharton   6653

Van Buren, Martin
Amistad: The Thunder of Freedom - David
   Pesci   4944
Burr - Gore Vidal   6485
Echo of Lions - Barbara Chase-Riboud   1004
Gone to Texas - Jason Manning   4074
The Land Where the Sun Dies - Henry Carlisle   896
Oregon! - Dana Fuller Ross   5484

The Slender Reed - Noel B. Gerson   2382
The Yankee From Tennessee - Noel B. Gerson   2388

Vane, Sir Henry
A Candle in the Wilderness - Irving A.
   Bacheller   256

Venable, Sabra
Cimarron - Edna Ferber   2061

Venizelos, Eleutherios
The Ashes of Smyrna - Richard Reinhardt   5294

Vignerot du Plessis, Louis-Francois-Armand de
Through a Glass Darkly - Karleen Koen   3531

Wade, Benjamin Franklin
*Woman with a Sword: The Biographical Novel of
   Anna Ella Carroll of Maryland* - Hollister
   Noble   4632

Wallace, Lew
Billy the Kid - Edwin Corle   1330

Walpole, Robert
Caroline the Queen - Jean Plaidy   5009
Now Face to Face - Karleen Koen   3530
Queen in Waiting - Jean Plaidy   5048

Walsingham, Sir Francis
The Shadow of the Earth - Lee Wichelns   6731

Warleggan, George
The Angry Tide - Winston Graham   2521
The Miller's Dance - Winston Graham   2528
The Stranger From the Sea - Winston Graham   2530

Warren, Joseph
Concord Bridge - Howard Horne   3035

Washington, Booker T.
Ragtime - E.L. Doctorow   1658

Washington, George
Alabama Empire - Welbourn Kelley   3392
Burr - Gore Vidal   6485
Give Me the Wind - Jan Jordan   3302
The Ironmaster - Anne Powers   5150
Lady Washington - Dorothy Clarke Wilson   6803
Man From Mt. Vernon - Burke Boyce   607
Manitou - Donald Clayton Porter   5120
Portrait of a Scoundrel - Nathaniel Benchley   438
The Seekers - John Jakes   3153
Seminole - Donald Clayton Porter   5126
Spirit Knife - Donald Clayton Porter   5128
Those Who Love - Irving Stone   6064
*Tidewater Dynasty: A Biographical Novel of the Lees
   of Stratford Hall* - Carey Roberts   5372
The Tree of Liberty - Elizabeth Page   4773

Webster, Daniel
Dolley - Rita Mae Brown   727
The Gorgeous Hussy - Samuel Hopkins Adams   30
Tamarack Tree - Howard Breslin   670

Wellesley, Arthur
Flashman - George MacDonald Fraser   2204
The Young Victoria - Tyler Whittle   6724

Wentworth, John
The Governor's Lady - Thomas H. Raddall   5228
Hangman's Beach - Thomas H. Raddall   5229
The Last Gentleman - Shirley Barker   312

Westfield, Thomas
Westfield - Roderick Thorp   6277

Weston, Aylmer
Statues in a Garden - Isabel Colegate   1198

Whitaker, Otis
While Rivers Flow - Glen H. Fleischmann   2125

White, John
Roanoke Hundred - Inglis Fletcher   2138

Whittington, Richard
Richard Whittington, London's Mayor - Gwynedd
   Sudworth   6112

Wilkes, John
Brimstone Club - F. van Wyck Mason 4147
The Vast Memory of Love - Malcolm Bosse 588

Wilkinson, James
The Fallon Pride - Reagan O'Neal 4742

Wilson, Woodrow
Hollywood: A Novel of America in the 1920s - Gore
  Vidal 6488
Lusitania - David Butler 819
A People Betrayed - Alfred Doblin 1654
Seven Days to Petrograd - Tom Hyman 3094
To the Honor of the Fleet - Robert H. Pilpel 5002

Winthrop, John
A Candle in the Wilderness - Irving A.
  Bacheller 256
The Greater Hunger - Barbara Dodge Borland 581
Hope Leslie; or, Early Times in Massachusetts -
  Catharine Maria Sedgewick 5714
The Winthrop Covenant - Louis Auchincloss 235
The Winthrop Woman - Anya Seton 5754

Witt, John de
The Queen's Husband - Samuel Edwards 1889

Witte, Sergei
Petersburg - Emily Hanlon 2677

Wolsey, Thomas
Anne Boleyn - Evelyn Anthony 158
Anne of the Thousand Days - Edward Fenton 2059
Windsor Castle - William Harrison Ainsworth 59

Worth, Anthony
Crimson Is the Eastern Shore - Don Tracy 6308

Wright, Silas
Light in the Clearing - Irving A. Bacheller 260

Yell, Archibald
A Man's Reach - Charles Morrow Wilson 6796

Young, Brigham
Children of God - Vardis Fisher 2106
For Time and All Eternity - Paul Bailey 268
Salt Lake City - A.R. Reife 5292

POLITICAL PRISONER

Manette, Alexander
A Tale of Two Cities - Charles Dickens 1642

PREHISTORIC HUMAN

Alane
The Reindeer Hunters - Joan Wolf 6841

Alin
Daughter of the Red Deer - Joan Wolf 6838

Amigigh
My Sister, the Moon - Sue Harrison 2750

Ashan
Children of the Dawn - Patricia Rowe 5516
Keepers of the Misty Time - Patricia Rowe 5517

Atlaw
Daughter of the Red Deer - Joan Wolf 6838

Attaroa
The Plains of Passage - Jean M. Auel 238

Ayla
The Clan of the Cave Bear - Jean M. Auel 236
The Mammoth Hunters - Jean M. Auel 237
The Plains of Passage - Jean M. Auel 238
The Valley of Horses - Jean M. Auel 239

Bad Belly/Still Water
People of the Earth - W. Michael Gear 2334

Balor
Wolves of the Dawn - William Sarabande 5604

Ban-Ya
The Edge of the World - William Sarabande 5597

Brave Man
People of the Earth - W. Michael Gear 2334

Brun
The Clan of the Cave Bear - Jean M. Auel 236

Catchstraw
People of the Sea - W. Michael Gear 2339

Cethlinn
Wolves of the Dawn - William Sarabande 5604

Cha-Kwena
The Edge of the World - William Sarabande 5597
Shadow of the Watching Star - William
  Sarabande 5601
Thunder in the Sky - William Sarabande 5602

Chagak
Mother Earth, Father Sky - Sue Harrison 2749

Deer Shadow
The Deer Dancers - Amanda Cockrell 1146

Doban
Shiva: An Adventure of the Ice Age - J.H.
  Brennan 657

Fifth, Brennis Gehan
The Flint Lord - Richard Herley 2857

Fomor
Wolves of the Dawn - William Sarabande 5604

Garroch
The Golden Strangers - Henry Treece 6328

Gotha
The Last Mammoth - Margaret Allan 89

Graylag
Reindeer Moon - Elizabeth Marshall Thomas 6244

Guidron, Lord
The Temple of the Sun - Moyra Caldecott 849

Heron
People of the Wolf - W. Michael Gear 2341

Hiram
Shiva: An Adventure of the Ice Age - J.H.
  Brennan 657

Hungry Bear
People of the Fire - W. Michael Gear 2335

Inanna
The Last Warrior Queen - Mary Mackey 3992

Isar
Shadows on the Stones - Moyra Caldecott 847

Isca
The Golden Strangers - Henry Treece 6328

Iza
The Clan of the Cave Bear - Jean M. Auel 236

Jhadel
Face of the Rising Sun - William Sarabande 5598

Jondalar
The Mammoth Hunters - Jean M. Auel 237
The Plains of Passage - Jean M. Auel 238
The Valley of Horses - Jean M. Auel 239

Karana
Beyond the Sea of Ice - William Sarabande 5595
Corridor of Storms - William Sarabande 5596
Forbidden Land - William Sarabande 5599

Kestrel
People of the Sea - W. Michael Gear 2339

Khu-Ren
Shadows on the Stones - Moyra Caldecott 847

Kiin
Brother Wind - Sue Harrison 2748
My Sister, the Moon - Sue Harrison 2750

Kori
The Animal Wife - Elizabeth Marshall Thomas 6243

Kosar-Eh
Shadow of the Watching Star - William
  Sarabande 5601

Krona
Sarum: The Novel of England - Edward
  Rutherfurd 5536

Kukutux
Brother Wind - Sue Harrison 2748

Kyra
The Tall Stones - Moyra Caldecott 848

Laena
Children of the Ice - Charlotte Prentiss 5166

Lark
Shadows on the Stones - Moyra Caldecott 847

Little Dancer
People of the Fire - W. Michael Gear 2335

Lok
The Inheritors - William Golding 2455

Lonit
Beyond the Sea of Ice - William Sarabande 5595
Corridor of Storms - William Sarabande 5596
Forbidden Land - William Sarabande 5599
Walkers of the Wind - William Sarabande 5603

Mah-Ree
The Edge of the World - William Sarabande 5597

Mal
The Inheritors - William Golding 2455

Maliwal
The Sacred Stones - William Sarabande 5600

Manaravak
Walkers of the Wind - William Sarabande 5603

Mar
Daughter of the Red Deer - Joan Wolf 6838

Mara
People of the Mesa - Charlotte Prentiss 5168

Marrah
The Year the Horses Came - Mary Mackey 3993

Masau
The Sacred Stones - William Sarabande 5600

Maya
The Mammoth Stone - Margaret Allan 90

Musselwhite
People of the Lightning - W. Michael Gear 2337

Nardo
The Reindeer Hunters - Joan Wolf 6841

Navahk
Corridor of Storms - William Sarabande 5596

Nel
The Horsemasters - Joan Wolf 6840

Nisha
Children of the Sun - Charlotte Prentiss 5167

Pondwader
People of the Lightning - W. Michael Gear 2337

Ranec
The Mammoth Hunters - Jean M. Auel 237

Raven Hunter
People of the Wolf - W. Michael Gear 2341

Rising Sun
The Last Mammoth - Margaret Allan 89

Ronan
The Horsemasters - Joan Wolf 6840

Running Deer
The Last Mammoth - Margaret Allan 89

Runs in Light
People of the Wolf - W. Michael Gear 2341

Samiq
Brother Wind - Sue Harrison   2748

Segle
The Stone Arrow - Richard Herley   2858

Sheck
Dance of the Tiger: A Novel of the Ice Age - Bjorn
    Kurten   3566

Shiva
Shiva: An Adventure of the Ice Age - J.H.
    Brennan   657

Shuganan
Mother Earth, Father Sky - Sue Harrison   2749

Stavan
The Year the Horses Came - Mary Mackey   3993

Sunchaser
People of the Sea - W. Michael Gear   2339

Swift
The Animal Wife - Elizabeth Marshall Thomas   6243
Reindeer Moon - Elizabeth Marshall Thomas   6244

Tagart
The Flint Lord - Richard Herley   2857
The Stone Arrow - Richard Herley   2858

Thonolan
The Valley of Horses - Jean M. Auel   239

Tiger
Dance of the Tiger: A Novel of the Ice Age - Bjorn
    Kurten   3566
Singletusk - Bjorn Kurten   3567

Tor
Children of the Dawn - Patricia Rowe   5516
Keepers of the Misty Time - Patricia Rowe   5517

Torka
Beyond the Sea of Ice - William Sarabande   5595
Corridor of Storms - William Sarabande   5596
Forbidden Land - William Sarabande   5599
Walkers of the Wind - William Sarabande   5603

Umak
Walkers of the Wind - William Sarabande   5603

Veyde
Dance of the Tiger: A Novel of the Ice Age - Bjorn
    Kurten   3566

Warakan
Face of the Rising Sun - William Sarabande   5598

Wardyke
The Tall Stones - Moyra Caldecott   848
The Temple of the Sun - Moyra Caldecott   849

White Ash
People of the Earth - W. Michael Gear   2334

Whitespear
Singletusk - Bjorn Kurten   3567

Wind Caller
The Deer Dancers - Amanda Cockrell   1146

Wolf
The Mammoth Stone - Margaret Allan   90

Yanan
Reindeer Moon - Elizabeth Marshall Thomas   6244

Ysuna
The Sacred Stones - William Sarabande   5600

PRINTER

Carey, Daniel
A Generation of Leaves - Robert S. Bloom   552

Estienne, Robert
The Sage and the Olive - Florence Whitfield
    Barton   369

Forty, Thomas
Thomas Forty - Edward Stanley   5982

Franklin, Benjamin
The Devil and Ben Franklin - Theodore
    Mathieson   4184
The Governor's Daughter - Denton Whitson   6718
A High Wind Rising - Elsie Singmaster   5867
The Indentured Heart - Gilbert Morris   4464

Halter, Abraham
The Book of Abraham - Marek Halter   2665

Winshore, Ordway
Remembrance Rock - Carl Sandburg   5583

PRISONER

Deans, Effie
The Heart of Midlothian - Sir Walter Scott   5698

Di Marco, Beltrame
The Borgia Prince - Pamela Bennetts   446

Di Marco, Bianca
The Borgia Prince - Pamela Bennetts   446

Dolliver, Eben
Andersonville - MacKinlay Kantor   3359

King Dick
The Lively Lady - Kenneth Roberts   5386

Nason, Richard
The Lively Lady - Kenneth Roberts   5386

Southfarer, Niall
The Price of Blood - Doris Sutcliffe Adams   24

Zhu Wong
The Golden Nineties - Lisa Mason   4166

PRIVATEER

Carter, Magnus
Magnus the Magnificent - Leslie Turner White   6688

Morgan, Jeremy
Yankee - Dana Fuller Ross   5495

Tucker, Richard
The Savage City - Jean Paradise   4787

PROFESSOR

Clayton, Alfred
Memories of the Ford Administration - John
    Updike   6391

Dash, Hannibal
Goldfield - Richard S. Wheeler   6660

Fenton, Nicholas
The Devil in Velvet - John Dickson Carr   909

Frankfurter, Felix
Murder in the Oval Office - Elliott Roosevelt   5450
Murder in the Red Room - Elliott Roosevelt   5451
*The Passion of Sacco and Vanzetti: A New England
    Legend* - Howard Fast   2040

Genovese, Christopher
Bay of Arrows - Jay Parini   4800

Jackson, Thomas Jonathan
Look Away - Harold Coyle   1395

Moriarty, James
*The Case of the Revolutionist's Daughter: Sherlock
    Holmes Meets Karl Marx* - Lewis S. Feuer   2076
*Enter the Lion: A Posthumous Memoir of Mycroft
    Holmes* - Michael P. Hodel   2961
Exit Sherlock Holmes - Robert Lee Hall   2657
The Return of Moriarty - John E. Gardner   2287

Sommerville, Robert
The Intrigue - Marion Chesney   1034

Stiles, Ezra
Strange Wives - Shirley Barker   317

Ware, Jonathan
The Sun Shines West - Nathan Schachner   5632

Xanthus
The Fabulist - John Vornholt   6512

PROSPECTOR

Arbuckle, Maude
Goldfield - Richard S. Wheeler   6660

Beaufort, Victor
Black Gold - Anita Richmond Bunkley   771

Blake, Frank
Pacific Destiny - Dana Fuller Ross   5487

Booth, Lemuel
The Smoky Hill - Don Coldsmith   1188

Burke, Hailey
The Treasure of Pleasant Valley - Frank Yerby   6928

Buttes, John
The Sweetwater - Jean Rikhoff   5333

Calvert, Leander
The American - Louis Dodge   1669

Carpenter, Harry
Journey - James A. Michener   4371

Clayton, Clark
Forty Pounds of Gold - Philip D. Stong   6066

Coit, Simon
Days of the Gold - Irwin R. Blacker   526

Fletcher, Zack
Wanderers Eastward, Wanderers West - Kathleen
    Winsor   6823

Grafton, Janse
The City of Gold - Francis Brett Young   6940

Hardy, Jim
The Goldseekers - William R. Burnett   794

Harkness, Bruce
The Treasure of Pleasant Valley - Frank Yerby   6928

Henslow, Philip
Journey - James A. Michener   4371

Hummel, John
Fools' Gold - Richard Wiley   6755

Kaneda
Fools' Gold - Richard Wiley   6755

King, Sam
Forefathers - Nancy Cato   960

Kyle, Jason
Judgment in July - Richard Fisher   2105

Macbean, Robert
The Adelita - Oakley Hall   2649

Mackenna, Glen
Mackenna's Gold - Will Henry   2845

Mason, Tolo
The Imperialists - William Stuart Long   3875

McCoy, Luff
City of Illusion - Vardis Fisher   2107

Milam, Andy
Forty Pounds of Gold - Philip D. Stong   6066

Morgan, Charles
Oh Glittering Promise - Anne Fisher   2099

Nilsson, Robert
The Settlers - Vilhelm Moberg   4424

O'Riley, Kathleen
Tomorrow's Dream - Peggy Hanchar   2674

O'Shea, Hogan
Tomorrow's Dream - Peggy Hanchar   2674

Randall, Walt
Treasure in Hell's Canyon - Bill Gulick   2619

Seadon, Val
The Seadon Fortune - Leonard St. Clair 5563

Shattuck, Tobin
The Big Lonesome - Will Bryant 737

Silva, Amador Flores da
Brazil - Errol Lincoln Uys 6395

Stopford, Anthony
The Golden Fool - David Divine 1649

Sutton
Seven Rivers West - Edward Hoagland 2959

Thicke, Hoxie
The Goldseekers - William R. Burnett 794

Tlingit, Tom
Days of the Gold - Irwin R. Blacker 526

Wallace, Finn
Fools' Gold - Richard Wiley 6755

Warrick, John
Forty Pounds of Gold - Philip D. Stong 6066

PROSTITUTE

Annie
Abigail - Malcolm Macdonald 3962

Bellebelle
Beloved Enemy: The Passions of Eleanor of Aquitaine - Ellen Jones 3288

Browne, Isabel
Clouds of Destiny - Lou Ellen Davis 1535

Cavanaugh, Kate
Storyville - Lois Battle 377

Drussard, Justine
Fallen Angel - Deborah Camp 872

Fortini, Colombia
Carnival of Saints - George Herman 2860

Gomer
The Valley of God - Irene Steinman Patai 4825

Greenpearl
Silk Road - Jeanne Larsen 3670

Hackabout-Jones, Fanny
Fanny: Being the True History of the Adventures of Fanny Hackabout-Jones - Erica Jong 3299

Harmony, Desire
Stars on the Sea - F. van Wyck Mason 4161

Hikenai
The Lion of England - Margaret Butler 824

Isaacs, Hannele
My Own Ground - Hugh Nissenson 4628

Jurer, Nancy
Winter Harvest - Norah Lofts 3863

Kelly, Marie
The Women of Whitechapel and Jack the Ripper - Paul West 6638

Khasturba
Silk and Steel - Stephen Alter 122

Latrec, Blue Rhonda
Southern Discomfort - Rita Mae Brown 730

Lotus Blossom
The Good Earth - Pearl S. Buck 754

Louise
The Age of Wonders - Aharon Appelfeld 173

La Marquesa
Sharpe's Honour - Bernard Cornwell 1344

Menendez, Coralita
Proud New Flags - F. van Wyck Mason 4156

Michaelmas, Charity
A World Too Wide - Susan Moore 4445

Monk, Mary
The Fireflower - Edith Layton 3687

Parker, Banana Mae
Southern Discomfort - Rita Mae Brown 730

Pickford, Ellen
The Abductors - Stuart Cloete 1121

Rahab
Scarlet Cord: A Novel of the Woman of Jericho - Frank G. Slaughter 5899

Ramirez, Angelica
Fool's Coach - Richard S. Wheeler 6659

Reynier, Gretje
The Drowning Room - Michael Kenneth Pye 5212

Riordan, Molly
Welcome to Hard Times - E.L. Doctorow 1660

St. Clair, Glory
The Great Alone - Janet Dailey 1454

Sally
Badenheim 1939 - Aharon Appelfeld 174

Scald Ibiz
The Tent of Orange Mist - Paul West 6636

Sewell, Celina
Sweetwater Fever - Robert H. Adelman 36

Shallot, Guenvere
St. John's Wood - Nancy Fitzgerald 2116

Stokes, Sally
A Broken Vessel - Kate Ross 5500

Tabor, Silver Dollar
All for Love: Baby Doe and Silver Dollar - John Vernon 6456

Turner, Fanny
The Girl From Storyville: A Victorian Novel - Frank Yerby 6919

Umegawa
Yedo - Lynn Guest 2609

Vignon, Claire de
The Blood Endures - Robert Inman 3107

Wilkinson, Esther
An Innocent Woman - Malcolm Macdonald 3967

Willinck, Susan
Flash for Freedom - George MacDonald Fraser 2203

Wood, Lorena
Lonesome Dove - Larry McMurtry 4298

PSYCHIC

Esther the Soothsayer
Cry of the Peacock - Gina Barkhordar Nahai 4552

Fox, Margaret
The Undiscovered Country - Jay Walz 6560

Harcombe, Timothy
English Music - Peter Ackroyd 18

Holmes, David J.
The Wizard's Daughter - Barbara Michaels 4362

Kyra
The Tall Stones - Moyra Caldecott 848
The Temple of the Sun - Moyra Caldecott 849

Pasquier, Genevieve
The Oracle Glass - Judith Merkle Riley 5335

Royland, Clare
Kingdom of Shadows - Barbara Erskine 1954

White Ash
People of the Earth - W. Michael Gear 2334

PSYCHOLOGIST

Kreizler, Dr. Lazlo
The Alienist - Caleb Carr 907

MacPherson, Stewart
Burden of Desire - Robert MacNeil 4023

Rivers, W.H.R.
The Eye in the Door - Pat Barker 307
Regeneration - Pat Barker 309

PUBLISHER

Bennett, James Gordon
Niagara - Robert Lewis Taylor 6189

Ellery, Francis
Ride with Me - Thomas B. Costain 1369

Hand, Carrie
Dutch Uncle - Marilyn Durham 1815

Hearst, William Randolph
The Americans - John Jakes 3143
California Gold - John Jakes 3145
Empire: A Novel - Gore Vidal 6487
Hollywood: A Novel of America in the 1920s - Gore Vidal 6488
Murder at San Simeon - Robert Lee Hall 2660
The Rough Rider - Gilbert Morris 4468
The Seventh Bullet - Daniel D. Victor 6483
Yellow: A Novel - Daniel Lynch 3932

Kent, Gideon
The Americans - John Jakes 3143

Kent, Gilbert
The Seekers - John Jakes 3153

Pulitzer, Joseph
The Americans - John Jakes 3143
Yellow: A Novel - Daniel Lynch 3932

Sanford, Blaise
Empire: A Novel - Gore Vidal 6487
Washington, D.C. - Gore Vidal 6493

Sorrell, William
Ladies Whose Bright Eyes - Ford Madox Ford 2162

Sternes, Jeremy
The Dedicated - Willa Gibbs 2399

Underwood, Ike
Paradise Falls - Don Robertson 5399

Vance, Logan
Black-Eyed Susan - Deborah Camp 871

RAILROAD WORKER

Boyle, Michael
The Warriors - John Jakes 3155

McGill, Cassie
The War Train: A Novel of 1916 - Brown Meggs 4324

Wright, Weatherby
The Road - John Ehle 1896

RAKE

Adderly, Mark
The Angry Tide - Winston Graham 2521

Amberley, Lord
The Parfit Knight - Juliet Blyth 555

Arundel, Christopher
Lord Libertine - Anthony Esler 1964

Atherton
Miss Philadelphia Smith - Paula Allardyce 91

Baron, Charles
Beau Barron's Lady - Helen Ashfield 204

Barry, Redmond
Barry Lyndon - William Makepeace Thackeray 6210

Belmanoir, Tracy
The Black Moth - Georgette Heyer 2877

Bemford, Lord
The Road and the Star - Berkely Mather 4182

Brooke, Joshua
The Rake and the Hussy - Robert W. Chambers 981

Calverleigh, Miles
Black Sheep - Georgette Heyer 2878

Carlton, Lord Guy
Rake's Progress - Marion Chesney 1047

Claibourne, Leigh
Rake's Ransom - Barbara Metzger 4347

Damerel, Jasper
Venetia - Georgette Heyer 2909

Gore, Bysshe
Vice Avenged: A Moral Tale - Lolah Burford 774

Granville, Alexis de
Lady Hellfire - Suzanne Robinson 5414

Guere, Jeffrey de
The Stanbroke Girls - Fiona Hill 2925

Harpcore, Dennison
The Parson's Daughter - Catherine Cookson 1286

Hawkhurst, Garret
Some Brief Folly - Patricia Veryan 6478

Jermyn, Sir Aubrey
A Fatal Assignation - Alice Chetwynd Ley 3764

Lethbridge, Robert
The Convenient Marriage - Georgette Heyer 2882

Lindley, Andrew
The Rake - Karen Lynn 3941

Mathieson, Roland Farleigh
The Dedicated Villain - Patricia Veryan 6461

Orloff, Sacha
The Rake and the Rebel - Ira J. Morris 4478

Roade, Kieron
Sarah Camberwell Tring - Janet Edmonds 1869

Roc-sur-Besbre, Comte de
Baneful Sorceries, or The Countess Bewitched - Joan Sanders 5585

St. Barbe, Alexander
Treason's Gift - Pamela Belle 434

Severn, Lord
Fleeting Fancy - Rosemary Edghill 1866

Striker, Frederick
Shadows on the Shore - Jessica Stirling 6048

Winthrop, Knight
Night Shadow - Catherine Coulter 1377

RANCHER

Allen, Buford
Warhorse - John Cunningham 1451

Anderson, Wil
The Cowboys - William Dale Jennings 3211

Bagnall, Clive
The Wisdom of Stones - Greg Matthews 4192

Baker, Ben
Filaree: A Novel of an American Life - Marguerite Noble 4633

Baron, Matt
The Grass Kingdom - Jory Sherman 5818

Bean, Ellis
Gone to Texas - Don Worcester 6871

Bent, Jerry
She Rode a Yellow Stallion - Walter Reed 5286

Brewton, Colonel Jim
The Sea of Grass - Conrad Richter 5323

Burnett, Andy
Folded Hills - Stewart Edward White 6701

Call, Woodrow F.
Lonesome Dove - Larry McMurtry 4298

Carlyon, John
Inherit the Sun - Maxwell Grant 2539

Casebolt, Tom
The Grass Kingdom - Jory Sherman 5818

Casta, Raphael de
The Place of Devils - Lucinda Baker 275

Chance, Sam
Sam Chance - Benjamin Capps 888

Channing, Jeb
Mirage - Helen Topping Miller 4390

Chisum, John
The Sons of Grady Rourke - Douglas Savage 5618

Clanton, Ike
Wyatt Earp - Matt Braun 653

Clay, Maggie
Lone Star Lady - Jill Gregory 2579

Croft, Art
The Ox-Bow Incident - Walter Van Tilburg Clark 1096

de la Rosa, Domingo
Promised Lands - Elizabeth Crook 1430

Dent, Abner
Montana Hitch - Richard S. Wheeler 6661

Dominguez, Ramon
A Shadow of Eagles - Jane Barry 360

Ewing, Mort
Arfive - A.B. Guthrie Jr. 2623
The Last Valley - A.B. Guthrie Jr. 2626

Farrands, Doug
The Wisdom of Stones - Greg Matthews 4192

Ferris, Colonel Virginius
Gold Is Where You Find It - Clements Ripley 5345

Fetchen, James Black
The Sky-Liners - Louis L'Amour 3629

Finn, Ben
The Grassman - Len Fulton 2256

Forbes, Josh
Forefathers - Nancy Cato 960

Freed, Vesper
The Far Canyon - Elmer Kelton 3404

Furniss, Hannah
The Garfield Honor - Frank Yerby 6918

Garfield, Roak
The Garfield Honor - Frank Yerby 6918

Garrett, Paul
Centennial - James A. Michener 4366

Goodnight, Charles
The Goodnight Trail - Ralph Compton 1227
Streets of Laredo - Larry McMurtry 4300

Grant, Augustus
A Mule for the Marquesa - Frank O'Rourke 4753

Hale, Andy
They Came to a Valley - Bill Gulick 2618

Hardy, Yule
The Bad Lands - Oakley Hall 2651

Harte, Joanna
San Antone - V.J. Banis 288

Harte, Lewis
San Antone - V.J. Banis 288

Hastings, Walter
Tamzen - Jane Gilmore Rushing 5530

Holt, Toby
Oregon Legacy - Dana Fuller Ross 5485

Horne, Jackson
Horne's Law - Jory Sherman 5819

Hunter, James
Colorado Ambush - Jess McCriede 4230

Ibarbo, Antonio
By the King's Command - Shirley Seifert 5723

Ives, John
Jubilee Trail - Gwen Bristow 698

Kincaid, Matt
Firewind - Bill Pronzini 5200

Knight, Charles
Crazy Fox Remembers - Don Preston 5174

Lacey, Ben Franklin
Border Line - Robert J. Conley 1238

Lansdowne, Valerie
The Wisdom of Stones - Greg Matthews 4192

Larkin, Liam
Redemption - Leon Uris 6393

Larrimore, Ed
Home Mountain - Jeanne Williams 6777

Layne, Jeff
The Far Canyon - Elmer Kelton 3404

Lockhart, Taisie
North of 36 - Emerson Hough 3042

MacClaren, Andrew
Women in the Wind - Margaret Ritter 5350

MacNamara, Paul
Where the Willows Weep - Patricia Shaw 5781

Manning, Jim
The Heart of the Continent - Nancy Cato 961

Martin, Kid
Born of the Sun - John H. Culp 1440

Masferrer, Cristobal
Daughter of Fortune - Carla Kelly 3398

Masferrer, Diego
Daughter of Fortune - Carla Kelly 3398

McCanless, Asa
No Roof but Heaven - Jeanne Williams 6782

McCaskill, Jick
English Creek - Ivan Doig 1683
Ride with Me, Mariah Montana - Ivan Doig 1684

McConles, Jesse
Duel in the Sun - Niven Busch 812

McCrae, Augustus
Lonesome Dove - Larry McMurtry 4298

McKenzie, Dan
Harry: A Novel of Australia - Robert Wales 6530

McLean, Trey
The Pumpkin Rollers - Elmer Kelton 3406

McLellan, Herd
The Long Trail North - Robert J. Conley 1245

Mores, Marquis de
Manifest Destiny - Brian Garfield 2290

O'Brien, Patrick
Lady of No Man's Land - Jeanne Williams 6780

O'Dare, Cord
Justice, My Brother - James Keene 3386

Odell, Roger
Brothers Three - John Oskison 4764

Olive, Isom Prenice "Print"
Rawhider - Gene Shelton 5802

O'Roarke, Ian
Devil's Backbone - Terry C. Johnston 3250

Parham, Billy
The Crossing - Cormac McCarthy 4221

Parham, Boyd
The Crossing - Cormac McCarthy 4221

Prescott, Matt
Live From the Devil - Wyatt Blassingame 542

Putnam, John Quincy
Winter Grass - Richard S. Wheeler 6665

Putnam, Lisa
The Snowblind Moon - John Byrne Cooke 1267

Randal, Percy
The Stars in Their Courses - Harry Brown 722

Redmond, Seth
Eye of the Hawk - David William Ross 5498

Reinhardt, Dan
Horne's Law - Jory Sherman 5819

Robbarde, Marc
The White Land - William Dieter 1643

Roosevelt, Theodore
Manifest Destiny - Brian Garfield 2290

Ross, Jeff
The Seventh Winter - Hal Borland 583

Roy, Gavin
The Valley - Clifford Irving 3114

Secombe, Oliver
Centennial - James A. Michener 4366

Sessions, John
Red Runs the River - Lewis B. Patten 4831

Severance, Stuart
Lights Along the Shore - Diane Austell 241

Severance, Vail
Lights Along the Shore - Diane Austell 241

Smith, Wesley
Diamond Six - William Fielding Smith 5932

Talon, Emily
Ride the Dark Trail - Louis L'Amour 3624

Templeton, Range
Divine Average - Elithe Hamilton Kirkland 3505

Tetley
The Ox-Bow Incident - Walter Van Tilburg
   Clark 1096

Tewkbury, Jonathan
The Feud - Amelia Bean 396

Tolliver, Nathan
The Predators - F.A. Parker 4804

Tyrrell, Martin
Honor Thy Father - Robert A. Roripaugh 5460

Uremay
A Shadow of Eagles - Jane Barry 360

Walker, Dhu
Border Line - Robert J. Conley 1238
The Long Trail North - Robert J. Conley 1245

Westbrook, Hugh
The Dreaming: A Novel of Australia - Barbara
   Wood 6848

White, Blanco
Glowstone - Macdonald Harris 2725

Winslow, Dan
The Valiant Gunman - Gilbert Morris 4474

RANGER

Hart, Matthew
Waltzing in Ragtime - Eileen Charbonneau 996

McCaskill, Varick
English Creek - Ivan Doig 1683

REBEL

Aske, Robert
A Trail of Blood - Jeremy Potter 5143

Balam Xoc
Tikal: A Novel about the Maya - Daniel Peters 4947

El Bilbanto
The Gun - C.S. Forester 2174

Carroll, Davy
Time and Chance - Anna Wibberley 6728

Connolly, James
An Excess of Love - Cathy Cash Spellman 5959

Enoch
The Brother - Chayym Zeldis 6958

Fawkes, Guy
Scapegoat for a Stuart - Kate Kirby 3504

FitzGibbon, Constance
An Excess of Love - Cathy Cash Spellman 5959

Grabeau
Amistad: The Thunder of Freedom - David
   Pesci 4944

Hereward the Wake
Harold Was My King - Hilda Lewis 3749
*The Last Englishman: The Story of Hereward the
   Wake* - Hebe Weenolsen 6596
The Saxon Tapestry - Sile Rice 5317

Iago
The Briar Rose - Linda Neale 4561

Oates, Titus
The Murder of Sir Edmund Godfrey - John Dickson
   Carr 913

O'Connor, Tierney
An Excess of Love - Cathy Cash Spellman 5959

Pearse, Patrick Henry
An Excess of Love - Cathy Cash Spellman 5959

Singbe-Pieh
Amistad: The Thunder of Freedom - David
   Pesci 4944

RECLUSE

Carpenter, Benjamin
A Sparkle From the Coal - Prudence Andrew 144

Cuthred
The Hermit of Eyton Forest - Ellis Peters 4961

Dickinson, Emily
Come Slowly Eden: A Novel about Emily Dickinson -
   Laura Benet 440
The Hesitant Heart - Anne Edwards 1882

Godric
Godric - Frederick Buechner 763

Old Man
Man of the Shadows - Don Coldsmith 1178

Wind River Kid
The Ghosts of Elkhorn - Kerry Newcomb 4589

REFUGEE

Baker, Annie Saunders
Sherman's March - Cynthia Bass 373

Carroway, Pete
Another Spring - Loula Grace Erdman 1948

Delcourt, Sophie
The Sugar Pavilion - Rosalind Laker 3600

Kercadiou, Aline de
Scaramouche the King-Maker - Rafael Sabatini 5555

Lohmann, Ernst
Death Squad London - Jack Gerson 2360

Nicols, Susan
Another Spring - Loula Grace Erdman 1948

Robiniere, Claire de la
Claire - Elizabeth Lyle 3931

Sauvigny, Guy de
The Wind From the Sea - Constance Heaven 2812

Sauvigny, Isabelle de
The Wind From the Sea - Constance Heaven 2812

Savigny, Isabella de
Nethergate - Norah Lofts 3854

RELATIVE

Debs, Theodore
Adversary in the House - Irving Stone 6053

Poldark, Jeremy
The Miller's Dance - Winston Graham 2528

Tussy, Eleanor
*The Case of the Revolutionist's Daughter: Sherlock
   Holmes Meets Karl Marx* - Lewis S. Feuer 2076

RELIGIOUS

Abelard, Peter
Peter Abelard: A Novel - Helen Waddell 6517
Strong as Death - Sharan Newman 4602

Abuyah, Elisha ben
As a Driven Leaf - Milton Steinberg 5992

Adams, Joel
Hope of Earth - Jane Gilmore Rushing 5528

Adi
Bundori - Laura Joh Rowland 5519

Agreda, Maria de
I, the King - Frances Parkinson Keyes 3479

Ailerman
In the Falcon's Claw: A Novel of the Year 1000 -
   Chet Raymo 5257

Ailroth, Father
The Raven in the Foregate - Ellis Peters 4969

Ainvar
Druids - Morgan Llywelyn 3817

Akiba ben Joseph
If I Forget Thee - Brenda Lesley Segal 5720
Prince of Israel - Elias Gilner 2422
The Soldier and the Sage: A Novel about Akiba -
   Richard G. Hubler 3065
The Source - James A. Michener 4374

Albrecht, Father
The Godforgotten - Gladys Schmitt 5642

Albriton, Charles
Cherished Enemy - Patricia Veryan 6460

Alcock, John
Crown of Roses - Valerie Anand 127

Aleaumes
The Seven Hills of Paradise - Rosemary
   Simpson 5859

Alexander III
My Life for My Sheep - Alfred Duggan 1772

Alexander VI
Carnival of Saints - George Herman 2860

City of God: A Novel of the Borgias - Cecelia Holland 2985
Daughter of Shadows - Miranda Seymour 5762
The Dogs of Paradise - Abel Posse 5141
Light on Lucrezia - Jean Plaidy 5029
Michelangelo the Florentine - Sidney Alexander 86
A Passion in the Blood - Genevieve Davis 1519
The Scarlet City - Hella S. Haasse 2632

Alexander VII
My Crown, My Love - Ruth Walgreen Stephan 5995

Aligorko
Time of Parting - Anton Donchev 1690

Ambrose
The Restless Flame - Louis De Wohl 1573
The Sinner of Saint Ambrose - Robert Raynolds 5275

Ambrosio
The Monk - Matthew Gregory Lewis 3756

Amergin
The Gods Are Not Mocked - Anna Taylor 6177

Amos
The Herdsman - Dorothy Clarke Wilson 6801

Anne of Nanteuil
The Seven Hills of Paradise - Rosemary Simpson 5859

Annianus
Dogheaded Death - Ray Faraday Nelson 4581

Anselm
The Spire - William Golding 2457

Aristander
Alexander the God - Maurice Druon 1731

Armitage, Charles
Diana the Huntress - Marion Chesney 1026
Frederica in Fashion - Marion Chesney 1032
Minerva - Marion Chesney 1037
The Taming of Annabelle - Marion Chesney 1052

Ashbery, Francis
Riders of the Long Road - Stephen E. Bransford 649

Askew, Anne
The Heretic - Alison Macleod 4002

Aspley, Meriet
The Devil's Novice - Ellis Peters 4958

Athanasios
The Beacon of Alexandria - Gillian Bradshaw 627

Athelstan, Brother
The Nightingale Gallery - Paul Harding 2684
Red Slayer: Being the Second of the Sorrowful Mysteries of Brother Athelstan - Paul Harding 2685

Aubrey
Atala - Francois Rene de Chateaubriand 1008

Audrey, Robin
Come Rack! Come Rope! - Robert Hugh Benson 458

Augustine
The Four Rivers of Paradise - Helen Constance White 6678
The Restless Flame - Louis De Wohl 1573
Son of Tears - Henry W. Coray 1320

Auriane
The Light Bearer - Donna Gillespie 2419

Avery, Ephraim
Avery's Knot - Mary Cable 843
The Tragedy at Tinkerton: An Historical Novel of Murder - Raymond Paul 4844

Ayscough, Adam
Dean's Watch - Elizabeth Goudge 2494

Bacon, Roger
The Black Rose - Thomas B. Costain 1363
Doctor Mirabilis - James Blish 550

Ball, John
Riot at Gravesend: A Novel of Wat Tyler's Rebellion - William Howard Woods 6864
Who Was Then the Gentleman - Charles E. Israel 3125

Balthazar
The Way - J.M. Hartley 2761

Balue, Cardinal Jean
Quentin Durward - Sir Walter Scott 5705

Balz, Guillaume
The Stones of the Abbey - Fernand Pouillon 5144

Bar Jonah, Simon
The Apostle - Sholem Asch 197

Barber, Nicholas
Morality Play - Barry Unsworth 6387

Bartholomew
I, Nathanael, Knew Jesus - William Gilbert Van Tassel Sutpen 6133

Batchelor, Barbara
The Towers of Silence - Paul Scott 5685

Beaton, David
A Stake in the Kingdom - Nigel Tranter 6321

Beaufort
The Bishop's Tale - Margaret Frazer 2215

Beaufort, Henry
Epitaph for Three Women - Jean Plaidy 5012
The Serpent Amongst the Lilies - P.C. Doherty 1678

Becket, Thomas
Beloved Enemy: The Passions of Eleanor of Aquitaine - Ellen Jones 3288
The Courts of Love - Jean Plaidy 5010
The Lion of Christ - Margaret Butler 823
The Lion of England - Margaret Butler 824
The Lion of Justice - Margaret Butler 825
My Life for My Sheep - Alfred Duggan 1772
The Pillars of the Earth - Ken Follett 2149
The Plantagenet Prelude - Jean Plaidy 5041
The Swords of December - Robert York 6933
Thomas: A Novel of the Life, Passions, and Miracles of Becket - Shelley Mydans 4538

Beecher, Henry Ward
Beecher: A Novel - Dan McCall 4218

Belknap, Thomas
The Fate of Princes - P.C. Doherty 1673

Bembo, Pietro
The Flame of the Borgias - Jean Briggs 680

Benaron, Jacob Chalif
The Emperor, the Sages and Death - Rachel Berdach 475

Benedict
Citadel of God: A Novel of Saint Benedict - Louis De Wohl 1563

Benkei
The Sword of Hachiman - Lynn Guest 2608

Berling, Gosta
The Story of Gosta Berling - Selma Lagerlof 3586

Bernadette Soubirous
The Song of Bernadette - Franz Werfel 6625

Bernard of Clairvaux
The Garden of Persephone - Cesar J. Rotondi 5510

Bernay, Odilon de
God's Equal - Alain Absire 14

Bevan, Hywel
Lord of Misrule - Gareth Jones 3290

Birdwell, Eliza
The Friendly Persuasion - Jessamyn West 6629

Bliss, John
Hunt for Heaven - Elsie Barber 298

Blount, Sulien
The Potter's Field - Ellis Peters 4968

Bonhoeffer, Dietrich
The Cup of Wrath - Mary Glazener 2429

Borgia, Rodrigo
Madonna of the Seven Hills - Jean Plaidy 5034
The Medici Guns - Martin Woodhouse 6852
The Memoirs of Christopher Columbus - Stephen Marlowe 4096
Mona Lisa: The Woman in the Portrait - Sara Mayfield 4206
The Naked Sword: The Story of Lucretia Borgia - F.W. Kenyon 3456

Braddee, David
The Delectable Country - Leland Dewitt Baldwin 280

Brebeuf, Jean de
Fathers and Crows - William T. Vollmann 6508
This Widowed Land - Kathleen O'Neal Gear 2331

Brendan the Navigator
Brendan - Frederick Buechner 762
Paradise - Dikkon Eberhart 1831

Bronte, Patrick
Bronte - Glyn Hughes 3073
Dark Quartet: The Story of the Brontes - Lynne Reid Banks 290
Path to the Silent Country - Lynne Reid Banks 291
Wild Decembers: A Biographical Portrait of the Brontes - Hilda Crystal White 6681

Broome, Arthur
The Year of the French - Thomas Flanagan 2121

Brown, Jacob
The View From Coyaba - Peter Abrahams 11

Brown, Jared
The Trembling Earth - Dale Van Every 6411

Bruno
The Miracle at St. Bruno's - Philippa Carr 925

Bungey, Friar
The Last of the Barons - Edward Bulwer-Lytton 769

Bunyan, John
The Pilgrim Prince - Gladys H. Barr 343

Burke, John
Blackfoot Massacre - David Thompson 6251

Cadfael, Brother
Brother Cadfael's Penance - Ellis Peters 4955
The Confessions of Brother Halvin - Ellis Peters 4956
Dead Man's Ransom - Ellis Peters 4957
The Devil's Novice - Ellis Peters 4958
An Excellent Mystery - Ellis Peters 4959
The Heretic's Apprentice - Ellis Peters 4960
The Hermit of Eyton Forest - Ellis Peters 4961
The Holy Thief - Ellis Peters 4962
The Leper of St. Giles - Ellis Peters 4963
Monk's Hood - Ellis Peters 4964
A Morbid Taste for Bones - Ellis Peters 4965
One Corpse Too Many - Ellis Peters 4966
The Pilgrim of Hate - Ellis Peters 4967
The Potter's Field - Ellis Peters 4968
The Raven in the Foregate - Ellis Peters 4969
The Rose Rent - Ellis Peters 4970
St. Peter's Fair - Ellis Peters 4971
The Sanctuary Sparrow - Ellis Peters 4972
The Summer of the Danes - Ellis Peters 4973
The Virgin in the Ice - Ellis Peters 4974

Calvalcanti, Inacio
Brazil - Errol Lincoln Uys 6395

Calverley, Paul
Prisoner of the Queen - Alison Macleod 4006

Calvin, John
City of Light - Alison Macleod 4001

God's Man: A Novel on the Life of John Calvin - Duncan Norton-Taylor 4650

Cameron, Gavin
The World, the Flesh, and the Devil - Reay Tannahill 6159

Campion, Edmund
All the Queen's Men - Evelyn Anthony 157
Come Rack! Come Rope! - Robert Hugh Benson 458
Edmund Campion - Evelyn Waugh 6585
Late Harvest - Olive White 6697
Tudor Underground - Denis Meadows 4320

Casaubon, Edward
Middlemarch - George Eliot 1909

Catherine of Siena
Lay Siege to Heaven: A Novel of Saint Catherine of Siena - Louis De Wohl 1570
The Saint - Fritz von Unruh 6385

Catton, Jeremiel
Bighorn Legacy - W. Michael Gear 2332

Cecily
The Corner That Held Them - Sylvia Townsend Warner 6568

Cera
Pride of Lions - Morgan Llywelyn 3823

Cerdic
A Wayside Tavern - Norah Lofts 3862

Cethlinn
Wolves of the Dawn - William Sarabande 5604

Chandler, Thomas
Miracles - Marcy Moran Heidish 2818

Clement VII
Anne Boleyn - Evelyn Anthony 158
A Cardinal of the Medici - Susan Hicks Beach 393
The Concubine - Norah Lofts 3839
The Image of Our Lord - Edward Burman 790

Clement VIII
The Anthem - Noel B. Gerson 2361
The Carmelite - Elgin Groseclose 2599

Coates, Eben
Show Me a Land - Clark McMeekin 4293

Coates, Rafael
The Marranos - Liliane Webb 6588

Cockley, Thomas
Ladysmead: A Novel in the Jane Austen Tradition - Jane Gillespie 2420

Coffman, Israel
The Border Men - Cameron Judd 3312

Coligny, Gaspard de
The Italian Woman - Jean Plaidy 5024
Queen Jezebel - Jean Plaidy 5049

Colley, Robert
Rites of Passage - William Golding 2456

Collingwood, Stephen
The Summer of the Royal Visit - Isabel Colegate 1199

Collins, William
Teverton Hall - Jane Gillespie 2421

Columba
Isle of Glory - Jane Oliver 4723

Cooke, Nicholas
The Physician of London - Stephanie Cowell 1394

Cotton, John
A Candle in the Wilderness - Irving A. Bacheller 256
Covenant of Grace - Jane Gilmore Rushing 5527
Uncharted Ways - Caroline Snedeker 5935
Witnesses - Marcy Moran Heidish 2820

Courtland, Charles
Palais-Royale - Richard Sennett 5747

Cowper, Christabel
The Man on a Donkey - H.F.M. Prescott 5170

Crane, Edwina
The Jewel in the Crown - Paul Scott 5684

Cranmer, Thomas
Anne Boleyn - Evelyn Anthony 158
Brief Gaudy Hour - Margaret Campbell Barnes 322
The Concubine - Norah Lofts 3839
The Fifth Queen - Ford Madox Ford 2161
The Heir of Allington - Philippa Wiat 6727
Henry VIII and His Six Wives - Maureen Peters 4975
I, Elizabeth - Rosalind Miles 4378
The King's Good Servant - Olive White 6696
The Man on a Donkey - H.F.M. Prescott 5170
My Lord of Canterbury - Godfrey Turton 6369
Queen Anne Boleyn - Francis Hackett 2634
The Ten-Day Queen - Lozania Prole 5199
The Wise Virgin - Hebe Elsna 1934
Young Bess - Margaret Irwin 3123

Crawford, Isabel
Light on the Mountain - Leonard Sanders 5589

Cromwell, Thomas
Henry VIII and His Six Wives - Maureen Peters 4975

Crozier, Columba
The World, the Flesh, and the Devil - Reay Tannahill 6159

da Burgos, Jorges
The Name of the Rose - Umberto Eco 1850

da Melck, Adso
The Name of the Rose - Umberto Eco 1850

Davenport, John
Until the Winds - Jean Clark 1089

Davey, Francis
Jamaica Inn - Daphne Du Maurier 1747

Davidson, Randall
The Widow of Windsor - Tyler Whittle 6723

Dawe, Gilbert
The Man on a Donkey - H.F.M. Prescott 5170

de Veuster, Joseph
Molokai - Oswald Andrew Bushnell 815

Deborah
The Sorceress - Nathaniel Norsen Weinreb 6602

Deming, Mark
Young Men See Visions - Mary Mian 4357

Dimmesdale, Arthur
Arthur Dimmesdale - Charles R. Larson 3671
Hester - Christopher Bigsby 496
The Scarlet Letter - Nathaniel Hawthorne 2786

Dodge, Anson
The Beloved Invader - Eugenia Price 5179

Dokyo
The Vermilion Bridge - Shelley Mydans 4539

Donne, John
Knaves Templar - Leonard Tourney 6300
Physician Extraordinary: A Novel of the Life and Times of William Harvey - David Weiss 6608

Dorn, Mahlon
Fire and the Hammer - Shirley Barker 311

Duprat, Antoine
The Chancellor - Lawrence Schoonover 5662

Dupre, Marc
This Widowed Land - Kathleen O'Neal Gear 2331

Dyer, Mary
Uncharted Ways - Caroline Snedeker 5935

Eadulf, Brother
Absolution by Murder - Peter Tremayne 6334

Eddy, Mary Baker
Live From Golgotha - Gore Vidal 6491

Edwards, Jonathan
The Indentured Heart - Gilbert Morris 4464
The Prospering - Elizabeth Speare 5954

Eilan
The Forest House - Marion Zimmer Bradley 625

Elijah
The Curse of Jezebel: A Novel of the Biblical Queen of Evil - Frank G. Slaughter 5884
Dara, the Cypriot - Louis Paul 4842
Jezebel - Dorothy Clarke Wilson 6802
The Painted Queen - Olga Hesky 2871

Elisha
Merari - Gloria Howe Bremkamp 656

Eluric, Brother
The Rose Rent - Ellis Peters 4970

Enfield, Mayhew
Crossings - Earl Rovit 5512

Escalona, Lorenzo de
The Franciscan - Forrester Blake 532

Evans, Emily
The Calling of Emily Evans - Janette Oke 4706

Fabri, Felix
A Stolen Tongue - Sheri Holman 3002

Farnese, Alessandro
Color From a Light Within: A Novel Based on the Life of El Greco - Donald Braider 641

Farr, Dr. Brockholst
Tenderloin - Samuel Hopkins Adams 33

Fell, Margaret
The Peaceable Kingdom - Jan de Hartog 2763

Fidelis, Brother
An Excellent Mystery - Ellis Peters 4959

Fidelma, Sister
Absolution by Murder - Peter Tremayne 6334

Field, Henry M.
All This, and Heaven Too - Rachel Field 2080

Fisher, John
The King's Good Servant - Olive White 6696
The King's Secret Matter - Jean Plaidy 5027
Queen Anne Boleyn - Francis Hackett 2634

Flambard, Ranulf
Flambard's Confession - Marilyn Durham 1816
Godric - Frederick Buechner 763
The Lion of Justice - Jean Plaidy 5031

Fleming, Samuel
The Witch and the Priest - Hilda Lewis 3754

Fletcher, Ralph
The Cage - Michael Weston 6650

Fleury, Andre Hercule de
Louis the Well-Beloved - Jean Plaidy 5032

Forbes, Martin
Drums of Change: The Story of Running Fawn - Janette Oke 4707

Fournier, Jacques
The Image of Our Lord - Edward Burman 790

Fox, George
The Peaceable Kingdom - Jan de Hartog 2763
Richard Carvel - Winston Churchill 1081

Francis of Assisi
Bird of Fire: A Tale of Francis of Assisi - Helen Constance White 6676
Blessed Are the Meek: A Novel about St. Francis of Assisi - Zofja Kossak-Szczucka 3542
The Joyful Beggar: A Novel of St. Francis of Assisi - Louis De Wohl 1568
My Beautiful White Roses - Michael Lechner 3703

The Perfect Joy of St. Francis - Felix
Timmermans 6281
Saint Francis - Nikos Kazantzakis 3385
Sing to the Sun - Lucille Borden 579

Frevisse, Sister
The Bishop's Tale - Margaret Frazer 2215
The Boy's Tale - Margaret Frazer 2216
The Novice's Tale - Margaret Frazer 2217
The Outlaw's Tale - Margaret Frazer 2218
The Servant's Tale - Margaret Frazer 2219

Frollo, Claude
The Hunchback of Notre Dame - Victor Hugo 3076

Fulbert, Pierre
Ordeal by Silence - Prudence Andrew 142

Furber, Jethro
Omensetter's Luck - William H. Gass 2317

Gabriel, Rabbi
Power - Lion Feuchtwanger 2074

Galbraith, James
Colliers Row - Jan Webster 6592

Gapon, George
Blood on the Snow - John Elliott 1916

Gapon, Georgi
Petersburg - Emily Hanlon 2677

Garces, Francisco
Dust on the King's Highway - Helen Constance
White 6677

Gardiner, Stephen
The King's Good Servant - Olive White 6696

Gasca, Pedro de la
I, the King - Howard Clewes 1112

Gaskell, Obadiah
The Forest Lord - Noel B. Gerson 2368

Gerbert
The Heretic's Apprentice - Ellis Peters 4960

Giraldus
Myself as Witness - James Goldman 2458

Glendinning, Edward
The Abbot - Sir Walter Scott 5688

Godric
Godric - Frederick Buechner 763

Godscale of Cologne
Scales of Gold - Dorothy Dunnett 1808

Granger, Henry
The Whip - Catherine Cookson 1291

Gregory, Brother
A Vision of Light - Judith Merkle Riley 5337

Gregory I
Gregory the Great - Gerhart Ellert 1913

Gregory VII
Not Built with Hands - Helen Constance White 6679

Gregory XI
*Lay Siege to Heaven: A Novel of Saint Catherine of
Siena* - Louis De Wohl 1570

Gregory the Great
The Unspeakables: A Tale of Lombardy - Laverne
Gay 2326

Guidron, Lord
The Temple of the Sun - Moyra Caldecott 849

Halvin, Brother
The Confessions of Brother Halvin - Ellis
Peters 4956

Harkfast
Harkfast: The Making of the King - Hugh C.
Rae 5238

Harmachis
Cleopatra - H. Rider Haggard 2637

Harmonia
Gate to the Sea - Bryher 743

Harrington, Edward Albert
Grandmother and the Priests - Taylor Caldwell 857

Haslam, Robert
For God and Glory - Tim Jeal 3171

Haworth, Ephraim
Jason McGee - Robert H. Fowler 2190

Heatherton, William
The Heatherton Heritage - Pamela Hill 2934

Helena
The Living Wood - Louis De Wohl 1571

Heloise
Death Comes as Epiphany - Sharan Newman 4598
The Devil's Door - Sharan Newman 4599
Peter Abelard: A Novel - Helen Waddell 6517
*Stealing Heaven: The Love Story of Heloise and
Abelard* - Marion Meade 4317

Henniker, John
The Rogue and the Witch - John Edward
Newton 4605

Henning, Johannes
Articles of Faith - Ronald Harwood 2770

Henri, Father
Dubu: A Novel of New Guinean Conquest - Maslyn
Williams 6789

Herlvin, Brother
The Holy Thief - Ellis Peters 4962

Hidalgo y Costilla, Miguel
The Cry of Dolores - Herbert Gorman 2492

Higginson, Thomas Wentworth
I Never Came to You in White - Judith Farr 2014

Hildegard of Bingen
The Journal of Hildegard of Bingen - Barbara
Lachman 3578

Hojo, Muchaku
Segaki - David Stacton 5975

Hooker, Richard
Roanoke Hundred - Inglis Fletcher 2138

Hopkins, Oscar
Oscar and Lucinda - Peter Carey 894

Hosea
The Valley of God - Irene Steinman Patai 4825

Humilis, Brother
An Excellent Mystery - Ellis Peters 4959

Hutchinson, Anne
Bear His Mild Yoke - Ethel White 6675
The Winthrop Covenant - Louis Auchincloss 235
The Winthrop Woman - Anya Seton 5754

Ide
Paradise - Dikkon Eberhart 1831

Ignatius Loyola
The Golden Thread - Louis De Wohl 1566
Set All Afire: A Novel of St. Francis Xavier - Louis De
Wohl 1574

Imhotep
Death Comes as the End - Agatha Christie 1076

Innocent III
Below the Salt - Thomas B. Costain 1362
*Blessed Are the Meek: A Novel about St. Francis of
Assisi* - Zofja Kossak-Szczucka 3542
The Joyful Beggar: A Novel of St. Francis of Assisi -
Louis De Wohl 1568
My Beautiful White Roses - Michael Lechner 3703

Innocent XI
The Anthem - Noel B. Gerson 2361
My Crown, My Love - Ruth Walgreen Stephan 5995

Istephan, Reb
The Apostle - Sholem Asch 197

Ixcawatzin
The Heart of Jade - Salvador de Madariaga 4024

Jackson, Horatio
Hellfire Jackson - Garland Roark 5355

Jackson, Sheldon
Alaska - James A. Michener 4364

James
*The Sins of Herod: A Novel of Rome and the Early
Church* - Frank G. Slaughter 5900

Jassa
A Quest for Love - Jacquetta Hawkes 2781

Jebu
Shike: Time of Dragons - Robert Shea 5784

Jeremiah
The Babylonians - Nathaniel Norsen Weinreb 6600

Jerome
The Converts: A Historical Novel - Rex
Warner 6564
The Four Rivers of Paradise - Helen Constance
White 6678

Jesus Christ
Brothers of Vengeance - LeGette Blythe 556
The Kingdom of the Wicked - Anthony Burgess 778
Man of Nazareth - Anthony Burgess 779

Joan of Arc
An Army of Angels: A Novel of Joan of Arc - Pamela
Marcantel 4079

Jocelin
The Spire - William Golding 2457

John
*The Sins of Herod: A Novel of Rome and the Early
Church* - Frank G. Slaughter 5900

John VIII
Joanna the Pope - Daniel Panger 4785
Pope Joan - Donna Woolfolk Cross 1433

John of the Cross
*Bold Encounter: A Novel Based on the Life of St. John
of the Cross* - Peter-Thomas Rohrbach 5433

Joseph, Brother
A Question of Choice - Prudence Andrew 143

Joshua
The Last Days - William Rayner 5272

Judd, Gerrit Parmalee
The White King - Samuel Bertram Harrison 2747

Julius II
The Agony and the Ecstasy - Irving Stone 6054

Kellner, Jakob
Peking: A Novel of China's Revolt - Anthony
Grey 2587

Kernunnos
The Horse Goddess - Morgan Llywelyn 3820

Khu-Ren
Shadows on the Stones - Moyra Caldecott 847

Knox, John
City of Light - Alison Macleod 4001
The Gay Galliard - Margaret Irwin 3119
Mary, Queen of Scotland and the Isles - Margaret
George 2356
The White Queen - Frederic Fallon 2011

Kordetzki
The Deluge - Henryk Sienkiewicz 5846

Kyra
Shadows on the Stones - Moyra Caldecott 847

Lacey, Pedro
Savages and Saints - Cora Older 4717

Laforgue
Black Robe - Brian Moore 4441

Lammas, Anthony
The Free Fishers - John Buchan 750

Landacta, Martin de
Cannibal Eliot and the Lost Histories of San Francisco - Hilton Obenzinger 4660

Langton, Stephen
The Barons of Runnymede - Pamela Bennetts 445

Las Casas, Bartolome de
Don Pedro and the Devil - Edgar Maas 3948
The Harp and the Shadow - Alejo Carpentier 905
The Indian Chronicles - Jose Barreiro 349
Takers of the City - Hoffman Reynolds Hays 2800

Latimer, Hugh
My Lord of Canterbury - Godfrey Turton 6369

Latour, Jean Marie
Death Comes for the Archbishop - Willa Cather 957

Laud, William
Exiled - Helene Holt 3007
The Golden Feather - Theda Kenyon 3462
John Inglesant - John Henry Shorthouse 5833
The Physician of London - Stephanie Cowell 1394

Laval, Honore
The Witch of Manga Reva - Garland Roark 5359

Leigh, Gervas
Towers in the Mist - Elizabeth Goudge 2495

Leo, Brother
Saint Francis - Nikos Kazantzakis 3385

Leo I
Throne of the World - Louis De Wohl 1575

Leo IV
The Right Line of Cedric - Alfred Duggan 1773

Leo X
A Cardinal of the Medici - Susan Hicks Beach 393
Leo Africanus - Amin Maalouf 3947
The Pope's Rhinoceros - Lawrence Norfolk 4642

Leo XII
Crown of Grass - Charles Andrew Brady 634

Livingstone, David
The Whales in Lake Tanganyika - Lennart Hagerfors 2636

Lockhart, David
The Asking Price - Jessica Stirling 6039
The Good Provider - Jessica Stirling 6043

Lothropp, John
Exiled - Helene Holt 3007

Low, Judah
The Sword of the Golem - Abraham Rothberg 5509

Lucat-mael
Druid's Enchantment - Millie J. Ragosta 5240

Luke
The Silver Chalice - Thomas B. Costain 1370

Luther, Martin
The Adventurer - Mika Waltari 6550
Flame of Fire - Jane Oliver 4722
Monk in Armour - Gladys H. Barr 342
Queen of the Reformation - Charles Ludwig 3922

Luttrell, Edmund
The Whyte Harte - P.C. Doherty 1681

mac Cainnech, Aidan
Byzantium - Stephen R. Lawhead 3680

Mackworth
Ravenshoe - Henry Kingsley 3500

MacLean, Alec
The Strange Brigade - John Edward Jennings 3209

Maia
The Other Sappho - Ellen Frye 2240

Malachi, Brother
In Pursuit of the Green Lion - Judith Merkle Riley 5334

Manentes, Diego
The Inquisitors - Jerzy Andrzejewski 153

Margaret of Metola
The Woman in the Cloak - Pamela Hill 2949

Marie Therese
The Song of Bernadette - Franz Werfel 6625

Mariette Baptiste
Mariette in Ecstasy - Ron Hansen 2682

Mark
Dogheaded Death - Ray Faraday Nelson 4581
Marcus - Laurene Chinn 1068

Mark, Brother
A Question of Choice - Prudence Andrew 143
The Summer of the Danes - Ellis Peters 4973

Marquette, Jacques
Blackrobe - Charles Corcoran 1323

Marrah
The Year the Horses Came - Mary Mackey 3993

Mather, Cotton
The Devil and the Mathers - Edward E. Elliott 1914
Gallows Hill - Frances Winwar 6831
Peace, My Daughters - Shirley Barker 314
The Prescott Chronicles - Albert Fried 2232
The Silver Oar - Howard Breslin 669

Mather, Increase
The Devil and the Mathers - Edward E. Elliott 1914
The Rogue and the Witch - John Edward Newton 4605

Mauro, Fra
A Mapmaker's Dream - James Cowan 1391

Mazarin, Jules
A Candle for D'Artagnan - Chelsea Quinn Yarbro 6895
The Cardinal and the Queen - Evelyn Anthony 159
My Crown, My Love - Ruth Walgreen Stephan 5995
Twenty Years After - Alexandre Dumas 1783

McArdle, James
The Forest and the Fort - Hervey Allen 100

McFadden, Hugh
The Dispossessed - Dell Shannon 5773

Medici, Giulio de'
A Brood of Vipers - Michael Clynes 1133

Medici, Ippolito de'
A Cardinal of the Medici - Susan Hicks Beach 393

Mehuru
A Respectable Trade - Philippa Gregory 2584

Mendoza
Torquemada - Howard Fast 2045

Meriamon
Lord of the Two Lands - Judith Tarr 6167

Micaiah
Jezebel - Dorothy Clarke Wilson 6802

Michael, Brother
An Unholy Alliance - Susanna Gregory 2586

Mohammed
The Voice of Allah - Edwin P. Hoyt 3062

Monk, Mordecai
The Peculiar People - Jan de Hartog 2764

Morris, Dinah
Adam Bede - George Eliot 1908

Muhlenburg, Henry Melchior
A High Wind Rising - Elsie Singmaster 5867

Mulkerin, Michael
The Californios - Louis L'Amour 3618

Mundelein, George
Organized Crime - Nicholas Von Hoffman 6511

Murphy, John
Sons of Thunder - Barbara Fitz Vroman 6516

Nachman of Bratslav
The Man Who Thought He Was Messiah - Curt Leviant 3735

Nathanael
I, Nathanael, Knew Jesus - William Gilbert Van Tassel Sutpen 6133

Nettleship, Lionel
Gentlemen in England - A.N. Wilson 6795

Newman, John Henry
Shadows and Images - Meriol Trevor 6344

Nicholas, Brother
Wandering Star - Steven Yount 6945

Oates, Titus
A Health Unto His Majesty - Jean Plaidy 5019
Traitor's Moon - Robert Neill 4574

Ocre, Pietro di
The Image of Our Lord - Edward Burman 790

O'Hara, Father Colum
Scarlett - Alexandra Ripley 5342

Oldcastle, John
The Whyte Harte - P.C. Doherty 1681

Origen Adamantius
Origen: A Historical Novel - Theodore Vrettos 6515

Owen
Beguiled - Alice Borchardt 577
Devoted - Alice Borchardt 578

Parker, Theodore
The Sin of the Prophet - Truman Nelson 4582

Parris, Samuel
Road to Lendor - Esther Hammon 1966

Patrick
Captive of Rome - Theodora McCormick Du Bois 1740
The Deer Cry - William Greenough Schofield 5650
Druid's Enchantment - Millie J. Ragosta 5240
The Lion and the Cross - Joan Lesley Hamilton 2669

Paul
Brothers of Vengeance - LeGette Blythe 556
The Eighth Veil - Ellis Kadison 3320
The Flames of Rome - Paul L. Maier 4033
The Glorious Folly: A Novel of the Time of St. Paul - Louis De Wohl 1565
God's Warrior - Frank G. Slaughter 5889
I, Paul - Rex Miller 4401
Man on Fire: A Novel on the Life of St. Paul - LeGette Blythe 558
Marcus - Laurene Chinn 1068
Saint Paul: A Historical Novel of His Life - Leon Poirier 5081
The Silver Chalice - Thomas B. Costain 1370
The Soothsayer - Laurene Chinn 1069
Upon This Rock: A Novel of Simon Peter, Prince of Apostles - Frank G. Slaughter 5906
Upon This Rock: The Life of St. Peter - Walter F. Murphy 4526

Paul III
The Venetian - David Weiss 6611

Paul V
The Samurai - Shusaku Endo 1941

Pennant, Robert
A Morbid Taste for Bones - Ellis Peters 4965

Persons, Robert
Tudor Underground - Denis Meadows 4320

Petar, Brother
Devil's Yard - Ivo Andric 152

Peter
The Eighth Veil - Ellis Kadison 3320
The Flames of Rome - Paul L. Maier 4033
Great Lion of God - Taylor Caldwell 858
The Last Athenian - Viktor Rydberg 5543

Peter, Brother
Lords of the Dance - Robin Lloyd-Jones 3815

Peter
Man on Fire: A Novel on the Life of St. Paul -
    LeGette Blythe 558
Marcus - Laurene Chinn 1068
The Master - Max Brod 702
Quo Vadis - Henryk Sienkiewicz 5848
The Silver Chalice - Thomas B. Costain 1370
*The Sins of Herod: A Novel of Rome and the Early
    Church* - Frank G. Slaughter 5900
*Upon This Rock: A Novel of Simon Peter, Prince of
    Apostles* - Frank G. Slaughter 5906
Upon This Rock: The Life of St. Peter - Walter F.
    Murphy 4526

Peyramale, Dean
The Song of Bernadette - Franz Werfel 6625

Philammon
Hypatia - Charles Kingsley 3498

Philip
The Pillars of the Earth - Ken Follett 2149

Philip of Evesham
Ordeal by Silence - Prudence Andrew 142

Pius IV
The Agony and the Ecstasy - Irving Stone 6054

Pius IX
Cock of the Walk - Roy Lewis 3762
The Harp and the Shadow - Alejo Carpentier 905

Pius XII
The Hangman's Crusade - James Barwick 370
Hitler Has Won - Frederic Mullally 4511

Plessis, Armand-Jean Du
The Anthem - Noel B. Gerson 2361
The Arm and the Darkness - Taylor Caldwell 850
A Candle for D'Artagnan - Chelsea Quinn
    Yarbro 6895
The Cardinal and the Queen - Evelyn Anthony 159
Cinq-Mars - Alfred Victor de Vigny 6495
An Epic Joy: A Novel Based on the Life of Rubens -
    Donald Braider 642
The Favourite - Francoise Mallet-Joris 4040
Louis the Well-Beloved - Jean Plaidy 5032
Louisiana Purchase - A.E. Hotchner 3039
The Three Musketeers - Alexandre Dumas 1782
Wife to Great Buckingham - Hilda Lewis 3751
World and Paradise - Edgar Maas 3953
The Young and Lonely King - Jane Lane 3659

Pole, Reginald
The Hireling - Alison Macleod 4003

Prescott, Francis
The Rector of Justin - Louis Auchincloss 233

Quintus
Upon This Rock: The Life of St. Peter - Walter F.
    Murphy 4526

Rabbi
The Brother - Chayym Zeldis 6958

Rasputin, Grigori Efimovich
Devoted Friends - Joe Poyer 5161
Love and Honor - Leslie Arlen 189
Rasputin's Revenge - John T. Lescroart 3725
Seance for a Vampire - Fred Saberhagen 5557
Time After Time - Allen Appel 171
White Nights, Red Dawn - Frederick Nolan 4634

Reardon, Francis
Brandywine - Jack Rowe 5513

Richepane, Louis
The Arm and the Darkness - Taylor Caldwell 850

Ridley, Nicholas
My Lord of Canterbury - Godfrey Turton 6369

Roberts, Oral
Live From Golgotha - Gore Vidal 6491

Rogers, Tiana
Walk in My Soul - Lucia St. Clair Robson 5418

Rohan, Louis de
The Queen's Confession - Victoria Holt 3019
The Queen's Necklace - Alexandre Dumas 1781

Romig, Jonathan
Shining Mountains - Steve Frazee 2214

Ruminez, Francisco
Master of Castile - Samuel Edwards 1888

Ryegate, Mark
If a Lion Could Talk - Mildred Walker 6532

Ryselius, Martin
Passion and the Sword - Harald Hornborg 3034

St. Agnes, Sister
St. Agnes' Stand - Tom Eidson 1900

Salammbo
Salammbo - Gustave Flaubert 2123

Samuel
David of Jerusalem - Louis De Wohl 1564
David: Warrior and King - Frank G. Slaughter 5885
King of Kings: A Novel of the Life of David - Malachi
    Martin 4134
The Prophet and the King - Shirley Watkins 6582
Rizpah - Charles E. Israel 3124

Sandor, Janos
Preacher on Horseback - Cecile Hulse
    Matschat 4186

Sanducci, Roberto
A Dancer in Darkness - David Stacton 5971

Santos, Fray Xavier
Ghost Woman - Lawrence Thornton 6275

Saul of Tarsus
Great Lion of God - Taylor Caldwell 858

Savonarola, Girolamo
The Florentine - Sandra Shulman 5840
The Palace - Chelsea Quinn Yarbro 6904
The Private Life of Mona Lisa - Pierre La
    Mure 3577
Romola - George Eliot 1910

Scarron, Father
A Rendezvous in Haiti - Stephen Becker 407

Sebastian, Father
Apache - Donald Clayton Porter 5114

Sebastian
Seek the Fair Land - Walter Macken 3989

Selkirk, John
The Great Valley - Mary Johnston 3234

Sergeant, John
The Prospering - Elizabeth Speare 5954

Serra, Junipero
A City for St. Francis - Evelyn Wells 6621
The Cross and the Sword - Jonreed Lauritzen 3674
Nine Days of Father Serra - Isabelle Gibson
    Ziegler 6961
The Road to Glory - Darwin Le Ora Teilhet 6199
This Promised Land - Robert Easton 1824

Seton, Elizabeth Ann
Heart in Pilgrimage - Evelyn Eaton 1827
Miracles - Marcy Moran Heidish 2818

Sheldon, Huldah
Crum Elbow Folks - Percy Raymond Barnes 332

Shonti
Shadow of a Star - Jamie Lee Cooper 1315

Siddhartha Gautama
The Yellow Robe: A Novel of the Life of Buddha -
    Robert Payne 4856

Sidmouth, Geoffrey
Jane and the Man of the Cloth - Stephanie
    Barron 355

Silverius
Count Belisarius - Robert Graves 2544

Simon Peter
Fisher of Men: A Novel of Simon Peter - Kurt
    Frieberger 2231

Sixtus IV
The Medici Emerald - Martin Woodhouse 6851
The Medici Guns - Martin Woodhouse 6852
The Medici Hawks - Martin Woodhouse 6853

Smith, Joseph
Children of God - Vardis Fisher 2106
The Devil's Rainbow - J.C. Furnas 2257
The Everlasting Fire - Jonreed Lauritzen 3675

Smith, Raccoon John
Raccoon John Smith - Louis Cochran 1145

Smith, Sydney
Come Be My Love - Diana Brown 717

Stacey, Sedley
Cousin Susannah - Hazel Hucker 3066

Starbuck, Elial
Battle Flag - Bernard Cornwell 1333

Sueer, Abbe
Death Comes as Epiphany - Sharan Newman 4598

Swift, Jonathan
*Fanny: Being the True History of the Adventures of
    Fanny Hackabout-Jones* - Erica Jong 3299
Violent Friends - Winston Clewes 1113

Sylvester II
In the Falcon's Claw: A Novel of the Year 1000 -
    Chet Raymo 5257

Symms, Edward
Orphan Train - James Magnuson 4029

Tamasrajasi
Path of the Eclipse - Chelsea Quinn Yarbro 6905

Taylor, John
Children of God - Vardis Fisher 2106

Tekakwitha, Kateri
Lily of the Mohawks - Jack Casey 952

Thackeray, William
Chase the Wind - E.V. Thompson 6264
Harvest of the Sun - E.V. Thompson 6265

Thaddeus, Juan
The Carmelite - Elgin Groseclose 2599

Theo
Theo and Matilda - Rachel Billington 498

Theobald
*Thomas: A Novel of the Life, Passions, and Miracles
    of Becket* - Shelley Mydans 4538

Theodore
Theo and Matilda - Rachel Billington 498

Theresa of Avila
*Bold Encounter: A Novel Based on the Life of St. John
    of the Cross* - Peter-Thomas Rohrbach 5433

Therese of Lisieux
*Love Is My Vocation: An Imaginative Study of St.
    Therese of Lisieux* - Tom Clarkson 1098

Thomas, Brother
A Trail of Blood - Jeremy Potter 5143

Thomas
Yeshua: The Gospel of St. Thomas - Alan Decker
    McNarie 4306

Thomas Aquinas
The Quiet Light - Louis De Wohl 1572

Thomas, Mark
Song of Wovoka - Earl Murray 4531

Thomas of Antioch
According to Thomas - Gladys Malvern 4053

Thomasine, Sister
The Novice's Tale - Margaret Frazer 2217
The Servant's Tale - Margaret Frazer 2219

Thoresby, John
The Apothecary Rose - Candace M. Robb 5364
The Lady Chapel - Candace M. Robb 5366

Thrand
This Land Fulfilled - Charles Andrew Brady 636

Thurston, Dame Louise
The Ladies of St. Hedwig's - E.M. Almedingen 117

Timothy
Live From Golgotha - Gore Vidal 6491
Man on Fire: A Novel on the Life of St. Paul -
  LeGette Blythe 558
The Soothsayer - Laurene Chinn 1069

Tirso de Molina
The Adventures of Don Juan - Richard Gardner 2289

Torquemada, Tomas de
Crown of Aloes - Norah Lofts 3840
The Dogs of Paradise - Abel Posse 5141
The Inquisitors - Jerzy Andrzejewski 153
The Memoirs of Christopher Columbus - Stephen
  Marlowe 4096
*The Queen's Cross: A Biographical Romance of
  Queen Isabella of Spain* - Lawrence
  Schoonover 5666
Torquemada - Howard Fast 2045

Torridon, Christopher
The King's Achievement - Robert Hugh Benson 459

Tour d'Auvergne, Michel de la
To the End of the World - Helen Constance
  White 6680

Treadup, David
The Call - John Hersey 2869

Trumbull, Nathaniel
The Greater Hunger - Barbara Dodge Borland 581

Tuck, Friar
The Good Yeomen - Jay Williams 6771

Turner, Nat
The Confessions of Nat Turner - William
  Styron 6106

Tutilo, Brother
The Holy Thief - Ellis Peters 4962

Urban VIII
The Star-Gazer - Zsolt de Harsanyi 2757

Vaillant, Joseph
Death Comes for the Archbishop - Willa Cather 957

Valliant, Martin
Martin Valliant - Warwick Deeping 1578

Vaughan, Maria
Luciano's Luck - Jack Higgins 2912

Vaughan, Penry
The Fox-Red Hills - Cynthia S. Roberts 5374

Velasco
The Samurai - Shusaku Endo 1941

Velasquez, Rodrigo
The Spanish Doctor - Matt Cohen 1159

Vilers, Gilbert de
In Pursuit of the Green Lion - Judith Merkle
  Riley 5334

Walter
The Corner That Held Them - Sylvia Townsend
  Warner 6568

Watson, John Selby
Watson's Apology - Beryl Bainbridge 271

Wayte, Cecilia
The Nunnery - Dorothy Charques 1001

Webster, Richard
The Standing Hills - Caroline Stickland 6038

Weems, Josiah
The Blood Seed - Andrew Ward 6561

Welles, Nathan
And Never Yield - Elinor Pryor 5204

Wentworth, Peter
Burden of Desire - Robert MacNeil 4023

Wesley, Charles
Dark Sails - Helen Topping Miller 4388

Wesley, John
Edward, Edward - Lolah Burford 772
The Holy Lover - Marie Oemler 4690
Jarrett's Jade - Frank Yerby 6923
Lord Vanity - Samuel Shellabarger 5796
A New Creature - Prudence Andrew 141
Take Her, Mr. Wesley - John W. Drakeford 1719

Whipple, John
Hawaii - James A. Michener 4370

Whitman, Marcus
Doctor in Buckskin - T.D. Allen 103
We Must March: A Novel of the Winning of Oregon -
  Honore Morrow 4491

Whitman, Narcissa
Doctor in Buckskin - T.D. Allen 103

Whitworth, Osborne
The Angry Tide - Winston Graham 2521
The Four Swans - Winston Graham 2525

Widowson, Alfred
The Golden Hand - Edith Simon 5856

Wilder, Marigold
The Blue Dragon - Diana Brown 716

Will, Silas
Riders of the Long Road - Stephen E. Bransford 649

William of Baskerville
The Name of the Rose - Umberto Eco 1850

Williams, Nash
Crossing the River - Caryl Phillips 4984

Williams, Roger
Ashes in the Wilderness - William Greenough
  Schofield 5649
Come Home at Even - Le Grand Cannon 884
The Greater Hunger - Barbara Dodge Borland 581
I Seek a City - Gilbert Rees 5289

Winslow, Gilbert
The Honorable Imposter - Gilbert Morris 4463

Wiseman, Nicholas
Cock of the Walk - Roy Lewis 3762

Wolsey, Thomas
Anne Boleyn - Evelyn Anthony 158
Anne of the Thousand Days - Edward Fenton 2059
The Autobiography of Henry VIII - Margaret
  George 2355
A Brood of Vipers - Michael Clynes 1133
Command of the King - Mary Lide 3773
The Concubine - Norah Lofts 3839
The Gallows Murder - Michael Clynes 1134
The Grail Murders - Michael Clynes 1135
Henry VIII and His Six Wives - Maureen
  Peters 4975
The King's Pleasure - Norah Lofts 3847
The King's Secret Matter - Jean Plaidy 5027
The Lady in the Tower - Jean Plaidy 5028

The Man on a Donkey - H.F.M. Prescott 5170
The Poisoned Chalice - Michael Clynes 1136
Queen Anne Boleyn - Francis Hackett 2634
The Reluctant Queen - Molly Costain Haycraft 2796
St. Thomas's Eve - Jean Plaidy 5060
The Serpent Garden - Judith Merkle Riley 5336
The Shadow of the Pomegranate - Jean Plaidy 5062
The Sword of Truth - Gilbert Morris 4472
The White Rose Murders - Michael Clynes 1137
Windsor Castle - William Harrison Ainsworth 59

Wycliffe, John
The Peacock and the Pearl - Jennifer Lang 3661

Xavier, Francis
The Golden Thread - Louis De Wohl 1566
Set All Afire: A Novel of St. Francis Xavier - Louis De
  Wohl 1574
So Far From Malabar - Joy DeWeese Wehen 6599

Ximenes de Cisneros, Francisco
The Shadow of the Pomegranate - Jean Plaidy 5062

Yechiel, Reb
Salvation - Sholem Asch 202

Young, Brigham
Children of God - Vardis Fisher 2106
The Devil's Rainbow - J.C. Furnas 2257
Dream Catcher - Terry C. Johnston 3251
The Everlasting Fire - Jonreed Lauritzen 3675
For Time and All Eternity - Paul Bailey 268
The Giant Joshua - Maurine Whipple 6673
Salt Lake City - A.R. Reife 5292
Sister Wives - Cleo Jones 3270

Young, Martin
The Pleasure Garden - Leon Garfield 2293

Ysuna
The Sacred Stones - William Sarabande 5600

Zumarraga, Juan de
Roses for Mexico - Ethel Cook Eliot 1907

RENEGADE

North, Rob
Red Cloud's Revenge - Terry C. Johnston 3255

Usher, Jubilee
Cry of the Hawk - Terry C. Johnston 3248
Dream Catcher - Terry C. Johnston 3251

REPAIRMAN

Varden, Gabriel
Barnaby Rudge: A Tale of the Riots of Eighty -
  Charles Dickens 1641

REVOLUTIONARY

Adams, Samuel
The Bastard - John Jakes 3144
Buckskin Baronet - Margaret Widdemer 6734
The Gentle Rebel - Gilbert Morris 4461
The Long Naked Descent into Boston - William
  Eastlake 1823
Sons of Liberty - Adam Rutledge 5540
Sound of the Trumpet - Gilbert Morris 4471
Yankee Doodle Dandy - Noel B. Gerson 2387

Adelita
The Adelita - Oakley Hall 2649

Anna
The Petersburg-Cannes Express - Hans Koning 3538

Antipov, Pavel
Doctor Zhivago - Boris Pasternak 4824

Ball, John
The Peacock and the Pearl - Jennifer Lang 3661
Riot at Gravesend: A Novel of Wat Tyler's Rebellion -
  William Howard Woods 6864

Who Was Then the Gentleman - Charles E. Israel 3125

Barabbas
The Eighth Veil - Ellis Kadison 3320

Barnabas
Shadows in Bronze - Lindsey Davis 1531

Barras, Paul
The Incorruptible - Marjorie Coryn 1357
Lady of Paris - William Vaughan Wilkins 6760
Mistress of Fortune - Sheila Lancaster 3651
Seed of Mischief - Willa Gibbs 2401

Batara, David
The View From Coyaba - Peter Abrahams 11

Batz, Baron Jean de
Scaramouche the King-Maker - Rafael Sabatini 5555

Bergeron, Maximilien
The Riven Heart - Genevieve Gennari 2354

Black, Christopher
The End of the Hunt - Thomas Flanagan 2119

Blood, Thomas
Peveril of the Peak - Sir Walter Scott 5703

Bolivar, Simon
The General in His Labyrinth - Gabriel Garcia Marquez 2282
The Splendor Stays: An Historic Novel Based on the Lives of the Seven Hart Sisters of Saybrook - Marguerite Allis 114

Bonaparte, Carlo
Good-Bye My Son - Marjorie Coryn 1356

Borowska, Wanda
White Eagle, Dark Skies - Jean Karsavina 3368

Brown, John
Flashman and the Angel of the Lord - George MacDonald Fraser 2205
House Divided - Ben Ames Williams 6765
The Slave of Frankenstein - Robert J. Myers 4549

Burenin, Paul
A House Divided - Michael Phillips 4988

Burke, Myles
The Killing Frost - Thomas Hayden 2799

Busson, Michel
The Glass-Blowers - Daphne Du Maurier 1745

Busson, Robert
The Glass-Blowers - Daphne Du Maurier 1745

Bustos, Baltasar
The Campaign - Carlos Fuentes 2245

Cartier, Paul
Coasts of Folly - Joel Williams 6784

Casement, Roger
Rebels: The Irish Rising of 1916 - Peter DeRosa 1622

Casey, Peadar
The Men That God Made Mad: A Novel about Ireland's Easter Rising - W.A. Ballinger 286

Castro, Fidel
Papa and Fidel - Karl Alexander 79

El Catolico
Sharpe's Gold - Bernard Cornwell 1343

Chabot, Francois
Scaramouche the King-Maker - Rafael Sabatini 5555

Christophe, Henri
Black Dawn - Christopher Nicole 4613
Drums of Destiny - Peter Bourne 593
Lydia Bailey - Kenneth Roberts 5387
Mistress of Darkness - Christopher Nicole 4617
A Time for Titans - Vina Delmar 1602

Cinque, Joseph
Echo of Lions - Barbara Chase-Riboud 1004

Clarke, Tom
Rebels: The Irish Rising of 1916 - Peter DeRosa 1622

Collins, Michael
The End of the Hunt - Thomas Flanagan 2119
High Heroic - Constantine FitzGibbon 2118

Condorcet, Nicholas
City of Darkness, City of Light - Marge Piercy 4998

Connolly, James
Heart of War - John Masters 4174
The Men That God Made Mad: A Novel about Ireland's Easter Rising - W.A. Ballinger 286
Rebels: The Irish Rising of 1916 - Peter DeRosa 1622
Saints and Scholars - Terrence Eagleton 1821

Connolly, Morgan
Across the Bitter Sea - Eilis Dillon 1646

Corday, Charlotte
Dr. Guillotine: The Eccentric Exploits of an Early Scientist - Herbert Lom 3867
To Spit Against the Wind - Benjamin H. Levin 3737

Cosette
Cosette: The Sequel to Les Miserables - Laura Kalpakian 3329

Couthon, Georges
The Incorruptible - Marjorie Coryn 1357

Cromwell, Oliver
Charles the King - Evelyn Anthony 160

Cruz, Artemio
The Death of Artemio Cruz - Carlos Fuentes 2246

Daley, Jamie
Gone the Rainbow, Gone the Dove - Joan Bagnel 264

Danton, Georges-Jacques
Citizen Tom Paine - Howard Fast 2028
City of Darkness, City of Light - Marge Piercy 4998
The Devil's Laughter - Frank Yerby 6913
The Gods Are Thirsty - Tanith Lee 3710
The Incorruptible - Marjorie Coryn 1357
The Incorruptible - Helma De Bois 1551
A Place of Greater Safety - Hilary Mantel 4077
Scaramouche - Rafael Sabatini 5554
To Spit Against the Wind - Benjamin H. Levin 3737
Veronique - Virginia Coffman 1158
The Way to the Lantern - Audrey Erskine Lindop 3790

Davitt, Michael
The Tenants of Time - Thomas Flanagan 2120

De Valera, Eamon
Rebels: The Irish Rising of 1916 - Peter DeRosa 1622

Delaney, Robert
The Tenants of Time - Thomas Flanagan 2120

Desmoulins, Camille
City of Darkness, City of Light - Marge Piercy 4998
The Devil's Laughter - Frank Yerby 6913
The Gods Are Thirsty - Tanith Lee 3710
The Incorruptible - Marjorie Coryn 1357
A Place of Greater Safety - Hilary Mantel 4077
Scaramouche the King-Maker - Rafael Sabatini 5555

Dessalines, Jean-Jacques
Drums of Destiny - Peter Bourne 593
Mistress of Darkness - Christopher Nicole 4617

Di Blasi, Francesco
The Council of Europe - Leonardo Sciascia 5678

Dineas, Daniel Bar
The Eighth Veil - Ellis Kadison 3320

Donovan, Sean
Chase Royal - Donald Seaman 5712

Erec
Kingdom of the Grail - A.A. Attanasio 226

Fabian, Adam
White Eagle, Dark Skies - Jean Karsavina 3368

Fay, Molly
Stranger in Two Worlds - Hugh Clevely 1111

Fierro, Rodolfo
The Friends of Pancho Villa - James Carlos Blake 535

Flores Magon, Ricardo
The Prison Notebooks of Ricardo Flores Magon - Douglas Day 1545

Fouche, Joseph
Captain Cut-Throat - John Dickson Carr 908
The Hastening Wind - Edward Grierson 2591
The Thousand Fires - Anne Powers 5155

Galban, Rafaela
Mingo Dabney - James H. Street 6078

Gallagher, Con
The Killing Frost - Thomas Hayden 2799

Garcia, Tomas
A Distant Thunder - Teresa de Luca 1561

Garcia y Inigues, Calixto
The Single Star - Walter Adolphe Roberts 5394

Glendower, Owen
Glendower Country - Martha Rofheart 5427
Owen Glendower - John Cowper Powys 5159

Goldman, Emma
Ragtime - E.L. Doctorow 1658

Gomez, Jose Miguel
The Single Star - Walter Adolphe Roberts 5394

Griffith, Arthur
High Heroic - Constantine FitzGibbon 2118
Rebels: The Irish Rising of 1916 - Peter DeRosa 1622

Guerro, Gasto
The Rebels - Alfred Neumann 4585

Guevara, Che
The Death of Che Guevara - Jay Cantor 886

Hale, Nathan
Sons of Liberty - Adam Rutledge 5540

Hancock, John
The Long Naked Descent into Boston - William Eastlake 1823

Heiden, Boris
Give Me the Daggers - Catherine Gavin 2321

Hereward the Wake
The Disputed Crown - Valerie Anand 128

Hidalgo y Costilla, Miguel
The Cry of Dolores - Herbert Gorman 2492

Holland, Frank
Beauty for Ashes - Timothy R. Wilson 6816

Howe, Tommy
From a Far Land - Robert S. Elegant 1903

Hung
Empire of Heaven - Linda Ching Sledge 5907

Ivanov, Oleg
Blood and Sable - Carol J. Kane 3350

Izquierdo, Conchita
Floodtide - Frank Yerby 6916

Kerensky, Alexandr Feodorovich
Lenin: The Novel - Alan Brien 679

Kim Yul-Chun
The Living Reed - Pearl S. Buck 756

Kokhba, Simon Bar
The Soldier and the Sage: A Novel about Akiba - Richard G. Hubler 3065

The Sword and the Promise - Benjamin Siegel 5845

Krakar, Janez
Pendragon. . .The Montenegran Plot - Robert
Trevelyan 6338

Krupskaya, Nadezhda Konstantinovna
Lenin in Zurich - Alexander Solzhenitsyn 5943

Kutebar, Izzat
Flashman at the Charge - George MacDonald
Fraser 2209

Lacombe, Claire
City of Darkness, City of Light - Marge Piercy 4998

Lacy, Frank
The End of the Hunt - Thomas Flanagan 2119

Larkin, Rory
Redemption - Leon Uris 6393

Lenin, Vladimir Ilich
Blood on the Snow - John Elliott 1916
The Dawning of Deliverance - Judith Pella 4892
Grishin - Hans Herlin 2859
Karl and Rosa - Alfred Doblin 1653
The King's Commissar - Duncan Kyle 3570
Lenin in Zurich - Alexander Solzhenitsyn 5943
The Revolutionist: A Novel of Russia - Robert
Littell 3810
Time After Time - Allen Appel 171
White Nights, Red Dawn - Frederick Nolan 4634

Leon, Pauline
City of Darkness, City of Light - Marge Piercy 4998

Liebknecht, Karl
Karl and Rosa - Alfred Doblin 1653
A People Betrayed - Alfred Doblin 1654

Lloyd, Stephen
The Single Star - Walter Adolphe Roberts 5394

Lu Mei-ling
Peking: A Novel of China's Revolt - Anthony
Grey 2587

Luxemburg, Rosa
Karl and Rosa - Alfred Doblin 1653
A People Betrayed - Alfred Doblin 1654

MacDonald, Flora
The Scotswoman - Inglis Fletcher 2140

Mackenzie, William Lyon
Bright to the Wanderer - Bruce Lancaster 3638

MacMahon, Hugh
The Tenants of Time - Thomas Flanagan 2120

Mao Tse-tung
High Road to China - Jon Cleary 1106
The Warlord - Malcolm Bosse 589

Marat, Jean-Paul
The Black Consul - Anatolii Vinogradov 6503
The Devil's Laughter - Frank Yerby 6913
*Dr. Guillotine: The Eccentric Exploits of an Early
Scientist* - Herbert Lom 3867
A Place of Greater Safety - Hilary Mantel 4077
To Spit Against the Wind - Benjamin H. Levin 3737
The Way to the Lantern - Audrey Erskine
Lindop 3790

Maria
The Edge of the Storm - Agustin Yanez 6893

Marita
Storm to the South - Thelma Strabel 6073

Markievicz, Constance
Rebels: The Irish Rising of 1916 - Peter
DeRosa 1622
Seasons - Anna Dillon 1645

Marsan, Gilles
Veronique - Virginia Coffman 1158

Martinez, Jorge
Not of War Only - Norman Zollinger 6966

Masson, Philippe
The Colors of Vaud - Bryher 741

McDermott, Sean
Rebels: The Irish Rising of 1916 - Peter
DeRosa 1622

Michales, Captain
Freedom or Death - Nikos Kazantzakis 3383

Moreau, Andre-Louis
Scaramouche - Rafael Sabatini 5554
Scaramouche the King-Maker - Rafael Sabatini 5555

Mortimer, Richard
The Prisoners of September - Leon Garfield 2294

Murdoc
Seek the Fair Land - Walter Macken 3989

Nolan, Ned
The Tenants of Time - Thomas Flanagan 2120

Oates, Titus
Peveril of the Peak - Sir Walter Scott 5703

O'Donovan, Declan
*The Men That God Made Mad: A Novel about
Ireland's Easter Rising* - W.A. Ballinger 286

O'Higgins, Bernardo
O'Higgins and Don Bernardo - Edna Deu Pree
Nelson 4578
Taste of Glory - Carleton Beals 394

Ormerod, Asa
The Golden Circle - Constance Robertson 5396

Paine, Thomas
Citizen Tom Paine - Howard Fast 2028
City of Darkness, City of Light - Marge Piercy 4998
The Long Naked Descent into Boston - William
Eastlake 1823

Pearse, Patrick Henry
High Heroic - Constantine FitzGibbon 2118
Rebels: The Irish Rising of 1916 - Peter
DeRosa 1622

Petion, Alexandre
Drums of Destiny - Peter Bourne 593

Philipon, Manon
City of Darkness, City of Light - Marge Piercy 4998

Plunkett, Joseph
Rebels: The Irish Rising of 1916 - Peter
DeRosa 1622

Poliakov, Sonya
Triptych - Dora Landey 3652

Polyxigis, Captain
Freedom or Death - Nikos Kazantzakis 3383

Pontmercy, Marius
Cosette: The Sequel to Les Miserables - Laura
Kalpakian 3329

Pougatcheff, Emelyan
The Captain's Daughter - Alexander Pushkin 5210

Princip, Gavrilo
The First Casualty - William Powell 5149

Pushchin, Ivan
The Year of December - Lucy Cores 1329

Rantzau, Irina
Petersburg - Emily Hanlon 2677

Riel, Louis
Drums of Change: The Story of Running Fawn -
Janette Oke 4707
The Half Breed - Maurice Constantin-Weyer 1261
Lord of the Plains - Alfred Silver 5852
The Magnificent Failure - Giles A. Lutz 3928

Riordan, Ian
Gone the Rainbow, Gone the Dove - Joan
Bagnel 264

Riqueti, Honore Gabriel
The Black Consul - Anatolii Vinogradov 6503
King's Masque - Evan John 3220
Mirabeau, Lover and Stateman - Pierre
Nezelof 4606

Robespierre, Maximilien Francois de
The Black Consul - Anatolii Vinogradov 6503
City of Darkness, City of Light - Marge Piercy 4998
The Devil's Laughter - Frank Yerby 6913
The Gods Are Thirsty - Tanith Lee 3710
The Incorruptible - Marjorie Coryn 1357
The Incorruptible - Helma De Bois 1551
The Man Who Killed the King - Dennis
Wheatley 6654
A Place of Greater Safety - Hilary Mantel 4077
Rasero - Francisco Rebolledo 5282
*The Rose of Malmaison: The Turbulent Life of the
Beautiful Josephine* - Gaby von Schonthan 5660
Scaramouche the King-Maker - Rafael Sabatini 5555
Tallien: A Brief Romance - Frederic Tuten 6370
La Vendee - Anthony Trollope 6346
Veronique - Virginia Coffman 1158

Saint-Just, Louis-Antoine-Leon de
A Place of Greater Safety - Hilary Mantel 4077
Scaramouche the King-Maker - Rafael Sabatini 5555

Sandino, Augusto Cesar
A Few Good Men - William Overgard 4768

Savenay, Henri de
The White Cockade - Charles James Louis
Gilson 2423

Shays, Daniel
The Sprig of Hemlock: A Novel about Shays' Rebellion
- Robert Muir 4509

Shen, Sun Lung
Blood Red Rose - Maxwell Grant 2538

Spartacus
Spartacus - Howard Fast 2044

Stalin, Joseph
Lenin: The Novel - Alan Brien 679

Starr, Padraic
The Rising of the Moon - William Martin 4140

Tallien, Jean-Lambert
Harp of a Thousand Strings - Harold Lenoir
Davis 1522

Tallien, Jean Lambert
The Incorruptible - Marjorie Coryn 1357
Lady of Paris - William Vaughan Wilkins 6760
Tallien: A Brief Romance - Frederic Tuten 6370

Teotl
Gods on Horseback - Samuel G. Baggett 263

Til, Alexander
The Revolutionist: A Novel of Russia - Robert
Littell 3810

Tolcheff, Andrew
The Petersburg-Cannes Express - Hans Koning 3538

Tolchin, Count Gregory
Triptych - Dora Landey 3652

Tone, Theobald Wolfe
The Year of the French - Thomas Flanagan 2121

Toussaint l'Ouverture, Pierre Dominique
All Souls' Rising - Madison Smartt Bell 422
The Black Consul - Anatolii Vinogradov 6503
Black Triumvirate: A Novel of Haiti - Benjamin H.
Levin 3736
Caribbean - James A. Michener 4365
*The Corsair: A Biographical Novel of Jean Lafitte,
Hero of the Battle of New Orleans* - Madeleine
Fabiola Kent 3444
Drums at Dusk - Arna Bontemps 575
Drums of Destiny - Peter Bourne 593
Lydia Bailey - Kenneth Roberts 5387
Mistress of Darkness - Christopher Nicole 4617

A Time for Titans - Vina Delmar 1602

Trotsky, Leon
Blood on the Snow - John Elliott 1916
The End of the World News - Anthony Burgess 777
Karl and Rosa - Alfred Doblin 1653
The King's Commissar - Duncan Kyle 3570
Lenin: The Novel - Alan Brien 679
Petersburg - Emily Hanlon 2677

Tyler, Blazely
Thunder Before Seven - Anna Brand 648

Tyler, Wat
Glendower Country - Martha Rofheart 5427
Katherine - Anya Seton 5752
Passage to Pontefract - Jean Plaidy 5038
The Peacock and the Pearl - Jennifer Lang 3661
Richard Whittington, London's Mayor - Gwynedd
  Sudworth 6112
Riot at Gravesend: A Novel of Wat Tyler's Rebellion -
  William Howard Woods 6864
The Ruthless Yeomen - Valerie Anand 134
Who Was Then the Gentleman - Charles E.
  Israel 3125
Within the Hollow Crown - Margaret Campbell
  Barnes 331

Ulyanov, Vladimir Ilich
Lenin: The Novel - Alan Brien 679
The Petrograd Consignment - Owen Sela 5739
Seven Days to Petrograd - Tom Hyman 3094

El Vago
El Vago - Laurence Gonzales 2474

Villa, Francisco
Blue Moon - Parris Afton Bonds 569
The Crimson Wind - Max Hennessy 2832
The Fifth Horseman - Jose Antonio Villarreal 6496
The Friends of Pancho Villa - James Carlos
  Blake 535
Last Reveille - David Morrell 4456
Not of War Only - Norman Zollinger 6966
Outlaw - Warren Kiefer 3482
Pancho And Black Jack - Fred Bean 398
The Prison Notebooks of Ricardo Flores Magon -
  Douglas Day 1545
Sergeant Gringo - Jack Cummings 1449
Tom Mix and Pancho Villa - Clifford Irving 3113
Under the Fifth Sun: A Novel of Pancho Villa - Earl
  Shorris 5832
El Vago - Laurence Gonzales 2474

Villa, Pancho
The Old Gringo - Carlos Fuentes 2247

Walker, Coalhouse
Ragtime - E.L. Doctorow 1658

Walker, William
The Journal of Colonel De Lancey - James Warner
  Bellah 426
The Lion's Skin - Darwin Le Ora Teilhet 6197

Wang Lee
Rebels of the Heavenly Kingdom - Katherine
  Paterson 4828

Zapata, Emiliano
The Crimson Wind - Max Hennessy 2832
Not of War Only - Norman Zollinger 6966
The Prison Notebooks of Ricardo Flores Magon -
  Douglas Day 1545
Tom Mix and Pancho Villa - Clifford Irving 3113
El Vago - Laurence Gonzales 2474

RODEO RIDER

Fletcher, George
Last Go Round - Ken Kesey 3473

Spain, Johnathan E. Lee
Last Go Round - Ken Kesey 3473

Sundown, Jackson
Last Go Round - Ken Kesey 3473

ROYALTY

Absalom
Bathsheba - Torgny Lindgren 3789
David: Warrior and King - Frank G. Slaughter 5885
Tamar - Ann Chamberlin 975

Adiawano
Savage Gentleman - Noel B. Gerson 2381

Agotime
Agotime, Her Legend - Judith Gleason 2430

Agrippina
Nero - Mary Teresa Ronalds 5437

Aidan
Alamut - Judith Tarr 6164

Albert Edward, Duke of Clarence
The Whitechapel Horrors - Edward B. Hanna 2678
The Women of Whitechapel and Jack the Ripper - Paul
  West 6638

Albert of Saxe-Coburg-Gotha
Albert's Victoria - Tyler Whittle 6719
Bertie, Albert Edward, Prince of Wales - Tyler
  Whittle 6720
The Captive of Kensington Palace - Jean
  Plaidy 5007
Castle of Foxes - Alanna Knight 3516
Consort for Victoria - William Vaughan
  Wilkins 6757
Flashman at the Charge - George MacDonald
  Fraser 2209
The Iron Roads - Forbes Bramble 644
The Prime Minister's Wife - Doris Leslie 3727
The Queen and Lord M - Jean Plaidy 5046
Queen Victoria's Bomb - Ronald Clark 1094
The Queen's Husband - Jean Plaidy 5052
Seven Tempest - William Vaughan Wilkins 6761
Swandowne - Daniel Farson 2024
Victoria and Albert - Evelyn Anthony 166
Victoria Victorious - Jean Plaidy 5073
The Young Victoria - Tyler Whittle 6724

Aldith
The Norman Pretender - Valerie Anand 132

Alexander
The Prince and the Pilgrim - Mary Stewart 6032

Alexandra
Valentina - Evelyn Anthony 165

Alexandra Feodorovna
And the Stars Shall Fall - True Bowen 603
The Dawning of Deliverance - Judith Pella 4892
Devoted Friends - Joe Poyer 5161
Elizabeth and Alexandra - Antony Lambton 3616
God Save the Tsar - Susanna Hoe 2976
Heirs of the Motherland - Judith Pella 4893
Love and Honor - Leslie Arlen 189
Rasputin's Revenge - John T. Lescroart 3725
Searching for the Emperor - Roberto Pazzi 4858
The Summer Day Is Done - R.T. Stevens 6001
Time After Time - Allen Appel 171

Alexandra of Denmark
Bertie, Albert Edward, Prince of Wales - Tyler
  Whittle 6720
Bertie and the Seven Bodies - Peter Lovesey 3908
Edward - Tyler Whittle 6721
The Second Sister - Leslie O'Grady 4701
The Widow of Windsor - Jean Plaidy 5076

Alexandrina Victoria
Blackstone - Richard Falkirk 2006

Alfred Atheling
Gildenford - Valerie Anand 130
The Proud Villeins - Valerie Anand 133

Alfrida
Avalon - Anya Seton 5748

Amleth
The Green Man - Henry Treece 6330

Amnon
Tamar - Ann Chamberlin 975

Andrew, Duke of York
Di and I - Peter Lefcourt 3714

Anjuli
The Far Pavilions - M.M. Kaye 3376

Anna Comnena
Count Robert of Paris - Sir Walter Scott 5695

Anne
The Elusive Crown - Hebe Elsna 1931
The Power and the Passion - Christina
  Nicholson 4609
The Queen's Husband - Samuel Edwards 1889

Anne of Austria
The Cardinal and the Queen - Evelyn Anthony 159
Cinq-Mars - Alfred Victor de Vigny 6495
The Three Musketeers - Alexandre Dumas 1782
Twenty Years After - Alexandre Dumas 1783
Wife to Great Buckingham - Hilda Lewis 3751

Anne of Bohemia
The Lords of Lancaster - Pamela Bennetts 452
Passage to Pontefract - Jean Plaidy 5038
Within the Hollow Crown - Margaret Campbell
  Barnes 331

Anne of Cleves
The Autobiography of Henry VIII - Margaret
  George 2355
The Fifth Queen - Ford Madox Ford 2161
Henry VIII and His Six Wives - Maureen
  Peters 4975
Kathryn: In the Court of Six Queens - Anne Merton
  Abbey 1
King's Fool - Margaret Campbell Barnes 325
My Lady of Cleves - Margaret Campbell Barnes 328
The Rose Without a Thorn - Jean Plaidy 5058
The Wise Virgin - Hebe Elsna 1934

Anne of Denmark
Daughter of Eve - Noel B. Gerson 2366
For My Great Folly - Thomas B. Costain 1365
Mine is the Kingdom - Jane Oliver 4726
The Murder in the Tower - Jean Plaidy 5035
Powhatan's Daughter - John Clarke Bowman 605
Unicorn Rampant - Nigel Tranter 6323

Antigone
The Eagle King - Henry Treece 6327

Ariadne
The King Must Die - Mary Renault 5298

Aricia
The Eagle and the Raven - Pauline Gedge 2344

Armstrong-Jones, Margaret
The Queen and I - Sue Townsend 6306

Arthur, Prince of Wales
Katharine: The Virgin Widow - Jean Plaidy 5025
The Prince of Darkness - Jean Plaidy 5044

Ashur, Tiglath
The Assyrian - Nicholas Guild 2610
The Blood Star - Nicholas Guild 2611

Aspasia
The Eagle's Daughter - Judith Tarr 6165

Astrov, Leonid
The Astrov Legacy - Constance Heaven 2802

d'Aubigne, Francoise
The Cat and the King - Louis Auchincloss 229
*The Crown and the Shadow: The Story of Francoise
  d'Aubigne, Marquise de Maintenon* - Pamela
  Hill 2930
The Gilded Torch - Iola Fuller 2252

The King's Way - Francoise Chandernagor 986
Ward of the Sun King - Mildred Allen Butler 826

Bahadur, Victor
Raj - Gita Mehta 4325

Bak-Isis
The River and the Stone: Moses' Early Years in Egypt - Kathleen Jenks 3192

Bathsheba
Bathsheba - Roberta Kells Dorr 1695
Bathsheba - Torgny Lindgren 3789
David at Olivet - Wallace Hamilton 2671
David of Jerusalem - Louis De Wohl 1564
David: Warrior and King - Frank G. Slaughter 5885
King David - Gwyn Jenkins 3191
King of Kings: A Novel of the Life of David - Malachi Martin 4134
Solomon and Sheba - Faye Levine 3740

Beatrice
Princess in Amber - Evelyn Wilde Mayerson 4205
The Widow of Windsor - Tyler Whittle 6723

Beaufort, Joan
James and Joan - Anne Fremantle 2221

Beaufort, Margaret
Women of Ashdon - Valerie Anand 135

Beauharnais, Hortense de
A Rose for Virtue - Norah Lofts 3858

Belshazzar
Babylon - Anthony Esler 1959

Ben Hur, Judah
Ben Hur: A Tale of the Christ - Lew Wallace 6536

Berengaria of Navarre
The Devil Is Loose - Graham Shelby 5790
The Heart of the Lion - Jean Plaidy 5020
The Kings of Vain Intent - Graham Shelby 5791
Lionheart!: A Novel of Richard I, King of England - Martha Rofheart 5428
The Lute Player - Norah Lofts 3852
My Lord Brother the Lionheart - Molly Costain Haycraft 2795
The Revolt of the Eaglets - Jean Plaidy 5057
The Talisman - Sir Walter Scott 5708

Berenice Basagrippa
Agrippa's Daughter - Howard Fast 2025

Blanche de Castille
The Battle of the Queens - Jean Plaidy 5005

Bogoljubov, Vassily
The Power and the Passion - Christina Nicholson 4609

Boguslav
The Deluge - Henryk Sienkiewicz 5846

Bohemond I
A Booke of Days: A Journal of the Crusade by Roger, Duke of Lunel - Stephen J. Rivele 5351

Boleyn, Anne
Anne Boleyn - Evelyn Anthony 158
Anne of the Thousand Days - Edward Fenton 2059
The Autobiography of Henry VIII - Margaret George 2355
Blood Royal - Mollie Hardwick 2690
Brief Gaudy Hour - Margaret Campbell Barnes 322
The Concubine - Norah Lofts 3839
The Heir of Allington - Philippa Wiat 6727
Henry VIII and His Six Wives - Maureen Peters 4975
In the Shadow of the Crown - Jean Plaidy 5022
Kathryn: In the Court of Six Queens - Anne Merton Abbey 1
King's Fool - Margaret Campbell Barnes 325
The King's Pleasure - Jean Plaidy 5026
The Lady in the Tower - Jean Plaidy 5028
The Man on a Donkey - H.F.M. Prescott 5170
Mistress Anne - Carolly Erickson 1952

Murder Most Royal - Jean Plaidy 5036
My Lord of Canterbury - Godfrey Turton 6369
Queen Anne Boleyn - Francis Hackett 2634
The Sword of Truth - Gilbert Morris 4472
Windsor Castle - William Harrison Ainsworth 59

Bolingbroke, Henry
Trumpet at the Gate - Jan Widgery 6739
Within the Hollow Crown - Margaret Campbell Barnes 331

Bolkonsky, Andrey
War and Peace - Leo Tolstoy 6295

Bonaparte, Caroline
My Brother Napoleon: The Confessions of Caroline Bonaparte - F.W. Kenyon 3455

Bonaparte, Jerome
The Amazing Mrs. Bonaparte - Harnett T. Kane 3351
My Dear Cousin - Peggy Hoffmann 2977

Bonaparte, Louis
A Rose for Virtue - Norah Lofts 3858

Bonaparte, Louis Napoleon
Rachel - Anne Powers 5153

Brighde
Swords in the North - Paul Lewis Anderson 138

Bruce, Marjorie
Marjorie of Scotland - Pamela Hill 2939

Brunahild
The Wolf and the Raven - Diana L. Paxson 4848

Burgh, Elizabeth de
Robert the Bruce: The Path of the Hero King - Nigel Tranter 6318
Robert the Bruce: The Price of the King's Peace - Nigel Tranter 6319
Robert the Bruce: The Steps to the Empty Throne - Nigel Tranter 6320

Caradoc
The Dark Island - Henry Treece 6326
The Eagle and the Raven - Pauline Gedge 2344

Carlos de Austria, Don
The Spanish Bridegroom - Jean Plaidy 5064

Carlota
The Breast of the Dove - Herbert Gorman 2491
The Cactus and the Crown - Catherine Gavin 2318
Chapultepec - Norman Zollinger 6965
Flames of Empire - Peter Bourne 594
The Grasshopper King - Elizabeth Boatwright Coker 1165
Passengers to Mexico: The Last Invasion of Mexico - Blair Niles 4627

Caroline-Matilda
The Lost Queen - Norah Lofts 3850
The Queen's Physician - Edgar Maas 3952

Caroline of Ansbach
Caroline the Queen - Jean Plaidy 5009
The Heart of Midlothian - Sir Walter Scott 5698
Queen in Waiting - Jean Plaidy 5048

Caroline of Brunswick
The Abandoned Woman - Richard Condon 1235
Brumaire - Mark Logan 3864
The Flight of the Eagle - Donald Thomas 6239
Footman in Powder - Helen Ashton 216
Regency Royal - Michael Hardwick 2687
The Regent's Daughter - Jean Plaidy 5055

Cassandra
Whom the Gods Would Destroy - Richard Powell 5148

Catherine I
Katrina - Jeramie Price 5190

Catherine, Grand Duchess of Russia
Far Flies the Eagle - Evelyn Anthony 162

Catherine of Aragon
Anne Boleyn - Evelyn Anthony 158
Anne of the Thousand Days - Edward Fenton 2059
The Autobiography of Henry VIII - Margaret George 2355
The Concubine - Norah Lofts 3839
Henry VIII and His Six Wives - Maureen Peters 4975
The Hireling - Alison Macleod 4003
I Am Mary Tudor - Hilda Lewis 3750
In the Shadow of the Crown - Jean Plaidy 5022
Katharine: The Virgin Widow - Jean Plaidy 5025
Kathryn: In the Court of Six Queens - Anne Merton Abbey 1
The King's Pleasure - Norah Lofts 3847
The King's Pleasure - Jean Plaidy 5026
The King's Secret Matter - Jean Plaidy 5027
The Lady in the Tower - Jean Plaidy 5028
The Man on a Donkey - H.F.M. Prescott 5170
Queen Anne Boleyn - Francis Hackett 2634
The Reluctant Queen - Molly Costain Haycraft 2796
The Shadow of the Pomegranate - Jean Plaidy 5062
The Sword of Truth - Gilbert Morris 4472
Uneasy Lies the Head - Jean Plaidy 5071
The White Rose Murders - Michael Clynes 1137

Catherine of Braganza
Catherine - Hilda Lewis 3746
A Health Unto His Majesty - Jean Plaidy 5019
The King's Bastard - Hebe Elsna 1932
The King's Brat - Constance Gluyas 2441
The Pleasures of Love - Jean Plaidy 5042
The Portingale - Alison Macleod 4005
With All My Heart - Margaret Campbell Barnes 330

Catherine of Valois
Crown in Candlelight - Rosemary Hawley Jarman 3166
Epitaph for Three Women - Jean Plaidy 5012
Fortune Made His Sword - Martha Rofheart 5426
Good King Harry - Denise Giardina 2393
Harry of Monmouth - A.M. Maughan 4199
The Queen's Secret - Jean Plaidy 5053
The Royal Pawn - Antonia Ridge 5327
The Star of Lancaster - Jean Plaidy 5065
Wife to Henry V - Hilda Lewis 3752

Ce Malinalli
Death of the Fifth Sun - Robert Somerlott 5944

Cea
Canis the Warrior - James Sinclair 5864

Ceawlin
Born of the Sun - Joan Wolf 6837

Chantra
Temple Bells - Marjorie McEvoy 4271

Charis
Taliesin - Stephen R. Lawhead 3683

Charles
Campion Towers - John Beatty 401
The Fortunes of Nigel - Sir Walter Scott 5696
Myself My Enemy - Jean Plaidy 5037
Unicorn Rampant - Nigel Tranter 6323
Woodstock; or, The Cavalier - Sir Walter Scott 5710

Charles II
Forever Amber - Kathleen Winsor 6822

Charles, Duke of Burgundy
Anne of Geierstein - Sir Walter Scott 5689

Charles, Prince of Wales
Di and I - Peter Lefcourt 3714
Miss Nobody - Caroline Ross 5465
The Queen and I - Sue Townsend 6306
Royal Escape - Georgette Heyer 2900

Charlotte of Mecklenburg-Strelitz
The Bonnet Laird's Daughter - Barbara Annandale 154
Goddess of the Green Room - Jean Plaidy 5016
Guillotine - Mark Logan 3865

Let the King Beware! - Honore Morrow 4489
Regency Royal - Michael Hardwick 2687
Sweet Lass of Richmond Hill - Jean Plaidy 5067
The Third George - Jean Plaidy 5068

Charlotte, Princess of Wales
The Girl Who Was Never Queen: A Biographical Novel of Princess Charlotte of Wales - Mary Main 4037
The Regent's Daughter - Jean Plaidy 5055

Clemence of Hungary
The Poisoned Crown - Maurice Druon 1734
The Royal Succession - Maurice Druon 1735

Cleopatra
Caesar - Allan Massie 4168

Clytemnestra
Amber Princess - Henry Treece 6325
Scandal in Troy - Eva Hemmer Hansen 2679

Commodus, Lucius Aelius Aurelius
Roman Nights - Ron Burns 803

Copilli
Copilli, Aztec Prince - Miguel Aleman Velasco 75

Corbera, Don Fabrizio
The Leopard - Giuseppe di Lampedusa 3634

Cridilla
The Serpent's Tooth - Diana L. Paxson 4846

d'Agrigente, Emma
1876: A Novel - Gore Vidal 6484

d'Asselnat, Marianne
Marianne and the Crown of Fire - Juliette Benzoni 467

David ap Gruffydd
The Brothers of Gwynedd - Edith Pargeter 4796

De Talmond, Prince
Hester - Brian Cleeve 1107

Dhruvadeva
Golden Fire - Jonathan Fast 2047

Diana, Princess of Wales
Di and I - Peter Lefcourt 3714
The Queen and I - Sue Townsend 6306

Domitillia
The Triumph - Ernest K. Gann 2280

Donough
Pride of Lions - Morgan Llywelyn 3823

Dubuc, Aimee
Sultana - Michael, Prince of Greece 4358

Edward
Hammer of the Scots - Jean Plaidy 5018
The She-Wolf of France - Maurice Druon 1736

Edward, Duke of Kent
The Little Victoria - Lozania Prole 5196

Edward, Duke of Windsor
Carnal Hours - Max Allan Collins 1210
A Royal Murder - Elliott Roosevelt 5456

Edward, Prince of Wales
Bertie, Albert Edward, Prince of Wales - Tyler Whittle 6720
Bertie and the Crime of Passion - Peter Lovesey 3907
Bertie and the Seven Bodies - Peter Lovesey 3908
Bertie and the Tinman - Peter Lovesey 3909
Buffalo Girls - Larry McMurtry 4296
Buller's Guns - Richard Hough 3048
Chariots of Fire - W.J. Weatherby 6586
Contessa - Helene Mansfield 4076
Dance on a Sinking Ship - Michael Kilian 3483
Death at Daisy's Folly - Robin Paige 4775
The Duchess of Duke Street - Mollie Hardwick 2693
Edward and Mrs. Simpson - A.C.H. Smith 5916
A Lady of Repute - Janice James 3158
Lillie - David Butler 818

Murder Makes an Entree - Amy Myers 4540
My Lady Hoyden - Jane Sheridan 5812
Oh! Where Are Bloody Mary's Earrings? - Robert Player 5079
The Prince of Darkness - P.C. Doherty 1675
Princess in Amber - Evelyn Wilde Mayerson 4205
The Queen's Husband - Jean Plaidy 5052
The Return of Moriarty - John E. Gardner 2287
The Robber Baroness - William Kendall Clarke 1097
A Season for Death - Ray Harrison 2743
The Second Sister - Leslie O'Grady 4701
Sergeant Verity and the Blood Royal - Francis Selwyn 5744
Sherlock Holmes Meets Annie Oakley - Stanley Shaw 5782
The Swan and the Rose - Francis W. Leary 3697
Victoria Victorious - Jean Plaidy 5073
The White Dove - Rosie Thomas 6246
The Whitechapel Horrors - Edward B. Hanna 2678
The Widow of Windsor - Jean Plaidy 5076
The Widow of Windsor - Tyler Whittle 6723

Edward, the Black Prince
By Right of Arms - Robyn Carr 937
Don Pedro's Captain - Pamela Bennetts 449
The Lady Royal - Molly Costain Haycraft 2794
The Lords of Vaumartin - Cecelia Holland 2992
Passage to Pontefract - Jean Plaidy 5038
The Vow on the Heron - Jean Plaidy 5074
The White Company - Sir Arthur Conan Doyle 1716

Edyth
The Wind From Hastings - Morgan Llywelyn 3825

Eleanor of Aquitaine
Banners of Gold - Pamela Kaufman 3371
Beloved Enemy: The Passions of Eleanor of Aquitaine - Ellen Jones 3288
Champion - L. Christian Balling 285
The Courts of Love - Jean Plaidy 5010
The Courts of Love: A Romance of Medieval France - Peter Bourne 592
The Devil Is Loose - Graham Shelby 5790
Eleanor the Queen - Norah Lofts 3842
The Heart of the Lion - Jean Plaidy 5020
Here Be Dragons - Sharon Kay Penman 4904
King's Man - C.M. Edmondston 1880
The Lion of Christ - Margaret Butler 823
The Lion of England - Margaret Butler 824
The Lion of Justice - Margaret Butler 825
Lionheart!: A Novel of Richard I, King of England - Martha Rofheart 5428
The Lute Player - Norah Lofts 3852
Mortal Love: A Novel of Eleanor of Aquitaine - Linda Hutchins 3090
The Plantagenet Prelude - Jean Plaidy 5041
The Queen's Man - Sharon Kay Penman 4905
The Queen's War: A Novel of Eleanor of Aquitaine - Jeanne Mackin 3996
The Revolt of the Eaglets - Jean Plaidy 5057
A Royal Quest - Mary Lide 3777
The Swords of December - Robert York 6933
The Troubadour's Romance - Robyn Carr 940
When Christ and His Saints Slept - Sharon Kay Penman 4908
The Wolf at the Door - Graham Shelby 5793

Eleanor of Provence
The Queen From Provence - Jean Plaidy 5047

Electra
Amber Princess - Henry Treece 6325

Elidan
Kingdom of Summer - Gillian Bradshaw 633

Elisabeth of Valois
The Spanish Bridegroom - Jean Plaidy 5064

Elissa
The Purple Quest: A Novel of Seafaring Adventure in the Ancient World - Frank G. Slaughter 5896

Elizabeth
In the Shadow of the Crown - Jean Plaidy 5022
Murder at the Palace - Elliott Roosevelt 5445

Elizabeth Fedorovna
By Command of the Viceroy - Duncan MacNeil 4010

Elizabeth, Grand Duchess Serge
Elizabeth and Alexandra - Antony Lambton 3616

Elizabeth of Bavaria
Imperial Waltz - William M. Abrahams 13

Elizabeth of Hungary
Elizabeth's Greetings - Rosemary Haughton 2774

Elizabeth of York
The Broken Sword - Rhoda S. Edwards 1885
The Daughter of Time - Josephine Tey 6209
Fire and Morning - Francis W. Leary 3696
The Queen's Sister - Sandra Wilson 6815
The Traitors of Bosworth - Robert Farrington 2021
Tudor Agent - Robert Farrington 2022
The Tudor Rose - Margaret Campbell Barnes 329
Uneasy Lies the Head - Jean Plaidy 5071
An Unknown Welshman - Jean Stubbs 6100

Elizabeth, the Queen Mother
Miss Nobody - Caroline Ross 5465
The Queen and I - Sue Townsend 6306

Elswyth
The Edge of Light - Joan Wolf 6839

Emma of Normandy
The Breath of Kings - Gene Farrington 2019
The Cunning of the Dove - Alfred Duggan 1765

Eric of Dubhlain
The Viking's Woman - Heather Graham 2520

Esharhamat
The Assyrian - Nicholas Guild 2610

Esmikan
Sofia - Ann Chamberlin 974

Esther
Esther: The Star and the Sceptre - Gina Andrews 146

Ethnea
Captive of Rome - Theodora McCormick Du Bois 1740

Eugenie
Banners of Silk - Rosalind Laker 3592
The Big Family - Vina Delmar 1600
Death Wore a Diadem - Iona McGregor 4277
Eugenie - Hester W. Chapman 989
Madeleine - Catherine Gavin 2323
The Passion of Letty Fox - Diana Saunders 5610
A Spy for Napoleon - Baroness Emma Orczy 4746
That Spanish Woman - F.W. Kenyon 3461

Falconeri, Tancredi
The Leopard - Giuseppe di Lampedusa 3634

Fara
The Big Fisherman - Lloyd C. Douglas 1702

Farag, Ahmed Hassan
In the Shadow of the Nile - Sara Hylton 3093

Fedorcenko, Katrina
The Crown and the Crucible - Michael Phillips 4987
A House Divided - Michael Phillips 4988

Fedorcenko, Sergei
The Dawning of Deliverance - Judith Pella 4892
Heirs of the Motherland - Judith Pella 4893
A House Divided - Michael Phillips 4988
Travail and Triumph - Michael Phillips 4991

Ferguson, Sarah Margaret
Di and I - Peter Lefcourt 3714

Fiann Sionna
The Emerald Crown - Theodora McCormick Du Bois 1741

Francois
Queen's Play - Dorothy Dunnett 1805

Francois II
Mary, Queen of Scotland and the Isles - Margaret George 2356

Franz Ferdinand
The Devil's Lieutenant - Maria Fagyas 1998
The First Casualty - William Powell 5149

Frederick
Waterloo - Bernard Cornwell 1350

Frederick III
The Girl Who Was Never Queen: A Biographical Novel of Princess Charlotte of Wales - Mary Main 4037

Frederick Augustus
The Duke's Mistress: The Story of Mary Ann Clarke - F.W. Kenyon 3447
Guillotine - Mark Logan 3865
Mary Anne - Daphne Du Maurier 1749
Regency Royal - Michael Hardwick 2687
The Regent's Daughter - Jean Plaidy 5055
Tricolour - Mark Logan 3866

Galitzine, Asya
Asya - Michael Ignatieff 3103

Galla Placidia
Heaven's Only Daughter - Kathleen Robinson 5406

Gaminini
The Winds of Sinhala - Colin De Silva 1562

George
Brumaire - Mark Logan 3864
Buller's Guns - Richard Hough 3048
Claire - Elizabeth Lyle 3931
The Duke's Mistress: The Story of Mary Ann Clarke - F.W. Kenyon 3447
Edward, Edward - Lolah Burford 772
The Girl Who Was Never Queen: A Biographical Novel of Princess Charlotte of Wales - Mary Main 4037
Goddess of the Green Room - Jean Plaidy 5016
Guillotine - Mark Logan 3865
Now Face to Face - Karleen Koen 3530
Perdita's Prince - Jean Plaidy 5040
The Prince and the Quakeress - Jean Plaidy 5043
Regency Royal - Michael Hardwick 2687
Sweet Lass of Richmond Hill - Jean Plaidy 5067
The Third George - Jean Plaidy 5068
Tricolour - Mark Logan 3866
Yankee - Dana Fuller Ross 5495

George V
Buller's Dreadnought - Richard Hough 3047

George Augustus
Queen in Waiting - Jean Plaidy 5048

George, Duke of Clarence
The Dragon Waiting: A Masque of History - John M. Ford 2165
The Sun in Splendour - Jean Plaidy 5066

George, Duke of York
Edward and Mrs. Simpson - A.C.H. Smith 5916

George, Prince of Wales
Footman in Powder - Helen Ashton 216
Lord Fancy - Leslie Turner White 6686
The Scarlet Pimpernel - Baroness Emma Orczy 4745
The Smile of the Stranger - Joan Aiken 53
The Stranger From the Sea - Winston Graham 2530

George, Prince Regent
Elyza - Clare Darcy 1486
The Flight of the Eagle - Donald Thomas 6239
Flying Colours - C.S. Forester 2173
A Love So Wild - Deborah Chester 1056

Regency Rogue - Helen Ashfield 212
The Regent's Daughter - Jean Plaidy 5055
Sanguinet's Crown - Patricia Veryan 6476
Sharpe's Regiment - Bernard Cornwell 1345
The Sugar Pavilion - Rosalind Laker 3600
Victoria in the Wings - Jean Plaidy 5072

Gintult, Prince
Ashes - Stefan Zeromski 6960

Giolitti-Crispi, Lorenzo
Summoned to Darkness - Anne-Marie Sheridan 5809

Glendower, Owen
Glendower Country - Martha Rofheart 5427

Godwinson, Fallon
Princess of Fire - Shannon Drake 1718

Golden Bells
Messer Marco Polo - Donn Byrne 840

Gormlaith
The Lion of Ireland - Morgan Llywelyn 3822
Pride of Lions - Morgan Llywelyn 3823

Grey, Lady Jane
My Lord of Canterbury - Godfrey Turton 6369
The Tower of London - William Harrison Ainsworth 58

Groa
King Hereafter - Dorothy Dunnett 1802

Gruoch
Lady of Moray - Bonnie Copeland 1318

Guenevere
Beloved Exile - Parke Godwin 2446
Firelord - Parke Godwin 2447
The Idylls of the Queen - Phyllis Ann Karr 3367
The Once and Future King - T.H. White 6705

Guinevere
Arthur Rex: A Legendary Novel - Thomas Berger 477
The Chessboard Queen - Sharan Newman 4597
Child of the Northern Spring - Persia Woolley 6867
The Emperor Arthur - Godfrey Turton 6368
First Knight - Elizabeth Chadwick 966
Guinevere Evermore - Sharan Newman 4601
Guinevere: The Legend in Autumn - Persia Woolley 6868
The King - Donald Barthelme 365
The Last Enchantment - Mary Stewart 6031
The Pendragon - Catherine Christian 1075
Queen of the Summer Stars - Persia Woolley 6869
The Queen's Knight - Marvin Borowsky 585
The Wicked Day - Mary Stewart 6033
The Winter King - Bernard Cornwell 1351
Witch of the North - Courtway Jones 3272

Gunarduilla
The Serpent's Tooth - Diana L. Paxson 4846

Gupta, Candra
Golden Fire - Jonathan Fast 2047

Gupta, Rama
Golden Fire - Jonathan Fast 2047

Guthfrid
Born of the Sun - Joan Wolf 6837

Gwenhwyfar
The Mists of Avalon - Marion Zimmer Bradley 626
Pendragon's Banner - Helen Hollick 3001

Gwenhwyvar
Arthur - Stephen R. Lawhead 3679

Gwinfreda
Artorius Rex - John Gloag 2432

Gwladys
The Captive Princess - Maxine Shore 5831

Gwynhwyfar
In Winter's Shadow - Gillian Bradshaw 632

Gwynmead, Cadwaladr
The Summer of the Danes - Ellis Peters 4973

Gwynmead, Owain
The Summer of the Danes - Ellis Peters 4973

Hadassah
Esther - Nathaniel Norsen Weinreb 6601

Hagan
Attila's Treasure - Stephan Grundy 2606

Hagar
Hagar - Cothburn O'Neal 4737

Harald
The Iron Crown - Clare Barroll 354

Harrap
The Seeking - Robert S. Elegant 1906

Hartburg, Aurora
A Castle in Bavaria - Prince Thibaut d'Orleans 1693

Hartburg, Gottfried von
A Castle in Bavaria - Prince Thibaut d'Orleans 1693

Hartburg, Ruprecht
A Castle in Bavaria - Prince Thibaut d'Orleans 1693

Hatshepsut
The Golden Balance - Arthur Dana Hall 2646

Helen of Troy
The Goddess - Miranda Seymour 5763
Paris of Troy - George Baker 273
The Private Life of Helen of Troy - John Erskine 1957

Helena
Julian - Gore Vidal 6489

Heliokleia
Horses of Heaven - Gillian Bradshaw 630

Henri of Anjou
Queen Margot - Alexandre Dumas 1780

Henrietta Anne of England
The Wandering Prince - Jean Plaidy 5075

Henrietta-Maria
Charles the King - Evelyn Anthony 160
Lady on the Coin - Margaret Campbell Barnes 326
My Lord Foxe - Constance Gluyas 2443
Myself My Enemy - Jean Plaidy 5037
Peveril of the Peak - Sir Walter Scott 5703
Twenty Years After - Alexandre Dumas 1783
Wife to Great Buckingham - Hilda Lewis 3751
The Young and Lonely King - Jane Lane 3659

Henry
The Bastard King - Jean Plaidy 5004
Katharine: The Virgin Widow - Jean Plaidy 5025
The Paladin - George Shipway 5830
The Star of Lancaster - Jean Plaidy 5065
The Thistle and the Rose - Jean Plaidy 5069
Uneasy Lies the Head - Jean Plaidy 5071

Henry II
The Earl - Cecelia Holland 2987

Henry of Battenburg
Princess in Amber - Evelyn Wilde Mayerson 4205

Henry of Monmouth
Harry of Monmouth - A.M. Maughan 4199

Henry of Wales
Di and I - Peter Lefcourt 3714

Henry the Navigator
The Mapmaker: A Novel of the Days of Prince Henry, the Navigator - Frank G. Slaughter 5893

Herod Agrippa I
I, Claudius - Robert Graves 2547

Herod Agrippa II
Claudius the God - Robert Graves 2543

Hilton, Andhra
Star of Randevi - Marjorie McEvoy 4270

Honoria
Throne of the World - Louis De Wohl 1575

Howard, Catherine
Here Comes the King - Philip Lindsay 3792
Katheryn, the Wanton Queen - Maureen Peters 4976
Kathryn: In the Court of Six Queens - Anne Merton Abbey 1
Murder Most Royal - Jean Plaidy 5036
The Red-Haired Brat - Joanna Dessau 1627
The Rose Without a Thorn - Jean Plaidy 5058

Howard, Katherine
The Fifth Queen - Ford Madox Ford 2161
Henry VIII and His Six Wives - Maureen Peters 4975
King's Fool - Margaret Campbell Barnes 325
The Wise Virgin - Hebe Elsna 1934

Ilchee
Columbia - Pamela Jekel 3184

Imogen
Roman Go Home! - Adam Fergusson 2065

Iona
Princess of the Veil - Helen Mittermeyer 4420

Irena of Moldavia
Flight From Bucharest - R.T. Stevens 6000

Isabeau
In a Dark Wood Wandering - Hella S. Haasse 2631
The Royal Pawn - Antonia Ridge 5327

Isabeau of Bavaria
Wife to Henry V - Hilda Lewis 3752

Isabel
The Lady Royal - Molly Costain Haycraft 2794

Isabel of Bourbon
I, the King - Frances Parkinson Keyes 3479

Isabel of France
Isabel the Fair - Margaret Campbell Barnes 323

Isabel of Hainault
The Rain Maiden - Jill M. Phillips 4985

Isabel of Portugal
Master of Castile - Samuel Edwards 1888

Isabella of Angouleme
The Barons of Runnymede - Pamela Bennetts 445
The Battle of the Queens - Jean Plaidy 5005
The Prince of Darkness - Jean Plaidy 5044
The Wolf at the Door - Graham Shelby 5793

Isabella of France
Braveheart - Randall Wallace 6538
The Death of a King - P.C. Doherty 1672
The Follies of the King - Jean Plaidy 5014
The Gentle Falcon - Hilda Lewis 3747
Harlot Queen - Hilda Lewis 3748
The Iron King - Maurice Druon 1732
The Lily and the Lion - Maurice Druon 1733
The Lion and the Leopard - Mary Ellen Johnson 3226
The Lords of Lancaster - Pamela Bennetts 452
Passage to Pontefract - Jean Plaidy 5038
The She-Wolf - Pamela Bennetts 456
The She-Wolf of France - Maurice Druon 1736
The Star of Lancaster - Jean Plaidy 5065
A Tapestry of Murders - C.L. Grace 2510
The Vow on the Heron - Jean Plaidy 5074
Vows of the Peacock - Alice Walworth Graham 2513

Isabelle de Bourbon
The Marranos - Liliane Webb 6588

Isca
The Golden Strangers - Henry Treece 6328

Isolde
The White Raven - Diana L. Paxson 4847

Itaz
Horses of Heaven - Gillian Bradshaw 630

Itchakoma
Jubal Sackett - Louis L'Amour 3620

Iveta
The Leper of St. Giles - Ellis Peters 4963

James
The Thistle and the Rose - Jean Plaidy 5069
The Three Crowns - Jean Plaidy 5070

Jayarajadevi
When God Slept - Peter Bourne 597

Jezebel
The Curse of Jezebel: A Novel of the Biblical Queen of Evil - Frank G. Slaughter 5884
Jezebel - Dorothy Clarke Wilson 6802
Merari - Gloria Howe Bremkamp 656

Joan
Harp into Battle - Cecil Maiden 4031
Here Be Dragons - Sharon Kay Penman 4904

Joan of Sicily
My Lord Brother the Lionheart - Molly Costain Haycraft 2795

Johann
The Ugly Duchess - Lion Feuchtwanger 2075

John
Banners of Gold - Pamela Kaufman 3371
Champion - L. Christian Balling 285
The Courts of Love - Jean Plaidy 5010
The Heart of the Lion - Jean Plaidy 5020
Ivanhoe - Sir Walter Scott 5699
The Lords of Vaumartin - Cecelia Holland 2992
The Rain Maiden - Jill M. Phillips 4985

John, Duke of Bedford
My Lord John - Georgette Heyer 2895

John Lackland
The Devil Is Loose - Graham Shelby 5790

John of Gaunt
Falstaff - Robert Nye 4653
Fortune Made His Sword - Martha Rofheart 5426
The Gentle Falcon - Hilda Lewis 3747
Good King Harry - Denise Giardina 2393
Harry of Monmouth - A.M. Maughan 4199
Katherine - Anya Seton 5752
The Lords of Lancaster - Pamela Bennetts 452
The Love Knot - Catherine Darby 1482
The Nightingale Gallery - Paul Harding 2684
Passage to Pontefract - Jean Plaidy 5038
The Peacock and the Pearl - Jennifer Lang 3661
Riddle Me a Murder - Duane Crowley 1435
The Star of Lancaster - Jean Plaidy 5065
The Vow on the Heron - Jean Plaidy 5074
Who Was Then the Gentleman - Charles E. Israel 3125
Within the Hollow Crown - Margaret Campbell Barnes 331

Josephine
Desiree - Annemarie Selinko 5741
The Eagle and the Rock - Frances Winwar 6830
The Emperor's Lady: A Novel Based on the Life of the Empress Josephine - F.W. Kenyon 3449
Far Flies the Eagle - Evelyn Anthony 162
Mirage - Ruth McKenney 4283
My Brother Napoleon: The Confessions of Caroline Bonaparte - F.W. Kenyon 3455
Napoleon Symphony - Anthony Burgess 780
The Raven and the Rose - Susan Wiggs 6746
A Rose for Virtue - Norah Lofts 3858
The Rose of Malmaison: The Turbulent Life of the Beautiful Josephine - Gaby von Schonthan 5660
So Great a Man - David Pilgrim 5000
Sultana - Michael, Prince of Greece 4358
Tom Burke of Ours - Charles James Lever 3732

Juan of Austria
The Last Crusader - Louis De Wohl 1569

Juan, Prince of the Asturias
Here Lies Margot - Pamela Hill 2935

Jujiro
Sakuran: A Novel of Medieval Japan - Edward Tolosko 6292

Julia
I Loved Tiberius - Elisabeth Dored 1692

Kassandra
The Firebrand - Marion Zimmer Bradley 624

Katherine of Aragon
King's Fool - Margaret Campbell Barnes 325
Mistress Anne - Carolly Erickson 1952

Khaemwaset
Mirage - Pauline Gedge 2346

Khana Tule Yasmin
Yankee - Dana Fuller Ross 5495

Kia
The River and the Stone: Moses' Early Years in Egypt - Kathleen Jenks 3192

Kurtsevich, Helena
With Fire and Sword - Henryk Sienkiewicz 5850

Lamsaloff, Mischa
The Only Sin - Julie Ellis 1923

Lassiter, Lakshmi
The Frog Earl - Carola Dunn 1792

Leopold of Saxe-Coburg
The Regent's Daughter - Jean Plaidy 5055

Lien
A House in Peiking - Robert Payne 4853

Livia
I Loved Tiberius - Elisabeth Dored 1692
Tiberius: The Memoirs of the Emperor - Allan Massie 4169

Llywelyn ap Gruffydd
The Brothers of Gwynedd - Edith Pargeter 4796
A Dragon for Edward - Pamela Bennetts 450
Falls the Shadow - Sharon Kay Penman 4903
Hammer of the Scots - Jean Plaidy 5018
The Heaven Tree Trilogy - Edith Pargeter 4797
The Reckoning - Sharon Kay Penman 4906
The Wind From Hastings - Morgan Llywelyn 3825

Llywelyn ap Iowerth
Here Be Dragons - Sharon Kay Penman 4904

Louis
Niccolo Rising - Dorothy Dunnett 1803

Louis XVII
Cockades: A Romance - Meade Minnigerode 4412
A King Reluctant - William Vaughan Wilkins 6759
Seed of Mischief - Willa Gibbs 2401
The Uncrowned King - Baroness Emma Orczy 4747

Louis Charles
Fear No More - Hester W. Chapman 990
The Man Who Killed the King - Dennis Wheatley 6654
The Prince Lost to Time - Ann Dukthas 1776

Louis, Comte de Provence
Scaramouche the King-Maker - Rafael Sabatini 5555

Louis de Valois
A Comedy of Murders - George Herman 2861

Lucia
Josephus and the Emperor - Lion Feuchtwanger 2073

Ludwig II
Sherlock in Love - Sena Jeter Naslund 4557

Lunyevitza-Mashin, Draga
Dance of the Assassins - Maria Fagyas 1997

Lusignan, James de
Race of Scorpions - Dorothy Dunnett 1806

Lusignon, Carlotta de
Race of Scorpions - Dorothy Dunnett   1806

Lygia
Quo Vadis - Henryk Sienkiewicz   5848

Madoc
The Children of the First Man - James Alexander
  Thom   6230

Madoc of Powys
A Moment in Time - Bertrice Small   5911

Maeve
Red Branch - Morgan Llywelyn   3824

Marcius
The Eagle and the Crown - Hubertus
  Loewenstein   3832

Marda
Druid's Enchantment - Millie J. Ragosta   5240

Margaret
Sing Morning Star - Jane Oliver   4727

Margaret of Anjou
Anne of Geierstein - Sir Walter Scott   5689
The Dragon Waiting: A Masque of History - John M.
  Ford   2165
Red Rose of Anjou - Jean Plaidy   5054
The Swan and the Rose - Francis W. Leary   3697

Margaret of Austria
The Gentle Fury: A Novel of Margaret of Austria -
  Paul Lewis   3758

Margaret Rose
Di and I - Peter Lefcourt   3714
Murder at the Palace - Elliott Roosevelt   5445

Margot
Evergreen Gallant - Jean Plaidy   5013
The Italian Woman - Jean Plaidy   5024
Queen Jezebel - Jean Plaidy   5049

Marguerite de Bourgogne
The Strangled Queen - Maurice Druon   1737

Marguerite de Valois
Queen Margot - Alexandre Dumas   1780
Young Henry of Navarre - Heinrich Mann   4062

Maria Louisa Victoria, Duchess of Kent
The Captive of Kensington Palace - Jean
  Plaidy   5007
The Queen and Lord M - Jean Plaidy   5046

Maria Theresa
The Shadow of the Sun - Sylvia Pell   4891

Mariana of Austria
I, the King - Frances Parkinson Keyes   3479

Marie Antoinette
Asylum for the Queen - Mildred A. Jordan   3303
City of Darkness, City of Light - Marge Piercy   4998
The Devil's Laughter - Frank Yerby   6913
*Dr. Guillotine: The Eccentric Exploits of an Early
  Scientist* - Herbert Lom   3867
*The Fatal Friendship: Marie Antoinette, Count Fersen
  and the Flight to Varennes* - Stanley Loomis   3895
Fear No More - Hester W. Chapman   990
The Frenchwoman - Jeanne Mackin   3995
I Thee Wed - Gilbert Wolf Gabriel   2267
King's Masque - Evan John   3220
The Man Who Killed the King - Dennis
  Wheatley   6654
Marie Antoinette - F.W. Kenyon   3453
Palaces of Desire - Kate Alexander   81
The Prince Lost to Time - Ann Dukthas   1776
The Queen's Confession - Victoria Holt   3019
The Queen's Necklace - Alexandre Dumas   1781
Sweet Marie-Antoinette - Lozania Prole   5198
To Dance with Kings - Rosalind Laker   3601
Tricolour - Mark Logan   3866

Marie de Guise
Mary, Queen of Scotland and the Isles - Margaret
  George   2356

Marie Louise of Austria
Emperor's Ladies - Noel B. Gerson   2367
Far Flies the Eagle - Evelyn Anthony   162
*My Brother Napoleon: The Confessions of Caroline
  Bonaparte* - F.W. Kenyon   3455

Marie-Therese
*The Crown and the Shadow: The Story of Francoise
  d'Aubigne, Marquise de Maintenon* - Pamela
  Hill   2930
The Oracle Glass - Judith Merkle Riley   5335

Marina
The Golden Princess - Alexander Baron   335

Marisco, Jasmine de
Wild Jasmine - Bertrice Small   5914

Mary
The Elusive Crown - Hebe Elsna   1931
The Three Crowns - Jean Plaidy   5070

Mary of Guise
The Game of Kings - Dorothy Dunnett   1801
Queen's Play - Dorothy Dunnett   1805
The Sword and the Flame - Pamela Hill   2945

Mary of Teck
Edward and Mrs. Simpson - A.C.H. Smith   5916
Murder at the Palace - Elliott Roosevelt   5445

Mary, Queen of Scots
The Abbot - Sir Walter Scott   5688

Matilda
The Lion of Justice - Jean Plaidy   5031
The Passionate Enemies - Jean Plaidy   5039
Stephen and the Sleeping Saints - Pamela
  Bennetts   457
Theo and Matilda - Rachel Billington   498

Matilda of Flanders
The Bastard King - Jean Plaidy   5004
The Disputed Crown - Valerie Anand   128
*Fortune's Knave: The Making of William the
  Conqueror* - Mary Lide   3774
The Golden Warrior: The Story of Harold and William
  - Hope Muntz   4517
The Saxon Tapestry - Sile Rice   5317
Sherwood - Parke Godwin   2449
Wife to the Bastard - Hilda Lewis   3753

Maud
The Fatal Crown - Ellen Jones   3289
When Christ and His Saints Slept - Sharon Kay
  Penman   4908

Maximilian
The Breast of the Dove - Herbert Gorman   2491
Passengers to Mexico: The Last Invasion of Mexico -
  Blair Niles   4627

Medici, Catherine de'
Courtesan - Diane Haeger   2635
Evergreen Gallant - Jean Plaidy   5013
The Faith and the Flame - June Dimmit
  Houston   3054
Immortal Queen - Elizabeth Byrd   834
The Italian Woman - Jean Plaidy   5024
The Longest Night - Ada Cook Lewis   3744
Madame Serpent - Jean Plaidy   5033
Mary, Queen of Scotland and the Isles - Margaret
  George   2356
The Negotiators - Francis Walder   6526
Les Quarant Cinq - Alexandre Dumas   1779
Queen Jezebel - Jean Plaidy   5049
Queen Margot - Alexandre Dumas   1780
Queen's Play - Dorothy Dunnett   1805

Medici, Marie de'
Evergreen Gallant - Jean Plaidy   5013

Mei Ling
Tournament of the Shadows - Nicholas Carnac   901

Meinhard
The Ugly Duchess - Lion Feuchtwanger   2075

Mendoza, Ana de
For One Sweet Grape - Kate O'Brien   4681

Meriamon
Lord of the Two Lands - Judith Tarr   6167

Michael
*The Curse of Jezebel: A Novel of the Biblical Queen of
  Evil* - Frank G. Slaughter   5884

Minerva
Curtains for the Cardinal - Elizabeth Eyre   1991

Mirana
Lord of Hawkfell Island - Catherine Coulter   1376

Mironov, Katya
Horses of War - Duff Hart-Davis   2760

Mixcatl
The Jaguar Princess - Clare Bell   421

Modred
Guinevere: The Legend in Autumn - Persia
  Woolley   6868

Monmouth, Harry
The Bloody Field - Edith Pargeter   4795
Glendower Country - Martha Rofheart   5427
The Hooded Falcon - Prudence Andrew   140
Royal Sword at Agincourt - Pamela Bennetts   455

Morgana
The Viking - Edison Marshall   4113

Moses
Moses - Sholem Asch   199

Murat, Joachim
Far Flies the Eagle - Evelyn Anthony   162
Valentina - Evelyn Anthony   165

Naksh-i-dil
Valide: A Novel of the Harem - Barbara Chase-
  Riboud   1007

Napoleon II
Napoleon and His Son - Pierre Nezelof   4607

Narouz
The Mamur Zapt and the Girl in the Nile - Michael
  Pearce   4867

Nausicaa
Homer's Daughter - Robert Graves   2546

Nefertiti
Akhnaton, King of Egypt - Dmitri
  Merezhkovski   4337
A God Against the Gods - Allen Drury   1738
King of the Two Lands: The Pharaoh Akhenaten -
  Jacquetta Hawkes   2780
King Tut's Private Eye - Lee Levin   3739
On a Balcony - David Stacton   5973
Pillar of Fire - Judith Tarr   6168
Return to Thebes - Allen Drury   1739
The Twelfth Transforming - Pauline Gedge   2347

Nero
Claudius the God - Robert Graves   2543

Neville, Anne
The Broken Sword - Rhoda S. Edwards   1885
Crouchback - Carola Oman   4732
Fire and Morning - Francis W. Leary   3696
The Reluctant Queen: The Story of Anne of York -
  Jean Plaidy   5056
Richard III: The Last Plantagenet - Tyler
  Whittle   6722
The White Queen - Lesley J. Nickell   4611

Ney, Michel
Valentina - Evelyn Anthony   165

Nezahual
The Jaguar and the Golden Stag - Dexter Allen   95

Niall Black-Knee
The Emerald Crown - Theodora McCormick Du
Bois   1741

Niniane
Born of the Sun - Joan Wolf   6837

O'Houlihan, Sean
O'Houlihan's Jest - Rohan O'Grady   4702

Olga, Grand Duchess of Russia
The Snow Mountain - Catherine Gavin   2324
The Summer Day Is Done - R.T. Stevens   6001

Olympias
Alexander of Macedon: The Journey to World's End -
Harold Lamb   3607
Fire From Heaven - Mary Renault   5296
Funeral Games - Mary Renault   5297

Orestes
Amber Princess - Henry Treece   6325

Orlov, Aleksey
The Man From St. Petersburg - Ken Follett   2148

O'Sullivan, Donal Cam
The Last Prince of Ireland - Morgan Llywelyn   3821

Oswy
Queen of the Lightning - Kathleen Herbert   2852

Otto of Brunswick
The Saracen Blade - Frank Yerby   6926

Ovinska, Casimir
Polonaise - Jane Aiken Hodge   2968

Ovinska, Isobel
Polonaise - Jane Aiken Hodge   2968

Owen
Bride of the Spear - Kathleen Herbert   2851

Paris
The Firebrand - Marion Zimmer Bradley   624
The Goddess - Miranda Seymour   5763
Paris of Troy - George Baker   273
Scandal in Troy - Eva Hemmer Hansen   2679
Whom the Gods Would Destroy - Richard
Powell   5148

Parr, Catherine
The Autobiography of Henry VIII - Margaret
George   2355
Henry VIII and His Six Wives - Maureen
Peters   4975
Kathryn: In the Court of Six Queens - Anne Merton
Abbey   1
The Queen's Grace - Jan Westcott   6646
The Red-Haired Brat - Joanna Dessau   1627
The Sixth Wife - Jean Plaidy   5063

Parr, Katherine
Her Royal Destiny - Carol Maxwell Eady   1820
The Heretic - Alison Macleod   4002
*The Ivy Crown: A Biographical Novel of Queen
Katherine Parr* - Mary M. Luke   3923
King's Fool - Margaret Campbell Barnes   325
The Young Elizabeth - Jennette Letton   3730

Petrovsky, Semyon
The World in His Arms - Rex Beach   392

Phaedra
The Bull From the Sea - Mary Renault   5295

Philip, Duke of Edinburgh
Di and I - Peter Lefcourt   3714
The Queen and I - Sue Townsend   6306

Philip the Handsome
The Prisoner of Tordesillas - Lawrence
Schoonover   5665

Philippa of Hainault
The Vow on the Heron - Jean Plaidy   5074

Philippe I, Duc d'Orleans
Angelique - Sergeanne Golon   2465

Royal Flush: The Story of Minette - Margaret
Irwin   3121

Philippe II, Duc d'Orleans
Through a Glass Darkly - Karleen Koen   3531

Plantagenet, Cicely
The Lady Cicely - Sandra Wilson   6813
Less Fortunate than Fair - Sandra Wilson   6814
The Queen's Sister - Sandra Wilson   6815

Plantagenet, Eleanor
The King's Daughters - Molly Costain
Haycraft   2793

Plantagenet, Elizabeth
The King's Daughters - Molly Costain
Haycraft   2793

Plantagenet, Henry
The Revolt of the Eaglets - Jean Plaidy   5057

Plantagenet, Joanna
The King's Daughters - Molly Costain
Haycraft   2793

Plantagenet, Mary
The King's Daughters - Molly Costain
Haycraft   2793

Plantagenet, Meg
The King's Daughters - Molly Costain
Haycraft   2793

Pulcheria
Imperial Purple - Gillian Bradshaw   631
Sign of the Pagan - Don Tracy   6312

Radegunde
Women in the Wall - Julia O'Faolain   4691

Radziwill, Yanush
The Deluge - Henryk Sienkiewicz   5846

Ram, Krishna
The Ravi Lancers - John Masters   4178

Ranjana
The Sleeping Tiger - Marjorie McEvoy   4269
Star of Randevi - Marjorie McEvoy   4270

Remizou, Katrina Fedorcenko
Travail and Triumph - Michael Phillips   4991

Richard, Duke of Gloucester
The Dragon Waiting: A Masque of History - John M.
Ford   2165
The Golden Yoke: A Novel of the War of the Roses -
Olive Eckerson   1837
The Heart Is a Traitor - Margaret Abbey   4
The Lodestar - Pamela Belle   432
The Son of York - Margaret Abbey   5
The Sun in Splendour - Jean Plaidy   5066
The Sunne in Splendour - Sharon Kay Penman   4907

Richard the Lionhearted
The Courts of Love: A Romance of Medieval France -
Peter Bourne   592
The Devil Is Loose - Graham Shelby   5790
King's Man - C.M. Edmondston   1880
The Queen's War: A Novel of Eleanor of Aquitaine -
Jeanne Mackin   3996
The Revolt of the Eaglets - Jean Plaidy   5057
A Royal Quest - Mary Lide   3777
The Unhurrying Chase - H.F.M. Prescott   5172

Riemmelth
Queen of the Lightning - Kathleen Herbert   2852

Rigana
The Serpent's Tooth - Diana L. Paxson   4846

Robert II Curthose
The Bastard King - Jean Plaidy   5004
The Lion of Justice - Jean Plaidy   5031
The Paladin - George Shipway   5830

Robert the Bruce
The Scottish Chiefs - Jane Porter   5135

Rodana
The Winds of Sinhala - Colin De Silva   1562

Romanov, Juliana
Circle in the Water - Susan Wiggs   6742

Rudolf, Crown Prince of Austria, Rudolf
The Archduke - Michael Arnold   194

Rupert
The Stranger Prince - Margaret Irwin   3122

Saheb, Nana
The Devil's Wind: Nana Saheb's Story - Manohar
Malgonkar   4039

Sekeeta
Winged Pharaoh - Joan Grant   2536

Selma
Regards From the Dead Princess: A Novel of a Life -
Kenize Mourad   4505

Serebryany, Prince
Prince of Outlaws - Alexey Tolstoy   6294

Serge, Grand Duke of Russia
Elizabeth and Alexandra - Antony Lambton   3616

Seymour, Jane
The Autobiography of Henry VIII - Margaret
George   2355
The Heir of Allington - Philippa Wiat   6727
Henry VIII and His Six Wives - Maureen
Peters   4975
Kathryn: In the Court of Six Queens - Anne Merton
Abbey   1
King's Fool - Margaret Campbell Barnes   325
The Lily and the Leopards - Alice Harwood   2765
The Queen's Grace - Jan Westcott   6646
*Shadow in the Sun: A Novel of Elizabeth I, the Virgin
Queen* - F.W. Kenyon   3460
So Merciful a Queen, So Cruel a Woman - Alice
Harwood   2769
Windsor Castle - William Harrison Ainsworth   59
The Wise Virgin - Hebe Elsna   1934

Shamala
The Carmelite - Elgin Groseclose   2599

Sidirov, Anya
Blood and Sable - Carol J. Kane   3350

Signy
The Iron Crown - Clare Barroll   354

Sigurdarson, Haraldr
Byzantium - Michael Ennis   1945

Singh, Jaya
Raj - Gita Mehta   4325

Singing Grass
Soldier in Buckskin - Ray Hogan   2981

Solomon
David at Olivet - Wallace Hamilton   2671
Solomon's Song - Roberta Kells Dorr   1697

Sophia Dorothea
The Princess of Celle - Jean Plaidy   5045

Stephen
The Vision of Stephen: An Elegy - Lolah
Burford   775

Stewart, James
The Riven Realm - Nigel Tranter   6317

Stolberg-Gedern, Louise de
The Queen of Hearts - Joan Rees   5290

Stuart, Charles
The King's General - Daphne Du Maurier   1748
The Phoenix Rising - Jean Evans   1984
Powhatan's Daughter - John Clarke Bowman   605
The Wandering Prince - Jean Plaidy   5075
Wife to Great Buckingham - Hilda Lewis   3751

Stuart, Charles Edward
Born to Be King - Constance Gluyas   2440
Candleshine No More - Jane Oliver   4721

Charlie Is My Darling - Mollie Hardwick   2691

Clandara - Evelyn Anthony   161

Commander of the Mists - D.L. Murray   4527

Crown Without Sceptre - William Vaughan
  Wilkins   6758

The Dark Mile - Dorothy Kathleen Broster   709

The Flight of the Heron - Dorothy Kathleen
  Broster   710

Highlands Rebel - Sally Watson   6584

I Came to the Highlands: A Novel of Suspense - Velda
  Johnston   3263

The Long Day Closes - Beatrice Tunstall   6360

Louis the Well-Beloved - Jean Plaidy   5032

A Prince, a Piper, and a Rose - John Scalzo   5628

Prince Charlie's Bluff - Donald Thomas   6241

The Queen of Hearts - Joan Rees   5290

Red Gauntlet - Sir Walter Scott   5706

The Scotswoman - Inglis Fletcher   2140

Waverley - Sir Walter Scott   5709

The Woman from The Glen - Chloe Gartner   2310

Stuart, Henrietta

Royal Flush: The Story of Minette - Margaret
  Irwin   3121

Stuart, Henry Frederick

Lion Rampant - Bernard Shrimsley   5836

The Murder in the Tower - Jean Plaidy   5035

Stuart, James

Mary of Scotland - F.W. Kenyon   3454

Stuart, James Francis Edward

Now Face to Face - Karleen Koen   3530

The Stuart Legacy - Robert Kerr   3472

Stuart, Mary

All the Queen's Men - Evelyn Anthony   157

The Queen's Husband - Samuel Edwards   1889

Sybilla

Jerusalem - Cecelia Holland   2990

Sybilla-Marie

A Finger to Her Lips - Evelyn Berckman   472

Tacara-Mi

The Last Princess - Charles O. Locke   3826

Taliesin

A Royal Quest - Mary Lide   3777

Tamasrajasi

Path of the Eclipse - Chelsea Quinn Yarbro   6905

Tania

The Death of Kings - Peter Danielson   1465

Taniu

Bride of the Spear - Kathleen Herbert   2851

Tatiana, Grand Duchess of Russia

Devoted Friends - Joe Poyer   5161

Thaissa

Alexander the God - Robert Payne   4849

Theodora

Against the Fall of Night - Michael Arnold   193

Basilissa: A Tale of the Empress Theodora - John
  Masefield   4142

The Female: A Novel of Another Time - Paul I.
  Wellman   6617

Theodora and the Emperor - Harold Lamb   3608

Theophano

The Eagle's Daughter - Judith Tarr   6165

Theresa-Maria of Pfaffenstein

Magic Flutes - Eva Ibbotson   3097

Theseus

The King Must Die - Mary Renault   5298

Theudelinda

The Unspeakables: A Tale of Lombardy - Laverne
  Gay   2326

Third Princess

Necklace and Calabash - Robert van Gulik   6419

Ti-Sar

Lot's Wife - Marie Ley-Piscator   3767

Tilla, Mona

The Sins of the Lion - Annette Motley   4503

Titus

The Iron Hand of Mars - Lindsey Davis   1528

The Silver Pigs - Lindsey Davis   1532

Venus in Copper - Lindsey Davis   1534

Tiye

The Twelfth Transforming - Pauline Gedge   2347

Tsepesh, Prince Vlad

*Children of the Vampire: The Diaries of the Family
  Dracul* - Jeanne Kalogridis   3326

*Covenant with the Vampire: The Diaries of the Family
  Dracul* - Jeanne Kalogridis   3327

*Lord of the Vampires: The Diaries of the Family
  Dracul* - Jeanne Kalogridis   3328

Tudor, Edward

The Bisley Boy - Christopher Hunt   3080

A Crown in Darkness: A Novel about Lady Jane Grey
  - Margaret Mullally   4512

*The Ivy Crown: A Biographical Novel of Queen
  Katherine Parr* - Mary M. Luke   3923

The Lily and the Leopards - Alice Harwood   2765

The Prince and the Pauper - Mark Twain   6373

The Queen's Grace - Jan Westcott   6646

The Red-Haired Brat - Joanna Dessau   1627

Tudor, Elizabeth

The Autobiography of Henry VIII - Margaret
  George   2355

A Crown in Darkness: A Novel about Lady Jane Grey
  - Margaret Mullally   4512

Elizabeth and the Prince of Spain - Margaret
  Irwin   3117

Elizabeth, Captive Princess - Margaret Irwin   3118

I, Elizabeth - Rosalind Miles   4378

*The Ivy Crown: A Biographical Novel of Queen
  Katherine Parr* - Mary M. Luke   3923

The Lily and the Leopards - Alice Harwood   2765

My Lord of Canterbury - Godfrey Turton   6369

Oh! Where Are Bloody Mary's Earrings? - Robert
  Player   5079

The Prince and the Pauper - Mark Twain   6373

The Queen's Grace - Jan Westcott   6646

The Red-Haired Brat - Joanna Dessau   1627

The Sixth Wife - Jean Plaidy   5063

The Spanish Bridegroom - Jean Plaidy   5064

The Strong Room - Jere Hungerford
  Wheelwright   6671

The Ten-Day Queen - Lozania Prole   5199

The Tower of London - William Harrison
  Ainsworth   58

Young Bess - Margaret Irwin   3123

The Young Elizabeth - Jennette Letton   3730

Tudor, Henry

The Tudor Rose - Margaret Campbell Barnes   329

Tudor, Margaret

Chain of Destiny - Nigel Tranter   6314

James, by the Grace of God - Nigel Tranter   6315

Merchant of the Ruby - Alice Harwood   2766

My Lady Glamis - Pamela Hill   2940

The Riven Realm - Nigel Tranter   6317

A Stake in the Kingdom - Nigel Tranter   6321

Sunset at Noon - Jane Oliver   4728

The Thistle and the Rose - Jean Plaidy   5069

The White Rose Murders - Michael Clynes   1137

Tudor, Mary

Anne Boleyn - Evelyn Anthony   158

The Autobiography of Henry VIII - Margaret
  George   2355

Brief Gaudy Hour - Margaret Campbell Barnes   322

Command of the King - Mary Lide   3773

A Crown in Darkness: A Novel about Lady Jane Grey
  - Margaret Mullally   4512

Elizabeth, Captive Princess - Margaret Irwin   3118

The Fifth Queen - Ford Madox Ford   2161

Henry VIII and His Six Wives - Maureen
  Peters   4975

I Am Mary Tudor - Hilda Lewis   3750

I, Elizabeth - Rosalind Miles   4378

*The Ivy Crown: A Biographical Novel of Queen
  Katherine Parr* - Mary M. Luke   3923

The King's Secret Matter - Jean Plaidy   5027

The Lily and the Leopards - Alice Harwood   2765

The Man on a Donkey - H.F.M. Prescott   5170

My Lord of Canterbury - Godfrey Turton   6369

The Prince and the Pauper - Mark Twain   6373

The Queen's Grace - Jan Westcott   6646

The Red-Haired Brat - Joanna Dessau   1627

The Reluctant Queen - Molly Costain Haycraft   2796

Royal Nonesuch: A Tudor Tapestry - Beatrice
  White   6674

The Serpent Garden - Judith Merkle Riley   5336

The Spanish Bridegroom - Jean Plaidy   5064

A Stake in the Kingdom - Nigel Tranter   6321

The Ten-Day Queen - Lozania Prole   5199

The White Rose Murders - Michael Clynes   1137

Young Bess - Margaret Irwin   3123

Tutankhamen

Return to Thebes - Allen Drury   1739

Tz'u-hsi

Twilight of the Dragon - Peter Bourne   596

Valenti, Leone da

The Sins of the Lion - Annette Motley   4503

Victoria

Albert's Victoria - Tyler Whittle   6719

The Captive of Kensington Palace - Jean
  Plaidy   5007

Victoria in the Wings - Jean Plaidy   5072

The Young Victoria - Tyler Whittle   6724

Victoria Adelaide Mary Louise

The Queen's Husband - Jean Plaidy   5052

Victoria, Duchess of Kent

The Little Victoria - Lozania Prole   5196

The Young Victoria - Tyler Whittle   6724

Vishnyevetski, Yeremi

With Fire and Sword - Henryk Sienkiewicz   5850

Volynski, Grisha

The Year of December - Lucy Cores   1329

Von Friedberg, Frederick

Meadowsweet - Gwendoline Butler   820

William, Duke of Clarence

Goddess of the Green Room - Jean Plaidy   5016

Regency Buck - Georgette Heyer   2898

Victoria in the Wings - Jean Plaidy   5072

William of Orange

The Elusive Crown - Hebe Elsna   1931

The Three Crowns - Jean Plaidy   5070

Treason's Gift - Pamela Belle   434

William's Wife - Jean Plaidy   5077

William of Wales

Di and I - Peter Lefcourt   3714

William Rufus

The Bastard King - Jean Plaidy   5004

Wise Coyote

The Jaguar Princess - Clare Bell   421

Woodville, Elizabeth

The Book of Shadows - C.L. Grace   2505

The Dragon Waiting: A Masque of History - John M.
  Ford   2165

The King's Grey Mare - Rosemary Hawley
  Jarman   3167

The Rose at Harvest End - Eleanor Fairburn   2003

The Summer Queen - Alice Walworth Graham   2512

The Sun in Splendour - Jean Plaidy   5066

Xuchitl

The Heart of Jade - Salvador de Madariaga   4024

Ygerma
Sword at Sunset - Rosemary Sutcliff 6125

Ypsilanti, Prince
Searching for the Emperor - Roberto Pazzi 4858

Yusupova, Lili
The Revolutionist: A Novel of Russia - Robert Littell 3810

RULER

Abdulhamid I
Valide: A Novel of the Harem - Barbara Chase-Riboud 1007

Abe No, Hime
The Vermilion Bridge - Shelley Mydans 4539

Aegeus
Medea - Miranda Seymour 5764

Affonso I
Lord of the Kongo - Peter Forbath 2155

Agamemnon
Amber Princess - Henry Treece 6325
The Greek Generals Talk: Memoirs of the Trojan War - Phillip Parotti 4817
Scandal in Troy - Eva Hemmer Hansen 2679
Whom the Gods Would Destroy - Richard Powell 5148

Ahab
The Curse of Jezebel: A Novel of the Biblical Queen of Evil - Frank G. Slaughter 5884
Jezebel - Dorothy Clarke Wilson 6802

Ahasuerus
So Great a Queen: The Story of Esther, Queen of Persia - Paul Frischauer 2235

Akbar
The Near and the Far - Leopold Hamilton Myers 4547

Akhenaton
Akhnaton, King of Egypt - Dmitri Merezhkovski 4337
The Egyptian - Mika Waltari 6552
A God Against the Gods - Allen Drury 1738
King of the Two Lands: The Pharaoh Akhenaten - Jacquetta Hawkes 2780
Murder in the Place of Anubis - Lynda S. Robinson 5409
On a Balcony - David Stacton 5973
Pillar of Fire - Judith Tarr 6168
Return to Thebes - Allen Drury 1739
The Twelfth Transforming - Pauline Gedge 2347

Alaric I
Bury Me in Ravenna - Agnes Carr Vaughan 6432
Captive of Rome - Theodora McCormick Du Bois 1740
The Last Romans - Teodor Jeske-Choinski 3216

Alexander I
The Angel: A Novel Based on the Life of Alexander I of Russia - William James Blech 543
Anna - Cynthia Harrod-Eagles 2752
Baltic Mission - Richard Woodman 6859
The Emperor Story: A Historical Romance - George Sava 5615
Far Flies the Eagle - Evelyn Anthony 162
Feast of the Jesters - Manuel Komroff 3533
The Gentleman From America - Paul Benton 464
Great Black Russian - John Oliver Killens 3484
Lustre in the Sky - R.G. Waldeck 6525
Madame Casanova - Gaby von Schonthan 5659
Napoleon and the Cossacks - Peter N. Krassnoff 3551
Napoleon Symphony - Anthony Burgess 780
Polonaise - Jane Aiken Hodge 2968
So Great a Man - David Pilgrim 5000

Alexander II
The Crown and the Crucible - Michael Phillips 4987

Alexander III
Alexander the Glorious - Jane Oliver 4719
Travail and Triumph - Michael Phillips 4991
True Thomas - Nigel Tranter 6322

Alexander of Serbia
Dance of the Assassins - Maria Fagyas 1997

Alexander the Great
Alexander in Babylon - Jakob Wassermann 6576
Alexander of Macedon: The Journey to World's End - Harold Lamb 3607
Alexander the God - Maurice Druon 1731
Alexander the God - Robert Payne 4849
The Conqueror: A Novel of Alexander the Great - Edison Marshall 4104
An Elephant for Aristotle - L. Sprague De Camp 1556
Fire From Heaven - Mary Renault 5296
Funeral Games - Mary Renault 5297
The Golden Lyre - Noel B. Gerson 2371
Lord of the Two Lands - Judith Tarr 6167
The Persian Boy - Mary Renault 5301
Star of Macedon - Karl V. Eiker 1901

Alexius I Comnenus
Count Robert of Paris - Sir Walter Scott 5695
The Lady for Ransom - Alfred Duggan 1768
Wine of Satan - Laverne Gay 2327

Alfred the Great
The Edge of Light - Joan Wolf 6839
The Flame in the Dark - Basil Bonallack 568
The King Liveth - Jeffrey Farnol 2013
The Marsh King - C. Walter Hodges 2975
The Price of Blood - Doris Sutcliffe Adams 24
Raven's Wind - Victor Canning 883
The Right Line of Cedric - Alfred Duggan 1773

Amenhotep III
The Twelfth Transforming - Pauline Gedge 2347

Amenhotep IV
The Goddess Queen: A Novel Based on the Life of Nefertiti - Nicole Vidal 6494

Amun
Child of the Morning - Pauline Gedge 2343

Andronicus I Comnenus
Against the Fall of Night - Michael Arnold 193
Their Most Serene Majesties - Ange Vlachos 6505
The Walking Drum - Louis L'Amour 3632

Anne
Exit Lady Masham - Louis Auchincloss 230
The Glory and the Dream - F.W. Kenyon 3450
Marlborough's Unfair Lady - Lozania Prole 5197
The Queen's Favourites - Jean Plaidy 5051
The Sachem - Donald Clayton Porter 5124

Antigonus I
The Bronze God of Rhodes - L. Sprague De Camp 1554

Arothgar
The Tower of Beowulf - Parke Godwin 2450

Artaxerxes I
Farewell Great King: A Novel of Ancient Greece - Jill Paton Walsh 4829

Arthur
Arthur - Stephen R. Lawhead 3679
Arthur Rex: A Legendary Novel - Thomas Berger 477
The Chessboard Queen - Sharan Newman 4597
Child of the Northern Spring - Persia Woolley 6867
The Coming of the King - Nikolai Tolstoy 6296
A Connecticut Yankee in King Arthur's Court - Mark Twain 6371
The Crimson Chalice - Victor Canning 882
The Emperor Arthur - Godfrey Turton 6368
Firelord - Parke Godwin 2447

First Knight - Elizabeth Chadwick 966
The Green Man - Henry Treece 6330
Guinevere Evermore - Sharan Newman 4601
Guinevere: The Legend in Autumn - Persia Woolley 6868
Hawk of May - Gillian Bradshaw 629
In the Shadow of the Oak King - Courtway Jones 3271
In Winter's Shadow - Gillian Bradshaw 632
The King - Donald Barthelme 365
Kingdom of Summer - Gillian Bradshaw 633
Kinsmen of the Grail - Dorothy James Roberts 5376
The Last Enchantment - Mary Stewart 6031
The Last Pendragon - Robert Rice 5316
The Mists of Avalon - Marion Zimmer Bradley 626
The Once and Future King - T.H. White 6705
The Pagan King - Edison Marshall 4109
The Pendragon - Catherine Christian 1075
Pendragon - Stephen R. Lawhead 3682
Pendragon's Banner - Helen Hollick 3001
Queen of the Summer Stars - Persia Woolley 6869
The Queen's Knight - Marvin Borowsky 585
The Road to Avalon - Joan Wolf 6842
The Wicked Day - Mary Stewart 6033
The Winter King - Bernard Cornwell 1351
Witch of the North - Courtway Jones 3272

Ashikaga Yoshimitsu
The House of Kanze - Nobuko Albery 64

Astyanax
The Shattered Horse - S.P. Somtow 5945

Ataulf
Bury Me in Ravenna - Agnes Carr Vaughan 6432
Captive of Rome - Theodora McCormick Du Bois 1740

Attila the Hun
Attila's Treasure - Stephan Grundy 2606
Darkness and the Dawn - Thomas B. Costain 1364
The Death of Attila - Cecelia Holland 2986
Sign of the Pagan - Don Tracy 6312
Throne of the World - Louis De Wohl 1575
The Twelve Pictures - Edith Simon 5857

Augustus
Augustus - Allan Massie 4167
Augustus - John Williams 6785
Golden Peacock - Gertrude Atherton 224
I, Claudius - Robert Graves 2547
I Loved Tiberius - Elisabeth Dored 1692
Roman Shadows - Ron Burns 804
Tiberius: The Memoirs of the Emperor - Allan Massie 4169

Augustus II
The Power and the Passion - Christina Nicholson 4609

Aurelian
Queen of the East - Alexander Baron 336

Authari
The Unspeakables: A Tale of Lombardy - Laverne Gay 2326

Axayacatl
Copilli, Aztec Prince - Miguel Aleman Velasco 75

Baldwin I
Sir Pagan - Henry John Colyton 1222

Baldwin II
Queen of Swords - Judith Tarr 6169

Baldwin IV
Alamut - Judith Tarr 6164
The Leper King - Zofja Kossak-Szczucka 3544

Baldwin V
The Firedrake - Cecelia Holland 2988

Bathory, Istvan
Darker Jewels - Chelsea Quinn Yarbro 6898

Batu Khan
Until the Sun Falls - Cecelia Holland 2998

Baudouin IV
Jerusalem - Cecelia Holland 2990

Bawajira
The Golden Honeycomb - Kamala Markandaya 4086

Bernadotte, Jean-Baptiste
Desiree - Annemarie Selinko 5741

Boadicea
The Eagle and the Raven - Pauline Gedge 2344
Red Queen, White Queen - Henry Treece 6332
Warrior Queen - James Sinclair 5865

Bolingbroke, Henry
The Lords of Lancaster - Pamela Bennetts 452

Bonaparte, Joseph
Sharpe's Honour - Bernard Cornwell 1344

Bonaparte, Louis Napoleon
The Big Family - Vina Delmar 1600
The Tontine - Thomas B. Costain 1371

Bonaparte, Napoleon
The Amazing Mrs. Bonaparte - Harnett T. Kane 3351
Anna - Cynthia Harrod-Eagles 2752
The Anthem - Noel B. Gerson 2361
Baltic Mission - Richard Woodman 6859
Being Met Together - William Vaughan Wilkins 6756
Blackstone and the Scourge of Europe - Richard Falkirk 2007
Brumaire - Mark Logan 3864
Captain Cut-Throat - John Dickson Carr 908
The Castle of Fratta - Ippolito Nievo 4625
Charles O'Malley - Charles James Lever 3731
Colossus: A Novel about Goya and a World Gone Mad - Stephen Marlowe 4093
Death at the French Creek - Raymond C. Borel 580
The Death of Napoleon - Simon Leys 3768
The Dedicated - Willa Gibbs 2399
Desiree - Annemarie Selinko 5741
Draw Near to Battle - Jere Hungerford Wheelwright 6667
The Eagle and the Rock - Frances Winwar 6830
Emperor's Ladies - Noel B. Gerson 2367
The Emperor's Lady: A Novel Based on the Life of the Empress Josephine - F.W. Kenyon 3449
Far Flies the Eagle - Evelyn Anthony 162
The Flight of the Eagle - Donald Thomas 6239
Good-Bye My Son - Marjorie Coryn 1356
A Great Lord - Paul Frischauer 2233
Holy Week - Louis Aragon 182
Imperial Venus: A Novel of Napoleon's Favorite Sister - Edgar Maas 3949
The Last Love - Thomas B. Costain 1367
The Limits of Glory: A Novel of Waterloo - James McDonough 4265
Madame Casanova - Gaby von Schonthan 5659
Marianne - Juliette Benzoni 466
Marianne and the Crown of Fire - Juliette Benzoni 467
Marianne and the Masked Prince - Juliette Benzoni 469
Marianne and the Privateer - Juliette Benzoni 470
Marianne and the Rebels - Juliette Benzoni 471
The Marriage of Josephine - Marjorie Coryn 1358
Mirage - Ruth McKenney 4283
My Brother Napoleon: The Confessions of Caroline Bonaparte - F.W. Kenyon 3455
Napoleon and His Son - Pierre Nezelof 4607
Napoleon and the Cossacks - Peter N. Krassnoff 3551
Napoleon Must Die - Quinn Fawcett 2054
Notorious Eliza - Basil Beyea 489
Palaces of Desire - Kate Alexander 81
The Raven and the Rose - Susan Wiggs 6746
The River Devils - Carter A. Vaughan 6437
The Rose and the Sword - Sandra Paretti 4792
A Rose for Virtue - Norah Lofts 3858

The Rose of Malmaison: The Turbulent Life of the Beautiful Josephine - Gaby von Schonthan 5660
Seven Men of Gascony - R.F. Delderfield 1589
Sharpe's Devil - Bernard Cornwell 1340
So Brief a Spring - Claude Manceron 4054
So Great a Man - David Pilgrim 5000
Tell Your Sons: A Novel of the Napoleonic Era - Willa Gibbs 2402
The Thousand Fires - Anne Powers 5155
Tide of Empire - Bates Baldwin 279
A Time for Titans - Vina Delmar 1602
Tom Burke of Ours - Charles James Lever 3732
Valentina - Evelyn Anthony 165
Valide: A Novel of the Harem - Barbara Chase-Riboud 1007
War and Peace - Leo Tolstoy 6295
Waterloo - Manuel Komroff 3536
Waterloo - Frederic E. Smith 5920
Why Waterloo? - Alan Patrick Herbert 2850

Brian Boru
The Kings in Winter - Cecelia Holland 2991
The Lion of Ireland - Morgan Llywelyn 3822

Caesar, Gaius Julius
Three's Company - Alfred Duggan 1774

Caligula
Brothers of Vengeance - LeGette Blythe 556
I Am a Barbarian - Edgar Rice Burroughs 807
I, Claudius - Robert Graves 2547
The Kingdom of the Wicked - Anthony Burgess 778
The Lost Legion - H. Warner Munn 4516
Man on Fire: A Novel on the Life of St. Paul - LeGette Blythe 558
No King but Caesar - Anne Powers 5151
Octavia: A Tale of Ancient Rome - Seymour Van Santvoord 6428
Pontius Pilate: A Biographical Novel - Paul L. Maier 4034
The Robe - Lloyd C. Douglas 1703
The Sins of Herod: A Novel of Rome and the Early Church - Frank G. Slaughter 5900
The Testament of Theophilus - Leonard Wibberley 6730
The Thorn of Arimathea - Frank G. Slaughter 5905
Tiberius: The Memoirs of the Emperor - Allan Massie 4169
The Word and the Sword - Theo Lang 3662

Cambyses II
The Prophet - Sholem Asch 201

Canute
King Hereafter - Dorothy Dunnett 1802

Caradoc
The Captive Princess - Maxine Shore 5831

Carlos II
Poison - Kathryn Harrison 2737

Catherine I
Peter the Great - Alexey Tolstoy 6293
Tsar's Woman - Pamela Hill 2946

Catherine II
The Captain's Daughter - Alexander Pushkin 5210
Rebel Princess - Evelyn Anthony 164
Valide: A Novel of the Harem - Barbara Chase-Riboud 1007
Young Catherine - E.M. Almedingen 118

Catherine the Great
The Incorruptible - Helma De Bois 1551
The Revolutionary - Lawrence Schoonover 5667
Russka: The Novel of Russia - Edward Rutherfurd 5535

Ceawlin
Born of the Sun - Joan Wolf 6837

Cetewayo
Yellowstone Kelly - Peter Bowen 602

Chaka
Great Elephant - Alan Scholefield 5654

Charles I
Call Lady Purbeck - Hilda Lewis 3745
Captain From Castile - Samuel Shellabarger 5794
Charles the King - Evelyn Anthony 160
An Epic Joy: A Novel Based on the Life of Rubens - Donald Braider 642
The Golden Feather - Theda Kenyon 3462
John Inglesant - John Henry Shorthouse 5833
Katherine Christian - Hugh Walpole 6546
The King Breaker - Elizabeth Linington 3797
Mary of Carisbrooke - Margaret Campbell Barnes 327
My Lord Foxe - Constance Gluyas 2443
Myself, Christopher Wren - David Weiss 6606
Myself My Enemy - Jean Plaidy 5037
The Phoenix Rising - Jean Evans 1984
Physician Extraordinary: A Novel of the Life and Times of William Harvey - David Weiss 6608
The Proud Servant: The Story of Montrose - Margaret Irwin 3120
The Quickenberry Tree - Annette Motley 4502
The Severed Crown - Jane Lane 3657
The Stranger Prince - Margaret Irwin 3122
Thanksgiving - Terry Coleman 1207
Twenty Years After - Alexandre Dumas 1783
The White Witch - Elizabeth Goudge 2496
Wife to Mr. Milton - Robert Graves 2553
The Young and Lonely King - Jane Lane 3659

Charles II
The Bellerose Bargain - Robyn Carr 934
Bennett's Welcome - Inglis Fletcher 2132
The Braeswood Tapestry - Robyn Carr 936
The Bride - Margaret Irwin 3116
Catherine - Hilda Lewis 3746
Chelynne - Robyn Carr 938
Countess Carrots - Molly Costain Haycraft 2792
Cutlass Empire - F. van Wyck Mason 4148
The Devil in Velvet - John Dickson Carr 909
The Golden Days - Robert Neill 4569
A Health Unto His Majesty - Jean Plaidy 5019
Here Lies Our Sovereign Lord - Jean Plaidy 5021
I, John Mordaunt - Virgil Scott 5687
The King's Bastard - Hebe Elsna 1932
The King's Brat - Constance Gluyas 2441
The King's Rogue - Max Peacock 4859
Lady on the Coin - Margaret Campbell Barnes 326
Lucy - Hester W. Chapman 992
Mary of Carisbrooke - Margaret Campbell Barnes 327
Masquerade for the King - Marina Oliver 4729
Mistress of the Boards - Richard Sumner 6118
Most Secret - John Dickson Carr 912
The Murder of Sir Edmund Godfrey - John Dickson Carr 913
My Lady Benbrook - Constance Gluyas 2442
Myself, Christopher Wren - David Weiss 6606
Old St. Paul's - William Harrison Ainsworth 57
Our Jo, or The Chronicle of a Coming Man - Kenneth M. Cameron 868
Peveril of the Peak - Sir Walter Scott 5703
The Pleasures of Love - Jean Plaidy 5042
The Portingale - Alison Macleod 4005
Restoration: A Novel of Seventeenth-Century England - Rose Tremain 6333
Royal Flush: The Story of Minette - Margaret Irwin 3121
The Spoils of Eden - Robert H. Fowler 2193
The Three Crowns - Jean Plaidy 5070
Traitor's Moon - Robert Neill 4574
With All My Heart - Margaret Campbell Barnes 330

Charles IV
The Naked Maja - Noel B. Gerson 2378
Rage in Silence: A Novel Based on the Life of Goya - Donald Braider 643
The She-Wolf - Pamela Bennetts 456

The She-Wolf of France - Maurice Druon 1736

Charles V
Against This Rock - Louis Zara 6948
I, the King - Howard Clewes 1112
In the House of the King - Louis Zara 6951
The Last Crusader - Louis De Wohl 1569
The Prisoner of Tordesillas - Lawrence
  Schoonover 5665

Charles VI
The Gentle Falcon - Hilda Lewis 3747
In a Dark Wood Wandering - Hella S. Haasse 2631
The Queen's Secret - Jean Plaidy 5053
The Royal Pawn - Antonia Ridge 5327
Royal Sword at Agincourt - Pamela Bennetts 455
The Spider King - Lawrence Schoonover 5668
Wife to Henry V - Hilda Lewis 3752

Charles VII
An Army of Angels: A Novel of Joan of Arc - Pamela
  Marcantel 4079
La Belle Sorel - Jacques Carton 949
The Burnished Blade - Lawrence Schoonover 5661
The Moneyman - Thomas B. Costain 1368
Personal Recollections of Joan of Arc - Mark
  Twain 6372
The Queen's Secret - Jean Plaidy 5053

Charles VIII
The Bride of Sforza - Miranda Seymour 5760
Duchess of Milan - Michael Ennis 1946
The Gentle Fury: A Novel of Margaret of Austria -
  Paul Lewis 3758
Here Lies Margot - Pamela Hill 2935
The Private Life of Mona Lisa - Pierre La
  Mure 3577
Romola - George Eliot 1910

Charles IX
The Longest Night - Ada Cook Lewis 3744
Queen Margot - Alexandre Dumas 1780

Charles XII
Peter the Great - Alexey Tolstoy 6293

Ch'ien Lung
A House in Peiking - Robert Payne 4853

Ch'in Shih Huang Ti
The Chinese Emperor - Jean Levi 3733

Christian II
The Fall of the King - Johannes Vilhelm
  Jensen 3214

Christian VII
The Lost Queen - Norah Lofts 3850
The Queen's Physician - Edgar Maas 3952

Christina
The Flight - Ruth Walgreen Stephan 5994
My Crown, My Love - Ruth Walgreen Stephan 5995

Christophe, Henri
Black Triumvirate: A Novel of Haiti - Benjamin H.
  Levin 3736
Drums of Destiny - Peter Bourne 593

Claudius I
Brothers of Vengeance - LeGette Blythe 556
Claudius the God - Robert Graves 2543
The Eagle and the Raven - Pauline Gedge 2344
The Eighth Veil - Ellis Kadison 3320
The Flames of Rome - Paul L. Maier 4033
The Glorious Folly: A Novel of the Time of St. Paul -
  Louis De Wohl 1565
I Loved Tiberius - Elisabeth Dored 1692
Octavia: A Tale of Ancient Rome - Seymour Van
  Santvoord 6428
Sarum: The Novel of England - Edward
  Rutherfurd 5536
Soul Flame - Barbara Wood 6850

Cleopatra
The Alexandrian - Martha Rofheart 5425
Augustus - Allan Massie 4167

Augustus - John Williams 6785
Cleopatra - H. Rider Haggard 2637
A Goddess to a God - John Lloyd Balderston 278
The Ides of March - Thornton Wilder 6753
The Mummy; or Ramses the Damned - Anne
  Rice 5315
Purple Pirate - Talbot Mundy 4514
That Egyptian Woman - Noel B. Gerson 2384
Throne of Isis - Judith Tarr 6170

Commodus, Lucius Aelius Aurelius
Between Eternities - Robert H. Pilpel 5001
*The Equinox: A Novel of Rome in the Time of
  Commodus* - Carol Saylor 5622
The Side of the Moon - Amanda Prantera 5162

Conachur, Mac Nessa
Deirdre - James Stephens 5996

Conchubar
A Shadow of Gulls - Patricia Finney 2096

Conn
Lady of Conquest - Teresa Medeiros 4322

Conor, Mac Nessa
Red Branch - Morgan Llywelyn 3824

Constantine I
Beyond the Aegean - Elia Kazan 3382
Constantine: The Miracle of the Flaming Cross -
  Frank G. Slaughter 5883
The Living Wood - Louis De Wohl 1571

Constantine XI Palaeologus
The Dark Angel - Mika Waltari 6551

Constantius II
The Death of the Gods - Dmitri Merezhkovski 4338

Constantius III
Bury Me in Ravenna - Agnes Carr Vaughan 6432

Croesus
Persian Conqueror - George Sidney Hellman 2822

Cunobelin
The Dark Island - Henry Treece 6326

Cynric
Born of the Sun - Joan Wolf 6837

Cyrus the Great
Persian Conqueror - George Sidney Hellman 2822
The Prophet - Sholem Asch 201

Darius
Alexander the God - Robert Payne 4849
Creation - Gore Vidal 6486
Farewell Great King: A Novel of Ancient Greece - Jill
  Paton Walsh 4829
The Persian Boy - Mary Renault 5301

David
Bathsheba - Roberta Kells Dorr 1695
Bathsheba - Torgny Lindgren 3789
David and Bathsheba - Ari Ibn-Sahav 3098
David at Olivet - Wallace Hamilton 2671
David of Jerusalem - Louis De Wohl 1564
David the King - Gladys Schmitt 5641
David: Warrior and King - Frank G. Slaughter 5885
David's Stranger - Moshe Shamir 5771
Giant Killer - Elmer Holmes Davis 1518
King David - Gwyn Jenkins 3191
The King David Report - Stefan Heym 2910
King of Kings: A Novel of the Life of David - Malachi
  Martin 4134
Rizpah - Charles E. Israel 3124
The Shining King - Peter Danielson 1476
Solomon and Sheba - Faye Levine 3740
Solomon and Sheba - Jay Williams 6774
Solomon's Song - Roberta Kells Dorr 1697
The Source - James A. Michener 4374
Tamar - Ann Chamberlin 975
The Trojan - Noel B. Gerson 2386
The Unanointed - Laurene Chinn 1070
*The Valley of Vision: A Novel of King Solomon and
  His Time* - Vardis Fisher 2113

Demetrius I
Besieger of Cities - Alfred Duggan 1761
The Bronze God of Rhodes - L. Sprague De
  Camp 1554

Dermot
Isle of Glory - Jane Oliver 4723
The Love of Fingin O'Lea - Theodora McCormick Du
  Bois 1743

Dessalines, Jean-Jacques
Black Triumvirate: A Novel of Haiti - Benjamin H.
  Levin 3736
Lydia Bailey - Kenneth Roberts 5387

Dido
Dido, Queen of Hearts - Gertrude Atherton 223

Diogenes, Romanus
The Lady for Ransom - Alfred Duggan 1768

Dionysios the Great
The Arrows of Hercules - L. Sprague De Camp 1553

Domitian
Gold for the Caesars - Florence A. Seward 5759
Josephus and the Emperor - Lion
  Feuchtwanger 2073
The Triumph - Ernest K. Gann 2280

Duncan I
King Hereafter - Dorothy Dunnett 1802
Lady of Moray - Bonnie Copeland 1318

Edgar
Avalon - Anya Seton 5748

Edward I
Angel of Death - P.C. Doherty 1670
The Black Rose - Thomas B. Costain 1363
The De Montfort Legacy - Pamela Bennetts 447
A Dragon for Edward - Pamela Bennetts 450
Hammer of the Scots - Jean Plaidy 5018
The King's Daughters - Molly Costain
  Haycraft 2793
The Lion of England - Eve Trevaskis 6336
The Prince of Darkness - P.C. Doherty 1675
The Reckoning - Sharon Kay Penman 4906
Robert the Bruce: The Steps to the Empty Throne -
  Nigel Tranter 6320
The Ruthless Yeomen - Valerie Anand 134
Sarum: The Novel of England - Edward
  Rutherfurd 5536
Satan in St. Mary's - P.C. Doherty 1676
Satan's Fire - P.C. Doherty 1677
The Scottish Chiefs - Jane Porter 5135
Spy in Chancery - P.C. Doherty 1680
Witness to Treason - Millie J. Ragosta 5244

Edward II
The Follies of the King - Jean Plaidy 5014
Harlot Queen - Hilda Lewis 3748
Isabel the Fair - Margaret Campbell Barnes 323
The Lion and the Leopard - Mary Ellen
  Johnson 3226
The She-Wolf - Pamela Bennetts 456
The She-Wolf of France - Maurice Druon 1736
Vows of the Peacock - Alice Walworth
  Graham 2513

Edward III
*Bodin, 1349: An Epic Novel of Christians and Jews in
  the Plague Years* - Roberta Kalechofsky 3322
By Right of Arms - Robyn Carr 937
The Death of a King - P.C. Doherty 1672
Harlot Queen - Hilda Lewis 3748
The King's Bishop - Candace M. Robb 5365
The Lady Chapel - Candace M. Robb 5366
The Lady Royal - Molly Costain Haycraft 2794
The Lily and the Lion - Maurice Druon 1733
Passage to Pontefract - Jean Plaidy 5038
The Peacock and the Pearl - Jennifer Lang 3661
The She-Wolf - Pamela Bennetts 456
The Vow on the Heron - Jean Plaidy 5074

Edward IV

The Book of Shadows - C.L. Grace 2505
Crown of Roses - Valerie Anand 127
The Dragon and the Rose - Roberta Gellis 2350
The Dragon Waiting: A Masque of History - John M. Ford 2165
The Eve of Saint Hyacinth - Kate Sedley 5716
Fortune's Wheel - Rhoda S. Edwards 1886
The Golden Yoke: A Novel of the War of the Roses - Olive Eckerson 1837
The Goldsmith's Wife - Jean Plaidy 5017
I Remember Love - Mollie Hardwick 2694
The Killing of Richard the Third - Robert Farrington 2020
The King's Grey Mare - Rosemary Hawley Jarman 3167
The Last of the Barons - Edward Bulwer-Lytton 769
The Lodestar - Pamela Belle 432
Merchant of the Ruby - Alice Harwood 2766
A Question of Choice - Prudence Andrew 143
Red Rose of Anjou - Jean Plaidy 5054
Richard III: The Last Plantagenet - Tyler Whittle 6722
The Rose at Harvest End - Eleanor Fairburn 2003
A Shrine of Murders - C.L. Grace 2509
The Summer Queen - Alice Walworth Graham 2512
The Sun in Splendour - Jean Plaidy 5066
The Sunne in Splendour - Sharon Kay Penman 4907
The Unicorn Hunt - Dorothy Dunnett 1811
The Warwick Heiress - Margaret Abbey 6
The White Queen - Lesley J. Nickell 4611
The White Rose - Jan Westcott 6648
The Winter Rose - Millie J. Ragosta 5243

Edward V

Crown of Roses - Valerie Anand 127

Edward VI

Feast in the Morning - Hugh Preston 5175
I, Elizabeth - Rosalind Miles 4378
The Ten-Day Queen - Lozania Prole 5199

Edward VII

Edward - Tyler Whittle 6721
Jewels - Robert Perrin 4917
The King Edward Plot - Robert Lee Hall 2658
Love at Sunset - Jane Sheridan 5811
Mr. American - George MacDonald Fraser 2211
The Revenge of the Hound - Michael Hardwick 2688

Edward VIII

The Plot to Kill Wallis Simpson: A Work of Faction - Graham Fisher 2104
That Vanderbilt Woman - Philip Van Rensselaer 6427
Wallis: The Novel - Anne Edwards 1883

Edward Longshanks

Braveheart - Randall Wallace 6538

Edward the Confessor

The Breath of Kings - Gene Farrington 2019
The Cunning of the Dove - Alfred Duggan 1765
Gildenford - Valerie Anand 130
The Golden Warrior: The Story of Harold and William - Hope Muntz 4517
King Hereafter - Dorothy Dunnett 1802
The Norman Pretender - Valerie Anand 132
The Saxon Tapestry - Sile Rice 5317

Elagabalus

Family Favorites - Alfred Duggan 1766

Elesing, Cerdric

Conscience of the King - Alfred Duggan 1763

Elizabeth

Rebel Princess - Evelyn Anthony 164

Elizabeth I

Absolute Elizabeth - Joanna Dessau 1624
All the Queen's Men - Evelyn Anthony 157
The Bartholomew Fair Murders - Leonard Tourney 6297
Beauvallet - Georgette Heyer 2876

Captain Bashful - Donald Barr Chidsey 1059
Captain for Elizabeth - Jan Westcott 6643
The Captive Queen of Scots - Jean Plaidy 5008
Chase the Heart - Maggie Osborne 4760
Court of Shadows - Cynthia Morgan 4450
Death of the Fox - George Garrett 2300
Deborah - Colette Davenat 1498
Deborah and the Many Faces of Love - Colette Davenat 1499
Deborah and the Siege of Paris - Colette Davenat 1500
Edmund Campion - Evelyn Waugh 6585
Elizabeth: Queen & Woman - Helen Thorpe 6279
Elizabeth, the Woman - Amanda Mae Ellis 1917
Envoy From Elizabeth - Pamela Bennetts 451
Fire over England - A.E.W. Mason 4143
The Firedrake's Eye - Patricia Finney 2095
The Flight of the Kestrel - Margaret Abbey 3
The Fourth Queen - Isabel Paterson 4827
Gay Lord Robert - Jean Plaidy 5015
Golden Admiral - F. van Wyck Mason 4150
Heart of a Queen - Josephine Delves-Broughton 1603
Her Majesty's Captain - Derek Wilson 6797
The Hounds of God - Rafael Sabatini 5551
Immortal Queen - Elizabeth Byrd 834
Kenilworth - Sir Walter Scott 5700
Kingdom of Gold - Susan Wiggs 6744
Lady in Waiting - Rosemary Sutcliff 6123
Lady Rich - Elizabeth Boatwright Coker 1166
Legacy - Susan Kay 3374
Mary, Queen of Scotland and the Isles - Margaret George 2356
The Master of Gray Trilogy - Nigel Tranter 6316
The Muscovite - Alison Macleod 4004
My Dear Lover England - Pamela Bennetts 453
My Enemy the Queen - Victoria Holt 3017
My Lord Essex - Olive Eckerson 1838
My Lord the Fox - Robert York 6932
Old Saxon Blood - Leonard Tourney 6302
Orlando - Virginia Woolf 6866
Physician Extraordinary: A Novel of the Life and Times of William Harvey - David Weiss 6608
The Proud Man - Elizabeth Linington 3800
The Queen and the Gypsy - Constance Heaven 2810
Queen of This Realm: The Story of Queen Elizabeth I - Jean Plaidy 5050
The Queen's Ward - Hebe Elsna 1933
Ralegh's Fair Bess: The Story of Bess Throckmorton - Judy Turner 6365
Reluctant Cavalier - Donald Barr Chidsey 1064
Roanoke Hundred - Inglis Fletcher 2138
The Robsart Affair - Jennette Letton 3729
Scapegoat for a Stuart - Kate Kirby 3504
The Scarlet Cloak - Jean Plaidy 5061
Shadow in the Sun: A Novel of Elizabeth I, the Virgin Queen - F.W. Kenyon 3460
So Merciful a Queen, So Cruel a Woman - Alice Harwood 2769
The Succession: A Novel of Elizabeth and James - George Garrett 2302
Sweet Will - Eric Malpass 4050
Take Heed of Loving Me: A Novel about John Donne - Elizabeth Gray Vining 6502
Tansy Taniard - Myrtle Strode-Jackson 6084
To Love a Queen - Lawrence Schoonover 5669
Too Near the Throne - Molly Costain Haycraft 2797
The Tower and the Dream - Jan Westcott 6647
Towers in the Mist - Elizabeth Goudge 2495
Trust and Treason - Margaret Birkhead 506
The White Queen - Frederic Fallon 2011
Will Shakespeare: The Untold Story - John Mortimer 4495
Women of Ashdon - Valerie Anand 135
You, My Brother - Philip Burton 809

Elizabeth II

Di and I - Peter Lefcourt 3714
Miss Nobody - Caroline Ross 5465

The Queen and I - Sue Townsend 6306

Esarhaddon

The Blood Star - Nicholas Guild 2611

Ethelred I

The Right Line of Cedric - Alfred Duggan 1773

Ethelred II the Unready

The Breath of Kings - Gene Farrington 2019

Ethelwulf

The Edge of Light - Joan Wolf 6839
The Right Line of Cedric - Alfred Duggan 1773

Ferdinand, Archduke

Rakossy - Cecelia Holland 2995

Ferdinand V

Caribbean - James A. Michener 4365
Columbus: A Romance - Rafael Sabatini 5549
Crown of Aloes - Norah Lofts 3840
The Dogs of Paradise - Abel Posse 5141
Ferdinand and Isabella - Hermann Kesten 3474
The Gentle Fury: A Novel of Margaret of Austria - Paul Lewis 3758
Here Lies Margot - Pamela Hill 2935
Katharine: The Virgin Widow - Jean Plaidy 5025
The Memoirs of Christopher Columbus - Stephen Marlowe 4096
Mercedes of Castile - James Fenimore Cooper 1304
The Prisoner of Tordesillas - Lawrence Schoonover 5665
The Queen's Cross: A Biographical Romance of Queen Isabella of Spain - Lawrence Schoonover 5666
The Shadow of the Pomegranate - Jean Plaidy 5062
Torquemada - Howard Fast 2045

Ferrante of Aragon

Duchess of Milan - Michael Ennis 1946

Francia, Jose Gaspar Rodriguez de

I, the Supreme - Augusto Antonio Roa Bastos 5353

Francis Joseph I

The Archduke - Michael Arnold 194

Francois I

Blood Royal - Mollie Hardwick 2690
The Chancellor - Lawrence Schoonover 5662
The King's Cavalier - Samuel Shellabarger 5795

Franz Josef I

The Emperor Franz Joseph - Ottokar Janetschek 3164
Imperial Waltz - William M. Abrahams 13
Poland - James A. Michener 4373
The Time of Murder at Mayerling - Ann Dukthas 1778
Winter of the Heart - Linda J. LaRosa 3665

Frederick II

Antichrist: A Novel of the Emperor Frederick II - Cecelia Holland 2982
Elizabeth's Greetings - Rosemary Haughton 2774
The Emperor, the Sages and Death - Rachel Berdach 475
The Great Infidel - Joseph Jay Deiss 1582
The Joyful Beggar: A Novel of St. Francis of Assisi - Louis De Wohl 1568
The Quiet Light - Louis De Wohl 1572
The Saracen Blade - Frank Yerby 6926

Frederick Barbarossa

The Kings of Vain Intent - Graham Shelby 5791

Frederick Leopold

A Castle in Bavaria - Prince Thibaut d'Orleans 1693

Frederick the Great

The Anthem - Noel B. Gerson 2361
Consuelo - George Sand 5582
The Days of the King - Bruno Frank 2200
Rebel Princess - Evelyn Anthony 164

Fulk

Queen of Swords - Judith Tarr 6169

Gadtsung
Lady Wu - Yutang Lin   3782

Galla Placidia
Bury Me in Ravenna - Agnes Carr Vaughan   6432

Genghis Khan
Orlok - Don Dandrea   1461

George I
Now Face to Face - Karleen Koen   3530
The Princess of Celle - Jean Plaidy   5045
Queen in Waiting - Jean Plaidy   5048

George II
Admiral of Fear - Victor Suthren   6126
Caroline the Queen - Jean Plaidy   5009
The Prince and the Quakeress - Jean Plaidy   5043

George III
The Bonnet Laird's Daughter - Barbara
    Annandale   154
Cato's War - Guy Wheeler   6655
The Duke's Mistress: The Story of Mary Ann Clarke -
    F.W. Kenyon   3447
Footman in Powder - Helen Ashton   216
Guillotine - Mark Logan   3865
The Lady From Yorktown - Eva McDonald   4260
Let the King Beware! - Honore Morrow   4489
Perdita's Prince - Jean Plaidy   5040
Regency Royal - Michael Hardwick   2687
The Regent's Daughter - Jean Plaidy   5055
*Sacred and Profane: A Novel of the Life and Times of
    Mozart* - David Weiss   6609
Sweet Lass of Richmond Hill - Jean Plaidy   5067
The Third George - Jean Plaidy   5068
Those Who Love - Irving Stone   6064

George IV
The Abandoned Woman - Richard Condon   1235
Blackstone and the Scourge of Europe - Richard
    Falkirk   2007
The Little Victoria - Lozania Prole   5196
The Young Victoria - Tyler Whittle   6724

George V
Attack the Lusitania! - Raymond Hitchcock   2956
The Buckingham Palace Connection - Ted
    Willis   6792
Edward and Mrs. Simpson - A.C.H. Smith   5916
The Faraway Drums - Jon Cleary   1104
God Save the Tsar - Susanna Hoe   2976

Gilgamesh
Gilgamesh the King - Robert Silverberg   5853

Go-Shirakawa
The Sword of Hachiman - Lynn Guest   2608

Godwinesson, Harold
The Saxon Tapestry - Sile Rice   5317

Grainne
This Land Fulfilled - Charles Andrew Brady   636

Grey, Lady Jane
A Crown in Darkness: A Novel about Lady Jane Grey
    - Margaret Mullally   4512
Elizabeth, Captive Princess - Margaret Irwin   3118
Feast in the Morning - Hugh Preston   5175
The Lily and the Leopards - Alice Harwood   2765
Sister to Jane: The Story of Lady Katharine Grey -
    Beatrice May   4202
The Sixth Wife - Jean Plaidy   5063
The Ten-Day Queen - Lozania Prole   5199

Gustav III
King's Masque - Evan John   3220

Gustavus II Adolphus
People of the Book - David Stacton   5974
World and Paradise - Edgar Maas   3953

Hadrian
The Crow Goddess - Patricia Finney   2094
Hadrian's Memoirs - Marguerite Yourcenar   6947
If I Forget Thee - Brenda Lesley Segal   5720
Prince of Israel - Elias Gilner   2422

The Soldier and the Sage: A Novel about Akiba -
    Richard G. Hubler   3065
The Sword and the Promise - Benjamin Siegel   5845

Harold II
The Bastard King - Jean Plaidy   5004
The Conqueror - Georgette Heyer   2881
The Conqueror's Wife - Noel B. Gerson   2363
The Golden Warrior: The Story of Harold and William
    - Hope Muntz   4517
Harold, the Last of the Saxon Kings - Edward Bulwer-
    Lytton   767
Harold Was My King - Hilda Lewis   3749
The Norman Pretender - Valerie Anand   132
The Wind From Hastings - Morgan Llywelyn   3825

Harold Harefoot
Gildenford - Valerie Anand   130
King Hereafter - Dorothy Dunnett   1802

Harun al Raschid
The Tyrant of Bagdhad - Glenn Pierce   4996

Hatshepsut
Child of the Morning - Pauline Gedge   2343
King and Goddess - Judith Tarr   6166
Pharaoh - Eloise Jarvis McGraw   4276

Hedh
Isle of Glory - Jane Oliver   4723

Henri I
*Fortune's Knave: The Making of William the
    Conqueror* - Mary Lide   3774

Henri II
Courtesan - Diane Haeger   2635
Immortal Queen - Elizabeth Byrd   834
The Italian Woman - Jean Plaidy   5024
Madame Serpent - Jean Plaidy   5033
Queen's Play - Dorothy Dunnett   1805
Royal Road to Fotheringay - Jean Plaidy   5059
Vagabond Prophet - Allene Symons   6149

Henri III
Les Quarant Cinq - Alexandre Dumas   1779
The Scarlet Cloak - Jean Plaidy   5061

Henri IV
The Anthem - Noel B. Gerson   2361
Deborah and the Siege of Paris - Colette
    Davenat   1500
Henry, King of France - Heinrich Mann   4061
Queen Margot - Alexandre Dumas   1780

Henry I
The Fatal Crown - Ellen Jones   3289
The Lion of Justice - Jean Plaidy   5031
The Passionate Enemies - Jean Plaidy   5039

Henry II
Ann of Cambray - Mary Lide   3772
Beloved Enemy: The Passions of Eleanor of Aquitaine
    - Ellen Jones   3288
Champion - L. Christian Balling   285
The Courts of Love - Jean Plaidy   5010
The Courts of Love: A Romance of Medieval France -
    Peter Bourne   592
The Devil Is Loose - Graham Shelby   5790
Eleanor the Queen - Norah Lofts   3842
Fitzempress' Law - Diana Norman   4644
King's Man - C.M. Edmondston   1880
The Lion of Christ - Margaret Butler   823
The Lion of England - Margaret Butler   824
The Lion of Justice - Margaret Butler   825
Lionheart!: A Novel of Richard I, King of England -
    Martha Rofheart   5428
My Life for My Sheep - Alfred Duggan   1772
Not Built with Hands - Helen Constance White   6679
Ordeal by Silence - Prudence Andrew   142
The Plantagenet Prelude - Jean Plaidy   5041
The Queen's War: A Novel of Eleanor of Aquitaine -
    Jeanne Mackin   3996
The Rain Maiden - Jill M. Phillips   4985
The Revolt of the Eaglets - Jean Plaidy   5057

A Royal Quest - Mary Lide   3777
The Swords of December - Robert York   6933
*Thomas: A Novel of the Life, Passions, and Miracles
    of Becket* - Shelley Mydans   4538
The Troubadour's Romance - Robyn Carr   940
When Christ and His Saints Slept - Sharon Kay
    Penman   4908

Henry III
Alexander the Glorious - Jane Oliver   4719
The Battle of the Queens - Jean Plaidy   5005
The De Montfort Legacy - Pamela Bennetts   447
Doctor Mirabilis - James Blish   550
Falconer's Judgement - Ian Morson   4494
Falls the Shadow - Sharon Kay Penman   4903
The Marriage of Meggotta - Edith Pargeter   4799
The Queen From Provence - Jean Plaidy   5047
Shield of Honor - Alice Walworth Graham   2511
The White Cutter - David Pownall   5158

Henry IV
The Bloody Field - Edith Pargeter   4795
The Dogs of Paradise - Abel Posse   5141
Glendower Country - Martha Rofheart   5427
Good King Harry - Denise Giardina   2393
Harry of Monmouth - A.M. Maughan   4199
In a Dark Wood Wandering - Hella S. Haasse   2631
My Lord John - Georgette Heyer   2895
Royal Sword at Agincourt - Pamela Bennetts   455
Simon the Coldheart - Georgette Heyer   2901
The Star of Lancaster - Jean Plaidy   5065
The Whyte Harte - P.C. Doherty   1681

Henry V
Crippled Splendour - Evan John   3219
Crown in Candlelight - Rosemary Hawley
    Jarman   3166
Falstaff - Robert Nye   4653
Fortune Made His Sword - Martha Rofheart   5426
Good King Harry - Denise Giardina   2393
In a Dark Wood Wandering - Hella S. Haasse   2631
The Lily and the Leopard - Susan Wiggs   6745
My Lord John - Georgette Heyer   2895
The Queen's Secret - Jean Plaidy   5053
The Royal Pawn - Antonia Ridge   5327
Simon the Coldheart - Georgette Heyer   2901
Walk with Peril - Dorothy V.S. Jackson   3132
Wife to Henry V - Hilda Lewis   3752

Henry VI
Crown in Candlelight - Rosemary Hawley
    Jarman   3166
Epitaph for Three Women - Jean Plaidy   5012
The Last of the Barons - Edward Bulwer-Lytton   769
The Queen's Secret - Jean Plaidy   5053
Red Rose of Anjou - Jean Plaidy   5054
The Royal Pawn - Antonia Ridge   5327
The White Rose - Jan Westcott   6648

Henry VII
The Dragon and the Rose - Roberta Gellis   2350
The Golden Knight - George Challis   971
Katharine: The Virgin Widow - Jean Plaidy   5025
The King's Grey Mare - Rosemary Hawley
    Jarman   3167
The Lady Cicely - Sandra Wilson   6813
The Queen's Sister - Sandra Wilson   6815
The Thistle and the Rose - Jean Plaidy   5069
The Traitors of Bosworth - Robert Farrington   2021
Tudor Agent - Robert Farrington   2022
The Tudor Rose - Margaret Campbell Barnes   329
Uneasy Lies the Head - Jean Plaidy   5071
The Wrong Plantagenet - Marian Palmer   4781

Henry VIII
Anne Boleyn - Evelyn Anthony   158
Anne of the Thousand Days - Edward Fenton   2059
The Autobiography of Henry VIII - Margaret
    George   2355
The Blanket of the Dark - John Buchan   749
Blood Royal - Mollie Hardwick   2690
Brief Gaudy Hour - Margaret Campbell Barnes   322

A Brood of Vipers - Michael Clynes 1133
Circle in the Water - Susan Wiggs 6742
Command of the King - Mary Lide 3773
The Concubine - Norah Lofts 3839
A Crown in Darkness: A Novel about Lady Jane Grey
   - Margaret Mullally 4512
Feast in the Morning - Hugh Preston 5175
The Fifth Queen - Ford Madox Ford 2161
Flame of Fire - Jane Oliver 4722
The Grail Murders - Michael Clynes 1135
The Green Salamander - Pamela Hill 2933
The Heir of Allington - Philippa Wiat 6727
Henry VIII and His Six Wives - Maureen
   Peters 4975
Her Royal Destiny - Carol Maxwell Eady 1820
Here Comes the King - Philip Lindsay 3792
The Heretic - Alison Macleod 4002
The Hireling - Alison Macleod 4003
I Am Mary Tudor - Hilda Lewis 3750
I, Elizabeth - Rosalind Miles 4378
In the Shadow of the Crown - Jean Plaidy 5022
The Ivy Crown: A Biographical Novel of Queen
   Katherine Parr - Mary M. Luke 3923
Katheryn, the Wanton Queen - Maureen Peters 4976
Kathryn: In the Court of Six Queens - Anne Merton
   Abbey 1
The King's Achievement - Robert Hugh Benson 459
King's Fool - Margaret Campbell Barnes 325
The King's Good Servant - Olive White 6696
The King's Pleasure - Norah Lofts 3847
The King's Pleasure - Jean Plaidy 5026
The King's Secret Matter - Jean Plaidy 5027
The Knight and the Dove - Lori Wick 6732
The Lady in the Tower - Jean Plaidy 5028
The Lily and the Leopards - Alice Harwood 2765
The Man on a Donkey - H.F.M. Prescott 5170
Mistress Anne - Carolly Erickson 1952
Murder Most Royal - Jean Plaidy 5036
My Lady Glamis - Pamela Hill 2940
My Lady of Cleves - Margaret Campbell Barnes 328
My Lord of Canterbury - Godfrey Turton 6369
The Poisoned Chalice - Michael Clynes 1136
The Prince and the Pauper - Mark Twain 6373
Queen Anne Boleyn - Francis Hackett 2634
Queen of This Realm: The Story of Queen Elizabeth I -
   Jean Plaidy 5050
The Queen's Grace - Jan Westcott 6646
The Red-Haired Brat - Joanna Dessau 1627
The Reluctant Queen - Molly Costain Haycraft 2796
The Rose Without a Thorn - Jean Plaidy 5058
Royal Nonesuch: A Tudor Tapestry - Beatrice
   White 6674
St. Thomas's Eve - Jean Plaidy 5060
The Serpent Garden - Judith Merkle Riley 5336
The Shadow of the Pomegranate - Jean Plaidy 5062
The Sixth Wife - Jean Plaidy 5063
Stage of Fools - Charles Andrew Brady 635
The Sword of Truth - Gilbert Morris 4472
The White Rose Murders - Michael Clynes 1137
Windsor Castle - William Harrison Ainsworth 59
The Wise Virgin - Hebe Elsna 1934
Women of Ashdon - Valerie Anand 135

Herod I
King Jesus - Robert Graves 2549

Herod Agrippa I
Agrippa's Daughter - Howard Fast 2025
The Kingdom of the Wicked - Anthony Burgess 778
Pontius Pilate: A Biographical Novel - Paul L.
   Maier 4034
The Sins of Herod: A Novel of Rome and the Early
   Church - Frank G. Slaughter 5900

Herod Agrippa II
The Glorious Folly: A Novel of the Time of St. Paul -
   Louis De Wohl 1565
Man on Fire: A Novel on the Life of St. Paul -
   LeGette Blythe 558

Herod Antipas
The Big Fisherman - Lloyd C. Douglas 1702
Brothers of Vengeance - LeGette Blythe 556
The Eighth Veil - Ellis Kadison 3320
The Good Tidings - William Sidney 5843
Hear Me, Pilate! - LeGette Blythe 557
Justus - Arthur L. Lapham 3663
The Last Temptation of Christ - Nikos
   Kazantzakis 3384
Pontius Pilate: A Biographical Novel - Paul L.
   Maier 4034
The Sins of Herod: A Novel of Rome and the Early
   Church - Frank G. Slaughter 5900

Herod the Great
A Love Divine - Alexandra Ripley 5340
Man of Nazareth - Anthony Burgess 779
The Source - James A. Michener 4374

Hippolita
The Bull From the Sea - Mary Renault 5295

Hohenstaufen, Henry
Banners of Gold - Pamela Kaufman 3371

Honorius
Bury Me in Ravenna - Agnes Carr Vaughan 6432
Captive of Rome - Theodora McCormick Du
   Bois 1740
Roman Go Home! - Adam Fergusson 2065
Threshold of Fire - Hella S. Haasse 2633

Horemheb
The Egyptian - Mika Waltari 6552
On a Balcony - David Stacton 5973

Hsien Feng
Imperial Woman - Pearl S. Buck 755

Hsuan-tsung
The Court of the Lion - Eleanor Cooney 1294

Hung Hsiu-Ch'uan
The Second Son of Heaven: A Novel of Nineteenth-
   Century China - C.Y. Lee 3707

Hypsipyle
Jason - Henry Treece 6331

Inanna
The Last Warrior Queen - Mary Mackey 3992

Irene
The Belt of Gold - Cecelia Holland 2984

Isabella
Columbus: A Romance - Rafael Sabatini 5549
The Prisoner of Tordesillas - Lawrence
   Schoonover 5665

Isabella I
1492 - Newton Frolich 2236
Crown of Aloes - Norah Lofts 3840
The Dogs of Paradise - Abel Posse 5141
Ferdinand and Isabella - Hermann Kesten 3474
The Gentle Fury: A Novel of Margaret of Austria -
   Paul Lewis 3758
Here Lies Margot - Pamela Hill 2935
The Memoirs of Christopher Columbus - Stephen
   Marlowe 4096
Mercedes of Castile - James Fenimore Cooper 1304
The Queen's Cross: A Biographical Romance of
   Queen Isabella of Spain - Lawrence
   Schoonover 5666
Torquemada - Howard Fast 2045

Ivan IV
Darker Jewels - Chelsea Quinn Yarbro 6898
The Muscovite - Alison Macleod 4004

Ivan the Terrible
Prince of Outlaws - Alexey Tolstoy 6294
The Ringed Castle - Dorothy Dunnett 1807
Russka: The Novel of Russia - Edward
   Rutherfurd 5535
Sir Rogue - Leslie Turner White 6691

James I
Call Lady Purbeck - Hilda Lewis 3745
The Cleopatra Boy - Eric Malpass 4048
Crippled Splendour - Evan John 3219
Daughter of Eve - Noel B. Gerson 2366
Death of the Fox - George Garrett 2300
For My Great Folly - Thomas B. Costain 1365
The Fortunes of Nigel - Sir Walter Scott 5696
James and Joan - Anne Fremantle 2221
Katherine Christian - Hugh Walpole 6546
The King James Version - Stanley N. Stewart 6035
Lady in Waiting - Rosemary Sutcliff 6123
Lion Rampant - Bernard Shrimsley 5836
The Murder in the Tower - Jean Plaidy 5035
Physician Extraordinary: A Novel of the Life and
   Times of William Harvey - David Weiss 6608
Pocahontas - Susan Donnell 1691
Powhatan's Daughter - John Clarke Bowman 605
Ralegh's Fair Bess: The Story of Bess Throckmorton -
   Judy Turner 6365
Scapegoat for a Stuart - Kate Kirby 3504
The Sea 'Venture - F. van Wyck Mason 4159
The Street of Kings - Charles Dexter 1637
The Succession: A Novel of Elizabeth and James -
   George Garrett 2302
Take Heed of Loving Me: A Novel about John Donne -
   Elizabeth Gray Vining 6502
To Love a Queen - Lawrence Schoonover 5669
Unicorn Rampant - Nigel Tranter 6323
Wife to Great Buckingham - Hilda Lewis 3751
The World, the Flesh, and the Devil - Reay
   Tannahill 6159
The Young and Lonely King - Jane Lane 3659

James II
The Elusive Crown - Hebe Elsna 1931
The Golden Days - Robert Neill 4569
James, by the Grace of God - Hugh Williamson
   Ross 5499
King's Agent - Justus Kent Clark 1090
Lillibullero - Robert Neill 4571
Log Cabin Noble - F. van Wyck Mason 4153
Lorna Doone - R.D. Blackmore 528
Silver Shoals - Hamilton Cochran 1142
Treason's Gift - Pamela Belle 434
William's Wife - Jean Plaidy 5077

James III
To Lie with Lions - Dorothy Dunnett 1810
The Unicorn Hunt - Dorothy Dunnett 1811

James IV
Chain of Destiny - Nigel Tranter 6314
Falcon: The Autobiography of His Grace James IV,
   King of Scots - A.J. Stewart 6021
The Hepburn - Jan Westcott 6645
The King's Vixen - Pamela Hill 2937
The Riven Realm - Nigel Tranter 6317
Sunset at Noon - Jane Oliver 4728
The Thistle and the Rose - Jean Plaidy 5069

James V
James, by the Grace of God - Nigel Tranter 6315
My Lady Glamis - Pamela Hill 2940
A Stake in the Kingdom - Nigel Tranter 6321

James VI
The Border Lord - Jan Westcott 6641
The Master of Gray Trilogy - Nigel Tranter 6316
Mine Is the Kingdom - Jane Oliver 4726
No Smoke Without Fire - Alice Harwood 2767

Jan II Kazimir
Poland - James A. Michener 4373

Jan III Sobieski
Poland - James A. Michener 4373

Jean de Brienne
Blessed Are the Meek: A Novel about St. Francis of
   Assisi - Zofja Kossak-Szczucka 3542

John
The Barons of Runnymede - Pamela Bennetts 445

The Battle of the Queens - Jean Plaidy 5005
The Falcon and the Flower - Virginia Henley 2826
Harp into Battle - Cecil Maiden 4031
Here Be Dragons - Sharon Kay Penman 4904
In the Shadow of Midnight - Marsha Canham 880
Lady of Hay - Barbara Erskine 1955
Leopards and Lilies - Alfred Duggan 1769
Myself as Witness - James Goldman 2458
The Prince of Darkness - Jean Plaidy 5044
The Sheriff of Nottingham - Richard Kluger 3512
This Bright Sword - Donald Barr Chidsey 1066
The Wolf at the Door - Graham Shelby 5793

John II
Their Most Serene Majesties - Ange Vlachos 6505

Juan II
The Dogs of Paradise - Abel Posse 5141
Master of Castile - Samuel Edwards 1888

Juan Carlos I
Di and I - Peter Lefcourt 3714

Juana I
The Prisoner of Tordesillas - Lawrence
   Schoonover 5665

Julian the Apostate
The Death of the Gods - Dmitri Merezhkovski 4338
Imperial Renegade - Louis De Wohl 1567
Julian - Gore Vidal 6489

Justinian I
Basilissa: A Tale of the Empress Theodora - John
   Masefield 4142
The Bearkeeper's Daughter - Gillian Bradshaw 628
Count Belisarius - Robert Graves 2544
The Female: A Novel of Another Time - Paul I.
   Wellman 6617
A Flame in Byzantium - Chelsea Quinn Yarbro 6899
Theodora - Samuel Edwards 1891
Theodora and the Emperor - Harold Lamb 3608
The Vandal - Richard O'Connor 4687

Kaahumanu
Lord of the Isles - Donald Barr Chidsey 1063

Kalakaua
Somewhere Within This House - Jean Francis
   Webb 6587

Kamehameha I
No Brighter Glory - Armstrong Sperry 5963

Kamehameha III
Ka'a'awa: A Novel about Hawaii in the 1850s -
   Oswald Andrew Bushnell 814
The White King - Samuel Bertram Harrison 2747

al-Kamil, al-Malik
Antichrist: A Novel of the Emperor Frederick II -
   Cecelia Holland 2982

Kamose
Sword of Glory - Peter Danielson 1477

Kanakoa
Hawaii - James A. Michener 4370

Kao Tsung
Empress - Evelyn McCune 4238

Khan, Akbar
Flashman - George MacDonald Fraser 2204

Kiwang Hsi
Imperial Woman - Pearl S. Buck 755

Kleomenes
The Corn King and the Spring Queen - Naomi
   Mitchison 4419

Kuang-Hsu
Twilight of the Dragon - Peter Bourne 596

Kublai Khan
Caravan to Kanadu: A Novel of Marco Polo - Edison
   Marshall 4103
Invisible Cities - Italo Calvino 867
The Journeyer - Gary Jennings 3194

Messer Marco Polo - Donn Byrne 840
Shike: Time of Dragons - Robert Shea 5784
*Sons of the Steppe: The Story of How the Conqueror
   Genghis Khan Was Overcome* - Hans
   Baumann 380

Leopold I
Seven Tempest - William Vaughan Wilkins 6761

Leopold II
The Gypsy From Cadiz - Tamsin Hamilton 2670
Lillie - David Butler 818

Liliuokalani
Carolina Courage - Dana Fuller Ross 5469

Liu Pang
The Dream of Confucius - Jean Levi 3734

Llywelyn the Great
Harp into Battle - Cecil Maiden 4031

Lobengula
Earthshaker - Robert Wilson Krepps 3553
On Trial for My Country - Stanlake Samkange 5578

Loth
Bride of the Spear - Kathleen Herbert 2851

Louis VI
Beloved Enemy: The Passions of Eleanor of Aquitaine
   - Ellen Jones 3288
The Dragon Waiting: A Masque of History - John M.
   Ford 2165

Louis VII
Beloved Enemy: The Passions of Eleanor of Aquitaine
   - Ellen Jones 3288
The Courts of Love - Jean Plaidy 5010
Eleanor the Queen - Norah Lofts 3842

Louis VIII
The Battle of the Queens - Jean Plaidy 5005

Louis IX
The Quiet Light - Louis De Wohl 1572

Louis X
The Poisoned Crown - Maurice Druon 1734
The Strangled Queen - Maurice Druon 1737

Louis XI
Fortune's Wheel - Rhoda S. Edwards 1886
The Golden Yoke: A Novel of the War of the Roses -
   Olive Eckerson 1837
The Hunchback of Notre Dame - Victor Hugo 3076
Quentin Durward - Sir Walter Scott 5705
The Spider King - Lawrence Schoonover 5668
To Lie with Lions - Dorothy Dunnett 1810
The Unicorn Hunt - Dorothy Dunnett 1811
The White Queen - Lesley J. Nickell 4611

Louis XII
The Golden Porcupine - Muriel Ray Bolton 567
The Reluctant Queen - Molly Costain Haycraft 2796
A Stake in the Kingdom - Nigel Tranter 6321

Louis XIII
The Arm and the Darkness - Taylor Caldwell 850
The Cardinal and the Queen - Evelyn Anthony 159
Cinq-Mars - Alfred Victor de Vigny 6495
The Three Musketeers - Alexandre Dumas 1782

Louis XIV
All the Golden Gifts - Iola Fuller 2251
All the King's Ladies - Janice Law 3678
Angelique - Sergeanne Golon 2465
Angelique and the King - Sergeanne Golon 2468
Angelique in Revolt - Sergeanne Golon 2471
The Anthem - Noel B. Gerson 2361
A Candle for D'Artagnan - Chelsea Quinn
   Yarbro 6895
The Cat and the King - Louis Auchincloss 229
*The Crown and the Shadow: The Story of Francoise
   d'Aubigne, Marquise de Maintenon* - Pamela
   Hill 2930
The Ghost of Monsieur Scarron - Janet Lewis 3755
The Gilded Torch - Iola Fuller 2252

The King's Way - Francoise Chandernagor 986
Louis the Well-Beloved - Jean Plaidy 5032
The Marquis - Joan Sanders 5586
The Oracle Glass - Judith Merkle Riley 5335
Royal Flush: The Story of Minette - Margaret
   Irwin 3121
The Secret Wife - Alice Acland 22
The Shadow of the Sun - Sylvia Pell 4891
The Shepherd's Crook - Paul Frischauer 2234
Sorrow by Day - Marjorie Coryn 1359
Three Came to Ville Marie - Alan Sullivan 6114
The Wandering Prince - Jean Plaidy 5075
Ward of the Sun King - Mildred Allen Butler 826

Louis XV
A Day of Battle - Vincent Sheean 5787
The French Bride - Evelyn Anthony 163
Golden Venus - David Mynders Smythe 5933
Louis the Well-Beloved - Jean Plaidy 5032
Louisiana Purchase - A.E. Hotchner 3039
Royal Merry-Go-Round - F.W. Kenyon 3459
To Dance with Kings - Rosalind Laker 3601
Tomahawk - Donald Clayton Porter 5129

Louis XVI
Asylum for the Queen - Mildred A. Jordan 3303
City of Darkness, City of Light - Marge Piercy 4998
The Devil's Laughter - Frank Yerby 6913
*Dr. Guillotine: The Eccentric Exploits of an Early
   Scientist* - Herbert Lom 3867
*The Fatal Friendship: Marie Antoinette, Count Fersen
   and the Flight to Varennes* - Stanley Loomis 3895
Fear No More - Hester W. Chapman 990
Hester - Brian Cleeve 1107
The Man Who Killed the King - Dennis
   Wheatley 6654
Marie Antoinette - F.W. Kenyon 3453
Palaces of Desire - Kate Alexander 81
The Queen's Confession - Victoria Holt 3019
Sweet Marie-Antoinette - Lozania Prole 5198
To Dance with Kings - Rosalind Laker 3601
Tricolour - Mark Logan 3866

Louis XVIII
Holy Week - Louis Aragon 182
Waterloo - Frederic E. Smith 5920

Louis Philippe
Disraeli Rising - Maurice Edelman 1852

Lusignan, James de
To Lie with Lions - Dorothy Dunnett 1810

Macbeth
King Hereafter - Dorothy Dunnett 1802
Lady of Moray - Bonnie Copeland 1318

Maelmordha
The Kings in Winter - Cecelia Holland 2991

Maeve
Fire Queen - Deborah Grabien 2503

Magnus Maximus
The Eagles Depart - John Gloag 2434

Mahmud II
Sultana - Michael, Prince of Greece 4358
Valide: A Novel of the Harem - Barbara Chase-
   Riboud 1007

Malcolm III
Sing Morning Star - Jane Oliver 4727

Manuel I
Their Most Serene Majesties - Ange Vlachos 6505

Marcus Aurelius
Between Eternities - Robert H. Pilpel 5001
*The Equinox: A Novel of Rome in the Time of
   Commodus* - Carol Saylor 5622
A Fig in Winter - Willa Gibbs 2400
Marius the Epicurean - Walter Pater 4826
Roman Nights - Ron Burns 803

Maria Theresa
Sacred and Profane: A Novel of the Life and Times of Mozart - David Weiss 6609
The Strange Case of Madamoiselle P. - Patrick Ireland 3109

Mark
The White Raven - Diana L. Paxson 4847

Mary I
The Bisley Boy - Christopher Hunt 3080
Elizabeth and the Prince of Spain - Margaret Irwin 3117
In the House of the King - Louis Zara 6951
In the Shadow of the Crown - Jean Plaidy 5022
Legacy - Susan Kay 3374
Oh! Where Are Bloody Mary's Earrings? - Robert Player 5079
Queen of This Realm: The Story of Queen Elizabeth I - Jean Plaidy 5050
The Ringed Castle - Dorothy Dunnett 1807
Shadow in the Sun: A Novel of Elizabeth I, the Virgin Queen - F.W. Kenyon 3460
So Merciful a Queen, So Cruel a Woman - Alice Harwood 2769
The Strong Room - Jere Hungerford Wheelwright 6671
The Tower of London - William Harrison Ainsworth 58
The Young Elizabeth - Jennette Letton 3730

Mary II
The Glory and the Dream - F.W. Kenyon 3450
The Power and the Passion - Christina Nicholson 4609
The Renegade - Donald Clayton Porter 5122
William's Wife - Jean Plaidy 5077

Mary, Queen of Scots
The Captive Queen of Scots - Jean Plaidy 5008
Checkmate - Dorothy Dunnett 1799
Come Rack! Come Rope! - Robert Hugh Benson 458
The Game of Kings - Dorothy Dunnett 1801
The Gay Galliard - Margaret Irwin 3119
The Green Salamander - Pamela Hill 2933
I, Elizabeth - Rosalind Miles 4378
Immortal Queen - Elizabeth Byrd 834
King in Hell: A Novel of Bothwell and Mary, Queen of Scots - Beverly Balin 282
The Lion and the Rose - Jane Oliver 4724
Maid of Honour: A Novel Set in the Court of Mary, Queen of Scots - Elizabeth Byrd 836
Mary of Scotland - F.W. Kenyon 3454
Mary, Queen of Scotland and the Isles - Margaret George 2356
The Master of Gray Trilogy - Nigel Tranter 6316
Mine Is the Kingdom - Jane Oliver 4726
No Smoke Without Fire - Alice Harwood 2767
Parcel of Rogues - Jane Lane 3656
The Proud Man - Elizabeth Linington 3800
Queen's Caprice - Marjorie Bowen 599
The Queen's Head - Edward Marston 4125
Queen's Play - Dorothy Dunnett 1805
Reluctant Cavalier - Donald Barr Chidsey 1064
Royal Road to Fotheringay - Jean Plaidy 5059
Seats of the Mighty: A Novel of James Stuart, Brother of Mary, Queen of Scots - Alice Harwood 2768
So Merciful a Queen, So Cruel a Woman - Alice Harwood 2769
The Sword and the Flame - Pamela Hill 2945
The Tower and the Dream - Jan Westcott 6647
The White Queen - Frederic Fallon 2011

Mauakes
Horses of Heaven - Gillian Bradshaw 630

Maud
Bond of Blood - Roberta Gellis 2349

Maximilian
The Breast of the Dove - Herbert Gorman 2491
The Cactus and the Crown - Catherine Gavin 2318
Chapultepec - Norman Zollinger 6965

Flames of Empire - Peter Bourne 594
The Grasshopper King - Elizabeth Boatwright Coker 1165
Passengers to Mexico: The Last Invasion of Mexico - Blair Niles 4627

Maximilian I
The Gentle Fury: A Novel of Margaret of Austria - Paul Lewis 3758

Medici, Lorenzo de
The Medici Emerald - Martin Woodhouse 6851
The Medici Guns - Martin Woodhouse 6852
The Medici Hawks - Martin Woodhouse 6853
The Time Returns - Alexandra Ripley 5343

Medici, Marie de'
The Young and Lonely King - Jane Lane 3659

Melisende
Queen of Swords - Judith Tarr 6169

Menelaus
The Goddess - Miranda Seymour 5763
The Private Life of Helen of Troy - John Erskine 1957

Minos
The King Must Die - Mary Renault 5298
The Maze Maker - Michael Ayrton 250

Mithridates VI
The Grass Crown - Colleen McCullough 4236

Monmouth, Harry
Royal Sword at Agincourt - Pamela Bennetts 455

Montezuma II
Aztec - Gary Jennings 3193
Captain From Castille - Samuel Shellabarger 5794
Copilli, Aztec Prince - Miguel Aleman Velasco 75
Cortez and Marina - Edison Marshall 4105
Death of the Fifth Sun - Robert Somerlott 5944
The Fair God - Lew Wallace 6537
The Golden Princess - Alexander Baron 335
The Great White Gods - Eduard Stucken 6102
The Heart of Jade - Salvador de Madariaga 4024
The Luck of Huemac: A Novel about the Aztecs - Daniel Peters 4946
The Sun, He Dies: A Novel about the End of the Aztec World - Jamake Highwater 2919
They Are Coming: The Conquest of Mexico - Jose Lopez Portillo y Pacheco 3896

Mor, Malachy
The Gallowglass - Howard Breslin 666

Moram
Ruan - Bryher 746

Mourad V
Regards From the Dead Princess: A Novel of a Life - Kenize Mourad 4505

Muhammad II
The Dark Angel - Mika Waltari 6551
The Medici Hawks - Martin Woodhouse 6853

Muhammad IV
Poland - James A. Michener 4373

Mulai Ismail
Angelique in Barbary - Sergeanne Golon 2469

Muwatallis I
The Hittite - Noel B. Gerson 2373

Napoleon I
Napoleon Symphony - Anthony Burgess 780

Napoleon III
Eugenie - Hester W. Chapman 989
Flames of Empire - Peter Bourne 594
The Gaudy Empire - Alfred Neumann 4584
I, Rachel - March Cost 1361
Imperial Courtesan - F.W. Kenyon 3452
The Passion of Letty Fox - Diana Saunders 5610
Quiet Lady - Norman Collins 1216
A Spy for Napoleon - Baroness Emma Orczy 4746

That Spanish Woman - F.W. Kenyon 3461

Narbonidus
The Prophet - Sholem Asch 201

Nebuchadnezzar II
The Babylonians - Nathaniel Norsen Weinreb 6600
Judith - Stella Wilchek 6748

Nefertiti
The Goddess Queen: A Novel Based on the Life of Nefertiti - Nicole Vidal 6494

Nero
The Apostle - Sholem Asch 197
Beware of Caesar - Vincent Sheean 5786
Bloody Poet - Deszo Kosztolanyi 3546
Brothers of Vengeance - LeGette Blythe 556
The Conspiracy - John Hersey 2870
The Eighth Veil - Ellis Kadison 3320
The Flames of Rome - Paul L. Maier 4033
The Glorious Folly: A Novel of the Time of St. Paul - Louis De Wohl 1565
Hortensius, Friend of Nero - Edith Pargeter 4798
The Illusionist - Anita Mason 4144
The Imperial Governor - George Shipway 5828
Josephus - Lion Feuchtwanger 2072
The Kingdom of the Wicked - Anthony Burgess 778
Man on Fire: A Novel on the Life of St. Paul - LeGette Blythe 558
Nero - Mary Teresa Ronalds 5437
Octavia: A Tale of Ancient Rome - Seymour Van Santvoord 6428
Quo Vadis - Henryk Sienkiewicz 5848
The Roman - Mika Waltari 6554
Scorpus the Moor - Leslie Turner White 6690
The Silver Chalice - Thomas B. Costain 1370
Upon This Rock: A Novel of Simon Peter, Prince of Apostles - Frank G. Slaughter 5906
The Wolf of Masada - John Fredman 2220

Nezahual
The Coil of the Serpent - Dexter Allen 94
Valley of Eagles - Dexter Allen 96

Nicholas I
The Fourth King - Glen Petrie 4979

Nicholas II
And the Stars Shall Fall - True Bowen 603
The Dawning of Deliverance - Judith Pella 4892
Devoted Friends - Joe Poyer 5161
Elizabeth and Alexandra - Antony Lambton 3616
Emily - Cynthia Harrod-Eagles 2753
God Save the Tsar - Susanna Hoe 2976
Heirs of the Motherland - Judith Pella 4893
Petersburg - Emily Hanlon 2677
Rasputin's Revenge - John T. Lescroart 3725
Searching for the Emperor - Roberto Pazzi 4858
The Snow Mountain - Catherine Gavin 2324
The Summer Day Is Done - R.T. Stevens 6001
Time After Time - Allen Appel 171
White Nights, Red Dawn - Frederick Nolan 4634

Oedipus
The Eagle King - Henry Treece 6327

O'Higgins, Bernardo
Taste of Glory - Carleton Beals 394

Oswy
Absolution by Murder - Peter Tremayne 6334

Otto II
The Eagle's Daughter - Judith Tarr 6165

Pasha, Husref Mehmed
Bosnian Chronicle - Ivo Andric 150

Pedro the Cruel
Don Pedro's Captain - Pamela Bennetts 449

Pericles
Alcibiades, Beloved of Gods - Vincenz Brun 735

Peter III
Rebel Princess - Evelyn Anthony 164

Peter the Great
Alaska - James A. Michener 4364
Jesters - David Markish 4090
Katrina - Jeramie Price 5190
Peter the Great - Alexey Tolstoy 6293
The Power and the Passion - Christina
  Nicholson 4609
Russka: The Novel of Russia - Edward
  Rutherfurd 5535
Tsar's Woman - Pamela Hill 2946

Philip II
Alexander of Macedon: The Journey to World's End -
  Harold Lamb 3607
The Barons of Runnymede - Pamela Bennetts 445
Beauvallet - Georgette Heyer 2876
The Bisley Boy - Christopher Hunt 3080
*Color From a Light Within: A Novel Based on the Life
  of El Greco* - Donald Braider 641
The Conqueror: A Novel of Alexander the Great -
  Edison Marshall 4104
The Devil Is Loose - Graham Shelby 5790
Elizabeth and the Prince of Spain - Margaret
  Irwin 3117
Elizabeth, Captive Princess - Margaret Irwin 3118
Fire From Heaven - Mary Renault 5296
For One Sweet Grape - Kate O'Brien 4681
The Heart of the Lion - Jean Plaidy 5020
The Hounds of God - Rafael Sabatini 5551
I, the King - Hermann Kesten 3475
In the House of the King - Louis Zara 6951
In the Shadow of the Crown - Jean Plaidy 5022
The Kings of Vain Intent - Graham Shelby 5791
The Last Crusader - Louis De Wohl 1569
Legacy - Susan Kay 3374
The Legend of Tyl Ulenspiegel - Charles Theodore
  Henri De Coster 1558
The Lute Player - Norah Lofts 3852
My Life for My Sheep - Alfred Duggan 1772
Oh! Where Are Bloody Mary's Earrings? - Robert
  Player 5079
The Rain Maiden - Jill M. Phillips 4985
The Revolt of the Eaglets - Jean Plaidy 5057
The Saracen Blade - Frank Yerby 6926
The Scarlet Cloak - Jean Plaidy 5061
Sea of Lentils - Antonio Benitez-Rojo 443
*Shadow in the Sun: A Novel of Elizabeth I, the Virgin
  Queen* - F.W. Kenyon 3460
The Spanish Bridegroom - Jean Plaidy 5064
Star of Macedon - Karl V. Eiker 1901
The Venetian - David Weiss 6611

Philip III
The Adventures of Don Juan - Richard Gardner 2289

Philip IV
Braveheart - Randall Wallace 6538
I, the King - Frances Parkinson Keyes 3479
The Iron King - Maurice Druon 1732
The Marranos - Liliane Webb 6588
The Prince of Darkness - P.C. Doherty 1675
Spy in Chancery - P.C. Doherty 1680

Philip VI
The Lily and the Lion - Maurice Druon 1733
The Lords of Vaumartin - Cecelia Holland 2992

Philip the Fair
The Image of Our Lord - Edward Burman 790

Priam
Scandal in Troy - Eva Hemmer Hansen 2679
The Trojan Generals Talk: Memoirs of the Greek War
  - Phillip Parotti 4818

Psin
Until the Sun Falls - Cecelia Holland 2998

Ptolemy I
The Bronze God of Rhodes - L. Sprague De
  Camp 1554

Pygmalion
*The Purple Quest: A Novel of Seafaring Adventure in
  the Ancient World* - Frank G. Slaughter 5896

Queen of Sheba
The Queen of Sheba - Roberta Kells Dorr 1696
Solomon and Sheba - Faye Levine 3740
Solomon and the Queen of Sheba - Czenzi
  Ormonde 4751

Quyuk
Until the Sun Falls - Cecelia Holland 2998

Ramses I
Pillar of Fire - Judith Tarr 6168

Ramses II
Ancient Evenings - Norman Mailer 4035
Mirage - Pauline Gedge 2346
Moses - Sholem Asch 199
Moses, Prince of Egypt - Howard Fast 2039
The Mummy; or Ramses the Damned - Anne
  Rice 5315

Ramses III
Lady of the Reeds - Pauline Gedge 2345

Ranavalona I
Flashman's Lady - George MacDonald Fraser 2210

Reza Shah Pahlavi
Cry of the Peacock - Gina Barkhordar Nahai 4552

Richard I
The Blue Falcon - Robyn Carr 935
Champion - L. Christian Balling 285
The Courts of Love - Jean Plaidy 5010
Eleanor the Queen - Norah Lofts 3842
The Golden Knight - George Challis 971
The Heart of the Lion - Jean Plaidy 5020
Ivanhoe - Sir Walter Scott 5699
Lionheart!: A Novel of Richard I, King of England -
  Martha Rofheart 5428
The Lute Player - Norah Lofts 3852
No Man's Son - Doris Sutcliffe Adams 23
Richard and the Knights of God - Pamela
  Bennetts 454
The Talisman - Sir Walter Scott 5708

Richard II
Fortune Made His Sword - Martha Rofheart 5426
The Gentle Falcon - Hilda Lewis 3747
Glendower Country - Martha Rofheart 5427
Good King Harry - Denise Giardina 2393
In a Dark Wood Wandering - Hella S. Haasse 2631
The Lords of Lancaster - Pamela Bennetts 452
My Lord John - Georgette Heyer 2895
Passage to Pontefract - Jean Plaidy 5038
Richard Whittington, London's Mayor - Gwynedd
  Sudworth 6112
Riot at Gravesend: A Novel of Wat Tyler's Rebellion -
  William Howard Woods 6864
The Ruthless Yeomen - Valerie Anand 134
Trumpet at the Gate - Jan Widgery 6739
Who Was Then the Gentleman - Charles E.
  Israel 3125
The Whyte Harte - P.C. Doherty 1681
Within the Hollow Crown - Margaret Campbell
  Barnes 331

Richard III
Blood of the Boar - Margaret Abbey 2
The Broken Sword - Rhoda S. Edwards 1885
Crouchback - Carola Oman 4732
The Daughter of Time - Josephine Tey 6209
The Dragon and the Rose - Roberta Gellis 2350
The Fate of Princes - P.C. Doherty 1673
Fire and Morning - Francis W. Leary 3696
The Killing of Richard the Third - Robert
  Farrington 2020
The King's Bed - Margaret Campbell Barnes 324
Less Fortunate than Fair - Sandra Wilson 6814
Merchant of the Ruby - Alice Harwood 2766
The Reluctant Queen: The Story of Anne of York -
  Jean Plaidy 5056

Richard III: The Last Plantagenet - Tyler
  Whittle 6722
An Unknown Welshman - Jean Stubbs 6100
We Speak No Treason - Rosemary Hawley
  Jarman 3168
The White Boar - Marian Palmer 4780
The White Queen - Lesley J. Nickell 4611

Richard the Lionhearted
Banners of Gold - Pamela Kaufman 3371
The Kings of Vain Intent - Graham Shelby 5791
Men Like Shadows - Dorothy Charques 1000
My Lord Brother the Lionheart - Molly Costain
  Haycraft 2795
The Rain Maiden - Jill M. Phillips 4985
A Search for a King: A 12th-Century Legend - Gore
  Vidal 6492
Shield of Three Lions - Pamela Kaufman 3372
Tomorrow's Fire - Jay Williams 6775

Robert I
The Follies of the King - Jean Plaidy 5014
Marjorie of Scotland - Pamela Hill 2939

Robert the Bruce
The Lion Is Come - Jane Oliver 4725
Robert the Bruce: The Path of the Hero King - Nigel
  Tranter 6318
Robert the Bruce: The Price of the King's Peace -
  Nigel Tranter 6319
Robert the Bruce: The Steps to the Empty Throne -
  Nigel Tranter 6320

Roger II
The Garden of Persephone - Cesar J. Rotondi 5510

Saladin
The Heart of the Lion - Jean Plaidy 5020
Jerusalem - Cecelia Holland 2990
The Kings of Vain Intent - Graham Shelby 5791
The Knights of Dark Renown - Graham Shelby 5792
Richard and the Knights of God - Pamela
  Bennetts 454
The Talisman - Sir Walter Scott 5708
Trail and Triumph: A Novel about Maimonides -
  Lester M. Morrison 4485

Saul
David at Olivet - Wallace Hamilton 2671
David of Jerusalem - Louis De Wohl 1564
David the King - Gladys Schmitt 5641
David: Warrior and King - Frank G. Slaughter 5885
The Death of Kings - Peter Danielson 1465
King David - Gwyn Jenkins 3191
King of Kings: A Novel of the Life of David - Malachi
  Martin 4134
The Prophet and the King - Shirley Watkins 6582
Rizpah - Charles E. Israel 3124

Selim III
Bosnian Chronicle - Ivo Andric 150
Lord Elgin's Lady - Theodore Vrettos 6514
Sultana - Michael, Prince of Greece 4358

Seti I
Return to Thebes - Allen Drury 1739

Shah Jehan
Blood Royal - Robert Payne 4850
The Dark Dancer - Frederic Prokosch 5193
The Young Emperor - Robert Payne 4857

Silkweb Empress
Bronze Mirror - Jeanne Larsen 3668

Singh, Jai
Raj - Gita Mehta 4325

Sokolovici, Mehmed Pasha
The Bridge on the Drina - Ivo Andric 151

Solomon
Bathsheba - Torgny Lindgren 3789
David of Jerusalem - Louis De Wohl 1564
David: Warrior and King - Frank G. Slaughter 5885
King David - Gwyn Jenkins 3191

The King David Report - Stefan Heym   2910
Love and Wisdom: A Novel about Solomon - Richard G. Hubler   3064
The Queen of Sheba - Roberta Kells Dorr   1696
Solomon and Sheba - Faye Levine   3740
Solomon and Sheba - Jay Williams   6774
Solomon and the Queen of Sheba - Czenzi Ormonde   4751
The Unanointed - Laurene Chinn   1070
The Valley of Vision: A Novel of King Solomon and His Time - Vardis Fisher   2113

Stephen
Brother Cadfael's Penance - Ellis Peters   4955
One Corpse Too Many - Ellis Peters   4966
The Passionate Enemies - Jean Plaidy   5039
To Keep This Oath - Hebe Weenolsen   6597

Stephen of Blois
When Christ and His Saints Slept - Sharon Kay Penman   4908

Stuart, Mary
Madame Serpent - Jean Plaidy   5033
The Queen's Husband - Samuel Edwards   1889
A Time for the Death of a King - Ann Dukthas   1777

Suleiman I
The Bride of Suleiman - Aileen Crawley   1421
Pawn in Frankincense - Dorothy Dunnett   1804
The Shadow of God - Aileen Crawley   1422

T'ai Tsung
Empress - Evelyn McCune   4238

Takakura
The Sword of Hachiman - Lynn Guest   2608

Tamatoa VI
Hawaii - James A. Michener   4370

Tancred
The Kings of Vain Intent - Graham Shelby   5791
My Lord Brother the Lionheart - Molly Costain Haycraft   2795

Tao Kuang
Mandarin Gold - James Leasor   3700

Temujin
Ruler of the Sky: A Novel of Genghis Khan - Pamela Sargent   5606

Theodora
The Bearkeeper's Daughter - Gillian Bradshaw   628
Theodora - Samuel Edwards   1891

Theodore II
The Hammer of God - Alan Scholefield   5655
When the Emperor Dies - Mason McCann Smith   5926

Theodosius II
Bury Me in Ravenna - Agnes Carr Vaughan   6432
Imperial Purple - Gillian Bradshaw   631
Sign of the Pagan - Don Tracy   6312

Theodosius the Great
The Last Romans - Teodor Jeske-Choinski   3216

Theseus
The Bull From the Sea - Mary Renault   5295

Thutmose II
King and Goddess - Judith Tarr   6166

Tiberius
Augustus - John Williams   6785
Brothers of Vengeance - LeGette Blythe   556
Dear and Glorious Physician - Taylor Caldwell   853
The Eagle and the Crown - Hubertus Loewenstein   3832
I, Claudius - Robert Graves   2547
I Loved Tiberius - Elisabeth Dored   1692
The Kingdom of the Wicked - Anthony Burgess   778
Man on Fire: A Novel on the Life of St. Paul - LeGette Blythe   558
No King but Caesar - Anne Powers   5151
The Robe - Lloyd C. Douglas   1703

The Testament of Theophilus - Leonard Wibberley   6730
Tiberius: The Memoirs of the Emperor - Allan Massie   4169
The Word and the Sword - Theo Lang   3662

Timur the Great
Master of the World - Cothburn O'Neal   4738

Titus
The Triumph - Ernest K. Gann   2280
The Voices of Masada - David Kossoff   3545

Tokugama Ieyasu
Daishi-San: A Novel - Robert P. Lund   3925
The Needle-Watcher - Richard Blaker   540

Toyotomi Hideyoshi
Taiko - Eiji Yoshikawa   6936

Trajan
The Soldier and the Sage: A Novel about Akiba - Richard G. Hubler   3065

Tsu Hsi
China Saga - C.Y. Lee   3706

Tudor, Henry
The Courts of Illusion - Rosemary Hawley Jarman   3165

Tung Chih
Imperial Woman - Pearl S. Buck   755

Tutankhamen
King Tut's Private Eye - Lee Levin   3739
Murder at the Feast of Rejoicing - Lynda S. Robinson   5407
Murder at the God's Gate - Lynda S. Robinson   5408
Murder in the Place of Anubis - Lynda S. Robinson   5409
Pillar of Fire - Judith Tarr   6168

Tutmose III
Pharaoh - Eloise Jarvis McGraw   4276

Tz'u-hsi
Forbidden City - Muriel Molland Jernigan   3215
Imperial Woman - Pearl S. Buck   755
Louisiana! - Dana Fuller Ross   5478
Manchu Empress - Bluebell Matilda Hunter   3081
The Time of the Dragon - Dorothy Eden   1863
White Poppy - Margaret Gaan   2261

Uther
Merlin - Stephen R. Lawhead   3681

Valdemar
The Trees of the Folkungs - Verner Von Heidenstam   2817

Valentinian III
Bury Me in Ravenna - Agnes Carr Vaughan   6432

Vercingetorix
Druids - Morgan Llywelyn   3817

Vespasian
The Iron Hand of Mars - Lindsey Davis   1528
The Jew of Rome - Lion Feuchtwanger   2071
Josephus - Lion Feuchtwanger   2072
The Kingdom of the Wicked - Anthony Burgess   778
Last Act in Palmyra - Lindsey Davis   1529
Shadows in Bronze - Lindsey Davis   1531
The Silver Pigs - Lindsey Davis   1532
The Source - James A. Michener   4374
The Tenth Measure - Brenda Lesley Segal   5721
Time to Depart - Lindsey Davis   1533
The Triumph - Ernest K. Gann   2280
The Voices of Masada - David Kossoff   3545
The Wolf of Masada - John Fredman   2220

Vespasianus, Titus Flavius
Agrippa's Daughter - Howard Fast   2025

Victoria
Anno-Dracula - Kim Newman   4595

Bertie, Albert Edward, Prince of Wales - Tyler Whittle   6720
Bertie and the Tinman - Peter Lovesey   3909
Beyond Desire: A Novel Based on the Life of Felix and Cecille Mendelssohn - Pierre La Mure   3574
By Command of the Viceroy - Duncan MacNeil   4010
Castle of Foxes - Alanna Knight   3516
Chase Royal - Donald Seaman   5712
Cock of the Walk - Roy Lewis   3762
Consort for Victoria - William Vaughan Wilkins   6757
The Day They Kidnapped Queen Victoria - H.K. Fleming   2127
Elizabeth and Alexandra - Antony Lambton   3616
Flashman - George MacDonald Fraser   2204
Follow the Drum - James Leasor   3699
Halfhyde and the Fleet Review - Philip McCutchan   4246
Halfhyde for the Queen - Philip McCutchan   4247
I, Victoria - Cynthia Harrod-Eagles   2755
The Iron Roads - Forbes Bramble   644
The List of Seven - Mark Frost   2237
The Little Victoria - Lozania Prole   5196
The Mudlark - Theodore Bonnet   573
Oh! Where Are Bloody Mary's Earrings? - Robert Player   5079
Pomp and Circumstance - Fred Mustard Stewart   6025
The Prime Minister's Wife - Doris Leslie   3727
Princess in Amber - Evelyn Wilde Mayerson   4205
The Queen and Lord M - Jean Plaidy   5046
Queen Victoria's Bomb - Ronald Clark   1094
The Queen's Husband - Jean Plaidy   5052
The Robber Baroness - William Kendall Clarke   1097
Sisters & Lovers - Nicola Thorne   6274
Swandowne - Daniel Farson   2024
That Spanish Woman - F.W. Kenyon   3461
This Old Bill - Loren D. Estleman   1980
The Vesey Inheritance - Gwendoline Butler   822
Victoria and Albert - Evelyn Anthony   166
Victoria Victorious - Jean Plaidy   5073
The Widow of Windsor - Jean Plaidy   5076
The Widow of Windsor - Tyler Whittle   6723
The Young Victoria - Tyler Whittle   6724

Wilhelm II
1901 - Robert Conroy   1258
Court of Honor - Maria Fagyas   1996
Lusitania - David Butler   819
To the Honor of the Fleet - Robert H. Pilpel   5002

William I
The Disputed Crown - Valerie Anand   128

William II
King of the Wood - Valerie Anand   131
Robin and the King - Parke Godwin   2448

William III
Dark Torrent of Glencoe - Edward Grierson   2590
The Glory and the Dream - F.W. Kenyon   3450
King's Agent - Justus Kent Clark   1090
The Power and the Passion - Christina Nicholson   4609
The Renegade - Donald Clayton Porter   5122

William IV
The Captive of Kensington Palace - Jean Plaidy   5007
Princess Pamela - Ray Russell   5534
Royal William - Doris Leslie   3728
The Young Victoria - Tyler Whittle   6724

William of Orange
The Bracegirdle - Burris Atkins Jenkins   3189

William Rufus
Death of the Red King - Pamela Bennetts   448
Flambard's Confession - Marilyn Durham   1816
The Lion of Justice - Jean Plaidy   5031
The Paladin - George Shipway   5830

William the Conqueror
The Bastard King - Jean Plaidy 5004
The Conqueror - Georgette Heyer 2881
The Firedrake - Cecelia Holland 2988
Harold, the Last of the Saxon Kings - Edward Bulwer-Lytton 767
Harold Was My King - Hilda Lewis 3749
Hereward the Wake - Charles Kingsley 3497
I Am England - Patricia Wright 6881
Robin and the King - Parke Godwin 2448
The Saxon Tapestry - Sile Rice 5317
Sherwood - Parke Godwin 2449
Wife to the Bastard - Hilda Lewis 3753

Wu Chao
Deception - Eleanor Cooney 1295
Empress - Evelyn McCune 4238
Green Dragon, White Tiger - Annette Motley 4501
The Jade Stalk - Jonathan Fast 2048
Lady Wu - Yutang Lin 3782

Xerxes I
Creation - Gore Vidal 6486
The Dragon of the Ishtar Gate - L. Sprague De Camp 1555
Esther - Nathaniel Norsen Weinreb 6601
Esther: The Star and the Sceptre - Gina Andrews 146
Farewell Great King: A Novel of Ancient Greece - Jill Paton Walsh 4829

Yannai
The King of Flesh and Blood - Moshe Shamir 5772

Yellow Emperor
Bronze Mirror - Jeanne Larsen 3668

Yenehala
Mandarin - Robert S. Elegant 1905

Zenobia
Queen of the East - Alexander Baron 336

Zoe
Byzantium - Michael Ennis 1945

RUNAWAY

Kestrel
People of the Sea - W. Michael Gear 2339

Kinsdale, Skye
A Pirate's Pleasure - Heather Graham 2518

Smith, Amanda
Sprig Muslin - Georgette Heyer 2903

SAILOR

Adams, John
East Indiaman - Frank Pollard 5087

Adams, William
Daishi-San: A Novel - Robert P. Lund 3925
The Needle-Watcher - Richard Blaker 540

Alvarez, Rodrigo
Friendly Cove - Irving Brant 651

Alysin, Garth
The Keys of England - William Victor Cooke 1271

Ancaeus
Hercules, My Shipmate - Robert Graves 2545

Anthony the Turk
The Drowning Room - Michael Kenneth Pye 5212

Ashton, Robert
Three Harbors - F. van Wyck Mason 4162

Bangs, Jonathon
The New Hope - Joseph C. Lincoln 3784

Barinthus
Paradise - Dikkon Eberhart 1831

Barney, Joshua
The Sea Eagles - John Edward Jennings 3206

Barraclough, Ira
Masts to Spear the Stars - Stephen Longstreet 3889

Battell, Andrew
Lord of Darkness - Robert Silverberg 5854

Baxter, August
Eye of the Hurricane - Fergus Reid Buckley 757

Beals, Dan
Look Away, Look Away - Leslie Turner White 6685

Bermejo, Juan Rodrigo
The Velvet Doublet - James H. Street 6082

Billinghurst, Surprise
Surprise - Brian Burland 785

Blackthorne, John
Shogun - James Clavell 1101

Blake, Benjamin
Benjamin Blake - Edison Marshall 4102

Blease, Roger
For My Great Folly - Thomas B. Costain 1365

Bond, Ezra
The Edge of Piracy - Donald Barr Chidsey 1060

Boone, Jonathan
The Barbarian - Willard Price 5191

Bowditch, Nathaniel
The Navigator: The Story of Nathaniel Bowditch - Alfred Stanford 5979

Boyd, Salathiel
The Wickedest Pilgrim - Donald Barr Chidsey 1067

Boyle, Kenny
The Sea Eagles - John Edward Jennings 3206

Braddee, David
The Delectable Country - Leland Dewitt Baldwin 280

Butler, Neal
Boon Island - Kenneth Roberts 5384

Cartwright, Bohannon
Run Me a River - Janice Holt Giles 2415

Cavanaugh, Kit
The Catherine - Robert S. MacDonald 3980

Coffyn, Hubert
Golden Admiral - F. van Wyck Mason 4150

Comstock, George
Captain Marooner - Louis B. Davidson 1504

Comstock, Sam
Captain Marooner - Louis B. Davidson 1504

Conal, Logan
The Feather and the Stone - Patricia Shaw 5780

Derker, Tom
Captain of the Sands - Keith Dewhurst 1636

Dingwall, Henry
Captain of the Sands - Keith Dewhurst 1636

Eliot, Cannibal
Cannibal Eliot and the Lost Histories of San Francisco - Hilton Obenzinger 4660

Erbin
Ruan - Bryher 746

Ericson, Magnus
The Island Harp - Jeanne Williams 6779

Folger, Tom
Captain Paul - Edward Ellsberg 1930

Forrest, John
The Return of Lono: A Novel of Captain Cook's Last Voyage - Oswald Andrew Bushnell 816

Gaskell, Obadiah
The Forest Lord - Noel B. Gerson 2368

Gill, Peter
The Greenlander - Mark Adlard 38

Grayson, Champ
On the Midnight Tide - Don Tracy 6310

Grimes, Matt
Benjamin Blake - Edison Marshall 4102

Griva, Roberto della
The Island of the Day Before - Umberto Eco 1849

Guerrero
A Signal Victory - David Stacton 5976

Hale, Elmer
Mighty Mountain - Archie Binns 502

Harwar, Simon Basil
Voyage: A Novel of 1896 - Sterling Hayden 2798

Hawkins, Jim
Treasure Island - Robert Louis Stevenson 6012

Howard, Julia
Jewel of the Sea - Ellen Argo 185

Huw
Grania: She-King of the Irish Seas - Morgan Llywelyn 3819

Hyatt, Stephen
The Southern Cross - Peter French 2226

Jewitt, John
Eagle Song - James Houston 3050

Jinsuke
Harpoon - C.W. Nicol 4612

Jones, Habakkuk
Stronghold - Donald Barr Chidsey 1065

Kakuktak
The White Dawn - James Houston 3053

Kennard, Alan
The Beckoning Waters - Robert Carse 944

Kinraid, Charley
Sylvia's Lovers - Elizabeth Gaskell 2312

Lamb, Johnny
Lord of the Isles - Donald Barr Chidsey 1063

Langman, Christopher
Boon Island - Kenneth Roberts 5384

Lavery, Dennis
Men of No Property - Dorothy Davis 1517

Lawe, Matthew
Darken Ship - Nicholas Monsarrat 4431
Running Proud - Nicholas Monsarrat 4432

Leigh, Amyas
Westward Ho! - Charles Kingsley 3499

Llewellyn, Davy
The Maid of Sker - R.D. Blackmore 529

Logan, Julia Howard
The Crystal Star - Ellen Argo 184

London, Jack
The Summer of Jack London - Andrew J. Fenady 2058

Loveday, Bob
The Trumpet Major - Thomas Hardy 2700

Mango, Peter
Fragments of the Ark - Louise Meriwether 4341

Marchena, Jayme De
1492 - Mary Johnston 3228

Marlowe, Thomas
The Glittering Strand - Judith Lennox-Smith 3716

Marsh, Abner
Fevre Dream - George R.R. Martin 4131

Marvin, Daniel
Captain Caution - Kenneth Roberts 5385

McGann, Toby
The Sea and the Sand - Christopher Nicole   4621

Mulkerin, Sean
The Californios - Louis L'Amour   3618

Myran, Lars
The Last of the Vikings - Johan Bojer   563

Oldsmith, Sebastian
Shout at the Devil - Wilbur Smith   5930

Pearson, Willard
You Rolling River - Archie Binns   503

Pilee
The White Dawn - James Houston   3053

Portagee
The White Dawn - James Houston   3053

Price, Ben
The Salem Frigate - John Edward Jennings   3205

Pytheas
*North to Thule: An Imagined Narrative of the Famous
   "Lost" Voyage of Pytheas of Massalla in the
   Fourth Century B.C.* - John Frye   2241

Rellison, John
Stronghold - Donald Barr Chidsey   1065

Richardson, Jim
The Greenlander - Mark Adlard   38

Ryan, John Clinton
El Lazo - L. Jay Martin   4132

Shaw, John
The Whales in Lake Tanganyika - Lennart
   Hagerfors   2636

Shaw, Jon
The Pepper Tree - John Edward Jennings   3203

Shea, Michael
My Pride, My Folly - Suzanne Butler   830

Sheridan, Rich
The Golden Coast - Philip Rooney   5441

Slater, Oliver
Long Pig - Russell Foreman   2168

Southfarer, Niall
The Price of Blood - Doris Sutcliffe Adams   24

Stanton, Dick
Swandowne - Daniel Farson   2024

Starbuck, Stephen
Nantucket Rebel - Edouard A. Stackpole   5970

Stockton, Edward
Letter of Marque - Andrew Hepburn   2849

Storm, Arthur
The Greenlander - Mark Adlard   38

Svenson
Runestone - Don Coldsmith   1186

Swain, David
Thread of Scarlet - Ben Ames Williams   6767

Thatcher, Jason
Jewel of the Sea - Ellen Argo   185

Thompson, John
Eagle Song - James Houston   3050

Tresize, Arthur
The Old Priory - Norah Lofts   3855

Trestane, Amoyot
Castle Dor - Sir Arthur Thomas Quiller-Couch   5226

Van Cleef, Jan
The Sea Beggars - Cecelia Holland   2996

Vandermark, Fred
The Magic Ship - Sandra Paretti   4791

Veniero, Giorgio
Sofia - Ann Chamberlin   974

Wade, Nathaniel
Manila Galleon - F. van Wyck Mason   4154

Wakefield, Luke
The Fall River Line - Daoma Winston   6824

Westing, Tom
Lisbon - Valerie Sherwood   5825

Whitman, Homer
American Captain - Edison Marshall   4101

William, William
The Glittering Strand - Judith Lennox-Smith   3716

Willoughby, Robin
Rogue's Harbor - Inglis Fletcher   2139

Wright, Jonathan
Eye of the Hurricane - Fergus Reid Buckley   757

Wyatt, Henry
Golden Admiral - F. van Wyck Mason   4150

SALOON HOSTESS

Bowe, Liza
Liza Bowe - Shirley Barker   313

Clements, Hannah
Storm the Last Rampart - David Taylor   6180

Daisy
Pacific Street - Cecelia Holland   2993

Flynn, Dinah
The Stallion Man - Judith Glover   2438

Mellish, Dolly
The Sea 'Venture - F. van Wyck Mason   4159

Perez, Catana
Captain From Castille - Samuel Shellabarger   5794

Tilden, Alicia
The Bellerose Bargain - Robyn Carr   934

Tryon, Katie
Three Harbors - F. van Wyck Mason   4162

SALOON KEEPER/OWNER

Alavedo, Olivio Fonseca
The White Rhino Hotel - Bartle Bull   765

Gifford, Jonathan
Liberty Tavern - Thomas Fleming   2129

Hardhardt, Frances
Pacific Street - Cecelia Holland   2993

King, Fergus
King's Royal - John Quigley   5224

Randolph, Marny
Calico Palace - Gwen Bristow   694

SCHOLAR

Abelard, Peter
*Stealing Heaven: The Love Story of Heloise and
   Abelard* - Marion Meade   4317

Albertus Magnus
Doctor Mirabilis - James Blish   550

Ascham, Roger
Elizabeth, Captive Princess - Margaret Irwin   3118

Bacon, Roger
Doctor Mirabilis - James Blish   550

Balthazar
How Far to Bethlehem? - Norah Lofts   3846

Bold Talent
Spring Moon: A Novel of China - Bette Bao
   Lord   3897

Casaubon, Edward
Middlemarch - George Eliot   1909

Eliazar
The Wandering Arm - Sharan Newman   4603

Erasmus, Desiderius
The Cloister and the Hearth - Charles Reade   5279
Flame of Fire - Jane Oliver   4722

Fineaux, Philip
Liza Bowe - Shirley Barker   313

FitzNigel, Julien
The Garden of Persephone - Cesar J. Rotondi   5510

Gamaliel the Elder
The Gospel According to Gamaliel - Gerald
   Heard   2801

Jacob
The Slave - Isaac Bashevis Singer   5866

James, William
The Haunting of Lamb House - Joan Aiken   48

Jastrow, Aaron
War and Remembrance - Herman Wouk   6875
The Winds of War - Herman Wouk   6876

Jerome
The Converts: A Historical Novel - Rex
   Warner   6564

Johnson, Samuel
Blind Justice - Bruce Alexander   76
The Bonnet Laird's Daughter - Barbara
   Annandale   154
Midwinter - John Buchan   751
Mr. Oddity, Samuel Johnson - Charles Norman   4643

Kerbouchard
The Walking Drum - Louis L'Amour   3632

Khaemwaset
Mirage - Pauline Gedge   2346

Lanyon, Aubrey
Venetia - Georgette Heyer   2909

Lempriere, John
Lempriere's Dictionary - Lawrence Norfolk   4641

Levendeur, Catherine
Death Comes as Epiphany - Sharan Newman   4598
The Devil's Door - Sharan Newman   4599

Maurepas
The Masked Man - P.C. Doherty   1674

Menetrier, Jacques
At the Sign of the Reine Pedauque - Anatole
   France   2198

Newman, John Henry
Shadows and Images - Meriol Trevor   6344

Oldbuck, Jonathan
The Antiquary - Sir Walter Scott   5690

Pater, Walter
The God of Mirrors - Robert Reilly   5293

Pentecost, Peter
The Blanket of the Dark - John Buchan   749

Romola
Romola - George Eliot   1910

Russell, Mary
A Letter of Mary - Laurie R. King   3488
A Monstrous Regiment of Women - Laurie R.
   King   3489

Segalla, Nicholas
The Prince Lost to Time - Ann Dukthas   1776
A Time for the Death of a King - Ann Dukthas   1777
The Time of Murder at Mayerling - Ann
   Dukthas   1778

Shen Wen-Ching
The Fabulous Concubine - Hsin-Hai Chang   987

Stiles, Ezra
Strange Wives - Shirley Barker   317

Tyndale, William
Flame of Fire - Jane Oliver 4722
The Sword of Truth - Gilbert Morris 4472

Vladomsky, Pan
The Nazarene - Sholem Asch 200

Webster, Noah
Portrait of a Scoundrel - Nathaniel Benchley 438

William of Baskerville
The Name of the Rose - Umberto Eco 1850

Wilson, Woodrow
Tolbecken - Samuel Shellabarger 5798

Yamamoto, Kenichi
Kagami - Elizabeth Kata 3369

SCIENTIST

Agassiz, Louis
McKay's Bees - Thomas McMahon 4289

Andree, Salomon August
The Flight of the Eagle - Per Olof Sundman 6119

Audubon, John James
The Iron Mistress - Paul I. Wellman 6618
Mr. Audubon's Lucy - Lucy Kennedy 3419

Bartram, John
Song of the Susquehanna - Herbert Stover 6071

Brahe, Tycho
Kepler: A Novel - John Banville 297

Brandon, Luke
Colorado! - Dana Fuller Ross 5471

Burke, Thad
Sassafras - Jack Matthews 4193

Charcot, Jean-Martin
The Secret Life of Laszlo, Count Dracula - Roderick Anscombe 156

Copernicus, Nicolaus
Doctor Copernicus - John Banville 296

Crispin, Gustave
The Balloonist - Macdonald Harris 2724

Darwin, Charles
Jemmy Button - Benjamin Subercaseaux 6107
The Origin - Irving Stone 6060

Dash, Hannibal
Goldfield - Richard S. Wheeler 6660

Downing, Samuel
The Greater Hunger - Barbara Dodge Borland 581

Du Pont, Lammot
Dominion - Jack Rowe 5514

Edison, Thomas Alva
A Peep into the 20th Century - Christopher Davis 1515

Einstein, Albert
A Family Matter - James Roosevelt 5458
Loving Little Egypt - Thomas McMahon 4288
Murder in the West Wing - Elliott Roosevelt 5453
Smart Moves - Stuart M. Kaminsky 3346
Till the End of Time - Allen Appel 170

Ellis, Havelock
The Crusader - Noel B. Gerson 2364
The Daughter: A Novel Based on the Life of Eleanor Marx - Judith Chernaik 1012

Fermi, Enrico
Beginning the World Again - Roberta Silman 5851
A Family Matter - James Roosevelt 5458

Fialka, Peter
Beginning the World Again - Roberta Silman 5851

Frankenstein, Victor
The Cross of Frankenstein - Robert J. Myers 4548
Frankenstein Unbound - Brian Aldiss 68

The Memoirs of Elizabeth Frankenstein - Theodore Roszak 5508
The Slave of Frankenstein - Robert J. Myers 4549

Franklin, Benjamin
Murder by the Waters - Robert Lee Hall 2661

Gabriel, Paul
Victim of the Aurora - Thomas Keneally 3417

Galilei, Galileo
Physician Extraordinary: A Novel of the Life and Times of William Harvey - David Weiss 6608
The Star-Gazer - Zsolt de Harsanyi 2757

Gassendi, Pierre
The Diary of William Harvey: The Imaginary Journal of the Physician Who Revolutionized Medicine - Jean Hamburger 2667

Goethe, Johann Wolfgang von
Sacred and Profane: A Novel of the Life and Times of Mozart - David Weiss 6609

Guillotin, Joseph Ignace
Dr. Guillotine: The Eccentric Exploits of an Early Scientist - Herbert Lom 3867

Hariot, Thomas
Nicholas Cooke: Actor, Soldier, Physician, Priest - Stephanie Cowell 1393
Roanoke Hundred - Inglis Fletcher 2138

Harvey, William
Physician Extraordinary: A Novel of the Life and Times of William Harvey - David Weiss 6608

Hubble, Edwin Powell
Hubble Time - Tom Bezzi 490

Huxley, Thomas Henry
The Origin - Irving Stone 6060

Huxtable, Franklin
Queen Victoria's Bomb - Ronald Clark 1094

Kepler, Johannes
Kepler: A Novel - John Banville 297
World and Paradise - Edgar Maas 3953

Kumlien, Thure
The Wolfling: A Documentary Novel of the 1870s - Sterling North 4648

Lavoisier, Antoine Laurent
The Black Consul - Anatolii Vinogradov 6503
Rasero - Francisco Rebolledo 5282

Lyell, Charles
The Origin - Irving Stone 6060

Melchior
How Far to Bethlehem? - Norah Lofts 3846

Mesmer, Franz Anton
The Strange Case of Madamoiselle P. - Patrick Ireland 3109

Morse, Elkanah
The Far Tribes - Richard S. Wheeler 6658

Morse, Samuel
All This, and Heaven Too - Rachel Field 2080

Newton, Isaac
Myself, Christopher Wren - David Weiss 6606

Oppenheimer, J. Robert
Beginning the World Again - Roberta Silman 5851
A Family Matter - James Roosevelt 5458
Stallion Gate - Martin Cruz Smith 5924

Pasteur, Louis
The Gypsy From Cadiz - Tamsin Hamilton 2670

Popple, Edward
The Rose Crossing - Nicholas Jose 3306

Saint-Victor, Remi
Mirage - Ruth McKenney 4283

Sheridan, Sir Charles
Death at Daisy's Folly - Robin Paige 4775

Death at Gallows Green - Robin Paige 4776

Swinbrooke, Kathryn
The Book of Shadows - C.L. Grace 2505
The Eye of God - C.L. Grace 2506
The Merchant of Death - C.L. Grace 2508
A Shrine of Murders - C.L. Grace 2509

Szilard, Leo
A Family Matter - James Roosevelt 5458

Tesla, Nikola
Loving Little Egypt - Thomas McMahon 4288

Van Helsing, Abraham
Children of the Vampire: The Diaries of the Family Dracul - Jeanne Kalogridis 3326
Lord of the Vampires: The Diaries of the Family Dracul - Jeanne Kalogridis 3328

Vold, Mourly
Loving Little Egypt - Thomas McMahon 4288

Walker, William
An Embarrassment of Riches - James Howard Kunstler 3565

Weitzman, Chaim
Behold the Fire - Michael Blankfort 541

Woodville, Loren
Joy in Mudville - Gordon McAlpine 4216

Wunderlich, Jacob
Beginning the World Again - Roberta Silman 5851

SCOUT

Baker, Jim
Kings of the Missouri - Hugh Pendexter 4895

Benteen, Dick
Wagons to Tucson - Ed Newsom 4604

Bowie, Henry
Carmen of the Rancho - Frank H. Spearman 5955

Bridger, Jim
Red Cloud's Revenge - Terry C. Johnston 3255

Brond, Black
The Red Road: A Romance of Braddock's Defeat - Hugh Pendexter 4898

Calendar, Miles
Last Reveille - David Morrell 4456

Clinton, Jim
The Devil Gun - William Syers 6148

Colt, Chris
Chief of Scouts - Don Bendell 439

Desportes, John
Mi Amigo - William R. Burnett 795

Donegan, Seamus
Black Sun - Terry C. Johnston 3242
Reap the Whirlwind - Terry C. Johnston 3254
Red Cloud's Revenge - Terry C. Johnston 3255
Sioux Dawn - Terry C. Johnston 3258
The Stalkers - Terry C. Johnston 3259

El Tigre
The Rose and the Flame - Jonreed Lauritzen 3676

Ferguson, James
Next to Valour - John Edward Jennings 3202

Frane, Adam
The Captive Witch - Dale Van Every 6407

Girty, Simon
Buckskin Cavalier - John Clagett 1082

Gowd, Skinner
Diamond Wedding - Wilbur Daniel Steele 5986

Grein, Walter
Adobe Walls: A Novel of the Last Apache Rising - William R. Burnett 791

Hale, Andy
They Came to a Valley - Bill Gulick   2618

Hardeman, Chris
The Snowblind Moon - John Byrne Cooke   1267

Jeffords, Thomas
Blood Brother - Elliott Arnold   190

Larkin, Timothy
Timothy Larkin - Jane Hutchens   3089

Marshall, Michael
Land for My Sons - Maribelle Cormack   1331

McDermott, Angus
Shadow of the Long Knives - Thomas Alexander
Boyd   615

Morgan, Matt
The Shining Mountains - Dale Van Every   6410

Paxton, Rush
A Land to Tame - Zola Helen Ross   5505

Phillips, Portugee John
North Against the Sioux - Kenneth Ulyatt   6376

Sieber, Al
Geronimo: An American Legend - Robert J.
Conley   1242

Smith, Jed
The Fancher Train - Amelia Bean   395

Walford, Gabe
Liveliest Town in the West - Bill Gulick   2615

Weiser, Conrad
A High Wind Rising - Elsie Singmaster   5867

SEA CAPTAIN

Adams, Enoch
The New England Story - Henry Beetle Hough   3046

Allson, Captain
The Hard to Catch Mercy - William Baldwin   281

Ammidon, Gerrit
Java Head - Joseph Hergesheimer   2854

Avery, Benjamin
The Pyrates - George MacDonald Fraser   2212

Bailey, Scon
Storm Tide - Allan R. Bosworth   590

Barnstable, Richard
The Pilot - James Fenimore Cooper   1306

Baxter, David
The Crystal Star - Ellen Argo   184
Jewel of the Sea - Ellen Argo   185
The Yankee Girl - Ellen Argo   186

Beaufort, Jason
Marianne - Juliette Benzoni   466
Marianne and the Lords of the East - Juliette
Benzoni   468
Marianne and the Privateer - Juliette Benzoni   470
Marianne and the Rebels - Juliette Benzoni   471

Beauvallet, Nicholas
Beauvallet - Georgette Heyer   2876

Belnatan
Fleet Surgeon to Pharaoh - Sheldon Jacobson   3140

Biddlescomb, Isaac
By Force of Arms - James L. Nelson   4579
The Maddest Idea - James L. Nelson   4580

Bilby, Jared
A Mirror for Witches - Esther Forbes   2157

Blamey, Captain Andrew
Demelza - Winston Graham   2524

Boll, Captain
Fair Wind to Java - Garland Roark   5354

Bolton, Isaac
Captain Bolton's Corpse - J.G. Jeffreys   3178

Brett, Jeremy
Brimstone Club - F. van Wyck Mason   4147

Brewster, Jonathan
The White Cockade - Henry Farrand Griffin   2592

Bright, Jonathan
Departure - Janet Stevenson   6004

Broadwinder, Philip
The Lady and the Deep Blue Sea - Garland
Roark   5356

Brown, Jeremiah H.
Star in the Rigging: A Novel of the Texas Navy -
Garland Roark   5358

Bryson, Raphael
Our Valiant Few - F. van Wyck Mason   4155

Butler, James
The Power and the Passion - Christina
Nicholson   4609

Cain, Nathan
Pride's Fancy - Thomas H. Raddall   5231

Calloway, Bart
Summer Thunder - Willie Snow Ethridge   1982

Campbell, Archibald
Restless Voyage - Stanley David Porteus   5138

Carew, Evan
Kingdom of Gold - Susan Wiggs   6744

Carrick, Alec
Night Storm - Catherine Coulter   1378

Carter, Magnus
Magnus the Magnificent - Leslie Turner White   6688

Cavarly, John
Annie's Captain - Kathryn Hulme   3077

Cavendish, Thomas
Captain for Elizabeth - Jan Westcott   6643

Challoner, James
Captain Ironhand - Rosamond Marshall   4116

Clark, Jonathan
The World in His Arms - Rex Beach   392

Coit, Shubael
The Pepper Tree - John Edward Jennings   3203

Colon, Cristobal
My Master Columbus - Cedric Belfrage   418

Columbus, Christopher
1492 - Newton Frolich   2236
Columbus: A Romance - Rafael Sabatini   5549
Crown of Aloes - Norah Lofts   3840
The Indian Chronicles - Jose Barreiro   349
Mercedes of Castile - James Fenimore Cooper   1304
To the Indies - C.S. Forester   2183
Torquemada - Howard Fast   2045

Cook, James
Charco Harbour - Godfrey Blunden   554
The Last Voyage: Captain Cook's Lost Diary -
Hammond Innes   3108

Dampier, William
Burning Gold - Robert Hardy Andrews   148

Dean, John
Boon Island - Kenneth Roberts   5384

DeBoer, Marinus
The Sable Lion - Jan Van Dorp   6405

Derker, William
Captain of the Sands - Keith Dewhurst   1636

Dodge, Jonas
Long Pennant - Oliver La Farge   3573

Dole, Isaiah
The New Hope - Joseph C. Lincoln   3784

Donovan, Andrew
Allegheny Captive - Caroline Bourne   591

Douglas, Richard
The Deadly Lady of Madagascar - C.V. Terry   6206

Dow, Caleb
Tide-Rode - Adelyn Bushnell   813

Drake, Sir Francis
Beauvallet - Georgette Heyer   2876
The Black Duchess - Alanna Knight   3514
Captain for Elizabeth - Jan Westcott   6643
Caribbean - James A. Michener   4365
Envoy From Elizabeth - Pamela Bennetts   451
The Hounds of God - Rafael Sabatini   5551
Kingdom of Gold - Susan Wiggs   6744
Reluctant Cavalier - Donald Barr Chidsey   1064
Westward Ho! - Charles Kingsley   3499

Drew, Hosea
The Great Steamboat Race - John Brunner   736

Early, Matthew
Matthew Early - Alexander Laing   3589

Elliott, Steven
Morning's Gate - Ann Victoria Roberts   5371

Endicott, Brand
The Fortress - Catherine Gavin   2320

Exforth, James
The Ravishers - Elizabeth Richards   5318

Faber, Walter
Time of the Unicorn - Barbara Jefferis   3176

Fallon, Robert
The Fallon Pride - Reagan O'Neal   4742

Fitz-Roy, Robert
Jemmy Button - Benjamin Subercaseaux   6107

Fitzhugh, Bernal
Buccaneer Surgeon - C.V. Terry   6205

Flinders, Matthew
My Love Must Wait: The Story of Matthew Flinders -
Ernestine Hill   2922

Frobisher, Martin
Beauvallet - Georgette Heyer   2876

Gallant, Paul
The Black Cockade - Victor Suthren   6127
In Perilous Seas - Victor Suthren   6130
A King's Ransom - Victor Suthren   6131

Gerardo, Kit
The Golden Hawk - Frank Yerby   6921

Grainger, Zadok
Pull Down to New Orleans - Zachary Ball   283

Grimes, Sinjin
In the Fire of Spring - Thomas Tryon   6355
The Wings of the Morning - Thomas Tryon   6356

Halfhyde, St. Vincent
Halfhyde and the Admiral - Philip McCutchan   4243
The Halfhyde Line - Philip McCutchan   4249
Halfhyde on the Amazon - Philip McCutchan   4250
Outward Bound - Philip McCutchan   4256

Harinxma, Martinus
The Centurion - Jan de Hartog   2762

Hart, Elisha
*The Splendor Stays: An Historic Novel Based on the
Lives of the Seven Hart Sisters of Saybrook* -
Marguerite Allis   114

Hawkes, Robert
The Pearl Pagoda - Susannah Broome   707

Hazlitt, Isaiah
The Yankee Brig - Carter A. Vaughan   6443

Hind, Jason
The Witch of Manga Reva - Garland Roark   5359

Hoxworth, Rafer
Hawaii - James A. Michener   4370

Hudson, Henry
Running Proud - Nicholas Monsarrat 4432

Inman, Dash
The Running of the Tide - Esther Forbes 2160

Jason
Hercules, My Shipmate - Robert Graves 2545

Jones, John Paul
Gallant Captain - Pearl Frye 2242
Give Me Liberty - Noel B. Gerson 2369

Jonsen
A High Wind in Jamaica - Richard Hughes 3074

Langley, Adam
I Know My Love - Catherine Gaskin 2315

Langrish, Malcolm
Pandora's Galley - Macdonald Harris 2727

Livingston, Tom
Dream Time - Parris Afton Bonds 570

Logan, Julia Howard
The Yankee Girl - Ellen Argo 186

Logan, Stephen
The Crystal Star - Ellen Argo 184
The Yankee Girl - Ellen Argo 186

Long, Adam
Captain Adam - Donald Barr Chidsey 1058

Loper, Richard Fanning
That Skipper From Stonington - Theda Kenyon 3464

Low, Charles Porter
Tall Ships to Cathay - Helen Augur 240

Ludlow, Captain
The Water Witch - James Fenimore Cooper 1311

MacBraugh, Jefferson
The Sinking of the Sarah Diamond - William Dale Jennings 3213

Martin, Mark
The Measure of the Years - Alice Mary Colver 1218

McGann, Harry
Old Glory - Christopher Nicole 4618

McGann, Jeremiah
Iron Ships, Iron Men - Christopher Nicole 4616

McGill, Bart
The Furies - John Jakes 3146

McLean, Brock
Sea Jade - Phyllis A. Whitney 6717

McLeod, Quentin
Biscayne - Barry Jay Kaplan 3365

McRae, Brant
Captain McRae: A Novel of the Northwest Frontier - William Heuman 2872

Meares, John
Friendly Cove - Irving Brant 651

Meiklejohn, Angus
Homeward Bound - Elizabeth Walter 6557

Meredith, Tyler
Captain Rebel - Frank Yerby 6910

Merlin, Christian
Lord of the River - Bernard Clavel 1099

Merrick, Elijah
This Is the House - Deborah Hill 2921

Montreuse, Felipe Flores y Lennox
The Black Duchess - Alanna Knight 3514

Morgan, Henry
Cutlass Empire - F. van Wyck Mason 4148
Windward Passage - Hamilton Cochran 1143

Morgan, Seth
Abigail - Joan Druett 1721

Musick, Adam
Long Storm - Ernest Haycox 2790

Myran, Kristaver
The Last of the Vikings - Johan Bojer 563

Nason, Richard
The Lively Lady - Kenneth Roberts 5386

Noyes, John
The Sea Stands Watch - Helen Parker Mudgett 4507

O'Cain, Michael
Golden Shore - George Shaftel 5769

Oleson, Anders
Lindeman's Daughters - Synnove Christensen 1073

Pacey, William
The Last Farewell - Philip McCutchan 4255

Paddock, Jedediah
Harpoon in Eden - F. van Wyck Mason 4152

Paddock, Micajah
Harpoon in Eden - F. van Wyck Mason 4152

Paddock, Obediah
Harpoon in Eden - F. van Wyck Mason 4152

Parbury, Miles
The Great Steamboat Race - John Brunner 736

Pendleton, Irons Saul
Voyage: A Novel of 1896 - Sterling Hayden 2798

Penmerry, Morgan
Scalpdancers - Kerry Newcomb 4592

Pennlyon, Jake
The Lion Triumphant - Philippa Carr 922

Perry, Geoffrey
The Bellerose Bargain - Robyn Carr 934

Phipps, William
Log Cabin Noble - F. van Wyck Mason 4153
Silver Shoals - Hamilton Cochran 1142

Polack, Charley
The Magic Ship - Sandra Paretti 4791

Pollard, George
The Jonah Man - Henry Carlisle 895

Quick, Bill
Rainbow in the Royals - Garland Roark 5357

Quick, James
Rainbow in the Royals - Garland Roark 5357

Raleigh, Sir Walter
Her Majesty's Captain - Derek Wilson 6797
The Voyage of the Destiny - Robert Nye 4657

Ravencroft, Brian
The Silver Dolphin - Velda Johnston 3264

Red Rover
The Red Rover - James Fenimore Cooper 1309

Riley, Cordellia
The River Witch - Margerie McIntyre 4278

Riley, Michael
The River Witch - Margerie McIntyre 4278

Rogers, Woodes
Lusty Wind for Carolina - Inglis Fletcher 2134

Ryall, Jeff
The Dram Tree - Hamilton Cochran 1140

Salter, Simon
The Ocean Mistress - Peter French 2225

Saudners, William
The Catherine - Robert S. MacDonald 3980

Scolvessen, Jon
Sea of Darkness - Roland Huntford 3086

Scott, David
The Slave Ship - Mary Johnston 3240

Scott-Hobey, Sir Raymond
On the Midnight Tide - Don Tracy 6310

Sharpentier, Quint
El Lazo - L. Jay Martin 4132

Shaw, Philander
The Private Adventures of Captain Shaw - Edith Shay 5783

Sherwood, Jonathon
Dragon Cove - Carter A. Vaughan 6434

Sissingen, Klaus von
Magnificent Enemies - Edgar Maas 3951

Skimmer of the Seas
The Water Witch - James Fenimore Cooper 1311

Slade, Lurman
Captain Caution - Kenneth Roberts 5385

Smith, John
For My Great Folly - Thomas B. Costain 1365

Snow, Benjamin
Storm Signals - Joseph C. Lincoln 3785

Spilsbury, Harriet
Yankee Woman - Frederic Baume 381

Staunton, Will
The Quickenberry Tree - Annette Motley 4502

Steel, Matthew
Praise at Morning - Mildred Masterson McNeilly 4310

Stone, Caleb
The Great Alone - Janet Dailey 1454

Strake, Eric
The Happy Parrot - Robert W. Chambers 977

Straton
The Purple Quest: A Novel of Seafaring Adventure in the Ancient World - Frank G. Slaughter 5896

Talburt, Wyck
Sail the Dark Tide - Davenport Steward 6017

Terentius, Titus
Fourth King - Norbert Coulehan 1373

Thorpe, Jake
Tarnished Angel - Phyllis Leonard 3723

Thorsson, Nils
Runestone - Don Coldsmith 1186

Turner, Nathan
Yankee Trader - Stanley Morton 4496

Turner, Will
Lusitania - David Butler 819

Utrecht, Simon Vann
Magnificent Enemies - Edgar Maas 3951

Vail, Ben
Jonathan Dearborn: A Novel of the War of 1812 - Willard Wallace 6540

Valmy, Nick
Tide of Empire - Bates Baldwin 279

Veres-Vorne, Nathan de
Mandalay - Alexandra Jones 3269

Ward, John
For My Great Folly - Thomas B. Costain 1365

West, Morgan
The Wings of Morning - Karen Harper 2714

Wilson, Samuel
The Southern Cross - Peter French 2226

Woodley, Cato
The Great Steamboat Race - John Brunner 736

Zafortezas, Sebastian
Spanish Bayonet - Stephen Vincent Benet 441

SEAMSTRESS

Castleman, Caroline
The Michaelmas Tree - Helen Ashfield 209

Courtney, Miranda
Autumn Lace - Eileen Jackson   3133

Eliott, Beatrice
The House of Eliott - Jean Marsh   4100

Eliott, Evangeline
The House of Eliott - Jean Marsh   4100

Garth, Celia
Celia Garth - Gwen Bristow   695

Howard, Devon
Mistress Devon - Virginia Coffman   1156

Julienne
The Frenchwoman - Jeanne Mackin   3995

Khurrem
The Bride of Suleiman - Aileen Crawley   1421

Lazar, Hannah
The Enduring Years - Claire Rayner   5263

Leguay, Gay
I Thee Wed - Gilbert Wolf Gabriel   2267

Louise
Banners of Silk - Rosalind Laker   3592

Mordal, Kirsten
Lady of No Man's Land - Jeanne Williams   6780

O'Neill, Sharon
Pride's Castle - Frank Yerby   6925

Tregellan, Emily
Emerald - Helen Ashfield   206

Van Meeteren, Analisa
Sunflower - Jill Marie Landis   3653

SECRETARY

Cabot, Wentworth
A Connecticut Yankee in Criminal Court - Peter J. Heck   2814
Death on the Mississippi - Peter J. Heck   2815

Carew, Charity
The Winter Bride - Carola Salisbury   5572

Conte, Sieur Louis de
Personal Recollections of Joan of Arc - Mark Twain   6372

Damianus
Gregory the Great - Gerhart Ellert   1913

Hori
Death Comes as the End - Agatha Christie   1076

Howard, Sara
The Alienist - Caleb Carr   907

Jones, Caroline Fremont
The Strange Files of Fremont Jones - Dianne Day   1544

Kasim, Ahmed
The Day of the Scorpion - Paul Scott   5682

Mervyn, Francis
The Melancholy Virgin - Annabel Laine   3587

O'Dowd, Molly
Molly - Teresa Crane   1417

Rush-Hodgeborn, Pamela
Murder and the First Lady - Elliott Roosevelt   5444

Short, William
Jefferson: A Novel - Max Byrd   838

SERVANT

Anicah, Sparrow
Mary's Land - Lucia St. Clair Robson   5415

Annie
Abigail - Malcolm Macdonald   3962

Aulirios, Niklos
A Candle for D'Artagnan - Chelsea Quinn Yarbro   6895
Crusader's Torch - Chelsea Quinn Yarbro   6897
A Flame in Byzantium - Chelsea Quinn Yarbro   6899

Baines, Timothy
Timothy Baines - John H. Culp   1445

Benno
Axe for an Abbot - Elizabeth Eyre   1989
Bravo for the Bride - Elizabeth Eyre   1990
Curtains for the Cardinal - Elizabeth Eyre   1991
Death of the Duchess - Elizabeth Eyre   1992

Bernay, Michael de
When God Slept - Peter Bourne   597

Biraygue, Pe de
The Golden Chain - Jean Gamo   2275

Bradford, Daniel
Sound of the Trumpet - Gilbert Morris   4471

Brand
Gildenford - Valerie Anand   130

Branwen
The White Raven - Diana L. Paxson   4847

Broughton, Abigail
Turn of the Dice - Janet Edmonds   1870

Brown, Harriet
The American Heiress - Dorothy Eden   1854

Brown, John
The Widow of Windsor - Jean Plaidy   5076
The Widow of Windsor - Tyler Whittle   6723

Burenin, Anna Yevnovna
The Crown and the Crucible - Michael Phillips   4987
A House Divided - Michael Phillips   4988
Travail and Triumph - Michael Phillips   4991

Burns, Molly
The Indentured Heart - Gilbert Morris   4464

Callant, John
The Boyds of Black River - Walter D. Edmonds   1871

Caprice, Mary
Christopher Humble - Charles Burnet Judah   3310

Carne, Demelza
The Renegade: A Novel of Cornwall, 1783-1787 - Winston Graham   2529

Chandon, Claire
Eden's Gate - Karen Harper   2711

Chrysaphos
Imperial Purple - Gillian Bradshaw   631

Church, Christopher
The Long Day Closes - Beatrice Tunstall   6360

Claus, Jeffry
The Eagle and the Wind - Herbert Stover   6068

Cleander
The Equinox: A Novel of Rome in the Time of Commodus - Carol Saylor   5622

Coe, Abbott
Eagle Fur - Robert Newton Peck   4884

Connelly, Ian
Nobody's Angel - Karen Robards   5363

Cooke, Mary
Amanda/Miranda - Richard Peck   4882

Coombes, Jane
Lady Jane - Norma Lee Clark   1092

Courtney, Miranda
Autumn Lace - Eileen Jackson   3133

Coventry
Fallen Skies - Philippa Gregory   2581

Danver, Marietta
Love's Tender Fury - Jennifer Wilde   6749

Dipper
A Broken Vessel - Kate Ross   5500
Cut to the Quick - Kate Ross   5501

Dugald, Davy
The Highland Hawk - Leslie Turner White   6682

Duvet, Berthe
The Porcelain Dove - Delia Sherman   5815

Eanes, Gil
Lord of the Kongo - Peter Forbath   2155

Edgar
The Cunning of the Dove - Alfred Duggan   1765

Elave
The Heretic's Apprentice - Ellis Peters   4960

Fairservice, Andrew
Rob Roy - Sir Walter Scott   5707

Fallon, Michael
The Fallon Blood - Reagan O'Neal   4741

Faraji, Osman
Angelique in Barbary - Sergeanne Golon   2469

Fenwolf, Morgan
Windsor Castle - William Harrison Ainsworth   59

Floyd, Mary
Mary of Carisbrooke - Margaret Campbell Barnes   327

Fogarty, Tim
Journey - James A. Michener   4371

Franklin, Toby
The Legion of the Lost - Donald Barr Chidsey   1062

Free, Henry
Free Man - Conrad Richter   5320

Gaillard, Diantha
The Judas Tree - Neil Harmon Swanson   6139

Gilmore, Martha
Whom the Gods Love - Kate Ross   5502

Godolphin, Lizzie
In the Shadow of the Brontes - Louise Brindley   690

Graeme, Roland
The Abbot - Sir Walter Scott   5688

Gregorio
The Lady in the Mask - Anne Green   2564

Hagar
Hagar - Cothburn O'Neal   4737

Hale, Jared
The Silver Saber - Carter A. Vaughan   6441
Yankee Rogue - Dana Fuller Ross   5496

Haredon, Caroline
Beyond the Blue Mountains - Jean Plaidy   5006

Harmonie, Gennie
Gennie the Huguenot Woman - Bette M. Ross   5464

Hartwell, Jane
Version and Diversion - Judith Terry   6207

Hawthorne, Cecily
Chelsea - Nancy Fitzgerald   2114

Heath, Keziah
Kezzy - Patricia Burns   799

Helios
Whom the Gods Would Destroy - Richard Powell   5148

Her-Bak
Her-Bak: The Living Face of Ancient Egypt - Isha Schwaller de Lubicz   5676

Hillaby
The Bondswoman - Caryl Ledner   3705

Hintermayer, Berchtold
The Heidenmauer - James Fenimore Cooper   1301

Holt, Daisy
The Days of the Butterfly - Norah Lofts   3841

Holt, Jellis
Man Cannot Tell - Philip Lightfoot Scruggs   5711

Horton, William
Ravenshoe - Henry Kingsley   3500

Howarth, Lance
Turn of the Dice - Janet Edmonds   1870

Hudson, Angus
Upstairs Downstairs - John Hawkesworth   2782

Hurst, Simon
The Frog Earl - Carola Dunn   1792

Huw
The Hooded Falcon - Prudence Andrew   140

Jarvis, Molly
The Vines of Yarrabee - Dorothy Eden   1864

Jenny
The Sound of Coaches - Leon Garfield   2295

Katerina
Katerina - Aharon Appelfeld   177

Kelso, Clare
Lantern for the Dark - Jessica Stirling   6045

Kephaolos
The Blood Star - Nicholas Guild   2611

Lawson, Sanchia
Masquerade for the King - Marina Oliver   4729

Leach
Lady Jane - Norma Lee Clark   1092

Lewellyn, David
A Place of Ravens - Pamela Hill   2942

Li Lien Ying
Imperial Woman - Pearl S. Buck   755

Libby
Mary of Carisbrooke - Margaret Campbell Barnes   327

Locke, Marianne
This Other Eden - Marilyn Harris   2733

Lundy, Katherine
Seasons - Anna Dillon   1645

MaCartney, Jenny
A Leaf in the Wind - Marie Joseph   3307

MacClaine, Jessica
The Explorers - William Stuart Long   3872

MacGregor, Kirsten
The Slow Awakening - Catherine Marchant   4082

Martha
The Still Storm - Francoise Sagan   5562

Matilda, Caroline
Freedom's Way - Theodora McCormick Du Bois   1742

Maum, Anna
The Hard to Catch Mercy - William Baldwin   281

Merridew, Jack
The King Edward Plot - Robert Lee Hall   2658

Michaelmas, Charity
A World Too Wide - Susan Moore   4445

Millican, Biddy
The Black Velvet Gown - Catherine Cookson   1274

Millican, Maria
The Black Velvet Gown - Catherine Cookson   1274

Moynahan, Ellen
One Small Candle - Mary Linehan MacKinnon   3998

Narses
The Bearkeeper's Daughter - Gillian Bradshaw   628

Nemo, Adam
Frobisher's Savage - Leonard Tourney   6299

Nofret
Pillar of Fire - Judith Tarr   6168

Osric
Red Lion and Gold Dragon - Rosemary Sprague   5969

Penelope
Gold for the Caesars - Florence A. Seward   5759

Philip of Evesham
Ordeal by Silence - Prudence Andrew   142

Philo of Crete
A Time for Judas - Morley Callaghan   866

Phinney, Desiree
Inherit the Earth - Margaret Shaw   5778

Pritchard, Anne-Louise
The Marigold Field - Diane Pearson   4876

Proctor, Jeremy
Blind Justice - Bruce Alexander   76
Murder in Grub Street - Bruce Alexander   77
Watery Grave - Bruce Alexander   78

Quo, Dinah
Lady Jane - Leslie O'Grady   4699

Rainbird, John
The Adventuress - Marion Chesney   1014
The Miser of Mayfair - Marion Chesney   1038
Rainbird's Revenge - Marion Chesney   1046
Rake's Progress - Marion Chesney   1047
The Wicked Godmother - Marion Chesney   1053

Rake
Under Two Flags - Ouida   4767

Ranulf
Angel of Death - P.C. Doherty   1670
The Crown in Darkness - P.C. Doherty   1671
The Prince of Darkness - P.C. Doherty   1675
Satan in St. Mary's - P.C. Doherty   1676

Rao, Balbeer
The Blood Seed - Andrew Ward   6561

Reilly, Mary
Mary Reilly - Valerie Martin   4136

Ross, Georgiana
The Wings of the Morning - Thomas Tryon   6356

Sarge
Invading Tibet - Mark Frutkin   2239

Sawby
The Lormes of Castle Rising - Fanny Cradock   1409
Wind of Change at Castle Rising - Fanny Cradock   1412

Scarlett, Nancy
The Heretic - Alison Macleod   4002

Scot, Micheal
Lady of Monkton - Elizabeth Byrd   835

Shallot, Roger
A Brood of Vipers - Michael Clynes   1133
The Gallows Murder - Michael Clynes   1134
The Grail Murders - Michael Clynes   1135
The Poisoned Chalice - Michael Clynes   1136

Shannon, Diana
A Daughter of Liberty - Allan Cole   1196

Snow, Robert
Pageant - G.B. Lancaster   3650

Spencer, Hugh
Scoundrels' Brigade - Carter A. Vaughan   6439

Spencer, Susan
The Woodsman - Don Wright   6880

Stewart, Eleanor
Death Wore a Diadem - Iona McGregor   4277

Sunil
The Barrier - Robin Maugham   4195

Teotochi, Mira
The Dark Palazzo - Virginia Coffman   1151

Tesseyman, Anne
The Heart of the Rose - June Barraclough   346

Toole, Milly
Beyond the Shadowlands - Georgina Fleming   2126

Tregellan, Emily
Emerald - Helen Ashfield   206

Tremorney, Lilith
Lilith - Jean Plaidy   5030

Trotter, Augustus
The Duchess of Duke Street - Mollie Hardwick   2693

Twillow, Philly
Enough Good Men - Charles Mercer   4336

Ulf
The Cross - Sigrid Undset   6380

Vane, Richard
Weep in the Sun - Jeanne Wilson   6809

Varney, Richard
Kenilworth - Sir Walter Scott   5700

Vaughan, Tom
City of Light - Alison Macleod   4001
The Hireling - Alison Macleod   4003

Waggett, Janie
The Gambling Man - Catherine Cookson   1276

Wagner, Christopher
Faust - Robert Nye   4654

Warne, Annie
Annie - Gloria Jahoda   3141

White, Polly
The Silver Saber - Carter A. Vaughan   6441

Whitman, Rebecca
Bound Girl - Everett Webber   6591

Wilson, Elizabeth "Lily"
Lady's Maid - Margaret Forster   2188

Woodson, Sylvester
A Story of Deep Delight - Thomas McNamee   4305

Woollatt, Margaret
The Son of York - Margaret Abbey   5

Wyatt, Jeffrey
Savage Gentleman - Noel B. Gerson   2381

Wyatt, Jem
Footman in Powder - Helen Ashton   216

Wynne, Jeremy
The King's Passenger - Nathan Schachner   5631

Yayael
My Master Columbus - Cedric Belfrage   418

Zeb
A Journey to Matecumbe - Robert Lewis Taylor   6188

SETTLER

Adams, Joel
Come Spring - Ben Ames Williams   6764

Agnew, Peter
The Sea 'Venture - F. van Wyck Mason   4159

Alden, John
Legacy - Robert Vaughan   6448
The Plymouth Adventure - Ernest Gebler   2342

Aletta
Watch for the Dawn - Stuart Cloete   1128

Ames, Joel
Valley in Arms: A Novel of the Settlement of Connecticut - Earl Schenck Miers   4376

Bainbridge, Rose
The Cabin at the Trail's End - Sheba
  Hargreaves 2706

Baker, Boniface
The Peaceable Kingdom - Jan de Hartog 2763

Ballantyne, Zouga
Men of Men - Wilbur Smith 5927

Beaton, David
Free Land - Rose Lane 3660

Bezvidenhout, Frederik
Watch for the Dawn - Stuart Cloete 1128

Bickley, Charles
Delilah's Mountain - Gloria Jahoda 3142

Billips, Priscilla Ann
The Long Sun - Janice Lucas 3920

Blackstone, William
The Disturber - L.S. Davidson Jr. 1505

Blennerhasset, Harman
The Rock Cried Out - Edward Stanley 5981

Bonwell, John
John Bonwell - Charles K. Pulse 5208

Borst, Gertje
*Valley in Arms: A Novel of the Settlement of
  Connecticut* - Earl Schenck Miers 4376

Bradford, William
The Plymouth Adventure - Ernest Gebler 2342

Bradley, Roger
The Quiet Shore - Walter Havighurst 2775

Bray, John
All Ye People - Merle Estes Colby 1167

Breen, Pat
The Ungodly: A Novel of the Donner Party - Richard
  Rhodes 5311

Brent, Margaret
Margaret Brent, Adventurer - Dorothy Grant 2533

Brightwood, Joshua
The Brightwood Expedition - Kay L.
  McDonald 4261

Brightwood, Marlette
The Brightwood Expedition - Kay L.
  McDonald 4261

Bristol, Saul
Ka'a'awa: A Novel about Hawaii in the 1850s -
  Oswald Andrew Bushnell 814

Brooks, Winsome
Rascal's Heaven - F. van Wyck Mason 4157

Broome, Jenny
The Traitors - William Stuart Long 3879

Brown, Humility
Daughter of Satan - Jean Plaidy 5011

Burke, Hailey
The Treasure of Pleasant Valley - Frank Yerby 6928

Burnett, Rice
The Earthbreakers - Ernest Haycox 2789

Buttes, Odder
Buttes Landing - Jean Rikhoff 5331

Buys, Coenraad de
King of the Bastards - Sarah Gertrude Millin 4405

Cambrin, Ma'am
Reckon with the River - Clark McMeekin 4292

Cameron, Bethany
The Edge of Time - Loula Grace Erdman 1949

Cameron, Wade
The Edge of Time - Loula Grace Erdman 1949

Carver, Cean
Lamb in His Bosom - Caroline Miller 4380

Carver, Lonzo
Lamb in His Bosom - Caroline Miller 4380

Catton, Gideon
Salt Lake City - A.R. Reife 5292

Chalmers, Richard
Gentlemen From England - Maude Hart
  Lovelace 3905

Chapman, Dick
Cormorant's Brood - Inglis Fletcher 2133

Chesney, Old Sergeant Bobby
Shadow of the Moon - Douglas C. Jones 3284

Chisholm, Hadley
The Chisholms - Evan Hunter 3082

Clare, Charles
Paradise - Sarah Neilan 4566

Clare, Rose
Paradise - Sarah Neilan 4566

Clayborn, Lance
*Forest Cavalier: A Romance of America's First
  Frontier and of Bacon's Rebellion* - Roy Catesby
  Flannagan 2122

Cockrell, Alexander
Destiny in Dallas - Shirley Seifert 5725

Coffin, Kathrin
The Strange Death of Mistress Coffin - Robert J.
  Begiebing 415

Coffyn, Dencey
The Beckoning Road - Caroline Snedeker 5934

Collins, Martin
Jornada - Robert L. Duffus 1754

Conway, John
That Callahan Spunk! - Francis Ames 124

Cooper, Garvin
Pillar of Cloud - Jackson Burgess 782

Cooper, Richard
The Believers - Janice Holt Giles 2409

Coopersand, Louise Danielle
Kansas Blue - Dylan Harson 2758

Copp, Dolly
The Pilgrim Soul - Anne Miller Downes 1711

Copp, Hayes
The Pilgrim Soul - Anne Miller Downes 1711

Cozad, John Jackson
Son of the Gamblin' Man: The Youth of an Artist -
  Mari Sandoz 5593

Crabtree, Robert
Certain People of Importance - Kathleen
  Norris 4647

Crawford, Melancthon
Harp of a Thousand Strings - Harold Lenoir
  Davis 1522

Crick, Harley
Sister Wives - Cleo Jones 3270

Dare, Virginia
Croatan - Mary Johnston 3231
The Lost Colony - Edison Marshall 4108

Dawson, Anthony
Cormorant's Brood - Inglis Fletcher 2133

Delahunty, Sibell
The Feather and the Stone - Patricia Shaw 5780

Delanay, Mary
Dark Sails - Helen Topping Miller 4388

Delusson, Jean Baptiste
The Delusson Family - Jacques Ducharme 1753

Donelson, John
Journey to Nashville - Alfred Leland Crabb 1402

Donner, George
The Mothers - Vardis Fisher 2109

Donner, Tamsen
The Mothers - Vardis Fisher 2109

Douglas, Maddy
Seattle Green - Jane Adams 26

Dunavant, Grady
Hill of the Hawk - Scott O'Dell 4689

Dupre, Blacky
Wagons West - Leslie Turner White 6692

Ellis, Nathan
A Fair Wind Home - Ruth Moore 4443

Erickson, Guri
Big Ember - Edward Havill 2778

Evans, Lije
The Way West - A.B. Guthrie Jr. 2628

Fairchild, Helen
O Genesee - Janet O'Daniel 4688

Fairchild, Nathan
Harvest of Dreams - Jaroldeen Edwards 1884

Fawley, Boone
This Savage Race - Douglas C. Jones 3285

Fawley, Molly
This Savage Race - Douglas C. Jones 3285

Fentress, Jeffrey
On the Long Tide - Laura Krey 3555

Field, Ashbel
Brave Pursuit - Marguerite Allis 107
To Keep Us Free - Marguerite Allis 115

Field, Connie
Brave Pursuit - Marguerite Allis 107

Field, Eve
Free Soil - Marguerite Allis 110

Field, Faith
To Keep Us Free - Marguerite Allis 115

Field, Lafayette
Free Soil - Marguerite Allis 110

Flagg, Abby-Delight
The Bright Land - Janet Fairbank 2000

Fletcher, William
Hope Leslie; or, Early Times in Massachusetts -
  Catharine Maria Sedgewick 5714

Forrester, Roland
Nick of the Woods; or, The Jibbenainosay - Robert
  Montgomery Bird 505

Forsyth, Heather
Summer Thunder - Willie Snow Ethridge 1982

Fowler, Hannah Moore
Hannah Fowler - Janice Holt Giles 2411

Freyling, Clara
Of Lizards and Angels: A Saga of Sioux Land -
  Frederick F. Manfred 4058

Freyling, Tunis
Of Lizards and Angels: A Saga of Sioux Land -
  Frederick F. Manfred 4058

Gardner, Rowland
Spirit Lake - MacKinlay Kantor 3363

Gentry, Kitty
Oh, Kentucky! - Betty Layman Receveur 5284

Gentry, Roman
Oh, Kentucky! - Betty Layman Receveur 5284

Gilbert, Joseph
Old Misery - Hugh Pendexter 4896

Glenny, Dave
Winter Harvest - Norah Lofts 3863

Graves, John
Juniata Valley - Virginia C. Cassel   954

Gray, Judith
Forest of the Night - Madison Jones   3291

Greer, Tamzen
Tamzen - Jane Gilmore Rushing   5530

Hale, Abner
Hawaii - James A. Michener   4370

Hale, Elmer
Mighty Mountain - Archie Binns   502

Hale, Lisette
Mighty Mountain - Archie Binns   502

Halifax, Jan
Wild Orchid - Isabel Dick   1640

Hancock, Leah
Deepwater: A Novel of the Carolinas - Pamela Jekel   3185

Hansa, Beret
Giants in the Earth - O.E. Rolvaag   5434

Hansa, Per
Giants in the Earth - O.E. Rolvaag   5434

Hapgood, Nathaniel
Beneath the Blue Mountain - Richard S. Wheeler   6656

Harkness, Bruce
The Treasure of Pleasant Valley - Frank Yerby   6928

Harman, Perry
The Salt and the Savor - Howard William Troyer   6354

Harper, Henry
Ghost Woman - Lawrence Thornton   6275

Harrison, Gabriel
The Yemassee - William Gilmore Simms   5855

Harrison, Tinkler
The Land Breakers - John Ehle   1895

Haseman, Karen
White Man - Peter Freuchen   2228

Haseman, Peter
White Man - Peter Freuchen   2228

Hawley, Jenny
The Explorers - William Stuart Long   3872

Heathcote, Mark
The Wept of Wish-Ton-Wish - James Fenimore Cooper   1312

Higgins, Elizabeth
The Strange Death of Mistress Coffin - Robert J. Begiebing   415

Hilyard, Jack
Cape Cod - William Martin   4139

Hollister, Althea
The Women at Pine Creek - Allis McKay   4279

Hollister, Mary
The Women at Pine Creek - Allis McKay   4279

Holm, Beret
Peder Victorious - O.E. Rolvaag   5435

Honer, Minta
The Living - Annie Dillard   1644

Howland, Robert
The Captive Bride - Gilbert Morris   4457

Ingledew, Jacob
The Architecture of the Arkansas Ozarks - Donald Harington   2708

Ingledew, Noah
The Architecture of the Arkansas Ozarks - Donald Harington   2708

Jayson, Robert
In Those Days - Harvey Fergusson   2068

Jeffreys, Anne
Western: A Saga of the Great Plains - Frank Yerby   6930

Johnson, Sir William
Wilderness Empire - Allen W. Eckert   1847

Jordan, Bethia
The Kentuckians - Janice Holt Giles   2413

Keene, Thomas
The Tree of Life - Hugh Nissenson   4629

King, Euphemia Texas Ashby
True Women - Janice Woods Windle   6820

Knight, Jabez
No Other Place - John Gould   2497

Lankester, Judith
Judith Lankester - Marjorie Allee   93

Le Moyne, Charles
High Towers - Thomas B. Costain   1366

Le Moyne, Jean-Baptiste
High Towers - Thomas B. Costain   1366

Le Moyne, Pierre
High Towers - Thomas B. Costain   1366

Lincoln, Thomas
The Matrix - Maria Thompson Daviess   1509

Lisa, Manuel
Those Who Go Against the Current - Shirley Seifert   5734

Livingstone, Harry
Wives of the Wind - Marjorie Jarrett   3170

Lockwood, Wayne
Song of Years - Bess Streeter Aldrich   72

Lockyear, Cal
The Earthbreakers - Ernest Haycox   2789

Lorimer, Paul de
Three Came to Ville Marie - Alan Sullivan   6114

Lovejoy, Ethan
Western: A Saga of the Great Plains - Frank Yerby   6930

Lowell, Wolsey
Thanksgiving - Terry Coleman   1207

Lucie
Honey in the Horn - Harold Lenoir Davis   1523

Lyte, Catherwood
Catherwood - Marly Youmans   6937

MacDonald, Flora
Raleigh's Eden - Inglis Fletcher   2137

MacDougall, Jack
Nebraska Coast - Clyde Brion Davis   1516

MacIntyre, Abijah
The Giant Joshua - Maurine Whipple   6673

Magoffin, Samuel
The Turquoise Trail - Shirley Seifert   5736

Magoffin, Susan Shelby
The Turquoise Trail - Shirley Seifert   5736

Maitland, Keith
Strife Before Dawn - Mary Schumann   5675

Martin, Caleb
The Peaceable Kingdom - Jan de Hartog   2763

Martin, Jeremiah
Song of Years - Bess Streeter Aldrich   72

Martin, Mark
The Measure of the Years - Alice Mary Colver   1218

Martin, Suzanne
Song of Years - Bess Streeter Aldrich   72

Mason, Daisy
Pilgrims: A Novel of the Mayflower - Gerard Mac   3955

Masters, Joline
Montana Woman - Rosanne Bittner   513

Mayhew, Bartholomey
Young Titan - F. van Wyck Mason   4165

Mayhew, Megan
Young Titan - F. van Wyck Mason   4165

McAlpine, Paul
Star of the Wilderness - Karle Wilson Baker   274

McCutcheon, Elias
The Raider - Jesse Hill Ford   2164

McDougal, Caleb
Columbia - Pamela Jekel   3184

McNeil, Amelie
First the Blade - May Miller   4400

McVey, Bob
Pillar of Cloud - Jackson Burgess   782

Meier, Matthias
Spring Came on Forever - Bess Streeter Aldrich   73

Melander
The Sea Runners - Ivan Doig   1685

Mellish, Dolly
The Sea 'Venture - F. van Wyck Mason   4159

Moore, Samuel
Hannah Fowler - Janice Holt Giles   2411

Mullins, Priscilla
The Wickedest Pilgrim - Donald Barr Chidsey   1067

Murray, Sam
The Day Must Dawn - Agnes Sligh Turnbull   6362

Nathoy, Lalu
Thousand Years of Gold - Ruthanne Lum McCunn   4239

Neilson, Gunnar
A Circle of Trees - Dana Faralla   2012

Neilson, Kersti
A Circle of Trees - Dana Faralla   2012

Norris, Jacqueline
Strife Before Dawn - Mary Schumann   5675

Oakes, Orrange
American Beauty - Edna Ferber   2060

Ollenshaw, Philip
Blossom Like the Rose - Norah Lofts   3836

O'Malley, Katie
The Adventurers - William Stuart Long   3869

O'Toole, Frances Melissa
Toward the Morning - Hervey Allen   101

Parre, Jude
Paradise - Esther Forbes   2158

Peck, Caleb
White Rising - Zane Kotker   3548

Percy, Ralph
To Have and to Hold - Mary Johnston   3241

Peridot, Evangeline
Greenstone - Yvonne Kalman   3324

Phelps, Amoret
Hope of Earth - Jane Gilmore Rushing   5528

Phelps, Stephen
Hope of Earth - Jane Gilmore Rushing   5528

Prawl, David
Trumpets Calling - Dora Aydelotte   248

Prawl, Martha
Trumpets Calling - Dora Aydelotte   248

Prescott, Samuel
The Prescott Chronicles - Albert Fried   2232

Prinsloo Willem, Oom
The Fiercest Heart - Stuart Cloete   1122

Purdy, Zillah
The Proselyte - Susan Ertz   1958

Quill, Kevin
Tomorrow the New Moon - Shirley Barker   319

Quimper, Jubal
Texas - James A. Michener   4375

Randolph, Martha
Crossing the River - Caryl Phillips   4984

Reed, Gabriel
Gabriel's Search - Della Lutes   3927

Reed, James Frazier
The Mothers - Vardis Fisher   2109
The Ungodly: A Novel of the Donner Party - Richard Rhodes   5311

Reed, Margaret
The Mothers - Vardis Fisher   2109

Reeves, Clint
Montana Woman - Rosanne Bittner   513

Reilly, Cat
The Bear Flag: A Novel of the Birth of California - Cecelia Holland   2983

Rennie, Lisabeth
Mists of Heaven - Yvonne Kalman   3325

Revell, Bartholomew
Massachusetts: A Novel - Nancy Zaroulis   6956

Riggs, Fred
Born Strangers - Helen Topping Miller   4384

Rivers, Reno
Leafy Rivers - Jessamyn West   6630

Robbins, Philip
Come Spring - Ben Ames Williams   6764

Roberts, Obadiah
Fruit in His Season - Helen C. Barney   333

Robertson, James
Journey to Nashville - Alfred Leland Crabb   1402

Rolfe, John
Daughter of Eve - Noel B. Gerson   2366
A Durable Fire - Virginia Bernhard   480
Pocahontas; or, The Nonparell of Virginia - David Garnett   2297
Powhatan's Daughter - John Clarke Bowman   605
The Sea 'Venture - F. van Wyck Mason   4159

Sackett, Abigail
To the Far Blue Mountains - Louis L'Amour   3630

Sackett, Barnabas
Sackett's Land - Louis L'Amour   3628
To the Far Blue Mountains - Louis L'Amour   3630

Safford, Joel
That Bennington Mob - Henry Barnard Safford   5558

Saltwood, Nicholas
The Covenant - James A. Michener   4368

Scarlock, Joan
Rivers Parting - Shirley Barker   315

Scarlock, John
Rivers Parting - Shirley Barker   315

Scarlock, Will
Rivers Parting - Shirley Barker   315

Schantz, Anna Sabilla
A High Wind Rising - Elsie Singmaster   5867

Shepherd, Catherine
Fairacres - Gladys Waters   6579

Shepherd, James
Fairacres - Gladys Waters   6579

Sheramy, Judith
Deep Summer - Gwen Bristow   696

Sheridan, Allegra
Oklahoma Run - Alberta Constant   1260

Sheridan, Bushrod
Oklahoma Run - Alberta Constant   1260

Sheridan, Mark
The Adventurers - Ernest Haycox   2787

Skiles, Jacob
Peace at Bowling Green - Alfred Leland Crabb   1405

Smith, John
Daughter of Eve - Noel B. Gerson   2366
Pocahontas - Susan Donnell   1691
Pocahontas; or, The Nonparell of Virginia - David Garnett   2297
Powhatan's Daughter - John Clarke Bowman   605
The Sea 'Venture - F. van Wyck Mason   4159
The Sot-Weed Factor - John Barth   364

Smollett, Arthur
Courting Emma Howe - Margaret A. Robinson   5410

Somers, George
The Sea 'Venture - F. van Wyck Mason   4159

Southgate, John
Wild Dog Running - Alan Scholefield   5658

Spence, Frances O'Riordan
The Settlers - William Stuart Long   3878

Stafford, Charles
Mists of Heaven - Yvonne Kalman   3325

Stafford, Linnie
The Lieutenant's Lady - Bess Streeter Aldrich   70

Standish, Miles
The Plymouth Adventure - Ernest Gebler   2342

Steed, Edmund
Chesapeake - James A. Michener   4367

Sterling, Will
A Durable Fire - Virginia Bernhard   480

Stoltz, Amelia
Spring Came on Forever - Bess Streeter Aldrich   73

Stonecypher, Elizabeth
Give Us This Valley - Tom Ham   2666

Stonecypher, George Washington
Give Us This Valley - Tom Ham   2666

Strong, Mama
White Rising - Zane Kotker   3548

Sutter, John A.
The American River - Gary McCarthy   4222
The Bear Flag: A Novel of the Birth of California - Cecelia Holland   2983
Captain Sutter's Gold - Jonreed Lauritzen   3673

Sutton, Martyn
The Lost Colony - Edison Marshall   4108

Tadlock
The Way West - A.B. Guthrie Jr.   2628

Taggart, Jenny
The Settlers - William Stuart Long   3878

Tante, Maria
The Fiercest Heart - Stuart Cloete   1122

Tempest, Rick
The Adventurers - William Stuart Long   3869

Thompson, Richard
Articles of Faith - Ronald Harwood   2770

Thorbjornsdottir, Gudrid
Gudrid's Saga - Constance Irwin   3115

Torry, Damaris
Legacy - Robert Vaughan   6448

Tower, Henry
The Grandmothers - Glenway Westcott   6640

Tower, Rose
The Grandmothers - Glenway Westcott   6640

Trask, Eldridge
Trask - Don Berry   483

Trefor, Will
Pilgrims: A Novel of the Mayflower - Gerard Mac   3955

Truman, Ellen
Free Soil - Margaret Lynn   3943

Truman, John
Free Soil - Margaret Lynn   3943

Van Buren, Joseph
The Colonists - William Stuart Long   3870

Van der Berg, Hendrik
The Turning Wheels - Stuart Cloete   1127

Van der Berg, Kaspar
Watch for the Dawn - Stuart Cloete   1128

Van Doorn, Willem
The Covenant - James A. Michener   4368

Van Reenen, Sannie
The Turning Wheels - Stuart Cloete   1127

Vicker, Charlotte
Wild Dog Running - Alan Scholefield   5658

Vicotte, Jules
Three Came to Ville Marie - Alan Sullivan   6114

Walden, Richard
Richard Walden's Wife - Eleanor Kelly   3399

Ward, Martin
New Road - Merle Estes Colby   1168

Ware, Jonathan
The Sun Shines West - Nathan Schachner   5632

Warne, Ewen
Beulah Land - Harold Lenoir Davis   1520

Warner, Edward
Caribee - Christopher Nicole   4614

Warner, Tom
Caribee - Christopher Nicole   4614

Warren, Cordy
Winter Harvest - Norah Lofts   3863

Warren, Esek
To Fame Unknown - Clifford Lindsey Alderman   67

Warrington, Charles
The Green Mountain Boys - Daniel Pierce Thompson   6249

Wheatley, Lena
The Family of Women - Richard Peck   4883

Wheaton, Francis
Thanksgiving - Terry Coleman   1207

Whyte, Catherine
By Reason of Strength - Gerald White Johnson   3225

Williams, Ephraim
The Prospering - Elizabeth Speare   5954

Willoughby, Robert
The Colonists - William Stuart Long   3870

Wilson, Francis
Juniata Valley - Virginia C. Cassel   954

Windrow, Oliver
Remembrance Rock - Carl Sandburg   5583

Winfield, Delilah
Delilah's Mountain - Gloria Jahoda   3142

Winslow, Brent
Blue Camellia - Frances Parkinson Keyes   3477

Winslow, Gilbert
The Captive Bride - Gilbert Morris   4457
The Honorable Imposter - Gilbert Morris   4463

Winslow, Margaret
Here I Stay - Elizabeth Coatsworth   1138

Winthrop, Elizabeth Fones
The Winthrop Woman - Anya Seton   5754

Woodbridge, Jonathan
The Bounty Lands - William Donohue Ellis   1927

Wright, Mooney
The Land Breakers - John Ehle   1895

Yardley, Temperance
A Durable Fire - Virginia Bernhard   480

Zachary, Ben
The Unforgiven - Alan Le May   3692

Zachary, Cassius
The Unforgiven - Alan Le May   3692

Zachary, Rachel
The Unforgiven - Alan Le May   3692

Zendt, Levi
Centennial - James A. Michener   4366

SHAMAN

Andiora
This Widowed Land - Kathleen O'Neal Gear   2331

Born Underwater
Fathers and Crows - William T. Vollmann   6508

Cha-Kwena
The Edge of the World - William Sarabande   5597
Shadow of the Watching Star - William
   Sarabande   5601
Thunder in the Sky - William Sarabande   5602

Deer Shadow
The Deer Dancers - Amanda Cockrell   1146

Digging Owl
Quest for the White Bull - Don Coldsmith   1182

El-i-chi
Sachem's Son - Donald Clayton Porter   5125

Ghostwind
Thunder in the Dawn - Earl Murray   4532

Gotha
The Last Mammoth - Margaret Allan   89

Heron
People of the Wolf - W. Michael Gear   2341

Hodano
Manitou - Donald Clayton Porter   5120
Spirit Knife - Donald Clayton Porter   5128

Hungry Bear
People of the Fire - W. Michael Gear   2335

Island Woman
The Firekeeper - Robert Moss   4498
The Interpreter - Robert Moss   4499

Jhadel
Face of the Rising Sun - William Sarabande   5598

Karana
Corridor of Storms - William Sarabande   5596
Forbidden Land - William Sarabande   5599

Kokopelli
She Who Remembers - Linda Lay Shuler   5838

Kwani
Voice of the Eagle - Linda Lay Shuler   5839

Lone Walker
Scalpdancers - Kerry Newcomb   4592

Looks Far
The Sacred Hills - Don Coldsmith   1187

Makwa-Ikwa
Shaman - Noah Gordon   2483

Maya
The Mammoth Stone - Margaret Allan   90

Navahk
Corridor of Storms - William Sarabande   5596

Nightshade
People of the River - W. Michael Gear   2338

Old Lodge
Song of the Cheyenne - Jory Sherman   5822

Old White Buffalo
Buffalo Medicine - Don Coldsmith   1171

Pope
Taos - Irwin R. Blacker   527

Red Horse
Quest for the White Bull - Don Coldsmith   1182

Singing Wolf
Track of the Bear - Don Coldsmith   1191

Standing-in-the-Doorway
The Dark Way - Robert J. Conley   1241
The Way of the Priests - Robert J. Conley   1253

Sunchaser
People of the Sea - W. Michael Gear   2339

Tay-Bodal
Death at Rainy Mountain - Mardi Oakley
   Medawar   4321

White Buffalo
Scalpdancers - Kerry Newcomb   4592

White Fox
Fort De Chastaigne - Don Coldsmith   1177

Wolf's Head
The Sacred Hills - Don Coldsmith   1187

Wounded Bear
Sand in the Wind - Kathleen O'Neal Gear   2329

Wovoka
The Day the Sun Died - Dale Van Every   6408
Song of Wovoka - Earl Murray   4531

Yellow Bird
Whisper of the Wolf - Terry C. Johnston   3261

SHEPHERD

Ismene
Earth Giant - Edison Marshall   4106

Shulamit
Solomon's Song - Roberta Kells Dorr   1697

SHIPOWNER

Bolderman, Martyn
The Sinking of the Sarah Diamond - William Dale
   Jennings   3213

Bourlotas, Kosmas
The Bourlotas Fortune - Nicholas Gage   2268

Cartwright, George
The Lady and the Deep Blue Sea - Garland
   Roark   5356

Clavier, Jacques
Those the Sun Has Loved - Rose Jourdain   3309

Conquy, Judah
The Rock: A Novel about Gibraltar - John
   Masters   4179

Malitas, Demo
The Bourlotas Fortune - Nicholas Gage   2268

Stuart, Tom
The Stuart Women - Matt Braun   652

Tyler, Tina
The Dram Tree - Hamilton Cochran   1140

Venetis, Jason
The Bourlotas Fortune - Nicholas Gage   2268

West, Morgan
The Wings of Morning - Karen Harper   2714

Whipple, Abiezar
The Pepper Tree - John Edward Jennings   3203

SIDEKICK

Giraud, Jules
Rasputin's Revenge - John T. Lescroart   3725

O'Gilroy, Conall
Spy's Honour - Gavin Lyall   3929

Watson, John H.
The Disappearance of Edwin Drood - Peter
   Rowland   5521
*Sherlock Holmes and the Mysterious Friend of Oscar
   Wilde* - Russell A. Brown   731
Sherlock Holmes and the Red Demon - Larry
   Millett   4404
Sherlock Holmes Meets Annie Oakley - Stanley
   Shaw   5782

SINGER

Adler, Irene
The Canary Trainer - Nicholas Meyer   4348
Good Morning, Irene - Carole Nelson Douglas   1698
Good Night, Mr. Holmes - Carole Nelson
   Douglas   1699
Irene at Large - Carole Nelson Douglas   1700
Irene's Last Waltz - Carole Nelson Douglas   1701

Broschi, Carlo
The Castrato - Lawrence Goldman   2459

Capello, Rachele
Creole Dusk - Walter Adolphe Roberts   5392

Caruso, Enrico
A Cadenza for Caruso - Barbara Paul   4834
A Chorus of Detectives - Barbara Paul   4835
Herma - Macdonald Harris   2726
Prima Donna at Large - Barbara Paul   4838

Casson-Perceval, Edwina
The Ring Master - David Gurr   2622

Consuelo
Consuelo - George Sand   5582

Daae, Christine
Phantom - Susan Kay   3375

Danby, April
Albuquerque - Sara Orwig   4757

Daniels, Kitty
Sweet Songbird - Teresa Crane   1418

d'Asselnat, Marianne
Marianne and the Masked Prince - Juliette
   Benzoni   469

Destinn, Emmy
A Cadenza for Caruso - Barbara Paul   4834
A Chorus of Detectives - Barbara Paul   4835

Dunkaldir, Kevin
Dominic - Kathleen Robinson   5405

Farrar, Geraldine
A Chorus of Detectives - Barbara Paul   4835
Prima Donna at Large - Barbara Paul   4838

Guiletta
Fairoaks - Frank Yerby   6915

Guthrie, Woody
Joy in Mudville - Gordon McAlpine   4216

Herma
Herma - Macdonald Harris   2726

Kelly, Michael
The Irish Boy: A Romantic Biography - Naomi
   Jacob   3137

Kenwood, Katharine
The Melancholy Virgin - Annabel Laine   3587

Kerr, Daniel
The Lion's Way - Lewis Orde   4750

Lind, Jenny
Jenny and Barnum: A Novel of Love - Roderick Thorp 6276
The Swedish Nightingale: Jenny Lind - Elizabeth Kyle 3571

Linley, Elizabeth
Perdita's Prince - Jean Plaidy 5040

Lorimer, Alexa
Alexa - Anne Melville 4330
Blaize - Anne Melville 4331

Lyse, Clementine
The Monterant Affair - Richard Grayson 2560

MacLeod, Katie
Home Mountain - Jeanne Williams 6777

Maffeo, Guido
Cry to Heaven - Anne Rice 5313

Malibran, Maria Felicita
Signorina - Henry Myers 4542

Martin, Sarah
Paiute - Sessions S. Wheeler 6666

Montressor, Letty
Letty - Clare Darcy 1491

Orsini, Orso
Familiar Acts - June Barraclough 345

Porteous, Flora
The Heroine's Sister - Frances Murray 4536

Preswald, Caitlin
Mississippi Belle - Clements Ripley 5346

Randall, Lilly
Tarnished Angel - Phyllis Leonard 3723

Ransom, Marianne
The Wizard's Daughter - Barbara Michaels 4362

Sala, Maria
Beyond Desire: A Novel Based on the Life of Felix and Cecille Mendelssohn - Pierre La Mure 3574

Sappho
My Name Is Sappho - Martha Rofheart 5429

Treschi, Tonio
Cry to Heaven - Anne Rice 5313

Valence, Lily
Fallen Skies - Philippa Gregory 2581

Volkman, Magda
The Career of Magda V. - Joseph Machlis 3982

Worth, Maddie
Mountain Laurel - Jude Deveraux 1632

SLAVE

Andrasta
The Wolf of Masada - John Fredman 2220

Anichis
The Trojan - Noel B. Gerson 2386

Anna
The Walk into Morning - Mildred Barger Herschler 2867

Attiba
Caribbee - Thomas Hoover 3025

Auria
Anabasis: A Journey to the Interior - Ellen Gilchrist 2408

Bagoas
The Persian Boy - Mary Renault 5301

Banks, Boy "Muddy"
Muddy Banks - Ruby C. Tolliver 6291

Basil of Antioch
The Silver Chalice - Thomas B. Costain 1370

Beauty Beast
Beauty Beast - MacKinlay Kantor 3361

Beeljie
Fairoaks - Frank Yerby 6915

Ben
Tell Me a Tale: A Novel of the Old South - James McEachin 4266

Ben Hur, Judah
Ben Hur: A Tale of the Christ - Lew Wallace 6536

Bernay, Michael de
When God Slept - Peter Bourne 597

Black Eunuch
Valide: A Novel of the Harem - Barbara Chase-Riboud 1007

Brendan
By Love Enslaved - Phoebe Conn 1255

Brittanicus
I Am a Barbarian - Edgar Rice Burroughs 807

Burns, Anthony
The Sin of the Prophet - Truman Nelson 4582

Cambridge
Cambridge - Caryl Phillips 4983

Carrick, Johnathan
Theory of War - Joan Brady 637

Cedonius
Behold, We Live - Charles Dunscomb 1812

Celisma
Bayou - Pamela Jekel 3183

Chap
The Walk into Morning - Mildred Barger Herschler 2867

Christophe, Henri
Lydia Bailey - Kenneth Roberts 5387

Cinque, Joseph
Echo of Lions - Barbara Chase-Riboud 1004

Clora
Family - J. California Cooper 1297

Coatl
Captain From Castille - Samuel Shellabarger 5794

Corax
The Gospel of Corax - Paul Park 4802

Cudjo
Chesapeake - James A. Michener 4367

De Clairpont, Ivon
The Proud Villeins - Valerie Anand 133

Demetrius
The Robe - Lloyd C. Douglas 1703

Dessalines, Jean-Jacques
Lydia Bailey - Kenneth Roberts 5387

Di-Peachy
High Hearts - Rita Mae Brown 728

Drum
Drum - Kyle Onstott 4744

Drumson
Drum - Kyle Onstott 4744

Eber
Abram, Son of Terah - Florence M. Bauer 378

Eri
Departed Glory - Peter Danielson 1466

Gabriel
Black Thunder - Arna Bontemps 574

Grabeau
Amistad: The Thunder of Freedom - David Pesci 4944

Grammy
Kingdom Coming - Roark Bradford 622

Gunnor
The Proud Villeins - Valerie Anand 133

Gwanga
Freedom's Dues - Robert H. Abel 9

Gyges
Star of Macedon - Karl V. Eiker 1901

Hagar
Children of the Lion - Peter Danielson 1464
Hagar - Lois T. Henderson 2824

Hemings, Sally
Arc d'X - Steve Erickson 1953
The President's Daughter - Barbara Chase-Riboud 1005
Sally Hemings - Barbara Chase-Riboud 1006

Hillaby
The Bondswoman - Caryl Ledner 3705

Hwesuhunu
The African - Harold Courlander 1386

Indian John
I, Tituba, Black Witch of Salem - Maryse Conde 1233

Jackson, Gideon
Freedom Road - Howard Fast 2031

Jacob
The Slave - Isaac Bashevis Singer 5866

Jim
The Further Adventures of Huckleberry Finn - Greg Matthews 4189

Justus
Raven's Wind - Victor Canning 883

Khurrem
The Bride of Suleiman - Aileen Crawley 1421

La Jeune, Charlotte
Daughter of Strangers - Elizabeth Boatwright Coker 1164

Lacer, Gaius Julius
Gold for the Caesars - Florence A. Seward 5759

Little David
Wind Like a Bugle - Leonard Nathan 3722

Lovey
Beulah Land - Lonnie Coleman 1202

Lykaina
The Other Sappho - Ellen Frye 2240

Lykos
Gate to the Sea - Bryher 743

Mango, Peter
Fragments of the Ark - Louise Meriwether 4341

Maum, Anna
The Hard to Catch Mercy - William Baldwin 281

McCloud, Georgia
Crossing over Jordan - Linda Beatrice Brown 725

McCutcheon, Peter
The White Slave - Fanny Howe 3059

Mehuru
A Respectable Trade - Philippa Gregory 2584

Moses
Tell Me a Tale: A Novel of the Old South - James McEachin 4266

Nairn, Alexander
Westward to Laughter - Colin MacInnes 3984

Naksh-i-dil
Valide: A Novel of the Harem - Barbara Chase-Riboud 1007

Nathoy, Lalu
Thousand Years of Gold - Ruthanne Lum McCunn 4239

O-Lan
The Good Earth - Pearl S. Buck   754

Ogier
The Viking - Edison Marshall   4113

Ookumi
The African - Harold Courlander   1386

Otto
Signals of Distress - Jim Crace   1408

Paloma
Jewel of the Sea - Susan Wiggs   6743

Parks, Wes
A Darkness at Ingraham's Crest: A Tale of the Slaveholding South - Frank Yerby   6912

Pruitt, October
All God's Children - Alston Anderson   136

Quasheba
Die the Long Day - Orlando Patterson   4833

Quickskill, Raven
Flight to Canada - Ishmael Reed   5285

Quintus, Julian
A Fig in Winter - Willa Gibbs   2400

Raanah
Charioteer: A Story of Old Egypt in the Days of Joseph - Gertrude Eberle   1835

Rachel of Rome
The Lives of Rachel - Joel Gross   2601

Raven
The Big Drum - Elizabeth Boatwright Coker   1162

Red Jade
A House in Peiking - Robert Payne   4853

Reed, Jackey
Ratoon - Christopher Nicole   4619

Ricky, Melinda Blake
The Slave Stealer - Boyd Upchurch   6390

Rizpah
Rizpah - Charles E. Israel   3124

Ruth
Street of the Sandalmakers: A Tale of Rome in the Time of Marcus Aurelius - Nis Peterson   4977

Sahak
Barabbas - Par Lagerkvist   3585

Samson
The View From Coyaba - Peter Abrahams   11

Sanchia
The Wind Dancer - Iris Johansen   3218

Shipman, Lettiele
The Tree of Life - Hugh Nissenson   4629

Singbe-Pieh
Amistad: The Thunder of Freedom - David Pesci   4944

Sosylos
Hannibal of Carthage - Mary Dolan   1686

Spartacus
Arena: A Novel of Spartacus and Crassus - Maurice Ghnassia   2391
Fortune's Favorite - Colleen McCullough   4235
Spartacus - Howard Fast   2044

Starr, Amantha
Band of Angels - Robert Penn Warren   6572

Steele, Mandrake
A Promise Unbroken - Al Lacy   3582

Taita
River God - Wilbur Smith   5928

Tamboura
Drum - Kyle Onstott   4744

Theophilus
The Testament of Theophilus - Leonard Wibberley   6730

Ti Noel
Kingdom of This World - Alejo Carpentier   906

Tilaki
When God Slept - Peter Bourne   597

Till, Nancy
Sapphira and the Slave Girl - Willa Cather   958

Tituba
I, Tituba, Black Witch of Salem - Maryse Conde   1233
Peace, My Daughters - Shirley Barker   314

Toussaint l'Ouverture, Pierre Dominique
Lydia Bailey - Kenneth Roberts   5387

Trudeau, Young Bone
Shadow of the Moon - Douglas C. Jones   3284

Tubman, Harriet
A Woman Called Moses - Marcy Moran Heidish   2821

Turner, Nat
The Confessions of Nat Turner - William Styron   6106
Ol' Prophet Nat - Daniel Panger   4786

Valli
So Far From Malabar - Joy DeWeese Wehen   6599

Varinia
Spartacus - Howard Fast   2044

Ware, Vyry
Jubilee - Margaret Walker   6531

Williamsburg
The Journey of August King - John Ehle   1894

Woodson, Sylvester
A Story of Deep Delight - Thomas McNamee   4305

Zeb
A Journey to Matecumbe - Robert Lewis Taylor   6188

Zenobia
The Saracen Blade - Frank Yerby   6926

SMUGGLER

Barnabas, Robert
Judith - Brian Cleeve   1108

De la Motte, Chevalier
Denis Duval - William Makepeace Thackeray   6211

Devant, James
Clouds of Destiny - Lou Ellen Davis   1535

Exforth, James
The Ravishers - Elizabeth Richards   5318

Foxhill, Tom
The Sugar Pavilion - Rosalind Laker   3600

Hovey, Matt
Blue Hurricane - F. van Wyck Mason   4146

Lavenham, Ludovic
The Talisman Ring - Georgette Heyer   2905

Northrup, Job
Pelican Coast - Alan Le May   3690

Paris, George
Judith Paris - Hugh Walpole   6545

Sauvigny, Guy de
The Wind From the Sea - Constance Heaven   2812

Squire, The
Kate - Brian Cleeve   1109

Trelcar, Davy
Farewell the Tranquil - R.F. Delderfield   1585

SOCIAL WORKER

Keele, Christopher
The Michaelmas Girls - John Barry   362

SOCIALITE

Adams, Marian "Clover"
Refinements of Love: A Novel about Clover and Henry Adams - Sarah Booth Conroy   1259

Arbor, Louise
Young Mrs. Cavendish and the Kaiser's Men - K.K. Beck   405

Archibald, Allan
Organized Crime - Nicholas Von Hoffman   6511

Blanchard, Catherine
Seattle Green - Jane Adams   26

Brassova, Annastatia
A Token of Jewels - Diane Cory   1353

Bristed, Georgia
The Book Class - Louis Auchincloss   228

Brummell, George Bryan
Rebel Heiress - Jane Aiken Hodge   2969

Bryant, Julie
While the Music Lasts - Suzanne Goodwin   2477

Cassidy, Brooke
Death on the Cliff Walk - Mary Kruger   3562
No Honeymoon for Death - Mary Kruger   3564

Devlin, Brooke
Masterpiece of Murder - Mary Kruger   3563

Fitzgerald, Zelda
One Last Glimpse - James Aldridge   74

Howard, Dulcima
The Ladies of Hanover Square - Rona Randall   5249

Jumel, Eliza
The Golden Mistress - Basil Beyea   488
Notorious Eliza - Basil Beyea   489

Karlotte, Anna-Marie Elsbet
The Blood Order - Jack D. Hunter   3084

Lavette, Jean
The Immigrants - Howard Fast   2034

Lee, Leila
The Book Class - Louis Auchincloss   228

McAllister, Ward
Tassels on Her Boots - Arthur Cheney Train   6313

Nash, Richard
Monsieur Beaucaire - Booth Tarkington   6163

Nesbit, Evelyn
Ragtime - E.L. Doctorow   1658

Richardson, Lesley Aymes
The Eleventh Year - Monique Raphel High   2914

Sherwood, Anson
The Normandie Affair - Elizabeth Villars   6497

Simpson, Wallis Warfield
Edward and Mrs. Simpson - A.C.H. Smith   5916
Wallis: The Novel - Anne Edwards   1883

Spencer, Christabel
The Millionaire's Daughter - Dorothy Eden   1858

Tabor, Elizabeth "Baby Doe"
Wilde West - Walter Satterthwait   5609

Taliafero, Vivian
Murder in the Rose Garden - Elliott Roosevelt   5452

Vanderbilt, Gloria Morgan
That Vanderbilt Woman - Philip Van Rensselaer   6427

SONGWRITER

Foster, Stephen
Banished Children of Eve - Peter Quinn   5227

Guthrie, Woody
Joy in Mudville - Gordon McAlpine   4216

SORCERER

Aldulf
Hawk of May - Gillian Bradshaw   629

Chimalman
The Luck of Huemac: A Novel about the Aztecs -
   Daniel Peters   4946

Karella
Pillar of the Sky - Cecelia Holland   2994

Maximus
Julian - Gore Vidal   6489

Merlin
Arthur - Stephen R. Lawhead   3679
The Coming of the King - Nikolai Tolstoy   6296
A Connecticut Yankee in King Arthur's Court - Mark
   Twain   6371
The Crimson Chalice - Victor Canning   882
The Crystal Dove - Mollie Hardwick   2692
The Emperor Arthur - Godfrey Turton   6368
The Hollow Hills - Mary Stewart   6030
The Last Enchantment - Mary Stewart   6031
Merlin - Stephen R. Lawhead   3681
The Pagan King - Edison Marshall   4109
Pendragon - Stephen R. Lawhead   3682
The Road to Avalon - Joan Wolf   6842
The Winter King - Bernard Cornwell   1351

Wardyke
The Tall Stones - Moyra Caldecott   848
The Temple of the Sun - Moyra Caldecott   849

SORCERESS

Becca
The Gods Are Not Mocked - Anna Taylor   6177

Circe
The Voyage Home - Ernst Schnabel   5644

Deveron, Andra
Swear by Apollo - Shirley Barker   318

Erif Der
The Corn King and the Spring Queen - Naomi
   Mitchison   4419

Gruffydd, Wynne ab
Where Magic Dwells - Rexanne Becnel   411

Luti
Prophets and Warriors - Peter Danielson   1473
The Trumpet and the Sword - Peter Danielson   1479

Medea
Jason - Henry Treece   6331
The King Must Die - Mary Renault   5298
Medea - Miranda Seymour   5764

Merza
The Soothsayer - Laurene Chinn   1069

Montvoisin, Catherine
The Oracle Glass - Judith Merkle Riley   5335

Morgan Le Fay
The Prince and the Pilgrim - Mary Stewart   6032

Morgan Le Fey
Witch of the North - Courtway Jones   3272

Morgawse
Hawk of May - Gillian Bradshaw   629

Muirheal
The Saxon Tapestry - Sile Rice   5317

SOUTHERN BELLE

Acklen, Adelicia
Dinner at Belmont - Alfred Leland Crabb   1398
Lodging at the Saint Cloud - Alfred Leland
   Crabb   1403

Allen, Delicia
Miss Delicia Allen - Mary Johnston   3237

Barringer, Lelia
Roses From the South - Perceval Reniers   5304

Berrien, Angelica
Blood Red Roses - Elizabeth Boatwright Coker   1163

Bibbs, Pamela
*A Darkness at Ingraham's Crest: A Tale of the
   Slaveholding South* - Frank Yerby   6912

Billingsley, Lettie
The Last Plantation - Don Wright   6879

Boozer, Marie
La Belle - Elizabeth Boatwright Coker   1161

Brittany, Morgan
Floodtide - Frank Yerby   6916

Browning, Natalie
To See Your Face Again - Eugenia Price   5188

Cannon, Gabrielle
Twilight of the Dawn - Elizabeth Nell Dubus   1752

Carvel, Virginia
The Crisis - Winston Churchill   1079

Chantrell, Cordelia
Cordelia Chantrell - Meade Minnigerode   4413

Chastain, Marcy
The Bayou Road - Mignon G. Eberhart   1832

Chevillon, Denise
The Moreland Legacy - Diana Haviland   2777

Clay, Margaret
Trumpet in the Sky - Helen Topping Miller   4397

Cleave, Linden
Thunder on the Chesapeake - David Divine   1650

Coberley, Brandon
The Laughing Stranger - Vina Delmar   1601

Cohran, Caline
The Great Tide - Rubylea Hall   2662

Coombs, Eulalie
Miami: A Saga - Evelyn Wilde Mayerson   4204

Currain, Cinda
House Divided - Ben Ames Williams   6765

D'Antoni, Ursula
The Golden Circle - John Edward Ames   125

Davis, Varina Howell
The Proud Way - Shirley Seifert   5731

Day, Eden
Yankee Stranger - Elswyth Thane   6217

Drake, Susan
Captain Rebel - Frank Yerby   6910

Drake, Susanna
Raintree County - Ross Lockridge Jr.   3827

Dubois, Dulcie
The Dram Tree - Hamilton Cochran   1140

Ferro, Jane
Jim Mundy: A Novel of the American Civil War -
   Robert H. Fowler   2192

Field, Eve
Free Soil - Marguerite Allis   110

Forrester, Dallas
Wagons to Tucson - Ed Newsom   4604

Fox, Odalie
The Foxes of Harrow - Frank Yerby   6917

Gaillard, Desiree
Cease Firing - Mary Johnston   3230

Gordon, Temple
The Proud and the Free - Janet Dailey   1456

Herrick, Emmeline
The Wilderness Brigade - Phyllis Gordon
   Demarest   1605

Kirby, Elizabeth
Bugles Blow No More - Clifford Dowdey   1704

Kittering, Alexandra
A Hundred Hills - Howard Breslin   667

Latimer, Natalie Browning
Before Darkness Falls - Eugenia Price   5178

Lawrence, Anne
Natchez: A Novel of the Deep South - Pamela
   Jekel   3186

Lawrence, Arden
Natchez: A Novel of the Deep South - Pamela
   Jekel   3186

Leche, Elaine de
Wild Is the River - Louis Bromfield   704

MacKay, Kieran
One Wore Blue - Heather Graham   2517

Manning, Margaret
Bates House - Clarence Benadum   437

McKensie, Rosa Ann
McKensie's Hundred: A Tale of the Old Dominion -
   Frank Yerby   6924

O'Hara, Scarlett
Gone with the Wind - Margaret Mitchell   4415

Paxton, Susanna
Song of the Bayou - Elinor Lynley   3936

Prevost, Steward
Marching On - James Boyd   612

Randall, Phoebe
Ask My Brother - Constance Wagner   6518

Rawls, Delcie
The Proud Retreat - Clifford Dowdey   1706

Ruffin, Abby
A Promise Unbroken - Al Lacy   3582

Rutland, Mary Marie
Bride of the River - Laura B. Harris   2723

Rutledge, Samantha
Niagara - Robert Lewis Taylor   6189

Saxon, Frankie-Julia
The Legacy of Beulah Land - Lonnie Coleman   1203

Seabright, Terry
Caleb Pettengill U.S.N. - George Fielding Eliot   1912

Selby, Lorena
Lorena - Frank G. Slaughter   5892

Seymour, Sylvia
Proud New Flags - F. van Wyck Mason   4156

Shover, Felicia Lee Cary Thornton
Untold Glory - Cothburn O'Neal   4739

Standish, Francesca
From Fields of Gold - Alexandra Ripley   5339

Steppleton, Charlotte
Old Miss - Thomas Campbell   877

Storm, Valerie
Storm Haven - Frank G. Slaughter   5903

Terraine, Dana
Show Me a Land - Clark McMeekin   4293

Todd, Mavis
West of Appomattox - Harley Duncan   1785

Tradd, Elizabeth
Charleston - Alexandra Ripley   5338

Woodling, Alexandra
Oklahoma! - Dana Fuller Ross   5482

Woods, Georgia Virginia Lawshe
True Women - Janice Woods Windle   6820

SPINSTER

Borden, Lizzie
Miss Lizzie - Walter Satterthwait   5608

Bright, Iphigenia
Mistress - Amanda Quick   5215

Clively, Miranda
Clively Close: Dead as Dead Can Be - Ann
   Crowleigh   1434

Crowbetter, Athene
The Brocken - Pamela Hill   2929

Dorring, Sophy
Seduction - Amanda Quick   5220

Faringdon, Emily
Scandal - Amanda Quick   5219

Herbert, Clarissa
The Shadowed Spring - Carola Salisbury   5571

Howe, Emma
Courting Emma Howe - Margaret A. Robinson   5410

Huntington, Victoria
Surrender - Amanda Quick   5221

Knight, Nan
Rivers Parting - Shirley Barker   315

Morrison, Charlotte
Rhine Journey - Ann Schlee   5639

Pomeroy, Harriet
Ravished - Amanda Quick   5216

Redman, Susannah
Nobody's Angel - Karen Robards   5363

Tonks, Miss
Back in Society - Marion Chesney   1017
Miss Tonks Turns to Crime - Marion Chesney   1041

Tribble, Amy
Animating Maria - Marion Chesney   1015
Enlightening Delilah - Marion Chesney   1028
Finessing Clarissa - Marion Chesney   1029
Marrying Harriet - Marion Chesney   1036
Perfecting Fiona - Marion Chesney   1044
Refining Felicity - Marion Chesney   1048

Tribble, Effy
Animating Maria - Marion Chesney   1015
Enlightening Delilah - Marion Chesney   1028
Finessing Clarissa - Marion Chesney   1029
Marrying Harriet - Marion Chesney   1036
Perfecting Fiona - Marion Chesney   1044
Refining Felicity - Marion Chesney   1048

Wingfield, Olympia
Deception - Amanda Quick   5214

SPIRIT

Clora
Family - J. California Cooper   1297

Eirik
*The Angel of the Opera: Sherlock Holmes Meets the
   Phantom of the Opera* - Sam Siciliano   5842

Herne the Hunter
Windsor Castle - William Harrison Ainsworth   59

Mama Yaya
I, Tituba, Black Witch of Salem - Maryse
   Conde   1233

Tusser, Ursula
Familiar Spirits - Leonard Tourney   6298

Walford, John
Walford's Oak - Jill M. Phillips   4986

SPORTS FIGURE

Abrahams, Harold
Chariots of Fire - W.J. Weatherby   6586

Boruchowicz, Shmuel
Heritage - Lewis Orde   4749

Butler, Jeremy
Catch a Falling Star - Stuart M. Kaminsky   3333
Down for the Count - Stuart M. Kaminsky   3336
The Fala Factor - Stuart M. Kaminsky   3337
Poor Butterfly - Stuart M. Kaminsky   3345

Celer, Lucius
Between Eternities - Robert H. Pilpel   5001

Cobb, Ty
Hoopla - Harry Stein   5990
Murder at Fenway Park - Troy Soos   5948

Cole, Doc
Flanagan's Run - Tom McNab   4303

Dean, Jay Hanna
Mr. Vertigo - Paul Auster   244

Fielder, Andrew Jackson
Fielder's Choice - Rick Norman   4646

Gotch, Frank
Last Go Round - Ken Kesey   3473

Heenan, John Carmel
Bread and Circus - Morris Renek   5303

Huai-i
The Jade Stalk - Jonathan Fast   2048

Jackson, Shoeless Joe
Murder at Wrigley Field - Troy Soos   5949

Jago, Henry
The Detective Wore Silk Drawers - Peter
   Lovesey   3911

Jeffries, Jim
Hoopla - Harry Stein   5990

Johnson, Jack
Hoopla - Harry Stein   5990
Yellowstone Kelly - Peter Bowen   602

Johnson, Walter
Murder at Fenway Park - Troy Soos   5948

Liddell, Eric
Chariots of Fire - W.J. Weatherby   6586

Louis, Joe
Down for the Count - Stuart M. Kaminsky   3336

Lovelock, Jack
Lovelock - James McNeish   4311

Mack, Connie
The Celebrant - Eric Rolfe Greenberg   2572

Marquard, Rube
Murder at Ebbets Field - Troy Soos   5947

Mathewson, Christy
The Celebrant - Eric Rolfe Greenberg   2572
Murder at Ebbets Field - Troy Soos   5947

McGraw, John
The Celebrant - Eric Rolfe Greenberg   2572
Murder at Ebbets Field - Troy Soos   5947

Merkle, Fred
Murder at Wrigley Field - Troy Soos   5949

Miller, Buck
The Fast Men - Tom McNab   4302

Morphy, Paul
The Chess Player: A Novel of New Orleans and Paris
   - Frances Parkinson Keyes   3478

Morrissey, John
Bread and Circus - Morris Renek   5303

Ranjitsinhji, K.S.
Playing the Game - Ian Buruma   810

Rawlings, Mickey
Murder at Ebbets Field - Troy Soos   5947
Murder at Fenway Park - Troy Soos   5948
Murder at Wrigley Field - Troy Soos   5949

Ross, Barney
True Detective - Max Allan Collins   1215

Ruth, George Herman
Joy in Mudville - Gordon McAlpine   4216
The Veracruz Blues - Mark Winegardner   6821

Scott, Darcy
Lord Fancy - Leslie Turner White   6686

Smith, Theolic "Fireball"
The Veracruz Blues - Mark Winegardner   6821

Speed, Billy Joe
The Fast Men - Tom McNab   4302

Stengel, Casey
Murder at Ebbets Field - Troy Soos   5947

Sullivan, John L.
Hoopla - Harry Stein   5990

Wagner, Honus
The Celebrant - Eric Rolfe Greenberg   2572

Warwyck, Daniel
Warwyck's Woman - Rosalind Laker   3604

Weatherby, Clint
The Great Blizzard - Albert E. Idell   3101

Weaver, George "Buck"
Hoopla - Harry Stein   5990

Winslow, Barney
The Final Adversary - Gilbert Morris   4460

Wright, George
If I Never Get Back - Darryl Brock   700

SPOUSE

Adams, Abigail
The Braintree Mission - Nicholas E. Wyckoff   6887
Jefferson: A Novel - Max Byrd   838
Sally Hemings - Barbara Chase-Riboud   1006
Seneca - Donald Clayton Porter   5127
Those Who Love - Irving Stone   6064
Yankee Doodle Dandy - Noel B. Gerson   2387

Adams, Louisa
Echo of Lions - Barbara Chase-Riboud   1004

Ahgavni
Mamigon - Jack Hashian   2772

Allen, Eliza
The Raven's Bride - Elizabeth Crook   1431

Andrewes, Hester
Kenya - John Halkin   2645

Anne
The Barrier - Robin Maugham   4195

Anoud
Blood and Sand - Rosemary Sutcliff   6121

Archer, Ann
A Dangerous Innocence - Victoria Lincoln   3787

Archer, Lucie
The Lady Chapel - Candace M. Robb   5366

Arinna
The Hittite - Noel B. Gerson   2373

Armagh, Bernadette
Captains and the Kings - Taylor Caldwell   851

Armour, Jean
Wonder of All the Gay World - James Barke   306

Armstrong, Merrin
The Dark Pasture - Jessica Stirling   6042

Arnold, Margaret Shippen
The Exquisite Siren - Edwin Haines   2639
Mars' Butterfly - Henry Pleasants   5080

Ashted, Rose Thompson
Threescore and Ten - Walter Allen   105

d'Aubigne, Francoise
The Anthem - Noel B. Gerson   2361

Aubrey, Sophie
The Commodore - Patrick O'Brian   4661
The Mauritius Command - Patrick O'Brian   4670
The Yellow Admiral - Patrick O'Brian   4680

Audubon, Lucy Blackwell
Mr. Audubon's Lucy - Lucy Kennedy   3419

Baker, Melissa
Filaree: A Novel of an American Life - Marguerite Noble   4633

Bale, Morganna
The General's Lady - Esther Forbes   2156

Barnard, Julia
The Flint Anchor - Sylvia Townsend Warner   6569

Barnes, Kate
Jubilee - John Brick   672

Barry, Jannion
The Covenant - Brigid Knight   3521

Bartlett, Adelaide Blanche
Sweet Adelaide - Julian Symons   6152

Bathsheba
The Unanointed - Laurene Chinn   1070

Beauharnais, Hortense de
A Rose for Virtue - Norah Lofts   3858

Beaumaris, Lallage
Midnight Moon - Jeanne Montague   4436

Bell, Jane
Red Morning - Ruby Frazier Frey   2230

Bellnap, Martha
Troubled Spring - John Brick   678

Bennett, Elizabeth
An Unequal Marriage; or Pride and Prejudice Twenty Years Later - Emma Tennant   6202

Bernay, Martha
The Passions of the Mind - Irving Stone   6062

Berrien, Angelica
The Grasshopper King - Elizabeth Boatwright Coker   1165

Berthois, Nicole
The Wine Widow - Tessa Barclay   301

Bibikov, Caroline
Devil Child - Jo Germany   2359

Bittersweet
Bittersweet - Leslie Li   3769

Blair, Susan
The Quality of Mercy - Anne Miller Downes   1712

Blake, Cathy Van Ayl
Texas! - Dana Fuller Ross   5490

Blakeslee, Love Simpson
Cold Sassy Tree - Olive Ann Burns   797

Blennerhasset, Margaret
The Rock Cried Out - Edward Stanley   5981

Bliss, Savanna
Deep River - Henrietta Buckmaster   760

Bolitho, Belinda
Success to the Brave - Alexander Kent   3441

Bonaparte, Maria Letizia
Good-Bye My Son - Marjorie Coryn   1356
In What Torn Ship - Evelyn Eaton   1828

Boone, Rebecca
Never No More: The Story of Rebecca Boone - Shirley Seifert   5730

Boswell, Margaret
Dear Mrs. Boswell - Marie Muir   4508

Boyd, Harriet
Bide Me Fair - Harvey Howells   3060

Bracken, Harriat
Wild Orchid - Isabel Dick   1640

Brady, Julia
The Gallery of His Dreams - Kristine Kathryn Rusch   5525

Brandt, Kirstina
My Pride, My Folly - Suzanne Butler   830

Braun, Eva
Eva - Ib Melchior   4329
Last Man to Die - Michael Dobbs   1652

Bright, Amanda
Departure - Janet Stevenson   6004

Broadwinder, Jenny
The Lady and the Deep Blue Sea - Garland Roark   5356

Broome, Kitty
The Empire Builders - William Stuart Long   3871
The Seafarers - William Stuart Long   3877

Brown, Emma
I Know My Love - Catherine Gaskin   2315

Browning, Caroline
Savannah - Eugenia Price   5186

Brules, Melisande
The Scout - Harry Combs   1224

Burden, Jane
Willowwood - Elizabeth Savage   5619

Burling, Susan
Angle of Repose - Wallace Stegner   5989

Burnett, Carmel
Folded Hills - Stewart Edward White   6701

Bush, Sally
Lincoln's Mothers: A Story of Nancy and Sally Lincoln - Dorothy Clarke Wilson   6804

Butler, Melissa
Look to the Mountain - Le Grand Cannon   885

Buttes, Emily Guthrie
Buttes Landing - Jean Rikhoff   5331

Cardenas, Carlota de
Apache Autumn - Robert Skimin   5875

Carey, Clementina
Up She Rises - David Garnett   2298

Carlyle, Jane
Neighboring Lives - Thomas M. Disch   1648

Carlyon, Anne
Inherit the Sun - Maxwell Grant   2539

Carpenter, Elizabeth
The Laughing Stranger - Vina Delmar   1601

Cassidy, Brooke
No Honeymoon for Death - Mary Kruger   3564

Catherine of Valois
Crown in Candlelight - Rosemary Hawley Jarman   3166

Cenci, Lucrezia
A Tale for Midnight - Frederic Prokosch   5195

Chatfield, Geneva
High Hearts - Rita Mae Brown   728

Chesney, Nalambigi
Shadow of the Moon - Douglas C. Jones   3284

Chester, Elizabeth
Knight's Honor - Roberta Gellis   2351

Chisholm, Miverva
The Chisholms - Evan Hunter   3082

Clark, Ann Rogers
From Sea to Shining Sea - James Alexander Thom   6232

Claudia
The Bride of Pilate - Esther Kellner   3393
Hear Me, Pilate! - LeGette Blythe   557
Man on Fire: A Novel on the Life of St. Paul - LeGette Blythe   558

Claudia Procula
First the Blade - Drayton Mayrant   4212

Clemence, Celia
Restoration: A Novel of Seventeenth-Century England - Rose Tremain   6333

Clemm, Virginia
Black Plume: The Supressed Memoirs of Edgar Allan Poe - David Madsen   4027
The Raven - Chancellor Williams   6769
Very Young Mrs. Poe - Cothburn O'Neal   4740

Cobb, Charis
An Ice-Cream War - William Boyd   616

Cockrell, Sarah
Destiny in Dallas - Shirley Seifert   5725

Coffield, Victoria Manning
A Heart Divided - Al Lacy   3580

Coke, Frances
Call Lady Purbeck - Hilda Lewis   3745

Cole, Sarah
Shaman - Noah Gordon   2483

Colmer, Amelia
Murder in the Oval Office - Elliott Roosevelt   5450

Conway, Clara
That Callahan Spunk! - Francis Ames   124

Cortlandt, Roxanne
Eagles Where I Walk - Stephen Longstreet   3885
A Few Painted Feathers - Stephen Longstreet   3886

Cosway, Antoinette Bertha
Wide Sargasso Sea - Jean Rhys   5312

Cowen, Jim
The Cup of Strength - Charlotte Paul   4840

Cowen, Merrie
The Cup of Strength - Charlotte Paul   4840

Crabtree, Ella
Certain People of Importance - Kathleen Norris   4647

Crispin, Anna
Heir to Kuragin - Constance Heaven   2807

Crittenden, Elizabeth
Action at Aquila - Hervey Allen   97

Crockett, Elizabeth
Crockett of Tennessee: A Novel Based on the Life and Times of David Crockett - Cameron Judd   3314

Cross, John Walter
Johnnie Cross - Terence de Vere White   6704

Crozier, Laura
Dear Laura - Jean Stubbs   6094

Cruz, Catalina
The Death of Artemio Cruz - Carlos Fuentes   2246

Cunningham, Sarah
Sarah Cobb - Catherine M. Rae   5236

Currie, Jessica
The Raid - John Brick   673

Curtis, Sarah
Hiwassee: A Novel of the Civil War - Charles F. Price   5176

Custer, Elizabeth Bacon
The Court-Martial of George Armstrong Custer -
  Douglas C. Jones 3276
*The Last Stand: A Novel about George Armstrong
  Custer and the Indians of the Plains* - Edwin P.
  Hoyt 3061
Libbie - Judy Alter 121
Marching to Valhalla: A Novel of Custer's Last Days -
  Michael Blake 538
Shadow on the Valley - Kirk Mitchell 4414

Dalton, Melody
Joy From Ashes - Al Lacy 3581

Dandridge, Dorothea
Give Me Liberty - Noel B. Gerson 2369

Davis, Varina Howell
Bride of Fortune - Harnett T. Kane 3352
The Lady of Arlington - Harnett T. Kane 3354
While the Music Plays - Diane Austell 242

Dawson, Angel
My Lady Benbrook - Constance Gluyas 2442

de Long, Laurel
The Valley - Clifford Irving 3114

De Salis, Sarah
Cashelmara - Susan Howatch 3058

Delaford, Laura
The Standing Hills - Caroline Stickland 6038

Delancey, Fiona
Dead Reckoning - C. Northcote Parkinson 4809

Delusson, Cecile
The Delusson Family - Jacques Ducharme 1753

Dent, Eve
Montana Hitch - Richard S. Wheeler 6661

Dernent, Claire
A Horseman Riding By - R.F. Delderfield 1588

Dickens, Kate
Charles - Victoria Lincoln 3786

Dickinson, Edna
Time in Its Flight - Susan Fromberg Schaeffer 5636

Dmitreyevna, Anna
Journey into Fire - Patricia Wright 6882

Dobrejcak, Mary
Out of This Furnace - Thomas Bell 425

Dodge, Anna
The Beloved Invader - Eugenia Price 5179

Dodge, Ellen
The Beloved Invader - Eugenia Price 5179

Donahoe, Cathlin
The Seadon Fortune - Leonard St. Clair 5563

Donegan, Samantha
Trumpet on the Land - Terry C. Johnston 3260

Donner, Tamsen
Tamsen - David Galloway 2273

Douglas, Addie Cutts
The Senator's Lady - Shirley Seifert 5733

Douglass, Ruth
These Latter Days - Laura Kalpakian 3330

Dousman, Jane
The House on the Mound - August Derleth 1616

Dow, Delight
Tide-Rode - Adelyn Bushnell 813

Dowland, Elizabeth
Torn Covenants - Lois Swann 6136

Dumont, Madeline
Lord of the Plains - Alfred Silver 5852

Durer, Agnes
Written in the Stars: A Novel about Albrecht Durer -
  Frances Hope Fisher 2103

Eaton, Anne
Until the Winds - Jean Clark 1089

Edwards, Madeleine
A Question of Honour - Clifford Dowdey 1707

Eisenstadt, Jullienne
Winter of the Heart - Linda J. LaRosa 3665

Elswyth
The Edge of Light - Joan Wolf 6839

Enfield, Elizabeth
Crossings - Earl Rovit 5512

d'Este, Beatrice
The Lady in the Mask - Anne Green 2564

Eugenie
Banners of Silk - Rosalind Laker 3592

Eurgain
The Eagle and the Raven - Pauline Gedge 2344

Evans, Maria
Maria - Eugenia Price 5184

Evans, Mary Ann
The Prime Minister's Wife - Doris Leslie 3727

Everden, Mary
Corner the Moon - Shirley Barker 310

Evesham, Roger
A Dangerous Innocence - Victoria Lincoln 3787

Fairchild, Rosalie
Watchfires - Louis Auchincloss 234

Fairfax, Anne
Rider on a White Horse - Rosemary Sutcliff 6124

Falkenhorst, Tessa von
Falkenhorst - Mark Rascovich 5254

Fayerdon, Beatrice
The Darkness of Corn - Caroline Stickland 6037

Fedorcenko, Anna
The Dawning of Deliverance - Judith Pella 4892
Heirs of the Motherland - Judith Pella 4893

Fenton, Clarissa
Lord of Ravensley - Constance Heaven 2809

Fenwick, Lizzie
The Old Enchantment - Sarah Neilan 4565

Ferguson, Cordelia
Cordelia - Winston Graham 2523

Fialka, Lisa
Beginning the World Again - Roberta Silman 5851

Flaherty, Alice
Across the Bitter Sea - Eilis Dillon 1646

Flecker, Helle
Dreaming of Samarkand - Martin Booth 576

Fleming, Mary
Born with the Century - William Kinsolving 3501

Forest, Camilla
Marry in Haste - Jane Aiken Hodge 2967

Forge, Fonella
The Running Iron - Rachel Ann Fish 2097

Forrest, Catherine
The Bluestocking - David Delman 1598

Fournois, Sabrina
The Vixens - Frank Yerby 6929

Fowler, Janice
Voyage to Santa Fe - Janice Holt Giles 2418

Fowler, Rebecca
The Believers - Janice Holt Giles 2409

Frane, Evelyn
Gamble's Hundred - Clifford Dowdey 1705

Fraser, Anne Couper
Where Shadows Go - Eugenia Price 5189

Fraser, Claire
Drums of Autumn - Diana Gabaldon 2263

Fraser, Jamie
Drums of Autumn - Diana Gabaldon 2263

Frasquita
The Three-Cornered Hat - Pedro Antonio de
  Alarcon 62

Fremont, Jessie Benton
Dream West - David Nevin 4587
Immortal Wife - Irving Stone 6057
*Jessie: A Novel Based on the Life of Jessie Benton
  Fremont* - Judy Alter 120

Gallagher, Abigail
Vision of the Eagle - Kay L. McDonald 4263

Galvan, Susana
A City for St. Francis - Evelyn Wells 6621

Gautier, Susannah
The Chateau - Stephen Coulter 1383

Genovese, Susan
Bay of Arrows - Jay Parini 4800

Gentry, Kitty
Kentucky Home - Betty Layman Receveur 5283

Geoffrey of Anjou
When Christ and His Saints Slept - Sharon Kay
  Penman 4908

Gibson, Amelia
Murder in the East Room - Elliott Roosevelt 5448

Gifford, Sarah
Liberty Tavern - Thomas Fleming 2129

Glendower, Lindsey
Beckoning Ridge - Emerson Waldman 6527

Glenroy, Jennie
Jennie Glenroy - Elisabeth Ogilvie 4695

Gordon, Eleanor Kinzie
Look to the Rose - Shirley Seifert 5728

Gould, Deborah
New Moon Rising - Eugenia Price 5185

Gould, Jane Harris
Lighthouse - Eugenia Price 5182

Grant, Julia Dent
Captain Grant - Shirley Seifert 5724
Ulysses: A Biographical Novel - Robert Skimin 5878

Gray, Effie
John Ruskin's Wife - Eva McDonald 4259

Greene, Catherine
Let My Name Stand Fair - Shirley Seifert 5727

Gromeko, Antonina "Tonia"
Doctor Zhivago - Boris Pasternak 4824

Grunewald, Juditha
Echo of the Flute - Mildred A. Jordan 3304

Gruoch
Lady of Moray - Bonnie Copeland 1318

Guishar, Larisa "Lara"
Doctor Zhivago - Boris Pasternak 4824

Hafise
The Bride of Suleiman - Aileen Crawley 1421
The Shadow of God - Aileen Crawley 1422

Halder, Julie
Still Is the Summer Night - August Derleth 1619

Hale, Lisette
Mighty Mountain - Archie Binns 502

Hamilton, Lady Emma
The Blacksmith's Daughter - Joanna Dessau 1625
Emma - F.W. Kenyon 3448
H.M.S. Cockerel - Dewey Lambdin 3611
Lord Elgin's Lady - Theodore Vrettos 6514
Shadow of a Lady - Jane Aiken Hodge 2971
The Volcano Lover - Susan Sontag 5946

Hammond, Annabella
The Far Side of Home - Maggie Davis   1536

Hampton, Tina
The Hampton Heritage - Julie Ellis   1920

Hanks, Nancy
Lincoln's Mothers: A Story of Nancy and Sally Lincoln - Dorothy Clarke Wilson   6804
The Matrix - Maria Thompson Daviess   1509

Hardacre, Mary
Hardacre - C.L. Skelton   5872

Harinxma, Sylvia
The Centurion - Jan de Hartog   2762

Harper, Elizabeth
Ghost Woman - Lawrence Thornton   6275

Harrigan, John
Julia's Last Hope - Janette Oke   4708

Harrigan, Julia
Julia's Last Hope - Janette Oke   4708

Harte, Julia
The Ways of Women - Elaine Crowley   1436

Haseman, Karen
White Man - Peter Freuchen   2228

Hathaway, Anne
The Best House in Stratford - Edward Fisher   2100
The Cleopatra Boy - Eric Malpass   4048
A House of Women - Eric Malpass   4049
Mrs. Shakespeare: The Complete Works - Robert Nye   4656
Nothing Like the Sun - Anthony Burgess   781
Shakespeare & Son - Edward Fisher   2102
Sweet Will - Eric Malpass   4050
Two Loves Have I - Clara Longworth de Chambrun   985
Will Shakespeare: The Untold Story - John Mortimer   4495

Hawke, Roberta
The Medicine Horn - Jory Sherman   5820

Haynow, Anna
The Drums of Winter - Sandra Paretti   4790

Helena
Julian - Gore Vidal   6489

Henderson, Mattie
Freedom's Banner - Teresa Crane   1415

Henderson, Simon
Private Knowledge - Betty Palmer Nelson   4576

Hepburn, James
Immortal Queen - Elizabeth Byrd   834
The Lion and the Rose - Jane Oliver   4724
Maid of Honour: A Novel Set in the Court of Mary, Queen of Scots - Elizabeth Byrd   836

Herodias
The Good Tidings - William Sidney   5843

Hildreth, Anne
The Lotus and the Wind - John Masters   4175

Hill, Caroline
The Caretaker Wife - Barbara Whitehead   6706

Hilton, Andhra
Star of Randevi - Marjorie McEvoy   4270

Holt, Caroline Brandon
Washington! - Dana Fuller Ross   5491

Holt, Clarissa
Tennessee! - Dana Fuller Ross   5489

Holt, Elizabeth
Pacific Destiny - Dana Fuller Ross   5487

Hoosen, Annetje
Forever Possess - Alexandra Phillips   4982

Hornblower, Barbara
Admiral Hornblower in the West Indies - C.S. Forester   2169
Commodore Hornblower - C.S. Forester   2172
Lord Hornblower - C.S. Forester   2179

Hornblower, Maria
Hornblower and the Atropos - C.S. Forester   2175
Hornblower and the Hotspur - C.S. Forester   2176
Ship of the Line - C.S. Forester   2182

Hoshi, Itoko
Chikara! - Robert Skimin   5876

Howard, Hannah Maria
The Plums Hang High - Gertrude E. Finney   2091

Huntington, Beth
Manitou - Donald Clayton Porter   5120
Spirit Knife - Donald Clayton Porter   5128

Hutchins, Eliza
The Land Where the Sun Dies - Henry Carlisle   896

Ifort, Gerda von
Foundation Stone - Lella Warren   6571

Indian John
I, Tituba, Black Witch of Salem - Maryse Conde   1233

Isabella of Angouleme
The Barons of Runnymede - Pamela Bennetts   445

Jackson, Anna Morrison
The Gallant Mrs. Stonewall - Harnett T. Kane   3353

Jackson, Rachel
1812 - David Nevin   4586
The Cavalier of Tennessee - Meredith Nicholson   4610
The Gorgeous Hussy - Samuel Hopkins Adams   30
Her Christmas at the Hermitage: A Tale about Rachel and Andrew Jackson - Helen Topping Miller   4389
Home to the Hermitage - Alfred Leland Crabb   1401
Jackson: A Novel - Max Byrd   837
Magnificent Destiny - Paul I. Wellman   6619
Old Hickory - Noel B. Gerson   2379
The President's Lady - Irving Stone   6063
Young Hickory - Stanley Young   6942

Jacova
The Gila River - Gary McCarthy   4223

Jansen, Anna
Wild Conquest - Peter Abrahams   12

Jaramillo, Josefa
Soldier in Buckskin - Ray Hogan   2981

Jardine, Margaret
Ain't Goin' to Glory - David Delman   1597

Jastrow, Natalie
War and Remembrance - Herman Wouk   6875

Jefferson, Martha
My Thomas: A Novel of Martha Jefferson's Life - Roberta Grimes   2593
Sally Hemings - Barbara Chase-Riboud   1006

Jenson, Esther
And the Desert Shall Bloom - Phyllis Barber   299

Johnson, Emily
War Drums - Donald Clayton Porter   5133

Josephine
Alone Among Men - Marjorie Coryn   1355
Far Flies the Eagle - Evelyn Anthony   162
Forty Centuries Look Down - Frederick Britten Austin   245
The Marriage of Josephine - Marjorie Coryn   1358
Mistress of Fortune - Sheila Lancaster   3651

Jumel, Eliza
The Conqueror: Being the True and Romantic Story of Alexander Hamilton - Gertrude Atherton   222
Painted Lady: Eliza Jumel, Her Life and Times - Leonard Falkner   2009

Kaminsky, Sarah
Trumpets of Silver - Norma Harris   2735

Kendrick, Deborah
Beulah Land - Lonnie Coleman   1202

Kennedy, Jacqueline
Flying into Love - D.M. Thomas   6236

Kent, Ann
The Rebels - John Jakes   3152

Keturah
The Sea Peoples - Peter Danielson   1474

King, Winona
Apache Blood - David Thompson   6250
Blood Truce - David Thompson   6253
Hawken Fury - David Thompson   6254
Tenderfoot - David Thompson   6259
Tomahawk Revenge - David Thompson   6260
Trapper's Blood - David Thompson   6261
Winterkill - David Thompson   6262

Lacey, Sal
O Beulah Land - Mary Lee Settle   5756

Landis, Leah
Piccadilly - Claire Rayner   5267

Lane, Polly
The Quiet Life of Mrs. General Lane - Victoria Case   951

Langlinais, Mathilde
Cajun - Elizabeth Nell Dubus   1751

Latham, Reva
Fort Worth - Leonard Sanders   5588

Lawson, Lucy
Season for War - P.F. Kluge   3510

Le Vendeur, Catherine
Strong as Death - Sharan Newman   4602

LeClerc, Pauline
Black Triumvirate: A Novel of Haiti - Benjamin H. Levin   3736

Lee, Mary Custis
Christmas with Robert E. Lee - Helen Topping Miller   4387
The Lady of Arlington - Harnett T. Kane   3354

Lester, Leonie
The Second Sister - Leslie O'Grady   4701

Levy, Sarah
Esau - Meir Shalev   5770

Lightbody, Eleanor
The Road to Wellville - T. Coraghessan Boyle   618

Lincoln, Mary Todd
Christmas for Tad: A Story of Mary and Abraham Lincoln - Helen Topping Miller   4386
The Dixie Widow - Gilbert Morris   4459
Forever Free - Honore Morrow   4487
Henry and Clara - Thomas Mallon   4042
Hoffman's Row - Walter Carnahan   902
Lincoln: A Novel - Gore Vidal   6490
Love Is Eternal - Irving Stone   6058
Mr. Lincoln's Wife - Anne Colver   1221
The Trial of Mary Todd Lincoln - James A. Rhodes   5309

Ling-ling
Red Barbarian - Margaret Gaan   2260

Linthorne, Sara
The Earth Abideth - George Dell   1595

Little Hoop
The Legend of Ben Tree - Paul Hawkins   2784

Livia
Augustus - Allan Massie   4167

Livingstone, Charlotte
Wives of the Wind - Marjorie Jarrett   3170

Livingstone, Kolfinna
Wives of the Wind - Marjorie Jarrett   3170

Livingstone, Mellie
Wives of the Wind - Marjorie Jarrett   3170

Livingstone, Sybil
Wives of the Wind - Marjorie Jarrett   3170

Lloyd, Constance
I Give You Oscar Wilde - Desmond Hall   2647

Logan, Carrie
Star of Empire: A Novel of Old San Antonio - Leonard Sanders   5590

Lorme, Christine
War Comes to Castle Rising - Fanny Cradock   1411

Lovell, Grace
A Horseman Riding By - R.F. Delderfield   1588

Luceiia
The Singing Sword - Jack Whyte   6725

Luther, Katie
Queen of the Reformation - Charles Ludwig   3922

MacClaren, Reanna
Women in the Wind - Margaret Ritter   5350

MacDonald, Mary Rose
The Blind Bend - Lorn MacIntyre   3985

Mackenzie, Mary
The Ginger Tree - Oswald Wynd   6890

Maclean, Elaine
The Powder River - Winfred Blevins   546

MacLeod, Lucy
Bridle the Wind - Julia Davis   1525
Cloud on the Land - Julia Davis   1526

MacWain, Fiona
The Silver Dolphin - Velda Johnston   3264

Madison, Dolley
1812 - David Nevin   4586
Back Bay - William Martin   4138
Burr - Gore Vidal   6485
A Daughter of Liberty - Allan Cole   1196
Dolley - Rita Mae Brown   727
My Dear Cousin - Peggy Hoffmann   2977
My Theodosia - Anya Seton   5753
Queen Dolley: The Life and Times of Dolley Madison - Dorothy Clarke Wilson   6806

Mago
Hannibal of Carthage - Mary Dolan   1686

Magoffin, Susan Shelby
The Turquoise Trail - Shirley Seifert   5736

Maimiti
Pitcairn's Island - Charles Nordhoff   4640

Maitland, Hope
Strife Before Dawn - Mary Schumann   5675

Mandelkern, Malkeh
Malkeh and Her Children - Marjorie Edelson   1853

Manette, Lucie
A Tale of Two Cities - Charles Dickens   1642

Mango, Rain
Fragments of the Ark - Louise Meriwether   4341

Manners, Catherine
Wife to Great Buckingham - Hilda Lewis   3751

Manning, Elizabeth
The Fires of July - Sharon Salvato   5576

Manning, Gwynne
The Drums of December - Sharon Salvato   5575

Maplethorpe, Ada
The Scottish Marriage - Karen Lynn   3942

Mara
Sword of Glory - Peter Danielson   1477

March, Catherine
The Imagination of the Heart - Judith Glover   2437

Marian
Robin and the King - Parke Godwin   2448

Markham, Elizabeth
The Rage of the Vulture - Barry Unsworth   6388

Markland, Sue
After the Glory - Helen Topping Miller   4383

Marsdon, Celia
Green Darkness - Anya Seton   5751

Marsdon, Stephen
Green Darkness - Anya Seton   5751

Martin, Beth
Dakota! - Dana Fuller Ross   5472

Martin, Lana
Drums Along the Mohawk - Walter D. Edmonds   1874

Marwood, Elizabeth
To Serve Them All My Days - R.F. Delderfield   1591

Mary
Before My Time - Niccolo Tucci   6358

Masa, Lady
Kagami - Elizabeth Kata   3369

Mason, Java Gordon
The Imperialists - William Stuart Long   3875

Matilda
The Lady for Ransom - Alfred Duggan   1768

Matilda of Flanders
The Conqueror's Wife - Noel B. Gerson   2363
The Disputed Crown - Valerie Anand   128

McAlpine, Jesse
Star of the Wilderness - Karle Wilson Baker   274

McDougal, Suzanne
Columbia - Pamela Jekel   3184

McGann, Marguerite
Iron Ships, Iron Men - Christopher Nicole   4616

McMahon, Mary
They Were Dreamers - James F. Murphy Jr.   4525

McQueen, Anne
Don Juan McQueen - Eugenia Price   5181

Mead, Caroline
The Green Land - Zola Helen Ross   5504

Mendelssohn, Cecille
Beyond Desire: A Novel Based on the Life of Felix and Cecille Mendelssohn - Pierre La Mure   3574

Mendes, Magdalena
The Conquest of Don Pedro - Harvey Fergusson   2066

Mendoza, Racquel
The Dutchman's Dilemma - Maan Meyers   4352

Mercybright, Linn
Seedtime and Harvest - Mary E. Pearce   4864

Mereet
The Golden Pharaoh - Peter Danielson   1468

Merewether, Caroline
For King and Company - Ellis K. Meacham   4314

Micay
The Incas - Daniel Peters   4945

Milbanke, Isabella
The Absorbing Fire: The Byron Legend - F.W. Kenyon   3445

Millbanke, Annabella
Lord of the Ladies - Joanna Dessau   1626

Millhouser, Hedwig
Ourselves to Know - John O'Hara   4704

Moncey, Caroline
Guillotine - Mark Logan   3865

Moorhouse, Bel
Aunt Bel - Guy McCrone   4231
Red Plush: The Story of the Moorhouse Family - Guy McCrone   4232

Morane, Matilda
The Traitors of Bosworth - Robert Farrington   2021
Tudor Agent - Robert Farrington   2022

Morelli, Roberta
I, Roberta - Elizabeth Gray Vining   6501

Mores, Medora de
Manifest Destiny - Brian Garfield   2290

Morgan, Jessie
Cry of the Rain Bird - Patricia Shaw   5779

Morning Sky
High Country - Jason Manning   4075

Mowbray, Ellen
A Father and His Fate - Ivy Compton-Burnett   1228

Mumtaz Mahal
The Dark Dancer - Frederic Prokosch   5193

Murray, Martha
The Day Must Dawn - Agnes Sligh Turnbull   6362

Newberry, Catherine
Blood of the Boar - Margaret Abbey   2

Nilsson, Kristina
The Emigrants - Vilhelm Moberg   4422
Last Letter Home - Vilhelm Moberg   4423
The Settlers - Vilhelm Moberg   4424
Unto a Good Land - Vilhelm Moberg   4425

Noyes, Julia
The Sea Stands Watch - Helen Parker Mudgett   4507

Octavia
Octavia: A Tale of Ancient Rome - Seymour Van Santvoord   6428

Ogilvie, Angela
The Restless Frontier - Duncan MacNeil   4018

Ogilvie, Kitty
The Case of Kitty Ogilvie - Jean Stubbs   6093

Oleson, Anne Pernille
Lindeman's Daughters - Synnove Christensen   1073

O'Rourke, Olivia
The Veil of Illusion - Rebecca Ryman   5545

Otis, Deborah
The Assassination of Mozart - David Weiss   6604

O'Toole, Frances Melissa
Toward the Morning - Hervey Allen   101

Page, Lucy
Steamboat Gothic - Frances Parkinson Keyes   3481

Patterson, Anna
Creature Comforts - Jessica Stirling   6041

Patterson, Elizabeth
The Amazing Mrs. Bonaparte - Harnett T. Kane   3351
Tide of Empire - Bates Baldwin   279

Patterson, Elspeth
Creature Comforts - Jessica Stirling   6041
Hearts of Gold - Jessica Stirling   6044

Peck, Evaline
The Crowded Hill - Le Roy MacLeod   4008
Years of Peace - Le Roy MacLeod   4009

Peck, Tyler
The Crowded Hill - Le Roy MacLeod   4008
Years of Peace - Le Roy MacLeod   4009

Penelope
Return to Ithaca - Eyvind Johnson   3224

Phaedra
The Bull From the Sea - Mary Renault   5295

Pinkney, Charlotte
A Visit to Highbury - Joan Austen-Leigh 243

Pitt, Charlotte
Ashworth Hall - Anne Perry 4918
Belgrave Square - Anne Perry 4919
Bethlehem Road - Anne Perry 4920
Bluegate Fields - Anne Perry 4921
Callander Square - Anne Perry 4923
Cardington Crescent - Anne Perry 4924
Death in the Devil's Acre - Anne Perry 4927
Farriers' Lane - Anne Perry 4930
Highgate Rise - Anne Perry 4931
Paragon Walk - Anne Perry 4932
Pentecost Alley - Anne Perry 4933
Resurrection Row - Anne Perry 4934
Rutland Place - Anne Perry 4935
Silence in Hanover Close - Anne Perry 4936
Traitors Gate - Anne Perry 4939

Poldark, Demelza
The Angry Tide - Winston Graham 2521
The Black Moon - Winston Graham 2522
Demelza - Winston Graham 2524
The Four Swans - Winston Graham 2525
The Last Gamble - Winston Graham 2527
The Miller's Dance - Winston Graham 2528
The Stranger From the Sea - Winston Graham 2530
The Twisted Sword - Winston Graham 2531
Venture Once More - Winston Graham 2532

Poldark, Elizabeth
Demelza - Winston Graham 2524
The Last Gamble - Winston Graham 2527
The Renegade: A Novel of Cornwall, 1783-1787 -
   Winston Graham 2529
Venture Once More - Winston Graham 2532

Pollard, Mary
The Jonah Man - Henry Carlisle 895

Polventon, Julie
Heir to Polventon - Marjorie Watson 6583

Pompeia
The Sacrilege - John Maddox Roberts 5380

Porter, Ellen Watson
Ceremony of the Innocent - Taylor Caldwell 852

Preele, Catherine
Morgan's Woman - Iris Gower 2500

Prescott, Harriet
The Rector of Justin - Louis Auchincloss 233

Procula
Pontius Pilate: A Biographical Novel - Paul L.
   Maier 4034

Prynne, Hester
Arthur Dimmesdale - Charles R. Larson 3671
Hester - Christopher Bigsby 496
Pearl - Christopher Bigsby 497
The Scarlet Letter - Nathaniel Hawthorne 2786

Purchis, Josephine
Savannah Purchase - Jane Aiken Hodge 2970

Purchis, Mercy
Wide Is the Water - Jane Aiken Hodge 2973

Pushkin, Natalya
The Fourth King - Glen Petrie 4979

Racon, Madeleine de
The Bastard - Brigitte Von Tessin 6208

Randolph, Judith
The Bizarre Sisters - Jay Walz 6559

Randolph, Nancy
A Generation of Leaves - Robert S. Bloom 552

Rathbone, Clara Harris
Henry and Clara - Thomas Mallon 4042

Raven, Lucy
All Desires Known - Malcolm Macdonald 3963

Redmond, Isabelle
Eye of the Hawk - David William Ross 5498

Reed, Kate
The Town House - Norah Lofts 3861

Rendell, Maria
The Lion and the Leopard - Mary Ellen
   Johnson 3226

Richardson, Esther
The Measure of the Years - Alice Mary Colver 1218

Rising, Florence
April Rising - Susan Sallis 5574

Roberts, Patience
Fruit in His Season - Helen C. Barney 333

Robsart, Amy
Gay Lord Robert - Jean Plaidy 5015
The Queen and the Gypsy - Constance Heaven 2810

Rochdale, Eustacia
Dragonmede - Rona Randall 5246

Rochechouart de Mortemart, Francoise Athenais
The Marquis - Joan Sanders 5586

Roet, Philippa de
Katherine - Anya Seton 5752

Rogers, Augustina
Bridge to Brooklyn - Albert E. Idell 3099
Centennial Summer - Albert E. Idell 3100
The Great Blizzard - Albert E. Idell 3101

Roosevelt, Alice Lee
*Alice and Edith: A Biographical Novel of the Two
   Wives of Theodore Roosevelt* - Dorothy Clarke
   Wilson 6798

Roosevelt, Edith
*Alice and Edith: A Biographical Novel of the Two
   Wives of Theodore Roosevelt* - Dorothy Clarke
   Wilson 6798
Speak Softly - Lawrence Alexander 83
TR - Noel B. Gerson 2385

Roosevelt, Eleanor
Eleanor: A Novel - Rhoda Lerman 3724
The Fala Factor - Stuart M. Kaminsky 3337
A First Class Murder - Elliott Roosevelt 5442
Hollywood: A Novel of America in the 1920s - Gore
   Vidal 6488
The Hyde Park Murder - Elliott Roosevelt 5443
Murder and the First Lady - Elliott Roosevelt 5444
Murder at the Palace - Elliott Roosevelt 5445
Murder in the Blue Room - Elliott Roosevelt 5446
Murder in the East Room - Elliott Roosevelt 5448
Murder in the Executive Mansion - Elliott
   Roosevelt 5449
Murder in the Oval Office - Elliott Roosevelt 5450
Murder in the Red Room - Elliott Roosevelt 5451
Murder in the Rose Garden - Elliott Roosevelt 5452
Murder in the West Wing - Elliott Roosevelt 5453
A Royal Murder - Elliott Roosevelt 5456
The White House Pantry Murder - Elliott
   Roosevelt 5457

Ross, Loretta
The Seventh Winter - Hal Borland 583

Rouault, Louise
Kingkill - Thomas Gavin 2325

Royland, Paul
Kingdom of Shadows - Barbara Erskine 1954

Rutledge, Ann
Queen's Gift - Inglis Fletcher 2136

Ryall, Peggy
The Richlands - Agnes Sligh Turnbull 6364

Ryegate, Harriet
If a Lion Could Talk - Mildred Walker 6532

Salter, Carolina
The Ocean Mistress - Peter French 2225

Salter, Sarah
The Cup, the Blade or the Gun - Mignon G.
   Eberhart 1833

Sandor, Rica
Preacher on Horseback - Cecile Hulse
   Matschat 4186

Sarah
Hagar - Cothburn O'Neal 4737

Sarton, Olivia
Sarton Kell - Kate Mallory 4043

Saxton, Glen Ellen
Tyrone of Kentucky - Clark McMeekin 4294

Scacerini, Dosolina
The Mill on the Po - Riccardo Bacchelli 254

Schliemann, Sophia
The Greek Treasure - Irving Stone 6056

Schumann, Clara Wieck
Spring Symphony - Eleanor Painter 4777

Schuyler, Elizabeth
Alexander Hamilton's Wife - Alice Curtis
   Desmond 1623

Selkirk, Jeannie
The Great Valley - Mary Johnston 3234

Sessions, Elena
The Lady - Conrad Richter 5321

Sevendor, Jemima
Cain's Daughters - Doris Shannon 5776

Shea, Kitty
A River Town - Thomas Keneally 3415

Shelmadine, Linda
Afternoon of a Autocrat - Norah Lofts 3834

Sheridan, Allegra
Oklahoma Run - Alberta Constant 1260

Sheridan, Emmy
Massacre at Cawnpore - Vivian Stuart 6089

Shining Moon
Expedition! - Dana Fuller Ross 5473
Outpost! - Dana Fuller Ross 5486
Westward! - Dana Fuller Ross 5492

Shipman, Laura
Listen for the Voices - Anne Colver 1220

Sinclair, Clarissa
Montana! - Dana Fuller Ross 5479

Singing Brook
Mohawk Woman - Barbara Riefe 5329

Skiles, Ella
Peace at Bowling Green - Alfred Leland Crabb 1405

Sky Toucher
Mohawk Woman - Barbara Riefe 5329

Smith, Ann
The Smiths - Janet Fairbank 2002

Sorensen, Margretta
Winds of Spring - Walter Havighurst 2776

Stafford, Gwynne
Mists of Heaven - Yvonne Kalman 3325

Stahl, Hanna
The Rainbird - Sara Lidman 3780

Stanhope, Abigail
The Bondswoman - Caryl Ledner 3705

Stanton, Sarah
Drums of War - Roy Clews 1114

Stapleton, Cynthia Legrand
The Spoils of War - Thomas Fleming 2131

Stenhouse, Helen
Whitton's Folly - Pamela Hill 2948

Stevenson, Emma
Kimberley - Colin Burke   784

Stewart, Henry
The Gay Galliard - Margaret Irwin   3119
Immortal Queen - Elizabeth Byrd   834
The Lion and the Rose - Jane Oliver   4724
Queen's Caprice - Marjorie Bowen   599

Stock, Joan
The Bartholomew Fair Murders - Leonard
   Tourney   6297
Familiar Spirits - Leonard Tourney   6298
Frobisher's Savage - Leonard Tourney   6299
Knaves Templar - Leonard Tourney   6300
Low Treason - Leonard Tourney   6301
Old Saxon Blood - Leonard Tourney   6302
The Players' Boy Is Dead - Leonard Tourney   6303
Witness of Bones - Leonard Tourney   6304

Swann, Henrietta
Theirs Was the Kingdom - R.F. Delderfield   1590

Tabor, Elizabeth "Baby Doe"
All for Love: Baby Doe and Silver Dollar - John
   Vernon   6456

Tairo Tamako
The Sword of Hachiman - Lynn Guest   2608

Tallboys, Sybilla
The Homecoming - Norah Lofts   3844
Knight's Acre - Norah Lofts   3848

Tarakandu, Larissa
The Great Alone - Janet Dailey   1454

Tedelli, Bianca
Bianca - Mabel Conquist   1257

Thais
The Golden Lyre - Noel B. Gerson   2371

Theodora
The Bearkeeper's Daughter - Gillian Bradshaw   628

Throckmorton, Bess
Lady in Waiting - Rosemary Sutcliff   6123
Ralegh's Fair Bess: The Story of Bess Throckmorton -
   Judy Turner   6365

Tirwell, Robert
Old Miss - Thomas Campbell   877

Tolonqua
Voice of the Eagle - Linda Lay Shuler   5839

Tolstoy, Sofya Andreyevna
The Last Station - Jay Parini   4801

Tonneman, Marianna
The High Constable - Maan Meyers   4353

Tower, Emma
The Lost Wagon - James Arthur Kjelgaard   3509

Treadup, Emily
The Call - John Hersey   2869

Treloar, Edith
Look Away! - George Nauman Shuster   5841

Trenchard, Constance
Painting the Darkness - Robert Goddard   2445

Tyler, Lora
The Quicksilver Pool - Phyllis A. Whitney   6716

Valence, Lily
Fallen Skies - Philippa Gregory   2581

Van Ayl, Cathy
Colorado! - Dana Fuller Ross   5471
Oregon! - Dana Fuller Ross   5484

Vanneau, Marie
The Heatherton Heritage - Pamela Hill   2934

Vayle, Charlotte
Lisbon - Valerie Sherwood   5825

Vernet, Victoire
Napoleon Must Die - Quinn Fawcett   2054

Von Bock, Eeva
The Czar's Madman - Jaan Kross   3560

Wade, Hannah
The Pride of Hannah Wade - Janet Dailey   1455

Wagner, Cosima
Hungarian Rhapsody: The Life of Franz Liszt - Jean
   Rousselot   5511
Magic Fire: Scenes around Richard Wagner - Bertita
   Harding   2683

Wainwright, Ellen
Cast a Long Shadow - Mary E. Pearce   4861

Walden, Aurora
Richard Walden's Wife - Eleanor Kelly   3399

Walton, Lucie
The Nun's Tale - Candace M. Robb   5367

Ware, Delia
The Sun Shines West - Nathan Schachner   5632

Warleggan, Elizabeth
The Angry Tide - Winston Graham   2521
The Black Moon - Winston Graham   2522
The Four Swans - Winston Graham   2525

Washington, Martha
Christmas at Mount Vernon - Helen Topping
   Miller   4385
Janice Meredith - Paul Leicester Ford   2166
Lady Washington - Dorothy Clarke Wilson   6803
Man From Mt. Vernon - Burke Boyce   607
Seneca - Donald Clayton Porter   5127
Valley Forge - MacKinlay Kantor   3364

Watson, Anne
Watson's Apology - Beryl Bainbridge   271

Wayman, Gwen
The Land Endures - Mary E. Pearce   4862

Weddle, Clorinda
The Corinthians - Nicholas E. Wyckoff   6888

Weissenberg, Catherine
The Firekeeper - Robert Moss   4498

Wells, Constance
The Head Waters - Archie Binns   500

Wentworth, Frances
The Governor's Lady - Thomas H. Raddall   5228

Westbrook, Harriet
*The Golden Years: A Novel Based on the Life and
   Loves of Percy Bysshe Shelley* - F.W.
   Kenyon   3451
Love's Children - Judith Chernaik   1013

Whipple, Jessie
The Pepper Tree - John Edward Jennings   3203

Whitaker, Rene Jo
While Rivers Flow - Glen H. Fleischmann   2125

Whiteoak, Adeline
Morning at Jalna - Mazo de la Roche   1560

Whitman, Narcissa
Doctor in Buckskin - T.D. Allen   103
To Heaven on Horseback - Paul F. Cranston   1419
We Must March: A Novel of the Winning of Oregon -
   Honore Morrow   4491

Whitmead, Lucy-Anne
The Cherished Wives - Valerie Anand   126

Whitworth, Morwenna
The Angry Tide - Winston Graham   2521
The Four Swans - Winston Graham   2525

Wickersham, Victoria
Eden - Julie Ellis   1918

Wilcox, Bella
The Wedding Journey - Walter D. Edmonds   1878

Wilder, Leela
Black Gold - Anita Richmond Bunkley   771

Wilson, Edith
Hollywood: A Novel of America in the 1920s - Gore
   Vidal   6488

Winslow, Mary
Blue Camellia - Frances Parkinson Keyes   3477

Winslow, Rachel
The Captive Bride - Gilbert Morris   4457

Winslow, Rebekah
The Last Confederate - Gilbert Morris   4466

Winster, Remember
Peace, My Daughters - Shirley Barker   314

Woburn, Nora
The Artist's Daughter - Leslie O'Grady   4698

Woods, Grace
The Land Was Ours: A Novel of the Great Plains -
   Charles W. Bailey   266

Woolf, Leonard
*The Shadow of the Moth: A Novel of Espionage with
   Virginia Woolf* - Ellen Hawkes   2779

Worth, Patience
To Have and to Hold - Mary Johnston   3241

Xanthippe
The Private and Public Life of Socrates - Rene
   Kraus   3552

Yasodhara
Lady of the Lotus - William E. Barrett   353

Yorke, Aurelia
Galleon - Dudley Pope   5095

Young, Lauren
Heaven's Gold - Giles Tippette   6282

Zenger, Anna
Anna Zenger: Mother of Freedom - Kent
   Cooper   1316

SPY

Adams, Laura
Defiant Hearts - Janelle Taylor   6185

Allison, Anthony
Toil of the Brave - Inglis Fletcher   2141

Anacrites
Last Act in Palmyra - Lindsey Davis   1529

Andre, John
Eagles Where I Walk - Stephen Longstreet   3885
The Exquisite Siren - Edwin Haines   2639
Hugh Wynne, Free Quaker - Silas Weir
   Mitchell   4416
Mars' Butterfly - Henry Pleasants   5080
The Secret Road - Bruce Lancaster   3646
Storm the Last Rampart - David Taylor   6180
The Sunshine Patriot: A Novel of Benedict Arnold -
   Norman Partington   4822
Trumpets at Dawn - Cyril Harris   2719
*The Twisted Saber: A Biographical Novel of Benedict
   Arnold* - Philip Vail   6398

Andrews, James
Rebel Run - Louis Zara   6952

ap-Maddox, Ivor
The King Breaker - Elizabeth Linington   3797

Archer, Frank
Company Q - Richard O'Connor   4684

Arnold, Margaret Shippen
Mars' Butterfly - Henry Pleasants   5080

Asher, Faith Mary
Faith and Honor - Robin Maderich   4025

Aubrey, John
Fire over England - A.E.W. Mason   4143

Avery, Charity
Monmouth - Charles Bracelen Flood   2144

Bauer, Harry
Seven Days to Petrograd - Tom Hyman   3094

Becket, Eleanora
Lady Gallant - Suzanne Robinson   5413

Belknap, Thomas
The Fate of Princes - P.C. Doherty   1673

Bent, Tristram
Tristram Bent - Henry Barnard Safford   5560

Bertomy, Haidee
The Wilderness - Carter A. Vaughan   6442

Birch, Harvey
The Spy: A Tale of the Neutral Ground - James
   Fenimore Cooper   1310

Blake, Giletta
Three Fields to Cross - Francis Tysen Nutt   4651

Blake, Henry
Arizona! - Dana Fuller Ross   5466
Homecoming - Dana Fuller Ross   5474
Illinois! - Dana Fuller Ross   5475
Kentucky! - Dana Fuller Ross   5477
Wisconsin! - Dana Fuller Ross   5493

Blakely, Morgan
Bride of the Unicorn - Kasey Michaels   4363

Blanchard, Marie
The Charlatan - Carter A. Vaughan   6433

Blue Feather, Peter
A Few Painted Feathers - Stephen Longstreet   3886

Bosola
A Dancer in Darkness - David Stacton   5971

Bowman, Toby
A Few Painted Feathers - Stephen Longstreet   3886

Boyd, Belle
The Smiling Rebel - Harnett T. Kane   3357

Braide, Simon
Men in Buckskin - Herbert Stover   6069

Brook, Roger
The Man Who Killed the King - Dennis
   Wheatley   6654

Butter, Amaziah
American Falls - John Calvin Batchelor   376

Cameron, Alexander
The Blood of Roses - Marsha Canham   879
The Pride of Lions - Marsha Canham   881

Captain S.
A Clear Road to Archangel - Geoffrey Rose   5461

Champion, John
Brother to the Enemy - Bart Spicer   5964

Chandler, Laura
While the Music Plays - Diane Austell   242

Chaucer, Geoffrey
The Nun's Tale - Candace M. Robb   5367

Clements, Hannah
Storm the Last Rampart - David Taylor   6180

Correnes, Victor de
The Gilded Torch - Iola Fuller   2252

Craig, Mary
The Long March - Jane Barry   358

Crockett, Hume
Home to Tennessee - Alfred Leland Crabb   1400
Lodging at the Saint Cloud - Alfred Leland
   Crabb   1403
Mockingbird Sang at Chickamauga - Alfred Leland
   Crabb   1404

D'Ancours, Diane
The Mohawk Ladder - Noel B. Gerson   2377

Danin, Vassily
Tournament of the Shadows - Nicholas Carnac   901

Darragh, Roxanne
Rebel Guns - Adam Rutledge   5539

Dawson, Anthony
Cormorant's Brood - Inglis Fletcher   2133

Dawson, Nicholas
City of God: A Novel of the Borgias - Cecelia
   Holland   2985

de Winter, Milady
The Three Musketeers - Alexandre Dumas   1782

Dexter, David
Armored Giants: A Novel of the Civil War - F. van
   Wyck Mason   4145

Donovan, William J. "Wild Bill"
Murder in the Chateau - Elliott Roosevelt   5447

Donsky, Saul
The Devil's Spy - Michael Hastings   2773

Ducos, Pierre
Sharpe's Honour - Bernard Cornwell   1344

Eldridge, Cyril
Stars and Stripes - Adam Rutledge   5541

Evans, Wilberforce
Chase Royal - Donald Seaman   5712

Fabius
Dead Reckoning - C. Northcote Parkinson   4809

Ferrand, Paul
The Wilderness - Carter A. Vaughan   6442

Fitzstephen, Blade
Lady Defiant - Suzanne Robinson   5412

Fleming, Harry
Rendezvous - Amanda Quick   5218

Frayne, John
Retreat and Recall - Joseph G.E. Hopkins   3029

Frontoni, Jacopo
The Bravo - James Fenimore Cooper   1298

Galliard, Jack
Secret Service Operator 13 - Robert W.
   Chambers   982

Garth, Celia
Celia Garth - Gwen Bristow   695

Gaudeans, Captain Richard
Captain Wonder - Donald Thomas   6238

Gibbs, John
The Iron Chain - Jim DeFelice   1579

Girard, Chase
While the Music Plays - Diane Austell   242

Graeme, Roland
The Abbot - Sir Walter Scott   5688

Grainger, Penn
No Bugles Blow - Bruce Lancaster   3642

Granger, Zachary
The Golden Circle - Constance Robertson   5396

Griewson, Eliza
Pancho And Black Jack - Fred Bean   398

Grishin, Mikhail
Grishin - Hans Herlin   2859

Grove, Matty
The Traitor - Dan Sherman   5814

Grunowski, Valentina
Valentina - Evelyn Anthony   165

Hammond, Sarah
Ironclads: Man-of-War - Larry D. Names   4554

Hart, Amy
The Storm Witch - Elisabeth Barr   339

Heatherton, Robin
Thin Moon and Cold Mist - Kathleen O'Neal
   Gear   2330

Hepburn, Allan
Captain Cut-Throat - John Dickson Carr   908

Herold, David
Lincoln: A Novel - Gore Vidal   6490

Heywood, Charley
Conspiracy of Knaves - Dee Brown   711

Hines, Henry Thomas
In the Season of the Wild Rose - Clara Rising   5347

Hussey, Johnny
A Nest of Simple Folk - Sean O'Faolain   4692

Irons, Forest
Scarlet Ribbons - Judith E. French   2224

Jankyn, Matthew
The Serpent Amongst the Lilies - P.C. Doherty   1678
The Whyte Harte - P.C. Doherty   1681

Jinsuke
Harpoon - C.W. Nicol   4612

Juan
Captain General - John P. Stevenson   6007

Justice, John Valcourt
A Balance of Dangers - Anthony Forrest   2184
Captain Justice - Anthony Forrest   2185
The Pandora Secret - Anthony Forrest   2186

Key, Jacob
Oh, Valley Green - John H. Culp   1443

Kimball, Jonathan
Farewell to Valley Forge - David Taylor   6178

King, Ranyard
The Unterrified - Constance Robertson   5397

Kirby, John
The Summer Day Is Done - R.T. Stevens   6001

Kischessinsky, Feliks
The Man From St. Petersburg - Ken Follett   2148

Ladd, Elizabeth
Farewell to Valley Forge - David Taylor   6178

Langalieve, Roger
Tory Tavern - Henry Barnard Safford   5559

Lawba, Spemica
Johnny Logan: Shawnee Spy - Allen W. Eckert   1843

Le Clerc, Maritza
The Passionate Rebel - Frank G. Slaughter   5894

Leyland, Francis
The White Witch - Elizabeth Goudge   2496

Lorendana, Juanita
A Spy for Napoleon - Baroness Emma Orczy   4746

Loveless, Gail
Secret Service Operator 13 - Robert W.
   Chambers   982

Lunt, Henry
Henry Lunt and the Ranger - Tom McNamara   4304

MacKellar, Patrick
The White Cockade - Vincent O'Brien   4683

Madden, Felicity
Valiant Libertine - John Gordon Bryson   748

Malmedy-Armagnac, Eugenie de
Concord Bridge - Howard Horne   3035

Maretzka, Olga
Dance on a Sinking Ship - Michael Kilian   3483

Markham, Elliott
Life and Liberty - Adam Rutledge   5538

Markham, Will
Fortress Fury - Carter A. Vaughan   6435

Marlowe, Christopher
A Dead Man in Deptford - Anthony Burgess   776
Strange Devices of the Sun and Moon - Lisa
   Goldstein   2463

Martin, Thomas
When the War Is Over - Stephen Becker   408

Mason, Deborah
Deborah - Colette Davenat   1498
Deborah and the Many Faces of Love - Colette
   Davenat   1499

Mata Hari
The Bloody Red Baron - Kim Newman   4596
*The Eye of the Lion: A Novel Based on the Life of
   Mata Hari* - Lael Tucker Wertenbaker   6626
The Man Who Loved Mata Hari - Dan
   Sherman   5813

Maturin, Stephen
The Commodore - Patrick O'Brian   4661
Desolation Island - Patrick O'Brian   4662
The Far Side of the World - Patrick O'Brian   4663
The Fortune of War - Patrick O'Brian   4664
H.M.S. Surprise - Patrick O'Brian   4666
The Ionian Mission - Patrick O'Brian   4667
The Letter of Marque - Patrick O'Brian   4668
Master and Commander - Patrick O'Brian   4669
The Mauritius Command - Patrick O'Brian   4670
The Nutmeg of Consolation - Patrick O'Brian   4671
Post Captain - Patrick O'Brian   4672
The Reverse of the Medal - Patrick O'Brian   4673
The Surgeon's Mate - Patrick O'Brian   4674
The Thirteen Gun Salute - Patrick O'Brian   4675
Treason's Harbour - Patrick O'Brian   4676
The Truelove - Patrick O'Brian   4677
The Wine-Dark Sea - Patrick O'Brian   4679
The Yellow Admiral - Patrick O'Brian   4680

McDaniel, Sharon
No Bugles Blow - Bruce Lancaster   3642

McKensie, Rosa Ann
McKensie's Hundred: A Tale of the Old Dominion -
   Frank Yerby   6924

McLeod, Margaretha Geertruida Zelle
The Last Summer of Mata Hari - Edward
   Huebsch   3067

Mendelson, Ruth
The Devil's Spy - Michael Hastings   2773

Mendoza, Racquel
The Dutchman - Maan Meyers   4351

Montez, Lola
Royal Flash - George MacDonald Fraser   2213

Morgan, Jeremy
Yankee - Dana Fuller Ross   5495

Morgan, Polly
The Secret Road - Bruce Lancaster   3646

Nichol, Beasley
Home to Tennessee - Alfred Leland Crabb   1400
Lodging at the Saint Cloud - Alfred Leland
   Crabb   1403
Mockingbird Sang at Chickamauga - Alfred Leland
   Crabb   1404

Nihoa, Hiram
Ka'a'awa: A Novel about Hawaii in the 1850s -
   Oswald Andrew Bushnell   814

Norland, Deborah
Deborah and the Siege of Paris - Colette
   Davenat   1500

O'Hara, Kimball
The Imperial Agent - T.N. Murari   4518

Oliphant, John
American Falls - John Calvin Batchelor   376

Page, Dick
Mr. Arnold - Francis Lynde   3935

Paige, Bennett
Storm the Last Rampart - David Taylor   6180

Paisley, Diccon
Lanterns - Patricia Veryan   6465

Pascali, Basil
The Idol Hunter - Barry Unsworth   6386

Pascoe, Tristram
Armada - Charles Gidley   2404

Pendragon, John Hawkdale
Pendragon: Late of Prince Albert's Own - Robert
   Trevelyan   6337
Pendragon. . .The Montenegran Plot - Robert
   Trevelyan   6338

Philby, Harold "Kim"
Gentleman Traitor - Alan Williams   6763

Pierce, Frederick
Blood Red Roses - Elizabeth Boatwright Coker   1163

Pollard, Cynthia
Squadron Shilling - Arch Whitehouse   6712

Pomeroy, John Stockley
Pomeroy - Gordon Williams   6770

Pryne, Richard
Richard Pryne: A Novel of the American Revolution -
   Cyril Harris   2718

Pym, Nicholas
A Firework for Oliver - John Sanders   5587

Quinn, Anthony
The Drums of April - Charles Mergendahl   4340

Ranklin, Matthew
Spy's Honour - Gavin Lyall   3929

Ravenel, Martin
Flames of Empire - Peter Bourne   594

Riebeck, Jean
Before the Glory Ended - Ursula Zilinsky   6963

River, Christian de
Lady Gallant - Suzanne Robinson   5413

Rokesby, Nicholas
Envoy From Elizabeth - Pamela Bennetts   451

Rosenberg, Ethel
Ethel: The Fictional Autobiography - Tema
   Nason   4558

Rosenberg, Julius
Ethel: The Fictional Autobiography - Tema
   Nason   4558

Rutledge, Belle
Conspiracy of Knaves - Dee Brown   711

Sheldon, Whipple
No Bugles Blow - Bruce Lancaster   3642

Shipov
*The Extraordinary Adventures of Secret Agent Shipov
   in Pursuit of Count Leo Tolstoy in the Year 1862* -
   Bulat Okudzhava   4712

Shover, Felicia Lee Cary Thornton
Untold Glory - Cothburn O'Neal   4739

Starr, Belle
Dim the Flaring Lamps - Jan Jordan   3301

Sterling, Amanda
Love Not a Rebel - Heather Graham   2516

Striecher, Paul
The Man on the Train - W.J. Chaput   995

Talbot, Holly
Dragon Cove - Carter A. Vaughan   6434

Tarranti, Sandra
Eagle in the Sun - Hoffman Birney   508

Townsend, Robert
The Culper Spy Ring - Lynn Groh   2596
The Secret Road - Bruce Lancaster   3646

Treloar, Robert
Look Away! - George Nauman Shuster   5841

Tryon, Richard
Hearts of Fire - Christina Savage   5616

Van Lew, Elizabeth
Weep No More - Janet Stevenson   6006

Vaughan, Tom
City of Light - Alison Macleod   4001
The Hireling - Alison Macleod   4003

Vinolas
The Witches - Jay Williams   6776

Walsingham, Sir Francis
All the Queen's Men - Evelyn Anthony   157
Women of Ashdon - Valerie Anand   135

Whipple, Dora
Confederates - Thomas Keneally   3412

Wickham, Belle
The Dixie Widow - Gilbert Morris   4459

Willetti, Tom
The Drums of April - Charles Mergendahl   4340

Wogan, Mrs.
Desolation Island - Patrick O'Brian   4662

Woodcott, Anthony
My Lord the Fox - Robert York   6932

Wormset, Richard Oliver
Seventeen of Leyden - John James   3160

Wyatt, Jonathan
The Golden Eagle - Noel B. Gerson   2370

Wynne, Hugh
Hugh Wynne, Free Quaker - Silas Weir
   Mitchell   4416

STEP-PARENT

Gale, Bob
The Nancy Flyer - Ernest Poole   5091

Lansdon, Benedict
The Changeling - Philippa Carr   918

STEWARD

Benchly, Roger
Evil Mark - Graham Miles   4377

Brown, Arnold
Cambridge - Caryl Phillips   4983

Frant, Theodore
The Quiet Gentleman - Georgette Heyer   2897

Ringan, Captain
Wilford's Daughter - Alexandra Manners   4071

STOCK BROKER

Bedford, Charles
Banished Children of Eve - Peter Quinn   5227

STORE OWNER

Blakeslee, E. Rucker
Cold Sassy Tree - Olive Ann Burns   797

Bloundel, Stephen
Old St. Paul's - William Harrison Ainsworth   57

Bradley, Garnet
Garnet - Helen Ashfield   207

Corry, Basil
Crystal - Helen Ashfield   205

Lampassas
North to Yesterday - Robert Flynn   2145

McKie, John
The Far Side of the Hill - Nancy Livingston   3811
The Land of Our Dreams - Nancy Livingston   3812

Mendes, Leo
The Conquest of Don Pedro - Harvey
    Fergusson 2066

Shea, Tom
A River Town - Thomas Keneally 3415

Turner, Ann
For My Great Folly - Thomas B. Costain 1365

Weber, Susanna
Madensky Square - Eva Ibbotson 3096

STREETPERSON

Canty, Tom
The Prince and the Pauper - Mark Twain 6373

Dawson, Angel
The King's Brat - Constance Gluyas 2441

Hathaway, Bess
Beau Barron's Lady - Helen Ashfield 204

Jamie
The Street Sparrows - Rose Ayers 249

Kropotka, Katerina
The House of Cards - Leon Garfield 2292

Leonie
These Old Shades - Georgette Heyer 2906

Pangersbourne, Amelia
The Pangersbourne Murders - J.G. Jeffreys 3179

Pinfold
Funny Papers - Tom De Haven 1559

Price, Ria
London's Child - Philip Boast 560

Smith, Meg
The Street Sparrows - Rose Ayers 249

Yorke, Crystal
Crystal - Helen Ashfield 205

STUDENT

Archibald, Allan
Organized Crime - Nicholas Von Hoffman 6511

Burnside, Alison
The Marrying Kind - Jessica Stirling 6046
The Penny Wedding - Jessica Stirling 6047

Bustos, Baltasar
The Campaign - Carlos Fuentes 2245

Carrill, Charles
Thunder on St. Paul's Day - Jane Lane 3658

Clement, Alvey
If I Were You - Joan Aiken 49

Clement, Juliette de
Storm Winds - Iris Johansen 3217

Conway, Jessie
The Wingless Bird - Catherine Cookson 1292

Denver, Annabelinda
A Time for Silence - Philippa Carr 930

Fallon, Peter
Back Bay - William Martin 4138

Giron, Irena
Organized Crime - Nicholas Von Hoffman 6511

Greenham, Lucinda
A Time for Silence - Philippa Carr 930

Griffen, Tristram
The Black Rose - Thomas B. Costain 1363

Hartwell, Amaryllis
Miss Hartwell's Dilemma - Carola Dunn 1796

Heron of Foix
A Walk with Love and Death - Hans Koning 3539

Higgins, Gerald
Ourselves to Know - John O'Hara 4704

Jochanan
The Nazarene - Sholem Asch 200

Lao Chen
The Examination - Malcolm Bosse 587

Mackenzie, Christabel
Death Wore a Diadem - Iona McGregor 4277

McKie, Luke
The Land of Our Dreams - Nancy Livingston 3812

Mitchell, Parris
Kings Row - Henry Bellamann 428

Pamphilius
Woman of Andros - Thornton Wilder 6754

Princip, Gavrilo
Death of a Schoolboy - Hans Koning 3537

Ramelius, Andreas
Land of the Beautiful River - Helmer
    Linderholm 3788

Reed, Daniel
Sons of Liberty - Adam Rutledge 5540

Ross, Hildebrand
Sprig Muslin - Georgette Heyer 2903

Rowntree, Elizabeth
Forbidden City - Anthony Esler 1962

Russell, Mary
*The Beekeeper's Apprentice, or, On the Segregation of
    the Queen* - Laurie R. King 3487

Shaw, Harriet
Swing, Swing Together - Peter Lovesey 3915

Stalker, Andrew
Call Home the Heart - Jessica Stirling 6040

Thoegersen, Mikkel
The Fall of the King - Johannes Vilhelm
    Jensen 3214

Tolbecken, Jared
Tolbecken - Samuel Shellabarger 5798

Traherne, Ada
Doubting Castle - Rebecca Kavaler 3373

Walter of Gurnie
The Black Rose - Thomas B. Costain 1363

Winship, Louisa
If I Were You - Joan Aiken 49

STUDENT—COLLEGE

Andrews, Will
Butcher's Crossing - John Williams 6786

Bannon, James
Look Away - Harold Coyle 1395

Bannon, Kevin
Look Away - Harold Coyle 1395

Bashford, Hendon
The Steps of the Sun - Joanna Trollope 6350

Brewster, Philip
Three Sides of Agiochook - Eric Kelly 3400

Carpenter, Benjamin
A Sparkle From the Coal - Prudence Andrew 144

Gilman, Roger
Gilman of the Redford - William Stearns Davis 1541

Hamilton, Richard
The Morning River - W. Michael Gear 2333

Nickerson, Ross
A Roaring in the Wind - Robert Lewis Taylor 6191

Paget, Matthew
The Steps of the Sun - Joanna Trollope 6350

Ramsay, Alex
Strathgallant - Laura Black 523

Roosevelt, Theodore
The Adventure of the Stalwart Companions - H. Paul
    Jeffers 3177

Sigourney, Corbet
The Willing Maid - C.T. Ritchie 5349

Symon, Thomas
Falconer's Crusade - Ian Morson 4493

STUDENT—HIGH SCHOOL

Grossberg, Sharon
The Year of Our War - Gloria Goldreich 2462

SUFFRAGETTE

Addams, Jane
The Dream Seekers - Grace Mark 4085

Anthony, Susan B.
Beecher: A Novel - Dan McCall 4218
Woman of Justice - Georgia Di Donato 1639

Belmont, Alva
Rivington Street - Meredith Tax 6175

Bray, Nell
Crown Witness - Gillian Linscott 3803
Dead Man's Sweetheart - Gillian Linscott 3804
An Easy Day for a Lady - Gillian Linscott 3805
Hanging on the Wire - Gillian Linscott 3806
Sister Beneath the Sheet - Gillian Linscott 3808
Stage Fright - Gillian Linscott 3809

Emory, Elizabeth
Sierra Triumph - Dana Fuller Ross 5488

Fieldfare, Bobbie
Sister Beneath the Sheet - Gillian Linscott 3808

Holt, Elizabeth
Pacific Destiny - Dana Fuller Ross 5487

Ivory, Florence
Bethlehem Road - Anne Perry 4920

Marsh, Margaret
Chicago Girls - Edith Freund 2229

Pankhurst, Emmeline
Sister Beneath the Sheet - Gillian Linscott 3808

Stanton, Elizabeth Cady
Seneca Falls Inheritance - Miriam Grace
    Monfredo 4429
Through a Gold Eagle - Miriam Grace
    Monfredo 4430

SURVEYOR

Ballard, Christopher
Gamble's Hundred - Clifford Dowdey 1705

Barry, Alan
Rebel in Blue - Herman Toepperwein 6289

Collins, Leslie
*The Kentucky Trace: A Novel of the American
    Revolution* - Harriette Simpson Arnow 195

Ruff, Alan
I Thee Wed - Gilbert Wolf Gabriel 2267

Washington, George
War in the Golden Weather - Stephen
    Longstreet 3892

SURVIVOR

Leonora
The Sea Treasure - Elisabeth Barr 338

TAILOR

Mandelkern, Yoysef
Malkeh and Her Children - Marjorie Edelson 1853

Nils
Arne - Bjornstjerne Bjornson 518

Rising, Will
April Rising - Susan Sallis 5574

Win, Philip
The Hooded Falcon - Prudence Andrew 140

TEACHER

Abbott, Jim
The Penny Wedding - Jessica Stirling 6047

Abelard, Peter
Death Comes as Epiphany - Sharan Newman 4598

Akeham, Henry
Ramillies - Barbara Whitehead 6708

Alcock, J.D.
To Serve Them All My Days - R.F. Delderfield 1591

Alden, Susanna
No Roof but Heaven - Jeanne Williams 6782

Anna
The Petersburg-Cannes Express - Hans Koning 3538

Aram, Eugene
Eugene Aram - Edward Bulwer-Lytton 766

Aristotle
The Conqueror: A Novel of Alexander the Great - Edison Marshall 4104
An Elephant for Aristotle - L. Sprague De Camp 1556
Fire From Heaven - Mary Renault 5296

Ascham, Roger
Elizabeth, Captive Princess - Margaret Irwin 3118

Batchelor, Barbara
The Towers of Silence - Paul Scott 5685

Becker, Friedrich
Karl and Rosa - Alfred Doblin 1653
A People Betrayed - Alfred Doblin 1654

Bethune, Mary McLeod
Murder in the Rose Garden - Elliott Roosevelt 5452

Bishop, Ella
Miss Bishop - Bess Streeter Aldrich 71

Black, Gideon
The Land Is Bright - Archie Binns 501

Bright, Iphigenia
Mistress - Amanda Quick 5215

Britewell, Jennifer
A Shadow's Bliss - Patricia Veryan 6477

Buchanan
Rogue's Harbor - Inglis Fletcher 2139

Burchard, Sela
Run of the Stars - Dora Aydelotte 247

Burlingame, Henry
The Sot-Weed Factor - John Barth 364

Cannon, Jonathan
Forest of the Night - Madison Jones 3291

Carlyon, Beth Brennan
Inherit the Sun - Maxwell Grant 2539

Chamberlain, Joshua Lawrence
Gods and Generals - Jeff Shaara 5765

Chrysis
Woman of Andros - Thornton Wilder 6754

Clare, Hannah
Ramillies - Barbara Whitehead 6708

Collingsworth, Benton
Arfive - A.B. Guthrie Jr. 2623
The Last Valley - A.B. Guthrie Jr. 2626

Cornwall, Charlotte
Out of the Dark - Norah Lofts 3856

Day, Julian
Dawn's Early Light - Elswyth Thane 6215

Dexter, Kate
Remnants of Glory - Teresa Miller 4403

Drum, Betina
Blood on the Divide - William W. Johnstone 3265

Duncan, Katherine
Gold Mountain - Charlotte Paul 4841

Falconer, William
Falconer's Crusade - Ian Morson 4493
Falconer's Judgement - Ian Morson 4494

Favoury, Willa Mae
Arrest Sitting Bull - Douglas C. Jones 3273

Goddard, Mary
A Visit to Highbury - Joan Austen-Leigh 243

Grant, Cordelia
The Time of the Hunter's Moon - Victoria Holt 3022

Grant, Sapphire
Sapphire - Helen Ashfield 214

Hall, Eliza
The Proud and the Free - Janet Dailey 1456

Hart, Nathan
Genesee Fever - Carl Lamson Carmer 898

Hartnett, Emily
Mamigon - Jack Hashian 2772

Heindrichs, Gwendolyn
The Garfield Honor - Frank Yerby 6918

Herbert, Clarissa
The Shadowed Spring - Carola Salisbury 5571

Izzard, Betony
The Land Endures - Mary E. Pearce 4862

Jabalwan
Wyvern - A.A. Attanasio 227

Jesus Christ
Great Lion of God - Taylor Caldwell 858

Jewel, Margaret
The Snake River - Winfred Blevins 547

Klein, Sanna
Leaving Cold Sassy - Olive Ann Burns 798

Lowell, Judith
Johnny Osage - Janice Holt Giles 2412

MacAllister, Malcolm
The Strange Brigade - John Edward Jennings 3209

MacDonald, Laurel
Trail of Tears - Frances Patton Statham 5983

Maclean, Elaine
The Powder River - Winfred Blevins 546

MacMahon, Hugh
The Tenants of Time - Thomas Flanagan 2120

Maddox, Minella
The Devil on Horseback - Victoria Holt 3014

Maxwell, John
Children of the Dust - Carlile Clancy 1084

McCarthy, Owen
The Year of the French - Thomas Flanagan 2121

McLeod, Hannah
A Heritage of Shadows - Madeleine Brent 660

Miller, Hacey
The Way to Fort Pillow - James Sherburne 5807

Montgomery, Dougless
A Knight in Shining Armor - Jude Deveraux 1631

Montgomery, Lacie
Thief of My Heart - Rexanne Becnel 410

Morrow, Tom
Follow the River - Albert Mayer 4203

Napier, Margaret
Death Wore a Diadem - Iona McGregor 4277

Osborn, Samuel
Tomorrow the New Moon - Shirley Barker 319

Pearse, Patrick Henry
Rebels: The Irish Rising of 1916 - Peter DeRosa 1622

Perkins, Sarah
The Revolt of Sarah Perkins - Marian Cockrell 1148

Pharos
Fires in the Sky - Phillip Parotti 4816

Philokrates
Anabasis: A Journey to the Interior - Ellen Gilchrist 2408

Pinto, Adolph
Pinto and Sons - Leslie Epstein 1947

Porpora
Consuelo - George Sand 5582

Powlett-Jones, David
To Serve Them All My Days - R.F. Delderfield 1591

Prescott, Francis
The Rector of Justin - Louis Auchincloss 233

Purbeck, Sandy
Always a River - Drayton Mayrant 4211

Randolph, Bruce
Griffin's Way - Frank Yerby 6922

Ransome, Christina
A Revolutionary Woman - Sheila Fugard 2248

Rodana
The Winds of Sinhala - Colin De Silva 1562

Ross, Georgiana
In the Fire of Spring - Thomas Tryon 6355

Selkirk, Olivia
Legacy of the Wolf - Jean Raynes 5274

Servetus, Antonio
Divine Mistress - Frank G. Slaughter 5886

Seton, Elizabeth Ann
Heart in Pilgrimage - Evelyn Eaton 1827
Miracles - Marcy Moran Heidish 2818

Sharp, John
The Living - Annie Dillard 1644

Shawnessy, John Wickliff
Raintree County - Ross Lockridge Jr. 3827

Shepherd, Beth
For Us the Living - Antonia Van-Loon 6424

Sherman, Ruth
Rogue's Kingdom - John Brick 676

Socrates
Goat Song: A Novel of Ancient Greece - Frank Yerby 6920
The Immortal Marriage - Gertrude Atherton 225

Washington, Booker T.
Ragtime - E.L. Doctorow 1658

Weatherby, Mark
Windover - Jane Aiken Hodge 2974

Whitby, Mary
The Woman Question - Dorothea Malm 4046

Winton, Leslie
Mills of the Gods - Daoma Winston 6828

Yehudi
Mr. Vertigo - Paul Auster 244

TEENAGER

Banner, Libbie
Northwest Passage - David Thompson 6258

Barnsby, Horace "Horse"
The Adventure of "Horse" Barnsby - Philip D. Stong 6065

Bass, Titus
Dance on the Wind - Terry C. Johnston 3249

Benton, Scot
The Bright Feathers - John H. Culp 1441

Blair, Todd
A Bright Tragic Thing - L.D. Clark 1091

Blake, Frank
Sierra Triumph - Dana Fuller Ross 5488

Blake, Peter
Oklahoma Pride - Dana Fuller Ross 5483

Blakeslee, Will Tweedy
Cold Sassy Tree - Olive Ann Burns 797

Bodeen, Ladd
The Horse Hunters - Robert Newton Peck 4887

Burnie, Davey
A Journey to Matecumbe - Robert Lewis Taylor 6188

Burnside, Alison
The Penny Wedding - Jessica Stirling 6047

Burton, Amanda
Miss Lizzie - Walter Satterthwait 5608

Cameron, Martin
The Restless Land - John H. Culp 1444

Champelle, Hank
The Last Boat out of Cincinnati - Don Tracy 6309

Chap
The Walk into Morning - Mildred Barger Herschler 2867

Clinton, Isabella
The Gentle Falcon - Hilda Lewis 3747

Crawford, Bill
Boy with a Pack - Stephen Warren Meader 4319

Dahlberg, Chris
Swift Rivers - Cornelia Meigs 4328

Dawes, David
Black Jack Davy - John Oskison 4763

Dawkins, Scrape
The Bright Feathers - John H. Culp 1441

Deane, John
Swords of Steel - Elsie Singmaster 5870

Dimon, Jeremiah
The Adventures of Jeremiah Dimon: The Novel of Old East Hampton - Everett Rattray 5255

Easter, Buddy
Joy in Mudville - Gordon McAlpine 4216

Fairchild, Pepper
Hard on the Road - Barbara Moore 4440

Fairfax, Ingrid
The Age of Miracles - Catherine MacCoun 3960

Fergusson, Davy
The Shadow and the Glory - John Edward Jennings 3207

Gaar, Thorold
Sandoval: A Romance of Bad Manners - Thomas Beer 414

Gao
Father and Son - Donald Clayton Porter 5117

Gatewood, Tenny
Pioneer Breed - Glenn R. Vernam 6453

Glen, Owen
Owen Glen - Ben Ames Williams 6766

Goforth, Billy
Bugle in the Wilderness - John Burress 805

Graves, Thomas "Grubber"
Me and Gallagher - Jack Farris 2023

Grayle, David
Sudden Country - Loren D. Estleman 1979

Greenleaf, Kitty
The Road to Bunker Hill - Shirley Barker 316

Greer, Tom
Wandering Star - Steven Yount 6945

Grossberg, Sharon
The Year of Our War - Gloria Goldreich 2462

Hallam, Lesley
Blood Kin - Barbara Anne Pauley 4845

Hampton, Elizabeth
The Hampton Women - Julie Ellis 1921

Harding, Rance
Pioneer Breed - Glenn R. Vernam 6453

Hatton, Glen
Poor Boy and a Long Way Home - James Sherburne 5806

Hawke, Morgan
Trapper's Moon - Jory Sherman 5823

Heath, Jessie
The Pilgrimage - Ann B. Ross 5463

Hervey, Penitence
Campion Towers - John Beatty 401

Honeycutt, Charlie "Slim"
The Cowboys - William Dale Jennings 3211

Hume, Sam
Sweetwater Fever - Robert H. Adelman 36

Jed
Look to the River - William A. Owens 4771

Jensie
Rockspring - R.G. Vliet 6506

Jonathan
An Army of Children - Evan H. Rhodes 5306

Kennedy, John F.
A First Class Murder - Elliott Roosevelt 5442

Killefer, Owen
The Canebrake Men - Cameron Judd 3313

King, Nathaniel
King of the Mountain - David Thompson 6255
Lure of the Wind - David Thompson 6256

Kronkhyte, Abe
If Not Victory - Frank Olney Hough 3043

Lanyon, Aubrey
Venetia - Georgette Heyer 2909

Laurelle
An Army of Children - Evan H. Rhodes 5306

Leaf, Dorney
Good Morning, Young Lady - Ardyth Kennelly 3424

Lucas
Midnight Is a Place - Joan Aiken 52

MacIntosh, Meggy
Meggy MacIntosh - Elizabeth Janet Gray 2555

MacLeod, Katie
Home Mountain - Jeanne Williams 6777

Mariah, Pete
Walk Like a Man - Donald Honig 3024

Mason, Daisy
Pilgrims: A Novel of the Mayflower - Gerard Mac 3955

McGee, Jason
Jason McGee - Robert H. Fowler 2190

McGook, Ham Esposita
The Bright Feathers - John H. Culp 1441

Miller, Hacey
Hacey Miller - James Sherburne 5805

Murgatroyd, Anna-Marie
Midnight Is a Place - Joan Aiken 52

Nettleship, Maudie
Gentlemen in England - A.N. Wilson 6795

O'Shea, Timmie
The Cotton Road - Frank Feuille 2077

Pale Star
Pale Star - Don Coldsmith 1181

Parham, Billy
The Crossing - Cormac McCarthy 4221

Pomponia
Golden Peacock - Gertrude Atherton 224

Pondwader
People of the Lightning - W. Michael Gear 2337

Porteous, Jim
Retreat From the Dolphin - Darwin Le Ora Teilhet 6198

Proctor, Jeremy
Blind Justice - Bruce Alexander 76
Murder in Grub Street - Bruce Alexander 77
Watery Grave - Bruce Alexander 78

Rabbit
Moon of Thunder - Don Coldsmith 1180

Roger
An Army of Children - Evan H. Rhodes 5306

Ross, Mattie
True Grit - Charles Portis 5139

Running Elk
Man on Two Ponies - Don Worcester 6872

Sager, John
On to Oregon! - Honore Morrow 4490

Scald Ibiz
The Tent of Orange Mist - Paul West 6636

Shelby, Sam
The Roads to Guadalupe - Robert Lewis Taylor 6190

Sima
The Snake River - Winfred Blevins 547

Slover, Betsey
Scarlet Feather - Dale Van Every 6409

Smith, Bud
Mi Amigo - William R. Burnett 795

Smith, Charlie
The Cowboys - William Dale Jennings 3211

Sunday, Billy
Billy Sunday - Rod Jones 3295

Ta-Na
Father and Son - Donald Clayton Porter 5117

Taylor, Jeff
Walk Like a Man - Donald Honig 3024

Tom
The Closest Possible Union - Joanna Scott 5680

Townsend, Sally Rose
The Road to Bunker Hill - Shirley Barker 316

Trowbridge, Little Ax
Captain Little Ax - James H. Street 6077

Ulric
The Trumpet of God - David Duncan 1784

Walden, Jenny
Buffalo Coat - Carol Brink 691

White, Juan
The Men of Gonzales - John H. Culp 1442

Woodlawn, Caddie
Caddie Woodlawn - Carol Brink 692

Yanan
Reindeer Moon - Elizabeth Marshall Thomas 6244

TERRORIST

McGee, Rossanna
The Tick of Death - Peter Lovesey 3916

THIEF

Agar, Robert
The Great Train Robbery - Michael Crichton 1426

Barabbas
Barabbas: A Novel of the Time of Jesus - Emery
  Bekessy 417
Brothers of Vengeance - LeGette Blythe 556
The Gospel of Corax - Paul Park 4802

Braaf
The Sea Runners - Ivan Doig 1685

Brodie, William
The Strange Case of Deacon Brodie - Forbes
  Bramble 646

Cobbold, Charley
The Rookery: A Novel of the Victorian Underworld -
  Hugh C. Rae 5239

Cooney
The Rookery: A Novel of the Victorian Underworld -
  Hugh C. Rae 5239

Daniels, Matt
Sweet Songbird - Teresa Crane 1418

Disbrow, Packy
Blue Russell - Will Bryant 738

Dunne, Jimmy
Banished Children of Eve - Peter Quinn 5227

Etcher
Arc d'X - Steve Erickson 1953

Gregson, Badger
The Rookery: A Novel of the Victorian Underworld -
  Hugh C. Rae 5239

Jankyn, Matthew
The Serpent Amongst the Lilies - P.C. Doherty 1678

Luttrell, Edmund
The Whyte Harte - P.C. Doherty 1681

Peveral, Luke
Sweet Songbird - Teresa Crane 1418

Pierce, Edward
The Great Train Robbery - Michael Crichton 1426

Rackham, Jacob
The Masters of Bow Street - John Creasy 1423

Ranulf
Angel of Death - P.C. Doherty 1670
The Crown in Darkness - P.C. Doherty 1671
The Prince of Darkness - P.C. Doherty 1675
Satan in St. Mary's - P.C. Doherty 1676

Rise, Ned
Water Music - T. Coraghessan Boyle 619

Sanchia
The Wind Dancer - Iris Johansen 3218

Shackleton, Frank
Jewels - Robert Perrin 4917

Shannon, Opal
Opal - Helen Ashfield 210

Stokes, Sally
A Broken Vessel - Kate Ross 5500

TIME TRAVELLER

Balfour, Alex
Till the End of Time - Allen Appel 170
Time After Time - Allen Appel 171
Twice upon a Time - Allen Appel 172

Blackwood, Pryor Deyhle
Riding Shotgun - Rita Mae Brown 729

Bondenland, Joe
Frankenstein Unbound - Brian Aldiss 68

Cheviot, John
Fire, Burn! - John Dickson Carr 910

Clifford, Jo
Lady of Hay - Barbara Erskine 1955

Fenton, Nicholas
The Devil in Velvet - John Dickson Carr 909

Fowler, Sam
If I Never Get Back - Darryl Brock 700

Fraser, Claire
Drums of Autumn - Diana Gabaldon 2263

Kenbrook, Gloriana
Knights - Linda Lael Miller 4399

Metzner, Helen
From Time to Time - Jack Finney 2092

Morley, Simon
From Time to Time - Jack Finney 2092
Time and Again - Jack Finney 2093

Padway, Martin
Lest Darkness Fall - L. Sprague De Camp 1557

Pruitt, Jessica
Serenissima: A Novel of Venice - Erica Jong 3300

Steward, Benjamin
The Lincoln Hunters - Wilson Tucker 6359

Wolf, Michael
A Whisper on the Wind - Madeline Baker 276

Zhu Wong
The Golden Nineties - Lisa Mason 4166

TRADER

Astor, John Jacob
Bright Journey - August Derleth 1614

Ayrton, Christy
Silver Nutmeg - Norah Lofts 3860

Bailly, Joseph
Wolves Against the Moon - Julia Cooley
  Altrocchi 123

Baranov, Aleksandr
Ashana - E.P. Roesch 5424

Benet, Skinner
Eagle Fur - Robert Newton Peck 4884

Bennett, Gill
Hong Kong - Mona Gardner 2288

Berg, Simon Van der
The Mask - Stuart Cloete 1125

Bishop, Joshua
Trade Imperial - Alan Lloyd 3814

Boudreau, Paul
West of the River - Charlton Laird 3591

Bravo, Ruben
Strange Wives - Shirley Barker 317

Brock, Tyler
Tai-Pan - James Clavell 1102

Campbell, Angus
The Fur Masters - Alan Sullivan 6113

Chafin
A Whistle in the Wind - John H. Culp 1447

Chain, John
Eagle in the Sun - Hoffman Birney 508

Charron, Pierre
Shadows on the Rock - Willa Cather 959

Chen, Gordon
Tai-Pan - James Clavell 1102

Chouteau, Auguste
Savanna - Janice Holt Giles 2416

Cole, Josiah
A Respectable Trade - Philippa Gregory 2584

Cotter, James
The Wayfarer - Shirley Seifert 5738

Da Silva, Francisco
The Viceroy of Ouidah - Bruce C. Chatwin 1009

Dasius
The Coin of Carthage - Bryher 740

Demetrius
Roman Wall - Bryher 745

Denton, John
Shanghai - Christopher New 4588

Dousman, Hercules
Bright Journey - August Derleth 1614
The House on the Mound - August Derleth 1616

Duclos, Paul
Thunder in the Wilderness - Charles Granville
  Hamilton 2668

Flood, Matthew
The Sun Is My Undoing - Marguerite Steen 5988

Flood, Wick
Montana Road - Harry Sinclair Drago 1717

Fowler, Johnny
The Great Adventure - Janice Holt Giles 2410
Voyage to Santa Fe - Janice Holt Giles 2418

Frazier, John
Red Morning - Ruby Frazier Frey 2230

Frost, Rory
Trade Wind - M.M. Kaye 3378

Fultz, Mark
The Eagle and the Wind - Herbert Stover 6068

Galmon, Jack
Dubu: A Novel of New Guinean Conquest - Maslyn
  Williams 6789

Gunn, Robert
Mandarin Gold - James Leasor 3700

Haan, Evert
Silver Nutmeg - Norah Lofts 3860

Hale, Oliver
Jubilee Trail - Gwen Bristow 698

Heggie, Calvin
The Kidnapped Surgeon - Alexander Knox 3527

Hook, Marcus
O Genesee - Janet O'Daniel 4688

Horsey, Jerome
The Muscovite - Alison Macleod 4004

Ives, John
Jubilee Trail - Gwen Bristow 698

Jardine, William
Mandarin Gold - James Leasor 3700

Jones, Big Sam
Goldfield - Richard S. Wheeler 6660

Juggins, Robert
The Doom Trail - Arthur Douglas Smith 5917

Kinzie, John
Gateway to Empire - Allen W. Eckert 1842

Kipp, Peter
The Two Medicine River - Richard S. Wheeler 6663

Lamb, Richard
Richard Lamb - Richard S. Wheeler 6662

Lamont, Baptiste
The Loon Feather - Iola Fuller 2253

Leslie, Arnett
The Judas Tree - Neil Harmon Swanson 6139

Lisa, Manuel
Those Who Go Against the Current - Shirley Seifert 5734

MacGregor, Baril
The Forbidden Ground - Neil Harmon Swanson 6138

Maclean, Robert Burns
The Yellowstone - Winfred Blevins 549

Main, Charles
Heaven and Hell - John Jakes 3147

Matheson, James
Mandarin Gold - James Leasor 3700

Matyeh
Shadow of a Star - Jamie Lee Cooper 1315

Moreland, Jason
The Moreland Legacy - Diana Haviland 2777

Morton, Thomas
The Disturber - L.S. Davidson Jr. 1505

Musgrove, John
Rascal's Heaven - F. van Wyck Mason 4157

Old Pine
Eight April Days - Scott Hart 2759

Ormerod, Harry
The Doom Trail - Arthur Douglas Smith 5917

O'Rourke, Rocheblave Xavier
River to the West: A Novel of the Astor Adventure - John Edward Jennings 3204

Osage, Johnny Fowler
Johnny Osage - Janice Holt Giles 2412

Otter
People of the Lakes - W. Michael Gear 2336

Page, Jasper
Early Candlelight - Maude Hart Lovelace 3904

Pasquinel
Centennial - James A. Michener 4366

Polo, Marco
The Journeyer - Gary Jennings 3194

Prevost, Etienne
Kings of the Missouri - Hugh Pendexter 4895

Ramsay, Gavin
The Proud Breed - Celeste De Blasis 1547

Retallick, Josh
Harvest of the Sun - E.V. Thompson 6265

Ridley, Gilbert
The Lady Chapel - Candace M. Robb 5366

Roussillon, Gaspard
Alice of Old Vincennes - Maurice Thompson 6268

Sekloong, Jonathan
Dynasty - Robert S. Elegant 1902

Shaw, Rodney
Black Feather - Harold Titus 6283

Simo
Woman of Andros - Thornton Wilder 6754

Smart, Colonel Wiley
Dodging Red Cloud - Richard S. Wheeler 6657

Straun, Tess
Gai-Jin: A Novel of Japan - James Clavell 1100

Struan, Dirk
Tai-Pan - James Clavell 1102

Struan, Malcolm
Gai-Jin: A Novel of Japan - James Clavell 1100

Thorfinn Karlsefni
Gudrid's Saga - Constance Irwin 3115

Thorne, Robin
Warm Wind, West Wind - Anne Irwin Matthew 4188

Veres-Vorne, Nathan de
Mandalay - Alexandra Jones 3269

Westmoreland, Ed
Six-Horse Hitch - Janice Holt Giles 2417

Willard, Eli
The Architecture of the Arkansas Ozarks - Donald Harington 2708

Winslow, Knox
The Holy Warrior - Gilbert Morris 4462

York, Jeremiah
Eagles of Destiny - Jory Sherman 5817

Zonas
The Coin of Carthage - Bryher 740

TRAITOR

Arnold, Benedict
The Exquisite Siren - Edwin Haines 2639
The Lure of the Falcon - Juliette Benzoni 465
Major Andre - Anthony Bailey 265
Mr. Arnold - Francis Lynde 3935
Proceed, Sergeant Lamb - Robert Graves 2550
The Secret Road - Bruce Lancaster 3646
Treason - Robert Gessner 2389

Ashville, Felice
Royal Sword at Agincourt - Pamela Bennetts 455

Judas Iscariot
I, Judas - Taylor Caldwell 859

TRAPPER

Boissart, Paul
Heritage of the River - Muriel Elwood 1937

Breckenridge, Hunter
Fur Brigade - Hal George Evarts 1985

Cadwell, Christopher
Jason McGee - Robert H. Fowler 2190

Campbell, Dylan
The High Missouri - Winfred Blevins 545

Crews, John
John Crews - Arthur Chapman 988

Driant, Pierre
The Great Adventure - Janice Holt Giles 2410

Garrett, J.C.
The Pilgrimage - Ann B. Ross 5463

Holt, Jefferson
Expedition! - Dana Fuller Ross 5473
Outpost! - Dana Fuller Ross 5486

King, Ezekiel
King of the Mountain - David Thompson 6255

King, Nathaniel
Apache Blood - David Thompson 6250
Blackfoot Massacre - David Thompson 6251
Blood Fury - David Thompson 6252
Blood Truce - David Thompson 6253
Hawken Fury - David Thompson 6254
Mountain Devil - David Thompson 6257
Northwest Passage - David Thompson 6258
Tenderfoot - David Thompson 6259
Tomahawk Revenge - David Thompson 6260
Trapper's Blood - David Thompson 6261
Winterkill - David Thompson 6262

Livingston, Whit
Look to the Mountain - Le Grand Cannon 885

Locke, Dan
Fire in the Sky - J.A. Shears 5785

McNair, Shakespeare
Apache Blood - David Thompson 6250
King of the Mountain - David Thompson 6255
Lure of the Wind - David Thompson 6256
Tomahawk Revenge - David Thompson 6260
Trapper's Blood - David Thompson 6261

Menteen, Milo
Mountain Devil - David Thompson 6257

Pasquinel
Centennial - James A. Michener 4366

Patche
Shadow of a Star - Jamie Lee Cooper 1315

Rapaho
Rapaho - Jamie Lee Cooper 1314

Reeshar, Jesse
Chant of the Hawk - John Harris 2720

Roebuck, Thomas
Gennie the Huguenot Woman - Bette M. Ross 5464

Slaughter, Nathan
Nick of the Woods; or, The Jibbenainosay - Robert Montgomery Bird 505

Stroud, George
Chant of the Hawk - John Harris 2720

Watley, Sam
Shadows on the Long House - Mike Roarke 5360
Silent Drums - Mike Roarke 5361
Thunder in the East - Mike Roarke 5362

Watley, Thad
Shadows on the Long House - Mike Roarke 5360
Silent Drums - Mike Roarke 5361
Thunder in the East - Mike Roarke 5362

Wilde, Sam
The Predators - F.A. Parker 4804

TRAVELLER

Dow, Margaret
The Lost Giants - Alan Scholefield 5657

Rhun
The Pilgrim of Hate - Ellis Peters 4967

Smith, Honoria
The Rake and the Rebel - Ira J. Morris 4478

TWIN

Boissart, Marguerite
Heritage of the River - Muriel Elwood 1937

Boissart, Paul
Heritage of the River - Muriel Elwood 1937

Cooke, Anna
The Sot-Weed Factor - John Barth 364

Cooke, Ebenezer
The Sot-Weed Factor - John Barth 364

Danver, George
Double Masquerade - Karen Lynn 3938

Danver, Georginna
Double Masquerade - Karen Lynn 3938

Dukay, Albert
Century in Scarlet - Lajos Zilahy 6962

Dukay, Antal
Century in Scarlet - Lajos Zilahy 6962

Fancot, Christopher "Kit"
False Colours - Georgette Heyer 2886

Fancot, Evelyn
False Colours - Georgette Heyer 2886

Field, Lafayette
The Rising Storm - Marguerite Allis 113

Field, Lancelot
The Rising Storm - Marguerite Allis 113

Furneau, Caroline
Stranger at the Wedding - Frances Lynch 3934

Furneau, Katherine
Stranger at the Wedding - Frances Lynch 3934

Landor, Angelet
Saraband for Two Sisters - Philippa Carr 928

Landor, Bersaba
Saraband for Two Sisters - Philippa Carr 928

MacAllan, Jennie
The Woman from The Glen - Chloe Gartner 2310

MacAllan, Pollux
The Woman from The Glen - Chloe Gartner 2310

Manaravak
Walkers of the Wind - William Sarabande 5603

Remus
Children of the Wolf - Alfred Duggan 1762

Romulus
Children of the Wolf - Alfred Duggan 1762

Tarconti, Andrea
Wings of the Falcon - Barbara Michaels 4361

Tarconti, Stefano
Wings of the Falcon - Barbara Michaels 4361

Umak
Walkers of the Wind - William Sarabande 5603

VAGRANT

Perrell, John
Escape From Sonora - Will Bryant 739

Verne, Martin
Stranger at Wildings - Madeleine Brent 663

VAMPIRE

Clemens, Atta Olivia
A Candle for D'Artagnan - Chelsea Quinn
    Yarbro 6895
Crusader's Torch - Chelsea Quinn Yarbro 6897
Darker Jewels - Chelsea Quinn Yarbro 6898
A Flame in Byzantium - Chelsea Quinn Yarbro 6899
The Palace - Chelsea Quinn Yarbro 6904

Dieudonne, Genevieve
Anno-Dracula - Kim Newman 4595

Dracula
The Bloody Red Baron - Kim Newman 4596
The Revenge of Dracula - Peter Tremayne 6335
Seance for a Vampire - Fred Saberhagen 5557
Sherlock Holmes vs. Dracula - Loren D.
    Estleman 1976

Montalia, Madelaine de
Hotel Transylvania - Chelsea Quinn Yarbro 6900
Out of the House of Life - Chelsea Quinn
    Yarbro 6903
Tempting Fate - Chelsea Quinn Yarbro 6906

Reed, Kate
The Bloody Red Baron - Kim Newman 4596

Saint-Germain, Comte de
Better in the Dark - Chelsea Quinn Yarbro 6894
Darker Jewels - Chelsea Quinn Yarbro 6898
Hotel Transylvania - Chelsea Quinn Yarbro 6900
Mansions of Darkness - Chelsea Quinn Yarbro 6902
Out of the House of Life - Chelsea Quinn
    Yarbro 6903
The Palace - Chelsea Quinn Yarbro 6904
Path of the Eclipse - Chelsea Quinn Yarbro 6905
Tempting Fate - Chelsea Quinn Yarbro 6906

Tsepesh, Arkady
*Children of the Vampire: The Diaries of the Family
    Dracul* - Jeanne Kalogridis 3326

Tsepesh, Prince Vlad
*Children of the Vampire: The Diaries of the Family
    Dracul* - Jeanne Kalogridis 3326
*Covenant with the Vampire: The Diaries of the Family
    Dracul* - Jeanne Kalogridis 3327
*Lord of the Vampires: The Diaries of the Family
    Dracul* - Jeanne Kalogridis 3328

York, Joshua
Fevre Dream - George R.R. Martin 4131

VAMPIRE HUNTER

Van Helsing, Abraham
*Children of the Vampire: The Diaries of the Family
    Dracul* - Jeanne Kalogridis 3326
*Lord of the Vampires: The Diaries of the Family
    Dracul* - Jeanne Kalogridis 3328

VETERAN

Abbot, Jim
The Marrying Kind - Jessica Stirling 6046

Allson, Colonel
The Hard to Catch Mercy - William Baldwin 281

Aramis
Twenty Years After - Alexandre Dumas 1783

Archer, Owen
The King's Bishop - Candace M. Robb 5365
The Nun's Tale - Candace M. Robb 5367

Armbrecht, Kurt
Hitler Has Won - Frederic Mullally 4511

Ashleigh, Gilliard
A Question of Honour - Emma Drummond 1726

Ashwood, Harry
Gentlemen, Hush! - Jere Hungerford
    Wheelwright 6668

Athos
Twenty Years After - Alexandre Dumas 1783

Becker, Friedrich
Karl and Rosa - Alfred Doblin 1653
A People Betrayed - Alfred Doblin 1654

Bellnap, Samuel
Troubled Spring - John Brick 678

Benteen, Dick
Wagons to Tucson - Ed Newsom 4604

Blake, John
Three Fields to Cross - Francis Tysen Nutt 4651

Blakeslee, E. Rucker
Cold Sassy Tree - Olive Ann Burns 797

Bodine, Captain
Shanghai Tango: A Novel of China - William
    Overgard 4769

Bourke, Austin
Kansas Blue - Dylan Harson 2758

Buckstone, Bion B.
The Buckstones - Paul I. Wellman 6615

Burke, Myles
The Killing Frost - Thomas Hayden 2799

Burnie, Jim
A Journey to Matecumbe - Robert Lewis
    Taylor 6188

Cain, Macaulay
Fair is the Rose - Meagan MacKinney 3997

Caldwell, Ward
On a Lonesome Porch - Ovid Williams Pierce 4997

Cantrell, Edward
Gone to Texas - John Williams Thomason 6247

Carey, Robert
Rebel Heiress - Robert Neill 4573

Carpenter, Brett
The Laughing Stranger - Vina Delmar 1601

Censorinus
Poseidon's Gold - Lindsey Davis 1530

Chance, Sam
Sam Chance - Benjamin Capps 888

Channing, Dickson
Mirage - Helen Topping Miller 4390

Coventry
Fallen Skies - Philippa Gregory 2581

Crabb, Joe
To the Ends of the Earth - Michael Talbot 6155

Craddock, Paul
A Horseman Riding By - R.F. Delderfield 1588

Cresap, Bill
Mignon - James M. Cain 845

Crown, Joseph
Homeland - John Jakes 3148

Currain, Travis
The Unconquered - Ben Ames Williams 6768

Daly, Barney
The Ways of Women - Elaine Crowley 1436

Danford, Owen
Dark Thicket - Elmer Kelton 3402

Darcy, Cavin
And Tell of Time - Laura Krey 3554

Devlin, Gavin
The Rising of the Moon - Peter Berresford Ellis 1926

Devlin, John-Joe
The Rising of the Moon - Peter Berresford Ellis 1926

Dodge, Anson
The Beloved Invader - Eugenia Price 5179

Donegan, Seamus
Black Sun - Terry C. Johnston 3242

Doubleday, Abner
Joy in Mudville - Gordon McAlpine 4216

Dunbar, Munro
They Had a Glory - Davenport Steward 6018

Edge, Zachary
Spangle - Gary Jennings 3196

Edwards, Ballard
A Question of Honour - Clifford Dowdey 1707

Ellis, Peter
A Princess in Berlin - Arthur R.G. Solmssen 5939

Fairbrother, Tolley
The Fairbrothers - Clark McMeekin 4291

Fleming, Tom
Give Me the Daggers - Catherine Gavin 2321

Flynn, Jonathan
Sudden Country - Loren D. Estleman 1979

Folland, Robert
The Lords of Loone - John James 3159

Forge, Robert
The Running Iron - Rachel Ann Fish 2097

Forrest, Nathan Bedford
Supper at the Maxwell House - Alfred Leland
    Crabb 1407

Fournois, Laird
The Vixens - Frank Yerby 6929

Franklin, John
The Hammer of God - Alan Scholefield 5655

Gauntry, Crawford
The House in Ruins - Robert S. Weekley 6595

Giuliani, Alessandro
A Soldier of the Great War - Mark Helprin 2823

Grail, Edmund
Death at the French Creek - Raymond C. Borel 580

Grobart, Jay
The Man Who Loved Cat Dancing - Marilyn
    Durham 1817

Harris, Stacey
Gentlemen, Hush! - Jere Hungerford
    Wheelwright 6668

Harte, Jack
The Ways of Women - Elaine Crowley 1436

Hascott, Warren
The Regulators - William Degenhard 1580

Haversham, Reed
The Haversham Legacy - Daoma Winston 6827

Hawley, Theron
Morning Time - Charles Kendall O'Neill 4743

Hazard, George
Heaven and Hell - John Jakes 3147

Holt, Toby
Washington! - Dana Fuller Ross 5491

Hook, Jonah
Cry of the Hawk - Terry C. Johnston 3248
Dream Catcher - Terry C. Johnston 3251
Winter Rain - Terry C. Johnston 3262

Hunter, James
Colorado Ambush - Jess McCriede 4230

Jackson, Travis
Cold War - Robert Vaughan 6446
The Iron Curtain - Robert Vaughan 6447

Josselyn, Daniel
Hearts and Bones - Margaret Lawrence 3685

Keith, Christoph
A Princess in Berlin - Arthur R.G. Solmssen 5939

Kensal, Aidan
Kentucky Pride - Gene Markey 4087

Kensal, Jared
That Far Paradise - Gene Markey 4088

Kilbourne, Dan
West of Appomattox - Harley Duncan 1785

Layne, Jeff
The Far Canyon - Elmer Kelton 3404
Slaughter - Elmer Kelton 3407

Ledbetter, Brian
The Coming of Rain - Richard Marius 4084

Lilly, Max Cary de
Vardy - John Harris 2721

Linwood, Martin
Some Far Elusive Dawn - Emma Drummond 1727

Longstreet, James
1901 - Robert Conroy 1258
The Unconquered - Ben Ames Williams 6768

Macko
The Teutonic Knights - Henryk Sienkiewicz 5849

Malone, Tim
The Far Down - Elizabeth Corbett 1321

Markland, Jack
After the Glory - Helen Topping Miller 4383

Markland, William
After the Glory - Helen Topping Miller 4383

Marsden, Willie
Oldest Living Confederate Widow Tells All - Allan
    Gurganus 2621

McCready, Spanish
Candle of the Wicked - Manly Wade Wellman 6612

McLaughlin, Willy
The Able McLaughlins - Margaret Wilson 6812

McQueen, John
Don Juan McQueen - Eugenia Price 5181

North, Rob
Red Cloud's Revenge - Terry C. Johnston 3255

Orton, Sir Giles
Rebel Heiress - Robert Neill 4573

Paulus
A Wayside Tavern - Norah Lofts 3862

Poldark, Captain Ross
The Renegade: A Novel of Cornwall, 1783-1787 -
    Winston Graham 2529

Porthos
Twenty Years After - Alexandre Dumas 1783

Preele, David
Morgan's Woman - Iris Gower 2500

Preston, Wayne
Fire on the Wind - David Garth 2304

Proops, Elias
Chad Hanna - Walter D. Edmonds 1873

Roche, Louis
A Question of Honour - Clifford Dowdey 1707

Sharp, Jeff
Seward's Folly - Edison Marshall 4111

Shays, Daniel
The Regulators - William Degenhard 1580

Smith, Tennessee
Tennessee Smith - James E. Hitt 2957

Smith, Wesley
Diamond Six - William Fielding Smith 5932

Stapleton, Jonathan
The Spoils of War - Thomas Fleming 2131

Starr, Ellery
Roll, Shenandoah - Bruce Lancaster 3644

Stewart, Tom
Gentlemen, Hush! - Jere Hungerford
    Wheelwright 6668

Swann, Adam
Give Us This Day - R.F. Delderfield 1586

Travis, David
Spanish Gold - Kevin D. Randle 5252

Tucker, Birch
A Thousand Shall Fall - Bodie Thoene 6227

Tyrone, David
Tyrone of Kentucky - Clark McMeekin 4294

Von Bock, Timotheus
The Czar's Madman - Jaan Kross 3560

Wade, Duncan
Rebellion Road - Helen Topping Miller 4392

Warden, Denis
Beyond Surrender - Marian Sims 5860

Wheeler
The Terrible Teague Bunch - Gary Jennings 3197

Wheeler, Joe
1901 - Robert Conroy 1258

Winslow, Thomas
The Crossed Sabres - Gilbert Morris 4458

Winslow, Zack
The Wounded Yankee - Gilbert Morris 4475

Winter, Stephen
Fallen Skies - Philippa Gregory 2581

Woodbridge, Jonathan
The Bounty Lands - William Donohue Ellis 1927

VETERINARIAN

Rose, Olan
The War Train: A Novel of 1916 - Brown
    Meggs 4324

VILLAIN

Randolph, Miles
Dream Time - Parris Afton Bonds 570

WAGONMASTER

Banner, Simon
Northwest Passage - David Thompson 6258

Bourke, Austin
Kansas Blue - Dylan Harson 2758

Brentwood, Sam
Independence! - Dana Fuller Ross 5476

WAITER/WAITRESS

Barclay, Frances
Niagara - Robert Lewis Taylor 6189

Biggs, Hazel
The Harvey Girls - Samuel Hopkins Adams 31

McLeod, Hannah
A Heritage of Shadows - Madeleine Brent 660

Rapalje, Deborah
The Harvey Girls - Samuel Hopkins Adams 31

Seelye, Alma "Cricket"
The Harvey Girls - Samuel Hopkins Adams 31

WANDERER

Aeneas
Dido, Queen of Hearts - Gertrude Atherton 223

Aesop
The Fabulist - John Vornholt 6512

Alice
The Prince and the Pilgrim - Mary Stewart 6032

Applegate, Luke
The Limner - Paul Darcy Boles 564

Balor
Wolves of the Dawn - William Sarabande 5604

Baxter, Thad
The Odyssey of Thaddeus Baxter - Robert P.
    Lund 3926

ben Kition, Dara
Dara, the Cypriot - Louis Paul 4842

Bleddyn, Morgan
The High Missouri - Winfred Blevins 545

Boone, Ray
The Gallows Land - Bill Pronzini 5201

Campbell, Dylan
The High Missouri - Winfred Blevins 545

Delahanty, Mick
O'Houlihan's Jest - Rohan O'Grady 4702

Drew, Jonathan
Strange Adventure of Jonathan Drew - Christopher
    Ward 6562
Yankee Rover - Christopher Ward 6563

Eshkal
The Miracle Hater - Shulamith Hareven 2704

Iri
The Promised Land - Peter Danielson 1471

King, Nathaniel
King of the Mountain - David Thompson 6255

Kwani
She Who Remembers - Linda Lay Shuler   5838

Liklik
The Echoing Cliffs - Hjalmar P. Thesen   6219

Menenhetet
Ancient Evenings - Norman Mailer   4035

Mina
For Every Sin - Aharon Appelfeld   175

Odysseus
The Voyage Home - Ernst Schnabel   5644

Ormandy, Blaize
So Free We Seem - Helen Todd   6286

Patterson, Gaddy
Treasures on Earth - Jessica Stirling   6049

Philemon
The Island of the Innocent: A Novel of Greek and Jew in the Time of the Maccabees - Vardis Fisher   2108

Pike, Noah
Heart of the Country - Greg Matthews   4190

Pilgermann
Pilgermann - Russell Hoban   2960

Rao, Balbeer
The Blood Seed - Andrew Ward   6561

Sanderlin, Claiborne
Solitudes - R.G. Vliet   6507

Strauss, Rudi
To the Land of the Cattails - Aharon Appelfeld   179

Strauss, Toni
To the Land of the Cattails - Aharon Appelfeld   179

Theo
For Every Sin - Aharon Appelfeld   175

Ulenspiegel, Tyl
The Legend of Tyl Ulenspiegel - Charles Theodore Henri De Coster   1558

Vogel
The Last Valley - J.B. Pick   4992

Wandering Jew
A Night with Casanova - Wolf Mankowitz   4060

Warakan
Face of the Rising Sun - William Sarabande   5598

WARD

Alba
Black Body - H.C. Turk   6361

Beethoven, Karl
Nephew to the Emperor: A Novel Based on the Life of Beethoven - Jacques Brenner   658

Catalina
Envoy From Elizabeth - Pamela Bennetts   451

Clare, Edward
Edward, Edward - Lolah Burford   772

Clervaux, Nicole de
Palaces of Desire - Kate Alexander   81

De Jeneau, Antoine
The Sugar Pavilion - Rosalind Laker   3600

Deirdre
Deirdre - James Stephens   5996

Doone, Lorna
Lorna Doone - R.D. Blackmore   528

Falconeri, Tancredi
The Leopard - Giuseppe di Lampedusa   3634

Grafton, Persephone
A London Season - Anthea Bell   420

Gurney, Hester
The Railway King - Margaret Mayhew   4207

Halay, Felicite-Anne
High Towers - Thomas B. Costain   1366

Hanard, Audrey
Audrey - Mary Johnston   3229

Ingham, Jane
The Nunnery - Dorothy Charques   1001

Ione
The Last Days of Pompeii - Edward Bulwer-Lytton   768

Lorimer, Alexa
Alexa - Anne Melville   4330

Lovell, Tina
The Old Maid - Edith Wharton   6652

Mallen, Barbara
The Mallen Girl - Catherine Cookson   1280

Medbeth
The Ravishers - Elizabeth Richards   5318

Mer, Katherine de
Witness to Treason - Millie J. Ragosta   5244

Newberry, Catherine
The Heart Is a Traitor - Margaret Abbey   4

Newcombe, Honoria
Sweet's Folly - Fiona Hill   2926

Sal
Fitzempress' Law - Diana Norman   4644

Shelton, Dick
The Black Arrow - Robert Louis Stevenson   6008

Sinclair, Fiona
The Miser of Mayfair - Marion Chesney   1038

Steane, Cherry
Charity Girl - Georgette Heyer   2879

Surriage, Agnes
Be My Love - Harriet Hinsdale   2955

Taverner, Judith
Regency Buck - Georgette Heyer   2898

Taverner, Sir Peregrine
Regency Buck - Georgette Heyer   2898

Trevenna, Morag
The Queen's Ward - Hebe Elsna   1933

vander Poele, Claes
Niccolo Rising - Dorothy Dunnett   1803

Vlassevna, Laisha
Tempting Fate - Chelsea Quinn Yarbro   6906

Voyle, Simon
Familiar Acts - June Barraclough   345

WARLORD

Geraint
The Man on the White Horse - Warwick Deeping   1577

Oda Nobunaga
Taiko - Eiji Yoshikawa   6936

Shan-Teh Tang
The Warlord - Malcolm Bosse   589

T'en Chih-Yu
Path of the Eclipse - Chelsea Quinn Yarbro   6905

Tokugama Ieyasu
Taiko - Eiji Yoshikawa   6936

Toranaga, Lord Yoshi
Shogun - James Clavell   1101

Yoshi
Gai-Jin: A Novel of Japan - James Clavell   1100

WARRIOR

Abh Allah
The Lord of the Last Days: Visions of the Year 1000 - Homero Aridjis   188

Abimelech
Prophets and Warriors - Peter Danielson   1473

Achates
Paris of Troy - George Baker   273

Achilles
The Greek Generals Talk: Memoirs of the Trojan War - Phillip Parotti   4817
The Invaders - Peter Danielson   1469
Troy - Richard Matturro   4194
Whom the Gods Would Destroy - Richard Powell   5148

Aeneas
Whom the Gods Would Destroy - Richard Powell   5148

Alaric I
The Sinner of Saint Ambrose - Robert Raynolds   5275

Andru
Taras Bulba - Nikolai V. Gogol   2451

Arik-Buka
Sons of the Steppe: The Story of How the Conqueror Genghis Khan Was Overcome - Hans Baumann   380

Ariston
Goat Song: A Novel of Ancient Greece - Frank Yerby   6920

Arthur
The Crimson Chalice - Victor Canning   882
The Duke of War - Walter O'Meara   4734
The Kingmaking - Helen Hollick   3000

Artos the Bear
The Great Captains - Henry Treece   6329
Sword at Sunset - Rosemary Sutcliff   6125

Atarho
Father of Waters - Donald Clayton Porter   5118

Atawulf
Heaven's Only Daughter - Kathleen Robinson   5406

Atretes
As Sure as the Dawn - Francine Rivers   5352

Auriane
The Light Bearer - Donna Gillespie   2419

Bardiya
The Year of the Horsetails - R.F. Tapsell   6162

Batu Khan
Poland - James A. Michener   4373

Bear Paws
Bride of the Morning Star - Don Coldsmith   1170

Beowulf
The Coming of the King - Nikolai Tolstoy   6296
The Green Man - Henry Treece   6330
The Tower of Beowulf - Parke Godwin   2450

Black Skull
People of the Lakes - W. Michael Gear   2336

Blood Hawk
Eye of the Hawk - David William Ross   5498

Brand
The Hammer and the Cross - Harry Harrison   2736

Brunahild
The Wolf and the Raven - Diana L. Paxson   4848

Bulba, Taras
Taras Bulba - Nikolai V. Gogol   2451

Canis
Canis the Warrior - James Sinclair   5864
Warrior Queen - James Sinclair   5865

Chaske
The Shining Trail - Iola Fuller 2254

Cochise
Geronimo - Bill Dugan 1758

Conn
Lady of Conquest - Teresa Medeiros 4322

Connal
Fire Queen - Deborah Grabien 2503

Cormac
Finn Mac Cool - Morgan Llywelyn 3818

Coyote
The Elk-Dog Heritage - Don Coldsmith 1174
Trail of the Spanish Bit - Don Coldsmith 1193

Crazy Horse
Buffalo Woman - Dorothy M. Johnson 3223
Crazy Horse - Bill Dugan 1757
Creek Mary's Blood - Dee Brown 712
A Good Day to Die - Del Barton 368
Kelly Blue - Peter Bowen 601
No Survivors - Will Henry 2846
Reap the Whirlwind - Terry C. Johnston 3254
*A Road We Do Not Know: A Novel of Custer at the
Little Bighorn* - Frederick J. Chiaventone 1057
Sitting Bull - Bill Dugan 1760
Stone Song: A Novel of the Life of Crazy Horse -
Winfred Blevins 548
Thunder in the Dawn - Earl Murray 4532
The Winter War - William Wister Haines 2640

Crow Feather
The Far Canyon - Elmer Kelton 3404
Slaughter - Elmer Kelton 3407

Cuchulain
Red Branch - Morgan Llywelyn 3824

Cusi Huaman
The Incas - Daniel Peters 4945

Dietric
The Death of Attila - Cecelia Holland 2986

Duatha
Red Queen, White Queen - Henry Treece 6332

Dull Knife
The Last Warpath - Will Henry 2844

Eagle
Man of the Shadows - Don Coldsmith 1178

Eagle Woman
Daughter of the Eagle - Don Coldsmith 1173

Edohi
The Dark Way - Robert J. Conley 1241
The Way of the Priests - Robert J. Conley 1253
The White Path - Robert J. Conley 1254

Edred
I Am England - Patricia Wright 6881

El-Hadj Omar
The Children of Segu - Maryse Conde 1232

Eri
Departed Glory - Peter Danielson 1466

Eric
The Iron Crown - Clare Barroll 354

Eric of Dubhlain
The Viking's Woman - Heather Graham 2520

Esarhaddon
The Assyrian - Nicholas Guild 2610

Filbyter, Folke
The Trees of the Folkungs - Verner Von
Heidenstam 2817

Flaminius, Marcus
The Scarlet Beast - Francis Gerard 2357

Flat Nose
Chiricahua - Will Henry 2839

Flat Warclub
The Manly-Hearted Woman - Frederick F.
Manfred 4057

Fly Catcher
People of the River - W. Michael Gear 2338

Gall
*A Road We Do Not Know: A Novel of Custer at the
Little Bighorn* - Frederick J. Chiaventone 1057

Gaspar
How Far to Bethlehem? - Norah Lofts 3846

Genghis Khan
*The Earth Is the Lord's: A Tale of the Rise of Genghis
Khan* - Taylor Caldwell 855
Poland - James A. Michener 4373
*Sons of the Steppe: The Story of How the Conqueror
Genghis Khan Was Overcome* - Hans
Baumann 380

Geronimo
Chiricahua - Will Henry 2839
City of Widows - Loren D. Estleman 1969
Paint the Wind - Cathy Cash Spellman 5960

Ghonkaba
Ambush - Donald Clayton Porter 5113
War Cry - Donald Clayton Porter 5132

Golem
The Sword of the Golem - Abraham Rothberg 5509

Goyah
The Pecos River - Fred Bean 399

Gray Fox
Tomahawk - Donald Clayton Porter 5129

Grey Horse Running
The Wolf and the Buffalo - Elmer Kelton 3408

Grey Wolf
A Good Day to Die - Del Barton 368

Guthorn
The Marsh King - C. Walter Hodges 2975

Hakon
Beguiled - Alice Borchardt 577

Hanshiro, Tosano
The Tokaido Road: A Novel of Feudal Japan - Lucia
St. Clair Robson 5417

Hasekura, Rokuemon
The Samurai - Shusaku Endo 1941

Hawk, John
The Overmountain Men - Cameron Judd 3315

Hawk's Shadow
This Land Is Mine - Frances Casey Kerns 3470

Hector
The Trojan Generals Talk: Memoirs of the Greek War
- Phillip Parotti 4818
Troy - Richard Matturro 4194
Whom the Gods Would Destroy - Richard
Powell 5148

Heraldsson, Rorik
Lord of Hawkfell Island - Catherine Coulter 1376

Herger
Eaters of the Dead - Michael Crichton 1425

Heyets
From Where the Sun Now Stands - Will Henry 2841

Hiram
The Trojan - Noel B. Gerson 2386

Huemac
The Luck of Huemac: A Novel about the Aztecs -
Daniel Peters 4946

Hunter of the Wolf
Comanche Moon - Catherine Anderson 137

Ichiro, Sano
Bundori - Laura Joh Rowland 5519

Shin Ju - Laura Joh Rowland 5520

Ironfist, Wulf
To Love Again - Bertrice Small 5913

Ivar
The Hammer and the Cross - Harry Harrison 2736

Ixcawatzin
The Heart of Jade - Salvador de Madariaga 4024

Ja-Gonh
Tomahawk - Donald Clayton Porter 5129
War Cry - Donald Clayton Porter 5132

Jo-Gonh
Renno - Donald Clayton Porter 5123

Joan of Arc
The Burnished Blade - Lawrence Schoonover 5661
Epitaph for Three Women - Jean Plaidy 5012
In a Dark Wood Wandering - Hella S. Haasse 2631
Personal Recollections of Joan of Arc - Mark
Twain 6372
The Queen's Secret - Jean Plaidy 5053
The Serpent Amongst the Lilies - P.C. Doherty 1678
The Voice and the Light - Edwin Fadiman 1995

Jocita
War Eagles - Frank Burleson 788

Joshua
The Sea Peoples - Peter Danielson 1474

Kazhak
The Horse Goddess - Morgan Llywelyn 3820

Keokotah
Jubal Sackett - Louis L'Amour 3620

Kicking Bird
Dances with Wolves - Michael Blake 537

Kinich Kakmoo
Tikal: A Novel about the Maya - Daniel Peters 4947

Krona
Sarum: The Novel of England - Edward
Rutherfurd 5536

Launcelot
The Duke of War - Walter O'Meara 4734

Little Hawk
War Clouds - Donald Clayton Porter 5131

Long Walker
Daughter of the Eagle - Don Coldsmith 1173

Ludona
Ambush - Donald Clayton Porter 5113

Lutero
The Pride of Hannah Wade - Janet Dailey 1455

Mac Cool, Finn
Finn Mac Cool - Morgan Llywelyn 3818

MacRomain, Lugh
The Crow Goddess - Patricia Finney 2094
A Shadow of Gulls - Patricia Finney 2096

MacSualtim, Cuchulain
The Crow Goddess - Patricia Finney 2094
A Shadow of Gulls - Patricia Finney 2096

Mar
Daughter of the Red Deer - Joan Wolf 6838

Massai
Broncho Apache - Paul I. Wellman 6614

McMahon, Angus
The Gentle Conqueror - Mary Ellen Gronau 2597

McMahon, Dorcas
Passionate Warriors - Mary Ellen Gronau 2598

McNeil, Neil
Passionate Warriors - Mary Ellen Gronau 2598

Meromic
The Conquered - Naomi Mitchison 4418

Mgobozi
Great Elephant - Alan Scholefield 5654

Michael
The Curse of Jezebel: A Novel of the Biblical Queen of Evil - Frank G. Slaughter 5884

Minamoto Yoshitshune
The Sword of Hachiman - Lynn Guest 2608

Miyamoto Musashi
Musashi: An Epic Novel of the Samurai Era - Eiji Yoshikawa 6935

Musselwhite
People of the Lightning - W. Michael Gear 2337

Nakoa
The Second Kiss - Gayle Rogers 5432

Night Wind
Night Wind's Woman - Shirl Henke 2825

No Name
Conquering Horse - Frederick F. Manfred 4055

Nyasanu
The Dahomean - Frank Yerby 6911

Odysseus
Troy - Richard Matturro 4194
Whom the Gods Would Destroy - Richard Powell 5148

O'Monoghan, Gelina
Lady of Conquest - Teresa Medeiros 4322

Otap
Taras Bulba - Nikolai V. Gogol 2451

Pa-nayo-tishn
Chiricahua - Will Henry 2839

Quasia
The Buffalo Soldiers - John Prebble 5165

Rafe
The Fourteenth of October - Bryher 742

Rattlesnake
Choctaw - Donald Clayton Porter 5116

Raven Hunter
People of the Wolf - W. Michael Gear 2341

Red Cloud
Dodging Red Cloud - Richard S. Wheeler 6657

Red Hawk
Thunder in the East - Mike Roarke 5362

Red Orm
The Long Ships - Frans Gunnar Bengtsson 442

Red Wolf
Sioux Splendor - Rosanne Bittner 515

Renno
Choctaw - Donald Clayton Porter 5116
The Renegade - Donald Clayton Porter 5122
The Sachem - Donald Clayton Porter 5124
Seminole - Donald Clayton Porter 5126
War Chief - Donald Clayton Porter 5130
White Indian - Donald Clayton Porter 5134

Ronin
The Ronin - William Dale Jennings 3212

St. Castine, Joseph de
The Golden Wildcat - Margaret Widdemer 6735

Saladin
Jerusalem - Cecelia Holland 2990

Santana, Vitorio
The Gila River - Gary McCarthy 4223

Sheck
Dance of the Tiger: A Novel of the Ice Age - Bjorn Kurten 3566

Shoz-Dijiji
Apache Devil - Edgar Rice Burroughs 806

Sibindi
The Tune That They Play - William Clive 1120

Siegfried
The Twelve Pictures - Edith Simon 5857

Sigfrid
The Wolf and the Raven - Diana L. Paxson 4848

Sigifrith
Rhinegold - Stephan Grundy 2607

Sitting Bear
Blood Fury - David Thompson 6252

Sosepsis
Indian Brother - Hubert Coryell 1354

Stavan
The Year the Horses Came - Mary Mackey 3993

Sun Runner
Song of the Cheyenne - Jory Sherman 5822

Sunu
The Shining King - Peter Danielson 1476
Triumph of the Lion - Peter Danielson 1478

Tagart
The Flint Lord - Richard Herley 2857
The Stone Arrow - Richard Herley 2858

Tall Bull
Bride of the Morning Star - Don Coldsmith 1170

Talus
Prophets and Warriors - Peter Danielson 1473

Tecante
Lakota - G. Clifton Wisler 6833

Tecolote
Eagles of Destiny - Jory Sherman 5817

Temujin
Ruler of the Sky: A Novel of Genghis Khan - Pamela Sargent 5606

Thorsten
The Winter Servant - M.H. Davis 1537

Three Owls
Pale Star - Don Coldsmith 1181

Thunzi
Wizards' Country - Daphne Rooke 5438

Tiger
Dance of the Tiger: A Novel of the Ice Age - Bjorn Kurten 3566

Titokowaru
Monday's Warriors - Maurice Shadbolt 5767

Toke
The Long Ships - Frans Gunnar Bengtsson 442

Tombul
Isle of Glory - Jane Oliver 4723

Tros
The Trojan - Noel B. Gerson 2386

Turms, Lars
The Etruscan - Mika Waltari 6553

Turning Hawk
Dance Back the Buffalo - Milton Lott 3899

Two Eagles
For Love of Two Eagles - Barbara Riefe 5328
Mohawk Woman - Barbara Riefe 5329
The Woman Who Fell From the Sky - Barbara Riefe 5330

Two Robes
Song of Wovoka - Earl Murray 4531

Two Sleep
Dream Catcher - Terry C. Johnston 3251

Ulf
The Iron Crown - Clare Barroll 354

Ulysses
Scandal in Troy - Eva Hemmer Hansen 2679

U'nkomo
Bush War! - William Moore 4447

Ute Killer
A Woman of the People - Benjamin Capps 893

Varrus, Caius Publius
The Singing Sword - Jack Whyte 6725

Vercingetorix
Druids - Morgan Llywelyn 3817

Waguli
Mountain Windsong - Robert J. Conley 1246

Wakwa Manunnappu
The Mists of Manittoo - Lois Swann 6135
Torn Covenants - Lois Swann 6136

White Bird
The Fleet Rabble: A Novel of the Nez Perce War - Frank Borden Hanes 2675

Wolf
The Mammoth Stone - Margaret Allan 90

Wulf
The Fourteenth of October - Bryher 742

Young Hunter
Dawn Land - Joseph Bruchac III 734

WIDOW(ER)

Adair, Abigail
The Wings of Morning - Karen Harper 2714

Allington, Ruth
Ask Me No Questions - Patricia Veryan 6459

Amesley, Nellanor
Chase the Heart - Maggie Osborne 4760

Anderson, Jane
In a Dark Garden - Frank G. Slaughter 5891

Andrews, Murray
City of the Flags - Clark McMeekin 4290

Asher, Faith Mary
Faith and Honor - Robin Maderich 4025

Aspasia
The Eagle's Daughter - Judith Tarr 6165

Avery, Charity
Monmouth - Charles Bracelen Flood 2144

Baker, Annie Saunders
Sherman's March - Cynthia Bass 373

Banks, Bethel
Muddy Banks - Ruby C. Tolliver 6291

Bishop, Bridget
Gallows Hill - Frances Winwar 6831

Blackwood, Charles
The Folly - Marion Chesney 1031

Blackwood, Pryor Deyhle
Riding Shotgun - Rita Mae Brown 729

Blenkinsop, Sue Ellen
Wind of Change at Castle Rising - Fanny Cradock 1412

Boone, Ray
The Gallows Land - Bill Pronzini 5201

Bowden, Kate
Mountain Man - Vardis Fisher 2110

Brandon, Margaretta
The Merrymaid - Mollie Hardwick 2696

Bransom, Penelope
The Sandalwood Fan - Diana Brown 720

Budge, Mary
Sir Philip's Folly - Marion Chesney 1051

Budley, Eliza
Mrs. Budley Falls From Grace - Marion Chesney 1042

Carlow, Fanny
Bath Tangle - Georgette Heyer   2875

Carr, Rosie
The Green Leaves of Summer - Ted Willis   6793

Carter, Lady Harriet
The Stranger From the Sea - Winston Graham   2530

Cauder, Janie
The Wide House - Taylor Caldwell   864

Chalmers, Stephanie
Echoes From the Past - Marjorie McEvoy   4268

Champlittle, Sophie de
The Brotherhood of the Red Poppy - Henri
   Troyat   6353

Chandler, Laura
While the Music Plays - Diane Austell   242

Charetty, Marian de
Niccolo Rising - Dorothy Dunnett   1803
The Spring of the Ram - Dorothy Dunnett   1809

Childe, Barbara
An Infamous Army - Georgette Heyer   2892

Clarke, Mary
Forget the Glory - Emma Drummond   1725

Clemence of Hungary
The Royal Succession - Maurice Druon   1735

Clively-Murdoch, Clare
Clively Close: Dead as Dead Can Be - Ann
   Crowleigh   1434

Craig, Kate
River of Sky - Karen Harper   2713

Craven, Taylor
The Woman of Catawba - Hilda Stahl   5978

Croston, Kate
Here Comes a Candle - Jane Aiken Hodge   2964

Cullen, Rose Mary O'Driscoll
Grandmother and the Priests - Taylor Caldwell   857

d'Agrigente, Emma
1876: A Novel - Gore Vidal   6484

Dallet, Susanna
The Serpent Garden - Judith Merkle Riley   5336

Daventry, Julia
Caroline and Julia - Clare Darcy   1484

Davis, Jefferson
The Proud Way - Shirley Seifert   5731

De Salis, Edward
Cashelmara - Susan Howatch   3058

Dean, Rachel
Passage Home - Alison McLeay   4286

Devane, Barbara
Now Face to Face - Karleen Koen   3530

Di Castelloni, Lucy
Claudine's Daughter - Rosalind Laker   3594

Dobson, Julia Turner
The Rainbow Promise - Lisa Gregory   2580

Dorman, Nell
The Wind Brings Up the Rain - Eric Malpass   4051

Drummond, Amelia
Bertie and the Seven Bodies - Peter Lovesey   3908

Drummond, Sir Daniel
Reckless Angel - Jane Feather   2056

Durris, Tanya
Castle of Foxes - Alanna Knight   3516

Elliott, Caroline
The Floral Companion - Anthea Bell   419

Fairbrother, Jenny
The Fairbrothers - Clark McMeekin   4291

Falkland, Barbara
Whom the Gods Love - Kate Ross   5502

Flael, Lissa de
Masques of Gold - Roberta Gellis   2352

Fleming, Jocelyn
Savage Thunder - Johanna Lindsey   3795

Fowler, Savanna
Savanna - Janice Holt Giles   2416

Fraser, Anne Couper
Beauty From Ashes - Eugenia Price   5177

Gilchrist, Jennie
The World of Jennie G. - Elisabeth Ogilvie   4696

Graham, Caroline Agnes
Bertie and the Tinman - Peter Lovesey   3909

Gray, Ellen
On a Lonesome Porch - Ovid Williams Pierce   4997

Gray, Lucy
On a Lonesome Porch - Ovid Williams Pierce   4997

Hartburg, Aurora
A Castle in Bavaria - Prince Thibaut d'Orleans   1693

Henley, Susan
Logic of the Heart - Patricia Veryan   6466

Heron, Maeve
This Willing Passion - Patricia Cloud   1132

Heulwen
The Running Vixen - Elizabeth Chadwick   968

Holcomb, Amelia
Too Long at the Dance - Mike Blakely   539

Howarth, Charlotte
An Imperfect Joy - Jean Stubbs   6097

Humphries, Claudia
Independence! - Dana Fuller Ross   5476

Irvine, Isabella
Ravenburn - Laura Black   522

Isabella of France
The Lily and the Lion - Maurice Druon   1733

Jebeau, Arthur
My Beloved Son - Catherine Cookson   1285

Jebeau, Ellen
My Beloved Son - Catherine Cookson   1285

Jones, Elizabeth
The Stars of the South - Julian Green   2568

Jordan, Betsy
Mrs. Betsy, or Widowed and Wed - Francis
   Marton   4141

Jordan, Felicia
The Brooks Legend - William Donohue Ellis   1928

Jourdain, Nicholas
Song of the Bayou - Elinor Lynley   3936

Judith
Judith - Stella Wilchek   6748

Karlin, Anna
Quiet Lady - Norman Collins   1216

Kincross, Colin
The Heiress Bride - Catherine Coulter   1375

Kriemhild
The Twelve Pictures - Edith Simon   5857

Kukutux
Brother Wind - Sue Harrison   2748

Lanyon, Jessica
To the End of Her Days - Malcolm Macdonald   3975

Lathbury, Sara
Prophecies - Helena Soister   5937

Lattimer, Kate
The Lattimer Legend - Ann Hebson   2813

Lindsay, Gloria
The Magic Ship - Sandra Paretti   4791

Linton, Emma
The Last Summer of Innocence - Linda Sole   5938

Lowell, Adam
Blood and Sable - Carol J. Kane   3350

MacKay, Kieran
One Wore Blue - Heather Graham   2517

MacKinder, Mary Beth
Oregon Bride - Rosanne Bittner   514

MacNamara, Paul
Where the Willows Weep - Patricia Shaw   5781

Madselin
Madselin - Norah Lofts   3853

Main, Madelaine
Heaven and Hell - John Jakes   3147

Margaret of Ashbury
In Pursuit of the Green Lion - Judith Merkle
   Riley   5334

La Marquesa
Sharpe's Honour - Bernard Cornwell   1344

Marsden, Lucy
Oldest Living Confederate Widow Tells All - Allan
   Gurganus   2621

Marsham, Beatrice
Beatrice Goes to Brighton - Marion Chesney   1019

Marston, Yates
The Woman of Catawba - Hilda Stahl   5978

Marwick, Bess
Prophecies - Helena Soister   5937

Mary of Guise
The Game of Kings - Dorothy Dunnett   1801
Queen's Play - Dorothy Dunnett   1805

Masters, Joline
Montana Woman - Rosanne Bittner   513

Mathewson, Ann
Lord of the Isles - Donald Barr Chidsey   1063

McClure, Hardee
Trumpet in the Sky - Helen Topping Miller   4397

McEverside, Stella
Tennessee Smith - James E. Hitt   2957

McKenzie, Jarrett
Runaway - Heather Graham   2519

Middleton, Nina
The Mighty and Their Fall - Ivy Compton-
   Burnett   1230

Millican, Maria
The Black Velvet Gown - Catherine Cookson   1274

Molloy, Charles
Passage West - Dallas Miller   4382

Mortimer, Amelia
Evil Mark - Graham Miles   4377

Mulkerin, Eileen
The Californios - Louis L'Amour   3618

Nanconou, Aurora
The Grandissimes - George W. Cable   842

Norvall, Annie
The Buffalo Soldiers - John Prebble   5165

O'Connell, Maura Dooley
Maura's Dream - Joel Gross   2602

O'Connor, Roseen
Tigerlilies - Judith Glover   2439

Orr, Susan
Wind Like a Bugle - Leonard Nathan   3722

Ostneige, Gudrun
Tempting Fate - Chelsea Quinn Yarbro   6906

Parrish, Rebecca
The Wagered Widow - Patricia Veryan 6481

Payne, Isobel
Jane and the Unpleasantness at Scargrave Manor - Stephanie Barron 356

Peony
The Red Peony - Yutang Lin 3783

Perle, Judith
The Rose Rent - Ellis Peters 4970

Perry, Sarah
Too Long a Stranger - Janette Oke 4710

Petrovna, Sophia
Blood on the Snow - John Elliott 1916

Pingree, Kitty
Proud New Flags - F. van Wyck Mason 4156

Pitborough, Charles
A Most Romantic City - Mary Ann Gibbs 2396

Platt, Elizabeth
By Antietam Creek - Don Robertson 5398

Polk, Sarah
Breakfast at the Hermitage - Alfred Leland Crabb 1397
Dinner at Belmont - Alfred Leland Crabb 1398
Home to Tennessee - Alfred Leland Crabb 1400
Lodging at the Saint Cloud - Alfred Leland Crabb 1403
Supper at the Maxwell House - Alfred Leland Crabb 1407

Pourure, Aurelie de
By Right of Arms - Robyn Carr 937

Preswald, Caitlin
Mississippi Belle - Clements Ripley 5346

Pryde, Clotilda
Weathercock - Constance Dodge 1668

Quarrendon, Neville
Limmerston Hall - Hester W. Chapman 991

Quill, Celia
The Rationalist - Warwick Collins 1217

Randall, Claire
Dragonfly in Amber - Diana Gabaldon 2262

Rao, Natholi
The Blood Seed - Andrew Ward 6561

Raoul, Jonathan
The Horn and the Forest - Jamie Lee Cooper 1313

Raven, Nora
Lord Raven's Widow - Leslie O'Grady 4700

Reade, Clara
Biscayne - Barry Jay Kaplan 3365

Reilly, Cat
The Bear Flag: A Novel of the Birth of California - Cecelia Holland 2983

Renisenb
Death Comes as the End - Agatha Christie 1076

Rizpah
As Sure as the Dawn - Francine Rivers 5352

Rogers, Hope
The Valiant Gunman - Gilbert Morris 4474

Rugger, Caressa
Caressa - Linda Lang Bartell 363

Running Deer
Child of the Dead - Don Coldsmith 1172

Ryder, Grizel
The Lonely Strangers - Charity Blackstock 531

St. Michael, Valentine
Lost Love Found - Bertrice Small 5910

Sancreed, Lorna
To the End of Her Days - Malcolm Macdonald 3975

Savarin-Decker, Claire
Glowstone - Macdonald Harris 2725

Sawtrey, Honor
Daneclere - Pamela Hill 2931

Scott, Mrs.
The Alien Light - Iain Crichton Smith 1427

Sedley, Amelia
Vanity Fair - William Makepeace Thackeray 6213

Shannon, Mark
Georgina - Clare Darcy 1488

Sinclair, Julian
Seduction - Amanda Quick 5220

Somerset, Larla
Midsummer Moon - Karen Lynn 3940

Southwick, Silence
Portrait of Emma - Lillian Cheatham 1010

Stair, Diana
Diana Stair - Floyd Dell 1594

Strong, Mama
White Rising - Zane Kotker 3548

Sybilla
Jerusalem - Cecelia Holland 2990

Thatcher, Lorna
Longleaf - Rose Brock 701

Tolworthy, Arabella
Lament for a Lost Lover - Philippa Carr 921

Tonneman, Pieter
The Dutchman - Maan Meyers 4351

Tring, Sarah Camberwell
Sarah Camberwell Tring - Janet Edmonds 1869

Troy, Elizabeth
On a Far Wide Shore - Malcolm Macdonald 3970

Van Ayl, Cathy
Nebraska! - Dana Fuller Ross 5480
Wyoming! - Dana Fuller Ross 5494

Van Gogh-Bonger, Johanna
Johanna: A Novel of the Van Gogh Family - Claire Cooperstein 1317

Verringer, Jason
The Time of the Hunter's Moon - Victoria Holt 3022

Volland, Anna
Vollands - Pamela Hill 2947

Wade, Caroline
Hard Road to Gettysburg - Ted Jones 3298

Walker, Margaret
The Weaver's Tale - Kate Sedley 5719

Ward, Hagar
New Road - Merle Estes Colby 1168

Warner, Jerd
Farewell the Stranger - Saliee O'Brien 4682

Whipple, Dora
Confederates - Thomas Keneally 3412

Wickham, Belle
The Dixie Widow - Gilbert Morris 4459

Woodbury, Randall
Swear by Apollo - Shirley Barker 318

Wright, Jedediah
The Taste of Time - Ferol Egan 1892

Yealm, Anna
Brumaire - Mark Logan 3864
Guillotine - Mark Logan 3865

York, Veronica
Silence in Hanover Close - Anne Perry 4936

Zelter, Rebekka
Shadow on the Valley - Kirk Mitchell 4414

WITCH

Alba
Black Body - H.C. Turk 6361

Alys
Hellbane - Anthony Esler 1963

de Villanegas, Matilda
The Monk - Matthew Gregory Lewis 3756

Doll
A Mirror for Witches - Esther Forbes 2157

Flower, Joan
The Witch and the Priest - Hilda Lewis 3754

Hywelis
Crown in Candlelight - Rosemary Hawley Jarman 3166

Lamia
Lamia: A Witch - Georgia Elizabeth Taylor 6183

Laveau, Marie
Voodoo Dreams: A Novel of Marie Laveau - Jewell Parker Rhodes 5310

Margery
Strange Devices of the Sun and Moon - Lisa Goldstein 2463

McGregor, Anne
Child of the Mist - Kathleen Morgan 4451

Morgan
The Mists of Avalon - Marion Zimmer Bradley 626

Morgause
The Last Enchantment - Mary Stewart 6031
The Wicked Day - Mary Stewart 6033

Murdockson, Meg
The Heart of Midlothian - Sir Walter Scott 5698

Slade, Alice
Malefice - Leslie Wilson 6810

Tamar
Daughter of Satan - Jean Plaidy 5011

Tituba
I, Tituba, Black Witch of Salem - Maryse Conde 1233
Peace, My Daughters - Shirley Barker 314

Tusser, Ursula
Familiar Spirits - Leonard Tourney 6298

Wulfrunt
Gilded Spurs - Grace Ingram 3105

WORKER

Alwyn, Chid
The Fleet in the Forest - Carl Daniel Lane 3654

Arne
Arne - Bjornstjerne Bjornson 518

Bannon, Millie
Thy Tears Might Cease - Michael Farrell 2018

Barlow, Ben
Law of the Land - Marguerite Allis 111

Barrington, Ruby
Stand We at Last - Zoe Fairbairns 1999

Barton, Joe
Maggie Craig - Marie Joseph 3308

Ben
The Rag Nymph - Catherine Cookson 1287

Blacksmith, Jimmie
The Chant of Jimmie Blacksmith - Thomas Keneally 3411

Bok, Yakov
The Fixer - Bernard Malamud 4038

Character Description Index

Boudreaux
The Terrible Teague Bunch - Gary Jennings 3197

Briggs, Nelly
Lovers - Suzanne Goodwin 2476

Buckerel, Dick
Liza Bowe - Shirley Barker 313

Cody, Ellery
My Sister's Keeper - Beverly Butler 817

Conway, Agnes
The Wingless Bird - Catherine Cookson 1292

Cooper, Rachel
The Standing Hills - Caroline Stickland 6038

Cornell, Sarah Maria
Avery's Knot - Mary Cable 843
The Tragedy at Tinkerton: An Historical Novel of Murder - Raymond Paul 4844

Cullen, Arthur
Day Is Coming - William Cameron 869

Diamond, Laura
Monday's Child - Mollie Hardwick 2697

Dobrejcak, Mike
Out of This Furnace - Thomas Bell 425

Dremont, Jeanne
To Dance with Kings - Rosalind Laker 3601

Eli
Tracker - David Wagoner 6521

Fayerdon, Daniel
The Darkness of Corn - Caroline Stickland 6037

Fowler, Jerry
Erie Water - Walter D. Edmonds 1875

Gibson, Mark
The Drayton Legacy - Rona Randall 5247

Gray, Rhian
Spinners' Wharf - Iris Gower 2502

Green, Perry
Charity Strong - Marguerite Allis 109

Hanna, Chad
Chad Hanna - Walter D. Edmonds 1873

Hardacre, Sam
Hardacre - C.L. Skelton 5872

Harker, Tom
The Shooting Party - Isabel Colegate 1197

Herleve
Fortune's Knave: The Making of William the Conqueror - Mary Lide 3774

Holland, Frank
Beauty for Ashes - Timothy R. Wilson 6816

Jenson, Alfred
And the Desert Shall Bloom - Phyllis Barber 299

Jim
The Two Farms - Mary E. Pearce 4865

Kaminsky, Shmuel
Trumpets of Silver - Norma Harris 2735

Kasane
The Tokaido Road: A Novel of Feudal Japan - Lucia St. Clair Robson 5417

Kelly, Jim
Home Station - Jeanne Williams 6778

Kendall, Simon
The Drayton Legacy - Rona Randall 5247

Lloyd, Martin
Morgan's Woman - Iris Gower 2500

Lucas
The Three-Cornered Hat - Pedro Antonio de Alarcon 62

MaCartney, Jenny
A Leaf in the Wind - Marie Joseph 3307

Montague, Michael
Madame Geneva - Jane Lane 3655

Mort
The Chant of Jimmie Blacksmith - Thomas Keneally 3411

Mortymer, Hywel
The Rape of the Fair Country - Alexander Cordell 1325

Mortymer, Iestyn
The Rape of the Fair Country - Alexander Cordell 1325

Mosher, Emmeline
Emmeline - Judith Rossner 5507

Musgrave, Freddie
The Harrogate Secret - Catherine Cookson 1278

Olszak, Orrange
American Beauty - Edna Ferber 2060

Oxley, Freddy
For They Shall Inherit - Malcolm Macdonald 3964

Palfrey, Sabra
Call the Darkness Light - Nancy Zaroulis 6954

Phelan, Edward
While England Sleeps - David Leavitt 3702

Ryan, Michael
Sunshine and Shadow - Antonia Van-Loon 6426

Ryder, Sara
Bride of Ae - Pamela Hill 2928

Salani, Metello
Metello - Vasco Pratolini 5163

Scacerini, Lazzaro
The Mill on the Po - Riccardo Bacchelli 254

Scacerni, Giovanni
Nothing New under the Sun - Riccardo Bacchelli 255

Skinner, Joseph
The Black Candle - Catherine Cookson 1273

Spiggy
The Queen and I - Sue Townsend 6306

Stanton, Jethro
The Valiant and the Daunted - Roy Clews 1115

Stanton, Peter
The Valiant and the Daunted - Roy Clews 1115

Stevenson, Nora
The World From Rough Stones - Malcolm Macdonald 3979

Sung Wing On
Lotus Land - Monica Highland 2917

Tallentire, John
The Hired Man - Melvyn Bragg 639

Tidmarsh, Miss
The Beano - Rony Robinson 5411

Tyler, Wat
Within the Hollow Crown - Margaret Campbell Barnes 331

Walford, Harry
Harry: A Novel of Australia - Robert Wales 6530

Weaver, Alice
The Pilgrim of Hate - Ellis Peters 4967

Webb, Becky
Sunrise to Sunset - Samuel Hopkins Adams 32

Whitman, Jonathan
The Marigold Field - Diane Pearson 4876

Will
Bodin, 1349: An Epic Novel of Christians and Jews in the Plague Years - Roberta Kalechofsky 3322

Wyse, Francis
I Am England - Patricia Wright 6881

Yechiel, Rivke
Salvation - Sholem Asch 202

WRITER

Abraham
The Book of Abraham - Marek Halter 2665

Adams, Henry
Empire: A Novel - Gore Vidal 6487
Hollywood: A Novel of America in the 1920s - Gore Vidal 6488
Panama - Eric Zencey 6959
The Raiders: A Novel of the Civil War at Sea - Willard Wallace 6541
Refinements of Love: A Novel about Clover and Henry Adams - Sarah Booth Conroy 1259

Adams, Marian "Clover"
Refinements of Love: A Novel about Clover and Henry Adams - Sarah Booth Conroy 1259

Addison, Joseph
Henry Esmond - William Makepeace Thackeray 6212

Aesop
The Fabulist - John Vornholt 6512
My Name Is Sappho - Martha Rofheart 5429
Persian Conqueror - George Sidney Hellman 2822

Alcott, Louisa May
Love and War - John Jakes 3150

Alfieri, Vittorio
Crown Without Sceptre - William Vaughan Wilkins 6758
The Queen of Hearts - Joan Rees 5290

Alkaios
My Name Is Sappho - Martha Rofheart 5429

Amergin
Bard: The Odyssey of the Irish - Morgan Llywelyn 3816

Andersen, Hans Christian
Flight of the Swan - Margaret Ann Hubbard 3063
The Swedish Nightingale: Jenny Lind - Elizabeth Kyle 3571

Apollinaire, Guillaume
The Burning Man - Stephen Longstreet 3883
The Young Men of Paris - Stephen Longstreet 3893

Ardleigh, Kathryn
Death at Daisy's Folly - Robin Paige 4775
Death at Gallows Green - Robin Paige 4776

Aretino, Pietro
The Scarlet City - Hella S. Haasse 2632

Aristophanes
Alcibiades, Beloved of Gods - Vincenz Brun 735
Goat Song: A Novel of Ancient Greece - Frank Yerby 6920
Goatsong - Tom Holt 3009

Armbrecht, Kurt
Hitler Has Won - Frederic Mullally 4511

Arnold, Matthew
The Buried Self: A Background to the Poems of Matthew Arnold - Isobel MacDonald 3961

Arouet, Francois Marie
Adrienne - Barbara Levy 3742
The Anthem - Noel B. Gerson 2361
A Day of Battle - Vincent Sheean 5787
Rasero - Francisco Rebolledo 5282
Voltaire! Voltaire! - Guy Endore 1943

Austen, Jane
Antipodes Jane: A Novel of Jane Austen in Australia - Barbara Ker Wilson 3468

Jane and the Man of the Cloth - Stephanie
   Barron   355
Jane and the Unpleasantness at Scargrave Manor -
   Stephanie Barron   356
Parson Austen's Daughter - Helen Ashton   219

Aveling, Edward
*The Daughter: A Novel Based on the Life of Eleanor
   Marx* - Judith Chernaik   1012

Bacon, Sir Francis
*Physician Extraordinary: A Novel of the Life and
   Times of William Harvey* - David Weiss   6608

Balzac, Honore de
I Am Vidocq - Vincent McConnor   4225
Wine of Life - Charles Orson Gorham   2489

Banner, Gabriel
Reckless - Amanda Quick   5217

Bantham, Jane
Kindred Spirits - June Barraclough   347

Barlow, Joel
To Spit Against the Wind - Benjamin H. Levin   3737

Barrett, Elizabeth
Lady's Maid - Margaret Forster   2188

Baudelaire, Charles Pierre
The Midnight Gardener: A Novel about Baudelaire -
   Max White   6694
A Singular Conspiracy - Barry Perowne   4915

Beaumarchais, Pierre Augustin Caron de
Poor Richard's Game - G.J.A. O'Toole   4766

Beaumont, Francis
The Player's Boy - Bryher   744

Beckford, William
Fonthill - Aubrey Menen   4335

Behn, Aphra
The Portingale - Alison Macleod   4005
*Purple Passage: A Novel about a Lady Both Famous
   and Fantastic* - Emily Hahn   2638

Bell, Clive
*The Shadow of the Moth: A Novel of Espionage with
   Virginia Woolf* - Ellen Hawkes   2779

Benchley, Robert
The Dorothy Parker Murder Case - George
   Baxt   384

Benson, E.F.
The Haunting of Lamb House - Joan Aiken   48

Bentley, E.C.
Dorothy and Agatha - Gaylord Larsen   3667

Bierce, Ambrose
The Old Gringo - Carlos Fuentes   2247
Yellow: A Novel - Daniel Lynch   3932

Blake, William
Vindication - Frances Sherwood   5824

Bloy, Leon
The Harp and the Shadow - Alejo Carpentier   905

Bold Talent
Spring Moon: A Novel of China - Bette Bao
   Lord   3897

Bonhoeffer, Dietrich
The Cup of Wrath - Mary Glazener   2429

Boswell, James
Blind Justice - Bruce Alexander   76
The Bonnet Laird's Daughter - Barbara
   Annandale   154
Dear Mrs. Boswell - Marie Muir   4508

Botsford, Brian
While England Sleeps - David Leavitt   3702

Brandt, Naftali
Behold the Fire - Michael Blankfort   541

Brecht, Bertold
The Howard Hughes Affair - Stuart M.
   Kaminsky   3340

Bronte, Anne
Bronte - Glyn Hughes   3073
Dark Quartet: The Story of the Brontes - Lynne Reid
   Banks   290
In the Shadow of the Brontes - Louise Brindley   690
These Were the Brontes - Dorothy Helen
   Cornish   1332
*Wild Decembers: A Biographical Portrait of the
   Brontes* - Hilda Crystal White   6681

Bronte, Charlotte
Bronte - Glyn Hughes   3073
Dark Quartet: The Story of the Brontes - Lynne Reid
   Banks   290
*H.—: The Story of Heathcliff's Journey Back to
   Wuthering Heights* - Lin Haire-Sargeant   2641
In the Shadow of the Brontes - Louise Brindley   690
Path to the Silent Country - Lynne Reid Banks   291
These Were the Brontes - Dorothy Helen
   Cornish   1332
*Wild Decembers: A Biographical Portrait of the
   Brontes* - Hilda Crystal White   6681

Bronte, Emily
Bronte - Glyn Hughes   3073
Dark Quartet: The Story of the Brontes - Lynne Reid
   Banks   290
In the Shadow of the Brontes - Louise Brindley   690
These Were the Brontes - Dorothy Helen
   Cornish   1332
*Wild Decembers: A Biographical Portrait of the
   Brontes* - Hilda Crystal White   6681

Browning, Elizabeth Barrett
How Do I Love Thee - Lucille Iremonger   3110

Browning, Robert
How Do I Love Thee - Lucille Iremonger   3110
Lady's Maid - Margaret Forster   2188
Neighboring Lives - Thomas M. Disch   1648

Bryant, William Cullen
1876: A Novel - Gore Vidal   6484
All This, and Heaven Too - Rachel Field   2080
The Furies - John Jakes   3146

Bulwer-Lytton, Edward
The Prime Minister's Wife - Doris Leslie   3727

Buntline, Ned
Buffalo Girls - Larry McMurtry   4296
This Old Bill - Loren D. Estleman   1980

Bunyan, John
The Pilgrim Prince - Gladys H. Barr   343

Burgoyne, John
Guns of Burgoyne - Bruce Lancaster   3640
The Long Naked Descent into Boston - William
   Eastlake   1823

Burney, Fanny
The Bonnet Laird's Daughter - Barbara
   Annandale   154
Sweet Lass of Richmond Hill - Jean Plaidy   5067
The Third George - Jean Plaidy   5068

Burns, Robert
Crest of the Broken Wave - James Barke   302
Song in the Green Thorn Tree - James Barke   303
Well of the Silent Harp - James Barke   304
The Wind That Shakes the Barley - James Barke   305
Wonder of All the Gay World - James Barke   306

Burton, Sir Richard Francis
Burton and Speke - William Harrison   2751

Byron, George Gordon
The Absorbing Fire: The Byron Legend - F.W.
   Kenyon   3445
The Blue Heaven Bends Over All - Jane Oliver   4720
Byron: A Novel - Sigrid Combuchen   1225
Count Manifred - Miranda Seymour   5761

Frankenstein Unbound - Brian Aldiss   68
*The Golden Years: A Novel Based on the Life and
   Loves of Percy Bysshe Shelley* - F.W.
   Kenyon   3451
Haunted Summer - Anne Edwards   1881
Lord Byron's Doctor - Paul West   6634
Lord of the Dead: The Secret History of Byron - Tom
   Holland   2999
Lord of the Ladies - Joanna Dessau   1626
Love's Children - Judith Chernaik   1013
The Memoirs of Lord Byron - Robert Nye   4655
The Missolonghi Manuscript - Frederic
   Prokosch   5194
My Sister, My Love - Lucille Iremonger   3111
The Secret Memoirs of Lord Byron - Christopher
   Nicole   4622
A Single Summer with Lord B. - Derek
   Marlowe   4092
The Stress of Her Regard - Tim Powers   5157
Teresa, or Her Demon Lover - Austin K. Gray   2554

Cable, George Washington
A Connecticut Yankee in Criminal Court - Peter J.
   Heck   2814

Campion, Edward
English Music - Peter Ackroyd   18

Carlyle, Jane
Neighboring Lives - Thomas M. Disch   1648

Carlyle, Thomas
Caribbean - James A. Michener   4365
Cock of the Walk - Roy Lewis   3762
The Consuming Flame: The Story of George Eliot -
   F.W. Kenyon   3446
Neighboring Lives - Thomas M. Disch   1648

Carradine, Brent
The Daughter of Time - Josephine Tey   6209

Carroll, Anna Ella
*Woman with a Sword: The Biographical Novel of
   Anna Ella Carroll of Maryland* - Hollister
   Noble   4632

Carroll, Lewis
Neighboring Lives - Thomas M. Disch   1648

Carsons, Kim
The Place of Dead Roads - William S.
   Burroughs   808

Casanova, Giovanni Jacopo
A Night with Casanova - Wolf Mankowitz   4060

Cathcart, Colin
Johnnie Cross - Terence de Vere White   6704

Catullus, Gaius Valerius
Chantefable - Eldorous L. Dayton   1546
The City of Libertines - W.G. Hardy   2702
Clodia - Robert DeMaria   1606
Farewell, Catullus - Pierson Dixon   1651
The Gods Are Not Mocked - Anna Taylor   6177
The Ides of March - Thornton Wilder   6753
The Key - Benita Kane Jaro   3169
The Venus Throw - Steven Saylor   5627

Caussinade, Gildas
The Still Storm - Francoise Sagan   5562

Celine, Louis-Ferdinand
The Exile of Celine - Tom Clark   1095

Cellini, Benvenuto
The Chancellor - Lawrence Schoonover   5662
The Florentine - Carl J. Spinatelli   5968

Cervantes, Miguel de
The Death and Life of Miguel De Cervantes - Stephen
   Marlowe   4094
A Man Called Cervantes - Bruno Frank   2201

Chandler, Raymond
Murder on the Yellow Brick Road - Stuart M.
   Kaminsky   3343

Chase, David
Jackson: A Novel - Max Byrd 837

Chateaubriand, Francois Rene de
Crown of Grass - Charles Andrew Brady 634

Chatterton, Thomas
Chatterton - Peter Ackroyd 17

Chaucer, Geoffrey
The Gentle Knight - Philip Lindsay 3791
Glendower Country - Martha Rofheart 5427
Katherine - Anya Seton 5752
The Love Knot - Catherine Darby 1482
The Nun's Tale - Candace M. Robb 5367
Riddle Me a Murder - Duane Crowley 1435
A Tapestry of Murders - C.L. Grace 2510
Within the Hollow Crown - Margaret Campbell
Barnes 331

Chenier, Andre
The Black Consul - Anatolii Vinogradov 6503

Christie, Agatha
Agatha - Kathleen Tynan 6374
The Bette Davis Murder Case - George Baxt 383
Dorothy and Agatha - Gaylord Larsen 3667

Cibber, Colley
Peg Woffington - Charles Reade 5281

Claudianus, Claudius
Threshold of Fire - Hella S. Haasse 2633

Claudius I
I, Claudius - Robert Graves 2547

Clayton, John
Murder in Grub Street - Bruce Alexander 77

Cleland, John
*Fanny: Being the True History of the Adventures of
Fanny Hackabout-Jones* - Erica Jong 3299

Clemens, Samuel L.
A Connecticut Yankee in Criminal Court - Peter J.
Heck 2814
Death on the Mississippi - Peter J. Heck 2815

Cleveland, John
The Shadow Flies - Rose Macaulay 3956

Coleridge, Samuel Taylor
Eliza's Daughter - Joan Aiken 44
Mister Christian - William Kinsolving 3502
Walford's Oak - Jill M. Phillips 4986

Collins, Wilkie
The Detective and Mr. Dickens - William J.
Palmer 4782
The Highwayman and Mr. Dickens - William J.
Palmer 4783
The Hoydens and Mr. Dickens - William J.
Palmer 4784
The Hungry Goblin: A Victorian Detective Novel -
John Dickson Carr 911

Commines, Philippe de
Quentin Durward - Sir Walter Scott 5705

Congreve, William
The Bracegirdle - Burris Atkins Jenkins 3189

Cooke, Ebenezer
The Sot-Weed Factor - John Barth 364

Cooper, James Fenimore
*The Splendor Stays: An Historic Novel Based on the
Lives of the Seven Hart Sisters of Saybrook* -
Marguerite Allis 114

Copperfield, David
The Real David Copperfield - Robert Graves 2551

Coward, Noel
The Noel Coward Murder Case - George Baxt 387

Cowley, Abraham
The Shadow Flies - Rose Macaulay 3956

Cox-Neville, Alexandra
Come Be My Love - Diana Brown 717

Crane, Stephen
Dark Rider - Louis Zara 6950
The Rough Rider - Gilbert Morris 4468
The Year of the Spaniard - Henry Castor 956

Crashaw, Richard
The Shadow Flies - Rose Macaulay 3956

Critias
Goat Song: A Novel of Ancient Greece - Frank
Yerby 6920

Crossley, Stephen
Cordelia - Winston Graham 2523

D'Annunzio, Gabriele
Eleanora Duse - Jean Stubbs 6095
The Lion of Pescara - George MacBeth 3958

Dante Alighieri
The Wanderer: A Novel of Dante and Beatrice -
Nathan Schachner 5633

d'Astarac, Sybille
Sybille - Marion Meade 4318

De Quincey, Thomas
The Prince of Eden - Marilyn Harris 2732

De Rhetoree, Germaine
The Girl From Paris - Joan Aiken 47

Defoe, Daniel
Burning Gold - Robert Hardy Andrews 148

Delahanty, Mick
O'Houlihan's Jest - Rohan O'Grady 4702

Dickens, Charles
Charles - Victoria Lincoln 3786
The Consuming Flame: The Story of George Eliot -
F.W. Kenyon 3446
The Detective and Mr. Dickens - William J.
Palmer 4782
English Music - Peter Ackroyd 18
The Highwayman and Mr. Dickens - William J.
Palmer 4783
The Hoydens and Mr. Dickens - William J.
Palmer 4784
The Mutual Friend - Frederick Busch 811
The Romance of Charles Dickens - Ursula
Bloom 553

Dickinson, Emily
Come Slowly Eden: A Novel about Emily Dickinson -
Laura Benet 440
The Diary of Emily Dickinson: A Novel - Jamie
Fuller 2255
The Hesitant Heart - Anne Edwards 1882
I Never Came to You in White - Judith Farr 2014
Peter Doyle - John Vernon 6457

Diderot, Denis
Rasero - Francisco Rebolledo 5282

Disraeli, Benjamin
Disraeli in Love - Maurice Edelman 1851

Donne, John
Knaves Templar - Leonard Tourney 6300
*Physician Extraordinary: A Novel of the Life and
Times of William Harvey* - David Weiss 6608
Take Heed of Loving Me: A Novel about John Donne -
Elizabeth Gray Vining 6502

Dostoevsky, Feodor Mikhailovich
The Devil Inside: A Novel of Dostoevsky's Life -
Stephen Coulter 1385

Douglas, Lord Alfred Bruce
The God of Mirrors - Robert Reilly 5293

Douglass, Frederick
The Furies - John Jakes 3146

Doyle, Arthur Conan
The List of Seven - Mark Frost 2237
Nevermore - William Hjortsberg 2958
The Night of the Ripper - Robert Bloch 551
The Six Messiahs - Mark Frost 2238

Drayton, Michael
Two Loves Have I - Clara Longworth de
Chambrun 985

Dryden, John
The Bracegirdle - Burris Atkins Jenkins 3189
The Golden Days - Robert Neill 4569
The Renegade - Donald Clayton Porter 5122

Du Maurier, George
To Seize the Passing Dream - Ted Berkman 479

Dumas, fils, Alexandre
The Blood Endures - Robert Inman 3107
King of Paris - Guy Endore 1942

Dumas, pere, Alexandre
I Am Vidocq - Vincent McConnor 4225
King of Paris - Guy Endore 1942
Passionate Rebel: The Story of Hector Berlioz - F.W.
Kenyon 3457
Rachel - Anne Powers 5153

Edgeworth, Maria
The Year of the French - Thomas Flanagan 2121

Eliot, George
Gentlemen in England - A.N. Wilson 6795
Johnnie Cross - Terence de Vere White 6704

Emerson, Ralph Waldo
The Jonah Man - Henry Carlisle 895
Listen for the Voices - Anne Colver 1220
The Prescott Chronicles - Albert Fried 2232
Walt Whitman's Secret - Ben Aronin 196

Erasmus, Desiderius
Warm Wind, West Wind - Anne Irwin Matthew 4188

Eschenbach, Wolfram von
Elizabeth's Greetings - Rosemary Haughton 2774

Ethan
The King David Report - Stefan Heym 2910

Eupolis
Goatsong - Tom Holt 3009
The Walled Orchard - Tom Holt 3010

Euripides
Goat Song: A Novel of Ancient Greece - Frank
Yerby 6920
Goatsong - Tom Holt 3009
The Shining - Stephen Marlowe 4097

Evans, Mary Ann
The Consuming Flame: The Story of George Eliot -
F.W. Kenyon 3446
The Hoydens and Mr. Dickens - William J.
Palmer 4784

Faulkner, William
Murder in the Executive Mansion - Elliott
Roosevelt 5449
Never Cross a Vampire - Stuart M. Kaminsky 3344
Rommel and the Rebel - Lawrence Wells 6622

Field, Henry M.
All This, and Heaven Too - Rachel Field 2080

Fielding, Henry
The Masters of Bow Street - John Creasy 1423
The Vast Memory of Love - Malcolm Bosse 588

Fitzgerald, F. Scott
One Last Glimpse - James Aldridge 74

FitzGibbon, Beth
An Excess of Love - Cathy Cash Spellman 5959

Fitzpercy, Charles
Kindred Spirits - June Barraclough 347

Flaubert, Gustave
The Girl From Paris - Joan Aiken 47

Flecker, James Elroy
Dreaming of Samarkand - Martin Booth 576

Fleming, Ian
You Bet Your Life - Stuart M. Kaminsky 3349

Fletcher, John
The Player's Boy - Bryher 744

Freneau, Philip
The Drums of Monmouth - Emma Gelders
 Sterne 5998

Freud, Sigmund
*Minna's Story: The Secret Love of Doctor Sigmund
 Freud* - Kathleen Daniels 1463

Gardner, Erle Stanley
Carnal Hours - Max Allan Collins 1210

Gaskell, Elizabeth
Path to the Silent Country - Lynne Reid Banks 291

Genovese, Christopher
Bay of Arrows - Jay Parini 4800

Gissing, George
*The Trial of Elizabeth Cree: A Novel of the Limehouse
 Murders* - Peter Ackroyd 21

Glass, Jason
The Legacy of Ladysmith - John Kenny Crane 1413

Godwin, Mary Wollstonecraft
The Absorbing Fire: The Byron Legend - F.W.
 Kenyon 3445
Frankenstein Unbound - Brian Aldiss 68
*The Golden Years: A Novel Based on the Life and
 Loves of Percy Bysshe Shelley* - F.W.
 Kenyon 3451
A Most Extraordinary Pair - Jean Detre 1628
My Sister, My Love - Lucille Iremonger 3111
A Single Summer with Lord B. - Derek
 Marlowe 4092
Vindication - Frances Sherwood 5824

Godwin, William
A Most Extraordinary Pair - Jean Detre 1628
Vindication - Frances Sherwood 5824

Goethe, Johann Wolfgang von
Angelica - Samuel A. Schreiner Jr. 5671
The Anthem - Noel B. Gerson 2361
*Sacred and Profane: A Novel of the Life and Times of
 Mozart* - David Weiss 6609

Gogol, Nikolai
Great Black Russian - John Oliver Killens 3484

Goldoni, Carlo
Lord Vanity - Samuel Shellabarger 5796

Goldsmith, Oliver
Angelica - Samuel A. Schreiner Jr. 5671
Dr. Johnson's Dear Mistress - Winifred Carter 948

Goncourt, Edmond de
The Gypsy From Cadiz - Tamsin Hamilton 2670

Gorky, Maxim
Blood on the Snow - John Elliott 1916
Petersburg - Emily Hanlon 2677

Graves, Robert
Regeneration - Pat Barker 309

Greene, Robert
The Shadow of the Earth - Lee Wichelns 6731

Gunderode, Karoline von
No Place on Earth - Christa Wolf 6836

Halleck, Fritz-Greene
*The Splendor Stays: An Historic Novel Based on the
 Lives of the Seven Hart Sisters of Saybrook* -
 Marguerite Allis 114

Hammett, Dashiell
The Black Mask Murderers - William F. Nolan 4635
Buried Caesars - Stuart M. Kaminsky 3332
Hammett: A Novel - Joseph N. Gores 2487
The William Powell and Myrna Loy Murder Case -
 George Baxt 390

Harris, Frank
The God of Mirrors - Robert Reilly 5293
The West End Horror - Nicholas Meyer 4350

Harte, Bret
The Mississippi Run - Paul Darcy Boles 565

Hawthorne, Nathaniel
Memories of the Ford Administration - John
 Updike 6391

Hearn, Lafcadio
The Blue Dragon - Diana Brown 716
*Mortal Hunger: A Novel Based on the Life of Lafcadio
 Hearn* - Harry E. Wedeck 6594

Hellman, Lillian
The William Powell and Myrna Loy Murder Case -
 George Baxt 390

Hemingway, Ernest
High Midnight - Stuart M. Kaminsky 3339
Murder in the Executive Mansion - Elliott
 Roosevelt 5449
One Last Glimpse - James Aldridge 74
Papa and Fidel - Karl Alexander 79
The Veracruz Blues - Mark Winegardner 6821
Walter Winchell: A Novel - Michael Herr 2863

Henneker, Victor
Victim of the Aurora - Thomas Keneally 3417

Herrick, Robert
The Shadow Flies - Rose Macaulay 3956

Hitchcock, Alma
The Alfred Hitchcock Murder Case - George
 Baxt 382

Hoode, Edmund
The Roaring Boy - Edward Marston 4127
The Silent Woman - Edward Marston 4128

Horace
Golden Peacock - Gertrude Atherton 224

Howe, Julia Ward
Banners Against the Wind - John Edward
 Jennings 3198

Hubble, Jane
Hubble Time - Tom Bezzi 490

Hugo, Victor
Naked Came I: A Novel of Rodin - David
 Weiss 6607
Palais-Royale - Richard Sennett 5747

Hung Tu
Go Ask the River - Evelyn Eaton 1826

Hunt, Leigh
*The Golden Years: A Novel Based on the Life and
 Loves of Percy Bysshe Shelley* - F.W.
 Kenyon 3451
Love's Children - Judith Chernaik 1013
Neighboring Lives - Thomas M. Disch 1648

Hurrocks, Thalia
St. John's Wood - Nancy Fitzgerald 2116

Irving, Washington
John Howard Payne, Skywalker - Maude
 Barragan 348
River to the West: A Novel of the Astor Adventure -
 John Edward Jennings 3204

James, Henry
Empire: A Novel - Gore Vidal 6487
The Haunting of Lamb House - Joan Aiken 48
Henry James' Midnight Song - Carol de Chellis
 Hill 2920
*Refinements of Love: A Novel about Clover and Henry
 Adams* - Sarah Booth Conroy 1259

James, William
The Haunting of Lamb House - Joan Aiken 48

Jerrold, Douglas
Princess Pamela - Ray Russell 5534

John of the Cross
*Bold Encounter: A Novel Based on the Life of St. John
 of the Cross* - Peter-Thomas Rohrbach 5433

Johnson, Ben
Powhatan's Daughter - John Clarke Bowman 605

Johnson, Samuel
Angelica - Samuel A. Schreiner Jr. 5671
Blind Justice - Bruce Alexander 76
The Bonnet Laird's Daughter - Barbara
 Annandale 154
Dr. Johnson's Dear Mistress - Winifred Carter 948
Midwinter - John Buchan 751
Mr. Oddity, Samuel Johnson - Charles Norman 4643

Jones, Orpheus
The Pleasure Garden - Leon Garfield 2293

Jonson, Ben
The Best House in Stratford - Edward Fisher 2100
The Cleopatra Boy - Eric Malpass 4048
The Disturber - L.S. Davidson Jr. 1505
Entered From the Sun - George Garrett 2301
Ralegh's Fair Bess: The Story of Bess Throckmorton -
 Judy Turner 6365
Take Heed of Loving Me: A Novel about John Donne -
 Elizabeth Gray Vining 6502
Two Loves Have I - Clara Longworth de
 Chambrun 985
You, My Brother - Philip Burton 809

Kaufman, George S.
The Dorothy Parker Murder Case - George
 Baxt 384

Keats, John
The Remarkable Young Man - Cecil Roberts 5373
The Stress of Her Regard - Tim Powers 5157

Key, Francis Scott
Crimson Is the Eastern Shore - Don Tracy 6308

Kleist, Heinrich von
No Place on Earth - Christa Wolf 6836

Kyd, Thomas
A Dead Man in Deptford - Anthony Burgess 776
Liza Bowe - Shirley Barker 313
The Shadow of the Earth - Lee Wichelns 6731
To Be a King - Robert DeMaria 1607

Laclos, Pierre Choderlos de
A Place of Greater Safety - Hilary Mantel 4077

Lamb, Charles
John Howard Payne, Skywalker - Maude
 Barragan 348
So Perish the Roses - Neil Bell 423

Lamb, Mary Ann
So Perish the Roses - Neil Bell 423

Landon, Letitia Elizabeth
Letty - Helen Ashton 218

Lardner, Ring
Blue Ruin: A Novel of the 1919 World Series -
 Brendan Boyd 610
Hoopla - Harry Stein 5990

Lavette, Barbara
The Establishment - Howard Fast 2030
The Immigrant's Daughter - Howard Fast 2035
The Legacy - Howard Fast 2037
Second Generation - Howard Fast 2043

Lawrence, D.H.
Daughter of Time - Nelia Gardner White 6695

Lawrence, T.E.
The Murder of Lawrence of Arabia - Matthew
 Eden 1865

Learmouth, Thomas
True Thomas - Nigel Tranter 6322

Leo Africanus
Leo Africanus - Amin Maalouf 3947

Levy, Esau
Esau - Meir Shalev 5770

Character Description Index

Lewes, George Henry
The Consuming Flame: The Story of George Eliot - F.W. Kenyon   3446

Lewis, Matthew Gregory
The Flight of the Eagle - Donald Thomas   6239

Lindsay, David
James, by the Grace of God - Nigel Tranter   6315

London, Jack
The Summer of Jack London - Andrew J. Fenady   2058

Lucan
The Conspiracy - John Hersey   2870

Lykaina
The Other Sappho - Ellen Frye   2240

Machiavelli, Niccolo
Michelangelo the Florentine - Sidney Alexander   86
The Scarlet City - Hella S. Haasse   2632
Then and Now - William Somerset Maugham   4198
Web of Lucifer: A Novel of the Borgia Fury - Maurice Samuel   5580

MacLaine, Shirley
Live From Golgotha - Gore Vidal   6491

Mansfield, Katherine
Daughter of Time - Nelia Gardner White   6695

Marcellus
Street of the Sandalmakers: A Tale of Rome in the Time of Marcus Aurelius - Nis Peterson   4977

Marcus Aurelius
A Fig in Winter - Willa Gibbs   2400

Marlow, Phoebe
Sylvester; or, The Wicked Uncle - Georgette Heyer   2904

Marlowe, Christopher
A Dead Man in Deptford - Anthony Burgess   776
Liza Bowe - Shirley Barker   313
Mermaid Tavern - George William Cronyn   1429
Nicholas Cooke: Actor, Soldier, Physician, Priest - Stephanie Cowell   1393
The Shadow of the Earth - Lee Wichelns   6731
The Slicing Edge of Death - Judith Cook   1263
Strange Devices of the Sun and Moon - Lisa Goldstein   2463
To Be a King - Robert DeMaria   1607
Will Shakespeare: The Untold Story - John Mortimer   4495

Maro, Publius Vergilius
The Death of Virgil - Hermann Broch   699

Martineau, Harriet
Path to the Silent Country - Lynne Reid Banks   291
Sisters & Lovers - Nicola Thorne   6274

Marvell, Andrew
The Portingale - Alison Macleod   4005

Marx, Karl
Sisters & Lovers - Nicola Thorne   6274

Maupassant, Guy de
Damned Shall Be Desire: The Passionate Life of Guy de Maupassant - Stephen Coulter   1384
The Gypsy From Cadiz - Tamsin Hamilton   2670

McCarthy, Owen
The Year of the French - Thomas Flanagan   2121

McManus, Philip
Julie - Jane Kesner Morris   4479

Meleager
The Master - Max Brod   702

Melville, Herman
The Robber Baroness - William Kendall Clarke   1097
Walt Whitman's Secret - Ben Aronin   196

Meng Chaio
Go Ask the River - Evelyn Eaton   1826

Meredith, George
Chatterton - Peter Ackroyd   17

Merimee, Prosper
The Questing Heart: A Romantic Novel about George Sand - F.W. Kenyon   3458

Mill, John Stuart
Caribbean - James A. Michener   4365
Neighboring Lives - Thomas M. Disch   1648

Milne, A.A.
Dorothy and Agatha - Gaylord Larsen   3667

Milton, John
John Inglesant - John Henry Shorthouse   5833
John Milton - Edmund Fuller   2249
Milton in America - Peter Ackroyd   20
Myself, Christopher Wren - David Weiss   6606
The Shadow Flies - Rose Macaulay   3956
Sporting with Amaryllis - Paul West   6635
The Tree of Knowledge - Eva Figes   2085
Wife to Mr. Milton - Robert Graves   2553

Moliere
Monsieur Moliere - Michael O'Shaughnessy   4762

Moller, Peder Ludwig
The Seducer - Henrik Stangerup   5980

Moore, George
The Year of the French - Thomas Flanagan   2121

Moore, Thomas
Come Be My Love - Diana Brown   717

More, Sir Thomas
The King's Good Servant - Olive White   6696
Stage of Fools - Charles Andrew Brady   635
Warm Wind, West Wind - Anne Irwin Matthew   4188

Morris, May
The Daughter: A Novel Based on the Life of Eleanor Marx - Judith Chernaik   1012

Morris, William
Day Is Coming - William Cameron   869

Murry, John Middleton
Daughter of Time - Nelia Gardner White   6695

Musset, Alfred de
Hungarian Rhapsody: The Life of Franz Liszt - Jean Rousselot   5511
The Questing Heart: A Romantic Novel about George Sand - F.W. Kenyon   3458
Rachel - Anne Powers   5153

Nash, Thomas
Liza Bowe - Shirley Barker   313

Nietzsche, Friedrich
When Nietzsche Wept: A Novel of Obsession - Irvin D. Yalom   6892

Nine-Lizard
The Jaguar Princess - Clare Bell   421

Norris, William
Neighboring Lives - Thomas M. Disch   1648

O'Casey, Sean
An Excess of Love - Cathy Cash Spellman   5959

Odell, Henry
Brothers Three - John Oskison   4764

Overbury, Thomas
The Murder in the Tower - Jean Plaidy   5035
The Street of Kings - Charles Dexter   1637

Ovid
God Was Born in Exile - Vintila Horia   3033
An Imaginary Life - David Malouf   4047

Owen, Wilfred
The Ghost Road - Pat Barker   308

Paine, Thomas
City of Darkness, City of Light - Marge Piercy   4998
The Rebels - John Jakes   3152

Parker, Dorothy
The Dorothy Parker Murder Case - George Baxt   384
The Noel Coward Murder Case - George Baxt   387

Pater, Walter
Gentlemen in England - A.N. Wilson   6795
The God of Mirrors - Robert Reilly   5293

Patridge, Edgar Allen
The Strange Files of Fremont Jones - Dianne Day   1544

Payne, John Howard
John Howard Payne, Skywalker - Maude Barragan   348

Peacock, Thomas Love
Love's Children - Judith Chernaik   1013

Pemberton, Martin
The Waterworks - E.L. Doctorow   1659

Penfield
Loon Lake - E.L. Doctorow   1657

Pepys, Samuel
Mr. Pepys of Seething Lane - Cecil Abernethy   10
The Portingale - Alison Macleod   4005
Thanksgiving - Terry Coleman   1207

Phillips, Wendell
The Sin of the Prophet - Truman Nelson   4582

Piozzi, Hester Lynch Thrale
Dr. Johnson's Dear Mistress - Winifred Carter   948

Poe, Edgar Allan
Black Plume: The Supressed Memoirs of Edgar Allan Poe - David Madsen   4027
The Bloody Red Baron - Kim Newman   4596
Evermore - Barbara Steward   6014
The Fever Called Living - Barbara Moore   4439
The Last Mystery of Edgar Allan Poe - Manny Meyers   4356
The Lighthouse at the End of the World - Stephen Marlowe   4095
The Lincoln Diddle - Barbara Steward   6015
My Savage Muse: The Story of My Life: Edgar Allan Poe, an Imaginative Work - Bernhardt J. Hurwood   3087
The Raven - Chancellor Williams   6769
A Singular Conspiracy - Barry Perowne   4915
Very Young Mrs. Poe - Cothburn O'Neal   4740

Porter, William Sydney
The Heart of O. Henry - Dale Kramer   3550

Potter, Beatrix
Death at Gallows Green - Robin Paige   4776

Pound, Ezra
The King - Donald Barthelme   365

Prentiss, Patrick
The Tenants of Time - Thomas Flanagan   2120

Proust, Marcel
Herma - Macdonald Harris   2726
To Seize the Passing Dream - Ted Berkman   479

Pushkin, Aleksandr Sergeyevich
The Fourth King - Glen Petrie   4979
Great Black Russian - John Oliver Killens   3484

Racine, Jean
Monsieur Moliere - Michael O'Shaughnessy   4762

Revesby, Martin
The Winter Bride - Carola Salisbury   5572

Rilke, Martin
A Future Arrived - Phillip Rock   5420

Rilke, Rainer Maria
Naked Came I: A Novel of Rodin - David Weiss   6607

Rimbaud, Arthur
Savage Prodigal - Konrad Bercovici   474

Rogers, Samuel
Come Be My Love - Diana Brown   717

Ronzha
The Revolutionist: A Novel of Russia - Robert
   Littell   3810

Ross, Robert
The Eye in the Door - Pat Barker   307

Rossetti, Dante Gabriel
Cock of the Walk - Roy Lewis   3762
The Golden Veil - Paddy Kitchen   3507
The Hoydens and Mr. Dickens - William J.
   Palmer   4784
I, James McNeill Whistler - Lawrence
   Williams   6787
Willowwood - Elizabeth Savage   5619

Rousseau, Jean Jacques
Rasero - Francisco Rebolledo   5282
Voltaire! Voltaire! - Guy Endore   1943

Runyon, Damon
The Ham Reporter - Robert J. Randisi   5251
Walter Winchell: A Novel - Michael Herr   2863

Ruskin, John
The Golden Veil - Paddy Kitchen   3507
I, James McNeill Whistler - Lawrence
   Williams   6787
The Invention of Truth - Marta Morazzoni   4449
John Ruskin's Wife - Eva McDonald   4259
Sisters & Lovers - Nicola Thorne   6274
Willowwood - Elizabeth Savage   5619

Sacher-Masoch, Leopold Ritter von
Reigning Passions - Kathrin Perutz   4940

Sadoc
The Kingdom of the Wicked - Anthony Burgess   778

Saint-Germain, Alain
Vagabond Prophet - Allene Symons   6149

Saint-Just, Louis-Antoine-Leon de
A Place of Greater Safety - Hilary Mantel   4077

Salome, Lou
When Nietzsche Wept: A Novel of Obsession - Irvin D.
   Yalom   6892

Sand, George
Hungarian Rhapsody: The Life of Franz Liszt - Jean
   Rousselot   5511
*The Questing Heart: A Romantic Novel about George
   Sand* - F.W. Kenyon   3458

Sappho
The Laughter of Aphrodite - Peter Green   2570
My Name Is Sappho - Martha Rofheart   5429
The Other Sappho - Ellen Frye   2240

Sassoon, Siegfried
The Eye in the Door - Pat Barker   307
Regeneration - Pat Barker   309

Sayers, Dorothy L.
Dorothy and Agatha - Gaylord Larsen   3667

Scarron, Paul
*The Crown and the Shadow: The Story of Francoise
   d'Aubigne, Marquise de Maintenon* - Pamela
   Hill   2930

Schecter, Leonard
Di and I - Peter Lefcourt   3714

Schiller, Friedrich
The Harp and the Shadow - Alejo Carpentier   905

Schuyler, Charlie
1876: A Novel - Gore Vidal   6484

Scott, Sir Walter
The Blue Heaven Bends Over All - Jane Oliver   4720
Bright Captivity - Eugenia Price   5180

Scrope, Harriet
Chatterton - Peter Ackroyd   17

Seneca, Lucius Annaeus
Beware of Caesar - Vincent Sheean   5786
The Conspiracy - John Hersey   2870
The Kingdom of the Wicked - Anthony Burgess   778
Nero - Mary Teresa Ronalds   5437

Shakespeare, William
*All the Living: A Novel of One Year in the Life of
   William Shakespeare* - Henrietta Buckmaster   758
The Best House in Stratford - Edward Fisher   2100
The Cleopatra Boy - Eric Malpass   4048
A Dead Man in Deptford - Anthony Burgess   776
Entered From the Sun - George Garrett   2301
Gentleman of Stratford - John Brophy   708
A House of Women - Eric Malpass   4049
Liza Bowe - Shirley Barker   313
Love's Labour's Won - Edward Fisher   2101
Mrs. Shakespeare: The Complete Works - Robert
   Nye   4656
No Bed for Bacon - Caryl Brahms   640
Nothing Like the Sun - Anthony Burgess   781
*Physician Extraordinary: A Novel of the Life and
   Times of William Harvey* - David Weiss   6608
The Quality of Mercy - Faye Kellerman   3391
Serenissima: A Novel of Venice - Erica Jong   3300
Shakespeare & Son - Edward Fisher   2102
Shakespeare's Dog - Leon Rooke   5439
Sweet Will - Eric Malpass   4050
Three Years to Play - Colin MacInnes   3983
To Be a King - Robert DeMaria   1607
Two Loves Have I - Clara Longworth de
   Chambrun   985
Will Shakespeare: The Untold Story - John
   Mortimer   4495
You, My Brother - Philip Burton   809

Shaw, George Bernard
*The Daughter: A Novel Based on the Life of Eleanor
   Marx* - Judith Chernaik   1012
The God of Mirrors - Robert Reilly   5293
Naked Came I: A Novel of Rodin - David
   Weiss   6607
The Night of the Ripper - Robert Bloch   551
Stage Fright - Gillian Linscott   3809
The West End Horror - Nicholas Meyer   4350

Shelley, Mary Wollstonecraft
Count Manifred - Miranda Seymour   5761
Gothic Romance - Emmanuel Carrere   942
Haunted Summer - Anne Edwards   1881
Lord Byron's Doctor - Paul West   6634
Love's Children - Judith Chernaik   1013
The Olympians - Guy Bolton   566
The Stress of Her Regard - Tim Powers   5157

Shelley, Percy Bysshe
The Absorbing Fire: The Byron Legend - F.W.
   Kenyon   3445
Count Manifred - Miranda Seymour   5761
Frankenstein Unbound - Brian Aldiss   68
*The Golden Years: A Novel Based on the Life and
   Loves of Percy Bysshe Shelley* - F.W.
   Kenyon   3451
Gothic Romance - Emmanuel Carrere   942
Haunted Summer - Anne Edwards   1881
Lord Byron's Doctor - Paul West   6634
Lord of the Dead: The Secret History of Byron - Tom
   Holland   2999
Lord of the Ladies - Joanna Dessau   1626
Love's Children - Judith Chernaik   1013
The Memoirs of Lord Byron - Robert Nye   4655
The Missolonghi Manuscript - Frederic
   Prokosch   5194
My Sister, My Love - Lucille Iremonger   3111
The Olympians - Guy Bolton   566
A Single Summer with Lord B. - Derek
   Marlowe   4092
The Stress of Her Regard - Tim Powers   5157

Sheridan, Richard Brinsley
Goddess of the Green Room - Jean Plaidy   5016
Perdita's Prince - Jean Plaidy   5040

Regency Royal - Michael Hardwick   2687

Sidney, Sir Philip
The Constant Star - Dorothy Norris Foote   2151
The Firedrake's Eye - Patricia Finney   2095
Lady Rich - Elizabeth Boatwright Coker   1166
The Master of Gray Trilogy - Nigel Tranter   6316
Roanoke Hundred - Inglis Fletcher   2138

Simonides
The Praise Singer - Mary Renault   5302

Sippy, Ben
Anything for Billy - Larry McMurtry   4295

Smith, Matthew
The Millionaire's Daughter - Dorothy Eden   1858

Smith, Sydney
Come Be My Love - Diana Brown   717

Sophocles
Farewell Great King: A Novel of Ancient Greece - Jill
   Paton Walsh   4829
Glory and the Lightning - Taylor Caldwell   856
Goat Song: A Novel of Ancient Greece - Frank
   Yerby   6920
Goatsong - Tom Holt   3009
The Immortal Marriage - Gertrude Atherton   225

Spencer, Herbert
The Consuming Flame: The Story of George Eliot -
   F.W. Kenyon   3446

Stael, Anne Louise Germaine de
The Missolonghi Manuscript - Frederic
   Prokosch   5194

Steele, Sir Richard
Henry Esmond - William Makepeace
   Thackeray   6212

Stein, Gertrude
The Burning Man - Stephen Longstreet   3883
The Caravaggio Shawl - Samuel M. Steward   6019
Murder in the Chateau - Elliott Roosevelt   5447
Murder Is Murder Is Murder - Samuel M.
   Steward   6020

Stoker, Bram
Good Morning, Irene - Carole Nelson Douglas   1698
Good Night, Mr. Holmes - Carole Nelson
   Douglas   1699
The West End Horror - Nicholas Meyer   4350

Stowe, Harriet Beecher
All This, and Heaven Too - Rachel Field   2080
Beecher: A Novel - Dan McCall   4218
The Cup Trembling - Karl Brown   723

Strassburg, Gottfried von
Elizabeth's Greetings - Rosemary Haughton   2774

Strickland, Clive
Scandal at High Chimneys: A Victorian Melodrama -
   John Dickson Carr   915

Suckling, Sir John
The Golden Feather - Theda Kenyon   3462

Swift, Jonathan
Exit Lady Masham - Louis Auchincloss   230
*Fanny: Being the True History of the Adventures of
   Fanny Hackabout-Jones* - Erica Jong   3299
Henry Esmond - William Makepeace
   Thackeray   6212
Violent Friends - Winston Clewes   1113

Swinburne, Algernon
To Seize the Passing Dream - Ted Berkman   479

Tabor, Silver Dollar
All for Love: Baby Doe and Silver Dollar - John
   Vernon   6456

Tennyson, Alfred, Lord
Caribbean - James A. Michener   4365
The Day They Kidnapped Queen Victoria - H.K.
   Fleming   2127
The Hedge of Thorns - Helen Ashton   217

Queen Victoria's Bomb - Ronald Clark   1094

Thackeray, William Makepeace
Memoirs of a Victorian Gentleman: William Makepeace Thackeray - Margaret Forster   2189
Path to the Silent Country - Lynne Reid Banks   291

Thoreau, Henry David
God's Angry Man - Leonard Ehrlich   1898
Listen for the Voices - Anne Colver   1220
The Prescott Chronicles - Albert Fried   2232
Walt Whitman's Secret - Ben Aronin   196

Tirso de Molina
The Adventures of Don Juan - Richard Gardner   2289

Toklas, Alice B.
The Caravaggio Shawl - Samuel M. Steward   6019
Murder Is Murder Is Murder - Samuel M. Steward   6020

Tolstoy, Leo
The Extraordinary Adventures of Secret Agent Shipov in Pursuit of Count Leo Tolstoy in the Year 1862 - Bulat Okudzhava   4712
The Last Station - Jay Parini   4801

Tramont, Philippe de
The Wine Widow - Tessa Barclay   301

Trollope, Anthony
Gentlemen in England - A.N. Wilson   6795
Princess Pamela - Ray Russell   5534

Twain, Mark
1876: A Novel - Gore Vidal   6484
A Bloodsmoor Romance - Joyce Carol Oates   4658
If I Never Get Back - Darryl Brock   700
The Robber Baroness - William Kendall Clarke   1097
Sister Wives - Cleo Jones   3270
Twice upon a Time - Allen Appel   172

Vaughan, Henry
The Swan of Usk - Helen Ashton   220

Verlaine, Paul
Savage Prodigal - Konrad Bercovici   474

Verne, Jules
The Harp and the Shadow - Alejo Carpentier   905
King of Paris - Guy Endore   1942

Villon, Francois
The Dragon Waiting: A Masque of History - John M. Ford   2165
Rogue's Legacy: A Novel about Francois Villon - Babette Deutsch   1629

Wallace, Lew
Billy the Kid - Edwin Corle   1330
City of Widows - Loren D. Estleman   1969

Walpole, Horace
Richard Carvel - Winston Churchill   1081

Walpole, Hugh
The Haunting of Lamb House - Joan Aiken   48

Watson, John H.
Exit Sherlock Holmes - Robert Lee Hall   2657

Wells, H.G.
Time After Time - Karl Alexander   80

Wharton, Edith
The Haunting of Lamb House - Joan Aiken   48
Henry James' Midnight Song - Carol de Chellis Hill   2920

Wheeler, Chancey
The Town - Conrad Richter   5325

Whitman, Walt
Peter Doyle - John Vernon   6457
Walt Whitman's Secret - Ben Aronin   196

Wilde, Oscar
All for Love: Baby Doe and Silver Dollar - John Vernon   6456
Chelsea - Nancy Fitzgerald   2114

Day Is Coming - William Cameron   869
Farriers' Lane - Anne Perry   4930
The God of Mirrors - Robert Reilly   5293
Good Night, Mr. Holmes - Carole Nelson Douglas   1699
I Give You Oscar Wilde - Desmond Hall   2647
Irene at Large - Carole Nelson Douglas   1700
The Last Testament of Oscar Wilde - Peter Ackroyd   19
Lillie - David Butler   818
The Night of the Ripper - Robert Bloch   551
Playing the Game - Ian Buruma   810
A Season for Death - Ray Harrison   2743
Sherlock Holmes and the Mysterious Friend of Oscar Wilde - Russell A. Brown   731
To Seize the Passing Dream - Ted Berkman   479
The West End Horror - Nicholas Meyer   4350
Wilde West - Walter Satterthwait   5609

Woolcott, Alexander
The Dorothy Parker Murder Case - George Baxt   384

Woolf, Virginia
The Shadow of the Moth: A Novel of Espionage with Virginia Woolf - Ellen Hawkes   2779

Wordsworth, Dorothy
Mister Christian - William Kinsolving   3502

Wordsworth, William
Eliza's Daughter - Joan Aiken   44
Mister Christian - William Kinsolving   3502

Wyatt, Sir Thomas
Blood Royal - Mollie Hardwick   2690
Brief Gaudy Hour - Margaret Campbell Barnes   322
The Heir of Allington - Philippa Wiat   6727
The King's Pleasure - Jean Plaidy   5026
Mistress Anne - Carolly Erickson   1952
Queen Anne Boleyn - Francis Hackett   2634
The Sword of Truth - Gilbert Morris   4472
The Tower of London - William Harrison Ainsworth   58
Windsor Castle - William Harrison Ainsworth   59

Wychwood, Charles
Chatterton - Peter Ackroyd   17

Yeats, William Butler
An Excess of Love - Cathy Cash Spellman   5959
High Heroic - Constantine FitzGibbon   2118

Yezierska, Anzia
John and Anzia: An American Romance - Norma Rosen   5462

Zeami, Fujiwaka Motokiyo
The House of Kanze - Nobuko Albery   64

Zhivago, Yurii Andreievich
Doctor Zhivago - Boris Pasternak   4824

Zola, Emile
Lust for Life - Irving Stone   6059
Naked Came I: A Novel of Rodin - David Weiss   6607

YOUNG MAN

Abram
The King's Persons - Joanne Greenberg   2573

Alexander, Keith
Tap Roots - James H. Street   6080

Alexias
The Last of the Wine - Mary Renault   5299

Apfegrun, Otto
The Battle of Wagram - Gilles Lapouge   3664

Applegarth, Ingram
Out on Any Limb - John Myers   4545

Archias
Years of the City - George Rippey Stewart   6028

Arnvid
The Foster Brothers - Edward Frankland   2202

Arthur
The Hollow Hills - Mary Stewart   6030

Asgeirsson, Gunnar
The Greenlanders - Jane Smiley   5915

Barratt, Jonathan
Riders of the Long Road - Stephen E. Bransford   649

Bathory-Kereshtur, Drake
The Blood Countess - Andrei Codrescu   1149

Bathurst, Roger Fitzroy
Intrigue in Baltimore - Janet Whitney   6715

Baynes, Barton
Light in the Clearing - Irving A. Bacheller   260

Beard, Andrew
Spanish Bayonet - Stephen Vincent Benet   441

Beatty, Haywood
Looking After Lily - Cindy Bonner   572

Beatty, Marion
Lily - Cindy Bonner   571

Beckwith, Sam
The Coming of Rain - Richard Marius   4084

Berg, Dirk Van der
The Hill of Doves - Stuart Cloete   1123

Beric
Blood of the Martyrs - Naomi Mitchison   4417

Bertrand, Cyril
The Uncrowned King - Baroness Emma Orczy   4747

Black, Robbie
Great Elephant - Alan Scholefield   5654

Blakeslee, Will Tweedy
Leaving Cold Sassy - Olive Ann Burns   798

Bolderman, Martyn
The Sinking of the Sarah Diamond - William Dale Jennings   3213

Born, Bertran de
Cross, Sword, and Arrow - Gladys H. Barr   340

Boruchowicz, Lazar
Heritage - Lewis Orde   4749

Boyd, Doone
The Boyds of Black River - Walter D. Edmonds   1871

Bradford, Jonathan
The Drums of Morning - Philip Van Doren Stern   5997

Braxton, Richard
Mistress of the Forge - David Taylor   6179

Bundy, Andrew
A Kind of Justice - Benjamin Siegel   5844

Campbell, Neil
The Fur Masters - Alan Sullivan   6113

Carlile, John
Walnut Grove - Jane Gilmore Rushing   5531

Catherwood, Lyle
A Vein of Riches - John Knowles   3526

Catlett, Johnny
Know Nothing - Mary Lee Settle   5755

Cheston, James
Kentucky Stand - Jere Hungerford Wheelwright   6670

Church, Jonathan
Prisons - Mary Lee Settle   5757

Cimber, Lucius
If I Forget Thee - Robert S. Deropp   1621

Cloud, Adam
Bound for the Promised Land - Richard Marius   4083

Conway, Tom
That Callahan Spunk! - Francis Ames 124

Corlaer, Adam
Reluctant Rebel - Frederic F. Van de Water 6403

Crandall, Lew
A Rage Against Heaven - Fred Mustard Stewart 6026

Crane, John
Distant Trails - Bill Gulick 2612

Crazy Walking
Dance Back the Buffalo - Milton Lott 3899

Cree, Lucius
The Velvet Horn - Andrew Lytle 3946

Curry, Jeff
The Hider - Loren D. Estleman 1972

Dain
The Road to San Jacinto - Leonard L. Foreman 2167

Dalyrymple, Jim
Perilous Journey: A Tale of the Mississippi River and the Natchez Trace - Clifford Sublette 6109

Damon
O Western Wind - John Anthony Devon 1634

Darby, Quint
River's Run - Jane Ludlow Abbot 7

D'Arcy, Dermod
Tide of Empire - Peter S. Kyne 3572

Darling, Miles
Croatan - Mary Johnston 3231

De Salis, Patrick
Cashelmara - Susan Howatch 3058

Denys, Paul
River and Empty Sea - Louis Vaczek 6396

d'Este, Gervase
The Longest Night - Ada Cook Lewis 3744

Dorman, Benbow
The Wind Brings Up the Rain - Eric Malpass 4051

Douay, Paul
Daniel Du Luth - Everett McNeil 4307

Douglas, Malcolm
Borrasca - Octavus Roy Cohen 1160

Dousmann, Otto
Tie My Bones to Her Back - Robert F. Jones 3294

Dow, John
Tide-Rode - Adelyn Bushnell 813

Doyle, Peter
Peter Doyle - John Vernon 6457

Dubelsky, Kolya
Imperial Winds - Priscilla Napier 4555

Dubelsky, Misha
Imperial Winds - Priscilla Napier 4555

Durant, Adrian
Westward the Sun - Brigid Knight 3524

Duriez, Colin
The Enchantress - Suyin Han 2673

Dye, Danny
The Fortune Road - James McCague 4217

Enfield, Prentiss
Crossings - Earl Rovit 5512

Enfield, Tyson
The Very Best People - Elizabeth Villars 6499

Eyring, Rafael
The Everlasting Fire - Jonreed Lauritzen 3675

Falconer, Rane
Wild Swan - Celeste De Blasis 1550

Farrill, David
Give Me Liberty: The Story of an Innocent Man - John Erskine 1956

Feldstein, Shimon
Jerusalem Interlude - Bodie Thoene 6223

Field, Buddy
The Longest Road - Jeanne Williams 6781

Fitch, Ned
Stuyvesant Square - Margaret Lewerth 3743

French, Jared
The Arch of Stars - Clifford Lindsey Alderman 66

Frye, Michael
Trumpet at the Gate - Jan Widgery 6739

Gad
Unto the Soul - Aharon Appelfeld 181

Gilchrist, Alick
Jennie about to Be - Elisabeth Ogilvie 4694
The World of Jennie G. - Elisabeth Ogilvie 4696

Glaucus
The Last Days of Pompeii - Edward Bulwer-Lytton 768

Gonzalo
Among the Innocent - Elizabeth Borton de Trevino 6339

Gorion
The Last Days - William Rayner 5272

Guemont, Marc de
The Incorruptible - Helma De Bois 1551

Gunnar
The Foster Brothers - Edward Frankland 2202

Guriandio, Adriano
Sing to the Sun - Lucille Borden 579

Hallam, Christopher
The King's Rogue - Max Peacock 4859

Haraldsson, Sweyn
The Cross and the Sword - Evangeline Walton 6558

Harper, William
Sing One Song - Helen Topping Miller 4394

Harrington, Lee
The History of Rome Hanks - Joseph Stanley Pennell 4909

Haskell, Fred
Where Is My Wandering Boy Tonight? - David Wagoner 6522

Havenell, Francis
The Bright Face of Danger - Clifford Sublette 6108

Haward, Marmaduke
Audrey - Mary Johnston 3229

Henry, Byron
The Winds of War - Herman Wouk 6876

Hewitt, Thomas
Look to Your Geese: A Novel of the Deflowering of New England - Jacquin Sanders 5584

Hiero of Marathon
The Shining - Stephen Marlowe 4097

Hilary of Bordeaux
The Four Rivers of Paradise - Helen Constance White 6678

Hilton, Matt
Mistress of Darkness - Christopher Nicole 4617

Holcomb, Arthur Jackson Jr.
Where Is My Wandering Boy Tonight? - David Wagoner 6522

Holt, Richard
The Redemptioner - Isaac Rusling Pennypacker 4910

Holt, Tim
Oregon Legacy - Dana Fuller Ross 5485

Holt, Toby
Louisiana! - Dana Fuller Ross 5478

Hope, Randall
Father Abraham - Irving A. Bacheller 258

Hubbard, Sam
The Nancy Flyer - Ernest Poole 5091

Icarus
The Maze Maker - Michael Ayrton 250

Ines, Heraclio
The Fifth Horseman - Jose Antonio Villarreal 6496

Jared
Called Away - Perdita Buchan 753

Jonathan of Cyrene
Behold Your King - Florence M. Bauer 379

Kalner, Jacob
Warsaw Requiem - Bodie Thoene 6229

Kay, Arthur
The Kays - Margaret Deland 1583

Keating, Simon
Stacey's Flyer - Patricia Burns 800

Killigrew, Maugan
The Grove of Eagles - Winston Graham 2526

Kornowski, Stefan
Polonaise - Piers Paul Read 5278

Kozlowski, David
The House of Cards - Leon Garfield 2292

Lackland, Jonah
The Haymarket - Claire Rayner 5265

Laird, Dave
The Kingdom Carver - E.G. Perrault 4916

Landerson, Roberto "Blanco"
The Color of Blood - E. Ralph Rundell 5524

Lao Hong
The Examination - Malcolm Bosse 587

Larkin, Conor
Trinity - Leon Uris 6394

Larsen, Lars
People of the Book - David Stacton 5974

Latimer, Burke
To See Your Face Again - Eugenia Price 5188

Lawley, John
Black William - Robert Neill 4567

Lazender, Toby
A Crowning Mercy - Susannah Kells 3396

Liddiard, Gerald
Eugenia - Clare Darcy 1487

Liddiard, Richard
Eugenia - Clare Darcy 1487

Longyan
Ming: A Novel of Seventeeth Century China - Robert B. Oxnam 4772

Luovitch, Yakov "Yasha"
Between Two Worlds - Monique Raphel High 2913

Lyle, Mark
The Road to San Jacinto - James F. Davis 1524

Lysis
The Last of the Wine - Mary Renault 5299

MacAllan, Pollux
The Woman from The Glen - Chloe Gartner 2310

MacDonald, Alasdair Og
Lady of the Glen - Jennifer Roberson 5369

Mackay, Philip
Against the Tide - Muriel Elwood 1935

MacMahon, Dominick
Seek the Fair Land - Walter Macken 3989

MacVey, Lint
A Fistful of Stars - Sarah Lockwood   3828

Malone, Michael
Through the Green Valley - Barbara Gowdy   2498

Manning, Andrew
The Fires of July - Sharon Salvato   5576

Marbot, Felix
So Great a Man - David Pilgrim   5000

Marsdon, Stephen
Green Darkness - Anya Seton   5751

Martin, Michael
Captain Lightfoot - William R. Burnett   792

Massy, Raymond
A Bride for New Orleans - Edward Francis
   Murphy   4522

Matlock, Craig
Tenants of the Earth - Sandra Paretti   4793

McConkey, Fremont
The Hawkeye - Herbert Quick   5222

McConnell, Hugh
The Day Must Dawn - Agnes Sligh Turnbull   6362

McKie, Davie
The Far Side of the Hill - Nancy Livingston   3811

Meion
Anabasis: A Journey to the Interior - Ellen
   Gilchrist   2408

Middleton, Egbert
The Mighty and Their Fall - Ivy Compton-
   Burnett   1230

Mitchell, Parris
Kings Row - Henry Bellamann   428

Moffatt, Andrew
The Nonsuch Lure - Mary M. Luke   3924

Morpain, Paul de
Restless Are the Sails - Evelyn Eaton   1830

Mountain, Colin
The Secret of Saramount - Lillian Cheatham   1011

Muller, Jonathan
Patriot's Dream - Barbara Michaels   4360

Munro, Donald
Greenyards - Joan Lingard   3796

Nardo
The Reindeer Hunters - Joan Wolf   6841

Nellis, Oskar
The Life and Times of Captain N. - Douglas
   Glover   2436

Nicanor
*Nicanor of Athens: The Autobiography of an Unknown
   Citizen* - Owen Francis Grazebrook   2563

Nicolas
Darkness and the Dawn - Thomas B. Costain   1364

Novak, Thad
The Last Confederate - Gilbert Morris   4466

Obregon, Juan
Far Mountains - Frank O'Rourke   4752

O'Connor, Matthew
All Their Kingdoms - Madeleine Polland   5084

O'Murray, Stewart
A Georgian Love Story - Ernest Raymond   5258

Opalgate, Marcus
Night Wind - Roberta Jean Mountjoy   4504

Opalgate, Richard
Night Wind - Roberta Jean Mountjoy   4504

Orme
The Battle-Ax of God - Le Roy MacLeod   4007

Orso, Giacomo
Web of Lucifer: A Novel of the Borgia Fury - Maurice
   Samuel   5580

Owens, Horace
Steamboat on the River - Darwin Le Ora
   Teilhet   6200

Pader, Benjamin
Private Knowledge - Betty Palmer Nelson   4576

Palfrey, John
Fire Bell in the Night - Constance Robertson   5395

Pasha, Abdullah
The Ashes of Smyrna - Richard Reinhardt   5294

Paulus, Marcus Lucius
The Pirate From Rome - John V.D.
   Southworth   5952

Pay, Duny Gene
Weedy Rough - Douglas C. Jones   3286

Peabody, Jeremy
An American, Sir - Corwin Root   5459

Pentecost, Owen
Great Day in the Morning - Robert Hardy
   Andrews   149

Pigge, Johnny
Paradise - Esther Forbes   2158

Pirrip, Philip "Pip"
Estella - Alanna Knight   3519

Pitcher, Tresham
Captain Vinegar's Commission - Philip
   Glazebrook   2428

Prince, Henry
The Rebel and the Turncoat - Malcolm Decker   1576

Randolph, Peter
Let the Spring Come - Henry Schindall   5637

Raoul, Nathan
The Horn and the Forest - Jamie Lee Cooper   1313

Ridgeway, Joel
Charming Sally - Maude Hart Lovelace   3903

Rogers, Jesse
Rogers' Folly - Albert E. Idell   3102

Rourke, Liam
The Sons of Grady Rourke - Douglas Savage   5618

Rourke, Patrick
The Sons of Grady Rourke - Douglas Savage   5618

Rourke, Sean
The Sons of Grady Rourke - Douglas Savage   5618

Rowntree, Burr
Iron Land - Dorothy Ogley   4697

Rowntree, Ethan
Iron Land - Dorothy Ogley   4697

Roy, Clayton
The Valley - Clifford Irving   3114

Royden, Olin
Catch a Falling Star - Frederic F. Van de
   Water   6401

Sackett, Kin-Ring
The Warrior's Path - Louis L'Amour   3633

Sackett, Yance
The Warrior's Path - Louis L'Amour   3633

Ste. Marie, Marcel
The Feast of All Saints - Anne Rice   5314

Sartoris, Bayard
The Unvanquished - William Faulkner   2050

Sauny, Gideon
Seminole - Theodore Pratt   5164

Scott, George
A House Behind the Mint - Laurie Huffman   3072

Senmut
The Golden Balance - Arthur Dana Hall   2646

Seton, John
The Dark Command - William R. Burnett   793

Severus
The Lost Eagles - Ralph Graves   2542

Sheriden, Ben
The Promise of Light - Paul Watkins   6581

Sigismund
The Headsman; or, The Abbaye des Vignerons - James
   Fenimore Cooper   1300

Silver Fox
Drums of Change: The Story of Running Fawn -
   Janette Oke   4707

Smith, Calhoun
The Post of Honor - David Coxe Cooke   1266

Stacey, Ajax
The Golden Feather - Theda Kenyon   3462

Stacey, Gerald
The Golden Feather - Theda Kenyon   3462

Staples, Peter
The Highwayman - Noel B. Gerson   2372

Stark, Beau
The Road to Baltimore - Robert S. Harper   2716

Stewart, Ian
The Dark Mile - Dorothy Kathleen Broster   709

Strang, Davy
His Majesty's Yankees - Thomas H. Raddall   5230

Tacios
The Last Princess - Charles O. Locke   3826

Talcott, Ray
Bitter Creek - Al Cody   1150

Taylor, Clay
Walk Like a Man - Donald Honig   3024

Tenatos
The Altar and the Crown - Marian Niven   4631

Thyloss
The Lily and the Bull - Moyra Caldecott   846

Tizzo
The Bait and the Trap - George Challis   970

Toussaint, Paul
So Brief a Spring - Claude Manceron   4054

Trant, Anthony
Sioux City - John Hyatt Downing   1714

Traore, Tiekoro
The Children of Segu - Maryse Conde   1232

Tregaran, John
The Legacy of Tregaran - Mary Lide   3776

Trowbridge, Robert
The Neutral Ground - Frank Olney Hough   3044

Tucker, Enoch
The Sprig of Hemlock: A Novel about Shays' Rebellion
   - Robert Muir   4509

Tudor, Jared
As Runs the Glass - Evan John David   1502

Tyrrell, Ira
Honor Thy Father - Robert A. Roripaugh   5460

Tyrrell, Mart
Honor Thy Father - Robert A. Roripaugh   5460

Valerius, Manlius
*The Equinox: A Novel of Rome in the Time of
   Commodus* - Carol Saylor   5622

Van Zandt, Dirk
Shad Run - Howard Breslin   668

Van Zyl, Joachim
The Great Sky and the Silence - James S. Rand   5245

Victorevitch, Kyril "Gredka"
Between Two Worlds - Monique Raphel High   2913

Wallich, Peter
Danzig Passage - Bodie Thoene   6221
Warsaw Requiem - Bodie Thoene   6229

Weddle, Simon
The Corinthians - Nicholas E. Wyckoff   6888

Westfall, Blake
This Land Is Mine - Frances Casey Kerns   3470

White, Perry Poer
Red Lanterns on St. Michael's - Thornwell
    Jacobs   3139

Wilcox, Roger
The Wedding Journey - Walter D. Edmonds   1878

Winslow, Cassidy
The Yukon Queen - Gilbert Morris   4476

Young, Dirk
Venture in the East - Bruce Lancaster   3648

Zbyszko
The Teutonic Knights - Henryk Sienkiewicz   5849

YOUNG WOMAN

Abel, Jennie
The Moneyman - Judith Liederman   3781

Aeshia
The Gentle Infidel - Lawrence Schoonover   5663

Ahearn, Kate
They Were Dreamers - James F. Murphy Jr.   4525

Ahuna
Children of the Lion - Peter Danielson   1464

Aimesley, Dorothy
Power - Howard Fast   2041

Airmid
The Crows of War - Steven Rayson   5276

Alane
The Reindeer Hunters - Joan Wolf   6841

Alin
Daughter of the Red Deer - Joan Wolf   6838

Aline
One Corpse Too Many - Ellis Peters   4966

Allen, Lindsey
And Never Yield - Elinor Pryor   5204

Alleyn, Philobeth
The Darkening Leaf - Caroline Stickland   6036

Allison, Georgiana
The Wanton Fires - Meriol Trevor   6345

Alwin, Deborah
White Indian - Donald Clayton Porter   5134

Amalia
Unto the Soul - Aharon Appelfeld   181

Anderson, Sarah Kent
Chapultepec - Norman Zollinger   6965

Angelica
The Gentle Infidel - Lawrence Schoonover   5663

Antonia
The Monk - Matthew Gregory Lewis   3756

Anysworth, Lillian
The Drummer Was the First to Die - Liza Pennywitt
    Taylor   6186

Appleton, Margaret
Hangman's Cliff - Robert Neill   4570

Arnold, Althea
The Firelands - Karen Harper   2712

Asa
The Pecos River - Fred Bean   399

Asgeirsdottir, Margaret
The Greenlanders - Jane Smiley   5915

Ashby, Henrietta
Reckless Angel - Jane Feather   2056

Aslalfetch
The Name of Hero - Richard Seltzer   5742

Aspinal, Samantha
The Magnificent Savages - Fred Mustard
    Stewart   6024

Astrid
The Foster Brothers - Edward Frankland   2202

Atala
Atala - Francois Rene de Chateaubriand   1008

Athelson, Justine
The Athelsons - Jocelyn Kettle   3476

Atherton, Emily
The Normandie Affair - Elizabeth Villars   6497

Ausonia, Fausta
The Last Romans - Teodor Jeske-Choinski   3216

Austin, Melody
Hue and Cry - Elizabeth Yates   6907

Balcombe, Betsy
The Last Love - Thomas B. Costain   1367

Baldwin, Maggie
The Last Ride - Tom Eidson   1899

Bancroft, Marianna
Cargo of Brides - Helen Rucker   5522

Bancroft, Mercy
The Gold Seekers - William Stuart Long   3874

Barrett, Evelyn
The House of War - Catherine Gavin   2322

Bartel, Adrienne
The Renegade - Donald Clayton Porter   5122

Bartleet, Abigail
The Valiant and the Daunted - Roy Clews   1115

Barton, Judith
The Pioneers - Courtney Ryley Cooper   1296

Bashinskey, Galina
The Summer of the Bashinskeys - Diane
    Pearson   4877

Bawn, Molly
O'Houlihan's Jest - Rohan O'Grady   4702

Becker, Claire
Galveston - Suzanne Morris   4482

Bedham, Cassie
Lucifer Land - Mildred B. Davis   1538

Bellarmi, Lucia
Divine Mistress - Frank G. Slaughter   5886

Benedetto, Diana
1915: A Novel - Roger McDonald   4264

Benton, Sarah
Benton's Row - Frank Yerby   6908

Beresford, Lydia
Some Far Elusive Dawn - Emma Drummond   1727

Best, Lydia
The Peculiar People - Jan de Hartog   2764

Beynon, Nerys
Fiddler's Ferry - Iris Gower   2499

Billings, Wichita
Apache Devil - Edgar Rice Burroughs   806

Billips, Priscilla Ann
The Long Sun - Janice Lucas   3920

Bishop, Mary
Gallows Hill - Frances Winwar   6831

Bishop, Tamsen
The Hills Stand Watch - August Derleth   1615

Blake, Beth
Washington! - Dana Fuller Ross   5491

Blanchard, Holly
Sound of the Trumpet - Gilbert Morris   4471

Blevins, Ruth
Reunion at Chattanooga - Alfred Leland Crabb   1406

Blood, Kate
Blood & Dreams - Leslie Waller   6543

Bloundel, Amabel
Old St. Paul's - William Harrison Ainsworth   57

Blythe, Annie
Kingdom of Gold - Susan Wiggs   6744

Blythe, Lally
The Secret Years - Judith Lennox-Smith   3718

Boller, Melissa
The Fancher Train - Amelia Bean   395

Borden, Lizzie
Lizzie - Evan Hunter   3083

Borelli, Augustina
Rogers' Folly - Albert E. Idell   3102

Borowska, Wanda
White Eagle, Dark Skies - Jean Karsavina   3368

Boruchowicz, Leah
Heritage - Lewis Orde   4749

Bowers, Eilley
City of Illusion - Vardis Fisher   2107

Braddon, Eleanor
Night Shall Overtake Us - Kate Saunders   5611

Bradford, Fiona
The Dedicated Villain - Patricia Veryan   6461

Bradley, Page
My Love, My Enemy - Jan Cox Speas   5958

Brandt, Margaret
The Cloister and the Hearth - Charles Reade   5279

Brawne, Cathie
The Dollar Gold Piece - Virginia Swain   6134

Bray, Ellen
Ellen Bray - Jane Julian   3319

Brendan, Alicia
The Hedge of Thorns - Helen Ashton   217

Brinton, Clarissa
The Golden Feather - Theda Kenyon   3462

Brook, Marisa Estrada
The House on Bitterness Street - Elizabeth Borton de
    Trevino   6340

Brooke, Margaret
Rogue's March - Maristan Chapman   993

Broome, Francia
The Mississippi Run - Paul Darcy Boles   565

Broome, Jenny
The Gallant - William Stuart Long   3873

Brown, Harriet
Whispering - Jane Aiken Hodge   2972

Brown, Stacey
Stacey's Flyer - Patricia Burns   800

Brown, Tracy
The Medicine Whip - Max Hennessy   2835

Brusilov, Nadja
The Jade Alliance - Elizabeth Darrell   1497

Bryant, Evangeline
Promises to Keep - Jocelyn Stirling   6051

Buckstone, Prudence
The Buckstones - Paul I. Wellman   6615

Buckwell, Kathleen
Crimson Creek: A Novel of the Early West - Robert
    McCraig   4228

Burgey, Joanna
The Peacock and the Pearl - Jennifer Lang   3661

Butterfield, Elizabeth
A Rage Against Heaven - Fred Mustard
   Stewart   6026

Button, Susannah
Dark Inheritance - Carola Salisbury   5568

Bzik, Wanda
The Slave - Isaac Bashevis Singer   5866

Cadman, Emma
Silver Linings - Shirley Davies-Owens   1508

Cameron, Caroline
Wind From the Carolinas - Robert Wilder   6751

Cameron, Christa
And One Rode West - Heather Graham   2514

Cameron, Clarissa
The Thing about Clarissa - Roberta St. Clair
   Cook   1264

Cameron, Garnet
Jubilee Trail - Gwen Bristow   698

Cameron, Lauren
Highlands Rebel - Sally Watson   6584

Camillina, Sosia
The Silver Pigs - Lindsey Davis   1532

Campbell, Catriona
Lady of the Glen - Jennifer Roberson   5369

Campbell, Olivia
The Dark Mile - Dorothy Kathleen Broster   709

Candish, Lilian
Angels Falling - Janice Elliott   1915

Cannaway, Charlotte
The Cannaway Concern - Graham Shelby   5788

Cantillon, Rosamund
Red Cloak Flying - Margaret Widdemer   6737

Canynges, Crede
Warm Wind, West Wind - Anne Irwin Matthew   4188

Cape, Hannah
The Massacre at Fall Creek - Jessamyn West   6631

Care, Maggie
Polsinney Harbour - Mary E. Pearce   4863

Carlington, Aurora
Night Shall Overtake Us - Kate Saunders   5611

Carroll, Caithlin
Time and Chance - Anna Wibberley   6728

Carrolton, Sue
Shaggy Legion - Hal George Evarts   1986

Cart, Denna
Timothy Baines - John H. Culp   1445

Carteret, Charlessie
Michael Beam - Richard Hallet   2663

Cartwright, Pearl
Pearl - Helen Ashfield   211

Catlett, Melinda
Know Nothing - Mary Lee Settle   5755

Cecilia
In the Wilderness - Sigrid Undset   6381
The Son Avenger - Sigrid Undset   6384

Cera
Pride of Lions - Morgan Llywelyn   3823

Chambon, Anne du
Restless Are the Sails - Evelyn Eaton   1830

Chambord, India de
No Brighter Glory - Armstrong Sperry   5963

Channing, Barbara
Matthew Early - Alexander Laing   3589

Channing, Victoria
Mirage - Helen Topping Miller   4390

Chappelle, Constance
Walk with Peril - Dorothy V.S. Jackson   3132

Charbonneau, Julia
Time and Again - Jack Finney   2093

Charetty, Catherine de
The Spring of the Ram - Dorothy Dunnett   1809

Charles, Holly
Gray Canaan - David Garth   2305

Chase, Miranda
When the Music Changed - Marie R. Reno   5305

Chavez, Pearl
Duel in the Sun - Niven Busch   812

Chernik, Hannah
The Dream Seekers - Grace Mark   4085

Chiswick, Caroly
The French Admiral - Dewey Lambdin   3609

Chodorov, Kala
Remember This Time - Gloria Kurian Broder   703

Cicely
The Tower of London - William Harrison
   Ainsworth   58

Clare, Quality
Paradise - Sarah Neilan   4566

Clarke, Clara
The Revenge of Dracula - Peter Tremayne   6335

Clarkson, Penninah
The Power and the Glory - Phyllis Bentley   462

Clavier, Isabella
Those the Sun Has Loved - Rose Jourdain   3309

Cleo
The Road to San Jacinto - Leonard L.
   Foreman   2167

Clerc, Lorelei Du
The Raven and the Rose - Susan Wiggs   6746

Clodagh
Time of the Unicorn - Barbara Jefferis   3176

Clover
Called Away - Perdita Buchan   753

Coale, Susan
Green Rose of Furley - Helen C. Barney   334

Cochrane, Charnisay
Grand Parade - G.B. Lancaster   3649

Cody, Clara
My Sister's Keeper - Beverly Butler   817

Coffin, Damaris
Thread of Scarlet - Ben Ames Williams   6767

Cohen, Rachel
The Books of Rachel - Joel Gross   2600

Coleman, Gretel
Telluride - Susan Clark Schofield   5648

Collins, Venetia
Street of the Madwoman - Isabel Ortega   4756

Comfort, Mary
Hang for Treason - Robert Newton Peck   4886

Comyn, Jenny
Pageant - G.B. Lancaster   3650

Conybeare, Julian
The Shadow Flies - Rose Macaulay   3956

Cooke, Flora
Farewell, My General - Shirley Seifert   5726

Cooper, Deborah
Gabriel's Search - Della Lutes   3927

Cooper, Eve
Yorktown - Burke Davis   1513

Corbeau, Jeanne
Song of a Strange Child - Gilbert Morris   4470

Corleone, Maria
The Rebels - Alfred Neumann   4585

Corley, Dinah
The Running Thread - Drayton Mayrant   4215

Cottrell, Sally
Bride of a Thousand Cedars - Bruce Lancaster   3637

Courville-Boissart, Elise de
Deeper the Heritage - Muriel Elwood   1936

Covington, Siobonna
Sons of Thunder - Barbara Fitz Vroman   6516

Craig, Maggie
Maggie Craig - Marie Joseph   3308

Croasdale, Leonie
Hand of Glory - Glen Petrie   4980

Crocker, Elizabeth Allen
A Southern Woman - Elena Yates Eulo   1983

Cromwell, Tacey
Tacey Cromwell - Conrad Richter   5324

Crosby, Mariana
The Castle of the Winds - Jeanne Montague   4434

Cuheno, Rachel
The Books of Rachel - Joel Gross   2600

Culhaney, Margaret
Gone the Rainbow, Gone the Dove - Joan
   Bagnel   264

Culpepper, India
Full of Thy Riches - Elizabeth Ferrell   2070

Currain, Lucy
The Unconquered - Ben Ames Williams   6768

Curtis, Abigail
Marblehead - Joan Thompson   6267

Cutler, Jocelyn
The Braeswood Tapestry - Robyn Carr   936

Cutterfield, Annie Bee
Pursuit of Bliss - Betty Palmer Nelson   4577

Dabney, Morna
Tap Roots - James H. Street   6080

Dagshaw, Anna
The Love Child - Catherine Cookson   1279

d'Aire, Thalia
The Longest Night - Ada Cook Lewis   3744

Dalgleish, Jenny
Night Shall Overtake Us - Kate Saunders   5611

Dalsgaard, Hanne
Kingdom Come - Virginia Sorensen   5950

Damao, Bonita
The Deadly Lady of Madagascar - C.V. Terry   6206

Dare, Jeannie
The Land Is Bright - James Arthur Kjelgaard   3508

Davelle, Victoria
Mills of the Gods - Daoma Winston   6828

Dawson, Spicy
The Labyrinth - Thomas William Duncan   1787

De Chartes, Anne
Touched with Fire - John William Tebbel   6195

Dean, Sara
Scoundrels' Brigade - Carter A. Vaughan   6439

Deane, Amelie
Paloverde - Jacqueline Briskin   693

Deems, Molly
This Is the House - Deborah Hill   2921

Deirdre
Red Branch - Morgan Llywelyn   3824

Delahousse, Juliette
The French Woman - Barbara Paul 4837

Delanay, Mary
Dark Sails - Helen Topping Miller 4388

Delancey, Clytie
The Governor's Daughter - Denton Whitson 6718

Delisle, Yvonne
A Bride for New Orleans - Edward Francis Murphy 4522

DeLong, Lily
Lily - Cindy Bonner 571
Looking After Lily - Cindy Bonner 572

Delorme, Julie
By Dim and Flashing Lamps - Alan Le May 3689

Demaury, Meg
Summoned to Darkness - Anne-Marie Sheridan 5809

Dennetry, Sophia
Drums of War - Roy Clews 1114

Derwent-Jones, Caroline
The Nightingale Legacy - Catherine Coulter 1379

Derwent, Marina
Damnation Reef - Jill Tattersall 6172

Deschaumes, Constance
The Riven Heart - Genevieve Gennari 2354

Desmond, Lizzie
Pomp and Circumstance - Fred Mustard Stewart 6025

Devera, Camille
Keeping Secrets - Suzanne Morris 4483

Deverell, Fancy
Paint the Wind - Cathy Cash Spellman 5960

Deveron, Ellen
Swear by Apollo - Shirley Barker 318

Devigne, Sophia
Starrbelow - China Thompson 6248

Devlin, Lisette
Wanderers Eastward, Wanderers West - Kathleen Winsor 6823

Dewar, Ellen
Hangman's Beach - Thomas H. Raddall 5229

Deyo, Gina
The Golden Circle - Constance Robertson 5396

Dixon, Kathy
The Master of Oakwindsor - Douglas Kent Hall 2648

Doane, Isabel
Winds of Blame - Jane Gilmore Rushing 5532

Doane, Joanna
Winds of Blame - Jane Gilmore Rushing 5532

Doireann
The Winter Servant - M.H. Davis 1537

Doll, Hannah
The Man on the Train - W.J. Chaput 995

Dominguez, Cayetana
A Shadow of Eagles - Jane Barry 360

Dorman, Corunna
Captain Caution - Kenneth Roberts 5385

Doucet, Olivia
Bayou - Pamela Jekel 3183

Dousmann, Jenny
Tie My Bones to Her Back - Robert F. Jones 3294

Dove, Mary
Mary Dove - Jane Gilmore Rushing 5529

Dowland, Elizabeth
The Mists of Manittoo - Lois Swann 6135

Downing, Hetty
The Greater Hunger - Barbara Dodge Borland 581

Drake, Deborah
River to the West: A Novel of the Astor Adventure - John Edward Jennings 3204

Drake, Sarah
Sons of Fire - Max McCoy 4227

Draper, Ellen
Lovers All Untrue - Norah Lofts 3851

Draper, Marion
Lovers All Untrue - Norah Lofts 3851

Drosis
Son of Judah - Dan Levin 3738

Drummond, Elizabeth
Born to Be King - Constance Gluyas 2440

Drummond, Yolande
The Noblest Frailty - Patricia Veryan 6474

Duchesne, Judith
Judith Duchesne - Lynda Sargent 5605

DuGay, Delia
Early Candlelight - Maude Hart Lovelace 3904

Dulaine, Clio
Saratoga Trunk - Edna Ferber 2062

Dunham, Mabel
The Pathfinder; or, The Inland Sea - James Fenimore Cooper 1305

Dupre, Merry
Wagons West - Leslie Turner White 6692

Durant, Charlotte
Westward the Sun - Brigid Knight 3524

Duriez, Bea
The Enchantress - Suyin Han 2673

Duval, Sophie
The Glass-Blowers - Daphne Du Maurier 1745

Dye, Nancy
The Fortune Road - James McCague 4217

Dyer, Mary
Bear His Mild Yoke - Ethel White 6675

Easton, Hannah
The Holder of the World - Bharati Mukherjee 4510

Eilan
The Forest House - Marion Zimmer Bradley 625

Eisner, Letty
The Limner - Paul Darcy Boles 564

Eleanor
The Unholy Pilgrim - R.F. Tapsell 6161

Elfreda
This January Tale - Bryher 747

Elin
Beguiled - Alice Borchardt 577
Devoted - Alice Borchardt 578

Elliot, Bronwen
The Valiant and the Daunted - Roy Clews 1115

Ellis, Guinevere
The Sea Scape - Mary Lide 3778

Emerton, Lucy
Count Manifred - Miranda Seymour 5761

Emine
Freedom or Death - Nikos Kazantzakis 3383

Enfield, Clovis
Crossings - Earl Rovit 5512

Epona
The Horse Goddess - Morgan Llywelyn 3820

Erdman, Lisa
The White Hotel - D.M. Thomas 6237

Estrada, Carmen
Carmen of the Rancho - Frank H. Spearman 5955

Estrada, Magdalena
This Land I Hold - Virginia Myers 4550

Etain
Return of the Stranger - Dorothy James Roberts 5377

Evans, Angela
Afterward - Catherine M. Rae 5234

Evans, Gwyneth
Bygones - Frank Wilkinson 6762

Evans, Maud
Afterward - Catherine M. Rae 5234

Evans, Molly
His Majesty's Highwayman - Donald Barr Chidsey 1061

Eyring, Myra
The Everlasting Fire - Jonreed Lauritzen 3675

Fairchild, Helen
O Genesee - Janet O'Daniel 4688

Fallon, Maud
Quinn's Book - William Kennedy 3423

Farebrother, Ellen
The Darkening Leaf - Caroline Stickland 6036

Farland, Catherine
The Lion Triumphant - Philippa Carr 922

Farringdon, Kate
Warwyck's Woman - Rosalind Laker 3604

Favor, Delia
Goldfield - Richard S. Wheeler 6660

Fay, Morgan
Silver Cross - Mary Johnston 3239

Feeney, Noreen
Brandywine - Jack Rowe 5513

Feldstein, Leah
Jerusalem Interlude - Bodie Thoene 6223
Munich Signature - Bodie Thoene 6224
Prague Counterpoint - Bodie Thoene 6225

Ferenc, Eva
Csardas - Diane Pearson 4875

Ferenc, Malie
Csardas - Diane Pearson 4875

Ferguson, Ellen
The Ship's Clock - Catherine M. Rae 5237

Fernald, Kate
Time out of Mind - Rachel Field 2081

Ferris, Serena
Gold Is Where You Find It - Clements Ripley 5345

Field, Laurie
The Longest Road - Jeanne Williams 6781

Finn, Corinna
Spy's Honour - Gavin Lyall 3929

Fitzgerald, Magheen
Gerait's Daughter - Millie J. Ragosta 5241

Flowers, Fanny Rosa
Hungry Hill - Daphne Du Maurier 1746

Flowers, Molly
Ballenrose - Mallory Burgess 783

Fong Yun, Brigid
China Saga - C.Y. Lee 3706

Fontaine, Myra
The Hunting Shirt - Mary Johnston 3235

Forrester, Mary
Hawthorn Hill - Doris Shannon 5777

Forster, Polly
An Air of Glory - Sarah Neilan 4563

Fowler, Iris
Born with the Century - William Kinsolving 3501

Fraser, Katrine
Mistress of The Highlands - Chloe Gartner 2309

Frazier, Willa
Galveston - Suzanne Morris 4482

Frey, Meta
The Heidenmauer - James Fenimore Cooper 1301

Frosbie, Ellen
Ho, the Fair Wind - I.A.R. Wylie 6889

Frost, Isabella
No Price Too High - Madeleine Polland 5085

Gadney, Deborah
Seventeen of Leyden - John James 3160

Gallus, Diana
The Robe - Lloyd C. Douglas 1703

Gamble, Libby
Tidewater - Clifford Dowdey 1709

Garland, Anne
The Trumpet Major - Thomas Hardy 2700

Garland, Francesca
Night Shall Overtake Us - Kate Saunders 5611

Garrega, Leonor de
Eagle of the Gredos - Claude Jack Osgood 4761

Garret, Serena
Galveston - Suzanne Morris 4482

Gates, Tamar
The Land Beyond the Tempest - Drayton Mayrant 4213

Gatewood, Kitty
Each Bright River - Mildred Masterson McNeilly 4308

Gentry, Marin
Lights Along the Shore - Diane Austell 241

Genville, Mary
The Devil in Velvet - John Dickson Carr 909

Ghislaine
The Courts of Love: A Romance of Medieval France - Peter Bourne 592

Gilmour, Marietta
The Fires of Glenlochy - Constance Heaven 2806

Glasman, Ronya Von
The Candlesticks and the Cross - Ruth Freeman Solomon 5940

Golden Orchard
The Fabulous Concubine - Hsin-Hai Chang 987

Gomez, Caterina
Whispering - Jane Aiken Hodge 2972

Gomez, Francisca de
Against the Tide - Muriel Elwood 1935

Goodacre, Joanna
The Pride of the Trevallions - Carola Salisbury 5570

Gordon, Faith
Flight From Avatchez - Frank G. Slaughter 5887

Grailhe, Eloise
The Comancheros - Paul I. Wellman 6616

Grainger, Zoe
Never Doubt I Love - Patricia Veryan 6473

Gray, Catherine
Not by Any Single Man - Brigid Knight 3522

Greenleaf, Laura
Distant Trumpet - Paul Horgan 3032

Greenway, Damask
Afternoon of a Autocrat - Norah Lofts 3834

Gregson, Sarah
The Rookery: A Novel of the Victorian Underworld - Hugh C. Rae 5239

Griggs, Devora
Farewell the Stranger - Saliee O'Brien 4682

Gross, Alice
Gettysburg - Stephen Longstreet 3887

Gudrid
A Viking's Daughter - John Andrews 147

Guerrero, Estrella
The Franciscan - Forrester Blake 532

Guerrero, Josepha
Tide of Empire - Peter S. Kyne 3572

Guidmar
Among the Innocent - Elizabeth Borton de Trevino 6339

Guinevere
Guinevere - Sharan Newman 4600

Gwyn, Viola
Viola Gwyn - George Barr McCutcheon 4258

Hale, Ann
Railroad West - Cornelia Meigs 4327

Haleevie, Fronah
Mandarin - Robert S. Elegant 1905

Hamilton, Mary
The Far Side of the Hill - Nancy Livingston 3811

Hampton, Merit
Angel with Spurs - Paul I. Wellman 6613

Hampton, Molly
Private Knowledge - Betty Palmer Nelson 4576

Harbin, Joan
A Question of Honour - Clifford Dowdey 1707

Harbourne, Grizelda
The Holy Innocents - Kate Sedley 5717

Harding, Caroline
Mistaken Virtues - Joanna Trollope 6349

Hare, Margaret
In the Days of Poor Richard - Irving A. Bacheller 259

Harley, Arabella
Castle Malindine - Hilary Ford 2163

Harris, Honor
The King's General - Daphne Du Maurier 1748

Harrison, Abigail
Abigail - Mary Louise Aswell 221

Hasdai, Gabriela
The Spanish Doctor - Matt Cohen 1159

Haslewood, Jenny
The White Witch - Elizabeth Goudge 2496

Hastings, Marilyn
An American, Sir - Corwin Root 5459

Haversham, Miranda
The Haversham Legacy - Daoma Winston 6827

Havisham, Estella
Estella - Alanna Knight 3519

Hawthorne, Jennie
Jennie about to Be - Elisabeth Ogilvie 4694

Healey, Celia
All Their Kingdoms - Madeleine Polland 5084

Henderson, Ral
Pursuit of Bliss - Betty Palmer Nelson 4577

Hermione
The Private Life of Helen of Troy - John Erskine 1957

Heron, Sabrina
Sabrina - Madeleine Polland 5086

Hill, Sophia
Princess Sophia - Edison Marshall 4110

Hilton, Andhra
The Sleeping Tiger - Marjorie McEvoy 4269

Hilton, Hope
Tavern in the Town - Cecile Hulse Matschat 4187

Hilton, Meg
Sunset - Christopher Nicole 4623

Hingham, Judith
East of the Giants - George Rippey Stewart 6027

Hobbs, Maria Zion
The Fairbrothers - Clark McMeekin 4291

Hollis, Hero
Trade Wind - M.M. Kaye 3378

Holm, Dina
Dina's Book - Herbjorg Wassmo 6577

Holt, Cindy
Louisiana! - Dana Fuller Ross 5478

Holt, Hannah
Dodging Red Cloud - Richard S. Wheeler 6657

Hopkins, Faith
Dragon Cove - Carter A. Vaughan 6434

Horn, Damaris
In Adam's Fall - Constance Dodge 1666

Howard, Ann
For They Shall Inherit - Malcolm Macdonald 3964

Howard, Jane
Blake's Reach - Catherine Gaskin 2313

Howard, Kirsty
A Falcon for a Queen - Catherine Gaskin 2314

Howard, Nancy Ann
The Parson's Daughter - Catherine Cookson 1286

Howarth, Anna
The Vivian Inheritance - Jean Stubbs 6101

Howe, Emily
From a Far Land - Robert S. Elegant 1903

Howell, Tempy Ann
The Perilous Night - Burke Boyce 609

Hunt, Louise
The Post of Honor - David Coxe Cooke 1266

Hunter, Teresa
No Tears for Christmas - Helen Topping Miller 4391

Hussey, Sara
Armada - Charles Gidley 2404

Hyde, Merideth
Hyde Place - Virginia Coffman 1154

Ibsen, Lori
Warsaw Requiem - Bodie Thoene 6229

Idaho, Harriet
Harry Idaho - Hugh Pendexter 4894

Ierii
The Lily and the Bull - Moyra Caldecott 846

Ildico
Darkness and the Dawn - Thomas B. Costain 1364

Isabel of Northfield
The Ruthless Yeomen - Valerie Anand 134

Iscariot, Judith
Barabbas: A Dream of the World's Tragedy - Marie Corelli 1327

Ivanovna, Maria
The Captain's Daughter - Alexander Pushkin 5210

Jackson, Marietta
The Ancestors Cry Out - Eugenia Lovett West 6627

Jackson, Rebekah
The Reluctant Bridegroom - Gilbert Morris 4467

Jahn, Trudy
Chicago Girls - Edith Freund 2229

James, Mary
My Sister's Keeper - Beverly Butler 817

Jara
If I Forget Thee - Brenda Lesley Segal 5720

Jardine, Camille
Wychwood - Nicole St. John 5564

Jardine, Nell
Wychwood - Nicole St. John 5564

Jastrow, Natalie
The Winds of War - Herman Wouk 6876

Jenkins, Mary
Proud Mary - Iris Gower 2501

Johns, Alenn
Plume Rouge: A Novel of the Pathfinders - John Upton
   Terrell 6203

Johnson, Mary
The Golden Wildcat - Margaret Widdemer 6735

Jones, Amelia
The Latter Adventures of Tom Jones - Bob
   Coleman 1200

Jones, Amity
Rivers of Gold - Janet Edmonds 1868

Jones, Megan
The Pearl Pagoda - Susannah Broome 707

Jordan, Jenny
Beloved Enemy - Al Lacy 3579

Jumelle, Justine
The Alpha Raid - Alan Scholefield 5651

Jupiter, Mona
Organized Crime - Nicholas Von Hoffman 6511

Kane, Rachel
The Books of Rachel - Joel Gross 2600

Kane, Tara
Tara Kane - George Markstein 4091

Karlin, Anna
Quiet Lady - Norman Collins 1216

Kartright, Becky
Night of Decision: A Novel of Colonial New York -
   Dorothy Grant 2534

Kemp, Hannah
The Sword of Truth - Gilbert Morris 4472

Kendrick, Stella
The Valiant - Sigman Byrd 839

Kenner, Katie
Promised Lands - Elizabeth Crook 1430

Kerr, Cindy Holt
Celebration! - Dana Fuller Ross 5470

Kieq Lan
Saigon - Anthony Grey 2588

Kilgour, Sandia
Saturday City - Jan Webster 6593

Kincaid, Augusta
The Fall River Line - Daoma Winston 6824

Kincaid, Soledad
Solitudes - R.G. Vliet 6507

King, Bettie Moss
True Women - Janice Woods Windle 6820

Knight, Elzada
No Other Place - John Gould 2497

Kornowski, Krystyna
Polonaise - Piers Paul Read 5278

Kortenaer, Dorande van
Phantom Fortress - Bruce Lancaster 3643

Kwiknee
The Echoing Cliffs - Hjalmar P. Thesen 6219

La-ena
Wyoming! - Dana Fuller Ross 5494

La Jeune, Charlotte
Daughter of Strangers - Elizabeth Boatwright
   Coker 1164

La Salle, Claire
Mission to Mackinac - Myron David Orr 4755

Lackland, Lettice
Chelsea Reach - Claire Rayner 5261

Lackland, Phoebe
Soho Square - Claire Rayner 5268

Ladland, Katie
For My Great Folly - Thomas B. Costain 1365

Lamoreaux, Madeleine
Touched with Fire - John William Tebbel 6195

Landers, Becky
Becky Landers, Frontier Warrior - Constance
   Skinner 5879

Landry, Mignon
Mignon - James M. Cain 845

Lane, Jane
Royal Escape - Georgette Heyer 2900

Laney, Garnet
For the Love of Robert E. Lee - M.A. Harper 2715

Langdon, Alicia
Golden Destiny - June Wyndham Davies 1506

Lange, Chris de
The Covenant - Brigid Knight 3521

Langley, Penelope
Traitor's Moon - Robert Neill 4574

Lansing, Jill
The Ironmaster - Anne Powers 5150

Lao-ke
Roanoke Warrior - Carter A. Vaughan 6438

Larsen, Hannale
People of the Book - David Stacton 5974

Laury, Ann
Soul of Abe Lincoln - Bernie Babcock 251

Lavelle, Adrienne
Ward of the Sun King - Mildred Allen Butler 826

Lavinia
The Bond and the Free - Charles Dunscomb 1813

Lawley, Molly
Black William - Robert Neill 4567

Lawton, Dolly
Brimstone Club - F. van Wyck Mason 4147

Layton, Sarah
The Day of the Scorpion - Paul Scott 5682

Leah
Babylon - Anthony Esler 1959

Lee, Mary Ellen
The Bannaman Legacy - Catherine Cookson 1272

Leguay, Gay
I Thee Wed - Gilbert Wolf Gabriel 2267

Leighton, Amelia
One Night in Newport - Elizabeth Villars 6498

Lenoir, Nicole
Always a River - Drayton Mayrant 4211

Lescure, Marie de
La Vendee - Anthony Trollope 6346

Leslie, Ann
The King's Rebel - James David Horan 3030

Levinson-Gore, Laura
In the Shadow of the Nile - Sara Hylton 3093

Lewarne, Linnet
Castle Dor - Sir Arthur Thomas Quiller-Couch 5226

Libba
Scorpus the Moor - Leslie Turner White 6690

Lichen
People of the River - W. Michael Gear 2338

Liddiard, Eugenia
Eugenia - Clare Darcy 1487

Lightfoot, Hannah
The Prince and the Quakeress - Jean Plaidy 5043

Lilia
The Lost Legion - H. Warner Munn 4516

Lily
The Mountain of Immoderate Desires - Leslie
   Wilson 6811

Lin Kwong
The House That Tai Ming Built - Virginia Lee 3711

Lindhelm, Elisa
Prague Counterpoint - Bodie Thoene 6225
Vienna Prelude - Bodie Thoene 6228

Lindsay, Hannah
Brave Kingdom - Frances Murray 4534

Linton, Kate
The Last Summer of Innocence - Linda Sole 5938

Llewelyn, Gwen
The White Rhino Hotel - Bartle Bull 765

Locke, Jane
This Other Eden - Marilyn Harris 2733

Locker, Sarah
The Price of Liberty - Joseph G.E. Hopkins 3028

Logan, Kendra
Calico Palace - Gwen Bristow 694

Lopez, Rebecca
The Quality of Mercy - Faye Kellerman 3391

Lorimer, Sally
The Cactus and the Crown - Catherine Gavin 2318

Lorne, Raurie
And the Wild Birds Sing - Lola Irish 3112

Lospe
This Promised Land - Robert Easton 1824

Lostris
River God - Wilbur Smith 5928

Lotus
Manchu Palaces - Jeanne Larsen 3669

Luarca, Francisca de
Poison - Kathryn Harrison 2737

Lucas, Celia
The Haymarket - Claire Rayner 5265

Luisa
The Balloonist - Macdonald Harris 2724

Lyle, Rena
Cottonwoods Grow Tall - Margaret Bell
   Houston 3055

Lynch, Dorothea
The Lovely Lynchs - Magdalen King-Hall 3490

Lynch, Ella
Young Vargas Lewis - Robert Brainard Pearsall 4874

Lynch, Jenny
The Lovely Lynchs - Magdalen King-Hall 3490

MacAllan, Jennie
The Woman from The Glen - Chloe Gartner 2310

Maceachern, Darthula
Commander of the Mists - D.L. Murray 4527

MacIan, Fiona
Dark Torrent of Glencoe - Edward Grierson 2590

MacIntosh, Sarah
The Glass Dove - Sally Carrighar 943

MacIntyre, Clory
The Giant Joshua - Maurine Whipple 6673

MacLean, Jeannie
The Strange Brigade - John Edward Jennings 3209

MacLeod, Mairi
The Island Harp - Jeanne Williams 6779

Macmillan, Sophie
In Still and Stormy Waters - Reay Tannahill 6157

Macpherson, Nancy
Give Me the Daggers - Catherine Gavin 2321

Macy, Abigail
Diamond Head - Houston Branch 647

Maeve
Isle of Glory - Jane Oliver 4723
Spy in Chancery - P.C. Doherty 1680

Maguire, Rose
I Know My Love - Catherine Gaskin 2315

Malatesta, Concordia
Concordia - Frances Fleetwood 2124

Malone, Madge
The Far Down - Elizabeth Corbett 1321

Malone, Rowan
Beyond the Shining Mountains - Doris Shannon 5775

Malone, Tessie
The Far Down - Elizabeth Corbett 1321

Manners, Daphne
The Jewel in the Crown - Paul Scott 5684

March, Hannah
Beauty for Ashes - Timothy R. Wilson 6816

Marcia
The Pirate From Rome - John V.D. Southworth 5952

Marian
Sherwood - Parke Godwin 2449

Marianne
Son of Judah - Dan Levin 3738

Mariot, Lisle
The Sounds of Chariots: A Novel of John Sevier and the State of Franklin - Helen Topping Miller 4396

Marquand, Mary
Golden Shore - George Shaftel 5769

Marsdon, Celia
Green Darkness - Anya Seton 5751

Marsh, Tansy
The King's Bed - Margaret Campbell Barnes 324

Marshall, Faith
Catch a Falling Star - Frederic F. Van de Water 6401

Martin, Beth
Montana! - Dana Fuller Ross 5479

Martin, Jenny
The Drums of April - Charles Mergendahl 4340

Martin, Mary
There Is a Season - Alice Mary Colver 1219

Martinez, Anita
The Golden Valley - Daoma Winston 6826

Marvayne, Lass
Fire and the Hammer - Shirley Barker 311

Marvin, Phoebe
Arundel - Kenneth Roberts 5383

Mary, Mary
The Tall One - Barbara Jefferis 3175

Mascarenhas, Leonora
The Pagoda Tree - Berkely Mather 4181

Maskey, Laura
Where the Willows Weep - Patricia Shaw 5781

Mason, Daisy
The Maltese Angel - Catherine Cookson 1283

Mason, Ella
Lord Raven's Widow - Leslie O'Grady 4700

Mason, Wendy
His Majesty's Highlanders - Leslie Turner White 6683

Masters, Beigh
The Holder of the World - Bharati Mukherjee 4510

Maud
This Bright Sword - Donald Barr Chidsey 1066

Maxwell, Rachel
Children of the Dust - Carlile Clancy 1084

McCann, Margot
She Rode a Yellow Stallion - Walter Reed 5286

McCloud, Mary
The Dark Command - William R. Burnett 793

McConnell, Rose
Grandmother and the Priests - Taylor Caldwell 857

McGrath, Ada
The Piano - Jane Campion 878

McKenna, Kit
Captain Ironhand - Rosamond Marshall 4116

McKensie, Kate
The Seventh Girl: A Romantic Tale of Civil War Texas - Tom Pendleton 4900

McNair, Christie
The Able McLaughlins - Margaret Wilson 6812

Mei Lin
Rebels of the Heavenly Kingdom - Katherine Paterson 4828

Meihua
Ming: A Novel of Seventeeth Century China - Robert B. Oxnam 4772

Meinhardt, Maria
The Copperheads - William James Blech 544

Mendoza, Mariana
The Kingsbridge Plot - Maan Meyers 4355

Merari
Merari - Gloria Howe Bremkamp 656

Mercer, Penelope
Pargeters - Norah Lofts 3857

Meredith, Janice
Janice Meredith - Paul Leicester Ford 2166

Merewyn
Avalon - Anya Seton 5748

Merrill, Colleen
Sand in the Wind - Kathleen O'Neal Gear 2329

Michaelson, Callie
And One Wore Gray - Heather Graham 2515

Middleton, Lavinia
The Mighty and Their Fall - Ivy Compton-Burnett 1230

Milholme, Denise
The Prize Master - Harvey Haislip 2642

Ming Sen
Treasure in Hell's Canyon - Bill Gulick 2619

Mitla
Gods on Horseback - Samuel G. Baggett 263

Mohini
The Golden Honeycomb - Kamala Markandaya 4086

Molloy, Molly
Rogue's Holiday - Hamilton Cochran 1141

Mompesson, Polly
The Running of the Tide - Esther Forbes 2160

Monckton, May
Lady Jane - Leslie O'Grady 4699

Montez, Lola
The Union Belle - Gilbert Morris 4473

Moore, Megan Byers
Megan - Kathleen Magill 4028

Morel, Charlotte
Charlotte Morel - Maria Lodi 3829
Charlotte Morel: The Dream - Maria Lodi 3830
Charlotte Morel: The Siege - Maria Lodi 3831

Morel, Jeanne
A Tale of the Wind: A Novel of Nineteenth-Century France - Kay Nolte Smith 5922

Morgan, Jane
West of Appomattox - Harley Duncan 1785

Morland, Lesley
Home Station - Jeanne Williams 6778

Morse, Remembrance
Trumpet to Arms - Bruce Lancaster 3647

Mortimer, Charlotte
Electricity: A Novel - Victoria Glendinning 2431

Moss, Elizabeth
The Three Lives of Elizabeth - Shirley Seifert 5735

Mountain, Sarah
The Secret of Saramount - Lillian Cheatham 1011

Munro, Alice
The Last of the Mohicans - James Fenimore Cooper 1302

Munro, Cora
The Last of the Mohicans - James Fenimore Cooper 1302

Murdoch, Jill
The Silver Oar - Howard Breslin 669

Murphy, Elisa
Munich Signature - Bodie Thoene 6224

Murray, Violet
The Day Must Dawn - Agnes Sligh Turnbull 6362

Musson, Clara
For God and Glory - Tim Jeal 3171

Naomi
Daughter of Jairus - Paul Hervey Fox 2196

Niccola
Leonardo's Judas - Leo Perutz 4941

Nicola
The Ruthless Yeomen - Valerie Anand 134

North, Mahalia
Fire Bell in the Night - Constance Robertson 5395

Nuala
The Gallowglass - Howard Breslin 666

Oakley, Harriet
The Golden Fleece - Norah Lofts 3843

Oakley, Myrtle
The Golden Fleece - Norah Lofts 3843

O'Brien, Elayna
A Whisper on the Wind - Madeline Baker 276

O'Carroll, Kathleen
Tassels on Her Boots - Arthur Cheney Train 6313

Oconechee
Mountain Windsong - Robert J. Conley 1246

Oenone
Paris of Troy - George Baker 273

Ojarra, Angelica
The Crimson Wind - Max Hennessy 2832

O'Neill, Maeve
The Black Duchess - Alanna Knight 3514

O'Rourke, Olivia
Olivia and Jai - Rebecca Ryman 5544

Ortiz, Magdalena
Lotus Land - Monica Highland 2917

Osgood, Jeanne
The Wilderness - Carter A. Vaughan 6442

Osgood, Mary
Dynasty - Robert S. Elegant 1902

Osmanagic, Fata
The Bridge on the Drina - Ivo Andric 151

Otter
A Shadow of Gulls - Patricia Finney 2096

Owen, Kathryn
The Very Best People - Elizabeth Villars 6499

Paget, Anne
Rebel Heiress - Robert Neill 4573

Paget, Barbara
Rebel Heiress - Robert Neill 4573

Paget, Emily
Emily - Cynthia Harrod-Eagles 2753

Paget, Frances
The Steps of the Sun - Joanna Trollope 6350

Pappentheim, Bertha
When Nietzsche Wept: A Novel of Obsession - Irvin D. Yalom 6892

Parolles, Rodriga de
No Man's Son - Doris Sutcliffe Adams 23

Parr, Rebecca
Lady in the Briars - Carola Dunn 1793

Parsons, Ann
The Yankee Brig - Carter A. Vaughan 6443

Parvati
The Last Victory - T.N. Murari 4519

Pasquelle, Marie
The Citadel of the Lakes - Myron David Orr 4754

Paston, Margery
Beloved Lady - Barbara Jefferis 3174

Patterson, Anna
Hearts of Gold - Jessica Stirling 6044

Pavernen, Julia
From a Far Land - Robert S. Elegant 1903

Paxton, Marcella
Scarborough House - Sharon Salvato 5577

Peat, Flora
Belgrave Square - Rachel Summerson 6117

Pendleton, Nancy
Sing for a Penny - Clifford Dowdey 1708

Peniston, Darthea
Hugh Wynne, Free Quaker - Silas Weir Mitchell 4416

Penn, Victoria
Halfhyde and the Fleet Review - Philip McCutchan 4246

Pennyform, Nokomis
Too Late! Too Late! The Maiden Cried - Joan Fleming 2128

Pepperell, Mercy
The Highwayman - Noel B. Gerson 2372

Peridot, Juliette
Greenstone - Yvonne Kalman 3324

Perrin, Sophie
The Colors of Vaud - Bryher 741

Perry, Althea
The Anatolian - Elia Kazan 3381

Perry, Elizabeth
The Willing Maid - C.T. Ritchie 5349

Perry, Rebecca
Too Long a Stranger - Janette Oke 4710

Petenera
The Memoirs of Christopher Columbus - Stephen Marlowe 4096

Peverel, Jenny
Polonaise - Jane Aiken Hodge 2968

Peyton, Jane
The Tree of Liberty - Elizabeth Page 4773

Phillips, Mercy
Judas Flowering - Jane Aiken Hodge 2965

Photina
A Woman of Samaria - James W. Ingles 3104

Pieteria
Cross, Sword, and Arrow - Gladys H. Barr 340

Plattner, Sophronia
The Paper Mistress - Dorothea Malm 4045

Pomegranate
Bronze Mirror - Jeanne Larsen 3668

Pontifrac, Berry
Loving Heart - Elsie Singmaster 5869

Porteous, Mary
The Heroine's Sister - Frances Murray 4536

Potter, Maggie
Masters of Illusion: A Novel of the Connecticut Circus Fire - Mary-Ann Tirone Smith 5925

Prinsloo, Lisbet
They Seek a Country - Francis Brett Young 6941

Prior, Juliet
The Wildcliffe Bird - Constance Heaven 2811

Pruitt, Lottie
Chihuahua 1916 - Otis Carney 903

Purchis, Juliet
Savannah Purchase - Jane Aiken Hodge 2970

Quinlaw, Sarah
The Ways of Women - Elaine Crowley 1436

Quist, Lancey
Shad Run - Howard Breslin 668

Rachel
The Rock: A Novel about Gibraltar - John Masters 4179

Ramsay, Catherine
Fortress Fury - Carter A. Vaughan 6435

Ramsay, Margaret
The Fortunes of Nigel - Sir Walter Scott 5696

Raventhorne, Maya
The Veil of Illusion - Rebecca Ryman 5545

Rebecca
If I Forget Thee - Robert S. Deropp 1621
Ivanhoe - Sir Walter Scott 5699

Regan, Kate
Westfield - Roderick Thorp 6277

Reil, Roxana
Yankee Pasha - Edison Marshall 4115

Reilly, Frances
1915: A Novel - Roger McDonald 4264

Renard, Margot
Baneful Sorceries, or The Countess Bewitched - Joan Sanders 5585

Renfro, Spring
The Good Old Boys - Elmer Kelton 3405

Retallick, Miriam
Harvest of the Sun - E.V. Thompson 6265

Rettig, Elizabeth
Elizabeth, By Name - Will Cook 1265

Riada
Raven's Wind - Victor Canning 883

Rian
The Earth Goddess - Richard Herley 2856

Rider, Kate
Three Roads to Valhalla - Catherine Pomeroy Stewart 6022

Ridley, Betsy
War Chief - Donald Clayton Porter 5130

Riesling, Margrethe
Blood Winter - William Patrick 4830

Rising, April
April Rising - Susan Sallis 5574

Ritter, Caroline
Rebel in Blue - Herman Toepperwein 6289

Rivera, Rose de
Dillinger - Harry Patterson 4832

Roberts, Amelia
Where the Willows Weep - Patricia Shaw 5781

Robertson, Julia
Burden of Desire - Robert MacNeil 4023

Robson, Sylvia
Sylvia's Lovers - Elizabeth Gaskell 2312

Rochdale, Eustacia
Dragonmede - Rona Randall 5246

Rodriguez, Micaela
The Edge of the Storm - Agustin Yanez 6893

Roebury, Wilhelmina
Black Angels - C.T. Ritchie 5348

Ronzie, Juliet de
The Charlatan - Carter A. Vaughan 6433

Rose
Miss Nobody - Caroline Ross 5465

Rose, Hannah
Shadowed Memories - Al Lacy 3583

Ross, Catriona
Greenyards - Joan Lingard 3796

Rosslyn, Kate
Daughters of England - Philippa Carr 919

Rowan, Letitia
A Calf for Venus - Norah Lofts 3838

Rulan
Empire of Heaven - Linda Ching Sledge 5907

Running Fawn
Drums of Change: The Story of Running Fawn - Janette Oke 4707

Rush, Ann
Bring Larks and Heroes - Thomas Keneally 3410

Rush, Neva
The Silver Mountain - Dan Cushman 1453

Rutledge, Ann
Comes an Echo on the Breeze - Edward J. Ryan 5542
The Soul of Ann Rutledge - Bernie Babcock 252

Sackett, Echo
Ride the River - Louis L'Amour 3625

St. Clair, Isabella
The Storm Witch - Elisabeth Barr 339

Salazar, Lola
Wolf Song - Harvey Fergusson 2069

Sancerre, Margot de
Papa La-Bas - John Dickson Carr 914

Sanford, Caroline
Empire: A Novel - Gore Vidal 6487

Sassoon, Dinah
Flowers in the Blood - Gay Courter 1387

Savarin-Decker, Hermine
Glowstone - Macdonald Harris 2725

Savigny, Annabelle de
Nethergate - Norah Lofts 3854

Sawyer, Melissa
Tomorrow the Harvest - Viola Paradise 4789

Schroeder, Tonia
Captain Wonder - Donald Thomas 6238

Scott, Brigid
Buckskin Baronet - Margaret Widdemer 6734

Scott, Ellen
A House Behind the Mint - Laurie Huffman 3072

Seabrook, Linda
Blossom Like the Rose - Norah Lofts 3836

Selden, Deborah
Captain Adam - Donald Barr Chidsey 1058

Seyawa
Long Pig - Russell Foreman 2168

Shackleton, Eve
The Legion of the Lost - Donald Barr Chidsey 1062

Shattuck, Star
Storm to the South - Thelma Strabel 6073

Shepard, Caroline
The Predators - F.A. Parker 4804

Sheramy, Ann
The Handsome Road - Gwen Bristow 697

Sheridan, Lainey
Oklahoma Run - Alberta Constant 1260

Sherwood, Felicity
Reluctant Rebel - Frederic F. Van de Water 6403

Shields, Harriet
Look Away - Harold Coyle 1395

Shinann
Bard: The Odyssey of the Irish - Morgan Llywelyn 3816

Shore, Jane
The Goldsmith's Wife - Jean Plaidy 5017

Shoshana
The Master - Max Brod 702

Silana, Marcella
The Second Crucifixion - Maurice Samuel 5579

Singer, Rachel
Behold the Fire - Michael Blankfort 541

Sinyosoglou, Taomna
America, America - Elia Kazan 3380

Slythe, Dorcas
A Crowning Mercy - Susannah Kells 3396

Snape, Rose
Aurora Rose - Anne Worboys 6870

Solomon, Leonora
Dreams of Gold - Lewis Orde 4748

South Wind
World of Silence - Don Coldsmith 1195

Spencer, Caledonia
Sister Wives - Cleo Jones 3270

Spencer, Connie
Sister Wives - Cleo Jones 3270

Spenser, Dorcas
Something Gleamed - Theda Kenyon 3463

Sprague, Lucy
In a Dark Garden - Frank G. Slaughter 5891

Sprague, Melissa
Wings of the Morning - Frederic F. Van de Water 6404

Spring Moon
Spring Moon: A Novel of China - Bette Bao Lord 3897

Stafford, Melissa
Montana Road - Harry Sinclair Drago 1717

Stahl, Linda
The Rainbird - Sara Lidman 3780

Stalker, Merrin
Call Home the Heart - Jessica Stirling 6040

Stands with a Fist
Dances with Wolves - Michael Blake 537

Stark, Sarah
The Pumpkin Rollers - Elmer Kelton 3406

Starke, Melissa
Melissa Starke - Annulet Andrews 145

Starr, Charlotte
Castle of Doves - Constance Heaven 2803

Sternwood, Carmen
Perchance to Dream - Robert B. Parker 4807

Stevens, Emily
For Love and Honor - Antonia Van-Loon 6423

Stewart, Jamie Lynne
The Eleventh Year - Monique Raphel High 2914

Stockdale, Lynn
Night March - Bruce Lancaster 3641

Stoddard, Roxanne Darragh
Stars and Stripes - Adam Rutledge 5541

Storey, Margaret
Lion in the Evening - Alan Scholefield 5656

Stratford, Julie
The Mummy; or Ramses the Damned - Anne Rice 5315

Stuart, Jane
Bed in Hell - Elfrida Vipont 6504

Su-Mei
Shanghai - Christopher New 4588

Sullivan, Tracy
Sunshine and Shadow - Antonia Van-Loon 6426

Summerbee, Kate
Sea Change - Alison McLeay 4287

Swenk, Vannie
The Golden Lady - Dorothy Gardiner 2283

Sykes, Jenny
The Trial of Jenny Sykes - Hebe Weenolsen 6598

Syon, Anne de
The Winter Rose - Millie J. Ragosta 5243

Talbott, Miriam
Panama - Eric Zencey 6959

Talcott, Aurora
The Wings of the Morning - Thomas Tryon 6356

Tana
The Homecoming - Norah Lofts 3844

Taniard, Tansy
Tansy Taniard - Myrtle Strode-Jackson 6084

Tarleton, Alice
Alice of Old Vincennes - Maurice Thompson 6268

Taylor, Angela
Lovers All Untrue - Norah Lofts 3851

Tempest, Elizabeth
The Gold Seekers - William Stuart Long 3874

Temple, Sadie
Crossing over Jordan - Linda Beatrice Brown 725

Temple, Story
Crossing over Jordan - Linda Beatrice Brown 725

Tewke, Beth
Apple Tree Lean Down - Mary E. Pearce 4860

Thaine, Alexandra
Wild Swan - Celeste De Blasis 1550

Thandelthur
Running West - James Houston 3052

Thayer, Silence
Wings of the Morning - Frederic F. Van de Water 6404

Thomas, Cottie
Tyrone of Kentucky - Clark McMeekin 4294

Thorman, Agnes
The Moth - Catherine Cookson 1284

Thorne, Thomasine
The Secret Years - Judith Lennox-Smith 3718

Thu
Lady of the Reeds - Pauline Gedge 2345

Titus, Phoebe
Arizona - Clarence Budington Kelland 3387

Toit, Lena du
The Hill of Doves - Stuart Cloete 1123

Trant, Helena
On the Night of the Seventh Moon - Victoria Holt 3018

Trefusis, Christina
Women of Ashdon - Valerie Anand 135

Tregaran, Alice
The Legacy of Tregaran - Mary Lide 3776

Trelawney, Sapphira
O Western Wind - John Anthony Devon 1634

Tresize, Lettice
The Old Priory - Norah Lofts 3855

Trevaine, Jacelyn
Rake's Ransom - Barbara Metzger 4347

Trigonis, Eleni
The Ashes of Smyrna - Richard Reinhardt 5294

Trotter, Tilly
Tilly - Catherine Cookson 1288
Tilly Wed - Catherine Cookson 1290

Tryon, Cassie
Hearts of Fire - Christina Savage 5616

Turnblow, Faye
The Last Days of Horse-Shy Halloran - Bill Pronzini 5203

Upford, Charlotte
The Lion at Sea - Max Hennessy 2834

Upjohn, Corrie May
The Handsome Road - Gwen Bristow 697

Upshall, Glory
The Rogue and the Witch - John Edward Newton 4605

Vallon, Louise du
Daughter of Marignac - Constance Heaven 2805

Van Ayl, Cathy
Independence! - Dana Fuller Ross 5476

Van Cleef, Hanneke
The Sea Beggars - Cecelia Holland 2996

Van Dyck, Margaretta
The Marriage Bed - Jean Clark 1088

Van Goens, Annabet
Silver Nutmeg - Norah Lofts 3860

Van Os, Trudi
Venture in the East - Bruce Lancaster 3648

Verendrye, Louise de La
My Blood and My Treasure - Mary Schumann   5674

Vernold, Emma
St. Peter's Fair - Ellis Peters   4971

Vestry, Caroline
Sisters & Lovers - Nicola Thorne   6274

Vestry, Emily
Sisters & Lovers - Nicola Thorne   6274

Vestry, Jane
Sisters & Lovers - Nicola Thorne   6274

Vezenobres, Isabeau
The Shepherd's Crook - Paul Frischauer   2234

Villars, Eleanora
The Notorious Angel - Patricia Maxwell   4201

Vredenburg, Stella
Floodtide - Suzanne Goodwin   2475

Wagenet, Haille
To the Swift - Anne Hawkins   2783

Walker, Lillis
The Weaver's Tale - Kate Sedley   5719

Walker, Nancy
Web of Destiny - Muriel Elwood   1939

Ware, Freedom
The Golden Season - Oriana Akinson   60

Warner, Sibyll
The Last of the Barons - Edward Bulwer-Lytton   769

Watson, Emma
Emma Watson - Joan Aiken   45

Watts, Deliverance
Stronghold - Donald Barr Chidsey   1065

Wayburn, Raney
A Georgian Love Story - Ernest Raymond   5258

Weir, Helen
The Buckskin Girl: A Novel of the California Trail in the Mid-Nineteenth Century - Gwen Moffat   4426

Wells, Miranda
Dragonwyck - Anya Seton   5750

Wendell, Charlotte
New Deal for Death - Elliott Roosevelt   5454

West, Alison
The Second Face of Valor - Ray Grant Toepfer   6288

Westburn, Maud
The Maclarens - C.L. Skelton   5873

Westlake, Gillian
Roll, Shenandoah - Bruce Lancaster   3644

Weston, Sophie
The Astrov Legacy - Constance Heaven   2802

Whipple, Jessie
The Pepper Tree - John Edward Jennings   3203

Whistlecraft, Judith
Blossom Like the Rose - Norah Lofts   3836

Whitaker, Margery
Elegant Witch - Robert Neill   4568

Whitby, Phoebe
The Woman Question - Dorothea Malm   4046

Whitmead, Susannah
Women of Ashdon - Valerie Anand   135

Wilde, Janice
Patriot's Dream - Barbara Michaels   4360

Wilford, Emma
Wilford's Daughter - Alexandra Manners   4071

Willett, Dorcas
Tomorrow the Harvest - Viola Paradise   4789

Williams, Constancy
The Lord's Anointed - Ruth Eleanor McKee   4282

Williams, Elizabeth
The Prospering - Elizabeth Speare   5954

Willoughby, Lizzie
Siege in the Sun - Mary Paradise   4788

Wilson, Katherine
Katherine - Antonia Van-Loon   6425

Wilton, Lucie
The Apothecary Rose - Candace M. Robb   5364

Windsor, Ainsley
Harvest of Dreams - Jaroldeen Edwards   1884

Winslow, Harriet
The Old Gringo - Carlos Fuentes   2247

Winslow, Lavinia
Blue Camellia - Frances Parkinson Keyes   3477

Winston, Cassandra Dell
They Called Her Mrs. Doc - Janette Oke   4709

Winter Cherry
Winter Cherry - Keith West   6632

Withers, Damaris
A Woman Named Damaris - Janette Oke   4711

Wood-Lacy, Jennifer
A Future Arrived - Phillip Rock   5420

Wood-Lacy, Victoria
A Future Arrived - Phillip Rock   5420

Woodruff, Sarah
The French Lieutenant's Woman - John Fowles   2194

Worth, Gracellen
Crimson Is the Eastern Shore - Don Tracy   6308

Wright, Stella
Flight From Avatchez - Frank G. Slaughter   5887

Wulfhild
The Disputed Crown - Valerie Anand   128

Wyman, Phyllida
The Rival Shores - Arthur Beverly-Giddings   487

Yarico
Caribee - Christopher Nicole   4614

Yates, Theophilius
A Land to Tame - Zola Helen Ross   5505

Yellan, Mary
Jamaica Inn - Daphne Du Maurier   1747

York, Meg
The Devil in Velvet - John Dickson Carr   909

Yorke, Deborah
The Ladies of Hanover Square - Rona Randall   5249

Yorke, Sara
*Passengers to Mexico: The Last Invasion of Mexico - Blair Niles   4627

Younger, Pearl
Pearl - Anne Leaton   3701

Ziani, Vittoria
Sing to the Sun - Lucille Borden   579

Zinn, Constance Philippa
A Bloodsmoor Romance - Joyce Carol Oates   4658

Zinn, Deirdre
A Bloodsmoor Romance - Joyce Carol Oates   4658

Zubaran, Luz de
Hill of the Hawk - Scott O'Dell   4689

ZEALOT

Rasputin, Grigori Efimovich
Devoted Friends - Joe Poyer   5161
Seance for a Vampire - Fred Saberhagen   5557
White Nights, Red Dawn - Frederick Nolan   4634

Savonarola, Girolamo
The Florentine - Sandra Shulman   5840

Sutton, Silas
Pilgrims in Paradise - Frank G. Slaughter   5895

Character Description Index

Author Index

This index is an alphabetical listing of the authors of the featured titles. Also included are co-authors and real names of authors using pseudonyms. For each author, the titles of included books and their entry numbers are also provided.

A

Abbey, Anne Merton
Kathryn: In the Court of Six Queens 1

Abbey, Margaret
Blood of the Boar 2
The Flight of the Kestrel 3
The Heart Is a Traitor 4
The Son of York 5
The Warwick Heiress 6

Abbot, Jane Ludlow
River's Run 7

Abbott, Margot
The Last Innocent Hour 8

Abel, Robert H.
Freedom's Dues 9

Abernethy, Cecil
Mr. Pepys of Seething Lane 10

Abrahams, Doris Caroline
No Bed for Bacon 640

Abrahams, Peter
The View From Coyaba 11
Wild Conquest 12

Abrahams, William M.
Imperial Waltz 13

Absire, Alain
God's Equal 14
Lazarus 15

Achebe, Chinua
Things Fall Apart 16

Ackroyd, Peter
Chatterton 17
English Music 18
The Last Testament of Oscar Wilde 19
Milton in America 20
The Trial of Elizabeth Cree: A Novel of the Limehouse Murders 21

Acland, Alice
The Secret Wife 22

Adams, Doris Sutcliffe
No Man's Son 23
The Price of Blood 24

Adams, Harold
The Man Who Missed the Party 25

Adams, Jane
Seattle Green 26

Adams, Richard
Traveller 27

Adams, Samuel Hopkins
Banner by the Wayside 28
Canal Town 29
The Gorgeous Hussy 30
The Harvey Girls 31
Sunrise to Sunset 32
Tenderloin 33

Adamson, Mary Jo
Bridey's Mountain 34

Adamson, Yvonne
Bridey's Mountain 34

Adelman, Robert H.
The Bloody Benders 35
Sweetwater Fever 36

Adicks, Richard
A Court of Owls 37

Adlard, Mark
The Greenlander 38

Adler, Elizabeth
Fortune Is a Woman 39

Aggeler, Geoff
Confessions of Johnny Ringo 40

Aguilera Malta, Demetrio
Manuela, La Caballeresa Del Sol 41

Ahitani, Gamal
Zayni Barakat 42

Aiken, Joan
Castle Barebane 43
Eliza's Daughter 44
Emma Watson 45
The Five-Minute Marriage 46
The Girl From Paris 47
The Haunting of Lamb House 48
If I Were You 49
Jane Fairfax 50
Mansfield Revisited 51
Midnight Is a Place 52
The Smile of the Stranger 53
The Weeping Ash 54

Ainsworth, Edward Maddin
Eagles Fly West 55

Ainsworth, William Harrison
Jack Sheppard 56
Old St. Paul's 57
The Tower of London 58
Windsor Castle 59

Akinson, Oriana
The Golden Season 60

Aksyonov, Vassily
Generations of Winter 61

Alarcon, Pedro Antonio de
The Three-Cornered Hat 62

Albert, Bill
Castle Garden 63
Death at Daisy's Folly 4775
Death at Gallows Green 4776

Albert, Susan Wittig
Death at Daisy's Folly 4775
Death at Gallows Green 4776

Albery, Nobuko
The House of Kanze 64

Albright, Harry
Gettysburg: Crisis of Command 65

Alderman, Clifford Lindsey
The Arch of Stars 66
To Fame Unknown 67

Aldiss, Brian
Frankenstein Unbound 68

Aldrich, Bess Streeter
A Lantern in Her Hand 69
The Lieutenant's Lady 70
Miss Bishop 71
Song of Years 72
Spring Came on Forever 73

Aldridge, James
One Last Glimpse 74

Aleman Velasco, Miguel
Copilli, Aztec Prince 75

Alexander, Bruce
Blind Justice 76
Murder in Grub Street 77
Watery Grave 78

Alexander, Karl
Papa and Fidel 79
Time After Time 80

Alexander, Kate
Palaces of Desire 81

Alexander, Lawrence
The Big Stick 82
Speak Softly 83
The Strenuous Life 84

Alexander, Sidney
The Hand of Michelangelo 85
Michelangelo the Florentine 86
Nicodemus: The Roman Years of Michelangelo Buonarroti, 1534-1564 87

Alexander, William P.
Land for My Sons 1331

Alfriend, Mary Bethell
Juan Ortiz: Gentleman of Seville 88

Alington, Argentine Francis
Gentlemen—The Regiment! 6154

Allan, Margaret
The Last Mammoth 89
The Mammoth Stone 90

Allardyce, Paula
Miss Philadelphia Smith 91

Alldritt, Keith
Elgar on the Journey to Hanley 92

Allee, Marjorie
Judith Lankester 93

Allen, Dexter
The Coil of the Serpent 94
The Jaguar and the Golden Stag 95
Valley of Eagles 96

Allen, Don B.
Doctor in Buckskin 103
Troubled Border 104

Allen, Henry
Chiricahua 2839
Death of a Legend 2840
From Where the Sun Now Stands 2841
The Gates of the Mountains 2842
Journey to Shiloh 2843
The Last Warpath 2844
Mackenna's Gold 2845
No Survivors 2846
One More River to Cross 2847
San Juan Hill 2848

Allen, Hervey
Action at Aquila 97
Anthony Adverse 98
Bedford Village 99
The Forest and the Fort 100
Toward the Morning 101

Allen, Merrit Parmalee
Battle Lanterns 102

Allen, T.D.
Doctor in Buckskin 103
Troubled Border 104

Allen, Terry D.
Doctor in Buckskin 103
Troubled Border 104

Allen, Walter
Threescore and Ten 105

Allis, Marguerite
All in Good Time 106
Brave Pursuit 107
The Bridge 108
Charity Strong 109
Free Soil 110
Law of the Land 111
Now We Are Free 112
The Rising Storm 113
*The Splendor Stays: An Historic Novel
    Based on the Lives of the Seven Hart
    Sisters of Saybrook* 114
To Keep Us Free 115
Water over the Dam 116

Almedingen, E.M.
The Ladies of St. Hedwig's 117
Young Catherine 118

Alston, Mary Niven
The Altar and the Crown 4631

Alter, Judy
*Cherokee Rose: A Novel of America's
    First Cowgirl* 119
*Jessie: A Novel Based on the Life of
    Jessie Benton Fremont* 120
Libbie 121

Alter, Stephen
Silk and Steel 122

Altieri, Daniel
The Court of the Lion 1294
Deception 1295

Altrocchi, Julia Cooley
Wolves Against the Moon 123

Ames, Francis
That Callahan Spunk! 124

Ames, John Edward
The Golden Circle 125

Anand, Valerie
The Cherished Wives 126
Crown of Roses 127
The Disputed Crown 128
The Faithful Lovers 129
Gildenford 130
King of the Wood 131
The Norman Pretender 132
The Proud Villeins 133
The Ruthless Yeomen 134
Women of Ashdon 135

Anderson, Alston
All God's Children 136

Anderson, Catherine
Comanche Moon 137

Anderson, Paul Lewis
Swords in the North 138

Andrew, Prudence
The Constant Star 139
The Hooded Falcon 140
A New Creature 141
Ordeal by Silence 142
A Question of Choice 143
A Sparkle From the Coal 144

Andrews, Annulet
Melissa Starke 145

Andrews, Gina
Esther: The Star and the Sceptre 146

Andrews, John
A Viking's Daughter 147

Andrews, Robert Hardy
Burning Gold 148
Great Day in the Morning 149

Andric, Ivo
Bosnian Chronicle 150
The Bridge on the Drina 151
Devil's Yard 152

Andrzejewski, Jerzy
The Inquisitors 153

Annandale, Barbara
The Bonnet Laird's Daughter 154

Anness, Milford E.
*Song of Metamoris: A Story That
    Remains of a People Who Passed
    This Way* 155

Anscombe, Roderick
*The Secret Life of Laszlo, Count
    Dracula* 156

Ansle, Dorothy P.
The Elusive Crown 1931
The King's Bastard 1932
Lady on the Coin 326
The Queen's Ward 1933
The Wise Virgin 1934

Anthony, Evelyn
All the Queen's Men 157
Anne Boleyn 158
The Cardinal and the Queen 159
Charles the King 160
Clandara 161
Far Flies the Eagle 162
The French Bride 163
Rebel Princess 164
Valentina 165
Victoria and Albert 166

Anthony, Piers
Isle of Woman 167
Shame of Man 168
Tatham Mound 169

Appel, Allen
Till the End of Time 170
Time After Time 171
Twice upon a Time 172

Appelfeld, Aharon
The Age of Wonders 173
Badenheim 1939 174
For Every Sin 175
The Healer 176
Katerina 177
The Retreat 178
To the Land of the Cattails 179
Tzili: The Story of a Life 180
Unto the Soul 181

Aragon, Louis
Holy Week 182

Archer, Jeffrey
As the Crow Flies 183

Ardmore, Jane Kesner
Julie 4479

Argo, Ellen
The Crystal Star 184
Jewel of the Sea 185
The Yankee Girl 186

Aridjis, Homero
*1492: The Life and Times of Juan
    Cabezon of Castile* 187
*The Lord of the Last Days: Visions of
    the Year 1000* 188

Arlen, Leslie
Love and Honor 189

Armstrong, David
Violent Friends 1113

Armstrong, Tilly
Palaces of Desire 81

Arnold, Elliott
Blood Brother 190
The Camp Grant Massacre 191
*Deep in My Heart: A Story Based on
    the Life of Sigmund Romberg* 192

Arnold, Michael
Against the Fall of Night 193
The Archduke 194

Arnow, Harriette Simpson
*The Kentucky Trace: A Novel of the
    American Revolution* 195

Aronin, Ben
Walt Whitman's Secret 196

Asch, Sholem
The Apostle 197
Mary 198
Moses 199
The Nazarene 200
The Prophet 201
Salvation 202

Ashcroft, Mary Ellen
The Magdalene Gospel 203

Ashfield, Helen
Beau Barron's Lady 204
Crystal 205
Emerald 206
Garnet 207
The Marquis and Miss Jones 208
The Michaelmas Tree 209
Opal 210
Pearl 211
Regency Rogue 212
Ruby 213
Sapphire 214
Topaz 215

Ashton, Helen
Footman in Powder 216
The Hedge of Thorns 217
Letty 218
Parson Austen's Daughter 219
The Swan of Usk 220

Ashton, Winifred
He Brings Great News 1462

Aswell, Mary Louise
Abigail 221

Atherton, Gertrude
*The Conqueror: Being the True and
    Romantic Story of Alexander
    Hamilton* 222
Dido, Queen of Hearts 223
Golden Peacock 224
The Immortal Marriage 225

Atkey, Philip
A Singular Conspiracy 4915

Attanasio, A.A.
Kingdom of the Grail 226
Wyvern 227

Attenborough, Bernard
The Great Sky and the Silence 5245

Auchincloss, Louis
The Book Class 228
The Cat and the King 229
Exit Lady Masham 230
The House of Five Talents 231
Portrait in Brownstone 232
The Rector of Justin 233

Watchfires 234
The Winthrop Covenant 235

Auel, Jean M.
The Clan of the Cave Bear 236
The Mammoth Hunters 237
The Plains of Passage 238
The Valley of Horses 239

Augur, Helen
Tall Ships to Cathay 240

Austell, Diane
Lights Along the Shore 241
While the Music Plays 242

Austen-Leigh, Joan
A Visit to Highbury 243

Auster, Paul
Mr. Vertigo 244

Austin, Frederick Britten
Forty Centuries Look Down 245
The Road to Glory 246

Aydelotte, Dora
Run of the Stars 247
Trumpets Calling 248

Ayers, Rose
The Street Sparrows 249

Ayrton, Michael
The Maze Maker 250

B

Babbs, W. Ken
Last Go Round 3473

Babcock, Bernie
Soul of Abe Lincoln 251
The Soul of Ann Rutledge 252

Babson, Naomi Lane
I Am Lidian 253

Bacchelli, Riccardo
The Mill on the Po 254
Nothing New under the Sun 255

Bacheller, Irving A.
A Candle in the Wilderness 256
D'ri and I 257
Father Abraham 258
In the Days of Poor Richard 259
Light in the Clearing 260
A Man for the Ages 261
The Master of Chaos 262

Baggett, Samuel G.
Gods on Horseback 263

Bagnel, Joan
*Gone the Rainbow, Gone the
    Dove* 264

Bailey, Anthony
Major Andre 265

Bailey, Charles W.
*The Land Was Ours: A Novel of the
    Great Plains* 266

Bailey, Henry Christopher
The Merchant Prince 267

Bailey, Paul
For Time and All Eternity 268

Bainbridge, Beryl
The Birthday Boys 269
Every Man for Himself 270
Watson's Apology 271
Young Adolf 272

Baker, George
Paris of Troy 273

Baker, Karle Wilson
Star of the Wilderness 274

Baker, Lucinda
The Place of Devils 275

Baker, Madeline
A Whisper on the Wind 276

Balchin, Nigel
Borgia Testament 277

Balderston, John Lloyd
A Goddess to a God 278

Baldwin, Bates
Tide of Empire 279

Baldwin, Leland Dewitt
The Delectable Country 280

Baldwin, William
The Hard to Catch Mercy 281

Balin, Beverly
King in Hell: A Novel of Bothwell and Mary, Queen of Scots 282

Ball, Zachary
Pull Down to New Orleans 283

Ballard, Todhunter
The Californian 284

Balling, L. Christian
Champion 285

Ballinger, W.A.
The Men That God Made Mad: A Novel about Ireland's Easter Rising 286

Banis, V.J.
The Earth and All It Holds 287
San Antone 288
This Splendid Earth 289

Banks, Lynne Reid
Dark Quartet: The Story of the Brontes 290
Path to the Silent Country 291

Banks, Polan
Black Ivory 292
The Gentleman From America 293

Bannister, Don
Long Day at Shiloh 294

Bannister, Patricia V.
Ask Me No Questions 6459
Cherished Enemy 6460
The Dedicated Villain 6461
Feather Castles 6462
Had We Never Loved 6463
Journey to Enchantment 6464
Lanterns 6465
Logic of the Heart 6466
Love Alters Not 6467
Love's Duet 6468
Married Past Redemption 6469
Men Were Deceivers Ever 6470
Mistress of Willowvale 6471
Nanette 6472
Never Doubt I Love 6473
The Noblest Frailty 6474
Practice to Deceive 6475
Sanguinet's Crown 6476
A Shadow's Bliss 6477
Some Brief Folly 6478
Time's Fool 6479
The Tyrant 6480
The Wagered Widow 6481

Banti, Anna
Artemesia 295

Banville, John
Doctor Copernicus 296
Kepler: A Novel 297

Bar-Zohar, Michael
The Devil's Spy 2773

Barber, Elsie
Hunt for Heaven 298

Barber, Phyllis
And the Desert Shall Bloom 299

Barchilon, John
The Crown Prince 300

Barclay, Tessa
The Wine Widow 301

Barke, James
Crest of the Broken Wave 302
Song in the Green Thorn Tree 303
Well of the Silent Harp 304
The Wind That Shakes the Barley 305
Wonder of All the Gay World 306

Barker, Pat
The Eye in the Door 307
The Ghost Road 308
Regeneration 309

Barker, Shirley
Corner the Moon 310
Fire and the Hammer 311
The Last Gentleman 312
Liza Bowe 313
Peace, My Daughters 314
Rivers Parting 315
The Road to Bunker Hill 316
Strange Wives 317
Swear by Apollo 318
Tomorrow the New Moon 319

Barnard, Robert
The Skeleton in the Grass 320

Barnes, Joanna
Pastora 321

Barnes, Margaret Campbell
Brief Gaudy Hour 322
Isabel the Fair 323
The King's Bed 324
King's Fool 325
Lady on the Coin 326
Mary of Carisbrooke 327
My Lady of Cleves 328
The Tudor Rose 329
With All My Heart 330
Within the Hollow Crown 331

Barnes, Percy Raymond
Crum Elbow Folks 332

Barney, Helen C.
Fruit in His Season 333
Green Rose of Furley 334

Baron, Alexander
The Golden Princess 335
Queen of the East 336

Barr, Elisabeth
Castle Heritage 337
The Sea Treasure 338
The Storm Witch 339

Barr, Gladys H.
Cross, Sword, and Arrow 340
The Master of Geneva: A Novel Based on the Life of John Calvin 341
Monk in Armour 342
The Pilgrim Prince 343

Barr, Pat
Jade 344

Barraclough, June
Familiar Acts 345

The Heart of the Rose 346
Kindred Spirits 347

Barragan, Maude
John Howard Payne, Skywalker 348

Barreiro, Jose
The Indian Chronicles 349

Barrett, Julia
Presumption: An Entertainment 350
The Third Sister 351

Barrett, Monte
Tempered Blade 352

Barrett, William E.
Lady of the Lotus 353

Barroll, Clare
The Iron Crown 354

Barron, Stephanie
Jane and the Man of the Cloth 355
Jane and the Unpleasantness at Scargrave Manor 356

Barry, Jane
The Carolinians 357
The Long March 358
Maximilian's Gold 359
A Shadow of Eagles 360
A Time in the Sun 361

Barry, John
The Michaelmas Girls 362

Bartell, Linda Lang
Caressa 363

Barth, John
The Sot-Weed Factor 364

Barthelme, Donald
The King 365

Bartlett, Lanier
Adios! 366

Bartlett, Paul
When the Owl Cries 367

Barton, Del
A Good Day to Die 368

Barton, Florence Whitfield
The Sage and the Olive 369

Barwick, Anthony
The Hangman's Crusade 370
Shadow of the Wolf 371

Barwick, James
The Hangman's Crusade 370
Shadow of the Wolf 371

Bass, Cynthia
Maiden Voyage 372
Sherman's March 373

Bassan, Jean
The Wrong Horse 374

Bassett, Ronald
Dando on Delhi Ridge 1119
The Tune That They Play 1120

Basso, Hamilton
The Light Infantry Ball 375

Batchelor, John Calvin
American Falls 376

Battle, Lois
Storyville 377

Battye, Gladys Starkey
Free Soil 3943

Bauer, Florence M.
Abram, Son of Terah 378
Behold Your King 379

Baumann, Hans
Sons of the Steppe: The Story of How the Conqueror Genghis Khan Was Overcome 380

Baume, Frederic
Yankee Woman 381

Bausher, Mildred Jordan
Asylum for the Queen 3303
Echo of the Flute 3304
One Red Rose Forever 3305

Baxt, George
The Alfred Hitchcock Murder Case 382
The Bette Davis Murder Case 383
The Dorothy Parker Murder Case 384
The Greta Garbo Murder Case 385
The Mae West Murder Case 386
The Noel Coward Murder Case 387
The Talking Pictures Murder Case 388
The Tallulah Bankhead Murder Case 389
The William Powell and Myrna Loy Murder Case 390

Baylis, Sarah
Utrillo's Mother 391

Beach, Rex
The World in His Arms 392

Beach, Susan Hicks
A Cardinal of the Medici 393

Beals, Carleton
Taste of Glory 394

Bean, Amelia
The Fancher Train 395
The Feud 396
Time for Outrage 397

Bean, Fred
Pancho And Black Jack 398
The Pecos River 399
Trail's End 400

Beatty, John
Campion Towers 401

Beatty, Patricia
Campion Towers 401

Beaty, Betty
Wings of the Morning 402

Beaty, David
Wings of the Morning 402

Beck, K.K.
Death in a Deck Chair 403
Peril under the Palms 404
Young Mrs. Cavendish and the Kaiser's Men 405

Becker, Beril
Whirlwind in Petticoats 406

Becker, Stephen
A Rendezvous in Haiti 407
When the War Is Over 408

Becnel, Rexanne
My Gallant Enemy 409
Thief of My Heart 410
Where Magic Dwells 411

Bedford, Donald F.
John Barry 412

Bee, David
Curse of Magira 413

Beer, Thomas
Sandoval: A Romance of Bad Manners 414

Begiebing, Robert J.
*The Strange Death of Mistress
    Coffin* 415

Begley, Louis
Wartime Lies 416

Bekessy, Emery
*Barabbas: A Novel of the Time of
    Jesus* 417

Belfrage, Cedric
My Master Columbus 418

Bell, Anthea
The Floral Companion 419
A London Season 420

Bell, Clare
The Jaguar Princess 421

Bell, Madison Smartt
All Souls' Rising 422

Bell, Neil
So Perish the Roses 423

Bell, Sallie
Marcel Armand 424

Bell, Thomas
Out of This Furnace 425

Bellah, James Warner
*The Journal of Colonel De
    Lancey* 426
The Valiant Virginians 427

Bellamann, Henry
Kings Row 428

Belle, Pamela
Alethea 429
The Chains of Fate 430
A Falling Star 431
The Lodestar 432
The Moon in the Water 433
Treason's Gift 434
Wintercombe 435

Bellonci, Maria
Private Renaissance 436

Benadum, Clarence
Bates House 437

Benchley, Nathaniel
Portrait of a Scoundrel 438

Bendell, Don
Chief of Scouts 439

Benet, Laura
*Come Slowly Eden: A Novel about
    Emily Dickinson* 440

Benet, Stephen Vincent
Spanish Bayonet 441

Bengtsson, Frans Gunnar
The Long Ships 442

Benitez-Rojo, Antonio
Sea of Lentils 443

Bennett, John
So Shall They Reap 444

Bennetts, Pamela
The Barons of Runnymede 445
Beau Barron's Lady 204
The Borgia Prince 446
Crystal 205
The De Montfort Legacy 447
Death of the Red King 448
Don Pedro's Captain 449
A Dragon for Edward 450
Emerald 206
Envoy From Elizabeth 451
Garnet 207
The Lords of Lancaster 452
The Marquis and Miss Jones 208

The Michaelmas Tree 209
My Dear Lover England 453
Opal 210
Pearl 211
Regency Rogue 212
Richard and the Knights of God 454
Royal Sword at Agincourt 455
Ruby 213
Sapphire 214
The She-Wolf 456
Stephen and the Sleeping Saints 457
Topaz 215

Benson, Robert Hugh
Come Rack! Come Rope! 458
The King's Achievement 459

Bentley, Barbara
Mistress Nancy 460

Bentley, Phyllis
Freedom, Farewell 461
The Power and the Glory 462

Benton, Kenneth
Death on the Appian Way 463

Benton, Paul
The Gentleman From America 464

Benzoni, Juliette
The Lure of the Falcon 465
Marianne 466
Marianne and the Crown of Fire 467
*Marianne and the Lords of the
    East* 468
Marianne and the Masked Prince 469
Marianne and the Privateer 470
Marianne and the Rebels 471

Berckman, Evelyn
A Finger to Her Lips 472

Bercovici, Konrad
The Exodus 473
Savage Prodigal 474

Berdach, Rachel
*The Emperor, the Sages and
    Death* 475

Beresford-Howe, Constance
My Lady Greensleeves 476

Berger, Thomas
Arthur Rex: A Legendary Novel 477
Little Big Man 478

Berkman, Ted
To Seize the Passing Dream 479

Bernhard, Virginia
A Durable Fire 480

Berry, Don
Moontrap 481
To Build a Ship 482
Trask 483

Berry, Jim
The Moon Stallion 484

Berstl, Julius
*Kean: The Imaginary Memoirs of an
    Actor* 485
The Tentmaker 486

Beverly-Giddings, Arthur
The Rival Shores 487

Beyea, Basil
The Golden Mistress 488
Notorious Eliza 489

Beyle, Henri
The Charterhouse of Parma 5993

Bezzi, Tom
Hubble Time 490

Bidwell, Marjory Elizabeth
The Admiral's Lady 2395
A Most Romantic City 2396
The Tempestuous Petticoat 2397

Biggins, John
The Emperor's Coloured Coat 491
A Sailor of Austria 492
The Two-Headed Eagle 493

Biggle, Lloyd Jr.
The Glendower Conspiracy 494
The Quallsford Inheritance 495

Bigsby, Christopher
Hester 496
Pearl 497

Billington, Rachel
Theo and Matilda 498
A Woman's Age 499

Binns, Archie
The Head Waters 500
The Land Is Bright 501
Mighty Mountain 502
You Rolling River 503

Bird, Horace
Don't Tread on Me 3366

Bird, Robert Montgomery
The Hawks of Hawk-Hollow 504
*Nick of the Woods; or, The
    Jibbenainosay* 505

Birkhead, Margaret
Trust and Treason 506

Birney, Hoffman
The Dice of God 507
Eagle in the Sun 508
Grim Journey 509

Bishcoff, Ilse
Proud Heritage 510

Bittner, Rosanne
Arizona Ecstasy 511
Embers of the Heart 512
Montana Woman 513
Oregon Bride 514
Sioux Splendor 515
Sweet Mountain Magic 516
Thunder on the Plains 517

Bjornson, Bjornstjerne
Arne 518

Black, Laura
Albany 519
Falls of Gard 520
Glendraco 521
Ravenburn 522
Strathgallant 523
Wild Cat 524

Blackburn, Thomas Wakefield
A Good Day to Die 525

Blacker, Irwin R.
Days of the Gold 526
Taos 527

Blackmore, R.D.
Lorna Doone 528
The Maid of Sker 529

Blackstock, Charity
The English Wife 530
The Lonely Strangers 531

Blake, Forrester
The Franciscan 532
Johnny Christmas 533
Wilderness Passage 534

Blake, James Carlos
The Friends of Pancho Villa 535
The Pistoleer 536

Blake, Michael
Dances with Wolves 537
*Marching to Valhalla: A Novel of
    Custer's Last Days* 538

Blake, William J.
*The Angel: A Novel Based on the Life
    of Alexander I of Russia* 543
The Copperheads 544

Blakely, Mike
Too Long at the Dance 539

Blaker, Richard
The Needle-Watcher 540

Blankfort, Michael
Behold the Fire 541

Blassingame, Wyatt
Live From the Devil 542

Blech, William James
*The Angel: A Novel Based on the Life
    of Alexander I of Russia* 543
The Copperheads 544

Blevins, Winfred
The High Missouri 545
The Powder River 546
The Snake River 547
*Stone Song: A Novel of the Life of
    Crazy Horse* 548
The Yellowstone 549

Blish, James
Doctor Mirabilis 550

Bloch, Robert
The Night of the Ripper 551

Bloom, Robert S.
A Generation of Leaves 552

Bloom, Ursula
The Little Victoria 5196
Marlborough's Unfair Lady 5197
The Romance of Charles Dickens 553
Sweet Marie-Antoinette 5198
The Ten-Day Queen 5199

Blunden, Godfrey
Charco Harbour 554

Blyth, Juliet
The Parfit Knight 555

Blythe, LeGette
Brothers of Vengeance 556
Hear Me, Pilate! 557
*Man on Fire: A Novel on the Life of St.
    Paul* 558
A Tear for Judas 559

Boast, Philip
London's Child 560

Bojer, Johan
The Emigrants 561
The Great Hunger 562
The Last of the Vikings 563

Boles, Paul Darcy
The Limner 564
The Mississippi Run 565

Bolitho, Sybil
A Goddess to a God 278

Bolton, Guy
The Olympians 566

Bolton, Muriel Ray
The Golden Porcupine 567

Bonallack, Basil
The Flame in the Dark 568

Bonds, Parris Afton
Blue Moon 569
Dream Time 570

Bonner, Cindy
Lily 571
Looking After Lily 572

Bonnet, Theodore
The Mudlark 573

Bontemps, Arna
Black Thunder 574
Drums at Dusk 575

Booth, Martin
Dreaming of Samarkand 576

Booth, Rosemary Frances
The Belchamber Scandal 4533
Brave Kingdom 4534
Castaway 4535
The Heroine's Sister 4536

Borchardt, Alice
Beguiled 577
Devoted 578

Borden, Lucille
Sing to the Sun 579

Borel, Raymond C.
Death at the French Creek 580

Borland, Barbara Dodge
The Greater Hunger 581

Borland, Hal
The Amulet 582
The Seventh Winter 583
When the Legends Die 584

Borowsky, Marvin
The Queen's Knight 585

Borton, Elizabeth
The Greek of Toledo: A Romantic Narrative of El Greco 586

Bosse, Malcolm
The Examination 587
The Vast Memory of Love 588
The Warlord 589

Bosworth, Allan R.
Storm Tide 590

Boucolon, Maryse
The Children of Segu 1232
I, Tituba, Black Witch of Salem 1233
Segu 1234

Bourne, Caroline
Allegheny Captive 591

Bourne, Peter
The Courts of Love: A Romance of Medieval France 592
Drums of Destiny 593
Flames of Empire 594
Soldiers of Fortune 595
Twilight of the Dragon 596
When God Slept 597

Bowden, Jean
The Bonnet Laird's Daughter 154
The Wine Widow 301

Bowen, Marjorie
The Lady and the Arsenic 598
Queen's Caprice 599

Bowen, Peter
Imperial Kelly 600
Kelly Blue 601
Yellowstone Kelly 602

Bowen, True
And the Stars Shall Fall 603

Bowering, George
Shoot! 604

Bowman, John Clarke
Powhatan's Daughter 605

Boyce, Burke
Cloak of Folly 606
Man From Mt. Vernon 607
Morning of a Hero 608
The Perilous Night 609

Boyd, Brendan
Blue Ruin: A Novel of the 1919 World Series 610

Boyd, James
Drums 611
Marching On 612

Boyd, Martin
Lucinda Brayford 613

Boyd, Thomas Alexander
Samuel Drummond 614
Shadow of the Long Knives 615

Boyd, William
An Ice-Cream War 616
The New Confessions 617

Boyle, T. Coraghessan
The Road to Wellville 618
Water Music 619

Boyne, Walter J.
Eagles at War 620

Brackett, Leigh
Follow the Free Wind 621

Bradford, Roark
Kingdom Coming 622
Three-Headed Angel 623

Bradley, Marion Zimmer
The Firebrand 624
The Forest House 625
The Mists of Avalon 626

Bradshaw, Gillian
The Beacon of Alexandria 627
The Bearkeeper's Daughter 628
Hawk of May 629
Horses of Heaven 630
Imperial Purple 631
In Winter's Shadow 632
Kingdom of Summer 633

Brady, Charles Andrew
Crown of Grass 634
Stage of Fools 635
This Land Fulfilled 636

Brady, Joan
Theory of War 637

Bragg, Bill
Drumm's War 638

Bragg, Melvyn
The Hired Man 639

Brahms, Caryl
No Bed for Bacon 640

Braider, Donald
Color From a Light Within: A Novel Based on the Life of El Greco 641
An Epic Joy: A Novel Based on the Life of Rubens 642
Rage in Silence: A Novel Based on the Life of Goya 643

Bramble, Forbes
The Iron Roads 644
Regent Square 645
The Strange Case of Deacon Brodie 646

Branch, Houston
Diamond Head 647

Brand, Anna
Thunder Before Seven 648

Bransford, Stephen E.
Riders of the Long Road 649

Branson, Henry C.
Salisbury Plain 650

Brant, Irving
Friendly Cove 651

Braun, Matt
The Stuart Women 652
Wyatt Earp 653

Breem, Wallace
Eagle in the Snow 654
The Leopard and the Cliff 655

Bremkamp, Gloria Howe
Merari 656

Brennan, J.H.
Shiva: An Adventure of the Ice Age 657

Brenner, Jacques
Nephew to the Emperor: A Novel Based on the Life of Beethoven 658

Brent, Madeleine
The Capricorn Stone 659
A Heritage of Shadows 660
Moonraker's Bride 661
Stormswift 662
Stranger at Wildings 663

Brentano, Lowell
Bride of a Thousand Cedars 3637

Breslin, Howard
The Bright Battalions 664
Concert Grand 665
The Gallowglass 666
A Hundred Hills 667
Shad Run 668
The Silver Oar 669
Tamarack Tree 670

Brick, John
Eagle of Niagara: The Story of David Harper and His Indian Captivity 671
Jubilee 672
The Raid 673
The Richmond Raid 674
The Rifleman 675
Rogue's Kingdom 676
The Strong Men 677
Troubled Spring 678

Brien, Alan
Lenin: The Novel 679

Briggs, Jean
The Flame of the Borgias 680

Brightwell, Emily
The Ghost and Mrs. Jeffries 681
The Inspector and Mrs. Jeffries 682
Mrs. Jeffries and the Missing Alibi 683
Mrs. Jeffries Dusts for Clues 684
Mrs. Jeffries on the Ball 685
Mrs. Jeffries on the Trail 686
Mrs. Jeffries Plays the Cook 687
Mrs. Jeffries Stands Corrected 688
Mrs. Jeffries Takes Stock 689

Brindley, Louise
In the Shadow of the Brontes 690

Brink, Carol
Buffalo Coat 691
Caddie Woodlawn 692

Briskin, Jacqueline
Paloverde 693

Bristow, Gwen
Calico Palace 694
Celia Garth 695
Deep Summer 696
The Handsome Road 697
Jubilee Trail 698

Broch, Hermann
The Death of Virgil 699

Brock, Darryl
If I Never Get Back 700

Brock, Rose
Longleaf 701

Brod, Max
The Master 702

Broder, Bill
Remember This Time 703

Broder, Gloria Kurian
Remember This Time 703

Bromfield, Louis
Wild Is the River 704

Brooke, Teresa
Under the Winter Moon 705

Brooker, Bertram
The Robber: A Tale of the Time of the Herods 706

Brooks, Jean
Kathryn: In the Court of Six Queens 1

Broome, Susannah
The Pearl Pagoda 707

Brophy, John
Gentleman of Stratford 708

Broster, Dorothy Kathleen
The Dark Mile 709
The Flight of the Heron 710

Brown, Anthony
A Balance of Dangers 2184
Captain Justice 2185
The Pandora Secret 2186

Brown, Dee
Conspiracy of Knaves 711
Creek Mary's Blood 712
Killdeer Mountain 713
Wave High the Banner 714
Yellowhorse 715

Brown, Diana
The Blue Dragon 716
Come Be My Love 717
The Emerald Necklace 718
The Hand of a Woman 719
The Sandalwood Fan 720

Brown, Esther Fisher
Gaul Is Divided 721

Brown, Harry
The Stars in Their Courses 722

Brown, Karl
The Cup Trembling 723

Brown, Katharine Holland
The Father 724

Brown, Linda Beatrice
Crossing over Jordan 725

Brown, Mary
Playing the Jack 726

Brown, Rita Mae
Dolley 727
High Hearts 728
Riding Shotgun 729
Southern Discomfort 730

Brown, Russell A.
Sherlock Holmes and the Mysterious Friend of Oscar Wilde 731

Brown, Wesley
Darktown Strutters 732

Browne, Howard
Scotch on the Rocks 733

Broxholme, John Franklin
The King's Commissar 3570

Bruchac, Joseph III
Dawn Land 734

Brun, Vincenz
Alcibiades, Beloved of Gods 735

Brunner, John
The Great Steamboat Race 736

Bryant, Will
The Big Lonesome 737
Blue Russell 738
Escape From Sonora 739

Bryher
The Coin of Carthage 740
The Colors of Vaud 741
The Fourteenth of October 742
Gate to the Sea 743
The Player's Boy 744
Roman Wall 745
Ruan 746
This January Tale 747

Bryson, John Gordon
Valiant Libertine 748

Buchan, John
The Blanket of the Dark 749
The Free Fishers 750
Midwinter 751
Salute to Adventurers 752

Buchan, Perdita
Called Away 753

Buck, Pearl S.
The Good Earth 754
Imperial Woman 755
The Living Reed 756

Buckley, Fergus Reid
Eye of the Hurricane 757

Buckmaster, Henrietta
All the Living: A Novel of One Year in the Life of William Shakespeare 758
And Walk on Love: A Novel Based on the Life of the Apostle Paul 759
Deep River 760
Fire in the Heart 761

Buechner, Frederick
Brendan 762
Godric 763
The Son of Laughter 764

Bull, Bartle
The White Rhino Hotel 765

Bulwer-Lytton, Edward
Eugene Aram 766
Harold, the Last of the Saxon Kings 767
The Last Days of Pompeii 768
The Last of the Barons 769
Rienzi, or The Last of the Tribunes 770

Bunch, Chris
A Daughter of Liberty 1196

Bunkley, Anita Richmond
Black Gold 771

Burford, Lolah
Edward, Edward 772
MacLyon 773
Vice Avenged: A Moral Tale 774
The Vision of Stephen: An Elegy 775

Burgess, Anthony
A Dead Man in Deptford 776
The End of the World News 777
The Kingdom of the Wicked 778
Man of Nazareth 779
Napoleon Symphony 780
Nothing Like the Sun 781

Burgess, Jackson
Pillar of Cloud 782

Burgess, Mallory
Ballenrose 783

Burke, Colin
Kimberley 784

Burland, Brian
Surprise 785

Burleson, Frank
Desert Hawks 786
Savage Frontier 787
War Eagles 788

Burlingame, Roger
Whittling Boy: The Story of Eli Whitney 789

Burman, Edward
The Image of Our Lord 790

Burnett, William R.
Adobe Walls: A Novel of the Last Apache Rising 791
Captain Lightfoot 792
The Dark Command 793
The Goldseekers 794
Mi Amigo 795
Saint Johnson 796

Burns, Olive Ann
Cold Sassy Tree 797
Leaving Cold Sassy 798

Burns, Patricia
Kezzy 799
Stacey's Flyer 800

Burns, Ron
Enslaved 801
The Mysterious Death of Meriwether Lewis 802
Roman Nights 803
Roman Shadows 804

Burress, John
Bugle in the Wilderness 805

Burroughs, Edgar Rice
Apache Devil 806
I Am a Barbarian 807

Burroughs, William S.
The Place of Dead Roads 808

Burton, Philip
You, My Brother 809

Buruma, Ian
Playing the Game 810

Busch, Frederick
The Mutual Friend 811

Busch, Niven
Duel in the Sun 812

Bushnell, Adelyn
Tide-Rode 813

Bushnell, Oswald Andrew
Ka'a'awa: A Novel about Hawaii in the 1850s 814
Molokai 815
The Return of Lono: A Novel of Captain Cook's Last Voyage 816

Butler, Beverly
My Sister's Keeper 817

Butler, David
Lillie 818
Lusitania 819

Butler, Gwendoline
Meadowsweet 820
Sarsen Place 821
The Vesey Inheritance 822

Butler, Margaret
The Lion of Christ 823
The Lion of England 824
The Lion of Justice 825

Butler, Mildred Allen
Ward of the Sun King 826

Butler, Ragan
Captain Nash and the Honour of England 827
Captain Nash and the Wroth Inheritance 828

Butler, Richard
The Men That God Forgot 829

Butler, Suzanne
My Pride, My Folly 830
Vale of Tyranny 831

Butterworth, Michael
An Autumn in Araby 5565
A Certain Splendour 5566
Count Vronsky's Daughter 5567
Dark Inheritance 5568
Dolphin Summer 5569
The Pride of the Trevallions 5570
The Shadowed Spring 5571
The Winter Bride 5572

Byers, Cordia
Desire and Deceive 832

Byrd, Elizabeth
The Famished Land 833
Immortal Queen 834
Lady of Monkton 835
Maid of Honour: A Novel Set in the Court of Mary, Queen of Scots 836

Byrd, Max
Jackson: A Novel 837
Jefferson: A Novel 838

Byrd, Sigman
The Valiant 839

Byrne, Donn
Messer Marco Polo 840

Byrne, John Keyes
Parnell and the Englishwoman 3721

C

Cabell, James Branch
The First Gentleman of America: A Comedy of Conquest 841

Cable, George W.
The Grandissimes 842

Cable, Mary
Avery's Knot 843

Cabries, Jean
Jacob 844

Cain, James M.
Mignon 845

Caldecott, Moyra
The Lily and the Bull 846
Shadows on the Stones 847
The Tall Stones 848
The Temple of the Sun 849

Caldwell, Taylor
The Arm and the Darkness 850
Captains and the Kings 851
Ceremony of the Innocent 852
Dear and Glorious Physician 853
Dynasty of Death 854
The Earth Is the Lord's: A Tale of the Rise of Genghis Khan 855
Glory and the Lightning 856
Grandmother and the Priests 857
Great Lion of God 858
I, Judas 859
Never Victorious, Never Defeated 860
A Pillar of Iron 861
A Prologue to Love 862
Testimony of Two Men 863
The Wide House 864

Calitri, Charles J.
The Goliath Head 865

Callaghan, Morley
A Time for Judas 866

Calvino, Italo
Invisible Cities 867

Cameron, Kenneth M.
Our Jo, or The Chronicle of a Coming Man 868

Cameron, William
Day Is Coming 869

Camp, Candace
The Rainbow Promise 2580

Camp, Deborah
Belle Starr 870
Black-Eyed Susan 871
Fallen Angel 872

Campbell, Grace
Torbeg 873

Campbell, Margaret
The Lady and the Arsenic 598
Queen's Caprice 599

Campbell, Patricia
Cedarhaven 874
The Royal Ann Tree 875
Silver Fruit 876

Campbell, Thomas
Old Miss 877

Campion, Jane
The Piano 878

Canham, Marsha
The Blood of Roses 879
In the Shadow of Midnight 880
The Pride of Lions 881

Canning, Victor
The Crimson Chalice 882
Raven's Wind 883

Cannon, Le Grand
Come Home at Even 884
Look to the Mountain 885

Cantor, Jay
The Death of Che Guevara 886

Capps, Benjamin
The Brothers of Uterica 887
Sam Chance 888
The Trail to Ogallala 889
The True Memoirs of Charley Blankenship 890
The White Man's Road 891
Woman Chief 892
A Woman of the People 893

Carey, Peter
Oscar and Lucinda 894

Carlisle, Henry
The Jonah Man 895
The Land Where the Sun Dies 896
Voyage to the First of December 897

Carmer, Carl Lamson
Genesee Fever 898

Carmichael, Emily
Visions of a Heart 899

Carnac, Nicholas
Indigo 900
Tournament of the Shadows 901

Carnahan, Walter
Hoffman's Row 902

Carney, Otis
Chihuahua 1916 903

Carothers, Annabel
Kilcaraig 904

Carpentier, Alejo
The Harp and the Shadow 905
Kingdom of This World 906

Carr, Caleb
The Alienist 907

Carr, John Dickson
Captain Cut-Throat 908
The Devil in Velvet 909
Fire, Burn! 910
*The Hungry Goblin: A Victorian
  Detective Novel* 911
Most Secret 912
*The Murder of Sir Edmund
  Godfrey* 913
Papa La-Bas 914
*Scandal at High Chimneys: A Victorian
  Melodrama* 915

Carr, Philippa
The Adulteress 916
The Black Swan 917
The Changeling 918
Daughters of England 919
Knave of Hearts 920
Lament for a Lost Lover 921
The Lion Triumphant 922
The Love Child 923
Midsummer's Eve 924
The Miracle at St. Bruno's 925
The Pool of St. Branok 926
The Return of the Gypsy 927
Saraband for Two Sisters 928
The Song of the Siren 929
A Time for Silence 930
Voices in a Haunted Room 931
Will You Love Me in September? 932
The Witch From the Sea 933

Carr, Robyn
The Bellerose Bargain 934
The Blue Falcon 935
The Braeswood Tapestry 936
By Right of Arms 937
Chelynne 938
The Everlasting Covenant 939
The Troubadour's Romance 940
Woman's Own 941

Carrere, Emmanuel
Gothic Romance 942

Carrighar, Sally
The Glass Dove 943

Carse, Robert
The Beckoning Waters 944

Carter, Forrest
Gone to Texas 945
*The Vengeance Trail of Josey
  Wales* 946
Watch for Me on the Mountain 947

Carter, Winifred
Dr. Johnson's Dear Mistress 948

Carton, Jacques
La Belle Sorel 949

Case, Josephine
Written in Sand 950

Case, Victoria
*The Quiet Life of Mrs. General
  Lane* 951

Casey, Jack
Lily of the Mohawks 952

Cashman, John
The Gentleman From Chicago 953

Cassel, Virginia C.
Juniata Valley 954

Cassill, R.V.
After Goliath 955

Castor, Henry
The Year of the Spaniard 956

Cather, Willa
Death Comes for the Archbishop 957
Sapphira and the Slave Girl 958
Shadows on the Rock 959

Cato, Nancy
Forefathers 960
The Heart of the Continent 961
North-West by South 962

Catton, Bruce
Banner at Shenandoah 963

Caudill, Harry M.
Dark Hills to Westward 964

Cecchi, Dario
Titian 965

Chadwick, Elizabeth
First Knight 966
The Leopard Unleashed 967
The Running Vixen 968
The Wild Hunt 969

Challans, Mary
The Bull From the Sea 5295
Fire From Heaven 5296
Funeral Games 5297
The King Must Die 5298
The Last of the Wine 5299
The Mask of Apollo 5300
The Persian Boy 5301
The Praise Singer 5302

Challis, George
The Bait and the Trap 970
The Golden Knight 971

Chalmers, Harvey
Drums Against Frontenac 972
West to the Setting Sun 973

Chamberlin, Ann
Sofia 974
Tamar 975

Chambers, Robert W.
Cardigan 976
The Happy Parrot 977
Hidden Children 978
Little Red Foot 979
Painted Minx 980
The Rake and the Hussy 981
Secret Service Operator 13 982
War Paint and Rouge 983
Whistling Cat 984

Chambrun, Clara Longworth de
Two Loves Have I 985

Chandernagor, Francoise
The King's Way 986

Chang, Hsin-Hai
The Fabulous Concubine 987

Chapman, Arthur
John Crews 988

Chapman, Hester W.
Eugenie 989
Fear No More 990
Limmerston Hall 991
Lucy 992

Chapman, John Higham Stanton
Rogue's March 993
Tennessee Hazard 994

Chapman, Maristan
Rogue's March 993
Tennessee Hazard 994

Chapman, Mary
Rogue's March 993
Tennessee Hazard 994

Chaput, W.J.
The Man on the Train 995

Charbonneau, Eileen
Waltzing in Ragtime 996

Charbonneau, Louis
Down From the Mountain 997
*Trail: The Story of the Lewis and Clark
  Expedition* 998

Charques, Dorothy
The Dark Stranger 999
Men Like Shadows 1000
The Nunnery 1001

Charters, Samuel
*Jelly Roll Morton's Last Night at the
  Jungle Inn: An Imaginary
  Memoir* 1002

Chase, Nicholas
Locksley 1003

Chase-Riboud, Barbara
Echo of Lions 1004
The President's Daughter 1005
Sally Hemings 1006
Valide: A Novel of the Harem 1007

Chateaubriand, Francois Rene de
Atala 1008

Chatwin, Bruce C.
The Viceroy of Ouidah 1009

Cheatham, Lillian
Portrait of Emma 1010
The Secret of Saramount 1011

Chernaik, Judith
*The Daughter: A Novel Based on the
  Life of Eleanor Marx* 1012
Love's Children 1013

Chesney, Marion
The Adventuress 1014
Animating Maria 1015
*At the Sign of the Golden
  Pineapple* 1016
Back in Society 1017
The Banishment 1018
Beatrice Goes to Brighton 1019
Belinda Goes to Bath 1020
Colonel Sandhurst to the Rescue 1021
Daphne 1022
Deborah Goes to Dover 1023
Deirdre and Desire 1024
The Desirable Duchess 1025
Diana the Huntress 1026
Emily Goes to Exeter 1027
Enlightening Delilah 1028
Finessing Clarissa 1029
The First Rebellion 1030
The Folly 1031

Frederica in Fashion 1032
Her Grace's Passion 1033
The Intrigue 1034
Lady Fortescue Steps Out 1035
Marrying Harriet 1036
Minerva 1037
The Miser of Mayfair 1038
Miss Davenport's Christmas 1039
Miss Fiona's Fancy 1040
Miss Tonks Turns to Crime 1041
Mrs. Budley Falls From Grace 1042
Penelope Goes to Portsmouth 1043
Perfecting Fiona 1044
Plain Jane 1045
Rainbird's Revenge 1046
Rake's Progress 1047
Refining Felicity 1048
The Scandalous Lady Wright 1049
The Scandalous Marriage 1050
Sir Philip's Folly 1051
The Taming of Annabelle 1052
The Wicked Godmother 1053
Yvonne Goes to York 1054

Chester, Deborah
French Slippers 1055
A Love So Wild 1056

Chiaventone, Frederick J.
*A Road We Do Not Know: A Novel of
  Custer at the Little Bighorn* 1057

Chidsey, Donald Barr
Captain Adam 1058
Captain Bashful 1059
The Edge of Piracy 1060
His Majesty's Highwayman 1061
The Legion of the Lost 1062
Lord of the Isles 1063
Reluctant Cavalier 1064
Stronghold 1065
This Bright Sword 1066
The Wickedest Pilgrim 1067

Childers, James
Tomorrow We Reap 6081

Chinn, Laurene
Marcus 1068
The Soothsayer 1069
The Unanointed 1070

Chisholm, P.F.
A Famine of Horses 1071
A Season of Knives 1072

Christensen, Synnove
Lindeman's Daughters 1073

Christgau, John
Spoon 1074

Christian, Catherine
The Pendragon 1075

Christie, Agatha
Death Comes as the End 1076

Christilian, J.D.
Scarlet Women 1077

Churchill, Winston
Coniston 1078
The Crisis 1079
The Crossing 1080
Richard Carvel 1081

Clagett, John
Buckskin Cavalier 1082
Cradle of the Sun 1083

Clancy, Carlile
Children of the Dust 1084

Clark, Dorothy Park
City of the Flags 4290
The Fairbrothers 4291
Reckon with the River 4292

Show Me a Land 4293
Tyrone of Kentucky 4294

Clark, Gail
The Baroness of Bow Street 1085
Dulcie Bligh 1086

Clark, Howard
The Mill on Mad River 1087

Clark, Jean
The Marriage Bed 1088
Until the Winds 1089

Clark, Justus Kent
King's Agent 1090

Clark, L.D.
A Bright Tragic Thing 1091

Clark, Norma Lee
Lady Jane 1092
The Tynedale Daughters 1093

Clark, Ronald
Queen Victoria's Bomb 1094

Clark, Tom
The Exile of Celine 1095

Clark, Walter Van Tilburg
The Ox-Bow Incident 1096

Clarke, Brenda
Death and the Chapman 5715
The Eve of Saint Hyacinth 5716
The Holy Innocents 5717
The Plymouth Cloak 5718
The Weaver's Tale 5719

Clarke, William Kendall
The Robber Baroness 1097

Clarkson, Tom
Love Is My Vocation: An Imaginative Study of St. Therese of Lisieux 1098

Clavel, Bernard
Lord of the River 1099

Clavell, James
Gai-Jin: A Novel of Japan 1100
Shogun 1101
Tai-Pan 1102

Clayton, Paul
Flight of the Crow 1103

Cleary, Jon
The Faraway Drums 1104
The Golden Sabre 1105
High Road to China 1106

Cleeve, Brian
Hester 1107
Judith 1108
Kate 1109
Sara 1110

Clemens, Samuel
A Connecticut Yankee in King Arthur's Court 6371
Personal Recollections of Joan of Arc 6372
The Prince and the Pauper 6373

Clevely, Hugh
Stranger in Two Worlds 1111

Clewes, Howard
I, the King 1112

Clewes, Winston
Violent Friends 1113

Clews, Roy
Drums of War 1114
The Valiant and the Daunted 1115

Cliff, Michelle
Free Enterprise 1116

Clifford, Nicholas R.
The House of Memory: A Novel of Shanghai 1117

Clift, Charmian
The Big Chariot 1118

Clive, William
Dando on Delhi Ridge 1119
The Tune That They Play 1120

Cloete, Stuart
The Abductors 1121
The Fiercest Heart 1122
The Hill of Doves 1123
How Young They Die 1124
The Mask 1125
Rags of Glory 1126
The Turning Wheels 1127
Watch for the Dawn 1128

Closs, Hannah
Deep Are the Valleys 1129
High Are the Mountains 1130
The Silent Tarn 1131

Cloud, Patricia
This Willing Passion 1132

Clynes, Michael
A Brood of Vipers 1133
The Gallows Murder 1134
The Grail Murders 1135
The Poisoned Chalice 1136
The White Rose Murders 1137

Coatsworth, Elizabeth
Here I Stay 1138
A Toast to the King 1139

Cochran, Hamilton
The Dram Tree 1140
Rogue's Holiday 1141
Silver Shoals 1142
Windward Passage 1143

Cochran, Louis
Fool of God: A Novel Based on the Life of Alexander Campbell 1144
Raccoon John Smith 1145

Cockrell, Amanda
The Deer Dancers 1146

Cockrell, Marian
The Misadventures of Bethany Price 1147
The Revolt of Sarah Perkins 1148

Codrescu, Andrei
The Blood Countess 1149

Cody, Al
Bitter Creek 1150

Coffman, Virginia
The Dark Palazzo 1151
Dark Winds 1152
The Gaynor Women 1153
Hyde Place 1154
Marsanne 1155
Mistress Devon 1156
Pacific Cavalcade 1157
The Passion of Letty Fox 5610
Veronique 1158

Coghlan, Margaret M.
The Asking Price 6039
Call Home the Heart 6040
Creature Comforts 6041
The Dark Pasture 6042
The Good Provider 6043
Hearts of Gold 6044
Lantern for the Dark 6045
The Marrying Kind 6046
The Penny Wedding 6047
Shadows on the Shore 6048
Treasures on Earth 6049

The Welcome Light 6050

Cohen, Matt
The Spanish Doctor 1159

Cohen, Octavus Roy
Borrasca 1160

Coker, Elizabeth Boatwright
La Belle 1161
The Big Drum 1162
Blood Red Roses 1163
Daughter of Strangers 1164
The Grasshopper King 1165
Lady Rich 1166

Colby, Merle Estes
All Ye People 1167
New Road 1168

Coldsmith, Don
Bearer of the Pipe 1169
Bride of the Morning Star 1170
Buffalo Medicine 1171
Child of the Dead 1172
Daughter of the Eagle 1173
The Elk-Dog Heritage 1174
The Flower in the Mountains 1175
Follow the Wind 1176
Fort De Chastaigne 1177
Man of the Shadows 1178
Medicine Knife 1179
Moon of Thunder 1180
Pale Star 1181
Quest for the White Bull 1182
Return of the Spanish 1183
Return to the River 1184
River of Swans 1185
Runestone 1186
The Sacred Hills 1187
The Smoky Hill 1188
Song of the Rock 1189
Thunderstick 1190
Track of the Bear 1191
Trail From Taos 1192
Trail of the Spanish Bit 1193
Walks in the Sun 1194
World of Silence 1195

Cole, Allan
A Daughter of Liberty 1196

Colegate, Isabel
The Shooting Party 1197
Statues in a Garden 1198
The Summer of the Royal Visit 1199

Coleman, Bob
The Latter Adventures of Tom Jones 1200

Coleman, Jane Candia
Doc Holliday's Woman 1201

Coleman, Lonnie
Beulah Land 1202
The Legacy of Beulah Land 1203
Look Away, Beulah Land 1204
Mark 1205

Coleman, Terry
Southern Cross 1206
Thanksgiving 1207

Collett, Bill
The Last Mutiny: The Further Adventures of Captain Bligh 1208

Collin, Richard Oliver
Contessa 1209

Collins, Max Allan
Carnal Hours 1210
The Dark City 1211
Murder by the Numbers 1212
Stolen Away 1213
True Crime 1214

True Detective 1215

Collins, Norman
Quiet Lady 1216

Collins, Warwick
The Rationalist 1217

Colver, Alice Mary
The Measure of the Years 1218
There Is a Season 1219

Colver, Anne
Listen for the Voices 1220
Mr. Lincoln's Wife 1221

Colyton, Henry John
Sir Pagan 1222

Combs, Harry
Brules 1223
The Scout 1224

Combuchen, Sigrid
Byron: A Novel 1225

Comfort, Will
Apache 1226

Compton, D.G.
The Fine and Handsome Captain 3933
Stranger at the Wedding 3934

Compton, Ralph
The Goodnight Trail 1227

Compton-Burnett, Ivy
A Father and His Fate 1228
A Heritage and Its History 1229
The Mighty and Their Fall 1230
Mother and Son 1231

Conde, Maryse
The Children of Segu 1232
I, Tituba, Black Witch of Salem 1233
Segu 1234

Condon, Richard
The Abandoned Woman 1235

Conley, Robert J.
The Actor 1236
Back to Malachi 1237
Border Line 1238
Colfax 1239
Crazy Snake 1240
The Dark Way 1241
Geronimo: An American Legend 1242
Go-Ahead Rider 1243
Killing Time 1244
The Long Trail North 1245
Mountain Windsong 1246
Ned Christie's War 1247
Nickajack 1248
Quitting Time 1249
The Saga of Henry Starr 1250
Strange Company 1251
To Make a Killing 1252
The Way of the Priests 1253
The White Path 1254

Conn, Phoebe
By Love Enslaved 1255

Connell, Evan S.
The Alchymist's Journal 1256

Conquist, Mabel
Bianca 1257

Conroy, Robert
1901 1258

Conroy, Sarah Booth
Refinements of Love: A Novel about Clover and Henry Adams 1259

Constant, Alberta
Oklahoma Run 1260

Constantin-Weyer, Maurice
The Half Breed 1261

Coogan, Beatrice
The Big Wind 1262

Cook, Judith
The Slicing Edge of Death 1263

Cook, Roberta St. Clair
The Thing about Clarissa 1264

Cook, Will
Elizabeth, By Name 1265

Cooke, David Coxe
The Post of Honor 1266

Cooke, John Byrne
The Snowblind Moon 1267
South of the Border 1268

Cooke, John Esten
The Virginia Comedians 1269

Cooke, John Peyton
Torsos 1270

Cooke, William Victor
The Keys of England 1271

Cookson, Catherine
The Bannaman Legacy 1272
The Black Candle 1273
The Black Velvet Gown 1274
The Cinderpath 1275
The Gambling Man 1276
The Girl 1277
The Harrogate Secret 1278
The Love Child 1279
The Mallen Girl 1280
The Mallen Lot 1281
The Mallen Streak 1282
The Maltese Angel 1283
Miss Martha Mary Crawford 4081
The Moth 1284
My Beloved Son 1285
The Parson's Daughter 1286
The Rag Nymph 1287
The Slow Awakening 4082
Tilly 1288
Tilly Alone 1289
Tilly Wed 1290
The Whip 1291
The Wingless Bird 1292

Coolidge, Dane
Gringo Gold 1293

Cooney, Eleanor
The Court of the Lion 1294
Deception 1295

Cooper, Courtney Ryley
The Pioneers 1296

Cooper, J. California
Family 1297

Cooper, James Fenimore
The Bravo 1298
The Deerslayer 1299
The Headsman; or, The Abbaye des Vignerons 1300
The Heidenmauer 1301
The Last of the Mohicans 1302
Lionel Lincoln; or, The Leaguer of Boston 1303
Mercedes of Castile 1304
The Pathfinder; or, The Inland Sea 1305
The Pilot 1306
The Pioneers; or, The Sources of the Susquehanna 1307
The Prairie 1308
The Red Rover 1309
The Spy: A Tale of the Neutral Ground 1310

The Water Witch 1311
The Wept of Wish-Ton-Wish 1312

Cooper, Jamie Lee
The Horn and the Forest 1313
Rapaho 1314
Shadow of a Star 1315

Cooper, Kent
Anna Zenger: Mother of Freedom 1316

Cooperstein, Claire
Johanna: A Novel of the Van Gogh Family 1317

Copeland, Bonnie
Lady of Moray 1318

Coppel, Alfred
The Marburg Chronicles 1319

Coray, Henry W.
Son of Tears 1320

Corbett, Elizabeth
The Far Down 1321
Faye's Folly 1322

Corcoran, Charles
Blackrobe 1323

Corcoran, William
Golden Horizons 1324

Cordell, Alexander
The Rape of the Fair Country 1325
This Sweet and Bitter Earth 1326

Corelli, Marie
Barabbas: A Dream of the World's Tragedy 1327

Cores, Lucy
Katya 1328
The Year of December 1329

Corle, Edwin
Billy the Kid 1330

Cormack, Maribelle
Land for My Sons 1331

Cornish, Dorothy Helen
These Were the Brontes 1332

Cornwell, Bernard
Battle Flag 1333
The Bloody Ground 1334
Copperhead 1335
Rebel 1336
Redcoat 1337
Sharpe's Battle 1338
Sharpe's Company 1339
Sharpe's Devil 1340
Sharpe's Eagle 1341
Sharpe's Enemy 1342
Sharpe's Gold 1343
Sharpe's Honour 1344
Sharpe's Regiment 1345
Sharpe's Revenge 1346
Sharpe's Rifles 1347
Sharpe's Siege 1348
Sharpe's Sword 1349
Waterloo 1350
The Winter King 1351

Corrington, John William
And Wait for the Night 1352

Cory, Diane
A Token of Jewels 1353

Coryell, Hubert
Indian Brother 1354

Coryn, Marjorie
Alone Among Men 1355
Good-Bye My Son 1356
The Incorruptible 1357

The Marriage of Josephine 1358
Sorrow by Day 1359

Cost, March
The Countess 1360
I, Rachel 1361

Costain, Thomas B.
Below the Salt 1362
The Black Rose 1363
Darkness and the Dawn 1364
For My Great Folly 1365
High Towers 1366
The Last Love 1367
The Moneyman 1368
Ride with Me 1369
The Silver Chalice 1370
The Tontine 1371

Cotton, Ralph W.
While Angels Dance 1372

Coulehan, Norbert
Fourth King 1373

Coulter, Catherine
Earth Song 1374
The Heiress Bride 1375
Lord of Hawkfell Island 1376
Night Shadow 1377
Night Storm 1378
The Nightingale Legacy 1379
Rosehaven 1380
Secret Song 1381
The Sherbrooke Bride 1382

Coulter, Stephen
The Chateau 1383
Damned Shall Be Desire: The Passionate Life of Guy de Maupassant 1384
The Devil Inside: A Novel of Dostoevsky's Life 1385

Courlander, Harold
The African 1386

Courter, Gay
Flowers in the Blood 1387
The Midwife 1388
The Midwife's Advice 1389
River of Dreams 1390

Cowan, James
A Mapmaker's Dream 1391

Cowdrey, A.E.
Elixir of Life 1392

Cowell, Stephanie
Nicholas Cooke: Actor, Soldier, Physician, Priest 1393
The Physician of London 1394

Coyle, Harold
Look Away 1395
Until the End 1396

Crabb, Alfred Leland
Breakfast at the Hermitage 1397
Dinner at Belmont 1398
Home to Kentucky: A Novel of Henry Clay 1399
Home to Tennessee 1400
Home to the Hermitage 1401
Journey to Nashville 1402
Lodging at the Saint Cloud 1403
Mockingbird Sang at Chickamauga 1404
Peace at Bowling Green 1405
Reunion at Chattanooga 1406
Supper at the Maxwell House 1407

Crace, Jim
Signals of Distress 1408

Cradock, Fanny
The Lormes of Castle Rising 1409

Shadows over Castle Rising 1410
War Comes to Castle Rising 1411
Wind of Change at Castle Rising 1412

Crane, John Kenny
The Legacy of Ladysmith 1413

Crane, Stephen
The Red Badge of Courage 1414

Crane, Teresa
Freedom's Banner 1415
The Hawthorne Legacy 1416
Molly 1417
Sweet Songbird 1418

Cranston, Paul F.
To Heaven on Horseback 1419

Crawford, Max
Lords of the Plains 1420

Crawley, Aileen
The Bride of Suleiman 1421
The Shadow of God 1422

Creasy, John
The Masters of Bow Street 1423

Creed, Will
The Sword of Il Grande 1424

Crichton, Michael
Eaters of the Dead 1425
The Great Train Robbery 1426

Crichton Smith, Iain
The Alien Light 1427

Cronyn, George William
The Fool of Venus 1428
Mermaid Tavern 1429

Crook, Elizabeth
Promised Lands 1430
The Raven's Bride 1431

Cross, Charlene
Masque of Enchantment 1432

Cross, Donna Woolfolk
Pope Joan 1433

Crowe, Amanda Cockrell
The Deer Dancers 1146

Crowleigh, Ann
Clively Close: Dead as Dead Can Be 1434

Crowley, Duane
Riddle Me a Murder 1435

Crowley, Elaine
The Ways of Women 1436

Crownfield, Gertrude
Where Glory Waits 1437

Croy, Homer
Wheels West 1438

Crozier, William
The Fates Are Laughing 1439

Culp, John H.
Born of the Sun 1440
The Bright Feathers 1441
The Men of Gonzales 1442
Oh, Valley Green 1443
The Restless Land 1444
Timothy Baines 1445
The Treasure of the Chisos 1446
A Whistle in the Wind 1447

Cummings, Barbara
Clively Close: Dead as Dead Can Be 1434

Cummings, Betty Sue
Say These Names (Remember Them) 1448

Cummings, Jack
Sergeant Gringo 1449

Cunningham, John
The Rainbow Runner 1450
Warhorse 1451

Curwood, James Oliver
The Plains of Abraham 1452

Cushman, Dan
The Silver Mountain 1453

D

Dailey, Janet
The Great Alone 1454
The Pride of Hannah Wade 1455
The Proud and the Free 1456

Dakers, Elaine
Madame Geneva 3655
Parcel of Rogues 3656
The Severed Crown 3657
Thunder on St. Paul's Day 3658
The Young and Lonely King 3659

Daley, Joseph A.
Exit with Drums 1457

Dalkey, Kara
Goa 1458

Daly, Robert Welter
Broadsides 1459
Soldier of the Sea 1460

Dandrea, Don
Orlok 1461

Dane, Clemence
He Brings Great News 1462

Daniels, Kathleen
*Minna's Story: The Secret Love of
    Doctor Sigmund Freud* 1463

Danielson, Peter
Children of the Lion 1464
The Death of Kings 1465
Departed Glory 1466
The Exodus 1467
The Golden Pharaoh 1468
The Invaders 1469
The Lion in Egypt 1470
The Promised Land 1471
The Prophecy 1472
Prophets and Warriors 1473
The Sea Peoples 1474
The Shepherd Kings 1475
The Shining King 1476
Sword of Glory 1477
Triumph of the Lion 1478
The Trumpet and the Sword 1479
Vengeance of the Lion 1480

Dann, Jack
*The Memory Cathedral: A Secret
    History of Leonardo Da Vinci* 1481

Darby, Catherine
The Love Knot 1482

Darcy, Clare
Allegra 1483
Caroline and Julia 1484
Cressida 1485
Elyza 1486
Eugenia 1487
Georgina 1488
Gwendolen 1489
Lady Pamela 1490
Letty 1491
Lydia, or Love in Town 1492

Victoire 1493

Dark, Eleanor
Storm of Time 1494
The Timeless Land 1495

Darrell, Elizabeth
Beyond All Frontiers 1722
*The Bridge of a Hundred
    Dragons* 1723
A Captive Freedom 1724
Forget the Glory 1725
The Gathering Wolves 1496
The Jade Alliance 1497
A Question of Honour 1726
Some Far Elusive Dawn 1727
That Sweet and Savage Land 1728

Darwin, Timothy
The Gentleman From Chicago 953

Davenat, Colette
Deborah 1498
*Deborah and the Many Faces of
    Love* 1499
Deborah and the Siege of Paris 1500

Davenport, Gwen
Time and Chance 1501

David, Evan John
As Runs the Glass 1502

Davidson, Diane
Feversham 1503

Davidson, Louis B.
Captain Marooner 1504

Davidson, L.S. Jr.
The Disturber 1505

Davies, John Evan Weston
The Midnight Gun 4180
The Pagoda Tree 4181
The Road and the Star 4182

Davies, June Wyndham
Golden Destiny 1506
Storm Before Sunrise 1507

Davies-Owens, Shirley
Silver Linings 1508

Daviess, Maria Thompson
The Matrix 1509

Daviot, Gordon
The Privateer 1510

Davis, Burke
The Ragged Ones 1511
*To Appomattox: Nine April Days,
    1865* 1512
Yorktown 1513

Davis, Christopher
*Belmarch: A Legend of the First
    Crusade* 1514
A Peep into the 20th Century 1515

Davis, Clyde Brion
Nebraska Coast 1516

Davis, Dorothy
Men of No Property 1517

Davis, Elmer Holmes
Giant Killer 1518

Davis, Genevieve
A Passion in the Blood 1519

Davis, Harold Lenoir
Beulah Land 1520
Distant Music 1521
Harp of a Thousand Strings 1522
Honey in the Horn 1523

Davis, James F.
The Road to San Jacinto 1524

Davis, Julia
Bridle the Wind 1525
Cloud on the Land 1526
Eagle on the Sun 1527

Davis, Lindsey
The Iron Hand of Mars 1528
Last Act in Palmyra 1529
Poseidon's Gold 1530
Shadows in Bronze 1531
The Silver Pigs 1532
Time to Depart 1533
Venus in Copper 1534

Davis, Lou Ellen
Clouds of Destiny 1535

Davis, Maggie
The Far Side of Home 1536

Davis, M.H.
The Winter Servant 1537

Davis, Mildred B.
Lucifer Land 1538

Davis, Paxton
The Seasons of Heroes 1539

Davis, W.E.
The Gathering Storm 1540

Davis, William Stearns
Gilman of the Redford 1541

Dawes, Edna
The Gathering Wolves 1496
The Jade Alliance 1497

Dawkins, Cecil
The Live Goat 1542

Day, Dianne
Fire and Fog 1543
*The Strange Files of Fremont
    Jones* 1544

Day, Douglas
*The Prison Notebooks of Ricardo Flores
    Magon* 1545

Dayton, Eldorous L.
Chantefable 1546

De Blasis, Celeste
The Proud Breed 1547
A Season of Swans 1548
Swan's Chance 1549
Wild Swan 1550

De Bois, Helma
The Incorruptible 1551

De Born, Edith
Felding Castle 1552

De Camp, L. Sprague
The Arrows of Hercules 1553
The Bronze God of Rhodes 1554
The Dragon of the Ishtar Gate 1555
An Elephant for Aristotle 1556
Lest Darkness Fall 1557

De Coster, Charles Theodore Henri
The Legend of Tyl Ulenspiegel 1558

De Haven, Tom
Funny Papers 1559

de la Ramee, Marie Louise
Under Two Flags 4767

de la Roche, Mazo
Morning at Jalna 1560

de Luca, Teresa
A Distant Thunder 1561

De Silva, Colin
The Winds of Sinhala 1562

De Wohl, Louis
*Citadel of God: A Novel of Saint
    Benedict* 1563
David of Jerusalem 1564
*The Glorious Folly: A Novel of the
    Time of St. Paul* 1565
The Golden Thread 1566
Imperial Renegade 1567
*The Joyful Beggar: A Novel of St.
    Francis of Assisi* 1568
The Last Crusader 1569
*Lay Siege to Heaven: A Novel of Saint
    Catherine of Siena* 1570
The Living Wood 1571
The Quiet Light 1572
The Restless Flame 1573
*Set All Afire: A Novel of St. Francis
    Xavier* 1574
Throne of the World 1575

Decker, Malcolm
The Rebel and the Turncoat 1576

Deeping, Warwick
The Man on the White Horse 1577
Martin Valliant 1578

DeFelice, Jim
The Iron Chain 1579

Degenhard, William
The Regulators 1580

Dehon, Theodora
Heroic Dust 1581

Deiss, Joseph Jay
The Great Infidel 1582

Deland, Margaret
The Kays 1583

Delblanc, Sven
Speranza 1584

Delderfield, R.F.
Farewell the Tranquil 1585
Give Us This Day 1586
God Is an Englishman 1587
A Horseman Riding By 1588
Seven Men of Gascony 1589
Theirs Was the Kingdom 1590
To Serve Them All My Days 1591

Delibes, Miguel
The Stuff of Heroes 1592

DeLillo, Don
Libra 1593

Dell, Floyd
Diana Stair 1594

Dell, George
The Earth Abideth 1595

Dellin, Genell
Cherokee Dawn 1596

Delman, David
Ain't Goin' to Glory 1597
The Bluestocking 1598

Delmar, Vina
Beloved 1599
The Big Family 1600
The Laughing Stranger 1601
A Time for Titans 1602

Delves-Broughton, Josephine
Heart of a Queen 1603
Officer and Gentleman 1604

Demarest, Phyllis Gordon
The Wilderness Brigade 1605

DeMaria, Robert
Clodia 1606
To Be a King 1607

Dempsey, Al
Path of the Sun 1608
What Law There Was 1609

Denker, Henry
The Healers 1610
Salome, Princess of Galilee 1611

Denti di Pirajno, Alberto
Ippolita 1612

Denuziere, Maurice
Bagatelle 1613

Derleth, August
Bright Journey 1614
The Hills Stand Watch 1615
The House on the Mound 1616
Restless Is the River 1617
The Shadow in the Glass 1618
Still Is the Summer Night 1619
Wind over Wisconsin 1620

Deropp, Robert S.
If I Forget Thee 1621

DeRosa, Peter
Rebels: The Irish Rising of 1916 1622

Desmond, Alice Curtis
Alexander Hamilton's Wife 1623

Dessau, Joanna
Absolute Elizabeth 1624
The Blacksmith's Daughter 1625
Lord of the Ladies 1626
The Red-Haired Brat 1627

Detre, Jean
A Most Extraordinary Pair 1628

Deutsch, Babette
Rogue's Legacy: A Novel about Francois Villon 1629

Deveraux, Jude
The Conquest 1630
A Knight in Shining Armor 1631
Mountain Laurel 1632
The Taming 1633

Devon, John Anthony
O Western Wind 1634

Devon, Louis
Aide to Glory 1635

Dewhurst, Keith
Captain of the Sands 1636

Dexter, Charles
The Street of Kings 1637

Dexter, Pete
Deadwood 1638

Di Donato, Georgia
Woman of Justice 1639

Dick, Isabel
Wild Orchid 1640

Dickens, Charles
Barnaby Rudge: A Tale of the Riots of Eighty 1641
A Tale of Two Cities 1642

Dieter, William
The White Land 1643

Dieterle, William
The Good Tidings 5843

Dillard, Annie
The Living 1644

Dillon, Anna
Seasons 1645

Dillon, Eilis
Across the Bitter Sea 1646
Wild Geese 1647

Disch, Thomas M.
Clara Reeve 2705
Neighboring Lives 1648

Divine, Arthur Durham
The Golden Fool 1649
Thunder on the Chesapeake 1650

Divine, David
The Golden Fool 1649
Thunder on the Chesapeake 1650

Dixon, Pierson
Farewell, Catullus 1651

Dobbs, Michael
Last Man to Die 1652

Doblin, Alfred
Karl and Rosa 1653
A People Betrayed 1654

Dobraczynski, Jan
The Letters of Nicodemus 1655

Doctorow, E.L.
Billy Bathgate 1656
Loon Lake 1657
Ragtime 1658
The Waterworks 1659
Welcome to Hard Times 1660
World's Fair 1661

Dodd, Christina
Candle in the Window 1662

Dodd, Susan
Mamaw 1663

Dodge, Constance
The Dark Stranger 1664
Graham of Claverhouse 1665
In Adam's Fall 1666
The Pointless Knife 1667
Weathercock 1668

Dodge, Louis
The American 1669

Doherty, Eddie
Captain Marooner 1504

Doherty, P.C.
An Ancient Evil 2504
Angel of Death 1670
The Book of Shadows 2505
A Brood of Vipers 1133
The Crown in Darkness 1671
The Death of a King 1672
The Eye of God 2506
The Fate of Princes 1673
The Gallows Murder 1134
The Golden Wind 2507
The Grail Murders 1135
The Masked Man 1674
The Merchant of Death 2508
The Nightingale Gallery 2684
The Poisoned Chalice 1136
The Prince Lost to Time 1776
The Prince of Darkness 1675
Red Slayer: Being the Second of the Sorrowful Mysteries of Brother Athelstan 2685
Satan in St. Mary's 1676
Satan's Fire 1677
The Serpent Amongst the Lilies 1678
A Shrine of Murders 2509
The Song of a Dark Angel 1679
Spy in Chancery 1680
A Tapestry of Murders 2510
A Time for the Death of a King 1777
The Time of Murder at Mayerling 1778
The White Rose Murders 1137
The Whyte Harte 1681

Doig, Ivan
Dancing at the Rascal Fair 1682
English Creek 1683
Ride with Me, Mariah Montana 1684
The Sea Runners 1685

Dolan, Mary
Hannibal of Carthage 1686

Dolbier, Maurice
Benjy Boone 1687
The Mortal Gods 1688

Donald, James
The Hangman's Crusade 370
Shadow of the Wolf 371

Donauer, Friedrich
Swords Against Carthage 1689

Donchev, Anton
Time of Parting 1690

Donn Byrne, Brian Oswald
Messer Marco Polo 840

Donnell, Susan
Pocahontas 1691

Donnelly, Gabrielle
Presumption: An Entertainment 350
The Third Sister 351

Dored, Elisabeth
I Loved Tiberius 1692

d'Orleans, Princess Marion
A Castle in Bavaria 1693

d'Orleans, Prince Thibaut
A Castle in Bavaria 1693

Dorr, Roberta Kells
Abraham and Sarah: The Long Journey 1694
Bathsheba 1695
The Queen of Sheba 1696
Solomon's Song 1697

Douglas, Carole Nelson
Good Morning, Irene 1698
Good Night, Mr. Holmes 1699
Irene at Large 1700
Irene's Last Waltz 1701

Douglas, Lloyd C.
The Big Fisherman 1702
The Robe 1703

Dowdey, Clifford
Bugles Blow No More 1704
Gamble's Hundred 1705
The Proud Retreat 1706
A Question of Honour 1707
Sing for a Penny 1708
Tidewater 1709
Where My Love Sleeps 1710

Downes, Anne Miller
The Pilgrim Soul 1711
The Quality of Mercy 1712

Downing, John Hyatt
Anthony Trant 1713
Sioux City 1714

Doyle, Sir Arthur Conan
Micah Clarke 1715
The White Company 1716

Drago, Harry Sinclair
Montana Road 1717

Drake, Shannon
Princess of Fire 1718

Drakeford, John W.
Take Her, Mr. Wesley 1719

Dreiser, Theodore
The Financier 1720

Drexler, Janice
The Long Sun 3920

Druett, Joan
Abigail 1721

Drummond, Emma
Beyond All Frontiers 1722
The Bridge of a Hundred Dragons 1723
A Captive Freedom 1724
Forget the Glory 1725
A Question of Honour 1726
Some Far Elusive Dawn 1727
That Sweet and Savage Land 1728

Drummond, June
The Bluestocking 1729
The Unsuitable Miss Pelham 1730

Druon, Maurice
Alexander the God 1731
The Iron King 1732
The Lily and the Lion 1733
The Poisoned Crown 1734
The Royal Succession 1735
The She-Wolf of France 1736
The Strangled Queen 1737

Drury, Allen
A God Against the Gods 1738
Return to Thebes 1739

Du Bois, Theodora McCormick
Captive of Rome 1740
The Emerald Crown 1741
Freedom's Way 1742
The Love of Fingin O'Lea 1743

Du Maurier, Daphne
Castle Dor 5226
Frenchman's Creek 1744
The Glass-Blowers 1745
Hungry Hill 1746
Jamaica Inn 1747
The King's General 1748
Mary Anne 1749

Du Maurier, George
Peter Ibbetson 1750

Dubus, Elizabeth Nell
Cajun 1751
Twilight of the Dawn 1752

Ducharme, Jacques
The Delusson Family 1753

Duffus, Robert L.
Jornada 1754

Duffy, Bruce
The World as I Found It 1755

Dugan, Bill
Chief Joseph 1756
Crazy Horse 1757
Geronimo 1758
Quanah Parker 1759
Sitting Bull 1760

Duggan, Alfred
Besieger of Cities 1761
Children of the Wolf 1762
Conscience of the King 1763
Count Bohemond 1764
The Cunning of the Dove 1765
Family Favorites 1766
Knight with Armour 1767
The Lady for Ransom 1768
Leopards and Lilies 1769
The Little Emperors 1770
Lord Geoffrey's Fancy 1771
My Life for My Sheep 1772
The Right Line of Cedric 1773
Three's Company 1774
Winter Quarters 1775

Dukthas, Ann
The Prince Lost to Time 1776
A Time for the Death of a King 1777
The Time of Murder at Mayerling 1778

Dumas, Alexandre
Les Quarant Cinq 1779
Queen Margot 1780
The Queen's Necklace 1781
The Three Musketeers 1782
Twenty Years After 1783

Dumke, Glenn S.
The Tyrant of Bagdhad 4996

Duncan, David
The Trumpet of God 1784

Duncan, Harley
West of Appomattox 1785

Duncan, Thomas William
Big River, Big Man 1786
The Labyrinth 1787
The Sky and Tomorrow 1788

Dunlap, Katharine
The Glory and the Dream 1789

Dunlop, Agnes M.R.
The Swedish Nightingale: Jenny Lind 3571

Dunn, Carola
Angel 1790
The Black Sheep's Daughter 1791
The Frog Earl 1792
Lady in the Briars 1793
Lavender Lady 1794
Lord Iverbrook's Heir 1795
Miss Hartwell's Dilemma 1796
Two Corinthians 1797

Dunn, Olav
The People of Juvik 1798

Dunnett, Dorothy
Checkmate 1799
The Disorderly Knights 1800
The Game of Kings 1801
King Hereafter 1802
Niccolo Rising 1803
Pawn in Frankincense 1804
Queen's Play 1805
Race of Scorpions 1806
The Ringed Castle 1807
Scales of Gold 1808
The Spring of the Ram 1809
To Lie with Lions 1810
The Unicorn Hunt 1811

Dunscomb, Charles
Behold, We Live 1812
The Bond and the Free 1813

Dupin, Armandine
Consuelo 5582

Durbin, Charles
The Mercenary 1814

Durham, Marilyn
Dutch Uncle 1815
Flambard's Confession 1816
The Man Who Loved Cat Dancing 1817

Durych, Jaroslav
The Descent of the Idol 1818

Dykeman, Wilma
The Tall Woman 1819

E

Eady, Carol Maxwell
Her Royal Destiny 1820

Eagleton, Terrence
Saints and Scholars 1821

Early, Tom
Sons of Texas 1822

Eastlake, William
The Long Naked Descent into Boston 1823

Easton, Robert
This Promised Land 1824

Eaton, Evelyn
Give Me Your Golden Hand 1825
Go Ask the River 1826
Heart in Pilgrimage 1827
In What Torn Ship 1828
Quietly My Captain Waits 1829
Restless Are the Sails 1830

Ebel, Suzanne
Floodtide 2475
Lovers 2476
While the Music Lasts 2477

Eberhart, Dikkon
Paradise 1831

Eberhart, Mignon G.
The Bayou Road 1832
The Cup, the Blade or the Gun 1833
Family Fortune 1834

Eberle, Gertrude
Charioteer: A Story of Old Egypt in the Days of Joseph 1835

Eccles, Frank
Mutiny Run 1836

Eckerson, Olive
The Golden Yoke: A Novel of the War of the Roses 1837
My Lord Essex 1838

Eckert, Allen W.
The Conquerors 1839
The Court Martial of Daniel Boone 1840
The Frontiersmen 1841
Gateway to Empire 1842
Johnny Logan: Shawnee Spy 1843
A Sorrow in Our Heart 1844
That Dark and Bloody River 1845
Twilight of Empire 1846
Wilderness Empire 1847
The Wilderness War 1848

Eco, Umberto
The Island of the Day Before 1849
The Name of the Rose 1850

Edelman, Maurice
Disraeli in Love 1851
Disraeli Rising 1852

Edelson, Marjorie
Malkeh and Her Children 1853

Eden, Dorothy
The American Heiress 1854
An Important Family 1855
Lady of Mallow 1856
Melbury Square 1857
The Millionaire's Daughter 1858
Never Call It Loving 1859
Ravenscroft 1860
The Salamanca Drum 1861
Speak to Me of Love 1862
The Time of the Dragon 1863
The Vines of Yarrabee 1864

Eden, Matthew
The Murder of Lawrence of Arabia 1865

Edghill, Rosemary
Fleeting Fancy 1866
Two of a Kind: An English Trifle 1867

Edmonds, Janet
Rivers of Gold 1868
Sarah Camberwell Tring 1869
Turn of the Dice 1870

Edmonds, Walter D.
The Boyds of Black River 1871
Cadmus Henry 1872
Chad Hanna 1873
Drums Along the Mohawk 1874
Erie Water 1875
In the Hands of the Senecas 1876
Rome Haul 1877
The Wedding Journey 1878
Young Ames 1879

Edmondston, C.M.
King's Man 1880

Edwards, Anne
Haunted Summer 1881
The Hesitant Heart 1882
Wallis: The Novel 1883

Edwards, F.H.M.
Indigo 900
Tournament of the Shadows 901

Edwards, Jaroldeen
Harvest of Dreams 1884

Edwards, Rhoda S.
The Broken Sword 1885
Fortune's Wheel 1886

Edwards, Samuel
The King's Messenger 1887
Master of Castile 1888
The Queen's Husband 1889
The Scimitar 1890
Theodora 1891

Egan, Ferol
The Taste of Time 1892

Egan, Judith
Elena 1893

Ehle, John
The Journey of August King 1894
The Land Breakers 1895
The Road 1896
Time of Drums 1897

Ehrlich, Leonard
God's Angry Man 1898

Eidson, Tom
The Last Ride 1899
St. Agnes' Stand 1900

Eiker, Karl V.
Star of Macedon 1901

Elegant, Robert S.
Dynasty 1902
From a Far Land 1903
Manchu 1904
Mandarin 1905
The Seeking 1906

Eliot, Ethel Cook
Roses for Mexico 1907

Eliot, George
Adam Bede 1908
Middlemarch 1909
Romola 1910
Silas Marner 1911

Eliot, George Fielding
Caleb Pettengill U.S.N. 1912

Ellenbech, Rosemary
Affairs of Love 6272
Cashmere 6273
Sisters & Lovers 6274

Ellerman, Annie Winifred
The Coin of Carthage 740
The Colors of Vaud 741
The Fourteenth of October 742
Gate to the Sea 743
The Player's Boy 744
Roman Wall 745
Ruan 746
This January Tale 747

Ellert, Gerhart
Gregory the Great 1913

Elliott, Edward E.
The Devil and the Mathers 1914

Elliott, Janice
Angels Falling 1915

Elliott, John
Blood on the Snow 1916

Ellis, Amanda Mae
Elizabeth, the Woman 1917

Ellis, Julie
Eden 1918
Glorious Morning 1919
The Hampton Heritage 1920
The Hampton Women 1921
The Magnolias 1922
The Only Sin 1923
Savage Oaks 1924

Ellis, Kenneth M.
Guns Forever Echo 1925

Ellis, Peter Berresford
Absolution by Murder 6334
The Revenge of Dracula 6335
The Rising of the Moon 1926

Ellis, William Donohue
The Bounty Lands 1927
The Brooks Legend 1928
Jonathan Blair, Bounty Lands Lawyer 1929

Ellsberg, Edward
Captain Paul 1930

Elsna, Hebe
The Elusive Crown 1931
The King's Bastard 1932
Lady on the Coin 326
The Queen's Ward 1933
The Wise Virgin 1934

Elwood, Muriel
Against the Tide 1935
Deeper the Heritage 1936
Heritage of the River 1937
So Much as Beauty Does 1938
Web of Destiny 1939

Emmons, Della F.
Sacajawea of the Shoshones 1940

Endo, Shusaku
The Samurai 1941

Endore, Guy
King of Paris 1942
Voltaire! Voltaire! 1943

Engstrom, Elizabeth
Lizzie Borden 1944

Engstrom, Lynn Gutzmer
Lizzie Borden 1944

Ennis, Michael
Byzantium 1945
Duchess of Milan 1946

Ensley, Evangeline
The Cross and the Sword 6558

Epstein, Leslie
Pinto and Sons 1947

Erdman, Loula Grace
Another Spring 1948
The Edge of Time 1949
The Far Journey 1950
Many a Voyage 1951

Erickson, Carolly
Mistress Anne 1952

Erickson, Steve
Arc d'X 1953

Erskine, Barbara
Kingdom of Shadows 1954
Lady of Hay 1955

Erskine, John
*Give Me Liberty: The Story of an
    Innocent Man* 1956
*The Private Life of Helen of
    Troy* 1957

Ertz, Susan
The Proselyte 1958

Esler, Anthony
Babylon 1959
The Blade of Castlemayne 1960
For Love of a Pirate 1961
Forbidden City 1962
Hellbane 1963
Lord Libertine 1964

Espey, John
Lotus Land 2917

Estey, Norbert
*All My Sins: A Novel of the Life and
    Loves of Ninon de Lenclos* 1965

Esther, Hammon
Road to Lendor 1966

Estleman, Loren D.
*Aces and Eights: A Novel of the Legend
    of Wild Bill Hickok* 1967
Bloody Season 1968
City of Widows 1969
Dr. Jekyll and Mr. Holmes 1970
Gunman 1971
The Hider 1972
The High Rocks 1973
Mister St. John 1974
Murdock's Law 1975
Sherlock Holmes vs. Dracula 1976
Stamping Ground 1977
The Stranglers 1978
Sudden Country 1979
This Old Bill 1980
Whiskey River 1981

Ethridge, Willie Snow
Summer Thunder 1982

Eulo, Elena Yates
A Southern Woman 1983

Evans, Jean
The Phoenix Rising 1984

Evans, Mary Ann
Adam Bede 1908
Middlemarch 1909
Romola 1910
Silas Marner 1911

Evarts, Hal George
Fur Brigade 1985
Shaggy Legion 1986

Everitt, David
*The Story of Pat Garrett and Billy the
    Kid* 1987
The Story of the Sundance Kid 1988

Eyre, Elizabeth
Axe for an Abbot 1989
Bravo for the Bride 1990
Curtains for the Cardinal 1991
Death of the Duchess 1992

F

Fabricius, Johan
Mortal Pageant 1993

Fackler, Elizabeth
*Billy the Kid: The Legend of El
    Chivato* 1994

Fadiman, Edwin
The Voice and the Light 1995

Fagyas, Maria
Court of Honor 1996
Dance of the Assassins 1997
The Devil's Lieutenant 1998

Fairbairns, Zoe
Stand We at Last 1999

Fairbank, Janet
The Bright Land 2000
*The Cortlandts of Washington
    Square* 2001
The Smiths 2002

Fairburn, Eleanor
The Rose at Harvest End 2003

Fairchild, William
No Man's Land 2004

Falkirk, Richard
Beau Blackstone 2005
Blackstone 2006
*Blackstone and the Scourge of
    Europe* 2007
Blackstone's Fancy 2008

Falkner, Leonard
*Painted Lady: Eliza Jumel, Her Life
    and Times* 2009

Fall, Thomas
The Justicer 2010

Fallon, Frederic
The White Queen 2011

Faralla, Dana
A Circle of Trees 2012

Farnol, Jeffrey
The King Liveth 2013

Farr, Judith
I Never Came to You in White 2014

Farrar, Rowena Rutherford
Bend Your Heads All 2015

Farrell, J.G.
The Siege of Krishnapur 2016
Troubles 2017

Farrell, Michael
Thy Tears Might Cease 2018

Farrington, Gene
The Breath of Kings 2019

Farrington, Robert
The Killing of Richard the Third 2020
The Traitors of Bosworth 2021
Tudor Agent 2022

Farris, Jack
Me and Gallagher 2023

Farson, Daniel
Swandowne 2024

Fast, Howard
Agrippa's Daughter 2025
The American 2026
April Morning 2027
Citizen Tom Paine 2028
Conceived in Liberty 2029
The Establishment 2030
Freedom Road 2031
Haym Solomon, Son of Liberty 2032
The Hessian 2033
The Immigrants 2034
The Immigrant's Daughter 2035
The Last Frontier 2036
The Legacy 2037
Max 2038
Moses, Prince of Egypt 2039
*The Passion of Sacco and Vanzetti: A
    New England Legend* 2040
Power 2041
The Proud and the Free 2042
Second Generation 2043
Spartacus 2044
Torquemada 2045
The Unvanquished 2046

Fast, Jonathan
Golden Fire 2047
The Jade Stalk 2048

Faulkner, William
Absalom, Absalom! 2049
The Unvanquished 2050

Faulks, Sebastian
Birdsong 2051

Faure, Raoul Cohen
Lady Godiva and Master Tom 2052

Faust, Frederick
The Bait and the Trap 970
The Golden Knight 971

Faust, Irvin
Foreign Devils 2053

Fawcett, Quinn
Napoleon Must Die 2054

Fearing, Kenneth
John Barry 412

Feather, Jane
Brazen Whispers 2055
Reckless Angel 2056

Federspiel, Jurg
The Ballad of Typhoid Mary 2057

Feldman, Ellen
The Normandie Affair 6497
One Night in Newport 6498
The Very Best People 6499

Fenady, Andrew J.
The Summer of Jack London 2058

Fenton, Edward
Anne of the Thousand Days 2059

Ferber, Edna
American Beauty 2060
Cimarron 2061
Saratoga Trunk 2062
Show Boat 2063

Ferbridge, Philippa
The Heir of Allington 6727

Fergus, Charles
Shadow Catcher 2064

Fergusson, Adam
Roman Go Home! 2065

Fergusson, Hannah Doris
The Prime Minister's Wife 3727
Royal William 3728

Fergusson, Harvey
The Conquest of Don Pedro 2066
Grant of Kingdom 2067
In Those Days 2068
Wolf Song 2069

Ferrell, Elizabeth
Full of Thy Riches 2070

Ferrell, Margaret
Full of Thy Riches 2070

Feuchtwanger, Lion
The Jew of Rome 2071
Josephus 2072
Josephus and the Emperor 2073
Power 2074
The Ugly Duchess 2075

Feuer, Lewis S.
*The Case of the Revolutionist's
    Daughter: Sherlock Holmes Meets
    Karl Marx* 2076

Feuille, Frank
The Cotton Road 2077

Field, Bradda
Bride of Glory 2078

Field, Dawn Stewart
Luise 2079

Field, Rachel
All This, and Heaven Too 2080
Time out of Mind 2081

Fifield, William
The Devil's Marchioness 2082

Figes, Eva
Light 2083
The Seven Ages 2084
The Tree of Knowledge 2085

Finch, Merton
*Simon Bar Cochba: Rebellion in
    Judea* 2086

Finch, Phillip
Birthright 2087

Fineman, Irving
Jacob: An Autobiography 2088
Ruth 2089

Fink, Merton
*Simon Bar Cochba: Rebellion in
    Judea* 2086

Finlay, Lucile
The Coat I Wore 2090

Finney, Gertrude E.
The Plums Hang High 2091

Finney, Jack
From Time to Time 2092
Time and Again 2093

Finney, Patricia
The Crow Goddess 2094
The Firedrake's Eye 2095
A Shadow of Gulls 2096

Finney, Walter Braden
From Time to Time 2092
Time and Again 2093

Fish, Rachel Ann
The Running Iron 2097

Fish, Robert L.
Rough Diamond 2098

Fisher, Anne
Oh Glittering Promise 2099

Fisher, Edward
The Best House in Stratford 2100
Love's Labour's Won 2101
Shakespeare & Son 2102

Fisher, Frances Hope
Written in the Stars: A Novel about Albrecht Durer 2103

Fisher, Graham
The Plot to Kill Wallis Simpson: A Work of Faction 2104

Fisher, Richard
Judgment in July 2105

Fisher, Vardis
Children of God 2106
City of Illusion 2107
The Island of the Innocent: A Novel of Greek and Jew in the Time of the Maccabees 2108
The Mothers 2109
Mountain Man 2110
Pemmican 2111
Tale of Valor 2112
The Valley of Vision: A Novel of King Solomon and His Time 2113

Fitzgerald, Nancy
Chelsea 2114
Mayfair 2115
St. John's Wood 2116

Fitzgerald, Valerie
Zemindar 2117

FitzGibbon, Constantine
High Heroic 2118

Flanagan, Thomas
The End of the Hunt 2119
The Tenants of Time 2120
The Year of the French 2121

Flannagan, Roy Catesby
Forest Cavalier: A Romance of America's First Frontier and of Bacon's Rebellion 2122

Flaubert, Gustave
Salammbo 2123

Fleetwood, Frances
Concordia 2124

Fleischmann, Glen H.
While Rivers Flow 2125

Fleming, Georgina
Beyond the Shadowlands 2126

Fleming, H.K.
The Day They Kidnapped Queen Victoria 2127

Fleming, Joan
Too Late! Too Late! The Maiden Cried 2128

Fleming, Thomas
Liberty Tavern 2129
Over There 2130
The Spoils of War 2131

Fletcher, Inglis
Bennett's Welcome 2132
Cormorant's Brood 2133
Lusty Wind for Carolina 2134
Men of Albemarle 2135
Queen's Gift 2136
Raleigh's Eden 2137
Roanoke Hundred 2138
Rogue's Harbor 2139
The Scotswoman 2140
Toil of the Brave 2141
Wicked Lady 2142
The Wind in the Forest 2143

Flood, Charles Bracelen
Monmouth 2144

Flynn, Robert
North to Yesterday 2145

Fogazzaro, Antonio
The Patriot 2146

Follett, Ken
A Dangerous Fortune 2147
The Man From St. Petersburg 2148
The Pillars of the Earth 2149
A Place Called Freedom 2150

Foote, Dorothy Norris
The Constant Star 2151

Foote, Shelby
Jordan County: A Landscape in Narrative 2152
Shiloh 2153

Forbath, Peter
The Last Hero 2154
Lord of the Kongo 2155

Forbes, Esther
The General's Lady 2156
A Mirror for Witches 2157
Paradise 2158
Rainbow on the Road 2159
The Running of the Tide 2160

Ford, Ford Madox
The Fifth Queen 2161
Ladies Whose Bright Eyes 2162

Ford, Hilary
Castle Malindine 2163

Ford, Jesse Hill
The Raider 2164

Ford, John M.
The Dragon Waiting: A Masque of History 2165

Ford, Paul Leicester
Janice Meredith 2166

Foreman, Leonard L.
The Road to San Jacinto 2167

Foreman, Russell
Long Pig 2168

Forester, C.S.
Admiral Hornblower in the West Indies 2169
Beat to Quarters 2170
The Captain From Connecticut 2171
Commodore Hornblower 2172
Flying Colours 2173
The Gun 2174
Hornblower and the Atropos 2175
Hornblower and the Hotspur 2176
Hornblower During the Crisis 2177
Lieutenant Hornblower 2178
Lord Hornblower 2179
Mr. Midshipman Hornblower 2180
Rifleman Dodd 2181
Ship of the Line 2182
To the Indies 2183

Forrest, Anthony
A Balance of Dangers 2184
Captain Justice 2185
The Pandora Secret 2186

Forrest, Williams
Trail of Tears 2187

Forrest-Webb, Robert
Pendragon: Late of Prince Albert's Own 6337
Pendragon...The Montenegran Plot 6338

Forster, Margaret
Lady's Maid 2188
Memoirs of a Victorian Gentleman: William Makepeace Thackeray 2189

Foulds, Elfrida Vipont
Bed in Hell 6504

Fowler, Robert H.
Jason McGee 2190
Jeremiah Martin: A Revolutionary War Novel 2191
Jim Mundy: A Novel of the American Civil War 2192
The Spoils of Eden 2193

Fowles, John
The French Lieutenant's Woman 2194

Fox, John
Erskine Dale, Pioneer 2195

Fox, Paul Hervey
Daughter of Jairus 2196

Foxell, Nigel
Loving Emma 2197

France, Anatole
At the Sign of the Reine Pedauque 2198

Frances, Stephen D.
La Guerra: A Spanish Saga 2199

Frank, Bruno
The Days of the King 2200
A Man Called Cervantes 2201

Frankland, Edward
The Foster Brothers 2202

Fraser, George MacDonald
Flash for Freedom 2203
Flashman 2204
Flashman and the Angel of the Lord 2205
Flashman and the Dragon 2206
Flashman and the Mountain of Light 2207
Flashman and the Redskins 2208
Flashman at the Charge 2209
Flashman's Lady 2210
Mr. American 2211
The Pyrates 2212
Royal Flash 2213

Frazee, Steve
Shining Mountains 2214

Frazer, Margaret
The Bishop's Tale 2215
The Boy's Tale 2216
The Novice's Tale 2217
The Outlaw's Tale 2218
The Servant's Tale 2219

Fredman, John
The Wolf of Masada 2220

Freedgood, Morton
Yankee Trader 4496

Freedgood, Stanley
Yankee Trader 4496

Fremantle, Anne
James and Joan 2221

French, Judith E.
Lovestorm 2222
Moonfeather 2223
Scarlet Ribbons 2224

French, Peter
The Ocean Mistress 2225
The Southern Cross 2226

Freuchen, Peter
The Law of Larion 2227
White Man 2228

Freund, Edith
Chicago Girls 2229

Frey, Ruby Frazier
Red Morning 2230

Frieberger, Kurt
Fisher of Men: A Novel of Simon Peter 2231

Fried, Albert
The Prescott Chronicles 2232

Friede, Donald
John Barry 412

Frischauer, Paul
A Great Lord 2233
The Shepherd's Crook 2234
So Great a Queen: The Story of Esther, Queen of Persia 2235

Frolich, Newton
1492 2236

Frost, Mark
The List of Seven 2237
The Six Messiahs 2238

Frutkin, Mark
Invading Tibet 2239

Frye, Ellen
The Other Sappho 2240

Frye, Harriet
North to Thule: An Imagined Narrative of the Famous "Lost" Voyage of Pytheas of Massalla in the Fourth Century B.C. 2241

Frye, John
North to Thule: An Imagined Narrative of the Famous "Lost" Voyage of Pytheas of Massalla in the Fourth Century B.C. 2241

Frye, Pearl
Gallant Captain 2242
A Game for Empires 2243
The Sleeping Sword: A Biographical Novel 2244

Fuentes, Carlos
The Campaign 2245
The Death of Artemio Cruz 2246
The Old Gringo 2247

Fugard, Sheila
A Revolutionary Woman 2248

Fuller, Edmund
John Milton 2249
A Star Pointed North 2250

Fuller, Iola
All the Golden Gifts 2251
The Gilded Torch 2252
The Loon Feather 2253
The Shining Trail 2254

Fuller, Jamie
The Diary of Emily Dickinson: A Novel 2255

Fulton, Len
The Grassman 2256

Furnas, J.C.
The Devil's Rainbow 2257

Furnas, Marthedith
The Far Country 2258

G

Gaan, Margaret
Little Sister 2259
Red Barbarian 2260
White Poppy 2261

Gabaldon, Diana
Dragonfly in Amber 2262
Drums of Autumn 2263
Outlander 2264
Voyager 2265

Gabriel, Gilbert Wolf
I, James Lewis 2266
I Thee Wed 2267

Gage, Nicholas
The Bourlotas Fortune 2268

Gaines, Diana
Nantucket Woman 2269

Gaines, Ernest J.
The Autobiography of Miss Jane Pittman 2270

Gaither, Frances
Double Moscadine 2271
The Red Cock Crows 2272

Galloway, David
Tamsen 2273

Galvan, Manuel de Jesus
The Cross and the Sword 2274

Gamo, Jean
The Golden Chain 2275

Gann, Ernest K.
The Antagonists 2276
The Aviator 2277
Gentlemen of Adventure 2278
In the Company of Eagles 2279
The Triumph 2280

Garbo, Norman
The Artist 2281

Garcia Marquez, Gabriel
The General in His Labyrinth 2282

Gardiner, Dorothy
The Golden Lady 2283
The Great Betrayal 2284
Snow-Water 2285

Gardiner, John Rolfe
Great Dream From Heaven 2286

Gardner, John E.
The Return of Moriarty 2287

Gardner, Mona
Hong Kong 2288

Gardner, Richard
The Adventures of Don Juan 2289

Garfield, Brian
Manifest Destiny 2290
Wild Times 2291

Garfield, Leon
The House of Cards 2292
The Pleasure Garden 2293
The Prisoners of September 2294
The Sound of Coaches 2295

Garland, Hamlin
Trail-Makers of the Middle Border 2296

Garnett, David
Pocahontas; or, The Nonparell of Virginia 2297
Up She Rises 2298

Garratt, Mary A.
The Asherwood Protegee 2299

Garrett, George
Death of the Fox 2300
Entered From the Sun 2301
The Succession: A Novel of Elizabeth and James 2302

Garrison, Omar V.
Balboa: Conquistador 2303

Garth, David
Fire on the Wind 2304
Gray Canaan 2305

Gartner, Chloe
Anne Bonny 2306
Drums of Khartoum 2307
The Infidels 2308
Mistress of The Highlands 2309
The Woman from The Glen 2310

Garwood, Julie
The Bride 2311

Gaskell, Elizabeth
Sylvia's Lovers 2312

Gaskin, Catherine
Blake's Reach 2313
A Falcon for a Queen 2314
I Know My Love 2315
Sara Dane 2316

Gass, William H.
Omensetter's Luck 2317

Gavin, Catherine
The Cactus and the Crown 2318
The Devil in Harbour 2319
The Fortress 2320
Give Me the Daggers 2321
The House of War 2322
Madeleine 2323
The Snow Mountain 2324

Gavin, Thomas
Kingkill 2325

Gay, Laverne
The Unspeakables: A Tale of Lombardy 2326
Wine of Satan 2327

Gay, Margaret Cooper
Hatchet in the Sky 2328

Gear, Kathleen O'Neal
The Morning River 2333
People of the Earth 2334
People of the Fire 2335
People of the Lakes 2336
People of the Lightning 2337
People of the River 2338
People of the Sea 2339
People of the Silence 2340
People of the Wolf 2341
Sand in the Wind 2329
Thin Moon and Cold Mist 2330
This Widowed Land 2331

Gear, W. Michael
Bighorn Legacy 2332
The Morning River 2333
People of the Earth 2334
People of the Fire 2335
People of the Lakes 2336
People of the Lightning 2337
People of the River 2338
People of the Sea 2339
People of the Silence 2340
People of the Wolf 2341

Gebler, Ernest
The Plymouth Adventure 2342

Gedge, Pauline
Child of the Morning 2343
The Eagle and the Raven 2344
Lady of the Reeds 2345

Mirage 2346
The Twelfth Transforming 2347

Gelb, Alan
Mussolini 2348

Gellis, Roberta
Bond of Blood 2349
The Dragon and the Rose 2350
Knight's Honor 2351
Masques of Gold 2352
A Silver Mirror 2353

Gennari, Genevieve
The Riven Heart 2354

George, Margaret
The Autobiography of Henry VIII 2355
Mary, Queen of Scotland and the Isles 2356

Gerard, Francis
The Scarlet Beast 2357

Germany, Jo
City of Golden Cages 2358
Devil Child 2359

Gerson, Jack
Death Squad London 2360

Gerson, Noel B.
The Anthem 2361
The Charlatan 6433
Clear for Action! 2362
The Conqueror's Wife 2363
The Crusader 2364
The Cumberland Rifles 2365
Daughter of Eve 2366
Dragon Cove 6434
Emperor's Ladies 2367
The Forest Lord 2368
Fortress Fury 6435
The Gentle Fury: A Novel of Margaret of Austria 3758
Give Me Liberty 2369
The Golden Eagle 2370
The Golden Lyre 2371
The Highwayman 2372
The Hittite 2373
I'll Storm Hell 2374
The Imposter 2375
The Invincibles 6436
The King's Messenger 1887
The Land Is Bright 2376
Master of Castile 1888
The Mohawk Ladder 2377
The Naked Maja 2378
The Nelson Touch 3759
Old Hickory 2379
The Queen's Husband 1889
The River Devils 6437
Roanoke Warrior 6438
Sam Houston 2380
Savage Gentleman 2381
The Scimitar 1890
Scoundrels' Brigade 6439
The Sea Panther: A Novel about the Commander of the U.S.S. Constitution 6397
The Seneca Hostage 6440
The Silver Saber 6441
The Slender Reed 2382
The Swamp Fox, Francis Marion 2383
That Egyptian Woman 2384
Theodora 1891
TR 2385
The Trojan 2386
The Twisted Saber: A Biographical Novel of Benedict Arnold 6398
The Wilderness 6442

The Yankee Brig 6443
Yankee Doodle Dandy 2387
The Yankee From Tennessee 2388
The Yankee Rascals 6444

Gessner, Robert
Treason 2389

Getz, William
Sam Patch: Ballad of a Jumping Man 2390

Ghnassia, Maurice
Arena: A Novel of Spartacus and Crassus 2391

Ghose, Zulfikar
The Incredible Brazilian: The Native 2392

Giardina, Denise
Good King Harry 2393
Storming Heaven 2394

Gibbs, Mary Ann
The Admiral's Lady 2395
A Most Romantic City 2396
The Tempestuous Petticoat 2397

Gibbs, Willa
According to Mary: A Novel of the Magdalene 2398
The Dedicated 2399
A Fig in Winter 2400
Seed of Mischief 2401
Tell Your Sons: A Novel of the Napoleonic Era 2402
The Twelfth Physician 2403

Gidley, Charles
Armada 2404

Gilbert, Anna
Flowers for Lilian 2405
The Long Shadow 2406
The Wedding Guest 2407

Gilchrist, Ellen
Anabasis: A Journey to the Interior 2408

Giles, Janice Holt
The Believers 2409
The Great Adventure 2410
Hannah Fowler 2411
Johnny Osage 2412
The Kentuckians 2413
The Land Beyond the Mountains 2414
Run Me a River 2415
Savanna 2416
Six-Horse Hitch 2417
Voyage to Santa Fe 2418

Giles, John Clifford
Horseshoe Bend 4779

Gillespie, Donna
The Light Bearer 2419

Gillespie, Jane
Ladysmead: A Novel in the Jane Austen Tradition 2420
Teverton Hall 2421

Gilner, Elias
Prince of Israel 2422

Gilson, Charles James Louis
The White Cockade 2423

Giono, Jean
The Horseman on the Roof 2424
The Straw Man 2425

Glancy, Diane
Pushing the Bear: A Novel of the Trail of Tears 2426

Glasgow, Alice
The Twisted Tendril 2427

Glazebrook, Philip
Captain Vinegar's Commission 2428

Glazener, Mary
The Cup of Wrath 2429

Gleason, Judith
Agotime, Her Legend 2430

Glendinning, Victoria
Electricity: A Novel 2431

Gloag, John
Artorius Rex 2432
Caesar of the Narrow Seas 2433
The Eagles Depart 2434

Gloss, Molly
The Jump-Off Creek 2435

Glover, Douglas
The Life and Times of Captain N. 2436

Glover, Judith
The Imagination of the Heart 2437
The Stallion Man 2438
Tigerlilies 2439

Gluyas, Constance
Born to Be King 2440
The King's Brat 2441
My Lady Benbrook 2442
My Lord Foxe 2443

Goddard, Robert
In Pale Battalions 2444
Painting the Darkness 2445

Godtsenhoven, Oscar van
The Sable Lion 6405

Godwin, Parke
Beloved Exile 2446
Firelord 2447
Robin and the King 2448
Sherwood 2449
The Tower of Beowulf 2450

Gogol, Nikolai V.
Taras Bulba 2451

Golding, Michael
Simple Prayers 2452

Golding, Morton
El Lazo 4132
Rush to Destroy 4133

Golding, William
Close Quarters 2453
Fire Down Below 2454
The Inheritors 2455
Rites of Passage 2456
The Spire 2457

Goldman, James
Myself as Witness 2458

Goldman, Lawrence
The Castrato 2459

Goldreich, Gloria
Leah's Journey 2460
West to Eden 2461
The Year of Our War 2462

Goldstein, Lisa
Strange Devices of the Sun and Moon 2463

Goldston, Robert
1901 1258

Goldthorpe, John
The Same Scourge 2464

Golon, Anne
Angelique 2465
Angelique and the Demon 2466
Angelique and the Ghosts 2467
Angelique and the King 2468

Golon, Serge
Angelique 2465
Angelique and the Demon 2466
Angelique and the Ghosts 2467
Angelique and the King 2468
Angelique in Barbary 2469
Angelique in Love 2470
Angelique in Revolt 2471
The Countess Angelique 2472
The Temptation of Angelique 2473

Golon, Sergeanne
Angelique 2465
Angelique and the Demon 2466
Angelique and the Ghosts 2467
Angelique and the King 2468
Angelique in Barbary 2469
Angelique in Love 2470
Angelique in Revolt 2471
The Countess Angelique 2472
The Temptation of Angelique 2473

Gonzales, Laurence
El Vago 2474

Goode, Ruth
Don Gaucho 5088

Goodwin, Suzanne
Floodtide 2475
Lovers 2476
While the Music Lasts 2477

Gordon, Caroline
None Shall Look Back 2478
Penhally 2479

Gordon, Charles William
The Rebel Loyalist 2480

Gordon, Dan
Wyatt Earp 2481

Gordon, Leo V.
Powderkeg 6482

Gordon, Noah
The Physician 2482
Shaman 2483

Gordon, Richard
Jack the Ripper 2484
The Private Life of Florence Nightingale 2485
The Sleep of Life 2486

Gores, Joseph N.
Hammett: A Novel 2487

Gorham, Charles Orson
Gold of Their Bodies: A Novel about Gauguin 2488
Wine of Life 2489

Gorman, Herbert
Brave General 2490
The Breast of the Dove 2491
The Cry of Dolores 2492
The Wine of San Lorenzo 2493

Goudge, Elizabeth
Dean's Watch 2494
Gilded Spurs 3105
Red Adam's Lady 3106
Towers in the Mist 2495
The White Witch 2496

Gould, John
No Other Place 2497

Gowdy, Barbara
Through the Green Valley 2498

Gower, Iris
Fiddler's Ferry 2499
Morgan's Woman 2500
Proud Mary 2501
Spinners' Wharf 2502

Graber, George Alexander
The Rape of the Fair Country 1325
This Sweet and Bitter Earth 1326

Grabien, Deborah
Fire Queen 2503

Grace, C.L.
An Ancient Evil 2504
The Book of Shadows 2505
The Eye of God 2506
The Golden Wind 2507
The Merchant of Death 2508
A Shrine of Murders 2509
A Tapestry of Murders 2510

Graham, Alice Walworth
Shield of Honor 2511
The Summer Queen 2512
Vows of the Peacock 2513

Graham, Heather
And One Rode West 2514
And One Wore Gray 2515
Love Not a Rebel 2516
One Wore Blue 2517
A Pirate's Pleasure 2518
Runaway 2519
The Viking's Woman 2520

Graham, Winston
The Angry Tide 2521
The Black Moon 2522
Cordelia 2523
Demelza 2524
The Four Swans 2525
The Grove of Eagles 2526
The Last Gamble 2527
The Miller's Dance 2528
The Renegade: A Novel of Cornwall, 1783-1787 2529
The Stranger From the Sea 2530
The Twisted Sword 2531
Venture Once More 2532

Grant, Dorothy
Margaret Brent, Adventurer 2533
Night of Decision: A Novel of Colonial New York 2534

Grant, Joan
Life as Carola 2535
Winged Pharaoh 2536

Grant, Laurie
Emerald Fire 2537

Grant, Maxwell
Blood Red Rose 2538
Inherit the Sun 2539

Grass, Gunther
The Tin Drum 2540

Grasso, Patricia
Highland Belle 2541

Graves, Ralph
The Lost Eagles 2542

Graves, Robert
Claudius the God 2543
Count Belisarius 2544
Hercules, My Shipmate 2545
Homer's Daughter 2546
I, Claudius 2547
Islands of Unwisdom 2548
King Jesus 2549
Proceed, Sergeant Lamb 2550
The Real David Copperfield 2551
Sergeant Lamb's America 2552

Wife to Mr. Milton 2553

Gray, Austin K.
Teresa, or Her Demon Lover 2554

Gray, Elizabeth Janet
Meggy MacIntosh 2555

Grayson, Richard
Crime Without Passion 2556
Death En Voyage 2557
Death Off Stage 2558
Death on the Cards 2559
The Monterant Affair 2560
The Montmarte Murders 2561
The Murder at Impasse Louvaine 2562

Grazebrook, Owen Francis
Nicanor of Athens: The Autobiography of an Unknown Citizen 2563

Green, Anne
The Lady in the Mask 2564

Green, Gerald
Murfy's Men 2565
The Sword and the Sun: The Story of the Spanish Civil Wars in Peru 2566

Green, Julian
The Distant Lands 2567
The Stars of the South 2568

Green, Peter
Achilles His Armour 2569
The Laughter of Aphrodite 2570
Sword of Pleasure: Being the Memoirs of the Most Illustrious Lucius Cornelius Sulla 2571

Greenberg, Eric Rolfe
The Celebrant 2572

Greenberg, Joanne
The King's Persons 2573

Greene, Liz
The Dreamer of the Vine 2574

Greenough, Malcolm W. Jr.
Dear Lily 2575

Greenwood, L.B.
Sherlock Holmes and the Case of Sabina Hall 2576
Sherlock Holmes and the Case of the Raleigh Legacy 2577
Sherlock Holmes and the Thistle of Scotland 2578

Greenwood, Lillian Bethel
Sherlock Holmes and the Case of Sabina Hall 2576
Sherlock Holmes and the Case of the Raleigh Legacy 2577
Sherlock Holmes and the Thistle of Scotland 2578
The Street Sparrows 249

Gregory, Jill
Lone Star Lady 2579

Gregory, Lisa
The Rainbow Promise 2580

Gregory, Philippa
Fallen Skies 2581
The Favored Child 2582
Meridon 2583
A Respectable Trade 2584
Wideacre 2585

Gregory, Susanna
An Unholy Alliance 2586

Grey, Anthony
Peking: A Novel of China's Revolt 2587

Saigon 2588

Grey, Zane
Western Union 2589

Grierson, Edward
Captain General 6007
Dark Torrent of Glencoe 2590
The Hastening Wind 2591

Griffin, Henry Farrand
The White Cockade 2592

Grimes, Roberta
*My Thomas: A Novel of Martha
    Jefferson's Life* 2593

Grimmelshausen, J.J.C.
Simplicissimus the Vagabond 2594

Grindal, Richard
Crime Without Passion 2556
Death En Voyage 2557
Death Off Stage 2558
Death on the Cards 2559
The Monterant Affair 2560
The Montmarte Murders 2561
*The Murder at Impasse
    Louvaine* 2562

Griswold, Francis
The Tides of Malvern 2595

Groh, Lynn
The Culper Spy Ring 2596

Gronau, Mary Ellen
The Gentle Conqueror 2597
Passionate Warriors 2598

Groseclose, Elgin
The Carmelite 2599

Gross, Joel
The Books of Rachel 2600
The Lives of Rachel 2601
Maura's Dream 2602
Sarah 2603

Grubb, Davis
A Dream of Kings 2604

Grun, Bernard
*The Golden Quill: A Novel Based on
    the Life of Mozart* 2605

Grundy, Stephan
Attila's Treasure 2606
Rhinegold 2607

Gudjonsson, Halldor Kiljan
Paradise Reclaimed 3686

Guest, Lynn
The Sword of Hachiman 2608
Yedo 2609

Guild, Nicholas
The Assyrian 2610
The Blood Star 2611

Gulick, Bill
Distant Trails 2612
Gathering Storm 2613
The Hallelujah Train 2614
Liveliest Town in the West 2615
Lost Wallowa 2616
The Moon-Eyed Appaloosa 2617
They Came to a Valley 2618
Treasure in Hell's Canyon 2619

Gulick, Grover C.
Distant Trails 2612
Gathering Storm 2613
The Hallelujah Train 2614
Liveliest Town in the West 2615
Lost Wallowa 2616
The Moon-Eyed Appaloosa 2617
They Came to a Valley 2618
Treasure in Hell's Canyon 2619

Gunn, Neil
Butcher's Broom 2620

Gurganus, Allan
*Oldest Living Confederate Widow Tells
    All* 2621

Gurr, David
The Ring Master 2622

Guthrie, A.B. Jr.
Arfive 2623
The Big Sky 2624
Fair Land, Fair Land 2625
The Last Valley 2626
These Thousand Hills 2627
The Way West 2628

H

Haas, Ben
The Chandler Heritage 2629
The Foragers 2630

Haasse, Hella S.
In a Dark Wood Wandering 2631
The Scarlet City 2632
Threshold of Fire 2633

Hackett, Francis
Queen Anne Boleyn 2634

Haeger, Diane
Courtesan 2635

Hagerfors, Lennart
The Whales in Lake Tanganyika 2636

Haggard, H. Rider
Cleopatra 2637

Hahn, Emily
*Purple Passage: A Novel about a Lady
    Both Famous and Fantastic* 2638

Haines, Edwin
The Exquisite Siren 2639

Haines, William Wister
The Winter War 2640

Haire-Sargeant, Lin
*H.—: The Story of Heathcliff's Journey
    Back to Wuthering Heights* 2641

Haislip, Harvey
The Prize Master 2642
Sailor Named Jones 2643
Sea Road to Yorktown 2644

Halkin, John
Kenya 2645

Hall, Arthur Dana
The Golden Balance 2646

Hall, Desmond
I Give You Oscar Wilde 2647

Hall, Douglas Kent
The Master of Oakwindsor 2648

Hall, James Norman
Botany Bay 4637
Men Against the Sea 4638
Mutiny on the Bounty 4639
Pitcairn's Island 4640

Hall, Oakley
The Adelita 2649
Apaches 2650
The Bad Lands 2651
The Children of the Sun 2652
Warlock 2653

Hall, Robert Lee
*Benjamin Franklin and a Case of Artful
    Murder* 2654

*Benjamin Franklin and a Case of
    Christmas Murder* 2655
*Benjamin Franklin Takes the
    Case* 2656
Exit Sherlock Holmes 2657
The King Edward Plot 2658
Murder at Drury Lane 2659
Murder at San Simeon 2660
Murder by the Waters 2661

Hall, Rubylea
The Great Tide 2662

Hallet, Richard
Michael Beam 2663

Hallstead, William F.
Conqueror of the Clouds 2664

Halter, Marek
The Book of Abraham 2665

Ham, Tom
Give Us This Valley 2666

Hamburger, Jean
*The Diary of William Harvey: The
    Imaginary Journal of the Physician
    Who Revolutionized Medicine* 2667

Hamilton, Charles Granville
Thunder in the Wilderness 2668

Hamilton, Joan Lesley
The Lion and the Cross 2669

Hamilton, Tamsin
The Gypsy From Cadiz 2670

Hamilton, Wallace
David at Olivet 2671

Hamilton-Paterson, James
Gerontius 2672

Han, Suyin
The Enchantress 2673

Hanchar, Peggy
Tomorrow's Dream 2674

Hanes, Frank Borden
*The Fleet Rabble: A Novel of the Nez
    Perce War* 2675

Hanks, Lindsey
Outlaw Lover 2676

Hanlon, Emily
Petersburg 2677

Hanna, Edward B.
The Whitechapel Horrors 2678

Hansen, Eva Hemmer
Scandal in Troy 2679

Hansen, Joseph
Longleaf 701

Hansen, Ron
*The Assassination of Jesse James by the
    Coward Robert Ford* 2680
Desperadoes 2681
Mariette in Ecstasy 2682

Harding, Bertita
*Magic Fire: Scenes around Richard
    Wagner* 2683

Harding, Paul
The Nightingale Gallery 2684
*Red Slayer: Being the Second of the
    Sorrowful Mysteries of Brother
    Athelstan* 2685

Hardman, Richard Lynden
Fifteen Flags 2686

Hardwick, Michael
Regency Royal 2687
The Revenge of the Hound 2688

Hardwick, Mollie
Beauty's Daughter 2689
Blood Royal 2690
Charlie Is My Darling 2691
The Crystal Dove 2692
The Duchess of Duke Street 2693
I Remember Love 2694
Lovers Meeting 2695
The Merrymaid 2696
Monday's Child 2697
The Shakespeare Girl 2698
Willowwood 2699

Hardy, Thomas
The Trumpet Major 2700

Hardy, W.G.
*All the Trumpets Sounded: A Novel
    Based on the Life of Moses* 2701
The City of Libertines 2702
Turn Back the River 2703

Hareven, Shulamith
The Miracle Hater 2704

Hargrave, Leonie
Clara Reeve 2705

Hargreaves, Sheba
The Cabin at the Trail's End 2706
*Heroine of the Prairies: A Romance of
    the Oregon Trail* 2707

Harington, Donald
*The Architecture of the Arkansas
    Ozarks* 2708
The Choiring of the Trees 2709

Harper, Karen
Circle of Gold 2710
Eden's Gate 2711
The Firelands 2712
River of Sky 2713
The Wings of Morning 2714

Harper, M.A.
For the Love of Robert E. Lee 2715

Harper, Robert S.
The Road to Baltimore 2716
Trumpet in the Wilderness 2717

Harris, Cyril
*Richard Pryne: A Novel of the
    American Revolution* 2718
Trumpets at Dawn 2719

Harris, John
Back to Battle 2828
Blunted Lance 2829
The Bright Blue Sky 2830
The Challenging Heights 2831
Chant of the Hawk 2720
The Crimson Wind 2832
The Dangerous Years 2833
The Lion at Sea 2834
The Medicine Whip 2835
Once More the Hawks 2836
Soldier of the Queen 2837
Vardy 2721

Harris, Julie
The Longest Winter 2722

Harris, Laura B.
Bride of the River 2723

Harris, Macdonald
The Balloonist 2724
Glowstone 2725
Herma 2726
Pandora's Galley 2727

Harris, Margaret
Chant of the Hawk 2720

Harris, Marilyn
American Eden 2728

Author Index

Eden and Honor 2729
The Eden Passion 2730
Eden Rising 2731
The Prince of Eden 2732
This Other Eden 2733
The Women of Eden 2734

Harris, Norma
Trumpets of Silver 2735

Harrison, Harry
The Hammer and the Cross 2736

Harrison, Kathryn
Poison 2737

Harrison, Ray
Counterfeit of Murder 2738
Death of a Dancing Lady 2739
Deathwatch 2740
Harvest of Death 2741
Patently Murder 2742
A Season for Death 2743
Sphere of Death 2744
Tincture of Death 2745
Why Kill Arthur Potter? 2746

Harrison, Samuel Bertram
The White King 2747

Harrison, Sue
Brother Wind 2748
Mother Earth, Father Sky 2749
My Sister, the Moon 2750

Harrison, William
Burton and Speke 2751

Harrod-Eagles, Cynthia
Anna 2752
Emily 2753
Fleur 2754
I, Victoria 2755

Harsanyi, Zsolt de
Lover of Life 2756
The Star-Gazer 2757

Harson, Dylan
Kansas Blue 2758

Hart, Scott
Eight April Days 2759

Hart-Davis, Duff
Horses of War 2760

Hartley, J.M.
The Way 2761

Hartog, Jan de
The Centurion 2762
The Peaceable Kingdom 2763
The Peculiar People 2764

Harwood, Alice
The Lily and the Leopards 2765
Merchant of the Ruby 2766
No Smoke Without Fire 2767
Seats of the Mighty: A Novel of James
   Stuart, Brother of Mary, Queen of
   Scots 2768
So Merciful a Queen, So Cruel a
   Woman 2769

Harwood, Ronald
Articles of Faith 2770
Cesar and Augusta 2771

Hashian, Jack
Mamigon 2772

Hastings, Michael
The Devil's Spy 2773

Haughton, Rosemary
Elizabeth's Greetings 2774

Hausman, Gerald
Wilderness 6957

Havighurst, Walter
The Quiet Shore 2775
Winds of Spring 2776

Haviland, Diana
The Moreland Legacy 2777

Havill, Edward
Big Ember 2778

Hawkes, Ellen
The Shadow of the Moth: A Novel of
   Espionage with Virginia
   Woolf 2779

Hawkes, Jacquetta
King of the Two Lands: The Pharaoh
   Akhenaten 2780
A Quest for Love 2781

Hawkesworth, John
Upstairs Downstairs 2782

Hawkins, Anne
To the Swift 2783

Hawkins, Paul
The Legend of Ben Tree 2784

Hawthorne, Hildegarde
No Road Too Long 2785

Hawthorne, Nathaniel
The Scarlet Letter 2786

Haycox, Ernest
The Adventurers 2787
Bugles in the Afternoon 2788
The Earthbreakers 2789
Long Storm 2790
Trouble Shooter 2791

Haycraft, Molly Costain
Countess Carrots 2792
The King's Daughters 2793
The Lady Royal 2794
My Lord Brother the Lionheart 2795
The Reluctant Queen 2796
Too Near the Throne 2797

Hayden, Sterling
Voyage: A Novel of 1896 2798

Hayden, Thomas
The Killing Frost 2799

Hays, Hoffman Reynolds
Takers of the City 2800

Healey, Ben
Captain Bolton's Corpse 3178
The Pangersbourne Murders 3179
The Thieftaker 3180
The Thistlewood Plot 3181
A Wicked Way to Die 3182

Heard, Gerald
The Gospel According to
   · Gamaliel 2801

Heaven, Constance
The Astrov Legacy 2802
Castle of Doves 2803
Castle of Eagles 2804
Daughter of Marignac 2805
The Fires of Glenlochy 2806
Heir to Kuragin 2807
The House of Kuragin 2808
Lord of Ravensley 2809
The Queen and the Gypsy 2810
The Wildcliffe Bird 2811
The Wind From the Sea 2812

Hebson, Ann
The Lattimer Legend 2813

Heck, Peter J.
A Connecticut Yankee in Criminal
   Court 2814
Death on the Mississippi 2815

Hegi, Ursula
Stones From the River 2816

Heidenstam, Verner Von
The Trees of the Folkungs 2817

Heidish, Marcy Moran
Miracles 2818
The Secret Annie Oakley 2819
Witnesses 2820
A Woman Called Moses 2821

Heiney, Donald W.
The Balloonist 2724
Glowstone 2725
Herma 2726
Pandora's Galley 2727

Hellman, George Sidney
Persian Conqueror 2822

Helprin, Mark
A Soldier of the Great War 2823

Henderson, Lois T.
Hagar 2824

Henke, Shirl
Night Wind's Woman 2825

Henley, Virginia
The Falcon and the Flower 2826
The Pirate and the Pagan 2827

Hennessy, Max
Back to Battle 2828
Blunted Lance 2829
The Bright Blue Sky 2830
The Challenging Heights 2831
The Crimson Wind 2832
The Dangerous Years 2833
The Lion at Sea 2834
The Medicine Whip 2835
Once More the Hawks 2836
Soldier of the Queen 2837

Henri, Florette
Kings Mountain 2838

Henry, Will
Chiricahua 2839
Death of a Legend 2840
From Where the Sun Now
   Stands 2841
The Gates of the Mountains 2842
Journey to Shiloh 2843
The Last Warpath 2844
Mackenna's Gold 2845
No Survivors 2846
One More River to Cross 2847
San Juan Hill 2848

Henshar, Peggy
Tomorrow's Dream 2674

Hepburn, Andrew
Letter of Marque 2849

Herbert, Alan Patrick
Why Waterloo? 2850

Herbert, Kathleen
Bride of the Spear 2851
Queen of the Lightning 2852

Hergesheimer, Joseph
Balisand 2853
Java Head 2854
The Three Black Pennys 2855

Herley, Richard
The Earth Goddess 2856
The Flint Lord 2857
The Stone Arrow 2858

Herlin, Hans
Grishin 2859

Herman, George
Carnival of Saints 2860

A Comedy of Murders 2861
The Tears of the Madonna 2862

Herr, Michael
Walter Winchell: A Novel 2863

Herrin, Lamar
The Unwritten Chronicles of Robert E.
   Lee 2864

Hersch, Virginia Davis
The Seven Cities of Gold 2865
To Seize a Dream 2866

Herschler, Mildred Barger
The Walk into Morning 2867

Hersey, John
Antonietta 2868
The Call 2869
The Conspiracy 2870

Hesky, Olga
The Painted Queen 2871

Heuman, William
Captain McRae: A Novel of the
   Northwest Frontier 2872

Heyer, Georgette
April Lady 2873
Arabella 2874
Bath Tangle 2875
Beauvallet 2876
The Black Moth 2877
Black Sheep 2878
Charity Girl 2879
A Civil Contract 2880
The Conqueror 2881
The Convenient Marriage 2882
Cotillion 2883
Cousin Kate 2884
Devil's Cub 2885
False Colours 2886
Faro's Daughter 2887
The Foundling 2888
Frederica 2889
Friday's Child 2890
The Grand Sophy 2891
An Infamous Army 2892
Lady of Quality 2893
The Masqueraders 2894
My Lord John 2895
The Nonesuch 2896
The Quiet Gentleman 2897
Regency Buck 2898
The Reluctant Widow 2899
Royal Escape 2900
Simon the Coldheart 2901
The Spanish Bride 2902
Sprig Muslin 2903
Sylvester; or, The Wicked Uncle 2904
The Talisman Ring 2905
These Old Shades 2906
The Toll-Gate 2907
The Unknown Ajax 2908
Venetia 2909

Heym, Stefan
The King David Report 2910

Heyward, DuBose
Peter Ashley 2911

Hibbert, Eleanor
The Adulteress 916
The Bastard King 5004
The Battle of the Queens 5005
Beyond the Blue Mountains 5006
The Black Swan 917
The Captive 3011
The Captive of Kensington
   Palace 5007
The Captive Queen of Scots 5008
Caroline the Queen 5009

The Changeling 918
The Courts of Love 5010
The Curse of the King 3012
Daughter of Satan 5011
Daughters of England 919
The Demon Lover 3013
The Devil on Horseback 3014
Epitaph for Three Women 5012
Evergreen Gallant 5013
The Follies of the King 5014
Gay Lord Robert 5015
Goddess of the Green Room 5016
The Goldsmith's Wife 5017
Hammer of the Scots 5018
A Health Unto His Majesty 5019
The Heart of the Lion 5020
Here Lies Our Sovereign Lord 5021
In the Shadow of the Crown 5022
It Began in Vauxhall Gardens 5023
The Italian Woman 5024
The Judas Kiss 3015
Katharine: The Virgin Widow 5025
The King's Pleasure 5026
The King's Secret Matter 5027
Knave of Hearts 920
The Lady in the Tower 5028
Lament for a Lost Lover 921
Light on Lucrezia 5029
Lilith 5030
The Lion of Justice 5031
The Lion Triumphant 922
Lord of the Far Island 3016
Louis the Well-Beloved 5032
The Love Child 923
Madame Serpent 5033
Madonna of the Seven Hills 5034
Midsummer's Eve 924
The Miracle at St. Bruno's 925
The Murder in the Tower 5035
Murder Most Royal 5036
My Enemy the Queen 3017
Myself My Enemy 5037
On the Night of the Seventh Moon 3018
Passage to Pontefract 5038
The Passionate Enemies 5039
Perdita's Prince 5040
The Plantagenet Prelude 5041
The Pleasures of Love 5042
The Pool of St. Branok 926
The Prince and the Quakeress 5043
The Prince of Darkness 5044
The Princess of Celle 5045
The Queen and Lord M 5046
The Queen From Provence 5047
Queen in Waiting 5048
Queen Jezebel 5049
Queen of This Realm: The Story of Queen Elizabeth I 5050
The Queen's Confession 3019
The Queen's Favourites 5051
The Queen's Husband 5052
The Queen's Secret 5053
Red Rose of Anjou 5054
The Regent's Daughter 5055
The Reluctant Queen: The Story of Anne of York 5056
The Return of the Gypsy 927
The Revolt of the Eaglets 5057
The Rose Without a Thorn 5058
Royal Road to Fotheringay 5059
St. Thomas's Eve 5060
Saraband for Two Sisters 928
The Scarlet Cloak 5061
Secret for a Nightingale 3020
The Shadow of the Pomegranate 5062
The Sixth Wife 5063
The Song of the Siren 929
The Spanish Bridegroom 5064

The Spring of the Tiger 3021
The Star of Lancaster 5065
The Sun in Splendour 5066
Sweet Lass of Richmond Hill 5067
The Third George 5068
The Thistle and the Rose 5069
The Three Crowns 5070
A Time for Silence 930
The Time of the Hunter's Moon 3022
Uneasy Lies the Head 5071
Victoria in the Wings 5072
Victoria Victorious 5073
Voices in a Haunted Room 931
The Vow on the Heron 5074
The Wandering Prince 5075
The Widow of Windsor 5076
Will You Love Me in September? 932
William's Wife 5077
The Witch From the Sea 933

Higgins, Jack
Luciano's Luck 2912

High, Monique Raphel
Between Two Worlds 2913
The Eleventh Year 2914
Encore 2915
The Four Winds of Heaven 2916

Highland, Monica
Lotus Land 2917

Highwater, Jamake
Journey to the Sky: A Novel about the True Adventures of Two Men in Search of the Lost Maya Kingdom 2918
The Sun, He Dies: A Novel about the End of the Aztec World 2919

Hill, Carol de Chellis
Henry James' Midnight Song 2920

Hill, Deborah
This Is the House 2921

Hill, Ernestine
My Love Must Wait: The Story of Matthew Flinders 2922

Hill, Fiona
The Autumn Rose 2923
The Country Gentleman 2924
The Stanbroke Girls 2925
Sweet's Folly 2926

Hill, Pamela
Artemia 2927
Bride of Ae 2928
The Brocken 2929
The Crown and the Shadow: The Story of Françoise d'Aubigne, Marquise de Maintenon 2930
Daneclere 2931
Fire Opal 2932
The Green Salamander 2933
The Heatherton Heritage 2934
Here Lies Margot 2935
The House of Cray 2936
The King's Vixen 2937
The Malvie Inheritance 2938
Marjorie of Scotland 2939
My Lady Glamis 2940
Norah 2941
A Place of Ravens 2942
Stranger's Forest 2943
The Suthurys 2944
The Sword and the Flame 2945
Tsar's Woman 2946
Vollands 2947
Whitton's Folly 2948
The Woman in the Cloak 2949

Hill, Porter
The War Chest 2950

Hill, Reginald
Captain Fantom 6377

Hill, Ruth Beebe
Hanta Yo 2951

Hill, Susan
Strange Meeting 2952

Hine, Al
Brother Owl 2953

Hinger, Charlotte
Come Spring 2954

Hinsdale, Harriet
Be My Love 2955

Hitchcock, Raymond
Attack the Lusitania! 2956

Hitt, James E.
Tennessee Smith 2957

Hjortsberg, William
Nevermore 2958

Hoagland, Edward
Seven Rivers West 2959

Hoban, Russell
Pilgermann 2960

Hodel, Michael P.
Enter the Lion: A Posthumous Memoir of Mycroft Holmes 2961

Hodge, Jane Aiken
Escapade 2962
First Night 2963
Here Comes a Candle 2964
Judas Flowering 2965
The Lost Garden 2966
Marry in Haste 2967
Polonaise 2968
Rebel Heiress 2969
Savannah Purchase 2970
Shadow of a Lady 2971
Whispering 2972
Wide Is the Water 2973
Windover 2974

Hodges, C. Walter
The Marsh King 2975

Hoe, Susanna
God Save the Tsar 2976

Hoffmann, Peggy
My Dear Cousin 2977

Hogan, Ray
The Ghost Raider 2978
Mosby's Last Ride 2979
Night Raider 2980
Soldier in Buckskin 2981

Holland, Cecelia
Antichrist: A Novel of the Emperor Frederick II 2982
The Bear Flag: A Novel of the Birth of California 2983
The Belt of Gold 2984
City of God: A Novel of the Borgias 2985
The Death of Attila 2986
The Earl 2987
The Firedrake 2988
Great Maria 2989
Jerusalem 2990
The Kings in Winter 2991
The Lords of Vaumartin 2992
Pacific Street 2993
Pillar of the Sky 2994
Rakossy 2995
The Sea Beggars 2996
Two Ravens 2997
Until the Sun Falls 2998

Holland, Sheila
Mistress of Fortune 3651

Holland, Tom
Lord of the Dead: The Secret History of Byron 2999

Hollick, Helen
The Kingmaking 3000
Pendragon's Banner 3001

Holm, John
The Hammer and the Cross 2736

Holman, Sheri
A Stolen Tongue 3002

Holmes, Marjorie
The Messiah 3003
Three From Galilee: The Young Man From Nazareth 3004
Two From Galilee: A Love Story 3005

Holt, Felix
Dan'l Boone Kissed Me 3006

Holt, Helene
Exiled 3007

Holt, Kare
The Race: A Novel of Polar Exploration 3008

Holt, Tom
Goatsong 3009
The Walled Orchard 3010

Holt, Victoria
The Captive 3011
The Curse of the King 3012
The Demon Lover 3013
The Devil on Horseback 3014
The Judas Kiss 3015
Lord of the Far Island 3016
My Enemy the Queen 3017
On the Night of the Seventh Moon 3018
The Queen's Confession 3019
Secret for a Nightingale 3020
The Spring of the Tiger 3021
The Time of the Hunter's Moon 3022

Honig, Donald
The Sword of General Englund 3023
Walk Like a Man 3024

Hoover, Thomas
Caribbee 3025
The Moghul 3026

Hopkins, Joseph G.E.
Patriot's Progress 3027
The Price of Liberty 3028
Retreat and Recall 3029

Horan, James David
The King's Rebel 3030
Seek Out and Destroy 3031

Horgan, Paul
Distant Trumpet 3032

Horia, Vintila
God Was Born in Exile 3033

Hornborg, Harald
Passion and the Sword 3034

Horne, Howard
Concord Bridge 3035

Hotchkiss, Bill
Ammahabas 3036
The Medicine Calf 3037
To Fell the Giants 3038

Hotchner, A.E.
Louisiana Purchase 3039

Hough, Emerson
54-40 or Fight 3040
Covered Wagon 3041
North of 36 3042

Hough, Frank Olney
If Not Victory 3043
The Neutral Ground 3044
Renown 3045

Hough, Henry Beetle
The New England Story 3046

Hough, Richard
Buller's Dreadnought 3047
Buller's Guns 3048
Buller's Victory 3049

House, R.C.
Drumm's War 638

Houston, James
Eagle Song 3050
Ghost Fox 3051
Running West 3052
The White Dawn 3053

Houston, June Dimmit
The Faith and the Flame 3054

Houston, Margaret Bell
Cottonwoods Grow Tall 3055

Houston, Robert
Bisbee '17 3056
The Nation Thief 3057

Howatch, Susan
Cashelmara 3058

Howe, Fanny
The White Slave 3059

Howells, Harvey
Bide Me Fair 3060

Hoyt, Edwin P.
*The Last Stand: A Novel about George
  Armstrong Custer and the Indians of
  the Plains* 3061
The Voice of Allah 3062

Hubbard, Margaret Ann
Flight of the Swan 3063

Hubler, Richard G.
*Love and Wisdom: A Novel about
  Solomon* 3064
*The Soldier and the Sage: A Novel
  about Akiba* 3065
*Trail and Triumph: A Novel about
  Maimonides* 4485

Hucker, Hazel
Cousin Susannah 3066

Huebsch, Edward
The Last Summer of Mata Hari 3067

Hueston, Ethel
*Calamity Jane of Deadwood
  Gulch* 3068
The Man of the Storm 3069
Star of the West 3070

Huff, Tom E.
Love's Tender Fury 6749

Huffaker, Claire
The Cowboy and the Cossack 3071

Huffman, Laurie
A House Behind the Mint 3072

Hughes, Glyn
Bronte 3073

Hughes, Richard
A High Wind in Jamaica 3074

Hughes, Rupert
Stately Timber 3075

Hugo, Victor
The Hunchback of Notre Dame 3076

Hulme, Kathryn
Annie's Captain 3077

Hummel, George Frederick
Joshua Moore, American 3078

Humphrey, William
No Resting Place 3079

Hunt, Christopher
The Bisley Boy 3080

Hunter, Bluebell Matilda
Manchu Empress 3081

Hunter, Evan
The Chisholms 3082
Lizzie 3083

Hunter, Jack D.
The Blood Order 3084
The Blue Max 3085

Huntford, Roland
Sea of Darkness 3086

Hurwood, Bernhardt J.
*My Savage Muse: The Story of My Life:
  Edgar Allan Poe, an Imaginative
  Work* 3087

Husted, Darrell
Louisa Brancusi 3088

Hutchens, Jane
Timothy Larkin 3089

Hutchins, Linda
*Mortal Love: A Novel of Eleanor of
  Aquitaine* 3090

Hyatt, Betty Hale
The Shalimar 3091

Hyde, Anthony
Locksley 1003

Hyde, Christopher
A Gathering of Saints 3092

Hyde, M.L.F.
King's Man 1880

Hylton, Sara
In the Shadow of the Nile 3093

Hyman, Tom
Seven Days to Petrograd 3094

I

Ibbotson, Eva
A Company of Swans 3095
Madensky Square 3096
Magic Flutes 3097

Ibn-Sahav, Ari
David and Bathsheba 3098

Idell, Albert E.
Bridge to Brooklyn 3099
Centennial Summer 3100
The Great Blizzard 3101
Rogers' Folly 3102

Ignatieff, Michael
Asya 3103

Ingles, James W.
A Woman of Samaria 3104

Ingram, Grace
Gilded Spurs 3105
Red Adam's Lady 3106

Inman, Robert
The Blood Endures 3107

Innes, Hammond
*The Last Voyage: Captain Cook's Lost
  Diary* 3108

Ireland, Patrick
*The Strange Case of Madamoiselle
  P.* 3109

Iremonger, Lucille
How Do I Love Thee 3110
My Sister, My Love 3111

Irish, Lola
And the Wild Birds Sing 3112

Irving, Clifford
Tom Mix and Pancho Villa 3113
The Valley 3114

Irwin, Constance
Gudrid's Saga 3115

Irwin, Margaret
The Bride 3116
*Elizabeth and the Prince of
  Spain* 3117
Elizabeth, Captive Princess 3118
The Gay Galliard 3119
*The Proud Servant: The Story of
  Montrose* 3120
*Royal Flush: The Story of
  Minette* 3121
The Stranger Prince 3122
Young Bess 3123

Israel, Charles E.
Rizpah 3124
Who Was Then the Gentleman 3125

J

Jack, Donald
It's Me Again 3126
Me So Far 3127
Me Too 3128
That's Me in the Middle 3129
This One's on Me 3130
Three Cheers for Me 3131

Jackson, Dorothy V.S.
Walk with Peril 3132

Jackson, Eileen
Autumn Lace 3133
Lord Rivington's Lady 3134

Jackson, Marian J.A.
Diamond Head 3135
The Sunken Treasure 3136

Jacob, Naomi
*The Irish Boy: A Romantic
  Biography* 3137

Jacob, Piers Anthony Dillingham
Isle of Woman 167
Shame of Man 168
Tatham Mound 169

Jacobs, Helen Hull
Storm Against the Wind 3138

Jacobs, Thornwell
Red Lanterns on St. Michael's 3139

Jacobson, Sheldon
Fleet Surgeon to Pharaoh 3140

Jahoda, Gloria
Annie 3141
Delilah's Mountain 3142

Jakes, John
The Americans 3143
The Bastard 3144
California Gold 3145

The Furies 3146
Heaven and Hell 3147
Homeland 3148
The Lawless 3149
Love and War 3150
North and South 3151
The Rebels 3152
The Seekers 3153
The Titans 3154
The Warriors 3155

James, Deana
Masque of Sapphire 3156

James, Donald
Once a Gentleman 3157

James, Janice
A Lady of Repute 3158

James, John
The Lords of Loone 3159
Seventeen of Leyden 3160
Talleyman 3161
Votan 3162

James, Will
The American Cowboy 3163

Janas, Frankie-Lee
Farewell the Stranger 4682
Pull Down to New Orleans 283

Janetschek, Ottokar
The Emperor Franz Joseph 3164

Jarman, Rosemary Hawley
The Courts of Illusion 3165
Crown in Candlelight 3166
The King's Grey Mare 3167
We Speak No Treason 3168

Jaro, Benita Kane
The Key 3169

Jarrett, Marjorie
Wives of the Wind 3170

Jauchius, Dean
*The Court Martial of Commodore
  Perry* 5307
Johnny Shiloh 5308
The Trial of Mary Todd Lincoln 5309

Jeal, Tim
For God and Glory 3171
A Marriage of Convenience 3172
Until the Colors Fade 3173

Jefferis, Barbara
Beloved Lady 3174
The Tall One 3175
Time of the Unicorn 3176

Jeffers, Graham
*The Courts of Love: A Romance of
  Medieval France* 592
Drums of Destiny 593
Flames of Empire 594
Soldiers of Fortune 595
Twilight of the Dragon 596
When God Slept 597

Jeffers, H. Paul
*The Adventure of the Stalwart
  Companions* 3177

Jeffreys, J.G.
Captain Bolton's Corpse 3178
The Pangersbourne Murders 3179
The Thieftaker 3180
The Thistlewood Plot 3181
A Wicked Way to Die 3182

Jekel, Pamela
Bayou 3183
Columbia 3184
*Deepwater: A Novel of the
  Carolinas* 3185

Natchez: A Novel of the Deep South 3186
Sea Star: The Private Life of Anne Bonny, Pirate 3187

Jelusich, Mirko
Caesar 3188

Jenkins, Burris Atkins
The Bracegirdle 3189

Jenkins, Elizabeth
Dr. Gully's Story 3190

Jenkins, Gwyn
King David 3191

Jenks, Kathleen
The River and the Stone: Moses' Early Years in Egypt 3192

Jennings, Gary
Aztec 3193
The Journeyer 3194
Sow the Seeds of Hemp 3195
Spangle 3196
The Terrible Teague Bunch 3197

Jennings, John Edward
Banners Against the Wind 3198
Call the New World 3199
Coasts of Folly 6784
Gentleman Ranker 3200
The Golden Eagle 3201
Next to Valour 3202
The Pepper Tree 3203
River to the West: A Novel of the Astor Adventure 3204
The Salem Frigate 3205
The Sea Eagles 3206
The Shadow and the Glory 3207
Shadows in the Dusk 3208
The Strange Brigade 3209
Tide of Empire 279
The Wind in His Fists 3210

Jennings, William Dale
The Cowboys 3211
The Ronin 3212
The Sinking of the Sarah Diamond 3213

Jensen, Johannes Vilhelm
The Fall of the King 3214

Jernigan, Muriel Molland
Forbidden City 3215

Jeske-Choinski, Teodor
The Last Romans 3216

Johansen, Iris
Storm Winds 3217
The Wind Dancer 3218

Johansen, Margaret Alison
Dark Possession 3771

John, Evan
Crippled Splendour 3219
King's Masque 3220
Ride Home Tomorrow 3221

Johnson, David
The Proud Canaries 3222

Johnson, Dorothy M.
Buffalo Woman 3223

Johnson, Ellen Argo
The Crystal Star 184
Jewel of the Sea 185
The Yankee Girl 186

Johnson, Eyvind
Return to Ithaca 3224

Johnson, Gerald White
By Reason of Strength 3225

Johnson, Mary Ellen
The Lion and the Leopard 3226

Johnson, Pamela Hansford
Catherine Carter 3227

Johnston, George
The Big Chariot 1118

Johnston, Mary
1492 3228
Audrey 3229
Cease Firing 3230
Croatan 3231
Drury Randall 3232
Foes 3233
The Great Valley 3234
The Hunting Shirt 3235
The Long Roll 3236
Miss Delicia Allen 3237
Prisoners of Hope: A Tale of Colonial Virginia 3238
Silver Cross 3239
The Slave Ship 3240
To Have and to Hold 3241

Johnston, Terry C.
Black Sun 3242
Blood Song 3243
Borderlords 3244
Buffalo Palace 3245
Carry the Wind 3246
A Cold Day in Hell 3247
Cry of the Hawk 3248
Dance on the Wind 3249
Devil's Backbone 3250
Dream Catcher 3251
Long Winter Gone 3252
One-Eyed Dream 3253
Reap the Whirlwind 3254
Red Cloud's Revenge 3255
Seize the Sky 3256
The Shadow Riders 3257
Sioux Dawn 3258
The Stalkers 3259
Trumpet on the Land 3260
Whisper of the Wolf 3261
Winter Rain 3262

Johnston, Velda
I Came to the Highlands: A Novel of Suspense 3263
The Silver Dolphin 3264

Johnstone, William W.
Blood on the Divide 3265
Eyes of Eagles 3266
Forty Guns West 3267
Talons of Eagles 3268

Jones, Alexandra
Mandalay 3269

Jones, Cleo
Sister Wives 3270

Jones, Courtway
In the Shadow of the Oak King 3271
Witch of the North 3272

Jones, Douglas C.
Arrest Sitting Bull 3273
The Barefoot Brigade 3274
Come Winter 3275
The Court-Martial of George Armstrong Custer 3276
A Creek Called Wounded Knee 3277
Elkhorn Tavern 3278
Gone the Dreams and the Dancing 3279
Remember Santiago 3280
Roman 3281
The Search for Temperance Moon 3282
Season of Yellow Leaf 3283

Shadow of the Moon 3284
This Savage Race 3285
Weedy Rough 3286
Winding Stairs 3287

Jones, Ellen
Beloved Enemy: The Passions of Eleanor of Aquitaine 3288
The Fatal Crown 3289

Jones, Gareth
Lord of Misrule 3290

Jones, H. Bedford
John Barry 412

Jones, Madison
Forest of the Night 3291

Jones, Mervyn
Joseph 3292
Lord Richard's Passion 3293

Jones, Robert F.
Tie My Bones to Her Back 3294

Jones, Rod
Billy Sunday 3295

Jones, Ted
The Fifth Conspiracy 3296
Grant's War 3297
Hard Road to Gettysburg 3298

Jong, Erica
Fanny: Being the True History of the Adventures of Fanny Hackabout-Jones 3299
Serenissima: A Novel of Venice 3300

Jordan, Jan
Dim the Flaring Lamps 3301
Give Me the Wind 3302

Jordan, Mildred A.
Asylum for the Queen 3303
Echo of the Flute 3304
One Red Rose Forever 3305

Jose, Nicholas
The Rose Crossing 3306

Joseph, Marie
A Leaf in the Wind 3307
Maggie Craig 3308

Jourdain, Rose
Those the Sun Has Loved 3309

Judah, Charles Burnet
Christopher Humble 3310

Judd, Cameron
Boone: A Novel Based on the Life and Times of Daniel Boone 3311
The Border Men 3312
The Canebrake Men 3313
Crockett of Tennessee: A Novel Based on the Life and Times of David Crockett 3314
The Overmountain Men 3315
Passage to Natchez 3316

Judd, Denis
The Adventures of Long John Silver 3317
Return to Treasure Island 3318

Julian, Jane
Ellen Bray 3319

K

Kadison, Ellis
The Eighth Veil 3320

Kagawa, Toyohiko
Behold the Man 3321

Kalechofsky, Roberta
Bodin, 1349: An Epic Novel of Christians and Jews in the Plague Years 3322

Kalman, Yvonne
After the Rainbow 3323
Greenstone 3324
Mists of Heaven 3325

Kalogridis, Jeanne
Children of the Vampire: The Diaries of the Family Dracul 3326
Covenant with the Vampire: The Diaries of the Family Dracul 3327
Lord of the Vampires: The Diaries of the Family Dracul 3328

Kalpakian, Laura
Cosette: The Sequel to Les Miserables 3329
These Latter Days 3330

Kaminsky, Stuart M.
Bullet for a Star 3331
Buried Caesars 3332
Catch a Falling Star 3333
Dancing in the Dark 3334
The Devil Met a Lady 3335
Down for the Count 3336
The Fala Factor 3337
He Done Her Wrong 3338
High Midnight 3339
The Howard Hughes Affair 3340
The Man Who Shot Lewis Vance 3341
The Melting Clock 3342
Murder on the Yellow Brick Road 3343
Never Cross a Vampire 3344
Poor Butterfly 3345
Smart Moves 3346
Think Fast, Mr. Peters 3347
Tomorrow Is Another Day 3348
You Bet Your Life 3349

Kane, Carol J.
Blood and Sable 3350

Kane, Harnett T.
The Amazing Mrs. Bonaparte 3351
Bride of Fortune 3352
The Gallant Mrs. Stonewall 3353
The Lady of Arlington 3354
New Orleans Woman: A Biographical Novel of Myra Clark Gaines 3355
Pathway to the Stars 3356
The Smiling Rebel 3357

Kane, Harriet
The Scandalous Mrs. Blackford 3358

Kantor, MacKinlay
Andersonville 3359
Arouse and Beware 3360
Beauty Beast 3361
Long Remember 3362
Spirit Lake 3363
Valley Forge 3364

Kaplan, Barry Jay
Biscayne 3365

Karig, Walter
Don't Tread on Me 3366

Karr, Phyllis Ann
The Idylls of the Queen 3367

Karsavina, Jean
White Eagle, Dark Skies 3368

Kata, Elizabeth
Kagami 3369

Kaufman, Fred S.
Custer Passed Our Way 3370

Kaufman, Pamela
Banners of Gold 3371
Shield of Three Lions 3372

Kavaler, Rebecca
Doubting Castle 3373

Kay, Susan
Legacy 3374
Phantom 3375

Kaye, M.M.
The Far Pavilions 3376
Shadow of the Moon 3377
Trade Wind 3378

Kaye-Smith, Sheila
Superstition Corner 3379

Kazan, Elia
America, America 3380
The Anatolian 3381
Beyond the Aegean 3382

Kazantzakis, Nikos
Freedom or Death 3383
The Last Temptation of Christ 3384
Saint Francis 3385

Keene, James
Justice, My Brother 3386

Kelland, Clarence Budington
Arizona 3387
Gold 3388
Hard Money 3389
The Jealous House 3390

Kellerman, Faye
The Quality of Mercy 3391

Kelley, Welbourn
Alabama Empire 3392

Kellner, Esther
The Bride of Pilate 3393
Mary of Nazareth 3394
The Promise 3395

Kells, Susannah
A Crowning Mercy 3396
The Fallen Angels 3397

Kelly, Carla
Daughter of Fortune 3398

Kelly, Eleanor
Richard Walden's Wife 3399

Kelly, Eric
Three Sides of Agiochook 3400

Kelly, Jack
Mad Dog 3401

Kelsey, Joan Marshall
Life as Carola 2535
Winged Pharaoh 2536

Kelton, Elmer
Dark Thicket 3402
The Day the Cowboys Quit 3403
The Far Canyon 3404
The Good Old Boys 3405
The Pumpkin Rollers 3406
Slaughter 3407
Sons of Texas 1822
The Wolf and the Buffalo 3408

Kendall, Lisa See
Lotus Land 2917

Kendrick, Baynard
The Flames of Time 3409

Keneally, Thomas
Bring Larks and Heroes 3410
The Chant of Jimmie Blacksmith 3411
Confederates 3412

Gossip From the Forest 3413
The Playmaker 3414
A River Town 3415
Schindler's List 3416
Victim of the Aurora 3417

Kennedy, John P.
Horseshoe Robinson, a Tale of the Tory Ascendancy 3418

Kennedy, Lucy
Mr. Audubon's Lucy 3419

Kennedy, Margaret
A Night in Cold Harbor 3420
Troy Chimneys 3421

Kennedy, William
Legs 3422
Quinn's Book 3423

Kennelly, Ardyth
Good Morning, Young Lady 3424
The Spur 3425

Kennett, Frances
A Woman by Design 3426

Kent, Alexander
Colors Aloft! 3427
Command a King's Ship 3428
Enemy in Sight! 3429
The Flag Captain 3430
Form Line of Battle! 3431
Honor This Day 3432
In Gallant Company 3433
The Inshore Squadron 3434
Midshipman Bolitho and the Avenger 3435
Passage to Mutiny 3436
Richard Bolitho—Midshipman 3437
Signal—Close Action! 3438
Sloop of War 3439
Stand into Danger 3440
Success to the Brave 3441
To Glory We Steer 3442
A Tradition of Victory 3443

Kent, Madeleine Fabiola
The Corsair: A Biographical Novel of Jean Lafitte, Hero of the Battle of New Orleans 3444

Kenyon, F.W.
The Absorbing Fire: The Byron Legend 3445
The Consuming Flame: The Story of George Eliot 3446
The Duke's Mistress: The Story of Mary Ann Clarke 3447
Emma 3448
The Emperor's Lady: A Novel Based on the Life of the Empress Josephine 3449
The Glory and the Dream 3450
The Golden Years: A Novel Based on the Life and Loves of Percy Bysshe Shelley 3451
Imperial Courtesan 3452
Marie Antoinette 3453
Mary of Scotland 3454
My Brother Napoleon: The Confessions of Caroline Bonaparte 3455
The Naked Sword: The Story of Lucretia Borgia 3456
Passionate Rebel: The Story of Hector Berlioz 3457
The Questing Heart: A Romantic Novel about George Sand 3458
Royal Merry-Go-Round 3459
Shadow in the Sun: A Novel of Elizabeth I, the Virgin Queen 3460
That Spanish Woman 3461

Kenyon, Theda
The Golden Feather 3462
Something Gleamed 3463
That Skipper From Stonington 3464

Keppel, Charlotte
Loving Sands, Deadly Sands 3465
My Name Is Clary Brown 3466
The Villains: A Haunting Tale of the Marshes 3467

Ker Wilson, Barbara
Antipodes Jane: A Novel of Jane Austen in Australia 3468
The Quade Inheritance 3469

Kerns, Frances Casey
This Land Is Mine 3470

Kerr, Philip
The Pale Criminal 3471

Kerr, Robert
The Stuart Legacy 3472

Kesey, Ken
Last Go Round 3473

Kessler, Julia Braun
Presumption: An Entertainment 350
The Third Sister 351

Kesten, Hermann
Ferdinand and Isabella 3474
I, the King 3475

Kettle, Jocelyn
The Athelsons 3476

Keyes, Frances Parkinson
Blue Camellia 3477
The Chess Player: A Novel of New Orleans and Paris 3478
I, the King 3479
Madame Castel's Lodger 3480
Steamboat Gothic 3481

Kiefer, Warren
Outlaw 3482

Kilian, Michael
Dance on a Sinking Ship 3483

Killens, John Oliver
Great Black Russian 3484

King, Grace
La Dame De Sainte Hermine 3485

King, Joan
Impressionist: A Novel of Mary Cassatt 3486

King, Laurie R.
The Beekeeper's Apprentice, or, On the Segregation of the Queen 3487
A Letter of Mary 3488
A Monstrous Regiment of Women 3489

King-Hall, Magdalen
Gay Crusader 3528
The Lovely Lynchs 3490

Kingsbury, Kate
Check-Out Time 3491
Do Not Disturb 3492
Eat, Drink, and Be Buried 3493
Grounds for Murder 3494
Room with a Clue 3495
Service for Two 3496

Kingsley, Charles
Hereward the Wake 3497
Hypatia 3498
Westward Ho! 3499

Kingsley, Henry
Ravenshoe 3500

Kinsolving, William
Born with the Century 3501
Mister Christian 3502

Kinstler, Ceysta
The Moon under Her Feet 3503

Kirby, Kate
Scapegoat for a Stuart 3504

Kirkland, Elithe Hamilton
Divine Average 3505
Love Is a Wild Assault 3506

Kitchen, Paddy
The Golden Veil 3507

Kjelgaard, James Arthur
The Land Is Bright 3508
The Lost Wagon 3509

Klein, Elinor
Triptych 3652

Kluge, P.F.
Season for War 3510

Kluger, Richard
Members of the Tribe 3511
The Sheriff of Nottingham 3512

Knaggs, John R.
The Bugles Are Silent: A Novel of the Texas Revolution 3513

Knight, Alanna
The Black Duchess 3514
Blood Line 3515
Castle of Foxes 3516
Deadly Beloved 3517
Enter Second Murderer 3518
Estella 3519
Killing Cousins 3520

Knight, Brigid
The Covenant 3521
Not by Any Single Man 3522
The Valiant Lady 3523
Westward the Sun 3524

Knight, Ruth Adams
Certain Harvest: A Novel of the Time of Peter Cooper 3525

Knowles, John
A Vein of Riches 3526

Knox, Alexander
The Kidnapped Surgeon 3527

Knox, Cleone
Gay Crusader 3528

Koch, Werner
Pontius Pilate Reflects 3529

Koen, Karleen
Now Face to Face 3530
Through a Glass Darkly 3531

Koestler, Arthur
The Gladiators 3532

Komroff, Manuel
Feast of the Jesters 3533
The Magic Bow 3534
Two Thieves 3535
Waterloo 3536

Koning, Hans
Death of a Schoolboy 3537
The Petersburg-Cannes Express 3538
A Walk with Love and Death 3539

Koningsberger, Hans
Death of a Schoolboy 3537
The Petersburg-Cannes Express 3538
A Walk with Love and Death 3539

Korda, Michael
The Immortals 3540

Korman, Keith
Secret Dreams 3541

Kossak-Szczucka, Zofja
Blessed Are the Meek: A Novel about St. Francis of Assisi 3542
The Covenant: A Novel of the Life of Abraham the Prophet 3543
The Leper King 3544

Kossoff, David
The Voices of Masada 3545

Kosztolanyi, Deszo
Bloody Poet 3546

Kotker, Norman
Herzl the King 3547

Kotker, Zane
White Rising 3548

Kotzwinkle, William
Fata Morgana 3549

Kramer, Dale
The Heart of O. Henry 3550

Krassnoff, Peter N.
Napoleon and the Cossacks 3551

Kraus, Rene
The Private and Public Life of Socrates 3552

Krentz, Jayne Ann
Dangerous 5213
Deception 5214
Mistress 5215
Ravished 5216
Reckless 5217
Rendezvous 5218
Scandal 5219
Seduction 5220
Surrender 5221

Krepps, Robert Wilson
Earthshaker 3553

Krey, Laura
And Tell of Time 3554
On the Long Tide 3555

Krokosz, Emily
Visions of a Heart 899

Kroll, Harry Harrison
Darker Grows the Valley 3556
Fury in the Earth: A Novel of the New Madrid Earthquake 3557
The Keeper of the House 3558
Perilous Journey: A Tale of the Mississippi River and the Natchez Trace 6109
Rogues' Company: A Novel of John Murrell 3559

Kross, Jaan
The Czar's Madman 3560

Krotkov, Yuri
The Red Monarch: Scenes From the Life of Stalin 3561

Kruger, Mary
Death on the Cliff Walk 3562
Masterpiece of Murder 3563
No Honeymoon for Death 3564

Kunstler, James Howard
An Embarrassment of Riches 3565

Kurten, Bjorn
Dance of the Tiger: A Novel of the Ice Age 3566
Singletusk 3567

Kurtz, Katherine
Two Crowns for America 3568

Kurzweil, Allen
A Case of Curiosities 3569

Kyle, Duncan
The King's Commissar 3570

Kyle, Elizabeth
The Swedish Nightingale: Jenny Lind 3571

Kyne, Peter S.
Tide of Empire 3572

L

La Farge, Oliver
Long Pennant 3573

La Mure, Pierre
Beyond Desire: A Novel Based on the Life of Felix and Cecille Mendelssohn 3574
Clair De Lune: A Novel about Claude Debussy 3575
Moulin Rouge: A Novel Based on Henri de Toulouse-Lautrec 3576
The Private Life of Mona Lisa 3577

Lachman, Barbara
The Journal of Hildegard of Bingen 3578

Lacy, Al
Beloved Enemy 3579
A Heart Divided 3580
Joy From Ashes 3581
A Promise Unbroken 3582
Shadowed Memories 3583

Lagard, Garald
Scarlet Cockerel 3584

Lagerkvist, Par
Barabbas 3585

Lagerlof, Selma
The Story of Gosta Berling 3586

Laine, Annabel
The Melancholy Virgin 3587
The Reluctant Heiress 3588

Laing, Alexander
Matthew Early 3589

Laird, Charlton
Thunder on the River 3590
West of the River 3591

Laker, Rosalind
Banners of Silk 3592
Circle of Pearls 3593
Claudine's Daughter 3594
Gilded Splendour 3595
The Golden Tulip 3596
Jewelled Path 3597
Ride the Blue Riband 3598
The Silver Touch 3599
The Sugar Pavilion 3600
To Dance with Kings 3601
Tree of Gold 3602
The Venetian Mask 3603
Warwyck's Woman 3604
What the Heart Keeps 3605

Lamb, F. Bruce
Kid Curry: The Life and Times of Harvey Logan and the Wild Bunch 3606

Lamb, Harold
Alexander of Macedon: The Journey to World's End 3607
Theodora and the Emperor 3608

Lambdin, Dewey
The French Admiral 3609
The Gun Ketch 3610
H.M.S. Cockerel 3611
The King's Coat 3612
A King's Commander 3613
The King's Commission 3614
The King's Privateer 3615

Lambert, Derek
Beau Blackstone 2005
Blackstone 2006
Blackstone and the Scourge of Europe 2007
Blackstone's Fancy 2008

Lambton, Antony
Elizabeth and Alexandra 3616

L'Ami, C.E.
The Green Madonna 3617

L'Amour, Louis
The Californios 3618
The Daybreakers 3619
Jubal Sackett 3620
Lonely on the Mountain 3621
The Man From Broken Hills 3622
Mustang Man 3623
Ride the Dark Trail 3624
Ride the River 3625
Rivers West 3626
The Sackett Brand 3627
Sackett's Land 3628
The Sky-Liners 3629
To the Far Blue Mountains 3630
Treasure Mountain 3631
The Walking Drum 3632
The Warrior's Path 3633

Lampedusa, Giuseppe di
The Leopard 3634

Lancaster, Bruce
The Big Knives 3635
Blind Journey 3636
Bride of a Thousand Cedars 3637
Bright to the Wanderer 3638
For Us the Living 3639
Guns of Burgoyne 3640
Night March 3641
No Bugles Blow 3642
Phantom Fortress 3643
Roll, Shenandoah 3644
The Scarlet Patch 3645
The Secret Road 3646
Trumpet to Arms 3647
Venture in the East 3648

Lancaster, G.B.
Grand Parade 3649
Pageant 3650

Lancaster, Sheila
Mistress of Fortune 3651

Landey, Dora
Triptych 3652

Landis, Jill Marie
Sunflower 3653

Lane, Carl Daniel
The Fleet in the Forest 3654

Lane, Jane
Madame Geneva 3655
Parcel of Rogues 3656
The Severed Crown 3657
Thunder on St. Paul's Day 3658
The Young and Lonely King 3659

Lane, Kenneth Westmacott
Winter Cherry 6632

Lane, Rose
Free Land 3660

Lang, Jennifer
The Peacock and the Pearl 3661

Lang, Theo
The Word and the Sword 3662

Lapham, Arthur L.
Justus 3663

Lapouge, Gilles
The Battle of Wagram 3664

LaRosa, Linda J.
Winter of the Heart 3665

Larreta, Antonio
The Last Portrait of the Duchess of Alba 3666

Larsen, Gaylord
Dorothy and Agatha 3667

Larsen, Jeanne
Bronze Mirror 3668
Manchu Palaces 3669
Silk Road 3670

Larson, Charles R.
Arthur Dimmesdale 3671

Laughlin, Ruth
The Wind Leaves No Shadow 3672

Lauritzen, Jonreed
Captain Sutter's Gold 3673
The Cross and the Sword 3674
The Everlasting Fire 3675
The Rose and the Flame 3676

Lavender, David
Red Mountain 3677

Law, Janice
All the King's Ladies 3678

Lawhead, Stephen R.
Arthur 3679
Byzantium 3680
Merlin 3681
Pendragon 3682
Taliesin 3683

Lawrence, Joan
The Scapegoat: A Life of Moses 3684

Lawrence, Margaret
Hearts and Bones 3685

Laxness, Halldor
Paradise Reclaimed 3686

Layton, Edith
The Fireflower 3687

Lazarus, Marguerite
Flowers for Lilian 2405
The Long Shadow 2406
The Wedding Guest 2407

Le Fanu, Joseph Sheridan
The House by the Churchyard 3688

Le May, Alan
By Dim and Flashing Lamps 3689
Pelican Coast 3690
The Searchers 3691
The Unforgiven 3692

Le Porrier, Herbert
The Doctor From Cordova: A Biographical Novel about the Great Philosopher Maimonides 3693

Lea, Tom
The Hands of Cantu 3694
The Wonderful Country 3695

Leary, Francis W.
Fire and Morning 3696
The Swan and the Rose 3697
This Dark Monarchy 3698

Leasor, James
Follow the Drum 3699
Mandarin Gold 3700

Leaton, Anne
Pearl 3701

Leavitt, David
While England Sleeps 3702

Lechner, Michael
My Beautiful White Roses 3703

Leckie, Ross
Hannibal 3704

Ledner, Caryl
The Bondswoman 3705

Lee, Barbara
The Fever Called Living 4439
Hard on the Road 4440

Lee, C.Y.
China Saga 3706
The Second Son of Heaven: A Novel of Nineteenth-Century China 3707

Lee, Edna
The Web of Days 3708

Lee, Lilian
Farewell to My Concubine 3709

Lee, Tanith
The Gods Are Thirsty 3710

Lee, Virginia
The House That Tai Ming Built 3711

Lee, Wendi
The Overland Trail 3712

Leekley, John
The Blue and the Gray 3713

Lefcourt, Peter
Di and I 3714

Leland, John Adams
Othniel Jones 3715

Lenanton, Carola M.
Crouchback 4732

Lennox-Smith, Judith
The Glittering Strand 3716
The Italian Garden 3717
The Secret Years 3718
Till the Day Goes Down 3719

Lentz, Perry
The Falling Hills 3720

Leonard, Hugh
Parnell and the Englishwoman 3721

Leonard, Nathan
Wind Like a Bugle 3722

Leonard, Phyllis
Tarnished Angel 3723

Lerman, Rhoda
Eleanor: A Novel 3724

Lescroart, John T.
Rasputin's Revenge 3725
Son of Holmes 3726

Leslie, Doris
The Prime Minister's Wife 3727
Royal William 3728

Letton, Francis
The Robsart Affair 3729
The Young Elizabeth 3730

Letton, Jennette
The Robsart Affair 3729
The Young Elizabeth 3730

Lever, Charles James
Charles O'Malley 3731
Tom Burke of Ours 3732

Levi, Jean
The Chinese Emperor 3733
The Dream of Confucius 3734

Leviant, Curt
The Man Who Thought He Was Messiah 3735

Levin, Benjamin H.
Black Triumvirate: A Novel of Haiti 3736
To Spit Against the Wind 3737

Levin, Dan
Son of Judah 3738

Levin, Lee
King Tut's Private Eye 3739

Levine, Faye
Solomon and Sheba 3740

Levitin, Sonia
The No-Return Trail 3741

Levy, Barbara
Adrienne 3742

Lewars, E.S.
A High Wind Rising 5867
I Speak for Thaddeus Stevens 5868
Loving Heart 5869
Swords of Steel 5870

Lewerth, Margaret
Stuyvesant Square 3743

Lewis, Ada Cook
The Longest Night 3744

Lewis, Hilda
Call Lady Purbeck 3745
Catherine 3746
The Gentle Falcon 3747
Harlot Queen 3748
Harold Was My King 3749
I Am Mary Tudor 3750
Wife to Great Buckingham 3751
Wife to Henry V 3752
Wife to the Bastard 3753
The Witch and the Priest 3754

Lewis, Janet
The Ghost of Monsieur Scarron 3755

Lewis, Mary
Starrbelow 6248

Lewis, Matthew Gregory
The Monk 3756

Lewis, Oscar
The Lost Years: A Biographical Fiction 3757

Lewis, Paul
The Gentle Fury: A Novel of Margaret of Austria 3758
The Nelson Touch 3759

Lewis, Preston
The Demise of Billy the Kid 3760
The Lady and Doc Holliday 3761

Lewis, Roy
Cock of the Walk 3762

Lewis, Sinclair
The God-Seeker 3763

Ley, Alice Chetwynd
A Fatal Assignation 3764
Masquerade of Vengeance 3765
A Reputation Dies 3766

Ley-Piscator, Marie
Lot's Wife 3767

Leys, Simon
The Death of Napoleon 3768

Li, Leslie
Bittersweet 3769

Liddon, Eloise S.
Some Lose Their Way 3770

Lide, Alice Alison
Dark Possession 3771

Lide, Mary
Ann of Cambray 3772
Command of the King 3773
Fortune's Knave: The Making of William the Conqueror 3774
Isobelle 3775
The Legacy of Tregaran 3776
A Royal Quest 3777
The Sea Scape 3778
Tregaran 3779

Lidman, Sara
The Rainbird 3780

Liederman, Judith
The Moneyman 3781

Lin, Yutang
Lady Wu 3782
The Red Peony 3783

Lincoln, Freeman
The New Hope 3784
Storm Signals 3785

Lincoln, Joseph C.
The New Hope 3784
Storm Signals 3785

Lincoln, Victoria
Charles 3786
A Dangerous Innocence 3787

Linderholm, Helmer
Land of the Beautiful River 3788

Lindgren, Torgny
Bathsheba 3789

Lindop, Audrey Erskine
The Way to the Lantern 3790

Lindsay, Philip
The Gentle Knight 3791
Here Comes the King 3792

Lindsey, Dawn
The Duchess of Vidal 3793

Lindsey, Johanna
Defy Not the Heart 3794
Savage Thunder 3795

Lingard, Joan
Greenyards 3796

Linington, Elizabeth
The Dispossessed 5773
The King Breaker 3797
The Long Watch 3798
Monsieur Janvier 3799
The Proud Man 3800
The Scalpel and the Sword 5774

Link, Gail
Wolf's Embrace 3801

Linklater, Eric
Husband of Delilah 3802

Linscott, Gillian
Crown Witness 3803
Dead Man's Sweetheart 3804
An Easy Day for a Lady 3805
Hanging on the Wire 3806
Murder, I Presume 3807
Sister Beneath the Sheet 3808
Stage Fright 3809

Littell, Robert
The Revolutionist: A Novel of Russia 3810

Livingston, Nancy
The Far Side of the Hill 3811
The Land of Our Dreams 3812

Llewellyn, Richard
How Green Was My Valley 3813

Lloyd, Alan
Trade Imperial 3814

Lloyd-Jones, Robin
Lords of the Dance 3815

Llywelyn, Morgan
Bard: The Odyssey of the Irish 3816
Druids 3817
Finn Mac Cool 3818
Grania: She-King of the Irish Seas 3819
The Horse Goddess 3820
The Last Prince of Ireland 3821
The Lion of Ireland 3822
Pride of Lions 3823
Red Branch 3824
The Wind From Hastings 3825

Locke, Charles O.
The Last Princess 3826

Lockridge, Ross Jr.
Raintree County 3827

Lockwood, Sarah
A Fistful of Stars 3828

Lodi, Maria
Charlotte Morel 3829
Charlotte Morel: The Dream 3830
Charlotte Morel: The Siege 3831

Loewenstein, Hubertus
The Eagle and the Crown 3832
The Lance of Longinus 3833

Lofts, Norah
Afternoon of a Autocrat 3834
Bless This House 3835
Blossom Like the Rose 3836
The Brittle Glass 3837
A Calf for Venus 3838
The Concubine 3839
Crown of Aloes 3840
The Days of the Butterfly 3841
Eleanor the Queen 3842
The Golden Fleece 3843
The Homecoming 3844
The House at Old Vine 3845
How Far to Bethlehem? 3846
The King's Pleasure 3847
Knight's Acre 3848
The Lonely Furrow 3849
The Lost Queen 3850
Lovers All Untrue 3851
The Lute Player 3852
Madselin 3853
Nethergate 3854
The Old Priory 3855
Out of the Dark 3856
Pargeters 3857
A Rose for Virtue 3858
Scent of Cloves 3859
Silver Nutmeg 3860
The Town House 3861
A Wayside Tavern 3862
Winter Harvest 3863

Logan, Mark
Brumaire 3864
Guillotine 3865
Tricolour 3866

Lom, Herbert
Dr. Guillotine: The Eccentric Exploits of an Early Scientist 3867

Long, Jeff
Empire of Bones: A Novel of Sam Houston and the Texas Revolution 3868

Long, William Stuart
The Adventurers 3869
The Colonists 3870
The Empire Builders 3871
The Explorers 3872
The Gallant 3873
The Gold Seekers 3874
The Imperialists 3875
The Nationalists 3876
The Seafarers 3877
The Settlers 3878
The Traitors 3879

Longman, M.B.
The Power of Black 3880

Longstreet, Ethel
Man of Montmartre: A Novel Based on the Life of Maurice Utrillo 3888

Longstreet, Stephen
All or Nothing 3881
The Bank 3882
The Burning Man 3883
The Dream Seekers 3884
Eagles Where I Walk 3885
A Few Painted Feathers 3886
Gettysburg 3887
Man of Montmartre: A Novel Based on the Life of Maurice Utrillo 3888
Masts to Spear the Stars 3889
Our Father's House 3890
Three Days 3891
War in the Golden Weather 3892
The Young Men of Paris 3893

Loomis, Noel M.
The Twilighters 3894

Loomis, Stanley
The Fatal Friendship: Marie Antoinette, Count Fersen and the Flight to Varennes 3895

Lopez Portillo y Pacheco, Jose
They Are Coming: The Conquest of Mexico 3896

Lopresti, Lucia
Artemesia 295

Lord, Bette Bao
Spring Moon: A Novel of China 3897

Lothar, Ernst
The Angel with the Trumpet 3898

Lott, Milton
Dance Back the Buffalo 3899
The Last Hunt 3900

Lottman, Eileen
The Brahmins 3901

Lovelace, Maude Hart
The Black Angels 3902
Charming Sally 3903
Early Candlelight 3904
Gentlemen From England 3905

Lovesey, Peter
Abracadaver 3906
Bertie and the Crime of Passion 3907
Bertie and the Seven Bodies 3908
Bertie and the Tinman 3909
A Case of Spirits 3910
The Detective Wore Silk Drawers 3911
The False Inspector Dew 3912
Keystone 3913
Mad Hatter's Holiday 3914
Swing, Swing Together 3915

The Tick of Death 3916
Waxwork 3917
Wobble to Death 3918

Lowden, Leone
Proving Ground: A Novel of Civil War Days in the North 3919

Lucas, Janice
The Long Sun 3920

Ludwig, Charles
Levi Coffin and the Underground Railroad 3921
Queen of the Reformation 3922

Luke, Mary M.
The Ivy Crown: A Biographical Novel of Queen Katherine Parr 3923
The Nonsuch Lure 3924

Lund, Robert P.
Daishi-San: A Novel 3925
The Odyssey of Thaddeus Baxter 3926

Lutes, Della
Gabriel's Search 3927

Lutz, Giles A.
The Magnificent Failure 3928

Lyall, Gavin
Spy's Honour 3929

Lyle, Elizabeth
Cassy 3930
Claire 3931

Lynch, Daniel
Yellow: A Novel 3932

Lynch, Frances
The Fine and Handsome Captain 3933
Stranger at the Wedding 3934

Lynde, Francis
Mr. Arnold 3935

Lynley, Elinor
Song of the Bayou 3936

Lynn, Jack
The Hallelujah Flight 3937

Lynn, Karen
Double Masquerade 3938
Dual Destiny 3939
Midsummer Moon 3940
The Rake 3941
The Scottish Marriage 3942

Lynn, Margaret
Free Soil 3943

Lytle, Andrew
At the Moon's Inn 3944
The Long Night 3945
The Velvet Horn 3946

Lyttleton, Edith J.
Grand Parade 3649
Pageant 3650

M

Maalouf, Amin
Leo Africanus 3947

Maas, Edgar
Don Pedro and the Devil 3948
Imperial Venus: A Novel of Napoleon's Favorite Sister 3949
A Lady at Bay 3950
Magnificent Enemies 3951
The Queen's Physician 3952

World and Paradise 3953

Mabie, Mary Louise
Prepare Them for Caesar 3954

Mac, Gerard
Pilgrims: A Novel of the Mayflower 3955

Macaulay, Rose
The Shadow Flies 3956

MacBeth, George
Dizzy's Woman 3957
The Lion of Pescara 3958

MacClure, Victor
A Certain Woman: The Story of Mary Magdalene 3959

MacCoun, Catherine
The Age of Miracles 3960

MacDonald, Isobel
The Buried Self: A Background to the Poems of Matthew Arnold 3961

Macdonald, Malcolm
Abigail 3962
All Desires Known 3963
For They Shall Inherit 3964
Goldeneye 3965
Honour and Obey 3966
An Innocent Woman 3967
Kernow & Daughter 3968
A Notorious Woman 3969
On a Far Wide Shore 3970
The Rich Are with You Always 3971
The Silver Highways 3972
Sons of Fortune 3973
Tessa d'Arblay 3974
To the End of Her Days 3975
The Trevarton Inheritance 3976
A Woman Possessed 3977
A Woman Scorned 3978
The World From Rough Stones 3979

MacDonald, Robert S.
The Catherine 3980

MacDonald, William Colt
California Caballero 3981

Machlis, Joseph
The Career of Magda V. 3982

MacInnes, Colin
Three Years to Play 3983
Westward to Laughter 3984

MacIntyre, Lorn
The Blind Bend 3985
Cruel in the Shadow 3986

Mackay, Margaret
The Wine Princes 3987

Mackay, Mary
Barabbas: A Dream of the World's Tragedy 1327

Macken, Walter
The Scorching Wind 3988
Seek the Fair Land 3989
The Silent People 3990

Mackensie, Norman
A Balance of Dangers 2184
Captain Justice 2185
The Pandora Secret 2186

Mackey, Mary
A Grand Passion 3991
The Last Warrior Queen 3992
The Year the Horses Came 3993

Mackin, Jeanne
Dreams of Empire 3994
The Frenchwoman 3995

The Queen's War: A Novel of Eleanor of Aquitaine 3996

MacKinney, Meagan
Fair is the Rose 3997

MacKinnon, Mary Linehan
One Small Candle 3998

Mackintosh, Elizabeth
The Daughter of Time 6209
The Privateer 1510

MacLean, Alistair
Breakheart Pass 3999

Macleod, Alison
The Changeling 4000
City of Light 4001
The Heretic 4002
The Hireling 4003
The Muscovite 4004
The Portingale 4005
Prisoner of the Queen 4006

MacLeod, Le Roy
The Battle-Ax of God 4007
The Crowded Hill 4008
Years of Peace 4009

MacNeil, Duncan
By Command of the Viceroy 4010
Charge of Cowardice 4011
Cunningham's Revenge 4012
Drums Along the Khyber 4013
The Gates of Kunara 4014
Lieutenant of the Line 4015
The Mullah From Kashmir 4016
The Red Daniel 4017
The Restless Frontier 4018
Sadhu on the Mountain Peak 4019
Subaltern's Choice 4020
The Train at Bundarbar 4021
Wolf in the Fold 4022

MacNeil, Robert
Burden of Desire 4023

Madariaga, Salvador de
The Heart of Jade 4024

Maderich, Robin
Faith and Honor 4025

Madl, Linda
Sweet Ransom 4026

Madsen, David
Black Plume: The Supressed Memoirs of Edgar Allan Poe 4027

Magill, Kathleen
Megan 4028

Magnuson, Dorothy Petrie
Orphan Train 4029

Magnuson, James
Orphan Train 4029

Maher, Mary
The Devil's Card 4030

Maiden, Cecil
Harp into Battle 4031
Man Before the Morning 4032

Maier, Paul L.
The Flames of Rome 4033
Pontius Pilate: A Biographical Novel 4034

Mailer, Norman
Ancient Evenings 4035
The Executioner's Song 4036

Main, Mary
The Girl Who Was Never Queen: A Biographical Novel of Princess Charlotte of Wales 4037

Malamud, Bernard
The Fixer 4038

Malgonkar, Manohar
The Devil's Wind: Nana Saheb's Story 4039

Mallet-Joris, Francoise
The Favourite 4040

Malliol, William
Slave 4041

Mallon, Thomas
Henry and Clara 4042

Mallory, Kate
Sarton Kell 4043

Mally, Emma Louise
The Tides of Dawn 4044

Malm, Dorothea
The Paper Mistress 4045
The Woman Question 4046

Malouf, David
An Imaginary Life 4047

Malpass, Eric
The Cleopatra Boy 4048
A House of Women 4049
Sweet Will 4050
The Wind Brings Up the Rain 4051

Malterre, Elona
Mistress of the Eagles 4052

Malvern, Gladys
According to Thomas 4053

Manceron, Claude
So Brief a Spring 4054

Manfred, Frederick F.
Conquering Horse 4055
Lord Grizzly 4056
The Manly-Hearted Woman 4057
Of Lizards and Angels: A Saga of Sioux Land 4058
Riders of Judgment 4059

Mankowitz, Wolf
A Night with Casanova 4060

Mann, Heinrich
Henry, King of France 4061
Young Henry of Navarre 4062

Mann, Helen R.
Gallant Warrior 4063

Mann, Klaus
Pathetic Symphony: A Novel about Tchaikovsky 4064

Mann, Thomas
Joseph of Egypt 4065
Joseph the Provider 4066
Tables of the Law 4067
The Tales of Jacob 4068
Young Joseph 4069

Manners, Alexandra
Cardigan Square 4070
Wilford's Daughter 4071

Manning, Jason
The Border Captains 4072
Flintlock 4073
Gone to Texas 4074
High Country 4075

Mansfield, Helene
Contessa 4076

Manso, Peter
The Shadow of the Moth: A Novel of Espionage with Virginia Woolf 2779

Mantel, Hilary
A Place of Greater Safety 4077

Manzoni, Alessandro
The Betrothed 4078

Marcantel, Pamela
An Army of Angels: A Novel of Joan of Arc 4079

Marchal, Lucien
Sage of Canudos 4080

Marchant, Catherine
Miss Martha Mary Crawford 4081
The Slow Awakening 4082

Marius, Richard
Bound for the Promised Land 4083
The Coming of Rain 4084

Mark, Grace
The Dream Seekers 4085

Markandaya, Kamala
The Golden Honeycomb 4086

Markey, Gene
Kentucky Pride 4087
That Far Paradise 4088

Markey, Morris
The Band Plays Dixie 4089

Markish, David
Jesters 4090

Markstein, George
Tara Kane 4091

Marlowe, Derek
A Single Summer with Lord B. 4092

Marlowe, Stephen
Colossus: A Novel about Goya and a World Gone Mad 4093
The Death and Life of Miguel De Cervantes 4094
The Lighthouse at the End of the World 4095
The Memoirs of Christopher Columbus 4096
The Shining 4097

Marsh, Ellen
If This Be Magic 4098

Marsh, George Tracy
Ask No Quarter 4099

Marsh, Jean
The House of Eliott 4100

Marshall, Edison
American Captain 4101
Benjamin Blake 4102
Caravan to Kanadu: A Novel of Marco Polo 4103
The Conqueror: A Novel of Alexander the Great 4104
Cortez and Marina 4105
Earth Giant 4106
The Infinite Woman 4107
The Lost Colony 4108
The Pagan King 4109
Princess Sophia 4110
Seward's Folly 4111
The Upstart 4112
The Viking 4113
West with the Vikings 4114
Yankee Pasha 4115

Marshall, Evelyn
The House of Eliott 4100

Marshall, Rosamond
Captain Ironhand 4116

Marshall, William
Faces in the Crowd 4117

Marshall-Andrews, Bob
The Palace of Wisdom 4118

Marston, Edward
The Dragons of Archenfield 4119
The Laughing Hangman 4120
The Lions of the North 4121
The Mad Courtesan 4122
The Merry Devils 4123
The Nine Giants 4124
The Queen's Head 4125
The Ravens of Blackwater 4126
The Roaring Boy 4127
The Silent Woman 4128
The Trip to Jerusalem 4129
The Wolves of Savernake 4130

Martin, George R.R.
Fevre Dream 4131

Martin, L. Jay
El Lazo 4132
Rush to Destroy 4133

Martin, Malachi
King of Kings: A Novel of the Life of David 4134

Martin, Sylvia
I, Madame Tussaud 4135

Martin, Valerie
Mary Reilly 4136

Martin, William
Annapolis 4137
Back Bay 4138
Cape Cod 4139
The Rising of the Moon 4140

Marton, Francis
Mrs. Betsy, or Widowed and Wed 4141

Masefield, John
Basilissa: A Tale of the Empress Theodora 4142

Mason, A.E.W.
Fire over England 4143

Mason, Anita
The Illusionist 4144

Mason, F. van Wyck
Armored Giants: A Novel of the Civil War 4145
Blue Hurricane 4146
Brimstone Club 4147
Cutlass Empire 4148
Eagle in the Sky 4149
Golden Admiral 4150
Guns for Rebellion 4151
Harpoon in Eden 4152
Log Cabin Noble 4153
Manila Galleon 4154
Our Valiant Few 4155
Proud New Flags 4156
Rascal's Heaven 4157
Rivers of Glory 4158
The Sea 'Venture 4159
Silver Leopard 4160
Stars on the Sea 4161
Three Harbors 4162
Trumpets Sound No More 4163
Wild Horizon 4164
Young Titan 4165

Mason, Lisa
The Golden Nineties 4166

Massie, Allan
Augustus 4167
Caesar 4168
Tiberius: The Memoirs of the Emperor 4169

Masson, Rene
Landru 4170

Masters, John
By the Green of the Spring 4171
Coromandel! 4172
The Deceivers 4173
Heart of War 4174
The Lotus and the Wind 4175
Nightrunners of Bengal 4176
Now, God Be Thanked 4177
The Ravi Lancers 4178
The Rock: A Novel about Gibraltar 4179

Mather, Berkely
The Midnight Gun 4180
The Pagoda Tree 4181
The Road and the Star 4182

Mathewson, Janet
Michael Torey 4183

Mathieson, Theodore
The Devil and Ben Franklin 4184

Mathiessen, Peter
Killing Mister Watson 4185

Matschat, Cecile Hulse
Preacher on Horseback 4186
Tavern in the Town 4187

Matthew, Anne Irwin
Warm Wind, West Wind 4188

Matthews, Greg
The Further Adventures of Huckleberry Finn 4189
Heart of the Country 4190
Power in the Blood 4191
The Wisdom of Stones 4192

Matthews, Jack
Sassafras 4193

Matturro, Richard
Troy 4194

Maugham, Robert C.R.
The Barrier 4195
The Last Encounter 4196

Maugham, Robin
The Barrier 4195
The Last Encounter 4196

Maugham, William Somerset
Catalina 4197
Then and Now 4198

Maughan, A.M.
Harry of Monmouth 4199
Young Pitt 4200

Maxfield, Karen
Double Masquerade 3938
Dual Destiny 3939
Midsummer Moon 3940
The Rake 3941
The Scottish Marriage 3942

Maxwell, Patricia
The Notorious Angel 4201

May, Beatrice
Sister to Jane: The Story of Lady Katharine Grey 4202

Mayer, Albert
Follow the River 4203

Mayerson, Evelyn Wilde
Miami: A Saga 4204
Princess in Amber 4205

Mayfield, Sara
Mona Lisa: The Woman in the Portrait 4206

Mayhew, Margaret
The Railway King 4207

Maynard, Kenneth
First Lieutenant 4208
Lamb in Command 4209
Lieutenant Lamb 4210

Mayrant, Drayton
Always a River 4211
First the Blade 4212
The Land Beyond the Tempest 4213
The Red Doe 4214
The Running Thread 4215

McAlpine, Gordon
Joy in Mudville 4216

McCague, James
The Fortune Road 4217

McCall, Dan
Beecher: A Novel 4218

McCann, Hugh Wray
''Utmost Fish!'' 4219

McCarry, Charles
The Bride of the Wilderness 4220

McCarthy, Cormac
The Crossing 4221

McCarthy, Gary
The American River 4222
The Gila River 4223
The Russian River 4224

McClelland, Diane
Csardas 4875
The Marigold Field 4876
The Summer of the Bashinskeys 4877

McConnor, Vincent
I Am Vidocq 4225

McCord, Christian
Across the Shining Mountains 4226

McCoy, Iola Fuller
All the Golden Gifts 2251
The Gilded Torch 2252
The Loon Feather 2253
The Shining Trail 2254

McCoy, Max
Sons of Fire 4227

McCraig, Robert
Crimson Creek: A Novel of the Early West 4228

McCreary, Lew
Mount's Mistake 4229

McCriede, Jess
Colorado Ambush 4230

McCrone, Guy
Aunt Bel 4231
Red Plush: The Story of the Moorhouse Family 4232

McCullough, Colleen
Caesar's Women 4233
The First Man in Rome 4234
Fortune's Favorite 4235
The Grass Crown 4236
The Ladies of Missalonghi 4237

McCune, Evelyn
Empress 4238

McCunn, Ruthanne Lum
Thousand Years of Gold 4239

McCutchan, Philip
Apprentice to the Sea 4240
Beware, Beware the Bight of Benin 4241
By Command of the Viceroy 4010
Charge of Cowardice 4011

Cunningham's Revenge 4012
Drums Along the Khyber 4013
The Gates of Kunara 4014
The Guns of Arrest 4242
Halfhyde and the Admiral 4243
Halfhyde and the Chain Gang 4244
Halfhyde and the Flag Captain 4245
Halfhyde and the Fleet Review 4246
Halfhyde for the Queen 4247
Halfhyde Goes to War 4248
The Halfhyde Line 4249
Halfhyde on the Amazon 4250
Halfhyde on Zanatu 4251
Halfhyde Ordered South 4252
Halfhyde to the Narrows 4253
Halfhyde's Island 4254
The Last Farewell 4255
Lieutenant of the Line 4015
The Mullah From Kashmir 4016
Outward Bound 4256
The Red Daniel 4017
The Restless Frontier 4018
Sadhu on the Mountain Peak 4019
The Second Mate 4257
Subaltern's Choice 4020
The Train at Bundarbar 4021
Wolf in the Fold 4022

McCutcheon, George Barr
Viola Gwyn 4258

McDonald, Eva
John Ruskin's Wife 4259
The Lady From Yorktown 4260

McDonald, Kay L.
The Brightwood Expedition 4261
The Vision Is Fulfilled 4262
Vision of the Eagle 4263

McDonald, Roger
1915: A Novel 4264

McDonough, James
The Limits of Glory: A Novel of Waterloo 4265

McEachin, James
Tell Me a Tale: A Novel of the Old South 4266

McEvoy, Marjorie
Camelot Country 4267
Echoes From the Past 4268
The Sleeping Tiger 4269
Star of Randevi 4270
Temple Bells 4271

McFarland, Philip
Seasons of Fear 4272

McGehee, Thomasine
Journey Proud 4273

McGerr, Patricia
Martha, Martha 4274

McGorian, Gladys
The Prince Regent's Silver Bell 4275

McGraw, Eloise Jarvis
Pharaoh 4276

McGregor, Iona
Death Wore a Diadem 4277

McInenly, William
Slave 4041

McIntyre, Margerie
The River Witch 4278

McKay, Allis
The Women at Pine Creek 4279

McKee, Alexander
H.M.S. Bounty 4280

McKee, Ruth Eleanor
Christopher Strange 4281
The Lord's Anointed 4282

McKenney, Ruth
Mirage 4283

McKeown, Martha Ferguson
Mountains Ahead 4284

McLeave, Hugh
A Man and His Mountain: The Life of Paul Cezanne 4285

McLeay, Alison
Passage Home 4286
Sea Change 4287

McMahon, Thomas
Loving Little Egypt 4288
McKay's Bees 4289

McMeekin, Clark
City of the Flags 4290
The Fairbrothers 4291
Reckon with the River 4292
Show Me a Land 4293
Tyrone of Kentucky 4294

McMeekin, Isabel
City of the Flags 4290
The Fairbrothers 4291
Reckon with the River 4292
Show Me a Land 4293
Tyrone of Kentucky 4294

McMurtry, Larry
Anything for Billy 4295
Buffalo Girls 4296
Dead Man's Walk 4297
Lonesome Dove 4298
Pretty Boy Floyd 4299
Streets of Laredo 4300
Zeke and Ned 4301

McNab, Tom
The Fast Men 4302
Flanagan's Run 4303

McNamara, Tom
Henry Lunt and the Ranger 4304

McNamee, Thomas
A Story of Deep Delight 4305

McNarie, Alan Decker
Yeshua: The Gospel of St. Thomas 4306

McNeil, Everett
Daniel Du Luth 4307

McNeilly, Mildred Masterson
Each Bright River 4308
Heaven Is Too High 4309
Praise at Morning 4310

McNeilly, Wilfred
The Men That God Made Mad: A Novel about Ireland's Easter Rising 286

McNeish, James
Lovelock 4311

McSpadden, Joseph Walker
Storm Center: A Novel about Andy Johnson 4312

Meacham, Ellis K.
The East Indiaman 4313
For King and Company 4314
On the Company's Service 4315

Mead, Robert Douglas
Heartland 4316

Meade, Marion
Stealing Heaven: The Love Story of Heloise and Abelard 4317
Sybille 4318

Meader, Stephen Warren
Boy with a Pack 4319

Meadows, Denis
Tudor Underground 4320

Medawar, Mardi Oakley
Death at Rainy Mountain 4321

Medeiros, Teresa
Lady of Conquest 4322

Meeker, Arthur
The Silver Plume 4323

Meggs, Brown
The War Train: A Novel of 1916 4324

Mehta, Gita
Raj 4325

Meigs, Cornelia
Call of the Mountains 4326
Railroad West 4327
Swift Rivers 4328

Melchior, Ib
Eva 4329

Melville, Anne
Alexa 4330
Blaize 4331
The Lorimer Line 4332

Melville, Herman
Billy Budd 4333
Israel Potter 4334

Menen, Aubrey
Fonthill 4335

Mercer, Charles
Enough Good Men 4336

Merezhkovski, Dmitri
Akhnaton, King of Egypt 4337
The Death of the Gods 4338
The Romance of Leonardo Da Vinci 4339

Mergendahl, Charles
The Drums of April 4340

Meriwether, Louise
Fragments of the Ark 4341

Merle, Robert
Vittoria 4342

Merliss, Reuben R.
The Year of the Death 4343

Merritt, Emma
Masque of Jade 4344

Mertz, Barbara
The Curse of the Pharaohs 4948
The Deeds of the Disturber 4949
Greygallows 4359
The Hippopotamus Pool 4950
The Last Camel Died at Noon 4951
Lion in the Valley 4952
The Mummy Case 4953
Patriot's Dream 4360
The Snake, the Crocodile, and the Dog 4954
Wings of the Falcon 4361
The Wizard's Daughter 4362

Metzger, Barbara
The Earl and the Heiress 4345
My Lady Innkeeper 4346
Rake's Ransom 4347

Meyer, Nicholas
The Canary Trainer 4348
The Seven-Per-Cent Solution 4349
The West End Horror 4350

Meyers, Annette
The Dutchman 4351

Author Index

The Dutchman's Dilemma 4352
The High Constable 4353
The House on Mulberry Street 4354
The Kingsbridge Plot 4355

Meyers, Maan
The Dutchman 4351
The Dutchman's Dilemma 4352
The High Constable 4353
The House on Mulberry Street 4354
The Kingsbridge Plot 4355

Meyers, Manny
The Last Mystery of Edgar Allan
    Poe 4356

Meyers, Martin
The Dutchman 4351
The Dutchman's Dilemma 4352
The High Constable 4353
The House on Mulberry Street 4354
The Kingsbridge Plot 4355

Mian, Mary
Young Men See Visions 4357

Michael, Prince of Greece
Sultana 4358

Michaels, Barbara
Greygallows 4359
Patriot's Dream 4360
Wings of the Falcon 4361
The Wizard's Daughter 4362

Michaels, Kasey
Bride of the Unicorn 4363

Michener, James A.
Alaska 4364
Caribbean 4365
Centennial 4366
Chesapeake 4367
The Covenant 4368
The Eagle and the Raven 4369
Hawaii 4370
Journey 4371
Mexico 4372
Poland 4373
The Source 4374
Texas 4375

Miers, Earl Schenck
Valley in Arms: A Novel of the
    Settlement of Connecticut 4376

Miles, Graham
Evil Mark 4377

Miles, Rosalind
I, Elizabeth 4378

**Milkomane, George Alexis
Milkomanovich**
The Emperor Story: A Historical
    Romance 5615

Millar, George
A Crossbowman's Story of the First
    Exploration of the Amazon 4379

Miller, Caroline
Lamb in His Bosom 4380

Miller, Cissie
Tish 4381

Miller, Dallas
Passage West 4382

Miller, Helen Topping
After the Glory 4383
Born Strangers 4384
Christmas at Mount Vernon 4385
Christmas for Tad: A Story of Mary
    and Abraham Lincoln 4386
Christmas with Robert E. Lee 4387
Dark Sails 4388

Her Christmas at the Hermitage: A Tale
    about Rachel and Andrew
    Jackson 4389
Mirage 4390
No Tears for Christmas 4391
Rebellion Road 4392
Shod with Flame 4393
Sing One Song 4394
Slow Dies the Thunder 4395
The Sounds of Chariots: A Novel of
    John Sevier and the State of
    Franklin 4396
Trumpet in the Sky 4397

Miller, Isabel
Patience and Sarah 4398

Miller, Linda Lael
Knights 4399

Miller, May
First the Blade 4400

Miller, Rex
I, Paul 4401

Miller, Stanley
Mr. Christian! 4402

Miller, Teresa
Remnants of Glory 4403

Millett, Larry
Sherlock Holmes and the Red
    Demon 4404

Millin, Sarah Gertrude
King of the Bastards 4405

Mills, Carla J.
Three Rivers 4406

Mills, Charles K.
A Mighty Afternoon 4407

Mills, James R.
The Gospel According to Pontius
    Pilate 4408

Milne, Roseleen
Borrowed Plumes 4409
The Ninth Statue 4410

Minnigerode, Meade
Black Forest 4411
Cockades: A Romance 4412
Cordelia Chantrell 4413

Mitchell, Kirk
Shadow on the Valley 4414

Mitchell, Margaret
Gone with the Wind 4415

Mitchell, Silas Weir
Hugh Wynne, Free Quaker 4416

Mitchison, Naomi
Blood of the Martyrs 4417
The Conquered 4418
The Corn King and the Spring
    Queen 4419

Mittermeyer, Helen
Princess of the Veil 4420

Mo, Timothy
An Insular Position 4421

Moberg, Vilhelm
The Emigrants 4422
Last Letter Home 4423
The Settlers 4424
Unto a Good Land 4425

Moffat, Gwen
The Buckskin Girl: A Novel of the
    California Trail in the Mid-
    Nineteenth Century 4426

Monfredo, Miriam Grace
Blackwater Spirits 4427

North Star Conspiracy 4428
Seneca Falls Inheritance 4429
Through a Gold Eagle 4430

Monsarrat, Nicholas
Darken Ship 4431
Running Proud 4432
The White Rajah 4433

Montague, Jeanne
The Castle of the Winds 4434
The Clock Tower 4435
Midnight Moon 4436

Monterosso, Carlo
The Salt of the Earth 4437

Montgomery, Yvonne
Bridey's Mountain 34

Montupet, Janine
The Lacemaker 4438

Moore, Barbara
The Fever Called Living 4439
Hard on the Road 4440

Moore, Brian
Black Robe 4441

Moore, John Trotwood
Hearts of Hickory 4442

Moore, Ruth
A Fair Wind Home 4443

Moore, Susan
Paths of Fortune 4444
A World Too Wide 4445

Moore, William
Bayonets in the Sun 4446
Bush War! 4447

Moorhouse, Frank
Grand Days 4448

Morazzoni, Marta
The Invention of Truth 4449

Morgan, Cynthia
Court of Shadows 4450

Morgan, Kathleen
Child of the Mist 4451

Morgan, Robert
The Truest Pleasure 4452

Morgan, Speer
Belle Starr 4453

Morike, Eduard Friedrich
Mozart on the Way to Prague 4454

Morley, Iris
We Stood for Freedom 4455

Morrell, David
Last Reveille 4456

Morris, Gilbert
The Captive Bride 4457
A City Not Forsaken 4480
The Crossed Sabres 4458
The Dixie Widow 4459
The Final Adversary 4460
The Gentle Rebel 4461
The Holy Warrior 4462
The Honorable Imposter 4463
The Indentured Heart 4464
The Jewelled Spur 4465
The Last Confederate 4466
The Reluctant Bridegroom 4467
The Rough Rider 4468
The Saintly Buccaneer 4469
Shadow of the Mountains 4481
Song of a Strange Child 4470
Sound of the Trumpet 4471
The Sword of Truth 4472
The Union Belle 4473

The Valiant Gunman 4474
The Wounded Yankee 4475
The Yukon Queen 4476

Morris, Ira J.
The Fortune Hunter 4477
The Rake and the Rebel 4478

Morris, Jane Kesner
Julie 4479

Morris, Kathrine
Death in a Deck Chair 403
Peril under the Palms 404
Young Mrs. Cavendish and the Kaiser's
    Men 405

Morris, Lynn
A City Not Forsaken 4480
Shadow of the Mountains 4481

Morris, Suzanne
Galveston 4482
Keeping Secrets 4483

Morrison, Gerry
Unvexed to the Sea: A Novel of the
    Vicksburg Campaign 4484

Morrison, Lester M.
Trail and Triumph: A Novel about
    Maimonides 4485

Morrison, Margaret Mackie
The Countess 1360
I, Rachel 1361

Morrow, Honore
Beyond the Blue Sierra 4486
Forever Free 4487
The Last Full Measure 4488
Let the King Beware! 4489
On to Oregon! 4490
We Must March: A Novel of the
    Winning of Oregon 4491
With Malice Toward None 4492

Morson, Ian
Falconer's Crusade 4493
Falconer's Judgement 4494

Mortimer, John
Will Shakespeare: The Untold
    Story 4495

Morton, Stanley
Yankee Trader 4496

Moss, Robert
Fire Along the Sky: A Novel of
    America 4497
The Firekeeper 4498
The Interpreter 4499

Mossinsohn, Igal
Judas 4500

Motley, Annette
Green Dragon, White Tiger 4501
The Quickenberry Tree 4502
The Sins of the Lion 4503

Mountjoy, Roberta Jean
Night Wind 4504

Mourad, Kenize
Regards From the Dead Princess: A
    Novel of a Life 4505

Moxon, Lloyd M.
Before the Wind 4506

Mudgett, Helen Parker
The Sea Stands Watch 4507

Muir, Marie
Dear Mrs. Boswell 4508

Muir, Robert
The Sprig of Hemlock: A Novel about
    Shays' Rebellion 4509

Mukherjee, Bharati
The Holder of the World 4510

Mullally, Frederic
Hitler Has Won 4511

Mullally, Margaret
*A Crown in Darkness: A Novel about
Lady Jane Grey* 4512

Mullins, Edwin
The Master Painter 4513

Mundy, Talbot
Purple Pirate 4514
Tros of Samothrace 4515

Munn, H. Warner
The Lost Legion 4516

Muntz, Hope
*The Golden Warrior: The Story of
Harold and William* 4517

Murari, T.N.
The Imperial Agent 4518
The Last Victory 4519

Murphy, Clyde Francis
Glittering Hill 4520

Murphy, Edward Francis
Angel of the Delta 4521
A Bride for New Orleans 4522
Road From Olivet 4523
The Scarlet Lily 4524

Murphy, James F. Jr.
They Were Dreamers 4525

Murphy, Walter F.
*Upon This Rock: The Life of St.
Peter* 4526

Murray, D.L.
Commander of the Mists 4527
Trumpeter, Sound! 4528

Murray, Earl
Free Flows the River 4529
High Freedom 4530
Song of Wovoka 4531
Thunder in the Dawn 4532

Murray, Frances
The Belchamber Scandal 4533
Brave Kingdom 4534
Castaway 4535
The Heroine's Sister 4536

Murray, Linda
The Dark Fire 4537

Mydans, Shelley
*Thomas: A Novel of the Life, Passions,
and Miracles of Becket* 4538
The Vermilion Bridge 4539

Myers, Amy
Murder Makes an Entree 4540

Myers, Henry
Our Lives Have Just Begun 4541
Signorina 4542

Myers, John
The Harp and the Blade 4543
I, Jack Swilling 4544
Out on Any Limb 4545
The Wild Yazoo 4546

Myers, Leopold Hamilton
The Near and the Far 4547

Myers, Robert J.
The Cross of Frankenstein 4548
The Slave of Frankenstein 4549

Myers, Virginia
This Land I Hold 4550

N

Nagaya, Yoshiro
Bronze Christ 4551

Nahai, Gina Barkhordar
Cry of the Peacock 4552

Names, Larry D.
The Cowboy Conspiracy 4553
Ironclads: Man-of-War 4554

Napier, Priscilla
Imperial Winds 4555

Nash, N. Richard
Behold the Man 4556

Naslund, Sena Jeter
Sherlock in Love 4557

Nason, Tema
*Ethel: The Fictional
Autobiography* 4558

Nathan, Robert
The Fair 4559

Naylor, Charles
Neighboring Lives 1648

Neagoe, Peter
*The Saint of Montparnasse: A Novel
Based on the Life of Constantin
Brancusi* 4560

Neale, Linda
The Briar Rose 4561

Neider, Charles
*The Authentic Death of Hendry
Jones* 4562

Neilan, Sarah
An Air of Glory 4563
The Braganza Pursuit 4564
The Old Enchantment 4565
Paradise 4566

Neill, Robert
Black William 4567
Elegant Witch 4568
The Golden Days 4569
Hangman's Cliff 4570
Lillibullero 4571
The Mills of Colne 4572
Rebel Heiress 4573
Traitor's Moon 4574

Neilson, Frances Fullerton
Edge of Greatness 4575

Neilson, Winthrop
Edge of Greatness 4575

Nelson, Betty Palmer
Private Knowledge 4576
Pursuit of Bliss 4577

Nelson, Edna Deu Pree
O'Higgins and Don Bernardo 4578

Nelson, James L.
By Force of Arms 4579
The Maddest Idea 4580

Nelson, Ray Faraday
Dogheaded Death 4581

Nelson, Truman
The Sin of the Prophet 4582
The Surveyor 4583

Neumann, Alfred
The Gaudy Empire 4584
The Rebels 4585

Nevin, David
1812 4586
Dream West 4587

New, Christopher
Shanghai 4588

Newcomb, Kerry
The Ghosts of Elkhorn 4589
Hearts of Fire 5616
In the Season of the Sun 4590
Ride of the Panther 4591
Scalpdancers 4592
Sword of Vengeance 4593
Warriors of the Night 4594

Newman, Kim
Anno-Dracula 4595
The Bloody Red Baron 4596

Newman, Sharan
The Chessboard Queen 4597
Death Comes as Epiphany 4598
The Devil's Door 4599
Guinevere 4600
Guinevere Evermore 4601
Strong as Death 4602
The Wandering Arm 4603

Newsom, Ed
Wagons to Tucson 4604

Newton, John Edward
The Rogue and the Witch 4605

Nezelof, Pierre
Mirabeau, Lover and Stateman 4606
Napoleon and His Son 4607

Ngagoyeanes, Nicholas
The Bourlotas Fortune 2268

Nicholas, Roland
Who Came by Night 4608

Nicholson, Christina
The Power and the Passion 4609

Nicholson, Meredith
The Cavalier of Tennessee 4610

Nickell, Lesley J.
The White Queen 4611

Nicol, C.W.
Harpoon 4612

Nicole, Christopher
Black Dawn 4613
Brumaire 3864
Caribee 4614
The Devil's Own 4615
Guillotine 3865
Iron Ships, Iron Men 4616
Love and Honor 189
Mistress of Darkness 4617
Old Glory 4618
The Power and the Passion 4609
Ratoon 4619
The Regiment 4620
The Sea and the Sand 4621
*The Secret Memoirs of Lord
Byron* 4622
Sunset 4623
Tricolour 3866
Wind of Destiny 4624

Nicolson, Catherine
Miss Nobody 5465

Nievo, Ippolito
The Castle of Fratta 4625

Niles, Blair
East by Day 4626
*Passengers to Mexico: The Last
Invasion of Mexico* 4627

Nissenson, Hugh
My Own Ground 4628
The Tree of Life 4629

Nisser, Peter William
The Red Marten 4630

Niven, Marian
The Altar and the Crown 4631

Noble, Hollister
*Woman with a Sword: The Biographical
Novel of Anna Ella Carroll of
Maryland* 4632

Noble, Marguerite
*Filaree: A Novel of an American
Life* 4633

Nolan, Frederick
White Nights, Red Dawn 4634

Nolan, William F.
The Black Mask Murderers 4635

Noonan, Michael
The Sun Is God 4636

Nordhoff, Charles
Botany Bay 4637
Men Against the Sea 4638
Mutiny on the Bounty 4639
Pitcairn's Island 4640

Norfolk, Lawrence
Lempriere's Dictionary 4641
The Pope's Rhinoceros 4642

Norman, Charles
Mr. Oddity, Samuel Johnson 4643

Norman, Diana
Fitzempress' Law 4644
The Morning Gift 4645

Norman, Rick
Fielder's Choice 4646

Norris, Kathleen
Certain People of Importance 4647

North, Sterling
*The Wolfling: A Documentary Novel of
the 1870s* 4648

Norton, Andre
Empire of the Eagle 4649

Norton-Taylor, Duncan
*God's Man: A Novel on the Life of
John Calvin* 4650

Nutt, Francis Tysen
Three Fields to Cross 4651

Nye, Nelson Coral
Pistols for Hire 4652

Nye, Robert
Falstaff 4653
Faust 4654
The Memoirs of Lord Byron 4655
*Mrs. Shakespeare: The Complete
Works* 4656
The Voyage of the Destiny 4657

O

Oates, Joyce Carol
A Bloodsmoor Romance 4658
Mysteries of Winterthurn 4659

Obenzinger, Hilton
*Cannibal Eliot and the Lost Histories of
San Francisco* 4660

O'Brian, Patrick
The Commodore 4661
Desolation Island 4662
The Far Side of the World 4663
The Fortune of War 4664
The Golden Ocean 4665

H.M.S. Surprise 4666
The Ionian Mission 4667
The Letter of Marque 4668
Master and Commander 4669
The Mauritius Command 4670
The Nutmeg of Consolation 4671
Post Captain 4672
The Reverse of the Medal 4673
The Surgeon's Mate 4674
The Thirteen Gun Salute 4675
Treason's Harbour 4676
The Truelove 4677
The Unknown Shore 4678
The Wine-Dark Sea 4679
The Yellow Admiral 4680

O'Brien, Kate
For One Sweet Grape 4681

O'Brien, Saliee
Farewell the Stranger 4682

O'Brien, Vincent
The White Cockade 4683

O'Connor, Richard
Company Q 4684
Guns of Chickamauga 4685
Officers and Ladies 4686
The Vandal 4687

O'Daniel, Janet
O Genesee 4688

O'Dell, Scott
Hill of the Hawk 4689

O'Doherty, Brian
The Strange Case of Madamoiselle P. 3109

Oemler, Marie
The Holy Lover 4690

O'Faolain, Julia
Women in the Wall 4691

O'Faolain, Sean
A Nest of Simple Folk 4692

O'Flaherty, Liam
Famine 4693

Ogilvie, Elisabeth
Jennie about to Be 4694
Jennie Glenroy 4695
The World of Jennie G. 4696

Ogley, Dorothy
Iron Land 4697

O'Grady, Leslie
The Artist's Daughter 4698
Lady Jane 4699
Lord Raven's Widow 4700
The Second Sister 4701

O'Grady, Rohan
O'Houlihan's Jest 4702

O'Hara, John
From the Terrace 4703
Ourselves to Know 4704

Oke, Janette
A Bride for Donnigan 4705
The Calling of Emily Evans 4706
Drums of Change: The Story of Running Fawn 4707
Julia's Last Hope 4708
They Called Her Mrs. Doc 4709
Too Long a Stranger 4710
A Woman Named Damaris 4711

Okudzhava, Bulat
The Extraordinary Adventures of Secret Agent Shipov in Pursuit of Count Leo Tolstoy in the Year 1862 4712

Oldenbourg, Zoe
Cities of the Flesh 4713
The Cornerstone 4714
Destiny of Fire 4715
The Heirs of the Kingdom 4716

Older, Cora
Savages and Saints 4717

Olds, Bruce
Raising Holy Hell 4718

Oliver, Jane
Alexander the Glorious 4719
The Blue Heaven Bends Over All 4720
Candleshine No More 4721
Flame of Fire 4722
Isle of Glory 4723
The Lion and the Rose 4724
The Lion Is Come 4725
Mine Is the Kingdom 4726
Sing Morning Star 4727
Sunset at Noon 4728

Oliver, Marina
Masquerade for the King 4729

Olsen, Theodore
There Was a Season: A Biographical Novel of Jefferson Davis 4730

Olson, Toby
The Life of Jesus: An Apocryphal Novel 4731

Oman, Carola
Crouchback 4732

O'Meara, Walter
The Devil's Cross 4733
The Duke of War 4734
The Spanish Bride 4735

Ondaatje, Michael
Coming through Slaughter 4736

O'Neal, Cothburn
Hagar 4737
Master of the World 4738
Untold Glory 4739
Very Young Mrs. Poe 4740

O'Neal, Reagan
The Fallon Blood 4741
The Fallon Pride 4742

O'Neill, Charles Kendall
Morning Time 4743

Onstott, Kyle
Drum 4744

Orczy, Baroness Emma
The Scarlet Pimpernel 4745
A Spy for Napoleon 4746
The Uncrowned King 4747

Orde, Lewis
Dreams of Gold 4748
Heritage 4749
The Lion's Way 4750

Ormonde, Czenzi
Solomon and the Queen of Sheba 4751

O'Rourke, Frank
Far Mountains 4752
A Mule for the Marquesa 4753

Orr, Myron David
The Citadel of the Lakes 4754
Mission to Mackinac 4755

Ortega, Isabel
Street of the Madwoman 4756

Orwig, Sara
Albuquerque 4757

Osborn, Karen
Between Earth and Sky 4758

Osborne, Anne
Wind From the Main 4759

Osborne, Maggie
Chase the Heart 4760

Osgood, Claude Jack
Eagle of the Gredos 4761

O'Shaughnessy, Michael
Monsieur Moliere 4762

Oskison, John
Black Jack Davy 4763
Brothers Three 4764

Ossana, Diana
Pretty Boy Floyd 4299
Zeke and Ned 4301

Ostlere, Gordon
Jack the Ripper 2484
The Private Life of Florence Nightingale 2485
The Sleep of Life 2486

O'Toole, G.J.A.
The Cosgrove Report 4765
Poor Richard's Game 4766

Ouida
Under Two Flags 4767

Overgard, William
A Few Good Men 4768
Shanghai Tango: A Novel of China 4769

Ovstedal, Barbara
Banners of Silk 3592
A Cadenza for Caruso 4834
A Chorus of Detectives 4835
Circle of Pearls 3593
Claudine's Daughter 3594
Devil's Fire, Love's Revenge 4836
The French Woman 4837
Gilded Splendour 3595
The Golden Tulip 3596
Jewelled Path 3597
Prima Donna at Large 4838
Ride the Blue Riband 3598
The Silver Touch 3599
The Sugar Pavilion 3600
To Dance with Kings 3601
To Love a Stranger 4839
Tree of Gold 3602
The Venetian Mask 3603
Warwyck's Woman 3604
What the Heart Keeps 3605

Owen, Dean
The Sam Houston Story 4770

Owens, William A.
Look to the River 4771

Oxnam, Robert B.
Ming: A Novel of Seventeeth Century China 4772

P

Page, Elizabeth
The Tree of Liberty 4773
Wilderness Adventure 4774

Paige, Robin
Death at Daisy's Folly 4775
Death at Gallows Green 4776

Paine, Lauran
Exiled 3007

Painter, Eleanor
Spring Symphony 4777

Pall, Ellen Jane
The Autumn Rose 2923
The Country Gentleman 2924
The Stanbroke Girls 2925
Sweet's Folly 2926

Palliser, Charles
The Quincunx 4778

Palmer, Bruce
Horseshoe Bend 4779

Palmer, John Leslie
So Great a Man 5000

Palmer, Marian
The White Boar 4780
The Wrong Plantagenet 4781

Palmer, William J.
The Detective and Mr. Dickens 4782
The Highwayman and Mr. Dickens 4783
The Hoydens and Mr. Dickens 4784

Panger, Daniel
Joanna the Pope 4785
Ol' Prophet Nat 4786

Paradise, Jean
The Savage City 4787

Paradise, Mary
Siege in the Sun 4788

Paradise, Viola
Tomorrow the Harvest 4789

Paretti, Sandra
The Drums of Winter 4790
The Magic Ship 4791
The Rose and the Sword 4792
Tenants of the Earth 4793
The Wishing Tree 4794

Pargeter, Edith
The Bloody Field 4795
Brother Cadfael's Penance 4955
The Brothers of Gwynedd 4796
The Confessions of Brother Halvin 4956
Dead Man's Ransom 4957
The Devil's Novice 4958
An Excellent Mystery 4959
The Heaven Tree Trilogy 4797
The Heretic's Apprentice 4960
The Hermit of Eyton Forest 4961
The Holy Thief 4962
Hortensius, Friend of Nero 4798
The Leper of St. Giles 4963
The Marriage of Meggotta 4799
Monk's Hood 4964
A Morbid Taste for Bones 4965
One Corpse Too Many 4966
The Pilgrim of Hate 4967
The Potter's Field 4968
The Raven in the Foregate 4969
The Rose Rent 4970
St. Peter's Fair 4971
The Sanctuary Sparrow 4972
The Summer of the Danes 4973
The Virgin in the Ice 4974

Parini, Jay
Bay of Arrows 4800
The Last Station 4801

Park, Paul
The Gospel of Corax 4802

Parker, Cornelia Stratton
Fabulous Valley 4803

Parker, F.A.
The Predators 4804

Parker, Gilbert
The Power and the Glory 4805

Parker, Norton S.
Table in the Wilderness 4806

Parker, Robert B.
Perchance to Dream 4807

Parker, Thomas Trebitsch
Anna, Ann, Annie 4808

Parkinson, C. Northcote
Dead Reckoning 4809
Devil to Pay 4810
The Fireship 4811
The Guernseyman 4812
The Life and Times of Horatio Hornblower 4813
So Near So Far 4814
Touch and Go 4815

Parotti, Phillip
Fires in the Sky 4816
The Greek Generals Talk: Memoirs of the Trojan War 4817
The Trojan Generals Talk: Memoirs of the Greek War 4818

Parrish, Anne
A Clouded Star 4819

Parry, Richard
The Winter Wolf: Wyatt Earp in Alaska 4820

Partington, Norman
Master of Bengal: A Novel of Robert Clive of India 4821
The Sunshine Patriot: A Novel of Benedict Arnold 4822

Partridge, Bellamy
The Big Freeze 4823

Pasternak, Boris
Doctor Zhivago 4824

Patai, Irene Steinman
The Valley of God 4825

Pater, Walter
Marius the Epicurean 4826

Paterson, Isabel
The Fourth Queen 4827

Paterson, Katherine
Rebels of the Heavenly Kingdom 4828

Paton Walsh, Gillian
Farewell Great King: A Novel of Ancient Greece 4829

Paton Walsh, Jill
Farewell Great King: A Novel of Ancient Greece 4829

Patrick, William
Blood Winter 4830

Patten, Lewis B.
Red Runs the River 4831

Patterson, Harry
Dillinger 4832
Luciano's Luck 2912

Patterson, Orlando
Die the Long Day 4833

Paul, Barbara
A Cadenza for Caruso 4834
A Chorus of Detectives 4835
Devil's Fire, Love's Revenge 4836
The French Woman 4837
Prima Donna at Large 4838
To Love a Stranger 4839

Paul, Charlotte
The Cup of Strength 4840
Gold Mountain 4841

Paul, Louis
Dara, the Cypriot 4842

Paul, Raymond
The Thomas Street Horror 4843
The Tragedy at Tinkerton: An Historical Novel of Murder 4844

Pauley, Barbara Anne
Blood Kin 4845

Paxson, Diana L.
The Serpent's Tooth 4846
The White Raven 4847
The Wolf and the Raven 4848

Payne, Robert
Alexander the God 4849
Blood Royal 4850
Caravaggio 4851
The Chieftain: A Story of the Nez Perce People 4852
Concord Bridge 3035
A House in Peiking 4853
The Lord Jesus 4854
O Western Wind 1634
The Shepherd 4855
The Yellow Robe: A Novel of the Life of Buddha 4856
The Young Emperor 4857

Pazzi, Roberto
Searching for the Emperor 4858

Peacock, Max
The King's Rogue 4859

Pearce, Mary E.
Apple Tree Lean Down 4860
Cast a Long Shadow 4861
The Land Endures 4862
Polsinney Harbour 4863
Seedtime and Harvest 4864
The Two Farms 4865

Pearce, Michael
The Mamur Zapt and the Donkey-Vous 4866
The Mamur Zapt and the Girl in the Nile 4867
The Mamur Zapt and the Men Behind 4868
The Mamur Zapt and the Night of the Dog 4869
The Mamur Zapt and the Return of the Carpet 4870
The Mamur Zapt and the Spoils of Egypt 4871

Pearce, Richard
The Impudent Rifle 4872
The Restless Border 4873

Pearsall, Robert Brainard
Young Vargas Lewis 4874

Pearson, Diane
Csardas 4875
The Marigold Field 4876
The Summer of the Bashinskeys 4877

Pearson, John
The Bellamy Saga 4878

Pearson, Michael
The Store 4879

Peattie, Donald Culross
Forward the Nation 4880
Up Country: A Story of the Vanguard 4881

Peck, Richard
Amanda/Miranda 4882
The Family of Women 4883

Peck, Robert Newton
Eagle Fur 4884

Fawn 4885
Hang for Treason 4886
The Horse Hunters 4887
The King's Iron 4888

Peeples, Samuel Anthony
The Dream Ends in Fury 4889

Pei, Mario
Swords of Anjou 4890

Pell, Sylvia
The Shadow of the Sun 4891

Pella, Judith
The Crown and the Crucible 4987
The Dawning of Deliverance 4892
Heirs of the Motherland 4893
A House Divided 4988
My Father's World 4989
Travail and Triumph 4991

Pendexter, Hugh
Harry Idaho 4894
Kings of the Missouri 4895
Old Misery 4896
Red Belts 4897
The Red Road: A Romance of Braddock's Defeat 4898
A Virginia Scout 4899

Pendleton, Tom
The Seventh Girl: A Romantic Tale of Civil War Texas 4900

Penfield, Wilder
No Other Gods 4901
The Torch 4902

Penman, Sharon Kay
Falls the Shadow 4903
Here Be Dragons 4904
The Queen's Man 4905
The Reckoning 4906
The Sunne in Splendour 4907
When Christ and His Saints Slept 4908

Pennell, Joseph Stanley
The History of Rome Hanks 4909

Pennypacker, Isaac Rusling
The Redemptioner 4910

Perenyi, Eleanor
The Bright Sword 4911

Perez Galdos, Benito
Saragossa 4912

Perkins, Jacob Randolph
Antioch Actress: A Novel of Pagan Against Christian 4913
The Emperor's Physician 4914

Perowne, Barry
A Singular Conspiracy 4915

Perrault, E.G.
The Kingdom Carver 4916

Perreard, Suzanne Butler
My Pride, My Folly 830
Vale of Tyranny 831

Perrin, Robert
Jewels 4917

Perry, Albert
The Scandalous Mrs. Blackford 3358

Perry, Anne
Ashworth Hall 4918
Belgrave Square 4919
Bethlehem Road 4920
Bluegate Fields 4921
Cain and His Brother 4922
Callander Square 4923
Cardington Crescent 4924
The Cater Street Hangman 4925

A Dangerous Mourning 4926
Death in the Devil's Acre 4927
Defend and Betray 4928
The Face of a Stranger 4929
Farriers' Lane 4930
Highgate Rise 4931
Paragon Walk 4932
Pentecost Alley 4933
Resurrection Row 4934
Rutland Place 4935
Silence in Hanover Close 4936
The Sins of the Wolf 4937
A Sudden, Fearful Death 4938
Traitors Gate 4939

Perutz, Kathrin
Reigning Passions 4940

Perutz, Leo
Leonardo's Judas 4941
The Marquis of Bolibar 4942
The Swedish Cavalier 4943

Pesci, David
Amistad: The Thunder of Freedom 4944

Peters, Daniel
The Incas 4945
The Luck of Huemac: A Novel about the Aztecs 4946
Tikal: A Novel about the Maya 4947

Peters, Elizabeth
The Curse of the Pharaohs 4948
The Deeds of the Disturber 4949
The Hippopotamus Pool 4950
The Last Camel Died at Noon 4951
Lion in the Valley 4952
The Mummy Case 4953
The Snake, the Crocodile, and the Dog 4954

Peters, Ellis
Brother Cadfael's Penance 4955
The Confessions of Brother Halvin 4956
Dead Man's Ransom 4957
The Devil's Novice 4958
An Excellent Mystery 4959
The Heretic's Apprentice 4960
The Hermit of Eyton Forest 4961
The Holy Thief 4962
The Leper of St. Giles 4963
Monk's Hood 4964
A Morbid Taste for Bones 4965
One Corpse Too Many 4966
The Pilgrim of Hate 4967
The Potter's Field 4968
The Raven in the Foregate 4969
The Rose Rent 4970
St. Peter's Fair 4971
The Sanctuary Sparrow 4972
The Summer of the Danes 4973
The Virgin in the Ice 4974

Peters, Maureen
Henry VIII and His Six Wives 4975
Katheryn, the Wanton Queen 4976
The Love Knot 1482

Peterson, Nis
Street of the Sandalmakers: A Tale of Rome in the Time of Marcus Aurelius 4977

Petrie, Glen
The Branch-Bearers 4978
The Fourth King 4979
Hand of Glory 4980
Marianne 4981

Phillips, Alexandra
Forever Possess 4982

Phillips, Caryl
Cambridge 4983
Crossing the River 4984

Phillips, Jill M.
The Rain Maiden 4985
Walford's Oak 4986

Phillips, Michael
The Crown and the Crucible 4987
A House Divided 4988
My Father's World 4989
Sea to Shining Sea 4990
Travail and Triumph 4991

Pick, J.B.
The Last Valley 4992

Pick, Robert
The Escape of Socrates 4993

Pickerell, Rodney R.
Across the Shining Mountains 4226

Pidoll, Carl von
Eroica: A Novel about Beethoven 4994

Pier, Arthur Stanwood
The Young Man From Mount Vernon 4995

Pierce, Glenn
The Tyrant of Bagdhad 4996

Pierce, Ovid Williams
On a Lonesome Porch 4997

Piercy, Marge
City of Darkness, City of Light 4998

Pietri, Arturo Uslar
The Red Lances 4999

Pilgrim, David
So Great a Man 5000

Pilpel, Robert H.
Between Eternities 5001
To the Honor of the Fleet 5002

Pinckney, Josephine
Hilton Head 5003

Plaidy, Jean
The Bastard King 5004
The Battle of the Queens 5005
Beyond the Blue Mountains 5006
The Captive of Kensington Palace 5007
The Captive Queen of Scots 5008
Caroline the Queen 5009
The Courts of Love 5010
Daughter of Satan 5011
Epitaph for Three Women 5012
Evergreen Gallant 5013
The Follies of the King 5014
Gay Lord Robert 5015
Goddess of the Green Room 5016
The Goldsmith's Wife 5017
Hammer of the Scots 5018
A Health Unto His Majesty 5019
The Heart of the Lion 5020
Here Lies Our Sovereign Lord 5021
In the Shadow of the Crown 5022
It Began in Vauxhall Gardens 5023
The Italian Woman 5024
Katharine: The Virgin Widow 5025
The King's Pleasure 5026
The King's Secret Matter 5027
The Lady in the Tower 5028
Light on Lucrezia 5029
Lilith 5030
The Lion of Justice 5031
Louis the Well-Beloved 5032
Madame Serpent 5033
Madonna of the Seven Hills 5034
The Murder in the Tower 5035

Murder Most Royal 5036
Myself My Enemy 5037
Passage to Pontefract 5038
The Passionate Enemies 5039
Perdita's Prince 5040
The Plantagenet Prelude 5041
The Pleasures of Love 5042
The Prince and the Quakeress 5043
The Prince of Darkness 5044
The Princess of Celle 5045
The Queen and Lord M 5046
The Queen From Provence 5047
Queen in Waiting 5048
Queen Jezebel 5049
Queen of This Realm: The Story of Queen Elizabeth I 5050
The Queen's Favourites 5051
The Queen's Husband 5052
The Queen's Secret 5053
Red Rose of Anjou 5054
The Regent's Daughter 5055
The Reluctant Queen: The Story of Anne of York 5056
The Revolt of the Eaglets 5057
The Rose Without a Thorn 5058
Royal Road to Fotheringay 5059
St. Thomas's Eve 5060
The Scarlet Cloak 5061
The Shadow of the Pomegranate 5062
The Sixth Wife 5063
The Spanish Bridegroom 5064
The Star of Lancaster 5065
The Sun in Splendour 5066
Sweet Lass of Richmond Hill 5067
The Third George 5068
The Thistle and the Rose 5069
The Three Crowns 5070
Uneasy Lies the Head 5071
Victoria in the Wings 5072
Victoria Victorious 5073
The Vow on the Heron 5074
The Wandering Prince 5075
The Widow of Windsor 5076
William's Wife 5077

Plain, Belva
Crescent City 5078

Player, Robert
Oh! Where Are Bloody Mary's Earrings? 5079

Pleasants, Henry
Mars' Butterfly 5080

Poirier, Leon
Saint Paul: A Historical Novel of His Life 5081

Poldermans, Joost
Vincent: A Novel Based on the Life of Van Gogh 5082

Poling, Daniel A.
He Came From Galilee 5083

Polland, Madeleine
All Their Kingdoms 5084
No Price Too High 5085
Sabrina 5086

Pollard, Frank
East Indiaman 5087

Pollock, Alyce
Don Gaucho 5088

Ponce de Leon, Napoleon Baccino
Five Black Ships: A Novel of Discoverers 5089

Ponicsan, Darryl
Tom Mix Died for Your Sins 5090

Poole, Ernest
The Nancy Flyer 5091

Poole, Gray
The Magnificent Traitor: A Novel of Alcibiades and the Golden Age of Pericles 5092

Poole, Lynn
The Magnificent Traitor: A Novel of Alcibiades and the Golden Age of Pericles 5092

Pope, Dudley
Buccaneer 5093
Drumbeat 5094
Galleon 5095
Governor Ramage, R.N. 5096
Ramage 5097
Ramage and the Dido 5098
Ramage and the Guillotine 5099
Ramage and the Rebels 5100
Ramage and the Saracens 5101
Ramage at Trafalgar 5102
The Ramage Touch 5103
Ramage's Devil 5104
Ramage's Diamond 5105
Ramage's Mutiny 5106
Ramage's Prize 5107
Ramage's Signal 5108
Ramage's Trial 5109
The Triton Brig 5110

Pope, Edith
River in the Wind 5111

Porter, Donald
Jubilee Jim and the Wizard of Wall Street 5112

Porter, Donald Clayton
Ambush 5113
Apache 5114
Cherokee 5115
Choctaw 5116
Father and Son 5117
Father of Waters 5118
Hawk's Journey 5119
Manitou 5120
Red Stick 5121
The Renegade 5122
Renno 5123
The Sachem 5124
Sachem's Son 5125
Seminole 5126
Seneca 5127
Spirit Knife 5128
Tomahawk 5129
War Chief 5130
War Clouds 5131
War Cry 5132
War Drums 5133
White Indian 5134

Porter, Jane
The Scottish Chiefs 5135
Thaddeus of Warsaw 5136

Porter, Margaret Evans
Heiress of Ardara 5137

Porteus, Stanley David
Restless Voyage 5138

Portis, Charles
True Grit 5139

Posse, Abel
Daimon 5140
The Dogs of Paradise 5141

Potter, Jeremy
The Dance of Death 5142
A Trail of Blood 5143

Potter, Margaret
Alexa 4330
Blaize 4331
The Lorimer Line 4332

Pouillon, Fernand
The Stones of the Abbey 5144

Pound, Arthur
Hawk of Detroit 5145

Powell, Deborah
Bayou City Secrets 5146

Powell, Richard
I Take This Land 5147
Whom the Gods Would Destroy 5148

Powell, William
The First Casualty 5149

Powers, Anne
The Ironmaster 5150
No King but Caesar 5151
No Wall So High 5152
Rachel 5153
Ride East! Ride West!: A Romance of the Hundred Years' War 5154
The Thousand Fires 5155

Powers, Tim
On Stranger Tides 5156
The Stress of Her Regard 5157

Pownall, David
The White Cutter 5158

Powys, John Cowper
Owen Glendower 5159

Poyer, David
The Only Thing to Fear 5160

Poyer, Joe
Devoted Friends 5161

Pozzessere, Heather Graham
And One Rode West 2514
And One Wore Gray 2515
Love Not a Rebel 2516
One Wore Blue 2517
A Pirate's Pleasure 2518
Princess of Fire 1718
Runaway 2519
The Viking's Woman 2520

Prantera, Amanda
The Side of the Moon 5162

Pratolini, Vasco
Metello 5163

Pratt, Theodore
Seminole 5164

Prebble, John
The Buffalo Soldiers 5165

Prentiss, Charlotte
Children of the Ice 5166
Children of the Sun 5167
People of the Mesa 5168

Prescott, H.F.M.
The Lost Flight 5169
The Man on a Donkey 5170
Son of Dust 5171
The Unhurrying Chase 5172

Prescott, John
Journey by the River 5173

Preston, Don
Crazy Fox Remembers 5174

Preston, Hugh
Feast in the Morning 5175

Preston, Sue
Crazy Fox Remembers 5174

Price, Charles F.
Hiwassee: A Novel of the Civil War 5176

Price, Eugenia
Beauty From Ashes 5177

Before Darkness Falls 5178
The Beloved Invader 5179
Bright Captivity 5180
Don Juan McQueen 5181
Lighthouse 5182
Margaret's Story 5183
Maria 5184
New Moon Rising 5185
Savannah 5186
Stranger in Savannah 5187
To See Your Face Again 5188
Where Shadows Go 5189

Price, Jeramie
Katrina 5190

Price, Willard
The Barbarian 5191

Pridgen, Tim
West Goes the Road 5192

Priley, Margaret Hubbard
Flight of the Swan 3063

Prokosch, Frederic
The Dark Dancer 5193
The Missolonghi Manuscript 5194
A Tale for Midnight 5195

Prole, Lozania
The Little Victoria 5196
Marlborough's Unfair Lady 5197
Sweet Marie-Antoinette 5198
The Ten-Day Queen 5199

Pronzini, Bill
Firewind 5200
The Gallows Land 5201
The Hangings 5202
*The Last Days of Horse-Shy
    Halloran* 5203

Pryor, Elinor
And Never Yield 5204
The Double Man 5205

Pugh, John J.
Captain of the Medici 5206
High Carnival 5207

Pullinger, Kate
The Piano 878

Pulse, Charles K.
John Bonwell 5208

Purtscher-Wydenbruch, Nora
Woman Astride 5209

Pushkin, Alexander
The Captain's Daughter 5210

Putnam, Nina Wilcox
The Inner Voice 5211

Pye, Michael Kenneth
The Drowning Room 5212

Q

Quick, Amanda
Dangerous 5213
Deception 5214
Mistress 5215
Ravished 5216
Reckless 5217
Rendezvous 5218
Scandal 5219
Seduction 5220
Surrender 5221

Quick, Herbert
The Hawkeye 5222
Vandemark's Folly 5223

Quigley, John
King's Royal 5224
Queen's Royal 5225

Quiller-Couch, Sir Arthur Thomas
Castle Dor 5226

Quinn, Peter
Banished Children of Eve 5227

Quoirez, Francoise
The Still Storm 5562

R

Raddall, Thomas H.
The Governor's Lady 5228
Hangman's Beach 5229
His Majesty's Yankees 5230
Pride's Fancy 5231
Roger Sudden 5232

Radin, Max
Epicurus My Master 5233

Rae, Catherine M.
Afterward 5234
Flight From Fifth Avenue 5235
Sarah Cobb 5236
The Ship's Clock 5237

Rae, Hugh C.
The Asking Price 6039
Call Home the Heart 6040
Creature Comforts 6041
The Dark Pasture 6042
The Good Provider 6043
*Harkfast: The Making of the
    King* 5238
Hearts of Gold 6044
Lantern for the Dark 6045
The Marrying Kind 6046
The Penny Wedding 6047
*The Rookery: A Novel of the Victorian
    Underworld* 5239
Shadows on the Shore 6048
Treasures on Earth 6049
The Welcome Light 6050

Ragosta, Millie J.
Druid's Enchantment 5240
Gerait's Daughter 5241
The House on Curtin Street 5242
The Winter Rose 5243
Witness to Treason 5244

Rand, James S.
The Great Sky and the Silence 5245

Randall, Rona
Dragonmede 5246
The Drayton Legacy 5247
The Eagle at the Gate 5248
The Ladies of Hanover Square 5249
The Mating Dance 5250

Randisi, Robert J.
The Ham Reporter 5251

Randle, Kevin D.
Spanish Gold 5252

Ransmayr, Christoph
*The Last World: A Novel with an
    Ovidian Repertory* 5253

Rascovich, Mark
Falkenhorst 5254

Rattray, Everett
*The Adventures of Jeremiah Dimon:
    The Novel of Old East
    Hampton* 5255

Rayford, Julian Lee
*Child of the Snapping Turtle, Mike
    Fink* 5256

Raymo, Chet
*In the Falcon's Claw: A Novel of the
    Year 1000* 5257

Raymond, Ernest
A Georgian Love Story 5258

Rayner, Claire
Bedford Row 5259
Charing Cross 5260
Chelsea Reach 5261
Covent Garden 5262
The Enduring Years 5263
Gower Street 5264
The Haymarket 5265
Paddington Green 5266
Piccadilly 5267
Soho Square 5268
The Strand 5269

Rayner, D.A.
The Long Fight 5270

Rayner, William
*The Knifeman: A Novel of Judas
    Iscariot* 5271
The Last Days 5272
The World Turned Upside Down 5273

Raynes, Jean
Legacy of the Wolf 5274

Raynolds, Robert
The Sinner of Saint Ambrose 5275

Rayson, Steven
The Crows of War 5276

Read, Piers Paul
The Free Frenchman 5277
Polonaise 5278

Reade, Charles
The Cloister and the Hearth 5279
Griffith Gaunt 5280
Peg Woffington 5281

Reasoner, James M.
Cannon's Call 5537
Life and Liberty 5538
Rebel Guns 5539
Sons of Liberty 5540
Stars and Stripes 5541

Reasoner, Livia
Dead-Stick 6574
Dog Heavies 6575

Rebolledo, Francisco
Rasero 5282

Receveur, Betty Layman
Kentucky Home 5283
Oh, Kentucky! 5284

Reed, Ishmael
Flight to Canada 5285

Reed, Walter
She Rode a Yellow Stallion 5286

Reeman, Douglas E.
Badge of Glory 5287
Colors Aloft! 3427
Command a King's Ship 3428
Enemy in Sight! 3429
The First to Land 5288
The Flag Captain 3430
Form Line of Battle! 3431
Honor This Day 3432
In Gallant Company 3433
The Inshore Squadron 3434
*Midshipman Bolitho and the
    Avenger* 3435
Passage to Mutiny 3436

Richard Bolitho—Midshipman 3437
Signal—Close Action! 3438
Sloop of War 3439
Stand into Danger 3440
Success to the Brave 3441
To Glory We Steer 3442
A Tradition of Victory 3443

Rees, Gilbert
I Seek a City 5289

Rees, Helen Christina
Alexander the Glorious 4719
*The Blue Heaven Bends Over
    All* 4720
Candleshine No More 4721
Flame of Fire 4722
Isle of Glory 4723
The Lion and the Rose 4724
The Lion Is Come 4725
Mine Is the Kingdom 4726
Sing Morning Star 4727
Sunset at Noon 4728

Rees, Joan
The Queen of Hearts 5290

Reid, Victor Stafford
New Day 5291

Reife, A.R.
Salt Lake City 5292

Reilly, Robert
The God of Mirrors 5293

Reinhardt, Richard
The Ashes of Smyrna 5294

Renault, Mary
The Bull From the Sea 5295
Fire From Heaven 5296
Funeral Games 5297
The King Must Die 5298
The Last of the Wine 5299
The Mask of Apollo 5300
The Persian Boy 5301
The Praise Singer 5302

Rendell, Ruth
Anna's Book 6500

Renek, Morris
Bread and Circus 5303

Reniers, Perceval
Roses From the South 5304

Reno, Marie R.
When the Music Changed 5305

Rhodes, Evan H.
An Army of Children 5306

Rhodes, James A.
*The Court Martial of Commodore
    Perry* 5307
Johnny Shiloh 5308
The Trial of Mary Todd Lincoln 5309

Rhodes, Jewell Parker
*Voodoo Dreams: A Novel of Marie
    Laveau* 5310

Rhodes, Richard
*The Ungodly: A Novel of the Donner
    Party* 5311

Rhys, Jean
Wide Sargasso Sea 5312

Rice, Anne
Cry to Heaven 5313
The Feast of All Saints 5314
*The Mummy; or Ramses the
    Damned* 5315

Rice, Robert
The Last Pendragon 5316

Rice, Sile
The Saxon Tapestry 5317

Richards, Elizabeth
The Ravishers 5318

Richter, Conrad
The Fields 5319
Free Man 5320
The Lady 5321
The Light in the Forest 5322
The Sea of Grass 5323
Tacey Cromwell 5324
The Town 5325
The Trees 5326

Ridge, Antonia
The Royal Pawn 5327

Riefe, Barbara
For Love of Two Eagles 5328
Mohawk Woman 5329
*The Woman Who Fell From the
  Sky* 5330

Rigney, James O.
The Fallon Blood 4741
The Fallon Pride 4742

Rikhoff, Jean
Buttes Landing 5331
One of the Raymonds 5332
The Sweetwater 5333

Riley, Judith Merkle
In Pursuit of the Green Lion 5334
The Oracle Glass 5335
The Serpent Garden 5336
A Vision of Light 5337

Ripley, Alexandra
Charleston 5338
From Fields of Gold 5339
A Love Divine 5340
New Orleans Legacy 5341
Scarlett 5342
The Time Returns 5343

Ripley, Clements
*Clear for Action: A Novel about John
  Paul Jones* 5344
Gold Is Where You Find It 5345
Mississippi Belle 5346

Rising, Clara
In the Season of the Wild Rose 5347

Ritchie, C.T.
Black Angels 5348
The Willing Maid 5349

Ritter, Margaret
Women in the Wind 5350

Rivele, Stephen J.
*A Booke of Days: A Journal of the
  Crusade by Roger, Duke of
  Lunel* 5351

Rivers, Francine
As Sure as the Dawn 5352

Roa Bastos, Augusto Antonio
I, the Supreme 5353

Roark, Garland
Fair Wind to Java 5354
Hellfire Jackson 5355
*The Lady and the Deep Blue
  Sea* 5356
Rainbow in the Royals 5357
*Star in the Rigging: A Novel of the
  Texas Navy* 5358
The Witch of Manga Reva 5359

Roarke, Mike
Shadows on the Long House 5360
Silent Drums 5361
Thunder in the East 5362

Robards, Karen
Nobody's Angel 5363

Robb, Candace M.
The Apothecary Rose 5364
The King's Bishop 5365
The Lady Chapel 5366
The Nun's Tale 5367

Robbins, David L.
Apache Blood 6250
Blackfoot Massacre 6251
Blood Fury 6252
Blood Truce 6253
Hawken Fury 6254
King of the Mountain 6255
Lure of the Wind 6256
Mountain Devil 6257
Northwest Passage 6258
Tenderfoot 6259
Tomahawk Revenge 6260
Trapper's Blood 6261
Winterkill 6262

Roberson, Jennifer
Lady of the Forest 5368
Lady of the Glen 5369

Roberts, Ann Victoria
Louisa Elliott 5370
Morning's Gate 5371

Roberts, Carey
*Tidewater Dynasty: A Biographical
  Novel of the Lees of Stratford
  Hall* 5372

Roberts, Cecil
The Remarkable Young Man 5373

Roberts, Cynthia S.
The Fox-Red Hills 5374

Roberts, Dorothy James
Fire in the Ice 5375
Kinsmen of the Grail 5376
Return of the Stranger 5377

Roberts, Elizabeth Madox
The Great Meadow 5378

Roberts, John Maddox
The Catiline Conspiracy 5379
The Sacrilege 5380
SPQR 5381
The Temple of the Muses 5382

Roberts, Kenneth
Arundel 5383
Boon Island 5384
Captain Caution 5385
The Lively Lady 5386
Lydia Bailey 5387
Northwest Passage 5388
Oliver Wiswell 5389
Rabble in Arms 5390

Roberts, Richard Emery
The Gilded Rooster 5391

Roberts, Walter Adolphe
Creole Dusk 5392
Royal Street 5393
The Single Star 5394

Robertson, Constance
Fire Bell in the Night 5395
The Golden Circle 5396
The Unterrified 5397

Robertson, Don
By Antietam Creek 5398
Paradise Falls 5399
Prisoner of Twilight 5400
The River and the Wilderness 5401
The Three Days 5402

Robinson, Chaille Howard
Dominic 5405
Heaven's Only Daughter 5406

Robinson, Derek
Goshawk Squadron 5403
War Story: A Novel 5404

Robinson, Kathleen
Dominic 5405
Heaven's Only Daughter 5406

Robinson, Lynda S.
*Murder at the Feast of
  Rejoicing* 5407
Murder at the God's Gate 5408
Murder in the Place of Anubis 5409

Robinson, Margaret A.
Courting Emma Howe 5410

Robinson, Rony
The Beano 5411

Robinson, Suzanne
Lady Defiant 5412
Lady Gallant 5413
Lady Hellfire 5414

Robson, Lucia St. Clair
Mary's Land 5415
Ride the Wind 5416
*The Tokaido Road: A Novel of Feudal
  Japan* 5417
Walk in My Soul 5418

Rock, Phillip
Flickers 5419
A Future Arrived 5420
The Passing Bells 5421

Rocquet, Claude Henri
*Bruegel, or, The Workshop of
  Dreams* 5422

Rodman, Howard A.
Destiny Express 5423

Roesch, E.P.
Ashana 5424

Roesch, Ethel
Ashana 5424

Roesch, Paul
Ashana 5424

Rofheart, Martha
The Alexandrian 5425
Fortune Made His Sword 5426
Glendower Country 5427
*Lionheart!: A Novel of Richard I, King
  of England* 5428
My Name Is Sappho 5429
The Savage Brood 5430

Rogers, Garet
Lancet 5431

Rogers, Gayle
The Second Kiss 5432

Rogers, Marian H.
Diamond Head 3135
The Sunken Treasure 3136

Rohrbach, Peter-Thomas
*Bold Encounter: A Novel Based on the
  Life of St. John of the Cross* 5433

Rolvaag, O.E.
Giants in the Earth 5434
Peder Victorious 5435
Their Fathers' God 5436

Ronalds, Mary Teresa
Nero 5437

Rooke, Daphne
Wizards' Country 5438

Rooke, Leon
Shakespeare's Dog 5439

Roome, Katherine A. Davis
Lucifer Land 1538

Rooney, Philip
*Captain Boycott, a Romantic
  Novel* 5440
The Golden Coast 5441

Roosevelt, Elliott
A First Class Murder 5442
The Hyde Park Murder 5443
Murder and the First Lady 5444
Murder at the Palace 5445
Murder in the Blue Room 5446
Murder in the Chateau 5447
Murder in the East Room 5448
*Murder in the Executive
  Mansion* 5449
Murder in the Oval Office 5450
Murder in the Red Room 5451
Murder in the Rose Garden 5452
Murder in the West Wing 5453
New Deal for Death 5454
The President's Man 5455
A Royal Murder 5456
*The White House Pantry
  Murder* 5457

Roosevelt, James
A Family Matter 5458

Root, Corwin
An American, Sir 5459

Roripaugh, Robert A.
Honor Thy Father 5460

Rose, Geoffrey
A Clear Road to Archangel 5461

Rosen, Norma
*John and Anzia: An American
  Romance* 5462

Ross, Ann B.
The Pilgrimage 5463

Ross, Bette M.
Gennie the Huguenot Woman 5464

Ross, Caroline
Miss Nobody 5465

Ross, Dana Fuller
Arizona! 5466
California! 5467
California Glory 5468
Carolina Courage 5469
Celebration! 5470
Colorado! 5471
Dakota! 5472
Expedition! 5473
Homecoming 5474
Illinois! 5475
Independence! 5476
Kentucky! 5477
Louisiana! 5478
Montana! 5479
Nebraska! 5480
Nevada! 5481
Oklahoma! 5482
Oklahoma Pride 5483
Oregon! 5484
Oregon Legacy 5485
Outpost! 5486
Pacific Destiny 5487
Sierra Triumph 5488
Tennessee! 5489
Texas! 5490
Washington! 5491
Westward! 5492
Wisconsin! 5493
Wyoming! 5494

Yankee 5495
Yankee Rogue 5496

Ross, David William
Beyond the Stars 5497
Eye of the Hawk 5498

Ross, Hugh Williamson
James, by the Grace of God 5499

Ross, Kate
A Broken Vessel 5500
Cut to the Quick 5501
Whom the Gods Love 5502

Ross, Malcolm
The Dukes: A Novel 5503

Ross, Robert
The Medici Emerald 6851
The Medici Guns 6852
The Medici Hawks 6853

Ross, Zola Helen
The Green Land 5504
A Land to Tame 5505

Ross-Macdonald, Malcolm
The Dukes: A Novel 5503

Rossiter, Leonard
Bernadin, My Love 5506

Rossner, Judith
Emmeline 5507

Roszak, Theodore
The Memoirs of Elizabeth Frankenstein 5508

Rothberg, Abraham
The Sword of the Golem 5509

Rotondi, Cesar J.
The Garden of Persephone 5510

Rousselot, Jean
Hungarian Rhapsody: The Life of Franz Liszt 5511

Routsong, Alma
Patience and Sarah 4398

Rovit, Earl
Crossings 5512

Rowe, Jack
Brandywine 5513
Dominion 5514
Fortune's Legacy 5515

Rowe, Patricia
Children of the Dawn 5516
Keepers of the Misty Time 5517

Rowell, Adelaide C.
On Jordan's Stormy Banks 5518

Rowland, Laura Joh
Bundori 5519
Shin Ju 5520

Rowland, Peter
The Disappearance of Edwin Drood 5521

Rucker, Helen
Cargo of Brides 5522

Rudigoz, Roger
French Dragoon 5523

Rundell, E. Ralph
The Color of Blood 5524

Rundle, Anne
Cardigan Square 4070
Wilford's Daughter 4071

Rusch, Kristine Kathryn
The Gallery of His Dreams 5525

Rush, William
Red Fox of the Kinapoo 5526

Rushing, Jane Gilmore
Covenant of Grace 5527
Hope of Earth 5528
Mary Dove 5529
Tamzen 5530
Walnut Grove 5531
Winds of Blame 5532

Russell, Pamela Redford
The Woman Who Loved John Wilkes Booth 5533

Russell, Ray
Princess Pamela 5534

Rutherfurd, Edward
Russka: The Novel of Russia 5535
Sarum: The Novel of England 5536

Rutledge, Adam
Cannon's Call 5537
Life and Liberty 5538
Rebel Guns 5539
Sons of Liberty 5540
Stars and Stripes 5541

Ryan, Edward J.
Comes an Echo on the Breeze 5542

Ryckmans, Pierre
The Death of Napoleon 3768

Rydberg, Viktor
The Last Athenian 5543

Ryman, Rebecca
Olivia and Jai 5544
The Veil of Illusion 5545

S

Sabatini, Rafael
Captain Blood 5546
The Carolinian 5547
Chivalry 5548
Columbus: A Romance 5549
The Gamester 5550
The Hounds of God 5551
King's Minion 5552
Master-At-Arms 5553
Scaramouche 5554
Scaramouche the King-Maker 5555
Venetian Masque 5556

Saberhagen, Fred
Seance for a Vampire 5557

Safford, Henry Barnard
That Bennington Mob 5558
Tory Tavern 5559
Tristram Bent 5560

Safire, William
Freedom 5561

Sagan, Francoise
The Still Storm 5562

St. Clair, Leonard
The Seadon Fortune 5563

St. John, Nicole
Wychwood 5564

Salisbury, Carola
An Autumn in Araby 5565
A Certain Splendour 5566
Count Vronsky's Daughter 5567
Dark Inheritance 5568
Dolphin Summer 5569
The Pride of the Trevallions 5570
The Shadowed Spring 5571
The Winter Bride 5572

Sallaska, Georgia
Three Ships and Three Kings 5573

Sallis, Susan
April Rising 5574

Salvato, Sharon
The Drums of December 5575
The Fires of July 5576
Scarborough House 5577

Samkange, Stanlake
On Trial for My Country 5578

Samuel, Maurice
The Second Crucifixion 5579
Web of Lucifer: A Novel of the Borgia Fury 5580

Sanchez, Thomas
Rabbit Boss 5581

Sand, George
Consuelo 5582

Sandburg, Carl
Remembrance Rock 5583

Sanders, Jacquin
Look to Your Geese: A Novel of the Deflowering of New England 5584

Sanders, Joan
Baneful Sorceries, or The Countess Bewitched 5585
The Marquis 5586

Sanders, John
A Firework for Oliver 5587

Sanders, Lawrence
The Dream Lover 6392

Sanders, Leonard
Fort Worth 5588
Light on the Mountain 5589
Star of Empire: A Novel of Old San Antonio 5590

Sandmel, Samuel
Alone Atop the Mountain 5591

Sandoz, Mari
Miss Morissa: Doctor of the Gold Trail 5592
Son of the Gamblin' Man: The Youth of an Artist 5593

Sanford, John A.
Song of the Meadowlark 5594

Sarabande, William
Beyond the Sea of Ice 5595
Corridor of Storms 5596
The Edge of the World 5597
Face of the Rising Sun 5598
Forbidden Land 5599
The Sacred Stones 5600
Shadow of the Watching Star 5601
Thunder in the Sky 5602
Walkers of the Wind 5603
Wolves of the Dawn 5604

Sargent, Lynda
Judith Duchesne 5605

Sargent, Pamela
Ruler of the Sky: A Novel of Genghis Khan 5606

Sass, Herbert Ravenel
Look Back to Glory 5607

Satterthwait, Walter
Miss Lizzie 5608
Wilde West 5609

Saunders, Diana
The Passion of Letty Fox 5610

Saunders, Kate
Night Shall Overtake Us 5611

Saunders, Raymond M.
Fenwick Travers and the Forbidden Kingdom 5612
Fenwick Travers and the Panama Canal 5613
Fenwick Travers and the Years of Empire 5614

Sava, George
The Emperor Story: A Historical Romance 5615

Savage, Christina
Hearts of Fire 5616

Savage, Douglas
The Court Martial of Robert E. Lee 5617
The Sons of Grady Rourke 5618

Savage, Elizabeth
Willowwood 5619

Savage, Les Jr.
Doniphan's Ride 5620
The Royal City 5621

Saxton, Judith
Ralegh's Fair Bess: The Story of Bess Throckmorton 6365

Saylor, Carol
The Equinox: A Novel of Rome in the Time of Commodus 5622

Saylor, Steven
Arms of Nemesis 5623
Catalina's Riddle 5624
A Murder on the Appian Way 5625
Roman Blood 5626
The Venus Throw 5627

Scalzo, John
A Prince, a Piper, and a Rose 5628

Scarfoglio, Carlo
The True Cross 5629

Schachner, Nathan
By the Dim Lamps 5630
The King's Passenger 5631
The Sun Shines West 5632
The Wanderer: A Novel of Dante and Beatrice 5633

Schaefer, Frank
The Ghosts of Elkhorn 4589
Hearts of Fire 5616

Schaefer, Jack
Company of Cowards 5634
Monte Walsh 5635

Schaeffer, Susan Fromberg
Time in Its Flight 5636

Schemm, Mildred W.
If a Lion Could Talk 6532

Schindall, Henry
Let the Spring Come 5637

Schlee, Ann
The Proprietor 5638
Rhine Journey 5639

Schmirger, Gertrud
Gregory the Great 1913

Schmitt, Gladys
Confessors of the Name 5640
David the King 5641
The Godforgotten 5642
Rembrandt 5643

Schnabel, Ernst
The Voyage Home 5644

Schoell, Yvonne
The Argonauts 5645

Schoeman, Karel
Another Country 5646

Schofield, Susan Clark
Refugio, They Named You Wrong 5647
Telluride 5648

Schofield, William Greenough
Ashes in the Wilderness 5649
The Deer Cry 5650

Scholefield, Alan
The Alpha Raid 5651
The Eagles of Malice 5652
Fire in the Ice 5653
Great Elephant 5654
The Hammer of God 5655
Lion in the Evening 5656
The Lost Giants 5657
Wild Dog Running 5658

Schonthan, Gaby von
Madame Casanova 5659
The Rose of Malmaison: The Turbulent Life of the Beautiful Josephine 5660

Schoonover, Lawrence
The Burnished Blade 5661
The Chancellor 5662
The Gentle Infidel 5663
The Golden Exile 5664
The Prisoner of Tordesillas 5665
The Queen's Cross: A Biographical Romance of Queen Isabella of Spain 5666
The Revolutionary 5667
The Spider King 5668
To Love a Queen 5669

Schorr, Mark
Bully! 5670

Schreiner, Samuel A. Jr.
Angelica 5671
Thine Is the Glory 5672

Schultz, Duane Philip
Glory Enough for All: The Battle of the Crater 5673

Schumann, Mary
My Blood and My Treasure 5674
Strife Before Dawn 5675

Schwaller de Lubicz, Isha
Her-Bak: The Living Face of Ancient Egypt 5676

Schwartz, Anne Powers
The Ironmaster 5150
No King but Caesar 5151
No Wall So High 5152
Rachel 5153
Ride East! Ride West!: A Romance of the Hundred Years' War 5154
The Thousand Fires 5155

Schwartz, George
Minna's Story: The Secret Love of Doctor Sigmund Freud 1463

Schwartz, Kathleen
Minna's Story: The Secret Love of Doctor Sigmund Freud 1463

Schwartz, Susan
Shards of Empire 5677

Sciascia, Leonardo
The Council of Europe 5678

Scott, Joanna
Arrogance 5679
The Closest Possible Union 5680

Scott, Leslie
Tombstone Showdown 5681

Scott, Paul
The Day of the Scorpion 5682
A Division of the Spoils 5683
The Jewel in the Crown 5684
The Towers of Silence 5685

Scott, Reva
Samuel Brannan and the Golden Fleece 5686

Scott, Virgil
I, John Mordaunt 5687

Scott, Sir Walter
The Abbot 5688
Anne of Geierstein 5689
The Antiquary 5690
The Betrothed 5691
The Black Dwarf 5692
The Bride of Lammermoor 5693
Castle Dangerous 5694
Count Robert of Paris 5695
The Fortunes of Nigel 5696
Guy Mannering 5697
The Heart of Midlothian 5698
Ivanhoe 5699
Kenilworth 5700
The Monastery 5701
Old Mortality 5702
Peveril of the Peak 5703
The Pirate 5704
Quentin Durward 5705
Red Gauntlet 5706
Rob Roy 5707
The Talisman 5708
Waverley 5709
Woodstock; or, The Cavalier 5710

Scruggs, Philip Lightfoot
Man Cannot Tell 5711

Seaman, Donald
Chase Royal 5712

Sebestyen, Ouida
Words by Heart 5713

Sedgewick, Catharine Maria
Hope Leslie; or, Early Times in Massachusetts 5714

Sedley, Kate
Death and the Chapman 5715
The Eve of Saint Hyacinth 5716
The Holy Innocents 5717
The Plymouth Cloak 5718
The Weaver's Tale 5719

See, Carolyn
Lotus Land 2917

Seely, Rebecca
Fire in the Ice 5375
Tidewater Dynasty: A Biographical Novel of the Lees of Stratford Hall 5372

Segal, Brenda Lesley
If I Forget Thee 5720
The Tenth Measure 5721

Seidick, Kathryn
Bride of the Unicorn 4363

Seidman, Robert J.
One Smart Indian 5722

Seifert, Shirley
By the King's Command 5723
Captain Grant 5724
Destiny in Dallas 5725
Farewell, My General 5726
Let My Name Stand Fair 5727
Look to the Rose 5728
The Medicine Man 5729
Never No More: The Story of Rebecca Boone 5730

The Proud Way 5731
River out of Eden 5732
The Senator's Lady 5733
Those Who Go Against the Current 5734
The Three Lives of Elizabeth 5735
The Turquoise Trail 5736
Waters of the Wilderness 5737
The Wayfarer 5738

Sela, Owen
The Petrograd Consignment 5739

Selby, John
Elegant Journey 5740

Selinko, Annemarie
Desiree 5741

Seltzer, Richard
The Name of Hero 5742

Selwyn, Francis
Cracksman on Velvet 5743
Sergeant Verity and the Blood Royal 5744
Sergeant Verity and the Imperial Diamond 5745
Sergeant Verity Presents His Compliments 5746

Sennett, Richard
Palais-Royale 5747

Seton, Anya
Avalon 5748
Devil Water 5749
Dragonwyck 5750
Green Darkness 5751
Katherine 5752
My Theodosia 5753
The Winthrop Woman 5754

Settle, Mary Lee
Know Nothing 5755
O Beulah Land 5756
Prisons 5757
The Scapegoat 5758

Seward, Florence A.
Gold for the Caesars 5759

Seymour, Miranda
The Bride of Sforza 5760
Count Manifred 5761
Daughter of Shadows 5762
The Goddess 5763
Medea 5764

Shaara, Jeff
Gods and Generals 5765

Shaara, Michael
The Killer Angels 5766

Shadbolt, Maurice
Monday's Warriors 5767
Season of the Jew 5768

Shaftel, George
Golden Shore 5769

Shalev, Meir
Esau 5770

Shamir, Moshe
David's Stranger 5771
The King of Flesh and Blood 5772

Shannon, Dell
The Dispossessed 5773
The Scalpel and the Sword 5774

Shannon, Doris
Beyond the Shining Mountains 5775
Cain's Daughters 5776
Hawthorn Hill 5777

Shaw, Margaret
Inherit the Earth 5778

Shaw, Patricia
Cry of the Rain Bird 5779
The Feather and the Stone 5780
Where the Willows Weep 5781

Shaw, Stanley
Sherlock Holmes Meets Annie Oakley 5782

Shay, Edith
The Private Adventures of Captain Shaw 5783

Shea, Robert
Shike: Time of Dragons 5784

Shears, J.A.
Fire in the Sky 5785

Sheean, Vincent
Beware of Caesar 5786
A Day of Battle 5787

Shelby, Graham
The Cannaway Concern 5788
The Cannaways 5789
The Devil Is Loose 5790
The Kings of Vain Intent 5791
The Knights of Dark Renown 5792
The Wolf at the Door 5793

Shellabarger, Samuel
Captain From Castile 5794
The King's Cavalier 5795
Lord Vanity 5796
Prince of Foxes 5797
Tolbecken 5798

Shelton, Gene
Brazos Dreamer 5799
Captain Jack 5800
Last Gun: The Legend of John Selman 5801
Rawhider 5802
Tascosa Gun: The Story of Jim East 5803

Sheppard, Stephen
The Four Hundred 5804

Sherburne, James
Hacey Miller 5805
Poor Boy and a Long Way Home 5806
The Way to Fort Pillow 5807

Sheridan, Anne-Marie
The Far-Off Rhapsody 5808
Summoned to Darkness 5809

Sheridan, Jane
Damaris 5810
Love at Sunset 5811
My Lady Hoyden 5812

Sherman, Dan
The Man Who Loved Mata Hari 5813
The Traitor 5814

Sherman, Delia
The Porcelain Dove 5815

Sherman, Jory
The Arkansas River 5816
Eagles of Destiny 5817
The Grass Kingdom 5818
Horne's Law 5819
The Medicine Horn 5820
Rio Grande 5821
Song of the Cheyenne 5822
Trapper's Moon 5823

Sherwood, Frances
Vindication 5824

Sherwood, Valerie
Lisbon 5825

Shine, Frances L.
Conjuror's Journal 5826

Shipway, George
Free Lance 5827
The Imperial Governor 5828
The Knight 5829
The Paladin 5830

Shore, Maxine
The Captive Princess 5831

Shorris, Earl
Under the Fifth Sun: A Novel of Pancho Villa 5832

Shorthouse, John Henry
John Inglesant 5833

Shrake, Edwin
Blessed McGill 5834

Shreve, Susan Richards
Daughters of the New World 5835

Shrimsley, Bernard
Lion Rampant 5836

Shuler, Linda Lay
Let the Drum Speak: A Novel of Ancient America 5837
She Who Remembers 5838
Voice of the Eagle 5839

Shulman, Sandra
The Florentine 5840

Shuster, George Nauman
Look Away! 5841

Shwartz, Susan
Empire of the Eagle 4649

Siciliano, Sam
The Angel of the Opera: Sherlock Holmes Meets the Phantom of the Opera 5842

Sidney, William
The Good Tidings 5843

Siegel, Benjamin
A Kind of Justice 5844
The Sword and the Promise 5845

Sienkiewicz, Henryk
The Deluge 5846
Fire in the Steppe 5847
Quo Vadis 5848
The Teutonic Knights 5849
With Fire and Sword 5850

Silman, Roberta
Beginning the World Again 5851

Silver, Alfred
Lord of the Plains 5852

Silverberg, Robert
Gilgamesh the King 5853
Lord of Darkness 5854

Simms, William Gilmore
The Yemassee 5855

Simon, Edith
The Golden Hand 5856
The Twelve Pictures 5857

Simon, S.J.
No Bed for Bacon 640

Simonhoff, Harry
And Abram Journeyed 5858

Simons, Katherine Drayton Mayrant
Always a River 4211
First the Blade 4212
The Land Beyond the Tempest 4213
The Red Doe 4214
The Running Thread 4215

Simpson, Evan John
Crippled Splendour 3219
King's Masque 3220
Ride Home Tomorrow 3221

Simpson, Rosemary
The Seven Hills of Paradise 5859

Sims, Marian
Beyond Surrender 5860

Sinclair, Harold
The Cavalryman 5861
The Horse Soldiers 5862
Westward the Tide 5863

Sinclair, James
Canis the Warrior 5864
Warrior Queen 5865

Sinclair, Kathleen H.
The Covenant 3521
Not by Any Single Man 3522
The Valiant Lady 3523
Westward the Sun 3524

Singer, Isaac Bashevis
The Slave 5866

Singmaster, Elsie
A High Wind Rising 5867
I Speak for Thaddeus Stevens 5868
Loving Heart 5869
Swords of Steel 5870

Sizer, Mona Young
Masque of Sapphire 3156

Skelton, C.L.
Beloved Soldiers 5871
Hardacre 5872
The Maclarens 5873
The Regiment 5874

Skimin, Robert
Apache Autumn 5875
Chikara! 5876
Gray Victory 5877
Ulysses: A Biographical Novel 5878

Skinner, Constance
Becky Landers, Frontier Warrior 5879

Skinner, June O'Grady
O'Houlihan's Jest 4702

Skvorecky, Josef
The Bride of Texas 5880
Dvorak in Love 5881

Slate, Sam J.
As Long as the Rivers Run 5882

Slaughter, Frank G.
Buccaneer Surgeon 6205
Constantine: The Miracle of the Flaming Cross 5883
The Curse of Jezebel: A Novel of the Biblical Queen of Evil 5884
David: Warrior and King 5885
The Deadly Lady of Madagascar 6206
Divine Mistress 5886
Flight From Avatchez 5887
The Galileans 5888
God's Warrior 5889
Golden Isle 5890
In a Dark Garden 5891
Lorena 5892
The Mapmaker: A Novel of the Days of Prince Henry, the Navigator 5893
The Passionate Rebel 5894
Pilgrims in Paradise 5895
The Purple Quest: A Novel of Seafaring Adventure in the Ancient World 5896

The Road to Bithynia: A Novel of Luke, the Beloved Physician 5897
Sangaree 5898
Scarlet Cord: A Novel of the Woman of Jericho 5899
The Sins of Herod: A Novel of Rome and the Early Church 5900
The Song of Ruth: A Love Story of the Old Testament 5901
The Stonewall Brigade: A Novel of the American Civil War 5902
Storm Haven 5903
The Stubborn Heart 5904
The Thorn of Arimathea 5905
Upon This Rock: A Novel of Simon Peter, Prince of Apostles 5906

Sledge, Linda Ching
Empire of Heaven 5907

Slotkin, Richard
The Crater 5908
The Return of Henry Starr 5909

Small, Bertrice
Lost Love Found 5910
A Moment in Time 5911
The Spitfire 5912
To Love Again 5913
Wild Jasmine 5914

Smiley, Jane
The Greenlanders 5915

Smith, A.C.H.
Edward and Mrs. Simpson 5916

Smith, Arthur Douglas
The Doom Trail 5917
Hate 5918

Smith, Chard Powers
Artillery of Time 5919

Smith, Frederic E.
Waterloo 5920

Smith, Herbert Francis
Hidden Victory: A Novel of Jesus 5921

Smith, Katharine
The Private Adventures of Captain Shaw 5783

Smith, Kay Nolte
A Tale of the Wind: A Novel of Nineteenth-Century France 5922

Smith, Martin Cruz
Rose 5923
Stallion Gate 5924

Smith, Mary-Ann Tirone
Masters of Illusion: A Novel of the Connecticut Circus Fire 5925

Smith, Mason McCann
When the Emperor Dies 5926

Smith, Wilbur
Men of Men 5927
River God 5928
The Roar of the Thunder 5929
Shout at the Devil 5930
When the Lion Feeds 5931

Smith, William Fielding
Diamond Six 5932

Smythe, David Mynders
Golden Venus 5933

Snedeker, Caroline
The Beckoning Road 5934
Uncharted Ways 5935

Snelling, Lauraine
An Untamed Land 5936

Snow, Donald Clifford
The Justicer 2010

Sohl, Jerry
Night Wind 4504

Soister, Helena
Prophecies 5937

Sole, Linda
The Last Summer of Innocence 5938

Solmssen, Arthur R.G.
A Princess in Berlin 5939

Solomon, Ruth Freeman
The Candlesticks and the Cross 5940

Solon, Gregory
The Three Legions 5941

Solzhenitsyn, Alexander
August 1914 5942
Lenin in Zurich 5943

Somerlott, Robert
Death of the Fifth Sun 5944

Somtow, S.P.
The Shattered Horse 5945

Sontag, Susan
The Volcano Lover 5946

Soos, Troy
Murder at Ebbets Field 5947
Murder at Fenway Park 5948
Murder at Wrigley Field 5949

Sorensen, Virginia
Kingdom Come 5950

Southon, Arthur E.
On Eagles' Wings 5951

Southwold, Stephen
So Perish the Roses 423

Southworth, John V.D.
The Pirate From Rome 5952

Spalding, Albert
A Fiddle, a Sword, and a Lady 5953

Speare, Elizabeth
The Prospering 5954

Spearman, Frank H.
Carmen of the Rancho 5955

Speas, Jan Cox
Bride of the MacHugh 5956
My Lord Monleigh 5957
My Love, My Enemy 5958

Spellman, Cathy Cash
An Excess of Love 5959
Paint the Wind 5960

Spence, Hartzell
Bride of the Conqueror 5961
Vain Shadow 5962

Sperry, Armstrong
No Brighter Glory 5963

Spicer, Bart
Brother to the Enemy 5964
The Day Before Thunder 5965
The Wild Ohio 5966

Spinatelli, Carl J.
Baton Sinister 5967
The Florentine 5968

Sprague, Rosemary
Red Lion and Gold Dragon 5969

Springer, Marilyn Harris
American Eden 2728
Eden and Honor 2729
The Eden Passion 2730
Eden Rising 2731
The Prince of Eden 2732

This Other Eden 2733
The Women of Eden 2734

Stackpole, Edouard A.
Nantucket Rebel 5970

Stacton, David
A Dancer in Darkness 5971
The Judges of the Secret Court 5972
On a Balcony 5973
People of the Book 5974
Segaki 5975
A Signal Victory 5976
Sir William 5977

Stahl, Hilda
The Woman of Catawba 5978

Stanford, Alfred
The Navigator: The Story of Nathaniel Bowditch 5979

Stangerup, Henrik
The Seducer 5980

Stanley, Edward
The Rock Cried Out 5981
Thomas Forty 5982

Staples, Reginald Thomas
Canis the Warrior 5864
Flight From Bucharest 6000
The Summer Day Is Done 6001
Warrior Queen 5865
A Woman of Texas 6002

Statham, Frances Patton
Trail of Tears 5983

Staynes, Jill
Axe for an Abbot 1989
Bravo for the Bride 1990
Curtains for the Cardinal 1991
Death of the Duchess 1992

Stearn, Jess
I, Judas 859

Steedman, Marguerite
Refuge in Avalon 5984

Steel, Danielle
Zoya 5985

Steele, Wilbur Daniel
Diamond Wedding 5986

Steelman, Robert
Call of the Arctic 5987

Steen, Marguerite
The Sun Is My Undoing 5988

Stegner, Wallace
Angle of Repose 5989

Stein, Harry
Hoopla 5990

Steinbeck, John
Cup of Gold 5991

Steinberg, Milton
As a Driven Leaf 5992

Stendhal
The Charterhouse of Parma 5993

Stephan, Ruth Walgreen
The Flight 5994
My Crown, My Love 5995

Stephens, Henrietta Henkle
All the Living: A Novel of One Year in the Life of William Shakespeare 758
And Walk on Love: A Novel Based on the Life of the Apostle Paul 759
Deep River 760
Fire in the Heart 761

Stephens, James
Deirdre 5996

Stern, Philip Van Doren
The Drums of Morning 5997

Sterne, Emma Gelders
The Drums of Monmouth 5998
No Surrender 5999

Stevens, R.T.
Flight From Bucharest 6000
The Summer Day Is Done 6001
A Woman of Texas 6002

Stevenson, Janet
The Ardent Years 6003
Departure 6004
Sisters and Brothers 6005
Weep No More 6006

Stevenson, John P.
Captain General 6007

Stevenson, Robert Louis
The Black Arrow 6008
Catriona 6009
Kidnapped 6010
The Master of Ballantrae: A Winter's Tale 6011
Treasure Island 6012

Stevenson, William
The Ghosts of Africa 6013

Steward, Barbara
Evermore 6014
The Lincoln Diddle 6015

Steward, Davenport
Rainbow Road 6016
Sail the Dark Tide 6017
They Had a Glory 6018

Steward, Dwight
Evermore 6014
The Lincoln Diddle 6015

Steward, Samuel M.
The Caravaggio Shawl 6019
Murder Is Murder Is Murder 6020

Stewart, A.J.
Falcon: The Autobiography of His Grace James IV, King of Scots 6021

Stewart, Catherine Pomeroy
Three Roads to Valhalla 6022

Stewart, Fred Mustard
Ellis Island 6023
The Magnificent Savages 6024
Pomp and Circumstance 6025
A Rage Against Heaven 6026

Stewart, George Rippey
East of the Giants 6027
Years of the City 6028

Stewart, Mary
The Crystal Cave 6029
The Hollow Hills 6030
The Last Enchantment 6031
The Prince and the Pilgrim 6032
The Wicked Day 6033

Stewart, Ramona
Casey 6034

Stewart, Stanley N.
The King James Version 6035

Stickland, Caroline
The Darkening Leaf 6036
The Darkness of Corn 6037
The Standing Hills 6038

Stirling, Jessica
The Asking Price 6039

Call Home the Heart 6040
Creature Comforts 6041
The Dark Pasture 6042
The Good Provider 6043
Hearts of Gold 6044
Lantern for the Dark 6045
The Marrying Kind 6046
The Penny Wedding 6047
Shadows on the Shore 6048
Treasures on Earth 6049
The Welcome Light 6050

Stirling, Jocelyn
Promises to Keep 6051

Stone, Grace Zaring
The Cold Journey 6052

Stone, Irving
Adversary in the House 6053
The Agony and the Ecstasy 6054
Depths of Glory 6055
The Greek Treasure 6056
Immortal Wife 6057
Love Is Eternal 6058
Lust for Life 6059
The Origin 6060
The Passionate Journey 6061
The Passions of the Mind 6062
The President's Lady 6063
Those Who Love 6064

Stong, Philip D.
The Adventure of "Horse" Barnsby 6065
Forty Pounds of Gold 6066

Storey, Margaret
Axe for an Abbot 1989
Bravo for the Bride 1990
Curtains for the Cardinal 1991
Death of the Duchess 1992

Stover, Herbert
Copperhead Moon 6067
The Eagle and the Wind 6068
Men in Buckskin 6069
Powder Mission 6070
Song of the Susquehanna 6071

Stowe, Harriet Beecher
Oldtown Folks 6072

Strabel, Thelma
Storm to the South 6073

Straight, Michael Whitney
Carrington 6074
A Very Small Remnant 6075

Street, James H.
By Valour and Arms 6076
Captain Little Ax 6077
Mingo Dabney 6078
Oh, Promised Land 6079
Tap Roots 6080
Tomorrow We Reap 6081
The Velvet Doublet 6082

Stribling, Thomas S.
The Forge 6083

Strode-Jackson, Myrtle
Tansy Taniard 6084

Strother, Pat Wallace
This Willing Passion 1132

Stuart, Frank Stanley
Caravan to China 6085

Stuart, Vivian
The Adventurers 3869
Brave Captains 6086
The Colonists 3870
The Empire Builders 3871
The Explorers 3872
The Gallant 3873

The Gold Seekers 3874
Hazard of Huntress 6087
Hazard's Command 6088
The Imperialists 3875
Massacre at Cawnpore 6089
The Nationalists 3876
The Seafarers 3877
The Settlers 3878
The Traitors 3879
The Valiant Sailors 6090
Victory at Sebastopol 6091

Stubbs, Jean
By Our Beginnings 6092
The Case of Kitty Ogilvie 6093
Dear Laura 6094
Eleanora Duse 6095
The Golden Crucible 6096
An Imperfect Joy 6097
My Grand Enemy 6098
The Northern Correspondent 6099
An Unknown Welshman 6100
The Vivian Inheritance 6101

Stucken, Eduard
The Great White Gods 6102

Styles, Showell
The Frigate Captain 6103
His Was the Fire 6104
The Sea Officer 6105

Styron, William
The Confessions of Nat Turner 6106

Subercaseaux, Benjamin
Jemmy Button 6107

Sublette, Clifford
The Bright Face of Danger 6108
Perilous Journey: A Tale of the Mississippi River and the Natchez Trace 6109
Scarlet Cockerel 6110

Sucharitkul, Somtow
The Shattered Horse 5945

Suckow, Ruth
Country People 6111

Sudworth, Gwynedd
Richard Whittington, London's Mayor 6112

Sullivan, Alan
The Fur Masters 6113
Three Came to Ville Marie 6114

Sullivan, Walter
Sojourn of a Stranger 6115

Summers, Richard
Vigilante 6116

Summerson, Rachel
Belgrave Square 6117

Sumner, Richard
Mistress of the Boards 6118

Sundman, Per Olof
The Flight of the Eagle 6119

Suskind, Patrick
Perfume: The Story of a Murderer 6120

Sutcliff, Rosemary
Blood and Sand 6121
The Flowers of Adonis 6122
Lady in Waiting 6123
Rider on a White Horse 6124
Sword at Sunset 6125

Sutherland, John
The Valiant 839

Suthren, Victor
Admiral of Fear 6126

The Black Cockade 6127
Captain Monsoon 6128
The Golden Galleon 6129
In Perilous Seas 6130
A King's Ransom 6131
Royal Yankee 6132

Sutpen, William Gilbert Van Tassel
I, Nathanael, Knew Jesus 6133

Swain, Virginia
The Dollar Gold Piece 6134

Swann, Lois
The Mists of Manittoo 6135
Torn Covenants 6136

Swanson, Neil Harmon
The First Rebel 6137
The Forbidden Ground 6138
The Judas Tree 6139
The Phantom Emperor 6140
The Silent Drum 6141
The Unconquered 6142

Swarthout, Glendon
The Homesman 6143
The Old Colts 6144
The Shootist 6145
The Tin Lizzie Troup 6146

Sweeney, Veronica Geoghegan
The Emancipist: An Unforgettable Epic of Australia 6147

Syers, William
The Devil Gun 6148

Symons, Allene
Vagabond Prophet 6149

Symons, Julian
The Blackheath Poisonings 6150
The Detling Secret 6151
Sweet Adelaide 6152

Szczypiorski, Andrzej
Mass for Arras 6153

T

Talbot, Hugh
Gentlemen—The Regiment! 6154

Talbot, Michael
To the Ends of the Earth 6155
A Wilful Woman 6156

Tannahill, Reay
In Still and Stormy Waters 6157
Return of the Stranger 6158
The World, the Flesh, and the Devil 6159

Tanner, Janet
The Hours of Light 6160

Tapsell, R.F.
The Unholy Pilgrim 6161
The Year of the Horsetails 6162

Tarkington, Booth
Monsieur Beaucaire 6163

Tarr, Judith
Alamut 6164
The Eagle's Daughter 6165
King and Goddess 6166
Lord of the Two Lands 6167
Pillar of Fire 6168
Queen of Swords 6169
Throne of Isis 6170

Tate, Allen
The Fathers 6171

Tattersall, Jill
Damnation Reef 6172
Dark at Noon 6173
Midsummer Masque 6174

Tax, Meredith
Rivington Street 6175
Union Square 6176

Taylor, Anna
The Gods Are Not Mocked 6177

Taylor, David
Farewell to Valley Forge 6178
Mistress of the Forge 6179
Storm the Last Rampart 6180
Sycamore Men 6181

Taylor, Georgia Elizabeth
The Infidel 6182
Lamia: A Witch 6183

Taylor, Janelle
Chase the Wind 6184
Defiant Hearts 6185

Taylor, Kamala
The Golden Honeycomb 4086

Taylor, Liza Pennywitt
The Drummer Was the First to Die 6186

Taylor, Lynn
Double Masquerade 3938
Dual Destiny 3939
Midsummer Moon 3940
The Rake 3941
The Scottish Marriage 3942

Taylor, Robert
Loving Belle Star 6187

Taylor, Robert Lewis
A Journey to Matecumbe 6188
Niagara 6189
The Roads to Guadalupe 6190
A Roaring in the Wind 6191

Taylor, Thomas
Born of War 6192

Taylor, Winchombe
Ram: Being the Tale of One Ramillies Anstruther 6193

Tebbel, John William
The Conqueror 6194
Touched with Fire 6195
A Voice in the Streets 6196

Teilhet, Darwin Le Ora
The Lion's Skin 6197
Retreat From the Dolphin 6198
The Road to Glory 6199
Steamboat on the River 6200

Tennant, Emma
Pemberley, or Pride and Prejudice Continued 6201
An Unequal Marriage; or Pride and Prejudice Twenty Years Later 6202

Terrell, John Upton
Plume Rouge: A Novel of the Pathfinders 6203

Terrot, Charles
The Passionate Pilgrim 6204

Terry, C.V.
Buccaneer Surgeon 6205
The Deadly Lady of Madagascar 6206

Terry, Judith
Version and Diversion 6207

Tessin, Brigitte Von
The Bastard 6208

Tey, Josephine
The Daughter of Time 6209

Thackeray, William Makepeace
Barry Lyndon 6210
Denis Duval 6211
Henry Esmond 6212
Vanity Fair 6213
The Virginians 6214

Thane, Elswyth
Dawn's Early Light 6215
Ever After 6216
Yankee Stranger 6217

Thayer, Steve
Saint Mudd 6218

Thesen, Hjalmar P.
The Echoing Cliffs 6219

Thibault, Jacques-Anatole-Francois
At the Sign of the Reine Pedauque 2198

Thirkell, Angela
Coronation Summer 6220

Thoene, Bodie
Danzig Passage 6221
In My Father's House 6222
Jerusalem Interlude 6223
Munich Signature 6224
Prague Counterpoint 6225
Say to This Mountain 6226
A Thousand Shall Fall 6227
Vienna Prelude 6228
Warsaw Requiem 6229

Thom, James Alexander
The Children of the First Man 6230
Follow the River 6231
From Sea to Shining Sea 6232
Long Knife 6233
Panther in the Sky 6234

Thomas, D.M.
Eating Pavlova 6235
Flying into Love 6236
The White Hotel 6237

Thomas, Donald
Captain Wonder 6238
The Flight of the Eagle 6239
Jekyll, Alias Hyde 6240
Prince Charlie's Bluff 6241
The Ripper's Apprentice 6242

Thomas, Elizabeth Marshall
The Animal Wife 6243
Reindeer Moon 6244

Thomas, Michael M.
Hanover Place 6245

Thomas, Rosie
The White Dove 6246

Thomason, John Williams
Gone to Texas 6247

Thompson, China
Starrbelow 6248

Thompson, Daniel Pierce
The Green Mountain Boys 6249

Thompson, David
Apache Blood 6250
Blackfoot Massacre 6251
Blood Fury 6252
Blood Truce 6253
Hawken Fury 6254
King of the Mountain 6255
Lure of the Wind 6256
Mountain Devil 6257
Northwest Passage 6258
Tenderfoot 6259
Tomahawk Revenge 6260

Trapper's Blood 6261
Winterkill 6262

Thompson, E.V.
Ben Retallick 6263
Chase the Wind 6264
Harvest of the Sun 6265
Republic: A Novel of Texas 6266

Thompson, Joan
Marblehead 6267

Thompson, Maurice
Alice of Old Vincennes 6268

Thompson, Morton
The Cry and the Covenant 6269

Thompson, Thomas
Crompton Way 6270

Thomsen, Robert
Carriage Trade 6271

Thorne, Nicola
Affairs of Love 6272
Cashmere 6273
Sisters & Lovers 6274

Thornton, Lawrence
Ghost Woman 6275

Thorp, Roderick
Jenny and Barnum: A Novel of Love 6276
Westfield 6277

Thorpe, Adam
Ulverton 6278

Thorpe, Helen
Elizabeth: Queen & Woman 6279

Tilsley, Frank
Mutiny 6280

Timmermans, Felix
The Perfect Joy of St. Francis 6281

Tippette, Giles
Heaven's Gold 6282

Titus, Harold
Black Feather 6283

Todd, Catherine
Bond of Honour 6284

Todd, Helen
A Man Called Grant 6285
So Free We Seem 6286

Toepfer, Ray Grant
The Scarlet Guidon 6287
The Second Face of Valor 6288

Toepperwein, Herman
Rebel in Blue 6289

Tolbert, Frank Xavier
The Staked Plain 6290

Tolliver, Ruby C.
Muddy Banks 6291

Tolosko, Edward
Sakuran: A Novel of Medieval Japan 6292

Tolstoy, Alexey
Peter the Great 6293
Prince of Outlaws 6294

Tolstoy, Leo
War and Peace 6295

Tolstoy, Nikolai
The Coming of the King 6296

Toperoff, Sam
A Family Matter 5458

Topping, John Dewey
Rebellion Road 4392

Torday, Ursula
The English Wife 530
The Lonely Strangers 531
Loving Sands, Deadly Sands 3465
Miss Philadelphia Smith 91
My Name Is Clary Brown 3466
The Villains: A Haunting Tale of the Marshes 3467

Tourney, Leonard
The Bartholomew Fair Murders 6297
Familiar Spirits 6298
Frobisher's Savage 6299
Knaves Templar 6300
Low Treason 6301
Old Saxon Blood 6302
The Players' Boy Is Dead 6303
Witness of Bones 6304

Tournier, Michel
Friday 6305

Townsend, Sue
The Queen and I 6306

Tracy, Don
Carolina Corsair 6307
Crimson Is the Eastern Shore 6308
The Last Boat out of Cincinnati 6309
On the Midnight Tide 6310
Roanoke Renegade 6311
Sign of the Pagan 6312

Train, Arthur Cheney
Tassels on Her Boots 6313

Tranter, Nigel
Chain of Destiny 6314
James, by the Grace of God 6315
The Master of Gray Trilogy 6316
The Riven Realm 6317
Robert the Bruce: The Path of the Hero King 6318
Robert the Bruce: The Price of the King's Peace 6319
Robert the Bruce: The Steps to the Empty Throne 6320
A Stake in the Kingdom 6321
True Thomas 6322
Unicorn Rampant 6323

Trease, Geoffrey
Snared Nightingale 6324

Trecker, Janice Law
All the King's Ladies 3678

Treece, Henry
Amber Princess 6325
The Dark Island 6326
The Eagle King 6327
The Golden Strangers 6328
The Great Captains 6329
The Green Man 6330
Jason 6331
Red Queen, White Queen 6332

Tremain, Rose
Restoration: A Novel of Seventeenth-Century England 6333

Tremayne, Peter
Absolution by Murder 6334
The Revenge of Dracula 6335

Trevaskis, Eve
The Lion of England 6336

Trevelyan, Robert
Pendragon: Late of Prince Albert's Own 6337
Pendragon. . .The Montenegran Plot 6338

Trevino, Elizabeth Borton de
Among the Innocent 6339

The Greek of Toledo: A Romantic Narrative of El Greco 586
The House on Bitterness Street 6340

Trevor, Elleston
Bury Him Among Kings 6341

Trevor, Meriol
The Fortunate Marriage 6342
Last of Britain 6343
Shadows and Images 6344
The Wanton Fires 6345

Trollope, Anthony
La Vendee 6346

Trollope, Joanna
Eliza Stanhope 6347
Leaves From the Valley 6348
Mistaken Virtues 6349
The Steps of the Sun 6350
The Taverners' Place 6351

Trotter, William R.
Winter Fire 6352

Troyat, Henri
The Brotherhood of the Red Poppy 6353

Troyer, Howard William
The Salt and the Savor 6354

Tryon, Thomas
In the Fire of Spring 6355
The Wings of the Morning 6356

Tsuji, Kunio
The Signore: Shogun of the Warring States 6357

Tucci, Niccolo
Before My Time 6358

Tucker, Wilson
The Lincoln Hunters 6359

Tunstall, Beatrice
The Long Day Closes 6360

Turk, H.C.
Black Body 6361

Turnbull, Agnes Sligh
The Day Must Dawn 6362
The King's Orchard 6363
The Richlands 6364

Turner, Judy
Ralegh's Fair Bess: The Story of Bess Throckmorton 6365

Turner, William Oliver
Call the Beast Thy Brother 6366

Turtledove, Harry N.
The Guns of the South 6367

Turton, Godfrey
The Emperor Arthur 6368
My Lord of Canterbury 6369

Tuten, Frederic
Tallien: A Brief Romance 6370

Twain, Mark
A Connecticut Yankee in King Arthur's Court 6371
Personal Recollections of Joan of Arc 6372
The Prince and the Pauper 6373

Tyler-Whittle, Michael
Albert's Victoria 6719
Bertie, Albert Edward, Prince of Wales 6720
Edward 6721
Richard III: The Last Plantagenet 6722
The Widow of Windsor 6723
The Young Victoria 6724

Tynan, Kathleen
Agatha 6374

Tyrrel, Mabel L.
The Affairs of Nicholas Culpepper 6375

U

Ulyatt, Kenneth
North Against the Sioux 6376

Underhill, Charles
Captain Fantom 6377

Undset, Sigrid
The Axe 6378
The Bridal Wreath 6379
The Cross 6380
In the Wilderness 6381
The Mistress of Husaby 6382
The Snake Pit 6383
The Son Avenger 6384

Unruh, Fritz von
The Saint 6385

Unsworth, Barry
The Idol Hunter 6386
Morality Play 6387
The Rage of the Vulture 6388
Sacred Hunter 6389

Upchurch, Boyd
The Slave Stealer 6390

Updike, John
Memories of the Ford Administration 6391

Upton, Mark
The Dream Lover 6392

Uris, Leon
Redemption 6393
Trinity 6394

Uys, Errol Lincoln
Brazil 6395

V

Vaczek, Louis
River and Empty Sea 6396

Vail, Philip
The Sea Panther: A Novel about the Commander of the U.S.S. Constitution 6397
The Twisted Saber: A Biographical Novel of Benedict Arnold 6398

Van Ash, Cay
The Fires of Fu Manchu 6399
Ten Years Beyond Baker Street 6400

Van de Water, Frederic F.
Catch a Falling Star 6401
Day of Battle 6402
Reluctant Rebel 6403
Wings of the Morning 6404

Van Dorp, Jan
The Sable Lion 6405

Van Every, Dale
Bridal Journey 6406
The Captive Witch 6407
The Day the Sun Died 6408
Scarlet Feather 6409
The Shining Mountains 6410
The Trembling Earth 6411

The Voyagers 6412

van Gulik, Robert
The Chinese Nail Murders 6413
The Emperor's Pearl 6414
The Haunted Monastery 6415
The Lacquer Screen 6416
The Monkey and the Tiger 6417
Murder in Canton 6418
Necklace and Calabash 6419
The Phantom of the Temple 6420
The Red Pavilion 6421
The Willow Pattern 6422

Van-Loon, Antonia
For Love and Honor 6423
For Us the Living 6424
Katherine 6425
Sunshine and Shadow 6426

Van Rensselaer, Philip
That Vanderbilt Woman 6427

Van Santvoord, Seymour
Octavia: A Tale of Ancient Rome 6428

Vansittart, Peter
A Choice of Murder 6429
The Lost Lands 6430
The Siege 6431

Vaughan, Agnes Carr
Bury Me in Ravenna 6432

Vaughan, Carter A.
The Charlatan 6433
Dragon Cove 6434
Fortress Fury 6435
The Invincibles 6436
The River Devils 6437
Roanoke Warrior 6438
Scoundrels' Brigade 6439
The Seneca Hostage 6440
The Silver Saber 6441
The Wilderness 6442
The Yankee Brig 6443
The Yankee Rascals 6444

Vaughan, Matthew
Major Stepton's War 6445

Vaughan, Robert
Cold War 6446
The Iron Curtain 6447
Legacy 6448
Over There 6449

Venable, Clarke
All the Brave Rifles 6450

Verissimo, Erico
Time and the Wind 6451

Vernam, Glenn R.
Indian Hater 6452
Pioneer Breed 6453
The Talking Rifle 6454

Vernon, Frances
Privileged Children 6455

Vernon, John
All for Love: Baby Doe and Silver Dollar 6456
Peter Doyle 6457
La Salle 6458

Veryan, Patricia
Ask Me No Questions 6459
Cherished Enemy 6460
The Dedicated Villain 6461
Feather Castles 6462
Had We Never Loved 6463
Journey to Enchantment 6464
Lanterns 6465
Logic of the Heart 6466
Love Alters Not 6467

Love's Duet 6468
Married Past Redemption 6469
Men Were Deceivers Ever 6470
Mistress of Willowvale 6471
Nanette 6472
Never Doubt I Love 6473
The Noblest Frailty 6474
Practice to Deceive 6475
Sanguinet's Crown 6476
A Shadow's Bliss 6477
Some Brief Folly 6478
Time's Fool 6479
The Tyrant 6480
The Wagered Widow 6481

Vetterli, Richard
Powderkeg 6482

Victor, Daniel D.
The Seventh Bullet 6483

Vidal, Gore
1876: A Novel 6484
Burr 6485
Creation 6486
Empire: A Novel 6487
Hollywood: A Novel of America in the 1920s 6488
Julian 6489
Lincoln: A Novel 6490
Live From Golgotha 6491
A Search for a King: A 12th-Century Legend 6492
Washington, D.C. 6493

Vidal, Nicole
The Goddess Queen: A Novel Based on the Life of Nefertiti 6494

Vigny, Alfred Victor de
Cinq-Mars 6495

Villarreal, Jose Antonio
The Fifth Horseman 6496

Villars, Elizabeth
The Normandie Affair 6497
One Night in Newport 6498
The Very Best People 6499

Vine, Barbara
Anna's Book 6500

Vining, Elizabeth Gray
I, Roberta 6501
Meggy MacIntosh 2555
Take Heed of Loving Me: A Novel about John Donne 6502

Vinogradov, Anatolii
The Black Consul 6503

Vipont, Elfrida
Bed in Hell 6504

Vlachos, Ange
Their Most Serene Majesties 6505

Vliet, R.G.
Rockspring 6506
Solitudes 6507

Vollmann, William T.
Fathers and Crows 6508
The Ice Shirt 6509
The Rifles 6510

Von Hoffman, Nicholas
Organized Crime 6511

Vornholt, John
The Fabulist 6512

Voynich, Ethel Lillian
Put Off Thy Shoes 6513

Vrettos, Theodore
Lord Elgin's Lady 6514
Origen: A Historical Novel 6515

Vroman, Barbara Fitz
Sons of Thunder 6516

W

Waddell, Helen
Peter Abelard: A Novel 6517

Wagner, Constance
Ask My Brother 6518

Wagner, Esther
The Gift of Rome 6520

Wagner, Geoffrey
Sophie 6519

Wagner, John
The Gift of Rome 6520

Wagoner, David
Tracker 6521
Where Is My Wandering Boy Tonight? 6522
Whole Hog 6523

Waldeck, R.G.
The Emperor's Duchess 6524
Lustre in the Sky 6525

Walder, Francis
The Negotiators 6526

Waldman, Emerson
Beckoning Ridge 6527

Waldo, Anna Lee
Prairie 6528
Sacajawea 6529

Wales, Robert
Harry: A Novel of Australia 6530

Walker, Margaret
Jubilee 6531

Walker, Mildred
If a Lion Could Talk 6532

Wall, Robert E.
Birthright 6533
Blackrobe 6534
Bloodbrothers 6535

Wallace, Lew
Ben Hur: A Tale of the Christ 6536
The Fair God 6537

Wallace, Randall
Braveheart 6538

Wallace, Willard
East to Bagaduce 6539
Jonathan Dearborn: A Novel of the War of 1812 6540
The Raiders: A Novel of the Civil War at Sea 6541

Wallach, Ira Jan
The Horn and the Roses: A Novel Based on the Life of Peter Paul Rubens 6542

Waller, Leslie
Blood & Dreams 6543

Walmsley, Arnold R.
Who Came by Night 4608

Walpole, Hugh
The Fortress 6544
Judith Paris 6545
Katherine Christian 6546
Rogue Herries 6547
Vanessa 6548

Walsh, Maurice
The Dark Rose 6549

Waltari, Mika
The Adventurer 6550
The Dark Angel 6551
The Egyptian 6552
The Etruscan 6553
The Roman 6554
The Secret of the Kingdom 6555
The Wanderer 6556

Walter, Elizabeth
Homeward Bound 6557

Walton, Evangeline
The Cross and the Sword 6558

Walz, Audrey
The Bizarre Sisters 6559
The Undiscovered Country 6560

Walz, Jay
The Bizarre Sisters 6559
The Undiscovered Country 6560

Ward, Andrew
The Blood Seed 6561

Ward, Christopher
Strange Adventure of Jonathan Drew 6562
Yankee Rover 6563

Ward-Thomas, Evelyn
All the Queen's Men 157
Anne Boleyn 158
The Cardinal and the Queen 159
Charles the King 160
Clandara 161
Far Flies the Eagle 162
The French Bride 163
Rebel Princess 164
Valentina 165
Victoria and Albert 166

Warner, Rex
The Converts: A Historical Novel 6564
Imperial Caesar 6565
Pericles the Athenian 6566
The Young Caesar 6567

Warner, Sylvia Townsend
The Corner That Held Them 6568
The Flint Anchor 6569

Warren, Charles Marquis
Valley of the Shadow 6570

Warren, Lella
Foundation Stone 6571

Warren, Robert Penn
Band of Angels 6572
Wilderness: A Tale of the Civil War 6573

Washburn, L.J.
Dead-Stick 6574
Dog Heavies 6575

Wassermann, Jakob
Alexander in Babylon 6576

Wassmo, Herbjorg
Dina's Book 6577

Waters, Frank
Diamond Head 647
Wild Earth's Nobility 6578

Waters, Gladys
Fairacres 6579

Watkins, Paul
In the Blue Light of African Dreams 6580
The Promise of Light 6581

Watkins, Shirley
The Prophet and the King 6582

Watson, Marjorie
Heir to Polventon 6583

Watson, Sally
Highlands Rebel 6584

Waugh, Evelyn
Edmund Campion 6585

Weatherby, W.J.
Chariots of Fire 6586

Webb, Jean Francis
Somewhere Within This House 6587

Webb, Liliane
The Marranos 6588

Webb, Lucas
Eli's Road 6589

Webb, Mary
Precious Bane 6590

Webber, Everett
Bound Girl 6591

Webber, Olga
Bound Girl 6591

Webster, Jan
Colliers Row 6592
Saturday City 6593

Wedeck, Harry E.
Mortal Hunger: A Novel Based on the Life of Lafcadio Hearn 6594

Weekley, Robert S.
The House in Ruins 6595

Weenolsen, Hebe
The Last Englishman: The Story of Hereward the Wake 6596
To Keep This Oath 6597
The Trial of Jenny Sykes 6598

Wehen, Joy DeWeese
So Far From Malabar 6599

Weinreb, Nathaniel Norsen
The Babylonians 6600
Esther 6601
The Sorceress 6602

Weiser, Theresa
Music for God 6603

Weiss, David
The Assassination of Mozart 6604
I, Rembrandt 6605
Myself, Christopher Wren 6606
Naked Came I: A Novel of Rodin 6607
Physician Extraordinary: A Novel of the Life and Times of William Harvey 6608
Sacred and Profane: A Novel of the Life and Times of Mozart 6609
The Spirit and the Flesh: A Novel Inspired by the Life of Isadora Duncan 6610
The Venetian 6611

Wellman, Manly Wade
Candle of the Wicked 6612

Wellman, Paul I.
Angel with Spurs 6613
Broncho Apache 6614
The Buckstones 6615
The Comancheros 6616
The Female: A Novel of Another Time 6617
The Iron Mistress 6618
Magnificent Destiny 6619
Ride the Red Earth 6620

Wells, Evelyn
A City for St. Francis 6621

Wells, Lawrence
Rommel and the Rebel 6622

Welty, Eudora
The Robber Bridegroom 6623

Wendorf, Patricia
Double Wedding Ring 6624

Werfel, Franz
The Song of Bernadette 6625

Wertenbaker, Lael Tucker
*The Eye of the Lion: A Novel Based on
the Life of Mata Hari* 6626

West, Eugenia Lovett
The Ancestors Cry Out 6627

West, Jessamyn
Except for Me and Thee 6628
The Friendly Persuasion 6629
Leafy Rivers 6630
The Massacre at Fall Creek 6631

West, Keith
Winter Cherry 6632

West, Pamela Elizabeth
Madeleine 6633

West, Paul
Lord Byron's Doctor 6634
Sporting with Amaryllis 6635
The Tent of Orange Mist 6636
*The Very Rich Hours of Count von
Stauffenberg* 6637
*The Women of Whitechapel and Jack
the Ripper* 6638

West, Rebecca
The Fountain Overflows 6639

Westcott, Glenway
The Grandmothers 6640

Westcott, Jan
The Border Lord 6641
Captain Barney 6642
Captain for Elizabeth 6643
Condottiere 6644
The Hepburn 6645
The Queen's Grace 6646
The Tower and the Dream 6647
The White Rose 6648
A Woman of Quality 6649

Weston, Michael
The Cage 6650

Wetherell, June
The Glorious Three 6651

Wharton, Edith
The Old Maid 6652
The Valley of Decision 6653

Wheatley, Dennis
The Man Who Killed the King 6654

Wheeler, Gidley
Armada 2404

Wheeler, Guy
Cato's War 6655

Wheeler, Richard S.
Beneath the Blue Mountain 6656
Dodging Red Cloud 6657
The Far Tribes 6658
Fool's Coach 6659
Goldfield 6660
Montana Hitch 6661
Richard Lamb 6662
The Two Medicine River 6663
Where the River Runs 6664
Winter Grass 6665

Wheeler, Sessions S.
Paiute 6666

Wheelwright, Jere Hungerford
Draw Near to Battle 6667
Gentlemen, Hush! 6668
The Gray Captain 6669
Kentucky Stand 6670
The Strong Room 6671
Wolfshead 6672

Whipple, Maurine
The Giant Joshua 6673

White, Beatrice
*Royal Nonesuch: A Tudor
Tapestry* 6674

White, Charles W.
In the Blazing Light 6693
*The Midnight Gardener: A Novel about
Baudelaire* 6694

White, Ethel
Bear His Mild Yoke 6675

White, Helen Constance
*Bird of Fire: A Tale of Francis of
Assisi* 6676
Dust on the King's Highway 6677
The Four Rivers of Paradise 6678
Not Built with Hands 6679
To the End of the World 6680

White, Hilda Crystal
*Wild Decembers: A Biographical
Portrait of the Brontes* 6681

White, Jude Gilliam
The Conquest 1630
A Knight in Shining Armor 1631
Mountain Laurel 1632
The Taming 1633

White, Leslie Turner
The Highland Hawk 6682
His Majesty's Highlanders 6683
Log Jam 6684
Look Away, Look Away 6685
Lord Fancy 6686
Lord Johnnie 6687
Magnus the Magnificent 6688
Monsieur Yankee 6689
Scorpus the Moor 6690
Sir Rogue 6691
Wagons West 6692

White, Max
In the Blazing Light 6693
*The Midnight Gardener: A Novel about
Baudelaire* 6694

White, Nelia Gardner
Daughter of Time 6695

White, Olive
The King's Good Servant 6696
Late Harvest 6697

White, Patrick
Voss 6698

White, Simon
Clear for Action! 6699
The English Captain 6700

White, Stewart Edward
Folded Hills 6701
The Long Rifle 6702
Ranchero 6703

White, Terence de Vere
Johnnie Cross 6704

White, T.H.
The Once and Future King 6705

Whitehead, Barbara
The Caretaker Wife 6706
Quicksilver Lady 6707
Ramillies 6708

Whitehouse, Arch
The Casket Crew 6709
Playboy Squadron 6710
Squadron Forty-Four 6711
Squadron Shilling 6712
Wings for the Chariots 6713

Whitehouse, Arthur George
The Casket Crew 6709
Playboy Squadron 6710
Squadron Forty-Four 6711
Squadron Shilling 6712
Wings for the Chariots 6713

Whitlock, Brand
The Strangers on the Island 6714

Whitney, Janet
Intrigue in Baltimore 6715

Whitney, Phyllis A.
The Quicksilver Pool 6716
Sea Jade 6717

Whitson, Denton
The Governor's Daughter 6718

Whittle, Tyler
Albert's Victoria 6719
*Bertie, Albert Edward, Prince of
Wales* 6720
Edward 6721
*Richard III: The Last
Plantagenet* 6722
The Widow of Windsor 6723
The Young Victoria 6724

Whyte, Jack
The Singing Sword 6725
*The Skystone: The Forging of Arthur's
Britain* 6726

Wiat, Philippa
The Heir of Allington 6727

Wibberley, Anna
Time and Chance 6728

Wibberley, Leonard
The Centurion 6729
The Testament of Theophilus 6730

Wichelns, Lee
The Shadow of the Earth 6731

Wick, Lori
The Knight and the Dove 6732

Wicker, Tom
Unto This Hour 6733

Widdemer, Mabel Cleland
Iron Land 4697

Widdemer, Margaret
Buckskin Baronet 6734
The Golden Wildcat 6735
Lady of the Mohawks 6736
Red Cloak Flying 6737

Widgery, Jan
The Adversary 6738
Trumpet at the Gate 6739

Wiegand, William
*The Chester A. Arthur
Conspiracy* 6740

Wiener, Willard
Morning in America 6741

Wiggs, Susan
Circle in the Water 6742
Jewel of the Sea 6743
Kingdom of Gold 6744
The Lily and the Leopard 6745
The Raven and the Rose 6746

Wight, Frederick
Verge of Glory 6747

Wignall, Anne
The Secret Wife 22

Wilchek, Stella
Judith 6748

Wilde, Jennifer
Love's Tender Fury 6749

Wilder, Robert
Bright Feather 6750
Wind From the Carolinas 6751

Wilder, Thornton
The Bridge of San Luis Rey 6752
The Ides of March 6753
Woman of Andros 6754

Wiley, Richard
Fools' Gold 6755

Wilkins, William Vaughan
Being Met Together 6756
Consort for Victoria 6757
Crown Without Sceptre 6758
A King Reluctant 6759
Lady of Paris 6760
Seven Tempest 6761

Wilkinson, Frank
Bygones 6762

Williams, Alan
Gentleman Traitor 6763

Williams, Ben Ames
Come Spring 6764
House Divided 6765
Owen Glen 6766
Thread of Scarlet 6767
The Unconquered 6768

Williams, Chancellor
The Raven 6769

Williams, Gordon
Pomeroy 6770

Williams, Jay
The Good Yeomen 6771
The Rogue From Padua 6772
The Siege 6773
Solomon and Sheba 6774
Tomorrow's Fire 6775
The Witches 6776

Williams, Jeanne
Home Mountain 6777
Home Station 6778
The Island Harp 6779
Lady of No Man's Land 6780
The Longest Road 6781
No Roof but Heaven 6782
The Unplowed Sky 6783

Williams, Joel
Coasts of Folly 6784

Williams, John
Augustus 6785
Butcher's Crossing 6786

Williams, Lawrence
I, James McNeill Whistler 6787

Williams, Mary Floyd
Fortune, Smile Once More 6788

Williams, Maslyn
*Dubu: A Novel of New Guinean
Conquest* 6789

Williamson, Thames Ross
The Gladiator 6790

Williman, Anne C.
Mary of Magdala 6791

Willis, Ted
*The Buckingham Palace
Connection* 6792

The Green Leaves of Summer 6793
Spring at The Winged Horse 6794

Wilson, A.N.
Gentlemen in England 6795

Wilson, Charles Morrow
A Man's Reach 6796

Wilson, Derek
Her Majesty's Captain 6797

Wilson, Dorothy Clarke
*Alice and Edith: A Biographical Novel
of the Two Wives of Theodore
Roosevelt* 6798
The Brother 6799
*The Gifts: A Story of the Boyhood of
Jesus* 6800
The Herdsman 6801
Jezebel 6802
Lady Washington 6803
*Lincoln's Mothers: A Story of Nancy
and Sally Lincoln* 6804
Prince of Egypt 6805
*Queen Dolley: The Life and Times of
Dolley Madison* 6806

Wilson, Erle
Adams of the Bounty 6807

Wilson, Jeanne
The Golden Harlot 6808
Weep in the Sun 6809

Wilson, John Burgess
A Dead Man in Deptford 776
The End of the World News 777
The Kingdom of the Wicked 778
Man of Nazareth 779
Napoleon Symphony 780
Nothing Like the Sun 781

Wilson, Leslie
Malefice 6810
*The Mountain of Immoderate
Desires* 6811

Wilson, Margaret
The Able McLaughlins 6812

Wilson, Sandra
The Lady Cicely 6813
Less Fortunate than Fair 6814
The Queen's Sister 6815

Wilson, Timothy R.
Beauty for Ashes 6816
Master of Morholm 6817

Wilson, William Edward
Abe Lincoln of Pigeon Creek 6818
The Raiders 6819

Windle, Janice Woods
True Women 6820

Winegardner, Mark
The Veracruz Blues 6821

Winslow, Pauline Glen
Damaris 5810
Love at Sunset 5811
My Lady Hoyden 5812

Winsor, Kathleen
Forever Amber 6822
*Wanderers Eastward, Wanderers
West* 6823

Winston, Daoma
The Fall River Line 6824
Gallows Way 6825
The Golden Valley 6826
The Haversham Legacy 6827
Mills of the Gods 6828

Wintle, Francis Edward
Russka: The Novel of Russia 5535

Sarum: The Novel of England 5536

Winwar, Frances
Ardent Flame 6829
The Eagle and the Rock 6830
Gallows Hill 6831
Last Love of Camille 6832

Wiseman, David
Ellen Bray 3319

Wisler, G. Clifton
Lakota 6833

Wittlin, Tadeusz
*Modigliani: Prince of
Montparnasse* 6834

Wohl, Burton
Soldier in Paradise 6835

Wolf, Christa
No Place on Earth 6836

Wolf, Joan
Born of the Sun 6837
Daughter of the Red Deer 6838
The Edge of Light 6839
The Horsemasters 6840
The Reindeer Hunters 6841
The Road to Avalon 6842

Wolfe, Gene
Soldier of the Mist 6843

Wolford, Nelson
The Southern Blade 6844

Wolford, Shirley
The Southern Blade 6844

Wolpert, Stanley
An Error of Judgment 6845
Nine Hours to Rama 6846

Wood, Barbara
Domina 6847
*The Dreaming: A Novel of
Australia* 6848
Green City in the Sun 6849
Soul Flame 6850

Woodhouse, Martin
The Medici Emerald 6851
The Medici Guns 6852
The Medici Hawks 6853

Woodhouse, Sarah
The Native Air 6854
The Peacock's Feather 6855
A Season of Mists 6856

Woodman, Richard
1805 6857
Arctic Treachery 6858
Baltic Mission 6859
The Bomb Vessel 6860
Decision at Trafalgar 6861
In Distant Waters 6862
A Private Revenge 6863

Woods, William Howard
*Riot at Gravesend: A Novel of Wat
Tyler's Rebellion* 6864

Woodward, Ann
The Exile Way 6865

Woolf, Virginia
Orlando 6866

Woolley, Persia
Child of the Northern Spring 6867
*Guinevere: The Legend in
Autumn* 6868
Queen of the Summer Stars 6869

Worboys, Anne
Aurora Rose 6870

Worcester, Don
Gone to Texas 6871
Man on Two Ponies 6872

Wouk, Herman
The Glory 6873
The Hope 6874
War and Remembrance 6875
The Winds of War 6876

Wright, Constance
A Chance for Glory 6877

Wright, Don
The Captives 6878
The Last Plantation 6879
The Woodsman 6880

Wright, Patricia
I Am England 6881
Journey into Fire 6882
The Near and Distant Place 6883
A Space of the Heart 6884
The Storms of Fate 6885
While Paris Danced 6886

Wright, Sean M.
*Enter the Lion: A Posthumous Memoir
of Mycroft Holmes* 2961

Wyckoff, Nicholas E.
The Braintree Mission 6887
The Corinthians 6888

Wylie, I.A.R.
Ho, the Fair Wind 6889

Wynd, Oswald
The Ginger Tree 6890

Wynne, Annabel
A Lady in Doubt 6891

Y

Yalom, Irvin D.
*When Nietzsche Wept: A Novel of
Obsession* 6892

Yanez, Agustin
The Edge of the Storm 6893

Yarbro, Chelsea Quinn
Better in the Dark 6894
A Candle for D'Artagnan 6895
Charity, Colorado 6896
Crusader's Torch 6897
Darker Jewels 6898
A Flame in Byzantium 6899
Hotel Transylvania 6900
The Law in Charity 6901
Mansions of Darkness 6902
Napoleon Must Die 2054
Out of the House of Life 6903
The Palace 6904
Path of the Eclipse 6905
Tempting Fate 6906

Yarde, Jeanne
The Castle of the Winds 4434
The Clock Tower 4435
Midnight Moon 4436

Yates, Elizabeth
Hue and Cry 6907

Yerby, Frank
Benton's Row 6908
Bride of Liberty 6909
Captain Rebel 6910
The Dahomean 6911
*A Darkness at Ingraham's Crest: A
Tale of the Slaveholding
South* 6912

The Devil's Laughter 6913
Devilseed 6914
Fairoaks 6915
Floodtide 6916
The Foxes of Harrow 6917
The Garfield Honor 6918
*The Girl From Storyville: A Victorian
Novel* 6919
*Goat Song: A Novel of Ancient
Greece* 6920
The Golden Hawk 6921
Griffin's Way 6922
Jarrett's Jade 6923
*McKensie's Hundred: A Tale of the Old
Dominion* 6924
Pride's Castle 6925
The Saracen Blade 6926
Serpent and Staff 6927
The Treasure of Pleasant Valley 6928
The Vixens 6929
*Western: A Saga of the Great
Plains* 6930
A Woman Called Fancy 6931

York, Margaret Elizabeth
Blood of the Boar 2
The Flight of the Kestrel 3
The Heart Is a Traitor 4
The Son of York 5
The Warwick Heiress 6

York, Robert
My Lord the Fox 6932
The Swords of December 6933

Yoshikawa, Eiji
The Heike Story 6934
*Musashi: An Epic Novel of the Samurai
Era* 6935
Taiko 6936

Youd, Samuel
Castle Malindine 2163

Youmans, Marly
Catherwood 6937

Young, Agatha
The Hospital 6938
I Swear by Apollo 6939

Young, Francis Brett
The City of Gold 6940
They Seek a Country 6941

Young, Stanley
Young Hickory 6942

Young, Stark
Heaven Trees 6943
So Red the Rose 6944

Yount, Steven
Wandering Star 6945

Yourcenar, Marguerite
The Abyss 6946
Hadrian's Memoirs 6947

Z

Zara, Louis
Against This Rock 6948
Blessed Is the Land 6949
Dark Rider 6950
In the House of the King 6951
Rebel Run 6952
This Land Is Ours 6953

Zaroulis, Nancy
Call the Darkness Light 6954
The Last Waltz 6955
Massachusetts: A Novel 6956

Zelazny, Roger
Wilderness 6957

Zeldis, Chayym
The Brother 6958

Zencey, Eric
Panama 6959

Zeromski, Stefan
Ashes 6960

Ziegler, Isabelle Gibson
Nine Days of Father Serra 6961

Zilahy, Lajos
Century in Scarlet 6962

Zilinsky, Ursula
Before the Glory Ended 6963
The Long Afternoon 6964

Zimmermann, Samuel
Sir Pagan 1222

Zollinger, Norman
Chapultepec 6965
Not of War Only 6966

Title Index

This index alphabetically lists all featured titles. Each title is followed by the author's name and its entry number.

54-40 or Fight
Hough, Emerson   3040

1492
Frolich, Newton   2236
Johnston, Mary   3228

1492: The Life and Times of Juan Cabezon of Castile
Aridjis, Homero   187

1805
Woodman, Richard   6857

1812
Nevin, David   4586

1876: A Novel
Vidal, Gore   6484

1901
Conroy, Robert   1258

1915: A Novel
McDonald, Roger   4264

A

The Abandoned Woman
Condon, Richard   1235

The Abbot
Scott, Sir Walter   5688

The Abductors
Cloete, Stuart   1121

Abe Lincoln of Pigeon Creek
Wilson, William Edward   6818

Abigail
Aswell, Mary Louise   221
Druett, Joan   1721
Macdonald, Malcolm   3962

The Able McLaughlins
Wilson, Margaret   6812

Abracadaver
Lovesey, Peter   3906

Abraham and Sarah: The Long Journey
Dorr, Roberta Kells   1694

Abram, Son of Terah
Bauer, Florence M.   378

Absalom, Absalom!
Faulkner, William   2049

Absolute Elizabeth
Dessau, Joanna   1624

Absolution by Murder
Tremayne, Peter   6334

The Absorbing Fire: The Byron Legend
Kenyon, F.W.   3445

The Abyss
Yourcenar, Marguerite   6946

According to Mary: A Novel of the Magdalene
Gibbs, Willa   2398

According to Thomas
Malvern, Gladys   4053

Aces and Eights: A Novel of the Legend of Wild Bill Hickok
Estleman, Loren D.   1967

Achilles His Armour
Green, Peter   2569

Across the Bitter Sea
Dillon, Eilis   1646

Across the Shining Mountains
McCord, Christian   4226

Action at Aquila
Allen, Hervey   97

The Actor
Conley, Robert J.   1236

Adam Bede
Eliot, George   1908

Adams of the Bounty
Wilson, Erle   6807

The Adelita
Hall, Oakley   2649

Adios!
Bartlett, Lanier   366

Admiral Hornblower in the West Indies
Forester, C.S.   2169

Admiral of Fear
Suthren, Victor   6126

The Admiral's Lady
Gibbs, Mary Ann   2395

Adobe Walls: A Novel of the Last Apache Rising
Burnett, William R.   791

Adrienne
Levy, Barbara   3742

The Adulteress
Carr, Philippa   916

The Adventure of "Horse" Barnsby
Stong, Philip D.   6065

The Adventure of the Stalwart Companions
Jeffers, H. Paul   3177

The Adventurer
Waltari, Mika   6550

The Adventurers
Haycox, Ernest   2787
Long, William Stuart   3869

The Adventures of Don Juan
Gardner, Richard   2289

The Adventures of Jeremiah Dimon: The Novel of Old East Hampton
Rattray, Everett   5255

The Adventures of Long John Silver
Judd, Denis   3317

The Adventuress
Chesney, Marion   1014

The Adversary
Widgery, Jan   6738

Adversary in the House
Stone, Irving   6053

Affairs of Love
Thorne, Nicola   6272

The Affairs of Nicholas Culpepper
Tyrrel, Mabel L.   6375

The African
Courlander, Harold   1386

After Goliath
Cassill, R.V.   955

After the Glory
Miller, Helen Topping   4383

After the Rainbow
Kalman, Yvonne   3323

Afternoon of a Autocrat
Lofts, Norah   3834

Afterward
Rae, Catherine M.   5234

Against the Fall of Night
Arnold, Michael   193

Against the Tide
Elwood, Muriel   1935

Against This Rock
Zara, Louis   6948

Agatha
Tynan, Kathleen   6374

The Age of Miracles
MacCoun, Catherine   3960

The Age of Wonders
Appelfeld, Aharon   173

The Agony and the Ecstasy
Stone, Irving   6054

Agotime, Her Legend
Gleason, Judith   2430

Agrippa's Daughter
Fast, Howard   2025

Aide to Glory
Devon, Louis   1635

Ain't Goin' to Glory
Delman, David   1597

An Air of Glory
Neilan, Sarah   4563

Akhnaton, King of Egypt
Merezhkovski, Dmitri   4337

Alabama Empire
Kelley, Welbourn   3392

Alamut
Tarr, Judith   6164

Alaska
Michener, James A. 4364

Albany
Black, Laura 519

Albert's Victoria
Whittle, Tyler 6719

Albuquerque
Orwig, Sara 4757

The Alchymist's Journal
Connell, Evan S. 1256

Alcibiades, Beloved of Gods
Brun, Vincenz 735

Alethea
Belle, Pamela 429

Alexa
Melville, Anne 4330

Alexander Hamilton's Wife
Desmond, Alice Curtis 1623

Alexander in Babylon
Wassermann, Jakob 6576

**Alexander of Macedon: The Journey
to World's End**
Lamb, Harold 3607

Alexander the Glorious
Oliver, Jane 4719

Alexander the God
Druon, Maurice 1731
Payne, Robert 4849

The Alexandrian
Rofheart, Martha 5425

The Alfred Hitchcock Murder Case
Baxt, George 382

**Alice and Edith: A Biographical
Novel of the Two Wives of
Theodore Roosevelt**
Wilson, Dorothy Clarke 6798

Alice of Old Vincennes
Thompson, Maurice 6268

The Alien Light
Crichton Smith, Iain 1427

The Alienist
Carr, Caleb 907

All Desires Known
Macdonald, Malcolm 3963

**All for Love: Baby Doe and Silver
Dollar**
Vernon, John 6456

All God's Children
Anderson, Alston 136

All in Good Time
Allis, Marguerite 106

**All My Sins: A Novel of the Life and
Loves of Ninon de Lenclos**
Estey, Norbert 1965

All or Nothing
Longstreet, Stephen 3881

All Souls' Rising
Bell, Madison Smartt 422

All the Brave Rifles
Venable, Clarke 6450

All the Golden Gifts
Fuller, Iola 2251

All the King's Ladies
Law, Janice 3678

**All the Living: A Novel of One Year
in the Life of William Shakespeare**
Buckmaster, Henrietta 758

All the Queen's Men
Anthony, Evelyn 157

**All the Trumpets Sounded: A Novel
Based on the Life of Moses**
Hardy, W.G. 2701

All Their Kingdoms
Polland, Madeleine 5084

All This, and Heaven Too
Field, Rachel 2080

All Ye People
Colby, Merle Estes 1167

Allegheny Captive
Bourne, Caroline 591

Allegra
Darcy, Clare 1483

Alone Among Men
Coryn, Marjorie 1355

Alone Atop the Mountain
Sandmel, Samuel 5591

The Alpha Raid
Scholefield, Alan 5651

The Altar and the Crown
Niven, Marian 4631

Always a River
Mayrant, Drayton 4211

Amanda/Miranda
Peck, Richard 4882

The Amazing Mrs. Bonaparte
Kane, Harnett T. 3351

Amber Princess
Treece, Henry 6325

Ambush
Porter, Donald Clayton 5113

America, America
Kazan, Elia 3380

The American
Dodge, Louis 1669
Fast, Howard 2026

American Beauty
Ferber, Edna 2060

American Captain
Marshall, Edison 4101

The American Cowboy
James, Will 3163

American Eden
Harris, Marilyn 2728

American Falls
Batchelor, John Calvin 376

The American Heiress
Eden, Dorothy 1854

The American River
McCarthy, Gary 4222

An American, Sir
Root, Corwin 5459

The Americans
Jakes, John 3143

Amistad: The Thunder of Freedom
Pesci, David 4944

Ammahabas
Hotchkiss, Bill 3036

Among the Innocent
Trevino, Elizabeth Borton de 6339

The Amulet
Borland, Hal 582

Anabasis: A Journey to the Interior
Gilchrist, Ellen 2408

The Anatolian
Kazan, Elia 3381

The Ancestors Cry Out
West, Eugenia Lovett 6627

Ancient Evenings
Mailer, Norman 4035

An Ancient Evil
Grace, C.L. 2504

And Abram Journeyed
Simonhoff, Harry 5858

And Never Yield
Pryor, Elinor 5204

And One Rode West
Graham, Heather 2514

And One Wore Gray
Graham, Heather 2515

And Tell of Time
Krey, Laura 3554

And the Desert Shall Bloom
Barber, Phyllis 299

And the Stars Shall Fall
Bowen, True 603

And the Wild Birds Sing
Irish, Lola 3112

And Wait for the Night
Corrington, John William 1352

**And Walk on Love: A Novel Based
on the Life of the Apostle Paul**
Buckmaster, Henrietta 759

Andersonville
Kantor, MacKinlay 3359

Angel
Dunn, Carola 1790

**The Angel: A Novel Based on the Life
of Alexander I of Russia**
Blech, William James 543

Angel of Death
Doherty, P.C. 1670

Angel of the Delta
Murphy, Edward Francis 4521

**The Angel of the Opera: Sherlock
Holmes Meets the Phantom of the
Opera**
Siciliano, Sam 5842

Angel with Spurs
Wellman, Paul I. 6613

The Angel with the Trumpet
Lothar, Ernst 3898

Angelica
Schreiner, Samuel A. Jr. 5671

Angelique
Golon, Sergeanne 2465

Angelique and the Demon
Golon, Sergeanne 2466

Angelique and the Ghosts
Golon, Sergeanne 2467

Angelique and the King
Golon, Sergeanne 2468

Angelique in Barbary
Golon, Sergeanne 2469

Angelique in Love
Golon, Sergeanne 2470

Angelique in Revolt
Golon, Sergeanne 2471

Angels Falling
Elliott, Janice 1915

Angle of Repose
Stegner, Wallace 5989

The Angry Tide
Graham, Winston 2521

The Animal Wife
Thomas, Elizabeth Marshall 6243

Animating Maria
Chesney, Marion 1015

Ann of Cambray
Lide, Mary 3772

Anna
Harrod-Eagles, Cynthia 2752

Anna, Ann, Annie
Parker, Thomas Trebitsch 4808

Anna Zenger: Mother of Freedom
Cooper, Kent 1316

Annapolis
Martin, William 4137

Anna's Book
Vine, Barbara 6500

Anne Boleyn
Anthony, Evelyn 158

Anne Bonny
Gartner, Chloe 2306

Anne of Geierstein
Scott, Sir Walter 5689

Anne of the Thousand Days
Fenton, Edward 2059

Annie
Jahoda, Gloria 3141

Annie's Captain
Hulme, Kathryn 3077

Anno-Dracula
Newman, Kim 4595

Another Country
Schoeman, Karel 5646

Another Spring
Erdman, Loula Grace 1948

The Antagonists
Gann, Ernest K. 2276

The Anthem
Gerson, Noel B. 2361

Anthony Adverse
Allen, Hervey 98

Anthony Trant
Downing, John Hyatt 1713

Antichrist: A Novel of the Emperor Frederick II
Holland, Cecelia 2982

Antioch Actress: A Novel of Pagan Against Christian
Perkins, Jacob Randolph 4913

Antipodes Jane: A Novel of Jane Austen in Australia
Ker Wilson, Barbara 3468

The Antiquary
Scott, Sir Walter 5690

Antonietta
Hersey, John 2868

Anything for Billy
McMurtry, Larry 4295

Apache
Comfort, Will 1226
Porter, Donald Clayton 5114

Apache Autumn
Skimin, Robert 5875

Apache Blood
Thompson, David 6250

Apache Devil
Burroughs, Edgar Rice 806

Apaches
Hall, Oakley 2650

The Apostle
Asch, Sholem 197

The Apothecary Rose
Robb, Candace M. 5364

Apple Tree Lean Down
Pearce, Mary E. 4860

Apprentice to the Sea
McCutchan, Philip 4240

April Lady
Heyer, Georgette 2873

April Morning
Fast, Howard 2027

April Rising
Sallis, Susan 5574

Arabella
Heyer, Georgette 2874

Arc d'X
Erickson, Steve 1953

The Arch of Stars
Alderman, Clifford Lindsey 66

The Archduke
Arnold, Michael 194

The Architecture of the Arkansas Ozarks
Harington, Donald 2708

Arctic Treachery
Woodman, Richard 6858

Ardent Flame
Winwar, Frances 6829

The Ardent Years
Stevenson, Janet 6003

Arena: A Novel of Spartacus and Crassus
Ghnassia, Maurice 2391

Arfive
Guthrie, A.B. Jr. 2623

The Argonauts
Schoell, Yvonne 5645

Arizona
Kelland, Clarence Budington 3387

Arizona!
Ross, Dana Fuller 5466

Arizona Ecstasy
Bittner, Rosanne 511

The Arkansas River
Sherman, Jory 5816

The Arm and the Darkness
Caldwell, Taylor 850

Armada
Gidley, Charles 2404

Armored Giants: A Novel of the Civil War
Mason, F. van Wyck 4145

Arms of Nemesis
Saylor, Steven 5623

An Army of Angels: A Novel of Joan of Arc
Marcantel, Pamela 4079

An Army of Children
Rhodes, Evan H. 5306

Arne
Bjornson, Bjornstjerne 518

Arouse and Beware
Kantor, MacKinlay 3360

Arrest Sitting Bull
Jones, Douglas C. 3273

Arrogance
Scott, Joanna 5679

The Arrows of Hercules
De Camp, L. Sprague 1553

Artemesia
Banti, Anna 295

Artemia
Hill, Pamela 2927

Arthur
Lawhead, Stephen R. 3679

Arthur Dimmesdale
Larson, Charles R. 3671

Arthur Rex: A Legendary Novel
Berger, Thomas 477

Articles of Faith
Harwood, Ronald 2770

Artillery of Time
Smith, Chard Powers 5919

The Artist
Garbo, Norman 2281

The Artist's Daughter
O'Grady, Leslie 4698

Artorius Rex
Gloag, John 2432

Arundel
Roberts, Kenneth 5383

As a Driven Leaf
Steinberg, Milton 5992

As Long as the Rivers Run
Slate, Sam J. 5882

As Runs the Glass
David, Evan John 1502

As Sure as the Dawn
Rivers, Francine 5352

As the Crow Flies
Archer, Jeffrey 183

Ashana
Roesch, E.P. 5424

The Asherwood Protegee
Garratt, Mary A. 2299

Ashes
Zeromski, Stefan 6960

Ashes in the Wilderness
Schofield, William Greenough 5649

The Ashes of Smyrna
Reinhardt, Richard 5294

Ashworth Hall
Perry, Anne 4918

Ask Me No Questions
Veryan, Patricia 6459

Ask My Brother
Wagner, Constance 6518

Ask No Quarter
Marsh, George Tracy 4099

The Asking Price
Stirling, Jessica 6039

The Assassination of Jesse James by the Coward Robert Ford
Hansen, Ron 2680

The Assassination of Mozart
Weiss, David 6604

The Assyrian
Guild, Nicholas 2610

The Astrov Legacy
Heaven, Constance 2802

Asya
Ignatieff, Michael 3103

Asylum for the Queen
Jordan, Mildred A. 3303

At the Moon's Inn
Lytle, Andrew 3944

At the Sign of the Golden Pineapple
Chesney, Marion 1016

At the Sign of the Reine Pedauque
France, Anatole 2198

Atala
Chateaubriand, Francois Rene de 1008

The Athelsons
Kettle, Jocelyn 3476

Attack the Lusitania!
Hitchcock, Raymond 2956

Attila's Treasure
Grundy, Stephan 2606

Audrey
Johnston, Mary 3229

August 1914
Solzhenitsyn, Alexander 5942

Augustus
Massie, Allan 4167
Williams, John 6785

Aunt Bel
McCrone, Guy 4231

Aurora Rose
Worboys, Anne 6870

The Authentic Death of Hendry Jones
Neider, Charles 4562

The Autobiography of Henry VIII
George, Margaret 2355

The Autobiography of Miss Jane Pittman
Gaines, Ernest J. 2270

An Autumn in Araby
Salisbury, Carola 5565

Autumn Lace
Jackson, Eileen 3133

The Autumn Rose
Hill, Fiona 2923

Avalon
Seton, Anya 5748

Avery's Knot
Cable, Mary 843

The Aviator
Gann, Ernest K. 2277

The Axe
Undset, Sigrid 6378

Axe for an Abbot
Eyre, Elizabeth 1989

Aztec
Jennings, Gary 3193

B

Babylon
Esler, Anthony 1959

The Babylonians
Weinreb, Nathaniel Norsen 6600

Back Bay
Martin, William 4138

Back in Society
Chesney, Marion 1017

Back to Battle
Hennessy, Max 2828

Back to Malachi
Conley, Robert J. 1237

The Bad Lands
Hall, Oakley 2651

Badenheim 1939
Appelfeld, Aharon 174

Badge of Glory
Reeman, Douglas E. 5287

Bagatelle
Denuziere, Maurice 1613

The Bait and the Trap
Challis, George 970

A Balance of Dangers
Forrest, Anthony 2184

Balboa: Conquistador
Garrison, Omar V. 2303

Balisand
Hergesheimer, Joseph 2853

The Ballad of Typhoid Mary
Federspiel, Jurg 2057

Ballenrose
Burgess, Mallory 783

The Balloonist
Harris, Macdonald 2724

Baltic Mission
Woodman, Richard 6859

Band of Angels
Warren, Robert Penn 6572

The Band Plays Dixie
Markey, Morris 4089

Baneful Sorceries, or The Countess Bewitched
Sanders, Joan 5585

Banished Children of Eve
Quinn, Peter 5227

The Banishment
Chesney, Marion 1018

The Bank
Longstreet, Stephen 3882

The Bannaman Legacy
Cookson, Catherine 1272

Banner at Shenandoah
Catton, Bruce 963

Banner by the Wayside
Adams, Samuel Hopkins 28

Banners Against the Wind
Jennings, John Edward 3198

Banners of Gold
Kaufman, Pamela 3371

Banners of Silk
Laker, Rosalind 3592

Barabbas
Lagerkvist, Par 3585

Barabbas: A Dream of the World's Tragedy
Corelli, Marie 1327

Barabbas: A Novel of the Time of Jesus
Bekessy, Emery 417

The Barbarian
Price, Willard 5191

Bard: The Odyssey of the Irish
Llywelyn, Morgan 3816

The Barefoot Brigade
Jones, Douglas C. 3274

Barnaby Rudge: A Tale of the Riots of Eighty
Dickens, Charles 1641

The Baroness of Bow Street
Clark, Gail 1085

The Barons of Runnymede
Bennetts, Pamela 445

The Barrier
Maugham, Robin 4195

Barry Lyndon
Thackeray, William Makepeace 6210

The Bartholomew Fair Murders
Tourney, Leonard 6297

Basilissa: A Tale of the Empress Theodora
Masefield, John 4142

The Bastard
Jakes, John 3144
Tessin, Brigitte Von 6208

The Bastard King
Plaidy, Jean 5004

Bates House
Benadum, Clarence 437

Bath Tangle
Heyer, Georgette 2875

Bathsheba
Dorr, Roberta Kells 1695
Lindgren, Torgny 3789

Baton Sinister
Spinatelli, Carl J. 5967

The Battle-Ax of God
MacLeod, Le Roy 4007

Battle Flag
Cornwell, Bernard 1333

Battle Lanterns
Allen, Merrit Parmalee 102

The Battle of the Queens
Plaidy, Jean 5005

The Battle of Wagram
Lapouge, Gilles 3664

Bay of Arrows
Parini, Jay 4800

Bayonets in the Sun
Moore, William 4446

Bayou
Jekel, Pamela 3183

Bayou City Secrets
Powell, Deborah 5146

The Bayou Road
Eberhart, Mignon G. 1832

Be My Love
Hinsdale, Harriet 2955

The Beacon of Alexandria
Bradshaw, Gillian 627

The Beano
Robinson, Rony 5411

The Bear Flag: A Novel of the Birth of California
Holland, Cecelia 2983

Bear His Mild Yoke
White, Ethel 6675

Bearer of the Pipe
Coldsmith, Don 1169

The Bearkeeper's Daughter
Bradshaw, Gillian 628

Beat to Quarters
Forester, C.S. 2170

Beatrice Goes to Brighton
Chesney, Marion 1019

Beau Barron's Lady
Ashfield, Helen 204

Beau Blackstone
Falkirk, Richard 2005

Beauty Beast
Kantor, MacKinlay 3361

Beauty for Ashes
Wilson, Timothy R. 6816

Beauty From Ashes
Price, Eugenia 5177

Beauty's Daughter
Hardwick, Mollie 2689

Beauvallet
Heyer, Georgette 2876

Beckoning Ridge
Waldman, Emerson 6527

The Beckoning Road
Snedeker, Caroline 5934

The Beckoning Waters
Carse, Robert 944

Becky Landers, Frontier Warrior
Skinner, Constance 5879

Bed in Hell
Vipont, Elfrida 6504

Bedford Row
Rayner, Claire 5259

Bedford Village
Allen, Hervey 99

Beecher: A Novel
McCall, Dan 4218

The Beekeeper's Apprentice, or, On the Segregation of the Queen
King, Laurie R. 3487

Before Darkness Falls
Price, Eugenia 5178

Before My Time
Tucci, Niccolo 6358

Before the Glory Ended
Zilinsky, Ursula 6963

Before the Wind
Moxon, Lloyd M. 4506

Beginning the World Again
Silman, Roberta 5851

Beguiled
Borchardt, Alice 577

Behold the Fire
Blankfort, Michael 541

Behold the Man
Kagawa, Toyohiko 3321
Nash, N. Richard 4556

Behold, We Live
Dunscomb, Charles 1812

Behold Your King
Bauer, Florence M. 379

Being Met Together
Wilkins, William Vaughan 6756

The Belchamber Scandal
Murray, Frances 4533

Belgrave Square
Perry, Anne 4919
Summerson, Rachel 6117

The Believers
Giles, Janice Holt 2409

Belinda Goes to Bath
Chesney, Marion 1020

The Bellamy Saga
Pearson, John 4878

La Belle
Coker, Elizabeth Boatwright 1161

La Belle Sorel
Carton, Jacques 949

Belle Starr
Camp, Deborah 870
Morgan, Speer 4453

The Bellerose Bargain
Carr, Robyn 934

Belmarch: A Legend of the First Crusade
Davis, Christopher 1514

Beloved
Delmar, Vina 1599

Beloved Enemy
Lacy, Al 3579

Beloved Enemy: The Passions of Eleanor of Aquitaine
Jones, Ellen 3288

Beloved Exile
Godwin, Parke 2446

The Beloved Invader
Price, Eugenia 5179

Beloved Lady
Jefferis, Barbara 3174

Beloved Soldiers
Skelton, C.L. 5871

Below the Salt
Costain, Thomas B. 1362

The Belt of Gold
Holland, Cecelia 2984

Ben Hur: A Tale of the Christ
Wallace, Lew 6536

Ben Retallick
Thompson, E.V. 6263

Bend Your Heads All
Farrar, Rowena Rutherford 2015

Beneath the Blue Mountain
Wheeler, Richard S. 6656

Benjamin Blake
Marshall, Edison 4102

Benjamin Franklin and a Case of Artful Murder
Hall, Robert Lee 2654

Benjamin Franklin and a Case of Christmas Murder
Hall, Robert Lee 2655

Benjamin Franklin Takes the Case
Hall, Robert Lee 2656

Benjy Boone
Dolbier, Maurice 1687

Bennett's Welcome
Fletcher, Inglis 2132

Benton's Row
Yerby, Frank 6908

Bernadin, My Love
Rossiter, Leonard 5506

Bertie, Albert Edward, Prince of Wales
Whittle, Tyler 6720

Bertie and the Crime of Passion
Lovesey, Peter 3907

Bertie and the Seven Bodies
Lovesey, Peter 3908

Bertie and the Tinman
Lovesey, Peter 3909

Besieger of Cities
Duggan, Alfred 1761

The Best House in Stratford
Fisher, Edward 2100

Bethlehem Road
Perry, Anne 4920

The Betrothed
Manzoni, Alessandro 4078
Scott, Sir Walter 5691

The Bette Davis Murder Case
Baxt, George 383

Better in the Dark
Yarbro, Chelsea Quinn 6894

Between Earth and Sky
Osborn, Karen 4758

Between Eternities
Pilpel, Robert H. 5001

Between Two Worlds
High, Monique Raphel 2913

Beulah Land
Coleman, Lonnie 1202
Davis, Harold Lenoir 1520

Beware, Beware the Bight of Benin
McCutchan, Philip 4241

Beware of Caesar
Sheean, Vincent 5786

Beyond All Frontiers
Drummond, Emma 1722

Beyond Desire: A Novel Based on the Life of Felix and Cecille Mendelssohn
La Mure, Pierre 3574

Beyond Surrender
Sims, Marian 5860

Beyond the Aegean
Kazan, Elia 3382

Beyond the Blue Mountains
Plaidy, Jean 5006

Beyond the Blue Sierra
Morrow, Honore 4486

Beyond the Sea of Ice
Sarabande, William 5595

Beyond the Shadowlands
Fleming, Georgina 2126

Beyond the Shining Mountains
Shannon, Doris 5775

Beyond the Stars
Ross, David William 5497

Bianca
Conquist, Mabel 1257

Bide Me Fair
Howells, Harvey 3060

The Big Chariot
Clift, Charmian 1118

The Big Drum
Coker, Elizabeth Boatwright 1162

Big Ember
Havill, Edward 2778

The Big Family
Delmar, Vina 1600

The Big Fisherman
Douglas, Lloyd C. 1702

The Big Freeze
Partridge, Bellamy 4823

The Big Knives
Lancaster, Bruce 3635

The Big Lonesome
Bryant, Will 737

Big River, Big Man
Duncan, Thomas William 1786

The Big Sky
Guthrie, A.B. Jr. 2624

The Big Stick
Alexander, Lawrence 82

The Big Wind
Coogan, Beatrice 1262

Bighorn Legacy
Gear, W. Michael 2332

Billy Bathgate
Doctorow, E.L. 1656

Billy Budd
Melville, Herman 4333

Billy Sunday
Jones, Rod 3295

Billy the Kid
Corle, Edwin 1330

Billy the Kid: The Legend of El Chivato
Fackler, Elizabeth 1994

Bird of Fire: A Tale of Francis of Assisi
White, Helen Constance 6676

Birdsong
Faulks, Sebastian 2051

The Birthday Boys
Bainbridge, Beryl 269

Birthright
Finch, Phillip 2087
Wall, Robert E. 6533

Bisbee '17
Houston, Robert 3056

Biscayne
Kaplan, Barry Jay 3365

The Bishop's Tale
Frazer, Margaret 2215

The Bisley Boy
Hunt, Christopher 3080

Bitter Creek
Cody, Al 1150

Bittersweet
Li, Leslie 3769

The Bizarre Sisters
Walz, Jay 6559

The Black Angels
Lovelace, Maude Hart 3902

Black Angels
Ritchie, C.T. 5348

The Black Arrow
Stevenson, Robert Louis 6008

Black Body
Turk, H.C. 6361

The Black Candle
Cookson, Catherine 1273

The Black Cockade
Suthren, Victor 6127

The Black Consul
Vinogradov, Anatolii 6503

Black Dawn
Nicole, Christopher 4613

The Black Duchess
Knight, Alanna 3514

The Black Dwarf
Scott, Sir Walter 5692

Black-Eyed Susan
Camp, Deborah 871

Black Feather
Titus, Harold 6283

Black Forest
Minnigerode, Meade 4411

Black Gold
Bunkley, Anita Richmond 771

Black Ivory
Banks, Polan 292

Black Jack Davy
Oskison, John 4763

The Black Mask Murderers
Nolan, William F. 4635

The Black Moon
Graham, Winston 2522

The Black Moth
Heyer, Georgette 2877

Black Plume: The Supressed Memoirs of Edgar Allan Poe
Madsen, David 4027

Black Robe
Moore, Brian 4441

The Black Rose
Costain, Thomas B. 1363

Black Sheep
Heyer, Georgette 2878

The Black Sheep's Daughter
Dunn, Carola 1791

Black Sun
Johnston, Terry C. 3242

The Black Swan
Carr, Philippa 917

Black Thunder
Bontemps, Arna 574

Black Triumvirate: A Novel of Haiti
Levin, Benjamin H. 3736

The Black Velvet Gown
Cookson, Catherine 1274

Black William
Neill, Robert 4567

Blackfoot Massacre
Thompson, David 6251

The Blackheath Poisonings
Symons, Julian 6150

Blackrobe
Corcoran, Charles 1323
Wall, Robert E. 6534

The Blacksmith's Daughter
Dessau, Joanna 1625

Blackstone
Falkirk, Richard 2006

Blackstone and the Scourge of Europe
Falkirk, Richard 2007

Blackstone's Fancy
Falkirk, Richard 2008

Blackwater Spirits
Monfredo, Miriam Grace 4427

The Blade of Castlemayne
Esler, Anthony 1960

Blaize
Melville, Anne 4331

Blake's Reach
Gaskin, Catherine 2313

The Blanket of the Dark
Buchan, John 749

Bless This House
Lofts, Norah 3835

Blessed Are the Meek: A Novel about St. Francis of Assisi
Kossak-Szczucka, Zofja 3542

Blessed Is the Land
Zara, Louis 6949

Blessed McGill
Shrake, Edwin 5834

The Blind Bend
MacIntyre, Lorn 3985

Blind Journey
Lancaster, Bruce 3636

Blind Justice
Alexander, Bruce 76

Blood & Dreams
Waller, Leslie 6543

Blood and Sable
Kane, Carol J. 3350

Blood and Sand
Sutcliff, Rosemary 6121

Blood Brother
Arnold, Elliott 190

The Blood Countess
Codrescu, Andrei 1149

The Blood Endures
Inman, Robert 3107

Blood Fury
Thompson, David 6252

Blood Kin
Pauley, Barbara Anne 4845

Blood Line
Knight, Alanna 3515

The Blood of Roses
Canham, Marsha 879

Blood of the Boar
Abbey, Margaret 2

Blood of the Martyrs
Mitchison, Naomi 4417

Blood on the Divide
Johnstone, William W. 3265

Blood on the Snow
Elliott, John 1916

The Blood Order
Hunter, Jack D. 3084

Blood Red Rose
Grant, Maxwell 2538

Blood Red Roses
Coker, Elizabeth Boatwright 1163

Blood Royal
Hardwick, Mollie 2690
Payne, Robert 4850

The Blood Seed
Ward, Andrew 6561

Blood Song
Johnston, Terry C. 3243

The Blood Star
Guild, Nicholas 2611

Blood Truce
Thompson, David 6253

Blood Winter
Patrick, William 4830

Bloodbrothers
Wall, Robert E. 6535

A Bloodsmoor Romance
Oates, Joyce Carol 4658

The Bloody Benders
Adelman, Robert H. 35

The Bloody Field
Pargeter, Edith 4795

The Bloody Ground
Cornwell, Bernard 1334

Bloody Poet
Kosztolanyi, Deszo 3546

The Bloody Red Baron
Newman, Kim 4596

Bloody Season
Estleman, Loren D. 1968

Blossom Like the Rose
Lofts, Norah 3836

The Blue and the Gray
Leekley, John 3713

Blue Camellia
Keyes, Frances Parkinson 3477

The Blue Dragon
Brown, Diana 716

The Blue Falcon
Carr, Robyn 935

The Blue Heaven Bends Over All
Oliver, Jane 4720

Blue Hurricane
Mason, F. van Wyck 4146

The Blue Max
Hunter, Jack D. 3085

Blue Moon
Bonds, Parris Afton 569

Blue Ruin: A Novel of the 1919 World Series
Boyd, Brendan 610

Blue Russell
Bryant, Will 738

Bluegate Fields
Perry, Anne 4921

The Bluestocking
Delman, David 1598
Drummond, June 1729

Blunted Lance
Hennessy, Max 2829

Bodin, 1349: An Epic Novel of Christians and Jews in the Plague Years
Kalechofsky, Roberta 3322

Bold Encounter: A Novel Based on the Life of St. John of the Cross
Rohrbach, Peter-Thomas 5433

The Bomb Vessel
Woodman, Richard 6860

The Bond and the Free
Dunscomb, Charles 1813

Bond of Blood
Gellis, Roberta 2349

Bond of Honour
Todd, Catherine 6284

The Bondswoman
Ledner, Caryl 3705

The Bonnet Laird's Daughter
Annandale, Barbara 154

The Book Class
Auchincloss, Louis 228

The Book of Abraham
Halter, Marek 2665

The Book of Shadows
Grace, C.L. 2505

A Booke of Days: A Journal of the Crusade by Roger, Duke of Lunel
Rivele, Stephen J. 5351

The Books of Rachel
Gross, Joel 2600

Boon Island
Roberts, Kenneth 5384

Boone: A Novel Based on the Life and Times of Daniel Boone
Judd, Cameron 3311

The Border Captains
Manning, Jason 4072

Border Line
Conley, Robert J. 1238

The Border Lord
Westcott, Jan 6641

The Border Men
Judd, Cameron 3312

Borderlords
Johnston, Terry C. 3244

The Borgia Prince
Bennetts, Pamela 446

Borgia Testament
Balchin, Nigel 277

Born of the Sun
Culp, John H. 1440
Wolf, Joan 6837

Born of War
Taylor, Thomas 6192

Born Strangers
Miller, Helen Topping 4384

Born to Be King
Gluyas, Constance 2440

Born with the Century
Kinsolving, William 3501

Borrasca
Cohen, Octavus Roy 1160

Borrowed Plumes
Milne, Roseleen 4409

Bosnian Chronicle
Andric, Ivo 150

Botany Bay
Nordhoff, Charles 4637

Bound for the Promised Land
Marius, Richard 4083

Bound Girl
Webber, Everett 6591

The Bounty Lands
Ellis, William Donohue 1927

The Bourlotas Fortune
Gage, Nicholas 2268

Boy with a Pack
Meader, Stephen Warren 4319

The Boyds of Black River
Edmonds, Walter D. 1871

The Boy's Tale
Frazer, Margaret 2216

The Bracegirdle
Jenkins, Burris Atkins 3189

The Braeswood Tapestry
Carr, Robyn 936

The Braganza Pursuit
Neilan, Sarah 4564

The Brahmins
Lottman, Eileen 3901

The Braintree Mission
Wyckoff, Nicholas E. 6887

The Branch-Bearers
Petrie, Glen 4978

Brandywine
Rowe, Jack 5513

Brave Captains
Stuart, Vivian 6086

Brave General
Gorman, Herbert 2490

Brave Kingdom
Murray, Frances 4534

Brave Pursuit
Allis, Marguerite 107

Braveheart
Wallace, Randall 6538

The Bravo
Cooper, James Fenimore 1298

Bravo for the Bride
Eyre, Elizabeth 1990

Brazen Whispers
Feather, Jane 2055

Brazil
Uys, Errol Lincoln 6395

Brazos Dreamer
Shelton, Gene 5799

Bread and Circus
Renek, Morris 5303

Breakfast at the Hermitage
Crabb, Alfred Leland 1397

Breakheart Pass
MacLean, Alistair 3999

The Breast of the Dove
Gorman, Herbert 2491

The Breath of Kings
Farrington, Gene 2019

Brendan
Buechner, Frederick 762

The Briar Rose
Neale, Linda 4561

Bridal Journey
Van Every, Dale 6406

The Bridal Wreath
Undset, Sigrid 6379

The Bride
Garwood, Julie 2311
Irwin, Margaret 3116

A Bride for Donnigan
Oke, Janette 4705

A Bride for New Orleans
Murphy, Edward Francis 4522

Bride of a Thousand Cedars
Lancaster, Bruce 3637

Bride of Ae
Hill, Pamela 2928

Bride of Fortune
Kane, Harnett T. 3352

Bride of Glory
Field, Bradda 2078

The Bride of Lammermoor
Scott, Sir Walter 5693

Bride of Liberty
Yerby, Frank 6909

The Bride of Pilate
Kellner, Esther 3393

The Bride of Sforza
Seymour, Miranda 5760

The Bride of Suleiman
Crawley, Aileen 1421

The Bride of Texas
Skvorecky, Josef 5880

Bride of the Conqueror
Spence, Hartzell 5961

Bride of the MacHugh
Speas, Jan Cox 5956

Bride of the Morning Star
Coldsmith, Don 1170

Bride of the River
Harris, Laura B. 2723

Bride of the Spear
Herbert, Kathleen 2851

Bride of the Unicorn
Michaels, Kasey 4363

The Bride of the Wilderness
McCarry, Charles 4220

Bridey's Mountain
Adamson, Yvonne 34

The Bridge
Allis, Marguerite 108

The Bridge of a Hundred Dragons
Drummond, Emma 1723

The Bridge of San Luis Rey
Wilder, Thornton 6752

The Bridge on the Drina
Andric, Ivo 151

Bridge to Brooklyn
Idell, Albert E. 3099

Bridle the Wind
Davis, Julia 1525

Brief Gaudy Hour
Barnes, Margaret Campbell 322

The Bright Battalions
Breslin, Howard 664

The Bright Blue Sky
Hennessy, Max 2830

Bright Captivity
Price, Eugenia 5180

The Bright Face of Danger
Sublette, Clifford 6108

Bright Feather
Wilder, Robert 6750

The Bright Feathers
Culp, John H. 1441

Bright Journey
Derleth, August 1614

The Bright Land
Fairbank, Janet 2000

The Bright Sword
Perenyi, Eleanor 4911

Bright to the Wanderer
Lancaster, Bruce 3638

A Bright Tragic Thing
Clark, L.D. 1091

The Brightwood Expedition
McDonald, Kay L. 4261

Brimstone Club
Mason, F. van Wyck 4147

Bring Larks and Heroes
Keneally, Thomas 3410

The Brittle Glass
Lofts, Norah 3837

Broadsides
Daly, Robert Welter 1459

The Brocken
Hill, Pamela 2929

The Broken Sword
Edwards, Rhoda S. 1885

A Broken Vessel
Ross, Kate 5500

Broncho Apache
Wellman, Paul I. 6614

Bronte
Hughes, Glyn 3073

Bronze Christ
Nagaya, Yoshiro 4551

The Bronze God of Rhodes
De Camp, L. Sprague 1554

Bronze Mirror
Larsen, Jeanne 3668

A Brood of Vipers
Clynes, Michael 1133

The Brooks Legend
Ellis, William Donohue 1928

The Brother
Wilson, Dorothy Clarke 6799
Zeldis, Chayym 6958

Brother Cadfael's Penance
Peters, Ellis 4955

Brother Owl
Hine, Al 2953

Brother to the Enemy
Spicer, Bart 5964

Brother Wind
Harrison, Sue 2748

The Brotherhood of the Red Poppy
Troyat, Henri 6353

The Brothers of Gwynedd
Pargeter, Edith 4796

The Brothers of Uterica
Capps, Benjamin 887

Brothers of Vengeance
Blythe, LeGette 556

Brothers Three
Oskison, John 4764

Bruegel, or, The Workshop of Dreams
Rocquet, Claude Henri 5422

Brules
Combs, Harry 1223

Brumaire
Logan, Mark 3864

Buccaneer
Pope, Dudley 5093

Buccaneer Surgeon
Terry, C.V. 6205

The Buckingham Palace Connection
Willis, Ted 6792

Buckskin Baronet
Widdemer, Margaret 6734

Buckskin Cavalier
Clagett, John 1082

The Buckskin Girl: A Novel of the California Trail in the Mid-Nineteenth Century
Moffat, Gwen 4426

The Buckstones
Wellman, Paul I. 6615

Buffalo Coat
Brink, Carol 691

Buffalo Girls
McMurtry, Larry 4296

Buffalo Medicine
Coldsmith, Don 1171

Buffalo Palace
Johnston, Terry C. 3245

The Buffalo Soldiers
Prebble, John 5165

Buffalo Woman
Johnson, Dorothy M. 3223

Bugle in the Wilderness
Burress, John 805

The Bugles Are Silent: A Novel of the Texas Revolution
Knaggs, John R. 3513

Bugles Blow No More
Dowdey, Clifford 1704

Bugles in the Afternoon
Haycox, Ernest 2788

The Bull From the Sea
Renault, Mary 5295

Buller's Dreadnought
Hough, Richard 3047

Buller's Guns
Hough, Richard 3048

Buller's Victory
Hough, Richard 3049

Bullet for a Star
Kaminsky, Stuart M. 3331

Bully!
Schorr, Mark 5670

Bundori
Rowland, Laura Joh 5519

Burden of Desire
MacNeil, Robert 4023

Buried Caesars
Kaminsky, Stuart M. 3332

The Buried Self: A Background to the Poems of Matthew Arnold
MacDonald, Isobel 3961

Burning Gold
Andrews, Robert Hardy 148

The Burning Man
Longstreet, Stephen 3883

The Burnished Blade
Schoonover, Lawrence 5661

Burr
Vidal, Gore 6485

Burton and Speke
Harrison, William 2751

Bury Him Among Kings
Trevor, Elleston 6341

Bury Me in Ravenna
Vaughan, Agnes Carr 6432

Bush War!
Moore, William 4447

Butcher's Broom
Gunn, Neil 2620

Butcher's Crossing
Williams, John 6786

Buttes Landing
Rikhoff, Jean 5331

By Antietam Creek
Robertson, Don 5398

By Command of the Viceroy
MacNeil, Duncan 4010

By Dim and Flashing Lamps
Le May, Alan 3689

By Force of Arms
Nelson, James L. 4579

By Love Enslaved
Conn, Phoebe 1255

By Our Beginnings
Stubbs, Jean 6092

By Reason of Strength
Johnson, Gerald White 3225

By Right of Arms
Carr, Robyn 937

By the Dim Lamps
Schachner, Nathan 5630

By the Green of the Spring
Masters, John 4171

By the King's Command
Seifert, Shirley 5723

By Valour and Arms
Street, James H. 6076

Bygones
Wilkinson, Frank 6762

Byron: A Novel
Combuchen, Sigrid 1225

Byzantium
Ennis, Michael 1945
Lawhead, Stephen R. 3680

C

The Cabin at the Trail's End
Hargreaves, Sheba 2706

The Cactus and the Crown
Gavin, Catherine 2318

Caddie Woodlawn
Brink, Carol 692

A Cadenza for Caruso
Paul, Barbara 4834

Cadmus Henry
Edmonds, Walter D. 1872

Caesar
Jelusich, Mirko 3188
Massie, Allan 4168

Caesar of the Narrow Seas
Gloag, John 2433

Caesar's Women
McCullough, Colleen 4233

The Cage
Weston, Michael 6650

Cain and His Brother
Perry, Anne 4922

Cain's Daughters
Shannon, Doris 5776

Cajun
Dubus, Elizabeth Nell 1751

Calamity Jane of Deadwood Gulch
Hueston, Ethel 3068

Caleb Pettengill U.S.N.
Eliot, George Fielding 1912

A Calf for Venus
Lofts, Norah 3838

Calico Palace
Bristow, Gwen 694

California!
Ross, Dana Fuller 5467

California Caballero
MacDonald, William Colt 3981

California Glory
Ross, Dana Fuller 5468

California Gold
Jakes, John 3145

The Californian
Ballard, Todhunter 284

The Californios
L'Amour, Louis 3618

The Call
Hersey, John 2869

Call Home the Heart
Stirling, Jessica 6040

Call Lady Purbeck
Lewis, Hilda 3745

Call of the Arctic
Steelman, Robert 5987

Call of the Mountains
Meigs, Cornelia 4326

Call the Beast Thy Brother
Turner, William Oliver 6366

Call the Darkness Light
Zaroulis, Nancy 6954

Call the New World
Jennings, John Edward 3199

Callander Square
Perry, Anne 4923

Called Away
Buchan, Perdita 753

The Calling of Emily Evans
Oke, Janette 4706

Cambridge
Phillips, Caryl 4983

Camelot Country
McEvoy, Marjorie 4267

The Camp Grant Massacre
Arnold, Elliott 191

The Campaign
Fuentes, Carlos 2245

Campion Towers
Beatty, John 401

Canal Town
Adams, Samuel Hopkins 29

The Canary Trainer
Meyer, Nicholas 4348

A Candle for D'Artagnan
Yarbro, Chelsea Quinn 6895

A Candle in the Wilderness
Bacheller, Irving A. 256

Candle in the Window
Dodd, Christina 1662

Candle of the Wicked
Wellman, Manly Wade 6612

Candleshine No More
Oliver, Jane 4721

The Candlesticks and the Cross
Solomon, Ruth Freeman 5940

The Canebrake Men
Judd, Cameron 3313

Canis the Warrior
Sinclair, James 5864

The Cannaway Concern
Shelby, Graham 5788

The Cannaways
Shelby, Graham 5789

Cannibal Eliot and the Lost Histories of San Francisco
Obenzinger, Hilton 4660

Cannon's Call
Rutledge, Adam 5537

Cape Cod
Martin, William 4139

The Capricorn Stone
Brent, Madeleine 659

Captain Adam
Chidsey, Donald Barr 1058

Captain Barney
Westcott, Jan 6642

Captain Bashful
Chidsey, Donald Barr 1059

Captain Blood
Sabatini, Rafael 5546

Captain Bolton's Corpse
Jeffreys, J.G. 3178

Captain Boycott, a Romantic Novel
Rooney, Philip 5440

Captain Caution
Roberts, Kenneth 5385

Captain Cut-Throat
Carr, John Dickson 908

Captain Fantom
Underhill, Charles 6377

Captain for Elizabeth
Westcott, Jan 6643

Captain From Castille
Shellabarger, Samuel 5794

The Captain From Connecticut
Forester, C.S. 2171

Captain General
Stevenson, John P. 6007

Captain Grant
Seifert, Shirley 5724

Captain Ironhand
Marshall, Rosamond 4116

Captain Jack
Shelton, Gene 5800

Captain Justice
Forrest, Anthony 2185

Captain Lightfoot
Burnett, William R. 792

Captain Little Ax
Street, James H. 6077

Captain Marooner
Davidson, Louis B. 1504

Captain McRae: A Novel of the Northwest Frontier
Heuman, William 2872

Captain Monsoon
Suthren, Victor 6128

Captain Nash and the Honour of England
Butler, Ragan 827

Captain Nash and the Wroth Inheritance
Butler, Ragan 828

Captain of the Medici
Pugh, John J. 5206

Captain of the Sands
Dewhurst, Keith 1636

Captain Paul
Ellsberg, Edward 1930

Captain Rebel
Yerby, Frank 6910

Captain Sutter's Gold
Lauritzen, Jonreed 3673

Captain Vinegar's Commission
Glazebrook, Philip 2428

Captain Wonder
Thomas, Donald 6238

Captains and the Kings
Caldwell, Taylor 851

The Captain's Daughter
Pushkin, Alexander 5210

The Captive
Holt, Victoria 3011

The Captive Bride
Morris, Gilbert 4457

A Captive Freedom
Drummond, Emma 1724

The Captive of Kensington Palace
Plaidy, Jean 5007

Captive of Rome
Du Bois, Theodora McCormick 1740

The Captive Princess
Shore, Maxine 5831

The Captive Queen of Scots
Plaidy, Jean 5008

The Captive Witch
Van Every, Dale 6407

The Captives
Wright, Don 6878

Caravaggio
Payne, Robert 4851

The Caravaggio Shawl
Steward, Samuel M. 6019

Caravan to China
Stuart, Frank Stanley 6085

Caravan to Kanadu: A Novel of Marco Polo
Marshall, Edison 4103

Cardigan
Chambers, Robert W. 976

Cardigan Square
Manners, Alexandra 4070

The Cardinal and the Queen
Anthony, Evelyn 159

A Cardinal of the Medici
Beach, Susan Hicks 393

Cardington Crescent
Perry, Anne 4924

The Career of Magda V.
Machlis, Joseph 3982

Caressa
Bartell, Linda Lang 363

The Caretaker Wife
Whitehead, Barbara 6706

Cargo of Brides
Rucker, Helen 5522

Caribbean
Michener, James A. 4365

Caribbee
Hoover, Thomas 3025

Caribee
Nicole, Christopher 4614

The Carmelite
Groseclose, Elgin 2599

Carmen of the Rancho
Spearman, Frank H. 5955

Carnal Hours
Collins, Max Allan 1210

Carnival of Saints
Herman, George 2860

Carolina Corsair
Tracy, Don 6307

Carolina Courage
Ross, Dana Fuller 5469

Caroline and Julia
Darcy, Clare 1484

Caroline the Queen
Plaidy, Jean 5009

The Carolinian
Sabatini, Rafael 5547

The Carolinians
Barry, Jane 357

Carriage Trade
Thomsen, Robert 6271

Carrington
Straight, Michael Whitney 6074

Carry the Wind
Johnston, Terry C. 3246

A Case of Curiosities
Kurzweil, Allen 3569

The Case of Kitty Ogilvie
Stubbs, Jean 6093

A Case of Spirits
Lovesey, Peter 3910

*The Case of the Revolutionist's
   Daughter: Sherlock Holmes Meets
   Karl Marx*
Feuer, Lewis S. 2076

Casey
Stewart, Ramona 6034

Cashelmara
Howatch, Susan 3058

Cashmere
Thorne, Nicola 6273

The Casket Crew
Whitehouse, Arch 6709

Cassy
Lyle, Elizabeth 3930

Cast a Long Shadow
Pearce, Mary E. 4861

Castaway
Murray, Frances 4535

Castle Barebane
Aiken, Joan 43

Castle Dangerous
Scott, Sir Walter 5694

Castle Dor
Quiller-Couch, Sir Arthur
   Thomas 5226

Castle Garden
Albert, Bill 63

Castle Heritage
Barr, Elisabeth 337

A Castle in Bavaria
d'Orleans, Prince Thibaut 1693

Castle Malindine
Ford, Hilary 2163

Castle of Doves
Heaven, Constance 2803

Castle of Eagles
Heaven, Constance 2804

Castle of Foxes
Knight, Alanna 3516

The Castle of Fratta
Nievo, Ippolito 4625

The Castle of the Winds
Montague, Jeanne 4434

The Castrato
Goldman, Lawrence 2459

The Cat and the King
Auchincloss, Louis 229

Catalina
Maugham, William Somerset 4197

Catalina's Riddle
Saylor, Steven 5624

Catch a Falling Star
Kaminsky, Stuart M. 3333
Van de Water, Frederic F. 6401

The Cater Street Hangman
Perry, Anne 4925

Catherine
Lewis, Hilda 3746

The Catherine
MacDonald, Robert S. 3980

Catherine Carter
Johnson, Pamela Hansford 3227

Catherwood
Youmans, Marly 6937

The Catiline Conspiracy
Roberts, John Maddox 5379

Cato's War
Wheeler, Guy 6655

Catriona
Stevenson, Robert Louis 6009

The Cavalier of Tennessee
Nicholson, Meredith 4610

The Cavalryman
Sinclair, Harold 5861

Cease Firing
Johnston, Mary 3230

Cedarhaven
Campbell, Patricia 874

The Celebrant
Greenberg, Eric Rolfe 2572

Celebration!
Ross, Dana Fuller 5470

Celia Garth
Bristow, Gwen 695

Centennial
Michener, James A. 4366

Centennial Summer
Idell, Albert E. 3100

The Centurion
Hartog, Jan de 2762
Wibberley, Leonard 6729

Century in Scarlet
Zilahy, Lajos 6962

Ceremony of the Innocent
Caldwell, Taylor 852

*Certain Harvest: A Novel of the Time
   of Peter Cooper*
Knight, Ruth Adams 3525

Certain People of Importance
Norris, Kathleen 4647

A Certain Splendour
Salisbury, Carola 5566

*A Certain Woman: The Story of Mary
   Magdalene*
MacClure, Victor 3959

Cesar and Augusta
Harwood, Ronald 2771

Chad Hanna
Edmonds, Walter D. 1873

Chain of Destiny
Tranter, Nigel 6314

The Chains of Fate
Belle, Pamela 430

The Challenging Heights
Hennessy, Max 2831

Champion
Balling, L. Christian 285

A Chance for Glory
Wright, Constance 6877

The Chancellor
Schoonover, Lawrence 5662

The Chandler Heritage
Haas, Ben 2629

The Changeling
Carr, Philippa 918
Macleod, Alison 4000

The Chant of Jimmie Blacksmith
Keneally, Thomas 3411

Chant of the Hawk
Harris, John 2720

Chantefable
Dayton, Eldorous L. 1546

Chapultepec
Zollinger, Norman 6965

Charco Harbour
Blunden, Godfrey 554

Charge of Cowardice
MacNeil, Duncan 4011

Charing Cross
Rayner, Claire 5260

*Charioteer: A Story of Old Egypt in
   the Days of Joseph*
Eberle, Gertrude 1835

Chariots of Fire
Weatherby, W.J. 6586

Charity, Colorado
Yarbro, Chelsea Quinn 6896

Charity Girl
Heyer, Georgette 2879

Charity Strong
Allis, Marguerite 109

The Charlatan
Vaughan, Carter A. 6433

Charles
Lincoln, Victoria 3786

Charles O'Malley
Lever, Charles James 3731

Charles the King
Anthony, Evelyn 160

Charleston
Ripley, Alexandra 5338

Charlie Is My Darling
Hardwick, Mollie 2691

Charlotte Morel
Lodi, Maria 3829

Charlotte Morel: The Dream
Lodi, Maria 3830

Charlotte Morel: The Siege
Lodi, Maria 3831

Charming Sally
Lovelace, Maude Hart 3903

The Charterhouse of Parma
Stendhal 5993

Chase Royal
Seaman, Donald 5712

Chase the Heart
Osborne, Maggie 4760

Chase the Wind
Taylor, Janelle 6184
Thompson, E.V. 6264

The Chateau
Coulter, Stephen 1383

Chatterton
Ackroyd, Peter 17

Check-Out Time
Kingsbury, Kate 3491

Checkmate
Dunnett, Dorothy 1799

Chelsea
Fitzgerald, Nancy 2114

Chelsea Reach
Rayner, Claire 5261

Chelynne
Carr, Robyn 938

Cherished Enemy
Veryan, Patricia 6460

The Cherished Wives
Anand, Valerie 126

Cherokee
Porter, Donald Clayton 5115

Cherokee Dawn
Dellin, Genell 1596

*Cherokee Rose: A Novel of America's
   First Cowgirl*
Alter, Judy 119

Chesapeake
Michener, James A. 4367

*The Chess Player: A Novel of New
   Orleans and Paris*
Keyes, Frances Parkinson 3478

The Chessboard Queen
Newman, Sharan 4597

The Chester A. Arthur Conspiracy
Wiegand, William 6740

Chicago Girls
Freund, Edith 2229

Chief Joseph
Dugan, Bill 1756

Chief of Scouts
Bendell, Don 439

*The Chieftain: A Story of the Nez
   Perce People*
Payne, Robert 4852

Chihuahua 1916
Carney, Otis 903

Chikara!
Skimin, Robert 5876

Child of the Dead
Coldsmith, Don 1172

Child of the Mist
Morgan, Kathleen 4451

Child of the Morning
Gedge, Pauline 2343

Child of the Northern Spring
Woolley, Persia 6867

Child of the Snapping Turtle, Mike Fink
Rayford, Julian Lee 5256

Children of God
Fisher, Vardis 2106

The Children of Segu
Conde, Maryse 1232

Children of the Dawn
Rowe, Patricia 5516

Children of the Dust
Clancy, Carlile 1084

The Children of the First Man
Thom, James Alexander 6230

Children of the Ice
Prentiss, Charlotte 5166

Children of the Lion
Danielson, Peter 1464

The Children of the Sun
Hall, Oakley 2652

Children of the Sun
Prentiss, Charlotte 5167

Children of the Vampire: The Diaries of the Family Dracul
Kalogridis, Jeanne 3326

Children of the Wolf
Duggan, Alfred 1762

China Saga
Lee, C.Y. 3706

The Chinese Emperor
Levi, Jean 3733

The Chinese Nail Murders
van Gulik, Robert 6413

Chiricahua
Henry, Will 2839

The Chisholms
Hunter, Evan 3082

Chivalry
Sabatini, Rafael 5548

Choctaw
Porter, Donald Clayton 5116

A Choice of Murder
Vansittart, Peter 6429

The Choiring of the Trees
Harington, Donald 2709

A Chorus of Detectives
Paul, Barbara 4835

Christmas at Mount Vernon
Miller, Helen Topping 4385

Christmas for Tad: A Story of Mary and Abraham Lincoln
Miller, Helen Topping 4386

Christmas with Robert E. Lee
Miller, Helen Topping 4387

Christopher Humble
Judah, Charles Burnet 3310

Christopher Strange
McKee, Ruth Eleanor 4281

Cimarron
Ferber, Edna 2061

The Cinderpath
Cookson, Catherine 1275

Cinq-Mars
Vigny, Alfred Victor de 6495

Circle in the Water
Wiggs, Susan 6742

Circle of Gold
Harper, Karen 2710

Circle of Pearls
Laker, Rosalind 3593

A Circle of Trees
Faralla, Dana 2012

Citadel of God: A Novel of Saint Benedict
De Wohl, Louis 1563

The Citadel of the Lakes
Orr, Myron David 4754

Cities of the Flesh
Oldenbourg, Zoe 4713

Citizen Tom Paine
Fast, Howard 2028

A City for St. Francis
Wells, Evelyn 6621

A City Not Forsaken
Morris, Lynn 4480

City of Darkness, City of Light
Piercy, Marge 4998

City of God: A Novel of the Borgias
Holland, Cecelia 2985

The City of Gold
Young, Francis Brett 6940

City of Golden Cages
Germany, Jo 2358

City of Illusion
Fisher, Vardis 2107

The City of Libertines
Hardy, W.G. 2702

City of Light
Macleod, Alison 4001

City of the Flags
McMeekin, Clark 4290

City of Widows
Estleman, Loren D. 1969

A Civil Contract
Heyer, Georgette 2880

Clair De Lune: A Novel about Claude Debussy
La Mure, Pierre 3575

Claire
Lyle, Elizabeth 3931

The Clan of the Cave Bear
Auel, Jean M. 236

Clandara
Anthony, Evelyn 161

Clara Reeve
Hargrave, Leonie 2705

Claudine's Daughter
Laker, Rosalind 3594

Claudius the God
Graves, Robert 2543

Clear for Action!
Gerson, Noel B. 2362
White, Simon 6699

Clear for Action: A Novel about John Paul Jones
Ripley, Clements 5344

A Clear Road to Archangel
Rose, Geoffrey 5461

Cleopatra
Haggard, H. Rider 2637

The Cleopatra Boy
Malpass, Eric 4048

Clively Close: Dead as Dead Can Be
Crowleigh, Ann 1434

Cloak of Folly
Boyce, Burke 606

The Clock Tower
Montague, Jeanne 4435

Clodia
DeMaria, Robert 1606

The Cloister and the Hearth
Reade, Charles 5279

Close Quarters
Golding, William 2453

The Closest Possible Union
Scott, Joanna 5680

Cloud on the Land
Davis, Julia 1526

A Clouded Star
Parrish, Anne 4819

Clouds of Destiny
Davis, Lou Ellen 1535

Coasts of Folly
Williams, Joel 6784

The Coat I Wore
Finlay, Lucile 2090

Cock of the Walk
Lewis, Roy 3762

Cockades: A Romance
Minnigerode, Meade 4412

The Coil of the Serpent
Allen, Dexter 94

The Coin of Carthage
Bryher 740

A Cold Day in Hell
Johnston, Terry C. 3247

The Cold Journey
Stone, Grace Zaring 6052

Cold Sassy Tree
Burns, Olive Ann 797

Cold War
Vaughan, Robert 6446

Colfax
Conley, Robert J. 1239

Colliers Row
Webster, Jan 6592

Colonel Sandhurst to the Rescue
Chesney, Marion 1021

The Colonists
Long, William Stuart 3870

Color From a Light Within: A Novel Based on the Life of El Greco
Braider, Donald 641

The Color of Blood
Rundell, E. Ralph 5524

Colorado!
Ross, Dana Fuller 5471

Colorado Ambush
McCriede, Jess 4230

Colors Aloft!
Kent, Alexander 3427

The Colors of Vaud
Bryher 741

Colossus: A Novel about Goya and a World Gone Mad
Marlowe, Stephen 4093

Columbia
Jekel, Pamela 3184

Columbus: A Romance
Sabatini, Rafael 5549

Comanche Moon
Anderson, Catherine 137

The Comancheros
Wellman, Paul I. 6616

Come Be My Love
Brown, Diana 717

Come Home at Even
Cannon, Le Grand 884

Come Rack! Come Rope!
Benson, Robert Hugh 458

Come Slowly Eden: A Novel about Emily Dickinson
Benet, Laura 440

Come Spring
Hinger, Charlotte 2954
Williams, Ben Ames 6764

Come Winter
Jones, Douglas C. 3275

A Comedy of Murders
Herman, George 2861

Comes an Echo on the Breeze
Ryan, Edward J. 5542

The Coming of Rain
Marius, Richard 4084

The Coming of the King
Tolstoy, Nikolai 6296

Coming through Slaughter
Ondaatje, Michael 4736

Command a King's Ship
Kent, Alexander 3428

Command of the King
Lide, Mary 3773

Commander of the Mists
Murray, D.L. 4527

The Commodore
O'Brian, Patrick   4661

Commodore Hornblower
Forester, C.S.   2172

Company of Cowards
Schaefer, Jack   5634

A Company of Swans
Ibbotson, Eva   3095

Company Q
O'Connor, Richard   4684

Conceived in Liberty
Fast, Howard   2029

Concert Grand
Breslin, Howard   665

Concord Bridge
Horne, Howard   3035

Concordia
Fleetwood, Frances   2124

The Concubine
Lofts, Norah   3839

Condottiere
Westcott, Jan   6644

Confederates
Keneally, Thomas   3412

The Confessions of Brother Halvin
Peters, Ellis   4956

Confessions of Johnny Ringo
Aggeler, Geoff   40

The Confessions of Nat Turner
Styron, William   6106

Confessors of the Name
Schmitt, Gladys   5640

Coniston
Churchill, Winston   1078

Conjuror's Journal
Shine, Frances L.   5826

*A Connecticut Yankee in Criminal
    Court*
Heck, Peter J.   2814

*A Connecticut Yankee in King
    Arthur's Court*
Twain, Mark   6371

The Conquered
Mitchison, Naomi   4418

Conquering Horse
Manfred, Frederick F.   4055

The Conqueror
Heyer, Georgette   2881
Tebbel, John William   6194

*The Conqueror: A Novel of
    Alexander the Great*
Marshall, Edison   4104

*The Conqueror: Being the True and
    Romantic Story of Alexander
    Hamilton*
Atherton, Gertrude   222

Conqueror of the Clouds
Hallstead, William F.   2664

The Conquerors
Eckert, Allen W.   1839

The Conqueror's Wife
Gerson, Noel B.   2363

The Conquest
Deveraux, Jude   1630

The Conquest of Don Pedro
Fergusson, Harvey   2066

Conscience of the King
Duggan, Alfred   1763

Consort for Victoria
Wilkins, William Vaughan   6757

The Conspiracy
Hersey, John   2870

Conspiracy of Knaves
Brown, Dee   711

The Constant Star
Andrew, Prudence   139
Foote, Dorothy Norris   2151

*Constantine: The Miracle of the
    Flaming Cross*
Slaughter, Frank G.   5883

Consuelo
Sand, George   5582

*The Consuming Flame: The Story of
    George Eliot*
Kenyon, F.W.   3446

Contessa
Collin, Richard Oliver   1209
Mansfield, Helene   4076

The Convenient Marriage
Heyer, Georgette   2882

The Converts: A Historical Novel
Warner, Rex   6564

Copilli, Aztec Prince
Aleman Velasco, Miguel   75

Copperhead
Cornwell, Bernard   1335

Copperhead Moon
Stover, Herbert   6067

The Copperheads
Blech, William James   544

Cordelia
Graham, Winston   2523

Cordelia Chantrell
Minnigerode, Meade   4413

The Corinthians
Wyckoff, Nicholas E.   6888

Cormorant's Brood
Fletcher, Inglis   2133

The Corn King and the Spring Queen
Mitchison, Naomi   4419

The Corner That Held Them
Warner, Sylvia Townsend   6568

Corner the Moon
Barker, Shirley   310

The Cornerstone
Oldenbourg, Zoe   4714

Coromandel!
Masters, John   4172

Coronation Summer
Thirkell, Angela   6220

Corridor of Storms
Sarabande, William   5596

*The Corsair: A Biographical Novel of
    Jean Lafitte, Hero of the Battle of
    New Orleans*
Kent, Madeleine Fabiola   3444

Cortez and Marina
Marshall, Edison   4105

The Cortlandts of Washington Square
Fairbank, Janet   2001

Cosette: The Sequel to Les Miserables
Kalpakian, Laura   3329

The Cosgrove Report
O'Toole, G.J.A.   4765

Cotillion
Heyer, Georgette   2883

The Cotton Road
Feuille, Frank   2077

Cottonwoods Grow Tall
Houston, Margaret Bell   3055

The Council of Europe
Sciascia, Leonardo   5678

Count Belisarius
Graves, Robert   2544

Count Bohemond
Duggan, Alfred   1764

Count Manifred
Seymour, Miranda   5761

Count Robert of Paris
Scott, Sir Walter   5695

Count Vronsky's Daughter
Salisbury, Carola   5567

Counterfeit of Murder
Harrison, Ray   2738

The Countess
Cost, March   1360

The Countess Angelique
Golon, Sergeanne   2472

Countess Carrots
Haycraft, Molly Costain   2792

The Country Gentleman
Hill, Fiona   2924

Country People
Suckow, Ruth   6111

*The Court Martial of Commodore
    Perry*
Rhodes, James A.   5307

The Court Martial of Daniel Boone
Eckert, Allen W.   1840

*The Court-Martial of George
    Armstrong Custer*
Jones, Douglas C.   3276

The Court Martial of Robert E. Lee
Savage, Douglas   5617

Court of Honor
Fagyas, Maria   1996

A Court of Owls
Adicks, Richard   37

Court of Shadows
Morgan, Cynthia   4450

The Court of the Lion
Cooney, Eleanor   1294

Courtesan
Haeger, Diane   2635

Courting Emma Howe
Robinson, Margaret A.   5410

The Courts of Illusion
Jarman, Rosemary Hawley   3165

The Courts of Love
Plaidy, Jean   5010

*The Courts of Love: A Romance of
    Medieval France*
Bourne, Peter   592

Cousin Kate
Heyer, Georgette   2884

Cousin Susannah
Hucker, Hazel   3066

The Covenant
Knight, Brigid   3521
Michener, James A.   4368

*The Covenant: A Novel of the Life of
    Abraham the Prophet*
Kossak-Szczucka, Zofja   3543

Covenant of Grace
Rushing, Jane Gilmore   5527

*Covenant with the Vampire: The
    Diaries of the Family Dracul*
Kalogridis, Jeanne   3327

Covent Garden
Rayner, Claire   5262

Covered Wagon
Hough, Emerson   3041

The Cowboy and the Cossack
Huffaker, Claire   3071

The Cowboy Conspiracy
Names, Larry D.   4553

The Cowboys
Jennings, William Dale   3211

Cracksman on Velvet
Selwyn, Francis   5743

Cradle of the Sun
Clagett, John   1083

The Crater
Slotkin, Richard   5908

Crazy Fox Remembers
Preston, Don   5174

Crazy Horse
Dugan, Bill   1757

Crazy Snake
Conley, Robert J.   1240

Creation
Vidal, Gore   6486

Creature Comforts
Stirling, Jessica   6041

A Creek Called Wounded Knee
Jones, Douglas C.   3277

Creek Mary's Blood
Brown, Dee   712

Creole Dusk
Roberts, Walter Adolphe   5392

Crescent City
Plain, Belva 5078

Cressida
Darcy, Clare 1485

Crest of the Broken Wave
Barke, James 302

Crime Without Passion
Grayson, Richard 2556

The Crimson Chalice
Canning, Victor 882

Crimson Creek: A Novel of the Early West
McCraig, Robert 4228

Crimson Is the Eastern Shore
Tracy, Don 6308

The Crimson Wind
Hennessy, Max 2832

Crippled Splendour
John, Evan 3219

The Crisis
Churchill, Winston 1079

Croatan
Johnston, Mary 3231

Crockett of Tennessee: A Novel Based on the Life and Times of David Crockett
Judd, Cameron 3314

Crompton Way
Thompson, Thomas 6270

The Cross
Undset, Sigrid 6380

The Cross and the Sword
Galvan, Manuel de Jesus 2274
Lauritzen, Jonreed 3674
Walton, Evangeline 6558

The Cross of Frankenstein
Myers, Robert J. 4548

Cross, Sword, and Arrow
Barr, Gladys H. 340

A Crossbowman's Story of the First Exploration of the Amazon
Millar, George 4379

The Crossed Sabres
Morris, Gilbert 4458

The Crossing
Churchill, Winston 1080
McCarthy, Cormac 4221

Crossing over Jordan
Brown, Linda Beatrice 725

Crossing the River
Phillips, Caryl 4984

Crossings
Rovit, Earl 5512

Crouchback
Oman, Carola 4732

The Crow Goddess
Finney, Patricia 2094

The Crowded Hill
MacLeod, Le Roy 4008

The Crown and the Crucible
Phillips, Michael 4987

The Crown and the Shadow: The Story of Francoise d'Aubigne, Marquise de Maintenon
Hill, Pamela 2930

Crown in Candlelight
Jarman, Rosemary Hawley 3166

The Crown in Darkness
Doherty, P.C. 1671

A Crown in Darkness: A Novel about Lady Jane Grey
Mullally, Margaret 4512

Crown of Aloes
Lofts, Norah 3840

Crown of Grass
Brady, Charles Andrew 634

Crown of Roses
Anand, Valerie 127

The Crown Prince
Barchilon, John 300

Crown Without Sceptre
Wilkins, William Vaughan 6758

Crown Witness
Linscott, Gillian 3803

A Crowning Mercy
Kells, Susannah 3396

The Crows of War
Rayson, Steven 5276

Cruel in the Shadow
MacIntyre, Lorn 3986

Crum Elbow Folks
Barnes, Percy Raymond 332

The Crusader
Gerson, Noel B. 2364

Crusader's Torch
Yarbro, Chelsea Quinn 6897

The Cry and the Covenant
Thompson, Morton 6269

The Cry of Dolores
Gorman, Herbert 2492

Cry of the Hawk
Johnston, Terry C. 3248

Cry of the Peacock
Nahai, Gina Barkhordar 4552

Cry of the Rain Bird
Shaw, Patricia 5779

Cry to Heaven
Rice, Anne 5313

Crystal
Ashfield, Helen 205

The Crystal Cave
Stewart, Mary 6029

The Crystal Dove
Hardwick, Mollie 2692

The Crystal Star
Argo, Ellen 184

Csardas
Pearson, Diane 4875

The Culper Spy Ring
Groh, Lynn 2596

The Cumberland Rifles
Gerson, Noel B. 2365

The Cunning of the Dove
Duggan, Alfred 1765

Cunningham's Revenge
MacNeil, Duncan 4012

Cup of Gold
Steinbeck, John 5991

The Cup of Strength
Paul, Charlotte 4840

The Cup of Wrath
Glazener, Mary 2429

The Cup, the Blade or the Gun
Eberhart, Mignon G. 1833

The Cup Trembling
Brown, Karl 723

The Curse of Jezebel: A Novel of the Biblical Queen of Evil
Slaughter, Frank G. 5884

Curse of Magira
Bee, David 413

The Curse of the King
Holt, Victoria 3012

The Curse of the Pharaohs
Peters, Elizabeth 4948

Curtains for the Cardinal
Eyre, Elizabeth 1991

Custer Passed Our Way
Kaufman, Fred S. 3370

Cut to the Quick
Ross, Kate 5501

Cutlass Empire
Mason, F. van Wyck 4148

The Czar's Madman
Kross, Jaan 3560

D

The Dahomean
Yerby, Frank 6911

Daimon
Posse, Abel 5140

Daishi-San: A Novel
Lund, Robert P. 3925

Dakota!
Ross, Dana Fuller 5472

Damaris
Sheridan, Jane 5810

La Dame De Sainte Hermine
King, Grace 3485

Damnation Reef
Tattersall, Jill 6172

Damned Shall Be Desire: The Passionate Life of Guy de Maupassant
Coulter, Stephen 1384

Dance Back the Buffalo
Lott, Milton 3899

The Dance of Death
Potter, Jeremy 5142

Dance of the Assassins
Fagyas, Maria 1997

Dance of the Tiger: A Novel of the Ice Age
Kurten, Bjorn 3566

Dance on a Sinking Ship
Kilian, Michael 3483

Dance on the Wind
Johnston, Terry C. 3249

A Dancer in Darkness
Stacton, David 5971

Dances with Wolves
Blake, Michael 537

Dancing at the Rascal Fair
Doig, Ivan 1682

Dancing in the Dark
Kaminsky, Stuart M. 3334

Dando on Delhi Ridge
Clive, William 1119

Daneclere
Hill, Pamela 2931

Dangerous
Quick, Amanda 5213

A Dangerous Fortune
Follett, Ken 2147

A Dangerous Innocence
Lincoln, Victoria 3787

A Dangerous Mourning
Perry, Anne 4926

The Dangerous Years
Hennessy, Max 2833

Daniel Du Luth
McNeil, Everett 4307

Dan'l Boone Kissed Me
Holt, Felix 3006

Danzig Passage
Thoene, Bodie 6221

Daphne
Chesney, Marion 1022

Dara, the Cypriot
Paul, Louis 4842

The Dark Angel
Waltari, Mika 6551

Dark at Noon
Tattersall, Jill 6173

The Dark City
Collins, Max Allan 1211

The Dark Command
Burnett, William R. 793

The Dark Dancer
Prokosch, Frederic 5193

The Dark Fire
Murray, Linda 4537

Dark Hills to Westward
Caudill, Harry M. 964

Dark Inheritance
Salisbury, Carola 5568

The Dark Island
Treece, Henry 6326

The Dark Mile
Broster, Dorothy Kathleen 709

The Dark Palazzo
Coffman, Virginia   1151

The Dark Pasture
Stirling, Jessica   6042

Dark Possession
Lide, Alice Alison   3771

Dark Quartet: The Story of the Brontes
Banks, Lynne Reid   290

Dark Rider
Zara, Louis   6950

The Dark Rose
Walsh, Maurice   6549

Dark Sails
Miller, Helen Topping   4388

The Dark Stranger
Charques, Dorothy   999
Dodge, Constance   1664

Dark Thicket
Kelton, Elmer   3402

Dark Torrent of Glencoe
Grierson, Edward   2590

The Dark Way
Conley, Robert J.   1241

Dark Winds
Coffman, Virginia   1152

Darken Ship
Monsarrat, Nicholas   4431

The Darkening Leaf
Stickland, Caroline   6036

Darker Grows the Valley
Kroll, Harry Harrison   3556

Darker Jewels
Yarbro, Chelsea Quinn   6898

Darkness and the Dawn
Costain, Thomas B.   1364

A Darkness at Ingraham's Crest: A Tale of the Slaveholding South
Yerby, Frank   6912

The Darkness of Corn
Stickland, Caroline   6037

Darktown Strutters
Brown, Wesley   732

The Daughter: A Novel Based on the Life of Eleanor Marx
Chernaik, Judith   1012

Daughter of Eve
Gerson, Noel B.   2366

Daughter of Fortune
Kelly, Carla   3398

Daughter of Jairus
Fox, Paul Hervey   2196

A Daughter of Liberty
Cole, Allan   1196

Daughter of Marignac
Heaven, Constance   2805

Daughter of Satan
Plaidy, Jean   5011

Daughter of Shadows
Seymour, Miranda   5762

Daughter of Strangers
Coker, Elizabeth Boatwright   1164

Daughter of the Eagle
Coldsmith, Don   1173

Daughter of the Red Deer
Wolf, Joan   6838

The Daughter of Time
Tey, Josephine   6209

Daughter of Time
White, Nelia Gardner   6695

Daughters of England
Carr, Philippa   919

Daughters of the New World
Shreve, Susan Richards   5835

David and Bathsheba
Ibn-Sahav, Ari   3098

David at Olivet
Hamilton, Wallace   2671

David of Jerusalem
De Wohl, Louis   1564

David the King
Schmitt, Gladys   5641

David: Warrior and King
Slaughter, Frank G.   5885

David's Stranger
Shamir, Moshe   5771

Dawn Land
Bruchac, Joseph III   734

The Dawning of Deliverance
Pella, Judith   4892

Dawn's Early Light
Thane, Elswyth   6215

The Day Before Thunder
Spicer, Bart   5965

Day Is Coming
Cameron, William   869

The Day Must Dawn
Turnbull, Agnes Sligh   6362

A Day of Battle
Sheean, Vincent   5787

Day of Battle
Van de Water, Frederic F.   6402

The Day of the Scorpion
Scott, Paul   5682

The Day the Cowboys Quit
Kelton, Elmer   3403

The Day the Sun Died
Van Every, Dale   6408

The Day They Kidnapped Queen Victoria
Fleming, H.K.   2127

The Daybreakers
L'Amour, Louis   3619

The Days of the Butterfly
Lofts, Norah   3841

Days of the Gold
Blacker, Irwin R.   526

The Days of the King
Frank, Bruno   2200

The De Montfort Legacy
Bennetts, Pamela   447

A Dead Man in Deptford
Burgess, Anthony   776

Dead Man's Ransom
Peters, Ellis   4957

Dead Man's Sweetheart
Linscott, Gillian   3804

Dead Man's Walk
McMurtry, Larry   4297

Dead Reckoning
Parkinson, C. Northcote   4809

Dead-Stick
Washburn, L.J.   6574

Deadly Beloved
Knight, Alanna   3517

The Deadly Lady of Madagascar
Terry, C.V.   6206

Deadwood
Dexter, Pete   1638

Dean's Watch
Goudge, Elizabeth   2494

Dear and Glorious Physician
Caldwell, Taylor   853

Dear Laura
Stubbs, Jean   6094

Dear Lily
Greenough, Malcolm W. Jr.   2575

Dear Mrs. Boswell
Muir, Marie   4508

The Death and Life of Miguel De Cervantes
Marlowe, Stephen   4094

Death and the Chapman
Sedley, Kate   5715

Death at Daisy's Folly
Paige, Robin   4775

Death at Gallows Green
Paige, Robin   4776

Death at Rainy Mountain
Medawar, Mardi Oakley   4321

Death at the French Creek
Borel, Raymond C.   580

Death Comes as Epiphany
Newman, Sharan   4598

Death Comes as the End
Christie, Agatha   1076

Death Comes for the Archbishop
Cather, Willa   957

Death En Voyage
Grayson, Richard   2557

Death in a Deck Chair
Beck, K.K.   403

Death in the Devil's Acre
Perry, Anne   4927

Death of a Dancing Lady
Harrison, Ray   2739

The Death of a King
Doherty, P.C.   1672

Death of a Legend
Henry, Will   2840

Death of a Schoolboy
Koning, Hans   3537

The Death of Artemio Cruz
Fuentes, Carlos   2246

The Death of Attila
Holland, Cecelia   2986

The Death of Che Guevara
Cantor, Jay   886

The Death of Kings
Danielson, Peter   1465

The Death of Napoleon
Leys, Simon   3768

Death of the Duchess
Eyre, Elizabeth   1992

Death of the Fifth Sun
Somerlott, Robert   5944

Death of the Fox
Garrett, George   2300

The Death of the Gods
Merezhkovski, Dmitri   4338

Death of the Red King
Bennetts, Pamela   448

The Death of Virgil
Broch, Hermann   699

Death Off Stage
Grayson, Richard   2558

Death on the Appian Way
Benton, Kenneth   463

Death on the Cards
Grayson, Richard   2559

Death on the Cliff Walk
Kruger, Mary   3562

Death on the Mississippi
Heck, Peter J.   2815

Death Squad London
Gerson, Jack   2360

Death Wore a Diadem
McGregor, Iona   4277

Deathwatch
Harrison, Ray   2740

Deborah
Davenat, Colette   1498

Deborah and the Many Faces of Love
Davenat, Colette   1499

Deborah and the Siege of Paris
Davenat, Colette   1500

Deborah Goes to Dover
Chesney, Marion   1023

The Deceivers
Masters, John   4173

Deception
Cooney, Eleanor   1295
Quick, Amanda   5214

Decision at Trafalgar
Woodman, Richard   6861

The Dedicated
Gibbs, Willa   2399

The Dedicated Villain
Veryan, Patricia 6461

The Deeds of the Disturber
Peters, Elizabeth 4949

Deep Are the Valleys
Closs, Hannah 1129

Deep in My Heart: A Story Based on the Life of Sigmund Romberg
Arnold, Elliott 192

Deep River
Buckmaster, Henrietta 760

Deep Summer
Bristow, Gwen 696

Deeper the Heritage
Elwood, Muriel 1936

Deepwater: A Novel of the Carolinas
Jekel, Pamela 3185

The Deer Cry
Schofield, William Greenough 5650

The Deer Dancers
Cockrell, Amanda 1146

The Deerslayer
Cooper, James Fenimore 1299

Defend and Betray
Perry, Anne 4928

Defiant Hearts
Taylor, Janelle 6185

Defy Not the Heart
Lindsey, Johanna 3794

Deirdre
Stephens, James 5996

Deirdre and Desire
Chesney, Marion 1024

The Delectable Country
Baldwin, Leland Dewitt 280

Delilah's Mountain
Jahoda, Gloria 3142

The Deluge
Sienkiewicz, Henryk 5846

The Delusson Family
Ducharme, Jacques 1753

Demelza
Graham, Winston 2524

The Demise of Billy the Kid
Lewis, Preston 3760

The Demon Lover
Holt, Victoria 3013

Denis Duval
Thackeray, William Makepeace 6211

Departed Glory
Danielson, Peter 1466

Departure
Stevenson, Janet 6004

Depths of Glory
Stone, Irving 6055

The Descent of the Idol
Durych, Jaroslav 1818

Desert Hawks
Burleson, Frank 786

The Desirable Duchess
Chesney, Marion 1025

Desire and Deceive
Byers, Cordia 832

Desiree
Selinko, Annemarie 5741

Desolation Island
O'Brian, Patrick 4662

Desperadoes
Hansen, Ron 2681

Destiny Express
Rodman, Howard A. 5423

Destiny in Dallas
Seifert, Shirley 5725

Destiny of Fire
Oldenbourg, Zoe 4715

The Detective and Mr. Dickens
Palmer, William J. 4782

The Detective Wore Silk Drawers
Lovesey, Peter 3911

The Detling Secret
Symons, Julian 6151

The Devil and Ben Franklin
Mathieson, Theodore 4184

The Devil and the Mathers
Elliott, Edward E. 1914

Devil Child
Germany, Jo 2359

The Devil Gun
Syers, William 6148

The Devil in Harbour
Gavin, Catherine 2319

The Devil in Velvet
Carr, John Dickson 909

The Devil Inside: A Novel of Dostoevsky's Life
Coulter, Stephen 1385

The Devil Is Loose
Shelby, Graham 5790

The Devil Met a Lady
Kaminsky, Stuart M. 3335

The Devil on Horseback
Holt, Victoria 3014

Devil to Pay
Parkinson, C. Northcote 4810

Devil Water
Seton, Anya 5749

Devil's Backbone
Johnston, Terry C. 3250

The Devil's Card
Maher, Mary 4030

The Devil's Cross
O'Meara, Walter 4733

Devil's Cub
Heyer, Georgette 2885

The Devil's Door
Newman, Sharan 4599

Devil's Fire, Love's Revenge
Paul, Barbara 4836

The Devil's Laughter
Yerby, Frank 6913

The Devil's Lieutenant
Fagyas, Maria 1998

The Devil's Marchioness
Fifield, William 2082

The Devil's Novice
Peters, Ellis 4958

The Devil's Own
Nicole, Christopher 4615

The Devil's Rainbow
Furnas, J.C. 2257

The Devil's Spy
Hastings, Michael 2773

The Devil's Wind: Nana Saheb's Story
Malgonkar, Manohar 4039

Devil's Yard
Andric, Ivo 152

Devilseed
Yerby, Frank 6914

Devoted
Borchardt, Alice 578

Devoted Friends
Poyer, Joe 5161

Di and I
Lefcourt, Peter 3714

Diamond Head
Branch, Houston 647
Jackson, Marian J.A. 3135

Diamond Six
Smith, William Fielding 5932

Diamond Wedding
Steele, Wilbur Daniel 5986

Diana Stair
Dell, Floyd 1594

Diana the Huntress
Chesney, Marion 1026

The Diary of Emily Dickinson: A Novel
Fuller, Jamie 2255

The Diary of William Harvey: The Imaginary Journal of the Physician Who Revolutionized Medicine
Hamburger, Jean 2667

The Dice of God
Birney, Hoffman 507

Dido, Queen of Hearts
Atherton, Gertrude 223

Die the Long Day
Patterson, Orlando 4833

Dillinger
Patterson, Harry 4832

Dim the Flaring Lamps
Jordan, Jan 3301

Dina's Book
Wassmo, Herbjorg 6577

Dinner at Belmont
Crabb, Alfred Leland 1398

The Disappearance of Edwin Drood
Rowland, Peter 5521

The Disorderly Knights
Dunnett, Dorothy 1800

The Dispossessed
Shannon, Dell 5773

The Disputed Crown
Anand, Valerie 128

Disraeli in Love
Edelman, Maurice 1851

Disraeli Rising
Edelman, Maurice 1852

The Distant Lands
Green, Julian 2567

Distant Music
Davis, Harold Lenoir 1521

A Distant Thunder
de Luca, Teresa 1561

Distant Trails
Gulick, Bill 2612

Distant Trumpet
Horgan, Paul 3032

The Disturber
Davidson, L.S. Jr. 1505

Divine Average
Kirkland, Elithe Hamilton 3505

Divine Mistress
Slaughter, Frank G. 5886

A Division of the Spoils
Scott, Paul 5683

The Dixie Widow
Morris, Gilbert 4459

Dizzy's Woman
MacBeth, George 3957

Do Not Disturb
Kingsbury, Kate 3492

Doc Holliday's Woman
Coleman, Jane Candia 1201

Doctor Copernicus
Banville, John 296

The Doctor From Cordova: A Biographical Novel about the Great Philosopher Maimonides
Le Porrier, Herbert 3693

Dr. Guillotine: The Eccentric Exploits of an Early Scientist
Lom, Herbert 3867

Dr. Gully's Story
Jenkins, Elizabeth 3190

Doctor in Buckskin
Allen, T.D. 103

Dr. Jekyll and Mr. Holmes
Estleman, Loren D. 1970

Dr. Johnson's Dear Mistress
Carter, Winifred 948

Doctor Mirabilis
Blish, James 550

Doctor Zhivago
Pasternak, Boris 4824

Dodging Red Cloud
Wheeler, Richard S. 6657

Dog Heavies
Washburn, L.J. 6575

Dogheaded Death
Nelson, Ray Faraday 4581

The Dogs of Paradise
Posse, Abel 5141

The Dollar Gold Piece
Swain, Virginia 6134

Dolley
Brown, Rita Mae 727

Dolphin Summer
Salisbury, Carola 5569

Domina
Wood, Barbara 6847

Dominic
Robinson, Kathleen 5405

Dominion
Rowe, Jack 5514

Don Gaucho
Pollock, Alyce 5088

Don Juan McQueen
Price, Eugenia 5181

Don Pedro and the Devil
Maas, Edgar 3948

Don Pedro's Captain
Bennetts, Pamela 449

Doniphan's Ride
Savage, Les Jr. 5620

Don't Tread on Me
Karig, Walter 3366

The Doom Trail
Smith, Arthur Douglas 5917

Dorothy and Agatha
Larsen, Gaylord 3667

The Dorothy Parker Murder Case
Baxt, George 384

The Double Man
Pryor, Elinor 5205

Double Masquerade
Lynn, Karen 3938

Double Moscadine
Gaither, Frances 2271

Double Wedding Ring
Wendorf, Patricia 6624

Doubting Castle
Kavaler, Rebecca 3373

Down for the Count
Kaminsky, Stuart M. 3336

Down From the Mountain
Charbonneau, Louis 997

The Dragon and the Rose
Gellis, Roberta 2350

Dragon Cove
Vaughan, Carter A. 6434

A Dragon for Edward
Bennetts, Pamela 450

The Dragon of the Ishtar Gate
De Camp, L. Sprague 1555

The Dragon Waiting: A Masque of History
Ford, John M. 2165

Dragonfly in Amber
Gabaldon, Diana 2262

Dragonmede
Randall, Rona 5246

The Dragons of Archenfield
Marston, Edward 4119

Dragonwyck
Seton, Anya 5750

The Dram Tree
Cochran, Hamilton 1140

Draw Near to Battle
Wheelwright, Jere Hungerford 6667

The Drayton Legacy
Randall, Rona 5247

Dream Catcher
Johnston, Terry C. 3251

The Dream Ends in Fury
Peeples, Samuel Anthony 4889

The Dream Lover
Upton, Mark 6392

The Dream of Confucius
Levi, Jean 3734

A Dream of Kings
Grubb, Davis 2604

The Dream Seekers
Longstreet, Stephen 3884
Mark, Grace 4085

Dream Time
Bonds, Parris Afton 570

Dream West
Nevin, David 4587

The Dreamer of the Vine
Greene, Liz 2574

The Dreaming: A Novel of Australia
Wood, Barbara 6848

Dreaming of Samarkand
Booth, Martin 576

Dreams of Empire
Mackin, Jeanne 3994

Dreams of Gold
Orde, Lewis 4748

D'ri and I
Bacheller, Irving A. 257

The Drowning Room
Pye, Michael Kenneth 5212

Druids
Llywelyn, Morgan 3817

Druid's Enchantment
Ragosta, Millie J. 5240

Drum
Onstott, Kyle 4744

Drumbeat
Pope, Dudley 5094

The Drummer Was the First to Die
Taylor, Liza Pennywitt 6186

Drumm's War
Bragg, Bill 638

Drums
Boyd, James 611

Drums Against Frontenac
Chalmers, Harvey 972

Drums Along the Khyber
MacNeil, Duncan 4013

Drums Along the Mohawk
Edmonds, Walter D. 1874

Drums at Dusk
Bontemps, Arna 575

The Drums of April
Mergendahl, Charles 4340

Drums of Autumn
Gabaldon, Diana 2263

Drums of Change: The Story of Running Fawn
Oke, Janette 4707

The Drums of December
Salvato, Sharon 5575

Drums of Destiny
Bourne, Peter 593

Drums of Khartoum
Gartner, Chloe 2307

The Drums of Monmouth
Sterne, Emma Gelders 5998

The Drums of Morning
Stern, Philip Van Doren 5997

Drums of War
Clews, Roy 1114

The Drums of Winter
Paretti, Sandra 4790

Drury Randall
Johnston, Mary 3232

Dual Destiny
Lynn, Karen 3939

Dubu: A Novel of New Guinean Conquest
Williams, Maslyn 6789

The Duchess of Duke Street
Hardwick, Mollie 2693

Duchess of Milan
Ennis, Michael 1946

The Duchess of Vidal
Lindsey, Dawn 3793

Duel in the Sun
Busch, Niven 812

The Duke of War
O'Meara, Walter 4734

The Dukes: A Novel
Ross, Malcolm 5503

The Duke's Mistress: The Story of Mary Ann Clarke
Kenyon, F.W. 3447

Dulcie Bligh
Clark, Gail 1086

A Durable Fire
Bernhard, Virginia 480

Dust on the King's Highway
White, Helen Constance 6677

Dutch Uncle
Durham, Marilyn 1815

The Dutchman
Meyers, Maan 4351

The Dutchman's Dilemma
Meyers, Maan 4352

Dvorak in Love
Skvorecky, Josef 5881

Dynasty
Elegant, Robert S. 1902

Dynasty of Death
Caldwell, Taylor 854

E

Each Bright River
McNeilly, Mildred Masterson 4308

The Eagle and the Crown
Loewenstein, Hubertus 3832

The Eagle and the Raven
Gedge, Pauline 2344
Michener, James A. 4369

The Eagle and the Rock
Winwar, Frances 6830

The Eagle and the Wind
Stover, Herbert 6068

The Eagle at the Gate
Randall, Rona 5248

Eagle Fur
Peck, Robert Newton 4884

Eagle in the Sky
Mason, F. van Wyck 4149

Eagle in the Snow
Breem, Wallace 654

Eagle in the Sun
Birney, Hoffman 508

The Eagle King
Treece, Henry 6327

Eagle of Niagara: The Story of David Harper and His Indian Captivity
Brick, John 671

Eagle of the Gredos
Osgood, Claude Jack 4761

Eagle on the Sun
Davis, Julia 1527

Eagle Song
Houston, James 3050

Eagles at War
Boyne, Walter J. 620

The Eagle's Daughter
Tarr, Judith 6165

The Eagles Depart
Gloag, John 2434

Eagles Fly West
Ainsworth, Edward Maddin 55

Eagles of Destiny
Sherman, Jory 5817

The Eagles of Malice
Scholefield, Alan 5652

Eagles Where I Walk
Longstreet, Stephen 3885

The Earl
Holland, Cecelia 2987

The Earl and the Heiress
Metzger, Barbara 4345

Early Candlelight
Lovelace, Maude Hart 3904

The Earth Abideth
Dell, George 1595

The Earth and All It Holds
Banis, V.J. 287

Earth Giant
Marshall, Edison 4106

The Earth Goddess
Herley, Richard 2856

The Earth Is the Lord's: A Tale of the
Rise of Genghis Khan
Caldwell, Taylor 855

Earth Song
Coulter, Catherine 1374

The Earthbreakers
Haycox, Ernest 2789

Earthshaker
Krepps, Robert Wilson 3553

East by Day
Niles, Blair 4626

The East Indiaman
Meacham, Ellis K. 4313

East Indiaman
Pollard, Frank 5087

East of the Giants
Stewart, George Rippey 6027

East to Bagaduce
Wallace, Willard 6539

An Easy Day for a Lady
Linscott, Gillian 3805

Eat, Drink, and Be Buried
Kingsbury, Kate 3493

Eaters of the Dead
Crichton, Michael 1425

Eating Pavlova
Thomas, D.M. 6235

Echo of Lions
Chase-Riboud, Barbara 1004

Echo of the Flute
Jordan, Mildred A. 3304

Echoes From the Past
McEvoy, Marjorie 4268

The Echoing Cliffs
Thesen, Hjalmar P. 6219

Eden
Ellis, Julie 1918

Eden and Honor
Harris, Marilyn 2729

The Eden Passion
Harris, Marilyn 2730

Eden Rising
Harris, Marilyn 2731

Eden's Gate
Harper, Karen 2711

Edge of Greatness
Neilson, Winthrop 4575

The Edge of Light
Wolf, Joan 6839

The Edge of Piracy
Chidsey, Donald Barr 1060

The Edge of the Storm
Yanez, Agustin 6893

The Edge of the World
Sarabande, William 5597

The Edge of Time
Erdman, Loula Grace 1949

Edmund Campion
Waugh, Evelyn 6585

Edward
Whittle, Tyler 6721

Edward and Mrs. Simpson
Smith, A.C.H. 5916

Edward, Edward
Burford, Lolah 772

The Egyptian
Waltari, Mika 6552

Eight April Days
Hart, Scott 2759

The Eighth Veil
Kadison, Ellis 3320

Eleanor: A Novel
Lerman, Rhoda 3724

Eleanor the Queen
Lofts, Norah 3842

Eleanora Duse
Stubbs, Jean 6095

Electricity: A Novel
Glendinning, Victoria 2431

Elegant Journey
Selby, John 5740

Elegant Witch
Neill, Robert 4568

Elena
Egan, Judith 1893

An Elephant for Aristotle
De Camp, L. Sprague 1556

The Eleventh Year
High, Monique Raphel 2914

Elgar on the Journey to Hanley
Alldritt, Keith 92

Eli's Road
Webb, Lucas 6589

Elixir of Life
Cowdrey, A.E. 1392

Eliza Stanhope
Trollope, Joanna 6347

Elizabeth and Alexandra
Lambton, Antony 3616

Elizabeth and the Prince of Spain
Irwin, Margaret 3117

Elizabeth, By Name
Cook, Will 1265

Elizabeth, Captive Princess
Irwin, Margaret 3118

Elizabeth: Queen & Woman
Thorpe, Helen 6279

Elizabeth, the Woman
Ellis, Amanda Mae 1917

Elizabeth's Greetings
Haughton, Rosemary 2774

Eliza's Daughter
Aiken, Joan 44

The Elk-Dog Heritage
Coldsmith, Don 1174

Elkhorn Tavern
Jones, Douglas C. 3278

Ellen Bray
Julian, Jane 3319

Ellis Island
Stewart, Fred Mustard 6023

The Elusive Crown
Elsna, Hebe 1931

Elyza
Darcy, Clare 1486

The Emancipist: An Unforgettable
Epic of Australia
Sweeney, Veronica Geoghegan 6147

An Embarrassment of Riches
Kunstler, James Howard 3565

Embers of the Heart
Bittner, Rosanne 512

Emerald
Ashfield, Helen 206

The Emerald Crown
Du Bois, Theodora McCormick 1741

Emerald Fire
Grant, Laurie 2537

The Emerald Necklace
Brown, Diana 718

The Emigrants
Bojer, Johan 561
Moberg, Vilhelm 4422

Emily
Harrod-Eagles, Cynthia 2753

Emily Goes to Exeter
Chesney, Marion 1027

Emma
Kenyon, F.W. 3448

Emma Watson
Aiken, Joan 45

Emmeline
Rossner, Judith 5507

The Emperor Arthur
Turton, Godfrey 6368

The Emperor Franz Joseph
Janetschek, Ottokar 3164

The Emperor Story: A Historical
Romance
Sava, George 5615

The Emperor, the Sages and Death
Berdach, Rachel 475

The Emperor's Coloured Coat
Biggins, John 491

The Emperor's Duchess
Waldeck, R.G. 6524

Emperor's Ladies
Gerson, Noel B. 2367

The Emperor's Lady: A Novel Based
on the Life of the Empress
Josephine
Kenyon, F.W. 3449

The Emperor's Pearl
van Gulik, Robert 6414

The Emperor's Physician
Perkins, Jacob Randolph 4914

Empire: A Novel
Vidal, Gore 6487

The Empire Builders
Long, William Stuart 3871

Empire of Bones: A Novel of Sam
Houston and the Texas Revolution
Long, Jeff 3868

Empire of Heaven
Sledge, Linda Ching 5907

Empire of the Eagle
Norton, Andre 4649

Empress
McCune, Evelyn 4238

The Enchantress
Han, Suyin 2673

Encore
High, Monique Raphel 2915

The End of the Hunt
Flanagan, Thomas 2119

The End of the World News
Burgess, Anthony 777

The Enduring Years
Rayner, Claire 5263

Enemy in Sight!
Kent, Alexander 3429

The English Captain
White, Simon 6700

English Creek
Doig, Ivan 1683

English Music
Ackroyd, Peter 18

The English Wife
Blackstock, Charity 530

Enlightening Delilah
Chesney, Marion 1028

Enough Good Men
Mercer, Charles 4336

Enslaved
Burns, Ron 801

Enter Second Murderer
Knight, Alanna 3518

Enter the Lion: A Posthumous
Memoir of Mycroft Holmes
Hodel, Michael P. 2961

Entered From the Sun
Garrett, George 2301

Envoy From Elizabeth
Bennetts, Pamela 451

An Epic Joy: A Novel Based on the
Life of Rubens
Braider, Donald 642

Epicurus My Master
Radin, Max 5233

Epitaph for Three Women
Plaidy, Jean 5012

The Equinox: A Novel of Rome in the Time of Commodus
Saylor, Carol 5622

Erie Water
Edmonds, Walter D. 1875

Eroica: A Novel about Beethoven
Pidoll, Carl von 4994

An Error of Judgment
Wolpert, Stanley 6845

Erskine Dale, Pioneer
Fox, John 2195

Esau
Shalev, Meir 5770

Escapade
Hodge, Jane Aiken 2962

Escape From Sonora
Bryant, Will 739

The Escape of Socrates
Pick, Robert 4993

The Establishment
Fast, Howard 2030

Estella
Knight, Alanna 3519

Esther
Weinreb, Nathaniel Norsen 6601

Esther: The Star and the Sceptre
Andrews, Gina 146

Ethel: The Fictional Autobiography
Nason, Tema 4558

The Etruscan
Waltari, Mika 6553

Eugene Aram
Bulwer-Lytton, Edward 766

Eugenia
Darcy, Clare 1487

Eugenie
Chapman, Hester W. 989

Eva
Melchior, Ib 4329

The Eve of Saint Hyacinth
Sedley, Kate 5716

Ever After
Thane, Elswyth 6216

Evergreen Gallant
Plaidy, Jean 5013

The Everlasting Covenant
Carr, Robyn 939

The Everlasting Fire
Lauritzen, Jonreed 3675

Evermore
Steward, Barbara 6014

Every Man for Himself
Bainbridge, Beryl 270

Evil Mark
Miles, Graham 4377

The Examination
Bosse, Malcolm 587

An Excellent Mystery
Peters, Ellis 4959

Except for Me and Thee
West, Jessamyn 6628

An Excess of Love
Spellman, Cathy Cash 5959

The Executioner's Song
Mailer, Norman 4036

The Exile of Celine
Clark, Tom 1095

The Exile Way
Woodward, Ann 6865

Exiled
Holt, Helene 3007

Exit Lady Masham
Auchincloss, Louis 230

Exit Sherlock Holmes
Hall, Robert Lee 2657

Exit with Drums
Daley, Joseph A. 1457

The Exodus
Bercovici, Konrad 473
Danielson, Peter 1467

Expedition!
Ross, Dana Fuller 5473

The Explorers
Long, William Stuart 3872

The Exquisite Siren
Haines, Edwin 2639

The Extraordinary Adventures of Secret Agent Shipov in Pursuit of Count Leo Tolstoy in the Year 1862
Okudzhava, Bulat 4712

The Eye in the Door
Barker, Pat 307

The Eye of God
Grace, C.L. 2506

Eye of the Hawk
Ross, David William 5498

Eye of the Hurricane
Buckley, Fergus Reid 757

The Eye of the Lion: A Novel Based on the Life of Mata Hari
Wertenbaker, Lael Tucker 6626

Eyes of Eagles
Johnstone, William W. 3266

F

The Fabulist
Vornholt, John 6512

The Fabulous Concubine
Chang, Hsin-Hai 987

Fabulous Valley
Parker, Cornelia Stratton 4803

The Face of a Stranger
Perry, Anne 4929

Face of the Rising Sun
Sarabande, William 5598

Faces in the Crowd
Marshall, William 4117

The Fair
Nathan, Robert 4559

The Fair God
Wallace, Lew 6537

Fair is the Rose
MacKinney, Meagan 3997

Fair Land, Fair Land
Guthrie, A.B. Jr. 2625

A Fair Wind Home
Moore, Ruth 4443

Fair Wind to Java
Roark, Garland 5354

Fairacres
Waters, Gladys 6579

The Fairbrothers
McMeekin, Clark 4291

Fairoaks
Yerby, Frank 6915

Faith and Honor
Maderich, Robin 4025

The Faith and the Flame
Houston, June Dimmit 3054

The Faithful Lovers
Anand, Valerie 129

The Fala Factor
Kaminsky, Stuart M. 3337

The Falcon and the Flower
Henley, Virginia 2826

A Falcon for a Queen
Gaskin, Catherine 2314

Falcon: The Autobiography of His Grace James IV, King of Scots
Stewart, A.J. 6021

Falconer's Crusade
Morson, Ian 4493

Falconer's Judgement
Morson, Ian 4494

Falkenhorst
Rascovich, Mark 5254

The Fall of the King
Jensen, Johannes Vilhelm 3214

The Fall River Line
Winston, Daoma 6824

Fallen Angel
Camp, Deborah 872

The Fallen Angels
Kells, Susannah 3397

Fallen Skies
Gregory, Philippa 2581

The Falling Hills
Lentz, Perry 3720

A Falling Star
Belle, Pamela 431

The Fallon Blood
O'Neal, Reagan 4741

The Fallon Pride
O'Neal, Reagan 4742

Falls of Gard
Black, Laura 520

Falls the Shadow
Penman, Sharon Kay 4903

False Colours
Heyer, Georgette 2886

The False Inspector Dew
Lovesey, Peter 3912

Falstaff
Nye, Robert 4653

Familiar Acts
Barraclough, June 345

Familiar Spirits
Tourney, Leonard 6298

Family
Cooper, J. California 1297

Family Favorites
Duggan, Alfred 1766

Family Fortune
Eberhart, Mignon G. 1834

A Family Matter
Roosevelt, James 5458

The Family of Women
Peck, Richard 4883

Famine
O'Flaherty, Liam 4693

A Famine of Horses
Chisholm, P.F. 1071

The Famished Land
Byrd, Elizabeth 833

The Fancher Train
Bean, Amelia 395

Fanny: Being the True History of the Adventures of Fanny Hackabout-Jones
Jong, Erica 3299

The Far Canyon
Kelton, Elmer 3404

The Far Country
Furnas, Marthedith 2258

The Far Down
Corbett, Elizabeth 1321

Far Flies the Eagle
Anthony, Evelyn 162

The Far Journey
Erdman, Loula Grace 1950

Far Mountains
O'Rourke, Frank 4752

The Far-Off Rhapsody
Sheridan, Anne-Marie 5808

The Far Pavilions
Kaye, M.M. 3376

The Far Side of Home
Davis, Maggie 1536

The Far Side of the Hill
Livingston, Nancy 3811

The Far Side of the World
O'Brian, Patrick 4663

The Far Tribes
Wheeler, Richard S. 6658

The Faraway Drums
Cleary, Jon 1104

Farewell, Catullus
Dixon, Pierson 1651

Farewell Great King: A Novel of Ancient Greece
Paton Walsh, Jill 4829

Farewell, My General
Seifert, Shirley 5726

Farewell the Stranger
O'Brien, Saliee 4682

Farewell the Tranquil
Delderfield, R.F. 1585

Farewell to My Concubine
Lee, Lilian 3709

Farewell to Valley Forge
Taylor, David 6178

Faro's Daughter
Heyer, Georgette 2887

Farriers' Lane
Perry, Anne 4930

The Fast Men
McNab, Tom 4302

Fata Morgana
Kotzwinkle, William 3549

A Fatal Assignation
Ley, Alice Chetwynd 3764

The Fatal Crown
Jones, Ellen 3289

The Fatal Friendship: Marie Antoinette, Count Fersen and the Flight to Varennes
Loomis, Stanley 3895

The Fate of Princes
Doherty, P.C. 1673

The Fates Are Laughing
Crozier, William 1439

The Father
Brown, Katharine Holland 724

Father Abraham
Bacheller, Irving A. 258

A Father and His Fate
Compton-Burnett, Ivy 1228

Father and Son
Porter, Donald Clayton 5117

Father of Waters
Porter, Donald Clayton 5118

The Fathers
Tate, Allen 6171

Fathers and Crows
Vollmann, William T. 6508

Faust
Nye, Robert 4654

The Favored Child
Gregory, Philippa 2582

The Favourite
Mallet-Joris, Francoise 4040

Fawn
Peck, Robert Newton 4885

Faye's Folly
Corbett, Elizabeth 1322

Fear No More
Chapman, Hester W. 990

Feast in the Morning
Preston, Hugh 5175

The Feast of All Saints
Rice, Anne 5314

Feast of the Jesters
Komroff, Manuel 3533

The Feather and the Stone
Shaw, Patricia 5780

Feather Castles
Veryan, Patricia 6462

Felding Castle
De Born, Edith 1552

The Female: A Novel of Another Time
Wellman, Paul I. 6617

Fenwick Travers and the Forbidden Kingdom
Saunders, Raymond M. 5612

Fenwick Travers and the Panama Canal
Saunders, Raymond M. 5613

Fenwick Travers and the Years of Empire
Saunders, Raymond M. 5614

Ferdinand and Isabella
Kesten, Hermann 3474

The Feud
Bean, Amelia 396

The Fever Called Living
Moore, Barbara 4439

Feversham
Davidson, Diane 1503

Fevre Dream
Martin, George R.R. 4131

A Few Good Men
Overgard, William 4768

A Few Painted Feathers
Longstreet, Stephen 3886

A Fiddle, a Sword, and a Lady
Spalding, Albert 5953

Fiddler's Ferry
Gower, Iris 2499

Fielder's Choice
Norman, Rick 4646

The Fields
Richter, Conrad 5319

The Fiercest Heart
Cloete, Stuart 1122

Fifteen Flags
Hardman, Richard Lynden 2686

The Fifth Conspiracy
Jones, Ted 3296

The Fifth Horseman
Villarreal, Jose Antonio 6496

The Fifth Queen
Ford, Ford Madox 2161

A Fig in Winter
Gibbs, Willa 2400

Filaree: A Novel of an American Life
Noble, Marguerite 4633

The Final Adversary
Morris, Gilbert 4460

The Financier
Dreiser, Theodore 1720

The Fine and Handsome Captain
Lynch, Frances 3933

Finessing Clarissa
Chesney, Marion 1029

A Finger to Her Lips
Berckman, Evelyn 472

Finn Mac Cool
Llywelyn, Morgan 3818

Fire Along the Sky: A Novel of America
Moss, Robert 4497

Fire and Fog
Day, Dianne 1543

Fire and Morning
Leary, Francis W. 3696

Fire and the Hammer
Barker, Shirley 311

Fire Bell in the Night
Robertson, Constance 5395

Fire, Burn!
Carr, John Dickson 910

Fire Down Below
Golding, William 2454

Fire From Heaven
Renault, Mary 5296

Fire in the Heart
Buckmaster, Henrietta 761

Fire in the Ice
Roberts, Dorothy James 5375
Scholefield, Alan 5653

Fire in the Sky
Shears, J.A. 5785

Fire in the Steppe
Sienkiewicz, Henryk 5847

Fire on the Wind
Garth, David 2304

Fire Opal
Hill, Pamela 2932

Fire over England
Mason, A.E.W. 4143

Fire Queen
Grabien, Deborah 2503

The Firebrand
Bradley, Marion Zimmer 624

The Firedrake
Holland, Cecilia 2988

The Firedrake's Eye
Finney, Patricia 2095

The Fireflower
Layton, Edith 3687

The Firekeeper
Moss, Robert 4498

The Firelands
Harper, Karen 2712

Firelord
Godwin, Parke 2447

Fires in the Sky
Parotti, Phillip 4816

The Fires of Fu Manchu
Van Ash, Cay 6399

The Fires of Glenlochy
Heaven, Constance 2806

The Fires of July
Salvato, Sharon 5576

The Fireship
Parkinson, C. Northcote 4811

Firewind
Pronzini, Bill 5200

A Firework for Oliver
Sanders, John 5587

The First Casualty
Powell, William 5149

A First Class Murder
Roosevelt, Elliott 5442

The First Gentleman of America: A Comedy of Conquest
Cabell, James Branch 841

First Knight
Chadwick, Elizabeth 966

First Lieutenant
Maynard, Kenneth 4208

The First Man in Rome
McCullough, Colleen 4234

First Night
Hodge, Jane Aiken 2963

The First Rebel
Swanson, Neil Harmon 6137

The First Rebellion
Chesney, Marion 1030

First the Blade
Mayrant, Drayton 4212
Miller, May 4400

The First to Land
Reeman, Douglas E. 5288

Fisher of Men: A Novel of Simon Peter
Frieberger, Kurt 2231

A Fistful of Stars
Lockwood, Sarah 3828

Fitzempress' Law
Norman, Diana 4644

Five Black Ships: A Novel of Discoverers
Ponce de Leon, Napoleon Baccino 5089

The Five-Minute Marriage
Aiken, Joan 46

The Fixer
Malamud, Bernard 4038

The Flag Captain
Kent, Alexander 3430

Flambard's Confession
Durham, Marilyn 1816

A Flame in Byzantium
Yarbro, Chelsea Quinn 6899

The Flame in the Dark
Bonallack, Basil 568

Flame of Fire
Oliver, Jane 4722

The Flame of the Borgias
Briggs, Jean 680

Flames of Empire
Bourne, Peter 594

The Flames of Rome
Maier, Paul L. 4033

The Flames of Time
Kendrick, Baynard 3409

Flanagan's Run
McNab, Tom 4303

Flash for Freedom
Fraser, George MacDonald 2203

Flashman
Fraser, George MacDonald 2204

Flashman and the Angel of the Lord
Fraser, George MacDonald 2205

Flashman and the Dragon
Fraser, George MacDonald 2206

Flashman and the Mountain of Light
Fraser, George MacDonald 2207

Flashman and the Redskins
Fraser, George MacDonald 2208

Flashman at the Charge
Fraser, George MacDonald 2209

Flashman's Lady
Fraser, George MacDonald 2210

The Fleet in the Forest
Lane, Carl Daniel 3654

The Fleet Rabble: A Novel of the Nez Perce War
Hanes, Frank Borden 2675

Fleet Surgeon to Pharaoh
Jacobson, Sheldon 3140

Fleeting Fancy
Edghill, Rosemary 1866

Fleur
Harrod-Eagles, Cynthia 2754

Flickers
Rock, Phillip 5419

The Flight
Stephan, Ruth Walgreen 5994

Flight From Avatchez
Slaughter, Frank G. 5887

Flight From Bucharest
Stevens, R.T. 6000

Flight From Fifth Avenue
Rae, Catherine M. 5235

Flight of the Crow
Clayton, Paul 1103

The Flight of the Eagle
Sundman, Per Olof 6119
Thomas, Donald 6239

The Flight of the Heron
Broster, Dorothy Kathleen 710

The Flight of the Kestrel
Abbey, Margaret 3

Flight of the Swan
Hubbard, Margaret Ann 3063

Flight to Canada
Reed, Ishmael 5285

The Flint Anchor
Warner, Sylvia Townsend 6569

The Flint Lord
Herley, Richard 2857

Flintlock
Manning, Jason 4073

Floodtide
Goodwin, Suzanne 2475
Yerby, Frank 6916

The Floral Companion
Bell, Anthea 419

The Florentine
Shulman, Sandra 5840
Spinatelli, Carl J. 5968

The Flower in the Mountains
Coldsmith, Don 1175

Flowers for Lilian
Gilbert, Anna 2405

Flowers in the Blood
Courter, Gay 1387

The Flowers of Adonis
Sutcliff, Rosemary 6122

Flying Colours
Forester, C.S. 2173

Flying into Love
Thomas, D.M. 6236

Foes
Johnston, Mary 3233

Folded Hills
White, Stewart Edward 6701

The Follies of the King
Plaidy, Jean 5014

Follow the Drum
Leasor, James 3699

Follow the Free Wind
Brackett, Leigh 621

Follow the River
Mayer, Albert 4203
Thom, James Alexander 6231

Follow the Wind
Coldsmith, Don 1176

The Folly
Chesney, Marion 1031

Fonthill
Menen, Aubrey 4335

Fool of God: A Novel Based on the Life of Alexander Campbell
Cochran, Louis 1144

The Fool of Venus
Cronyn, George William 1428

Fool's Coach
Wheeler, Richard S. 6659

Fools' Gold
Wiley, Richard 6755

Footman in Powder
Ashton, Helen 216

For Every Sin
Appelfeld, Aharon 175

For God and Glory
Jeal, Tim 3171

For King and Company
Meacham, Ellis K. 4314

For Love and Honor
Van-Loon, Antonia 6423

For Love of a Pirate
Esler, Anthony 1961

For Love of Two Eagles
Riefe, Barbara 5328

For My Great Folly
Costain, Thomas B. 1365

For One Sweet Grape
O'Brien, Kate 4681

For the Love of Robert E. Lee
Harper, M.A. 2715

For They Shall Inherit
Macdonald, Malcolm 3964

For Time and All Eternity
Bailey, Paul 268

For Us the Living
Lancaster, Bruce 3639
Van-Loon, Antonia 6424

The Foragers
Haas, Ben 2630

Forbidden City
Esler, Anthony 1962
Jernigan, Muriel Molland 3215

The Forbidden Ground
Swanson, Neil Harmon 6138

Forbidden Land
Sarabande, William 5599

Forefathers
Cato, Nancy 960

Foreign Devils
Faust, Irvin 2053

The Forest and the Fort
Allen, Hervey 100

Forest Cavalier: A Romance of America's First Frontier and of Bacon's Rebellion
Flannagan, Roy Catesby 2122

The Forest House
Bradley, Marion Zimmer 625

The Forest Lord
Gerson, Noel B. 2368

Forest of the Night
Jones, Madison 3291

Forever Amber
Winsor, Kathleen 6822

Forever Free
Morrow, Honore 4487

Forever Possess
Phillips, Alexandra 4982

The Forge
Stribling, Thomas S. 6083

Forget the Glory
Drummond, Emma 1725

Form Line of Battle!
Kent, Alexander 3431

Fort De Chastaigne
Coldsmith, Don 1177

Fort Worth
Sanders, Leonard 5588

The Fortress
Gavin, Catherine 2320
Walpole, Hugh 6544

Fortress Fury
Vaughan, Carter A. 6435

The Fortunate Marriage
Trevor, Meriol 6342

The Fortune Hunter
Morris, Ira J. 4477

Fortune Is a Woman
Adler, Elizabeth 39

Fortune Made His Sword
Rofheart, Martha 5426

The Fortune of War
O'Brian, Patrick 4664

The Fortune Road
McCague, James 4217

Fortune, Smile Once More
Williams, Mary Floyd 6788

Fortune's Favorite
McCullough, Colleen 4235

Fortune's Knave: The Making of William the Conqueror
Lide, Mary 3774

Fortune's Legacy
Rowe, Jack 5515

The Fortunes of Nigel
Scott, Sir Walter 5696

Fortune's Wheel
Edwards, Rhoda S. 1886

Forty Centuries Look Down
Austin, Frederick Britten 245

Forty Guns West
Johnstone, William W. 3267

Forty Pounds of Gold
Stong, Philip D. 6066

Forward the Nation
Peattie, Donald Culross 4880

The Foster Brothers
Frankland, Edward 2202

Foundation Stone
Warren, Lella 6571

The Foundling
Heyer, Georgette 2888

The Fountain Overflows
West, Rebecca 6639

The Four Hundred
Sheppard, Stephen 5804

The Four Rivers of Paradise
White, Helen Constance 6678

The Four Swans
Graham, Winston 2525

The Four Winds of Heaven
High, Monique Raphel 2916

Title Index

The Fourteenth of October
Bryher 742

Fourth King
Coulehan, Norbert 1373

The Fourth King
Petrie, Glen 4979

The Fourth Queen
Paterson, Isabel 4827

The Fox-Red Hills
Roberts, Cynthia S. 5374

The Foxes of Harrow
Yerby, Frank 6917

Fragments of the Ark
Meriwether, Louise 4341

The Franciscan
Blake, Forrester 532

Frankenstein Unbound
Aldiss, Brian 68

Frederica
Heyer, Georgette 2889

Frederica in Fashion
Chesney, Marion 1032

Free Enterprise
Cliff, Michelle 1116

The Free Fishers
Buchan, John 750

Free Flows the River
Murray, Earl 4529

The Free Frenchman
Read, Piers Paul 5277

Free Lance
Shipway, George 5827

Free Land
Lane, Rose 3660

Free Man
Richter, Conrad 5320

Free Soil
Allis, Marguerite 110
Lynn, Margaret 3943

Freedom
Safire, William 5561

Freedom, Farewell
Bentley, Phyllis 461

Freedom or Death
Kazantzakis, Nikos 3383

Freedom Road
Fast, Howard 2031

Freedom's Banner
Crane, Teresa 1415

Freedom's Dues
Abel, Robert H. 9

Freedom's Way
Du Bois, Theodora McCormick 1742

The French Admiral
Lambdin, Dewey 3609

The French Bride
Anthony, Evelyn 163

French Dragoon
Rudigoz, Roger 5523

The French Lieutenant's Woman
Fowles, John 2194

French Slippers
Chester, Deborah 1055

The French Woman
Paul, Barbara 4837

Frenchman's Creek
Du Maurier, Daphne 1744

The Frenchwoman
Mackin, Jeanne 3995

Friday
Tournier, Michel 6305

Friday's Child
Heyer, Georgette 2890

Friendly Cove
Brant, Irving 651

The Friendly Persuasion
West, Jessamyn 6629

The Friends of Pancho Villa
Blake, James Carlos 535

The Frigate Captain
Styles, Showell 6103

Frobisher's Savage
Tourney, Leonard 6299

The Frog Earl
Dunn, Carola 1792

From a Far Land
Elegant, Robert S. 1903

From Fields of Gold
Ripley, Alexandra 5339

From Sea to Shining Sea
Thom, James Alexander 6232

From the Terrace
O'Hara, John 4703

From Time to Time
Finney, Jack 2092

From Where the Sun Now Stands
Henry, Will 2841

The Frontiersmen
Eckert, Allen W. 1841

Fruit in His Season
Barney, Helen C. 333

Full of Thy Riches
Ferrell, Elizabeth 2070

Funeral Games
Renault, Mary 5297

Funny Papers
De Haven, Tom 1559

Fur Brigade
Evarts, Hal George 1985

The Fur Masters
Sullivan, Alan 6113

The Furies
Jakes, John 3146

**The Further Adventures of
Huckleberry Finn**
Matthews, Greg 4189

**Fury in the Earth: A Novel of the
New Madrid Earthquake**
Kroll, Harry Harrison 3557

A Future Arrived
Rock, Phillip 5420

G

Gabriel's Search
Lutes, Della 3927

Gai-Jin: A Novel of Japan
Clavell, James 1100

The Galileans
Slaughter, Frank G. 5888

The Gallant
Long, William Stuart 3873

Gallant Captain
Frye, Pearl 2242

The Gallant Mrs. Stonewall
Kane, Harnett T. 3353

Gallant Warrior
Mann, Helen R. 4063

Galleon
Pope, Dudley 5095

The Gallery of His Dreams
Rusch, Kristine Kathryn 5525

The Gallowglass
Breslin, Howard 666

Gallows Hill
Winwar, Frances 6831

The Gallows Land
Pronzini, Bill 5201

The Gallows Murder
Clynes, Michael 1134

Gallows Way
Winston, Daoma 6825

Galveston
Morris, Suzanne 4482

Gamble's Hundred
Dowdey, Clifford 1705

The Gambling Man
Cookson, Catherine 1276

A Game for Empires
Frye, Pearl 2243

The Game of Kings
Dunnett, Dorothy 1801

The Gamester
Sabatini, Rafael 5550

The Garden of Persephone
Rotondi, Cesar J. 5510

The Garfield Honor
Yerby, Frank 6918

Garnet
Ashfield, Helen 207

Gate to the Sea
Bryher 743

The Gates of Kunara
MacNeil, Duncan 4014

The Gates of the Mountains
Henry, Will 2842

Gateway to Empire
Eckert, Allen W. 1842

A Gathering of Saints
Hyde, Christopher 3092

The Gathering Storm
Davis, W.E. 1540

Gathering Storm
Gulick, Bill 2613

The Gathering Wolves
Darrell, Elizabeth 1496

The Gaudy Empire
Neumann, Alfred 4584

Gaul Is Divided
Brown, Esther Fisher 721

Gay Crusader
Knox, Cleone 3528

The Gay Galliard
Irwin, Margaret 3119

Gay Lord Robert
Plaidy, Jean 5015

The Gaynor Women
Coffman, Virginia 1153

The General in His Labyrinth
Garcia Marquez, Gabriel 2282

The General's Lady
Forbes, Esther 2156

A Generation of Leaves
Bloom, Robert S. 552

Generations of Winter
Aksyonov, Vassily 61

Genesee Fever
Carmer, Carl Lamson 898

Gennie the Huguenot Woman
Ross, Bette M. 5464

The Gentle Conqueror
Gronau, Mary Ellen 2597

The Gentle Falcon
Lewis, Hilda 3747

**The Gentle Fury: A Novel of
Margaret of Austria**
Lewis, Paul 3758

The Gentle Infidel
Schoonover, Lawrence 5663

The Gentle Knight
Lindsay, Philip 3791

The Gentle Rebel
Morris, Gilbert 4461

The Gentleman From America
Banks, Polan 293
Benton, Paul 464

The Gentleman From Chicago
Cashman, John 953

Gentleman of Stratford
Brophy, John 708

Gentleman Ranker
Jennings, John Edward 3200

Gentleman Traitor
Williams, Alan 6763

Gentlemen From England
Lovelace, Maude Hart 3905

Gentlemen, Hush!
Wheelwright, Jere Hungerford 6668

Gentlemen in England
Wilson, A.N.   6795

Gentlemen of Adventure
Gann, Ernest K.   2278

Gentlemen—The Regiment!
Talbot, Hugh   6154

A Georgian Love Story
Raymond, Ernest   5258

Georgina
Darcy, Clare   1488

Gerait's Daughter
Ragosta, Millie J.   5241

Geronimo
Dugan, Bill   1758

Geronimo: An American Legend
Conley, Robert J.   1242

Gerontius
Hamilton-Paterson, James   2672

Gettysburg
Longstreet, Stephen   3887

Gettysburg: Crisis of Command
Albright, Harry   65

The Ghost and Mrs. Jeffries
Brightwell, Emily   681

Ghost Fox
Houston, James   3051

The Ghost of Monsieur Scarron
Lewis, Janet   3755

The Ghost Raider
Hogan, Ray   2978

The Ghost Road
Barker, Pat   308

Ghost Woman
Thornton, Lawrence   6275

The Ghosts of Africa
Stevenson, William   6013

The Ghosts of Elkhorn
Newcomb, Kerry   4589

The Giant Joshua
Whipple, Maurine   6673

Giant Killer
Davis, Elmer Holmes   1518

Giants in the Earth
Rolvaag, O.E.   5434

The Gift of Rome
Wagner, John   6520

The Gifts: A Story of the Boyhood of Jesus
Wilson, Dorothy Clarke   6800

The Gila River
McCarthy, Gary   4223

The Gilded Rooster
Roberts, Richard Emery   5391

Gilded Splendour
Laker, Rosalind   3595

Gilded Spurs
Ingram, Grace   3105

The Gilded Torch
Fuller, Iola   2252

Gildenford
Anand, Valerie   130

Gilgamesh the King
Silverberg, Robert   5853

Gilman of the Redford
Davis, William Stearns   1541

The Ginger Tree
Wynd, Oswald   6890

The Girl
Cookson, Catherine   1277

The Girl From Paris
Aiken, Joan   47

The Girl From Storyville: A Victorian Novel
Yerby, Frank   6919

The Girl Who Was Never Queen: A Biographical Novel of Princess Charlotte of Wales
Main, Mary   4037

Give Me Liberty
Gerson, Noel B.   2369

Give Me Liberty: The Story of an Innocent Man
Erskine, John   1956

Give Me the Daggers
Gavin, Catherine   2321

Give Me the Wind
Jordan, Jan   3302

Give Me Your Golden Hand
Eaton, Evelyn   1825

Give Us This Day
Delderfield, R.F.   1586

Give Us This Valley
Ham, Tom   2666

The Gladiator
Williamson, Thames Ross   6790

The Gladiators
Koestler, Arthur   3532

The Glass-Blowers
Du Maurier, Daphne   1745

The Glass Dove
Carrighar, Sally   943

The Glendower Conspiracy
Biggle, Lloyd Jr.   494

Glendower Country
Rofheart, Martha   5427

Glendraco
Black, Laura   521

Glittering Hill
Murphy, Clyde Francis   4520

The Glittering Strand
Lennox-Smith, Judith   3716

The Glorious Folly: A Novel of the Time of St. Paul
De Wohl, Louis   1565

Glorious Morning
Ellis, Julie   1919

The Glorious Three
Wetherell, June   6651

The Glory
Wouk, Herman   6873

The Glory and the Dream
Dunlap, Katharine   1789
Kenyon, F.W.   3450

Glory and the Lightning
Caldwell, Taylor   856

Glory Enough for All: The Battle of the Crater
Schultz, Duane Philip   5673

Glowstone
Harris, Macdonald   2725

Go-Ahead Rider
Conley, Robert J.   1243

Go Ask the River
Eaton, Evelyn   1826

Goa
Dalkey, Kara   1458

Goat Song: A Novel of Ancient Greece
Yerby, Frank   6920

Goatsong
Holt, Tom   3009

A God Against the Gods
Drury, Allen   1738

God Is an Englishman
Delderfield, R.F.   1587

The God of Mirrors
Reilly, Robert   5293

God Save the Tsar
Hoe, Susanna   2976

The God-Seeker
Lewis, Sinclair   3763

God Was Born in Exile
Horia, Vintila   3033

The Goddess
Seymour, Miranda   5763

Goddess of the Green Room
Plaidy, Jean   5016

The Goddess Queen: A Novel Based on the Life of Nefertiti
Vidal, Nicole   6494

A Goddess to a God
Balderston, John Lloyd   278

The Godforgotten
Schmitt, Gladys   5642

Godric
Buechner, Frederick   763

Gods and Generals
Shaara, Jeff   5765

God's Angry Man
Ehrlich, Leonard   1898

The Gods Are Not Mocked
Taylor, Anna   6177

The Gods Are Thirsty
Lee, Tanith   3710

God's Equal
Absire, Alain   14

God's Man: A Novel on the Life of John Calvin
Norton-Taylor, Duncan   4650

Gods on Horseback
Baggett, Samuel G.   263

God's Warrior
Slaughter, Frank G.   5889

Gold
Kelland, Clarence Budington   3388

Gold for the Caesars
Seward, Florence A.   5759

Gold Is Where You Find It
Ripley, Clements   5345

Gold Mountain
Paul, Charlotte   4841

Gold of Their Bodies: A Novel about Gauguin
Gorham, Charles Orson   2488

The Gold Seekers
Long, William Stuart   3874

Golden Admiral
Mason, F. van Wyck   4150

The Golden Balance
Hall, Arthur Dana   2646

The Golden Chain
Gamo, Jean   2275

The Golden Circle
Ames, John Edward   125
Robertson, Constance   5396

The Golden Coast
Rooney, Philip   5441

The Golden Crucible
Stubbs, Jean   6096

The Golden Days
Neill, Robert   4569

Golden Destiny
Davies, June Wyndham   1506

The Golden Eagle
Gerson, Noel B.   2370
Jennings, John Edward   3201

The Golden Exile
Schoonover, Lawrence   5664

The Golden Feather
Kenyon, Theda   3462

Golden Fire
Fast, Jonathan   2047

The Golden Fleece
Lofts, Norah   3843

The Golden Fool
Divine, David   1649

The Golden Galleon
Suthren, Victor   6129

The Golden Hand
Simon, Edith   5856

The Golden Harlot
Wilson, Jeanne   6808

The Golden Hawk
Yerby, Frank   6921

The Golden Honeycomb
Markandaya, Kamala   4086

Golden Horizons
Corcoran, William   1324

Golden Isle
Slaughter, Frank G.   5890

The Golden Knight
Challis, George   971

The Golden Lady
Gardiner, Dorothy 2283

The Golden Lyre
Gerson, Noel B. 2371

The Golden Mistress
Beyea, Basil 488

The Golden Nineties
Mason, Lisa 4166

The Golden Ocean
O'Brian, Patrick 4665

Golden Peacock
Atherton, Gertrude 224

The Golden Pharaoh
Danielson, Peter 1468

The Golden Porcupine
Bolton, Muriel Ray 567

The Golden Princess
Baron, Alexander 335

The Golden Quill: A Novel Based on the Life of Mozart
Grun, Bernard 2605

The Golden Sabre
Cleary, Jon 1105

The Golden Season
Akinson, Oriana 60

Golden Shore
Shaftel, George 5769

The Golden Strangers
Treece, Henry 6328

The Golden Thread
De Wohl, Louis 1566

The Golden Tulip
Laker, Rosalind 3596

The Golden Valley
Winston, Daoma 6826

The Golden Veil
Kitchen, Paddy 3507

Golden Venus
Smythe, David Mynders 5933

The Golden Warrior: The Story of Harold and William
Muntz, Hope 4517

The Golden Wildcat
Widdemer, Margaret 6735

The Golden Wind
Grace, C.L. 2507

The Golden Years: A Novel Based on the Life and Loves of Percy Bysshe Shelley
Kenyon, F.W. 3451

The Golden Yoke: A Novel of the War of the Roses
Eckerson, Olive 1837

Goldeneye
Macdonald, Malcolm 3965

Goldfield
Wheeler, Richard S. 6660

The Goldseekers
Burnett, William R. 794

The Goldsmith's Wife
Plaidy, Jean 5017

The Goliath Head
Calitri, Charles J. 865

Gone the Dreams and the Dancing
Jones, Douglas C. 3279

Gone the Rainbow, Gone the Dove
Bagnel, Joan 264

Gone to Texas
Carter, Forrest 945
Manning, Jason 4074
Thomason, John Williams 6247
Worcester, Don 6871

Gone with the Wind
Mitchell, Margaret 4415

Good-Bye My Son
Coryn, Marjorie 1356

A Good Day to Die
Barton, Del 368
Blackburn, Thomas Wakefield 525

The Good Earth
Buck, Pearl S. 754

Good King Harry
Giardina, Denise 2393

Good Morning, Irene
Douglas, Carole Nelson 1698

Good Morning, Young Lady
Kennelly, Ardyth 3424

Good Night, Mr. Holmes
Douglas, Carole Nelson 1699

The Good Old Boys
Kelton, Elmer 3405

The Good Provider
Stirling, Jessica 6043

The Good Tidings
Sidney, William 5843

The Good Yeomen
Williams, Jay 6771

The Goodnight Trail
Compton, Ralph 1227

The Gorgeous Hussy
Adams, Samuel Hopkins 30

Goshawk Squadron
Robinson, Derek 5403

The Gospel According to Gamaliel
Heard, Gerald 2801

The Gospel According to Pontius Pilate
Mills, James R. 4408

The Gospel of Corax
Park, Paul 4802

Gossip From the Forest
Keneally, Thomas 3413

Gothic Romance
Carrere, Emmanuel 942

Governor Ramage, R.N.
Pope, Dudley 5096

The Governor's Daughter
Whitson, Denton 6718

The Governor's Lady
Raddall, Thomas H. 5228

Gower Street
Rayner, Claire 5264

Graham of Claverhouse
Dodge, Constance 1665

The Grail Murders
Clynes, Michael 1135

Grand Days
Moorhouse, Frank 4448

Grand Parade
Lancaster, G.B. 3649

A Grand Passion
Mackey, Mary 3991

The Grand Sophy
Heyer, Georgette 2891

The Grandissimes
Cable, George W. 842

Grandmother and the Priests
Caldwell, Taylor 857

The Grandmothers
Westcott, Glenway 6640

Grania: She-King of the Irish Seas
Llywelyn, Morgan 3819

Grant of Kingdom
Fergusson, Harvey 2067

Grant's War
Jones, Ted 3297

The Grass Crown
McCullough, Colleen 4236

The Grass Kingdom
Sherman, Jory 5818

The Grasshopper King
Coker, Elizabeth Boatwright 1165

The Grassman
Fulton, Len 2256

Gray Canaan
Garth, David 2305

The Gray Captain
Wheelwright, Jere Hungerford 6669

Gray Victory
Skimin, Robert 5877

The Great Adventure
Giles, Janice Holt 2410

The Great Alone
Dailey, Janet 1454

The Great Betrayal
Gardiner, Dorothy 2284

Great Black Russian
Killens, John Oliver 3484

The Great Blizzard
Idell, Albert E. 3101

The Great Captains
Treece, Henry 6329

Great Day in the Morning
Andrews, Robert Hardy 149

Great Dream From Heaven
Gardiner, John Rolfe 2286

Great Elephant
Scholefield, Alan 5654

The Great Hunger
Bojer, Johan 562

The Great Infidel
Deiss, Joseph Jay 1582

Great Lion of God
Caldwell, Taylor 858

A Great Lord
Frischauer, Paul 2233

Great Maria
Holland, Cecelia 2989

The Great Meadow
Roberts, Elizabeth Madox 5378

The Great Sky and the Silence
Rand, James S. 5245

The Great Steamboat Race
Brunner, John 736

The Great Tide
Hall, Rubylea 2662

The Great Train Robbery
Crichton, Michael 1426

The Great Valley
Johnston, Mary 3234

The Great White Gods
Stucken, Eduard 6102

The Greater Hunger
Borland, Barbara Dodge 581

The Greek Generals Talk: Memoirs of the Trojan War
Parotti, Phillip 4817

The Greek of Toledo: A Romantic Narrative of El Greco
Borton, Elizabeth 586

The Greek Treasure
Stone, Irving 6056

Green City in the Sun
Wood, Barbara 6849

Green Darkness
Seton, Anya 5751

Green Dragon, White Tiger
Motley, Annette 4501

The Green Land
Ross, Zola Helen 5504

The Green Leaves of Summer
Willis, Ted 6793

The Green Madonna
L'Ami, C.E. 3617

The Green Man
Treece, Henry 6330

The Green Mountain Boys
Thompson, Daniel Pierce 6249

Green Rose of Furley
Barney, Helen C. 334

The Green Salamander
Hill, Pamela 2933

The Greenlander
Adlard, Mark 38

The Greenlanders
Smiley, Jane 5915

Greenstone
Kalman, Yvonne 3324

Greenyards
Lingard, Joan 3796

Gregory the Great
Ellert, Gerhart 1913

The Greta Garbo Murder Case
Baxt, George   385

Greygallows
Michaels, Barbara   4359

Griffin's Way
Yerby, Frank   6922

Griffith Gaunt
Reade, Charles   5280

Grim Journey
Birney, Hoffman   509

Gringo Gold
Coolidge, Dane   1293

Grishin
Herlin, Hans   2859

Grounds for Murder
Kingsbury, Kate   3494

The Grove of Eagles
Graham, Winston   2526

Gudrid's Saga
Irwin, Constance   3115

The Guernseyman
Parkinson, C. Northcote   4812

La Guerra: A Spanish Saga
Frances, Stephen D.   2199

Guillotine
Logan, Mark   3865

Guinevere
Newman, Sharan   4600

Guinevere Evermore
Newman, Sharan   4601

Guinevere: The Legend in Autumn
Woolley, Persia   6868

The Gun
Forester, C.S.   2174

The Gun Ketch
Lambdin, Dewey   3610

Gunman
Estleman, Loren D.   1971

Guns for Rebellion
Mason, F. van Wyck   4151

Guns Forever Echo
Ellis, Kenneth M.   1925

The Guns of Arrest
McCutchan, Philip   4242

Guns of Burgoyne
Lancaster, Bruce   3640

Guns of Chickamauga
O'Connor, Richard   4685

The Guns of the South
Turtledove, Harry N.   6367

Guy Mannering
Scott, Sir Walter   5697

Gwendolen
Darcy, Clare   1489

The Gypsy From Cadiz
Hamilton, Tamsin   2670

H

H.—: The Story of Heathcliff's Journey Back to Wuthering Heights
Haire-Sargeant, Lin   2641

Hacey Miller
Sherburne, James   5805

Had We Never Loved
Veryan, Patricia   6463

Hadrian's Memoirs
Yourcenar, Marguerite   6947

Hagar
Henderson, Lois T.   2824
O'Neal, Cothburn   4737

The Half Breed
Constantin-Weyer, Maurice   1261

Halfhyde and the Admiral
McCutchan, Philip   4243

Halfhyde and the Chain Gang
McCutchan, Philip   4244

Halfhyde and the Flag Captain
McCutchan, Philip   4245

Halfhyde and the Fleet Review
McCutchan, Philip   4246

Halfhyde for the Queen
McCutchan, Philip   4247

Halfhyde Goes to War
McCutchan, Philip   4248

The Halfhyde Line
McCutchan, Philip   4249

Halfhyde on the Amazon
McCutchan, Philip   4250

Halfhyde on Zanatu
McCutchan, Philip   4251

Halfhyde Ordered South
McCutchan, Philip   4252

Halfhyde to the Narrows
McCutchan, Philip   4253

Halfhyde's Island
McCutchan, Philip   4254

The Hallelujah Flight
Lynn, Jack   3937

The Hallelujah Train
Gulick, Bill   2614

The Ham Reporter
Randisi, Robert J.   5251

The Hammer and the Cross
Harrison, Harry   2736

The Hammer of God
Scholefield, Alan   5655

Hammer of the Scots
Plaidy, Jean   5018

Hammett: A Novel
Gores, Joseph N.   2487

The Hampton Heritage
Ellis, Julie   1920

The Hampton Women
Ellis, Julie   1921

The Hand of a Woman
Brown, Diana   719

Hand of Glory
Petrie, Glen   4980

The Hand of Michelangelo
Alexander, Sidney   85

The Hands of Cantu
Lea, Tom   3694

The Handsome Road
Bristow, Gwen   697

Hang for Treason
Peck, Robert Newton   4886

Hanging on the Wire
Linscott, Gillian   3806

The Hangings
Pronzini, Bill   5202

Hangman's Beach
Raddall, Thomas H.   5229

Hangman's Cliff
Neill, Robert   4570

The Hangman's Crusade
Barwick, James   370

Hannah Fowler
Giles, Janice Holt   2411

Hannibal
Leckie, Ross   3704

Hannibal of Carthage
Dolan, Mary   1686

Hanover Place
Thomas, Michael M.   6245

Hanta Yo
Hill, Ruth Beebe   2951

The Happy Parrot
Chambers, Robert W.   977

Hard Money
Kelland, Clarence Budington   3389

Hard on the Road
Moore, Barbara   4440

Hard Road to Gettysburg
Jones, Ted   3298

The Hard to Catch Mercy
Baldwin, William   281

Hardacre
Skelton, C.L.   5872

Harkfast: The Making of the King
Rae, Hugh C.   5238

Harlot Queen
Lewis, Hilda   3748

Harold, the Last of the Saxon Kings
Bulwer-Lytton, Edward   767

Harold Was My King
Lewis, Hilda   3749

The Harp and the Blade
Myers, John   4543

The Harp and the Shadow
Carpentier, Alejo   905

Harp into Battle
Maiden, Cecil   4031

Harp of a Thousand Strings
Davis, Harold Lenoir   1522

Harpoon
Nicol, C.W.   4612

Harpoon in Eden
Mason, F. van Wyck   4152

The Harrogate Secret
Cookson, Catherine   1278

Harry: A Novel of Australia
Wales, Robert   6530

Harry Idaho
Pendexter, Hugh   4894

Harry of Monmouth
Maughan, A.M.   4199

Harvest of Death
Harrison, Ray   2741

Harvest of Dreams
Edwards, Jaroldeen   1884

Harvest of the Sun
Thompson, E.V.   6265

The Harvey Girls
Adams, Samuel Hopkins   31

The Hastening Wind
Grierson, Edward   2591

Hatchet in the Sky
Gay, Margaret Cooper   2328

Hate
Smith, Arthur Douglas   5918

The Haunted Monastery
van Gulik, Robert   6415

Haunted Summer
Edwards, Anne   1881

The Haunting of Lamb House
Aiken, Joan   48

The Haversham Legacy
Winston, Daoma   6827

Hawaii
Michener, James A.   4370

Hawk of Detroit
Pound, Arthur   5145

Hawk of May
Bradshaw, Gillian   629

Hawken Fury
Thompson, David   6254

The Hawkeye
Quick, Herbert   5222

Hawk's Journey
Porter, Donald Clayton   5119

The Hawks of Hawk-Hollow
Bird, Robert Montgomery   504

Hawthorn Hill
Shannon, Doris   5777

The Hawthorne Legacy
Crane, Teresa   1416

Haym Solomon, Son of Liberty
Fast, Howard   2032

The Haymarket
Rayner, Claire   5265

Hazard of Huntress
Stuart, Vivian   6087

Hazard's Command
Stuart, Vivian   6088

He Brings Great News
Dane, Clemence 1462

He Came From Galilee
Poling, Daniel A. 5083

He Done Her Wrong
Kaminsky, Stuart M. 3338

The Head Waters
Binns, Archie 500

The Headsman; or, The Abbaye des Vignerons
Cooper, James Fenimore 1300

The Healer
Appelfeld, Aharon 176

The Healers
Denker, Henry 1610

A Health Unto His Majesty
Plaidy, Jean 5019

Hear Me, Pilate!
Blythe, LeGette 557

A Heart Divided
Lacy, Al 3580

Heart in Pilgrimage
Eaton, Evelyn 1827

The Heart Is a Traitor
Abbey, Margaret 4

Heart of a Queen
Delves-Broughton, Josephine 1603

The Heart of Jade
Madariaga, Salvador de 4024

The Heart of Midlothian
Scott, Sir Walter 5698

The Heart of O. Henry
Kramer, Dale 3550

The Heart of the Continent
Cato, Nancy 961

Heart of the Country
Matthews, Greg 4190

The Heart of the Lion
Plaidy, Jean 5020

The Heart of the Rose
Barraclough, June 346

Heart of War
Masters, John 4174

Heartland
Mead, Robert Douglas 4316

Hearts and Bones
Lawrence, Margaret 3685

Hearts of Fire
Savage, Christina 5616

Hearts of Gold
Stirling, Jessica 6044

Hearts of Hickory
Moore, John Trotwood 4442

The Heatherton Heritage
Hill, Pamela 2934

Heaven and Hell
Jakes, John 3147

Heaven Is Too High
McNeilly, Mildred Masterson 4309

The Heaven Tree Trilogy
Pargeter, Edith 4797

Heaven Trees
Young, Stark 6943

Heaven's Gold
Tippette, Giles 6282

Heaven's Only Daughter
Robinson, Kathleen 5406

The Hedge of Thorns
Ashton, Helen 217

The Heidenmauer
Cooper, James Fenimore 1301

The Heike Story
Yoshikawa, Eiji 6934

The Heir of Allington
Wiat, Philippa 6727

Heir to Kuragin
Heaven, Constance 2807

Heir to Polventon
Watson, Marjorie 6583

The Heiress Bride
Coulter, Catherine 1375

Heiress of Ardara
Porter, Margaret Evans 5137

The Heirs of the Kingdom
Oldenbourg, Zoe 4716

Heirs of the Motherland
Pella, Judith 4893

Hellbane
Esler, Anthony 1963

Hellfire Jackson
Roark, Garland 5355

Henry VIII and His Six Wives
Peters, Maureen 4975

Henry and Clara
Mallon, Thomas 4042

Henry Esmond
Thackeray, William Makepeace 6212

Henry James' Midnight Song
Hill, Carol de Chellis 2920

Henry, King of France
Mann, Heinrich 4061

Henry Lunt and the Ranger
McNamara, Tom 4304

The Hepburn
Westcott, Jan 6645

Her-Bak: The Living Face of Ancient Egypt
Schwaller de Lubicz, Isha 5676

Her Christmas at the Hermitage: A Tale about Rachel and Andrew Jackson
Miller, Helen Topping 4389

Her Grace's Passion
Chesney, Marion 1033

Her Majesty's Captain
Wilson, Derek 6797

Her Royal Destiny
Eady, Carol Maxwell 1820

Hercules, My Shipmate
Graves, Robert 2545

The Herdsman
Wilson, Dorothy Clarke 6801

Here Be Dragons
Penman, Sharon Kay 4904

Here Comes a Candle
Hodge, Jane Aiken 2964

Here Comes the King
Lindsay, Philip 3792

Here I Stay
Coatsworth, Elizabeth 1138

Here Lies Margot
Hill, Pamela 2935

Here Lies Our Sovereign Lord
Plaidy, Jean 5021

The Heretic
Macleod, Alison 4002

The Heretic's Apprentice
Peters, Ellis 4960

Hereward the Wake
Kingsley, Charles 3497

Heritage
Orde, Lewis 4749

A Heritage and Its History
Compton-Burnett, Ivy 1229

A Heritage of Shadows
Brent, Madeleine 660

Heritage of the River
Elwood, Muriel 1937

Herma
Harris, Macdonald 2726

The Hermit of Eyton Forest
Peters, Ellis 4961

Heroic Dust
Dehon, Theodora 1581

Heroine of the Prairies: A Romance of the Oregon Trail
Hargreaves, Sheba 2707

The Heroine's Sister
Murray, Frances 4536

Herzl the King
Kotker, Norman 3547

The Hesitant Heart
Edwards, Anne 1882

The Hessian
Fast, Howard 2033

Hester
Bigsby, Christopher 496
Cleeve, Brian 1107

Hidden Children
Chambers, Robert W. 978

Hidden Victory: A Novel of Jesus
Smith, Herbert Francis 5921

The Hider
Estleman, Loren D. 1972

High Are the Mountains
Closs, Hannah 1130

High Carnival
Pugh, John J. 5207

The High Constable
Meyers, Maan 4353

High Country
Manning, Jason 4075

High Freedom
Murray, Earl 4530

High Hearts
Brown, Rita Mae 728

High Heroic
FitzGibbon, Constantine 2118

High Midnight
Kaminsky, Stuart M. 3339

The High Missouri
Blevins, Winfred 545

High Road to China
Cleary, Jon 1106

The High Rocks
Estleman, Loren D. 1973

High Towers
Costain, Thomas B. 1366

A High Wind in Jamaica
Hughes, Richard 3074

A High Wind Rising
Singmaster, Elsie 5867

Highgate Rise
Perry, Anne 4931

Highland Belle
Grasso, Patricia 2541

The Highland Hawk
White, Leslie Turner 6682

Highlands Rebel
Watson, Sally 6584

The Highwayman
Gerson, Noel B. 2372

The Highwayman and Mr. Dickens
Palmer, William J. 4783

The Hill of Doves
Cloete, Stuart 1123

Hill of the Hawk
O'Dell, Scott 4689

The Hills Stand Watch
Derleth, August 1615

Hilton Head
Pinckney, Josephine 5003

The Hippopotamus Pool
Peters, Elizabeth 4950

The Hired Man
Bragg, Melvyn 639

The Hireling
Macleod, Alison 4003

His Majesty's Highlanders
White, Leslie Turner 6683

His Majesty's Highwayman
Chidsey, Donald Barr 1061

His Majesty's Yankees
Raddall, Thomas H. 5230

His Was the Fire
Styles, Showell 6104

The History of Rome Hanks
Pennell, Joseph Stanley 4909

Hitler Has Won
Mullally, Frederic 4511**

The Hittite
Gerson, Noel B.   2373

Hiwassee: A Novel of the Civil War
Price, Charles F.   5176

H.M.S. Bounty
McKee, Alexander   4280

H.M.S. Cockerel
Lambdin, Dewey   3611

H.M.S. Surprise
O'Brian, Patrick   4666

Ho, the Fair Wind
Wylie, I.A.R.   6889

Hoffman's Row
Carnahan, Walter   902

The Holder of the World
Mukherjee, Bharati   4510

The Hollow Hills
Stewart, Mary   6030

Hollywood: A Novel of America in
   the 1920s
Vidal, Gore   6488

The Holy Innocents
Sedley, Kate   5717

The Holy Lover
Oemler, Marie   4690

The Holy Thief
Peters, Ellis   4962

The Holy Warrior
Morris, Gilbert   4462

Holy Week
Aragon, Louis   182

Home Mountain
Williams, Jeanne   6777

Home Station
Williams, Jeanne   6778

Home to Kentucky: A Novel of
   Henry Clay
Crabb, Alfred Leland   1399

Home to Tennessee
Crabb, Alfred Leland   1400

Home to the Hermitage
Crabb, Alfred Leland   1401

The Homecoming
Lofts, Norah   3844

Homecoming
Ross, Dana Fuller   5474

Homeland
Jakes, John   3148

Homer's Daughter
Graves, Robert   2546

The Homesman
Swarthout, Glendon   6143

Homeward Bound
Walter, Elizabeth   6557

Honey in the Horn
Davis, Harold Lenoir   1523

Hong Kong
Gardner, Mona   2288

Honor This Day
Kent, Alexander   3432

Honor Thy Father
Roripaugh, Robert A.   5460

The Honorable Imposter
Morris, Gilbert   4463

Honour and Obey
Macdonald, Malcolm   3966

The Hooded Falcon
Andrew, Prudence   140

Hoopla
Stein, Harry   5990

The Hope
Wouk, Herman   6874

Hope Leslie; or, Early Times in
   Massachusetts
Sedgewick, Catharine Maria   5714

Hope of Earth
Rushing, Jane Gilmore   5528

The Horn and the Forest
Cooper, Jamie Lee   1313

The Horn and the Roses: A Novel
   Based on the Life of Peter Paul
   Rubens
Wallach, Ira Jan   6542

Hornblower and the Atropos
Forester, C.S.   2175

Hornblower and the Hotspur
Forester, C.S.   2176

Hornblower During the Crisis
Forester, C.S.   2177

Horne's Law
Sherman, Jory   5819

The Horse Goddess
Llywelyn, Morgan   3820

The Horse Hunters
Peck, Robert Newton   4887

The Horse Soldiers
Sinclair, Harold   5862

The Horseman on the Roof
Giono, Jean   2424

A Horseman Riding By
Delderfield, R.F.   1588

The Horsemasters
Wolf, Joan   6840

Horses of Heaven
Bradshaw, Gillian   630

Horses of War
Hart-Davis, Duff   2760

Horseshoe Bend
Palmer, Bruce   4779

Horseshoe Robinson, a Tale of the
   Tory Ascendancy
Kennedy, John P.   3418

Hortensius, Friend of Nero
Pargeter, Edith   4798

The Hospital
Young, Agatha   6938

Hotel Transylvania
Yarbro, Chelsea Quinn   6900

The Hounds of God
Sabatini, Rafael   5551

The Hours of Light
Tanner, Janet   6160

The House at Old Vine
Lofts, Norah   3845

A House Behind the Mint
Huffman, Laurie   3072

The House by the Churchyard
Le Fanu, Joseph Sheridan   3688

A House Divided
Phillips, Michael   4988

House Divided
Williams, Ben Ames   6765

A House in Peiking
Payne, Robert   4853

The House in Ruins
Weekley, Robert S.   6595

The House of Cards
Garfield, Leon   2292

The House of Cray
Hill, Pamela   2936

The House of Eliott
Marsh, Jean   4100

The House of Five Talents
Auchincloss, Louis   231

The House of Kanze
Albery, Nobuko   64

The House of Kuragin
Heaven, Constance   2808

The House of Memory: A Novel of
   Shanghai
Clifford, Nicholas R.   1117

The House of War
Gavin, Catherine   2322

A House of Women
Malpass, Eric   4049

The House on Bitterness Street
Trevino, Elizabeth Borton de   6340

The House on Curtin Street
Ragosta, Millie J.   5242

The House on Mulberry Street
Meyers, Maan   4354

The House on the Mound
Derleth, August   1616

The House That Tai Ming Built
Lee, Virginia   3711

How Do I Love Thee
Iremonger, Lucille   3110

How Far to Bethlehem?
Lofts, Norah   3846

How Green Was My Valley
Llewellyn, Richard   3813

How Young They Die
Cloete, Stuart   1124

The Howard Hughes Affair
Kaminsky, Stuart M.   3340

The Hoydens and Mr. Dickens
Palmer, William J.   4784

Hubble Time
Bezzi, Tom   490

Hue and Cry
Yates, Elizabeth   6907

Hugh Wynne, Free Quaker
Mitchell, Silas Weir   4416

The Hunchback of Notre Dame
Hugo, Victor   3076

A Hundred Hills
Breslin, Howard   667

Hungarian Rhapsody: The Life of
   Franz Liszt
Rousselot, Jean   5511

The Hungry Goblin: A Victorian
   Detective Novel
Carr, John Dickson   911

Hungry Hill
Du Maurier, Daphne   1746

Hunt for Heaven
Barber, Elsie   298

The Hunting Shirt
Johnston, Mary   3235

Husband of Delilah
Linklater, Eric   3802

The Hyde Park Murder
Roosevelt, Elliott   5443

Hyde Place
Coffman, Virginia   1154

Hypatia
Kingsley, Charles   3498

I

I Am a Barbarian
Burroughs, Edgar Rice   807

I Am England
Wright, Patricia   6881

I Am Lidian
Babson, Naomi Lane   253

I Am Mary Tudor
Lewis, Hilda   3750

I Am Vidocq
McConnor, Vincent   4225

I Came to the Highlands: A Novel of
   Suspense
Johnston, Velda   3263

I, Claudius
Graves, Robert   2547

I, Elizabeth
Miles, Rosalind   4378

I Give You Oscar Wilde
Hall, Desmond   2647

I, Jack Swilling
Myers, John   4544

I, James Lewis
Gabriel, Gilbert Wolf   2266

I, James McNeill Whistler
Williams, Lawrence   6787

I, John Mordaunt
Scott, Virgil   5687

I, Judas
Caldwell, Taylor   859

I Know My Love
Gaskin, Catherine 2315

I Loved Tiberius
Dored, Elisabeth 1692

I, Madame Tussaud
Martin, Sylvia 4135

I, Nathanael, Knew Jesus
Sutpen, William Gilbert Van Tassel 6133

I Never Came to You in White
Farr, Judith 2014

I, Paul
Miller, Rex 4401

I, Rachel
Cost, March 1361

I, Rembrandt
Weiss, David 6605

I Remember Love
Hardwick, Mollie 2694

I, Roberta
Vining, Elizabeth Gray 6501

I Seek a City
Rees, Gilbert 5289

I Speak for Thaddeus Stevens
Singmaster, Elsie 5868

I Swear by Apollo
Young, Agatha 6939

I Take This Land
Powell, Richard 5147

I, the King
Clewes, Howard 1112
Kesten, Hermann 3475
Keyes, Frances Parkinson 3479

I, the Supreme
Roa Bastos, Augusto Antonio 5353

I Thee Wed
Gabriel, Gilbert Wolf 2267

I, Tituba, Black Witch of Salem
Conde, Maryse 1233

I, Victoria
Harrod-Eagles, Cynthia 2755

An Ice-Cream War
Boyd, William 616

The Ice Shirt
Vollmann, William T. 6509

The Ides of March
Wilder, Thornton 6753

The Idol Hunter
Unsworth, Barry 6386

The Idylls of the Queen
Karr, Phyllis Ann 3367

If a Lion Could Talk
Walker, Mildred 6532

If I Forget Thee
Deropp, Robert S. 1621
Segal, Brenda Lesley 5720

If I Never Get Back
Brock, Darryl 700

If I Were You
Aiken, Joan 49

If Not Victory
Hough, Frank Olney 3043

If This Be Magic
Marsh, Ellen 4098

I'll Storm Hell
Gerson, Noel B. 2374

Illinois!
Ross, Dana Fuller 5475

The Illusionist
Mason, Anita 4144

The Image of Our Lord
Burman, Edward 790

An Imaginary Life
Malouf, David 4047

The Imagination of the Heart
Glover, Judith 2437

The Immigrants
Fast, Howard 2034

The Immigrant's Daughter
Fast, Howard 2035

The Immortal Marriage
Atherton, Gertrude 225

Immortal Queen
Byrd, Elizabeth 834

Immortal Wife
Stone, Irving 6057

The Immortals
Korda, Michael 3540

An Imperfect Joy
Stubbs, Jean 6097

The Imperial Agent
Murari, T.N. 4518

Imperial Caesar
Warner, Rex 6565

Imperial Courtesan
Kenyon, F.W. 3452

The Imperial Governor
Shipway, George 5828

Imperial Kelly
Bowen, Peter 600

Imperial Purple
Bradshaw, Gillian 631

Imperial Renegade
De Wohl, Louis 1567

Imperial Venus: A Novel of Napoleon's Favorite Sister
Maas, Edgar 3949

Imperial Waltz
Abrahams, William M. 13

Imperial Winds
Napier, Priscilla 4555

Imperial Woman
Buck, Pearl S. 755

The Imperialists
Long, William Stuart 3875

An Important Family
Eden, Dorothy 1855

The Imposter
Gerson, Noel B. 2375

Impressionist: A Novel of Mary Cassatt
King, Joan 3486

The Impudent Rifle
Pearce, Richard 4872

In a Dark Garden
Slaughter, Frank G. 5891

In a Dark Wood Wandering
Haasse, Hella S. 2631

In Adam's Fall
Dodge, Constance 1666

In Distant Waters
Woodman, Richard 6862

In Gallant Company
Kent, Alexander 3433

In My Father's House
Thoene, Bodie 6222

In Pale Battalions
Goddard, Robert 2444

In Perilous Seas
Suthren, Victor 6130

In Pursuit of the Green Lion
Riley, Judith Merkle 5334

In Still and Stormy Waters
Tannahill, Reay 6157

In the Blazing Light
White, Max 6693

In the Blue Light of African Dreams
Watkins, Paul 6580

In the Company of Eagles
Gann, Ernest K. 2279

In the Days of Poor Richard
Bacheller, Irving A. 259

In the Falcon's Claw: A Novel of the Year 1000
Raymo, Chet 5257

In the Fire of Spring
Tryon, Thomas 6355

In the Hands of the Senecas
Edmonds, Walter D. 1876

In the House of the King
Zara, Louis 6951

In the Season of the Sun
Newcomb, Kerry 4590

In the Season of the Wild Rose
Rising, Clara 5347

In the Shadow of Midnight
Canham, Marsha 880

In the Shadow of the Brontes
Brindley, Louise 690

In the Shadow of the Crown
Plaidy, Jean 5022

In the Shadow of the Nile
Hylton, Sara 3093

In the Shadow of the Oak King
Jones, Courtway 3271

In the Wilderness
Undset, Sigrid 6381

In Those Days
Fergusson, Harvey 2068

In What Torn Ship
Eaton, Evelyn 1828

In Winter's Shadow
Bradshaw, Gillian 632

The Incas
Peters, Daniel 4945

The Incorruptible
Coryn, Marjorie 1357
De Bois, Helma 1551

The Incredible Brazilian: The Native
Ghose, Zulfikar 2392

The Indentured Heart
Morris, Gilbert 4464

Independence!
Ross, Dana Fuller 5476

Indian Brother
Coryell, Hubert 1354

The Indian Chronicles
Barreiro, Jose 349

Indian Hater
Vernam, Glenn R. 6452

Indigo
Carnac, Nicholas 900

An Infamous Army
Heyer, Georgette 2892

The Infidel
Taylor, Georgia Elizabeth 6182

The Infidels
Gartner, Chloe 2308

The Infinite Woman
Marshall, Edison 4107

Inherit the Earth
Shaw, Margaret 5778

Inherit the Sun
Grant, Maxwell 2539

The Inheritors
Golding, William 2455

The Inner Voice
Putnam, Nina Wilcox 5211

An Innocent Woman
Macdonald, Malcolm 3967

The Inquisitors
Andrzejewski, Jerzy 153

The Inshore Squadron
Kent, Alexander 3434

The Inspector and Mrs. Jeffries
Brightwell, Emily 682

An Insular Position
Mo, Timothy 4421

The Interpreter
Moss, Robert 4499

The Intrigue
Chesney, Marion 1034

Intrigue in Baltimore
Whitney, Janet 6715

The Invaders
Danielson, Peter 1469

Invading Tibet
Frutkin, Mark 2239

The Invention of Truth
Morazzoni, Marta   4449

The Invincibles
Vaughan, Carter A.   6436

Invisible Cities
Calvino, Italo   867

The Ionian Mission
O'Brian, Patrick   4667

Ippolita
Denti di Pirajno, Alberto   1612

Irene at Large
Douglas, Carole Nelson   1700

Irene's Last Waltz
Douglas, Carole Nelson   1701

The Irish Boy: A Romantic Biography
Jacob, Naomi   3137

The Iron Chain
DeFelice, Jim   1579

The Iron Crown
Barroll, Clare   354

The Iron Curtain
Vaughan, Robert   6447

The Iron Hand of Mars
Davis, Lindsey   1528

The Iron King
Druon, Maurice   1732

Iron Land
Ogley, Dorothy   4697

The Iron Mistress
Wellman, Paul I.   6618

The Iron Roads
Bramble, Forbes   644

Iron Ships, Iron Men
Nicole, Christopher   4616

Ironclads: Man-of-War
Names, Larry D.   4554

The Ironmaster
Powers, Anne   5150

Isabel the Fair
Barnes, Margaret Campbell   323

The Island Harp
Williams, Jeanne   6779

The Island of the Day Before
Eco, Umberto   1849

The Island of the Innocent: A Novel of Greek and Jew in the Time of the Maccabees
Fisher, Vardis   2108

Islands of Unwisdom
Graves, Robert   2548

Isle of Glory
Oliver, Jane   4723

Isle of Woman
Anthony, Piers   167

Isobelle
Lide, Mary   3775

Israel Potter
Melville, Herman   4334

It Began in Vauxhall Gardens
Plaidy, Jean   5023

The Italian Garden
Lennox-Smith, Judith   3717

The Italian Woman
Plaidy, Jean   5024

It's Me Again
Jack, Donald   3126

Ivanhoe
Scott, Sir Walter   5699

The Ivy Crown: A Biographical Novel of Queen Katherine Parr
Luke, Mary M.   3923

J

Jack Sheppard
Ainsworth, William Harrison   56

Jack the Ripper
Gordon, Richard   2484

Jackson: A Novel
Byrd, Max   837

Jacob
Cabries, Jean   844

Jacob: An Autobiography
Fineman, Irving   2088

Jade
Barr, Pat   344

The Jade Alliance
Darrell, Elizabeth   1497

The Jade Stalk
Fast, Jonathan   2048

The Jaguar and the Golden Stag
Allen, Dexter   95

The Jaguar Princess
Bell, Clare   421

Jamaica Inn
Du Maurier, Daphne   1747

James and Joan
Fremantle, Anne   2221

James, by the Grace of God
Ross, Hugh Williamson   5499
Tranter, Nigel   6315

Jane and the Man of the Cloth
Barron, Stephanie   355

Jane and the Unpleasantness at Scargrave Manor
Barron, Stephanie   356

Jane Fairfax
Aiken, Joan   50

Janice Meredith
Ford, Paul Leicester   2166

Jarrett's Jade
Yerby, Frank   6923

Jason
Treece, Henry   6331

Jason McGee
Fowler, Robert H.   2190

Java Head
Hergesheimer, Joseph   2854

The Jealous House
Kelland, Clarence Budington   3390

Jefferson: A Novel
Byrd, Max   838

Jekyll, Alias Hyde
Thomas, Donald   6240

Jelly Roll Morton's Last Night at the Jungle Inn: An Imaginary Memoir
Charters, Samuel   1002

Jemmy Button
Subercaseaux, Benjamin   6107

Jennie about to Be
Ogilvie, Elisabeth   4694

Jennie Glenroy
Ogilvie, Elisabeth   4695

Jenny and Barnum: A Novel of Love
Thorp, Roderick   6276

Jeremiah Martin: A Revolutionary War Novel
Fowler, Robert H.   2191

Jerusalem
Holland, Cecilia   2990

Jerusalem Interlude
Thoene, Bodie   6223

Jessie: A Novel Based on the Life of Jessie Benton Fremont
Alter, Judy   120

Jesters
Markish, David   4090

The Jew of Rome
Feuchtwanger, Lion   2071

The Jewel in the Crown
Scott, Paul   5684

Jewel of the Sea
Argo, Ellen   185
Wiggs, Susan   6743

Jewelled Path
Laker, Rosalind   3597

The Jewelled Spur
Morris, Gilbert   4465

Jewels
Perrin, Robert   4917

Jezebel
Wilson, Dorothy Clarke   6802

Jim Mundy: A Novel of the American Civil War
Fowler, Robert H.   2192

Joanna the Pope
Panger, Daniel   4785

Johanna: A Novel of the Van Gogh Family
Cooperstein, Claire   1317

John and Anzia: An American Romance
Rosen, Norma   5462

John Barry
Bedford, Donald F.   412

John Bonwell
Pulse, Charles K.   5208

John Crews
Chapman, Arthur   988

John Howard Payne, Skywalker
Barragan, Maude   348

John Inglesant
Shorthouse, John Henry   5833

John Milton
Fuller, Edmund   2249

John Ruskin's Wife
McDonald, Eva   4259

Johnnie Cross
White, Terence de Vere   6704

Johnny Christmas
Blake, Forrester   533

Johnny Logan: Shawnee Spy
Eckert, Allen W.   1843

Johnny Osage
Giles, Janice Holt   2412

Johnny Shiloh
Rhodes, James A.   5308

The Jonah Man
Carlisle, Henry   895

Jonathan Blair, Bounty Lands Lawyer
Ellis, William Donohue   1929

Jonathan Dearborn: A Novel of the War of 1812
Wallace, Willard   6540

Jordan County: A Landscape in Narrative
Foote, Shelby   2152

Jornada
Duffus, Robert L.   1754

Joseph
Jones, Mervyn   3292

Joseph of Egypt
Mann, Thomas   4065

Joseph the Provider
Mann, Thomas   4066

Josephus
Feuchtwanger, Lion   2072

Josephus and the Emperor
Feuchtwanger, Lion   2073

Joshua Moore, American
Hummel, George Frederick   3078

The Journal of Colonel De Lancey
Bellah, James Warner   426

The Journal of Hildegard of Bingen
Lachman, Barbara   3578

Journey
Michener, James A.   4371

Journey by the River
Prescott, John   5173

Journey into Fire
Wright, Patricia   6882

The Journey of August King
Ehle, John   1894

Journey Proud
McGehee, Thomasine   4273

Journey to Enchantment
Veryan, Patricia   6464

A Journey to Matecumbe
Taylor, Robert Lewis   6188

Journey to Nashville
Crabb, Alfred Leland   1402

Journey to Shiloh
Henry, Will 2843

Journey to the Sky: A Novel about the True Adventures of Two Men in Search of the Lost Maya Kingdom
Highwater, Jamake 2918

The Journeyer
Jennings, Gary 3194

Joy From Ashes
Lacy, Al 3581

Joy in Mudville
McAlpine, Gordon 4216

The Joyful Beggar: A Novel of St. Francis of Assisi
De Wohl, Louis 1568

Juan Ortiz: Gentleman of Seville
Alfriend, Mary Bethell 88

Jubal Sackett
L'Amour, Louis 3620

Jubilee
Brick, John 672
Walker, Margaret 6531

Jubilee Jim and the Wizard of Wall Street
Porter, Donald 5112

Jubilee Trail
Bristow, Gwen 698

Judas
Mossinsohn, Igal 4500

Judas Flowering
Hodge, Jane Aiken 2965

The Judas Kiss
Holt, Victoria 3015

The Judas Tree
Swanson, Neil Harmon 6139

The Judges of the Secret Court
Stacton, David 5972

Judgment in July
Fisher, Richard 2105

Judith
Cleeve, Brian 1108
Wilchek, Stella 6748

Judith Duchesne
Sargent, Lynda 5605

Judith Lankester
Allee, Marjorie 93

Judith Paris
Walpole, Hugh 6545

Julian
Vidal, Gore 6489

Julia's Last Hope
Oke, Janette 4708

Julie
Morris, Jane Kesner 4479

The Jump-Off Creek
Gloss, Molly 2435

Juniata Valley
Cassel, Virginia C. 954

Justice, My Brother
Keene, James 3386

The Justicer
Fall, Thomas 2010

Justus
Lapham, Arthur L. 3663

K

Ka'a'awa: A Novel about Hawaii in the 1850s
Bushnell, Oswald Andrew 814

Kagami
Kata, Elizabeth 3369

Kansas Blue
Harson, Dylan 2758

Karl and Rosa
Doblin, Alfred 1653

Kate
Cleeve, Brian 1109

Katerina
Appelfeld, Aharon 177

Katharine: The Virgin Widow
Plaidy, Jean 5025

Katherine
Seton, Anya 5752
Van-Loon, Antonia 6425

Katherine Christian
Walpole, Hugh 6546

Katheryn, the Wanton Queen
Peters, Maureen 4976

Kathryn: In the Court of Six Queens
Abbey, Anne Merton 1

Katrina
Price, Jeramie 5190

Katya
Cores, Lucy 1328

The Kays
Deland, Margaret 1583

Kean: The Imaginary Memoirs of an Actor
Berstl, Julius 485

The Keeper of the House
Kroll, Harry Harrison 3558

Keepers of the Misty Time
Rowe, Patricia 5517

Keeping Secrets
Morris, Suzanne 4483

Kelly Blue
Bowen, Peter 601

Kenilworth
Scott, Sir Walter 5700

The Kentuckians
Giles, Janice Holt 2413

Kentucky!
Ross, Dana Fuller 5477

Kentucky Home
Receveur, Betty Layman 5283

Kentucky Pride
Markey, Gene 4087

Kentucky Stand
Wheelwright, Jere Hungerford 6670

The Kentucky Trace: A Novel of the American Revolution
Arnow, Harriette Simpson 195

Kenya
Halkin, John 2645

Kepler: A Novel
Banville, John 297

Kernow & Daughter
Macdonald, Malcolm 3968

The Key
Jaro, Benita Kane 3169

The Keys of England
Cooke, William Victor 1271

Keystone
Lovesey, Peter 3913

Kezzy
Burns, Patricia 799

Kid Curry: The Life and Times of Harvey Logan and the Wild Bunch
Lamb, F. Bruce 3606

Kidnapped
Stevenson, Robert Louis 6010

The Kidnapped Surgeon
Knox, Alexander 3527

Kilcaraig
Carothers, Annabel 904

Killdeer Mountain
Brown, Dee 713

The Killer Angels
Shaara, Michael 5766

Killing Cousins
Knight, Alanna 3520

The Killing Frost
Hayden, Thomas 2799

Killing Mister Watson
Mathiessen, Peter 4185

The Killing of Richard the Third
Farrington, Robert 2020

Killing Time
Conley, Robert J. 1244

Kimberley
Burke, Colin 784

A Kind of Justice
Siegel, Benjamin 5844

Kindred Spirits
Barraclough, June 347

The King
Barthelme, Donald 365

King and Goddess
Tarr, Judith 6166

The King Breaker
Linington, Elizabeth 3797

King David
Jenkins, Gwyn 3191

The King David Report
Heym, Stefan 2910

The King Edward Plot
Hall, Robert Lee 2658

King Hereafter
Dunnett, Dorothy 1802

King in Hell: A Novel of Bothwell and Mary, Queen of Scots
Balin, Beverly 282

The King James Version
Stewart, Stanley N. 6035

King Jesus
Graves, Robert 2549

The King Liveth
Farnol, Jeffrey 2013

The King Must Die
Renault, Mary 5298

The King of Flesh and Blood
Shamir, Moshe 5772

King of Kings: A Novel of the Life of David
Martin, Malachi 4134

King of Paris
Endore, Guy 1942

King of the Bastards
Millin, Sarah Gertrude 4405

King of the Mountain
Thompson, David 6255

King of the Two Lands: The Pharaoh Akhenaten
Hawkes, Jacquetta 2780

King of the Wood
Anand, Valerie 131

A King Reluctant
Wilkins, William Vaughan 6759

King Tut's Private Eye
Levin, Lee 3739

The Kingdom Carver
Perrault, E.G. 4916

Kingdom Come
Sorensen, Virginia 5950

Kingdom Coming
Bradford, Roark 622

Kingdom of Gold
Wiggs, Susan 6744

Kingdom of Shadows
Erskine, Barbara 1954

Kingdom of Summer
Bradshaw, Gillian 633

Kingdom of the Grail
Attanasio, A.A. 226

The Kingdom of the Wicked
Burgess, Anthony 778

Kingdom of This World
Carpentier, Alejo 906

Kingkill
Gavin, Thomas 2325

The Kingmaking
Hollick, Helen 3000

The King's Achievement
Benson, Robert Hugh 459

King's Agent
Clark, Justus Kent 1090

The King's Bastard
Elsna, Hebe 1932

The King's Bed
Barnes, Margaret Campbell 324

The King's Bishop
Robb, Candace M.   5365

The King's Brat
Gluyas, Constance   2441

The King's Cavalier
Shellabarger, Samuel   5795

The King's Coat
Lambdin, Dewey   3612

A King's Commander
Lambdin, Dewey   3613

The King's Commissar
Kyle, Duncan   3570

The King's Commission
Lambdin, Dewey   3614

The King's Daughters
Haycraft, Molly Costain   2793

King's Fool
Barnes, Margaret Campbell   325

The King's General
Du Maurier, Daphne   1748

The King's Good Servant
White, Olive   6696

The King's Grey Mare
Jarman, Rosemary Hawley   3167

The Kings in Winter
Holland, Cecelia   2991

The King's Iron
Peck, Robert Newton   4888

King's Man
Edmondston, C.M.   1880

King's Masque
John, Evan   3220

The King's Messenger
Edwards, Samuel   1887

King's Minion
Sabatini, Rafael   5552

Kings Mountain
Henri, Florette   2838

Kings of the Missouri
Pendexter, Hugh   4895

The Kings of Vain Intent
Shelby, Graham   5791

The King's Orchard
Turnbull, Agnes Sligh   6363

The King's Passenger
Schachner, Nathan   5631

The King's Persons
Greenberg, Joanne   2573

The King's Pleasure
Lofts, Norah   3847
Plaidy, Jean   5026

The King's Privateer
Lambdin, Dewey   3615

A King's Ransom
Suthren, Victor   6131

The King's Rebel
Horan, James David   3030

The King's Rogue
Peacock, Max   4859

Kings Row
Bellamann, Henry   428

King's Royal
Quigley, John   5224

The King's Secret Matter
Plaidy, Jean   5027

The King's Vixen
Hill, Pamela   2937

The King's Way
Chandernagor, Francoise   986

The Kingsbridge Plot
Meyers, Maan   4355

Kinsmen of the Grail
Roberts, Dorothy James   5376

Knave of Hearts
Carr, Philippa   920

Knaves Templar
Tourney, Leonard   6300

**The Knifeman: A Novel of Judas
    Iscariot**
Rayner, William   5271

The Knight
Shipway, George   5829

The Knight and the Dove
Wick, Lori   6732

A Knight in Shining Armor
Deveraux, Jude   1631

Knight with Armour
Duggan, Alfred   1767

Knights
Miller, Linda Lael   4399

Knight's Acre
Lofts, Norah   3848

Knight's Honor
Gellis, Roberta   2351

The Knights of Dark Renown
Shelby, Graham   5792

Know Nothing
Settle, Mary Lee   5755

L

The Labyrinth
Duncan, Thomas William   1787

The Lacemaker
Montupet, Janine   4438

The Lacquer Screen
van Gulik, Robert   6416

The Ladies of Hanover Square
Randall, Rona   5249

The Ladies of Missalonghi
McCullough, Colleen   4237

The Ladies of St. Hedwig's
Almedingen, E.M.   117

Ladies Whose Bright Eyes
Ford, Ford Madox   2162

The Lady
Richter, Conrad   5321

The Lady and Doc Holliday
Lewis, Preston   3761

The Lady and the Arsenic
Bowen, Marjorie   598

The Lady and the Deep Blue Sea
Roark, Garland   5356

A Lady at Bay
Maas, Edgar   3950

The Lady Chapel
Robb, Candace M.   5366

The Lady Cicely
Wilson, Sandra   6813

Lady Defiant
Robinson, Suzanne   5412

The Lady for Ransom
Duggan, Alfred   1768

Lady Fortescue Steps Out
Chesney, Marion   1035

The Lady From Yorktown
McDonald, Eva   4260

Lady Gallant
Robinson, Suzanne   5413

Lady Godiva and Master Tom
Faure, Raoul Cohen   2052

Lady Hellfire
Robinson, Suzanne   5414

A Lady in Doubt
Wynne, Annabel   6891

Lady in the Briars
Dunn, Carola   1793

The Lady in the Mask
Green, Anne   2564

The Lady in the Tower
Plaidy, Jean   5028

Lady in Waiting
Sutcliff, Rosemary   6123

Lady Jane
Clark, Norma Lee   1092
O'Grady, Leslie   4699

The Lady of Arlington
Kane, Harnett T.   3354

Lady of Conquest
Medeiros, Teresa   4322

Lady of Hay
Erskine, Barbara   1955

Lady of Mallow
Eden, Dorothy   1856

Lady of Monkton
Byrd, Elizabeth   835

Lady of Moray
Copeland, Bonnie   1318

Lady of No Man's Land
Williams, Jeanne   6780

Lady of Paris
Wilkins, William Vaughan   6760

Lady of Quality
Heyer, Georgette   2893

A Lady of Repute
James, Janice   3158

Lady of the Forest
Roberson, Jennifer   5368

Lady of the Glen
Roberson, Jennifer   5369

Lady of the Lotus
Barrett, William E.   353

Lady of the Mohawks
Widdemer, Margaret   6736

Lady of the Reeds
Gedge, Pauline   2345

Lady on the Coin
Barnes, Margaret Campbell   326

Lady Pamela
Darcy, Clare   1490

Lady Rich
Coker, Elizabeth Boatwright   1166

The Lady Royal
Haycraft, Molly Costain   2794

Lady Washington
Wilson, Dorothy Clarke   6803

Lady Wu
Lin, Yutang   3782

Lady's Maid
Forster, Margaret   2188

**Ladysmead: A Novel in the Jane
    Austen Tradition**
Gillespie, Jane   2420

Lakota
Wisler, G. Clifton   6833

Lamb in Command
Maynard, Kenneth   4209

Lamb in His Bosom
Miller, Caroline   4380

Lament for a Lost Lover
Carr, Philippa   921

Lamia: A Witch
Taylor, Georgia Elizabeth   6183

The Lance of Longinus
Loewenstein, Hubertus   3833

Lancet
Rogers, Garet   5431

The Land Beyond the Mountains
Giles, Janice Holt   2414

The Land Beyond the Tempest
Mayrant, Drayton   4213

The Land Breakers
Ehle, John   1895

The Land Endures
Pearce, Mary E.   4862

Land for My Sons
Cormack, Maribelle   1331

The Land Is Bright
Binns, Archie   501
Gerson, Noel B.   2376
Kjelgaard, James Arthur   3508

The Land of Our Dreams
Livingston, Nancy   3812

Land of the Beautiful River
Linderholm, Helmer   3788

A Land to Tame
Ross, Zola Helen   5505

The Land Was Ours: A Novel of the Great Plains
Bailey, Charles W. 266

The Land Where the Sun Dies
Carlisle, Henry 896

Landru
Masson, Rene 4170

Lantern for the Dark
Stirling, Jessica 6045

A Lantern in Her Hand
Aldrich, Bess Streeter 69

Lanterns
Veryan, Patricia 6465

Last Act in Palmyra
Davis, Lindsey 1529

The Last Athenian
Rydberg, Viktor 5543

The Last Boat out of Cincinnati
Tracy, Don 6309

The Last Camel Died at Noon
Peters, Elizabeth 4951

The Last Confederate
Morris, Gilbert 4466

The Last Crusader
De Wohl, Louis 1569

The Last Days
Rayner, William 5272

The Last Days of Horse-Shy Halloran
Pronzini, Bill 5203

The Last Days of Pompeii
Bulwer-Lytton, Edward 768

The Last Enchantment
Stewart, Mary 6031

The Last Encounter
Maugham, Robin 4196

The Last Englishman: The Story of Hereward the Wake
Weenolsen, Hebe 6596

The Last Farewell
McCutchan, Philip 4255

The Last Frontier
Fast, Howard 2036

The Last Full Measure
Morrow, Honore 4488

The Last Gamble
Graham, Winston 2527

The Last Gentleman
Barker, Shirley 312

Last Go Round
Kesey, Ken 3473

Last Gun: The Legend of John Selman
Shelton, Gene 5801

The Last Hero
Forbath, Peter 2154

The Last Hunt
Lott, Milton 3900

The Last Innocent Hour
Abbott, Margot 8

Last Letter Home
Moberg, Vilhelm 4423

The Last Love
Costain, Thomas B. 1367

Last Love of Camille
Winwar, Frances 6832

The Last Mammoth
Allan, Margaret 89

Last Man to Die
Dobbs, Michael 1652

The Last Mutiny: The Further Adventures of Captain Bligh
Collett, Bill 1208

The Last Mystery of Edgar Allan Poe
Meyers, Manny 4356

Last of Britain
Trevor, Meriol 6343

The Last of the Barons
Bulwer-Lytton, Edward 769

The Last of the Mohicans
Cooper, James Fenimore 1302

The Last of the Vikings
Bojer, Johan 563

The Last of the Wine
Renault, Mary 5299

The Last Pendragon
Rice, Robert 5316

The Last Plantation
Wright, Don 6879

The Last Portrait of the Duchess of Alba
Larreta, Antonio 3666

The Last Prince of Ireland
Llywelyn, Morgan 3821

The Last Princess
Locke, Charles O. 3826

Last Reveille
Morrell, David 4456

The Last Ride
Eidson, Tom 1899

The Last Romans
Jeske-Choinski, Teodor 3216

The Last Stand: A Novel about George Armstrong Custer and the Indians of the Plains
Hoyt, Edwin P. 3061

The Last Station
Parini, Jay 4801

The Last Summer of Innocence
Sole, Linda 5938

The Last Summer of Mata Hari
Huebsch, Edward 3067

The Last Temptation of Christ
Kazantzakis, Nikos 3384

The Last Testament of Oscar Wilde
Ackroyd, Peter 19

The Last Valley
Guthrie, A.B. Jr. 2626
Pick, J.B. 4992

The Last Victory
Murari, T.N. 4519

The Last Voyage: Captain Cook's Lost Diary
Innes, Hammond 3108

The Last Waltz
Zaroulis, Nancy 6955

The Last Warpath
Henry, Will 2844

The Last Warrior Queen
Mackey, Mary 3992

The Last World: A Novel with an Ovidian Repertory
Ransmayr, Christoph 5253

Late Harvest
White, Olive 6697

The Latter Adventures of Tom Jones
Coleman, Bob 1200

The Lattimer Legend
Hebson, Ann 2813

The Laughing Hangman
Marston, Edward 4120

The Laughing Stranger
Delmar, Vina 1601

The Laughter of Aphrodite
Green, Peter 2570

Lavender Lady
Dunn, Carola 1794

The Law in Charity
Yarbro, Chelsea Quinn 6901

The Law of Larion
Freuchen, Peter 2227

Law of the Land
Allis, Marguerite 111

The Lawless
Jakes, John 3149

Lay Siege to Heaven: A Novel of Saint Catherine of Siena
De Wohl, Louis 1570

Lazarus
Absire, Alain 15

El Lazo
Martin, L. Jay 4132

A Leaf in the Wind
Joseph, Marie 3307

Leafy Rivers
West, Jessamyn 6630

Leah's Journey
Goldreich, Gloria 2460

Leaves From the Valley
Trollope, Joanna 6348

Leaving Cold Sassy
Burns, Olive Ann 798

The Legacy
Fast, Howard 2037

Legacy
Kay, Susan 3374
Vaughan, Robert 6448

The Legacy of Beulah Land
Coleman, Lonnie 1203

The Legacy of Ladysmith
Crane, John Kenny 1413

Legacy of the Wolf
Raynes, Jean 5274

The Legacy of Tregaran
Lide, Mary 3776

The Legend of Ben Tree
Hawkins, Paul 2784

The Legend of Tyl Ulenspiegel
De Coster, Charles Theodore Henri 1558

The Legion of the Lost
Chidsey, Donald Barr 1062

Legs
Kennedy, William 3422

Lempriere's Dictionary
Norfolk, Lawrence 4641

Lenin in Zurich
Solzhenitsyn, Alexander 5943

Lenin: The Novel
Brien, Alan 679

Leo Africanus
Maalouf, Amin 3947

Leonardo's Judas
Perutz, Leo 4941

The Leopard
Lampedusa, Giuseppe di 3634

The Leopard and the Cliff
Breem, Wallace 655

The Leopard Unleashed
Chadwick, Elizabeth 967

Leopards and Lilies
Duggan, Alfred 1769

The Leper King
Kossak-Szczucka, Zofja 3544

The Leper of St. Giles
Peters, Ellis 4963

Less Fortunate than Fair
Wilson, Sandra 6814

Lest Darkness Fall
De Camp, L. Sprague 1557

Let My Name Stand Fair
Seifert, Shirley 5727

Let the Drum Speak: A Novel of Ancient America
Shuler, Linda Lay 5837

Let the King Beware!
Morrow, Honore 4489

Let the Spring Come
Schindall, Henry 5637

Letter of Marque
Hepburn, Andrew 2849

The Letter of Marque
O'Brian, Patrick 4668

A Letter of Mary
King, Laurie R. 3488

The Letters of Nicodemus
Dobraczynski, Jan 1655

Letty
Ashton, Helen 218
Darcy, Clare 1491

Levi Coffin and the Underground Railroad
Ludwig, Charles   3921

Libbie
Alter, Judy   121

Liberty Tavern
Fleming, Thomas   2129

Libra
DeLillo, Don   1593

Lieutenant Hornblower
Forester, C.S.   2178

Lieutenant Lamb
Maynard, Kenneth   4210

Lieutenant of the Line
MacNeil, Duncan   4015

The Lieutenant's Lady
Aldrich, Bess Streeter   70

Life and Liberty
Rutledge, Adam   5538

The Life and Times of Captain N.
Glover, Douglas   2436

The Life and Times of Horatio Hornblower
Parkinson, C. Northcote   4813

Life as Carola
Grant, Joan   2535

The Life of Jesus: An Apocryphal Novel
Olson, Toby   4731

Light
Figes, Eva   2083

The Light Bearer
Gillespie, Donna   2419

Light in the Clearing
Bacheller, Irving A.   260

The Light in the Forest
Richter, Conrad   5322

The Light Infantry Ball
Basso, Hamilton   375

Light on Lucrezia
Plaidy, Jean   5029

Light on the Mountain
Sanders, Leonard   5589

Lighthouse
Price, Eugenia   5182

The Lighthouse at the End of the World
Marlowe, Stephen   4095

Lights Along the Shore
Austell, Diane   241

Lilith
Plaidy, Jean   5030

Lillibullero
Neill, Robert   4571

Lillie
Butler, David   818

Lily
Bonner, Cindy   571

The Lily and the Bull
Caldecott, Moyra   846

The Lily and the Leopard
Wiggs, Susan   6745

The Lily and the Leopards
Harwood, Alice   2765

The Lily and the Lion
Druon, Maurice   1733

Lily of the Mohawks
Casey, Jack   952

The Limits of Glory: A Novel of Waterloo
McDonough, James   4265

Limmerston Hall
Chapman, Hester W.   991

The Limner
Boles, Paul Darcy   564

Lincoln: A Novel
Vidal, Gore   6490

The Lincoln Diddle
Steward, Barbara   6015

The Lincoln Hunters
Tucker, Wilson   6359

Lincoln's Mothers: A Story of Nancy and Sally Lincoln
Wilson, Dorothy Clarke   6804

Lindeman's Daughters
Christensen, Synnove   1073

The Lion and the Cross
Hamilton, Joan Lesley   2669

The Lion and the Leopard
Johnson, Mary Ellen   3226

The Lion and the Rose
Oliver, Jane   4724

The Lion at Sea
Hennessy, Max   2834

The Lion in Egypt
Danielson, Peter   1470

Lion in the Evening
Scholefield, Alan   5656

Lion in the Valley
Peters, Elizabeth   4952

The Lion Is Come
Oliver, Jane   4725

The Lion of Christ
Butler, Margaret   823

The Lion of England
Butler, Margaret   824
Trevaskis, Eve   6336

The Lion of Ireland
Llywelyn, Morgan   3822

The Lion of Justice
Butler, Margaret   825
Plaidy, Jean   5031

The Lion of Pescara
MacBeth, George   3958

Lion Rampant
Shrimsley, Bernard   5836

The Lion Triumphant
Carr, Philippa   922

Lionel Lincoln; or, The Leaguer of Boston
Cooper, James Fenimore   1303

Lionheart!: A Novel of Richard I, King of England
Rofheart, Martha   5428

The Lions of the North
Marston, Edward   4121

The Lion's Skin
Teilhet, Darwin Le Ora   6197

The Lion's Way
Orde, Lewis   4750

Lisbon
Sherwood, Valerie   5825

The List of Seven
Frost, Mark   2237

Listen for the Voices
Colver, Anne   1220

Little Big Man
Berger, Thomas   478

The Little Emperors
Duggan, Alfred   1770

Little Red Foot
Chambers, Robert W.   979

Little Sister
Gaan, Margaret   2259

The Little Victoria
Prole, Lozania   5196

Live From Golgotha
Vidal, Gore   6491

Live From the Devil
Blassingame, Wyatt   542

The Live Goat
Dawkins, Cecil   1542

Liveliest Town in the West
Gulick, Bill   2615

The Lively Lady
Roberts, Kenneth   5386

The Lives of Rachel
Gross, Joel   2601

The Living
Dillard, Annie   1644

The Living Reed
Buck, Pearl S.   756

The Living Wood
De Wohl, Louis   1571

Liza Bowe
Barker, Shirley   313

Lizzie
Hunter, Evan   3083

Lizzie Borden
Engstrom, Elizabeth   1944

Locksley
Chase, Nicholas   1003

The Lodestar
Belle, Pamela   432

Lodging at the Saint Cloud
Crabb, Alfred Leland   1403

Log Cabin Noble
Mason, F. van Wyck   4153

Log Jam
White, Leslie Turner   6684

Logic of the Heart
Veryan, Patricia   6466

A London Season
Bell, Anthea   420

London's Child
Boast, Philip   560

Lone Star Lady
Gregory, Jill   2579

The Lonely Furrow
Lofts, Norah   3849

Lonely on the Mountain
L'Amour, Louis   3621

The Lonely Strangers
Blackstock, Charity   531

Lonesome Dove
McMurtry, Larry   4298

The Long Afternoon
Zilinsky, Ursula   6964

Long Day at Shiloh
Bannister, Don   294

The Long Day Closes
Tunstall, Beatrice   6360

The Long Fight
Rayner, D.A.   5270

Long Knife
Thom, James Alexander   6233

The Long March
Barry, Jane   358

The Long Naked Descent into Boston
Eastlake, William   1823

The Long Night
Lytle, Andrew   3945

Long Pennant
La Farge, Oliver   3573

Long Pig
Foreman, Russell   2168

Long Remember
Kantor, MacKinlay   3362

The Long Rifle
White, Stewart Edward   6702

The Long Roll
Johnston, Mary   3236

The Long Shadow
Gilbert, Anna   2406

The Long Ships
Bengtsson, Frans Gunnar   442

Long Storm
Haycox, Ernest   2790

The Long Sun
Lucas, Janice   3920

The Long Trail North
Conley, Robert J.   1245

The Long Watch
Linington, Elizabeth   3798

Long Winter Gone
Johnston, Terry C.   3252

The Longest Night
Lewis, Ada Cook   3744

The Longest Road
Williams, Jeanne   6781

The Longest Winter
Harris, Julie 2722

Longleaf
Brock, Rose 701

Look Away
Coyle, Harold 1395

Look Away!
Shuster, George Nauman 5841

Look Away, Beulah Land
Coleman, Lonnie 1204

Look Away, Look Away
White, Leslie Turner 6685

Look Back to Glory
Sass, Herbert Ravenel 5607

Look to the Mountain
Cannon, Le Grand 885

Look to the River
Owens, William A. 4771

Look to the Rose
Seifert, Shirley 5728

Look to Your Geese: A Novel of the Deflowering of New England
Sanders, Jacquin 5584

Looking After Lily
Bonner, Cindy 572

The Loon Feather
Fuller, Iola 2253

Loon Lake
Doctorow, E.L. 1657

Lord Byron's Doctor
West, Paul 6634

Lord Elgin's Lady
Vrettos, Theodore 6514

Lord Fancy
White, Leslie Turner 6686

Lord Geoffrey's Fancy
Duggan, Alfred 1771

Lord Grizzly
Manfred, Frederick F. 4056

Lord Hornblower
Forester, C.S. 2179

Lord Iverbrook's Heir
Dunn, Carola 1795

The Lord Jesus
Payne, Robert 4854

Lord Johnnie
White, Leslie Turner 6687

Lord Libertine
Esler, Anthony 1964

Lord of Darkness
Silverberg, Robert 5854

Lord of Hawkfell Island
Coulter, Catherine 1376

Lord of Misrule
Jones, Gareth 3290

Lord of Ravensley
Heaven, Constance 2809

Lord of the Dead: The Secret History of Byron
Holland, Tom 2999

Lord of the Far Island
Holt, Victoria 3016

Lord of the Isles
Chidsey, Donald Barr 1063

Lord of the Kongo
Forbath, Peter 2155

Lord of the Ladies
Dessau, Joanna 1626

The Lord of the Last Days: Visions of the Year 1000
Aridjis, Homero 188

Lord of the Plains
Silver, Alfred 5852

Lord of the River
Clavel, Bernard 1099

Lord of the Two Lands
Tarr, Judith 6167

Lord of the Vampires: The Diaries of the Family Dracul
Kalogridis, Jeanne 3328

Lord Raven's Widow
O'Grady, Leslie 4700

Lord Richard's Passion
Jones, Mervyn 3293

Lord Rivington's Lady
Jackson, Eileen 3134

Lord Vanity
Shellabarger, Samuel 5796

The Lord's Anointed
McKee, Ruth Eleanor 4282

The Lords of Lancaster
Bennetts, Pamela 452

The Lords of Loone
James, John 3159

Lords of the Dance
Lloyd-Jones, Robin 3815

Lords of the Plains
Crawford, Max 1420

The Lords of Vaumartin
Holland, Cecelia 2992

Lorena
Slaughter, Frank G. 5892

The Lorimer Line
Melville, Anne 4332

The Lormes of Castle Rising
Cradock, Fanny 1409

Lorna Doone
Blackmore, R.D. 528

The Lost Colony
Marshall, Edison 4108

The Lost Eagles
Graves, Ralph 2542

The Lost Flight
Prescott, H.F.M. 5169

The Lost Garden
Hodge, Jane Aiken 2966

The Lost Giants
Scholefield, Alan 5657

The Lost Lands
Vansittart, Peter 6430

The Lost Legion
Munn, H. Warner 4516

Lost Love Found
Small, Bertrice 5910

The Lost Queen
Lofts, Norah 3850

The Lost Wagon
Kjelgaard, James Arthur 3509

Lost Wallowa
Gulick, Bill 2616

The Lost Years: A Biographical Fiction
Lewis, Oscar 3757

Lot's Wife
Ley-Piscator, Marie 3767

The Lotus and the Wind
Masters, John 4175

Lotus Land
Highland, Monica 2917

Louis the Well-Beloved
Plaidy, Jean 5032

Louisa Brancusi
Husted, Darrell 3088

Louisa Elliott
Roberts, Ann Victoria 5370

Louisiana!
Ross, Dana Fuller 5478

Louisiana Purchase
Hotchner, A.E. 3039

Love Alters Not
Veryan, Patricia 6467

Love and Honor
Arlen, Leslie 189

Love and War
Jakes, John 3150

Love and Wisdom: A Novel about Solomon
Hubler, Richard G. 3064

Love at Sunset
Sheridan, Jane 5811

The Love Child
Carr, Philippa 923
Cookson, Catherine 1279

A Love Divine
Ripley, Alexandra 5340

Love Is a Wild Assault
Kirkland, Elithe Hamilton 3506

Love Is Eternal
Stone, Irving 6058

Love Is My Vocation: An Imaginative Study of St. Therese of Lisieux
Clarkson, Tom 1098

The Love Knot
Darby, Catherine 1482

Love Not a Rebel
Graham, Heather 2516

The Love of Fingin O'Lea
Du Bois, Theodora McCormick 1743

A Love So Wild
Chester, Deborah 1056

Lovelock
McNeish, James 4311

The Lovely Lynchs
King-Hall, Magdalen 3490

Lover of Life
Harsanyi, Zsolt de 2756

Lovers
Goodwin, Suzanne 2476

Lovers All Untrue
Lofts, Norah 3851

Lovers Meeting
Hardwick, Mollie 2695

Love's Children
Chernaik, Judith 1013

Love's Duet
Veryan, Patricia 6468

Love's Labour's Won
Fisher, Edward 2101

Love's Tender Fury
Wilde, Jennifer 6749

Lovestorm
French, Judith E. 2222

Loving Belle Star
Taylor, Robert 6187

Loving Emma
Foxell, Nigel 2197

Loving Heart
Singmaster, Elsie 5869

Loving Little Egypt
McMahon, Thomas 4288

Loving Sands, Deadly Sands
Keppel, Charlotte 3465

Low Treason
Tourney, Leonard 6301

Luciano's Luck
Higgins, Jack 2912

Lucifer Land
Davis, Mildred B. 1538

Lucinda Brayford
Boyd, Martin 613

The Luck of Huemac: A Novel about the Aztecs
Peters, Daniel 4946

Lucy
Chapman, Hester W. 992

Luise
Field, Dawn Stewart 2079

The Lure of the Falcon
Benzoni, Juliette 465

Lure of the Wind
Thompson, David 6256

Lusitania
Butler, David 819

Lust for Life
Stone, Irving 6059

Lustre in the Sky
Waldeck, R.G. 6525

Lusty Wind for Carolina
Fletcher, Inglis 2134

The Lute Player
Lofts, Norah 3852

Lydia Bailey
Roberts, Kenneth 5387

Lydia, or Love in Town
Darcy, Clare 1492

M

Mackenna's Gold
Henry, Will 2845

The Maclarens
Skelton, C.L. 5873

MacLyon
Burford, Lolah 773

The Mad Courtesan
Marston, Edward 4122

Mad Dog
Kelly, Jack 3401

Mad Hatter's Holiday
Lovesey, Peter 3914

Madame Casanova
Schonthan, Gaby von 5659

Madame Castel's Lodger
Keyes, Frances Parkinson 3480

Madame Geneva
Lane, Jane 3655

Madame Serpent
Plaidy, Jean 5033

The Maddest Idea
Nelson, James L. 4580

Madeleine
Gavin, Catherine 2323
West, Pamela Elizabeth 6633

Madensky Square
Ibbotson, Eva 3096

Madonna of the Seven Hills
Plaidy, Jean 5034

Madselin
Lofts, Norah 3853

The Mae West Murder Case
Baxt, George 386

The Magdalene Gospel
Ashcroft, Mary Ellen 203

Maggie Craig
Joseph, Marie 3308

The Magic Bow
Komroff, Manuel 3534

**Magic Fire: Scenes around Richard
Wagner**
Harding, Bertita 2683

Magic Flutes
Ibbotson, Eva 3097

The Magic Ship
Paretti, Sandra 4791

Magnificent Destiny
Wellman, Paul I. 6619

Magnificent Enemies
Maas, Edgar 3951

The Magnificent Failure
Lutz, Giles A. 3928

The Magnificent Savages
Stewart, Fred Mustard 6024

**The Magnificent Traitor: A Novel of
Alcibiades and the Golden Age of
Pericles**
Poole, Lynn 5092

The Magnolias
Ellis, Julie 1922

Magnus the Magnificent
White, Leslie Turner 6688

**Maid of Honour: A Novel Set in the
Court of Mary, Queen of Scots**
Byrd, Elizabeth 836

The Maid of Sker
Blackmore, R.D. 529

Maiden Voyage
Bass, Cynthia 372

Major Andre
Bailey, Anthony 265

Major Stepton's War
Vaughan, Matthew 6445

Malefice
Wilson, Leslie 6810

Malkeh and Her Children
Edelson, Marjorie 1853

The Mallen Girl
Cookson, Catherine 1280

The Mallen Lot
Cookson, Catherine 1281

The Mallen Streak
Cookson, Catherine 1282

The Maltese Angel
Cookson, Catherine 1283

The Malvie Inheritance
Hill, Pamela 2938

Mamaw
Dodd, Susan 1663

Mamigon
Hashian, Jack 2772

The Mammoth Hunters
Auel, Jean M. 237

The Mammoth Stone
Allan, Margaret 90

**The Mamur Zapt and the Donkey-
Vous**
Pearce, Michael 4866

**The Mamur Zapt and the Girl in the
Nile**
Pearce, Michael 4867

**The Mamur Zapt and the Men
Behind**
Pearce, Michael 4868

**The Mamur Zapt and the Night of
the Dog**
Pearce, Michael 4869

**The Mamur Zapt and the Return of
the Carpet**
Pearce, Michael 4870

**The Mamur Zapt and the Spoils of
Egypt**
Pearce, Michael 4871

**A Man and His Mountain: The Life of
Paul Cezanne**
McLeave, Hugh 4285

Man Before the Morning
Maiden, Cecil 4032

A Man Called Cervantes
Frank, Bruno 2201

A Man Called Grant
Todd, Helen 6285

Man Cannot Tell
Scruggs, Philip Lightfoot 5711

A Man for the Ages
Bacheller, Irving A. 261

The Man From Broken Hills
L'Amour, Louis 3622

Man From Mt. Vernon
Boyce, Burke 607

The Man From St. Petersburg
Follett, Ken 2148

**Man of Montmartre: A Novel Based
on the Life of Maurice Utrillo**
Longstreet, Stephen 3888

Man of Nazareth
Burgess, Anthony 779

Man of the Shadows
Coldsmith, Don 1178

The Man of the Storm
Hueston, Ethel 3069

The Man on a Donkey
Prescott, H.F.M. 5170

**Man on Fire: A Novel on the Life of
St. Paul**
Blythe, LeGette 558

The Man on the Train
Chaput, W.J. 995

The Man on the White Horse
Deeping, Warwick 1577

Man on Two Ponies
Worcester, Don 6872

The Man Who Killed the King
Wheatley, Dennis 6654

The Man Who Loved Cat Dancing
Durham, Marilyn 1817

The Man Who Loved Mata Hari
Sherman, Dan 5813

The Man Who Missed the Party
Adams, Harold 25

The Man Who Shot Lewis Vance
Kaminsky, Stuart M. 3341

**The Man Who Thought He Was
Messiah**
Leviant, Curt 3735

Manchu
Elegant, Robert S. 1904

Manchu Empress
Hunter, Bluebell Matilda 3081

Manchu Palaces
Larsen, Jeanne 3669

Mandalay
Jones, Alexandra 3269

Mandarin
Elegant, Robert S. 1905

Mandarin Gold
Leasor, James 3700

Manifest Destiny
Garfield, Brian 2290

Manila Galleon
Mason, F. van Wyck 4154

Manitou
Porter, Donald Clayton 5120

The Manly-Hearted Woman
Manfred, Frederick F. 4057

A Man's Reach
Wilson, Charles Morrow 6796

Mansfield Revisited
Aiken, Joan 51

Mansions of Darkness
Yarbro, Chelsea Quinn 6902

Manuela, La Caballeresa Del Sol
Aguilera Malta, Demetrio 41

Many a Voyage
Erdman, Loula Grace 1951

**The Mapmaker: A Novel of the Days
of Prince Henry, the Navigator**
Slaughter, Frank G. 5893

A Mapmaker's Dream
Cowan, James 1391

Marblehead
Thompson, Joan 6267

The Marburg Chronicles
Coppel, Alfred 1319

Marcel Armand
Bell, Sallie 424

Marching On
Boyd, James 612

**Marching to Valhalla: A Novel of
Custer's Last Days**
Blake, Michael 538

Marcus
Chinn, Laurene 1068

Margaret Brent, Adventurer
Grant, Dorothy 2533

Margaret's Story
Price, Eugenia 5183

Maria
Price, Eugenia 5184

Marianne
Benzoni, Juliette 466
Petrie, Glen 4981

Marianne and the Crown of Fire
Benzoni, Juliette 467

Marianne and the Lords of the East
Benzoni, Juliette 468

Marianne and the Masked Prince
Benzoni, Juliette 469

Marianne and the Privateer
Benzoni, Juliette 470

Marianne and the Rebels
Benzoni, Juliette 471

Title Index

Marie Antoinette
Kenyon, F.W.   3453

Mariette in Ecstasy
Hansen, Ron   2682

The Marigold Field
Pearson, Diane   4876

Marius the Epicurean
Pater, Walter   4826

Marjorie of Scotland
Hill, Pamela   2939

Mark
Coleman, Lonnie   1205

Marlborough's Unfair Lady
Prole, Lozania   5197

The Marquis
Sanders, Joan   5586

The Marquis and Miss Jones
Ashfield, Helen   208

The Marquis of Bolibar
Perutz, Leo   4942

The Marranos
Webb, Liliane   6588

The Marriage Bed
Clark, Jean   1088

A Marriage of Convenience
Jeal, Tim   3172

The Marriage of Josephine
Coryn, Marjorie   1358

The Marriage of Meggotta
Pargeter, Edith   4799

Married Past Redemption
Veryan, Patricia   6469

Marry in Haste
Hodge, Jane Aiken   2967

Marrying Harriet
Chesney, Marion   1036

The Marrying Kind
Stirling, Jessica   6046

Mars' Butterfly
Pleasants, Henry   5080

Marsanne
Coffman, Virginia   1155

The Marsh King
Hodges, C. Walter   2975

Martha, Martha
McGerr, Patricia   4274

Martin Valliant
Deeping, Warwick   1578

Mary
Asch, Sholem   198

Mary Anne
Du Maurier, Daphne   1749

Mary Dove
Rushing, Jane Gilmore   5529

Mary of Carisbrooke
Barnes, Margaret Campbell   327

Mary of Magdala
Williman, Anne C.   6791

Mary of Nazareth
Kellner, Esther   3394

Mary of Scotland
Kenyon, F.W.   3454

Mary, Queen of Scotland and the Isles
George, Margaret   2356

Mary Reilly
Martin, Valerie   4136

Mary's Land
Robson, Lucia St. Clair   5415

The Mask
Cloete, Stuart   1125

The Mask of Apollo
Renault, Mary   5300

The Masked Man
Doherty, P.C.   1674

Masque of Enchantment
Cross, Charlene   1432

Masque of Jade
Merritt, Emma   4344

Masque of Sapphire
James, Deana   3156

Masquerade for the King
Oliver, Marina   4729

Masquerade of Vengeance
Ley, Alice Chetwynd   3765

The Masqueraders
Heyer, Georgette   2894

Masques of Gold
Gellis, Roberta   2352

Mass for Arras
Szczypiorski, Andrzej   6153

Massachusetts: A Novel
Zaroulis, Nancy   6956

Massacre at Cawnpore
Stuart, Vivian   6089

The Massacre at Fall Creek
West, Jessamyn   6631

The Master
Brod, Max   702

Master and Commander
O'Brian, Patrick   4669

Master-At-Arms
Sabatini, Rafael   5553

The Master of Ballantrae: A Winter's Tale
Stevenson, Robert Louis   6011

Master of Bengal: A Novel of Robert Clive of India
Partington, Norman   4821

Master of Castile
Edwards, Samuel   1888

The Master of Chaos
Bacheller, Irving A.   262

The Master of Geneva: A Novel Based on the Life of John Calvin
Barr, Gladys H.   341

The Master of Gray Trilogy
Tranter, Nigel   6316

Master of Morholm
Wilson, Timothy R.   6817

The Master of Oakwindsor
Hall, Douglas Kent   2648

Master of the World
O'Neal, Cothburn   4738

The Master Painter
Mullins, Edwin   4513

Masterpiece of Murder
Kruger, Mary   3563

The Masters of Bow Street
Creasy, John   1423

Masters of Illusion: A Novel of the Connecticut Circus Fire
Smith, Mary-Ann Tirone   5925

Masts to Spear the Stars
Longstreet, Stephen   3889

The Mating Dance
Randall, Rona   5250

The Matrix
Daviess, Maria Thompson   1509

Matthew Early
Laing, Alexander   3589

Maura's Dream
Gross, Joel   2602

The Mauritius Command
O'Brian, Patrick   4670

Max
Fast, Howard   2038

Maximilian's Gold
Barry, Jane   359

Mayfair
Fitzgerald, Nancy   2115

The Maze Maker
Ayrton, Michael   250

McKay's Bees
McMahon, Thomas   4289

McKensie's Hundred: A Tale of the Old Dominion
Yerby, Frank   6924

Me and Gallagher
Farris, Jack   2023

Me So Far
Jack, Donald   3127

Me Too
Jack, Donald   3128

Meadowsweet
Butler, Gwendoline   820

The Measure of the Years
Colver, Alice Mary   1218

Medea
Seymour, Miranda   5764

The Medici Emerald
Woodhouse, Martin   6851

The Medici Guns
Woodhouse, Martin   6852

The Medici Hawks
Woodhouse, Martin   6853

The Medicine Calf
Hotchkiss, Bill   3037

The Medicine Horn
Sherman, Jory   5820

Medicine Knife
Coldsmith, Don   1179

The Medicine Man
Seifert, Shirley   5729

The Medicine Whip
Hennessy, Max   2835

Megan
Magill, Kathleen   4028

Meggy MacIntosh
Gray, Elizabeth Janet   2555

The Melancholy Virgin
Laine, Annabel   3587

Melbury Square
Eden, Dorothy   1857

Melissa Starke
Andrews, Annulet   145

The Melting Clock
Kaminsky, Stuart M.   3342

Members of the Tribe
Kluger, Richard   3511

Memoirs of a Victorian Gentleman: William Makepeace Thackeray
Forster, Margaret   2189

The Memoirs of Christopher Columbus
Marlowe, Stephen   4096

The Memoirs of Elizabeth Frankenstein
Roszak, Theodore   5508

The Memoirs of Lord Byron
Nye, Robert   4655

Memories of the Ford Administration
Updike, John   6391

The Memory Cathedral: A Secret History of Leonardo Da Vinci
Dann, Jack   1481

Men Against the Sea
Nordhoff, Charles   4638

Men in Buckskin
Stover, Herbert   6069

Men Like Shadows
Charques, Dorothy   1000

Men of Albemarle
Fletcher, Inglis   2135

The Men of Gonzales
Culp, John H.   1442

Men of Men
Smith, Wilbur   5927

Men of No Property
Davis, Dorothy   1517

The Men That God Forgot
Butler, Richard   829

The Men That God Made Mad: A Novel about Ireland's Easter Rising
Ballinger, W.A.   286

Men Were Deceivers Ever
Veryan, Patricia   6470

Merari
Bremkamp, Gloria Howe   656

Mercedes of Castile
Cooper, James Fenimore   1304

The Mercenary
Durbin, Charles 1814

The Merchant of Death
Grace, C.L. 2508

Merchant of the Ruby
Harwood, Alice 2766

The Merchant Prince
Bailey, Henry Christopher 267

Meridon
Gregory, Philippa 2583

Merlin
Lawhead, Stephen R. 3681

Mermaid Tavern
Cronyn, George William 1429

The Merry Devils
Marston, Edward 4123

The Merrymaid
Hardwick, Mollie 2696

Messer Marco Polo
Byrne, Donn 840

The Messiah
Holmes, Marjorie 3003

Metello
Pratolini, Vasco 5163

Mexico
Michener, James A. 4372

Mi Amigo
Burnett, William R. 795

Miami: A Saga
Mayerson, Evelyn Wilde 4204

Micah Clarke
Doyle, Sir Arthur Conan 1715

Michael Beam
Hallet, Richard 2663

Michael Torey
Mathewson, Janet 4183

The Michaelmas Girls
Barry, John 362

The Michaelmas Tree
Ashfield, Helen 209

Michelangelo the Florentine
Alexander, Sidney 86

Middlemarch
Eliot, George 1909

The Midnight Gardener: A Novel about Baudelaire
White, Max 6694

The Midnight Gun
Mather, Berkely 4180

Midnight Is a Place
Aiken, Joan 52

Midnight Moon
Montague, Jeanne 4436

Midshipman Bolitho and the Avenger
Kent, Alexander 3435

Midsummer Masque
Tattersall, Jill 6174

Midsummer Moon
Lynn, Karen 3940

Midsummer's Eve
Carr, Philippa 924

The Midwife
Courter, Gay 1388

The Midwife's Advice
Courter, Gay 1389

Midwinter
Buchan, John 751

A Mighty Afternoon
Mills, Charles K. 4407

The Mighty and Their Fall
Compton-Burnett, Ivy 1230

Mighty Mountain
Binns, Archie 502

Mignon
Cain, James M. 845

The Mill on Mad River
Clark, Howard 1087

The Mill on the Po
Bacchelli, Riccardo 254

The Miller's Dance
Graham, Winston 2528

The Millionaire's Daughter
Eden, Dorothy 1858

The Mills of Colne
Neill, Robert 4572

Mills of the Gods
Winston, Daoma 6828

Milton in America
Ackroyd, Peter 20

Mine Is the Kingdom
Oliver, Jane 4726

Minerva
Chesney, Marion 1037

Ming: A Novel of Seventeeth Century China
Oxnam, Robert B. 4772

Mingo Dabney
Street, James H. 6078

Minna's Story: The Secret Love of Doctor Sigmund Freud
Daniels, Kathleen 1463

Mirabeau, Lover and Stateman
Nezelof, Pierre 4606

The Miracle at St. Bruno's
Carr, Philippa 925

The Miracle Hater
Hareven, Shulamith 2704

Miracles
Heidish, Marcy Moran 2818

Mirage
Gedge, Pauline 2346
McKenney, Ruth 4283
Miller, Helen Topping 4390

A Mirror for Witches
Forbes, Esther 2157

The Misadventures of Bethany Price
Cockrell, Marian 1147

The Miser of Mayfair
Chesney, Marion 1038

Miss Bishop
Aldrich, Bess Streeter 71

Miss Davenport's Christmas
Chesney, Marion 1039

Miss Delicia Allen
Johnston, Mary 3237

Miss Fiona's Fancy
Chesney, Marion 1040

Miss Hartwell's Dilemma
Dunn, Carola 1796

Miss Lizzie
Satterthwait, Walter 5608

Miss Martha Mary Crawford
Marchant, Catherine 4081

Miss Morissa: Doctor of the Gold Trail
Sandoz, Mari 5592

Miss Nobody
Ross, Caroline 5465

Miss Philadelphia Smith
Allardyce, Paula 91

Miss Tonks Turns to Crime
Chesney, Marion 1041

Mission to Mackinac
Orr, Myron David 4755

Mississippi Belle
Ripley, Clements 5346

The Mississippi Run
Boles, Paul Darcy 565

The Missolonghi Manuscript
Prokosch, Frederic 5194

Mistaken Virtues
Trollope, Joanna 6349

Mister Christian
Kinsolving, William 3502

Mister St. John
Estleman, Loren D. 1974

Mistress
Quick, Amanda 5215

Mistress Anne
Erickson, Carolly 1952

Mistress Devon
Coffman, Virginia 1156

Mistress Nancy
Bentley, Barbara 460

Mistress of Darkness
Nicole, Christopher 4617

Mistress of Fortune
Lancaster, Sheila 3651

The Mistress of Husaby
Undset, Sigrid 6382

Mistress of the Boards
Sumner, Richard 6118

Mistress of the Eagles
Malterre, Elona 4052

Mistress of the Forge
Taylor, David 6179

Mistress of The Highlands
Gartner, Chloe 2309

Mistress of Willowvale
Veryan, Patricia 6471

The Mists of Avalon
Bradley, Marion Zimmer 626

Mists of Heaven
Kalman, Yvonne 3325

The Mists of Manittoo
Swann, Lois 6135

Mockingbird Sang at Chickamauga
Crabb, Alfred Leland 1404

Modigliani: Prince of Montparnasse
Wittlin, Tadeusz 6834

The Moghul
Hoover, Thomas 3026

The Mohawk Ladder
Gerson, Noel B. 2377

Mohawk Woman
Riefe, Barbara 5329

Molly
Crane, Teresa 1417

Molokai
Bushnell, Oswald Andrew 815

A Moment in Time
Small, Bertrice 5911

Mona Lisa: The Woman in the Portrait
Mayfield, Sara 4206

The Monastery
Scott, Sir Walter 5701

Monday's Child
Hardwick, Mollie 2697

Monday's Warriors
Shadbolt, Maurice 5767

The Moneyman
Costain, Thomas B. 1368
Liederman, Judith 3781

The Monk
Lewis, Matthew Gregory 3756

Monk in Armour
Barr, Gladys H. 342

The Monkey and the Tiger
van Gulik, Robert 6417

Monk's Hood
Peters, Ellis 4964

Monmouth
Flood, Charles Bracelen 2144

Monsieur Beaucaire
Tarkington, Booth 6163

Monsieur Janvier
Linington, Elizabeth 3799

Monsieur Moliere
O'Shaughnessy, Michael 4762

Monsieur Yankee
White, Leslie Turner 6689

A Monstrous Regiment of Women
King, Laurie R. 3489

Montana!
Ross, Dana Fuller 5479

Montana Hitch
Wheeler, Richard S. 6661

Montana Road
Drago, Harry Sinclair   1717

Montana Woman
Bittner, Rosanne   513

Monte Walsh
Schaefer, Jack   5635

The Monterant Affair
Grayson, Richard   2560

The Montmarte Murders
Grayson, Richard   2561

The Moon-Eyed Appaloosa
Gulick, Bill   2617

The Moon in the Water
Belle, Pamela   433

Moon of Thunder
Coldsmith, Don   1180

The Moon Stallion
Berry, Jim   484

The Moon under Her Feet
Kinstler, Ceysta   3503

Moonfeather
French, Judith E.   2223

Moonraker's Bride
Brent, Madeleine   661

Moontrap
Berry, Don   481

Morality Play
Unsworth, Barry   6387

A Morbid Taste for Bones
Peters, Ellis   4965

The Moreland Legacy
Haviland, Diana   2777

Morgan's Woman
Gower, Iris   2500

Morning at Jalna
de la Roche, Mazo   1560

The Morning Gift
Norman, Diana   4645

Morning in America
Wiener, Willard   6741

Morning of a Hero
Boyce, Burke   608

The Morning River
Gear, W. Michael   2333

Morning Time
O'Neill, Charles Kendall   4743

Morning's Gate
Roberts, Ann Victoria   5371

The Mortal Gods
Dolbier, Maurice   1688

*Mortal Hunger: A Novel Based on
  the Life of Lafcadio Hearn*
Wedeck, Harry E.   6594

*Mortal Love: A Novel of Eleanor of
  Aquitaine*
Hutchins, Linda   3090

Mortal Pageant
Fabricius, Johan   1993

Mosby's Last Ride
Hogan, Ray   2979

Moses
Asch, Sholem   199

Moses, Prince of Egypt
Fast, Howard   2039

A Most Extraordinary Pair
Detre, Jean   1628

A Most Romantic City
Gibbs, Mary Ann   2396

Most Secret
Carr, John Dickson   912

The Moth
Cookson, Catherine   1284

Mother and Son
Compton-Burnett, Ivy   1231

Mother Earth, Father Sky
Harrison, Sue   2749

The Mothers
Fisher, Vardis   2109

*Moulin Rouge: A Novel Based on
  Henri de Toulouse-Lautrec*
La Mure, Pierre   3576

Mountain Devil
Thompson, David   6257

Mountain Laurel
Deveraux, Jude   1632

Mountain Man
Fisher, Vardis   2110

The Mountain of Immoderate Desires
Wilson, Leslie   6811

Mountain Windsong
Conley, Robert J.   1246

Mountains Ahead
McKeown, Martha Ferguson   4284

Mount's Mistake
McCreary, Lew   4229

Mozart on the Way to Prague
Morike, Eduard Friedrich   4454

Mr. American
Fraser, George MacDonald   2211

Mr. Arnold
Lynde, Francis   3935

Mr. Audubon's Lucy
Kennedy, Lucy   3419

Mr. Christian!
Miller, Stanley   4402

Mr. Lincoln's Wife
Colver, Anne   1221

Mr. Midshipman Hornblower
Forester, C.S.   2180

Mr. Oddity, Samuel Johnson
Norman, Charles   4643

Mr. Pepys of Seething Lane
Abernethy, Cecil   10

Mr. Vertigo
Auster, Paul   244

Mrs. Betsy, or Widowed and Wed
Marton, Francis   4141

Mrs. Budley Falls From Grace
Chesney, Marion   1042

Mrs. Jeffries and the Missing Alibi
Brightwell, Emily   683

Mrs. Jeffries Dusts for Clues
Brightwell, Emily   684

Mrs. Jeffries on the Ball
Brightwell, Emily   685

Mrs. Jeffries on the Trail
Brightwell, Emily   686

Mrs. Jeffries Plays the Cook
Brightwell, Emily   687

Mrs. Jeffries Stands Corrected
Brightwell, Emily   688

Mrs. Jeffries Takes Stock
Brightwell, Emily   689

*Mrs. Shakespeare: The Complete
  Works*
Nye, Robert   4656

Muddy Banks
Tolliver, Ruby C.   6291

The Mudlark
Bonnet, Theodore   573

A Mule for the Marquesa
O'Rourke, Frank   4753

The Mullah From Kashmir
MacNeil, Duncan   4016

The Mummy Case
Peters, Elizabeth   4953

The Mummy; or Ramses the Damned
Rice, Anne   5315

Munich Signature
Thoene, Bodie   6224

Murder and the First Lady
Roosevelt, Elliott   5444

Murder at Drury Lane
Hall, Robert Lee   2659

Murder at Ebbets Field
Soos, Troy   5947

Murder at Fenway Park
Soos, Troy   5948

The Murder at Impasse Louvaine
Grayson, Richard   2562

Murder at San Simeon
Hall, Robert Lee   2660

Murder at the Feast of Rejoicing
Robinson, Lynda S.   5407

Murder at the God's Gate
Robinson, Lynda S.   5408

Murder at the Palace
Roosevelt, Elliott   5445

Murder at Wrigley Field
Soos, Troy   5949

Murder by the Numbers
Collins, Max Allan   1212

Murder by the Waters
Hall, Robert Lee   2661

Murder, I Presume
Linscott, Gillian   3807

Murder in Canton
van Gulik, Robert   6418

Murder in Grub Street
Alexander, Bruce   77

Murder in the Blue Room
Roosevelt, Elliott   5446

Murder in the Chateau
Roosevelt, Elliott   5447

Murder in the East Room
Roosevelt, Elliott   5448

Murder in the Executive Mansion
Roosevelt, Elliott   5449

Murder in the Oval Office
Roosevelt, Elliott   5450

Murder in the Place of Anubis
Robinson, Lynda S.   5409

Murder in the Red Room
Roosevelt, Elliott   5451

Murder in the Rose Garden
Roosevelt, Elliott   5452

The Murder in the Tower
Plaidy, Jean   5035

Murder in the West Wing
Roosevelt, Elliott   5453

Murder Is Murder Is Murder
Steward, Samuel M.   6020

Murder Makes an Entree
Myers, Amy   4540

Murder Most Royal
Plaidy, Jean   5036

The Murder of Lawrence of Arabia
Eden, Matthew   1865

The Murder of Sir Edmund Godfrey
Carr, John Dickson   913

A Murder on the Appian Way
Saylor, Steven   5625

Murder on the Yellow Brick Road
Kaminsky, Stuart M.   3343

Murdock's Law
Estleman, Loren D.   1975

Murfy's Men
Green, Gerald   2565

*Musashi: An Epic Novel of the
  Samurai Era*
Yoshikawa, Eiji   6935

The Muscovite
Macleod, Alison   4004

Music for God
Weiser, Theresa   6603

Mussolini
Gelb, Alan   2348

Mustang Man
L'Amour, Louis   3623

Mutiny
Tilsley, Frank   6280

Mutiny on the Bounty
Nordhoff, Charles   4639

Mutiny Run
Eccles, Frank   1836

The Mutual Friend
Busch, Frederick   811

My Beautiful White Roses
Lechner, Michael 3703

My Beloved Son
Cookson, Catherine 1285

My Blood and My Treasure
Schumann, Mary 5674

My Brother Napoleon: The Confessions of Caroline Bonaparte
Kenyon, F.W. 3455

My Crown, My Love
Stephan, Ruth Walgreen 5995

My Dear Cousin
Hoffmann, Peggy 2977

My Dear Lover England
Bennetts, Pamela 453

My Enemy the Queen
Holt, Victoria 3017

My Father's World
Phillips, Michael 4989

My Gallant Enemy
Becnel, Rexanne 409

My Grand Enemy
Stubbs, Jean 6098

My Lady Benbrook
Gluyas, Constance 2442

My Lady Glamis
Hill, Pamela 2940

My Lady Greensleeves
Beresford-Howe, Constance 476

My Lady Hoyden
Sheridan, Jane 5812

My Lady Innkeeper
Metzger, Barbara 4346

My Lady of Cleves
Barnes, Margaret Campbell 328

My Life for My Sheep
Duggan, Alfred 1772

My Lord Brother the Lionheart
Haycraft, Molly Costain 2795

My Lord Essex
Eckerson, Olive 1838

My Lord Foxe
Gluyas, Constance 2443

My Lord John
Heyer, Georgette 2895

My Lord Monleigh
Speas, Jan Cox 5957

My Lord of Canterbury
Turton, Godfrey 6369

My Lord the Fox
York, Robert 6932

My Love Must Wait: The Story of Matthew Flinders
Hill, Ernestine 2922

My Love, My Enemy
Speas, Jan Cox 5958

My Master Columbus
Belfrage, Cedric 418

My Name Is Clary Brown
Keppel, Charlotte 3466

My Name Is Sappho
Rofheart, Martha 5429

My Own Ground
Nissenson, Hugh 4628

My Pride, My Folly
Butler, Suzanne 830

My Savage Muse: The Story of My Life: Edgar Allan Poe, an Imaginative Work
Hurwood, Bernhardt J. 3087

My Sister, My Love
Iremonger, Lucille 3111

My Sister, the Moon
Harrison, Sue 2750

My Sister's Keeper
Butler, Beverly 817

My Theodosia
Seton, Anya 5753

My Thomas: A Novel of Martha Jefferson's Life
Grimes, Roberta 2593

Myself as Witness
Goldman, James 2458

Myself, Christopher Wren
Weiss, David 6606

Myself My Enemy
Plaidy, Jean 5037

Mysteries of Winterthurn
Oates, Joyce Carol 4659

The Mysterious Death of Meriwether Lewis
Burns, Ron 802

N

Naked Came I: A Novel of Rodin
Weiss, David 6607

The Naked Maja
Gerson, Noel B. 2378

The Naked Sword: The Story of Lucretia Borgia
Kenyon, F.W. 3456

The Name of Hero
Seltzer, Richard 5742

The Name of the Rose
Eco, Umberto 1850

The Nancy Flyer
Poole, Ernest 5091

Nanette
Veryan, Patricia 6472

Nantucket Rebel
Stackpole, Edouard A. 5970

Nantucket Woman
Gaines, Diana 2269

Napoleon and His Son
Nezelof, Pierre 4607

Napoleon and the Cossacks
Krassnoff, Peter N. 3551

Napoleon Must Die
Fawcett, Quinn 2054

Napoleon Symphony
Burgess, Anthony 780

Natchez: A Novel of the Deep South
Jekel, Pamela 3186

The Nation Thief
Houston, Robert 3057

The Nationalists
Long, William Stuart 3876

The Native Air
Woodhouse, Sarah 6854

The Navigator: The Story of Nathaniel Bowditch
Stanford, Alfred 5979

The Nazarene
Asch, Sholem 200

The Near and Distant Place
Wright, Patricia 6883

The Near and the Far
Myers, Leopold Hamilton 4547

Nebraska!
Ross, Dana Fuller 5480

Nebraska Coast
Davis, Clyde Brion 1516

Necklace and Calabash
van Gulik, Robert 6419

Ned Christie's War
Conley, Robert J. 1247

The Needle-Watcher
Blaker, Richard 540

The Negotiators
Walder, Francis 6526

Neighboring Lives
Disch, Thomas M. 1648

The Nelson Touch
Lewis, Paul 3759

Nephew to the Emperor: A Novel Based on the Life of Beethoven
Brenner, Jacques 658

Nero
Ronalds, Mary Teresa 5437

A Nest of Simple Folk
O'Faolain, Sean 4692

Nethergate
Lofts, Norah 3854

The Neutral Ground
Hough, Frank Olney 3044

Nevada!
Ross, Dana Fuller 5481

Never Call It Loving
Eden, Dorothy 1859

Never Cross a Vampire
Kaminsky, Stuart M. 3344

Never Doubt I Love
Veryan, Patricia 6473

Never No More: The Story of Rebecca Boone
Seifert, Shirley 5730

Never Victorious, Never Defeated
Caldwell, Taylor 860

Nevermore
Hjortsberg, William 2958

The New Confessions
Boyd, William 617

A New Creature
Andrew, Prudence 141

New Day
Reid, Victor Stafford 5291

New Deal for Death
Roosevelt, Elliott 5454

The New England Story
Hough, Henry Beetle 3046

The New Hope
Lincoln, Joseph C. 3784

New Moon Rising
Price, Eugenia 5185

New Orleans Legacy
Ripley, Alexandra 5341

New Orleans Woman: A Biographical Novel of Myra Clark Gaines
Kane, Harnett T. 3355

New Road
Colby, Merle Estes 1168

Next to Valour
Jennings, John Edward 3202

Niagara
Taylor, Robert Lewis 6189

Nicanor of Athens: The Autobiography of an Unknown Citizen
Grazebrook, Owen Francis 2563

Niccolo Rising
Dunnett, Dorothy 1803

Nicholas Cooke: Actor, Soldier, Physician, Priest
Cowell, Stephanie 1393

Nick of the Woods; or, The Jibbenainosay
Bird, Robert Montgomery 505

Nickajack
Conley, Robert J. 1248

Nicodemus: The Roman Years of Michelangelo Buonarroti, 1534-1564
Alexander, Sidney 87

A Night in Cold Harbor
Kennedy, Margaret 3420

Night March
Lancaster, Bruce 3641

Night of Decision: A Novel of Colonial New York
Grant, Dorothy 2534

The Night of the Ripper
Bloch, Robert 551

Night Raider
Hogan, Ray 2980

Night Shadow
Coulter, Catherine 1377

Night Shall Overtake Us
Saunders, Kate 5611

Night Storm
Coulter, Catherine 1378

Night Wind
Mountjoy, Roberta Jean 4504

Night Wind's Woman
Henke, Shirl 2825

A Night with Casanova
Mankowitz, Wolf 4060

The Nightingale Gallery
Harding, Paul 2684

The Nightingale Legacy
Coulter, Catherine 1379

Nightrunners of Bengal
Masters, John 4176

Nine Days of Father Serra
Ziegler, Isabelle Gibson 6961

The Nine Giants
Marston, Edward 4124

Nine Hours to Rama
Wolpert, Stanley 6846

The Ninth Statue
Milne, Roseleen 4410

No Bed for Bacon
Brahms, Caryl 640

No Brighter Glory
Sperry, Armstrong 5963

No Bugles Blow
Lancaster, Bruce 3642

No Honeymoon for Death
Kruger, Mary 3564

No King but Caesar
Powers, Anne 5151

No Man's Land
Fairchild, William 2004

No Man's Son
Adams, Doris Sutcliffe 23

No Other Gods
Penfield, Wilder 4901

No Other Place
Gould, John 2497

No Place on Earth
Wolf, Christa 6836

No Price Too High
Polland, Madeleine 5085

No Resting Place
Humphrey, William 3079

The No-Return Trail
Levitin, Sonia 3741

No Road Too Long
Hawthorne, Hildegarde 2785

No Roof but Heaven
Williams, Jeanne 6782

No Smoke Without Fire
Harwood, Alice 2767

No Surrender
Sterne, Emma Gelders 5999

No Survivors
Henry, Will 2846

No Tears for Christmas
Miller, Helen Topping 4391

No Wall So High
Powers, Anne 5152

The Noblest Frailty
Veryan, Patricia 6474

Nobody's Angel
Robards, Karen 5363

The Noel Coward Murder Case
Baxt, George 387

None Shall Look Back
Gordon, Caroline 2478

The Nonesuch
Heyer, Georgette 2896

The Nonsuch Lure
Luke, Mary M. 3924

Norah
Hill, Pamela 2941

The Norman Pretender
Anand, Valerie 132

The Normandie Affair
Villars, Elizabeth 6497

North Against the Sioux
Ulyatt, Kenneth 6376

North and South
Jakes, John 3151

North of 36
Hough, Emerson 3042

North Star Conspiracy
Monfredo, Miriam Grace 4428

*North to Thule: An Imagined
    Narrative of the Famous "Lost"
    Voyage of Pytheas of Massalla in
    the Fourth Century B.C.*
Frye, John 2241

North to Yesterday
Flynn, Robert 2145

North-West by South
Cato, Nancy 962

The Northern Correspondent
Stubbs, Jean 6099

Northwest Passage
Roberts, Kenneth 5388
Thompson, David 6258

Not Built with Hands
White, Helen Constance 6679

Not by Any Single Man
Knight, Brigid 3522

Not of War Only
Zollinger, Norman 6966

Nothing Like the Sun
Burgess, Anthony 781

Nothing New under the Sun
Bacchelli, Riccardo 255

The Notorious Angel
Maxwell, Patricia 4201

Notorious Eliza
Beyea, Basil 489

A Notorious Woman
Macdonald, Malcolm 3969

The Novice's Tale
Frazer, Margaret 2217

Now Face to Face
Koen, Karleen 3530

Now, God Be Thanked
Masters, John 4177

Now We Are Free
Allis, Marguerite 112

The Nunnery
Charques, Dorothy 1001

The Nun's Tale
Robb, Candace M. 5367

The Nutmeg of Consolation
O'Brian, Patrick 4671

O

O Beulah Land
Settle, Mary Lee 5756

O Genesee
O'Daniel, Janet 4688

O Western Wind
Devon, John Anthony 1634

The Ocean Mistress
French, Peter 2225

Octavia: A Tale of Ancient Rome
Van Santvoord, Seymour 6428

The Odyssey of Thaddeus Baxter
Lund, Robert P. 3926

*Of Lizards and Angels: A Saga of
    Sioux Land*
Manfred, Frederick F. 4058

Officer and Gentleman
Delves-Broughton, Josephine 1604

Officers and Ladies
O'Connor, Richard 4686

Oh Glittering Promise
Fisher, Anne 2099

Oh, Kentucky!
Receveur, Betty Layman 5284

Oh, Promised Land
Street, James H. 6079

Oh, Valley Green
Culp, John H. 1443

*Oh! Where Are Bloody Mary's
    Earrings?*
Player, Robert 5079

O'Higgins and Don Bernardo
Nelson, Edna Deu Pree 4578

O'Houlihan's Jest
O'Grady, Rohan 4702

Oklahoma!
Ross, Dana Fuller 5482

Oklahoma Pride
Ross, Dana Fuller 5483

Oklahoma Run
Constant, Alberta 1260

Ol' Prophet Nat
Panger, Daniel 4786

The Old Colts
Swarthout, Glendon 6144

The Old Enchantment
Neilan, Sarah 4565

Old Glory
Nicole, Christopher 4618

The Old Gringo
Fuentes, Carlos 2247

Old Hickory
Gerson, Noel B. 2379

The Old Maid
Wharton, Edith 6652

Old Misery
Pendexter, Hugh 4896

Old Miss
Campbell, Thomas 877

Old Mortality
Scott, Sir Walter 5702

The Old Priory
Lofts, Norah 3855

Old St. Paul's
Ainsworth, William Harrison 57

Old Saxon Blood
Tourney, Leonard 6302

*Oldest Living Confederate Widow
    Tells All*
Gurganus, Allan 2621

Oldtown Folks
Stowe, Harriet Beecher 6072

Oliver Wiswell
Roberts, Kenneth 5389

Olivia and Jai
Ryman, Rebecca 5544

The Olympians
Bolton, Guy 566

Omensetter's Luck
Gass, William H. 2317

On a Balcony
Stacton, David 5973

On a Far Wide Shore
Macdonald, Malcolm 3970

On a Lonesome Porch
Pierce, Ovid Williams 4997

On Eagles' Wings
Southon, Arthur E. 5951

On Jordan's Stormy Banks
Rowell, Adelaide C. 5518

On Stranger Tides
Powers, Tim 5156

On the Company's Service
Meacham, Ellis K. 4315

On the Long Tide
Krey, Laura 3555

On the Midnight Tide
Tracy, Don 6310

On the Night of the Seventh Moon
Holt, Victoria 3018

On to Oregon!
Morrow, Honore 4490

On Trial for My Country
Samkange, Stanlake 5578

Once a Gentleman
James, Donald 3157

The Once and Future King
White, T.H. 6705

Once More the Hawks
Hennessy, Max 2836

One Corpse Too Many
Peters, Ellis 4966

One-Eyed Dream
Johnston, Terry C. 3253

One Last Glimpse
Aldridge, James 74

One More River to Cross
Henry, Will 2847

One Night in Newport
Villars, Elizabeth 6498

One of the Raymonds
Rikhoff, Jean 5332

One Red Rose Forever
Jordan, Mildred A. 3305

One Small Candle
MacKinnon, Mary Linehan 3998

One Smart Indian
Seidman, Robert J. 5722

One Wore Blue
Graham, Heather 2517

The Only Sin
Ellis, Julie 1923

The Only Thing to Fear
Poyer, David 5160

Opal
Ashfield, Helen 210

The Oracle Glass
Riley, Judith Merkle 5335

Ordeal by Silence
Andrew, Prudence 142

Oregon!
Ross, Dana Fuller 5484

Oregon Bride
Bittner, Rosanne 514

Oregon Legacy
Ross, Dana Fuller 5485

Organized Crime
Von Hoffman, Nicholas 6511

Origen: A Historical Novel
Vrettos, Theodore 6515

The Origin
Stone, Irving 6060

Orlando
Woolf, Virginia 6866

Orlok
Dandrea, Don 1461

Orphan Train
Magnuson, James 4029

Oscar and Lucinda
Carey, Peter 894

The Other Sappho
Frye, Ellen 2240

Othneil Jones
Leland, John Adams 3715

Our Father's House
Longstreet, Stephen 3890

Our Jo, or The Chronicle of a Coming Man
Cameron, Kenneth M. 868

Our Lives Have Just Begun
Myers, Henry 4541

Our Valiant Few
Mason, F. van Wyck 4155

Ourselves to Know
O'Hara, John 4704

Out of the Dark
Lofts, Norah 3856

Out of the House of Life
Yarbro, Chelsea Quinn 6903

Out of This Furnace
Bell, Thomas 425

Out on Any Limb
Myers, John 4545

Outlander
Gabaldon, Diana 2264

Outlaw
Kiefer, Warren 3482

Outlaw Lover
Hanks, Lindsey 2676

The Outlaw's Tale
Frazer, Margaret 2218

Outpost!
Ross, Dana Fuller 5486

Outward Bound
McCutchan, Philip 4256

Over There
Fleming, Thomas 2130
Vaughan, Robert 6449

The Overland Trail
Lee, Wendi 3712

The Overmountain Men
Judd, Cameron 3315

Owen Glen
Williams, Ben Ames 6766

Owen Glendower
Powys, John Cowper 5159

The Ox-Bow Incident
Clark, Walter Van Tilburg 1096

P

Pacific Cavalcade
Coffman, Virginia 1157

Pacific Destiny
Ross, Dana Fuller 5487

Pacific Street
Holland, Cecelia 2993

Paddington Green
Rayner, Claire 5266

The Pagan King
Marshall, Edison 4109

Pageant
Lancaster, G.B. 3650

The Pagoda Tree
Mather, Berkely 4181

Paint the Wind
Spellman, Cathy Cash 5960

Painted Lady: Eliza Jumel, Her Life and Times
Falkner, Leonard 2009

Painted Minx
Chambers, Robert W. 980

The Painted Queen
Hesky, Olga 2871

Painting the Darkness
Goddard, Robert 2445

Paiute
Wheeler, Sessions S. 6666

The Palace
Yarbro, Chelsea Quinn 6904

The Palace of Wisdom
Marshall-Andrews, Bob 4118

Palaces of Desire
Alexander, Kate 81

The Paladin
Shipway, George 5830

Palais-Royale
Sennett, Richard 5747

The Pale Criminal
Kerr, Philip 3471

Pale Star
Coldsmith, Don 1181

Paloverde
Briskin, Jacqueline 693

Panama
Zencey, Eric 6959

Pancho And Black Jack
Bean, Fred 398

The Pandora Secret
Forrest, Anthony 2186

Pandora's Galley
Harris, Macdonald 2727

The Pangersbourne Murders
Jeffreys, J.G. 3179

Panther in the Sky
Thom, James Alexander 6234

Papa and Fidel
Alexander, Karl 79

Papa La-Bas
Carr, John Dickson 914

The Paper Mistress
Malm, Dorothea 4045

Paradise
Eberhart, Dikkon 1831
Forbes, Esther 2158
Neilan, Sarah 4566

Paradise Falls
Robertson, Don 5399

Paradise Reclaimed
Laxness, Halldor 3686

Paragon Walk
Perry, Anne 4932

Parcel of Rogues
Lane, Jane 3656

The Parfit Knight
Blyth, Juliet 555

Pargeters
Lofts, Norah 3857

Paris of Troy
Baker, George 273

Parnell and the Englishwoman
Leonard, Hugh 3721

Parson Austen's Daughter
Ashton, Helen 219

The Parson's Daughter
Cookson, Catherine 1286

Passage Home
McLeay, Alison 4286

Passage to Mutiny
Kent, Alexander 3436

Passage to Natchez
Judd, Cameron 3316

Passage to Pontefract
Plaidy, Jean 5038

Passage West
Miller, Dallas 4382

Passengers to Mexico: The Last Invasion of Mexico
Niles, Blair 4627

The Passing Bells
Rock, Phillip 5421

Passion and the Sword
Hornborg, Harald 3034

A Passion in the Blood
Davis, Genevieve 1519

The Passion of Letty Fox
Saunders, Diana 5610

The Passion of Sacco and Vanzetti: A New England Legend
Fast, Howard 2040

The Passionate Enemies
Plaidy, Jean 5039

The Passionate Journey
Stone, Irving 6061

The Passionate Pilgrim
Terrot, Charles 6204

The Passionate Rebel
Slaughter, Frank G. 5894

Passionate Rebel: The Story of Hector Berlioz
Kenyon, F.W. 3457

Passionate Warriors
Gronau, Mary Ellen 2598

The Passions of the Mind
Stone, Irving 6062

Pastora
Barnes, Joanna 321

Patently Murder
Harrison, Ray 2742

Path of the Eclipse
Yarbro, Chelsea Quinn 6905

Path of the Sun
Dempsey, Al 1608

Path to the Silent Country
Banks, Lynne Reid 291

Pathetic Symphony: A Novel about Tchaikovsky
Mann, Klaus 4064

The Pathfinder; or, The Inland Sea
Cooper, James Fenimore 1305

Paths of Fortune
Moore, Susan 4444

Pathway to the Stars
Kane, Harnett T. 3356

Patience and Sarah
Miller, Isabel 4398

The Patriot
Fogazzaro, Antonio 2146

Patriot's Dream
Michaels, Barbara 4360

Patriot's Progress
Hopkins, Joseph G.E. 3027

Pawn in Frankincense
Dunnett, Dorothy 1804

Peace at Bowling Green
Crabb, Alfred Leland 1405

Peace, My Daughters
Barker, Shirley 314

The Peaceable Kingdom
Hartog, Jan de 2763

The Peacock and the Pearl
Lang, Jennifer 3661

The Peacock's Feather
Woodhouse, Sarah 6855

Pearl
Ashfield, Helen 211
Bigsby, Christopher 497
Leaton, Anne 3701

The Pearl Pagoda
Broome, Susannah 707

The Pecos River
Bean, Fred 399

The Peculiar People
Hartog, Jan de 2764

Peder Victorious
Rolvaag, O.E. 5435

A Peep into the 20th Century
Davis, Christopher 1515

Peg Woffington
Reade, Charles 5281

Peking: A Novel of China's Revolt
Grey, Anthony 2587

Pelican Coast
Le May, Alan 3690

Pemberley, or Pride and Prejudice Continued
Tennant, Emma 6201

Pemmican
Fisher, Vardis 2111

The Pendragon
Christian, Catherine 1075

Pendragon
Lawhead, Stephen R. 3682

Pendragon: Late of Prince Albert's Own
Trevelyan, Robert 6337

Pendragon's Banner
Hollick, Helen 3001

Pendragon...The Montenegran Plot
Trevelyan, Robert 6338

Penelope Goes to Portsmouth
Chesney, Marion 1043

Penhally
Gordon, Caroline 2479

The Penny Wedding
Stirling, Jessica 6047

Pentecost Alley
Perry, Anne 4933

A People Betrayed
Doblin, Alfred 1654

The People of Juvik
Dunn, Olav 1798

People of the Book
Stacton, David 5974

People of the Earth
Gear, W. Michael 2334

People of the Fire
Gear, W. Michael 2335

People of the Lakes
Gear, W. Michael 2336

People of the Lightning
Gear, W. Michael 2337

People of the Mesa
Prentiss, Charlotte 5168

People of the River
Gear, W. Michael 2338

People of the Sea
Gear, W. Michael 2339

People of the Silence
Gear, W. Michael 2340

People of the Wolf
Gear, W. Michael 2341

The Pepper Tree
Jennings, John Edward 3203

Perchance to Dream
Parker, Robert B. 4807

Perdita's Prince
Plaidy, Jean 5040

The Perfect Joy of St. Francis
Timmermans, Felix 6281

Perfecting Fiona
Chesney, Marion 1044

Perfume: The Story of a Murderer
Suskind, Patrick 6120

Pericles the Athenian
Warner, Rex 6566

Peril under the Palms
Beck, K.K. 404

Perilous Journey: A Tale of the Mississippi River and the Natchez Trace
Sublette, Clifford 6109

The Perilous Night
Boyce, Burke 609

The Persian Boy
Renault, Mary 5301

Persian Conqueror
Hellman, George Sidney 2822

Personal Recollections of Joan of Arc
Twain, Mark 6372

Peter Abelard: A Novel
Waddell, Helen 6517

Peter Ashley
Heyward, DuBose 2911

Peter Doyle
Vernon, John 6457

Peter Ibbetson
Du Maurier, George 1750

Peter the Great
Tolstoy, Alexey 6293

Petersburg
Hanlon, Emily 2677

The Petersburg-Cannes Express
Koning, Hans 3538

The Petrograd Consignment
Sela, Owen 5739

Peveril of the Peak
Scott, Sir Walter 5703

Phantom
Kay, Susan 3375

The Phantom Emperor
Swanson, Neil Harmon 6140

Phantom Fortress
Lancaster, Bruce 3643

The Phantom of the Temple
van Gulik, Robert 6420

Pharaoh
McGraw, Eloise Jarvis 4276

The Phoenix Rising
Evans, Jean 1984

The Physician
Gordon, Noah 2482

Physician Extraordinary: A Novel of the Life and Times of William Harvey
Weiss, David 6608

The Physician of London
Cowell, Stephanie 1394

The Piano
Campion, Jane 878

Piccadilly
Rayner, Claire 5267

Pilgermann
Hoban, Russell 2960

The Pilgrim of Hate
Peters, Ellis 4967

The Pilgrim Prince
Barr, Gladys H. 343

The Pilgrim Soul
Downes, Anne Miller 1711

The Pilgrimage
Ross, Ann B. 5463

Pilgrims: A Novel of the Mayflower
Mac, Gerard 3955

Pilgrims in Paradise
Slaughter, Frank G. 5895

Pillar of Cloud
Burgess, Jackson 782

Pillar of Fire
Tarr, Judith 6168

A Pillar of Iron
Caldwell, Taylor 861

Pillar of the Sky
Holland, Cecelia 2994

The Pillars of the Earth
Follett, Ken 2149

The Pilot
Cooper, James Fenimore 1306

Pinto and Sons
Epstein, Leslie 1947

Pioneer Breed
Vernam, Glenn R. 6453

The Pioneers
Cooper, Courtney Ryley 1296

The Pioneers; or, The Sources of the Susquehanna
Cooper, James Fenimore 1307

The Pirate
Scott, Sir Walter 5704

The Pirate and the Pagan
Henley, Virginia 2827

The Pirate From Rome
Southworth, John V.D. 5952

A Pirate's Pleasure
Graham, Heather 2518

The Pistoleer
Blake, James Carlos 536

Pistols for Hire
Nye, Nelson Coral 4652

Pitcairn's Island
Nordhoff, Charles 4640

A Place Called Freedom
Follett, Ken 2150

The Place of Dead Roads
Burroughs, William S. 808

The Place of Devils
Baker, Lucinda 275

A Place of Greater Safety
Mantel, Hilary 4077

A Place of Ravens
Hill, Pamela 2942

Plain Jane
Chesney, Marion 1045

The Plains of Abraham
Curwood, James Oliver 1452

The Plains of Passage
Auel, Jean M. 238

The Plantagenet Prelude
Plaidy, Jean 5041

Playboy Squadron
Whitehouse, Arch 6710

The Player's Boy
Bryher 744

The Players' Boy Is Dead
Tourney, Leonard 6303

Playing the Game
Buruma, Ian 810

Playing the Jack
Brown, Mary 726

The Playmaker
Keneally, Thomas 3414

The Pleasure Garden
Garfield, Leon 2293

The Pleasures of Love
Plaidy, Jean 5042

The Plot to Kill Wallis Simpson: A Work of Faction
Fisher, Graham 2104

Plume Rouge: A Novel of the Pathfinders
Terrell, John Upton 6203

The Plums Hang High
Finney, Gertrude E. 2091

The Plymouth Adventure
Gebler, Ernest 2342

The Plymouth Cloak
Sedley, Kate 5718

Pocahontas
Donnell, Susan 1691

Pocahontas; or, The Nonparell of Virginia
Garnett, David 2297

The Pointless Knife
Dodge, Constance 1667

Poison
Harrison, Kathryn 2737

The Poisoned Chalice
Clynes, Michael 1136

The Poisoned Crown
Druon, Maurice 1734

Poland
Michener, James A. 4373

Polonaise
Hodge, Jane Aiken 2968
Read, Piers Paul 5278

Polsinney Harbour
Pearce, Mary E. 4863

Pomeroy
Williams, Gordon 6770

Pomp and Circumstance
Stewart, Fred Mustard 6025

Pontius Pilate: A Biographical Novel
Maier, Paul L. 4034

Pontius Pilate Reflects
Koch, Werner 3529

The Pool of St. Branok
Carr, Philippa 926

Poor Boy and a Long Way Home
Sherburne, James 5806

Poor Butterfly
Kaminsky, Stuart M. 3345

Poor Richard's Game
O'Toole, G.J.A. 4766

Pope Joan
Cross, Donna Woolfolk 1433

The Pope's Rhinoceros
Norfolk, Lawrence 4642

The Porcelain Dove
Sherman, Delia 5815

The Portingale
Macleod, Alison 4005

Portrait in Brownstone
Auchincloss, Louis 232

Portrait of a Scoundrel
Benchley, Nathaniel 438

Portrait of Emma
Cheatham, Lillian 1010

Poseidon's Gold
Davis, Lindsey 1530

Post Captain
O'Brian, Patrick 4672

The Post of Honor
Cooke, David Coxe 1266

The Potter's Field
Peters, Ellis 4968

Powder Mission
Stover, Herbert 6070

The Powder River
Blevins, Winfred 546

Powderkeg
Vetterli, Richard 6482

Power
Fast, Howard 2041
Feuchtwanger, Lion 2074

The Power and the Glory
Bentley, Phyllis 462
Parker, Gilbert 4805

The Power and the Passion
Nicholson, Christina 4609

Power in the Blood
Matthews, Greg 4191

The Power of Black
Longman, M.B. 3880

Powhatan's Daughter
Bowman, John Clarke 605

Practice to Deceive
Veryan, Patricia 6475

Prague Counterpoint
Thoene, Bodie 6225

The Prairie
Cooper, James Fenimore 1308

Prairie
Waldo, Anna Lee 6528

Praise at Morning
McNeilly, Mildred Masterson 4310

The Praise Singer
Renault, Mary 5302

Preacher on Horseback
Matschat, Cecile Hulse 4186

Precious Bane
Webb, Mary 6590

The Predators
Parker, F.A. 4804

Prepare Them for Caesar
Mabie, Mary Louise 3954

The Prescott Chronicles
Fried, Albert 2232

The President's Daughter
Chase-Riboud, Barbara 1005

The President's Lady
Stone, Irving 6063

The President's Man
Roosevelt, Elliott 5455

Presumption: An Entertainment
Barrett, Julia 350

Pretty Boy Floyd
McMurtry, Larry 4299

The Price of Blood
Adams, Doris Sutcliffe 24

The Price of Liberty
Hopkins, Joseph G.E. 3028

The Pride of Hannah Wade
Dailey, Janet 1455

The Pride of Lions
Canham, Marsha 881

Pride of Lions
Llywelyn, Morgan 3823

The Pride of the Trevallions
Salisbury, Carola 5570

Pride's Castle
Yerby, Frank 6925

Pride's Fancy
Raddall, Thomas H. 5231

Prima Donna at Large
Paul, Barbara 4838

The Prime Minister's Wife
Leslie, Doris 3727

A Prince, a Piper, and a Rose
Scalzo, John 5628

The Prince and the Pauper
Twain, Mark 6373

The Prince and the Pilgrim
Stewart, Mary 6032

The Prince and the Quakeress
Plaidy, Jean 5043

Prince Charlie's Bluff
Thomas, Donald 6241

The Prince Lost to Time
Dukthas, Ann 1776

The Prince of Darkness
Doherty, P.C. 1675
Plaidy, Jean 5044

The Prince of Eden
Harris, Marilyn 2732

Prince of Egypt
Wilson, Dorothy Clarke 6805

Prince of Foxes
Shellabarger, Samuel 5797

Prince of Israel
Gilner, Elias 2422

Prince of Outlaws
Tolstoy, Alexey 6294

The Prince Regent's Silver Bell
McGorian, Gladys 4275

Princess in Amber
Mayerson, Evelyn Wilde 4205

A Princess in Berlin
Solmssen, Arthur R.G. 5939

The Princess of Celle
Plaidy, Jean 5045

Princess of Fire
Drake, Shannon 1718

Princess of the Veil
Mittermeyer, Helen 4420

Princess Pamela
Russell, Ray 5534

Princess Sophia
Marshall, Edison 4110

The Prison Notebooks of Ricardo Flores Magon
Day, Douglas 1545

Prisoner of the Queen
Macleod, Alison 4006

The Prisoner of Tordesillas
Schoonover, Lawrence 5665

Prisoner of Twilight
Robertson, Don 5400

Prisoners of Hope: A Tale of Colonial Virginia
Johnston, Mary 3238

The Prisoners of September
Garfield, Leon 2294

Prisons
Settle, Mary Lee 5757

The Private Adventures of Captain Shaw
Shay, Edith 5783

The Private and Public Life of Socrates
Kraus, Rene 3552

Private Knowledge
Nelson, Betty Palmer 4576

The Private Life of Florence Nightingale
Gordon, Richard 2485

The Private Life of Helen of Troy
Erskine, John 1957

The Private Life of Mona Lisa
La Mure, Pierre 3577

Private Renaissance
Bellonci, Maria 436

A Private Revenge
Woodman, Richard 6863

The Privateer
Daviot, Gordon 1510

Privileged Children
Vernon, Frances 6455

The Prize Master
Haislip, Harvey 2642

Proceed, Sergeant Lamb
Graves, Robert 2550

A Prologue to Love
Caldwell, Taylor 862

The Promise
Kellner, Esther 3395

Title Index

The Promise of Light
Watkins, Paul   6581

A Promise Unbroken
Lacy, Al   3582

The Promised Land
Danielson, Peter   1471

Promised Lands
Crook, Elizabeth   1430

Promises to Keep
Stirling, Jocelyn   6051

Prophecies
Soister, Helena   5937

The Prophecy
Danielson, Peter   1472

The Prophet
Asch, Sholem   201

The Prophet and the King
Watkins, Shirley   6582

Prophets and Warriors
Danielson, Peter   1473

The Proprietor
Schlee, Ann   5638

The Proselyte
Ertz, Susan   1958

The Prospering
Speare, Elizabeth   5954

The Proud and the Free
Dailey, Janet   1456
Fast, Howard   2042

The Proud Breed
De Blasis, Celeste   1547

The Proud Canaries
Johnson, David   3222

Proud Heritage
Bishcoff, Ilse   510

The Proud Man
Linington, Elizabeth   3800

Proud Mary
Gower, Iris   2501

Proud New Flags
Mason, F. van Wyck   4156

The Proud Retreat
Dowdey, Clifford   1706

The Proud Servant: The Story of Montrose
Irwin, Margaret   3120

The Proud Villeins
Anand, Valerie   133

The Proud Way
Seifert, Shirley   5731

Proving Ground: A Novel of Civil War Days in the North
Lowden, Leone   3919

Pull Down to New Orleans
Ball, Zachary   283

The Pumpkin Rollers
Kelton, Elmer   3406

Purple Passage: A Novel about a Lady Both Famous and Fantastic
Hahn, Emily   2638

Purple Pirate
Mundy, Talbot   4514

The Purple Quest: A Novel of Seafaring Adventure in the Ancient World
Slaughter, Frank G.   5896

Pursuit of Bliss
Nelson, Betty Palmer   4577

Pushing the Bear: A Novel of the Trail of Tears
Glancy, Diane   2426

Put Off Thy Shoes
Voynich, Ethel Lillian   6513

The Pyrates
Fraser, George MacDonald   2212

Q

The Quade Inheritance
Ker Wilson, Barbara   3469

The Quality of Mercy
Downes, Anne Miller   1712
Kellerman, Faye   3391

The Quallsford Inheritance
Biggle, Lloyd Jr.   495

Quanah Parker
Dugan, Bill   1759

Les Quarant Cinq
Dumas, Alexandre   1779

The Queen and I
Townsend, Sue   6306

The Queen and Lord M
Plaidy, Jean   5046

The Queen and the Gypsy
Heaven, Constance   2810

Queen Anne Boleyn
Hackett, Francis   2634

Queen Dolley: The Life and Times of Dolley Madison
Wilson, Dorothy Clarke   6806

The Queen From Provence
Plaidy, Jean   5047

Queen in Waiting
Plaidy, Jean   5048

Queen Jezebel
Plaidy, Jean   5049

Queen Margot
Dumas, Alexandre   1780

The Queen of Hearts
Rees, Joan   5290

The Queen of Sheba
Dorr, Roberta Kells   1696

Queen of Swords
Tarr, Judith   6169

Queen of the East
Baron, Alexander   336

Queen of the Lightning
Herbert, Kathleen   2852

Queen of the Reformation
Ludwig, Charles   3922

Queen of the Summer Stars
Woolley, Persia   6869

Queen of This Realm: The Story of Queen Elizabeth I
Plaidy, Jean   5050

Queen Victoria's Bomb
Clark, Ronald   1094

Queen's Caprice
Bowen, Marjorie   599

The Queen's Confession
Holt, Victoria   3019

The Queen's Cross: A Biographical Romance of Queen Isabella of Spain
Schoonover, Lawrence   5666

The Queen's Favourites
Plaidy, Jean   5051

Queen's Gift
Fletcher, Inglis   2136

The Queen's Grace
Westcott, Jan   6646

The Queen's Head
Marston, Edward   4125

The Queen's Husband
Edwards, Samuel   1889
Plaidy, Jean   5052

The Queen's Knight
Borowsky, Marvin   585

The Queen's Man
Penman, Sharon Kay   4905

The Queen's Necklace
Dumas, Alexandre   1781

The Queen's Physician
Maas, Edgar   3952

Queen's Play
Dunnett, Dorothy   1805

Queen's Royal
Quigley, John   5225

The Queen's Secret
Plaidy, Jean   5053

The Queen's Sister
Wilson, Sandra   6815

The Queen's War: A Novel of Eleanor of Aquitaine
Mackin, Jeanne   3996

The Queen's Ward
Elsna, Hebe   1933

Quentin Durward
Scott, Sir Walter   5705

A Quest for Love
Hawkes, Jacquetta   2781

Quest for the White Bull
Coldsmith, Don   1182

The Questing Heart: A Romantic Novel about George Sand
Kenyon, F.W.   3458

A Question of Choice
Andrew, Prudence   143

A Question of Honour
Dowdey, Clifford   1707
Drummond, Emma   1726

The Quickenberry Tree
Motley, Annette   4502

Quicksilver Lady
Whitehead, Barbara   6707

The Quicksilver Pool
Whitney, Phyllis A.   6716

The Quiet Gentleman
Heyer, Georgette   2897

Quiet Lady
Collins, Norman   1216

The Quiet Life of Mrs. General Lane
Case, Victoria   951

The Quiet Light
De Wohl, Louis   1572

The Quiet Shore
Havighurst, Walter   2775

Quietly My Captain Waits
Eaton, Evelyn   1829

The Quincunx
Palliser, Charles   4778

Quinn's Book
Kennedy, William   3423

Quitting Time
Conley, Robert J.   1249

Quo Vadis
Sienkiewicz, Henryk   5848

R

Rabbit Boss
Sanchez, Thomas   5581

Rabble in Arms
Roberts, Kenneth   5390

Raccoon John Smith
Cochran, Louis   1145

The Race: A Novel of Polar Exploration
Holt, Kare   3008

Race of Scorpions
Dunnett, Dorothy   1806

Rachel
Powers, Anne   5153

The Rag Nymph
Cookson, Catherine   1287

A Rage Against Heaven
Stewart, Fred Mustard   6026

Rage in Silence: A Novel Based on the Life of Goya
Braider, Donald   643

The Rage of the Vulture
Unsworth, Barry   6388

The Ragged Ones
Davis, Burke   1511

Rags of Glory
Cloete, Stuart   1126

Ragtime
Doctorow, E.L.   1658

The Raid
Brick, John   673

The Raider
Ford, Jesse Hill   2164

The Raiders
Wilson, William Edward   6819

The Raiders: A Novel of the Civil War at Sea
Wallace, Willard   6541

Railroad West
Meigs, Cornelia   4327

The Railway King
Mayhew, Margaret   4207

The Rain Maiden
Phillips, Jill M.   4985

The Rainbird
Lidman, Sara   3780

Rainbird's Revenge
Chesney, Marion   1046

Rainbow in the Royals
Roark, Garland   5357

Rainbow on the Road
Forbes, Esther   2159

The Rainbow Promise
Gregory, Lisa   2580

Rainbow Road
Steward, Davenport   6016

The Rainbow Runner
Cunningham, John   1450

Raintree County
Lockridge, Ross Jr.   3827

Raising Holy Hell
Olds, Bruce   4718

Raj
Mehta, Gita   4325

The Rake
Lynn, Karen   3941

The Rake and the Hussy
Chambers, Robert W.   981

The Rake and the Rebel
Morris, Ira J.   4478

Rake's Progress
Chesney, Marion   1047

Rake's Ransom
Metzger, Barbara   4347

Rakossy
Holland, Cecelia   2995

Ralegh's Fair Bess: The Story of Bess Throckmorton
Turner, Judy   6365

Raleigh's Eden
Fletcher, Inglis   2137

Ram: Being the Tale of One Ramillies Anstruther
Taylor, Winchombe   6193

Ramage
Pope, Dudley   5097

Ramage and the Dido
Pope, Dudley   5098

Ramage and the Guillotine
Pope, Dudley   5099

Ramage and the Rebels
Pope, Dudley   5100

Ramage and the Saracens
Pope, Dudley   5101

Ramage at Trafalgar
Pope, Dudley   5102

The Ramage Touch
Pope, Dudley   5103

Ramage's Devil
Pope, Dudley   5104

Ramage's Diamond
Pope, Dudley   5105

Ramage's Mutiny
Pope, Dudley   5106

Ramage's Prize
Pope, Dudley   5107

Ramage's Signal
Pope, Dudley   5108

Ramage's Trial
Pope, Dudley   5109

Ramillies
Whitehead, Barbara   6708

Ranchero
White, Stewart Edward   6703

Rapaho
Cooper, Jamie Lee   1314

The Rape of the Fair Country
Cordell, Alexander   1325

Rascal's Heaven
Mason, F. van Wyck   4157

Rasero
Rebolledo, Francisco   5282

Rasputin's Revenge
Lescroart, John T.   3725

The Rationalist
Collins, Warwick   1217

Ratoon
Nicole, Christopher   4619

The Raven
Williams, Chancellor   6769

The Raven and the Rose
Wiggs, Susan   6746

The Raven in the Foregate
Peters, Ellis   4969

Ravenburn
Black, Laura   522

The Raven's Bride
Crook, Elizabeth   1431

The Ravens of Blackwater
Marston, Edward   4126

Raven's Wind
Canning, Victor   883

Ravenscroft
Eden, Dorothy   1860

Ravenshoe
Kingsley, Henry   3500

The Ravi Lancers
Masters, John   4178

Ravished
Quick, Amanda   5216

The Ravishers
Richards, Elizabeth   5318

Rawhider
Shelton, Gene   5802

The Real David Copperfield
Graves, Robert   2551

Reap the Whirlwind
Johnston, Terry C.   3254

Rebel
Cornwell, Bernard   1336

The Rebel and the Turncoat
Decker, Malcolm   1576

Rebel Guns
Rutledge, Adam   5539

Rebel Heiress
Hodge, Jane Aiken   2969
Neill, Robert   4573

Rebel in Blue
Toepperwein, Herman   6289

The Rebel Loyalist
Gordon, Charles William   2480

Rebel Princess
Anthony, Evelyn   164

Rebel Run
Zara, Louis   6952

Rebellion Road
Miller, Helen Topping   4392

The Rebels
Jakes, John   3152
Neumann, Alfred   4585

Rebels of the Heavenly Kingdom
Paterson, Katherine   4828

Rebels: The Irish Rising of 1916
DeRosa, Peter   1622

Reckless
Quick, Amanda   5217

Reckless Angel
Feather, Jane   2056

Reckon with the River
McMeekin, Clark   4292

The Reckoning
Penman, Sharon Kay   4906

The Rector of Justin
Auchincloss, Louis   233

Red Adam's Lady
Ingram, Grace   3106

The Red Badge of Courage
Crane, Stephen   1414

Red Barbarian
Gaan, Margaret   2260

Red Belts
Pendexter, Hugh   4897

Red Branch
Llywelyn, Morgan   3824

Red Cloak Flying
Widdemer, Margaret   6737

Red Cloud's Revenge
Johnston, Terry C.   3255

The Red Cock Crows
Gaither, Frances   2272

The Red Daniel
MacNeil, Duncan   4017

The Red Doe
Mayrant, Drayton   4214

Red Fox of the Kinapoo
Rush, William   5526

Red Gauntlet
Scott, Sir Walter   5706

The Red-Haired Brat
Dessau, Joanna   1627

The Red Lances
Pietri, Arturo Uslar   4999

Red Lanterns on St. Michael's
Jacobs, Thornwell   3139

Red Lion and Gold Dragon
Sprague, Rosemary   5969

The Red Marten
Nisser, Peter William   4630

The Red Monarch: Scenes From the Life of Stalin
Krotkov, Yuri   3561

Red Morning
Frey, Ruby Frazier   2230

Red Mountain
Lavender, David   3677

The Red Pavilion
van Gulik, Robert   6421

The Red Peony
Lin, Yutang   3783

Red Plush: The Story of the Moorhouse Family
McCrone, Guy   4232

Red Queen, White Queen
Treece, Henry   6332

The Red Road: A Romance of Braddock's Defeat
Pendexter, Hugh   4898

Red Rose of Anjou
Plaidy, Jean   5054

The Red Rover
Cooper, James Fenimore   1309

Red Runs the River
Patten, Lewis B.   4831

Red Slayer: Being the Second of the Sorrowful Mysteries of Brother Athelstan
Harding, Paul   2685

Red Stick
Porter, Donald Clayton   5121

Redcoat
Cornwell, Bernard   1337

Redemption
Uris, Leon   6393

The Redemptioner
Pennypacker, Isaac Rusling   4910

Refinements of Love: A Novel about Clover and Henry Adams
Conroy, Sarah Booth   1259

Refining Felicity
Chesney, Marion   1048

Refuge in Avalon
Steedman, Marguerite   5984

Refugio, They Named You Wrong
Schofield, Susan Clark 5647

Regards From the Dead Princess: A Novel of a Life
Mourad, Kenize 4505

Regency Buck
Heyer, Georgette 2898

Regency Rogue
Ashfield, Helen 212

Regency Royal
Hardwick, Michael 2687

Regeneration
Barker, Pat 309

Regent Square
Bramble, Forbes 645

The Regent's Daughter
Plaidy, Jean 5055

The Regiment
Nicole, Christopher 4620
Skelton, C.L. 5874

The Regulators
Degenhard, William 1580

Reigning Passions
Perutz, Kathrin 4940

The Reindeer Hunters
Wolf, Joan 6841

Reindeer Moon
Thomas, Elizabeth Marshall 6244

The Reluctant Bridegroom
Morris, Gilbert 4467

Reluctant Cavalier
Chidsey, Donald Barr 1064

The Reluctant Heiress
Laine, Annabel 3588

The Reluctant Queen
Haycraft, Molly Costain 2796

The Reluctant Queen: The Story of Anne of York
Plaidy, Jean 5056

Reluctant Rebel
Van de Water, Frederic F. 6403

The Reluctant Widow
Heyer, Georgette 2899

The Remarkable Young Man
Roberts, Cecil 5373

Rembrandt
Schmitt, Gladys 5643

Remember Santiago
Jones, Douglas C. 3280

Remember This Time
Broder, Gloria Kurian 703

Remembrance Rock
Sandburg, Carl 5583

Remnants of Glory
Miller, Teresa 4403

Rendezvous
Quick, Amanda 5218

A Rendezvous in Haiti
Becker, Stephen 407

The Renegade
Porter, Donald Clayton 5122

The Renegade: A Novel of Cornwall, 1783-1787
Graham, Winston 2529

Renno
Porter, Donald Clayton 5123

Renown
Hough, Frank Olney 3045

Republic: A Novel of Texas
Thompson, E.V. 6266

A Reputation Dies
Ley, Alice Chetwynd 3766

A Respectable Trade
Gregory, Philippa 2584

Restless Are the Sails
Eaton, Evelyn 1830

The Restless Border
Pearce, Richard 4873

The Restless Flame
De Wohl, Louis 1573

The Restless Frontier
MacNeil, Duncan 4018

Restless Is the River
Derleth, August 1617

The Restless Land
Culp, John H. 1444

Restless Voyage
Porteus, Stanley David 5138

Restoration: A Novel of Seventeenth-Century England
Tremain, Rose 6333

Resurrection Row
Perry, Anne 4934

The Retreat
Appelfeld, Aharon 178

Retreat and Recall
Hopkins, Joseph G.E. 3029

Retreat From the Dolphin
Teilhet, Darwin Le Ora 6198

The Return of Henry Starr
Slotkin, Richard 5909

The Return of Lono: A Novel of Captain Cook's Last Voyage
Bushnell, Oswald Andrew 816

The Return of Moriarty
Gardner, John E. 2287

The Return of the Gypsy
Carr, Philippa 927

Return of the Spanish
Coldsmith, Don 1183

Return of the Stranger
Roberts, Dorothy James 5377
Tannahill, Reay 6158

Return to Ithaca
Johnson, Eyvind 3224

Return to the River
Coldsmith, Don 1184

Return to Thebes
Drury, Allen 1739

Return to Treasure Island
Judd, Denis 3318

Reunion at Chattanooga
Crabb, Alfred Leland 1406

The Revenge of Dracula
Tremayne, Peter 6335

The Revenge of the Hound
Hardwick, Michael 2688

The Reverse of the Medal
O'Brian, Patrick 4673

The Revolt of Sarah Perkins
Cockrell, Marian 1148

The Revolt of the Eaglets
Plaidy, Jean 5057

The Revolutionary
Schoonover, Lawrence 5667

A Revolutionary Woman
Fugard, Sheila 2248

The Revolutionist: A Novel of Russia
Littell, Robert 3810

Rhine Journey
Schlee, Ann 5639

Rhinegold
Grundy, Stephan 2607

The Rich Are with You Always
Macdonald, Malcolm 3971

Richard III: The Last Plantagenet
Whittle, Tyler 6722

Richard and the Knights of God
Bennetts, Pamela 454

Richard Bolitho—Midshipman
Kent, Alexander 3437

Richard Carvel
Churchill, Winston 1081

Richard Lamb
Wheeler, Richard S. 6662

Richard Pryne: A Novel of the American Revolution
Harris, Cyril 2718

Richard Walden's Wife
Kelly, Eleanor 3399

Richard Whittington, London's Mayor
Sudworth, Gwynedd 6112

The Richlands
Turnbull, Agnes Sligh 6364

The Richmond Raid
Brick, John 674

Riddle Me a Murder
Crowley, Duane 1435

Ride East! Ride West!: A Romance of the Hundred Years' War
Powers, Anne 5154

Ride Home Tomorrow
John, Evan 3221

Ride of the Panther
Newcomb, Kerry 4591

Ride the Blue Riband
Laker, Rosalind 3598

Ride the Dark Trail
L'Amour, Louis 3624

Ride the Red Earth
Wellman, Paul I. 6620

Ride the River
L'Amour, Louis 3625

Ride the Wind
Robson, Lucia St. Clair 5416

Ride with Me
Costain, Thomas B. 1369

Ride with Me, Mariah Montana
Doig, Ivan 1684

Rider on a White Horse
Sutcliff, Rosemary 6124

Riders of Judgment
Manfred, Frederick F. 4059

Riders of the Long Road
Bransford, Stephen E. 649

Riding Shotgun
Brown, Rita Mae 729

Rienzi, or The Last of the Tribunes
Bulwer-Lytton, Edward 770

The Rifleman
Brick, John 675

Rifleman Dodd
Forester, C.S. 2181

The Rifles
Vollmann, William T. 6510

The Right Line of Cedric
Duggan, Alfred 1773

The Ring Master
Gurr, David 2622

The Ringed Castle
Dunnett, Dorothy 1807

Rio Grande
Sherman, Jory 5821

Riot at Gravesend: A Novel of Wat Tyler's Rebellion
Woods, William Howard 6864

The Ripper's Apprentice
Thomas, Donald 6242

The Rising of the Moon
Ellis, Peter Berresford 1926
Martin, William 4140

The Rising Storm
Allis, Marguerite 113

Rites of Passage
Golding, William 2456

The Rival Shores
Beverly-Giddings, Arthur 487

The Riven Heart
Gennari, Genevieve 2354

The Riven Realm
Tranter, Nigel 6317

River and Empty Sea
Vaczek, Louis 6396

The River and the Stone: Moses' Early Years in Egypt
Jenks, Kathleen 3192

The River and the Wilderness
Robertson, Don 5401

The River Devils
Vaughan, Carter A. 6437

River God
Smith, Wilbur 5928

River in the Wind
Pope, Edith   5111

River of Dreams
Courter, Gay   1390

River of Sky
Harper, Karen   2713

River of Swans
Coldsmith, Don   1185

River out of Eden
Seifert, Shirley   5732

*River to the West: A Novel of the
Astor Adventure*
Jennings, John Edward   3204

A River Town
Keneally, Thomas   3415

The River Witch
McIntyre, Margerie   4278

Rivers of Glory
Mason, F. van Wyck   4158

Rivers of Gold
Edmonds, Janet   1868

Rivers Parting
Barker, Shirley   315

River's Run
Abbot, Jane Ludlow   7

Rivers West
L'Amour, Louis   3626

Rivington Street
Tax, Meredith   6175

Rizpah
Israel, Charles E.   3124

The Road
Ehle, John   1896

The Road and the Star
Mather, Berkely   4182

Road From Olivet
Murphy, Edward Francis   4523

The Road to Avalon
Wolf, Joan   6842

The Road to Baltimore
Harper, Robert S.   2716

*The Road to Bithynia: A Novel of
Luke, the Beloved Physician*
Slaughter, Frank G.   5897

The Road to Bunker Hill
Barker, Shirley   316

The Road to Glory
Austin, Frederick Britten   246
Teilhet, Darwin Le Ora   6199

Road to Lendor
Esther, Hammon   1966

The Road to San Jacinto
Davis, James F.   1524
Foreman, Leonard L.   2167

The Road to Wellville
Boyle, T. Coraghessan   618

*A Road We Do Not Know: A Novel
of Custer at the Little Bighorn*
Chiaventone, Frederick J.   1057

The Roads to Guadalupe
Taylor, Robert Lewis   6190

Roanoke Hundred
Fletcher, Inglis   2138

Roanoke Renegade
Tracy, Don   6311

Roanoke Warrior
Vaughan, Carter A.   6438

The Roar of the Thunder
Smith, Wilbur   5929

The Roaring Boy
Marston, Edward   4127

A Roaring in the Wind
Taylor, Robert Lewis   6191

Rob Roy
Scott, Sir Walter   5707

*The Robber: A Tale of the Time of
the Herods*
Brooker, Bertram   706

The Robber Baroness
Clarke, William Kendall   1097

The Robber Bridegroom
Welty, Eudora   6623

The Robe
Douglas, Lloyd C.   1703

*Robert the Bruce: The Path of the
Hero King*
Tranter, Nigel   6318

*Robert the Bruce: The Price of the
King's Peace*
Tranter, Nigel   6319

*Robert the Bruce: The Steps to the
Empty Throne*
Tranter, Nigel   6320

Robin and the King
Godwin, Parke   2448

The Robsart Affair
Letton, Jennette   3729

The Rock: A Novel about Gibraltar
Masters, John   4179

The Rock Cried Out
Stanley, Edward   5981

Rockspring
Vliet, R.G.   6506

Roger Sudden
Raddall, Thomas H.   5232

Rogers' Folly
Idell, Albert E.   3102

The Rogue and the Witch
Newton, John Edward   4605

The Rogue From Padua
Williams, Jay   6772

Rogue Herries
Walpole, Hugh   6547

*Rogues' Company: A Novel of John
Murrell*
Kroll, Harry Harrison   3559

Rogue's Harbor
Fletcher, Inglis   2139

Rogue's Holiday
Cochran, Hamilton   1141

Rogue's Kingdom
Brick, John   676

*Rogue's Legacy: A Novel about
Francois Villon*
Deutsch, Babette   1629

Rogue's March
Chapman, Maristan   993

Roll, Shenandoah
Lancaster, Bruce   3644

Roman
Jones, Douglas C.   3281

The Roman
Waltari, Mika   6554

Roman Blood
Saylor, Steven   5626

Roman Go Home!
Fergusson, Adam   2065

Roman Nights
Burns, Ron   803

Roman Shadows
Burns, Ron   804

Roman Wall
Bryher   745

The Romance of Charles Dickens
Bloom, Ursula   553

The Romance of Leonardo Da Vinci
Merezhkovski, Dmitri   4339

Rome Haul
Edmonds, Walter D.   1877

Rommel and the Rebel
Wells, Lawrence   6622

Romola
Eliot, George   1910

The Ronin
Jennings, William Dale   3212

*The Rookery: A Novel of the
Victorian Underworld*
Rae, Hugh C.   5239

Room with a Clue
Kingsbury, Kate   3495

Rose
Smith, Martin Cruz   5923

The Rose and the Flame
Lauritzen, Jonreed   3676

The Rose and the Sword
Paretti, Sandra   4792

The Rose at Harvest End
Fairburn, Eleanor   2003

The Rose Crossing
Jose, Nicholas   3306

A Rose for Virtue
Lofts, Norah   3858

*The Rose of Malmaison: The
Turbulent Life of the Beautiful
Josephine*
Schonthan, Gaby von   5660

The Rose Rent
Peters, Ellis   4970

The Rose Without a Thorn
Plaidy, Jean   5058

Rosehaven
Coulter, Catherine   1380

Roses for Mexico
Eliot, Ethel Cook   1907

Roses From the South
Reniers, Perceval   5304

Rough Diamond
Fish, Robert L.   2098

The Rough Rider
Morris, Gilbert   4468

The Royal Ann Tree
Campbell, Patricia   875

The Royal City
Savage, Les Jr.   5621

Royal Escape
Heyer, Georgette   2900

Royal Flash
Fraser, George MacDonald   2213

Royal Flush: The Story of Minette
Irwin, Margaret   3121

Royal Merry-Go-Round
Kenyon, F.W.   3459

A Royal Murder
Roosevelt, Elliott   5456

Royal Nonesuch: A Tudor Tapestry
White, Beatrice   6674

The Royal Pawn
Ridge, Antonia   5327

A Royal Quest
Lide, Mary   3777

Royal Road to Fotheringay
Plaidy, Jean   5059

Royal Street
Roberts, Walter Adolphe   5393

The Royal Succession
Druon, Maurice   1735

Royal Sword at Agincourt
Bennetts, Pamela   455

Royal William
Leslie, Doris   3728

Royal Yankee
Suthren, Victor   6132

Ruan
Bryher   746

Ruby
Ashfield, Helen   213

*Ruler of the Sky: A Novel of Genghis
Khan*
Sargent, Pamela   5606

Run Me a River
Giles, Janice Holt   2415

Run of the Stars
Aydelotte, Dora   247

Runaway
Graham, Heather   2519

Runestone
Coldsmith, Don   1186

The Running Iron
Fish, Rachel Ann   2097

The Running of the Tide
Forbes, Esther   2160

Running Proud
Monsarrat, Nicholas　4432

The Running Thread
Mayrant, Drayton　4215

The Running Vixen
Chadwick, Elizabeth　968

Running West
Houston, James　3052

Rush to Destroy
Martin, L. Jay　4133

The Russian River
McCarthy, Gary　4224

Russka: The Novel of Russia
Rutherfurd, Edward　5535

Ruth
Fineman, Irving　2089

The Ruthless Yeomen
Anand, Valerie　134

Rutland Place
Perry, Anne　4935

S

The Sable Lion
Van Dorp, Jan　6405

Sabrina
Polland, Madeleine　5086

Sacajawea
Waldo, Anna Lee　6529

Sacajawea of the Shoshones
Emmons, Della F.　1940

The Sachem
Porter, Donald Clayton　5124

Sachem's Son
Porter, Donald Clayton　5125

The Sackett Brand
L'Amour, Louis　3627

Sackett's Land
L'Amour, Louis　3628

Sacred and Profane: A Novel of the Life and Times of Mozart
Weiss, David　6609

The Sacred Hills
Coldsmith, Don　1187

Sacred Hunter
Unsworth, Barry　6389

The Sacred Stones
Sarabande, William　5600

The Sacrilege
Roberts, John Maddox　5380

Sadhu on the Mountain Peak
MacNeil, Duncan　4019

The Saga of Henry Starr
Conley, Robert J.　1250

The Sage and the Olive
Barton, Florence Whitfield　369

Sage of Canudos
Marchal, Lucien　4080

Saigon
Grey, Anthony　2588

Sail the Dark Tide
Steward, Davenport　6017

Sailor Named Jones
Haislip, Harvey　2643

A Sailor of Austria
Biggins, John　492

The Saint
Unruh, Fritz von　6385

St. Agnes' Stand
Eidson, Tom　1900

Saint Francis
Kazantzakis, Nikos　3385

St. John's Wood
Fitzgerald, Nancy　2116

Saint Johnson
Burnett, William R.　796

Saint Mudd
Thayer, Steve　6218

The Saint of Montparnasse: A Novel Based on the Life of Constantin Brancusi
Neagoe, Peter　4560

Saint Paul: A Historical Novel of His Life
Poirier, Leon　5081

St. Peter's Fair
Peters, Ellis　4971

St. Thomas's Eve
Plaidy, Jean　5060

The Saintly Buccaneer
Morris, Gilbert　4469

Saints and Scholars
Eagleton, Terrence　1821

Sakuran: A Novel of Medieval Japan
Tolosko, Edward　6292

The Salamanca Drum
Eden, Dorothy　1861

Salammbo
Flaubert, Gustave　2123

The Salem Frigate
Jennings, John Edward　3205

Salisbury Plain
Branson, Henry C.　650

La Salle
Vernon, John　6458

Sally Hemings
Chase-Riboud, Barbara　1006

Salome, Princess of Galilee
Denker, Henry　1611

The Salt and the Savor
Troyer, Howard William　6354

Salt Lake City
Reife, A.R.　5292

The Salt of the Earth
Monterosso, Carlo　4437

Salute to Adventurers
Buchan, John　752

Salvation
Asch, Sholem　202

Sam Chance
Capps, Benjamin　888

Sam Houston
Gerson, Noel B.　2380

The Sam Houston Story
Owen, Dean　4770

Sam Patch: Ballad of a Jumping Man
Getz, William　2390

The Same Scourge
Goldthorpe, John　2464

Samuel Brannan and the Golden Fleece
Scott, Reva　5686

Samuel Drummond
Boyd, Thomas Alexander　614

The Samurai
Endo, Shusaku　1941

San Antone
Banis, V.J.　288

San Juan Hill
Henry, Will　2848

The Sanctuary Sparrow
Peters, Ellis　4972

Sand in the Wind
Gear, Kathleen O'Neal　2329

The Sandalwood Fan
Brown, Diana　720

Sandoval: A Romance of Bad Manners
Beer, Thomas　414

Sangaree
Slaughter, Frank G.　5898

Sanguinet's Crown
Veryan, Patricia　6476

Sapphira and the Slave Girl
Cather, Willa　958

Sapphire
Ashfield, Helen　214

Sara
Cleeve, Brian　1110

Sara Dane
Gaskin, Catherine　2316

Saraband for Two Sisters
Carr, Philippa　928

The Saracen Blade
Yerby, Frank　6926

Saragossa
Perez Galdos, Benito　4912

Sarah
Gross, Joel　2603

Sarah Camberwell Tring
Edmonds, Janet　1869

Sarah Cobb
Rae, Catherine M.　5236

Saratoga Trunk
Ferber, Edna　2062

Sarsen Place
Butler, Gwendoline　821

Sarton Kell
Mallory, Kate　4043

Sarum: The Novel of England
Rutherfurd, Edward　5536

Sassafras
Matthews, Jack　4193

Satan in St. Mary's
Doherty, P.C.　1676

Satan's Fire
Doherty, P.C.　1677

Saturday City
Webster, Jan　6593

The Savage Brood
Rofheart, Martha　5430

The Savage City
Paradise, Jean　4787

Savage Frontier
Burleson, Frank　787

Savage Gentleman
Gerson, Noel B.　2381

Savage Oaks
Ellis, Julie　1924

Savage Prodigal
Bercovici, Konrad　474

Savage Thunder
Lindsey, Johanna　3795

Savages and Saints
Older, Cora　4717

Savanna
Giles, Janice Holt　2416

Savannah
Price, Eugenia　5186

Savannah Purchase
Hodge, Jane Aiken　2970

The Saxon Tapestry
Rice, Sile　5317

Say These Names (Remember Them)
Cummings, Betty Sue　1448

Say to This Mountain
Thoene, Bodie　6226

Scales of Gold
Dunnett, Dorothy　1808

Scalpdancers
Newcomb, Kerry　4592

The Scalpel and the Sword
Shannon, Dell　5774

Scandal
Quick, Amanda　5219

Scandal at High Chimneys: A Victorian Melodrama
Carr, John Dickson　915

Scandal in Troy
Hansen, Eva Hemmer　2679

The Scandalous Lady Wright
Chesney, Marion　1049

The Scandalous Marriage
Chesney, Marion　1050

The Scandalous Mrs. Blackford
Kane, Harriet　3358

The Scapegoat
Settle, Mary Lee　5758

The Scapegoat: A Life of Moses
Lawrence, Joan 3684

Scapegoat for a Stuart
Kirby, Kate 3504

Scaramouche
Sabatini, Rafael 5554

Scaramouche the King-Maker
Sabatini, Rafael 5555

Scarborough House
Salvato, Sharon 5577

The Scarlet Beast
Gerard, Francis 2357

The Scarlet City
Haasse, Hella S. 2632

The Scarlet Cloak
Plaidy, Jean 5061

Scarlet Cockerel
Lagard, Garald 3584
Sublette, Clifford 6110

*Scarlet Cord: A Novel of the Woman
    of Jericho*
Slaughter, Frank G. 5899

Scarlet Feather
Van Every, Dale 6409

The Scarlet Guidon
Toepfer, Ray Grant 6287

The Scarlet Letter
Hawthorne, Nathaniel 2786

The Scarlet Lily
Murphy, Edward Francis 4524

The Scarlet Patch
Lancaster, Bruce 3645

The Scarlet Pimpernel
Orczy, Baroness Emma 4745

Scarlet Ribbons
French, Judith E. 2224

Scarlet Women
Christilian, J.D. 1077

Scarlett
Ripley, Alexandra 5342

Scent of Cloves
Lofts, Norah 3859

Schindler's List
Keneally, Thomas 3416

The Scimitar
Edwards, Samuel 1890

The Scorching Wind
Macken, Walter 3988

Scorpus the Moor
White, Leslie Turner 6690

Scotch on the Rocks
Browne, Howard 733

The Scotswoman
Fletcher, Inglis 2140

The Scottish Chiefs
Porter, Jane 5135

The Scottish Marriage
Lynn, Karen 3942

Scoundrels' Brigade
Vaughan, Carter A. 6439

The Scout
Combs, Harry 1224

The Sea and the Sand
Nicole, Christopher 4621

The Sea Beggars
Holland, Cecelia 2996

Sea Change
McLeay, Alison 4287

The Sea Eagles
Jennings, John Edward 3206

Sea Jade
Whitney, Phyllis A. 6717

Sea of Darkness
Huntford, Roland 3086

The Sea of Grass
Richter, Conrad 5323

Sea of Lentils
Benitez-Rojo, Antonio 443

The Sea Officer
Styles, Showell 6105

*The Sea Panther: A Novel about the
    Commander of the U.S.S.
    Constitution*
Vail, Philip 6397

The Sea Peoples
Danielson, Peter 1474

Sea Road to Yorktown
Haislip, Harvey 2644

The Sea Runners
Doig, Ivan 1685

The Sea Scape
Lide, Mary 3778

The Sea Stands Watch
Mudgett, Helen Parker 4507

*Sea Star: The Private Life of Anne
    Bonny, Pirate*
Jekel, Pamela 3187

Sea to Shining Sea
Phillips, Michael 4990

The Sea Treasure
Barr, Elisabeth 338

The Sea 'Venture
Mason, F. van Wyck 4159

The Seadon Fortune
St. Clair, Leonard 5563

The Seafarers
Long, William Stuart 3877

Seance for a Vampire
Saberhagen, Fred 5557

*A Search for a King: A 12th-Century
    Legend*
Vidal, Gore 6492

The Search for Temperance Moon
Jones, Douglas C. 3282

The Searchers
Le May, Alan 3691

Searching for the Emperor
Pazzi, Roberto 4858

A Season for Death
Harrison, Ray 2743

Season for War
Kluge, P.F. 3510

A Season of Knives
Chisholm, P.F. 1072

A Season of Mists
Woodhouse, Sarah 6856

A Season of Swans
De Blasis, Celeste 1548

Season of the Jew
Shadbolt, Maurice 5768

Season of Yellow Leaf
Jones, Douglas C. 3283

Seasons
Dillon, Anna 1645

Seasons of Fear
McFarland, Philip 4272

The Seasons of Heroes
Davis, Paxton 1539

*Seats of the Mighty: A Novel of
    James Stuart, Brother of Mary,
    Queen of Scots*
Harwood, Alice 2768

Seattle Green
Adams, Jane 26

The Second Crucifixion
Samuel, Maurice 5579

The Second Face of Valor
Toepfer, Ray Grant 6288

Second Generation
Fast, Howard 2043

The Second Kiss
Rogers, Gayle 5432

The Second Mate
McCutchan, Philip 4257

The Second Sister
O'Grady, Leslie 4701

*The Second Son of Heaven: A Novel
    of Nineteenth-Century China*
Lee, C.Y. 3707

The Secret Annie Oakley
Heidish, Marcy Moran 2819

Secret Dreams
Korman, Keith 3541

Secret for a Nightingale
Holt, Victoria 3020

*The Secret Life of Laszlo, Count
    Dracula*
Anscombe, Roderick 156

The Secret Memoirs of Lord Byron
Nicole, Christopher 4622

The Secret of Saramount
Cheatham, Lillian 1011

The Secret of the Kingdom
Waltari, Mika 6555

The Secret Road
Lancaster, Bruce 3646

Secret Service Operator 13
Chambers, Robert W. 982

Secret Song
Coulter, Catherine 1381

The Secret Wife
Acland, Alice 22

The Secret Years
Lennox-Smith, Judith 3718

The Seducer
Stangerup, Henrik 5980

Seduction
Quick, Amanda 5220

Seed of Mischief
Gibbs, Willa 2401

Seedtime and Harvest
Pearce, Mary E. 4864

Seek Out and Destroy
Horan, James David 3031

Seek the Fair Land
Macken, Walter 3989

The Seekers
Jakes, John 3153

The Seeking
Elegant, Robert S. 1906

Segaki
Stacton, David 5975

Segu
Conde, Maryse 1234

Seize the Sky
Johnston, Terry C. 3256

Seminole
Porter, Donald Clayton 5126
Pratt, Theodore 5164

The Senator's Lady
Seifert, Shirley 5733

Seneca
Porter, Donald Clayton 5127

Seneca Falls Inheritance
Monfredo, Miriam Grace 4429

The Seneca Hostage
Vaughan, Carter A. 6440

Serenissima: A Novel of Venice
Jong, Erica 3300

Sergeant Gringo
Cummings, Jack 1449

Sergeant Lamb's America
Graves, Robert 2552

Sergeant Verity and the Blood Royal
Selwyn, Francis 5744

*Sergeant Verity and the Imperial
    Diamond*
Selwyn, Francis 5745

*Sergeant Verity Presents His
    Compliments*
Selwyn, Francis 5746

The Serpent Amongst the Lilies
Doherty, P.C. 1678

Serpent and Staff
Yerby, Frank 6927

The Serpent Garden
Riley, Judith Merkle 5336

The Serpent's Tooth
Paxson, Diana L. 4846

The Servant's Tale
Frazer, Margaret 2219

Service for Two
Kingsbury, Kate 3496

Set All Afire: A Novel of St. Francis Xavier
De Wohl, Louis 1574

The Settlers
Long, William Stuart 3878
Moberg, Vilhelm 4424

The Seven Ages
Figes, Eva 2084

The Seven Cities of Gold
Hersch, Virginia Davis 2865

Seven Days to Petrograd
Hyman, Tom 3094

The Seven Hills of Paradise
Simpson, Rosemary 5859

Seven Men of Gascony
Delderfield, R.F. 1589

The Seven-Per-Cent Solution
Meyer, Nicholas 4349

Seven Rivers West
Hoagland, Edward 2959

Seven Tempest
Wilkins, William Vaughan 6761

Seventeen of Leyden
James, John 3160

The Seventh Bullet
Victor, Daniel D. 6483

The Seventh Girl: A Romantic Tale of Civil War Texas
Pendleton, Tom 4900

The Seventh Winter
Borland, Hal 583

The Severed Crown
Lane, Jane 3657

Seward's Folly
Marshall, Edison 4111

Shad Run
Breslin, Howard 668

The Shadow and the Glory
Jennings, John Edward 3207

Shadow Catcher
Fergus, Charles 2064

The Shadow Flies
Macaulay, Rose 3956

The Shadow in the Glass
Derleth, August 1618

Shadow in the Sun: A Novel of Elizabeth I, the Virgin Queen
Kenyon, F.W. 3460

Shadow of a Lady
Hodge, Jane Aiken 2971

Shadow of a Star
Cooper, Jamie Lee 1315

A Shadow of Eagles
Barry, Jane 360

The Shadow of God
Crawley, Aileen 1422

A Shadow of Gulls
Finney, Patricia 2096

The Shadow of the Earth
Wichelns, Lee 6731

Shadow of the Long Knives
Boyd, Thomas Alexander 615

Shadow of the Moon
Jones, Douglas C. 3284
Kaye, M.M. 3377

The Shadow of the Moth: A Novel of Espionage with Virginia Woolf
Hawkes, Ellen 2779

Shadow of the Mountains
Morris, Lynn 4481

The Shadow of the Pomegranate
Plaidy, Jean 5062

The Shadow of the Sun
Pell, Sylvia 4891

Shadow of the Watching Star
Sarabande, William 5601

Shadow of the Wolf
Barwick, James 371

Shadow on the Valley
Mitchell, Kirk 4414

The Shadow Riders
Johnston, Terry C. 3257

Shadowed Memories
Lacy, Al 3583

The Shadowed Spring
Salisbury, Carola 5571

Shadows and Images
Trevor, Meriol 6344

A Shadow's Bliss
Veryan, Patricia 6477

Shadows in Bronze
Davis, Lindsey 1531

Shadows in the Dusk
Jennings, John Edward 3208

Shadows on the Long House
Roarke, Mike 5360

Shadows on the Rock
Cather, Willa 959

Shadows on the Shore
Stirling, Jessica 6048

Shadows on the Stones
Caldecott, Moyra 847

Shadows over Castle Rising
Cradock, Fanny 1410

Shaggy Legion
Evarts, Hal George 1986

Shakespeare & Son
Fisher, Edward 2102

The Shakespeare Girl
Hardwick, Mollie 2698

Shakespeare's Dog
Rooke, Leon 5439

The Shalimar
Hyatt, Betty Hale 3091

Shaman
Gordon, Noah 2483

Shame of Man
Anthony, Piers 168

Shanghai
New, Christopher 4588

Shanghai Tango: A Novel of China
Overgard, William 4769

Shards of Empire
Schwartz, Susan 5677

Sharpe's Battle
Cornwell, Bernard 1338

Sharpe's Company
Cornwell, Bernard 1339

Sharpe's Devil
Cornwell, Bernard 1340

Sharpe's Eagle
Cornwell, Bernard 1341

Sharpe's Enemy
Cornwell, Bernard 1342

Sharpe's Gold
Cornwell, Bernard 1343

Sharpe's Honour
Cornwell, Bernard 1344

Sharpe's Regiment
Cornwell, Bernard 1345

Sharpe's Revenge
Cornwell, Bernard 1346

Sharpe's Rifles
Cornwell, Bernard 1347

Sharpe's Siege
Cornwell, Bernard 1348

Sharpe's Sword
Cornwell, Bernard 1349

The Shattered Horse
Somtow, S.P. 5945

She Rode a Yellow Stallion
Reed, Walter 5286

She Who Remembers
Shuler, Linda Lay 5838

The She-Wolf
Bennetts, Pamela 456

The She-Wolf of France
Druon, Maurice 1736

The Shepherd
Payne, Robert 4855

The Shepherd Kings
Danielson, Peter 1475

The Shepherd's Crook
Frischauer, Paul 2234

The Sherbrooke Bride
Coulter, Catherine 1382

The Sheriff of Nottingham
Kluger, Richard 3512

Sherlock Holmes and the Case of Sabina Hall
Greenwood, L.B. 2576

Sherlock Holmes and the Case of the Raleigh Legacy
Greenwood, L.B. 2577

Sherlock Holmes and the Mysterious Friend of Oscar Wilde
Brown, Russell A. 731

Sherlock Holmes and the Red Demon
Millett, Larry 4404

Sherlock Holmes and the Thistle of Scotland
Greenwood, L.B. 2578

Sherlock Holmes Meets Annie Oakley
Shaw, Stanley 5782

Sherlock Holmes vs. Dracula
Estleman, Loren D. 1976

Sherlock in Love
Naslund, Sena Jeter 4557

Sherman's March
Bass, Cynthia 373

Sherwood
Godwin, Parke 2449

Shield of Honor
Graham, Alice Walworth 2511

Shield of Three Lions
Kaufman, Pamela 3372

Shike: Time of Dragons
Shea, Robert 5784

Shiloh
Foote, Shelby 2153

Shin Ju
Rowland, Laura Joh 5520

The Shining
Marlowe, Stephen 4097

The Shining King
Danielson, Peter 1476

Shining Mountains
Frazee, Steve 2214

The Shining Mountains
Van Every, Dale 6410

The Shining Trail
Fuller, Iola 2254

Ship of the Line
Forester, C.S. 2182

The Ship's Clock
Rae, Catherine M. 5237

Shiva: An Adventure of the Ice Age
Brennan, J.H. 657

Shod with Flame
Miller, Helen Topping 4393

Shogun
Clavell, James 1101

Shoot!
Bowering, George 604

The Shooting Party
Colegate, Isabel 1197

The Shootist
Swarthout, Glendon 6145

Shout at the Devil
Smith, Wilbur 5930

Show Boat
Ferber, Edna 2063

Show Me a Land
McMeekin, Clark 4293

A Shrine of Murders
Grace, C.L. 2509

The Side of the Moon
Prantera, Amanda 5162

The Siege
Vansittart, Peter 6431
Williams, Jay 6773

Siege in the Sun
Paradise, Mary 4788

The Siege of Krishnapur
Farrell, J.G. 2016

Sierra Triumph
Ross, Dana Fuller 5488

Sign of the Pagan
Tracy, Don 6312

Signal—Close Action!
Kent, Alexander 3438

A Signal Victory
Stacton, David 5976

Signals of Distress
Crace, Jim 1408

The Signore: Shogun of the Warring States
Tsuji, Kunio 6357

Signorina
Myers, Henry 4542

Silas Marner
Eliot, George 1911

Silence in Hanover Close
Perry, Anne 4936

The Silent Drum
Swanson, Neil Harmon 6141

Silent Drums
Roarke, Mike 5361

The Silent People
Macken, Walter 3990

The Silent Tarn
Closs, Hannah 1131

The Silent Woman
Marston, Edward 4128

Silk and Steel
Alter, Stephen 122

Silk Road
Larsen, Jeanne 3670

The Silver Chalice
Costain, Thomas B. 1370

Silver Cross
Johnston, Mary 3239

The Silver Dolphin
Johnston, Velda 3264

Silver Fruit
Campbell, Patricia 876

The Silver Highways
Macdonald, Malcolm 3972

Silver Leopard
Mason, F. van Wyck 4160

Silver Linings
Davies-Owens, Shirley 1508

A Silver Mirror
Gellis, Roberta 2353

The Silver Mountain
Cushman, Dan 1453

Silver Nutmeg
Lofts, Norah 3860

The Silver Oar
Breslin, Howard 669

The Silver Pigs
Davis, Lindsey 1532

The Silver Plume
Meeker, Arthur 4323

The Silver Saber
Vaughan, Carter A. 6441

Silver Shoals
Cochran, Hamilton 1142

The Silver Touch
Laker, Rosalind 3599

Simon Bar Cochba: Rebellion in Judea
Finch, Merton 2086

Simon the Coldheart
Heyer, Georgette 2901

Simple Prayers
Golding, Michael 2452

Simplicissimus the Vagabond
Grimmelshausen, J.J.C. 2594

The Sin of the Prophet
Nelson, Truman 4582

Sing for a Penny
Dowdey, Clifford 1708

Sing Morning Star
Oliver, Jane 4727

Sing One Song
Miller, Helen Topping 4394

Sing to the Sun
Borden, Lucille 579

The Singing Sword
Whyte, Jack 6725

The Single Star
Roberts, Walter Adolphe 5394

A Single Summer with Lord B.
Marlowe, Derek 4092

Singletusk
Kurten, Bjorn 3567

A Singular Conspiracy
Perowne, Barry 4915

The Sinking of the Sarah Diamond
Jennings, William Dale 3213

The Sinner of Saint Ambrose
Raynolds, Robert 5275

The Sins of Herod: A Novel of Rome and the Early Church
Slaughter, Frank G. 5900

The Sins of the Lion
Motley, Annette 4503

The Sins of the Wolf
Perry, Anne 4937

Sioux City
Downing, John Hyatt 1714

Sioux Dawn
Johnston, Terry C. 3258

Sioux Splendor
Bittner, Rosanne 515

Sir Pagan
Colyton, Henry John 1222

Sir Philip's Folly
Chesney, Marion 1051

Sir Rogue
White, Leslie Turner 6691

Sir William
Stacton, David 5977

Sister Beneath the Sheet
Linscott, Gillian 3808

Sister to Jane: The Story of Lady Katharine Grey
May, Beatrice 4202

Sister Wives
Jones, Cleo 3270

Sisters and Brothers
Stevenson, Janet 6005

Sisters & Lovers
Thorne, Nicola 6274

Sitting Bull
Dugan, Bill 1760

Six-Horse Hitch
Giles, Janice Holt 2417

The Six Messiahs
Frost, Mark 2238

The Sixth Wife
Plaidy, Jean 5063

The Skeleton in the Grass
Barnard, Robert 320

The Sky and Tomorrow
Duncan, Thomas William 1788

The Sky-Liners
L'Amour, Louis 3629

The Skystone: The Forging of Arthur's Britain
Whyte, Jack 6726

Slaughter
Kelton, Elmer 3407

Slave
Malliol, William 4041

The Slave
Singer, Isaac Bashevis 5866

The Slave of Frankenstein
Myers, Robert J. 4549

The Slave Ship
Johnston, Mary 3240

The Slave Stealer
Upchurch, Boyd 6390

The Sleep of Life
Gordon, Richard 2486

The Sleeping Sword: A Biographical Novel
Frye, Pearl 2244

The Sleeping Tiger
McEvoy, Marjorie 4269

The Slender Reed
Gerson, Noel B. 2382

The Slicing Edge of Death
Cook, Judith 1263

Sloop of War
Kent, Alexander 3439

The Slow Awakening
Marchant, Catherine 4082

Slow Dies the Thunder
Miller, Helen Topping 4395

Smart Moves
Kaminsky, Stuart M. 3346

The Smile of the Stranger
Aiken, Joan 53

The Smiling Rebel
Kane, Harnett T. 3357

The Smiths
Fairbank, Janet 2002

The Smoky Hill
Coldsmith, Don 1188

The Snake Pit
Undset, Sigrid 6383

The Snake River
Blevins, Winfred 547

The Snake, the Crocodile, and the Dog
Peters, Elizabeth 4954

Snared Nightingale
Trease, Geoffrey 6324

The Snow Mountain
Gavin, Catherine 2324

Snow-Water
Gardiner, Dorothy 2285

The Snowblind Moon
Cooke, John Byrne 1267

So Brief a Spring
Manceron, Claude 4054

So Far From Malabar
Wehen, Joy DeWeese 6599

So Free We Seem
Todd, Helen 6286

So Great a Man
Pilgrim, David 5000

So Great a Queen: The Story of Esther, Queen of Persia
Frischauer, Paul 2235

So Merciful a Queen, So Cruel a Woman
Harwood, Alice 2769

So Much as Beauty Does
Elwood, Muriel 1938

So Near So Far
Parkinson, C. Northcote 4814

So Perish the Roses
Bell, Neil 423

So Red the Rose
Young, Stark 6944

So Shall They Reap
Bennett, John 444

Sofia
Chamberlin, Ann 974

Soho Square
Rayner, Claire 5268

Sojourn of a Stranger
Sullivan, Walter 6115

The Soldier and the Sage: A Novel about Akiba
Hubler, Richard G. 3065

Soldier in Buckskin
Hogan, Ray 2981

Soldier in Paradise
Wohl, Burton 6835

A Soldier of the Great War
Helprin, Mark 2823

Soldier of the Mist
Wolfe, Gene 6843

Soldier of the Queen
Hennessy, Max 2837

Soldier of the Sea
Daly, Robert Welter 1460

Soldiers of Fortune
Bourne, Peter 595

Solitudes
Vliet, R.G. 6507

Solomon and Sheba
Levine, Faye 3740
Williams, Jay 6774

Solomon and the Queen of Sheba
Ormonde, Czenzi 4751

Solomon's Song
Dorr, Roberta Kells 1697

Some Brief Folly
Veryan, Patricia 6478

Some Far Elusive Dawn
Drummond, Emma 1727

Some Lose Their Way
Liddon, Eloise S. 3770

Something Gleamed
Kenyon, Theda 3463

Somewhere Within This House
Webb, Jean Francis 6587

The Son Avenger
Undset, Sigrid 6384

Son of Dust
Prescott, H.F.M. 5171

Son of Holmes
Lescroart, John T. 3726

Son of Judah
Levin, Dan 3738

The Son of Laughter
Buechner, Frederick 764

Son of Tears
Coray, Henry W. 1320

Son of the Gamblin' Man: The Youth of an Artist
Sandoz, Mari 5593

The Son of York
Abbey, Margaret 5

Song in the Green Thorn Tree
Barke, James 303

The Song of a Dark Angel
Doherty, P.C. 1679

Song of a Strange Child
Morris, Gilbert 4470

The Song of Bernadette
Werfel, Franz 6625

Song of Metamoris: A Story That Remains of a People Who Passed This Way
Anness, Milford E. 155

The Song of Ruth: A Love Story of the Old Testament
Slaughter, Frank G. 5901

Song of the Bayou
Lynley, Elinor 3936

Song of the Cheyenne
Sherman, Jory 5822

Song of the Meadowlark
Sanford, John A. 5594

Song of the Rock
Coldsmith, Don 1189

The Song of the Siren
Carr, Philippa 929

Song of the Susquehanna
Stover, Herbert 6071

Song of Wovoka
Murray, Earl 4531

Song of Years
Aldrich, Bess Streeter 72

Sons of Fire
McCoy, Max 4227

Sons of Fortune
Macdonald, Malcolm 3973

The Sons of Grady Rourke
Savage, Douglas 5618

Sons of Liberty
Rutledge, Adam 5540

Sons of Texas
Early, Tom 1822

Sons of the Steppe: The Story of How the Conqueror Genghis Khan Was Overcome
Baumann, Hans 380

Sons of Thunder
Vroman, Barbara Fitz 6516

The Soothsayer
Chinn, Laurene 1069

Sophie
Wagner, Geoffrey 6519

The Sorceress
Weinreb, Nathaniel Norsen 6602

Sorrow by Day
Coryn, Marjorie 1359

A Sorrow in Our Heart
Eckert, Allen W. 1844

The Sot-Weed Factor
Barth, John 364

Soul Flame
Wood, Barbara 6850

Soul of Abe Lincoln
Babcock, Bernie 251

The Soul of Ann Rutledge
Babcock, Bernie 252

The Sound of Coaches
Garfield, Leon 2295

Sound of the Trumpet
Morris, Gilbert 4471

The Sounds of Chariots: A Novel of John Sevier and the State of Franklin
Miller, Helen Topping 4396

The Source
Michener, James A. 4374

South of the Border
Cooke, John Byrne 1268

The Southern Blade
Wolford, Nelson 6844

Southern Cross
Coleman, Terry 1206

The Southern Cross
French, Peter 2226

Southern Discomfort
Brown, Rita Mae 730

A Southern Woman
Eulo, Elena Yates 1983

Sow the Seeds of Hemp
Jennings, Gary 3195

A Space of the Heart
Wright, Patricia 6884

Spangle
Jennings, Gary 3196

Spanish Bayonet
Benet, Stephen Vincent 441

The Spanish Bride
Heyer, Georgette 2902
O'Meara, Walter 4735

The Spanish Bridegroom
Plaidy, Jean 5064

The Spanish Doctor
Cohen, Matt 1159

Spanish Gold
Randle, Kevin D. 5252

A Sparkle From the Coal
Andrew, Prudence 144

Spartacus
Fast, Howard 2044

Speak Softly
Alexander, Lawrence 83

Speak to Me of Love
Eden, Dorothy 1862

Speranza
Delblanc, Sven 1584

Sphere of Death
Harrison, Ray 2744

The Spider King
Schoonover, Lawrence 5668

Spinners' Wharf
Gower, Iris 2502

The Spire
Golding, William 2457

The Spirit and the Flesh: A Novel Inspired by the Life of Isadora Duncan
Weiss, David 6610

Spirit Knife
Porter, Donald Clayton 5128

Spirit Lake
Kantor, MacKinlay 3363

The Spitfire
Small, Bertrice 5912

The Splendor Stays: An Historic Novel Based on the Lives of the Seven Hart Sisters of Saybrook
Allis, Marguerite 114

The Spoils of Eden
Fowler, Robert H. 2193

The Spoils of War
Fleming, Thomas 2131

Spoon
Christgau, John 1074

Sporting with Amaryllis
West, Paul 6635

SPQR
Roberts, John Maddox 5381

Sprig Muslin
Heyer, Georgette 2903

The Sprig of Hemlock: A Novel about Shays' Rebellion
Muir, Robert 4509

Spring at The Winged Horse
Willis, Ted 6794

Spring Came on Forever
Aldrich, Bess Streeter 73

Spring Moon: A Novel of China
Lord, Bette Bao 3897

The Spring of the Ram
Dunnett, Dorothy 1809

The Spring of the Tiger
Holt, Victoria 3021

Spring Symphony
Painter, Eleanor 4777

The Spur
Kennelly, Ardyth 3425

The Spy: A Tale of the Neutral Ground
Cooper, James Fenimore 1310

A Spy for Napoleon
Orczy, Baroness Emma 4746

Spy in Chancery
Doherty, P.C. 1680

Spy's Honour
Lyall, Gavin 3929

Squadron Forty-Four
Whitehouse, Arch 6711

Squadron Shilling
Whitehouse, Arch 6712

Stacey's Flyer
Burns, Patricia 800

Stage Fright
Linscott, Gillian 3809

Stage of Fools
Brady, Charles Andrew 635

A Stake in the Kingdom
Tranter, Nigel 6321

The Staked Plain
Tolbert, Frank Xavier 6290

The Stalkers
Johnston, Terry C. 3259

Stallion Gate
Smith, Martin Cruz   5924

The Stallion Man
Glover, Judith   2438

Stamping Ground
Estleman, Loren D.   1977

The Stanbroke Girls
Hill, Fiona   2925

Stand into Danger
Kent, Alexander   3440

Stand We at Last
Fairbairns, Zoe   1999

The Standing Hills
Stickland, Caroline   6038

The Star-Gazer
Harsanyi, Zsolt de   2757

*Star in the Rigging: A Novel of the
   Texas Navy*
Roark, Garland   5358

*Star of Empire: A Novel of Old San
   Antonio*
Sanders, Leonard   5590

The Star of Lancaster
Plaidy, Jean   5065

Star of Macedon
Eiker, Karl V.   1901

Star of Randevi
McEvoy, Marjorie   4270

Star of the West
Hueston, Ethel   3070

Star of the Wilderness
Baker, Karle Wilson   274

A Star Pointed North
Fuller, Edmund   2250

Starrbelow
Thompson, China   6248

Stars and Stripes
Rutledge, Adam   5541

The Stars in Their Courses
Brown, Harry   722

The Stars of the South
Green, Julian   2568

Stars on the Sea
Mason, F. van Wyck   4161

Stately Timber
Hughes, Rupert   3075

Statues in a Garden
Colegate, Isabel   1198

*Stealing Heaven: The Love Story of
   Heloise and Abelard*
Meade, Marion   4317

Steamboat Gothic
Keyes, Frances Parkinson   3481

Steamboat on the River
Teilhet, Darwin Le Ora   6200

Stephen and the Sleeping Saints
Bennetts, Pamela   457

The Steps of the Sun
Trollope, Joanna   6350

Still Is the Summer Night
Derleth, August   1619

The Still Storm
Sagan, Francoise   5562

Stolen Away
Collins, Max Allan   1213

A Stolen Tongue
Holman, Sheri   3002

The Stone Arrow
Herley, Richard   2858

*Stone Song: A Novel of the Life of
   Crazy Horse*
Blevins, Winfred   548

Stones From the River
Hegi, Ursula   2816

The Stones of the Abbey
Pouillon, Fernand   5144

*The Stonewall Brigade: A Novel of
   the American Civil War*
Slaughter, Frank G.   5902

The Store
Pearson, Michael   4879

Storm Against the Wind
Jacobs, Helen Hull   3138

Storm Before Sunrise
Davies, June Wyndham   1507

*Storm Center: A Novel about Andy
   Johnson*
McSpadden, Joseph Walker   4312

Storm Haven
Slaughter, Frank G.   5903

Storm of Time
Dark, Eleanor   1494

Storm Signals
Lincoln, Joseph C.   3785

Storm the Last Rampart
Taylor, David   6180

Storm Tide
Bosworth, Allan R.   590

Storm to the South
Strabel, Thelma   6073

Storm Winds
Johansen, Iris   3217

The Storm Witch
Barr, Elisabeth   339

Storming Heaven
Giardina, Denise   2394

The Storms of Fate
Wright, Patricia   6885

Stormswift
Brent, Madeleine   662

A Story of Deep Delight
McNamee, Thomas   4305

The Story of Gosta Berling
Lagerlof, Selma   3586

*The Story of Pat Garrett and Billy the
   Kid*
Everitt, David   1987

The Story of the Sundance Kid
Everitt, David   1988

Storyville
Battle, Lois   377

The Strand
Rayner, Claire   5269

Strange Adventure of Jonathan Drew
Ward, Christopher   6562

The Strange Brigade
Jennings, John Edward   3209

The Strange Case of Deacon Brodie
Bramble, Forbes   646

The Strange Case of Madamoiselle P.
Ireland, Patrick   3109

Strange Company
Conley, Robert J.   1251

The Strange Death of Mistress Coffin
Begiebing, Robert J.   415

*Strange Devices of the Sun and
   Moon*
Goldstein, Lisa   2463

The Strange Files of Fremont Jones
Day, Dianne   1544

Strange Meeting
Hill, Susan   2952

Strange Wives
Barker, Shirley   317

Stranger at the Wedding
Lynch, Frances   3934

Stranger at Wildings
Brent, Madeleine   663

The Stranger From the Sea
Graham, Winston   2530

Stranger in Savannah
Price, Eugenia   5187

Stranger in Two Worlds
Clevely, Hugh   1111

The Stranger Prince
Irwin, Margaret   3122

Stranger's Forest
Hill, Pamela   2943

The Strangers on the Island
Whitlock, Brand   6714

The Strangled Queen
Druon, Maurice   1737

The Stranglers
Estleman, Loren D.   1978

Strathgallant
Black, Laura   523

The Straw Man
Giono, Jean   2425

The Street of Kings
Dexter, Charles   1637

Street of the Madwoman
Ortega, Isabel   4756

*Street of the Sandalmakers: A Tale of
   Rome in the Time of Marcus
   Aurelius*
Peterson, Nis   4977

The Street Sparrows
Ayers, Rose   249

Streets of Laredo
McMurtry, Larry   4300

The Strenuous Life
Alexander, Lawrence   84

The Stress of Her Regard
Powers, Tim   5157

Strife Before Dawn
Schumann, Mary   5675

Strong as Death
Newman, Sharan   4602

The Strong Men
Brick, John   677

The Strong Room
Wheelwright, Jere Hungerford   6671

Stronghold
Chidsey, Donald Barr   1065

The Stuart Legacy
Kerr, Robert   3472

The Stuart Women
Braun, Matt   652

The Stubborn Heart
Slaughter, Frank G.   5904

The Stuff of Heroes
Delibes, Miguel   1592

Stuyvesant Square
Lewerth, Margaret   3743

Subaltern's Choice
MacNeil, Duncan   4020

Success to the Brave
Kent, Alexander   3441

*The Succession: A Novel of Elizabeth
   and James*
Garrett, George   2302

Sudden Country
Estleman, Loren D.   1979

A Sudden, Fearful Death
Perry, Anne   4938

The Sugar Pavilion
Laker, Rosalind   3600

Sultana
Michael, Prince of Greece   4358

The Summer Day Is Done
Stevens, R.T.   6001

The Summer of Jack London
Fenady, Andrew J.   2058

The Summer of the Bashinskeys
Pearson, Diane   4877

The Summer of the Danes
Peters, Ellis   4973

The Summer of the Royal Visit
Colegate, Isabel   1199

The Summer Queen
Graham, Alice Walworth   2512

Summer Thunder
Ethridge, Willie Snow   1982

Summoned to Darkness
Sheridan, Anne-Marie   5809

*The Sun, He Dies: A Novel about the
   End of the Aztec World*
Highwater, Jamake   2919

The Sun in Splendour
Plaidy, Jean   5066

The Sun Is God
Noonan, Michael   4636

The Sun Is My Undoing
Steen, Marguerite 5988

The Sun Shines West
Schachner, Nathan 5632

Sunflower
Landis, Jill Marie 3653

The Sunken Treasure
Jackson, Marian J.A. 3136

The Sunne in Splendour
Penman, Sharon Kay 4907

Sunrise to Sunset
Adams, Samuel Hopkins 32

Sunset
Nicole, Christopher 4623

Sunset at Noon
Oliver, Jane 4728

Sunshine and Shadow
Van-Loon, Antonia 6426

The Sunshine Patriot: A Novel of
    Benedict Arnold
Partington, Norman 4822

Superstition Corner
Kaye-Smith, Sheila 3379

Supper at the Maxwell House
Crabb, Alfred Leland 1407

The Surgeon's Mate
O'Brian, Patrick 4674

Surprise
Burland, Brian 785

Surrender
Quick, Amanda 5221

The Surveyor
Nelson, Truman 4583

The Sutburys
Hill, Pamela 2944

The Swamp Fox, Francis Marion
Gerson, Noel B. 2383

The Swan and the Rose
Leary, Francis W. 3697

The Swan of Usk
Ashton, Helen 220

Swandowne
Farson, Daniel 2024

Swan's Chance
De Blasis, Celeste 1549

Swear by Apollo
Barker, Shirley 318

The Swedish Cavalier
Perutz, Leo 4943

The Swedish Nightingale: Jenny Lind
Kyle, Elizabeth 3571

Sweet Adelaide
Symons, Julian 6152

Sweet Lass of Richmond Hill
Plaidy, Jean 5067

Sweet Marie-Antoinette
Prole, Lozania 5198

Sweet Mountain Magic
Bittner, Rosanne 516

Sweet Ransom
Madl, Linda 4026

Sweet Songbird
Crane, Teresa 1418

Sweet Will
Malpass, Eric 4050

Sweet's Folly
Hill, Fiona 2926

The Sweetwater
Rikhoff, Jean 5333

Sweetwater Fever
Adelman, Robert H. 36

Swift Rivers
Meigs, Cornelia 4328

Swing, Swing Together
Lovesey, Peter 3915

The Sword and the Flame
Hill, Pamela 2945

The Sword and the Promise
Siegel, Benjamin 5845

The Sword and the Sun: The Story of
    the Spanish Civil Wars in Peru
Green, Gerald 2566

Sword at Sunset
Sutcliff, Rosemary 6125

The Sword of General Englund
Honig, Donald 3023

Sword of Glory
Danielson, Peter 1477

The Sword of Hachiman
Guest, Lynn 2608

The Sword of Il Grande
Creed, Will 1424

Sword of Pleasure: Being the
    Memoirs of the Most Illustrious
    Lucius Cornelius Sulla
Green, Peter 2571

The Sword of the Golem
Rothberg, Abraham 5509

The Sword of Truth
Morris, Gilbert 4472

Sword of Vengeance
Newcomb, Kerry 4593

Swords Against Carthage
Donauer, Friedrich 1689

Swords in the North
Anderson, Paul Lewis 138

Swords of Anjou
Pei, Mario 4890

The Swords of December
York, Robert 6933

Swords of Steel
Singmaster, Elsie 5870

Sybille
Meade, Marion 4318

Sycamore Men
Taylor, David 6181

Sylvester; or, The Wicked Uncle
Heyer, Georgette 2904

Sylvia's Lovers
Gaskell, Elizabeth 2312

T

Table in the Wilderness
Parker, Norton S. 4806

Tables of the Law
Mann, Thomas 4067

Tacey Cromwell
Richter, Conrad 5324

Tai-Pan
Clavell, James 1102

Taiko
Yoshikawa, Eiji 6936

Take Heed of Loving Me: A Novel
    about John Donne
Vining, Elizabeth Gray 6502

Take Her, Mr. Wesley
Drakeford, John W. 1719

Takers of the City
Hays, Hoffman Reynolds 2800

A Tale for Midnight
Prokosch, Frederic 5195

A Tale of the Wind: A Novel of
    Nineteenth-Century France
Smith, Kay Nolte 5922

A Tale of Two Cities
Dickens, Charles 1642

Tale of Valor
Fisher, Vardis 2112

The Tales of Jacob
Mann, Thomas 4068

Taliesin
Lawhead, Stephen R. 3683

The Talisman
Scott, Sir Walter 5708

The Talisman Ring
Heyer, Georgette 2905

The Talking Pictures Murder Case
Baxt, George 388

The Talking Rifle
Vernam, Glenn R. 6454

The Tall One
Jefferis, Barbara 3175

Tall Ships to Cathay
Augur, Helen 240

The Tall Stones
Caldecott, Moyra 848

The Tall Woman
Dykeman, Wilma 1819

Talleyman
James, John 3161

Tallien: A Brief Romance
Tuten, Frederic 6370

The Tallulah Bankhead Murder Case
Baxt, George 389

Talons of Eagles
Johnstone, William W. 3268

Tamar
Chamberlin, Ann 975

Tamarack Tree
Breslin, Howard 670

The Taming
Deveraux, Jude 1633

The Taming of Annabelle
Chesney, Marion 1052

Tamsen
Galloway, David 2273

Tamzen
Rushing, Jane Gilmore 5530

Tansy Taniard
Strode-Jackson, Myrtle 6084

Taos
Blacker, Irwin R. 527

Tap Roots
Street, James H. 6080

A Tapestry of Murders
Grace, C.L. 2510

Tara Kane
Markstein, George 4091

Taras Bulba
Gogol, Nikolai V. 2451

Tarnished Angel
Leonard, Phyllis 3723

Tascosa Gun: The Story of Jim East
Shelton, Gene 5803

Tassels on Her Boots
Train, Arthur Cheney 6313

Taste of Glory
Beals, Carleton 394

The Taste of Time
Egan, Ferol 1892

Tatham Mound
Anthony, Piers 169

Tavern in the Town
Matschat, Cecile Hulse 4187

The Taverners' Place
Trollope, Joanna 6351

A Tear for Judas
Blythe, LeGette 559

The Tears of the Madonna
Herman, George 2862

Tell Me a Tale: A Novel of the Old
    South
McEachin, James 4266

Tell Your Sons: A Novel of the
    Napoleonic Era
Gibbs, Willa 2402

Telluride
Schofield, Susan Clark 5648

Tempered Blade
Barrett, Monte 352

The Tempestuous Petticoat
Gibbs, Mary Ann 2397

Temple Bells
McEvoy, Marjorie 4271

The Temple of the Muses
Roberts, John Maddox 5382

The Temple of the Sun
Caldecott, Moyra 849

The Temptation of Angelique
Golon, Sergeanne 2473

Tempting Fate
Yarbro, Chelsea Quinn 6906

The Ten-Day Queen
Prole, Lozania 5199

Ten Years Beyond Baker Street
Van Ash, Cay 6400

Tenants of the Earth
Paretti, Sandra 4793

The Tenants of Time
Flanagan, Thomas 2120

Tenderfoot
Thompson, David 6259

Tenderloin
Adams, Samuel Hopkins 33

Tennessee!
Ross, Dana Fuller 5489

Tennessee Hazard
Chapman, Maristan 994

Tennessee Smith
Hitt, James E. 2957

The Tent of Orange Mist
West, Paul 6636

The Tenth Measure
Segal, Brenda Lesley 5721

The Tentmaker
Berstl, Julius 486

Teresa, or Her Demon Lover
Gray, Austin K. 2554

The Terrible Teague Bunch
Jennings, Gary 3197

Tessa d'Arblay
Macdonald, Malcolm 3974

The Testament of Theophilus
Wibberley, Leonard 6730

Testimony of Two Men
Caldwell, Taylor 863

The Teutonic Knights
Sienkiewicz, Henryk 5849

Teverton Hall
Gillespie, Jane 2421

Texas
Michener, James A. 4375

Texas!
Ross, Dana Fuller 5490

Thaddeus of Warsaw
Porter, Jane 5136

Thanksgiving
Coleman, Terry 1207

That Bennington Mob
Safford, Henry Barnard 5558

That Callahan Spunk!
Ames, Francis 124

That Dark and Bloody River
Eckert, Allen W. 1845

That Egyptian Woman
Gerson, Noel B. 2384

That Far Paradise
Markey, Gene 4088

That Skipper From Stonington
Kenyon, Theda 3464

That Spanish Woman
Kenyon, F.W. 3461

That Sweet and Savage Land
Drummond, Emma 1728

That Vanderbilt Woman
Van Rensselaer, Philip 6427

That's Me in the Middle
Jack, Donald 3129

Their Fathers' God
Rolvaag, O.E. 5436

Their Most Serene Majesties
Vlachos, Ange 6505

Theirs Was the Kingdom
Delderfield, R.F. 1590

Then and Now
Maugham, William Somerset 4198

Theo and Matilda
Billington, Rachel 498

Theodora
Edwards, Samuel 1891

Theodora and the Emperor
Lamb, Harold 3608

Theory of War
Brady, Joan 637

There Is a Season
Colver, Alice Mary 1219

There Was a Season: A Biographical Novel of Jefferson Davis
Olsen, Theodore 4730

These Latter Days
Kalpakian, Laura 3330

These Old Shades
Heyer, Georgette 2906

These Thousand Hills
Guthrie, A.B. Jr. 2627

These Were the Brontes
Cornish, Dorothy Helen 1332

They Are Coming: The Conquest of Mexico
Lopez Portillo y Pacheco, Jose 3896

They Called Her Mrs. Doc
Oke, Janette 4709

They Came to a Valley
Gulick, Bill 2618

They Had a Glory
Steward, Davenport 6018

They Seek a Country
Young, Francis Brett 6941

They Were Dreamers
Murphy, James F. Jr. 4525

Thief of My Heart
Becnel, Rexanne 410

The Thieftaker
Jeffreys, J.G. 3180

Thin Moon and Cold Mist
Gear, Kathleen O'Neal 2330

Thine Is the Glory
Schreiner, Samuel A. Jr. 5672

The Thing about Clarissa
Cook, Roberta St. Clair 1264

Things Fall Apart
Achebe, Chinua 16

Think Fast, Mr. Peters
Kaminsky, Stuart M. 3347

The Third George
Plaidy, Jean 5068

The Third Sister
Barrett, Julia 351

The Thirteen Gun Salute
O'Brian, Patrick 4675

This Bright Sword
Chidsey, Donald Barr 1066

This Dark Monarchy
Leary, Francis W. 3698

This Is the House
Hill, Deborah 2921

This January Tale
Bryher 747

This Land Fulfilled
Brady, Charles Andrew 636

This Land I Hold
Myers, Virginia 4550

This Land Is Mine
Kerns, Frances Casey 3470

This Land Is Ours
Zara, Louis 6953

This Old Bill
Estleman, Loren D. 1980

This One's on Me
Jack, Donald 3130

This Other Eden
Harris, Marilyn 2733

This Promised Land
Easton, Robert 1824

This Savage Race
Jones, Douglas C. 3285

This Splendid Earth
Banis, V.J. 289

This Sweet and Bitter Earth
Cordell, Alexander 1326

This Widowed Land
Gear, Kathleen O'Neal 2331

This Willing Passion
Cloud, Patricia 1132

The Thistle and the Rose
Plaidy, Jean 5069

The Thistlewood Plot
Jeffreys, J.G. 3181

Thomas: A Novel of the Life, Passions, and Miracles of Becket
Mydans, Shelley 4538

Thomas Forty
Stanley, Edward 5982

The Thomas Street Horror
Paul, Raymond 4843

The Thorn of Arimathea
Slaughter, Frank G. 5905

Those the Sun Has Loved
Jourdain, Rose 3309

Those Who Go Against the Current
Seifert, Shirley 5734

Those Who Love
Stone, Irving 6064

The Thousand Fires
Powers, Anne 5155

A Thousand Shall Fall
Thoene, Bodie 6227

Thousand Years of Gold
McCunn, Ruthanne Lum 4239

Thread of Scarlet
Williams, Ben Ames 6767

The Three Black Pennys
Hergesheimer, Joseph 2855

Three Came to Ville Marie
Sullivan, Alan 6114

Three Cheers for Me
Jack, Donald 3131

The Three-Cornered Hat
Alarcon, Pedro Antonio de 62

The Three Crowns
Plaidy, Jean 5070

Three Days
Longstreet, Stephen 3891

The Three Days
Robertson, Don 5402

Three Fields to Cross
Nutt, Francis Tysen 4651

Three From Galilee: The Young Man From Nazareth
Holmes, Marjorie 3004

Three Harbors
Mason, F. van Wyck 4162

Three-Headed Angel
Bradford, Roark 623

The Three Legions
Solon, Gregory 5941

The Three Lives of Elizabeth
Seifert, Shirley 5735

The Three Musketeers
Dumas, Alexandre 1782

Three Rivers
Mills, Carla J. 4406

Three Roads to Valhalla
Stewart, Catherine Pomeroy 6022

Three Ships and Three Kings
Sallaska, Georgia 5573

Three Sides of Agiochook
Kelly, Eric 3400

Three Years to Play
MacInnes, Colin 3983

Three's Company
Duggan, Alfred 1774

Threescore and Ten
Allen, Walter 105

Threshold of Fire
Haasse, Hella S. 2633

Throne of Isis
Tarr, Judith 6170

Throne of the World
De Wohl, Louis 1575

Through a Glass Darkly
Koen, Karleen 3531

Through a Gold Eagle
Monfredo, Miriam Grace 4430

Through the Green Valley
Gowdy, Barbara 2498

Thunder Before Seven
Brand, Anna 648

Thunder in the Dawn
Murray, Earl 4532

Thunder in the East
Roarke, Mike 5362

Thunder in the Sky
Sarabande, William 5602

Thunder in the Wilderness
Hamilton, Charles Granville 2668

Thunder on St. Paul's Day
Lane, Jane 3658

Thunder on the Chesapeake
Divine, David 1650

Thunder on the Plains
Bittner, Rosanne 517

Thunder on the River
Laird, Charlton 3590

Thunderstick
Coldsmith, Don 1190

Thy Tears Might Cease
Farrell, Michael 2018

Tiberius: The Memoirs of the Emperor
Massie, Allan 4169

The Tick of Death
Lovesey, Peter 3916

Tide of Empire
Baldwin, Bates 279
Kyne, Peter S. 3572

Tide-Rode
Bushnell, Adelyn 813

The Tides of Dawn
Mally, Emma Louise 4044

The Tides of Malvern
Griswold, Francis 2595

Tidewater
Dowdey, Clifford 1709

Tidewater Dynasty: A Biographical Novel of the Lees of Stratford Hall
Roberts, Carey 5372

Tie My Bones to Her Back
Jones, Robert F. 3294

Tigerlilies
Glover, Judith 2439

Tikal: A Novel about the Maya
Peters, Daniel 4947

Till the Day Goes Down
Lennox-Smith, Judith 3719

Till the End of Time
Appel, Allen 170

Tilly
Cookson, Catherine 1288

Tilly Alone
Cookson, Catherine 1289

Tilly Wed
Cookson, Catherine 1290

Time After Time
Alexander, Karl 80
Appel, Allen 171

Time and Again
Finney, Jack 2093

Time and Chance
Davenport, Gwen 1501
Wibberley, Anna 6728

Time and the Wind
Verissimo, Erico 6451

A Time for Judas
Callaghan, Morley 866

Time for Outrage
Bean, Amelia 397

A Time for Silence
Carr, Philippa 930

A Time for the Death of a King
Dukthas, Ann 1777

A Time for Titans
Delmar, Vina 1602

Time in Its Flight
Schaeffer, Susan Fromberg 5636

A Time in the Sun
Barry, Jane 361

Time of Drums
Ehle, John 1897

The Time of Murder at Mayerling
Dukthas, Ann 1778

Time of Parting
Donchev, Anton 1690

The Time of the Dragon
Eden, Dorothy 1863

The Time of the Hunter's Moon
Holt, Victoria 3022

Time of the Unicorn
Jefferis, Barbara 3176

Time out of Mind
Field, Rachel 2081

The Time Returns
Ripley, Alexandra 5343

Time to Depart
Davis, Lindsey 1533

The Timeless Land
Dark, Eleanor 1495

Time's Fool
Veryan, Patricia 6479

Timothy Baines
Culp, John H. 1445

Timothy Larkin
Hutchens, Jane 3089

The Tin Drum
Grass, Gunther 2540

The Tin Lizzie Troup
Swarthout, Glendon 6146

Tincture of Death
Harrison, Ray 2745

Tish
Miller, Cissie 4381

The Titans
Jakes, John 3154

Titian
Cecchi, Dario 965

To Appomattox: Nine April Days, 1865
Davis, Burke 1512

To Be a King
DeMaria, Robert 1607

To Build a Ship
Berry, Don 482

To Dance with Kings
Laker, Rosalind 3601

To Fame Unknown
Alderman, Clifford Lindsey 67

To Fell the Giants
Hotchkiss, Bill 3038

To Glory We Steer
Kent, Alexander 3442

To Have and to Hold
Johnston, Mary 3241

To Heaven on Horseback
Cranston, Paul F. 1419

To Keep This Oath
Weenolsen, Hebe 6597

To Keep Us Free
Allis, Marguerite 115

To Lie with Lions
Dunnett, Dorothy 1810

To Love a Queen
Schoonover, Lawrence 5669

To Love a Stranger
Paul, Barbara 4839

To Love Again
Small, Bertrice 5913

To Make a Killing
Conley, Robert J. 1252

To See Your Face Again
Price, Eugenia 5188

To Seize a Dream
Hersch, Virginia Davis 2866

To Seize the Passing Dream
Berkman, Ted 479

To Serve Them All My Days
Delderfield, R.F. 1591

To Spit Against the Wind
Levin, Benjamin H. 3737

To the End of Her Days
Macdonald, Malcolm 3975

To the End of the World
White, Helen Constance 6680

To the Ends of the Earth
Talbot, Michael 6155

To the Far Blue Mountains
L'Amour, Louis 3630

To the Honor of the Fleet
Pilpel, Robert H. 5002

To the Indies
Forester, C.S. 2183

To the Land of the Cattails
Appelfeld, Aharon 179

To the Swift
Hawkins, Anne 2783

A Toast to the King
Coatsworth, Elizabeth 1139

Toil of the Brave
Fletcher, Inglis 2141

The Tokaido Road: A Novel of Feudal Japan
Robson, Lucia St. Clair 5417

A Token of Jewels
Cory, Diane 1353

Tolbecken
Shellabarger, Samuel 5798

The Toll-Gate
Heyer, Georgette 2907

Tom Burke of Ours
Lever, Charles James 3732

Tom Mix and Pancho Villa
Irving, Clifford 3113

Tom Mix Died for Your Sins
Ponicsan, Darryl 5090

Tomahawk
Porter, Donald Clayton 5129

Tomahawk Revenge
Thompson, David 6260

Tombstone Showdown
Scott, Leslie 5681

Tomorrow Is Another Day
Kaminsky, Stuart M. 3348

Tomorrow the Harvest
Paradise, Viola 4789

Tomorrow the New Moon
Barker, Shirley 319

Tomorrow We Reap
Street, James H. 6081

Tomorrow's Dream
Hanchar, Peggy 2674

Tomorrow's Fire
Williams, Jay 6775

The Tontine
Costain, Thomas B. 1371

Too Late! Too Late! The Maiden Cried
Fleming, Joan 2128

Too Long a Stranger
Oke, Janette 4710

Too Long at the Dance
Blakely, Mike 539

Too Near the Throne
Haycraft, Molly Costain 2797

Topaz
Ashfield, Helen 215

Torbeg
Campbell, Grace 873

The Torch
Penfield, Wilder 4902

Torn Covenants
Swann, Lois 6136

Torquemada
Fast, Howard 2045

Torsos
Cooke, John Peyton 1270

Tory Tavern
Safford, Henry Barnard 5559

Touch and Go
Parkinson, C. Northcote 4815

Touched with Fire
Tebbel, John William 6195

Tournament of the Shadows
Carnac, Nicholas 901

Toward the Morning
Allen, Hervey 101

The Tower and the Dream
Westcott, Jan 6647

The Tower of Beowulf
Godwin, Parke 2450

The Tower of London
Ainsworth, William Harrison 58

Towers in the Mist
Goudge, Elizabeth 2495

The Towers of Silence
Scott, Paul 5685

The Town
Richter, Conrad 5325

The Town House
Lofts, Norah 3861

TR
Gerson, Noel B. 2385

Track of the Bear
Coldsmith, Don 1191

Tracker
Wagoner, David 6521

Trade Imperial
Lloyd, Alan 3814

Trade Wind
Kaye, M.M. 3378

A Tradition of Victory
Kent, Alexander 3443

**The Tragedy at Tinkerton: An
  Historical Novel of Murder**
Paul, Raymond 4844

**Trail and Triumph: A Novel about
  Maimonides**
Morrison, Lester M. 4485

Trail From Taos
Coldsmith, Don 1192

Trail-Makers of the Middle Border
Garland, Hamlin 2296

A Trail of Blood
Potter, Jeremy 5143

Trail of Tears
Forrest, Williams 2187
Statham, Frances Patton 5983

Trail of the Spanish Bit
Coldsmith, Don 1193

**Trail: The Story of the Lewis and
  Clark Expedition**
Charbonneau, Louis 998

The Trail to Ogallala
Capps, Benjamin 889

Trail's End
Bean, Fred 400

The Train at Bundarbar
MacNeil, Duncan 4021

The Traitor
Sherman, Dan 5814

The Traitors
Long, William Stuart 3879

Traitors Gate
Perry, Anne 4939

Traitor's Moon
Neill, Robert 4574

The Traitors of Bosworth
Farrington, Robert 2021

Trapper's Blood
Thompson, David 6261

Trapper's Moon
Sherman, Jory 5823

Trask
Berry, Don 483

Travail and Triumph
Phillips, Michael 4991

Traveller
Adams, Richard 27

Treason
Gessner, Robert 2389

Treason's Gift
Belle, Pamela 434

Treason's Harbour
O'Brian, Patrick 4676

Treasure in Hell's Canyon
Gulick, Bill 2619

Treasure Island
Stevenson, Robert Louis 6012

Treasure Mountain
L'Amour, Louis 3631

The Treasure of Pleasant Valley
Yerby, Frank 6928

The Treasure of the Chisos
Culp, John H. 1446

Treasures on Earth
Stirling, Jessica 6049

Tree of Gold
Laker, Rosalind 3602

The Tree of Knowledge
Figes, Eva 2085

The Tree of Liberty
Page, Elizabeth 4773

The Tree of Life
Nissenson, Hugh 4629

The Trees
Richter, Conrad 5326

The Trees of the Folkungs
Heidenstam, Verner Von 2817

Tregaran
Lide, Mary 3779

The Trembling Earth
Van Every, Dale 6411

The Trevarton Inheritance
Macdonald, Malcolm 3976

**The Trial of Elizabeth Cree: A Novel
  of the Limehouse Murders**
Ackroyd, Peter 21

The Trial of Jenny Sykes
Weenolsen, Hebe 6598

The Trial of Mary Todd Lincoln
Rhodes, James A. 5309

Tricolour
Logan, Mark 3866

Trinity
Uris, Leon 6394

The Trip to Jerusalem
Marston, Edward 4129

Triptych
Landey, Dora 3652

Tristram Bent
Safford, Henry Barnard 5560

The Triton Brig
Pope, Dudley 5110

The Triumph
Gann, Ernest K. 2280

Triumph of the Lion
Danielson, Peter 1478

The Trojan
Gerson, Noel B. 2386

**The Trojan Generals Talk: Memoirs
  of the Greek War**
Parotti, Phillip 4818

Tros of Samothrace
Mundy, Talbot 4515

The Troubadour's Romance
Carr, Robyn 940

Trouble Shooter
Haycox, Ernest 2791

Troubled Border
Allen, T.D. 104

Troubled Spring
Brick, John 678

Troubles
Farrell, J.G. 2017

Troy
Matturro, Richard 4194

Troy Chimneys
Kennedy, Margaret 3421

True Crime
Collins, Max Allan 1214

The True Cross
Scarfoglio, Carlo 5629

True Detective
Collins, Max Allan 1215

True Grit
Portis, Charles 5139

**The True Memoirs of Charley
  Blankenship**
Capps, Benjamin 890

True Thomas
Tranter, Nigel 6322

True Women
Windle, Janice Woods 6820

The Truelove
O'Brian, Patrick 4677

The Truest Pleasure
Morgan, Robert 4452

The Trumpet and the Sword
Danielson, Peter 1479

Trumpet at the Gate
Widgery, Jan 6739

Trumpet in the Sky
Miller, Helen Topping 4397

Trumpet in the Wilderness
Harper, Robert S. 2717

The Trumpet Major
Hardy, Thomas 2700

The Trumpet of God
Duncan, David 1784

Trumpet on the Land
Johnston, Terry C. 3260

Trumpet to Arms
Lancaster, Bruce 3647

Trumpeter, Sound!
Murray, D.L. 4528

Trumpets at Dawn
Harris, Cyril 2719

Trumpets Calling
Aydelotte, Dora 248

Trumpets of Silver
Harris, Norma 2735

Trumpets Sound No More
Mason, F. van Wyck 4163

Trust and Treason
Birkhead, Margaret 506

Tsar's Woman
Hill, Pamela 2946

Tudor Agent
Farrington, Robert 2022

The Tudor Rose
Barnes, Margaret Campbell 329

Tudor Underground
Meadows, Denis 4320

The Tune That They Play
Clive, William 1120

Turn Back the River
Hardy, W.G. 2703

Turn of the Dice
Edmonds, Janet 1870

The Turning Wheels
Cloete, Stuart 1127

The Turquoise Trail
Seifert, Shirley 5736

The Twelfth Physician
Gibbs, Willa 2403

The Twelfth Transforming
Gedge, Pauline 2347

The Twelve Pictures
Simon, Edith 5857

Twenty Years After
Dumas, Alexandre 1783

Twice upon a Time
Appel, Allen 172

Twilight of Empire
Eckert, Allen W. 1846

Twilight of the Dawn
Dubus, Elizabeth Nell 1752

Twilight of the Dragon
Bourne, Peter 596

The Twilighters
Loomis, Noel M. 3894

The Twisted Saber: A Biographical Novel of Benedict Arnold
Vail, Philip 6398

The Twisted Sword
Graham, Winston 2531

The Twisted Tendril
Glasgow, Alice 2427

Two Corinthians
Dunn, Carola 1797

Two Crowns for America
Kurtz, Katherine 3568

The Two Farms
Pearce, Mary E. 4865

Two From Galilee: A Love Story
Holmes, Marjorie 3005

The Two-Headed Eagle
Biggins, John 493

Two Loves Have I
Chambrun, Clara Longworth de 985

The Two Medicine River
Wheeler, Richard S. 6663

Two of a Kind: An English Trifle
Edghill, Rosemary 1867

Two Ravens
Holland, Cecelia 2997

Two Thieves
Komroff, Manuel 3535

The Tynedale Daughters
Clark, Norma Lee 1093

The Tyrant
Veryan, Patricia 6480

The Tyrant of Bagdhad
Pierce, Glenn 4996

Tyrone of Kentucky
McMeekin, Clark 4294

Tzili: The Story of a Life
Appelfeld, Aharon 180

U

The Ugly Duchess
Feuchtwanger, Lion 2075

Ulverton
Thorpe, Adam 6278

Ulysses: A Biographical Novel
Skimin, Robert 5878

The Unanointed
Chinn, Laurene 1070

Uncharted Ways
Snedeker, Caroline 5935

The Unconquered
Swanson, Neil Harmon 6142
Williams, Ben Ames 6768

The Uncrowned King
Orczy, Baroness Emma 4747

Under the Fifth Sun: A Novel of Pancho Villa
Shorris, Earl 5832

Under the Winter Moon
Brooke, Teresa 705

Under Two Flags
Ouida 4767

The Undiscovered Country
Walz, Jay 6560

Uneasy Lies the Head
Plaidy, Jean 5071

An Unequal Marriage; or Pride and Prejudice Twenty Years Later
Tennant, Emma 6202

The Unforgiven
Le May, Alan 3692

The Ungodly: A Novel of the Donner Party
Rhodes, Richard 5311

An Unholy Alliance
Gregory, Susanna 2586

The Unholy Pilgrim
Tapsell, R.F. 6161

The Unhurrying Chase
Prescott, H.F.M. 5172

The Unicorn Hunt
Dunnett, Dorothy 1811

Unicorn Rampant
Tranter, Nigel 6323

The Union Belle
Morris, Gilbert 4473

Union Square
Tax, Meredith 6176

The Unknown Ajax
Heyer, Georgette 2908

The Unknown Shore
O'Brian, Patrick 4678

An Unknown Welshman
Stubbs, Jean 6100

The Unplowed Sky
Williams, Jeanne 6783

The Unspeakables: A Tale of Lombardy
Gay, Laverne 2326

The Unsuitable Miss Pelham
Drummond, June 1730

An Untamed Land
Snelling, Lauraine 5936

The Unterrified
Robertson, Constance 5397

Until the Colors Fade
Jeal, Tim 3173

Until the End
Coyle, Harold 1396

Until the Sun Falls
Holland, Cecelia 2998

Until the Winds
Clark, Jean 1089

Unto a Good Land
Moberg, Vilhelm 4425

Unto the Soul
Appelfeld, Aharon 181

Unto This Hour
Wicker, Tom 6733

Untold Glory
O'Neal, Cothburn 4739

The Unvanquished
Fast, Howard 2046
Faulkner, William 2050

Unvexed to the Sea: A Novel of the Vicksburg Campaign
Morrison, Gerry 4484

The Unwritten Chronicles of Robert E. Lee
Herrin, Lamar 2864

Up Country: A Story of the Vanguard
Peattie, Donald Culross 4881

Up She Rises
Garnett, David 2298

Upon This Rock: A Novel of Simon Peter, Prince of Apostles
Slaughter, Frank G. 5906

Upon This Rock: The Life of St. Peter
Murphy, Walter F. 4526

Upstairs Downstairs
Hawkesworth, John 2782

The Upstart
Marshall, Edison 4112

"Utmost Fish!"
McCann, Hugh Wray 4219

Utrillo's Mother
Baylis, Sarah 391

V

Vagabond Prophet
Symons, Allene 6149

El Vago
Gonzales, Laurence 2474

Vain Shadow
Spence, Hartzell 5962

Vale of Tyranny
Butler, Suzanne 831

Valentina
Anthony, Evelyn 165

The Valiant
Byrd, Sigman 839

The Valiant and the Daunted
Clews, Roy 1115

The Valiant Gunman
Morris, Gilbert 4474

The Valiant Lady
Knight, Brigid 3523

Valiant Libertine
Bryson, John Gordon 748

The Valiant Sailors
Stuart, Vivian 6090

The Valiant Virginians
Bellah, James Warner 427

Valide: A Novel of the Harem
Chase-Riboud, Barbara 1007

The Valley
Irving, Clifford 3114

Valley Forge
Kantor, MacKinlay 3364

Valley in Arms: A Novel of the Settlement of Connecticut
Miers, Earl Schenck 4376

The Valley of Decision
Wharton, Edith 6653

Valley of Eagles
Allen, Dexter 96

The Valley of God
Patai, Irene Steinman 4825

The Valley of Horses
Auel, Jean M. 239

Valley of the Shadow
Warren, Charles Marquis 6570

The Valley of Vision: A Novel of King Solomon and His Time
Fisher, Vardis 2113

The Vandal
O'Connor, Richard 4687

Vandemark's Folly
Quick, Herbert 5223

Vanessa
Walpole, Hugh 6548

Vanity Fair
Thackeray, William Makepeace 6213

Vardy
Harris, John 2721

The Vast Memory of Love
Bosse, Malcolm 588

The Veil of Illusion
Ryman, Rebecca 5545

A Vein of Riches
Knowles, John 3526

The Velvet Doublet
Street, James H. 6082

The Velvet Horn
Lytle, Andrew 3946

La Vendee
Trollope, Anthony 6346

Venetia
Heyer, Georgette 2909

The Venetian
Weiss, David 6611

The Venetian Mask
Laker, Rosalind 3603

Venetian Masque
Sabatini, Rafael 5556

Vengeance of the Lion
Danielson, Peter 1480

The Vengeance Trail of Josey Wales
Carter, Forrest 946

Venture in the East
Lancaster, Bruce 3648

Venture Once More
Graham, Winston 2532

Venus in Copper
Davis, Lindsey 1534

The Venus Throw
Saylor, Steven 5627

The Veracruz Blues
Winegardner, Mark 6821

Verge of Glory
Wight, Frederick 6747

The Vermilion Bridge
Mydans, Shelley 4539

Veronique
Coffman, Virginia 1158

Version and Diversion
Terry, Judith 6207

The Very Best People
Villars, Elizabeth 6499

The Very Rich Hours of Count von Stauffenberg
West, Paul 6637

A Very Small Remnant
Straight, Michael Whitney 6075

Very Young Mrs. Poe
O'Neal, Cothburn 4740

The Vesey Inheritance
Butler, Gwendoline 822

Vice Avenged: A Moral Tale
Burford, Lolah 774

The Viceroy of Ouidah
Chatwin, Bruce C. 1009

Victim of the Aurora
Keneally, Thomas 3417

Victoire
Darcy, Clare 1493

Victoria and Albert
Anthony, Evelyn 166

Victoria in the Wings
Plaidy, Jean 5072

Victoria Victorious
Plaidy, Jean 5073

Victory at Sebastopol
Stuart, Vivian 6091

Vienna Prelude
Thoene, Bodie 6228

The View From Coyaba
Abrahams, Peter 11

Vigilante
Summers, Richard 6116

The Viking
Marshall, Edison 4113

A Viking's Daughter
Andrews, John 147

The Viking's Woman
Graham, Heather 2520

The Villains: A Haunting Tale of the Marshes
Keppel, Charlotte 3467

Vincent: A Novel Based on the Life of Van Gogh
Poldermans, Joost 5082

Vindication
Sherwood, Frances 5824

The Vines of Yarrabee
Eden, Dorothy 1864

Viola Gwyn
McCutcheon, George Barr 4258

Violent Friends
Clewes, Winston 1113

The Virgin in the Ice
Peters, Ellis 4974

The Virginia Comedians
Cooke, John Esten 1269

A Virginia Scout
Pendexter, Hugh 4899

The Virginians
Thackeray, William Makepeace 6214

The Vision Is Fulfilled
McDonald, Kay L. 4262

A Vision of Light
Riley, Judith Merkle 5337

The Vision of Stephen: An Elegy
Burford, Lolah 775

Vision of the Eagle
McDonald, Kay L. 4263

Visions of a Heart
Carmichael, Emily 899

A Visit to Highbury
Austen-Leigh, Joan 243

Vittoria
Merle, Robert 4342

The Vivian Inheritance
Stubbs, Jean 6101

The Vixens
Yerby, Frank 6929

The Voice and the Light
Fadiman, Edwin 1995

A Voice in the Streets
Tebbel, John William 6196

The Voice of Allah
Hoyt, Edwin P. 3062

Voice of the Eagle
Shuler, Linda Lay 5839

Voices in a Haunted Room
Carr, Philippa 931

The Voices of Masada
Kossoff, David 3545

The Volcano Lover
Sontag, Susan 5946

Vollands
Hill, Pamela 2947

Voltaire! Voltaire!
Endore, Guy 1943

Voodoo Dreams: A Novel of Marie Laveau
Rhodes, Jewell Parker 5310

Voss
White, Patrick 6698

Votan
James, John 3162

The Vow on the Heron
Plaidy, Jean 5074

Vows of the Peacock
Graham, Alice Walworth 2513

Voyage: A Novel of 1896
Hayden, Sterling 2798

The Voyage Home
Schnabel, Ernst 5644

The Voyage of the Destiny
Nye, Robert 4657

Voyage to Santa Fe
Giles, Janice Holt 2418

Voyage to the First of December
Carlisle, Henry 897

Voyager
Gabaldon, Diana 2265

The Voyagers
Van Every, Dale 6412

W

The Wagered Widow
Veryan, Patricia 6481

Wagons to Tucson
Newsom, Ed 4604

Wagons West
White, Leslie Turner 6692

Walford's Oak
Phillips, Jill M. 4986

Walk in My Soul
Robson, Lucia St. Clair 5418

The Walk into Morning
Herschler, Mildred Barger 2867

Walk Like a Man
Honig, Donald 3024

A Walk with Love and Death
Koning, Hans 3539

Walk with Peril
Jackson, Dorothy V.S. 3132

Walkers of the Wind
Sarabande, William 5603

The Walking Drum
L'Amour, Louis 3632

Walks in the Sun
Coldsmith, Don 1194

The Walled Orchard
Holt, Tom 3010

Wallis: The Novel
Edwards, Anne 1883

Walnut Grove
Rushing, Jane Gilmore 5531

Walt Whitman's Secret
Aronin, Ben 196

Walter Winchell: A Novel
Herr, Michael 2863

Waltzing in Ragtime
Charbonneau, Eileen 996

The Wanderer
Waltari, Mika 6556

The Wanderer: A Novel of Dante and Beatrice
Schachner, Nathan 5633

Wanderers Eastward, Wanderers West
Winsor, Kathleen 6823

The Wandering Arm
Newman, Sharan 4603

The Wandering Prince
Plaidy, Jean 5075

Wandering Star
Yount, Steven 6945

The Wanton Fires
Trevor, Meriol 6345

War and Peace
Tolstoy, Leo 6295

War and Remembrance
Wouk, Herman 6875

The War Chest
Hill, Porter 2950

War Chief
Porter, Donald Clayton 5130

War Clouds
Porter, Donald Clayton 5131

War Comes to Castle Rising
Cradock, Fanny 1411

War Cry
Porter, Donald Clayton 5132

War Drums
Porter, Donald Clayton 5133

War Eagles
Burleson, Frank 788

War in the Golden Weather
Longstreet, Stephen 3892

War Paint and Rouge
Chambers, Robert W. 983

War Story: A Novel
Robinson, Derek 5404

The War Train: A Novel of 1916
Meggs, Brown 4324

Ward of the Sun King
Butler, Mildred Allen 826

Warhorse
Cunningham, John 1451

Warlock
Hall, Oakley 2653

The Warlord
Bosse, Malcolm 589

Warm Wind, West Wind
Matthew, Anne Irwin 4188

Warrior Queen
Sinclair, James 5865

The Warriors
Jakes, John 3155

Warriors of the Night
Newcomb, Kerry 4594

The Warrior's Path
L'Amour, Louis 3633

Warsaw Requiem
Thoene, Bodie 6229

Wartime Lies
Begley, Louis 416

The Warwick Heiress
Abbey, Margaret 6

Warwyck's Woman
Laker, Rosalind 3604

Washington!
Ross, Dana Fuller 5491

Washington, D.C.
Vidal, Gore 6493

Watch for Me on the Mountain
Carter, Forrest 947

Watch for the Dawn
Cloete, Stuart 1128

Watchfires
Auchincloss, Louis 234

Water Music
Boyle, T. Coraghessan 619

Water over the Dam
Allis, Marguerite 116

The Water Witch
Cooper, James Fenimore 1311

Waterloo
Cornwell, Bernard 1350
Komroff, Manuel 3536
Smith, Frederic E. 5920

Waters of the Wilderness
Seifert, Shirley 5737

The Waterworks
Doctorow, E.L. 1659

Watery Grave
Alexander, Bruce 78

Watson's Apology
Bainbridge, Beryl 271

Wave High the Banner
Brown, Dee 714

Waverley
Scott, Sir Walter 5709

Waxwork
Lovesey, Peter 3917

The Way
Hartley, J.M. 2761

The Way of the Priests
Conley, Robert J. 1253

The Way to Fort Pillow
Sherburne, James 5807

The Way to the Lantern
Lindop, Audrey Erskine 3790

The Way West
Guthrie, A.B. Jr. 2628

The Wayfarer
Seifert, Shirley 5738

The Ways of Women
Crowley, Elaine 1436

A Wayside Tavern
Lofts, Norah 3862

We Must March: A Novel of the Winning of Oregon
Morrow, Honore 4491

We Speak No Treason
Jarman, Rosemary Hawley 3168

We Stood for Freedom
Morley, Iris 4455

Weathercock
Dodge, Constance 1668

The Weaver's Tale
Sedley, Kate 5719

The Web of Days
Lee, Edna 3708

Web of Destiny
Elwood, Muriel 1939

Web of Lucifer: A Novel of the Borgia Fury
Samuel, Maurice 5580

The Wedding Guest
Gilbert, Anna 2407

The Wedding Journey
Edmonds, Walter D. 1878

Weedy Rough
Jones, Douglas C. 3286

Weep in the Sun
Wilson, Jeanne 6809

Weep No More
Stevenson, Janet 6006

The Weeping Ash
Aiken, Joan 54

The Welcome Light
Stirling, Jessica 6050

Welcome to Hard Times
Doctorow, E.L. 1660

Well of the Silent Harp
Barke, James 304

The Wept of Wish-Ton-Wish
Cooper, James Fenimore 1312

The West End Horror
Meyer, Nicholas 4350

West Goes the Road
Pridgen, Tim 5192

West of Appomattox
Duncan, Harley 1785

West of the River
Laird, Charlton 3591

West to Eden
Goldreich, Gloria 2461

West to the Setting Sun
Chalmers, Harvey 973

West with the Vikings
Marshall, Edison 4114

Western: A Saga of the Great Plains
Yerby, Frank 6930

Western Union
Grey, Zane 2589

Westfield
Thorp, Roderick 6277

Westward!
Ross, Dana Fuller 5492

Westward Ho!
Kingsley, Charles 3499

Westward the Sun
Knight, Brigid 3524

Westward the Tide
Sinclair, Harold 5863

Westward to Laughter
MacInnes, Colin 3984

The Whales in Lake Tanganyika
Hagerfors, Lennart 2636

What Law There Was
Dempsey, Al 1609

What the Heart Keeps
Laker, Rosalind 3605

Wheels West
Croy, Homer 1438

When Christ and His Saints Slept
Penman, Sharon Kay 4908

When God Slept
Bourne, Peter 597

When Nietzsche Wept: A Novel of Obsession
Yalom, Irvin D. 6892

When the Emperor Dies
Smith, Mason McCann 5926

When the Legends Die
Borland, Hal 584

When the Lion Feeds
Smith, Wilbur 5931

When the Music Changed
Reno, Marie R. 5305

When the Owl Cries
Bartlett, Paul 367

When the War Is Over
Becker, Stephen 408

Where Glory Waits
Crownfield, Gertrude 1437

Where Is My Wandering Boy Tonight?
Wagoner, David 6522

Where Magic Dwells
Becnel, Rexanne 411

Where My Love Sleeps
Dowdey, Clifford 1710

Where Shadows Go
Price, Eugenia 5189

Where the River Runs
Wheeler, Richard S. 6664

Where the Willows Weep
Shaw, Patricia 5781

While Angels Dance
Cotton, Ralph W. 1372

While England Sleeps
Leavitt, David 3702

While Paris Danced
Wright, Patricia 6886

While Rivers Flow
Fleischmann, Glen H. 2125

While the Music Lasts
Goodwin, Suzanne 2477

While the Music Plays
Austell, Diane 242

The Whip
Cookson, Catherine 1291

Whirlwind in Petticoats
Becker, Beril 406

Whiskey River
Estleman, Loren D. 1981

Whisper of the Wolf
Johnston, Terry C. 3261

A Whisper on the Wind
Baker, Madeline 276

Whispering
Hodge, Jane Aiken 2972

A Whistle in the Wind
Culp, John H. 1447

Whistling Cat
Chambers, Robert W. 984

The White Boar
Palmer, Marian 4780

The White Cockade
Gilson, Charles James Louis 2423
Griffin, Henry Farrand 2592
O'Brien, Vincent 4683

The White Company
Doyle, Sir Arthur Conan 1716

The White Cutter
Pownall, David 5158

The White Dawn
Houston, James 3053

The White Dove
Thomas, Rosie 6246

White Eagle, Dark Skies
Karsavina, Jean 3368

The White Hotel
Thomas, D.M. 6237

The White House Pantry Murder
Roosevelt, Elliott 5457

White Indian
Porter, Donald Clayton 5134

The White King
Harrison, Samuel Bertram 2747

The White Land
Dieter, William 1643

White Man
Freuchen, Peter 2228

The White Man's Road
Capps, Benjamin 891

White Nights, Red Dawn
Nolan, Frederick 4634

The White Path
Conley, Robert J. 1254

White Poppy
Gaan, Margaret 2261

The White Queen
Fallon, Frederic 2011
Nickell, Lesley J. 4611

The White Rajah
Monsarrat, Nicholas 4433

The White Raven
Paxson, Diana L. 4847

The White Rhino Hotel
Bull, Bartle 765

White Rising
Kotker, Zane 3548

The White Rose
Westcott, Jan 6648

The White Rose Murders
Clynes, Michael 1137

The White Slave
Howe, Fanny 3059

The White Witch
Goudge, Elizabeth 2496

The Whitechapel Horrors
Hanna, Edward B. 2678

*Whittling Boy: The Story of Eli
    Whitney*
Burlingame, Roger 789

Whitton's Folly
Hill, Pamela 2948

Who Came by Night
Nicholas, Roland 4608

Who Was Then the Gentleman
Israel, Charles E. 3125

Whole Hog
Wagoner, David 6523

Whom the Gods Love
Ross, Kate 5502

Whom the Gods Would Destroy
Powell, Richard 5148

Why Kill Arthur Potter?
Harrison, Ray 2746

Why Waterloo?
Herbert, Alan Patrick 2850

The Whyte Harte
Doherty, P.C. 1681

The Wicked Day
Stewart, Mary 6033

The Wicked Godmother
Chesney, Marion 1053

Wicked Lady
Fletcher, Inglis 2142

A Wicked Way to Die
Jeffreys, J.G. 3182

The Wickedest Pilgrim
Chidsey, Donald Barr 1067

The Wide House
Caldwell, Taylor 864

Wide Is the Water
Hodge, Jane Aiken 2973

Wide Sargasso Sea
Rhys, Jean 5312

Wideacre
Gregory, Philippa 2585

The Widow of Windsor
Plaidy, Jean 5076
Whittle, Tyler 6723

Wife to Great Buckingham
Lewis, Hilda 3751

Wife to Henry V
Lewis, Hilda 3752

Wife to Mr. Milton
Graves, Robert 2553

Wife to the Bastard
Lewis, Hilda 3753

Wild Cat
Black, Laura 524

Wild Conquest
Abrahams, Peter 12

*Wild Decembers: A Biographical
    Portrait of the Brontes*
White, Hilda Crystal 6681

Wild Dog Running
Scholefield, Alan 5658

Wild Earth's Nobility
Waters, Frank 6578

Wild Geese
Dillon, Eilis 1647

Wild Horizon
Mason, F. van Wyck 4164

The Wild Hunt
Chadwick, Elizabeth 969

Wild Is the River
Bromfield, Louis 704

Wild Jasmine
Small, Bertrice 5914

The Wild Ohio
Spicer, Bart 5966

Wild Orchid
Dick, Isabel 1640

Wild Swan
De Blasis, Celeste 1550

Wild Times
Garfield, Brian 2291

The Wild Yazoo
Myers, John 4546

The Wildcliffe Bird
Heaven, Constance 2811

Wilde West
Satterthwait, Walter 5609

The Wilderness
Vaughan, Carter A. 6442

Wilderness
Zelazny, Roger 6957

Wilderness: A Tale of the Civil War
Warren, Robert Penn 6573

Wilderness Adventure
Page, Elizabeth 4774

The Wilderness Brigade
Demarest, Phyllis Gordon 1605

Wilderness Empire
Eckert, Allen W. 1847

Wilderness Passage
Blake, Forrester 534

The Wilderness War
Eckert, Allen W. 1848

Wilford's Daughter
Manners, Alexandra 4071

A Wilful Woman
Talbot, Michael 6156

Will Shakespeare: The Untold Story
Mortimer, John 4495

Will You Love Me in September?
Carr, Philippa 932

*The William Powell and Myrna Loy
    Murder Case*
Baxt, George 390

William's Wife
Plaidy, Jean 5077

The Willing Maid
Ritchie, C.T. 5349

The Willow Pattern
van Gulik, Robert 6422

Willowwood
Hardwick, Mollie 2699
Savage, Elizabeth 5619

The Wind Brings Up the Rain
Malpass, Eric 4051

The Wind Dancer
Johansen, Iris 3218

The Wind From Hastings
Llywelyn, Morgan 3825

Wind From the Carolinas
Wilder, Robert 6751

Wind From the Main
Osborne, Anne 4759

The Wind From the Sea
Heaven, Constance 2812

The Wind in His Fists
Jennings, John Edward 3210

The Wind in the Forest
Fletcher, Inglis 2143

The Wind Leaves No Shadow
Laughlin, Ruth 3672

Wind Like a Bugle
Leonard, Nathan 3722

Wind of Change at Castle Rising
Cradock, Fanny 1412

Wind of Destiny
Nicole, Christopher 4624

Wind over Wisconsin
Derleth, August 1620

The Wind That Shakes the Barley
Barke, James 305

Winding Stairs
Jones, Douglas C. 3287

Windover
Hodge, Jane Aiken 2974

Winds of Blame
Rushing, Jane Gilmore 5532

The Winds of Sinhala
De Silva, Colin 1562

Winds of Spring
Havighurst, Walter 2776

The Winds of War
Wouk, Herman 6876

Windsor Castle
Ainsworth, William Harrison 59

Windward Passage
Cochran, Hamilton 1143

The Wine-Dark Sea
O'Brian, Patrick 4679

Wine of Life
Gorham, Charles Orson 2489

The Wine of San Lorenzo
Gorman, Herbert 2493

Wine of Satan
Gay, Laverne 2327

The Wine Princes
Mackay, Margaret 3987

The Wine Widow
Barclay, Tessa 301

Winged Pharaoh
Grant, Joan 2536

The Wingless Bird
Cookson, Catherine 1292

Wings for the Chariots
Whitehouse, Arch 6713

The Wings of Morning
Harper, Karen 2714

Wings of the Falcon
Michaels, Barbara 4361

Wings of the Morning
Beaty, David 402

The Wings of the Morning
Tryon, Thomas 6356

Wings of the Morning
Van de Water, Frederic F. 6404

The Winter Bride
Salisbury, Carola 5572

Winter Cherry
West, Keith 6632

Winter Fire
Trotter, William R. 6352

Winter Grass
Wheeler, Richard S. 6665

Winter Harvest
Lofts, Norah 3863

The Winter King
Cornwell, Bernard 1351

Winter of the Heart
LaRosa, Linda J. 3665

Winter Quarters
Duggan, Alfred 1775

Winter Rain
Johnston, Terry C. 3262

The Winter Rose
Ragosta, Millie J. 5243

The Winter Servant
Davis, M.H. 1537

The Winter War
Haines, William Wister 2640

*The Winter Wolf: Wyatt Earp in
    Alaska*
Parry, Richard 4820

Wintercombe
Belle, Pamela 435

Winterkill
Thompson, David 6262

The Winthrop Covenant
Auchincloss, Louis 235

The Winthrop Woman
Seton, Anya 5754

Wisconsin!
Ross, Dana Fuller 5493

The Wisdom of Stones
Matthews, Greg 4192

The Wise Virgin
Elsna, Hebe 1934

The Wishing Tree
Paretti, Sandra 4794

The Witch and the Priest
Lewis, Hilda 3754

The Witch From the Sea
Carr, Philippa 933

The Witch of Manga Reva
Roark, Garland 5359

Witch of the North
Jones, Courtway 3272

The Witches
Williams, Jay 6776

With All My Heart
Barnes, Margaret Campbell 330

With Fire and Sword
Sienkiewicz, Henryk 5850

With Malice Toward None
Morrow, Honore 4492

Within the Hollow Crown
Barnes, Margaret Campbell 331

Witness of Bones
Tourney, Leonard 6304

Witness to Treason
Ragosta, Millie J. 5244

Witnesses
Heidish, Marcy Moran 2820

Wives of the Wind
Jarrett, Marjorie 3170

Wizards' Country
Rooke, Daphne 5438

The Wizard's Daughter
Michaels, Barbara 4362

Wobble to Death
Lovesey, Peter 3918

The Wolf and the Buffalo
Kelton, Elmer 3408

The Wolf and the Raven
Paxson, Diana L. 4848

The Wolf at the Door
Shelby, Graham 5793

Wolf in the Fold
MacNeil, Duncan 4022

The Wolf of Masada
Fredman, John 2220

Wolf Song
Fergusson, Harvey 2069

The Wolfling: A Documentary Novel of the 1870s
North, Sterling 4648

Wolf's Embrace
Link, Gail 3801

Wolfshead
Wheelwright, Jere Hungerford 6672

Wolves Against the Moon
Altrocchi, Julia Cooley 123

The Wolves of Savernake
Marston, Edward 4130

Wolves of the Dawn
Sarabande, William 5604

Woman Astride
Purtscher-Wydenbruch, Nora 5209

A Woman by Design
Kennett, Frances 3426

A Woman Called Fancy
Yerby, Frank 6931

A Woman Called Moses
Heidish, Marcy Moran 2821

Woman Chief
Capps, Benjamin 892

The Woman from The Glen
Gartner, Chloe 2310

The Woman in the Cloak
Hill, Pamela 2949

A Woman Named Damaris
Oke, Janette 4711

Woman of Andros
Wilder, Thornton 6754

The Woman of Catawba
Stahl, Hilda 5978

Woman of Justice
Di Donato, Georgia 1639

A Woman of Quality
Westcott, Jan 6649

A Woman of Samaria
Ingles, James W. 3104

A Woman of Texas
Stevens, R.T. 6002

A Woman of the People
Capps, Benjamin 893

A Woman Possessed
Macdonald, Malcolm 3977

The Woman Question
Malm, Dorothea 4046

A Woman Scorned
Macdonald, Malcolm 3978

The Woman Who Fell From the Sky
Riefe, Barbara 5330

The Woman Who Loved John Wilkes Booth
Russell, Pamela Redford 5533

Woman with a Sword: The Biographical Novel of Anna Ella Carroll of Maryland
Noble, Hollister 4632

A Woman's Age
Billington, Rachel 499

Woman's Own
Carr, Robyn 941

The Women at Pine Creek
McKay, Allis 4279

Women in the Wall
O'Faolain, Julia 4691

Women in the Wind
Ritter, Margaret 5350

Women of Ashdon
Anand, Valerie 135

The Women of Eden
Harris, Marilyn 2734

The Women of Whitechapel and Jack the Ripper
West, Paul 6638

Wonder of All the Gay World
Barke, James 306

The Wonderful Country
Lea, Tom 3695

The Woodsman
Wright, Don 6880

Woodstock; or, The Cavalier
Scott, Sir Walter 5710

The Word and the Sword
Lang, Theo 3662

Words by Heart
Sebestyen, Ouida 5713

World and Paradise
Maas, Edgar 3953

The World as I Found It
Duffy, Bruce 1755

The World From Rough Stones
Macdonald, Malcolm 3979

The World in His Arms
Beach, Rex 392

The World of Jennie G.
Ogilvie, Elisabeth 4696

World of Silence
Coldsmith, Don 1195

The World, the Flesh, and the Devil
Tannahill, Reay 6159

A World Too Wide
Moore, Susan 4445

The World Turned Upside Down
Rayner, William 5273

World's Fair
Doctorow, E.L. 1661

The Wounded Yankee
Morris, Gilbert 4475

Written in Sand
Case, Josephine 950

Written in the Stars: A Novel about Albrecht Durer
Fisher, Frances Hope 2103

The Wrong Horse
Bassan, Jean 374

The Wrong Plantagenet
Palmer, Marian 4781

Wyatt Earp
Braun, Matt 653
Gordon, Dan 2481

Wychwood
St. John, Nicole 5564

Wyoming!
Ross, Dana Fuller 5494

Wyvern
Attanasio, A.A. 227

Y

Yankee
Ross, Dana Fuller 5495

The Yankee Brig
Vaughan, Carter A. 6443

Yankee Doodle Dandy
Gerson, Noel B. 2387

The Yankee From Tennessee
Gerson, Noel B. 2388

The Yankee Girl
Argo, Ellen 186

Yankee Pasha
Marshall, Edison 4115

The Yankee Rascals
Vaughan, Carter A. 6444

Yankee Rogue
Ross, Dana Fuller 5496

Yankee Rover
Ward, Christopher 6563

Yankee Stranger
Thane, Elswyth 6217

Yankee Trader
Morton, Stanley 4496

Yankee Woman
Baume, Frederic 381

The Year of December
Cores, Lucy 1329

The Year of Our War
Goldreich, Gloria 2462

The Year of the Death
Merliss, Reuben R. 4343

The Year of the French
Flanagan, Thomas 2121

The Year of the Horsetails
Tapsell, R.F. 6162

The Year of the Spaniard
Castor, Henry 956

The Year the Horses Came
Mackey, Mary 3993

Years of Peace
MacLeod, Le Roy 4009

Years of the City
Stewart, George Rippey 6028

Yedo
Guest, Lynn 2609

Yellow: A Novel
Lynch, Daniel 3932

The Yellow Admiral
O'Brian, Patrick 4680

The Yellow Robe: A Novel of the Life of Buddha
Payne, Robert 4856

Yellowhorse
Brown, Dee 715

The Yellowstone
Blevins, Winfred 549

Yellowstone Kelly
Bowen, Peter 602

The Yemassee
Simms, William Gilmore 5855

Yeshua: The Gospel of St. Thomas
McNarie, Alan Decker 4306

Yorktown
Davis, Burke 1513

You Bet Your Life
Kaminsky, Stuart M. 3349

You, My Brother
Burton, Philip 809

You Rolling River
Binns, Archie 503

Young Adolf
Bainbridge, Beryl 272

Young Ames
Edmonds, Walter D. 1879

The Young and Lonely King
Lane, Jane 3659

Young Bess
Irwin, Margaret 3123

The Young Caesar
Warner, Rex 6567

Young Catherine
Almedingen, E.M. 118

The Young Elizabeth
Letton, Jennette 3730

The Young Emperor
Payne, Robert 4857

Young Henry of Navarre
Mann, Heinrich 4062

Young Hickory
Young, Stanley 6942

Young Joseph
Mann, Thomas 4069

The Young Man From Mount Vernon
Pier, Arthur Stanwood 4995

The Young Men of Paris
Longstreet, Stephen 3893

Young Men See Visions
Mian, Mary 4357

Young Mrs. Cavendish and the Kaiser's Men
Beck, K.K. 405

Young Pitt
Maughan, A.M. 4200

Young Titan
Mason, F. van Wyck 4165

Young Vargas Lewis
Pearsall, Robert Brainard 4874

The Young Victoria
Whittle, Tyler 6724

The Yukon Queen
Morris, Gilbert 4476

Yvonne Goes to York
Chesney, Marion 1054

Z

Zayni Barakat
Ahitani, Gamal 42

Zeke and Ned
McMurtry, Larry 4301

Zemindar
Fitzgerald, Valerie 2117

Zoya
Steel, Danielle 5985